VOLUME 9

Desert to Egret

THE ENCYCLOPEDIA
AMERICANA
INTERNATIONAL EDITION

COMPLETE IN THIRTY VOLUMES
FIRST PUBLISHED IN 1829

GROLIER INCORPORATED

International Headquarters: Danbury, Connecticut 06816

COPYRIGHT © 1985 BY GROLIER INCORPORATED

COPYRIGHT © BY GROLIER INCORPORATED:
1984, 1983, 1982, 1981

COPYRIGHT © BY AMERICANA CORPORATION:
1980, 1979, 1978, 1977, 1976, 1975, 1974, 1973,
1972, 1971, 1970, 1969, 1968, 1967, 1966, 1965,
1964, 1963, 1962, 1961, 1960, 1959, 1958, 1957,
1956, 1955, 1954, 1953, 1952, 1951, 1950, 1949,
1948, 1947, 1946, 1945, 1944, 1943, 1942, 1941,
1940, 1939, 1938, 1937, 1936, 1932, 1931, 1929,
1927

COPYRIGHT BY ENCYCLOPEDIA AMERICANA CORPORATION:
1924, 1922, 1920, 1918

COPYRIGHT PHILIPPINES: 1972, 1979, 1980, 1984, 1985 BY
GROLIER INTERNATIONAL, INC.

COPYRIGHT UNDER INTERNATIONAL COPYRIGHT CONVENTIONS AND UNDER
PAN AMERICAN COPYRIGHT CONVENTIONS

ALL RIGHTS RESERVED UNDER INTER-AMERICAN COPYRIGHT UNION

Library of Congress Cataloging in Publication Data
Main entry under title:

THE ENCYCLOPEDIA AMERICANA.

   Includes bibliographies and index.
   1. Encyclopedias and dictionaries.
AE5.E333   1985   031   84-22553
ISBN 0-7172-0116-3 (set)

PRINTED AND MANUFACTURED IN THE U.S.A.

Desert sand dunes such as these in California's Death Valley form and migrate under the action of winds.
JOSEPH MUENCH

DESERT, any area that, because of dryness or cold, may be characterized as having low potential as a human habitat. Specifically, the term is applied to two kinds of areas: (1) most commonly, areas with arid climate, sparse vegetation or no vegetation, angular landforms, and an absence of full-flowing rivers; and (2) the lands on the polar fringes of the Northern Hemisphere continents and the ice-covered wastes of Greenland and Antarctica. These two kinds of deserts may be spoken of as *deserts of dryness* and *deserts of cold*. Deserts of dryness cover about 18% of the earth's land areas, and deserts of cold cover 16%.

CONTENTS

Section	Page	Section	Page
Deserts of Dryness	1	Human Habitation of	
Climate	1	the Desert	5
Landforms	2	Desert Animals	6
Water	3	Desert Plants	12
Deserts of Cold	4		

DESERTS OF DRYNESS

Deserts of dryness are found wherever precipitation is regularly too light to support either a forest or a complete grass cover. The different kinds of dry deserts are characterized by particular combinations of climate, native vegetation, landforms, water features, and soils. The ways in which man has come to use these areas are likewise distinctive.

Dry deserts are systematically distributed over most of the world. Typically, they occur on continental west coasts between approximately 20° and 30° of latitude in both the Northern and Southern hemispheres. From this location, they extend inland, curving toward the poles to reach into the higher middle latitudes in the continental interiors. This generalized position should not be considered precise, principally because of interruption by mountains and because of the detailed direction of coastlines. The generalized distribution of deserts is the result, primarily, of the circulation of the earth's atmosphere. Either the winds are offshore and hence bring no rain, or they have traveled so far from a water source that no moisture remains in them to be condensed and precipitated.

Climate. The outstanding features of all desert or arid climates are meagerness and uncertainty of precipitation. The amount of rain does not equal the potential evaporation. Even the small amount that does fall is subject to great variation from year to year. Rain comes at infrequent and irregularly spaced intervals in all areas of arid climate. Generally, there is no definite season of rains, and widespread rain is uncommon. Storms are localized so that effects are not felt over any considerable area. Months or even years may pass between storms; but when they do occur they are often so violent as to cause extensive damage to any of the works of man. The few, normally dry stream channels fill rapidly to overflowing, destroying villages and oasis gardens lying near them. On the other hand, the storms replenish the scanty supplies of groundwater that make life possible in the desert. On the occasion of a very rare gentle shower, the rain barely moistens the surface and is soon evaporated. At times, clouds form, and one can see rain beginning to fall from them, only to be reevaporated before it reaches the ground. Thus an average yearly precipitation figure is almost meaningless. It can only suggest meagerness. The uncertainty and irregularity of precipitation in desert areas must be understood, as well.

Temperatures within arid climates vary all the way from those characteristic of the tropics to those of the high latitudes. The only common element is great range, both annual and daily. In the low latitudes, the difference between the coolest and warmest months amounts to 15° to 30° F (about 8° to 17° C); in the middle latitudes, the yearly range usually amounts to 40° to 50° F (22° to 28° C). Where arid climates extend to continental west coasts, as they do near the margins of the low latitudes, relatively low temperatures and annual ranges are encountered as a result of the presence of offshore cold ocean currents in these latitudes.

Daily temperature ranges are usually large in most deserts. In the low latitudes and on the margins of the tropics have been recorded the highest air temperatures known anywhere in the world. Azizia, southwest of Tripoli in Libya, has registered a shade temperature of 136.4° F (58° C). Even higher air temperatures have been reported unofficially from northeastern Ethiopia, and Death Valley in California has reported fractionally over 134° F (56.7° C). At Wadi Halfa on the Nile River in the Sudan, 100° F (37.8° C) has been reported in every month except January, and that month has had a maximum of 99° F. In the Australian desert, temperature has risen over 100° F for over 60 days consecutively. At Yuma, Ariz., during one summer, the daily maximum passed 100° F in 79 out of 80 days. In spite of very high daytime temperatures, those at night may be very low. The oasis of In-Salah in the central Sahara has had a range of 100° F (55.5° C) within a 24-hour period: from 126° to 26° F (52.2° to −3.3° C). On Christmas Day in 1878, Bir Milrha, south of Tripoli in Libya, recorded a high of 99° and a low of 31° F (37.2° to −0.5° C). Most commonly, the daily range is between 25° and 30° F (between about 14° and 17° C), but frequently it is more.

All arid climates are characterized by two other features, sunshine and wind. In the low-latitude continental interiors, over 80% of the possible sunshine is received. In cooler areas, as along the low-latitude west coast and in the higher middle latitudes, cloudiness is greater. High winds, producing dust storms of great violence, are also a distinguishing feature of arid climates.

Landforms. Unlike the surface in regions in which plentiful rainfall creates a heavy cover of vegetation, the great detail of desert surface is not masked and is, therefore, all the more striking. Sharp, angular landforms are the rule, as are valleys without streams. Great accumulations of rock waste are present at the base of steep slopes, and in the valleys and other low areas. In humid lands with full-flowing streams, water carries away the accumulation of rock fragments; in the desert only the wind and intermittent streams can transport them. Wind moves only the finest dusts, and the streams seldom reach beyond the desert. Hence, little of the weathered rock material is removed.

So far as major types are concerned, there are two principal kinds of dry deserts. These are the mountain and bolson desert, and the hammada (or hamada) and erg desert. On each of these major types of surface there are distinctive detailed landforms.

Mountain and Bolson Desert. A mountain and bolson surface is characterized by a series of hill or mountain ranges separated by broad basins, called bolsons, like the surface of the Great Basin of the United States, particularly in Nevada and Utah. In South America, the Peruvian desert, the Atacama Desert in Chile, and the Bolivian plateau are mountain and bolson deserts. In such a desert, rainfall is greatest in amount and more frequently on the mountain ranges. Because the falls are usually of the cloudburst type and because of the steep slopes, most of the water runs rapidly off the mountains and down into the bolsons. Thus, the mountain slopes are cut by ravines and gorges, and weathered rock material is moved along them into the bolson. When the stream reaches the bolson, the slope of its bed is decreased, and its ability to carry the rock materials is therefore lessened. Consequently, there is built up at the foot of the mountain and at the margin of the bolson a deposit sloping gradually down from the mountain front—an *alluvial fan*. Very gradually, over a long period of time, the fan grows along the mountain face and toward the center of the bolson. Where many mountain torrents lead down into one bolson, that bolson may eventually be filled as the mountains are worn down.

During and for a short time after a cloudburst, streams may reach across the fans to spread water over the lowest part of the bolson, forming a temporary shallow lake. The water is soon evaporated, however, and there remains a white deposit of salts. This is known as a *playa*, or salt flat. If a sufficiently large number of streams carry water to the bolson, and at least some of it is derived from a reliable source in better-watered mountains, a permanent shallow salt lake, like Great Salt Lake in Utah, is formed. The saltiness of the lake results from the fact that it has no outlet, and the salts are concentrated under constant strong evaporation of water from the lake's surface.

Hammada and Erg Desert. Hammada and erg deserts present striking contrasts to mountain and bolson deserts. Hammada is rocky desert, and erg is sandy desert; the names "hammada" and "erg" are Anglicized forms of the Berber terms for such features in the western Sahara. Extensive rocky surfaces of generally low relief alternate irregularly with relatively smaller sandy wastes. In every instance, the rocky surfaces lie at higher elevations than the sandy areas. Often hammadas represent nearly horizontal layers of resistant rock, but sometimes they are erosion surfaces of domed rocks of varying resistance. With this kind of structure, less resistant rocks are worn away, leaving more resistant layers standing as asymmetric ridges, or cuestas. Facing inward toward the center of doming, the surface is a cliff; away from the center the slope is gradual. If erosion proceeds far enough to expose a very resistant crystalline core at the center of the dome, isolated craggy mountains may stand up prominently above the general level of the hammada. To these the descriptive name *inselberge*, or island mountains, is given. Often, too, fragments of the hammada are detached from the edges of the main mass by the erosive force of streams, either permanent or intermittent. The remaining mass is flat topped, with cliffs dropping away on all sides and a heavy mantle of rock fragments lying steeply up against the base of the cliffs. This type of landform is known as a *mesa;* sometimes, if the summit area is small, the remnant is called a *butte*. On some hammadas where physical

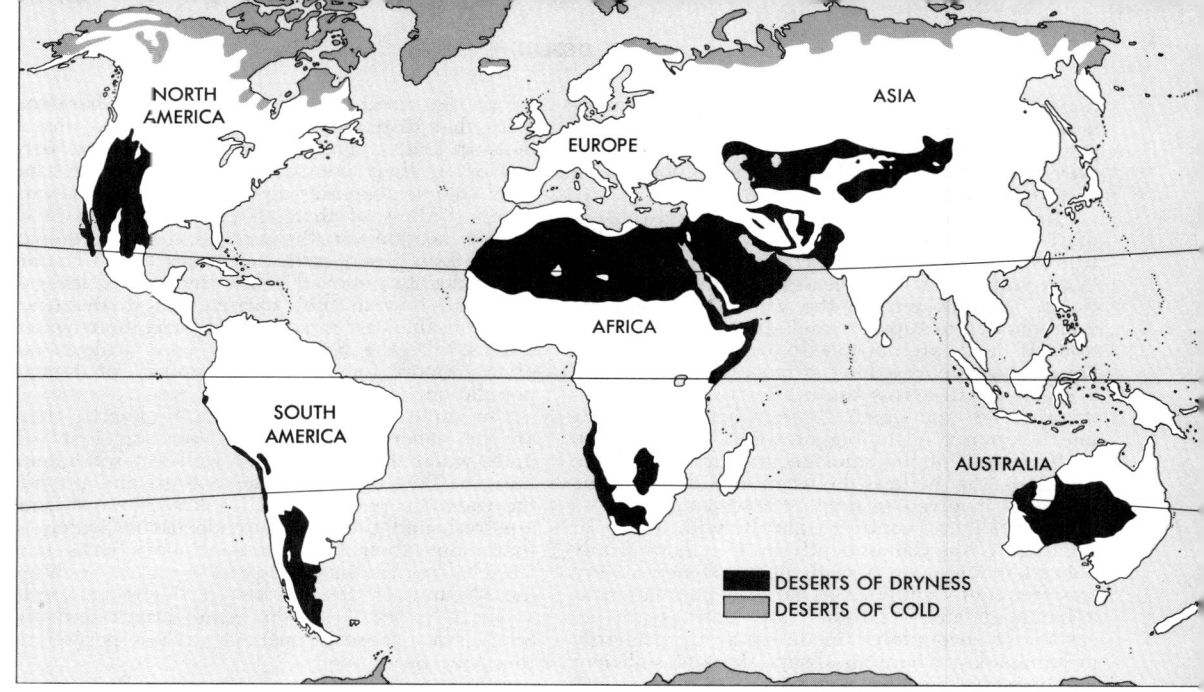

Deserts of dryness and cold together constitute about 34% of the world's total land area.

weathering is very active, a covering of angular rock fragments of varying size is encountered; this is known as *desert pavement*. If the fragments are of small size, the surface is spoken of as *gravelly desert*, or *reg*. In some instances, the hammada may represent geologically ancient mountains of a former mountain and bolson desert, and erg may represent the bolson completely filled with the detrital material worn from the mountains.

The surface of most hammadas is creased by the usually dry stream channels that have been formed by the torrential runoff following the infrequent storms. The erosive power of the steams, exerted downward, cuts vertical-sided valleys; but since the flow of water is of short duration, the materials that are carried by the flood are dropped on the valley floor. Thus, after the valley has again become dry, the valley floor is seen to be flat. Such trenchlike channels of intermittent streams are known as *wadis* (as in North Africa) or *arroyos* (as in southwestern United States). All of them lead from the higher parts of the hammada toward the lower parts of erg. While the erg is reached, the wadi as a distinctive form disappears, for any water reaching the sand quickly sinks below the surface.

Material worn from the hammadas supplies the sand of the erg. The extent of erg is a measure of the size and the degree of erosion of nearby hammadas, and of the number of wadis that lead into it. Wind is the agent responsible for the formation of dunes on the sandy surface. Where winds blow constantly from one direction, dunes arrange themselves in rows at right angles to the wind, with gentler slopes on the windward side and steeper slopes on the lee side. Any individual row of dunes is not continuous over long distances, but rather is a line of sand hills separated by low segments. Usually the rows are arranged *en echelon*. That is, the highest parts of one row are opposite the lower sections of the adjacent row. Unless checked by vegetation or by human control, the whole dune field tends to migrate leeward. No other detailed landforms characterize areas of erg.

Throughout the whole belt of deserts in northern Africa and Asia, the desert is essentially of the hammada and erg type, only a small part of it being erg. South of the equator in Africa, the Kalahari Desert is almost entirely hammada, as is the desert of Australia. A few areas in North America, such as the Colorado Plateau, and the Patagonian desert in South America, are hammada deserts.

Water. By far the most important factor for life in the desert is the availability of fresh water. The human population that a desert can support is very closely proportional to the amount of water that can be obtained. This may be (1) groundwater, obtained from wells or, in rare instances, from springs; (2) artesian water, obtained through artesian wells or artesian springs; or (3) river water, obtained from the few streams that flow from mountains to salt lakes in bolsons, or from a so-called exotic river (a river that rises in a humid area and flows across a desert, either into the sea or back into a humid land).

Groundwater. There is groundwater in most deserts, as there is in most humid lands; but there is less of it, and it usually lies at considerably greater depth below the surface. The supply is occasionally replenished by downward-percolating water after a storm, and there is also some underground seepage from more moist areas adjacent to the desert. In mountain and bolson deserts, even when there is no permanent stream flowing from the mountains to the alluvial fans, groundwater is usually available in the valley bottoms within the mountains and near the apexes of alluvial fans. Wells dug in these locations can usually be depended upon for a permanent, though often small, supply; but the farther one goes from the mountains toward the center of the bolson, the smaller is the supply and the deeper it lies beneath the surface. The water of the playa or salt lake is unsuitable for crops, animals, and human beings because of its saltiness. Where permanent streams issue from the mountains, they may provide a source for irrigation of all except the lower slopes of a fan.

In hammada and erg deserts, groundwater is most likely to be found in the gravel fill of the wadis and in the hollows between the dunes. Where numerous wadis lead into an erg, the supply from wells dug in the wadi floors may be great enough to support a relatively large population. If floods are not too frequent, a single wadi floor may support a long string of oases, making a green swath across the otherwise brown landscape. The amount of water in an erg depends mostly upon the number of wadis draining into it, the depth of the sand accumulation, and the depth of the hollows between the dunes. The problems involved in digging a well in the loose sand of an erg contrast sharply with those of digging to the same depth in the more firmly packed material on a wadi floor. Hence an erg less frequently supports as large a population as a hammada does. Groundwater springs are occasionally encountered in desert areas, primarily in hammadas, where an abrupt slope of sufficient height intersects the water table (the upper limit of the zone of saturation in the soil).

Artesian Water. The presence of an artesian structure may provide a water source. An artesian structure requires a system of sedimentary rocks dipping in such a way as to bring a porous layer, like a coarse sandstone, to the surface in a moist climatic area beyond the desert. Overlying the porous layer there must be an impervious stratum. Rain falling on the porous outcrop seeps downward into and along the dip of the rocks and cannot rise to the surface except where the impervious rock layer is broken. Such breaks occur naturally where the rock layers are faulted, so there are natural artesian springs. Many of the Saharan oases receive their water from this source, as do many points in the Australian desert. The impervious layer may also be pierced by drilling to bring water to the surface. The water supply from a groundwater source may thus be increased, or an entirely new water source may be provided.

Streams. Streams provide the third source of water in the desert. These are of two kinds: exotic streams and permanent streams leading to a salt lake. Exotic streams usually spread out into a maze of small shallow channels; there are shifting sandbars where they enter the desert in poorly defined valleys. Often they continue as multiple-channeled streams, called braided streams. If the valley is sharply enough defined, they may continue in a single course across the desert. The Niger River in western Africa flows northeastward from the Guinea Highlands out beyond the southern margin of the Sahara. As it enters the desert, it spreads out into many channels and then turns again to the southeast and makes its way back into humid lands, where it resumes a single channel normal to streams in moist areas. In its northward bend through the desert it is an exotic river. The White Nile leaves the moist tropical uplands of Uganda and flows northward into the Sahara. On the nearly flat plain of southern Sudan, it adopts a winding braided course, finding its way sluggishly to a structural valley where it again becomes single channeled as it flows across the desert to the Mediterranean Sea.

Exotic streams have two special characteristics that distinguish them from the streams of moister lands. They have relatively few tributaries in their courses across the desert, and their volume decreases downstream through evaporation. Many of them, like the Colorado in its canyon section, or the Loa River that crosses the Chilean desert from the Andes to the Pacific, are so deeply trenched below the general level of land and flow in such narrow valleys that they are unusable as a source of irrigation water. Others, like the Nile, flow in wide valleys and offer support for very large groups of human population.

In some mountain and bolson deserts, there are permanent streams that have sufficient volume, when they issue from well-watered mountains, to flow out into large bolsons and provide the water for permanent salt lakes. These streams are fresh and therefore provide usable water, so that along their banks a continuous oasis may stretch from the mountains to the lake. Such are the streams of the Turkestan desert of southwestern Soviet Asia, the Amu Darya and the Sir Darya. These permanent streams perpetuate the Aral Sea.

DESERTS OF COLD

On the Arctic fringe of North America and Eurasia, the long-continued cold produces a situation in which plants grow with great difficulty, if at all. The northern coniferous forest gives way to a stunted growth of miniature trees and bushes, and this, in turn, yields to a mixture of plants such as mosses, sedges, lichens, and a few grasses. This is called *tundra*. Northward, even the tundra ceases to be continuous, occurring in patches separated by stretches completely devoid of vegetation. To this spottily covered zone, the name *desert tundra* or *cold desert* is applied. Beyond the limit of any vegetation, ice covers the land, as in the interior of Greenland. To such an extensive region the name *ice desert* is sometimes applied.

During most of the year, water is present only in the form of ice and hence is not available to plants. In the short period when temperatures are high enough to allow plant growth, there is usually an excess of water, resulting primarily from poor drainage and low evaporation. Since the surface of much of the tundra is flat, surface drainage is poor, and temperatures are seldom high enough for a long period to bring about thawing of the subsoil and thus allow adequate soil drainage.

Excess quantities of water about plant roots act to impede growth, with much the same results as are encountered where there is too little water. Hence, plants of the cold deserts are xerophytic (structurally adapted to limited supplies of water) as are the plants found in deserts of dryness, but they are xerophytic for different reasons and in different ways from plants of a desert of dryness.

Most of the tundra occurs on the Arctic margins of North America and Eurasia. In addition, long fingers of tundra stretch southward along highland zones. Most of Greenland and a large part of Ellesmere Island to the west are ice covered. Hence there is an appreciable extent of cold desert in the Northern Hemisphere; the total extent of this cold desert area approximates the size of the United States without Alaska and Hawaii.

The jutting rock pinnacles (*above*) in the Sahara of northern Africa are the eroded remains of a plateau.

HAMMADA AND ERG DESERTS

The terms *hammada* (meaning rocky) and *erg* (sandy) are derived from Berber words for such features of the western Sahara.

In southern Libya (*above*), centuries of wind and sand storms have worn away the desert rocks into odd shapes.

Ayers Rock (*right*) in the desert of central Australia is a single rock 7 miles (11 km) around at the base.

MAJOR DESERTS OF DRYNESS

Desert	Location	Approximate Area in Sq Mi (1 sq mi = 2.59 sq km)
Sahara	northern Africa	3,500,000
Great Australian	central and western Australia	1,300,000
Great Arabian	Arabian peninsula	950,000
Turkestan	southwestern	750,000
North American	southwestern North America	500,000
Gobi	Mongolia	500,000
Patagonian	eastern Argentina	260,000
Great Indian (Thar)	northwestern India and Pakistan	230,000
Kalahari	southern Africa	220,000
Takla Makan	Sinkiang Province, China	200,000
Iranian	Iran	150,000
Atacama	Peru and Chile	140,000

HUMAN HABITATION OF THE DESERT

The deserts of the world are inhabited by approximately 4% of the world's people. By far the largest number of them live by agriculture. Where water is available, it can be led onto the land, and crops can be adequately watered; but these spots are limited in area and are separated by great distances. The kind of site that is occupied in one type of desert is very different from that which can be occupied in another. Early desert occupancy was of the subsistence-agricultural type; where there has been Euro-American contact, commercial agriculture has largely replaced it.

The controlling factor in type and extent of agriculture is the presence of an adequate and continuing source of water. Sunshine is normally to be expected, and if water is accessible, there are few crops that the desert cannot produce. The range is from truly tropical plants to those that will grow in the very short growing season on the margins of the high latitudes. A few plants with deep taproots (like the date palm), when once established, can reach far below the surface and draw needed moisture from groundwater supplies, but usually the plants grown as crops require some form of irrigation. Everywhere the limit is established by the amount of water available. Historically, this has meant that the deserts of the world have been occupied most successfully by peoples whose culture included knowledge of ways to increase the supply of water.

The earliest settlements were in the deserts of the Old World, particularly Africa. It has been well established that the earliest inhabitants of the Saharan area were Negroid peoples from the tropical part of Africa. They attached themselves to wet spots in the Sahara at a very early time, probably during the concluding phase of the great Ice Age, when the climate was more moist than it is at present. Even then, attachment to the wet spots was imperative. These people learned that the number of inhabitants who could be supported was in strict proportion to the actual supply of water. Through technological progress, the ways of making the desert produce have changed, the ways of increasing the water supply at any given place have improved, but the absolute limit to what the desert can support is still measured in terms of water.

Hammada and Erg Regions. In hammada and erg deserts, settlement is limited to three kinds of places: the wadi bottoms or the hammada surface adjacent to wadi bottoms; the hollows between the dunes; and the banks of exotic streams. Wadi bottoms are ordinarily the sites of oasis gardens. Under usual conditions, wells supply sufficient water for crop irrigation, and the wadi floors are intensively cultivated. The dwellings of the inhabitants are normally constructed on the hammada at the side of the wadi and above the level where occasional floods may be destructive. In some instances, as along the Wadi Saura in the western Sahara (where floods are rare), cultivated land is practically continuous for a distance of over 600 miles (960 km), from the Atlas Mountains of Morocco out toward the center of the Sahara. In hammadas that are cut by numerous wadis, a relatively high density of population may be encountered, as in the area just south of the Saharan Atlas Mountains in Algeria. In a few places, as again in the western Sahara, the peoples have advanced to the stage of building retention dams in the upper courses of the wadis to stop the sudden flash floods and to retain a reserve of water for use at times of unusually little rain.

Oases in ergs are less numerous and are usually smaller than those in hammadas for two reasons: the hollows between the dunes offer relatively restricted sites, and the supply of water in ergs is usually smaller than in hammadas. Furthermore, occupancy of the erg is usually more difficult because of the constant shifting of the sands. Nevertheless, some erg oases support a surprisingly high density of population, as in the Erg Oriental (Great Eastern Erg) in eastern Algeria.

Some of the highest population densities to be found anywhere in the world occur where exotic streams in wide valleys cut across the desert. The prime example is the valley of the Nile River, especially its Egyptian portion. There, diversion of the river water for irrigation is easily possible. Actually, in ancient Egypt, the natural regime of the river sufficed to produce one of the garden spots of the world. Because of the climatic character of the areas in which the two major sources of the Nile have their beginning, one branch, the White Nile from tropical Africa, provides a steady year-round flow; the other, the Blue Nile, flowing from the highlands of Ethiopia, has a season of flood and a season of low water. The two join at Khartoum in the Sudan, and from there downstream the Nile proper has alternately a period of high water and a period of low water. In the past, part of the plain on either side of the river was subject to yearly inundation. This was counted upon to provide a new deposit of silt, and also to create a supply of soil moisture sufficient to permit the growth of crops immediately following the recession of the flood. For most of the year, the land of the valley lay dry and brown. This was followed by a period when water covered nearly all of the valley floor. Then came the short fruitful period of green crops and intensive cultivation.

All of this changed when the Nile Valley was brought into the sphere of commercial agriculture. Then the problem became one of making the land produce as much as possible. Dams were built to retain the waters of the flood period; canals were built to distribute the waters to parts of the valley floor not formerly covered by the floods. Instead of one watering and one resultant crop, the land was constantly watered, and several crops were grown through the year. But the beneficial layering of the cultivated land with fresh silt no longer occurred. The consequence was soil deterioration and the need for artificial fertilizers and soil nutrients. Still, with a guaranteed supply of water, the desert offers a livelihood for agricultural people; a population density of over 1,000 per square mile (nearly 400 per sq km) occurs throughout much of the Nile Valley in Egypt.

Mountain and Bolson Regions. In mountain and bolson deserts, the sites of human settlement are very different. The availability of water is still the determining factor, both as to size and location of oases. Normally, the apex of an alluvial fan is the site chosen. How far down the slopes of the fan the land may be utilized is strictly a matter of the amount of water. In deserts that are particularly deficient in moisture, the oasis may actually be confined to the stream valley within the mountains and may not extend into the bolson at all. In others, where the amount of water draining from the mountains permits the stream to flow permanently out onto the lower levels to a salt lake, irrigated agriculture may produce a narrow belt of cultivated land on either side of the stream.

Nomadic Groups. While sedentary, irrigated agriculture is the most common form of occupation in deserts, there are some regions in which nomadic groups maintain a precarious existence. The desert margin is more characteristically their habitat, but occasional groups migrate over the desert in search of pasture for their flocks. Mobility is the key word for these groups, since they must constantly seek new food sources for their animals. The uncertainty of rain and, consequently, the uncertainty of even meager pasture makes such livelihood very difficult. Because the agricultural oasis dweller is relatively so well able to supply his needs and even to amass surplus, he is the natural enemy of the pastoral nomad when pasture cannot be found. Conflict between oasis dwellers and nomads has been a dominating theme in the Old World deserts.

The deserts of the Americas and of Australia are devoid of nomadic groups. This is so because these deserts never had the horse or the camel as animals upon which the nomad could depend until after European exploration and colonization. No nomadic group has been able to eke out an existence without fleet-footed animals. In some deserts, as in northern Nevada and central Utah, the vegetation cover is heavy enough to provide scanty pasture. Though of very low carrying capacity, this range makes possible a livestock economy. Seasonal use of mountain pastures is usually a supplementary measure to such grazing.

STOPPELMAN, FROM PIX

(Above) A chinchilla ranch operates on a high plateau in a mountain and bolson desert area of northern Chile. *(Below)* This tundra is part of the great desert of cold that extends along Canada's northern coastline.

ANNAN PHOTOS

Mining Oases. Occasionally one encounters mining oases, as in the desert of northern Chile. These exist because of the high value of the minerals that they produce. All of the necessities of life must be brought into such oases, the desert itself does not support the human beings who make up this kind of settlement. In northern Chile, even water is carried as much as 50 miles (80 km) from the Andes Mountains by means of pipeline. In contrast to the oases dependent upon subsistence agriculture, those that result from mining are ephemeral features of the landscape. The true desert dweller is the agriculturist, taking full advantage of every known source of water.

Deserts of Cold. Very few inhabitants are now to be found in either the North American or the Eurasian tundra. Eskimos, who managed a carefully adjusted, seminomadic life by hunting, fishing, and gathering wild plant foods, occupied an area from eastern Siberia across North America to Greenland. Other groups, such as the Lapps and the Samoyeds, occupied the Eurasian fringes, basing their living on the reindeer. Most of the Eurasian peoples occupied the tundra only in summer, withdrawing to the forests during the winter. Contacts with the Occidental culture world destroyed the precarious balance by which the Eskimos lived, simply by providing better hunting and fishing equipment. Hunting of the hair seal, especially, which was the backbone of Eskimo economy, became so easy that this animal was all but exterminated. There remained no solid base for the Eskimo way of life. Similarly, the less delicate balance has been destroyed for most of the Eurasian tribes. Though no accurate count has been made, it is probable that Eskimos have declined in number to approximately 40,000. Eurasian tundra-dwelling groups have declined in numbers similarly.

In the Southern Hemisphere there is very little tundra, since ice covers nearly all of Antarctica. This continent is totally without permanent inhabitants.

HENRY M. KENDALL, *Coauthor of "Introduction to Physical Geography"*

Bibliography

Bowman, Isaiah, *Desert Trails of the Atacama* (New York 1924).
Cressey, George B., *Crossroads: Land and Life in Southwest Asia* (Philadelphia 1960).
Fisher, William B., *The Middle East: A Physical, Social, and Regional Geography*, 5th ed. (New York 1953).
Gautier, Émile F., *Sahara: The Great Desert*, tr. by Dorothy F. Mayhew (New York 1935).
James, Preston E., and Kline, H. V., *A Geography of Man*, 3d ed. (Boston 1966).
Kimble, George H. T., and Good, Dorothy, eds., *Geography of the Northlands* (New York 1955).
Leopold, A. Starker, *The Desert*, rev. ed. (New York 1967).
Nesbitt, Lewis M., *Hell-Hole of Creation: The Exploration of Abyssinian Danakil* (New York 1935).
Zierer, Clifford M., ed., *California and the Southwest* (New York 1956).

DESERT ANIMALS

The desert can be successfully inhabited only by animals possessing some suitable means of dealing with the intense heat and the scarcity of water. The high desert temperatures and the limited water supply inevitably produce a conflict within the animal between retaining water for bodily functions and transpiring (evaporating) it for cooling purposes. Excessive transpiration usually results in desiccation (drying) and death. The rate at which water is lost through transpiration depends largely upon the size of the body's surface: the larger the surface, the greater the rate. Because small animals have a large body surface compared to their size, they are very susceptible to desiccation. At high rates of transpiration the loss of body water in small animals quickly reaches lethal extremes.

If a flea, for example, transpired at the rate of 5 milligrams per square cm per hour (roughly, an hourly loss of 1/1,000 of an ounce of water per square inch of body surface) for a period of 15 minutes, it would lose 10% of its body water. A man would have to transpire 4,500 times as fast to lose the same percentage in the same period of time.

Small animals, therefore, can exist in the desert only by avoiding climatic extremes. This they achieve by sheltering or burrowing underground during the day and coming out at night when the temperature falls and the relative humidity of the air increases. In larger forms the prevention of water loss by transpiration is less important, because a given rate of transpiration can proceed for much longer before the content of body water falls to a lethal level. So, although large animals are unable to escape the rigors of the desert climate in the same way as smaller ones, they can better afford to lose water through evaporative cooling.

Insects and Arachnids. The animals principally represented in arid regions are insects, arachnids (spiders, scorpions, and others), reptiles, birds, and mammals. The adaptations of insects and arachnids to hot, dry environments consist of heat-avoiding behavior, remarkable hardiness, and an efficient utilization of available water.

The adaptive behavior includes burrowing, nocturnal habits, seasonal rhythms of activity, and a dormant stage during development that coincides with the dry season. The uncommon hardiness involves the ability to withstand extremes of starvation, dehydration, and high temperatures. The efficient utilization of available water is achieved in various ways: most commonly, there is the ability to conserve metabolic water (water formed during the oxidation and breakdown of food molecules); many desert species also transpire more slowly than their relatives in moister parts of the world; and some, by a remarkable process that is not fully understood, are actually able to absorb moisture from unsaturated air through their body surface (integument).

Reptiles. Reptiles are conspicuous and comparatively numerous desert animals. They have a relatively impervious, scaly skin that greatly reduces the loss of body water by evaporation and effectively restricts such water loss to the saturated breath expelled from the lungs during breathing. Their urinary wastes are usually eliminated as a pulpy, semisolid mass, predominantly of uric acid, with little accompanying water. The reptiles' diet supplies adequate water, and evaporation can be greatly reduced by daily or seasonal periods of rest within a cool, humid burrow.

Reptiles can regulate their body temperature, but they do so by behavior rather than physiological means. The animals sun themselves until their body temperature has risen to its optimum; then they hide away in holes or crevices to prevent overheating. When it is very hot, the African tortoise *Testudo sulcata* can maintain a body temperature of about 105° F (40.5° C) by copious salivation, which wets the head, neck, and front legs. This draws heavily upon the tortoise's body water, however, and cannot be sustained for prolonged periods.

The lizards of sandy regions show two kinds of adaptation to the environment, according to whether they are "sand runners" or "sand swimmers." In the former, the toes of both the front and the hind feet are fringed with elongated scales. These scales, functioning like snowshoes, widen the surface that presses on the loose sand. When not running, a sand runner stands alert, with head held high and the front part of the body raised on the forelimbs so that it clears the hot sand. In motion, the animal holds its tail well above the ground as a counterpoise. Such adaptations are found in many unrelated species from different parts of the world.

Sand swimmers include skinks and other lizards, as well as some snakes that are adapted for rapid burrowing in loose sand. In these, the nose is pointed and shovel-like, and the nostrils tend to be directed upward instead of forward. In most of these snakes the nostrils are shielded from the sand by complicated valves, or they are reduced to pinhole size. Some species of sand swimmers dive headfirst into loose sand as though it were water. Others have widened bodies for burrowing by lateral and vertical movements instead of plowing forward into the sand. Some snakes, such as the American sidewinder (*Crotalus cerastes*) and African and Asiatic horned vipers of the genus *Aspis*, progress across the sand by utilizing a helical (spiral) side-winding movement.

Birds. Although many species of birds live in desert regions, most of these inhabit the fringe of the desert and never go far from water. The most serious physiological factor limiting the distribution and dispersion of desert birds is water loss by evaporation. Small birds lose water by evaporation very much more rapidly than mammals of comparable size, and most of this is lost in panting rather than through skin transpiration. It has been suggested that this greater evaporation loss in birds occurs because their body temperatures are higher that those of most mammals. The air expired from the bird's lungs is therefore warmer and can and does hold a higher moisture content. Thus, small birds can survive in the desert only by drinking or by eating very succulent food.

To conserve body water, birds utilize shade to protect themselves from the full heat of the sun, but they are also physiologically adapted to tolerate a rise in body temperature without ill effects. This allows them to retain body water that would otherwise be used to dissipate accumulated body heat. Desert birds also can quickly make up severe water loss by drinking, in contrast to some animals that may suffer ill effects in attempting to drink enough at one time to compensate fully for the loss.

Thus the capacity of the American mourning dove (*Zenaidra macroura*) to endure elevated body temperature and extensive dehydration, combined with the ability to make up water deficit and to fly long distances, allows this species to meet the demands of a desert existence.

The large, flightless ostrich (*Struthio camelus*), though it must drink water or eat very succulent food for adequate water intake, possesses special salt-excreting glands that enable it to live off brackish or even salty water without ill effects. These glands, located in the head near the eyes, remove salt from the blood and discharge it through the nasal passages. The ostrich also can rapidly make good the loss in weight resulting from dehydration.

Besides physiological specializations, the adaptations of birds to arid habitats include behavioral and ecological factors. Sandgrouse (*Pterocles*), common inhabitants of African and Asiatic deserts, feed and nest far away from rivers and lakes. These birds have adopted an extraordinary method of providing moisture for their young. As the sun rises, great flocks of these small birds fly many miles to water. Before reaching the watering sites, the male birds rub their breasts on the ground until the feathers are awry and easily saturated while they are drinking. They then fly back to the nesting area, where the young take turns in passing the wet feathers through their beaks until the supply of moisture is exhausted. Before they can fly, the young take water in no other way.

The eggs of birds that nest on the desert surface are rapidly killed by heat if left uncovered during the day. Only the largest egg, that of the ostrich, can survive prolonged exposure to the desert sun. Many desert birds, therefore, nest in the shelter of bushes, in holes, caves, or crevices, or under boulders.

Mammals. The mammals most independent of water are the desert rodents known as kangaroo rats (*Dipodomys*), gerbils (*Gerbillus* and others), and jerboas (*Jaculus* and others). These can subsist solely on the metabolic water obtained from the oxidation and breakdown of dry food. The use of burrows as living sites by these rodents is of special significance in this regard. Microclimatic measurements of temperature and humidity within the burrows have shown that, although the air is not saturated, its moisture content is higher than that of the air outside. Consequently, the rate of water evaporation from the rodents' lungs is considerably reduced. If the animals were to breathe the air outside their burrows continually, the rate of evaporation from the lungs would exceed the rate of formation of metabolic water.

The burrows, in addition to being moist content, are relatively cool. The coolness of the burrow reduces the temperature, and hence the moisture-carrying capacity, of the expired air as it leaves the nose. Because of these humidifying and cooling effects, the rodents inhabiting burrows have a lower rate of water evaporation from the lungs than that of most other mammals.

These rodents also possess physiological specializations for the conservation of body water. They produce both an extremely concentrated urine, enabling them to use less water in excreting waste products, and have dry feces. The North African sand rat (*Psammomys obesus*), which lives on succulent but salty plants found on intermittently dry stream beds, is the most exceptional in this respect: it can produce a urine nearly four times as salty as seawater, enabling it to utilize the saline water contained within its plant diet.

Desert rodents, like other small mammals, do not sweat. It seems likely that the general absence of sweat glands in small mammals results from the necessity to reduce the high rate of water loss caused by their relatively large surface areas. A kangaroo rat or jerboa, for example, in order to maintain a constant, normal body temperature when the surrounding temperature is

104° F (40° C), would have to lose 20% of its body weight in water each hour. Though they do not sweat, such mammals have an emergency temperature-regulating process: if the body temperature approaches the lethal level, about 107.5° F (42° C), the animal salivates copiously, wetting the fur of its chin and throat. The cooling effect of this procedure may keep experimental animals alive for up to half an hour at temperatures fatal to other small rodents.

Aestivation, the summertime equivalent of hibernation, occurs in a number of desert rodents. The ground squirrel (*Citellus*), for example, becomes torpid and aestivates during the summer and early autumn. Its body temperature falls to that of the air, and its metabolic rate, respiration, and other physiological processes are reduced, permitting the animal to live without food and decreasing the evaporation of water from the lungs. Especially important is the fact that with a lowered body temperature, less water is required to saturate the expired air.

Little is known about carnivorous desert mammals, but there is no doubt that they obtain considerable quantities of water from their food. The fennec fox, in addition to its catholic diet of insects, lizards, rodents, and plant material, exhibits a number of characteristics typical of a desert inhabitant. It is much smaller than its relatives from temperate climates; it has large eyes and ears; and it spends the day in a burrow, thus avoiding extremes of heat.

Large desert mammals, such as antelopes and camels, cannot escape daytime heat by burrowing: they must either endure a rise in body temperature or expend water for heat regulation, and, in fact, they do both. Camels, besides tolerating a wide range of body temperatures, can also lose about 30% of their weight in body water without ill effects and can make up the loss at one drinking without suffering water intoxication (see CAMEL). The gazelle, however, has become adapted to the desert not so much physiologically as by its speed and ability to travel great distances to obtain food and water.

Strictly behavioral responses to the intensity of the sun are seen in large desert animals. Any available shade is utilized, and camels, as well as sheep and goats, orient their bodies to reduce the area of body surface exposed to the sun's rays. When an animal's head faces the sun, a smaller area of its body is heated than if the sun were shining on its side.

J. L. CLOUDSLEY-THOMPSON
University of Khartoum, Sudan

Further Reading: Buxton, Patrick A., *Animal Life in Deserts* (London 1923; reprinted 1955); Cloudsley-Thompson, John L., *Desert Life* (Oxford 1965); Cloudsley-Thompson, John L., and Chadwick, M. J., *Life in Deserts* (London and Philadelphia 1964); Dill, D. B., ed., *Adaptation to the Environment* (Baltimore 1964); Leopold, A. Starker, *The Desert*, rev. ed. (New York 1967); Schmidt-Nielsen, K., *Desert Animals: Physiological Problems of Heat and Water* (London 1964).

DESERT PLANTS

The world's vegetation can be divided into three major categories: (1) forests, with soil moisture throughout the year; (2) grasslands, with soil moisture available only during part of the year; and (3) arid lands, or deserts, with only periodic moisture. These three types of vegetation form a continuum—a gradual change of one into another—in which the larger trees are at one end and desert plants are at the other.

As the vegetation shifts from one type to another, transitional forms are encountered. In the change from forests to grasslands, for example, one transitional form is woodland, where individual trees are separated by expanses of grassy areas. The transitional vegetation between grasslands and deserts, however, is more difficult to define. In essence, as less and less water is available, fewer and fewer kinds of plants are able to adapt themselves to the stresses imposed by aridity. To survive in arid lands, plants must possess adaptations geared to the severely restricted water supply.

Such adaptations may be viewed in terms of (1) tolerance to dehydration, (2) methods of obtaining and storing water, and (3) the prevention, avoidance, or reduction of water loss.

Dehydration Tolerance. The ultimate water stress suffered by desert plants may be regarded as the dehydration of the protoplasm in the plant's cells. The tolerance to such dehydration—that is, the amount of water that can be lost at the cellular level before irreversible dehydration and death occur—varies greatly among different species of plants. A number of desert plants display a high tolerance. In the creosote bush (*Larrea tridentata*) the water content of the leaves may drop to 50% of the leaves' dry weight, but the plant will recover when adequate water is supplied. In comparison, the water content of leaves of forest trees generally ranges from 100% to 300% of the leaves' dry weight.

Obtaining Water. The main absorbing areas of the plant are the surfaces of the roots, mainly the epidermal cell layers, and the root hairs, which are extensions of the root epidermal cells. Howard J. Dittmer, an American plant physiologist, has measured the remarkable extent of root surface area—a quantity often underestimated. A single plant of the winter rye grass (*Secale cereale*)—when grown in a well-watered container, 12 x 12 x 22 inches deep (30 x 30 x 55 cm deep), filled with dark loam soil—had nearly 14 million roots, with a total surface area of about 2,500 square feet (about 230 sq meters), and more than 14 billion root hairs, with a total surface area of about 4,300 square feet (about 400 sq meters). The total root surface of nearly 6,900 square feet (640 sq meters) was more than 2,000 square feet (185 sq meters) larger than a standard collegiate basketball court. If placed end-to-end, the roots and root hairs of this single rye plant would have spanned nearly 390 miles (630 km).

Extensive root systems, presumably even more elaborate than those of plants from areas of higher moisture, are a special feature of arid-land plants. They may be wide-spreading, as in the saguaro cactus (*Carnegiea gigantea*), or deep-penetrating, as in the mesquite (*Prosopis juliflora*), whose roots have been collected as deep as 175 feet (53 meters). The effectiveness of these root systems in securing water sometimes results in a markedly uniform spacing between plants, giving them a cultivated appearance. In such instances, each plant, requiring a given amount of soil area for its survival, so thoroughly absorbs the moisture that no other plant can grow near it.

Water Storage. Many desert plants, such as the cacti and agaves, are termed succulents, that is, plants with fleshy tissues used for water storage. Water is stored in the roots, stems, and leaves, from which it can be drawn during periods of no soil moisture. The barrel cactus (*Ferocactus wislizeni*) stores so much liquid that it has been used as an emergency source of drinking water by Indians and other desert inhabitants.

Water Loss. Water loss in plants is primarily a function of transpiration—an evaporation process that allows water to diffuse from the plant into the atmosphere. Transpiration occurs from the stems and leaves of the plant, with the greatest amount taking place from the pores, or stomata, in the surface layer of the leaves. It is through the stomata that carbon dioxide and oxygen, the gases necessary for the processes of respiration and photosynthesis, pass into and out of the plant. When the stomata are open for the necessary exchange of gases, water from within the plant passes to the outside. Because transpiration is a universal feature, many suggestions have been made as to its value. However, many biologists now believe it has no special value at all: transpiration is simply a necessary evil, a byproduct of the gaseous exchange occurring during respiration and photosynthesis.

In arid lands, water loss from transpiration is a very serious matter. To lessen the extent of this water loss, desert plants often have small, thick leaves, which reduce both the amount of surface area from which evaporation can take place and the amount of cell-wall area exposed to air spaces within the leaves. Another common feature of desert plants is the presence of a thick waxy cuticle (outer covering) on the stems and leaves that retards water diffusion. In addition, downy hairlike growths on the stems and leaves and the placement of the stomata in sunken pockets may also serve to slow water passage. Some plants have the stomata placed only on the underside of the leaf, while others, such as the succulents, may open the stomata only at night during the driest weather.

Xerophytes. Desert plants are often referred to as xerophytes. This is an ecological description based on the scarcity of water in the plants' environment. This classification also recognizes hydrophytes, or water plants, and mesophytes, or plants that live on dry land but not in arid places. This terminology reflects the continuum of moist to dry mentioned earlier.

Xerophytes can be further divided into four classes: (1) drought-escaping, (2) drought-evading, (3) drought-enduring, and (4) drought-resisting.

Drought-escaping plants are those with life cycles so short that the cycle is completed before extreme drought conditions are in force. These include most of the annuals that lay over the driest periods as seeds. Bladderpod mustard (*Lesquerella gordoni*), for example, is a very fast-growing plant that is able to complete its life cycle from seed to seed in the remarkably short time of 10 to 20 days. Because of their short life cycle and rapid disappearance, drought-escaping plants are also called *ephemerals*. Drought-escaping plants are the basis for the phenemonon "desert in bloom," in which seeds germinate and the plants quickly flower during the brief rains.

Drought-evading plants are those that conserve the little water available by virtue of their small size and restricted growth. In this category are plants with bulbs or enlarged roots or stems, such as the night-blooming cereus (*Peniocereus*

JOSEF MUENCH
DESERT VEGETATION in the foothills of the Kofa Mountains of Arizona includes the ocotillo, with its thorny, whiplike branches, and small shrubs and cacti.

greggii), which has underground stems up to 85 pounds (38.5 kg) in weight.

Drought-enduring plants are those shrubby plants, such as the creosote bush, which, when soil moisture is absent, cease their growth and shed leaves (the site of greatest transpiration loss) and even portions of the stems (self-pruning). Drought-enduring plants continue to live during the driest season but are very inactive.

Drought-resisting plants include the cacti and other succulents, in which water reserves are accumulated in the plant's tissues.

Parallel Evolution. The growth forms of desert plants are quite similar throughout the world, a feature referred to as parallel evolution. This is the result of plants of different families being exposed to similar environment conditions and responding to these conditions in a similar way. Thus certain plants of the spurge family (Euphorbiaceae) and the milkweed family (Asclepiadaceae) from arid lands in South Africa look like and are often mistaken for cacti (family Cactaceae), which are native to the Americas.

WALTER S. PHILLIPS
University of Arizona

Bibliography

Cloudsley-Thompson, J. L., and Chadwick, M. J., *Life in Deserts* (London and Philadelphia 1964).
Jaeger, Edmund C., *The North American Deserts* (Palo Alto 1961).
Leopold, A. Starker, *The Desert*, rev. ed. (New York 1967).
Pickwell, Gayle, *Deserts* (New York 1939).
Shreve, Forrest, *Vegetation of the Sonoran Desert*, vol. 1, Carnegie Institution of Washington, Publication No. 591 (Washington 1951).

DESERTED VILLAGE, a narrative poem, by the British writer Oliver Goldsmith (q.v.). The best known of Goldsmith's poems, it appeared in May 1770 and went into a 5th edition in August of that year.

The Deserted Village exposes the harm done by rich men who enlarged their private grounds by buying up neighboring farms or villages and driving out the inhabitants. Doubtless, the poem is melodramatic, but while Goldsmith used a poet's weapons against selfish luxury, argument is not the essential merit of the work. Goldsmith's rhymed couplets achieve a flowing rhythm that matches the deeper rhythm of his emotion. Images of the prosperous days of the village—the evening sports on the green, the parsonage, the schoolhouse, the inn—are presented with a felicity that makes the poem memorable, regardless of its social purpose.

DESERTER, a member of an armed force who quits his service or his place of duty without authority, intending not to return or to avoid important or hazardous duty. Long absence tends to prove intent to remain away. In some countries in wartime, however, unauthorized absence of even a few hours may be considered desertion, punishable by death.

In United States practice a wartime deserter is subject to trial by court-martial at any time. Charges for peacetime desertion must be filed within three years after the offense, unless the deserter has been beyond the reach of U. S. jurisdiction. A peacetime deserter from the U. S. armed forces who goes to another country cannot be extradited, because treaties do not require the return of military offenders, but he is subject to trial if he later returns to U. S. control.

A U. S. serviceman convicted as a deserter may be punished by dishonorable discharge, loss of rank and all pay, and confinement for two years, if he returns voluntarily; if he is apprehended, confinement can be for three years; if he deserted to avoid hazardous duty, confinement can be for five years. A declaration of war automatically lifts these limits, permitting a wartime deserter to be sentenced to death or any lesser penalty.

HAROLD E. PARKER, *Brig. General, USA
Assistant Judge Advocate General, U. S. Army*

DESERTION, or willful abandonment, is a ground for the legal separation of married couples in every state of the United States. In 45 states it is a ground for divorce. In most states a separation may be secured without regard to the duration of the desertion, but state laws vary as to the time required when desertion is offered as a ground for divorce.

A healthy spouse's prolonged refusal to cohabit may constitute abandonment, even without physical separation. Some states also recognize imprisonment for a period of time (involuntary desertion) or disappearance under mysterious circumstances as grounds for dissolution of marriage. But the more general definition of desertion is unjustified voluntary departure. There is no abandonment if the departure is justified, that is, by cruelty, adultery, or other marital offense.

Offer to Return. Desertion ceases with a bona fide offer to return, and the deserted spouse is obliged to accept it unless there is justification for refusal. Thus, although one is not obliged to condone serious marital offenses, a returning husband or wife, whose only fault was unjustified departure from the home, is entitled to full restoration of conjugal rights. Refusal to reconcile in such cases reverses the roles; the deserted becomes the deserter.

Marital Consequences. Because of the legal consequences that ensue from desertion, it becomes important to establish which spouse is guilty of abandonment. A deserting wife is generally deprived of the right to alimony. (See also ALIMONY.) Rights of inheritance may be lost by a deserting spouse.

Finally, domicile of the wife follows that of the husband, and a wife cannot establish her own domicile unless she can justify her departure. Thus she may find it impossible to secure a divorce for desertion in a state other than that of the marital domicile, particularly when her grounds for divorce would not be considered legal grounds in the home state. All such cases involving jurisdiction raise highly complex questions of conflict of law, so that competent legal counsel should be sought.

Desertion of Children. In most states, desertion of young children by a parent responsible for their support is a crime. Most states do not require consent of the deserter if the deserted spouse wishes to offer their children for adoption. A deserting parent may be forced to support deserted children under the 1950 Uniform Support of Dependents Law, which, as amended in one form or another, has been adopted by every U. S. state, territory, and dependency. These laws set up procedures for compelling support when the responsible parent resides elsewhere. The person claiming support need not physically leave home. The complainant appears in the court of her jurisdiction; if she shows a prima facie case, that court communicates with the courts of the place where the respondent resides. Hearings are held and orders issued without requiring either party to seek counsel in the other's jurisdiction, thus providing an inexpensive, effective remedy.

JULIA PERLES
*Chairman, Special Committee on Matrimonial Law
New York County Lawyers Association*

DE SEVERSKY, də sə-vûr′skē, **Alexander Procofieff** (1894–1974), Russian-American aviator and aeronautical engineer. He was born in Tiflis, Russia, on June 7, 1894. After serving in the Russian naval air service during World War I, he went to the United States. From 1918 to 1922, he was a test pilot and consulting engineer to the U. S. government. In 1922 he founded the Seversky Aero Corporation. He later headed several aeronautical firms (including Seversky Aircraft Corporation, 1931–1939) and served as aeronautical consultant to the U. S. government and various universities and businesses. He became an American citizen in 1927.

De Seversky's patents include one for an automatic bombsight, which was purchased by the U. S. government. In 1936 he designed a cantilever all-metal trainer and a high-speed fighter plane, and in 1938 he designed a fighter with a turbo-supercharged air-cooled engine, which was the prototype of the P-47. Besides many technical articles, he wrote several books, including *Victory Through Air Power* (1942). He died in New York City on Aug. 24, 1974.

ROBERT S. WOODBURY
Massachusetts Institute of Technology

DESHOULIÈRES, dā-zōō-lyâr′, **Antoinette** (1638–1694), French poet and social leader. She was born Antoinette du Ligier de La Garde in Paris on Jan. 1, 1638. During the war of the Fronde she followed her husband, Seigneur Deshoulières, who was in the service of the Prince of Condé, to Rocroi, near Brussels, and was rescued by him after she had been imprisoned by Spanish authorities. After her return to Paris she became hostess of a literary salon.

Influenced by the poetry and philosophy of Pierre Gassendi (q.v.), she soon became a celebrated writer, sometimes called the "10th Muse." Voltaire praised her work, which included idylls, eclogues, odes, elegies, madrigals, and the tragedy *Génseric* (1680). She died in poverty in Paris on Feb. 17, 1694. Her collected works were published posthumously by her daughter in 1695.

DESIDERIO DA SETTIGNANO, dā-sē-dâ′ryō dä sät-tē-nyä′nō (1428?–1464), Italian sculptor, who was one of the leading Florentine artists of the Renaissance. He was born at Settignano, near Florence. Strongly influenced by Donatello, who may have been his teacher, Desiderio attained an original style of great delicacy and technical virtuosity.

Desiderio's major works are marble monuments and busts and reliefs of women and children. His chief monumental works are the tomb of the humanist scholar Carlo Marsuppini (about 1455; Church of Santa Croce, Florence) and the marble *Tabernacle of the Sacrament* (completed 1461; Church of San Lorenzo, Florence). Examples of his low-relief carvings are the *Madonna and Child* (Bargello, Florence) and the *Infant Christ and John the Baptist* (Louvre, Paris). The National Gallery, in Washington, D. C., has four of his portrait busts. Desiderio died in Florence on Jan. 16, 1464.

DESIDERIUS, des-i-dir′ē-əs (reigned 757–774), was the last Lombard king of northern Italy. His ambition was to recover those Italian lands taken from his predecessor and bestowed upon the pope by the Franks in 756. For this purpose, he allied himself with Bavaria and in 770 married his daughter to Charlemagne, one of the two kings of the Franks.

In 771, when Charlemagne became the sole king on the death of his brother, he no longer needed the friendship of Desiderius. When the Lombards began their advance into central Italy, Charlemagne responded to a papal appeal for aid, repudiated his wife, and invaded Italy in 773. Desiderius withstood a long Frankish siege of his capital, Pavia. He was finally forced to capitulate, and was banished to a monastery, while Charlemagne assumed the Lombard crown.

JOHN HENNEMAN
McMaster University, Hamilton, Ontario

DESIRE UNDER THE ELMS is a play by the American dramatist Eugene O'Neill (q.v.), produced and published in 1924. The play's setting is a New England farm in 1850. The principal characters are Ephraim Cabot, a farmer; his three sons, Simeon, Peter, and Eben; and his young third wife, Abbie Putnam. Ephraim struggles to keep his place as absolute owner and undisputed master. The two older sons seek escape from his domination by departing for California. Eben, born of his father's second wife, wishes to avenge the mistreatment that hastened his mother's death and to secure possession of the farm that originally was hers. The new wife also schemes to inherit the property through her illegitimate child by Eben, whom she seduced. The drama culminates in Abbie's strangling the child and the imprisonment of Eben and Abbie, leaving a lonely and embittered Ephraim in undisputed possession of the land.

DÉSIRÉE, dā-zē-rā′ (1777–1860), fiancée of Napoleon, and later the queen of Sweden. Désirée Clary was born in Marseille, France, the daughter of François Clary, a wealthy merchant. She met Napoleon and became his fiancée after her sister, Julia, married his brother, Joseph Bonaparte, in 1794. Although Napoleon, then a young and ambitious army officer, wanted to marry her, Désirée hesitated. Her father, who is reputed to have said, "One Bonaparte in the family is enough," strongly opposed their marriage.

Napoleon's attention soon turned to Josephine de Beauharnais, whom he married in 1796. Napoleon retained his interest in Désirée, however, and tried to arrange an advantageous marriage for her. In 1798 she married General Bernadotte, one of France's leading generals. Her connections with Napoleon also benefited Bernadotte, who received rapid promotions.

During 1810–1811, after Bernadotte had been elected crown prince of Sweden, Désirée visited Sweden with her husband. Bernadotte succeeded to the throne as Charles XIV in 1818, and Désirée became his queen consort but did not return to Sweden until 1823. She played a minor role in Swedish affairs. Her son, whose godfather was Napoleon, became king as Oscar I in 1844. She died in Stockholm in 1860.

DESK, a piece of furniture of table or cabinet form that is used primarily for writing or reading. The earliest desk was probably a box that had a sloping lid for writing, under which there was storage space for writing materials. Boxes of this type were used in the *scriptorium* (writing room) of medieval monasteries. Eventually, these boxes came to be mounted on specially constructed stands—the form of the desk, or writing table, that lasted into the 18th century. In France the tops of such writing tables were covered with a woolen cloth (baize) called *bure*. By the 17th century, drawers were added to the table frames. This addition produced a chest of drawers, from which the kneehole desk was later evolved.

In the 18th century a bookcase or cabinet top and a hinged writing surface were added to the chest of drawers, to form the *secrétaire* (secretary). Also in the 18th century, when letter and memoir writing thrived in France and England, small desks, often called "ladies' desks," were placed throughout the house. These pieces had either lids or sliding doors (often of tambour construction), or cylinders that rolled back. (The 19th century rolltop desk was an outgrowth of cylinder construction.)

In the early 19th century, straight drop-front cabinets of Empire style replaced the more elaborate architectural forms of the earlier secretaries. Modern desks, constructed of synthetic material as well as wood, are designed in both new and traditional forms.

JOSEPH T. BUTLER
Author of "American Antiques, 1800–1900"

DESMAN, dez'mən, an aquatic member (*Desmana moschata*) of the mole family (Talpidae), native to southeastern Europe and central western Asia. This species, also called the Russian desman, has a body about 8 inches (20 cm) long and an equally long sideways-flattened tail. It has partially webbed forefeet and fully webbed hind feet. Man hunts the desman for its reddish brown fur. The desman feeds on insects, crayfish, snails, clams, fish, and amphibians.

The closely related but smaller Pyrenean, or Spanish, desman (*Galemys pyranaicus*) is found in the Pyrenees and Portugal.

FREDERICK S. SZALAY
The American Museum of Natural History

DESMARETS, dā-mȧ-rā', **Nicolas** (1648–1721), French controller general (minister of finance) under Louis XIV. He was born in Paris on Sept. 10, 1648. Trained in the controller general's office from the age of 16 by his uncle, the great Jean Baptiste Colbert, Desmarets seemed the logical successor to the office when Colbert died in 1683. Instead, he was exiled to his estates.

Subsequent controllers general, however, urgently needed Desmaret's expert advice. From 1699 to 1708, he was virtual minister of finance. He finally became controller general in 1708 and proved immensely resourceful in nursing the economy through the worst years of the War of the Spanish Succession.

Desmarets was dismissed, along with other ministers, after Louis XIV's death in 1715. He died in Paris on May 4, 1721.

LIONEL ROTHKRUG, *University of Michigan*

DESMARETS DE SAINT-SORLIN, dā-mȧ-rā' də saN sôr-laN', **Jean** (1595–1676), French author. A native of Paris, he became a protégé of Cardinal Richelieu and began to write plays at his patron's request. After gaining a reputation with the romantic novel *Ariane* (1632), Desmarets was admitted to the group that later became the Académie Française. His works include the comedy *Les Visionnaires* (1637), the prose tragedy *Erigone* (1638), the verse tragedy *Scipion* (1639), and the epic *Clovis* (1657). He died in Paris on Oct. 28, 1676.

DE SMET, də smet', **Pierre Jean** (1801–1870), Jesuit missionary among the American Indians. He was born in Dendermonde (Termonde), Belgium, on Jan. 30, 1801. He went to the United States and joined the Society of Jesus in 1821. Ordained a priest in 1827, he was among a group sent west to found the Missouri Province of the Jusuits, but poor health forced him to retire to Belgium for four years. Returning to the American West, De Smet founded a mission among the Potawatomi Indians at Council Bluffs, Iowa, in 1838. In 1840 he visited tribes in the Rocky Mountains and a year later founded St. Mary's Mission near Missoula, Mont. In 1843 he made the first of 16 journeys to Europe to seek funds and personnel for the misions. On his return in 1844 he founded a central mission on the Willamette River in Oregon.

Recalled from active missionary work in 1846 to serve as treasurer and secretary of the Jesuit province of St. Louis, De Smet continued to make periodic journeys among the Indians until his death on May 23, 1870. His rapport with the Indians often enabled him to act as peacemaker and agent for the government. In 1868 he was instrumental in starting peace negotiations with Chief Sitting Bull of the Sioux. His books include *New Indian Sketches* (1865) and *Western Missions and Missionaries* (1863).

CLEMENT J. ARMITAGE, S.J.
Jesuit Missions, New York

DES MOINES, də moin, is the capital of Iowa and county seat of Polk county. It is the most populous city in Iowa and is situated near the center of the state, at the confluence of the Raccoon and Des Moines rivers. The city is a major center for manufacturing and for the insurance, publishing, banking, jobbing, and retailing businesses.

Des Moines took its first steps toward an urban renewal program in 1955, and in 1968 it was one of the first cities in the United States to receive model cities planning grants from the federal government. It is a member of the Central Iowa Regional Planning Commission, which hopes eventually to represent a 9-county area. Several suburbs, including West Des Moines, Urbandale, Windsor Heights, and Clive, have grown up to the west of the city.

The Economy. More than 50 insurance companies have their home offices in Des Moines. The city's industries include the manufacture of agricultural implements, plastics, chemicals, outdoor clothing, automobile accessories and tires, and printing. Several truck, bus, air, and rail lines provide Des Moines with transportation, and the city is on two interstate highways.

Education and Cultural Life. A broad program of public school adult education was developed in the early 1930's, growing out of the Des Moines Public Forum. Smouse Opportunity School provides facilities for physically handicapped elementary school children. Drake University, the College of Osteopathic Medicine and Surgery, Open Bible College, Grand View College, and the American Institute of Business are some of the institutions for higher and specialized education.

The Des Moines Art Center, designed by the Finnish architect Eliel Saarinen and opened in 1958, has an active education program as well as a fine museum collection and library. The Public Library of Des Moines has special collections in the fields of music, business, and local history. The state libraries, including those in law, medicine, genealogy, and Iowa history, are located in or near the capitol. The Iowa Commission for the Blind has the largest collection of materials for the blind in the nation.

The Des Moines Community Playhouse and the Drama Workshop provide the city with active community theater programs. KRNT Theater, one of the largest legitimate theaters in the United States, is used by touring companies. The programs of the Civic Music Association and the Des Moines Symphony attract large audiences.

The morning *Register* and some national periodicals are published in the city. The evening *Tribune* ceased publication in 1982.

Points of Interest. The state capitol and the nearby State Historical Museum contain many items of artistic, historical, and scientific interest. One of the most unusual buildings in Des Moines is Salisbury House, patterned after a 16th century Tudor mansion. Outstanding modern buildings include the American Republic Insurance

DES MOINES is situated on the Des Moines River (top right). The Raccoon River cuts across the city from the left. Its confluence with the larger river is shown at top center.

GREATER DES MOINES CHAMBER OF COMMERCE

Building, designed by the architectural firm of Skidmore, Owings, & Merrill, and the Home Federal Savings and Loan Building, designed by noted architect Mies van der Rohe.

Ewing Park, with its lilacs, and Water Works Park, with its flowering crab trees, are two of the city's most beautiful parks in springtime. There are facilities for golf, tennis, swimming, boating, and skating. A children's zoo was opened in 1965. Professional hockey is represented by the Oak Leafs. The Iowa State Fair is held annually in Des Moines in the latter part of August.

History. Fort Des Moines, named after the river, was built on the site in 1843. Some historians think the name comes from the French word *moyen*, meaning "middle," referring to the Des Moines as the largest river between the Mississippi and Missouri. Others think it derives from French *moines*, meaning "monks," recalling the early French missionaries, or from Moingona, the name of an Indian tribe whose village was on the river. Fort Des Moines was evacuated in 1846 after the Sac and Fox Indians, whom it was intended to protect, moved west. The city of Des Moines was incorporated in 1857 and became the state capital the following year.

A new Fort Des Moines was established in 1901 on land given to the government by Des Moines citizens. Since 1962, sections of the fort have been turned over to the city, the school board, and the College of Osteopathic Medicine and Surgery.

Government. Des Moines adopted the council-manager-ward system of government in 1968. The mayor and two councilmen are elected at large, and four councilmen are elected to represent the wards in which they live. The council determines policy for the city, and administration is under the direction of the city manager. Population: (city) 191,003, (standard metropolitan statistical area) 338,048.

DAN A. WILLIAMS
The Public Library of Des Moines

DES MOINES RIVER, the longest river in Iowa, flowing about 500 miles (800 km) from northwest to southeast across the state. The West Fork and the East Fork rise in southwestern Minnesota. They join near Humboldt, Iowa, to form the main stream, which empties into the Mississippi River near Keokuk in the southeastern corner of Iowa. The Des Moines drains about a fourth of the land area of the state.

DESMOND, dez'mənd, **Earls of,** an Anglo-Irish noble family, notorious for its infidelity to the English crown. Maurice Fitzthomas (died 1356) was created 1st Earl of Desmond (east Kerry and west Cork) in 1329, and his heirs, the Fitzgeralds of Munster, retained the title until 1601.

During the 14th century the earls of Desmond were leaders of Anglo-Irish resistance to the claims of the English crown, and they established alliances with the Gaelic Irish chieftains to achieve their purposes. The Fitzgeralds gradually assimilated into the cultural structure of Gaelic Ireland and established a tradition of marrying the daughters of Gaelic chieftains.

Thomas, the 8th Earl (1426?–1468), was executed for concluding alliances with the native Irish. After his death, the Leinster Fitzgeralds, earls of Kildare, became the dominant branch of the family in Anglo-Irish politics. In the 16th century the earls of Desmond were once more active in anti-English combinations, and Gerald, the 15th Earl (died 1583), became the focal point of the Munster revolt against Queen Elizabeth's political and religious policies. He received some aid in the form of men and equipment from Spain and money from the pope, but by 1581 the rebellion was under control, with Gerald on the run. He was captured and killed in 1583. Three years later the Desmond estates were forfeited to the crown.

In 1600, Elizabeth released Gerald's son James (1570?–1601) from the Tower of London and sent him to Ireland to enlist the allegiance of the Munster Geraldines for the crown's Irish policy. But James failed in the attempt. With him the title became extinct, but in 1598, while James was in the Tower, James Fitzthomas Fitzgerald had assumed the Desmond title. The "straw" Earl was captured as a rebel in 1601 and seven years later died insane in the Tower.

LAWRENCE J. McCAFFREY
University of Maine

DESMOULINS, dā-mōō-laN', **Camille** (1760–1794), French revolutionary journalist and pamphleteer. He was born on March 2, 1760, in Guise, the son of a local royal official. He was an unsuccessful lawyer in Paris when he was suddenly lifted to fame by his forceful street-corner speeches to the Parisian crowds during the great events of July 12–14, 1789, which ended with the fall of the Bastille. In November 1789 he launched a popular newspaper, *Révolutions de France et de Brabant,* which he published until

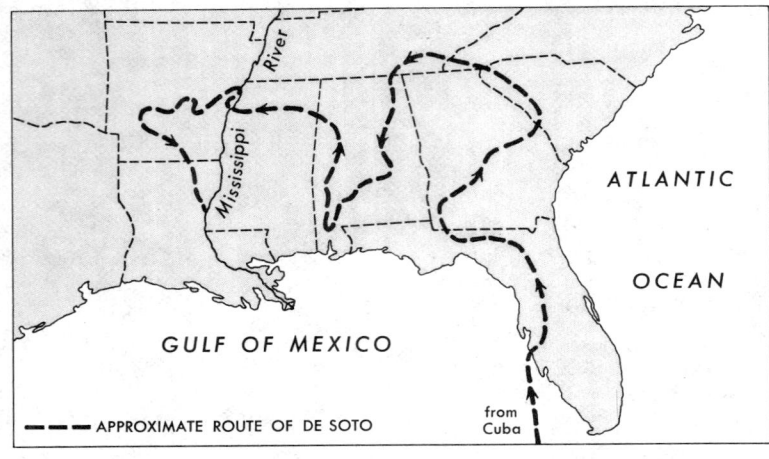

DE SOTO'S ROUTE through the southeastern portion of what is now the United States is not known precisely. The route on the map is only an approximation based on historical study.

1791. Like his fellow journalist Marat, Desmoulins contributed to the radicalization of public opinion.

Elected to the National Convention from Paris in September 1792, Desmoulins proved to be an ineffective deputy and received no important assignments. Gradually he became disaffected with revolutionary measures that he once had supported. Late in 1793 he published the first of a series of pamphlets, *Le vieux cordelier,* that criticized the harsh policies of the convention. Urging a spirit of moderation, he associated himself with Danton and other so-called "indulgents." When Robespierre suppressed the "indulgents," Desmoulins shared Danton's fate. After a perfunctory trial he was executed on April 5, 1794.

ISSER WOLOCH
University of California at Los Angeles

DE SOTO, dā sō'tō, **Hernando** (1500–1542), Spanish conquistador and explorer in the Americas, who discovered the Mississippi River in 1541. He was born in Jérez de los Caballeros, Spain. After completing his education at the University of Salamanca, he went to Panama in 1519 to join his patron, Governor Pedrarias. De Soto campaigned in Panama and then went to Nicaragua to win that province for Pedrarias against Gil González Dávila in 1525–1526. For several years thereafter, in partnership with Hernán Ponce de León, he carried on a profitable trade in Indian captives. Late in 1530 he lent his two ships to Pizarro for the venture to Peru.

Conquest of Peru. From 1531 to 1535 De Soto was prominent in the conquest of the Inca empire. The first European to meet Atahualpa (q.v.), he awed the Inca emperor and his entourage with his horsemanship. He was the first European to enter Cuzco, the Inca capital, with its magnificent buildings and Temple of the Sun.

Following the imprisonment of Atahualpa, De Soto became the emperor's friend and protector. He was off on a mission when, in 1533, the Spaniards determined to execute Atahualpa after collecting the fantastic tribute that his subjects had gathered to ensure his release. On his return, De Soto was very angry, and his respect for Pizarro cooled notably. He stayed on, however, and was able to mediate between the two rivals, Pizarro and Diego de Almagro. But a day came, in 1535, when the situation proved impossible. De Soto went back to Spain, now a very wealthy man.

Exploration and Discovery. De Soto was held in much honor in Spain, and he made a successful marriage in late 1536 to a daughter of Pedrarias, Isabella de Bobadilla. But life in Spain began to pall on Hernando, and he yearned to return to an active life. He hoped to lead an expedition of conquest inland from the kingdom of Quito (Ecuador) to serve as governor of Guatemala. Instead, he was named *adelantado* (royal deputy) of the Floridas in 1537. It was a challenge, for Juan Ponce de León and Pánfilo de Narváez had already failed to conquer the area. The explorer Cabeza de Vaca (q.v.) had returned to Spain, and De Soto tried to enlist him as his second in command; but Cabeza de Vaca had his own plans and merely shared his knowledge of North America with De Soto.

On May 25, 1539, De Soto led the van of his party ashore at Charlotte Harbor in "La Tierra Florida." The next months were spent in futile searching for riches in Florida. In the process Juan Órtiz was turned up, a survivor of the Narváez expedition who had been saved from death by a chieftain's daughter many years before the questionable Pocahontas–John Smith incident; Órtiz proved valuable as an interpreter. But the closest the Spaniards came to great treasure were the pearls at Cutifachiqui, in the realm of the Carolina chieftainess, after they had crossed Georgia. Later they lost the pearls.

De Soto's scouts probably went as far as Tennessee. Then the army moved through Alabama toward the Gulf of Mexico, hoping to make contact with the fleet, which had returned to the Caribbean islands for supplies. At Mabilla (near Mobile) the Indians enticed the Spaniards into a fortified town and very nearly killed them. After that close escape, De Soto's story is one of a frantic search for wealth that was never found.

Moving northward and westward through Mississippi in 1541, the Spaniards came to the banks of the great river, which they called Río del Espíritu Santo. Then they probed into Louisiana and Arkansas, and possibly into Oklahoma. Meanwhile, fever and disappointment had broken the health and spirit of De Soto, and on May 21, 1542, he died and was buried in his river.

Before his death De Soto named Luis de Moscoso to lead the party back to civilization. The survivors reached Mexico in 1543. But even De Soto's failure was not without reward—fame as one of the conquistadors of North America and discoverer of its greatest river, the Mississippi.

JOHN FRANCIS BANNON, *St. Louis University*

Further Reading: Bourne, Edward G., ed., *Narratives of the Career of Hernando de Soto,* 2 vols., reprint (New York 1923); Maynard, Theodore, *De Soto and the Conquistadores* (New York 1930).

DE SOTO NATIONAL MEMORIAL, di sōt'ō, in western Florida, is situated on Tampa Bay, about 5 miles (8 km) west of Bradenton. It commemorates the landing of Hernando de Soto in the vicinity in 1539 and the first major European expedition into the interior of what is now the United States. A stone marker set on an Indian mound indicates the start of the explorer's trail. The memorial has an area of 30 acres (12 hectares). It became a national memorial in 1949.

DESOXYRIBONUCLEIC ACID. See DNA.

DESPENSER was the name of an English baronial family that was active in politics between 1258 and 1400. The family's most famous member, Hugh III, virtually ruled England and Wales between 1322 and 1326, maintaining one of the most oppressive and unpopular governments in British history.

Hugh I was chief justiciar of England three times between 1260 and 1265. He acted in behalf of the baronial opposition to King Henry III and was killed with Simon de Montfort in the rout of Simon's party at Evesham on Aug. 4, 1265.

Hugh II (1261?–1326), Hugh I's son, was protected by his grandfather, Philip Basset, who was Henry III's chief justiciar in 1261–1263. In the 1290's, Hugh II, called the Elder, became a councillor of King Edward I. After Edward I's death in 1307, Hugh was one of the few barons Edward II could depend on for support, and Hugh thus antagonized the leader of the baronial opposition, Thomas, Earl of Lancaster.

In 1317, Hugh II's son, Hugh III (c. 1285–1326), called the Younger, inherited through his wife one third of the immense estates of the earls of Gloucester. The next year Edward II appointed him royal chamberlain, and he thus secured exceptional opportunities for influencing the King, whose favorite he gradually became. He used his position to oust the other claimants to the Gloucester inheritance, which he then tried to extend into a vast principality, covering most of South Wales. As a result the threatened Welsh marcher lords formed a coalition; their forces overran Glamorganshire; and in August 1321 the King had to banish both Hugh III and his father.

Divisions among Edward's opponents, however, enabled him to destroy them piecemeal in a skilful campaign (December 1321–March 1322) that may have been planned by the Despensers. But the victors exploited their victory so ruthlessly that they ruined their chances of establishing an enduring regime. Hugh III, a very suspicious dictator, instituted a reign of terror.

In 1325, in an effort to end a series of disasters in Gascony, Hugh II and Hugh III sent Edward's Queen, Isabella (q.v.), to negotiate with her brother, King Charles IV of France. It was a desperate measure, for Isabella was an irreconcilable enemy of the younger Hugh. After concluding a truce, the Queen organized an invasion of England with a group of fellow exiles and, finding no resistance, captured both Despensers, and had them put to death.

The Despenser family became extinct with Hugh III's great-grandson, Thomas (1373–1400), Earl of Gloucester. He joined a conspiracy to assassinate King Henry IV and was executed.

E. B. FRYDE
University College of Wales, Aberystwyth

DESPIAU, des-pē-ō' **Charles** (1874–1946), French sculptor, whose portrait busts and female nudes are composed of large, simple forms related in style to the work of his contemporary Aristide Maillol. Despiau was born at Mont-de-Marsan, Landes, and studied at the École des Beaux-Arts in Paris. An early work, *Paulette* (1907; Musée d'Art Moderne, Paris), attracted the attention of Rodin, who employed Despiau as his assistant from 1907 to 1914. Despiau's work as this time shows the influence of Rodin, but he gradually turned toward solider, simpler forms influenced by archaic Greek art.

Despiau's *Apollon* (1946) stands in front of the Musée d'Art Moderne in Paris. His other works include a war memorial (1920–1922) for his native town, the portrait bust of Antoinette Schulte (1934; Tate Gallery, London), and *Assia*, a standing female nude (1938; Museum of Modern Art, New York). He died in Paris, on Oct. 30, 1946.

DES PLAINES, des plānz', a city in northeastern Illinois, in Cook county, is situated on the Des Plaines River, 18 miles (29 km) northwest of Chicago, of which it is a suburb. It is primarily a residential community with some light industry, including manufactures of electrical equipment, radio parts, and greenhouse specialties. O'Hare International Airport, one of the world's busiest airports, is just south of Des Plaines. Glenview Naval Air Station is 3 miles (5 km) to the northeast.

Founded in the 1830's, the community was originally known as Rand. It was renamed Des Plaines in 1869 and was incorporated as a city in 1925. Government is by a mayor and council. Population: 53,568.

DESPORTES, dā-pôrt', **Alexandre François** (1661–1743), French artist, who was noted as a painter of animals and hunting scenes. He was born in Champigneulles. Desportes was largely self-taught but he received some instruction from the Flemish animal painter Nicasius Bernaerts. In 1695 he went to Poland for two years to paint portraits of the royal family and members of the court. When he returned to France, he devoted himself to painting animals and scenes of the chase.

A favorite of Louis XIV and Louis XV, Desportes became an official painter to the court. He aided in the decoration of Versailles, Fontainebleau, and the Château Marly, where he painted portraits of the most valuable royal hunting dogs. He also painted still lifes and designed Gobelin and Savonnerie tapestries. The Louvre, in Paris, has many of his works, including *Self-Portrait in Hunting Costume.* Desportes died in Paris in 1743.

DESPORTES, dā-pôrt', **Philippe** (1546–1606), French court poet, who wrote graceful, delicate sonnets and elegies. A native of Chartres, Desportes was appointed court poet by Henry III, who gave him the abbeys of Tiron and Josaphat (although Desportes never took holy orders).

Desportes' early poems, *Premières oeuvres* (1573), which emulate the style of Petrarch and other Italians, have been compared with works of Pierre de Ronsard. His *Dernières oeuvres* (1583) marked his transition from a secular to a religious poet. Desportes died at Pont-de-l'Arche, in Normandy, on Oct. 5, 1606.

DESPOT, des′pət, an absolute ruler, autocrat, dictator. The term generally is used in a pejorative sense, conveying the idea of tyranny, oppression, and even brutality. Because absolute power tends to be abused, so-called "benevolent despots" have been rare.

The word despot is derived from the Greek *despotēs*, meaning a lord or master of the house. The Byzantine emperors used it as an honorary title bestowed on their sons and sons-in-law when named governors of provinces. Alexius III Angelus (reigned 1195–1205) reportedly introduced this title and made it first in rank after that of emperor. See also DICTATORSHIP.

DESROCHES ISLAND, dā-rôsh′, is a tropical coral island in the Indian Ocean, 140 miles (225 km) southwest of the Seychelles Islands. It belonged to the Seychelles until 1965, when it became part of the new British Indian Ocean Territory. Desroches is 4 miles (6 km) long, forming the southern side of an atoll. Copra is produced. Population: (1965) 112.

DESSALINES, dā-sȧ-lēn′, **Jean Jacques** (1758–1806), emperor of Haiti. Born a slave in Grande Rivière, Haiti, he adopted the surname of his Negro master. In the early 1790's he joined the slave uprising in the colony and became one of Toussaint L'Ouverture's chief lieutenants. When the French attempted to reconquer the island in 1802, Dessalines led one of the most ferocious rearguard actions, burning towns and executing Frenchmen who fell into his hands. Soon, however, Dessalines and other Negro chieftains surrendered with a promise of amnesty.

The French shortly betrayed their guarantee and arrested L'Ouverture. In mid-October 1802 the blacks and mulattoes once more raised the standard of revolt. The native forces had a powerful ally in yellow fever. Fighting was brutal and vicious on both sides, but slowly the rebel army under Dessalines' overall command began to defeat the French. On Jan. 1, 1804, Dessalines proclaimed independence; his generals named him governor-general for life. One month later he decreed, and carried out, the annihilation of almost all Frenchmen on the island.

In September 1804, Dessalines proclaimed himself emperor as Jacques I. Despite his authority he was unable to restore order or prosperity, and some of his own lieutenants rebelled. He was killed in an ambush near Port-au-Prince on Oct. 17, 1806.

KARL M. SCHMITT, *University of Texas*

DESSAU, des′ou, is a city in East Germany, in Halle district. It lies 34 miles (55 km) north of Leipzig on the west bank of the Mulde River, 2 miles (3 km) above its junction with the Elbe. It is an industrial city in which the mechanical engineering industries, especially the manufacture of railroad, electrical, and cement-making equipment, are particularly developed. Sugar is prepared from the beets grown on the rich farmland that surrounds the city. Before World War II, Dessau was the center of the Junkers aircraft industry, and the city retains large armament factories. It is also an important railroad junction on the Berlin-Leipzig line.

Established by German settlers, probably in the 12th century, in an area inhabited mainly by Slavs, Dessau received a city charter in the early 13th century. At the beginning of the 17th century it became the seat of one of the branches of the Anhalt family and later was the residence of the dukes of Anhalt. During the 18th and 19th centuries the city became a minor center of art and culture. From 1925 to 1933 it was the home of the famous Bauhaus (q.v.), the school of architectural design founded by Walter Gropius. The old town contained a number of Renaissance and baroque buildings and was a place of great beauty before its almost complete destruction in World War II. Population: (1966 est.) 96,300.

NORMAN J. G. POUNDS, *Indiana University*

DESSYE, des′yā, one of the largest towns in Ethiopia, is situated on the edge of an escarpment of the Great Rift Valley, 8,868 feet (2,703 meters) above sea level. Dessye, also spelled *Dessie*, is the capital of Wallo province. It is a trade center and has some handicraft industry.

Dessye was of strategic importance during the war between Italy and Ethiopia in the 1930's. It was captured by the Italians in 1936 but was restored to Ethiopia in 1941. In the 1950's the town prospered as a center along the road to the thriving port of Assab. However, most Ethiopian foreign trade was rerouted to Djibouti in French Somaliland in 1958, and Dessye's economy suffered. Population: (1963 est.) 56,400.

HUGH C. BROOKS
St. John's University, New York

D'ESTE. See ESTE.

DESTINN, des′tin, **Emmy** (1878–1930), Bohemian operatic soprano, who was noted for her range and control of voice and for her acting skill. She was born Ema Kittlová in Prague on Feb. 26, 1878. She studied voice under Marie Loewe-Destinn, whose name she adopted.

Destinn made her debut as Santuzza in Mascagni's *Cavalleria rusticana* in Berlin in 1898, and she remained associated with the Royal Opera House there for 10 years. She also sang in London, where her Cio-Cio San in Puccini's *Madama Butterfly* was a great success in 1905. Richard Strauss chose her for the premieres of his *Salome* in Berlin in 1906 and in Paris in 1907.

Following her New York debut in *Aïda* in 1908, Destinn sang for eight years with the Metropolitan Opera. In 1910 she created the role of Minnie in Puccini's *Girl of the Golden West*. She retired in 1921 and died at Ceské, Budějovice, Czechoslovakia, on Jan. 28, 1930.

DESTOUCHES, dā-tōosh′, **Philippe** (1680–1754), French playwright, who wrote sentimental comedies of the type known as *comédie larmoyante* (a genre between comedy and tragedy). In these works he sought to emulate Molière.

Destouches was born Philippe Néricault, at Tours, on April 9, 1680. A member of the diplomatic service, he served for a time in Switzerland and from 1717 to 1723 in London. He died at Fortoiseau, near Melun, on July 4, 1754.

Destouches' first play, *Le curieux impertinent*, produced with success in 1710, was followed by *L'Ingrat* (1712), *L'Irrésolu* (1713), and *Le Médisant* (1715). His masterpiece, *Le Glorieux* (1732), deals with the conflict between the old nobility and the nouveaux riches. Among his numerous other plays are *L'Ambitieux* (1737), and *Le Dissipateur* (1753). Destouches was the first to translate scenes from the works of Shakespeare into French.

FOUR-STACK U. S. DESTROYER of a type built during World War I and leased to Britain in World War II.

IMPERIAL WAR MUSEUM, LONDON

DESTROYER, a small, fast warship that constitutes the bulk of modern navies. Antisubmarine warfare (ASW) has been the main task of destroyers since World War II, but they are also used for surface torpedo and gun action, gunfire support of amphibious operations, shore bombardment, guided-missile fire, radar picket functions, mine warfare, aircraft fighter direction, pilot recovery, helicopter operation, and, in peace, "showing the flag."

High speed of 30 to 40 knots (56-74 km/hr) is required of destroyers. Their size varies greatly, from about 250 to 600 feet (75-180 meters) in length and about 1,000 to over 9,000 tons displacement. Most are around 3,000 tons and 300 to 400 feet (90-120 meters) long. In the U.S. Navy the largest destroyers are called *destroyer leaders* (DL) or *frigates*, and smaller, slower destroyers are called *escort ships* or *destroyer escorts* (DE). In the British and Commonwealth navies, however, the frigate is the smallest destroyer type. The slang term for destroyer is "can" or "tincan."

The world's first nuclear-powered destroyer was the frigate U.S.S. *Bainbridge*, commissioned in 1962, which was larger than some light cruisers of World War II. Able to cruise 16 times around the world without refueling, this type proved the value of nuclear power for destroyers, always plagued by low fuel capacity.

Propulsion by gas turbines has an exceptional advantage for ASW work—acceleration from 0 to 30 knots (0-56 km/hr) in 5 minutes. In the 1960's, gas turbines drove the larger destroyers of Britain, Canada, the USSR, and other European countries, but not those of the U.S. Navy.

History. The designation "destroyer" is a shortened form of "torpedo-boat destroyer." The automobile torpedo, developed by 1876, was launched from small, swift torpedo boats. Sir Alfred F. Yarrow, British shipbuilder, countered them with the destroyer, over 200 feet (60 meters) long, with new watertube boilers capable of 31 knots (57 km/hr). Destroyers soon replaced torpedo boats as torpedo launchers. The first true destroyers in the U.S. Navy were the 420-ton *Bainbridge* class, launched in 1900, with 2 torpedo tubes and 2 small guns, capable of 29 knots (54 km/hr).

Destroyers were not very effective as torpedo launchers in World War I, but in World War II the Japanese were successful with oxygen-powered long-range torpedoes, launched from cruisers and destroyers. The ASW role for destroyers began in World War I, and in World War II it became their primary mission. A single-purpose ASW type, the destroyer escort, was designed; 450 of these were built for the U.S. Navy.

The best-known U.S. destroyers between the world wars were the 1,200-ton 4-stackers, 242 of which were built between 1918 and 1922. In 1940, 50 of these were exchanged for base rights on six British islands in the Western Atlantic. Others were converted into minesweepers, minelayers, seaplane tenders, and small, fast troop transports.

New designs appeared in 1934 with the *Farragut* class. The World War II American destroyers were the 2,000-ton Fletcher and 2,200-ton *Allen M. Sumner* classes, 245 of which were built between 1942 and 1945. Postwar types were larger, the *Forrest Sherman* class of 1955 displacing 2,850 tons. See also WARSHIPS.

JOHN D. HAYES
Rear Admiral, U.S. Navy (Retired)

NUCLEAR-POWERED FRIGATE, the guided-missile destroyer U. S. S. *Bainbridge*, was commissioned in 1962.

BETHLEHEM STEEL

DESTUTT DE TRACY, des-tüt' də trå-sē', **Count** (1754–1836), French philosopher, whose sensationalistic, antiauthoritarian doctrine, called "ideology," reflected the philosophy that underlay the French Revolution. Antoine Louis Claude Destutt de Tracy was born in Paris on July 20 1754, into a noble family of Scottish descent. He was well read in the rationalist works of the *philosophes* and in the sensationalist philosophy of Condillac. He had a successful military career and was a reform-minded deputy of the nobility to the States-General. Imprisoned for a year during the Terror, he developed his own philosophy, presented in *Eléments d'idéologie* (1801–1815).

Destutt divided mental processes into four categories—perceiving, remembering, judging, and desiring—and attempted to reduce them all to different sorts and mixtures of sensations. Holding philosophy to be only a branch of physiology or zoology, he believed men should be free to discover empirical truth unhampered by religious or other authority. The foremost of the *idéologues*, as he and his followers were called, Destutt became an influential member of the newly founded Institut de France. He was a senator under Napoleon but proposed the Emperor's dethronement to the Senate in 1814 and regained his title, lost during the Revolution, under the Restoration. He died in Paris on March 9, 1836.

F. X. J. COLEMAN, *University of Pittsburgh*

DETECTIVE, one who is employed to investigate persons suspected of crime, or to get other evidence that is not readily available. Generally, the work of a detective involves at least the possibility of legal action. In criminal cases, his work may help establish guilt or prove innocence. In civil cases, no major law firm operates without a skilled investigator.

Most detectives are employed by governments for criminal investigations or other security procedures in connection with regular police service, and are therefore public policemen assigned to detective duty on a temporary or permanent basis. So-called "private detectives" (or *private investigators*—the preferred term) are engaged and paid by firms or individuals.

The term "detective" was originally applied to various members of the police establishment who operated in plain clothes, and whose task was to infiltrate criminal gangs and conduct surveillances of suspected and known criminals. Because the detective's mode of operation often involved fraud and misrepresentation, "detectives" developed a dubious public image. They were often held up to ridicule in literature, although famous "detectives" in fiction include the great Sherlock Holmes.

Use of the term "detective" has diminished. It is often replaced in the United States by terms such as *special agent* (Federal Bureau of Investigation), *agent* (Treasury or Secret Service), *investigator* (state bureaus of investigation), *criminalist* (chemist in a crime laboratory), *operative* (private investigator), *examiner* (government fact finder), or *inspector* (arson squad).

Detective Work. Regardless of what he is called, the detective should be a fact finder. If he is on the homicide squad in a large police department, he may interview witnesses at the scene. A detective on the burglary detail may take plaster casts of jimmy marks on a window that has been pried open, for subsequent comparison with a suspect's pry bar. A Secret Service agent may "tail" persons suspected of passing counterfeit money, or he may examine the medical records of a person who has threatened the life of the president of the United States.

A private investigator working for a private law firm may follow a spouse in a divorce case or discreetly investigate a key witness.

The training of detectives combines practical investigation with modern police science. A detective's work in a crime detection laboratory may range from the comparison of signatures on forged checks to employment of neutron activation analysis to see whether hairs at the scene of a robbery are from the head of the suspect. See also CRIMINAL INVESTIGATION.

MARSHALL HOUTS
Author of "From Evidence to Proof"

DETECTIVE STORIES. See MYSTERY STORIES.

DETECTOR. See RADIO—*Radio Theory and Technology.*

DÉTENTE, dā-tänt', is a French word for the easing of international tensions. It was popularized in the world media after President Nixon's trips to Peking and Moscow in 1972, which seemed to evince a new flexibility in relations between the United States and the Communist powers. After 1972 the United States and the Soviet Union maintained a policy of negotiating on major issues, such as strategic arms limitation; of avoiding confrontations, as in the Middle East; and of cooperating in various other areas of mutual interest, such as trade, scientific programs, and cultural exchanges. This policy continued after President Ford expressed his disapproval of "détente" as the word for it early in 1976.

Since the death of Stalin, brief détentes in U. S.-Soviet relations had occurred after the Geneva Agreement of 1954 on Indochina and following the Cuban missile crisis of 1962. The détente of the 1970's was not expected to end U. S.-Soviet rivalry, but, at least in the American view, it implied more restraint and cooperation than had the policy of peaceful coexistence in the 1960's.

DETERDING, dā'tər-ding, **Sir Henri Wilhelm August** (1866–1939), Dutch business leader, who became a magnate in the world oil industry. He was born in Amsterdam, on April 19, 1866, the son of a master mariner. He entered business at 16 as a bank clerk and later worked for the Netherlands Trading Society in the Dutch East Indies. In 1896 he joined the Royal Dutch Petroleum Co., which was then a small new concern.

Deterding became managing director of Royal Dutch in 1900 and began a policy of amalgamation with competitors to coordinate production and marketing. In 1903 the firm headed a group of closely cooperating companies, including the Shell Transport and Trading Co. of Britain. An agreement between Royal Dutch and Shell in 1907, while not effecting an outright merger, consolidated their finances and formed subsidiaries to handle their production and marketing.

Deterding became director general of the Royal Dutch-Shell group, which eventually included about 200 companies. He died in St. Moritz, Switzerland, on Feb. 4, 1939.

ELEANOR S. BRUCHEY, *Michigan State University*

DETERGENT, di-tûr′jent, a material that increases the cleaning effect of water on soiled objects. There are also nonaqueous detergents that enhance the cleaning power of organic solvents; for example, they are used in dry cleaning and in engine oils to prevent dirt and gummy decomposition products from depositing on the metal. However, this article will discuss only those detergents that are effective in water.

Composition. Detergents vary in composition, depending on the cleaning task for which they are intended. Those that are used for laundering usually contain several basic kinds of ingredients. There are *surface active agents*, or *surfactants*, which are substances that greatly lower the surface tension of water. This physical effect is important in detergency, and many surfactants are effective detergents by themselves. There are also *builders*, which are generally inorganic salts or alkalis that enhance the cleaning action of the surfactant, although they themselves may not be good detergents. Detergents may also contain auxiliary components that impart special performance characteristics to the material.

Soap, which is made from fats or fatty acids, is a detergent. However, in common usage the term "detergent" is not applied to soap but only to the synthetic non-soap substances first introduced in the 1930's.

Surfactants. Surfactants have elongated molecules, one end of which is a water-insoluble nonpolar hydrocarbon, while the other end is a water-soluble polar radical, which may or may not be capable of ionizing. Thus there are anionic (negatively charged), cationic (positively charged), and nonionic surfactants. The anionic and nonionic types are commonly used as detergent components.

Soap is an anionic surfactant in which the polar group is a carboxyl group. Both the free-acid form of soap and its salts with heavy metals are insoluble. Therefore, soap does not perform well in hard or acid water. The synthetic anionic surfactants that have either sulfonate or sulfate polar groups form soluble heavy metal salts and acids. Their ability to perform well in hard water and at low pH is a major advantage.

Most nonionic surfactants are liquids. They tend to be poor foamers and are favored where low foam is desirable. The nonionic surfactants perform well over a wide range of water hardness and pH.

Builders. The most effective builders for synthetic laundering formulations are the condensed phosphates, particularly sodium tripolyphosphate, which is a deflocculant and water softener that contributes greatly to the overall detergent effect. In many detergents, builders serve special functions other than cleaning. For example, silicates boost the cleaning power of soap but contribute little to that of the synthetic surfactants; however, they are used in synthetic formulations to inhibit the corrosion of metal washing-machine parts.

Auxiliary Agents. Among the auxiliary agents used in detergents the most important are the foam stabilizers, the optical brighteners or whiteners, and the antiredeposition agents. Foam stabilizers are organic materials that are closely related to surfactants. Optical brighteners are colorless dyes that are deposited more or less irreversibly on the fabric during washing; they fluoresce in sunlight, thereby producing a brighter than normal appearance. During washing, some components of the removed dirt tend to redeposit on the fabric. An antiredeposition agent strongly inhibits this effect and is an essential ingredient in synthetic laundering formulations.

Types of Detergents. The major categories of detergents are those for personal use, laundering, hard-surface cleaning, and specialized industrial cleaning.

Detergents for personal use seldom contain builders. Soap bars consist essentially of pure soap, aside from coloring and perfume and normal moisture. Synthetic surfactant bars contain binding materials as well as active surfactant. The binders give the bar the desired mechanical properties. Shampoos are usually solutions of synthetic surfactants together with foam-boosting ingredients. They often contain special auxiliaries for controlling dandruff or conditioning hair.

The largest single use of detergents is in laundering. Laundering detergents are most commonly found in the form of spray-dried beads. Such detergents contain 15% to 25% synthetic surfactant, 30% to 40% condensed phosphate, 5% anticorrosive silicate, and 1% or less of antiredeposition agent and optical brightener. The remainder, except for other special auxiliaries, consists of inert inorganic salt, which gives the dried product good physical and mechanical properties. Liquid laundering detergents contain essentially the same active ingredients as the bead type, but in place of the inert salt they have solubilizers and water. Cold-water detergents contain surfactant auxiliaries that soften and loosen the dirt rapidly at low temperatures.

Detergents for hard-surface cleaning contain less organic surfactant and more builder than laundering detergents. The builders vary according to the alkalinity desired and the type of cleaning to be done. Condensed phosphates and orthophosphate are effective, versatile hard-surface cleaners and are used in many different formulations. Sodium silicates are used in machine dishwashing compounds. Scouring powders contain a large proportion of abrasive together with builders, such as ammonia and borax. Window cleaners and fast-acting, liquid general-purpose cleaners may also contain organic solvents.

Most industrial cleaning involves hard-surface substrates. The operations include the cleaning of metal parts during fabrication and before plating or painting; maintenance cleaning of vehicles; and janitorial cleaning. The detergents used are usually high in builder content and contain low-foaming surfactants of high cleaning power. Foam is objectionable because it lowers the efficiency of most cleaning machines.

Detergents and Water Pollution. Early synthetic detergents caused water pollution because their surfactant components were not susceptible to breakdown by bacteria in the soil and in sewage treatment plants. The detergent foam persisted in streams and impeded the operation of sewage disposal plants. This situation has been almost entirely corrected by the adoption of biodegradable surfactants, which are attacked and broken down readily by sewage and soil bacteria. However, there is still concern over the possible damaging effects of the phosphate component of detergents when it is discharged into streams and lakes. Phosphate can stimulate the growth of algae and upset the ecological balance of large bodies of water.

ANTHONY M. SCHWARTZ
Gillette Research Institute, Washington, D. C.

DETERMINANT

DETERMINANT, a square array of quantities, called elements, that symbolizes the sum of specified products of these elements. The theory of determinants is a part of matrix theory (see MATRIX), which in turn is a branch of algebra. Determinants are important in solving systems of linear equations. They also are a useful notational tool in such areas as analytic geometry, calculus, and differential equations.

History. The origin of determinants lies in the solution of linear equations. While Leibniz is most frequently credited with the discovery (1693), some historians indicate that Seki Kowa in Japan knew of their existence prior to 1683. Determinants were forgotten until, in 1750, Gabriel Cramer rediscovered them while working on the analysis of curves. Early developments in the theory were given by A. T. Vandermonde (1771). Laplace (1772), Lagrange (1773), and K. F. Gauss (1801) extended these results.

A firm foundation for modern determinant theory was provided by the works of Augustin Louis Cauchy of France (1815) and Carl Jacobi of Germany (1841). In the following years there was a proliferation of writings in determinant theory. Many other names can be cited, including J. J. Sylvester (1814–1897), Arthur Cayley of England (1821–1895), Karl Weierstrass (1815–1897), and Leopold Kronecker of Germany (1823–1891). Subsequent research interest has shifted from determinant theory to the more general theory of matrices.

Determinants of Second Order. The square array

$$\begin{vmatrix} a_1 & b_1 \\ a_2 & b_2 \end{vmatrix}$$

of four elements a_1, b_1, a_2, b_2 arranged in two rows and two columns is called a second-order determinant. It has the value

$$a_1 b_2 - a_2 b_1. \quad (1)$$

Thus: $\begin{vmatrix} 3 & -5 \\ 6 & 4 \end{vmatrix} = (3)(4) - (6)(-5) = 42.$

Simultaneous Linear Equations in Two Unknowns. Suppose that the following system of equations is to be solved for x and y:

$$a_1 x + b_1 y = c_1 \text{ and } a_2 x + b_2 y = c_2 \quad (2)$$

Ordinary algebra yields the solutions

$$x = \frac{c_1 b_2 - c_2 b_1}{a_1 b_2 - a_2 b_1}; \quad y = \frac{a_1 c_2 - a_2 c_1}{a_1 b_2 - a_2 b_1}. \quad (3)$$

Comparing these results with equation (1), the definition of the second-order determinant, equation (3) becomes:

$$x = \frac{\begin{vmatrix} c_1 & b_1 \\ c_2 & b_2 \end{vmatrix}}{\begin{vmatrix} a_1 & b_1 \\ a_2 & b_2 \end{vmatrix}} \equiv \frac{D_x}{D}; \quad y = \frac{\begin{vmatrix} a_1 & c_1 \\ a_2 & c_2 \end{vmatrix}}{\begin{vmatrix} a_1 & b_1 \\ a_2 & b_2 \end{vmatrix}} \equiv \frac{D_y}{D}, \quad (4)$$

provided $D = a_1 b_2 - a_2 b_1 \neq 0$. When $D = 0$, the given system of equations may either have no solution or an infinite number of solutions.

Since the elements of determinant D are the coefficients of x and y given in equation (2), D is called the coefficient determinant. The determinants D_x and D_y are obtained from D by replacing the coefficients of the indicated unknown with the constant terms in the given equations.

This procedure for solving two linear equations in two unknowns is called Cramer's rule. It can be generalized to the solution of n linear equations in n unknowns.

Determinants of Third Order. The square array of nine elements arranged in three rows and columns is a determinant of third order:

$$\begin{vmatrix} a_1 & b_1 & c_1 \\ a_2 & b_2 & c_2 \\ a_3 & b_3 & c_3 \end{vmatrix}.$$

It symbolizes the sum:

$$a_1 b_2 c_3 + a_2 b_3 c_1 + a_3 b_1 c_2 - a_1 b_3 c_2 - a_2 b_1 c_3 - a_3 b_2 c_1. \quad (5)$$

This rather complicated expression is made up of all possible products of three factors such that no two factors are in the same row or column. To remember which of the terms are preceded by a negative sign, note that terms in which the subscripts are in *cyclic order* (that is, 123, 231, and 312) are positive; the others are negative. Thus:

$$\begin{vmatrix} 1 & 3 & -2 \\ 2 & -1 & -4 \\ 4 & -3 & 5 \end{vmatrix} = (-5) + (12) + (-48) - (12) - (30) - (8) = -91.$$

A double subscript notation is frequently used to locate the individual elements in a determinant. Thus a_{ij} designates an element lying in the ith row and jth column. For example, a_{32} is the element in the third row, second column.

Determinants of Order n. The square array of n^2 elements arranged in n rows and n columns

$$\begin{vmatrix} a_{11} & a_{12} & \cdots & a_{1n} \\ a_{21} & a_{22} & \cdots & a_{2n} \\ & & \cdots & \\ a_{n1} & a_{n2} & \cdots & a_{nn} \end{vmatrix} \quad (6)$$

is called a determinant of order n. The expansion of this array is the algebraic sum of all possible terms consisting of n factors selected so that one and only one factor comes from each row and each column. There are thus $n! = 1 \cdot 2 \cdot 3 \ldots (n-1) \cdot n$ terms in the expansion.

Each term has associated with it an algebraic sign. A rule for establishing the sign may be expressed in terms of subscript inversions. An inversion of positive integers occurs whenever one integer precedes a smaller integer. For example, in the sequence 2,1,6,5,4 the integer 2 precedes 1, 6 precedes 5 and 4, and 5 precedes 4. Therefore, there are 4 inversions. To determine the proper sign prefixing any term, arrange the factors in the term so that row subscripts are in natural order. If an even number of inversions (or none) appears in the column subscripts, a plus sign is used. Otherwise, a minus sign is affixed.

Expansion by Minors. Instead of explicitly determining each of the $n!$ terms that comprise the expansion of an nth-order determinant, it is possible to find the value using minors. The minor A_{ij} of an element a_{ij} in an nth-order determinant is the resulting determinant of order $n - 1$ obtained when both the ith row and jth column are removed. In a 3d-order determinant:

$$\begin{vmatrix} a_{11} & a_{12} & a_{13} \\ \cancel{a_{21}} & \cancel{a_{22}} & \cancel{a_{23}} \\ a_{31} & a_{32} & a_{33} \end{vmatrix}$$

the minor of a_{23} is

$$\begin{vmatrix} a_{11} & a_{12} \\ a_{31} & a_{32} \end{vmatrix} \equiv A_{23}.$$

The cofactor of a_{ij} is equal to the minor A_{ij} with a prefixed sign determined by summing the indices of a_{ij}. If the sum is odd, the sign is $-$; if even, the sign is $+$. For example, the cofactor of $a_{23} = -A_{23}$ since $2 + 3 = 5$ is odd.

To find the expansion of an nth-order determinant, select any row (or column). Then, take the algebraic sum of each element in that row (or column) multiplied by its cofactor. For example, selecting the third row:

$$\begin{vmatrix} 1 & -2 & 1 \\ 2 & -3 & -1 \\ -1 & 2 & -1 \end{vmatrix} = (-1)\begin{vmatrix} -2 & 1 \\ -3 & -1 \end{vmatrix}$$
$$- (2)\begin{vmatrix} 1 & 1 \\ 2 & -1 \end{vmatrix} + (-1)\begin{vmatrix} 1 & -2 \\ 2 & -3 \end{vmatrix}.$$

Expansion by minors reduces the computation of a determinant of order n to the computation of n determinants of order $n-1$. Each of these can then in turn be evaluated by computing $n-1$ determinants of order $n-2$ and so on. Whenever an element in the row (or column) selected is zero, the number of determinants of order $n-1$ that need be calculated is decreased.

Properties. Certain properties are useful in simplifying numerical computations:
(1) If all the corresponding rows and columns of a determinant are interchanged, the value of the determinant is unchanged.

Example: $\begin{vmatrix} a_{11} & a_{12} & a_{13} \\ a_{21} & a_{22} & a_{23} \\ a_{31} & a_{32} & a_{33} \end{vmatrix} = \begin{vmatrix} a_{11} & a_{21} & a_{31} \\ a_{12} & a_{22} & a_{32} \\ a_{13} & a_{23} & a_{33} \end{vmatrix}.$

(2) If all elements in a row (or column) are zero, the value of the determinant is zero.
(3) If any two rows (or columns) are interchanged, the sign of the determinant changes.
(4) If two rows (or columns) have corresponding elements equal or proportional, the value of the determinant is zero.
(5) If each element in a row (or column) is multiplied by the same number p, the determinant is multiplied by p.

Example: $\begin{vmatrix} pa_1 & b_1 \\ pa_2 & b_2 \end{vmatrix} = p\begin{vmatrix} a_1 & b_1 \\ a_2 & b_2 \end{vmatrix}.$

(6) If numbers are added to the elements of a given row (or column), the results may be expressed as the sum of two determinants:

$$\begin{vmatrix} a_1+p & b_1 \\ a_2-q & b_2 \end{vmatrix} = \begin{vmatrix} a_1 & b_1 \\ a_2 & b_2 \end{vmatrix} + \begin{vmatrix} p & b_1 \\ q & b_2 \end{vmatrix}.$$

(7) If to each element of a row (or column) is added p times the corresponding element of any other row (or column), the value of the determinant remains unchanged.

Example: $\begin{vmatrix} a_1+pb_1 & b_1 \\ a_2+pb_2 & b_2 \end{vmatrix} = \begin{vmatrix} a_1 & b_1 \\ a_2 & b_2 \end{vmatrix}.$

Numerical Evaluation. These properties can be used with the expansion by minors to take much of the work out of evaluating a determinant. In particular, property (7) may be used as often as necessary to reduce all but one of the elements in some convenient row (or column) to zero. Expanding by minors of that row or column will then reduce the determinant to the next smaller order. For example, the following determinant of order 4, which would require 24 additions and 72 multiplications for a straightforward solution, may be reduced to a single determinant of order 2 by this method.

$$\begin{vmatrix} 1 & -2 & 1 & 4 \\ 2 & -3 & -1 & 6 \\ -1 & 2 & -1 & -2 \\ 4 & 1 & -1 & -6 \end{vmatrix} = \begin{vmatrix} 1 & -2 & 1 & 4 \\ 2 & -3 & -1 & 6 \\ 0 & 0 & 0 & 2 \\ 4 & 1 & -1 & -6 \end{vmatrix}.$$

The determinant on the right is achieved by adding the first row to the third. Expanding by the minors of the third row results in:

$$-(2)\begin{vmatrix} 1 & -2 & 1 \\ 2 & -3 & -1 \\ 4 & 1 & -1 \end{vmatrix}.$$

Adding the first row to the second and third rows and then expanding by minors of the last column:

$$-2\begin{vmatrix} 1 & -2 & 1 \\ 3 & -5 & 0 \\ 5 & -1 & 0 \end{vmatrix}$$
$$= (-2)(1)\begin{vmatrix} 3 & -5 \\ 5 & -1 \end{vmatrix} = -44.$$

Systems of Linear Equations. Cramer's rule for the solution of n linear equations in n unknowns is a generalization of solution (4), where $n=2$. Suppose that the following n linear equations are to be solved for the n unknowns $x_1, x_2, \ldots, x_n$:

$$a_{11}x_1 + a_{12}x_2 + \ldots + a_{1n}x_n = c_1$$
$$a_{21}x_1 + a_{22}x_2 + \ldots + a_{2n}x_n = c_2$$
$$\ldots$$
$$a_{n1}x_1 + a_{n2}x_2 + \ldots + a_{nn}x_n = c_n.$$

Let D (equal to determinant (6) above) be the coefficient determinant of $x_1, x_2, \ldots, x_n$, and let D_k be the determinant of D with the kth column (i.e., the column corresponding to the coefficients of x_k) replaced by the column of constants $c_1, c_2, \ldots, c_n$ in the given equations. Then, there is a unique solution, provided $D \neq 0$:

$$x_1 = D_1/D;\ x_2 = D_2/D;\ \ldots;\ x_n = D_n/D.$$

If $D = 0$, the equations may be inconsistent (that is, there is no solution) or dependent (that is, there are an infinite number of solutions).

Other Applications. In analytic geometry many equations occur that can be simply expressed in determinant notation. For example, a circle through the points $(2,3)\ (4,-7)$ and $(1,-3)$ has as its equation:

$$\begin{vmatrix} [x^2+y^2] & x & y & 1 \\ [2^2+3^2] & 2 & 3 & 1 \\ [4^2+(-7)^2] & 4 & -7 & 1 \\ [1^2+(-3)^2] & 1 & -3 & 1 \end{vmatrix} = 0.$$

In calculus and differential equations a determinant called the Jacobian is used to test for functional relationships among n functions in n variables. The Wronskian is another determinant used in testing a set of n functions in a single variable for linear independence.

LOUISE GRINSTEIN
Kingsborough Community College, N.Y.

Further Reading: Aitken, Alexander C., *Determinants and Matrices* (Edinburgh 1939); Muir, Thomas, *The Theory of Determinants in the Historical Order of Development*, 4 vols. (London 1906–1923); Hart, William L., *College Algebra* (Boston 1966); Uspensky, James V., *Theory of Equations* (New York 1948).

DETERMINISM. See FREE WILL AND DETERMINISM.

DETONATOR. See BLASTING; EXPLOSIVES.

DETRITUS, di-trī'təs, is a term applied in geology to the rock waste formed by disintegration of rocks, and to accumulations of such waste. Detritus may consist of fragments showing little or no sign of weathering, debris, or more or less water-worn materials such as gravel, sand, or clay, or an admixture of these. The term is especially applicable to fragments that, if consolidated, would form the rock known as breccia.

Civic Center in downtown Detroit. Cars park on the roof of Cobo Hall; just beyond is the round Convention Arena.

DETROIT, di-troit', a city in southeastern Michigan, seat of Wayne county, is the most populous city in the state and the sixth largest in the United States. It is situated across the Detroit River from the Canadian city of Windsor, Ontario. Detroit stretches along the river for 11 miles (18 km). The city, on the western bank of the river, is shaped roughly like a half-circle. Two independent cities, Highland Park and Hamtramck, lie entirely within Detroit's boundaries. As the birthplace of the automobile industry in the United States, and still the contry's largest producer of motor vehicles, Detroit is popularly known as the Motor City.

Skyscrapers rise along the busy riverfront in downtown Detroit and cluster at the foot of Woodward Avenue, the main highway northward from the city. Nearby, on the river, is the Detroit Civic Center, including Cobo Hall, the Convention Arena, Veterans Memorial, and the Ford Auditorium. The 73-story Detroit Plaza Hotel, centerpiece of the Renaissance Center on the riverfront, was opened in mid-March 1977. Here too are the Detroit-Windsor vehicular tunnel entrance and the Ambassador Bridge, both important links between the United States and Canada.

Streets in the downtown section of Detroit radiate from Grand Circus Park following a plan adapted from that of Pierre Charles L'Enfant for Washington, D. C. Considerable rehabilitation has been necessary in this part of the city. In the residential districts, the old blends with the new as 19th century houses are dwarfed by new highrise apartment buildings.

The Detroit metropolitan area is the fifth most populous in the United States. It extends southwestward into Monroe county, on Lake

INFORMATION HIGHLIGHTS

Population: (1980 census) city, 1,203,339; metropolitan area (including Wayne county and parts of Monroe, Oakland, and Macomb counties), 4,353,413.
Land Area: City, 139.6 square miles (360 sq km).
Elevation: 581 feet (177 meters), measured at the Detroit River.
Climate: Mean temperatures—January, 26.2° F (−4° C); July, 73.3° F (23° C). Normal precipitation—31.03 inches (775 mm) annually.
Government: Mayor and 9-member city council.
Date of Founding: July 24, 1701.

Erie, and covers Wayne county. It also includes much of Oakland county and Macomb county on Lake St. Clair. Lake St. Clair lies just north of Detroit and is connected with Lake Erie by the Detroit River and with Lake Huron by the St. Clair River.

The city's name, given to the site in 1701 by the original French settlers there, is taken from the French word *détroit,* meaning "strait" or "narrows", since the French considered the Detroit River to be a strait on the Great Lakes.

The city's cosmopolitan character was established in the 19th century when large numbers of English, Irish, Canadians, Germans, and French migrated to Detroit and other parts of Michigan. By 1900 the percentage of foreign-born had reached 34%. Migration of Russians, Austrians, and Hungarians highlighted the first decade of the 20th century, followed by a Polish migration in the 1910-1920 period. As a result of the immigration laws of the 1920's the foreign-born percentage dropped steadily.

Housing and Urban Renewal. Detroit is a city of homeowners. Of the city's total dwelling units, approximately 30% are single homes, and owners occupy over 75% of the dwellings. However, in some sections of the city, once well-kept residential districts have deteriorated. Measures taken to clear these areas and convert the land to profitable use were started in 1946 and were expanded in 1949, when the National Housing Act provided federal assistance. In recent years the city has undertaken further rehabilitation projects at its own expense.

The Detroit Housing Commission is the official urban renewal agency for the city. It operates more than 8,000 permanent low-rent public housing units. When a blighted area is cleared of homes, the housing commission assists displaced persons to become relocated. By the late 1960's, more than 8,000 families and 1,000 businesses had been successfully relocated. By that time, too, 24 federally assisted and 6 city-funded redevelopment projects were under way.

Typical of the redevelopment projects in Detroit is the Gratiot project that was completed in 1963. Before the ground was cleared in 1954, it was a typical slum area where 1,958 families and 989 individuals lived in deplorable conditions. Today the area has 1,700 tower and townhouse apartments in eight residential developments. A new elementary school, a shopping center, and a park serve the project's 4,000 residents. It is also the site of the Lafayette Clinic, Wayne State University School of Medicine, and the Detroit Housing Commission.

Fourteen conservation projects, which differ from the redevelopment program because they attempt to fight blight rather than to remove it and replace it, were under way in Detroit in the late 1960's. Five of these were federally assisted, and nine were city financed. These voluntary neighborhood projects have "grass roots" leadership but work closely with the Mayor's Committee for Human Resources Development, Keep Detroit Beautiful, Inc., and the Mayor's Committee for Neighborhood Conservation and Improved Housing. They are assisted by city departments, citizens, businesses, and religious and educational groups.

Suburban Changes. Despite the phenomenal growth of some Detroit suburbs between 1940 and 1970, particularly of certain suburbs north and west of the city, many suburban cities showed a marked decrease in population in the 1970's. Dearborn, in Wayne county, dropped from 104,199 in 1970 to 90,660 in 1980; while Warren, in Macomb county, dropped from 179,260 to 151,134 in the same period. Livonia declined from 110,109 in 1970 to 104,814 in 1980. In the entire Detroit metropolitan area, the population decreased from 4,435,051 in 1970 to 4,353,413 in 1980.

The Economy. Detroit's prominence as a manufacturing center dates back to the mid-19th century. Following the decline of the fur trade in the 1820's, Detroit became one of the leading shipbuilding cities on the Great Lakes and an important flour and grain center. By 1860, Detroit also produced steam engines, railroad cars, boilers, stoves, furnaces, and other machinery. These industries expanded in the post-Civil War decades and were joined by the manufacture of drugs, tobacco products, and paint. With the discovery of huge beds of salt under the Detroit area in the late 19th century, a flourishing chemical industry sprang up.

THE HORACE H. RACKHAM MEMORIAL is the center for many engineering societies in the Motor City.

By the turn of the 20th century, Detroit was deeply involved in a new industry—the manufacture of automobiles. With experience gained in the production of carriages and bicycles and an ample supply of skilled and semiskilled mechanics, Detroit was able to take an early lead in automobile production. Under the capable and imaginative leadership of Ransom E. Olds, Henry Ford, John and Horace Dodge, Henry Leland, and other Detroiters, the city had captured 20% of the auto market by 1904. It continued to expand its control until the name "Detroit" came to signify the automobile industry in general.

The manufacture and assembly of motor vehicles have been spread to subsidiary plants throughout the United States, but the headquarters of the principal companies remain in Detroit. As a result of this dispersion, the labor force employed by the automobile companies in Detroit has been reduced drastically from that of its peak years.

The city also ranks high in the production of machine tools and accessories, gray iron, foundry items, hardware, metal stampings, industrial inorganic chemicals, drugs, paints and varnishes, wire, office machinery, and rubber tires. Detroit has a higher percentage of manufacturing employment (84%) in the metal and metal products industries than any other area in the United States.

Detroit is the headquarters of the United Automobile Workers, one of the largest labor

ASSEMBLY LINE techniques speed production at one of Detroit's principal automobile manufacturing plants.

town Detroit and connects with the highway to Lansing, Grand Rapids, and Muskegon in west central Michigan on the shore of Lake Michigan. The Walter P. Chrysler Expressway, providing a direct, limited-access freeway to the Straits of Mackinac in northern Michigan, and the Jeffries Expressway, connecting Detroit with Toledo and other cities of the south, are the latest in Michigan's Detroit-centered highways.

Within the city limits, Detroit depends on motor transportation. The city never has had a subway or elevated transit system. Trolley cars have given way to buses, although the agency operating the municipal bus system is still called the Department of Street Railways. Rush-hour traffic in Detroit, in the mornings and evenings, presents many problems for commuters and residents alike.

Education and Cultural Life. There are more than 300 public schools in Detroit, including senior high schools, junior high schools, and trade schools. Colleges and universities in the Detroit metropolitan area include Wayne State University, with an enrollment of more than 30,000 students; the University of Detroit, operated by Jesuits; Oakland University, in nearby Rochester; and the Dearborn branch of the University of Michigan. The Merrill-Palmer School in Detroit and the Cranbrook schools in Bloomfield Hills are well-known private schools in the Detroit area.

The Detroit Public Library, one of the largest in the United States, holds more than 2 million volumes. Two new wings completed in 1963 doubled the size of the library. About 30 branch libraries and 400 deposit collections in public buildings facilitate the use of the library's resources. There are special collections relating to automotive history and labor. The Burton Historical Collection, specializing in books and manuscripts on the old Northwest Territory and on early French and British colonies in North America, is a distinguished research collection.

The libraries of Wayne State University, adjacent to the Detroit Public Library, increase the available research facilities in Detroit. The Labor History Archives of the university, established in 1960, contains records relating to the American labor movement, particularly industrial unions, and related reform movements in America. The Archives of American Art, located in the Detroit Institute of Arts, collects and preserves information relating to American artists.

The Detroit Historical Museum is one of the finest municipal museums in the United States. Its changing historical exhibits tell the story of life in Detroit during the city's 250-year history. The Kresge wing of the museum was opened in July 1968. The museum also administers the Ulysses S. Grant House on the Michigan State Fair Grounds, the Dossin Great Lakes Museum on Belle Isle in the Detroit River, and the Fort Wayne Military Museum.

The Ford Museum and Greenfield Village are popular attractions in Dearborn, which adjoins Detroit on the southwest. The Detroit Institute of Arts, in the Cultural Center near Wayne State University and the Detroit Historical Museum, was forced to add two wings to accommodate its ever-increasing collection of masterpieces. The Cranbrook Institute in Bloomfield Hills operates a science museum and a planetarium.

Detroit has long been closely associated with the development of modern architecture and de-

unions in the world. Founded in 1936, the UAW represents 1,700,000 workers in 1,500 local unions in the United States and Canada. The UAW has contributed substantially to the high standard of living in the Detroit metropolitan area.

Transportation. Detroit's transportation services include domestic and international airlines, nationwide bus lines, major railroads, and foreign and domestic steamship lines. Detroit Metropolitan Airport, in western Wayne county, handles domestic and international flights, while Detroit City Airport, within city limits, provides shorter flights, to midwestern cities. Fifty domestic and foreign steamship lines serve the city. Passenger, cruise, and excursion boats operate between Detroit and other Great Lakes ports. International shipping reaches the port of Detroit via the St. Lawrence Seaway. During the ice-free seasons cargo vessels, including grain, coal, and iron-ore carriers, line the Detroit River piers.

Limited-access expressways speed vehicular traffic in and out of Detroit. The Edsel Ford Expressway runs east-west through the city and connects Detroit with the southwestern tip of Michigan via one of the longest toll-free roads in the United States. The John Lodge Expressway runs northwest from the Civic Center in down-

Renaissance Center, with four office towers surrounding the 73-story Detroit Plaza Hotel, was completed in 1977.

sign. In the 1920's the Cranbrook Foundation in Bloomfield Hills obtained the services of the great Finnish architect Eliel Saarinen to design the Cranbrook buildings and to head the Cranbrook Academy of Art. Saarinen, whose son Eero Saarinen also was a famous architect, attracted a number of artists to Bloomfield Hills, including Carl Milles, the Swedish sculptor.

Entertainment and Communications. Detroiters enjoy the Detroit Symphony Orchestra in the Ford Auditorium of the Civic Center. Concert artists, ballet and dance troupes, and symphony orchestras perform at Detroit's Masonic Temple. Each spring the Grand Opera Association presents the New York Metropolitan Opera Company, and in summer months band concerts are performed under the stars on Belle Isle and at the Michigan State Fair Grounds. The Meadowbrook concerts at Oakland University are also popular.

Theatrical entertainment in Detroit includes New York productions at the Fisher Theatre, as well as professional summer stock and amateur groups. Wayne State University sponsors two theaters, the Jessie Bonstelle Theatre, which produces contemporary plays, and the Hilberry Classic Theatre devoted to Shakespearean productions. Oakland University also sponsors professional theater productions.

Detroit is served by two metropolitan newspapers, the morning *Free Press* and the evening *News*, as well as by major television and radio stations.

Places of Interest. Few buildings remain from Detroit's early history because the disastrous fire of 1805 razed much of the city. Subsequent industrial expansion and urban renewal have also taken their toll. The Detroit Historical Museum reconstructed the J. Bell Moran House, the home of an early French settler. The museum also has a comprehensive display depicting "The Streets of Old Detroit."

Fort Wayne, now a military museum, is said to be the best preserved pre-Civil War fort in the Middle West. It was authorized by the Congress in 1841 and was completed 10 years later. Greenfield Village, built by Henry Ford and opened in 1929, contains 100 reproductions or restorations of historic buildings, including the homes of Thomas Edison, Daniel Webster, Luther Burbank, Orville Wright, and Henry Ford, and the Logan County Court House and the Clinton Inn. Cranbrook Institute has the largest collection of works by the noted Swedish sculptor Carl Milles to be found anywhere outside of Sweden.

Tiger Stadium in downtown Detroit is the home of the Detroit Tigers baseball team. The Detroit Olympia Arena serves as headquarters for the Detroit Red Wings hockey team and Cobo Arena for the Detroit Pistons basketball team. The Detroit Lions football team moved to Pontiac Stadium in suburban Pontiac.

Detroit has undergone a building boom since World War II. Hundreds of new buildings, public and private, have been erected, including many skyscrapers. The 26-story Detroit Bank and Trust Building (1964) was built on the site of Fort Lernoult, a British fort. The Detroit Civic Center, built on the downtown riverfront, offers large convention facilities in Cobo Hall and the Convention Arena. The McGregor Memorial Center, designed by the American architect Minoru Yamasaki, was completed in 1958 on the campus of Wayne State University. More recent buildings are the Renaissance Center (four 39-story office buildings surrounding the 73-story Detroit Plaza Hotel, opened in 1977) and the Medical Center, with four major hospitals.

Parks and Zoos. Detroit has many parks, playfields, and playgrounds covering more than 6,000 acres (2,400 hectares). These facilities, as well as golf courses, driving ranges, artificial ice-skating rinks, outdoor swimming pools, and rec-

THE FORD AUDITORIUM, home of the Detroit Symphony Orchestra, is at the eastern end of the Civic Center. Skyline of Windsor, Canada, is in the background.

CITY OF DETROIT

reation centers are under the jurisdiction of Detroit's Parks and Recreation Department. Kensington Metropolitan Park, 35 miles (56 km) to the northwest, Stoney Creek Metropolitan Park, 30 miles (48 km) to the north, and six other parks operated by the Five-County Huron-Clinton Metropolitan Authority provide recreational facilities for the metropolitan area. Metropolitan Beach, on Lake St. Clair, is one of the largest freshwater public beaches in the world.

The Detroit Zoological Park, located in southern Oakland County, was a pioneer in the display of animals in natural settings. The Holden Museum of Living Reptiles and a penguin house, both opened in the 1960's, are special attractions. A children's zoo and aquarium located on Belle Isle are also city operated.

Belle Isle, about 2 miles (3.2 km) long and 1 mile (1.6 km) wide, lies in the middle of the Detroit River about 2 miles northeast of the Civic Center and less than a half-mile offshore. It was purchased by the city in 1879 and its area of approximately 1,000 acres (400 hectares) has been developed with rose gardens, picnic and playground areas, an athletic field, bridle paths, and a municipal golf course.

Government. Detroit has a strong mayor-type government. The mayor and nine-man council are elected in a nonpartisan contest held every four years, the year following the U.S. presidential election. The city clerk and treasurer are also elected on the same ballot. The councilmen are all elected at large. The man receiving the highest vote automatically becomes the council president and acting mayor in the absence of the elected mayor. The city charter was adopted in 1918.

The chief sources of revenue for the city are a property tax, and an income tax on persons living and working in Detroit.

History. Antoine de la Mothe Cadillac, a French colonial administrator, founded Detroit on July 24, 1701. Leading a flotilla of 25 canoes carrying 50 French soldiers, 50 artisans, and about 100 friendly Indians, he selected a site on a bluff overlooking a narrow strait on the Detroit River. In the weeks that followed, he and his men built Fort Pontchartrain, named after Louis XIV's minister of colonies, and later established a palisaded village on the riverfront, near the present site of Cobo Hall. Cadillac's objective in selecting this site was to control the river traffic and, thus, the rich fur trade of the upper Great Lakes.

The village grew slowly. Cadillac had difficulty recruiting settlers, and the nearby Indians were a constant menace. A series of wars with England threatened the village's existence. On November 29, 1760, the French surrendered Detroit to Maj. Robert Rogers, who led a force of British soldiers against the settlement.

Warfare dominated most of the period during which the British occupied Detroit. In 1763 the Indian tribes, restive under British rule and led by the Ottawa chieftain Pontiac, conspired to capture Detroit by surprise. When this plot failed, the Indians laid siege to the fort for several months. During the American Revolution, Detroit was the headquarters for the murderous British-led Indian raids on the white settlements in Kentucky, Ohio, and western Virginia. Fort Lernoult was built in 1778–1779 to protect Detroit against a threatened attack by Americans under Col. George Rogers Clark.

Although the Treaty of Paris, ending the American Revolution in 1783, provided that Detroit and the rest of Michigan be turned over to the Americans, the British refused to withdraw. It was not until 1796, two years after Gen. Anthony Wayne defeated the Indians at the Battle of Fallen Timbers, that the British at last evacuated the city.

The 19th Century. Under American rule, Detroit prospered. In 1802 the village was incorporated and in 1805 it became the capital of Michigan Territory. On June 5, 1805, a fire completely leveled the city. The new city was laid out on a plan derived from Pierre Charles

L'Enfant's plans for Washington, D.C., with wide streets, squares, and circles. Campus Martius and Grand Circus Park still remain a part of the original Detroit. The city changed hands twice during the War of 1812. Gen. William Hull, governor of Michigan Territory, surrendered to the British in 1812, but the Americans recaptured Detroit in 1813. The Rush-Bagot Agreement of 1817, prohibiting armed vessels on the Great Lakes, marked a new era of harmony between the United States and Canada.

After the opening of the Erie Canal in 1826 and favorable publicity about Michigan, settlement increased the state's population from 31,640 in 1830 to 212,267 in 1840, and to 341,591 in 1850. Most of these settlers arrived at Detroit on their way into interior sections of Michigan. From 1837, when Michigan became a state, until 1847, Detroit was the capital of Michigan.

Meanwhile, cultural activities also flourished. The Detroit *Gazette*, the city's first newspaper, was published in 1817, and in the same year the University of Michigan was founded in Detroit. Literary clubs, lending libraries, and other social organizations were formed in the 1820's.

In the two decades prior to the Civil War, Detroit served as a major station on the Underground Railroad, the route by which hundreds of Negro slaves escaped to Canada. Thousands of Detroiters served in the Union ranks during the Civil War.

The 20th Century. Detroiters also made substantial contributions during World War I—in army volunteers, aircraft, boats, and tanks. Although the economy prospered after the war, Detroit suffered during the depression of the 1930's. Unemployment was widespread, with one third of the work force out of work in 1933. Unions were established and with the aid of federal legislation, won bargaining rights. Following the historic sit-down strikes in Detroit and Flint, Mich., in 1937, the United Automobile Workers was recognized by General Motors in February 1937. The Chrysler Corporation recognized the union in April 1937 and the Ford Motor Company in 1941.

During World War II, Detroit again contributed greatly to the war effort. The Ford Motor Company opened the Willow Run bomber plant at nearby Ypsilanti, and Chrysler Corporation became a leading producer of tanks. Detroit earned the title "arsenal of democracy."

Other wartime developments in Detroit revealed the deep-seated social problems that faced the city. In 1943, racial tensions erupted into a full-scale riot, resulting in death to 35 and injury to more than 1,000 persons. Public officials, business and labor leaders, the clergy, and private citizens worked to solve the acute problems of relations between the races. Substantial progress was made; in fact, Detroit became known as a racially "model city." The United States, therefore, was shocked at the civil disturbance that erupted into a major disorder in July 1967. For five days extremely destructive rioting paralyzed Detroit. Forty-three persons were killed and several hundred injured. Portions of the city were burned to the ground. Black and white leaders, through the New Detroit Committee and other organizations, subsequently joined forces to find lasting solutions to the problems of racial injustice that remained.

PHILIP P. MASON, *Wayne State University*

Bibliography

Bald, F. Clever, *Detroit's First American Decade, 1796–1805* (Ann Arbor, Mich., 1948).
Bald, F. Clever, *Michigan in Four Centuries*, rev. ed. (New York 1961).
Burton, Clarence, *The City of Detroit, Michigan*, 5 vols. (Detroit 1922).
Catlin, George, *The Story of Detroit* (Detroit 1923).
Dain, Floyd, *Every House a Frontier* (Detroit 1956).
Detroit Public Library, *Detroit in its World Setting* (Detroit 1953).
Farmer, Silas, *The History of Detroit and Michigan*, 2 vols. (Detroit 1884).
Glazer, Sidney, *Detroit: A Study in Urban Development*, (New York 1965).
Greater Detroit Board of Commerce, *Facts and Figures About the Greater Detroit Area* (Detroit 1968).
Pound, Arthur, *Detroit, Dynamic City* (New York 1940).

DETROIT'S PUBLIC LIBRARY, one of the largest in the United States, is part of the city's Cultural Center. It has special collections on automobile history and labor.

DETROIT, University of, di-troit, a Catholic coeducational university in Detroit, Mich., conducted by the Society of Jesus. It was founded in 1877 as Detroit College and received its present name in 1911. It maintains three campuses in Detroit as well as Colombiere College, a Jesuit seminary in Clarkston, Mich.

The university comprises colleges of arts and sciences, commerce and finance, and engineering; schools of law, dentistry, and architecture; two evening divisions; and a graduate school offering master's degrees in many subjects and doctorates in chemistry. Degrees in engineering, architecture, accounting, and some other courses are earned through cooperative plans requiring the student to alternate terms of study with terms of training assignments in his professional field. Other special programs include a legal clinic for the poor, which enables student lawyers to plead in courts; programs in Jewish studies and in pastoral counseling; and courses in Canadian and Afro-American history. Total enrollment exceeds 10,000.

WILMER T. RABE, *University of Detroit*

DETROIT INSTITUTE OF ARTS, di-troit', a museum of art in Detroit, Mich., operated as a city department. It was founded as a private corporation—the Detroit Museum of Art—in 1885 and was acquired by the city in 1919. Its present building on Woodward Avenue was opened in 1927. The Founders Society, a membership organization, helps to finance the museum's various services and the purchase of new works.

The institute's collection, which provides a survey of art history from the Stone Age to contemporary times, includes outstanding Flemish 15th century paintings, Dutch 17th century paintings, and American art from the colonial period to the present. Among famous works are *St. Jerome in His Study* by Jan van Eyck, *The Wedding Dance* by Pieter Bruegel the Elder, *The Cemetery* by Jacob van Ruisdael, and murals by Diego Rivera depicting the automotive industry.

WILLIAM H. PECK
The Detroit Institute of Arts

DETROIT RIVER, di-troit', between southeastern Michigan and southwestern Ontario, forming part of the international boundary between the United States and Canada. It connects Lake St. Clair on the north with Lake Erie on the south. It is about 31 miles (49 km) long, and its maximum width is about 3 miles (5 km). Its current is slow, and its depth will accommodate large vessels. As a link in the waterway through the Great Lakes to the Atlantic Ocean by the St. Lawrence Seaway, the river carries large amounts of shipping traffic.

The city of Detroit is on the west shore at the northern end, with Windsor, Ontario, on the opposite shore. Wyandotte, Mich., and Amherstburg, Ontario, are other important cities on the river.

DETROIT SYMPHONY ORCHESTRA, a musical organization in Detroit, Mich., founded in 1914 with Weston Gales as its first director. The orchestra attained national prominence under his successor, the eminent pianist Ossip Gabrilowitsch, who became conductor in 1918. After Gabrilowitsch's death in 1936, the orchestra declined, and concerts were suspended for the 1942–1943 season. Concerts were resumed the following season under Karl Krueger; however, friction marred his tenure, and six years later concerts were again suspended.

The orchestra was reorganized in 1951 under conductor Paul Paray, and in 1956 it occupied the new Ford Auditorium in the Civic Center. Sixten Ehrling was conductor in 1963–1973. He was followed by Aldo Ceccato in 1973–1977. Antal Dorati became music director in 1977.

DETT, Robert Nathaniel (1882–1943), American conductor and composer. Dett, a Negro, was born in Drummondville, Quebec, Canada, on Oct. 11, 1882. After graduating from the Oberlin Conservatory of Music in 1908, he studied at Harvard, Columbia, and the Eastman School of Music and in Paris. He was director of music at the Hampton Institute in Virginia from 1913 to 1935 and conductor of the Hampton Choir on tours of the United States, Canada, and Europe.

Dett was one of the first composers to use Negro folk music in classical forms, notably in his two oratorios, *The Chariot Jubilee* (1921) and *The Ordering of Moses* (1937). His 4-volume *Collection of Negro Spirituals* was published in 1937. Dett died on Oct. 2, 1943, in Battle Creek, Mich.

DEUCALION, doo-kāl'yən, in Greek mythology, was the son of Prometheus and, with his wife Pyrrah, the sole survivor of the flood with which Zeus punished mankind's impiety. When the waters subsided, Deucalion and Pyrrah offered a sacrifice to Zeus. They were told to repopulate the earth by casting their mother's bones behind them. Interpreting this to mean stones, the bones of Mother Earth, they brought forth a new race of man.

DEUS EX MACHINA, dā'əs eks mak'ə-nə, is a Latin phrase, translated from the Greek, meaning "a god from a machine." When the plot of classical Greek drama became so involved that no realistic solution seemed possible, an actor in the role of a god would fly onto the stage in a basket to bring an abrupt end to the action. The basket was actually operated by a crane (*mēchanē*), thus giving rise to the expression, which has come to denote any contrived or extraordinary agency introduced in literature or drama to resolve a difficulty.

DEUS RAMOS, dā'ōōsh ra'mōōsh, **João de** (1830–1896), Portuguese poet, who ranks as one of the best lyric poets in Portugal since Camões. His poems are characterized by sincerity and spontaneity and a simplicity of language.

Deus Ramos was born in São Bartholomeu de Messines, Algarve province, on March 8, 1830. After graduating from the University of Coimbra in 1859, he practiced law briefly and then worked as an editor in Beja for several years. He moved to Lisbon in 1866.

Deus Ramos began writing poetry during his undergraduate days. *Campo de flores*, the first comprehensive collection of Deus Ramos' poems, was published in 1893. His prose writings were collected in *Prosas*, published posthumously in 1898. A new primer, *Cartilha maternal* (1876), which he wrote to replace the old-fashioned ones used in Portuguese schools, was officially adopted in 1888. Deus Ramos died in Lisbon on Jan. 11, 1896.

DEUSDEDIT I, dē-əs-ded'it, **Saint** (died 618), pope from 615 to 618. Little is known of his early life except that he was a native Roman and the son of Stephen, a subdeacon. During his reign as pope he was occupied primarily with disturbances in Italy. The murder of the exarch John of Ravenna in 616 prompted Emperor Heraclius to send Eleutherius to restore order. Deusdedit supported the imperial legate in this effort and also in his successful campaign against John of Compsa, who had seized Naples and declared it independent of Constantinople.

In church affairs Deusdedit tended to favor the secular clergy by appointing them to papal offices that had been held by monks under his predecessors. His feast is celebrated on November 8.

ROBERT SENKEWICZ, S. J.
Loyola Seminary, Shrub Oak, N. Y.

DEUTERIUM, dōō-tir'ē-əm, is a stable isotope of hydrogen. The deuterium atom has one neutron and one proton in its nucleus, while hydrogen has only a proton. About 0.015% of naturally occurring hydrogen is deuterium. Deuterium, often represented by the symbol D, was first isolated by the American chemist Harold C. Urey in 1931.

Deuterium is used as a tracer element in chemical research; in the form of heavy water, D_2O, it is used as a moderator in nucleur reactors to slow down fast fission neutrons. It is produced by electrolytic separation from hydrogen, by distillation of water or liquid hydrogen, and by chemical exchange processes.

Because the atomic mass of deuterium (2.014735 amu) is almost twice that of hydrogen (1.008142 amu), there is a marked difference in their chemical behavior. The principal difference is in the greater stability of the bond between atoms of deuterium in the deuterium molecule, D_2. In biological systems, the decrease in reactivity inhibits cell division and interrupts reproductive processes. Also, the boiling point, density, viscosity, thermal conductivity, and dielectric constant of deuterium are higher than the respective values of hydrogen.

HERBERT LIEBESKIND
The Cooper Union

DEUTERON, dōō'tər-on, the nucleus of the deuterium atom, which is an isotope of hydrogen. The deuteron is composed of a proton and a neutron in a stable but rather loosely bound combination. The two particles of this nucleus are held together by a binding energy of only 2.23 Mev, whereas the average nuclear binding energy per particle in heavier nuclei is about 7 Mev. Because the spins of the protron and the neutron are parallel to each other, the deuteron has a spin of 1. The shape of the nucleus is almost spherical.

The deuteron has been used extensively in studies of the strength and range of nuclear forces and the structure of atomic nuclei. It is especially useful because the internal behavior of only two particles is relatively easy to describe mathematically. As a target or as a projectile in nuclear research using a particle accelerator, the deuteron often serves as a convenient carrier of a neutron. In many experiments using the deuteron as a target, the effects of the proton and the neutron can be considered separately, yielding a first approximation to a neutron target. See also DEUTERIUM.

CLIFFORD E. SWARTZ
State University of New York, Stony Brook

DEUTERONOMY, dōō-tə-ron'ə-mē, the fifth book of the Pentateuch, the opening books of the Bible traditionally attributed to Moses. Deuteronomy, unlike many other parts of the Pentateuch, is largely given to law, not narrative. The word "Deuteronomy" is an English form of the Greek word "second law" used in the Septuagint version of Deuteronomy 17:18 for the Hebrew "copy of the law."

Structure and Style. Almost all the book is cast in the form of speeches by Moses. The first of these (1:6 to 4:43), generally admitted to consist of secondary additions to the book, tells of the journey from Horeb (Sinai) up to the Promised Land and emphasizes the conquest of Transjordania. The second speech (4:44 to 28:68), the heart of the book, has distinct subdivisions: 4:44 to 11:32 is a fervent exhortation to give oneself to the God of the Covenant with one's whole heart; 12:1 to 26:15 is the law of this Covenant; 26:16 to 27:26 recounts various covenant-making rites; chapter 28 lists the blessings and curses that depend upon obedience to the Covenant law. Moses' third speech (29 to 30; also, with 31 to 34, a secondary addition) is a renewed appeal for fidelity. The book ends with a narrative of Moses' last words and acts.

The style of Deuteronomy, even in its laws, is oratorical, but fresh and vigorous. At one time scholars attributed this to prophetic influence. Now, without rejecting all connection with the prophets, they recognize that much in the style is unique. Its rhetorical tendencies and its concern with cult and interior religion reflect the preaching of the priests and Levites, the ancient custodians of Torah (usually translated "law"). See PENTATEUCH.

Theme. The whole aim of Deuteronomy is to persuade one to a total commitment to the God of Israel, which means a total love of God (6:5). Such a commitment is to be lived out not only according to certain basic general laws, the Ten Commandments (5:6-21), but also according to the elaborate religious legislation, the "Deuteronomic Code," in chapters 12 to 26. In the context, no legal formalism is implied. It emphasizes total union with Yahweh. One must worship Him only, and in the proper way. Hence there is an emphasis upon ritual. The negative aspect of this total commitment to Yahweh is that Israel must turn away from anything that smacks of heathenism. This aspect is expressed in a manner harsh to modern ears. However, the positive side, social justice and pure love of the sovereign God, more often receives fervent encouragement.

Authorship. Behind such concerns are the problems of a stratified community settled amid worshipers of other gods, not those of an isolated and classless nomadic group such as Moses would have led. Thus it is unlikely that Moses composed Deuteronomy. But Deuteronomy can be called Mosaic in the sense that all Hebrew law grew out of the basic traditions (for example, the worship of Yahweh alone) that go back to the times in which Moses appears as leader and teacher. The Deuteronomic Code represents this living tradition of law as an adaptable source of guidance in the ever-changing circumstances of life. In fact, Deuteronomy itself represents Moses as giving a new interpretation of law for life in Canaan at the very moment when Israel was changing from nomadic to settled life (29:1), and the Deuteronomic Code shows concrete adaptations of older law to much later conditions.

Deuteronomic Code. Modern scholarship agrees on the hypothesis that the Deuteronomic Code (Deuteronomy 12 to 26) is essentially the same as the book of the law found in the temple under King Josiah of Judah in 621 B.C. (II Kings 22). However, scholars have abandoned the old theory of a pious fraud by which the Code was produced at the time to be "discovered," and so influence the King's politico-religious policy. Josiah's aims were clear well before the book was discovered. Even the total centralization of worship in Jerusalem seems not to stem from Deuteronomy, as is usually supposed, but from a policy that sought political unity through religious centralization. Deuteronomy demands worship in shrines devoted to Yahweh alone; but apart from interpolations in chapter 12, this means not a single shrine but proper shrines devoted only to Yahweh, whatever their number.

In many ways Deuteronomy summarizes the doctrines of the great prophets of the 8th century B.C. They also preached the absolute sovereignty of God, and Israel's special relation to Him, with the consequent condemnation of idolatry. They spoke of God's mercy and love with the consequent demand for justice toward one's neighbor. In addition some believe Deuteronomy (or its nucleus) to be a compendium of doctrine saved from Samaria after its fall in 721 B.C. Even those who argue that its place of origin was Jerusalem hold to an 8th century date.

The exact form of the book of Deuteronomy discovered by King Josiah has been much discussed. The parts of the present book of Deuteronomy certainly had at one time been separate. The question is: When were these elements put together? Since reading the Law frightened Josiah (II Kings 22:11–13), the document probably contained at least some curses like those in the present chapter 28. More important, the basic structure of Deuteronomy—hortatory introduction with historical allusions, then stipulations (that is, the laws), and finally blessings or curses conditioned upon obeying the stipulations—clearly reflects a well-known form for an ancient treaty or covenant. Such a document was ratified by a ceremony, and Josiah's lawbook led him to renew ceremonially the covenant between Yahweh and Israel. This is a further indication that the document had the familiar treaty structure, which called for such a rite. Thus, it would have resembled the present Deuteronomy with all of its basic parts.

Deuteronomy had an immense influence. In the interpretation that allowed worship in Jerusalem alone, it supplied the theology of the historian who gave definitive form to the history of Israel in Joshua-Kings and explained the fall of the Hebrew kingdoms. Its insistence on worship and its insistence that worship was possible only at Jerusalem gave the Judaism that grew up after the Exile its special form and character.

DENNIS J. MCCARTHY, S. J.
St. Louis University Divinity School

Further Reading: Nicholson, Ernest W., *Deuteronomy and Tradition* (Philadelphia 1967); McCarthy, Dennis J., *Treaty and Covenant* (Rome 1963); Rad, Gerhard von, *Deuteronomy* (Philadelphia 1966); Welch, Adam C., *Deuteronomy, the Framework of the Code* (Oxford 1932).

DEUTZIA, dōōt'sē-ə, any of a small group of mostly Asian, shrubby plants of the saxifrage family (Saxifragaceae). Deutzia flowers are white, sometimes tinged with pink, and each one has five petals. They usually appear in the spring or early summer, occurring in long spikes or short, broad clusters. The leaves are opposite, toothed, and often covered with stiff hairs. Deutzias are readily cultivated.

Deutzia gracilis

Deutzia gracilis is a small shrub, often with arching branches bearing large white flowers and bright green leaves. *D. scabra* grows to 6 feet (1.8 meters) and has rough dull green leaves, reddish branches, and white flowers often tinged with pink. A double-flowered form known as Pride of Rochester is very popular.

FRANCES SHERBURNE
Massachusetts Audubon Society

DEUX-SÈVRES, dü sā'vrə, is a department in west central France, the northwesternmost of the four departments that make up the administrative region of Poitou-Charentes. The name of the department is derived from its two rivers. The Sèvre-Nantaise rises in the center of the department and runs northwest for about 80 miles (130 km) to join the Loire River at Nantes. The Sèvre-Niortaise starts in the southeast and flows west some 95 miles (153 km), through the department seat, Niort, and down through the swampy coastal lowlands, emptying into the Bay of Biscay about 10 miles (16 km) north of La Rochelle. The southwestern part of Deux-Sèvres is lowlands, entirely below 500 feet (150 meters), but the northern and eastern sections, comprising the Vendée Hills, are more rugged and higher.

The department is rather sparsely populated. Agricultural pursuits occupy most of the labor force, with considerable production of cereals, vegetables, and some fruit. South of the Loire Valley wine district, the department has a sizable cider production. Livestock are very important, and milk, butter, and cheese are major sources of income. Cattle are the most important, but sheep and goats are numerous in the south.

Niort is a manufacturing center, especially known for its leatherworking and gloves. It also has some light engineering and logging. Melle has some chemical production, and Parthenay, an old fortress town, has assorted food, engineering, metallurgy, and timber industries. Population of the department: (1962) 321,100.

HOMER PRICE, *Hunter College*

DE VALERA, dev-ə-ler'ə, **Eamon** (1882–1975), the outstanding political figure of modern Ireland, De Valera was born in New York City on Oct. 14, 1882. His mother was Irish, his father a Spanish artist. On his father's death in 1885, Eamon was sent to Ireland, where he was reared by his mother's brother at Bruree, County Limerick. He was educated by the Christian Brothers at Charleville and then sent to Blackrock College, Dublin, in 1898. At the Royal University, which he entered in 1901, he was an outstanding student, especially in mathematics. Following his graduation in 1904, he taught mathematics, Latin, and French in various Catholic colleges. In 1910 he married Sinead Flanagan, who bore him five sons and two daughters.

Revolutionist and President in Exile. About 1907, de Valera joined the Gaelic League and later the Irish Republican Brotherhood, a secret nationalist society condemned by the Catholic Church. In 1913 he joined the National Volunteers. During the Easter Rising of 1916 he commanded a battalion of volunteers that inflicted heavy losses on British forces and was the last to surrender.

His court-martial sentence of death was commuted to penal servitude for life, but he was released from prison in England under an amnesty in 1917 and was almost immediately elected a member of Parliament for Clare and national president of Sinn Fein. In 1918, however, he was rearrested for alleged complicity in a (fictitious) German plot and spent nearly another year in jail.

In April 1919, while still in prison, de Valera was elected president of Ireland by Dail Eireann (the revolutionary parliament under which Ireland went to war with Britain). In May he escaped and entered New York as a stowaway. During 18 months in the United States he traveled from coast to coast and raised $6 million for Irish independence.

Opposition Leader at Home. In July 1921 a truce ended the Anglo-Irish War. Although de Valera went to London to confer with Prime Minister Lloyd George, he did not take part in the final negotiations, and he repudiated the treaty signed in December by Arthur Griffith and Michael Collins because it required Irish officeholders to take an oath to the crown and excluded Northern Ireland from the projected Free State. Despite de Valera's vehement opposition, the treaty was ratified by the Dail in January 1922. In the short but bitter civil war that ensued, de Valera's followers were defeated, and he was imprisoned for nearly a year by the government. In 1926 he broke with Sinn Fein and founded a new party, Fianna Fail, which in 1927 became the official opposition. In order to reenter the Dail he had to subscribe to the oath that he had repudiated five years earlier.

Prime Minister. In 1932, Fianna Fail won a majority at the polls, and de Valera became prime minister. He held that office for 21 years —from 1932 to 1948, from 1951 to 1954, and from 1957 to 1959. In 1933 he abolished the oath of loyalty to the British crown and refused to pay further land annuities to Britain. Westminster retaliated by rising tariffs on Irish imports, and there followed an "economic war" (1933–1938), in which Irish agriculture suffered severely. By agreement in 1938, Ireland paid £10 million in settlement of the annuities, and Britain evacuated the three Irish harbors it had occupied since 1922.

Eamon de Valera

WIDE WORLD

In domestic politics, de Valera sought to encourage the development of new industries behind protective tariffs. He was forced to suppress the Irish Republican Army (q.v.). In 1937 he drew up a new constitution, which was ratified by plebiscite. It replaced the Free State with the "independent, sovereign state" of Eire.

On the outbreak of World War II in 1939, de Valera at once declared Irish neutrality—a policy he followed unswervingly despite considerable pressure from Britain and the United States. Neutrality was popular in Ireland, which experienced prosperity through Britain's dependence on Irish agricultural produce.

In 1959 ill health and threatened blindness forced de Valera to retire from active politics. He was elected president (a largely ceremonial office) for a 7-year term, and in 1966 he was reelected. He retired to a nursing home in 1973, and died in Dublin on Aug. 29, 1975.

GIOVANNI COSTIGAN, *University of Washington*

DE VALOIS, də val-wä', **Dame Ninette** (1898–   ), English choreographer and dancer, who, as founder of the Royal Ballet, was a leader in the upsurge of British ballet in the 20th century. She was born Edris Stannus at Blessington, County Wicklow, Ireland, on June 6, 1898. After training with such teachers as Enrico Cecchetti, she was accepted as a soloist in Diaghilev's Ballets Russes in 1923. Two years later she left the company to found, in London, the Academy of Choreographic Art, where students performed her works, as well as opera ballets and other dances, with de Valois as ballerina.

When Lilian Baylis, director of the Old Vic Theatre, reopened the Sadler's Wells Theatre in 1931, she invited de Valois to organize a resident ballet company, the Vic-Wells Ballet. It later became the Sadler's Wells Ballet, and in 1946 it moved to Covent Garden as the Royal Ballet. De Valois, who was created a Dame of the British Empire in 1951, retired as director of the company in 1963.

De Valois' ballets, sturdily wrought examples of dramatic dance, were the backbone of the early Sadler's Wells repertoire. They include *Job* (1931), *The Rake's Progress* (1935), *Checkmate* (1937), and *The Prospect Before Us* (1940). Her books include *Invitation to the Ballet* (1937) and *Come Dance with Me* (1957).

DORIS HERING, *"Dance Magazine"*

DEVALUATION

DEVALUATION is an official decrease in the par value of a currency. Most countries that are members of the International Monetary Fund have registered the par value of their currencies with the IMF. The par value is expressed in terms of gold or of the U. S. dollar, and the countries agree to maintain it within plus or minus 1%. Also, each country has agreed not to devalue its currency by more than 10% without the prior concurrence of the directors of the fund.

The U. S. dollar has a par value of 0.02857 ounces of gold; inversely, one ounce of gold is worth $35. The British pound was worth 0.11514 ounces of gold, or $4.03, in 1948. The first post-war devaluation of the British pound, in September 1949, resulted in a new value of 0.07799 ounces of gold, or $2.80. A second devaluation, in November 1967, resulted in a par value of 0.06851 ounces of gold, or $2.40.

Causes. The price of a currency, like the price of other things, depends primarily upon supply and demand. Supply and demand for different currencies meet on the foreign exchange markets. How do different currencies get into the foreign exchange markets?

Take the example of a manufacturer in Boston who sells a tractor for $4,800 to a tractor dealer in London. The British dealer pays for it with a check written on his own bank in London, in British pounds. At an exchange rate of £1 = $2.40, his check would be in the amount of £2,000. But the Boston manufacturer wants dollars, and so he sells the check in the foreign exchange market (that is, to a large bank, perhaps in New York or Chicago) for $4,800. On the other hand, the British dealer might have been required to make the payment in dollars. In that case, he could buy dollars from the London foreign exchange market (that is, a large London bank), obtaining $4,800 with his own £2,000 and sending the dollars to Boston. The first method increased the supply of pounds in the U. S. foreign exchange market; the second decreased the supply of dollars in London.

(Tourism, private investment abroad, foreign military expenditures, and other factors also affect the supply of different currencies in different foreign exchange markets. See BALANCE OF PAYMENTS.)

If, over the years, the British keep buying far more goods from the United States than the latter buys from them, there would be a surplus of pounds available in New York and a shortage of dollars in London. When London banks start running short of dollars, they will wish to buy more from New York banks, paying for them, as usual, with British pounds, at the rate of £1 = $2.40. But the New York banks may accumulate too many British pounds and will then offer less than $2.40 per pound. When they begin to offer too much less—for example, $2.37—the Bank of England will attempt to prevent the exchange rate from falling below $2.38 per pound. The Bank of England will sell its dollar reserves on the London foreign exchange market to increase the dollar supply in England, and it will sell dollars in New York in exchange for pounds to decrease the supply of pounds in the United States. It will also sell its gold reserves for dollars and follow the same procedure. If the Bank of England runs out of both dollars and gold, it may borrow dollars from the IMF or from the United States or some other country. However, if the Bank of England can borrow no more dollars and so cannot support the price of the pound, the price will begin to go down below $2.38. At that point Britain may decide to devalue its currency.

Effects. The usual cause of a devaluation is that a country continually imports more goods and services than it exports (for some countries, such as the United States, other factors such as heavy foreign military expenditures cause the balance of payments deficit). A major reason for imports exceeding exports may be that the prices of a country's goods are too high in terms of other currencies. For example, if a British motorcycle sells for £100 at an exchange rate of $2.40 per pound, it would cost a Chicago motorcycle dealer $240. If he can buy an equivalent motorcycle from Japan for $225, he probably would do so. However, if the British devalue their currency to $2.00 per pound, the Chicago dealer can buy the £100 motorcycle for $200. So the Chicago dealer may change direction and begin buying British motorcycles, thus increasing British exports.

Devaluation has the reverse effect for the British tractor dealer who paid £2,000 for a U. S. tractor when the pound was worth $2.40. If the pound were devalued to $2.00, the $4,800 tractor would cost £2,400. But if a similar tractor were manufactured and sold in England for £2,200, the British dealer, after such a devaluation, would buy the British tractor rather than the one from Boston, thereby decreasing British imports. It is obvious, then, that a devaluation should result in decreased imports and increased exports, leading to a surplus in the balance of trade.

A government faced with continual deficits in its balance of payments could adopt fiscal and monetary measures and changes in foreign policy that might solve the problem without devaluation. Devaluation alone is only a temporary relief from a balance of payments deficit. For example, an increase in exports and a decrease in imports will tend to cause an economic boom and lead to inflation. In addition, if a country depends upon imports for a large part of its supply of food and raw materials, as Britain does, these supplies will cost more in terms of the country's currency than before devaluation. The cost of food goes up, and the cost of manufactured goods increases, again resulting in inflation. If this inflation is not controlled by the government through fiscal and monetary policies and other measures, the country will lose the benefits of its previous devaluation and will have to devalue again, leading to another round of inflation.

Diversity of Effects. Many underdeveloped countries do not benefit from a devaluation. This is because, even after the devaluation, they continue to import the same goods as previously, and they may not be able to increase their exports.

Among the developed countries, some have a great dependence on imported food and raw materials and therefore benefit less from a devaluation. If a key country such as the United States were to devalue its currency, many other countries probably would devalue their currencies by a like amount, and the United States would lose most of the potential benefits of the devaluation.

LEE C. NEHRT, *Indiana University*
Author of "International Finance for Multinational Business"

DEVELOPMENTAL PSYCHOLOGY is the study of behavioral changes accompanying the growth and development of organisms throughout their life spans. The human life span is conventionally divided into five periods: infancy (birth to about 1 year), childhood (1 to about 12), adolescence (12 to 21), maturity (21 to 65), and old age (65 and over). The critical factors distinguishing these periods are stages in bodily growth and change, intellectual abilities, and general behavior; thus the study of physiology and sociology is essential to developmental psychology.

Developmental psychology originated in late 19th century studies of infant and child behavior. Because these fields remain (with adolescent behavior) the most important areas of developmental psychology, it is often confused with child psychology and adolescent psychology. However, its scope includes behavior at all ages; the psychology of old age, for example, is an important field. See also ADOLESCENCE; CHILD DEVELOPMENT; INFANCY AND INFANT CARE; SENILITY.

DEVENS, dev′ənz, **Charles** (1820–1891), American lawyer, soldier, and cabinet officer. Born in Charlestown, Mass., on April 4, 1820, he graduated from Harvard in 1838 and became a lawyer and politician in Massachusetts. As a U. S. marshal (1849–1853), he delivered a runaway slave to his master under the Fugitive Slave Act but then worked to obtain the slave's freedom.

Devens joined the Union Army as a major at the outbreak of the Civil War and was mustered out as a major general in 1866. In 1867 he was named to the Massachusetts superior court and in 1873 to the state supreme court. After serving as U. S. attorney general (1877–1881), he was reappointed to the Massachusetts supreme court, where he served until his death in Boston on Jan. 7, 1891. The U. S. Army camp at Ayer, Mass., was named for him in 1917.

JOSEPH LOGSDON
Louisiana State University in New Orleans

DEVENTER, dā′vən-tər, is an industrial town in the Netherlands, in the province of Overijssel, on the right bank of Ijssel River. It contains many 11th to 16th century structures, including parts of the city walls, the municipal library (*Athenaeum*), which contains manuscripts and archives, and the Groote Kerk, a 15th–16th century church with an 11th century crypt and a Gothic tower. The town hall dates from 1694.

Deventer's industries include the manufacture of chemicals, carpets and tapestries, textiles, flour, confectionery (notably the famous honey gingerbread, *Deventer koek*), and light engineering products and the printing of books. The town is also a marketing and servicing center for the surrounding agricultural lands. Its port was once accessible to small ships but is now used only by barges and pleasure craft.

Founded in the 8th century, Deventer became an important commercial center in the Middle Ages and was a member of the Hanseatic League. It was the birthplace of the 14th century Dutch religious reformer Gerhard Groote and the center of his religious movement, the Brethren of the Common Life (q.v.). Deventer was a center of the early printing industry, and both Desiderius Erasmus and Thomas à Kempis were educated there. Population: (1978) 64,607.

F. J. MONKHOUSE
Author of "Geography of Northwestern Europe"

DEVERS, dev′ərz, **Jacob Loucks** (1887–1979), American general, who led the Allied forces in the invasion of southern France in World War II. He was born in York, Pa., on Sept. 8, 1887. He graduated from the U. S. Military Academy and became an expert in mechanized and armored warfare.

Early in World War II, Devers supervised the rapid expansion of the American armored force and then commanded U. S. forces assembling in Britain before the invasion of France. Sent to the Mediterranean theater of operations, he served as deputy supreme Allied commander, among other assignments. He then commanded the 6th Army Group, which landed in southern France in mid-August 1944 and drove swiftly northward to link with other Allied forces that had come ashore in Normandy. Composed of the Seventh U. S. and First French armies, Devers' command attacked through Germany and into Austria as the right wing of the Allied Expeditionary Force.

Promoted to full general in the spring of 1945, Devers was commanding general of U. S. Army ground forces until he retired in 1949 to head the American Battle Monuments Commission. He died in Washington, D. C., on Oct. 15, 1979.

CHARLES B. MACDONALD
Deputy Chief Historian
U. S. Department of the Army

DEVI, dā′vē, is a name that is applied to a number of goddesses and to a special ideology in Hinduism. The god Shiva (Siva) is often shown with a consort. This "wife," or Devi, usually becomes a powerful deity in her own right. Shiva is regarded as a withdrawn or merely potential form of the divine, while the Devi manifests his tremendous creative energy. Through her the whole world comes into existence, and the good and evil in life fall to the lot of man.

Devi has several forms. In relation to Shiva she appears in her most benign form, as Uma, the gracious. As Parvati, she represents queenly majesty. As Durga, she is the fierce power of religious wrath. As Kali, she is "the horrible one." The term Devi can refer to all the manifested power of the universe, equivalent to the combined energy of Brahma (q.v.), Vishnu, and Shiva, the Hindu trinity.

Indications of the worship of a feminine power appear in India in the artifacts of the Indus Valley civilization (3250–2750 B.C.). Several seals show a goddess with symbols that may relate to the contemporary notion of the cosmos or may be agricultural or fertility symbols. It is possibly this old form of worship that persists now in rural parts of India in the cult of the Gramadevata—frightening village goddesses usually depicted by crude images or uncarved stones.

The sophisticated worship of the goddess was slow to gain ground during the earliest phase of Indian religious history (the Vedic period, 1500–800 B.C.), which emphasized warlike male gods of the atmosphere. Later developments in Hinduism, originating in the northeastern part of India, brought forth a full-blown system of goddess worship together with complex ideological interpretations of the nature of the goddess.

CHARLES S. J. WHITE, *University of Pennsylvania*

DEVIATION, Standard. See STATISTICS—*Measures of Dispersion*.

THE DEVIL holds a prayerbook for St. Wolfgang, in an Austrian altarpiece by Michael Pacher (about 1483).

DEVIL, The, in Christian belief, the evil spirit, Satan. The word "devil" is derived from the Greek *diabolos* ("slanderer"), while "Satan" is taken from the Hebrew word *shatan* ("adversary").

The view of Satan as the Evil One was developed in the New Testament and in Christian theology. It was largely based on an earlier extracanonical and apocalyptic literature of the 2d and 1st centuries B.C., which in turn appears to have been heavily influenced by Babylonian, Chaldean, and Persian sources. The Zoroastrians of Persia held a dualistic conception of the world as a struggle between the powers of light and the powers of darkness, with neither having supremacy. This Zoroastrian doctrine later became the basis for the Manichaean sect in early Christian times.

The figure of the Devil resembles somewhat the Zoroastrian spirit of Evil, Ahriman. As Lord of the Underworld, or Hell, and caretaker of the souls of the wicked dead, the Devil of Christian tradition also bears resemblances to other underworld spirits of ancient mythology, such as the Egyptian Seth and the Greek god Pluto.

In the apocryphal and apocalyptic literature of the pre-Christian and early Christian periods an elaborate demonology was introduced, containing many names for Satan and referring to hundreds of demons. One such demon, Asmodeus, derived from Persian mythology, appears in the Book of Tobit, which presumably dates from the 2d century B.C. The first clear reference to Satan in the Old Testament appears in the Book of Job. There, however, he is represented as the accuser who is admitted into the presence of God with the heavenly host and who tests men, with the permission of God. Neither the name Lucifer nor the account of the fallen angels appears in the Old Testament, although New Testament statements such as those in Jude 6 and II Peter 2:4, appear to refer to such a tradition. The fall of Lucifer is an important part of Christian teachings, for it explains the origin of the Devil and depicts evil as prideful disobedience to Divine Will. Further, the Old Testament concept of Sheol as the abode of the dead involves no ideas of punishment or connection with Satan.

Early Christian Beliefs. The Christian conception of the Devil as the supreme evil spirit and tempter of mankind emerges through fragmentary references in the New Testament. Beelzebub (Lord of the Flies), originally a Philistine deity, becomes Beelzebul (Lord of Dung) and is called the prince of demons (Matthew 10:25; 12:24–27; Mark 3:22–23; Luke 11:15–18). Also, the serpent of Genesis is identified with Satan in several passages in the New Testament (Romans 16:20; Revelations 12:9; 20:2). (Such a connection between the serpent and the Devil still persists in contemporary American snake-handling cults.) The great red dragon and the Beast of Revelations are equated with Satan. Satan is also seen as the ruler of this world and as the tempter who offers power not only to men but even to Jesus (Matthew 4:5–7; Luke 4:9–12). In the Gospels are a number of references to demoniac possession, or possession by "unclean spirits," whom Jesus exorcised. These spirits have also been identified with the Devil, as disembodied evil spirits.

The early Christians identified all pagan gods and spirits with the Devil and thus considered their worship devil worship. This tendency has continued to the present in Christian missionary work. Baptism into the Christian community often includes a ritual of exorcism with the individual forswearing the service of Satan.

Medieval Beliefs. During the Middle Ages the Devil was often represented as horned, tailed, hairy, and cloven-hoofed, thus showing resemblances to the ancient Greek god Pan and the satyrs. He was also represented as a deformed human being, or as any of a variety of more or less fabulous animals, sometimes winged. Much of the earlier demonology was taken over, and as Christianity spread to new regions, additional pagan gods and spirits, such as the fairies of northern Europe, were converted into demons. Remnants of pagan religious practices were linked to devil worship, which was held to be a major feature of witchcraft and heresy. A denial of the existence of the Devil was also considered to be heretical.

It was believed that the Devil could take on any form he wished, of animals as well as of persons. Among these manifestations were black cats, as witches' familiars, and incubi and succubi. Witches were thought to gather at "witches' Sabbaths" to worship, by means of obscene rites, the Devil in the form of a black goat. Another example of devil worship or Satanism was the Black Mass. This is said to consist of a blasphemous performance of the Mass in honor of the Devil. A description of the Black Mass has been given by the French novelist J. K. Huysmans in his novel *Là-bas* (*Down There*); the authenticity of his version has been disputed, however. The Black Mass is supposed to involve the desecration of a consecrated host. Such an attempted desecration is the subject of the legend of the "Miracle du Saint-Sacrement," depicted in stained-glass windows of the Cathedral of St.

Michael and Ste. Gudule in Brussels, Belgium. According to the legend, Satanists stole a host and pierced it with a knife. Miraculously, the host began to bleed; the men, who could not stop this great flow of blood, were caught and punished. This miracle is still celebrated in Brussels in an annual procession.

The Devil was the subject of many medieval legends, the central theme of which was the diabolic pact: the Devil promises wealth, power, youth, or beauty to a man or woman in exchange for the sale of his or her soul after a given term, usually seven years. The pact was signed in blood. As proof of such a pact, witches were thought to have a "Devil's mark" on their bodies. The intervention of the Devil in everyday life was felt to be a concrete reality, and such a pact could be an explanation for the worldly success of some men and the failure of others. Furthermore, it was believed that the Devil could be conjured up easily by drawing his picture or speaking his name. Thus, many innocuous substitute names were developed, such as the dickens and Mr. Scratch. Many famous persons were believed to have had contact with the Devil and to have been tempted by him, a frequent theme in the legends of medieval saints. The fact that many Gothic cathedrals were never finished, such as those not having two complete towers, is also attributed to the Devil in a number of legends. Among these are the cathedrals of Vienna and Antwerp.

It was believed in medieval times that the philosophers of antiquity were demonologists; alchemists and astrologers were also suspected of dealings with the Devil. The legend of Dr. Faustus expresses this suspicion.

While folkloric representations of the Devil may be humorous at times in the way they manifest the triumph of good over evil and the dangers of sin, the medieval view of the Devil was utterly serious. It formed the central concept in the activities of the Inquisition, in the widespread persecution of witches and heretics. In 1489 two German Dominican monks, Heinrich Krämer and Jakob Sprenger, published the *Witches' Hammer* (*Malleus maleficarum*), in which they showed how to make witches confess their dealings with the Devil. The book constitutes a veritable handbook for prosecutors and witch-hunters. The witch-hunts, which led to the death of tens of thousands of persons over a period of some 200 years, attest to the seriousness with which belief in the existence and activity of the Devil was taken. It is noteworthy that the period of most intense persecution of witches coincided with the Renaissance and the Reformation. See also WITCHCRAFT.

Another example of the reality of these beliefs is found in the many cases of demoniac possession, which, on occasion, could turn into veritable epidemics, as in the case of the possession of Sister Marie-des-Anges of Loudun, France, in the 17th century. While rare nowadays, such cases still appear occasionally, and exorcism is still practiced by various Christian churches.

Persistence in Folklore. The Devil is also evident in European folklore and folk customs. In Austria he supposedly accompanies St. Nicholas on December 6, to punish wicked children, while the saint rewards the good ones. In this custom the Devil is called Krampus and his impersonator wears a mask, horns, black tights, and a long tail as specific diabolic attributes. Representations of dragons in folk pageantry are also interpreted as references to the Devil. Many place-names, names of animals, plants, and objects contain references to the Devil: Devil's Bridge, Devil's Island, Devil's Lake, and Spuyten Duyvil Creek, as well as devil's darning needle, devil's dung, and devil's food cake.

In Art and Literature. Since the Devil was a very real part of the experience of the men of the Middle Ages, it is not surprising that he was represented with great frequency in the art of the period. The Apocalypse formed a frequent subject of illuminated manuscripts and cathedral sculpture, and in both of these the Devil appeared in varied and grotesque forms. Among the manuscripts of this type is that of the 8th century monk Beatus, a work of which several versions have been preserved, and the famous Apocalypse of Saint-Sever (11th century). The sculptures of the great cathedrals, especially those built during the 11th and 12th centuries, abound in figurations of the Devil, both inside the sanctuaries and outside. Undoubtedly the best known are the gargoyles and the Portal of the Last Judgment at the Cathedral of Notre Dame, Paris. Similar sculptures adorn the cathedrals at Autun, Chartres, and Vézelay.

The medieval legend of Dr. Faustus has been a recurrent theme in Western literature, the most famous versions being by Marlowe and Goethe, and in the 20th century by Paul Valéry and Thomas Mann. According to the legend, Faustus employed magical incantations to conjure up the Devil, with whom he then made a compact, offering his soul in return for unworldly knowledge and pleasure. Goethe's *Faust* has been the basis for operas and choral works by Gounod, Berlioz, Schumann, and Boito.

Other famous representations of the Devil in literature are found in Dante's *Divine Comedy* (Inferno, Canto 34), where Lucifer is depicted as a hideous being with three heads, and where Hell and its denizens are given their fullest description. Vondel's *Lucifer* and Milton's *Paradise Lost* may be cited as other examples in world literature. Modern literary representations of the Devil appear in G. B. Shaw's *Don Juan in Hell*, S. V. Benét's *The Devil and Daniel Webster*, C. S. Lewis' *Screwtape Letters*, and in Stravinsky's *L'histoire du soldat* (based on a play by the Swiss writer C. F. Ramuz) and his opera *The Rake's Progress*. The Broadway musical and film *Damn Yankees* was a popular version of the Faustus theme.

In the graphic and plastic arts the Devil continued as a frequent subject into the Renaissance and more recent periods. He is found in various renderings of the Temptation of St. Anthony, as in works by Matthias Grünewald, Hieronymus Bosch, and the modern painter James Ensor.

ERIKA BOURGUIGNON
The Ohio State University

Bibliography

Corte, Nicolas, *Who Is the Devil?*, tr. by D. Pryce (New York 1958).
Grivot, Denis, *Le Diable dans la cathédrale* (Paris 1960).
Huxley, Aldous, *The Devils of Loudun* (New York 1952).
Kelly, Bernard J., *God, Man, and Satan* (Westminster, Md., 1950).
North, Sterling, and Boutell, C. B., *Speak of the Devil* (New York 1945).
Oesterreich, Traugott K., *Possession, Demoniacal and Other*, 2d ed. (New York 1966).
Thorndike, Lynn, *History of Magic and Experimental Science* (New York 1934).

DEVIL AND DANIEL WEBSTER, The, a short story by Stephen Vincent Benét (q.v.), originally published in the *Saturday Evening Post* and then included in *Thirteen O'Clock* (1937), a volume of Benét's stories. In the story, Jabez Stone, a New Hampshire farmer, has sold his soul to the Devil, called Mr. Scratch, in return for 10 years of prosperity. When Mr. Scratch comes to Stone's wedding to collect the debt, Stone appeals to his guest, Daniel Webster, to defend him. The eloquence of the great American statesman wins an acquittal for Stone from a jury of notorious American villains selected by the Devil. The story, now an American folk classic, has been made into a play, a one-act opera with music by Douglas Moore, and a motion picture, *All That Money Can Buy* (1941).

DEVILFISH, any of a group of very large rays. See also RAY.

DEVIL'S ADVOCATE, in popular use, is one who upholds an unpopular or even erroneous position in order to stimulate argument. The term is a translation of the Latin *advocatus diaboli*, a name applied to the official in the Roman Catholic Church's Congregation of Rites who examines all the evidence in causes for beatification or canonization. Properly, this official is called *promoter of the faith*. See ADVOCATUS DIABOLI.

DEVIL'S BIT, a perennial herb found in moist woods and bogs of the eastern United States and occasionally cultivated in shady gardens. Devil's bit, also called *blazing star* and *fairywand*, produces many small flowers in slender spikelike clusters (racemes) at the ends of unbranched stems. The flowers have three sepals and three petals, both of which are initially white but turn yellowish with age. Male and female flowers are borne on separate plants.

The staminate, or male, plants grow to 1½ or 2 feet (45–60 cm) high, with flower clusters that tend to nod gracefully. The pistillate, or female, plants may reach 4 feet (120 cm) in height and have erect flower clusters. In both, the lower leaves are spoon-shaped, 3 to 8 inches (8–20 cm) long, and occur in a basal rosette. Other leaves grow singly along the stem, becoming smaller and narrower as they approach the top.

Devil's bit (*Chamaelirium luteum*) is a member of the lily family (Liliaceae). See also BLAZING STAR.

JOAN E. RAHN
Author of "Experiments in Science"

DEVIL'S DISCIPLE, a comedy by George Bernard Shaw, published in his *Three Plays for Puritans* (1897). The setting of *The Devil's Disciple* is New Hampshire in the winter of 1777, during the American Revolution. The title character, Dick Dudgeon, takes sides with the Devil against the excesses of Puritan respectability. His effect on the lives of others, especially on Parson Anderson, lends humor to the plot and also demonstrates that people make startling discoveries about themselves during a crisis. In one episode Shaw brilliantly portrays a historical personage in "Gentleman Johnny" Burgoyne, the British general, and makes particular fun of both the British military mentality and the religious Puritanism of the Americans.

DEVIL'S ISLAND, one of the three Iles du Salut, 8 miles (13 km) off the coast of French Guiana, South America. The island, about 16 square miles (40 sq km) in area, is dry, rocky, and sandy. A possession of France, it formerly was notorious as the site of a penal colony. Its most famous prisoner was Capt. Alfred Dreyfus (q.v.), who was sent there for alleged treason in 1895. After wide publicity about the harsh conditions on the island, the colony was abandoned, beginning in 1938. The last of the prisoners was repatriated by 1951.

DEVIL'S PAINTBRUSH. See HAWKWEED.

DEVILS POSTPILE NATIONAL MONUMENT, in eastern California, in Madera county, about 30 miles (48 km) east of Yosemite National Park. The feature of the site is a mass of symmetrical blue-gray rock columns rising as high as 60 feet (18 meters), the remnant of a basaltic lava flow that cooled in columnar form. Piles of broken columns lies at the base of the cliff. The monument was establshed in 1911.

JOSEF MUENCH

THE DEVILS POSTPILE NATIONAL MONUMENT in the Sierra Nevadas of eastern California is named for its formations of closely spaced postlike basaltic columns rising to 60 feet high.

DEVILS TOWER NATIONAL MONUMENT, in northeastern Wyoming, in Crook county, is on the bank of the Belle Fourche River. It is a tower of columnar rock, 865 feet (259 meters) high, the remains of a volcanic intrusion. The columns are a fine example of the prismatic structure that some igneous rocks assume in cooling. The Sioux Indians called it "the bad god's tower." It was established as a national monument (the first in the United States) on Sept. 24, 1906. The monument reservation covers 1,346 acres (545 hectares).

DE VINNE, də-vin'ē, **Theodore Low** (1828–1914), American printer, who made important contributions to the development of typography as a fine art. He was born in Stamford, Conn., on Dec. 25, 1828. After serving his apprenticeship with the Newburgh (N. Y.) *Gazette,* he went to New York City in 1850 and worked for the printer Francis Hart, who made him a partner in 1858. When Hart died in 1877, De Vinne became the owner of the business, changing its name first to Theodore L. De Vinne and Company and in 1908 to the De Vinne Press.

A founder of the Grolier Club, De Vinne printed many of its books, as well as such publications as *Century Magazine.* For distinction in the field of printing he received honorary M. A. degrees from Yale and Columbia universities in 1901. A style of type, "De Vinne type," was named for him. His books include *The Practice of Typography,* in four manuals (1900–1904). He died in New York City on Feb. 16, 1914.

DEVON. See CATTLE—*2. Breeds of Cattle.*

DEVONIAN PERIOD, di-vō'nē-ən, a period of geologic time, represented by the Devonian system of rocks. The name "Devonian" derives from Devonshire, England, where the geologists Sir Roderick Murchison and Adam Sedgwick discovered a great sequence of fossiliferous rocks in 1839. They proposed the Devonian system to include these and all contemporaneous rocks. The Devonian period is the middle one of seven periods that make up the Paleozoic era. It is now known to have begun about 400 million years ago and to have lasted for about 50 million years.

Geology. In Devonshire the Devonian system is 10,000 to 12,000 feet (3,000 to 3,200 meters) thick. It consists largely of graywacke and slate, with lesser amounts of conglomerate and of limestone, and much volcanic ash (tuff) and many lava flows. The rocks have been extensively altered by igneous intrusions and are intensely deformed by the compression that produced a bold mountain range across southern England and Ireland during later Paleozoic time. (This range is referred to as the Variscan Alps.) As a result, the original bedding is commonly obscured by foliation, its fossils are largely obliterated or poorly preserved, and the succession of strata is badly broken and locally inverted. The Devonshire rocks are therefore a poor standard for comparison with Devonian rocks elsewhere.

Europe and North America. More important is the large area of Devonian rocks that forms the highlands of Ardennes in northeastern France and strikes eastward across southern Belgium into west central Germany, centering about Coblenz on the Rhine River. Here the Devonian system is thick, relatively complete, richly fossiliferous, and mostly unmetamorphosed. Although

ERA	PERIOD	
CENOZOIC	QUATERNARY	
	TERTIARY	
MESOZOIC	CRETACEOUS	
	JURASSIC	
	TRIASSIC	
PALEOZOIC	PERMIAN	
	CARBON-IFEROUS	PENNSYLVANIAN
		MISSISSIPPIAN
	DEVONIAN	
	SILURIAN	
	ORDOVICIAN	
	CAMBRIAN	
PRE-CAMBRIAN TIME		

considerably deformed, the rocks fall readily into their natural sequence. They have been accepted as the standard Devonian section for Europe and, indeed, for the world. The system is divided into three series and seven stages, as follows (beginning with the oldest rocks): Lower Devonian series—Gedinnian, Coblenzian, and Emsian stages; Middle Devonian series—Eifelian and Givetian stages; and Upper Devonian series—Frasnian and Framnian stages.

Devonian rocks are known in many other parts of the world and are exceptionally well developed in North America. A geosynclinal facies is displayed in the central part of the Appalachian region, where the Devonian system reaches a maximum exposure of at least 9,000 feet (3,000 meters), and is well exposed in the fold belt of Pennsylvania and along the northern margin of the Allegheny Plateau. Here the system is essentially complete, structurally simple, and richly fossiliferous. Ever since the classical study of the area by the Geological Survey of New York (1836–1842), the New York section has been accepted as the standard for North America. The Devonian system in North America is divided as follows: Lower Devonian—Helderbergian, Oriskanian, and Ulsterian stages; Middle Devonian—Erian stage; Upper Devonian—Senecan, Chautauquan, and Bradfordian stages. The Bradfordian stage may be transitional into the Mississippian period that follows.

Old Red Sandstone. Special interest attaches to a nonmarine kind of rock that is widely distributed in the British Isles and is commonly known as Old Red Sandstone. Abundant land plants and many freshwater fish preserved in these deposits afford a record of the rapidly developing land life of the time. The "Old Red" is a complex of interbedded sandstone, siltstone, and shale. It represents the sediment spread by flooded streams across subsiding lowlands in a series of structural basins. It was laid down under a warm and humid climate, probably with marked wet and dry seasons. Although red is the conspicuous color, and in part the dominant one, considerable portions of the "Old Red" are gray or greenish gray. The red portions represent deposits formed on surfaces that were well drained, at least during the dry season; the gray beds were formed in swampy or humid lowlands, where decaying plant debris caused reduction of the red pigment.

Similar red beds in North America—in eastern New York and central Pennsylvania—are recognized as the landward part of a great compound delta (the Catskill delta) that was building west-

DEVONIAN LANDSCAPE, as reconstructed in a mural by Charles R. Knight. The trees in the lowlands are typical of the middle Devonian period.

AMERICAN MUSEUM OF NATURAL HISTORY

ward into the geosyncline during Middle and Late Devonian time. Early geologists named these the Catskill redbeds and believed them to be the youngest division of the Devonian system, resting on the gray marine or Chemung sandstone. The redbeds are now known to be an eastward, marginal, nonmarine rock representing nearly all of the Middle and Late Devonian time and grading westward into (and intertonguing with) the gray marine strata. The redbeds represent the lowlands of the Catskill delta front; the gray sandstones are the shallow sea floor. Traced westward, the beds at each horizon become finer in grain. Thus each time-stratigraphic unit in the region grades laterally from redbeds in the east through gray marine sandstone and siltstone into gray shale, and finally grades toward the west into black shale.

Devonian formations are generally thin and irregularly distributed across the central part of North America but are thick in parts of Nevada and Utah and from there northward through the Canadian Rocky Mountains. In this region they generally contain limestone. Devonian redbeds are thick also in central East Greenland.

Fauna and Flora. Devonian fossils reveal the life of the Paleozoic era at its fullest. In the seas, brachiopods were the dominant shellfish, but clams and gastropods were abundant on the muddy and sandy floors. On the cleaner sea floors the two great groups of Paleozoic corals, the tetracorals and tabulata, were at their climax and made extensive reefs. Bryozoans and crinoids also were abundant, but the trilobites were on a great decline. Primitive fish had appeared earlier, but now more advanced fish appeared in great numbers and variety. Most noteworthy were the lungfish (*Choanichthyes*), which near the end of the period gave rise to the first land vertebrates. In very late Devonian time in Greenland, among an amazing fauna of lungfish, have been found two species of amphibians (*Ichthyostegia*); these are the oldest known air-breathing, four-footed vertebrates.

Equally striking was the spread of land plants. Early in the period, primitive plants such as ferns appeared. By the middle of the period, however, forests of spore-bearing trees with trunks as much as 2 or 3 feet (nearly 1 meter) in diameter were spreading over the lowlands.

CARL O. DUNBAR, *Director Emeritus
Peabody Museum of Natural History
Yale University*

Further Reading: Cooper, G. A., and others, "Correlation of the Devonian Sedimentary Formations of North America," *Geological Society of America Bulletin*, vol. 53 (New York 1942); Dunbar, Carl O., *Historical Geology* (New York 1960); Gignoux, M., *Géologie stratigraphique*, 4th ed. (Paris 1950).

DEVONPORT, dev′ən-pôrt, a seaport of Australia, in northern Tasmania, is situated at the mouth of the Mersey River, on Devonport Harbour, 45 miles (72 km) northwest of Launceston. Its harbor is one of the best in Tasmania, and the city is also a popular beach resort.

Devonport's chief exports are agricultural products, cement, and lime. The city was created in 1890 by the merging of Torquay, east of the Mersey, with Formby, on the west bank. Population: 16,757.

DEVONSHIRE, dev′ən-shər, **8th Duke of** (1833–1908), British political leader. He was born Spencer Compton Cavendish, at Holker Hall, Lancashire, England, on July 23, 1833. His family was one of the most distinguished in the English peerage, and he bore the courtesy title Marquess of Hartington until he inherited his father's dukedom in 1891.

Cavendish was elected to Parliament as a Liberal in 1857 and entered Lord Russell's cabinet in 1866, shortly before its fall. He was a leading member of the Liberal government of 1868–1874 and, on William Ewart Gladstone's resignation in 1875, became leader of the party. When Queen Victoria invited him to form a government after the election of 1880, however, he stepped aside in favor of Gladstone, who had returned from retirement.

In Gladstone's second cabinet Hartington was secretary of state for India (1880–1882), secretary of state for war (1882–1885), and in general the main spokesman for the right wing of the party. In particular, he consistently urged strong action to maintain order in Ireland.

In 1885, Hartington resigned his cabinet office shortly before Gladstone's conversion to home rule became known. He refused to join Gladstone's brief third ministry of 1886 and opposed its attempt to pass a home rule bill. He, rather than Joseph Chamberlain, influenced the Liberals who voted with the Conservatives to defeat the bill in the Commons, and when the dissidents set up the Liberal Unionist party, he was unanimously elected its leader. After the 1886 election he refused to form a government with Conservative support; instead, until 1892, his party gave moral support to a purely Conservative ministry.

Devonshire led the majority in the House of Lords that rejected the second home rule bill in 1893. In 1895 he accepted office in a Unionist government and remained in the cabinet until 1903, when he resigned in protest at Chamberlain's attack on free trade. He died at Cannes, France, on March 24, 1908.

JOHN BROWN, *University of Edinburgh*

DEVONSHIRE, dev'ən-shir, **9th Duke of** (1868–1938), governor general of Canada. He was born Victor Christian William Cavendish, in London, on May 31, 1868. He entered Commons in 1891 as a Liberal Unionist but moved to the House of Lords in 1908 on succeeding to the dukedom. He was governor general of Canada, 1916–1921.

He served through the most difficult years of World War I, notably during the conscription crisis of 1917–1918. This called for restraint on his part—the more so because Canada, under Prime Minister Borden, was then in rapid transition to much fuller control over its own affairs. During Devonshire's term the Borden government greatly enhanced Canadian influence in imperial matters. He was briefly colonial secretary in the Bonar Law government of 1922–1923. He died at Chatsworth, England, on May 6, 1938.

J. M. S. CARELESS, *University of Toronto*

DEVONSHIRE, dev'ən-shir, a county of southwestern England, extends north from the English Channel to the Bristol Channel and east from Cornwall to Somerset and Dorset. It is England's third-largest county, with an area of 2,612 square miles (6,765 sq km). Devonshire is among the richest agricultural counties in England and is extremely popular with vacationists. The county is also known as *Devon*.

The land is dominated by two areas of high ground, both designated as national parks: Dartmoor in the southwest, a bleak granite plateau averaging 1,200 feet (365 meters) with points rising to 2,000 feet (610 meters), and Exmoor, less wild but rising to 1,700 feet (520 meters) near the cliffbound north coast. The south coast has many vacation centers, notably Torquay.

The most important industries are stock raising, dairy farming, and tourism. Plymouth is Devon's chief industrial center. China clay is worked on the southern fringe of Dartmoor, and pottery is made at Barnstaple, Watcombe, and a few other villages. There is some fishing.

Buckland Abbey near Yelverton was founded in the 13th century and was once owned by Sir Francis Drake; it is now a naval and folk museum. At Buckfastleigh, Benedictine monks have rebuilt the ruined pre-Norman abbey. Dartmouth is the site of the Royal Naval College. Exeter, the county seat, and Plymouth were both devastated in World War II but have achieved a new prosperity. Exeter University received its charter in 1955. Population: (1961) 823,751.

GORDON STOKES
Author of "English Place-Names"

DE VOTO, də vō'tō, **Bernard Augustine** (1897–1955), American editor, critic, novelist, and historian, who took a special interest in frontier America. He was born in Ogden, Utah, on Jan. 11, 1897. After serving in the infantry during World War I, he graduated from Harvard College in 1920. He rapidly built a reputation as a writer of controversial social and literary criticism, as an authority on the life and works of Mark Twain, and, under the name of "John August," as the author of popular thrillers.

De Voto served for a time as editor of the *Saturday Review of Literature*, and from 1935 to 1952 he wrote the "Easy Chair" column for *Harper's* magazine, where he addressed himself to a great variety of contemporary problems. *Across the Wide Missouri* (1947) received the 1948 Pulitzer Prize for history. *The Course of Empire* (1952), a history of the exploration of the American continent before 1850, is one of the best books ever written about the American West. De Voto died in New York City on Nov. 13, 1955.

DAVID GALLOWAY
Case Western Reserve University

DE VRIENDT, Frans. See FLORIS, FRANS.

DEVRIENT FAMILY, də-vrēnt', a German family of actors, directors, and producers, prominent in the theater throughout the 19th century. One of the Devrients' pivotal contributions was producing Shakespeare unbowdlerized.

LUDWIG DEVRIENT (1784–1832) abandoned business in 1804 to join a provincial troupe of actors in Thuringia. He become a favorite comedian and tragedian in court theaters at Dessau, Breslau, and Berlin, specializing in Shakespeare (particularly the roles of Richard III, Lear, Shylock, and Falstaff) and Schiller (notably Franz Moor in *Die Räuber*).

KARL AUGUST DEVRIENT (1797–1872) was the eldest of Ludwig's three nephews representing the second generation of Devrients. Karl acted at Dresden, Karlsruhe, and Hannover in both romantic and character parts in Shakespeare (Lear, Shylock) and Schiller (the title role in *Wallenstein*, Philip II in *Don Carlos*).

PHILIPP EDUARD DEVRIENT (1801–1877), Karl's brother, started as an actor and singer, then directed productions at Dresden, organized and directed the grand duke's theater at Karlsruhe, and produced his friend Mendelssohn's revival of Bach's *St. Matthew Passion* (1829). He also published translations of Shakespeare and wrote plays and a fact-packed, 5-volume history of the German theater, *Geschichte der deutschen Schauspielkunst* (1848–1874).

GUSTAVE EMIL DEVRIENT (1803–1872), the third nephew of Ludwig, was as famous an actor as his uncle. For a third of a century he was associated with the court theater in Dresden, also specializing in Shakespeare and Schiller. His Hamlet, played in London in 1852 and 1853, was compared favorably with Edmund Kean's.

OTTO DEVRIENT (1838–1894), son of Philipp, represented the third generation of the Devrient family. After studying acting with his father, Otto became an outstanding director at Oldenburg, Karlsruhe, Frankfurt, Weimar, and Berlin. With his father he edited and published translations from Shakespeare (1872–1876).

J. SHERWOOD WEBER
Pratt Institute

DE VRIES, də vrēs, **David Pietersen** (1592?–?1655), Dutch sea captain, who was involved in a series of ill-fated attempts to plant colonies in North America. He was born in La Rochelle, France, of Dutch parents. As a merchant-navigator, he sailed the Mediterranean Sea, the Atlantic Ocean, and to the Dutch East Indies. In 1631 he planted a colony in New Netherland on the Delaware River near the site of modern Lewes, Del. The Indians destroyed that colony and others De Vries planted on Staten Island, N.Y., and on the Hudson River near the site of Tappan, N.Y., in the years from 1638 to 1643. In 1655, De Vries published *Korte historiael, ende journaels aenteyckeninge van verscheyden voyagiens in de vier deelen des wereldts-ronde*, describing his travels and enterprises. It is a valuable source of information about New Netherland.

CARL UBBELOHDE
Case Western Reserve University

DE VRIES, də vrēs, **Hugo** (1848–1935), Dutch botanist, who rediscovered Mendel's laws of heredity and advanced the theory of hereditary mutations. Darwin's theory of evolution did not explain how individuals inherit the variations on which natural selection depends. De Vries devised a scheme describing how different characteristics might persist from generation to generation, combining and recombining to produce any number of distinct individuals. He supported his view with careful studies of plant heredity.

In 1900, as De Vries was preparing to publish his work, he discovered that Gregor Mendel, an Austrian monk, had advanced a similar theory in 1866 but had been completely ignored. De Vries referred to Mendel's theory in detail in his paper and advanced his own work as mere confirmation. In the same year, two other scientists, Karl Correns and Erich Tschermak, also reported the discovery of Mendel's work.

De Vries was able to go beyond Mendel in one respect. In 1886 he accidentally noticed widely different varieties of the American evening primrose growing together in a close-knit colony that must surely have sprung from a single ancestral plant. De Vries found that each variety bred true in general but would occasionally produce a "sport." Such "sports," or sudden radical changes in characteristics that subsequently bred true, had long been known to herdsmen and farmers, but De Vries began to study them scientifically. He suggested that evolution proceeded as a result of these sudden changes, or *mutations*, that were sometimes quite sizable. Later evidence supported this view, and mutation became important in evolution theory.

De Vries was born in Haarlem, the Netherlands, on Feb. 16, 1848. He studied at the universities of Leiden, Heidelberg, and Würzburg. In 1878 he became professor of botany at the University of Amsterdam. In 1918 he retired to Lunteren, where he continued to study plant mutations. He died in Amsterdam on May 21, 1935.

ISAAC ASIMOV
Boston University School of Medicine

DE VRIES, də vrēs, **Peter** (1910–   ), American author, noted for his good-humored satirical novels and stories. The son of Dutch immigrants, he was born in Chicago, Ill., on Feb. 27, 1910. After graduating from Calvin College in 1931, he became a free-lance writer and the editor of a community newspaper in Chicago. He joined the staff of *Poetry* magazine as associate editor in 1938 and became coeditor in 1942. From 1944 he was on the editorial staff of the *New Yorker*.

No, But I Saw the Movie (1952) is a collection of De Vries' *New Yorker* stories. His novels, many of which are concerned with the absurdities of suburban life, include *Tunnel of Love* (1954) which he dramatized in collaboration with Joseph Fields in 1957; *Comfort Me with Apples* (1959); *Reuben, Reuben* (1964; adapted by Herman Shumlin for the stage as *Spofford*, 1967); and *Vale of Laughter* (1967).

DEW is a condensation of atmospheric moisture on objects that are colder than the dew-point temperature of the surrounding air. (Dew point is the temperature at which air of a given water vapor content and at a given pressure becomes saturated—that is, when its relative humidity is 100%.) The term "dew" is generally restricted to meteorological conditions, but the "sweating" of pipes, the deposit of moisture on the outside of drinking glasses containing ice, and the condensation of water from steam, are all caused by the same physical process.

Formation of Dew. Meteorologists recognize several kinds of weather conditions that lead to condensation of moisture from the air onto exposed surfaces. The most common form of dew is the deposit that forms during calm clear nights. The droplets are often so numerous and tightly packed that they may cover exposed surfaces with an extended film of water. The essential process in this kind of dew formation is the cooling of a surface at night by heat radiation to a clear sky. The dew forms only on those surfaces whose temperature falls below the dew-point temperature of the adjacent air.

A second, less common kind of dew formation sometimes occurs when a brisk, warm, moist wind blows over a cold ground, usually under a cloudy sky. The ground becomes visibly damp or even wet, but the moisture does not stand out in tiny droplets (the usual concept of dew).

Certain objects acquire dew while others do not. For example, the dew often covers only the upper portions of blades of grass, dry leaves, small plants, boards, fences, or roofs; on the bare ground, on sidewalks and stones, and at the base of the grass it is absent. The explanation lies in the differing heat conductivity of the objects. Thus, objects in extensive contact with the ground can draw at night upon the heat stored up in the ground during the day. If they are good conductors, their temperature will not fall so fast during the night. Isolated small objects and poor conductors cool more rapidly than others and thus will sooner reach the dew-point temperature of the adjacent air.

If the moisture content of the air is too low, its saturation point will not be reached, and dew will not be formed, despite cooling. Although the maximum water vapor content of the air for a given temperature determines the quantity of dew deposit possible, it is not usually a critical factor in determining whether dew will or will not form. The probability of dew formation is best indicated by the spread between actual air temperatures in the preceding afternoon and the dew-point temperature of the air, provided the sky remains clear and the wind light or calm. The larger the spread between these temperatures, the more cooling is required for dew to form.

Evaporation from the ground and transpiration from vegetation are not likely to change the outlook for dew once night has begun, because the amounts of moisture thus added to the air are negligible at night. Wind during the night tends to delay or prevent the formation of dew by mixing warm air from above into the lower atmospheric layers, so that the surfaces cool less rapidly. The wind also evaporates any dew that forms.

Climatic Differences. The right combination of conditions for dew formations occurs frequently in middle latitudes and in most parts of the tropics, but is rare or impossible in polar regions. In middle latitudes, the favorable weather situation is usually found in the central regions of transient high-pressure areas, or anticyclones, where winds are light and skies are clear. However, in winter the air may be too dry; and, when the temperature of the surfaces falls below freezing, hoarfrost forms instead of dew. In tropical latitudes, dew forms at night during the dry season and in the deserts. In some deserts, dew may form only on the scattered plants, whose growth depends to a considerable degree on this source of moisture.

Measurement of Dew. It is possible to measure the quantity of dew deposited by means of special gauges. The *Duvdevani dew gauge*, which is the most widely used, consists of specially prepared sticks of wood exposed from sunset to sunrise at standard heights over standard plots of ground. The dew accumulated on the stick by sunrise is photographed and, from a previous calibration, the photographs are interpreted in terms of millimeters of water per stick per night. Other gauges, called *drosometers*, weigh the amount of dew deposited on a suitably exposed plate. See also FROST.

ROBERT G. STONE, *Air Weather Service*
U.S. Military Airlift Command

DEW LINE, a net of Distant Early Warning radar stations near the parallel of 69° north latitude, from northwestern Alaska to northeastern Canada, to give warning of hostile aircraft approaching from the north. The name DEW is an abbreviation of Distant Early Warning. Built and operated jointly by the United States and Canada, it was begun in 1954 and became operational on July 31, 1957. It was extended to the Aleutian Islands in 1959 and across Greenland in 1961. The DEW Line was designed to alert the back-up defenses of the North American Air Defense Command, including the Mid-Canada (along the 55th parallel) and Pine Tree (along the 49th parallel) radar warning and control lines. It provides up to six hours of advance warning of aircraft which may penetrate the Northern Hemisphere, and is complementary to the Ballistic Missile Early Warning System (BMEWS) which since June 1961 has been on guard to detect approaching ballistic missiles. See also RADAR— *Uses and Types*.

JOHN W. CARPENTER, III
Lt. Gen. USAF; Commander, Air University

DEW POND, an artificial pond used to provide water for cattle on streamless uplands, such as the chalk downs of southern England. In making a dew pond, a shallow, saucer-shaped depression is dug in the ground and lined with layers of straw and wet clay. The lining provides insulation from the heat of the earth and holds moisture. The banks are built up sufficiently to prevent destruction by animal hoofs. Loose flints are laid on the bottom of the dew pond and some water is poured in to make a start. The night mists and dews then readily condense on the surface of the pond. The supply of water in dew ponds does not fail, even during hot summers.

No archaeological evidence has yet been found to support the long-held view that dew ponds were a common feature of the Iron Age hilltop strongholds of pre-Roman Britain. It is likely that the water table in the chalk downs was higher then, so that springs were available in valleys that are now waterless. A dew pond at Orna Mere in Wiltshire survives from the 9th century A.D., but most dew ponds located near archaeological sites are quite modern. For example, the ancient Chanctonbury Ring in Sussex is adjoined by a dew pond that was constructed in 1874.

THOMAS KINGSTON DERRY
Coauthor of "A Short History of Technology"

DEWAR, dū′ər, **Sir James** (1842–1923) British chemist, who is best known for his experimental techniques in the production of high vacuums and low temperatures. He was born in Kincardine, Scotland, on Sept. 20, 1842. He was educated at Edinburgh University and taught there and at the Royal Veterinary College. Dewar became Jacksonian professor at Cambridge in 1875 and Fullerian professor at the Royal Institution in London in 1877, holding both posts until his death, in London, on March 27, 1923.

Dewar proposed a structural formula for benzene in 1867. While working on calorimetry in 1872, he invented the famous vacuum jacket, called *Dewar's flask*. It became an essential tool in low temperature science, and later a modification, commonly known as a thermos bottle, found wide use. Had he patented his invention, he might have made a fortune.

Dewar's chief work was on the liquefaction of gases. He was the first to liquefy oxygen fully (1884), and he showed the magnetic properties of oxygen and ozone in 1891. Dewar liquefied hydrogen in 1898 and solidified it in 1899. He also liquefied and solidified fluorine. Dewar's use of liquid-air temperature charcoal for producing extremely high vacuums was a major contribution to atomic physics techniques. He also worked with Sir Frederick Abel in the development of the propellant-explosive cordite.

FRANK GREENAWAY, *Science Museum, London*

DEWAS, dä-wäs′, a former princely state of India, is now a district in western Madhya Pradesh state. Dewas, which has an area of 2,765 square miles (7,160 sq km), is situated on the western slopes of the Vindhya Hills.

In the 10th century the area was controlled by Bundela Rajputs, but between the 14th and 18th centuries Dewas was tributary to the Muslim rulers of Malwa. In 1728 Ponwar Marathas, claiming Rajput descent, reasserted Hindu control. In 1841, under the British, two principalities, Dewas Senior and Dewas Junior, emerged. Both merged into independent India in 1948, and together form the present district.

The town of Dewas, the former princely capital, lies 22 miles (35 km) northeast of Indore, at the foot of Chamunda hill. Atop the hill is the famous Devivasini shrine. Population: (1961) of the town, 34,577.

BRIJEN K. GUPTA, *Brooklyn College*

Dewdrop (*Dalibarda repens*)

DEWBERRY is the name given to certain trailing species of blackberries and also to the sweet edible fruits of these plants. Dewberries are perennial plants, but the individual canes flower and fruit during their second year and then die at the end of that season.

Several principal species of dewberries grow in North America. The northern dewberry (*Rubus flagellaris*) ranges from Nova Scotia and Quebec to Minnesota and south to Tennessee and Texas. A few cultivated varieties, including the popular Lucretia, appear to belong to this species. The southern dewberry (*R. trivialis*) ranges as far north as Virginia and as far west as Oklahoma. The Gregg, Houston, and Manatee varieties are thought to be of this species. The California dewberry (*R. vitifolius*) grows in California and is found along stream banks and in other moist places. A popular variety of this species, the Mammoth Blackberry, has large fruits and leaves. Closely related to the California dewberry is *R. macropetalus*, which ranges from northern California to British Columbia. It is the source of the varieties known as Skagit Chief, Zelinski, and Washington Climbing.

LAWRENCE ERBE
University of Southwestern Louisiana

DEWDNEY, dūd'nē, **Edgar** (1835–1916), Canadian political leader and administrator. He was born in Devonshire, England, and went to British Columbia in 1859. He was chosen by Gov. James Douglas to plan New Westminster as capital of the new colony; then, to bring gold-rush miners to British rather than American territory, he laid a trail to Wild Horse Creek.

Elected as a Conservative to the British Columbia legislature (1869) and then to the federal House of Commons (1872), Dewdney consistently supported Prime Minister John A. Macdonald. As both Indian commissioner and lieutenant governor of the Northwest Territories during the Riel rebellion of 1885, he curbed serious Indian unrest. After being Macdonald's interior minister (1888–1892), Dewdney served four years as lieutenant governor of British Columbia. He died in Victoria on Aug. 8, 1916.

GORDON R. ELLIOTT
Simon Fraser University

DEWDROP, a creeping perennial herb of eastern North America, with rounded long-stalked leaves and two types of flowers. One or two small, white, and usually sterile flowers are borne at the tips of slender stems, 2½ to 5 inches (6–13 cm) high. Numerous flowers without petals occur on shorter stems and produce a few dry, 1-seeded fruits (drupelets) enclosed in the sepals, which are fused into a cup. Dewdrop (*Dalibarda repens*) grows in bogs and woods, where it flowers in the summer. It is a member of the rose family (Rosaceae).

JOAN E. RAHN
Author of "Experiments in Science"

D'EWES, dūz, **Sir Simonds** (1602–1650), English chronicler and antiquarian. He was born in Coxden, England, on Dec. 18, 1602. Educated at St. John's College, Cambridge, and at the Middle Temple, London, where he was trained for the bar, he began to practice law in 1623. In 1640 he was a member of the Long Parliament, from which in 1648 he was expelled in Pride's Purge (q.v.). He died in Suffolk on April 8, 1650.

D'Ewes kept diaries and collected transcripts of various records, including journals of all the parliaments that met during the reign of Elizabeth I. His major work, *A Journal of All the Parliaments of the Reign of Queen Elizabeth*, was edited and published by Paul Bowes in 1682 and reedited by Wallace Notestein as *The Journal of Sir Simonds D'Ewes* (1923).

DE WET, də vet', **Christiaan Rudolph** (1854–1922), South African military and political leader, who led a guerrilla campaign against the British during the South African War. He was born in Smithfield, Orange Free State, on Oct. 7, 1854. He later moved to the Transvaal, where he fought in the first Anglo-Boer War (1880–1881). He became a member of the Transvaal Volksraad (parliament) in 1885 but soon resigned and resettled in the Orange Free State, where he was also elected to parliament.

During the South African War (second Anglo-Boer War, 1899–1902), De Wet won fame in the Battle of Nicholson's Nek, when, with 300 men, he killed 200 British soldiers and captured 800. Promoted to the rank of general, he served under Gen. Pieter Cronjé on the western front. After the British captured Cronjé, De Wet became commander in chief of the Orange Free State forces. He organized guerrilla warfare and became famous for his mobility and many close escapes. His description of these campaigns was published in *The Three Years of War* (1902).

De Wet signed the Vereeniging Peace Treaty, ending the war, on May 31, 1902. The Orange Free State was made a British colony, and De Wet was elected to its parliament and appointed minister of agriculture, although he continued to oppose British rule. He served in the National Convention that unified South Africa in 1910.

To advance the cause of separation from Britain, De Wet helped found the National party under the leadership of James Hertzog in 1914. During World War I, he led an abortive revolt against the South African government and was sentenced to 6 years' imprisonment, but was released 11 months later after pledging to refrain from political agitation. He died in Dewetsdorp, Orange Free State, on Feb. 3, 1922.

F. A. VAN JAARSVELD
Rand Afrikaans University, South Africa

PAINTING BY MILLER, FROM U.S. NAVAL ACADEMY MUSEUM
Admiral George Dewey

DEWEY, George (1837–1917), American admiral, whose victory at the Battle of Manila Bay ended Spanish power in the Philippine Islands. He was born in Montpelier, Vt., on Dec. 26, 1837, the son of a doctor. He graduated from the U.S. Naval Academy in 1858. During the Civil War he took part in the battles of New Orleans and Port Hudson, La., the North Atlantic blockade, and attacks on Fort Fisher, N.C. His peacetime service was varied.

Dewey took command of the Asiatic Squadron in January 1898, and on February 25, Assistant Secretary of the Navy Theodore Roosevelt instructed him to proceed to Hong Kong and prepare for action in the Philippines. The United States declared war against Spain on April 21. On April 25, Dewey was ordered to proceed at once to the Philippines and to capture or destroy the Spanish fleet there. His squadron, consisting of six cruisers, one revenue cutter, and two support ships, headed south on April 27 after the arrival from Manila of the U.S. consul with the first intelligence report on the Philippines the Navy had had since 1876.

Dewey's ships entered Manila Bay on May 1, shortly after midnight, through mined waters and in the face of numerous guns on islands at the entrance. Only a few guns opened fire, and without effect. At 5:40 A.M. Dewey spoke the famous order to the captain of his flagship: "You may fire when you are ready, Gridley." Dewey's squadron, in an ellipse, steamed back and forth at a range of 2,000 yards (1.8 km), its rapid-fire guns demolishing the Spanish fleet of seven weaker ships that were drawn up in line off Cavite Island. When he withdrew at 7:35 A.M., the Spanish fleet was destroyed. Cavite surrendered about noon, but Manila could not be occupied until troops arrived. Dewey established a blockade, but a larger German fleet, sympathetic to Spain, landed supplies. Dewey announced that the U.S. fleet was ready to fight, and the Germans retired.

Congress created for Dewey the rank of admiral of the navy, and he was chairman of the General Board, advising the navy secretary. He died in Washington, D.C., on Jan. 16, 1917.

JOHN D. HAYES
Rear Admiral, U.S. Navy (Retired)

DEWEY, John (1859–1952), American philosopher and educator, who was the most influential American thinker of his time. His philosophy of "instrumentalism," and his writing and teaching in general, profoundly affected not only philosophy and educational theory and practice but also psychology, law, and political science.

Life. Dewey was born on a farm near Burlington, Vt., on Oct. 20, 1859. After graduating from the University of Vermont in 1879, he spent three years teaching in schools in Pennsylvania and Vermont. During this period he published, in the *Journal of Speculative Philosophy*, his first philosophical articles.

Inspired by the philosophical guidance of Professor H. A. P. Torrey of the University of Vermont, Dewey decided in 1882 to continue his studies at the newly opened Johns Hopkins University. On the acceptance of his dissertation, "The Psychology of Kant," he was awarded a doctorate there in 1884. In the same year he became an assistant professor of philosophy at the University of Michigan.

After an interval of one year (1888–1889) as a professor of philosophy at the University of Minnesota, Dewey served as chairman of the philosophy department at the University of Michigan from 1889 to 1894. During this period he published several books, as well as articles on philosophy, psychology, and education. In 1886 he married his first wife, Alice Chipman, who later became a professional educator; they had six children.

Recognition of Dewey as an important educator dates from his work as chairman of the department of philosophy, psychology, and pedagogy at the University of Chicago (1894–1904). In 1896 he organized the university's laboratory school, which he directed with the help of his wife until 1903. There he pioneered in experimenting with curricula, methods, and organization, effectively combining educational theory and practice. His success in persuading parents to participate with teachers in the educational process led to the publication of his first influential educational work, *The School and Society* (1899), a series of lectures to parents of the pupils in the school. During his tenure at Chicago he also published many other books and served (1899–1900) as president of the American Psychological Association.

Because of disagreements with the administration of the University of Chicago over the laboratory school, Dewey left Chicago in 1904 to become a professor of philosophy at Columbia University. There he attained the full measure of his national and international reputation as a philosopher, educator, writer, and leader in public affairs. Through his teaching and writing Dewey reached out to the minds of philosophers and educators all over the world. His concern transcended the academic; he labored incessantly for the betterment of human life everywhere. Through his own work and that of his disciples, the foremost of whom in the field of education was William Heard Kilpatrick, Dewey affected educational thought and practice in many lands.

During this period Dewey was active in many organizations. He served as president of the American Philosophical Association in 1905–1906. In 1915 he became the founder and first president of the American Association of University Professors. The next year he became a charter member of the Teachers' Union, which he was to leave in

JOHN DEWEY examines a Chinese statuette that he received in honor of his 90th birthday, October 1949.

the 1930's because of what he felt were leftist tendencies. In 1920 he helped organize the American Civil Liberties Union. On the international scene, Dewey made tours of the Far East in 1919 and 1931. He also surveyed education in Turkey (1924), Mexico (1926), and the USSR (1928), recording his observations in *Impressions of Soviet Russia and the Revolutionary World, Mexico—China—Turkey* (1929).

After his retirement in 1930, Dewey concentrated on writing and on public affairs. He was active in advancing adult education, especially in the fields of political and international understanding. His political activities included the presidency of the People's Lobby in Washington (after 1929) and the chairmanships of the League for Independent Political Action and the League for Industrial Democracy. He also served as chairman (1937–1938) of the commission of inquiry into the charges made against Leon Trotsky in the Moscow trials; its finding, that Trotsky was innocent, subjected Dewey to a storm of vituperation from the Soviet and American Communist parties.

Dewey's first wife died in 1927, and in 1946 he married Mrs. Roberta Grant. He died in New York City on June 1, 1952.

Philosophy. Although Dewey's early philosophy followed the idealism of Hegel, he gradually drifted away toward the pragmatism of William James. This meant that he came to reject the view that truth is fixed and unchanging in favor of the view that truth is determined on the basis of the consequences of ideas. Dewey's philosophy, usually known as "instrumentalism" or "experimentalism," is reflected in his educational theory in its emphasis on the importance of "learning by doing" and its opposition to the stress on dogmatic and authoritarian teaching methods and on rote learning. He advocated laboratory and workshop courses, which he felt would foster creativity and cooperation among the students. Dewey held that the democratic society must instill in its citizens the habit of free inquiry and an antipathy to rigid and dictatorial methods. Typical of his view that education, to be most meaningful, must have a practical outcome is his statement, in *Democracy and Education* (1916), that "men have to *do*

something to the things when they wish to find out something; they have to alter conditions."

Dewey's ideas were adopted and often distorted by the "progressive education" movement, with the result that, to cater to the whims of students or teachers, subject matter was often neglected in favor of disorganized entertainment or reduced to mere vocational training. The spread of such abuses ultimately forced Dewey to protest them in his *Experience and Education* (1938), which affirmed the importance of the cultural heritage and cautioned against deriving education from experience alone: "The belief that all genuine education comes about through experience does not mean that all experiences are genuinely or equally educative. Experience and education cannot be directly related to each other. For some experiences are mis-educative."

Influence. Without a doubt, Dewey was the best-known American educator of all time, both at home and abroad. To some of his admirers he was the greatest educator who ever lived. On the other hand, there are many who attribute all the ills of education in the United States to the influence of his ideas. Certain specific influences of Dewey's include his emphasis on the avoidance of "either-or" arguments in thinking; he taught generations of readers and students to examine ideas dispassionately before deciding on a course of action. Dewey also championed the philosophy of legal realism, according to which the judge plays an active role in the making of the law and should therefore be made more conscious of the inevitable social consequences of his decisions. But perhaps Dewey's greatest contribution lay in his insistence that the true function of philosophy is to solve human problems and his demonstration that it can be made to do so. Retaining his fundamental viewpoints in the face of bitter opposition, Dewey never ceased his struggle to better the lot of humanity in all parts of the world.

WILLIAM W. BRICKMAN
Coeditor of "John Dewey: Master Educator"

Bibliography

Dewey's books include *Psychology* (1887), *The Ethics of Democracy* (1888), *Applied Psychology: An Introduction to the Principles and Practice of Education* (1889), *Interest As Related to Will* (1896), *My Pedagogical Creed* (1897), *Ethical Principles Underlying Education* (1897), *The School and Society* (1899), *The Child and the Curriculum* (1902), *The Educational Situation* (1902), *Studies in Logical Theory* (with others, 1903), *Ethics* (with James H. Tufts, 1908), *Moral Principles in Education* (1909), *How We Think* (1910), *Interest and Effort in Education* (1913), *Schools of Tomorrow* (with his daughter Evelyn, 1915), *Democracy and Education: An Introduction to the Philosophy of Education* (1916), *Reconstruction in Philosophy* (1920), *Experience and Nature* (1925), *The Public and Its Problems* (1927), *Characters and Events* (1929), *The Quest for Certainty* (1929), *Impressions of Soviet Russia and the Revolutionary World, Mexico—China—Turkey* (1929), *Philosophy and Civilization* (1931), *Art as Experience* (1934), *A Common Faith* (1934), *Liberalism and Social Action* (1935), *Logic: The Theory of Inquiry* (1938), *Experience and Education* (1938), *Freedom and Culture* (1939), and *Knowing and the Known* (with Arthur Bentley, 1949).

Archambault, Reginald D., ed., *Dewey on Education: Appraisals* (New York 1966).
Baker, Melvin C., *Foundations of John Dewey's Educational Theory* (New York 1955).
Blewett, John, ed., *John Dewey: His Thought and Influence* (New York 1960).
Brickman, William W., and Lehrer, Stanley, eds., *John Dewey: Master Educator*, 2d ed. (New York 1965).
Handlin, Oscar, *John Dewey's Challenge to Education* (New York 1959).
Lawson, Douglas E., and Lean, Arthur E., eds., *John Dewey and the World View* (Carbondale, Ill., 1964).
Thomas, Milton H., *John Dewey, a Centennial Bibliography* (Chicago 1962).

DEWEY, dōō′ē, **Melvil** (1851–1931), American librarian, who devised the Dewey Decimal System for classifying books in libraries and probably had more influence on the development of librarianship as a profession in the United States than any other individual.

Life. He was born Melville Louis Kossuth Dewey in Adams Center, N. Y., on Dec. 10, 1851. After graduating from Amherst College in 1874, he served as acting librarian there for two years. His system of classification was first published in a 42-page booklet in 1876 as *A Classification and Subject Index for Cataloguing and Arranging the Books and Pamphlets of a Library*, of which 1,000 copies were printed.

For the next seven years Dewey lived in Boston, where he was active in various organizations for the improvement of library services and for the promotion of spelling reform and of the use of the metric system of measurement. From 1883 to 1888 he was librarian at Columbia College, where he started the first professional library school (1887) in the United States. When Dewey moved to Albany in 1888 to become director of the New York State Library, the school was continued in Albany as the New York State Library School. (It returned to Columbia University in 1926.) While in Albany, Dewey also served (1888–1906) as secretary of the Board of Regents of the University of the State of New York.

In 1895, Dewey organized the Lake Placid Club in the Adirondacks as a membership resort, and he founded a similar club in Florida in 1927. He died at Lake Placid, Fla., on Dec. 26, 1931.

Dewey was a founder of the American Library Association (1876) and served at various times as its secretary and president. He was also active in the organization of the Children's Library Association (1888), the Association of State Librarians (1890), and the American Library Institute (1905). In addition, he served as editor of the *Library Journal* (1876–1881) and of *Library Notes* (1886–1898).

The Dewey Decimal System. Dewey's book on his classification system, revised and enlarged, reached its 17th edition in 1965 under the title *Dewey Decimal Classification and Relative Index*, in two volumes totaling 2,153 pages. The system is now used in libraries throughout the world. The basic plan of the system is the division of all recorded knowledge into ten classes, which in turn are divided into ten divisions and further subdivided into ten sections. The main classes are: 000–099, General Works; 100–199, Philosophy, Psychology, Ethics; 200–299, Religion and Mythology; 300–399, Social Sciences; 400–499, Philology; 500–599, Science; 600–699, Technology; 700–799, Fine Arts; 800–899, Literature; 900–999, History, Geography, Biography, Travel. The system also provides divisions that can be used with any subject to denote the form (such as essays, history, dictionary) in which the subject is presented. The relative index to the system is arranged alphabetically and attempts to include all topics contained in the various classes, together with the Dewey class number. If a topic is treated in more than one class, the number it takes in each class is indicated. See also LIBRARIES—5. *Library Service and Organization*.

JOHN DAVID MARSHALL
Editor of "Books—Libraries—Librarians"

Further Reading: Rider, Fremont, *Melvil Dewey* (Chicago 1944).

DEWEY, dōō′ē, **Thomas Edmund** (1902–1971), American lawyer and political leader. He was born on March 24, 1902, in Owosso, Mich., the son of the local newspaper publisher. He received his B. A. degree from the University of Michigan in 1923 and graduated from Columbia University Law School in 1925. From 1931 to 1933 he served as chief assistant to the U. S. attorney for the southern district of New York and then as U. S. attorney.

Although Dewey was a Republican, Herbert H. Lehman, Democratic governor of New York, appointed him special prosecutor to root out racketeering in 1935. In 1937 he was elected district attorney of New York county. His successful prosecution of the criminal syndicate Murder, Inc., brought him national fame. In 1938 he ran for governor of New York against Lehman but lost. Two years later he made an unsuccessful bid for the Republican presidential nomination. But in 1942 he was elected governor, and he won reelection in 1946 and 1950.

Thomas E. Dewey

HENRY GRANT COMPTON

As governor, Dewey exercised firm control over the legislature and gave the state an efficient, businesslike administration. Among his leading achievements were a large-scale highway building program, the first state law anywhere against racial or religious discrimination in employment, improved unemployment and disability benefits, and an effective labor mediation board. His record was sufficiently progressive to keep the Democrats on the defensive, while his skill in handling patronage and his fiscal conservatism prevented any potential Republican split.

In 1944, Dewey had won the Republican presidential nomination but was defeated by President Franklin D. Roosevelt. In 1948 he was again his party's standard-bearer, but the wide lead given him by the public opinion polls led to fatal over-confidence. His own lackluster campaign, Democratic President Harry S Truman's attacks on the "do-nothing" Republican 80th Congress, and the country's prosperity gave Truman an upset victory. In 1952, Dewey played a major role in securing the Republican presidential nomination for Dwight D. Eisenhower. After 1954, he practiced law in New York City. Dewey died on March 16, 1971, in Bal Harbour, Fla.

JOHN BRAEMAN, *University of Nebraska*

DEWEY DECIMAL SYSTEM. See DEWEY, MELVIL.

DEWING, dū'ing, **Francis** (1700?–?1765), English engraver, who did the first important copper-engraving work in America. Very little is known of his life. He sailed in 1716 from London to Boston, where he was active until about 1723. He carved designs in wood for printing fabrics, engraved devices on silver, and made copper engravings of maps and coats of arms. In 1718 he was arrested on suspicion of counterfeiting but was apparently soon cleared of this charge. He made engravings of Cyprian Southack's maps *Seacoast of English America and the New French Settlements* (1716), *Canso Harbor* (1720), and *Casco Bay* (1720) and of Capt. John Bonner's map *The Town of Boston* (1722).

DEWING, dū'ing, **Thomas Wilmer** (1851–1938), American painter, whose delicate style was influenced by French impressionism. He was one of the "Ten American Artists," a group of progressive painters that included John H. Twachtman, J. Alden Weir, Edmund C. Tarbell, and Willard Metcalf.

Dewing was born in Boston on May 4, 1851. He studied in Paris from 1876 to 1879. When he returned to the United States, he settled in New York City, where he soon gained recognition for his delicate figure studies and portraits of women. In 1897 he resigned from the rather academic Society of American Artists and joined the "Ten." His paintings include *The Letter* (Canajoharie Art Gallery, Canajoharie, N. Y.) and *Portrait of a Young Girl* (Addison Gallery of American Art, Andover, Mass.). Dewing died in New York City on Nov. 6, 1938.

DE WITT, də vit, **Cornelis** (1623–1672), Dutch political leader, brother of Johan De Witt (q.v.). He was born on June 25, 1623, in Dordrecht, Holland. His father was imprisoned by William II of Orange (1650), and both sons became implacable enemies of the house of Orange.

Cornelis De Witt became alderman and burgomaster of Dordrecht (1666–1667) and, during the Second and Third Dutch Wars against England, he was attached to the navy as a representative of the States General. In 1672, after the downfall of his brother, Cornelis was accused of conspiring to murder William III of Orange. He was acquitted, but he and his brother were murdered by an Orangist mob in The Hague on Aug. 20, 1672.

JACOB W. SMIT, *Columbia University*

DE WITT, də vit, **Johan** (1625–1672), Dutch political leader. Born on Sept. 24, 1625, in Dordrecht, Holland, De Witt belonged to one of the hereditary governing families of the city, and his political rise was rapid. In 1650 he was appointed a pensionary of his native city and its representative in the provincial estates of Holland; in 1653 he was elected grand pensionary of the province, a position that virtually entailed leadership of the United Netherlands.

De Witt came to power in a difficult situation. In 1652 the first war with England had begun (see DUTCH WARS), and Dutch trade was suffering. Moreover, the war was complicated by the internal party strife between the republicans and the house of Orange. De Witt was a republican, and he managed to keep the Oranges out of office until his downfall (1672). But he had to overcome strong opposition in the official Calvinist ministry and in the other provinces of the republic, especially in 1654, when it appeared that he had concluded a peace with the English containing a secret guarantee that the Oranges would be excluded from their offices in Holland.

De Witt's foreign policy initially reflected the neutralist concepts of his party, but later it developed into a more active interventionist diplomacy. After the Dutch victory in the second Anglo-Dutch war (1665–1667), he sided with England against French expansionism in the Spanish Netherlands, but an Anglo-French alliance, leading to the Third Dutch War (1672), brought about his downfall. Orangist enthusiasm had been rising as William III approached adulthood; De Witt also met increasing opposition within his own party. After an Orangist revolt, he resigned (Aug. 4, 1672) and was murdered with his brother by an Orangist mob in The Hague on Aug. 20, 1672.

JACOB W. SMIT, *Columbia University*

DE WITT, də wit, **Simeon** (1756–1834), American cartographer, who made maps for the Continental Army in the American Revolution and for New York state. He was born in Wawarsing, N. Y., on Dec. 25, 1756, and attended Queens College (now Rutgers—the State University, New Jersey). He served in a Continental battalion at the Battle of Saratoga in October 1777. His ability as a surveyor prompted his uncle, Gen. James Clinton, to recommend him to General Washington, who was seeking assistants for his geographer, Col. Robert Erskine.

De Witt joined Erskine in July 1778 and succeeded him in October 1780. He made surveys for Washington's staff until the end of the war. About 130 manuscript maps made for the Army are in the New-York Historical Society.

De Witt was surveyor general of New York state for 50 years from 1784. He was one of the three New York commissioners who surveyed part of the New York-Pennsylvania boundary in 1786–1787. His large New York state map of 1802 was one of the earliest official state maps. De Witt helped to plan the expansion of New York City beyond the settled area, and he began supervising the construction of the Erie and Champlain canals in 1808. He died in Ithaca, N. Y., on Dec. 3, 1834.

CLARA E. LEGEAR
Geography and Map Division, Library of Congress

DE WOLFE, də woolf, **Elsie** (1865–1950), American actress and society leader. Her married name was Lady Mendl. She was born in New York City on Dec. 20, 1865, and was presented at court and introduced to London society at the age of 17. In the 1880's she began a professional stage career, playing in Charles Frohman's productions opposite John Drew. She retired from the stage in the early 1900's to embark on a successful career as an interior decorator.

A prominent member of international society, she was active in many charitable enterprises during World Wars I and II. In 1917, France conferred on her the Croix de Guerre and membership in the Legion of Honor. She gave up her American citizenship in 1926 to marry Sir Charles Mendl, a British diplomat, but regained it in 1940 by special act of Congress. Her memoirs, *After All*, appeared in 1935. She died in Versailles, France, on July 12, 1950.

DEXEDRINE. See AMPHETAMINE.

DEXTER, Timothy (1747–1806), American merchant and eccentric. He was born in Malden, Mass., on Jan. 22, 1747. At an early age he became an apprentice at leather dressing, and he progressed so rapidly that he soon owned his own establishment. Speculating in currency and a variety of commercial ventures, he succeeded in amassing a large fortune.

Dexter's eccentric efforts to attain social prominence gave him great notoriety. He assumed the title of "Lord" Timothy Dexter and constructed bizarre residences in Newburyport, Mass., and Chester, N. H. The grounds of the former house were adorned with over 40 colossal wooden statues of famous men. He included himself in the number, adding the inscription "I am first in the East." He assembled an extensive library of books, notable chiefly for their expensive bindings, and an extraordinary collection of worthless paintings, and he subsidized a poet, who composed verses in his honor. Dexter himself wrote a pamphlet called *A Pickle for the Knowing Ones* (1802), with all the punctuation marks printed on the last page—there being none in the text proper—and instructions to readers to "peper and solt it as they plese."

Dexter was able and shrewd in business, but he was extremely dissipated and was regarded as probably mentally deranged. He died in Newburyport, Mass., on Oct. 23, 1806.

DEXTRAN, dek'strən, is a complex polysaccharide synthesized by certain microorganisms. It is important medically because of its use as a plasma substitute or extender in the treatment of shock. Dextran is also used at a "molecular sieve" in the purification of proteins, as a food additive, and in lacquers.

Dextran is synthesized from sucrose (cane sugar) by some strains of bacteria of the genus *Leuconostoc* and by certain other microorganisms. It is found on fermenting dairy products and vegetables. There are various types of dextrans, some with molecular weights as high as 4,000,-000; they occur as ropy slimes. Dextran that is used as a plasma substitute is partially broken down to form chains with molecular weights of about 75,000. Dextran is very stable and is easily stored. It is soluble in water and forms very viscous solutions.

DEXTRIN, dek'strən, is an intermediate product of the breakdown of starch. Dextrin, which is also called *artificial gum* or *vegetable gum*, is used commercially in the manufacture of adhesives, for sizing paper and textiles, as a thickening agent, and in various food products such as corn syrup.

Dextrins consist of complex mixtures of molecules of varying structure and size. Some dextrins have branched chains, while others are unbranched. They are produced by the action on starch of heat, acids, enzymes (α- and β-amylases), or oxidizing agents such as peroxide. The commercial production of dextrin involves the heat treatment of starch containing a trace of acid. Dextrins are white or yellow amorphous powders that are soluble in water but insoluble in alcohol or ether.

Dextrins are found in honey and in the leaves of starch-producing plants. In plants they occur either as intermediates in the production of starch from glucose or as intermediate products of the breakdown of starch.

In living organisms the starch molecule is enzymatically broken down by hydrolysis. Plants contain both α- and β-amylases and a debranching enzyme ("R-enzyme"), while animals have pancreatic and salivary α-amylase and a debranching enzyme. In the degradation of starch the enzymes progressively split off sugar (maltose) units by breaking specific chemical bonds in the chains. With amylopectin, which is a branched glucose polymer that makes up the outer portion of starch granules, the enzymatic breakdown is stopped at the points of branching of the chains; approximately half of the starch molecule is degraded to maltose, while the remaining portion, the *limit dextrin*, is left intact.

ARNOLD E. S. GUSSIN
Smith College

DEXTROSE, dek'strōs, also known as *-D-glucose* or *grape sugar*, is a common sugar found in both plants and animals. The stepwise breakdown of glucose to carbon dioxide and water is the main source of energy for most living organisms. This sugar is also the basic structural unit of most of the important polysaccharides, including starch, cellulose, and glycogen.

The formula for dextrose is $C_6H_{12}O_6$. It is a white crystalline substance that has a sweet taste and is soluble in water. See also GLUCOSE.

ARNOLD E. S. GUSSIN
Smith College

DEY, dā, was a title given to the rulers of the Ottoman provinces of Algeria and Tunisia. It derives from the Turkish *dayı*, meaning "maternal uncle." This was used as a term of respect for elders and specifically for the Janissary and corsair chiefs who seized power in Algeria and Tunisia, and governed them in semi-independence of the Ottomans. The corsair ruler of Algiers was officially styled "dey" from 1671 to the French conquest in 1830. In Tunisia, "dey" was the title used by the Janissary rulers from 1594 to 1705.

JOHN R. WALSH
University of Edinburgh

DEZFUL. See DIZFUL.

DEZHNEV, dezh-nyôf', **Semyon Ivanovich** (1605?–?1672), Russian navigator and explorer, who was the first European to prove the separation of Asia and North America. He was born about 1605, but nothing is known of his early life except that he served with the Yakut Cossacks.

In 1641 he began the explorations of Siberia for which he is famous. He started his most notable voyage in 1647, sailing east from the Kolyma River around the northeastern tip of Asia, now Cape Dezhnev, to the mouth of the Anadyr River. This journey proved the existence of what is now known as the Bering Strait and of a sea route around northern Siberia. It yielded descriptions of the Chukchi Peninsula and the Anadyr River basin. He continued his voyages into the 1660's, exploring the Yana and Lena rivers.

Dezhnev explored during a time of rising interest in Siberia, but his potentially valuable descriptions remained undiscovered until 1736, so that navigators in the early 18th century, notably Vitus Bering, believed that they were the first explorers of Siberia. He died in Moscow.

PETER CZAP, JR., *Amherst College*

DHAHRAN, dä-rän', is an oil town in eastern Saudi Arabia, located at the center of a small headland jutting into the Persian Gulf. Bahrain Island lies close offshore. Dhahran (also *az-Zahran*) is situated in an arid region that has few natural features. The town is linked by a railway to Riyadh and by a highway to Riyadh and Jidda. There is an international commercial airport and a U.S. Air Force base.

Prior to oil exploration in 1938, Dhahran was a tiny hamlet, but today it is impressively modern. It is the headquarters of the Arabian American Oil Company, containing the company's main offices and the living quarters for personnel employed in the adjacent oil fields. Oil is shipped through Dammam, a port about 10 miles (16 km) north of Dhahran, and Dhahran is the starting point of the Trans Arabian Pipeline to the Mediterranean. Population: (1968 est.) 12,500.

W. B. FISHER, *University of Durham*

DHAR, där, a former princely state of India, is now a district in Madhya Pradesh state. Another form of this district's name is *Dhara*. Situated on the northern slopes of the Vindhya Hills, Dhar's area of 3,150-square miles (8,155 sq km) is dotted with lakes and commands the entrance to the Narmada (Narbada) River valley.

Between the 9th century and the 13th century the area was the center of Parmar Rajput power. Raja Bhoja (reigned 1018–1060) was the most illustrious ruler. In the 14th century the territory came under Muslim domination. However, in 1730, Ponwar Marathas, claiming descent from the Rajputs, gained control. Dhar accepted British paramountcy in 1819, retaining local autonomy. In 1948 the state was ceded to India.

The town of Dhar is the former princely capital. Here Raja Bhoja founded a Sanskrit college, inscribing rules of grammar on slabs of stone. In the 14th century the college was converted into a mosque with the slabs intact. Other historic remains are the red sandstone fort at nearby Mandu and the Lat Mosque, built out of the remains of a Jain temple. Population: (1961) of the town, 28,325.

BRIJEN K. GUPTA, *Brooklyn College*

DHARMA, dur'mə, in Indian thought, means the proper course of action in a particular context. The earliest Hindus believed that the design, motion, and purpose of the universe are governed by abstract fundamental law (*rita*). From this developed the belief in a law for human behavior, also referred to as *dharma*. The precepts of *dharma* are embodied in a group of Hindu semicanonical writings called *Smriti*, or (*Human*) *Tradition*. They include such books of law as the *Dharma Shastra*, or *Sacred Law*, which codifies *dharma*, and the *Dharma Sutras*, or *Aphorisms on Dharma*.

Dharma is regarded as one of the four goals of human life in Hinduism. Each man, the Hindus say, is governed by the desire for wealth (*artha*), pleasure (*kama*), righteousness (*dharma*), and spiritual liberation (*moksha*). Ideally, each individual will see the need to integrate the desire for wealth and pleasure into the socio-religious obligations of his caste and sect, and thus will seek righteousness and virtue, or *dharma*, the way of living appropriate to his particular status. Finally, all men, to be truly fulfilled, must seek spiritual liberation, which can properly be found only through an ascetic life and the foregoing of wealth, pleasure, and one's role in society.

Although it is only one of the aspects of man's life fulfillment, the concept of *dharma* has had very far-reaching effects on Hindu society. It has led to the goal of perfect conformity to one's caste rules and barriers, vocation, and traditional religious observance. In thus defining and limiting the individual's role and actions in life, the concept of *dharma* has served to buttress the extremely complex regulation of status and all aspects of human behavior in Hindu society and has acted as a strong deterrent to radical reform and innovation.

CHARLES S. J. WHITE
University of Pennsylvania

DHARWAR, där-wär', a town in southeastern India, the capital of Dharwar district, is located in Mysore state, 290 miles (470 km) southeast of Bombay and 80 miles (130 km) east of Goa. Dharwar is an important railroad junction and a trade center for the cotton, timber, and grain of the surrounding region. It has cotton, rice, and oilseed mills. The town is the seat of Karnatak University, founded in 1949, which includes colleges of arts, sciences, law, and education. Old Karnatak College became the university's college of arts. Population: (1960) 77,163.

DHAULAGIRI, dou-lə-gi'rē, **Mount,** a section of the Himalaya in north central Nepal, about 130 miles (200 km) northwest of Katmandu. Its eastern and western slopes give rise to the headwaters of the Ganges, Gandak, and Ghagura rivers. Mt. Dhaulagiri has several summits with an altitude of over 25,000 feet (7,600 meters). Dhaulagiri I, which rises to 26,810 feet (8,171 meters), is the seventh-highest mountain peak in the world. The peak was first scaled on May 13, 1960, by a 6-man Swiss expedition led by Max Eiselin.

DHOLE, dōl, a member (*Cuon alpinus*) of the dog family (Canidae). The dhole, also known as the red dog or the Indian, Siberian, or Asiatic wild dog, occurs in east central Russia, Nepal, Burma, northern China, Malaysia, Sumatra, Java, and India. It is now becoming rare over much of its range. Slightly larger than the coyote, the powerfully built dhole is about 4½ feet (1.5 meters) in length, about a third of which is bushy tail, and up to 46 pounds (21 kg) in weight. Its body is covered with reddish hair.

Like most wild canids, dholes feed mainly on rodents and rabbits. They sometimes hunt in small packs and are reputed to run down deer and even force tigers and leopards from their kill. The young are born in the late spring after a gestation period of about 9 weeks. There are usually 2 to 6 young in a litter.

E. LENDELL COCKRUM, *University of Arizona*

DHOLPUR, dōl'po͝or, a former princely state of India, is now a subdivision of Bharatpur district in the state of Rajasthan. It occupies an area of 232 square miles (600 sq km), washed by the Chambal River (q.v.). The quarrying of fine-grained red sandstone is the area's major economic activity.

The area was settled by Deswali Jats in the 11th century. It felt Muslim pressures in the 14th century, but in 1449, under Surjan Deo, the Jats reestablished themselves. In 1805 the British took the princely state under protection. The quasi-independent status of Dholpur came to an end in 1948 when it merged into India.

The town of Dholpur, formerly the capital of the princely state, lies 34 miles (55 km) south of Agra. It has a magnificent fortified caravan-serai, dating back to the 16th century. The town is a center of marble-carving, brass, and hand-loom-weaving industries. Population: (1961) of the town, 27,412.

BRIJEN K. GUPTA, *Brooklyn College*

DHOW, dou, a seagoing Arab vessel with one or two lateen (triangular) sails, a sharp long bow, and a decorated poop copied from 18th century European merchantmen. In the 18th and 19th centuries, dhows were used by slave traders and pirates. Now they are employed to seek fish,

ARAB DHOW has a lateen rig. This large dhow is known as a baggala; the small dhow is a sambuk.

ILLUSTRATION BY CECIL G. TREW, FROM "THE STORY OF SAIL," BY G. S. LAIRD CLOWES (EYRE AND SPOT-TISWOODE LTD.)

shells, and pearls around Arabia and northeastern Africa. Many are built in Masqat (Muscat), Oman, of imported wood.

DHRANGADHRA, dräng′gə-drä, a former princely state of India, is now a subdivision of Gujarat state. Dhrangadhra's territory of 399 square miles (1,035 sq km) borders on the Little Rann of Kutch, whose deposits of alkalies support a flourishing chemical industry. The state was established by the Jhala Rajputs in the 8th century A.D. During most of its existence it was tributary to either Hindu or Muslim overlords. It came under direct British control in 1924 and was merged into independent India in 1948.

The town of Dhrangadhra, the former capital of the princely state, is the home of the Dhrangadhra Chemical Works. Population: (1961) of the town, 32,197.

BRIJEN K. GUPTA, *Brooklyn College*

DIABASE, dī′ə-bās, is a compact crystalline igneous rock that is found most commonly in dikes. Its essential constituents are plagioclase feldspar (see FELDSPAR) and augite (see PYROXENE). The augite fills the interstices between the long, narrow plagioclase crystals. Diabase is chemically equivalent to gabbro but is more finely grained. Diabases are of common occurrence in the United States, forming dikes and laccoliths (lens-shaped masses of igneous rock between sedimentary beds) along the Atlantic seaboard. Other diabases are found around Lake Superior and in the Rocky Mountains.

The field name "greenstone" is often given to diabases. In Britain the term "dolerite" is used in preference to diabase.

DIABELLI, dē-ä-bel′ē, **Antonio** (1781–1858), Austrian composer and music publisher. Antonio (or Anton) Diabelli was born in Mattsee, near Salzburg, on Sept. 6, 1781. He studied for the priesthood before moving to Vienna in 1803, where he became a teacher of piano and guitar. In 1818 he entered into partnership with the music publisher Peter Cappi, and he continued the firm alone, under the name of Diabelli & Co., from 1824 to 1852, publishing works by Franz Schubert, Johann Strauss, and other composers. Diabelli died in Vienna on April 7, 1858.

Diabelli's works include songs, piano pieces, masses, and the operetta *Adam in der Klemme* (1809). He is remembered today primarily because Beethoven's *Thirty-three Variations* (Opus 120), known as the "Diabelli Variations," is based on a waltz theme by Diabelli.

DIABETES, dī-ə-bēt′ēz, is a medical term applied to two different, unrelated diseases: diabetes mellitus and diabetes insipidus.

DIABETES MELLITUS

Diabetes mellitus occurs when the body's cells are unable to obtain or utilize adequate amounts of the hormone insulin. Insulin is secreted by special cells, called beta cells, that are found in certain cell groups, the islets of Langerhans, in the pancreas. When insulin is present in the bloodstream, it normally enables the body cells to absorb and metabolize (burn) the sugar glucose, a major constituent of carbohydrate foods. In most diabetics, the amount of insulin in the blood is higher than in normal people, but the effectiveness of the hormone is impaired, either by the presence of insulin antagonists or by tissue resistance to the hormone's action. Furthermore, the release of insulin from the pancreas after eating is delayed in diabetics. Although the body's inability to handle carbohydrates is the major characteristic of diabetes mellitus, the disease may also involve practically every organ of the body without an overt disturbance of glucose metabolism.

It is estimated that there are 4 million diabetics in the United States, in half of whom the disease has not yet been diagnosed. Diabetes may occur at any age, but most cases are diagnosed in people between the ages of 40 and 60. Although both sexes are affected by the disease, females are generally more susceptible.

Causes. Susceptibility to diabetes mellitus is inherited as a recessive autosomal (nonsex-linked) trait. In order for the disorder to develop in a susceptible person, certain factors must usually be present. Among these are obesity, menopause, pregnancy, infection, trauma, severe emotional shock, and various glandular disorders. In some cases, diabetes is not related to heredity, but is due to other causes, including destruction of the pancreas by cancer.

Types. There are two basic forms of diabetes mellitus. One form is known as the *adult*, or *mature*, form because it usually does not occur before the age of 40. The second form is called *juvenile*, or *youthful*, diabetes because it begins early in life. Once they occur, both adult and juvenile diabetes persist throughout the individual's life.

One major difference between juvenile and adult diabetes is that only in the juvenile form is there clear evidence of disease in the pancreas. In people with juvenile diabetes the islets of Langerhans have a marked reduction in the number of beta cells, and the beta cells that are present contain fewer granules than normal cells. These granules are believed to be either insulin itself or its precursor. Because of these changes, the islets produce very little insulin. In patients with adult diabetes, the pancreas may contain the usual number of beta cells and granules, and production of insulin may be normal. In some patients, however, some islets may be replaced by scar tissue or a glassy tissue that is called hyaline.

Another major difference between juvenile and adult diabetes mellitus is that the characteristic symptoms of the disease are much more severe in the juvenile form. In the adult form there may be no symptoms at all.

Besides the juvenile and adult forms of diabetes, there is a condition known as *prediabetes* or *diabetes premellitus*. This condition is often associated with the eventual development of overt diabetes. Among the people said to be prediabetic are those who are known to be genetically susceptible—either because an identical twin or both parents have the disease. A woman may also be considered prediabetic if she gives birth to very large babies (over 9 pounds, or 4 kg) or if she has many miscarriages or stillbirths.

Pathology and Symptoms. When carbohydrates are eaten, a hormone secreted from the upper gastrointestinal tract sends out a preliminary call for insulin. From the small intestine, glucose, the major end product of carbohydrate digestion, is absorbed into the blood, bringing about an increase in the sugar content of the blood. This rise in the blood sugar level acts as a stimulus to the beta cells, which then secrete large amounts of insulin into the blood. Although the exact mechanism by which insulin affects the cells is not clearly understood, it apparently facilitates the intake of glucose into each body cell where it is metabolized to form large quantities of adenosine triphosphate (ATP), the cell's major source of energy. In liver and muscle cells, insulin also aids in the conversion of glucose into a storage form, called glycogen, and in the liver, insulin is also required for the conversion of glucose into fat.

In people with diabetes mellitus, the deficiency or unavailability of insulin prevents much of the glucose from entering the body cells, and the glucose accumulates in the blood. Upon reaching a certain level, some of the excess glucose is excreted by the kidneys in the urine. When large amounts of sugar are thus excreted, the patient produces larger quantities of urine and has to urinate frequently. In addition, he develops a great thirst, complains of a dry mouth, becomes weaker, and loses weight. In females, the presence of excess sugar in the urine sometimes encourages the growth of fungi in the genital area, producing intense inflammation and itching. Sometimes, the excess sugar in the blood also enters the eye fluids and produces blurring of vision.

When the body cannot metabolize enough glucose to meet its energy needs, fatty acids are released from fat deposits in the body, and they are broken down into smaller units to provide energy. Because of the overproduction of these units, excessive amounts of substances known as ketone bodies are produced. As these substances accumulate in the blood, their acidity produces a condition known as acidosis. The patient becomes markedly dehydrated, is usually vomiting, and has deep labored breathing. If the patient's condition is not alleviated, he sinks into diabetic coma and may die.

Diagnosis. The discovery of sugar in the urine does not automatically indicate the presence of diabetes mellitus. Sometimes, the urine sugar is lactose, fructose, or some other type of sugar, indicating a different type of disorder. Even when the urine sugar is identified as glucose, the diagnosis of diabetes is not confirmed. Some people normally excrete a certain amount of glucose in their urine, a harmless condition known as renal diabetes. Glucose may also appear in the urine as a result of certain glandular disorders, such as hyperthyroidism. To distinguish diabetes from these other conditions, the physician determines the level of sugar in the patient's blood after a period of fasting. If an abnormally high blood sugar is confirmed, the diagnosis of diabetes can be made. However, even if the blood sugar is normal after fasting, diabetes cannot be ruled out, and the doctor then measures the blood sugar level after the patient has ingested some glucose. In this test, called a glucose-tolerance test, glucose is administered in a palatable solution to the fasting patient and his blood sugar level is measured every hour for 3 to 5 hours. In a diabetic patient, the blood sugar level will rise higher and remain elevated longer than in a normal person.

Treatment. There is no known cure for diabetes, and all therapeutic measures are aimed at limiting the disease and relieving the patient's symptoms. Of chief importance in the control of diabetes mellitus are a proper diet, sufficient exercise, and the administration of drugs to reduce the blood sugar level. Sometimes only a slight restriction of carbohydrates is all that is necessary. In other cases, a very strict curtailment in the diet is required. In general, all diabetics should avoid candy, cake, jam, and ice cream. Other carbohydrate-rich foods, such as bread, cereal, fruits, and certain vegetables, should be limited. A common error made by diabetics is the drinking of canned fruit juices to which no sugar has been added. The patient often forgets that fruit juices contain natural sugar. Sugar-free hard candies and chewing gum are permissible, as are sugarless carbonated beverages. Alcohol in moderate quantities is very useful to elderly people and should not be forbidden.

The adult form of diabetes often requires the administration of oral drugs that stimulate the beta cells to produce more insulin. These drugs are known collectively as sulfonylureas. In juvenile diabetes they are of very little value, and even in adult diabetes they are not always successful, especially if the patient neglects his diet. Sometimes, these drugs work for only one or two years. DBI is a useful drug often used to supplement the sulfonylureas.

The most powerful and reliable antidiabetic agent known is insulin itself. A major drawback of insulin, however, is that it can be administered only by injection, a problem for many blind and other handicapped persons. Commercial preparations of insulin are made in two forms: a clear, quick-acting form and a cloudy suspension that has a delayed, although prolonged action. When insulin is used in treating diabetes, it is important that meals be eaten on time. If a meal is delayed and there is not enough glucose in the bloodstream, the patient may suffer severe reactions, including trembling, cold sweats, hunger, dizziness, and bizarre behavior. These reactions may be corrected by drinking a sweet beverage.

Exercise, such as swimming or walking briskly, is almost as good as a shot of insulin and is very useful in controlling diabetes. When a person exercises, the increased muscle activity allows additional amounts of glucose to be metabolized. Thus, if a diabetic is about to exercise strenuously, he must either reduce his insulin intake or eat more carbohydrates.

Prognosis. Although most diabetics, especially those with adult diabetes, can live normal, healthy lives, others, despite proper treatment, develop serious complications. Sometimes, severe premature atherosclerosis attacks the coronary arteries leading to a heart attack. The blood vessels of the legs may also be affected, producing difficulty in walking and eventually leading to painful ulcers and infections of the feet. In such cases, gangrene sometimes develops and the patient's foot may be amputated.

Diabetes mellitus may also lead to a special type of nephritis and, in the eyes, it may cause cataracts, hemorrhages, spots in the retina, and paralysis of the eye muscles. A painful neuritis may occur temporarily in the legs.

IRVING SOLOMON, M.D.
Mount Sinai School of Medicine, New York

DIABETES INSIPIDUS

Diabetes insipidus is a disorder characterized by the excretion of very dilute urine. As in diabetes mellitus, there is an excessive output of urine accompanied by extreme thirst. Unlike diabetes mellitus, however, there is no sugar in the urine and the blood sugar level is normal.

The substance that normally influences the kidney's capacity to conserve water and form concentrated urine is the antidiuretic hormone called vasopressin. This hormone is secreted by the hypothalamus, a small area of the brain located just above and in front of the pituitary gland. When the hypothalamus or the pituitary gland is diseased or injured, the secretion of vasopressin is decreased or stopped. As a result, large amounts of water are lost from the body, usually 10 quarts (9 liters) or more a day. If the patient does not counteract this loss by drinking much water, his blood volume falls, and shock, dehydration, and death may follow.

The known causes of diabetes insipidus include tumors in or near the base of the brain, head injury, and certain brain diseases, such as meningitis or encephalitis. In many cases, however, the cause of the disease is unknown. The diagnosis of diabetes insipidus is based on giving the patient vasopressin and then performing tests to see if the urine becomes more concentrated. If the vasopressin fails to work, the underlying disease may be a kidney disorder known as renal diabetes insipidus.

Once diabetes insipidus is diagnosed, it may be treated by administering a powdered form of the posterior pituitary gland. Another effective agent is the drug pitressin tannate, and a modern preparation of synthetic vasopressin is available in the form of a nasal spray.

NICHOLAS P. CHRISTY, M.D.
The Roosevelt Hospital, New York

DIACRITICAL MARKS, dī-ə-krit′i-kəl, are marks added above, below, beside, or through a letter or pair of letters to signal a difference in sound, accent, or intonation from the unmarked form. They are also called "diacritics." The term is derived from Greek *diakrinein* ("to distinguish").

Such marks are of very ancient use in Semitic and Indic writing as vowel symbols, but their modern use is largely to adapt the Roman alphabet to the sounds of languages having non-Latin phonemes.

In English the marks are found chiefly in various systems of phonetic respelling, as in the respelling above to show pronunciation; occasionally to separate the sounds of identical vowels (zoölogy, preëminent); in foreign words taken into English (façade, naïve); and in poetry to signal an abnormal pronunciation ("in virtue clothèd").

Standard Diacritical Marks

Acute Accent (´).—In Portuguese, Spanish, and ancient Greek this mark indicates the accented syllable. In Czech, French, Hungarian, Icelandic, Irish, and Lithuanian it signals the "long" (more accurately the tenser or more closed) sound of a vowel. In Polish it functions much as the háček does in Czech (see Háček).

Bar (-).—In Icelandic, đ sounds like *th* in *then*. In Serbo-Croatian, đ sounds like *dy* in *had you*.

Breve (˘).—Turkish ğ sounds like g in German *sagen*. It is a voiced dorsovelar fricative that does not occur in any dialect of English anymore (though it once did). In Rumania, ă has the neutral sound of *o* in *bacon*.

Cedilla (¸).—In French and Portuguese, ç sounds like *s* in *sit*; in Turkish, like *ch* in *chow*. In Rumanian and Turkish, ş sounds like *sh* in *show*, in Rumanian, ţ sounds like *ts* in *its*. In Latvian a form of cedilla on *k, l, n,* and *r* indicates the "soft" or palatalized sound of these consonants.

Circumflex (ˆ).—In French, â is pronounced like the *a* in *father*, ô like the *o* in *go*, and ê like the *e* in *bet*. In Rumanian, both â and î are pronounced somewhat like *i* in *smith*. In Portuguese the circumflex indicates accent.

Diaeresis (¨).—In German and Swedish, ä sounds like the *e* in *bet*; in Finnish, German, Hungarian, Swedish, and Turkish, ö sounds like *eu* in French *feu*; and in German and Turkish, ü sounds like the *u* in French *rue*. In French, Portuguese, and English, the diaeresis separates the sounds of adjoining identical vowels. A modified diaeresis (˝) is used over *o* and *u* in Hungarian to signal a long ö and ü.

Dot (˙).—In Polish and Lithuanian, ż sounds like *su* in *measure*. In Lithuanian, ė is "long." In Irish a dotted consonant is aspirated.

Grave Accent (`).—This mark is used chiefly to indicate accent, as in Italian, Lithuanian, Portuguese, and ancient Greek. In French, è is pronounced like the *e* in *bet*. In French and Italian the grave accent sometimes signals a difference of meaning rather than sound, as in the word *à* versus *a* or *è* versus *e*.

Háček or Wedge (ˇ).—In Czech, č sounds like *ch* in *church*, ď like *dy* in *did you*, ň like *ny* in *win you*, ř like *rsi* in *version*, š like *sh* in *shirt*, ť like *ty* in *get you*, and ž like *su* in *measure*. It functions similarly in Serbo-Croatian, Lithuanian, and Latvian.

Hook (˛).—In Polish the hook nasalizes *a* and *e*. In Lithuanian it indicates that ą, ę, į, and ų were formerly nasal vowels.

Macron (ˉ).—In Lithuanian ū sounds like *oo* in *soon*. In Latvian the macron marks four "long" vowels.

Ring (˚).—In Swedish, å sounds like the *o* in *hope*. In Czech, ů sounds like *oo* in *soon*.

Slash or Solidus or Virgule (/).—In Danish and Norwegian, ø sounds like *eu* in French *feu*. In Polish, ł is like English *l*, or sometimes like *w*.

Tilde (˜).—In Spanish, ñ sounds like *ny* in *canyon*. In Portuguese the tilde nasalizes *a* and *o*.

ROBERT L. CHAPMAN,
Drew University

DIADEM. See CROWNS AND CORONETS.

DIADOCHI, dī-ad′ə-kī, a Greek word meaning "successors," is used to refer to the chief lieutenants of Alexander the Great, who tried to partition his empire or obtain all of it for themselves after his death in 323 B.C. It is possible to speak of an "age of the Diadochi," extending from Alexander's death to the Battle of Ipsus (301), where the last major attempt to gain all of the empire ended with the death of Antigonus I; or to the Battle of Corupedion (281), where the boundaries of the main states of the Hellenistic age became roughly fixed.

There were six chief contenders for the empire. Among them Antipater and his friend Antigonus I tried to hold the vast empire together, while Ptolemy, Seleucus, Lysimachus, and Cassander favored dividing it. The almost constant wars of the successors made this an age remarkable for the complexity of its politics and for the striking character of its personalities.

HARRY J. DELL
University of Virginia

DIAERESIS. See DIACRITICAL MARKS.

DIAGHILEV, dyä′gyi-lyəf, **Sergei Pavlovich** (1872–1929), Russian impresario and founder of the Ballets Russes, the dance company that revitalized ballet in the early 20th century when it had become a ponderous and stereotyped theatrical form. His organizational genius brought together the foremost of Russia's academically trained dancers and choreographers and the best contemporary musicians and artists.

Diaghilev was born in Novgorod on March 19, 1872. He turned from the study of law to music, graduating from the St. Petersburg Conservatory in 1892. Art and theater interested him almost as much as music. He organized several exhibitions of modern European art in St. Petersburg, and became editor of the *World of Art,* an illustrated journal published by a group of artists and writers that included the painters Léon Bakst and Alexandre Benois.

After a brief tenure as assistant to the director of the Imperial Theaters, Diaghilev, with more imagination than money, organized an exhibit of Russian art in Paris in 1906, followed by concerts of Russian music and a production of the opera *Boris Godunov*. In 1909, Paris witnessed the spectacularly successful first performances of the Ballets Russes de Sergei Diaghilev.

For the next 20 years the major cities of Europe and the Western Hemisphere saw Diaghilev's brilliant amalgam of choreography, decor, music, and dance. The company went through three periods: the first dominated by sumptuous Asian ballets; the second, by chic French works; and the third, by severe, stylized ballets. During World War I, Diaghilev made Monte Carlo his headquarters. After his death in Venice on Aug. 19, 1929, the company soon dispersed, and his choreographers and dancers carried his ideas to other companies in Europe and the United States. See also BALLETS RUSSES DE SERGEI DIAGHILEV.

DORIS HERING, *"Dance Magazine"*

Further Reading: Buckle, Richard, *In Search of Diaghilev* (New York 1961); Fokine, Vitale, *Fokine, Memoirs of a Ballet Master* (Boston 1961); Grigoriev, Sergei L., *The Diaghilev Ballet (1909–1929)* (London 1953); Haskell, Arnold, and Nouvel, Walter, *Serge Diaghilev* (New York 1935).

DIAGNOSIS. See DISEASE—*Methods of Diagnosis*.

DIAL, The, a quarterly review, published from 1840 to 1844, that was a highly influential organ of the transcendentalist movement in New England. Its first editor was Margaret Fuller, who was followed in 1842 by Ralph Waldo Emerson. A second magazine of the same name was edited for a year (1860–1861) in Cincinnati by Moncure Conway, a clergyman. A third *Dial*, founded in 1880 in Chicago as a conservative journal of literary criticism, moved to New York in 1918 and became an important literary review, noted for presenting the work of avant-garde writers and distinguished scholars. It ceased publication in 1929. A fourth *Dial*, a literary quarterly edited by James Silberman, was published in New York from 1959 to 1962.

DIALECT, dī′ə-lekt, the way a language is spoken in a particular region (for example, the "Southern dialect" of the United States). Although dialects exist in writing, and there are dialect literary works (the poetry of Robert Burns, for example), dialect is, in the main, confined to speech.

All languages have dialects, but it is important to note that the difference between a dialect and a language is relative, not absolute; arbitrary, not logical. In Italy the Tuscan dialect became Standard Italian, but there is still a wide difference between the Italian spoken in northern Italy and that spoken, for example, in Sicily. Dutch and Flemish are dialects of the same language, the differences between them arising out of the geographical, political, and even religious differences between the Netherlands and Belgium. In Spain, Castilian is Standard Spanish, but there are other important dialects and even other languages, especially Catalan, spoken by large numbers of people. And in Norway, where Danish was once the language of educated people, a standard Norwegian language is evolving from a synthesis of several Norwegian dialects.

The use of the word "dialect" to mean a *regional dialect*—as in the phrase "that ancient dialect Ionic Greek"—is the oldest and the one that still predominates. A regional dialect is a variation, peculiar to a district or region, from the norm of standard speech; it is a regional language within a language. As early as the 1570's, however, "dialect" also meant the speech either of a social class or of a profession or trade. But in the sense of "occupational dialect" the term is being discarded in favor of "jargon" (see JARGON).

Not even regional dialects are solely regional: the influences of class and occupation are often noticeable, especially in rural speech. And, as scholars have fully recognized only in the 20th century, even some cities possess dialects as distinct, for example, as the English dialects of Essex, Lancashire, or County Cork, or of Maine, Tennessee, or Oklahoma.

The word "dialect" has subtle differences of meaning, according to its application. For example, some scholars contend that in the phrase "the dialect of the upper classes," dialect means something different from what it means in "the Yorkshire dialect" or "the Southern dialect of the United States." And in the expression "the Negro dialect and subdialects of North America," dialect has both "class" and ethnic relevance.

Since the publication of Joseph Wright's *English Dialect Dictionary* (1898–1905), the subject of dialect has been undergoing a searching reconsideration and a salutary refocusing, especially in Britain and the United States. The result is that scholars have acquired relatively clear ideas about what dialect is, how to study dialects in general, and the nature of a particular dialect or group of dialects.

Dialects of English. George L. Brook's *English Dialects* (1963), a leading general work on the subject, deals globally with all the dialects and the principal subdialects of English. It lists the three main dialects as British English, American English, and the varieties of English spoken in the Commonwealth (outside Britain). To these should be added those varieties of English, British and American, spoken in other parts of the world.

Within each of these groups there are subdialects, such as the regional dialects of Britain; the regional dialects of the United States; Canadian (with a large admixture of American English), South African, Australian, and New Zealand; and the subdialects of India, Pakistan, Malaysia, Hong Kong, and other places where English is an official or second language.

England. Of the dialects spoken in the British Isles, the most important are those spoken in England. The four main dialects of Old English —Northumbrian, Mercian, West Saxon, and Kentish—became five in Middle English: Northern, East Midland, West Midland, Southwestern, and Southeastern. By the end of the 14th century, the East Midland dialect, not surprisingly, predominated. Midlanders were favorably situated geographically, commercially, professionally, and culturally. The Midlands possessed two great centers of learning—Oxford and Cambridge—and three of culture—Oxford, Cambridge, and London. As explained by McKnight and Emsley in *Modern English in the Making* (1928): "In the nature of things the language of London was bound to exert wide influence. An East Midland dialect, . . . it enjoyed with the Midland speech used at Oxford the advantage . . . of being something of a happy mean. Its use, too, in governmental activities and its gradual adoption into use in the aristocratic circles of English court life lent it prestige. To London even more generally than to Oxford were drawn people from different parts of the country, and the form of English there met with naturally became widely known." The authors rightly add that even without the powerful example of Chaucer, the East Midland dialect would have achieved supremacy. Less because of its inherent merits than because of favoring circumstances, this dialect became accepted as Standard English.

The United States. Although it is true that the dialects and subdialects of the United States are less numerous and distinct than in England, since the late 1930's it has become increasingly evident that they are more numerous and distinct than had previously been supposed. Allowing for the great differences of time, place, and distance, much the same sort of process as took place in England occurred in the United States. The speech of New England, especially of Massachusetts and Connecticut, became the dominant speech of the new nation. From the very beginning, New England had an advantage in education and learning, in literature and general culture.

However, what finally emerged as a rather vague and much disputed approximation of a Standard American is not a single predominant dialect but three dialects—Northern, Midland, and Southern—and all three have subdialects. (Rather than speak of subdialects of Northern, however, it might be more accurate to speak of two main branches: the New England and the rest of the Northern.)

Other Dialect Areas. Less important, in the mass, than the British English and American English dialects, yet notable, are the dialects of Australia and Canada. Australian speech is especially distinctive, sounding much like the Cockney dialect of London. Australian dialects, moreover, are enriched by an admixture of words from the language of the aborigines. Canadian dialects include the English spoken in the French provinces of Canada.

Research. In England since 1873, when the English Dialect Society was formed, there has been lively, continuous, progressive interest in dialect study. The English Dialect Society ceased operations in 1896, but in the 1940's its work was undertaken by the Philological Society, which instituted a general linguistic survey and atlas under the direction of Harold Orton.

In addition to this general study, valuable information has been published by regional dialect societies in their annual journals. The academic study of dialects has been centered in the universities of Leeds and Edinburgh. In 1952, Angus McIntosh of the University of Edinburgh published *An Introduction to a Survey of Scottish Dialects*, and in 1962, Harold Orton, at the University of Leeds, published the first volume of a projected multivolume study entitled *Survey of English Dialects*.

The American Dialect Society was founded in 1889, and its *Dialect Notes* published valuable findings from 1890 to 1925, the year the linguistic quarterly *American Speech* first appeared. From 1925, both *American Speech* and the American Dialect Society's bulletins and other publications continued the work. The compilation of a linguistic atlas of the United States and Canada was begun in the 1930's under the direction of Hans Kurath.

Regional dialect research in the United States has consisted chiefly of independent but related projects carried forward at several universities. Research on the Middle Atlantic and South Atlantic regions was under the direction of Raven I. McDavid at the University of Chicago. The preparation of linguistic atlases was directed by Harold B. Allen at the University of Minnesota (for the Upper Midwest) and David W. Reed at the University of California, Berkeley (for the Pacific Coast and the Northwest). At Emory University, Lee Pederson directed research on dialects of the Gulf and Inner South states.

ERIC PARTRIDGE, *Author of "A Dictionary of Slang and Unconventional English"*

Bibliography

Brook, George Leslie, *English Dialects* (London 1963).
Craigie, Sir William A., and Hulbert, James R., eds., *A Dictionary of American English*, 4 vols. (Chicago 1938–1943).
Grose, Francis, *A Provincial Glossary* (London 1787).
McKnight, George H., and Emsley, Bert, *Modern English in the Making* (New York 1928).
Mathews, Mitford M., ed., *A Dictionary of Americanisms*, 2 vols. (Chicago 1951).
Mencken, Henry L., *The American Language*, 4th ed., rev. and enl. (New York 1936; supplement, 1, 1945; supplement 2, 1948).
Wentworth, Harold, *American Dialect Dictionary* (New York 1944).
Wright, Joseph, *The English Dialect Dictionary*, 6 vols. (London 1898–1905).

DIALECTIC has meant different things to different philosophers. No single definition can cover all legitimate uses of this term.

Before 1800. Originally, dialectic was the method employed by Zeno of Elea in the 5th century B.C. to show that the position of his opponents gave rise to paradoxes. These paradoxes are still widely discussed.

Influenced by Zeno and Socrates (see DIALOGUE), Plato called dialectic the supreme science and contrasted it with deduction. His dialectic moves upward from premises to presuppositions and ultimately to the eternal Forms. Dialectic is needed for, but does not always lead to, the mystical vision of the highest Form, the Good. This fusion of intellectual training and mysticism also characterized Neoplatonism, which associated dialectic with three stages. The world was said to be governed by a pattern of unity—going out of, and returning into, oneself.

In Kant's *Critique of Pure Reason* (1781) dialectic becomes "the logic of illusion," while "Transcendental Dialectic" (half of the book) is defined as "a critique of this dialectical illusion." Under this heading Kant offered his epoch-making attacks on dogmatical psychology and cosmology and on attempts to prove God's existence. To show how reason becomes involved in contradictions when it transcends experience, he offered four theses and four antitheses on facing pages. Soon Fichte introduced the three-step of thesis, antithesis, and synthesis; and Schelling took up these terms. Hegel did not.

Since 1800. Nevertheless, it is widely assumed that Hegel invented the dialectic in which every thesis generates an antithesis, and then a synthesis (a fusion of both) that becomes the thesis of another triad. In fact, Hegel derided such mechanical formalism, and his triads cannot be reduced to such terms. His dialectic is neither a law nor a rigorous method. He insisted that everything spiritual must be comprehended through its development, and he established the historical approach to philosophy, religion, and art. He stressed conflict and ironical reversals. Pushed to their limits, concepts and views change strikingly, but not in any precise sense into their opposites.

Marx rejected Hegel's emphasis on spirit and stressed economic factors, while consciously adopting Hegel's dialectic (see DIALECTICAL MATERIALISM). Kierkegaard attacked Hegel from a Christian point of view but also prized his dialectic; and neoorthodox Protestant theology has been called "dialectical theology."

Today "dialectic" usually suggests some subtle ironical development, and not sophistry. But when no meaning is specified and no historical reference implied, the term lacks precision.

WALTER KAUFMANN, *Author of "Hegel"*

DIALECTICAL MATERIALISM is the philosophical theory developed by Karl Marx and Friedrich Engels (qq.v.) and adopted as the official philosophy of the Soviet Union.

Marx formulated his theory of dialectical materialism by combining the traditional view of a universe composed solely of matter with the dialectic of G. W. F. Hegel (q.v.). Marx's analysis of capitalism, which asserts that economic forces are in the last analysis the determining ones in history, is the supreme example of his use of the dialectical method. See also MARXISM.

DIALLAGE. See PYROXENE.

DIALOGUE as a literary form was developed in the 5th century B.C. in Greek tragedy. Long passages in Aeschylus' *Eumenides* and in many of Euripides' plays influenced Plato's dialogues. But Plato also owed much to Socrates, who had actually engaged other men in conversation and developed philosophical arguments through questions and answers. Socrates was less concerned to present theories than to criticize the views of others by bringing out hidden premises and unforeseen implications that would prove unacceptable. Plato, who had tried writing tragedies, decided upon meeting Socrates to write philosophical dialogues. This device allowed Plato to deal with objections, to leave some uncertainty about his own positions, and to initiate his readers into the life of thought.

The literary form fashioned by Plato was later taken up by George Berkeley in *Three Dialogues Between Hylas and Philonous* (1713). Philonous defends the author's idealism against Hylas' objections. David Hume's *Dialogues Concerning Natural Religion* (1779) are more elusive, but most scholars consider the character Philo to be Hume's mouthpiece. The dialogue form is still used occasionally. George Santayana published *Dialogues in Limbo* (1926), and Walter Kaufmann's *Critique of Religion and Philosophy* (1958) includes three dialogues between Satan and a theologian, a Christian, and an atheist.

In Martin Buber's books, the term "dialogue" does not necessarily involve words; it is a way of recognizing another being as no mere object or It, but as a Thou. Buber's views have had considerable influence on contemporary theologians. Dialogue was a way of life for Socrates, too; but Buber lacked Socrates' faith in argument.

WALTER KAUFMANN
Author of "Tragedy and Philosophy"

Further Reading: Buber, Martin, *Between Man and Man*, tr. by Ronald Gregor Smith (London 1947); id., *I and Thou*, tr. by Ronald Gregor Smith (New York 1937); Morgan, Charles, *Dialogue in Novels and Plays* (Philadelphia 1954).

DIALOGUES OF LEOPARDI, lä-ō-pär′dē, the philosophical writings, mostly in dialogue form, of the Italian poet Giacomo Leopardi (q.v.), published in 1827 as the *Operette morali*. These "little works" contain expositions of Leopardi's attitude toward life, restating many of the themes of his poems. His sarcasm is merciless, violent, and despairing. The dialogues—models of clarity and conciseness—also include the author's meditations on aesthetic theory and his ideas on prose forms.

Often overestimated for their philosophical value, the dialogues contain phrases borrowed from the 18th century French deists, but Leopardi denies the humanitarianism that logically springs from the doctrines of French rationalism. His sarcasm is merciless and violent as he attacks man and nature in a despair that permits no escape. He considers ideas of progress, social reform, and scientific discovery as delusions with which men console themselves because they are afraid to face the unredeemable lot of mankind. He regards mankind's struggle for happiness as hopelessly beyond its reach, and from his solitude he looks forward to a time when men will have become extinct.

DIALOGUES OF PLATO. See PLATO.

DIALYSIS, dī-al'ə-səs, is a method for separating chemical substances by means of diffusion through a semipermeable membrane. The membrane acts as a sieve with small holes that let small molecules and ions pass but keep back large ones. The term *dialysis* was first used by the Scottish chemist Thomas Graham, who in 1866 used a membrane to separate sugar from gum arabic.

A typical use of dialysis is for the removal of salt from protein preparations. An impure protein solution is placed in a sack, which is then dipped in pure water. The salts diffuse out of the sack into the surrounding water, while the protein stays in the sack.

The interaction of the membrane material with the solvent is important. For example, a membrane of rubber does not allow water to pass through it, but benzene, which has larger molecules than water, does pass. This is explained by the fact that the benzene molecules are attracted to the molecular chains of the rubber and cause the rubber to swell, with the result that the spaces between the chains are also enlarged.

Electrodialysis. A different kind of separation is achieved by placing ionic charges on the membrane. Such membranes may be composed of collodion or cellulose acetate that has been treated chemically to introduce sulfonate or carboxylate ions, or the membranes may be fabricated from ion-exchange resins. (SEE ION EXCHANGE.) The molecular chains of the membrane carry fixed positive or negative electrical charges, depending on the ionic groups present. Because electrical neutrality must be conserved, the ionic groups on the membrane have small mobile ions of opposite charge associated with them; thus a membrane with fixed negative sulfonate ions might carry an equal number of positive sodium ions. A membrane with this structure would allow positive ions to pass through it because these would merely change places with other ions already in the membrane. However, negative ions would be virtually excluded because they would have to bring positive ions into the membrane with them, and the resultant crowding would take much energy. In the same way, a membrane with fixed positive charges would allow negative ions to pass across, but not positive ions.

In one type of electrodialysis a cell is constructed that is divided into three compartments by the presence of one negative and one positive membrane. A salt solution fills all three compartments and an electric current is passed through the solution. The current causes the positive ions to pass out of the central compartment through the negative membrane, while the negative ions leave it through the positive membrane.

Electrodialysis is widely used in biochemistry. It is faster than ordinary dialysis and allows the selective removal of salts from uncharged molecules. An important use of electrodialysis is in the purification of saline water. The cells used for desalting water have many parallel compartments with alternate cation-exchange and anion-exchange membranes; when the current passes, salt is removed from alternate compartments and concentrated in the others.

HAROLD F. WALTON, *University of Colorado*

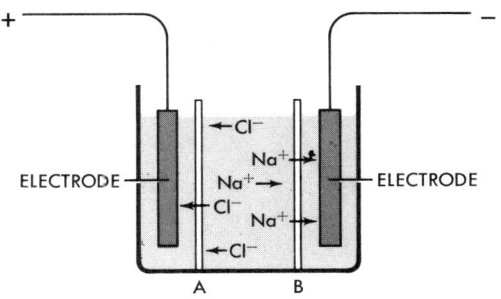

THE ELECTRODIALYSIS CELL is divided into three compartments by two membranes. A is an anion-exchange membrane with fixed positive charges. B is a cation-exchange membrane with fixed negative charges.

DIAMAGNETISM, dī-ə-mag'nə-tiz-əm, is a classification for substances, such as bismuth, that magnetize in a direction opposite to that of an applied magnetic field and that have a magnetic permeability less than that of a vacuum. See MAGNETISM—*Diamagnetism and Paramagnetism.*

DIAMANTINA, dē-ə-maNN-tē'nə, is an inland city in Brazil, in northern Minas Gerais state, about 310 miles (500 km) north of Rio de Janeiro. Diamonds were discovered here in 1729, and by 1735 the influx of miners from the gold-rush area of Ouro Prêto, a few miles to the south, had swelled the town's population to 30,000. The gold and diamonds from this region helped Rio de Janeiro to outstrip Bahía, the sugar-exporting center to the north, as Brazil's major port and, ultimately, as its principal city.

With smuggling and thievery rampant in the diamond fields, Diamantina acquired a reputation for lawlessness. By the mid-1800's the jewel-diamond industry was dead, for no diamonds remained to be mined by individuals at surface level. Nevertheless, in the 1960's $3 million worth of industrial diamonds (used as drills in machinery) were still being mined annually by hydraulic methods. Population: (1960) 14,252.

HELEN MILLER BAILEY
East Los Angeles College

DIAMOND, David (1915–   ), American composer, whose neoromantic music employs disciplined chromaticism, animated rhythms, and original contrapuntal devices.

Life. Diamond was born in Rochester, N. Y., on July 9, 1915. His family moved to Cleveland, Ohio, and he studied there at the Cleveland Institute of Music (1927–1929). He then studied at the Eastman School with composer Bernard Rogers (1930–1934), with Roger Sessions in New York (1934–1936), and with Nadia Boulanger in Paris (1937–1938). Diamond was awarded two Guggenheim fellowships (1938 and 1941). In 1943 he received the New York Music Critics Circle Award for his Symphony No. 1. He went to Florence, Italy, on a Fulbright grant in 1951 and remained there until 1965, returning to the United States from time to time to teach.

Works. Diamond's work includes eight symphonies; orchestral, choral, chamber, and solo instrumental works; and music for the ballet, the theater, and motion pictures. His most frequently performed works are his *Rounds* (1944), for string orchestra; Symphony No. 4 (1945); and *Music for Romeo and Juliet* (1947). Among his later compositions are *To Music* (1968), for tenor, bass baritone, chorus, and orchestra.

W. THOMAS MARROCCO
Coauthor of "Music in the United States"

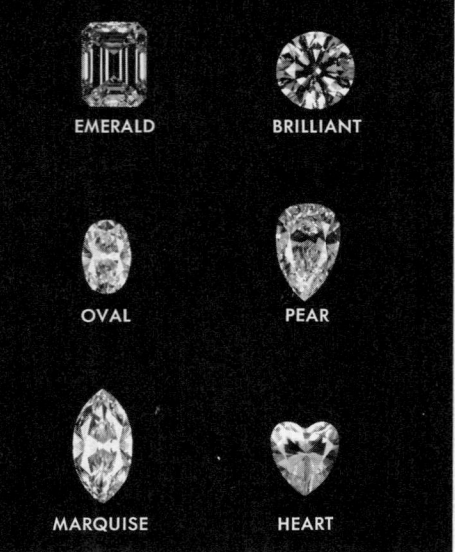

CUT DIAMONDS (left), shown in some of the more popular shapes, and rough diamonds (right) of several sizes and shapes as they occur in their natural state.

DIAMOND, di′ə-mənd, the hardest of all known substances, is a mineral composed solely of carbon. The word "diamond" is a corruption of the Greek word *adamas,* which means "unconquerable." The ancient Greeks probably gave this name to a variety of hard bright substances, including metals. It was first applied to the substance known today as diamond by writers such as the Roman naturalist Pliny, because of the hardness of the mineral and the mistaken belief that it could not be shattered by a blow—a test often used for diamonds in the past, with sad results.

USES OF DIAMOND

Diamond is the best-known gem and the one that is most commonly used in engagement rings. It is the birthstone for April. Because the mineral is the hardest substance known, diamond dust has long been used to cut diamond crystals into gems. In the 20th century the mineral has become the most important industrial abrasive; it is virtually indispensable as a grinding material in a wide range of industrial applications. Diamond today is monetarily one of the major items in the international mineral trade. Some of the demand for the abrasive is being met by the production of synthetic diamond.

Use as a Gem. The first known discoveries of diamonds were in ancient India. These early finds were kept loose or were mounted in their natural state, except when lapidaries occasionally ground a flat surface or shaped a crystal according to whim. It was the rarity of the stones, their exceptional hardness, and at times the presence of a delicate color that made the people of India value them. Most diamonds were owned by rulers.

The beauty and hardness of diamonds gave rise to the notion that they enabled their wearers to acquire certain virtues. For example, a diamond was supposed by some people to impart invulnerability to its owner and to protect a warrior in battle. Other legends were that possession of a diamond would prevent mental illness or ward off the effects of a poison.

In medieval times, diamond was ranked below several other gem materials—especially ruby, emerald, and pearl. Also, diamond was only known to occur in India, so that its availability elsewhere was limited. The full beauty of the stone was not really recognized until the development of the gem shape called the "brilliant cut," toward the end of the 17th century, by the Italian lapidary Vincenzo Peruzzi.

With the application of regularly shaped designs that revealed the brilliancy of the gem, diamond came into its own. Then, in the early part of the 18th century, the mineral was found in greater abundance in Brazil; this discovery brought it to the attention of a much larger market as a gem material. The general adoption of diamond as the chief material for engagement rings developed gradually thereafter.

Industrial Uses. Diamonds for industrial uses are more important than gem diamonds, although they are less profitable. Industrial diamonds are a by-product and depend on a prosperous gem industry to justify their recovery; the industrial varieties represent 75% to 80% of output by weight, but only 25% to 30% by value, of the total diamond market.

Industrial Classifications. Industrial diamonds are used in several forms. Crystals having no special name range in size from 200 crystals per carat to single crystals of 10 carats or more. The smaller ones (mostly under half a carat) are rather regular in shape; the larger ones may have various shapes and properties that suit them for special uses. Some of the specialized applications are for bearings, knife edges, ruling tools, phonograph needles, hardness-testing devices, and glass cutters.

Crushing bort is a low-grade natural diamond material of indefinite size and shape. It is broken into small fragments or crushed to a powder, and is used for grinding, cutting, and polishing operations; synthetic diamond is also much used for these purposes. Originally, the diamond craftsman was the sole user of such powder and grit, and he crushed his own bort by rough means. Sieves now separate the coarser sizes, and the finer ones are separated by sedimentation, elutriation (lifting by the flow of water), or centrifuge. These methods grade the particles according to their mass.

Two other familiar kinds of industrial diamond are *ballas* and *carbonado* (or simply *car-*

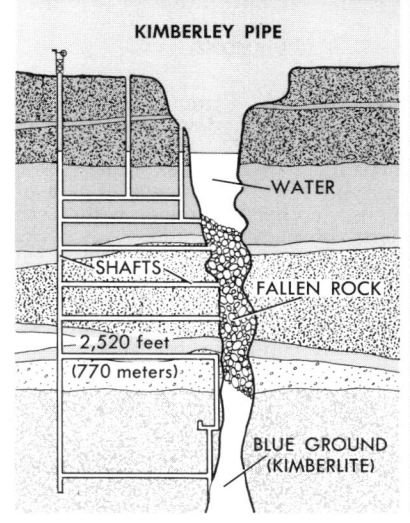

KIMBERLITE, the primary mineral source of diamonds, occurs typically in narrow pipes extending down into the earth. The famous South African Kimberley mine was worked first as an open pit and then from deep shafts sunk alongside the pipe. Kimberley was mined out in 1914, and the pit is now filling up with water.

PHOTO FROM N. W. AYER AND SON, INC.

bon). Ballas is nearly round but may have to be split before being used to shape—to "true" —abrasive wheels. Carbonado, found almost solely in Brazil, occurs as an irregular mass that lacks the consistent crystal structure (and hence the cleavage weakness) of other diamonds.

Kinds of Industries. Henry Ford was the first to discover that, on a large scale, diamond is actually the cheapest industrial abrasive for long-term use in spite of its high initial cost. Today the automotive industry is the principal buyer of industrial diamond, and Detroit has more diamond-tool dealers than any other city in the world. Indeed, there are more than 15 different uses for the mineral in an automobile factory. Aircraft production has parallel opportunities for the use of this unexcelled abrasive.

The machine-tool industry is in the forefront of diamond research. Antifriction bearings involve uses similar to those for automobiles and machine tools. The glass and optical industries were early users of diamonds, as for grinding mirrors or for sawing spectacles. A major application of larger diamonds is in diamond drills used in prospecting for minerals, in mining ores, and in drilling oil and gas wells.

The electronics industry and the electrical industry are both users of industrial diamonds. Textile printers use them to cut patterns. Dentists and physicians use diamonds to cut delicate bone and tissue, and jewelers use them to fashion gems—including other diamonds. Finally, the manufacture of many common household products involves the use of diamonds that are too flawed or discolored to appear in jewelry.

PROPERTIES

The most distinctive characteristic of diamond is its hardness, which serves as the highest point—number 10—on Mohs' scale of hardness used in mineralogy. This means that diamond is able to scratch or abrade every other mineral. In fact, a greater difference exists in this respect between diamond and corundum (number 9 on Mohs' scale) than between corundum and talc (number 1). Other scales of hardness used in science and industry likewise show the superiority of diamond. Its hardness makes it valuable as an industrial tool and also enables it to withstand wear as a gem. The diamond crystal, however, is not equally hard in all directions. In practice, the crystals are set singly for use in cutting tools. In this way they can be oriented correctly to within one degree, by X-rays and gamma radiation, with respect to the crystal direction of greatest hardness.

Crystal Appearance and Structure. Diamond crystallizes in the isometric system. The crystals, which range from white or colorless to brown or black, are most often octahedrons that resemble two square-based pyramids placed base to base. The next most common form is the dodecahedron, which has 12 faces. Cubes are less abundant. As is true of most natural crystals, these forms often occur rounded, flattened, or otherwise distorted. Twin crystals are found frequently, especially the so-called *spinel twin* of double octahedrons.

Both the crystal shape and the hardness of diamond reflect the 3-dimensional pattern in which the carbon atoms are arranged within the crystal. An atom of another element may take the place of a carbon atom in this crystal lattice structure, but there is seldom more than one such atom for every 10,000 carbon atoms; and the finest natural diamonds contain only one foreign part for about 100,000 carbon atoms.

The atomic structure in turn influences the way that diamond breaks. Despite ancient legends to the contrary, diamond has a perfect cleavage parallel to the octahedron faces of the diamond—that is, there are four directions of cleavage. This property is used to divide large crystals and spinel twins, and to shape the finished gem.

Owing to the relatively close packing of the carbon atoms in the crystal lattice, diamond has a fairly high density; its specific gravity is 3.52. Hardness and heaviness combine to make diamond an ideal placer mineral—that is, one separable from other surface deposits by processes such as washing.

Optical Properties. The optical properties of diamond give it the beauty that makes it desirable as a gem. First is its luster, which is termed *adamantine* (from the ancient name for diamond); the crystal has a very bright, slightly oily surface reflection. Diamond has a high refractive index of 2.417 as well, which means that a properly cut stone can return to the eye of the beholder a large proportion of the light that enters the stone. Its light dispersion—the breaking up of white light into its component colors—also is high; this is called *fire*.

Diamonds are classified as type I or type II according to the way they absorb radiation in the visible as well as the infrared and ultraviolet regions of the spectrum. (A few intermediate specimens are of different types in different regions of the spectrum.) Type II, the only kind that occurs blue in nature, seems to be a more nearly perfect kind of crystal lattice that has fewer crystal defects than type I.

Color, or the absence of color, is another and a most important optical property of gem diamond, strongly affecting its commercial value. See section on *Grading*.

Conductivity. Most diamonds are extremely good electrical insulators. Some crystals of type II are semiconductors, however. The heat conductivity of gem-quality diamonds at room temperature, on the other hand, is greater than that of any other known substance. For this reason, diamond can be cut at high speeds without being damaged by the heat generated.

OCCURRENCE

In only one rock, *kimberlite* (named for the diamond-mining city of Kimberley, South Africa), does diamond occur originally. All other occurrences are secondary. That is, diamond found in other rocks was eroded from a primary source (presumably kimberlite) and incorporated in some kind of sedimentary rock, which then may have been more or less changed by metamorphism.

Kimberlite does not always contain diamond. Even when it does, the proportion averages only about 1 part in 40 million parts of rock and probably never has exceeded 1 part in 8 million parts. Diamond thus is a so-called accessory mineral and would be of little interest except for its economic significance.

Mineralogy of Kimberlite. Kimberlite is an altered and brecciated (broken) form of peridotite. Peridotite, in turn, is a heavy, high-temperature igneous rock of basic composition (high iron and magnesium content). The form known as kimberlite consists of large corroded crystals of high-pressure minerals, including diamond, in a matrix of calcite and a distinctive group of basic minerals, most of which are green. Kimberlite usually contains inclusions of dense rocks of various kinds, some brought up from considerable depths and others dragged down from above.

Kimberlite occurs typically in diatremes, or *pipes*. These somewhat cylindrical bodies of rock are of volcanic origin, although their connection with actual surface volcanoes is uncertain. Any evidence of such association has been eroded away. The explosive origins of kimberlite pipes is shown, nevertheless, by the abundant indications of shattering upward movement and downward or inward collapse in the pipes. At greater depths the pipes become narrow and take on the shapes of dikes.

As kimberlite weathers and its iron oxidizes, the color of the rock changes from bluish green (when it is called *blue ground*) to yellowish (*yellow ground*). The weathering of kimberlite frees the diamonds it contains. They are carried away by streams and other agents of erosion and finally come to rest in placer deposits. Later stages of erosion may move the diamonds again. They are recovered from stream gravels, from windblown deposits (dunes), and from beach deposits, and offshore mining of submarine beds is conducted along the Atlantic Ocean coast of Africa. Conglomerate, sandstone, and other sedimentary rocks yield diamond in various parts of the world. An especially interesting host rock is the flexible sandstone called *itacolumite*. Schist and related metamorphic rocks also contain diamonds.

The minerals found with diamond depend on where it occurs. In kimberlite the associations are so typical that the prospector can depend on them. Olivine, garnet, phlogopite, mica, pyroxene, ilmenite, serpentine, chlorite, and calcite are the usual minerals. In placer and other secondary deposits, however, the accompanying minerals are not necessarily related to a kimberlite origin; they may be minerals characteristic of placers—such as magnetite and gold—as well as locally derived minerals.

Diamond Sites. The first great source of diamond was India, although production there today is very small. The prominent Golconda mines used a name that concealed the mines'

SOME FAMOUS DIAMONDS

BRAZIL

PRESIDENT VARGAS The 727-carat° Vargas is the largest diamond yet found in South America. Discovered in 1938 in the San Antonio River by a prospector, it was cut into 29 stones, the largest of which is about 48 ct.
STAR OF THE SOUTH Found in the Bagagem mines in 1853, the uncut crystal weighed about 262 ct. The brilliant that was shaped from it weighs nearly 129 ct.

INDIA

FLORENTINE This pale yellow diamond was acquired in the early 17th century by the Duke of Tuscany and later became one of the Austrian crown jewels. The present location of the 137-ct diamond is unknown.
GREAT MOGUL Found about 1650, the 280-ct Great Mogul was the largest diamond cut in India. The original stone may have weighed nearly 800 ct. It was last seen about 1665 and may have been cut into smaller gems.
KOH-I-NOOR "The Mountain of Light." This gem has the oldest verifiable history of all diamonds and has been traced back to 1304. After changing hands many times it was purchased by Britain in 1849 and is now in the Queen Mother's crown. The recut stone weighs approximately 108 ct.
ORLOV The 200-ct rose-cut Orlov, according to legend, was stolen from an Indian temple where it formed one of the eyes of an idol. Eventually bought by a Russian prince, it is now in the USSR diamond treasury.
REGENT or PITT Discovered in 1701, the 410-ct Regent was cut into a brilliant of about 140 ct and sold to the regent of France. Stolen in 1792 (with the Sancy and Hope gems) and then recovered, it is in the Louvre.

REPUBLIC OF SOUTH AFRICA

CULLINAN The Cullinan, the largest diamond yet found, weighed 3,106 ct when discovered in the Premier mine in 1905. It was presented to Britain's Edward VII in 1907 and was cut into nine large stones (now part of the British crown jewels) and nearly 100 gems.
EXCELSIOR Found in the Jagersfontein mine in 1893 as a 995-ct rough diamond crystal, the Excelsior was cut into 21 stones, the largest of which is about 70 ct.
JONKER The 726-ct Jonker was found at Elandsfontein in 1934 and was bought by Harry Winston, Inc., of New York City. It was cut into 12 gems.
JUBILEE Discovered in 1895, the 650-ct rough diamond was named in honor of Queen Victoria's jubilee of 1897. It was cut to form a gem of about 245 ct.
TIFFANY The deep yellow, 128-ct Tiffany was discovered in the Kimberley mine as a 287-ct rough crystal.

Other famous cut diamonds include the **REGENT OF PORTUGAL** (Brazil), 221 ct—which may be a topaz, however; **VICTORIA** (South Africa), 185 ct; **SHAH** (India), 89 ct; **STAR OF SOUTH AFRICA** (South Africa), 48 ct; **SANCY** (India), 55 ct; **HOPE** (India; the largest blue diamond), 44 ct; and **DRESDEN GREEN** (India), 41 ct.

°Weights are expressed in metric carats; 1 ct equals 0.2 gram (about 0.007 ounce). Figures are rounded because value of carat has varied and weights are often approximate.

CUTTING A DIAMOND

ALL PHOTOGRAPHS BY N. W. AYER AND SON, INC.

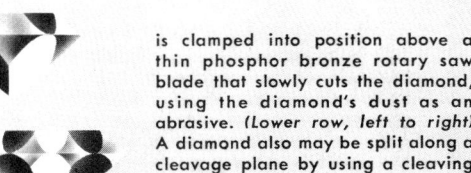

Steps in cutting and polishing a diamond—from the octahedral shape of a typical crystal to a finished brilliant cut having 58 facets—are shown in the diagrams. The actual process of diamond cutting is shown in the photographs above. (Upper row, left to right) The rough stone is examined through a powerful magnifying glass and marked with ink for cutting. Stones to be cut are mounted in holders, called dops, in preparation for sawing. The dop is clamped into position above a thin phosphor bronze rotary saw blade that slowly cuts the diamond, using the diamond's dust as an abrasive. (Lower row, left to right) A diamond also may be split along a cleavage plane by using a cleaving knife. The diamond is then girdled—that is, shaped at its greatest width. Finally, its facets are precisely ground as the stone is held against a revolving iron disk impregnated with oil and diamond dust.

---

true locations, for Golconda (now a deserted fort near Hyderabad) was merely the trading center. The mining was done over a wide area on the eastern side of the Deccan plateau and extended into the Bundelkhand district, where present operations take place. Mining practically ceased in the 17th century, not long after all the historic stones except the *Koh-i-noor* were found. One ancient kimberlite mine has again been worked in central India, but the rest are in secondary deposits.

South America. In 1727, not long after production declined in India, diamonds were found in Brazil. In spite of political interference and poor trade practices, Brazil maintained a leading position in diamond production for a century and a half. Three states—Minas Gerais (the mining center is Diamantina), Bahia, and Mato Grosso—are the most important producers, but six others have yielded some diamonds. The average grade of the stones is very high, and a few large crystals have been found.

Guyana has diamond beds across its entire width, but until recently they were not sufficiently accessible; today exports are substantial. Venezuela has become another large exporter.

Africa. The first recognized diamond in South Africa was picked up by children of a Boer farmer in 1867. It weighed 22 carats. A second large crystal was found in 1869 by a shepherd boy. A diamond rush began the next year and spread across South Africa, changing its character as wealth from diamonds opened up the gold-mining industry. Certain mines have become famous, such as the Kimberley, Dutoitspan, Bultfontein, Premier, Wesselton, Jagersfontein, and De Beers mines. In most mining history the mother lode has been sought long after the working of placer deposits began, but in Africa the secondary alluvial diamond deposits became important only after the working of kimberlite pipes.

Southwest Africa began to produce diamonds in 1908. Operations expanded in surges;

PROPORTIONS OF A CUT DIAMOND

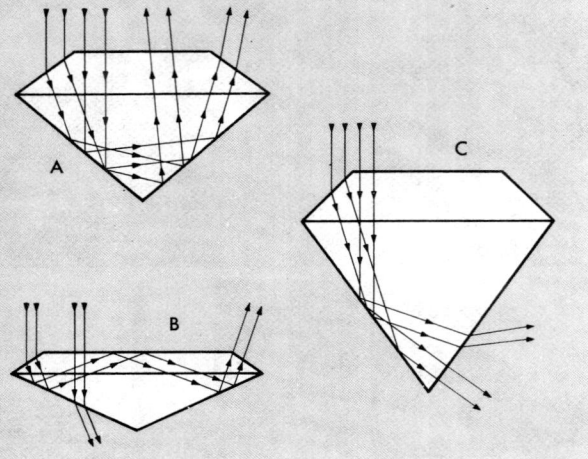

In a properly cut diamond (A), the light that enters it is reflected back through the top. If it is cut too shallow (B), some light passes through the gem; if it is cut too deep (C), much light leaks out the sides.

now they extend offshore and involve the use of barges that suck up debris from the sea floor. On land, the beach deposits yield one part diamond to 100 million parts sand.

Nearly all the new nations of southern Africa and even nations and territories farther north have some deposits of diamonds, especially Sierra Leone, Ghana, Guinea, Angola, Liberia, Ivory Coast, and the Central African Republic. The Congo region has been a heavy producer of industrial diamonds since 1910. The largest kimberlite pipe yet known, the Williamson, is in Tanzania (another large producer of diamonds).

United States. A kimberlite pipe in Pike county, Ark., has yielded 40,000 diamonds weighing up to 40 carats each. Discovered in 1906, it had been operated by a succession of owners, none of whom made it profitable until it was turned into a tourist attraction where visitors may explore for a fee. Many dozens of crystals have been picked up in the Great Lakes states, where they evidently were transported from Canada by the glaciers of the Pleistocene ice age. More puzzling are the crystals found in California, in regions of the Appalachian Mountains that never experienced glaciation, and in a few other areas, because their original sources are completely unknown. Kimberlite, nevertheless, has been noted in various sites in the United States and Canada.

Other Areas. Borneo and Indonesia furnish some diamonds and have done so for centuries. Most of them are small but of good quality. New South Wales and—to a lesser extent—other states in Australia have yielded diamonds. Details about diamond deposits in the Soviet Union are lacking. They are of major rank, however, and include both gem and industrial stones. The largest locations are in kimberlite deposits in Siberia, which were discovered after 1954.

PRODUCTION

The mining of diamonds is similar to the mining of other minerals. However, the crystals are never abundant in any secondary occurrence and are so widely scattered through the kimberlite that the grade of rock seldom can be determined in advance—as can often be done with metal-bearing ores, for example.

Recovery. Both open-pit (surface) mining and underground mining of diamonds are conducted. The Kimberley pit went down more than 1,000 feet (300 meters), after which shafts were sunk to a depth of 3,520 feet (1,050 meters). During slack times the recovered rock may be crushed, spread over the ground, and allowed to weather for some months. Usually, however, the rock is put through a series of mechanical operations that have been developed in the past 100 years.

After the rock is broken into pieces underground, the pieces that are still too large are removed when they fail to pass through sets of iron bars collectively called a *grizzly*. The large pieces are crushed again and join the smaller rock that has passed through the grizzly.

Washing frees the rock of clay, grit, and sand, and the two fractions thus obtained are treated differently. The coarser material is given a sink-and-float treatment. It is placed in a conical tank containing a dense fluid, where the heavier material sinks to the bottom; a second treatment of the same kind but in a still denser medium isolates the diamonds. The finer material (clay, grit, and sand) is placed in a bed of pebbles lying on a sieve and is shaken up and down by a pulse of water forcing diamonds to the bottom of the bed.

The diamond concentrate obtained by these processes goes next to *grease tables*. These tables, which utilize diamond's peculiar property of adhering to grease but not to water, are sloping, vibrating sheets of metal. The sheets are covered with petroleum jelly, and they hold the loose diamonds until they are scraped off and boiled free. Lastly, the crystals are hand-picked and carefully cleaned. Sorting and grading take place before any cutting is done.

Diamonds in secondary deposits may be recovered in different ways. A great thickness of overburden may have to be removed, and the bedrock may even be hand-brushed or vacuum-cleaned. Electrostatic methods sometimes are used to recover tiny diamonds. Lone prospectors employ a simple gold pan or some local substitute.

Cutting and Polishing. Diamond is the only mineral that can be cut and polished in the same operation. The process is one of simple abrasion. The octahedral shape of most crystals lends itself perfectly to the popular "brilliant" cut, but many stones are cut without regard to this relationship of shapes.

The chief complication in cutting has to do with the presence of the octahedral cleavage. The cleavage makes possible the easy trimming of a specimen to reduce its size and eliminate flaws, but it also makes necessary a careful orientation of the crystal. No facet can be placed exactly parallel to a cleavage surface, because such surfaces have a pearly luster. Separation in any direction except along a cleavage plane is accomplished by sawing. A crystal may be cleaved several times, or cleaving may be combined with sawing operations.

A crystal selected for cutting must first be examined carefully to determine its shape and cleavage. Before cleaving, a small groove is cut into an edge of the crystal with a diamond cutting tool. A thin blunt knife called a *cleaving iron* is then set in the groove, parallel to the desired cleavage, and is struck a sharp blow; the crystal breaks apart. Before sawing, the desired cuts are outlined in ink on the crystal. The diamond saw is a thin disk of phosphor bronze that is rotated vertically at high speed and fed with a mixture of diamond powder and olive oil. After cleaving and sawing, the diamond is roughly ground to shape it; a lathelike machine is used for this purpose.

The placing of facets on a diamond is done with a rotating horizontal disk called a *lap*, made of soft iron and treated with diamond powder and oil. The stone is placed in a holder called a *dop*, to which it is attached with solder or held with steel claws. Mechanical devices enable the cutter to set the diamond in various positions against the lap, to give it the desired facets. The stone is boiled in acid to clean it.

The most popular diamond cut is the *diamond brilliant*. This familiar rounded cut has 58 facets. There are 33 facets in the *crown* above the equatorial line (or *girdle*) and 25 in the *pavilion* below. The top facet, called the *table*, is the largest. It is surrounded by 24 triangular facets and 8 four-sided facets. The bottom facet, called the *culet*, which is needed only to prevent chipping, is surrounded by 16 triangular and 8 five-sided facets. The brilliant cut follows standardized laws of mathematical optics fairly closely. Additional facets or special patterns occasionally are applied to large or otherwise unusual stones.

Begun in India and perfected in Italy, diamond cutting is one of the most skilled and highly paid crafts. Belgium, Luxembourg, and the Netherlands are well known for their diamond-cutting establishments, which are concentrated in Antwerp and Amsterdam. France and West Germany ship nearly as many cut diamonds to the United States as the Netherlands does. Diamond-cutting now has spread to Israel, India, and the Republic of South Africa. Some cutting, especially of better stones, also is done in London, New York, and elsewhere.

Grading. Gem diamonds are graded and priced according to four factors: perfection, color, cutting, and size. The absence of flaws is important because cracks, inclusions, and so-called carbon spots (which may be places where the carbon has failed to crystallize or has become graphite) prevent the free passage of light. Some carbon spots have proved to be places where nitrogen atoms substitute for carbon in the crystal lattice. *Perfect diamond* is generally an unacceptable trade term, because perfection is impossible to attain, but it is permitted for a stone that reveals no flaws to the trained eye under a 10-power magnifier.

Color is an essential factor in grading, because it is directly related to the degree of rarity. A yellow or brown cast is undesirable unless the hue is distinctive enough to be favorably regarded as a "fancy" color. Pink, bluish, violet, green, and other attractive hues bring premium prices. Blue-white is another trade term that is not much in favor, but it can properly be used to mean the absence of yellow.

Cutting can bring out the best features of a diamond, so it is always a substantial part of the cost of a gem diamond. Finally, size is an obvious factor in the price of a diamond. A two-carat stone is worth more than twice as much as a one-carat stone of equal quality, and the price ratio increases rapidly with the size.

Marketing. Control of about 80% of the world's production is in the hands of the De Beers Central Selling Organisation, which combines three seperate groups that deal in gemstones, industrial stones, and the output of independent producers. The producers of the other 20% sell to whomever they please. About 150 individuals and companies handle the marketing of diamonds; they buy the rough diamonds in parcels and allot sales to cutters and others. (Switzerland is a major middleman in the sale of rough stones.) The distribution of diamonds is a rather tightly held monopoly, a system that is favored by the miners and the governments concerned. Certainly it has the effect of maintaining stable prices.

SYNTHETIC DIAMONDS

In the United States in 1954 the General Electric Company succeeded in crystallizing diamonds synthetically. There is some evidence, however, that this remarkable feat was achieved a little earlier in Sweden; still older claims have not been adequately verified. Synthetic diamonds are now also produced in Ireland, South Africa, the USSR, Czechoslovakia, and Japan.

The basis for the General Electric experiments was the work of the American physicist Percy W. Bridgman on high-pressure physics. Bridgman showed that when high temperatures and high pressures are combined, diamond rather than graphite is the stable form of carbon; the reverse is true at high temperatures and low pressures. In producing synthetic diamonds, extremely high values are obtained for both heat and pressure, and the raw material can be any convenient form of carbon (even the carbon in peanut butter has been used). The presence of nickel or other metallic elements speeds the reaction.

Another method of synthetic diamond production was developed through study of the presence of diamonds in meteorites. Such diamonds apparently originate either in an explosion or in a collision of the parent body in space, or else in the impact of the meteorite on the earth's surface. New minerals have been found associated with meteorite craters, and this association has encouraged the further study of meteoritic diamonds. As a result, a hexagonal form of diamond was discovered in 1967 and given the name *lonsdaleite*. In 1968 the Du Pont company put on the market a synthetic diamond powder made under a blanket of high-velocity plastic explosive, producing alternating layers of isometric and hexagonal diamond.

RICHARD M. PEARL
Colorado College

Bibliography

Berman, Robert, ed., *Physical Properties of Diamond* (London 1965).
Copeland, Lawrence L., *Diamonds* (Los Angeles 1966).
Dickinson, Joan Younger, *The Book of Diamonds* (New York 1965).
Gemological Institute of America, *The Diamond Dictionary* (Los Angeles 1960).
Smith, Norman R., *Industrial Applications of the Diamond* (London 1965).
Wagner, P. A., *The Diamond Fields of South Africa* (Johannesburg 1914).
Webster, Robert, *Gems: Their Sources, Descriptions, and Identification*, 2 vols. (London 1962).
Williams, Alpheus F., *The Genesis of the Diamond*, 2 vols. (London 1932).

DIAMOND HEAD, a promontory in Hawaii, is at the southeastern tip of the island of Oahu, about 5 miles (8 km) southeast of Honolulu. Its sharp peak, rising to 761 feet (about 230 meters), is a conspicuous sight from Honolulu and from Waikiki Beach.

Diamond Head is an extinct volcano; the floor of the ancient crater makes a hollow behind the summit. Fort Ruger military reservation, formerly a site for coast artillery emplacements, is at the north end of the promontory. A highway skirts the seaward edge of the summit. The U.S. Department of the Interior has conditionally approved the designation of a scenic portion of Diamond Head, from the rim of the crater to the sea at the base of the volcanic cone, as a registered natural landmark.

DIAMOND NECKLACE AFFAIR, a sensational incident at the court of Louis XVI in 1785 that seriously discredited the French monarchy. The names of Queen Marie Antoinette and of a diamond thief, an adventuress, a prostitute, and a cardinal were exposed in a public trial.

The affair arose out of the desire of Cardinal de Rohan, grand almoner of France and a member of one of the most illustrious noble families, to be restored to the favor of the Queen, whom he had previously alienated. The cardinal met and had intimate relations with the Countess de la Motte, a pauperized descendant of a bastard of Henry II, who claimed she enjoyed the Queen's favor. With the aid of forged papers the countess persuaded Rohan that the Queen was in love with him. Utterly infatuated after a secret rendezvous in the garden at Versailles with a prostitute disguised as the Queen, Rohan agreed to act as surety to acquire a fabulously expensive diamond necklace for Marie Antoinette. Rohan told the jewelers that the purchase was authorized by the Queen and delivered the necklace, in the Countess' house, to a man who posed as the Queen's valet. The countess' husband carried the necklace to London, where he sold it stone by stone.

On Aug. 15, 1785, Rohan was arrested and charged with falsely procuring the necklace in the Queen's name without paying for it. He demanded to be tried before the Paris Parlement. The Baron de Breteuil, a royal minister, foolishly agreed to prosecute the cardinal before that body, which was bitterly hostile to the monarchy. In the trial the cardinal was acquitted; he was, however, stripped of his offices and exiled from court. Jeanne de la Motte, the chief figure in the affair, was sentenced to be flogged, branded, and imprisoned for life. She escaped, however, in nine months.

The Countess' escape and Rohan's exile only intensified public rumor that the Queen had sold her favors to Rohan for a diamond necklace and then balked at paying the price. The countess explicitly made the charge against the Queen in her memoirs. Napoleon, for one, dated the beginning of the French Revolution from this affair. Although his judgment was an exaggeration, it is true that the affair seriously damaged the reputation of Marie Antoinette and the monarchy.

LIONEL ROTHKRUG, *University of Michigan*

DIAMOND WEDDING, the 75th anniversary of a wedding. Diamonds are traditional gifts on this occasion. See WEDDING ANNIVERSARY.

JACK DERMID

Diamondback terrapin

DIAMONDBACK TERRAPIN, ter′ə-pən, a turtle of the brackish and salt marshes of eastern North America from Massachusetts to Mexico. During the last part of the 19th century it became such a popular food that the species was in danger of becoming extinct. In the early 20th century, however, the U.S. Bureau of Fisheries developed artificial propagation that resulted in the production of about a quarter of a million young diamondbacks, and several states passed laws to protect the species.

The diamondback terrapin can be recognized by its spotted skin and the appearance of the horny plates of its upper shell, or carapace. These plates are slightly conical and have concentric growth rings that produce conspicuous grooves. Males are smaller than females; in fact, the size difference between the sexes is greater than in any other known North American turtle. The carapace of the female is usually from 6 to 8 inches (15–20 cm) long; that of the male is only 5 or 6 inches (12–15 cm) long.

An omnivorous species, the diamondback terrapin devours such animals as crustaceans, mollusks, fishes, and even insects; little is known, however, about the plant food it consumes. Most females lay a clutch of from 7 to 12 eggs three or four times a year. The eggs hatch in about 3 months. Like other turtles, the female diamondback can store sperm and produce fertile eggs 3 or 4 years after contact with a male.

Diamondback terrapins make up the genus *Malaclemys* of the family Emydidae. The only species is *M. terrapin,* but there are 7 geographic subspecies.

CLIFFORD POPE, *Author, "The Reptile World"*

DIANA, dī-an′ə, in Roman mythology, was a goddess identified with the Greek Artemis (q.v.). Her name probably meant "Bright One," referring to her association with the moon. She was commonly worshipped in groves and forests, and her connection with human fertility probably developed from her role as mother and protectress of wildlife. Although she was the goddess of young maidens, she was also worshipped by women for success in marriage and childbirth.

One of Diana's most celebrated shrines was at Aricia (modern Ariccia) in a grove on the shore of Lake Nemi, then known as "Diana's Mirror." In the 6th century B.C., King Servius Tullius established the headquarters of her cult in Rome and built the Temple of Diana on the Aventine. One of the Seven Wonders of the ancient world was the Temple of Diana at Ephesus, in Asia Minor, described by Pliny the Elder as having had 100 columns, 54 feet (15.4 meters) high.

ROBERT G. RUSSO, *Queens College, New York*

DIANA, dē-ä′nä, is a pastoral romance written in Spanish by the 16th century Portuguese poet Jorge de Montemayor (q.v.) and published in Valencia about 1559. A masterpiece of its genre, it met with immense international success, inspiring several sequels and imitations. The work, in both prose and poetry, is the first example of its kind in Spain, and it greatly strengthened the Renaissance vogue for pastoral literature.

Diana relates the loves of the shepherd Sireno and the shepherdess Diana. Although structurally indebted to Sannazzaro's *Arcadia* (1481), it is original in its avoidance of Sannazzaro's elaborate mythology and erudition and in its emphasis on the free flow of emotion. Portuguese in feeling, despite its language, *Diana* was inspired by the old national bucolic tradition and is pervaded by *saudade*, the peculiarly Lusitanian brand of melancholy and longing. The amatory casuistry of the plot is subordinated to a deep psychological analysis of the pangs of unrequited love, and the whole is suffused with a Platonic idealism bordering on a quietistic mysticism.

ERNESTO G. DA CAL
City University of New York

DIANA OF THE CROSSWAYS is a novel by the English novelist George Meredith (q.v.), published in 1885. In this social comedy of 19th century England, Diana Warwick, a beautiful and brilliant Irish girl, becomes a social rebel after an early disastrous marriage forces her to leave her husband. Despite gossip and scandal, she tries to earn a living by writing. She falls in love with Sir Percy Dacier, a rising young politician, but angered at his compromising advances, she betrays his confidence by selling a government secret to a newspaper. Shortly afterward her husband is killed in an accident, but the Dacier episode has made her so disgusted with herself that she is almost unable to take advantage of her freedom. By the end of the novel, however, she regains her self-respect by marrying her old friend Tom Redworth.

The novel satirizes the gossip-mongering hypocrisy common in high society life. It addresses itself not only to the woman question but also to issues of parliamentary and agrarian reform in England and Ireland.

LAWRENCE GRAVER, *Williams College*

DIANE DE FRANCE, dyȧn də fräɴs (1538–1619), Duchess d'Angoulême and Châtellerault, was the daughter of Henry II of France by a Piedmontese, Filippa Duci, whom he had raped. Diane was legitimated in 1547 and married in 1553 to Orazio Farnese, son of the Duke of Parma. Farnese was killed six months later at the Battle of Hesdin, and on May 4, 1557, Diane was married to Marshal François de Montmorency.

During the Wars of Religion, François was a leader of the Politiques, a group that tried to find a middle course between the Catholic and Protestant parties. After his death in 1579, Diane continued to work for the same goal and was instrumental in reconciling Henry III with the future Henry IV in 1589. In 1610 she had the bodies of Catherine de Médicis and Henry III brought to St.-Denis for burial. She died in Paris on Jan. 11, 1619.

FREDRIC L. CHEYETTE, *Amherst College*

DIANE DE POITIERS, dyȧn də pwȧ-tyā′ (1499–1566), Duchess de Valentinois, a woman of legendary beauty, was a favorite of Henry II of France. She was born on Sept. 3, 1499, the daughter of Jean de Poitiers, Sire de St.-Vallier, and Jeanne de Baternay. Brought up in the court of Anne de Beaujeu, Louis XI's daughter, she was married in 1515 to Louis de Brézé, grand seneschal of Normandy. The marriage soon brought her within the circle of the powerful Montmorency family and helped save her father when he was implicated in the treason of Charles III, Duke de Bourbon, against Francis I.

Soon after her husband's death in 1531, Diane became the mistress of the future Henry II, who was 20 years her junior. Her influence over him lasted until his death. When Henry ascended the throne in 1547, she became part of his inner council, skillfully playing the two major factions, the Guise and the Montmorency families, against each other. She allied herself with both families through the marriages of her daughter and granddaughter. Pious and intolerant, she used her influence to combat the Protestants and was instrumental in getting Henry to accept the Treaty of Cateau-Cambrésis (1559), which ended the long war between France and Spain. The wealth that she accumulated from the royal treasury enabled her to rebuild the châteaus of Chenonceaux (acquired as a royal gift) and Anet.

Even after Henry's death (1559), her influence with the factions at court protected her from reprisal. Henry's widow, Catherine de Médicis, who had lived in obscurity throughout her husband's reign, obtained some revenge by forcing her to give up Chenonceaux, but Diane was allowed to retire to Anet, where she died on April 22, 1566.

FREDRIC L. CHEYETTE, *Amherst College*

DIAPASON, dī-ə-pāz′ən, in music, is the name used for the basic sets of stops that give the great organ of the pipe organ its characteristic sound. The term *open diapason* describes a set of metal pipes open at the top and gradated in length. The open diapason pipe that is 8 feet (2.4 meters) in length and about 6 inches (15 cm) in diameter sounds the C two octaves below middle C. The 16-foot (4.8-meter) pipe sounds the C three octaves below middle C and is usually the lowest pedal note of the modern pipe organ.

The *stopped diapason* is a set of graduated wooden pipes closed at the top by tompions (stoppers). A stopped diapason pipe of 4 feet (1.2 meters) in length emits the same pitch as the 8-foot open diapason pipe, but of different quality.

Diapason normal is a term that originated in France in the 19th century to identify the pitch of the A above middle C produced by a tuning fork vibrating at 435 double vibrations per second. Today, however, the A produced at 440 double vibrations per second is widely accepted as the standard ("international") pitch.

HELEN N. MORGAN
North Shore Branch, New England Conservatory

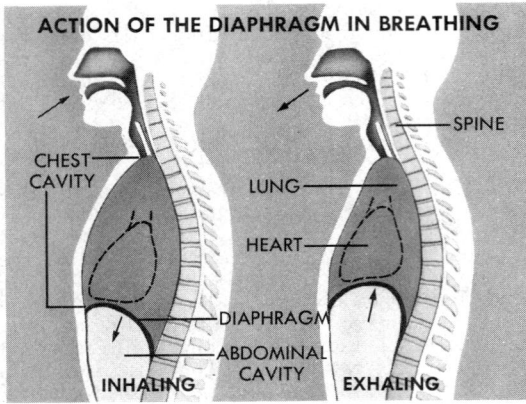

ACTION OF THE DIAPHRAGM IN BREATHING

As a person inhales, the diaphragm contracts and moves downward, expanding the chest cavity. As he exhales, the diaphragm relaxes and moves upward, decreasing the chest cavity and helping force air from the lungs.

DIAPHRAGM, dī'ə-fram, the thin, dome-shaped muscular sheet that separates the chest cavity from the abdominal cavity. Three openings in the diaphragm allow three major structures to pass through it—the aorta, the esophagus, and the inferior vena cava, the large vein that empties into the heart.

The diaphragm plays an important role in breathing. During inspiration, the diaphragm contracts and the rib cage rises, increasing the volume of the chest cavity. As a result, the lungs expand and air rushes into them. During expiration, the diaphragm relaxes and the rib cage lowers, forcing air out of the lungs.

JEFFREY WENIG, *ENDO Laboratories*

DIARRHEA, dī-ə-rē'ə, a condition in which bowel movements are more liquid than normal. The more watery and more frequent the movements, the more severe the diarrhea. Diarrhea may pass in a few hours or persist for years. It may be only a minor inconvenience, or it may be severe enough to cause death within several hours.

As recently as the beginning of the 20th century, diarrhea was a major health problem in all areas of the world. In developed countries, such as the United States, the generally high level of sanitation has reduced diarrhea to a minor health problem, but in developing countries diarrhea is still the main cause of death in children under five years of age.

Diarrhea is a major contributor to malnutrition in small children in developing regions. One reason is that children tend to lose their appetites when they are ill with diarrhea. In addition, food is often withheld by mothers who think it may make the diarrhea worse. Moreover, during an episode of diarrhea the food that is eaten is not absorbed normally by the intestines. This further reduces the child's intake of calories and nutrients.

Causes. Diarrhea has many causes. Sudden brief episodes of diarrhea are usually caused by bacterial, viral, or parasitic infections. The bacteria include toxin-producing strains of *Escherichia coli* and *Vibrio cholerae*, and strains of *Salmonella*, *Shigella*, and *Campylobacter*. The viruses include rotaviruses and Norwalk agent viruses, while the parasites include *Entameba histolytica* and *Giardia lamblia*. Mild and chronic diarrheas usually are due to noninfectious or unknown causes, as in the irritable bowel syndrome or ulcerative colitis.

Course of a Diarrheal Episode. The bacteria, viruses, or parasites that cause diarrhea are ingested by way of contaminated food or water. As the organisms multiply in the intestine, they produce diarrhea by either of two mechanisms, depending on the type of organism. They may invade and destroy the cells that line the intestine, thus reducing the intestine's ability to absorb liquid, or they may produce toxins that cause the intestine to secrete excessive amounts of fluids. In either case bowel movements are more liquid than normal. Eventually the body's immune system eliminates the infecting agent and the episode of diarrhea ends. Most episodes of this type last for two to five days and may be accompanied by abdominal discomfort, nausea, vomiting, and fever. The only treatment required is replacement of fluids and electrolytes lost in the diarrheal stool. This usually can be done simply with a solution of glucose and electrolytes (such as salt) that the patient can drink. This effective and inexpensive "oral rehydration therapy" forms the basis for diarrhea treatment programs around the world. In severe cases, however, intravenous fluids may be necessary. For most types of diarrhea antibiotics usually are not necessary.

How Diarrhea Spreads. Infectious diarrhea is a serious health problem in developing regions because the infectious organisms are easily spread by contaminated food and water in the unsanitary environments common in such regions. This is especially true in hot weather. Children are particularly susceptible because they have not yet developed immunity to the infectious organisms and are especially vulnerable to losses of body fluids in diarrhea.

Diarrhea is usually sporadic. Occasionally epidemics cause many people in a community to become ill within a few days or weeks. The most common cause of such epidemics in developing countries is cholera, a diarrhea-causing infection by *Vibrio cholerae*. In the United States and other developed countries epidemics are uncommon. The small outbreaks that do occur can usually be traced to a single source: for example, contaminated food eaten at a community picnic, or a contaminated community water supply.

Travelers' Diarrhea. People who travel from the United States and other developed countries to regions with inadequate sanitation frequently contract diarrhea—so frequently that the disorder has been called "travelers' diarrhea." The most common cause of this illness is the bacterium *Escherichia coli*, which provides a toxin in the intestines. The bacterium is ingested by way of contaminated water and food, usually uncooked vegetables. The main reason visitors are susceptible is that, not having been previously exposed to the diarrhea-causing bacterium, they have not developed immunity to it.

Travelers' diarrhea sometimes can be prevented by avoiding foods that are likely to be contaminated. In some cases preventive treatment with antibiotics, begun before leaving home, is helpful. The antibiotic most commonly prescribed for this purpose is doxycycline or trimethoprim-sulfamethoxazole.

R. BRADLEY SACK, M.D., *Johns Hopkins University School of Medicine*

DIARY, a written record of daily experiences. The diary (from the Latin *dies*, meaning "day") had very practical origins but has in the course of time taken on literary, social, and even philosophical dimensions. It is one of the most flexible of literary forms and consequently has attracted authors of an exceptionally wide range of interests and varying degrees of talent.

Greek and Roman Antecedents. The earliest ancestor of the diary was probably the Greek *ephēmerides* (from *ephēmeros*, meaning "lasting for one day"), an almanac in which the positions of the planets and other heavenly bodies were recorded. The almanac, then as now, had obvious value to an agricultural and pastoral people that depended for their well-being on a proper anticipation of the various seasonal cycles. But it was not only the agrarian economy that was served by the *ephēmerides*; early Greek religion, too, was based to a large extent on seasonal change, and religious customs and observances were related to specific times of the year. Hence, these earliest forms of the diary came to include details of daily religious and civic ceremony. But the *ephēmerides* were not personal accounts like modern diaries; they were altogether public and utilitarian records.

The Romans, with their characteristic practicality, extended the use of such daily records further than the Greeks. As early as the 4th century B.C., *annales* (annals), or yearbooks, were kept by official historians in Rome appointed to record daily events ranging from the details of domestic housekeeping to an accounting of public administration and the activities of magistrates.

The Romans not only broadened the range of the Greek almanac but were also the first to recognize its historical and literary potential. The first Roman epic and the first Roman history were based on *annales*. Quintus Ennius (239–?169 B.C.), generally recognized as one of the founders of Roman literature, wrote an epic of the founding of Rome in 18 books, entitled *Annals*, only fragments of which survive. Ennius' poem, the earliest example of Latin hexameter verse, clearly reflects the influence of the antique Greek almanacs—a fact perhaps explained by his having been a teacher of Greek and a translator of Greek plays. Marcus Porcius Cato (234–149 B.C.), better known as Cato the Censor or Cato the Elder, produced the first history of Rome, which, like Ennius' poem, survives only in fragments. Entitled *Origins*, Cato's work derived from the almanac tradition. Livy (Titus Livius, 59 B.C.–17 A.D.) used *Annals* as the title of his panoramic history of Rome from Aeneas to Tiberius, as did Cornelius Tacitus (55?–?117 A.D.) for his history of the Roman emperors from Tiberius to Nero.

To the practical and literary aspects of these prototypes of the diary, the Romans added the distinctive note of personality, a quality not found in the *ephēmerides* or *annales* but recognized today as an ingredient of any successful diary. It would be difficult to overestimate the contribution in this regard of Julius Caesar (100–44 B.C.), whose *Commentaries* on the Gallic wars combined historical accuracy with personal response to immediate events.

The Modern Diary. By the beginning of the Christian era the two essential ingredients of the modern diary were in existence—the tradition of day-to-day recording of experience and an appreciation of expressions of personal awareness. Once these characteristics were established, the diary was recognizable as a unique literary form. On the one hand, its very dailiness distinguished it from such related forms as the memoir or autobiography, which are recollective rather than immediate. They look backward from a completed experience, whereas the diary looks forward into an experience whose structure cannot be determined in advance. On the other hand, the personal aspect of the diary distinguishes it from the account book, the logbook, or the memorandum, which record external events without expressions of individual involvement.

It was not until the Renaissance, however, that fully formed examples of the diary were produced. As postclassical society became more complex and governmental operations more diffuse, almanacs and daily public records multiplied. The seasonal liturgy of early and medieval Christianity demanded calendars and yearbooks, breviaries and missals, to coordinate religious ceremonies all over Christendom. But there was relatively little emphasis in these on the psychology of the individual, who was considered less essential than the civic or ecclesiastical unit of which he was a member. That the names of few pre-Renaissance artists have survived is an indication of the general acceptance of anonymity that discouraged the creation of such personal literature as the diary.

The contrast between medieval communalism and Renaissance individualism can be oversimplified and exaggerated, but certainly the intimacy of the portrayal by Dante (1265–1321) of his love for Beatrice in the *Vita nuova* and by Petrarch (1304–1374) of his love for Laura in the *Canzoniere* signals a new emphasis on the personal element in literature. Impelled by this new climate of self-awareness, the diary was free to develop beyond the restrained commentaries of earlier ages.

Famous Diaries. From the Renaissance to contemporary times the diary has ranged from records of society and scandal, such as the *Journal d'un bourgeois de Paris* (1409–1449), the Marquis de Dangeaux's diary (1684–1720) of the reign of Louis XIV, and Charles Collé's journal (1748–1777); through sensational or informative exposures, such as Alastair Moray's *Diary of a Rum-Runner* (1927) and David Lawrence's *Diary of a Washington Correspondent* (1942); to the quietly intense aesthetic and philosophic speculation of André Gide's distinguished *Journals* (1889–1951).

The finest examples of the diary have been produced, as might be expected, by literary figures such as Jonathan Swift, James Boswell, Sir Walter Scott, Ralph Waldo Emerson, Edmond and Jules de Goncourt, and Katherine Mansfield. But important diaries also have been produced by religious leaders (John Wesley, Cotton Mather, Pope John XXIII), political figures (George Washington, John Quincy Adams, Harold Nicholson), adventurers (William Parry, Capt. James Cook), and representatives of practically every other segment of society.

Still the undisputed classic of all diaries in the English language is the first diary of Samuel Pepys (q.v.; 1633–1703). He began keeping his diary in 1660 (the end of the Cromwellian era in England), threatened, as he believed, by blindness. He ended the first diary in 1669. He kept other journals and diaries later in life, but nothing equal to the first. His account of the years 1660–1669 is one of the most fascinating and valuable accounts of life under the restored monarch, Charles II.

An interesting combination of piety, sensuality, and sharp-eyed awareness of the world, Pepys' diary was kept in a code that was not deciphered until 1825. No complete, unexpurgated edition was published until the 20th century. Unlike his famous contemporary John Evelyn, who carefully revised and corrected his diary, Pepys recorded his experiences directly and without elaboration, thus gaining in immediacy what he lost in elegance. Though a diary, unlike a memoir or autobiography, cannot be structured according to a predetermined governing principle (the unforeseen accidents of time are the *sine qua non* of the diary), Pepys' accounts of the Great Plague (1665) and the Great Fire of London (1666) achieve remarkable dramatic coherence and tension. The surprising way in which passing events coalesce into an artistic whole has been witnessed again in our own day in Anne Frank's moving *Diary of a Young Girl* (1942–1944), which was successfully adapted both as a stage play and as a motion picture. (See DIARY OF ANNE FRANK.)

Instances of writers deliberately making use of the diary form in fictional narrative are Daniel Defoe's *Journal of the Plague Year* (1722) and Georges Bernanos' *Journal d'un curé de Campagne* (1936; *Diary of a Country Priest*). They prove, in an intentionally artistic way, what diarists have long recognized—that the sequential revelation of a private life may have a strong public appeal.

RICHARD E. HUGHES, *Boston College*

Further Reading: Matthews, William, *British Diaries: An Annotated Bibliography of British Diaries Written Between 1442–1942* (Berkeley, Calif., 1950); Matthews, William, and Pearce, R. H., *American Diaries: An Annotated Bibliography of American Diaries Written Prior to the Year 1861* (Berkeley, Calif., 1945).

DIARY OF ANNE FRANK, the personal journal of a young German-Dutch girl, Anne Frank (1929–1945), originally published in Dutch as *Het achterhuis* in 1947. It was later translated into English and published as *The Diary of a Young Girl* in 1952. Anne kept the diary between the years 1942 and 1944 when she, her family, and some friends were hiding out in a warehouse in Amsterdam, Netherlands, in an unsuccessful attempt to escape the persecution of the Jews by the Nazis during World War II. Written with skill, humor, and great insight, the work is a monument to the courage and strength of the human spirit.

Surrounded outside by death and destruction, and within by the nightmare reality of eight persons crowded into tiny living quarters in mortal fear of being discovered, she set down simply and movingly the hopes, dreams, conflicts, and feelings of a young girl on the verge of womanhood. A few days after the last entry, the Nazis ferreted out the group, and Anne was sent to the extermination camp at Bergen-Belsen, where she died in 1945 at the age of 15. The journal was successfully dramatized by Frances Goodrich and Albert Hackett and presented in New York as *The Diary of Anne Frank* in 1956. It was adapted as a motion picture in 1959.

DIAS, Antônio Gonçalves. See GONÇALVES DIAS, ANTÔNIO.

DIAS, dē'ash, **Bartholomeu** (died 1500), Portuguese navigator, who discovered the Cape of Good Hope and the sea route to India. His name is also spelled *Diaz*.

In 1486, King John II of Portugal commissioned Dias to sail down the African coast to search for Prester John (q.v.) and for the sea route to India. Dias left Portugal with two caravels and a storeship in August 1487. After reaching Cape Cross (22° S), then the southern limit of Portuguese exploration, he left the coast. Sailing farther south and then east and north, he struck land at Mossel Bay, about 200 miles (370 km) east of the Cape of Good Hope, which he had not sighted. He traveled farther east until (probably at the Great Fish River) his crews and officers demanded that he return to Portugal. On the return trip he sighted the Cape of Good Hope, which he probably named.

Dias reached Lisbon in December 1488, after a remarkable voyage of over 16 months in which he had opened the way to India and had discovered about 1,400 miles (2,250 km) of African coast previously unknown to Europeans. However, he was passed over in favor of Vasco da Gama for command of the expedition that reached India in 1498. Dias died at sea when his ship—part of Pedro Álvares Cabral's fleet that discovered Brazil—was sunk in a squall in the South Atlantic Ocean in May 1500.

HARRISON M. WRIGHT
Swarthmore College

DIAS, dē'əs, **Henrique** (1600?–?1662), Brazilian leader of an army of slaves and freemen who conducted a revolt against Dutch control of the province of Pernambuco in colonial Brazil. The Dutch had captured this coastal area in 1630 during a period when the Brazilian colonies were claimed by Spain. The colony was administered by the Dutch East India Company, with no Portuguese protest, until the colonial people—white, black, and Indian—revolted in 1641. The bravest and most continuous fighting was carried on by the army of Dias, a free black man.

A literate man, he wrote a letter to the Dutch saying that his troops were fierce and tireless black fighters who maintained their tribal identities from West Africa. Though the Dutch considered him "merely a slave and not worth capturing," he was able to defeat their armies by 1654 and remained a local hero.

HELEN M. BAILEY, *East Los Angeles College*

DIASPORA, dī-as'pə-rə, is a term used by historians to refer to those settlements inhabited by Jews in all parts of the world outside the state of Israel. It comes from a Greek term meaning a scattering or dispersion. Although it is sometimes used as a synonym for exile, this is not its primary meaning. Diaspora originally referred to the dispersion of the Jews outside Palestine during the Greek and Roman period. Small Jewish communities outside of Palestine have existed as far back as the time of the separate states of Israel and Judah.

The Diaspora, as the term is now used, began in the 4th century B.C. with the settlement of Jews in Alexandria, Egypt, and Antioch, Syria. By the 2d century B.C. the Diaspora extended over a wide area—to Asia Minor, North Africa, and Rome. Cicero, the Roman orator, speaking in 55 B.C., mentions Jews who had acquired citizenship rights in Rome. It has been established that Jewish communities in parts of Europe existed in pre-Christian centuries, before the destruction of the second Temple in Jerusalem (70 A.D.). Eventually, the Diaspora extended to Spain, France, England, the Rhineland, and later to Poland, Russia, parts of India and China, as well as to the Western Hemisphere.

All the areas of dispersion created by forced captivity and exile, whose people were often subject to persecution and discrimination, were held together by a common religion, customs, and the hope of a "return to Zion," the homeland of the Jewish people.

EDWARD T. SANDROW
Rabbi, Temple Beth El, Cedarhurst, N.Y.

DIASPORE, dī'ə-spōr, is a mineral consisting of hydrogen aluminum oxide. It commonly occurs in emery rock in association with corundum. Formerly, diaspore was of mineralogical interest only, but it is now recognized as an important constituent of clays with a high alumina (aluminum oxide) content. The principal use of such clays is in the manufacture of high-temperature brick; the ability of brick to resist high temperatures increases with its diaspore content. Diaspore clays have interest as a potential source of aluminum, but at present they cannot compete economically with bauxite. In the United States the best deposits of the clays are in Missouri, between Gerard and Belle; and in Clearfield county, Pennsylvania.

Composition, $HAlO_2$; hardness, 6.5-7; specific gravity, 3.35-3.45; crystal system, orthorhombic.

GEORGE SWITZER
Smithsonian Institution

DIASTROPHISM, dī-as'trə-fiz-əm, in geology, is a term applied to the processes that deform the crust of the earth. The two broadest kinds of deformation processes are epeirogeny and orogeny.

Epeirogeny involves the relative rise and fall of broad segments of the crust with little or no folding. An example of epeirogenic movement is the warping of crustal rocks to form plateaus or broad domes and basins. The breaking of the upper crust into blocks bordered by faults is known as *taphrogeny*. The latter process results in features such as *grabens* and *horsts*—that is, down-faulted and relatively risen blocks of crust. The Basin and Range geographic province of the southwestern United States consists of grabens, horsts, and tilted blocks.

Orogeny involves conventional crustal shortening in which folds and thrust faults are produced, resulting in changes in relative distances on the earth's surface. Thrust faults are widely spread in the Rocky Mountains of western North America, for example. Orogenic movements include mountain building, but in many cases the structures produced by these movements are superficial rather than deeply penetrating. (The term "thrust" carries the misleading implication of a physical push, whereas it may be a gliding of crustal rocks down tectonic planes due to the earth's gravitational pull.)

A form of diastrophism that has been prevalent over wide areas involves the lateral shifting of crustal blocks against such other blocks. The shifting takes place along high-angle faults called *wrench faults* (nearly vertical strike-slip or transcurrent faults). The most famous wrench faults are the Great Glen Fault that runs along a topographic trench through Loch Ness in northern Scotland and the San Andreas Fault that extends from the Gulf of California to the California coast north of San Francisco.

Diastrophism also includes another important process—the spreading of parts of the earth's crust. An example is the spreading that occurs along the mid-Atlantic ridge of the Atlantic Ocean and elsewhere in ocean basins. The separation takes place along a grabenlike trench or rift in the ridge and may represent an upwelling of material from deep within the mantle. This process is associated with the concept of continental drift. See also CONTINENT.

In the early years of geological studies, the concept arose that the earth's history was marked by a number of worldwide and synchronous diastrophic events. The events were assumed to be associated with and to account for the ends of geological periods. This theory eventually was discarded, however. It is now generally accepted that diastrophism does not take place continually at a constant magnitude. Instead there are pulses of activity at frequent intervals, some of them of sufficient magnitude to be called *orogenic revolutions*. Perhaps no geological revolution of this nature has been truly worldwide; each of them has affected only narrowed mobile belts of the earth's crust.

Eustatic movements—worldwide changes in the level of the sea—may result from diastrophism. That is, earth movements may increase or decrease the volumes of ocean basins enough to cause water to encroach on or retreat from all land surfaces simultaneously. Eustatic changes also can be produced by other means, however, such as the growth or the melting of glaciers.

MARSHALL KAY, *Columbia University*

DIATHERMY, dī'ə-thûr-mē, is a form of heat therapy in which microwaves are transmitted to various body tissues below the surface of the skin. Diathermy employs high-frequency microwaves from a single vacuum tube, and every diathermy transmitter, whether in a hospital or doctor's office, must be registered with the Federal Communications Commission since it may interfere with broadcasts from other shortwave transmitters.

Diathermy is generally considered to be a safe, effective method of treating many types of muscle and tendon pain. It is used in treating bursitis, tendonitis, tension headaches, backaches, stiff shoulders, and tennis elbow (muscle strain in the forearm). The exposure time is usually 20 minutes, and the treatment is generally repeated daily for three to nine days. The treatment level is usually kept at 1.5 million microwaves per second to avoid burning the patient's skin. The patient usually feels only a slight sensation of warmth, and after treatment the exposed skin is warm to the touch. After treatment it is important that the patient not be exposed to changes in temperature.

The term "diathermy" was first used in 1907 by the German physician Carl F. Nagelschmidt. His work was based on earlier research by the French scientist Jacques Arsène d'Arsonval (1851–1940), who was one of the first experimenters to use high-frequency waves on humans.

REAUMUR S. DONNALLY, M.D.
Washington Hospital Center

DIATOM

DIATOM, dī'ə-tom, any of the microscopic one-celled plants constituting the class Bacillariophycae of the division, or phylum, Bacillariophyta. Diatoms are either solitary and free, attached to a substrate by gelatinous extrusions, or joined to each other in chains of varying lengths. Many species are capable of active movement but others are merely free floating and depend on currents for transport. Individual diatoms range in size from about 2 microns (less than $1/10,000$ of an inch) to more than 2,000 microns (nearly $1/10$ of an inch), although there are few species that exceed 200 microns (about $1/100$ of an inch) in length.

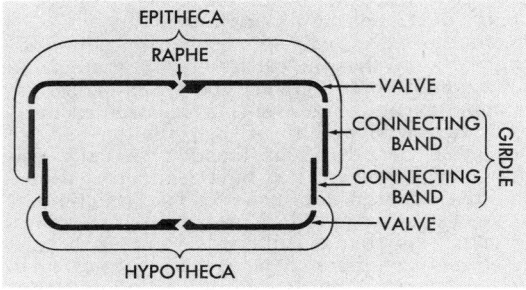

A diatom frustule, or shell.

Diatoms are distributed throughout the world in aquatic, semiaquatic, and moist habitats. They are found in the sea, estuaries, freshwater lakes, ponds, streams, and ditches. More rigorous habitats—such as moist rocks or soil or damp bark—sometimes support lush growths of diatoms. The actual number of diatom species is unknown, but estimates range from 2,000 to over 10,000. The uncertainty of this number is compounded by the 80,000 to 95,000 names that have been applied to the various diatoms.

Though individual cells are microscopic, masses of diatoms can often be seen on stream bottoms and elsewhere as a brownish film. Free-floating (planktonic) diatoms can impart a brownish discoloration to the water.

Structure. The diatom cell differs from other algal cells chiefly in the nature of its cell wall (frustule). The wall is made of silicon and is constructed of two halves (thecae) that fit together, one inside the other, like a box. Each half (outer: epitheca; inner: hypotheca) consists of a plate, called the valve, and a connecting band that joins the thecae to each other. The connecting bands of the two thecae are usually referred to as girdle bands. The valves are intricately designed, having holes, slits, and chambers forming definite patterns, which are used to distinguish the species. A long, narrow opening, called the raphe, also may be present in the valve.

Reproduction. Diatoms reproduce principally by ordinary cell division (asexually). Although sexual reproduction occurs in many species, it is not the usual mode of reproduction. In ordinary cell division each daughter cell formed contains one of the two different-size thecae of the original mother cell plus a newly formed half to fit inside it. With some exceptions, one daughter cell is thus smaller than the original cell, making the average cell size smaller as the population increases. To return to the maximum size, a "rejuvenation" cell, called an auxospore, is produced. Auxospores may be formed asexually or sexually. In asexual auxospore formation, the protoplasm escapes from its wall, expands by forming large internal liquid-filled vacuoles, and then deposits a new cell wall. Sexual auxospore formation is similar but involves the additional process of meiosis (reduction to one-half of the chromosome number) followed by fusion of the sex cells, which restores the original chromosome number.

Fossil Diatoms. The earliest records of fossil diatoms are from Eocene marine deposits about 60 million years old. Freshwater diatoms have been found as far back as the Miocene, about 25 million years ago.

CHARLES W. REIMER
The Academy of Natural Sciences, Philadelphia

DIATOMS, shown here enlarged 200 times, occur in a variety of forms.

CARL STRUEWE, FROM MONKMEYER

DIATOMACEOUS EARTH, dī-ət-ə-mā′shəs, is a fine-grained, porous material consisting of opaline silica, a hydrous and noncrystalline form of silica. The chalklike material is usually white or cream-colored. Diatomaceous earth is also known as *diatomite* and *kieselguhr.*

Deposits of diatomaceous earth were formed by the slow accumulation on ocean floors of the shells of minute algae called diatoms (see DIATOM), which occur in immense numbers in the sea. Such deposits, overlain by later sediments, are sometimes hundreds of feet thick and may cover large areas. Diatomaceous earth is mined and purified for use as an abrasive, a filter, an absorbent, and an insulating material.

DIATONIC, dī-ə-ton′ik, in music, is a term used in Western tonality to describe any scale, or portion thereof, consisting of a varying order of whole or half steps within the compass of an octave. By using the whole and half steps in different sequences, a variety of scales may be created; the most widely used are the *major, minor, whole-tone, pentatonic* (five-tone), and *gapped.* A gapped scale, of which the pentatonic is an example, is one in which the interval is larger than a whole step.

Early scales called "modes" were also based on a series of whole and half steps. These modal scales, which comprise eight successive white keyboard notes beginning on each of the white notes in the octave from C to C, are derived from formulas that were codified by the medieval church and used in Gregorian chant. See MODES.

Before about 1875, all diatonic scales were thought to have key centers, or tonic notes, and certain steps of the scale were said to have strong or weak melodic and harmonic tendencies. Composers since 1900, however, have tended to de-emphasize the importance of any single note in the scale, and modern atonal (no key) and polytonal (multikeyed) music, having no tonic note, give equal importance to all 12 semitones, or half steps, of the diatonic scale.

HELEN N. MORGAN
North Shore Branch, New England Conservatory

DIATRYMA, dī-ə-trī′mə, any of a group of extinct, giant, flightless, predatory birds now known only from fossil deposits dating from the early Eocene period, some 60 million years ago. Diatryma fossils have been found in western North America and possibly in Europe.

The diatryma was a powerfully built bird with sturdy legs, very small wings, a thick neck, and a massive head. It was one of the largest land animals of its time—the beginning of the age of mammals.

The largest species of diatryma, *Diatryma steini,* known from the finding of a nearly complete skeleton, stood almost 7 feet (2.1 meters) high. Its skull, about 17 inches (43 cm) long, was mostly beak. This beak—a formidable, laterally compressed weapon—was 9 inches (23 cm) long and 6 inches (15 cm) high. The bird's legs were more than 4 feet (1.2 meters) long. The diatryma is thought to have been a flesh-eating predator that could run down and kill prey.

Diatrymas are classified in the family Diatrymidae of the order Diatryiformes and are placed near the living cariamas that are found in South America.

GEORGE E. WATSON, *Smithsonian Institution*

DÍAZ, dē′äs, **Adolfo** (1874–1964), president of Nicaragua. A Conservative, Díaz became provisional president in 1911 during a troubled time. He was backed by the United States, which wanted to ensure collection of private American loans made to Nicaragua. A Liberal revolt against Díaz was quelled by U.S. marines in 1912, and he was elected president the same year, serving until 1916. During his term the Bryan-Chamorro Treaty was signed (1914) and ratified (1916), giving the United States rights in perpetuity to build a canal across Nicaragua.

The United States withdrew its marines in 1925. Civil war ensued, the marines returned, and Díaz, again with American support, assumed the presidency from 1926 to 1928. He then retired from public life. Díaz died in San José, Costa Rica, on Jan. 27, 1964.

HELEN MILLER BAILEY
East Los Angeles College

DÍAZ, dē′äs, **Porfirio** (1830–1915), Mexican president, who has been called the "maker of modern Mexico." His long rule (1876–1880, 1884–1911) brought political peace and economic progress to a nation that had enjoyed neither since colonial times. But his dictatorial regime stunted political growth in Mexico and laid new burdens on the common people, and in 1910 the nation exploded in revolution.

José de la Cruz Porfirio Díaz was born on Sept. 15, 1830, in the city of Oaxaca. The young mestizo studied law, coming under the influence of the great liberal Indian leader Benito Juárez. After serving in Oaxaca during the war with the United States (1846–1848), Porfirio joined the liberal revolt against the dictator Santa Anna in 1854 and fought with distinction in the struggles against the conservatives and against the French invaders supporting Maximilian. He rose to the rank of general and helped restore Juárez to the presidency.

Díaz was a man of prodigious physical energy, military talent, and political ambition. In 1871–1872 his ambition led him to revolt unsuccessfully against his old teacher Juárez and four years later—successfully—against Juárez's successor, Sebastián Lerdo de Tejada. Díaz was provisional president in 1876–1877 and elected president from 1877 to 1880. He then served seven consecutive terms from 1884 to 1911.

Diatryma (reconstruction)
FIELD MUSEUM OF NATURAL HISTORY

Porfirio Díaz

The Porfirian Era. Confronted by the task of welding the nation into a tranquil unit, Díaz performed political and economic miracles. He observed constitutional forms in the main, but in reality ruled as an absolute monarch.

Díaz accomplished much because the country was weary of strife. He rewarded the cooperative and suppressed the recalcitrant. He played political rivals and factions against each other, so that elements formerly in conflict—petty local chiefs, liberal and conservative political factions, the army, the Roman Catholic Church, and the landowners—became pillars of the regime. To these were added the expanded bureaucracy, the intellectuals, and foreign interests.

The regime made a significant contribution to the economic progress of the country. Previously there had been confusion, bankruptcy, and debt, but now revenues rose, reserves were created, and the nation's credit improved, so that it was possible to borrow at reasonable rates and, for example, to finance the consolidation of the railroads. But under Díaz the Mexican people failed to advance politically. The major beneficiaries were selected Mexicans and the foreigners. The masses were unaffected except adversely. The old institutional burdens—the *hacienda* (large landed estate), the privileged position of church and army, the rigid class system—all were reinforced under Díaz. Concentration of land ownership increased, often at the expense of the Indian villages.

The Fall of Díaz. By 1910, Mexicans had many grievances, and the situation was explosive. Remarkably, the break came in political form, and Díaz himself set the match to the tinder pile. In an interview in 1908, he expressed his desire not to stand for reelection, and Mexico witnessed a tremendous political effervescence. The opposition gradually coalesced behind the candidacy of Francisco I. Madero. Díaz had himself reelected in 1910 after all, but Madero led an armed rebellion, which by May 1911 had forced the antiquated regime to capitulate.

The Mexican Revolution had begun. Díaz went into exile in Paris. Until his death there on July 2, 1915, he remained convinced that his was the only way to rule Mexico.

STANLEY R. ROSS, *University of Texas*

DIAZ DE LA PEÑA, dyȧz' də lȧ pä-nyȧ', **Narcisse Virgile** (1808–1876), French painter of the Barbizon school. Born of Spanish parents at Bordeaux on Aug. 20, 1808, Diaz became an apprentice in porcelain painting at Sèvres when he was 15. He was largely self-taught as a painter. He began exhibiting his early romantic paintings, which reflect the influence of Eugène Delacroix, at the Paris Salon of 1831. After he joined the Barbizon painters in Fontainebleau, about 1840, Diaz' painting acquired more realism, mainly through his association with Théodore Rousseau. He died at Menton, France, on Nov. 18, 1876.

Diaz is best known for his landscape paintings, which are often peopled with mythological figures, but he is also noted for his exquisite flower pieces.

DÍAZ DEL CASTILLO, dē'äth thel käs-tē'lyō, **Bernal** (1496?–?1584), Spanish soldier and historian. He was born in Medina del Campo, Spain. At the age of 18 he joined an expedition to the New World. He went first to Panama, then to Cuba, and in 1517–1518 made two voyages of discovery to Yucatán. In 1519 he embarked on the greatest event of his life: the conquest of Mexico led by Hernán Cortés (q.v.). In 1541 he moved to Guatemala, where he remained until his death.

Bernal Díaz is famous for his *Historia verdadera de la conquista de la Nueva España* (*The True History of the Conquest of New Spain*), a colorful eyewitness account of the conquest. He wrote it in about 1568 partly to counteract the scholarly work of Francisco López de Gómara, which, Díaz maintained, praised only Cortés and gave little credit to the soldiers. Friends who read the manuscript thought it was too simply written, and it was not published until 1632. It is claimed that this first edition had many deletions. In 1904 the Mexican historian Genaro García brought out a new edition based on the Díaz manuscript in the Guatemalan archives. Although this manuscript is only a copy, it has corrections and changes in Díaz' handwriting. The original manuscript used for the first edition was never found.

In 1908, Alfred P. Maudslay published, in London, an English translation based on García's work. Since then there have been many other translations and editions, so that, next to Cervantes, Bernal Díaz is probably the most widely read Spanish author.

HERBERT CERWIN, *Author of "Bernal Díaz: Historian of the Conquest"*

DÍAZ ORDAZ, dē'äs ôr-däs', **Gustavo** (1911–1979), president of Mexico, who continued the tradition of stable, moderate civilian rule introduced into Mexican political life in 1946. He was born in what is now Ciudad Serdán, Puebla state, on March 12, 1911. In 1937 he received a law degree from Puebla University.

His career in government service followed the basic pattern of holding a succession of state and national offices on the road to the presidency. In 1946 he ran for senator from Puebla and, owing to the dominance of the official party, easily won the seat. When his friend Adolfo López Mateos became president in 1958, Díaz Ordaz was made minister of government.

In this crucial post, he earned a reputation as a representative of the right wing of the party. He cracked down hard on politically inspired strikes and imprisoned several prominent leftists and Communists.

After becoming president in 1964, he generally followed the moderate policies of his predecessors. He frequently voiced his concern over poverty and illiteracy in the rural areas, and he expanded education, welfare, and industrial training programs. During his term, however, the country underwent some of the most serious student revolts in its history. On Oct. 2, 1968, Díaz Ordaz directed the suppression by police of a riot in which an unknown number of students were killed. He was succeeded by Luis Echeverría Álvarez on Dec. 1, 1970, and in 1977 was appointed ambassador to Spain. He died in Mexico City on July 15, 1979.

KARL M. SCHMITT*, *University of Texas*

DIAZO COMPOUNDS, dī-az'ō, any of a group of compounds containing the RN_2^+ structure. The R group is usually an aromatic ring. Diazo compounds, which are extensively used in the synthesis of organic compounds, are generally prepared by treating aromatic amines with nitrous acid.

$$\text{C}_6\text{H}_5\text{NH}_2 \xrightarrow[\text{H}^+ + \text{Cl}^-]{\text{NO}_2^-} \text{C}_6\text{H}_5\text{N}_2^+\text{Cl}^-$$

DIAZONIUM SALT

The diazonium ion can undergo substitution, reduction, or coupling reactions, and so makes possible a wide range of products. Coupling reactions are the most important of the diazonium reactions, since this type of reaction is used in the manufacture of a large number of azo dyes.

$$\text{C}_6\text{H}_5\text{N}_2^+\text{Cl}^- - \text{C}_6\text{H}_5\text{NH}_2 \rightarrow \text{C}_6\text{H}_5\text{N}=\text{N}\text{C}_6\text{H}_4\text{NH}_2$$

ANILINE YELLOW

Aniline yellow, which is used in wood stains and lacquers, is the simplest example.

OTTO W. NITZ
Stout State University, Menomonie, Wis.

DIBDIN, dib'din, **Charles** (1745–1814), English playwright, actor, and songwriter, who wrote many ballad operas. His two sons, Charles (1768–1833) and Thomas (1771–1841), were also actors, singers, and composers, and the works of the three are frequently confused.

The father was born in Southampton in March 1745 and died in London on July 25, 1814. His two sons were illegitimate, and at first called themselves after their mother, the actress Harriet Pitt. But when the father (who saw little of either son) became celebrated as a writer and composer, the boys adopted his name—to their father's annoyance and posterity's confusion.

It is certain that the elder Charles Dibdin wrote *Tom Bowling* and *The Lass That Loved a Sailor*, perhaps the most universally known of his huge output of sea songs. It is practically certain, also, that he wrote the music as well as the words of most of his ditties. His two sons put words to the music of other composers or to traditional tunes.

ALAN DENT
Author of "Mrs. Patrick Campbell"

DICE GAMES are contests of chance and skill, in which players wager on the outcome of casting marked cubes, the oldest gambling implements known to man. The cubes, or dice, are symmetrical, with edges equally rounded and faces marked with spots numbering from 1 to 6. The sum of the spots on opposite faces always totals 7. In casting, or rolling, a die, the chance or *odds* that a specified spot will appear is 1 in 6, or 5 to 1 against its showing. With two dice, the spots can appear in 36 ways (6×6), and with three dice they can show in 216 ways. Mathematical probabilities applying to dice are constant, and a player can calculate the risk before placing his bet.

Craps. Any number can play this game, one always being the shooter who rolls two dice. Bets on the outcome are made before each series of rolls. The shooter puts up his *stake* (any sum) to win and invites each player to *fade it* (match, or cover, it). Then he removes uncovered sums and starts his series of rolls. On his first roll, if the sum of the tops is 7 or 11, it is a *natural*, and he wins; if the total is 2, 3, or 12, it is *craps*, and he loses. In either case the bets are settled, and he keeps the dice and repeats the procedure. If, however, he rolls 4, 5, 6, 8, 9, or 10, the number becomes his *point*, and he continues to roll. Bets are settled after he either *passes* (wins) by repeating his point, or *misses* by rolling a 7, thereby losing the dice to the player next in turn.

The odds against the shooter passing are 251 to 244 at the start. If his point is 4 or 10, the odds are 2 to 1 against him. Odds are 3 to 2 against making 5 or 9, and 6 to 5 against

TYPICAL BANK CRAPS LAYOUT

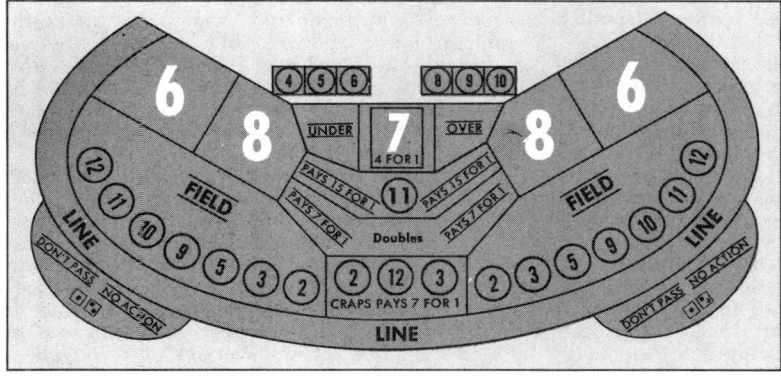

The layout shown here is typical of those found in gambling houses. The odds for and against the shooter, and the house percentages, appear in the table on page 74. Details of betting are explained in the accompanying text. A player can bet against the shooter, but in that case the 1:2 roll is a standoff. Bets quoted as 7 "for" 1 are at odds 6 to 1, because the payoff of 7 includes the original stake.

making 6 or 8. In addition to betting against the shooter, players bet with each other, seeking such bets at odds favorable to themselves.

Bank Craps. This game is played in gambling houses. Players surround a *layout*, or craps table, that shows the available bets and the odds offered by the house. Players place bets on the table (against the house) and roll their own dice. On the roll, the dice must either bounce off a wall or go over a wire stretched across the table. Each house keeps a certain percentage of whatever money is wagered against it.

The accompanying table shows the common bets that can be made playing on a typical layout (see illustration). A bet on the *line* is a bet that the shooter passes; on the *field*, that a number covered there will come up on the next roll. A *come* bet is a bet that the shooter will win a series starting with his next roll. *Hard way* means he must make his point by doubles.

Bets against	Chances Against	Chances For	House pays	House percentage
Shooter and come bets	251	244	even	1.42
Making point 6 or 8	6	5	even	4.54
Making point 5 or 9	3	2	7–5	4.00
Making point 4 or 10	2	1	5–3	11.11
Making hard way 4 or 10	8	1	7–1	11.11
Making hard way 6 or 8	10	1	9–1	9.09
Making field number, next roll	19	17	even	5.56
Making any doubles, next roll	5	1	4–1	16.67
Making under or over 7, next roll	21	15	even	16.67
Making craps (2, 3, or 12), next roll	16	2	7–1	11.11
Making 11, next roll	17	1	15–1	11.11
Don't pass (1:2 barred)	488	447	even	4.38

Chuck-a-Luck (Bird Cage). Three dice are used, and bets are placed on a layout that varies with the house. The basic bet is that a selected number will show up. Dice are turned over in a wire cage to expose new faces. If the chosen number shows once in the three dice, the bettor collects the amount of his bet; twice, he receives double; three times, he gets triple the amount. Some houses have bets on odd, even, low (4–10), or high (11–17). If triplets (*raffles*) show, the house collects all bets. On single numbers, the house percentage is 7.5; with most combinations the percentage is higher.

Poker Dice. Using five dice, players try to make the best poker "hand" in three rolls or less. A player may set aside any number of dice in each of his first two rolls, rolling the others to try to improve the hand. Hands rank in value as in poker (q.v.), except that there are no flushes, and straights do not count. Low hand loses the bet.

FRANK K. PERKINS, *Boston "Herald"*

DICHROISM, dī′krō-iz-əm, is an optical effect observed in certain crystalline materials, in which two different colors are seen when the crystals are viewed in different directions in plane polarized light (light whose waves are restricted to a single direction of vibration). Dichroism is observed only in colored materials, and it is more pronounced in deeply colored than in pale substances.

Optically, crystals belong to two classes: isotropic and anisotropic. Light that passes through an isotropic crystal is absorbed in the same way in all directions by the crystal. In an anisotropic crystal the light is absorbed differently, depending on its direction of travel through the crystal. Isotropic colored crystals show no color change as they are rotated in plane polarized light, whereas anisotropic crystals exhibit a change in color when they are viewed in different directions. An anisotropic crystal may produce a number of different colors in this way. The general effect is known as *pleochroism;* when only two colors are observed it is called dichroism. Colored materials that crystallize in the tetragonal and hexagonal systems exhibit dichroism.

GEORGE SWITZER
Smithsonian Institution

DICHROITE. See CORDIERITE.

DICK, George Frederick (1881–1967), and **Gladys Henry** (1881–1963), American physicians who, working as a husband-and-wife team, made important discoveries about scarlet fever. In 1923, George and Gladys Dick inoculated volunteers with hemolytic streptococci taken from a scarlet fever victim and successfully produced the disease in some of the volunteers. They thus demonstrated that some streptococcal organisms cause scarlet fever. The Dicks also developed a test for gauging an individual's susceptibility to scarlet fever. In this "Dick test," a small amount of the streptococcal toxin is injected under the skin. If a bright red flush appears at the injection site within a few hours, the individual is known to be susceptible to scarlet fever.

George Dick was born in Fort Wayne, Ind., on July 12, 1881, and received his M.D. from Rush Medical College at Chicago in 1905. After studying in Europe, he returned to Chicago and worked at the McCormick Institute of Infectious Diseases with his wife (married 1914). From 1933 to 1946 he was chairman of the University of Chicago's Department of Medicine. He died in Palo Alto, Calif., on Oct. 14, 1967.

Gladys Dick was born in Pawnee City, Nebr., on Dec. 18, 1881, and received her M.D. from Johns Hopkins University in 1907. She died in Menlo Park, Calif., on Aug. 24, 1963.

L. R. C. AGNEW
University of California at Los Angeles

DICK TEST, a medical test for determining susceptibility to scarlet fever. It was first devised in 1924 by George and Gladys Dick (q.v.).

DICKCISSEL, dik-sis′əl, a small finch of the meadows and pastures of central North America between the Rocky Mountains and the Allegheny Mountains from the U.S.-Canadian border to the Gulf coast.

About 6 or 7 inches (15–18 cm) long, the dickcissel is approximately the same size as the common house sparrow, but it has a slimmer body and a heavier beak. Resembling a meadowlark, it has a black and brown streaked back, white chin, yellow breast, and prominent black patch on the throat. The female's plumage is duller than the male's.

Dickcissels are valuable as eaters of insects, especially grasshoppers, and of weed seeds. They build sturdy nests on the ground or in shrubs and small trees. The nests are made of coarse grasses and leaves and are lined with fine grasses or hair. The female lays 3 to 5 pale blue eggs.

The dickcissel, *Spiza americana*, belongs to the family Fringillidae, order Passeriformes.

CARL WELTY, *Beloit College*

DICKENS, dik'ənz, **Charles** (1812–1870), English novelist, who holds an outstanding position in the history of literature because of the breadth of his appeal and the fertility of his invention. Many of the characters he created—such as Sam Weller, Uriah Heep, Mr. Micawber, Mrs. Gamp, and Mr. Pecksniff—have entered popular mythology, and many of his sayings have become part of everyday language. Translations of his works have proliferated; his novels have been dramatized, filmed, and adapted into musicals.

Dickens' unique combination of humor, pathos, and humanitarian purpose made him the most popular writer of his day—a national figure read and esteemed by people in all walks of life. A later generation, reacting against him, labeled him "one of those Victorian scarecrows with ludicrous Freudian flaws," and saw him as a showman wallowing in facile jokes and sickly sentimentality. In more recent times, however, he has been taken very seriously, both as a literary artist and as a social analyst. Literary criticism has emphasized the symbolical, surrealist, and at times almost hallucinatory qualities of his novels, which connect him with modernist trends and with such masters of fiction as Dostoyevsky and Kafka. Dickens' anatomy of Victorian society—industrialized, money-oriented, and self-important—has given him a place in the great tradition of morally and socially responsible novelists.

Charles Dickens

LIFE

Early Years. Charles Dickens was born at Portsea, near Portsmouth, on Feb. 7, 1812, the second child and eldest son of John and Elizabeth Dickens, neither of whom had any literary inclinations. The somewhat ambiguous social position of his parents has led to the supposition that Dickens suffered from social maladjustment throughout his life. His mother was of middle-class origin; both his paternal grandparents were domestic servants. His father, a clerk in the Navy Pay Office, was, however, only too anxious to be a gentleman. Easygoing and amiable, he was unable to handle money—a fault that up to his death in 1851 was to blight his son's life.

Dickens' earliest years were happy, particularly those, between the ages of five and nine, which he spent at Chatham, where the family had moved after a short spell in London. A delicate, precocious, and imaginative boy, he roamed the country of the Thames and Medway estuaries (later the setting of so many scenes in his novels). He fed his voracious reading appetite on the *Arabian Nights*, on Shakespeare, and on a store of 18th century novels that he found in the attic. At school he was keen to learn and to distinguish himself.

This childhood world was shattered in 1822 with the transfer of Dickens' father to London, where he soon found himself in financial difficulties. When Charles, who had been left at Chatham to finish his school term, joined the family, he found them living in poverty in a small house in Camden Town. There was no more schooling for the boy, only household chores. Instead of the Kentish marshes he roamed the London streets, often on errands to the pawnshops. The severest blow fell in February 1824, when his father was arrested for debts and taken to Marshalsea prison. Charles, then barely 12, was sent to work, pasting labels on bottles in a blacking warehouse for a wage of six shillings a week, with which he had to support himself. (The rest of the family had taken up residence in the Marshalsea.) His father received a legacy and was released in May 1824, but the parents, who were unaware of the extent of Charles' despair, let him continue working for a few weeks longer.

These months of social humiliation and the resulting apparent defeat of all his personal ambition left Dickens with a lifelong wound, so painful that his own wife and children did not learn of this episode until after his death. It was a formative experience, however, steeling him into the relentless drive that ever after characterized him—an experience reflected in the many suffering children—often orphans—and other victims of injustice in his stories.

After a few more years of study, at Wellington House Academy, Dickens became, at 15, an office boy in the Holborn law firm of Ellis and Blackmore. Before long, however, he became dissatisfied with this dull and unpromising work and turned to journalism. With ardent determination he learned shorthand and pursued opportunities in his chosen career. By 1832 he was general reporter for the *True Sun* and also parliamentary reporter on his uncle's newspaper, the *Mirror of Parliament*. As a sideline he began to write small fictional sketches, based on observations of London life, for magazines. Almost at once they attracted attention by their acute and lively humor, and with the publication of a 2-volume collection, *Sketches by Boz*, in February 1836, Dickens was launched as a promising author.

By this time Dickens' first novel, *Pickwick Papers* (1836–1837), was well under way. He had originally been asked merely to provide the text for a series of comic sporting plates, but with his characteristic determination he took over the project, remolded it to his own design, and gave the world the immortal Mr. Pickwick and his associates. The first of its 20 monthly numbers appeared in April 1836.

This event coincided with Dickens' marriage to Catherine Hogarth. His first romance, with Maria Beadnell, had been an unhappy affair, the memory of which remained painful throughout his life. In Catherine Hogarth, who came of a family with literary interests—her father was the editor of the *Evening Chronicle* and had been a friend of Sir Walter Scott—he found a placid, though not very imaginative, wife. She bore him 10 children in 15 years, but their relationship became increasingly uncongenial, and in 1858 the couple separated.

Middle Years. *Pickwick Papers,* which after a slow start provoked a rage of enthusiasm, brought Dickens fame. His ambition drove him on to consolidate and extend his renown, and in the next eight years, during which his family rapidly increased, his social life became more lavish, and his circle of famous friends expanded, he produced an amazing number of works. These included five novels, miscellaneous stories and essays, works for the stage, and several Christmas books, notably *A Christmas Carol* (1843), which became one of the world's classics.

Monthly or weekly serialization of his novels —sometimes in magazines edited by himself— kept him in close touch with his reading public. Occasionally he bowed to the pressure of his readers, as when sales of *Martin Chuzzlewit* (1843–1844) began to fall off and he quickly provided new interest by sending his hero on a trip to America. More often, however, he educated public taste and taught his readers to expect new and different things from him. The criminal underworld in *Oliver Twist* (1837–1839), the industrial wastes of the Black Country in *The Old Curiosity Shop* (1840), and the storming of Newgate prison in *Barnaby Rudge* (1841) are a far cry from the cozy and humorous world of Mr. Pickwick.

With the attack on the Poor Law in *Oliver Twist* and on the notorious Yorkshire schools for unwanted children in *Nicholas Nickleby* (1838–1839), Dickens earned a reputation as a social reformer—a reputation that he supported by deeds as well as words. Together with the rich heiress Angela Burdett Coutts, later Baroness Burdett-Coutts, he engaged in welfare work, involving himself in such projects as slum clearance, the Ragged Schools for poor children, and a home for the rehabilitation of fallen women.

The public, which he had made laugh, he now also made cry. The whole nation wept for the death of little Nell in *The Old Curiosity Shop,* a scene that came right from Dickens' heart. The character of Nell was based on his sister-in-law, Mary Hogarth, whom he had worshiped. She had joined the Dickenses soon after their marriage, and in 1837, when she was only 17, she was suddenly taken ill and died in Dickens' arms. His grief verged on the pathological, and the memory of her haunted him for years.

In January 1842, Dickens and his wife went on a 6-month tour of the United States, with a brief visit to Canada. They were lionized in Boston and New York and then continued amid physical discomforts to Philadelphia, Washington, Pittsburgh, Cincinnati, and down the Ohio River, passing the city of Cairo, Ill., which was to become the model for "Eden" in *Martin Chuzzlewit.* Dickens had gone to the United States in the hope of disproving the gloomy accounts of that country given by earlier British travelers. However, his attitude was soured by violent attacks on him in the American press (partly brought about by his own outspokenness on the issue of copyright laws) and by certain features of American life, particularly slavery, which he found uncouth and repulsive. He returned to England, in his own words, "a Lover of Freedom disappointed." The travel book *American Notes* (1842) was fair and innocuous enough, but the sharp and somewhat biased satire of America and its people that appeared in his next novel, *Martin Chuzzlewit,* made him many enemies on the other side of the Atlantic.

By the mid-1840's, the pressure under which Dickens was working was making him increasingly restless. One of the ways in which he sought to release his nonliterary energies was through further travel, and the whole family lived for two years in Italy and Switzerland. Another main outlet was his dramatic activities. From childhood, Dickens had been a great lover of the theater, enjoying the production and stage management aspects as much as the acting. There were frequent and elaborate private theatricals in his house in London, and between 1847 and 1857 the amateur company that he formed and led with unflagging zest appeared in public more than 60 times, in London and the provinces, and even performed before Queen Victoria.

Meanwhile, though Dickens now found novel writing a slower and more demanding process than in his early days as an author, he was reaching the peak of his creative power, working from a deepened understanding of himself as well as of his society. In 1847–1849 he tried to write an autobiography but, after struggling with the episode in the blacking factory, abandoned it as too painful. Instead, he turned to *David Copperfield* (1849–1850), his "favourite child" and his most autobiographical novel. David Copperfield's career touches that of Charles Dickens at many key points, apart from the childhood sufferings. Behind David's "child-wife" Dora, there is Maria Beadnell; behind the history of Little Emily is Dickens' work for the home for fallen women; and, as Dickens himself pointed out, the model for Mr. Micawber was his own father. No doubt Mrs. Micawber bore a likeness to his mother, though Dickens only confessed to having featured her in the giddy and inane mother of the hero in *Nicholas Nickleby.*

In *Dombey and Son* (1846–1848), which immediately preceded *David Copperfield,* Dickens had dissected a society ruled by commercial interests rather than by human feelings. This heartlessness of a system pitted against man is the chief concern of the novels of the 1850's: *Bleak House* (1852–1853), *Hard Times* (1854), and *Little Dorrit* (1855–1857). In *Little Dorrit* there is a complete fusion of autobiography and social criticism, as the Marshalsea debtors' prison is transmuted into a symbol of England's condition. *Hard Times,* in which Dickens was most directly concerned with industry, was inspired by an actual weavers' strike in Preston, Lancashire. It appeared in *Household Words,* a weekly magazine that Dickens had begun in 1850. Work on this periodical and on its successor, *All the Year Round* (begun 1859), involved Dickens in unceasing editorial activity for the last 20 years of his life. *A Tale of Two Cities* (1859) and *Great Expectations* (1860–1861) were both first published in *All the Year Round.*

That the Dickens of these later novels was a more somber, less exuberant person than young "Boz" had been was a matter partly of social disillusionment and partly of personal and domestic circumstances. Dickens was not a happy man despite his literary successes—"there is no writing against such power as this—one has no chance," said Thackeray, his greatest rival, after reading the chapter in *Dombey and Son* that told of the death of little Paul. Dickens' marriage was falling apart, and in the spring of 1859 he and his wife separated. Catherine Dickens went to live in a house of her own with their eldest son. Dickens, with those of his children who still remained at home, resided from this time more or less permanently at Gad's Hill Place, the country house in Kent that he had dreamt of owning in his childhood and that he had acquired in 1856. His household was managed, as it had already been for many years, by his sister-in-law Georgina Hogarth. Undoubtedly her competent presence in the house, aided by the fact that she strongly resembled the much-mourned Mary Hogarth, had been one source of friction between husband and wife. The immediate reason for the breakup, however, was Dickens' growing attraction to the young actress Ellen Lawless Ternan.

Last Years. Dickens' last decade was one of continued professional success undermined by personal unhappiness, spiritual unrest, and failing health. The scandal brought on by his separation probably had its effect on him; but, more important, no real happiness seems to have resulted from his relationship with Ellen Ternan, the exact nature of which is not known. Some of its emotional bearings can be seen in the Pip-Estella relationship in *Great Expectations*, and in the obsessed and thwarted passions of Bradley Headstone in Dickens' last completed novel, *Our Mutual Friend* (1864–1865), and of Jasper Drood in the unfinished *Mystery of Edwin Drood*.

There were other personal worries, too: his sons, given all the advantages that he had lacked, were not turning out as well as he had hoped. One or two of them seemed to have inherited their grandfather's cavalier attitude toward money and seemed destined for lives of useless snobbery, much in the manner of the early Pip in *Great Expectations*.

Partly to ensure that he should leave a fortune to his large family, and partly because he loved the stage, Dickens spent much of his energy, from 1858 onward, in a series of public readings from his own works. He scored tremendous successes throughout England, and in 1867, though his health was giving cause for concern, he revisited the United States, where he performed before enraptured audiences. He left the United States in April 1868, this time in a blaze of mutual goodwill. However, he also left as a man in irreparably broken health. A last series of readings in England had to be suspended midway because of his physical breakdown; but he persisted in giving a farewell series in London, from January to March 1870. For this he prepared a rendering of the murder of Nancy in *Oliver Twist*, so powerful that it wrung every ounce of strength out of him and left scores of women fainting in the audience.

Burning his candle at both ends, Dickens persevered in his editorial and creative work. He was halfway through his last novel, *The Mystery of Edwin Drood* (6 out of 12 planned numbers were issued in 1870), when he had a stroke and died, at Gad's Hill, on June 9, 1870. He was buried five days later in Westminster Abbey.

Dickens' death was felt as a national calamity. The London *Times* summed up what he had meant to the English-speaking world: "Statesmen, men of science, philanthropists, the acknowledged benefactors of their race, might pass away and yet not leave the void which will be caused by the death of Dickens . . . . It needs an extraordinary combination of intellectual and moral qualities . . . before the world will consent to enthrone a man as their unassailable and enduring favourite. This is the position which Mr. Dickens has occupied with the English and also with the American public for the third of a century."

WRITINGS

In the case of Charles Dickens, the man and the artist, his life and his writings, are particularly closely bound up. Not only do details of his own life appear under fictional guise in his novels and stories; but, more important, the energy and exuberance that characterized him as a human being are reflected in the extraordinary vividness of all he wrote, and especially in his comic figures. Yet, he suffered hurts and humiliations in his life, and underneath his cheerfulness and exhilaration there was an undertone of sadness. Out of these conflicting elements of his own personality, he created fiction with a uniquely wide and varied range of emotions.

Perhaps more than anything else it is Dickens' control of the reader's emotions that distinguishes him as an author. Just as he was both literally and metaphorically a great stage manager in life, so he manipulates the reader's sympathies with a theatrical flair in his novels. Whether he is seen as an entertainer, a social critic, or a poet with a vision of his own to communicate—and he is all of these—the first and last impression of any work of his is that it is the product of a very strong personality.

Entertainer and Critic. Although Dickens did not live to a great age by modern standards, his life spanned a time of one of the great social and cultural changes in English history: from the Regency, with its still predominantly agricultural society and its cultural center in an extravagant aristocracy, to the mid-Victorian commercial and industrial era, dominated by a wealthy middle class. The span of Dickens' own work is a barometer of this change, ranging from the world of leisurely stagecoach travel and rural idylls in *Pickwick Papers*, through the London business world and the train journeys in *Dombey and Son*, to the "grey, dusty, withered evening in London city" and the dustheaps, symbols of the human waste in a materialistic society, in *Our Mutual Friend*. This development alone is an indication of Dickens' strong conviction that the function of the novelist was to be an interpreter of his age as well as a public entertainer. The immense success of *Pickwick Papers* was due to its comedy and good-humored satire, and many people felt that, as Dickens moved from his first novel toward works which were darker in mood and in which the comedy was more savage and the criticism more radical, he was betraying his own genius. However, Dickens himself refused to accept and stick to a success formula.

Dickens' energetic exploration of new subject matter and new modes of expression suggests, too, a kind of artistic integrity which, on the face of it, may appear to be contradicted by the method of publication of his novels. Not one of the novels was published in its entirety before all (or in the case of *Oliver Twist*, the greater part) of it had appeared in monthly or weekly serial numbers. This practice necessarily involved a certain amount of hand-to-mouth writing and an eye to the public, which had to have its interest sustained from number to number. Dickens' earlier novels in particular bear traces of improvisation. In many of these works, the watchful reader may be conscious of each number as a separate unit of composition. Also in the early novels, characters that were obviously going down well, like Mrs. Gamp in *Martin Chuzzlewit*, or those that gradually took hold of Dickens' imagination, like Fagin in *Oliver Twist*, tend to run away with the story. But, with time, Dickens became increasingly careful to build each work according to a preconceived design. This overall plan usually existed only in his own mind—hence the amount of conjecture as to how *The Mystery of Edwin Drood* would have been completed and resolved. However, recent studies of Dickens at work have shown that, from the time of *Dombey and Son* onward, he wrote down detailed plans for each number of a novel. The most striking evidence of Dickens' artistic progress in terms of his increased sense of design is a comparison of his first and last novels. *Pickwick Papers* is almost without plot, its structure simply a series of incidents loosely held together by the figures of the "hero" and his companions. *Edwin Drood* has a plot as carefully constructed as that of a detective story, and everything is subordinated to that central "mystery," which was never resolved.

However, Dickens' growing concern for form and structure was not merely a matter of plot; it also involved thematic unity. Seriousness of social and moral comment goes hand in hand with control of the artistic medium. When Dickens began to write, his masters were the novelists who had written before the dark satanic mills encroached on the beauty of "merrie olde" England. He looked to the picaresque novels of Fielding and Smollett and the sentimental tradition of Goldsmith and Sterne. In their spirit he fashioned *Pickwick Papers* as a comic epic in which, apart from some interpolated melodramatic tales, seriousness intrudes only toward the end, when Mr. Pickwick is thrown into debtor's prison—the first hint of what was to be a recurring theme of injustice in his novels.

Nicholas Nickleby is typical of the picaresque structure of Dickens' early novels, organized as it is only by the adventures of Nicholas. Its plot separates into a set of romantic love stories, and its moral world is a scheme of black-and-white, good-and-evil opposites. The wicked uncle, Ralph Nickleby, and the miser, Arthur Gride, are obvious villains contrasted with the noble hero, his virtuous sister, and the impossibly good Cheeryble brothers. In such a world, social criticism must be incidental and directed toward specific evils, as in the Dotheboys Hall episode, and even there Mr. Squeers, the Yorkshire schoolmaster, is a comic, rather than a threatening caricature. In *Martin Chuzzlewit* the story for the first time is shaped by a clearly discernible theme: "the love of self" in its various forms, most gruesomely seen in the distintegrating mind of the murderer Jonas Chuzzlewit. Evil, too, has become less melodramatic and more multilayered, as in the hypocritical Mr. Pecksniff.

With *Dombey and Son*, Dickens became a structural innovator, creating the novel dealing with a social group. The whole work centers on the big London business house of Dombey (who never realizes his dream of becoming Dombey and Son), and the interlinking sets of characters are all related to it and to the mercantile ideal for which it stands. Dickens used the same technique in *Bleak House*, in which the focus of the structure, as well as of the social criticism, is the Court of Chancery. All the main groups of characters—from the proud Lady Dedlock to the inhabitants of Tom-all-Alone's, the rotting London slum—are involved in an exasperating Chancery suit. Nor is the focus on a specific social evil as it is in the early novels. Chancery stands for the whole system of antiquated and dehumanized institutions under which England was stifling and rotting away. As in *Bleak House*, evil is no longer restricted to particular, well-defined villains; it has spread into the whole system. Similarly, in *Little Dorrit* the whole social system becomes symbolic of a prison, made concrete in the hated Marshalsea, which plays a central part in the lives of all the principal characters.

David Copperfield, written between these more obviously social novels, is an apparent return to the picaresque style of *Nicholas Nickleby*. Its form is determined by the things that happen to David, Dickens' alter ego. The important difference, however, is that they happen *to* David, changing and modifying him as a person, so that the work is unified, by the process of growth, into a psychological epic. In *Great Expectations*, regarded by many as Dickens' greatest novel, this technique is combined with that of the social novels. The stages of Pip's, the hero's, "expectations," are firmly organized to embody his growth and development, into and out of snobbery, but at the same time the institutions and ideals of contemporary society are scrutinized and evaluated. Here, and even more in Dickens' last completed work, *Our Mutual Friend*, social issues are woven into the very fabric of the novel, and into the minds of his ever more subtly realized characters.

Yet, it would be a gross oversimplification to see Dickens' development as a steady move from entertainer to social critic. *Oliver Twist*, with its attack on the Poor Law, probably made a more direct social impact than any of his late novels, and there is glorious comedy even in his darkest and bitterest work, *Our Mutual Friend*. Indeed, his force as social critic and his power as an entertainer had the same source: his ability to perceive the oddities of human behavior and to recreate them, on a magnified scale, in fiction. It was because the critic spoke with the entertainer's voice that he could reach a wider public than any novelist before or after. One can hardly overestimate the way in which his work influenced the emotional attitudes of Victorians to social problems, especially in the 1840's, when a preacher is quoted as saying: "There have been at work among us three great social agencies: the London City Mission; the novels of Dickens; the cholera." Yet, he was not a practical politician initiating reforms; nor was he a profound thinker or a social or moral theorist. Basically, his ethics remained those of orthodox Christianity, and basically—though, in recent times, Marxist critics have wanted to see him as a spokesman of the proletariat—he wrote from a Victorian middle-class position. His reaction against a capitalist society, as his reaction against stultifying institutions, was on the simple thesis that it fosters man's inhumanity to man. Basically, his novels speak up for man as an individual, against the dehumanizing forces of institutionalized society. The greater artistic integrity of the later novels is a matter of the imagination: as he saw deeper into the mind of men, his vision became more unified.

Dickens' Imagination. In *Hard Times*, within a framework of industrial problems, Capital vs. Labor, Dickens' real concern is with Imagination vs. Fact. He protests against the suppression of the human spirit, the repression of human feelings, by the forces of utilitarianism. This novel might be seen as a paradigm of his own art, in which—from the beginning to the end of his career—imagination reigns supreme. It is an imagination that enabled him to bring alive images of his own contemporary England, particularly the London scene, as well as past history (the Gordon riots in *Barnaby Rudge;* the French Revolution in *A Tale of Two Cities*). Above all, it enabled him to bring alive characters which, as T. S. Eliot has described them, are "of greater intensity than human beings." Dickens' art is one of great caricature; his characters are seen in terms of their obsessions. Often their grotesqueness serves a comic purpose, and often the comedy has a satirical bite, as when Mr. Pecksniff warms his hands before the fire "as benevolently as if they were somebody else's, not his." But there is also another side to his characterizations—his imaginative identification with the dark depths of the human soul: the guilt-ridden, the criminal, the rebel. It has often been pointed out that Dickens' point of view tends to be that of an insecure and undernourished child roving the London streets, and some of the finest parts of his novels are those—in *David Copperfield* and *Great Expectations*, for example—in which he rendered the fearful and almost hallucinated visions of such children.

The chief tool of Dickens' imagination is his style, a style that has little to do with ordinary colloquial prose. Like his art as a whole, it draws attention to itself by its blatant theatricality; overstatements, chanted repetitions, reiterated catchphrases and imagery, dramatically unexpected metaphors in which people and things merge grotesquely (so that the "tight-clenched" bureau of a miser has a "bad and secret forehead"). At its worst, his style strikes the reader as excessively rhetorical. His death scenes and other pathetic episodes, especially those involving the tender emotions, tend to be embarrassing to a modern reader. At its best, however, his style acts on us as poetry, as in the opening paragraphs of *Great Expectations*.

Dickens' symbolism, finally, is the aspect of his art that pulls its separate strands together. There is incidental symbolism throughout his work, but each of the mature novels is unified by a predominant symbol, often obvious enough and often socially weighted, like the train in *Dombey and Son*, the prison in *Little Dorrit*, and the dustheaps in *Our Mutual Friend*. The fog that envelops the Chancery-ridden world of *Bleak House*, the dark and threatening river that runs through *Our Mutual Friend*, the misty and haunted marshes of *Great Expectations*—these are not only effective structural devices setting the social atmosphere, they also embody states of the mind and of the soul. To pay serious attention to such features of Dickens' writings is to realize that his greatest achievement is as entertainer, social critic, and poet—all in one.

INGA-STINA EWBANK
University of London

Bibliography
Butt, John, and Tillotson, Kathleen, *Dickens at Work* (Methuen 1957).
DeVries, Duane, *Dickens' Apprentice Years: The Making of a Novelist* (Barnes & Noble 1976).
Dickens, Charles, *The Letters of Charles Dickens*, ed. by Madelaine House, Graham Storey, and others (Oxford 1965–).
Dickens, Charles, *Speeches*, ed. by Kenneth J. Fielding (Oxford 1965).
Fielding, Kenneth J., *Charles Dickens: A Critical Introduction*, rev. ed. (Houghton 1962).
Ford, George, and Lane, Lauriat, Jr., eds., *The Dickens Critics* (Cornell Univ. Press 1961).
Garis, Robert, *The Dickens Theatre: A Re-Assessment of the Novels* (Oxford 1965).
House, Arthur Humphrey, *The Dickens World* (Oxford 1941).
Johnson, Edgar, *Charles Dickens: His Tragedy and Triumph*, 2 vols. (Little 1965).
Miller, Joseph H., Jr., *Charles Dickens: The World of His Novels* (Harvard Univ. Press 1959).
Price, Martin, ed., *Dickens: A Collection of Critical Essays* (Prentice-Hall 1967).
Slater, Michael, ed., *Dickens on America and the Americans* (Univ. of Texas Press 1978).
Wilson, Edmund, "Dickens: The Two Scrooges," in *The Wound and the Bow* (Houghton 1941).

DICKEY, dik'ē, **Bill** (1907–), American baseball player, who was the outstanding catcher in the game for more than 15 years. A career-long player for the New York Yankees (1928–1946), he was elected to the Baseball Hall of Fame in 1954.

William Malcolm Dickey was born in Bastrop, La., on June 6, 1907. He joined the Yankees in 1928, after six years of minor league baseball, and became their regular catcher in 1929. During the next 13 years he caught more than 100 games a season. He was named to all-star teams six times and played in eight World Series, seven of which the Yankees won. A left-handed batter, he hit .313 during his career.

Dickey served in the U.S. Navy in 1944–1945. In 1946 he managed the Yankees from May 24 to September 12 after Joseph V. McCarthy resigned. He piloted Little Rock (Southern Association) in 1947, returning to the Yankees as a coach until 1957.

BILL BRADDOCK, *New York "Times"*

DICKINSON, Edwin (1891–1978), American painter, who explored his own highly individual path of fantasy in a period dominated by nonobjective painting. His work did not gain wide recognition until the 1950's, although it had long been admired by other artists, both realists and abstractionists.

Dickinson was born at Seneca Falls, N.Y., on Oct. 11, 1891. He studied in New York City at the Pratt Institute and at the Art Students League, where he spent most of his life teaching. He died in Orleans, Mass., on Dec. 2, 1978.

Dickinson's mature paintings, on each of which he worked years, are large, intricate and mysterious compositions of figures set within an inexplicable environment of light and dark shadow. A typical example is *Composition with Still Life* (1933–1937; Museum of Modern Art, New York), in which two nude bodies, or corpses, lie grotesquely within the shadowed atmospheric space that seems to be part interior and part landscape. Later works, such as *Ruin at Daphne* (1943–1953; Metropolitan Museum of Art, New York), have intricate architectural perspective, but the strong feeling for fantasy persists.

H. H. ARNASON
The Solomon R. Guggenheim Foundation

Further Reading: Goodrich, Lloyd, *Edwin Dickinson* (Praeger 1966).

Emily Dickinson

ROBERT FROST LIBRARY, AMHERST COLLEGE

DICKINSON, Emily (1830–1886), American poet, who is now recognized as one of the greatest poets of 19th century America. Her verse, along with that of Emerson and Whitman, best defines the distinctive qualities of the American experience.

Life. Emily Elizabeth Dickinson, the second of three children of Edward and Emily Dickinson, was born on Dec. 10, 1830, in Amherst, Mass., and lived an outwardly uneventful life there. She was educated at Amherst Academy and spent a year (1847–1848) at nearby Mount Holyoke College, then called Mount Holyoke Female Seminary. When Emily was growing up, Amherst was a country town remote from the intellectual ferment of Boston and Concord, where Emerson was formulating his transcendental doctrines. Until her maturity, there was only one church in the town, the Congregational, firmly Trinitarian and evangelical; even Amherst College (across the street from the Dickinson mansion, built by Emily's grandfather in 1810) exhibited the religious conservatism that had long characterized towns in the Connecticut Valley. Though she was deeply moved by a religious revival during the winter of 1845–1846 and again while at Mount Holyoke in 1848, Emily found herself unable to "convert"—that is, to experience a conviction of faith and to testify to her experience before the assembled church.

Emily's father, one of the wealthiest and most respected citizens of the town, was a leader of the church and a zealous defender of its orthodoxy against the currents of "New Thought" emanating from Concord. "Squire" Dickinson, as he was often called by humbler neighbors, saw to it that his family attended Sunday meeting, and he bought religious books for them to read. But he was unable to protect them completely from the "latest infidelity," transcendentalism, for Ben Newton, a law student in his office, gave Emerson's *Poems* to Emily for Christmas in 1850. Thereafter she had two "fathers," Edward Dickinson in Amherst, to whom she was tied by the strongest bonds of love and gratitude, and Ralph Waldo Emerson in Concord, her intellectual "validator," who assured her that her religious doubts were not unreasonable and who inspired her to pursue religious intuitions that could not be fitted into Amherst's orthodoxy. For the rest of her life she bought, read, and reread all of Emerson's books, which inspired many of her poems.

Denied most of the comforts and satisfactions that sustain humanity, particularly love and marriage and a secure religious faith, Emily lived intensely, finding in her books, her garden, and the friends with whom she corresponded the possibilities of rich experience and fulfillment. After her father's death in 1874, she went into the seclusion that led to her being called "the nun of Amherst." She died there on May 15, 1886.

Poetry. Over a thousand poems were discovered in Emily Dickinson's bureau after her death. In all, she wrote nearly 1,800 poems, several hundred of which are among the finest ever written by any American poet. She gave only 24 of the poems titles, and only seven were printed during her lifetime.

The earliest surviving verse by the poet's hand was embroidered on a sampler when she was 15. Its interest lies chiefly in its relation to her later religious development. It begins "Jesus Permit Thy Gracious Name to stand/ As the First efforts of an infants hand" and ends with the prayer that He may write His name upon her heart. Many of her late religious poems treat Jesus, whom her father called the divine Son of God, as an avatar and validator who taught the difficulty and necessity of faith and "endorsed the sheen" of life. They suggest that in the end, after all her doubts, His name was written on her heart.

Form. Emily Dickinson's earliest surviving poem (written in 1852) is a comic valentine that exhibits the wit that would later be so prominent a feature of her mature verse. In verse form, too, it foreshadows her mature work, being written in a variation of one of the hymn forms described and illustrated in Isaac Watts' *Christian Psalmody* and in *Psalms, Hymns, and Spiritual Songs*, 19th century editions of which were used for congregational singing in her church and copies of which were also in her father's library. Of the several variations of this meter, the most frequently used, "the common meter," which the poet chose for most of her work, is the same as that of most of the older folk ballads, the nursery rhymes, and modern jingles. Like Emerson before her, but more consistently, she chose the most "nonliterary" form available for the majority of her poems. For the rest, she chose one of the traditional variations. Often she denied church doctrine in the form the church had chosen as its vehicle for teaching it:

> We hated Death and hated Life
> And nowhere was to go
> Than Sea and continent there is
> A larger—it is Woe.

Emily's most creative period, from 1858 to 1862, ended with her "nervous breakdown." After this, she composed less often but not less well; some of her latest poems are among her greatest; for example, *A Route of Evanescence*, *How Brittle Are the Piers*, and *The Road Was Lit with Moon and Star*.

Thought. Apart from the occasional verse and the small number of pure love poems, about which there has been too much fruitless speculation concerning who was meant, her single complex subject was the self and its ultimate destiny. Having failed, despite the religious revivals, to find the comfort of her father's faith, she settled for a while for Emerson's. But then Emerson, though he continued to be valued as a spiritual guide, came to seem to her not to have taken sufficient account of the fact of suffering. After this she carried on a running debate with both her "fathers" on the possibility of any valid faith, Christian or transcendental.

Emily Dickinson sometimes anticipated the naturalism characteristic of the 20th century. She epitomized the history of American religious development—from Jonathan Edwards to Emerson and then to Wallace Stevens, Conrad Aiken, Robinson Jeffers, and other naturalistic poets who came to maturity in the 1920's.

Important to the poet's development was a series of men that Emily often called her "mentors." Ben Newton, who introduced her to Emerson, was the first of these and was never forgotten after his early death. Her next mentor was the Rev. Charles Wadsworth, who was pastor of a Philadelphia church when she met him. In 1862, when he moved to California and she could never expect to see him again, she suffered the first of her several emotional crises. After her recovery that same year she solicited advice from Thomas Wentworth Higginson, a clergyman and author living in Cambridge, Mass., with whom she corresponded regularly for some 20 years and who meant less to her personally but was still a resource in time of need. After her father's death she turned to an old family friend, Judge Otis Lord, not, as with Higginson, for advice about poetry (advice she never took) but for consolation. After the death of Lord's wife, she allowed affectionate respect for him to develop into love, and considered marriage, but then he died too, and there were no more men, or mentors either, in her life.

Sources. Emily Dickinson's poetry exhibits four primary influences, if we count as one influence the Bible and the Protestant hymns—which retold the Biblical story, usually in Biblical images, and gave her her meter. Next come Shakespeare, Emerson, and Hawthorne. Of these four, the Bible and Emerson were crucial to her; without them her poetry would have been entirely different or, more likely, would not have been written at all. Shakespeare was for her, as for most of her contemporaries, a linguistic and imagistic resource. Hawthorne she might have done without, though we should not then have had some of her finest poems, among them *I Heard a Fly Buzz—When I Died*, which takes off from the "Governor Pyncheon" chapter in *The House of Seven Gables*.

Some four years after Emily's death, Mabel Loomis Todd, a friend and neighbor whose aid Emily's sister Lavinia had enlisted, managed to persuade Higginson, who had publishing connections, to join her in editing and "correcting" a selection of the poems. Thereafter, friends and relatives continued to publish additional edited selections from the manuscripts until, in 1955, Thomas H. Johnson published a complete, 3-volume edition, including variant readings, of the poems as the poet had written them.

HYATT H. WAGGONER, *Author of "American Poets, from the Puritans to the Present"*

Bibliography
Bianchi, Martha D., *The Life and Letters of Emily Dickinson* (Houghton 1924).
Gelpi, Albert J., *Emily Dickinson: The Mind of the Poet* (1965; reprint, Norton 1971).
Johnson, Thomas H., *Emily Dickinson: An Interpretative Biography* (1955; reprint, Atheneum 1967).
Leyda, Jay, *The Years and Hours of Emily Dickinson*, 2 vols. (Yale Univ. Press 1960).
Whicher, George F., *This Was a Poet: A Critical Biography of Emily Dickinson* (Scribner 1938).

DICKINSON, John (1732–1808), American political leader and writer. He held important posts in the Revolutionary and post-Revolutionary periods but is best known for his so-called "Farmer's Letters," a series of political tracts denouncing British taxation policy in the American colonies, which effectively aroused public opinion in both England and America.

Dickinson was born in Talbot county, Md., on Nov. 8, 1732. In 1740 he moved with his family to Delaware. He studied law in Philadelphia and at the Middle Temple in London, and in 1757 he began to practice law in Philadelphia. In 1760 he was elected to the Delaware Assembly and two years later to the Pennsylvania Assembly. He served there with distinction until 1765 and again from 1770 to 1776.

During the pre-Revolutionary years, Dickinson wrote a large number of papers and pamphlets, including the influential *Letters from a Pennsylvania Farmer to the Inhabitants of the British Colonies* (1767) and the *Essay on Constitutional Power of Great Britain over the American Colonies* (1774). A member of the Continental Congress from 1774 to 1776, he was responsible for its *Address to the Inhabitants of Quebec* and its *Petitions to the King*, and he probably also drew up the *Declaration of the Causes of Taking up Arms*. Conservatively clinging to hopes of reconciliation with Britain, however, he opposed the Declaration of Independence and refused to sign it. By then the radicals were in the ascendancy, and his influence waned somewhat on that account.

Nevertheless, Dickinson served in the American Army during the Revolution, attaining the rank of brigadier general in the Delaware militia. He also wrote the first draft of the Articles of Confederation and, as a delegate from Delaware, was prominent in the debates of the Constitutional Convention of 1787, strongly advocating adoption of the Constitution. He served as president of Delaware (1781–1782) and governor of Pennsylvania (1782–1785).

After 1787, Dickinson held no further public office, but he maintained his interest in public affairs for the rest of his life and continued to write on political subjects. He published two volumes of his writings in 1801. He died in Wilmington, Del., on Feb. 14, 1808.

DICKINSON, Preston (1889–1930), American painter, who was one of the pioneers of modern art in the United States. He was born in New York City on Sept. 9, 1889. After studying at the Art Students League in New York from 1905 to 1910, he spent the next five years in Europe, mostly studying the old masters in the Louvre. Following World War I he developed a style that contained cubist elements with Oriental overtones, deriving some of his inspiration from Cézanne's paintings and from Japanese prints. Dickinson traveled widely, particularly in Europe, and died in Hendaye, France, on Nov. 30, 1930.

Although Dickinson worked in oil and watercolor, he became especially noted for his pastels—both still lifes and landscapes. His pastel portrayals of industrial and urban scenes, notably those of New York City bridges and scenes of Quebec, have a surprising delicacy in comparison with the frequently harsh colors of his still lifes. His work is represented in the major museums of the United States.

DICKINSON, a city in southwestern North Dakota, the seat of Stark county, is 100 miles (161 km) west of Bismarck. It is an agricultural and wholesale center. The manufacture of lignite briquettes is an important industry. Dickinson State College is situated here.

Dickinson was founded in 1882, after the railroad reached the site. In the following years it was a forwarding point for supplies to the gold fields in the Black Hills. It was incorporated as a village in 1899 and as a city in 1919. Government is by commission. Population: 15,924.

DICKSON, Leonard Eugene (1874–1951), American mathematician, who made contributions to the theory of finite and infinite groups, the theory of numbers, algebras and their arithmetics, and the history of mathematics. He was born in Independence, Iowa, on Jan. 22, 1874, and received his bachelor's and master's degrees at the University of Texas in 1893 and 1894 and his Ph. D. at the University of Chicago in 1896. From 1900 to 1939, Dickson taught mathematics at the University of Chicago, from 1910 as full professor. He died in Harlingen, Texas, on Jan. 17, 1954.

Dickson's many papers and books deal with algebras and their invariants, the theory of Galois, and number theory; his *History of the Theory of Numbers* (3 vols., 1919–1923) is the standard work on the subject. His other books include *Linear Algebras* (1914), *Theory and Applications of Finite Groups* (1916), *Algebras and Their Arithmetics* (1923), and *Introduction to the Theory of Numbers* (1929). Subjects of Dickson's special attention were the Waring problem, the last theorem of Fermat, and the arithmetic theory of quadratic forms.

DIRK J. STRUIK
Author, "A Concise History of Mathematics"

DICOTYLEDONS. See PLANTS AND PLANT SCIENCE—*1. Classification* (Pteropsida).

DICTATING MACHINES are instruments for recording and reproducing dictation. They are used mostly for business correspondence and other business communications. Letters or other messages are dictated into the microphone of a recording unit. They are later transcribed by a typist, who plays back the recording on a reproducing unit at any desired speed. Though the recording and reproducing functions are usually performed by separate units, combination units are available. Dictating machines have become standard office equipment because they are versatile and greatly increase efficiency.

Dictating machines range in size from large central units to small portable units. Some of the smallest machines are battery-powered or can be connected to the electrical systems of cars, trains, or airplanes. There is also a variety of recording media, including magnetic tape, plastic discs and plastic belts, and loops. The plastic media are cut, like phonograph records, with an embossing stylus.

Thomas Edison, in 1877, was the first to record the human voice. Alexander Graham Bell improved the recorder, using a wax mixture of 50% beeswax and 50% paraffin as the recording medium. In 1886, the first machine for recording and reproducing sound, the Tainter Graphophone, was patented.

LEILA H. LITTLE
Dictaphone Corporation

DICTATORSHIP is a form of government in which a person or group possesses absolute power without effective constitutional limitations. The term "dictatorship" is derived from the Latin title *dictator,* designating a magistrate given extraordinary power for a limited period in an emergency. But the meaning of the term has changed since Roman times. The essential ingredient of modern dictatorships is power; an emergency is not necessarily present.

Related Terms. A number of terms have been used to denote nondemocratic or antidemocratic regimes, and often they are synonymous with dictatorship. The least extreme of these terms is *authoritarianism.* Authority denotes a legal or rightful power and implies the right to command by virtue of an office or trust; authoritarianism suggests a regime that stresses authority rather than individual liberty and in which traditional institutions and groups are dominant. A stronger term is *autocracy,* which implies an absolute sovereign, a monarch ruling without restriction. Similarly, *absolutism* implies a system in which a ruler has unconditional power, bases his claim to legitimacy on the principle of hereditary or divine right, and claims that the sovereignty of the state is vested in him—though he also claims that he rules for the common good.

The term *despotism,* derived from the Greek word *despotēs* (meaning "master" or "lord") and formerly applied to Byzantine emperors, Italian princes, and the petty Christian rulers in the Turkish Empire, generally refers to a regime in which an absolute ruler exercises power arbitrarily or tyrannically. *Tyranny* in early Greece meant simply a regime in which power had been obtained by irregular, nonconstitutional methods and in which the tyrant was not a legitimate or hereditary monarch. However, in his *Politics,* Aristotle characterized tyranny as the worst of all political systems and as a regime that was perverted because the ruler was interested only in his own welfare. History has accepted Aristotle's judgment.

In the 20th century the term *totalitarianism* was coined to apply especially to three regimes: the Soviet Union during the period of Joseph Stalin's rule (and, to a lesser extent, thereafter), Fascist Italy under Benito Mussolini, and Nazi Germany under Adolf Hitler. In all three regimes no political party other than the ruling party was permitted. Totalitarianism meant the concentration of power in the rulers and especially in the leader of the party, the total subordination of all organizations to the state, the destruction of all possible opposition groups, and the heightened use of censorship, propaganda and indoctrination, and terror.

These three totalitarian regimes were distinguished from absolutist regimes because of their unique destruction of the lines of activity between society and the state; the existence of a one-party regime; their reliance on lawlessness, the secret police, and murder; and the almost complete subjection of everything to the will of the rulers. By contrast, the absolute monarch was a legitimate ruler, who did not act arbitrarily or greatly interfere in many areas of life.

CAUSES OF DICTATORSHIP

Dictatorships have come into existence for a number of reasons:

(1) Some such regimes have been established in the belief that dictatorship is the only way that a regime can be founded or its stability can be maintained. In medieval Italy, Machiavelli argued that the founding of a new republic must be the work of one man only, and in France the revolutionist Robespierre believed that liberty would be achieved through a dictatorship.

(2) Dictatorships have been created to install in power the man or group regarded as indispensable to save the state or to respond to a real or imaginary crisis. In 1922, Mussolini, the head of the Fascist party, was called to power by the king of Italy, who saw him as the representative of order capable of dealing with Bolshevism, anarchy, and industrial unrest.

(3) Ambitious figures have pretended to discern dangers in order to rationalize a coup d'etat. In ancient Greece, Pisistratus and Dionysius the Elder each feigned to be targets of assassination attempts in order to capture power. Supposed emergencies or extremist plots, such as the 18th Brumaire (Nov. 9, 1799) in France or the burning of the Reichstag in Germany in 1933 or a Communist threat in Greece in 1936, allowed Napoleon, Hitler, and Gen. Ioannes Metaxas, respectively, to take power or to strengthen their positions.

(4) Dictatorial regimes also have arisen in response to the incompetence or corruption of governments, to financial difficulties or social upheavals, or to the vacuum created by the decline in the acceptance of the legitimacy of traditional authorities and institutions.

(5) Some dictatorships have claimed to be based on divine will—as in Japan, where emperors were said to have descended from the Heaven Shining Goddess.

(6) Dictatorships often have resulted from humiliation in war, disruptions caused by war, or a military crisis that could not be met by available forces. Control over military forces or victory in war have often been the way to power. This was shown in ancient Israel, and it was the path by which many of the Greek tyrants, the Renaissance *podestas*, Napoleon, various war commanders, Latin American despots, and many contemporary dictators were able to take control.

(7) Dictatorships have been set up to introduce dramatic changes and modernization. Thus, the benevolent dictator Kemal Atatürk transformed Turkey into a secular state with civil codes of law, set up a free and compulsory educational system, and forbade polygamy.

(8) Dictatorships have been created to achieve reformist, revolutionary, or counterrevolutionary objectives. In the first instance, dictators have arisen when dissatisfied, dispossessed, or disfranchised groups demand consideration, as happened in England under Oliver Cromwell or in France during the first part of the French Revolution. Revolutionary dictatorship occurs with the attempt to change economic and social systems, as was the case with the Gracchi in ancient Rome, in the latter part of the French Revolution, or in the 1917 revolution in Russia.

Counterrevolutionary dictatorships seek to preserve the existing system or to allow a traditional group to regain its influence, as in Sparta, in Spain under Gen. Francisco Franco, Portugal under Antonio de Salazar, and Hungary under Nicholas Horthy. Many have resulted from the ambition or demagoguery of an individual, as in the case of Dionysius of Syracuse whose attacks on government and army leaders led to his being made sole general and dictator.

ELEMENTS IN DICTATORIAL RULE

The pattern and methods of dictatorial rule have remained constant. All dictators have reduced the power of other institutions in the political system, especially representative assemblies and independent judiciaries. All have limited personal liberties and have dispensed with constitutional restraints and the rule of law. All have wielded censorship to reduce criticism or to uphold official beliefs. All have hindered—and many have physically eliminated—opponents of the regime.

Many dictators have used religion or myths to gain support or to uphold their authority. Communications media, mass meetings, and music and drama also have been utilized for purposes of indoctrination. Modern dictatorships have encouraged youth organizations to aid in the process of propaganda.

Some dictators have ruled by coercion only; others have sought to win popular approval: by acclamation as did the rulers of Verona; by plebiscites as did Agathocles in Syracuse, Napoleon, and Hitler; or by elections as do many modern rulers. Many have sought to distract the attention of the populace by spectacular internal displays, public works, or ceremonies, or have engaged in foreign adventures and fostered heightened nationalism to gain support. Some dictators, such as Napoleon, have encouraged a cult of personality and have tried to appear as charismatic figures; others, such as Salazar, have been content to remain relatively obscure or the power behind the throne.

Yet all dictatorships suffer from similar problems. Competent subordinates are less available to the dictator than to a democratic leader. Administrators are likely to be cautious in taking any initiative that might be disapproved, and error is likely to persist if the will of the dictator always prevails and a few dare to offer critical advice. Above all, no dictatorship has been able to solve the problem of succession without internal dissension and machination.

EARLY DICTATORSHIPS

Ancient history in the Middle East and in Greece is largely an account of tyrannies. There was rarely a time when dictatorships were not present in the Greek territories.

Greece. The best known of the early dictators were the Athenians. Solon, who was given power in 594 B.C. to deal with civil strife in Attica, has come down in history as a wise lawgiver. He canceled debts, encouraged trade, revised the coinage, and extended citizenship. Although he revised the constitution and remained in power for 22 years, he refused to make himself a permanent dictator.

Pisistratus, a relative of Solon, seized power in Athens in 560 B.C. with the support of guards given to him after he claimed to have been wounded by enemies of the people. After two expulsions he regained power and ruled as dictator for 19 years.

Rome. Dictatorships in ancient Rome usually resulted from a crisis or public emergency. The dictator, or *magister populi*, was invested by the consuls, and later by the senate, with absolute power to take measures necessary to preserve public safety in the interests of the whole community. He controlled most administrative matters and the functioning of all other magistrates and was free of the restrictions imposed on the consuls themselves. But his powers ordinarily were limited in time. The dictator was bound to surrender power when his task was ended, and he could exercise control for a maximum period of six months, after which he had to render an account of his actions. Many dictators not only maintained order and upheld the state religion, but also encouraged trade, reformed taxes and land distribution, reduced or abolished debts, and built public works.

Among the more prominent Roman dictators were Marius, Sulla, and Julius Caesar. Marius, who had risen from humble origins to become a distinguished soldier, was chosen consul seven times beginning in 107 B.C. Regarded as the tribune of the plebs, he introduced social and political reforms, including the creation of a volunteer professional army. His rivalry with Sulla, the leader of the Roman aristocracy, caused a civil war.

Sulla took control in 82 B.C. His appointment differed from that of previous dictators in that he was not limited either in time or in competence. As ruthless in politics as he had been on the battlefield, he ordered some 40 senators and 5,000 opponents killed, and many others were banished or had their property confiscated. Sulla restored the power of the Senate, ruling that no measure could be put before the assembly except by consent of the Senate, and he returned to senators the exclusive right to serve as jurors in the higher courts. He also limited the veto rights of the tribunes. However, after two years of dictatorship, he resigned unexpectedly.

One of the younger opponents spared by Sulla was Julius Caesar. After holding various political and military offices, Caesar was appointed dictator in 49 B.C. He resigned after a few days but resumed power in 46 B.C. Two years later he was appointed dictator for life, and he assumed the title of "Imperator." Caesar, who differed from previous dictators in sparing his opponents, intervened in both political and economic affairs. Politically, he controlled the Assembly, reduced the role of the Senate, vetoed the decisions of tribunes and consuls, and proposed and executed laws. In economic matters he controlled finance, established a stable currency, reduced debts and lowered interest rates, took a census, sponsored a building program, and distributed land to soldiers and the poor. He also controlled religion in his role as *pontifex maximus*.

DICTATORSHIPS IN THE MODERN WORLD

After Renaissance tyrants, absolute monarchs in the 17th century, and enlightened despots in the 18th century, the modern type of dictatorship began to emerge with the French Revolution. Since that time dictators have found it desirable to provide at least the trappings of democracy.

Origins in the French Revolution. Fearing a rightest revolt, the French Convention in 1793 granted exceptional powers to the Committee of Public Safety, authorizing it to control prices and wages and subject all bachelors of ages 18 to 25 to military draft. More or less officially, this committee also wielded the Reign of Terror during which anyone accused of unpatriotic or counter-revolutionary action was arrested. Some 300,000 citizens were seized, of whom about 35,000 were killed or died in prison.

Robespierre, the Jacobin leader and dictator, wanted to create "a republic of virtue" by "a despotism of liberty." Napoleon continued this fusion of democracy and dictatorship. In 1802 the French Senate voted him the office of first consul for ten years, but he held a plebiscite of the people, which gave him the office for life. In 1804 the permanent consul crowned himself emperor. Since the French Revolution many dictatorships have pretended to be democratic and to embody the will of the people, or have used the institutions and processes of democratic systems, such as political parties and elections, for their own ends.

Modern Dictatorships. Modern dictatorships can be classified in various ways, but a useful method is to distinguish between traditional authoritarian dictatorships, Latin American strong rulers, totalitarian regimes, military dictatorships, guided democracies, and reforming dictatorships.

Traditional Dictatorships. Modern dictatorships of the orthodox, authoritarian order were established in Portugal under Salazar, in Spain under Franco, and in pre-world War II central Europe (as in Poland under Marshal Józef C. Pilsudski, in Hungary under Gen. Gyula von Gömbös and Admiral Horthy, and in Greece under General Metaxas). All these dictators reacted in response to a fear of revolution and upheld the traditional authorities. In the New Order set up by Salazar, for example, all parties other than the National Union party were outlawed, education was closely controlled, and a corporative chamber was given only advisory powers. The regime emphasized patriotism, service, obedience, discipline, and order, all frequently at the expense of personal liberty.

Latin Strong Men. Latin America has been the scene of countless struggles of ambitious and ruthless men to capture power in nations that were economically backward, dominated by the Roman Catholic Church, and divided by racial and cultural differences, were a few property owners controlled most of the land, and where there was a heritage of violent rule. Dictators, known as *caudillos*, emerged as would-be liberators or saviors of the country. Most were military men, though some were civilians supported by the army. A few were dedicated to public service, such as the great Simón Bolívar, Porfirio Díaz, in his early years as dictator of Mexico, and Juan Gómez in Venezuela. But most were actuated by personal venality, preoccupied with building grandiose public monuments, concerned about titles and ceremony, and frequently engaged in personal excesses. Dictatorships of this kind were held together not by devotion to impersonal objectives, but by attachment to the person of the dictator.

Totalitarian Regimes. The most extreme version of modern dictatorship is the totalitarianism experienced in the Soviet Union, Italy, and Germany, all characterized by an ideology, a single party and a dictator, a secret police and terror, and control over communication.

After the initial period in which Lenin held political power on behalf of the "dictatorship of the proletariat," the history of the Soviet Union was dominated by Stalin from 1924 to 1952. As secretary-general of the Communist party Stalin controlled the levers of political power; purged and liquidated suspected personal and political opponents from the party, government, armed forces, and police; and imposed ideological conformity on the country and on the international Communist movement. The Stalinist regime served as a model totalitarian system for Communist China.

The Facist and Nazi dictatorships were reactions against the threat of Marxism and international communism. Both Italy and Germany had suffered severely in World War I. In the postwar period Italy had been plagued by industrial unrest, civil disorder, and governmental instability. Germany thought itself humiliated by the Versailles treaty, the separatist movement in the Rhineland, the occupation forces, the invasion of the Ruhr, and the amount of reparations due.

Communist ideology encompasses social equality, internationalism, humanitarianism, rational thought, and—at least in theory—a dictatorship that would exist only temporarily. By contrast, Mussolini and Hitler stressed the need for a strong state, the importance of authority, the inequality of men and races, and the value of discipline and sacrifice for the good of the whole. Both regimes were highly nationalistic and belligerent in foreign affairs. Both outlawed all competing parties, tolerated no political opponents, and ended the rights of free assembly and communication. But the regime of Hitler was far more bestial, with its violent and arbitrary terror, concentration camps, and genocide policies.

Military Dictatorships. Military dictatorial regimes have existed from the time of Artaxerxes of Persia. But they have become more numerous in the contemporary world, where the army in many of the underdeveloped nations considers itself best qualified to act as the agent of political unity. Theoretically, a military coup is a temporary interruption of civilian rule, but frequently the military remains in power if no other group can maintain stability.

Guided Democracies and Reforming Dictatorships. In some underdeveloped nations, as in Ghana and Guinea, dictatorship was defended as necessary to unite divisive groups and achieve national integration. "Reforming" dictatorships, such as that of Fidel Castro in Cuba, generally have an ideological orientation and are pledged to vaguely socialist policies of land redistribution, industrialization, and nationalization of resources.

See also COMMUNISM; FASCISM; GOVERNMENT; NAZISM; and articles on countries and individuals mentioned.

MICHAEL R. CURTIS
Rutgers—The State University (N. J.)

Bibliography

Andrewes, Antony, *The Greek Tyrants* (New York 1963).
Arendt, Hannah, *The Origins of Totalitarianism*, new ed. (New York 1966).
Brinton, C. Crane, *The Anatomy of Revolution*, rev. ed. (New York 1952).
Cobban, Alfred, *Dictatorship: Its History and Theory* (New York 1939).
Friedrich, Carl J., and Brzezinski, Zbigniew K., *Totalitarian Dictatorship and Autocracy*, 2d ed. (New York 1966).
Hallgarten, George W. F., *Why Dictators?* (New York 1954).
Hamill, Hugh M., ed., *Dictatorship in Spanish America* (New York 1966).
Kohn, Hans, *Revolutions and Dictatorships* (Cambridge, Mass., 1941).
Palmer, Robert, *Twelve Who Ruled: The Committee of Public Safety During the Terror* (Princeton 1941; reprinted New York 1965).
Ure, Percy, *The Origins of Tyranny* (London 1922).

DICTIONARY, dik′shə-ner-ē, is the term most frequently used in English to designate a reference book that gives chiefly linguistic information about a set of forms (words, names, phrases, abbreviations and symbols, prefixes, suffixes, and other word elements) listed in a systematic way, usually in alphabetical order. The basic type is the general dictionary of a particular language. The primary aim of this kind of dictionary is to explain the meanings (denotations) of the forms entered and to give information as to spelling, syllabification, pronunciation, synonyms, etymology, facts of usage, and derived forms.

Special dictionaries of restricted scope are also common and of ancient vintage. They tend to be of four types: (1) the glossary, or vocabulary, of a field that has a distinctive terminology—cookery, mining, sports, chemistry; (2) the dictionary of a single aspect of linguistics—etymology, pronunciation, synonyms, dialect, slang, rare words; (3) the so-called "dictionary" that is in actuality an encyclopedia more concerned with factual information than with linguistic information—*Grove's Dictionary of Music and Musicians* and the *Dictionary of American Biography* are outstanding examples of the type; and (4) the bilingual dictionary, which enters the forms in one language and defines them, or more often merely gives their equivalents, in another language. This last type is the immediate predecessor of the modern European general dictionary.

INTRODUCTION

"Dictionaries," said Samuel Johnson, "are like watches; the worst is better than none, and the best cannot be expected to go quite true." Every honest lexicographer agrees, knowing that no matter how keenly he strives to make his book "go true," he will inevitably lose the battle with what might be called "linguistic indeterminacy." Since indeterminacy will be the prime fact of his professional life, he will often be tempted to deny and resent, like the grammarians of the 17th and 18th centuries, the radical instability of languages.

Lexicography. The aim of general lexicography is to produce the most accurate, useful, and up-to-date census of the language that refined methodology and trained linguistic sensibility can yield, and to publish revisions as often as possible to ensure that linguistic indeterminacy does not hopelessly outrun the book. In practice a modern dictionary of less than unabridged size will be heavily revised every two or three years and renewed every ten years.

Denotation. In the fundamental problem of denotation, that is, of writing definitions, indeterminacy impinges in four ways. First, if it is theoretically true that no word has ever been used with precisely the same meaning more than once, then the defining statement, in very brief scope, must attempt to cover an infinitude of meanings without being fatally abstract. Second, meanings change as time passes; hence, the definer must also take account of new meanings and warn of the obsolescence of old ones. Third, meanings vary from place to place, region to region, field to field, class to class, and the variants must be sorted out and labeled. And, fourth, new forms are constantly being added to the language as old ones perish, and dictionaries are properly expected to record and define them.

Methodology. A lexicographer depends on a carefully selected reference library and on a "citation file," which includes thousands of copied-out instances of words and phrases as they have actually been used both in writing and in speaking. If the sources for the file are wisely selected, the slips may be used for both the determination of new definitions and the improvement of old ones. The file covers all kinds of linguistic information—not merely meaning, but usage, pronunciation, regional or local occurrence, and the like. The modern file is kept on punch cards, magnetic tape, or other input media for computer use. Dictionary entries based on a sound reference collection and a sizable citation file will respond more nearly to the objective facts of the language than will entries based on guesswork and impression or whim and prejudice.

Other Considerations. In spite of exact methodology, however, the lexicographer neither can nor would wish to claim that his pursuit is a science. Many decisions must be made on the basis of linguistic sensitivity and tact, or on the basis of infirm predictions about the immediate future of the language.

Since dictionaries are not meant to be read but to be spot-consulted, the lexicographer must present his material in a concise, convenient, and consistent style. He must plan every detail of presentation and typography so that ideally a consulter can find at once, in one place, the information he needs. The typefaces, symbols, and intricate systems of order needed for ready usefulness make modern dictionaries both technically complex and expensive to produce.

The Authority of a Dictionary. Although the foregoing view of lexicography has been standard doctrine among dictionary makers since early in the 19th century, many dictionary users persist in regarding these books not as careful descriptive records but rather as authoritative prescriptive compilations intended to preserve the "purity" of the language. They believe that the dictionary editor should be a censor and excluder and that the mere fact of a word's entry in a dictionary confers legitimacy or approval.

But this is to misunderstand the responsibility of the lexicographer, which is not to condemn certain words and phrases by banishment, but to explain by labeling (slang, informal, substandard) and other means the social and linguistic appropriateness of each entry. Such appropriateness is judged from the same sort of evidence as is denotation, is equally subject to change, and is equally vital to the total meaning of a word or phrase. The authority of a good dictionary rests upon its accuracy in recording the language as actually used in various ambiences, not upon its adherence to some ideal "pure" state of the language.

ENGLISH-LANGUAGE DICTIONARIES

The dictionary as a ubiquitous reference book found beside the Bible in every home is, like the inexpensive Bible itself, a product of modern times. This is not to say that dictionaries themselves were a novel phenomenon. Hellenistic Greece had dictionaries of all sorts. The Chinese had the *Shuo Wen*, a very extensive work, as early as 150 B.C. The Muslims had a highly developed science of lexicography, expounded in the *Fiah al-lugha* (*Science of Lexicography*) in the 10th century A.D. The English grammarian John of Garland made a classified list of words in the early 13th century and called it *Dictionarius*, the first known use of the word.

17th Century. In 1604, Robert Cawdrey published his *A Table Alphabeticall* of "hard usuall English wordes" for the "benefit and helpe of Ladies, Gentlewomen, or any other unskilfull persons," and thereby gained the credit of initiating the modern period of English dictionaries. Cawdrey gave brief definitions of about 2,500 words like "commotrix," "concinnate," and "glacitate." The "hard words" pattern persisted for about a century after Cawdrey's pioneering work and includes Henry Cockeram's *The English Dictionarie* (1623), the first to be called a "dictionary," and the *New World of Words* (1658) by Edward Phillips, nephew of the poet John Milton.

18th Century. The first wordbook to break with the hard-words tradition was *A New English Dictionary* (1702), signed by a certain "J. K." (perhaps John Kersey). Whether or not he was J. K., John Kersey in his own name truly inaugurated the modern tradition by bringing out the first dictionary of considerable scope (38,000 entries), with a clear and consistent defining style, in his 1706 revision of Phillips' *New World of Words*. Two years later, Kersey published the *Dictionarium Anglo-Britannicum*, a small, cheap dictionary that is the direct ancestor of the modern "desk" or "college" dictionary.

Had he not been eclipsed by Samuel Johnson, the laborious and systematic Nathan Bailey would surely be considered the greatest lexicographer of the 18th century. Bailey made three dictionaries of increasing scope and mastery, published between 1721 and 1736. He was the first to perfect a methodology of word collection and compilation, to feature etymologies, and to mark the stress and syllabification of the entry words.

Between the work of Bailey and that of Johnson there need be mentioned only Thomas Dyche's *A New General English Dictionary* (1735), which introduced the practice of showing pronunciation and included a brief grammar of English; and Benjamin Martin's *Lingua Britannica Reformata* (1749), which was a model of analytical defining, with the various senses of each word separated and numbered.

Johnson's Dictionary. In 1747, Samuel Johnson contracted with a group of London booksellers to produce *A Dictionary of the English Language*; the fee was £1,575. In 1755, after eight years of towering and morose effort, the book was published in two folio volumes; it was over 2,300 pages long and defined about 50,000 words.

Johnson's dictionary had only one technical innovation, the printing of quotations containing the word being defined, and even this had already been done by several European dictionaries, and suggested earlier by Joseph Addison and others.

The 20th century remembers Johnson's *Dictionary* only for a few definitions that reflect his prejudices (*oats, pension, whig*) or his ponderousness ("*network*: Any thing reticulated or decussated, at equal distances, with interstices between the intersections"), or for the reply he made when a lady asked him why he had defined *pastern* as "The knee of a horse": "Ignorance, Madam, pure ignorance." These lapses do not represent the general quality of the book, however, and its *Preface* is the finest thing ever written in English on lexicography.

The Pronouncing Dictionaries. The next stage of British lexicography dealt with pronunciation, or "orthoepy," as it was then called. Many specialized pronouncing dictionaries were brought out. William Kenrick, in 1773, was the first to divide the words into syllables and indicate phonetic quality with diacritical marks. Thomas Sheridan's aim in his 1780 dictionary was "to establish a Standard of Pronunciation," although Johnson quarreled with his right to, Sheridan having "the disadvantage of being an Irishman."

19th Century. For most Americans, "Noah Webster" means "dictionary." Webster, a Connecticut Yankee, saw that in the early 1800's Johnson's dictionary was seriously out of date, especially in the burgeoning fields of science, technology, and political economy, and judged that the United States would develop its own form of English. He was also well in advance of Johnson, and more akin to modern dictionary makers, in his conviction that it "is our business to find out what the English language *is*, and not, how it *might have been made*."

Webster's Dictionary. Webster set to work in 1807 on the great *American Dictionary of the English Language*, published in 1828. Webster's dictionary defined about 75,000 terms in 1,936 pages. He managed the 2d edition (1840) and did some work, before his death in 1843, on the 3d (1847), which was first published by the firm of G. and C. Merriam.

The 5th edition (1846), called "the Unabridged," represents the definitive break with Webster's own work. The etymologies and the history of English brought this book abreast of linguistic science. Successors in this excellent tradition are the *New International* (1909), the *New International, Second Edition* (1934), and *Webster's Third New International* (1961).

Joseph Worcester. Although his reputation has been eclipsed by Webster's, Joseph Worcester prepared dictionaries that were in no respect inferior to Webster's. Worcester's best achievement was his dictionary of 1860, which culminated more than 30 years of lexicography and was superior to the 4th edition of Webster's (1859). Worcester's dictionary was the first to include illustrations and synonyms in the text, and the first to be made by a fairly large staff of editors and a corps of expert consultants.

The Oxford English Dictionary (OED). Not until 1857, when Richard Chenevix Trench read a paper "On Some Deficiencies in Our English Dictionaries" before the Philological Society, was the next and immortal work of British lexicography launched. Partly stimulated by Charles Richardson's curious *New Dictionary of the English Language* (1835–1837), which was in effect a violent attack on Johnson's dictionary, Trench proposed what became *A New English Dictionary on Historical Principles* (*NED*), called since 1894 the *Oxford English Dictionary* (*OED*).

The *OED* is in 12 volumes totaling 15,487 pages. The first volume was published in 1884 and the 12th in 1928, with a supplement in 1933. The work is based on about 5 million citation slips, of which about 2 million citations are printed in the text. It defines and shows the complete history of some 250,000 English words (in a total entry list of about 414,000), strictly from evidence of actual use. The *OED* is the prime monument of English lexicography, and stimulated a number of similar works.

Other 19th Century Dictionaries. The colossal and masterly *OED* dominates the 19th century, but John Ogilvie's *Imperial Dictionary* (1851) was a workmanlike job, and James Stormonth's *The Etymological and Pronouncing Dictionary* (1871) was entirely admirable, the equal in many respects of the American dictionaries of the tradition of Webster and Worcester. Stormonth was the first to respell the words to indicate pronunciation, rather than merely marking the printed entry word as his predecessors had done.

In this period the term "encyclopedic" began to be used for certain dictionaries, indicating that they "explain not only words but things, . . . give an explanation of the things to which such words are applied." Charles Annandale's 1882 revision of Ogilvie's dictionary was the first to be called "encyclopedic," and the best British exemplar of the type was John Hunter's 14-volume *The Encyclopedic Dictionary* (also called *Cassell's*; 1879–1888). Hunter's work was inspired not by the *OED*, which proclaimed itself nonencyclopedic, but by Pierre Larousse's *Grand dictionnaire universel* (1866–1876).

The concept of the encyclopedic dictionary is important because it continued to be a debated point in lexicographical theory and because it became the hallmark of the American unabridged books, as opposed to the typical British dictionaries. The greatest American encyclopedic dictionary is the *Century Dictionary and Cyclopedia* (1889–1899), which defines about 200,000 terms and identifies 250,000 biographical and geographical names.

In 1894 the Funk and Wagnalls Company published its *Standard Dictionary* under the editorship of Isaac K. Funk, president of the company. The book introduced four policies, all based on the declared purpose of immediate helpfulness, that have been very generally adopted in American dictionaries: (1) arrangement of definitions in the order of current frequency rather than the order of historical occurrence; (2) placement of the etymologies at the end rather than the beginning of definitions; (3) use of one alphabetical listing for all entries, instead of separate sections for biography and the like; and (4) use of lowercase instead of capital letters at the beginning of all words except proper nouns. The *Standard* was revised and enlarged in 1903 and entirely reedited as the *New Standard* in 1913.

Funk was especially interested in spelling reform and accurate phonetic representation. The *New Standard* used two separate alphabets for showing pronunciation, one with a simple diacritical system, the "textbook key," and the other a relatively advanced "Revised Scientific Alphabet."

20th Century. In the early 1900's, as the *OED* neared completion, the Oxford University Press commissioned a condensed dictionary based on the *OED* but having better commercial possibilities. *The Concise Oxford Dictionary of Current English* (1911) went into its 5th edition in 1964 and has been the standard desk dictionary for British users. It apparently stimulated the compilation of Henry Cecil Wyld's *Universal Dictionary of the English Language* (1932).

The Shorter Oxford English Dictionary (1932; is an abridgment of the *OED*, defining about 195,000 terms. It has been the chief British dictionary in the "semiunabridged" category, midway in size between the unabridged (450,000–650,000 entries) and the desk, or college, type.

The "historical principles" of the *OED*, and a great many of its citation slips, have since been used for several specialized scholarly dictionaries. Sir William Craigie (1867–1957), editor of the *OED* from 1901 to 1933, provided continuity between the *OED* and its offspring by editing the 4-volume *A Dictionary of American English* (*DAE;* 1938–1944) and initiating *The Dictionary of the Older Scottish Tongue* (1931–). The smaller *Dictionary of Americanisms* (*DA;* 1951) restricted itself to terms originating in the United States.

Besides these "second-generation" *OED* books, a handful of other specialized dictionaries deserve mention. Joseph Wright's *English Dialect Dictionary*, 6 volumes (1898–1905), is invaluable in its field. Walter W. Skeat's *Etymological Dictionary of the English Language* (1881; revised 1909) was unmatched until the appearance of Eric Partridge's *Origins* (1958), followed rather soon, as these matters go, by C. T. Onions' *The Oxford Dictionary of English Etymology* (1966) and Ernst Klein's superb 2-volume *Comprehensive Etymological Dictionary of the English Language* (1966–1967). Walter S. Avis was chief of a group of Canadian scholars who produced the important *Dictionary of Canadianisms* in 1967.

American Semiunabridged Dictionaries. In the intermediate size, 180,000 to 250,000 entries, notable dictionaries are the Funk and Wagnalls *Standard Dictionary of the English Language, International Edition* (1958 with revision), Clarence Barnhart's excellent *World Book Encyclopedia Dictionary* (1963), and the *Random House Dictionary* (1966).

American Desk or College Dictionaries. One of the most impressive developments in lexicography has been the lavish scale on which American publishers produce the smaller dictionaries of widest use. These include not only desk, or college, dictionaries but also elementary and secondary school dictionaries, usually published in graded series.

Clarence Barnhart's *American College Dictionary* (1947) was historically the first monument of this development. *Webster's New World Dictionary* (1953), edited by Joseph Friend and David Guralnik and distinguished by the etymological work of Harold Whitehall, was the next important book. A legal decision finally established the unprotected status of the word "Webster" for dictionaries entirely unconnected with the legal successors of Noah Webster.

Webster's Ninth New Collegiate Dictionary (1983) continued the Merriam-Webster series, and the Funk and Wagnalls *Standard College Dictionary* (1963) had major revisions in 1966 and 1968. The college edition of the *Random House Dictionary* appeared in 1968, and the *American Heritage Dictionary* was published in 1969.

NON-ENGLISH-LANGUAGE DICTIONARIES

In addition to the classical Greek, ancient Chinese, and medieval Arabic dictionaries mentioned earlier in this article, there are important modern dictionaries of European and Oriental languages. Many of these are works of high scholarship that required many years to compile.

Romance Languages. Historically the most important French dictionary is the 2-volume *Dictionnaire de l'Académie Française* (1931–1935), the first version of which was published in 1694. The *Dictionnaire de la langue française* (1956–1958), in 7 volumes, is a modernization of Émile Littré's great work of 1873–1878. Among the other celebrated French dictionaries are *Petit Larousse illustré* (1959) and *Dictionnaire alphabétique et analogique*, begun in 1951.

In Italy, the *Vocabolario degli Accademici della Crusca* (1863–1923) is the dictionary (still incomplete) of the oldest European academy, which brought out its first dictionary in 1612. *Grande dizionario della lingua italiana* (1961–1964) is a 3-volume dictionary that supersedes the excellent 4-volume work (1861–1879) that had been the standard Italian dictionary.

The dictionary of the Spanish Academy, first published in 1726–1739, is *Diccionario de la lengua española* (1956). Other Spanish dictionaries include *Diccionario historico de la lengua española*, begun in 1960, and the 3-volume *Enciclopedia del idioma* (1958).

Among the most important dictionaries in Portuguese is the 12-volume *Grande dicionário da língua portuguesa* (1st ed., 1789; 10th ed., 1949–1959), published in Lisbon. The 5-volume *Grande e novissimo dicionário da língua portuguesa* (1939–1944) was published in Rio de Janeiro.

Germanic Languages. There are two notable Dano-Norwegian dictionaries, the 2-volume *Norsk riksmålordbok* (1930–1957), published in Oslo, and the *Ordbog over det danske Sprog* (27 vols., 1919–1954), published in Copenhagen. The Swedish Academy dictionary, *Ordbok över svenska språket*, was begun in 1898.

There are several fine German dictionaries, including the 16-volume *Deutsches Wörterbuch* (1854–1960), which was begun by the 19th century philologists Jacob and Wilhelm Grimm; *Wörterbuch der deutschen Gegenwartssprache*, begun in 1961; and the 8-volume *Trübners deutsches Wörterbuch* (1936–1957).

Slavic Languages. There are two important Russian dictionaries, the 4-volume *Slovar russkovo yazyka* (1957–1961) and *Slovar sovremennovo russkovo literaturnovo yazyka*, begun in 1950.

The dictionary of the Czech Academy is *Příručni slovnik jazyka coského* (8 vols., 1935–1957). The outstanding Polish dictionary is the 8-volume *Słownik jezyka polskiego* (1930–1935). Serbo-Croatian is represented by *Rječnik hrvatskoga ili srpskoga jezika, na svijet izdaje Jugoslavenska Akademija*, begun in 1880.

Oriental Languages. *Tz'ŭ Hai*, the encyclopedic Chinese dictionary, appeared in 1915, with a supplement in 1931. There are three notable Japanese dictionaries: *Dai jiten*, a 26-volume work, published in 1934–1936; *Dai genkai* (1932–1935), in 4 volumes, an important dictionary that registers etymologies in the Western tradition; and *Dai nihon kokugo jiten* (1928–1929), a 4-volume work first published in 1921.

ROBERT L. CHAPMAN, *Drew University*

Bibliography

Collison, R. L., *Dictionaries of English and Foreign Languages*, 2d ed. (Hafner 1971).
Landau, Sidney I., *The Art and Craft of Lexicography* (Scribner 1984).
Mathews, Mitford M., *A Survey of English Dictionaries* (Oxford 1933).
Sledd, James H., and Kolb, Gwin J., *Dr. Johnson's Dictionary* (Univ. of Chicago Press 1955).
Wells, Ronald A., *Dictionaries and the Authoritarian Tradition: A Study in English Usage and Lexicography* (Mouton 1973).

DICTUM OF KENILWORTH. See BARONS' WAR.

DICTYS CRETENSIS, dik'tis krē-ten'sis, is the reputed author of a diary of the Trojan War. He is supposed to have been from Knossos, Crete, and to have followed Idomeneus to Troy. The Latin version of the diary (*Ephemeris belli Troiani*) has an introduction relating how the narrative, inscribed in Phoenician characters on bark, was found during the reign of the Roman emperor Nero, who had it translated into Greek. Actually, the work was probably written in Greek in the 2d or 3d century A. D. and translated into Latin in the 4th century.

This story of the Trojan War has little intrinsic value, but it had considerable importance during the Middle Ages, when it was considered an eyewitness account of the war. It frequently appeared with an equally spurious account attributed to Dares Phrygius.

DIDACHE, did'a-kē, an early Christian document. The full Greek title is the "Teaching of the (Twelve) Apostles." The *Didache* contains 16 paragraphs of instruction for catechumens, dealing with morality, baptism, the Eucharist, and church life and organization. These are valuable sources of information on early church faith and practice.

Until Philotheos Bryennios, the Archbishop of Nicomedia, discovered a manuscript of the text (dated 1056) in 1873 and published it in 1883, it had been known only through references in early church writings. Its present form is probably a result of editing of early materials. When and where it was originally composed is uncertain. Some scholars date it as early as 70 A. D.; others, as late as the 3d century. Syria, Palestine, Egypt, and Asia Minor have all been proposed as the place of composition.

JOHN T. FORD, C. S. C.
The Catholic University of America

DIDACTIC LITERATURE, dī-dak-tik, is literature that has as its major purpose the instruction or guidance of the reader, particularly in moral or religious matters, but also in politics, science, and other affairs. All literature may be considered didactic to some degree in that it exists to communicate some emotion, fact, or idea, but a work is called "didactic" if what the author intends to communicate takes precedence over artistic quality.

A basic controversy in literary criticism centers on the question of whether a work should be judged primarily by its didactic qualities or by its artistic qualities. Plato insisted that art should be judged on its didactic qualities; he banished Homer from the ideal state outlined in the *Republic* for Homer's unflattering portrayal of the gods. Aristotle, on the other hand, insisted in his *Poetics* on the primacy of the self-consistent work of art. Critics have since tended to espouse either Plato's or Aristotle's position. The Roman poet Horace, in his *Ars poetica*, tried to reconcile the two views by giving art a dual function—to instruct and to please.

Among the great didactic masterpieces are Lucretius' *De rerum natura* and Virgil's *Georgics*, both written in the 1st century B. C. Most medieval literature was didactic, and didactic works flourished again in the 18th and 19th centuries. The 20th century saw a reaction against didacticism in the triumph of "art for art's sake."

C. HUGH HOLMAN
Coauthor of "A Handbook of Literature"

MUSÉE D'ART ET D'HISTOIRE, GENEVA
Denis Diderot (portrait by Dmitri Grigorievich Levitsky).

DIDEROT, dē-drō', **Denis** (1713–1784), French encyclopedist, philosopher, and man of letters, who was one of the most dynamic leaders of the Enlightenment. During his lifetime he was best known as chief editor of the *Encyclopédie* (1751–1772). This great publishing enterprise, the largest attempted up to that time, was more than simply a comprehensive work of reference. It was also intended, in Diderot's own words, "to change the general way of thinking" and to bring about "a revolution in men's minds."

The 20th century, while continuing to recognize Diderot's importance in the Enlightenment, especially esteems him as the author of a number of posthumously published works of extraordinary originality and daring. They have a vitality, an experimental quality, and a sense of life's ambivalences and ambiguities that particularly engage the modern taste.

Early Life and Works. Diderot was born at Langres, on Oct. 5, 1713. He studied at the Jesuit college there, probably attended the Jansenist Collège d'Harcourt in Paris, and received a master of arts degree from the University of Paris. After 10 bohemian years, he married Anne Toinette Champion in 1743.

The world of letters first knew Diderot as a translator of English works: Temple Stanyan's *Grecian History* (1743), Lord Shaftesbury's *Inquiry Concerning Virtue and Merit* (1745), and Robert James' *Medicinal Dictionary* (6 vols., 1746–1748). In 1746, Diderot published anonymously his own *Pensées philosophiques*, an influential book of deistic aphorisms, which was condemned to be burned by the public executioner. In 1748 he brought out anonymously a slightly obscene "philosophical" novel, *Les bijoux indiscrets* and, under his own name, a slender volume on physics and mathematics, *Mémoires sur différents sujets de mathématiques*. He was imprisoned for three months in the Château de Vincennes in 1749 for having written the *Lettre sur les aveugles*, a book on the behavior of the blind, which also opened up questions of philosophical materialism and of the existence of God.

"Encyclopédie." In 1747, Diderot, aided by Jean d'Alembert, became editor of the *Encyclopédie*. Originally it was intended to be a translation of Ephraim Chambers' *Cyclopaedia* (1728), but Diderot greatly expanded it. Its prospectus appeared in 1750, and the work itself was published from 1751 to 1772 in 17 volumes of text and 11 volumes of engravings.

Diderot was a materialist. Questioning tradition and authority, he believed in the power of human reason, guided by sense experience, to increase human knowledge and well-being. He gathered like-minded writers and scientists to contribute to the *Encyclopédie* and himself wrote hundreds of articles for it. The most notable are those dealing with the history of philosophy and the crafts and industries of France.

The *Encyclopédie*, reflecting its editor's point of view, frequently embodied proposals for social change and implicitly challenged much in the contemporary political and religious establishment. It was subject to censorship by the government and was a target of conservatives and reactionaries. Thus, the long struggle to bring the *Encyclopédie* to completion was part of the agitation for greater tolerance and greater freedom of expression that was an important element in the Enlightenment. In 1752 the government suspended the work for almost a year, and in 1759 it revoked Diderot's license to publish. Subsequently, the work was allowed to proceed surreptitiously, but even so Diderot was not spared heartsickening disappointment: his publisher, Le Breton, secretly altered many of the articles after Diderot had finished with them. Though Diderot discovered the deceit in 1764, he decided not to expose it; but he wrote to Le Breton, "I shall bear the wound until I die."

Other Works. Although Diderot complained that the *Encyclopédie* had used up—in writing, editing, proofreading, supervising of engravings, and other editorial tasks—fully 25 years of his life, he found time to write many other works that amply demonstrate the great range and versatility of his mind. *Lettre sur les sourds et muets* (1751), a book primarily on the behavior and psychology of deaf-mutes, also discussed poetics, aesthetics, and linguistics. *Pensées sur l'interprétation de la nature* (1753) was an influential short treatise on scientific method. His two plays, *Le fils naturel* (1757) and *Le père de famille* (1758), greatly influenced the theater in their naturalistic portrayal of everyday middle-class life. Diderot accompanied these plays with important supplementary essays on the theory of playwriting and production—*Entretiens sur Le fils naturel* (1757) and *De la poésie dramatique* (1758).

Many works that Diderot judged likely to be suppressed by the censors were published posthumously. In the novel *La religieuse* (1760; published 1796) he portrayed the distressing experiences of a young nun who wishes to renounce her vows. In *Le neveu de Rameau* (1761; published in German, 1805) he showed his mastery of the dialogue form, brilliantly satirizing his enemies while discussing music, creativity, genius, and ethics. For his *Salons*, a series of critiques of the Royal Academy of Art's biennial art exhibition, Diderot is often regarded as a founder of modern art criticism.

Le rêve de d'Alembert (1769; published 1830) is a dialogue that treats the origin of organized matter and of life without presupposing a creator. It contains prophetic insights into chemistry and biology, which propel the reader into the 20th century world of genes and amino acids. The theory of acting is dealt with in *Le paradoxe sur le comédien* (1773; published 1830). The *Supplément au Voyage de Bougainville* (1772; published 1796), while ostensibly discussing the mores of the Tahitians, actually criticizes the laws and mores of contemporary Europe. The novel *Jacques le fataliste et son maître* (1771–1773; published 1796), long regarded as a bizarre and undisciplined effusion, has come to be considered a masterpiece that explores various levels of meaning and various kinds of novelistic techniques. *Éléments de physiologie* (1774–1784; published 1875) shows Diderot's remarkable familiarity with the medical and scientific researches of his day and especially reveals his insights into neurophysiology.

A defense of the Roman philosopher Seneca, published in 1779 and enlarged in 1782, was a kind of apology for his own life. It was followed by an autobiographical play, *Est-il bon? Est-il méchant?* (1781; published 1834), whose hero, with the best of intentions, minds everyone's business but his own. Diderot also wrote several important philosophical tales, various lengthy memoranda, and some clever light verse.

Character and Later Life. Among his many friends Diderot numbered the philosophers Holbach, Rousseau, Hume, Helvétius, and the Abbé Raynal; the literary figures Laurence Sterne, Marmontel, and Sedaine; the criminologist Beccaria; the economist Galiani; the political leader John Wilkes; the actor David Garrick; and the sculptor E. M. Falconet, with whom he exchanged heated letters about immortality and posterity. In his relations with these friends Diderot was warmhearted, generous, somewhat absentminded, and slightly inclined to be self-righteous. These qualities were especially evident in his friendship with the difficult Rousseau, which ended in 1757. His friends greatly admired Diderot's eloquent conversational powers. He loved to participate in the famous discussions at Holbach's salon, where Horace Walpole found him "a very lively old man and great talker."

Chronically neglectful of his wife, Diderot lavished greater affection on Sophie Volland, his liaison with her lasting from about 1755 until her death in 1784. His letters to her are universally regarded as one of the most fascinating and dazzling revelations of an era and a personality that the art of letter writing can provide.

Diderot doted on his only surviving child, Angélique, and to increase her dowry he sold his library in 1765 to Catherine II of Russia for 15,000 livres. The Empress stipulated that Diderot retain the use of the library and gave him 1,000 livres a year to improve it. In 1766, when Diderot was 53, she paid him a lump sum of 50,000 livres in advance for another half century of similar services. Diderot traveled to St. Petersburg in 1773–1774 to thank Catherine personally, and after this long and difficult journey his health was never robust. He died in Paris on July 31, 1784.

ARTHUR M. WILSON
Author of "Diderot: The Testing Years"

Further Reading: Crocker, Lester G., *Diderot: The Embattled Philosopher*, rev. ed. (New York 1966); Gordon, Douglas H., and Torrey, Norman L., *Censoring of Diderot's "Encyclopédie" and the Re-established Text* (New York 1947); Proust, Jacques, *Diderot et l'Encyclopédie* (Paris 1962); Wilson, Arthur M., *Diderot: The Testing Years, 1713–1759* (New York 1957).

DIDIUS JULIANUS, did′ē-əs jōō-lē-ā′nəs, **Marcus** (c. 133–193 A.D.), Roman emperor. He was probably born in 133 at Milan. Although he had held various high offices in the Roman state before becoming emperor, his principal distinction was his wealth. Accordingly, when he learned that the Praetorian Guards, who had murdered Emperor Pertinax, were auctioning the empire to the highest bidder, Didius hastened to their camp and won the bidding by offering a huge sum to each guardsman. He became emperor on March 28, 193.

News of his accession provoked the ambition of three commanders of major provincial armies, including Septimius Severus, who was then in Pannonia (roughly, part of modern Hungary). Hated by the populace of Rome and by the Senate, Didius would appear in public only if surrounded by a huge bodyguard of the Praetorians, who also despised him. Attempts to prepare a defense of Rome or to negotiate with the approaching Severus failed. Severus persuaded the Praetorians to betray Didius, and the Senate proclaimed Didius deposed and Severus emperor. Deserted in his palace, Didius was killed on June 1, 193.

STEWART IRVIN OOST, *University of Chicago*

DIDO, dī′dō, in Greek legend, was the founder of Carthage. She is best known from the account of her in the Roman poet Virgil's *Aeneid*, which differs from earlier versions of her story. According to the older legends, she was born Elissa, the daughter of Belus (Agenor), king of Tyre. Her brother Pygmalion, who succeeded their father on the throne, slew her husband Acerbas in an attempt to obtain his wealth. Elissa escaped to Libya, where she founded Carthage (in what is now Tunisia) and became its queen, taking the name Dido, "the Wanderer." When the Libyan king Iarbas demanded, under threat of war, that Dido marry him, she was forced by her subjects to consent. However, Dido resolved to escape her fate by leaping onto the flaming nuptial pyre.

In the *Aeneid* version, Aeneas, shipwrecked off the coast of Libya after the Trojan War, becomes the object of Dido's affections. When Aeneas departs, commanded by the gods to forsake her and pursue his destiny, the distraught queen mounts a funeral pyre to die. This account constitutes the fourth book of Virgil's *Aeneid*.

ROBERT G. RUSSO
Queens College, City University of New York

DIDO AND AENEAS, dī′dō, i-nē′əs, is a tragic opera in three acts by Henry Purcell (q.v.), with the libretto by Nahum Tate. The first true opera (that is, using music throughout) by an English composer, *Dido and Aeneas* had its premiere in 1689 at a London girls' school.

Based on incidents from book 4 of Virgil's *Aeneid*, the plot tells of the love of the widowed Carthaginian queen Dido (soprano) for the Trojan prince Aeneas (tenor). Assured by her lady-in-waiting Belinda (soprano) that Aeneas returns her affection, Dido receives the prince in state. Meanwhile, an unfriendly sorceress contrives to ruin Dido's happiness by sending Aeneas a false message that Jove has commanded him to depart from Carthage. Although Aeneas offers to defy the request, Dido counsels him not to neglect his duty. When the Trojans leave Carthage, Dido, in despair, kills herself.

Although it is conceived on a small scale, *Dido and Aeneas* contains some of Purcell's most deeply felt music. The characterization of Dido is particularly effective, and the work as a whole anticipates the operas of Gluck and Mozart.

ERIC D. MACKERNESS
Author of "A Social History of English Music"

DIDOT, dē-dō′, a family of French publishers, who made important contributions to printing, publishing, typefounding, and papermaking. The company of F. Didot was established in Paris in the 18th century and continues in operation there.

FRANÇOIS DIDOT (1689–1757), who founded the firm in 1713, was a Parisian printer and bookseller. In 1747 he published Abbé Prévost's 20-volume account of his travels—*Histoire générale des voyages*.

FRANÇOIS AMBROISE DIDOT (1730–1804), son of François, specialized in typefounding and is credited with being the first to print on vellum (1780). He prepared to the order of Louis XVI a 32-volume set of French classics.

PIERRE FRANÇOIS DIDOT (1732?–?1795), the brother of François Ambroise, was also an innovator in typefounding and papermaking. In 1788 he published a folio edition of Thomas à Kempis' *Imitation of Christ*.

PIERRE DIDOT (1761–1853), eldest son of Françoise Ambroise, specialized in deluxe editions of the classics, particularly the works of Virgil, Horace, and Racine.

FIRMIN DIDOT (1764–1836), also a son of François Ambroise, was the first to print books from stereotype plates. He also was proficient as a typefounder. Firmin Didot wrote two plays.

AMBROISE FIRMIN DIDOT (1790–1876) and HYACINTHE FIRMIN DIDOT (1794–1880), Firmin's sons, assumed control of the firm on their father's death and published several important bibliographic works.

JOHN TEBBEL, *New York University*

DIDRIKSON, Babe. See ZAHARIAS, MILDRED ELLA.

DIDYMA, did′i-mə, an ancient town located 12 miles (19 km) south of Miletus on the western coast of Asia Minor, was the site of a famous oracle and temple of Apollo (the Didymaeum). The town was also called *Branchidae*.

According to the geographer Pausanias, the oracle existed even before the Ionian migration to Asia Minor from Greece. The first temple, built in the 6th century B.C., was destroyed in 494 B.C. by the Persians, who exiled the Branchidae, the priestly family that had guarded the temple, and carried off the cult statue of Apollo by Canachus of Sicyon. (The statue was finally recovered by Seleucus I in 295 B.C.) The oracle and cult revived after Alexander the Great captured Miletus in 334 B.C.; the oracle gained fame because it was believed to have announced Alexander's divine origin and prophesied his victory over Persia.

A new temple was begun on an ambitious scale about 300 B.C. Though the temple was never completed, Strabo regarded it as the greatest among Greek temples. Imposing remains survive. The vast structure was in Ionic style; the shrine housing the cult statue lay in a sunken open-air court. The cult survived into late antiquity.

D. J. BLACKMAN, *University of Bristol*

DIDYMIUM, dī-dim'ē-əm, is an alloy of rare-earth elements. The metal consists principally of neodymium (72%) and praseodymium (27%), with small amounts of lanthanum and other metals. Most didymium is used in flints for lighters; small amounts are added as alloying agents to steel castings, stainless steels, and zirconium-magnesium alloys. Didymium is also used as a substitute for misch metal, which is another alloy of rare-earth metals.

Didymium is produced commercially by electrolysis of a mixture of fused anhydrous chlorides at a temperature of about 850°C (1562°F). The liquid metal is collected in the bottom of the cell, and after a suitable amount accumulates, it is ladled off and cast into ingots.

Douglas V. Keller, Jr.
Syracuse University

DIDYMUS OF ALEXANDRIA, did'i-məs (313–398), early Christian theologian. Blinded as a young child, Didymus is often called *Didymus the Blind*. He was never in ecclesiastical orders, but his influence as a teacher and writer was considerable. He headed the famed Catechetical School of Alexandria and taught St. Jerome and Rufinus of Aquileia. Jerome made extensive use of Didymus' *Commentary on Zachariah* in his own monumental Scripture commentaries.

Didymus defended the Council of Nicaea (325) against the Arians and Macedonians; hence his doctrine is, in the main, orthodox. But he was condemned posthumously (Council of Constantinople, 553) for allegedly teaching the eternal pre-existence of created souls and the eventual return of all souls, even those of the damned, to perfect union with God. Of his many writings, little more than a few Scripture commentaries, Jerome's translation of his work *The Holy Spirit*, and certain works of doubtful authenticity have survived. He died in Alexandria in 398.

Robert Barr, S. J., *John XXIII Center for Eastern Christian Studies, New York*

DIE, a device for forming materials into a desired shape. Dies are used in a wide variety of manufacturing processes, such as forging, sheet-metal forming, blanking, extrusion, and wire-drawing. Dies have been an important factor in the growth of manufacturing because they make possible the production of identical parts at a high rate. Furthermore, parts that are produced with dies usually have a good surface finish and high dimensional accuracy, and thus little or no surface material has to be removed by subsequent machining.

In all die operations there is a deformation of material to conform to the shape of a cavity or contour in the die. When a material is deformed, its mechanical strength is usually enhanced. However, if the deformation becomes excessive, cracks develop. Therefore, a major problem in the use of dies is the design of the die geometry so that the material being deformed will flow into every part of the die without the occurrence of cracks. Because of the danger of cracks in the finished product there are certain limits on the shapes and surface contours for proper die design.

During a die operation, the dies are subjected to high impact forces and friction between the die surfaces and the deforming material. Frequently, high temperatures are also present from heat initially contained in the material to be deformed and from heat generated during the forming process. As a result, the material from which dies are made must be strong at high temperatures, and it must also resist the wearing down of the contours on the die surfaces. Common die materials include tool steels and cemented carbides.

Forging Dies—Open Forging Dies. Forging is the compression of material between two die blocks. Forging dies that have a flat surface or a surface that is slightly contoured and allows the material to spread freely as it is compressed are called open forging dies (Fig. 1). Open-die forging is generally used to carry out the initial deformation of ingots and to produce large parts with simple shapes.

Closed Forging Dies. Closed forging dies contain cavities that control the spreading of the material as it is compressed. At the end of a stroke in closed-die forging the material is completely surrounded in the die cavity (Fig. 2). Since it is impossible to match exactly the amount of material before it is deformed to that in the final shape, a *flash gutter* is provided into which the small amount of excess material flows. The resulting flash extending from the finished part is subsequently trimmed off the final product.

Designs for closed forging dies must facilitate the proper flow of material in the die cavity. The parting line—the line of separation between die blocks—should be near the center line of the finished part so that the deformation in each half of the cavity is equal. Sharp corners must be avoided, because they develop tensile stresses that are conducive to cracking. Small pockets and recesses are not permissible, because the material will not flow into them. Usually a slight taper is required in each half of the die cavity; this design permits the easy removal of the finished part from the dies.

Closed-die forging is used to produce parts of complex shape, such as wrenches, connecting rods, and axles. Most parts cannot be forged in one step, but require the formation of several intermediate shapes prior to the final shape. In this case, open dies are frequently used for the initial steps, with the final forgings being made with closed dies.

Heading is a closed-die operation that is used to produce bolts, rivets, and other cylindrical parts. The dies used in heading consist of a pair of gripping dies, which hold the length of wire or rod to be forged. Then a ram, containing a cavity with the inverse shape of the head to be formed, is impacted on the end of the wire or rod.

Coining is another type of closed-die operation, which is used to produce coins and similar small articles of jewelry. Coining dies contain a shallow impression of the design to be stamped on the material. Dies of this type do not contain a flash gutter.

Cylindrical Dies. Cylindrical dies perform a function similar to closed forging dies, except that a rolling action is employed. The die cavities are machined into the periphery of two semicylinders that compress and roll the material. In this way, long parts that are not easily forged in conventional closed-die operations can be produced.

The concept of using cylindrical dies to forge parts of long length has been extended to the formation of a regular surface profile on shafts. The dies used in these operations are complete

TYPES OF DIES

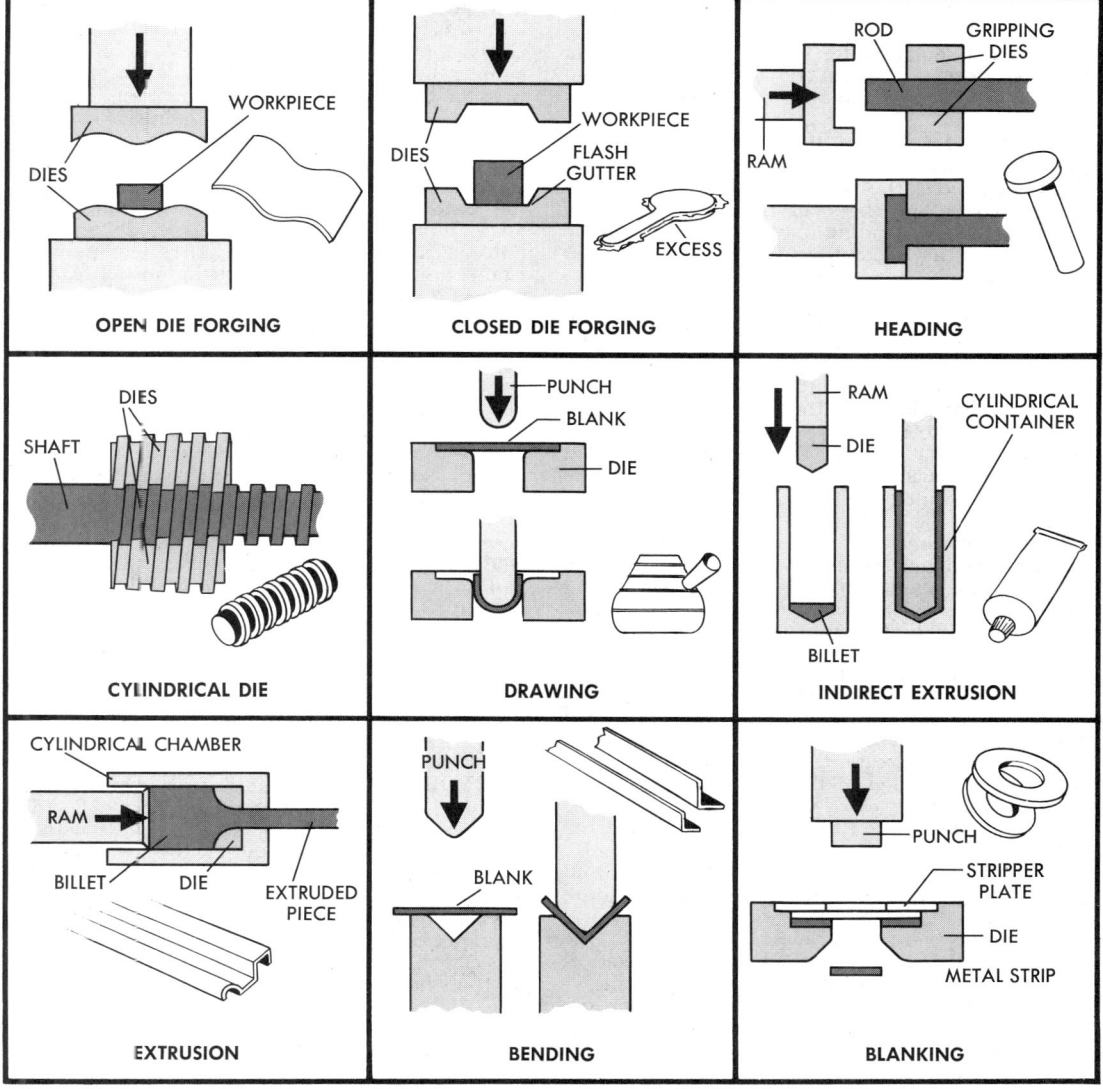

cylinders with a profile machined on them corresponding to the profile to be formed on the shaft. Two such dies are placed on opposite sides of a shaft with the axes of the die cylinders and the shaft parallel. As the dies rotate, they are pressed against the shaft and deform the surface to conform to the profile of the dies. Examples of the profiles that can be formed on shafts are helical grooves, as in threaded shafts, and raised ribs parallel to the axis, as in splined shafts. A current use of cylindrical dies is in the production of gears. The gears are made by rolling the profile of the gear teeth on a shaft and then cutting it in transverse sections to form individual gears.

Extrusion Dies. Parts with long length and a constant cross section are produced by extrusion. An extrusion die assembly consists of a cylindrical container fitted at one end with a die block containing an opening whose cross-sectional area is much less than that of the cylinder. A billet of material is placed in the cylinder and forced to deform through the die opening by a ram or high-pressure fluid at the other end (Fig. 3). The emerging material has the same cross section as the die opening. Extrusion is used to produce beams of practically any shape, such as channels, T-sections, and rails.

Indirect Extrusion. Indirect, or backward, extrusion involves a type of extrusion device in which the die is forced into the material rather than the material's being forced through the die. The die assembly in this case consists of a cylindrical container that is closed at one end; the billet is placed in this container. A die attached to the end of a ram is then pushed into the open end of the cylinder, forcing the metal to deform through the die opening. Long, thin-walled tubes, such as tooth-paste tubes, are produced in this way.

Sheet Metalworking Dies. These dies have the action of a punch (a ram with a cross-sectional shape or contour on its end), forcing the metal to be deformed into an opening or cavity in the die. Dies for sheet metalworking operations may act to deform the metal from its original flat shape, such as a circular plate, into a form, such as a cup, or they may shear off metal along some closed curve to form holes or to trim away excess material.

In sheet forming by bending, the end of the punch and the die have mating contours. As the punch forces the sheet into the die, the sheet bends to take the shape of the die and punch. An example of bending dies is the right-angle bend shown in Fig. 4.

Deep-Drawing Dies. In deep-drawing die assemblies, the punch and the die opening have the same cross-sectional shape. The bottom rim of the punch and the inside rim of the die opening are rounded (Fig. 5). The punch descends into the die opening, thereby drawing the originally flat blank on the die face down over the die rim into the opening, and the sheet takes the shape of the punch. The clearance provided between the outside of the punch and the inside of the die opening is approximately equal to the thickness of the material.

Deep-drawing dies are usually equipped with a clamp, or blank holder, which presses the rim of the blank against the die face as it is being drawn. This is necessary to prevent the blank rim from wrinkling as it is drawn in toward the opening.

The ability of deep-drawing dies to form a blank into the desired shape witnout defects is dependent largely on the curvatures of the punch and the rim of the die opening. Curvatures that are too small increase the stresses in the sheet and lead to cracking of the material. Curvatures that are too large can lead to wrinkling of the rim of the blank, even in the presence of a blank holder.

Blanking and Punching Dies. Blanking and punching dies are similar to deep-drawing dies, except that the punch and die rims are sharp, and there is very little clearance between the punch and the die opening (Fig. 6). Instead of being drawn over the die rim, as in deep-drawing, the sheet of material is sheared off along the die rim. Such operations are used to cut out blanks for use in subsequent forming, to trim off excess material from finished shapes, or to punch holes in the sheet.

Combination and Progressive Dies. Combination dies and progressive dies perform two or more sheet-forming operations simultaneously or in rapid succession on one die set. For example, a blank may be sheared from a sheet by a blanking punch; the blank is then immediately drawn into a cup by a drawing punch, with the blanking and drawing dies being part of the same die block. Flat washers are formed by first punching out the hole and then blanking out the washer from the sheet. This is done with two successive strokes of a progressive die.

Other Die Operations. Dies are widely used in other manufacturing operations, including embossing, ironing, sizing, swagging, thread rolling, wiredrawing, tube drawing, stretch forming, powder compaction, and die casting. All of these processes involve putting solid, granular, or liquid material into a shaped die and forcing the material to adopt the shape of the die cavity.

HOWARD A. KUHN and RICHARD W. HECKEL
Drexel Institute of Technology

DIEBITSCH, dē'bich, **Hans Karl Anton Friedrich von** (1785–1831), German-born Russian field marshal. In Russia his title was Count Ivan Ivanovich Dibich-Zabalkansky. He was born at Grossleippe, Silesia, on May 13, 1785. After joining the Berlin Cadet Corps, he shifted to the Russian Semenov Guards Regiment in 1801.

In the Napoleonic Wars, Diebitsch rose rapidly as a staff officer after the Battle of Austerlitz in 1805. In 1812 he was a major general, and in 1813 he served brilliantly, especially at the Battle of Leipzig in October. Alexander I made him a lieutenant general at 28 and took him as his adviser in the 1814 campaign in France. In March, Diebitsch induced Alexander to occupy Paris, thereby dethroning Napoleon.

Diebitsch, now chief of staff of the First Army, became adjutant general to the czar in 1818. In 1821, Alexander took him to the Congress of Laibach (Ljubljana, Yugoslavia), where he showed diplomatic ability. After Alexander's death in 1825, Diebitsch scotched an officers' plot and won the favor of Nicholas I and the rank of general of infantry. In the Russo-Turkish War of 1828–1829 he defeated the Turks, crossed the Balkan Mountains, and made peace at Adrianople (Edirne, Turkey). The czar made him a field marshal and Count Zabalkansky (Transbalkan). In 1831 he defeated the Polish insurgents, but failed to take Warsaw. He died of cholera on June 10, 1831, at Kleczewo, near Pułtusk, Poland.

JOHN S. CURTISS
Duke University; Author of "The Russian Army Under Nicholas I, 1825–1855"

DIEFENBAKER, dē'fən-bā-kər, **John George** (1895–1979), prime minister of Canada from 1957 to 1963. He was born on Sept. 18, 1895, in Grey county, Ontario. Moving west with his parents, he was educated at the University of Saskatchewan. He served overseas in World War I, and afterward became a prominent trial lawyer in Prince Albert, Saskatchewan. His early attempts to obtain elective office, although unsuccessful, made him well known, and from 1936 to 1940 he served as leader of the Conservative

John George Diefenbaker

party in Saskatchewan. In 1940 he was elected to the federal House of Commons. Highly effective in opposition, he won the party leadership in 1956.

Prime Minister. Diefenbaker's party won a plurality of Commons seats in the election of 1957, and he took office on June 21, 1957, as prime minister in a minority government. When he went to the people again in 1958, his party won an unprecedented 208 of the 265 House seats.

Apart from obtaining some valuable agricultural legislation, notably the Agricultural Rehabilitation Development Act (ARDA) of 1961, Diefenbaker was much less successful in office than on the campaign trail. Circumstances were partly to blame. The postwar tide of prosperity was receding by 1957 as other nations became competitive on the international market and as major construction projects, such as the St. Lawrence Seaway, ended. But Diefenbaker was also to blame. His concern for the rights of individuals and minorities—for "the average Canadian"—overrode his understanding of broad national and international issues. Indecisiveness regarding such issues constituted the major weakness of his government.

As a result, Diefenbaker's position by 1962 was vastly different from that of the happy days of 1958. Devaluation of the dollar, a general election in which the loss of 92 House seats reduced his government once again to a minority, the announcement of an austerity program, and the October Cuban missile crisis all followed in rapid succession. The Cuban crisis revealed that the Diefenbaker government, which had earlier agreed to build Bomarc missile sites in Canada, could not make up its mind to arm the missiles with nuclear warheads. It widened rifts with the American government and within the cabinet. A nuclear arms debate in the House of Commons in January 1963 and a press release by the U.S. State Department challenging statements made by Diefenbaker brought the crisis to a head.

The Government's Defeat. The minister of national defense resigned. Other ministers plotted Diefenbaker's overthrow and only with difficulty were brought back into line. On Feb. 5, 1963, the government was defeated in the House of Commons. A general election was called, and, following defeat at the polls, Diefenbaker submitted his government's resignation on April 17.

Always a tenacious fighter, Diefenbaker struggled to retain the leadership of a Conservative party rapidly turning against him. In 1965 he campaigned with his old vigor and succeeded in keeping the Liberal government in a minority. Even when his rebelling party called a convention to choose a new leader in September 1967, he did not acknowledge defeat until the votes were counted. He was elected to the Commons a record 13 times and still represented his district of Prince Albert, Saskatchewan, at the time of his death, in Ottawa, on Aug. 17, 1979.

D. G. G. Kerr, *University of Western Ontario*

DIEFFENBACHIA, dĕf-ən-bak'ē-ə, is a genus of tropical American plants belonging to the arum family (Araceae). Members of the genus are characterized by tiny flowers crowded on a fleshy stalk called the spadix. Surrounding the spadix is a leaflike bract called the spathe. The entire structure is similar to that of the jack-in-the-pulpit and the calla.

There are 30 known species of *Dieffenbachia*,

Dieffenbachia

T. H. EVERETT

and two of them—*D. picta* and *D. seguine*—are often cultivated as houseplants. Both have large shiny leaves with irregularly scattered patches of white or yellow. The leaves are about 2 feet (60 cm) long and are attached to the stem by a clasping petiole. The plants range in height from 3 to 6 feet (0.9–1.8 meters) and their stems are about ½ inch (13 mm) in diameter. Often, the lower portion of the stem is horizontal, resting on the ground. The name "dumb cane" is sometimes applied to *D. seguine* because chewing the plant causes the tongue to swell, making speech very difficult.

Sydney C. Bausor
California State College (Pa.)

DIEGO GARCIA. See Chagos Archipelago.

DIEGO-SUAREZ, dyä'gō swä'räs, a seaport and bay in the northernmost part of Madagascar. The port, formerly called Antsirana, is situated on the south shore of Diégo-Suarez Bay, an inlet of the Indian Ocean, and is one of the finest natural harbors in the world. However, as there is no rail service from the city and only a small portion of the road to the national capital, Tananarive, is paved, the port directly serves only a small hinterland. It is mainly a port of call and a transshipment point between oceangoing ships and coastal vessels. The town's economy also depends on the French naval base there. Salt extracted and processed in Diégo-Suarez supplies most of Madagascar's needs.

The town was discovered in 1500 by Diogo Dias, sailing for Prince Henry of Portugal. In the 17th century a French pirate founded the short-lived Republic of Libertalia there. The Malagasy Merina kingdom fought French penetration in the 19th century, but in 1885, Diégo-Suarez was named the capital of a separate French colony. It became part of Madagascar in 1896. Population: (1972) 45,487.

Hugh C. Brooks, *St. Johns University, N.Y.*

DIELDRIN, dēl'drən, an insecticide with the formula $C_{12}H_8OCl_6$, used principally on corn, citrus, and other crops, and for mothproofing fabrics. Production for most uses was banned in 1975 because of its cancer-causing properties.

Dieldrin is a very toxic chemical and should be handled with care. It is poisonous if swallowed or inhaled, and since it is absorbed through the skin, contact with the substance may also prove dangerous.

Dieldrin is a flaky, light tan solid that is insoluble in water. However, it is soluble in most of the common organic solvents other than methanol. It is prepared by the oxidation of aldrin, $C_{12}H_8Cl_6$, which is a closely related insecticide. Endrin, which is also used as an insecticide, is a stereoisomer of dieldrin.

DIELECTRIC, dī-ə-lek′trik, a material that is a poor conductor of electricity. Usually a dielectric is a solid, but it may be a liquid, a gas such as air, or a composite material such as paper impregnated with mineral oil.

Dielectrics are widely used as electrical insulation. (The word "dielectric" often is used synonymously with "electrical insulation.") They are also used in capacitors to store electrical energy. The early dielectrics—amber, sulfur, wood, glass, asphalt, mica, paper, and rubber— were made of natural materials. With the development of man-made plastics, many new ones have become available.

Solid dielectric is used to separate conductors in electrical equipment and prevent the flow of electricity along undesired paths. It is needed and used in all electrical equipment. The exposed covering for appliance leads is a familiar example, but insulation also is present in television sets, radios, electric clocks, toasters, motors, and other electrical equipment even though it may not be exposed to view.

All dielectrics will puncture or break down if the voltage exceeds a certain value for a given thickness of material. The ratio of the puncture voltage to the thickness is the breakdown strength at that thickness. See also CAPACITOR; INSULATION.

A. HARRY SHARBAUGH, *General Electric Company*

DIELECTRIC HEATING, dī-ə-lek′trik, is the process of heating a dielectric (electrical insulator such as wood, rubber, or a plastic) by placing it in a radio-frequency electric field. The dielectric to be heated is positioned between flat or contoured electrodes connected to an oscillator, which produces a radio frequency in the range of from 1 to 100 megahertz (Mhz) with the electrodes at a potential of 1 to 20 kilovolts. Some of the energy of the electric field between the electrodes is absorbed by the dielectric and appears as heat generated by the molecular friction of charges moving back and forth under the influence of the rapidly alternating field. Because the heat is generated within the material, dielectrics can be heated rapidly and uniformly by this method. It is difficult to do so with an external heat source because dielectrics usually are poor conductors of heat.

Uses. Dielectric heating is widely used in industry for tasks such as removing moisture from wood, hardening thermosetting glues for laminated wood, curing foam rubber, and heating thermoplastic plastics before molding them. Dielectric heating also is used for electronic cooking at microwave frequencies (several thousand Mhz). The food is cooked in an oven with a resonant cavity, which provides microwave power that penetrates the food. See also DIELECTRIC.

A. HARRY SHARBAUGH, *General Electric Company*

DIELS, dēls, **Otto Paul Hermann** (1876–1954), German chemist, who received the Nobel Prize for his part in the discovery of the Diels-Alder reaction. Diels was born in Hamburg on Jan. 23, 1876. He studied chemistry under Emil Fischer at the University of Berlin, where he received his doctorate in 1899. He remained at Berlin until 1916, when he accepted a call to the University of Kiel as head of the chemistry department.

In 1906, Diels discovered a new oxide of carbon, intermediate between the monoxide and the dioxide; it was somewhat inappropriately named carbon suboxide, C_2O_3. During his work on the chemical nature of cholesterol, started in 1911, he found a generally applicable method for reducing a complex organic compound to its fundamental component by heating it with selenium.

Work that they began in 1925 led Diels and his assistant, Kurt Alder, to a unifying rule underlying several known addition reactions. This type of reaction, known as the Diels-Alder reaction (q.v.), proved to be of great importance in the synthesis of a large class of compounds. In 1950, Diels and Alder were awarded the Nobel Prize in chemistry for this work. Diels, who had lost two sons and seen his institute destroyed during World War II, died at Kiel on March 7, 1954.

EDUARD FARBER
Editor of "Great Chemists"

DIELS-ALDER REACTION, dēls äl′dər, an important method for synthesizing many carbon compounds containing six-membered rings. It was developed by the German chemists Otto Diels and Kurt Alder, who shared the 1950 Nobel Prize in chemistry for its discovery.

A basic requirement of the Diels-Alder reaction is the presence of a diene such as 1,3-butadiene, $CH_2=CH-CH=CH_2$. The substance added to the diene must have a double or triple bond. The reaction usually proceeds with the addition of only a small amount of heat. The double bond of the adding substance breaks, leaving a single bond, and the freed valences link to the diene. A compound with a six-membered ring with one double bond is formed.

OTTO W. NITZ
Stout State University, Menomonie, Wis.

DIEMEN, Anton van. See VAN DIEMEN, ANTON.

DIEN BIEN PHU, dyen byen fōō, is a town and military outpost in North Vietnam, almost 200 miles (322 km) west of Hanoi, near the Laotian border. It was the scene in 1954 of the final defeat of France in its unsuccessful 8-year war to retain control of Indochina.

Dien Bien Phu was a large village at the junction of several routes to the north and to Laos, which the French decided in 1953 was the place to stop the Vietminh thrust into Laos. However, the French forces, concentrated in this exposed fortress surrounded by enemy-held highlands, could not withstand the attacking Vietminh commanded by Gen. Vo Nguyen Giap. Vietnamese weapons and supplies were transported over long distances, many of them on the backs of thousands of Vietnamese. Attempts to help the besieged garrison failed. The French, under Gen. Christian de Castries, held out from March 13 to May 7. They lost over 15,000 men, killed, wounded, imprisoned, and missing.

The defeat discouraged France from continuing the war. Negotiations already begun in Geneva led, on July 21, 1954, to a cease-fire and to the international recognition of the independence of Vietnam, Laos, and Cambodia.

ELLEN J. HAMMER
Author of "Vietnam: Yesterday and Today"

DIENCEPHALON. See BRAIN—2. *Major Divisions of the Brain.*

DIENTZENHOFER, dēn′tsən-hō-fər, a family of baroque architects, active in Bavaria and Bohemia during the late 17th and early 18th centuries.

JOHANN DIENTZENHOFER (1665?–?1726), called "Dientzenhofer of Bamberg," designed three major early 18th century works. The Cathedral of Fulda (1701–1712), Hesse, is a rather severe design, derived from Roman baroque work of the early 17th century. The abbey church at Banz (1710–1719), Franconia, is much more venturesome, with a plan based on a series of overlapping ovals. Only portions of the third work, the baroque Castle of Weissenstein (1711–1718), at Pommersfelden, are attributed to him.

CHRISTOPH DIENTZENHOFER (1655–1722), brother of Johann, designed the Margarethenkirche (1708–1715), at Prague, a good example of a figure 8 plan, with heavily emphasized diagonal vaulting ribs. His facade for the Church of St. Nicholas in the Little Town (1703–1711), Prague, has an undulating plan that divides the west front into three concave elements.

KILIAN IGNAZ DIENTZENHOFER (1698–1751), son of Christoph, was the most talented of the family. He settled in Prague about 1720. Among his major works in Prague are the Villa Amerika (1720), a mansard-roofed house with delicate ornamentation; the Church of St. Johann Nepomuk am Felsen (1730), with towers set at angles to the facade; and the Church of St. Nicholas in the Old Town (finished 1737), with a vertical, almost cramped facade. His finest work is the completion (1737–1752) of his father's St. Nicholas in the Little Town, in which he repeated the undulations of the facade in the illusionistically painted nave vaults. The cupola, placed close to a single slender tower, is one of the finest compositions of the baroque period.

WALTER KIDNEY, *"Progressive Architecture"*

DIEPPE, dyep, is a city in France, on the English Channel, 105 miles (170 km) northwest of Paris, in the Seine-Maritime department of Haute-Normandie. Lying in a break in the chalk cliffs of the Caux coast, astride the Arques River, Dieppe is an important commercial and fishing port. It has daily ferry service to the English port of Newhaven. Its location at the point on the Channel coast nearest to Paris has aided the city's commercial development and its popularity as a seaside resort. Dieppe's commercial port handles a large turnover of such varied goods as wood, fibers, fuels, fruits, wines and spirits, and machinery. Its brisk trade has led to the establishment of considerable manufacturing.

The interesting historical past of Dieppe is evoked by its many churches and monuments, its fortress, and its museum. The 15th century fortress, which houses the museum, overlooks the town from a cliff and is partially surrounded by walls dating from the 16th century. Though severely damaged in 1944, it has been repaired. The museum contains many sculptures from the Middle Ages and Renaissance, some maritime maps of the 16th and 17th centuries, and a beautiful collection of Dieppe ivory ware. The most notable churches are those of St. Jacques (13th and 14th centuries) and St. Rémy.

Dieppe has figured prominently in French military history. Its first castle was probably built by Charlemagne in 800. An important naval base in the 17th century, the town was destroyed by the English and Dutch in 1694. It was occupied by the Germans both in 1870–1871 and in World War II. On Aug. 19, 1942, Dieppe was raided by the Allies in the first, costly expedition to test German coastal defenses. Population: (1968) 29,829.

HOMER PRICE, *Hunter College*

DIES, dīz, **Martin, Jr.** (1901–1972), American congressman from Texas, who was the first chairman (1938–1945) of the House Committee on Un-American Activities. A Democrat, he served in the House in 1931–1945 and 1953–1959.

Dies was born on Nov. 5, 1901, in Colorado, Texas. Like his father, who had served in Congress for a decade, he represented a constituency which was suspicious of the changes wrought by the Roosevelt administration. The reiterated charge of the Dies committee was that the New Deal and the Congress of Industrial Organizations (CIO) was infiltrated by Communists and that liberals were being duped by Communist-controlled organizations. Dies exposed Communist influence in many areas, but he weakened his own case by his publicity seeking, his vendetta against New Deal programs and personalities, and his pioneering use of the technique of guilt by association.

Although his committee won support around the country—notably from veteran and fundamentalist groups—Dies' political career never advanced. He failed in a try for a Senate seat in 1941; the U. S.-Soviet wartime alliance undermined his anticommunism theme, and he resigned from the House in 1944. On his return in 1953, he was denied a place on the committee he had sired. His apologia, *The Martin Dies Story*, was published in 1963. He died on Nov. 14, 1972, in Lufkin, Texas.

WALTER GOODMAN, *Author of "The Committee"*

DIES IRAE, dē′ās ē′rā, is a sequence (hymn said or sung between the Epistle and Gospel at Mass) of the Roman Catholic Church. It was formerly appointed for masses for the dead but is now optional. It is named for its opening words, meaning "Day of Wrath," and is a description of the day of judgment and a prayer for mercy. It was probably first used for private devotion, and some have thought its original liturgical use was for Advent. Thomas of Celano, a 13th century Franciscan, is generally given as the author, but this is now contested. Many composers have written settings for the poem.

DIESEL, dē′zəl, **Rudolf** (1858–1913), German inventor, who developed the internal combustion engine that bears his name. He was born in Paris on March 18, 1858. Diesel studied at Augsburg and Munich and later became an assistant to the German physicist Karl P. G. von Linde. He was exposed to applications of thermodynamics through Linde's work in refrigeration machines. In 1879, Diesel joined Sulzer Brothers, a Swiss machine building company, and after gaining practical experience there, moved to Baron Maurice de Hirsch's company in Munich, which was manufacturing Linde's machines.

Diesel was granted a German patent on Feb. 28, 1892, for designs of compression-ignition engines to be operated with coal dust as the fuel. His patent was not unique, however, with respect to the compression-ignition process, since the English inventor Charles Akroyd-Stuart had patented a compression-ignition engine in 1888.

In 1893, Diesel published *Theory and Design of a Rational Heat Engine,* a theoretical analysis of an internal combustion engine with high efficiency. The book and his ideas came under strong attack from his contemporaries, but he was sufficiently persuasive to acquire the combined backing of Maschienenfabrik Augsbern Nürnberg and Friedrich Krupp to build a practical engine.

Diesel's intent was to utilize the constant-temperature heat addition of the Carnot cycle, feeding coal dust into the combustion chamber. However, the impracticability of coal dust was soon recognized, and it was abandoned in favor of fuel oil, with air injection. Diesel's wisdom in compromising his own theories and his perseverance in the face of continuous criticism led to success and the construction of large numbers of engines for worldwide use. He derived considerable profit from his development, but his poor investments led to severe monetary losses. Diesel disappeared from a channel steamer on Sept. 30, 1913, while crossing from England to Belgium.

ERNEST S. STARKMAN
University of California at Berkeley

DIESEL ENGINE, dē′zəl, an internal combustion engine named for Rudolf Diesel (q.v.). It differs from other internal combustion engines mainly in its method of introducing fuel and ignition. In the diesel engine the fuel is sprayed directly into the combustion chamber and ignited by the high temperature to which the air in the combustion chamber has been heated during the compression process. In other internal combustion engines, such as the gasoline engine, fuel and air are mixed before entering the combustion chamber and are spark-ignited. See INTERNAL COMBUSTION ENGINE—Plate 6.

How the Diesel Engine Works. The diesel engine operates on a cycle that consists of compression of air in the combustion chamber, injection of fuel into the chamber, combustion and expansion of the hot gases (power stroke), and exhaust. The cycle then begins again with the intake of a new charge. Combustion is considered to take place at constant pressure. This cycle, as well as the engine, is named for Rudolf Diesel, even though the principles were advanced by the French engineer Alphonse Beau de Rochas in 1862.

The manner of fuel introduction is the key to satisfactory and efficient operation. A high-pressure pump is used for fuel introduction. Fuel must be injected at precisely the proper moment in the stroke, accurately metered in rate and total quantity and properly atomized. This necessitates relatively expensive fuel-injection components of extremely closely controlled manufacturing tolerance.

Because of its characteristic fuel supply and combustion system and its use of heavy fuels, the diesel engine has certain limitations. Smoking occurs in the exhaust if an attempt is made to use more than 60% to 70% of the air in the cylinder during the combustion process. This smoking determines the maximum power that will be produced by the engine. A gasoline engine, the spark-ignition counterpart of the diesel engine, with the same airflow rate, will produce much more power. Consequently, a diesel engine producing the same power as its counterpart is much bulkier and heavier.

Both 2- and 4-stroke cycle engines are in equally successful applications. Most 2-stroke versions are characterized by the use of either mechanically driven or exhaust-driven superchargers. These superchargers have been used partly to aid in providing a new charge of air to the cylinder that will be free of burned gas from the previous cycle. This is to help overcome the smoking tendency of the engine. More recently, the supercharger has been used for the additional function of raising the pressure in the cylinder at the start of compression to a level greater than atmospheric pressure.

Although relatively costly, the diesel engine has high efficiency and long life and needs servicing infrequently. Large numbers of diesel engines are used where these factors are important, as in motor vehicles, where fuel is expensive, and in locomotives, trucks and buses, where high reliability and long life are important.

Types of Diesel Engines. The modern diesel engine for use in trucks, buses, tractors and locomotives is available in almost 400 different variations of size, number of cylinders, and power output. These range from single-cylinder models with a bore and stroke of little more than 3 inches (8 cm), weighing 200 pounds (90 kg), and producing 7 horsepower at 2400 rpm to versions with 16 cylinders with a bore of 9 inches (23 cm), a stroke of 10.5 inches (27 cm), weighing 41,000 pounds (18,000 kg), and producing 3600 horsepower at 1100 rpm.

The largest engines are to be found in facilities for generating electricity and for propelling ships; these are typically very heavy because weight is not a restrictive consideration. These engines usually have a 30-inch (76-cm) bore and a 40-inch (102 cm) stroke, and produce up to 10,000 horsepower from their 12 cylinders at a speed of about 200 rpm.

History. By present standards the early diesel engine was a clumsy and slow-running engine. At the beginning of the 20th century the commercial diesel engine produced about 25 horsepower for each of its 12-inch (30-cm) diameter cylinders while operating at a maximum of 200 rpm. Fuel was injected into the combustion chamber by means of a compressed-air jet. The necessity to provide compressed air for fuel injection was bothersome and a source of mechanical breakdown. Mechanical injection was adopted after 1910. Present diesel engines, except for very large units, are exclusively equipped with the mechanical, or solid, injection system.

ERNEST S. STARKMAN
University of California at Berkeley

DIET, the daily allowance of food and drink. In order to grow and function properly, the body needs certain essential nutrients. These nutrients are supplied through the diet, and a nutritionally adequate diet is one that provides these nutrients in the specific amounts required by the individual. An adequate diet is one that is made up of a variety of foods, for there is no single food, nor even any combination of a few foods, that supplies adequate amounts of all the essential nutrients.

Five basic types of nutrients are essential, either for themselves or for materials supplied through their metabolism. These five nutrients are protein, fat, carbohydrate, vitamins, and certain minerals. Water, although not considered a nutrient, is also essential for life because it is necessary for all the biochemical activities that occur in the body. In addition to requiring each of the essential nutrients, the body needs sufficient amounts of nutrients to supply it with enough energy to carry on all of the vital life processes. Food energy, which is measured in units called calories, is supplied mainly by fat and carbohydrate, but may also be supplied by protein. (In this article the term "calorie" refers to the larger, or kilogram, calorie, which equals 1,000 small, or gram, calories.)

Specific amounts of essential nutrients recommended for healthy individuals in the United States have been established by the Food and Nutrition Board of the National Research Council. To meet these recommendations, a person must eat several basic types of foods each day. According to the U.S. Department of Agriculture's plan entitled *A Daily Food Guide*, there are four main food groups that should be represented in the daily diet. These groups are known as the milk group, the meat group, the vegetable and fruit group, and the bread and cereal group. In addition, sufficient calories to meet the needs of the individual must be furnished, either from the foods in these groups or from foods not included in the groups. For adults, the food guide recommends a daily intake of at least two glasses of milk (or its equivalent), two servings from the meat group, four servings from the vegetable and fruit group (including one dark green or yellow vegetable and a citrus fruit or tomatoes), and four servings from the bread and cereal group. For children under 9 years of age, the guide recommends a daily intake of 2 to 3 cups of milk; for those 9 to 12 years old, 3 or more cups; and for teen-agers, at least 4 cups. The rest of the food group recommendations for children and teen-agers are the same as for adults, with modifications in amounts made to meet individual caloric and nutrient needs. See also NUTRITION OF MAN.

Modified Diets. Certain diseases may cause an individual's requirements for essential nutrients to be considerably higher than those of healthy individuals. Diets designed for treating diseases, therefore, are planned as modifications of the normal diet. The basic premise of such diets is that normal allowances be met whenever possible and if the diet modification is such that these allowances cannot be met by foods alone, other measures must be taken.

The treatment of disease through diet is referred to as diet therapy, or therapeutic nutrition. Diet therapy has always been a part of medicine; one of the earliest mentions of diet therapy is found in the writings of the ancient Greek physician Hippocrates. Over the years, diet therapy has undergone many changes, and today it is an integral part of the treatment of a great variety of diseases.

One of the basic principles of diet therapy is that any modification of the normal diet should relate to a specific physiological condition. Accordingly, a single diet may then be used to treat any disease in which the same physiological condition exists. A diet restricted in sodium, for example, may be prescribed for a person with any disease in which there is an abnormal retention of fluid in the body, since sodium normally aids in the retention of fluid in the body tissues.

Therapeutic diets may be classified into two broad groups: those in which the modifications are qualitative and those in which they are quantitative. Qualitative modifications are used in treating disorders that are not as yet directly related to food metabolism. Most of the gastrointestinal diseases, such as ulcers, fall into this category. Quantitative modifications are used for treating disorders that are directly related to food metabolism. These disorders include obesity, underweight, diabetes, and the many diseases involving inborn errors of metabolism, such as phenylketonuria (PKU) and galactosemia. In many of these disorders, the deficiency or complete absence of a particular hormone or metabolic enzyme has been found to be the causative factor.

Whenever the normal diet is modified quantitatively, a specific level of nutrient or calorie intake should always be indicated. Thus, the phrase "low calorie diet" should never be used. Instead, the specific level of calories should be indicated, as in a "1,200 calorie diet."

Therapeutic diets should never be undertaken except when prescribed and supervised by a physician. Once a therapeutic diet is prescribed, qualified dietitians and nutritionists can help the individual in interpreting the prescribed diet to meet his particular needs. A well-planned therapeutic diet is one that adjusts to the individual's religious, ethnic, social, and economic background as well as to his personal preferences.

One of the first diseases to be treated through diet was diabetes. The need to control the patient's intake of carbohydrate was recognized for many years, and until the discovery and general availability of insulin, the restriction of carbohydrate was extremely strict. Today, however, a more liberal diet is possible for diabetics, and they are able to consume a nutritionally adequate diet made up of a wide variety of foods.

When doctors and dietitians were developing special diets for diabetics, a committee representing the American Dietetic Association, the American Diabetes Association, and the U.S. Public Health Service devised special lists, called exchange lists, to aid in meal planning. There are six different exchange lists, each one corresponding to a basic food group—milk, vegetables, fruits, breads, meat, and fats. The foods in each group are roughly equivalent in composition and caloric value. The use of these lists allows an individual to plan a varied and interesting diet that assures adequate nutrition. (Copies of these lists may be obtained from the American Dietetic Association at 620 N. Michigan Avenue, Chicago, Ill., 60611. The cost is 15¢ and all orders must be placed through a dietitian or a doctor.)

DIETS TO CONTROL WEIGHT

Losing Weight. Obesity results when a person's intake of calories is greater than the amount needed by the body for energy. Fat supplies about twice as many calories as carbohydrate and protein, and except for alcohol, these three nutrients are the body's only source of calories. Whenever any of these substances are not used for energy, they can be converted into fat and stored in the body. Therefore, two factors must be considered in controlling overweight: the intake of calories and the expenditure of energy. Normal body weight is maintained when these two factors are balanced. To bring about a loss of weight, fewer calories must be taken in and more energy may need to be expended. By the proper regulation of diet and exercise a negative calorie balance can be achieved, and as a result, the energy, or fat, stores in the body will be drawn upon to supply the body's energy needs and produce a loss of weight.

Only a very small percentage of obese individuals can attribute their overweight to endocrine gland disturbances that affect their metabolism. All other overweight people have only their lack of activity and excess food intake to blame.

The desired rate of weight loss for most people is considered to range from 1½ to 2 pounds (0.7 to 0.9 kg) per week. However, this rate may vary depending on such factors as water balance, activity, heat loss, and the presence of disease. For most women, diets ranging between 1,200 and 1,500 calories a day will bring about a satisfactory weight loss. For men, the range is between 1,500 and 2,000 calories a day. An intake of less than 1,200 calories is generally not advised since it is likely to be nutritionally inadequate. Because the needs of teen-agers and young children vary greatly from one individual to the next, no general rule can be applied to them and calorie levels should be prescribed individually by a dietitian or doctor.

Pursuing a weight-reduction regimen is difficult for many individuals, and they must be highly motivated in order to persist in the regimen and to maintain a caloric level low enough to bring about a loss of weight. Appetite-depressing drugs, known as anorexigenic drugs, have been used in the management of obesity by some physicians to help the individual reduce his calorie intake to the prescribed level. The use of these drugs, however, should be considered only a part of the overall treatment, which entails re-educating the patient in proper eating and exercise while treating any other factors, such as neuroses, which may be a major cause of the individual's problem. By themselves anorexigenic drugs will not control obesity, and reliance on such drugs, rather than on proper diet, leads to failure in a weight-reduction regimen. Also, there are indications that the unsupervised use of some anorexigenic drugs may be harmful.

In addition to appetite-depressing drugs there are many other products available to overweight people to help them in their attempt to lose weight. These products include methyl cellulose wafers, various high-priced harmless materials often accompanied with bizarre diet plans and other, sometimes not so harmless, materials, usually sold in pill form. By themselves none of these products will cause a reduction in weight.

A variety of special, rather unusual diets have also been reported to be effective in weight reduction. These diets have been known under such names as the grapefruit diet, the drinking man's diet, the 10-day diet, and others. Naturally, if these diets are low enough in calories, and if the individual stays on the diet long enough, he will lose weight. However, the problem with the vast majority of these diets is that they are often made up of only a few foods or a strange assortment of foods, so that they are not nutritionally adequate. Another fault of these fad diets is that certain foods or combinations of foods are erroneously believed to have certain nutritional properties. For example, proponents of the grapefruit diet claim that eating grapefruit before a meat dish helps one lose weight because the acid in the grapefruit will destroy some of the calories of the meat.

Gaining Weight. In the treatment of people who are underweight, the diet must include more calories than the body needs for energy so that the excess calories can be stored in the body as fat. If the underweight person also suffers from a wasting away of body tissues, a diet high in protein as well as calories may be prescribed.

As a rule, the addition of 500 calories a day above the energy needs of the individual will bring about a gain in weight of about 1 pound (0.5 kg) per week. Sometimes, the daily intake of food may need to be divided into six or eight separate meals in order to reach the desired calorie level.

OTHER THERAPEUTIC DIETS

Sodium-Restricted Diets. A sodium-restricted diet is one in which the sodium intake is kept at a specified level. This type of diet is used in treating such diseases as cirrhosis of the liver, toxemia of pregnancy, hypertension (high blood pressure), cardiac insufficiency, and kidney disorders. The average daily intake of sodium for most people is between 5 and 10 grams, most of which is eaten in the form of table salt (sodium chloride). People on sodium-restricted diets, therefore, must greatly reduce their salt intake; this often necessitates a modification in the foods they normally eat. Sometimes a sodium-restricted diet is erroneously described as a "salt-free" or
(continued on page 104)

RECOMMENDED CALORIE ALLOWANCES

The following table indicates the recommended daily allowances of calories for healthy persons living in the United States. These allowances, however, are average figures and should be modified according to the individual's activity. A 25-year-old construction worker, for example, may require as much as 4,000 calories a day, while a sedentary office worker the same age may need only 2,500 calories each day.

	Age Group	Calories
Children:	1– 3	1,300
	3– 6	1,600
	6– 9	2,100
Boys:	9–12	2,400
	12–15	3,000
	15–18	3,400
Girls:	9–12	2,200
	12–15	2,500
	15–18	2,300
Men:	18–35	2,900
	35–55	2,600
	55–75	2,200
Women:	18–35	2,100
	35–55	1,900
	55–75	1,600

CALORIC VALUES OF COMMON FOODS

The following table lists the approximate calorie content of many common foods. Where canned products are listed, the given caloric value applies to popular brands.

FOOD	CALORIES
Almonds, dried shelled, unsalted, ½ cup	425
unsalted, 9–10 nuts	60
salted, 9–10 nuts	62
Anchovies, canned, 5 fillets	35
Anchovy paste, 1 T	42
Apple juice, canned or bottled 6 oz	81
Apples, raw, peeled, 1 avg (2½″ diameter)	66
raw, unpeeled, 1 avg	80
frozen slices, swt, ½ cup	93
Applesauce, canned, swt, ½ cup	100
canned, unswt, ½ cup	49
Apricot nectar, canned, 6 oz	96
Apricots, raw, 3 avg (12 per lb)	55
candied, 1 oz	95
canned, 4 halves w/2 T hvy syrup	105
dried, 1 cup	390
Artichoke hearts, frozen, 3 hearts	22
Artichokes, boiled, 1 avg	53
Asparagus, boiled, 1 cup cut spears	35
canned, 6 spears	20
frozen, 5 spears	23
Avocadoes, Calif., peeled, ½ avg	185
Florida, peeled, ½ avg	157
Bacon, cooked, 2 slices	98
Canadian, cooked, 1 slice	58
Bananas, raw, 1 avg (6¾″ long)	87
Barley, pearled, dry, ¼ cup	175
Bass, sea, 4 oz	116
striped, 4 oz	120
Beans, baked, in molasses sauce, 1 cup	332
in tomato sauce, 1 cup	270
Beans, green, boiled, ½ cup	16
frozen, cut or whole, ½ cup	23
frozen, w/butter sauce, ½ cup	63
Beans, kidney, navy, pea boiled, ½ cup	95
Beans, lima, boiled, ½ cup	89
frozen, ½ cup	100
frozen, w/butter sauce, ½ cup	117
Beans, wax, boiled, ½ cup	16
frozen, ½ cup	25
Beef, choice grade cuts, 4-oz portions:	
chuck, pot roasted, lean and fat	329
chuck, pot roasted, lean only	220
club steak, broiled, lean and fat	517
club steak, broiled, lean only	278
flank steak, braised	223
ground, regular	326
ground, lean	250
porterhouse steak, broiled, lean and fat	530
porterhouse steak, broiled, lean only	255
rib, roasted, lean and fat	502
rib, roasted, lean only	275
round, broiled	297
rump, roasted, lean and fat	395
rump, roasted, lean only	237
sirloin steak, broiled, lean and fat	450
sirloin steak, broiled, lean only	240
t-bone steak, broiled, lean and fat	539
t-bone steak, broiled, lean only	254
Beef, corned, boiled, 4 oz	424
canned, 4 oz	246
canned hash, 1 cup	405
Beef goulash, canned, 7¾ oz	183
Beef pie, frozen, 8-oz pie	443
Beef stew, canned, 8 oz	182
Beer, 12 oz can or bottle	173
Beet greens, boiled, ½ cup	18
Beets, boiled, ½ cup	27
canned, ½ cup	31
Blackberries, raw, ½ cup	42
canned in hvy syrup, ½ cup	114
frozen, swt, ½ cup	70
Blueberries, raw, ½ cup	43
canned in hvy syrup, ½ cup	126
frozen, swt, ½ cup	95
Bluefish, baked or broiled w/butter, 4 oz	181
Bologna, all meat, ¼ lb	312
w/cereal, ¼ lb	299
Brazil nuts, 1 nut	50
Bread:	
Boston brown, 1 slice (3″ x ¾″)	101
corn, 1 piece (2″ x 2″ x 1″)	139
cracked wheat, 1 slice (20 per 1 lb loaf)	60
French or Vienna, 1 slice (3¼″ x 2″ x 1″)	58
Gluten, 1 slice (20 per 8 oz loaf)	35
Hollywood Diet, 1 slice (20 per 14 oz loaf)	46
Italian, 1 slice (3¼″ x 2″ x 1″)	55
Profile, 1 slice (20 per 1 lb loaf)	55
pumpernickel, 1 slice (3¾″ x ⅛″)	74
raisin, 1 slice (20 per 1 lb loaf)	60
Rite Diet, 1 slice (20 per 14 oz loaf)	56
rye, light, 1 slice (20 per 1 lb loaf)	56

FOOD	CALORIES
rye, light, party, 1 slice (3″ x 2″ x ½″)	36
white, 1 slice (20 per 1 lb loaf)	62
white, 1 slice (26 per 1 lb loaf)	46
whole wheat, 1 slice (20 per 1 lb loaf)	56
Broccoli, raw, trimmed, ½ lb	227
boiled, 1 cup spears	150
frozen, chopped, ½ cup	94
frozen spears, 1 spear	94
Brownies, 1 piece (2″ x 2″ x ¾″)	140
Brussels sprouts, boiled, ½ cup	23
frozen, ½ cup	34
Butter, 1 cup (½ lb)	1,625
1 T	100
Cabbage, raw, shredded, 1 cup	24
Cakes:	
angel food, 1/12 of 8″ cake	110
cheesecake, 2″ wedge	250
chocolate w/choc icing, 1/16 of 10″ cake	445
fruitcake, dark, 1 slice ½″ thick	142
gingerbread, 1 piece (2″ x 2″ x 2″)	175
plain, 1 piece (3″ x 2″ x 1½″)	200
plain w/choc icing, 1/16 of 10″ cake	370
pound, 1 piece (2¾″ x 3″ x ⅝″)	140
sponge, 1/12 of 8″ cake	120
Candies:	
almonds, chocolate covered, 1 piece	10
butterscotch, 1 oz	111
caramel, chocolate, 1 oz	114
chocolate, milk, bar, 1 oz	154
chocolate, milk, kisses, 1 piece	47
chocolate, unsweetened, 1 oz	175
chocolate cream, 1 small	51
coconut, chocolate covered, 1 oz	122
fondant, 1 oz	102
fudge, chocolate or vanilla, 1 oz	112
gumdrops, 2 large (1″ diameter each)	97
jelly beans, 10 beans (1 oz)	102
Life Saver, fruit flavor, 1 piece	9
marshmallow, 1 medium (1¼″ diameter)	26
mint wafers, 3.5 oz	587
peanut brittle, 1 oz	122
peppermint patties, 3.5 oz	432
Sugar Daddy, 1 piece	145
Cantaloupe, ½ melon, 5″ diameter	58
Carrots, raw, 1 medium (5½″ long)	21
boiled, diced, ½ cup	23
Cashew nuts, roasted, 1 cup	760
Catsup, 1 T	21
Cauliflower, raw, trimmed, ½ lb	61
boiled, ½ cup	13
frozen, ½ cup	21
Caviar, granular, 1 oz	74
pressed, 1 oz	89
Celery, raw, 1 outer stalk	6
raw or boiled, ½ cup	9
Cereals:	
All-Bran, ½ cup	96
bran flakes, ¾ cup	104
Cheerios, 1 cup	100
cornflakes, 1⅓ cups	105
cornmeal, enriched, ¼ cup	130
Cream of Wheat, 1 oz (uncooked)	100
farina, 1 oz (uncooked)	106
Grape-Nuts, ¼ cup	100
hominy grits, ¾ cup (cooked)	90
oat flakes, ⅔ cup	110
oatmeal, ½ cup (cooked)	75
Post Toasties, 1 cup	110
puffed rice, 1 cup	51
puffed wheat, 1 cup	43
raisin bran, ⅔ cup	100
Rice Krispies, 1 cup	106
shredded wheat, 2 biscuits	126
Special K, 1½ cups	109
Sugar Frosted Flakes, ¾ cup	107
Total, 1 cup	108
Wheaties, 1 cup	108
Chard, Swiss, raw, 1 lb	104
cooked, ½ cup	14
Cheeses:	
American, processed, 1 oz	105
blue, 1 oz	99
Camembert, 1 oz	86
Cheddar, 1 oz	113
cottage, creamed, ⅓ cup	80
cottage, uncreamed, ⅓ cup	65
cream, 1 oz	96
cream, whipped, 1 oz	101
Edam, 1 oz	105
Gorgonzola, 1 oz	112
Gouda, 1 oz	108
Gruyère, 1 oz	110
Limburger, 1 oz	98

(continued on next page)

FOOD	CALORIES
mozzarella, 1 oz	79
Munster, 1 oz	100
Parmesan, grated, 1 T	31
Provolone, 1 oz	99
Romano, grated, 1 T	31
Roquefort, 1 oz	105
Swiss, 1 oz	104
Cherries, fresh, sour, 1 cup	70
fresh, sweet, 1 cup	82
candied, 1 large	17
canned, sour, in hvy syrup, 1 cup	231
canned, sweet, in hvy syrup, 1 cup	211
Chewing gum—see Gum, chewing	
Chicken, broiled, meat only, 4 oz	155
fried, ½ breast (3.3 oz)	154
fried, drumstick (2.1 oz)	89
roasted, meat only, 4 oz	210
stewed, meat only, 4 oz	237
canned, boned, 4 oz	226
Chicken a la king, frozen, ¾ cup	90
Chicken gizzards, boiled, 2 oz	84
Chicken pie, frozen, 8 oz pie	503
Chick-peas, dry, ½ cup	360
Chili, canned, w/beans, 8 oz	270
Chili sauce, bottled, 1 T	20
Chives, raw, ¼ lb	32
Chocolate, cooking, semisweet, 2 sqs	260
unswt, 2 sqs	280
Chocolate candy—see Candy	
Chocolate syrup, 1 T	51
Chop suey, canned, w/meat, 8 oz	141
Chow mein, chicken, canned, 8 oz	86
Clams, raw, meat only, 8 oz	182
canned, 4 oz	112
Cocoa, 1 cup	235
Coconut, fresh, shredded, ½ cup	170
fresh, 1 piece (2" x 2" x ½")	156
dry, grated, ½ cup	300
Cod, broiled w/butter, 4 oz	194
frozen, fillets, 2 fillets	84
frozen fish sticks, 5 sticks	276
Coffee, black, 1 cup	2
Cookies: 1 piece	
animal cracker	10
arrowroot	15
creme sandwich	50
chocolate chip	51
chocolate wafer	13
date and nut	78
Fig Newton	59
gingersnap	32
graham, chocolate	55
graham cracker	17
macaroon, coconut	81
oatmeal	60
peanut	33
sugar or vanilla wafer	18
Corn, kernels, boiled, ½ cup	69
canned, cream style, ½ cup	94
on cob, cooked, 1 ear (5" long)	71
frozen, cream style, ½ cup	85
frozen, cut, ½ cup	77
frozen, on cob, 1 ear	82
frozen, w/butter sauce, ½ cup	101
Corn chips, 1 oz	166
Cornstarch, 2 T	60
Crabmeat, steamed, 3½ oz	93
Cracker meal, 1 T	44
Crackers, 1 cracker:	
Melba toast, 4 gm	16
onion, 2 gm	11
oyster, 1 gm	4
Ritz, 3 gm	18
saltine, 3 gm	14
soda, 6 gm	26
zwieback, 7 gm	31
Cranberry juice cocktail, 6 oz	124
Cranberry sauce, jellied, 2 oz	92
whole, 2 oz	96
Cream, light, ½ cup	253
half and half, ½ cup	150
whipping, light, ½ cup unwhipped	358
whipping, heavy, ½ cup unwhipped	419
Cream, sour, 2 T	57
Creamer, non-dairy, 1 tsp	11
Cucumber, peeled, 1 medium (7½" long)	29
Currants, red or white, raw, ¾ cup	50
Dates, 4 avg	76
Dips, commercially prepared:	
blue cheese, 2 oz	138
clam, 2 oz	134
onion, 2 oz	92
Duck, domestic, roasted, meat only, 4 oz	352
Egg, chicken, raw or boiled, 1 large	81
Eggnog, 4.7% fat, ½ cup	138
8.8% fat, ½ cup	195
Eggplant, raw, diced, ½ cup	50
Endive, raw, 10 small leaves	5

FOOD	CALORIES
Escarole, 7 small leaves	4
Figs, raw, 3 small (1½" diameter)	91
canned, 3 figs w/2 T hvy syrup	96
dried, 1 large (2" x 1")	57
Filberts, 10 – 12 nuts	95
Frankfurter, all meat, cooked, 1 avg	151
Fruit cocktail, canned, ½ cup	84
Fruit salad, in jars, 3½ oz	60
Garlic, raw, 5 cloves	14
Gelatin dessert, all flavors, ½ cup	81
Gelatin, dry, 1 T	34
Gin—see Liquor	
Goose, roasted, meat only, 4 oz	266
Gooseberries, raw, ¼ lb	114
Grapefruit, pink, ½ medium (4½" diameter)	58
white, ½ medium (4½" diameter)	52
white, sections, 1 cup	76
Grapefruit drink, 8 oz	107
Grapefruit juice, 6 oz	72
canned, swt, 6 oz	100
canned, unswt, 6 oz	76
Grape drink, canned, 8 oz	117
Grape juice, canned, 6 oz	133
frozen, diluted, 6 oz	99
Grapes, American varieties, 1 cup	153
European varieties, 1 cup	160
Gravy, thick, 3 T	180
Gum, chewing, 1 stick	8
dietetic, 1 stick	5
Haddock, smoked, 4 oz	117
frozen fillets, 2 fillets	88
frozen fish sticks, 5 sticks	280
Halibut, broiled w/butter, 4 oz	195
frozen steak, ½ steak	144
Ham, boiled, 4 oz	266
fresh roasted, medium fat, 4 oz	426
light-cure, roasted, medium fat, 4 oz	329
picnic, roasted, medium fat, 4 oz	368
Hazlenuts, 10 – 12 nuts	95
Herring, raw, Atlantic, 2 oz	100
raw, Pacific, 2 oz	56
pickled, 2 oz	127
Hollandaise sauce, 1 T	65
Honey, 1 T	64
Honeydew melon, 1 wedge (2" x 7")	49
diced, ½ cup	40
Ice cream, chocolate, ⅓ pint	191
strawberry, ⅓ pint	174
vanilla, 10.2% fat, ⅓ pint	176
vanilla, 12.1% fat, ⅓ pint	186
Ice cream bar, chocolate coated, 1 bar	162
Ice cream sandwich, 1 sandwich	208
Ice milk, vanilla, ⅓ pint	135
Jams and preserves, all flavors, 1 T	54
Jellies, all flavors, 1 T	55
Kale, chopped, frozen, ½ cup	29
Kidney, beef, 4 oz	287
Knockwurst, ¼ lb	317
Kohlrabi, boiled, ½ cup	19
Lamb chop, loin, 1 chop (4.8 oz):	
boiled, lean and fat	402
broiled, lean only	140
Lamb, leg, roasted, lean and fat, 4 oz	318
roasted, lean only, 4 oz	212
Lamb, shoulder, roasted, lean and fat, 4 oz	385
roasted, lean only, 4 oz	234
Lard, 1 cup	1,984
1 T	124
Lemonade, 8 oz	104
frozen, diluted, 8 oz	98
Lemon juice, fresh, ½ cup	30
Lemons, fresh, 1 avg (2⅕" diameter)	19
Lentils, whole, cooked, ½ cup	102
Lettuce, Boston, 1 head (4" diameter)	31
iceberg, 1 head (4¾" diameter)	59
romaine, 3 leaves (8" long)	5
Lime juice, fresh, ½ cup	32
Limes, 1 avg (1½" long)	19
Liquor, 1 oz:	
100 proof	86
86 proof	74
80 proof	69
Liver, beef, fried, 6 oz	389
calf, fried, 6 oz	444
chicken, simmered, 6 oz	280
Liverwurst, fresh, ¼ lb	350
smoked, ¼ lb	364
Lobster meat, cooked, 8 oz	216
Macadamia nuts, roasted, 6 nuts	104
Macaroni, cooked, 1 cup	168
Mackerel, broiled w/butter, 4 oz	269
Manhattan cocktail, 3 oz undiluted	160
Maple syrup, 1 T	55
Margarine, 1 T	100
Marmalade, citrus, 1 T	51
Martini, 3 oz undiluted, 86 proof gin	
5:1 proportions	190
10:1 proportions	205

FOOD	CALORIES
Mayonnaise, 1 T	100
Milk, fluid, whole, 3.5% fat, 8 oz	151
whole, 3.7% fat, 8 oz	159
buttermilk, 1% fat, 8 oz	100
buttermilk, 2% fat, 8 oz	122
skim, 8 oz	81
skim, fortified, 8 oz	137
Milk, canned, condensed, swt, ½ cup	500
evaporated, ½ cup	174
Milk, dry, whole, 4 T	141
nonfat, reconstituted, 8 oz	82
Molasses, light, 1 T	50
blackstrap, 1 T	43
Muffin, corn, 1 muffin	180
English, 1 muffin	140
Mushrooms, raw, ½ lb	61
canned, 1 cup	61
Mussels, raw, meat only, 4 oz	108
Mustard, prepared, 1 tsp	10
Mustard greens, boiled, 1 cup	140
Nectarine, 1 avg	30
Noodles, egg, cooked, ½ cup	100
Nuts—see individual listings	
Oil, corn, cottonseed, safflower, 1 T	128
olive, 1 T	125
Okra, boiled, 8 pods (3" long)	25
frozen, ½ cup	36
Olives, canned or bottled, 1 large	5
Onions, raw, 1 avg (2½" diameter)	40
boiled, 1 cup	60
Orange drink, 8 oz	106
Orange-grapefruit juice, 6 oz	76
Orange juice, navel, 6 oz	90
most Florida varieties, 6 oz	80
canned, 6 oz	81
dried, reconstituted, 6 oz	86
Oranges, navel, raw, 1 orange	60
most Florida varieties, 1 orange	75
Oyster meat, raw, 1 medium	20
Pancakes, 4" diameter:	
regular	61
buttermilk	71
Parsley, raw, chopped, 1 T	2
Parsnips, boiled, 1 cup	102
Peaches, raw, 1 avg (2" diameter)	35
frozen, ⅓ cup	99
Peanut butter, 1 T	72
Peanuts, roasted, salted, 1 cup halves	842
chopped, 1 T	54
Pears, raw, 1 avg (2½" diameter)	100
canned, 2 halves w/2 T hvy syrup	78
Peas, green, boiled, ½ cup	57
frozen, ½ cup	70
frozen w/butter sauce, ½ cup	97
Pecans, 1 cup halves	742
chopped, 1 T	51
Perch, baked w/butter, 4 oz	134
Pickles, dill, 1 avg (4" long)	12
sweet, 1 avg (2¾" long)	29
Pies, 1 wedge, 1/7 of 9" pie:	
apple	346
cherry	355
custard	280
lemon meringue	305
mince	365
pumpkin	275
Pineapple, raw, diced, 1 cup	73
canned, swt, 1 cup chunks	168
canned, swt, 1 slice	74
Pineapple juice, canned, 6 oz	102
Pineapple-grapefruit drink, 8 oz	125
Pistachio nuts, shelled, ¼ lb	673
Plums, raw, 1 avg (2" diameter)	36
Popcorn, unbuttered, 1 cup	42
Pork chop, 3½ oz:	
broiled, lean and fat	260
broiled, lean only	130
Pork roast, loin, 3½ oz:	
lean and fat	353
fat only	244
Potato chips, 2 oz	312
Potatoes, baked, 1 small (incl. skin)	93
boiled in skin, 1 small	76
boiled, peeled, 1 small	65
French-fried, 10 pieces (2" long)	156
mashed, ½ cup	93
Potatoes, sweet, baked, peeled, 1 avg	155
boiled, peeled, 1 avg	125
candied, ½ cup	204
Pretzels, 3-ring, 1 pretzel	12
sticks, 1 stick	3
Prune juice, 8 oz	170
Prunes, dried, 12 large	280
Puddings:	
Jello, all flavors except lemon, ½ cup	145
Jello, lemon flavored	125
Radishes, raw, 4 small	7
Raisins, ¼ cup	90

FOOD	CALORIES
Raspberries, black, raw, 1 cup	90
red, raw, 1 cup	70
red, frozen, ½ cup	138
Rhubarb, raw, trimmed, ½ lb	31
Rice, brown, cooked, 1 cup	183
white, cooked, 1 cup	187
Rum, 1 oz	73
Salad dressings, commercially prepared, 1 T:	
cheese	67
French	70
Russian	55
Thousand Island	65
Salad dressing mixes, prepared, 1 T	85
Salmon, chinook, canned, 3 oz	178
Salmon steak, baked w/butter, 3½ oz	140
broiled w/butter, 3½ oz	210
Salmon, smoked, 3½ oz	176
Sardines, canned in oil, bristling, 3¾ oz	360
sild, 3¾ oz	380
Sardines, canned in tomato sauce, 3½ oz	197
Sauerkraut, ⅔ cup	27
Sausage, pork, 4 oz	538
Scallops, fried, 5 – 6 medium scallops	427
Sherbet, ½ cup	135
Shrimp, boiled, 5 large	70
Soft drinks, 8 oz:	
bitter lemon	128
cola flavored, regular	96
Fresca	2
ginger ale	88
quinine water	88
root beer	96
Seven-Up	97
Sole, fillets, 2 fillets	88
Soups, canned, diluted, 1 cup:	
beef broth	26
chicken noodle	65
consommé, chicken	23
minestrone	100
onion	35
split pea	150
tomato	83
vegetable	74
Soy sauce, 1 T	9
Spaghetti, cooked, 1 cup	159
Spinach, cooked, 1 cup	41
canned, 1 cup	43
frozen, 1 cup	48
Squash, cooked, 1 cup:	
acorn	113
butternut	139
hubbard	102
scallop	34
yellow	31
zucchini	25
Steak—see Beef	
Strawberries, raw, ½ cup	28
frozen, halves, ½ cup	155
frozen, whole, ½ cup	98
Succotash, frozen, ½ cup	90
Sugar, beet or cane:	
brown, 1 cup	821
brown, 1 T	51
granulated, 1 cup	770
granulated, 1 T	42
granulated, 1 lump	25
Swordfish steak, broiled w/butter, 5 oz	241
Tangerine juice, canned, swt, 6 oz	93
canned, unswt, 6 oz	80
Tangerines, 1 avg (2½" diameter)	39
Tartar sauce, 1 T	75
Tea, 1 cup	1
Tomato sauce, ½ cup	35
Tomato paste, ⅓ cup	82
Tomatoes, raw, 1 avg (2½" diameter)	33
canned, ½ cup	25
Tongue, beef, braised, 3½ oz	244
Tuna, canned in oil, 7 oz	333
Turkey, roasted, 3½ oz:	
dark meat	203
light meat	176
Turnips, boiled, ½ cup	18
Veal chop, loin, broiled, 3½ oz	234
cutlet, broiled, 3½ oz	216
roast, 3½ oz	248
Vegetable juice, canned, 6 oz	31
Vodka—see Liquor	
Walnuts, shelled, 1 cup halves	654
chopped, 1 T	49
Watermelon, 1 wedge (4" x 8")	111
Whiskey—see Liquor	
Whitefish, smoked, ¼ lb	176
Wines:	
port, 2 oz	100
sherry, 2 oz	80
table red or white, 4 oz	95
Yogurt, plain or vanilla, 1 cup	167
strawberry, 1 cup	260

"low-salt" diet. However, many foods, including milk, are natural sources of sodium, so that a diet may be low in salt but not low in sodium.

A person following a sodium-restricted diet must also be aware of the many sources of sodium other than foods. In many communities, the drinking water is high enough in sodium to make a sodium-restricted diet worthless. In such cases, distilled water may have to be used for cooking and drinking purposes. Many medicines also contain sodium, and the continual use of such medicines by a person on a sodium-restricted diet may invalidate the diet. Among the medicines that contain large amounts of sodium are alkalizers and antacids.

As in other quantitatively modified diets, a sodium-restricted diet must always specify the level of sodium. Three sodium-restriction levels have been established by the American Heart Association: severe restriction (500 mg), moderate restriction (1,000 mg), and mild restriction (2,400–4,500 mg). In the most severely restricted sodium diets all salt must be eliminated, so that even the usual canned vegetables must be excluded from the diet. An invaluable aid to people on highly restricted sodium diets are the various commercially prepared foods, including milk and canned vegetables, that are low in sodium. These foods, like other foods prepared to meet the requirements of certain modified diets, are called "Dietetic Foods," and they are regulated by the Federal Food and Drug Administration. The labels on these foods must state the level of the substance for which they have been modified. For example, canned vegetables that are advertised to be low in sodium must state on the label the exact amount of sodium per 100 grams or per serving. Therefore, it is important to read the labels on all foods to be included in modified diets, especially in sodium-restricted diets.

Fat-Controlled Diets. A fat-controlled diet is one in which the amount of cholesterol as well as the amount and type of fat are indicated in specific amounts. This type of diet is aimed at reducing the cholesterol level of the blood, and it is often used in the prevention and treatment of atherosclerosis, a major factor in heart disease.

The average American consumes between 40% and 45% of the calories in his diet in the form of fat. In a fat-controlled diet, this percentage is reduced to 35% or less. In addition, the relative amounts of saturated fat and polyunsaturated fats in the diet are carefully regulated. (For an explanation of the differences between saturated and unsaturated fats, see the article FATTY ACIDS.) Scientific evidence indicates that saturated fats tend to increase the normal blood cholesterol level, while polyunsaturated fats tend to lower the blood cholesterol level. In general, polyunsaturated fats are found in vegetable oils, such as those obtained from safflower, cottonseed, corn, soybeans, and sesame seed. Saturated fats are found in animal foods, such as meat, milk, and milk products such as cheese and butter.

For a fat-controlled diet to be effective in lowering the blood cholesterol level, it must contain less saturated fat than polyunsaturated fat. At a 1,200 calorie level, the usual ratio of polyunsaturated fat to saturated fat is 1.1 to 1. At a 1,800 calorie level, the ratio is about 1.3 to 1, and at a 2,400 calorie level, the ratio is about 1.5 to 1.

Although the body does synthesize a certain amount of cholesterol, reducing the patient's intake of cholesterol is extremely important in a fat-controlled diet. Among the foods highest in cholesterol are egg yolk, liver, brain, kidney, sweetbread (thymus), and shellfish. These foods must be either severely restricted or entirely eliminated in order to obtain the best results from a fat-controlled diet. Egg whites may be eaten as much as desired, but egg yolks are usually limited to three or four a week.

Foods to be included in a fat-controlled diet must be prepared without the use of saturated fats, substituting polyunsaturated fats in their place. For example, special margarines high in polyunsaturated fats should be used instead of butter in cooking and eating. Special salad dressings made with oils that are high in polyunsaturated fats should also be used. Meats must be lean and well trimmed of fat, and poultry must have the skin removed. Fresh fish and fish that is not packed in oil are excellent protein-rich foods that should be included in the diet. Skim milk and cheeses made from skim milk are also important in a fat-controlled diet.

Diets for Inborn Errors of Metabolism. Diets for the treatment of inborn errors of metabolism are designed to reduce greatly or eliminate foods containing the particular substance that cannot be properly metabolized by the body. In phenylketonuria (PKU), the amino acid phenylalanine cannot be metabolized normally because the body lacks the enzyme phenylalanine hydroxylase. As a result, phenylalanine and abnormal metabolites accumulate in the body, causing brain damage. In controlling phenylketonuria, the diet is designed to keep the phenylalanine content as low as possible without affecting the growth and development of the infant. In galactosemia, another inborn error of metabolism, the body lacks one of the enzymes necessary in the metabolism of galactose, a component of lactose (milk sugar). In the treatment of this disorder, all foods containing galactose are greatly reduced or completely eliminated from the diet.

Diets for Treating Intestinal Ulcers. Certain disorders of the gastrointestinal tract, such as ulcers and ulcerative colitis, are generally treated with modified diets in which the amount of cellulose and other fibrous material is greatly reduced. This type of diet, known as a low-fiber diet, is designed to reduce the amount of mechanical irritation to the upper gastrointestinal tract (the stomach and small intestine) while also reducing the amount of fecal residue in the large intestine. In the treatment of duodenal and gastric ulcers, however, it has been found that the disorder may be effectively controlled regardless of the type of diet. In these disorders, other factors may be considerably more important than the kind of food ingested. For example, neutralizing gastric acidity with antacid tablets and avoiding stressful situations may control the patient's condition well enough to allow him to eat a normal diet.

DORIS JOHNSON, PH.D.
Yale-New Haven Hospital

Further Reading: Johnson, Doris, "Present Concepts in Diet Therapy" in *World Review of Nutrition and Dietetics*, vol. 5, 1965. Robinson, C. H., *Proudfit-Robinson's Normal and Therapeutic Nutrition*, 13th ed. (New York 1967); id., *Basic Nutrition and Diet Therapy* (New York 1965); Turner, D. H., *Handbook of Diet Therapy*, 4th ed. (Chicago 1965); Wohl, M. G., and Goodhart, R. S., *Modern Nutrition in Health and Disease*. 3d ed. (Philadelphia 1964).

THE JAPANESE DIET, convened for an opening ceremony, stands respectfully for the arrival of the emperor.

WIDE WORLD

DIET, an assembly of delegates or dignitaries meeting for political, administrative, or ecclesiastical purposes. The legislative assemblies of Germany, Austria, Hungary, Poland, Sweden, Denmark, Switzerland, and Japan have been called diets; but as a general term, "diet" implies the governing body of a loose confederation and is most often used to refer to the formal assemblies of the estates of the Holy Roman Empire (q.v.).

The Diet of the Holy Roman Empire was formally established by the Golden Bull of Charles IV in 1356. It was originally a feudal body in which only lords could appear, but by 1500 the imperial cities had secured the right to participate in all Diets beside the higher estates of electors (see ELECTOR) and princes. Each estate deliberated by itself as a college, the agreement of all three and the assent of the emperor being necessary for taking action. The best-known meetings were the Diets at Nuremberg in 1467, Worms in 1521, Speyer in 1529, and Augsburg in 1530.

After the Treaty of Westphalia (1648), which ended the Thirty Years' War, the Diet lost its legislative authority. The emperor was obliged to convoke the Diet every ten years, but these meetings, held at Regensburg (Ratisbon), were merely conferences of ambassadors from the various principalities. The Holy Roman Empire was dissolved in 1806, and the Diet gave way to the various legislatures (often called diets) of the German Confederation, the German Empire, the Weimar Republic, the Third Reich, and the postwar republics.

MARTIN GRUBERG
Wisconsin State University, Oshkosh

DIETARY LAWS are laws indicating which foods or combinations of foods may be eaten or must be abstained from, according to certain religious principles. Although such laws are generally associated with the Jewish tradition, their origin is pre-Israelitic, and their practice was known to the ancient Babylonians, Egyptians, and Hindus.

Most scholars are convinced that the dietary laws of the Old Testament, known as *Kashrut*, were established to stress holiness, discipline, or moral sensitivity, rather than for hygienic reasons. They identify which foods are *kosher*, or suitable for eating; forbidden foods are known as *trayfah*, or unfit, a term originally referring to an animal that had been torn apart by predatory beasts. The laws are specifically described in Deuteronomy 14. Listed among the "abominable" or "unclean" foods are fish without scales or fins (such as shellfish), birds of prey, insects, and reptiles. Among mammals, only those that have cloven hoofs and chew their cud are permitted; hares and pigs are among the animals specifically forbidden.

The laws of the *Kashrut* dictate not only which animals may be eaten but the method of slaughter as well. The animal must be killed by an expertly trained and religiously observant Jew (a *shohet*), using a clean, sharp knife to sever the animal's windpipe with a single stroke. Blood, as a symbol of life, cannot be eaten, and is to be drained out of the animal; traces of blood are removed by washing and salting. Animals that die from natural causes or have been killed by wild beasts cannot be eaten, because of ethical considerations.

The commandment "You shall not boil a kid in its mother's milk" (Exodus 23:19) is thought to be the origin of the Talmudic prohibition against having meat and milk or milk products at the same meal. Meat and milk products are prepared in separate pots and served on dishes that are carefully differentiated. Foods that are designated as *parve*, or neutral, such as fish, eggs, vegetables, and fruits, can be eaten with either meat or dairy dishes.

Traditional Jews—Orthodox and Conservative —continue to follow the dietary commandments. Some Reform Jews consider them as a means of separation and tend to disregard them.

The New Testament rejected dietary laws as a means of separation or of establishing religious identity. In Mark 7:19, all foods are declared clean. Food laws have been retained, however, by certain Christian sects, as well as by Muslims. Other dietary laws, seemingly unrelated to those of the Old Testament though possibly also springing from an effort to instill holiness and discipline, are found throughout the world— among Hindus, for example. See also JEWISH HISTORY AND SOCIETY—*19. Religious Traditions and Customs.*

EDWARD T. SANDROW
Rabbi, Temple Beth El, Cedarhurst, N.Y.

Further Reading: Finkelstein, Louis, *The Jews: Their History, Culture, and Religion* (New York 1949); Gaster, Theodor H., *Customs and Folkways of Jewish Life*, rev. ed. (New York 1966); Heller, Abraham M., *The Jew and His World* (New York 1965); Karp, Abraham J., *Jewish Way of Life* (Englewood Cliffs, N.J., 1962).

DIETETICS is the art and science that deals with the application of the principles of nutrition to the feeding of individuals or groups of individuals under various cultural, economic, sociological, and health conditions.

The science of dietetics deals with the nutritional needs of the body for food energy (calories), proteins, vitamins, and minerals, and relates these needs to the nutritional elements supplied by foods. It is also concerned with the nutritional needs of the body when certain diseases are present. Furthermore, modern dietetics involves a knowledge and understanding of the reactions of individuals and groups to different foods, and of the cultural, economic, psychological, and sociological factors that affect these reactions.

The art of dietetics is concerned with the knowledge and skills involved in planning diets to meet the needs of various individuals and groups. It includes the efficient and economic purchasing of food and the preparation and serving of food in an attractive and appealing manner.

CAREERS IN DIETETICS

The field of dietetics offers a wide variety of job opportunities for qualified people. The American Dietetic Association, which is the major professional organization for dietetics in the United States, is largely responsible for setting the training requirements for professional dietitians.

Opportunities. For many years the work of trained dietitians was largely confined to hospitals, particularly to the needs of patients on special diets. Gradually, the dietitian's responsibility expanded to include the feeding of all patients as well as of hospital personnel. As the profession grew, the concern of the dietitian extended to many groups outside the hospital and finally to the public as a whole.

Hospitals. Approximately 65% of all qualified dietitians are associated with hospitals. The three major branches of hospital dietetics are scientific, administrative, and educational. In a small hospital, a single dietitian may handle all three aspects of the work, but in a large hospital there may be several dietitians, each specializing in a particular branch.

The scientific, or therapeutic, area of specialization concentrates on the planning of the normal and modified diets for the individual needs of those patients for whom a physician has prescribed certain requirements. The administrative dietitian deals with the normal nutrition of the other patients and of all persons who work at the hospital. Such a dietitian plans menus that are attractive, nutritious, and economical; hires, trains, and supervises employees; buys or requisitions all food and equipment; supervises the preparation of the food; and controls the finances of the dietary department. The dietitian concerned with education teaches student nurses, patients, and employees, and in some institutions also teaches dietetic interns and medical students. In the hospital clinic, the clinic dietitian teaches and guides clinic patients, particularly those who have been placed on special diets by their physicians.

Schools. About 10% of all dietitians are employed in the administrative aspect of college and university food service. Their work is much the same as the administrative hospital dietitian, although their title may be food service director or food service manager. A relatively recent aspect of dietetics concerns the management of the school lunch service in elementary and high schools.

Business. A smaller number of dietitians, about 4%, are employed by various hotel, restaurant, and industrial food service companies. Some airlines, railroad dining-car services, and steamship companies also employ dietitians, particularly to develop menus and serving methods appropriate for the requirements of each mode of transportation.

Research. About 5% of all qualified dietitians are employed in consulting, writing, editing, and research. These specialists are employed in the home economics divisions of food equipment and utility companies, advertising agencies, and food manufacturing, processing, and distribution firms. Their work is largely promotional in nature and includes relating information on nutrition to the public so that it ties in with the firm's products, writing recipe books and standardizing recipes for publication, maintaining experimental kitchens where the firm's products are developed into menu items, conducting radio or television programs, and helping in the preparation of advertising copy.

A small but increasing number of dietitians devote their time to nutrition research in medical centers, colleges, universities, and business organizations. An advanced academic degree, with special stress on science, is necessary preparation for employment in this particular type of research work.

Instruction. College teaching, in foods, nutrition, or institution management, is the concern of about 10% of all dietitians. Advanced academic training to the level of a master's degree or a doctoral degree is required for most teaching opportunities in colleges.

Community Work. A growing field in dietetics is that of community nutrition. About 6% of all dietitians are engaged in this work, which is devoted to helping members of the community live healthier lives through an understanding of nutrition. Workers in this area are recommended to have postgraduate work in nutrition as well as public health and social work in order to qualify as nutritionists. They are employed by international, national, state, county, and city health agencies, both public and private.

Community nutritionists are concerned with translating scientific information into simple specific instructions that the public can understand and follow. Most of their time is spent giving talks and demonstrations, and preparing written material on nutrition. They also serve as consultants to physicians, nurses, dentists, and social workers.

Training. Preparation for work in the field of dietetics has been carefully outlined by the American Dietetic Association. In addition to requiring certain academic studies, the association strongly recommends a hospital internship or advanced academic degrees in nutrition or public health for all students wanting to become dietitians.

Academic Requirements. Students preparing for the profession of dietetics must receive a bachelor's degree from an accredited college or university and must complete, either during or after their college years, certain courses required by the Executive Board of the American Dietetic Association. These academic requirements represent a wide variety of subjects, including human physiology, bacteriology, chemistry, food selection, meal preparation and planning, and nutrition. In addition to the basic course requirements, the student may take certain other courses to prepare for a specialty in dietetics.

Internship. After receiving a bachelor's degree with a suitable background of courses, the student dietitian continues his training with a hospital internship. The internship enables the student dietitian to put into practice under skilled guidance what he has learned in college and to acquire further knowledge and skill before he can be qualified for professional work.

There are about 60 hospitals in the United States that offer dietetic internships, and nine different internship programs are available. In most of these programs the emphasis is placed on hospital food service administration and therapeutics dietetics. However, in one type of program only administration is emphasized, and in another program only nutrition education and therapeutics are stressed.

Most internship programs are one year in length; four programs are longer. Three of these programs offer a coordinated internship and master's degree program in various branches of dietetics. One program is combined with training at the master's degree level in public health nutrition, and another internship provides both a bachelor's degree in medical dietetics and an internship in a four-year period. Most internship programs provide the student with an educational stipend as well as sufficient funds to cover expenses.

In all internships, the student dietitians attend classes and seminars and participate in the planning, preparing, and serving phases of food production. The hospital dietetic interns also attend medical conferences, visit patients, and may participate in community health programs as well. Upon completion of the internship, with the recommendation of members of the American Dietetic Association, the student becomes a fullfledged professional dietitian with the right to membership in the organization as a certification of his readiness to contribute to the profession of dietetics.

HISTORY

The field of dietetics has developed so much since World War I that it is sometimes regarded as a recent field even though its beginnings can be traced back to the dawn of medical history. The Ebers papyrus, which was written in Egypt around 1500 B.C., contains what may be considered to be the first recorded diet prescription. The ancient Greek philosopher Pythagoras, who lived during the 6th century B.C., was the first to advocate the exact measurement of food and drink, and the Greek physician Hippocrates (c. 460–c. 377 B.C.) was among the first to emphasize the treating of disease through diet. According to the Roman encyclopedist Aulus Cornelium Celsus, who lived during the 1st century A.D., diseases could be divided into three groups: diseases treated by diet, diseases treated by medicines, and diseases treated by manual manipulation.

During the Renaissance, the English scientist Thomas Moffett (1553–1604) defined diet as "an orderly, due course observed in the use of bodily nourishment for the Preservation, Recovery, and Continuance of the Health of Mankind." Moffett, as well as others, speculated on the role of food in the cause, cure, and prevention of disease, but it was not until the development of the science of nutrition, which began in the late 1700's, that the study of dietetics emerged as a science.

The art of dietetics began with the work of Florence Nightingale (1820–1910), who is also credited as the founder of the nursing profession. In 1854, while at Scutari, Turkey, during the Crimean War, Miss Nightingale established two extra "diet kitchens" and arranged more suitable facilities for preparing food for the sick. In her books *Notes on Nursing* (1860) and *Notes on Hospitals* (1859), she stressed the importance of the proper cooking of foods for the sick and the preparation of a variety of foods for nurses. From the time of Miss Nightingale's first nursing efforts until the 1890's, the nursing profession was largely responsible for the preparation of foods in hospitals, and the nurse to whom this work was assigned was called a "dietist."

United States. The basis for the profession of dietetics in the United States was established from the 1870's to the 1890's, when several cooking schools were founded. Mrs. Sarah Tyson Rorer (1847–1937), who presided over one of these cooking schools, is believed to qualify as the first American dietitian. Around 1890, several hospitals began placing their kitchens in the charge of women who had been trained at these schools. Johns Hopkins Hospital in Baltimore was the first hospital to use such a woman to teach its nurses how to prepare food for patients. Shortly afterward, another hospital, the Presbyterian Hospital in Philadelphia, hired a graduate of a cooking school to instruct its nurses in the preparation of food for patients. This woman was known as the superintendent of diet. It is believed that the term "dietitian" came into use in 1899 and was applied to a person who specialized in the study of food and could meet the demands of the medical profession for implementing prescribed diets.

A major factor in the development and recognition of modern dietetics in the United States has been the American Dietetic Association. During World War I, Americans were faced with the problem of conserving food, and the need for trained food experts arose. In response to this need, the American Dietetic Association was founded in October 1917. It was established by an organization of 58 dietitians whose purpose was "to improve the nutritional status of human beings; to raise the standards of dietary service; and to foster cooperation between members and workers in allied fields." Today, the American Dietetic Association has a membership of more than 20,000 dietitians and is largely responsible for setting the standards of the dietetics profession. Its headquarters is in Chicago, Ill.

CHARLOTTE YOUNG
School of Nutrition, Cornell University

Bibliography

American Dietetic Association, *Dietetics as a Profession* (Chicago 1966).
American Dietetic Association, *Requirements for Membership in the American Dietetic Association* (Chicago 1965).
Barber, Mary I., ed., *History of the American Dietetic Association, 1917–1959* (Philadelphia 1959).
Pike, R. L., and Brown, M. L., *Nutrition: An Integrated Approach* (New York 1967).
Robinson, C. H., *Proudfit-Robinson's Normal and Therapeutic Nutrition*, 13th ed. (New York 1967).
Wilson, E. D., Fisher, K. H., and Fuqua, M. E., *Principles of Nutrition*, 2d ed. (New York 1965).

JOHN SPRINGER/BETTMANN

MARLENE DIETRICH with Charles Boyer in a scene from the motion picture *The Garden of Allah* (1936).

DIETHYLSTILBESTROL, dī-eth-əl-stil-bes′trōl, or D. E. S., a synthetic estrogen, or sex hormone, formerly used to help prevent threatened miscarriages. Between 500,000 and 2 million pregnant women were given D. E. S., or a hormone of similar composition, in the years 1940 to 1971. In the latter year the use of D. E. S. was found to be associated with the later appearance, in female offspring exposed to the drug in their mother's womb, of a type of cancer called clear cell cancer of the vagina. In the same year the Registry of Clear Cell Adenocarcinoma of the Genital Tract in Young Females was established to keep track of the occurrence of these tumors in women born in 1940 or later. By February 1978 the condition had been reported in approximately 360 patients, 60% of whom were found to have been exposed to D. E. S., or a similar estrogen, before the 18th week of their mothers' pregnancies. By the 18th week the development of the genital tract is complete in female babies, and from then on the tract is much less likely to be harmed by drugs or other agents. Clear cell cancer is rare, even in women exposed to D. E. S. before they were born.

D. E. S. also has been associated with vaginal adenosis, a benign condition affecting the upper front wall of the vagina and the cervix. Vaginal adenosis is common in women exposed to D. E. S. prior to the 18th week of their mothers' pregnancy. While it sometimes occurs together with clear cell cancer, no case of proven progression from adenosis to cancer has been reported.

Vaginal adenosis usually requires no treatment, but patients with this condition should be kept under close observation. They should have vaginal and cytological examinations every six months to one year, so that if a malignant change should occur it can be diagnosed and treated promptly. In addition to such changes in the vagina and cervix, some patients with vaginal adenosis develop uterine abnormalities that often can be detected by special X-ray examinations. Clear cell cancer of the vagina is treated with radiotherapy or radical surgery, depending on how far the disease has progressed.

DENIS CAVANAUGH, M. D.
Director of Gynecologic Oncology, University of South Florida College of Medicine

DIETRICH, dē′trĭкн, **Marlene** (1904–   ), German-American film actress and singer, who projected a mysterious, sensual image throughout a long career. She was born Marie Magdalene von Losch in Berlin, Germany, on Dec. 27, 1904. She studied violin until a wrist injury made a musical career impossible. Deciding to be an actress, she had minor roles on the stage and in films from 1923 to 1929 but attracted little attention until the director Josef von Sternberg cast her as Lola Lola, a nightclub entertainer, in the German film *The Blue Angel* (1930). Her performance brought her worldwide fame.

Marlene Dietrich and von Sternberg made numerous Hollywood films together, among them *Morocco* (1930), *Shanghai Express* (1932), *Blond Venus* (1932), and *The Scarlet Empress* (1934). Her later pictures included *Destry Rides again* (1939), *A Foreign Affair* (1948), *Witness for the Prosecution* (1957), and *Judgment at Nuremberg* (1961).

Marlene Dietrich became an American citizen in 1937. Noted for her throaty voice and blasé singing style, she made many recordings and toured extensively as an entertainer—in nightclubs and concerts.

HOWARD SUBER
University of California at Los Angeles

DIETRICH VON BERN, dē′trĭкн fôn bern, a heroic figure in medieval Germanic literature. Historically he corresponds to Theodoric the Great, king of the Ostrogoths (reigned 474–526). However, many of the tales about Dietrich were purely fictional, emphasizing his supernatural ancestry, his exploits against giants, trolls, and other formidable adversaries, and his ultimate disappearance on a black horse. After years of exile from his kingdom of Bern (Verona), Dietrich returns with a Hun army to defeat and kill his enemy Ermanarich. His adventures were the subject of a number of German songs and of the 13th century Icelandic *Thidrekssaga*.

DIEU ET MON DROIT, dyü ā môn drwȧ (French for "God and my right"), the motto of the arms of England, first assumed by Richard I, who flung this battle cry at his French adversaries in the engagement at Gisors, France, in 1198. It was revived by Edward III in 1340, when he claimed the French throne. Except during the reigns of Elizabeth I and Anne, who used the motto *Semper eadem*, and of William III, who used *Je maintiendray* as his motto (with *Dieu et mon droit* on the great seal), it has remained the royal motto of England.

DIEZ, dēts, **Friedrich Christian** (1794–1876), German philologist, who laid the foundations of Romance linguistics. He was born in Giessen, Hesse-Darmstadt, on March 15, 1794. As a result of a meeting with Goethe in 1818, Diez became interested in Provençal literature and took up the study of Romance languages. In 1822 he became a lecturer at Bonn University, where he was appointed professor of modern languages in 1830.

Diez devoted most of his life to two great works on Romance languages—a grammar (3 vols., 1836–1843) and a dictionary (1853), both of which were translated into English. He died in Bonn on May 29, 1876.

DIFFERENTIAL CALCULUS. See CALCULUS.

DIFFERENTIAL EQUATIONS are equations that involve derivatives. The solution of a differential equation is a function or a collection of functions.

The following is a somewhat oversimplified example. Suppose an object is dropped from the top of a building; let s be the distance in feet that the object falls in t seconds. The velocity of the object may be written $v = ds/dt$ where ds/dt means the instantaneous rate of change of distance with respect to time. Because the object falls with a continually increasing velocity, one may express the velocity by the mathematical statement $ds/dt = 32t$, where 32 is the acceleration caused by gravity. This equation is by definition a differential equation. Since the right side is a function of the independent variable t, one can use the techniques of the calculus to integrate at once and state that the *general solution* is $s = 16t^2 + C$, where C thus far is any constant. If we agree to measure the distance fallen from the spot at which the object is when $t = 0$, then $s = 0$ when $t = 0$. If we substitute these values, called *initial conditions*, we find that $C = 0$, so that the function $s = 16t^2$ is the solution. From it we can calculate how far the body falls in any number of seconds.

The differential equation we have just examined is commonly considered to fall within the province of the calculus rather than of differential equations because the solution is obtained at once by a direct integration. However, the motion of pendulums, the motion of the planets under the gravitational attraction of the sun, the shapes assumed by rods and bars when subjected to pressures at the ends, the propagation of sound in space, and many other physical phenomena, all involve more complicated differential equations that cannot be solved by direct integration. Significant differential equations are generally the mathematical statements of fundamental physical principles.

Ordinary Differential Equations. One such principle is known as Newton's law of cooling. It states that the rate of change of the temperature of an object is continuous and proportional to the difference between the temperature of the object and that of the surrounding medium. Let us suppose that the object is initially at a temperature of $100°$ and that it is immersed in an atmosphere kept at the constant temperature of $0°$. Now the object loses temperature continuously. The rate of change of temperature T with time t is denoted by dT/dt. Since the difference between the temperature of the object and the surrounding medium is always $T - 0$, or T, Newton's law states that $dT/dt = -kT$. Here k is the proportionality constant, and the negative sign enters because the rate of change is negative, that is, T decreases.

This differential equation differs from the previous one in that the right-hand side is a function of the dependent variable (T) instead of the independent variable. There is a systematic procedure for solving a differential equation of this form, but mathematicians often can avoid a laborious procedure by using their knowledge of functions encountered in the calculus. One can ask what function possesses the property that its derivative equals $-k$ times the function itself. The only such function is the exponential function e^{-kt}. Thus the answer is $T = De^{-kt}$, where D is any constant and e is the number that is approximately 2.718, also known as the base of the Naperian logarithm system. We can determine D, as before, from the initial conditions. If time is measured from the instant when $T = 100$, then $T = 100$ when $t = 0$. If we substitute these values in the answer and use the fact that $e^0 = 1$, then the final solution is $T = 100e^{-kt}$. The quantity k depends on the object. Some objects lose heat rapidly (k large) and others slowly (k small). The precise value of k can be determined by measuring the temperature at one additional instant of time, say one minute after $t = 0$.

The differential equation for the cooling of a body is called a *first-order differential* equation because the derivative that enters into it (dT/dt) is a first derivative.

Second-Order Differential Equation. Let us examine another differential equation that arose in the work of the physicist Robert Hooke, who studied the action of springs for the purpose of designing a spring-driven watch. Imagine a frictionless table on which lies a spring fastened to the table at one end with a weight of mass m attached to the other end of the spring (see diagram). If the spring is extended or compressed by the weight, the spring exerts what is called a restoring force. Hooke discovered the physical principle still known as Hooke's law, which states that the restoring force is proportional to the amount by which the spring is extended or compressed. If the origin of the x-axis is at the free end of the unstretched spring, and x is the position of the weight at any time, then it is clear that the force exerted on the weight will be to the left (or negative) when x is positive, and conversely. This force can then be written as $F = -kx$, in which k is a constant.

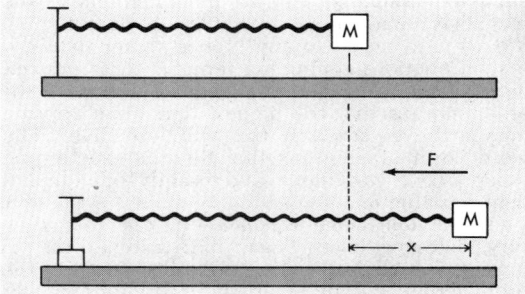

To obtain the differential equation of the motion of the weight we must call upon a second physical principle, namely, Newton's second law of motion. This states that when a force is applied to an object, the force equals the mass of the object times the acceleration. In symbols, $F = ma$. The force in the case of the weight on the spring is the restoring force. Moreover, the acceleration, as one learns in the calculus, is d^2x/dt^2. Hence the differential equation for the force exerted by the spring is

$$m(d^2x/dt^2) = -kx.$$

This is a second-order differential equation, and there is a systematic technique for solving it. However, in this case, too, the mathematician can ask what function possesses the property that (ignoring the k and m for the moment) its second derivative is the negative of the function. The answer is $\sin t + \cos t$. To take into account the presence of the k and m one modifies these functions slightly so that the solution becomes

$$x = A \sin \frac{k}{m} t + B \cos \frac{k}{m} t.$$

The quantities A and B are any constants. However, their values can be determined if one makes some agreement on how time is measured. For example, if time is measured from the instant the weight is released, then x equals some length x_0 when $t = 0$. Since $\sin 0 = 0$, and $\cos 0 = 1$, this means that B must equal x_0. If the spring is simply released (not given some initial impulse), it can be shown that $A = 0$. Thus the final solution is $x = x_0 \cos \frac{k}{m} t$. Here x_0 is called the amplitude of the motion. It is of great significance physically, as the mathematical solution shows, that the motion is oscillatory, and the period of one complete oscillation is $2\pi \frac{m}{k}$.

Hooke's results became the basis for the design of all pocket watches.

Linear nth-Order Differential Equation. The variety of differential equations is considerable, and to avoid seeking separate methods of solving each one as it arises mathematicians have sought and devised methods of treating general forms that comprise numerous physically interesting cases. The most important single class of equation is

$$A \frac{d^n y}{dx^n} + B \frac{d^{n-1} y}{dx^{n-1}} + \ldots + M \frac{dy}{dx} + Ny = f(x),$$

where the coefficients $A, B, \ldots N$ may be either constants or functions of x. This equation is known as the linear nth-order ordinary differential equation. The term "linear" refers to the fact that none of the variables $y, dy/dx, \ldots d^n y/dx^n$ are raised to any higher power than the first. Equations containing terms such as $y\,dy/dx$ or $(dy/dx)^2$ are called nonlinear. The term "nth-order" means that the highest derivative appearing in the equation is the nth derivative. The word "ordinary" means that there is exactly one independent variable x and exactly one dependent variable y.

Partial Differential Equation. In the 18th century, mathematicians began to investigate the vibrations of strings (such as violin strings), the propagation in space of the vibrations of air caused by the vibrating string, the oscillation of columns of air in organ pipes and wind instruments of various shapes, and the flow of liquids and gases. In the 19th century they turned primarily to electrical and magnetic phenomena. After unearthing the appropriate physical principles, the mathematical physicists were unable to formulate the differential equations for the respective phenomena. However, all of these problems differ in an essential respect from the ordinary differential equations described above. In both of the above examples, once the time was known the dependent variable (temperature in one case, distance in the other) was uniquely determined. However, to study the motion of the vibrating string one wishes to know the displacement of all points on the string as a function of time. That is, we need to know not only the time but also which point on the string we are discussing before we can determine the dependent variable (displacement). To specify the various points one regards the straight line segment

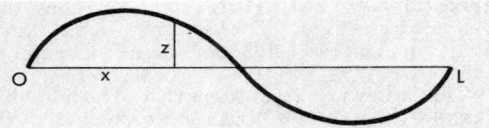

formed by the string when it is at rest as a coordinate axis, and to each point from 0 to L one attaches an x-value that is its distance from 0 (see diagram). The displacement of that point at any particular time t is the length denoted by z. Then the displacement of the entire string is given by z as a function of x and t. Here x and t are the independent variables, and z is the dependent variable. The differential equation that describes the motion of the string is

$\partial^2 z / \partial t^2 = a^2 (\partial^2 z / \partial x^2)$, where a is a constant.

The special symbol ∂ denotes that the second derivative of z is being taken with respect to one variable only, the other being treated as a constant. Both $\frac{\partial^2 z}{\partial t^2}$ and $\frac{\partial^2 z}{\partial x^2}$ are called partial derivatives, and the differential equation is called a partial differential equation. There are many classes of such equations, just as there are of ordinary differential equations. Once again, the solution to a particular problem involving partial differential equations depends on supplementary information analogous to the initial conditions in the examples of ordinary differential equations described above. In the case of partial differential equations, however, the supplementary information must usually be more extensive; it consists of both initial and boundary conditions. Thus, in the problem of the vibrating string one must take into account that the ends of the string are fixed at all times; these are boundary conditions. The initial conditions in this problem give information as to how the string is set into motion at $t = 0$.

Systems of Differential Equations. Beyond individual differential equations there are systems of differential equations, just as there can be systems of algebraic equations. These systems will consist of two or more interrelated differential equations involving two or more dependent variables. An example of such a system is Maxwell's equations summarizing all electromagnetic phenomena.

Importance of Differential Equations. The creation of methods for solving ordinary and partial differential equations has stimulated a vast amount of mathematical work. The subject is considered by many to be the heart of mathematics, and it also comprises the substance of the major theories of physics, since most important physical principles, when mathematically formulated, appear as differential equations.

MORRIS KLINE
Courant Institute, New York University

Bibliography

Boyce, William E., and Di Prima, Richard C., *Elementary Differential Equations and Boundary Value Problems* (New York 1965).

Brauer, Fred, and Nobel, John A., *Elementary Differential Equations: Principles, Problems and Solutions* (New York 1968).

Greenspan, Donald, *Introduction to Partial Differential Equations* (New York 1961).

Leighton, Walter, *Ordinary Differential Equations* (New York 1952).

Ritger, Paul D., and Rose, Nicholas J., *Differential Equations with Applications* (New York 1968).

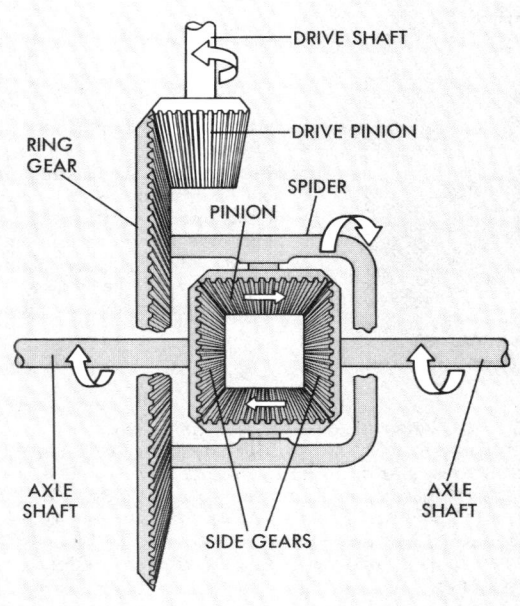

A DIFFERENTIAL GEAR is shown operating while an automobile is rounding a left curve. It allows the right axle to rotate faster than the left.

DIFFERENTIAL GEAR, an assembly of gears that connects a divided shaft and permits the two sections of the shaft to rotate at different speeds or varying relative speeds. The most common application of the differential gear is in the automobile differential. It connects the divided rear axle, giving equal driving force to the two rear wheels while permitting them to rotate at different speeds when the automobile rounds a curve and the outer wheel tracks a longer arc than the inner wheel. This prevents undue slippage of the tires on the pavement, which would cause excessive tire wear, and reduces strain on the axle.

An ordinary automobile differential is shown in the accompanying diagram. The driving wheels are mounted on the outer ends of the divided rear axle. Power is transmitted to them from the drive shaft through the differential. As the drive shaft rotates, its pinion gear turns the ring gear and the spider, which is rigidly attached to the ring gear. As the spider rotates, its pinion gears turn the side gears, which are rigidly fixed to the inner ends of the divided rear axle.

When the automobile is moving straight ahead, the side gears and the spider's pinion gears do not move relatively to each other but rotate as a unit. However, when the automobile is rounding a curve, the side gears turn at different speeds, allowing one wheel to turn faster than the other. The difference in the speeds of the side gears is compensated for by the spider's pinion gears, which rotate so that the increase in speed of one side gear is offset by a corresponding decrease in speed of the other. The spider's pinion gears rotate at speeds that are the algebraic sum of the rotation speeds of the side gears.

JOSEPH DATSKO, *University of Michigan*

DIFFERENTIAL GEOMETRY. See GEOMETRY—7. *Differential Geometry*.

DIFFERENTIAL PSYCHOLOGY is the study of psychological differences between individuals and between groups. Study of such differences has been greatly advanced by the use of statistical techniques. Information on the amount, causes, and effects of individual differences is essential in fields such as education and employment managing. See also EDUCATION—10. *Educational Psychology;* PSYCHOLOGY—*Special Psychological Fields*.

DIFFERENTIATION, in embryology, is the process by which undifferentiated embryonic material gradually changes and becomes specialized for adult structure and function. The early changes that determine the general form of the developing embryo are known as *morphogenesis;* the later changes that result in tissues specialized for a specific function in an organ are known as *histogenesis.* See also EMBRYOLOGY; PLANTS AND PLANT SCIENCE—3. *Embryology*.

DIFFRACTION, the deflection and subsequent spreading of a beam of radiation when the beam grazes the edge of an obstacle or passes through a narrow aperture. Diffraction applies to radiation in the form of light waves, sound waves, and all other kinds of waves. Scientists make use of diffraction effects in spectroscopic work and in studies of the atomic structure of solids.

History. The first observation of diffraction is attributed to Francesco Grimaldi (1618–1663), who discovered it by observing sunlight passed through a pinhole aperture. An explanation of diffraction was furnished by Christian Huygens (1629–1695); according to Huygens' principle, the progress of a light wave can be predicted by assuming that each point in a wave front acts as the source of a secondary wavelet that spreads out in all directions. The envelope of all the secondary waves produced by all of the points is the new wave front. This principle not only explains diffraction but also the basic laws of refraction and reflection.

Diffraction of Light. Diffraction is easily demonstrated by using a point source of light, an object, and a white screen. When the object is placed between the light source and the screen, the shadow cast by the object is not perfectly sharp because some of the light spreads into the geometric shadow region (see figure on the following page).

When an opaque partition containing a small pinhole or slit is used, the light from a point source spreads out after passing through the slit. In this case, the finer the slit, the greater is the angle of spread.

When the aperture consists of a number of regularly spaced openings, as in a fine mesh screen, a combination of diffraction and interference occurs. The light passing through the screen is broken up into a definite pattern, and each part of the pattern is dispersed into a spectrum of colors. Optical diffraction gratings for spectroscopy make use of this effect. Such gratings are made by ruling many fine lines on a glass plate, typically 50,000 or more over a width of 2 or 3 inches (5 or 7.6 cm). The parallelism and spacing of the rulings must be accurate within a few millionths of an inch to be useful for precise spectroscopic work.

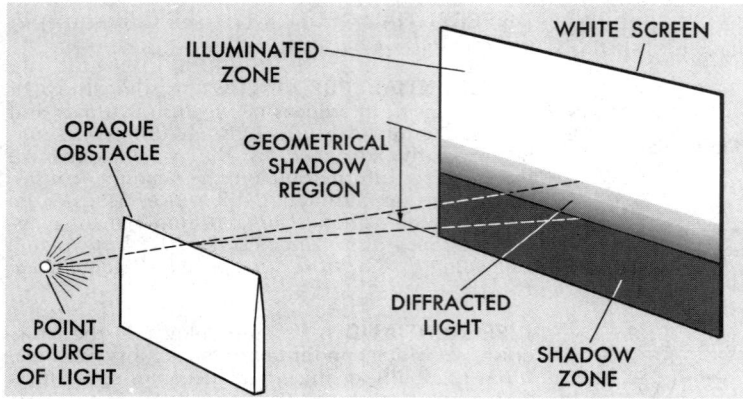

DIFFRACTION OF LIGHT

When a light beam from a point source grazes the edge of the opaque obstacle, some light rays are deflected and spread downward, illuminating a part of the region in back of the opaque obstacle.

Diffraction of X-Rays. In a crystalline solid, the atoms occur in a regular periodic arrangement called a lattice. The lattice acts much the same as a grating when radiation passes through the crystal or is reflected from its surface; however, the crystal structure must be studied with very short wavelength radiation, namely, X-rays, because of the extremely small spacing between adjacent rows of atoms. The precise arrangement of atoms in a crystal is now known as a result of X-ray diffraction studies.

Diffraction of Electrons. Diffraction effects are also observed when a beam of electrons is sent through matter. Electron diffraction, like X-ray diffraction, is useful in the study of the atomic makeup of solids. See also LIGHT—*1. Introduction* (Diffraction) and *5. Instruments and Applications* (Diffraction); X-RAYS—*1. Physics of X-Rays*.

GRANT R. FOWLES
University of Utah

DIFFUSION, dif-ū′zhən, is the spontaneous spreading or movement of matter caused by the random motion of molecules. Diffusion occurs down a concentration gradient—that is, the molecules move from a region where they are in high concentration to areas in which their concentration is lower.

Diffusion occurs most rapidly in gases and at a much slower rate in liquids. Diffusion may also occur in solids; this is possible because of imperfections in crystal lattices that allow atoms to move around one another and change places. However, the rate is so slow that two solids show no visible signs of mixing even after years of close contact.

The rate of diffusion is governed by the concentration gradient. The greater the difference in concentration between two areas, the more rapidly molecules diffuse from the area of the higher to the lower concentration. The presence of various types of forces, such as electrical and magnetic fields, may also strongly influence the movement of the molecules.

The diffusion rate is also directly related to temperature—an increase in temperature increases the diffusion rate because it causes the molecules to move faster. In gases, the diffusion rate is inversely proportional to molecular weight because light molecules travel faster than heavy ones. This phenomenon is of practical importance and is used to separate the isotopes of uranium, ^{235}U and ^{238}U.

HAROLD F. WALTON
University of Colorado

DIGESTION, dī-jes′chən, is the breakdown and conversion of food into materials that can be absorbed and assimilated into the body. The following discussion is limited to a consideration of human digestion. For information about digestion in other animals, see ANATOMY, COMPARATIVE—*Body Systems of Vertebrates* (Digestive System).

As food passes through the digestive tract, it is broken down mechanically and chemically into smaller and smaller particles. The food is acted upon by digestive secretions from the salivary glands, stomach, liver, pancreas, and small intestine.

Unabsorbed residues pass through the small intestine into the large intestine, where they are stored for variable periods before being eliminated from the body. Most of the digestive process is controlled by a complex series of reflexes and by hormones produced in various parts of the gastrointestinal tract.

The chemical phase of digestion involves a series of hydrolytic reactions—all catalyzed by specific enzymes—in which the nutrient molecules are split with water. Water is an important part of the digestive process. It acts as a solvent as well as being one of the main reactants. As a result of digestion, proteins are broken down into amino acids, carbohydrates are broken down into glucose, and fats into fatty acids and glycerol. These comparatively simple substances are used by the body for energy, for replacement of cells, and for growth.

Digestion in the Mouth. Digestion begins with chewing, which softens the food and exposes it to the digestive enzyme produced by the salivary glands. The food is also mixed with saliva, which increases the water content and facilitates transport of the food mass through the esophagus.

Saliva is produced by three pairs of salivary glands: the parotid glands, which lie in front and below the ears; the submaxillary glands, which are under the jaw; and the sublingual glands, which lie under the forepart of the floor of the mouth.

A watery secretion is produced by the parotid glands and a mucous secretion by the submaxillary and sublingual glands. The total amount of saliva produced daily in man ranges from 1,000 to 1,500 ml (30–45 oz).

The most important digestive component of saliva is the enzyme amylase. Salivary amylase, or ptyalin, breaks down starch and glycogen molecules, first to dextrins, which are complex polysaccharides, and finally to a mixture of maltose

DIGESTION

DIGESTIVE SECRETIONS AND THEIR FUNCTIONS

Secretion	Site of Production	Site of Activity	Action
Salivary amylase	Mouth	Mouth and stomach	Breaks down starch and glycogen to glucose and maltose.
Gastric Juice	Stomach	Stomach, small intestine	
Hydrochloric acid			Activates pepsin and secretin.
Pepsin			Breaks down protein to peptides.
Gastrin	Stomach	Stomach	Stimulates gastric secretion.
Secretin	Small intestine	Pancreas	Stimulates pancreatic secretion.
Pancreozymin	Small intestine	Pancreas	Stimulates pancreatic secretion.
Cholecystokinin	Small intestine	Gallbladder	Stimulates contraction of gallbladder.
Intracellular intestinal enzymes	Small intestine	Small intestine	
Peptidases			Break down peptides to amino acids.
Lipases			Break down long-chain fatty acids.
Disaccharidases			Break down sugars.
Trypsin	Pancreas	Small intestine	Breaks down proteins to peptides.
Chymotrypsin	Pancreas	Small intestine	Breaks down proteins to peptides.
Elastase	Pancreas	Small intestine	Breaks down peptides to amino acids.
Procarboxypeptidase	Pancreas	Small intestine	Breaks down peptides to amino acids.
Pancreatic lipase	Pancreas	Small intestine	Breaks down fats to gylcerides, glycerol, and fatty acids.
Pancreatic amylase	Pancreas	Small intestine	Breaks down starch, glycogen, and dextrins to sugars.
Bile	Liver	Small intestine	Breaks down and absorbs fats.

and glucose. Saliva also flushes the mouth and makes possible the tasting of food.

Swallowing. Food that is mixed with saliva and chewed becomes a *bolus* (a soft ball of food) ready to be swallowed. The food is moved backward in the mouth by the tongue toward the pharynx (the back of the throat). As soon as the bolus of food reaches the back wall of the pharynx, neuromuscular reflexes cause the muscles of the pharynx to contract; the contraction propels the food bolus into the esophagus.

During the process of swallowing, breathing stops because a flap of tissue—the epiglottis—covers the upper opening of the windpipe, or trachea, and thus prevents food from entering the lungs.

The Esophagus. The esophagus is a simple tubular structure consisting of two layers of muscular tissue and extending from the pharynx to the stomach. The upper third of the esophagus has striated muscle similar to the voluntary muscles of the extremities; the lower portion consists of smooth muscle. Both ends of the esophagus are closed by sphincter muscles (rings of muscle). The upper esophageal sphincter is located at the level of the larynx, while the lower sphincter is at the junction of the esophagus and the stomach.

Food is propelled down the esophagus by a wave of contraction. Passage through the esophagus takes approximately 8 seconds. Early in the act of swallowing, the sphincter between the esophagus and the stomach relaxes so that the bolus of food can pass from the esophagus into the stomach. After the food enters the stomach, the sphincter closes, thereby preventing the food from reentering the esophagus.

Digestion in the Stomach. The stomach is a muscular J-shaped organ that is connected to the esophagus and the small intestine. It is separated from the small intestine by the pyloric sphincter muscle.

The stomach has both motor and secretory functions. The upper portion of the stomach serves as a storage organ, permitting further digestion of carbohydrates by salivary amylase. The motor functions of the stomach include division of the food into smaller particles and propulsion of the contents from the stomach into the small intestine. Little motor activity occurs in the upper part of the stomach. However, in the lower half the contractions exert powerful pressures on the contents of the stomach, both kneading them and mixing them.

The lower, or antral, section of the stomach has a pumping mechanism that allows a small amount of the gastric contents to be discharged into the first portion of the small intestine, with each contraction. After consumption of a meal it takes several hours for the stomach to empty completely.

The tissues of the stomach lining secrete gastric juice, which consists of water, hydrochloric acid, and pepsin and other enzymes; it also contains mucus, which forms a protective layer over the cells of the gastric mucosa. The glands that secrete mucus are in the upper part of the stomach. The pyloric glands, which are in the lower part of the stomach, secrete a hormone called gastrin that stimulates gastric secretion. The fundic glands, which are found in the mid-portion of the stomach, consist of parietal cells, chief cells, and mucous neck cells. Parietal cells secrete hydrochloric acid; the chief cells produce pepsinogen, a precursor, or inactive form, of the digestive enzyme pepsin. Pepsinogen is activated into pepsin by hydrochloric acid. Pepsin attacks proteins and breaks them down into smaller units called peptides.

Gastric secretion is controlled by the central nervous system and by the hormone gastrin. Gastrin is a polypeptide that is secreted into the bloodstream, from which it is returned to the stomach and stimulates the secretion of acid. Gastrin formation is inhibited when the concentration of acid in the lower part of the stomach becomes sufficiently great. The secretion of gastric juice is inhibited by the hormone secretin, which is secreted by the cells of the lining of the small intestine.

The control of the central nervous system over the secretions of the stomach is through the vagus nerve (one of the cranial nerves originating in the brain). Secretion can be initiated by the thought of eating, but normally there is little or no secretion between meals. However, secretion is markedly increased in response to the entrance of food into the stomach. When the products of gastric digestion are in the proper form, they are discharged into the small intestine. Food in this stage of digestion is called *chyme*. Chyme is highly acid because of the presence of the hydrochloric acid of gastric juice.

Digestion in the Small Intestine. The small intestine is the most important part of the digestive tract. Digestion is completed in the intestine and the nutrients are absorbed into the cells of the intestinal lining; from these cells the nutrients are absorbed into the bloodstream and lymphatic system and carried to all the cells of the body.

The small intestine is divided into three parts. The uppermost section, the duodenum, is the shortest and widest part of the small intestine and is from 20 to 25 cm (8–10 inches) long. The jejunum, or middle section, and the ileum, or terminal section, have a combined length of from 7 to 9 meters (21 to 27 feet). There are both anatomic differences and physiologic differences between the various parts of the small intestine.

The inner surface of the small intestine, particularly in the duodenum and upper jejunum, is covered with fingerlike projections called villi, which greatly increase the absorptive surface of the intestinal lining. There are about 5 million villi in the intestine of man. The villi are covered by a layer of epithelial cells. The border of these cells resembles a brush and is made up of hundreds of microvilli. These structures also increase the absorptive surface of the small intestine.

In the depressions between the villi are the openings of small glands called the crypts of Lieberkühn. These structures are the site of much mitotic activity, and it is thought that they produce new cells to replace those that are worn off or shed from the villi. The duodenum also contains glandular structures called Brunner's glands, which secrete mucus. These glands are located around the area where the pancreatic juice and bile enter the duodenum, and the large amount of mucus they produce protects the intestinal wall from the action of the digestive juices.

The duodenum is the site for the mixing of food from the stomach with secretions from the liver and pancreas. Both the duodenum and jejunum are characterized by circular folds of tissue that extend into the intestinal lumen. These folds, which are known as valvulae conniventes, are covered with villi. In addition to increasing the surface area of the intestine these structures form a transverse barrier that slows down the passage of food through the small intestine.

The jejunum is the main site for the homogenization and mixing of the intestinal contents and the formation of intestinal enzymes. It is also an important site for absorption of nutrients, including sugars, amino acids, and fats.

The ileum is the site of absorption of vitamin B_{12}, bile acids, and remaining portions of amino acids and fats. Both the jejunum and ileum are responsible for the absorption of water and electrolytes.

The hormones secretin and pancreozymin, both of which stimulate pancreatic secretion, are produced in the small intestine, along with cholecystokinin, which stimulates the gallbladder. In addition to the hormones, the intestinal wall is the site of formation and storage of histamine and serotonin. Histamine is produced in the mast cells of the gastrointestinal tract and may play a role in gastric secretion. Serotonin comes from the argentaffine cells. It stimulates intestinal motility, and it may be a regulator of the transit of food through the intestine.

The cells lining the small intestine contain the intestinal enzymes. Some of the cells are shed into the intestinal lumen, or cavity, and their enzymes become mixed with the contents of the intestine, thereby adding to the digestive capacities of the intestinal juice. Some digestion, particularly of carbohydrates, occurs with the cells of the intestinal lining after the nutrients have been absorbed from the lumen. The intracellular enzymes include peptidases, lipases, and disaccharidases. The peptidases are responsible for splitting of peptides into absorbable amino acids; the lipases attack long-chain fatty acids; and the disaccharidases act on various types of sugars.

The motor activities of the small intestine mix the food and facilitate action by the digestive enzymes; slow the downward movement of chyme; and facilitate intestinal absorption. The most characteristic form of motor activity of the small intestine is that of segmentation, in which adjacent segments alternately contract and relax, thereby kneading and mixing the chyme. The movement of chyme through the small intestine is very slow; it takes about 4 hours for a meal to pass through.

The Pancreas. The pancreas secretes important enzymes and electrolytes into the small intestine. It is connected to the duodenum by the main pancreatic duct; a sphincter muscle separates the two parts. Pancreatic secretion is controlled primarily by hormonal stimulation. The two hormones that effect the pancreas are secretin and pancreozymin, which are secreted by the small intestine. Secretin is a polypeptide formed in the tissues of the duodenal lining when the acid contents of the stomach enter the small intestine. The hormone is then absorbed into the bloodstream and carried to the pancreas, where it stimulates the pancreas to produce a watery juice that is high in bicarbonate but low in enzyme content. The high content of bicarbonate is of great importance for neutralizing the acidity of the gastric juice in the food from the stomach. Pancreozymin, another hormone formed in the duodenum, stimulates the release of enzymes from the pancreas. Pancreatic secretion is also stimulated by the passage through the duodenum of the breakdown products of protein. Gastrin also increases the output of enzymes from the pancreas. The average daily production of pancreatic juice is about 2,000 ml (60 oz).

Pancreatic enzymes break down proteins, fats, and carbohydrates. The pancreas secretes trypsinogen and chymotrypsinogen, which are the inactive forms of the enzymes trypsin and chymotrypsin. Trypsinogen is activated to trypsin in the small intestine by the action of the enzyme enterokinase, which is produced by the small intestine. The trypsin itself then acts as a catalyst and activates both more trypsinogen and also chymotrypsinogen. Both of these enzymes split proteins into small units. There are other pancreatic enzymes, such as elastase and procarboxypeptidase, that are activated in the small intestine and act to break down peptides and similar groups to amino acids. Pancreatic lipase breaks down fats. Lipase is produced in a relatively inactive form and is activated in the small intestine by bile acids and salts. The breakdown products of fat include diglycerides and monoglycerides and a small amount of glycerol and fatty acids. Pancreatic amylase, or amylopsin, acts on starch, glycogen, and dextrins, splitting them into sugars.

The Liver and Gallbladder. Bile is formed by the cells of the liver and flows through a duct into the gallbladder, where it is concentrated five or six times and stored. The hepatic ducts together with the cystic ducts from the gallbladder form the common bile duct, which opens into the duodenum. In the absence of the gallbladder, bile is discharged continuously from the liver into the gastrointestinal tract. However, in the presence of an intact gallbladder, emptying occurs only after eating. The gallbladder is stimulated to contract by cholecystokinin, a hormone formed in the wall of the duodenum in response to the presence of fats.

Bile is a complex solution containing about 3% solids and 97% water (before it is concentrated). The yellow-green color of bile is the result of its content of bilirubin, which is a breakdown product of red blood cells.

The major digestive components of the bile are the bile salts. The bile salts include salts of four bile acids, of which glycocholic acid is the most important in man. The physiologic functions of bile acids include activation of lipases; emulsification of fats by decreasing their surface tension; promotion of absorption of fatty acids; stimulation of bile formation and flow; and stimulation of motor activity of the small intestine.

The bile salts are secreted with the bile into the small intestine where they combine with fats to form micelles, which are absorbed in the lower part of the small intestine. After absorption, bile salts are released from the cells of the intestinal lining and circulate in the blood; they are taken up in the liver, which again secretes them into the bile.

Absorption. Absorption of the breakdown products of digestion is the prime function of the small intestine. Absorption may be divided into three stages: transport of material from the lumen of the intestine into the cells of the intestinal lining; metabolism of the nutrients within the cells; and removal of the material from the intestinal cells into the bloodstream or lymphatic system.

There are marked differences in the rate of absorption of various substances from the intestinal lumen. Water, glucose, amino acids, and certain fats are absorbed in large quantities, while only small amounts of iron and vitamin B_{12} are absorbed.

In man about 8.5 liters (8.9 quarts) of fluid enter the gastrointestinal tract per day. Of this about 1.5 liters (1.57 quarts) are taken in through the mouth, while the rest is secreted into the tract from other parts of the body. Since only about 150 ml of water are lost in the feces daily, more than 8 liters (8.4 quarts) of fluid are absorbed from the gastrointestinal tract.

There are two types of transport across the membrane of the intestinal lining. The first is by simple diffusion, or passive transport. In this case transport of material across the membrane is based upon the physical-chemical processes of diffusion and osmosis and does not proceed against electrochemical gradients and does not utilize energy. Active transport, on the other hand, proceeds against an electrical or chemical gradient and requires the expenditure of energy.

Water, chloride, ascorbic acid, pyridoxine, and riboflavin move mostly or exclusively by passive transport from the lumen of the intestine into the cells of the intestinal lining. On the other hand, most nutrients, including sugars, fats, amino acids, bile acids, vitamin B_{12}, thiamin, and calcium, are absorbed by an active transport mechanism.

Active transport may occur through the use of a "membrane carrier system," in which the molecules of nutrient combine with a "carrier." The carrier then reacts with the cell membrane at special reactive sites, thereby enabling the nutrient-carrier complex to enter the cell.

Different sugars are absorbed at different rates, with glucose and galactose being absorbed most rapidly. These sugars are actively absorbed through the cell membranes, particularly in the upper portion of the small intestine. Intact proteins are not absorbed from the intestinal lumen but instead are broken down to their constituent amino acids, which are then absorbed. The protein found in the small intestine is from the food in the diet and endogenous protein, which is derived from the enzymes of digestive secretions and from the tissue shed from the lining of the gastrointestinal tract. The dietary intake of protein is about 50 grams a day, while endogenous protein is at least three times as great. The absorption of amino acids is also thought to depend on a carrier mechanism.

Fats are emulsified in the intestinal lumen. The more complex fats are hydrolyzed by pancreatic lipase to their component parts. These substances, along with fatty acids, form fat micelles. Because the micelles are fat soluble, the fatty acids penetrate the lipid-containing cellular membrane of the intestinal absorbing cells. The fats are resynthesized within the cells of the intestinal lining. Fats leave the cells in the form of chylomicrons, which are small fat droplets in conjunction with phospholipids and proteins.

The Large Intestine. The large intestine, or colon, does not have a digestive function; it serves to store undigested food residues and to convert the liquid contents from the small intestine into a solid fecal mass. In the process, between 250 and 350 ml (7.5–10.5 oz) of water are absorbed daily. There is also an exchange of sodium chloride for bicarbonates and a loss of potassium into the lumenal contents.

E. Clinton Texter, Jr.
Scott and White Clinic, Temple, Texas

Bibliography

Best, Charles H., and Taylor, Norman B., *The Physiological Basis of Medical Practice* (New York 1966).
Davenport, Horace W., *Physiology of the Digestive Tract* (Chicago 1966).
Gregory, Roderic A., *Secretory Mechanisms of the Gastro-Intestinal Tract* (Baltimore 1962).
Guyton, Arthur C., *Textbook of Medical Physiology* (Philadelphia 1966).
Texter, E. Clinton, Jr., *Physiology of the Gastrointestinal Tract* (St. Louis 1968).

DIGESTIVE SYSTEM. See Anatomy, Comparative—*Body Systems of Vertebrates* (Digestive System); Anatomy, Human—*Systems of the Body* (The Alimentary Canal).

DIJON contains many monuments of the rule of the Dukes of Burgundy. The tomb of Philip the Bold, with its recumbent figure guarded by angels on the top and its procession of mourners around the sides, was executed between 1385 and 1411. It is now in the Salle des Gardes of the Musée des Beaux-Arts.

MUSÉE DES BEAUX-ARTS, DIJON

DIGGERS, dig′ərz, an extreme radical group during the English Civil War, who believed in a classless society and common land. Their leaders were William Everard, a soldier in the New Model Army, and Gerard Winstanley, a writer and visionary. Beginning at St. George's Hill, Weybridge, they challenged landlords and cultivated the ancient commons of the manorial estates. Oliver Cromwell and the Council of State frequently used force against them, which for religious and philosophical reasons they would not resist, and the movement was soon broken.

The Diggers were linked with the Levelers (q.v.) in the minds of prosperous Englishmen. In fact, the Diggers called themselves "True Levelers" to distinguish themselves from the less radical group. Their opponents called them "Diggers" from the opening line of their freedom song: "You noble Diggers, all, stand up now, stand up now."

STUART E. PRALL
Queens College, New York

DIGITAL COMPUTER. See COMPUTERS.

DIGITALIS, dij-ə-tal′əs, is a drug widely used in the treatment of heart disease. It is obtained from the dried leaf of the purple foxglove plant (*Digitalis purpurea*). The term "digitalis," however, is used to refer to a whole class of glycosides found in various plants, all having characteristic pharmacological effects on the heart.

Digitalis is most commonly used to treat congestive heart failure; it is particularly effective when the congestive heart failure is caused by hypertension or arteriosclerotic heart disease. Digitalis is also used to slow the abnormally rapid cardiac rate found in cases of atrial fibrillation.

The most important action of digitalis is to increase the contractile power of the heart by acting directly on the heart muscle, or myocardium. This increase in the contractility of the heart muscle has no advantage in a normal person or animal, but in patients with heart disease in which the contractile power of the heart cannot keep up with the body's demand for heart action, digitalis has a most useful and strengthening effect on cardiac action. Other effects of digitalis include a slowing of the cardiac rate, an increase in cardiac output, and a decrease in the size of the heart. Digitalis will also increase urine secretion in patients who have edema caused by heart disease.

Only very small doses of digitalis are necessary to increase the contractile power of the heart. When the therapeutic doses are exceeded, digitalis can produce distinctly undesirable effects and even death.

Because digitalis also acts on enzymes that regulate ion transport across cellular membranes, it is of considerable interest to molecular biologists.

ANDRES GOTH, M. D.
University of Texas Southwestern Medical School

DIJON, dē-zhôn′, is a city in east central France, in the Burgundy region, 168 miles (270 km) southeast of Paris. The Ouche River and the Canal de Bourgogne flow through the southwestern part of the city; the Suzon River enters from the north. Dijon is the seat of government of the Côte d'Or department and has been the seat of a bishopric since 1731. The city has a court of appeals and a university, which was founded in 1722.

Dijon is the principal market center for a rich surrounding agricultural area. Its wine trade is especially important because Dijon is at the northern end of the famous Burgundy wine districts—the Côte d'Or, Chalonnais, Mâconnais, and Beaujolais—which stretch from the outskirts of Dijon south along the western edge of the Saône Valley. The city is also a major industrial and transportation center. It is important for the manufacture of leather goods, electrical equipment, chemicals, and many food products. It is famous for a black currant liqueur called *cassis,* and for its mustard.

History. Dijon is historically and culturally one of the most interesting French cities. Founded as a Roman military camp, it became part of the kingdom of Burgundy in the 5th century, then passed in the 6th century to the Merovingian rulers of France. It became the capital of the dukes of Burgundy in 1016. Soon after the death of Duke Charles the Bold in 1477, Dijon passed under the control of the French crown. In 1870, during the Franco-Prussian War, the Germans occupied the city twice. In World War II, Dijon, occupied by the Germans after the fall of France, was liberated on Sept. 11, 1944.

Places of Interest. Among the many notable buildings of Dijon is the old palace of the dukes of Burgundy. Only the guard room, the kitchen, the arched rooms of the ground floor, and two towers remain of the medieval structure, which was rebuilt in the 14th and 15th centuries. The rest of the palace was rebuilt during the 17th century according to the plans of Louis XIV's famous architect, Jules Hardouin-Mansart. Today it houses the town hall and the Musée des Beaux-Arts, one of the best collections of painting and sculpture in France, with examples of early Italian, Flemish, and French painters.

The early 15th century palace of justice was the seat of the Burgundian parliament. Nearby is the house in which St. Jane de Chantal was born in 1572. The Church of St. Michael, which was built between 1499 and 1540, has one of the most beautiful Romanesque facades of all French churches. The Cathedral of St. Bénigne, an old Benedictine abbey, which was reconstructed between 1281 and 1325, possesses a curious crypt and an attractive main doorway. Nearby is an archaeological museum, which features prehistoric and Gallo-Roman remains and artifacts and sculpture of the Middle Ages and Renaissance.

The most famous of Dijon's churches is Notre Dame. Built between 1229 and 1240, and still possessing its original facade, with its three ranks of gargoyles, it is the outstanding example of the Burgundian Gothic style. Its south steeple is topped by a 14th century clock. The interior has some beautiful 13th century stained glass windows, a 12th century wooden sculpture of the Virgin, and a stone sculpture of the Assumption by Paul Dubois. Population: (1962) 133,975.

Homer Price, *Hunter College*

DIK-DIK, dik′dik, one of the smallest African antelopes, 14 to 16 inches (35–40 cm) high and about 8 pounds (3.5 kg) in weight. The females are hornless and slightly larger than the males. Coat color varies from grayish to brownish. The four to five species of dik-diks are classified in the genus *Madoqua*. Dik-diks are found in the arid thornbush regions of northeastern and southwestern Africa but not in the areas between. They are adapted to living on water obtained from dew and the shrubs they eat. Individual males defend a territory that is marked off by deposits of secretions from glands in front of the eyes and by sites regularly used to deposit dung.

Richard D. Estes, *Museum of Comparative Zoology, Harvard University*

DIKE, an embankment that holds back the waters of a sea or a river. See Levee.

DIKE, in geology, a kind of igneous rock structure. (The British spelling is *dyke*.) Dikes usually are formed by the intrusion of magma into rock fissures; the cooling magma takes the flat, narrow shape of the fissures. They range in size from very thin intrusions to those that are many yards wide. In contrast to sills, which are emplaced parallel to rock strata or other geological structures, dikes cut across surrounding structures. They also differ from veins in that veins sometimes are filled by minerals that were precipitated from descending fluids.

Dikes are made of a great variety of intrusive rocks, ranging from the most silicic (such as aplite) to the most mafic (such as peridotite). They commonly are found in *swarms* in a region and often are dominantly parallel within such swarms, although sometimes they radiate outward from a central intrusion. The term *ring dike*, or cone sheet, is given to intrusions that have a conical form.

Marshall Kay, *Columbia University*

DILKE, dilk, **Charles Wentworth** (1843–1911), British political leader. Dilke was born in London on Sept. 4, 1843. He graduated from Cambridge University in law in 1866 and inherited a baronetcy and a substantial fortune in 1869. Meanwhile, in 1868, he had published *Greater Britain,* in which he expressed a belief in empire and a hatred of racism.

Dilke was elected to Parliament as a Liberal in 1868. By the time of Gladstone's second government (1880–1885) he and Joseph Chamberlain were recognized as leaders of the party's left wing. Dilke was undersecretary at the foreign office from 1880 to 1882 and president of the local government board from 1882 to 1885, when he was cited as correspondent in a sensational divorce. Although the case against him was dismissed, the publicity destroyed his career. He was defeated in the election of 1886, and although he returned to Parliament in 1892, he never held cabinet office again. He died in London on Jan. 26, 1911.

John Brown, *University of Edinburgh*

DILL, Sir John Greer (1881–1944), British field marshal, who was chief of the Imperial General Staff during World War II and led the British Military Mission in Washington. He was born at Lurgan, Northern Ireland, on Dec. 25, 1881. Commissioned into the Leinster Regiment, he campaigned in South Africa (1901–1902). In World War I he showed great ability in France on the staff of a Canadian corps and a British division and at general headquarters.

Dill commanded the 1st Corps in the British Expeditionary Force in 1939, but before the campaign began in France, he was appointed vice chief and then chief of the Imperial General Staff. In 1941 he was promoted to field marshal and went to Washington, where he quickly gained the trust of President Franklin D. Roosevelt and Gen. George C. Marshall. By his integrity and breadth of vision he became a vital link between the British and American high commands; few men did more to further the Allied cause. Dill died in Washington on Nov. 5, 1944.

Antony Brett-James
Royal Military Academy Sandhurst

A dike of granite cuts through darker Precambrian rock.
MARSHALL KAY IN "STRATIGRAPHY AND LIFE HISTORY" (JOHN WILEY & SONS, INC.)

DILL is the common name of a Eurasian annual or biennial herb (*Anethum graveolens*) belonging to the parsley family (Umbelliferae). It is widely used for seasoning food. The dill plant grows up to 3 or 4 feet (90–120 cm) high and has a long, spindle-shaped root, a branched stem, finely divided leaves, and compound clusters (umbels) of yellow flowers. Although the entire plant is aromatic, the largest amount of the volatile oil of dill (oleum anethi) is present in the seeds. Dill oil, a minor essential oil, is produced by steam distillation from the herb

Dill

PAUL E. GENEREUX

and from the mature fruit. The main constituent —some 43% to 63%—is carvone ($C_{10}H_{14}O$).

Dill has been cultivated in the Mediterranean area since ancient times. It is now also grown in many other parts of Europe, in the United States, and in India. In the United States, where it is grown mostly in Ohio, Indiana, Michigan, Oregon, and Idaho, commercial plantings were begun in 1930. The young leaves and the seeds are used for seasoning foods. Dill vinegar, made by steeping the seeds in vinegar for several days, is used for flavoring and pickling. Dill seeds are also used medicinally, for their carminative, or gas-expelling, properties. India dill fruit (*Anethum sowa*), introduced in the European market as a substitute for *A. graveolens* and caraway, contains less carvone than dill.

THEODOR JUST
Editor of "Plant and Animal Communities"

DILLARD, dil'ərd, **Harrison** (1923–   ), American track star, who was an Olympic champion in the dash, relays, and hurdles. He once won 82 consecutive hurdles races. He held records at several distances, including 13.6 seconds for the 120-yard high hurdles and 22.3 for the 220-yard low hurdles. William Harrison Dillard was born in Cleveland, Ohio, on July 8, 1923. As a student at Baldwin Wallace College, he won all national hurdle championships in 1947. His string of 82 victories ended in June 1948, when he stumbled over a hurdle in the Olympic trials. However, he qualified in the 100-meter dash and won the event in the London Olympics. In 1952 at Helsinki he won the Olympic gold medal in his specialty, the 110-meter high hurdles. In the 1948 and 1952 Olympics he won gold medals in the 400-meter relay. In 1955, Dillard was voted the Sullivan Award as the outstanding American amateur athlete.

BILL BRADDOCK, *New York "Times"*

DILLINGER, dil'in-jər, **John** (1903–1934), American criminal. He represented the new kind of criminal that appeared in the United States, particularly in the Midwest, as the Depression of the 1930's deepened.

Unlike organization mobsters, such as Al Capone, the Dillinger-type criminals did their own shooting. Made mobile by the motorcar, they would rob a bank, then race across a state line to safety. Their daring impudence in those days of disorganized law enforcement led to the strengthening of the Federal Bureau of Investigation. Among them were Baby Face Nelson and Bonnie Parker and Clyde Barrow, but it was Dillinger who most captured public imagination.

He was born in Indianapolis, Ind., on June 22, 1903. After spending nine years in a reformatory and prison for a youthful crime, he emerged, embittered and schooled in crime by professionals, to become in 13 hectic months the most notorious bank robber since the James brothers. He was captured twice, escaped jail twice, and fought his way out of numerous traps. Finally he was shot down on July 22, 1934, outside Chicago's Biograph Theatre by federal agents tipped off by his girl friend's landlady, "the woman in red."

JOHN TOLAND, *Author, "The Dillinger Days"*

DILLINGHAM, dil'ing-ham, **Charles Bancroft** (1868–1934), American theatrical producer, who presented over 200 plays on Broadway, most of them musicals, and managed over 50 prominent American and foreign performers. He was born in Hartford, Conn., on May 30, 1868. Before becoming a producer, he worked as a journalist and as drama critic on the New York *Sun*. In 1910 he opened the Globe Theatre in New York, and for more than 20 years he managed the productions there, many of them musical shows starring Fred Stone. In 1914 he took over the management of the Hippodrome, where his vaudeville shows ran the gamut from trained animal acts to the dancing of Anna Pavlova. He also headed the Dillingham Theatre Corporation.

Dillingham's fortunes were seriously affected by the Depression and he became bankrupt in 1933. He died in New York City on Aug. 30, 1934.

DILLON, dil'ən, **C. Douglas** (1909–   ), American financier and public official. Clarence Douglas Dillon was born in Geneva, Switzerland, on Aug. 21, 1909, to American parents. After graduating from Groton School in 1927, he received a B. A. degree from Harvard in 1931. Except for service in the Navy from 1941 to 1945, Dillon spent his life in financial and political activities and became an expert in international finance. He was a member of the New York Stock Exchange at the age of 22.

In 1953, Dillon joined the Eisenhower administration as U. S. ambassador to France. Later he was undersecretary of state for economic affairs (1958–1959) and undersecretary of state (1959–1960). In 1961, Democratic President John F. Kennedy selected Dillon, a Republican, as his secretary of the treasury. Dillon proved to be a master of detail, a persuasive but flexible administrator, and an advocate of aggressive and innovative foreign and domestic economic policies. He remained in his cabinet post until 1965, when he resigned.

DONALD B. JOHNSON, *University of Iowa*

DILLON, John (1851–1927), Irish nationalist, who was perhaps Charles Stewart Parnell's ablest lieutenant in the 1880's. Dillon was born in Blackrock, County Dublin, on Sept. 4, 1851, and was trained as a surgeon. He entered politics as a disciple of the extremist John Mitchel but transferred his allegiance to Parnell in 1879. Dillon was prominent in the agrarian aspects of Irish nationalism and was jailed three times. After the divorce scandal that ruined Parnell, Dillon joined the anti-Parnellite wing of the Irish party, and in 1896 he became its chairman. In 1900 he supported John Redmond, a Parnellite, as chairman of a reunited party. Thereafter Dillon served as Redmond's right-hand man in running the nationalist movement.

Although Dillon was pro-British in World War I, he defended the patriotism of the Easter Monday rebels, and in 1918, after he succeeded Redmond as party chairman, he opposed applying conscription to Ireland. The Sinn Fein victory in the general election of 1918, however, liquidated the Irish party, and Dillon lost his East Mayo seat to Eamon de Valera. Dillon died in London on Aug. 4, 1927.

LAWRENCE J. McCAFFREY
University of Maine

DILTHEY, dil'tī, **Wilhelm** (1833–1911), German philosopher, who held that philosophy, "the critique of historical reason," should study human life as expressed in history. He had great influence on theology, sociology, existentialism, and education.

Dilthey was born in Biebrich on Nov. 19, 1833. After studies at Heidelberg and Berlin, he taught philosophy at the universities of Basel, Kiel, Breslau, and Berlin. His many works include *Introduction to the Human Studies* (1883) and *The Essence of Philosophy* (1907; Eng. tr., 1954). He died in Seis on Oct. 1, 1911.

To prevent the reduction of all learning to a description of physical phenomena, as contemporary positivism proposed, Dilthey distinguished between objective natural sciences and subjective human studies (*Geisteswissenschaften*). The human studies, including economics, law, politics, art, religion, psychology, history, and philosophy, focus on life, or human meaning, and involve freedom, intentions, and institutions as they concern all "humanity, or human-social-historical reality." Such studies require the correlation of three elements: the "lived experience" of the student himself, a distinctive attitude of "understanding" (*Verstehen*), and the "expression" of the human spirit—the ideas, or intended personal and social meaning—in the words, gestures, works of art, and institutions of man's history. Dilthey's method of study took the historicist approach that any such expression must be seen in historical context. In opposition, however, to the skepticism of universal values that such a relativist view might entail, he found in the flow of life through various periods or cultures some recurrent structural forms, or categories, including being, cause, value, and purpose. Each period or culture achieves a comprehensive world view (*Weltanschauung*) in terms of these categories.

JAMES D. COLLINS
Author of "The Existentialists"

Further Reading: Hodges, Herbert Arthur, *The Philosophy of Wilhelm Dilthey* (New York 1952); Kluback, William, *Wilhelm Dilthey's Philosophy of History* (New York 1956).

JOE DIMAGGIO at bat in June 1941, during the streak in which he hit safely in 56 consecutive games.

DIMAGGIO, di-mä'jē-ō, **Joe** (1914–   ), American baseball player, who was one of the greatest outfielders in the history of the game. His feat of hitting safely in 56 consecutive games between May 15 and July 16, 1941, set a major league record.

Joseph Paul DiMaggio was born in Martinez, Calif., on Nov. 25, 1914. His career began with San Francisco (Pacific Coast League) in 1932. He was purchased by the New York Yankees of the American League in 1936 and played with the Yankees until he retired in 1951. He was nicknamed the Yankee Clipper by his fans; his appeal was his perfection and languid grace.

A fine defensive center fielder and a powerful right-handed hitter, DiMaggio won the American League batting championship in 1939 with an average of .381 and in 1940 with .352. He was voted the league's most valuable player in 1939, 1941, and 1947. In 13 playing years, despite many physical ailments, he compiled a batting average of .325. (He missed the 1943, 1944, and 1945 seasons because of Army service.) He hit 361 home runs in 1,736 games. He played in 10 World Series and 11 All-Star contests. DiMaggio was elected to baseball's Hall of Fame in 1955.

BOB McCORMICK
Associated Features Inc.

DIME NOVELS were paperbound melodramatic tales of adventure that were popular in the United States from 1860 to about 1900. Although the earliest publisher, Beadle and Adams, sold the novels for 10 cents apiece, many other "dime" novels actually sold for 5 cents. The first Beadle and Adams novel, Ann S. Stephens' *Malaeska: The Indian Wife of the White Hunter* (1860), had a sale of 300,000 copies in its first year.

Action-filled tales of the American Revolution, the Civil War, and Indian warfare were the most popular dime novels. The books were generally regarded as a disreputable form of writing, although the majority of them were highly moralistic, with an obvious villain and hero. Dime novels were gradually displaced by pulp magazines, and today they are collectors' items.

DIMENSIONAL ANALYSIS

DIMENSIONAL ANALYSIS is a branch of mathematical physics that concerns itself with analyzing physical problems in terms of such relatively simple concepts as mass, length, time, and electric charge. Every physical entity may be assigned two distinct kinds of values—number value and dimension value. For example, the phrase "sixty miles per hour" has the number value 60 and the dimensional value of velocity (the units being miles per hour). Every unit in physics implies a dimension, but the dimension of a physical entity does not imply any particular unit. For example, length is a primary dimensionality, but its number value may be given in inches, meters, or light-years.

All physical entities, such as mechanical force, heat energy, magnetic induction density, electric field, and many others, may be expressed in terms of a relatively small group of simple and familiar factors such as mass, length, time, and electric charge. Such factors are called *primary*. Symbols for mass, length, time, and electric charge are usually written as M, L, T, and Q, respectively. For example, acceleration, a, has the dimensions of length divided by time twice. This may be written $[a] = L/T^2 = LT^{-2}$. The symbol [ ] is read as: "the dimensions of" (the contained letter). Other sets of primary factors may be used, depending on circumstances. But in all cases these primary factors must be few in number and independent of one another. All other physical entities are called *secondary factors*. The dimensionality of magnetic induction density, B (in webers per square meters), is an example of a secondary factor. It may be written as: $[B] = MQ^{-1}T^{-1}$.

Dimensional analysis has several uses, one of which is checking the validity of physical relationships expressed in mathematical form, to see whether each term has the same dimension. For example, in uniformly accelerated motion we have
$$s = s_0 + v_0 t + \tfrac{1}{2}at^2 \qquad (1)$$
In this case each term has the dimensions of length. For instance the dimensions of $\tfrac{1}{2}at^2 = (LT^{-2})T^2 = L$. Other uses are found in aerodynamics and modern physics, particularly in problems involving changes of scale.

Foundations. A set of definitions and closely knit principles and theorems—somewhat overlapping in content—form the foundations of dimensional analysis.

(I) *Dimensional homogeneity:* In general, physically valid equations are those for which each term has the same dimensionality. For example, in the equation relating the work done on a body to the energy it receives, $F \cdot s = \tfrac{1}{2}mv^2$, $[F\ s] = (MLT^{-2})(L) = ML^2T^{-2}$ and $[\tfrac{1}{2}mv^2] = M(LT^{-1})^2 = ML^2T^{-2}$. Thus the dimensions of work and energy are identical.

(IIa) *Absolute significance of relative magnitude:* The ratio of the measured lengths of two rigid rods, relatively at rest, is independent of the size of the unit of length. If we extend this principle to any two physical factors of the same dimensionality, it follows that:

(IIb) *Physically valid relations do not change their mathematical form when the units are changed.*

(III) *The π-theorem:* If we divide each term of Equation (1) by s, there results:
$$s_0 s^{-1} + v_0 t s^{-1} + \tfrac{1}{2}at^2 s^{-1} - 1 = 0 \qquad (2)$$
Each term of (2) is a dimensionless product; e.g.:
$$[\tfrac{1}{2}at^2 s^{-1}] = (LT^{-2})(T^2)(L^{-1}) = 1$$

Now this simple process may be generalized, thus: Represent all such products by the symbols π_1, π_2, etc. Suppose we have a total of n physical factors. Let us choose p primary and independent factors for our dimensional analysis. Then the π-theorem may be stated: Any valid physical relation may be expressed as a function of $n-p$ independent dimensionless products, each product involving physical factors, both primary and secondary, in general. Formally, this π-theorem becomes:
$$F(\pi_1, \pi_2, \ldots) = 0 \qquad (3)$$
in which the π's are independent dimensionless products of physical factors. Thus, for (Equation 2), $\pi_1 = s_0 s^{-1}$; $\pi_2 = v_0 t s^{-1}$, etc. We now illustrate the use of this theorem by a simple example. *A dimensional analysis of the simple pendulum*—Our problem is to determine the period of a simple pendulum without friction of any kind. Since this is a problem in mechanics, the primary factors may be taken as mass, length, and time. We make the knowledgeable assumption that the relevant physical factors will be the pendulum length, l; the mass of the bob, m; the initial angular displacement θ_0; the acceleration due to earth's gravitational field, g; and, of course, the period, P, to be determined. We have a total of five physical factors; three of these—mass, length, and period—are primary factors with the dimensionalities M, L, T. The number of independent π's are then $n-p = 5-3 = 2$. θ_0 is one of the π's; it is dimensionless. Thus $\pi_1 = 0 = $ constant. For the other π we set $\pi_2 = m^\alpha l^\beta g^\gamma P^\delta$ in which $\alpha, \beta, \gamma, \delta$ are exponents to be found under the condition that π_2 shall be dimensionless. Thus our F-function is written: $F(\pi_1, \pi_2) = F(\theta_0; m^\alpha l^\beta g^\gamma P^\delta) = 0$. Solve this for π_2. Thus
$$\pi_2 \equiv m^\alpha l^\beta g^\gamma P^\delta = f(\theta_0) \qquad (4)$$
in which $f(\theta_0)$ is dimensionless. Reducing π_2 to its primary factors M, L, T we have
$$M^\alpha L^\beta (LT^{-2})^\gamma T^\delta = M^\alpha L^{\beta+\gamma} T^{\delta-2\gamma} \qquad (5)$$
If this product is to be dimensionless, *each exponent must be zero*. Thus $\alpha = 0$, $\beta + \gamma = 0$, $\delta - 2\gamma = 0$, giving us 3 equations in 4 unknowns. One of these unknowns is thus arbitrary—for example, say δ. Thus, $\alpha = 0$; $\beta = -\delta/2$; $\gamma = \delta/2$. Therefore Equation 4 becomes $l^{-\delta/2}g^{\delta/2}P^\delta = f(\theta_0)$ from which
$$P = \{f(\theta_0)\}^{1/\delta} \sqrt{l/g} \qquad (6)$$
free of m, the mass of the pendulum bob. Since the pendulum is frictionless, θ_0 remains constant so the $f(\theta_0)^{1/\delta} = $ constant. Thus, finally
$$P = \text{const.} \sqrt{l/g} \qquad (7)$$

Dimensional analysis thus confirms what we get from the corresponding differential equations but the constant cannot be determined straightforwardly from the present state of the art of dimensional analysis.

Scientific intuition and considerable preknowledge are frequently necessary for a satisfactory dimensional analysis. This can only mean that dimensional analysis, despite its many successes, needs much more development on the formal side. Such developments are being made steadily.

WILLIAM BENDER
Western Washington University

Further Reading: Bridgman, Percy W., *Dimensional Analysis* (New Haven, Conn., 1931); Bender, William, *Introduction to Scale Coordinate Physics* (Minneapolis 1958).

DIMETHYL SULFOXIDE, dī-meth′əl sul-fok′sīd, is an organic compound derived from lignin, a constituent of wood. Its chemical formula is $(CH_3)_2SO$, and it is commonly known by the abbreviation DMSO. It has many chemical and industrial uses and possible medical uses.

DMSO is a colorless liquid at room temperatures. It is a powerful solvent, and it is also freely mixable with water, oils, and organic solvents. Industrially, DMSO is used to extract materials from mixtures, to speed chemical processes and as a solvent in spinning synthetic fibers.

DMSO also has some interesting and potentially useful effects on living tissues. It has a remarkable ability to penetrate plant and animal tissues and to carry another substance along with it. Thus, a substance that ordinarily cannot pass through intact skin will pass through rapidly if it is dissolved in DMSO and then placed on the skin. Laboratory tests with aqueous solutions of DMSO have also revealed that DMSO helps to preserve living cells during freezing.

Preliminary tests have shown that DMSO has low toxicity, and it has possible medical uses in the topical application of drugs. It is considered an experimental drug, and it cannot be administered in the United States, except in a government-approved experiment.

SOLOMON GARB, M.D.
University of Missouri School of Medicine

DIMINISHING RETURNS. In economics, the law of diminishing returns describes a technologically determined relationship between productive resources inputs (such as land, laborers, factories, equipment, and raw materials) and output. It was stated first in the 18th century writings of economists A.R.J. Turgot in France and Thomas Malthus and David Ricardo in England. These economists utilized the law to explain changes in agricultural production arising from increasing the intensity of cultivation on one land plot. Currently, it is also known to economists as the law of variable proportions or the law of diminishing marginal production.

The law of diminishing returns assumes unchanging technology and states: when a producer augments output by employing additional units of one productive resource (for example, labor) with a fixed quantity of other resources, he will find that eventually in this process the output added by one more input unit (laborer) will be less than the output produced by the just previously added input unit. This is the stage of diminishing returns. Diminishing returns begin because the larger number of workers reduces the amount of land, machinery, equipment, and raw materials available to each worker. This stage ordinarily is preceded by a brief stage of *increasing returns* where each successive input unit (laborer) adds more units to output than did the immediately preceding input unit. The stage of diminishing returns ends when an additional input unit reduces total production, thus beginning the stage of *negative returns*.

Diminishing returns is an important economic phenomenon because it causes costs of production to rise as output is increased within a short period of time. (Over a longer period of time a producer can alter the quantity of several or all resources and avoid diminishing returns.) A producer subject to diminishing returns will produce and market a larger output only if he is offered a higher price to cover his increasing costs of production. Diminishing returns is thus the basis for the economic law of short-run supply—that is, as the price offered on a market is raised, the quantity of a commodity producers will bring to the market increases.

THOMAS E. WENZLAU, *Lawrence University*

DIMITRI. For Russians by this name, see DMITRI.

DIMITRIJEVIĆ, di-mē′trē-ye-vĕt-yə, **Dragutin** (1876–1917), Serbian army officer, known as Apis. He was born August 1876 in Belgrade, and was commissioned as an officer in 1895. Apis took part in the assassination of King Alexander Obrenović in 1903 and he soon became a powerful figure in the army and in Serbian politics. In 1911 he founded the secret society known as the Black Hand or Union or Death (Ujedinjenje ili Smrt), which aimed at the unification of all Serbs. In 1913 he became intelligence chief of the general staff.

Apis was involved in the assassination of the Austrian Archduke Franz Ferdinand in Sarajevo in 1914, but his role is controversial. Many scholars believe that he planned the assassination, but others admit only that he provided weapons for the young Bosnian nationalists. He was tried and executed at Thessaloniki on June 27, 1917, for plotting to kill the Serbian regent, Prince Alexander, there—a charge never fully proved.

BARBARA JELAVICH and CHARLES JELAVICH
Indiana University

DIMITROV, di-mē′trof, **Georgi** (1882–1949), Bulgarian Communist leader. He was born on June 18, 1882, in Kovachevtsi, Bulgaria. He began to work at the age of 12 but continued his education by reading widely. In 1902 he joined the Social Democratic party, and when the party split in 1903, he went with the left wing. In 1908 he was made secretary of the left-wing party, which became the Communist party in 1919, and from 1909 was a member of its central committee. Dimitrov was also active in the trade unions and as a journalist. In 1913 he was elected to parliament.

Imprisoned in 1918 for his opposition to Bulgarian participation in World War I, Dimitrov resumed his revolutionary activities after the war. He attended the third congress of the Comintern in 1921 and was one of the leaders of the abortive Communist uprisings in Bulgaria in 1923. Fleeing to Yugoslavia, he was sentenced to death in absentia. He remained abroad until 1945.

Dimitrov gained world attention in 1933 when he was arrested in connection with the burning of the German Reichstag. At the trial, he defended his own views ably and courageously and attacked the Nazi party. Acquitted, he left in 1934 for the USSR, where he received Soviet citizenship. He was active in the Comintern and was elected a deputy to the Supreme Soviet.

During World War II, he played a major part in organizing the Bulgarian resistance movement. In November 1945 he returned to Bulgaria, where he became head of the government and thereafter presided over the change to complete Communist rule. Under Dimitrov's leadership, Bulgaria retained close ties with the USSR. He died on July 2, 1949 near Moscow.

BARBARA JELAVICH and CHARLES JELAVICH
Indiana University

DINAGAT ISLAND, dē-nä′gät, in the Philippines, is a part of North Surigao province, lying 5 miles (8 km) northeast of Mindanao. The island is 309 square miles (800 sq km) in area. Half of its population lives in the town of Dinagat, on the southwest coast. The island commands the entrance to Leyte Gulf.

Dinagat and its neighbors, mainland North Surigao and Nonoc Island, are the mainstay of the Philippines ferronickel industry, with deposits of nickel in excess of 1 billion tons, as well as supplies of iron, chromite, and manganese. Dinagat also produces abaca, copra, and timber. Population: (1963 est.) 24,320.

LEONARD CASPER, *Boston College*

DINAN, dē-näN′, is a city in northwestern France, in the Côtes-du-Nord department of Brittany. It is situated about 15 miles (24 km) from the Gulf of St. Malo on the left bank of the Rance River. Dinan is a minor seaport as well as a commercial and tourist center. Its industries include brewing, cider distilling, and the manufacture of hosiery and farm machinery.

Located on a steep bluff, Dinan is a picturesque city, with walls and a fortress-castle dating from the Middle Ages, old houses, and winding streets. The imposing castle was built between 1382 and 1387. At the southwest corner of its ramparts stands a great oval-shaped turret, which commands a wide panorama. Inside the castle there is a museum of archaeology and history. The Church of St. Sauveur, with its tall spire built in 1779, is a mixture of Gothic and Romanesque styles; parts of it date back to the 12th century. A cenotaph inside the church contains the heart of Bertrand du Guesclin, who defended Dinan in 1359, when it was besieged by the English Duke of Lancaster. An English garden behind the church offers a fine view of the river and the Lanvallay Viaduct that crosses it. The 15th century Church of St. Malo is also noteworthy. Population: (1962) 12,730.

HOMER PRICE, *Hunter College*

DINANT, dē-näN′, is a town in Belgium, in the province of Namur, on the east bank of the Meuse River, 15 miles (24 km) north of the French border and 17 miles (28 km) south of Namur. Dinant owes its importance to its position in the Meuse Valley, which is the main north-south corridor across the Ardennes. The town is a road and rail junction and a tourist center for the Meuse Valley and the Ardennes.

In the Middle Ages, Dinant was an industrial center. It was renowned for chased copper and brass ware, which are still produced on a small scale. Modern industries include the making of textiles, beer, and chocolate and the quarrying of limestone for lime and cement.

Founded in the 6th century, Dinant was rebuilt in 1040 and again in 1818–1821. With its citadel (now a museum) perched on top of a limestone cliff, it has been a fortress town with a stormy history. It was destroyed by the Burgundians in 1466 and by the French in 1554; it was captured by the French in 1675 and remained in their hands until 1705 and again during the Napoleonic Wars; and it was badly damaged during the German invasion in World War I (August 1914) and to a lesser extent during World War II. Population: (1966 est.) 9,700.

F. J. MONKHOUSE
Author of "Geography of Northwestern Europe"

DINAR, dē-när′, the national currency unit in several countries, including Algeria, Iraq, Jordan, Kuwait, Tunisia, and Yugoslavia. In Iran it is a subdivision of the basic monetary unit, the rial. First struck in 696, the dinar was the standard gold coin of the Muslims and one of the great commercial currencies of the Middle Ages. It generally was inscribed with religious formulas and, later, with the names of the mint, the official responsible for the coinage, and the caliph.

DINARCHUS, dī-när′kəs (c. 360–c. 290 B.C.), was a Greek orator, and the leading Athenian speech writer from 322 to 307 B.C. Dinarchus (also spelled *Deinarchus*) was born in Corinth. Prevented as a foreigner from speaking in the Athenian courts or assembly, he wrote speeches for others. His surviving orations, *Against Demosthenes*, *Against Aristogiton*, and *Against Philocles*, were used to prosecute the three men, charged with accepting bribes from the Macedonian noble Harpalus. With the fall of the oligarchy in 307 B.C., Dinarchus, charged with conspiracy against the new government, fled to Chalcis in Euboea. He is thought to have died soon after his return to Athens in 292 B.C.

DINARD, dē-nàr′, is a city in northwestern France, in Ille-et-Vilaine, the easternmost department of Brittany. It is situated on the English Channel at the entrance to the wide Rance River estuary, across from the cities of St.-Malo and St.-Servan. On the west Dinard has merged with the village of St.-Énogat, and on many maps it appears as Dinard-St.-Énogat.

Since the middle of the 19th century Dinard has been an elegant seaside resort. It is well equipped with elaborate accommodations for tourists, including beaches, pools, tennis courts, golf courses, and sailing facilities, and beautiful parks and public gardens. There is also a casino and an aquarium and maritime museum. The Clair de Lune Promenade along the base of a dike on the Rance estuary is a pleasant walk, and a magnificent panorama of the Breton coast from Cape Fréhel to beyond St.-Malo can be seen from Moulinet Point.

In November 1966 a hydroelectric project, including a dam that serves as a bridge across the Rance River estuary, was completed near Dinard. Population: (1962) 7,944.

DINARIC ALPS, di-nar′ik, a range of limestone mountains and plateaus in western Yugoslavia. Linked in the north with the main Alpine system, the range extends some 400 miles (640 km) along the Adriatic coast from Istria to Albania and comprises most of the provinces of Bosnia, Hercegovina, and Montenegro.

Toward the south the mountains become increasingly wild and rugged, and several peaks are over 8,000 feet (2,400 meters) in height.

D'INDY, daN-dē′, **Vincent** (1851–1931), French composer. Paul Marie Théodore Vincent d'Indy was born in Paris on March 27, 1851, of an aristocratic family. He manifested an interest in music at an early age, and in 1862 he began to study piano with Diémer and (later) Marmontel and harmony with Lavignac. After serving in the Franco-Prussian War (1870–1871), he obtained an interview with César Franck, who offered to teach him composition. D'Indy became Franck's pupil at the Paris Conservatory in 1872 and was strongly influenced by him. In the same year, in order to gain practical knowledge of instrumentation, d'Indy joined the Colonne Orchestra as a tympanist. He was also becoming known as a composer through the performance of his *Piccolomini Overture* (1874) and other symphonic works.

Deeply impressed by Wagner's *Ring* cycle, the premier of which he attended at Bayreuth, Germany, in 1876, d'Indy aspired to be the "French Wagner." Although he wrote several music dramas. including *Le chant de la cloche* (1879–1883) and *La légende de Saint-Christophe* (1908–1915), his success in the theater was limited. He is best known for his orchestral music, notably the fresh and charming *Symphonie sur un chant montagnard* (1886; *Symphony on a French Mountain Air*), for orchestra and piano, based on a folk song from the mountainous region of the Cévennes. Other major works include the Suite in D Major for trumpet, two flutes, and string quartet (1886); the symphonic variations *Istar* (1896); and the tone poem *Jour d'été à la montagne* (1905). He also wrote songs, and solo works for piano and organ. His music is brilliantly orchestrated and rich in melodies.

D'Indy wrote biographies of Beethoven (1906) and Franck (1911). An influential teacher and theorist, he helped found the famous Schola Cantorum in Paris in 1894. Originally intended for the study of church music, it was transformed into a general music school in 1900. D'Indy taught composition there until his death. He died in Paris on Dec. 2, 1931.

GILBERT CHASE, *Tulane University*

DINESEN, dē'nə-sən, **Isak** (1885–1962), Danish author, who wrote highly polished short stories, many of which have a supernatural background. A member of an aristocratic Danish family, Karen Christence Dinesen was born on April 17, 1885, at Rungstedlund, north of Copenhagen. She lived on a coffee plantation in Nairobi, Kenya, from 1914 to 1931. Her marriage in 1914 to her cousin, Bror Blixen-Finecke, a Swedish baron, ended in divorce in 1922. When a world depression in coffee prices in 1931 caused the bankruptcy of her plantation, she returned to Denmark and lived there until her death on Sept. 7, 1962, in Copenhagen.

Karen Blixen's first stories appeared in Danish journals under the pen name "Osceola," but she used the pseudonym "Isak Dinesen" for all but one of her books, written in both English and Danish. *Seven Gothic Tales* (1934) first gained her an international reputation. *Out of Africa* (1937), an account of her years in Kenya, is generally regarded as her best work. This was followed by various collections of stories—*Winter's Tales* (1942), *Last Tales* (1957), and *Anecdotes of Destiny* (1958)—and more African sketches in *Shadows on the Grass* (1960). She published *The Angelic Avengers* (1947), a novel that takes place in England in 1841, under the pen name "Pierre Andrézel." Her novel *Ehrengard* (1963) and *Essays* (1965) were published posthumously.

ELIAS BREDSDORFF
University of Cambridge, England

Further Reading: Johannesson, Eric O., *The World of Isak Dinesen* (Seattle, Wash., 1961); Langbaum, Robert, *The Gayety of Vision: A Study of Isak Dinesen's Art* (New York 1965); Migel, Parmenia, *Titania: The Biography of Isak Dinesen* (New York 1967).

DINGANE, ding'gan (1790?–1840), was king of the Zulu from 1828 to 1840. His name is also spelled *Dingaan*. He became king after taking part in the assassination of his half brother, Chaka (Shaka), the founder of the Zulu kingdom.

Dingane tried to maintain Chaka's policy of military expansion but met increasing internal opposition and external pressure. From the first, he had trouble with British traders at Port Natal (now Durban), who provided a refuge for deserters from his kingdom. Later, he was confronted with Afrikaner *voortrekkers*, who had left Cape Colony to found an independent state in Natal, south of Zululand. Dingane signed a treaty ceding Natal to Piet Retief in February 1838 but then had Retief's party massacred and sent his *impis* (regiments) to attack the main body of *voortrekkers*. The Zulu army was defeated on Dec. 16, 1838, at what became known as Blood River.

Dingane's half brother, Mpande, with Boer assistance, inflicted a second defeat on him in January 1840. Dingane fled and was killed by Africans in Swaziland in March 1840.

LEONARD M. THOMPSON
University of California at Los Angeles

DINGHY, ding'ē, a small boat, with pointed or rounded bow, flat or round bottom, and square stern, used mainly as a tender to a ship or yacht. The naval dinghy is up to 20 feet (6 meters) long; the yacht dinghy may be less than half that length. The term *dinghy* may be applied to many types of auxiliary craft.

DINGO, ding'gō, the Australian wild dog, the only carnivorous placental mammal native to Australia at the time of European settlement. The dingo is frequently considered a subspecies (*Canis familiaris dingo*) of the domestic dog, but it is also often classified as a separate species (*Canis dingo*). It is generally assumed that the dingo came from somewhere in Southeast Asia and reached Australia with the aborigines several thousand years ago. The oldest genuinely dated dingo remains are 3,000 years old.

Dingoes are widely distributed throughout Australia but are not found in Tasmania or New

Dingo
ARTHUR AMBLER, FROM NATIONAL AUDUBON SOCIETY

Guinea. They average about 24 inches (60 cm) high at the shoulders and are usually creamy or reddish yellow in color, but other color varieties from black to white occur. Dingoes breed once a year; litters of up to eight pups are born during the winter after a gestation period of about 9 weeks. The average number of surviving pups, however, is probably no more than three. Pups captured by the aborigines are domesticated and used for hunting game.

Besides killing small mammals such as rats, the dingo attacks animals much larger than itself, such as kangaroos. In sheep and cattle areas, dingoes may cause serious economic loss.

A. G. LYNE, *Author of*
Marsupials and Monotremes of Australia

DINIZ (also spelled *Dinis*). See DENIS, king of Portugal.

DINIZ DA CRUZ E SILVA, dē-nēzh' thə krōoz ē sil'və, **António** (1731–1799), Portuguese poet, who wrote the famous satiric poem *O Hissope*. Born in Lisbon on July 4, 1731, he was trained in law at the University of Coimbra and held various provincial judicial posts. In Lisbon, Diniz da Cruz e Silva helped found the Arcádia Lusitana, a society dedicated to reviving Portuguese poetry by basing it on classical rather than Spanish models. Because he introduced the Pindaric ode to Portugal he is known as the "Portuguese Pindar." In 1776 he was sent to Rio de Janeiro, Brazil, as counsel to the superior court. He died there on Oct. 5, 1799.

Among Diniz da Cruz e Silva's sonnets, eclogues, elegies, and odes, the most outstanding work is *O Hissope* (published posthumously, 1802), a spirited mock-heroic poem, pervaded, like his other poetry, by local color. It realistically paints the vanities and intrigues of a provincial town whose loyalties are divided between the bishop and the dean.

DINIZULU, din-i-zōō'lōō (1869–1913), was the last king of Zululand. He was the son of King Cetshwayo, after whose death in 1884 he was proclaimed king. Afrikaner farmers helped Dinizulu established his position in return for the cession of territory in northern Zululand, where they created the "New Republic" of Vryheid.

After the British annexed Zululand in 1887, Dinizulu tried to prevent them from taking power out of the hands of the chiefs. He was arrested, convicted of treason, and exiled to St. Helena in 1889. He was allowed to return home in 1898, but only as headman of the Usutu district.

Dinizulu was suspected of being an instigator of the Natal African rebellion of 1906 and was again charged with treason. Found innocent of fomenting the rebellion but guilty of harboring rebels, he was sentenced to four years' imprisonment. He was released from prison in 1910 and spent his last years quietly in the Transvaal, where he died on Oct. 18, 1913.

LEONARD M. THOMPSON
University of California at Los Angeles

DINKA, ding'kə, a tall, slender Nilotic people who inhabit the southern Sudan just west of the White Nile River, a region they probably settled about the 10th century A.D. They number more than 500,000. Culturally related to the Anuak, Meban, Shilluk, and Nuer peoples, the Dinka speak a language belonging to the Eastern Sudanic branch of the Chari-Nile subfamily of the Nilo-Saharan family.

The Dinka are primarily a seminomadic pastoral people. They possess an egalitarian social system. Their traditional political system, relatively simple in form, relies for the maintenance of social control primarily on "spear chiefs," who serve as rainmakers, sacrificial priests, and peacemakers between feuding groups.

The area inhabited by the Dinka was subjected to slave raids by various Arab and Egyptian groups during much of the 19th century. In the 1960's the southern Sudan was the site of bitter political violence as the Sudanese government attempted to integrate the region with the culturally Arabic, politically dominant north.

ROBERT A. LYSTAD
The Johns Hopkins University

DINOFLAGELLATE, dī-nō-flaj'ə-lat, any of a group of microscopic, unicellular organisms possessing two flagella. Dinoflagellates are an important part of the food chain, being a major constituent of plankton.

The classification of dinoflagellates is controversial, since some contain a photosynthetic pigment, while other members of the group are heterotropic. Dinoflagellates may be classified as algae belonging to the plant division Pyrrophyta, or they may be classified as animals belonging to the Protozoa.

Except for their flagella, which are slender, whiplike organelles, dinoflagellates exhibit great diversity in appearance. Some are bounded only by a thin cell membrane, while others possess a tough outer layer called a theca. The theca consists of cellulose, which may be toughened by impregnation with minerals. It may consist of one or two pieces or be constructed of numerous plates. Dinoflagellates that do not have a theca are often brightly colored, and some are phosphorescent.

Some dinoflagellates, such as *Gonyaulax* of the Gulf of Mexico, are known to cause "red tides," which result in the widespread destruction of fish. These red tides are caused by a red pigment secreted by the organisms, and it is this pigment that is toxic to the fish.

DAVID A. OTTO, *Stephens College*

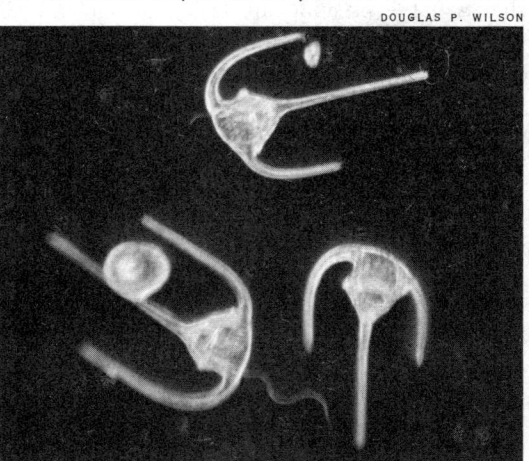

DINOFLAGELLATE *Ceratium tripos* is a minute organism that occurs as part of the plankton of the oceans.

DOUGLAS P. WILSON

Herds of 30-foot-long hadrosaurs, like giant kangaroos, roamed the Northern Hemisphere in the late Cretaceous. Their tails, like those of most other dinosaurs, were used as balancing organs and did not drag on the ground.

DINOSAUR, dī'nə-sôr, any of a large and successful group of reptiles that included the largest land animals that ever lived. The dinosaurs thrived for more than 175 million years. The earliest fossils are found in the rocks of the early Triassic period, some 243 million years ago, and the latest are found in deposits formed at the end of the Cretaceous period, about 65 million years ago. Dinosaurs were the dominant vertebrate land animals of their time, and their remains have been found on every continent except Antarctica.

The term Dinosauria, meaning "terrible lizards," was coined by the English comparative anatomist Richard Owen in 1842 to describe a newly recognized group of giant reptiles that had been discovered in fossil deposits during the previous 20 years. Later, in 1887, the English paleontologist Harry Seeley recognized that two distinct orders of reptiles, the Saurischia and the Ornithischia, were included in Owen's Dinosauria, but the name dinosaur has continued to be applied to both groups.

Size. The first few fossil dinosaurs found in England were large species, estimated to be 40 feet (12 meters) or more in length. Later, paleontologists tended to emphasize the large dinosaurs in their press reports, and the idea became common that all dinosaurs were big. This is not true, however.

Many of the plant-eating dinosaurs, especially those known as sauropods, did grow to gigantic dimensions. The longest of all terrestrial animals was a slender Jurassic sauropod named *Diplodocus*, which attained a length of 87.5 feet (27 meters) and an estimated weight of 12 tons. Its well-known relative *Brontosaurus* was not as long (67 feet, or 20 meters) but much bulkier, having an estimated weight of 30 tons. (A large African elephant weighs about 8 tons.) Even larger was the less well-known *Brachiosaurus*, which attained a length of about 80 feet (24 meters) and could have put its head into a fourth-story window. It was a massive creature whose weight is estimated at 50 to 70 tons—the largest of all land animals of any age.

On the other hand, most dinosaurs were considerably smaller than these giants, and some, such as the coelurosaur *Compsognathus*, were hardly larger than a common barnyard chicken. Coelurosaurs in general tended to be small, with few exceeding 8 feet (2.4 meters) in length.

Discovery of Dinosaur Fossils. In the first half of the 19th century no one could conceive that the earth might have been inhabited in the past by animals that were entirely different from those found at that time. It was not surprising, therefore, that the first indications of dinosaurs discovered were ascribed to more familiar kinds of animals. Thus the first-known dinosaur bones that are still available for confirmation are those collected in the Connecticut Valley by Solomon Ellsworth, Jr., in 1818. They were identified as "possible remains of human beings." Similarly, the dinosaur tracks found in the same area by Pliny Moody in 1800 were attributed to "Noah's raven."

The first dinosaur fossil to be recognized as a new kind of creature was *Megalosaurus*, or the "Great Fossil Lizard of Stonesfield," described by the English geologist William Buckland in 1824. In the following year another description of a dinosaur, genus *Iguanodon*, appeared. This description might have appeared earlier had not the discoverer and describer, the English physician Gideon Mantell, been discouraged from it by "higher authority." Mantell was convinced that he had discovered a completely new kind of reptile, but his contemporaries at the Geological Society in London as well as the noted Baron Cuvier of Paris identified various bones and teeth as belonging to fishes, hippopotamuses, and rhinoceroses. Cuvier admitted his error after the description appeared. It remained only for the British zoologist Richard Owen to recognize in 1842 that these and a number of subse-

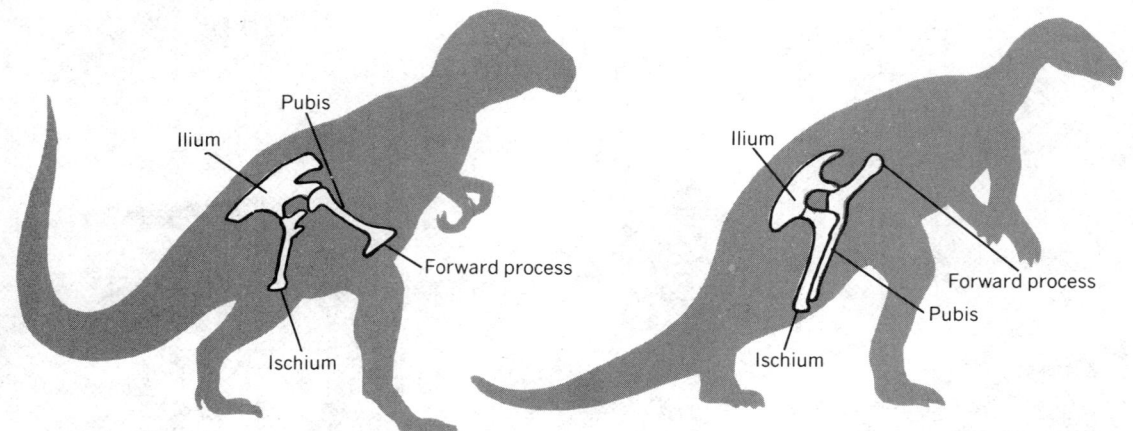

Allosaurus, a saurischian dinosaur   **Camptosaurus, an ornithischian dinosaur**

Saurischian and ornithischian dinosaurs had very different pelvic, or hip, bones. The saurischian pelvis (left) was a three-pronged structure consisting of ilium, ischium, and pubis. In the ornithischian pelvis (right), the pubis had rotated back parallel to the ischium and developed a forward-pointing process, giving it a four-pronged structure.

quently described fossils represented a previously unknown group of reptiles—the dinosaurs.

In 1856 the Philadelphia anatomist Joseph Leidy described some teeth collected in western North America, identifying one group as *Trachodon*, a "herbivorous lacertilian reptile allied to the *Iguanodon*," and another as *Deinodon*, a reptile resembling *Megalosaurus*. He later was able to describe a much more complete skeleton found in Haddonfield, N.J., as *Hadrosaurus*, another relative of the English *Iguanodon*.

In 1877 two American paleontologists, Edward D. Cope and Othniel C. Marsh, began operating separate and competing field parties in Colorado and Wyoming. These parties dug up tons of dinosaur bones, and within 10 years this gigantic dinosaurian fauna of the Mesozoic was made known to all through dozens, perhaps hundreds, of popular and scientific papers.

Meanwhile, an entire herd of *Iguanodon* was found in a Belgian mine, apparently having fallen into a narrow ravine during the Cretaceous period. More than 30 specimens were removed from the mine and prepared and described by Louis Dollo in hundreds of scientific papers from 1882 until 1900. The papers by Dollo, Cope, and Marsh laid the basis for the modern era of dinosaur study.

ORIGINS OF THE DINOSAURS

Dinosaurs belong to the large group of reptiles called archosaurs ("ruling reptiles"). This group of advanced reptiles includes, besides the two dinosaur orders (Saurischia and Ornithischia), the dinosaur ancestors (Thecodontia), extinct flying reptiles (Pterosauria), the crocodilians (Crocodylia), and the ancestral stock of the modern birds. The archosaurs differ from most other reptilian groups in having a two-arched temporal region of the skull (diapsid), usually a skull opening in front of the eye (antorbital fenestra), and a similar opening on the exterior surface of the lower jaw (mandibular fenestra). These openings are believed to allow greater areas for muscle attachment and contraction. The teeth are set in separate sockets (thecodont), rather than being attached to the surface of the jaw, as in lizards and snakes. The crocodilians, with their depressed (flattened) heads, have lost the antorbital fenestra.

The crocodilians and birds, living descendants of the early archosaurs, have a number of advanced morphological, physiological, and behavioral features that are not found in other modern reptiles. These include an advanced circulatory system with a four-chambered heart, nesting and care of the young, and (in birds) feathers and homeothermy (maintenance of a constant body temperature). It is widely believed that many dinosaurs shared these traits.

Dinosaur Ancestors. A large number of the ancient groups of reptiles became extinct at the end of the Permian period, about 245 million years ago. However, one group of relatively light-bodied, partially bipedal reptiles, the thecodonts (order Thecodontia), survived and formed the ancestral group from which all later archosaurs were derived. *Euparkeria*, a slender lizardlike reptile about 3 feet (0.9 meter) long from the early Triassic of South Africa is a well-known representative of this group.

Euparkeria retained some primitive features of the skull as well as having teeth in the palate, but its hind limbs were distinctly longer than its forelimbs, and the reduced fifth toe in the hind foot presaged the four-toed foot of early dinosaurs. As in most archosaurs, there was some body armor, but it was restricted to a pair of bony plates down the middle of the back. The proportions of its limbs suggest that the animal could both walk as a quadruped and run as a biped, with the long tail acting to balance the body weight. It was able to run rapidly, rather than waddle as most lizards do, because its legs were drawn up under the body in birdlike fashion and not projected to the side as in primitive reptiles.

From a thecodont such as *Euparkeria*, it is only a short step to the true dinosaurs. In fact such seemingly intermediate Triassic reptiles as *Scleromochlus* and *Ornithosuchus* have been classified by different scientists as either thecodonts or saurischian dinosaurs. The transition from the thecodonts to the early dinosaurs involved the acquisition of true bipedalism, with the necessary adjustments in the pelvic girdle and hind limbs to support the full weight of the body, the reduction of the forelimbs, and the loss of such primitive features as teeth on the palate.

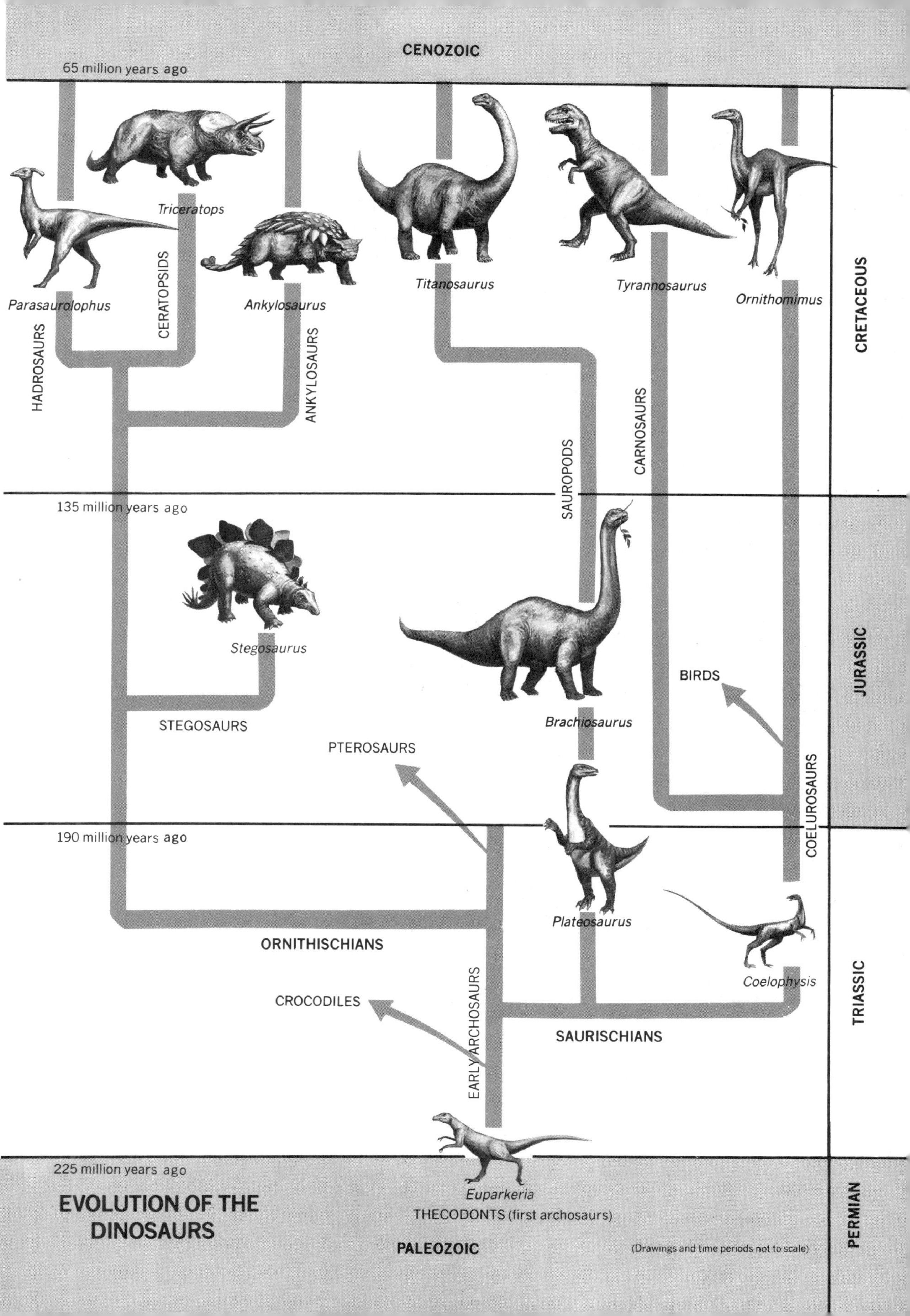

EVOLUTION OF THE DINOSAURS

CENOZOIC
65 million years ago

CRETACEOUS

Parasaurolophus — HADROSAURS
Triceratops — CERATOPSIDS
Ankylosaurus — ANKYLOSAURS
Titanosaurus — SAUROPODS
Tyrannosaurus — CARNOSAURS
Ornithomimus

135 million years ago

JURASSIC

Stegosaurus — STEGOSAURS
Brachiosaurus
BIRDS
COELUROSAURS

190 million years ago

PTEROSAURS
Plateosaurus
Coelophysis
ORNITHISCHIANS
CROCODILES
EARLY ARCHOSAURS
SAURISCHIANS

TRIASSIC

225 million years ago

Euparkeria
THECODONTS (first archosaurs)

PALEOZOIC

PERMIAN

(Drawings and time periods not to scale)

Homeothermy. A continuing controversy in paleontology involves questions such as whether dinosaurs were "cold-blooded" (poikilothermic), like modern reptiles, or "warm-blooded" (homeothermic), like birds and mammals. The body temperature of poikilotherms varies with that of their surroundings, while that of homeotherms remains constant despite environmental variations.

One reason for posing this question is that it has become increasingly evident that dinosaurs —unlike modern reptiles—were not the sprawling, slow-moving beasts that they have long been thought to be. Rather, most of them were swift-footed, birdlike animals—even the large carnivores such as *Allosaurus* and *Tyrannosaurus*. The dinosaur's tail did not drag on the ground, as visualized in most early reconstructions; instead, it stuck straight out behind, stiffened by masses of ligaments, and probably functioned as a balancing organ.

A great deal more energy is required to maintain such a bipedal position than the "rush and rest" belly-down stance of modern lizards and crocodilians. Modern terrestrial reptiles cannot maintain any sustained activity for more than a few minutes. The lungs and circulatory systems of poikilotherms do not furnish sufficient oxygen to the muscles to allow it. By this reasoning, therefore, dinosaurs must have been homeotherms, and a number of paleontologists have brought forward observations that support this view.

The American paleontologists John Ostrom and Robert Bakker have been major proponents of the theory that dinosaurs were warm-blooded animals. The theory is supported by the following observations: (1) Besides dinosaurs, the only known bipeds (birds and some mammals) are homeotherms. (2) The predator-prey relationships of some fossil faunas (relatively few predators) suggest that the predators had a high metabolic rate (with a correspondingly high food intake) and must therefore have been homeotherms. (3) The bones of dinosaurs, unlike those of modern reptiles, possess the Haversian canal systems (for the rapid flow of nutrients and oxygen) typical of homeotherms.

Perhaps even more impressive is the recognition that the Jurassic fossil "bird" *Archaeopteryx* is merely a coelurosaur with feathers. If the outlines of its feathers had not been so well preserved in the lithographic limestone of Solnhofen, Bavaria, *Archaeopteryx* would have been classified as just another of these small, light-bodied dinosaurs. Some other fossils have helped to substantiate the idea that feathers are modified reptile scales (as indicated by their development) and that they were useful primarily as insulation and only later became important as a mechanism of flight. Since homeotherms typically need insulation to help them maintain their body temperature, the presence of insulating feathers is strong evidence that *Archaeopteryx* was a homeotherm.

A small theocodont, *Longisquamata,* from the middle Triassic of Russia is unusually well preserved and appears to show a transitional state between scales and feathers. It has enlarged, loosely overlapping scales that may have provided insulation between the animal and the outside world. For these and other reasons, many paleontologists now visualize at least some dinosaurs not only as homeotherms but also as covered with feathers.

SAURISCHIAN DINOSAURS

The saurischian dinosaurs made their appearance shortly before the ornithischian dinosaurs, and there are no known links between the two. Each may have been derived from a different thecodontian ancestor. The key element that distinguishes the two is the kind of pelvic girdle they have.

The members of the order Saurischia retained the triradiate pelvis (similar to that of modern reptiles) found in the thecodonts but modified to better accommodate the head of the femur. All the early members were bipedal and carnivorous, and all carnivorous dinosaurs belong to this order. By the late Triassic, however, some of this group (Prosauropoda) had become large and heavy herbivores and had slumped to a four-footed gait. Still later (in the Jurassic) these evolved into the huge herbivorous dinosaurs (Sauropoda), the largest animals ever to walk on land.

The carnivorous dinosaurs (Theropoda) were divided among small, lightly built runners (Coelurosauria) and heavier, more massively built large predators (Carnosauria).

Coelurosaurs. Coelurosaurs had many birdlike features. Many of their long bones were hollow, suggesting that perhaps the respiratory system had been improved by the addition of the air sacs found in modern birds. The hind limbs were very birdlike, with the reduction or loss of the fifth digit and the rotation of the first digit toward the rear of the foot. The forelimbs were no longer used for locomotion but were modified for grasping prey. The neck was long and flexible and bore a relatively small, elongate head with large eyes. If, as some think, these small dinosaurs were covered with feathers, only the long tail would have been distinctively dinosaurian at a distance.

The coelurosaurs of the Triassic were quite small. *Saltopus* and *Podokesaurus* were little larger than house cats, and the "larger" ones such as *Coelophysis* were only 6 to 8 feet (1.8–2.4 meters) long. *Coelurus*, of the Jurassic, was about 6 feet long, and the ostrichlike *Ornithomimus* of the Cretaceous was about 8 feet long. All of these appear to have been swift-running little predators with grasping forelimbs. Some of the later ones lost their teeth, presumably having a beak, thus giving an even more birdlike appearance. These small carnivorous dinosaurs are believed to have fed on insects as well as lizards and other small vertebrates.

By the late Triassic these lightly built carnivorous dinosaurs had given off a branch of heavy-bodied carnivores, the carnosaurs, that presumably fed on the large herbivores of that era. They also had given off another branch of lightly built, hollow-boned, beaked dinosaurs that became what we call birds.

Carnosaurs. While the coelurosaurs were evolving toward more speedy predators of small animals, another branch of theropod dinosaurs was developing toward predators of large animals. These carnosaurs were more massively built animals that presumably fed on the large herbivorous dinosaurs. Unlike the coelurosaurs, the carnosaurs had a short strong neck with a large head and well-toothed jaws. One of the first definitely known is *Ornithosuchus* from the late Triassic of Scotland. It was about 12 feet (3.7 meters) long, not as specialized as some of the later carnosaurs but bipedal, hollow-boned, and with a mouthful of long sharp teeth.

In the Jurassic period the carnosaurs became the major predators of larger animals. Most of these are represented by incomplete specimens, but *Allosaurus* of western North America is a well-known reptile of the late Jurassic. It was only about 34 feet (10 meters) long, but its massive skull with wide gape and fearsome recurved teeth shows that it was capable of feeding on any of its larger contemporaries. The three-toed forelimbs were greatly reduced but still efficient grasping structures. The massive hind limbs were quite birdlike in structure, with three toes pointing forward and the fourth turned backward to form a prop.

These giant carnivores continued to evolve and become larger during the Cretaceous period. The massive *Tyrannosaurus*, the largest terrestrial carnivore ever to have existed, represents the end of the line. Its head, like that of *Allosaurus*, was large in comparison with the 47-foot (14-meter) body and had an enormous gape. Its saberlike teeth, some of them 6 inches (15 cm) in length, had serrated edges. *Tyrannosaurus* and its relatives did not appear until the late Cretaceous. Its brief existence, along with that of all other dinosaurs, was terminated at the end of that period.

Prosauropoda. While the early saurischians were all carnivores, some heavy-bodied mainly herbivorous species appeared before the end of the Triassic period. These are the prosauropods.

As a group, they were considerably larger than the early carnivores and had proportionately longer forelimbs than that group. Thus they were not strictly bipedal. The nails of the feet tended to be more hooflike than clawlike. The 20-foot (6-meter) *Plateosaurus* is one of the better-known representatives of this group. Unlike the coelurosaurs, the prosauropods were relatively clumsy creatures with solid rather than hollow bones. The head seems to have been absurdly small for an animal of its dimensions, and the teeth of *Plateosaurus* and its close relatives were flattened—adapted for stripping leaves off trees and bushes.

Presumably this group gave rise to the true sauropods of the Jurassic.

Sauropods. The sauropods consist of the massive four-footed herbivorous dinosaurs of the Jurassic and Cretaceous periods. They include such forms as the well-known *Brontosaurus*, *Apatosaurus*, and *Diplodocus*.

These dinosaurs had a small head on the end of a long neck, a massive body that presumably contained a complex digestive system, massive pillarlike legs, and a long tapering tail. For many years investigators disagreed on whether the elephantlike legs of the dinosaurs could have supported the enormous body weight of up to 50 tons or more, but that appears to be so. Many of the doubters suggested that the animals must have been aquatic or amphibious, so that the water could help support the weight. Such a life would provide even greater respiratory problems, however, and most paleontologists now believe that these animals did indeed walk about on dry ground, feeding on the leaves and needles from the tops of the Mesozoic trees.

The teeth, like those of the prosauropods, were flattened for stripping leaves from the branches. As in the coelurosaurs, many of the

Herds of brontosaurs, brachiosaurs, and other giant sauropods are now believed to have walked on dry land and fed on tree leaves. Previously they were thought to be marsh animals.

bones were hollow to reduce the enormous weight, and even the vertebrae enclosed large spaces that must have been penetrated by air sacs.

ORNITHISCHIAN DINOSAURS

Although saurischian dinosaurs appeared slightly earlier in the Triassic rocks, the ornithischians were not far behind. All the members of this group were herbivores, and although none ever reached the sizes of the sauropods, they are of considerable interest because of the varied and often bizarre kinds that appeared.

The structure that distinguishes this group is the pelvic girdle, which has a tetraradiate shape like that of a bird's pelvis because of a long anterior process on the pubic bone. In addition the lower jaw has a unique bone at the symphysis, the predentary. It is found in no other group of reptiles.

Only the primitive members of this group had teeth in the front of the mouth. All the more advanced kinds had a beak that is believed to have been used to cut off pieces of tough vegetation. On the sides of the jaws behind this beak were numerous rows of complex teeth that could chew such food into tiny pieces.

Although these dinosaurs are known from the late Triassic to the end of the Cretaceous, the early forms are represented only by scraps of bone that give little information about their structure. The group is divided into four subdivisions: (1) the Ornithopoda, primitive bipeds that presumably gave rise to the others; (2) the Stegosauria, quadrupeds with a double row of bony plates and spines down the back; (3) the Ankylosauria, heavily armored quadrupeds; and (4) the Ceratopsia, the horned dinosaurs, also quadrupeds.

Ornithopoda. Although there is no doubt that this group originated in the Triassic, the few fossils give no detailed information on the morphology of its early members. However, the group persisted through the Jurassic and Cretaceous,

Allosaurus, a 30-foot carnosaur that probably preyed on large plant-eating dinosaurs, such as *Brontosaurus*.

and some of the latter representatives are among the best known of dinosaurs.

The genus *Hypsilophodon*, from the early Cretaceous of Europe, is one of the most primitive known dinosaurs of this group. This 4-foot (1.2-meter) ornithopod had retained some teeth in the front of the mouth in spite of the apparent presence of a beak. Behind the beak was the series of closely packed cheek teeth typical of this group. It was a true biped, although the forelimbs were relatively large.

A larger and better-known ornithopod is *Camptosaurus* from late Jurassic and early Cretaceous beds in Europe and North America. It ranged from 6 to 20 feet (1.8–6.1 meters) in length. It had lost its front teeth but retained a bipedal posture.

The best known of this group were the hadrosaurs of the late Cretaceous. These bipedal herbivores were about 30 feet (9 meters) long, and they apparently ranged in herds throughout the Northern Hemisphere. They are among the most common of dinosaur fossils, and some are so well preserved that they show the texture of the leathery skin and the strong tendons that helped them to maintain their upright posture. In a few even the stomach was fossilized, together with the pine needles that they were feeding on. The beak had become flattened and ducklike, and the cheek teeth had been multiplied to form a multirowed grinding apparatus. The hadrosaurs, like the carnosaurs, suddenly became extinct at the end of the Cretaceous period.

Stegosaurs. The genus *Stegosaurus* of the late Jurassic had a distinctive high-arched body with rows of large flat plates projecting up from its back. Although it had reverted to a quadrupedal position, its hind limbs were much longer than the forelimbs. This, with its small elongate head, gave the animal a very unusual appearance, which was emphasized further by the two pairs of long spines near the end of the tail. It and a number of related forms were distributed over most of the Northern Hemisphere.

Ankylosaurs. The ankylosaurs were a heavily armored group of dinosaurs that lived during the Cretaceous. With their broad flattened body, short legs, and complete body armor, they looked something like enormous turtles.

Ceratopsids. The horned dinosaurs also appeared in the Cretaceous. Beginning after the middle of this period, with the small (8-foot, or 2.4-meter) hornless *Protoceratops*, they diversified into many kinds and larger sizes before they all suddenly became extinct at the end of the Cretaceous. *Triceratops* ranged up to 20 feet (6 meters) in length. Some had only one horn on the nose; others had one or more horns above each eye. All, however, had a bony "frill" that covered the neck region. Rather than being primarily for protection of that area, it seems to have provided room for attachment of the enormous jaw muscles. These animals carried the beaked snout and the massed cheek teeth to the ultimate extreme, giving the impression that they could have chewed their way through a large tree trunk.

EXTINCTION OF THE DINOSAURS

About 65 million years ago, at the end of the Cretaceous period (the last period of the Mesozoic era), the dinosaurs became extinct. For many years scientists could not reach agreement on the cause of the extinction. As knowledge of the earth's history increased, however, it gradually became clear that the dinosaurs died off suddenly. Thus none of the gradual changes that had been proposed—of climate or of oceanic temperatures, for example—could explain how the dinosaurs disappeared at the end of the Cretaceous and were replaced by the mammals in the following Paleocene period (the first period of the Cenozoic era).

About the same time that the dinosaurs died off, many other forms of life also came to a sudden end on the land and in the sea. On the land no animal that weighed more than about 55 pounds (25 kg) survived the close of the Cretaceous. The shallow seas that had teemed with gigantic lizards (mosasaurs), plesiosaurs, and dolphinlike ichthyosaurs were suddenly empty. In all seas and oceans even microscopic plankton disappeared and were replaced by new species in the Paleocene epoch.

The recognition that this sweeping extinction was a sudden event has come about only recently. Studies of cores of sedimentary rock drilled

---

CLASSIFICATION OF THE DINOSAURS

The dinosaurs make up two orders of the reptilian subclass Archosauria, which also includes the primitive thecodonts, the crocodylians, and the pterosaurs.

ORDER SAURISCHIA
(Lizard-hipped dinosaurs—carnivores and herbivores)

Suborder Theropoda. Beast-footed (four-toed) bipeds.
  Infraorder Coelurosauria. Small birdlike predators such as *Coelophysis* and *Ornithomimus*.
  Infraorder Carnosauria. Large massively built predators such as Megalosaurus, *Allosaurus*, and *Tyrannosaurus*.

Suborder Sauropodomorpha. Lizard-footed (five-toed) dinosaurs.
  Infraorder Prosauropoda. Primitive herbivores such as *Plateosaurus*.
  Infraorder Sauropoda. Giant, long-necked herbivores such as *Diplodocus, Brachiosaurus, Brontosaurus,* and *Titanosaurus*.

ORDER ORNITHISCHIA
(Bird-hipped dinosaurs—all herbivores)

Suborder Ornithopoda. Bird-footed (three-toed) bipeds, including *Iguanodon, Hadrosaurus,* and *Anatosaurus*.

Suborder Stegosauria. Plated quadrupeds with spikes at the ends of their tails, including *Stegosasurus* and similar genera.

Suborder Ankylosauria. Heavily armored quadrupeds, including *Ankylosaurus* and similar genera.

Suborder Ceratopsia. Horned, rhinoceroslike quadrupeds, including *Protoceratops, Torosaurus,* and *Triceratops*.

from the ocean beds between 1960 and 1980 showed the dramatic changes in microscopic animal life. The earlier limestones, made up of the skeletons of species characteristic of the Cretaceous, come to an abrupt end. Above them, the first, early layers of Paleocene limestones contain only a few species—apparently the survivors of a catastrophic extinction—but higher, later layers contain the decidedly different fossils characteristic of the Cenozoic era. The abrupt change from the Cretaceous to the Paleocene is marked by a thin bed of clay separating the two sequences of limestone layers.

In the late 1970's, Luis N. Alvarez and other scientists at the University of California in Berkeley began a chemical analysis of the clay as a possible means of dating it. The sample that they studied was taken from Gubbio, in central Italy. The scientists found unexpectedly that the concentration of rare heavy metals—especially iridium—was much higher than in the sedimentary rocks below and above it. The shallowness of the clay bed, which is only about 1 to 2 inches (25–50 mm) thick, indicates that the event that deposited the iridium was sudden and brief on the geological time scale. This feature—a high concentration of iridium in a thin clay bed—was first found at Gubbio, then in Denmark, and subsequently at other locations, including several in the western United States. In every case the unusual concentrations of heavy metals occur in the clay layer that marks the division between Cretaceous and Paleocene time periods—and nowhere else.

The peak concentrations of heavy metals found in the Cretaceous-Paleocene clay is much higher than those found in other sedimentary rocks on the earth. However, such concentrations are characteristic of many meteorites. This fact provides the basis for the most recent and certainly the most reasonable explanation of the extinction of Mesozoic life forms.

Alvarez and others calculated that a meteorite—probably an asteroid—with a diameter of about 6 miles (10 km) could provide the amount of heavy metals found in the Mesozoic-Cenozoic boundary layer worldwide. If such an object hit the earth, it would create a massive crater, disintegrate, and throw up a dust cloud that might obscure the sun for months. With their energy source cut off, green plants would die. This would lead to the death of many plant-eating animals and eventually to the death of the carnivores that feed on them. The absence of sunlight would also bring about an unusually cold winter that might kill off some of the surviving species. After such a climatic disaster, many plant species might be regenerated from seeds and underground roots. But it would be harder for most animal species to survive. Probably the only survivors would be small herbivores that could sustain themselves on roots and seeds and the small carnivores that prey on them.

Most biologists believe that a disaster of this kind, caused by the impact of a large asteroid, is the most likely explanation for the sudden disappearance of the dinosaurs. But even if the asteroid-impact hypothesis should be disproved, it is clear that some cataclysmic event closed the Mesozoic era, forever destroying the Age of Reptiles and leaving a nearly empty world open for the evolution of their small descendants, the birds and mammals.

HERNDON G. DOWLING, *New York University*

Bibliography

Charig, Alan, *A New Look at the Dinosaurs* (Heinemann 1979).
Colbert, E. H., *Dinosaurs: Their Discovery and Their World* (Hutchinson 1962).
Colbert, E. H., *The Age of Reptiles* (Norton 1966).
Colbert, E. H., *Men and Dinosaurs* (Dutton 1968).
Desmond, A. J., *The Hot-Blooded Dinosaurs* (Dial 1976).
Kurten, Bjorn, *The Age of the Dinosaurs* (McGraw 1968).
McLoughlin, J. C., *Archosauria: A New Look at the Old Dinosaur* (Viking 1979).
Romer, A. S., *Vertebrate Paleontology* (Univ. of Chicago Press 1966).
Simpson, G. G., *Fossils and the History of Life* (Scientific American Library 1983).
Thomas, R.T., and Olson, E.C., eds., *A Cold Look at the Warm-Blooded Dinosaurs* (Westview 1980).

DINOSAUR NATIONAL MONUMENT, dī′nə-sôr, in northwestern Colorado and northeastern Utah, about 200 miles (322 km) northwest of Denver, Colo. It was established in 1915 to preserve the spectacular canyons cut by the Green and Yampa rivers through mountains. A quarry containing fossil remains of dinosaurs and other forms of ancient life is an attraction.

The total area of the monument is about 312 square miles (811 sq km), of which about 75% is in Colorado.

DINUR, di-no͞or′, **Ben-Zion** (1884–1973), Israeli historian and educator. He was born in the Ukraine on June 2, 1884. After completing rabbinical studies in Russia he attended the universities of Berlin and Bern. In 1921 he emigrated to Israel, where he became principal of the teachers' seminary in Jerusalem. Dinur was made professor of Jewish history at the Hebrew University in 1947 and later headed its school of humanities. He was elected to the first Knesset (parliament) in 1949, and from 1951 to 1955 was minister of education and culture.

Dinur published essays and books on history, philosophy, and Zionism. He also served as president (1953–1959) of Yad Vashem, the national memorial to the victims of the Holocaust. Dinur was awarded the Israel Prize for Jewish studies in 1958 and for education in 1973. He died in Jerusalem on July 7, 1973.

EDWARD T. SANDROW
Rabbi, Temple Beth El, Cedarhurst, N.Y.

DINWIDDIE, din-wid′ē, **Robert** (1693–1770), British colonial administrator in America, who was lieutenant governor of Virginia during the early years of the French and Indian War. He was born in Scotland, apparently became a merchant, and entered British official service as collector of customs for Bermuda in 1727. Eleven years later he was promoted to surveyor general (of revenues) for all the southern colonies. He became a resident of Virginia at that time.

Dinwiddie was appointed lieutenant governor of Virginia in 1751 (the governor lived in England). His first years in office were marred by the controversy over the "pistole fee" that he imposed for securing land patents. This tax created hostility between Dinwiddie and the House of Burgesses at a time when cooperation was needed to counter French activities in the Ohio country claimed by Virginia.

Dinwiddie sent George Washington to warn the French away in 1753. He next dispatched Washington, with troops, to seize the site of what is now Pittsburgh. The French drove the Virginians away and, with Indian allies, defeated Gen. Edward Braddock's forces at the Battle of the Wilderness in 1755. Dinwiddie was then left to devise Virginia's own defenses against Indian attacks on the frontier. He was an able executive, but his health failed. He was granted a leave of absence to return to England, and Francis Fauquier succeeded him in 1758. Dinwiddie died at Clifton, England, on July 27, 1770.

CARL UBBELOHDE
Case Western Reserve University

DIO CASSIUS, dī'ō kash'-ē-əs (c. 163–after 229 A.D.), was a historian of ancient Rome. More properly called *Cassius Dio Cocceianus*, he was born in Nicaea, in the province of Bithynia (part of modern Turkey), of a distinguished family. Dio entered upon a Roman administrative career and attained the consulship in 211 and 229. After various minor literary projects, he began a history of Rome to about 229 A.D. in Greek, his native language. After 10 years of preliminary reading, he devoted 15 years to its writing.

Of this great work in 80 books, only books 36–54, covering the years 68–10 B.C., are extant; the rest is known only from various medieval Greek epitomes and extracts. Although the work was based on Livy, as well as on other works no longer extant, what remains is valuable to students of the Roman republic in its decline. The epitomes for the empire period are also useful, and the portions narrating the events of the last decades of Dio's life are important as the observations of a contemporary. Dio did not do research as modern scholars understand it; the speeches he inserts are his own. Nevertheless, the work is useful to modern historians of Rome.

STEWART IRVIN OOST, *University of Chicago*

DIO CHRYSOSTOM, dī'ō kris'əs-təm (c. 40–c. 112), Greek orator and philosopher. He was born at Prusa, Bithynia (now Bursa, Turkey), of a socially prominent family. Dio early became known as a skillful orator, acquiring the name *Chrysostomus*, which means "Golden-Mouthed" in Greek. Involved in a political intrigue in Rome in 82, he was banished from Bithynia and Italy, but in 96 he was permitted to return. He probably died in Rome after 112.

Some 80 of Dio's orations survive, many of them incomplete. They reveal his elegant and lofty evaluations of moral, social, political, and cultural issues. In his philosophy Dio combined elements of Stoicism and Cynicism.

DIOCESE, dī'ə-səs, a territorial division of the Christian church over which a bishop rules as its proper and ordinary pastor. The term was used to designate an administrative division of a country in the Roman Empire. In the early church the territorial divisions were known as "churches" and later as parishes, but by the 4th century the term "diocese" was already in use.

Every diocese is divided into parts called *parishes*, each with its own pastor and people assigned to it. The whole diocese is divided into larger segments called *deaneries*, made up of several parishes and presided over by a rural dean with limited supervisory authority.

In the Roman Catholic Church, several neighboring dioceses are usually united into an ecclesiastical *province;* the presiding bishop is known as an archbishop or metropolitan, and his diocese is called an *archdiocese* or *metropolitan see*. There is no essential difference between a diocese and an archdiocese; the distinction is mainly one of ceremonial precedence, but the archbishop has a limited authority over the so-called *suffragan dioceses*. In rare instances (for example, the archdiocese of Washington, D.C.) archdioceses are not metropolitan sees (having no suffragan dioceses) and are not under any metropolitan see.

Most of the post-Reformation churches that have kept a hierarchical or episcopal structure have also kept a diocesan structure. In the Oriental churches the diocese is known as an *eparchy* or *archeparchy*.

DAMIAN BLAHER, O.F.M.
Holy Name College, Washington, D.C.

DIOCLETIAN, dī-ə-klē'shən (c. 245–313 A.D.), Roman emperor and reformer. His full name as emperor was *Gaius Aurelius Valerius Diocletianus*. He was born in humble circumstances in the town of Dioclea in Dalmatia (now in Yugoslavia), and was named Diocles. The army was his path to greatness, and he distinguished himself in many military campaigns, eventually attaining senatorial rank and the consulate.

When, in 284, Emperor Numerian died, presumably as the result of foul play, the soldiers chose Diocles, who was commander of the emperor's bodyguards, to succeed to the throne. As emperor, he adopted the name Diocletian. His first act was to slay Aper, the praetorian prefect, to avenge the death of Numerian. He then marched at top speed against the hated Carinus, brother and co-emperor of Numerian. Carinus was slain by one of his own officers during the battle, and Diocletian was left sole master of the Roman world.

Diocletian's Reforms. Diocletian's principal concern was to assure the stability of state and throne, seriously threatened or reduced in dignity by a turbulent half century of secessionist movements, rebellions, imperial assassinations, and invasions. To accomplish this end, he devised, over the course of several years and probably not in accordance with a preconceived theory, a form of government called the tetrarchy (rule of four), which included two senior emperors (augusti) and two junior emperors (caesars) ruling simultaneously. Thus in 285 he appointed as caesar a stouthearted soldier named Maximian, who was proclaimed augustus by his troops and accepted as such by Diocletian in 286. Nevertheless, throughout their joint reign, Diocletian remained the superior of Maximian. Then, in 293, as emperor in the East, Diocletian took Galerius as caesar, while Constantius I became caesar to Maximian, emperor in the West. Each augustus adopted his caesar as his son; each caesar was married to a relative of his augustus. Thus Diocletian hoped to discourage conspiracies and rebellions by a united front of four emperors.

To the same end he caused many of the provinces of the empire to be subdivided, thus reducing the power of provincial governors. The activities of local governments as well as of individuals were increasingly regulated and Diocletian's system came to prescribe almost every phase of human activity in the hope of halting the decay of state and society. To restore the veneration in which emperors should be held by their subjects, Diocletian abolished the last vestiges of the old Roman republic's egalitarian forms, which had been preserved for 300 years, and largely completed the introduction of the servile etiquette of Oriental courts, a system toward which his predecessors had also been more and more inclined.

Military and Economic Affairs. Diocletian reformed the army and increased its numbers. The better troops were made into a mobile force to defend the empire more effectively. The coinage, which had been debased to almost worthless slugs in the course of the preceding century, was reformed and became more stable. But the attempt to fix maximum prices by an edict in 301 was foredoomed to failure by the operation of the laws of economics, then quite unknown. A method of collecting most taxes in kind instead of money was adopted.

While Diocletian dominated it, the system generally worked. Maximian successfully defended the Rhine frontier against the Germans and Africa against the desert nomads. Constantius put down Carausius and Allectus, who successively rebelled in Britain. In the East the Persians under their Great King Narses attacked the empire, but after an initial failure Galerius defeated them decisively. Diocletian himself put down a revolt in Egypt in 297.

Religious Persecutions. Diocletian was also desirous of reviving the ancient pagan religion of Rome. He himself took Jupiter as his patron, and Maximian chose Hercules. The Manichaeans, followers of a dualistic religion that stressed the conflict between good and evil, were persecuted under his regime. Their religion had been preached first in the 3d century by a Persian named Mani, and Diocletian probably persecuted them because he distrusted their eastern connections at the time of his campaign against Persia.

At the opening of the 4th century the Christians had been largely undisturbed by the imperial government for more than 40 years. But largely, it seems, at the instigation of Galerius, who came more and more to dominate the aging emperor, Diocletian, by a series of edicts commencing in 303, began the "Great Persecution" —the last, probably the bloodiest, and the longest of the persecutions of the church.

Retirement. In 304, Diocletian fell gravely ill, and in 305, compelling Maximian to follow his example, he abdicated. Galerius and Constantius succeeded as augusti, and new caesars were appointed. Diocletian retired to the magnificent fortified palace he had built at Split near the head of the Adriatic Sea. Without Diocletian to dominate it, the tetrarchic system broke down, and in 308, Diocletian briefly emerged from retirement at the request of Galerius to try in vain to restore order among his successors. His last years were saddened also by the persecution of his relatives by contenders for the throne.

STEWART IRVIN OOST, *University of Chicago*

Further Reading: Cook, Stanley Arthur, and others, eds., *Cambridge Ancient History*, vol. 12 (London 1939).

DIODE. See ELECTRIC CIRCUITS—*Circuit Elements (Diodes)*; ELECTRONICS—*Diodes*.

DIODORUS SICULUS, dī-ə-dôr′əs sik′ū-ləs, was a Greek historian of the 1st century B.C. He came from Agyrium (Agira) in Sicily and lived in Alexandria and Rome. Diodorus wrote a world history (*Bibliotheke*), in 40 books, from the mythical era down to 54 B.C. Books 1–5 and 11–20 are fully preserved; there are only fragments of the others. Diodorus relied on earlier historians, whom he copied liberally; but he had an overall chronological scheme and covered the Middle East as well as Greece and Rome.

CHESTER G. STARR, *University of Illinois*

DIOECIOUS, dī-ē′shəs, is a term (meaning literally "two houses") used for organisms in which the sexes are separate. In botany the term is applied to plants in which male and female flowers are borne on separate individuals.

The contrasting term, *monoecious* ("one house"), refers to organisms in which one individual bears the reproductive organs of both sexes.

DIOGENES LAERTIUS, dī-oj′ə-nēz lā-ûr′shē-əs, Greek biographer of the 3d century A.D., whose *Lives of Eminent Philosophers* has long been a major source of information for students of history and philosophy. Its 10 books contain valuable, if occasionally inaccurate, accounts of the lives of such important Greek sages as Socrates, Plato, Zeno, Pythagoras, Democritus, and Epicurus, as well as summaries of their philosophies and commentaries on their ideas. With the exception of a part of book 7, the manuscript has survived in its entirety. Diogenes included selections from the works of several philosophers, some of whose writings, long since destroyed, would otherwise have been lost to posterity. Among the most valuable of these inclusions are the texts of three letters of Epicurus.

DIOGENES OF APOLLONIA, dī-oj′ə-nēz, ap-ə-lō′-nē-ə, Greek philosopher of the 5th century B.C. He was born in the town of Apollonia, either in Phrygia (now in Turkey) or in Crete and probably lived in Athens for some time.

Diogenes wrote several works, the most important of which was *On Nature*. He searched for the first principle of the world and concluded, like Anaximenes of Miletus, that this great principle was air, "the origin of all things," endowed with consciousness and divinity. His theory that air was controlled and disseminated through the power of intelligence owes something to the ideas of his contemporary, Anaxagoras.

DIOGENES OF SINOPE, dī-oj′ə-nēz, sə-nō′pe (412 B.C.?–?323 B.C.), Greek philosopher, was the most famous and colorful of the Cynics (q.v.) and a forerunner of the Stoics. To the Stoics, Diogenes was the paradigm of virtue, embodying the Stoic ideals of dispassionate self-reliance and indifference to material goods and comforts.

A disciple of the Cynic philosopher Antisthenes, who taught that only virtue brings happiness, Diogenes exceeded his master in his contempt for possessions, the amenities, and everything else that might hinder the pursuit of virtue. He influenced the thought of Zeno of Citium and subsequent Stoic philosophers, especially through his pupil Crates of Thebes.

Diogenes was born at Sinope (now in Turkey) on the Black Sea, in the late 5th century B.C. Little is known of his life except apocryphal stories from such sources as Diogenes Laertius' *Lives of Eminent Philosophers* (3d century A.D.)—stories meant to be illustrative of Diogenes' character and views. Diogenes is said to have gone to Athens as an exile with his father, when either his father or he himself was accused of counterfeiting or tampering in some other way with the currency of Sinope. In Athens, Diogenes became a devoted disciple of Antisthenes and is reputed to have lived in a borrowed tub and to have discarded his only possession, a bowl, after seeing a boy drink from his hands. Other stories point up his contempt for pretentiousness, his hatred of philosophical speculation and argument, and his neglect of civic responsibility.

Diogenes is often depicted as having a cultivated hatred of men, but it would be more accurate to say that he simply could not find any man who qualified as "good" by his exceedingly high standards. It is said that he searched Athens with a lighted lamp in broad daylight, looking for a good man. We are told that when Alexander the Great offered Diogenes anything he wanted, Diogenes replied that he wished only that Alexander would step aside to prevent blocking the sunshine. Tradition relates that Alexander said, "If I were not Alexander, I would be Diogenes." Diogenes' biting sarcasm and his manner of life earned him the nickname "The Dog."

JAMES L. CELARIER, *University of Maryland*

DIOGNETUS, Epistle to, dī-og-nē′təs, an apology for Christianity, of uncertain date and origin. It treats three major themes: the nature of the Christian God; the secret of Christian love; and the reason that Christianity entered the world so late.

After contrasting Christianity with paganism and Judaism, the epistle glowingly describes the way of Christians. Christianity is not the product of man. It is God's revelation of Himself through the Son as Saviour. It is an expression of God's infinite loving mercy. In God's plan of salvation the lateness of Christianity shows sinful man his innate inability to save himself. The last two chapters differ greatly in style from the first 10, suggesting that they are a later addition.

The writer of the epistle is unknown. It was at one time attributed to St. Justin Martyr because it survived in a 13th–14th century manuscript with other works also attributed to him. The espistle was obviously intended for a wide readership. Addressing it to "Diognetus" may have been a common stylistic device, comparable to writing "an open letter to the editor" or "to the president." The name Diognetus may refer to the Emperor Hadrian. The letter is regarded as a masterpiece of Christian Greek literature.

ALFRED C. RUSH, C. SS. R.
Catholic University of America

DIOMEDE ISLANDS, dī′ə-mēd, two small islands in Bering Strait, 25 miles (40 km) west of Cape Prince of Wales, Alaska, and about the same distance from the mainland of Siberia. Big Diomede, or Ratmanov Island, belongs to the USSR; Little Diomede belongs to the United States. The international date line lies between the islands, which are about 2 miles (3 km) apart. Both islands are sparsely ihabited. They were discovered by Vitus Bering, a Danish navigator in the service of Russia, on St. Diomede's Day (August 16), 1728.

DIOMEDES, dī-ə-mēd′ēz, in Greek mythology, was a king of Argos and the son of Tydeus, one of the seven chiefs who attacked Eteocles of Thebes. Diomedes joined in the siege of Troy and was considered one of the bravest and mightiest of Greek heroes, having dared to wound even Aeneas, Aphrodite, and Ares. He and Odysseus satisfied the four conditions upon which the defeat of Troy depended. They killed King Rhesus and captured his horses; they secured the bow and arrows of Hercules; they persuaded Neoptolemus, son of Achilles, to fight against Troy; and they stole Athena's Palladium from the citadel of Troy. Diomedes was one of the warriors concealed in the Trojan Horse.

After the Trojan War, Diomedes married Euippe, daughter of King Daunus, and founded many cities in Italy. According to one legend, he was killed by Daunus and buried in the Diomede Islands.

Diomedes was also the name of a Thracian king, the owner of four man-eating mares. In the eighth of Hercules' 12 labors, Diomedes was slain and fed to the horses.

BERNARD MANDELBAUM
Bronx Community College, New York

DION, dī′on (c. 409–354 B.C.), was a political leader in Syracuse, Sicily, who was related to the rulers of the city. The influence of Plato, who visited Syracuse in 387, led Dion to oppose the reigning tyranny. After helping to make peace with Syracuse's old foe Carthage in 366, he secured an invitation for Plato to visit Syracuse again in an effort to make the ruler Dionysius II adopt more liberal policies. The effort failed and Dion fled to Athens, where he joined Plato's Academy.

In 357, Dion returned to Sicily with a small force, supported by the Carthaginians. The populace of Syracuse rose in revolt while Dionysius II was absent and forced the adherents of the tyrant to retreat to the island of Ortygia, the oldest portion of the city. Dion, however, as a conservative, aroused the distrust of the masses, who supported his former friend, the admiral Heraclides. Dion was soon expelled but then was recalled, and he took Ortygia in 355.

Dion dissolved the navy as the focus of the democratic elements and eventually allowed Heraclides to be assassinated. He reformed the Syracusan constitution on the lines of the Platonic ideal state but in practice became ever more a tyrant himself. In 354 he was murdered by soldiers under the orders of Callippus.

Plutarch wrote a life of Dion; Plato wrote his Seventh Letter to justify his relationship with Dion after hearing the news of Dion's death.

CHESTER G. STARR, *University of Illinois*

DIONNE, dē-ôn′, **Narcisse Eutrope** (1848–1917), French-Canadian physician, historian, and bibliographer. He was born in St.-Denis-de-Kamouraska, Lower Canada (Quebec), on May 18, 1848. In 1874 he received an M.D. degree from Laval University; he practiced medicine until 1880. In that year he became editor of the journal *Courrier du Canada* and redirected his career. As a student he had worked as a copyist for the historian Francis Parkman, an experience that gave him a special interest in historical and bibliographical research.

After 1880, Dionne published a number of historical studies, among them *Jacques Cartier* (1889), *La Nouvelle-France de Cartier à Champlain* (1891), the standard *Samuel Champlain* (2 vols., 1891–1906), and, with Arthur Doughty, *Quebec Under Two Flags* (1903). He was named librarian of the Quebec legislature in 1892. His *Inventaire chronologique* (4 vols., 1905–1909), an index of the books, brochures, maps, and periodicals published in or relating to Quebec, was a major contribution to Canadian bibliography. Dionne died in Quebec City on March 30, 1917.

MICHEL BRUNET, *University of Montreal*

DIONNE QUINTUPLETS, dyôn, the five daughters born in Callander, Ontario, on May 28, 1934, to Oliva and Elzire Dionne, who already had six children. The quintuplets, Annette, Émilie, Yvonne, Marie, and Cécile, were delivered at the Dionne farmhouse (now preserved and restored). They were cared for by Dr. Allan Roy Dafoe, a local general medical practitioner. The Canadian Red Cross provided them with incubators and nursing care, and the Dafoe Memorial Hospital was built nearby by public subscription as a nursery. In 1935 the Ontario legislature made them wards of the province to avoid exploitation by theatrical managers and show producers; their father regained custody in 1941.

In 1943 a new family home was built, and the quintuplets were educated there until they entered Nicolet College in 1952. Marie (Mrs. Florian Houle) died in Montreal on Feb. 27, 1970. Émilie died of an epileptic seizure on Aug. 6, 1954, in Ste.-Agathe-des-Monts, Quebec. Yvonne trained as a nurse and spent several years in convents. Annette married Germain Allard of Montreal, and Cécile married Philippe Langlois of Quebec.

CORNELIUS J. JAENEN, *University of Ottawa*

DIONYSIA, dī-ə-nish'ē-ə, were festivals in honor of the god Dionysus. They originated in ancient Attica, where two festivals bearing this name were celebrated annually.

The Greater, or City, Dionysia was held in Athens for six days near the end of March in honor of Dionysus Eleuthereus. It was introduced in Attica in the 6th century B.C. by the tyrant Pisistratus, who seems to have taken an interest in building up the festival. It began with a procession that conveyed the statue of the god to various temples, with singing and sacrifices, and ended in the Theater of Dionysus on the southern slope of the Acropolis. The celebration consisted principally of the production of tragedies, satyr plays, comedies, and lyric choruses, all presented in competition. In the 5th century this festival was the deadline for payment by Athens' subject allies, whose tribute was paraded before the full theater.

The Lesser, or Rural, Dionysia was celebrated in the demes throughout the countryside of Attica for four days about the third week of December. It consisted of processions, songs, and dances, mostly impromptu and usually riotous. One feature event was the *askoliasmos*, dancing or hopping on one leg on a full goatskin made slippery with oil. In imitation of the Greater Dionysia, dramatic performances were put on in the demes by groups of roving players and became a more important part of the celebration.

In Athens there were other festivals in honor of Dionysus: the Anthesteria, the Oschophoria, and the Lenaea. Only the last, however, was designated as Dionysia, apparently because it alone of this group featured performances of comedy and tragedy. The term "Dionysia" came more and more to be identified with dramatic festivals, and it spread throughout Greece.

DONALD W. BRADEEN, *University of Cincinnati*

DIONYSIUS, dī-ə-nish'ē-əs, **Saint** (died 268), pope from about 260 to 268. He became pope probably on July 22, 260. The historically reliable information about his pontificate centers on his supervision of doctrinal questions and his concern for the afflicted. In answer to an appeal from the priests of Alexandria, Pope Dionysius set forth the correct Trinitarian teaching and asked his namesake, Dionysius, bishop of Alexandria, to clarify his own position on the subject. The latter complied in his *Refutation and Apology*, which established his orthodoxy. St. Basil, in one of his letters, mentions the Pope's consoling letter to the church of Caesarea in Cappadocia when it suffered from a Persian invasion and the aid given to ransom the captives. Dionysius died in Rome on Dec. 26, 268. His feast is observed on December 30.

HERMIGILD DRESSLER, O. F. M.
Catholic University of America

DIONYSIUS I, dī-ə-nish'ē-əs (c.430–367 B.C.), was a powerful tyrant of Syracuse, in Sicily. When the Syracusan leaders failed to prevent the Carthaginian destruction of Agrigentum (Acragas) in 405, Dionysius first secured his election by the people as one of the generals and then became tyrant as "sole general," protected by a bodyguard. His career was marked both by wars with Carthage and by the expansion of Syracusan power in Sicily and southern Italy.

Wars with Carthage. After an initial defeat by the Carthaginians and an attempted revolt by conservatives at home, Dionysius made an unfavorable peace with Carthage and fortified the Syracusan island of Ortygia as a stronghold. Later, on the heights above the city, he built the great fortress of Euryalus. Dionysius also built a large fleet and siege machinery of new types, with which he renewed the struggle against Carthage in 398. Although he took the enemy base of Motya in western Sicily, he was defeated by sea and in 397 was driven back to Syracuse, where he was besieged until a plague forced the Carthaginian general Himilco to retreat.

After repelling another attack in 392, Dionysius made peace with Carthage. In the next war he was defeated at Cronium (either 382 or 375) and had to yield Selinus and Thermae to Carthage. His last war, in 368, was halted by the Carthaginians at their fortress of Lilybaeum.

Syracusan Expansion. Beginning in 403, Dionysius destroyed a number of neighboring Greek cities in Sicily, including Naxos and Leontini, and settled their inhabitants in Syracuse. He also freed slaves and made them citizens. From 388 on he gained power in southern Italy in alliance with the city of Locri and even founded colonies in the Adriatic. He also reduced Etruscan piracy, helped Sparta against Athens for a time, and may have had diplomatic relations with Rome. He relied largely on mercenaries, who were paid by exactions on his subjects. Dionysius was not able to weld his Greek subjects into an enduring union because of these onerous exactions.

Dionysius also wrote plays, one of which was given first prize at a festival in Athens. Plato visited him in 387, but they disagreed so completely that Plato had to leave Syracuse.

CHESTER G. STARR, *University of Illinois*

DIONYSIUS II, dī-ə-nish'ē-əs, the eldest son of Dionysius I, succeeded his father as tyrant of Syracuse in 367 B.C., at the age of about 30. Unlike his father, Dionysius II enjoyed court life. On his accession he immediately made peace with Carthage. He governed his realm weakly, though he founded two colonies in southern Italy. He also patronized philosophers and wrote poems and philosophic works himself.

Dionysius' relative Dion invited Plato to Syracuse in 366, but this effort to bend the young tyrant to more liberal ways failed. Thereafter the historian Philistus was his principal minister. When Plato visited Syracuse again in 361, his mission was even less successful than before, and he and Dionysius parted as enemies.

Dion returned to Sicily from exile in 357 with Carthaginian support and took the city of Syracuse while Dionysius II was absent with his fleet off southern Italy. In 355, Dionysius' son surrendered the Syracusan island stronghold of Ortygia to Dion, but Dionysius retained a base at the Italian town of Locri. In 347 he regained Syracuse briefly but lost Locri and then, in 345, mainland Syracuse to Hicetas, the master of Leontini, who besieged him in Ortygia with Carthaginian assistance. The next year Dionysius II yielded Ortygia to Timoleon from Corinth, and retired to Corinth, where he later died.

CHESTER G. STARR, *University of Illinois*

DIONYSIUS EXIGUUS, dī-ə-nis′ē-əs eg-zig′ū-əs (died c.526), was an Eastern monk and canonist, who went to Rome (possibly from Scythia) where he lived at the end of the 5th and the first part of the 6th century. He translated many of the decrees of the early Eastern ecumenical councils from Greek into Latin. He compiled the *Liber canonum*, which contained 50 of the so-called Canons of the Apostles; to these he added the Canons of the Eastern Councils and the legislation of the African Church.

His *Liber decretalium* constitutes the first real canonical collection. It contains 41 decretals of popes from Siricius (reigned 384–399) to Anastasius II (reigned 496–498) but consists mainly of the letters of Innocent I (401–417). A combination of the *Liber canonum* and the *Liber decretalium* in a revised form was given to Charlemagne in 774 by Pope Hadrian I when Charlemagne asked for laws of the Roman Church.

In his *Liber de Paschate*, Dionysius was the first to date the Christian era from the birth of Christ, but he made an error of several years.

DAMIAN J. BLAHER, O.F.M.
Holy Name College, Washington, D.C.

DIONYSIUS OF ALEXANDRIA, dī-ə-nis′ē-əs, **Saint** (died c. 265), bishop of Alexandria and a disciple of Origen. He is often called *Dionysius the Great*. A convert from paganism, he became head of the famed catechetical school of Alexandria in 232 and bishop of Alexandria in 247–248. In the Decian persecution (250) he fled the city, but returned in 251. In the Valerian persecution he was exiled to Libya (257), returning several years later.

Dionysius was deeply involved in disputes over theological terminology that was still evolving concerning the Trinity. He rejected the term *homoousios* (Greek for "consubstantial" with the Father) when referring to the Second Person of the Trinity, and he also called the Second Person "something made" by the Father from all eternity. Pope Dionysius (reigned 259–268) accused him of implying that the Son is inferior to the Father (subordinationism). Dionysius replied that homoousios was unscriptural and could be understood as meaning not only "one in substance," which would be orthodox, but also "one in Person," which would deny the distinction of Persons in the Trinity (Sabellianism). He explained that by "something made" he merely meant the orthodox "begotten" of the Father from all eternity, rather than creation out of nothing. Only a few remnants of Dionysius' extensive writings are extant, principally *Retort and Defense*, which defends his orthodoxy. He died in Alexandria about 265.

ROBERT BARR, S. J., *Fordham University*

DIONYSIUS OF CORINTH, dī-ə-nis′ē-əs, kor′inth, **Saint,** bishop of Corinth in the 2d century. He is known primarily for his letters, now lost, that are mentioned in Eusebius' *Ecclesiastical History*. Dionysius wrote seven letters on doctrine and other subjects to the churches of Athens, Lacedaemon, Nicomedia, Pontus, Knossos, Gortyna, and Rome, as well as a personal letter on spiritual life. In his letter to Rome, Dionysius thanked that church for its charity and mentioned the high regard in which the Corinthians held the letters from Popes Clement and Soter.

Dionysius' writings were apparently collected during his lifetime. His feast is April 8 in the West and November 29 in the East.

CONSTANTINE P. BELISARIUS, S. J.
Loyola Seminary, Shrub Oak, N.Y.

DIONYSIUS OF HALICARNASSUS, dī-ə-nis′ē-əs, hal-ə-kär-nas′əs, Greek historian and rhetorician of the 1st century B.C. He went to Rome from his native Halicarnassus about 30 B.C. and supported himself as a teacher of rhetoric while writing his chief work, *Roman Antiquities*, which was published (or began to be published) in 7 B.C. It consisted of 20 books, of which books 1 through 10, most of 11, and fragments of the rest are still extant.

In *Roman Antiquities*, a kind of paean of praise to early Rome, Dionysius defends the Romans against the usual Greek view of them as barbarians, even maintaining, erroneously, that the founders of Rome were of Greek origin. He voices also the contemporary belief, prominent in Livy and Virgil, that the gods chose the Romans for world dominion because of their uprightness and piety. The writing, however, is marred by a tendency to emphasize emotional and sensational details, and the story is frequently hampered by the insertion of factitious speeches, all composed according to the stereotypes of the rhetorical schools.

In 10 extant short works on rhetorical matters, Dionysius champions a classical style of speaking against the current florid "Asian" style, declaring Demosthenes to be the ideal orator. The fragmentary *On Imitations* shows how the Aristotelian doctrine of *mimēsis*, the philosophical imitation of nature, had degenerated into mere advice about copying older authors.

RICHMOND Y. HATHORN
Author of "Tragedy, Myth, and Mystery"

DIONYSIUS THE AREOPAGITE, dī-ə-nis′ē-əs, ar-ē-op′ə-jīt, an Athenian converted to Christianity by St. Paul (Acts 17:34). Nothing more is known with certainty, but an early tradition holds that he became the first bishop of Athens. Other early accounts say that he was martyred there under Domitian. His feast is kept October 3 by the Greeks and Syrians. Dionysius was once credited with mystical writings now assigned to a 5th century author (see DIONYSIUS THE PSEUDO-AREOPAGITE), and he was long confused with St. Denis of France (see DENIS, ST.).

DIONYSIUS THE PSEUDO-AREOPAGITE, dī-ə-nish'ē-əs, sōōd'ō-ar-ē-op'ə-jīt, often called *Pseudo-Dionysius*, the author of several theological works, claimed to be the convert of St. Paul mentioned in Acts 17:34. This claim made his works highly respected, but internal evidence indicates that he was a late 5th or 6th century Syrian writer. First mentioned by Severus, patriarch of Antioch from 512 to 518, the writings were used by Severian Monophysites in the theological conference at Constantinople (532). Hypatius (died after 536), bishop of Ephesus, questioned their value since they were not known to the early church fathers.

Dionysius was the author of the treatises *Divine Names, Mystical Theology, Celestial Hierarchy,* and *Ecclesiastical Hierarchy.* He used Neoplatonism to interpret theology, and his writings contain a complete theology, beginning with a transcendent God and working down through nine choirs of angels to the earthly church, which reflects the heavenly hierarchy. The whole order is conceived of as coming to a consummation in the resurrection. Although presented in an obscure style, his theology, with its triad of purgative, illuminative, and unitive ways, remains a classic.

Dionysius was influential in the West through the translation of John Scotus Erigena (c. 810–c. 877). Medieval and Renaissance writers produced a body of commentaries on Dionysius' works. Lorenzo Valla (died 1457) questioned their authenticity and began a controversy that lasted for centuries. Modern scholars are still unable to agree on the identity of Dionysius.

ALFRED C. RUSH, C.SS.R
Catholic University of America

DIONYSUS, dī-ə-nī'səs, in mythology, was the Greek god of fertility and vegetation. Although worshiped primarily as the god of wine, Dionysus, *Dionysos,* or *Bacchus* was more properly representative of many fluids in nature—the sap of the tree, the juice of the grape, and the blood of animals. Dionysus probably originated in Thraco-Phrygian legend. In Greek mythology he was the son of Zeus and Semele. His mother was consumed in the flames when Zeus appeared to her in all his Olympian radiance. Zeus saved the unborn Dionysus and sewed him up in his thigh until the time for his birth.

When he grew up, Dionysus wandered throughout the world teaching viticulture to mankind and spreading his worship, attended by a wine-frenzied troupe of nymphs and satyrs. Characteristic of the religion were orgiastic rites in which the votaries, chiefly women called maenads or bacchantes, roamed the mountains dressed in fawn skins, shrieking and brandishing torches. At the height of ecstasy they would seize wild animals, tearing them apart and devouring the flesh raw. Of the many cult legends telling of the god's irresistible invasion into Greece, the most famous concerned King Pentheus of Thebes, who intruded on a Dionysian orgy and was torn to pieces by his own mother. This story forms the subject of Euripides' *Bacchae.* See also BACCHUS.

ROBERT G. RUSSO
Queens College, City University of New York

DIOPHANTINE ANALYSIS, dī-ə-fan'tən, is the body of techniques used in determining the integral solutions of indeterminate algebraic equations or in proving that no such solutions exist. An equation with integral coefficients and more than one unknown, such as $2x = 3y$, is called indeterminate because it has infinitely many pairs of solution-values, only some of which are integers, such as $+3,+2$; $-3,-2$; $+6,+4$; $-6,-4$; $+9,+6$; $-9,-6$; and so on. When one seeks only these integral solutions, the equation becomes a Diophantine equation.

Isolating the integral solutions by Diophantine analysis usually precludes the use of many standard algebraic techniques, but it permits the use of methods not generally applicable in algebra.

Methods for Finding Solutions. As an example of Diophantine analysis, consider the equation $x^2 + y^2 = z^2$, for which one seeks integral solutions (called "Pythagorean number triples"). In this example, one may assume that x, y, $z > 0$, and that any two of x, y, z are coprime (have no common divisor). One of these, say x, must be even; hence, y and z are odd, $z + y$ and $z - y$ even, and $\frac{z+y}{2}$ and $\frac{z-y}{2}$ coprime. The original equation may be rewritten as $\left[\frac{x}{2}\right]^2 = \left[\frac{z+y}{2}\right] \cdot \left[\frac{z-y}{2}\right]$. Since the left side is a square integer, each of the coprime factors on the right must be a square integer. Hence $\frac{z+y}{2} = p^2$ and $\frac{z-y}{2} = q^2$, and so $x = 2pq$, $y = p^2 - q^2$, $z = p^2 + q^2$ ($p > q > 0$; p,q coprime, and one is odd and the other is even). Substitution of all suitable values of p and q into the last three equations yields all possible number triples x,y,z. As this solution shows, Diophantine analysis relies heavily on theorems that involve concepts such as "prime," "even," and "odd" and that therefore apply only to the domain of integers.

One property possessed only by integers leads to a very effective technique called the "method of infinite descent." Suppose a rational right triangle (a triangle the lengths of whose sides form a number triple) has an area equal to a square integer such as u^2. If that triangle has sides x,y,z, one can show that the equation $\frac{1}{2}xy = pq(p^2 - q^2) = u^2$ leads to another triple x', y', z', where x', y', z' are respectively less than x,y,z. Similarly, $\frac{1}{2}x'y' = u'^2$ leads to a third triple x'',y'',z'' smaller than x',y',z', and so on. But there is no infinite set of descending integers $x > x' > x''$, and so on; any such set must have a least element ≥ 1. Therefore, there is no rational right triangle with an area equal to a square integer. By the same method one can also show that the Diophantine equation $x^4 + y^4 = z^2$ has no solution, and hence neither does $x^4 + y^4 = z^4$. The last equation is a special case of Fermat's Theorem (q.v.), which states that the Diophantine equation $x^n + y^n = z^n$ has no solution for $n > 2$.

MICHAEL S. MAHONEY
Princeton University

Further Reading: Dickson, Leonard E., *History of the Theory of Numbers,* vol. 2 (reprinted New York 1950). Hardy, George H., and Wright, Edward M., *Introduction to the Theory of Numbers,* 3d ed. (New York 1954).

DIOPHANTUS OF ALEXANDRIA, dī-ō-fan′təs, al-ig-zan′drē-ə (c. 250 A.D.), was a Greek algebraist and number theorist. Nothing is known about him personally; even the date of his activity results from indirect evidence.

Diophantus' fame rests on his *Arithmetic*, of which only the first half has survived. It contains algebraic problems involving determinate (only one answer possible) and indeterminate (many answers possible) equations of the first and second degree, many of them involving particular number-theoretic conditions. The determinate problems and their solutions seem to belong to a tradition of Babylonian origin, but the indeterminate problems and their treatment may in part display Diophantus' originality. Although Diophantus devised a symbolic notation for the unknown and its powers, his problems still contain specific numerical values. Hence, the solutions proceed by paradigm rather than general formulation, and many of them, though skillful, have little applicability beyond the problem at hand. Diophantus usually produces only a single positive, rational solution, although often many exist. The *Arithmetic* exercised great influence on the development of symbolic algebra and number theory in the 17th century, especially in the work of Pierre de Fermat.

MICHAEL S. MAHONEY
Princeton University

Further Reading: Heath, Thomas L., *Diophantus of Alexandria* (New York 1964).

DIOPSIDE, dī-op′sīd, a calcium magnesium silicate, is a member of the pyroxene group of rock-forming minerals. Iron may replace the magnesium in all proportions; a complete series exists between diopside and hedenbergite (calcium iron silicate). Diopside characteristically is found in crystalline limestones in association with other silicates. It also is a major constituent of some igneous rocks, such as gabbros, peridotites, and pyroxenites. It is abundant and widespread but has no commercial use.

Composition, $CaMgSi_2O_6$; hardness, 5–6; specific gravity, 3.2–3.3; crystal system, monoclinic.

GEORGE SWITZER, *Smithsonian Institution*

DIOR, də-ôr′, **Christian** (1905–1957), French fashion designer, who brought out the controversial "New Look" after World War II. He was born on Jan. 21, 1905, in Granville, Manche department. Though he originally planned a career in diplomacy and studied political science at the University of Paris, he decided at the age of 23 to become an art dealer and was among the first to exhibit works by such artists as Salvador Dali and Jean Cocteau.

Dior was forced to give up his gallery in 1934 because of poor health. After working for a time as a magazine illustrator, he went into dress designing and was employed by such prominent Parisian designers as Robert Piguet and Lucien Lelong. In 1946, with the backing of France's leading textile manufacturer, Marcel Boussac, Dior established his own Paris salon and eventually had branches in 24 countries.

In reaction to economical wartime styles, Dior's New Look, introduced in 1947, emphasized long hemlines and full skirts. Among his later fashion innovations was the A-line (1955), which featured narrow shoulders and gently flaired hems. Dior died at Montecatini, Italy, on Oct. 24, 1957.

DIORAMA, dī-ə-ram′ə, a three-dimensional representation of a scene, in which figures and objects, usually life-sized, are grouped in front of a painted or modeled background that creates an illusion of depth. (A *cyclorama,* such as the Civil War cyclorama at Grant Park in Atlanta, Ga., is a two-dimensional representation that encircles the spectator. A *panorama* is a large flat or curved painting.)

The earliest dioramas were religious scenes, mostly of the Nativity, displayed in European churches during the Christmas season. The finest examples of these crèches were made in Naples during the 18th century. Dioramas were introduced at Edinburgh, Scotland, about 1788 by Robert Barker. Louis J. M. Daguerre, inventor of the daguerreotype, was the first to exhibit dioramas in Paris, in 1822.

Full-scale dioramas are used today in natural history museums to display animals, birds, and plants in their natural habitat. The Museum of the City of New York contains dioramas that depict events of the city's history.

LINO S. LIPINSKY, *Curator of History*
John Jay Homestead, Katonah, N.Y.

DIORI, di-o-ri, **Hamani** (1916–   ), political leader of Niger and first president of the country. He was born near Niamey on June 16, 1916. After teaching in Niamey, he went to Paris in 1938 as an instructor.

In 1946, Diori joined Félix Houphouët-Boigny and others to organize the African Democratic Rally and the Niger Progress party as its branch in Niger. He was elected to represent Niger in the French National Assembly in 1946 and again in 1956, and became vice president of the Assembly in 1957.

Diori became prime minister of the new Niger Republic in 1958, and two years later he was elected president of Niger. Reelected in 1965 and 1970, he became known as a moderate and a mediator in African disputes, but he was ousted in a military coup d'etat in April 1974, in which his wife was killed.

L. GRAY COWAN*, *Author of*
"The Dilemmas of African Independence"

DIORITE, dī′ə-rīt, is an igneous rock of coarse granular texture. It is composed of plagioclase feldspar and of one or more ferromagnesian minerals, such as biotite, hornblende, or pyroxene. Diorite is chemically similar to the volcanic rock andesite, but it is plutonic and has a coarser texture. Diabase also is somewhat finer-textured than diorite and is more basaltic.

Diorite generally is gray to dark gray. It consists of 50% to 65% silica, about 20% aluminum oxide, and as much as 15% iron oxide. It contains more calcium than magnesium and more sodium carbonate than potassium carbonate. In contrast to the somewhat darker gabbro, it has less than 50% calcic plagioclase (anorthite), while gabbro has less than 50% silica.

Diorite and gabbro commonly are intrusive rocks found in large dikes and in stocks or batholiths (bodies of igneous rock). The largest batholiths may contain the more silicic phases of diorite, such as granodiorite and quartz-diorite. For example, the principal rock of the Sierra Nevada in California is granodiorite, commonly with large phenocrysts (embedded crystals) of orthoclase feldspars.

MARSHALL KAY, *Formerly, Columbia University*

DIOSCORIDES PEDANIUS, dī-əs-kor'ə-dēz pə-dā'nē-əs, Greek botanist, physician, and pharmacologist, who wrote the oldest surviving text on drugs and their uses—*De materia medica.* Dioscorides was born in Anazarbos, near Tarsus, in Cilicia. His birth and death dates are uncertain, but he was active around 60 A.D. He probably served as a physician in the Roman legion in the Middle East.

De materia medica was the authoritative text on drugs until the late Renaissance. Divided into five books, it deals with drugs derived from plant, animal, and mineral origins and describes approximately 600 plants, 80 animals, and 50 minerals. The most important aspect of the text is the careful descriptions of plants. These descriptions were based on Dioscorides' personal knowledge and were used to identify plants. In *De materia medica,* Dioscorides also provided information on the preparation, dosage, and administration of drugs and on which drugs were reportedly beneficial for specific diseases.

Dioscorides wrote in Greek. His style was clear and succinct despite the use of many technical terms. *De materia medica* was an influential book that was translated into several languages. The best Greek edition is by Max Wellmann (3 vols., 1906–1914). A 17th century English translation, edited by R. T. Gunther, was published in London in 1934.

JERRY STANNARD, *University of Kansas*

DIOSCORUS, dī-os'kə-rəs (died 530), antipope in the early 6th century. A Greek born in Alexandria, Egypt, he went to Rome as a deacon. Pope St. Symmachus (reigned 498–514) sent him on an important mission to Theodoric the Ostrogoth at Ravenna, and Pope St. Hormisdas (reigned 514–523) appointed him legate to the court of Justinian in Constantinople.

Returning to Rome, Dioscorus became the leader of the Byzantine faction, which was opposed to that of the Goths. Pope St. Felix IV (reigned 526–530) favored the latter and before his death designated Boniface II (reigned 530–532) as his successor. Most of the Roman priests refused to accept Boniface and chose Dioscorus. The schism that resulted came to an end three weeks later, when Dioscorus died, on Oct. 14, 530, and the Roman priests submitted to Boniface II.

MARION A. HABIG, O. F. M.
St. Augustine's Friary, Chicago, Ill.

DIOSCORUS, dī-os'kə-rəs (died 454), patriarch of Alexandria. He served as archdeacon for St. Cyril of Alexandria and accompanied him to the Council of Ephesus (431). In 444 he succeeded Cyril as bishop of Alexandria. Dioscorus adopted the theological teachings of Cyril, but he does not seem to have understood them deeply.

Eutyches, an ardent anti-Nestorian, denied traditional orthodox teaching by asserting that the human nature in Christ was absorbed by the divine, an error usually called Monophysitism. Eutyches was denounced as a heretic by various bishops and finally by his own bishop, Flavin, who in 448 held a synod that condemned him. Eutyches appealed to Dioscorus in Alexandria and to Pope Leo I in Rome. Emperor Theodosius II, with papal approval, called a general council for 449, which was presided over by Dioscorus. The council has been called the *Latrocinium,* or Robber Synod, because Dioscorus and his friends managed to exclude nearly every bishop opposed to them and refused to allow the papal legates to read Pope Leo's teaching on the issue, stated in his *Tome,* or letter to Flavian. Flavian and several Antiochene bishops were deposed, and Eutyches was reinstated.

Flavian appealed to Rome, and after the death of Emperor Theodosius, a general council was held in Chalcedon in 451. Here the *Tome* of Leo was accepted as the orthodox teaching, and Dioscorus was deposed and exiled. He died in exile at Gangra, Paphlagonia, on Sept. 4, 454. Some of the Christians at Alexandria, however, refused to accept the teaching of the Council of Chalcedon. This was the beginning of a separate Monophysite church, once powerful in Egypt and the Middle East.

ROBERT HENNESSEY, O. P.
Dominican House of Studies, Washington, D.C.

DIOXIN, dī-ok'sən, any of a group of organic chemicals, especially a highly toxic compound formed as a by-product of the manufacture of the herbicide 2,4,5-T. This compound is more precisely called TCDD, from its scientific name 2,3,7,8-tetrachlorodibenzo-*p*-dioxin. Partly because of its extreme toxicity and its persistence in the environment, discoveries of soil levels of TCDD in excess of one part per billion have triggered government-sponsored community clean-up projects.

The lethal dose of TCDD in humans is unknown. Doses below 1 microgram per kilogram of body weight kill guinea pigs. However, hamsters are about 5,000 times less sensitive, and other animals respond between these values.

Long-term studies of the effects of TCDD on certain animals show that the chemical can cause cancer and can kill fetuses. In humans exposed to TCDD in industrial accidents, the only confirmed symptom has been chloracne, a serious skin rash. Other effects suggested but not confirmed include weight loss; behavioral, neurological, and reproductive impairment; porphyria; birth defects; and soft-tissue sarcoma.

ROBERT SNYDER
Rutgers University

DIP, in geology, the maximum angle that an inclined planar geological feature, such as a rock stratum or a vein, forms with the horizontal plane. The angle of dip is determined by an instrument called a clinometer (see CLINOMETER). The direction of the dip is the line of highest inclination and is expressed by compass bearing. The *strike*—the line of intersection of the dipping surface with the horizontal plane—is at right angles to the direction of dip.

DIPHILUS, dif'i-ləs (340?–291 B.C.), Greek poet, who was a leading writer of the New Comedy, the final period in the development of Greek comic drama. He was born in Sinope (now Sinop, Turkey) but lived and worked in Athens for many years. He died in Smyrna (now Izmir, Turkey) in 291 B.C. and was buried in Athens.

Of Diphilus' approximately 100 plays, only 50 titles and a few fragments survive; they indicate a style that is vigorous, simple, a full of sparkling imagery. His fondness for mythological subjects is shown in such plays as *Heracles* and *Theseus.* Diphilus' influence on the Roman theater is seen in the imitation and adaptation of many of his works by Plautus and Terence.

DIPHTHERIA, dif-thir′ē-ə, is an acute contagious infection that chiefly affects children. For many years it was one of the most serious contagious diseases, occurring in epidemic form throughout the world. In recent decades the disease has become much less prevalent in western Europe and North America, but in many other parts of the world it is still a serious problem.

Cause and Symptoms. Diphtheria is caused by the bacterium *Corynebacterium diphtheriae*. Although diphtheria bacteria may enter the body through the skin, genitals, eyes, or ears, the most common site of infection is the upper respiratory tract. Usually, the bacteria become lodged in the nose, throat, and windpipe, from which they can be easily transmitted to other people in droplets of respiratory secretions. Sometimes a person may harbor the bacteria without developing any recognizable symptoms, and he may spread the disease without knowing it.

After the bacteria become established in the respiratory tract, they begin multiplying and producing a poisonous substance known as diphtheria exotoxin. The exotoxin is then carried by the bloodstream to other parts of the body, where it produces characteristic symptoms. The onset of symptoms occurs suddenly, usually after an incubation period ranging from 1 to 4 days. Among these symptoms are moderate fever (usually less than 102°F, or 38°C), chills, general malaise, and a mild sore throat accompanied by a brassy cough. At this time, the mucous membrane lining the upper respiratory tract becomes coated with a layer made largely of dead cells and bacteria.

In response to the presence of diphtheria exotoxin, the body produces a neutralizing substance known as diphtheria antitoxin. If the antitoxin is produced promptly enough and in large enough amounts, it enables the patient to recover from the disease. The antitoxin also provides an immunity to the disease for at least several months and usually longer.

Although an uncomplicated recovery from diphtheria is the general rule, the exotoxin sometimes impairs the functioning of the heart and peripheral nerves. These complications usually arise 2 to 4 weeks after the onset of the disease. Involvement of the heart may produce myocarditis, or inflammation of the heart muscle. If the nerves are affected, a temporary paralysis may result.

Treatment. The only effective treatment of diphtheria is the prompt administration of antitoxin to neutralize any exotoxin still circulating in the bloodstream. The first effective diphtheria antitoxin was produced by the German scientist Emil von Behring in 1890. Although the commercial preparation of antitoxin today is slightly different from von Behring's method, the basic principle is the same.

In preparing diphtheria antitoxin, small amounts of diphtheria exotoxin are injected into horses. After several injections, diphtheria antitoxin appears in the horses' blood. The blood serum, which contains the antitoxin, is then separated from the other blood components and is processed under sterile conditions before it is administered to diphtheria patients. Because horse serum is a foreign protein in the human body, its administration is sometimes followed by severe sensitivity reactions (anaphylactic shock), and it is important that the antitoxin be injected only after the patient has been given special tests to determine his sensitivity to the serum.

In addition to administering antitoxin, the physician also treats any serious symptoms that develop during the course of the disease. If the layer coating the throat membrane becomes so thick that it completely obstructs the air passageway, the doctor performs a tracheotomy, making an incision in the throat and inserting a tube into the windpipe. Following the patient's recovery, the tube is removed and the incision is closed. In some cases the windpipe is not completely obstructed, and the doctor may enable the patient to breathe more easily by inserting a thin silver tube into the windpipe, a procedure known as intubation. In most cases, however, it is not necessary to resort to either tracheotomy or intubation.

The administration of antibiotics, such as penicillin and streptomycin, has not proved to be of any value in treating diphtheria. General supportive measures, such as bed rest and increasing the patient's intake of fluids, are helpful in making the patient comfortable.

Prevention. The only method of preventing diphtheria is to immunize susceptible people. The substance used in immunizing an individual is diphtheria toxoid, which is made by treating diphtheria exotoxin with formalin, a chemical that destroys the poisonous qualities of the exotoxin without impairing its ability to stimulate the body's formation of antitoxin. The immunity that results from administering diphtheria toxoid lasts for at least several months and usually longer. It is common practice to administer the toxoid to children before the age of 1. A booster dose is usually given 2 or 3 years later, and again when the child enters school.

Because a person may have had diphtheria without knowing it, the only way to determine if he has had the disease is to test his immunity to it. The most widely used test for determining a person's state of immunity to diphtheria is the Schick test, which was first developed in 1913 by the Hungarian-American pediatrician Béla Schick. In this test, a small amount of diphtheria exotoxin is introduced into the skin. If the area becomes reddish over a period of 3 or 4 days, the person is susceptible to diphtheria. If no reaction occurs, the level of antitoxin in the person's blood is high enough to protect against the disease.

FRANCIS S. CHEEVER, M.D.
University of Pittsburgh School of Medicine

DIPLOCOCCUS, dip-lō-kok′əs, a genus of bacteria that received its name from the fact that organisms of this genus usually occur in pairs. The term *diplococcus* is also used to describe the pairing of any spherical bacteria.

The only species of the genus *Diplococcus* is *D. pneumoniae*, which causes pneumonia, meningitis, and peritonitis. This species is transmitted from one person to another and is thought to be carried by as much as 50% of the world population. Normally, unless the body's defenses are weakened by illness, the bacterium's growth is held in check.

The individual diplococcus is surrounded by a structure called a capsule. The bacteria generally occur in pairs, but also singly and in short chains. The paired cocci appear as spindle-shaped units measurnig 0.5 by 1.25 microns. Unlike many other bacteria, they do not form spores.

DAVID A. OTTO, *Stephens College*

DIPLOMA. See DEGREE.

MODERN DIPLOMACY employs many principles founded at the Congress of Vienna (1814–1815). Among the negotiators were Prince Metternich of Austria (*seventh from left*), Count Nesselrode of Russia (*ninth from left*), Lord Castlereagh of Great Britain (*seated, eleventh from left*), and Talleyrand of France (*seated, fourth from right*).

CONTENTS

Section	Page	Section	Page
1. **Negotiation**	141	5. **Foreign Office**	145
2. **The Nation-State and Permanent Missions**	142	The Foreign Minister	145
		Organization of the Foreign Office	146
3. **Diplomacy as a Profession**	142	6. **Foreign Services**	148
		Aristocratic Diplomacy	148
Qualities of a Diplomat	143	The Merit System	148
		7. **The Embassy**	148
Selection of Diplomats	143	Privileges and Immunities	149
Languages of Diplomacy	143	Embassy Organization	149
4. **Open Diplomacy**	144	8. **International Diplomacy**	150

DIPLOMACY, də-plō′mə-sē, comprises the procedures and processes of negotiating agreements, usually between sovereign states. The word comes from the ancient Greek *diplōma*, denoting a folded document that was used for identification or conferred a favor or privilege. The classification and evaluation of such papers, most of which dealt with international matters, came to be known in French as "diplomatique" and later in English as "diplomatics." Eventually, the connection with documents disappeared. Edmund Burke first used the word in written English in 1796 when he referred to "the double diplomacy of France." Individuals who engage in diplomacy are called *diplomats* or *diplomatists*, the words being used interchangeably; such persons are usually members of the *diplomatic service* of their governments.

The word "diplomacy" has many different meanings. It is used by speakers and writers to mean what each intends at a given moment—foreign policy, international relations, or simply tact. Considerable confusion results from the tendency to equate diplomacy with some of the many tasks assigned to ambassadors, such as propaganda, espionage, and management of a large staff, many of whom are not engaged in the procedure or process of negotiation. Propaganda, economic pressure, and espionage may strengthen or weaken the position of a diplomat engaged in negotiations, but they are not part of the process of diplomacy.

Human beings organized in groups, whether tribes, kingdoms, nations, or city-states, have always had some kind of relationship with others, apart from war. The ancient kings of Babylonia, Assyria, and Egypt sent envoys to negotiate with other rulers as early as 1500 B.C. The Queen of Sheba visited King Solomon of Israel in 950 B.C. on what would today be called a diplomatic mission. In the 6th century B.C. the Greek city-states often sent representatives, known as heralds, to other cities to plead a cause before a public body. The Japanese were receiving emissaries from Korea in 33 B.C., not long after Cleopatra had visited Julius Caesar to promote the national interests of Egypt. Chinese representatives were negotiating in Japan in 13 B.C., and with countries bordering the Indian Ocean by 6 A.D. The Roman emperor Marcus Aurelius sent emissaries to the Han court of China in 166 A.D. By 1000 A.D. the Byzantine Empire and the Vatican had the rudiments of foreign offices, including extensive arrangements for the collection and analysis of information received from agents abroad.

Information concerning the development of diplomacy in Africa is scarce. There is material available on Egypt and Ethiopia, and it is known that Yusuf IV of Morocco had amicable relations with Europe and with neighboring Tunis. For Africa south of the Sahara, there is almost no published material other than what is available from anthropological studies, but it is safe to assume that there was some form of intertribal negotiation.

1. Negotiation

The tendency to equate diplomacy with foreign policy and international relations has resulted in an immense literature in which the process of diplomacy itself tends to become lost. An understanding of diplomacy involves an understanding of the decision-making process, the organization and machinery that assists in decision making and then transmits instructions to negotiators, and, finally, the nature of negotiation itself.

Studies of the organization and machinery of diplomacy were made during the 19th century, and the 15 years following the end of World War II witnessed the development of sophisticated analyses of decision making. But with few exceptions, such as the memoirs of the French diplomat Jules Cambon, the analyses in Sir Ernest Satow's *A Guide to Diplomatic Practice*, and some of Sir Harold Nicolson's books, there was little systematic study of the process of negotiation. Some of the pioneers in such work are Nathan Leites, Thomas Schelling, Kenneth Boulding, Klaus Knorr, Robert Bowie, Philip Mosely, Kenneth W. Thompson, and Fred Iklé. Iklé's *How Nations Negotiate* (1967) pulls together much of the best of current thinking on what is involved in negotiation. The book "is concerned with the process and effects of negotiation between governments; in particular, it seeks to relate the *process* of negotiation to the *outcome*." Iklé notes that while there are excellent studies of war and of the details of strategy and tactics involved in individual battles, "little has been written on the strategies and tactics of negotiation that would be equivalent in precision and coherence."

Iklé illustrates that in order for there to be negotiation, there must be a difference of values or national interest on the one hand, and on the other, some interests common to all parties. "The process by which two or more parties relate conflicting to common interests is the warp and woof not only of international relations but of human society; individuals, groups, and governments engage in it all the time.... Negotiation in a narrower sense denotes a process that is different from tacit bargaining or other behavior that regulates conflict," being "a process in which explicit proposals are put forward ostensibly for the purpose of reaching agreement on an exchange or on realization of a common interest where conflicting interests are present. Frequently, these proposals deal not only with the terms of agreement but also with the topics to be discussed (the agenda), with the ground rules that ought to apply, and with underlying technical and legal issues. It is the confrontation of explicit proposals that distinguishes negotiation (as here defined) from tacit bargaining and other types of conflict behavior."

2. The Nation-State and Permanent Missions

Diplomacy as it exists in the 20th century required first the development of the existing system of nation-states and then the creation of permanent diplomatic missions. The Peace of Westphalia (1648), which ended the Thirty Years' War, created a large number of nation-states with varying degrees of sovereignty, most of which quickly developed their own diplomatic services. The Peace of Westphalia was the result of two international conferences held in German cities—Münster and Osnabrück—30 miles (50 km) apart. The separation was necessary because France and Sweden both demanded precedence. The result was French precedence at Münster and Swedish precedence at Osnabrück; and a papal nuncio at Münster, but not at Osnabrück, because the Swedes would not accept a representative of the papacy as mediator. Taken together, these constituted one of the first of the great international conferences that were to become more and more frequent during the following 300 years —conferences attended by heads of state and foreign ministers from a considerable number of countries, in what is now called "international" or "summit" diplomacy.

During the 16th and 17th centuries, in what was developing as international law, distinguished statesmen, scholars, and lawyers such as Cardinal Richelieu, Hugo Grotius, and Albericus Gentilis began to recognize the need for more stable and reliable international agreements. Not until the beginning of the 19th century, however, were the first significant steps taken to achieve this end by establishing diplomacy as a profession. But before this was possible, there had to develop a system of permanent missions, or embassies, abroad.

Permanent missions appeared first in the Italian city-states, which, cramped together as they were in Italy, found it desirable to know as much as possible about one another and to find ways of settling certain disputes by negotiation rather than by war. Venice may have had the first permanent diplomatic missions abroad, because of its extensive commercial interests in the eastern Mediterranean and consequent long experience in negotiating with the Byzantine Empire, from which Venice received its first "diploma" in 584 A.D. There were permanent diplomatic missions in Genoa, Milan, Naples, Rome, and Venice by the middle of the 15th century. The major countries of Europe—England, France, Spain, and the Holy Roman Empire—followed suit within a century.

The creation of permanent embassies or legations of a foreign power within a national capital created problems resulting from what seems to be inherent human suspicion of foreigners. The early foreign embassies frequently faced rigid restrictions on freedom of movement not dissimilar to those experienced at various times in the 20th century by Western diplomats in the Soviet Union and China and by Communist diplomats in countries that retaliated. Among the embassies themselves, there were difficult problems, one of which was that of precedence. In 1661 the employees of the French and Spanish embassies in London fought a bloody street battle in order to determine which ambassador's carriage should be first in line for a royal procession. Such rivalries were due to the fact that the degree of precedence, given to or taken by one ambassador might mean more favorable treatment for his country on some matter of importance. Out of such struggles came elaborate rules governing precedence, protocol, extraterritoriality, and privileges and immunities.

3. Diplomacy as a Profession

As the total number of sovereign states increased, so did the complexities of the decision-making process, the machinery for conducting foreign relations, and the nature of the task of the diplomat. As the number of diplomats increased, problems arose as to how the representatives of large states should be treated, as compared with those from small states; whether the representative of a king in a country where the monarch was a relative should be treated the same as an ambassador from a king who was not a relative; or whether the representatives of kings should receive the same treatment as those from republics. A wide variety of practices and precedents developed during the 18th century, and the first steps were taken to regularize the system of diplomatic representation at the Congress of Vienna (1815) at the end of the Napoleonic Wars. Not until 1818, however, at Aix-la-Chapelle, was agreement reached on the first code of diplomatic behavior.

Four classes of diplomatic representatives were established. The first consisted of *ambassadors, papal nuncios,* and *legates,* who represented their heads of state and government and were accredited to, and entitled to, personal access to the chief magistrate of the host country. The ambassador was called "extraordinary" because he was the representative of the head of his state; he was "plenipotentiary" because he had full powers to negotiate.

The second category included *minister plenipotentiary* and *envoy extraordinary*; neither represented the person of the head of his state, but each was accredited to the head of the host country, without the right of personal access. The third category was the *minister resident,* who was accredited to the head of the host state but lacked the qualities of "extraordinary" or "plenipotentiary." The second and third categories were combined in the 1963 Vienna Convention on Diplomatic Relations. The fourth category, *chargé d'affaires,* was accredited only to the foreign minister.

The limitations of the international world in the early years of the 19th century are indicated by the fact that these categories of diplomatic agents were approved only by eight western European states—Austria, France, Britain, Portugal, Prussia, Russia, Spain, and Sweden. Not until 1896 was the United States sufficiently involved in foreign affairs to approve the diplomatic code. During the 20th century two other groups of persons became diplomatic agents: consuls and officers of the foreign office who had not made a career in service abroad.

Qualities of a Diplomat. There is general agreement among experienced practitioners of diplomacy on the qualities that the person who negotiates for his government must possess. Unfortunately, many critics of diplomacy use as a basis for their comments a pun written by a British ambassador early in the 17th century. Sir Henry Wotton wrote in Latin in a friend's notebook that "An ambassador is an honest man, sent to lie abroad for the good of his country." The humor was in the word "lie," which Wotton used to indicate that the serious role of an ambassador is to be sent to "reside" abroad, but the double meaning led critics to conclude that Wotton believed himself and other diplomats to be liars and spies.

François de Callières, an experienced French diplomat, was the author of *On the Manner of Negotiating With Princes* (1716), which has been called the "best manual of diplomatic method ever written." He wrote that "the good negotiator . . . will never found the success of his mission on promises which he cannot redeem or on bad faith. It is a capital error, which prevails widely, that a clever negotiator must be a master of deceit. Deceit indeed is but a measure of the smallness of mind of him who employs it, and simply shows that his intelligence is too meagerly equipped to enable him to arrive at his ends by just and reasonable means . . . a lie always leaves a drop of poison behind, and even the most dazzling diplomatic success gained by dishonesty stands on insecure foundations."

De Callières listed what he considered to be the personal qualities of a good negotiator. Among these were "an observant mind . . . a spirit of application which refuses to be distracted by pleasures . . . penetration which enables him to discover the thoughts of men . . . a mind so fertile in expedients as easily to smooth away the difficulties . . . presence of mind to find a quick and pregnant reply . . . and equable humor, a tranquil and patient nature . . . an address always open, genial, civil, agreeable . . . with easy and ingratiating manners." The negotiator should also be fluent in Latin and French.

Sir Harold Nicolson, the author of *Diplomacy* (first published in 1939), probably the most widely read book on the subject, believed that the qualities of an ideal diplomatist were, "truth, accuracy, calm, patience, good temper, modesty, and loyalty. They are also the qualities of an ideal diplomacy." Taken for granted were, "intelligence, knowledge, discernment, prudence, hospitality, charm, industry, courage, and even tact."

Selection of Diplomats. The number of men who can, or ought to, meet the above standards is very limited. For centuries diplomats were usually relatives of the king or members of the upper economic and social classes with interests closely related to his. There were exceptions, when certain monarchs believed ambassadors to be spies or so distrusted the nobility as to appoint commoners; King Henry VIII of England sent his barber as an ambassador to Spain. Under such circumstances, men of ability chose not to serve. By the 16th century the common practice was for ambassadors to be chosen from the aristocracy, but it was not always easy to get competent men to accept. Travel was difficult, life abroad was complicated and often unpleasant, and the difficulties of communication discouraged some who were unwilling to accept responsibility without authority. Kings were not apt to delegate authority and did not always condone or forgive mistakes made in their names.

By the 18th century the situation had changed, and the prestige and honor that went with being an ambassador representing the person of the king, together with the potential interest and excitement of the job itself, attracted men of high quality. Then, as now, the role of the diplomat in the making of foreign policy was ambiguous; then, as now, he was not always chosen because he was an experienced negotiator or likely to become one. On the one hand, he received instructions and carried them out; while at the same time influencing, and sometimes determining policy, by the manner in which he fulfilled his assignment. In selecting ambassadors account should be taken of the admonition of Ermolao Barbaro, the Venetian ambassador to Rome in 1490, who said, "The first duty of an ambassador is exactly the same as that of any servant of a government, that is to do, say, advise, and think, whatever may best serve the preservation and aggrandizement of his own state."

Languages of Diplomacy. In order to use his desirable qualities effectively, the diplomatist must be able to use the languages, or language, of diplomacy; and if the country where he is stationed uses still another language, he should understand it. Lacking such ability, he is forced to negotiate through interpreters, with the consequent decrease in mutual certainty of meaning and understanding. Until the 17th century, Latin was the language of diplomacy, as it was the universal language of discourse among edu-

CHIEF PARTICIPANTS at the 1919 Versailles Peace Conference were (seated, left to right): Prime Ministers Orlando (Italy), Lloyd George (Britain), and Clemenceau (France), and President Wilson of the United States.

cated men in Europe. It was replaced by French, which was considered a precise language, because French had become the tongue of educated Europeans, as well as of an increasing number of upper-class students from all over the world who had studied in Paris. Not until the Versailles Peace Conference in 1919 did English acquire approximate equality with French as the language of diplomacy.

The first real effort to develop multiple languages for diplomacy took place in Geneva at the League of Nations, where consecutive interpretations in either English or French were provided for all speeches. The United Nations has gone much farther in this direction, beginning with its Charter in 1945, of which Chinese, English, French, Russian, and Spanish texts are "equally authentic." Simultaneous interpretation in these five, and sometimes other languages, is available in meetings. Working papers are always provided in English and French, and sometimes in other languages, depending on the nature of the subject and the language of members particularly interested. There were few diplomats who did not speak and understand English by the late 1960's.

4. Open Diplomacy

The procedures and processes of negotiation between the representatives of governments were, until recent times, always carried on in private and often in great secrecy. The agreements, treaties, aide-mémoires, or protocols that resulted were seldom published, either because few persons were interested or in order to keep secret certain provisions for the advancement of the interests of two or more states at the expense of others. Examples were secret treaties of alliance and other understandings, which were thought to be the real reason why war could not be avoided in 1914. The belligerent governments, between 1914 and 1918, published such secret agreements as each thought would condemn its adversaries in the eyes of world public opinion.

President Woodrow Wilson addressed Congress on Jan. 18, 1918, and presented the broad outline for a peace plan known as the "Fourteen Points," one of which advocated "open covenants, openly arrived at, after which there shall be no private international undertakings of any kind but diplomacy shall proceed always frankly and in the public view." Wilson was criticized at the time and since for naïveté and worse. He even had to explain, on March 12, 1919, to Robert Lansing, his own secretary of state, that "when I pronounced for open diplomacy, I meant not that there should be no private discussions of delicate matters, but that no secret agreements of any sort should be entered into and that all international relations, when fixed should be open, above-board, and explicit." The President, despite his great knowledge of history and experience in politics, failed to realize that many people would not understand that he assumed that private negotiations would be taken for granted.

Wilson could not have foreseen the extent to which the records of diplomatic negotiations and agreements were, within 20 years, to be made currently available to anyone interested. Prior to 1920, treaties and other international acts were published when the governments concerned thought the time proper. The records of negotiations were seldom published, except in memoirs that usually appeared long after the event. There were privately published collections of treaties, the most famous of which was Georg Friedrich von Martens' *Recueil de traités*. It was actually several series of treaties covering the years from 1761 to 1806.

A revolutionary change in the publication of records of diplomatic negotiations and agreements took place after World War I, when the governments of Austria-Hungary, Germany, and Russia were destroyed. Their successors, eager to discredit the preceding governments, published the diplomatic correspondence, both secret and otherwise, of the years from 1870 to 1914. Between 1920 and 1926 the Germans published 40 volumes, and the Austrians 9. Individual Russians made available sufficient documents to fill 4 volumes. Thus, there were more than 50 volumes of diplomatic correspondence available by 1926. In self-defense, France published 43 volumes by 1936, and Britain 13 by 1938.

President Wilson's demand for open diplomacy, in part at least, resulted in Article 18 of the League of Nations Covenant, which stated that treaties would not be binding unless registered with the League. When the League was disbanded in 1946, there were 205 volumes in its Treaty Series. Article 102 of the United Nations Charter states that treaties may not be invoked unless registered. There were over 560 volumes in the Treaty Series in the late 1960's.

Under this kind of pressure for disclosure of agreements made by governments on behalf of their people, foreign offices decreased the gap between negotiation and agreement, and publication of the record. Although changes have taken place, completely open diplomacy does not exist: in 1957 public access to the papers of the British foreign office was available only up to 1902—55 years previous; and in 1967 the U.S. State Department files were open up to 1937—30 years previous. The officials of the Department of State who produce the *Foreign Relations of the United States* have reduced the gap slowly but steadily and in some instances have published the record within a few years. The Library of Congress, with State Department approval, published within 12 months the 16 volumes of mimeographed working documents of the San Francisco Conference that drafted the United Nations Charter.

5. Foreign Office

All countries have a unit of government that is assigned the responsibility for the conduct of foreign relations. Such a department is known by various titles, including the foreign office, the department of state, and the ministry of external affairs. It is this agency of government that supplies instructions for diplomats engaged in negotiations. In the 3d century B.C. the Han dynasty in China developed an office whose responsibility it was to collect and assess information concerning foreign lands in order to provide advice and counsel to the emperor. By 1000 A.D. the Byzantine Empire and the Vatican had similar units, and the Vatican was receiving information from legates serving extended terms abroad. Venice, because of its long experience with Byzantium, developed a unit that would now be called a foreign office. In western Europe, France in 1589 and Britain in 1782 had single offices for the handling of foreign affairs. The United States had a Department of Foreign Affairs in 1781, which became the Department of State in 1789.

The foreign office must be closely associated with the head of state, who is the first diplomat of his country whenever he chooses. Kings have negotiated with one another for centuries, but sometimes mutual distrust was such that elaborate security precautions were necessary. A famous example was Napoleon's meeting with the Russian Czar Alexander I in 1807, on a raft in the middle of the Niemen River. Woodrow Wilson was the first American president to engage in "summit," or "conference," diplomacy, when he went to Paris in 1919 to meet Premier Georges Clemenceau of France and Prime Minister David Lloyd George of Britain. Adolf Hitler and Neville Chamberlain met at Berchtesgaden, Germany, in 1938. Franklin Roosevelt, Winston Churchill, and Joseph Stalin met together at Teheran, Iran, in 1943 and at Yalta, in the Soviet Union, in 1945. Every American president since then has gone abroad at least once to engage in "summit" diplomacy, and there has been a steady stream of heads of state visiting the capitals of great powers, such as Moscow and Washington, D. C., since 1945.

The head of state himself, except when an absolute monarch or dictator such as Hitler, is not an independent agent, although he has control over all the departments of government concerned with foreign affairs. In Britain the prime minister is responsible to the majority party, or coalition, in the House of Commons. In the United States, according to the Constitution, the president is "head" of all executive departments and "commander in chief of the army and navy." But he cannot make a treaty without the "concurrence" of the Senate, nor spend money unless appropriated by the Congress; and only the Congress can declare war. In the dichotomy of state and Communist party in the Soviet Union, the central committee of the Communist party provides a powerful check on the power of the head of state.

The Foreign Minister. The primary function of the foreign minister is to serve as the principal adviser to the head of state on foreign affairs, and as such he is usually a significant policy maker. The foreign minister is responsible for the instructions that go out in cables and dispatches to embassies. If he is powerful enough, he may dominate policy making, as did Cardinal Richelieu in the 16th century and Talleyrand in the late 18th and early 19th centuries in France.

When the foreign minister issues policy statements they have usually been approved by his head of state, but these are not necessarily diplomacy. For example, U.S. Secretary of State George C. Marshall's suggestion in June 1947 for what was to become the Marshall Plan was a combination of practical and idealistic policies, but the diplomacy came later when the details had to be negotiated with the representatives of other governments. Secretary of State Dean Acheson's speech in 1949, suggesting that Korea might be outside the geographical limits of vital U.S. security interests, was an attempt to limit United States commitments and had to be followed by difficult negotiations. Secretary of State John Foster Dulles' statement that the United States might have to undergo an "agonizing reappraisal" of its policy toward the Soviet Union was meant to be a warning, which was thought to be necessary for the United States. In such statements lies the difference between foreign policy and diplomacy.

Politician. Closely related to the foreign minister's role as principal adviser on foreign relations to the head of state is his role as a politician. In the United States, the secretary of state is fourth in the line of presidential succession. Whether in parliamentary, republican, or Communist governments, the foreign minister must maintain working relationships with the power centers of the national legislature. In democratic countries, foreign ministers are often selected primarily because of their ability to influence legislators. President Franklin Roosevelt chose Cordell Hull, and President Harry Truman chose James F. Byrnes, as their secretaries of state because, among other reasons, each had great influence in the Senate. In cabinet-type governments, such as Britain, the foreign minister has a seat in Parliament and is one of the most influential members of his own party. In the Soviet Union the minister of foreign affairs has sometimes been a member of the secretariat of the central committee of the Communist party, as in the case of Vyacheslav A. Molotov, and sometimes not, as in the case of Andrei Gromyko, but he has always been a member of the party.

Negotiator. In addition to being policy maker and politician, the foreign minister engages in diplomatic negotiations with the ambassadors accredited to his head of state. The magnitude of the size of the diplomatic corps in any major capital is such that the foreign minister can see only a few ambassadors, except on state occasions or when he meets them in groups. The most that the foreign minister can hope to do is to conduct the most important negotiations with selected ambassadors. The main burden of day-to-day negotiations has to be carried by high-ranking officers such as assistant secretaries of state. In order not to affront the many representatives of heads of state, the foreign minister must engage in a tiring social schedule that permits him at least to meet the totality of the ambassadors in his capital.

As travel time has been reduced by the airplane, foreign ministers tend more and more to go to other capitals for direct negotiations with their opposite numbers, either individually or in conferences of foreign ministers. For example, British Foreign Minister Sir Anthony Eden before World War II and U.S. Secretary of State Dean Rusk in the 1960's engaged in such direct negotiations.

Administrator. An unavoidable responsibility for a foreign minister is the administration of the foreign office and of the service abroad. This was not difficult in 1661, when the Quai d'Orsay (the French foreign office) consisted of five persons, nor in 1685 when it had to supervise only 19 missions abroad. The foreign secretary in the foreign office in London had only 14 employees in 1793. For the modern foreign minister the problem is quite different: the secretary of state of the United States is responsible for some 25,000 employees, about 7,500 of whom are Americans in Washington, and 7,500 serving abroad, in addition to 10,000 foreigners employed in embassies and consulates.

UNITED STATES MISSIONS ABROAD, 1790–1960

	Embassies	Legations and other	Consular and commercial agencies	Total
1790	—	2	10	12
1840	—	20	152	172
1900	9	36	713	755
1950	58	16	207	281
1960	95	11	192	292

Organization of the Foreign Office. It would be impossible for a foreign minister, or a secretary of state, to manage effectively this many people and still carry on his primary functions of providing advice to his chief of state and negotiating with representatives of foreign powers, either in his own office, or abroad. Various forms of division of functions are used by different governments.

Britain. In Britain, Her Majesty's principal secretary for foreign affairs, the foreign minister, is supported by two ministers of state, and two parliamentary undersecretaries, who are members of Parliament. These four men, as members of the governing party, constitute the principle liaison with Parliament and have sufficient stature to negotiate with some ambassadors and visiting dignitaries. The foreign office itself is managed by a permanent undersecretary of state, who is a career civil servant and retains his post regardless of which political party is in power. He serves for an extended period of time and provides a desirable continuity to procedures and, where possible, to policy. Many countries organize their foreign offices along the lines of the British system.

United States. In the U.S. Department of State the secretary has no such assistants as the two ministers of state and the two parliamentary undersecretaries. Both the secretary of state and the undersecretary are political appointees of the president, leaving the continuity of management to third level officers—the deputy undersecretaries. There is no such thing as a permanent undersecretary chosen from the civil service, as in Britain. Even the deputy undersecretaries are often political rather than career officers.

Soviet Union. There have been countries that have had what amounted to dual foreign offices. The Nazis had their Brown House, which was separate from the foreign office on the Wilhelmstrasse. In the Soviet Union the pattern of parallel government and party structure is followed in the management of foreign affairs. The small (possibly 10-member) presidium of the government council of ministers, which is about the same size as, and has the same membership as, the secretariat of the Communist party, makes the major appointments in the ministry of foreign affairs. Within the ministry, there is the collegium, consisting of the foreign minister, a first deputy and several other deputy ministers—to which are added approximately an equal number of individuals without portfolio other than member of the collegium. The collegium advises the foreign minister, and assists in the first deputy's management of the diplomatic establishment. Thus the party, whether through the presidium, party secretariat, or collegium, has complete control of both policy and management.

Position Papers. Below the foreign minister and the second-ranking official, whatever his title, there are such offices as deputy undersecretaries, assistant secretaries, bureau heads, division chiefs, special assistants, and advisers. A primary function of many of these people is to prepare "position papers" for the foreign minister to use when advising the head of state, consulting with legislators, or negotiating with foreign powers. Before these people can prepare such papers, an immense amount of information and intelligence received each day has to be analyzed, evaluated, and organized in such a manner that it can be properly stored and readily made available when needed.

The British foreign minister in 1842 could say that he read every report from every consular officer, whereas today the foreign office receives upward of 600,000 dispatches each year. Based on this vast store of information, instructions have to be drafted for missions and embassies abroad to go out each night in cables, or in dispatches, usually over the signature of the foreign minister, who will actually see only the most important ones. To other senior officers has been delegated the authority to send certain kinds of instructions over the foreign minister's name. The magnitude of the task involved may be realized from the fact that the Department of State must provide whatever instructions are needed each day to 262 offices—more than 110 embassies in national capitals, more than 10 special missions to such agencies as the United Nations and NATO, and more than 135 consular offices not located in national capitals.

Geographic Desks and Functional Units. The structure of a foreign office involves various combinations of geographic "desks," functional departments, and service units. The designation of a geographic "desk" is a relic of the days when the foreign minister wrote most of the instructions going abroad or had the assistance of a man at a German "desk," for example. The officers in the geographic divisions are apt to be returned foreign service officers acquainted with the problems of the country or countries concerned. Because of the experience of these men, the geographic divisions tend to be very powerful in the intradepartmental structure.

The functional units include those that maintain liaison with the legislature; work with the nongovernmental public groups and individuals in developing understanding of foreign policy goals and policies; issue passports and visas; and supervise the work of missions to international intergovernmental organizations such as the United Nations. The functional units also include those whose business it is to follow relevant information in subject fields such as economics, social affairs, intercultural relations, and international law.

The Service Units. The negotiators, whether at the ambassadorial or consular level, must be freed from the day-to-day problems of administering the complexities of modern diplomatic establishments. In every foreign office there are service units for communications, personnel, travel, archives and files, research, security, and finance. Communications involves ciphers and coding and decoding of cables; movement of mail and couriers for handling very confidential papers; and arrangements for long-distance telephone lines to embassies abroad, including installation of "scramblers" and other devices to make interception meaningless. A personnel division, in the U.S. State Department, for example, maintains records for more than 25,000 employees; develops adequate policies for promotion, transfer, salaries, allowances for travel and living abroad; and administers provisions for sickness, and care of families in the event of the death of a foreign service officer while serving abroad. Very complicated arrangements have to be made for travel by every known method of transport, not only for the employee but for his family, his household goods, and even for his pets.

A staggering mass of papers has to be filed each day in such a manner that it can be retrieved when wanted. Files for current use have to be separated from those to be sent to archives because even the largest buildings, and the latest devices for microreproduction, will not hold indefinitely the papers of the foreign office of a large state. Separate buildings have to be planned and erected to hold such archives. Such publications as the *Foreign Relations of the United States* require research units constantly studying and writing the history of the foreign affairs of a nation. Heads of state and foreign ministers frequently call for historical summaries for use in speeches or public documents, and such calls are not usually made long in advance of need. The confidential and secret nature of many documents requires that there be adequate security provisions, including elaborate safes and alarm systems, as well as women and men trained to provide adequate protection. Personnel having access to particularly delicate and confidential matters and papers have to be checked because of the effective espionage systems maintained by many governments.

The unit that supervises consular affairs is large and very important. The Bureau of Security and Consular Affairs in the State Department issues some 1,500,000 passports annually, and is responsible for more than 300 consular offices and consular sections of embassies that provide over 1,000,000 visas.

Last but not least are the finance officers to whom the foreign minister delegates responsibility for seeing that expenditures do not exceed legislative appropriations. In 1784 this was not an impossible task for a foreign minister when the total cost of the British foreign service establishment was £107,056, of which only £14,178 represented the cost of the foreign office in London. The situation today is much different, when the budget for the U.S. Department of State in one year is over $400,000,000.

As the size of governments has expanded, it has been necessary to institute overall controls of expenditures; the treasury in Britain and the Bureau of the Budget in the United States have very great power in determining how, and for what, any department may spend money. In the United States, the deputy assistant secretary of state for budget works with the Bureau of the Budget to secure approval of sufficient funds for the implementation of policy. In democratic societies such as Britain and the United States, the power of the treasury or the Bureau of the Budget is immense, and the success of the negotiators abroad may depend on the ability of a budget officer in the Department of State to maintain smooth working relations with the Bureau of the Budget.

Planning Staff. In order to prepare adequate instructions, on almost every imaginable subject, for offices all over the world a foreign office needs a unit whose purpose it is to make long-range studies and develop proposals for courses of action, and bases for instructions. The issues and crises of the day are the province of the geographic and functional units, but policies are often inadequate if problems have not been considered in advance. The first important attempt in the United States to develop policy planners was the so-called "House Inquiry," initiated by President Wilson in 1917, under the leadership of Edward Mandel House, for the purpose of studying the interests of the United States in the ultimate peace settlement after World War I. The Department of State was not involved, and the inquiry was conducted entirely by a group advisory to the President.

The planning during World War II was quite different. In the autumn of 1939—two years before the United States entered the war—the Department of State began its *Post-war Foreign Policy Preparation*, the record of which has been published in a book of that name. The fact that the position papers prepared during the years from 1939 to 1945 were not always used in preparing instructions for negotiators does not detract from the fact that, for the first time, the United States entered important negotiations after careful sudy and consideration of almost every imaginable future issue. In 1944 it was recognized that some form of permanent long-range planning was desirable, with the result that the

Department of State established the Policy Planning Staff, headed by a senior officer. This was followed by the Policy Planning Council.

The difficulty has been to keep the long-range planners from becoming involved in day-to-day crises because their overall knowledge of U.S. policies and interests makes them invaluable when drafting instructions to diplomats working on a current issue. The country desk officers, and those from the functional divisions, consider and study subjects within their fields, whereas the planning officers are presumed to have studied the same problems in relation to a wide variety of others. The relationships between planning and operations officers are often strained.

6. Foreign Services

Finding men and women who meet the standards for diplomatic agents set by de Callières and Nicolson has not been an easy task, and the development of foreign services as they exist today has been a long process. One reason for this is that the foreign service officer, at whatever grade, from beginner to ambassador, has to engage in negotiations on behalf of his government, and to be an effective negotiator usually takes time and experience. Actually, several so-called foreign services have developed together: the diplomatic service, the foreign office staff, the consular service, the commercial service, and the information service. Of these, the consular service is usually the oldest, but until the 20th century it was considered to be socially inferior because consuls were "in trade," while those in the diplomatic service came from the aristocracy.

Aristocratic Diplomacy. The diplomatic service abroad was staffed by the aristocracy of Europe and Asia until the middle of the 19th century. Because these men came from similar social classes, and all usually spoke either Latin or French, the process of negotiation was relatively easy. All British foreign service officers who were university graduates came from Oxford or Cambridge, and all had attended private secondary schools, with about one third coming from Eton.

During the 19th century most persons entering the foreign service of the United States were the sons of wealthy men or had means of their own. Ambassadors were usually chosen from the ranks of businessmen who had supported the victorious presidential candidate. Three out of four men entering the U.S. foreign service as late as 1920 were graduates of "Ivy League" colleges, with about one third coming from Harvard, which led to complaints about the "Harvard clique."

The first changes in the background of diplomats came when entering secretaries of embassy were paid by the government instead of being selected and appointed by the ambassador and living as members of his household—usually with private incomes of their own. Indeed, from 1790 to 1919, men entering the British diplomatic service were required by law to have a private income of £400 assured for at least two years. Under such circumstances, a considerable proportion of the candidates were peers or the sons of peers. The British inaugurated a paid foreign service in 1822, and the United States followed suit in 1831.

The Merit System. During most of the 19th century there was agitation for reforms that would open the diplomatic services to men on the basis of merit rather than on their social connections. In 1856, France became the first state to initiate a system of competitive entrance examinations, followed by limited competition in Britain in 1880 and in the United States, in varying degrees, between 1906 and 1924. For the merit system to have real meaning, it was necessary to abolish the social distinctions between men who served in the diplomatic service abroad and those who either served abroad as consuls or at home in the foreign office. France combined the diplomatic and consular services in 1883, but the United States did not do so until 1924, and the British not until 1934. Amalgamation of the foreign office staff with the foreign service took place in Britain in 1919 and in the United States in 1947. The United States had a separate foreign service of the Department of Agriculture until it was combined with that of the State Department in 1939.

A merit system had little meaning unless it permitted competent men who did not have private financial resources to enter the foreign service. Annual salaries for Americans entering the service in 1790 were set at $1,350, increasing to $2,000 in 1810 and remaining at that figure until 1924, when they were increased to $2,500. Such remuneration did not attract competent men, unless they had private means. By 1962 the beginning salary was increased to $5,085, and, with the effective competitive examination system then in effect, the service was opened to any young man or woman who could qualify.

A career in the United States foreign service lacked attraction from 1790 to 1855, when the salary for an ambassador was set at a maximum of $9,000. A great change came in 1856, when salaries for ambassadors were increased to a minimum of $10,000 and a maximum of $17,500. In addition, the system of allowances for extra expenses was increased. Today the British ambassador in Washington, for example, receives expense allowances of more than $100,000.

Women, as in most professions in the 19th century, were not appointed to the diplomatic services. The first woman to be appointed to a foreign service was Lucille Atcherson in the United States in 1922. The first woman ambassador was Alexandra Kollontay, who was appointed ambassador to Mexico by the Soviet Union in 1926; the first woman ambassador from the United States was Ruth Bryan Owen, appointed to Denmark in 1934.

7. The Embassy

Most diplomatic negotiations takes place in embassies or legations abroad, or in the foreign offices of the countries to which ambassadors are accredited. The physical buildings and grounds where diplomats work are known as embassies, or as legations if of a secondary status. Included are the buildings needed to conduct the business of the mission and the residence of the ambassador, but not the consulate unless it is on the same premises as the embassy. The host states determine the areas that are to be included in the embassy.

What takes place in an embassy was described by the U.S. Department of State in *The American Ambassador* (1957). It declares that an ambassador is "charged with the four basic responsibilities that ranking diplomats have carried throughout history. These are: protection of his country's interests abroad; reporting to his government on conditions in the country of his assignment; negotiation of agreement; ceremonial

THE BIG-THREE (Great Britain, Russia, and the U. S.) meet at Potsdam in 1945. At the table are Winston Churchill (*upper left*), Joseph Stalin (*right*), and Harry S Truman (*foreground, back to camera*), with their staffs.

representation . . . . Until shortly before World War II, the ambassador's contacts were largely confined to a relatively small circle composed of high officials of the host government and his opposites of the diplomatic corps. . . . No longer can the diplomat confine his attention to politics and policies—important though they are. As executor of his country's foreign policy . . . his interests and his responsibilities range through politics, economics, commerce, industry, agriculture, finance, labor, standards of living, transport and communications, social welfare, education, science, art, religion—in fact, all aspects of life in the country of his assignment."

Other than the very broad directive to protect the interests of his country, the primary tasks of the diplomat are negotiation of agreements and reporting to his head of state or foreign minister. The latter task can be carried out by others; the negotiating function can not, unless by the head of state, the foreign minister, or a special representative.

In order to be effective in carrying out either of the two primary functions, or in representation, it is vital for the diplomat to participate in, and attend a wide variety of, official and private social functions. The development of friendships and acquaintanceships is necessary for effective negotiating or for gathering information for reporting purposes. An excellent example of the diplomat who knew the members of the government to which he was accredited was Prince Karl Lichnowsky, the German ambassador in London in 1914. He understood how official British thinking was developing during the last weeks before World War I and reported and pleaded with his government to realize that its diplomacy in July 1914 was certain to involve Britain in the war. That his advice was ignored was not the fault of the diplomat, but of the policy makers.

The ambassador has to be accredited by the government of the host country, and each member of his staff has to receive the same approval, but on a less formal basis. The ambassador and his professional staff are members of the diplomatic corps of the national capital where all reside. After centuries of confusion and argument, it was agreed that the senior diplomat with highest rank, usually ambassador, was to be the doyen of the corps and would take precedence over all others in the capital to which he was accredited. Seniority was determined by the ambassador whose date of accreditation to the head of state bore the earliest date.

Priviliges and Immunities. It is essential in the conduct of the relations between states for diplomatic agents to have certain privileges and immunities. Most important of these are the inviolability of the embassy, freedom of communication, and exemption from local jurisdiction.

The inviolability is usually known as "extraterritoriality" and has sometimes been said to spring from the idea that the embassy is the territory of the head of state represented by the ambassador. This is obviously not possible, but the degree of protection provided is very great and seldom violated. An example was the room in the attic of the imperial Chinese embassy in London where the republican revolutionary Sun Yat-sen was imprisoned in 1896, to be released only after repeated demands from the British government. The inviolability extends to the ambassador's staff, papers, family, servants, and vehicles. When two countries go to war, a caretaker embassy assumes responsibilites for the vacated embassy, as Switzerland did for the United States embassies in Tokyo and Berlin in 1941.

In times of domestic strife individuals may seek asylum in the embassy of a foreign power. The inviolability of the embassy extends to such persons, and it is rarely disregarded. Cardinal Mindszenty of Hungary, for example, lived in the United States embassy in Budapest for over a decade after 1956. Elaborate rules governing such matters exist in the 1963 United Nations Vienna Convention on Diplomatic Relations, which in turn is based on rules developed by the League of Nations, the United Nations Headquarters Agreement of 1946, and the Organization of American States Convention of 1954.

Embassy Organization. The organization for carrying on the functions of an embassy necessarily follows closely the organization of the foreign office it serves. The ambassador, or minister, stands at the head, with theoretical authority for all units. Actually, he is a coordinator, and in the case of military and some other attachés, his authority may be quite limited. In large embassies, the second man is a minister; in smaller embassies, a first secretary. When the ambassador or minister is absent, the senior officer remaining is known as a chargé d'affaires, who may be *ad interim* (temporary) or *en titre* (permanent), in which case he will usually be the third man in rank in the embassy.

In a large embassy there are political, economic, cultural, information, and administrative sections, and a consular agent or officer. In addition, there may be numerous attachés, such as those of army, navy, air force, labor, treasury, agriculture, and labor. Not only must the activities of the various attachés be coordinated, but some United States embassies are responsible for Peace Corps operations. In addition, there is the always present problem resulting from the fact that almost every major unit of a government such as the United States has foreign interests that do not always coincide with those of the Department of State. The extent to which an ambassador is cognizant of the espionage activities of his government within the country to which he is accredited varies greatly. It is this aspect of the duties of some ambassadors that still leads some people to consider an ambassador and his staff as spies. Most ambassadors would probably prefer not to know anything about the espionage activities of their own governments; lacking such knowledge, their honesty and credibilitary may be accepted to an extent not otherwise possible.

8. International Diplomacy

During the 19th century there developed what is known variously as "international diplomacy," "conference diplomacy," or "multilateral diplomacy," meaning that negotiations are conducted simultaneously with a group, rather than with one state, usually in an international congress or organization. Traditional diplomacy has not, as is sometimes claimed, been set aside when an ambassador has to negotiate with representatives of governments that support his position at the same time that he is negotiating with some who oppose him, and with still others who are uncommitted.

A United States ambassador at the United Nations in the 1950's, Ernest A. Gross, said that there are five rules for an ambassador operating within an international organization: "(1) be tough—act gentle; (2) do not negotiate with your friends in public; (3) don't close the front door without opening the back; (4) timely discussion is 'consulting'—discussion too late is 'insulting'; (5) lead—don't drive."

International diplomacy has as its emphasis the finding of the common interests of many states rather than those of only two. The long public debates in the United Nations usually are not diplomacy; the diplomacy is carried on quietly in the corridors and in the individual missions. A famous example was the private discussion at the United Nations between Ambassador Philip Jessup of the United States and Ambassador Jacob Malik of the Soviet Union, which resulted in the end of the Berlin blockade in 1949. The public speeches in the General Assembly of the United Nations are not entirely different from those of the ancient Greek heralds, when they pleaded in public the causes of their cities.

The concept of representation of something larger than the national interest is exemplified by the preamble to the United Nations Charter, which begins with the words, "We the peoples of the United Nations, determined to save succeeding generations from the scourge of war . . ." and ends with the words, "accordingly, our respective governments . . . have agreed to the present Charter." Thus "We the people" do not negotiate nor sign treaties; these are still the functions of diplomats.

The larger concept has seen its greatest fulfillment in the development of an international civil service, the principal officers of which are diplomats who sometimes negotiate on behalf of the world community rather than on behalf of the country of which they happen to be nationals. Sir Eric Drummond, the first secretary-general of the League of Nations, had been permanent undersecretary of the British Foreign Office, but as an international civil servant he played an important role in the negotiations for the pacific settlement of disputes during the decade of the 1920's. Albert Thomas, the first secretary-general of the International Labor Organization, was a dynamic Frenchman who led negotiations that set international standards that no single government, his own included, was willing or able to accomplish. Ralph Bunche of the UN Secretariat was able to negotiate armistices between Israel and the various Arab states in 1948 because he was not representing any of the great powers. The quiet negotiations of Dag Hammarskjöld, the second secretary-general of the United Nations, in Peking, Cairo, Jerusalem, London, Paris, and Washington were successful because all concerned knew that he represented the common interests of many nations. This kind of representation is far more common than is sometimes realized, for there are 199 international intergovernmental organizations with civil servants working steadily to develop, among other things, the concept of diplomatic representation of something larger than the national interest.

See also AMBASSADOR; ASYLUM; CONSULAR SERVICE; EXTRATERRITORIALITY; INTERNATIONAL LAW; INTERNATIONAL ORGANIZATION; PRIVILEGES AND IMMUNITIES; STATE, DEPARTMENT OF.

WALDO CHAMBERLIN, *Dartmouth College*

Bibliography

Bishop, Donald G., *The Administration of British Foreign Relations* (Syracuse, N. Y., 1961).
Callières, François de, *Traité de la manière de négocier avec les souverains* (1716); Eng. tr. by A. F. Whyte, *On the Manner of Negotiating with Princes* (Notre Dame, Ind., 1964).
Ilchman, Warren F., *Professional Diplomacy in the United States 1779–1939; a Study in Administrative History* (Chicago 1961).
Iklé, Fred C., *How Nations Negotiate* (New York 1967).
Mattingly, Garrett, *Renaissance Diplomacy* (Boston 1955).
Nicolson, Sir Harold, *Diplomacy* (London 1939).
Satow, Sir Ernest, *A Guide to Diplomatic Practice*, 4th ed. by Neville Brand (New York 1957).

DIPLOMATIC POUCH, an official mailbag transmitted through the regular post or by a special courier to and from a diplomatic mission abroad. To ensure the secrecy of diplomatic dispatches, the pouch is protected by international law and is not subject to customs inspection. Furthermore, diplomatic couriers carry special passports defining their status as official dispatch bearers. They are exempted from local jurisdiction and have the right of innocent passage (q.v.) through third states.

DIPOLE MOMENT, dī′pōl, the measure of the strength of an electric or magnetic dipole. An electric dipole consists of two equal but opposite electric charges, while a magnetic dipole consists of two equal magnetic poles of opposite polarity. The magnitude of the electric dipole moment (μ), or electric moment, is equal to the product of one of the charges and the distance between them ($\mu = ql$); the magnitude of the magnetic dipole moment (m), or magnetic moment, is the product of one of the poles and the distance between them ($m = pl$). Situations in which opposite electric charges are permanently or temporarily separated by small distances are so prevalent that it is convenient to consider the electric dipole as a special source of electrical influence. In the case of magnets, isolated poles do not exist, and so magnetism must be described in terms of magnetic dipoles.

The field strength, or influence, produced by a dipole is inversely proportional to the cube of the distance from the dipole and also depends on the angle between the dipole axis and the line to the dipole. The field can be pictured in terms of lines of force streaming from the positive charge of an electric dipole (or north pole of a magnet) and curving back to enter the negative charge (or south pole of a magnet).

If an electric dipole is in an electric field—or if a magnetic dipole is in a magnetic field—the dipole and the field interact, subjecting the dipole to a torque. For example, the torque that causes most electric motors to turn results from the interaction of a magnetic dipole and an ambient magnetic field.

Molecular Dipole Moment. Although a molecule has an equal number of positive and negative charges, their distribution within the molecule frequently is asymmetric. The uneven distribution of positive and negative charges is caused by the different electronegativities of the atoms or by the different sizes of the atoms. In either case the center of density of the negative electron charge does not coincide with the center of density of the positive proton charge, which is also the center of mass. A molecule with this structure has a permanent dipole moment; that is, it exists in the absence of an applied field.

Many molecules have permanent dipole moments. In a water molecule, for instance, the two hydrogen atoms and the oxygen atom are arranged in the form of an isosceles triangle. Most of the negative electron charge is grouped about the oxygen nucleus, leaving the positive protons exposed. This separation of charge produces a large electric dipole moment for the molecule.

In some molecules, such as H_2, CO_2, CH_4, and CCl_4, the distribution of positive and negative charges within the molecule is symmetrical; that is, the center of density of the negative electron charge coincides with the center of density of the positive proton charge. A molecule with this structure has no permanent dipole moment; however, a dipole moment can be induced in the molecule by subjecting it to an external electric field. The induced dipole moment exists only so long as the molecule is under the influence of an external field.

Studies of dipole behavior provide clues to the structure of molecules. See also MOLECULAR THEORY—*Forces Between Molecules* (Origin of the Attractive Forces).

CLIFFORD E. SWARTZ
State University of New York, Stony Brook

SCHUTZENHOFER, FROM ANNAN PHOTO FEATURES
European dipper

DIPPER, any of several small birds associated with fast-flowing mountain streams. Dippers occur in the western Americas from Alaska south to Argentina, in Europe from Scandinavia to northwest Africa, and in Asia from Siberia south to Taiwan.

Dippers are compact birds from 5½ to 7½ inches (14–19 cm) long. They have thin straight bills, relatively short wings, and short tails. They vary in color from gray to brown; the North American and Asiatic dippers are uniformly gray and brown respectively, but the South American species has a white head, and the European species has a white throat and chest. The sexes are alike in size and color.

Although not considered aquatic birds like loons or ducks, dippers are known for their unusual aquatic way of life. They are at home in a fast-flowing mountain stream where they swim and dive readily. Their feet are not, however, webbed for swimming, and they move rapidly underwater by means of their wings. Dippers can dive to a depth of 20 feet (6 meters), and they have been reported to "walk" on the stream bottom. In flight, they flutter rapidly from rock to rock, often close to the water surface. The food of dippers consists primarily of aquatic insects and their larvae, but dippers will also eat small crustaceans and snails as well as small salamanders and fish.

The dipper's nest is a large domed structure, made of moss and grass and lined with grass and leaves. Dippers usually place their nests close to water in the crevices of rocks, on ledges, between tree roots, or on trees fallen across streams. A favorite nest site is a ledge behind a waterfall. The nest structure is always on the side. The female lays usually four or five pure white eggs. She alone incubates the eggs, but the male aids in caring for the young.

There are four species of dippers making up the genus *Cinclus* of the family Cinclidae of the order Passeriformes.

KENNETH E. STAGER
Los Angeles County Museum of Natural History

DIPPER, BIG. See BIG DIPPER.

DIPPER, LITTLE. See URSA MINOR.

DIPTYCH showing in the left panel the Nativity and in the right panel the Crucifixion. The diptych was carved in France in the 14th century. Each of its ivory panels measures slightly under 4 inches by 5 inches.

DIPPING NEEDLE, an instrument used to show the tilt of the earth's magnetic field at a given point. At the magnetic equator the needle of the instrument is perfectly horizontal; at the magnetic poles it is vertical. The instrument has been referred to as a magnetic inclinometer and as an inclination compass because, when geographic north is known, the direction to magnetic north can easily be determined. Or, if the magnetic deviation for a given area is known, geographic north can be determined just as with a magnetic compass.

The most advanced instrument of this kind, which can show the azimuth as well as the tilt of the magnetic field, looks like a gyrocompass gimbaled on three axes, with one of the axes a light but highly magnetized bar. The same measurements can now be made much more rapidly with sensitive induction coils. The induction coil technique yields the magnitude of the magnetic field at the point of measurement as well, and it is thus the preferred method in modern geological and geophysical studies.

Laurence W. Fredrick, *University of Virginia*

DIPTERA, dip′tə-rə, is an order of insects in which only the fore wings are used for flight, the hind pair having been modified into balancing organs called halteres. The order Diptera, which includes all the true flies, is divided into three suborders: Nematocera, the most primitive flies, including the midges, gnats, crane flies, mosquitoes, and others with many-segmented antennae; Brachycera, made up of a number of archaic families, including the horseflies and robber flies; and Cyclorhapha, chiefly "muscoid" flies, that is, those that generally resemble the housefly *Musca domestica*.

All flies obtain their food by sucking and are unable to chew. Some, like the housefly, mop up their food through a sponge formed from the lobes of the labium (lower lip). Others use a tube formed from the elongate mandibles (primary jaws) and maxillae (secondary jaws) and suck nectar from flowers or blood from vertebrate animals by first piercing their skin (bloodsucking flies). Flies of several families catch other insects and suck their body fluids. The eyes of flies are often very large, and in males they may occupy the entire surface of the head.

Diptera, both as adults and as larvae (maggots), are among the insects most harmful to man. Mosquitoes, sandflies, biting midges, and tsetse flies transmit diseases (malaria, sleeping sickness, yellow fever, many viruses) when they suck blood. Maggots attack plants, animals, and man.

Harold Oldroyd
British Museum (Natural History), London

DIPTYCH, dip′tik, a folding rectangular tablet of wood, ivory, or metal, used in Greco-Roman times to record titles, offices, and greetings. Diptychs normally consisted of two leaves held together with hinges, rings, or cords. The early Christians adopted diptychs for liturgical use, recording on them the names of martyrs or other important persons. Gradually, a standard protocol for the liturgical diptych emerged. The absence of a name from its accustomed place among the honored implied a charge of heresy, since those who departed from the orthodox path had their names "stricken from the diptychs."

Many of the diptychs that have survived from the late Roman Empire were made to mark the beginning of a consul's term of office. The outer faces of the leaves of these diptychs were often decorated with figural scenes showing the consul opening the games. Other ornamental diptychs were made for Christian use. In the following centuries the custom of making such luxury diptychs fell into abeyance until the 13th century, when ivory diptychs gained new popularity. Ivory tablets were carved with religious scenes in the Gothic style for use as small altarpieces or for private devotion. The late Middle Ages also saw the creation of larger diptychs painted on wooden panels.

Wayne Dynes, *Columbia University*

DIRAC, di-rak′, **Paul Adrien Maurice** (1902–), British theoretical physicist, who made many contributions to the quantum mechanical description of atomic phenomena. He was awarded a share of the 1933 Nobel Prize in physics for his discovery of new forms of atomic theory.

Dirac was born at Bristol, England, on Aug. 8, 1902, and educated at the University of Bristol and St. John's College, Cambridge. While at Cambridge, Dirac worked under the guidance of R. H. Fowler and prepared a number of papers on relativistic dynamics and various aspects of the older quantum theory. It was shortly after a visit to Cambridge in 1925 by one of the founders of the new quantum mechanics, Werner Heisenberg, that Dirac became acquainted with the novel approaches which Heisenberg was then initiating. Dirac's first paper in quantum mechanics, "The Fundamental Equations of Quantum Mechanics," added greatly to the understanding of the foundations of the subject.

By 1928, Dirac had applied the techniques of relativistic mechanics to quantum theory. He suggested a relativistic form of Schrödinger's fundamental equation. The solutions for this relativistic wave equation possessed, however, a curious property: they included negative energy states as well as positive ones. Dirac interpreted this situation for the electron in the following manner. The negative energy states—in the absence of an external electrical field—are always filled, so that ordinarily they can be disregarded (no transitions are made into them). If, however, an appropriate field is applied, an electron may "jump" from a filled negative energy state into an unfilled positive state. The effect will be seen in the laboratory as the creation of *two* particles, an ordinary electron and a positron (a positively charged particle in all other respects exactly like an electron). Thus, Dirac predicted the first of the antiparticles in his theory of pair production. The positron was later experimentally discovered by C. D. Anderson and independently by P. M. S. Blackett and G. P. S. Occhialini in 1933.

Dirac also was co-inventor of the Fermi-Dirac statistics and pioneered in the quantum theory of radiation. His publications include *The Principles of Quantum Mechanics* (1930) and many papers.

ROBERT KARGON
The Johns Hopkins University

DIRCE, dûr'sē, in Greek mythology, was the second wife of Lycus, king of Thebes. According to one legend, Lycus abandoned his first wife, Antiope, who had borne him two sons, Amphion and Zethus. Dirce commanded the sons to bind Antiope to the horns of a wild bull so that she would be dragged to death. Upon discovering that Antiope was their mother, the brothers compelled Dirce to endure the fate she had designed for Antiope. The gods pitied her suffering and changed Dirce into a spring that flows near Thebes and still bears her name.

DIRE DAWA, dē'rä də-wä' is the principal commercial center of eastern Ethiopia. It is situated about 200 miles (320 km) east of Addis Ababa, the national capital, and 35 miles (56 km) northwest of the provincial capital, Harar, the center of Ethiopia's Muslim region. Dire Dawa lies on the railroad line that links Addis Ababa with Djibouti, capital of French Somaliland. Dire Dawa's airport is capable of handling jet traffic.

The area around the city produces pulses, coffee, and *chat* (a mild stimulant) for export. A cement factory and the country's oldest and largest textile mill are also located in Dire Dawa. Population: (1963 est.) 32,300.

DIRECT TAXES. See TAXATION.

DIRECT CURRENT, an electric current that flows in one direction only. A direct current may have either a constant magnitude or a varying magnitude, but it always flows in the same direction. See also ELECTRICITY.—3. *Direct Electric Current.*

DIRECTING, in the theatrical sense, means superintending the preparation of a dramatic work for the stage, films, television, or some other medium. Directing involves choosing the actors, coordinating their performances, and supervising the designers and makers of scenery, costumes, properties, wigs, and whatever else the production may require.

In the English-speaking theater there is some confusion between "director" and "producer," because in Britain the director is called the producer, whereas in the United States the producer is the person responsible for the financing and business organization of a theatrical enterprise. In Britain this person is known as the manager. Perhaps the function of the stage director is more clearly defined by the French equivalent: *metteur en scène* (the person who puts the play on the stage).

History. The director as an important member of the theatrical hierarchy is a relatively new development; until about 1920 the public was scarcely aware that such a person existed. Yet, like every other activity involving the cooperation of a number of people, theatrical productions have always had to be "directed." Even as long ago as 400 B.C. the chorus in Greek tragedy was directed, usually by the author. As a matter of fact, throughout the ages authors have, very properly, been closely concerned with the direction of their plays.

It was customary, until about the beginning of the 20th century, for the director's function to be entrusted to a company's leading actor. He bore the principal responsibility during a play's performance; he was frequently the most dominating personality present, the natural leader of the group. Also, he was probably the principal "draw" for the public. For all these reasons the actor–manager traditionally was the most logical person to direct the production of a play, and for the best part of two centuries—until the early 20th century—it was the usual custom for him to do so.

For 21 years, between 1878 and 1899, at the Lyceum Theatre, London, Sir Henry Irving did just this. Since that time, however, the theater's entire context—social, political, financial, and artistic—has changed, and, because theatrical business has become enormously more competitive, expensive, and complicated, the actor–manager has largely disappeared from the contemporary theater.

The modern theatrical manager, unlike his counterpart in earlier theatrical history, must grapple with the serious financial and administrative burdens posed by such things as income tax, employer's liability for the insurance of his staff, and the complex regulations and considerable demands of six or seven different trade unions. Consequently, it is no longer possible for one man to be responsible for a company of actors, a backstage staff, the box office, catering, cleaning, advertising, heating, insurance, and a hundred other administrative arrangements, and at the same time determine his theater's artistic policy, choose the plays, direct the rehearsals, and play most of the leading parts.

Play production came to be undertaken by a corps of specialists. Broadly speaking, there developed a business or administrative side, with a producer (in British usage, manager) in charge; and an artistic side, headed, no longer by the author or the leading actor, but by a director.

In the 20th century the director's status advanced, partly because the mass dramatic media (radio, television, and films) require a group of technicians—cameramen, lighting and sound engineers, cutters, and others—each with their own "satellites." The activities of these technicians were all coordinated under a director, and their importance added to his.

Function. The director bears to the preparation of a play much the same relation an orchestral conductor bears to the rehearsal of a symphony. However, the symphony is not only rehearsed but performed by the conductor, with the orchestra playing under his leadership. He interprets and guides the entire performance. The theatrical director's work ends before the first performance. He prepares the play, but, when the time comes to show it to the public, the performance goes on without him. Like Moses on Mount Nebo he can only watch the fulfillment of a dream in which he retains no active part.

Most of the really important directorial decisions are made before the actors even begin to rehearse. The director's interpretation of a play will be greatly conditioned by his casting of it. If A, B, and C are to play Othello, Iago, and Cassio, and if X and Y are to be Desdemona and Emilia, it will be fairly clear, even before a single rehearsal has been held, what the general attempt of a director is going to be in this particular production.

Conferences with those who are to design the scenery and costumes will determine how a production is to look. At these conferences a wise director will not dictate to his collaborators, although they will look to him for general guidance. Some designers like to work "on ruled lines," as it were; to others a wink or a nudge is as good as columns of closely typed instructions. If it is vital that designers' creative talents be encouraged, not frustrated, it is equally vital that other, and possibly more important, aspects of a production are not butchered to make a designer's holiday.

While the general shape and feeling of the production will have been settled before the actors assemble for the first rehearsal, the intensely interesting detailed work of interpretation begins with the rehearsals. It is usually at this point that the director communicates his ideas to the cast.

In theory, a director should not instruct competent actors in the detailed playing of their parts. He should make clear what he thinks are the important general aspects of a scene or a speech; he must explain why a particular passage must go fast in order to give weight to a slow passage following; he must determine precisely where, and how, the audience's attention must be focused. While there are many technical devices available to achieve all these things, they all depend upon the *directed* coordination of the actors.

In addition to this, every actor depends upon a director for advice and criticism, for the sort of assistance a writer expects from his editor. Furthermore, sometimes the less gifted or less experienced actors need positive instruction from a director: when to move, when to keep still, which word to stress, what a speech or a piece of "business" is intended to convey.

While a good director may often offer helpful criticism and valuable coaching or supply interesting, even thrilling, interpretative ideas, perhaps his most useful contribution to the work of rehearsal is not "artistic" at all but consists in being a good chairman. In this capacity he arranges the "agenda" of each day's rehearsal, sets the pace, and determines the amount of time to be devoted to each activity.

Above all, it is principally from the director that a rehearsal takes its tone, derives its atmosphere. It depends on him whether rehearsals are boring or exciting; whether they strike the happy medium between being too tense and too relaxed; and whether or not the proceedings are suffused with the degree of vitality and goodwill needed to bring anything into being.

If there were nothing more to directing than being a good chairman and a methodical organizer who possesses some degree of technical know-how, then theatrical direction would be no more than a craft, like good plain cooking. But there is more to it. Possibly the most significant relationship between director and players is established, not on the conscious, practical, rational level, but on a plane where communication is not articulated in words and where influence is exerted not by precept but by evocation. A similar process of evocation takes place when a great conductor is in charge of an orchestra. The story is told of an old orchestra player saying of Toscanini: "It isn't that he makes you play as well as you can. He makes you play better than you knew you could."

The conductor, or director, does not consciously try to pull the performance out of the players. He seeks only to interpret the work. Without the conscious intention of either party, however, a special relationship occasionally establishes itself between them. It is intermittent. It rarely lasts for more than a few seconds at a time. It is unpredictable. It certainly does not come by being sought. All artists know how vain it is to seek for inspiration. Nevertheless, in the field of creative imagination and of artistic communication an inspired relationship can occasionally be established between an idea and its expression; and an inspired personal relationship can come into being between those concerned, so that jointly they express an idea that none of them singly is aware of having originated.

Everyone, not just the artist, knows the experience of being taken in charge, carried away, by a force that apparently has nothing to do with the "usual self," whose power is far greater than anything of which the "usual self" is normally capable. It is impossible to be precise about what is vaguely and metaphorically called "inspiration," but it would be very rash on that account to deny its existence. It is when inspiration takes over that the competent and experienced craftsman becomes an artist.

A theatrical director must be a craftsman first and foremost. He must devote all his energy to learning the intricacies of this difficult and interesting trade. However, now and again all craftsmanship can be ennobled by inspiration; now and again a good plain cook will create a dish at which the mouths of archangels must water.

SIR TYRONE GUTHRIE
Author of "A Life in the Theatre"

Further Reading: Canfield, Fayette C., *Craft of Play Direction* (New York 1963); Cole, Toby, and Chinoy, Helen K., eds., *Directors on Directing*, 2d ed. (Indianapolis 1963); Hunt, Hugh, *Director in the Theatre* (New York 1954).

RADIO DIRECTION FINDER loop, shown above a radar antenna midway up a ship's mast (near right), and the direction finder receiver (far right), with compass degrees to mark the signal's bearing.

RCA RADIOMARINE PHOTOS

DIRECTION FINDER, an electronic device for determining the direction of arrival of radio waves sent from a distant radio transmitting station. Because it can locate the geographical direction, or *bearing*, of a distant station, the direction finder is used aboard ships, small boats, and aircraft as an aid in navigation. It is also used to locate illegal or enemy radio transmitting stations. Direction finders are used at radio frequencies ranging from about 15,000 to 500 million hertz (cycles per second).

Operation. In its simplest form the direction finder consists of a directive antenna, such as a loop of wire, and a radio receiver. In taking the bearing of a distant station the operator rotates the loop until the signal is weakest or completely last; this null condition occurs when the plane of the loop is broadside to the direction to the station. The *automatic direction finder* (ADF) for aircraft navigation has a motor to rotate the loop automatically to the proper null position and a pointer and scale to indicate the direction toward the distant transmitter.

Other direction finders have arrays of vertical wires, forming what is called an *Adcock antenna*. These vertical arrays are used at radio frequencies in the shortwave band where loop antennas are inaccurate.

History. Heinrich Hertz demonstrated the directive properties of a loop antenna about 1888. Practical direction finders were conceived shortly after 1900, and they were in wide use by World War I.

DONALD S. BOND, *RCA Laboratories*

Further Reading: Bond, Donald S., *Radio Direction Finders* (New York 1944); Keen, Ronald, *Wireless Direction Finding* (London 1947).

DIRECTOIRE STYLE, di-rek-twär', in interior decoration and in fashion, a style that emerged in France about the time of the Directory (1795–1799). It was a transitional style between the ornateness of the Louis XVI period and the neoclassicism of the Empire. The architects Charles Percier and Pierre Fontaine and the painter Louis David were important influences in the development of the Directoire style.

Directoire furniture is simpler than Louis XVI furniture, with more straight lines and less ornament. Plain surfaces of painted or waxed wood replace the elaborate inlaid designs of the preceding period. The taste for classical Greek and Roman details, which came to full flower during the Empire, began its revival in the Directoire period.

Women's dresses in Directoire style featured low necklines and straight skirts hanging from high waistlines. Men wore wide-lapeled coats and tight breeches laced at the knee.

DIRECTORY, the name of the government that ruled France from Nov. 3, 1795, to Nov. 9, 1799. The constitution of the Directory (French, Directoire) was written by the National Convention, and by its terms the Directory succeeded the Convention as the legal government of France.

The executive authority of the Directory was vested in a commission of five directors, who were elected by a bicameral legislature consisting of a Council of Ancients and a Council of Five Hundred. In an attempt to give stability to the government, only one of the directors and one third of the legislators were to be replaced each year. Before the National Convention disbanded, it had voted to place two thirds of its own members in the new legislature.

The Directory marked a retreat from the revolutionary fervor of the early years of the French Revolution and from the instability that marked the period after Robespierre's fall in 1794. Suffrage was restricted, and property qualifications for voting were established. Idealism gave way to avarice, and profiteering and corruption were widespread. After surviving several attempted coups d'etat, the Directory was overthrown in a coup led on behalf of Napoleon Bonaparte in 1799.

DIRICHLET, dē-rē-klä', **Gustav Peter Lejeune** (1805–1859), German mathematician, who was one of the founders of analytical number theory. He was born on Feb. 3, 1805, in Düren. During 1822–1825, Dirichlet was a tutor in Paris, where he met Jean Fourier and other leading French mathematicians. Fourier's work on the theory of heat and Karl F. Gauss' classic on number theory (*Disquisitiones arithmeticae*) strongly influenced Dirichlet's future mathematical work. After a short stay in Breslau he taught from 1831 to 1855 at the University of Berlin. He died at Göttingen on May 5, 1859.

Dirichlet developed new and powerful methods in analytical number theory, which he connected with the theory of infinite series and definite integrals. He provided the first rigorous convergence proofs for Fourier series, and thus contributed to a correct understanding of the concept of a function. A central problem in electrostatics and potential theory generally is the determination of a harmonic function satisfying certain boundary conditions; this is called *Dirichlet's problem* because of his work on it. His beautiful *Vorlesungen über Zahlentheorie* was published posthumously (1863; 4th ed., 1894).

D. J. STRUIK
Massachusetts Institute of Technology

DIRIGIBLE. See AIRSHIP.

DIRK HARTOGS ISLAND, dûrk här′togz, is in the Indian Ocean, just off the west coast of Australia. The island is located at the entrance of Shark Bay and forms the southern boundary of Naturaliste Channel.

Covering an area of 239 square miles (619 sq km), it is 48 miles (77 km) long and 3 to 7 miles (5–11 km) wide. The island is used as a sheep run.

DIRKSEN, dûrk′sən, **Everett McKinley** (1896–1969), American legislator who was elected leader of the Republican party in the U. S. Senate in 1959. One of the most persuasive and influential senators, he became known as a sensitive and shrewd negotiator. He was acclaimed as an orator for the range of his cadences and for the subtlety of his often quotable thrusts. Although usually classified as an independent conservative, he advised his party against merely negative opposition, remarking that America has "a dynamic economy ... and sometimes you have to change your position." His own position was often crucial.

Dirksen was born in Pekin, Ill., of German immigrant parents on Jan. 4, 1896. Working at many small-business jobs from his youth, he studied at the University of Minnesota for three years before joining the Army in World War I. He was elected to local office in Pekin in 1926 but was defeated for Congress in a 1930 primary. In 1932 he was overwhelmingly elected to the House of Representatives. Failing eyesight caused him to retire from Congress in 1948. When a quick recovery permitted him to campaign for the Senate in 1950, he defeated Scott W. Lucas, the Democratic majority leader, and began his long Senate career.

Dirksen's early record in the Senate was conservative. He supported Senator Robert A. Taft for the Republican presidential nomination in 1952 and was not always happy with the Eisenhower administration. On his election as leader of the Republican minority in the Senate, however, he cooperated vigorously with the president.

In the Kennedy administration, Dirksen supported the nuclear test ban treaty but opposed federal medical care for the aged. During the Johnson administration the Republican leader and the Democratic president formed a close working partnership that was unusual in American politics. Dirksen was a major architect of the Civil Rights Act of 1964 and of the Voting Rights Act of 1965. In 1965 and 1966 he blocked repeal of federal law authorizing state right-to-work laws against the union shop. The Senate shelved his proposals for constitutional amendments to approve voluntary public school prayers and to allow the apportionment of one house in a state legislature on a geographical basis—both aimed at overriding decisions of the U. S. Supreme Court. In 1966 he refused to allow open-occupancy housing legislation to come to a vote in the Senate, but in 1968 he helped push such a bill through Congress. Dirksen supported American goals and actions in Vietnam, but criticized President Johnson's offer of "negotiations without prior conditions."

Dirksen's album, *Gallant Men,* won a Grammy award for best documentary recording of 1967. He died in Washington, D. C., on Sept. 7, 1969.

FRANKLIN L. BURDETTE
University of Maryland

DISABILITY INSURANCE. See LIFE INSURANCE; SOCIAL SECURITY.

DISABLED AMERICAN VETERANS, an organization of veterans with service-connected ailments or disabilities. It provides for the welfare of the veterans and their dependents. The DAV was founded by a committee of disabled veterans, headed by Judge Robert S. Marx, in Cincinnati, Ohio, in 1921 and received a charter from the U. S. Congress in 1932.

The organization, administered by officers elected at annual conventions, supports a national service program and has a service office in each regional office of the Veterans Administration to assist its membership in obtaining VA benefits. Its chief activity is the production and sale of identotags (miniature automobile license plates for key chains).

In the late 1960's the DAV had 1,900 local chapters and a membership, including the ladies' auxiliary, of 300,000. The national headquarters are at Cold Spring, Ky.

DENVEL D. ADAMS, *National Adjutant, DAV*

Everett Dirksen

DISALLOWANCE, in Canadian political practice, is the authority of the executive to abrogate an act of a subordinate legislature. The British North America Act (1867) empowered the British government to disallow any act of the Canadian government within two years of its enactment. Always sparingly used, this power was declared obsolete in 1926. Although provincial statutes may still be disallowed by federal authority—usually because the provincial legislation conflicts with national interests or policies —disallowance has been rarely invoked since the 1920's.

DISARMAMENT, dis-är′mə-mənt, is the limitation, reduction, or elimination of national armaments or particular types of armaments, and the regulation of the use of armaments. The problem of disarmament has been called the heart of international politics; and doubtless increases and decreases in the armament programs of the principal powers measure the rise and fall of international tension. Disarmament agreements are recorded from the earliest times in Chinese, Mesopotamian, Indian, and classical history. Negotiations on the subject have been prominent in modern history, especially following major wars, and have occupied increasing attention in the 20th century. The relative size of a state's armament became the accepted measure of its power, and fluctuations in the relative size of armaments have had a primary influence on world politics.

Membership in the "nuclear club," which includes the United States, the Soviet Union, Britain, France, and China, has come to be the symbol of great power status. Furthermore, the increasing menace to civilian life of modern weapons, especially nuclear weapons, has induced widespread belief that the future of civilization itself depends on some form of disarmament.

It has been realized, however, that not only armaments, but such factors as military potential, the capacity of a nation to sustain diplomatic and military effort, and the ability of a nation to win the help of allies in time of emergency must also be considered in appraising the power or capability of the state. Consequently it has been difficult to separate disarmament from the regulation of industry, propaganda, and foreign policy. Such phrases as "industrial disarmament," "moral disarmament," and "political disarmament" have been used. The breadth of the problem has prevented general and enduring agreement. But numerous limited agreements have been made, such as unilateral arms restrictions, local demilitarizations, truces in building armament stockpiles, and regulations of trade in, and use of, armaments. The problem of general quantitative or qualitative disarmament has been a major preoccupation of the Hague Conferences, the League of Nations, and the United Nations, but little progress has been made.

Unilateral Disarmament. Unilateral disarmament normally occurs voluntarily as a result of taxpayers' pressure whenever the government feels there has been a reduction of international tension and an increase in security. That is the usual situation after wars. The United States, for example, greatly reduced its armaments and armed forces after World War II.

Unilateral disarmament has often been demanded of the defeated state in treaties of peace. Thus by the Treaty of Versailles, "in order to render possible the initiation of a general limitation of the armaments of all nations," Germany was compelled to accept severe limitations of its land, naval, and air forces.

After World War II the armament restrictions imposed on the defeated Axis powers were less severe. Treaties of peace with Italy, Hungary, Rumania, Bulgaria, and Finland did, however, impose unilateral restrictions. Complete German disarmament was an accepted occupation policy. However, Germany was divided into western and eastern zones, and though no treaty of peace had been drafted, the western zone, constituted as the Federal Republic of Germany, became a member of the North Atlantic Treaty Organization with requirements for rearmament rather than disarmament. Japan was required during the occupation to incorporate provisions for disarmament in its constitution.

Local Disarmament. Reciprocal disarmament by international agreement has been most effective in the case of local disarmament. By the Rush-Bagot Agreement of 1817, the United States and Britain agreed not to maintain warships of more than 100 tons on the Great Lakes. This pledge has been maintained ever since and constitutes the longest-lived disarmament agreement in history. Its spirit has extended to the land frontiers with the result that the 3,000-mile (4,828-km) boundary between the United States and Canada has not been the scene of fortification, mobilization, or war for nearly a century and a half. Some 50 local disarmament agreements have been made in the 20th century, including those affecting the Strait of Magellan, the Norwegian-Swedish frontier, the New Hebrides, Spitsbergen, and the insular possessions of the great powers in the Pacific.

Truces in Arms Races. The shorter the duration of a disarmament agreement, the easier it has proved to negotiate, but even a brief arms truce may stop a dangerous arms race likely to lead to war. By the Washington Naval Armaments treaties of 1921 and 1922, the United States, Britain, Japan, France, and Italy agreed to keep certain types of naval vessels below defined limits for 15 years, and this was extended to other types during the last 5 years of this term by the London Naval Treaty of 1931. In the same year, as a preparation for the proposed General Disarmament Conference, the Assembly of the League of Nations requested the states invited to that conference to accept a truce on all armament building for 1 year. The truce was accepted by 54 governments, including the United States.

Arms Trade. Imperial powers have often forbidden arms trade in colonial areas, and the Brussels Act of 1890, revised in the treaty of 1919, regulated such trade in colonial Africa. The League of Nations Covenant recognized that "the manufacture by private enterprise of munitions and implements of war is open to grave objections." In pursuance of this provision, a convention was drawn up at Geneva in 1925 for the regulation of arms trade, but the United States refused to ratify for constitutional reasons and because such agreement might make it impossible for countries without arms manufacture to provide for their defense.

The theory that arms manufacturers stimulate wars to create markets for their products developed in the interwar period and was supported by the Senate committee headed by Sen. Gerald Nye of North Dakota. The committee's report influenced American neutrality legislation from 1935 to 1937, forbidding the export of arms, ammunition, and implements of war to belligerent countries while the United States was neutral. The popularity of this theory declined when it appeared that the aggressive Axis powers were profiting by it, and the Neutrality Act was modified, at first to permit the export of arms on a "cash and carry" basis. Later, arms exports to the Allies were stimulated by the Lend-Lease Act of 1941 while the United States was still nominally neutral.

Use of Arms. In the Washington Naval Conference of 1921–1922, after the participants had failed to agree on a convention for limiting the manufacture and possession of submarines, a convention was agreed upon, though not ratified, prohibiting the use of submarines for attack on merchant vessels.

The history of war is full of efforts to forbid the use of certain types of weapons deemed particularly barbarous. The Lateran Council of 1215 prohibited the crossbow. Efforts were made to prohibit the use of grapeshot during the Napoleonic period, and declarations of the Hague Conference of 1899 prohibited the use of poison gases and the launching of projectiles from aircraft. Other Hague conventions of 1899 and 1907 sought to regulate bombardments from land, sea, or air and to prohibit the use of any weapon that "causes unnecessary suffering," thus carrying out the St. Petersburg Convention of 1868, which had prohibited the use of small explosive bullets. Subsequent conventions have reaffirmed prohibitions of the use of poison gases. Efforts to forbid the use of nuclear weapons or any weapons, including bacteria, which cause mass destruction, have failed. With the exception of those concerning poison gases, these agreements have not proved effective, and even the poison gas convention was violated by Italy in the Ethiopian War of 1935, when retaliation in kind was not to be feared.

Quantitative Disarmament. The ideal of disarmament is reduction of all national armaments to a level necessary only for the maintenance of internal order. It is assumed that armaments beyond this are for defense from external attack and so are related to the armament of others. Consequently, with a simultaneous proportionate reduction of all armaments leaving each state only enough for policing internal disorders, no state would be less secure. Difficulties arise, however, because armaments for policing can be used for external aggression. The policing and defense components of armament cannot be sharply distinguished. Therefore, general disarmament has been attempted by reducing categories of armament to assigned levels, as in the Washington Naval Armaments treaties of 1921 and 1922, or by reducing them by an assigned proportion, as proposed in the League conference of 1932 and by both the United States and the Soviet Union in the 1950's and 1960's. Such agreements, however, involve the problems of measurement, of ratios, and of guarantees. Should armaments be measured by budgetary expenditures, by numbers of effectives (fully equipped soldiers), or by quantity of various types of matériel? If by matériel, should reductions be equal in all categories or should the special needs of one country for particular types of armaments be balanced against the needs of others for different types? Unless reductions are made proportional to the existing situation, ratios of strength must be accepted, such as the 5:3:3 ratio between the United States, Britain, and Japan at the Washington Naval Conference. Such ratios involve political prestige and the power equilibrium and so are difficult to achieve. In any case the problem of mutual confidence in observance presents itself. Governments, jealous of territorial sovereignty and suspicious of the motives of visiting commissions, especially in a time of tension such as that which existed during the cold war after World War II, are reluctant to accept inspection that would ensure compliance.

The exchange of information, not only on armaments, but on the number, location, and movement of armed forces, is a recognized aid to the making and maintenance of armament agreements. In the League of Nations Covenant the members undertook "to interchange full and frank information as to the scale of their armaments, their military and naval programs, and the condition of such of their industries as are adaptable to warlike purposes" (Art. 8, par. 6). This resulted in publication of an armaments yearbook.

Qualitative Disarmament. The difficulties of general quantitative disarmament led to a concentration of attention on particular weapons in the League of Nations Conference of 1932. Efforts were made to distinguish between defensive and offensive armaments, the latter said to include heavy mobile artillery, large tanks, capital ships, aircraft carriers, submarines, bombing airplanes, poison gases, and bacteria. After World War II, special efforts were made to regulate atomic weapons and other "weapons of mass destruction," all of which were distinguished from "conventional armaments."

The Hague Conferences. The major purpose of the Czar of Russia in calling the first Hague Conference in 1899 was to effect the reduction of armaments, especially heavy artillery. A similar objective motivated the summoning of the second Hague Conference in 1907. No such reduction was effected, largely because of the objections of Germany. These conferences had to content themselves with efforts to facilitate settlement of international disputes, to regulate the use of armaments in war, and to codify the rules of war. A third Hague conference, with purposes similar to its predecessors, was in preparation for 1914, but the outbreak of World War I prevented its assembly. The Washington Conference of 1921–1922 and its successors, the abortive Geneva Conference of 1927, the more successful London Conference of 1930, and the less successful London Conference of 1936, initiated by the United States and held outside the League of Nations, may be regarded as continuances of the Hague system. These conferences did achieve a temporary success in checking rivalry among the great naval powers in the building of capital ships, and in providing for the disarmament of Pacific bases between Pearl Harbor and Singapore.

The League of Nations. A major objective of the League of Nations, which came into being in 1920, was disarmament. The fourth of President Wilson's 14 points of 1918 proposed that "adequate guarantees be given and taken that national armaments be reduced to the lowest point consistent with domestic safety." The Covenant restated this objective and required the Council, "taking account of the geographical situation and circumstances of each state," to "formulate plans for such reduction for the consideration and action of the several governments." Such plans were to be reconsidered at least every 10 years and, after reduction, the limits of armaments established could not be exceeded without "concurrence of the Council" (Art. 8). The League persistently sought to realize these provisions until the rise of Hitler and the failure of the disarmament conference of 1932 led to rearmament.

The League early appreciated the fact that the Permanent Armament Commission, established by the Covenant (Art. 9) and consisting of professional military men of the principal powers, was ineffective to advise on disarmament. It therefore established the Temporary Mixed Commission, with civilian members. Reports of this commission and resolutions of the Assembly established the interdependence of *disarmament, security,* and *arbitration,* the last term including adequate means for assuring international justice, even by "peaceful change."

The Geneva Protocol of 1924 sought, as prerequisites to disarmament, to elaborate Charter provisions on security and arbitration by defining aggression, establishing collective obligations of states to act against it, and providing means for the pacific settlement of all disputes. The protocol was defeated because of the reluctance of the Conservative government of Britain, successor to Ramsay MacDonald's Labour government, which had signed the protocol, to make such extensive commitments, especially as the policy of the United States, not a member of the League, was uncertain. After the more successful effort to increase security by the Locarno treaties and to develop pacific settlement by the Geneva General Act for the Pacific Settlement of International Disputes of 1928, and after the United States and the Soviet Union had begun to cooperate in the preparatory disarmament conference, hopes for disarmament ran high. A convention drafted by the preparatory commission in December 1930 indicated qualified agreement on six points: (1) the principle of budgetary limitation of armament expenditure; (2) limitation of periods of service; (3) limitation of number of effectives in land, sea, and air forces; (4) acceptance of the method of naval limitation of the London Agreement of 1930; (5) the reduction of chemical and bacteriological warfare; and (6) the establishment of a permanent disarmament commission.

In January 1931 the Council of the League summoned the general disarmament conference to open on Feb. 2, 1932. The representatives of 59 states attended, but the atmosphere had been adversely affected by the Japanese invasion of Manchuria, by the German rejection of the Draft Convention as too favorable to the status quo, and by the world economic depression. However, at Britain's suggestion, attention was soon turned to qualitative disarmament, and in July 1932 all parties except Germany and the Soviet Union reached an agreement to prohibit air attacks against civilian populations, to limit the size of artillery and tanks, and to abolish chemical warfare. Germany insisted on armament equality and elimination of the unilateral restrictions of the Versailles Treaty, and in December 1932 the United States, France, and Italy agreed that such equality should be granted in a system guaranteeing security for all. Germany was temporarily placated, but specific plans proposed by British Prime Minister Ramsay MacDonald, establishing schedules of disarmament, and by President Herbert Hoover, proposing proportionate reductions of the "defense component" of armaments, proved unacceptable to Germany, especially after Hitler came to power early in 1933. The conference continued and debated a proposal by the newly elected U. S. president, Franklin D. Roosevelt, for defining aggression and accepting nonaggression obligations, but Germany left the conference in October 1933, and its activity practically ceased.

The United Nations. The UN Charter is much less specific in its provisions concerning disarmament than the Covenant had been. Effective organization to prevent aggression was given priority, on the theory, accepted also by the League, that disarmament is contingent upon security and pacific settlement. The Atlantic Charter and the Yalta agreements had particularly stressed the unilateral disarmament of the Axis powers, but the 4-power Moscow Declaration of October 1943 had referred to "a practicable general agreement with respect to the regulation of armaments in the post-war period."

The Charter gives the General Assembly authority to discuss and make recommendations on "the principles governing disarmament and the regulation of armaments" (Art. 11). Also, "in order to promote the establishment of international peace and security with the least diversion for armaments of the world's human and economic resources" (repeating a provision in the Moscow Declaration), the Security Council was made "responsible for formulating, with the assistance of the Military Staff Committee, plans to be submitted to the Members for the establishment of a system for the regulation of armaments."

Shortly after the Charter had been negotiated in 1945, the first atomic bomb was exploded. One of the first acts of the UN General Assembly on meeting in January 1946 was to establish an Atomic Energy Commission to propose effective means for the regulation and control of the new weapon. The report of this commission, which appeared under the name of Bernard Baruch, the American representative, provided for the ownership and control by an international commission of fissionable and raw materials for the production of atomic energy. It was debated and approved by the General Assembly in December 1946, but without the consent of the Soviet Union. The same session of the Assembly recognized the distinction between atomic and conventional armaments, and asserted the necessity for "an early general regulation and reduction of armaments and armed forces." The Commission for Conventional Armaments, parallel to that on atomic energy, was established, but the unwillingness of the Western powers to reduce armaments without effective international control, and the refusal of the Soviet Union to permit adequate inspection and control in its territory, resulted, by 1949, in the failure of the Baruch proposal (Baruch Plan), and also of all proposals concerning conventional armaments.

In 1952, the two commissions were combined in a single Disarmament Commission, composed of all members of the Security Council and Canada. A subcommittee consisting of the countries principally involved—the United States, the Soviet Union, the United Kingdom, France, and Canada—was established in 1954, after the death of Stalin had given promise of a less obstructive policy in the Soviet Union. Three years later, following the Soviet Union's successful launching of two earth satellites in the fall of 1957, the USSR objected to the preponderance of North Atlantic Treaty Organization powers on the committees and announced its unwillingness to participate further in them. Though the Commission was enlarged from 11 (or 12) to 25 members in November 1957, and one year later to the entire UN membership, in order to satisfy Soviet demands, disarmament talks were not resumed until 1960. In that year a UN-sponsored disarmament conference was held in Geneva, with the 10 members divided between the Soviet and Western blocs. Though the conference was ended by the Russians on June 27, 1960, disarmament discussions were continued in the UN, and in March 1962 another UN-sponsored conference was held in Geneva, this time including nonaligned countries as well. Although this 18-member commission (in which France, though a member, did not participate) failed in its first year to establish areas of agreement between the great powers, both the USSR and the United States seemed interested in maintaining it as a permanent body.

During the course of these prolonged negotiations, the USSR and the United States agreed in principle on the need for fixing numerical limits to armed forces and armaments, and each sponsored plans for destroying stockpiles of fissionable materials, for terminating their production, and for destroying nuclear delivery vehicles. But these goals could not be implemented since the United States and the USSR maintained their opposed views on verification.

One mode of verification, proposed by U. S. President Dwight D. Eisenhower in 1955, was the establishment of "open skies"—complete aerial reconnaissance to lessen the danger of surprise attack. At first indicating interest in this proposal, the USSR later denounced it as merely a device for espionage. When the United States suggested the substitution of ground inspection, the USSR replied it would permit no more than three "symbolic" ground inspections a year.

In 1956 the Soviet Union seemed to be on the point of accepting simultaneous verification and disarmament. But by the early 1960's Russian negotiators had withdrawn to the position that the control organization should have free access to all objects of control only when total disarmament had been achieved; prior to that stage, the control organization might only inspect weapons destroyed, and not the weapons and armed forces retained at each stage of disarmament. They charged the West with refusing to agree that the succession from one stage to the next should be automatic, thus assuring that once the process was begun, total disarmament would be achieved. Fearing surprise attacks or incomplete fulfillment of earlier stages if control organs were not permitted to verify all phases of disarmament from the first, the United States rejected these Soviet proposals.

The West was also unwilling to accept the Soviet view that a ban on nuclear tests must apply to all environments and could be monitored by national detection systems, without any international supervision. In 1963, however, after dangerous confrontations over Berlin and Cuba, the United States, the Soviet Union, and the United Kingdom agreed to ban all but underground nuclear tests—and without on-site inspections. This first modest disarmament agreement was widely acclaimed. Besides preventing dangerous pollution of the atmosphere, it was expected to retard the spread of nuclear weapons to other countries; and it seemed to manifest a degree of confidence that might lead to further disarmament agreements. Most other nations joined in the test ban. Of the major powers only France and Communist China refused to sign.

A distinction developed between arms control and disarmament. The first seeks to regulate arms building and to maintain a system of mutual deterrence or balance of power—especially in nuclear weapons—to assure sufficient retaliatory second-strike capability to make a first strike suicidal. The attempt to control arms was furthered in 1968, when a majority of UN members endorsed a nuclear nonproliferation draft treaty. In July, more than 60 countries signed the treaty. Its main provision was that signatory countries not in possession of nuclear weapons would refrain from acquiring them. The United States, the USSR, and Britain pledged to help defend countries without nuclear weapons if they faced nuclear aggression.

General and complete disarmament seeks to reduce armaments to the level necessary for internal policing and for contributions to a UN peace force. The United States and the USSR agreed in 1961 on principles for disarmament negotiations (McCloy-Zorin agreement), stating that the goal of negotiation was to assure that war would not be used as an instrument to settle international problems, and to establish reliable processes for peaceful settlement of disputes and maintenance of peace. Armed forces (except those necessary for maintaining internal order and a UN peace force), arms production and stockpiles of weapons, military training and expenditure, and military establishments would all be reduced or eliminated. Disarmament would develop by stages, and with suitable verification so that at no stage would any state gain a military advantage. An international disarmament organization would supervise the process, accompanied by measures aimed at strengthening international peace-keeping institutions. This program led to the formation of draft treaties by the United States and the USSR in 1962.

Nevertheless, the two countries agreed on a "hot line" of communication to prevent retaliation in case of nuclear accident. They also approved a treaty, in accord with a 1963 General Assembly resolution, to refrain from using outer space for military purposes and, in particular, from putting weapons of mass destruction in orbit. Also of major importance was the beginning in late 1969 of the Strategic Arms Limitation Talks (SALT). The first arms control accord, signed in Moscow on May 26, 1972, by the United States and the USSR, was a treaty limiting antiballistic missile (ABM) systems of both powers, and the second was an interim agreement freezing offensive strategic missiles at current levels for up to five years. At a 1974 summit meeting between President Gerald Ford and Soviet leader Leonid Brezhnev, both sides agreed to set limits on numbers of strategic missiles, multiple missile delivery systems, and heavy bombers. The SALT II treaty was signed in Vienna on June 18, 1979, by Brezhnev and President Jimmy Carter. Ratification was delayed in the U. S. Senate, however, and later indefinitely postponed following the Soviet invasion of Afghanistan at the end of 1979. See also ATOMIC WEAPONS CONTROL; UNITED NATIONS.

QUINCY WRIGHT°, *Author of "The Role of International Law in the Elimination of War"*

Bibliography

Falk, Richard, and Mendlovitz, Saul, eds., *Disarmament and Economic Development* (World Law 1966).
Forbes, Henry W., *The Strategy of Disarmament* (Public Affairs Press 1962).
Henkin, Louis, ed., *Arms Control* (Oceana 1964).
Howard, Michael, *Studies in War and Peace* (Viking 1971).
Lefever, Ernest W., ed., *Arms and Arms Control* (Praeger 1962).
Osgood, Charles E., *An Alternative to War or Surrender* (Univ. of Ill. Press 1962).
Schelling, Thomas C., and Halperin, Morton H., *Strategy and Arms Control* (Twentieth Cent. Fund 1961).
Wright, Quincy, *Study of War*, 2d ed. (Univ. of Chicago Press 1965).
Wright, Quincy, and others, eds., *Preventing World War III: Some Proposals* (Simon & Schuster 1962).

DISASTERS. Following is a list of some memorable disasters in world history, most of them involving great loss of life. It includes earthquakes and volcanic eruptions; storms, such as hurricanes, tornadoes and typhoons; fires and explosions; mine disasters; aircraft accidents; marine disasters; and railroad accidents. For a listing of major floods, see FLOODS.

EARTHQUAKES AND VOLCANIC ERUPTIONS

79 A.D., Aug. 24–26—Pompeii and Herculaneum, Italy: destroyed by eruption of Mount Vesuvius.
521, Nov 29—Antioch, Syria: 4,870 die in earthquake.
526, May 20—Antioch, Syria: 250,000 die in earthquake.
543, July 9—Syria: Tyre, Sidon, Beirut, Tripolis, Byblos heavily damaged by earthquake; many thousands die.
546, Aug. 15–Sept. 23—Constantinople, Thrace (Istanbul, Turkey), and Nicomedia, Bithynia (Izmit, Turkey): heavy damage and much loss of life from recurring earthquakes. Nicomedia almost entirely razed.
550, Oct. 6–16—Constantinople, Thrace (Istanbul, Turkey): historic buildings destroyed by earthquakes.
551, July 9—Berytus, Syria (Beirut, Lebanon): destroyed by earthquake.
856, December—Corinth, Greece: 45,000 lives lost in earthquake.
1268—Cilicia, Asia Minor: earthquake kills 60,000.
1290, Sept. 27—Chihli (Hopeh), China: earthquake believed to have killed about 100,000 persons.
1293, May 20—Kamakura, Japan: dead in earthquake estimated 30,000.
1531, Jan. 26—Lisbon, Portugal: earthquake claims 30,000 lives.
1556, Jan. 24—Shensi, China: up to 800,000 dead in earthquake.
1631, Dec. 16—Vesuvius erupts, overwhelming 5 towns and taking 3,000 lives.
1669—Sicily: Mount Etna erupts; 27,000 homeless.
1693, Jan. 11—Sicily: over 60,000 perish after earthquake and eruption of Mount Etna; 40 towns partially or totally destroyed.
1703, Dec. 30—Edo (now Tokyo), Japan: 200,000 lives lost by earthquake.
1737, Oct. 11—Calcutta India: earthquake kills estimated 300,000.
1755, Nov. 1—Lisbon, Portugal: 60,000 persons dead and most of city destroyed in great earthquake.
1783, Feb. 4—Southern Italy and Sicily: earthquake ravages wide area, including city of Messina; 60,000–100,000 dead.
1797, Feb. 4—Cuzco, Peru, and Quito, Ecuador: cities destroyed; 40,000 buried in earthquake.
1828, Dec. 28—Honshu, Japan: earthquake kills an estimated 30,000.
1868, Aug. 13–16—Peru and Ecuador: severe quakes raze many towns in southern Peru and northern Ecuador; 25,000 perish; damage $300,000,000.
1875, May 16—Venezuela and Colombia: earthquakes kill about 16,000.
1883, Aug. 26–28—Java and neighboring islands of the Netherlands Indies: earthquakes and eruptions of several volcanoes, including Krakatau, kill 36,000.
1886, Aug. 31—Charleston, S. C.: earthquake, felt over a thousand-mile area, damages 90% of city.
1896, Aug. 16—Ecuador and Peru: estimated 70,000 dead in earthquake.
1902, May 8—Martinique, West Indies: Mount Pelée erupts; 40,000 dead; St. Pierre destroyed.
1906, April—Mount Vesuvius in eruption; several towns destroyed.
1906, April 16—Chile: large area affected by earthquake, principally Valparaiso and Santiago; 5,000 dead; estimated property loss $100 million.
1906, April 18—San Francisco, Calif., and neighboring towns: earthquake followed by fire; about 500 lives lost; property damage $350 million.
1907, Jan. 14—Kingston, Jamaica: earthquake kills 1,400.
1908, Dec. 28—Southern Italy and Sicily: 85,000 perish in earthquake.
1915, Jan. 13—Central Italy: earthquake kills 30,000.
1920, Dec. 16—Kansu, China: earthquake kills an estimated 180,000; 10 cities destroyed.
1923, Sept. 1—Tokyo district of Japan: Yokohama and about half of Tokyo destroyed by earthquake; some 143,000 killed, many thousands missing.
1932, Dec. 26—Kansu, China; earthquakes kill 70,000.
1935, May 31—Quetta, Baluchistan, India: earthquake kills over 50,000.
1939, Jan. 24—Chile: earthquake kills about 30,000 leaves 700,000 homeless.
1939, Dec. 27—Anatolia, Turkey: series of earthquakes, followed by floods and blizzards, kills about 45,000.
1946, Dec. 21—Japan: earthquake and six tidal waves cause damage in 60,000 square miles of southern Japan; over 1,000 persons die.
1948, June 28—Honshu, Japan: earthquake destroys 70% of Fukui; 3,200 dead, 7,500 injured.
1949, Aug. 5—Ecuador: earthquake destroys 50 towns; estimated 6,000 killed, 100,000 homeless.
1950, Aug. 15—Assam, India: severe earthquake affects 30,000 square miles; death toll about 1,500.
1951, Jan. 18–21—New Guinea: Mount Lamington erupts, devastating a wide area; 3,000 die.
1953, Feb. 12—Eastern Iran: earthquake takes about 1,100 lives, mostly in village of Trud.
1956, June 10–17—Afghanistan: series of earthquakes strikes northern regions, killing about 2,000.
1960, Feb. 29 and March 1—Agadir, Morocco: 20,000 die in two earthquakes, a tidal wave, and fire.
1960, May 21–29—Chile: earthquakes and seismic sea waves hit southern coast; estimated 5,700 die.
1962, Jan. 10—Peru: Avalanche from extinct volcano buries 16 villages, killing about 3,000 persons.
1962, Sept. 1—Iran: most destructive earthquake in Iran's history kills 12,403 persons.
1963, March 17–21—Bali, Indonesia: volcanic eruption of Mount Agung kills 1,584 persons.
1963, July 26—Skopje, Yugoslavia: mass quake devastates town; kills 1,011 and injures 3,350.
1968, Aug. 31–Sept. 1—Iran: 18,000 to 20,000 die in earthquakes in the province of Khurasan.
1969, July 25—China: About 3,000 die in earthquake in eastern China, south of Tientsin.
1970, May 31—Peru: About 70,000 persons are killed in an earthquake in northern Peru.
1972, April 10—Iran: earthquake levels 45 villages south of Teheran, killing 5,000 persons.
1972, Dec. 23—Managua, Nicaragua: earthquake levels Managua, killing 10,000, injuring 10,000 more.
1974, Dec. 28—Pakistan: earthquake destroys several villages, kills an estimated 5,200 persons.
1976, Feb. 4—Guatemala: earthquakes destroy parts of Guatemala City and nearby areas, leave 24,103 dead and 1,500,000 homeless.
1976, June 26—West Irian, Indonesia: earthquakes followed by landslides kill more than 8,000.
1976, July 28—Northern China: earthquakes centered in area bounded by Tangshan, Peking, and Tianjin leave estimated 242,000 dead and 164,000 seriously injured. City of Tangshan is virtually destroyed.
1976, Aug. 17—Philippines: earthquake and tidal wave leave estimated 8,000 dead in southern Mindanao.
1976, Nov. 24—Turkey: quakes in eastern Turkey leave estimated 4,000 dead in Van Province.
1977, March 4—Eastern Europe: quake destroys part of Bucharest, leaves over 1,500 dead.
1978, Sept. 17—Eastern Iran: severe quakes destroy city of Tabas; at least 25,000 killed.
1980, May 18—United States: Mt. Saint Helens in southwestern Washington erupts in first of a series of explosions; 36 people killed, 23 missing.
1980, Oct. 10—Algeria: Two earthquakes destroy most of city of Al Asnam; estimated 4,000–5,000 killed.
1980, Nov. 23—Southern Italy: earthquake and aftershocks destroy villages; leave estimated 4,500 dead.
1981, July 28—Southeastern Iran: earthquake in province of Kerman leaves estimated 8,000 dead.

STORMS

1703, Nov. 26–27—England: "Great Storm" kills 8,000.
1876, Oct. 31—Bakarganj, India (now East Pakistan): cyclone and storm wave kill 200,000.
1881, Oct. 8—Indochina: typhoon and tidal wave cause an estimated 300,000 deaths.
1882, June 5—Bombay, India: cyclone and tidal wave kill 100,000.
1884, Feb. 19—United States: tornadoes ranging from Illinois to Gulf of Mexico kill 800.
1893, Aug. 22–30—Caribbean and southern United States: hurricane ranges from Caribbean up Carolina coast, killing about 1,000; Charleston, S. C., ravaged.
1896, May 27—St. Louis, Mo.: 306 killed by tornado.
1900, Aug. 27–Sept. 8—Galveston, Texas: hurricane and tide wreck city; about 5,000 dead.
1925, March 18—United States: tornado tears through five states; 800 killed, 13,000 injured, 15,000 homeless; 35 towns totally destroyed.
1928, Sept. 12–17—Caribbean and Florida: hurricane ranging from Windward Islands to Florida kills about 4,000 (1,836 in Florida).
1930, Sept. 3—Santo Domingo, Dominican Republic: hurricane kills 2,000, injures 6,000.
1932, March 21–22—United States: five Southern states hit by series of tornadoes; at least 362 dead.
1934, Sept. 21—Honshu, Japan: typhoon kills about 4,000; property damage over $50 million.
1935, Oct. 21—Haiti: storm kills 2,000.
1936, April 5–6—United States: 421 die as tornadoes rip through five Southern states.

1938, Sept. 21—New England: hurricane kills about 680; property damage $400 million.
1942, Oct. 16—Bengal, India: cyclone devastates area; up to 40,000 believed dead.
1947, Sept. 15-19—Honshu Island, Japan: typhoon and flood kill about 1,000, injure 1,616; 984 missing.
1949, Oct. 31-Nov. 2—Philippine Islands: 1,000 believed dead as the result of a typhoon.
1952, March 21-22—United States: tornadoes hit six Mississippi Valley states; 239 dead, 1,202 injured.
1953, May 11—Texas: two tornadoes hit Waco and San Angelo; 124 killed, over 500 injured.
1954, Aug. 31—United States: northeastern seaboard hit by hurricane Carol; 68 deaths; $500 million damage.
1954, Sept. 26—Japan: typhoon in northern Japan kills 1,218, leaves 196 missing.
1954, Oct. 12-16—Haiti, United States, Canada: hurricane Hazel kills 410 in Haiti and moves northward; 99 die in United States, 85 in Canada.
1955, Aug. 18-19—United States: hurricane Diane ravages six Northeastern states, causing 180 deaths, $457 million damage.
1957, June 27-28—Louisiana and Texas: hurricane Audrey and tidal wave leave 531 dead or missing.
1958, Sept. 27-28—Japan: typhoon Ida hits central Honshu, south of Tokyo; 679 dead, 249 missing.
1959, Sept. 26-27—Japan: typhoon Vera sweeps across central Honshu; 4,464 killed, many missing.
1959, Oct. 27-28—Mexico: hurricane causes floods and mudslides in Pacific coast states of Jalisco and Colima; 1,452 reported dead.
1960, Oct. 10, 31—East Pakistan: two cyclones, each followed by tidal waves, kill respectively 6,000 and 4,000 in Bay of Bengal area.
1963, May 28-29—East Pakistan: storms and tidal waves in Bay of Bengal area kill about 12,000.
1963, Oct. 3-8—Caribbean: hurricane Flora kills an estimated 2,500 in Haiti and 1,000 in Cuba.
1964, Aug. 26-28—Caribbean: hurricane Cleo leaves 124 dead in Haiti and 14 on Guadeloupe.
1965, April 11—United States: 37 separate tornadoes rip across six states of the Midwest; 242 dead, 2,500 injured, $250 million damage.
1965, May 11-12, June 1-2—East Pakistan: two cyclones, followed by tidal waves, hit the Bay of Bengal area; up to 45,000 believed killed.
1967, July 9—Japan: typhoon Billie strikes Honshu and Kyushu; 347 are dead and 2,000 homeless.
1969, Aug. 17-19—United States: hurricane Camille batters Gulf coast and other Southern states; estimated 250 dead and $1.5 billion in damage.
1970, Nov. 13—East Pakistan: cyclone and sea wave leave death toll officially estimated at 200,000.
1971, Nov. 1—India: cyclone and sea wave strike Orissa state, killing at least 10,000 persons.
1974, Sept. 19-20—Honduras: hurricane destroys many towns and crops, leaves estimated 5,000 killed.
1974, Dec. 25—Australia: cyclone destroys 90% of the city of Darwin, kills at least 49.
1977, Nov. 21—India: cyclone strikes state of Andhra Pradesh, leaving at least 3,000 dead.
1979, Aug. 29-Sept. 7—Caribbean and U.S.: hurricane David leaves 1,000 or more dead in Dominica, Puerto Rico, Haiti, and the Dominican Republic.
1979, Sept. 4-14—Caribbean and U.S.: hurricane Frederic batters Caribbean islands and Gulf coast; damage in Alabama, Mississippi, and Florida estimated at $1.5 billion.
1983, Aug. 18—Texas: hurricane Alicia batters Galveston and Houston areas, leaving 17 dead and damage estimated at more than $1 billion.

FIRES AND EXPLOSIONS

64 A. D., July 19-24—Rome, Italy: great fire destroys 10 of the city's 14 wards; Christians executed as arsonists.
1666, Sept. 2-6—London, England: 89 churches burned, many public buildings, and 13,200 houses destroyed; 200,000 homeless.
1835, Dec. 16—New York City: 674 buildings burned; loss about $20 million.
1836, Feb. 14—St. Petersburg, Russia: theater fire; 700 lives lost.
1842, May 5-7—Hamburg, Germany: over 4,000 buildings and 100 lives lost; property damage about $35 million.
1845, May 25—Canton, China: theater fire; 1,670 lives lost.
1846, June 12—Quebec, Canada: 200 lives lost in theater fire.
1851, May 4—St. Louis, Mo.: large part of city burned; loss $15 million.
1863, Dec. 8—Santiago, Chile: Church of the Campania burned; loss of life 2,000, mostly women.
1866, July 4—Portland, Me.: almost completely destroyed; loss $10 million.
1866, Oct. 13—Quebec, Canada: 2,500 buildings burned.
1871, Oct. 8-9—Chicago, Ill.: 3½ square miles laid waste; 250 persons killed; nearly 100,000 homeless; 17,450 buildings destroyed; loss about $200 million.
1871, Oct. 8-14—Michigan and Wisconsin: one of the greatest forest fires in United States history destroys wide area; over 1,000 lives lost.
1872, Nov. 9-11—Boston, Mass.: more than 600 buildings burned; loss about $75 million.
1876, Dec. 5—Brooklyn, N.Y.: Conway's Theater burns; about 295 die.
1877, June 20—St. John, New Brunswick, Canada: 100 dead in fire; property loss about $12,500,000.
1881, Dec. 8—Vienna, Austria: Ring Theater fire; 640 lives lost.
1883, Jan. 13—Berdichev, Russia: nearly 270 persons killed in theater fire.
1887, May 25—Paris, France: 200 die in fire at Opéra Comique.
1887, Sept. 4—Exeter, England: theater fire kills 200.
1888, May 25—Oporto, Portugal: Baquet Theater burns, killing 200 persons.
1894, Sept. 1—Minnesota: forest fire in region of Hinckley burns over 160,000 acres; toll 418.
1900, June 30—Hoboken, N.J.: pier fire; more than 300 lives lost; property damage $4,627,000.
1902, Sept. 20—Birmingham, Ala.: 115 die in church blaze.
1903, Dec. 30—Chicago, Ill.: Iroquois Theater fire; about 600 killed.
1904, Feb. 7-8—Baltimore, Md.: 75 city blocks destroyed, covering 140 acres; loss $85 million.
1906, April 18—San Francisco, Calif.: four square miles burned in fire following earthquakes; 500 lives lost; property damage about $350 million.
1908, Jan. 13—Boyertown, Pa.: over 100 killed in Rhoades Opera House in blaze caused by explosion of motion-picture machine.
1908, March 4—Collinwood, Ohio: school fire in this Cleveland suburb kills 161 children and teachers.
1909, Feb. 15—Acapulco, Mexico: Flores Theater burns, killing 250.
1909, Nov. 13—Cherry, Ill.: fire in mine kills 259.
1911, March 25—New York City: Triangle Shirtwaist Factory fire; 145 lives lost.
1916, July 30—Jersey City, N.J.: war sabotage by Germany causes Black Tom Island explosion; loss $22 million.
1917, Dec. 6—Halifax, Nova Scotia, Canada: explosion of war materials and fire; 1,654 killed, over 4,000 injured; 20,000 homeless; property loss $35 million.
1918, Oct. 13-15—Minnesota and Wisconsin: forest fires kill about 1,000 persons; $100 million loss.
1921, Sept. 21—Oppau, Germany: explosion of ammonium nitrate kills about 600 persons.
1922, Sept. 13—Smyrna, Asia Minor: city almost completely destroyed; great loss of life; 100,000 homeless; loss about $100 million.
1929, May 15—Cleveland, Ohio: 125 suffocate in Crile Hospital Clinic as a result of poisonous fumes from burning X-ray film.
1930, April 21—Columbus, Ohio: 317 convicts in Ohio State Penitentiary are burned to death and 231 are injured when fire sweeps through 4 cell blocks.
1934, March 22—Hakodate, Japan: fire destroys city, 1,500 die; 1,000 are injured.
1937, March 18—New London, Texas: natural gas explosion destroys schoolhouse; 413 children and 14 teachers killed.
1938, Nov. 12-16—Changsha, China: fire razes city; 2,000 killed.
1939, March 1—Osaka, Japan: huge munitions dump explodes, wiping out village; 500 killed and injured; 800 houses destroyed; 8,313 homeless.
1939, July 10—Peñaranda de Bracamonte, Spain: approximately 100 killed, 1,500 injured; town demolished in explosion of munitions factory.
1939, Nov. 14—Langunillas, Venezuela: oil town built over Lake Maracaibo destroyed; over 500 killed.
1940, April 23—Natchez, Miss.: 198 killed in fire at dance hall.
1941, June 8—Smederevo, Yugoslavia: ammunition plant explodes, killing 1,000.
1942, May 1—Tessenderlo, Belgium: explosion in chemical works kills 250 workers, injures 1,000.
1942, Nov. 28—Boston, Mass.: Cocoanut Grove Night Club fire kills 493.
1942, Dec. 13—St. John's, Newfoundland: fire panic in Knights of Columbus hostel causes over 100 deaths and injures 100.
1943, May 7—Sandoná, Colombia: 103 killed, 125 injured in fire, which demolishes municipal palace.
1944, April 14—Bombay, India: 128 die in ship fire, which causes explosion in ammunition dump; 1,000 injured.
1944, July 6—Hartford, Conn.: audience stampedes in circus "big top" fire; 165 killed, 193 seriously burned.
1944, July 17—Port Chicago, Calif.: explosion at two ammunition dumps kill more than 300.

DISASTERS

1946, Dec. 7—Atlanta, Ga.: Winecoff Hotel fire kills 120; injures 100.
1947, April 16—Texas City, Texas: explosion of French vessel *Grandcamp* destroys most of city; more than 500 dead or missing.
1947, Aug. 20—Cádiz, Spain: 300 to 500 killed in explosion at shipyards.
1947, Oct. 25—Maine: forest fire destroys part of Bar Harbor, damages Acadia National Park.
1948, July 28—Ludwigshafen, Germany: explosions and fire wreck chemical works of I.G. Farben Company; 200 killed and several thousand injured.
1949, Sept. 4—Chungking, China: fire in central part of city causes 1,700 deaths; leaves 100,000 homeless.
1951, May 13—Kano, Nigeria: movie house burns, killing 100, injuring 300.
1956, Aug. 7—Cali, Colombia: seven trucks carrying dynamite explode; dead estimated at 1,100.
1958, Dec. 1—Chicago, Ill.: parochial school fire kills 90 children and 3 nuns.
1960, July 14—Guatemala City, Guatemala: about 200 die as fire sweeps hospital for mental cases.
1960, Nov. 13—Amude, Syria: 152 children die in fire in movie house.
1960, Dec. 19—New York City: fire on unfinished aircraft carrier *Constellation* kills 50 workmen and causes damages estimated at $58 million.
1961, Dec. 17—Niteroi, Brazil: circus tent fire kills 323.
1963, March 20-21—Saigon, South Vietnam: 300 children reported killed in waterfront fire.
1967, May 23—Brussels, Belgium: fire in L'Innovation department store kills 322 persons.
1970, Nov. 1—Grenoble, France: fire in dance hall near city kills 145 trapped behind locked exits.
1971, Dec. 25—Seoul, Korea: hotel fire kills 163.
1974, Feb. 1—São Paulo, Brazil: fire in top of 25-story bank building kills 227.
1975, Dec. 12—Saudi Arabia: fire sweeps tent camp of Muslim pilgrims near Mecca, killing 138.
1977, May 28—Southgate, Ky.: fire in supper club results in death of 164 persons.
1978, July 11—Tarragona, Spain: gas truck explodes at a beach, killing 170 campers and injuring hundreds.
1982, Nov. 2 or 3—Afghanistan: fire from fuel truck explosion in Salang Tunnel kills several hundred Afghan civilians and Soviet troops in a convoy.

MINE DISASTERS

1906, March 10—Courrières, France: 1,060 miners die in explosion.
1907, Dec. 6—Monongah, W. Va.: 361 killed in coal mine explosion.
1907, Dec. 19—Jacobs Creek, Pa.: mine blast kills 239.
1909, Nov. 13—Cherry, Ill.: fire in mine kills 259.
1913, Oct. 22—Dawson, N. Mex.: mine explosion kills 263.
1934, Sept. 22—Wrexham, Wales: coal mine explosion kills 265.
1942, April 26—Manchuria: worst mine disaster in history to date kills 1,549 at the Honkeiko Colliery.
1947, March 25—Centralia, Ill.: explosion in coal mine kills 111 miners.
1951, Dec. 21—West Frankfort, Ill.: explosion and resulting fire in coal mine take 119 lives.
1956, Aug. 8—Marcinelle, Belgium: coal mine fires kill 263 Belgian and Italian miners.
1958, Feb. 1—India: explosion in coal mine near Asansol kills more than 180 miners.
1960, Jan. 21—Coalbrook, South Africa: cave-ins, explosions kill 437 trapped in coal mine.
1960, Feb. 22—Zwickau, East Germany: explosion at Karl Marx mine; 123 dead.
1961, July 8—Dolna Suce, Czechoslovakia: gas explosion kills 108 coal miners.
1962, Feb. 7—Saar, Germany: mine explosion kills 299 coal miners.
1966, Oct. 21—Aberfan, Wales: avalanche of coal waste and mud engulfs mining town, killing 172.
1968, Nov. 20—Mannington, W. Va.: 78 miners die when trapped by explosions and fires in coal mine.
1969, March 31—Mexico: explosions in the Altos Hornos coal mines in northern Mexico kill 156 miners.
1972, May 2—Kellogg, Idaho: 91 miners killed in fire in Sunshine silver mine; 2 miners found alive May 9.
1972, June 6—Wankie, Rhodesia: explosion in coal mine kills 427 persons.
1975, Dec. 27—India: explosion and flood in coal mine northwest of Calcutta kill at least 431 miners.

AIRCRAFT ACCIDENTS

1908, Sept. 17—Fort Meyer, Va.: first airplane fatality. Orville Wright and Lt. Thomas E. Selfridge in airplane thrown out of control by hitting bracing wire; Selfridge killed and Wright badly injured.
1912, July 2—Atlantic City, N.J.: the first U.S. dirigible *Akron* explodes 2,000 feet over city; builder and crew of four killed.
1921, Aug. 24—England: British dirigible ZR-2 breaks in two on trial trip near Hull; 62 die.
1922, Feb. 21—Hampton, Va.: U.S. dirigible *Roma* explodes; 34 die.
1923, Dec. 21—French dirigible *Dixmude*, with 50 aboard, vanishes over Mediterranean Sea or Sahara Desert.
1925, Sept. 3—Caldwell, Ohio: U. S. dirigible *Shenandoah* breaks apart; 14 die.
1930, Oct. 5—Beauvais, France: world's largest airship to date, the British *R-101*, crashes; 47 killed.
1933, April 4—New Jersey: the second U. S. dirigible *Akron* forced down in violent storm, falls into sea and cracks up; 73 die.
1935, May 18—Russia: stunt flyer crashes into giant land plane *Maxim Gorky* over Moscow; 49 dead.
1935, Aug. 15—Alaska: Will Rogers and Wiley Post killed when their airplane crashes.
1937, May 6—Lakehurst, N. J.: German Zeppelin *Hindenburg* explodes at naval air station at moment of tying up to mast; falls in flames; 36 dead.
1937, July 2—Pacific Ocean: Amelia Earhart and her pilot, Capt. Fred Noonan, are lost on a round-the-world flight and never found.
1942, Jan. 16—Las Vegas Nev.: transport plane crash during cross-country tour for Victory Loan kills Carole Lombard, motion picture actress, 15 army ferry pilots, and 6 others.
1944, Aug. 23—Freckleton, England: United States bomber crashes into school and bursts into flames; 76 dead, including 51 children.
1945, July 28—New York, N. Y.: B-25 bomber crashes into Empire State Building (between 78th and 79th floors), killing 3 aboard plane and 10 in building.
1947, Jan. 26—Copenhagen, Denmark: Dutch airliner crashes at airport in takeoff; 22 dead, among them Grace Moore, popular concert singer, and Prince Gustavus Adolphus of Sweden.
1949, Nov. 1—Washington, D. C.: P-38 fighter collides with DC-4 airliner above airport; 55 persons die.
1950, June 24—Michigan: 58 die as plane explodes and falls into Lake Michigan.
1951, June 30—Rocky Mountain National Park, Colo.: 50 lost in crash of airliner northwest of Denver.
1951, Dec. 16—Elizabeth, N. J.: nonscheduled plane plunges into Elizabeth River after takeoff from Newark Airport; 56 dead.
1952, Jan. 22—Elizabeth, N. J.: airliner crashes in city; 30 dead, including 7 in homes.
1952, Feb. 11—Elizabeth, N. J.: third airline crash here in less than 2 months kills 33 (4 in homes).
1952, Dec. 20—Moses Lake, Wash.: Air Force plane falls and burns after takeoff from Larson Air Force Base; 87 servicemen killed, 28 injured.
1953, June 18—Japan: U. S. Air Force Globemaster crashes near Tokyo; 129 servicemen killed.
1954, Oct. 31—Atlantic Ocean: U. S. Navy plane disappears on flight from New Jersey to Azores with 42 aboard.
1955, March 22—Hawaii: U. S. Navy plane hits cliff near Honolulu, killing all 66 aboard.
1955, Aug. 11—Germany: 66 U. S. Air Force men lost as two Flying Boxcars collide in midair.
1955, Oct. 6—Wyoming: airliner crashes in mountains near Laramie, killing 66.
1955, Nov. 1—Colorado: bomb planted by passenger's son causes explosion of airliner near Longmont, killing 44 persons.
1956, June 20—Venezuelan airliner crashes in Atlantic 40 miles south of New York City, killing 74.
1956, June 30—Grand Canyon, Ariz.: midair collision of two airliners kills 128 in civil aviation's most disastrous crash to date.
1956, Oct. 10—Atlantic Ocean: U. S. Air Force transport disappears north of Azores; 59 servicemen lost.
1956, Dec. 9—British Columbia: Canadian airliner crashes in mountains near Vancouver, killing 62.
1957, March 17—Cebu Island, Philippines: Philippine Air Force transport crashes, killing President Ramón Magsaysay and 25 others.
1957, March 21—Pacific Ocean: U. S. Air Force plane is lost in ocean 250 miles from Tokyo; 64 servicemen and 3 civilians disappear.
1957, Aug. 11—Quebec: chartered Canadian airliner crashes near Quebec; 79 dead.
1958, April 21—Nevada: commercial airliner and U. S. Air Force supersonic jet collide near Las Vegas; 49 die.
1958, Aug. 14—North Atlantic: Dutch plane falls into ocean west of Ireland; 99 killed; worst disaster involving single commercial plane to date.
1959, Feb. 3—New York City: 65 are killed when turboprop airliner crashes into East River.
1960, Feb. 25—Rio de Janeiro, Brazil: U. S. Navy plane and Brazilian airliner collide, killing 61, including 19 Navy bandsmen on South American tour.

1960, Dec. 16—New York City: airliner and jet airliner collide in air, killing 134, including 6 on ground.
1962, June 3—Paris, France: French jet airliner crashes and kills 130.
1962, June 22—Guadeloupe, West Indies: French jet airliner crash kills all 113 abroad.
1963, Nov. 27—Montreal, Quebec: Canadian jet airliner crashes; all 118 aboard killed.
1965, May 20—Cairo, Egypt: 119 die in crash of Pakistani jetliner.
1966, Jan. 24—France: all 117 aboard die as Indian plane hits Mont Blanc.
1966, Feb. 4—Japan: Japanese airliner crashes into Tokyo Bay, killing all 133 persons aboard.
1966, March 5—Japan: British jetliner crashes at foot of Mount Fuji; all 124 persons aboard are killed.
1968, April 20—Windhoek, Southwest Africa: South African plane crashes, killing 129 persons.
1969, March 16—Venezuela: Venezuelan airliner carrying 83 persons crashes into Maracaibo suburb, killed a total of 155 persons and injuring 100.
1970, July 3—Spain: Chartered British airliner hits a mountain peak near Barcelona; 112 die.
1970, July 5—Toronto, Canada: Canadian airliner crashes near Toronto; 108 killed.
1970, Oct. 2—Silver Plume, Colo.: plane carrying Wichita (Kans.) State University football team crashes; 29 die.
1970, Nov. 14—Kenova, W. Va.: all 75 aboard die as plane carrying football team of Marshall University (Huntington, W. Va.) crashes in mountains.
1971, July 30—Japan: Japanese jet airliner struck by fighter plane over Japanese Alps; all 162 aboard die.
1972, June 18—England: British passenger jet crashes near London, killing all 118 aboard.
1972, Aug. 14—East Germany: all 156 aboard East German airliner die in crash in suburb of East Berlin.
1972, Oct. 13—USSR: Aeroflot Ilyushin-62 crashes near Moscow, killing 176.
1972, Dec. 3—Canary Islands: Chartered Spanish jetliner crashes after take-off, killing 155.
1973, Jan. 22—Nigeria: Jetliner carrying Muslim pilgrims from Mecca crashes in northern Nigeria, killing 176.
1973, July 11—France: Brazilian jetliner crashes just short of Orly airport near Paris, killing 122.
1974, March 3—Turkish jetliner crashes in forest after takeoff from Paris, killing all 346 aboard.
1974, Dec. 4—Dutch jetliner carrying Indonesian Muslim pilgrims to Mecca crashes in Sri Lanka, killing 191.
1975, April 4—U. S. Air Force plane carrying Vietnamese children crashes near Saigon, killing 172.
1975, June 24—Jetliner crashes outside Kennedy Airport, New York City, killing 113 of 124 aboard.
1975, Aug. 3—Jordanian jetliner crashes into mountain in Morocco, killing all 188 aboard.
1975, Aug. 20—Czechoslovak jetliner crashes on landing in Damascus, killing 126 of 128 aboard.
1976, Sept. 10—Midair collision of British and Yugoslav jet planes near Zagreb kills 176.
1976, Sept. 19—Turkish Airlines plane crashes into mountain in southwestern Turkey, killing 155.
1977, March 27—American and Dutch jets collide on runway at Santa Cruz de Tenerife, Canary Islands; 574 killed.
1978, Jan. 1—Indian jetliner explodes and plunges into sea near Bombay, killing all 213 aboard.
1978, Sept. 25—Private plane and jetliner collide near San Diego; 144 killed.
1978, Nov. 15—Jetliner carrying Indonesian Muslims home from pilgrimage to Mecca crashes at Colombo, Sri Lanka, killing 183 of 259 aboard.
1979, May 25—U. S. DC-10 jetliner crashes on takeoff in Chicago, killing 273 aboard and 2 on the ground.
1979, Aug. 11—Two Soviet jetliners collide over the Ukraine; 173 reported killed.
1980, Aug. 19—Saudi airliner lands in flames at airport in Riyadh, Saudi Arabia; 301 killed.
1981, Dec. 1—Yugoslav jetliner crashes into mountain on approach to Ajaccio, Corsica, killing 178.
1982, June 8—Brazilian airliner crashes into mountain near Fortaleza, Brazil, killing 137.
1982, July 9—Pan American jet crashes in Kenner, La., killing all 146 on board and 8 on the ground.

MARINE DISASTERS

1831, July 19—Immigrant vessel *Lady Sherbrooke*, bound from England to Quebec, wrecked off Cape Ray; 263 die.
1850, March 29—Steamer *Royal Adelaide* wrecked off Margate, England; 400 lost.
1852, March 26—Troopship *Birkenhead*, bound from Queenstown, South Africa, to Cape of Good Hope wrecked; 454 lost.
1853, Sept. 29—Immigrant vessel *Annie Jane* wrecked off Scotland; 348 die.
1854, March—*City of Glasgow*, bound for Philadelphia from Liverpool, vanishes with 450 aboard.
1858, Sept. 13—The *Austria*, a steamer headed for New York City from Hamburg, catches fire; 471 die.
1859, April 27—The *Pomona* is wrecked off Ireland en route to New York City from Liverpool; 386 lives lost.
1859, Oct. 25—The *Royal Charter* is wrecked and about 450 lives lost in Irish Sea off coast of Anglesea.
1860, Sept. 8—Lake Michigan excursion steamer *Lady Elgin* collides with lumber ship; 300 dead.
1865, April 27—River steamer *Sultana* explodes near Memphis, Tenn., and sinks; 1,450 dead.
1867, Oct. 29—Mail boats *Rhone* and *Wye* and many small vessels wrecked in storm at St. Thomas, West Indies; about 1,000 lost.
1870, Sept. 17—British warship *Captain* founders off Finistère in France; 472 die.
1873, April 1—British steamer *Atlantic* is wrecked off Nova Scotia; 547 aboard die.
1878, Sept. 3—English steamer *Princess Alice* sinks after collision in Thames; 700 persons killed.
1890, Sept. 19—Turkish frigate *Ertogrul* burns off Japanese coast; about 540 lost.
1891, March 17—British steamer *Utopia* sinks in collision off Gibraltar; 574 die.
1898, Feb. 15—U. S. battleship *Maine* blows up in harbor at Havana, Cuba; 264 killed.
1898, July 4—560 lives lost in collision of French liner *La Bourgogne* and British *Cromartyshire* near Sable Island, off Nova Scotia.
1904, June 15—Steamboat *General Slocum* burns in New York City's East River; more than 1,000 perish.
1904, June 28—Some 600 die in wreck of *Norge* on Rockall Reef, off Scotland.
1912, March 5—Spanish steamer *Principe de Asturias* wrecked on rocks off northern coast; about 500 drowned.
1912, April 15—Liner *Titanic* strikes iceberg in North Atlantic on maiden voyage from Southampton to New York City; toll variously estimated at 1,490, 1,502, and 1,517.
1912, Sept. 28—Japanese steamer *Kichemaru* sinks off coast of Japan; about 1,000 lost.
1914, May 29—Canadian Pacific liner *Empress of Ireland* sinks after collision with Norwegian collier in St. Lawrence River; lost 1,024.
1915, May 7—British passenger liner *Lusitania* sunk by German submarine in Atlantic Ocean off southwestern coast of Ireland; 1,195 (or 1,198) dead, including about 124 Americans.
1915, July 24—Excursion steamer *Eastland* capsizes in Chicago River, Illinois; more than 800 die.
1916, Aug. 29—Estimated 1,000 perish in sinking of *Hsin Yu* off coast of China.
1917, July 9—British warship *Vanguard* blows up at Scapa Flow dock; about 800 killed.
1919, Jan. 17—Wreck of French steamer *Chaonia* in Strait of Messina kills 460.
1921, March 18—Steamer *Hongkong* wrecked on rocks off Swatow, China; estimated 1,000 dead.
1926, Oct. 16—Chinese troopship explodes in Yangtze River, killing estimated 1,200.
1927, Oct. 25—About 326 perish in sinking of Italian ship *Principessa Mafalda* after explosion off Pôrto Segura, Bahia, Brazil.
1928, Nov. 12—British steamship *Vestris* founders off the Virginia capes; 113 lost.
1931, June 14—French excursion steamer overturns in gale off St.-Nazaire; approximately 450 lost.
1934, Sept. 8—S. S. *Morro Castle* burns off coast of New Jersey and is beached at Asbury Park; 137 dead.
1942, Oct. 2—*Queen Mary* rams and sinks British cruiser *Curaçao* off English coast; 338 on cruiser die.
1942, Oct. 26—More than 200 Jewish refugees from Bulgaria drown in shipwreck in Sea of Marmara.
1944, Dec. 17-18—Typhoon strikes task force of U. S. Third Fleet in Philippine Sea; almost 800 officers and men lost; 3 destroyers capsized, 6 or 7 other ships seriously damaged; 146 aircraft destroyed.
1945, April 9—United States Liberty ship explodes in harbor at Bari, Italy; 360 dead, 1,730 injured.
1946, Aug. 2—Steamer *Vitya* sinks in Lake Nyasa, Tanganyika; 295 drowned.
1947, Jan. 19—Greek steamer *Himara* strikes mine off Athens, sinks in 30 minutes; at least 392 die.
1948, Jan. 28—Freighter *Joo Maru* strikes mine and sinks in Japan's Inland Sea; 250 lost.
1948, Feb. 28—Steamer capsizes during pirate attack near Amoy, China; 160 die.
1948, June 11—Danish passenger ship *Kjoebenhavn* sinks after striking mine off coast of Jutland; at least 140 die.
1948, Dec. 3—Chinese steamer explodes and sinks south of Shanghai; 1,100 missing or dead.
1949, Jan. 27—Chinese liner and collier collide and sink off coast of southern China; at least 600 dead.
1949, Sept. 17—Great Lakes passenger ship *Noronic* burns at pier in Toronto, Canada, killing about 130 and injuring more than 100.

1951, April 16—British submarine *Affray* sunk off the Isle of Wight; 75 lost.
1952, April 26—United States destroyer-minesweeper *Hobson* sinks after colliding with aircraft carrier *Wasp* during Atlantic maneuvers; 176 lost.
1954, Sept. 26—Japanese ferry *Toya Maru* sinks in Tsugaru Strait; 1,172 drowned.
1956, July 26—Italian liner *Andrea Doria* sinks off Massachusetts coast after collision (July 25) with Swedish motor ship *Stockholm*; 52 killed or missing; 1,652 rescued.
1958, March 1—Ferryboat breaks up near Istanbul, Turkey, in Sea of Marmara; at least 238 die.
1961, April 8—212 persons lost as British liner *Dara* burns in Persian Gulf.
1961, July 8—Portuguese ship *Save* runs aground off Mozambique and explodes, killing 259.
1963, April 10—United States nuclear submarine *Thresher*, with 129 aboard, is lost in North Atlantic.
1963, May 4—Motor launch sinks in Upper Nile, at Maghagha, Egypt; 206 Muslim pilgrims drown.
1964, Feb. 10—Australian destroyer *Voyager* collides with aircraft carrier *Melbourne* off Uladulla, Australia, and sinks with loss of 82 seamen.
1967, March 18—U.S. tanker *Torrey Canyon* runs aground off Cornwall, England. Resulting oil spill contaminates marine life on French and English coasts.
1967, July 29—Fire and explosions on the U. S. aircraft carrier *Forrestal* off Vietnam kill 134 men.
1968, May 21—U. S. Navy nuclear submarine *Scorpion*, with crew of 99, is lost near the Azores.
1968, Oct. 10—From 300 to 500 perish as a ferry sinks in waters off Mindanao, the Philippines.
1969, June 2—74 men aboard the U. S. destroyer *Evans* die as the vessel is sliced in half by the Australian carrier *Melbourne* in the South China Sea.
1970, Dec. 15—More than 300 persons drown when Korean ferry sinks in Korea Strait.
1972, Jan. 9—Luxury liner *Queen Elizabeth* burns and capsizes in Hong Kong Harbor.
1972, May 11—Liberian oil tanker *Tien Chee* and British cargo ship *Royston Gorge* collide east of Buenos Aires, Argentina; 83 reported missing.
1973, Feb. 21—Rangoon, Burma: Collision between ferry boat and Japanese freighter kills more than 200.
1975, Aug. 3—Collision of two boats on West River near Canton, China, leaves estimated 500 dead.
1978, March 17—Supertanker *Amoco Cadiz* is wrecked off Brittany; oil spill contaminates French coast.
1980, April 20—About 230 persons are drowned when ferry capsizes on the Padma River, Bangladesh.
1981, Jan. 6—Boat capsizes on the Amazon River upstream from Macapá, Brazil; 230 killed.
1981, Sept. 19—More than 300 believed drowned as Amazon River boat capsizes at Obidos, Brazil.
1983, May 25—At least 272 killed as Nile River steamboat burns and sinks in Lake Nasser.
1983, June 5—Soviet sources report 240 killed as Russian ship rams a railway bridge across the Volga River at Ulyanovsk.

RAILROAD ACCIDENTS

1853, May 6—Norwalk, Conn.: 44 killed as train drops through open drawbridge.
1856, July 17—Philadelphia, Pa.: wreck near here takes lives of 66 children on Sunday school outing.
1857, March 17—Quebec, Canada: train derailment on bridge over Soulanges Canal causes about 60 deaths.
1864, July 15—Pennsylvania: train carrying Confederate prisoners collides with another, killing 65.
1876, Dec. 29—Ashtabula, Ohio: train bridge collapses in snowstorm, plummeting 92 aboard train to death.
1879, Dec. 28—Dundee, Scotland: about 78 persons are drowned as train plunges off Tay Bridge.
1881, June 24—Cuautla, Mexico: about 200 are lost as train plunges into river.
1887, Aug. 10—Chatsworth, Ill.: train wreck, caused by collapse of burning bridge, kills 81.
1889, June 12—Armagh, Ireland: collision kills 80.
1904, Aug. 7—Eden, Colo.: wreck claims 96 lives.
1910, March 1—Wellington, Wash.: avalanche sweeps 2 trains into 300-foot canyon, taking 96 lives.
1915, May 22—Gretna, Scotland: 228 killed at Quintinshill, near here, when troop train collides with local train, and passenger express plows into wreckage.
1917, Dec. 12—Modane, France: death toll estimated at nearly 550 as troop train is derailed.
1918, June 22—Ivanhoe, Ind.: empty troop train rams into rear of train carrying circus performers; 68 die.
1918, July 9—Nashville, Tenn.: head-on collision of 2 trains near here causes 92 deaths.
1918, Nov. 1—Brooklyn, N. Y.: 5-car train of Brooklyn Rapid Transit Line is derailed after hitting support at entrance to Malbone Street Tunnel; 92 killed.
1937, July 16—Patna, India: 107 killed in derailment of Delhi-Calcutta express near here.
1938, Dec. 25—Kishinev, Rumania: about 100 killed, 350 injured as passenger trains collide near here.
1939, Dec. 22—Germany: 2 express trains collide near Magdeburg killing at least 132; another wreck near Friedrichshafen on the same day takes 99 lives.
1940, Jan. 29—Osaka, Japan: passenger trains collide and burn; deaths estimated at 200.
1943, Sept. 6—Philadelphia, Pa.: 79 perish as 9 cars of *Congressional Limited* are derailed.
1943, Dec. 16—Lumberton, N.C.: 2 streamline trains collide near here; 73 die.
1944, Jan. 16—León Province, Spain: train wreck inside tunnel causes more than 500 deaths.
1944, March 2—Italy: passenger train stalls in tunnel near Salerno; 521 suffocate.
1944, July 6—High Bluff, Tenn.: locomotive and 2 cars of troop train plunge into gorge; 35 killed.
1944, Dec. 31—Ogden, Utah: crash of 2 sections of *Pacific Limited* west of city claims 50 lives.
1945, Feb. 1—Cazadero, Mexico: train with religious pilgrims struck by freight; about 100 lives lost.
1946, March 20—Aracaju, Brazil: train wreck near here kills 185.
1946, April 25—Naperville, Ill.: collision near Chicago causes 45 fatalities.
1947, Aug. 3—Sumatra, Netherlands East Indies: at least 400 killed in wreck near Pematangsiantar.
1949, April 28—Johannesburg, South Africa: 3 trains in collision near here; 74 killed.
1949, Oct. 22—Nowy Dwor, Poland: Danzig-Warsaw express jumps from tracks, resulting in 200 deaths.
1950, April 6—Brazil: 108 killed as train plunges into flooded Indios River, near Tanguá.
1950, May 7—Bihar State, India: crash of Punjab mail train near Jasidih kills 81; sabotage is blamed.
1950, Sept. 11—Newcomerstown, Ohio: passenger express rams rear of Pennsylvania National Guard troop train; 33 die.
1950, Nov. 22—Richmond Hill, N. Y.: 79 lives lost as standing commuter train is hit by another.
1951, Feb. 6—Woodbridge, N.J.: commuter train plunges through temporary overpass; 85 killed, 500 injured.
1951, June 7—Rio de Janeiro, Brazil: collision of train and gasoline truck at grade crossing near here (Nova Iguaça) takes 54 lives.
1952, March 4—Rio de Janeiro: 2 passenger trains crash near here; 119 die.
1952, July 12—Rzepin, Poland: 160 Soviet soldiers reported killed in wreck near here.
1952, Oct. 8—Harrow, England: 112 deaths result when 2 express trains crash into commuter train.
1953, Dec. 24—New Zealand: 155 lives lost as Wellington-Auckland express plunges into stream near Wairoa.
1954, Sept. 28—India: Express plunges from bridge 50 miles east of Hyderabad; 137 die.
1955, April 3—Guadalajara, Mexico: about 300 perish as train plunges into canyon near here.
1956, Sept. 2—India: 2 coaches plunge into river near Secunderabad as bridge collapses, causing 121 deaths.
1956, Nov. 23—India: 143 lose lives as express train dives down embankment of Marudaiyar River.
1957, Sept. 1—Jamaica, British West Indies: train plunges into ravine; 178 dead.
1957, Sept. 29—West Pakistan: 250 reported dead in crash of express into standing oil train.
1957, Oct. 20—Istanbul, Turkey: 89 killed as 2 trains collide at high speed near here.
1957, Dec. 4—London, England: 92 lose lives as commuter train hits rear of another in fog, near here.
1958, March 7—Santa Cruz, Brazil: 67 die in collision of 3 commuter trains.
1958, May 8—Rio de Janeiro, Brazil: 128 perish in head-on collision of 2 trains near here.
1958, Sept. 15—Bayonne, N. J.: train plunges through lift bridge into Newark Bay, near here; 48 dead.
1959, May 28—Java, Indonesia: 92 lives lost as train spills into ravine.
1959, June 5—São Paulo, Brazil: about 60 killed in head-on collision of 2 trains.
1960, May 15—Leipzig, Germany: collision of express train and local train takes 59 lives.
1960, Nov. 14—Pardubice, Czechoslovakia: 110 persons killed in collision of two passenger trains.
1962, Jan. 8—Woerden, Netherlands: collision of passenger trains kills 91.
1962, May 3—Tokyo, Japan: freight train and two commuter trains collide; 163 die.
1964, July 26—Oporto, Portugal: train wreck results in 94 deaths.
1970, Feb. 1—Argentina: express train hits a commuter train north of Buenos Aires, killing 139.
1970, Feb. 16—Train wreck in northern Nigeria kills at least 80; another 52 die in crash of truck en route to hospital.
1972, June 16—Two passenger trains collide in tunnel at Vierzy, France; at least 92 persons are killed.
1977, Jan. 18—Train is derailed near Sydney, Australia, and crashes into bridge; 82 killed.

DISCIPLE, one who learns anything from another; hence the follower of any teacher, philosopher, or head of a sect. Though it is sometimes used to refer to the follower of a political or artistic leader, the term usually has a religious connotation. Thus we read in the Scriptures of the disciples of the prophet Isaiah (Isaiah 8:16), of John the Baptist (Matthew 11:2), and of Jesus (John 6:66).

Often the word has specific reference to the followers of Jesus. In this connection all who received Jesus's doctrines are called disciples, but in a more limited sense it is applied to the 70 or 72 persons who were his immediate followers during his life. At other times it is used as synonymous with "apostle" and is thus applied to the inner circle of the Twelve (Matthew 10:1).

DISCIPLES OF CHRIST, an American Protestant religious body, formally named The Christian Church (Disciples of Christ). It developed simultaneously in Kentucky and Pennsylvania, moved westward with the American frontier, and has become one of the major denominations in the United States. Based on a desire for unity among all Christians, it has continued this major emphasis through the years.

Origin and History. In 1803, Barton W. Stone, a Presbyterian minister in Kentucky, formed a group he called by the Biblical term "Christians" and said they were "Christians only." He and his followers proclaimed freedom of thought in religion and turned to the Bible as their one source of authority. They believed that all Christians should be allowed to worship together if they wished and that all should recognize their oneness in Jesus Christ. As their concepts developed, they became a power for Christian unity.

In 1807, Thomas Campbell, a Presbyterian minister from Ireland, went to the United States in search of a new home for his family. He also sought freedom to worship where and how he wished and to be free of the strong denominational competition that separated Christians. He affiliated at first with the Presbyterians and then with the Baptists, but he was not satisfied. His "Declaration and Address," which sets forth his beliefs for his followers, became the basis of the new movement, the leadership of which was gradually passed into the hands of his son, Alexander Campbell.

The Campbell movement in Pennsylvania, going by the name "Disciples," and the Stone followers in Kentucky, calling themselves "Christians," joined forces in Lexington, Ky., in 1832. Walter Scott, a strong evangelist, drew great crowds to camp meetings. Alexander Campbell—scholar, preacher, writer, and theologian—won great respect for the movement and is still quoted by church leaders.

Over the years two divisions occurred. About 1900, one group that opposed the use of musical instruments in worship developed into the Churches of Christ. In 1927, another conservative group, protesting against the system of coordination of mission support, became independent as the North American Christian Convention.

From the beginning the leaders had avoided becoming a denomination. They called the new church "a movement," "a communion," or "a brotherhood" even though it increasingly took on the characteristics of a denomination. In a historic meeting of the church's International Convention Assembly at Kansas City, Mo., in 1968 the name *The Christian Church (Disciples of Christ)* became official, replacing the former name, *The Christian Churches (Disciples of Christ)*.

Ideals and Practices. The following ideals and practices have grown into an informal doctrine generally accepted but not considered to be rules of the church:

The church has no formal creed and is therefore free to update its emphases and convictions with the changing times.

The basis of authority is the Bible, with special emphasis on the New Testament and the life of Jesus Christ.

A positive answer to the minister's question, "Do you believe that Jesus is the Christ, the Son of the living God, and do you accept Him as your personal Savior?" followed by the rite of baptism (traditionally by immersion) is the accepted procedure for becoming a member.

Christ's church is by nature a unit and should be united; therefore a major emphasis is on the ecumenical movement.

An individual has access to God through personal prayer and does not need to pray through an intermediary priest or minister.

The Lord's Supper, signifying a desire for spiritual renewal on the part of the worshipers, serves as a reminder of the supreme sacrifice of Jesus Christ. It is open to all members of the church and is observed weekly in Disciples of Christ congregations.

Every congregation and every member have the privilege of individual opinion and are not bound by the general outlook of the church. Congregations may select their own ministers, make their own budgets, and own their own property.

Current Status. After more than 150 years of growth the Disciples of Christ have approximately 6,000 congregations and 1,200,000 members in the United States and Canada, and they work in some 16 other nations of the world. Major strength in the United States centers in the Midwest, Southwest, and on the Pacific coast. The church has 33 colleges and seminaries, 8 homes for children, and 11 homes for the aging. Its central office is located in Indianapolis, Ind.

The Disciples have two major periodicals. *World Call* is a monthly magazine that interprets the work of the church at home and abroad. *The Christian,* a weekly, is concerned with news and opinion. St. Louis, Mo., is the home of the Christian Board of Publication, the church's official publishing house.

At its 1968 Kansas City assembly, Disciples voted to adopt "A Provisional Design for The Christian Church (Disciples of Christ)." The "Design" provided for a change from a group of autonomous, individual congregations without an official top officer to a responsible body, more closely related and yet with the freedom of the local churches protected.

In addition to their strong support of church union, the Disciples have a major interest in the worldwide mission of the church, in evangelism, in vital social issues, and in personal Christian living. They support the National Council of Churches of Christ in the U. S. A. and the World Council of Churches.

SAMUEL F. PUGH, *Editor, "World Call"*

Further Reading: Adams, Hampton, *Why I Am a Disciple of Christ* (New York 1957); Garrison, Winfred E., and DeGroot, Alfred T., *The Disciples of Christ, a History* (St. Louis 1958); Pugh, Samuel F., ed., *Primer for New Disciples* (St. Louis 1963).

DISCIPLINE, Books of, two books issued by the Church of Scotland. The first was drawn up in 1560 by John Knox and five other Presbyterian ministers as a plan for church organization and administration. Based on the *Ordonnances* of the Reformed Church of Geneva, the first book was supported by Knox's followers, but the civil authorities failed to ratify it.

The second book, drawn up by Andrew Melville in 1578, was strongly antiepiscopal. It laid down principles governing the relation between church and state; defined the jurisdiction and duties of church officers and the mode of their election; and prescribed the operation of the General Assembly, synods, and presbyteries of the Church of Scotland. The book was endorsed by the General Assembly in 1581 but failed to receive civil sanction. Nevertheless, it came to be recognized as the authoritative standard in matters of church government and discipline.

DISCOUNT RATE, the rate that banks in the United States pay to borrow from the Federal Reserve. This rate, although set individually by each of the 12 Federal Reserve banks, is identical in all Federal Reserve districts most of the time.

Despite popular opinion to the contrary, the discount rate is not a major determinant of whether banks borrow from the Federal Reserve. Because the discount rate is invariably well below what banks in turn charge the public for money, banks would be delighted to obtain new funds by discounting when credit is tight and they have no more lendable funds. However, discounting at the Federal Reserve is reserved for emergency needs, such as an unexpected increase in the public's desire for cash or an unexpected adverse clearance (when more money flows from the specific bank into others than flows from others to it). Thus, despite the low level of the U. S. discount rate relative to other interest rates, bank borrowing is not motivated or deterred by changes in the discount rate.

The real significance of the discount rate in the United States is as a signal of Federal Reserve intentions. When the discount rate is raised, it usually indicates that the Federal Reserve will be tightening credit through its "open-market operations." These operations involve sopping up bank reserve funds through the Federal Reserve's sale of securities on the open market to banks and bank depositors, who pay with checks on banks that the banks in turn must honor.

Bank lending rates to the public generally rise when the discount rate goes up, but it is not because the banks must pay more for money. Rather it is because they expect that the Federal Reserve soon will make money scarce, and thus they raise business loan rates as a way to allocate available funds. But a rise in the discount rate does not mean bank lending rates will rise automatically, especially if bank loan demands are weak. A decline in the discount rate conversely means that the Federal Reserve probably will soon ease credit through open-market operations.

Penalty Rates. In some countries the discount rate is high enough to be a penalty rate, which forces the banks to follow a discount rate increase with higher lending charges themselves. In such cases, however, the central bank often provides a larger portion of bank funds than is the case in the United States.

Paul S. Nadler, *Rutgers University*

DISCOUNT RETAILING, the selling of merchandise—typically a large selection of well-known brands—at prices less than those suggested by manufacturers. It is conducted by retailing establishments known as *discount houses*. Unlike department stores, discount houses stress self-service. Often they also lower their operating costs by locating in buildings not as elaborate as other retail outlets. Thus, although other retailers may sell at less than manufacturer-suggested prices, the typical discounter offers still lower prices.

Discount houses usually carry a wide variety of merchandise, ranging from durables (hard goods) such as electrical appliances and furniture to nondurables (soft goods) such as clothing, blankets, linens, and, in some instances, even groceries. Some discounters, however, specialize in relatively limited lines of merchandise, and some rely mainly on private (their own) brands, priced to compete with "name" brands.

Rise of the Discount House. The popularity and growth of the discount house is a post-World War II phenomenon in the United States. By 1948 such operations had become widespread in major cities. The selling of consumer goods at less than full price has always been an American custom, but it was practiced only in a random way before World War II. It has been said that many consumers were "trained" to buy at discount at post exchanges while in military service or by receiving employee discounts at their places of employment.

The discount house is partly an outgrowth of the conditions brought about by the "fair trade" pricing laws. Under these laws, passed by individual states in the 1930's and later, manufacturers were permitted to require wholesalers and retailers to resell their products at or above prices set by the manufacturer. "Fair trade" supported high retail margins, thus making discounting attractive for many dealers who, ignoring the manufacturers, cut prices and achieved higher sales volumes.

The strong faith that consumers have in manufacturers' brands was another factor leading to the rise of the discount house. The brands of major manufacturers had become so well established from advertising that personal salesmanship and the various customer services found in department stores and other retail outlets were unnecessary. Thus consumers were more interested in price than in the prestige or attractiveness of the outlet.

Advantages and Disadvantages. Discount customers obtain name-brand merchandise at reduced prices and avoid paying for unwanted services. Some risk is involved, however. In some cases the customer finds that an unethical discounter has marked up prices fictitiously high and then "discounted" them to a level that does not represent a bargain.

For the store owner, a major advantage of discounting is the ability to achieve the high volume that results from lower prices offered for well-known merchandise. He meets rising competition, however, from many of the more conventional retailers, who match prices by reducing services and improving operational efficiency.

Neil M. Ford, *University of Wisconsin*

DISCRIMINATION. See Prejudice and Discrimination.

DISCUS. See Track and Field—*Field Events*.

DISEASE is the impairment of the health, or normal functioning, of an organism. Diseases may primarily affect a single organ or tissue, a group of organs or tissues, or the entire body. They may result from a wide variety of causes, including infectious organisms, such as bacteria, viruses and tapeworms; hereditary factors, such as those responsible for hemophilia and color blindness; and environmental hazards, such as radiation or toxic fumes. Some diseases are *acute,* usually producing severe symptoms lasting only a short time; others are *chronic,* lasting a long period of time, and still others are *recurrent,* returning periodically.

The term "disease" is sometimes defined as the failure of an organism to respond adaptively to its environment. This definition emphasizes the large number of factors that cause a disease; there is no single cause, and the prevention, control, and treatment of disease must be approached at all levels, from the molecular to the social. It is also important to note that no disease is an isolated entity; the expression, "There are no diseases, only sick people," emphasizes this point.

CONTENTS

Section	Page	Section	Page
Types of Disease	169	Physical Examination	174
Infectious Diseases	169	Laboratory Studies	174
Immunological Diseases	170	Specialized Tests and Procedures	174
Neoplasms	170	**Treatment of Disease**	175
Congenital and Metabolic Diseases	171	Symptomatic Drug Therapy	175
Diseases of Growth and Development	171	Specific Drug Therapy	175
Diseases Due to Chemical and Physical Agents	172	Surgery	176
Nutritional Diseases	172	Other Types of Therapy	176
Endocrine Diseases	173	**Prevention of Disease**	176
Circulatory Diseases	173	Eradicating Parasites	176
Mental Illness	173	Vaccination	177
Methods of Diagnosis	174	**Bibliography**	177
Medical History	174		

Diseases affect all living organisms. This article, however, deals with the diseases of particular kinds of animals appears in many of the separate articles on animals, such as CAT, CATTLE, DOG, and HORSE. A general discussion of diseases in animals appears in the article ANIMAL DISEASES, and plant diseases are covered in the article PLANT AND PLANT SCIENCES. In addition, many individual diseases of plants and animals, including man, are covered separately in such articles as BRUCELLOSIS, CANCER, DRY ROT, INFLUENZA, and TUBERCULOSIS. Other related articles include BLACK DEATH, CHEMOTHERAPY, DRUG, and MEDICINE, HISTORY OF.

Role of Disease in History. One of the most interesting aspects of the study of the relationship between man and his environment is the role of disease in history. Typhus, bubonic plague, malaria, smallpox, and other diseases have all affected the course of political and military, as well as social, history. Herodotus in the 5th century B. C. recorded a pestilence that swept through the Persian army of Xerxes when he entered Thessalia with about 800,000 men. The campaign had to be abandoned, and Xerxes returned to Persia after losing about 200,000 men. The sieges of Syracuse by the Carthaginians in 414 and 396 B. C. were relieved by a disease that was either plague or smallpox. Thus, in all likelihood, Hannibal was defeated not by the might of Rome but by disease. The course of history was also altered when Alexander the Great died at an early age, presumably from a type of malaria.

In 425 A. D. the Huns called off their advance on Constantinople because a disease decimated their forces, and the Abyssinians in the so-called Elephant War (570 B. C.) were turned back from Mecca by what may have been smallpox. Accounts of the various Crusades are replete with stories of battles that were complicated by epidemic diseases among the Western invaders. During the period from the 14th century through the 17th century, bubonic plague, then called the Black Death, was responsible for decreasing the population of Europe by at least one quarter. In 1812 the losses that Napoleon's army suffered as a result of typhus and dysentery, which the men contracted during their march through Poland and Russia, contributed to the disasters of the French campaign as much as the Russian armies and the severe Russian winter.

Throughout history, diseases that have been new to a population have always caused an unusually high mortality rate. Even today, measles is frequently fatal in Africa, parts of the Middle East, and elsewhere but is rarely fatal among Europeans and Americans. In the early 1500's smallpox was introduced into the Western Hemisphere by Spanish conquerors, and within a short time several million American Indians had succumbed to the disease. Syphilis was probably introduced into Europe by Columbus' men on their return from the New World. On the other hand, there is considerable evidence that malaria was unknown in the Americas before the arrival of Columbus and that subsequent migrations from the West, in addition to the slave trade, were instrumental in establishing this disease in the Western Hemisphere.

Although migration, crowding, and poverty have long been the most important factors in the initiation and propagation of epidemics, one disease—poliomyelitis—differs from other diseases in that it flourishes in highly advanced societies. This apparent mystery is explained by the fact that the disease produces only very mild effects in infants and very young children. Under conditions of poverty, most of the very young contract the disease and thus become immune to it. Children who are not exposed to the disease at a very early age remain susceptible to it during middle and late childhood, and if they contract poliomyelitis during those years, they are likely to suffer paralysis. Thus, until the advent of effective vaccines, poliomyelitis was epidemic in the United States, Britain, and Sweden and was relatively uncommon in Africa, the Middle East, and the Far East.

Today the greatest disease problems in many countries are those directly or indirectly related to the inadequate quality or quantity of food. In some parts of the world many contagious diseases have been eliminated, and the increasing population in these regions threatens to outstrip the available food supplies. In an effort to counteract this problem, many countries, particularly India, have instituted broad birth control programs. There are also programs for finding new sources of food from the sea, increasing crop yields, and developing inexpensive food supplements from plants and other sources, even petroleum.

THE BLACK DEATH, one of the world's most dreaded diseases, ravaged Europe in the 1300's and reappeared in later years. This engraving of 1679 shows victims of the black death plague in a Vienna hospital.

THE BETTMANN ARCHIVE

TYPES OF DISEASE

There are several different ways of classifying diseases. Probably the most widely used method divides diseases into ten major groups: infectious diseases, immunological diseases, neoplasms (tumors), genetic and metabolic diseases, diseases of growth and development, diseases due to chemical and physical agents, nutritional diseases, endocrine diseases, circulatory diseases, and mental disorders.

Infectious Diseases. Infectious diseases are caused by bacteria, viruses, rickettsiae, mycoplasmas, and parasitic organisms such as certain amebas and roundworms. The term "contagious" is sometimes used interchangeably with "infectious," but most often "contagious" is reserved for those diseases that can be spread from one person to another. Thus, influenza is said to be a contagious disease, but bubonic plague, which can be transmitted to man only through the bite of a flea, is not considered to be contagious.

Many disease-causing bacteria attack specific organs, while others attack organs and tissues throughout the body. Some bacteria invade the throat; the most important of these is a type of *Streptococcus* that is a frequent cause of pharyngitis. The bacterium *Neisseria meningitidis* chiefly affects the brain coverings (meninges), and a closely related species, *N. gonorrhoeae*, is the cause of the common venereal disease gonorrhea. Typhoid fever is caused by the bacterium *Salmonella typhosa*, which chiefly attacks the intestines but also affects other organs and tissues, such as bone.

In many bacterial diseases, the body is affected not by the bacteria themselves but by the toxins (poisons) they produce. Diphtheria is caused by the bacterium *Cornybacterium diphtheriae*, which characteristically infects the pharynx; however, the toxins produced by the bacterium affect the heart, kidneys, and nerves. *Staphylococcus aureus*, which is the causative agent of furuncles (boils), also grows readily in meats and creamed dishes that are not adequately refrigerated and produces a toxin that causes nausea, vomiting, severe abdominal cramps, and diarrhea. A more severe, often fatal, form of food poisoning is caused by the toxin of another bacterium, *Clostridium botulinum*. Fortunately, this type of poisoning, botulism, is rare because the toxin is destroyed by cooking.

Rickettsiae and viruses differ from bacteria in that they cannot grow outside living cells. Common rickettsial diseases are typhus, Q fever, and Rocky Mountain spotted fever. Common viral diseases include measles, chicken pox, influenza, poliomyelitis, and the common cold. Some of the viral diseases can be prevented by vaccinations, but there are no available drugs for treating viral diseases once they have been contracted. Rickettsial diseases can be treated with some antibiotics.

Parasitic organisms range in size from microscopic one-celled protozoans, such as the malaria-producing *Plasmodium vivax*, to the beef tapeworm (*Taenia saginata*), which may reach a length of 82 feet (25 meters). Malaria, one of the most important of all parasitic diseases in man, is caused by four species of *Plasmodium*. These organisms are transmitted from infected individuals to healthy ones through the bite of an *Anopheles* mosquito. The most severe form of malaria is caused by *P. falciparum*, which may kill the patient within 24 to 48 hours after he becomes infected. The form of malaria caused by *P. vivax* is characterized by multiple recurrences, but is rarely fatal.

Transmission. Infectious diseases are the only ones that can be transmitted. They may be spread by infected animals, infected people, or contaminated substances such as food and water. Infectious diseases that can be transmitted to humans from infected animals are known as *zoonoses*. Zoonoses may be transmitted by carriers, such as insects; by the bite of an infected animal; by direct contact with an infected animal or its excretions; or by eating animal products.

The term *vector* is applied to any animal that carries a disease-causing organism from one host to another. Vectors are generally divided into two types: mechanical vectors and biological vectors. Flies are an example of mechanical vectors in that they passively transfer disease-causing organisms to food. In a biological vector the disease-causing organism multiplies or passes through an essential part of its life cycle while in the body of the vector. Among the many diseases that are transmitted through vectors are malaria, yellow fever, typhus, bubonic plague, leishmaniasis, and schistosomiasis.

Rabies is an example of an infectious disease that is transmitted through the bite of an infected animal. The animals most commonly involved are the dog, wolf, and other members of the canine family, but the vampire bat may also transmit the disease. Diseases that are transmitted by contact with an infected animal or its excretions include brucellosis, tularemia, and psittacosis (ornithosis). Anthrax is transmitted by contact with animal products, such as wool. Tuberculosis, tapeworm infestation, and salmonella infection are transmitted by the consumption of animal products.

In diseases that are spread from person to person by direct body contact or by contact with body excretions, the person who spreads the disease may not actually suffer from the disease. This type of person is known as a *carrier*. Typhoid fever is a prominent example of a disease that is mainly transmitted through a healthy carrier. Often, the disease-causing bacteria reside in the carrier's gall bladder and are excreted with his feces. Viral hepatitis is another disease that may be transmitted by a healthy carrier. Staphylococcal diseases are frequently transmitted by healthy carriers of *Staphyloccus aureus*. Such carriers are particular hazardous in hospitals, where patients with pneumonia may develop a staphylococcal disease of the lungs, surgical wounds may become infected, and newborn babies may be affected to such an extent that the hospital nursery may have to be closed until the bacteria are eradicated.

Tuberculosis is transmitted not only through contaminated milk and other animal products but also through direct contact with an infected person. In countries where the pasteurization of milk and milk products is a common practice, human contact is the only way the disease is transmitted. Transmission is through the respiratory secretions, and contact with a carrier on a bus or in the theater may be sufficient to produce the disease. Other diseases that are highly contagious through contact with respiratory secretions include all of the usual childhood diseases, such as whooping cough, mumps, chicken pox, measles, and German measles.

Several important parasitic diseases may also be transmitted directly from one person to another without an intermediate host. Pinworms (*Enterobius vermicularis*) may be transmitted through contact with the feces of an infected person, and this infection is so contagious that if one member of a family is infected, all other family members may soon become infected. Pinworm infestation is common in institutions, such as mental institutions and schools, particularly nursery schools and kindergartens.

Contaminated food, water, and soil are common sources of infectious diseases. Staphylococcal food poisoning and botulism are transmitted through foods, and both food and water are common sources of salmonella infections and infections caused by Shigella bacteria, which cause a mild to severe dysentery. Even such usually harmless organisms as the coliform bacteria, which include *Escherichia coli* (the bacterium that normally inhabits the intestines), may contaminate milk that is used in hospital nurseries and produce epidemics of dysentery.

Schistosomiasis is due to three different species of parasitic flukes, and all three are generally transmitted through contact with water. The free-living larval forms of the flukes live in water. Upon finding a suitable host, they penetrate the skin and eventually reach the liver, gastrointestinal tract, or the urinary bladder, where they develop into adults. Schistosomiasis is a particularly hazardous infection in Egypt, where in some regions more than 90% of the population is infected. Unfortunately, the construction of dams for irrigation often spreads the parasites to such an extent that eradication of the disease in some regions is not possible in the foreseeable future.

Water can also be an important source of cholera, which occasionally occurs in epidemics in the Middle East, Far East, and Africa. Amebic dysentery, which is caused by the ameba *Entamoeba histolytica*, is transmitted through contact with infested food, water, or soil. In many countries, the spread of amebic dysentery and similar diseases is promoted by the use of human feces for fertilizer (night soil).

Often, travelers to foreign countries are affected by gastrointestinal disturbances. Although some of these infections may be identified as *Shigella* infections or amebic dysentery, some of them may be caused by viruses or simply by a change in diet. For example, the use of olive oil in many foods is a frequent cause of diarrhea in travelers to Italy.

Immunological Diseases. The natural reaction of the body to foreign proteins is called an immune response. The body usually reacts to a foreign protein by developing a local reaction at the site of invasion and by developing special chemical substances, called *antibodies*, which serve to neutralize the protein. During embryological development, all substances that come into contact with the embryo while the immune mechanism is developing will be tolerated by the body later on, and all substances that are introduced into the body after the immune mechanism has developed will be rejected. Thus, the organism will not normally form antibodies against its own proteins, but it will form antibodies against all other proteins, whether they are from other animals, plants, viruses, fungi, bacteria, or rickettsiae.

The body's response to a foreign protein varies greatly, depending on the type of protein. Fortunately, foreign materials do not always provoke a violent immune reaction, for if people developed antibodies to all foods, dust, and other agents, they would always be ill. The immune response is usually protective and is a very important part of the body's defenses against disease. On the other hand, the immune reaction may sometimes be more severe than the effect of the foreign protein on the body. This condition is called *hypersensitivity*, and it is probably responsible for such diseases as hay fever, asthma, eczema, and some types of contact dermatitis.

Hypersensitivity not only causes disease but may also occur as a complication of a disease. In tuberculosis, for example, the first exposure to the bacterium *Mycobacterium tuberculosis* produces a minor inflammation with no symptoms. Subsequent exposures to the bacterium, however, cause such a high degree of cellular inflammation that the hypersentitive reaction to the bacterium is as destructive as the actual bacterial invasion.

Collagen diseases are diseases of connective tissue that are believed to be caused by the production of autoantibodies—antibodies produced by the body against its own tissues. In most of these diseases, it is still unknown whether these antibodies actually cause the disease or whether they are merely a reflection of an underlying disease process. The collagen diseases include rheumatoid arthritis, lupus erythematosus,

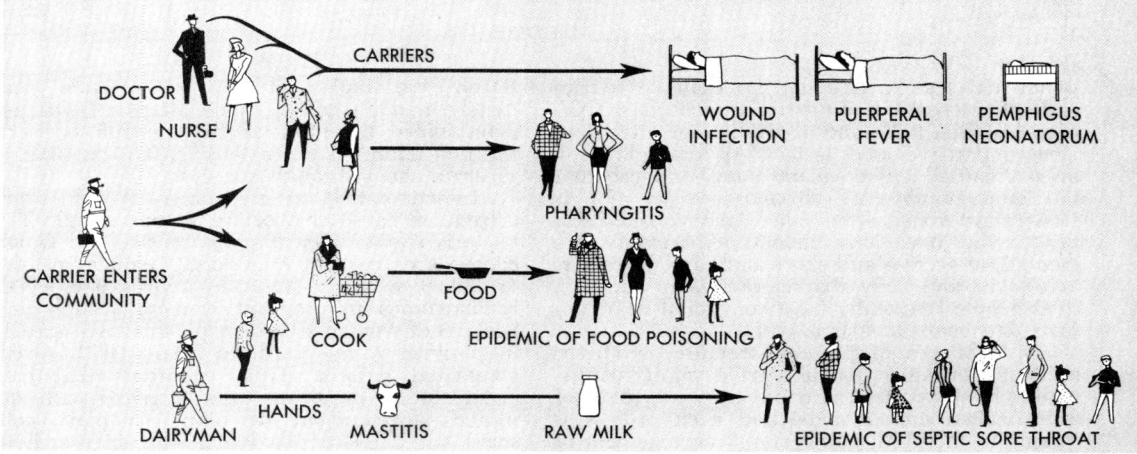

AN INFECTIOUS DISEASE spreading through a community can sometimes be traced to a single carrier. In this case, the healthy carrier is spreading streptococcal bacteria. Some of the persons who come into contact with him develop streptococcal diseases, while others become additional carriers, further spreading the bacteria.

dermatomyositis, scleroderma, and periarteritis nodosa. They are all generally characterized by inflammation of the small blood vessels, necrosis (death) of the vessel walls, and eventual occlusion of the vessels by thrombi (blood clots) and scar tissue.

Just as disease may result from a hyperactive immune response, disease may also result from an inadequate response of the body's immune mechanism. Patients who have agammaglobulinemia, an absence or deficiency of gamma globulins, cannot produce antibodies following exposure to foreign proteins and are very susceptible to viral infections. Again, if the reticuloendothelial system, the body's source of antibodies, is diseased, the person's immune response is depressed. This condition is frequently found in leukemia patients, who may die from infections that would ordinarily be tolerated by the body. Steroid therapy, which is used to treat certain diseases, also depresses the body's immune response.

Neoplasms. A neoplasm, or tumor, is the uncontrolled growth of abnormal tissue at the expense of normal tissue. Neoplasms are either *benign* or *malignant*, and they may arise in any tissue of the body. Benign tumors differ from malignant ones in many ways, but the most important difference is that malignant tumors metastasize, or spread, to other parts of the body. Metastasis may occur by direct invasion, or it may occur through the bloodstream or the lymphatic system.

Malignant tumors are known collectively as *cancer*. Cancers that originate in supporting tissues, such as bone or fat tissues, are called *sarcomas*. Cancers that arise from epithelial (surface) tissues, such as the skin or the lining of the gastrointestinal tract, are called *carcinomas*. Benign tumors are usually not fatal unless they interfere with the functioning of a vital organ. Most cancers, on the other hand, are fatal if not treated.

Although the cause of cancer is not known, certain environmental factors are known to influence the onset of the disease. The first reported industrial cancer was carcinoma of the scrotum, which was found by the 18th century English physician Percival Potts to occur in men who cleaned chimneys. Today, many other environmental factors, including radiation and some chemicals, are known to initiate certain types of cancer.

Many years ago it was common practice to apply X-ray therapy to the upper chest for infants who had respiratory difficulties. (It was erroneously believed at the time that the respiratory difficulties were due to an enlargement of the thymus gland.) Later, it was found that those people who had been exposed to radiation at an early age had a higher incidence of carcinoma of the thyroid gland than people who had never received X-ray therapy. In recent years, excessive exposure to sunlight has been found to induce cancer of the skin, and cigarette smoking has been found to be related to carcinoma of the lung. Although viruses have been discovered to be the causative agents of some animal cancers, efforts to implicate viruses as a cause of some human cancers have been inconclusive.

The signs and symptoms of cancer vary greatly and are largely determined by the location of the neoplasm and whether or not it has metastasized. Cancer of the skin may resemble a sore; cancer of the esophagus may cause difficulty in swallowing; cancer of the intestines may result in diarrhea or constipation; and cancer of the breast produces an abnormal lump in that organ. (Most lumps in the breast, however, are the result of benign tumors or normal physiological processes.)

Congenital and Metabolic Diseases. In the nucleus of every human cell are 23 pairs of chromosomes. Each chromosome consists largely of long chains of deoxyribonucleic acid (DNA). The DNA contains the hereditary material of the cell; each unit of heredity is called a *gene*. Genes control protein production and transmit inherited characteristics from a cell to its descendants. Thus, the genes and their effect on metabolism are important in health and disease.

The most frequently investigated genetic diseases are caused by alterations of chromosomes or defects in the synthesis, structure, or functioning of proteins. Of the 46 chromosomes in the nucleus of a human cell, two, the X chromosome and the Y chromosome, are the sex chromosomes. The remaining 44 chromosomes are called *autosomes*. Normally, a male has 44 autosomes, an X chromosome, and a Y chromosome, while a female has 44 autosomes and two X chromosomes. Any alteration in the number of chromosomes may lead to disease. For example, a man with 44 autosomes and the sex chromosomes XXY, may be thin, tall, and mentally defective and have underdeveloped testes. An example of a disease caused by too many autosomes (so that the total number of chromosomes is 47) is Down's syndrome, often called "mongolism." Patients who have this genetic abnormality are mentally defective and short and have characteristic facial and body characteristics. In addition, such people frequently have congenital heart defects and acute leukemia.

Disturbances of protein structure, synthesis, and function are found in a wide variety of diseases. Every protein is made up of a chain of units, called *amino acids*, and each protein is unique in the kind, number, and arrangement of its amino acids. If a particular amino acid is missing or is replaced by another amino acid, the protein will not function properly. For example, in sickle cell anemia the amino acid glutamic acid is replaced by the amino acid valine in the hemoglobin of the red blood cells.

This single amino acid alteration changes the shape of the red blood cells from the normal disk shape to an abnormal shape similar to that of a sickle. Sickling of the red blood cells is accompanied by plugging of the blood vessels by clots and severe anemia. Other important genetic or metabolic diseases include diabetes mellitus; phenylketonuria (PKU), a defect that may cause mental defficiency; and various disorders interfering with the metabolism of glycogen (a storage form of glucose), which cause the glycogen to accumulate in the liver, heart, or skeletal muscles.

Diseases of Growth and Development. Many diseases of growth and development are genetically determined. However, many congenital diseases —that is, diseases present at birth—are caused by factors in the embryo's environment, and still others are without any obvious cause. From the moment of conception, development of the embryo may be affected by many environmental as well as genetic factors. Approximately 5% of all infants have some obvious anomaly, or defect, although in only about 10% of these children is the defect serious.

Developmental defects may occur in every organ and region of the body. Some anomalies are so severe that an entire organ or region may not develop beyond early embryological stages. Organs or limbs may be absent (agenesis) or poorly developed (hypoplastic); tubular structures may fail to develop normal channels; and tissues and organs may appear in the wrong places (ectopia). The most common congenital defects involve the heart, gastrointestinal tract, and central nervous system.

Among the environmental factors that interfere with the normal development of the embryo are diseases of the placenta, the spongy organ through which the embryo receives food materials and oxygen. Sometimes the placenta is in an improper position and may interfere with the process of childbirth as well as the development of the infant. Premature separation of the placenta from the uterus may lead to the death of the mother or the baby.

The occurrence of twins is sometimes considered to be an abnormality of development, although the twins are usually normal children. Occasionally, the fertilized egg cell may divide into separate cells, producing identical twins. Rarely, the single cell does not separate completely, and the twins, called Siamese twins, remain joined together. If the junction between the two infants is not extensive, it is possible to separate them through surgery.

Infections that occur in pregnant women are a frequent cause of abortion or fetal death. The bacteria *Clostridium, Staphylococcus,* and *Gonococcus* are frequent offenders. German measles (rubella), which is caused by a virus, is especially dangerous in pregnant women; a high percentage of women who develop this disease early in pregnancy give birth to infants with severe congenital defects. Other disorders that may occur during pregnancy and interfere with the infant's development are herpes simplex (cold sore) and salivary gland inclusion disease, both of which are caused by viruses; and toxoplasmosis, which is caused by a parasitic protozoan.

Trauma at birth is another important cause of disease in early childhood. Head injuries causing hemorrhaging are the most serious type of birth trauma. Cerebral palsy, an affliction of children, may be the result of a brain hemorrhage, a virus infection of the brain, or oxygen deficiency (hypoxia), which frequently accompanies prolonged labor.

Dwarfism, the stunting of normal growth, may be the result of nutritional deficiencies, chronic infections, inborn errors of metabolism, hormone imbalances, or achondroplasia, a hereditary disease affecting the skeleton. Achondroplasia is inherited as a dominant trait and is characterized by short stature and abnormally short limbs. A similar inherited trait is found in a certain breed of dogs, the dachshund.

Diseases Due to Chemical and Physical Agents. Diseases in this category represent some of the most important causes of illness and death. When one realizes that automobile drivers have killed more people in the United States than were killed in all American wars since 1776, the magnitude of death by trauma is apparent. Trauma, or physical disease, may be caused by objects ranging from cars to bullets, blows from fists, body contact in sports, drowning, or falls in the bathtub. In the United States, accidents are the major cause of death in very young children.

Many years ago, most chemical disease resulted from poisons such as lye, acids, and arsenic. Today, the development and widespread use of drugs have created a new category of chemical diseases, called *iatrogenic diseases*. For example, patients who have been incorrectly treated for sore throat with the antibiotic chloramphenicol have died as a result of a severe depression of their white blood cell production, a condition caused entirely by the drug.

In recent decades, other causes of chemical and physical disease have become increasingly important. These include pollution of the air and water by industrial wastes, alteration of meat and other foods by insecticides and other agricultural chemicals, and contamination of the air, soil, and food by radioactive materials.

Nutritional Diseases. Nutritional disease results from a deficiency or absence of all or some of the essential food elements or from an excess of some or all of these elements. The three major constituents of food are carbohydrates, fats, and proteins. In addition, other food elements, such as vitamins and minerals, are vital to the diet. Malnutrition, or undernutrition, is most commonly due to a lack of protein in the diet.

Starvation, which is rare in many parts of the world, is due to the complete absence of all food. An isolated deficiency of protein, vitamins, or minerals is unusual because a deficiency of one of these elements is generally accompanied by an inadequate intake of other food elements.

Nutritional disease has its greatest effect in very young children. A frequent disease in Africa, the Middle East, the Far East, and some of the Caribbean Islands is kwashiorkor, which is caused by an inadequate intake of protein during the weaning period. Children with kwashiorkor suffer from an accumulation of fluid in the tissues and have an enlarged liver. In addition, their hair is sparse, fine, and frequently reddish in color.

Many nutritional diseases are caused by inadequate vitamin intake. A deficiency of vitamin B_1 (thiamine) results in beriberi, a disease most frequently seen in parts of the Far East where polished (hulled) rice is a major part of the diet. The disorder resulting from a deficiency of vitamin C is called scurvy, characterized by hemorrhages of the mucous membranes, particularly those of the gums. A deficiency of vitamin D leads to rickets, a disorder primarily affecting the bones.

In the United States and other advanced countries, the most common nutritional disease is obesity, which is often complicated by arteriosclerosis effecting the heart and major blood vessels. Although obesity may be caused by internal disorders, such as endocrine diseases, it is most commonly due to external factors, such as overeating.

Endocrine Diseases. The endocrine system consists of the pituitary gland, the thyroid gland, the parathyroid glands, the adrenal glands, the gonads, and the islets of Langerhans in the pancreas. The endocrine glands secrete elaborate chemical substances, called *hormones,* directly into the bloodstream, which carries them to the organs and tissues they affect.

Some diseases of the endocrine glands are characterized by an oversecretion of hormones. These diseases are often caused by hyperplasia (enlargement) of the gland or by the presence of a benign or malignant tumor of the gland. Other endocrine diseases are characterized by a deficiency of hormone secretion, due to the partial or complete destruction of the gland from a variety of causes, including tumors and infections.

The pituitary gland consists of two major parts, called the anterior pituitary gland and the posterior pituitary gland. The anterior pituitary gland is often called the master gland of the body, for its secretions affect other endocrine glands as well as nonglandular organs. One of the major functions of the anterior pituitary gland is to secrete hormones that regulate growth, so that diseases of this gland may result in giantism or dwarfism. The posterior pituitary gland stores antidiuretic hormone (ADH). Any disease that destroys this gland may result in a deficiency of ADH, which leads to diabetes insipidus.

The hormones of the thyroid gland regulate the metabolism of the body cells. A deficiency of these hormones, called *hypothyroidism,* occurs in several forms, the most important of which are cretinism and myxedema. Cretinism is hypothyroidism that is present at birth, while myxedema is a severe adult form of hypothyroidism. Myxedema may result from many causes, including a deficiency of iodine in the diet. *Hyperthyroidism,* the overproduction of thyroid hormones, usually results from an enlargement of the gland. The most prominent features of hyperthyroidism are exophthalmos (bulging of the eyes), increased basal metabolic rate, increased appetite, loss of weight, and intolerance to heat.

The adrenal gland consists of two different types of tissue: the cortex and the medulla. The cortex secretes hormones that control the metabolism of carbohydrates and the balance of salts and water in the body. It also secretes androgen (masculinizing hormone) and estrogen (femininizing hormone). Accordingly, an overactivity or underactivity of the various parts of the adrenal cortex produces a wide variety of syndromes. The adrenal medulla secretes epinephrine. There are no diseases associated with epinephrine deficiency and the only one associated with oversecretion is a type of tumor that may be either malignant or benign.

The islets of Langerhans secrete the hormone insulin. A deficiency of this hormone results in diabetes mellitus, a disorder in which the body cells are unable to absorb or metabolize sufficient amounts of the sugar glucose. The production of too much insulin results in hypoglycemia, a condition marked by profuse sweating, trembling, hunger, nausea, headache, rapid heartbeat, and other symptoms.

Circulatory Diseases. This category is made up of diseases of the heart and blood vessels. Circulatory diseases take many forms and are extremely important; for example, in the United States, they cause about 55% of all the deaths. The most important of these diseases are arteriosclerotic heart disease, cerebrovascular accident (stroke), and hypertensive heart disease. Other important circulatory diseases are congenital heart defects, rheumatic fever, and various other inflammations of the heart.

Arteriosclerotic heart disease is the result of atherosclerosis of the coronary arteries, the tiny blood vessels supplying the heart muscle. In this disease, the arteries become narrowed, the blood supply to the muscle is diminished, and fibrosis, or massive scarring (infarction) of the muscle results, sometimes accompanied by the presence of thrombi (clots) in the vessels. A stroke results from a decrease in the blood supply to the brain caused by atherosclerosis of the brain arteries. Other common causes of stroke, particularly in young people, are congenital aneurysms (weakened segments) of the brain arteries. In fact, this condition is one of the most frequent causes of sudden death in teen-agers.

Hypertension (high blood pressure) may be caused by kidney failure, tumors of the adrenal glands, pregnancy, tumors of the kidney, and obesity. However, in more than 90% of the patients with hypertension, no cause can be found. This type of high blood pressure is known as idiopathic, or essential, hypertension.

Mental Disorders. Mental, or psychiatric, disorders are generally classified into two major groups: those in which there is a disturbance in the mental functioning of the brain, and those which result from a difficulty of the individual to adapt and in which any associated brain malfunction is secondary. The first category includes acute and chronic brain disorders resulting from trauma, infection, drugs, poisons, tumors, and various hereditary or idiopathic mental deficiency syndromes. The second category includes various psychotic disorders, such as manic-depressive psychosis, schizophrenia, and paranoia. Also in this group are the psychophysiological disorders, which include reactions of the skin, muscles, respiratory system, gastrointestinal system, nervous system, and cardiovascular system. The second category also includes the very important psychoneuroses and other personality disorders.

METHODS OF DIAGNOSIS

The diagnosis of disease generally depends on three different types of examinations. First, the doctor examines the patient's medical history. Next, he performs a physical examination of the patient. And finally, he performs certain laboratory studies. In some cases he may perform specialized examinations and tests.

Medical History. The medical history of a patient is essential for the physician who is attempting to analyze the manifestations of a disease. The first items to be recorded are the patient's name, race, age, birthplace, sex, marital status, occupation, and residence. The patient's age is an important factor because certain diseases, including some contagious diseases, congenital heart disease, rheumatic fever, and acute leukemia, are found mainly in young people, while other diseases, including arteriosclerotic heart disease and degenerative diseases, are much more common in middle-aged and elderly people. The patient's occupation is also an important factor, especially if the patient's job exposes him to certain substances, such as aniline, benzene, silica, or lead in the form of bullets. In recent years, the widespread use of insecticides has caused disease in farmers, gardeners, and even housewives.

The next questions the doctor asks concern the patient's present symptoms, his illnesses, and the illnesses of family members. At the completion of a thorough medical history, the physician often has a good lead to the nature of the patient's disorder, or at least he can begin to categorize illness.

Physical Examination. Just as in history taking the doctor must exclude extraneous material, so the physical examination must concentrate on a logical exploration of the patient's physical abnormalities. The physical examination covers the whole body, even though all of the patient's complaints may be related to only one region or organ. A patient may seek the assistance of a doctor for a common cold, but a thorough examination may disclose cancer of the rectum. As part of the examination, the doctor measures the patient's height, weight, temperature, blood pressure, and pulse rate. He also examines the patient's skin, head, eyes, ears, nose, mouth and throat, neck, chest and lungs, heart, breasts, abdomen, genitalia, back and spine, nervous system, and rectum.

Laboratory Studies. The laboratory studies performed depend on the medical history and the findings of the physical examination. However, certain tests are performed on all patients regardless of the diagnosis. These include a urinalysis, an X-ray of the chest, a screening test for syphilis, a hematocrit (a test to determine the volume of red blood cells in the blood), and in women, a screening test for cancer of the uterus. A routine urinalysis includes tests for sugar and protein in the urine and may lead to a diagnosis of diabetes mellitus or a disorder of the kidneys or the pituitary gland. The chest X-ray is particularly important, for unsuspected tuberculosis may be found, and the hematocrit may detect an unsuspected anemia. Following the laboratory studies, the doctor usually arrives at his diagnosis. If necessary, he may order additional procedures and tests to confirm or reject his diagnosis.

Specialized Tests and Procedures. The blood is one of the most important body fluids readily available for study, and many diseases are reflected by alterations in the composition of the blood and the structure and number of the blood cells. Common blood tests include a red blood cell count, a white blood cell count, a differential analysis of the various kinds of white blood cells, a test to determine the blood's clotting ability, and a study of the structure of the red blood cells. If the doctor suspects an abnormality of the hemoglobin, he may have the hemoglobin analyzed by electrophoresis, a technique that involves the separation of proteins in an electrical field, using paper, agar, cellulose acetate, or starch as a medium. In addition to examining the blood hemoglobin, the doctor may wish to examine the red blood cell enzymes. Sometimes an examination of the blood may reveal the presence of the parasites that cause malaria, filariasis, and trypanosomiasis. In some cases the patient's bone marrow is also studied, sometimes leading to a diagnosis of leukemia, metastatic cancer, lymphoma, or pernicious anemia.

Bacteriological and immunological studies of blood are used for diagnosing various infections and immunological diseases. For example, a bacteriological culture of the blood is made when typhoid fever, paratyphoid fever, or brucellosis is suspected. Some of these and other bacterial diseases, as well as rickettsial diseases, are detected by immunological studies of blood. Syphilis is also detected through various immunological studies as well as through identification of the causative organism, *Treponema pallidum,* on a lesion of the genital organs or on the mucous membranes of the mouth.

Bacterial examinations are also frequently performed on sputum, bronchial secretions, vaginal and cervical secretions, urine, feces, spinal fluid, and pus from various organs. These studies include a microscopic examination of smears that are stained with special dyes for detecting bacteria or fungi, and the growing of the microorganisms in laboratory cultures. Feces may also be examined for parasite eggs, larvae, and adults.

Cytological (cellular) studies have their greatest use in detecting cancers of the uterus, lungs, gastrointestinal tract, kidneys, and the urinary bladder. In a cytological examination, cells scraped from these organs are examined under a microscope, and if malignant cells are seen or suspected, a biopsy is performed to confirm the diagnosis. A biopsy is the removal and examination of living tissue; it is used mostly to diagnose tumors before and during surgery. After the tissue is removed, it is stained and examined by a pathologist.

There are two basic methods the doctor can use to examine regions of the body not visible upon external examination. One method, called endoscopy, involves the use of various tube-shaped instruments that are designed to enter any natural body opening and allow the doctor to see the internal organs. The proctoscope and sigmoidoscope are used for examining the rectum and descending colon; the laryngoscope is used for the larynx; the bronchoscope is used for the bronchi; the cystoscope is used for the urinary bladder; the esophagoscope is used for the esophagus; and the gastroscope is used for the stomach.

The second method used for examining the interior of the body involves the use of X-ray photography. All regions of the body may be X-rayed for diagnostic purposes, and many structures that are not readily visible on X-ray photographs can be observed if they are first injected with a radio-opaque dye. For example, blood and lymphatic vessels are not normally seen on an X-ray photograph, but they can be seen if they are injected with certain dyes. This technique can be used for detecting abnormalities of any blood vessels, including the tiny arteries of the heart. To inject dye into these arteries, a narrow tube, called a catheter, is fed into a vessel in the arm and directed into the heart arteries. Once the catheter is in place, the dye is released into the arteries, and the area is X-rayed.

The electrical activity of both the heart and the brain may be recorded by special instruments. An electrocardiogram, which records the electrical impulses of the heart, can be used to detect various heart disorders, including enlargement of the ventricles, cardiac arrhythmias (irregular heart rates), and myocardial infarction, a common cause of heart attacks. The electroencephalogram, which records the electrical impulses of the brain, is useful in locating brain tumors or sites of destruction from hemorrhages or thrombosis (occlusion due to a clot).

Another specialized diagnostic technique involves the use of radioactive isotopes, which are most frequently used in detecting disorders of the thyroid gland, blood diseases, and tumors. Radioactive isotopes are also used to determine the volume of red blood cells and plasma in the blood.

TREATMENT OF DISEASE

The treatment of disease may involve the administration of drugs to relieve the patient's symptoms (symptomatic drug therapy) or cure the underlying cause of the disease (specific drug therapy). It may also entail various surgical procedures and other techniques, including psychotherapy. All types of therapy have hazards, and the doctor must weigh the dangers of therapy against the potential ill effects caused by the disease. If the physician decides that a specific disease may be self-limiting, he may prescribe only mild drug therapy aimed at relieving the patient's symptoms, or he may decide not to prescribe any therapy at all. For example, the best therapy for the common cold is simple bed rest and the relief of symptoms with aspirin and steam inhalation. Antibiotics should only be given if a bacterial infection arises. Unfortunately, some patients have been overtreated for this self-limited disease, sometimes with fatal complications.

Symptomatic Drug Therapy. Pain and discomfort are important symptoms of disease, but once the diagnosis is established, it is the duty of the physician to relieve suffering as much as possible. Sometimes the physician may not relieve the patient's pain immediately, for the character of the pain is often an important clue to the diagnosis of the disease. For example, if pain is relieved too soon in a patient with suspected appendicitis the most important indication of the disease may be abolished and the diagnosis may not be possible for several hours.

There is a wide range of drugs for the relief of pain, from aspirin to morphine and other narcotics. A major consideration for the physician is the knowledge that all drugs are toxic. Even aspirin, the drug most widely used and most commonly prescribed, has its dangers. Constant use of aspirin may produce small hemorrhages, inflammation of the stomach, and metabolic disturbances. The stronger pain-killers, such as morphine, are to be avoided as long as possible, but if they are needed, they are not withheld from a patient. However, when narcotics are prescribed, they are usually given for only a short period of time, to avoid narcotic addiction.

Sedatives and sleep-inducing drugs (hypnotics) are used in a wide variety of conditions. The most frequently used drugs in this group are the barbiturates, mainly to treat anxiety. Sedatives are also often given to relatives of critically ill patients. Barbiturates and other sedatives can be addicting if taken in large enough quantities over a long period of time. The withdrawal symptoms include delirium tremens and convulsions.

Nausea is a frequent, short-lived symptom that commonly results from a chemically induced inflammation of the stomach or intestine. This inflammation often results from excessive alcohol intake or an intestinal infection. Nausea is often so distressing that almost any external stimulus may produce vomiting. Often the most effective therapy for nausea is quiet bed rest. Sometimes, sedatives, such as phenobarbital, are administered. More severe nausea or vomiting may require an antihistamine with a strong antinausea and antimotion sickness effect. In some cases a derivative phenothiazine may be given, but the use of these drugs should be restricted because of their toxicity. Included among their toxic effects are severe hypotension (fall in blood pressure), neurological symptoms, jaundice due to obstruction of the small bile ducts, agranulocytosis (depressed production of the white blood cells), and various skin reactions. The phenothiazines are not used for self-limited gastrointestinal disturbances because the potential ill effects of the drugs may be much more severe than the disease symptoms. These drugs are also contraindicated for the nausea of early pregnancy because they may have an adverse effect on the developing embryo. Finally, except for promethazine, these drugs are not effective in treating the nausea and vomiting caused by motion sickness and other disturbances of the vestibular organs of the ear.

Specific Drug Therapy. The treatment of infectious diseases was revolutionized by the discovery of the sulfonamides and the antibiotics. Penicillin, the first important antibiotic to be discovered, has the highest therapeutic effectiveness and greatest safety of all these drugs. It is most useful in treating diseases caused by staphylococci, streptococci, gonococci, and pneumococci. However, penicillin is not without danger. A small percentage of patients are so sensitive to this drug that a severe skin reaction or even a fatal immune reaction may occur following the intake of penicillin. After penicillin, the next most useful drugs are the tetracyclines and other broad-spectrum antibiotics, which are useful in treating many diseases caused by certain bacteria that are not affected by penicillin. Tuberculosis

IMPORTANT DISEASES TRANSMITTED TO HUMANS FROM ANIMALS

Disease	Causative organisms	Principal animals involved	Transmitting agents
Anthrax	Bacteria	Domestic livestock	Animal products, soil
Brucellosis	Bacteria	Domestic livestock	Animal products, excretions
Bubonic plague	Bacteria	Rodents	Fleas, ticks
Influenza	Viruses	Horses, pigs	Respiratory secretions
Leptospirosis	Bacteria	Rodents, dogs, pigs, wild animals	Animal products, excretions
Leishmaniasis	Protozoans	Dogs, cats, rodents	Sand flies
Murine typhus	Rickettsiae	Rats	Rat fleas
Psittacosis	Viruses	Parrots, poultry, pigeons	Respiratory secretions, feces
Q fever	Rickettsiae	Domestic animals	Milk, dust
Rabies	Viruses	Dogs, other mammals	Saliva
Relapsing fevers	Bacteria	Cave-dwelling rodents	Ticks, lice
Rocky Mountain spotted fever	Rickettsiae	Rodents, dogs	Ticks
Salmonellosis	Bacteria	Rats, poultry, dogs	Flesh, eggs, excretions
Scrub typhus	Rickettsiae	Rodents	Mite larvae
Toxoplasmosis	Protozoans	Wild mammals, birds	Unknown
Tuberculosis	Bacteria	Domestic livestock	Milk, flesh
Tularemia	Bacteria	Wild rabbits	Flesh, deerflies, ticks

is treated by various combinations of two organic chemicals—isoniazid and para-aminosalicylic acid—and by the antibiotic streptomycin.

One of the most important considerations in antibiotic therapy, as well as in therapy with certain other drugs, is the danger of creating another disease by the use of the therapeutic agent. The prolonged use of antibiotics may alter the bacterial makeup inside the body enough to allow other organisms, which are normally kept in check by the bacteria being attacked, to grow and cause disease. For example, certain bacteria normally check the growth of the fungus *Candida albicans;* if these bacteria are eradicated by the prolonged use of penicillin, the fungus may cause disease of the mouth and throat. Similarly, staphylococci may cause disease of the gastrointestinal tract while the patient is under therapy with tetracyclines, antibiotics that destroy the normal flora (mostly *E. coli*) of the gastrointestinal tract. Another problem with antibiotics is that micro-organisms resistant to the drugs may develop.

Drugs are also used to treat other than infectious diseases. Antacids and antispasmodics are used for gastrointestinal disorders; iron and vitamin B_{12} are used for certain blood disorders; digitalis glycosides are used for cardiac insufficiency; and various other agents, such as methotrexate, nitrogen mustard, and vineblastine, are used for certain types of cancer.

Surgery. Surgical approaches to disease include the removal of organs or parts of organs, the repair of damaged or diseased tissues, the replacement of segments of organs by artificial devices, and the transplantation of whole organs from one person to another. The removal of an organ without replacing it depends on whether the organ is paired and whether the loss of one or both organs is compatible with life. For example, one kidney or lung can be removed without endangering the patient's life, but the heart cannot be removed without being replaced. The uterus is a single organ, but the loss of this structure will not adversely affect the patient. Both the adrenal glands may be removed, but the patient must continue to take daily doses of adrenal hormones.

The surgical removal of organs is necessary in a wide variety of cases. An appendectomy is required to treat acute appendicitis to prevent the appendix from becoming perforated or gangrenous. Surgical removal is also indicated in treating most cancers of the lung, stomach, intestines, breast, prostrate gland, kidney, and urinary bladder. Skin grafting is a form of reparative surgery that is used following severe burns, and injury to nerves, tendons, and blood vessels requires surgical repair in order to prevent their loss of function. Other wounds, ranging from skin cuts to knife and bullet wounds, may require a surgical restoration of the affected organs and tissues.

In recent years, the development of drugs that suppress the patient's immune mechanism has facilitated the transplantation of various organs, such as kidneys, lungs, and the heart. Although organ transplantation is still largely experimental, it may eventually become an established method of treating people whose organs are too damaged to be repaired or treated with drugs.

Other Types of Therapy. Radiation therapy is most widely used to eradicate various skin cancers and to relieve the symptoms of other types of cancer. This type of therapy includes the use of X-rays, radium, other sources of radiation, and radioactive isotopes of various elements that become concentrated in particular organs. For example, radioactive iodine is used in treating cancer of the thyroid because iodine in the body is concentrated in the thyroid gland.

Psychotherapy is directed toward treating the patient's total thinking–feeling–behaving pattern. The psychiatrist suggests, counsels, directs, supports, educates, interprets, and reorganizes the patient's environment or combines these procedures in order to free the patient from interfering stresses or from his pathological reactions to them.

Physical therapy involves the restoration of the function of limbs or other regions of the body by education, exercise, and manipulative measures. Heat may also be applied to the affected limb or region.

PREVENTION OF DISEASE

The methods used in preventing disease vary greatly depending on the type of disease. For example, diseases caused by tapeworms and other parasitic organisms can be prevented by eradicating the organisms in the environment. On the other hand, many bacterial, viral, and other infectious diseases may be prevented by the use of vaccines, which confer immunity against the invading organisms.

Important measures in preventing all diseases are periodic medical and dental checkups. With regular examinations, many disorders, including diabetes, dental decay, gum diseases, high blood pressure, heart diseases, urinary tract infections, tuberculosis, glaucoma, and some psychiatric illnesses may be detected and cured, or at least controlled, at an early stage. Diseases that are related to poverty, such as lead poisoning in children (the result of eating cracked paint), malnutrition, tuberculosis, and maternal and infant mortality, can only be eliminated by the eradication of the causes of poverty. Preventive measures and therapeutic medicines are only limited solutions.

Eradicating Parasites. Some of the major parasitic diseases, such as schistosomiasis and African sleeping sickness, are widespread in some parts of the world but have never been a problem in other countries, such as the United States, because of the absence of intermediate hosts. Other parasitic diseases, such as malaria, were eliminated in the United States and elsewhere as a result of the alteration of the environment and the general well-being of the population. Nevertheless, in these countries, the thousands of soldiers and other government personnel, businessmen, tourists, and students who have been exposed to parasitic diseases abroad become reservoirs of parasitic infection when they return home.

Parasitic diseases may be prevented by various means, such as installing a pure water supply, indoor toilets, and sewage facilities; inspecting and adequately cooking meat; periodically inspecting food handlers; periodically administering protective drugs; wearing protective clothing and shoes; and placing screens in windows and doors.

Malaria is a major public health problem in Central and South America, Africa, and the Middle and Far East. Nevertheless, this disease is rarely a problem in the major cities, because a major factor in the elimination of malaria is the development of the land, thereby removing pools of stagnant water in which the larvae of the carrier mosquitoes live. Efforts to eradicate malaria in rural areas have involved the use of insecticides, such as DDT and inorganic phosphate compounds, but in many places insecticide-resistant varieties of the parasite have appeared. Some antimalarial drugs, such as chloroquine and primaquine, are both therapeutic and prophylactic (preventive). However, attempts to use these drugs on a large scale have often failed because of lack of cooperation by the people. Drugs have been successful with soldiers and travelers abroad, but there are strains of *Plasmodium falciparum* in the Far East and South America that are resistant to many antimalarial drugs.

Infestations with the beef tapeworm and the pork tapeworm can be prevented by rigorous programs of meat inspection and by the adequate cooking of meat. Infestation with the pork tapeworm is no problem among religious Muslims and Jews, whose religions forbid the eating of pork. However, this infection is a major problem in Germany and in certain parts of the United States, where partially cooked pork products are considered to be delicacies.

The most important disease-causing intestinal protozoan is *Entamoeba histolytica*, the cause of amebic dysentery. This disease is widespread in people of all ages and races among both urban and rural populations in temperate and tropical climates. The most important preventive measure against this disease is to provide adequate safe supplies of water for drinking, bathing, and household purposes. In addition, food supplies must be protected against contamination by night soil, infected food handlers, and flies and other insects. Tourists who travel in regions where the water and food are not safe must take precautions to decrease the probability of illness. If the water is unsafe, the tourist should substitute reliable carbonated beverages, drink only water that has been boiled for at least one minute, or use iodinate compounds in the water to eliminate the microorganisms. Chlorinated compounds are not safe, since they will not kill the amebas. Tea is safe in most cases because the water has most likely been boiled. Coffee, however, may not always be made with boiled water, so that this beverage should be avoided. Milk and other dairy products, as well as salads and all uncooked foods, are also potentially dangerous. Fresh fruit and vegetables can be eaten raw only if they are first peeled.

Vaccination. Artificial immunization through the use of vaccines is effective in preventing many diseases. The decrease in incidence of such communicable diseases as smallpox, diphtheria, tetanus, and poliomyelitis in recent decades has been due to the widespread use of immunizing agents. Vaccines against measles, mumps, German measles, and influenza are in the early stages of development. The routine use of typhoid vaccines in the United States and some other countries has considerably diminished, because in most urban areas the infection is rare, the vaccine provides only partial protection, and the injection causes discomfort and inconvenience. However, typhoid vaccine is widely used in times of local disasters, such as fires and floods, where the safety of the water supply is endangered.

The vaccine against yellow fever is one of the most effective of all vaccines. It is not needed in the United States or Canada, for example, because yellow fever has disappeared from North America, but immunization is recommended for travelers to Central and South America and Africa. It is also required for all travelers to India. Although yellow fever has never been found in India, all of the conditions for propagating the disease, including the insect vector *Aedes aegypti*, are present. Other effective vaccines for adult travelers are those against smallpox and tetanus. Vaccines are also available for other diseases, such as cholera, plague, and typhus, but the effectiveness of these vaccines is generally low.

JAMES E. BOWMAN, M. D.
*Departments of Medicine and Pathology
University of Chicago*

Bibliography

Beason, Paul B., and McDermott, Walsh, eds., *Cecil-Loeb Textbook of Medicine*, 12th ed. (Philadelphia 1967).
Burack, Richard, *Handbook of Prescription Drugs* (New York 1967).
Clark, Duncan W., and MacMahon, Brian, eds., *Preventive Medicine* (Boston 1967).
Dubos, René, *Mirage of Health* (New York 1959).
Harrison, Tinsley R., and others, eds., *Principles of Internal Medicine*, 5th ed. (New York 1966).
Major, Ralph H., and Delp, Mahlon H., *Physical Diagnosis* (Philadelphia 1962).
Topley, William W. C., and Wilson, G. S., *Principles of Bacteriology and Immunity*, 4th ed., ed. by G. S. Wilson, and A. A. Miles (Baltimore 1964).
Van Peenan, H. J., *Essentials of Pathology* (Chicago 1966).

DISESTABLISHMENT is the withdrawal from a church of rights, privileges, or patronage accorded to it by the state. Churches that hold a privileged position in a state are usually referred to as *established churches*. Historically, established churches have varied from those supported or endowed and largely controlled by the state to those holding a privileged position not enjoyed by other churches in the same country.

Most church establishments have by now disappeared. Those that remain in the Scandinavian countries still display characteristics of the historic Reformation state church. In some Latin countries, notably Spain, the Roman Catholic Church is accorded a special status under the law and a concordat with the Vatican.

The Church of England is an established church, not financially supported by the state but accorded a special place in national life. Its association with the state is maintained by act of Parliament. The crown appoints bishops and some other dignitaries, and the assent of the crown is required for new church regulations to become ecclesiastical law. The Church of Ireland (Anglican) was disestablished in 1871. Similarly, the Church of England in Wales was separated from its state connection in 1920. Agitation for disestablishment in England itself arises periodically. See also CHURCH AND STATE.

POWEL MILLS DAWLEY
General Theological Seminary, New York

DISFRANCHISEMENT is the act of depriving a person of any right, privilege, or power. The term usually refers to depriving a citizen of the right to vote or hold office. Persons may be disfranchised if they lose their citizenship, if they fail to register when required, or if they are convicted of certain crimes. Many people are disfranchised temporarily when they move, until they meet new residence requirements.

Sometimes disfranchisement is the result of political manipulation (such as gerrymandering of electoral district boundaries) or intimidation of voters. It may also come about through the alteration of suffrage qualifications. Poll taxes and other discriminatory voting requirements have disfranchised many Negro citizens in the southern United States since the late 19th century. They were outlawed on the federal level by the 24th Amendment to the U. S. Constitution in 1964.

In Britain the term "disfranchisement" is often applied to Parliament's depriving a constituency of representation in the House of Commons, either through a redistribution of seats or because of corruption within the constituency.

MARTIN GRUBERG, *Wisconsin State University*

DISINFECTANT, a chemical that kills microorganisms—bacteria, viruses, protozoa, or fungi. Disinfectants are also often called *germicides*. Strictly speaking, disinfectants are used to kill pathogenic, or disease-causing, organisms, while germicides kill all organisms; however, this distinction is not essential, and substances known as disinfectants are used as preservatives and deodorizers to kill nonpathogenic organisms. A distinction may also be made between disinfectants, which kill microorganisms on inanimate objects, and *antiseptics*, which kill organisms on living tissues. This distinction between disinfectants and antiseptics is not rigid, however, and many chemicals are suitable for both uses; in fact, the application of germicides to unbroken skin to prevent infection is usually called disinfection.

Disinfectants may also be divided according to the particular class of microorganisms that they affect; for example, bactericides kill bacteria, and viricides kill viruses. The term "disinfectant" is an old one, and it does not include antimicrobial substances that are produced by living cells, that is, antibiotics.

Types. Hundreds of disinfectant chemicals are now available. They are found in many chemical classes and include phenolic compounds (phenols, cresols, halogenated phenols), alcohols (ethyl alcohol and propyl alcohol), aldehydes (formaldehyde), acids (propionic acid and benzoic acid), halogenated compounds (chlorine, hypochlorite, iodine, and organic iodine compounds), and the derivatives of heavy metals (copper and mercury salts, organic mercurials).

An important group of disinfectants synthesized in more recent years comprises the surface-active agents such as benzalkonium and cetylpyridinium. These disinfectants are similar to modern detergents. They combine penetrating and cleansing power with high germicidal potency and are widely used as hospital and home disinfectants. Many disinfectant cleansing preparations now contain a surface-active agent.

Iodine is a particularly effective disinfectant and antiseptic that has many desirable properties. Newly developed germicides that release iodine in solution have important industrial uses, particularly in dairies and other food-handling establishments.

Properties and Action. Several properties are desirable in disinfectants. To be efficient in killing microorganisms, disinfectants should have a broad antimicrobial spectrum, that is, the ability to destroy all types of microorganisms, including spore forms of bacteria and fungi, and rapid killing power. They should also have high potency (so that only small amounts are necessary), chemical stability and nonreactivity, and high penetrating power (low surface tension). The absence of staining, corrosive, or irritating properties is another desirable characteristic.

Of all the properties desirable for disinfectants, the most important is germicidal potency and speed of action. Great progress has been made in improving the methods of testing germicides, and some germicides that gained popularity as potential household disinfectants (e.g., the mercury compounds) have been found merely to inhibit bacterial growth rather than to kill the microorganisms. In modern testing procedures each of the desired properties is evaluated, and certain disinfectants are found to be best suited for specific uses.

The various disinfectant substances act differently. Many are protoplasmic poisons and are therefore toxic not only to microorganims but to all living tissues. The potential toxicity to man and animals of these disinfectants must be considered before they are widely used. A few other germicides are relatively harmless to man in doses that have effective antimicrobial concentrations. Among these are the food preservatives such as propionic and benzoic acids.

Uses. Inestimable contributions to public health have resulted from the widespread use of disinfectants in water purification (usually chlorine), in reducing the dissemination of infectious organisms in public washrooms and other facilities used by large numbers of people, in disinfecting the environment and utensils associated with the preparation and dispensing of food, and in hospital sanitation. The use of disinfectants in hospitals includes disinfection of waste materials, cleansing and disinfection of the environment, sterilization of instruments and materials used in surgical procedures, and disinfection of patients' skin prior to surgery. Disinfectants are also used to preserve food and drugs and to protect fabrics, wood, other porous materials, and moist surfaces from rot and fungi.

History. Disinfectant substances have been used for many centuries. The Egyptians used preservative spices and oils in their embalming practices, and the preservation value of certain materials in pickling and salting foods was also recognized empirically in ancient times. However, disinfectants have been in wide use for only about a century. In the 1850's, Ignaz P. Semmelweis, a Viennese obstetrician, dramatically reduced the incidence of childbed fever by requiring his assistants to wash their hands in chlorinated lime before examining a patient. The reason for this practice was not understood, however, and it did not spread until acceptance of the germ theory of disease in the late 19th century.

In 1867, Joseph Lister clearly showed the value of disinfectants by applying phenol (carbolic acid) to tissues in compound fractures, thus reducing the incidence of serious infection. He also advocated the use of carbolic acid vapor in operating rooms during surgery. Although this practice was unsatisfactory, it marked an initial step toward control of surgical infection.

DON W. ESPLIN
McGill University Faculty of Medicine

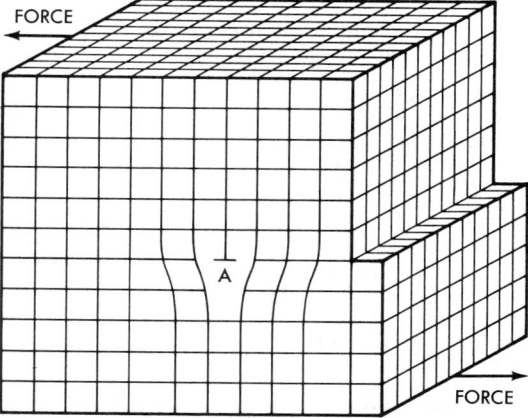

Fig. 1. In an edge dislocation, an extra plane of atoms is present in the lattice structure of the crystal. In this case the extra plane is found adjacent to area A.

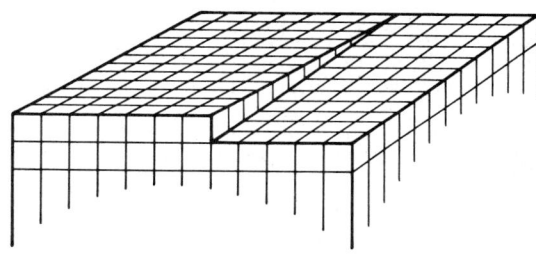

Fig. 2. In a screw dislocation, a plane of atoms forms a step in the crystal surface. Other atoms can then line up against this step as the crystal grows.

DISLOCATION, in medicine, often refers to the complete displacement of the bones forming a joint, with a stretching or tearing of the supporting ligaments and the enclosing fibrous capsule. A dislocation most commonly arises as a result of injury, but it may sometimes be present at birth as a congenital defect.

Types. *Congenital dislocations* most frequently involve the hip joint, and they occur in about 1.5 out of every 1,000 births. Girls are about 5 to 8 times more frequently affected than boys. Usually only one hip is involved.

Traumatic dislocations are those caused by injury. The joints most often affected are the shoulder, elbow, finger joints, hip, and ankle. The joint most frequently dislocated by force is the shoulder, and there is a distinct tendency for shoulder joint dislocations to become recurrent in young people, even after they have received proper treatment. Elbows and ankles are most often dislocated by falls, and finger joints are most often dislocated by blows received on an outstretched hand. Traumatic hip dislocations often result from car accidents.

Treatment. A congenital dislocation of the hip should be diagnosed and treated as soon after birth as possible, especially since the dislocation may lead to severe hip disability in adult life. Treatment consists of manipulating the joint by hand or placing the bones through surgery.

Joints that are dislocated by injury can almost always be treated by manipulation, with the patient under anesthesia. If manipulation is not successful, surgery is required.

JOHN J. GARTLAND, M. D.
Jefferson Medical College, Philadelphia

DISLOCATION is a type of defect in the atomic arrangement of a crystalline material. A material is classified as crystalline if there is a precise geometric order between its constituent atoms over distances of many hundreds of atomic diameters (see CRYSTAL). Most solid substances other than glass and plastic are crystalline in nature. Since dislocations are a disorder in the crystalline system, their presence in a material increases the internal energy, electrical conductivity, and hardness and influences many other physical properties.

Dislocations are classified as line defects, which are one of three types of crystal defects. They are to be distinguished both from plane defects, which may occur as grain boundaries and are visually evident in frost patterns on windows, and from point defects, which consist of atoms missing from their normal lattice site or of interstitial atoms that are present on sites not normal to the crystallography of the crystal.

The existence of dislocations was first proposed in 1934 by G. I. Taylor, E. Orowan, and M. Polanyi to account for the fact that the strength of single crystal materials was from 100 to 100,000 times less than that predicted by theory.

Perfect single crystals have been produced, but the process is exceedingly delicate and expensive. If extreme care is not utilized in the forming of the crystal, numerous defects are injected into the crystal lattice during growth.

Reactions of the material with the crucible or the atmosphere, impurities in the system, and small mechanical stresses are the main causes for the presence of defects.

Types of Dislocations. A dislocation is formed in a perfect crystal when an extra plane of atoms lying on the proper lattice sites terminates within the bulk of the crystal. Fig. 1 illustrates a simple cubic lattice into which an extra plane of atoms, adjacent to A, has been injected and terminates within the crystal. In this case the extra plane was generated by placing opposing forces along the direction of the arrows, causing the atoms to slip. The line of termination of this extra plane is called a dislocation line, and this specific defect is called an *edge dislocation*. Fig. 2 shows a screw dislocation, which is formed within the plane of atoms.

Under a shear force, as shown in Fig. 1, the dislocation will shift to the left, a step at a time, until the extra plane of atoms reaches the surface on the left. At that point the entire crystal is again perfect, but the top portion has been moved relative to the lower portion by one atomic distance. The important concept is that this process requires a smaller initiating force than if the shift occurred all at once and involved all of the atoms; hence, the material appears weaker than the atomic cohesive forces would suggest.

Generally, when dislocations can move, the material behaves as a plastic material. When the dislocations are locked, or pinned, the material resists plastic motion and remains rigid.

The number of dislocations in a unit mass can vary from near zero to a concentration of about 10^{12} dislocations intersecting a square centimeter of surface. The number of dislocations is a function of the state of disorder in the crystal; for example, an ordinary single crystal may contain as many as 10^6 dislocations per sq cm while a normal polycrystalline specimen or a piece of some cold-worked metal may have 10^8 dislocations per sq cm.

A pure metal that has been carefully cast and slowly cooled in a mold will usually contain single crystal grains several square millimeters in cross section. The grains contain about 10^{-7} dislocations per sq cm and numerous other point defects. Occasionally, the dislocations are lined up in parallel arrangement—as above and below point A in Fig. 1—to form a subboundary, or they are lined up in a horizontal fashion, blocked by another defect, such as a grain boundary. It is also possible that both vertical and horizontal configurations are interrelated to form a dislocation network.

If the cast ingot is subjected to any form of mechanical work, such as rolling, dislocations are moved about, lost at grain boundaries, and generated at other boundaries. After working, there are many more dislocations and other defects than before; consequently, the metal hardness has also increased. Careful heating of the metal to a point where the small grains tend to enlarge will tend to sweep the grain regions of dislocations and return the system to the original concentration of defects. The metal will once again be relatively soft.

Douglas V. Keller, Jr., *Syracuse University*

DISMAL SWAMP, in southeastern Virginia and northeastern North Carolina, extending about 40 miles (64 km) from near Suffolk, Va., to Elizabeth City, N. C. It covers about 600 square miles (1,550 sq km), principally in Nansemond county, Va., and Camden and Pasquotank counties, N. C. Formerly it was more than six times as large, but most of its area has been reclaimed as highly productive farmland. It sometimes is called the *Great Dismal Swamp*.

About three fourths of the swamp is a morass of highly acidic coffee-colored water, peat bogs, and expanses of rushes, which are known as the "green sea." The remainder is a dense timberland that yields valuable amounts of cypress, gum, cedar, and pine. In the center of the swamp is Lake Drummond, 6 miles long and 3 miles wide (9 by 4 km), discovered in 1677 by William Drummond, first colonial governor of North Carolina. The swamp supports abundant game and fish.

The swamp, known since earliest colonial times, has borne a sinister reputation. William Byrd, who surveyed it in 1728, first described it as "dismal." George Washington owned a large part of it, and in 1763 his slaves began building drainage canals to reclaim it. A waterway, the Dismal Swamp Canal, was begun in 1787 and opened in 1828 from Norfolk, Va., to Elizabeth City. It is used by small pleasure craft.

J. W. Schwendeman
Eastern Kentucky University

DISMAS, diz′məs, **Saint,** traditional name of the penitent thief who died on the Cross beside Jesus (Luke 23:39–43). He is also known as "The Good Thief" and his feast is March 25. The other thief is traditionally called *Gestas*.

DISNEY, diz′nē, **Walt** (1901–1966), American motion picture animator and producer, who created the world-famous cartoon character Mickey Mouse. Walter Elias Disney was born in Chicago, Ill., on Dec. 5, 1901. He began producing advertising films in Kansas City, Mo., in 1919, and then turned to animation, but with only limited success. He moved to Hollywood, Calif., where he and his brother Roy became partners. Their first two films featuring Mickey Mouse were silent, and the partners were unable to get them released commercially, but when Disney added a sound track to *Steamboat Willie* (1928), Mickey Mouse and Walt Disney became internationally famous. See also Cartoon, Animated.

Walt Disney

© WALT DISNEY PRODUCTIONS— WORLD RIGHTS RESERVED

Winner of a record 30 Academy Awards, Disney made not only cartoon shorts, such as the Mickey Mouse, Donald Duck, and *Silly Symphony* series, but also animated feature films, beginning with *Snow White and the Seven Dwarfs* (1937) and including *Pinocchio* (1938), *Fantasia* (1940), *Dumbo* (1941), and *Bambi* (1942). When the cost of making animated features became prohibitive, he began to make such "true-life adventures" as *Seal Island* (1948), *Beaver Valley* (1950), *Nature's Half Acre* (1951), and *The Living Desert* (1953). Later, he made live-action family films, including *Davy Crockett* (1955) and *Mary Poppins* (1965).

Disney introduced a new method for synchronizing sound with animation and was the first to use the three-color process (in *Flowers and Trees*, 1932). In addition, he produced the first feature-length animated picture (*Snow White and the Seven Dwarfs*) and the first television series in color (*Walt Disney's Wonderful World of Color*, beginning in 1961). He also launched two amusement parks, Disneyland and Disney World, in California and Florida, respectively. Disney died in Los Angeles on Dec. 15, 1966.

HOWARD SUBER
University of California, Los Angeles

DISNEYLAND AND DISNEY WORLD are two large, lavish amusement parks in the United States. The first, located in Anaheim, Calif., opened in 1955. The second, officially called Walt Disney World, is southwest of Orlando, Fla. It opened in 1971. Epcot Center, a section of the latter, opened in 1982. The parks are intended to appeal to both children and adults.

The inspiration behind Disneyland and Disney World was the film producer Walt Disney. It was Disney's idea that the parks should be built around specific themes. As a result, Disneyland, for example, has such theme areas as Fantasyland, Adventureland, and Frontierland. The parks are noted for their careful upkeep and extensive facilities. See also EPCOT CENTER.

DISORDERLY CONDUCT may be defined generally as conduct that disturbs the peace or endangers the morals, safety, or health of the community. The precise definition depends on the terms of the applicable state or municipal law. Because of the obvious difficulty of specifying all the types of conduct to be classified as disorderly, and the constitutional due-process requirement that statutes be specific enough to provide adequate notice of what conduct is criminal, enforcement of these statutes may invade constitutional rights. Police decisions, necessarily subjective because of the breadth of the legislation, often give rise to charges of police harassment. Derelicts, demonstrators, prostitutes, vagrants, and agitators all have been stigmatized at times as disorderly persons.

The application of disorderly conduct statutes in the United States became especially controversial in the 1960's with the increase of sit-ins and peace demonstrations. The Supreme Court, in *Cox v. Louisiana* (1965), held that a breach-of-the-peace statute could not be applied to conduct—in this case, peaceful picketing—that was protected by 1st Amendment free-speech guaranties.

The American Law Institute's draft Model Penal Code (1962) defines disorderly conduct as engaging in violent behavior, unreasonable noise, or abusive language or other hazardous conduct that serves no legitimate purpose. The person charged, however, must be shown to have acted with a "purpose to cause public inconvenience."

LINDA ALDEN MOODY, *Columbia Law School*

DISPENSATION, in canon, or church, law, the relaxation of a law in a particular case. Through a dispensation one is exempted from the obligation of the law without ceasing to remain habitually subject to the law. In canonical jurisprudence the granting of a dispensation is justified by the common good, which must take into consideration individual cases that could scarcely be considered in a general law. There is no question of dispensation from divine law but only from human ecclesiastical law.

The act of dispensing is an act of jurisdiction and can be exercised only in favor of one's subjects, for example, the pope over the whole church or the bishop over those who are subject to him. The power to dispense belongs to those who are empowered to make laws, for example, the pope or the bishop of a diocese. A dispensation may also be granted by those to whom the lawmaker has given the power in particular cases. A just and reasonable cause proportionate to the gravity of the law is required for the granting of a dispensation. A dispensation granted by the lawmaker himself without such a justifying cause is illicit but valid; one granted by an official in virtue of delegated authority is, in the same circumstances, illicit and invalid. When the cause for the dispensation is doubtful, it may be licitly sought and granted.

DAMIAN J. BLAHER, O. F. M.
Holy Name College, Washington, D. C.

DISPERSION is the separation of a beam of radiation into a spectrum of its component wavelengths. For example, when a beam of white light is sent through a glass prism, light emerges from the prism as a fan-shaped beam of rainbow colors, each color being produced by a different narrow band of wavelengths contained in the white light.

The dispersion of light by a transparent medium results from the fact that the speed of light in any given material is not the same for all wavelengths but varies for different wavelengths in a regular manner. By the laws of refraction, the larger the index of refraction of a material medium, the greater is the deflection of a light beam on entering the medium. (The index of refraction is the ratio of the speed of light in a vacuum to its speed in the medium.) The index of refraction of most materials increases as the wavelength decreases, and thus the index is greater for violet light than for red light. As a result, rays in the violet end of the spectrum are refracted more than rays at the red end: this is called *normal dispersion*. The order of the spectral colors is red, orange, yellow, green, blue, and violet.

In certain materials, such as a dye that exhibits absorption bands, the index of refraction decreases as the wavelength decreases; this is called *anomalous dispersion*. A prism made of such a material produces a reversed spectrum of colors, ranging from violet to red. See also COLOR; LIGHT; SPECTROSCOPY.

GRANT R. FOWLES, *University of Utah*

Benjamin Disraeli, the 1st earl of Beaconsfield, from a photograph taken during his second ministry.

DISRAELI, diz-rā′lē, **Benjamin** (1804–1881), British statesman and writer, who was prime minister of Britain in 1868 and 1874–1880. Disraeli, also known as the 1st earl of Beaconsfield, was the architect of the modern Conservative party and one of the most brilliant parliamentarians in the history of the House of Commons.

Disraeli was born in London on Dec. 21, 1804. His grandfather, Benjamin D'Israeli, emigrated to London in 1748 from a colony of Spanish Jews living near Venice. He prospered as a trader and stockbroker and married Sarah Shiprut, who was related to the prominent Portuguese Jewish family of Villareal. Their only son, Isaac D'Israeli, became a respected man of letters in London. He married Maria Basevi, a descendant of Italian Jews. They had a daughter and subsequently four sons, the eldest of whom was Benjamin. In 1817, Isaac D'Israeli abandoned Judaism and in the same year his daughter and three surviving sons were baptized in the Anglican Church. Benjamin was educated at private schools at Blackheath and Epping Forest. He did not attend a university.

Early Career. When he was 17, Disraeli was apprenticed to a firm of London solicitors to study law. Although his name was entered on the roll at Lincoln's Inn three years later, he never practiced law. From 1824 to 1826 he engaged in stock market and publishing ventures that proved disastrous and left him with debts he was unable or unwilling to pay.

Embittered but still full of confidence, he announced his intention to become a writer. Isaac D'Israeli's position gave Benjamin entrance to literary society, and the young man's dress and manner assured him attention there. Benjamin played the dandy. He was variously regarded as brilliant, clever, impudent, and vulgar.

His first novel, *Vivian Grey*, appeared anonymously in two volumes in 1826 and 1827. Its crude but lively satire of the activities of well-known contemporaries attracted considerable attention. Its author's identity was soon disclosed, and the harsh ripostes directed at him contributed to the anxieties that brought on a nervous collapse in 1828. Disraeli retired to his father's house in Buckinghamshire and avoided the spotlight entirely for the next three years. During that time he published an inferior novel, *The Young Duke* (1830). Following a 16-month trip to the Mediterranean in 1830–1831, he returned to Buckinghamshire and shortly announced his candidacy for Parliament as a Conservative from High Wycombe.

Entry into Politics. Between 1832 and 1835, Disraeli offered himself as a candidate three times at High Wycombe and once at Taunton and lost all four elections. He bided his time but did a prodigious amount of writing, including numerous bombastic political pamphlets and the novels *Contarini Fleming* (1832) and *Alroy* (1833). Thereafter he published *Vindication of the English Constitution* (1835), an analysis of English history in which he first expressed his theory of popular Toryism as an alliance of the crown, the church, and the people against the Whig oligarchy. He wrote several other political works, mostly pamphlets, and two more novels: *Henrietta Temple* (1837), a love story based on his own liaison with Henrietta, the wife of Sir Francis Sykes; and *Venetia* (1837).

Election to Parliament. In 1837, King William IV died. The accession of Victoria and the consequent formation of a new Parliament afforded Disraeli his long-awaited opportunity. The borough of Maidstone returned two members to Parliament, one of whom, Wyndham Lewis, held an assured seat. Through the influence of important friends, Disraeli was invited to enter the bitter contest for the other seat.

During the ensuing campaign Disraeli's character was attacked on both fair and specious grounds. His unpaid debts, his Jewish origins, his open liaison with Mrs. Sykes, and his fierce, often wounding speeches in the past were used against him. But he pressed his campaign and won the seat.

His maiden speech in the House of Commons on Dec. 7, 1837, was a disaster. The speech itself was overwrought, and the speaker was, in the opinion of most members, overdressed. The combination of his ringlets and ruffles and the extravagance of his oratorical style produced shouts of derision from opponents and, before the speech was finished, general laughter in the house. Shouting to be heard, Disraeli concluded the debacle with the defiant prophecy: "I will sit down now, but the time will come when you will hear me." Chastened by the experience, he gradually moderated his style.

Within a year, Wyndham Lewis, his conservative colleague from Maidstone, died, and on Aug. 28, 1839, Disraeli married Lewis' widow. She brought him wealth, which he was never able to acquire in his own right, and the semblance of a social position. Although the marriage was contracted largely for practical reasons—his wife was 12 years his senior—they became an extremely devoted couple. Years later she declared: "Dizzy married me for my money, but if he had the chance again he would marry me for love."

Rebellious Tory. After his marriage Disraeli resolved to establish a firmer political position for himself. His idealized vision of a common cause between the Tory monarchy and the workingman led him into sympathy with Chartism, the first great political movement of the British working class. His skeptical view of the Reform Law of 1832 placed principal blame for the miseries of labor on the Whigs, but the pragmatism of the Tories led by Sir Robert Peel also clashed with his own ideas. When Peel rather curtly declined Disraeli's irregular request to be included in the Tory ministry formed in 1841, Disraeli resolved to loosen his ties with the party leadership and veered toward more outspoken support of workmen's grievances.

Disraeli's sympathy with the industrial poor was undoubtedly sincere. In an effort to present his view of what he saw as a conspiracy against them, he wrote two of his most persuasive novels: *Coningsby* (1844) and *Sybil, or the Two Nations* (1845). *Coningsby* is a portrayal of the Young England movement that arose within Tory ranks in the 1840's and looked to Disraeli for leadership. The novel's effect was sensational. Its idealized view of conservatism's role in regenerating England gave Disraeli the instrument he needed to split the Tory party and eventually erect a new Conservative party.

The opportunity presented itself in 1845, when Peel, in response to a new famine in Ireland, came out in support of repealing the corn laws—protective tariffs on foreign grain that favored landowners and burdened poor consumers. In doing so, Peel reversed a long-standing policy of the party. Disraeli and other protectionists rebelled. The repeal bill passed, with the support of the Whigs, but the rebels brought down the government in June 1846.

Party Leader. The split and partial disintegration of the old Tory party inaugurated a long period of political confusion in which neither of the traditional parties had a clear majority. During the Whig administration (1846–1852) of Lord Russell, Disraeli advanced to the leadership of the Conservatives in Commons, but with the Peelites in active opposition to the party majority the prospect of a Conservative government seemed distant. Disraeli realized that the party's stand on protectionism was unpopular, but his recent attacks on Peel prevented him from reversing his position.

After Russell's government fell in 1852, Disraeli became chancellor of the exchequer in the minority government of the earl of Derby. Later in the year Derby's government fell, and the Conservatives returned to the opposition for six more years, during most of which a coalition of small parties ruled. In 1858 a setback for the emerging Liberal party permitted the Conservatives, still led by Derby, to form another short-lived government. Disraeli seized the opportunity the following year to introduce a moderate bill dealing with long-overdue electoral reform. The measure was defeated, and the Conservatives returned to the opposition for seven more years.

Already approaching 60 and his party's leader in Commons for more than a decade, Disraeli saw his chances slipping away. He was doubly cheated by the long survival of Derby. In 1866, when the Conservatives installed a third minority government, an aged and ailing Derby again became prime minister, and Disraeli was again his chancellor of the exchequer.

First Prime Ministry. Disraeli was determined that credit for electoral reform should go to the Conservatives. He introduced a bill in the House of Commons that became law in 1867, but the Liberals, whose majority in the House had attached important amendments to the bill, got most of the credit. In February 1868, Derby retired and Disraeli became prime minister. John Bright, a prominent Liberal, described the event as "a great triumph of intellect and courage and patience and unscrupulousness employed in the service of a party full of prejudices and selfishness and wanting in brains."

Disraeli remained prime minister only until November, for the first general elections based on the new reform law returned the Liberals to power. Their commanding new leader was William Ewart Gladstone, whose personal vendetta with Disraeli helped finally to polarize two modern parties in Britain. Before Disraeli left office, Queen Victoria, whose fondness for him became legend, offered him a peerage. At his request, the title was conferred on his wife so that he might remain in Commons.

Opposition. During the first few years of Gladstone's administration Disraeli luxuriated in the comparative ease of opposition. For the first time in more than 20 years he wrote a novel, *Lothair* (1870), a gaudy romance that did nothing to enhance his prestige. Restive party members questioned his leadership. Nothing seemed to erode the popularity of the Liberals.

But after 1870, Disraeli concentrated on party organization, and the fortunes of the Conservatives began gradually to rise. Liberal defeats in by-elections signaled discontent with Gladstone's concessions to Irish nationalism and with his accommodation to emerging Prussian and Russian power in Europe. Disraeli sensed the feeling of

QUEEN VICTORIA, in *Punch* cartoon, raises Disraeli to peerage after he added "Empress of India" to her title.

THE GRANGER COLLECTION

the country and shrewdly appealed to its damaged pride. On March 11, 1873, the Conservatives narrowly defeated a Liberal bill to create an Irish university for Catholics. Gladstone resigned and suggested that Disraeli form a minority government. Disraeli shrewdly refused, and Gladstone, whose popularity was rapidly declining, was forced to return. His mandate was exhausted. In January 1874 he dissolved Parliament, and in February the Conservatives won a majority of 83 seats—their first majority in a general election since 1841.

Second Prime Ministry. Disraeli, for the first time, formed a new government. He was nearly 70 and had led his party in Commons longer than any man in the history of the House. Tragically he had had to wait too long. Age and intermittent illness, and loneliness after his wife's death in 1872, denied him the vigor that he could have brought to the office earlier.

Disraeli formed a distinguished and able cabinet and set about redeeming his campaign promises to act on social welfare problems. In addition to landmark legislation on urban renewal and workers' housing, his administration enacted a trade union act more favorable to the unions than earlier acts, a drug act, and the comprehensive Public Health Act of 1875, which codified numerous existing laws on health and sanitation. These and other laws filled important gaps in welfare legislation left by the Liberals.

In foreign affairs, which dominated the later years of his administration, Disraeli devoted his efforts to bolstering Britain's declining prestige overseas. In 1875, acting entirely on his own initiative and against the advice of his foreign minister, he arranged government purchase of a substantial interest in the Suez Canal Company from the khedive of Egypt. Although not a controlling interest, it enhanced Britain's imperial power, secured the nation lower canal rates, and led to eventual British control of the waterway. Disraeli's secret canal transaction was both a diplomatic and political coup.

In 1876, the same year that Disraeli obtained from Parliament the addition of "Empress of India" to Queen Victoria's titles, she created him earl of Beaconsfield. In 1878, Beaconsfield successfully checked Russian imperialism in Turkey and the Balkans. Using the threat of intervention and exercising masterly control of the European delegates called at his urging to the Congress of Berlin in 1878, he engineered a revision, extremely favorable to Britain, of the treaty ending the Russo-Turkish War.

Disraeli's prestige was never higher, but he was rapidly failing in health. Against his wishes, he remained in office, but renewed problems at home and abroad brought defeat to his party in the general election of April 1880. He retired from politics to finish *Endymion*, his last novel. He died at his London house on April 19, 1881.

Bibliography
The complete fiction of Disraeli is collected in *Novels and Tales by the Earl of Beaconsfield*, 11 vols. (1881); several of the novels are available individually in later editions. A comprehensive selection of his correspondence is contained in *Lord Beaconsfield's Letters, 1830–1852*, ed. by R. Disraeli, 2d ed. (1928).
Blake, Robert, *Disraeli* (St. Martins 1967).
Jerman, B. R., *The Young Disraeli* (Princeton Univ. Press 1960).
Maurois, André, *Disraeli*, Eng. tr. (Blackie & Son 1947).
Monypenny, William F., and Buckle, G. E., *The Life of Benjamin Disraeli*, rev. ed., 4 vols. (Russell 1968).
Pearson, Hesketh, *Dizzy* (1951; reprint, Greenwood 1975).

DISSENTERS are those who refuse to adhere to an established church and who worship apart in accordance with their own religious convictions or allegiance. The word is applied almost exclusively to the Roman Catholics and Puritans who refused to give their allegiance to the Church of England after the religious settlement of Queen Elizabeth I.

With the rapid growth of sectarianism in the 17th century, "dissenter" was applied to Presbyterians, Congregationalists, Baptists, Quakers, and other Protestants, who also refused conformity to the Church of England. After the Restoration (1660) they were called Nonconformists.

DISSOCIATION, in psychology, is a state in which certain activities or ideas are isolated from the mainstream of consciousness. Essentially a defense mechanism, it typically occurs in individuals who are suffering severe emotional conflict because of strong impulses that are unacceptable to the conscious mind. When the conscious expression of such impulses would cause the individual intolerable guilt and anxiety, the impulses may detach themselves from the conscious standards by which they are inhibited and appear to exist independently in the personality. Once this dissociation has occurred, the individual can express such impulses without feeling anxiety, as the conscious mind remains in some way detached from the dissociated behavior. Together with conversion reactions, in which psychosomatic symptoms function as defense mechanisms, dissociative reactions make up the class of mental disorders known as hysteria.

Dissociation ranges from some forms of normal behavior to severe psychoses. In normal people it appears as two or more simultaneous activities, of which one is conscious and directed and the rest unconscious and seemingly involuntary. Thus a man who is concentrating heavily on what he is reading may make gestures or mutter responses to questions without seeming to be aware of anything but his reading. In cases of this sort the individual will often deny that such unconscious behavior occurred at all.

The abnormal patterns of behavior classified as dissociative include coma, stupor, narcolepsy, depersonalization, sleepwalking, amnesia, fugue, and multiple personality. Each of these involves a suppression of the sense of identity. Coma, stupor, and narcolepsy (abnormal inclination to sleep) may follow behavior that would arouse anxiety if the individual did not suppress his consciousness in some way. In depersonalization the individual feels detached from himself and regards his actions as unreal. In sleepwalking he may act out suppressed impulses.

Amnesia and fugue are responses to extremely stressful situations from which the individual can find no escape. Whole segments of personality are repressed along with the situation itself. In amnesia the individual often "forgets" who he is; in fugue, he leaves the stressful situation and establishes a different life in a new environment and often with a new identity, forgetting his earlier life. In multiple personality two or more relatively independent identities occur in the same person. This disorder invariably reflects a conflict between a desire to be proper and conforming and a desire to be wicked and uninhibited. Cases of multiple personality are dramatic but extremely rare.

AUSTIN E. GRIGG, *University of Richmond*

DISSONANCE, dis'ə-nəns, also called *discordance*, is the simultaneous sounding of two or more pitches that, when heard together, cause a feeling of unease or tension in the listener. Traditionally, theorists have always labeled certain intervals as dissonant in contrast to others agreeable to the ear that are labeled "consonant." However, intervals thought of as dissonant in one period have been known to find acceptance in the harmony of later periods. For example, the rules of 18th century harmony, which classified major and minor seconds, sevenths, and ninths and all augmented and diminished intervals as dissonant, have been virtually ignored by modern composers, who find many of these so-called "dissonances" naturally pleasing and exciting. On the other hand, in the 10th century, the augmented fourth, or tritone, was considered consonant, yet in the 16th century it was forbidden in strict counterpoint as a dissonance.

Dissonance can also be defined more technically as an acoustical phenomenon. Based on the Pythagorean system of numerical ratios for musical intervals, this definition explains dissonance as the simultaneous sounding of pitches whose fundamentals or overtones produce "beats" —alternate strengthening and weakening of sound waves that are disconcerting to the ear.

HELEN N. MORGAN
North Shore Branch, New England Conservatory

DISTANT EARLY WARNING SYSTEM. See DEW LINE; RADAR—*2. Uses and Types* (Military Radar).

DISTEMPER is any of several unrelated contagious diseases that affect dogs, cats, horses, and many other animals. There are several forms of distemper, all worldwide in distribution.

Canine distemper is a common disease caused by a virus. It occurs primarily in young dogs. Symptoms of the disease include fever, coughing, diarrhea, and discharges from the eyes and nose. Neurological complications may occur at any time, even following an apparent recovery, and the animal may die in convulsions. Sometimes the infected dog develops muscular twitching.

Feline distemper is caused by a different virus. It affects all members of the cat family, as well as the raccoon. Symptoms of feline distemper include marked weakness, fever, vomiting, and diarrhea. Other viral strains infect raccoons, foxes, and all members of the family Mustelidae, which includes the ferret, mink, marten, weasel, otter, badger, fisher, skunk, and wolverine.

Equine, or *horse, distemper* is caused by the bacterium *Streptococcus equi*. Young horses are primarily affected. They develop fever, marked depression, sneezing, coughing, and a profuse nasal discharge. Often the lymph glands in the throat become abscessed and drain.

The forms of distemper caused by viruses can generally be prevented by vaccines, and successfully immunized animals remain protected for life. However, once an animal is infected, the disease is difficult to treat. Equine distemper, on the other hand, can be treated effectively, especially if the disease is diagnosed early. Although vaccines against equine distemper are available, they are not as effective as the vaccines against canine and feline distemper.

KEITH WAYT, D.V.M.
Colorado State University

DISTEMPER, in art, is a painting medium in which powdered pigment is mixed with a simple glue size (the binder) and with water (the diluent). It differs from fresco, in which the dry colors are mixed with calcined plaster and water for application to a damp plaster surface; and from tempera, which combines pigment with a fatty binder and water.

Because it is inexpensive and impermanent, distemper is now used chiefly for painting stage scenery. Until the 15th century, however, when the more permanent oil and varnish mediums were developed, distemper was more widely used, particularly for wall decoration.

DISTILLATION is a technique for purifying liquids by collecting vapors from the boiling liquid and condensing them back to liquid form. Distillation processes are widely used in industry, particularly in the petroleum industry for the separation of crude-oil components. The process is also used in the production of alcoholic beverages and in the organic chemical industry. Liquid air is distilled to produce oxygen, nitrogen, and the inert gases, and distillation is one of the methods most frequently used for the production of fresh water from salt water. Distillation occurs in nature in the form of the water cycle, in which rainwater falls, then evaporates into the atmosphere, condenses, and falls again.

SIMPLE DISTILLATION

In the simplest kind of distillation only one substance vaporizes, while the impurities, which are nonvolatile, remain in the liquid. The desalting of water is an example of simple distillation. In this type of distillation the impure liquid is placed in a flask and boiled. The distillation apparatus (Fig. 1) contains a thermometer, which shows the temperature of the vapor. The vapor passes down the double-walled water-cooled condenser, which cools it and converts it back to a liquid. The purified liquid, which is called the *distillate,* accumulates in a receiving vessel.

Distillation of Water. Water is the liquid that is most often purified by distillation. Distilled water is used in the laboratory, in medicine, and in photography; for filling steam irons and automobile batteries; and for many other purposes. Ordinary water contains dissolved mineral salts that do not vaporize when the water is boiled. The only common impurity that does boil out, besides the dissolved air, is carbon dioxide gas, and this can easily be kept from boiling out by the addition of a little alkali to the water.

Stills to produce distilled water are available in all sizes and are generally made of glass or stainless steel. Tin or tin-lined copper is often used for the condenser to resist the solvent action of the hot distillate. An important design feature of these stills is the provision of *baffles* to hold back spray. Steam bubbles rising in the boiling water burst as they break the surface and scatter small droplets of impure water that would be carried over with the steam if the baffles were not present.

Desalting of Water. Distillation is carried out on a vast scale to obtain fresh water from seawater. To keep the operating cost of the process low, it is necessary to make the most efficient use of the great quantities of heat used.

Water has a high latent heat of evaporation—that is, it takes a great deal of heat to convert it from the liquid to the vapor state. The heat is released again when the vapor condenses. In a simple still the heat is transferred to the cooling water and is lost. However, the heat can be used to warm up the impure, or raw, water that is on its way to the still pot, or it may be used to boil a second batch of raw water under a lower pressure than that existing in the first pot. (The lower the pressure, the lower the boiling point.) To make the best use of the heat, 10 or more stages are employed with an elaborate system of pumps and heat exchangers. One experimental plant, using 12 stages, produces a million gallons of fresh water a day.

A somewhat different principle is used in *compression distillation*. In this technique a small motor-driven pump is used to compress the steam produced in the first boiling. The work of compression raises the temperature of the steam, which is then sent through a pipe to boil more water.

It is likely that nuclear power will eventually be used to supply heat for large-scale distillation of seawater. Solar heat is also being used in experimental plants. For desalting sea water, distillation is the most promising method at present, but other techniques are more economical for brackish waters of low salt content. See also DESALTING.

FRACTIONAL DISTILLATION

Fractional distillation is a technique used to separate a mixture of liquids that boil at different temperatures. Fractional distillation can be used for the separation of some very complex mixtures. For example, crude oil has been separated for research purposes into well over 100 constituents, with each constituent being recovered in essentially pure form.

When a mixture of two or more volatile liquids is boiled, the vapor will contain molecules of all the substances, but it will normally contain a higher concentration of the most volatile substance than of the others. The liquid obtained by condensing the vapor in a simple distillation apparatus would be enriched in the most volatile constituent, but even the first drops to distill would contain some of the other constituents, and the proportion of the less volatile constituents would increase as distillation proceeded. To achieve efficient separation of the mixture the simple distillation apparatus must be modified in two ways: first, there should be repeated redistillation of the product to concentrate the more volatile component; second, there should be a recycling, or return, of the intermediate distillates to conserve material. The process is called *multistage countercurrent distillation*.

The basic equipment for fractional distillation is shown in Fig. 2. The mixture to be separated is placed in a flask, or still-pot. Extending from the flask is a vertical column that is divided into horizontal segments, or plates, each of which retains a certain volume of liquid. The "bubble-cap" plate is commonly used in large industrial columns.

When the liquid in the flask is boiled at a fast rate, most of the vapor that is produced condenses in the column and runs back into the pot. This process is called *reflux distillation*, and the fraction of the vapor that returns to the pot as liquid is called the *reflux ratio*. If this ratio is one, it means that all the liquid is returning to the pot; this is called *total reflux*. If the ratio is zero, it means that none of the liquid returns to the pot, that it is all being distilled, and that there is no separation of substances. In practice, a compromise is made between efficient fractionation, which requires distillation with a high reflux ratio, and fast distillation, which requires distillation with a low reflux ratio.

At the lowest plate of the column in Fig. 2, the liquid has a composition approximating that of the first drops distilling from a simple, single-stage still. Vapor condensing on this plate releases latent heat and causes some of the liquid to evaporate again and pass up to the second plate of the column. The composition of the liquid on the second plate is the same as that which would have been obtained by taking the product of a simple distillation apparatus and distilling again with the same equipment. Each plate in the column corresponds to a small single-stage still, except that the liquid lost from the plate by vaporization is replenished by that which runs down from the plate above it, as well as by condensation of fresh vapor from below. This is the "countercurrent" feature of the distillation process.

In small-scale production, batch operations

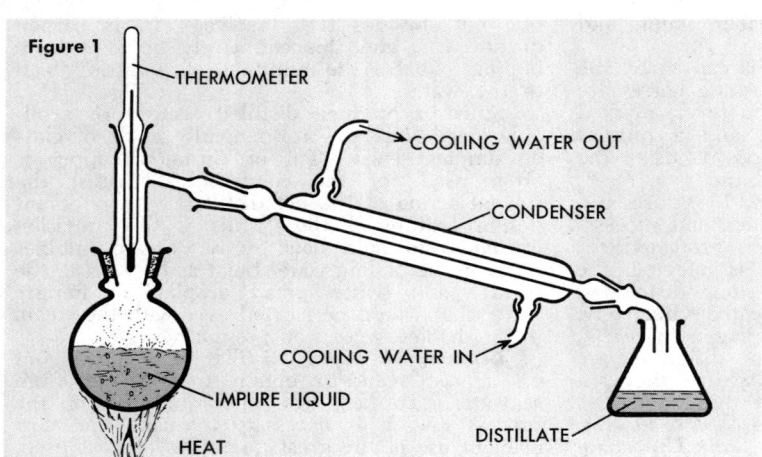

SIMPLE DISTILLATION

In simple distillation the impure liquid is heated. Vapors rise in the flask and pass through the condenser, where they liquefy, and then into the collecting flask.

are preferred. However, for large-scale fractional distillation the apparatus shown in Fig. 2 is modified to make it operate continuously. The mixture to be separated is run into the column somewhere near the middle, and the still-pot is provided with an exit tube. The high-boiling constituents of the mixture are drawn out of the bottom of the column, while the low-boiling constituents come out of the top.

Separations by fractional distillation become more efficient at reduced pressure, so that it is common practice to conduct distillations at pressures of one centimeter of mercury or below. There are two advantages to this technique: first, compounds of low volatility can be distilled at moderate temperatures with minimum danger of decomposition; second, the ratio of the vapor pressures of two liquids increases as the pressure, and therefore the temperature, is lowered.

Separation Efficiency. The ease of separating two liquids does not depend so much on the difference in their boiling points as on the separation between the liquid and vapor compositions. This separation depends on the interactions between molecules. If a molecule of substance A and a molecule of substance B attract each other less than the average attraction of molecules A or B for each other, the separation of the liquid and the vapor is enhanced.

The more plates or subdivisions a column has, the more effective it is in separating mixtures. Many columns do not have plates but are packed instead with objects such as short hollow cylinders, saddle-shaped pieces of glass or ceramic, or glass spirals or beads—all of which bring the descending liquid into intimate contact with the ascending vapor. Another arrangement, which is very effective on the laboratory scale, is the "spinning-band column" in which a long metal strip, twisted into a helix, spins rapidly on a vertical axis, just grazing the walls of an accurately formed, open cylindrical tube.

The effectiveness of all such columns is expressed in terms of the number of "theoretical plates." The number of theoretical plates can be expressed in terms of the equivalent number of simple distillations accomplished by the column. In other words, a column that accomplishes the same degree of separation as five successive simple distillations has five theoretical plates.

OTHER DISTILLATION PROCESSES

Azeotropic Distillation. Azeotropic distillation is a technique that is used to separate a mixture of liquids that are very close in volatility. It is also used for azeotropic mixtures, which are mixtures of liquids whose composition does not change on boiling—that is, the composition of the vapor is the same as that of the original liquid, and such a mixture cannot be separated by distillation alone.

Often, the simplest way to separate mixtures of these types is to add a substance that forms an azeotropic mixture with one of the substances to be separated. The azeotrope boils off first at a temperature below that of the original mixture. Azeotropic distillation is used in the production of pure ethyl alcohol. A solution of 95.57% alcohol with 4.43% water is an azeotropic mixture and therefore cannot be separated by distillation. However, if benzene is added to the solution, it forms an azeotropic mixture with

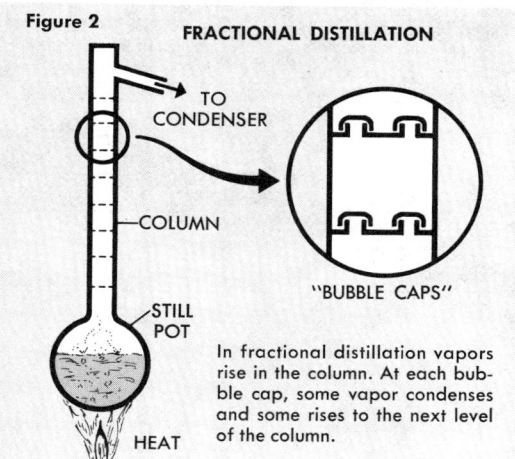

Figure 2

FRACTIONAL DISTILLATION

"BUBBLE CAPS"

In fractional distillation vapors rise in the column. At each bubble cap, some vapor condenses and some rises to the next level of the column.

the water. This mixture, plus a little of the alcohol, distills off at 65°C. The rest of the alcohol, which contains no water or benzene, distills off at 78°C.

Molecular Distillation. Molecular distillation is used with substances of very low volatility and high molecular weight, such as fats, steroids, and vitamins. Very low pressures of 0.001 mm of mercury and below are used. At such pressures it is possible to vaporize a substance and then condense it on a cold surface a few millimeters away before its molecules have had a chance to collide with other molecules. The distillation rate depends not only on the vapor pressure, but on the rate of travel of the molecules, which varies inversely with the square root of the molecular weight (Graham's law of diffusion). Thus, light molecules have a double advantage over heavy ones in speed of distillation, and separations of light molecules are doubly effective. However, separations of this type are only single-stage, equivalent to simple distillation.

Steam Distillation. Steam distillation is a long-established process that is used to purify liquids that have an appreciable vapor pressure at the temperature of boiling water and do not dissolve in water. In this technique the crude mixture is placed in a flask with water, and steam is passed through the flask. The vapor of the volatile constituent is carried with the steam and condenses in the receiving vessel as a separate layer. An example of a liquid that is purified in this way is aniline.

Sublimation. Sublimation is a phenomenon in which a solid changes directly to a vapor without first melting; the substance also condenses directly from a gas to a solid with no liquid phase. Iodine and arsenious oxide are purified in this way, as well as many other substances.

HAROLD F. WALTON
University of Colorado

Bibliography

Hengstebeck, Robert J., *Distillation: Principles and Design Procedures* (New York 1961).
Hoffman, Edward J., *Azeotropic and Extractive Distillation* (New York 1964).
Holland, Charles D., *Multicomponent Distillation* (Englewood Cliffs, N. J., 1963).
Krell, E., *Handbook of Laboratory Distillation* (New York 1963).
Van Winkle, Matthew, *Distillation* (New York 1968).

FERMENTATION takes place before distillation in the preparation of distilled spirits. These huge fermenting vats are made of cypress wood.

JOSEPH E. SEAGRAM AND SONS

DISTILLED SPIRITS are alcoholic beverages, commonly called simply spirits or liquors. They may be distilled from wine or from the fermented sugars or starches of grain, grapes or other fruit, sugarcane, potatoes, or many other less frequently utilized plants. Spirits may be flavored by the products from which they are distilled, or flavoring (and coloring) may be added. So-called neutral spirits are flavorless and are almost pure alcohol.

All spirits, regardless of their eventual color, come from the still as colorless as the primitive liquor that was distilled from wine and hailed by 12th century alchemists as *aqua vitae* (French; *eau-de-vie*), "water of life." This was described by the late 13th century Spanish philosopher Raymond Lully as "an element newly revealed to man but hid from antiquity because the human race was then too young to need this beverage destined to revive the energies of modern decrepitude." Thus, in the Middle Ages, *aqua vitae*, or brandy, as it is now called, was already obtainable on the continent of Europe, at about the same time that the Irish and Scots had perfected the art of distilling whiskey from grain. Cognac, which was to be the prototype of European brandies as we now know them, did not come until some centuries later.

BRANDY

The finest of all wine brandies are the French Cognac and Armagnac. Cognac is distilled in crook-necked pot stills, hardly changed since the early 17th century, when the acid Charente wines of the Cognac district in France were first converted to brandy. At that time, ships from countries bordering the North and Baltic seas would come into the French port of La Rochelle for cargoes of salt and would take on some of the local wines, too. Then, to save space in the ships and increase the value of a small cargo, the bulk of the wine was reduced by distillation. Originally, the idea was that by adding water, the liquor could be turned back into wine when it reached land again. But the customers soon decided they preferred Charente brandy to the rather acid wines it replaced. There are now many brandies, but the name Cognac is correct only when applied to those produced in the delimited district around the Charente River towns of Cognac and Jarnac.

Cognac and Armagnac. The soil of the Cognac area is chalky limestone, and the area is divided into seven districts. In descending order of quality of the brandy they produce, the districts are: Grande Champagne, Petite Champagne, Borderies, Fins Bois, Bons Bois, Bois Ordinaires, and Bois à Terroir. Grande Champagne is the heart of the region, with the other zones circling around it. The designation "Fine Champagne" is restricted to Cognacs made from wines of Grande or Petite Champagne; it has nothing to do with the wine of the Champagne region. Grapes throughout the Cognac region are white, with St.-Émilion now predominant.

The Cognac district grower is usually an independent farmer, who may distill his own wine under government control or may turn the process over to a distiller. After two distillations, the raw spirit is put in barrels to age. Traditionally, the barrels are of Limousin oak, but today other oaks, especially those from the Tronçais forest, may be used. The brandy "breathes" through the wood and draws color and flavor from it, but the brandy also suffers loss of volume by evaporation. The aging process is required by French law to last at least 5 years. Cognacs will often be older, of course, but it is no longer practical to tie up for many years the capital represented in a great store of brandy. Nor does the spirit necessarily improve after 40 or 50 years in wood. Overaging can make the best of Cognac taste too "woody." At the same time, spirits do not mature in glass, and the legendary quality of "Napoleon brandy" is a myth. If a bottle from Napoleon's time were still in existence, the brandy would not be any more mature than the day it was bottled.

Increasingly, Cognacs are blends of various ages and characteristics. By this system, brandies of peak vintages fill up the "valleys" of less good ones. A small amount of vintage Cognac is still kept for sale under the label of British Bonded, but this custom is dying out. Vintage brandies are not marketed in the United States because French aging certificates are not recognized by U.S. authorities. Every shipment of brandy is accompanied by a government certificate guaranteeing authenticity.

Armagnac, the other great French brandy, comes from wines grown, for the most part, in sandy soil near the towns of Eauze and Condom, in Tenarèze, in the Gascon region of southwest France. The finest tracts in this delimited area are Bas-Armagnac, Tenarèze, and Haut-Armagnac. The brandy, aged traditionally, if not universally, in black casks of native oak, is robust, pungent, and full of character. It is usually sold in flat-bottomed flagons known as *basquaises*. Vintage brandy is produced rather oftener here than in Cognac. In these and other wine areas, the French also distill from the pomace, or marc, that is the skins or leftovers of grapes after pressing. This type of brandy is known as *eau-de-vie-de-marc*, or simply as marc, and an old marc of Burgundy can be an excellent brandy. Grappa is the Italian term for pomace and it is also a term used in Spanish-speaking countries and in California for this type of brandy.

Brandies of Other Lands. Spain's distinctive brandies are distilled mainly from the sherry wines grown from the Palomino grape in the Jerez district. Some pure grape brandy is produced also in other districts. Spanish brandy, fuller in flavor and less dry than the French, has more or less replaced Cognac in popularity among Spaniards. Midway in type between the Spanish and the French are the muscat brandies of Portugal. No European country has been making brandy, or *acquavite*, longer than Italy, where the modern brandy tends to be dark and rather mellow. Greek brandies, made from white and red grapes, are produced in three styles: the youngest, claiming to be 5 years old; Five Star, 25 years old; and Seven Star, claiming to be aged more than 40 years. Probably the best-known brandy exported by Greece is a dry, light-colored spirit. Other Greek brandies are darker and sweeter, and are preferred as after-dinner liqueurs.

Some form of brandy is distilled in every country where grapes for wines are grown. After France, the United States is the chief producer of brandy, with over half a million acres (200,000 hectares) of vineyards growing wines for distillation—principally in California. About three quarters of the brandy consumed by Americans is distilled in the United States. Distillation of American wines was pioneered early in the 19th century in Ohio and California, using small pot stills. Later on, the modern continuous still was introduced. The distilling industry, aided by scientific studies at the University of California, has made great progress in the United States. American brandies produced from the grapes and soil most favorable to flavor and quality are not imitations of Cognac nor of any other foreign spirit. They are well-made, with characters of their own. About two thirds of the brandy distilled in the United States is produced in California.

Types of Fruit Brandies. Different types of spirits may be made from fruits other than the grape. In France, Alsace is famous for raspberry, pear, and greengage white brandies, and for kirsch, which is distilled from cherries and cherry stones. Kirsch is also made in Germany, Switzerland, and the United States. In the Balkans, the amber-colored plum slivovitz is traditional; while the Hungarians pride themselves on their apricot-flavored Barack Palinka. Finally, there is Calvados, the famous French apple brandy distilled from cider in pot stills—chiefly in Normandy—and aged for 4 to 20 years. The American version of this remarkable distillation is applejack, which has been known there since colonial times. In those days, however, New England farmers were apt to make it in a rough-and-ready way, by freezing fermented cider. Since water freezes at a higher temperature than alcohol, the ice, which may be skimmed off, is almost pure water and the liquid residue is almost pure alcohol. Nowadays, continuous stills turn out an apple brandy that requires only a few years in oak barrels to achieve smoothness. Often, the distilled cider is cut with distilled water and grain neutral spirits.

WHISKEY

In Ireland and Scotland, the Gaelic *uisge beatha* ("water of life"), was being made in the 12th century from malted barley, dried in a kiln over a peat fire. It was afterward "mashed" (diluted with water and cooked) and left to ferment into "distillers beer," which was then distilled in old-fashioned pot stills. In America, corn and rye are the principal whiskey grains, with some millet, sorghum, and barley used. Sweet mash whiskey is made by adding selected yeasts to the fermentation; sour mash by the introduction of a residue of spent beer or "draff." Both beer and draff are then poured into huge patent stills and the resultant spirit is diluted and aged in casks—in Scotland, in old sherry barrels, in the United States usually in new casks charred inside to accelerate the action of the oak.

American Whiskey. Unlike Scotch and Irish, American whiskeys are classified by type, not by origin. They range in character from well-matured, often magnificent spirits to harsher blends. Whiskey, so long established in Britain, was not the drink of the early American distillers; they were content with beer, rum, and New England applejack. It was the Scottish and Irish settlers in Pennsylvania who started to distill whiskey, as a farm industry. It was a product easier to transport and sell than the grain from which it was derived. Then, when the Congress in 1791 put an excise tax on whiskey (causing an uproar in 1794 known as the Whiskey Rebellion) many of the distillers moved to the uncharted West, preferring to face Indians rather than tax gatherers. Gradually, the home industry grew into big business.

Traditional American whiskey types are Bourbon (named after Bourbon county, Kentucky), rye, and corn. Under U.S. regulations, Bourbon must be distilled from a mash of at least 51% corn and rye from a mash of at least 51% rye. Both are aged in new charred oak barrels. Corn whiskey is distilled from a mash of at least 80% corn and aged in used or uncharred barrels. American "straight" whiskies must be distilled at not more than 160 proof, since higher proof would neutralize their flavor and character, and they are marketed at between 80 and 100 proof.

American whiskeys may be labeled as "straight" or "blended straight," meaning the whiskeys are at least 2 years old, or they may be labeled a "blend." The latter type must contain at least 20% straight whiskey. The remainder may be neutral spirits ("neutralized" at higher proof), aged in the same stills as the straight whiskey, plus some flavoring. The very

SAMPLING BRANDY aging in oak barrels in the Cognac district of France. Cognac ages for at least 5 years.
ROBERT DOISNEAU, FROM RAPHO GUILLUMETTE

popular "blends" have found favor because they are lighter and, of course, cheaper. Whiskey labeled "bottled in bond" is straight whiskey, at least 100 proof, warehoused under U.S. government custodianship for 4 to 8 years. The government, however, does not guarantee the whiskey's quality.

Canadian Whisky. (In Canada and Scotland the preferred spelling is "whisky.") The typically light-bodied Canadian whisky, usually at least 6 years old, is well respected in many countries of the world. Canadian government regulations require only that it be distilled from cereal grains, which means usually corn, rye, wheat, and barley malt, blended according to the prescription of the distiller. Different blends produce whiskies resembling American Bourbon and rye and having a delicacy like Scotch.

Irish Whiskey. Irish whiskey is dry and has a distinctive, rather austere flavor. The high-quality types, unblended, are triple-distilled in pot stills from pure Irish grain mash, mostly barley, malted and unmalted, with a little wheat, oats, and rye. These grains are not dried directly over peat fires, as in Scottish distilleries, and so lack the "smoky" taste of Scotch. Peter the Great of Russia (1672–1725) said: "Of all wine, Irish wine is the best," and the Irish are still of this opinion. But in exporting their nectar, they are up against hard competition from the Scots. At home, high taxes mean that many Irishmen cannot afford their favorite drink. This has led to the production of "poteen" (little pot) whiskey in illicit stills. Yet the Irish market abroad is growing, and the whiskey has its keen adherents everywhere.

Scotch Whisky. The quality of Scotch whisky depends on malted barley, the pure water of Highland streams, and the unique flavor given by heating the malt over peat fires. Pure malt whisky, made in traditional pot stills, can still be obtained, but most Scotch is now blended with grain whisky, bulk-produced in continuous stills. The modern tendency is to use less malt, thus producing a lighter spirit, which is aged in used sherry casks. In the old days, pure malt whisky was distilled in the Highlands, often at home, by the mistress of the house. When these domestic stills were suppressed by the English Parliament and heavy duties were imposed on spirits, the distillers took to the hills. In the early 18th century, more "moonshine" whisky was made (and seeped over the border to England) than the legal kind. Eventually the duty was lowered. Now, internal taxation has reached incredible heights.

RUM AND OTHER SPIRITS

Rum. The distillate of products of fermented sugarcane is rum. Of all spirits, rum retains best those natural taste factors derived from its base. Processing is simpler since (1) the step of turning starch into sugar is eliminated; (2) rum does not have to be distilled at very high proof, as do gin and vodka; (3) it receives the minimum of chemical treatment; and (4) rum can be matured in casks that have already been used for spirit aging. Sugar caramel may be added and, accordingly, the color of rum varies from colorless through amber to mahogany. The heaviest, most pungent type is Jamaican rum, although it is not so strong or so dark as some of the Demerara types. Cuban rum, on the other hand, is light and pale—a style emulated in Puerto Rico and the Virgin Islands. Other West Indian islands produce intermediate types of rum. The rums that were staple liquors of the New England colonists were made from molasses and were full-flavored and robust.

Gin and Aquavit. Gin is obtained by the distillation and rectification, or processing, of grain spirits—or it may be made from any kind of rectified spirit. The two principal types are London dry gin (like that made in the United States) and Dutch. Holland gins, which are often sold in stone crocks, retain a strong taste of juniper, the traditional gin flavoring. London dry gin is really a neutral spirit mildly flavored according to recipes that differ slightly with each maker.

Aquavit (Scandinavian, *Akvavit*) is distilled from either grain or potatoes and flavored with caraway. It is a favorite drink in Sweden, Norway, and Denmark.

Vodka. Generally distilled from grain, rather than from potatoes as formerly, vodka is the national drink of the USSR and Poland and is also very popular in the Western world. Vodka is distilled at quite high proof and rectified into a spirit without taste or aroma, although some of the Polish vodkas are flavored with fruit, flowers, or herbs. A favorite Polish type is *zubrowka*, which has a bison on the label because it tastes of the "holy" grass on which the animal loves to graze. Russian vodkas range from about 65 to 95 proof.

There is scarcely a region or an island in the world that has not developed its own type of distilled spirits: cloudy Greek ouzo; the various arracks and rakis of eastern Europe and the Middle East, which are derived from dates, figs, palms, or anything handy; South America's fiery tequila, distilled from the pulque that is made from Mexico's mysterious century plant; and many less well-known concoctions.

ALEXIS LICHINE, *Author of
"Encyclopedia of Wines and Spirits
of the World"*

Further Reading: Grossman, Harold J., *Grossman's Guide to Wines, Spirits, and Beers,* 4th ed. (New York 1964); Lafon, René, Lafon, Jean, and Couillard, Pierre, *Le Cognac: sa distillation,* 4th ed. (Paris 1964); Lichine, Alexis, *Encyclopedia of Wines and Spirits of the World* (New York 1967).

DISTRIBUTION, in economics, concerns the allocation of wealth or income in an economy. Distribution refers to the processes that determine the flow of wealth or income. The term also refers to statistical accounts of how ownership and control are divided among classes of individuals or geographically (for instance, comparing wealth in different regions within a country, or making a comparison of one country with other countries). See WEALTH—*Distribution of Wealth.*

In trade, the term "distribution" refers to the activities and organizations that make goods available to wholesale and retail purchasers. See MARKETING.

DISTRIBUTION, in law. See DESCENT AND DISTRIBUTION.

DISTRIBUTIVE LAW, in arithmetic, the fundamental law that multiplication may be "distributed" over addition: in symbols, $a(b+c) = ab+ac$; $(b+c)a = ba+ca$. That is, the product of a factor and a sum can be found by multiplying the factor into each element of the sum and then adding the products. The rule may be generalized to any number of terms. Thus, $a(b+c+d) = ab+ac+ad$; $(a+b)(c+d) = a(c+d) + b(c+d)$. However, addition is not distributive over multiplication; that is: $a + bc \neq (a + b)(a + c)$.

In the algebra of sets, each of the two operations is distributive over the other. The product AB is the set of elements in both A and B; the sum $A+B$ is the set of elements in A or in B, or in both. Thus $A(B+C) = AB+AC$, and $A+BC = (A+B)(A+C)$.

In logic, also, each operation is distributive over the other. If p and q are *propositions* (that is, statements which are true or false), $p \cdot q$ means p and q are both true; $p+q$ means that at least one is true. Thus $p \cdot (q+r) = (p \cdot q)+(p \cdot r)$, and $p+(q \cdot r) = (p+q) \cdot (p+r)$.

FRANCIS A. GREENE
Loyola Blakefield School, Towson, Md.

DISTRICT is a term often used to designate a geographical area having a distinct character or location, but without precise boundaries. In other cases, it refers to a definitely determined subdivision of a state, county, or municipality provided for judicial, political, or administrative purposes. In England, ecclesiastic districts exist for the registration and religious observance of births, deaths, and marriages.

In the United States, separate election districts often are established for the different kinds of public officials, with the result that federal, state, and local electoral districts overlap. Common public functions that operate on a district basis include schools, fire protection, public utilities, conservation, housing, social welfare, and taxation.

Most school districts are governed by elective boards; other specialized districts often are governed by appointive boards, which have no taxing power and must consequently depend on service charges.

See also APPORTIONMENT, LEGISLATIVE; COURT; EDUCATION—9. *Educational Organization;* ELECTIONS; INTERNAL REVENUE; MUNICIPAL GOVERNMENT; TAXATION; UNITED STATES—14. *State and Local Government* (School and Nonschool Special Districts).

DISTRICT ATTORNEY is the designation given in the United States to the public official, invariably a lawyer, who is responsible for prosecuting criminal cases locally in behalf of a state or the federal government. "District" refers to the fact that only a part of the territory of a state (or the United States) is within his charge. Usually that area is a county, and his official title may be *county attorney* or *county prosecutor.* In the federal system he is called the *United States attorney* for a particular district, as for the Southern District of New York. There are more than 2,700 state, and 93 federal, district attorneys in the United States.

In the federal system, the district attorney serves under the U.S. attorney general, and in a few states under the state attorney general. Most, however, are elected officials; and they, as well as many others appointed by a governor or the court, are not subject to control by any other government official. In practice a district attorney's power is often limited by the police, upon whom he normally must depend for assistance, and by the courts, which rule on the validity of the cases he brings and the way in which he may prosecute them.

In a rural area the district attorney may be only a part-time official who handles all phases of pertinent cases. In an urban area he may run a large office; for example, in Los Angeles county he is in charge of hundreds of assistant district attorneys and thus becomes largely an administrator and policymaker rather than a trial lawyer. Many county district attorneys also have responsibility for all kinds of matters other than criminal; and the U.S. attorneys are the local trial lawyers for the federal government in civil, as well as criminal, cases.

Powers. A district attorney exercises considerable discretion as to the consequences an individual may suffer as the result of an alleged criminal act. His willingness to prosecute vigorously certain kinds of cases, and not others, will frequently determine the patterns of police activity in a community. (See ARREST.) Moreover, once a person has been arrested, the district attorney will often decide initially whether there is enough legal evidence to warrant going further with the case. He must then decide what precise crime should be formally charged, a decision that may make considerable difference as to the punishment available. Because of the increasing volume of criminal cases, there is more emphasis on the district attorney's discretionary role to reach a just disposition without a trial, rather than on his role as the state's advocate against the accused.

District attorneys also have the power to initiate investigations. They do this federally, and in many states, by summoning witnesses before the grand jury (see JURY) and in other states by an information (q.v.). They are expected to use this power especially to guard against official corruption. Sometimes the district attorney's office leads to a higher political post, but most often, if the "D.A." goes into another public office, he becomes a judge. Young lawyers often seek service in district attorney's offices for this reason, as well as to gain a considerable amount of trial experience in a brief period of time.

RICHARD A. GREEN
Director, American Bar Association Project on Minimum Standards for Criminal Justice

DISTRICT OF COLUMBIA, a federal district coextensive in area with the city of Washington, D.C., the United States capital. Its population (1980 census) is 638,432. Congress authorized creation of a national capital on the Potomac River in July 1790. President Washington chose the site and Maj. Pierre Charles L'Enfant was commissioned to plan the future city. The cornerstone of the north wing of the Capitol was laid on Sept. 18, 1793. In June 1800, President John Adams and the entire staff of the federal government (less than 140 people) moved to the unfinished city from Philadelphia.

Initially laid out as a 10-mile (16-km) square, the District extended across the Potomac, occupying lands ceded in 1791 by Virginia and Maryland (see map below). In 1846 the portion given by Virginia—including the city of Alexandria and what is now the urban county of Arlington—was returned to that state, and the District has since comprised only the former Maryland territory on the north bank of the river, an area of 67 square miles (173.5 sq km).

Most Americans think of Washington only as the nation's capital, a picturesque city of gleaming monuments, famous buildings, impressive government complexes, museums, historical landmarks, and broad, tree-shaded avenues and malls. But to hundreds of thousands of persons, it is the place where they live, work, and raise families. The city confronts many problems common to most U.S. metropolises: traffic congestion, air and water pollution, rising taxes, slums, poverty, crime, and rapid population changes. Some of these problems are aggravated by special inner-city conditions—for example, Washington is the largest U.S. urban center with a majority of nonwhite residents. Other problems have resulted from the unusually rapid growth of the suburbs in neighboring Maryland and Virginia,

which strain the resources of an already crowded city as it attempts to function as the hub of a metropolitan area with over 3 million people.

The Penalties of Leadership. Washington is neither part of any state nor a federal territory, but a separate area composed of lands ceded by states to the federal government. Legally, it is an incorporated municipality like other cities, but created by federal rather than state law. It is governed by federal law, with final authority resting in the president and Congress. By law, its residents until 1974 were denied the privilege of electing officials of the city government. They had no representation in Congress (except for a brief three-year period in the 1870's) and, until the 23d Amendment to the federal Constitution was ratified in 1961, they had no voice in the election of U.S. presidents. (They had voted in presidential primaries for the first time in 1956.)

In 1970 the District was granted the right to have a nonvoting delegate in the House of Representatives. The delegate might introduce legislation and attend committee meetings, but could not participate in floor debates or vote. It was not until 1974 that the city was given a significant measure of home rule by the Congress.

The Early Years. When local government was first established in 1802, the capital of the United States, then known as the City of Washington, was governed by a "mayor-council" form of government, with a mayor appointed by the president of the United States and an 8-member board of aldermen and a 12-member council, both elected by the voters. By 1820, the voters' role had been considerably expanded. In 1812 the council was empowered to elect the mayor. In 1820 the voters were authorized to elect him.

The Middle Years. In the years following the Civil War both the city government and the voters' role in local affairs changed abruptly. At that time municipal governments were at a low ebb. Corruption was widespread. The Tweed Ring in New York City, the Gas Ring in Philadelphia, and notorious machines in other large cities were being exposed and reform movements initiated. The nation's capital was no exception. Its government at this time was characterized by graft, extravagance, and inefficiency.

In 1871, Congress changed the city's status to that of a federal territory and renamed it the "District of Columbia." As such, it was administered by a governor appointed by the president, an appointed board of public works, and a bicameral legislature—an 11-member council appointed by the president and a 22-member house of delegates elected by the voters. This structure lasted only three years, but during those years the District enjoyed direct representation in Congress (through an appointed, nonvoting delegate in the House of Representatives).

In 1874 territorial status was revoked and a new form of municipal government—a "commissioner government"—was established, consisting of a 3-member board of commissioners appointed by the president; two of the commissioners were civilians and one was an officer of the Army Corps of Engineers. Under this plan, city functions were assigned to the commissioners individually or jointly. Public works functions, including roads and construction, were assigned to the engineer commissioner. Public safety functions, including police and fire, were assigned to one civilian commissioner, and social programs,

The light area in the map covers the present District of Columbia. The dotted line bounds the original area, including the portion returned to Virginia in 1846.

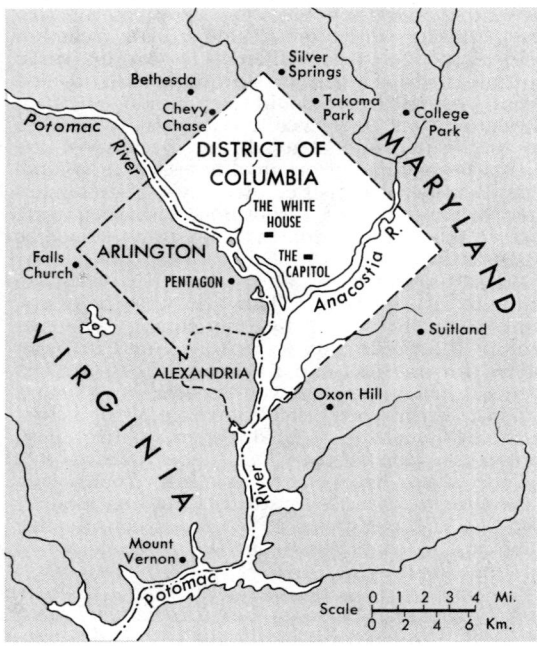

including health, welfare, and corrections, to the other. Joint functions included general administration and appeals. The commissioners' responsibilities were not all-inclusive, for many functions were assigned to federal agencies, and others to autonomous boards and commissions.

The commissioner government remained in effect for 89 years, while the city's population grew from 150,000 to over 800,000, its budget soared from $4 million to over $500 million, and the number of city employees rose from less than 500 to more than 30,000. During these nine decades, the weaknesses of the system became more and more apparent. At best, it represented government by divided authority. A more serious criticism, particularly when urban problems began to multiply in the 1950's and 1960's, pointed to the subordination of the commissioners to a few senior members of the U. S. Congress—most particularly, the chairmen of the House and Senate district committees. These powerful individuals, who represented constituencies that were usually distant or rural (or both) and who were immune to reprisal by the District's voteless residents, often exercised excessive authority over city affairs through their control of the purse strings; their approval was needed for virtually all city expenditures. They were frequently accused of being unresponsive to the real needs of the District's exploding population.

The Reorganization of 1967. After years of intensive study and debate, another form of government, providing for unified executive leadership in the office of a "mayor" and legislative action through a council, was established. Specifically, Reorganization Plan No. 3 of 1967 created the offices of commissioner (commonly called the "mayor" or "mayor–commissioner") and assistant to the commissioner (usually termed the "deputy commissioner"), both appointed by the president. At least one must be a resident of the city at the time of appointment and both must reside in the city during their term of office. The first incumbents were Walter E. Washington, commissioner, and Thomas W. Fletcher, deputy commissioner, whose terms were to run until 1969. Thereafter, appointees were to serve 4-year terms, subject to removal by the president.

The 1967 plan also provided for a council, officially called the District of Columbia Council. It was a 9-member body composed of a chairman, vice chairman, and seven other members, all appointed by the president. The 1967 law called for the council membership to be "broadly representative of the community" and required only that it be "nonpartisan," with no more than six members of any one political party. Each must have been an actual resident of the city for three years prior to appointment, and each could be removed by the president for cause. Terms were for three years and were staggered to ensure continuity. The council's primary role and its strength were in its powers to review budget requests of the city's agencies and to enact ordinances and regulations for the city.

The 1967 reorganization unified the executive function and provided for a clear separation of the city's executive and legislative powers. It consolidated under the mayor-commissioner many of the city's agencies and offices, including those of health, welfare, highways, traffic, police, fire, alcoholic beverage control, sanitary engineering, corrections and parole, and licensing and regulation. In addition, an executive office under the mayor brought together the budget, management, personnel, public affairs, and program development functions, providing an effective center for comprehensive program-planning and review. By an action of the first mayor, steps were also taken to bring various related executive functions together into "agencies," each under the direction of a single head. The public safety director, for example, coordinates all police, fire, and civil defense activities.

Unresolved Problems. The foregoing innovations, though substantial, were far from being final answers to the fundamental problems of District government. First, the 1967 plan did not increase the powers of the local government in local affairs, but simply reallocated the powers of the former board between new executive and legislative branches. Second, the city government was not fully unified, since most of the functions assigned to autonomous boards and commissions were still beyond its jurisdiction, as were many other functions—the district and federal district court systems, for example—which remained under the direct jurisdiction of federal agencies. Third, presidential appointees still held most of the city's key offices, and congressional action, as well as presidential approval, was still required to enact or amend city laws and to raise taxes or create new revenue sources. Fourth, there was little (aside from one later provision for the popular election of the board of education) to encourage the long-time proponents of "home rule," who had hoped for a new system of local elections that would dramatically increase direct citizen participation in city affairs. And finally, there was the unanswered question of what role District citizens should play in national affairs, particularly through direct representation in Congress.

Home Rule. Some of the problems of government were solved by a home-rule charter provided by Congress in 1974. Under this charter the District elects its mayor and 13-member District Council for 4-year terms. Although the District is empowered to raise money through taxation, Congress retains control over the budget and maintains the right to overrule most District decisions. With much of its real estate public property, and without the industry necessary for an adequate tax base, the District was required to draw much of its operating revenue from the U. S. Treasury. The home rule charter, however, authorized the city to turn to the Wall Street municipal bond market, where it might be able to obtain lower interest rates. The first home rule government in more than a century was elected in November 1974 and took office on Jan. 2, 1975. In consonance with the District's ethnic makeup, the mayor (Walter E. Washington) and 11 of the 13 members of the new District Council were black; and two thirds of the jobs in the city government, including more than a third of the top nonelective posts, were held by blacks.

Representation in Congress. Congress in 1970 authorized the District to have a nonvoting delegate in that body, and in 1978 approved a proposal for an amendment to the U. S. constitution that would give the District two Senate seats and at least one representative in the House. For ratification of the amendment, approval by three fourths, or 38, of the state legislatures is required within seven years.

See also WASHINGTON, D. C.

JEAN E. SPENCER*, *University of Maryland*

DISTRITO FEDERAL. See Mexico, Federal District of.

DISTURBANCE. See Nuisance.

DITHYRAMB, dith'i-ram, an ancient Greek song accompanied by a dance, performed originally at ceremonies honoring the god Dionysus but later secularized. Dithyrambs probably originated in the 6th century B.C. By the next century they were important parts of theatrical presentations and, at the great festivals held in Athens for Dionysus, shared the stage with tragedy and comedy. For these performances, such renowned poets as Pindar and Simonides wrote the words.

Like the dramas, the dithyrambs were staged as contests. Ten choruses of 50 persons each competed: five choruses were made up of boys and five of men, and each age group was awarded a prize. From the 4th century B.C. to the 2d century A.D., when the dithyramb died out, the words were generally secondary to the music. Although Aristotle asserted that there was a connection between dithyrambs and the choruses in Greek tragedy, which also arose as part of the worship of Dionysus, the point is seriously disputed by a number of modern classical scholars.

DITMARS, dit'märz, **Raymond Lee** (1876–1942), American naturalist, who made important contributions to the study of snakes. Ditmars was born in Newark, N.J., on June 20, 1876. He studied at Barnard Military Academy and graduated in 1891. After working for five years as an assistant in the department of entomology at the American Museum of Natural History in New York, he joined the staff of the New York *Times* as a court reporter.

In 1899, when the Bronx Zoo opened its reptile house, Ditmars became curator of reptiles, a position he held until his death. He achieved international fame for his work on reptiles. His books, most of which were written for amateur naturalists, include *The Reptile Book* (1907; revised as *The Reptiles of North America*, 1936), *Reptiles of the World* (1910), *Strange Animals I Have Known* (1931), *Wild Animals of the World* (1937), *A Field Book of North American Snakes* (1939), and *Animal Kingdom* (1941). He died in New York City on May 12, 1942.

Eldon J. Gardner, *Utah State University*

DITTANY, dit'ən-ē, any of a small group of low-growing plants of the mint family (Labiatae). Probably the best-known species is the common dittany (*Cunila origanoides*), which is also known as "sweet horsemint" or "stonemint." It is native to the eastern United States, growing in dry places as a much-branched perennial. Like other members of the mint family, its leaves are opposite, and its stems are square.

The small bell-shaped flowers of the common dittany are white or purple, with an erect, notched upper lip and a spreading 3-lobed lower lip. The flowers are borne in flat-topped clusters in which the inner flowers open before the outer ones. The plant has a fragrant odor and is pungent to the taste due to the presence of an oil that resembles the oil of the horsemint (*Monarda*). The leaves of the plant are sometimes used for making mint tea.

Sydney C. Bausor
California State College, Pa.

DITTERSDORF, dit'ərs-dôrf, **Karl Ditters von** (1739–1799), Austrian violinist and composer, whose charming and spirited music contains much interesting instrumentation and melodic inventiveness. He was born Karl Ditters in Vienna on Nov. 2, 1739. He early displayed talent as a violinist and performed in the orchestra of St. Stephen's Cathedral. At the age of 11 he joined the orchestra of the Prince von Hildburghausen. When the Prince dismissed his musicians in 1759, Ditters joined the Imperial Opera orchestra.

In 1761, Ditters toured Italy with Gluck, winning fame as a violin virtuoso. Returning to Vienna, where he became a close friend of Haydn, he found a potential rival in the Italian violinist Lolli. But the Viennese preferred Ditters, not only for his technique, but also because he knew how to "speak to the heart." From 1764 to 1769 he was *Kapellmeister* to the bishop of Grosswardein in Pressburg, where he wrote his first opera, *Amore in musica* (1767).

In 1770, Ditters was engaged by the prince bishop of Breslau and moved to the bishop's estate in Johannisberg, Silesia. There he organized an orchestra and opera house, and through the bishop's influence he was ennobled by Emperor Joseph II in 1773, receiving the name Ditters von Dittersdorf. He spent his last years at the castle of Baron von Stillfried near Neuhof, Bohemia, dictating his autobiography to his son. He died there on Oct. 24, 1799.

A prolific composer, Dittersdorf wrote numerous symphonies, violin concertos, chamber compositions, piano and violin sonatas, cantatas, oratorios, and stage works, mostly *Singspiele* (operettas). His best-known works include the Concerto in A Major for harp and orchestra and the operetta *Doktor und Apotheker* (1786).

Gilbert Chase, *Tulane University*

DIU, dē'ōō, is a district of western India situated on the Arabian Sea, 170 miles (275 km) northwest of Bombay. Administratively, it is a part of the Union Territory of Goa, Daman, and Diu, known formerly as Portuguese India. Along with Goa and Daman, Diu was annexed by the Republic of India on Dec. 18, 1961. Diu district (area: 15 square miles, or 41.5 sq km), at the southernmost point of Kathiawar Peninsula, comprises three units: Diu Island in the Arabian Sea, 7 miles (11 km) long and 2 miles (3.2 km) wide, near the mainland; Fort Simbor, on a smaller island, 14 miles (22.5 km) out at sea; and the village of Goghla (Gogola) and its environs on the mainland.

Occupied by the Portuguese in 1535, Diu was a flourishing seaport in the days of small sailing ships. However, it later faded into obscurity. Population: (1961) 14,280.

Robert C. Kingsbury, *Indiana University*

DIURETIC, dī-yōō-ret'ik, a drug that increases the flow of urine. Most of the useful diuretics also increase the salt content of urine.

The kidneys normally play an essential role in maintaining the constancy of the internal environment of the body by excreting appropriate amounts of water, inorganic salts, and organic waste products. When normal kidney function is disturbed, diuretics are often used to help restore an adequate output of water and solutes in urine. Diuretics are most commonly employed to treat edema, an accumulation of fluid in the body resulting from congestive heart failure or some other disease process. In eliminating salt and water from the body, diuretics help restore its normal salt and water balance.

There are many available diuretics of dissimilar chemical structure and varying potency. The most powerful diuretics, the organic mercurials and benzothiadiazides, block the reabsorption of salt and water from fluid in the renal, or kidney, tubules by inhibiting transport mechanisms in the tubules. This interference with reabsorption leads to increased urinary output. Mercurials, such as calomel, have long been known to produce diuresis, and various organic mercurials have been widely used since about 1920 whenever the use of potent diuretics was indicated.

In the late 1950's and early 1960's the benzothiadiazides (especially chlorothiazide) were synthesized and studied thoroughly; they then replaced most other diuretics in the treatment of most disorders. The benzothiadiazides are effective when given orally in tablet form—a practical advantage over many other diuretics. In addition to their use in cases of fluid retention, the benzothiadiazides are used to treat hypertension; they effectively aid in lowering high blood pressure, but how they produce this effect is not completely understood.

Other diuretics include osmotic diuretics and acid-forming salts. Osmotic diuretics, such as urea and mannitol, are substances that are reabsorbed partially or not at all from the renal tubules; they produce an increase in the volume of urine and electrolyte secretion. Acid-forming salts, such as ammonium chloride, interfere with the normal electrolyte balance in the kidneys, resulting in diuresis. These diuretics are no longer frequently used alone, but are occasionally used in combination with a mercurial diuretic.

Water also sometimes functions as a diuretic. The volume of urine is influenced by the secretion of the anti-diuretic hormone (ADH) from the posterior pituitary gland. The ingestion of water in amounts exceeding the needs of the body interferes with the secretion of the hormone and produces diuresis.

ANDRES GOTH, M. D.
University of Texas Southwestern Medical School

DIVAN, divan', a term that formerly was applied to the council of state in Muslim countries. It was used in Sassanid Persia (3d to 7th century A.D.) to denote both account books and offices of administration, and in the first of these meanings it was adopted by the Arabs (in the form *diwan*) during the reign of Caliph Umar (reigned 634–644) for the register of the early Muslims. In the first centuries of the Abbasid caliphate (750–1258), it designated various offices of the state (for example, those relating to finance and the army), but as the empire contracted, these departments were absorbed into a single divan presided over by the vizier (*wazir*). This was to be the prototype for the councils of state in the various independent sultanates that arose in the provinces.

In early Ottoman practice, the divan was a council consisting of the sultan and his chief ministers and was open to all who had business with the government. But from the time of Mehmed II (reigned 1451–1581), the sultan no longer attended in person, membership was regulated by protocol, and business was conducted in private. The divan assembled regularly in a domed hall in the center court of the palace in Istanbul, and the furnishings of this chamber became the model for Ottoman interior decoration. The elevated platform (*sedir*), extending around the walls and covered by a long flat cushion (*minder*), is the origin of the seat known as a "divan" in the Western world.

The collected verse of a poet is also designated by this term; for example, the *Divan of Hafiz*. In a divan, the poems are usually classified as to form and entered in alphabetical order according to the terminating letters of the lines.

JOHN R. WALSH
University of Edinburgh

Further Reading: Gibb, H. A. R., and Bowen, Harold, *Islamic Society and the West*, vol. 1, part 1 (London and New York 1950).

DIVERTICULITIS, dī-vər-tik-yə-lī'təs, is an inflammation of the diverticula, the small pouches that often form in the wall of the lower intestinal tract in middle aged people. Although diverticula may also form in other portions of the intestinal tract, such as the esophagus and small intestine, they occur mostly in the large intestine, particularly the sigmoid colon, which lies just above the rectum.

The diverticula are subject to irritation and infection from any alteration in the fecal matter, whether it be constipation or diarrhea. An attack of diverticulitis is usually accompanied by cramps, fever, lower abdominal discomfort, and sometimes by rectal bleeding. Complications of the disorder include obstruction of the bowel, abscess formation, hemorrhaging, and perforation of the intestinal wall.

In its early stages, diverticulitis generally responds to treatment with antispasmodics and antibiotics, usually a combination of penicillin and a tetracycline. The patient is also put on a bland diet and once the attack is over he is cautioned against eating nuts, seeds, and other coarse foods. In severe cases, diverticulitis may be treated through surgery.

REAUMUR S. DONNALLY, M. D.
Washington (D. C.) Hospital Center

DIVI-DIVI, dē-vē-dē'vē, is the trade name applied to the fruits (pods) of *Libidibia coriaria*, formerly known as *Caesalpinia coriaria*, of the pea family (Leguminosae). The species is native to tropical America, where it occurs on dry open sites as a large shrub or small bushy tree of some 15 to 30 feet (4.5–9 meters) in height and from 6 to more than 10 inches (15–25 cm) in diameter.

Divi-divi pods, which at maturity are about 3 inches (7.5 cm) long and 1 inch (2.5 cm) wide, are characteristically S-shaped when thoroughly dried. They contain a yellowish powdery substance that yields as much as 50% by weight of an exceptionally fine tannin (used in leather manufacture) when extracted with hot water. The tree is cultivated in tropical America, Ceylon, India, Java, and parts of tropical Africa for its rich, tanniferous fruits. The United States imports most of its divi-divi from Colombia and Venezuela.

The wood of this tree is the source of a red dye, but is otherwise of no value.

E. S. HARRAR, *Duke University*

DIVIDE, Great. See CONTINENTAL DIVIDE.

DIVIDEND, an appropriation, usually of current or accumulated earnings, that results in a distribution of corporate assets to stockholders. When the term "dividend" is used alone, the distribution usually is in cash. Payment, however, may be made in media other than cash (such as more shares of stock). Dividends are also paid on other types of ownership interests, such as life insurance policies and savings and loan shares.

When a dividend is in cash, a certain dollar amount is distributed per share of stock outstanding. For example, a $2.5 million dividend paid on 1 million shares outstanding would result in a distribution of $2.50 per share held.

Because corporate stock is normally of two basic types, common and preferred, dividends are normally payable to both. Each type need not receive an identical amount. Preferred shares receive their dividend before any is paid to the common, but they receive only up to a maximum amount agreed upon by contract. After preferred shareholders receive the contract amount, common shareholders have a claim on any remaining amounts to the extent that they are available and are declared payable by the board of directors.

Dividends paid on common shares can vary in amount from period to period, and sometimes they are skipped entirely. The amount paid each year depends on the size of earnings as well as their stability. Many companies with fluctuating earnings maintain regular dividends by paying modest dividends in prosperous years and using accumulated earnings as the basis for dividends in low-income years.

Information on dividends paid by corporations may be found in their annual reports, in the financial press (for example, the *Wall Street Journal* and *Barron's*) and, for longtime periods in the past, in *Moody's Industrial Manual* and other Moody's manuals.

DONALD E. FISCHER, *University of Connecticut*

DIVINATION is the attempt to discover events that do or will affect human beings for good or evil, but that are beyond their control and are believed to have a supernatural, mystical, or other-than-human cause. All known peoples of the world have practiced divination. Forms such as palmistry, dream interpretation, and astrology are popular in highly developed societies. The practice is particularly important in those areas of life where ignorance is great or where human control over events is weak.

The means of divination are many. In some instances the diviner undergoes changes in his physical or psychological condition so that he may serve the divinatory power as a medium or vehicle; in other instances, certain objects and events are considered to be signs of an external power and are used as divinatory mechanisms.

Types of Mediums. The most widespread form of internal power is that of diviners who act while in a state of "possession," often in a state of trance. Possession is thought to be by a divine or supernatural power, often a high god or a vehicle of divine power in the form of spirits, saints, or various animals. Diviners of this kind are often known as shamans, chiefly among indigenous peoples of North America and Siberia.

Shamans, prophets, seers, and mediums may act while in a state of possession. They often hold that their powers come direct to them from a high god, so that they are above petty interests and disputes and also above criticism by ordinary people who lack this direct contact. Prophets and seers may thus act as revolutionary political figures, with charismatic authority and often with mystical powers of healing.

Diviners of similar kinds include the many types of mediums who may communicate with the dead (the process known as necromancy), as well as crystal gazers, dream interpreters, divining-rod operators, and diviners by automatic writing, all of whom are popular in the Western world today. Even if they do not regard themselves as having supernatural powers, they usually claim a heightened psychological insight denied to ordinary people.

Interpreting Signs and Omens. Divination by the interpretation of phenomena without possession or supernatural powers is distinguished mainly by the nature of the objects used. The interpreters are considered to have an expertise that enables them to interpret signs or omens that are set before them. The reasoning behind this kind of divination is that human fate is not haphazard but is part of a wider cosmic pattern. The total pattern of the universe is known only to the divine power that established it; but certain signs are also part of this pattern and reflect an individual's fate. Thus, by interpreting these signs, the individual's place in the total scheme of things can be understood.

Signs and objects relating to the human body are most often used for divinatory purposes among the advanced and literate societies, while both literate and primitive peoples seek to interpret natural phenomena. Some means of divination based on the human body are linked with the belief that parts of the body are mystically related to the courses of the heavenly bodies, which ultimately decide human fate. Divination of this kind includes reading the palm of the hand (cheiromancy), the shoulder blades (scapulimancy), the distribution of moles on the body (neomancy), the lines on the forehead (metoposcopy), the lines on the feet (pedomancy), the eyes (ophthalmoscopy), and the fingernails (onychomancy). Other forms of divination are concerned mainly with discovering the moral and psychological nature of the individual, such as from the shape of the skull (phrenology). From the time of the Italian criminologist Cesare Lombroso (1836–1909), many theories have been put forward about the relationship between body features and temperament. These include the "scientific" theories of William Herbert Sheldon, E. A. Hooton, and Ernst Kretschmer, who divide people into a number of physical types, each with corresponding psychological characteristics. None of these theories is thoroughly convincing.

The best-known forms of divination based on the interpretation of natural phenomena are astrology and horoscopy, divination from the relationship of the heavenly bodies and human fate. Both have a long history and use highly sophisticated analyses. Other forms are divination from the pattern of earth and stones thrown onto the ground (geomancy), from flames (pyromancy), stones (lithomancy), water (hydromancy), and the casting of dice. Some divinatory practices involve the study of various objects associated with animals, such as entrails (haruspication), or of the cries and behavior of birds and animals (augury). There is also a category of divination that includes the use of man-made phenomena, such as the interpretation of the Bible or of the writings of Virgil.

Persistence of Divination. There is little, if any, evidence that divination reveals the actual truth. Nevertheless divination is found at all places and at all times. One reason is that divination is an effective way of giving confidence to people in trouble or uncertainty. Another reason is that the individual, in appealing to divination, wishes to confirm his own suspicions. Also, by the law of chance some divinatory statements, even if guesses, will be correct and thus support the faith held in them.

Although divination answers questions about events that are affecting an individual's life, the diviner is rarely asked an open question and often does not give a direct answer. The client does not ask, "Who is harming me?" but "One of the following, all of whom I have reason to think dislike me, is harming me. Which one is it?" The diviner then chooses one of the suggested names and thus cannot fail to satisfy the client. If the question is more general, the diviner may answer elliptically, often in a trance or uttering strange words, and the client himself interprets the reply to confirm his own beliefs.

Many diviners today claim to have powers of telepathy or extrasensory perception. Even if some do have these powers, it is likely that they would be in a minority of the practicing diviners. Until the existence of extrasensory perception and telepathy is scientifically determined, this question with regard to divination cannot be answered satisfactorily. See also ASTROLOGY; DIVINING ROD; MAGIC.

JOHN MIDDLETON, *New York University*

Further Reading: Lessa, W. A., and Vogt, E. Z., *Reader in Comparative Religion* (New York 1965); Middleton, John, *Magic, Witchcraft, and Curing* (New York 1967).

DIVINE, Father (c. 1875–1965), American Negro religious cult leader. He was born George Baker near Savannah, Ga., and began preaching in the South about 1900. About 1915 he moved to New York, where he founded his Peace Mission Movement and later adopted the name Father Divine.

The movement's salient features included: (1) the worship of Divine as God incarnate; (2) communal living—through cooperative labor without pay and the surrender of their possessions, members enabled Divine to provide them with food and shelter at little cost, thus strengthening their faith in his miraculous powers; (3) vows of strictest morality, celibacy, and charity —members were enjoined to make restitution for past sins, and remarkable acts of penance were reported; and (4) the observance of racial equality.

The movement's first communal dwelling, or "Heaven," was in Sayville, N. Y. Although Divine was forced to move to the Harlem section of New York and later to Philadelphia, his movement grew rapidly. At its height there were 178 "Heavens," most of them in New York City and Philadelphia. There are no figures on the membership, but it probably ran into the tens of thousands. It subsequently declined, especially after Divine's death—which was a great disillusionment to his followers—in Lower Merion Township, Pa., on Sept. 10, 1965.

HARRY V. RICHARDSON
Interdenominational Theological Center

DIVINE COMEDY, the supreme achievement of Italy's greatest poet, Dante Alighieri (q.v.). It is a narrative poem of 14,233 lines, written in terza rima (triple rhyme) in 14th century Italian. The work is divided into 100 cantos of approximately 142 lines each. The date of composition is uncertain: at the end of *La vita nuova*, written about 1292, Dante indicates that he had the concept of his great work already in mind. Probably the poem was not actually begun until 1306 at the earliest, and it was finished only shortly before the author's death in 1321.

The Divine Comedy (Italian, *La divina commedia*), written in the first person, relates the journey of Dante through the world of the dead, and the three major divisions, or *cantiche—Inferno* (Hell), *Purgatorio* (Purgatory), and *Paradiso* (Paradise)—indicate the realms of the afterlife the pilgrim visited. The work is superbly proportioned and rich in ornament. Santayana's verdict is as perceptive as it is succinct: "Dante ... has put his whole world into his canvas. Seen there, that world becomes complete, clear, beautiful and tragic. It is vivid and truthful in its detail, sublime in its march and in its harmony.... It has taught us to love and to renounce, to judge and to worship. What more could a poet do?"

The large number of extant manuscripts of *The Divine Comedy* (nearly 600) and of commentaries that appeared shortly after the poet's death attest to the impact of the poem in the 14th and 15th centuries. It has been repeatedly translated into all the languages of the West (there are 40 complete translations into English alone) and into many other tongues as well. The quantity and quality of the tributes offered the poet in 1965 on the 700th anniversary of his birth indicate that the 20th century is perhaps even more responsive to him than its predecessors had been.

The Story. In the first *cantica*, the *Inferno* (34 cantos), the poet meets Virgil in a dark wood and follows his classical mentor through the realm of the damned. The circles of Hell follow an ethical pattern, Aristotelian in essence. The poet first sees the souls of the incontinent, including the lustful, the gluttonous, and the avaricious; then the violent, broken down into the three categories of the violent against neighbor, against self, and against God; and finally the circles of the fraudulent. This latter area is subdivided into two regions: an upper one for those who have betrayed the common bond of humanity, and a lower one for those who have deceived intimates, such as kinsmen, friends, hosts, or political allies. At the center of Hell, Dante finds Lucifer, at once the lord and the ultimate victim of evil, in whose rapacious mouth are being chewed the souls of Brutus and Cassius, traitors to the Roman state, and of Judas, the arch-traitor of all time.

The *Inferno*, for many years the most widely read and most eagerly studied part of *The Divine Comedy*, is rich in characterizations, including such unforgettable portrayals as those of the pathetic Francesca da Rimini, the rugged Ghibelline partisan Farinata, and the self-confident Ulysses. Memorable too is the figure of Ugolino della Gherardesca, pictured as dwelling in the cold ice of the deepest circle, devouring the brain of his betrayer, Ruggieri degli Ubaldini. Such majestic archetypes of human passion and the realism with which their conditions are set forth give the *Inferno* its magnificent and terrible vitality.

In the second *cantica*, the *Purgatorio* (33 cantos), having surveyed the abode of sinners, Virgil leads Dante upward from the seat of Satan through the other side of the earth and emerges in the Southern Hemisphere, where Dante places the Mountain of Purgatory. The arrangement of the penitential mount follows a Christian pattern: after a rather large Antepurgatory, the mountain, rising sharply, is divided into seven successive terraces, on each of which the sins of the penitents are purged. These terraces, in order, are of pride, envy, wrath, sloth, avarice, gluttony, and lust. After Dante and Virgil have completed their ascent, they find at the summit of the mountain the earthly paradise. There they are received by a solemn ritualistic procession, at the end of which Dante's early love, Beatrice, appears. Virgil vanishes at her coming, and it is she who prepares Dante for the ascent to the spheres of Paradise.

In the third *cantica*, the *Paradiso* (33 cantos), the poet, under the tutelage of his love, Beatrice, moves through the successive Ptolemaic spheres, each of which contains representatives of a certain stage of heavenly bliss. In the lowest three, the moon, Mercury, and Venus, all under the earth's shadow, Dante encounters, respectively, the souls of the inconstant, the ambitious, and those whose love had some touch of the earthly. The higher spheres, of the sun, Mars, Jupiter, Saturn, the fixed stars, and the *primum mobile*, afford the poet the opportunity to meet, in turn, the souls of the great teachers, the pious crusaders, the just lawgivers, the contemplative spirits, and, in the last two regions, the saints and angels.

The final heaven, which Dante carefully points out is the only true one, is the empyrean. It is the scene of the last three cantos of the poem and brings Dante, thanks to the intervention of St. Bernard, the mystic, the privilege of the beatific vision. As the poet gropes for the meaning of his ultimate spiritual experience and as the ineffable revelation bursts upon him, the poem ends.

The last two divisions of the *Comedy* lack something of the vigor that characterizes the *Inferno*. But each of these kingdoms has its own special appeal. The *Purgatorio* is charged with a sense of light and hope and is full of passages of great descriptive beauty; it contains instructive digressions touching on various matters, such as the political state of the world, the nature of the human soul, and literary criticism. The *Paradiso*, filled with a kind of ethereal poetry in which light and movement take the place of the naturalistic detail found in the other divisions, also affords the poet an occasion for investigations of philosophical and theological matters.

World View. Fascinating though the narrative is, it is the lesser part of the poem, at least in the intention of the author. In a letter to Can Grande, Dante wrote that the subject of his work "taken in the literal sense only, is the state of souls after death," but that from the allegorical point of view it is "man, according as by his merits or demerits in the exercise of his free will he is deserving of reward or punishment by justice." It follows then that the poem is a study of men and movements in Dante's world, seen from an ethical point of view and surveyed against the background of the eternal.

Yet the *Comedy* is a very personal poem, too; the protagonist is the poet himself, openly expressing his convictions, his hopes, and his doubts and ever mindful of his first love, Beatrice, who, whatever she may symbolize, remains also the beloved woman of his early youth.

The Divine Comedy is a magnificent historical document. Dante examines the political, cultural, social, and literary currents of his time, penetrates to their essence with remarkable acuteness, and fearlessly pronounces his judgment on them. The rise of nationalism, the growth and prestige of the city-states, the decadence of the great religious orders, and the new movements in poetry are all woven into the substance of the poem. The dramatic effect of the work is enhanced by its vivid portraits of historical personalities: the lives of St. Francis and St. Dominic are depicted in the *Paradiso*; the figures of warrior princes and politicians are brought to life by the presentation of such characters as Guido da Montefeltro in the *Inferno* and Sordello in the *Purgatorio*; and frequent allusions bring into sharp focus the images of such great leaders as Pope Boniface VIII and King Philip the Fair of France. The *Comedy* contains catalogs of monarchs, poets, philosophers, and prominent citizens of Dante's native city, Florence.

Philosophy. To pass judgment on a society, especially the society made up of one's contemporaries, requires a firm philosophical and religious frame of reference, and the *Comedy* is an expression of Dante's deepest convictions and aspirations for humanity. It is a splendid exposition of orthodox medieval dogma, presented clearly, logically, and sympathetically. Yet Dante's faith, though unshakable, is not rigid, even as his basic conservatism is not without illumination and sympathetic understanding of dissent. Although he believes that salvation is dependent on baptism, he puts Cato, a suicide and a pagan, in the *Purgatorio* and even makes him guardian of its seven realms. To some extent the *Comedy* is a persistent and almost desperately intense groping after justice. Dante does not hesitate to question, in Paradise itself, the justice of condemning to an eternity of punishment the truly virtuous who have had no opportunity to embrace the faith. In part this springs from Dante's persistent and intense sense of justice.

Classical Allusions. Because of Dante's reverence for the classical tradition, the pagan figures in the poem are almost as numerous as the Christian. In the *Inferno*, classical figures are woven into the texture of the narrative: Dido stands beside Francesca; Dionysius and Alexander share the bath of boiling blood with the contemporary tyrant Obizzo d'Este; and the Roman Gaius Scribonius Curio, who encouraged Caesar to destroy the republic, is placed in the same category as the medieval mischief-maker Bertran de Born.

In the other *cantiche*, where non-Christians (except Cato) are excluded, classical personages are used as terms of reference or sometimes as illustrative embellishments to the narrative. Classical figures are paired with Christians in the *exempla* of the *Purgatorio*, where their case histories are employed as spurs to virtue or checks on the various sins being purged. The *Paradiso* is also rich in classical allusions; in fact at its most crucial and most human moment, portraying the meeting of Dante and his ancestor Cacciaguida, the poet compares himself to Aeneas.

Dogma aside, Dante seems to see the family of mankind as one and indivisible. The poet's fusion of the West's classical and Judeo-Christian inheritances is no mere literary strategem. Rather it articulates a concept enormously important to the development of Western culture.

THOMAS G. BERGIN, *Author of "Dante"*

Bibliography

The standard text of *The Divine Comedy* was edited by Giuseppe Vandelli in the *Opere di Dante*, 2d ed. (Florence 1960), published by the Società Dantesca Italiana. English prose translations include that in the Temple Classics by John Carlyle, Thomas Okey, and Philip Wicksteed (London 1899–1900) and one by John D. Sinclair (London 1939–1946). English poetic translations include the terza rima renderings by Dorothy L. Sayers (London 1962) and by Geoffrey L. Bickersteth (Cambridge, Mass., 1965) and a blank verse version by Thomas G. Bergin (New York 1955).

Auerbach, Erich, *Dante, Poet of the Secular World*, tr. by Ralph Manheim (Chicago 1961).
Brandeis, Irma, *The Ladder of Vision* (New York 1961).
Fergusson, Francis, *Dante's Drama of the Mind* (Princeton 1953).
Gilbert, Alan H., *Dante and His Comedy* (New York 1963).
Singleton, Charles S., *Dante Studies 1: Commedia, Elements of Structure* (Cambridge, Mass., 1954).
Singleton, Charles S., *Dante Studies 2: Journey to Beatrice* (Cambridge, Mass., 1958).
Stambler, Bernard, *Dante's Other World* (New York 1957).
Vernon, William W., *Readings in the Inferno, Purgatory and Paradise*, 6 vols. (London and New York 1889–1900).

DIVINE OFFICE, a compilation of Psalms, readings from Scripture and the early Fathers and Doctors of the Church, hymns, and prayers. Whether recited privately or recited or sung in common, the office is the official public liturgical prayer of the Roman Catholic Church. ("Office" comes from the Latin *officium*, "duty" or service.") Orthodox and other Eastern churches also have a divine office, whose structure varies among the different rites. The value and meaning of the Office stem from the belief of the church that the one praying the Office, either when deputed by the church or in union with a priest, is united to Christ. The Office becomes the very prayer that Christ himself, united to His church, gives to the Father. The clergy and certain others are obligated by church law to recite the Office daily.

The prayers and readings of the office are arranged according to the days of the week, the feasts and seasons of the liturgical year (for example, Lent, Easter, Pentecost), and the feast days of the saints. Each day's prayer is divided into seven parts, or "hours," corresponding to different times of the day. *Matins* is properly said during the night, but it is permissible to say it at other times. *Lauds* is the morning prayer. (*Prime*, a second morning prayer, was eliminated by order of the Second Vatican Council in 1963.) The brief hours of *Terce, Sext,* and *None* are named for the third, sixth, and ninth hours of the day (9 A.M., 12 noon, 3 P.M.). *Vespers* is the evening prayer. *Compline,* the bedtime prayer, completes the day. When Prime was included, the division of seven hours was maintained by considering matins and lauds as one hour. When the Office is recited privately, the times of the various hours need not be strictly followed.

History. The roots of the Divine Office reach back into Old Testament times, to the services of the synagogue. These services were held daily, morning, noon, and evening. Early Christians, who centered their worship on Eucharistic celebrations, also took part in the synagogue services.

By the 2d century, Christians had developed their own noneucharistic services of prayers and readings, modeled on the synagogue ritual. By the 3d century a cycle of prayer was developed, including prayers at dawn, 9 A.M., 12 noon, 3 P.M., evening, and midnight. Ascetic influences finally added two more times for prayer: Prime in the early morning and Compline before retiring.

The Rule of St. Benedict (died 547) gives a detailed arrangement of the monastic Office, a plan eventually accepted by the secular clergy for use whether prayed in common or privately. By the 13th century, with the rise of the mendicant orders, the recitation of the Office in private rather than in choir became acceptable. The designation of the Divine Office as the Breviary also became common in this period.

Although the structure of the Office has remained essentially the same since the time of St. Benedict, it has undergone numerous reforms and changes. A major revision was carried out under Pope Pius V in 1568. This edition was made mandatory for all churches with the exception of those with an office that had been in use for at least 200 years.

Breviary revisions called for by Vatican Council II have pruned the readings of doubtful saints' lives and will eventually double the readings from classic religious literature of all ages. The Council also decreed that the psalter, the whole of which was recited in the course of one week, be spread out over a longer period of time. The Council granted bishops the right to give permission to recite the Office in the vernacular instead of the traditional Latin to those bound to the recitation of the Office. The permission has been widely granted on the grounds that prayer in the vernacular would be more meaningful.

HENRY FEHREN
Moorhead State College, Minn.

Further Reading: Jungmann, Josef A., *Public Worship* (Collegeville, Minn., 1957); Salmon, Pierre, *The Breviary Through the Centuries* (Collegeville, Minn., 1962); Sheppard, Lancelot C., *The Liturgical Books* (New York 1962).

DIVINE RIGHT OF KINGS, a political doctrine widely used by royalists in England and, to a lesser extent, in France and other European countries in the 17th century to counteract revolutionary teaching aimed at undermining the governments of existing rulers. The doctrine contained four principles of faith: (1) monarchy is a divinely ordained institution; (2) hereditary right cannot be abolished; (3) kings are accountable only to God; and (4) subjects are charged by God not to resist their monarch but passively to obey him, even if, in their view, he is wicked.

Sources of the Doctrine. In Christian Europe throughout the Middle Ages political writers generally agreed that government, of whatever kind, was divinely inspired and approved. In theory the pope had supreme authority in all spiritual matters, and the Holy Roman emperor had supreme authority in all secular matters—according to Christ's teaching that men should render unto Caesar the things that are Caesar's. But in practice the pope was very nearly supreme in both spheres. In 1300, Pope Boniface VIII, maintaining that Christendom had become a body with two heads, declared himself both pope and emperor. Nearly a century earlier the submission of King John of England to Pope Innocent III had also shown that in the last resort the spiritual head of Christendom was paramount.

As popes became quarrelsome and sometimes corrupt, however, such writers as Dante, Marsiglio of Padua, William of Occam, and John Wycliffe began to question the doctrine of the divine right of the papacy in secular affairs. Finally the realistic materialist arguments of Machiavelli and the repudiation of the papacy by Protestants in the 16th century put an end to papal claims of worldly paramountcy, and the doctrine of divinely approved absolutism was transferred, at any rate in Protestant kingdoms, to monarchs.

In England and Scotland apologists for the papacy were entirely unwilling to admit that certain monarchs were absolute. The apologists resented the fact that Protestant kings could punish Roman Catholic subjects for practicing the ancient faith. Jesuits began to preach that subjects had a right to overthrow wicked monarchs. Calvinists revived in a somewhat different form the view that the church was omnipotent. The Scottish preacher Andrew Melville, for example, went so far as to call King James VI of Scotland (later James I of England) "God's silly vassal." A number of writings appeared at the end of the 16th century by Catholics like Juan de Mariana and Robert Bellarmine and Calvinists like John Knox and Thomas Cartwright that sanctioned the rebellion of discontented subjects against evil rulers. The theory of the divine rights of kings was perfected to counter such dangerously subversive propaganda.

Claims of James I of England. The divine right theory was put forward in England by a number of authors, notably by Church of England clergy who were affronted by Jesuit propaganda directed against Queen Elizabeth I because she had rejected papal supremacy. The doctrine may also be found in such various sources as a play written by Thomas Heywood in 1600 entitled *Royal King and Loyal Subject* and in the writings of Robert Sibthorpe, Roger Manwaring, John Cowell, and Richard Montague. But divine right has always been peculiarly associated with James I. It has been cynically observed that because James himself was not absolutely certain who his father was (it was asserted that he was not the son of Lord Darnley but of Queen Mary's secretary, David Rizzio), he compensated by proving that he ruled through divine right.

The king, James claimed, is God's representative on earth and is responsible to God alone for his conduct. Kings are "the breathing images of God upon earth"; they are "not only God's Lieutenants upon earth and sit upon God's throne, but even by God Himself they are called Gods." They derive their power through heredity, and even if their kingdoms were originally acquired by conquest, that was no usurpation, for God Himself had ordained it. The king, James insisted, is above the law.

The idea that the king was above the law was completely novel, for at least until the Reformation there was general agreement that kings were subject to the divine law—to "natural law" or the moral law or traditional customs of the land.

Patriarchy. To support his claims, King James employed argument by analogy, a device widely used by royalist political thinkers everywhere at the beginning of the 17th century. "I am the Husband," James told Parliament in 1603, "and all the whole Isle is my lawfull wife: I am the Head and it is my Body: I am the Shepherd and it is my flock." In a speech to the same Parliament in 1610, he argued that just as a father may dispose freely of his inheritance to his children so may a king deal freely with his subjects.

Sir Robert Filmer, a comparatively obscure country Englishman, whose works were published posthumously by friends of King Charles II to boost his shoddy reign, wrote the classic patriarchal argument for divine right in a book called *Patriarcha or a Defence of the Natural Power of Kings Against the Unnatural Liberty of the People* (1680). Filmer's basic premise was that the Bible is literally true. The Bible, he argued, shows that God intended all human beings to be subordinate to Adam and to his hereditary successors. God told Cain of his brother Abel: "his desires shall be subject to thine and thou shalt rule over him." Isaac instructed Jacob, "Be lord over thy brethren and let the sons of thy mother bow before thee." Political obligation, according to Filmer, was based on Scriptural patriarchy: God had never intended people to elect their own rulers or limit their rulers' powers.

Filmer's patriarchal theories were employed in the latter half of the 17th century to reinforce the doctrine that absolute monarchy was a divinely ordained institution. Advocates of constitutional monarchy and of the right of subjects to rebel against unjust kings, who included Algernon Sidney and John Locke, had first to clear the way for their revolutionary views by refuting the devoted Filmer.

Too much reliance on the divine right of kings—whether according to the prescription of James I or Louis XIV's belief that he *was* the state—helped indirectly to carry their successors, Charles I and Louis XVI, to their executions.

MAURICE ASHLEY
Author of "Life in Stuart England"

Further Reading: Figgis, John Neville, *The Divine Right of Kings* (London 1922); Filmer, Sir Robert, *Patriarcha*, ed. by P. Laslett (London 1949).

DIVINE WORD, Society of the, a Roman Catholic missionary congregation of men. It was founded in 1875 by the Rev. Arnold Janssen in Steyl, Holland. Originally intended to be a society of secular priests who would labor in the missions, it became a religious congregation with public vows in 1884.

The society's primary work is direct missionary activity, but it also maintains secondary schools and universities, and staffs seminaries, particularly those devoted to the training of native clergy. The society also has a particular interest in research in the missionary-related sciences of ethnology and cultural anthropology. Its publishing facility, Divine Word Publications, publishes and disseminates an extensive amount of Catholic literature.

The society is active in 36 countries on all continents. In the United States its first foundation, in 1899, was in Techny, Ill., which is still the headquarters for its operations in the country. In the four provinces of the congregation in the United States there is particular emphasis on involvement in inner city parishes and on recruitment and preparation of black youth for the ministry to black communities at home and abroad. Worldwide membership exceeds 5,000, including over 3,000 priests and 1,300 lay brothers.

JOSEPH M. CONNORS, S. V. D.
St. Mary's Mission Seminary, Techny, Ill.

DIVING is an athletic activity in which the participant leaps from a level above the water, executes maneuvers in the air, and descends into the water either head- or feet-first. As a competitive sport, diving requires coordinated movements, expertly timed and controlled.

Diving developed in the latter part of the 19th century, when Swedish and German gymnasts performed their acrobatic and tumbling routines in swimming areas. Competitions were first conducted in England about 1880, as a result of arguments among various swimming clubs that claimed to have the best divers. Diving has been an Olympic sport for men since 1904 and for women since 1912. Competitive diving on an international level has been governed by the Fédération Internationale de Natation Amateur (FINA) since the early competitions.

In the United States the first diving meet was held at the University of Pennsylvania in Philadelphia in 1907. Ernest Brandsten, a member of the 1908 Swedish Olympic diving team, who became coach at Stanford University in 1912, is credited with pioneering the sport in the United States. Governing organizations for the sport are the National Collegiate Athletic Association, which controls high school and college meets, and the Amateur Athletic Union, which governs outdoor and indoor contests for private and public clubs and for the YMCA, as well as any amateur athlete.

Equipment. Dives are executed from a flexible board or a fixed platform. For springboard diving an aluminum board 16 feet long and about 19½ inches wide is used in all major contests. It weights approximately 135 pounds, and its thickness tapers from about 2 inches at one end to under 1 inch at the diving end. The light weight and taper produce a snappy, springing action that helps the diver gain height. A nonskid material covers the surface of the board to prevent the diver from slipping.

The board is mounted on a steel or concrete standard that sets the height at 1 or 3 meters (about 3 to 10 feet) above water level. The fulcrum can be adjusted up to 2 feet to give the board more or less flexibility, depending on the individual diver's preference. The front edge of the board should overhang the edge of the pool by at least 6 feet. The 1-meter and 3-meter boards should be at least 10 feet from the sides of the pool. Water depth for springboard diving should be at least 12 feet.

Diving towers, most often constructed of cement wih reinforced steel, have platforms at levels of from 1 to 10 meters (about 3 to 33 feet) for platform diving. The lower levels are used for practice takeoffs, for lead-up dives, or for gradually working to the 10-meter level for the more difficult dives.

Platforms are generally no less than 20 feet long and 7 to 10 feet wide and are covered with a nonskid matting. The back and sides are surrounded by hand railings.

BASIC DIVING TECHNIQUES

Basic movements for a successful dive from the springboard or the tower include the starting position, the approach, the walk, the hurdle, if using the forward approach, the takeoff, the execution through the air, and the entry into the water.

Starting Position. Before attempting any dive, one must take a correct posture on the board or

DIVING requires precise timing and muscular control to blend fast actions into a graceful flowing movement.

platform. The diver stands with feet together and legs straight, abdomen drawn in, arms at his sides, and head erect, and he keeps his eyes on the far end of the board.

Approach and Takeoff. The approach and takeoff vary with the different dives. For a forward dive from the springboard, the approach includes a walk and hurdle (jump). The walk to the end of the board usually involves either three or four steps; in the three-step approach, the first step is taken on the foot from which the diver will hurdle. During the walk the diver keeps his arms near his sides, so that they may be placed in proper position for the hurdle.

The hurdle, the most important movement in the forward approach, begins as the last step is taken. The free leg is lifted as it comes forward and is bent so that the horizontal upper part of the leg forms a right angle with the lower part. Simultaneously, the diver's arms swing forward and upward, spreading slightly as they reach a position above his head, and he pushes hard off the other leg from the board, into the air. As the diver reaches the peak of the jump, he brings his two legs together—the bent one extends downward while the push-off leg moves forward to join it—and his toes reach for the end of the board. During this movement, the arms begin to circle slightly backward and downward. As the diver drops onto the end of the board from the hurdle, with arms first circling close to his sides and then forward and upward until they extend overhead, his legs push down on the board and he is forced into the air.

For a back dive from the springboard, the diver first walks to the end of the board and turns around. He lifts his arms to a position at shoulder level and shoulder width apart in front of his body. Then he places one foot at a time at the end of the board, heels extending beyond the end. When in complete balance, he drops his arms to the sides. In the takeoff he lifts his arms forward and laterally overhead to begin a circular swing backward and downward past his sides and upward in front of his body to a position overhead. His legs bend during the arm swing. As the arms lift upward, the legs and ankles extend, and the diver jumps up and away from the board.

Approaches and takeoffs for tower dives should be attempted under experienced supervision. For a forward dive the diver may use a standing takeoff from the end of the platform, a running approach with either a one- or two-foot takeoff, or a running skip approach with a one-foot takeoff. In back dives, the takeoff is quite similar to that used from the springboard.

In armstand dives from the tower, the diver may place his hands on the platform near the edge or may curl his fingers over the edge. He may assume the stand from a one-leg kick up, or a press up either in tuck or pike position. He must hold the stand for a few seconds, with legs straight and together, feet and toes extended.

Execution. Movements in executing the dive should be graceful, deliberate, and well defined. They may be performed in one or a combination of four positions: layout, tuck, pike, and free. When the body remains in a straight position, with the legs extended, the diver is in a *layout position*. In the *pike position*, his body is bent at the waist and his legs are straight; the position of the arms is optional. He is in *tuck position* when he has his legs drawn tightly to his chest, heels close to the buttocks, and hands clasping his shins to form a tight "ball." The *free position* occurs during a twisting somersault dive, where the body changes position two or three times during the execution of the dive.

Entry. Divers enter the water head first or feet first, depending on the dive. With the former, the diver enters slightly short of vertical, with the body straight, arms extended overhead, and hands clasped together. In the latter, the arms are at the sides, and the head is held erect. In either entry the line of flight (the path described by the center of body weight from the takeoff to the entry) should be projected directly down to the bottom of the pool so that every part of the body will pass through the same opening in the surface of the water.

TYPES OF DIVES

The more than 60 different springboard dives are grouped into five categories. The 50-odd tower dives fall into six categories, the additional classification being essential for armstand dives. A few elementary dives in the different groups are cited below, and one from each group is illustrated on pages 203 and 204. The more advanced dives are combinations of either the forward or backward movements with a somersault or a twist in layout, pike, tuck, or free positions. Basic tower dives are usually first attempted on the graduated platforms.

Group I: The Forward Dives. All dives executed with the diver facing the water and the body rotating toward a position in front when leaving the board or platform constitute those in this classification. The basic springboard dive is the *forward dive, layout, pike,* or *tuck,* commonly called the *swan*. Other elementary dives include the *forward somersault, tuck* and *forward somersault, pike*. The basic dive from the tower is the *running* or *standing front dive, pike* or *layout*.

Group II: The Backward Dives. All dives in this category are performed with the diver taking off with his back to the water and rotating backwards. The basic dive in this group is the *back dive, layout, pike,* or *tuck*. Another elementary dive is the *back somersault, tuck*. From the tower, a basic dive is the *back somersault, layout*.

Group III: The Reverse Dives. All dives in this group (formerly, the *gainer* group) start with a forward takeoff. Instead of progressing forward to the water, however, the diver rotates backward (reverses his direction as he leaves the board) and performs the dive in the same direction as those in the backward group. Basic dives include the *reverse dive, layout, pike,* or *tuck* and the *reverse somersault*.

Group IV: The Inward Dives. Dives in this classification (formerly, the *cutaways*) begin with a back takeoff. The body rotates in a direction toward the board or platform—just opposite to that in the backward dive. A basic springboard and tower dive is the *inward dive, layout* or *pike*.

Group V: The Twisting Dives. Any dive in which the body spirals laterally (rotates around its long axis) belongs in this group. It is the largest of all groups because a twist may be added to any dive in any direction. In a half twist a 180-degree turn is made so that the diver is facing in the opposite direction from which he starts. A full twist is a complete circle (360 degrees) so that the diver faces in the same way. An elementary dive from this group is the *forward dive with a half twist, layout*.

Group VI: The Armstand Dives. Dives in this group are done only from the tower, with an armstand approach and takeoff. An elementary dive is the armstand, *cut through, tuck*.

COMPETITIVE DIVING

There are two forms of diving contests: dual and championship meets. Dual meets involve two colleges, clubs, or schools, with no more than two divers representing each group. The winner is the competitor with the greatest number of points. In championships, three or more teams are represented (in National AAU meets representation is by individuals), and the winner is determined through an elimination process. Springboard contests usually include a preliminary, semifinal, and final session; tower contests, a preliminary and final round.

Dives used in competition are classified as compulsory (a dive that must be done under certain circumstances) and optional (a dive the competitor chooses, but not a repetition of a required dive). The compulsory dives are the basic dives in the five groups—forward, back, reverse, inward, and forward dive with a half twist—performed straight, piked, or tuck. These indicate a competitor's grace and control of basic

FRONT APPROACH

Diver first assumes a stance with good posture. He takes three walking steps and then lifts one leg, knee bent, to form a right angle, while he swings his arms forward and upward. He extends his bent knee as the other leg moves forward to meet it. His arms circle back, forward, and up as he lands on the end of the board before takeoff.

SWAN DIVE

Diver leaves the board with arms and legs fully extended, eyes fixed on a point at the far end of the pool. As his body rises, he lowers his arms at right angles to his body. On the descent his eyes spot the water 3 to 5 feet from the end of the board. He enters at this spot, arms overhead and head and body nearly vertical.

BACK DIVE, TUCK

As diver leaves the board, he drives his legs to his chest and bends his body slightly forward, arms fully extended. At the peak of the dive his hands grasp his knees above his shins. On the descent his hands release the knees and he extends his arms laterally and straightens his body. He enters with arms stretched overhead.

REVERSE DIVE, PIKE

Leaving the board with legs and arms extended, diver contracts his stomach and thigh muscles to lift legs quickly. At the peak of the dive he reaches slightly forward to touch his hands to his toes. On descending the body falls away from the legs, the arms move laterally overhead, and the head tilts back to fix the eyes on the entry spot.

INWARD DIVE, PIKE

Diver leaves the board with legs extended and arms swinging forward and upward. He lifts up with his hips and bends at the waist as he moves his arms and shoulders toward his legs. At the peak of the dive he touches his toes and fixes his eyes on the water. As his arms extend to the water he pushes his legs upward and enters vertical.

FORWARD ½ TWIST, LAYOUT
On takeoff diver lowers one shoulder and moves her arms laterally to turn the body on its side. At the peak, the arms are perpendicular to the water. They reach overhead to complete the half twist. Entry is vertical.

ARMSTAND, CUT THROUGH, TUCK
Diver holds an armstand several seconds before he leans away from tower. As he pushes off from platform he draws his legs to his chest and grasps his shins. From tuck position he extends his legs toward the water and lifts his arms to swan position. At the last instant he drops arms laterally to his sides and enters the water feet first.

diving skills. The optional dives, selected in national meets to include at least one dive from each of the five groups, are acrobatic feats involving intricate movements.

The number of dives a competitor must perform depends on the type of contest. In competitions for boys or girls 10 years old or younger, four compulsory and two optional dives are prescribed. The number of dives increases as the diver competes in the older brackets. In high school and college meets, a diver performs one required and five optionals. On the day of the meet the referee draws the required dive from the list of basic dives in the five groups.

In men's and women's championship meets (springboard and platform) all divers first execute a stipulated number of compulsory and optional dives in a preliminary session. The 16 divers with the highest total scores advance to a semifinal round, where further competition reduces the number to 12. In the finals the 12 contestants execute the remainder of the prescribed dives, and their rank in the contest is based on the total score they have received in all three rounds. In springboard competition each entrant normally performs 5 required and 6 optional dives. In platform diving, men's contests require 6 voluntary dives from the six diving groups with a total limit on the degree of difficulty, and another 6 dives with no limit on the total degree of difficulty; women's contests include 4 required (front, back, reverse, and inward) and 5 optional dives from different groups.

All dives are rated numerically, according to the relative difficulty of the dive. The rating, from 1.0 for the easiest dive (front dive, tuck) to 3.0 for the most difficult dive (forward 3½ somersault, pike) is called the *degree of difficulty*. The compulsory dives all have reasonably low degrees of difficulty. (Tables listing all recognized dives with their difficulty ratings are published annually by the national governing organizations.)

Judges evaluate a dive and award points in whole or half numbers ranging from 0 (completely failed) to 10 (perfect). Three judges are generally used in dual meets, five in championships, and seven in international diving contests. With five or more judges, the high and low scores are canceled; only the three middle scores are added. The total score for a particular dive is calculated by multiplying the degree of difficulty of the dive by the total of the three awards given by the judges.

Before a contest each diver enters on a form the names of the dives he plans to execute, the diving position in which he will perform each dive, and the degree of difficulty of each dive. On the same form are spaces for the points awarded by the judges, the total of these points, and the score for the dive when multiplied by its degree of difficulty. During the contest these forms are handled by an announcer who calls each diver by name and states the dive and its difficulty rating. He then passes the form to a clerk who fills in the awards and computes the scores as they are made.

HOBIE BILLINGSLEY, *Indiana University*

Further Reading: Armbruster, David A., Allen, Robert H., and Billingsley, Hobert Sherwood, *Swimming and Diving*, 5th ed. (St. Louis, Mo., 1968); Billingsley, Hobie, *Diving Illustrated* (New York 1965); Fairbanks, Anne Ross, *Teaching Springboard Diving* (Englewood Cliffs, N. J., 1963); Moriarty, Phil, *Springboard Diving* (New York 1959).

DIVING, Professional. Professional divers, using a variety of equipment, are employed in survey, construction, service and maintenance, chiefly of pipelines, drilling rigs and waterfront civil works, as well as of bridge moorings, dams, and other submerged or partly submerged structures. Divers also inspect or repair the undersides of ships, salvage sunken ships or other objects, and demolish underwater hazards. Military specialist divers are trained in underwater reconnaissance and hydrographic survey of port areas and landing beaches, the clearance of underwater obstacles and coastal defenses by demolition, clandestine underwater sabotage of enemy shipping, and the clearance of mines. Sports diving is described separately in the article UNDERWATER SWIMMING.

Professional diving may be classified as *shallow diving* or *deep diving*, although the two types overlap in several areas. There is no specific depth at which shallow diving stops and deep diving begins, but it is usually at 200 to 300 feet (60–90 meters). In this range of depth the diving supervisor considers changing from air as a breathing medium to a helium-oxygen or other mixture. Pure oxygen, mixed gas, or air may be used for shallow diving, while all deep diving is done using a mixed gas.

SHALLOW DIVING

Hard-Hat Outfit. The mention of diving in general conjures up an image of a so-called deep-sea diver clad in a canvas suit and a metal helmet and lead-soled boots, laden with a weighted belt, and trailing the air hose and lifeline that are his tenuous link to the surface. This is the classical "hard-hat" air diving outfit, or diving rig, for shallow diving. It has been in use for over a hundred years and is still used to a great extent, especially where the underwater work to be performed is in water of little or no visibility or in a swift current or other hazardous situation.

The typical tinned-copper helmet has several portholes of thick glass, weighs about 60 pounds (15 kg), and is connected through an interrupted screw at the neck ring to a breastplate, also of tinned copper. Fiber-glass hard-hat helmets with improved communication systems in them patterned after the astronauts' space helmets are also used. A watertight seal is made between the breastplate and rubber gasketing at the neck of a canvas dress. Compressed air from the surface is delivered to the diver through a hose. The diver regulates the flow of air into his helmet with a valve at his waist. Air is exhausted from the helmet to the surrounding sea through another valve that the diver can adjust. By choking down on the exhaust valve, the diver can increase the volume of air in his suit to make himself more buoyant. Though he cannot really swim, the diver can make himself light to facilitate movement, such as searching, and make himself heavy to facilitate the handling of tools at his work site.

While considered the safest of diving systems, the hard-hat rig is nonetheless subject to hazards. One of the chief hazards is called a *blow-up*. If the diver makes himself too light, or the exhaust valve becomes blocked, he can become so ballooned that his arms are outstretched. Unable to regulate either the supply valve or exhaust valve, he quickly rises to the surface. The rapid ascent can cost him his life. The diver wears heavy shoes and a weighted belt and laces the pants legs of the dress to restrict any tendency to balloon and especially to keep him from rising upside down.

Lightweight Outfits. Where diving conditions are such that the safety afforded by the hard-hat rig is not needed, the diver may choose one of the lightweight outfits that afford him greater mobility. These outfits can be supplied with a breathing gas through a hose from the surface or from gas bottles worn by the diver. The latter are called "self-contained underwater breathing apparatus," or *scuba*.

In cold or polluted water the diver may wear a constant-volume suit, which is a rubberized canvas dress similar to that worn with the hard-hat rig but considerably lighter and without as heavy shoes or weights. It has rubber flapper-type exhaust valves and is not likely to experience blow-up. Alternately, the diver may wear either of two types of tight-fitting, two-piece rubber suits with optional bootees, gloves, and head hood if needed. One is a *dry suit*, which keeps out water altogether, is difficult to don, and must fit well to be comfortable. The other is a *wet suit*, which is made of relatively thick sponge rubber and is fitted with zippers in the jacket and each lower leg and is easy to don. The entrapped layer of water against the diver's skin insulates against the cold. Sometimes only the jacket is worn if the water temperature is not too cold. Divers often prefer to wear no dress at all except for ordinary trunks or a suit of woolen diver's underwear. Swim fins can be worn with any of the lightweight dresses, but often sneakers, canvas coral shoes, or rubber galoshes are preferred if the task at hand involves walking on the bottom or entering a structure.

Jack Brown Rig. One of the commonest lightweight rigs consists of a simple triangular face mask with a simple air-control valve on its side. The mask is strapped over the diver's head and is supplied with air from the surface. This apparatus is called a Jack Brown rig. It, like the hard-hat rig, uses a free-flow air circuit—that is, air from the surface-supplied hose flows into the mask at all times and exhausts through a flapper valve. While being the safest type breathing circuit, it is rather wasteful of air.

Hookah Rig. Another type of lightweight diving apparatus is one that replaces the diver's air-control valve with a demand regulator, or a balanced valve device, that automatically opens as soon as the diver sucks or inhales, or "demands," air. The surface-supplied air flows until the diver ceases to inhale, and then the valve automatically shuts off. There is no bubbling or exhaust of air from the apparatus until the diver exhales. The demand valve is mounted on the diver's mask or strapped between his shoulder blades, in which case a separate face mask is worn. A light air hose brings the air from the surface to the valve. This type apparatus is known as a surface-supplied hookah rig.

Closed-Circuit Scuba. Clandestine military missions demand a breathing apparatus that leaves no telltale trail of bubbles. Missions involving the disarming of acoustic mines and bombs, as well as those involving stealth, require a breathing apparatus that also is free of the noise generated by the bubbling exhaust. One such rig is the closed-circuit oxygen scuba, which contains an inhalation and an exhalation bag. Carbon dioxide is removed from the exhaled air. Oxygen is carried in relatively small bottles on the diver's torso; it is metered into the inhalation bag. The consumption of oxygen is quite low.

Because the human body is quite susceptible to oxygen poisoning, closed-circuit oxygen scuba is very dangerous. Not all people can breath pure oxygen, even at surface pressure. Generally speaking, pure oxygen cannot be used as a breathing medium at pressures above 2 atmospheres (33 feet, or 10 meters) of seawater. Thus, this kind of scuba is depth-limited to about 33 feet. For this reason, mixed-gas scuba diving equipment, designed for minimum noise and minimum bubble trail, is also used. In mixed-gas scuba the breathing gas is a mixture of oxygen and an inert gas, such as helium or nitrogen.

Constant-Mass-Flow, Mixed-Gas Scuba. A compromise type of scuba that employs mixed gas is in wide use by military divers in all the major navies of the world as well as by some commercial divers. Neither a closed-circuit nor an open-circuit scuba, this apparatus is best described as a constant-mass-flow, mixed-gas scuba —generally referred to merely as a mixed-gas scuba. This apparatus is very much like the closed-circuit oxygen scuba described earlier, except that it is not as efficient in its use of oxygen as is the closed-circuit apparatus, and it leaves a bubble trail. However, the amount of gas exhausted is quite small and can be diffused so that bubble size and noise are minimal. Furthermore, the exhaust valve is designed so that the diver can gag it closed for short periods of time.

Although mixed gas theoretically can be used to almost any depth divers can attain, in practice mixed-gas scuba is generally considered to be limited to maximum depths of between 200 and 300 feet (60–90 meters).

DEEP DIVING

Helium Hard-Hat Rig. The original deep-diving rig, and the one still used extensively both by military and commercial divers, is known as the helium hard-hat rig. It is similar to the hard-hat rig except that oxygen-helium mixtures are used in place of air. The gas-flow circuitry in the helmet is considerably modified, and rather than being a free-flow system, it is best described as a semiclosed recirculating system. A large absorbent canister is mounted behind the helmet to absorb carbon dioxide. Since the volume of this canister adds considerable buoyancy to the overall rig, the diver wears extra-heavy shoes and a weighted belt.

One of the major problems associated with the helium-rich atmosphere is that of heat loss. Helium has a significantly higher coefficient of heat transfer than air. Consequently, the diver is not so well insulated, and he loses body heat at a more rapid rate. This is aggravated by the fact that deep diving is almost always done in very cold water. Diver heating systems, therefore, are essential in all deep diving. The preferred heating method is to pump hot water to the diver. The hot water is circulated through tubes in the wet suit or through special tubular underwear worn under a diver's canvas dress.

Deep Diving Systems. With the increase in offshore oil and gas drilling, and with offshore mining being contemplated, a more efficient system of diving deep has been developed. This system, called either deep dive system (DDS) or advanced dive system (ADS), incorporates a pressurized personnel transfer capsule (PTC), like an elevator, in which the divers ascend and descend rapidly to working depths. The divers, employing mixed-gas hookah breathing apparatus and wearing lightweight suits, emerge from the PTC and are brought up to the surface for decompression. Such capsules are also used to transport divers to the experimental habitats such as SEALAB and TEKTITE.

Deep dive systems exist that can support diving to depths as great as 1,000 feet (300 meters). Dives to this depth, however, are not common and are quite hazardous. Ventures into extreme depths beyond 1,000 feet are made in special capsules and submarinelike submersible vehicles. Such diving is better classified as a submarine operation and is described in the article *Deep Sea Exploration*.

SATURATION DIVING

There has been increased interest in the natural resources of the continental shelf—the flat, shallow portion of the ocean bottom adjacent to the continents, where the depth does not exceed about 1,000 feet. In order to exploit these resources more fully, it will be necessary for divers to spend long periods of time working on the bottom. Three experimental projects, the American SEALAB and TEKTITE, and the French CONSHELF, have demonstrated that divers, provided with habitats on the ocean floor and making use of special diving equipment, can live underwater for weeks and even months, diving outside their habitat in order to perform useful work. These divers are called *aquanauts,* and they practice a third diving technique called *saturation diving.*

In saturation diving, the body is under pressure so long that the body tissues absorb their full capacity of inert gas; that is, they become saturated. Once this has happened, at shallow or deep depths, the amount of decompression needed by the man in order to return to the surface does not change. In general terms, a saturated diver requires 24 hours of decompression for every 100 feet (30 meters) of depth at which he was saturated. An interesting aspect of saturation diving is that divers living in a habitat can make excursion dives to greater depths, more or less as if they were making a dive from the surface. On the other hand, saturated divers are not able to make excursions upward toward the surface for more than 33 feet (10 meters).

The breathing gas mixtures employed both inside and outside the habitat and the rigs used for diving are generally the same as would be employed for shallow or deep diving, depending on the depth of saturation. Most divers employ either a hookah-type mixed-gas rig or a true scuba rig, and a safety tether line, for it would be fatal if a saturated diver became lost outside the habitat, since he could not surface.

DIVING PROCEDURES AND HAZARDS

Physical Hazards. The profession of diving is filled with physical dangers: strong underwater currents, outcrops of rock or debris, hostile marine life, the possibility of accidents with tools, and the possible malfunctioning of life-support equipment. For this reason, stringent safety procedures are observed, and safety devices are provided. The nonreturn valve in the hard-hat rig and a similar check valve in all surface-supplied free-flow rigs are safety devices. All scuba rigs contain a reserve valve on at least one gas bottle. The reserve valve is closed during the beginning of a dive and must be opened manually if the diver finds he has exhausted his normal supply of breathing gas. Some scuba rigs also carry a small "come-home" bottle of gas; others carry special sensors to warn of oxygen depletion and carbon dioxide buildup in the breathing bags.

Oxygen Toxicity and Nitrogen Narcosis. Most men can breathe pure oxygen under pressures of less than 2 atmospheres. However, oxygen under higher pressure is toxic, causing convulsions and unconsciousness. Since oxygen composes about one fifth of the air by volume, it exerts about one fifth of the total air pressure. Thus the partial pressure of the oxygen in ordinary air surpasses 1 atmosphere at a total pressure of 5 atmospheres (at seawater depth of about 132 feet, or 40 meters). It is deemed to approach the danger point at 7 atmospheres. The usual practice is to reduce the percentage of oxygen in any diving mixture to a level where the partial pressure exerted by oxygen does not exceed 1 atmosphere.

At high pressures, nitrogen is absorbed into the bloodstream. At pressures of about 7 atmospheres, the nitrogen in solution in the blood begins to affect judgment in the way that nitrous oxide, or "laughing gas," does. There have been many cases of divers, affected by nitrogen narcosis, also called "rapture of the deep," who dived past safe depths to their deaths.

To avoid problems of oxygen toxicity and nitrogen narcosis, most dives deeper than 200 feet (60 meters), and all dives deeper than 300 feet (90 meters) employ a special breathing mixture consisting of a lowered percentage of oxygen and an inert gas, usually helium.

A curious side effect of using the high percentage helium gas mixtures for breathing is the "Donald Duck" effect. Because helium is significantly less dense than nitrogen, or air itself, the vocal chords vibrate much faster in it, resulting in a very high squeaky tone. This effect makes voice communication very difficult, and special electronic "voice unscramblers" are necessary in the diver's telephone circuit to make the diver's messages intelligible.

Decompression Sickness, or the Bends. The most serious physiological aspect in diving to depths at which the pressure exceeds 2 atmospheres is the possibility of decompression sickness, or the bends. As a diver descends, the inert gas (helium or nitrogen) of the compressed breathing mixture begins to be absorbed into his bloodstream and from there into the fatty tissues. If a significant amount of the gas is absorbed by the fatty tissues, the danger arises that as the diver ascends the gas will be released into the bloodstream in the form of bubbles, resulting in the bends (see BENDS). Decompression procedures are used to prevent the bends. The time that a diver may remain at a given depth without undergoing decompression procedures on his ascent varies with depth. For example, a diver may remain at 100 feet (30 meters) for 25 minutes and not require subsequent decompression procedures, but at 190 feet (58 meters) a dive of more than 5 minutes would require decompression procedures.

PROFESSIONAL DIVER in the traditional hard-hat outfit gathers sponges from the ocean floor with a rake.

SCUBA GEAR is used by divers shown tying a rope to an anchor so that it may be hauled to the surface.

Decompression consists simply of allowing time for the absorbed gas bubbles to come out of solution gradually enough so that they can be transferred through the lungs and exhaled. The diver stops at specified depths—called stages, or stops—in his ascent for a prescribed period of time before rising again.

If a diver develops bends after he has reached the surface, he must be placed into a recompression chamber and treated. Treatment consists of taking the diver back "down" until the symptoms disappear. He then is slowly decompressed, remaining inside the chamber and under medical observation. The U.S. Navy requires the presence of a decompression chamber for all dives exceeding 170 feet (52 meters), while many commercial firms have chambers for dives that exceed a depth of 100 feet (30 meters).

HISTORY

Early skin divers performed military tasks for the Greeks and the Alexandrians. Roman sources describe the first surface-supported diving outfits—leather helmets, with air hoses whose open ends floated in bladders at the surface. The next real advance in diving apparatus was not made until the early 18th century, when John Lethbridge of England invented a barrellike outfit with sleeves and an observation port. The outfit was only practicable at depths of 10 feet (3 meters) or less, but it made its inventor a fortune.

The air hard-hat outfit was invented in England in 1819 by the German inventor Augustus Siebe. This equipment was supplied with compressed air from a pump. The suit was open at the bottom, but the air pressure prevented water from rising into the outfit. The difficulty with the first outfit was that the diver could not bend over without the risk of drowning. Consequently, Siebe in 1830 invented the closed diving dress outfit that is still in use and is known today as the standard hard-hat.

Early divers were limited to less than 40 feet (12 meters) because of the high incidence of bends at greater depths. Studies of the bends were made by physiologists Paul Bert of France in about 1880 and John Scott Haldane of England in about 1910, and the technique of stage decompression was evolved. The hazards of diving with an air mixture continued to limit divers to 200 to 300 feet (60-90 meters) until studies by the U. S. Navy in the 1930's led to the use of a helium and oxygen mixture. Dives surpassing 1,000 feet (300 meters) have been made with this mixture.

Several different types of scuba equipment were invented in the late 19th and early 20th century. It was not until the advent of urgent military need in World War II that truly operational scuba was developed.

W. F. SEARLE, JR., *Captain, USN*
Supervisor of Salvage, U. S. Navy

Bibliography
Borghese, J. Valerio, *Sea Devils* (London 1952).
Burke, Edmund, *Diver's World: An Introduction* (New York 1966).
Cousteau, Jacques-Yves, *World Without Sun*, ed. by James Dugan (New York 1965).
Davis, Robert H., *Deep Diving and Submarine Operations* (London 1951).
U. S. Navy, *U. S. Navy Diving Manual* (3 parts), Navships 250–538 (Washington 1966).
U. S. Navy, *U. S. Navy Submarine Medicine Practice*, Navmed P-5054 (Washington 1956).

Diving beetle sucking the fluid from a captured tadpole.

DIVING BEETLE, any of a family of aquatic beetles found throughout the world. There are about 2,500 different species of diving beetles, and they make up the family Dytiscidae. They are usually shiny brownish black, sometimes marked with dull yellow, and their oval, flattened bodies range in length from about ½ inch to 1½ inches (12–38 mm).

Diving beetles live in pools, where they float with their heads hanging down and the tips of their abdomens at the water's surface. Mating and egglaying occur during the warm months; the eggs are deposited on the surface of floating vegetation. Both the larvae and adults are predatory, and the larvae are so voracious that they are sometimes a pest in fish hatcheries. Some species, when attacked, emit an irritating substance from special glands located on the front of the body.

R. H. ARNETT, JR., *Purdue University*

DIVINING ROD, an instrument used for finding subterranean water or minerals. It was originally used in the 15th century in the Harz Mountains of Germany for finding metals. In more recent times its main use has been in finding water. The rod consists of a forked stick, usually of hazel or willow, although a metal rod is sometimes used. It is held in the hands and twists downward when the holder is over water. The skill itself, known as dowsing, water witching, or rhabdomancy, is usually claimed by its practitioners to be a mystical power, although some claim unconscious stimulation from the presence of underlying water and "electricity."

Belief in the effectiveness of the divining rod is widespread, especially in areas where water is scarce and the geological rock structure is complex. There are an estimated 25,000 dowsers practicing in the United States. Studies indicate that although folk belief accepts the skill of dowsers, their successes in finding water are no more frequent than those gained by other methods. See also DIVINATION; DOWSING; MAGIC.

JOHN MIDDLETON, *New York University*
Further Reading: Hyman, Ray, and Vogt, E. Z., *Water Witching U. S. A.* (Chicago 1959).

DIVISION. See ARITHMETIC—*Fundamental Operations.*

DIVISION, Military, in modern field armies, the smallest unit capable of independent operations on the battlefield—about 15,000 men in balanced tactical and logistical forces. Several divisions are grouped under the command of a corps, which is subordinate to the field army.

In naval operations a division is a group of ships, usually four, in a fleet or task force; it is also a personnel administrative unit. In air force usage a division is a tactical command comparable to an army corps headquarters; the unit resembling the army division is the wing.

The infantry division (called the rifle division in the Soviet Army) has infantrymen as the basic fighting force, augmented and supported by tanks, artillery, engineers, signal and medical services, and others. The armored or mechanized division has tanks as the principal force, with additional infantry. The airborne division, with lighter weapons and less support, is transportable by air for parachute drops. The airmobile division, first used by the U. S. Army in Vietnam, has armed helicopters to deploy troops and to give them immediate and direct fire support. Besides their own elements, all divisions have attached units, such as truck companies, to supplement their capabilities.

The division came into being in 1794 when Lazare Carnot organized the military forces of the French Revolution into permanent divisions. By 1900 all leading armies could be measured in divisions. In World War I, European divisions had about 15,000 men while the U. S. "square" division had almost twice as many.

During World War II there were infantry, armored, modified armored, airborne, and mountain divisions, and in the Soviet Army, there were artillery divisions. The U. S. division was triangular: three infantry regiments of three battalions each, or three armored combat commands, or one glider and two infantry regiments (in the airborne division).

The United States formed the pentomic division of five battle groups in the 1950's. In 1963–1964 the U. S. Army converted to ROAD (Reorganization Objective Army Division), using a variable mix of elements for greater flexibility.

MARTIN BLUMENSON
Author of "Kasserine Pass"

DIVISION OF LABOR, in economics, is specialization to increase output of goods and services. Specialization has been carried in modern industry to much higher levels than in past centuries. There is, in the first place, a division of labor *among individuals.* Hundreds of distinct occupations may be observed in industry, government bureaus, and educational institutions, where any individual worker may perform only a very simple, special task. There is also a division of labor *among industries.* A steel lawn mower is the product of the iron ore miner, the railway worker, the seaman, the steelworker, and finally the processor who transmutes the raw steel into a finished and usable device. There is even a division of labor *among machines.* The development of single-purpose or limited-purpose machines for manufacture is an aspect of division of labor.

Finally, there is a *geographic division of labor.* Industries are located in certain geographical areas, for example, to reduce the cost of transporting raw materials or finished products. Thus, steel mills were initially placed near coal supplies.

Advantages and Limitations. Although others had observed that specialization leads to increasing output, Adam Smith in his *Wealth of Nations* (1776) was the first to enumerate and underline effectively the reasons for the gain in productivity that followed from this system of organizing work. In his view, concentration upon a single task increased proficiency and dexterity. Elimination of the need to shift from one task to another saved time. The worker's mastery of his single task led him to devise methods for saving labor. Smith saw specialization as a great boon.

Normally, division of labor leads to greater output and provision of goods and services, making possible an increase in the standard of living of large masses of people. Many people, on the other hand, have deplored the fact that concentration on minute tasks often carries with it a loss of craftsmanship and of joy in performing work. Against this valid criticism must be placed the great material benefits that have followed—the ability of ordinary people to have more comforts and conveniences—and, ultimately, to enjoy many nonmaterial benefits that were available in less productive societies to only the wealthy few.

Adam Smith suggested the existence of a point at which diminishing returns may set in when he made the observation that division of labor is limited by the size of the market. Experience has shown that unless a given number of units can be sold, it is often more profitable to use simple methods rather than the high-cost specialized machinery that may be technically available. One reason for this is the "indivisibility" of some types of productive equipment; that is, some equipment must be of a certain minimum size or complexity to perform effectively, and when operated at an efficient level, it may produce more goods than can be sold.

Scale of Industry. The division of labor is closely related to what is called the scale of industry. Production on a large scale makes possible the use of specialized machinery and thereby increases output. In many instances a large plant may be more efficient than a small plant because of the economies deriving from specialization. As an industry grows in size, it may come to utilize to advantage the technical knowledge previously available but not theretofore usable because of the limited market for the product or service. Increase in the scale of operations of the industry may also make possible economies that derive from the development of specialized services, such as engineering, marketing, and financing. Savings resulting from such services, if available to many firms, are called "external economies."

However, growth in the scale of operations and increase in the division of labor do not inevitably go together. There have been occasions, though rare, when the growth of an industry or plant has led to a reintegration of labor operations. Also, there are areas of business where small-scale production remains the rule, as in certain "increasing-cost" industries in which increase in the scale of output causes increase in the unit cost of the product. Even when an industry is dominated by giant concerns, a small firm may be able to survive and prosper. *See also* DIMINISHING RETURNS; INDUSTRY; MASS PRODUCTION.

PHILIP TAFT, *Brown University*
Author, "Organized Labor in American History"

DIVORCE is the legal dissolution of marriage. Divorce is distinguished from *annulment,* which declares a marriage void from the time of its celebration.

Nearly all societies provide some arrangement for divorce. Only the Incas are recorded as having had no provision for dissolving marriage. Comparing divorce rates of nonliterate societies with those in the United States, anthropologists have noted that perhaps half of the known societies have had permanent marital-disruption rates higher than current rates in the United States.

In some societies divorce is rare, while in others a permanent union is unusual. In most societies, public opinion tends to be opposed to divorce, but in a few societies social pressure serves to undermine the marital relationship. The general public view of most groups has been that divorce is unfortunate but often necessary.

DIVORCE IN THE UNITED STATES

A divorce in the United States is a civil action brought before a court. If the judge grants the divorce, he issues a divorce decree that includes the terms of the divorce, such as custody and financial support of the children, visitation rights for the parent not granted custody, financial support, if any, for one of the marriage partners, and division of property.

Fault Divorce. As in any court action, grounds are required for bringing suit. In some states divorces are granted only on fault grounds. The party seeking the divorce, the plaintiff, files a complaint giving grounds for the divorce in accordance with the state law. If the other party, the defendant, also wants the divorce, the defendant does not contest the complaint. If the defendant does not want the divorce, he or she may contest the complaint or may, as a plaintiff, file another complaint in which he or she gives grounds for seeking the divorce.

The traditional grounds for divorce in the laws of American states were cruelty, desertion, and adultery. A century ago, most divorces were granted on grounds of desertion and adultery. By 1950 these had become minor grounds, and more than half the divorces in the United States were granted on grounds of cruelty.

Although grounds for divorce now differ from one state to the next, certain grounds are found in nearly all states. Among these are abandonment or desertion, adultery, and physical cruelty. Other grounds for divorce in some states include nonsupport or neglect of duty, alcoholism, drug addiction, insanity, mental cruelty, cruel or inhuman treatment, or voluntary separation. The definitions of these terms are given within the law of the state and may differ from one state to another.

The plaintiff in a fault action for divorce must prove to the court that the spouse is "guilty" of actions specified in the complaint and that these actions constitute grounds for divorce in the state where the action is brought. If the complaint is contested, the spouse has the opportunity of answering the charges. The judge then decides whether the divorce will be granted and under what conditions.

No-Fault Divorce. Before the 1960's, most divorces in the United States were granted on the basis of adversary proceedings. Courts generally adhered to the theory that each divorce must be a contest. The divorce was predicated on the assumption that one of the parties must be guilty, a concept derived from the old ecclesiastical courts in which it was necessary that one party be found innocent and the other guilty in order for a legal separation to be granted. This assumption often forced the participants into absurd or hypocritical situations, since divorce actions had been prearranged by both parties.

Over a period of years there has been a tendency among the states toward "no-fault" divorce. In a no-fault divorce action neither spouse is considered the "guilty" party. As early as 1933, "incompatibility" was made a legal ground for divorce in New Mexico. Subsequently many states allowed divorce after a period of separation, although in many cases it was necessary to show an intent to desert.

In 1970 the National Conference of Commissioners on Uniform State Laws prepared a Uniform Marriage and Divorce Act (UMDA). This act provides for no-fault divorce if the court finds that the marriage is "irretrievably broken." Many state legislatures have adopted the UMDA and made it part of state law. "Irretrievable breakdown" is defined differently among the states but generally requires that both partners have lived separate and apart for a period of time that may be as long as 12 or 18 months, and that during that time they lived in accordance with a separation agreement.

In the decade beginning with 1967, divorce laws in the United States and many other countries underwent a profound change toward no-fault divorce. A precedent-setting step in this direction was taken in the California family law act of 1969, in which there are only two grounds for divorce: irreconcilable differences that have caused the irremediable breakdown of the marriage, and incurable insanity. If, from evidence at a hearing, the court finds that irreconcilable differences have caused the irremediable breakdown of the marriage, it orders the dissolution of the marriage or legal separation, whichever the participants are seeking. During these proceedings, any testimony or evidence of specific acts of misconduct are improper and inadmissible except in cases where child custody must be determined by the court, and evidence of serious misconduct on the part of a parent would be relevant.

A second important characteristic of the 1969 California law is that either husband or wife can be required to support the other, and either or both can be required to support their minor children, depending on the court's judgment.

In the decade beginning with 1967, nearly every state has altered its laws to provide either a short period of separation or a no-fault provision similar to that of the California law. Many of the new laws also incorporate the provision that either spouse may be required to support the other spouse and/or their minor children. Previously universal grounds for divorce such as adultery have actually been eliminated as legal grounds for terminating a marriage.

Separation Agreement. The separation agreement is often a part of an uncontested fault divorce or a no-fault divorce action. It is a legal civil contract between husband and wife that specifies how the two will divide the assets accumulated during the marriage and how the couple will handle such matters as support for the spouse and dependent children. It is not a court order unless it becomes part of the divorce decree issued by the court. Often the separation agreement serves as a basis for the judge's decision regarding matters covered by the agreement, although the judge need not follow its provisions.

Validity of State Decrees. The recognition of the divorce decrees of one state by the courts of other states is covered by Article IV, section 1, of the Constitution of the United States, which makes the following provision:

"Full Faith and Credit shall be given in each State to the public Acts, Records, and judicial Proceedings of every other State. And the Congress may by general Laws prescribe the Manner in which such Acts, Records and Proceedings shall be proved, and the Effect thereof."

In addition, in 1790, the Congress passed an act stating "the mode in which the public Acts, Records, and Judicial Proceedings in each State shall be authenticated so as to take effect in every other State."

The "Full Faith and Credit" clause has been interpreted by judges to obligate the courts of one state to recognize the divorce decree of another only if the latter properly had jurisdiction in the case. Thus in many instances such decisions effectually invalidate the "Full Faith and Credit" clause where divorce is concerned.

DIVORCE IN OTHER COUNTRIES

Western Europe. Divorce laws in western Europe have undergone the same kinds of changes as American divorce laws. The key concepts in the new laws are mutual consent, separation, and irretrievable breakdown. The trend is away from adversary proceedings and the listing of specific matrimonial offenses as grounds for divorce. Changes in the laws in the decade beginning in 1967 brought Britain, France, West Germany, and the Scandinavian countries to the point that separation, mutual consent, or some combination was the common basis for divorce proceedings. For example, in Britain, the sole grounds for divorce is irretrievable breakdown of the marriage, but separation by mutual consent for two years is accepted as demonstration of the irretrievable breakdown. Italy, without provision for divorce until 1970, now allows divorce on grounds of five years of separation. Among the countries of Europe, only Spain does not recognize divorce.

Eastern Europe. Divorce laws in the Soviet Union have been characterized by extreme swings of liberality and restrictiveness. In 1917, after the Bolshevik Revolution, all divorces became strictly private affairs, no longer requiring the involvement of the ecclesiastical courts or any public agency. In 1926 state registration of marriages merely consisted of a statement that a certain relationship existed, while divorce became merely a registration of the fact that it no longer existed. By 1944 divorce had been made nearly impossible, very expensive, and time consuming. In the 1960's several changes in procedure made divorce easier to obtain.

A more modern divorce law, effective in 1968, was built on the concept of irretrievable breakdown: "A marriage is dissolved if the court ascertains that a couple's continued cohabitation and preservation of the family have become impossible." Where there are no minor children, spouses may divorce by mutual consent without court proceedings, simply by registering the fact of divorce with the agencies for registration of documents pertaining to civil status. Where there are minor children, either spouse can be required to support them, and either spouse can be required to support the other as the court decides.

Other eastern European countries retain court proceedings as a necessary part of dissolution of the marriage. Generally, however, existing laws provide only the general grounds of incompatibility or a conclusion by the court that the marital relationship cannot be restored.

Muslim Countries. Persons who enter into a Muslim marriage in the following countries are subject to Muslim divorce laws: Aden, Brunei, Kenya, Malaysia, Pakistan, Singapore, Sri Lanka, Tanzania, Iraq, India, and Iran. In these societies the husband has the right to divorce his wife without assigning specific reasons. This type of divorce is effected when the husband, before two witnesses, simply pronounces *talaq*, or words of renunciation of the wife ("I divorce thee"). In Malaysia, however, *talaq* can be revoked for a small fee. Only the third *talaq* is irrevocable. Under Islamic law the wife has no redress to divorce by *talaq*.

In 1966 major reforms took effect in Egyptian divorce laws. The husband was required to go to court and state his reasons for wanting to divorce his wife. Furthermore, a wife was given the right to divorce or separation when abuse can be specified. In practice, however, a wife can initiate divorce only with difficulty. For the first time, a provision for alimony was included in the law, and the husband may now have to pay alimony up to four months. Any children of the marriage belong to the husband's family, and the children of divorced parents stay with their father after they reach the age of seven. The wife can take with her only the property she brought to the marriage. A divorce is almost always followed by a remarriage. Although the law still follows the Koran in allowing a man four wives, the first wife can now secure a divorce if the husband takes a second wife.

SOCIAL ASPECTS OF DIVORCE

It has been widely argued that expansion of the economic system through industrialization weakens the family and therefore raises divorce rates. Studies of the divorce rate among the developing nations show this belief to be false, however. Industrialization brings some countries rising divorce rates; in others, falling divorce rates.

Family Structure and Divorce Rates. Nearly every type of family structure is found in nonindustrial societies, and the divorce rates range from close to zero to almost 100%. It can be said that during the process of industrialization the family forms of diverse societies become more alike, and the nuclear family unit (composed of husband, wife, and children) becomes more independent of inclusive kinship groups. This type of family organization is associated with comparatively high divorce rates, but not so high as the rates of some nonindustrialized societies. In the process of industrialization, then, countries with very low divorce rates will usually experience a substantial rise, while countries with very high divorce rates will experience a reduction.

For example, during the first half of the 20th century the divorce rate (per 1,000 marriages contracted in the same year) in Japan fell from about 300 to 100, and in Algeria from over 300 to about 150, while the rate in the United States rose from about 80 to approximately 250 and in England and Wales from almost zero to about 80.

DIVORCE RATES PER 1,000 POPULATION, 1955 AND 1975, FOR SELECTED COUNTRIES

	1955	1975
Declining		
Egypt	2.64[1]	2.02[2]
Iran	1.45	0.64[2]
Israel	1.24	0.88
Stable		
France	0.72	0.95
Yugoslavia	1.10	1.17
Japan	0.85	1.04[2]
Increasing		
United States	2.30	4.80
England and Wales	0.60	2.14
Sweden	1.14	3.33
USSR	1.30	2.95
Czechoslovakia	1.05	2.18

[1] 1954. [2] 1974. Source: United Nations, *Demographic Yearbook* (annual).

Changes in Divorce Rates. Since 1965, divorce rates in many developed countries have risen dramatically. The accompanying table gives divorce rates for selected countries for 1955 and 1975. In the United States, for example, 2% of all existing marriages ended in divorce. It was estimated that more than half of the marriages contracted in the 1970's in the United States would end in divorce.

The increases in overall divorce rates are not associated solely with the increased instability of marriages. Marriages of more than 20 years duration have doubled their divorce rates. Approximately 25% of all divorces occur in marriages of more than 15 years duration, compared with only 4% in 1947. This indicates that the change is not associated with any change in selection of marriage partners in the younger generation nor with any change in attitudes toward marriage peculiar to those recently married.

While the United States has the highest divorce rate of any developed country, several others experienced a doubling of the divorce rate during the decade following 1965. It is more than a coincidence that the general increases in divorce rates occurred during the same period as a general relaxation of the divorce laws. It is not clear that the relaxation of the laws "caused" the increase in divorces, but it is clear that both the changes in the laws and the increase in divorces that the legal change facilitated were reflections of a change in attitude toward divorce.

Most divorced persons remarry. In the United States of all persons in their late 30's who were ever divorced, only about one in five has not remarried. Divorced males are more likely to remarry than females. Remarriage generally occurs within a short time after the termination of the previous marriage. In a 15-state sample of divorced persons who remarried, 25% did so within five months after obtaining their divorce. By the end of the first year, 50% had remarried. An unsuccessful first marriage evidently turns very few persons against marriage in general.

Studies based on interviews indicate that nearly all of those who remarry consider their second marriage an improvement over their first. The frequency, speed, and success of remarriage of divorced persons are taken by many family sociologists to indicate the basic soundness of the present marital institution.

It has been widely believed that the presence of children acts as a deterrent to divorce. When length of marriage is taken into account, it has been shown that divorcing couples actually have higher fertility rates than nondivorcing couples. Based on information from 29 states in the divorce registration area, the mean number of children involved in the number of divorces granted was 0.92 in 1955, 1.32 in 1965, and 1.08 in 1975. This rise and decline is merely a reflection of the high birthrates up to 1960, and the continuous decline in birthrates in the 1960's and early 1970's.

The strongest arguments against divorce are frequently made on behalf of the children of divorced parents. It has been believed that children are damaged by the divorce of their parents and that this predisposes them to delinquency and emotional maladjustment. A number of studies show that when children from broken marriages are compared with children from intact marriages, the latter are better adjusted and have better relationships with their parents. But the crucial comparison is between children from homes broken by divorce and those from homes that are intact but unhappy. When this comparison was made in one study of adolescents, those from divorced homes fared better in every comparison: they showed less delinquent behavior and better adjustment to parents than the adolescents from intact but unhappy homes.

From the evidence available it can no longer be maintained that divorce is entirely detrimental to children. The effects of divorce on children other than adolescents are not known. It can be concluded that marital conflict and disruption are disturbing to children and disorganize their lives. If divorce removes the source of conflict, then divorce is better for the children than living in conflict.

Children are thought to complicate the remarriage process, including the period of courtship. However, available data show that women with children are almost as likely to remarry, and that they do so as quickly as those without children at divorce.

Social Factors in Marital Instability. The probability of divorce is not spread evenly throughout the population. Socioeconomic status, race, religion, age at marriage, and geographical location are factors related to the risk of divorce.

In countries where attitudes and laws concerning divorce are restrictive, only the upper classes have enough money and influence to obtain a divorce. In countries where legislation and public opinion are more permissive, divorce is more common in the lower classes. In the United States the greater incidence of divorce among low-income families, as compared with high-income families, is well documented.

U. S. DIVORCE RATE

Year	Number of divorces	Divorces per 1,000 population
1900	56,000	0.5
1910	83,000	0.9
1920	171,000	1.6
1930	196,000	1.6
1940	264,000	2.0
1950	385,000	2.6
1955	377,000	2.3
1960	393,000	2.2
1965	481,000	2.5
1970	708,000	3.5
1975	1,026,000	4.8
1976	1,077,000	5.0

Source: *Statistical Abstract of the United States* and U. S. Census Bureau.

The adverse effect of low income on marital stability is greater than the divorce statistics indicate, since poor people often separate without obtaining a legal divorce. The circumstances of lower-class environments, with irregular employment, economic hardship, and a general inability of the individual to control his destiny impose great strains on marital stability. In most lower-class groups the marital relationship itself, compared with relationships with friends and relatives, is of less emotional significance than in groups of higher status. These factors combine to produce divorce rates among the poor that are two to five times higher than among the more affluent segments of society.

Divorce and separation rates of blacks in the United States are much higher than those of whites. It was formerly thought that this difference in rates was attributable to the low socio-economic status of blacks, but analysis of census data has shown that when blacks and whites of the same educational, occupational, or income level are compared, marital instability for blacks is one and a half to two times as great as for whites. Adequate explanations for the racial difference in divorce rates are not available.

Roman Catholics have lower divorce rates than non-Catholics. Among non-Catholics, Jewish couples have the lowest divorce rates and Protestants have the highest rates. Among the Protestants, Episcopalians have the highest divorce rates and Lutherans the lowest. Couples that do not belong to any denomination have the highest incidence of marital disruption. These differences are properly explained by the greater reluctance of Catholics and of religiously active persons in general to divorce, rather than by differences in marital happiness, although religious persons generally report better marital adjustment than the nonreligious. Studies show that interfaith marriages have a divorce rate that is only slightly higher than that of marriages in general.

Marriages contracted at early ages in the United States are subject to higher divorce rates than those undertaken at later ages. Generally, the divorce rates for women married under 18 and men under 20 are on the order of one and a half to two times the rate for those married in their 20's. A number of differences between young marriers and later marriers help to account for the relative instability of young marriages. Those who marry young generally have less education and lower income. There is a higher probability that the woman is pregnant at marriage, and the partners are readier to dissolve a marriage, should it be unhappy. Young marriers also have differences in personality from those who marry later. However, after these and other predisposing factors are accounted for, sheer youthfulness accounts for a substantial proportion of the difference in marital stability.

The divorce rate increases in times of economic prosperity and decreases during depressions. Marriage rates change even more dramatically with the economic conditions of the country, however, probably because it is easier to enter a marriage than to terminate one. Inflated divorce rates have followed major wars, beginning with the Civil War, in the United States. Most scholars believe this tendency is related to the fact that hasty and ill-conceived marriages are entered into under the stressful conditions of war but cannot withstand the years of normality following the war.

To some extent this is no doubt true, but data for the years around World War II show that the circumstances of the war years raised divorce rates for couples who were married 10 to 20 years before just as much as for couples married during the war years. The separations and disruptions of family life brought about by war and the estrangement that these separations frequently cause are devastating for all marriages, not just those of the wartime years.

Divorce rates are higher in urban than in rural populations. Today most of the urban-rural difference is doubtless due to the migration of divorced persons to cities. Married women who grew up on farms are just as likely to divorce as those who did not.

In general, while men who divorce and do not remarry experience a rise in standard of living, women who divorce and do not remarry experience a decline in standard of living. Lack of job training and loss of skills during childbearing work against the divorced woman.

Studies indicate that the no-fault divorce laws are leaving the wife worse off financially than under adversary law. She is no longer in a bargaining position for financial settlements—that is, alimony and child support. Only a few of the states with no-fault divorce laws have enacted provisions calling for a division of property and economic support based on recognition of the homemaker's contribution in the marriage.

The amount of welfare benefits paid to separated mothers with dependent children has increased, and it has been suggested that public-assistance payments might actually encourage divorce. Studies of AFDC (Aid to Families with Dependent Children) payments indicate that such benefits do not increase marital disruptions. However, there is some indication that financial aid acts as a deterrent to remarriage.

Attitudes Toward Divorce. In the United States, as in many other countries, attitudes toward divorce appear to have become increasingly permissive. In the 1920's the Methodist Church prohibited ministers from performing marriages for divorced persons unless they were innocent parties in divorces granted for adultery. By the 1960's, Methodist ministers were required only to satisfy themselves that the divorced person understood the reasons for the failure of the marriage and was prepared to do better the next time. Similar changes occurred in the doctrines of many other Protestant denominations during the same period. The Roman Catholic Church has steadfastly maintained the concept of indissoluble marriage.

Protestant acceptance of divorce as necessary or justifiable in particular cases has not spelled a decline of interest in the stability of marriage on the part of the clergy. Their counseling function has received steadily increased emphasis. Nearly as many Americans receive marriage counseling from the clergy as from all other professional sources combined.

Typical of the point of view of contemporary American Judaism is the following statement by a leading rabbi concerning a desirable uniform divorce law: "Such a law should be drafted with a sense of the realities of the situation with due regard to the frailties of human nature and the exigencies of modern society. Judaism, which always maintained a realistic view with respect to divorce, would be in favor of a liberal divorce law, which would safeguard the security of the family, but would provide for the dissolution of an intolerable marriage."

Urbanites are found to be more tolerant of divorce than rural people, men more tolerant than women, and those with more education more tolerant than those with less (in contradiction to their actual divorce record). The more religiously devout the person and the more doctrinally strict the group to which he claims affiliation, the more opposed to divorce he is likely to be.

Divorce and the Future of the Family. Few persons now suppose that increases in divorce rates signify a general decline in the happiness of marriages. High marital stability does not necessarily mean high levels of marital happiness. It may mean only that the emotional significance of the marital relationship for married individuals is not very great. Increases in the divorce rates of many countries are an indication of decreasing tolerance for emotionally unsatisfying marriages and the general acceptance of divorce as the solution to the problem. In many Western countries, cultural values appear to have abandoned the concept of marriage as a permanent commitment. Marriage is in the process of being defined as a temporary relationship, to be maintained only as long as it helps both partners get what they want out of life.

Current high divorce rates should not be seen as a sign of the impending destruction of marriage as a social institution. Rather they should be understood as a sign of the transformation of the traditional institution of marriage into an instrument for the realization of individual goals rather than emphasis on the service of broader social purposes.

HISTORICAL BACKGROUND

Among early civilizations marriage was considered a social contract to which the state was not party. Individuals and their families made and unmade such arrangements. An important exception was the theocratic government of the Jews, which regulated all of the affairs of society.

The lives of the ancient Hebrew women were rigidly circumscribed. The patriarch, or father of the household, theoretically had the power of absolute life and death over his daughters. Polygamy was practiced by men who could afford it. The bride, in the marriage arranged for her by her family, was given a dowry and thereafter served as a chattel of her husband. The word for wife, *beulah*, meant "owned," and the Scriptures instructed the wife: "Thy desire shall be to thy husband, and he shall rule over thee." The law provided that the man could divorce his wife as he wished. There were no restrictions upon his private conduct; he could live with whatever woman he wished as long as she was the property of no other man.

Under Athenian law, divorce could be granted to either spouse. It was more freely granted to the husband, who could dismiss his wife for any cause. The wife was not at liberty to leave her husband, but if she had the resources and initiative, she could present her cause before the archon on grounds of cruelty or degenerate behavior.

The most notable and modern-sounding aspect of Athenian divorce law was that divorce was available by common consent, formally expressed in open court before the archon. The children were always given to the father.

Although the early Roman republic gave women little control over their marriages, by 200 B.C. women were gaining power and influence and could divorce their husbands at will. Men of the propertied classes were always free to divorce their wives and often did. Men of highest rank had many wives. The Roman statesmen Sulla and Pompey were each married five times. The method of divorce was simple. The man simply presented his wife with a letter declaring their mutual freedom.

During the reign of Augustus Caesar (30 B.C.–14 A.D.), laws were passed restricting divorce. The most important of these were the Julian laws conceived by Augustus in his old age to reform the morals of the Romans. The Julian laws brought marriage and divorce under the regulation of the state for the first time in Roman history.

Christian Tradition. Early Christian groups followed the Pauline teaching of forbidding divorced persons to remarry unless one of the parties in the first marriage had not been converted to the faith. In the Christianized Byzantine Empire, church and secular laws continued to exist side by side. The Justinian Code, formulated in the 6th century, reflected the Christian ardor of the emperor. Justinian desired that the church's views on divorce should prevail, but this view departed drastically from the will of the people. Women had not been subject to the custodianship of their fathers and husbands for 200 years, and they joined the rest of the populace in protesting the stringent church laws. Thus, later Justinian legislation provided a number of allowable grounds for divorce.

The canon law of the Christian Church was organized, codified, and presented as an orderly body of law by the monk Gratian about 1150. Originally, the canon law was a disorganized body of scriptural passages, commentaries on the Scriptures, records of customs, opinions of ecclesiastics, ancient laws, and other codes, such as that of Justinian. All of these elements were redrawn by Gratian to accord with the views of the church at that time. Canon law covered every subject dealt with under any existing civil law plus the regulation of marriage, separation, and divorce. The church claimed the right to enforce the canon law wherever necessary and to impose penalties for its infraction.

Canon law provided that, upon proof of sufficiently serious grounds presented by the wife or husband, a separation could be granted by the church. These grounds were adultery, extreme cruelty, or withdrawal from the church by one of the partners. An annulment was the only method of securing complete freedom from one's spouse and the privilege of remarrying. Annulments were granted if it was found that the marriage had violated any of the canonical impediments to marriage. Over the years the canonical impediments came to be interpreted so broadly that some grounds could nearly always be found to terminate successfully the marriage of a person who possessed enough political power or influence.

Protestant Views. The greater freedom to obtain divorces was paralleled by an increased secularization of marriage, strengthened by the Protestant Reformation. Martin Luther had stated that marriage is "an external worldly thing, subject to secular jurisdiction, just like dress and food, home and field." Repudiation of the sacramental nature of marriage opened the way for divorce and for the transfer of legal responsibility from church to state. Marital cases were not generally handled by civil courts following the Reformation on the Continent, but church government was administered by members of royalty, ruling families, and others who possessed secular power. The practice of allowing divorces in these fundamentally secular courts for proven adultery, cruelty, and desertion became commonplace. There was also the new institution of executive divorce by the sovereign. This institution became the basis for divorce by legislative decree once prevalent in the United States, especially in early New England. Scandinavian divorces of the present day are arranged by administrative agencies that have their roots in divorce by executive decree.

The impact of the Protestant revolt was strongly felt in England, but did not quickly work toward the liberalizing of divorce laws. The Puritans, Separatists, and other liberals suffered, though not in silence, under the conservatism of the Restoration. The Puritan John Milton issued a tract in 1643, *The Doctrine and Discipline of Divorce*, in which he expressed his belief that divorce grounds should include contrariness, defects of disposition, and impediments to personal "solace and peace," and strongly urged the right of private divorce. In his *Tetrachordon*, published two years later, he examined the phrase from the marriage ceremony, "what therefore God hath joined together, let no man put asunder." Milton wrote, "Shall we say that God hath joined error, fraud, unfitness, wrath, contention, perpetual loneliness, perpetual discord; whatever lust, or wine or witchery, threat or incitement, avarice of ambition hath joined together, faithful and unfaithful, Christian with anti-Christian, hate with hate, or hate with love, shall we say this is God's joining?" His tracts had no immediate effects on public policy, and they even brought down on him the wrath of many of his fellow Puritans, who felt that in advocating private divorce he had gone too far. But he was widely read and quoted in the 19th and 20th centuries in the United States by many of those who wished to liberalize and standardize the profusion of divorce regulations.

In England between the years 1669 and 1850, only 229 divorces were granted, all but 3 or 4 of which were to men. Only in the mid-20th century did British divorce laws undergo further liberalization.

Development of Divorce Law in the United States. America received English common law by acts of the legislatures of the individual colonies, which adapted the law to the needs of the new land. The English Puritans who settled New England were still arguing about marriage and divorce as they had in England. But the conservative Anglicans dominated public affairs in Virginia and other Southern colonies. The statutes of the Southern colonies contained no laws pertaining to divorce.

Legal separations did not exist in the Southern colonies either, although unhappy couples often did separate through mutual consent, as they customarily have done in every society. Absolute divorce was not recognized, and no case of divorce prior to the American Revolution has been discovered. The colonies of New York, New Jersey, Delaware, and Pennsylvania occupied a middle position geographically and in attitude between those of Puritan New England and the Anglican South.

Lack of Uniformity. The Constitution of the United States left complete authority over marriage and divorce legislation to the separate states. The first state constitutions, by omitting the subject, left the matter of divorce to the legislatures. Each state was free to develop its own legislation with regard to divorce. Herein, of course, lie the roots of the jumble and variety of divorce legislation in the United States today. The problems caused by this diversity were early recognized. In 1884, constitutional amendments were introduced to empower Congress to regulate divorce. These first amendments were defeated, and for more than 60 years similar amendments were introduced and similarly defeated. None was ever put to a vote in either house. Essentially, there remain 51 different sets of conditions, or divorce laws—one for each state and for the District of Columbia. While unquestionably more uniform divorce laws are needed, a great deal of simplification, as well as liberalization, has been achieved during the last hundred years.

See also ANNULMENT OF MARRIAGE.

J. RICHARD UDRY
Carolina Population Center,
University of North Carolina

Bibliography

Council of State Governments, *The Book of the States* (annually).
Goode, William J., *World Revolution and Family Patterns* (Free Press 1970).
Howard, George Elliott, *A History of Matrimonial Institutions*, 3 vols. (Humanities Press 1964).
Jacobson, Paul H. and Pauline E., *American Marriage and Divorce* (Rinehart 1959).
Mayer, Michael F., *Divorce and Annulment in the Fifty States*, rev. ed. (Arc Bks 1975).
Moles, Oliver C. and Levinger, George, eds., "Divorce and Separation," *Journal of Social Issues*, vol. 32, no. 1 (1976).
Rheinstein, Max, *Marriage, Stability, Divorce and the Law* (Univ. of Chicago Press 1972).
Sachar, Abram Leon, *A History of the Jews* (Knopf 1967).
Udry, J. Richard, *The Social Context of Marriage*, 3d ed. (Lippincott 1974).
United Nations, *Demographic Yearbook, 1975* (1976).
U. S. Bureau of the Census, *U. S. Census of Population: 1970*, Subject Reports: Final Report PC(2)-4A (USGPO 1973).
U. S. Bureau of the Census, *U. S. Census of Population: 1970*, Subject Reports: Final Report PC(2)-4D (USGPO 1973).
U. S. Department of Labor, Bureau of Labor Statistics, *Women Who Head Families—A Socioeconomic Analysis*, Special Labor Report 190 (USGPO 1976).

DIWALI, di-wä′lē, the Hindu feast of lights, commemorates, among other things, the deity Rama's defeat of the demon Ravana, who desired to destroy the world. Diwali (also spelled *Divali* and *Dipavali*) also commemorates the return of light to the world after the rainy season, during which, according to Hindu myth, the heavens are obscured by a water spirit. It signals the resumption of such religious activities and rituals as pilgrimages, marriages, and initiations. A traditional feature of the festival is the illumination of Hindu homes with numerous tiny clay lamps.

The festival, celebrated in October–November, is a time of New Year observance for those Hindus who follow the Vikram era—a system of dating comparable to the Christian calendar. Offerings are made to Lakshmi (Laksmi), goddess of wealth, for prosperity in the coming year.

CHARLES S. J. WHITE
University of Pennsylvania

DIX, Dorothea (1802–1887), American social reformer, who campaigned for better conditions and treatment for prisoners and the mentally ill. She was born Dorothea Lynde Dix in Hampden, Me., on April 4, 1802. In 1816, at just 14 years of age, she began to teach school in Worcester, Mass.; in 1821 she opened a young ladies' school in Boston, where she taught until made inactive by weak health in 1835. In this period she also wrote many children's books.

In 1841, Miss Dix undertook to teach a Sunday school class in the East Cambridge (Mass.) house of correction. Horrified by the conditions there and especially by the mingling of prisoners with the mentally ill, she began a systematic survey of Massachusetts prisons, poorhouses, and insane asylums. Her shocking conclusions were delivered in 1843 in a "Memorial to the Legislature of Massachusetts," with the result that the state insane asylum at Worcester was improved. She then continued her crusade, eventually visiting every state east of the Rockies.

In 1848, Miss Dix went to Washington, D.C., hoping to secure passage of a bill to apportion land for the support of the mentally ill. Such a bill was finally approved by Congress but was vetoed by President Franklin Pierce in 1854. Miss Dix was heartbroken but continued her crusade. When the Civil War broke out in 1861, she was appointed Superintendent of Women Nurses in the Union Army, the highest office held by a woman during the war. In 1865 she turned once more to her reform work.

In all, Miss Dix was directly responsible for the founding or enlarging of 32 mental hospitals in 15 states, Canada, Britain, Europe, and Japan. In 1881 she retired to live at the New Jersey State Hospital in Trenton, the first mental hospital built as a direct result of her efforts. She died there on July 17, 1887.

JAMES F. WARREN
National Association for Mental Health

DIX, Dorothy (1861–1951), American newspaper columnist, who was the pioneer writer of "advice to the lovelorn" columns. Her real name was Elizabeth Meriwether Gilmer. She was born in Woodstock, Tenn., on Nov. 18, 1861. To support herself and her incurably ill husband, she became a writer for the women's page of the New Orleans *Picayune* in 1896 and began her advice column, "Dorothy Dix Talks." She continued her column after joining the staff of the New York *Journal* as a special writer in 1901.

The column eventually appeared in almost 300 newspapers, and its practical, down-to-earth advice kept pace with the times. Dorothy Dix's books include *How to Hold a Husband* (1939). She died on Dec. 16, 1951, in New Orleans, La.

DIX, John Adams (1798–1879), American political leader and general, who gave the famous order "If anyone attempts to haul down the American flag, shoot him on the spot." Dix was born at Boscawen, N. H., on July 24, 1798. As a boy he took part in the War of 1812, serving as a junior officer in the Army. A captain in 1828, he resigned to practice law at Cooperstown, N.Y. Dix served as adjutant general of New York state in 1830 and as secretary of state from 1833 to 1839. He was a member of the so-called "Albany Regency," which controlled New York state's Democratic party.

Elected in 1845 to fill a vacancy, Dix served as a United States senator until 1849. From January to March 1861 he was U.S. secretary of the treasury. He cleared a financial deadlock and obtained money to start fighting the Civil War. His order concerning the American flag was issued to a Treasury official in New Orleans shortly after Louisiana seceded from the Union.

In the Civil War, Dix was a major general, in command at Baltimore, Md., then at Fortress Monroe, Va. After the draft riots in New York City he went there to command the Department of the East. He was minister to France from 1866 to 1869. In 1872, although a Democrat, Dix was elected governor of New York on the Republican ticket. He died in New York City on April 21, 1879. Fort Dix, N. J., is named for him.

JOSEPH B. MITCHELL
Author of "Decisive Battles of the Civil War"

DIX, Otto (1891–1969), German painter, who was a leader of the "New Objectivity" (*Neue Sachlichkeit*), a form of social realism that emerged in Germany after World War I. Dix was born at Unterhausen, near Gera, on Dec. 2, 1891. He studied at the Dresden Academy of Art and served in the German Army during World War I. His early work was influenced by Dadaism and by the style of George Grosz. His paintings of World War I, depicting the horrors of war, were rooted in German Gothic art.

After the war, Dix reacted against the influence of cubism and Dada. His *Parents of the Artist* (1921; Kunstmuseum, Basel) goes beyond the usual 19th century realism into "magic realism," a mode of representation that takes on an aura of the fantastic through the exaggerated detail and honesty with which commonplace objects are pictured. From 1927 to 1933, Dix taught art in Dresden. He was forbidden to exhibit during the Nazi regime. After World War II he turned to a form of mystical religious expression. He died in Singen, West Germany, on July 25, 1969.

HARVARD ARNASON
The Solomon R. Guggenheim Foundation

DIXIE, dik′sē, is a name associated with the American South and is the title of a popular minstrel song. Though the origin of the term is uncertain, several theories have been advanced to explain it. During the Civil War, Southerners generally agreed that it was a corruption of "Mason and Dixon's Line," which divided free and slave states. Another version traced it to $10 bills issued by the Citizens Bank of New Orleans in the 1850's that bore the French word "dix" (ten) on the reverse. These bills were popularly referred to as "dixies," and the region in which they circulated was known as the "land of dixies."

A third version, supported by older tradition, derived the term from a kindhearted 18th century slave owner on Manhattan Island named Dixy or Dixie. When his slaves were forced to move South into less congenial circumstances, they longed for their old home and began to sing of "Dixie's Land" as a heaven on earth.

From these slave songs the term found its way into the music of the "black-face" minstrel shows. In 1859, Daniel Decatur Emmett composed a "walk-around" song for Bryant's Minstrels with the refrain, "I wish I was in Dixieland," and it was immediately popular all over the country. When Abraham Lincoln first heard it in 1860 at a

New York performance, he shouted, "Let's have it again," from his box. In January 1861 it was sung in New Orleans to a wildly enthusiastic audience. On Feb. 18, 1861, a band played *Dixie* at the inauguration of Jefferson Davis as president of the Confederate States of America, and the song became the favorite marching tune of the Confederate army.

So infectious was the melody that several lyrics were set to it. On May 30, 1861, a Confederate version by Gen. Albert Pike of Arkansas appeared in the Natchez (Miss.) *Courier;* Dan Emmett and T. M. Cooley composed Union words to the music. By 1863 it was reported that the tune was "as popular in New York as in Richmond," but the name "Dixie" was regarded as the peculiar designation of the South. Confederate sympathizers wrote other songs using the word, including a *Dixie Doodle* to replace *Yankee Doodle*, and Mrs. Marinda Branson Moore of North Carolina published a "Dixie Series" of school textbooks. Thus the name Dixie came to refer to the former Confederate States, but the song is part of the American heritage.

DAVID L. SMILEY
Wake Forest University

DIXIECRATS, dik'sē-krats, a splinter group of Southern Democrats in the U.S. elections of 1948, who rejected President Harry S. Truman's civil-rights program and revolted against the civil-rights plank adopted at the Democratic National Convention. A conference of states' rights leaders then met in Birmingham and suggested Gov. J. Strom Thurmond of South Carolina for president and Gov. Fielding Wright of Mississippi for vice president. The group hoped to force the election into the House of Representatives by preventing either Truman or his Republican opponent, Thomas E. Dewey, from obtaining a majority of the electoral votes.

The plan failed. Although Thurmond electors ran and won as the official Democratic candidates in four states—Alabama, Louisiana, Mississippi, and South Carolina—other Thurmond electors running as "States Rights Democrats" lost to Truman slates. Thurmond polled 22.5% of the total Southern vote to Truman's 50.1%. Nationally, Thurmond obtained 39 electoral votes with 1,169,032 popular votes. The Dixiecrat movement encouraged Northern blacks to vote for Truman, but it ultimately strengthened the Republican party in the South, for many Dixiecrats became Republicans.

DONALD B. JOHNSON, *University of Iowa*

DIXIELAND. See under JAZZ.

DIXON, Joseph, (1799–1869), American inventor and manufacturer, who founded one of the first lead-pencil factories in the United States. He was born at Marblehead, Mass., on Jan. 18, 1799. In spite of a skimpy education, he acquired a skill in chemistry that he later put to good use. His inventions included a photolithographic printing process, an improved camera for daguerreotypes, and an electric battery. But his main interest was developing products based on graphite—especially lead pencils, stove polish, and crucibles for the pottery and metal industries.

In 1827, Dixon established a pencil and stove-polish factory at Salem, Mass. In 1847, following the steady growth of business, he moved the factory to Jersey City, N.J. In 1867 he established a company to manufacture graphite crucibles, which he had first experimented with in his late teens—long before a commercial market for the product existed. He died in Jersey City on June 15, 1869.

DIXON, Thomas (1864–1946), American Baptist minister, novelist, and playwright. He was born in Shelby, N.C., on Jan. 11, 1864, and was educated at Wake Forest College. He studied law and was admitted to the bar. He resigned from the North Carolina state legislature in 1886 to become a Baptist minister.

After 1900 he devoted himself almost wholly to the writing of novels and melodramatic plays, a number of which enjoyed considerable success. The best remembered of his many works is *The Clansman* (1905), from which his friend D. W. Griffith, the early motion picture producer, made the sensational film *The Birth of a Nation* in 1915. Dixon died at Raleigh, N.C., April 3, 1946.

POWEL MILLS DAWLEY
General Theological Seminary, New York

DİYARBAKIR, dē-yär-be-kēr', the largest city of southeastern Turkey and the capital of Diyarbakır province. Situated in a fertile plain on the right bank of the Dicle (Tigris) River, it has since ancient times been of commercial and military importance owing to its position at the junction of the routes connecting Asia Minor with neighboring areas. Its former name, Amid (earlier Amida), is attested to as early as Assyrian times. The city was called Amid down to the beginning of the 20th century, when the name was changed to Diyarbakır.

The city was a key point in the wars of the Persians with the Romans (and later with the Byzantines), who in 349 A.D. erected the black basalt walls that still enclose the city. Taken by the Arabs in 638, it was held by a succession of minor Muslim powers until its absorption into the Ottoman Empire in 1517. Today the city is largely dominated by military installations belonging to Turkey and the North Atlantic Treaty Organization (NATO). Population: (1975) of the city, 235,617; of the province, 778,150.

JOHN R. WALSH
University of Edinburgh

DIZZINESS. See VERTIGO.

DJAKARTA. See JAKARTA.

DJENNÉ, je-nā', a historic town in Mali, on the Bani River. The site has a record of settlement going back to 200 B.C. At the height of its power in the 14th to 16th centuries, Djenné (Jenne) was a major center of Muslim learning. It rivaled Timbuktu in the investiture of imams and threatened to supplant it in commercial and political importance.

Nearly surrounded by water and with the appearance of a medieval fortified town, Djenné presents the most homogeneous and beautiful ensemble of traditional architecture in West Africa. Its streets have a unique, picturesque charm; its houses were built by generations of masons since the 14th century. The celebrated mosque of Djenné stands on 100 square pillars. Population: (1976) 10,251.

ALFRED GERTEINY, *University of Bridgeport*

The minaret of Hammoudi Mosque is a landmark of Djibouti, the capital of the Republic of Djibouti.

DJIBOUTI, ji-bōō′tē, a small country on the northeast coast of Africa, facing the strait of Bab el-Mandeb at the southern end of the Red Sea. Measuring only 8,410 square miles (21,783 sq km), it is wedged between Somalia and Ethiopia in the strategic region that is known as the Horn of Africa.

The Republic of Djibouti, formerly the French Territory of the Afars and Issas, gained its independence on June 27, 1977. As a political unit it dates from 1896, after the French had founded the port town of Djibouti to provide their overseas empire with a coaling station on the route to the East. Much of the town's later prosperity was due to its becoming the terminus of the railroad from Addis Ababa and hence Ethiopia's main trade outlet. Having no ethnic identity and almost no natural resources of its own, the Republic of Djibouti owes its existence to the competing commercial and strategic interests of other nations.

The Land. The republic covers the land to a perimeter of about 55 miles (90 km) around the Gulf of Tadjoura, a long inlet running westward from the Gulf of Aden (Indian Ocean). The terrain is volcanic in origin and largely desert. It consists mainly of plateaus broken by deep rift valleys and wide sunken plains, with salt lakes such as those of Assal and Alol, which lie below sea level. Pasture is sparse, and hardly any land is arable.

There are no permanent watercourses on the surface, but several subterranean rivers, and irrigation is possible by tapping the water table. The only permanent vegetation is found on the basaltic mountain range north of the Gulf of Tadjoura, where peaks reach elevations of more than 5,000 feet (1,500 meters).

The climate is among the hottest and driest in the world. The temperature averages 85° F (29° C) and can rise to 125° F (52° C). Annual rainfall is less than 5 inches (125 mm), though occasional rains can be extremely heavy and cause flooding.

The People. The population was estimated at 330,000 in 1983. Nearly half of the people are nomadic pastoralists. Most of the settled portion live in Djibouti town, the capital, with a population of 180,000; the remainder, in the towns of Dikhil, Ali Sabieh, Tadjoura, and Obock.

The two main ethnic groups, both indigenous to the area, are the Afar (Danakil), constituting about 35% of the population, and the Issa (a branch of the Somali people), some 40%. The two have in common their traditional life-style of nomadic pastoralism and their Muslim religion. They speak related languages and are ethnically similar. Large numbers of both groups live outside the borders of Djibouti. The Afar, who occupy the northern part of the country, have probably twice as many members in Ethiopia; the Issa, who inhabit the southern half of Djibouti, have perhaps an equal representation in Somalia (the Somali Democratic Republic). Somalis belonging to clan groups other than the Issa have migrated into Djibouti town since its foundation, in search of employment. Government estimates put these, together with the Arab population, at 25% of the population. The Arab immigrants, mainly from the Yemen, are traders, with a small number of market gardeners.

The French population is estimated at 12,000, of whom about a third are government and military personnel. Other small foreign groups in-

---

INFORMATION HIGHLIGHTS

Official Name: Republic of Djibouti.
Name of Nationals: Djiboutians.
Head of State: President.
Head of Governent: Premier.
Legislature: Chamber of Deputies (unicameral).
Area: 8,410 square miles (21,783 sq km).
Boundaries: *Northeast,* Bab el-Mandeb (strait); *east,* Gulf of Aden (Indian Ocean); *southeast,* Somalia; *south, west,* and *northwest,* Ethiopia.
Elevations: *Highest*—Moussa Ali (6,768 feet, or 2,063 meters); *lowest,* Lake Assal (509 feet, or 155 meters, below sea level).
Population: (1960–1961 census) 81,200; (1983 est.) 330,000.
Capital and Largest City: Djibouti.
Major Languages: French (official), Somali, Afar, Arabic.
Major Religious Group: Muslims.
Monetary Unit: Djibouti franc (= 100 centimes).
Flag: Two horizontal stripes, light blue over light green, extending from a white triangle at the hoist; centered in the triangle, a five-pointed red star. See also FLAG.

clude Greeks, Italians, and Indians. To these were added, in 1978–1979, some 45,000 to 50,000 refugees, mostly Somalis from the Ethiopian region of Ogaden.

Relations between the Afar and Somalis in precolonial times were conditioned by competition for scarce water and grazing, which often led to violent conflict. This rivalry was exacerbated during the colonial era and remains a problem of the independent state.

The literacy rate of the indigenous population is estimated at less than 9%, and expansion of education is a pressing concern of the government. The language of instruction is French, with Arabic gaining in importance.

Government. The president of the republic is elected by universal suffrage for a six-year term and may serve no more than two terms. The cabinet, headed by a premier, is called the Council of Ministers. The unicameral legislature, the Chamber of Deputies, is elected every five years.

The only legal political party, since 1981, is the Popular Rally for Progress (Rassemblement Populaire pour le Progrès, or RPP), which controls the selection of candidates for both the legislature and the presidency. Political life is shaped largely by the country's ethnic tensions and their interaction with the commercial and strategic interests of foreign powers. The paramount concern of both the colonial and independence governments was to balance these factors. For instance, the list of candidates for election to the Chamber of Deputies is designed to reflect in its proportions the ethnic composition of the population.

The Economy. The national economy depends on service industries, since the country has little primary production or manufacturing. Djibouti port and airport and the railroad from Addis Ababa make the capital a transshipment center. Banking is increasing in importance, and government policy is to maximize that sector through an open economy.

The port's prosperity was hit by the closure of the Suez Canal in 1967–1975, and its subsequent recovery was hampered by competition from other ports, such as Jidda in Saudi Arabia. The future is seen in containerization, and an enlarged modern container terminal was completed in the mid-1980's. Djibouti has been a free port since 1981.

The railroad from Addis Ababa, though remaining the basis for Ethiopia's interest in Djibouti, is a precarious avenue of trade. In 1977–1978 it was put out of action by political dissidents in Ethiopia, and it remains vulnerable to such attacks. In 1981 a new company for its management was formed by the governments of Ethiopia and Djibouti, which bought out the shares owned by the French government in the previous company. A modernization program was then begun.

Djibouti airport gained in importance as inland African countries increasingly air-freighted goods there for reexport.

Agriculture in Djibouti requires irrigation, but only 400 acres (100 hectares) are irrigated. Plans are to increase that total by boring more wells. The pastoralists herd camels, cattle, sheep, and goats, mainly for subsistence. However, they supply some live animals, meat, and skins for export to Arab countries, France, and Italy. These products are Djibouti's only ex-

© PAT MILLER/MONKMEYER PRESS

Donkey cart, auto, and bicycle all have a place in Djibouti's urban economy. The sign advertises groceries.

ports of domestic origin, although the development of fisheries has considerable potential.

The extraction of salt from abundant local deposits may again become economic. Exploitation of geothermal energy is promising, and major investment in this activity began in 1984.

Industrial plants process food, bottle mineral water, and make electrical and plastic items.

Imports vastly exceed exports in value. The visible trade deficit is offset by services and by foreign aid, mainly from France and Saudi Arabia. The chronically high rate of unemployment remains a serious problem.

History. Trading along the Red Sea coast goes back to classical times and before. The Somali and Afar peoples, though their earlier history remains controversial, have been in the area for over a thousand years. Links with the Arab world have always been strong, and the introduction of the Muslim religion, beginning in the 9th century, was crucial to the development of both peoples. The Afar are directly linked with the medieval Sultanate of Adal, and during the 19th century they were organized in three minor sultanates, which at least formally still exist. The Somali traditionally have had a looser and less hierarchical form of social organization.

The presence of the French on the coast began in 1862, when they occupied the small port of Obock on the northern shore of the Gulf of Tadjoura. During the 1880's they entered into treaties of protection with the Afar and Issa

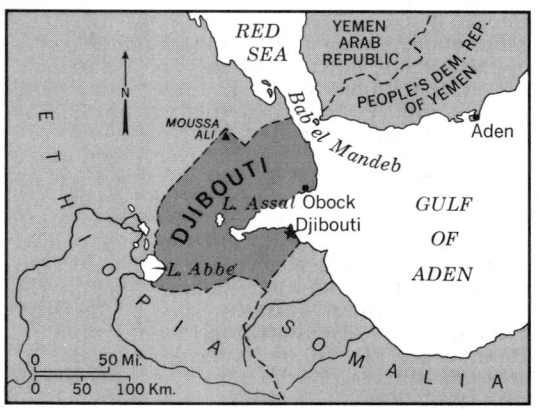

Men discuss local affairs at a curbside get-together in Djibouti. Custom excludes women from such gatherings.

tribespeople in the gulf area. Because of the inadequacy of Obock's harbor, the French began to develop the hitherto uninhabited site of Djibouti on the opposite side of the gulf. In 1896, Djibouti town was made the capital of the newly constituted colony of French Somaliland (Côte Française des Somalis). The frontiers drawn between the colony and Ethiopia on the one hand, and the then British Somaliland Protectorate on the other, had the effect of dividing the territories of both the Afar and the Issa Somalis.

A treaty between France and Ethiopia, signed in 1897, designated Djibouti the official outlet for Ethiopian trade. The railroad from Addis Ababa was completed in 1917.

During World War II the French authorities in Djibouti declared for the Vichy government, and the port suffered an Allied blockade that brought extreme hardship to the population. After the war, moves were made toward autonomy for the colony: in 1946 it acquired a representative council and returned a deputy to the French National Assembly, though indigenous voting rights remained restricted. Universal suffrage was introduced in 1957. Meanwhile, the tide of Somali nationalism had begun to rise. As independence and merger of the British and Italian Somali territories came into view, independence for the French colony seemed likely to mean its joining the "greater Somalia." Such an outcome was unacceptable to Ethiopia as to France. In general, it was also unacceptable to the Afar, who had previously shown little modern political consciousness but now began to play a dominant part on the national scene. In a referendum held in 1967, with the balloting strictly controlled by the French authorities, the Afar vote along with the French carried the day in favor of continued union with France. The country was then renamed the French Territory of the Afars and Issas.

Hardliners among the Somali nationalists went underground, and several terrorist episodes took place. Desire for independence within the territory increasingly was supported by the Organization of African States and world opinion, while France's loss of its Eastern empire and the uncertain situation of the Suez Canal made Djibouti port less essential to the metropolitan country. Political changes among the Afar population led to increased pressure for independence from that quarter also.

In 1977 the territory became formally independent, with the neutral name Republic of Djibouti. The new republic was led by the veteran Issa moderate Hassan Gouled Aptidon. Emphasizing traditional links with the Arab world, it became a member of the Arab League; and it depended for much of its finance on Saudi Arabia and other Arab countries. Somali nationalist aspirations remained unsatisfied, but the Somali Republic formally denied any territorial claims. France retained a military base in the port of Djibouti.

In 1978–1979, the problems of the new state were aggravated by the influx of perhaps 50,000 refugees, mainly Somalis escaping from the conflict between Somalia and Ethiopia in the latter's Ogaden region. International aid provided for the refugees temporarily, and a plan for their repatriation to Ethiopia was readily accepted by the Ethiopian and Djiboutian governments. However, it proved hard to implement.

Djibouti today has problems as a trading state situated in a strategically sensitive area of the globe. In order to survive, it must keep a balance between the rival claims of its two major ethnic groups, between the neighbor states of Ethiopia and the Somali Republic, and among France, the Arab countries, and the superpowers.

VIRGINIA LULING
Author of "A Somali Sultanate"

Further Reading: Lewis, I.M., *A Modern History of Somalia*, 2d ed. (Longmans 1980); Tholomier, Robert, *Djibouti, Pawn of the Horn of Africa* (Scarecrow 1981); Thompson, Virginia, and Adloff, Richard, *Djibouti and the Horn of Africa* (Stanford Univ. Press 1968).

DJIBOUTI, ji-bōō′tē, the capital of the Republic of Djibouti, in northeastern Africa. The city is a port on Gulf of Tadjoura, an inlet of the Indian Ocean just south of the entrance to the Red Sea. It was built during the French colonial period, largely in semi-Arab style. Unlike other ports on the coast, it has no "old town" or ancient monuments.

The population, estimated at 180,000 in 1981, is mixed. Its chief components are the two indigenous groups of the area, the Afar (Danakil) and the Issa Somalis; other Somalis; Yemeni Arabs; and a small but important French community.

Although Djibouti has some light industry, its economy depends on trade and financial services. The city is a free port and a center for transshipment. The railroad joining Djibouti to Addis Ababa makes the port Ethiopia's principal outlet to the sea, apart from Eritrea. The international airport is becoming increasingly important as a center for air freight. Djibouti also is the main French naval base on the Indian Ocean.

The port was built in 1892 by the French, chiefly as a station on the Suez Canal route to the East, corresponding to the British port of Aden. It became the official outlet for the trade of Ethiopia and grew rapidly. In 1896 it became the capital of French Somaliland, later called the French Territory of the Afars and Issas. In 1977 the territory gained independence as the Republic of Djibouti, with the city as its capital.

VIRGINIA LULING
Author of "A Somali Sultanate"

DJILAS, jē′läs, **Milovan** (1911–), Yugoslav Communist leader and writer, who was imprisoned for expressing his opposition to Communist policies in Yugoslavia. He was born in Polja, near Kolašin, Montenegro, on June 12, 1911. He became a Communist after obtaining his law degree in 1933. A close friend of Tito, Djilas was a leader of the Partisans in World War II and after the war held high government posts.

Djilas' criticism of the Communist regime in Yugoslavia began in 1953 and led to his resignation from the government, his expulsion from the party, and then his imprisonment in 1956. He received additional sentences for the controversial books he wrote in prison, but he was finally released on Dec. 31, 1966.

The New Class (1957), Djilas' best-known book, is a devastating explication of the failures of communism in practice. His essays in *Anatomy of a Moral* (1959) are highly critical of the bureaucracy and unethical behavior engendered by the Yugoslav Communist regime. *Conversations with Stalin* (1962) casts doubts on Stalin's moral integrity. Djilas' writings include his autobiographical *Land Without Justice* (1958); *Montenegro* (1963), history; *The Leper and Other Stories* (1964), fiction; *Njegos: Poet, Prince, Bishop* (1966), a study of the Serbian poet; and *Wartime* (1977), history.

VASA D. MIHAILOVICH
University of North Carolina

DLUGOSZ, dloo′gôsh, **Jan** (1415–1480), Polish historian and diplomat. He is also known by the Latin name Johannes Longinus. He was born in Brzeźnica in 1415. Head of the chancery of Cardinal Oleśnicki and a canon of Cracow, he undertook several missions to Italy, where he came under the influence of humanism. He participated in the diplomatic negotiations with the Teutonic Knights in the 1454–1466 war and, having gained the favor of King Casimir IV, was entrusted with the education of the royal princes in 1467. He died in Cracow in 1480, having just completed his most important work, a 12-volume history of Poland (*Historia Polonica*).

PIOTR S. WANDYCZ, *Yale University*

DMITRI, də-mē′trē, the name of Czar Ivan IV's son (1582–1591) and of several pretenders to the Russian throne during Russia's "Time of Troubles" (1605–1613). Dmitri Ivanovich died under mysterious circumstances in 1591. However, with the death of Czar Fyodor I, the last of the old dynasty, and the accession of Boris Godunov in 1598, there began the period of anarchy, social unrest, and foreign intervention known as the "Time of Troubles," in which at least four pretenders appeared, claiming to be Dmitri. The first, with Polish support, became czar in 1605, but he was killed in 1606. The second rallied Polish and peasant support in 1607–1610 before he too was killed. Two more claiming to be Dmitri or his son were executed by 1614.

Dmitri Ivanovich. Dmitri was born in 1582, the son of Ivan IV by his seventh wife, Maria Nagoy. After Ivan's death in 1584, Boris Godunov, who was regent for Dmitri's half brother Czar Fyodor I, exiled Dmitri to Uglich. Dmitri died in May 1591. According to Godunov, his death was due to an accidental knife wound during an epileptic fit. However, court circles suspected that Boris had murdered him to gain the throne for himself or for the offspring of Fyodor, whose wife was Boris' sister. When Fyodor died childless in 1598, Boris became czar.

First False Dmitri. Rumors soon spread that Dmitri was still alive. The first pretender appeared in Poland by 1601, became a Roman Catholic, and married a Polish noblewoman, Marina Mniszek. He was Russian, and tales unfavorable to him described him as one Grigori Otrepiev, a renegade church deacon. In 1605, Boris died, and many Russian army units joined the pretender's Polish and Cossack forces to crown him czar in Moscow. However, in May 1606, Prince Vasili Shuisky and a party of princes and boyars incited a Moscow mob to kill Dmitri and drive out his Catholic Polish advisers. Shuisky became czar.

Second False Dmitri. In 1607 another Dmitri, called the "Thief," arose, claiming that he had escaped Shuisky's mob. When he had secured Marina Mniszek's recognition of him as her husband, he won the support of Poles and Cossacks. He also received some aid from the Russian "service nobility" (the class whose titles were derived from service to the czars), who resented boyar dominance. Unable to take Moscow, Dmitri set up court in Tushino. In 1610 he lost his Polish support when King Sigismund of Poland claimed the Russian throne for his son Władysław. The Russian nobles deserted Dmitri because of his peasant following. Dmitri fled to Kaluga, where he was murdered in December 1610.

End of the "Troubles." Finally, in 1613, a national coalition, led by church, service nobility, burghers, and some Cossacks, elected Michael Romanov as czar. Cossack rebels still supported the second false Dmitri's son as czar, but the boy was taken and hanged in 1614.

The vitality of the claims of the false Dmitris was a symptom of the chaos of the period. The service nobility supported them in the name of legitimacy and the old order. The Poles used them as pawns for expansion. The peasantry and the Cossacks saw in them the "benevolent and just czar" who would give them land and freedom.

DAVID B. MILLER, *Roosevelt University*

DMITRI DONSKOY, də-mē′trē dun-skoi′ (1350–1389), prince of Moscow and grand prince of Vladimir, won the first victory by a Russian prince over the Tatars after the Tatar–Mongol invasion of Russia in the early 13th century. Succeeding his father Ivan II as prince of Moscow in 1359, Dmitri secured the title of grand prince of Vladimir from the Tatar khan of the Golden Horde in 1369 after a struggle with princes Michael of Tver and Olgerd of Lithuania. The war with Tver continued until 1375, when Prince Michael recognized the supremacy of Moscow. In 1367, Dmitri began construction of Moscow's Kremlin.

Dmitri is best remembered for his victory of 1380 over the Tatar khan Mamai on the Kulikovo plain beside the Don River; hence his sobriquet *Donskoy* ("of the Don"). The victory sparked an upsurge of patriotism, which saw in Moscow the unifier of Russia and its liberator from the Tatars. The poetic tale of Dmitri's victory, called the *Zadonshchina* (*Beyond the Don*), exemplifies this new patriotic spirit.

Although a new khan, Tokhtamysh, sacked Moscow in 1382 and forced it to pay tribute again, Dmitri passed his titles on to his son Vasili I without consulting the Horde. From this time onward Moscow was increasingly independent of the Tatars. Dmitri died on Sept. 8, 1389.

DAVID B. MILLER, *Roosevelt University*

DNA, *deoxyribonucleic acid*, is the genetic substance of all living cells and many viruses. The hereditary information transmitted from each generation to the next is encoded in the structures of the DNA molecules. These molecules are very long, essentially one-dimensional chains, composed of four types of subunits; the genetic information is conveyed in the sequence of the subunits (see NUCLEIC ACIDS).

DNA was first discovered by the German biochemist Friedrich Miescher in 1869. However, it was not until 1953 that the actual structure of the DNA molecules was finally determined. This was done in great part by the combined efforts of the American biochemist James D. Watson, the British molecular biologist Francis Crick, and the British biophysicist Maurice Wilkins.

Structure. The subunits of DNA, which are called *nucleotides*, are each composed of a carbohydrate residue (deoxyribose), a phosphate group, and a heterocyclic base. The chain is formed by coupling each deoxyribose to the deoxyribose of the next subunit through a phosphate group. There are four heterocyclic bases in DNA—adenine, guanine, cytosine, and thymine.

DNA molecules are most often found as double polynucleotide chains, intertwined to form a double helix. The nucleotides in the two chains of typical DNA are matched in such a way that adenine in one chain is always paired with thymine in the other, while guanine in one chain is always paired with cytosine in the other. Thus the two chains bear a precisely complementary relationship to each other, and the nucleotide sequence of either chain directly specifies the sequence of the other chain. In some viruses, however, DNA is present in a single-stranded form.

A virus particle contains only one DNA molecule, which ranges in length from 5,000 to over 200,000 subunits, depending on the virus. The number of molecules of DNA in the cell of a higher organism is unknown; the total length of DNA in a human cell would include 5 billion subunits. Over 99% of this DNA is found in the chromosomes in the cell nucleus. A small but distinct fraction is found in the mitochondria, and in plant cells DNA is also found in the chloroplasts.

Replication. As DNA molecules contain the hereditary instructions, a copy of each must be transmitted to each daughter cell at cell division. Replication of the DNA molecule is accomplished prior to division by a progressive separation of the two strands of the double helix, followed by the enzymatically catalyzed synthesis, from subunits, of complementary strands about each separated strand. The single strands act as a template during this process. The over-all result is the formation of two double helices, each identical to the original.

A partial replication can be used for repair of DNA. Maintenance of the fidelity of the hereditary instructions is of paramount importance to the cell and its progeny. If the damage is restricted to one strand of the double helix, it can be repaired in a two-stage process in which the damaged section is first removed by an enzyme and then replaced by resynthesis on the corresponding section of the undamaged complementary strand. Mechanisms for such repair are present in many types of cells.

In some viruses, DNA is present in a single-stranded form. During the replication a complementary double-stranded intermediate is formed, which replicates in the normal manner. A final stage of asymmetric replication provides the single strands for the progeny particles.

Mutation. Occasional mistakes occur in DNA replication as a consequence of radiation effects, thermal modifications of structure, or the presence in the cell of certain chemical substances. These result in a change in the nucleotide pattern and thereby in a genetic mutation. In the course of evolution increments of DNA content, accompanied by mutational changes in the DNA, have provided the hereditary variations from which new species could arise.

Function. A major portion of hereditary instructions of DNA is the set of specifications for the sequences of the amino acids of polypeptide chains. The polypeptides make up the protein molecules, which comprise the structural elements and catalytic agents (enzymes) of the cell. Each polypeptide chain is specified by a sequence of nucleotides in a DNA molecule. The nucleotides, taken consecutively in groups of three, specify through a code common to all forms of life the corresponding amino acid sequence. An elaborate machinery exists within the cell to synthesize protein according to the DNA instructions and to exert a variety of specific controls upon this process. This machinery involves RNA, ribonucleic acid, which is synthesized on the DNA template (see RNA).

Another portion of the total DNA blueprint is directly related to the process of control and specification of the initiation and termination points of message sequences for particular proteins. Although all cells of a higher organism contain the complete DNA complement, in any specialized cell only a small percentage of the messages are employed at any time. It is believed that means exist within the cell for the recognition of segments of DNA that in turn act as on-off switches of the function of the adjacent DNA tracts; controls are exerted through complex interactions of cellular components with such "operator" segments.

ROBERT L. SINSHEIMER
California Institute of Technology

DNEPRODZERZHINSK, dnyi-prə-dyer-zhinsk′, is a city in the USSR. It is situated on the Dnieper River, west of Dnepropetrovsk, in the Ukraine. The city is one of the Soviet Union's principal iron and steel centers, ranking third after Magnitogorsk in the Urals and Krivoi Rog in the Ukraine. In addition to the Dzerzhinsky steel mill, there are coke-chemical plants, a nitrogen fertilizer factory, and a major railroad-car manufacturing plant.

Electric power is supplied both by local coal-burning plants and by the Dneprodzerzhinsk hydroelectric station on the Dnieper River above the city. Construction of the 350,000-kw hydroelectric plant began in 1956, and its first turbines went into operation in 1963. Locks on the right bank of the river permit navigation.

Founded in the mid-18th century, the city, then called Kamenskoye, was a small steelworking town until the advent of Soviet rule. It has expanded greatly during the Soviet period. The present name was adopted in 1936 for the Dnieper River and Feliks Dzerzhinsky (1877–1926), a Soviet leader. Population: (1967 est.) 224,000.

THEODORE SHABAD
Editor of "Soviet Geography"

DNEPROPETROVSK, dnyi-prə-pye-trôfsk′, is a city in the USSR. It is the capital of Dnepropetrovsk oblast in the Ukraine. Situated at a point where several rail lines cross the Dnieper River, Dnepropetrovsk is an important transportation hub and one of the largest industrial centers in the USSR. The city has iron and steel mills, large metal-fabricating plants, and factories specializing in heavy industrial equipment. Among the products are blast furnaces and steel furnaces, portal cranes, excavators, machine tools, and farm equipment. The city derives much of its electric power from a 2.4 million-kw coal-burning station built in the 1960's at Pridneprovsk, which is on Chapli Island, in the Dnieper River just below Dnepropetrovsk.

Dnepropetrovsk is one of the Ukraine's educational and cultural centers, with specialized schools as well as a university. It has a concert hall and both a Russian and a Ukrainian theater.

The city was founded in 1786 by Grigori Potemkin, one of Catherine the Great's favorites, who named it Yekaterinoslav in honor of the empress. It flourished as an administrative center of New Russia, Russia's newly conquered southern territories. Modern development began in the 1880's when the city was reached by the railroad. The city was renamed Dnepropetrovsk in 1926, for the Dnieper River and Grigori Petrovsky, an early Soviet Ukrainian leader.

Dnepropetrovsk oblast, with an area of 12,317 square miles (31,900 sq km) is one of the principal industrial regions in the Ukraine. In addition to Dnepropetrovsk, the main cities are Dneprodzerzhinsk, Krivoi Rog, Nikopol, and Zheltye Vody. Population: (1967 est.) of the city, 816,000; of the oblast, 3,212,000.

THEODORE SHABAD
Editor of "Soviet Geography"

DNIEPER RIVER, nē′pər, the most important stream and waterway, after the Volga River, in the European part of the USSR. About 1,420 miles (2,285 km) long, the Dnieper (Russian, *Dnepr*) rises in the Valdai hills west of Moscow and flows generally south past Smolensk, Mogilev, Kiev, Kremenchug, Dnepropetrovsk, Zaporozhie, and Kherson to the Black Sea. Its upper reaches, in the forest zone, are partly swampy, but the middle and lower reaches of the Dnieper form a well-defined valley, 4 to 10 miles (6–16 km) wide. The principal tributaries in its drainage basin of 194,000 square miles (503,000 sq km) are, on the left, the Sozh, Desna, Psel, and Samara rivers and, on the right, the Berezina and Pripyat (Pripet) rivers.

During the relatively long shipping season (for Russian conditions) from March to December, the Dnieper functions as a major water transport route, carrying building materials and other bulk freight. The Dnieper basin is linked by old canal systems with the Western Dvina, Niemen (Neman), and Western Bug rivers, but these waterways accommodate only small barges.

The construction of a series of hydroelectric stations and reservoirs, which began in the 1930's, has greatly altered the course of the Dnieper River. The Dneproges Dam, at Zaporozhie, completed in 1932 and rebuilt in 1947 after destruction in World War II, flooded rapids that had formerly been an obstacle to navigation. Its hydroelectric station has a generating capacity of 650,000 kw. Downstream from Zaporozhie is a large reservoir created by the 343,000-kw Kakhovka station, which was opened in 1955 at Novaya Kakhovka. The 686,000-kw Kremenchug hydroelectric plant went into operation in 1959, followed by the 350,000-kw station at Dneprodzerzhinsk in 1963. The 526,000-kw Kiev plant, which uses the pumped storage principle, opened in 1965. Another major dam, with a generating capacity of 420,000 kw, was under construction at Kanev in the late 1960's.

THEODORE SHABAD
Editor of "Soviet Geography"

DNIESTER RIVER, nēs′tər, in the USSR, flowing in a generally southeast direction from the northern slopes of the Carpathian Mountains to the Black Sea. The Dniester (Russian, *Dnestr*) has a length of 845 miles (1,360 km) and, with its tributaries, drains a basin of 27,800 square miles (72,000 sq km). The river pursues a meandering course past the cities of Galich, Mogilev-Podolski, Bendery, and Tiraspol. Along part of its course, it forms the border between the two Soviet republics of the Ukraine and Moldavia.

Although the Dniester has only a light ice cover between December and March and does not freeze at all in some warm winters, it is of minor importance for navigation because of irregular water levels. In an effort to regulate the stream flow, several large storage dams have been planned, including a hydroelectric station, with a generating capacity of 500,000 kw, at Mogilev-Podolski. The only hydroelectric plant in operation in the 1960's was a small station inaugurated in 1954 at Dubossary. It has a capacity of 44,000 kw.

The Dniester was known to the ancient Greeks as the Tyras. Its modern name was first mentioned as Danastrus by the 6th century Gothic historian Jordanes. From 1919 to 1940 the Dniester marked the frontier between the USSR and Rumania.

THEODORE SHABAD
Editor of "Soviet Geography"

DOAB, dō'äb, a Hindustani term derived from Persian, means literally "two waters" but more freely denotes the land lying between two rivers. It refers specifically to the relatively flat, high lands that separate adjacent river valleys in northern India and West Pakistan.

In the Pakistani Punjab, the land between the Indus and the Chenab and Jhelum rivers is known as the Sind Sagar Doab. The area lying between the Jhelum and Chenab rivers is called the Jech or Chaj Doab; that between the Chenab and Ravi rivers is the Rechna Doab; and that between the Ravi and Sutlej is the Bari Doab. This last doab stretches across the Pakistan boundary into India.

Although a number of similar areas in northern India are also called doabs, there is one particular area of overriding importance known simply as The Doab. Lying between the Ganges and Yamuna (Jumna) rivers, The Doab has for centuries been a heartland of Indian culture and political power. It is bounded by such major cities as Delhi, Agra, Kanpur, and Allahabad, and in its center are Saharanpur and Meerut.

ROBERT C. KINGSBURY
Indiana University

DOBBS, Arthur (1689–1765), Irish government official, who encouraged the search for a Northwest Passage. He was born in Carrickfergus, Ireland, on April 2, 1689. Dobbs, a wealthy landowner, was a member of the Irish Parliament and surveyor general of Ireland. He believed strongly in the existence of a Northwest Passage from Hudson Bay to Asia and persuaded the British admiralty in 1741 to send an expedition to the bay to test his theory. The results were disappointing, and Dobbs launched an attack on the Hudson's Bay Company, claiming that its monopoly of the fur trade in the area made it hostile to exploration and sluggish in expanding westward.

In 1744, Dobbs published *An Account of the Countries Adjoining to Hudson's Bay*, which contained useful information on the bay's geography and resources. He organized his own expedition to the bay in 1746–1747, which again failed to find a passage. His attacks on the company led to a parliamentary inquiry in 1749, but it upheld the company's charter. In 1754, Dobbs was appointed governor of North Carolina. He died in Town Creek, N. C., on March 28, 1765.

D. M. L. FARR, *Carleton University*

DOBBS FERRY is a residential village in southern New York, in Westchester county, on the east bank of the Hudson River. It is 25 miles (40 km) north of downtown New York City, of which it is a suburb. The village is the home of the Children's Village, a rehabilitation school for boys.

The community received its name from the ferry operated here by William Dobbs and his son Jeremiah in the 18th century. Dobbs Ferry was occupied by both British and American troops during the American Revolution. The area was a part of the Philipse manorial estate that was forfeited to the state of New York after the war. In 1785, Philip Livingston purchased land here, including the house where Generals Washington and Rochambeau planned the Yorktown campaign.

Dobbs Ferry was incorporated in 1873. It is governed by a mayor and board of trustees. Population: 10,053.

DOBELL, dō-bel', **Sydney Thompson** (1824–1874), English poet and critic. He was born in Cranbrook, Kent, on April 5, 1824, and was educated by private tutors. A precocious youth, he viewed himself as a seer whose verse was metaphysically inspired. The stylistic extravagances of his best-known work, the dramatic poem *Balder* (1854), were parodied in *Firmilian* by William Aytoun, who labeled Dobell and his associates the "spasmodic" school. Dobell's poem *The Roman* (1850) expressed his sympathy for the Italian nationalists, and his *England in Time of War* (1856) contained descriptive verses on the Crimean War.

A semi-invalid during his last 20 years, Dobell died on Aug. 22, 1874, and was buried at Painswick, Gloucestershire. His miscellaneous prose was published posthumously in *Thoughts on Art, Philosophy, and Religion* (1876).

DOBELL, dō-bel', **Sir William** (1899–1970), Australian artist, who is noted for his fine craftsmanship and sense of color and for his Hogarthian realism. He was born on Sept. 24, 1899, in New Castle, New South Wales, and worked there as an architect before moving to Sydney to study art. In 1929 he received a traveling scholarship from the Australian Society of Arts and went to London, where he studied at the Slade School and later exhibited at the Royal Academy. Returning to Australia in 1939, he was the official artist of the Allied Works Council there during World War II.

In 1943, Dobell's portrait of a fellow artist, Joshua Smith, won the Archibald Prize for portraiture. His paintings are represented in the national galleries of Sydney and Adelaide, and in private collections.

Dobell was knighted in 1966. He died in Wangi, New South Wales, on May 14, 1970.

DÖBEREINER, dü'bə-rī-nər, **Johann Wolfgang** (1780–1849), German chemist who, with his theory of triads, introduced the idea that certain elements with similar properties can be arranged in natural groups. Döbereiner was born in Hof, Bavaria, on Dec. 13, 1780. At the age of 14 he began working in pharmacies, where he acquired a knowledge of chemistry. In 1810 he was appointed professor of chemistry at the University of Jena.

Döbereiner, inspired by Sir Humphry Davy's work with platinum, produced a platinum "sponge" in 1823 by decomposing a platinum salt with heat. When hydrogen gas was directed against a piece of this porous metal in air, the gas ignited. He incorporated the process into a lighter that became known as Döbereiner's lamp. His work was an important step in the use of platinum as a catalyst.

Between 1817 and 1829, Döbereiner sought experimental proof that chemically similar elements can be arranged in groups of three, or triads, in which the equivalent weights of the elements increase by equal amounts. His triads included calcium-strontium-barium and chlorine-bromine-iodine. Döbereiner thus produced the first evidence of the periodicity of the elements. Though his work was not considered important during his lifetime, it foreshadowed Mendeleyev's periodic table of the elements. Döbereiner died in Jena on March 24, 1849.

EDUARD FARBER
Editor of "Great Chemists"

DOBERMAN PINSCHER, dō′bər-mən pin′chər, a medium-sized dog trained for use in police and military work and as a protector-companion in the home. Doberman pinschers have the fire and lightning reaction of terriers and the power and intelligence of guard and herding breeds. It is also used as a hunting dog.

The breed originated in Germany in the late 19th century, but its ancestry is not certain. It derives its name from Louis Doberman of Apolda, Thuringia (a region of West Germany), whose experiments were reportedly involved in the early development of the breed, and from the German word for terrier. The breed's reputation for courage and its beauty made it popular in other lands, particularly the United States.

The Doberman pinscher has a short, shiny coat, clipped ears and tail, and very strong musculature. Its height at the shoulders is 24 to 28 inches (60–70 cm), and its weight may be 55 to 90 pounds (25–40 kg); males are larger than females. The Doberman pinscher's coat may be black, reddish-brown, bluish-gray, or silvery-beige with characteristic rust markings.

Doberman pinscher
EVELYN M. SHAFER

DOBIE, dō′bē, **J. Frank** (1888–1964), American writer. James Frank Dobie was born on a ranch in Live Oak county, Texas, on Sept. 26, 1888. Working as a newspaper reporter between terms, he graduated from Southwestern University in 1910 and received a master's degree from Columbia in 1914. During World War I he was an artillery officer. He taught English at several institutions, mainly at the University of Texas.

Noted as a collector and recorder of Southwestern folklore, he was for two decades secretary of the Texas Folklore Society and editor of its publications. His 20 books include *A Vaquero of the Brush Country* (1929), *Coronado's Children* (1930), *The Longhorns* (1941), and *The Mustangs* (1952). He died in Austin, Texas, on Sept. 18, 1964.

WAYNE GARD
Author of "Rawhide Texas"

Further Reading: Dobie, J. Frank, *Some Part of Myself* (Boston 1967).

DÖBLIN, dü blēn, **Alfred** (1878–1957), German writer of the expressionist school. He was born in Stettin, Pomerania, on Aug. 10, 1878, and was a physician in Berlin before critical acclaim for his novel *Die drei Sprünge des Wanglun* (1915), set in China. His later books include a historical novel, *Wallenstein* (1920); a Utopian satire, *Berge, Meere und Giganten* (1924); and his best-known work, *Berlin Alexanderplatz* (1929; Eng. tr., 1931), a novel whose interior monologues show the influence of Joyce.

After living in exile in France and the United States from 1933 to 1945, Döblin returned to Germany. His last novel, *Hamlet* (1956), was an expression of his hope for a new Europe. He died on June 26, 1957, at Emmendingen.

DOBRIZHOFFER, dō′brits-hôf-ər, **Martin** (1717–1791), Austrian Jesuit missionary in Paraguay. He was born in Friedberg, Bohemia, on Sept. 7, 1717, and joined the Society of Jesus in 1736. He was sent in 1749 to Paraguay, where he labored for 18 years among the Guarani and Abipón tribes. When the Jesuits were expelled from Paraguay and other Spanish possessions in 1767, he returned to Austria. He composed a 3-volume work, *Historia de Abiponibus* (1783–1784), based on his experiences and observations. The work provides a detailed description of the manners, customs, history, and life of the Paraguayan Indians and highlights the efforts of the missionaries to prevent the despoliation of the Indians by the civil authorities.

Dobrizhoffer was named preacher to the Imperial Court at Vienna in 1773. He held this post until his death in Vienna on July 17, 1791.

CLEMENT J. ARMITAGE, S. J.
Jesuit Missions, N. Y.

DOBROVSKÝ, dō′brôf-skē, **Joseph** (1753–1829), Czech philologist, who laid the foundations for the comparative study of Slavonic languages. He was born of Bohemian parents on Aug. 17, 1753, in Gyermet, near Györ, Hungary. For a brief time he was a Jesuit priest. After the dissolution of the Jesuit order in 1773, he devoted his life to scholarship. He died at Brno, Moravia, on Jan. 6, 1829.

Dobrovský wrote in Latin and German, but not in Czech. However, he helped revive the Czech national consciousness and, through his studies, inspired the revival of Czech as a literary language. His principal works are *Geschichte der böhmishcen Sprache und ältern Litteratur* (1792), a survey of the Czech language; *Ausführliches Lehrgebäude der böhmischen Sprache* (1809–1819), a study of Czech grammar; and *Institutiones linguae Slavicae dialecti veteris* (1822), the first scientific grammar of Old Slavonic.

DOBRUDJA, dô′broo-jä, is a historical region of the Balkan peninsula, now divided politically between Bulgaria and Rumania. It is bounded on the west and north by the Danube River and its estuary (the Kilia channel), on the east by the Black Sea, and on the south by a line running from the Danube near Tutrakan (Turtucaia) to Ekrene, south of Balchik, on the Black Sea. Dobrudja (or Dobruja) has an area of approximately 9,000 square miles (23,300 sq km). The Rumanian name for the region is Dobrogea.

The chief cities in the region are Silistra and Tolbukhin (Dobrich) in Bulgaria, and Constanţa, the major port of Rumania. The area is flat and semiarid, and it produces a high yield of cereal crops. A major industrial district was built up around Constanţa in the 1950's and 1960's. The area also has vineyards, and a fishing industry operates along the coast.

The Rumanian section of Dobrudja is now the center of that country's tourist industry. A se-

Dobrudja (dark shading) and nearby territory

ries of resorts with large, modern hotels stretch from Mamaia, near Constanța, in the north to Mangalia in the south. The center is Mamaia, which attracts visitors in large numbers from both eastern and western Europe. The facilities for water sports of all kinds are excellent. These resorts also offer a regular program of opera, folk dancing, ballet, and classical and popular music. From here it is possible to take excursions through Rumania and also to such places as Odessa, Istanbul, and Cairo. The traveler to Dobrudja should also take the opportunity to visit Constanta and two archaeological sites—the Greek city of Histria and the Roman monument at Adamclisi (Adam-Klissi), built by Emperor Trajan (reigned 98–117 A. D.) to commemorate a Roman victory over the Dacians in the 2d century A. D. In the Bulgarian section of Dobrudja, Balchik, a former residence of the Rumanian kings, is the principal tourist center.

History. The region has had a long and chaotic history. The original Geto-Dacian population was conquered in the 6th century B. C. by Greeks from Asia Minor. The principal settlements that they founded were Tomi (now Constanța), Histria, and Callatis (now Mangalia). In the 5th century B. C. the area was taken by the Scythians and in the 1st century B. C. by the Romans, who built a series of walled cities there. It later became a part of the Roman Empire. In this period it suffered from constant invasions by its neighbors and by the Goths, Huns, and Avars. It was also for a time a part of the Second Bulgarian Empire.

The name was probably acquired during the rule of Dobrotitch, a Rumanian prince who reigned briefly in the 14th century. In 1411, Dobrudja was conquered by the Ottoman Turks, who held it thereafter for over 400 years. This was a bleak period in its history. The region was virtually deserted, and its lands were scarcely cultivated.

In 1878 at the Congress of Berlin the first political partition of the area in modern times occurred. Rumania received the northern section, while the autonomous Bulgaria was given the south. The boundary was redrawn repeatedly as a result of the three wars that followed, in which Bulgaria was consistently on the losing side. After the Second Balkan War (1913), Rumania was able to extend its boundary southward to include almost the whole area. After World War I, by the Treaty of Neuilly, Rumania gained the entire region. The Treaty of Craiova in 1940 returned southern Dobrudja, including Silistra and Balchik, to Bulgaria. This settlement was confirmed by treaties made after World War II.

BARBARA JELAVICH and CHARLES JELAVICH
Indiana University

DOBSON, Austin (1840–1921), English poet, critic, and biographer. Henry Austin Dobson was born in Plymouth, England on Jan. 18, 1840, and was a civil servant with the Board of Trade from 1856 to 1901. Throughout his life he wrote prolifically. He died in Ealing, a suburb of London, on Sept. 2, 1921.

Dobson's poetry, much of it written in such French forms as the triolet and rondeau, is noted for its lightness and delicacy. His books of verse include *Proverbs in Porcelain* (1877), *Collected Poems* (1897), and *Carmina Votiva* (1901). Among his prose works, also graceful and delicate, are *Eighteenth Century Vignettes* (3 series; 1892–1894, and 1896) and biographies of William Hogarth (1879), Steele (1886), Horace Walpole (1890), and Fanny Burney (1903).

DOBSON, Frank (1888–1963), English sculptor, who was one of the forerunners of the modern art movement in Britain. He was born in London on Nov. 18, 1888. He first studied painting at art schools in Epping, Arbroath, and London but turned to sculpture in 1913. His early sculpture, with its geometric, abstract forms, aroused controversy because of its cubist style, which had not yet gained wide acceptance in Britain. His later work, although it retained a degree of abstraction, became more classical, in the manner of Maillol.

Dobson worked in many mediums—stone, bronze, brass, silver, glass, and concrete—and produced portraits of such well-known persons as Osbert Sitwell (1923). Appointed an associate of the Royal Academy in 1942, Dobson became a full member in 1953, and from 1946 to 1953 he was professor of sculpture at the Royal College of Art. He died on July 22, 1963, in London.

DOBSON, William (c. 1610–1646), English portrait painter. He was born in London and is believed to have been a student of the German artist Francis Cleyn and possibly a protégé of Sir Anthony Van Dyck. In 1642 he succeeded Van Dyck as court painter to Charles I at Oxford, where the King's headquarters were located during the Civil War. Containing only slight hints of Van Dyck's style, Dobson's portraits of various courtiers are painted in a robust Italianate manner that may have been derived from his study of the Venetian paintings in Charles I's collection.

Dobson's best painting is the full-length portrait of William Compton, in the collection of Castle Ashby, Northampton. In his painting *The Beheading of St. John*, the head of John is thought to be a portrait of Prince Rupert, Charles I's nephew. With Charles' fall from power, Dobson's fortunes declined. He was buried in London on Oct. 28, 1646.

Adult dobsonfly

DOBSONFLY, dob′sən-flī, the common name of the Corydalidae, a small family of insects whose aquatic larvae, called *hellgrammites,* are used by fishermen as bait, especially for bass. Dobsonflies are found in many regions of the world. The largest and most striking species in North America is *Corydalus cornutus,* which has two pairs of net-veined wings with a wingspan of 5 inches (13 cm). The adult male of this species is easily recognized by its curved protruding jaws, which may be an inch (2.5 cm) long. The female has jaws of normal size.

Members of the dobsonfly family have a 3-year life cycle. In early summer the adult female deposits masses of 2,000 or more white eggs on objects overhanging streams or other bodies of water. The larvae feed on small aquatic animals and are often eaten by fish.

RALPH H. DAVIDSON
Ohio State University

DOBZHANSKY, dob-zhän′skē, **Theodosius** (1900–1975), American biologist, whose detailed studies of fruit fly genetics have revealed important information concerning diversity within species. Initial genetic studies of fruit flies (*Drosophila*) in the early 1900's resulted in the idea that a population consists of a "normal" or "wild" strain, with fixed characteristics, and mutated individuals that form a small minority of abnormal and deformed variations from the norm. In the late 1920's, Dobzhansky, working with the American geneticist Thomas Hunt Morgan, showed that this was a grossly oversimplified view and that there is great genetic diversity within species. He showed that most individuals of a species possess one or more genes that are considered not normal or wild and are less useful at the time than the normal gene.

Dobzhansky went on to show that the "genetic load" of less useful or weakening genes is of use to the species. He found that successful species tend to have larger genetic loads than less successful species. The greater gene variability present in species with large genetic loads makes for greater diversity within the species and consequently a greater chance for the species to adapt to changing circumstances and be naturally selected in the process of evolution.

Dobzhansky was born in Nemirov, Russia, on Jan. 25, 1900. He studied zoology at the University of Kiev, graduating in 1921; he then taught zoology there and at the University of Leningrad. In 1927 he went to the United States to work with T. H. Morgan at Columbia University and at the California Institute of Technology. Later he was professor at Columbia (1940–1962), Rockefeller University (1962–1971), and the University of California at Davis, from 1971 until his death, at Davis, on Dec. 18, 1975. His books include *Genetics and the Origin of Species* (1937).

ISAAC ASIMOV
Boston University School of Medicine

DOCETISM, dō-sē′tiz-əm, was an early Christian heresy. The term is derived from the Greek *dokein,* meaning "to appear." Docetism proposed that Christ only "appeared" to have a real human body. This belief was a prevalent feature of Gnosticism, which held that matter and spirit are antagonistic. For the Gnostics, salvation consisted in liberation from the bondage of matter; consequently, while accepting Christ as Saviour, Gnosticism could not logically accept a real Incarnation. Another common Docetistic tenet was that Christ's sufferings on Calvary were an illusion or that someone else was substituted for Him.

The origins of Docetism are obscure. Some indications of its existence and repudiation are found in the New Testament. By the early 2d century, Ignatius of Antioch (died c. 110) had condemned it. More detailed refutations were given by Irenaeus (died c. 202) and Tertullian (died after 220). While Docetism exerted its major influence in the 2d and 3d centuries, tendencies occasionally appeared later in conjunction with sects such as the Manichees and Catharists.

JOHN FORD, C. S. C.
Catholic University of America

DOCK, the common name applied to various species of herbs of the genus *Rumex* in the buckwheat family (Polygonaceae). They are worldwide in distribution and are mainly hardy perennials, with strong deep roots and long clus-

Curled dock
(*Rumex crispus*)

ters (panicles) of small greenish flowers. The docks are distinguished from the sorrels in the same genus by having male and female reproductive structures in the same flower rather than in separate flowers. The tiny fruits are small, dry, three-cornered capsules (achenes), each containing a single seed.

A few species—such as herb patience, or spinach dock (*Rumex patientia*), and curled, or yellow, dock (*R. crispus*)—are used as greens and potherbs. They are sometimes cultivated for that purpose, since the leaves appear earlier than most plants used similarly. Some species have limited ornamental uses, especially for bold effects, but most are rather weedy and difficult to control, as any piece of root left in the ground produces plants. See also CANAIGRE; SORREL.

RICHARD M. STRAW
Los Angeles State College

DOCK, a berthing space for ships. There are two general kinds: in *wet docks*, ships are berthed afloat; in *dry docks*, ships are supported on blocking in the dry, except during entry and exit. This article deals only with wet docks; see also DRY DOCK.

Wet docks are large artificial basins bounded by berthing structures such as quay walls or piers. They include open and enclosed types.

Enclosed Docks. Enclosed docks have locks and gates that protect them from tidal action. They are mainly used in northern European ports, such as London and Liverpool, where the tidal range often exceeds 14 feet (4.3 meters). A deep-draft ship under full load enters a dock at high tide, and the entrance gates close to keep the high-water level inside as the tide recedes. An unloaded ship can depart through a lock at a lower tidal stage without disturbing the water depth of ships at other berths.

Open Docks. Generally, an open dock is the space between two adjacent piers. Open docks, which are exposed to tidal action, are used in ports in the United States, Australia, the Mediterranean Sea, and in many other ports where the tidal range is small.

Berthing Structures. Berthing structures accommodate ships and facilitate receiving or discharging cargoes or passengers. *Quay walls*, generally built parallel to the shore, retain earth on one face and accommodate ships on the other face. Solid quay walls are made of concrete or masonry. A pile-supported quay wall, often called a *marginal wharf*, has a sheet-pile bulkhead to retain earth along the rear face.

Piers project into the water at an angle and provide berthing space for ships on both faces. The typical open-structure pier consists of a reinforced concrete deck supported on vertical piles and braced laterally by batter piles. A cargo pier usually is more than 100 feet (30.5 meters) wide and has a transit shed mounted on the deck for receiving and transshipping cargo.

JAMES R. AYERS AND RALPH C. STOKES
Formerly, U. S. Navy Bureau of Yards and Docks

DOCTOR is a title signifying professional qualification or academic distinction. In modern use it is most often applied in the first sense to designate a person trained in medicine—a doctor of medicine (M. D.). The title is also given to those who hold the doctorate of philosophy (Ph. D.) or other academic degrees. The doctorate is the highest earned degree awarded by most universities. See DEGREE.

The term "doctor" comes from the Latin word meaning "teacher" (from *docere*, "to teach") and originally denoted anyone who taught. In the Middle Ages it came to mean a man renowned for learning. Some great theologians were called doctors. See DOCTOR OF THE CHURCH.

DOCTOR FAUSTUS, fou′stəs, is a verse tragedy by the English dramatist Christopher Marlowe (q.v.). It was one of the most popular Elizabethan plays and is recognized as a major contribution to drama. Its date is uncertain; some scholars place it soon after *Tamburlaine* (about 1587), Marlowe's first success in the theater, while others put it at the end of his short life.

Based on the English translation of the German *Faustbuch*, *The Tragicall History of Doctor Faustus* tells of a scholar who, dissatisfied with the limits of orthodox knowledge, sells his soul to the devil for 24 years of power and sensuality. The opening scenes, culminating in the signing of the bond; Faustus' address to the apparition of Helen of Troy; and his concluding soliloquy when the bond falls due—all show the splendor of Marlowe's verse and a high intellectual passion. There are also scenes of rather frigid comedy, in which another hand than Marlowe's may have been at work. The total effect is complex but unified, revealing Marlowe's fascination with human daring and a realization of its futility.

CLIFFORD LEECH, *Editor of
"Marlowe: A Collection of Critical Essays"*

DOCTOR JEKYLL AND MR. HYDE, a tale of horror and suspense by the Scottish writer Robert Louis Stevenson (q.v.), published in 1886. In *The Strange Case of Dr. Jekyll and Mr. Hyde*, Henry Jekyll, a prominent London doctor thought to be humane and generous, becomes mysteriously associated with the vicious Edward Hyde. Hyde's tyranny over Jekyll seems unaccountable until the end of the story reveals that Jekyll's scientific experiments had enabled him to change his identity at will and that he himself was Mr. Hyde. Jekyll, progressively less able to control these changes, eventually dies as Hyde. The tale is narrated by a lawyer, Mr. Utterson, who experiences first the terror of meeting Hyde and then the shock of realizing that Hyde, a murderer, and Dr. Jekyll are the same man.

The names of the story's protagonists have become bywords for persons suffering from a split personality—one side benevolent, the other evil. Despite supernatural overtones, Stevenson's tale dramatizes a psychological duality also explored in fiction by Poe, Dostoyevsky, and Conrad, and in psychology by Freud and Jung.

LAWRENCE GRAVER, *Williams College*

DOCTOR OF THE CHURCH is a title of honor for those Christian ecclesiastical writers who are outstanding in their witness to religious truths in their life and writings. Three requisites are usually enumerated: (1) eminent holiness—only canonized saints are recognized as doctors; (2) exceptional learning—their contribution to the Christian community must be outstanding; and (3) declaration by the church—the conferral of this title is distinguished from the medieval custom of giving an academic nickname to philosophers and theologians.

The teaching of a Doctor of the Church is not binding on the believer as such. However, the doctors have preeminence as teachers because of their grasp of the Christian mysteries and their expression of them in life and teaching.

Four writers of the early Latin Church—Saints Ambrose (died 397), Jerome (died 419), Augustine (died 430), and Gregory the Great (died 604)—were recognized as the great doctors of the West by Pope Boniface VIII in 1298.

Saints Basil the Great (died 379), Gregory of Nazianzus (died 390), and John Chrysostom (died 407) were recognized as the great doctors of the East. The Western church usually enumerated St. Athanasius (died 373) with the other Eastern doctors, although the Eastern churches hesitated to give him equal rank with the other three. No other writer was declared a Doctor of the Church until Pope Pius V so honored St. Thomas Aquinas in 1568. The number reached 30 when John XXIII gave this title to St. Lawrence of Brindisi in 1959.

ROBERT HENNESSEY, O. P.
Dominican House of Studies, Washington, D. C.

DOCTOR ZHIVAGO, zhi-vä'gō, is a novel by the Russian writer Boris Pasternak (q.v.). It was published in translation, first in Milan, Italy, in 1957 and then in other countries in 1958, and filmed by British director David Lean in 1965. Because of what Soviet editors called stylistic inadequacies and because of material considered hostile to the Soviet Union, the book was not published in the USSR.

The novel records the life and thought of a Russian physician and poet, Yuri Zhivago, from early 1903 to his death in 1929 (with an epilogue set in 1943). Although Zhivago is a product of upper-class, pre-Revolutionary Russian culture, he welcomes the revolution and its promise of universal justice. Later, his wife persuades him to avoid famine in Moscow by going on a dramatic journey to the family estate in the Ural Mountains, where he is caught in the middle of the civil war between the White and Red forces. He finally returns to Moscow, where he dies.

The main theme of *Doctor Zhivago* is the interdependence of human destinies. The story is told in 17 parts, the last of which is a sequence of 25 poems closely tied to the story's theme and events. Structured as a succession of scenes, dialogues, and descriptions, the novel mixes the real with the symbolic, shifting between the world of sensations and the world of ideas.

Pasternak began writing *Doctor Zhivago* in 1948, though the idea for the novel dates back to his autobiographical tale *A Safe Conduct* (1929–1931) and to a 1938 sketch *From a New Novel About 1905*. Some of the poems first appeared in 1954. In 1955, Pasternak submitted the manuscript to the literary magazine *Novy mir* and, with official permission, to the Milan publisher Feltrinelli. In September 1956 *Novy mir* rejected the manuscript, and the book, acclaimed in the West, was ignored in the USSR.

FRANKLIN D. REEVE
Author of "The Russian Novel"

DOCTORFISH. See SURGEONFISH.

DOCTOR'S DILEMMA, a play by George Bernard Shaw (q.v.), first acted in 1906. One of Shaw's most brilliant and controversial plays, it is seldom revived because of the large and proficient cast it requires. The play's longest run was in 1942–1943 at the Haymarket Theatre in London.

The *Doctor's Dilemma* begins with a group of amusingly different medical men who have met to celebrate the knighthood of one of their number. While together, they discuss the fate of a young genius whose paintings they admire but whose morals they deplore and whose wife Jennifer infatuates them all. Circumstances oblige the doctors to choose either saving the life of the artist or using their limited resources to sustain the life of a colleague who is otherwise doomed to die in poverty and misery. They choose the latter course, and the painter dies.

The Doctor's Dilemma is said to have been written as a reply to critic William Archer's taunt that Shaw could not claim the highest rank as a dramatist until he had written a death scene. The scene in which the painter dies caused readers of the play to accuse Shaw of not taking death seriously, and he inserted in the program of the first production: "Life does not cease to be funny when people die, any more than it ceases to be serious when people laugh."

ALAN DENT
Author of "Mrs. Patrick Campbell"

DOCTRINAIRES, dôk-trē-nâr', is the name adopted by a small group of French politicians active after the Bourbon restoration in 1815. Their leaders were Pierre Royer-Collard and François Guizot. Camille Jordan, Achille de Broglie, and the Baron de Barante were associated with the group. The Doctrinaires took their name from the colloquial name for a religious order whose school Royer-Collard had attended.

Attempting to strike a balance between revolution and reaction, the Doctrinaires favored a constitutional monarchy with parliamentary control. Until 1820 they supported the goals of the moderate Constitutional party, but later disagreements splintered their group. After 1830, the Doctrinaires formed a small faction in the Chamber of Deputies that supported Guizot. In present-day usage, the term "doctrinaire" denotes someone who holds to his principles in a rigid, uncompromising manner.

DOCTRINE means literally "teaching," usually a teaching of a religious group. It can be understood either in the active sense of imparting information or in the passive sense of what is taught. In a Christian context the purpose of doctrine is the conversion of life of the hearer and believer; thus, Christian doctrine should not be thought of as merely a system of religious teachings or a philosophy of religion. The subject presented is a person, Jesus Christ: His life, death, Resurrection, and Ascension, and His promise of eternal life to those who believe in Him with love.

The method and content of Christian doctrine change with different conditions—for example, from the relative simplicity of the apostolic age to the patristic period when Greek philosophy was used as the teaching instrument. Today, Biblical scholarship, historical consciousness, secularization, the rise of human and social sciences, and ecumenism have made new approaches necessary. However, the test of valid change is fidelity to the person of Jesus Christ. Even teachings formalized in creeds or defined in councils are subject to further exploration because a creed or definition is essentially a minimal statement, while the fundamental subject of Christian doctrine is God in Jesus Christ, who is beyond exhaustive understanding or knowledge.

CHARLES E. SHEEDY, C. S. C.
University of Notre Dame

DOCUMENTATION. See INFORMATION STORAGE AND RETRIEVAL.

DODD, Frank Howard (1844–1916), American publisher. He was born in Bloomfield, N. J., on April 12, 1844, and began to work in his father's bookstore and publishing house in New York as a boy of 15. Ten years later, with his cousin Edward S. Mead, he formed Dodd, Mead & Company. While Mead was primarily an editor and writer, Dodd was a highly enterprising businessman, obtaining popular American and British authors by offering them generous inducements. He was also the first to bring out inexpensive reprints of popular copyrighted works.

In 1884, Dodd bought Alden's *Library of Universal Knowledge*, which he published in a revised edition in 1890 as the *International Cyclopedia*. It was issued again in 1902 as the *New International Encyclopedia* in 17 volumes. He also started the *Bookman*, patterned after the London periodical of the same name, in 1895.

Dodd was president of the American Publishers Association for a number of years. He died in New York City on Jan. 10, 1916.

CHARLES A. MADISON
Author of "Book Publishing in America"

DODD, Thomas Joseph (1907–1971), American political leader. He was born in Norwich, Conn., on May 15, 1907. After graduating from Yale law school in 1933, he became a special agent for the Federal Bureau of Investigation. As special assistant to the attorney general (1938–1945) he helped establish a civil rights section in the U. S. Department of Justice and was its first director. He served as U. S. executive trial counsel at the Nuremberg trials.

A Democrat, Dodd served in the U. S. House of Representatives (1953–1957). He won election to the Senate in 1958 and 1964. Following charges by former members of Dodd's staff that he had diverted campaign funds for personal use, the Senate ethics committee recommended, after an investigation, that he be censured for his conduct. After a debate in the Senate in 1967, Dodd was censured by a 92-to-5 vote, and he failed to win reelection in 1970. He died in Old Lyme, Conn., on May 24, 1971.

DODD, William Edward (1869–1940), American historian and diplomat. He was born in Clayton, N. C., on Oct. 21, 1869. He graduated from Virginia Polytechnic Institute (B. S., 1895) and obtained his Ph. D. from the University of Leipzig in 1900. After occupying the chair of history at Randolph-Macon College, he transferred in 1908 to the University of Chicago, having already earned a reputation as an authority on the Old South. He wrote *Statesmen of the Old South* (1911) as well as biographies of Jefferson Davis (1907) and Woodrow Wilson (1920) and, with Ray Stannard Baker, edited *The Public Papers of Woodrow Wilson* (1925–1926).

Recalling his happy student years in Leipzig, Dodd accepted appointment as U. S. ambassador to Berlin in 1933. But the Germans and the Germany of his youth had vanished. Only a strong sense of duty induced him to retain his post for nearly five years in a country where personal and intellectual liberty was denied, race hatred was propagated, and Storm Troopers assaulted Americans who failed to render Nazi salutes. An account of his frustrating experiences in Germany was published posthumously as *Ambassador Dodd's Diary* (1941). Dodd died at Round Hill, Va., on Feb. 9, 1940.

DODDER, dod'ər, any of a group of widely distributed parasitic plants, related to the morning glory family, characterized by dense tangles of leafless threadlike stems, usually yellow or orange in color. Dodder parasitizes green plants, and though some forms show a distinct preference for certain hosts, many will attack a wide variety of plants. One species has been recorded as parasitizing 131 kinds of plants.

The dodder seed germinates in the ground, producing only a short root to anchor the stem. As the stem lengthens, it grows in a spiral fashion (nutation) until it makes contact with a host plant. After securing itself to the host by twining around it, the dodder develops modified roots, called haustoria, which penetrate and absorb water and nutrients from the host's tissues. The dodder's ground root then dies and shrivels away, leaving the parasite completely dependent on its host for survival. Dodder seedlings that do not reach a suitable host may live from 4 days to 5 weeks after germination.

The growing, branching dodder may attack other plants nearby, and a single dodder can parasitize several plants at once. In one study of dodder, the longest single stem piece was 6 feet 9 inches (2.06 meters) in length, and the total length of all the stem pieces was 2,406 feet (744 meters). Under ideal growing conditions, total stem lengths of more than a mile (1.6 km) are considered probable.

Clusters of minute, tubular, often white flowers are usually borne during the summer and fall. The mature flowers produce tiny seeds that remain viable (able to germinate) for up to 5

DODDER, a parasitic plant, appears as a tangled mass of leafless stems twining repeatedly around its host.

JACK DERMID

years. Dodder can also reproduce vegetatively from detached stem pieces.

Parasitism by dodder, which weakens and discolors the host plants, is particularly troublesome in alfalfa and clover agriculture. The production of clover seed in certain parts of Europe had to be abandoned because of this parasite. Control methods include prevention of accidental introduction of the seed, hand removal or destruction of the plant, and the rather expensive and somewhat unreliable application of chemicals.

The some 150 species of dodder are classified in the genus *Cuscuta* of the dodder family (Cuscutaceae).

RICHARD S. COWAN
Smithsonian Institution

DODDRIDGE, dod′rij, **Philip** (1701–1751), English Dissenting minister. He was born in London on June 26, 1701. Unable to attend Oxford or Cambridge because of laws requiring students to be members of the Church of England, he was trained by pious parents and in private schools. Doddridge began preparing for the ministry in 1723 at a seminary in Kibworth, Leicestershire. In 1729 he was called to a parish in Northampton, where he served as pastor and developed an influential academy.

Doddridge was a pious man given to study and self-examination. His commentary on the New Testament, *The Family Expositor* (6 vols., 1739–1756), became a household work in England. His devotional work, *The Rise and Progress of Religion in the Soul* (1745), was one of the most widely read books in Europe and America. Doddridge's books, which expressed a mild Calvinism, provided an incentive to faith. In a period of arid rationalism he stressed dependence upon divine assistance, grace, and illumination. Influenced by the tolerant ideas of John Locke, he was particularly sympathetic toward Wesley and the Methodists. After his death, about 170 of his hymns were published in a popular collection in 1755.

Continual illness caused him to seek a milder climate. He died in Lisbon, Portugal, on Oct. 26, 1751.

JAMES H. SMYLIE
Union Theological Seminary, Richmond, Va.

DODECAHEDRON, dō-dek-ə-hē′drən, a solid that has 12 plane faces. When the 12 faces are equal pentagons, the solid is called a *regular dodecahedron*. See also POLYHEDRON.

DODECANESE, dō-dek′ə-nēz, a collective name applied to the islands in the southeastern Aegean Sea between eastern Crete and Turkey. The islands, also known as the *Southern Sporades*, belong to Greece. The name Dodecanese means "the 12 islands."

The number 12 was fixed in the 16th century when 12 islands voluntarily submitted to Turkish rule and were granted local autonomy on payment of a fixed annual tribute. The 12 islands were, from south to north, Kasos, Karpathos, Chalke, Telos, Syme, Kastellorizo, Astypalaia, Nisyros, Kalymnos, Leros, Patmos, and Icaria. The two richest islands in the area, namely Rhodes and Kos, were excluded from the Turkish agreement. However, they are included in the present-day Dodecanese, and their inclusion raises the total of sizable islands in the group to 14.

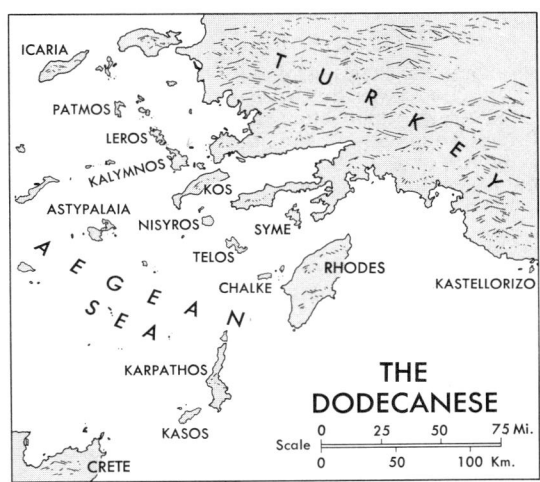

THE DODECANESE

Rhodes, Kos, and Icaria have good land and are richer than their neighbors. The other islands suffer from a deficiency of arable soil and often of water, so that the islanders have depended on fishing, sponge diving, and the shipping trade to supplement their income from crops of fruit, olives, and tobacco. Since 1945 the increasing use of artificial sponge and the decline in the use of small craft have impoverished most of the islands and led to much emigration.

History. The Dodecanese have often been controlled by outside powers. The Minoan rulers of Crete planted colonies at Ialysus in Rhodes and on Kalymnos about 1600 B.C. The great powers of the classical world—Athens, Sparta, the Hellenistic kings, and Rome—courted or subjugated the islands, especially Rhodes, which often fought for its independence. With the weakening of the Byzantine Empire, the Venetians, the Genoese, and the Crusaders in turn seized the islands, and in the 14th and 15th centuries the Knights of St. John administered a group of islands that extended from Leros to Rhodes, the Knights' headquarters.

The Turks honored their 16th century agreement with the Dodecanese. They retained them until 1912, when Italy occupied the islands. The occupation was confirmed by the Treaty of London in 1915 and the Treaty of Lausanne in 1923. After the Italian collapse in World War II, the islands were annexed to Greece (by treaty in April 1947).

N. G. L. HAMMOND
University of Bristol

DODECAPHONY. See ATONAL MUSIC.

DODGE, Grenville Mellen (1831–1916), American general and civil engineer, who built railroads in the western United States. He was born in Danvers, Mass., on April 12, 1831. He was a railroad engineer in Illinois and Iowa. In the Civil War, Dodge became a major general in the Union Army and commanded the XVI Corps at the siege of Atlanta in 1864. He resigned from the Army in 1866. In the next 15 years he supervised the construction of 9,000 miles (15,000 km) of track for the Union Pacific and other western railroads. His railroad surveys were said to have totaled some 60,000 miles (96,000 km). With Sir William Horne, he built a railroad in Cuba that was completed in 1903.

After the Spanish-American War (1898) he headed the Dodge Commission, named to investigate the conduct of the conflict. The report of this body was the basis of massive changes in U. S. Army organization after 1900. Dodge published volumes on the Battle of Atlanta, the building of the Union Pacific, and recollections of Lincoln, Grant, and Sherman. He died in Council Bluffs, Iowa, on Jan. 3, 1916.

COURTNEY R. HALL
Author, "History of American Industrial Science"

DODGE, Henry (1782–1867), American soldier and political leader. He was born in Vincennes, Ind., on Oct. 12, 1782. In 1805 he became a sheriff in the Missouri Territory, and he later was marshal of Missouri and a general in the territorial militia. After moving to southwestern Wisconsin (then part of the Michigan Territory) in 1827, he participated in the Winnebago and Black Hawk wars. In 1834 and 1835, as commander of a regiment of U. S. dragoons, he led patrol and pacification marches to the Red River and the Colorado Rockies.

Dodge was appointed governor of the new Territory of Wisconsin in 1836, and from 1841 to 1845 he represented that territory in Congress as a Democrat. In 1845 he was reappointed governor, and when Wisconsin achieved statehood in 1848, he was elected to the U. S. Senate. His son, Augustus C. Dodge (1812–1883), served in the Senate contemporaneously (1848–1854), representing the new state of Iowa. As a senator, Henry Dodge adhered to the predominantly free-soil views of his constituents. He retired in 1857 and died in Burlington, Iowa, on June 19, 1867.

HOWARD W. SMITH, Spring Hill College

DODGE, Mary Elizabeth Mapes (1831–1905), American writer and editor of juvenile literature, who is best known for *Hans Brinker; or the Silver Skates* (1865). She was born in New York City on Jan. 26, 1831. She married William Dodge in 1851, and after the death of her husband in 1858 she turned to writing to support her two small children. From the publication of *Irvington Stories* in 1864 her work found quick acceptance. She exercised considerable influence in moving children's literature from the morbid, sentimental, and didactic to more cheerful themes. *Hans Brinker*, her greatest success, combines an exciting story with much information on the history and social customs of Holland.

From 1873, Mrs. Dodge was editor of the children's monthly *St. Nicholas Magazine*. Her books include *A Few Friends and How They Amused Themselves* (1869), *Donald and Dorothy* (1883), *When Life Is Young* (1894), *The Land of Pluck* (1894), and two books compiled from her contributions to *St. Nicholas Magazine—Baby Days* (1876) and *Baby World* (1884). She died in Onteora Park, N. Y., on Aug. 21, 1905.

JEROME STERN, Florida State University

DODGE, Raymond (1871–1942), American experimental psychologist, who is best known for his studies of eye movements in reading. He was born in Woburn, Mass., on Feb. 20, 1871. He studied at Williams College and the University of Halle, receiving his Ph.D. in 1896. Dodge taught psychology at Wesleyan University from 1898 to 1924 and then joined the Institute of Psychology at Yale. In 1929 he became a director of the newly established Yale Institute of Human Relations, serving until his retirement in 1936. He died in Tryon, N. C., on April 8, 1942.

Using tachistoscopes of his own invention, Dodge was able to measure and record eye movements with unusual precision. His studies were put to practical use in the training of gunners during World War I. He also studied the physiological effects of alcohol, demonstrating its depressant characteristics, and contributed to the study of habituation and other forms of conditioning. His works include *The Elementary Conditions of Human Variability* (1927) and (with E. Kahn) *The Craving for Superiority* (1931).

MICHAEL G. ROTHENBERG
Columbia University

DODGE CITY, a city in southwestern Kansas, the seat of Ford county, is 150 miles (240 km) west of Wichita, on the Arkansas River. Situated in a wheat-growing and cattle-raising area, it is the trading center for southwestern Kansas. Industrial plants manufacture feed mixers, cattle-handling equipment, grain-drying and cleaning equipment, crop sprayers, tillage tools, and bale movers. Other industries include meat packing and the manufacture of athletic equipment and mobile homes. The city is the seat of St. Mary of the Plains College and the Dodge City Community Junior College, both coeducational institutions. Because of its colorful history, Dodge City is an important tourist center.

With the coming of the Sante Fe Railroad, huge herds of buffalo in the area were slaughtered and shipped east. By 1875 the cattle industry was thriving. Texas longhorns, driven from Texas to Dodge City by hundreds of cowboys and trail bosses, were shipped east on the railroad.

Fort Dodge, an army post built in 1864, is 5 miles (8 km) east. The fort provided protection for travelers and wagon trains on the Santa Fe Trail. Some of the original buildings are still in good condition. Dodge City has a commission form of government. Population: 18,001.

LOIS L. FLANAGAN
Dodge City Public Library

DODGSON, Charles Lutwidge. See CARROLL, LEWIS.

DODO, any of three species of extinct, heavy-bodied, flightless birds that inhabited the Mascarene Islands in the central Indian Ocean. The dodo's ungainly appearance, tameness, and demise have made it a symbol of stupidity and anachronism.

The true dodo (*Raphus cucullatus*) of Mauritius was of about the same bulk as a large domestic turkey. It had a huge head with a massive 9-inch (23 cm) strongly hooked bill, short yellow legs, heavy feet, yellowish white rudimentary wings, and short, curly tail feathers. The facial skin and the body plumage were ashy gray. The similar Réunion dodo, or solitaire (*R. solitarius*), was mostly white with some yellow on its plumage.

The Rodriguez solitaire (*Pezophaps solitaria*) was less heavily built than the other two dodos and had a longer neck and longer legs. It also had a smaller head and a shorter bill that was not hooked at the tip. Most Rodriguez solitaires were brownish gray or tan, but some were white. The wing tip had a heavy knob that was used as a club in fighting. The Rodriguez solitaire could run rapidly and was hard to capture. It ate seeds and leaves and ingested stones to help grind its food. It laid one egg in a palm-leaf nest.

Dodos became extinct on Mauritius soon after 1680 and on Réunion about 1750, but they remained on Rodriguez until 1800. Although thousands were slaughtered for meat, pigs and monkeys which destroyed dodo eggs were probably most responsible for the dodo's extinction.

Dodos are known today from the accounts and drawings of 17th and 18th century travelers and from fossil remains. Entire skeletons have been found on Mauritius and Rodriguez islands.

Dodos belong to the family Raphidae of the pigeon order Columbiformes.

GEORGE E. WATSON, *Smithsonian Institution*

DODOMA, dōd-ə-mä, is a region and city in central Tanzania. The region occupies a hilly area of 15,950 square miles (41,311 sq km). It is drained by the Great Ruaha and Mkondoa rivers. Sorghum, maize, peanuts, castor beans, coffee, and sisal are produced, and cattle are raised. Mineral resources include mica, gold, limestone, and salt. The regional administrative headquarters is the city of Dodoma, which also was declared the new national capital in 1973, replacing Dar es Salaam. A new, enlarged city was planned, to be constructed over the next several years. The government's move to the new capital was to be completed before 1990. The National Assembly met there for the first time in October 1974, but most of the government's offices remained in Dar es Salaam. Population: region (1975 est.) 847,000; city (1967 census) 23,559.

DODONA, dō-dō'nə, was the site of an ancient oracle to Zeus in the region of Epirus, Greece. According to the historian Herodotus, a black dove flew there from Thebes in Egypt, directing in human language that an oracle to Zeus be established. The oracle's responses were given in the rustling of a sacred oak tree and were interpreted by priests known as Selli.

The sanctuary at Dodona was destroyed by the Aetolians in 219 B.C., but 19th century excavations uncovered temples of Zeus and Aphrodite, as well as tablets containing sample questions asked of the oracle.

DODSWORTH, dodz'wûrth, is a novel by Sinclair Lewis. It was published in 1929. The title character, Samuel Dodsworth, is a retired automobile manufacturer from the Midwest who goes on a tour of Europe with his frivolous wife Fran. When his wife's infidelity and selfishness become evident to him, he decided to leave her for the more sympathetic companionship of Edith Cortright, an American widow whom he meets during the trip. Penetrating comments contrasting American and European attitudes are interwoven in the story.

DOENITZ, dû'nits, **Karl** (1891–1980), German admiral, who briefly succeeded Adolf Hitler as chancellor of the Third Reich. He was the leader of the U-boat offensive against Allied shipping during World War II and commander in chief of the German Navy from 1943 to 1945.

Doenitz was born at Grünau, near Berlin, on Sept. 16, 1891. A U-boat commander in World War I, he was captured by the British in October 1918 while attacking a convoy off Sicily and was held prisoner of war until repatriated in 1919. He served in the postwar German Navy and for one year commanded the cruiser *Emden*.

FIELD MUSEUM OF NATURAL HISTORY
Dodo (reconstruction)

In 1936, Doenitz was given the rank of commodore and the task of recreating the U-boat arm disallowed by the Treaty of Versailles but resanctioned under the Anglo-German Naval Agreement of 1935. He was enthusiastic about this assignment, and the resulting success of Germany's U-boats during the early years of World War II was due to his excellent training of submarine crews and to the wolf-pack tactics he applied. On Jan. 30, 1943, he was chosen by Hitler to relieve Grand Admiral Erich Raeder as commander in chief of the navy.

Hitler died on April 30, 1945, and on May 1 Doenitz became chancellor of Germany. He tried to negotiate a separate peace with the Western Allies at the expense of the USSR but was unsuccessful, and on May 7 he surrendered unconditionally. Later arrested and found guilty at the Nuremberg War Crimes Trial, he served ten years in prison. He was released in 1956 and his *Memoirs* appeared in 1959. He died in Hamburg, West Germany, on Dec. 24, 1980.

B. B. SCHOFIELD, *Vice Admiral, Royal Navy Author of "British Sea-Power"*

DOESBURG, dōōs'bûrкн, **Theo van** (1883–1931), Dutch painter, architect, and poet. His real name was Christian Émil Marie Küpper. He was born in Utrecht on Aug. 30, 1883, and was self-taught as a painter. Van Doesburg is most noted for his role as the leading spokesman of the group in the Netherlands called "de Stijl" (The Style). He, Piet Mondrian, and others founded the journal *de Stijl* in 1917 to promote their theory of art called "neoplasticism" (q.v.).

Although van Doesburg's knowledge of architecture was reputedly slight, he is thought to have influenced the work of Walter Gropius and Mies van der Rohe through some lectures he gave at the Bauhaus in 1921. During the 1920's he became interested in Dadaism, and some of his Dadaist poems were published under the name of I. K. Bonset in *de Stijl*. He died in Davos, Switzerland, on March 7, 1931.

DOG

Four Brittany spaniels stand staunchly on point, the rear dogs backing, or honoring, the forward dog's point.

EVELYN M. SHAFER

CONTENTS

Section	Page	Section	Page
1. Origin and History of the Dog	235	5. Dog Shows and Obedience Trials	242
2. Kinds of Dogs	235	Dog Shows	242
The Breed	235	Obedience Trials	242
Breed Categories	235	6. Field Competition	243
Table of Breeds	238	Field Trials	243
3. Selecting and Caring for a Dog	236	Racing, Coursing, and Fighting	243
The New Puppy	236	7. Kennel Clubs	244
Feeding	237	Dog Registries	243
Housing	237	8. Diseases	244
Grooming	237	9. Breeding	245
4. Training	240	Estrous Cycle	245
Equipment	241	The Newborn Puppies	246
Commands	241	Glossary of Terms	245
Housebreaking	241		

DOG, a carnivorous mammal, probably the first animal domesticated by man. How or when this domestication took place is not known with certainty, but the dog's association with man began at least 10,000 years ago.

Dogs are found throughout the world, wherever man lives. Statements as to the size of the world dog population are little better than guesses and vary widely, but informed estimates place the number between 120 million and 150 million. In the United States, according to estimates based on projections of market research reports for certain areas of the country, the dog population is probably between 29 million and 35 million.

General Characteristics. The dog (*Canis familiaris*) possesses great genetic variation, and widely differing breeds can be developed from the same stock within a relatively short time. This genetic plasticity has been utilized in producing the more than 400 distinct breeds in the world today.

These breeds vary from those that weigh as little as 1½ pounds (680 grams), such as the chihuahua, to those that exceed 200 pounds (90 kg) such as the St. Bernard. Breed heights also vary markedly. A toy poodle may stand only 8 inches (20 cm) high at the shoulders, whereas some great danes and Irish wolfhounds may reach 37 inches (94 cm).

The dog's coat, which ranges from short to long and from wiry to straight, may be almost entirely lacking, as in the Mexican hairless, or as luxuriant as that of the old English sheepdog, whose guard hairs may be 10 inches (25 cm) long.

Greyhounds and borzois are very long-muzzled, while pugs, pekingese, and bulldogs have "pushed-in" faces. Bulldogs have small, folded ears; German shepherds have large erect ones. A basset hound, which may be only 14 inches (35 cm) high at the shoulders may have ears that span 24 inches (60 cm) from tip to tip.

Dogs are digitigrade animals; that is, they walk on what is anatomically their four fingertips. The fifth finger, or thumb, known as the *dewclaw*, does not reach the ground. Most breeds lack dewclaws on their hind feet.

The dog, like man, has two sets of teeth. The 32 milk, or baby, teeth appear at about 3 to 5 weeks of age and fall out when the puppy is from 4 to 6 months old. The adult dog's teeth, which includes the molars, number 42.

The dog can hear pure tones of 35 kiloherz (kHz; 1 kHz = 1,000 cycles per second), whereas in man, 20 kHz appears to be the top limit. The dog's visual acuity is not especially sharp and is roughly comparable to man's. However, dogs probably cannot perceive colors and see only shades of gray. The dog's most important sense is that of smell. Exact measurements of this sense have been rather difficult to make, and there have been conflicting results; but it is unquestionable that the ability to track faint or old trails is an extremely sensitive one. For some substances the scenting ability of dogs is not very different from that of man, but in the detection of certain aliphatic ("fatty") acids—acids present in the skin secretions of mammals and left behind in their track—dogs have been shown to be more than a million times more perceptive than man.

Usefulness of Dogs. Man has used dogs for

many purposes, including hunting, guarding, racing, companionship, and leading the blind. Some applications have been quite odd. The French have used dogs to locate Perigord truffles—edible fungi that grow underground. Modern narcotic officers have used dogs trained to detect drug odors in luggage and packages. St. Bernards have been used to search out snow-covered trails and warn of hidden crevasses. They have also been used to locate people buried by snow avalanches.

In earlier centuries dogs worked as turnspits to keep meat revolving over a fire, and they served as footwarmers during services in unheated churches. The Spanish conquistadores are reported to have taught dogs to attack and kill Indians. Modern armies have used dogs to lead scouting patrols, locate wounded, carry messages and supplies, and guard bases. Sled dogs helped the Eskimos adapt to the rigors of Arctic life. The American Plains Indians used dogs to haul the travois, a primitive type of sled made by hooking two poles into the dog's harness.

The use of dogs in medical research and teaching has steadily increased. Testimony before committees of the U. S. Congress indicates that every year more than 3 million dogs are killed for this purpose. The demand for research dogs is so great that legislation has been enacted in both Britain and the United States to stem the traffic in stolen dogs and to foster more humane treatment of dogs in laboratories.

Maxwell Riddle, *Author of*
"Complete Book of Puppy Training and Care"

1. Origin and History of the Dog

The dog is a domesticated wolf, and its history must be traced through the ancestors of this carnivore. (It used to be thought that the jackal had contributed to the ancestry of the dog, but on anatomical and behavioral grounds this is no longer tenable.) The forerunners of the wolf, such as *Aelurodon*, were present in North America during the late Miocene and early Pliocene, roughly 15 million to 10 million years ago, but they are not commonly found in Europe until the Villafranchian, the earliest stage of the Pleistocene, about 2 million years ago. True wolves, however, appeared in Europe in the middle Pleistocene, some 1 million years ago, but are not recorded from the New World until some 700,000 years later.

In the Old World the earliest definite remains of the dog are a fossil jaw found in a cave at Palegawra, near Kirkuk in what is now Iraq. The jaw's age, as estimated from the amount of fluorine it had absorbed from groundwater, is about 14,000 years. The earliest New World fossil, found in Jaguar Cave in Idaho, is about 10,500 years old. Such early dogs were probably used for hunting and as a source of food.

Identification of very early domestic dogs remains a complex task, and the results are always open to interpretation, but it is probable that the dog was the first animal to be domesticated by man. These early dogs resembled the present-day dingo, the wild dog of Australia.

Following domestication, selective breeding produced dogs of divergent forms. The ancient Egyptians, as early as 7,000 years ago, had dogs of many distinct breeds, including the forerunners of the greyhound, mastiff, and dachshund.

Juliet Clutton-Brock
Institute of Archaeology, London

2. Kinds of Dogs

Very early in its history, the dog was bred into a variety of races, or breeds, depending on climate, certain environmental directions of selection, and the preferences of its masters.

The Breed. A more formal and systematic creation of bloodlines was developed when dog breeders recognized and accepted the concept of "breed" as formulated by the horsemen of Arabia. A breed may be defined as a group of animals bred by man to possess certain inheritable qualities, including a uniform appearance, that distinguish it from other members of the same species.

BREED CATEGORIES

The breeds of dogs are so varied in size, function, geographical origin, and other aspects that it is difficult to make an objective classification. However, by using original function as the main criterion, logical groupings can be made.

Sporting Dogs. This is a multifaceted group, which is best subdivided according to the manner in which the dogs hunt.

Pointing Breeds. These are breeds that follow wind-borne scents and are frequently used in the hunting of upland birds. When a pointer detects a suitable game bird, it stops, points its muzzle in the direction of the bird, and holds this pose until the hunter arrives to flush out and shoot the bird. Many pointing breeds are also required to retrieve the fallen bird.

Retrieving Breeds. Since pointing breeds are not always adept at retrieving and because certain kinds of hunting, such as for waterfowl, do not require game-finding dogs, hunters have developed the retriever. This is typically a very obedient dog that waits quietly by its master's side until instructed to bring in killed game.

Flushing Breeds. These dogs, unlike the field-hunting pointers, search underbrush and reedy areas to find and flush game for the hunter. Because they flush the game themselves and do

A Bushman's dogs hold an oryx at bay in South Africa.

N. R. FARBMAN, LIFE MAGAZINE © TIME INC.

not wait for the arrival of the hunter, they are close-ranging dogs, staying as near to the hunter as possible. In many instances, these flushing breeds are not required to retrieve the game.

Scent Hounds. These are breeds with an excellent sense of smell, and they generally trail ground-borne scents. According to their size and the game being pursued, they may keep the game running and circling toward the hunter or bring it to bay to await the hunter's gun. Though scent hounds may be used on ground-running birds, such as pheasants, they are primarily utilized in the tracking of mammals. Some breeds (the schweisshunde) are held on long leather leashes while following the blood trail of a wounded animal.

Sight Hounds. These dogs depend upon their vision rather than their scenting ability to locate and follow game. Sight hounds hunt far afield, and their high, narrow, supple bodies are built for speed. They were developed as hunters of swift-footed mammals.

Terriers. These are courageous, vivacious dogs that were originally developed to enter the ground dens of foxes, rabbits, and other animals and drive them out to the hunters. Terriers are still used on farms to kill rats and other vermin.

Mastiffs. The mastiffs are very large, heavily built breeds that were formerly used for a variety of purposes, but now mostly serve as guard dogs or pets. The Assyrians and Babylonians used mastiff breeds in lion hunting; the Romans used them as guard dogs; and the modern Japanese still use them as fighting dogs.

Northland-Type Dogs. This is a broad group, encompassing the sled dogs, the laikas, and the spitzes. These breeds all have stiff, erect ears and carry their tails curled up over their backs. The kinship with the wolf is very evident in the sled dogs, but the laikas, which are used as hunters and watchdogs, are lighter in build. The sled dogs make as little use of their voices as do the laikas, but the European spitzes—old, established watchdogs—give tongue willingly.

Herders. This is the largest and most comprehensive group. For many centuries man has used these dogs to guard sheep, cattle, goats, and pigs, and he has trained many of them to actually guide, or herd, groups of these animals. In Europe, when herds of cattle had to be driven over relatively great distances to grazing grounds or slaughterhouses, tough, robust droving dogs were used to sustain the ponderous forward progress of the cattle. Today the able herding dogs, such as the German shepherd, have been singled out and trained to do a variety of tasks.

Toys. Small pet dogs, probably dwarfs, were known in ancient China and among the Aztecs of Mexico. The modern toy dog is not a dwarf but a correctly proportioned miniature form developed from almost any one of the previously named breed groups—the pug, for example, from the mastiff.

ERICH SCHNEIDER-LEYER
Author of "Dogs of the World"

3. Selecting and Caring for a Dog

Adequate care of a dog begins with the selection of a suitable breed or mixed-breed dog that will fit comfortably into the home. Sedentary individuals should select one of the medium-small or toy breeds. People who are confirmed outdoor types will be happier with a medium or large dog or perhaps one of the sporting varieties. Great Danes, bullmastiffs, and St. Bernards are very decorative but require large areas to afford them adequate activity to maintain good muscle tone. The buyer should select a sleek, well-fed puppy with a clean coat; that is, one with no staining around the eyes, anus, or urinary orifice. Puppies under 4 months of age should be alert, active, and ready to romp. Avoid shy or withdrawn puppies: they may be either ill or very timid.

The dependable breeder will have a record of any inoculations the puppy has received, advice on his diet, and information regarding follow-up inoculations or worming. He will allow the puppy to be examined by a private veterinarian of the buyer's choice and to be returned should the veterinarian's findings indicate that the puppy is unwell.

The New Puppy. A newly acquired puppy should be given quiet sleeping quarters. The site should be comfortably warm and draft-free. A large carton or wooden box lined with shredded newspaper will suffice during the housebreaking period.

Puppies require vaccination against distemper, hepatitis, and leptospirosis, which can be started during the first trip to the veterinarian. Several methods of vaccination are available.

With few exceptions, worming is best left to the veterinarian. The new owner should bring a stool specimen in a tightly stoppered container to the doctor—at the first visit, if possible. Roundworms, hookworms, whipworms, and tapeworms may be present, either singly or in combination, and a stool specimen can pinpoint which if any of these parasites the puppy is harboring. Since hookworms and roundworms can on occasion be transmitted to young children, early detection is imperative.

If the puppy should be harboring fleas or ticks, obtain veterinary advice on their eradication. Some sprays or powders can be very toxic to young puppies if improperly applied or used with unwarranted frequency. They can also be hazardous to humans if they are inhaled excessively or contaminate food utensils.

Three border collies are given herding instructions.
CARL H. BRADFORD

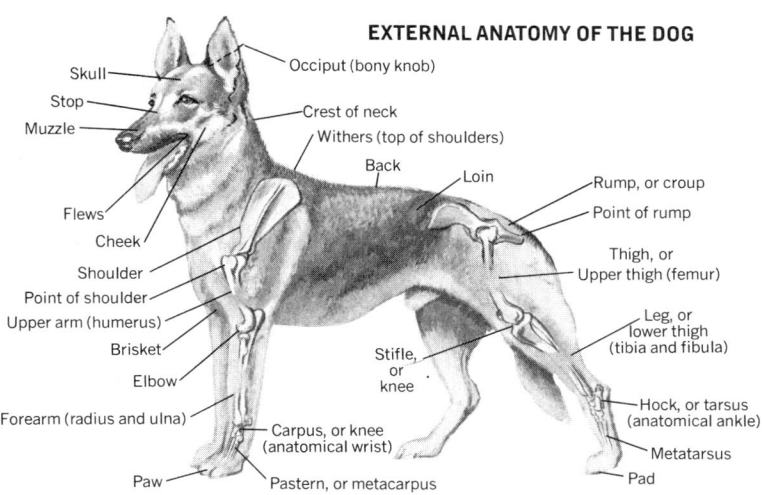

EXTERNAL ANATOMY OF THE DOG

Feeding. The dog's digestive tract is most efficient in utilizing concentrated protein foods, such as meat, fish, eggs, and cheese, and less so in converting starches and cereal-type foods. Fats are well utilized, and at least 5% to 7% of the diet should consist of animal fats.

Puppies less than 6 weeks old do best on four to five feedings daily; though it is possible to raise puppies under 6 weeks of age on fewer feedings, the longer intervals between meals result in ravenous puppies that are more likely to gorge and swallow air, with resulting distension and vomiting or diarrhea.

Puppies between 6 and 10 weeks old should have four feedings daily; from 10 weeks until 5 or 6 months of age three feedings daily will suffice. From 6 months to one year, most breeds will do well on two feedings daily. After one year of age one feeding daily is adequate except for the giant breeds, which are slower to mature and may require two feedings daily until they are 15 to 18 months old.

A typical menu for young puppies requiring four feedings could include:

Meal 1, 7–8 A.M.: ground or scraped beef 1 part and cottage cheese 1 part; mix and make into a paste consistency; feed at room temperature.

Meal 2, 12–1 P.M.: puppy meal 1 part and soup stock, water, or milk 1 part; allow to thicken; mix well prior to feeding.

Meal 3, 5–6 P.M.: repeat A.M. feeding or vary by adding cooked eggs or lamb in lieu of the ground beef.

Meal 4, 9–10 P.M.: puppy meal 1 part and meat 1 part; or substitute instant cereal and milk or cottage cheese.

Vitamin and mineral supplements may be added to any feeding upon veterinary recommendation. Puppies of the larger, fast-growing breeds often require supplementation with dicalcium phosphate and cod liver oil to prevent rickets. It is very important not to overdose with vitamin D or mineral supplements, as this can result in premature calcification of the bones with either stunting or deformity, or both. Large doses of vitamin C will occasionally correct a painful condition of the joints caused by oversupplementation in the rapidly growing giant breeds.

Feeding the older puppy and adult dog is simpler. There are many foods to choose from: dry meal or kibble, canned foods, the "soft moists," fresh meat, and a variety of human foods. No one food will be adequate for every dog. A herding dog or an outdoor sentry dog will have vastly different caloric requirements than a sedentary house pet.

Housing. The privately owned dog will generally sleep indoors. He can be trained to sleep on a folded blanket, dog mattress, or in a dog bed. The sleeping quarters should be draft-free and so situated that the dog is not underfoot. Unfinished basements or garages are usually unsatisfactory—they are either too damp, too cold, or too hot. The garage may also present a problem because of automobile exhaust fumes.

A long- or heavy-coated dog may be allowed to sleep outdoors. He must be gradually acclimated to doing so, however, and it is best to start this in the summer or early fall. He should have a well-constructed doghouse no more than 3 inches (7.5 cm) higher than his head. The floor should be double and raised at least 8 inches (20 cm) off the ground. The entrance should be situated to one side and barely large enough to admit the dog. In cold climates an inner partition near the entrance will serve to block cold drafts, and in severe weather a heavy blanket or rug can be tacked over the entry to keep snow and rain from entering. The interior can be filled to a depth of 8 to 10 inches (20–25 cm) with hay. Sawdust and cedar shavings are overrated as bedding and insulation, and they sometimes produce eye irritations from the abundant dust.

Grooming. All dogs at one time or another require a bath; however, with regular and proper brushing the bathing (except for medicinal reasons) may be kept to a minimum.

Dogs with profuse bangs and beards need special attention. Though some breed standards call for such hair styling, and despite the old wives' tale that removal of hair around the eyes of these breeds will lead to blindness, the trimming of both bangs and beards is medically advisable. Many of these dogs become victims of eye infections because the owners do not see the eyes often enough to notice accumulations of discharges and matted hair. They often bump against furniture because they do not see clearly. The beards frequently become saturated with saliva and food juices, which may result in halitosis and fungus infections around the lips

MARVIN J. SHEFFIELD, D.V.M.

DOG BREEDS OF THE WORLD
(Compiled by Erich Schneider-Leyer)

SPORTING DOGS

Pointing Breeds

Breed	Country[1]	Coat[2]	Weight[3] (lbs.)	Height[4] (in.)
Ariège pointer	France	s	63	25
Auvergne pointer	France	s	60	22
Barbet	France	w	55	20
Belgian pointer	Belgium	s	57	25
Bourbonnais pointer	France	s	60	22
Braco Navarro	Spain	s	61	23
Breton epagneul[5,6]	France	l	52	19
Brittany spaniel[5]	United States	l	35	19
Drentse partridge dog	Netherlands	l	69	23
Dupuy pointer	France	s	70	26
English pointer	England	s	70	23
English setter	England	l	70	25
Fousek pointer	Czechoslovakia	w	61	23
French pointer (large)	France	s	62	23
French pointer (small)	France	s	46	20
French epagneul[6]	France	l	60	22
German griffon	Germany	w	60	22
German longhaired (langhaar) pointer	Germany	l	62	24
German roughhaired (stichelhaar) pointer	Germany	w	62	24
German shorthaired (kurzhaar) pointer	Germany	s	61	23
German wirehaired (drahthaar) pointer	Germany	w	61	23
Gordon setter	Scotland	l	70	25
Griffon (longhaired)	France	w	59	21
Griffon (rough)	France	w	59	21
Griffon (wirehaired)	France	w	59	21
Irish setter	Ireland	l	70	25
Istrian pointer	Yugoslavia	s	45	19
Italian bracco	Italy	s	70	25
Münsterländer (large)	Germany	l	61	23
Münsterländer (small)	Germany	l	60	21
Pachon de Vitoria	Spain	s	60	21
Perdiguero Burgales	Spain	s	60	21
Picard epagneul[6] (standard)	France	l	61	22
Picard epagneul[6] (blue)	France	l	61	22
Pont Audemer epagneul[6]	France	l	60	22
Poodle pointer	Germany	w	61	23
Portuguese perdigeiro	Portugal	s	60	24
St. Germain pointer	France	s	60	22
Spinone	Italy	w	60	24
Staby	Netherlands	l	62	19
Vizsla (rough)	Hungary	w	60	23
Vizsla (shorthaired)	Hungary	s	60	23
Weimaraner	Germany	s	62	24
Welsh setter	Wales	l	70	25

Retrieving Breeds

Breed	Country[1]	Coat[2]	Weight[3] (lbs.)	Height[4] (in.)
American water spaniel	United States	c	32	17
Chesapeake Bay retriever	United States	c	60	23
Curly-coated retriever	England	c	70	24
Flat-coated retriever	England	l	65	23
Golden retriever	England	l	65	22
Irish water spaniel	Ireland	c	58	22
Labrador retriever	England	s	60	22
Nova Scotia duck tolling retriever	Canada	l	40	20
Portuguese water dog	Portugal	l	45	21

Flushing Breeds

Breed	Country[1]	Coat[2]	Weight[3] (lbs.)	Height[4] (in.)
American cocker spaniel	United States	l	27	14
Boykin spaniel	United States	l	35	16
Clumber spaniel	England	l	55	17
English cocker spaniel	England	l	32	16
English springer spaniel	England	l	50	20
Dutch water spaniel	Netherlands	c	57	21
Field spaniel	England	l	42	18
German spaniel (wachtelhund)	Germany	l	37	19
Sussex spaniel	England	l	42	16
Welsh springer spaniel	Wales	l	40	16

[1] Country in which most significant development occurred; it is usually the country of origin. [2] s = shorthaired; l = longhaired; w = wirehaired; c = curly coated; h = hairless. [3] Average breed weight. To convert pounds to kilograms, multiply given figure by 0.45. [4] Average breed height from shoulders (withers) to ground. To convert inches to centimeters, multiply given figure by 2.5. [5] Americans generally do not distinguish between the Breton epagneul and the Brittany spaniel. [6] "Epagneul," usually translated as "spaniel," actually means "longhaired pointer." [7] The basset hound is derived from the basset Artésien-Normand, modified by crosses with English bloodhounds. [8] "Schweisshund" is often translated as "bloodhound" because the word "schweiss," which means "sweat," refers to the blood dripped by a wounded game animal and trailed by the "schweisshund." The "blood" in the name of the English bloodhound refers to "full-blooded," or purebred.

SCENT HOUNDS

Breed	Country[1]	Coat[2]	Weight[3] (lbs.)	Height[4] (in.)
Alano	Spain	s	60	22
American foxhound	United States	s	59	22
Ariègeois	France	s	58	22
Artésien-Normand	France	s	59	22
Austrian bracke	Austria	s	54	19
Austrian dachsbracke	Austria	s	50	15
Balkan hound	Yugoslavia	s	56	20
Basenji	Central Africa	s	23	16
Basset Artésien-Normand	France	s	48	11
Basset bleu de Gascogne	France	s	50	14
Basset d'Artois	France	s	48	11
Basset fauve de Bretagne	France	s	49	13
Basset griffon Vendéen	France	w	51	16
Basset hound[7]	England	s	50	13
Bavarian Mountain schweisshund[8]	Germany	s	22	17
Beagle	England	s	51	14
Berner hound	Switzerland	s	36	17
Billy	France	s	58	22
Black-and-tan coonhound	United States	s	68	25
Bloodhound[8]	England	s	105	25
Bluetick hound	United States	s	68	25
Brazilian tracker	Brazil	s	67	25
Briquet griffon Vendéen	France	w	55	21
Catahoula stockdog	United States	s	58	22
Chambray	France	s	58	22
Chien d'Artois	France	s	59	22
Chien Français (blanc et noir)	France	s	100	26
Chien de St. Hubert	Belgium	s	102	26
Chinese hound	China	s	59	22
Cirnego dell'Etna	Italy	s	23	18
Dachshund (standard)	Germany	s, w, l	24	15
Dachshund (miniature)	Germany	s, w, l	17	11
Dalmatian	Yugoslavia	s	59	22
Dogo Argentino	Argentina	s	60	23
Drever (Swedish dachsbracke)	Sweden	s	21	13
Dunker	Norway	s	55	20
Dutch steenbrack	Netherlands	s	18	15
Elinikos Ichnilatis	Greece	s	42	20
English coonhound	United States	s	60	24
English foxhound	England	s	57	21
Estonian hound	Estonia	s	37	19
Fila Brasileiro	Brazil	s	107	27
Finnish hound	Finland	s	58	22
German bracke	Germany	s	18	15
Grand bleu de Gascogne	France	s	59	23
Grand Gascon Saintongeois	France	s	58	22
Grand griffon Nivernais	France	w	60	24
Grand griffon Vendéen	France	s	58	22
Halden hound	Norway	s	58	22
Hamilton hound	Sweden	s	58	22
Hannoverian schweisshund[8]	Germany	s	60	20
Harrier	England	s	56	20
Haut Poitou	France	s	58	22
Hungarian hound (large)	Hungary	s	57	21
Hungarian hound (small)	Hungary	s	24	16
Hygen hound	Norway	s	58	21
Illyrian hound	Yugoslavia	w	39	20
Istrian hound	Yugoslavia	s, w	45	20
Jura hound	Switzerland	w	36	17
Kaikadi	India	s	38	17
Kangaroo hound	Australia	s	70	28
Kerry beagle	Ireland	s	20	15
Levesque	France	s	58	22
Lucerne hound	Switzerland	s	36	17
Mha Si Savat	Thailand	s	37	22
Niam niam	Sudan	s	23	17
Otter hound	England	w	68	25
Petit bleu de Gascogne	France	s	58	20
Petit Gascogne-Saintongeois	France	s	55	19
Petit griffon bleu de Gascogne	France	w	54	18
Petit griffon fauve de Bretagne	France	w	55	19

English foxhounds — Keystone

SPORTING GROUP (HOUND)

Since Roman days, dogs have been classified according to use or size. For dog shows, the American Kennel Club divides the 115 breeds it registers into six groups: Sporting Dogs (Gun) and Sporting Dogs (Hound), Working Dogs, Terriers, Toys, and Nonsporting Dogs. On these pages are shown some of the more popular breeds in each group, with a note on each breed.

On this page are six of the best-known hounds —beagle, basset, dachshund, Afghan, borzoi, and English foxhound. The beagle and basset are scent hounds whose keen sense of smell enables them to follow the track of their quarry. The dachshund works like a terrier: when the track of the game he is following leads into a burrow, he follows underground and will fight his adversary in the narrow tunnel. The Afghan and borzoi work by sight. Afghans are used in Afghanistan to chase a variety of game. In Russia, borzoi hunted wolves. The English foxhounds at the top of the page are traditionally used in packs to hunt foxes. The slightly leggier American foxhound frequently hunts as a single dog.

Beagle — Taylor/Annan

PLATE 1

Dachshund — Taylor/Annan

Alpha — **Basset hound**

Borzoi
Mary Eleanor Browning/D.P.I.

Afghan hound — Walter Chandoha

SPORTING GROUP

On these two pages are 11 gun-dog breeds of the Sporting Group. German shorthaired pointers, pointers, Brittany spaniels, English setters, Irish setters, and Weimaraners locate and "point" at the quarry for the hunter. The cocker spaniel and English springer spaniel find and flush game so that the hunter can shoot. The Chesapeake Bay retriever, golden retriever, and Labrador retriever are specialists in retrieving ducks or upland birds that have been killed by the hunter.

German shorthaired pointer — F.P.G.

Pointer — Walter Chandoha

Chesapeake Bay retriever — H. Armstrong Roberts

Golden retriever — Walter Chandoha

Taylor/Annan

Labrador retriever

PLATE 2

Brittany spaniel

English setter

Irish setter

Cocker spaniel

English springer spaniel

Weimaraner

PLATE 3

WORKING GROUP

All the breeds on these two pages are members of the Working Group. The German shepherd was once associated with sheepherding, like the old English sheepdog, Shetland sheepdog, and collie. It has become better known since it has been trained for police and military service, like the boxer and Doberman pinscher. The Newfoundland is the world's greatest swimming dog; in the days of sail it was often used to rescue sailors swept overboard. Great Danes once hunted wild boar and were called "Boarhounds." The St. Bernard saved travelers lost in Alpine snow. The Alaskan Malamute, big and strong, is used to pull freight sledges.

German shepherd
Walter Chandoha

Boxer
H. Armstrong Roberts

Newfoundland
Walter Chandoha

Old English sheepdog
Taylor/Annan

Mary Eleanor Browning/D.P.I.
Doberman pinscher

PLATE 4

Shetland sheepdog — Walter Chandoha

Collie — Walter Chandoha

Great Dane — Bowden/Monkmeyer

Alaskan Malamute — Walter Chandoha

St. Bernard — Walter Chandoha

PLATE 5

Walter Chandoha
Bedlington terrier

TERRIER GROUP

Eight well-known breeds of the Terrier Group appear on this page and at the top of the facing page. Bedlingtons look like lambs but have great spirit. Bull terriers are more attracted to people than to other dogs. The miniature schnauzer was once Germany's favorite house and farm dog. Airedales are famous as big-game hunters. Scottish and cairn terriers come from the Scottish Highlands, where they hunt small predatory game. Fox terriers accompanied foxhound packs in England and entered dens to rout out the fox. Manchester terriers were once employed chiefly to kill rats in horse stables.

Miniature Schnauzer

Walter Chandoha

Taylor/Annan
Bull terrier

Taylor/Annan **Scottish terrier**

Airedale terrier Walter Chandoha

Taylor/Annan **Cairn terrier**

Wire Fox terrier

Manchester terrier (standard)

TOY GROUP

While many people believe that breeds in the Toy Group are only suited to be ladies' lapdogs, the majority of these tiny dogs possess all the admirable qualities of their larger cousins. In fact, many Toys have been purposely bred down from larger breeds, including the Pomeranian, toy poodle, Italian greyhound, toy Manchester terrier, and English toy spaniel.

Pekingese

Pug

Chihuahua

Miniature pinscher

Pomeranian

Italian greyhound

Toy poodle

Maltese

NONSPORTING GROUP

The poodle (counting all three varieties, toy, miniature, and standard) has been the favorite breed in the United States for many years. Possessing beauty and brains, it wins followers by its almost human sense of humor. Bulldogs baited bulls in the 18th and 19th centuries, but now are steadfast pets. Dalmatians were famous as "coach dogs," trotting beneath the rear axle of every coach-and-four in England. The Chow Chow, from China, was once a great hunting dog. The schipperke ("little skipper") was a watchdog on barges in the Low Countries. The popular Boston terrier was bred in the United States by crossing the bulldog and a terrier.

Poodle (standard) Mary Eleanor Browning/D.P.I.

Bulldog
Owen/Black Star

Dalmatian Walter Chandoha

Taylor/Annan **Boston Terrier**

Chow Chow Walter Chandoha

Walter Chandoha **Schipperke**

PLATE 8

DOG BREEDS OF THE WORLD (continued)

SCENT HOUNDS (cont.)

Breed	Country[1]	Coat[2]	Weight[3] (lbs.)	Height[4] (in.)
Petit griffon Nivernais	France	w	56	20
Pharaonenhund	Spain	s	62	25
Plott hound	United States	s	58	22
Podenco Espagnol	Spain	s	61	24
Podenco Ibicenco	Spain	s	62	24
Podenco Portuguese (large)	Portugal	s	63	26
Podenco Portuguese (small)	Portugal	s	40	24
Podenco Portuguese (miniature)	Portugal	s	19	11
Poitevin-Normand	France	s	59	22
Polski ogar	Poland	s	56	24
Porcelaine	France	s	57	21
Posavski hound	Yugoslavia	s	38	20
Redbone hound	United States	s	60	24
Rhodesian ridgeback	South Africa	s	70	25
Russian hound (fawn)	USSR	s	60	23
Russian hound (red)	USSR	s	60	23
Sabueso	Spain	s	57	20
Schiller hound	Sweden	s	59	22
Swiss hound	Switzerland	s	36	17
Swiss Niederlauf hound	Switzerland	s, w	28	14
Segugio	Italy	s	57	21
Slovakian hound	Czechoslovakia	s	36	18
Smaland hound	Sweden	s	42	19
Staghound	England	s	72	23
Styrian Mountain bracke	Austria	w	47	18
Tennessee brindle	United States	s	40	23
Treeing Walker hound	United States	s	60	24
Trigg hound	United States	s	60	24
Tyroler bracke (large)	Austria	s	46	17
Tyroler bracke (small)	Austria	s	40	14
Veadeiro Catarinense	Brazil	s	61	24
Welsh hound	Wales	w	75	23
Westphalian dachsbracke	Germany	s	15	13

SIGHT HOUNDS

Breed	Country[1]	Coat[2]	Weight[3] (lbs.)	Height[4] (in.)
Afghan hound	Afghanistan	l	55	26
Australian hound	Australia	s	60	28
Baganda hunting dog	Uganda	s	26	20
Banjara hound	India	s	57	27
Borzoi	USSR	l	90	28
Chika (large)	China	s	50	24
Chika (small)	China	s	45	20
Chippiparai hound	India	s	66	29
Chortay	USSR	s	53	25
Galgo Espagnol	Spain	s	90	30
Greek greyhound	Greece	s	60	25
Greyhound	England	s	65	29
Guanchen hound	Spain	s	28	20
Ibizan hound (Ivicene)	Balearic Is., Spain	s	50	24
Irish wolfhound	Ireland	w	120	31
Khampas hound	India	s	29	22
Kombai hound	India	s	29	20
Lurcher	England (Gypsy)	s	50	25
Magyar agar	Hungary	s	50	24
Mudhol hound	India	s	28	23
Rampur hound	India	s	60	28
Russian hunting courser	USSR	l	90	28
Russian steppe courser	USSR	s	52	25
Saluki	Iran	s	60	25
Scottish deerhound	Scotland	w	92	29
Shaky-i	Tibet	s	29	21
Siamese greyhound (phu quoc)	Thailand	s	40	21
Sloughi	North Africa	s	51	24
Tazy	USSR	s	54	26
Vaghari hound	India	s	28	23
Whippet	England	s	22	19

TERRIERS

Breed	Country[1]	Coat[2]	Weight[3] (lbs.)	Height[4] (in.)
African hairless dog	North Africa	h	12	22
Airedale terrier	England	w	61	23
Alunk	India	l	13	12
Australian terrier	Australia	l	13	10
Austrian terrier	Austria	s	33	16
Bedlington terrier	England	c	22	15
Border terrier	England-Scotland	w	13	10
Boston terrier	United States	s	20	14
Bull terrier (standard)	England	s	23	16
Bull terrier (small)	England	s	20	14
Cairn terrier	Scotland	w	13	10
Chinese crested dog	China	h, l	12	12
Czech terrier	Czechoslovakia	w	15	12
Dandie Dinmont terrier	Scotland	l	18	10
Doberman pinscher	Germany	s	70	26

TERRIERS (cont.)

Breed	Country[1]	Coat[2]	Weight[3] (lbs.)	Height[4] (in.)
Fox terrier (smooth)	England	s	17	14
Fox terrier (wire)	England	w	17	14
Giant schnauzer	Germany	w	72	26
Glen of Imaal terrier	Ireland	w	30	14
Harlequin pinscher	Germany	w	15	13
Irish terrier	Ireland	w	26	18
Jagdterrier	Germany	w	17	15
Kerry blue terrier	Ireland	w	36	18
Krohmofohrländer	Germany	w	18	16
Lakeland terrier	England	w	16	14
Manchester terrier	England	s	17	14
Mexican hairless dog	Mexico	h	11	11
Nihon terrier	Japan	s	17	14
Norfolk terrier	England	w	11	10
Norwich terrier	England	w	11	10
Parson Jack Russell terrier	England	w	15	13
Pinscher	Germany	s	40	18
Russian black terrier	USSR	w	72	26
Schnauzer (standard)	Germany	w	52	19
Scottish terrier	Scotland	w	21	10
Sealydale terrier	South Africa	s	20	11
Sealyham terrier	Wales	w	19	11
Silky terrier	Australia	l	10	9
Skye terrier	Scotland	l	25	10
Smoushond	Netherlands	s	31	15
Soft-coated wheaten terrier	Ireland	w	40	16
Staffordshire terrier (pit bull terrier)	England	s	40	18
Staffordshire bull terrier	England	s	30	16
Welsh terrier	Wales	w	20	15
West Highland white terrier	Scotland	s	13	10

MASTIFFS

Breed	Country[1]	Coat[2]	Weight[3] (lbs.)	Height[4] (in.)
Alangu	India	s	116	28
Bangara mastiff	India	l	81	23
Bordeaux mastiff	France	s	110	25
Boxer	Germany	s	63	23
Bullmastiff	England	s	115	26
English bulldog	England	s	53	18
Fila da Terceiro	Portugal	s	91	24
Great Dane (German mastiff)	Germany	s	145	30
Kuochi	India	s	73	24
Landseer[9]	England	l	140	28
Leonberger	Germany	l	151	29
Mastiff	England	s	150	29
Mastino Napoletano	Italy	s	142	27
Moscow mastiff	USSR	s	117	27
Moscow watchdog	USSR	l	120	25
Newfoundland[9]	England	l	140	27
Rajapalagam	India	s	142	29
St. Bernard	Switzerland	s, w	142	29
Sindh mastiff	India	s	141	29
Spanish mastiff	Spain	s	115	26
Tibetan mastiff	Tibet/India	l	165	25
Tosa-Inu	Japan	s	72	23

NORTHLAND-TYPE DOGS

Breed	Country[1]	Coat[2]	Weight[3] (lbs.)	Height[4] (in.)
Ainu-Ken	Japan	s	39	—
Akita-Inu	Japan	s	86	25
Alaskan malamute	United States	l	80	24
American spitz (Eskimo spitz)	United States	l	18	18
Chinese fighting dog	China	l	40	17
Chow chow	China	l	42	18
East Siberian laika	USSR	l	50	22
Escara-Inu	Japan	s	76	23
Eskimo dog	United States	l	75	23
European-Russian laika	USSR	l	43	20
Finnish spitz	Finland	l	42	17
German great spitz	Germany	l	39	15
German wolf spitz	Germany	l	42	17
Iceland spitz	Iceland	l	37	14
Italian spitz (volpino)	Italy	l	9	11
Japanese spitz	Japan	l	24	13
Karelian bear dog	Finland	l	49	20
Kuri	New Zealand	s	24	17
Keeshond	Netherlands	l	41	18
Kuchi	India	l	16	10
Lapland spitz	Sweden	l	42	18
Lundehund	Norway	s	17	10
Nihon-Ken	Japan	s	42	18
Norrbotten laika	Norway	l	40	16
Northeastern sleigh dog	Siberia-China	l	75	22

[9] In the United States the landseer and the Newfoundland are considered color variations of the same breed.

DOG BREEDS OF THE WORLD (continued)

NORTHLAND-TYPE DOGS (cont.)

Breed	Country[1]	Coat[2]	Weight[3] (lbs.)	Height[4] (in.)
North Russian Samoyed laika	USSR	l	46	19
Norwegian buhund	Norway	l	42	18
Norwegian elkhound	Norway	l	46	19
Russian-Finnish laika	USSR	l	42	17
Samoyed	United States	l	45	21
Sanshu-Ken	Japan	l	42	19
Schipperke	Belgium	s	12	11
Shiba-Inu	Japan	l	38	15
Siberian husky	United States	l	50	22
Swedish grähund	Sweden	l	48	20
Swedish herder (Västgöta spitz)	Sweden	s	26	14
Swedish jämthund	Sweden	l	51	23
Tahl-Tan bear dog	Canada	l	40	14
Tripuri	India	s	40	14
West Siberian laika	Siberia	l	46	21

HERDERS

Breed	Country[1]	Coat[2]	Weight[3] (lbs.)	Height[4] (in.)
Alentejo	Portugal	l	80	26
American farm shepherd	United States	l	50	19
Appenzeller herder dog	Switzerland	s	48	20
Armant	Egypt	s	45	18
Atlas sheepdog	Morocco	s	48	14
Australian cattle dog (heeler)	Australia	s	49	20
Australian shepherd	Australia	l	46	20
Bearded collie	Scotland	l	48	22
Beauceron	France	s	80	25
Bergamasko herder	Italy	l	52	23
Berner herder (Bernese mountain) dog	Switzerland	l	53	25
Bisten	India	l	72	27
Border collie	Scotland	w	46	18
Bothia	India	l	73	22
Bouvier des Ardennes	Belgium	w	60	23
Bouvier des Flandres	Belgium	w	62	17
Briard	France	l	56	24
Canaan dog (collielike)	Israel	l	48	22
Canaan dog (dingolike)	Israel	s	48	22
Castro Laboreiro	Portugal	s	60	22
Catalan	Spain	s, l	40	18
Caucasian owtscharka	USSR	l	79	25
Collie	Scotland	s, l	48	22
Croatian herder	Yugoslavia	l	53	22
Croatian (Illyrian) sheepdog	Yugoslavia	l	60	22
Cumberland sheepdog	England	l	51	22
Dhangari sheepdog	India	s	26	19
Dingo[10]	Australia	s	48	22
Dutch schapendoes	Netherlands	l	49	20
Dutch sheepdog	Netherlands	s,l,w	53	24
English shepherd	United States	l	50	20
Entlebucher herder dog	Switzerland	s	43	18
German shepherd (Alsatian)	Germany	s	54	24
Great Swiss herder dog	Switzerland	s	95	26
Greek sheepdog	Greece	l	59	22
Groenendael[11] (Belgian sheepdog)	Belgium	l	53	23
Hovawarth	Germany	l	70	25
Kanawar	India	l	70	24
Kelpie	Australia	s	45	16
Komondor	Hungary	l	60	23
Kuvasz	Hungary	l	52	22
Laekenois[11]	Belgium	w	53	23
Languedoc sheepdog	France	l	46	17
Lappland sheepdog	Finland	l	48	18

HERDERS (cont.)

Breed	Country[1]	Coat[2]	Weight[3] (lbs.)	Height[4] (in.)
Malinois[11]	Belgium	s	53	23
Maremaner herder dog	Italy	l	80	26
Matin Belge	Belgium	s	101	29
Middle Asiatic owtscharka	USSR	s, l	80	25
Mudi	Hungary	w	23	17
Nepal herder dog	India	l	64	25
Old English sheepdog	England	l	50	21
Pariah[12]	Orient	s, l, w	48	23
Patti sheepdog	India	s	61	22
Picardy sheepdog	France	l	54	23
Polish nizinny sheepdog	Poland	l	43	16
Polish Tatra herder	Poland	l	78	25
Poodle (standard)	France	w	45	16
Puli	Hungary	l	51	16
Pumi	Hungary	l	53	18
Pyrenean herder	Spain	l	100	29
Pyrenean sheepdog	France	l	45	18
Rottweiler	Germany	s	56	23
Rumanian herder	Rumania	l	58	24
Savoy sheepdog	France	l	50	19
Serra da Estrela herder	Portugal	s, l	80	25
Serra de Aires sheepdog	Portugal	l	32	17
Shaky-i	Tibet	l	60	21
Shetland sheepdog	Scotland	l	48	14
South Russian owtscharka	USSR	l	78	24
Tervueren[11]	Belgium	l	53	23
Tibetan terrier	Tibet/India	l	50	15
Vikha sheepdog	India	l	40	18
Welsh corgi (Cardigan)	Wales	l	24	12
Welsh corgi (Pembroke)	Wales	s	22	11
Welsh sheepdog	Wales	l	40	18
Yugoslavian herder	Yugoslavia	l	70	25

TOYS

Breed	Country[1]	Coat[2]	Weight[3] (lbs.)	Height[4] (in.)
Affenpinscher	Germany	w	11	9
Bichon (Bolognese)	France	l	10	11
Bichon (frisé)	France	l	16	11
Bichon (Havanese)	Cuba	l	10	12
Bichon (Löwchen)	France	l	10	11
Bichon (Teneriffe)	Canary Islands	l	10	11
Brabançon[13]	Belgium	s	10	8
Brussels griffon[13]	Belgium	w	10	8
Cavalier King Charles spaniel	England	l	14	10
Chihuahua	Mexico	s, l	4	5
English toy spaniel	England	l	11	10
French bulldog	France	s	25	11
Italian greyhound	Italy	s	8	8
Japanese spaniel (chin)	Japan	l	7	8
Lhasa apso	Tibet	l	17	10
Maltese	Italy	l	9	8
Papillon	France-Belgium	l	6	10
Pekingese	China	l	12	9
Pinscher (miniature)	Germany	s	14	10
Pomeranian	Germany	l	5	10
Poodle (miniature)	France	w	18	12
Poodle (toy)	France	w	15	10
Pug	England	s	16	10
Rabbit dachshund	Germany	s, l, w	16	14
Schnauzer (miniature)	Germany	w	18	13
Shi tzu	Tibet	l	16	10
Tibetan spaniel	Tibet	l	10	10
Toy fox terrier	United States	s	5	9
Toy Manchester terrier	England	s	9	10
Yorkshire terrier	England	l	7	6
Xoloitzcuintli	Mexico		35	20

[10] The dingo is actually a wild-living descendant of dogs brought to Australia by the aborigines. It is often considered a separate species from the domestic dog. [11] The shepherd dog of Belgium was developed into four recognized breeds on the basis of coat type and color. These were the groenendael (longhaired black), the malinois (shorthaired brindle-fawn), the tervueren (longhaired blackish fawn), and the laekenois (wirehaired brindle-brown). The first three were all registered as Belgian sheepdogs by the American Kennel Club until 1959, when this name was reserved for the groenendael. The malinois and tervueren were given separate breed status. [12] Pariahs are semiwild dogs of varying types. [13] In the United States the brabançon and the Brussels griffon are considered the same breed.

4. Training

Any untrained dog may be a nuisance, but a large untrained dog may be a danger. For a smooth and well-adjusted assimilation into its human family, a dog must receive at least a basic amount of training.

A dog receiving a sound foundation of training will be housebroken and will respond to the commands "No," "Heel," "Sit," "Stay," and "Come." The dog's obedience to these five commands will enable its handler to control the dog in almost any situation—and control of the dog is the essence of training. To establish this control, it is necessary to be consistent: the dog must always obey a learned command; if you are

A DALMATIAN is examined by judge at a dog show. The handler holds the lead taut to steady the dog. The judge will scrutinize the dog not only for its muscular and skeletal conformation but also for its body and leg movement, its overall condition, and its alertness.

I. DONALD BOWDEN

not prepared to enforce your command, do not give it.

Equipment for Training Dogs. It is important to use the correct equipment in training dogs. For the new puppy, a show lead is perhaps the most practical item. A show lead, with its adjustable collar, will fit any size dog, and the collar can be let out while the dog is growing. The training, or choke, collar should not be used until it is time for serious training. When the choke collar, or chain, is used, it is extremely important to allow for its quick release by placing it on the dog correctly. With the dog on your left side, the leash fastens to the ring of the choke chain that passes over the dog's neck. If placed correctly, the collar will loosen when you slacken it.

Commands—No. The most important single word any dog can learn is "no," and it should be used whenever the dog does something wrong or is about to do something wrong. The command is taught by using it simultaneously with some form of chastisement. For example, if the dog tries to chase other dogs, cats, or flying leaves, the leash should be jerked and the dog reprimanded with a sharply spoken "No!"

Heel. The more formal type of training should begin with the command "heel." "Heel" simply means that the dog walks on the handler's left side without pulling on the leash or lagging behind. The dog keeps its head aligned with the handler's legs.

Training is begun with the dog at your left side. Step off briskly on your left foot and give the command, "Heel!" The puppy will attempt to run ahead. This forward motion should be stopped by jerking on the leash or rapidly pivoting on your right foot and walking swiftly in the opposite direction, while repeating the command "Heel!" This right-about-turn will provide a sharp correction. Anytime the dog becomes unmanageable, repeat the right-about-turn. This rapid turn will also keep the dog on your left side. If the dog lags behind, it should be encouraged and coaxed forward and not jerked.

Sit. After the dog is heeling reasonably well, you may start working on the "sit." The trained dog will sit automatically every time his handler comes to a halt. To teach the dog to sit, walk at a brisk pace with the dog on your left and then gradually slow down. As you slow down, shorten up on the leash with your right hand and move your right hand directly over the dog's head; when you come to a halt, pull up on the leash with your right hand and push down on the dog's rump with your left hand. As you apply this pressure and force the dog into a sit position, use the command, "Sit!"

Stay. Once the dog will sit on command, you are ready to start working on the "stay." Start practicing this exercise with the dog sitting at your left side and the leash in your right hand. Place the palm of your left hand directly in front of the dog's nose and give the command "Stay!" in a long, drawn out, reassuring tone of voice. (If the dog attempts to lick or nuzzle your hand, jerk on the leash and say "No!") Repeat the command "Stay!" and then step directly in front of the dog by pivoting on your left foot. Repeat the command "Stay!" and pivot back to the dog's side. Repeat this exercise two or three more times.

After you have told the dog to stay and are standing directly in front of him, you may now start to slowly back away. If your dog starts to get up, jerk on the leash and command, "No! Sit! Staaay!" Return to your dog's side, pat him on the head and praise him. Gradually, extend the distance that you can move away from your dog, until you can reach the end of the leash.

Come. After your dog has learned the "Sit-Stay" well enough so you may move out to the end of the leash, you may start working on the recall, or the word "come." Use the dog's name followed by the word "come." Gently tug on the leash and encourage your dog to move toward you. If your dog seems apprehensive, squat down a bit, and repeat its name and the command in an encouraging tone. If it seems a little slow in responding, back away and repeat its name; encourage it toward you. As it comes toward you, gather the leash in your hands so you will have a minimum amount of slack when is reaches you. When the dog is directly in front of you, give the command "Sit!" and lavish it with praise as soon as it obeys.

Housebreaking. "Paper breaking" is teaching a dog to relieve itself indoors on paper rather than out-of-doors. "Housebreaking" is teaching a dog to relieve itself outside at all times. Many people believe that paper breaking is a prerequisite to housebreaking. This is incorrect. To paperbreak a dog before housebreaking merely increases the problems.

Housebreaking begins as soon as you get your puppy. Take it out early and often. It should be taken out first thing in the morning and last thing at night. Its outings should be frequent

LABRADOR RETRIEVER, competing in a field trial, returns to its handler with a downed duck. The field trial judges write their observations and decisions in notebooks. The gallery of spectators watches at a distance. The dog will be judged on how quickly it is able to locate and retrieve the bird, and on its obedience to its handler's instructions.

EVELYN M. SHAFER

and evenly spaced. It is an excellent idea to arrange an outing immediately after meals and after heavy exertion. Confine the dog to a small area. Dogs are basically clean animals and do not wish to soil their immediate areas. Therefore, the smaller the area, the better. You may limit the dog's space with some kind of obstacle.

ARTHUR J. HAGGERTY
Capt. Haggerty's School for Dogs

5. Dog Shows and Obedience Trials

Dog Shows. A dog show is an exhibition in which pure-bred dogs compete for points leading to championships and higher honors. Requests for entry into a licensed American Kennel Club show must be made on special forms and submitted at least 12 days in advance of the show. Entries at licensed shows range from 300 to more than 3,000 dogs, and more than ten of these annual shows regularly have over 2,000 entries. Puppies must be six months of age or older to compete, and since it is a licensed show, championship points are awarded to class winners. A dog earning 15 points in a prescribed manner is awarded the title of champion.

The regular AKC dog show classes are *puppy*, which may be divided into 6-to-9 and 9-to-12 months; *novice, American-bred; bred-by-exhibitor;* and *open*. Each breed competes separately in these classes, and except in very rare breeds, the classes are divided by sex. Winners of the regular classes receive a blue ribbon and compete in the winners class against other winners of the same sex. The best dog (winners dog) and best bitch (winners bitch) in the winners class get a purple ribbon and championship points. Winners dog, winners bitch, and champions then compete for best of breed. If either the winners dog or winners bitch is chosen best of breed, it is automatically also best of winners. If a champion is chosen best of breed, the winners dog and winners bitch then compete for best of winners. After the best-of-breed and best-of-winners judging, the dogs compete for best of opposite sex. If a bitch is chosen best of breed, the males compete for best of opposite sex; if a male is chosen best of breed, the bitches compete for best of opposite sex. The best-of-breed winners compete for first in their respective groups: sporting, hound, working, terrier, toy, and non-sporting. Group winners compete for best in show. The Canadian system is basically the same.

AKC championship points are awarded according to a complicated scale based on breed population and the amount of competition in a given geographical area over a period of years. In rare breeds, a winners dog or winners bitch chosen from among six entries can win the maximum of five points allowed at one show. Requirements for German shepherds are the highest, and it takes a group of 73 entries of one sex for the winners dog or winners bitch to win five points. Fifteen points are required for an AKC championship. At least 6 of these points must be won three or more at a time (a "major" win) at two different shows under two different judges. The Canadian Kennel Club requires 10 points for a championship.

The United Kennel Club, a smaller American registry, also sponsors shows. Class winners get 10 points; best of breed is awarded 15. To become a champion, a dog must win 100 points, plus one best male or female in show.

The Kennel Club in England confers championships on dogs winning three challenge certificates. A challenge certificate is awarded on the discretion of the judge to a dog winning best of sex in any of several breed classes in a KC licensed show. Australia, Hong Kong, and Japan use variations of the English system. Most South American countries use variations of the AKC system, but Brazil uses an English variation.

Obedience Trials. Obedience trials were accepted as formal competition by the American Kennel Club in 1936. These are tests of a dog's ability to take training rather than of its intelligence. The tests include walking at heel, sitting and lying among other dogs, standing for examination, retrieving, broad and high jumps, scent discrimination, seeking lost articles, and working on hand signals. Obedience titles, which are won by satisfactory performance in progressively more difficult classes, are Companion Dog (CD) in novice work, Companion Dog Excellent (CDX) in open classes, Utility Dog (UD) in utility classes, and Tracking (T). Except for tracking, which requires passing the test only once, a dog wins a title by scoring at least 170 out of a possible 200 points in three different trials under three different judges. Tracking tests are held in fields and are 440 yards (402 meters) in length.

MAXWELL RIDDLE, *Author*
"Complete Book of Puppy Training and Care"

6. Field Competition

Field Trials. These are formal contests conducted under simulated hunting or working conditions in which various breeds of dogs are rated on their ability to perform prescribed tasks. The purpose of field trials is to determine and select those strains of dogs that possess the natural ability and desire to hunt or work and an amenability to training and discipline.

Gun Dogs. In field trials of pointing breeds, the dogs are required to seek, locate, and point their quarry, usually quail or pheasant, within a prescribed time period over a designated course. Except in the trials of "continental" pointing breeds, such as the German shorthaired pointer, in which birds may be shot to demonstrate a dog's retrieving ability, the birds are not killed; only blanks are fired.

Flushing dogs, such as springer spaniels, must seek, find, and flush "planted," or set-out, birds on a designated course. The flushed birds are shot, and the dogs are required to retrieve them.

Both pointers and flushers are run in braces (pairs). Their performance is rated on how closely it approaches the judges' concept of excellence rather than by a comparison with the performances of other braces in the trial.

Retrievers, such as Labradors, must sit quietly at their handlers' sides until commanded to fetch a downed bird from land or water. The trials involve a series of tests, which include "marked retrieves," where dogs see the birds fall, and "blind retrieves," where the dogs are handled, or directed, to an unseen bird by whistle, hand, and voice signals.

Hounds must trail their quarry (rabbit, hare, fox, or raccoon) until the conclusion of the hunt or until ordered up by the judges. They may be run in braces or in packs and are rated on their ability to stay accurately with the scent line left by the quarry. Hounds compete directly with each other; they are required to beat their bracemates or lead the pack in order to increase their rating or to win.

Sheepdogs. In sheepdog trials, border collies or other herding breeds, working alone or in braces, are required to perform a variety of tasks with a small group of sheep under the direction of a handler. The dogs usually must gather the sheep, drive them through a gate, stop and turn back several of the flock, and then move them into a pen.

Cattledogs, such as the Australian cattle dog, sometimes compete in informal cattle-herding contests similar to sheepdog trials.

Racing, Coursing, and Fighting. In professional dog racing, greyhounds, which cover 18 feet (5.5 meters) with each running stride, chase a mechanical rabbit around an oblong track for various distances, the most popular in the United States being 5/16 mile (0.5 km). Betting is conducted as in horse racing. Whippets, smaller than greyhounds, race on straight tracks or on oblong tracks, similar to those used by greyhounds.

Coursing with "long dogs" (greyhound types) is probably the oldest form of hunting and competition involving dogs. These speedy dogs sight, chase, and dispatch hares in formal meets or may be used to run down wild game.

Dogfighting, when organized as a formal competition, is conducted under recognized rules, with referees and handlers. Where illegal, as in the United States, dogfights are carried on clandestinely. Mixed-breed dogs may be the protagonists, but in the United States, formal pittings involve a breed known variously as the Staffordshire terrier (AKC designation), pit bull terrier (UKC designation), or Yankee terrier. Three wins earn a fighting dog his championship. The Japanese use the tosa, a huge mastifflike dog, in their dogfights.

DAVID MICHAEL DUFFEY
Dog Editor, "Outdoor Life"

DOG REGISTRIES OF THE WORLD

Country	Registry
NORTH AMERICA	
Canada	Canadian Kennel Club
Mexico	Asociación Canofilia Mexicana
United States	American Coon Hunter's Registry (coonhounds)
	American Foxhound Breeders Association
	American Kennel Club
	Field Dog Stud Book
	National Coursing Assn. (greyhounds)
	United Kennel Club
SOUTH AMERICA	
Argentina	Argentine Kennel Club
Brazil	Brazil Kennel Club
Chile	Organización National de Clubs Caninos
Colombia	Club Canino Colombiano
Uruguay	Kennel Club Urugayo
EUROPE	
Austria	Österreicher Kynologen Verband
Belgium	Société Royal Saint-Hubert
Denmark	Dansk Kennelklub
Finland	Suomen Kennelliitto-Finska Kennelklubben
France	Société Centrale Canine
Germany	About 30 clubs, each devoted to a single breed or a small group of breeds
Ireland	The Irish Kennel Club
Italy	Ente Nazionale Della Cinofilia Italiana
Netherlands	Raad van Beheer op Kynologisch Gebied in Nederland
Norway	Norsk Kennel Klub
Spain	Real Sociedad Central de Fomento de las Razas en España
Sweden	Svenska Kennelklubben
Switzerland	Schweizerische Kynologische Gesellschaft
United Kingdom	The Kennel Club
	National Coursing Club (greyhounds only)
	Masters of Foxhounds Assn.
USSR	Klub Sluzhobnovo Sobakovodstva
	Otdel Okhotnichyevo Sobakovodstva pri Moskovskom Obshchestve Okhotnikov
	Sektsia Lyubiteley Komnatno-Dekorativnovo
AFRICA	
Kenya	East Africa Kennel Club
South Africa	Kennel Union of Southern Africa
ASIA	
India	Kennel Club of India
Pakistan	Kennel Club of Pakistan
AUSTRALASIA	
Australia	Australian National Kennel Council
New Zealand	New Zealand Kennel Club

7. Kennel Clubs

Kennel clubs basically have one or both of these functions: (1) to maintain a record (registry, or stud book) of lineage, or pedigree, to provide evidence of a given dog's lineage; (2) to regulate formal competition between dogs. One of the earliest kennel club registries was the *Foxhound Kennel Stud Book* of the Masters of Foxhounds Association, England, which was first published in 1844 and has appeared since at regular intervals; the first volume included the names of hounds going back to 1800.

Kennel clubs are organized on various bases. There are national clubs, local clubs, clubs for a single breed, and clubs for specialized interests such as trials or races. In the early 1930's the Fédération Cynologique Internationale was formed to develop uniform control over dog shows and dog breeding on an international basis.

Many kennel clubs publish magazines to keep their members informed of show and trial results. These magazines usually include articles relating to the breeding and care of dogs.

H. MALCOLM STEPHENS
"Dogs in Canada" Magazine

8. Diseases

Distemper. Canine distemper is an infectious, airborne viral disease characterized by respiratory infection, fever, diarrhea, and in severe cases by convulsions or muscular twitching. The symptoms appear usually 6 to 12 days, sometimes as soon as 4 days, after exposure to the virus. Infected dogs should be well isolated, and professional veterinary treatment is imperative. Effective vaccines are available to protect the dog from this disease.

Infectious Canine Hepatitis. This is a viral disease with a great affinity for the liver and the lining of the blood vessels. It is spread by contact with discharges or urine from an infected dog. The disease may have a peracute (very acute and violent) form, in which case the puppy may be listless and feverish for a day, then suddenly die. In the less acute form the incubation period is usually 6 to 9 days after exposure. Symptoms include abdominal pain, a fiery redness of the mucous membranes of the eye and mouth, listlessness, and fever.

Treatment consists of broad-spectrum antibiotics, blood transfusions, and general supportive therapy according to the needs of the animal. Modern preventive vaccines are frequently used in combination with distemper vaccine.

Leptospirosis. This is a bacterial disease of dogs and man generally produced by contact with urine from actively ill or convalescent animals. In acute cases the symptoms are vomiting, diarrhea, and rapid dehydration, leading to coma and death. Less acute cases show a visibly dejected dog, with a painful, drawn-up abdomen, high fever initially, with a rapid plunge to subnormal, vomiting of froth and bile, intense thirst, bloody dysentery, dehydration, and weakness.

Treatment consists of attempts to control the severe vomiting and dehydration and to aid kidney function. Short-term vaccines are helpful in reducing the risk of exposure.

Rabies. This is an acute viral infectious disease of warm-blooded animals transmitted through the bite of an afflicted animal, though there is now evidence of airborne infection from masses of bats in "bat caves." The incubation period of the virus, which has a special affinity for nervous tissue, is usually from 12 to 30 days, but it may be as long as 6 months or more.

Treatment of the afflicted dog, once the symptoms appear, is futile. The best barrier to the spread of rabies and the best safeguard for the dog is regular immunization. For people in high-risk groups, such as veterinarians, human vaccines are available. *See* RABIES.

Roundworms. These ascarid worms are about 5 to 8 inches (12–20 cm) in length when fully grown, usually white or yellowish white in color, and pointed at both ends. Infection is caused by swallowing the infective eggs of these worms, which hatch in the intestines. The newly hatched larvae penetrate the intestinal wall and migrate through the liver and lung tissues, finally returning to the intestinal tract. Unborn puppies can be infected by larvae migrating from the mother across the placenta. Since a dog can pick up the infective eggs on food or playthings dragged on the floor, the removal of all droppings and strict sanitation are necessary to prevent constant reinfection in puppies.

Roundworm infection in puppies is usually characterized by a potbelly, unthrifty appearance, capricious appetites, and intermittent vomiting and diarrhea. The worms may appear in the vomit or stool. Worming can be done at home, but since treatment is usually messy and proper dosages of the various drugs often difficult to gauge, professional veterinary care is preferable.

Tapeworms. The tapeworm is made up of a chain of body segments, or proglottids. The most posterior segments, which fill with eggs, break loose and are passed by the dog. These segments are commonly pinkish white in color, about ½ inch (12.5 mm) in length, and flat and fleshy in appearance. They are capable of movement. Dead and dried segments, looking like brown grains of rice, may adhere to the dog's coat or be found in the dog's sleeping quarters.

The most common dog tapeworm, *Dipylidium caninum*, requires partial development in the dog flea or dog louse before it becomes infective for the dog. The tapeworm eggs, passed by the dog, are ingested by fleas or lice that act as the intermediate host. Infected fleas or lice swallowed by the dog are digested, and the immature tapeworm is liberated.

Control of tapeworms is directed chiefly at eliminating the principal intermediate hosts—fleas and lice. Treatment for tapeworms is best attempted in a veterinary hospital.

Heartworms. The adult heartworm, which may be 10 to 12 inches (25–30 cm) in length, commonly lives in the right ventricle of the heart. The female worms produce larvae (microfilariae) that circulate in the bloodstream. When mosquitoes ingest the microfilariae by feeding on an infected dog, the larvae develop to an infective stage. When the infected mosquitos bite another dog, the larvae are transmitted to it, thereby renewing the cycle.

Symptoms produced vary with the number of worms in the heart or pulmonary artery. A chronic cough, labored respiration, and collapse can result from heavy infestation. Milder cases show early fatigue upon any attempts at exercise. Treatment may consist of surgical removal of the adult worms from the heart and the careful use of drugs to kill the microfilariae. Where the disease is endemic, dogs can be protected in mosquito season by drugs that kill microfilariae.

Hookworms. The most common dog hookworm is ⅜ to ¾ inch (10–19 mm) in length and lives by attaching its mouthparts to the small intestine of the host. The females deposit many eggs, which pass in the feces and hatch outside to become infective larvae.

The infective larvae may either be ingested or penetrate through the skin. In puppies, prenatal infection can occur when the larvae migrate through the tissues of the pregnant bitch. Larvae that are swallowed develop into adult worms within 2 to 3 weeks. Those larvae that penetrate the skin burrow into the blood capillaries and eventually get into the bronchi of the lungs and subsequently are coughed up and swallowed. They mature in the intestinal tract.

In puppies, large numbers of hookworms may cause profound anemia, leading to collapse. In less severe infections the puppies show a tarry and black diarrhea, anemia, and weakness.

Treatment of severely debilitated puppies consists of blood transfusions, administration of intestinal protectives and of liver and iron, and specific medication to kill the adult parasites. Strict sanitation is imperative.

Ticks. Ticks are external parasites that fasten themselves to their host and suck its blood. Isolated ticks on a dog can be removed with tweezers after stupefying the ticks with alcohol or acetone. For heavy infestations, periodic dipping of the dog is necessary. Owners of dogs with tick problems should obtain professional advice regarding sprays and dips—many of the sprays can result in poisoning if used improperly or too frequently.

Fleas. Dog fleas deposit their eggs in litter on the ground. The newly hatched larvae, which are wormlike and bristly, pupate (begin the change to adult form) after 3 months. The bites of fleas are extremely irritating, and their saliva produces intolerable itching. Dogs harboring many fleas become sensitized and may develop a severe dermatitis. Much of the so-called summer eczema can be traced to a heavy flea infestation.

Bathing the dog in emulsions of pine oil, rotenone, or pyrethrum will kill the fleas it is carrying. The premises can be treated with 2.5% malathion in a spray, using precautions to avoid contamination of feeding utensils.

9. Breeding

Estrous Cycle. Though a mature male dog can be bred at any time, the bitch can be bred only when in estrus. The bitch's estrous cycle has four stages. *Proestrus* lasts 7 to 10 days and is characterized by marked swelling of the external parts of the genitals (vulva) and commonly a clear, bright-red blood flow. This is followed by true *estrus*, when the flow persists but fades to paler red or straw color. Estrus lasts about 9 days and merges into *metestrus*, when the flow becomes scanty or absent and the swelling slowly subsides. If no conception has occurred, *metestrus* is followed by regressive changes in the uterus, known as *anestrus*, and the bitch is out of "season". The entire period from proestrus to metestrus is usually 18 to 22 days. Anestrus normally lasts a little more than 5 months, and most bitches pass through two estrous cycles per year.

The optimum time for breeding the bitch is between the 10th and 14th day of the cycle. The bitch while in estrus should be kept under

GLOSSARY OF TERMS

Action.—The way in which a dog moves forward.
Apple Head.—A domed skull.
Bat Ear.—An erect ear, broad at base, rounded at tip, with opening directly to the front.
Belton.—A white coat heavily flecked with colored hairs.
Bench Show.—A dog show; more specifically, one where the dogs are kept in stalls, or benches.
Bite.—The meeting of the teeth when the mouth is closed.
Blue Merle.—A coat of blue and gray hair mixed with black.
Brace.—A pair of dogs.
Breeching.—The tan-colored hair on the inside of the thighs.
Brindle.—A coat of mixed light and dark hairs, the latter usually black and forming irregular stripes.
Butterfly Nose.—A partially pigmented nose.
Button Ear.—An ear with the tip folding forward and lying close to the skull.
Cat Foot.—A short, round, compact foot with toes highly arched.
Clip.—The trimming style of the coat.
Cobby.—Short-bodied, compact.
Coupling.—The portion of the body between the front and hind legs.
Cowhocked.—The hock joints turned inward toward each other, causing rear feet to turn out.
Culotte.—The longer hair on the back of the thighs.
Dewclaw.—The rudimentary 5th toe on the inside of the leg.
Dewlap.—The loose skin under the throat.
Dock.—To cut (shorten) the tail.
Double Coat.—A coat consisting of a soft undercoat with an outer coat of long coarse guard hairs.
Drop Ears.—Long, soft, pendulous ears that hang flat and close to the head.
Dry Neck.—Taut skin, neither loose nor wrinkled.
Ewe Neck.—A neck that is concave rather than convex in outline along its upper surface.
Feathering.—The fringes of longer hairs on ears, legs or tail.
Flews.—The pendulous inner corners of the upper lips.
Gay Tail.—A tail that is carried over the back.
Harefoot.—An elongated narrow foot.
Harlequin.—A patched, or pied, color, usually black on white.

Haw.—The reddish third eyelid, located at the eyeball at the inner corner.
Height.—The measurement from the withers (highest point of shoulders) to the ground.
Hock.—The actual heel of the dog, located on the hind leg at the first joint above the foot.
Loaded Shoulders.—Excessive development of the shoulder muscles.
Occiput.—A bony protuberance at the rear of the skull.
Overshot.—A bite in which the front teeth of the upper jaw overlap the front teeth of the lower jaw so as not to touch.
Prick Ear.—A usually pointed ear carried erect.
Roan.—A dark-colored coat lightened by a mixture of white hairs.
Rose Ear.—A small ear folding over and away from the front to reveal the inner surface.
Sable.—A lacing of black hair in or over a lighter ground color.
Saddle.—A black marking extending over the back.
Scissors Bite.—A bite in which the front upper teeth close just over and in front of the lower teeth. The normal bite in most breeds of dogs.
Smooth Coat.—A short-haired coat, consisting of stiff hair lying flat and close to the body.
Stifle.—The true knee of the dog; the joint just above the hock.
Stop.—The step up from the muzzle to the skull or the indentation between the eyes.
Ticked.—A coat with comparatively small areas of colored hair isolated on a white background.
Topknot.—A tuft of hair on the top of the head.
Tricolor.—A coat consisting of black, white, and tan.
Tulip Ear.—An erect ear with slight forward curvature along the sides.
Undershot.—A bite in which the teeth of the lower jaw overlap and project beyond the front teeth of the upper jaw when the mouth is closed.
Walleye.—An eye with a pale, whitish, or colorless iris. Also called fisheye, glass eye, and pearl eye.
Wheaten.—A pale yellow or fawn color.
Wirehaired.—A coat of hard, crisp, or wiry hair.

H. MALCOLM STEPHENS
"Dogs in Canada" Magazine

strict surveillance, as it is possible for a bitch to breed with one or more dogs in a given day. This could result in a litter fathered by two or more dogs—though each individual puppy, of course, will have only one sire. This mixed litter would not ruin a valuable bitch, since previous matings do not affect the characteristics or qualities of later offspring.

The Newborn Puppies. The puppies are born after a gestation, or pregnancy, period of usually 62 to 63 days. One of the signs of approaching birth is repeated muscular contractions. The puppy usually emerges head first, right after passage of the glistening bubblelike "water bag," or amniotic sac. A second puppy is born shortly after the first. Then a rest period of several hours may occur, after which another puppy or two may be born. If the litter is a large one, the entire birth process may take up to 24 hours.

The puppies' eyes generally open between the 10th and 14th days and appear milky blue. The puppies should not be exposed to excessive glare or sun at this stage. At 3 weeks of age they toddle around, and at 4 weeks they begin to manifest canine behavioral responses. At 5 to 6 weeks they play by engaging in mock free-for-all attacks upon one another and the bitch. Supplemental feeding of scraped raw lean beef, cottage cheese, and baby cereals can be started at 5 weeks of age, or somewhat earlier, at about 4 weeks of age, if the bitch has a scanty milk flow.

Marvin J. Sheffield, D. V. M.

Bibliography
American Kennel Club, *The Complete Dog Book* (Howell 1975).
Bueller, Lois E., *Wild Dogs of the World* (Stein & Day 1973).
Cross, Jeanette W., and Saunders, Blanche, *New Standard Book of Dog Care and Training* (Hawthorn 1962).
Dangerfield, Stanley, and Howell, Elsworth, *The International Encyclopedia of Dogs* (Howell 1971).
Goodall, Charles S., *How to Train Your Own Gun Dog* (Howell 1978).
Howe, John, *Choosing the Right Dog* (Harper 1976).
Howell, Elsworth S., and others, *Howell Book of Dog Care and Training* (Howell 1963).
Lorenz, Konrad Z., *Man Meets Dog* (Penguin 1965).
Pfaffenberger, Clarence, *New Knowledge of Dog Behavior* (Howell 1963).
Riddle, Maxwell, *Complete Book of Puppy Training and Care*, rev. ed. (Coward 1963).
Saunders, Blanche, *The Complete Book of Dog Obedience*, 4th ed. (Howell·1978).
Schneider-Leyer, Erich, *Dogs of the World* (Arco 1970).
Whitney, Leon F., *Dog Psychology: The Basis of Dog Training*, 2d ed. (Howell 1971).

DOG DAYS is a term applied to the hottest season of the year. The term originated in ancient times, when what was usually the hottest season—a period of about 40 days—coincided with the time of year when Sirius, the Dog Star, rose just before the sun. The expression is still used, but owing to the precession of the equinoxes the hottest period of the year no longer coincides with this conjunction of the rising of the Dog Star and the sun.

DOG FAMILY, or Canidae, a group of essentially carnivorous mammals whose members are characterized by a long muzzle, large canine teeth, relatively long legs and tail, and blunt, nonretractile claws. All but a few species of canids have 42 teeth in the adult, five toes on the forefeet, and four toes on the hind feet. The bat-eared fox may normally have as many as 50 teeth, and the bush dog as few as 38. The African hunting dog has four toes on each foot.

The members of the dog family, including dogs, wolves, coyotes, jackals, foxes, zorros, dingoes, and dholes, range in size from 3¼ pounds (1.5 kg) for the fennec fox to 175 pounds (80 kg) for the gray wolf. Most are rather uniformly colored in tones of gray or brown, but the Arctic fox may be all white (in winter), the African hunting dog is varyingly blotched with black, yellow, and white, and the side-striped jackal carries striped markings.

Economic Value. Wild canids have little economic value except that the fur of some species is used in the clothing industry. In the United States, in a single year in the 1960's, about 4,000 coyotes, 200 wolves, and 113,000 foxes were trapped and sold for their fur. Some kinds of canids are also routinely raised in captivity for their furs. In past years, when fox fur was in vogue, fur farms specializing in foxes were numerous and profitable.

Behavior. Canids rely most on the senses of smell and vision for hunting. Some canids, like the foxes, hunt alone; others, such as wolves, hunt in packs, which may be little more than family groups. The locality regularly traversed by these animals, called the "home range," depends on many factors: the season of the year, the age and sex of the individual, the number of other individuals of the same species in the same area, and the availability of food, water, and shelter. In general, the smaller canids have home ranges of 200 to 300 acres (100–125 hectares). In contrast, some of the wolves of the western United States have home ranges as great as 50 miles (80 km) in diameter.

Studies of pet and captive wolves and foxes have shown that wild canids have an extensively developed "language." In addition to the vocal sounds—barks, growls, whimpers, yelps—the position of the body and of its parts also have meaning. The placement of the ears and tail, the ruffling of the hair on the neck, the expression of the face, and even the animal's stance are all involved in communication. Wolves may have a "vocabulary" of 30 or more "words."

Most canids try to avoid man, and unprovoked attacks are rare. However, if accidentally or deliberately cornered or wounded, these animals are ferocious fighters and can do considerable damage. Under conditions of extreme hunger, canids have been known to attack and kill humans, especially if the human involved is a child or is injured or exhausted. Animals infected with rabies, not an uncommon disease among the Canidae, may attack humans, domestic animals, and even inanimate objects.

Reproduction. Canids usually bear one litter of 3 to 12 young each year. The gestation period averages about 63 days, but it may be as short as 51 days, as in the fennec fox, or possibly as long as 80 days, as has been reported for the African hunting dog. The pups are generally born in a den in the ground. The eyes are closed at birth and open in about 10 days. The pups are nursed for 4 to 8 weeks. Adult size is reached in about 6 months; sexual maturity, at about one year. However, the coyote may take 2 years and the wolf 3 years to become sexually mature. In the wild, canids may reach 13 or more years of age.

Conservation. The importance of wild canids in the balance of nature is becoming increasingly recognized. Coyotes, for example, formerly thought to be responsible for the destruction

CLASSIFICATION OF THE DOG FAMILY (CANIDAE)

The dog family is classified in the superfamily Canoidea, in the order Carnivora, class Mammalia. It is divided into 38 species, which are grouped into 14 genera and placed in 3 subfamilies.

Subfamily CANINAE

1. Canis lupus — Gray Wolf — Europe, Asia, North America
2. Canis niger — Red Wolf — North America
3. Canis latrans — Coyote — North America
4. Canis aureus — Asiatic Jackal — Europe, Asia, Africa
5. Canis mesomelas — Black-Backed Jackal — Africa
6. Canis adustus — Side-Striped Jackal — Africa
7. Canis familiaris — Domestic Dog — Worldwide
8. Canis dingo — Dingo — Australia
9. Vulpes vulpes — Old World Red Fox — Europe, Asia
10. Vulpes fulva — North American Red Fox — North America
11. Vulpes velox — Swift, or Kit, Fox — North America
12. Vulpes macrotis — Kit, or Swift, Fox — North America
13. Vulpes ruppelli — Sand Fox — Asia, Africa
14. Vulpes ferrilata — Tibetan Sand Fox — Asia
15. Vulpes chama — Cape Fox — Africa
16. Vulpes cana — Blansford Fox — Europe, Asia
17. Vulpes corsac — Corsac Fox — Europe, Asia
18. Alopex lagopus — Arctic Fox — Europe, Asia, North America
19. Urocyon cinereoargenteus — Gray Fox — North America, Central America, South America

Subfamily CANINAE (Continued)

20. Urocyon littoralis — Island Gray Fox — North America
21. Fennecus zerda — Fennec Fox — Asia, Africa
22. Nyctereutes procyonoides — Raccoon Dog — Asia, Europe
23. Atelocynus microtis — Small-Eared Zorro — South America
24. Chrysocyon jubatus — Maned Wolf — South America
25. Cerdocyon thous — Crab-Eating Fox — South America
26. Dusicyon griseus — Patagonian Gray Fox — South America
27. Dusicyon gymnocercus — Pampas Gray Fox — South America
28. Dusicyon inca — Peruvian Gray Fox — South America
29. Dusicyon culpaeus — Colpeo Zorro — South America
30. Dusicyon fulvipes — Chiloé Zorro — South America
31. Dusicyon vetulus — Brazilian Zorro — South America
32. Dusicyon culpaeolus — (no common name) — South America
33. Dusicyon sechurae — (no common name) — South America

Subfamily SIMOCYONINAE

34. Cuon alpinus — Dhole — Asia
35. Lycaon pictus — African Hunting Dog — Africa
36. Speothos venaticus — Bush Dog — South America
37. Speothos panamensis — Bush Dog — Central America

Subfamily OTOCYONINAE

38. Otocyon megalotis — Bat-Eared Fox — Africa

of native game as well as domestic animals, feed on carrion, rodents, rabbits; and wild fruit and other vegetable material. Extensive efforts to eliminate coyotes, such as the killing of 60,000 coyotes in Kansas in the 1940's for bounties, often result in huge increases in the rabbit and rodent populations. Frequently the damage done to crops and grasslands by rabbits and rodents far outweighs the loss of the relatively few game and domestic animals taken by coyotes.

As a result of wildlife studies, modern programs of carnivore control tend to emphasize the elimination of specific troublesome individuals rather than the entire population.

DISTRIBUTION AND CLASSIFICATION

The dog family, which originated in late Eocene times, about 45 million years ago, is widely distributed. It is found in all parts of the world except Antarctica and some oceanic islands, and in a wide variety of habitats. The living members of the family are divided into at least 38 species grouped into 14 genera, which are placed in three subfamilies: Caninae, Simocyoninae, and Otocyoninae. One species, the Falkland Island dog, a reportedly trusting and friendly animal that inhabited the Falkland Islands off the southern coast of Argentina, was exterminated about 1876 by the island's settlers.

Caninae. The subfamily Caninae, containing at least 33 species grouped into 10 different genera, includes most of the living members of the family.

The true dogs (*Canis*) comprise 8 species: the gray, or timber, wolf (*Canis lupus*), which formerly ranged throughout the northern part of Europe, Asia, and North America; the red wolf (*C. niger*), of the southeastern United States; the coyote (*C. latrans*), found throughout most of North America from Alaska to central Mexico; the Asiatic, or golden, jackal (*C. aureus*), of eastern Europe, central and southern Asia, and northern Africa; the black-backed jackal (*C. mesomelas*), of central and southern Africa; the side-striped jackal (*C. adustus*), of eastern and southern Africa; the domestic dog (*C. familiaris*), formerly believed to have been derived from both the wolf and jackal but now considered to be solely descended from the wolf; and the Australian dingo (*C. dingo*), probably evolved from domestic dogs taken to Australia by early man. The dingo is sometimes considered only a subspecies of the domestic dog.

The true foxes (*Vulpes*) include 9 species: the Old World red fox (*Vulpes vulpes*), of northern and central Europe and Asia, and the North American red fox (*V. fulva*), which some zoologists believe is identical to the Old World species; the swift fox (*V. velox*), of the northern Great Plains of southern Canada and the northern United States; the kit fox (*V. macrotis*), of the southwestern United States and northern Mexico; the sand fox (*V. ruppelli*), of northern Africa and Arabia; the Tibetan sand fox (*V. ferrilata*), of Tibet and Nepal; the Cape fox (*V. chama*), of southern Africa; the Blansford fox (*V. cana*), of southwestern Russia and northeastern Iran; and the corsac fox (*V. corsac*), of southeastern Russia, Mongolia, North Korea, and northern China.

Related to the true foxes are four other fox-like caninids: the Arctic fox (*Alopex lagopus*), found in Arctic regions across the world; the gray fox (*Urocyon cinereoargenteus*), occurring from the eastern United States into northern

South America; the closely related island gray fox (*U. littoralis*), from the islands off the coast of southern California; and the fennec fox (*Fennecus zerda*), of northeastern Africa and western Arabia.

The raccoon dog (*Nyctereutes procyonoides*), of eastern Siberia, Japan, and China southward into North Vietnam, is, in general appearance, the least doglike member of the family. It has a raccoonlike face, a broad body, and a bushy tail. Its generally brownish fur is highly valued and is sold commercially as "ussurian raccoon" or "Japanese fox." The raccoon dog has been introduced into parts of Russia as a fur animal and is now found in certain areas of eastern Europe.

Eleven species in this subfamily are confined to South America. These are variously known as zorros (Spanish for "fox"), wolves, dogs, and foxes. The small-eared zorro (*Atelocynus microtis*), found in the Amazon basin of Brazil, Ecuador, Peru, and Colombia, is about 14 inches (35 cm) high at the shoulders and 30 inches (75 cm) in length, with a 12-inch (30-cm) tail.

The maned "wolf" (*Chrysocyon jubatus*), from the interior of Brazil south to northern Argentina, is second in height only to the gray wolf, although it is much lighter. It has exceptionally long legs and a characteristic mane of long hair on its neck. With its shaggy reddish coat, a foxlike head, and blackish legs, the maned wolf has been described as a giant fox on stilts.

The crab-eating fox (*Cerdocyon thous*) is widely distributed from Colombia and Venezuela to northern Argentina. Despite its name, the crab-eating fox seems to feed largely on small rodents.

The remaining South American members of this subfamily superficially resemble small coyotes and are generally grouped into a single genus, *Dusicyon*. The interrelationships of the eight species currently recognized within the genus are poorly understood. It is probable that at least some of the so-called species are simply geographic variants of a single species. The eight species include the Patagonian gray fox (*Dusicyon griseus*), of central Chile and western Argentina; the pampas gray fox (*D. gymnocercus*), from Argentina, Paraguay, and Uruguay; the Peruvian gray fox (*D. inca*), confined to Peru; and five species of zorros, distributed from Ecuador to Tierra del Fuego: the colpeo zorro (*D. culpaeus*), the Chiloé zorro (*D. fulvipes*), the Brazilian zorro (*D. vetulus*), and two species without common names, *D. culpaeolus* and *D. sechurae*. The Brazilian zorro, of southern Brazil and northern Argentina, does not appear to be as closely related to the other four species as those species are to one another. The extinct Falkland Island dog (*D. australis*) was a member of this group.

Simocyoninae. The subfamily Simocyoninae is a small group of Old World and South American dogs: the dhole (*Cuon alpinus*), of Asia; the African hunting dog (*Lycaon pictus*), from the Sudan and Ghana to southern Africa; and the bush dogs (*Speothos venaticus* and *S. panamensis*), of Panama and tropical South America.

Otocyoninae. The subfamily Otocyoninae is represented by a single species (*Otocyon megalotis*) from eastern and southern Africa. Known commonly as the bat-eared, or big-eared, fox, this inhabitant of arid regions feeds mainly on termites and other insects.

E. LENDELL COCKRUM, *University of Arizona*

DOG RACING is a sport in which greyhounds or other dogs of similar type compete in pursuit of a live or artificial animal. In *coursing*, which takes place in open fields or in enclosures on private estates, greyhounds pursue a hare that is given a head start of about 60 to 80 yards. The most familiar races, however, are those in which greyhounds chase a mechanical lure, which is maneuvered around an electrified rail on an oval track. Because of the greyhound's speed, competitive nature, endurance, keen sight, and instinct to pursue the hare, this dog is used exclusively in professional races. Eight-dog fields are run in the United States over sand-surfaced tracks. The British and Irish system uses six dogs in each race, and the run is over grass. Australia, Portugal, Spain, Mexico, Italy, France, Colombia, and Sweden also conduct races.

In the United States, racing with a mechanical lure is a popular pari-mutuel attraction with more than 30 dog tracks in seven states. Open-field coursing is a nonwagering sport in several states where rabbits are a severe menace to crops. In amateur competition, dogs that follow by scent are raced as well as those that pursue their quarry by sight.

Greyhounds are one of the oldest canine breeds and have been used for hunting and coursing since ancient times. For centuries in England they were dogs of the aristocracy; early British laws forbade commoners to own them. The first written code for coursing was formulated in England in 1776. Greyhounds were brought to America by the early settlers, and during the 19th century they were used mainly to chase jackrabbits and coyotes on the plains.

Development of Racing. In 1876 in England the first simulated rabbit was used in greyhound racing at Hendon, Middlesex, over a straight 400-yard course. The dogs eagerly pursued the lure, but owners lost interest in the venture.

An Arkansas promoter, Owen Patrick Smith, is credited with introducing greyhound racing in the United States. He invented an artificial lure and demonstrated his device at Salt Lake City, Utah, in 1907. Later attempts to use Smith's lure were made at Houston, Texas, in 1912, and at Emeryville, Calif., in 1919. Both ventures were failures, mainly because betting was not allowed. Attempts to introduce greyhound racing in Tulsa, Okla., in 1920 and Chicago in 1921 were more successful but short-lived.

Racing then moved to Florida, where a track opened at Hialeah in 1922, and more than 5,000 fans saw the first Miami Derby in March of that year. Hialeah closed in 1926, the year the St. Petersburg (Fla.) Kennel Club opened its track. Today the St. Petersburg track is the oldest greyhound course in the world operating on its original site, and its Derby and Gold Trophy races are the oldest continuously running events of their kind in the United States. The first English track opened at Belle Vue, Manchester, in 1926. In Australia the first greyhound track race was run in New South Wales in 1927.

In the 1920's, conditions for dog racing in the United States were crude, and the sport was held in disrepute. Because of gangster interest in racing and unsavory conditions at the tracks, some of the racecourses were raided. With the legalization of pari-mutuel betting, first in Florida in 1932 and later in Massachusetts and other states, greyhound racing was elevated to a higher plane. Now, tracks are licensed by the individual states and supervised and controlled by state racing commissions.

The American Greyhound Track Operators Association, founded in Florida in 1947, promotes the sport and sets up uniform practices for the industry. This association, together with the National Coursing Association (NCA), which began in Nebraska in 1906, established the Greyhound Hall of Fame at Abilene, Kans., in 1963 to honor the great track and coursing stars of the past. An All-American Greyhound Team of eight dogs is chosen annually.

Breeding and Identification. The first greyhound stud book was initiated in England in 1882. A separate Irish Coursing Club studbook was begun in 1923. In the United States the NCA has published its studbook since 1906. The association registers all U. S. litters and issues identification certificates for racers; these certificates must be presented to the state racing commission and the racecourse concerned before a dog can be entered in a race. Puppies are tattooed in the left ear with the month and year they were whelped, and this number appears on every racing greyhound's Bertillon card, which also shows the dog's age, breeding, owner, color, marks and scars, toenails, weight, and certificate number. A dog's Bertillon is checked and approved by a race official at the track before every race in which the dog is entered.

Principal breeding centers are at Abilene and Ocala, Fla. Although there are many great American sires and dams, most of the U. S. bloodlines contain strains of Irish, English, and Australian champions. Today Ireland is the largest supplier of greyhound imports to the United States.

Grading. The racing secretary of the track grades dogs as to ability and past performance and matches those of like grade for the various races. There are generally six grades: A, B, C, D, E, and M (Maiden, nonwinners). Grade A, or sometimes AA, is the best rating a dog can achieve. The winner of any race is advanced one grade until it reaches A. If a dog fails to finish first, second, or third in three consecutive starts, he is lowered one grade. This system of grading dogs was inaugurated in 1948.

Race Procedures. Dogs begin to race at 14 to 16 months of age; their racing careers last about three years. Strict track rules and regulations protect the dogs and the racing public. Security measures at the track prevent substitution of greyhounds or administration of any illegal medication. Once the dogs are brought to the track, they are locked in separate kennels, and no kennel personnel are allowed near them until race time. A dog is brought out from the lockout kennel just before his race, and an official weighs him, checks his Bertillon, and fits him with a muzzle and a racing blanket, the color of which is determined by his previously drawn post position.

When all the dogs are in the starting box, the lure operator starts the mechanical rabbit around the track. This opens the box, and the dogs are released for the chase. The lure is kept at a uniform distance and speed, just ahead of the lead dog. Ten or eleven races complete a program, and three judges have final authority on all matters affecting the outcome of the program.

Tracks and Classic Races. Tracks are generally about ¼ mile around, and race distances vary from ³⁄₁₆- and ⁵⁄₁₆-mile sprints to ⅜- or ⁷⁄₁₆-mile.

BISCAYNE KENNEL CLUB

RACING GREYHOUNDS in Miami, Fla., speed around an oval track pursuing a pair of artificial rabbits moving along an electrified rail on the inside of the track.

Famous national and international stakes races include the Wonderland Derby at Revere, Mass.; the St. Petersburg (Fla.) Derby; the Raynham (Mass.) International Derby; the Taunton (Mass.) American Derby; the Biscayne (Fla.) Irish-American Tri-Distance Championship; and the world's richest classic, the Flagler International at Miami. The English Derby at White City stadium in London is Britain's richest prize, and the Hobart (Tasmania) Thousand is Australia's most famous annual event.

Amateur Racing. Racing with sight hounds other than greyhounds—Afghans, Irish wolfhounds, salukis, Scottish deerhounds, and borzois—is an attraction at some dog shows. The Westbury (N. Y.) Kennel Show races Afghans.

Scent-hound races, in which hounds pursue a caged raccoon drawn across 100 yards of water, are held each year at Lake Hartwell near Anderson, S. C. In this event, the first dog passing a marker on shore is declared "line" winner, and the first hound to bark after entering a circle around the tree in which the quarry is held is declared "tree" winner.

ROBERT NIEMEYER
Editor of "The Greyhound Racing Record"

Further Reading: Clarke, H. Edwards, *The Greyhound* (London 1965); Florida State Racing Commission, *Greyhound Racing Rules and Regulations* (Miami 1968); Wimhurst, C. G. E., *The Book of the Greyhound* (London 1961).

DOG STAR. See SIRIUS.

Dogbane (Apocynum androsaemifolium)

DOGBANE, dŏg′bān, is the common name for the seven species of North American perennial herbs making up the genus *Apocynum*, in the dogbane family (Apocynaceae). The dogbanes are tall branching plants with fibrous stems and a poisonous milky juice. They bear loose clusters (cymes) of small, bell-shaped, white, pink, or greenish flowers. The flower is unusual because its pistil is composed of two free carpels (ovaries) that are fused into a single style and stigma; the style is extremely short, and the stigma rests directly on top of the two carpels. Each carpel matures into a podlike fruit (follicle).

Indian hemp, or hemp dogbane (*Apocynum cannabinum*) was once cultivated as a cordage plant for its tough stem fibers.

S. C. BAUSOR
California State College, California, Pa.

DOGE, dōj, was the title of the chief of state of the Venetian republic from its origins in the 8th century until its fall in 1797. The republic of Genoa was also ruled by elected doges from 1339 until the 18th century. The name is derived from the Latin *dux*, signifying "leader."

A tradition of uncertain accuracy names Paulicio Anafesto (died 727) as the first Venetian doge. The Byzantine emperors perhaps named the first holders of the office, but from the 8th century Venice was electing its own doges, who were drawn from patrician families, to serve for life. The doge represented the city in foreign affairs and presided over numerous councils and courts. But a series of constitutional reforms, concentrated in the two centuries from 1150 to 1350, curtailed his original powers. From the late 12th century, the Maggior Consiglio, or Great Council, replaced him as the state's supreme authority. From 1192 the doge had to take a coronation oath to respect established practices. The closing (1297) of the Great Council to all but descendants of old members and the growing power of the despotic Council of Ten (from 1310) confirmed the oligarchy's dominance and left the doge with little but ceremonial functions.

One doge was executed for treason (Marino Faliero, in 1355) and another was forced to resign (Francesco Foscari, in 1457), but Venice was on the whole well served by its titular leaders. The office of doge gave the Venetian constitution an aura of stability that was admired throughout Europe; it also provided political thinkers with an example of limited executive power.

DAVID HERLIHY, *University of Wisconsin*

DOGES' PALACE, dō′jəz, the former official residence of the doges of Venice, Italy. In Italian it it called the *Palazzo Ducale*. The original palace dates from the 9th century, but the present building, one of the unique glories of Venice, is the result of repeated reconstructions undertaken between the 14th and 17th centuries.

The southern façade, facing St. Mark's Canal, reveals a two-tiered open arcade dating from the 14th century; the upper tier, with its elegant marble tracery and graceful pointed arches, is a fine example of the Venetian Gothic style. In contrast, the wide expanse of marble-faced wall that rises above the arcade is interrupted only by a richly decorated central balcony window and six flanking Gothic windows.

The interior courtyard, one side of which backs onto St. Mark's Cathedral, dates from the Renaissance. The lower half of its façade consists of a two-tiered open arcade; the upper tier is reached from the courtyard by a splendid open stairway (Scala dei Giganti), which is flanked at the top by huge statues of Mars and Neptune. The walls and ceilings of the palace's apartments and council chambers are enriched by paintings, some by Tintoretto and Veronese. The famous Bridge of Sighs connects the palace with the neighboring state prison.

DONALD S. WALKER
Author of "A Geography of Italy"

DOGFISH, any of several sharks of the family Squalidae. The name "dogfish" is, however, most often applied to the species *Squalus acanthias*, a small shark found in the continental-shelf waters of the cooler parts of the temperate zones. This shark is also known as *spiny dogfish*, *grayfish*, *spotted dog*, and *piked dogfish*.

Range. The dogfish is seasonally abundant along the North American coasts: on the Atlantic coast from Newfoundland to the Virginia capes, and on the Pacific coast from southern Alaska to San Francisco Bay. Seasonal migrations occasionally extend its range.

Similar populations are present from Iceland and northern Norway southward along many European coasts, including the coasts of the Baltic, Mediterranean, and Black seas. Dogfish populations also occur from Japan to southern China, off the southern tips of Africa and South America, and around New Zealand and the southern coasts of Australia.

Description. Dogfish usually reach a length of about 3 feet (90 cm) and a weight of 6 to 10 pounds (2.7–4.5 kg), although mature females may be heavier and a little longer. The fish are gray above, white below, and usually marked on their upper surfaces with a few irregularly spaced, small white spots. Dogfish lack an anal fin but have two strong spines along the leading edge of each dorsal fin. These spines are defensive structures for the dogfish, and they may inflict painful wounds on fishermen.

Behavior. Dogfish usually form dense schools. They feed on many fishes, especially herring and herringlike species. The female's eggs are internally fertilized, and the dogfish has the longest gestation period—18 to 22 months—known for any vertebrate. The litter usually includes 6 "pups" but may number from 2 to 12. At birth the young are 9 to 12 inches (22–30 cm) long. The dogfish is believed to have a long life-span, estimated, through growth studies of tagged dogfish, at 25 to 30 years.

Spiny dogfish (*Squalus acanthias*)

Economic Importance. Although dogfish liver oil was once valued for its vitamin A content and dogfish supported a thriving fishery off Washington state and British Columbia, they are now rarely landed by North American fisheries. However, substantial quantities are marketed for human food in Europe and Asia.

When abundant, dogfish may become a serious pest and inflict severe economic losses on fisheries by damaging fishing gear and the catches of the more desirable fish. Furthermore, huge schools of dogfish sweeping over the sea bottom devour and all but eliminate the smaller fishes and invertebrates in their paths.

Classification. Dogfish sharks belong to the family Squalidae, order Selachii. Most of the other members of the family are poorly known species found at great depths in cool ocean waters.

STEWART SPRINGER
U. S. Fish and Wildlife Service

DOGGER BANK, an extensive area of sandbanks in the North Sea, about 100 miles (161 km) east of the coast of Yorkshire, England. It is about 160 miles (257 km) long and 70 miles (112 km) wide. The Dogger Bank is celebrated for its cod fisheries and its naval history.

On the night of Oct. 21, 1904, the Russian battle fleet, on its way to the Far East to engage the Japanese, opened fire on a fleet of British fishing trawlers. One trawler was sunk, and some lives were lost. The incident threatened war between the two countries, but an international commission resolved the dispute and awarded damages to the British. On Jan. 24, 1915, during World War I, a British cruiser force defeated a German squadron off the Dogger Bank.

DOGMA, dŏg'mə. In its original Greek usage, the word *dogma* meant either an authoritative decision or the opinions of a particular philosophical school or sect. In Christian theology the word gradually became a technical term for those doctrines officially taught by the church as expressions of divine revelation and, hence, binding on all orthodox Christians. In this sense, the Trinitarian doctrine formulated at the Council of Nicaea (325 A. D.) is generally accepted as the first clear instance of dogmatic definition. See also DOCTRINE.

The notion of dogma depends on a prior definition of the church's teaching authority. Christian churches differ in the emphasis that they give to dogma as binding on the individual and as to what is considered necessary for a doctrine to be regarded as dogma. Although Roman Catholics recognize as dogma all those revealed truths that are universally taught in the church, they tend in practice to limit the term to doctrines that have been solemnly defined by an ecumenical council or by the pope in an extraordinary (ex cathedra) decision. Thus not all papal decisions are regarded as dogma. The Eastern Orthodox churches similarly restrict dogma in its strictest sense to teachings of ecumenical councils that have been universally accepted in the church. Most Anglicans also regard the doctrinal decisions of the first seven ecumenical councils as normative in their theology. Protestant churches generally give less emphasis to dogma and derive its binding force primarily from its scriptural foundation rather than from the authority of the church.

JOHN W. HEALEY, S. J., *Woodstock College, Md.*

DOGON, dō'gon, a people of West Africa, who live east of the Niger River in western Mali. They number about 250,000. The language of the Dogon belongs to the Voltaic subfamily of the Congo-Kordofanian family.

The Dogon are primarily agriculturalists, using hoe cultivation, with crop rotation and some irrigation. Millet and sorghum are their staple foods. Dogon settlements consist of widely scattered family households, related through ties of common culture, language, and marriage rather than through centralized political institutions. Social control is exerted primarily by the head of the patrilineal household. Despite the apparent simplicity of their way of life, the Dogon's religion, philosophy, and world view are highly complex in their use of symbols.

ROBERT A. LYSTAD
The Johns Hopkins University

DOG-TOOTH VIOLET, any of a small group of plants of the lily family. Members of the group (genus *Erythronium*) are also commonly known as adder's-tongues. See ADDER'S-TONGUE.

DOGWOOD is a common name for several species of small trees in the genus *Cornus*, of the dogwood family (Cornaceae). One of the better-known species is the flowering dogwood (*Cornus florida*), which grows naturally beneath taller trees in forests from southern Canada to Florida and west to Kansas and Oklahoma. The flowering dogwood is a bushy tree seldom reaching more than 40 feet (12 meters) in height; at the northern limits of its range it often occurs as a shrub. The leaves are oval in general shape and sharply pointed at the tip; they grow opposite each other on the stem, and their margins are either entire or irregularly and inconspicuously toothed. The dogwood's leaves are among the first to turn color in autumn, changing from a bright green to a brilliant scarlet.

The flower buds appear in midsummer at the tips of twigs and open the next spring, before the leaves unfold. The flowers, which are small and inconspicuous, are arranged in dense heads surrounded by four large, white, petallike bracts,

(LEFT) PAUL E. GENEREUX; (CENTER) ROSS E. HUTCHINS; (RIGHT) SMITH

Flowering dogwood (*Cornus florida*), showing (*l. to r.*) the tree in bloom, the flower, and the fruit.

each of which is broader toward the notched tip. The combination of the green flower head and white bracts is often mistaken for a single blossom. The fruits are oval, becoming scarlet colored when they ripen in the autumn, and are relished by native birds.

The wood is close-grained and very hard, and has been used for bearings, tool handles, and engravers' blocks and for making charcoal. The bark contains some of the same chemical substances as quinine bark and has been used medicinally. It has also been used in making black ink, and the root bark yields a scarlet dye.

Because of the beauty of the tree, both in spring and autumn, the flowering dogwood is widely planted. In some areas, trees with faintly pink to deep red bracts occur naturally, and these have been brought into cultivation.

RICHARD S. COWAN, *Smithsonian Institution*

DOHA, dō′hə, also called ad-Dawhah, the capital of Qatar, on the southern coast of the Persian Gulf. Doha is situated on the east coast of the Qatar peninsula and forms a wide semicircle around the southern shore of Doha Bay. Since 1939, when oil was discovered in the Dukhan area nearby, the economy of Doha has depended on the huge oil royalties received by the ruling sheikh. The city is the home and urban center of many of the workers in the oil fields, and it is the residence and administrative center of the ruling family (al-Thami). Prior to 1939 the inhabitants had lived by pearling, fishing, and trading, and by slaving and smuggling.

Doha has undergone enormous changes since the opening of the Dukhan field. It has trebled in population and doubled in area and now contains three quarters of the total population of Qatar. The center of the city is dominated by the ruler's new palace. Nearby are closely packed houses in twisting alleys, contrasting with modern government offices, neat bungalows, a shopping center, and a mosque. To the south lie new government low-rent housing areas and to the east rise a hotel, clubs, and the new oil quay. The city is served by a modern airport. Population: (1971 est.) 95,000.

W. B. FISHER, *University of Durham*

DOHERTY, dŏ′ər-tē, **Charles Joseph** (1855–1931), Canadian public official. He was born in Montreal on May 11, 1855. Educated at St. Mary's College and McGill University (B. C. L., 1876), he was admitted to the bar as an advocate in 1877. He was professor of law at McGill University and served also as puisne judge of the superior court of Quebec from 1891 to 1906.

Doherty was elected to the Dominion House of Commons as a Conservative in 1908 and three years later become minister of justice in Sir Robert Borden's government, a post he held until 1921. A delegate to the Paris peace conference in 1919, he signed the Treaty of Versailles on his country's behalf and represented Canada at the assembly of the League of Nations during 1920–1921. Later he was retained by Mackenzie King's government as counsel in negotiations with Newfoundland over its title to Labrador. Doherty died in Westmount, Quebec, on July 28, 1931.

DOHNÁNYI, dō′nä-nyē, **Ernst von** (1877–1960), Hungarian pianist, composer, and conductor, whose most popular work is *Variation on a Nursery Song* (1913), for piano and orchestra. He was born in Pressburg, Hungary (now Bratislava, Czechoslovakia), on July 27, 1877, and studied piano and composition at the Royal Academy of Music in Budapest. His Symphony in F won the Hungarian Millennium Prize in 1896 and was first performed in 1897–the year he also made his successful debut as a pianist in Berlin.

Dohnányi was professor of piano at Berlin's Hochschule from 1908 to 1915. In 1916 he moved to Budapest, where he became director of the Conservatory in 1919 and was conductor of the Budapest Philharmonic from 1919 to 1944. Forced to leave Hungary for political reasons in 1948, he settled in the United States, and from 1949 until his death he was professor of piano and composition at Florida State University. He died in New York City on Feb. 9, 1960.

Donhányi's music was strongly influenced by Brahms, who had praised his early work; like Brahms, he used Hungarian folk elements to a limited extent, particularly in the suite *Ruralia Hungarica* (1924). He retained a respect for traditional forms and conventional harmonies and wrote opera, ballet music, symphonies, chamber pieces, songs, and various instrumental music.

SHIRLEY FLEMING, *Editor of "Musical America"*

DOISY, doi′zē, **Edward Adelbert** (1893–   ), American biochemist, who made important discoveries concerning the female sex hormones and vitamin K. For his discovery of the chemical nature of vitamin K, Doisy shared, with Henrik Dam, the 1943 Nobel Prize in physiology or medicine.

Contributions to Science. Doisy began research on the female sex hormones in the 1920's. Ovarian preparations were known to cause powerful physiological effects, but the actual chemical entity responsible had not been identified. After

Edgar Allen of the anatomy department of St. Louis University School of Medicine worked out an efficient method of assaying, or analyzing, the effects of hormone preparations, he and Doisy started to track down the ovarian hormone.

Beginning in 1922 they fractionated ovarian preparations by various methods. They repeatedly subdivided the fractions showing the highest concentrated activity until in 1929 they succeeded in isolating pure crystals of a female sex hormone—estrone, the chemical at least partially responsible for the effects of ovarian preparations. Soon thereafter Doisy and Allen went on to isolate two related female sex hormones—estriol and estradiol.

In 1936, Doisy turned his attention to a new field. A few years earlier, Henrik Dam had announced the discovery of a food factor (vitamin K) necessary for the proper coagulation of blood. Active preparations of the food factor were known, but the chemical itself had not been isolated. After three years of intensive work, Doisy and his colleagues at St. Louis University School of Medicine isolated two closely related compounds—vitamin K_1 and vitamin K_2. Vitamin K_1 was isolated from a plant source and vitamin K_2 from cultures of microorganisms. Doisy then went on to determine the chemical structure of both compounds and to synthesize vitamin K_1. This was the work for which he and Dam shared the Nobel Prize.

During World War II, Doisy began to study antibiotics. He was one of the first to isolate crystalline compounds that had antibiotic activities. However, his antibiotic compounds proved to be comparatively unimportant and were quickly overshadowed by penicillin. Doisy also worked on insulin, blood buffers, and bile acids.

Life. Doisy was born in Hume, Ill., on Nov. 13, 1893. He attended the University of Illinois, receiving his B. A. in 1914. After two years of army service during World War I, he continued his studies at Harvard University and received his Ph. D. in 1920. He taught for several years at Washington University School of Medicine in St. Louis and in 1923 joined the faculty of the St. Louis University of Medicine. His books include *Female Sex Hormones* (1941).

ISAAC ASIMOV
Boston University School of Medicine

DOKTOR FAUSTUS, dôk'tor fous'tōos, is a novel by the German author Thomas Mann (q.v.), first published in 1947. It is a powerful and moving work about the tragic career of a composer, Adrian Leverkühn, whose life and experiences, suggesting the Faustian legend, parallel and symbolize the rise and fall of Nazi Germany.

The story, set in Germany, is narrated by Leverkühn's friend Serenus Zeitblom. Leverkühn is a frail man of arrogant disposition and vivid imagination. One evening he is taken to a brothel by a mysterious stranger, and there contracts a venereal disease. The beginning of his physical disintegration, however, also marks the beginning of his brilliant musical career, which continues for the next 20 years. Tormented by demonic visions and hounded by tragedy, Leverkühn eventually dies, a broken and disillusioned man.

DOLABELLA, dol-ə-bel'ə, **Publius Cornelius** (died 43 B.C.), Roman political leader. He married Cicero's daughter Tullia in 50 B.C., over Cicero's objections, but indebtedness and unfaithfulness eventually produced a separation. When civil war erupted, Dolabella joined Caesar and fought for him without conspicuous success in 49 and 48. Although born a patrician, he had himself transferred to the plebs and elected to the tribunate for 47. Reckless and dissolute, he advocated abolition of debts and remission of rents, provoking riots that had to be suppressed by Antony.

His inconsistent behavior continued in succeeding years. After serving with Caesar in Africa and Spain, Dolabella was promised a consulship for 44. But after Caesar's assassination he joined the assassins and bargained with Antony to secure his consulship. He used the office in 44 to suppress worship of Caesar and to extort a governorship in Syria. Unconcerned with law or humanity, he delayed repayment of Tullia's dowry and in 43 ruthlessly slew Trebonius, the governor of Asia and partisan of Brutus and Cassius. He levied troops by force, but he was defeated by Cassius at Laodicea and committed suicide in July 43.

ERICH S. GRUEN
University of California at Berkeley

DOLCI, dōl'chē, **Carlo** (1618–1686), Italian baroque painter, who was among the last to display in his style the suavity and formal correctness of the Florentine High Renaissance. He was born on May 25, 1618, in Florence, where he worked throughout his life and where he died, on Jan. 17, 1686.

Dolci was a student of the late-mannerist painter Jacopo Vignali. He made his reputation at an early age by a series of strong, naturalistic portraits such at the likeness of Ainolfo dei Bardi (Pitti, Florence), painted when Dolci was only 16. But Dolci was deeply pious, and most of his paintings are of religious subjects. The most outstanding is perhaps the large *Martyrdom of St. Andrew* (1646; Pitti). Later he turned increasingly to small paintings, often on copper, of popular saints, the Madonna, or the Magdalen, in attitudes of rapt devotion. The overt piety, immaculately smooth surfaces, and soft sfumato of these cabinet paintings suited the taste of the late Medici court, while the scrupulous rendering of texture and detail delicately reflects a realism persistent in Florentine baroque painting.

BARRY HANNEGAN
University of Virginia

DOLDRUMS, dōl'drəmz, a belt of calm or light and variable winds in equatorial regions. The winds lie in the equatorial low-pressure zone that straddles the thermal equator (the line of highest mean temperature of the air at the earth's surface). On either side of the doldrums are the Northern Hemisphere's northeast trade winds and the Southern Hemisphere's southeast trade winds. These wind systems converge toward the thermal equator; the zone where they come together is called the Intertropical Convergence Zone (ITCZ). The system of doldrums and the ITCZ follow the thermal equator as it moves north and south with the sun throughout the year.

The doldrums are characterized by heavy precipitation from thunderstorms, and they create rainy seasons as they pass over tropical areas in their northward and southward migrations. Areas near the equator may have two rainy seasons; areas farther away have only one. When the ITCZ and the doldrums are 5 degrees latitude or more from the equator, the deflective force of the earth's rotation on atmospheric motions may produce tropical cyclones, some of which develop into hurricanes or typhoons. The doldrums are most apparent and persistent in a band from eastern equatorial Africa to the central Pacific Ocean, and in shorter bands off the west coasts of Africa and Central America.

JAMES E. MILLER, *New York University*

DOLE, Robert Joseph (1923–   ), American political leader, who was the Republican party's nominee for vice president in 1976. Dole was born in Russell, Kans., on July 22, 1923. While a platoon leader in the U.S. Army in Italy during World War II, he was injured by an exploding shell. After three years of intensive rehabilitation he could walk, but he permanently lost the use of his right arm.

Dole obtained B.A. and law degrees from Washburn University in 1952. Entering politics, he served in the state legislature, as Russell county attorney, and in the U.S. House from 1961 until his election to the U.S. Senate in 1968.

In Congress, Dole's record was generally conservative. But he voted for most civil-rights programs and supported the food stamp program and aid for the handicapped. Dole defended President Richard Nixon on the Cambodian invasion and on two controversial Supreme Court nominations. He headed the Republican National Committee from 1971 to 1973 but was not involved in the Watergate scandal.

Dole was reelected to the Senate in 1974 and 1980 and became a powerful figure, respected for his skills in negotiation. He was a major advocate of agricultural interests and, as chairman of the Senate Finance Committee, he engineered a significant 1982 tax bill. In public debate, he was renowned for his partisanship and for his wit and sarcasm.

President Gerald Ford chose Dole as his running mate in 1976. They lost to the Democratic ticket. In 1980, Dole unsuccessfully sought the Republican nomination for the presidency.

Dole's first marriage ended in divorce. In 1975 he was married to Elizabeth Hanford, a member of the Federal Trade Commission who in 1983 was appointed secretary of transportation by President Ronald Reagan. The Doles' combined influence and political expertise made them a formidable Washington couple.

DOLE, Sanford Ballard (1844–1926), American political leader and judge. He was born in Honolulu on April 23, 1844, the son of a New England missionary. After attending Williams College and studying law in Boston, he returned to Honolulu, where he practiced law and served in the legislature. In 1887 he was a leader of the uprising that forced King Kalakaua to grant a constitution reducing the crown's authority. Appointed an associate justice on Hawaii's supreme court in 1887, he resigned in 1893 to join the revolution that deposed Queen Liliuokalani.

Dole became the first president of the new Republic of Hawaii in 1894. He worked for Hawaii's acquisition by the United States and after annexation became the first territorial governor (1900). He served as judge of the U.S. district court for Hawaii in 1903–1915, and died in Honolulu on June 9, 1926.

DAVID LINDSEY*
California State College at Los Angeles

DOLE, dōl, a city in eastern France, on the Doubs River and the Rhine-Rhône Canal. Dole (also Dôle) is in Jura department in the Franche-Comté region, about 225 miles (360 km) southeast of Paris. Its principal products are metals, dairy goods, bicycles, and ceramics.

Historically a city of many allegiances, Dole was in the county of Burgundy (Franche-Comté) during the early Middle Ages. It then passed to the Holy Roman Empire, the duchy of Burgundy, and the Spanish Habsburgs, and finally was taken in 1674 by Louis XIV. Louis incorporated the Franche-Comté into France and transferred its capital from Dole to Besançon.

Among the main points of interest are the remains of the city's ramparts, a 16th century church, the Collège de l'Arc museum, and the birthplace of the scientist Louis Pasteur. Population: (1975) 29,295.

HOMER PRICE, *Hunter College*

DOLERITE. See DIABASE.

DOLET, dô-le′, **Etienne** (1509–1546), French humanist and printer, who made important contributions to Renaissance classical scholarship. He was born in Orléans on Aug. 3, 1509, and studied at the University of Paris and in Italy. He acquired a deep interest in humanism, with its love of the classics and indifference to the teachings of the church. In 1534 he settled in Lyon and a year later published his *Dialogus de imitatione Ciceroniana*, a defense of his devotion to the works of Cicero. From 1536 to 1538 he wrote the valuable *Commentarii linguae Latinae*, a discussion of the Latin language, and translated Cicero and other classical authors. In 1538 he set up a printing press and published works of such authors as Marot and Rabelais.

Hot-tempered and stubborn, Dolet was twice accused and acquitted of crimes—once of murder and once of heresy. Finally, however, he was convicted of heresy and burned at the stake in Paris on Aug. 3, 1546.

DOLIN, dō′lin, **Anton** (1904–1983), English ballet dancer and choreographer, who was one of England's first internationally famous danseurs nobles. Francis Patrick Healey-Kay was born in Slinfold, Sussex, on July 27, 1904. He studied ballet with the Russian ballerina Serafina Astafieva and the Polish choreographer Nijinska. He made his ballet debut in 1921 in Diaghilev's production of *The Sleeping Princess* and adopted his stage name in 1923.

Dolin spent several seasons with Diaghilev's Ballets Russes, becoming soloist in 1924. Roles were created for him by Nijinska in *Le Train Bleu* (1924) and by George Balanchine in *The Prodigal Son* (1929) and *Le Bal* (1929). From 1931 to 1935 he was a guest soloist in London's Vic-Wells Ballet. With the ballerina Alicia Markova he founded the Markova-Dolin Ballet Company in 1935 and directed it until 1938. In the 1940's, Dolin joined New York's Ballet Theatre as premier danseur and costarred with Markova in major productions. He choreographed classic ballets for several dance companies. From 1950 to 1961, Dolin was artistic director and principal dancer of the London Festival Ballet.

Dolin also was a teacher and choreographer and the author of seven books on ballet. He was knighted in 1981. He died in Paris, France, on Nov. 25, 1983.

KACHINA DOLLS, made by Hopi Indians from cottonwood root, represent kachinas, mythical ancestral spirits of the Hopi. The dolls are used in annual fertility ceremonies.

AMERICAN MUSEUM OF NATURAL HISTORY

DOLL, a figurine of a human being. The word was first used for the child's toy about 1700, possibly as a contraction of Greek *eidolon* ("idol"), but more probably from the girl's name "Doll," which was short for "Dorothy." Some authorities now use the word only to refer to the child's toy. Other classes of dolls include religious figurines, objects of art, and souvenirs.

Ancient Dolls. The earliest dolls were almost certainly endowed with religious significance. The oldest such figurines, dating from the Aurignacian period (about 40,000 B.C.) and found from France to the southern USSR, are female in form. Their exaggerated sexual characteristics suggest that they were fertility figures supposed to work through sympathetic magic. They are known as "Venuses"; the most famous is the Venus of Willendorf, found at Willendorf, Germany.

Most ancient dolls have been recovered from graves. Almost none are prehistoric; however, dolls dating from about 3000 B.C. have been found at Mohenjo-Daro, on the Indus River in what is now West Pakistan. These are simple clay figurines; other ancient dolls durable enough to have survived are made of bone, wood, stone, ivory, and other hard substances. There is evidence that ancient dolls were also made of perishable substances, but no such doll is extant.

In many societies dolls were entombed in order to provide the dead with servants and concubines in the afterworld; this was the case, for instance, in Egypt. Some Egyptian tomb figurines were made of baked clay; others, the so-called "paddle dolls," were made of simple flat pieces of wood and lacked feet. In China the ancient custom of sacrificing members of the dead man's household and interring them with the corpse was abandoned when dolls were substituted for the human victims.

In such societies, as well as in those where dolls served as religious icons, the figurines had great ceremonial significance, and children were sometimes enjoined against even touching them. On the other hand, the kachina dolls of the Hopi Indians, although religious in nature, were given to children as playthings. In any case, the presence of dolls in children's graves in Egypt suggests their use as toys, and in ancient Greece and Rome some dolls were certainly toys, although others were still used as religious offerings.

Later Dolls. Little is known about the dolls of the Middle Ages, although a few small figures, including representations of knights, survive. Perhaps the most important development of the Middle Ages was the crèche, with figures of the Holy Family and others. These attained their most elaborate development in Catholic Europe of the 17th and 18th centuries; during the same time there was a great vogue for dollhouses in Protestant Europe, where crèches had been abandoned because of the Reformation strictures against religious images.

Toward the end of the 14th century, dolls of the type known as "fashion babies" appeared in France—and, by 1391, in England. These were figures usually made of pasteboard and dressed in fashionable costumes, their purpose being to acquaint the wealthy with the current styles. In the early 1500's dollmaking was begun at Nuremberg, Germany, which remained for centuries the preeminent source of dolls. German craftsmen of the period sometimes made doll production a lifework—carving dolls (often with jointed limbs) from wood, painting them beautifully, and dressing them to resemble everything from peasant women to ladies of fashion. Other dolls were made of clay, ivory, stone, leather, terra-cotta, cloth, bone, and so on.

During the 17th and 18th centuries, dolls became so elaborate that many were presented at court; some were so costly that, in time of war, they were given safe transport to some peaceful refuge. Fashion dolls were also popular during this period, and children of the lower social classes had simpler dolls, usually made of cloth or leather and stuffed with some soft material.

North American dolls of the 18th century were imported from Europe, were modeled on European dolls, or were generally very simple in design. Most were made of perishable materials, and very few survive. Toward the end

An Egyptian paddle doll, dating from about 2000 B.C.
THE METROPOLITAN MUSEUM OF ART

of the century, dolls modeled on celebrities (such as George Washington) began to appear. But the industry did not develop significantly in the United States until many decades later.

The 19th Century. This was the period of greatest advance in dollmaking. Papier-mâché, which had been known in the Orient for centuries, was developed in Germany about 1810 and began to be used for dolls' heads. This innovation was followed about 1820 by the large-scale introduction for this purpose of bisque and china. All these techniques were developed primarily in Germany, and for many years the china factories at Meissen, Germany, supplied china heads and bodies for the entire world. In England the Montanari family in the 1840's perfected the use of wax for dolls' heads. Three techniques were developed: the wax might be poured directly into a mold of the head; it might be applied as the coating of a plaster core; or it might simply provide a finish for a head of papier-mâché.

Dolls of this period also reflected various mechanical improvements. Wigs, generally made of human hair, were widely used. Eyes designed to be closed by wires appeared about 1810, and the first doll that could say "Mama" and Papa" was invented in 1830. Dolls with more elaborate speech or with music boxes were developed throughout the century.

The United States began producing dolls on a large scale in the second half of the century. The first American doll patent was granted to Ludwig Greiner in 1858 for a method of making papier-mâché heads. Greiner's dolls were much indebted to European designs of the time. A more distinctively American product was the rag doll, such as those manufactured by Izannah Walker during the latter half of the century; these were followed in the 1890's by the rag dolls designed by Mrs. Martha Chase. Along with the wooden "Springfield" dolls, made in Vermont, these rag dolls were distinguished by fresh and original designs that in essence were inspired adaptations to the limitations imposed by the unsophisticated materials used.

The latter half of the century also saw the development of additional materials; various compositions were employed, rubber dolls were made by Charles Goodyear, and celluloid dolls were introduced in 1881. These last were very popular, but their inflammability finally led to general prohibition of their production. They are still produced, however, in some countries.

The new materials were accompanied by further mechanical improvements. The Montanaris began the first large-scale commercial production of "baby dolls." A walking doll was introduced in 1862, although such dolls were not perfected until the 1950's. A jointed doll was patented in 1873, and it quickly led to the development of more complex and realistic jointed dolls. Among these were the elegant bisque dolls produced by the Jumeau family in France, which were highly popular as fashion dolls throughout the second half of the century. In 1889, Thomas A. Edison invented a doll that used a miniature phonograph to sing nursery songs. In 1890 a drinking doll was introduced, and about the same time counterweighted "sleeping eyes" were developed.

The 20th Century. A popular new doll in the first decade of the century was the "Billikin," which was based on Japanese dolls by E. I. Horsman, an outstanding figure in the American doll industry, in 1908. It was followed in the next year by Rose O'Neill's "Kewpie," a small chubby doll with a topknot, which is perhaps the most popular doll of all time. Various other dolls were introduced about the same time or a few years later. Some were printed on sheets of cloth and designed to be cut out, sewn together, and stuffed at home. Other dolls, as in the past, were modeled on real or fictional celebrities. Among those so honored between 1900 and 1940 were Raggedy Ann and Andy, the "Pooh" characters, the Dionne quintuplets, Eloise, and Princess (now Queen) Elizabeth. By far the most successful of all such dolls was the one modeled on Shirley Temple in 1934.

Meanwhile there were other innovations in the world of dolls. Kathe Kruse, a German designer, introduced in the 1920's a line of dolls designed to resemble children very closely. Realism was also increasing constantly with various mechanical ingenuities: the addition of plastic hair in 1952 was a big step forward.

A revolutionary new doll was introduced in 1959; this was the "Barbie" doll, designed to resemble a teen-age girl fashion model and equipped over the years with scores of costumes. Regarded skeptically at first because it departed from the "baby doll" pattern that had controlled the market, it eventually proved itself immensely popular, bringing sales of more than $500 million within a decade. In the 1960's the trend toward increased realism continued. One of its results was the introduction of Negro dolls, both baby and adolescent. Another and far more controversial development was the French doll "Baby Brother," which was marketed in 1966 and entered the United States in 1967. This doll was made to resemble a male child of four months—complete with genitals.

Group of wooden dolls made by the Watutsi people of East Africa.

AVA HAMILTON

French doll made in the second half of the 19th century has a china head and a body of leather.
NEW YORK HISTORICAL SOCIETY

Cornhusk doll in dress studded with pins exemplifies use of simple materials in 19th century United States.
NEW YORK HISTORICAL SOCIETY

H. L. LINDQUIST PUBLICATIONS, NEW YORK
18th century French doll is clothed in bridal gown.

Parisian fashion doll in a lacy dress strewn with rosebuds dates from 1860's.
ESSEX INSTITUTE

257

"Raggedy Ann" doll has long been a favorite doll of children in the United States.

Contemporary Japanese doll in kimono.

20th century Italian doll, made in Milan, in a period costume.

Kewpie dolls, dating from 1909, have had immense popularity.

Attractions of Dolls. There seem to be three ways in which dolls are valued. Depending on what it resembles, a doll may seem to the little girl who plays with it to be a baby, a child, or an older person. The baby doll presumably appeals to the girl's developing sense of her own nature as a female, and by "mothering" the doll she strengthens her role identity. Some dolls, on the other hand, can be bought in the same size and "age" as the child, up to maxima usually of about 40 inches and 6 years of age; these dolls can actually wear the same clothes the little girl herself wears. Their appeal therefore seems to lie in a sort of companionship they provide in the girl's imagination. Finally, the dolls that represent older people presumably provide a focus for the child's ego ideal, appealing to his or her sense of a desired future identity. In Japan, for instance, where dolls have been very important for millennia, both boys and girls celebrate annual festivals during which they are presented with dolls that represent men and women outstanding in Japanese history; during the festivals manly and womanly virtues are praised for the children's edification.

The chief role of dolls in general seems to fluctuate from one period to another. The dolls most popular at the middle of the 19th century were lady dolls with extensive wardrobes; their appeal presumably lay in the child's identification with the lady of fashion represented by the doll. Toward the turn of the century the most popular kind of doll became the baby doll, its role being to emphasize and appeal to the girl's maternal values. Now, with the wide appeal of various adolescent dolls with large wardrobes, the pendulum appears to have swung back. However, the contrast can easily be exaggerated; in all cases the little girl adopts an imaginary role, in relationship to the doll, that presumably gratifies in some way her sense of herself.

Doll Manufacture. For many centuries Germany was the world center of doll production, and it ceased to be only in the early 20th century. The cessation during World War I of doll importation from Germany and Japan led the United States finally to develop its own industry to the full, and its production by the late 1960's totaled well over $100 million worth per year. A few million dollars' worth of dolls are exported yearly, and a much larger number are imported; the majority of these come from Japan, most of the rest from various European countries.

Doll Collecting. Collecting dolls is a very popular hobby. Collections often begin with the collector's own childhood toys. Later the collector may decide to specialize, for example, by collecting dolls in national costumes or dolls produced in a specific period or by a specific firm. It is not clear when adults began to collect dolls, but probably the most famous of all doll fanciers was Queen Victoria, whose collection included more than 100 dolls.

In the United States there are more than 10,000 private and public collections. Some of the most outstanding public collections are those of the Museum of the City of New York, the Metropolitan Museum of Art (New York), and the Wenham Museum (in Wenham, Mass.). Among the preeminent collections abroad are the State Museum of Toys in Zagorsk, USSR; the Germanisches Museum in Nuremberg, Germany; the Carnavalet Musée in Paris; and several important collections in England, including those at the London Museum and at the Bethnal Green Museum, both in London, and that at the Castle Museum in York.

Bibliography

Fawcett, Clara E., *Dolls: A New Guide for Collectors* (Newton Centre, Mass., 1964).
Fawcett, Clara E., *On Making, Mending, and Dressing Dolls* (Watkins Glen, N. Y., 1963).
Hillier, Mary, *Dolls and Dollmakers* (New York 1968).
Jacobs, Flora G., and Faurholt, Estrid, *Book of Dolls and Doll Houses* (Rutland, Vt., 1967).
Noble, John, *Dolls* (New York 1967).
Singleton, Esther, *Dolls* (Washington 1927).
Young, Helen, *The Complete Book of Doll Collecting* (New York 1967).

DOLLAR, dŏl'ər. The dollar became the standard monetary unit of the United States in 1792, on the recommendation of Thomas Jefferson. Jefferson favored a decimal system of coinage and monetary units, based on the Spanish milled "dolar" (which circulated widely in the colonies prior to the Revolutionary War), over the English nondecimal system of pounds sterling, shillings, and pence.

Values. The dollar was originally defined in the Coinage Act of 1792 as equivalent to either 371.25 grains of fine silver or 24.75 grains of fine gold. (See also COINS—*United States Coins: Establishment of the Coinage System.*) These values later changed several times. After 1873 the dollar was no longer defined in terms of silver. In 1934 it was devalued in terms of gold to 13.71 grains, yielding a $35-per-ounce price of gold for monetary use.

In earlier years, coins were minted at full weight—that is, they were "worth their weight in gold" (or silver)—and "representative" paper currency was freely redeemable in full-weight coin. Since 1934, however, all U. S. domestic circulating currency (including coinage) has been "fiat money," not redeemable in anything and deriving its value solely from purchasing power. The U. S. stock of monetary gold is held by the Treasury for use in settling deficits in the country's international financial accounts and thereby maintaining the gold convertibility of the dollar internationally. International gold convertibility is necessary to preserve the dollar's special status as an international "key currency" for the financing of world trade.

Stability of the Dollar. By far the largest part—over 90% by some estimates—of the total value of all domestic money payments in the United States is made through the use of commercial-bank checking accounts. So the dollar exists now primarily as a concept, a unit of account in terms of which the value of everything else is measured. Maintaining its value—the stability of its purchasing power—has therefore become an important objective of national economic policy. This objective is pursued through the influence of the central bank (the Federal Reserve System) on the money supply (monetary policy) and also through congressionally determined Treasury fiscal policy (taxing and spending).

The United States has not been especially successful in achieving the objective of stability. Between 1940 and 1980, for example, the dollar lost four fifths of its purchasing power. Between 1950 and 1980, the consumer price index rose approximately 300%. In the period from 1960 to 1965, prices advanced at a relatively low rate of less than 2% annually. But during the next two five-year periods the rate accelerated to more than 4% and 6%, respectively. During the 1970's and into the early 1980's the consumer price index reached "double-digit" levels of more than 10% annually.

This occurred because national economic objectives were viewed by several administrations as more important than price and purchasing-power stability. Domestically, these objectives were full employment of the labor force and satisfactory rates of national economic growth. Internationally, they included the filling of strategic needs for defense and foreign aid and the financing of wars in Korea and Vietnam.

CLIFTON H. KREPS, JR.*
University of North Carolina at Chapel Hill

DOLLAR DIPLOMACY is a term used originally to characterize aspects of U. S. diplomacy in President William Howard Taft's administration (1909–1913), which frankly supported U. S. business expansion in China and Central America. This method of extending American influence was eventually discredited, and "dollar diplomacy" is now used as a disapproving term.

Taft and Secretary of State Philander C. Knox hoped, in China, to undercut Japanese and Russian influence in Manchuria, increase American investment, and thus strengthen the Open Door (q.v.) policy and the feeble Chinese government. In Latin America, Taft and Knox hoped to secure the Panama Canal from potential European threats, strengthen democratic forces, and provide investment outlets for U. S. business.

The Taft administration insisted that American bankers be allowed to participate in a loan consortium to China. English, French, and German bankers consented reluctantly in May 1911. The administration also sponsored an unsuccessful plan to form an international syndicate to purchase the South Manchuria Railway and Chinese Eastern Railway (the former controlled by Japan, the latter by Russia).

Taft's intervention in Nicaragua is the clearest example of dollar diplomacy in action. Dictator José Santos Zelaya upset Knox by financing Nicaragua's debt through an international syndicate of European bankers. Taft and Knox waged diplomatic war against Zelaya, helping rebels to force Zelaya out. In the Knox-Castrillo Convention (1911), Nicaragua accepted an American loan and placed its customs collections under American control during the life of the loan. Although the U. S. Senate refused to approve the convention, the United States maintained a virtual protectorate over Nicaragua.

Judged by Taft and Knox's goals, dollar diplomacy was a partial success only in Latin America. Interventionist precedents were set, however, that troubled the hemisphere for 25 years.

MARVIN ZAHNISER, *Ohio State University*

Further Reading: Munro, Dana G., *Intervention and Dollar Diplomacy in the Caribbean, 1900–1921* (Princeton 1964); Nearing, Scott, and Freeman, Joseph, *Dollar Diplomacy: A Study in American Imperialism* (New York 1925).

DOLLARD DES ORMEAUX, dô-làr' dā zôr-mō', **Adam** (1635–1660), French soldier in Canada. He arrived in Canada from France perhaps in 1658 and became a garrison officer at Montreal. In 1660, leading 16 other young colonists, he set out to raid the Iroquois, intending to prove the colonists' determination to thwart their Indian enemies but also to seize furs from them. At the Long Sault on the Ottawa River the colonists were surprised by a large body of Indians. Deserted by most of their 40 Huron allies, the Frenchmen in a little fort held off the Indians, but after eight days (perhaps by May 10, 1660) all 17 had been slaughtered.

Dollard (sometimes also called *Daulac*) is a controversial figure in Canadian history. Some scholars have considered him an adventurer and fur thief. Others maintain that he led a heroic enterprise and that his courage caused the Indians to abandon temporarily their plans for an attack on Montreal and thus saved the colonists.

MICHEL BRUNET, *University of Montreal*

Further Reading: Vachon, André, "Dollard des Ormeaux, Adam," *Dictionary of Canadian Biography*, vol. 1 (Toronto 1966).

DOLLARFISH, a common name sometimes given to two species—*Peprilus alepidotus* and *P. paru*—of the butterfish family, Stromateidae. See BUTTERFISH.

DOLLFUSS, dōl'fōos, **Engelbert** (1892–1934), Austrian chancellor and dictator. He was born in Kirnberg on Oct. 4, 1892. Dollfuss was active in the conservative Christian Socialist party before becoming director of the Lower Austrian chamber of agriculture (1927) and agriculture minister (1931–1932).

Dollfuss became chancellor in May 1932 and bolstered Austria's fragile independence by obtaining loans from the League of Nations and political and economic support from Mussolini. A procedural error in voting enabled him to suspend parliamentary government in March 1933 and establish a dictatorship.

Dictatorship. Dollfuss fashioned a clerical-authoritarian regime based on an indigenous Fascist militia (Heimwehr), a consolidation of political groups (Fatherland Front), further support from Italy (Rome Protocols, 1934), and conservative Catholic ideology (papal encyclical *Quadragesimo anno*, 1931). He confronted the Austrian Nazis and incurred the wrath of Hitler, who boycotted the Austrian state and aided Austrian Nazi conspirators. Dollfuss jeopardized his regime by military action against the Austrian Socialists (February 1934) and subsequent imprisonment of Socialist leaders. On July 25, 1934, Nazi activists attempted to seize power and killed Dollfuss in his chancellory in Vienna.

HENRY CORD MEYER
University of California at Irvine

DÖLLINGER, dŭl'ing-ər, **Johannes Joseph Ignaz von** (1799–1890), German church historian and theologian. He was born in Bamberg, Germany, on Feb. 28, 1799. Döllinger studied at the University of Würzburg and the seminary in Bamberg and was ordained in 1822. In 1826 he received a doctorate from the University of Landshut and was appointed professor of church history at the University of Munich; there he associated himself with Catholics who sought to apply Catholic principles to social and political life.

In 1837 the king of Bavaria named him to membership in the Royal Bavarian Academy of Sciences and later to its presidency (1873). The king also named him a canon of the royal chapel of St. Cajetan (1839) and its provost (1847). As representative of the university in the Bavarian parliament, his protest against the dismissal of several professors resulted in his own dismissal (1847), although he was later reinstated. He was also a Bavarian representative at the Congress of Frankfurt (1848–1849).

A prolific writer of both general and specialized works on church history, he emphasized the ideas of "organic growth" and "consistent development"; his volumes *The Reformation* and *Luther* criticized Protestantism as a break with the historical continuity and development of Christianity.

In 1869, Döllinger entered the controversy concerning papal infallibility and supported the opponents of its definition during the First Vatican Council. When he later refused to accept the council's definition of infallibility, he was excommunicated and deprived of his professorship; however, he continued to enjoy the king's favor. Although in close contact with leaders of the Old Catholic Church, he never became a member but continued to attend Roman Catholic services. Despite efforts at reconciliation, he died in Munich on Jan. 10, 1890, unreconciled with Rome.

JOHN FORD, C. S. C.
Holy Cross College, Washington, D. C.

DOLLOND, dol'ənd, **John** (1706–1761), English optical instrument maker, who was the first to supply telescopes corrected for chromatic aberration. He was born on June 10, 1706, in London, of French Huguenot parents. Dollond earned a living as a silk weaver while devoting his leisure to the study of astronomy, optics, and classical languages.

Isaac Newton had supposed that the color around the image seen in a telescope could not be avoided; but in experiments with different kinds of glass, conducted during 1757–1758, Dollond proved that a composite lens made from two sorts of glass could give color-free (achromatic) images. The Royal Society awarded the Copley Medal to Dollond in 1758 for this invention. Chester Moor Hall had made the same discovery in 1733, but he did not publicize it.

In 1761, Dollond was elected a fellow of the Royal Society and appointed optician to King George III. He died in London on Nov. 30, 1761.

G. L'E. TURNER, *Oxford University*

DOLL'S HOUSE, a play by the Norwegian dramatist Henrik Ibsen (q.v.). It was a milestone in modern drama, the first serious play about a significant social problem. Written in 1879 and first performed in December of that year at the Royal Theater, Copenhagen, it began the series of skillfully structured, controversial dramas of Ibsen's "naturalistic" period.

In the "happy" marriage of the Helmers, Torvald, the husband, appears to be a paragon of strength and honesty. Actually, the family is prosperous only because Nora, his wife, once committed a fraud. When the fraud is later exposed, Torvald accuses her of ruining his reputation; when the threat of public exposure evaporates, he regrets his behavior. But Nora, now aware that their marriage is not founded on mutual respect and understanding, leaves her husband, children, and home for an uncertain future of self-discovery.

A Doll's House is frequently dismissed as a defense of feminism, centering on the courageous Nora's search for her human rights. But Ibsen's thesis is that in a sound marriage, husband and wife must be true to themselves as well as to each other. Both Helmers are dolls—lifelike puppets manipulated by complex social forces that Nora senses but that Torvald does not begin to comprehend even as the curtain falls.

Rolf Fjelde's English translation of *A Doll's House*, in *Ibsen: Four Major Plays* (1965), is faithful to Ibsen's style and meaning. It is also highly readable and actable.

J. SHERWOOD WEBER, *Pratt Institute*

DOLLY VARDEN TROUT. See TROUT.

DOLMEN, dōl'mən, a megalithic tomb of the Neolithic (New Stone Age) period. The term "cromlech" formerly was used interchangeably with "dolmen," but archaeologists now use "cromlech" in a loose, nontechnical sense to designate large upright stones, either single or arranged in a circle. "Dolmen" has come to mean a flat, tablelike structure consisting of a single slab of stone supported by three or more uprights, beneath which is a burial chamber. The structure was sometimes covered with earth.

There is some evidence that dolmens and similar large stone structures were associated with a megalithic religion that may have originated in the Aegean in the early Neolithic and then were carried to other shores of the Mediterranean by a seafaring people who also traveled to Portugal, Brittany, and the British Isles. Some of the best examples of dolmens are found at Carnac in Brittany.

PRISCILLA C. WARD
American Museum of Natural History

DOLMETSCH, dol'mech, **Arnold** (1858–1940), English authority on old music and musical instruments. He was born at Le Mans, France, on Feb 24, 1853. His father was a piano manufacturer and musician, and Arnold learned much from him about instrument making. In 1885, after studying violin in Brussels and London, Arnold became a violin teacher at Dulwich College in London. In 1889, excited and inspired by the discovery of 17th century English music for consorts of viols in the British Museum, Dolmetsch decided to devote his life to the study, restoration, and performance of old music.

From 1890, Dolmetsch appeared frequently in concerts with members of his family, performing early music on such instruments as the harpsichord, clavichord, lute, and viol. He also specialized in making and restoring such instruments. One of his chief contributions was the reintroduction of the recorder. In 1915 he published his authoritative book, *The Interpretation of the Music of the 17th and 18th Centuries*. The annual Haslemere Festival of old chamber music was established by him in 1925. Dolmetsch died at Haslemere, England, on Feb. 28, 1940.

GILBERT CHASE, *Tulane University*

DOLOMITE, dō'lə-mīt, is a carbonate of calcium and magnesium. It occurs most frequently as a massive gray or white rock, finely to coarsely granular, resembling limestone. It is found chiefly in widely extended rock masses as dolomitic limestone and dolomitic marble, often intimately mixed with calcite. It is used for many of the purposes for which limestone is used. It grades into limestone by imperceptible degrees.

The most important use of dolomite is in the manufacture of magnesia for making the refractory linings of the converters employed in steelmaking. (Limestone cannot be substituted for this purpose.) Other important uses include making high-magnesia lime and certain cements; as a flux in smelting iron, steel, and ferroalloys; and as a source for magnesium.

Composition, $CaMg(CO_3)_2$; hardness, 3.5–4.0; specific gravity, 2.85; crystal system, hexagonal.

GEORGE SWITZER, *Smithsonian Institution*

DOLOMITES, dō'lə-mīts, a mountain region of the Alps in northern Italy, bounded by the valleys of the upper Piave River in the east, the upper Brenta in the south, and the Adige and Isarco in the west. Covering about 1,600 square miles (4,100 sq km) in Belluno and Bolzano provinces, most of the Dolomites (Italian, I Dolomiti) belonged to Austria before the South Tyrol was annexed to Italy in 1918. German is widely spoken, particularly in Bolzano province, and Ladin, a language derived from Latin and similar to Swiss Romansh (Rumansch), also survives locally.

The area takes its name from the characteristic peaks of dolomite (magnesian limestone) that emerge spectacularly from high but accessible plateaus. Several of the peaks are over 10,000 feet (3,000 meters) high. The traditional occupations of the region are livestock raising and forestry, but the area is now chiefly important for its hydroelectric power and tourism. Cortina d'Ampezzo, Canazei, Ortisei, and San Martino di Castrozza are among the main resorts.

DONALD S. WALKER
Author of "Geography of Italy"

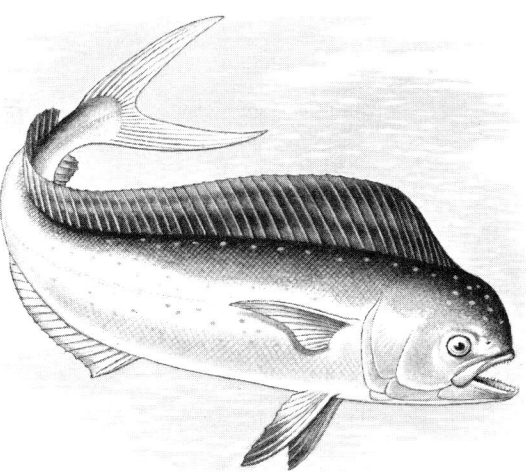

The common fish dolphin (*Coryphaena hippurus*)

DOLPHIN, dol'fən, an oceanic fish found in most warm seas. It is also known by the common name *dorado* and in the Hawaiian Islands by the name *mahimahi*. Mahimahi is a favorite food among Hawaiians, but it is not valued as food in other parts of the world. The term "dolphin" is also applied to certain marine cetaceans, which are air-breathing mammals. For these, see DOLPHIN (mammal).

The dolphin has a long triangular body with a soft, many-rayed (55–65 rays) dorsal fin that runs along the whole back. Its bluish color is complemented by vivid luminous shades of purple, green, and gold. The colors blend to form a changing color scheme when the fish is alive, but the luminous shades disappear soon after the fish dies.

The male dolphin has a characteristic squarish head; the female has a more rounded head. Adult males may attain a length of almost 6 feet (1.8 meters) and a weight of over 67 pounds (30.5 kg), but the female seldom weighs over 35 pounds (16 kg). Dolphins grow very rapidly, and their entire life-span may be no more than 3 years.

Occurring alone or in schools, the dolphin is a fast-moving fish that can swim up to 35 miles per hour. It often swims under its favorite prey, the flying fish, and seizes it as it returns to water. It also eats a wide variety of other fishes and invertebrates.

The dolphin, *Coryphaena hippurus*, is a member of the family Coryphaenidae. The only other member of the family is the pompano dolphin, *C. equisetis*, which seldom attains a length of over 35 inches (88 cm) and is often mature at 12 inches (30 cm). It also has fewer (48–55) rays than the common dolphin. Both species are in the order Percoidea.

Donald D. Zumwalt
John G. Shedd Aquarium, Chicago, Ill.

DOLPHIN, an aquatic mammal belonging to the whale family and found in all the oceans of the world, as well as in the estuaries of some large rivers. The name is usually reserved for members of the family Delphinidae, although it is sometimes applied to porpoises (family Phocaenidae). Dolphins are slender cetaceans characterized by a beaklike snout, while porpoises have a heavier body form and a blunt snout. (See Porpoise.) The name dolphin is also used for oceanic fishes of the family Coryphaenidae. See Dolphin (fish).

The freshwater or river dolphins make up the family Platanistidae, consisting of four genera and as many species. These dolphins are found in Asia and South America. The long-snouted dolphins (family Stenidae) have long, pointed jaws.

The mammalian dolphins are playful, intelligent creatures that can be trained to perform a great variety of exercises. They have become familiar entertainers at marinelands and aquariums, where they are often mislabeled porpoises.

The family Delphinidae contains 18 genera and about 62 species arranged in four subfamilies: the right whale dolphins, the true dolphins, the pilot and killer whales, and Commerson's dolphin. They range in length from 4 to 14 feet (1.2–2.4 meters) and weigh between 50 and 500 pounds (23–225 kg). Most species have numerous cone-shaped teeth in both the upper and lower jaws. The dorsal "blow hole," through which the animal exhales air and water vapor from its lungs, is located well back from the tip of the beak. Dolphins have a distinct dorsal fin, pectoral fins, and flippers.

Although they sometimes swim singly or in pairs, dolphins usually congregate in large herds, often numbering in the hundreds. These large schools feed on herring, sardines, and other fish. Dolphins are among the most maneuverable of the whales. They are capable of speeds of up to 25 knots and can leap high out of the water.

The bottle-nosed dolphin mates in spring and summer. Gestation lasts from 10 to 12 months, after which the young are nursed for 16 months. The life span is about 25 to 35 years in the wild, somewhat less in captivity.

The two most familiar and best-loved species are the common dolphin (*Delphinus delphis*) and the bottle-nosed dolphin (*Tursiops truncatus*). The common dolphin is black or brown on the back with lighter stripes on the sides and a white belly. This species is often sighted playing around the bow of oceangoing vessels, and is associated with schools of tuna, as are two species of spotted dolphin (genus *Stenella*). They are known to lead tuna to escape from purse-seine nets. Despite enactment by Congress of protective laws, great numbers of dolphins are killed annually when they are caught in the nets.

The bottle-nosed dolphin is the well-known "star" of aquariums and marine showplaces, such as Marineland in Florida, as well as of motion pictures and television. (The Pacific white-sided dolphin, *Lagenorhynchus obliquidens*, fills this role in California aquariums.) The bottle-nosed dolphin is black or slate blue above, lighter underneath, and with dark flippers. It ranges from 6 to 12 feet (1.75–3.6 meters) in length. The prominent snout or beak combines with the curvature of the mouth to produce a natural "smile" that is very appealing. Dolphins in shows have been trained to execute an astonishing number of feats, including acrobatics, jumping through flaming hoops or leaping in precise group formations, and other circus-type routines.

Classical literature provides numerous tales of dolphins and their relationship with man. Plutarch's account of a dolphin's rescue from drowning of Telemachus, son of Odysseus, is one of many examples in Greek and Roman lore of the creature's friendly attitude toward humans. Until the 20th century, these stories were dismissed as fantasy, but modern scientific research into the behavior of dolphins indicates that such ancient legends may have rested, in part at least, on factual grounds. Extensive studies are continuing into the intelligence of dolphins and also into their ability to communicate by means of a wide range of underwater sounds or pulses. These noises include mating calls and danger signals. One researcher has discovered that dolphins are able to imitate human speech. The ultrasonic sounds produced by dolphins apparently serve purposes of orientation by means of echolocation.

The bottle-nosed dolphin delights spectators at oceanariums throughout the world with its acrobatic tricks.

MIAMI SEAQUARIUM, J. W. LA TOURRETTE

DOLTON, dōl′tən, is a village in northeastern Illinois, in Cook county, 18 miles (29 km) south of Chicago, on the Calumet River. Its principal manufactured products are steel, chains, and paper bags. The community was settled in 1832 and was incorporated in 1892. Population: 24,766.

DOMAGK, dō′mäk, **Gerhard** (1895–1964), German chemist and physician, who was awarded the 1939 Nobel Prize in medicine or physiology for his discovery of prontosil, a precursor of the sulfa drugs. In 1930, while working in a German dye company, Domagk began to investigate the chemotherapeutic effects of various azo dyes. In 1935, after testing more than 1,000 of these dyes, he announced that one of them—prontosil (sulfonamide-crysoidin)—could cure experimentally induced streptococcal infections in mice.

Curiously, prontosil had no direct effect on streptococcal bacteria in test tubes but exerted its effect only in the body, where it was broken down to yield the active agent sulfanilamide, which acts directly on streptococci. This discovery introduced the first of the so-called sulfa drugs. Although the sulfa drugs have largely been replaced by the newer antibiotics, they are still used to treat some infections, such as urinary tract infections.

Domagk was born in Lagow, Brandenburg, Germany, on Oct. 30, 1895. He received his M.D. from the University of Kiel in 1921. When he was awarded the 1939 Nobel Prize, the German government would not allow him to accept it, and it was not until 1947 that he was able to receive the prize. Domagk died in Burberg, Baden-Württemberg, West Germany, on April 24, 1964.

L. R. C. AGNEW
University of California at Los Angeles

DOMBEY AND SON, dom′bē, a novel by Charles Dickens (q.v.), published in 1848. It was first issued in monthly parts from October 1846 to April 1848. The work's original title was *Dealings with the Firm of Dombey and Son, Wholesale, Retail, and for Exportation.*

Dombey and Son, the first Dickens novel to have a carefully designed plot, centers on Mr. Dombey, who believes that "the earth was made for Dombey and Son to trade in." The story reaches its first climax with the death of "Son," little Paul Dombey. Dombey, a widower, remarries, but his second wife soon runs away with his manager. Her flight, coinciding with the financial ruin of the firm, provides the second climax as Dombey is plunged into literal and metaphorical bankruptcy. Only then is Dombey united with his loving daughter Florence, whom he has previously rejected. She and the kindly group of people who surround her are contrasted with the Dombey world—as warm humanity against cold, mercenary inhumanity.

This work, with its attack on the mid-Victorian mercantile ideal, marks a new departure in Dickens' fiction, both artistically and in terms of social and psychological insight. Historically, it is important as initiating the novel of the social group, aimed at a critical analysis of the contemporary ethos, and thus anticipates novels like H. G. Wells' *Tono-Bungay* and Sinclair Lewis' *Babbitt.*

INGA-STINA EWBANK
University of Liverpool

DOME, in architecture, a hemispherically shaped vault (q.v.); by extension, a similar form not constructed as a vault. Often a dome may be slightly pointed or ovoid. A segmental dome is less than a hemisphere. In some buildings, such as Muslim mosques, the dome may be more than a hemisphere and terminate in a reverse curve; the dome is then onion-shaped.

Ancient and Byzantine Domes. Mesopotamian builders as early as the 3d millennium B.C. covered some rooms of palaces with domes. Since they used sun-baked brick, a weak material, no Mesopotamian domes survive, but they have been pictured in relief sculpture.

The Romans were the first to use domes in the West. The dome of the Pantheon (2d century A.D.) in Rome is one of the largest, measuring 142 feet (43.3 meters) in diameter. Its hemispherical form is supported by cylindrical walls that are about 20 feet (6.1 meters) thick. Because a dome, being a continuous vault, produces a diagonal thrust in the direction of its radius, it requires the support of a continuous ring of masonry above the wall on which it rests. Hence, the dome of the Pantheon, which is largely embedded in its cylindrical wall, has the added support of several steps above the wall that form weighted rings to contain the thrust. Consequently, while the full curve of the dome is visible from within, only a fragment can be seen on the exterior.

A dome lends itself to a single large circular chamber below, as in the Pantheon, but in most buildings the space is more complex. Since a circle does not combine with other shapes as readily as does the square, architects during the late Roman Empire devised the *pendentive* (q.v.), a spherical triangle whose lower point rests on a pier and whose upper edge, combined with those of three other pendentives, provides a circle on which the dome is constructed. The piers supporting the pendentives mark the corners of a square and need no connecting walls between them. Thus the space under the dome may be combined with other spaces covered by barrel or groin vaults or other domes. Such additional areas could be used as aisles, transepts, or for other purposes. The use of the pendentive was continued by medieval and Renaissance architects.

The Byzantine architects of the 6th century perfected the use of pendentives, as may be seen in Hagia Sophia (532–537) in Istanbul, designed by Anthemius of Tralles and Isidorus of Miletus. Here, massive buttresses support the four main pendentives, while a complex system of half domes and arches girdles the main dome to receive its thrust in all directions. Consequently, Hagia Sophia does not require thick walls. As in the Pantheon, only part of the dome's curve is visible externally, and weighted steps likewise encircle the lower part. Whereas the Pantheon is lighted by a circular *oculus,* or window, at the top of the dome, Hagia Sophia has a ring of small windows around the lower perimeter of the dome, a solution made possible in part by its nonmassive construction.

For a thousand years the dome remained basic to Byzantine architecture and to the Russian architecture adapted from it. Byzantine influence also shaped the five-domed St. Mark's (1063) in Venice and the Cathedral of St. Front (about 1120) at Périgueux, France, with its five domes on pendentives.

Michelangelo's dome for St. Peter's in Rome, completed by Giacomo della Porta in 1590.

PARTS OF A DOME

- LANTERN
- DOME
- DRUM
- PENDENTIVE

Brunelleschi's dome for the Cathedral of Santa Maria del Fiore, Florence.

Renaissance and Later Domes. Renaissance architecture virtually began with Filippo Brunelleschi's dome for the Cathedral of Santa Maria del Fiore (begun 1420) in Florence. His dome, about 140 feet (42.7 meters) in diameter, is partly inspired by the dome of the nearby Baptistery (8th to 13th centuries), but while the earlier dome is concealed under a roof, the full curve of Brunelleschi's dome, octagonal in plan and slightly pointed in profile, is visible externally. In order to achieve this striking effect, Brunelleschi had to substitute chains embedded in the masonry for the massive stepped buttressing of Roman domes.

Michelangelo, too, was concerned with external appearance when he designed the dome of St. Peter's in Rome, which is 138 feet (42.1 meters) in diameter. He raised his dome upon a drum or cylinder of masonry consisting of paired columns that appear to support the sixteen visible ribs of the dome. Since these columns do not provide the continuous buttressing required for a dome, Michelangelo also resorted to chains to contain the lateral thrust. He did not live to see his dome completed. It was built (1588–1590) by Giacomo della Porta, who gave its profile a slightly pointed shape instead of the hemisphere planned by Michelangelo.

In St. Paul's Cathedral (1675–1710) in London, built by Sir Christopher Wren, the dome has three structural parts—a dome visible on the outside, constructed of wood covered with lead; a pyramid inside the outer dome, which supports the lantern at the top; and an inner dome of masonry that is visible from the inside. Wren, like Michelangelo, used a drum, but he set his masonry dome within the drum, not upon it. Moreover, the drum is a ring of columns supporting a continuous entablature that more effectively buttresses the masonry dome than do Michelangelo's chains.

The visual unity of a dome has made it a commonly accepted symbol of the unity of government. When Charles Bulfinch designed the State House (1795) in Boston, Mass., he started the American tradition of state capitols culminating in domes. In this case the gilded dome seen on the exterior covers a dome below it that is visible from the inside. Some capitol domes have been inspired by St. Peter's (for example, the Minnesota state capitol in St. Paul, designed by Cass Gilbert) or by St. Paul's, London (for example, the Rhode Island Capitol, Providence, designed by McKim, Mead, and White).

The dome of the U. S. Capitol in Washington, D. C., as originally designed by Benjamin Latrobe, would have been of the Pantheon type with only a part of its curve visible above rings of steps, but Bulfinch, who built it, raised its profile somewhat. The resulting compromise form, as seen in old prints, was not entirely satisfactory, and the dome was replaced in 1856–1865 by Thomas U. Walter, who generally accepted the shape of St. Paul's for a better effect.

In the second quarter of the 20th century most historic styles of architecture were rejected, and styles based on traditional types of domes almost disappeared. However, domical forms cast in shell concrete were built. An example is the roof of the Kresge Auditorium (1951) at the Massachusetts Institute of Technology in Cambridge, Mass., designed by Eero Saarinen. It is only one eighth of a sphere, a triangular shell that rests on three points.

EVERARD M. UPJOHN, *Columbia University*

DOME OF THE ROCK, a 7th century mosque in Jerusalem. It stands on the traditional site of the Temple of Solomon and of the Temple built by the Jews after the Exile, and it enshrines the rock from which Mohammed is said to have ascended to heaven. Sometimes called the Mosque of Umar, from an erroneous tradition that it was built by Caliph Umar I, the Dome of the Rock was actually built by Caliph Abd al-Malik between 687 and 691.

The first domed mosque to be built, the Dome of the Rock is a masterpiece of Islamic architecture. The octagonal plan and the rotunda dome of wood are of Byzantine design. The Persian tiles on the exterior and the marble slabs that decorate the interior were added by Suleiman I in 1561. See also ISLAMIC ART AND ARCHITECTURE.

DOMENICHINO, dō-mā-nē-kē′nō (1581–1641), Italian painter, who developed a fine form of baroque classicism. Influenced by ancient art and by classical elements in the style of Annibale Carracci, Domenichino's work is distinguished by lucid composition, planar structure, a balanced arrangement of figures, restrained gesture and expression, clear and even light, and subdued or simple color. His many landscape paintings refined the classical landscape style that had been newly developed by Annibale, and led directly to the severe and monumental landscapes of Nicolas Poussin. Domenichino's careful, sober, intellectual manner was of the greatest importance in the development of the classical tradition in Europe during the 17th and 18th centuries.

He was born Domenico Zampieri, in Bologna, on Oct. 21 or 28, 1581, and studied there with Lodovico Carracci. In 1602 he went to Rome to aid Annibale Carracci in finishing the frescoes in the Farnese Palace. In Rome, Domenichino frequented a circle of writers and aestheticians who were supporters of a rigorous classicism. Important commissions soon came his way, and Domenichino produced some of the most significant works done in Rome during the first quarter of the 17th century. These include the *Last Communion of St. Jerome* (Vatican Museum, Rome); *Hunt of Diana* (Villa Borghese, Rome); the frescoes depicting the life of St. Cecilia, in the Church of San Luigi de'Francesi; and the fresco cycle in the Church of Sant'Andrea della Valle, which marks the apogee of his classical style. A shift in public taste toward the less classical, more properly baroque style of Lanfranco may have prompted Domenichino to move to Naples, where he worked from 1630 until his death there on April 3, 1641.

BARRY HANNEGAN
University of Virginia

DOMENICO VENEZIANO, dō-mā′nē-kō vā-nā-tsyä′nō (1405?–1461), Italian painter, who was one of the chief figures in the development of early Renaissance painting in Florence. With Fra Angelico, Uccello, and Fra Filipo Lippi, he contributed to the enrichment of the Florentine style after the innovations of Masaccio.

Domenico was probably born in Venice. (He sometimes signed his name "Domenico da Venezia.") It appears likely that he was brought up in the international Gothic style and came to maturity in the late 1430's under the influence of Fra Angelico. Although Domenico may have been in Florence some years before 1439, he is not recorded as being active there until that year, when he was working for the Medici, with the young Piero della Francesca as an assistant.

COURTESY OF THE TRUSTEES, NATIONAL GALLERY, LONDON
Domenico Veneziano's *Virgin Enthroned*

Most of Domenico's major commissioned works have been lost, but three impressive ones that survive clearly illustrate his style. The earliest, and possibly his first Florentine work, is a detached fresco, the *Carnesecchi Tabernacle* (1438; National Gallery, London). Its Renaissance characteristics may be attributed to the influence of Fra Angelico and Uccello. The second major surviving work is a tondo, *The Adoration of the Magi* (?1440; Staatliche Museen, Berlin). Its large and fully developed landscape background is unique in Florentine painting of the time and may indicate that Domenico had some knowledge of contemporary Flemish art.

The finest of Domenico's surviving works is the *Santa Lucia dei Magnoli Altarpiece* (1445–1448?; Uffizi, Florence). Two exquisite panels from its dismembered predella are in the National Gallery in Washington, D. C. Though ideas and motifs of Masaccio, Uccello, Donatello, and even traces of the international Gothic style can be discerned in this work, the strong white light that fills it is uniquely Domenico's own. The pale, cool colors—so unlike the bright tones used by his contemporaries—are clearly intended to render the appearance of daylight. Domenico was probably the first Renaissance painter who endeavored to give such a specific natural setting to his subjects. This attribute and a sweet, grave melancholy are the touchstones of his style. He died in Florence in 1461.

BARRY HANNEGAN, *University of Virginia*

DOMESDAY BOOK, dōōmz'dā, the record, written in Latin, of a survey made in England in 1086 to ascertain the holdings and rights of the crown and to list the economic resources of the country for accurate taxation. It was ordered by William the Conqueror in 1085, and was completed the following year. The accuracy and speed with which the survey was taken make it a unique achievement of medieval times.

The country was divided into units, or "hundreds," and each hundred was represented by a jury of 12 men who gave information under oath to royal officers. This information covered the crown's property in each district and all other castles, baronial estates, manors, and land holdings with a history of the ownership of each. The amount of arable land, pasture, forests, livestock, fisheries, mills, and other sources of income were recorded, and the overall value was estimated. The peasants were counted and classified. The information was condensed in book form, in two volumes. The larger one omits many details, such as the count of livestock, presumably to keep its size within reasonable limits.

A study of the Domesday Book shows the society described to be adjusting to the aftermath of the Norman Conquest. A great deal of land had changed hands, for William rewarded his supporters with grants, and the country was reorganizing along feudal lines.

The most interesting and historically valuable information is that given about the towns, which usually includes a description of native customs, military service records, and some political and social history. A few towns, however, including London, were not covered, and some northern counties were omitted.

The name *Domesday* (sometimes spelled *Doomsday*) means "day of judgment," in this case in a legal or economic sense. The Domesday Book was used as a final authority in the settlement of suits and disputes of ownership for centuries, and has occasionally been used as evidence in legal cases as late as the 20th century. It has been in official custody since it was finished and is kept in the public record office in London.

DOMESTIC RELATIONS. See COURT OF DOMESTIC RELATIONS; DIVORCE; FAMILY.

DOMESTICATED ANIMALS. See ANIMALS, DOMESTICATION OF; PETS AND THEIR CARE.

DOMICILE AND RESIDENCE are two contrasting legal terms that distinguish between permanent residence (*domicile*) and the mere act of dwelling or habitation (*residence*). Legally, one may have as many residences as his purse will allow, but only one domicile. He may winter on the French Riviera or in the Caribbean. But if he lives in San Francisco, votes there, and intends to continue living there permanently, San Francisco is his legal residence, or domicile.

Kinds of Domicile. A person's *domicile of origin* is the domicile of his parents, of the head of his family, or of the person on whom he was legally dependent at the time of his birth. A *domicile of choice* is the place a person has chosen for himself, with intent to replace his previous domicile. *Domicile by operation of law* is established independent of an individual's own intent or actual residence. Thus, the domicile of a child is that of his parents, especially that of his father. The domicile of a wife is that of her husband. A person living abroad without any intention of returning to his native country may acquire a foreign domicile.

Children of ambassadors to foreign countries, children born at sea, and, usually, those born on a trip abroad take the domicile of their parents. The domicile of an illegitimate child is that of its mother; of a legitimate child, that of its father.

Importance. Domicile is important in determining a person's right to vote, to divorce, to hold public office, and to dispose of personal and real property by will. Also, it governs such matters as school privileges, taxation, and court jurisdiction. Virtually every state of the United States requires that one be a legal resident (that is, be domiciled in that state) for a certain period of time before he can be the recipient of welfare payments of one kind or another. Domicile is of primary concern in determining the validity and interpretation of a will, the matter of inheritance taxes, and the respective rights of those claiming property.

Neither husband nor wife is legally permitted to change an existing domicile after committing a matrimonial offense that entitles either of them to a divorce. A deserted wife, however, may acquire a separate domicile, to enable her to sue for divorce in the state in which she takes up new residence.

Once a domicile is established, a mere temporary absence—no matter how long—with intent to return will not invalidate it. The legal presumption is in favor of continuance of domicile, unless specifically changed.

A commercial domicile is the principal place where a business firm has executive offices.

SAMUEL G. KLING, *Author of*
"The Complete Guide to Everyday Law"

DOMINGO, dō-min'gō, **Placido** (1941–   ), Spanish operatic tenor, who was equally at home in French and Italian roles. He was born in Madrid on Jan. 21, 1941. His parents were per-

Spanish tenor Placido Domingo sings the title role in the Metropolitan Opera production of Verdi's Otello.

METROPOLITAN OPERA

formers of *zarzuela*, a kind of musical play. When he was eight his family settled in Mexico. In Mexico City he majored in piano and voice at the conservatory and made his operatic debut in *La Traviata* in 1961. Later that year he appeared in a Dallas, Texas, production of *Lucia di Lammermoor* starring Joan Sutherland, which led to a two-year contract in Tel Aviv, Israel. He joined the New York City Opera in 1966, singing the title role in Ginastera's *Don Rodrigo*.

He joined the Metropolitan Opera Company in 1968, making his debut there four days earlier than planned when he substituted for the popular Franco Corelli in *Adriana Lecouvreur*. After that he sang annually at the Met but spent part of each year in Europe. Besides these performances, he conducted, often appeared on television, made varied complete operatic recordings, and starred in the Franco Zeffirelli film version of *La Traviata* (1983). An unusually well-grounded musician, Domingo has a dark, resonant voice that he uses with great security of style.

WILLIAM ASHBROOK
Author of "The Operas of Puccini"

DOMINIC, dom'ə-nik, **Saint** (c. 1171–1221), Spanish founder of the Friars Preachers, or Dominicans, a religious order that combines the contemplative life of the monk with the active apostolate of the evangelist. Dominic had an intense love for God and zeal for the salvation of men, both Christian and pagan; and, endowed with charm and compassion, he attracted many followers. He buttressed his preaching with asceticism, purity of life, and prayer.

Early Career. Dominic was born about 1171 at Caleruega, Spain, the son of Don Félix of Guzman and Juana of Aza. He studied liberal arts and theology in Palencia. About 1194 he became a canon regular in the cathedral chapter of Osma and was ordained priest.

In 1203 and 1204, Dominic accompanied his bishop, Didacus of Acebes, to Denmark on two diplomatic missions for Ferdinand VIII of Castile. On a trip to Rome in 1206, they became acutely aware of the difficulties of the church in southern France with the Albigensian heretics and decided to remain there to preach against, and debate with, the heretics. With monks from the Abbey of Cîteaux they devised a method of evangelical preaching in imitation of the apostles, going two by two on foot, carrying no money, and begging for their food. After the bishop died in 1207, Dominic continued the mission, directing bands of preachers working from Prouille.

Founding of the Preaching Order. Around 1214, Dominic began formulating plans to found a preaching order. By the spring he had received episcopal approval and by December of 1216 he had obtained confirmation for the order from Pope Honorius III. A month later the pope entrusted the order with general preaching.

Encouraged by papal approval and support, Dominic devoted the few remaining years of his life to organizing and extending the order. In August 1217 he sent four friars to Spain to preach and found houses and seven to Paris to make a foundation, preach, and enroll in the university. He himself established a priory and general headquarters in Bologna in 1218. During 1218-1219 he visited the priories in southern France, Spain, and Paris and sent friars out from these houses to make new foundations in other areas. He presided over the first two general chapters the order held in Bologna, in 1220 and 1221. With the collaboration of the friars, he added to the constitutions of the order. The first part of the constitution had been adopted, along with the Rule of St. Augustine, in 1216. The new section, which included a series of revolutionary innovations, structured the order's government, academic program, preaching work, and the observance of poverty.

During these years Dominic preached throughout Lombardy in collaboration with the papal legate, Cardinal Ugolino (the future Gregory IX). Worn out by his labors, he died in Bologna on Aug. 6, 1221. He had already seen the establishment of 4 monasteries, about 20 priories, and 8 provinces, and he had sent friars to establish provinces in England, eastern Europe, Greece, and Palestine. His friend Gregory IX, who canonized him in 1234, judged Dominic "had lived the life of the apostles to perfection." His feast day is August 8. See also DOMINICANS.

WILLIAM HINNEBUSCH, O. P.
Dominican House of Studies, Washington, D. C.

Further Reading: Lehner, Francis C., ed., *Saint Dominic, Biographical Documents* (Thomist Press 1964); Vicaire, Marie-Humbert, *St. Dominic and His Times*, tr. by K. Pond (Burns & MacEachern 1964).

DOMINICA, dom-ə-nē'kə, an island republic in the Windward group of the West Indies, between the islands of Martinique and Guadeloupe. Formerly an associated state of the United Kingdom, the Commonwealth of Dominica is an independent member of the Commonwealth of Nations.

Dominica is 29 miles (46 km) long and up to 16 miles (26 km) wide, covering 289.5 square miles (750 sq km). It is a fairly mountainous island of volcanic origin, with a rich soil that produces tropical fruit, cacao, vanilla beans, and spices. Most of the inhabitants are descendants of black slaves who worked the large sugar plantations in the 18th century. The capital is Roseau, on the southwest coast. About 500 pure Carib Indians remain in the interior.

The island was discovered on Nov. 3, 1493, by Columbus, who made his landfall there on his second voyage. The name of the island derives from the Latin *Dies Dominica* (Day of the Lord), commemorating the fact that the day of discovery was a Sunday. In 1660 a Franco-British treaty assigned Dominica to the Carib Indian inhabitants, but French settlers moved in anyway to establish plantations under a French governor. The island changed hands several times in the wars of the mid-1700's, with Britain gaining complete control only after 1805. The rural islanders now generally speak a French dialect, but English is the official language.

Dominica and five other Leeward and Windward island units agreed in 1966 to form the West Indies Associated States, in which each unit was a self-governing dominion with a British-appointed governor who served with the "guidance" of the prime minister. On Nov. 3, 1978, an independent republic, the Commonwealth of Dominica, came into being with a new constitution providing for a president and a unicameral House of Assembly of appointed senators and elected representatives.

The island was heavily damaged and 22 people killed by hurricane "David" on Aug. 29, 1979. Population: (1976 est.) 79,550.

HELEN MILLER BAILEY°
East Los Angeles College

SANTO DOMINGO, the site of the national capitol (*center*) is the nation's largest city, founded in 1496.

CONTENTS

Section	Page	Section	Page
1. The People	269	Transportation and Communications	270
Way of Life	269	Foreign Trade	270
The Cities	269	4. Education and Cultural Life	272
2. The Land	269		
3. The Economy	270	5. Government	272
Agriculture	270	6. History	272
Industry	270		

Coat of Arms

DOMINICAN REPUBLIC, də-min′i-kən, an independent nation in the West Indies, occupying the eastern two thirds of the island of Hispaniola, the other third being the Republic of Haiti. The Dominican Republic takes its name from Santo Domingo, its capital city, which was founded in 1496. The nation bears the cultural imprint of Spain, tempered by a strong African influence —the legacy of the many slaves brought to the island in colonial times.

Hispaniola, second only to Cuba in size among the Caribbean islands, was the first to be settled by the Spaniards; Santo Domingo is the oldest permanent European settlement in the New World. The city became an important center of colonial administration, but the island itself was neglected in favor of other, richer lands. As the French moved into the western part of Hispaniola in the 17th and 18th centuries, a handful of Spaniards concentrated their activities in the eastern section. In the early 1800's the Spanish colony was overshadowed by the young Haitian nation, whose large Negro population had rebelled against their French masters and whose leaders sought to control the entire island. When the Dominicans declared their independence in 1844, they were establishing their freedom less from Spain than from Haiti.

Since independence, the nation has had a turbulent history, characterized mainly by alternating periods of dictatorship and revolutionary anarchy. Peace and progress seldom have been possible except under the rule of ruthless dictators such as Ulises Heureaux in the late 1800's or Rafael Trujillo, who controlled the government from 1930 to 1961. The fall of a Dominican strongman has usually left the country stumbling through a period of violent civil discord. This led on two occasions (1916 and 1965) to armed intervention by the United States.

Despite its instability, the nation has some advantages. It is favored by a varied agricultural economy dominated by small producers and thus has been spared both the restrictive effects of a one-crop economy and the domination of large foreign-controlled interests. Its prospects have

---

INFORMATION HIGHLIGHTS

Official Name: República Domincana.
Head of State: President.
Head of Government: President.
Legislature: Congreso Nacional—*Senado* (27 members, elected for 4-year terms); *Cámara de Diputados* (91 members, elected for 4-year terms).
Area: 18,816 square miles (48,734 sq km).
Highest Elevation: Pico Duarte, 10,490 feet (3,197 meters).
Population: (1980) 5,430,879.
Capital: Santo Domingo (1980 population, 1,241,131).
Major Language: Spanish.
Major Religion: Roman Catholicism.
Monetary Unit: Peso (100 centavos).
Weights and Measures: Metric system.
Flag: White cross imposed on red and blue rectangles. Coat of arms at center. See also FLAG.
National Anthem: *Quisqueyanos valientes.*

been improved by new industries, but the republic must still cope with extensive pockets of dire poverty, a low level of literacy, and the uncertainty bred by too many years of political turmoil and repression.

1. The People

The language and culture of the Dominican Republic are Spanish, but the people represent a complex ethnic mixture in which the blood lines of European (mainly Spanish) colonial settlers have intermingled with those of Negro slaves and their descendants. Despite a sudden crowding of the cities in the 1960's, more than two thirds of the population is rural.

Ethnology. The population of Santo Domingo began to become racially mixed in the 1500's when the first of the Spanish colonizers mingled with the native Indians of Hispaniola. As the importation of African slaves increased and the Indian population declined and disappeared, the mixture acquired a darker hue, and when many of the descendants of the early colonizers were driven out after 1800 by the Haitian rebels, the African influence became even more pronounced.

Although an ethnic classification of the present population is hard to determine precisely, it can be estimated that nearly 70% are mulatto, with complexions varying from very light to very dark. The second-largest group, perhaps 20%, are of pure Negro stock, while about 10% are white. The African strain is particularly strong along the Haitian border and in the southern coastal area, where most of the sugar is grown.

Religion. About 90% of the people are nominally Roman Catholic, but the influence of the church is weaker than in other parts of Spanish America, particularly among the poor and in the rural hinterland. Religious cults echoing ancient African tribal beliefs can be found in remote areas and along the Haitian frontier.

Way of Life. The lower classes of the rural and urban areas are made up almost entirely of darker-skinned people, while the small middle and professional class and the even smaller upper class of landowners and wealthy businessmen are of much lighter coloring. Nevertheless, some individuals of pure African ancestry are to be found at every social level, and social conflict seldom takes the form of overt racial discrimination.

There is no doubt, however, that darker-skinned citizens have suffered from the general Dominican inclination to identify the nation and its culture as "Spanish," in contradistinction to French-African Haiti, which is viewed with some disdain and suspicion. European clothing and mores prevail in all of the cities, and in the countryside at large there is little evidence of the colorful African, Indian, and distinctively Latin American costumes that may be observed in other parts of the Caribbean and in Central America.

Although less so than in other Hispanic countries, society tends to be hierarchical and family life patriarchal and fairly rigid, particularly in its restrictive definition of the role of women. The typical dwelling in the rural areas, where most Dominicans live, is the small, thatched farmhouse, more often than not a one- or two-room structure without flooring. Cooking is often done in a separate shed. Poverty has been a major social problem, particularly among the landless peasants and in the urban slums, partly due to population growth. The population increased over two-and-one-half times during the 31 years of the Trujillo dictatorship, and it continued to increase during the 1960's at an annual rate of 4%, high even by Latin American standards.

The Cities. Santo Domingo, the ancient capital, with about one sixth of the nation's present population, is the economic, cultural, and political hub. Its busy harbor on the southern coast receives the bulk of the republic's imports and ships most of its sugar. The city is also being developed as a major Caribbean resort center.

The capital's only major metropolitan rival is Santiago de los Caballeros, a marketing and light industrial center that has prospered by virtue of its central location in the fertile northern farming region. Other noteworthy towns include Puerto Plata, La Vega, and San Francisco de Macorís, which also serve the agricultural northland, and the port cities of San Pedro de Marcorís and La Romana, along the southern coast.

While in power, Trujillo restricted the free movement of people within the republic. After his death in 1961, the principal cities were flooded by the rural poor who could no longer find enough agricultural land to support them. The populations of the two largest cities nearly doubled in seven years, that of Santo Damingo rising to nearly 600,000 and that of Santiago to more than 100,000. The smaller cities also experienced sudden rises, and none was able to provide adequate employment opportunities to integrate the new arrivals.

2. The Land

The terrain of the Dominican Republic is dominated by a central mountain chain and several lesser ranges. Despite the island's subtropical location, it enjoys a predominantly comfortable climate, well suited for agricultural production.

Physical Features. The Cordillera Central, formed mainly of igneous rock, rises gently in the eastern part of the island and runs westward through the center of the republic, gradually broadening out and increasing in elevation. In the west it boasts several high peaks, including Pico Duarte, which, at 10,490 feet (3,197 meters), is the highest mountain in the West Indies. Along the northern coast runs the less elevated Cordillera Septentrional. In the southwest are some lesser ranges, including the Sierra de Neiba and the Sierra de Bahoruco (where bauxite is mined). A very low-lying plain, called the Cul de Sac, separates the two southern ranges. Here is located the country's largest lake, Enriquillo, a saline body covering about 200 square miles (520 sq km) and nearly 150 feet (45 meters) below sea level. The republic's coastline is over 850 miles (1,370 km) long.

The nation's most important region is the Cibao in the northwest. It is formed by the northern, pine-covered slopes of the Cordillera Central, the southern limestone and shale slopes of the Cordillera Septentrional, and the wide valley that runs between the two chains for a distance of about 150 miles (240 km). In the east-central part of the Cibao is the so-called Vega Real, a plain of rich, thick loam that is one of the most fertile agricultural areas of the Caribbean. The Cibao is drained by the Yuna River and the Yaque del Norte.

A FARMER plows his rice paddy. Agriculture fills most domestic demands, but many methods still are primitive.

PAUL CONKLIN, FROM PIX

Climate. Lying just south of the Tropic of Cancer, the Dominican Republic's climate is moderated by constant trade winds from the Atlantic. Rainfall, which is heaviest from May to November, is abundant through most of the nation but quite scarce in a few regions, most notably in the Cul de Sac. The average temperatures in the valleys and coastal lowlands range from 75° to 80°F, (24°–27°C). The averages drop as the elevation increases; at the highest altitudes, freezing temperatures are occasionally registered during the winter months. The island is subject to infrequent visits by destructive hurricanes, usually in August or September.

Plant and Animal Life. Natural vegetation is extremely varied, owing to the many degrees of elevation and exposure produced by the mountainous terrain. Scrub brush and cacti may be found in the semiarid Cul de Sac, while savanna type plant life and dense rain forests thrive elsewhere. Stands of mahogany, logwood, and pine cover many mountain slopes, but depletion of forest reserves and the threat of land erosion have become matters of concern.

The fauna is also varied, including numerous reptiles and rodents and many species of birds, among them the flamingo. Offshore waters are rich in mackerel, mullet, and other fish.

3. The Economy

The Dominican economy is mainly agricultural, with small, individually operated farm units predominating. Roads, communications, and the service sector of the economy were markedly improved during the Trujillo era, but government controls and constant official interference hampered business growth. After Trujillo's death, the government sought to encourage foreign investment, particularly in the industrial and tourist sectors, and both the United States (through the Alliance for Progress) and the International Development Bank furnished extensive aid. The nation's economic potential is considerable, although it can hardly be realized unless political stability can be established.

Agriculture. The republic is fortunate in that its agricultural production is not so heavily export-oriented that it fails to supply most of the consumer needs of the home market. The leading export crop is sugar, followed by coffee, cacao, and tobacco. Export crops are grown on less than half of the cultivated land.

Under the quota system, the United States purchases about 60% of the sugar produced by the republic, and the rest is sold at much lower prices on the world market. There are large sugar plantations on the southern coast. Coffee and cacao (the major ingredient in chocolate) are cultivated in the foothills of the mountain ranges and in the Cibao. Tobacco, fruits, and legumes, along with some rice, corn (maize), tomatoes, eggplants, and other crops for domestic consumption are grown in the rich Vega Real. Unfortunately, the impressive herds of livestock built up by Trujillo were slaughtered shortly after his assassination. Since the mid-1960's, fresh efforts have been made to develop high-quality cattle.

Except for the large sugar plantations, which are highly mechanized and scientifically run, most farm agriculture does not use modern methods, fertilizers, or irrigation. Agricultural schools have been established, however, and the United States has stressed agricultural assistance in its overall technical aid. The Peace Corps has been especially effective in improving agricultural techniques on the smaller farms.

Industry. Aside from sugar refining, which is the largest single industry, and bauxite mining, almost all industrial activity is geared to the local consumer demand for manufactured products. A variety of consumer goods—textiles, glassware, light metalware, wood products, paint, and cement—are produced. Some of these light industries—for example, the beer industry of Santiago—have had much to do with the sound economic development of the towns or regions in which they have located.

The nation's industrial potential is somewhat hampered by the absence of fuels. Hydroelectric possibilities are not great, and most of the power needs are supplied by thermal plants.

Transportation and Communications. The Dominican Republic has an adequate system of roads, including a modern highway that connects Santo Domingo and Santiago. The principal ports are Santo Domingo, on the south coast, and Puerto Plata, serving Santiago and the Cibao, on the north coast. The modern airport near Santo Domingo is served by direct flights to the United States, Venezuela, Colombia, and neighboring Caribbean islands. Telephone and telegraph services are fairly well developed.

Labor. Only about one fourth of the economically active rural laborers who constitute the bulk of the Dominican labor force work for wages. Most are self-employed on their own or rented land. The sugar workers, by far the largest single wage-earning group, were long prevented from organizing by Tujillo's government and by plantation managers who could import large numbers of cane-cutters from Haiti. Since the return to a freer economy in 1961, labor groups have succeeded in raising wages by an overall average of 40%. This increase, though justified by the low level at which wages were previously held, has been inflationary.

Foreign Trade. Drought, political unrest, and falling prices on the world market contributed to the republic's unfavorable trade balances after the fall of Trujillo. Export earnings in the 1960's were covering only about 75% of the cost of imports, thus increasing foreign indebt-

DOMINICAN REPUBLIC Map Index

Population: 4,324,760   Area: 18,703 square miles

PROVINCES

Azua, 75,147	B 3
Baoruco, 52,343	A 3
Barahona, 79,880	A 3
Dajabón, 40,822	A 2
Distrito Nacional, 462,192	C 3
Duarte, 161,326	B 2
El Seibo, 115,604	C 3
Espaillat, 117,126	B 2
Independencia, 27,475	A 3
La Altagracia, 65,340	D 3
La Estrelleta, 43,266	A 3
La Romana, 39,047	D 3
La Vega, 248,069	B 3
María Trinidad Sánchez, 85,185	C 2
Monte Cristi, 59,240	A 2
Pedernales, 8,652	A 3
Peravia, 106,736	B 3
Puerto Plata, 163,896	B 2
Salcedo, 68,656	B 2
Samaná, 44,592	C 2
San Cristóbal, 249,776	B 3
San Juan, 148,206	A 3
San Pedro de Macorís, 68,953	C 3
Sánchez Ramírez 93,498	B 2
Santiago, 287,941	B 2
Santiago Rodríguez, 40,399	A 2
Valverde, 59,558	A 2

CITIES and TOWNS

Altamira, 1,336	B 2
Azua, 17,089	B 3
Bajos de Haina, 4,614	C 3
Baní, 17,952	B 3
Bánica, 633	A 2
Barahona, 24,550	B 3
Bayaguana, 1,848	C 3
Boca Chica, 7,692	C 3
Boca del Soco, 7,647	C 3
Bonao, 20,991	B 3
Cabral, 4,149	A 3
Carrera de Yeguas, 6,393	A 2
Castillo, 2,021	C 2
Cayacoa, 3,478	C 3
Constanza, 3,162	B 3
Cotuí, 4,706	B 2
Dajabón, 3,230	A 2
Duvergé, 6,701	A 3
El Cercado, 2,302	A 3
El Cuey, 6,310	D 3
El Guayabo, 8,684	C 2
El Pozo, 8,887	C 2
El Salado, 5,170	D 3
El Seibo, 4,621	D 3
Elías Piña, 2,890	A 3
Enriquillo, 3,485	A 4
Esperanza, 3,899	B 2
Hato Mayor, 5,775	C 3
Imbert, 2,325	B 2
Jarabacoa, 3,710	B 2
Jaragua, 3,828	A 3
Jima Abajo, 8,573	B 2
La Ciénaga, 4,424	B 3
La Romana, 29,255	D 3
La Vega, 24,019	B 3
Las Matas de Farfán, 3,585	A 3
Luperón, 1,548	B 2
Mata Palacio, 7,148	C 3
Miches, 3,110	D 3
Moca, 18,859	B 2
Montecristi, 5,912	A 2
Monte Plata, 2,202	C 3
Nagua, 9,337	C 2
Najayo Abajo, 3,183	B 3
Neiba, 7,322	A 3
Nizao, 2,574	B 3
Padre Las Cases, 3,026	B 3
Paraíso, 1,665	A 4
Pedernales, 2,466	A 3
Peña, 2,286	B 2
Peralta, 5,521	B 3
Piedra Blanca, 7,984	B 3
Pimentel, 5,258	B 2
Polo, 3,470	A 3
Puerto Plata, 21,070	B 2
Sabana de la Mar, 4,032	C 2
Sabana Grande, 2,857	C 3
Salcedo, 6,175	B 2
Salvaleón de Higüey, 15,656	D 3
Samaná, 3,309	C 2
San Cristóbal, 22,614	B 3
San Francisco de Macorís, 36,688	B 2
San José de las Matas, 2,305	A 2
San José de Ocoa, 5,591	B 3
San Juan, 34,250	A 3
San Pedro de Macorís, 23,005	C 3
Sánchez, 4,587	C 2
Santiago, 127,026	B 2
Santiago Rodríguez, 3,590	A 2
Santo Domingo (cap.), 577,371	C 3
Sosua, 1,808	B 2
Tamayo, 3,613	A 3
Tenares, 1,980	B 2
Valverde, 31,132	A 2
Veragua Abajo, 3,765	B 2
Villa Altagracia, 4,344	B 3
Villa Riva, 1,215	C 2
Yaguate, 1,440	B 3
Yamasá, 1,511	B 3
Yásica Abajo, 13,080	B 2

OTHER FEATURES

Alto Velo (chan.)	A 4
Alto Velo (isl.)	A 4
Balandra (point)	C 2
Baoruco, Sierra de (mts.)	A 3
Beata (cape)	A 4
Beata (chan.)	A 4
Beata (isl.)	A 4
Cabrón (cape)	C 2
Calderas (bay)	B 3
Cana (point)	D 3
Catalina (isl.)	D 3
Caucedo (cape)	C 3
Central, Cordillera	A 2
Duarte, Pico (mt.)	B 2
Engaño (cape)	D 3
Enriquillo (lake)	A 3
Escocesa (bay)	C 2
Espada (point)	D 3
Falso (cape)	A 4
Frailes, Los (isl.)	A 4
Francés Viejo (cape)	C 2
Gallo (mt.)	A 2
Isabela (bay)	A 2
Isabela (cape)	B 1
Los Frailes (isl.)	A 4
Macorís (cape)	B 2
Manzanillo (bay)	A 2
Mona (passage)	D 3
Neiba (bay)	B 3
Neiba, Sierra de (mts.)	A 3
Ocoa (bay)	B 3
Oriental, Cordillera (range)	C 3
Palenque (point)	B 3
Palmillas (point)	D 3
Rincón (bay)	C 2
Rucia (point)	A 2
Salinas (point)	B 3
Samaná (bay)	C 2
Samaná (cape)	D 2
San Rafael (cape)	D 2
Saona (isl.), 409	D 3
Septentrional, Cordillera (range)	B 2
Tina (mt.)	B 3
Yaque del Norte (river)	A 2
Yaque del Sur (river)	A 3
Yuma (bay)	D 3
Yuna (river)	C 2

Population years: Total—1970 off. est.; Santo Domingo—1967 off. est.; cities over 15,000—1966 off. est.; others—1966 off. est.

edness. Trade dependence on the United States has been excessive. Economists hope that by forming a Caribbean trade association, the republic can both increase its total trade and reduce the relative importance of the U.S. role.

4. Education and Cultural Life

Spain established the first university in the New World in Santo Domingo in 1538, and the nation can boast of a proud cultural heritage. Nevertheless, in the late 1960's hardly more than a third of the predominantly rural Dominican population could read and write, and the republic lacked the means to force any rapid reduction in this high rate of illiteracy.

Elementary and Secondary Education. A law requiring compulsory education for children from 7 to 14 exists, but its provisions are weakened by a shortage of teachers, facilities, and funds to attend to an unusually large school-age population, particularly in the remote rural areas and the teeming urban slums. Only 18,000 were attending school in the entire country when U.S. troops occupied the Dominican Republic in 1916. When the marines left eight years later, the school population had risen to over 100,000.

Trujillo did not completely ignore educational needs, but his yearly budgetary assignment for this purpose was one quarter of that for the military and police. Private and religious schools, which exist in all of the large towns and in some rural localities, have always been necessary to supplement state-financed public education.

Higher Education. There are three institutions of higher learning. The national university, oldest in the Americas, is autonomous though state-supported. Located in Santo Domingo, it has an associated school of medicine. Also in the capital and also state-supported is the Pedro Henríquez-Ureña University and its school of tropical agriculture. A Catholic University is located in Santiago.

Literature and the Arts. The Dominican Republic has produced several notable poets, the best known being Gastón Fernando Delingue (1861–1913) and Salome Ureña de Henríquez (1850–1897). The latter's sons, the cultural historians Pedro and Max Henríquez-Ureña, are among the most distinguished men of letters of the 20th century. Other modern giants are the essayist, novelist, and former president Juan Bosch and the historian E. Rodriguez Demorozi.

Dominican folk music, in its rhythmic and melodic sophistication, reflects an important African influence. The *merengue* is sufficiently popular to be considered a national dance. Art is produced in limited quantities, the best-known work being in the form of wood carvings from sturdy mahogany trunks or branches.

Santo Domingo contains several important buildings dating from the colonial era. Perhaps the most authentic is the cathedral, which may still contain the bones of Christopher Columbus. The famous Alcázar—the palace of the first viceroy, Diego Columbus—has been rebuilt.

5. Government

The Dominican Republic has been governed under a succession of democratic constitutions which have defined a tripartite division of powers and have guaranteed the rights of citizens. Unfortunately, their provisions have often been abrogated or ignored by ambitious political leaders, both military and civilian.

National Government. Under democratic conditions, which have seldom prevailed, the government is headed by a president elected by universal suffrage to a 4-year term. The president governs with the support of a bicameral legislative branch, also elected every four years.

A strong, independent judiciary is also provided for but is yet to be developed. Under Trujillo, judges and lawyers were completely subject to the strong man's orders, and, under his successors, lack of financial support has hindered the creation of an impartial legal system. Critics of the post-Trujillo governments have also complained of the lack of independence of certain departments of the executive branch, citing their heavy reliance on advice from the more than 600 consultants attached to the U.S. embassy in Santo Domingo.

Local Government. Mayors and other local officials are locally elected, but government at the more important provincial level is centralized in Santo Domingo by virtue of the president's power to appoint and remove governors. Joaquín Balaguer, who was elected president in 1966, surprised many by appointing women to the governorships of all of the 26 provinces, an unusual political maneuver by which he quelled any possible jealousies among aspiring local leaders, won feminine support, and increased his influence in local affairs.

Parties and Power Groups. Rafael Trujillo's Dominican party, which tolerated only token opposition during his years in power, was promptly disbanded after his death. By the late 1960's, its two most important successors were the Reformist party of Joaquín Balaguer, which won 22 of the 27 Senate seats in the 1966 election, and the somewhat more left-leaning Dominican Revolutionary party of Juan Bosch. Other political organizations included the Revolutionary Social Christian party and two Communist groups, the Dominican Communist party and the Popular Socialist party.

Industrial, labor, and landowning agrarian interests have all exerted political influence during the post-Trujillo years, but by far the most imposing pressure group is the army. Paradoxically, its power has increased since the days of Trujillo, who, until the year of his fall, could count on unquestioning support throughout the army ranks. The mild-mannered, scholarly Balaguer entered office in 1966 with army support but with no assurance of its continuing loyalty.

The Roman Catholic Church is also a significant force. Unlike its role in certain other Latin American nations, its influence in the Dominican Republic has been a liberalizing one, its efforts being directed to social reforms.

6. History

Christopher Columbus discovered the island of Hispaniola in December 1492. His flagship, the *Santa Maria*, ran aground on what is now the north coast of Haiti, forcing him to construct a small fort, called Navidad, to protect the sailors who could not be accommodated on the remaining two ships for the return voyage to Spain. When he returned in 1493 with several shiploads of Spanish settlers and fortune seekers, he found that the seemingly friendly Arawak Indians had destroyed the fort and murdered its occupants. A temporary peace was reestablished, but the Spaniards' lust for gold and silver could

ALMA MATER statue in the courtyard of the University of Santo Domingo, the oldest in the New World, which was founded by Spain in 1538.

not be satisfied unless the Indians could be forced to relinquish their freedom and work for the newcomers. Within 50 years, virtually all of the native population of Hispaniola—an estimated 100,000—was exterminated through mistreatment and disease.

The Colonial Era. Late in 1493, Columbus' companions established the first colony in the New World at Isabella (near present Puerto Plata) on the north coast of Hispaniola, but early in 1496 this site was abandoned for a healthier and better protected harbor on the south coast. Here the Spaniards established Santo Domingo (originally Santiago de Guzman), the administrative capital of their colonizing operations in the Caribbean. Under the viceroy Diego Columbus, son of the discoverer, a luxurious court with beautiful homes and a palace was created in the early 1500's. Although Santo Domingo continued for some 300 years to be a colonial administrative center and the site of the royal judicial court for the Caribbean, the splendor of the founding era was short-lived as the Spanish colonizers moved on to explore and exploit much richer lands such as Mexico and Peru.

However, French, Dutch, and English adventurers did not neglect the island colony in their search for the sources of Spanish wealth. John Hawkins surprised the Spaniards by delivering slaves to the struggling sugar plantations around Santo Domingo in 1563. Sir Francis Drake paid a much less welcome visit in 1586, when he sacked the city. In the early 1600's, the Spanish settlers were officially encouraged to abandon their farms and towns in the north and to congregate around the capital in the south. As a result, the north and west coasts were abandoned to buccaneers and foreign settlers, who eventually came under the protection of France. In 1697, by the Treaty of Ryswick, Spain was forced to recognize France's claims to the western third of the island.

Through the 1700's, the French colony—which was to become known as Saint Domingue, and later as Haiti—prospered, while the Spanish colony declined. Finally, in 1795, Spanish Hispaniola, too, was ceded to France. But the French were never to occupy Santo Domingo. Instead, it was invaded and captured in 1801 by the great Haitian Negro leader, Gen. Pierre Dominique Toussaint L'Ouverture, who had freed the slaves of Saint Domingue. When Haiti became the second independent nation in the New World in 1804, the former Spanish colony of Santo Domingo was included within its borders. Spain briefly recovered its colony in 1809, but in 1822 it fell again to the Haitians. In 1844, a triumvirate headed by the European-educated Juan Pablo Duarte established the Dominican Republic as an independent nation.

The Republic from 1844 to 1930. Forced to defend their freedom by force of arms in 1844, 1849, and 1855, the Dominicans were understandably preoccupied by the Haitian threat. In 1861, President Pedro Santana persuaded Spain to reinstate its sovereignty, but many Dominicans resisted the return of a Spanish administration, and Spain withdrew from the island for the last time in 1865. During the succeeding decade, President Buenaventura Báez asked U.S. presidents Andrew Johnson and Ulysses S. Grant to consider the possibility of taking over the insecure and impoverished nation. Opposition in the U.S. Congress prevented such a move.

President Ulises Heureaux, a Negro whom the Dominicans called "Lilís," ruled the Dominican Republic as a strong-willed military dictator during most of the period from 1882 until his assassination in 1897. Under his firm, often violent, exercise of authority, the republic experienced economic progress and some development of its agricultural potential, but it also saw a growth of its debt to foreign creditors. These debts continued to increase during the era of anarchic civil strife that followed Heureaux' death, and by an agreement concluded in 1905 the United States assumed control of the collection of Dominican customs duties (a right it was not to surrender until 1941).

In 1916, after several attempts to pacify the various Dominican political camps, President Woodrow Wilson sent the U.S. Marines into the violence-ridden nation. The occupation brought about some further economic development as well as progress in education and public health, but it also brough military rule, press censorship, and economic exploitation by U.S. business interests, and it was bitterly resented.

U.S. troops were finally withdrawn in 1924. Within five years, the Dominican Republic had lapsed again into political anarchy.

The Trujillo Years: 1930–1961. In 1930 another military strong man took over the reins of government. Rafael Leonidas Trujillo Molina was an offiicer trained by the occupation forces. Seizing the presidency in a time of crisis, he quickly became an absolute dictator.

The era of Trujillo was characterized, on the one hand, by political stability and economic growth, and, on the other, by corruption of public and private morality. No political opposition was permitted. Trujillo selected or approved all public officials and, while occasionally allowing other individuals to occupy the presidency, remained always in full command. The system of public highways was expanded. The capital city of Santo Domingo, which was virtually destroyed by a hurricane a few months after Trujillo seized power, was rebuilt and renamed Ciudad Trujillo. (The immodest generalissimo was also to authorize the erection of huge public signs honoring "God and Trujillo.") Sugar, coffee, and cacao plantations were reorganized and modernized and, at the same time, were brought under the personal control of the Trujillo family.

By 1947 the dictator had paid off all of the nation's outstanding foreign debts. By that time, too, he and his family were so completely identified with the government and the national economy that it was impossible to distinguish between the wealth of the state and the financial resources of the family. Though Trujillo himself tended toward austerity in his personal habits, he made no apparent effort to curb the excesses of his family and officials, allowing political and moral corruption to develop to the point that no citizen, however distinguished, was safe from arrest or personal degradation at the hands of Trujillo's intimates and his secret police.

Trujillo's fortunes began to turn in the late 1950's. In 1959 he had to fend off an invasion by Cuban-based Dominican exiles, and in 1960 he was censured and ostracized by the Organization of American States (OAS). On May 30, 1961, he was assassinated by elements of the army, the organization that had given him his strongest support for more than three decades.

The Republic After 1961. With the death of Trujillo, the task of reestablishing a free political and business climate fell to a generation with little experience in democracy. The army officers were generally in favor of a return to army dictatorship. The rural peasantry—the group perhaps least affected by Trujillo—were, in the main, either conservative or politically indifferent, though anxious to improve their lot and acquire more land. The urban middle class and professional groups were restless for the establishment of the democratic government of which they had long been deprived, and the upper-class economic and social elites that had been eclipsed by Trujillo and his entourage were impatient to recover their positions of leadership.

The transition was difficult, but in late 1962 the Dominican Republic finally held its first free election in 38 years. The winner, Juan Bosch, a writer and professor who had spent most of his life in exile, was elected primarily by the votes of farmers and the urban middle classes. He set out in February 1963 to establish a firmly independent government dedicated to political freedom, but his administration endured barely seven months. Unrest arising from left-wing agitation among the urban unemployed led to a bloodless coup staged by the military.

The new government was no more successful in quelling national unrest, and in the spring of 1965 young military officers precipitated a civil war, the apparent aim of which was the restoration of constitutional government under the deposed Juan Bosch. But the United States became alarmed at reports of Communist activity within the rebel ranks, and, although the extent of these influences was never established, it dispatched a sizable military force to terminate the war and pacify the country. The action was later sanctioned by the OAS, and military command was promptly turned over to an Inter-American Peace Force, but most political factions in the republic deplored the new act of intervention.

When civil strife had ended, a provisional president, Hector García Godoy, was installed. The election of June 1966 resulted in the defeat of Bosch by Joaquín Balaguer. A moderate conservative, he had served as president under Trujillo, who installed him in office shortly before his assassination to reduce criticism of his regime.

During his first years as president, Balaguer succeeded in calming the passions aroused by the civil war. He took members of the opposition into his government and won the confidence of business and the rural majority. Belaguer gave the nation a taste of political stability and was reelected in 1970 and 1974.

In 1978, Balaguer was defeated by Antonio Guzmán, candidate of the left-wing Dominican Revolutionary party (PRD). Two years later the PRD disassociated itself from Guzmán, who committed suicide on July 3, 1982. Meanwhile, the election of May 16, 1982, was won by PRD candidate Salvador Jorge Blanco, who took over the presidency from Vice President Jacobo Majluta Azar as scheduled, on Aug. 16, 1982.

THOMAS MATHEWS*
Institute of Caribbean Studies
University of Puerto Rico

HISTORICAL HIGHLIGHTS

1492	Hispaniola discovered by Christopher Columbus.
1496	First Spanish settlement in New World moved from Isabella on north coast to Santo Domingo on the south coast.
1509	Diego Columbus became governor of Santo Domingo.
1538	New World's first university founded in Santo Domingo.
1697	Western third of Hispaniola ceded to France.
1801	Toussaint L'Ouverture led Haitian invasion of Santo Domingo.
1844	Dominican Republic was established.
1897	The dictator Ulises Heureaux was assassinated.
1916	U. S. Marines began 8-year occupation of Dominican Republic.
1930	Rafael Leonidas Trujillo Molina seized power.
1961	Trujillo was assassinated (May 30).
1962	Juan Bosch won presidency in free election.
1963	Junta deposed Bosch (Sept. 25).
1965	U. S. troops invaded republic to quell civil war.
1966	Joaquín Balaguer elected president.
1978	Antonio Guzmán elected president.
1982	President Guzmán committed suicide (July 3); Salvador Jorge Blanco elected president.

Bibliography

Atkins, G. Pope, *Arms and Politics in the Dominican Republic* (Westview 1981).
Gordon, Raoul, ed., *Image of the Dominican Republic: The Dominican Miracle* (Gordon Press 1978).
Logan, Rayford W., *Haiti and the Dominican Republic* (Oxford 1968)
Lowenthal, Abraham F., *Dominican Intervention* (Harvard Univ. Press 1972).
Welles, Sumner, *Naboth's Vineyard: The Dominican Republic*, 2 vols. in 1 (1928; reprint, Arno 1972).

DOMINICANS, də-min′i-kənz, is the name popularly applied to the Roman Catholic religious order that St. Dominic founded in 1215 in order to preach the Gospels, instruct the people in sound morals, and combat vice and error. It is legally known as the Order of Friars Preachers (O.P.). Pope Honorius III confirmed the order on Dec. 22, 1216, and on Jan. 21, 1217, commissioned it to preach. The order's spirit and life stem from its preaching mission.

Organization. The Order of Friars Preachers comprises three orders. The First Order is made up of priests and brothers. The Second Order consists of cloistered nuns. The Third Order is divided into two branches: one comprising sisters who live in community and engage in teaching, foreign mission work, and social and charitable activities, and the other consisting of laymen and women, called tertiaries, who seek to live according to the Dominican pattern outside the organized communal life. The characteristic habit of the Dominicans who live in community consists of a white tunic, hood (a veil for nuns), and scapular (a black mantle), and a rosary.

The order's life in contemplative and apostolic and is modeled on that of earlier monastic communities. It follows the Rule of St. Augustine (supplemented by constitutions originally drawn up in 1216 and 1221) and stresses a solemn choir service (there is a Dominican liturgical rite), active community living, and a strict asceticism of silence. The long-standing requirements of fasting and of abstinence from meat have been eased in modern times. To reconcile this contemplative regime with active preaching and the study preparatory to it, St. Dominic introduced revolutionary concepts into monastic life: (1) he substituted systematic study for manual labor and meditative reading; (2) he excused students and preachers from ascetical and liturgical requirements when these impeded their work; (3) he freed the friars from parish work; (4) he required absolute poverty, thus freeing the friars from the management of personal and corporate possessions; (5) he abandoned the requirement that members of an order remain in the monastery they first joined; (6) he adopted a rule and constitution that are not binding under sin; and (7) he established a representative democratic government.

Based on the principle of representation, the order's government is composed of strongly empowered superiors (master general, provincials, and priors) who are elected by, and responsible to, chapters (general, provincial, and priory) for limited terms of office. Triennial general chapters (annual until 1370) of either provincials or elected delegates, have the power, and have constantly used it, to modify the law and details of Dominican life and work.

History. In 1221, six years after the order was founded, the Dominicans were divided in 8 provinces; by 1500 there were 22 provinces and over 600 priories. In 1256 there were 13,000 friars; before 1350 there were over 20,000. The Black Death in the 14th century caused membership to decline sharply, but a 15th century revival and reform movement accelerated membership growth. By the 18th century about 13,000 friars (no statistics available for 11 provinces) could be counted. The membership declined to only 3,000 friars in 1850, reflecting the turmoil in Europe. In modern times membership has again gained: from 1876 to 1968 the number of provinces jumped from 22 to 39; in 1968 there were 9,995 friars (U.S. 1,354) and 50,985 sisters (U.S. 16,100). A 1962 census showed 6,941 nuns (U.S. 436). No statistics are kept on tertiary membership.

Medieval Period. The order's preaching mission committed it to intellectual pursuits from its very beginnings. Its preoccupation with truth, especially scriptural and theological, led to the development of a well-integrated school system. St. Dominic laid the foundation for the system, and five friars, among them Albertus Magnus and Thomas Aquinas, elaborated its final details in 1259. Ranging upward, the schools went from priory schools of theology, through provincial schools of theology and philosophy, to the university-level general house of studies, which was usually incorporated into one of the general universities. The order held two chairs of theology at the University of Paris by 1230 and one at Oxford by 1248. After 1300 each major province had its own house of studies.

Preachers by calling, Dominicans founded houses in cities and towns, built large and open churches, preached twice on Sundays and daily in Advent and Lent, and sent out itinerant preachers. To cover territory systematically, each priory divided its area into preaching districts and erected preaching homes in remote areas. Preaching led to other apostolates. The convents of Dominican nuns, inspired and directed by such friars as Meister Eckhart and John Tauler, became centers of the 14th century mystical movement. The friars founded confraternities for the laity, most notably the Marian, Holy Name, and Rosary confraternities, and worked among the lay religious known as the Beghards and the Beguines.

Spanish friars penetrated into Morocco, and friars from Scandinavia, Poland, and Hungary went into unconverted Slavic lands. From Greece and Palestine others went to Syria, Mesopotamia, Asia, and India. The Congregation of Pilgrim Friars (founded about 1300) worked in southern Russia and southern Asia. Raymond of Peñafort (died 1275) founded schools for the study of Arabic and Hebrew in Spain; Thomas Aquinas and Raymond Martin wrote treatises to guide friars working among pagans; William of Tripoli and Ricoldo of Montecroce undertook the first European studies of the Muslim religion.

Decline in discipline began about 1300 and accelerated after 1349 because of difficulty over the observance of poverty, prevalent wars, decreasing membership, and unwise recruiting methods used after the Black Death. The original success of the Dominicans caused many pastors to question their privilege to preach and to hear confessions in local parishes, and in 1300, Boniface VIII restricted their privileges. But the conflict did not reach an equitable settlement until the Council of Trent (1545–1563).

The 16th to 18th Centuries. The rejuvenation of the Dominicans in the 16th century was exemplified in the vigorous revival of Thomism. In Spain this movement was led by Francisco de Vitoria (died 1546), and in Italy by Cajetan. The curriculum of studies was broadened and adapted to the age of humanism and Protestantism. Colleges were opened in Rome, in Salamanca and Valladolid, Spain, and in America and the Philippines. The order's scholars were occupied in controversies with Protestant and

Catholic theologians about grace, the Immaculate Conception, and probabilism. About 130 Dominican bishops and theologians, notably Melchior Cano and Domingo de Soto, participated in the Council of Trent.

Although the rise of Protestantism destroyed 3 provinces and crippled 14 others, and Turkish victories permanently weakened the Hungarian province, 11 new provinces and a congregation in Spanish and Portuguese overseas dominions were founded. The Philippine province (founded 1592) staffed missions throughout Asia.

Dominican government, while remaining basically unchanged, suffered from religious and political upheavals that made recourse to the master general or chapter meetings difficult. The spirit of the Enlightenment weakened discipline and impeded recruiting. Beginning in 1789 the suppression of religious orders in France, Spain, Portugal, and Latin America almost destroyed the order.

Since 1850. The Risorgimento in Italy, the Kulturkampf in Germany, the expulsion of religious orders from France in 1903, and the 1936 Spanish Civil War occasioned fresh setbacks, but the steady recovery begun in 1843 by Jean Baptiste Henri Lacordaire in France continued. Alexandre Vincent Jandel, master general of the order from 1850 to 1875, reorganized the government and the provinces, restored religious life, and revived studies. The order founded the theological faculty of the University of Fribourg in 1890, and in 1908 it reorganized the Angelicum (now the University of St. Thomas, Rome). J. M. Lagrange established St. Stephen's Biblical School of Jerusalem in 1890.

In the 20th century, activities spread to communications. Gilbert Hartke founded the speech and drama department of the Catholic University of America and Players Incorporated. Urban Nagle, playwright, and Thomas Carey organized Blackfriars Theater in New York City. Dominicans established institutes in Paris and Istanbul for the study of Eastern Christian churches, and in Cairo for Islamic studies, and founded the Instituto Boliviana de Estudio y Acción Sociales in Bolivia. French Dominicans were active in the worker-priest movement after World War II, and Henri Pire, a Belgian, received the Nobel Peace Prize in 1958 for his work among war refugees. The American Walter Farrell (died 1959) pioneered in introducing into college theology courses for laymen.

WILLIAM A. HINNEBUSCH
Dominican House of Studies, Washington, D.C.

Further Reading: Galbraith, Georgina R., *The Constitution of the Dominican Order 1216–1360* (Manchester, England, 1925); Hinnebusch, William A., *Early English Friars Preachers* (Rome 1951); id., *History of the Dominican Order*, vol. 1 (New York 1966).

DOMINION, də-min′yən, a territory controlled by, or owing allegiance to, a sovereign or other supreme authority. Formerly, in its best-known usage, the term was used to designate those countries associated with Britain as self-governing dominions in the British Commonwealth of Nations. However, on the grant of independence to India in 1949 and the admission of India to the Commonwealth, the name of the group was changed to Commonwealth of Nations ("British" being dropped), and the term "dominion" was discarded in favor of "member state"—a designation compatible with the independence of each member. See also COMMONWEALTH OF NATIONS.

DOMINION DAY, də-min′yən, the national holiday of Canada, celebrated on July 1 to commemorate the joining of Upper and Lower Canada, New Brunswick, and Nova Scotia as the Dominion of Canada. The British North America Act (q.v.), proclaimed by Queen Victoria, effected the union on July 1, 1867.

DOMINIS, dô′mē-nēs, **Marco Antonio** (1566–1624), Roman Catholic bishop and theologian. He was born at Arbe (modern Rab, Yugoslavia), an island off the Dalmatian coast. He joined the Jesuits as a young man and studied at the Illyrian College and the University of Padua. After ordination he served as professor of mathematics at Padua. He left the Jesuits in 1596 and was named bishop of Segni (Senj). He was promoted to the primatial see of Spalato (Split) in 1602.

Having incurred the displeasure of Pope Paul V for opposing the Holy See in its dispute with the republic of Venice, Dominis resigned his see in 1616 and went to England. King James I appointed him dean of Windsor and master of Savoy. In his principal work, *De republica ecclesiastica* (1617), Dominis bitterly attacked the monarchical constitution of the Roman Church. When his kinsman Gregory XV was elected pope in 1622, the apostate bishop returned to Rome and published a recantation of his earlier writings, *Sui reditus ex Anglia consilium* (1623). But Gregory died the following year, and Dominis was soon after indicted by the Inquisition. His case was pending when he died in Rome on Sept. 8, 1624. He was subsequently judged a relapsed heretic, and his corpse and writings were publicly burned.

CYPRIAN J. LYNCH, O.F.M.
Siena College, Loudonville, N.Y.

DOMINO, dom′ə-nō, in 18th century dress, a long hooded cloak, perhaps derived from a kind of clerical hood, or the half mask with which it was usually worn. The term was also applied to a person who wore such a costume.

The mask came into use with Italian Renaissance comedy, in which half masks were worn by such characters as Harlequin. The masks were later worn by aristocrats who did not wish to be recognized when taking part in plays, and the half mask developed into a disguise. Men and women who wore dominoes at masquerades and carnivals usually did so to remain incognito. The domino was also worn by women while traveling.

DOMINO THEORY, dom′ə-nō, the assumption that if one country in Southeast Asia were to fall to the Communists all the other countries in the region would fall, one after another, like dominoes. In the 1950's and 1960's this theory was usually invoked in reference to South Vietnam, a context in which it was first used by U.S. President Dwight D. Eisenhower in 1954.

In the belief that a non-Communist Southeast Asia was vital to the defense of the United States, Presidents Eisenhower, Kennedy, and Johnson all endorsed some form of commitment to South Vietnam in its fight against Communist North Vietnam. Critics of the theory held that loss of South Vietnam would not necessarily lead to a Communist Southeast Asia.

SERGIO BARZANTI
Fairleigh Dickinson University

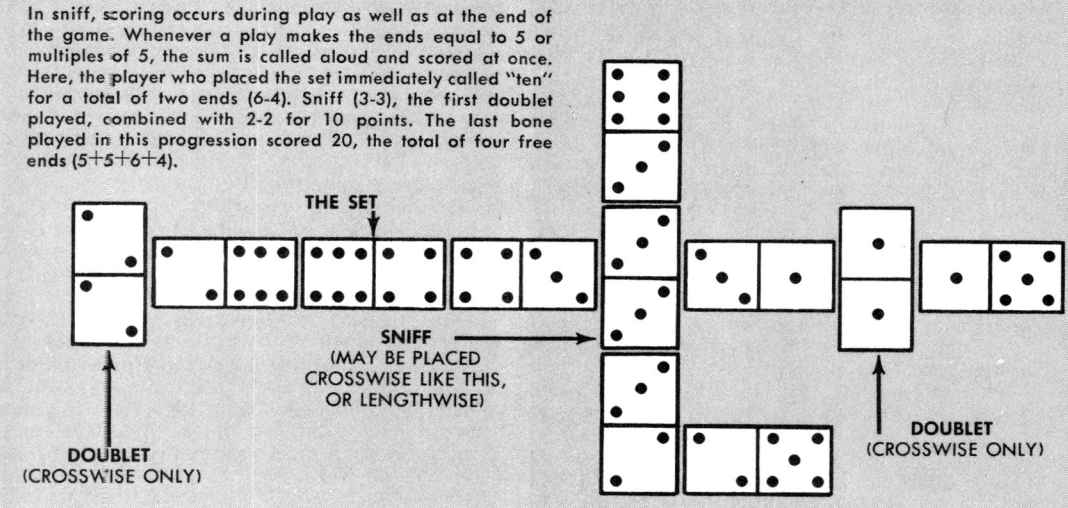

THE SNIFF GAME OF DOMINOES

In sniff, scoring occurs during play as well as at the end of the game. Whenever a play makes the ends equal to 5 or multiples of 5, the sum is called aloud and scored at once. Here, the player who placed the set immediately called "ten" for a total of two ends (6-4). Sniff (3-3), the first doublet played, combined with 2-2 for 10 points. The last bone played in this progression scored 20, the total of four free ends (5+5+6+4).

THE SET

SNIFF (MAY BE PLACED CROSSWISE LIKE THIS, OR LENGTHWISE)

DOUBLET (CROSSWISE ONLY)

DOUBLET (CROSSWISE ONLY)

DOMINOES, dom'ə-nōz, is any of several number-matching games for two or more persons. The games are played with flat, oblong blocks identified by the number of dots on the faces. Domino blocks in various forms appeared a thousand years ago in China, but these pieces were generally substitutes for dice. The modern game appeared about 1750 in Italy and France and gradually spread throughout Europe and to the United States. Of the many different games, draw, muggins, sniff, and matador are probably the most widely played.

The blocks used in dominoes, commonly called *bones*, are made of wood, bone, or similar materials. They are rectangular, with one face black and the other divided into halves, or *ends*, by a ridge across the center. The ends may be blank or marked by dots. In a standard set of 28 bones, the ends show every possible combination of two numbers from zero to 6. Bones with the same number of dots at each end are *doublets*, and each doublet belongs to one *suit*. (A suit consists of pieces with the same number of spots on an end.) Other bones belong to two suits, for example, 0–4 or 3–6. A 28-piece set has seven suits but eight ends of any one number.

Draw. The draw game is the basic version for two. Players shuffle the bones face down; then each takes seven from the pile, the remaining pieces forming the stock or *boneyard*. The leader, determined by a draw, places the first bone, known as *the set*, on the table. After that, turns alternate. A play is made by placing a bone adjacent to another with a free end, so that touching ends match (see illustration). Doublets are placed crosswise in the chain or *layout*, so that there are always two free ends. Only one end can be matched in a turn, and if a player is unable to make a match he must draw from the boneyard until he can. He must play if he is able. If he exhausts the boneyard and still cannot play, his turn lapses, but he may reenter the game if his adversary plays a bone he can match. The first to dispose of all of his pieces calls "Domino!" and scores the total count of his opponent's unplayed bones. If neither side can play, the game is *blocked*, and the player with the lowest count scores the total dots in his adversary's hand. If three or four play, each starts with five bones. Game is 50 to 100 points.

Muggins (All Fives). This is an elaboration of the draw game. In addition to the points scored by going *domino*, a player who makes the open ends of the layout total 5 or a multiple of 5 immediately tallies that number of points. Also, he does not have to play, if he prefers instead to draw. Game is 200 points.

Sniff. This variant of muggins makes the first doublet played, called *sniff*, matchable on four open areas (ends and sides), because it can be placed lengthwise or crosswise in the layout. Other doublets must be used crosswise. Game is 200 points. (See illustration for routine plays at sniff.)

Matador. In this variant of draw, the object is not to match touching dominoes but to total 7; for example, 2 would be played to a 5, or 3 to a 4. A blank is a block, except to any one of four *matadors*: 0–0, 6–1, 5–2, and 4–3. Either end of these bones may be played at any time. If a player cannot make a 7, he must draw from the boneyard until he can, but two bones must always be left in the boneyard. (It is often good strategy for a player to draw rather than to use his last matador.) Doublets count as single numbers only, that is, 2–2 can be played with a 5 and not with a 3; and therefore doublets are placed endwise in the layout. In scoring, the full number of doublet spots is counted. If the game is blocked, the player with the lowest count scores the number of the combined hands. With two or three players, seven dominoes are drawn to start; with four players, five dominoes make up the hand. The highest double or the one with the highest domino places the set. Game is 100 points.

Variations. Many variations in rules exist in dominoes. Some sets use bones up to 9–9 and others as high as 12–12. In draw, sometimes the player with the highest doublet starts the game; in some versions he is not required to make a play. In some games the last two bones may never be drawn from the boneyard. In scoring any variant, sometimes only the difference between the players' totals are counted when neither goes domino.

FRANK K. PERKINS, Boston *"Herald"*

DOMITIAN, dō-mish'ən (51–96 A.D.), Roman emperor from 81 to 96 A.D., was widely regarded in antiquity as one of the worst of the Roman emperors. The historian Tacitus blackened his memory in the *Agricola,* and Martial, the Younger Pliny, and Suetonius were all harsh in their treatment of him. Some modern historians have attempted to show that Domitian did not deserve much of this criticism, but they have not been entirely successful.

Titus Flavius Domitianus was born on Oct. 24, 51 A.D., the son of the future emperor Vespasian. He first came to the public eye when his father Vespasian became emperor late in 69. Vespasian gave Domitian important titles but little power. Instead, Vespasian seemed to favor his older son, Titus.

When Vespasian died in 79, Titus became emperor, and Domitian constantly insulted him. Titus died unexpectedly in 81. Some people suspected Domitian of treachery, but there is no evidence that he was involved in his brother's death. In any event, Domitian became emperor, but he lacked the training for this position that his father and brother had received.

Domitian sought autocratic power. During the first eight years of his reign, he appointed himself consul every year. In his lifetime he held the consulship 17 times, more than any Roman emperor before him. In 85 he named himself censor for life. He ignored the Roman Senate and alienated the senators.

However, Domitian did not become completely tyrannical until after the revolt, in 88, of one of his provincial governors, the senator Lucius Antonius Saturninus. Frightened by this revolt, Domitian afterward systematically purged the Senate of all those he suspected of disloyalty. Domitian also turned against the philosophers because they supported the Senate. In 89 he banished them from Rome and, in 95, from Italy. Among their number were Epictetus and Dio Chrysostom.

Domitian was assassinated on Sept. 18, 96, after his wife and his Praetorian prefect turned against him and plotted with members of the Senate to kill him. When he died, the Senate officially damned his memory.

Although Domitian was a tyrant, in many ways he was a good administrator. During his reign he strengthened the defenses of the frontiers and reorganized the governmental bureaucracy. He tried to stimulate the economy of the empire. He also attempted to restore the old Roman paganism by restricting the spread of the Oriental religions, Judaism, and Christianity. Although there is no evidence of widespread persecution of Christianity during his reign, there is some indication of a limited persecution at Rome. In early Christian literature, Domitian was frequently depicted as a persecutor.

There is no doubt that Domitian encouraged the spread of Roman paganism by building new temples and restoring old ones. He also promoted the arts and literature and retained the famous rhetorician Quintilian on the imperial payroll. Unfortunately, his reign was severely marred by his treatment of the senatorial aristocracy. If he had been more tolerant, he would have been one of Rome's better emperors.

ARTHER FERRILL, *University of Washington*

Further Reading: Salmon, E. T., *A History of the Roman World, 30 B.C.–A.D. 138,* 3d ed. (New York 1959).

DOMITILIA, dom-ə-til'ē-ə, **Saint Flavia,** a pagan Roman of noble birth, who embraced the Christian religion in the latter part of the 1st century. Few details of her life are known with certainty. She was closely related to the three Flavian emperors—Vespasian, Titus, and Domitian. Her husband, the Roman consul Flavius Clemens, died as a Christian martyr during the reign (81–96) of Domitian.

After Flavius' death she became a Christian and a church benefactor. According to one account, she was banished to one of the Pontine Islands off Naples. In another she and two foster sisters, Euphrosyne and Theodora, were put to death, because of their faith, at the seaport of Terracina, north of Naples. A cemetery on the Ardeatine Way, still used by Christians in the 4th century, was named for St. Domitilla (as her name is often spelled). Her feast is observed on May 12 with that of St. Achilleus and St. Nereus, who were martyred during the reign (54–68) of Nero.

MARION A. HABIG, O.F.M.
St. Augustine Friary, Chicago, Ill.

DOMRÉMY-LA-PUCELLE, dōn-rā-mē' là pü-sel', is a small village in eastern France, in the Vosges department of Lorraine. It is situated on the Meuse River, 175 miles (280 km) east of Paris. It was the birthplace of Joan of Arc (Jan. 6, 1412); the house in which she was born has been preserved, and there is a museum devoted to her life. The village church has been greatly modified, but it preserves the 12th century font where the heroine was baptized, and it contains a holy-water basin and a statue of St. Margaret, which date from the time of Joan of Arc. Near the village is the Basilica of St. Joan of Arc, built in the 1880's. Population: (1962) 171.

DON CARLOS, dôn kär'lōs, an opera in five acts by Giuseppe Verdi (q.v.), was introduced in Paris on March 11, 1867. The libretto by François Joseph Méry and Camille du Locle was based on Schiller's play *Don Carlos* (1787). In 1884, Verdi revised the opera in four acts; in 1887 he rearranged it in five acts.

The Spanish prince Don Carlos (tenor) loves the French princess Elizabeth (soprano), but their love is considered incestuous when a political marriage makes Elizabeth the wife of Carlos' father, Philip II (bass). When Princess Eboli (mezzo-soprano) falls in love with Carlos and is rejected by him, she reveals to Philip his son's love for Philip's wife. Rodrigo (baritone), a humanitarian and good friend to Carlos, sacrifices his life for Carlos, after the Grand Inquisitor (bass) has warned the King that both Carlos and Rodrigo are a threat to Spain and Catholicism. Carlos takes a last farewell of Elizabeth, but his grandfather, Charles V (bass), materializes as a monk and saves him from the fury of King and church.

The score, for all its unrelievedly somber color, reveals Verdi's profound understanding of human suffering. The opera contains six absorbing characters and some very powerful music. Particularly imposing are Philip's monologue, the scene between the King and the Inquisitor, Eboli's aria of repentance (*O don fatale!*), and Elizabeth's aria that opens the last act.

WILLIAM ASHBROOK, *Author of "Donizetti"*

DON COSSACKS. See COSSACKS.

DON GIOVANNI, don jō-vä'nē, is an opera in two acts by Wolfgang Amadeus Mozart, with a libretto by Lorenzo da Ponte. It was first performed on Oct. 29, 1787, in Prague, with Mozart conducting. Da Ponte was present at the opera's American première, in New York City, on May 23, 1826.

Don Giovanni is based on the story of the notorious Don Juan Tenorio. It is not certain that this person ever existed, but tales of his amorous adventures were circulating even before the appearance of the play *El burlador de Sevilla* (1630). Molère and Goldoni also wrote plays on Don Juan, as did Mozart's contemporary Giovanni Bertati, whose work was turned into an opera by Giuseppe Gazzaniga shortly before Mozart wrote his version.

Don Giovanni is a triumphant fusion of tragic and comic elements—Mozart's own designation, "dramma giocoso" ("merry drama"), is extraordinarily apt. The opera, whose appeal is universal, reveals an astonishing variety of human emotions, frailties, and philosophies. It is a long work with many scene changes, but because of the flashing contrasts of comic and tragic, dark and light, sublime and frivolous, audience interest never slackens.

Musically, *Don Giovanni* is so rich in superlative inspiration that most listeners agree with Richard Wagner's judgment that every passage in the opera is perfect. Among the outstanding 20th century interpreters of the title role have been Victor Maurel, Maurice Renaud, Antonio Scotti, Ezio Pinza, and Cesare Siepi.

The Story. *Don Giovanni* takes place about the middle of the 17th century. In the first scene, the licentious Don is compelled to make a hasty retreat from the Commendatore's palace, where he has failed in his attempted seduction of Donna Anna, the Commendatore's daughter. Challenged to a duel by the Commendatore, the Don slays the gallant old man and escapes, then immediately embarks on an adventure with the fetching peasant girl Zerlina. This affair is thwarted, however, by the unexpected appearance of Donna Elvira, an early and steadfast flame of Giovanni's, who does not want Zerlina to fall victim to the Don's perfidious ways. The Don invites the townspeople to a feast in his palace, hoping that there he will have an opportunity to complete his conquest. Zerlina, however, resists him, and her screams attract the guests, among them Donna Anna, her suitor Don Ottavio, and Donna Elvira —all in disguise. Giovanni fails to divert their suspicion to his rascally servant Leporello and is forced to fight his way through the angry crowd.

In Act II, Don Giovanni meets Leporello in a cemetery, where the statue of the dead Commendatore suddenly speaks, demanding silence. Giovanni, undaunted, orders his frightened servant to invite the statue to dinner that evening. To the Don's consternation and Leporello's absolute horror, the statue nods his acceptance. A few hours later, the Don is enjoying a sumptuous meal to the accompaniment of gay music. He turns a deaf ear to Elvira's plea that he mend his ways. Suddenly, amid terrifying sounds, the statue enters and in sepulchral tones orders Giovanni to repent his sins. Giovanni refuses, whereupon flames engulf the house and the seducer is dragged into hell. The opera ends with the other principals rejoicing in his fate.

GEORGE JELLINEK
Music Director, Radio Station WQXR, New York

DON JUAN, dôn hwän, a legendary hero, who symbolizes the dashing, dissolute, and irresistible lover, driven by boundless lust to conquer one woman after another. He has appeared in more literary reincarnations than any of the other three great heroes in world fiction—Hamlet, Faust, and Don Quixote.

Don Juan never pauses to fall in love, for to do so would be to destroy the very nature of his being. After each seduction, he abandons the woman and promptly goes on to another adventure. Erotic, virile, and passionate, Don Juan embodies the universal triumph of sensuality.

Early Dramatic Treatments. Don Juan was a figure in the folklore of many European countries before he first appeared in literature in the play *El burlador de Sevilla y convidado de piedra* (1630), probably by the Spanish monk Tirso de Molina. In this drama, Don Juan has four amorous adventures. Three end in seduction; the fourth ends in the slaying by the Don of the father of an aristocratic girl who barely escapes being seduced. At the play's close, the stone statue of the murdered man grasps Don Juan's hand and casts him into Hell without giving him time to have a priest called for confession. A 17th century Spanish audience would have been sympathetic toward this Don, a believer in God but a bad Christian for thinking that the reckoning for his actions would be postponed indefinitely. He is also honorable, according to Spanish tradition, because he keeps his word to men.

From Spain, the Don Juan legend passed to Italy, where it became popular in the repertoires of the *commedia dell'arte*. Gradually, as the comic elements rather than the religious and moral aspects of the legend were stressed, the figure of Don Juan deteriorated. In France, Molière restored some dignity to Don Juan's image in his play *Dom Juan ou le festin de pierre* (1665). Unlike Tirso de Molina's hero, who is purely a man of action, Molière's Don Juan analyzes his deeds and is less passionate.

Later Literary Treatments. In the 19th century, Don Juan was viewed as a more responsible individual, who was at least capable of love. Among the most famous 19th century literary interpretations of the legend are E. T. A. Hoffmann's tale *Don Juan* (1813), Byron's satirical epic poem *Don Juan* (1819–1824), and José Zorrilla's play *Don Juan Tenorio* (1844). In Zorrilla's version, Don Juan is saved through the love of a noble and generous woman.

One of the most important 20th century literary versions of the legend is Shaw's *Man and Superman* (1903). In the play's "Don Juan in Hell" sequence, the libertine is shown as a wit and philosopher, expounding on the forces behind love and marriage. Another 20th century interpretation, Max Frisch's drama *Don Juan, or the Love of Geometry* (1953), turns the Don into a misogynist.

The "Don" in Music and Art. The most famous treatment of Don Juan in music is Mozart's operatic masterpiece *Don Giovanni* (1787). Another important musical portrayal is Richard Strauss' tone poem *Don Juan* (1889). The 19th century artist Delacroix painted scenes from the legend, notably *La barque de Don Juan*.

DONALD W. BLEZNICK, *University of Cincinnati*

Further Reading: Mandel, Oscar, ed., *The Theatre of Don Juan: A Collection of Plays and Views, 1630–1963* (Lincoln, Nebr., 1963); Weinstein, Leo, *The Metamorphoses of Don Juan* (Stanford 1959).

DON JUAN, don jōō'ən, is a mock-epic verse satire by the English romantic poet Lord Byron (q.v.), first published between 1819 and 1824. The looseness of the ottava rima form (borrowed from the Italian satiric writers Casti, Berni, and Pulci) allowed the author free scope for facetious comments on life and manners while narrating picaresque adventures. Byron converted the rake of the original Don Juan legend into an innocent who serves as a norm against which the absurdities of the world are to be viewed. *Don Juan* runs the gamut of Byronic attitudes. From the deepest melancholy and the highest flights of romantic longing it descends to the most outrageous deflation of sentiment and the frankest realism in the exposure of hypocrisy in love, war, and religion. The colloquial ease and unpretentious sincerity of the poem lift it in modern critical esteem above Byron's outpourings of the romantic ego in *Childe Harold,* and it is generally acknowledged as his masterpiece.

The Story. The adventures of the hero begin in his native Seville, where his platonic adolescent love for the slightly older Donna Julia ends in a farcical seduction not without pathos. Juan, sent on his travels to escape the scandal, is shipwrecked, witnesses but does not participate in cannibalism, and is cast on an Aegean island where he has an idyllic love affair with a pirate's daughter, Haidée—"Half-naked, loving, natural, and Greek." The beauty of this "natural love" comes to an end when the pirate returns and sends Juan in a galley to the slave market at Constantinople. He is purchased for the pleasure of the Sultana, spends a night in the harem disguised as an odalisque, then escapes to join the Russian army besieging the Turks at Ismail. Having become hero more by accident than design, he is sent with dispatches to Catherine the Great of Russia, who lavishes her favors on him. But he languishes in "Royalty's vast arms" and, after an illness, is sent by Catherine on a diplomatic mission to England. There Juan has an opportunity to observe "those haughty tradesmen," and the unfinished story leaves him the center of various intrigues at an English country house. Byron broke off with the 14th stanza of the 17th canto, concluding, "I leave the thing a problem, like all things."

Critique. The true value of *Don Juan* is in the digressions, and as a slice of life it is complete. Byron had begun the poem with the express purpose of being "a little quietly facetious upon every thing." But he soon took it more seriously as a "satire upon abuses" in society. He deliberately took his hero into various situations and climates in order to "show the different ridicules of the society in each of those countries."

But Juan for the most part is only a puppet, albeit one with some of the idealized qualities Byron ascribed to his own innocent youth, and the author steps on the stage so often as to steal the show and become himself the protagonist, a philosophical and humorous puppeteer, who adds his commentary with a disarming frankness and a sharp wit. The poem reflects every mood of Byron's mobile mind. The themes are as varied as those in his vivacious letters: his dislike for learned ladies ("Oh! ye lords of ladies intellectual,/Inform us truly, have they not henpecked you all?"); his skeptical view of love and marriage ("Think you, if Laura had been Petrarch's wife,/He would have written sonnets all his life?"); his picture of martial glory as the romantically cloaked business of butchery; his war with "all who war/ With thought"; his recollections of the delights, as well as the boredom and hypocrisy, of English society.

The eight lines of the ottava rima stanza permitted the freedom that Byron needed for his mock epic, giving pliancy to the ironic deflation of commonly accepted attitudes and sentiments. The conversational idiom, the unheroic portraits of the characters, the epigrammatic wit, the comic rhymes in the final couplets (which heighten the satiric effect)—all endow his verse with a living freshness in sharp contrast with the poetic conventions of his day.

More than Wordsworth, Byron spoke the language of men—not the language of inspired poetry, but that of reason and honest feeling. When his friends urged him to write some serious work worthy of his talents, he replied: "You have so many '*divine*' poems, is it nothing to have written a *Human* one? without any of your worn-out machinery." He eschewed the "grand style" and wrote something more flexible and human. It is as an epic of modern man, who, despite romantic longings, has reluctantly come to terms with the world as it is—and has found it amusing—that *Don Juan* takes its place as a classic among the works of the 19th century.

LESLIE A. MARCHAND
Author of "Byron: A Biography"

DON JUAN, dôn zhü-än', is a play by the French dramatist Molière (q.v.). It was composed in haste in 1664 and first acted in February 1665. Its performance was stopped the following month when strong opposition to the allegedly impious comedy developed in conservative and clerical circles in Paris.

Molière was probably unaware of the original Spanish play (published 1630) by the monk Tirso de Molina and of an Italian adaptation of the Spanish work, but he may have been familiar with two French adaptations of the Italian version—by Claude de Villiers in 1659 and Nicolas Dorimond in 1661. When the court forbade performances of Molière's *Tartuffe* as a danger to religion, the playwright hurriedly put together the loose scenes that make up *Don Juan* (in full, as Molière spelled it, *Dom Juan ou le festin de pierre*). He retained the supernatural elements of the legend and the libertine Don's final punishment when the Commander's statue upbraids him and hell engulfs him. But he made the character comical as well and placed him in a French context as a libertine seducing simple women with fine words, carrying off Elvire, saving her brother from bandits, insulting his own father, and mocking piety. He also made Sganarelle, the earthy, superstitious servant, an entertaining foil to his impious master.

The supernatural element in the play and the mystery with which Molière endowed Don Juan—the seeker after an eternal feminine ideal never to be possessed on earth—are largely responsible for the drama's continued hold on audiences. Molière's protagonist is not merely a sadist and a conqueror of the other sex but also an unbeliever asserting an Epicurean view of life against both religious hypocrisy and true piety.

HENRI PEYRE
Yale University

Further Reading: Guicharnaud, Jacques, *Molière: une aventure théâtrale* (Paris 1963); Moore, Will G., *Molière: A New Criticism* (New York 1949).

DON QUIXOTE, dôn kē-hô'te, a novel by the Spanish author Miguel de Cervantes Saavedra (see CERVANTES), published in two parts in 1605 and 1615. The full title is *El ingenioso hidalgo Don Quixote de la Mancha* (*The Ingenious Gentleman Don Quixote de la Mancha*). It is one of the world's greatest and best-loved books and has been reprinted, in Spanish and in translation, more often than any other novel in history. A social satire, philosophic tale, adventure story, comedy, and portrait of an eccentric, idealistic, and delightful man, *Don Quixote* is appealing on various levels, to adults and to children. With his compassionate, humorous, and warmly human portrayal of Don Quixote and his squire Sancho Panza, Cervantes not only penetrated the reality of Spanish life in his time but created two supremely real characters, who live out the universal problems of human experience.

The first part, published in Madrid in January 1605, was an immediate success. During Cervantes' lifetime, 16 editions were published, including translations into English (1612) and French (1614). The publication of a spurious continuation in 1614, by a certain Avellaneda, spurred Cervantes to finish the second part of the work, which was published at the end of 1615.

Background and Sources. In many ways, Cervantes' life would be deemed a failure if judged by worldly standards. For much of his life he held a variety of ill-paid administrative posts and was continually plagued with financial reversals, some of which resulted in imprisonment. Although he had earlier written poetry and moderately successful plays, Cervantes did not start on his masterpiece until he was well into middle age. Disillusioned, worldly-wise, but unembittered, he probably began to compose *Don Quixote* while in prison in 1597.

Cervantes' original intent was most likely to parody the novels of chivalry that had achieved great popularity in the 16th century. The prologue to Part 1 of the work announces that it is "an invective against books of chivalry," and Cervantes' indebtedness to chivalric romances, including Montalvo's *Amadis of Gaul* and Francisco de Moraes' *Palmerin of England*, is obvious in the work. Several 19th century critics suggested that the Don may have been modeled after a real person. Critics in the 20th century have adduced literary antecedents for the Don. Ramón Menéndez Pidal traced the source of the novel's main character to the anonymous short play *Entremés de los romances*, in which the protagonist, Bartolo, becomes mad as a result of reading Spanish ballads.

Plot. Don Quixote, a 50-year-old gentleman of modest means and an avid reader of romances, fancies himself a knight errant and decides to right injustice in the world. Swearing allegiance to his lady, whom he calls Dulcinea del Toboso though she actually is a local farm girl named Aldonza Lorenzo, he sets out mounted on Rocinante, an old horse. During his first adventure, he stops at an inn believing it to be a castle, is beaten by a servant there, and is finally taken home by a farmer from his own town. Undaunted, he sets out again, this time with the peasant Sancho Panza, who thereafter serves as his squire.

Don Quixote distorts reality in order to have all episodes conform to a chivalric mold. He mistakes windmills for giants and is beaten when he attacks them. He sees two flocks of sheep as

FRITZ HENLE, FROM PHOTO RESEARCHERS

DON QUIXOTE and Sancho Panza, with Cervantes above them: a sculpture group in Plaza de España, Madrid.

two contending armies and enters the fray. The outraged shepherds shower him with stones and knock him off his horse. When he liberates a chain of galley slaves, who he thinks are unjustly condemned, they insult Dulcinea and stone him to the ground. At the end of Part 1, Don Quixote, imprisoned in a wooden cage, is taken back home.

Following the literary conventions of his time, Cervantes inserted several extraneous narrative episodes into Part 1. These include the pastoral story of Marcela and Crisóstomo and the exemplary tale about foolish curiosity. In response to readers' criticism, Cervantes decided to omit digressive tales in the second part.

In Part 2, Sampson Carrasco, a neighbor, in order to cure Don Quixote of his madness, urges him to undertake a third sally. He plans to conquer the Don in knightly combat and thus require him to return home. This time he meets a real lion, but the lion fails to attack and will not cooperate with Quixote in his effort to display his valor. Master Peter's puppet show seems so real that the Don's knightly zeal impels him to attack those puppets that he believes to be heathen Moors. Several practical jokes are played on Don Quixote and Sancho in the palace of the Duke and Duchess, who permit the squire to govern the imaginary Island of Barataria, actually a village under their rule. Meanwhile, the well-intentioned Carrasco, disguising himself as the Knight of the Mirrors, confronts the Don but is defeated. Inspired now more by a desire for revenge than by charity, Carrasco, toward the end of the novel, disguises himself as the Knight of the White Moon, again encounters the Don, and defeats him. Carrasco then imposes upon him the condition that he renounce his adventures for a year. After arriving home in the midst of sad thoughts, Don Quixote becomes ill. To the sorrow and dismay of Sancho, he confesses the folly of his past adventures just before he dies.

Characterization and Style. The 20th century critic Angel del Río, in commenting on the duality that exists in *Don Quixote,* pointed out the tension and equilibrium in such dichotomies as being-seeming, madness-sanity, drama-comedy, and reality-fantasy. The quintessence of the antithetical duality that informs the novel is found in the relationship between the Don and Sancho. Don Quixote is the noble and selfless reformer completely devoted to the ideals of knight errantry. Materialism, on the other hand, motivates Sancho's actions during most of the novel. However, he also exhibits sterling moral qualities in his loyalty to his master, in his concern for his family's welfare, and in his sincerity and generosity. The two characters affect and complement each other, and viewed together they are a composite of every human being, since all men possess "quixotic" and materialistic elements in varying degrees. At the novel's end the two men reverse their roles, as the master renounces his life of chivalry and Sancho, now thoroughly imbued with quixotic ideals, pleads with the Don to resume his knightly career.

The minor characters, drawn from all levels of Spanish society, are also superbly realized. While most of the novel is written in a simple, realistic, and stately style, Cervantes at times affects the archaic style of the romances of chivalry.

Critical Interpretation and Influence. English literary critics of the 18th century admired *Don Quixote,* and the influence of Cervantes' satire is discernible in the novels of Fielding and Smollett. German romanticists, such as the Schlegel brothers, considered Don Quixote the supreme example of the romantic man in this world. In the 19th century, the influence of Cervantes can be detected in the novels of many authors, including Dickens, Balzac, Flaubert, Galdós, Dostoyevsky, and Tolstoy. The Spanish writers of the "Generation of 1898" accorded a racial symbolism to the figure of Don Quixote. For Ortega y Gasset, the noted 20th century Spanish philosopher, the Don embodied the problem of Spanish destiny. In the 20th century, rigorous scholarship has shed new light on the genesis, structure, and style of *Don Quixote.* Notable 20th century critics of the work have included Manuel Durán, Mark Van Doren, Leo Spitzer, Richard L. Predmore, and Aubrey F. G. Bell.

Don Quixote in the Arts. Among the artists who have depicted scenes from the novel are Daumier, Goya, Doré, and Picasso. Noteworthy musical compositions include Richard Strauss' tone poem *Don Quixote,* Massenet's opera *Don Quichotte,* and Manuel de Falla's opera *Retablo de maese Pedro.* There have been outstanding cinematic productions of *Don Quixote* in Spain (1947) and Russia (1957). A notable American representation of Cervantes' immortal work was Dale Wasserman's musical play, *Man of La Mancha* (1965), a highly successful interpretation of the novel in which the identities of Cervantes and Don Quixote are interwoven and merged. In the same year the choreographer George Balanchine masterfully performed the title role in the ballet *Don Quixote,* his full-length version of the shorter Petipa-Minkus work (1869).

DONALD W. BLEZNICK
University of Cincinnati

Further Reading: *Don Quixote* has been published in a critical edition by F. Rodríguez Marín, rev. ed., 10 vols. (Madrid 1947–1949). English translations include those by Samuel Putnam (New York 1949) and John M. Cohen (London 1950). See also bibliography for CERVANTES, MIGUEL DE.

DON RIVER, dôn, in the USSR, in the European part of the Russian republic. Its drainage basin of 160,000 square miles (414,400 sq km) lies between the Volga in the east and the Dnieper in the west. About 1,200 miles (1,900 km) in length, the Don rises south of Moscow near the city of Novomoskovsk and flows southeast until it approaches to within 35 miles (56 km) of the Volga at Volgograd; then it curves away to the southwest and flows past Rostov into the Sea of Azov. A typical, lazy-flowing steppe river, the Don rises at an elevation of only 630 feet (190 meters); because of its gentle slope, it has become known as the "quiet Don."

The Don freezes over for 100 to 125 days, from November to March. During the navigation season, shallow-draft vessels can go 840 miles (1,350 km) up the river and, during the spring floods, 150 miles (240 km) beyond to the area of Voronezh. The great Tsimlyansk Reservoir, completed in 1952 at the bend in the river near the Volga, has regularized the annual flow of the river, which has a low stage in August and September. The reservoir and the Volga-Don Canal, also opened in 1952, have made the lower course of the Don a major shipping artery. It carries lumber from the upper Volga Basin and coal from the Donets Basin, to which it is linked by its chief tributary, the Donets. The Don's lower reaches, especially its delta on the Sea of Azov, have valuable fisheries.

The ancient name of the river was the Tanaïs, and the Tatars knew it as the Duna. The Don Basin lay in the path of the Tatars and other nomadic peoples who swept from Asia into Europe in the Middle Ages. In the 16th century, the Don Basin began to be settled by the Cossacks, Russian adventurers who sought to escape czarist control in the still undeveloped steppe. The Don Cossacks later became a military caste who furthered Russian expansion. After the revolution of 1917, the independent-minded Don Cossacks resisted Soviet rule until early 1920.

THEODORE SHABAD, *Editor of "Soviet Geography"*

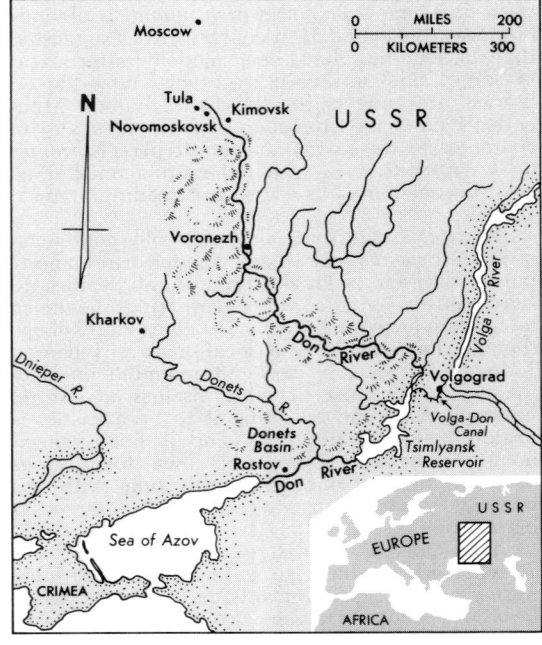

DONALD, David Herbert (1920–   ), American historian. He was born on Oct. 1, 1920, in Goodman, Miss. He received his B. A. (1941) from Millsaps College and his Ph. D. (1946) from the University of Illinois. A dynamic undergraduate lecturer, he also earned the profound loyalty of his graduate students at Columbia, Princeton, and, after 1962, at Johns Hopkins University.

Donald demonstrated his competence in both the traditional and more innovative techniques of historical writing. His works include *Lincoln's Herndon* (1948), *Lincoln Reconsidered* (1956), *Charles Sumner and the Coming of the Civil War* (1960), and, with J. G. Randall, *The Civil War and Reconstruction* (1961). While imaginative in their application of the techniques of social science to history, Donald's writings reveal a conservative bias. His craftsmanship in combining literary style with probing analysis won him the Pulitzer Prize for his life of Sumner, but he was criticized for his hostility toward Sumner and other antislavery reformers. But a later book, *The Politics of Reconstruction, 1863–1867* (1965), escaped controversy.

BERTRAM WYATT-BROWN
Case Western Reserve University

DONATELLO, dō-nä-tel'lō (1386?–1466), Florentine sculptor, who, with Lorenzo Ghiberti and Nanni di Banco, was one of the founders of Italian Renaissance sculpture. Of the three, Donatello most fully investigated such basic artistic problems of the time as the relationship of form to space and the opposing claims of realism and idealism. His strongly independent solutions of these problems exerted great influence on the general development of Renaissance art.

Early Career. Precise details of Donatello's personal life and early career are scarce. His real name was Donato; he was born in Florence, probably in 1386, the son of Niccolò di Betto di Bardo, a wool comber. Donatello was trained initially as a goldsmith, but at 17 he was working in the studio of Lorenzo Ghiberti, where he assisted in finishing the famous bronze north doors of the Baptistery in Florence. In 1407 he went to the workshop of the Duomo (cathedral), where the presence of Nanni di Banco and Brunelleschi did much to orient his style and interests.

The refined elegance of Donatello's first authenticated work, the marble *David* (1408; Bargello, Florence), reflects his apprenticeship to Ghiberti and Nanni. Yet it also asserts Donatello's greater concern for realism, a characteristic that continued to develop throughout his career. Other works of his early career in Florence are the series of monumental figures for the Duomo and the Orsanmichele. A trip to Rome with Brunelleschi, probably in 1409, exposed Donatello to classical art with its use of movement and handling of light and shade. The result is apparent in his *St. George* (1415–1417; Museo Nazionale, Florence), executed for the Orsanmichele. Classical in attitude but not classicistic in style, the saint stands alert and tense, independent of all architectural support. A physical reality, involved with the space around him, he is also the ideal Renaissance champion.

In the relief *St. George Slaying the Dragon* (Orsanmichele), originally part of the base of the statue of St. George, Donatello introduced a revolutionary way of handling space. Although the carving is very shallow, it gives the illusion

ALINARI—ART REFERENCE BUREAU
DONATELLO'S *Dancing Putti* (a detail appears above) adorns the Singing Gallery of the Duomo of Florence.

of great depth through subtle and varied surface modulations. It is one of the early Renaissance experiments with perspective in relief sculpture, although its depth is determined by shades of light and dark rather than by the mathematically plotted perspective that was being formulated by Brunelleschi.

For the campanile of the Duomo, Donatello executed a series of figures that includes *Il Pensieroso, Prophet with a Scroll, Il Zuccone, Sacrifice of Isaac,* and *Habukkuk.* In these works he explored the whole range of tragic expression to such depths that their often cruelly realistic portrayals acquire great universal significance. Because they were executed over a long period of time—from about 1416 to 1439—they show the development of Donatello's interest in chiaroscuro, which was already evident in his *St. John the Evangelist* (commissioned 1408; Museo dell'-Opera del Duomo) and in *St. Mark* (commissioned 1411; Orsanmichele). For the later prophets, Donatello seems to have relied both on Roman prototypes and on some Gothic sculpture with its agitated, deeply carved draperies.

Middle Career. In the years between 1420 and 1430, Donatello tried to reconcile his interest in the classical style of Brunelleschi with his own greater realism. He shared a workshop with Michelozzo di Bartolommeo and received many commissions for monumental tombs and for statues in architectural settings. The détente in Donatello's growing realism is best exemplified in the *St. Louis of Toulouse* (about 1423–1425; Museo dell'Opera, Santa Croce), originally executed for the Orsanmichele. The carving is softer, subtler, and more subdued than in the prophets to harmonize better with its architectural setting. Quiet, rather dreamy emotional qualities also predominate in the *Tomb of Baldassare Coscia* (1425–1427; Baptistery, Florence) and in the *Tomb of Rinaldo Brancacci* (1427; Church of Sant'Angelo a Nilo, Naples).

Donatello's relief sculpture of this period also pays stricter heed to the perspective theories of Brunelleschi. But eventually these theories proved too restrictive, and for *Il Zuccone* (1423–1425), also called "Pumpkin Head," and *Habakkuk* (about 1427–1435; Museo dell'Opera del Duomo), the last of the campanile prophets, he returned to agitated forms and a great play of light and dark. This movement and irrational balance finally developed into an outright opposition to Brunelleschi's theories in the work executed by Donatello between 1430 and 1440.

A second trip to Rome, with Michelozzo in 1432–1433, reinforced Donatello's new direction. In Rome he and Michelozzo worked on the reliefs for the tabernacle of the sacrament in the Sacristy of the Beneficiati in St. Peter's. He studied early Christian, medieval, Romanesque, and Byzantine frescoes and mosaics, and he may have met Leon Battista Alberti, whose recently published treatise on painting defined form as motion—a definition that conformed to Donatello's concept of sculptural form.

When he returned to Florence, Donatello executed the wildly dancing cherub reliefs for the cantoria of the Duomo (1433–1439; Museo dell'Opera del Duomo) and the outdoor pulpit for the Prato Cathedral (1433–1438). These works illustrate his renewed interest in the expressive properties of light and movement, his divergence from the contemporary attitude toward classical art, and his new interest in high relief. The sculpture he did for Brunelleschi's Old Sacristy of the Church of San Lorenzo (1435–1443) also reflects his Roman experience and his break with Brunelleschi's theories. His four stucco tondi of the evangelists are full of classical decorative motifs, but their arrangement recalls medieval compositions. The same is true of Donatello's bronze *Door of the Apostles* and *Door of the Martyrs*, also at San Lorenzo. The energetic modeling disrupts the quiet classicism of the surrounding architecture in the same way as the restless play of light on the surface of his bronze *David* (c. 1432; Bargello, Florence) distracts from its classical source.

Padua. At the peak of his success, Donatello quit Florence for Padua, where he stayed from 1443 to 1454. His Paduan works are perhaps his most ambitious in scale. In the giant sculptural-architectural group for the high altar of St. Anthony, he presents *The Virgin and Child with Saints* (1450) with the formality and piety of a medieval altarpiece. Dismantled in the 16th century, it originally combined shallow reliefs and freestanding sculpture, in marble and in bronze. In this work Donatello set forth his religious philosophy of the attainment of the sublime through death.

The Gattamelata monument (1447–1453) in Padua, a portrait statue of the Venetian condottiere Erasmo da Narni, reintroduced into Renaissance art the equestrian monument used by the Romans for the glorification of heroes. Its classical model perhaps explains the greater degree of idealism to which Donatello reverted for this work.

Return to Florence. When Donatello returned to Florence in 1454, the artistic climate had changed and was alien to his style. In contrast to the graceful and polished styles of Ghiberti, Antonio Rosellino, and Desiderio da Settignano, Donatello's work seems ruggedly expressionistic, complex, and deeply introspective. The *Magdalene* (1455; Baptistery, Florence) is typical. Siena, unchanged since the Middle Ages, provided him with a more sympathetic environment, and from 1457 to 1461 he worked there.

The bronze reliefs for the two pulpits in the Church of San Lorenzo are typical of Donatello's last Florentine works. They were unfinished when he died in Florence on Dec. 13, 1466. Their realism is exaggerated, almost abstracted, the better to express the absolute tragedy and soul-wrenching emotion of the Passion.

Donatello's concept of naturalism, which embodied both lyrical and expressionistic qualities, together with his theory that light and motion are inherent attributes of form, had a great influence on painters and architects as well as on sculptors. Such diverse artists as Fra Filippo Lippi, Domenico Veneziano, Botticelli, and Andrea del Verrochio benefited from his example. It was with Michelangelo, however, that his entire achievement came to fruition.

MERRIBELL PARSONS
Institute of Fine Arts, New York

Bibliography

Castelfranco, Giorgio, *Donatello*, tr. by R. H. Boothroyd (Clifton, N. J., 1965).
Cecchi, Emilio, *Donatello* (Rome 1942).
Cruttwell, Maud, *Donatello* (London 1911).
Goldscheider, Ludwig, *Donatello* (New York 1941).
Janson, Horst W., *The Sculpture of Donatello*, 2d ed. (Princeton 1963).
Planiscig, Leo, *Donatello* (Vienna 1939).
Schubring, Paul, *Donatello*, 2d ed. (Stuttgart 1922).

DONATI, dō-nä′tē, **Giovanni Battista** (1826–1873), Italian astronomer, who is noted for his work on comets. Born in Pisa on Dec. 16, 1826, he went to Florence in 1852 as assistant in the observatory where he was to spend his whole working life. There he discovered the brilliant comet of 1858, which bears his name, and five other comets.

Following the epochal establishment of the principles of spectroscopy by Gustav Kirchhoff and Robert Bunsen in 1859, Donati sought to apply the new tool to astronomical purposes. His pioneering attempt to analyze starlight in 1860 was a comparative failure, but it stimulated others and guided them in making the instrumental improvements necessary to accomplish the task. In 1864 he performed the first spectroscopic analysis of a comet and proved from its bright-band spectrum that it was composed of glowing gas, rather than shining by reflected light as had previously been assumed. In the same year he was appointed director of the Florence observatory. He served as its director until his death in Florence on Sept. 20, 1873.

VICTOR E. THOREN, *Indiana University*

DONATION OF CONSTANTINE, kon′stən-tēn, is the spurious document by which Emperor Constantine I (reigned 306–337) was presumed to have granted Pope Sylvester I and his successors the Lateran Palace in Rome, imperial dignities and insignia, "and likewise all provinces, palaces, and districts of the city of Rome and Italy and of the regions of the West."

The Latin form of the title is *Constitutum Constantini*. The grant to the popes of imperial authority in the West was made supposedly on the occasion of Constantine's withdrawal to the new Eastern capital of Constantinople, and in gratitude to Sylvester for both baptizing him in Christianity and miraculously curing him of leprosy. That Sylvester had done these things for the Emperor was attested to by a late 5th century apocryphal *Legenda S. Silvestri*. It was this legend apparently that gave credence to the fabricated document.

The most famous forgery of the early Middle Ages, the Donation was probably produced between 750 and 800. There is considerable doubt about its origin. Internal evidence seems to indicate that it was the work of a cleric in the Roman Curia, but the fact that the earliest use made of it was by Frankish authors suggests that it may have originated in the Frankish Empire. The first pope to make use of the document was Leo IX in a letter to Michael Cerularius, patriarch of Constantinople, in 1054. The document lent support to papal claims of temporal lordship over central Italy and was accepted as genuine by both friends and enemies of the papacy throughout most of the Middle Ages. Because Rome was also the capital of the old Roman Empire, the popes at times were tempted to confuse theological claims and limited territorial rights with a pretended jurisdiction over the entire political order of Europe. Such pretensions appeared in the 8th century and reached their height during the reigns of Innocent IV (1243–1254) and Boniface VIII (1294–1303).

Emperor Otto III reigned (983–1002) was the first to repudiate the Donation as a fabrication. Innocent III (reigned 1198–1216) also dispensed with the charter as unnecessary. But critical rejection of the document did not come until the Renaissance, when Lorenzo Valla published his *De falso credita et ementita Constantini donatione declamatio* (1440). Although there were defenders of the Donation's authenticity as late as the 18th century, the falsity of the document is accepted at present by all authorities.

MICHAEL V. GANNON, *University of Florida*

Further Reading: Coleman, Christopher B., ed. and tr., *The Treatise of Lorenzo Valla on the Donation of Constantine* (New York 1922); Ullman, Walter, *Growth of Papal Government in the Middle Ages*, 2d ed., pp. 74–86 (London 1962).

DONATISM, don'ə-tiz-əm, was a 4th and 5th century Christian schismatic movement in North Africa. Theologically, Donatism claimed that the validity of a sacrament depended upon the state of grace of the minister who dispensed it.

The election of Caecilian as bishop of Carthage in 312 triggered the controversy. A rigorous minority charged that his consecration was invalid because Felix of Aptunga, one of the consecrating bishops, was a *traditor*, that is, one who escaped martyrdom during the Diocletian persecution by handing over the sacred books of the church. No *traditor*, in their view, could confer valid orders. The Numidian bishops rejected Caecilian and consecrated Majorinus in 312 and then Donatus, the moving spirit of Donatism, in 315.

Donatism raised the question of the relation of the empire to religious controversy, because the Donatists appealed three times to Emperor Constantine. He had three synods appointed (313, 314 and 316) to hear the case, and all of them found in favor of Caecilian. Rejecting these decisions, the Donatists questioned the right of the emperor to interfere in the church. Donatus appealed to the native North African population, and the controversy took on anti-Roman aspects. Constantine exiled the Donatist bishops, confiscated their property, and sent in an army.

When repressive policies failed, a tolerant attitude was adopted in 321. Thereafter, repression depended upon the policy of the incumbent emperor and the violence of the Donatists. Terrorist bands called Circumcellions roamed about, forcing conversions to Donatism. The controversy caused St. Augustine to clarify the theology of the church and the sacraments in order to reply properly to the Donatists. After fruitless conversations in Carthage to settle the dispute, the Donatists were outlawed by the empire again in 411. With the Vandal invasion of North Africa in the 5th century, Donatism began to decline. However, it continued to exist until the Muslim conquest of Africa in the 7th century.

ALFRED RUSH, C.SS.R.
Catholic University of America

DONATUS, dō-nā'təs, **Aelius,** Roman grammarian of the 4th century A.D. His famous *Ars grammatica* served as a standard elementary textbook for the study of Latin in the Middle Ages, when the word *Donet* or *Donat* came to be synonymous with any Latin grammar or other elementary treatise on the subject. He also wrote commentaries on the works of Terence and Virgil and was the teacher of St. Jerome, who made the Vulgate translation of the Bible.

DONAU. See DANUBE RIVER.

DONBAS. See DONETS BASIN.

DONCASTER, dong'kə-stər, in England, is a county borough in the West Riding of Yorkshire, on the Don River, 30 miles (48 km) south of York, in a coal-mining region. It has railroad shops and manufactures electrical equipment, agricultural machinery, and man-made fibers. Doncaster has been a transportation center since the Roman period, when it was called Danum. There has been horse racing at Doncaster since the 17th century; the St. Leger Stakes, dating from 1776, is run here in September. Population: (1961) 86,402.

DONEGAL, don'ē-gôl, in the northwestern corner of Ireland, is one of three counties of the province of Ulster that did not become part of Northern Ireland when Ireland was divided in 1920. Much of the county is mountainous, the granite Blue Stack Range being the most prominent hill formation. The soil is not rich; oats and potatoes are the main crops. There are a number of Irish-speaking areas along the rugged west coast of the county where the cottage industries noted for handmade woolens and handwoven tweeds are centered. Bacon curing and flour milling are leading industries of the county.

Donegal had a long association with the O'Donnell clan, whose castle was in the town of Donegal, a small seaport on the west coast. The castle, which is a national monument, has a square tower dating from 1505. Just south of the town are the ruins of the abbey of the Franciscan friars who in the early 17th century wrote the *Annals of the Four Masters*, a major chronicle of Irish history and legend. The county had a population of 113,842 in 1961. Population: (1966) 108,486.

THOMAS FITZGERALD
Formerly of Department of Education, Dublin

DONELSON, don'-əl-sən, **Andrew Jackson** (1799–1871), American political leader. He was born near Nashville, Tenn., on Aug. 25, 1799, and was brought up by his uncle, Andrew Jackson. After graduating from the U. S. Military Academy in 1820, he served as an aide to Jackson in Florida, then practiced law in Nashville. From 1829 to 1837 he was President Jackson's private secretary, and until her death in 1836, Donelson's wife, Emily, was the White House hostess.

Donelson conducted the negotiations to annex Texas (1844–1845). From 1846 to 1849 he was minister to Prussia, and in 1856 he was the vice-presidential candidate of the Know Nothing party. He opposed secession and refused to support the South in the Civil War. He died in Memphis on June 23, 1871.

DONETS BASIN, də-nyets', a major industrial region of the USSR, in the Ukraine and the Rostov oblast of the Russian republic. Situated south of the Donets River, for which it is named, the Donets Basin has an area of 12,000 square miles (30,000 sq km) and a population of about 10 million. It is one of the most highly urbanized areas of the USSR. The largest cities are Donetsk (formerly Stalino), Lugansk (formerly Voroshilovgrad), Gorlovka, Makeyevka, Zhdanov (formerly Mariupol), Kramatorsk, Konstantinovka, Kadiyevka (formerly Sergo), Kommunarsk (formerly Voroshilovsk), and Shakhty.

Geologically a coalfield, the Donets Basin produces both bituminous coal and anthracite. Coal production (more than 200 million tons a year in the late 1960's) has in turn fostered the development of iron and steel centers, based on coking coal from the Donets Basin and iron ore from Krivoi Rog. The basin accounts for about 20% of the Soviet Union's production of pig iron and steel. The steel industry supplies important fabricating and machine-building plants. There are also large chemical plants, based on local salt deposits, on coal-tar products, and on natural gas, which is brought in by pipeline. Other mineral resources include mercury (at Gorlovka), limestone (used for smelting), and building materials. Large coal-burning power plants provide electricity for the basin's industries.

The industrial development of the Donets Basin began in the 1870's, when coking coal began to replace charcoal as the fuel for iron and steel making. In the Soviet period, the Donets Basin remained the USSR's principal center of heavy industry despite the development of new industrial districts in the Urals, in Siberia, and in Kazakhstan.

THEODORE SHABAD
Editor of "Soviet Geography"

DONETS RIVER, də-nyets', in the USSR, in southern European Russia and the Ukraine. The Donets, which is 650 miles (1,050 km) long, is a tributary of the Don River (q.v.). It rises in the middle Russian uplands, north of Belgorod, and flows generally southeast along the northern edge of the Donets Basin to the Don. The Donets is significant principally as a source of water for the industries of the Donets Basin.

Navigation of the Donets (mainly for coal barges) is limited to the lower 130 miles (210 km) of the course, which is ice-free from March through October.

THEODORE SHABAD
Editor of "Soviet Geography"

DONETSK, də-nyetsk' is the capital of Donetsk oblast in the Ukrainian republic of the USSR. It is the largest city in the Donets Basin and a center of heavy industry, with coal mines, a large iron and steel plant, chemical plants, and metal-fabricating factories. The city's products include construction steel and mining equipment. Donetsk was affected by an industrial water shortage before the construction of a canal from the Donets River to the city in 1957–1958.

The industrial character of Donetsk is reflected in its educational institutions, which, in addition to a university, include a mining school and a coal research institute. The city also has theaters for opera, ballet, drama, and puppet shows, as well as a concert hall.

The modern development of Donetsk began in 1870, when a British entrepreneur named John Hughes founded the original ironworks. The city was called Yuzovka (a phonetic derivative of Hughes) until 1924, when it was renamed Stalino. The present name dates from 1961, when places named for Stalin were redesignated as part of the de-Stalinization policy.

Donetsk oblast, a political subdivision of the Ukraine, has an area of 10,800 square miles (26,500 sq km). It includes the western third of the Donets Basin and is one of the Soviet Union's principal heavy industrial districts, producing coal, iron and steel, chemicals, and machinery. The largest iron and steel center is Zhdanov (the former Mariupol), a port on the Sea of Azov. Other steel mills are at Donetsk, Makeyevka, Yenakiyevo (the former Ordzhonikidze), Kramatorsk, and Konstantinovka. Slavyansk and Artemovsk have salt-based chemical industries. Population: (1967 est.) of the city, 840,000; of the oblast, 4,856,000.

THEODORE SHABAD
Editor of "Soviet Geography"

DONGAN, dong'gən, **Thomas** (1634–1715), American colonial governor. Dongan was born in Castletown, Ireland, in 1634. He served in the English and French armies and as lieutenant governor of Tangier before James, Duke of York (the future James II), commissioned him governor of New York in 1682. An energetic administrator, Dongan provided defenses against French expansion and pursued English interests in establishing a protectorate over the Iroquois Indians, who controlled much of the North American fur trade. He also instituted a representative assembly, which was abolished by King James in 1685 after New York became a royal province.

Dongan's governorship was terminated in 1688, when the colony was incorporated into the Dominion of New England under Gov. Edmund Andros. Dongan remained in New York where, because he was a Roman Catholic, his presence helped spread rumors of a Catholic plot at the time of the "Glorious Revolution" in England. He returned to England in 1691, became Earl of Limerick in 1698, and died in London on Dec. 14, 1715.

CARL UBBELOHDE
Case Western Reserve University

DONGEN, dông'ən, **Kees van** (1877–1968), Dutch-born French painter. Cornélius van Dongen ("Kees" is a nickname) was born in Delfshaven, the Netherlands, on Jan. 26, 1877. Settling in Paris in 1897, he worked at various jobs while training himself as a painter. He contributed drawings to satirical papers, and from 1905 was influenced by the Fauvists in his paintings.

By the end of World War I, van Dongen had become a fashionable portraitist, though his portraits were generally unflattering and often cruel. Among the celebrated persons whose pictures he painted were Anatole France, King Leopold II of Belgium, Maurice Chevalier, and Brigitte Bardot.

In his landscapes, van Dongen used violent colors and a simple technique that reduced nature to its essential forms. He also illustrated books, including the complete works of Proust. He died at Monte Carlo on May 28, 1968.

DONGOLA, dong'gō-lə, is a town in Sudan, in the north central part of the country, on the west bank of the Nile River. The present town lies 90 miles (145 km) north of the site of old Dongola, which was situated on a hill overlooking the east bank of the Nile just above the great bend at Debba. Dongola was also the name of a former African kingdom. The Arabic form of the name is *Dunqulah*.

History. The strategic importance of old Dongola's commanding position on the Nile was recognized by the ancient Egyptians, who established a settlement there during the New Kingdom (1570–1075 B.C.). Old Dangola became prominent as the capital of Maqurra (also known as Dongola), one of the three Nubian kingdoms that appeared after the breakup of the larger kingdom of Meroë in the 4th century A.D. The Nubian kingdoms were Christianized between 543 and 575, and in the following century Maqurra absorbed the neighboring kingdom of Nobatia to the north.

The town was besieged in 652 by Islamic Arabs from Egypt under the leadership of Abd Allah Ibn Sad Ibn Abi Sarh. The Christian cathedral was destroyed, but the king of Maqurra and the Arab leader agreed to an armistice. Arab–Nubian relations were subsequently regularized by trade relations and an understanding that no Muslims were to settle in Nubia and no Nubians in Egypt. This peaceful relationship lasted for nearly six centuries.

So long as the Arabs ruled Egypt, peace was maintained on the Nubian frontier. But when the Mamlukes (Mamelukes) acquired control of the Nile delta, the Arab nomads settled in Upper Egypt and raided along the Maqurra border. Mamluke military expeditions devastated Maqurra in the 13th and 14th centuries, and Christian political authority was supplanted by the Mamlukes' Muslim institutions by 1400.

In the 16th century a mysterious people, the Funj, established control over the middle Nile, with the headquarters of their northern province at Dongola. However, Funj power gradually diminished, and by the end of the 18th century old Dongola was deserted.

In 1821 the forces of Mohammed Ali, the viceroy of Egypt, conquered the Sudan, eliminating the remnants of the Mamlukes who had taken refuge in Nubia with their headquarters at Ordu, commonly known as new Dongola. After the Egyptian conquest, new Dongola became the seat of local Egyptian administration and a principal frontier town of the Mahdist state.

ROBERT O. COLLINS
University of California at Santa Barbara

DONIPHAN'S EXPEDITION, don'i-fənz, a U.S. foray during the Mexican War. After Gen. Stephen W. Kearney captured Santa Fe in 1846, Col. Alexander William Doniphan and his 1st Regiment of Missouri Mounted Volunteers, who had marched on Santa Mounted, were ordered southward. At the end of 1846, Doniphan's motley army of 856 men left the Rio Grande. On Feb. 28, 1847, at Sacramento, 20 miles (32 km) north of Chihuahua, they encountered 4,200 Mexicans. Doniphan's forces charged and cut through the Mexican lines, which could not regroup. The Americans then occupied Chihuahua. The American victory at Sacramento, with few losses, reduced the Army of Central Mexico and relieved pressure on U.S. troops elsewhere in Mexico.

Doniphan then turned east toward Saltillo, where eventually he joined Gen. John E. Wool's army. Once in Saltillo, the Missourians were ordered to the Gulf coast to be transported by boat to New Orleans. During the entire expedition (beginning in Missouri), Doniphan and his men marched 3,600 miles (5,800 km).

THOMAS D. CLARK, *Indiana University*

DONIZETTI, dō-nē-dzāt'tē, **Gaetano** (1797–1848), Italian composer of operas, who, with Rossini and Bellini, dominated the opera houses of his day. He was born on Nov. 29, 1797, in Bergamo. He received his first musical instruction there and then went to Bologna in 1815 to complete his training. The tradition that he served in the army is unfounded.

From 1822 to 1838, Donizetti made Naples the center of his activities, though he frequently wrote for the opera houses of other Italian cities. When his opera *Poliuto* was forbidden by the Neapolitan censors in 1838, Donizetti moved to Paris, where he brought out *Les Martyrs* (1840), a revision of the *Poliuto* score. From 1842 he lived part of the time in Paris, the rest in Vienna, where he introduced *Linda di Chamounix* (1842). The last significant premieres (*Don Pasquale* and *Dom Sébastien*) of his career took place in 1843. In 1845, Donizetti was stricken with paresis and, paralyzed in body and mind, died in Bergamo on April 8, 1848.

Works. Donizetti's first opera, *Enrico di Borgogna*, went unnoticed when it was produced in 1818. His first success was at Rome with *Zoraide di Granata* (1822). He composed more than two dozen operas before 1830, all strongly indebted to the work of Rossini, though some contain highly individual passages. These apprentice works established Donizetti as a composer equally proficient in comic and serious veins. Following *Anna Bolena* (1830), which introduced him to audiences in London and Paris, he composed his best-known operas: *L'elisir d'amore* (1832), *Lucrezia Borgia* (1833), *Lucia di Lammermoor* (1835), *La fille du régiment* (1840), and *La Favorita* (1840).

Too frequently Donizetti is summarily dismissed as a composer. Although he never attained the stature of the mature Verdi, a striking feature of his later style is a fondness for straightforward melodies of the type usually associated with Verdi's music. Donizetti's melodic romanticism and his skill at composing intensely moving ensembles have been reassessed as the result of a number of revivals of his less familiar operas, such as *Parisina* (1833), *Maria Stuarda* (1834), and *Roberto Devereux* (1837).

WILLIAM ASHBROOK, *Author of "Donizetti"*

ADULT DONKEY (left) and half-grown offspring. The donkey is still widely used as a beast of burden.

DONKEY, dong'kē, a domesticated member (*Equus asinus*) of the horse family (Equidae). It is generally agreed that the donkey, now found throughout the world, is a descendant of the African wild ass. Related to the donkey is the domesticated white ass (*Equus hemionus*), a descendant of Asian ancestors. Domestication of both occurred in Neolithic times, some 5,000 years ago, and both played important roles in the development of early civilizations in Africa and Asia. In rough undeveloped areas they are unequaled as beasts of burden.

Donkeys are usually 3 to 5 feet (90–150 cm) tall at the shoulders and have large ears, a mane of short erect hairs, and a tufted tail. Coat color varies from grayish through brownish to black. Miniature donkeys, about 30 inches (75 cm) high, are now raised and sold as pets.

Small donkeys, known by their Spanish name of *burro*, were once widely used as pack animals in the southwestern United States and Mexico. Many of these either escaped or were turned loose, and now a large population of feral (wild) burros exists in the desert areas of that region.

Donkeys breed throughout the year. Commonly, one young is born after a gestation period of about 12 months, one month longer than the gestation period for horses. Donkeys can be bred with horses, but the offspring are generally sterile. The offspring of a female donkey (jennet or jenny) and a male horse (stallion) is known as a hinny. Hinnies are smaller and less adaptable to training than mules, the offspring of a male donkey (jackass) and a female horse (mare). Donkeys live to more than 25 years of age.

E. LENDELL COCKRUM, *University of Arizona*

DONNACONA, don-ə-kō′nə, a town in southeastern Quebec, Canada, is on the north bank of the St. Lawrence River, at the mouth of the Jacques Cartier River, 31 miles (50 km) west of Quebec city. The principal industry is a large paper mill, for which the Jacques Cartier River supplies hydroelectric power.

The town is named for the Indian chief Donnacona, whom the explorer Jacques Cartier took with him to France in 1535. It was incorporated as a town in 1920. Population: 5,731.

DONNE, dun, **John** (1572–1631), English poet, preacher, and prose writer, who was the chief exponent of the "metaphysical" style in poetry and a towering figure in 17th century English literature. Little of his poetry was published during his lifetime. His love lyrics, both cynical and passionate, together with the elegies and satires of his early youth, did not see print but were circulated widely in manuscript among the courtly wits and intellectuals of Elizabethan and Jacobean London.

Rediscovered in the 20th century after 200 years of relative neglect, Donne has enjoyed among modern readers a remarkable popularity that shows no sign of diminishing. His influence on 20th century English and American poetry has been incalculable. His example was instrumental in forging the poetic styles of Yeats and T. S. Eliot, the two dominant forces in modern English poetry, and literary historians and critics agree in ranking Donne as one of the greatest of English poets. Future generations are unlikely to revise this estimate.

Life. Born in London of a firmly Roman Catholic family, Donne studied at Oxford and possibly also at Cambridge but did not take a degree at either university; his faith made it impossible for him to swear the required oath of allegiance to the Protestant queen. He studied law at Lincoln's Inn in London during the 1590's and began an intensive study of theology in order to investigate the opposing claims of Protestantism and Catholicism. He had other pursuits as well: a contemporary describes him at that time as "very neat, a great visitor of ladies, a great frequenter of plays, a great writer of conceited verses."

Donne seems to have traveled on the Continent at some point during these years, and he took part in the Earl of Essex's military expeditions against Spain in 1596 and 1597. The fact that, in 1598, Donne became secretary to Sir Thomas Egerton, lord keeper of the great seal, makes it probable that by then the poet had become at least nominally an Anglican. In 1601, Donne fell in love with Anne More, niece of Sir Thomas More and daughter of Sir George More, chancellor of the Garter. They were secretly married, and Sir George's displeasure led to Donne's dismissal from his post, imprisonment for a brief period, and the ruin of his hopes for a career in public life.

The next 10 years of Donne's life were marked by penury and desperation. Until Sir George finally relented to some degree, Donne and his growing family were obliged to depend largely on the charity of friends and the generosity of patrons, the chief of whom was Sir Robert Drury, in memory of whose daughter Donne wrote the great *Anniversarie* poems. Other patrons included some of the great ladies of Jacobean England, most importantly Lucy, Countess of Bedford. In this period Donne also published works in which he supported the Anglican position against that of the Catholics.

Friends had often urged Donne to take holy orders, but he had been reluctant to do so—perhaps because of feelings of unworthiness as a result of the sexual indiscretions of his youth, perhaps because of lingering doubts as to the identity of the true church. But in 1615, after repeated pressures from King James I, Donne was ordained a minister of the Church of England. He rapidly established himself as one of the greatest preachers of the age, was almost immediately made chaplain to the king, and in 1621 was appointed Dean of St. Paul's Cathedral in London, a post he retained the rest of his life.

Donne's death, in London on March 31, 1631, was as vivid and theatrical as his life. After preaching his last sermon—described by his friend Isaak Walton as "his own funeral sermon"—he took to his bed and had his portrait painted in his shroud, keeping the picture for his contemplation until he died a few days later.

Poetry. Some of Donne's early poetry shows the Renaissance trait of classical imitation. His elegies (which are not elegies in the modern sense of being poems of lament) are modeled on the *Amores* of Ovid, and his satires show the influence of Juvenal and Persius.

For a long time it was believed that all of Donne's love poetry was composed during his youth and that his later years were given over to the writing of religious verse and prose, but modern scholarship has established that some of the *Songs and Sonets* (as they were called in the posthumous editions) were written as late as 1617 and that the great sequence *Holy Sonnets* was written for the most part as early as 1609. The pattern that thus emerges is more in accord with what is known of Donne's complex yet strangely unified personality. In their own way, the *Holy Sonnets*, too, are love poems: the speaker has changed his object from an earthly mistress to a transcendent Deity, but in the divine poems, as in the profane ones, a desperate desire for absolute union finds expression in witty intellectual analogies that attempt to bestow a unity on the scattered fragments of experience. It is significant that whereas the amorous poems are permeated with religious imagery, the devotional poems operate largely through erotic imagery.

There is little physical description of any sort in Donne's poetry. Specifically intellectual quality manifests itself in the structure of his poems, which is typically logical or argumentative, and in their figuration, which depends heavily on the device of the "conceit," or farfetched metaphor. Donne's conceits, unlike those of some other baroque poets, are usually based not on an extravagant perception of physical resemblance but rather on an intellectually perceived resemblance of function or inner nature. Such is the case in the famous lines from *A Valediction: Forbidding Mourning*, in which he addresses his beloved (according to tradition, his wife Anne) from whom he is about to be separated. Referring to their two souls, he writes:

> If they be two, they are two so
> As stiffe twin compasses are two,
> Thy soule the fixt foot, makes no show
> To move, but doth, if the other doe.
>
> And though it in the center sit,
> Yet when the other far doth rome,
> It leanes, and hearkens after it,
> And growes erect, as that comes home.

Donne's reputation as a poet suffered many vicissitudes after his death. For more than a generation he remained the chief influence on English lyric poetry, but with the coming of neoclassicism his vogue began to wane. A succession of important English poets, however, honored his memory, although with reservations. Dryden admired his wit but was troubled by his flouting of decorum; Pope found him worthy of imitation; Dr. Johnson esteemed his learning but censured him for what he felt was a lack of taste. In the 19th century Coleridge praised him, and Donne

John Donne (after a portrait by Isaac Oliver)

is probably to be regarded as one of Browning's sources for his conception of the dramatic monologue. The rehabilitation of Donne's poetic reputation was completed in the 20th century.

Love Poems. Donne's love lyrics, or *Songs and Sonets*, are strikingly original and among the most widely read of his works. Such poems as *The Good-Morrow*, *The Canonization*, and *Lovers Infinitenesse* depart from the conventions of Elizabethan love poets like Spenser, Sidney, and Drayton in a number of significant ways. Donne's love poems are dramatic rather than descriptive: instead of delineating the beauties of his beloved or recounting the pangs of his desire, he characteristically speaks directly to his beloved, to some other individual, or to himself.

Donne is perhaps the greatest of English love poets. His eminence in this field rests not only on the intensity of his expression and the completeness with which he explores the entire range of amorous experience and its manifold moods but also on the nobility of his conception of sexual love. This conception, derived from Plato and influenced by Petrarch, departs from its sources in refusing to separate spiritual love from the bodily love in which, for Donne, it is rooted. His attitude is summed up in *The Extasie*, his most sustained presentation of an amorous philosophy.

The "Anniversaries." Donne's interest in Copernican astronomy shows itself in the two *Anniversaries* (1611, 1612), the only important poetic works to see print during his lifetime. The 14-year-old daughter of Sir Robert Drury died in December 1610, and in the next year Donne published *The First Anniversarie: An Anatomy of the World*, accompanied by *A Funerall Elegie*. *The Second Anniversarie: Of the Progress of the Soule* appeared in 1612.

In these bizarre but very great works, the dead little girl is identified with some kind of vital female principle, the destruction of which means nothing less than the death of the world. In *The First Anniversarie* the disturbing implications of the new science (Copernicanism), with its abolition of the orderly world view inherited from previous ages, are adduced to symbolize the decay of the Creation. In *The Second Anniversarie*, Donne's obsessive theme of transcendence finds eloquent expression as he visualizes the soul of the dead girl, identified with the human soul in general, rising beyond all earthly concerns to experience the bliss of union with God.

Devotional Poems. Among the poems written after Donne's ordination, the most important are the three great *Hymnes*, three additional *Holy Sonnets* found in the Westmoreland Manuscript, which the critic Edmund Gosse purchased from the estate of the Earl of Westmoreland in 1892, and, possibly, *A Nocturnall upon St. Lucies Day, Being the Shortest Day*. The last-mentioned poem, one of the most complex and powerful of the *Songs and Sonets*, is believed by some scholars to have as its subject the death of the poet's wife in 1617. Of the Westmoreland verses (which may be dated after 1617), one poem betrays continuing uncertainty about the nature of the true church and another poem contrasts the poet's desperate love for his dead wife with the absolute love of God that he is trying to achieve. A similar concern announces itself in the earliest of the *Hymnes*, *A Hymne to Christ at the Authors Last Going into Germany*, in which, with a characteristically imperative violence, the poet urges God to compel him to love Him alone.

There is some uncertainty concerning the dates of the composition of Donne's last two great poems. *A Hymne to God the Father*, in which, typically, the poet puns on his own name, was probably occasioned by the same illness that elicited the prose *Devotions*. According to Izaak Walton, Donne's earliest biographer, the *Hymne to God my God, in my Sicknesse* was composed by Donne on his deathbed, but some modern scholars believe it to be contemporaneous with the *Hymne to God the Father* and identical in inspiration.

Whatever the truth of the matter, the *Hymne to God, my God, in my Sicknesse* is reminiscent of Donne's religious prose in its sobriety of tone and singleness of purpose. The poem recalls both the *Holy Sonnets* and the more passionate of the *Songs and Sonets* in its combination of emotional intensity and ingenious and playful wit. Its exploitation of the imagery of geography and exploration reminds the reader of such amorous poems as *The Good-Morrow* and *The Sunne Rising*. And its last line, a characteristic theological paradox, sums up the tortured complexity of Donne's personality and of the vision his works express: "Therefore that He may raise the Lord throws down."

Prose. Donne's middle years saw the production of a wide variety of works. In addition to the two meditative sequences of *Holy Sonnets*, he wrote many verse letters, witty and often obscure, addressed usually to fellow intellectuals or to his courtly patronesses. Some time around 1608 he wrote *Biathanatos*, a prose tract attempting to prove that suicide "is not so naturally a sinne, that it may never be otherwise." This work, an indication of the writer's distress at that time, was not published until 1646. *Pseudo-Martyr*, a learned treatise arguing the Anglican position against the Roman Catholic, was published in 1610, and in the next year appeared *Ignatius His Conclave*, a hilarious prose satire against the Jesuits. A minor theme of *Ignatius* is Donne's interest in the new heliocentric astronomy espoused originally by Copernicus and supported in Donne's own day by the findings of Kepler and Galileo.

After his ordination Donne devoted himself largely to religious writings, for the most part in prose. His more than 160 sermons, published in great folio editions in 1640, 1649, and 1660, constitute an extraordinary body of prose. Related to his poetry by their qualities of imagination, extravagance, and wit, Donne's *Sermons* recall the poems also in their characteristic themes and emphasis. Unusual in an age of virulent religious controversy by virtue of their broad viewpoint and moderate tone, they concentrate on the essentials of Christianity rather than on controversial points of dogma. A recurrent theme is divine love; another, typically Donnesque, is the inevitable death and dissolution of the body, on the details of which Donne's imagination dwells with disturbing power. He shows no contempt for the body, however; and the vision of physical decay is consistently balanced by his dwelling on the doctrine of the resurrection of the body, destined, for those who are saved, to be glorified and reunited with the soul. Donne the preacher is the same man who, years before, had written *The Extasie*.

Devotions Upon Emergent Occasions, published in 1624, ranks with the *Sermons* in assuring Donne's immortality among writers of English prose. In 1623, Donne suffered a near fatal illness; the *Devotions* are the psychological and spiritual fruit of that attack and his recovery from it. In a series of 23 units, each consisting of a "Meditation," an "Expostulation," and a "Prayer," Donne traces the various steps of his disease and its cure, expending his full imaginative energy on drawing witty analogies between the situation of man in sickness and the general situation of man in his sinfulness and his need for divine mercy.

A prominent example of the general European spiritual practice of formal meditation, the *Devotions* are notable for their psychological perceptions, powerful expression of the theme of brotherhood, and demonstration of the rhetorical strength of baroque prose—a kind of prose that, eschewing the more formal style and structure of typical Renaissance works, aims at achieving dramatic and colloquial immediacy. Donne's prose, like that of other prominent prose-writers of the time, suggests not the polished and persuasive presentation of conclusions arrived at some time in the past, but rather the illusion of thought in the very process of being thought.

FRANK J. WARNKE, *Coeditor of "Seventeenth Century Prose and Poetry"*

Bibliography

The standard edition of Donne's poetry is by Sir Herbert J. C. Grierson, 2 vols. (1912). Helen Gardner edited the *Divine Poems* (1952), and Frank Manly edited *The Anniversaries* (1963). Donne's sermons were edited by George R. Potter and Evelyn M. Simpson, 10 vols. (1953–1962).

Coffin, Charles M., *John Donne and the New Philosophy* (New York 1937).
Hughes, Richard E., *The Progress of the Soul: The Interior Career of John Donne* (New York 1968).
Hunt, James Clay, *Donne's Poetry* (New Haven 1954).
Kermode, Frank, *John Donne* (London 1957).
Leishman, James B., *The Monarch of Wit* (London 1951).
Martz, Louis L., *The Poetry of Meditation*, rev. ed. (New Haven 1962).
Simpson, Evelyn M., *A Study of the Prose Works of John Donne*, rev. ed. (London 1948).
Stein, Arnold, *John Donne's Lyrics* (Minneapolis 1962).
Webber, Joan, *Contrary Music* (Madison, Wis., 1963).
White, Helen C., *The Metaphysical Poets* (New York 1936).
Williamson, George, *The Donne Tradition* (Cambridge, Mass., 1930).

DONNELLY, don'əl-ē, **Ignatius** (1831–1901), American political leader and writer. He was born in Philadelphia, Pa., on Nov. 3, 1831. After training for the law in Pennsylvania, he moved to Minnesota in 1856. His hopes of making a fortune there were blasted by the panic of 1857, but he had a gift for politics and at the age of 28 became lieutenant governor of the state.

Donnelly was a member of Congress from 1863 to 1869. Originally a Republican, he became a Greenback Democrat and eventually a Populist, achieving considerable personal popularity and a reputation as a radical reformer. He edited two political journals (the *Anti-Monopolist* and the *Representative*), served in the Minnesota state senate from 1874 to 1878, and was nominated for vice president of the United States in 1900 by the Populists.

Donnelly's love of the bold and controversial idea was reflected in an unusual literary career that began when he was past 50. One of his works, *Caesar's Column: A Story of the Twentieth Century* (1891), was an extremely popular novel. He is best remembered, however, for *The Great Cryptogram* (1888), in which he endeavored to prove by an elaborate word cipher that Francis Bacon wrote the plays of William Shakespeare. Donnelly died in Minneapolis on Jan. 1, 1901.

DONNER, dôn'ər, **Georg Raphael** (1693–1741), Austrian sculptor, who was his country's leading sculptor of the baroque period. He was born in Esslingen on May 24, 1693. The influence of Italian baroque art is seen in his early work, and it is often assumed that Donner traveled and studied in northern Italy sometime before 1715. He worked in Salzburg from 1725 to 1728, in Pressburg until 1738, and finally in Vienna, where he died on Feb. 15, 1741.

Donner's early, baroque style is exemplified by his sculptural decorations for the staircase at Schloss Mirabell, Salzburg. His later work, influenced by 17th century French sculpture and by ancient art, leans more toward neoclassicism. Among Donner's best works are the large castlead *St. Martin* (1735) in the Pressburg cathedral and a fountain built in 1737–1739 for the Mehlmarkt, Vienna, but later moved to the city's Barockmuseum.

DONNER PARTY, don'ər, a group of pioneers traveling to California by wagon train, led by George Donner. Their misfortune was the most spectacular catastrophe of the overland crossings.

The party left Illinois in April 1846. On July 20, Donner led 20 wagons onto the untried Hastings Cutoff around the south side of Great Salt Lake. They encountered difficulties that delayed their desert crossing and arrived at Truckee (Donner) Lake in the eastern Sierras on October 31. Snow blocked the pass, and they were forced to encamp. One group built cabins at the lake, while the others, including the Donners, located at Alder Creek, 5 miles distant.

Faced with starvation, 17 members attempted to cross the Sierras on snowshoes in December. Seven survived. From January through April, four relief parties brought out the remaining survivors. Death by starvation had been averted by cannibalism. In all, 40 of the 87 emigrants survived their terrible agonies.

H. BRETT MELENDY
San Jose State College, Calif.

DONNYBROOK, don'ē-brŏŏk, is a residential district of Dublin, Ireland, about 3 miles (5 km) southeast of the center of the city, of which it forms a part. It is on the main road from Dublin to the seaside resorts of Bray and Greystones. Donnybrook was once well known for its fair, established in 1204. The fair grew in importance and popularity over the centuries, but it began to attract elements given more to riot and disorder than to buying and selling, and the government finally suppressed the fair in 1855. The term "Donnybrook" is still sometimes used to denote a brawl.

In neighboring Belfield on the Stillorgan Road to Bray, a 250-acre (100-hectare) university campus was under construction in the late 1960's for University College, Dublin. The college was to move eventually from its old confined buildings in Earlsfort Terrace to the new campus. Donnybrook is also the principal television transmission center in Ireland.

THOMAS FITZGERALD
Formerly, Department of Education, Dublin

DONORA, də-nôr'ə, is a borough in southwestern Pennsylvania, in Washington county, on the Monongahela River, 19 miles (30 km) southeast of Pittsburgh. It is situated in an area of varied industry and agriculture. On Oct. 30–31, 1948, Donora was covered by a poisonous smog that caused the death of 20 persons and the illness of about 5,000. The borough was incorporated in 1901. It is administered by a mayor and council. Population: 7,524.

DONOVAN, don'ə-vən, **Richard Frank** (1891–1970), American composer, conductor, and educator, whose music is characterized by complex rhythms and subtle harmonic textures. He wrote orchestral, chamber, choral, and keyboard works.

Donovan was born on Nov. 29, 1891, in New Haven, Conn. After graduating from Yale, he continued his studies at the Institute of Musical Art (now part of the Juilliard School of Music) in New York City and with composer Charles Widor in Paris. He joined the Yale faculty in 1928 and became conductor of New Haven's Bach Cantata Club (1933–1944), assistant conductor of the New Haven Orchestra (1936–1951), and organist and choirmaster at Christ Church (1928–1966). He died in Middletown, Conn., on Aug. 22, 1970.

DONOVAN, don'ə-vən, **William Joseph** (1883–1959), American public official, who organized and directed the Office of Strategic Services (OSS) during World War II. He was born in Buffalo, N.Y., on Jan. 1, 1883, and became an attorney there. Serving in the U.S. Army during World War I, he rose to the rank of colonel and earned the Medal of Honor, and acquired the nickname "Wild Bill" for his daring. He then resumed law practice and became active in New York Republican politics. He was assistant U.S. attorney general in 1924–1925.

After observing military strength and intelligence in Europe, Donovan was commissioned to plan a new U.S. intelligence service. From 1942 to 1945 he was director of the wartime OSS, the military precursor of the Central Intelligence Agency, and rose to the rank of major general. In 1953–1954 he was U.S. ambassador to Thailand. He died in Washington, D.C., on Feb. 8, 1959.

DONUS, do'nəs (died 678), was pope from 676 to 678. A native of Rome, he was consecrated pope on Nov. 2, 676. Donus (or *Domnus*) received the submission of Archbishop Reparatus of Ravenna, ending the schism begun by his predecessor Archbishop Maurus, who tried to make Ravenna an independent see. It is said that Donus solved the problem of the Nestorian monks in the monastery of Boethius by assigning them to other religious houses in the city and giving the monastery to Roman monks. He died on April 11, 678, and was buried in St. Peter's Basilica in the Vatican.

Marion A. Habig, O. F. M.
St. Augustine Friary, Chicago, Ill.

DOODLEBUG. See Ant Lion.

DOOLEY, Mr. See Dunne, Finley Peter.

DOOLEY, doo'lē, **Thomas Anthony, III** (1927–1961), American doctor and author, who won fame for his humanitarian work in southeast Asia. Dooley was born in St. Louis, Mo., on Jan. 17, 1927. He interrupted his studies at Notre Dame to serve as a Navy medical corpsman from 1944 to 1946. After graduating from Notre Dame, he entered the St. Louis University School of Medicine, receiving an M. D. degree in 1953.

In 1954, Dooley rejoined the Navy as an intern, serving on the U. S. S. *Montague*, off Vietnam, and later in Haiphong. There he supervised camps housing 600,000 refugees before their evacuation to South Vietnam to escape the Viet Minh. This experience he recorded in his book *Deliver Us from Evil* (1956). In 1956, Dooley resigned from the Navy to lead a private medical unit to Laos, where he established several village hospitals. In 1958 he founded, with Dr. Peter Comanduras, the Medical International Cooperation Organization (MEDICO). MEDICO, later a service of CARE, Inc., was largely supported by sales of his books. Dooley died of cancer in New York City on Jan. 18, 1961.

Sam Kaufman
Director of Public Relations, CARE, Inc.

DOOLITTLE, doo'lit-əl, **Hilda** (1886–1961), American poet, who was a member of the imagist movement, but whose finest verse is to be found in her postimagist volumes. All of her work appeared under her pen name "H. D."

Life. Hilda Doolittle was born in Bethlehem, Pa., on Sept. 10, 1886. When she was 8 years old, her father, the astronomer Charles Leander Doolittle, moved to the outskirts of Philadelphia, where he was director of the Flower Observatory. H. D. entered Bryn Mawr in 1904 but left in her sophomore year because of ill health. In 1911 she went to Europe, expecting to stay for the summer, but she spent most of the rest of her life abroad, mainly in England and Switzerland. In 1913 she married Richard Aldington, an English poet and novelist who was also a member of the imagist group. They were later divorced. She died on Sept. 27, 1961, in Zürich.

Writings. H. D.'s first poems were printed in the magazine *Poetry* (published in Chicago) in 1913. Her work next appeared in *Des imagistes* (1914), an anthology published by the imagist leader Ezra Pound. *Collected Poems* (1925), probably her most widely read work, was still characterized by the spare, noncommittal observations of detail associated with imagist verse, but *Red Roses for Bronze* (1931) showed her moving in the direction of her later work, toward a more discursive expression of psychic and religious archetypes. In *The Walls Do Not Fall* (1944) she bade farewell to the modernist school, of which imagism had been the opening phase. Thereafter, H. D.'s verse tended to concentrate on mythical themes—sometimes, as in *Helen in Egypt* (1961), her last work, seeing all myths as ultimately one. Her prose works include the novels *Hedylus* (1928) and *Palimpsest* (1936) and her autobiographical *Tribute to Freud* (1956).

Hyatt H. Waggoner, *Author of "American Poets, from the Puritans to the Present"*

DOOLITTLE, doo'lit-əl, **James Harold** (1896–   ), American general, who led the first air attack on Tokyo in World War II. He was born at Alameda, Calif., on Dec. 14, 1896, and began his military aviation career in the Army Air Service in 1917. He earned the doctor of science degree at Massachusetts Institute of Technology in 1925. In 1922 he became the first to fly across the continent of North America in less than 24 hours. As a racing pilot, he set speed records and won the Schneider (1925), Mackay (1926), Bendix (1931), and Thompson (1932) trophies. As an experimental engineer in the Air Corps Materiel Division, he played a leading role in developing aircraft instruments and made the first successful blind flight. For contributions to instrument flying he received the Harmon Trophy (1930). Leaving the active Air Corps in 1930, he was an aviation specialist for an oil company until 1940, when he was recalled to duty as a major and worked to convert the automobile industry to aircraft production.

On April 18, 1942, Doolittle voluntarily led a raid by 16 B-25 bombers from the U. S. S. *Hornet* in a daring attack against Tokyo. This action bolstered U. S. morale, slowed the Japanese offensive, and won him the Medal of Honor. He then commanded air forces in North Africa, Europe, and the Pacific. After retiring as a U. S. Air Force lieutenant general in 1946, he was chairman of the Air Force Scientific Advisory Board (1955) and National Advisory Committee for Aeronautics (1956).

John W. Carpenter, III
Lt. Gen., USAF; Commander, Air University

DOOMSDAY BOOK. See Domesday Book.

DOOR AND DOORWAY. A door is a relatively solid surface, opaque or wholly or partly glazed, that closes an entrance to a building or a room. In contrast, gates, which serve a similar purpose, are often open grillwork. A doorway includes the door and its frame, both of which are sometimes richly decorated.

In antiquity, doors frequently swung on pivots set in the lintel and threshold of the doorway. Later doors are almost always hinged to the jamb on one side. Some doors, usually between rooms, slide horizontally in grooves. Most doors consist of a single slab or leaf, but large doors may have two leaves hinged to both jambs. The "Dutch" door is divided horizontally, so that the upper section may be open while the lower is closed.

Ancient and Medieval Periods. Few doors have been preserved from the period of antiquity. Those of some important buildings were of bronze, but it seems unlikely that most doors could have

(Left) Ghiberti's highly decorated 15th century bronze baptistry doors, Florence, Italy. *(Above)* Neoclassic doorway of the early 19th century at the rear of the Essex Institute in Salem, Mass.

been so costly. Much attention, however was paid to the doorway. That of the north porch of the Erechtheum (about 421–406 B.C.) in Athens is exquisite in its proportions and in the delicacy of its carved moldings. A cornice resting on consoles, or brackets, crowns the doorway.

In churches of the Romanesque period (11th and 12th centuries) in Europe, the principal doorway is commonly splayed; that is, the jambs of the door spread out diagonally on each side of the opening. Colonnettes support a series of concentric arches, each larger than the one below, the outermost serving to support the thick wall. The doors of the main entrance are often paired, and separated by a *trumeau*, or post of stone. Since the doors are rectangular but set under an arch, a semicircular area called a "tympanum" remains above them. The tympanum, which holds no weight, may be richly carved. Some of the finest sculpture of the Romanesque period in France is concentrated in the tympanums of St. Pierre at Moissac and of St. Lazare at Autun, both of the 12th century.

The same type of doorway continued, with modifications, in the Gothic period. On the west front of Chartres cathedral (late 12th century), the pointed arch replaces the Romanesque round arch. Also, slender elongated figures of kings and queens in part supplant the earlier colonnettes. In 13th century structures, as in Amiens cathedral, buttresses at the corners of the twin towers project from the plane of the facade. Hence the splayed doorways become porches set between the buttresses, visually emphasizing through their depth the function of the door as an entrance. Because of the pointed arch, the Gothic tympanum is higher in proportion to its width than the semicircular Romanesque one. Whereas the sculpture of an earlier tympanum presents a single subject, filling the whole area, a Gothic tympanum is divided into horizontal bands, making it possible to present several related subjects, one above the other.

Gothic doors were commonly made of planks set vertically and nailed to a frame within. Because they were heavy, they required massive hinges of wrought iron, often in the form of long straps extending over more than half the door. In some important doorways, plain hinges were replaced by elaborate scroll designs.

Renaissance. Renaissance architects in the 15th century and later rejected Gothic architecture as barbaric. They returned to the Roman round arch or to a plain rectangle spanned by a *lintel*, or beam. Also, the doors began to be paneled, which tended to lighten the door and prevented warping. Paneling also offered a field for rich decoration in the size and arrangement of the panels and the carving of the moldings that defined them.

Roman architectural elements enframe Renaissance doorways in a great variety of designs to emphasize the doorway's importance. In the simplest form the moldings of the jambs and lintels are continuous, as in a plain picture frame. A more or less elaborate cornice may project above the lintel. *Pilasters*, or engaged columns, of one of the five orders of architecture may flank the jambs and support an entablature. Finally, a full or broken pediment, of triangular, segmental, or scroll form, may crown the entablature. The pediment discharges rainfall to the sides of the door instead of allowing it to drip down in front. Doorways of these types appeared in the Renaissance during the 15th century in Italy and continued in later styles through the early 20th century. A fairly elaborate example is the door of Il Gesù (1568–1575) in Rome, by Giacomo della Porta, where a triangular pediment is set within a larger segmental pediment.

American Styles. The door of American colonial houses of the 17th century, like the rest of the building, preserves medieval tradition. That of the Parson Capen House (1683) at Topsfield, Mass., is typical. Vertical boards are nailed to an inner frame, the nails driven in a diamond pattern. Since hardware was costly, little was used, though perhaps a wrought iron handle and a knocker appear. Such doors were secured by a latch fitting into a socket on the inner jamb. A thong was attached to the movable end of the latch and then threaded through a small hole above it. When the thong was pulled, the latch would rise and the door swung open.

In the Georgian period in the 18th century, the doors and doorways followed the Renaissance types. Thus paneled doors replaced plank doors. Interior doors of this period commonly have six panels, one pair below the level of the handle, a somewhat taller pair above, and square panels at the top. Outside doors, being larger, often have more panels, the top row sometimes being glazed to help light the hall. An alternative solution was a glazed transom between the door and its main lintel. The latch string gave way to box locks, perhaps in wrought iron but often encased in polished brass.

The doorways are varied and rich. Thus a cornice resting on consoles tops the door of the Vassall (Longfellow) House (1759) at Cambridge, Mass. The Cabot-Endicott-Low House (about 1750) at Salem, Mass., has a triangular pediment. A segmental pediment completes the door on the west front of the Royall House (1747) at Medford, Mass., while Westover (1726), near Williamsburg, Va., has one of the first scroll pediments.

The porch appears first in the Federal style that began after the Revolution and continued until about 1825. Samuel McIntire created the exquisite porched doorway of the Gideon Tucker House (1808–1809) at Salem. The slender columns of its semicircular porch suggest at once his appreciation of the delicacy of his material (wood) and his admiration of the English style associated with the Adam brothers. The door itself is crowned with an elliptical fanlight and flanked by narrow sidelights, both with patterns of leaded glass.

In the second quarter of the 19th century the Greek Revival turned for its details generally to Hellenic architecture. The Greek Doric or Ionic orders replaced the Roman or Adamesque types. Doors with two slender panels replaced the six- or eight-paneled form, perhaps for simplicity since no Greek precedent is known.

The austerity of modern architecture eliminated the decorative aspects of doors and doorways, until the door became occasionally a sliding panel of glass hardly distinguishable from the glass walls of the house or public building.

EVERARD M. UPJOHN, *Columbia University*

DOPPLER, dôp′lər, **Christian Johann** (1803–1853), Austrian physicist and mathematician, who was the first to explain the "Doppler effect" (q.v.). He was born in Salzburg on Nov. 29, 1803. He studied at the Polytechnic Institute in Vienna and was appointed assistant in mathematics there in 1829. He later became professor of mathematics and physics at the *Realschule* in Prague, the School of Mines in Chemnitz (Saxony) and the University of Vienna. Doppler died in Venice on March 17, 1853.

Although Doppler wrote only one book (on arithmetic and algebra), he was the author of dozens of important scientific papers. The most important of these, published in 1842, explains what is now known as the Doppler effect. This work, which connects the frequency of a wave with the relative motion between the source of the wave and the observer, had an immediate impact on acoustics and optics. By the 1850's it was widely used to explain several puzzling astronomical phenomena.

L. LAUDAN, *University College, London*

DOPPLER EFFECT, dop′lər, an apparent shift in the frequency of waves received by an observer, depending on the relative motion between the observer and the source of the waves. The effect, named after Christian Johann Doppler (q.v.), applies to water waves, sound waves, light waves, and all other wave phenomena.

Perhaps the most familiar example of the Doppler effect is the decrease in pitch of a locomotive whistle as the train passes by the listener. When the train approaches, the frequency of the sound measured by a stationary observer is higher than the rest frequency that he would measure if the train were standing still. As the train recedes, the observer measures the sound of the whistle at a frequency lower than the rest frequency.

Applications. The Doppler effect has perhaps found its most spectacular applications in astronomy. By examining the frequency shift of spectroscopic lines in the light from the stars, astronomers have determined the velocities of these stars relative to our sun, and by measuring the frequency shifts of radio waves emitted by clouds of hydrogen gas in our galaxy, they have been able to analyze the motions of these clouds. In 1929, E. P. Hubble examined the frequency shift of the light from distant galaxies. He found that the light was red shifted (its frequency decreased) as he looked at increasingly distant galaxies, and thus he was the first to verify that the galaxies are receding from us with relative velocities that increase in proportion to the distance.

Doppler Effect in a Material Medium. Sound waves (and water waves) require a material medium, such as the atmosphere, for their propagation. If both the source of the waves and the observer are stationary in the medium, then in a time, t, the number of wave crests that pass by the observer is ct/λ, where c is the *phase velocity* of the waves (the speed with which individual crests propagate through the medium), and λ is the *wavelength*, or distance between two successive crests. The *rest frequency*, v, which is equal to c/λ, is the number of crests that pass the observer per unit time. In the case of sound waves, the observer measures the rest frequency of the sound when he and the sound source are stationary in the medium.

When the observer moves toward a sound source that is stationary in the medium, he hears a sound at a frequency v' that differs from the rest frequency v because he encounters an additional number of wave crests in time t. In this case, the sound heard by the observer has a frequency given by

$$v' = v(1 + v_r/c) \qquad (1)$$

where v_r is the velocity of the observer relative to the medium. This velocity is taken positive in the direction from the observer to the sound source.

When the sound source moves toward an observer who remains stationary in the medium, the observer again will encounter an additional number of wave crests in time t. In this case, the sound heard by the observer has a frequency

$$v' = v/(1 - v_r/c) \qquad (2)$$

where v_r is the velocity of the sound source relative to the medium. As long as v_r is much less than c, the frequency v' measured by the observer in case (1) is only slightly different from what it is in case (2).

Relativistic Doppler Effect. Electromagnetic radiation (radio waves, infrared waves, light waves, ultraviolet waves, X-rays, and gamma rays) does not require a material medium for its propagation. It travels in a vacuum with a phase velocity, c, of 186,000 miles per second (3×10^{10} cm/sec). This phase velocity is a constant, independent of the relative motion between source and observer.

An important consequence of Einstein's special theory of relativity is that there can be no meaningful way for an observer to measure whether he is traveling at some constant velocity with respect to the vacuum through which light propagates. Hence, only relative motions between the light source and observer are meaningful. Einstein showed that the correct formula for the Doppler shift (the frequency shift from v to v') in the light encountered by the observer in this case is

$$v' = v(\sqrt{1 - v^2/c^2}/1 - v_r/c) \qquad (3)$$

where $v = \sqrt{v_r^2 + v_t^2}$ is the total relative velocity, including the component v_r along the line joining the source and the observer, and the component of velocity, v_t, perpendicular to this line. As long as v is much less than c, the numerical difference between (3) and Doppler's formulas (1) and (2) is very small, but the difference becomes important when v is not much less than c. See also ELECTROMAGNETIC RADIATION—*Doppler Effect.*

HAROLD S. ZAPOLSKY, *University of Maryland*

DOPPLERITE, dop'lər-īt, is an amorphous mineral consisting of organic acids derived from humus. It occurs in elastic or jellylike masses in peat bogs or where solutions from low-rank coal deposits accumulate. The fresh material is brownish black and has a greasy luster; it becomes black and brittle when dehydrated. On the average, dopplerite contains 56.5% carbon, 36% oxygen, 5.5% hydrogen, and 2% nitrogen. It may also contain calcium, iron, or magnesium.

DORAT, dō-rá', **Jean** (1508–1588,) French scholar and poet. Dorat (also spelled *Daurat*) was born in Limoges, France, but his exact birthday is unknown. He became director of the Collège de Coqueret in 1547, and there gathered around himself a group of young poets who became famous as the Pléiade. Although Dorat wrote poetry, mostly in Greek and Latin, his importance for French literature lies primarily in the influence he exerted on other members of the group, such as Pierre de Ronsard and Joachim du Bellay, especially in the direction of learning from classical models. In 1560 he became professor of Greek at the Collège de France and later was made poet royal by Charles IX. He died in Paris on Nov. 1, 1588.

DORBEETLE, dôr'bēt-əl, a name sometimes applied to various insects that produce a buzzing sound while flying. The true dorbeetle (*Geotrupes* of the scarab family) is a large black beetle with an oval body about an inch (25 mm) long, ridges on the wing covers, spines on the front legs, and short antennae with three large leaflike terminal segments. While flying, it produces a loud, low-pitched sound. Both the adult dorbeetle and the larva also stridulate, producing a rasping noise by rubbing the hind legs across ridges on the base of the middle legs. This noise is usually a warning.

The true dorbeetle is also sometimes called the "dung beetle" because the female lays her eggs in balls of dung, which serve as food for the developing larvae. Larval growth takes place during the summer, and when fully grown, the larvae burrow into the soil and construct cases in which they then undergo pupation. The adult dorbeetles emerge in the spring or early summer.

R. H. ARNETT, JR., *Purdue University*

DORCHESTER, dôr'chə-stər, a municipal borough in England, the county town of Dorsetshire, is situated 115 miles (185 km) southwest of London. It is an agricultural market center for the surrounding area. Dorchester was the site of the chief settlement of the Belgic tribe, the Durotriges. Maiden Castle, a tribal fortress and the largest prehistoric earthwork in England, is 2 miles (3 km) to the southwest.

Dorchester was called Durnovaria by the Romans, who captured Maiden Castle in 43 A.D. Population: (1961) 12,266.

DORCHESTER, dôr'chə-stər, in eastern Massachusetts, is a part of Boston, 5 miles (8 km) south of the center of the city. The first settlement of the Massachusetts Bay Company within the boundaries of Suffolk county was made here. Dorchester was a township until 1870, when it was annexed to Boston. Historic landmarks include the Roger Clap house (1633), the Robert Pierce house (1640), the James Blake house (1648), and the Old North Burying Ground (1634).

Dorchester was settled in 1630. Its situation on the Neponset River made it a major port for domestic trade and a center for fishing and manufacturing. A grist mill was established in 1633; a powder mill in 1675; a paper mill in 1727; and the first chocolate mill in the United States in 1765. Dorchester originated the town meeting form of local government and founded the first free public school supported by direct taxation.

On March 4, 1776, colonial forces occupied Dorchester Heights, a hill overlooking Boston Harbor, thus forcing the evacuation of British troops from Boston on March 17. The hill was designated a national historic site in 1951.

LINDA M. IVERS, *Dorchester Branch Library of the Boston Public Library*

DORDOGNE, dôr-dôn′yə, is a department of southwestern France, situated at the west central edge of the Central Massif. It has an area of 3,561 square miles (9,263 sq km). Périgueux, the department seat, is on the Isle River near the central part of the department.

Dordogne is crossed by a series of rivers flowing northeast-southwest, including the Dordogne, the Isle, the Auvézère, the Dronne, and the Vézère. Between the river valleys is a series of small plateaus. The valleys contain most of the population and fertile land, and produce wheat, grapes, vegetables, and fruit in abundance, as well as some tobacco and nuts. The sparsely populated uplands are drier, with thin soils; they sustain some cereals and flocks of sheep. About 25% of the department is forested.

Dordogne, which corresponds roughly to the historic province of Périgord, is one of France's most beautiful and interesting regions. Its cuisine is world-famous, especially the goose liver pâté with black truffles. In the south lies the spectacular scenery of the Dordogne River valley. Prehistoric remains and cave paintings (the most famous being those of Lascaux) testify to one of the earliest prehistoric civilizations known. Museums containing prehistoric remains are found at Périgueux and Eyzies. Population: (1962) 375,455.

HOMER PRICE, *Hunter College*

DORDOGNE RIVER, dôr-dôn′yə, one of France's longest rivers. It runs southwest and west from its source in the north central part of the Central Massif until it joins the Garonne River just north of Bordeaux to form the Gironde River. The river's principal tributaries along its 300-mile (480–km) course are the Vézère and the Isle.

The varied and spectacular natural scenery and the interesting architecture along upper and middle course make the Dordogne Valley a prime tourist region. Between the Trémolat meander and Souillac, upstream from Argentat, there are many reservoir lakes created behind dams harnessed for hydroelectric power.

HOMER PRICE, *Hunter College*

DORDRECHT, dôr′dreκнt, is a town in the Netherlands, in the province of South Holland. It is situated near the mouth of the Rhine River at the junction of several natural and artificial waterways. The old town, founded in 1008 and granted its charter about 1220, lies mainly on the south bank of the Oude Maas (a branch of a distributary of the Rhine); it has numerous attractive buildings, including a 14th-16th century church, old courtyards, and gabled houses. The new town has grown beyond, with large housing developments.

For a long period Dordrecht's position on the waterways made it a leading port, but silting and the increasing size of ships enabled Rotterdam, 15 miles (25 km) nearer the North Sea, to surpass it. Deepening of the Oude Maas, however, has helped Dordrecht to maintain some maritime and inland waterway trade, and the town has benefited from the vast growth of the Rotterdam complex, of which it is part. Its industries include shipbuilding, marine and other engineering, and the manufacture of chemicals. Population: (1966)) 88,547.

F. J. MONKHOUSE
Author of "Geography of Northwestern Europe"

DORÉ, dô-rā′, **Gustave** (1832–1883), French illustrator, many of whose dramatic engravings have become almost as well known as the literary classics they illustrate. His wood engravings for an 1861 edition of Dante's *Inferno* were a major factor in the 19th century revival of interest in Dante. Doré's works are characterized by rather overcrowded compositions, theatrical lighting, and dramatic emotional appeal—effects that endeared him to his Victorian contemporaries. His ability to make real the characters of literary fantasy has ensured his lasting fame.

Paul Gustave Doré was born in Strasbourg on Jan. 6, 1832. He went to Paris in 1848 and began his career drawing caricatures for the *Journal pour rire*. He was only 22 when he became famous for his illustrations of the 1854 edition of Rabelais' works. The demand for Doré's work grew to the point that he sometimes had to employ more than 40 artisans to help engrave his designs. He illustrated nearly 100 books, including Balzac's *Droll Stories* (1855), Perrault's *Fairy Tales* (1862), Cervantes' *Don Quixote* (1863), Milton's *Paradise Lost* (1865), the Bible (1866), Tennyson's *Idylls of the King* (1868–1869), and Coleridge's *The Rime of the Ancient Mariner* (1875).

Doré's paintings, mostly of religious and historical subjects, never achieved the recognition afforded his graphic work. Of his sculptures, the best known is the statue of Alexandre Dumas *père* in the Place Malesherbes, Paris. Doré died in Paris on Jan. 23, 1883.

COLTA FELLER IVES
Metropolitan Museum of Art, New York

Further Reading: Jerrold, Blanchard, *Life of Gustave Doré* (London 1891); Lehmann-Haupt, Hellmut, *The Terrible Gustave Doré* (New York 1943); Roosevelt, Blanche, *Life and Reminiscences of Gustave Doré* (New York 1885).

Gustave Doré: engraving for Dante's *Inferno*, Canto XIX.

BROWN BROTHERS

DORGON, dô-'gon', was a Manchu prince who was the actual founder of the Ch'ing dynasty (1644–1912) of China. He was born on Nov. 17th, 1612, in Hetu Ala, Manchuria, the 14th son of Nurhaci. In 1636, Dorgon became instead one of the coregents of the infant ruler Shun Chih. He commanded the armies that conquered North China in 1644 and supervised the conquest of South China that followed. After deposing his coregent, he established the forms of Manchu rule in China.

When Dorgon died suddenly on a hunting trip in Jehol, on Dec. 31, 1650, he left a legacy of hatred among Manchus who had suffered under his power. His followers were soon punished, and Dorgon was posthumously denounced for his "crimes." His achievements in the Manchu cause were not again officially recognized until more than a century later, when Emperor Ch'ien Lung restored his family to rank and privilege.

JAMES SHIRLEY, *Northern Illinois University*

DORIA, dô'ryä, **Andrea** (1466–1560), a Genoese soldier of fortune, admiral, and statesman. He was born on Nov. 30, 1466, at Oneglia, on the Gulf of Genoa, of a prominent Genoese family then in exile. Orphaned at an early age and forced to make his own fortune, he embarked on a spectacular military and diplomatic career. He changed masters frequently, at various times serving the popes, the French, the Habsburgs, and various princes. His career was largely governed by four goals: his own personal advance and that of his family, the welfare of his ancestral city of Genoa, the expulsion of the French from Italy, and the defense of Christendom against the fleets of the Barbary pirates and the Turks.

Career. As a young soldier, Doria served the popes and several other Italian princes. He helped the French, who were then in control of Genoa, to subdue Corsica (1503–1506), and after the French were expelled from Italy in 1512, he became captain general of the Genoese fleet and checked the Barbary pirates.

When Genoa was taken by the troops of the Habsburg Emperor Charles V in 1522, Doria entered the service of France. His galleys were chiefly responsible for saving Marseille from imperial capture in 1524, and in 1527 he recovered Genoa for the French. However, French policies and meager pay led him to abandon French service for that of the emperor in 1528. With imperial support, Doria returned to Genoa in triumph and showed his ability as a statesman by reforming the Genoese constitution, giving it a distinctly aristocratic cast. (Doria's constitution was retained until 1798.) He refused the office of doge but accepted the title "Liberator and Father of His Country." The grateful Emperor Charles made him Prince of Melfi.

In the last years of his life, rival Genoese families organized several conspiracies against him. In 1547 the Fieschi assassinated his nephew and apparent heir, Giannettino. The aged Doria punished the plotters ruthlessly, and his commanding position at Genoa remained unshaken. Even in his nineties, and in spite of domestic distractions, Doria continued his maritime expeditions against his old enemies, the Turks and the French. He died on Nov. 25, 1560, in Genoa.

Evaluation. A valorous and resourceful as well as ambitious leader, Doria could be treacherous and cruel, as shown in his merciless reprisals against the Fieschi family. But he served Genoa well both as a military leader and as a statesman and profoundly influenced the political events of his day. He played a major role in frustrating the French ambitions to dominate Italy and was a principal instrument in winning for Charles V's Mediterranean policies their considerable measure of success. His exploits as a seaman won him his reputation as one of the great admirals of history. By the princely palaces he built, which other nobles imitated, he helped impart to Genoa its Renaissance splendor.

DAVID HERLIHY, *University of Wisconsin*

DORIANS, dôr'ē-ənz, a major division of the ancient Greek people. Traditionally they were led into the Peloponnesus by the descendants of Heracles (Hercules) soon after the Trojan War (12th century B.C.). Archaeological and linguistic evidence suggests that the Dorians came into Greece from the lower Balkans (modern Albania and Macedonia) about this time and attacked in particular the rich but declining centers of the Mycenaean and Minoan cultures; they did not bring with them any major cultural achievements. Argos, near Mycenae, became one of their centers. They also occupied Megara and, in the Peloponnesus, Corinth, Sparta, and Messenia.

About the same time the Dorians moved out into the Aegean, where they dominated Thera, Melos, Crete, Rhodes, and Cos. This sweep led them as far as Halicarnassus and Cnidus in southwestern Asia Minor. During the great wave of later colonization after 750 B.C., Dorian colonies were established at Cyrene in Africa and Tarentum in Italy, and also at Syracuse in Sicily.

The Dorians were a cultural and linguistic group who shared Greek civilization with the Ionians, Aeolians, and other groups. Dorian city-states were usually divided into three political sections or tribes, called Hylleis, Dymanes, and Pamphyli, whereas Ionian cities often had four tribes bearing quite different names. Such Dorian centers as Sparta, Argos, and Corinth were prominent in the 7th and 6th centuries B.C. in bronzework, sculpture, pottery, and architecture; the "Doric" column was generally used throughout the Greek world in temples until the late 5th century B.C. Corinth and Aegina were very active in commerce. In Sparta and Crete warrior brotherhoods and exploitation of the peasants as virtual serfs lasted longer than elsewhere in Greece.

During the struggles between Sparta and Athens in the 5th century, the distinction between Dorian and Ionian took on some of the characteristics of the later division between Latin and Teutonic. Since Athens became the cultural center of Greece, its dialect, akin to Ionian, grew to be the literary language of Greek civilization, and very little was written in pure Doric.

CHESTER G. STARR, *University of Illinois*

Further Reading: Myres, John, *Who Were the Greeks?* (Berkeley 1930); Will, E., *Doriens et ioniens* (Paris 1956).

DORIC ORDER. See CAPITAL; COLUMN.

DORION, dô-ryôn', **Sir Antoine Aimé** (1818–1891), Canadian political leader and judge. He was born on Jan. 17, 1818, in Ste.-Anne-de-la-Pérade, Lower Canada (Quebec). After studying law at Nicolet College, he was called to the bar in 1842 and practiced law in Montreal. An anticlerical member of the Rouge party, he vociferously opposed Confederation.

Dorion represented Montreal in the legislature of United Canada from 1854 to 1861, when George E. Cartier defeated him. He held the crown lands portfolio in the three-day Brown-Dorion administration in 1858. He represented Hochelaga in the legislature from 1862 to 1867 and was provincial secretary in J. S. Macdonald's government (1862–1863) and then Lower Canadian leader and attorney general (1863–1864). He came to accept Confederation and served in the Canadian House of Commons from 1867 to 1874, when he was appointed chief justice of Quebec. In 1873–1874 he had been minister of justice in Alexander Mackenzie's government. Dorion died in Montreal on May 31, 1891.

CORNELIUS J. JAENEN, *University of Ottawa*

DORION, dô'ry-ôN', a town in southern Quebec, Canada, is on the south bank of the Ottawa River near its junction with the St. Lawrence River. The Ottawa-Montreal and Toronto-Montreal highways join here. The town shares a post office with Vaudreuil, and the name sometimes is listed as Dorion-Vaudreuil. A number of summer homes are situated in Dorion.

The town was named for Sir Antoine Aimé Dorion, joint premier of United Canada (1858 and 1863–1864. It was incorporated as a village in 1891 and as a town in 1916. Population: 5,749.

DORIS, dôr'is, was a small district in the central part of ancient Greece where the headwaters of the Cephisus River rise. Although a road ran through the district from Thermopylae on the north to Phocis and Delphi on the south, Doris played a secondary part in Greek history. It was organized into four small communes or city-states, namely, Boeum, Cytinium, Erineus, and Pindus, which formed a league or tetrapolis. Doris held membership in the Delphic Amphictyony, which directed the great shrine of Apollo. The Dorians as a whole came from farther north, but one small group may have settled in Doris during the Dorian migrations and so may have given the district its name.

CHESTER G. STARR
University of Illinois

DORKING, dôr'king, is an urban district in Surrey, England, 22 miles (35 km) southwest of London, at the foot of Box Hill. It is primarily a residential center and market town but also has several small industries, including the manufacture of electric cables and the burning of lime; it is noted for a special breed of poultry. There are several fine mansions here, one of which is Deepdene.

Dorking was the home of Thomas Malthus and George Meredith; Ralph Vaughn Williams, another resident, founded the annual Leith Hill music festival here. Once situated on an old Roman road between London and the Sussex coast, Dorking was a popular stop in England's coaching days. Population: (1961) 22,594.

DORMONT is a borough in southwestern Pennsylvania, in Allegheny county, directly across the Monongehela River from the downtown business section of Pittsburgh. The borough is principally residential.

The first settlement on the site was made before 1790. Dormont was incorporated as a borough in 1909. Government is by manager and council. Population: 11,275.

DE WYS

Dormouse

DORMOUSE, a small nocturnal rodent resembling a squirrel, native to Europe, Asia, and Africa. Dormice have well-developed eyes, rounded ears, soft fur, and a bushy tail. Their usual coloration is brown or gray above and white or buff below. Dormice range in length from about 4 inches to 14 inches (10–35 cm), including the tail, which accounts for almost half the length. Dormice are good climbers, and most species live in trees. They also inhabit brush, rocky areas, and buildings. Their diet consists of fruit, nuts, eggs, small birds, and insects; some kinds will kill and eat smaller rodents.

In the late summer and fall, dormice store food in their nests and put on large amounts of fat. In most habitats they are dormant in winter, with body temperatures dropping to barely above freezing. At times they arouse themselves, eat some of the stored food, and then become dormant again.

Tropical species may breed throughout the year, but northern forms appear to have only one or sometimes two litters per year. Litter size ranges from 2 to 10 young, which are born blind and hairless after a gestation period of 21 to 28 days. Dormice live from 2 to 5 years.

The dormice constitute the family Gliridae, which is made up of 7 genera divided into 23 living species. Fossil dormice have been found from as far back as the Oligocene epoch of Europe, some 30 million years ago.

There are two species of dormice in the family Platacanthomidae; these are distinguished from the other dormice mainly by differences in the teeth and skull. The spiny dormouse (*Platacanthomys lasiurus*) is native to southern India; the Chinese pygmy dormouse (*Typhlomys cinereus*) is from southern China.

WALTER A. SHEPPE, JR., *University of Zambia*

DORN, dôrn, **Friedrich Ernst** (1848–1916), German physicist, who discovered the element radon. Dorn was born in Guttstadt, East Prussia (Polish, Dobre Miasto), on July 27, 1848. He was professor of physics at Breslau (1873–1881), Darmstadt (1881–1886), and Halle (1886–1916). He died in Halle on June 13, 1916.

Dorn's work contributed to some of the great advances made between 1880 and 1910 in electricity, radioactivity, radiation, and optics. In 1878 he found that the motion of charged particles through a liquid creates an electric voltage, a phenomenon called the *Dorn effect*. Between 1883 and 1895, Dorn developed a standard of reference for the precise value of the ohm, the unit of electric resistance. In 1897 he determined what part of the energy of electrons striking target atoms is converted to X-rays, and in 1900 he showed how to find the velocity of secondary electron emissions produced when X-rays hit heavy metals. Dorn's discovery in 1900 that radium decays into radon was probably the first proof that in radioactive processes one element is transmuted into another.

HOMER STARR
"Chemical Week"

DORONICUM, də-ron′i-kəm, is a small genus of European and Asian plants popularly known as "leopard's-bane." The most popular species is

Doronicum

Doronicum plantagineum, a hardy herbaceous European perennial widely grown in American gardens. It grows about 2 feet (60cm) tall and bears handsome yellow daisylike flowers that are 2 to 3 inches (50–75 mm) wide and bloom in April and May. The plant grows readily in sun or shade and requires no attention whatsoever. After flowering, it is easily divided to make new clumps. Like the daisy, the leopard's-bane belongs to the composite family (Compositae).

DONALD WYMAN
Arnold Aboretum, Harvard University

DORPAT. See TARTU.

DÖRPFELD, dûrp′felt, **Wilhelm** (1853–1940), German archaeologist. He was born in Barmen (now Wuppertal) on Dec. 26, 1853. He began his career by training at the Architectural Academy of Berlin, where he studied classical architecture under Friedrich Adler. He accompanied Adler on his excavations at Olympia, in the Peloponnesus, in 1877–1881. The following year, Dörpfeld was appointed secretary of the German Archaeological Institute in Berlin. He later became director, holding this post until 1911. He assisted Heinrich Schliemann in his work at Troy, Mycenae, and Tiryns. In 1896, Dörpfeld published, with Emil Reisch, the first authoritative book on the ancient Greek theater.

A major effort in Dörpfeld's work was to trace the location of places mentioned in Homeric literature. In 1900 he identified modern Leukas as Ithaca, the home of Odysseus, and later asserted that Homer's Pylos was the modern town of Kakovatos. Although Dörpfeld's contribution to the science of excavation was of great importance, many of his interpretations have been opposed by other scholars. Dörpfeld died in Leukas on April 26, 1940.

CLIFFORD J. JOLLY, *New York University*

DORR, Thomas Wilson. See DORR'S REBELLION.

DORREGO, dôr-rä′gō, **Manuel** (1787–1828), early federalist in Argentina, who served as governor of Buenos Aires province. His overthrow and execution by Gen. Juan Lavalle, a leader of the opposing centralist or unitary faction, led to civil war and the eventual rise to power of the federalist dictator of Juan Manuel de Rosas.

Born in Buenos Aires on June 11, 1787, Dorrego studied law there and in Chile. He participated in the struggle for Argentine independence from 1811 to 1817, when he earned the wrath of the Unitary Director who sent him into exile (1817–1820). On his return he was briefly provisional governor of Buenos Aires. When he became governor eight years later (1828), he signed a treaty ending the war with Brazil over the territory that became independent Uruguay. The passions surrounding this war resulted in an uprising led by Lavalle, who ordered Dorrego shot on Dec. 13, 1828.

JOHN J. FINAN, *The American University*

DORR'S REBELLION was an uprising against the government of Rhode Island in 1842, led by Thomas W. Dorr (1805–1854). The Dorrites took up arms after having failed to obtain a liberal state constitution. Their rebellion was quickly crushed, but some of their proposals for reform were adopted in the constitution of 1843.

From 1834, Dorr, a member of the Rhode Island General Assembly, had led the struggle to extend voting rights, reapportion legislative seats, enact a bill of rights, and make the judiciary independent. Most of these issues stemmed from the fact that Rhode Island was still being governed under principles laid down in the charter of 1663. Only adult male landowners and their eldest sons could vote; the northern industrial towns were grossly underrepresented in the legislature; citizens were denied such basic American guarantees as freedom of assembly and speech; and there was no real separation of powers in the government.

Sporadic attempts at reform culminated in the fall of 1841 in the calling of two constitutional conventions: one by the legislature, the other by the Dorrites. The Dorrites' extralegal convention drafted a so-called "People's Constitution" and submitted it to an enlarged electorate, which ratified it by an overwhelming margin. In a special election sponsored by the Dorrites in the spring of 1842 the voters elected a slate of state officers headed by Dorr as governor.

Meanwhile, a coalition of Dorrites and ultraconservatives had voted down a constitution framed by the other convention. Both sides then appealed for support from outside the state.

Dorr was backed by New York City's Democratic Tammany Hall, and the regularly elected governor, Samuel Ward King, received from Whig President John Tyler a promise of federal intervention in the event of an armed uprising.

Federal support proved unnecessary, for the revolt was a fiasco. Dorr foolishly attempted to seize the state armory in Providence in May 1842. However, many Dorrites rejected his call to arms or were deterred by the severe penalties threatened for those who attempted to hold office or to exercise power under the "People's Constitution." With his forces in disarray, Dorr fled the state. He returned briefly in June with a small band of New York volunteers, but fled once more when Governor King called out the state militia.

The King government declared martial law. Hundreds of arrests were made, and Dorrite homes were ransacked for evidence. Once the government had consolidated its power, it convened another constitutional convention, which drafted a document incorporating many Dorrite proposals. Approved by the voters, it went into effect in 1843.

Dorr returned to Rhode Island later in 1843. He was convicted of treason and served one year (1844–1845) of a life sentence. Democratic legislatures in 1851 and 1854 reversed the treason conviction and restored his civil and political rights.

Dorr's Rebellion may be considered a partial success as it brought constitutional reform. But the Dorrites achieved less than they wanted, and their movement intensified the animosity among conflicting interest groups in the state. Nationally, the rebellion attracted Democratic support and Whig opposition and raised questions about such issues as majority rule and minority rights and the basis of suffrage.

PETER J. COLEMAN
University of Illinois at Chicago Circle

Further Reading: Coleman, Peter J., *The Transformation of Rhode Island, 1790–1860* (Providence 1963).

D'ORSAY, dôr-sā', **Count** (1801–1852), French society figure and patron of the arts, who became well known through his association with the English Countess of Blessington (q.v.). Alfred Guillaume Gabriel d'Orsay was born in Paris on Sept. 4, 1801, and in 1819 began a career in the bodyguard of Louis XVIII. The course of his life was changed, however, in 1821, when he met the Earl and Countess of Blessington in London. In 1822 he left his post to travel with them, and in 1827, to please the Earl, he married the 15-year-old Lady Harriet Gardiner, Blessington's daughter by a previous marriage.

When the Earl died in 1829, d'Orsay and his wife settled in London with the Countess. His wife left him in 1831, but d'Orsay remained with the Countess, and their household became a center of fashion and the arts and a source of aid for French exiles, including Louis Napoleon. D'Orsay became bankrupt in 1849 and fled to Paris, where Louis Napoleon, after regaining power, made him director of fine arts in 1852. D'Orsay died that same year, on August 4, in Paris.

DORSET, 1st Earl of. See SACKVILLE, THOMAS.

DORSET, 6th Earl of. See SACKVILLE, CHARLES.

DORSET, dôr'sət, a county in southwest England, is on the English Channel between Devonshire on the west and Hampshire on the east, extending inland as far as Salisbury Plain. It is a county of high downs, with Pilsdon Pen rising to 907 feet (276 meters), and lush valleys of arable and pasture land. Dorset is predominantly dairy farming country, producing large quantities of milk and butter.

The Dorset coast exhibits a variety of formations, including Purbeck stone, Kimmeridge clay, fuller's earth, lias, and Portland stone. The strip of shingle known as the Chesil Beach links the Isle of Portland to the mainland at Weymouth, and the narrow ridge of the Purbeck Hills produces the nearly circular Lulworth Cove and strange eroded rocks near Swanage. Dorset is of great archaeological importance. Ichthyosaur and plesiosaur remains have been found in the cliffs at Lyme Regis. Numerous burial mounds have been excavated on the downs. Maiden Castle, a Bronze Age hill fortress, is the largest and one of the best documented earthworks in Britain.

The county has few large-scale industries. Poole makes pottery, chiefly from Purbeck materials. Weymouth has engineering works. There is widespread stone quarrying in Portland. The Dragon nuclear reactor, a joint project of 12 European nations, was opened at Winfrith in 1968.

Dorchester, the county town, is a busy road center. Weymouth and Poole are the largest centers of population. Shaftesbury, Sherborne, Wareham, Blandford, and Bridport are typical Dorset county towns. Notable buildings include the 12th century minster at Wimborne and the abbey at Sherborne, part of which is occupied by a boys' school first founded in the 8th century. At Shaftesbury, there are remains of an abbey founded by Alfred the Great.

Thomas Hardy, whose novels portray Dorset and its people, is the county's chief literary figure. Jane Austen visited Lyme Regis on the coast and wrote of it in *Persuasion*. Population: (1961) 313,460.

GORDON STOKES
Author of "English Place-Names"

DORSEY BROTHERS, dôr'sē, American dance band leaders, who were dominant figures in the golden age of "big bands" in the 1930's and 1940's. Jimmy Dorsey, a saxophone player and clarinetist, was born in Shenandoah, Pa., on Feb. 29, 1904. His brother Tommy, a trombonist, was born in Mahonoy Plains, Pa., on Nov. 19, 1905. They received their first music lessons from their father, and through their teens they performed in parades and at local functions, frequently with bands that they themselves had organized. They joined the Paul Whiteman Orchestra in the late 1920's.

In 1933 the Dorseys formed their famous Dorsey Brothers Orchestra, but they parted a year later and formed separate bands. The brothers starred with their bands in their screen biography *The Fabulous Dorseys* (1947), but were not actually reunited until 1953, when they formed a band called "The Fabulous Dorseys." Tommy Dorsey died on Nov. 26, 1956, in Greenwich, Conn. Jimmy Dorsey died on June 12, 1957, in New York City.

DAVID EWEN
Author of "History of Popular Music"

DORT, Synod of, dôrt, a synod of the Reformed Church convened by the States General of the Netherlands in 1618 at Dordrecht (Dort) to settle the theological dispute over Arminianism, a less stringent form of Calvinism. On the one side were the followers of the deceased Dutch theologian Jacobus Arminius, who were called Arminians or Remonstrants (after the Remonstrance of 1610, which expressed their position); on the other were Franciscus Gomarus and his followers, called Gomarists or Counter-Remonstrants. The synod held 154 meetings, from Nov. 13, 1618, to May 9, 1619. Most of those present were Dutch, but theologians from England, Switzerland, and Germany also attended.

The Arminian position was rejected by the synod with the assertion of five points that became the hallmark of Calvinism. They were: the fall of man leaves him no natural light to effect his salvation; election is founded on God's purpose "before the foundation of the world"; the efficacy of Christ's atonement extends only to the elect; regeneration is an inward renewal that is wholly the work of God; and God so preserves the elect that they cannot fall from grace. Some visiting theologians tried unsuccessfully to exert a moderating influence upon the predominant Gomarists. The theological debate was clouded by politics, since the Arminians had been instrumental in concluding an unpopular truce with Spain. See also ARMINIANISM.

JAMES H. SMYLIE
Union Theological Seminary, Richmond, Va.

DORTMUND, dôrt'mŏont, is a West German industrial city in the Ruhr industrial region, in the state of North Rhine-Westphalia. It is situated on the small Emscher River, a tributary of the Rhine, 46 miles (74 km) northeast of Cologne.

Dortmund has been an important center for iron and steel working since the mid-19th century and has been important for coal mining a great deal longer. Today it is the site of three large iron-smelting and steelmaking works, and despite a decline in the coal-mining industry since World War II, there are still a number of active pits close to the city. The iron-smelting industry, which developed on the basis of local fuel and ore, now relies exclusively on imported iron ore. The Dortmund-Ems Canal, opened in 1898, links the city with the North Sea port of Emden and also, by way of the Herne Canal, with the Rhine. This canal system is intensively used to transport ore, fuel, and other bulky commodities.

In addition to its primary iron and steel production, Dortmund manufactures a wide range of mechanical and engineering goods. It has a chemical industry and is a brewing center.

History. Dortmund owed its rise during the Middle Ages to its location in a fertile agricultural region on an ancient route, known as the Hellweg, which ran from the Rhine eastward into Saxony. The city was first mentioned in the 9th century, but its development came chiefly in the later Middle Ages, when it was a member of the Hanseatic League and played an important role in the commerce of northern Germany. It grew little from this time until the 19th century, when the local fuel and mineral resources began to be exploited. It then grew rapidly and became an important communications center. It suffered extensive damage during World War II but was later rebuilt. Population: (1965 est.) 657,000.

NORMAN J. G. POUNDS, *Indiana University*

DORVAL, dôr-vàl', a city in southwestern Quebec, Canada, is 13 miles (21 km) west of Montreal, on the south shore of Montreal Island, where the St. Lawrence River widens into Lake St. Louis. Dorval is principally residential. The summer resort of Dorval Island is opposite the city. The Montreal airport is in Dorval.

A mission was begun on the site in 1666, and in 1670 the Sulpicians built the Fort de la Présentation. The community was incorporated as a town in 1903 and a city in 1956. Pop.: 17,722.

DOSIMETER. See RADIATION.

DOS PASSOS, dəs pas'əs, **John** (1896–1970), American novelist, essayist, and historian, who wrote the celebrated novel *U. S. A.,* a massive trilogy covering three decades of American life. He was born in Chicago, Ill., on Jan. 14, 1896. After spending much of his childhood in Europe, he entered Harvard College, graduating in 1916. During World War I he served successively with a voluntary ambulance unit in France, the Red Cross in Italy, and the U. S. Army Medical Corps. His wartime experiences were incorporated in the novel *Three Soldiers* (1921), which provoked considerable controversy because of its critically realistic treatment of army life.

This and other early novels set the mood of social consciousness that characterized all of Dos Passos' work and reflected the disillusionment of his generation. Because of his idealism and his proletarian sympathies, he was at first attracted to Marxism, but in later years his political orientation became increasingly conservative. During World War II he traveled in Europe and the Pacific, writing a series of articles eventually collected as *Tour of Duty* (1946). His travels and writing continued until his death, in Baltimore, Md., on Sept. 28, 1970.

Writings. Dos Passos first emerged as a major writer with the publication of *Manhattan Transfer* (1925), a kaleidoscopic, cross-sectional view of New York life. Even more experimental in form and ambitious in scope is the trilogy *U. S. A.* (1937), which includes *The 42nd Parallel* (1930), *1919* (1932), and *The Big Money* (1936). In this painstakingly detailed portrait of industrial America between 1898 and 1929, he developed three experimental techniques for capturing the change and disorder of the decades the novel treats: the "newsreel," which juxtaposes newspaper headlines with popular songs, advertisements, and fragments of news articles; the "biographies," which vividly portray real Americans who played prominent national roles; and the "camera eye," which represents the author's own poetic, stream-of-consciousness response to the American scene. His second trilogy, *District of Columbia* (1939, 1943, 1949), is less interesting, but he returned with some success to his more experimental methods in the novel *Midcentury* (1961).

Dos Passos published more than 40 volumes, all directly or indirectly concerned with American life. In addition to novels, his works include a volume of verse, *A Pushcart at the Curb* (1922); three plays; collections of sociological, travel, and political essays; the biography *The Head and Heart of Thomas Jefferson* (1954); and such historical works as *The Men Who Made the Nation* (1957) and *Mr. Wilson's War* (1962).

DAVID GALLOWAY
Case Western Reserve University

DOSSO DOSSI, dôs'sō dôs'sē (1479?–1542), Italian painter, who was a member of the school of Ferrara, although some aspects of his work—his brilliant color, loose brushwork, and interest in landscape—are more closely related to Venetian painting. Dosso's distinctive style has a poetic intensity akin to that of Giorgione, but the strain of waywardness and fantasy in his best works reveals his affiliation with the highly individualistic tradition of Ferrara.

He was born Giovanni de Lutero in the vicinity of Mantua and probably grew up there, at the extravagant Gonzaga court, where his father held a minor post. Little is known of his training (possibly in Ferrara), and a presumed sojourn in Rome from 1517 to 1524 would have come too late to change his style. With his less talented brother Battista he produced, in the region around Ferrara, Modena, and Pesaro, many altarpieces, allegories, and frescoes of uneven quality. He died in Ferrara.

Perhaps the most engaging of Dosso's works are those illustrating episodes from ancient history and legend, such as *Circe* (Borghese Gallery, Rome). These works combine a delight in the fabulous with an air of mystery and reverie that is reminiscent of the late works of Giovanni Bellini. The sense of enchantment is heightened in Dosso's work by the unreal colors that create effects of smoldering iridescence.

BARRY HANNEGAN
University of Virginia

Further Reading: Mezzetti, Amalia, *Il Dosso e Battista Ferraresi* (Milan 1965).

DOST MOHAMMED KHAN, dōst mō-hum'məd ᴋʜän (1789–1863), was a founder of modern Afghanistan and first ruler of the Mohammedzai dynasty. The 20th son of the vizier Payindah Khan, he early gained the nickname "Little Wolf" because of his impetuous nature and his bravery. During his youth, Dost Mohammed witnessed the decline of the Sadozai dynasty and the division of the Afghan empire into petty principalities. In 1826 he fought and maneuvered his way to control of the principality of Kabul, and he took the title of amir in 1834.

When Peshawar (in present-day Pakistan) was lost to Ranjit Singh, Sikh ruler of the Punjab, Dost Mohammed sought British help. The British, however, alarmed at Russian activity in central Asia, wanted a docile ruler in Kabul. When Dost Mohammed received a Russian envoy, the British recalled the mission they had sent and used the incident as a pretext to invade Afghanistan. In the ensuing First Afghan War (1839–1842), Dost Mohammed Khan was driven from Kabul. He surrendered to the British in 1840 and was exiled to India.

In 1843, after the assassination of the British-supported ruler Shah Shuja and the British withdrawal from Afghanistan, Dost Mohammed was able to return and resume the throne. He sided with the Sikhs in the Anglo-Sikh War (1848–1849) and attempted in vain to take Peshawar. Nevertheless, he concluded treaties of friendship with the British in 1855 and 1857. Dost Mohammed was able to add to Kabul the region of Kandahar (1855), the Uzbek state south of the Amu Darya (1850–1859), and Herat (1863). He died on June 9, 1863. His reunification of Afghan territory and his reforms led to the emergence of modern Afghanistan.

KENNETH A. LUTHER, *The University of Michigan*

DOSTOYEVSKY, dôs-tə-yef'skē, **Fyodor Mikhailovich** (1821–1881), Russian novelist and one of the most seminal writers in European literature. He has profoundly influenced not only the modern novel but also the thought of modern man. His role as iconoclastic thinker has been so potent because it found expression in creative rather than abstract thought. "I am weak in philosophy," he wrote to a friend on June 6, 1870, a statement that becomes all too obvious when he tries to make his heroes into the mouthpieces of his own extreme views.

Life. Dostoyevsky was born in Moscow on Nov. 11 (Oct. 30, Old Style), 1821, the second son of a former army doctor, who was at the time attached to the Mariinsky Hospital for the Poor and Aged. The boy was educated at a Moscow private boarding school and, shortly after the death of his mother in February 1837, was sent to St. Petersburg, where he entered the Army Engineering College. He received a commission in 1843 and was attached to the Army Engineering Corps in St. Petersburg. In 1844 he resigned his commission to devote himself to literature.

In the spring of 1846, Dostoyevsky joined the group of utopian socialists led by Mikhail Butashevich-Petrashevsky, a disciple of François Marie Charles Fourier (q.v.). In April 1849, Dostoyevsky and other members of the group were arrested and imprisoned for eight months in the Petropavlovsk Fortress in St. Petersburg. On November 16, Dostoyevsky was sentenced to death, but the death sentence was commuted to four years hard labor in a Siberian prison. However, he and the other prisoners were not informed of their reprieve. Instead, on Dec. 22, 1849, they were taken to a parade ground and made to endure the ceremonies preliminary to their execution before their reprieve was read to them. After his release from prison in February 1854, he did his compulsory army service in Siberia. On Feb. 6, 1857, he married Maria Isaev, a 29-year old widow.

In March 1859, Dostoyevsky resigned from the army and was granted permission to return to European Russia. Two years after his return to St. Petersburg, at the end of 1859, he founded the monthly periodical *Time* under the nominal editorship of his elder brother Mikhail. In June 1862 he went abroad for the first time. He returned to St. Petersburg that August, and in May of the following year *Time* was suppressed because of an article on the Polish uprising. In August 1863 he went abroad again, returning in October to join his dying wife in Moscow. In January 1864 he founded his second periodical, *Epoch*, which lasted only one year. The death of his brother Mikhail in July 1865 involved Dostoyevsky in debts that drove him abroad to seek refuge from his creditors. In February 1867, Dostoyevsky married Anna Snitkin, his 22-year old stenographer; the couple went abroad and stayed until July 1871. From January 1873 to February 1874 he was editor of the conservative weekly *Citizen*. In 1876 he founded and edited his own monthly, *The Writer's Diary*. An epileptic all his life, Dostoyevsky died in St. Petersburg on Feb. 9 (Jan. 28, Old Style), 1881, from a burst blood vessel in his lungs aggravated by an attack of epilepsy.

Works. Between 1844, when he resigned his army commission, and 1849, when he was imprisoned, Dostoyevsky wrote 10 long and short stories. The first, *Poor People* (1845), was acclaimed by the influential critic Vissarion Belinsky as "the first attempt at a Russian social novel." Belinsky singled out three most characteristic features of Dostoyevsky's fiction: the minute accuracy of the descriptions of everyday life, the masterly delineation of character and social conditions, and the profound, intuitive understanding of the tragic element in life. Dostoyevsky's second story, *The Double* (1846), a brilliant study of schizophrenia, was not appreciated by either Belinsky or a reading public that found it too obscure and diffuse. His third story, *Mr. Prokharchin* (1846), was a desperate attempt to match the success of *Poor People* by a return to the same environment of the St. Petersburg slums. It met with the annihilating criticism of Belinsky, as did his next story, *The Landlady* (1847). There followed several other stories that were equally unsuccessful. In 1848 he published four other stories: *White Nights*, a sentimental tale of a young dreamer, remarkable for its gentle humor and touches of genuine feeling; *The Honest Thief*, the embryo of the idea that was to be fully developed in *Crime and Punishment*; the satirical story *The Christmas Tree and the Wedding*, a savage indictment of success in an acquisitive society; and an unfinished novel *Netochka Nezvanova*.

While imprisoned in the Petropavlovsk fortress, Dostoyevsky wrote *The Little Hero*, a story remarkable for its analysis of the mentality of an 11-year-old boy and for its deeply sympathetic characterization of a young erring wife. Immediately on his release from the Siberian prison, Dostoyevsky wrote two long short stories: *My Uncle's Dream*, a lighthearted comic picture of socialites in a remote provincial town; and *The Village of Stepanchikovo*, whose hero was a first sketch of "a perfect man" who, 10 years later, was to be given a much more satisfactory embodiment in Prince Myshkin, the hero of *The Idiot*. Both these stories show signs of Dostoyevsky's desire to ingratiate himself with the authorities and reveal all too clearly the change in his political orientation from a red radicalism to a dyed-in-the-wool conservatism. The most important works published after his return to St. Petersburg were the novel *The Insulted and the Injured* (1861) and the autobiographical *The House of the Dead* (1861–1862), a vivid description of the nightmare world of the Siberian prison. In the latter work, Dostoyevsky for the first time developed the theme of spiritual regeneration through suffering and expressed his admiration for religious meekness and "active" love, the two qualities that were to become the distinguishing characteristics of Myshkin in *The Idiot* and Alyosha in *The Brothers Karamazov*.

Dostoyevsky continued his attack on the liberals in his short story *An Unpleasant Incident* (1862). In his *Winter Notes on Summer Impressions* (1863) he described life in London and Paris and set down the conclusion that Russia alone could bring about "the brotherhood of man." He continued his attack on Western civilization in *Notes from the Underground* (1864), in which he rejected the panaceas of the utilitarians and claimed that redemption could be achieved by religion alone.

Crime and Punishment. Between 1864 and 1866, Dostoyevsky worked on *Crime and Punishment* and, to meet a publisher's deadline, dashed off *The Gambler*, a melodramatic and superficial

Fyodor Dostoyevsky

work in which he tried to give an account of his own mania for gambling. Dostoyevsky intended *Crime and Punishment* (1866) as "a psychological study of crime" as well as "a novel of contemporary life." He began to write the novel in the first person, in the form of a confession. But in November 1865 he decided to jettison that plan and start again. He expanded his original idea, that happiness could be "bought" only by suffering, and conceived of Raskolnikov, the central figure, as a man of immense pride who, although he has only contempt for society, wants to acquire power over society for its own good. This leads to Raskolnikov's plan of murder for money and Dostoyevsky's exploration of the Napoleonic theme—the theory that there are a few extraordinary men who stand above the law.

Dostoyevsky's first intention was that Raskolnikov should accept his punishment to expiate his crime. But because this was not a decision Raskolnikov would logically have taken, Dostoyevsky introduced Sonia to embody the Christian concept of penance through suffering.

Dostoyevsky used the mechanism of dreams to add a fourth dimension to his novel. Raskolnikov dreams of a peasant whipping an old horse and is horrified by the violence; at that very moment he is planning to murder the money lender. Raskolnikov also dreams prophetically of a world in which the Napoleonic idea, if realized, leads to dictatorships and ideological warfare.

The Idiot. During his four years abroad between February 1867 and July 1871, Dostoyevsky wrote his two great novels *The Idiot* and *The Devils*. He finished *The Idiot* in January 1869. "The main idea of the novel," he wrote to a correspondent, "is to depict a positively perfect man. There is nothing more difficult in the world than this." In his notebooks, Dostoyevsky describes Prince Myshkin, the hero of *The Idiot*, as "Prince-Christ." The Christian virtues of meekness and humility are most characteristic of him. He is an epileptic and the first impression he produces is that of "an idiot." At the same time, everyone he comes across feels Myshkin's moral superiority. This inspires love in some of the characters, such as Nastasya Filippovna, one of the most powerful characters created by Dostoyevsky, and intense hatred in others, particularly Rogozhin, the embodiment of destructive, egoistic passion, who is madly in love with Nastasya Filippovna and in the end murders her. The contact with a Christlike figure such as Prince Myshkin does not, therefore, result in anything but tragedy; both saint and sinner are in the end turned into incurable lunatics.

Dostoyevsky was dissatisfied with *The Idiot* because it had failed as a convincing vehicle for his ideas. Realizing that some of these ideas were so extreme that he would make himself ridiculous if he advocated them seriously, he put them into the mouths of his avowedly ridiculous characters. It was only when he felt very strongly about a subject that he did not hesitate to make his hero the exponent of his own ideas. Thus, Prince Myshkin, contrary to his character, is made to deliver a violent diatribe against the Roman Catholic Church. He enlarged on these ideas in his *Writer's Diary* and in the speech he delivered at the unveiling of the Pushkin memorial in Moscow shortly before his death.

The Devils. The political ferment in Russia, culminating in the murder of a young student by a terrorist organization in Moscow, led Dostoyevsky to write his "tendentious" novel, *The Devils* (also called *The Possessed*; 1872). Its two chief characters, Nikolai Stavroghin and Pyotr Verkhovensky, are pegs on which Dostoyevsky hung his two most violent dislikes, his dislike of the Russian aristocracy and his dislike of the revolutionaries. The other conspirators in the novel are quite terrifyingly alive as people but only caricatures as revolutionaries. It was only in a character like Shatov, who like Dostoyevsky himself had turned his back on his liberal past and embraced a philosophy based on autocracy and the church, that Dostoyevsky saw the possibility of salvation for a world rent by discord and hatred. Dostoyevsky cut out the vision of the Golden Age, originally assigned to Stavroghin, and transferred it partly to his next novel, *The Adolescent* (also called *The Raw Youth*, 1875), and partly to his fantastic "science fiction" story *The Dream of a Ridiculous Man* (1877).

Dostoyevsky's hatred not only of his opponents but also of all imaginary "enemies" of Russia was entirely in line with his religious views. He was not able to overcome this feeling in *The Devils*, as is shown by his lampoon of Ivan Turgenev. This is a serious blot on a novel that, in spite of its structural and artistic blemishes, possesses a tremendous vitality as well as moments of great tenderness. Therefore, while it would be absurd to take seriously Dostoyevsky's political views as expressed in *The Devils*, it would be no less absurd to overlook his moments of great illumination, his amazing insight into the human heart, and his shattering criticism of those aspects of man's character that profoundly affect human thought and behavior.

A Writer's Diary. In 1873, Dostoyevsky began publishing his *Writer's Diary*, a commentary on politics and life. In it he also included some of his finest short stories, such as *A Gentle Creature*, remarkable for the immense pity he felt for the meek and the helpless, and *The Peasant Marey*, whose hero is an idealized peasant figure from the author's early childhood. Dostoyevsky's attitude toward the Russian peasants, as it appears from the *Writer's Diary*, was somewhat ambivalent. On the one hand, he depicted the peasant as an inhuman beast in his description of the flogging of a peasant woman by her husband, and, on the other, as a human being "whose only love is Christ whose image he adores to the point of suffering." He did his best, however, to reestablish himself in the eyes of the liberal and left-wing writers, whom he had alienated by *The Devils*, by offering his next novel, *The Adolescent*, for serialization in *Home Annals*, the left-wing monthly published by the poet Nikolai Nekrasov.

The Adolescent. The main theme of *The Adolescent* was formulated by Dostoyevsky as "the disintegration of family life." As usual, Dostoyevsky made use of some of the more sensational court cases, including the trial in 1874 of the members of a small revolutionary group, but he treated it with a great deal less rancor than he did the trial of the revolutionaries in *The Devils*. In his notes to the novel, however, his argument against the utilitarians is much more outspoken. He makes Versilov say to his adolescent son: "Even if you discovered the secrets of the exact sciences... the question would still remain: What shall we do then? With that amount of comfort what is there to live for? What is to be our aim? Mankind would still yearn for a great idea. I admit that, so far as the feeding of mankind is concerned, to feed and share out equally is at the moment also a great idea. But it is a minor and a subsidiary one, for after man has been fed he will most surely ask what he has to live for." This argument had not so far been formulated as profoundly as it would be four years later in "The Legend of the Grand Inquisitor" in *The Brothers Karamazov* (1878–1880).

The Brothers Karamazov. During 1876 and 1877, Dostoyevsky was wholly occupied with the publication of *The Writer's Diary*. He embarked on it mainly because, as he explained, he was getting ready to write *The Brothers Karamazov* and wished "to immerse himself in the study of the details of current life." He was also anxious to thrash out his argument against the theories of the materialists, whom he identified more and more with the "seminarists," such as Rakitin in *The Brothers Karamazov*—that is to say, the extreme radical writers, most of whom were the sons of priests and former seminarians.

"You understand, of course," he wrote in one of the issues of the *Diary*, "that science is still in its infancy... but what if all knowledge, the scientific discoveries which our sages don't even dream of, were suddenly disclosed to mankind? ...At first they would feel that they had been showered with blessings.... [We are told that] there would no longer be any need for continuous labor to earn the bare necessities of life.... I doubt, however, if all these ecstasies would last for one generation. Men would suddenly discover that they had no life, no freedom of spirit, no freedom of will and personality..., and man would realize that he had become a brute. Man would be covered with festering sores and would bite his tongue in torment when he saw that life had been taken from him for bread, for 'stones made into bread.'... People would become depressed and bored, everything had been done and there was nothing more left to do, everything was known and there was nothing more left to know.... Then perhaps men would cry out to God: 'Thou art right, O Lord. Man shall not live by bread alone.'"

The central idea of *The Brothers Karamazov*, embodied in the parable "The Legend of the Grand Inquisitor," had, therefore, already taken shape in Dostoyevsky's mind at the beginning of 1876. Dostoyevsky continued the argument, later expressed in artistic form in the parable, in his reply to a correspondent who asked him the meaning of his reference to "stones made into bread." It was, Dostoyevsky explained, the first temptation the Evil Spirit presented to Christ. Contemporary socialism in Europe eliminated Christ and was concerned above all with bread. It maintained that the cause of all men's troubles was poverty, the struggle for existence, and the bad influence of the environment. To that, Christ replied that man did not live by bread alone, that is, he propounded the axiom of the spiritual origin of man. If man had no spiritual life, no ideal of beauty, he fell into a state of boredom and was in danger of becoming insane, of "indulging in all sorts of pagan fantasies."

Other themes in *The Brothers Karamazov* deal with the disintegration of family life and the maltreatment of children, "the universal disorder" reigning everywhere in the leading ideas and convictions of society, the twilight of the Roman Catholic Church, the claim that socialism is a union of mankind brought about by force, and trial by jury, which Dostoyevsky ridiculed. In this novel Dostoyevsky seems also to have drawn a line between the Orthodox faith and the Orthodox Church, as personified by its priests. Zosima, the idealized holy man, is neither priest nor monk, but an "elder" (*starets*, a somewhat suspect figure in the Orthodox world), whom Dostoyevsky took great pains to put across as one of God's chosen spirits.

The towering characters of *The Brothers Karamazov* are a more compact and condensed variation of a whole number of his most important characters: the perfect man (Zosima); the great sinner (Fyodor Karamazov); the man of unrestrained passion and honesty, selfishness and self-torture (Dmitri); the young thinker and iconoclast (Ivan); the embodiment of Christian meekness and active love (Alyosha); the nihilist seminarist (Rakitin); the tragic courtesan (Grushenka); the proud and haughty fiancée (Katerina); and the hysterical girl (Lise). But what makes this novel so monumental a work of fiction is that in it Dostoyevsky succeeded in achieving his greatest triumph both as a creative artist and as a profound and fearless thinker.

See also BROTHERS KARAMAZOV; CRIME AND PUNISHMENT.

DAVID MAGARSHACK
Author of "Dostoevsky"

Bibliography
Standard English Translations of Dostoyevsky's works include those by Constance Garnett and David Magarshack.
Berdyaev, Nikolai, *Dostoievsky, an Interpretation*, tr. by Donald Attwater (London 1934).
Carr, Edward H., *Dostoevsky* (New York and London 1931).
Gide, André, *Dostoevsky*, tr. and with an introd. by Arnold Bennett (New York and London 1926).
Lavrin, Janko, *Dostoevsky, a Study* (London 1943).
Magarshack, David, *Dostoevsky* (New York and London 1962).
Murry, J. Middleton, *Fyodor Dostoevsky, a Critical Study* (London 1916).
Powys, John Cowper, *Dostoievsky* (London 1947).
Troyat, Henri, *Firebrand; the Life of Dostoevsky*, tr. by Norbert Guterman (New York 1946).
Yarmolinsky, Avrahm, *Dostoevsky, a Life*, 2d ed. (Toronto 1957).

DOTHAN, dō'thən, is a city in southeastern Alabama, the seat of Houston county, 95 miles (155 km) southeast of Montgomery. It is an important transportation and trade center for a large livestock and farming area. Dothan has lumber, meat-packing, and fertilizer industries, and it manufactures hosiery, clothing, furniture, peanut and cottonseed oil, chemicals, cigars, and toys. Dothan was settled in 1885. It has a commission form of government. Population: 48,750.

DOU, dou, **Gerard** (1613–1675), Dutch painter, who studied with Rembrandt and later succeeded him as the leading painter in the city of Leiden. His name is also spelled *Dow* or *Douw*.

He was born on April 7, 1613, in Leiden, the Netherlands, where he spent his entire life. After early training under the engraver Bartholomeus Dolendo and the glass painter Pieter Couwenhorn, Dou began his studies with Rembrandt. When Rembrandt moved to Amsterdam in 1632, Dou became Leiden's chief artist and contributed to the city's cultural growth by building a school and establishing a painters' guild there. He died in Leiden in early February 1675.

Dou is best known for his portraiture and genre painting, including such works as *Woman with Dropsy* and *Poulterer's Shop*. While his early paintings are reminiscent of Rembrandt in their free brushstroke and strong contrasts of light and shade, his later work is characterized by a smooth, enamel-like finish and shows a meticulous attention to detail.

DOUAI, dwä', is a city in northern France, in Nord department, in what was once the province of Flanders. It is on the Scarpe River, 19 miles (31 km) south of Lille and 125 miles (200 km) northeast of Paris. Douai's industrial growth has been greatly spurred by its proximity to the valuable Pas-de-Calais coalfield. It is primarily a commercial and industrial city, with its major activities in metallurgy, chemicals, and textiles. A famous educational center until its main faculties were transferred to Lille in 1887, it still has specialized schools.

The most notable building is the Town Hall, built half in the 15th century and half in 1860, with a splendid belfry 210 feet (65 meters) tall. The municipal museum contains Roman and medieval objects and a good collection of Flemish, Dutch, Italian, and French paintings, including the famous polyptych of Jean Bellegambe (1470–1534).

History. Known in ancient times as Duacum, the city came under the control of the counts of Flanders during the Middle Ages and prospered as a cloth center. Its importance declined after the Hundred Years' War, and it was later ruled by the dukes of Burgundy. In 1667, Louis XIV captured the city, which was ceded to France the next year. Douai suffered a great deal of damage during World Wars I and II, when it was occupied by the Germans.

In 1568, English Roman Catholics dedicated to revitalizing English Catholicism founded a college at Douai. Scholars at the college began working on an English version of the Latin Vulgate Bible, and a complete text was issued at Douai in 1609–1610. The Douay Bible soon became the Bible of English-speaking Roman Catholics. Population: (1972 est.) 49,187.

HOMER PRICE
Hunter College

DOUALA, doo-ä′lə, the largest city and port of Cameroon, situated about 20 miles (32 km) upstream from the Bight of Biafra. Located on the left bank of the Wouri River, Douala handles most of Cameroon's foreign trade and also serves the landlocked Central African Republic. It ships a variety of hardwoods, as well as coffee and palm products. The city has an international airport and is linked by rail north to N'Kongsamba and east to Yaoundé, Cameroon's capital, and M'Balmayo. Douala's industries include lumbering and the manufacture of aluminum products and consumer goods such as beer and textiles.

Situated about four degrees north of the equator, near the West African coast, Douala is hot and humid all year, with rainfall averaging 160 inches (406 cm) annually. The area around the city is forested; except for pockets of rubber and banana plantations and palm groves, it is unproductive agriculturally.

Douala was under German control from 1884 to 1916, and was the capital of the German protectorate of Kamerun. It was occupied by France in World War I and remained under French control until 1960, when the French Cameroons became independent. Population: (1976) 458,426.

HUGH C. BROOKS
St. Johns University, N.Y.

DOUAY BIBLE, doo-ā′, the first official Roman Catholic English version of the Bible. It is a translation of the Latin Vulgate Bible made at the English College of Douai (Douay; now in France) by Gregory Martin, assisted by William Allen and others. The New Testament was published in 1582 at Reims, where the college was temporarily located. The Old Testament was finished shortly afterward but not printed until 1609–1610, at Douai.

The translation retained many Latinisms unintelligible to many English readers. To make it more readily understandable, Bishop Richard Challoner issued a series of revisions (1749–1772) on which nearly all later editions have been based. See also BIBLE—*History of the English Bible.*

DOUBLE BASS, bās, or *contrabass,* the largest instrument of the violin family and the lowest in range. The instrument dates from the 16th century. Early Italian versions are bowed like the cello, from the palm downward, but the modern instrument generally is bowed from the palm upward. Its strings, usually four, are tuned in fourths (E-A-D-G), distinguishing it from other members of the violin family, all of which are tuned in fifths.

The double bass sounds tones an octave lower than the written notes; its range extends from E two octaves and a sixth below middle C to about A above middle C. Originally the instrument was used to reinforce, or "double," an octave lower, the cello parts. Today it can function independently and is particularly effective in "pizzicato," or plucked, passages.

DOUBLE BASSOON. See CONTRABASSOON.

DOUBLE-CROSTIC. See ACROSTIC.

DOUBLE INDEMNITY. See LIFE INSURANCE—*Optimal Coverage.*

DOUBLE JEOPARDY, jep′ər-dē, a legal defense available to an American criminal defendant (built into the 5th and 14th Amendments to the U.S. Constitution to protect basic rights) if he or she is prosecuted a second time for the same crime or crimes. This defense would apply after a first trial has started and then been concluded—either by an acquittal, by a conviction not overturned by an appeals court, or (under some circumstances) by an improper termination of the trial ("mistrial") by the judge without either conviction or acquittal.

Interpretation of the double-jeopardy rule is complicated by the issue of what constitutes retrial for the same crime. If a person kills several others at once, even with only one explosion of a single weapon, each death, if criminal, constitutes a separate homicide. Thus mass murderers may be tried many times for the same killing incident (one trial for each victim). Similarly, unlawfully killing a person by arson of the victim's house generally constitutes at least two crimes (arson and murder), although there is one victim.

Because of separation of jurisdiction in the U.S. federal system, the double-jeopardy rule does not prevent successive trials before a state court and a federal court for conduct that is criminal under both state and federal law.

RICHARD B. CHILD
New England School of Law

DOUBLE STAR. See BINARY STAR.

DOUBLE TAXATION, the levying of two taxes on the same object of taxation. The duplication may arise from either one or two governments. The term generally applies to any of four tax situations.

(1) A double listing of an item may appear on the tax roll, as when a railroad bridge is taxed as a bridge and again as part of a railroad. This is a consequence of inept or arbitrary administration.

(2) The state may levy on two aspects of or interests in a taxable object, as when it collects both a license tax and a motor fuel tax on an automobile. This type of multiplicity need involve no inequities if the basis of classification is reasonable. It has involved such controversies as those associated with the double listing of real property and mortgages for property taxation and the double listing of corporate incomes and dividends for income taxation.

(3) A territorial species of double taxation arises from independent and frequently non-uniform rules of jurisdiction among countries or states. This is a grievous problem that has been attacked by negotiating treaties, by allowing credits, and by promoting uniform legislation. It is generally agreed that a taxpayer whose income arises in more than one jurisdiction should not be required to pay more taxes than another who confines himself to one jurisdiction.

(4) More than one layer of government (such as state and federal) may impose "overlapping" taxes. This double taxation entails complications but need not involve inequities. (It is possible, for example, that two kinds of taxes at each of two levels of government can add up to exactly the same result as one kind of tax at each level.)

It is established legal doctrine that "the power to tax twice is as ample as the power to tax once." However, the multiplicity of taxes on the same object or person by the same or different governments adds enormously to the complication of the tax system and to the problems of preserving equity in the system.

HAROLD M. GROVES, *University of Wisconsin*

DOUBLE TENTH is a Chinese national holiday that falls on the 10th day of the 10th month, that is, October 10th. It honors the revolution against the Ch'ing dynasty, beginning with the Wuchang insurrection on Oct. 10, 1911, which brought about the establishment of the first republic in Asia.

A legal holiday in Taiwan, it is celebrated there with a military review and public speeches. Double Tenth is not celebrated in Communist China, where it has been replaced by October 1, honoring the establishment of the Chinese People's Republic in 1949. Among overseas Chinese, the celebration of either of these holidays has taken on the character of a political act.

JAMES R. SHIRLEY, *Northern Illinois University*

DOUBLEDAY, Abner (1819–1893), American army officer, who was once credited with inventing baseball. Doubleday was born in Ballston Spa, N.Y., on June 26, 1819. He worked as a surveyor from 1836 to 1838 and graduated from the U.S. Military Academy in 1842. He served under Gen. Zachary Taylor in the war with Mexico (1846–1848).

At the outbreak of the Civil War, Doubleday fired the first Union gun in defense of Fort Sumter, S.C., on April 12, 1861. He fought in many battles, including Bull Run and Antietam. His heroic work at Gettysburg in 1863 is commemorated by a bronze statue on the battlefield. Doubleday retired from active service in 1873. He died in Mendham, N.J., on Jan. 26, 1893.

In 1980 a commission formed by Albert G. Spalding credited Doubleday with inventing baseball, but this report was discredited. See also BASEBALL—*The History of Baseball*.

BOB MCCORMICK, *Associated Features, Inc.*

DOUBLEDAY, Frank Nelson (1862–1934), American book publisher. He was born in Brooklyn, N.Y., on Jan 8, 1862. At 15 he began to work at Charles Scribner's Sons, and he remained there for 20 years, becoming manager of *Scribner's Magazine* in 1887. In 1897, with Samuel S. McClure, Doubleday started the book publishing firm of Doubleday & McClure, which Doubleday and Walter Hines Page reorganized in 1900 as Doubleday, Page & Company. Ten years later he moved the firm to Garden City, Long Island, and also started a chain of bookshops.

When William Heinemann, the English publisher, died in 1920, Doubleday bought his business. Then, in 1927, Doubleday merged his American firm with George H. Doran & Company, renaming it Doubleday, Doran & Company. It became Doubleday & Company in 1946. Doubleday died in Coconut Grove, Fla., on Jan. 30, 1934, after which his son, Nelson Doubleday (1889–1949), headed the firm.

Frank Doubleday was primarily a businessman, highly aggressive in promoting his publications. However, he loved good books and attracted a number of popular authors, including Conrad, Tarkington, Sinclair Lewis, and Kipling.

CHARLES A. MADISON
Author of "Book Publishing in America"

DOUBLET, dub'lət, is a term applied to both an undergarment and an outergarment worn by men in Europe from the Middle Ages to the beginning of the 17th century. Doublets had sleeves and were fastened in front, first by thongs and later by buttons. As an undergarment, the doublet was padded and was worn, along with hip-length hose, under armor.

As an outergarment, the doublet, worn over an inner tunic, made its first appearance in the 13th century in Italy. (A jerkin, similar to the doublet but sleeveless, was sometimes worn over both the tunic and doublet.) In Elizabethan times the doublet extended far below the waist. By the late 16th century, doublet sleeves were decorated with lacings, ribbons, and slashings and sometimes were puffed out at the shoulder. By the early 17th century, the doublet was gored and began to resemble the modern suit jacket. It was worn partly open in front to show the shirt, and the sleeves had fancy lace cuffs.

DOUBS, dōō, a department in eastern France on the Swiss border, in the administrative region of Franche-Comté. The department takes its name from the Doubs River, which cuts through it on its way to join the Saône.

Most of the department lies in the Jura Mountains and is hence quite rugged and high. Only a small area in the Doubs Valley near the northwest border lies below 1,000 feet (300 meters) The city of Besançon, an important manufacturing center, is the capital of the department. Other towns include Audincourt and Montbéliard. The department's area is 2,021 square miles (5,234 sq km). Population: (1980 est.) 492,500.

HOMER PRICE, *Hunter College*

DOUBS RIVER, dōō, a tributary of the Saône in eastern France. It rises in the Jura Mountains near the Swiss border and flows northeast to form the French-Swiss border for some distance, then into Switzerland and back into France. Turning west, then southwest, it passes through the cities of Besançon and Dole to join the Saône a few miles north of Chalon. Many canals have been constructed from the river, among them the Canal du Rhône au Rhin, linking the Rhône and Rhine rivers near Montbéliard.

HOMER PRICE, *Hunter College*

DOUC, dook, a leaf-eating langur monkey (*Pygathrix nemaeus*) native to the forests of North and South Vietnam and Laos. Its numbers are thought to have been seriously reduced in the 1960's as a result of the Vietnam war.

DOUGHBOY, dō'boi, is a slang term for a soldier of the U.S. Army in World War I. In its first recorded application to soldiers, in 1867, "doughboy" was a derogatory name applied to infantrymen, particularly by cavalrymen. The most commonly accepted origin of the word is the fact that the Union infantry uniform in the Civil War had large globular brass buttons resembling a doughboy, a flour dumpling cooked in soup.

At the start of World War I, American soldiers in France resented being called "Sammies" and "Teddies." Maj. Gen. William Sibert asked for suggestions, and a consensus chose "doughboy." In World War II the U.S. enlisted man was called a "G.I." (for "government issue," applied to army supplies), although "dogface" and other names were used.

DOUGHERTY, dô′ərt-ē, **Dennis Joseph** (1865–1951), American Roman Catholic archbishop and cardinal. He was born in Girardville, Pa., on Aug. 16, 1865. After studying in Canada, he entered St. Charles Seminary, Overbrook, Pa., but transferred to the North American College in Rome, where he was ordained on May 31, 1890. He went back to St. Charles as professor and treasurer. In 1903 he was named missionary bishop to the Philippines, where he served successively at Nueva Segovia and Jaro.

Dougherty became bishop of Buffalo, N. Y., in 1915 and archbishop of Philadelphia in 1918. As archbishop he created 112 parishes, 145 parochial schools, 53 high schools, 4 colleges, 12 hospitals, and 11 homes for the aged in a 30-year building campaign. He was named a cardinal in 1921 and aided in the canonization of St. Thérèse de Lisieux (1925). He died in Philadelphia on May 31, 1951.

HARRY J. SIEVERS, S. J.
Loyola Seminary, Shrub Oak, N. Y.

DOUGHERTY, DOKH′ər-tē, **Paul** (1877–1947), American painter. He was born in Brooklyn, N. Y., on Sept. 6, 1877. He had an early interest in art, but, following his father's wishes, he obtained a law degree from New York Law School in 1898.

Dougherty's main concern soon reverted to art, however, and from 1900 to 1905 he painted and studied in London, Florence, Paris, and Munich. When he returned to the United States, his paintings, mostly landscapes, began to attract favorable attention. But it was his marine paintings, done on trips along the New England coast, that made his reputation. A typical example is his *October Seas* (1910) in the Metropolitan Museum of Art, New York City. His later work includes mountain scenes, watercolor landscapes, figure paintings, and still lifes. He died at Palm Springs, Calif., on Jan. 9, 1947.

DOUGHTY, dou′tē, **Sir Arthur George** (1860–1936), Canadian archivist and historian. He was born in Maidenhead, England, on March 22, 1860. After emigrating to Canada in 1886, he worked as a clerk in a Montreal mercantile firm and became music, drama, and literary critic for the Montreal *Gazette*. In 1897 he entered the Quebec civil service and by 1901 was joint librarian of the Quebec legislative library with N. E. Dionne, with whom he wrote *Quebec Under Two Flags* (2 vols., 1903). He became archivist of the Dominion of Canada in 1904, serving until his death, in Ottawa, on Dec. 1, 1936.

Doughty played an important role in the Quebec tercentenary in 1908, editing the 2-volume *King's Book of Quebec*. He compiled *The Siege of Quebec and the Battle of the Plains* (6 vols., 1901–1902) with G. W. Parmelee, and *The Oxford Encyclopedia of Canadian History* (1926) with L. J. Burpee, and edited *Canada and Its Provinces* (23 vols., 1913–1917) with Adam Shortt. He also wrote *The Fortress of Quebec* (1904), *The Cradle of New France* (1909), and *The Acadian Exiles* (1916). As dominion archivist, he organized systematic searching for historical records and founded the archival publications *Documents Relating to the Constitutional History of Canada* and *The Elgin-Grey Papers*.

CORNELIUS J. JAENEN
University of Ottawa

DOUGHTY, dou′tē, **Charles Montagu** (1843–1926), English traveler and author. He was born at Theberton Hall, Suffolk, on Aug. 19, 1843, and studied geology at Cambridge. In 1870, motivated by interest in the origins of English culture, he started on a prolonged journey through Europe and the Middle East, culminating in his spectacular wanderings in northwestern Arabia. He lived both in towns and in the desert with the nomads and endured great privation and danger—experiences he described in *Travels in Arabia Deserta* (1888). The book received little attention until it was reissued in 1921 with an introduction by T. E. Lawrence.

Most of Doughty's other work is poetry. He took special pride in his epic *The Dawn of Britain* (6 vols., 1906–1907), which is an attempt to trace the rise of the national consciousness. Doughty died at Sissinghurst, Kent, on Jan. 20, 1926.

THOMAS J. ASSAD
Author of "Three Victorian Travellers"

Further Reading: Assad, Thomas J., *Three Victorian Travellers* (London 1964); Fairley, Barker, *Charles M. Doughty* (London 1927); Hogart, David G., *The Life of Charles Montagu Doughty* (London 1928).

DOUGHTY, dou′tē, **Thomas** (1793–1856), American landscape painter, who was a founder of the Hudson River school (q.v.). He was one of the first American painters to devote himself exclusively to landscape painting and one of the first to achieve international recognition. His idealized scenes of woodlands, river valleys, and lakes are valued for the "silvery tone" that was much admired in romantic landscapes and for their detailed sky effects.

Doughty was born in Philadelphia, on July 19, 1793. After a period of apprenticeship to a leather currier, he turned to painting. Although he was almost entirely self-taught, success came rapidly. He lived at various times in Philadelphia, New York, and Boston, and from 1837 to 1839 in England. Among his best-known works are *On the Hudson* and *A River Glimpse*, both in the Metropolitan Museum, New York. Doughty died in New York City on July 22, 1856.

DOUGLAS is the name of a Scottish family, first mentioned in the 12th century. Its history was for three centuries inseparable from the history of Scotland.

Sir James Douglas (c. 1286–1330), the son of a patriot who died in the Tower of London, joined the Scottish resistance under Robert the Bruce (see BRUCE) and with him is joint hero of John Barbour's poem *The Bruce*. After helping Bruce win his kingdom at Bannockburn, Sir James, called "the Black" because of his swarthy complexion, made a series of brilliant raids on the north of England that consolidated the victory. He was rewarded with wide estates. On Bruce's death in 1329, Sir James was given Bruce's heart, to be borne in battle against the infidel. Douglas died fighting the Moors in Spain on Aug. 25, 1330, and the circumstance of his death led to the addition of a bloody heart to the Douglas arms.

The Black Douglases, Earls of Douglas. Nine successive Douglases, drawn from four generations, held the earldom of Douglas for a century from 1358, when David II created the title for Sir James' nephew, William (1327?–1384). Renowned through Europe for their warlike exploits, the Douglases acquired huge estates.

James (c. 1358–1388), 2d Earl, was the "dead man who won a fight." Mortally wounded in battle at Chevy Chase (Otterburn), he instructed his comrades to raise his standard and hide the fact of his death until the battle was won. After the victory his title and estates passed to Archibald the Grim (1328?–1400), the illegitimate son of the first Sir James. His son Archibald (1369?–1424), 4th Earl, fought valiantly for Charles VII of France.

A dynastic feud led to the downfall of the Black Douglases. Archibald (1391?–1439), who succeeded his father as 5th Earl, had claims through his mother and wife to the royal succession by descent from both of King Robert II's marriages, whereas the Stuart kings were descended only from Robert's first and legally dubious marriage. Archibald's son William (1423?–1440), 6th Earl, was murdered at a dinner arranged in Edinburgh Castle by courtiers of the 6-year-old King James II, and the family estates were divided between William's sister Margaret and his great-uncle James (1371?–1443), 7th Earl. However, the latter's son William (1425?–1452), 8th Earl, married Margaret, thereby reuniting the Douglas lands and regaining the claim to the throne. But his ambition proved fatal. William was stabbed to death by James II at Stirling, and his brother James (1426–1488), 9th Earl, who then married Margaret, fled to England and was deprived of his title and estates in 1455.

The Red Douglases, Earls of Angus. William, 1st Earl of Douglas, had an illegitimate son, George (1380?–1403), by Margaret Stuart, Countess of Angus. When George married King Robert III's daughter Mary in 1397, he became Earl of Angus. On the fall of the Black Douglases, the Angus branch received some of the Black Douglases' estates.

Archibald (1449?–1514), 5th Earl, led the nobles against James III in 1482. His grandson and successor, Archibald (1489?–1557), 6th Earl, married Margaret Tudor, widow of James IV, and their daughter was mother of Lord Darnley and grandmother of James VI (James I of England). The 6th Earl ruled Scotland for two years at the end of James V's minority but was banished to England in 1528. He returned in 1543 and was politically active in the minority of Mary, Queen of Scots. The title was briefly held by his nephew David (died 1557), whose son, Archibald (1555–1588), succeeded. Both the 8th Earl of Angus and his uncle James Douglas, Earl of Morton, who was regent during the minority of James VI, continued the Protestant and pro-English tradition of the house that the 6th Earl had established.

William (1589–1660), 11th Earl, was created Marquess of Douglas in 1633, and Archibald (1694–1761), 3d Marquess, became Duke of Douglas in 1703. On his death there ensued the "Douglas Cause" to settle the succession to the titles and estates. The estates went to a nephew, from whom they passed by marriage to the earls of Home, and most of the titles went to the dukes of Hamilton, who are still marquesses of Douglas and earls of Angus.

GORDON DONALDSON, *University of Edinburgh*

DOUGLAS, Lord Alfred (1870–1945), British editor and poet, who is remembered primarily for his controversial friendship with Oscar Wilde. He was born Alfred Bruce Douglas, in Worcester, England, on Oct. 22, 1870, the third son of the 8th Marquess of Queensberry. He was educated at Winchester and Oxford, which he left without a degree. Douglas, who was known as "Bosie" throughout his life, was introduced to Oscar Wilde in July 1891. A romantic friendship, opposed by the Queensberrys, developed, culminating in the Queensberry-Wilde libel suit, which led to Wilde's 2-year imprisonment. The friendship nevertheless continued until Wilde's death in 1900.

On March 4, 1902, Douglas married Olive Custance, who separated from him in 1913. He had become a Roman Catholic in 1911. He edited the *Academy, Plain English,* and *Plain Speech,* but he always identified himself as a poet. Besides his volumes of verse, he published two books about Wilde, *Oscar Wilde and Myself* (1914) and *Oscar Wilde: A Summing Up* (1940). Douglas died at Lancing, near London, on March 20, 1945.

ARTHUR C. YOUNG, *Russell Sage College*

DOUGLAS, Gavin (1474?–1522), Scottish poet and bishop, who was the first person to translate a major Latin classic, Virgil's *Aeneid,* into English. As a younger son of the 5th Earl of Angus, Gavin (or Gawain) Douglas was educated for the church. In 1514 his nephew married Henry VIII of England's sister, the widowed queen of James IV of Scotland. The marriage enabled Douglas to exert political pressure to have himself appointed bishop of Dunkeld in 1515. When the marriage collapsed in 1521, Douglas went to the English court to defend his nephew against a charge of treason. Douglas was deprived of his bishopric while in London and died there in September 1522.

Writings. Douglas' chief work is his forceful and exuberant translation (1513) of the *Aeneid* in rhymed pentameter couplets. To Virgil's 12 books he added a 13th by the Italian humanist Mapheus Vegius and 13 prologues, including some that vigorously describe Scottish scenery, some that develop critical theories, and some that moralize tediously. His own poetry includes a moral dream allegory, *The Palise of Honour* (first published ?1533). Another allegory, *King Hart* (first printed 1786), has been attributed to him.

DAVID F. C. COLDWELL
Author of "Gavin Douglas"

DOUGLAS, dug'ləs, **Sir Howard** (1776–1861), British general and colonial governor. He was born at Gosport, England and had a military career. While governing New Brunswick (1823–1831) he preserved peace with Maine despite provocative incidents. When the United States and Britain agreed in 1827 to submit the border dispute to the King of the Netherlands for arbitration, Douglas prepared Britain's case; the issue was not settled, however, until the Webster-Ashburton Treaty of 1842. He died at Tunbridge Wells, England, on Nov. 9, 1861.

DOUGLAS, Sir James (1803–1877), Canadian trader and public official, known as "the father of British Columbia." He was born in Demerara (now in Guyana) on Aug. 15, 1803, and went to Canada as a fur trade clerk in 1819.

Douglas became chief factor at Fort Victoria in 1849. When he was also appointed governor of Vancouver Island (1851–1863), he held positions of conflicting interest. With the gold rush of

1858, he severed his commercial ties to serve also as governor (1858–1864) of the mainland colony of British Columbia. Douglas feared the influence of gold-seeking Americans. With the aid of the Royal Engineers, good magistrates, a strong judge, and the Royal Navy, he built roads, ensured law and order, and made the Fraser River rather than the Columbia the main entry to the gold colony—all to hold the territory for the British crown. He was knighted for his successes and retired in 1864. He died in Victoria on Aug. 2, 1877.

GORDON R. ELLIOTT, *Simon Fraser University*

DOUGLAS, Lloyd Cassel (1877–1951), American clergyman and author, who wrote popular inspirational novels dramatizing Christian faith and morals. The most successful of these books was *The Robe* (1942).

Douglas was born in Columbia City, Ind., on Aug. 27, 1877, and was educated at Wittenberg University in Springfield, Ohio. He was chaplain and director of religious work at the University of Illinois from 1911 to 1915 and spent many years as the pastor of churches in the United States and Canada. After retiring from the ministry in 1933, Douglas devoted his life to writing and lecturing. He died on Feb. 15, 1951, in Los Angeles.

After his best-selling first novel, *Magnificent Obsession* (1929), Douglas wrote such books as *Invitation to Live* (1940), *Green Light* (1935) and *Disputed Passage* (1939). He completed only the beginning of his autobiography in *Time to Remember* (1951), but his life story was continued by his two daughters in *The Shape of Sunday* (1952).

DOUGLAS, Melvyn (1901–1981), American actor, who in a long career went from debonair leading man to distinguished dramatic actor. Melvyn Hesselberg was born in Macon, Ga., on April 5, 1901. In 1919 he made his debut (as Melvyn Douglas) with a stock company in Chicago, Ill., and later joined Jessie Bonstelle's stock company there. For a short time he had his own stock company in Madison, Wis.

In 1928, Douglas made his Broadway debut. In 1930 he played opposite Helen Gahagan in David Belasco's last production, *Tonight or Never*. In 1931 they were married, and that year *Tonight or Never* was filmed with Gloria Swanson. Douglas was hired to play opposite her, and except for occasional appearances or directorial stints in New York, he remained in Hollywood as a leading man until World War II. He made the classic *Ninotchka* with Greta Garbo in 1939. He enlisted in the U. S. Army as a private in 1942 and was demobilized as a major in 1945.

From 1947 to 1949 he again made films. He returned to the stage in *Time Out for Ginger* in 1952 and toured in it until 1955. He appeared in *The Waltz of the Toreadors* in 1959, and in 1960 he received the "Tony" Award as best actor for his performance in *The Best Man*.

As a character man, Douglas won Academy Awards as best supporting actor for his work in the motion pictures *Hud* (1963) and *Being There* (1979) and the 1968 "Emmy" award as best actor for his performance in the television play *Do Not Go Gentle into That Good Night*. He also played character roles in *The Americanization of Emily* (1964) and *The Candidate* (1972). He died in New York City on Aug. 4, 1981.

DOUGLAS, Norman (1868–1952), British novelist and author of travel books. George Norman Douglas was born on Dec. 8, 1868, at Thüringen, Vorarlberg, Austria, a descendant, on his paternal side, of Scottish lairds, and, on his maternal side, of Scottish and German aristocrats. He spent his early childhood in Austria, where his family owned cotton mills. He received his first schooling in England and completed his formal education at the gymnasium in Karlsruhe, Germany. He then prepared for the British diplomatic service, entered the foreign office in London in 1893, and was posted to St. Petersburg (now Leningrad) in 1894. He quit diplomacy in 1896, and thereafter lived chiefly in Italy. In 1898 he married his cousin, Elsa FitzGibbon, from whom he was divorced in 1903. Douglas died at Capri, Italy, on Feb. 9, 1952.

Douglas is best known for his first novel, *South Wind* (1917), a philosophic work with a Capri-like setting, and for his travel books, especially those on southern Italy—*Siren Land* (1911) and *Old Calabria* (1915). His books, written in a precise and easy style, are pervaded by his interests in geology and biology, languages, and the ancient world. They also reflect his affection for the landscape and people of the Mediterranean and his prejudice against middle-class morality and religion, which he associated particularly with northern Europe.

J. K. JOHNSTONE
University of Saskatchewan

DOUGLAS, Paul Howard (1892–1976), American economist and senator. He was born in Salem, Mass., on March 26, 1892, graduated from Bowdoin College in 1913, and received a Ph. D. in economics from Columbia in 1921. After serving on several economic faculties, he went to the University of Chicago in 1920, becoming a full professor of economics in 1925. He won national recognition as an economist with the publication of *Wages and the Family* (1925). His later works, including *Real Wages in the United States 1890–1926* (1930), *The Theory of Wages* (1934), *Ethics in Government* (1952), and *Economy in the National Government* (1952), further enhanced his reputation.

In the 1920's and 1930's, Douglas served in various consultative capacities. He was adviser to state commissions on unemployment in Pennsylvania and New York, and in Illinois he drafted state legislation on unemployment, public utility regulation, old age pensions, and housing, while serving (1925–1942) as chairman of the arbitration board for the newspaper industry. During the New Deal days in Washington, he acted as adviser to the National Recovery Administration.

He served as a Chicago alderman from 1939 to 1942. In World War II he enlisted as a marine private in 1942, at the age of 50, and rose to the rank of lieutenant colonel. He was wounded at Okinawa. In 1948 he was elected to the U. S. Senate as a Democrat, and was reelected in 1954 and 1960, but lost in 1966 to Charles Percy. As a senator, Douglas was active and constructive in formulating legislation in the fields of labor, social security, and banking and currency, and he urged a code of ethics for all members of Congress. His memoirs, *In the Fullness of Time*, appeared in 1972. He died in Washington, D. C., on Sept. 24, 1976.

DAVID LINDSEY
California State College at Los Angeles

DOUGLAS, dug'ləs, **Stephen Arnold** (1813–1861), American political leader. A U. S. senator for 14 years and a contender for the presidency, Douglas was a major force in American politics before the Civil War. However, he often is remembered primarily for his association with Abraham Lincoln, whom he defeated for the Senate in 1859 following the famous Lincoln-Douglas debates. Much literature extolling Lincoln has depicted Douglas as an unscrupulous politician who conspired with the South to make slavery a national institution. But scholarship has revealed that Douglas' motives were not Machiavellian and that his contribution was of positive importance. He was considerably more than a "foil" for Lincoln.

Early Life. Douglas was born in Brandon, Vt., on April 23, 1813. After serving an apprenticeship to a Vermont cabinetmaker, he attended Canandaigua Academy in New York. Restlessness drove him westward as a young man, first to Cleveland, then to St. Louis, and finally to Jacksonville, Ill., where he studied law. He was admitted to the bar at the age of 20. His meteoric rise in politics paralleled the growth of the Democratic party in Illinois. By the time he was 27, Douglas was on the Illinois supreme court.

Political Career. Douglas was elected to the Illinois General Assembly in 1836 but was unsuccessful in his first bid for Congress two years later. He also served briefly as secretary of state of Illinois (1840) before his term as a judge (1841–1843). In 1842 he was elected to Congress for the first of two consecutive terms. Four years later he became a U. S. senator and was immediately thrust into the potentially influential position of chairman of the Senate Committee on Territories.

Also in 1847, Douglas married Martha Denny Martin, who bore him two sons. She died in 1853, and three years later he married Adèle Cutts, the great-niece of Dolley Madison.

In keeping with northward population shifts in Illinois, Douglas moved to Chicago in 1847 and became deeply involved in the city's development. As a senator he was instrumental in securing passage in 1850 of the Illinois Central Railroad Bill, which provided that Chicago be the railroad's northern terminus. During this period he played a major, though behind-the-scenes, role in enacting the Compromise of 1850 (q.v.). By 1852 he had distinguished himself sufficiently to become the presidential candidate of the "Young America" wing of the Democratic party. He lost the nomination but won reelection to the Senate.

The Slavery Issue. In 1854, Douglas was the principal architect of the controversial Kansas-Nebraska Act (q.v.), which organized the territories of Kansas and Nebraska in preparation for statehood. According to Douglas' principle of "popular sovereignty," which would allow the people to declare their wishes on slavery by local "friendly" or "unfriendly" legislation, the law provided that the people in these territories decide for themselves on issues concerning slavery. Many Northerners, including Abolitionists, Democrats, and Whigs, vigorously opposed this position. Consequently, the Kansas-Nebraska Act was a principal factor in the birth of the Republican party, which adopted as its goal the nonextension of slavery to the territories.

In 1857, Douglas' position on slavery again came under fire when Kansas' proslavery Lecompton Constitution (q.v.) was submitted to Congress. Despite President Buchanan's support of this constitution, Douglas opposed it as a violation of "popular sovereignty," thereby causing a breach within the Democratic party.

Stephen A. Douglas

Also in 1857 the U. S. Supreme Court handed down the Dred Scott decision, which guaranteed Southerners the right to take slave property westward. Confronted with the dilemma of reconciling "popular sovereignty" with this ruling, Douglas declared that Kansans still could exclude slavery through "unfriendly" legislation. This position cost him much support in the South.

Douglas v. Lincoln. In 1858, Senator Douglas returned to Illinois to seek reelection. He accepted the challenge of Abraham Lincoln, his Republican opponent, to a series of political debates on the Kansas slavery issue. The debates marked the high point of "stump speaking" in America. The "Little Giant," barely 5 feet tall, with a massive head, thick neck, and barrel chest, was dwarfed on the platform by the tall, lean Lincoln, but his voice was deep and resonant, in contrast with Lincoln's shrill delivery. Douglas continued to defend "popular sovereignty" although Lincoln repeatedly pointed out the inconsistency of this stand with the Dred Scott decision. The Republicans won a popular majority, but apportionment proved advantageous to the Democrats, and Douglas was returned to the Senate by the state legislature. See also LINCOLN, ABRAHAM—*Lincoln-Douglas Debates.*

The two Illinois politicians met again in 1860 with the presidency at stake. Douglas won the Democratic nomination, but the Southern wing bolted and nominated a separate candidate, a decision that was instrumental in Lincoln's victory.

As the Civil War neared, Douglas worked tirelessly in the Senate to preserve the Union and gave President Lincoln his firm support. While on a speaking tour to rally the nation behind its government, Douglas was stricken with typhoid fever and died in Chicago on June 3, 1861.

RICHARD ALLEN HECKMAN, *Berea College, Ky.*

Further Reading: Heckman, Richard A., *Lincoln vs. Douglas: The Great Debates Campaign* (Washington 1967); Johannsen, Robert W., ed., *The Letters of Stephen A. Douglas* (Urbana, Ill., 1961); Johnson, Allen, *Stephen A. Douglas* (New York 1908); Milton, George Fort, *The Eve of Conflict: Stephen A. Douglas and the Needless War* (Boston 1934).

DOUGLAS, Thomas Clement (1904–   ), first leader of Canada's New Democratic party. He was born in Falkirk, Scotland, on Oct. 20, 1904, and grew up in Winnipeg. By 1931, "Tommy" Douglas was a Baptist minister in Weyburn, Saskatchewan. Appalled by depression conditions, he joined the Saskatchewan Independent Labour party, which in 1932 helped form the Cooperative Commonwealth Federation (CCF), composed of farmer, labor, and socialist movements in various parts of Canada. From 1935 to 1944 he was a CCF member of the Canadian Parliament.

In 1944, Douglas became the first CCF premier of Saskatchewan. The accomplishments of his administration included compulsory government health insurance, government medicare, government automobile insurance, and rural electrification and distribution of natural gas at cost. When in 1961 the CCF joined with the Canadian Labour Congress to form the New Democratic party, Douglas became that party's first national leader, resigning his Saskatchewan premiership. He reentered the Parliament of Canada, representing Burnaby-Coquitlam, British Columbia, from 1962 to 1968.

G. O. ROTHNEY, *Lakehead University*

DOUGLAS, William Orville (1898–1980), American public official and judge, who served an unprecedented 36½ years (1939–1975) as associate justice of the U. S. Supreme Court. A dedicated naturalist and conservationist, he was author of some 30 books, mainly on these subjects.

Born in Maine, Minn., on Oct. 16, 1898, Douglas was raised in Yakima, Wash., by his widowed mother. Afflicted at an early age with poliomyelitis, he resolved to recover his strength by hiking in the nearby Cascade Mountains. This marked the beginning of his lifelong interest in nature. He graduated in 1920 from Whitman College in Walla Walla, Wash., and in 1925 from the Columbia University Law School. After practice in New York City and Yakima and teaching at Columbia, he joined the law faculty of Yale University in 1928. His specialty was business law, and he published leading casebooks on the law of business organizations.

Douglas was appointed a member of the Securities and Exchange Commission (SEC) on Jan. 21, 1936, and on Sept. 21, 1937, he became its chairman. On March 20, 1939, President Roosevelt nominated him to the Supreme Court, one of the youngest justices ever appointed to that post. He was sworn in on April 17, 1939.

On Dec. 31, 1974, Douglas suffered a stroke from which he was unable to recover fully. Although he returned to the Supreme Court in the fall of 1975, his failing health forced him to retire on Nov. 12, 1975, after serving a record 36 years and 7 months.

As a justice, Douglas consistently voted for a broad exercise of the court's powers. For example, in the fall of 1967 he dissented from the court's decision not to review several cases that might have raised the issue of the legality of the Vietnam War. Always advocating a strong interpretation of the Bill of Rights, he led the struggle to apply these rights to those accused of crimes in state courts. At first in dissent, he argued that the Bill of Rights was applicable to the states through the due process clause of the 14th Amendment, but after *Mapp* v. *Ohio* (1961), which held the 4th Amendment prohibiting unreasonable searches and seizures applicable to the states, a majority of the court tended to vote with him on this issue.

While carrying out his duties for the court, Douglas traveled widely and wrote prolifically. His books include *Of Men and Mountains* (1950), *Beyond the High Himalayas* (1952), *An Almanac of Liberty* (1954), *Russian Journey* (1956), *Democracy's Manifesto* (1962), and *A Wilderness Bill of Rights* (1965). In 1966, Douglas married for the fourth time. He died in Washington, D. C., on Jan. 19, 1980, and was buried in Arlington National Cemetery.

EDMUND W. KITCH, *University of Chicago*

DOUGLAS FIR
(Pseudotsuga taxifolia)

DOUGLAS FIR, a graceful, cone-bearing tree, frequently 200 feet (60 meters) tall, with a trunk measuring 12 feet (3.5 meters) or more in diameter. The Douglas fir (*Pseudotsuga taxifolia*), a member of the pine family (Pinaceae), is naturally distributed from British Columbia south through the Rocky Mountains to western Texas and northern Mexico. It is found from sea level to elevations above 11,000 feet (3,300 meters). The Douglas fir is often planted in the northern and eastern United States for the beauty of its form and has been introduced into Europe.

The red-brown bark of mature trees is up to 12 inches (30 cm) thick and is divided into large, ridged, oblong plates. The wood is soft and red or yellow in color, with an almost white sapwood. It is variable in density and quality, but it is one of the most important woods in the United States, especially in the Northwest, where it is used for construction lumber, fuel, rail ties, and pilings. The bark is sometimes used for tanning leathers.

The horizontal branches and their pendulous branchlets are densely clothed with spirally arranged needle leaves, spreading into two opposite rows. The straight, linear, blunt-tipped needles are up to 1¼ inches (3 cm) long and about 1⁄16 inch (1.5 mm) wide and are usually dark yellow-green in color. The male (staminate) and female (pistillate) reproductive parts occur in separate, drooping flower cones on the same tree: the staminate cones are orange-red; the pistillate cones, reddish. The flower cones mature into woody fruits with rounded scales, which are dark blue-green on the underside, purplish toward the tips, and bright red along the edge. Three-pointed bracts project as much as ½ inch (13 mm) from between the scales. The seeds are about ¼ inch (6 mm) long, with a light brown-red wing that catches air currents for dispersal of the seed.

Because of its symmetry and rapid growth, the Douglas fir is widely planted, thriving best in a porous, sandy loam. Unlike the spruces, which it resembles in cultural requirements, it usually should be planted in groups because the soft, thin needles are easily broken and dessicated by hot winds. The Douglas fir's many fibrous roots suit it well for transplanting, even when the tree is of considerable size, as well as for growth in shallow soils. Seeds for planting should be collected at maturity and, after overwintering, set first in beds or flats and then into nursery rows. Seeds from trees on the Pacific slope produce plants subject to frost damage, but trees from high elevations bear cold-resistant seeds. Layering and grafting are used to propagate unusual varieties and forms.

RICHARD S. COWAN, *Smithsonian Institution*

DOUGLAS-HOME, dug'ləs hūm, **Sir Alec** (1903–), British prime minister from October 1963 to October 1964. Alexander Frederick Douglas-Home was born in Scotland on July 2, 1903, the son of the 13th Earl of Home. After attending Eton and Oxford, he entered the House of Commons (with the courtesy title Lord Dunglass) as a Conservative in 1931. Until World War II, his interest lay in domestic issues, in which he emphasized the need to mitigate class divisions.

When Neville Chamberlain became prime minister in 1937, Dunglass was made his parliamentary private secretary, with administrative rather than policy-making duties. He was omitted from the Churchill government that replaced Chamberlain's in 1940. He became a joint parliamentary undersecretary at the foreign office in May 1945 but lost his Commons seat in the 1945 election and did not return until 1950.

In 1951, Dunglass succeeded his father as the 14th Earl of Home. Although forced to leave the house of Commons, he made rapid progress politically. He became minister of state for Scotland in 1951, Commonwealth secretary in 1955, and leader of the House of Lords in 1957. In 1930 he was appointed foreign secretary by Prime Minister Macmillan. This appointment aroused criticism, but Home proved to be diplomatically skillful and forthright.

Macmillan resigned in October 1963, and Home, to general surprise, succeeded him as prime minister, as a compromise candidate least likely to split the party. He renounced his peerage and became Sir Alec Douglas-Home. As prime minister, he was an excellent chairman and dispatcher of business rather than a "powerhouse of ideas."

After the Conservative defeat in 1964, Douglas-Home surprised many by his effectiveness as leader of the opposition. But because of his distaste for political intrigue, he refused to fight to save his position and resigned as Conservative leader in July 1965 in response to internal party criticism. In 1970, Prime Minister Edward Heath named him foreign secretary. Douglas-Home's political career revealed him as a man who acted instinctively on the basis of somewhat rigidly held beliefs, rather than as the possessor of a well-formulated ideology.

A. J. BEATTIE, *London School of Economics*

DOUGLASS, Andrew Ellicott (1867–1962), American astronomer and dendrochronologist, who originated the science of dendrochronology in 1901. He was born in Windsor, Vt., on July 5, 1867, graduated from Trinity College, Hartford, Conn., in 1889, and was appointed professor of physics and astronomy at the University of Arizona in 1906. He was the director of its Steward Observatory from 1918 to 1938. He died in Tucson, Ariz., on March 20, 1962.

Douglass developed dendrochronology as a result of an investigation of the theory that the sun affects the weather and the weather affects tree growth. Later, he established parallel patterns between the tree ring growth, climatic cycles, and sunspot variations, and he constructed an exact chronology of climatic variations over a period of nearly 2,000 years. His technique of dating events by rings in aged wood also proved useful in determining the dates of archaeological sites.

ALAN D. COVEY, *Arizona State University*

DOUGLASS, David (died 1786), English actor and theater manager, who established America's first permanent theater, the Southwark, in Philadelphia in 1766. He also directed (1767) his American Company in Thomas Godfrey's *The Prince of Parthia*, the first professional production of an American play.

Little is known about Douglass' early life. In 1758, while on an acting tour in Jamaica, he married the widow of the English theater manager Lewis Hallam, Sr. Douglass combined Hallam's company with his own to form the American Company and took his actors to the American colonies. In spite of opposition from the Puritans, he built several theaters there, including the historic Southwark and another permanent theater, the John Street, which he established in New York in 1767. At the onset of the American Revolution, he returned to Jamaica, where he held a British government post until his death.

DOUGLASS, Frederick (1817–1895), American Negro abolitionist and reformer. He was born in February 1817 near Easton, Md. Intelligent and spirited, he escaped from slavery in 1838 and settled in New Bedford, Mass. In 1841 at an abolitionist meeting in Nantucket he related his slave experiences, and for the next four years, despite many indignities, he lectured throughout the East for antislavery groups. In 1845 he published *The Narrative of the Life of Frederick Douglass,* which revealed his master's identity and endangered Douglass' liberty. The tall, handsome, and articulate Douglass took refuge in England, where friendly liberals purchased his freedom from his master.

From 1847, after his return to the United States, he published his own abolitionist newspaper, the *North Star,* in Rochester, N.Y., until 1863. It also supported women's rights, a cause that Douglass championed from his participation in the first women's rights convention (1848).

Frederick Douglass

Gradually he broke with William Lloyd Garrison's "moral suasionist" policy and became a political abolitionist, ultimately supporting the Republican party. He used his lecture fees to aid fugitive slaves and headed the Rochester station of the underground railroad. He was forced by a lack of funds to abandon his scheme for an industrial college for Negroes. Despite his opposition to the Harpers Ferry raid (1859), Douglass fled to Canada because he had raised money for the ventures of his friend and confidant John Brown.

During the Civil War he recruited Negroes for the Union Army, pushed for emancipation and enfranchisement, and then supported congressional Reconstruction. He campaigned for the postwar Republican presidential candidates and was rewarded with various federal appointments including that of minister to Haiti (1889–1891). He died in Washington on Feb. 20, 1895.

JAMES J. KENNEALLY, *Stonehill College*

Further Reading: Douglass, Frederick, *Life and Writings*, ed. by P. S. Foner, 4 vols. (New York 1950–1955); Quarles, Benjamin, *Frederick Douglass* (Washington 1948).

DOUHET, dōō-e′, **Giulio** (1869–1930), Italian army air officer, who forecast the impact of air power and bombardment on military strategy. He was born at Caserta, Italy, on May 30, 1869, and began his career as an artillery officer in the Italian army. An early advocate of the airplane, he commanded an air battalion from 1912 to 1914. In 1915, during World War I, he unsuccessfully urged that Italy build a fleet of Caproni bombers and destroy vital areas in Austria. Imprisoned for a year in 1916–1917 for criticizing his superiors, he was later vindicated by the Italian defeat at Caporetto, which occurred much as he had predicted, and was appointed director of aeronautical technical services. Douhet retired as a lieutenant colonel in 1918 but was given post-service rank as major general in 1921. He died at Rome on Feb. 14, 1930.

Douhet published *The Command of the Air* in 1921, and another major work, *The War of 19--*, appeared posthumously in 1931. In these books, Douhet visualizes a purely defensive role for surface forces, with almost sole reliance on aerial offensives to command the air and destroy enemy capabilities. See also AIR WARFARE.

JOHN W. CARPENTER, III
Lt. General, USAF; Commander, Air University

DOUKHOBORS, dōō′kə-bôrz, a nonconformist Christian sect that originated in Russia in the 18th century and whose members later emigrated to Canada. The total population of Doukhobors in Canada is estimated at about 20,000. The name "Doukhobors" derives from the Russian *dukhobortsy*, meaning "spirit fighters."

Beliefs. In doctrine and practice the Doukhobors resemble somewhat the Quakers, Mennonites, and other dissenting religious movements that arose at the same time. They seek to restore the simplicity of worship of the early Christian church. The church, priests, sacraments, and icons are therefore rejected. The altar holds only water, bread, and salt.

The Doukhobors seek inner inspiration, which must come from direct revelation. God is conceived as the Soul of the World, living in the human heart, teaching wisdom, and giving happiness. The soul does not enter the body at the moment of birth; it develops gradually during childhood and adolescence. It is shaped by the memory and reason of the "Living Book," which is a tradition that is believed to derive from Christ and is expressed in a large number of hymns, meditations, precepts, and commentaries. The doctrine of original sin is also denied. The fall of Adam is understood as having no degenerating influence on his descendants.

All Doukhobors are vegetarians. They are also pacifists and refuse to be inducted into military service. Family ties are based on mutual affection and not on parental authority.

History. The Doukhobors sect was first discovered in 1750 by the czarist authorities in the villages along the Dnieper River in the Ukraine. The sect was by then already fully organized with a clearly defined creed and a large membership. Members opposed the Orthodox Church and rejected the authority of the czar and government. They also refused to bear arms. The Doukhobors were severely persecuted by Catherine the Great and later by her son, Paul I, who in 1799 commanded that all members of the sect be banished to Siberian mines and given the hardest work. They were permitted to return by Czar Alexander I but were again exiled in the reign of Nicholas I.

One of the first notable leaders of the sect was Saveli Kapustin. Like Doukhobor leaders after him, he was acknowledged to be the reincarnation of Christ. The most influential leader was Peter Verigin, under whose guidance the Doukhobors accomplished their exodus from Russia to Canada. With the financial help of Count Leo Tolstoy and the English Quakers, 8,000 Doukhobors emigrated in 1898. Verigin was held in exile in Siberia but was permitted to join the sect in Saskatchewan in 1902. Many Doukhobors later settled in British Columbia.

In Canada the sect divided into three colonies, which soon differed from one another in creed and economic organization. The most radical group is called the Sons of Freedom. They refuse to send their children to public schools, reject modern technology, and generally oppose the Western way of life. They have used violent methods, such as arson, to coerce fellow members who have strayed from the creed. They have also held nude parades to demonstrate their desire to return to primitive simplicity. Most Doukhobors, however, are being assimilated into Canadian life.

SULA BENET, *Hunter College, New York*

DOULTON WARE, dōl'tən, is a 19th century stoneware pottery made in England. Throughout the 18th century, beer jugs and mugs of stoneware decorated in crude relief were made at Fulham (London). This tradition was continued by the firm of Doulton & Watts of Lambeth, which was founded in 1815 by John Doulton and John Watts. Among the typical early products are gin bottles of stoneware in various forms, ranging from pistols to portraits of political figures.

In 1854 the firm became Doulton & Co., and in the 1860's it began to experiment with decorative pottery, employing students from the Lambeth School of Art. These included George Tinworth, known for vases with relief patterns and amusingly modeled figures; Hannah Barlow, for incised drawings of animals on vases; and Mary Mitchell, for incised figure subjects.

Doulton introduced several new ceramic bodies, including a creamware misleadingly called "faience." The company started porcelain manufacture at Burslem in 1882 and discontinued its stoneware products at London about 1956.

GEORGE SAVAGE
Author of "Porcelain Through the Ages"

Further Reading: Eyles, Desmond, *Royal Doulton, 1815–1965* (London 1965).

DOUMERGUE, dōō-merg', **Gaston** (1863–1937), president and premier of France. He was born at Aigues-Vives on April 1, 1863. After studying law and holding various judicial appointments in the colonies, he served in the Chamber of Deputies (1893–1910) as a Radical and after 1910 in the Senate. He also held several cabinet posts before World War I and in 1913–1914 served as premier for six months.

In 1923 he was elected president of the Senate and actively supported France's occupation of the Ruhr when Germany defaulted on reparations payments. He was elected president of France in June 1924 as a moderate who would place national interests above party politics.

A skillful and prudent president, he became increasingly conservative. After completing his term in 1931, he retired but was recalled as premier to form a national unity cabinet after the antiparliamentary riots in February 1934. His proposals to reform the constitution by increasing the executive powers alarmed the left and led to the fall of his cabinet in November 1934. He died at Aigues-Vives on June 18, 1937.

JOEL COLTON, *Duke University*

DOURO RIVER, dō'rōō, a major river of northern Spain and Portugal. Rising in Spain in the Sierra de Urbión, the Douro (Spanish, *Duero*) flows westward for 480 miles (770 km) into the Atlantic Ocean near Oporto, Portugal. For about 70 miles (110 km) it forms the Spanish-Portuguese border.

Along the frontier the river plunges over the Castilian tableland in a series of gorges. The waterpower of this area is being developed jointly by Spain and Portugal. The Spanish hydroelectric plant at the Aldeadávila Dam is the largest in western Europe and produced about one tenth of Spain's hydroelectric power in the late 1960's. The Bernposta Dam in Portugal was planned to provide power for the development of large iron-ore reserves at Moncorvo. The vineyards of the lower Douro Valley produce port wines.

JAMES M. HOUSTON
Hertford College, Oxford University

ROY PINNEY, FROM PHOTO-LIBRARY
Douroucouli

DOUROUCOULI, dōō-rə-kōō'lē, a medium-sized South American monkey that is widely distributed in the forests south of the Orinoco River, in the Amazon Basin, in the foothills of the Andes, and in the Gran Chaco region. The douroucouli (*Aotus*) is a nocturnal primate and hence is sometimes also known as the "night monkey."

The douroucouli's body (including the head) is 12 to 15½ inches (300–400 mm) long, and its tail may be equally long. The short soft fur is usually silvery gray to dark gray above and pale gray or brown below. The large rounded eyes of the douroucouli are directed forward and are surrounded by white crescent-shaped areas that resemble open eyes when the animal is asleep.

Douroucoulis are wholly tree-living and subsist on a diet of fruit and insects. They live in small family groups consisting of two adults and the young.

JOHN R. NAPIER
Author of "A Handbook of Living Primates"

DOUW, Gerard. See DOU, GERARD.

DOVE, duv, **Arthur Garfield** (1880–1946), American painter, who is usually considered the first abstract artist in the United States, though some suggestion of subject matter is evident in his paintings. Dove was born at Canandaigua, N. Y., on Aug. 2, 1880. He was an illustrator until 1907, when he decided to study painting in Paris. His long association with Alfred Stieglitz and the young modern painters in Stieglitz' circle began in 1912, the year in which Dove had his first exhibition at Stieglitz' Photo-Secession gallery in New York.

Dove's early "abstractions," such as *Pagan Philosophy* (1913; Metropolitan Museum of Art, New York), were followed by more representational works in the 1920's. A strain of fantasy, influenced by surrealism and by the works of Albert Ryder and Odilon Redon, reached a peak in Dove's paintings of the 1930's. In *Rise of the Full Moon* (1937; Phillips Collection, Washington, D. C.) the landscape is suggestive of a looming monster, and the moon is transformed into a great Cyclops eye. Dove died at Huntington, N. Y., on Nov. 23, 1946.

H. H. ARNASON
The Solomon R. Guggenheim Foundation

DOVE, duv, a small pigeon. Though there is no technical difference between the terms "dove" and "pigeon" and the names are sometimes used interchangeably, "dove" is usually applied to small, more graceful pigeons with pointed tails. Doves are found throughout the world except in the Arctic, subarctic, Antarctic, and subantarctic regions and some oceanic islands. The domestic pigeon (*Columba livia*), a direct descendant of the rock dove of Europe, western Asia, India, and North Africa, was probably the first bird domesticated by man.

Doves and pigeons have plump, compact bodies and rather small heads. They are usually from 6 to 33 inches (15–84 cm) long and have dense plumage. They vary in color from dull gray and brown to bright yellow, green, orange, and lavender. Doves feed almost entirely on vegetable matter such as seeds, acorns, grains, and fruits, but a few species also eat insects, worms, and grubs. Doves and pigeons, like the sandgrouse, drink water by means of a sucking action that is unusual among birds.

Doves' nests usually consist of a flimsy platform of sticks. Doves most often place their nests in trees, but some place them on the ground or on cliff ledges or buildings, and a few species nest in holes in trees or burrows in the ground. The eggs, generally one or two in number, are usually pale white and have no markings. Both sexes incubate the eggs for 14 to 19 days. The female incubates the eggs during the night and the male incubates them during the day.

Young doves are fed by both parents. The

THE MOURNING DOVE (*Zenaidura macroura*) is the most common species of dove found in North America.

food consists of "pigeon's milk," a substance produced by a thickening of the lining of the parents' crops during incubation. This "pigeon's milk" sloughs off as whitish curds that are regurgitated into the mouths of the young.

There are about 289 species of pigeons and doves making up the family Columbidae in the order Columbiformes.

KENNETH E. STAGER
Los Angeles County Museum of Natural History

DOVEKIE, a small auk. See AUK.

DOVER, dō'vər, a city in central Delaware, is the capital of the state and the seat of Kent county. It is located on the St. Jones River, 45 miles (72 km) south of Wilmington. Besides being a center of government, it is a center of commerce and industry and a residential city. The city contains notable examples of Georgian colonial architecture.

Dover is the site of several large plants of major U.S. corporations. A gelatin food products plant is one of the largest single-plant users of sugar in the world. A prime contractor to the National Aeronautics and Space Administration makes space suit equipment. Another plant manufactures synthetic polymers, adhesives, elastomers, latex, chemical coatings, resins, and specialty chemicals. Employment at the Dover Air Force Base, the principal air cargo terminal supplying U. S. forces around the world, contributes largely to the city's economy.

Delaware State College, a 4-year, coeducational land-grant institution, is just north of the city. Wesley College, a 2-year coeducational Methodist institution, is on North State Street. Buildings of interest in the city include Woodburn (the governor's house), the Delaware state museum, the Ridgely house, and the Bradford-Lockerman house.

On Aug. 11, 1683, William Penn, proprietor of the "Three Lower Counties" on the Delaware River, issued a warrant to lay out the town of Dover. The town was platted in 1717, centered on The Green, which is still the focus of official activities. "Dover Days" are held annually on the first weekend in May. Government is by mayor and council. Population: 23,507.

VIRGINIA K. BOWLES
Dover Public Library

DOVER has been the capital of Delaware since 1777. The Old State House, pictured without later additions, is still used by some branches of the state government.

Dover, England, is dominated by its castle that stands on a steep cliff facing France across the Strait of Dover.

DOVER, a municipal borough and seaport in Kent, England, is 22 miles (35 km) across the Strait of Dover from Calais, France. For centuries, Dover has been known as the gateway to Britain. The busiest ferry service across the English Channel is based here. Trial borings for the Channel Tunnel, which was finally approved in 1966, were begun many years before at the foot of the white cliffs of Dover.

Dover spreads across the Dour River valley, which cuts through the high chalk cliffs facing the strait. The town has ben extensively rebuilt since its heavy bombing and shelling in World War II and presents a modern appearance, but it is an ancient place. The Romans built a castle and a lighthouse (which still stands) on the cliff to the east. In the 11th century the Normans erected a castle and Dover became one of the original Cinque Ports, organized for the protection of England. A Benedictine priory, built by the Normans, forms part of the buildings of Dover College, a boys' public school. Dover was incorporated in 1278.

Industries in Dover include papermaking and engineering, but the chief employment is in the operation of the harbor and its docks. A naval base was built here between 1898 and 1909, but in 1923 the British admiralty relinquished it to the harbour board for civilian use. Population: (1961) 35,215.

GORDON STOKES
Author of "English Place-Names"

DOVER, a city in southeastern New Hampshire, the seat of Strafford county, is situated on the Cocheco River, 11 miles (17 km) north of Portsmouth. The city's industries include the manufacture of shoes, electronic products, printing presses, synthetic rubber, and wood and aluminum products. The Woodman Institute, a historical museum, consists of the Damme Garrison building, built of logs about 1674 as a protection against Indians, with the Woodman House (1818) and the Sen. John P. Hale house (1813) on either side. The Tuttle and Roberts farms in Dover, dating from the 1640's, still are occupied by descendants of the first owners. A library society, the first in New Hampshire, was organized in Dover before 1776.

Dover was settled in 1623. In 1662, Capt. Richard Waldron, a governor's deputy, ordered that Quakers should be whipped out of town. This incident was described in John Greenleaf Whittier's verses *How the Women Went from Dover*. Not long afterward, one third of the residents became Quakers.

Dover was known at various times as Wecohannet, Bristol, and Northam. It received its present name in 1651, and was incorporated in 1855. Government is by council-manager. Population: 22,377.

MILDRED E. MORRISON
The Dover Public Library

DOVER, a city in northern New Jersey, is in Morris county, on the Rockaway River, 23 miles (37 km) northwest of Newark. The city manufactures metal products, metal window and door frames, picture frames, sportswear, women's and children's apparel, and ribbons. The federal Picatinny Arsenal and a powder mill are nearby. The extraction of building stone and iron ore was important in Dover in the early 19th century.

Dover was settled in 1722. It became a village in 1826 and a town in 1869. It was chartered in 1875 and became a city in 1896. Government is by a mayor and a board of aldermen. Population: 14,681.

DOVER, a city in eastern Ohio, is in Tuscarawas county, 70 miles (113 km) south of Cleveland. It fabricates steel and manufactures tubs, garbage cans, vacuum cleaners, flooring, chemicals, and clothing. The Warther Museum in Dover contains hand-fashioned models of railroad locomotives and steam engines. Dover was founded in 1807. It was incorporated as a village in 1867 and as a city in 1903. It is governed by a mayor and council. Population: 11,526.

DOVER, Strait of, the narrow passage between England and France, connecting the English Channel and the North Sea. It is 19 miles (30 km) wide at its narrowest point. Its southern limit extends from Dungeness, England, to Cape Gris-Nez, France, and its northern limit from the North Foreland, England, to Calais, France.

The strip of turbulent water has proved to be one of Britain's surest defenses. Sir Winston Churchill called it "the world's best tank trap." A memorial at St. Margaret's Bay in Kent commemorates the Dover Patrol, the small Anglo-American naval force of World War I that kept enemy submarines from passing from the North Sea to the Atlantic. Allied forces were evacuated from Dunkirk across the strait in 1940.

The first recorded swim across the strait was made by Capt. Matthew Webb, an Englishman, in 1875. The first woman to perform the feat, Gertrude Ederle of the United States, crossed in 1926. In 1785 a balloon crossing was made by Jean Pierre Blanchard and John Jefferies. The first heavier-than-air crossing was that of Louis Blériot in 1909.

GORDON STOKES
Author of "English Place-Names"

DOVER, Treaty of, the name given to two agreements, one secret (June 1, 1670), the other camouflage (Dec. 31, 1670), in which Louis XIV of France and Charles II of England resolved to make war on the Dutch.

In the earlier or "Catholic" accord, concluded after secret talks between the English King and his sister, the Duchess of Orléans, Louis promised to pay Charles £166,000 for a declaration of war against the Dutch, a naval alliance, and Charles' conversion to Roman Catholicism. Moreover, Louis agreed to provide 6,000 troops for use in England in the event that the announcement of Charles' conversion resulted in an uprising. In addition, England was to receive the Dutch islands of Walcheren and Kadzand and the Dutch inland port of Sluis.

Realizing that the time was not ripe for Charles to join the Roman Church, the parties negotiated the camouflage treaty, which differed from its counterpart in that it made no mention of the English King's religion and added the Dutch islands of Goedereede and Voorne to the list of spoils. Neither treaty was ratified, although the English did cooperate with the French in a war against the Dutch in 1672, and the principal effect of both agreements was to widen religious and political divisions in England.

JOHN FERGUSON, *Smith College*

DOVETAIL. See WOODWORKING—*Joinery* (Dovetail Joint).

DOW, dou, **Charles Henry** (1851–1902), American journalist and editor, who founded Dow Jones & Co., Inc., a news agency that pioneered in the dissemination of fast, accurate, and trustworthy financial information. He was also the first editor and publisher of the *Wall Street Journal*, and one of the earliest analysts of the forces that influence trends in stock and commodity markets.

Born in Sterling, Conn., on Nov. 6, 1851, Dow joined the Springfield (Mass.) *Daily Republican* as a reporter in 1872 and rose to be assistant editor. Subsequently he joined the Providence (R.I.) *Journal* and there began to write editorials and articles on economic and financial subjects, leaving in 1880 to try his hand in New York City.

In 1882 with two associates, Edward D. Jones and Charles M. Bergstresser, he formed Dow Jones & Co., which periodically during the business day collected and distributed to brokers the available news affecting business. On July 8, 1889, appeared the first issue of the *Wall Street Journal*, which began as merely a collection of the news bulletins gathered during the day.

Dow's work on this newspaper firmly established his reputation as a financial journalist. He was the first to attempt a statistical measure of the New York stock market. He evolved a theory that the market tended to move in broad patterns, like the waves of the ocean, and he distinguished between the intermediate ripples and the main tides. His analysis was the forerunner of what is now known as the "Dow theory," although others elaborated its details.

Although a successful businessman, Dow remained a working reporter, editor, and commentator until his death in New York on Dec. 4, 1902.

VERMONT ROYSTER, *"Wall Street Journal"*

DOW, dou, **Herbert Henry** (1866–1930), American chemist, who revolutionized the bromine industry by developing a new process for extracting bromine from brine. He was born on Feb. 26, 1866, in Belleville, Ontario, Canada, where his father was managing a sewing machine factory. The family soon moved to Cleveland, Ohio, where Dow received a scholarship from Case School of Applied Science (now Case Western Reserve University). His original ambition to study architecture was thwarted because Case offered no courses in that subject. Consequently, he enrolled in chemistry.

Dow's interest in brine research began while he was preparing his senior year thesis, and it continued into his chemistry teaching days at the Huron Street Hospital College in Cleveland. There, by the spring of 1889, he developed his "blowing-out" process, which frees bromine from brine through electrolysis and uses air blown through the vapor to stimulate the bromine's exit. On this invention he founded, on May 18, 1897, what became one of the world's largest and most diversified chemical firms, The Dow Chemical Company.

Working with homemade equipment, Dow first made bromides and then chlorine. He led the way for the first American synthesis of indigo, the creation of cheap synthetic phenol, and the extraction of magnesium and bromine from seawater.

Dow was an active horticulturist and a friend of Luther Burbank. He died in Rochester, Minn., on Oct. 15, 1930.

DAVID K. WINSTON
The Dow Chemical Company

DOW, dou, **Neal** (1804–1897), American temperance leader. He was born in Portland, Me., on March 20, 1804, to a Quaker family. After attending the Friends' Academy in New Bedford, Mass., he entered his father's tanning business in Portland. Dow devoted much of his life to the temperance movement, convinced that drinking kept the poor from becoming self-sufficient.

In 1838 he organized the Maine Temperance Union, and in 1846, largely through its influence, Maine passed a prohibition law, which proved to be unenforceable. Elected mayor of Portland in 1851, Dow secured passage of a stronger state measure, known as the Maine Law. After his reelection in 1855, the Maine Law was repealed, but he obtained its reenactment in 1858.

Dow served in the Civil War as a brigadier general of volunteers. In 1880 he was the presidential candidate of the Prohibition party. He died in Portland on Oct. 2, 1897.

DOWDEN, dou′dən, **Edward** (1843–1913), Irish literary critic, noted for his studies of the life and works of Shakespeare and Shelley. Dowden was born in Cork, Ireland, on May 3, 1843. He studied at Queen's College, Cork, and at Trinity

College, Dublin, where he became professor of oratory and English literature in 1867. He later lectured at Oxford and Cambridge. He died in Dublin on April 4, 1913.

Dowden approached literature from biographical and historical standpoints. His most important book is *Shakespeare: A Critical Study of His Mind and Art* (1875), the first comprehensive study in English of Shakespeare's works.

DOWDING, dou'ding, Sir Hugh Caswall Tremenheere (1882–1970), British air commander, who was an early champion of radar and strong air defenses. He was born at Moffat, Dumfries, Scotland, on April 24, 1882, and was graduated from the Royal Military Academy, Woolwich, in 1900. In World War I he commanded a Royal Flying Corps Wing in France. From 1930 he headed research and development in the Royal Air Force, and in 1936 he took charge of Fighter Command.

Expecting a German air offensive against Britain in 1940, he husbanded RAF fighters and opposed a heavy commitment of them on the Continent. Gaining Churchill's agreement and given a 6-week respite after the fall of France, Dowding prepared for the expected Nazi air attack. His skill and resolution in directing Fighter Command during the crucial phase of the Battle of Britain (July–October 1940) were decisive in achieving a great air victory. He retired in 1942 as air chief marshal, and was created 1st Baron Dowding of Bentley Priory in 1943. He died in Tunbridge Wells, Kent, England, on Feb. 15, 1970.

JOHN W. CARPENTER, III
Lt. Gen., USAF; Commander, Air University

DOWIE, dou'ē, John Alexander (1847–1907), American religious leader and founder of the Christian Catholic Church in Zion. He was born in Edinburgh, Scotland, on May 25, 1847. He moved with his parents to Australia, but returned to Edinburgh to study theology. Ordained to the Congregational ministry in 1870, he preached in Australia for a while and became known for his crusading zeal against tobacco and alcohol and for his claim to the power of healing. He went to the United States in 1888, settling in San Francisco, and moved to Chicago in 1890.

Dowie organized the Christian Catholic Church in 1896, and in 1901 he built Zion City for his followers on the shore of Lake Michigan, some 40 miles (64 km) north of Chicago. He designated himself "overseer" of the new church and subsequently expanded his role, calling himself "Messenger of the Covenant," "Elijah the Restorer" and the "First Apostle."

Full of missionary zeal, Dowie, along with several thousand followers, attempted to convert New York City in 1903. The trip was a fiasco and was costly financially, and Dowie found himself in trouble with his followers. He aggravated his situation by using autocratic means to gather funds to pay his debts and by the "Round the World Visitation" on which more funds were wasted. Finally he was deposed. He died in Chicago on March 9, 1907.

A small group of Dowieites still live in Zion, which is no longer an exclusive city. They publish the *Theocrat* and *Leaves of Healing* and annually present a Passion play.

JAMES H. SMYLIE
Union Theological Seminary, Richmond, Va.

ANNAN PHOTO FEATURES
Short-billed dowitcher

DOWITCHER, dow'i-chər, a small, long-billed wading bird of arctic North America. Dowitchers are migratory and annually winter from California to Peru on the west and from Cuba and Jamaica to eastern Brazil on the east.

Dowitchers are small, heavyset birds from 10½ to 12½ inches (27–32 cm) long. They have a straight bill that may be as much as four times the length of the head. During the fall and winter, dowitchers are a mottled gray with a patch of white on the rump and upper back, but during the spring and summer, the gray plumage is replaced by rich chestnut-red feathers, and the birds are then often called red-breasted snipes.

When migrating, dowitchers form large flocks, and they frequent exposed mudflats and sand flats of bays and sheltered estuaries or the margins of small freshwater ponds and marshes. In these areas they feed by thrusting their long bills deep into the soft mud or sand. Their food consists of small invertebrate animal life obtained from the mud or sand. The dowitcher's nest is a depression in the moist moss-covered ground of the Arctic. It is lined with a few dry grasses and leaves. The female lays four olive-green eggs that are marked with fine spots of dark brown. The female alone incubates the eggs, but the male alone cares for the young birds.

Dowitchers are classified in the genus *Limnodromus* of the family Scolopacidae, which also includes curlews, snipes, woodcocks, and sandpipers, of the order Charadriiformes.

KENNETH E. STAGER
Los Angeles County Museum of Natural History

DOWLAND, dou'lənd, John (1563?–?1626), British composer and virtuoso lutanist, who was England's greatest songwriter before Purcell. Dowland was probably born in Ireland and spent some years in Paris before attending Oxford, from which he graduated in 1588. Unable to obtain a suitable post in England, he toured the Continent, where he became a performer of high repute. He was lutenist to King Christian IV of Denmark from 1598 to 1606. On his return to England in 1606, Dowland enjoyed the patronage of Lord Howard de Walden and King James I. From 1612 he was a court "Musician for the Lutes." He died in London.

Dowland's settings of song lyrics reveal an exquisite sensitivity to language and a subtle employment of chromatic harmonies. His *In Darkness Let Me Dwell* and *Weep You No More, Sad Fountains* are splendid examples of his advanced achievements in the art song, a form in which he was a pioneer. Also famous are his three books of *Songes or Ayres* (1597–1603) and his *Lacrymae* (1604), a set of "seven passionate Pavans" for instruments.

Eric D. Mackerness
Author of "A Social History of English Music"

DOWLING, dou'ling, **Eddie** (1894–1976), American theatrical producer, director, and actor, who started his career as a song-and-dance man and became an important force in the American theater. He was born Joseph Nelson Goucher on Dec. 9, 1894, in Woonsocket, R. I. Beginning in vaudeville with his wife, Ray Dooley, he later appeared in the Ziegfeld *Follies* and in 1922 starred in the hit musical *Sally, Irene and Mary*, which he wrote with Cyrus Woods.

Dowling's highly acclaimed production of *Richard the Second* (1937) helped establish Maurice Evans on the American stage. Four Dowling productions won New York Drama Critics Circle awards: *Shadow and Substance* (1938) and *The White Steed* (1939) for best foreign plays, and *The Time of Your Life* (1940) and *The Glass Menagerie* (1945), both of which he codirected and starred in. In 1946, Dowling directed O'Neill's *The Iceman Cometh*. He remained active in the theater until the 1960's. He died in Smithfield, R. I., on Feb. 18, 1976.

Myron Matlaw, *Queens College of the City University of New York*

DOWN, a county in Northern Ireland, extends from Carlingford Lough in the south to Belfast Lough in the north and fronts on the Irish Sea. In the south are the Mourne Mountains, an area of great scenic interest. There is mixed farming throughout the county; oats and barley are the main tillage crops. Sheep are raised on the dry hillsides. Down's principal towns include Bangor, Newtownards, and Newry. Bangor, once the site of one of Ireland's most famous abbeys, is the chief seaside resort of the north. The county's northern towns form the environs of Belfast. Linen, woolens, textiles, and sacks are the principal manufactures. Kilkeel is one of the most important fishing centers in Northern Ireland.

The capital of the county is Downpatrick, where, according to tradition, St. Patrick is buried in the cathedral grounds. Ballynahinch was the scene of a battle in the insurrection of the United Irishmen in 1798. Population: (1971) 311,266.

Thomas FitzGerald
Department of Education, Dublin

DOWNERS GROVE is a village in northeastern Illinois, in Du Page county, 21 miles (35 km) west of Chicago. Its industries produce bearings, gears, construction tools and equipment, copper wire, electrical components, plastics, hospital and scientific instruments, food products, and office equipment. The Avery Coonley School is in Downers Grove, and the Argonne National Laboratory and the Morton Arboretum are near by. Downers Grove was settled in 1832 and incorporated in 1873. It has a council-manager form of government. Population: 39,274.

DOWNEY, a city in southwestern California, is in Los Angeles county, about 10 miles (16 km) southeast of the center of the city of Los Angeles. It is situated between the San Gabriel Mountains and the Pacific Ocean. Freeways provide easy access to ocean and mountains.

Downey is primarily a residential community, but it has several aerospace-related industries. The city is the home of Ranch Los Amigos, the county hospital for chronic diseases, which is known for its pioneering techniques and its equipment for the treatment of crippled patients.

Downey was named for John Gately Downey, governor of California during the Civil War, who bought the land in 1873 and sold parts of it for farms. It was incorporated as a city in 1956, with a council-manager government, and became a chartered city in 1963. Population: 82,602.

Ruth Miller, *Downey City Librarian*

DOWNING, Sir George (1623–1684), British diplomat and financier, for whom Downing Street (q. v.) is named. Born in Dublin, Ireland, in August 1623, he was sent by his uncle, Gov. John Winthrop of Massachusetts, to Harvard College and became its second graduate (1642). Back in England by 1646, he joined the Parliamentary army. He was a member of Parliament under Cromwell but later served the monarchy.

As envoy to The Hague, his aggressiveness in promoting England's commercial interests against those of the Dutch, coupled with such measures as the Navigation Act of 1651, hastened the outbreak of the First and Second Dutch Wars. Appointed secretary to the treasury in 1667, he made important reforms. He died in Cambridgeshire, in July 1684.

DOWNING STREET, in London, England, is a short, narrow street that runs from Whitehall to St. James Park. On the north side are three small houses. One of these, which is called Number 10 from the days when it was one of a row, is the official residence of the prime minister of Great Britain. Number 11, next door, is the offiicial residence of the chancellor of the exchequer, and Number 12, adjoining it, is used as offices for the government whips. The south side of the street is occupied by the foreign office.

Downing Street was named for Sir George Downing (q.v.), secretary to the treasury in the late 1660's, who bought property in Whitehall in 1681 and built four houses. In 1735, Robert Walpole, then prime minister, accepted Number 10 from the crown as the official residence for himself and all of his successors.

DOWNPATRICK, an urban district in Northern Ireland, the county seat of County Down, is situated near the mouth of the Quoile River, at the southern end of Strangford Lough, 21 miles (35 km) south of Belfast. Downpatrick is a market center and also manufactures linen, cotton textiles, leather, and liquors. Its cathedral was restored in 1790. The original church, erected in 1412, was sacked and severely damaged in 1538.

Downpatrick was a residence of the kings of ancient Ulster and was a place of importance even before the arrival in the 5th century of St. Patrick, who built the Abbey of Saul, 2 miles (3 km) to the northeast. St. Patrick is reputedly buried beside the cathedral at Downpatrick. Population: (1971) 8,401.

DOWNS, in England, are uplands of chalk, but the term is commonly applied only to the North Downs and South Downs of Kent and Surrey and the highlands of Wiltshire and Berkshire. The name is derived from *dūn*, the Old English word for "hill," though the typical down has a rather ridgelike form. Downs are covered with short springy turf on which sheep and cattle are raised. Where sufficient soil overlies the chalk, barley and other crops are grown.

From early times travelers and settlers were attracted to the dry and open downs, which rose out of undrained swampy forests. Remains indicate that the Wiltshire Downs were once among the most populous parts of Britain. Many downs are marked by figures of men and horses that were fashioned by cutting away turf and exposing the white chalk. White Horse Hill in Berkshire is identified by the figure of a horse 374 feet (114 meters) long cut in prehistoric times.

GORDON STOKES
Author of "English Place-Names"

DOWNS, The, an anchorage for ships off the southeast coast of Kent, England, between the North and South Forelands. It is a natural harbor, about 9 miles long and 6 miles wide (14 by 9 km), with a depth of 25 to 70 feet (4–12 fathoms). The Goodwin Sands, a natural breakwater, protects the harbor from the sea. In the days of sail, it was an important naval base. Three castles—Deal, Walmer, and Sandown—were built by Henry VIII in 1540 to protect the anchored shipping; Deal and Walmer castles are still standing.

DOWN'S SYNDROME. See MONGOLISM.

DOWRY, dou′rē, is the property that the bride's family gives to the groom or his family upon marriage. In many primitive cultures, the dowry is part of a complicated series of exchanges of wealth between intermarrying families and is fundamental to the social and economic functioning of the society. It is often accompanied with the payment of bridewealth—property given by the husband's family to the bride's. In this way interfamilial alliances are cemented. This form of exchange of wealth is developed to a high degree in African cultures, where the full payment of dowry and bridewealth may continue over a long period and the marriage is considered fully ratified only when it is completed.

The European dowry system has certain similarities to the dowry systems in primitive societies, particularly in the aspect of marriage contracts serving to forge family alliances. However, in Europe and the United States the primary function of the dowry is to provide the wife with some equity in the property of the marriage.

The manner in which the dowry is administered differs according to the legal traditions of the country and local custom. Under British law, or common law, as found in Britain, most of the Commonwealth nations, and the United States (with the exception of Louisiana), a married woman in the past was under the "disabilities of coverture." This meant that her dowry and any other possessions became the property of her husband, who was also responsible for any legal rights or obligations she might have. As a widow she was entitled to a life interest in one third of her husband's estate, but otherwise she could own nothing in her own right. Her situation was mitigated by settlements made by courts of chancery, and in England some provision to safeguard the dowry was made by placing in the hands of trustees the property brought to the marriage by either party; thus, while the wife owned nothing, she had some equity. The first real improvement came with the married women's property act of 1839, in Mississippi. A similar act was passed in England in 1870. American marital property laws differ from state to state, and there are variations in Britain and other Commonwealth nations.

Under civil, or Napoleonic, law, as found in the Latin countries, the state of Louisiana, and Quebec, the concept of the dowry (French, *dot*) is somewhat different. The dowry was traditionally managed by the husband, but he never had unlimited rights to it. In Roman times he had to return it if the marriage ended in divorce. Later, in medieval Europe, when divorce was impossible, there were various ways to safeguard the wife's equity. In modern Europe, couples choose at marriage which property system they want—dowry, community property, or complete separation of property. Community property is the system usually chosen.

PRISCILLA C. WARD
American Museum of Natural History

DOWSING, dous′ing, is a method of locating objects—liquids, minerals, or living organisms—by the use of a forked stick or other implement that is reputed to move in the presence of the object sought.

History. Great antiquity is imputed to the practice of dowsing. Moses, who brought forth water by striking a rock with a rod (Numbers 20:9–11), has been called the first water dowser. The Romans supplied the name *virgula divina* (divining rod), but they employed the rod in a form of divination unrelated to dowsing.

The first authenticated evidence of dowsing with a forked stick comes from medieval Germany: in 1556, Georgius Agricola published, in his *De re metallica*, a description of dowsing by Teutonic miners to locate minerals and ores. Martin Luther and other clerics felt dowsing had possible satanic relationships. In spite of church injunctions, dowsing spread from Germany to other European countries. It was introduced into England during the reign of Queen Elizabeth I by German miners working in Cornwall. Exploration and colonization by Europeans carried dowsing to Africa, Asia, and the New World.

Methods. Today considerable variation exists in the equipment used in dowsing. The traditional device, and still the most popular instrument, is a Y-shaped forked stick. One fork of the stick is held in each hand. The palms of the hand are held upward. The end of the stick is pointed forward and maintained in a horizontal or slightly raised position. When the end of the stick bends down, the presence of the desired object is indicated. In the past, rods of hazelwood were preferred. Now a variety of woods are employed, as are rods made of whalebone, nylon, and metal. The leading alternative dowsing instrument is a pendulum suspended from a string or chain. The end of the string is held with the thumb and first finger or is sometimes attached to a Bible held by the dowser. The presence of an object is indicated by gyration of the pendulum weight. A third method of dowsing involves the use of a pair of L-shaped angle rods. One rod is grasped in each hand. The short leg of the rod is kept in a vertical position, while the long leg projects forward in a horizontal plane. The projecting legs will cross or swing outward to indicate the presence of an object. Finally, some dowsers claim to be able to detect objects with their hands alone, while others are famous for dowsing over maps.

Dowsers claim the instrument they are using moves of its own accord in locating an object. Careful observation shows that animation of the instrument is due to minute muscular movement by the dowser, generally on a subconscious level. Controlled field and laboratory tests have failed to establish the validity of dowsing, and judged by scientific standards the practice has little basis in fact. Believers in dowsing impute negative test results to supposed inadequacies in the scientific approach, or argue that the practice cannot be expected to work in the artificial environment of the laboratory.

E. Z. VOGT and L. K. BARRETT
Harvard University

DOWSON, dous'ən, **Ernest** (1867–1900), English poet of the *fin de siècle* decadent school, who is remembered for his exquisite and fragile, sensuous yet refined, lyrics on the pathos and brevity of life and the agony of unrequited love. Ernest Christopher Dowson was born at Lee, Kent, on Aug. 2, 1867. After travel on the Continent, mostly in France, he entered Queen's College, Oxford, in 1886, but left in 1888 without taking a degree. He began to write short stories and poems while working on the London docks and in 1880 became a member of the Pre-Raphaelite Rhymers' Club.

Dowson was shattered by the death of his father in 1894 and his mother's suicide six months later. These horribly painful experiences were heightened by his great but unrequited passion for a young girl, Adelaide Foltinowicz, the daughter of a Polish café owner. To her he dedicated his *Verses* (1896). Ill with consumption and despairing, he sought escape in alcohol. He died in London on Feb. 23, 1900.

Dowson's fame rests on the poem *Non Sum Qualis Eram Bonae sub Regno Cynarae*, containing the well-known line, "I have been faithful to thee, Cynara! in my fashion." He also wrote the book of poems *Decorations* (1899); a volume of short stories *Dilemmas* (1895); and a poetic drama, *The Pierrot of the Minute* (1897).

NORTON B. CROWELL
University of New Mexico

DOXOLOGY, doks-ol'ə-jē, a kind of hymn or formula of praise, generally brief, addressed to God in public worship. It is usually sung or chanted, but it may be said in unison by the congregation. The *Gloria in excelsis* is sometimes called the greater doxology; the *Gloria Patri,* the lesser doxology.

The *Gloria in excelsis* is based on the song of the angels in Luke 2:14, "Glory to God in the highest, and on earth peace, good will towards men." It was an early 4th century Eucharistic hymn and is still sung at the beginning of the Roman and Eastern rites and read frequently in Protestant services. The usual translation begins, "Glory be to God on high."

The *Gloria Patri,* "Glory be to the Father, and to the Son, and to the Holy Ghost . . . ," is commonly added at the end of psalms, thus adapting them to Christian worship; and Christian sermons often close with a doxology.

To most Protestants, "the doxology" means the words that form the concluding stanza of two of Bishop Thomas Ken's hymns:

> Praise God, from whom all blessings flow;
> Praise Him, all creatures here below;
> Praise Him above, ye heavenly host;
> Praise Father, Son, and Holy Ghost.

Doxologies conclude several psalms in Jewish worship and are also used to end public prayers. The Eighteen Benedictions (the *shemoneh esreh*) close with a *berakah,* or blessing, such as "Blessed art Thou, O Lord, the Shield of Abraham."

The New Testament contains numerous examples of doxologies, such as in Romans 11:36 and 16:27, and, above all, in the early addition to the Lord's Prayer (Matthew 6:13: "For thine is the kingdom, and the power, and the glory, for ever and ever. Amen.") found in many good manuscripts, a sentence based on I Chronicles 29:11-13. The Book of Revelation also has passages reflecting the use of doxologies in heavenly worship, as in Revelation 4:11.

FREDERICK C. GRANT
Union Theological Seminary, N.Y.

DOYLE, Sir Arthur Conan (1859–1930), British author and crusader for spiritualism. He is famous as the creator of Sherlock Holmes, the most renowned detective in fiction, who solves crimes of the utmost complexity through brilliant deductive reasoning. Conan Doyle was born on May 22, 1859, in Edinburgh, Scotland. He was educated in the Jesuit colleges of Stonyhurst in Lancashire and Feldkirch in Austria and received an M.D. from Edinburgh University in 1885. After two voyages as a ship's doctor, he established a medical practice in Southsea, England.

Creation of Sherlock Holmes. In 1885, Conan Doyle began writing a detective novel, *A Study in Scarlet.* He first named his detective "Sherringford Holmes" and then "Sherlock Holmes." He endowed him with an inquisitive, bungling, good-natured friend, Dr. Watson, and installed him in fictional quarters at 221b Baker Street, London. Purchased by Ward, Locke for £25, *A Study in Scarlet* appeared in *Beaton's Christmas Annual* for 1887 and in *Lippincott's Magazine* in the United States. After publication of a second Holmes novel, *The Sign of the Four* (1890), Conan Doyle abandoned medicine for full-time writing.

Arthur Conan Doyle

A Scandal in Bohemia and six more stories about Holmes published in the *Strand Magazine* made the detective famous, but in 1893, growing to hate him, Conan Doyle "drowned" him in the Reichenbach Falls in Switzerland. But Holmes' millions of admirers raised such an outcry that Conan Doyle "revived" him in *The Hound of the Baskervilles* (1902) and contributed more Holmes stories to the *Strand*. Holmes became the object of a cult of hero-worshippers, some of whom called themselves "Baker Street Irregulars" (q.v.). The American actor William Gillette wrote *Sherlock Holmes* (1899), a play based on Conan Doyle's stories, and starred in it for years. See also SHERLOCK HOLMES, ADVENTURES OF.

Other Writings. Although Conan Doyle's fame rests on his creation of Sherlock Holmes, he also wrote plays and several historical romances. He was knighted in 1902 for two works defending British policy in the Boer War, in which he served as a civilian doctor. In 1917, Sir Arthur, believing that he had received personal messages from a son killed in World War I, embarked on a worldwide crusade for spiritualism, refusing payment for his spiritualist lectures and for his 2-volume *History of Spiritualism* (1926). The last Holmes book, *The Casebook of Sherlock Holmes*, was published in 1927. Conan Doyle died in Crowborough, Sussex, on July 7, 1930.

DOROTHY GARDINER, *Author, "West of the River"*

Further Reading: Carr, John Dickson, *The Life of Sir Arthur Conan Doyle* (New York 1949); Nordon, Pierre, *Conan Doyle, a Biography*, tr. by Frances Partridge (New York 1967); Pearson, Hesketh, *Conan Doyle* (London 1961).

DOYLE, Richard (1824–1883), English caricaturist and watercolor painter, noted for his elflike, whimsical designs and sketches. He was born in London in September 1824. After learning his craft from his father, John Doyle (1797–1868), a political caricaturist who was known as "HB," he became at the age of 19 an illustrator for the new weekly *Punch*. His contributions to *Punch* included the series *Manners and Customs of ye Englyshe*, and in 1849 the magazine adopted his cover design.

A devout Roman Catholic, Doyle left *Punch* in 1850 because of its anti-Catholic opinions. He then turned to watercolor painting and also gained recognition as an illustrator of books, among them Thackeray's *The Newcomes*, Ruskin's *King of the Golden River*, three of Dickens' *Christmas Books*, and his own pleasantly comic *Foreign Tour of Messrs. Brown, Jones, and Robinson*. Doyle died in London on Dec. 11, 1883.

DOYLESTOWN, a borough in southeastern Pennsylvania, the seat of Bucks county, is about 23 miles (37 km) north of Philadelphia. It is principally a residential community, but clothing, textiles, rubber products, building materials, and electronic products are made. Fruit, vegetables, corn, poultry, and cattle are raised in the region. Delaware Valley College of Science and Agriculture is at Doylestown. Font Hill, the château-like home of the archaeologist Henry C. Mercer (1856–1930), is of interest. The Bucks County Historical Society museum has a large collection of early tools and machines.

Doylestown was settled in 1735 and was named for William Doyle, an innkeeper. It was incorporated in 1838. Government is by council and manager. Population: 8,717.

D'OYLY CARTE, doi'lē kärt, **Richard** (1844–1901), English opera impresario, who achieved world fame as the producer of the comic masterworks of Gilbert and Sullivan. D'Oyly Carte was born in London on May 3, 1844. Educated at University College in London, he began his career in music as a composer and had three of his operettas produced between 1868 and 1871. He soon turned to theater management, handling individual artists (including the composer Charles Gounod) and producing French opéra bouffes in London. In 1875 he commissioned William S. Gilbert and Arthur Sullivan (qq.v.) to write the one-act opera *Trial by Jury*. The production was a great success and initiated a historic producer-composer-librettist association.

In 1881, D'Oyly Carte built the Savoy Theatre for his productions of "Gilbert and Sullivan." The first electrically lit theater in London, it became popular as the home of such Gilbert and Sullivan masterpieces as *Patience* (1881), *The Mikado* (1885), and *The Gondoliers* (1889). Much to the dissatisfaction of Gilbert, however, D'Oyly Carte, backed by Sullivan, established a different theater for productions of English grand opera. Disputes concerning this undertaking led to a three-year hiatus in the Gilbert and Sullivan partnership, and D'Oyly Carte's Royal English Opera House was a fiasco, opening and closing in 1891 with Sullivan's *Ivanhoe*. After Gilbert and Sullivan began to collaborate again, D'Oyly Carte produced their last two comic operas, *Utopia Limited* (1893) and *The Grand Duke* (1896). He died on Aug. 3, 1901, in London.

Following D'Oyly Carte's death, the D'Oyly Carte company, popularly known as the "Savoyards," was managed until 1913 by his wife, Helen, and later by his son Rupert and granddaughter Bridgit. It folded on Feb. 27, 1982.

DAVID EWEN
Author of "The Book of European Light Opera"

DOZOKU, dō-zō-kōō, is a Japanese sociological term used to designate a lineage or an extended family group. In traditional Japanese society the *dozoku* consisted of a main family and any number of collateral or branch families. Its chief characteristics were its rigid hierarchical structure and its custom of adopting outside households whose members, although not related by blood to the rest of the *dozoku*, were given fictive kinship designations.

The *dozoku* pattern of organization has been imitated in many areas of Japanese society, including industry, politics, labor, and the performing arts. It has provided considerable social stability in the past, but since its emphasis has been on loyalty and submission to the group, such stability has been achieved only at the expense of individual rights and freedom.

H. PAUL VARLEY, *Columbia University*

DPN. See NAD.

DRA, Wadi, drä, an intermittent river in Morocco. Formed by the junction of the Imini and Dadès rivers east of Ouarzazate on the southern slope of the High Atlas Mountains, it crosses the Anti-Atlas Mountains, flows southwest, then veers southwest, and continues to the Atlantic Ocean near Cape Dra. The length of the riverbed is about 700 miles (1,125 km), but it is generally waterless except in its upper course.

DRACAENA is popular as a house plant because of its colorful foliage. The two species shown are *D. sanderiana* (left) and *D. fragrans*.

DRACAENA, drə-sē′nə, is a genus of plants native to wide areas of the tropics and grown indoors in northern temperate regions for their colorful foliage. The genus comprises more than 50 species and belongs to the lily family (Liliaceae).

The leaves of the plants are sword-shaped and are often marked with stripes, bands, or dots of yellow or white. The small white, red, or greenish yellow flowers and the small berries seldom appear in cultivated specimens. The name of the genus is derived from the Greek word *drakaina*, meaning female dragon, and the juice of one species, the dragon tree (*Dracaena draco*), is supposed to resemble dragon's blood. The dragon tree, which is native to the Canary Islands, can reach a height of 60 feet (18 meters), but other species are much shorter.

DONALD WYMAN
Arnold Arboretum, Harvard University

DRACHENFELS, dräkн′ən-fels, is the most southerly of the range of volcanic hills known as the Siebengebirge (Seven Mountains) in Germany. Lying on the east bank of the Rhine just southeast of Bonn, the hill rises steeply from the river to a height of 1,053 (321 meters). On its summit are a 19th century "castle" and the ruins of a 12th century fortress. According to legend, the hill is where Siegfried slew the dragon; hence the name, "Dragon Mountain."

DRACHMA, drak′mə, the basic monetary unit of modern Greece. It is divided into 100 lepta. Until 1928 the drachma was equivalent to the franc, but in that year wide fluctuations in its value caused it to become linked to sterling. After World War II another period of fluctuation occurred, and in 1954 a new issue of notes and coins was put into circulation, with 1 new drachma equaling 1,000 old drachmas.

In ancient Greece the drachma was both a monetary unit and a basic unit of weight for silver. At Athens it weighed 4.37 grams, and the standard coin was a 4-drachma piece. Weights and measures were not widely standardized at that time, however, and at nearby Corinth the drachma weighed 2.8 grams, and the major coin was a 3-drachma piece called a stater. Generally, the drachma was divided into 6 obols; 100 drachmas equaled 1 mina of silver; and 60 minas equaled 1 talent.

DRACHMANN, draкн′män, **Holger Henrik Herholdt** (1846–1908), Danish poet, playwright, and novelist, who attained a high place in Danish literature as a lyric poet. He was born on Oct. 9, 1846, in Copenhagen. Starting out as a marine painter, Drachmann took a painting trip in 1871 to London, where his meeting with English trade unionists and refugees from the Paris Commune of that year strengthened his own revolutionary tendencies. On his return to Denmark in 1872 he became closely associated with the new radical literary movement led by Georg Brandes.

Digte (1872), Drachmann's first volume of poems, reflects his youthful rebelliousness and his disgust with conservative bourgeois ideals. This and four other volumes of poems in the 1870's firmly established him as the leading lyric poet of Denmark. But he had an unstable temperament, and after the dissolution of his first marriage and a remarriage, he praised, in his poetry of the 1880's, all the conventional values he had previously scorned. An affair with a music hall singer made him turn his back once again on bourgeois respectability, and he put on the mantle of a Bohemian poet. His third and last marriage brought him back to a more settled existence but also to less inspired poetry. He died on Jan. 14, 1908, at Hornbæk, Denmark.

Drachmann's best poetry—personal, passionate, and musical—is of very high quality. *Vølund Smed* (1894), his best play, contains undertones of both the Edda and Shakespeare. His best novel, *Forskrevet* (1890), personifies the two aspects of his nature in two characters, a vagabond poet and a diligent artist-writer.

ELIAS BREDSDORFF
University of Cambridge, England

DRACO, drā′kō, was an Athenian lawgiver of the 7th century B.C. He was the first to codify and write down the laws of Athens, which previously had been interpreted and administered arbitrarily by aristocratic magistrates. His code, written about 621 B.C., became famous for its harshness; death was the penalty for almost all crimes. One advance was in the laws of homicide, which recognized the responsibility of the state, not the victim's family, in punishing a murderer; thus blood feuds were to be avoided.

Draco did not change the constitution; innovations attributed to him by Aristotle in the *Constitution of the Athenians* do not fit the 7th century, and the attribution is now recognized as false. All of his laws were repealed by Solon in the early 6th century B.C. except those on homicide, which remained in force and exist on stone as part of the code as revised at the end of the 5th century B.C.

DONALD W. BRADEEN
University of Cincinnati

DRACO, drā'kō, the Dragon, in astronomy, is an ancient constellation of the Northern Hemisphere. In mythology, Draco is the dragon slain either by Hercules or Cadmus. The constellation contains no first magnitude stars and is somewhat difficult to trace. However, it occupies an interesting position in the sky near the north celestial pole, with a portion of the dragon's "tail" lying between Ursa Major and Ursa Minor. In about 3500 B.C. one star of the constellation—Thuban, or α Draconis—was the Pole Star and was worshiped by the Egyptians. Since that time, Polaris has become the Pole Star because of the precession of the equinoxes. The star γ Draconis also is of interest because observations of this star in the early 18th century led to the discovery of the aberration of light in 1729. See also CONSTELLATION (table).

DRACULA, drak'yə-lə, is a novel by the British author Bram Stoker (q.v.), published in 1897. It was produced as a play in 1927 and first filmed in 1931.

Count Dracula, a centuries-old vampire of the Transylvania region of eastern Europe, is a corpse during the day but comes to life at night. He lives by sucking the blood from living persons (who then also become vampires). In a series of horrifying adventures, Count Dracula pursues his victims relentlessly. He is in turn pursued by others until his body, on its way to his castle, is overtaken, and a stake is driven through its heart, thus ending the count's nocturnal forays.

DRACUT, drā'kət, is a town in northeastern Massachusetts, in Middlesex county, on the Merrimack River, 2 miles (3 km) north of Lowell. Industries include a textile mill and plants for textile products, chemical products, and missile systems. Among the town's historic buildings are the Stephen Russell House (1680), the Cutter Homestead (1720), and the Old Yellow Meeting House (1794, remodeled 1897).

The town site was a center of the Merrimack Valley Indians. The origin of the name Dracut is uncertain. It appears first in a deed of 1664, where it is spelled "Dracutt." The town was incorporated in 1701. It has a town meeting form of government administered by three selectmen. Population 21,249.

DRAFT, Military. See CONSCRIPTION.

DRAFTING. See DRAWING, ENGINEERING.

DRAGO, drä'gō, **Luis María** (1859–1921), Argentine diplomat, author, and jurist, who is best known as the originator and foremost advocate of the so-called Drago Doctrine. He was born in Buenos Aires on May 6, 1859. Drago served his country in a number of important positions, including minister of foreign affairs in 1902. In 1909 he was appointed to the tribunal of arbitration established by the United States and Britain to resolve the North Atlantic fisheries controversy. Shortly before his death he was invited by the Council of the League of Nations to help draft the statute of the Permanent Court of International Justice. Drago died in Buenos Aires on Jan. 9, 1921.

The Drago Doctrine was embodied in a letter of Dec. 29, 1902, to the Argentine minister in Washington, D. C., for delivery to the U. S. Department of State. Intended as a logical corollary to the Monroe Doctrine, it was formulated in protest to the blockade of Venezuelan ports by Britain, Italy, and Germany as a means of enforcing their demands for payment of public debts owed by Venezuela. The doctrine stated that, "the public debt of an American State cannot occasion armed intervention, nor even the actual occupation of the territory of American nations by a European power."

Although this principle was not widely accepted by the major powers, a limited version of it, the Porter Convention, was sponsored by the United States at the Hague Peace Conference of 1907 and adopted by a vote of 39 to 5. The Porter Convention prohibited the use of force for the collection of any contract debt except when the debtor state refused or neglected to reply to an offer of arbitration or, after accepting the offer, prevented an arbitration tribunal from being established, or refused to carry out an award. These exceptions, strongly opposed by the Latin American states, largely nullified the real significance of the renunciation of the use of force. Subsequent inter-American treaties, however, and United Nations Charter restrictions on the use of force have superseded the limitations of the Porter Convention. Thus the principle of the Drago Doctrine may now be considered incorporated into general international law.

DONALD R. SHEA
University of Wisconsin—Milwaukee

DRAGOMAN, drag'ə-mən, was a term used to designate the interpreter through whom affairs were conducted by foreigners in the Middle East, principally in the Ottoman Empire. The term derives from the Arabic *tarjuman.*

While there never was an official with this title in the Ottoman government, individuals from among the resident subject minorities did act as translators in negotiations with foreigners. In the European embassies, the dragoman was an officer on whose loyalty and abilities so much depended that from the middle of the 17th century some European countries trained their own nationals for this function instead of relying on local recruitment.

With the increase in Middle Eastern travel in the mid-19th century, the name was also applied to the Levantine escorts and tour organizers operating in the principal cities of Syria and Egypt.

JOHN R. WALSH
University of Edinburgh

DRAGON, a mythical animal, composed of diverse elements but generally including the body of a snake, wings, lion's claws, and a crocodile's head, often represented as spitting fire. Dragons and dragonlike creatures appear in the myths, folklore, and art of many peoples, taking on various forms and playing a variety of roles. In Egyptian mythology the dragon (or serpent) Apophis was the enemy of the sun god Re. Babylonian myths of the creation tell of the monster Tiamat, whom some scholars interpret as a dragon. Various dragons are found in the art and mythology of the Canaanite peoples. In the Bible there are numerous references to dragons (Hebrew, Tannin), the most important being the Leviathan (Psalm 74:13; Isaiah 27:1, 51:9; Job 41) and the great red dragon of Revelations 12, which is identified with Satan.

DRAGON

A detail from the *Nine Dragon Scroll* by Ch'en Jung, Sung dynasty, 13th century.

MUSEUM OF FINE ARTS, BOSTON—FRANCIS GARDNER CURTIS FUND

There are also numerous references to dragons in Greek and Roman mythology. Various Greek heroes—such as Hercules in the Garden of the Hesperides and Perseus liberating Andromeda—battled these monsters. The Roman legions used a dragon standard that was taken over from the barbarian troops they fought. During the Middle Ages dragon standards were filled with burning oil and thus fire-spitting dragons could precede the fighting men. See also DRAGOONS.

Christian legends combine the Satanic image of the dragon with elements of Greek and other pagan legends. The struggle of the archangel Michael with Satan in the shape of a dragon (Revelations) and the struggles of the Greek heroes with dragons provided the pattern for various accounts, most notably that of St. George, who freed the daughter of the king of Libya from a dragon that daily required human sacrifice; St. George tamed the monster with the sign of the Cross before killing him. The same tale is told of St. Martha, who freed a region of Provence from a dragon called La Tarasque. This struggle is reenacted in an annual pageant in the French town of Tarascon. (A satirical view is found in Alphonse Daudet's novel *Tartarin de Tarascon*, 1872.) The struggle of St. George against the dragon is represented at Mons, Belgium, in the pageant of the Combat du Lumeçon.

A Nordic example of the dragon legend is found in the story of the Lindwurm, the guardian of the treasure of the Rheingold, who is killed by the hero Siegfried. This theme was used by Richard Wagner in his opera *Siegfried*.

A very different picture of the dragon is presented in Chinese tradition, as in the ancient book of *I Ching*, although its general physical similarity to Middle Eastern and European types is notable. In Chinese tradition and art the dragon is the ancient symbol of power, fertility, and well-being. It appears as a motif in art, as in ancient pottery decorations, and in folk pageantry, such as the masked dancing processions of Chinese New Year's celebrations.

In Bali, dragonlike representations of mythical creatures may be seen in the animal mask of Barong, a central character in ritual dramatic presentations, where he is the good force opposing the witch Rangda. Other hybrid monsters are found in the art and mythology of many peoples, such as the plumed serpent of the Aztecs of Mexico and the cannibal monster shown on the pottery of the ancient Nazca culture of Peru.

ERIKA BOURGUIGNON, *The Ohio State University*

DRAGONBOAT FESTIVAL, or *Upright Sun Festival*, is a traditional Chinese holiday celebrated on the fifth day of the fifth moon and associated with the summer solstice. The festival was generally observed by exchanging rice cakes, wearing yellow strips on the back, and posting yellow banners to ward off the "five evils" (centipedes, scorpions, snakes, lizards, and toads). In some places, rice in bamboo tubes was placed in rivers to honor the spirit of the 3d century B.C. poet Ch'ü Yüan, who was said to have drowned himself when his reform proposals were ignored by the emperor. In some parts of South China, dragon-prowed boats representing villages or guilds were raced.

JAMES R. SHIRLEY
Northern Illinois University

DRAGONET, any of a family of small saltwater fishes that inhabit the bottom of tropical and temperate waters. Dragonets are chiefly Old World fishes, but three Atlantic species occur in coastal waters from Florida southward.

Dragonets are small slender fishes, usually 4 to 8 inches (10–20 cm) long. They have a short first dorsal fin; a long second dorsal fin; a long anal fin; broad, fan-shaped pectoral fins; and rounded or pointed tail fins that are often as long as the body. They also have a strong spine on each cheek. The general body color of dragonets is brown, but the pattern is often bizarre, with spots, mottlings, and marblings of bright colors. Males are brighter than females and have much higher dorsal fins. Dragonets are adapted to life on the ocean bottom. For example, they lack swim bladders; their gill openings are high; their heads are broad and flattened; and their eyes are large, high on the head, and often directed upward.

Dragonets are one of the few temperate marine species to practice a spawning ritual, called a "nuptial flight." The male swims around the female with his fins and gill covers erected, and then both male and female swim close together toward the surface, and the eggs are extruded and fertilized. The European dragonet (*Callionymus lyra*) spawns in February or March. The eggs float freely and hatch in about two weeks. After hatching, the larvae form part of the pelagic plankton, but later settle to the bottom.

Dragonets make up the family Callionymidae of the order Perciformes.

E. J. CROSSMAN
University of Toronto

DRAGONFLY is the common name for the graceful long-bodied insects that are most often seen flying swiftly along the borders of lakes and streams. The name is applied particularly to insects of the suborder Anisoptera, but it is also used as a general name for the entire order Odonata, which includes the damselflies. Dragonflies are also called "darning needles."

The Adult Insect. The head of the adult dragonfly is characterized by two huge compound eyes that occupy more than half of the head's surface. These eyes are composed of numerous facets and produce a mosaic, or checkerboardlike, type of vision that is very sensitive to moving objects. Small single-faceted eyes, called ocelli, are also present. The dragonfly's antennae are small and bristlelike, and its mouthparts are modified for biting.

The dragonfly's thorax, like that of other insects, is composed of three segments. The first segment has two legs and is separate from the other two segments, which are fused together into a large pterothorax bearing two pairs of legs and two pairs of membranous wings. The legs are placed far to the front and are well adapted for perching but not for walking. Their many bristles help to capture small insects in flight. The wings are held horizontally outspread when at rest (in contrast to the damselflies, which hold them vertically above the body).

The long slender abdomen is composed of 10 well-marked segments. The last one in the male ends in three caudal appendages, one below and two above. The lower appendage is often divided, and the two upper ones are modified in various ways. The male genitalia, including the penis, are in a pocket on the underside of the second segment from the thorax, far from the opening of the sperm duct on the ninth segment. This characteristic of the order Odonata is a unique feature among insects. The female abdomen is stouter, ending in two, usually cylindrical appendages, with the genital opening on the ventral side of the eighth segment. Some females have a complicated ovipositor for inserting eggs singly into soft plant tissues.

Mating. During mating, the male transfers sperm to the penis and clasps the head of the female with his caudal appendages. In some species the two fly in tandem during egg laying, but in others the female oviposits alone, repeatedly dipping the end of the abdomen in the water and washing off some eggs each time. The total number of eggs laid by a female in one batch varies from a few hundred to a few thousand. The largest authentic published count of eggs found in a female is 5,200. Because in a few species a number of females will lay eggs in closely associated gelatinous strings, masses of 100,000 eggs have been erroneously credited to one female.

Flight. Flight habits vary with the species. Some rarely alight during hours of flight, but others occupy favorite perches from which they go forth to capture food or explore. Some males defend a definite territory over a stretch of water where eggs will be laid, often patrolling back and forth across this area. Most species fly only in bright sunlight, and instantly stop when the sun is darkened by clouds. A few fly only briefly at dawn or dusk. The complete flight period of most individuals lasts only a few weeks. Some species have an explosive annual emergence in temperate climates and soon disappear, while in other species individuals will continue to emerge throughout the summer, or all year long in the tropics.

Nymph. The immature form of the dragonfly is called a larva, a naiad, or, most commonly, a nymph. Nymphs live almost exclusively in fresh water, their body form and legs being adapted to specific habitats. Some species burrow in sand or mud, some sprawl on the silt bottom, while others cling to vegetation.

The most remarkable feature of the nymph is the labium, or lower lip. It is folded upon itself at the middle like a hinge and turned backward between the legs. There are two movable lobes at the front end of the labium that are armed with teeth, spines, and hooks for capturing prey. The labium can be shot forward with lightning speed to grasp a food organism, which is then drawn back to the biting jaws.

The nymphal stage lasts from a few weeks to about five years, depending upon the species, being much shorter for some species living in the tropics. The nymph passes through 10 to 15 instars, or developmental stages, each beginning

HERMES, FROM NATIONAL AUDUBON SOCIETY

DRAGONFLY'S wings are reinforced by a network of veins. At the far right a dragonfly is shown with the nymphal shell from which the insect has just emerged.

False dragonhead (*Physostegia pulchella*)

with a molt of the outside skin. The wing pads, which appear after the third or fourth molt, are noticeably swollen in the last instar, indicating imminent emergence.

Metamorphosis. Dragonflies are said to have incomplete metamorphosis because there is no true pupal, or resting, stage; however, prior to emergence the nymph does not eat for several days and may extend part of its body above water for more oxygen while great changes are occurring within it. The nymph then leaves the water and crawls up a plant, log, or rock, to which it attaches itself by its legs. Soon a split develops on the upper side of the head and thorax of the nymphal skin, and the head and thorax of the adult, followed by the abdomen, appear. The newly emerged insect, soft and helpless—a condition referred to as "teneral"—begins to expand its wings and lengthen its abdomen. Many dragonflies emerge during the night and are ready to fly by daylight. Others emerge during the day.

Food and Enemies. Adult dragonflies eat flying insects of any kind found in sufficient numbers and of the proper size, such as mosquitoes and midges. Large adults may eat the bees near a hive, but most dragonflies are decidedly beneficial, and all are harmless to man. Nymphs at first feed on protozoans and minute crustaceans and then, as they grow in size, on mosquito, midge, and other insect larvae, small worms, and even other dragonfly nymphs. Large nymphs have been observed to eat small fish.

Nymphs are eaten by fish, and even the adults may be caught as they dip into the water. Birds, frogs, and spiders consume many young or teneral adults.

History and Distribution. Dragonflies appeared early in the history of insects. In fossil deposits of the upper Carboniferous (Pennsylvanian), which are about 320 million years of age, large dragonflylike insects have been found with a wingspan of over 30 inches (75 cm). Today, dragonflies occur on all major land masses, with species and individuals most numerous in the tropics. Some species have a limited distribution, but at least one species is found on all continents except Europe.

MINTER J. WESTFALL, JR.
University of Florida

DRAGONHEAD is the common name for some 45 species of annual and perennial herbs constituting the genus *Dracocephalum* of the mint family (Labiatae). Except for the North American species *D. parviflorum,* the genus is native to Europe and Asia. Dragonheads bear small purple, blue, or occasionally white flowers crowded into dense spikes at the top of the stem or into dense heads in the axils of the leaves.

False Dragonhead. The approximately 15 species of false dragonheads (*Physostegia*), also members of the mint family, are all native to North America. These are slender perennial herbs that bear purple, rose, or white flowers in a spike at the top of the stem. The species *P. virginiana* is sometimes called the "obedient plant" because its stem can be bent into almost any desired position.

S. C. BAUSOR
California State College, Pa.

DRAGOON, drə-gōōn', a mounted soldier trained to fight either on horseback or on foot. Dragoons were so called because their muskets were said to spit fire in the fashion of a dragon.

The first dragoons, called *arquebusiers à cheval,* were organized in France by Piero Strozzi in 1537 for Francis I. From 1668, when the first full regiment was created under Louis XV, until 1831, when they were combined with the line cavalry, they formed a major force in the French military complement. Frederick the Great of Prussia (1712–1786) used them in his military plan of an army, which served as a standard pattern of armies throughout the world for more than 150 years.

In the United States the Continental Army had four regiments of light dragoons, and dragoon units served in wars until they were finally consolidated with the cavalry at the beginning of the Civil War (1861).

DRAINAGE, in agriculture, is the removal of excess water from the soil. Surface drainage is the removal of water from the top of the soil, and subsurface drainage is the removal of water from beneath the soil surface.

There are two major reasons why excess water should be removed from the soil. One reason is that waterlogged soils are deficient in oxygen, and since plant roots require oxygen for respiration, the plants cannot thrive. A ponding of water on the surface of the soil also cuts off the supply of oxygen to the roots. The need for oxygen is particularly critical when the plants are germinating, or sprouting. In the midwestern and eastern sections of the United States, for example, waterlogging is most likely to occur during the spring rainy season, just when many crops are sprouting. According to the U.S. Agricultural Research Service, crop damage due to excess water in the soil is the dominant problem in 14% of the country's cropland.

The second major reason for draining cultivated land is that it helps control the salinity (salt content) of the soil. This problem is most acute in regions where rainfall is supplemented with irrigation water. In these areas the salt in the irrigation water tends to become concentrated in the soil after the water has been used by the plants or has evaporated. Additional irrigation water seeping downward through the soil dissolves the salt, but it must be carried off through a system of drains.

POORLY DRAINED LAND becomes waterlogged and allows rainwater to form huge puddles on the surface.

SOIL CONSERVATION SERVICE, USDA

An example of the use of drainage to control soil salinity is seen in the Imperial Valley in California. In the Imperial Valley the water used for irrigation comes from the Colorado River, and it contains about 1 ton (0.9 metric ton) of salt per acre-foot of water. (An acre-foot is the amount of water needed to cover 1 acre, or 0.4 hectare, to the depth of 1 foot, or 30 cm.) During the growing season, each acre of land receives about 7 acre-feet of irrigation water, and because the growing plants use up only about 150 pounds (68 kg) of the 7 tons (6.3 metric tons) of the salt in the water, the rest of the salt remains in the soil. In order to remove this salt, additional irrigation water is applied after the growing season, but because of the stratification of the soil, which traps the water, a system of drains is needed to carry off the water containing the dissolved salt.

If salt concentrations are not leached out of soil, the land becomes too saline, and reclamation procedures are needed to restore the land's productivity. The first step in reclamation is the provision of adequate drainage. The soil is then leached by ponding water on the surface or by frequently applying irrigation water, which escapes through the drainage.

Drainage Systems. In the Imperial Valley and other sizable regions that are under irrigation, a typical drainage system consists of main, secondary, and tertiary drains that carry water away from the individual farms. The major channels are generally open drains, or ditches, but on each farm closed, or covered, drains are used. Open drains are relatively inexpensive to install, and can carry larger amounts of water. However, they are rarely used for on-farm drainage because of the large amount of land that would be removed from cultivation and because of the difficulty of conducting farming operations between closely spaced open drains.

Covered drains often consist of concrete or tile pipe segments buried in the soil. The pipes are laid end to end, and the water enters them through the cracks between adjacent pipes. Sometimes, perforated plastic pipes are used. The perforations may be drilled holes or sawed slots, and the pipe may be smooth-walled or corrugated. In the United States the smallest pipes that are used have a diameter of 4 inches (10 cm), but in Europe the most commonly used type of pipe has a diameter of 2 inches (5 cm).

A TYPICAL AGRICULTURAL DRAINAGE SYSTEM. The principal drains of a region (top) are shown as they relate to the drains of a small farm (shaded).

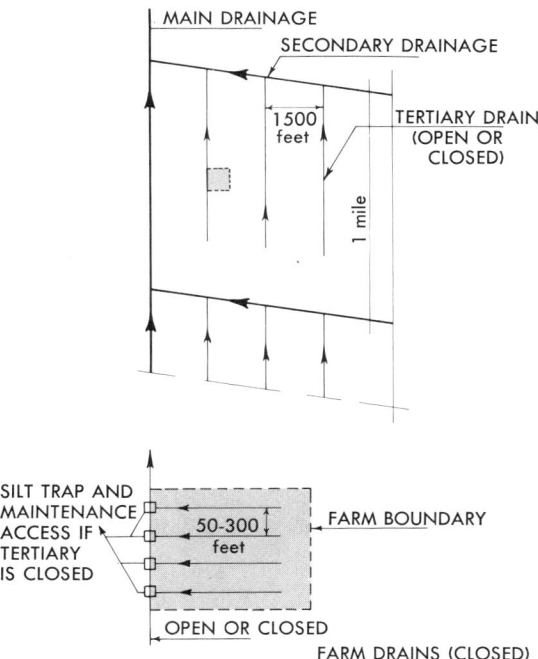

Distances are approximate for purpose of illustration

OPEN DRAINS, sometimes lined with concrete, are used as main and secondary drains, while the tertiary and on-farm drains are often underground.

SOIL CONSERVATION SERVICE, USDA

The depth and spacing of covered drains vary according to the climate and the type of soil. In humid regions the depth of the drains ranges from 2 to 3½ feet (60–105 cm), and they may be from 30 to 100 feet (9–30 meters) apart. In arid regions that are irrigated, the minimum depth of covered drains is 5 feet (1½ meters), although most are installed at a depth of 6 feet (1.8 meters) or more. The spacing of the drains in irrigated regions ranges from about 50 to 300 feet (15–90 meters), depending on the soil's hydraulic conductivity, that is, its ability to conduct, or transmit, water. In irrigated regions it is customary to surround a closed drain pipe with a gravel envelope or filter to prevent soil particles from entering the pipe along with the water. In humid regions, where the soil is generally more cohesive, it is not necessary to use a gravel filter.

Although most drainage systems involve the use of drains, in some irrigated areas it is possible to lower a shallow water table by pumping water from a well. For successful well drainage the soil must be waterlogged from the shallow soil layers to the aquifer (underground water source), which may be from 50 to 300 feet (15–90 meters) below the soil surface.

In many areas the slope and topography of the land do not permit excess rainfall to run off into a natural outlet. These conditions are often associated with soils that have a low hydraulic conductivity, and in order to remove the water it is necessary to provide ditches or to improve natural channels to carry the water out of the area. In addition, it is necessary to shape and grade the land surface so that the water may flow freely into the channel.

History. The construction of drains for agricultural purposes started long before recorded history. Some of the earliest recorded instructions for building and spacing drains are found in the writings of Cato the Elder (234–149 B.C.) and Varro (116–27 B.C.). The recommendations of these and other writers were followed for more than a thousand years.

Drainage systems have been designed in accordance with the properties of soil only in relatively recent times. In 1856, Henry Darcy of France described the law governing the flow of water through soil and other porous materials, and in 1938, S. B. Hooghoudt of the Netherlands published the first comprehensive analyses of drainage problems, including a field method for measuring the soil's hydraulic conductivity. The development of drainage systems is still the subject of much research.

JAMES N. LUTHIN
University of California at Davis

DRAKE, Edwin Laurentine (1819–1880), American oil producer, who drilled the first oil well. He was born near Greenville, N. Y., on March 19, 1819. After many years as hotel clerk, steamboat employee, and railway conductor, he became a key figure in the birth of the giant petroleum industry. Drake was induced to invest $200 in the stock of the Pennsylvania Rock Oil Company, which was formed in 1854 to market surface oil from a farm near Titusville, Pa. While tests had proved the quality of the oil, little had been done to obtain it in quantity.

Drake had no experience to guide him when he arrived at Titusville in 1857 to look into the possibilities of obtaining profitable quantities of rock oil. However, on the way to the area, he had studied salt well drilling operations in Pittsburgh and Syracuse. What he saw there proved to be the key to high production.

Drake leased the land from the company and formed a subsidiary, the Seneca Oil Co. It took him many months to obtain equipment and operators before drilling began in June 1859. He endured much ridicule for his apparently vain efforts to bring up oil, but "Drake's Folly" came in on August 27, 1859, with 25 barrels daily from a depth of 69 feet (21 meters), proving the existence of underground reservoirs of oil. It was the first time such stores had been tapped at their source. A factor in Drake's success, besides his persistence, was his device of sinking a pipe casing to protect the drill from sand and clay. Drake lost his savings in a stock deal and died in poverty, at Bethlehem, Pa., on Nov. 8, 1880.

COURTNEY R. HALL
Queens College, City University of New York
Author, "History of American Industrial Science"

SIR FRANCIS DRAKE and the 100-ton *Golden Hind* (right), in which he sailed around the world in 1577–1580.

NATIONAL PORTRAIT GALLERY, LONDON
MAP ROOM, BRITISH MUSEUM

DRAKE, Sir Francis (c. 1543–1596), English admiral, whose circumnavigation of the earth and predatory attacks on Spanish shipping made him a legend during his lifetime. His life spanned the "heroic" age of English maritime enterprise, the period in which the English first became a "nation of sailors."

Drake's family were yeomen farmers in Devon, in southwestern England. They had some pretensions to gentility but no great means. Edmund Drake, Francis' father, was an early adherent and lay preacher of the reformed, rather than the established, religion. For this reason he and his family had to leave Devon in 1549 for the east coast.

Young Francis grew up in an atmosphere of relative poverty and religious persecution. Although he learned to read and write and inherited his father's eloquence, he had little formal education. He was apprenticed early to the master of a coasting bark, became a skipper in his turn, and learned his mastery of ship handling and pilotage in the Thames estuary and the English Channel.

Early Ventures. In 1566, Drake shipped as seaman with John Lovell on a slaving venture to the Spanish West Indies. The following year he sailed with John Hawkins, a master in the slave trade, in the *Jesus of Lübeck*. In the course of this voyage he was given command of the 50-ton *Judith*. Drake was present at the Battle of San Juan de Ulúa (now Veracruz, Mexico), where Hawkins, trapped in harbor by the Spanish viceroy Martín Enríquez, lost three of his five ships and much treasure. The circumstances in which Drake and his *Judith* "foresook us in our great misery" (in Hawkins' words) have never been fully explained. The episode added to Drake's hatred of Spanish officialdom and bolstered his Protestant convictions.

In 1570, 1571, and 1572, Drake himself commanded small private raiding expeditions to the West Indies to recoup his fortunes. All three expeditions had the Isthmus of Panama as their principal goal, but the first two achieved little. On the third voyage, early in 1573, Drake's party, reinforced by French Huguenot pirates and guided by *cimarrones* (runaway Negro slaves), successfully ambushed a mule train carrying Peruvian silver to Nombre de Dios, Panama, for shipment to Spain. Enough bullion was captured and taken back to England to "make" the voyage and Drake's reputation. His return, however, coincided with an attempt by England's Elizabeth I and Philip II of Spain to compose their differences. Though no action was taken against Drake, he was probably warned to lie low.

Circumnavigation of the World. The objects of Drake's circumnavigation voyage of 1577–1580 included exploration and trade in the Pacific and possibly a search for Ptolemy's *Terra Australis* (Southern Land)) or for the "Strait of Anian," believed to connect the Atlantic and Pacific north of America. With Drake in command, plunder must also have been expected. The Queen gave verbal consent and probably invested in the venture, though secretly—the voyage was almost wholly one of private enterprise.

Five ships left Plymouth carrying about 160 men. Only one ship completed the voyage—the flagship, *Pelican,* which Drake in the course of the voyage renamed *Golden Hind* in compliment to his patron Sir Christopher Hatton, whose crest was a golden deer. She was not a big ship by contemporary standards but was very strongly built and exceptionally well armed. Drake's fleet cruised down the African coast, taking several ships as prizes; crossed to Brazil; and refitted in Port St. Julian (Puerto San Julián) on the Patagonian coast, where two ships were abandoned. Here occurred the trial and execution, or "judicial murder," of Thomas Doughty, a gentleman volunteer whom Drake suspected of treachery.

The three remaining ships made a rapid passage—16 days—through the Strait of Magellan, but in the Pacific they were separated by storms. One ship disappeared; another put back into the strait and then returned to England. Drake himself was driven to the south of Tierra del Fuego and found there nothing but open sea—an important discovery about the Antarctic region that received little attention at the time.

When the weather abated, Drake embarked on a piratical cruise up the Pacific coast of South America, raiding both harbors and shipping and collecting a large quantity of silver and other booty. This was the first English incursion into the Pacific, and it caused great indignation and alarm in Spain. Drake refitted his ship in a bay on the coast of California. A brass plate purporting to record his stay there was found north of San Francisco in 1936. (Historians are divided about its authenticity.) From California, Drake set off across the Pacific, guided by captured Spanish pilots. He visited the Moluccas—the first English captain to do so—and loaded several tons of cloves. He returned to England by way of the Cape of Good Hope.

331

Drake was the first English captain to sail around the world. The Queen, in answer to Spanish protests, ordered a token portion of his loot to be restored to the Spaniards. But in 1581, Elizabeth condoned Drake's piracies by knighting him on board the *Golden Hind*. The ship itself was preserved for many years as a monument.

War with Spain. Drake was now both a popular hero and a man of means. In 1584 he was elected a member of Parliament. His maritime depredations and those of many imitators, however, had contributed to a steady deterioration of Anglo-Spanish relations. In 1585 the Spanish government seized English ships in Iberian harbors. Queen Elizabeth replied by letters of reprisal, and Drake was sent off to the West Indies on an authorized cruise, with a fleet of more than 20 sail, including two of the Queen's ships. The expedition captured and sacked Santo Domingo and Cartagena, took a number of small prizes, but missed the homeward-bound Spanish treasure fleet. On the way home Drake destroyed the Spanish fort at St. Augustine, Florida, and stopped at Roanoke Colony, in Virginia, where he picked up Ralph Lane's discouraged settlers.

The physical damage caused by Drake's operations in the West Indies was not crucial, but the effect on English and (conversely) Spanish morale was very great. The cruise off the Spanish coast that Drake next commanded, in 1587, was more important from a strategic point of view. His fleet destroyed more than 20 ships in Cádiz harbor and disrupted, for several months, supplies converging on Lisbon to outfit the Armada, with which Spain planned to sail against England. Drake caused the Spanish naval offensive to be postponed until the following year. When in 1588 the Armada finally sailed, Drake served dutifully and ably as vice admiral under Lord Howard of Effingham in the fleet that defeated the Armada in the English Channel.

The rest of Drake's career was anticlimactic. The expedition against Lisbon in 1589—150 ships, the biggest fleet Drake ever commanded—was a failure, and Drake was blamed for it. He was not again employed until 1595, in joint command with John Hawkins in another large-scale raid on the Spanish West Indies. It was a disaster. The Spanish defenses had been greatly strengthened since 1585. The English suffered from hesitation and divided counsels. The commanders were aging and past their best. Both Drake and Hawkins died in the course of the voyage—Drake on Jan. 28, 1596—and were buried at sea.

Importance. Drake was admired in his own day as a great corsair rather than as a great admiral. He never thought of himself as a pirate, though toward Spaniards he often behaved like one. But even toward Spaniards he could be magnanimous. He was significant, not as the founder of a naval tradition, but as a focus of admiration and envy. He stimulated the predatory instincts of the aristocracy and gentry, the financial and commercial ambitions of businessmen, and the adventurousness and professional competence of seamen. More than any other, he "inflamed the whole country with a desire to adventure into the seas."

JOHN H. PARRY, *Harvard University*

Further Reading: Corbett, Julian S., *Drake and the Tudor Navy*, 2 vols., 2d ed. (New York 1965); Nuttall, Zelia, ed., *New Light on Drake* (New York 1914); Williamson, James A., *The Age of Drake*, 4th ed. (New Yc-k 1960).

DRAKE, Joseph Rodman (1795–1820), American poet and satirist, who, in collaboration with his close friend Fitz-Greene Halleck, published the famous *Croaker Papers*. Drake was born in New York City on Aug. 7, 1795. After studying medicine, he toured Europe for two years and, on his return to the United States in 1818, became a druggist.

In 1819 Drake began to publish light satirical verse in the New York *Evening Post* under the pseudonym "Croaker." Later, joined by Halleck in these writings, he changed the signature to "Croaker and Company." Drake died in New York City on Sept. 21, 1820.

Drake's only published book of serious poetry, *The Culprit Fay and Other Poems*, was issued posthumously in abridged form in 1835. In addition to the title poem, which is based on the folklore of the Hudson River highlands, the *Culprit Fay* volume includes the patriotic eulogy *The American Flag* as well as two nature poems, *Bronx* and *Niagara*.

DRAKE, a male duck. See DUCK.

DRAKE UNIVERSITY is a private coeducational institution located in Des Moines, Iowa. Founded in 1881 by the Disciples of Christ, it is named for Francis Marion Drake, the first president of the board of trustees. The university comprises colleges of fine arts, liberal arts, business administration, pharmacy, and education. It also has schools of journalism, divinity, and law; a graduate division; and University College (for adult education).

The university cooperates with the city of Des Moines in operating an observatory and a symphony orchestra, and since 1910 it has sponsored the Drake Relays, a major annual U.S. track and field meet. Drake has approximately 7,000 students.

DRAKENSBERG, drä'kənz-bûrg, mountain range in South Africa, extending from northeastern Transvaal province to southern Cape province and forming the border with Lesotho. It is actually a steep, seaward-facing scarp. Part of the Great Escarpment of southern Africa, it separates the extensive higher plateau areas from the lower marginal lands.

The Natal Drakensberg, along the Natal-Lesotho border, is the most abrupt and prominent part of the mountain range. Its highest point is 11,425 feet (3,482 meters) at Thabana Ntlenyana in Lesotho.

The Natal Drakensberg constitutes a formidable barrier to communication, with a 160-mile (260-km) stretch that no road crosses. Rainfall distribution also is affected because the mountains act as barriers to the moisture-laden easterly winds. Farther north, in the Transvaal Drakensberg, elevations are somewhat lower, and there are mountain passes that permit road and rail construction.

EDWARD J. MILES
University of Vermont

DRAM, a unit of volume or a unit of mass. As a unit of fluid volume, the drama is equal to ⅛ fluid ounce. As a unit of mass in the avoirdupois system, the dram is equal to $\frac{1}{16}$ avoirdupois ounce. As a unit of mass in the apothecaries' weights, the dram is ⅛ of the apothecaries' ounce. See also WEIGHTS AND MEASURES.

DRAMA

Modern production of Sophocles' *Oedipus Rex* (chorus in front) indicates austere quality of classical tragedy.

CONTENTS

Section	Page
Western Drama	334
1. Greek Drama	334
2. Roman Drama	336
3. Medieval Drama	337
4. Renaissance Tragedy	338
5. Renaissance Comedy	343
6. Restoration Comedy	345
7. Modern Realism	346
8. German Romanticism	346
9. Naturalism	347
10. Ibsen and Symbolism	347
11. Modern Russian Drama	348
12. Modern Italian Drama	349
13. Modern Spanish Drama	350
14. 20th Century Trends	350
Oriental Drama	352
15. India	352
16. China	354
17. Japan	356

DRAMA is a form of literature intended for performance by actors. In general the subject matter is narrative in character and, in the type of story traditionally considered suitable for presentation on the stage, the interplay of opposing elements usually results in a conflict. In European drama the phases of this situation are generally depicted in a sequence of scenes arranged so that each is the consequence of the preceding, until the conflicting elements reach a point of climax, after which the conflict is resolved and the play ends. This principle of design, sometimes attributed to Sophocles, corresponds with the general norms of storytelling in Europe. In Asia acceptable modes of narrative are simpler. Eastern plays are often tissues of episodes connected chiefly by the presence of the principal characters, without any special terminal principle.

In ancient Athens the word "drama" (from *dran*, "to do") would recall the distinction between the *dromenon* (the "thing done") in the course of the Eleusinian mysteries, and the *mythos* (the "thing said"). But while ritual appears always to include dramatic elements, the difference between drama and ritual is fundamental. Ritual is essentially practical in purpose. It is a ceremony designed to enlist the support of the higher powers, to avert their wrath, or to facilitate the passage of individuals through the successive stages of life, maturity, and death. Ancient Greek drama never lost its connection with the cult of Dionysus, and Indian plays were always given under the banner of Indra. But it seems clear that in the theater for which Aeschylus wrote the *Oresteia*, the efficient purposes of the ceremony were pretty well overshadowed by considerations of an aesthetic and intellectual nature. The purpose of the Bacchic ritual was doubtless the enhancement of fertility and the perpetuation of life, and the plays given in the course of the rites were dedicated to this end. But by the time of Aeschylus, drama had acquired a certain autonomy, and it was soon to acquire another purpose. For Aristotle the purpose of drama was to give pleasure. For Horace, it was to delight and to instruct. For Molière, the end of comedy was to make good people laugh.

The most obvious connection of Greek drama with Greek ritual is seen in the orgiastic nature of the Bacchic cult and the capacity of drama to arouse a common emotional experience in many people. The momentary deliverance of the individual from the consciousness of self and the consequent merging of the psyche in the vital stream of our common humanity is probably the highest pleasure the theater can afford, and the ultimate goal of dramatic art. When, at rare moments, something of the sort is achieved, it is obvious to everyone that the play is blessed. When, on the contrary, the spectator experiences no empathy, the play is likely to seem a pointless and unprofitable mummery.

Western Drama

Drama in the Western countries has had an interesting and varied growth, but in all its history it has flowered only three times, and then only briefly. Its first great period was in ancient Greece, in Attica, in the century preceding the Peloponnesian War. The second expression of Western dramatic genius came in the Renaissance, during the cultural transition between the Christian Middle Ages and the modern world. In Italy this period corresponded with the political expansion of Florence, and the artistic development of Ferrara and Venice (1475–1600). In England, it came in the time of Elizabeth (1533–1603); in France, in the age of Louis XIV (1638–1715); and in Spain, in the Golden Age, during the reign of Philip II (1556–1598) and his immediate successors. The third great period of the drama is the age of Ibsen (1828–1906). It has its roots in the Second French Empire, and in the social and intellectual ferments associated with the revolutionary ideas of Schopenhauer, Darwin, and Marx.

1. Greek Drama

Tragedy and comedy are forms peculiar to the Attic stage, and to the drama later written in imitation of the Greek. There is nothing comparable in the Eastern tradition, and nothing precisely corresponding to these forms in modern drama in the West, although the terms are used loosely to distinguish plays that make a sad impression from those intended to evoke laughter. The distinction between tragedy and comedy in classical times, however, had no essential relation to the nature of the outcome. The difference was a matter of style. Tragedy was written in high style, and dealt with characters to whom high style was appropriate—gods, kings, and heroes. Comedy was in low style, and dealt with characters of a low order. There was no style appropriate to everyday reality; consequently, there was no realistic drama.

Tragedy. There is every likelihood that tragedy originated, as Aristotle says, in the dithyramb, a choral song, accompanied by the flute, sung ceremonially in honor of the god Dionysus. It has been conjectured that the participants wore goatskins and pretended to be satyrs. If true, this would account for the term "tragedy," which means goat-song. At a certain point, it is thought, the leader of the chorus, the *coryphaeus*, was detached from the group, and played a special role in connection with it. The tradition is that at the Dionysia of 534 B.C., in the time of Pisistratus, a certain Thespis, who was then coryphaeus, added to the chorus an "answerer" (*hypocritēs*) with whom he carried on a dialogue. *Hypocritēs* became the Greek word for "actor." It is for this reason that Thespis is usually credited by historians of the theater with the invention of tragedy. Aristotle informs us that it was Aeschylus (524?–456 B.C.) who added a second actor to the chorus, and that Sophocles (495–405 B.C.) added the third. This was the extent of the Greek cast. Presumably there were never more than three masked characters on the stage at once.

While there can be, in the present state of knowledge, no certainty as to the origin of tragedy, there is little doubt that there was a close relation originally between tragedy and the Dionysian ritual. It has been amply demonstrated that Dionysus was a year spirit, or vegetation god. But the tragic hero is never Dionysus, and it is only in the *Bacchae* of Euripides that we are afforded an actual glimpse of the god's role in the Bacchic sacrifices. Early in the 20th century, Sir William Ridgeway provoked much discussion by denying that tragedy had anything to do with Dionysus. It was his conjecture that tragedy originated in the commemorative rites at the grave of a hero. But the evidence of Aristotle, and the close connection of the drama with the Dionysian cult, makes his proposal difficult to accept. The Greek plays, in any event, were performed in Athens at the Great Dionysia in early spring; at the Lenaea, the festival of the wine vats, in January; and throughout Greece at the Rustic Dionysia in December. In the great spring festival, the entire urban population came to the theater of Dionysus on the slope of the Acropolis. The plays were given in the form of a contest. Three poets were chosen yearly to compete on each of three consecutive days, and normally each presented a trilogy of plays, followed, it is said, by a satyr play.

In the early period of Greek drama, the principal element of the production was the masked chorus, the size of which appears to have varied considerably. In *The Suppliants* of Aeschylus it numbers 50; but in most of Aeschylus' plays, it seems to have numbered only 12, and Sophocles is said to have increased this number to 15. The size of the chorus apparently diminished in the 5th century, perhaps because its function was lyrical rather than dramatic, perhaps because it was too expensive to maintain. Its role is difficult to define. It can hardly be considered the ideal spectator. In many plays it is deeply concerned in the action. Where it is not, it creates an emotional climate for the play, reacting to the deeds of the principals in a manner that may be thought to approximate the feelings of the audience, defining a prudent standard of behavior that gives scale to the action, and commenting sententiously on what is done. The chorus thus provides a norm by which to judge the action. Against this background of unremarkable people, singularly articulate, to whom nothing happens, the remarkable people of the drama move through their extraordinary course.

The theatrical practice of the Greeks is fairly clear. All parts were played by men. The actors wore masks. They sang certain lyric passages, either by themselves or with the aid of the chorus. In tragedy they walked about on high clogs (*kothornoi*) and wore long gowns and lofty headdresses. They played their parts on a low platform, raised slightly above the circular area (*orchestra*) in which the chorus danced, and were thus exalted by a foot or more above the common run of humanity.

In the *Poetics*, Aristotle speaks of tragedy and epic in the same breath, remarking that

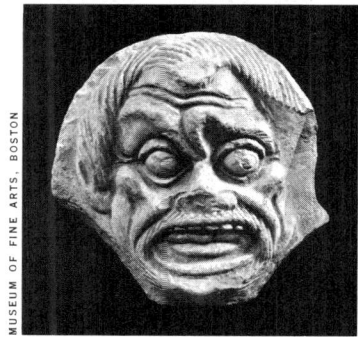

IN ANCIENT THEATER, actors wore masks, such as Greek mask (*top left*) and Roman mask (*bottom left*). Pompeian mural (*right*) is a scene from a Roman comedy.

they differ chiefly with respect to the magnitude of the action they represent. Epics, intended for recital, might be of considerable length and might involve a complex story. But it would be unreasonable, in his opinion, to expect an audience to believe that an action represented in a couple of hours actually spans a period of years. For this curious reason, he limited the permissible duration of the dramatic action to the space of a single day. The Renaissance critics called this limitation the unity of time and added to it, in the name of verisimilitude, two other "rules"—unity of place and unity of action. This meant that the action of a tragedy must take place in a single day and in a single place, and must converge upon a single event. In fact most Greek tragedies, though by no means all, conform to this scheme, and the consequence is a tightly knit story, the enactment of which entails a lengthy exposition and the services of messengers to describe what, because of the unities, cannot be represented. In the name of credibility, also, it was considered that deeds of violence could not be performed before the eyes of the audience, since actors could hardly be slaughtered on the stage. It was customary, therefore, to exhibit only the results of violence. Thus, after the murder of Agamemnon is described in the *Oresteia*, the body itself is wheeled out on a wagon-stage, called the *ekkyklēma*, so that the audience might see for itself that the deed has been done.

Aristotle sees tragedy in terms of a wrong choice, an error in judgment. The word he uses in the *Poetics* is *hamartia*, a miss in shooting at a target. This was interpreted in the Renaissance as a characterological defect, or moral flaw, and this idea did much to develop the subsequent concept of drama as an interplay of action and character. But we look in vain for flaws in the characters of most of the Greek tragic heroes. A more fruitful approach to the Greek idea of tragedy may perhaps be found in the doctrine of Herodotus (484?–425 B.C.), whose *History* thoroughly illustrates the unhappy consequences of *hybris*. This term, often translated as pride, designates the trait that attracts *nemesis*, or retribution. To be unusually fortunate among mortals is hybristic and a sure way of attracting the envy (*phthonos*) of the gods. The consequence is disaster. Tragedy is, accordingly, the occupational disease of heroes. To be undistinguished among men is to be safe. The Greek chorus never tires of extolling the advantages of obscurity. Trapped between his desire for distinction and the limitations of the human condition, man's lot is generally not happy. Certain men, however, are doomed by fate (*moira*), by necessity, or by a superior power, as in the case of Oedipus or Hippolytus; or, like Creon in *Antigone*, caught in a dilemma that offers no acceptable alternative. Such men are the special subjects of tragedy. In such cases, it is the sense of claustrophobia, together with the feeling of indignation at the injustice of the human condition, that gives tragedy its peculiar savor, and it was stories of this sort, apparently, that chiefly attracted the attention of the Greek tragic writers.

In these circumstances the pleasure of tragedy must be ascribed to a very special sort of empathy. Aristotle intimates that the purgation of emotion—specifically pity and fear—is pleasurable in itself. What he meant, precisely, by tragic catharsis has never been entirely clear. Plato had excluded drama from his ideal commonwealth on the ground that it aroused passions that defied rational control. It is likely that Aristotle intended to justify tragedy on the basis of the psychic purification it brought about. Presumably, the spectator, having spent his emotions in the course of the play, would leave the theater in the calm and rational state that befitted the citizen of a well-ordered republic.

Greek drama, in the main, is Attic. During and after the Macedonian empire, theaters sprang up everywhere, but the great tragedies belong to the relatively short period of Athenian supremacy in the Aegean. Of the precursors of the great age—Choerilus, Phrynicus, and Pratinas—we know little beyond their names. The Attic drama in effect begins with Aeschylus, and it ends with Euripides (c.485–406 B.C.). The high period of Greek drama is thus something less than a century, from 499 to 405 B.C., a period that spans the greatness of Athens from the generation after Solon, through the age of Pericles, to the fall of Athens at the hands of the Spartans in 405. It is possible to see a certain organic development of the art from Aeschylus, who is often said to be austerely simple in his thinking, though a lover of long words, to Euripides, who seems to some critics, because of his obvious skepticism, his humane attitude, and his easy style, as well as his complex plots, to reflect in some way the decay of Attic culture. From this viewpoint Sophocles marks the high point of the art. But in recent years, the questioning spirit and the manifest humanity of Euripides have made him increasingly the subject of admiration; indeed, of all the writers of his time, he seems nearest to the modern age and the most comprehensible.

Comedy. Comedy is somewhat less mysterious in its origins than tragedy. Aristotle tersely ascribes its source to "the leaders of the phallic songs" (*ta phallika*). The word "comedy," *kōmoidia*, is clearly derived from *kōmos* (a "revel"), and there is every reason to suppose that this dramatic genre had its beginnings in the procession of revelers who carried the phallus in the Dionysian festivals, singing and shouting appropriate ribaldries at the onlookers. It is these scurrilities, apparently, that developed into the personal ridicule that was a feature of Old Comedy until, in 414 B.C., the practice was forbidden as demoralizing in time of war.

Comedy in ancient Greece went through a development so considerable that the Old and New Comedy seem to have nothing in common. Before Aristophanes (c.450–c.385 B.C.), we hear of Cratinus, Crates, and Eupolis; and fragments of the mimes of Epicharmus and Sophron have been painfully reconstructed; but little is known of any of these writers, save that in their time they were highly regarded. What we know of Old Comedy is substantially the work of Aristophanes, an amazing monument to the Greek comic spirit.

In form, comedy differed from tragedy chiefly in the use of the chorus. This was larger than the tragic chorus; possibly it numbered 24. At the end of the traditional dispute between the protagonist and the second actor, the chorus moved to a position facing the audience and delivered the anapestic strophes of the *parabasis*, a complex lyrical composition ending with an ode and a satiric speech of good counsel on some subject of current interest. The second part of the comedy followed, consisting of a number of episodes with short choral interludes, in which the plot elements set forth in the first part were brought to a successful conclusion. The *exodos* (conclusion) was invariably joyful, and ended in a revel and often in a marriage. The choral dances, unlike the staid measures of tragedy, were apparently vigorous and sometimes included the *cordax*, a southern dance associated with drunkenness and regarded as especially indecent.

While tragedy confined its subject matter to myth and historical legend, the comic poet was expected to give his imagination the fullest scope. Aristophanes' comedies include all sorts of delightful extravagances, sparing neither gods nor men. *Ecclesiazusae* (c.392 B.C.) is the last of the great plays of this genre. It clearly reflects the sober mood of the postwar period and represents the institution of a new political order in which women take over the management of Athens, after the mess that men have made of it.

New Comedy apparently developed quite naturally from the older form. After legal restrictions were placed on the satiric extravagances of Aristophanic comedy, it became necessary to devise a more polite genre, without political implications and without personal attacks. Instead of exercising his imagination in spectacular flights of fancy, the playwright now exerted his ingenuity in devising intricate plots and detailed character types. This kind of play is mainly associated with Menander (c.342–292 B.C.), whose work has survived only in fragments. But the Roman playwrights Plautus and Terence imitated him carefully, and through them New Comedy, with its stock masks, mistaken identities, reversals, and discoveries, was transmitted to the modern world, in which it has had a long and significant history.

2. Roman Drama

Roman taste apparently inclined much more to spectacle than to drama. In the drama, Roman genius was limited to a relatively small number of writers, all of whom wrote in imitation of the Greek.

Livy (59 B.C.–17 A.D.) notes that the drama in Rome began with the importation of *ludi scenici* (theatrical games) from Etruria in 364 B.C. to dispel the wrath of the gods in the course of a plague. There was, in early times, a form of rustic farce performed in Atella in Campania. This developed into the *fabulae Atellanae*, acted by amateurs in the 3d century B.C. and by professional comedians in the 1st century. These farces presented a cast of stock characters—the fool Maccus; the old man Pappus; the glutton Mandacus; the hunchback Dossenus—in what must have been broadly comic situations. In 240 B.C. a Greek tragedy and a comedy were translated into Latin by Livius Andronicus (c. 284–c.204 B.C.) for performance at the Roman games that year. This was the first step in the introduction of Greek drama into Rome. It was followed by similar adaptations by Naevius (active 235–201 B.C.) and later by Ennius (239–169 B.C.), but their work has survived only in bits. Plautus (c.254–c.184 B.C.) was the first Roman playwright to achieve distinction in comedy. Toward the end of the Second Punic War, he wrote a series of comedies adapted from the Greek, mainly imitations of Menander, Philemon, and Diphilus. These were played with masks and the Greek cloak (*pallium*) and were called *fabulae palliatae* to distinguish them from comedies on Italian subjects in which the actors wore Roman togas (*fabulae togatae*). There were 130 comedies attributed to Plautus; 20 are extant, enough to give an excellent idea of his style. Among the better known are the *Menaechmi*, the *Amphitryo*, the *Aulularia*, and the *Captivi*.

Plautus handled his models freely, weaving together themes and scenes from different plays to suit his purpose—a practice called "contamination"—and adapting his material to Roman customs wherever he deemed it useful. In this manner he naturalized New Comedy in Rome, preserving and perhaps enhancing the high spirits and boisterous humor of his originals. The form of his plays reflected late Greek practice. The chorus was practically eliminated; episodes in dialogue *(diverbia)* were spoken in an iambic meter; and there were lyrical passages *(canticae)*, which the actors declaimed over music, or sang, solo or in duet, to the sound of the flute. Substantially, therefore, the Plautine form was a kind of musical comedy, in which ingenuity and broad humor were the main ingredients.

The work of Plautus was continued by Terence (P. Terentius Afer, c.190–c.159 B.C.). Terence was originally a Carthaginian slave. He died young, leaving only six plays which he had written over a period of six years. The *Andria* was produced in 166 B.C.; his last play, the *Adelphi*, in 160. Terence evidently aimed at a more sophisticated audience than had Plautus. In comparison, his style shows a very considerable refinement, with a corresponding lack of vigor. Terence's plots are intricate, his dialogue witty rather than funny, and his style so highly cultivated that his plays were used as models of elegant speech throughout Europe in the Middle Ages and Renaissance.

After Terence, comedy patterned on Greek models degenerated rapidly in Rome, and during the Empire, comedy dwindled rapidly into ribald farce and mime. This in turn gave way to musical shows with indecent dances, which apparently enjoyed great popularity until at last they succumbed to the strictures of the Christian church.

Tragedy, on the other hand, was never popular in Rome. Since it had no religious connotations, as in Greece, it was esteemed mainly as a medium of moral instruction on the one hand, and as a vehicle for the display of eloquence on the other. Such, at any rate, seems to be Horace's idea of the goal of dramatic poetry—the fusion of the didactic and the delightful. The only Roman tragic poet of any importance was Lucius Annaeus Seneca (c.4 B.C.–65 A.D.), to whom are attributed nine tragedies—*Hercules Furens, Phoenissae, Troades, Medea, Phaedra, Oedipus, Agamemnon, Thyestes,* and *Hercules Oetaeus.* To these, *Octavia,* in which Seneca is a character, is sometimes added, though it is clear he could not have written it. Like Plautus and Terence, he borrowed his material from Greek sources, but he did not translate the Greek plays. He used the Greek themes for a type of tragic play that is distinctly not Greek. It is doubtful that his tragedies were intended for the stage. The likelihood is that they were written to be declaimed by a single *rhetor,* perhaps with the aid of a chorus, although Seneca used the chorus with great restraint. It is possibly because they were not meant for production that these plays dwell so luridly on the gruesome aspects of the Greek myths. Aristotle had spoken of tragedy in relation to its ability to evoke feelings of pity and terror. Seneca evidently regarded this statement as prescriptive, but where Euripides had emphasized the pathetic aspects of his heroes, Seneca developed chiefly the horrible. His tragic heroes are monsters who are not only inhumanly cruel but also unnaturally articulate. It was this pungent blend of sadism and sententiousness that formed Renaissance ideas of tragedy.

Although tragedy was given official sanction, and even imperial patronage, as late as the reign of Hadrian (reigned 117–138 A.D.), as soon as Christianity was officially established in Rome, the antagonism of the church toward everything that smacked of the stage rapidly drove the actors into vagabondage. Roman drama had, in any case, from first to last a tentative character. The permanent stone theater built by Pompey dates back only to 55 B.C. For a long time, plays were performed exclusively by amateurs. It was only in the 2d century A.D. that managers appeared with troupes of professional slave-actors available for hire at festivals. Actors generally, even when free men, were without civil status in Rome, although famous professionals like Roscius and Aesopus were able to achieve social position through their genius. Under the interdiction of the church, the mimes and dancers became itinerant players hounded by the bishops and harassed by civil authorities, and, in this unlikely fashion, the classic tradition was transmitted through the Middle Ages until once again it came to light in the popular farces and mummeries of the Renaissance.

3. Medieval Drama

Our knowledge of the medieval theater is gleaned largely from episcopal edicts directed against the *joculatores* and *histriones* who earned a precarious livelihood trudging the roads from court to court and town to town. The pagan festivals offered a knottier problem, which the church solved by absorbing them. The rites of May Day and midsummer, the St. George combats, the Feasts of Fools and Feasts of Asses, with their ancient ribaldries, all took on Christian color and were allowed to survive.

The early religious drama was fostered directly by the church. As early as the 5th century, Bible stories were made vivid by means of live tableaux accompanied by singing. Some time before the 10th century, significant portions of the liturgy at Christmas and Easter were expanded into "tropes," such as the Nativity antiphonies and the *Quem quaeritis?* These tropes came to include, in time, rudimentary representations of the Resurrection at the sepulcher, mimed by the priests along with the choir that sang the service.

From about the 11th century, plays on Biblical subjects—the Easter story, Daniel, the raising of Lazarus, and the Fall—were acted by the clergy, first in Latin, later in the vernacular. As these little plays were expanded in scope, they were gradually secularized and appropriated by guilds and other trade associations for their own purposes: the water carriers made a specialty of Noah's Flood, and the bakers' guild presented the Last Supper. The festival of Corpus Christi (ordered in 1264 but not established until 1311–1312) served to integrate these dramatic activities into an acceptable religious framework. (See CORPUS CHRISTI, Feast of.) But the popular drama eluded official control and, about 1500, clerical opposition to the plays stiffened. In time, the religious drama was completely disavowed, and eventually it was forbidden.

One reason for this reaction was the rapidity with which this drama developed secular characteristics, particularly motifs derived from popular farce. The *Jeu de Saint Nicolas* by Jean Bodel, an early 13th century French *trouvère*, affords some charming glimpses of tavern life in medieval Arras. *Le miracle de Théophile,* by his contemporary Rutebeuf, is an early version of the Faust story and includes a good bit of contemporary realism. Such plays foreshadow the wide-ranging *Miracles de Notre-Dame,* which deal realistically, and often humorously, with all sorts of interesting situations amenable to the intervention of the Blessed Virgin, who figures in them as a sort of *dea ex machina.* By the end of the 13th century, Passion plays were being performed in many French towns. In Paris a dramatic society called La Confrérie de la Passion was licensed in 1402 by Charles VI and developed an acting tradition that ended only in 1548, when, under pressure from both the clergy and the humanists, the Confrérie was forbidden to play the Passion.

The French mysteries, as the Biblical plays came to be called (from *mysterium,* "service" or "office"), were written in strophic verse, in pedestrian style, but often rhymed with considerable ingenuity. They were played usually on a multiple set, with the various localities, or "mansions," arranged in linear fashion so that the action could move back and forth in space in accordance with the exigencies of the play. Far from observing unities of time, place, or action, these plays ranged freely through Scriptural history from the Creation to the Day of Judgment. The technique was remarkably realistic, and not always controllable. Devils frequently caught fire; the audience was sometimes inundated by the Deluge; and in Metz, in 1437, according to reliable sources, the priest who played Christ was taken from the Cross more dead than alive. In the course of the 16th century, the mystery plays became vast and splendid spectacles with magnificent costumes and intricate machinery. *The Acts of the Apostles* performed at Bourges toward the middle of the century had 494 speaking parts. It made use of artificial canals; devils flew through the air; two tigers were transformed into sheep; and St. Barnabas was burned alive. Also of this order was *Le Mystère du Vieil Testament,* performed in Abbeville in 1548 and two years later in Paris.

In the first decades of the 15th century, secular plays of an allegorical nature began to be performed in France by students and law clerks. These plays, written by *trouvères* and called moralities, depicted moral conflicts, particularly the struggle of good and evil forces in the individual soul, in terms of personified abstractions. The moralities soon spread over the Continent and to England, together with their indispensable adjuncts, the Devil and his unruly servant the Vice. These characters, dedicated to mischief, became a prime source of amusement, if not of edification. Plays of this type, of which the 15th century English *Everyman* is the foremost example, brought a whole new subject matter into the drama. Beginning with religious and moral questions, these plays soon entered every field of debate, and were rapidly extended into farce and satire. Eventually they became indistinguishable from the short nonallegorical plays called interludes, which often had a polemical tone. John Skelton's *Magnifycence* (about 1516) is an attack on extravagance; *Respublica* (1553; author unknown) attacks reformers; John Redford's *Wit and Science* (1548) criticizes the humanists; Sir David Lindsay's *Three Estates* (1540) includes a sharp satire on both church and state. The medieval farces, on the other hand, have no serious aim. The anonymous French *Farce du Cuvier* and *Farce du pâté et de la tarte* are purely amusing pieces. The masterpiece in this genre is, without doubt, *Maître Pierre Pathelin* (about 1464), a pleasant piece which is still eminently stageworthy. In England, interludes such as John Heywood's *Johan Johan* and the *Four P's* are of much the same sort.

The English mystery plays appear to have originated in Chester soon after the middle of the 13th century. By the 16th century, mysteries were being performed in many English towns in cycles of considerable length. Four main collections of this type are extant—the York cycle, the Towneley or Wakefield cycle, the Chester cycle, and the so-called Coventry cycle. (See MIRACLE AND MYSTERY PLAYS.) These cycles were not performed on stationary stages as in France, but on movable floats called pageants. In Chester, in the 16th century, each guild prepared its pageant in anticipation of the festival, and, on the appointed days, the two-tiered wagons rolled in succession through the town, stopping to perform in each street.

The mysteries, boisterous and realistic in character, did much to shape public taste in England. *The Second Shepherds' Play* of the Towneley cycle, for example, makes the transition from farce to seriousness in a manner that clearly foreshadows the great drama of the Elizabethan age. It was the morality plays, however, that developed directly into the plays of the coming period. In these plays, written by men of letters such as John Rastell, Henry Medwall, and John Heywood, the popular taste for comedy and realism merged with considerations of a more distinctly intellectual nature. Evil Counsel in *Johan the Evangelist* (about 1560; author unknown) is a typical ne'er-do-well of Tudor times. In *Nice Wanton* (1560; author unknown) the good children are efficiently distinguished from the bad by the Vice Iniquity. *Gammer Gurton's Needle* (about 1560; author unknown) offers an unforgettable picture of domestic life in the 16th century. In John Bale's *King John* (about 1548) abstractions coexist with flesh and blood personages drawn from history.

4. Renaissance Tragedy

It was not until the middle of the 16th century that the classical influence asserted itself in the English drama. Medieval scholars had derived what they knew of comedy largely from the plays of Terence, whose works were regularly studied in connection with the commentary of the grammarian Aelius Donatus (4th century A.D.). His analysis of comedic structure into protasis, epitasis, and catastrophe—that is to say, exposition, complication, and denouement—served as the basis of dramaturgy for centuries. But it took some time for these ideas to permeate dramatic practice, especially in England. School plays like Nicholas Udall's *Ralph Roister Doister* (q.v.) show the influence of Plautus, but Udall appears to have had no idea of the way to construct a play. The first English prose

Medieval strolling players performed outdoors on movable platforms, which in England were called "pageants."

comedy, George Gascoigne's *The Supposes* (1566), is a remarkably inept version of Ariosto's *I suppositi*, a fairly free adaptation of Latin comedy.

Tragedy fared no better in this period. Early in the 14th century Nicolas Trivet wrote a commentary on the tragedies of Seneca. It had wide currency, and was soon followed by a number of Senecan imitations by contemporary writers. As early as 1315, Albertino Mussato composed a tragedy in Latin on a contemporary subject, the *Ecerinis*, using Senecan technique with considerable originality. Giangiorgio Trissino inaugurated tragedy in Italian with *Sofonisba* in 1515. The nine tragedies of Giraldi Cinzio or Cinthio (1504–1573), all in Italian and in Senecan style, were already famous when Thomas Norton and Thomas Sackville produced the first regular tragedy in English, *Gorboduc*, in 1562. The early humanists had derived their idea of the classic mode in tragedy, however, not only from Seneca but from Horace's *Ars poetica* and the fragmentary treatises of the classical grammarians Donatus, Evanthius, and Diomedes, which hinted at still more authoritative sources. In 1498 the humanist Giorgio Valla at last translated into Latin and published the text of Aristotle's *Poetics*. It had little influence; but when Francesco Robortelli (Robortello) published his edition and its commentary in 1548, the world was ready for it, and the *Poetics* was enshrined as the chief authority on classical practice in tragedy. An impressive body of interpretation soon grew up around this terse little manual, and its "rules" became the laws of literary composition.

But as humanism became increasingly fashionable, the Senecan models posed a question as to the proper mode of classical imitation. By the beginning of the 16th century, although the works of Sophocles—the greatest of the classical masters of play construction—were available for imitation, many Renaissance dramatists preferred to follow Seneca. But in England the stiff blank verse of *Gorboduc*, with its cumbrous apparatus of messengers and chorus, its lack of visible action, and its pedantic rigidity, was obviously not suited to public taste. The alternative was to play the classical subject matter with medieval realism. This was done in Thomas Preston's *Cambises* (about 1570), a morality play adapted from an episode in Herodotus' *History* that mixes horror with "pleasant mirth" in truly hair-raising fashion. In the course of the 16th century a firm distinction was established between the two dramatic styles that were to dominate the European stage for the next two centuries. In Italy and, after some hesitation, in France, "regular" drama became the established mode, and serious writers vied with one another in the effort to be, above all, classically correct. But in England and Spain dramatists adapted the classic mode to the native traditions. Each style gave rise to masterpieces, but until well into the 19th century these styles did not merge.

Two things chiefly distinguished the "regular" from the so-called "romantic" drama of England and Spain—the observance of the unities and the restriction against the mixing of genres. The unities were not simply an arbitrary set of conventions; they were a shaping principle. The extraordinary ingenuity required to compress a considerable body of narrative into an action that ran its course in one place in one day provided an element of craftsmanship that was prized by the French, but quite foreign to English play making. Plot normally involves the idea of a time sequence. In the regular drama, the unity of time made it necessary to focus the story so sharply that the narrative element was virtually eliminated from the action, and all the emphasis fell on the declamation. The Senecan models were in fact full of long poetic tirades, alternating with stichomythic passages crackling with literary wit. Since in these plays it was the scene of horror that was important, and not the means by which one arrived at it, the catastrophe was prepared for by means of ghosts, recitals, foreshadowing dreams, and premonitions. And since it was considered indecorous for royal personages to quarrel in public, the French dramatists went to considerable trouble to prevent the antagonists from arriving at a confrontation. Accordingly, their feelings were expressed exclusively to their confidants and nurses, the indispensable agencies of the classic stage.

The tragedies written in Italy along these lines are of interest mainly to the scholar. None of the Italian playwrights of the period 1500–1600 succeeded in writing a viable tragedy. The age was inclined rather to the epic, in connection with which the classical restrictions were often discussed, but seldom observed. The best that could be done in Italian tragedy at this time barely transcended the limits of melodrama. There was little basis in the classics for tragicomedy, a genre that presumably would admit the use of comic scenes in a serious play. Giovanni Battista Guarini (q.v.) crystallized this form in *Il pastor fido* (about 1590), a daring innovation he spent a good part of his life defending. This was the most important contribution of Italy to the dramatic literature of the Renaissance, so far as tragedy was concerned. The Italian short story, the *novella*, provided a veritable mine for the exploitation of European dramatists in this period, but the great development of regular drama took place in France.

French Tragedy. French dramatic practice dominated the Continental stage, except in Spain, from about 1550 to about 1800. Étienne Jodelle's *Cléopâtre captive* (1552) was the first tragedy in French, and it initiated a period of wide experimentation in works by Jean de la Taille, Jacques Grévin, and Robert Garnier. But the early French playwrights hardly brought their plays to the stage. It was not until Alexandre Hardy (c.1575–c.1631) expanded the classical style into something resembling the popular mode that the regular forms became other than literary exercises.

Hardy stopped writing in 1628. In 1636 Pierre Corneille (q.v.) wrote *Le Cid* (produced 1637), the play that established the tragic mode that was to rule the Continental stage until after the time of Napoleon. *Le Cid* was written as a tragicomedy; only later was it called a tragedy. In discussing its success, in the 1649 edition, Corneille emphasized the fact that he had followed Aristotle's precept in the *Poetics*: "In tragedy the persecution and the danger do not come from an enemy . . . but from a person who must love the one who suffers, and be loved by him." This idea shifted the emphasis in tragedy from the contemplation of a grim spectacle to a much more highly refined and complex conception. Psychology thus became a central element in serious drama, and motivation a matter of primary interest.

The psychic situation that Corneille found primarily interesting for tragic purposes was the conflict of mind and heart in a noble nature. The tragic hero, in his conception, was one who was at odds not so much with an external power, as with himself. In a remarkable series of tragedies after *Le Cid*—*Horace* (1640), *Cinna* (1640 or 1641), *Polyeucte* (1642), *Pompée* (1643), and *Rodogune* (1644 or 1645)—Corneille developed to the full the character of the dynamic hero—strong-willed, self-mastered, noble, glorious, but not happy. The tendency of these plays was therefore toward a type of serious drama in which the hero, having proved himself worthy, ultimately attains the object of his desire. Such is the typical outcome of serious comedy. But for Corneille the sense of life's injustice was an essential element of tragedy, and his plays demonstrate vividly his sense of the absurd in the contrast between the greatness of man and the hopelessness of the human situation.

Like his older contemporary Shakespeare, Corneille was mainly concerned with the behavior of remarkable people in remarkable situations. His tragedies were designed to excite wonder and admiration, and they involved an ingeniously logical arrangement of scenes of high excitement in formal patterns that accorded with ideas of beauty, symmetry, and harmony current in the other arts. He also exhibited a taste for the complex and marvelous that is characteristic of the age of the baroque. The same may be said of English dramatists from Shakespeare to Webster. But the vogue of the baroque did not outlast the 17th century. In France a neoclassical movement led by the critics René Rapin, Nicolas Boileau-Despréaux, and Dominique Bouhours developed a strong reaction against Italian fantasy and Spanish exaggeration. A new wave of classicism swept over Europe in the closing decades of the 17th century. Among the first to sense this reaction was Jean Racine (1639–1699). Racine did not restore the tragic plot to the classic simplicity that Boileau-Despréaux advocated. What he did was to push the focus of tragedy from the external circumstances more deeply into the inner world of his characters. For Racine, motives are never simple, and drama resides mainly in the individual soul. Racine's protagonists are, typically, neurotic characters sick with love. Placed in a hopeless situation, they strive desperately to make a rational choice; but they are usually not equal to the effort. They are moved by passion, not reason, and in this we see their humanity, and also the source of their tragedy.

Of the great dramatists, Racine was perhaps the least fortunate on the stage. In 1667 his *Andromaque* was enormously successful. Three years later, *Bérénice* encountered resistance. *Bajazet* (1672) was an attempt to write a tragedy in the style of Corneille, and both this and *Mithridate* (1673) were quite successful, while *Iphigénie* (1674) enjoyed a spectacular success. But *Phèdre* (1677) was a disaster, though artistically it is his masterpiece. Racine wrote it for his mistress, La Champmeslé, who is said to have surpassed herself in the role, the most profound study of feminine psychology before the time of Ibsen. The play was a failure, and had to be withdrawn, while Nicolas Pradon's mediocre *Phèdre et Hippolyte*, produced two days later under the patronage of Racine's enemies, was a great success. It is easy to see why, quite independently of the machinations of the anti-Racine cabal, Racine's play failed and Pradon's did not. Racine relied for his effect on the subtle interplay of passions exquisitely expressed in verse; Pradon, on an ingenious plot full of turns and surprises. It was in this direction that public taste was tending, and would continue to tend, for another two centuries.

Racine's popularity lasted a decade. After this the looser form of tragedy associated with Corneille once again came into fashion. Antoine Houdar de La Motte (1672–1731) rebelled vociferously against the restrictions of the classical form, but his only innovation was the suppression of the confidante in *Inès de Castro* (1723). His advanced views did not find favor with Voltaire, the most influential French dramatist of the next age. During his three-year stay in England, Voltaire had acquired some knowledge of English drama. He appreciated its vigor, but considered it barbarous. Nevertheless he made some concession to English practice in *Brutus* (1730), *Zaïre* (1732), *La mort de César* (1735), and *Sémiramis* (1748); and in 1759 he succeeded in clearing the spectators from the stage at the Comédie Française, so as to give the actors some freedom of movement. Under the Empire, the actor Lekain introduced period costume, and the great Talma added what sparkle an actor could to the classical productions. In *Christophe Colomb* (1809), Népomucène Lemercier (1771–1840) for the first time disregarded the unities entirely—and provoked a riot in the theater. But, for all these efforts to revive it, tragedy was now beyond rescue, and the competition of the opera, with its vast scenic possibilities, was overwhelming. The classical rules withstood the attacks of Gotthold Lessing and August and Friedrich Schlegel in Germany, and of Alessandro Manzoni in Italy, but their days were numbered. The idea of romanticism was as yet undefined, but the way was obviously open for a new type of dramatic art. In 1822, Stendhal in the essays *Racine et Shakespeare* declared energetically that classic art was dead. The day of Racine was over. The watchword of the avant-garde was Shakespeare. Johann Friedrich Schiller's *Die Räuber* (1781) had already indicated the path that romantic drama was to take. In 1827, Charles Kemble took an English company to Paris with a repertory of Shakespearean plays and was an enormous success. In 1829, Alexandre Dumas *père* (1803–1870) initiated the new style in Paris with *Henri III et sa cour* at the Comédie Française. The following year Victor Hugo produced *Hernani*.

There was no essential difference between the idea of romantic tragedy and that of the older form. Its characters were much like those of classical drama—they were unbelievably heroic and impressively noble, and spoke in exalted verse, but, released from their classic inhibitions, they were free to bustle about the stage. Masked and caped in Spanish fashion, sword in hand, they vanished into secret passages, appeared in caverns, made love beautifully, and died with memorable lines on their lips. Unhappily, the romantic tragedies did not capture the Shakespearean manner. The result was a series of swashbuckling plays, ending in 1843 with the miserable failure of Hugo's *Les Burgraves*. The entire romantic adventure in tragedy lasted only a dozen years.

English Tragedy. The Shakespearean manner, in fact, was something that only Shakespeare could manage. There had been nothing in English dramatic literature to announce his coming; and there is nothing after him that really extends his tradition in any but a formal way. Christopher Marlowe (1564–1593) is often spoken of as Shakespeare's forerunner, though Shakespeare's affinity with Thomas Kyd seems more obvious. Shakespeare evidently borrowed from everyone. He invented few plots, if any; he adapted whatever he needed for his purposes. But time has eroded the matrix. Through the work of Robert Greene (1560–1592), Thomas Nashe (1567–1601), Henry Chettle (1560–1607), and Anthony Munday (1553–1633) a glimpse may be caught of the bustling theatrical atmosphere in which Shakespeare worked. It is possible to come a little closer to Shakespeare through Thomas Dekker (1572–1641), John Marston (c.1576–1634), George Chapman (1559–1634), and John Webster (c.1580–c.1634). But only Ben Jonson (1572–1637), who practiced another and more classical style than Shakespeare's, in any way compares with him in the golden age of English drama.

Christopher Marlowe's *Tamburlaine Part I* (1587) and *Part II* (1588) foreshadowed the course of English drama in the next generation. It was intended as a vast spectacle of many episodes connected chiefly by the presence of the principal character, whose life and death are the subject of the play. There is a minimum of plot and no easily discernible theme. The characterization is rudimentary. *Tamburlaine*'s relation to the earlier chronicle-histories would be entirely clear were it written in the jigging rhymes of the more popular drama instead of in a smooth and lofty style of blank verse. Marlowe's *Tragical History of Doctor Faustus* (1588–1589) has survived in sadly mutilated condition. As it stands, it is chiefly interesting for two fine verse passages. *The Jew of Malta* (about 1590) and *Edward II* (1591–1592) show a considerable advance in plotting and characterization, and it is probable that had Marlowe lived longer, he would have produced a masterpiece.

There is no reason to doubt that Shakespeare saw *Tamburlaine*, since it was revived frequently after he came to London two years or so after its first production. From this play he may well have learned something of the dramatic uses of massive blocks of run-on rhythmic verse, and something of the flamboyant rhetoric appropriate to a scene that had to be built largely of words. In fact, Shakespeare began his career with a series of history plays in which traces of Marlowe's manner are apparent. To find a style for tragedy was more difficult. It seems clear that Shakespeare knew the classical rules, and that he chose to disregard them. *Titus Andronicus* (about 1594), in which Shakespeare had at least a hand, indicates that his first idea of tragedy was related to the Senecan tradition of horror illustrated in such plays as *Cambises*. By this time, however, he had certainly mulled over the virtues of *The Spanish Tragedy* (1589?), the most popular play of its time. This tragedy, usually attributed to Thomas Kyd (c.1558–c.1594), was the first play in English in which there is real dramatic motivation, a real attempt at characterization, and a sequence of events inexorably meshed so as to bring about an inevitable conclusion. It is a play of revenge, extravagantly bloody, and burdened with Senecan trappings, but for all its excesses and its occasional naïveté, it clearly outlined an acceptable style for English tragedy.

ELIZABETHAN PLAYS were performed on simple stages with little scenery and few stage properties.

Romeo and Juliet (about 1595) burst upon the English stage like a meteor. It was a lyrical drama, the first of its kind, which presented the tragic opposition of love and social obligation in a way totally new to the European stage. The seven Shakespearean tragedies that followed, from *Hamlet* (1601?) to *Coriolanus* (1608?), mark the ultimate achievement of modern drama in the tragic genre.

The fundamental difference between ancient tragedy and the tragedy of modern times rests in the nature of the tragic conflict. The Greek tragic writers had manifested no special concern with the inner life of the tragic hero—it is only in *Oedipus at Colonus* that there is an attempt to give psychic insight beyond the ordinary. For the ancients the source of tragedy was the collision of the individual with an external force of unreasonable character. But for the great dramatists of the Renaissance—Shakespeare, Corneille, and Racine—tragedy was the consequence of the soul's illness. This was an idea traceable in part to the Platonic psychology of the age and in part to the intense concentration on the individual soul in Christian times. The consequence in serious drama was to throw the main emphasis on characterization, rather than on plot, as Aristotle indicated; and this developed the rigorously analytic tendency that distinguishes modern drama. Shakespeare's characteristic irony and his lack of message are a result of his interest in the individual rather than in the archetype. He was above all not a preacher. Like Corneille he was keenly aware of the absurdity of human behavior, and, like Racine, deeply conscious of its pathos, but he had no wish to read a sermon or to moralize his tale, and in this also he demonstrated the universal quality of his genius.

The distinctive characteristics of English tragedy as Shakespeare left it are a very free and vigorous treatment of a complex plot, with a full representation of thrilling scenes; a penetrating and detailed characterization of the principal characters; logical motivation; and remarkably fluid and sonorous poetry, rich in metaphor and vivid imagery. The conditions of the Elizabethan stage were consonant with this type of play. The lack of scenery and the relative paucity of stage properties made it possible to play a sequence of scenes with great fluidity. The ready availability of fine tragic actors and of gifted clowns challenged the utmost capacity of the writer to create fine roles, and the existence of fine permanent acting companies made it possible to compose plays for actors with whose talents the author was entirely familiar. Not the least important of the predisposing elements was the Elizabethan audience, which was either remarkable to begin with or soon became so.

The Elizabethan mode in tragedy was carried on after Shakespeare by a group of prolific writers who would seem more remarkable were they not so completely overshadowed by Shakespeare: George Chapman (c.1559–1634), John Marston (c.1575–1634), Francis Beaumont (1584–1616), John Fletcher (1579–1625), Philip Massinger (1583–1640), John Ford (1586–c.1639), John Webster (c.1580–c.1625), and Cyril Tourneur (c. 1576–1626). The last of these carried the Shakespearean tradition into the sphere of the macabre as far as absurdity; but plays like Webster's *The White Devil* (c.1612) and *The Duchess of Malfi* (c. 1614) occasionally glow with something of the fire of the dying age. By the time the Puritans closed the London theaters in 1642, the Elizabethan mode in tragedy was spent. When in 1660 the theaters reopened, a new age had dawned and a new playhouse had taken shape.

William Davenant (1606–1668) opened the new era in English drama in 1656 with *The Siege of Rhodes*, an entertainment with scenery and music that he later called an opera. Three years later, two theatrical companies were playing in London, one under Davenant, the other headed by Thomas Killigrew. Both secured patents from Charles II. The companies went through several viscissitudes and finally were established at Covent Garden and Drury Lane. In 1737, when the royal prerogative to license theaters was revoked by Parliament, these two theaters, together with Vanbrugh's theater in the Haymarket, were the only legitimate theaters in London. Until the Theatre Regulation Act of 1843, the two patent houses in Covent Garden and Drury Lane claimed a monopoly of legitimate drama—that is, of tragedy and comedy—and the many "minor" theaters that sprang up in the meantime had to rely on all sorts of interesting subterfuges to carry on any sort of theatrical enterprise.

After the Restoration, English drama came under strong French influence, and there was an earnest attempt to regularize English tragedy. This resulted in a great deal of critical literature and one noteworthy play, *All for Love* (1677), by John Dryden. But the dramatists of the Restoration had no great gift for tragedy. The spirit of the time was expressed rather in two curiously extravagant forms, the heroic play and the comedy of manners.

The heroic play was a form adapted by Roger Boyle, 1st Earl of Orrery (1621–1679), and John Dryden (1631–1700) from Continental sources in an attempt to express in rhymed couplets the expansive idioms of such Renaissance heroic poems as *Orlando furioso* (q.v.). It therefore represented a natural but unfortunate extension of the romantic tragicomedy of Beaumont and Fletcher in the direction of Spanish extravagance. All the tendency of these plays was toward theatrical excess and operatic effectiveness; the characters were monolithic and larger than life, and the plots turned typically on questions of love and honor. The heroic plays came as close to the puppet theater of Japan as anything in English drama. Everything that is noteworthy in this genre was written by Dryden—*The Indian Queen* (1664), *Tyrannic Love* (1669), and the two parts of *The Conquest of Granada* (1670, 1671). Heroic drama barely survived Buckingham's satire on it in *The Rehearsal* (1671); but Dryden had a last fling at it with *Aureng-Zebe* (1675) before he turned to tragedy in classic style. Save for the work of Nicholas Rowe (1674–1718) and Thomas Otway (1652–1685), and a wooden effort by Joseph Addison to write a regular tragedy, *Cato* (1713), English tragedy produced nothing of note after the 17th century. Thereafter the tragic mode was kept alive mainly by the frequent revivals of Shakespeare and the vain efforts of the romantic poets to imitate his style. The chief dramatic manifestation of the age was comedy.

5. Renaissance Comedy

The ancient authorities had not discussed comedy, but the comedies of Terence were known throughout the Middle Ages, and in 1427, Nicholas of Cusa brought a manuscript of 12 plays of Plautus to Rome. In 1433, Donatus' commentaries on Terence were brought to light, and a theory of comedy was cobbled up in accordance with Cicero's supposed description of comedy as "the imitation of life, the mirror of custom, and the image of truth." It thus became customary to speak of comedy as the art of imitating "pleasing and amusing happenings" for the purpose of criticizing the follies of mankind: *castigat ridendo mores*.

The mimetic tradition that had survived the dark ages came to light early in the Italian Renaissance in the practice of professional actors called *comici dell'arte*, who were adept at improvising farces on a preconceived plot *(scenario)*. The style for written comedy, *commedia erudita*, was fixed at the beginning of the 16th century by Lodovico Ariosto and Niccolò Machiavelli. There was at first some uncertainty as to correct form. The first two comedies of Ariosto —*La Cassaria* (1508) and *I suppositi* (1509)— were originally written in prose and later revised, in accordance with the classic models, in verse. But Machiavelli's *La Mandragola* (about 1518) was written in prose, and as it was generally accounted the best comedy of the age, the use of prose in comedy was at least tacitly sanctioned thereafter.

The subject matter of comedy was usually drawn from the classics or from popular *novelle*. The usual plot involved an amorous intrigue in the style of Plautus or Terence, some piece of trickery involving disguises, mistaken identities, and stratagems devised by the mastermind of a servant or parasite, as in the *Mostellaria* or the *Menaechmi* of Plautus. Apart from *Mandragola* the best example of this style is Giordano Bruno's *Il Candelaio* (about 1582). In general, comic plots tended to be bawdy, in imitation of the Latin works; and the characters, derived from the Latin plays, were stock types—the gallant, the old man, the pretty lady, the more or less clever servant, the parasite, the braggart soldier. The *commedia dell'arte* (q.v.) transformed these types into a cast of provincial *personae*—Pantalone, the Venetian shopkeeper; Dottor Graziano, the Bolognese lawyer; Capitano Spaventa, the Spanish bravo; the various clowns; and the indispensable soubrette *(servetta)*. The devising of a comic plot was thus largely a matter of ingenuity in arranging the relations of stock characters, each of which had, like a chessman, his special worth and type of movement. In time the methods of these professional farceurs infiltrated the *commedia erudita*, and the contrary also took place, so that by the time of Aretino *commedia dell'arte* and *commedia erudita* were virtually indistinguishable in form.

Since the narrative possibilities of comedy conceived along the lines of *commedia dell'arte* were limited, the desire for novelty resulted in a progressive complication of the plot by combining in a single story a number of different themes related by interlocking characters and converging on a common conclusion. Characterization, however, being fixed by type, stayed simple. In comedy it remained largely a matter of the exaggeration of typical idiosyncrasies—the shopkeeper's miserliness, the parasite's greed, and the soldier's swashbuckling.

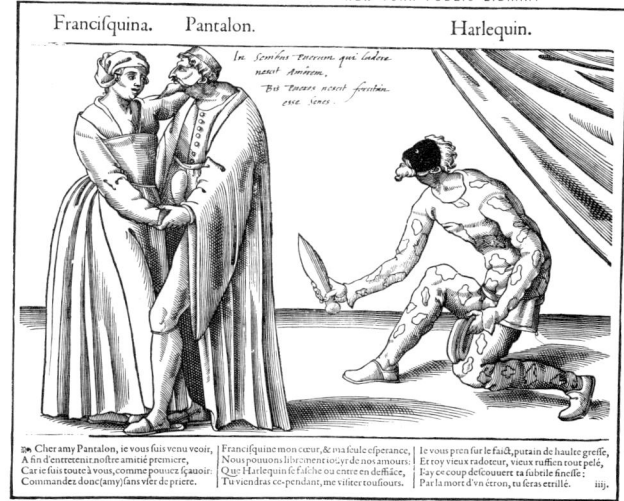

COMMEDIA DELL'ARTE, Renaissance Italy's popular comedy, used stock characters in improvised situations.

NEW YORK PUBLIC LIBRARY

Out of this practice grew the concept of "humors-characters," an idea based on the physiology of Galen, according to which eccentricities of character were the result of an imbalance in the bodily humors. Eventually this tradition resulted in characterization according to a dominant trait, a *faculté maîtresse*, so that individuals might be classified readily through the predominant characterological tendency that determined their behavior. This was the customary mode of characterization until the end of the 19th century and, though modified by modern psychological insight, is still a common method of distinguishing basic character types.

One of the consequences of the Council of Trent (1545–1563) was a decisive change in the nature of Italian comedy. During the Counter-Reformation the Inquisition effectively discouraged the bawdiness of early Renaissance comedy, as well as the comedic representation of filial disobedience, gulling and cheating, and the successful intrigue of illicit love. This fairly well disposed of the Roman tradition, and writers of comedy were forced, somewhat against their will, to take for their themes romantic love and honest courtship on the one hand, and the satiric depiction of antisocial traits on the other. From Italy these influences spread to all countries affected either by Protestant puritanism, such as Shakespeare's England, or by the Counter-Reformation itself, such as France and Spain.

The language of love did not exist in classical drama, but a proper syntax had been elaborated in the medieval lyric and the romances. The system of courtly love was thus available for dramatic purposes. By the end of the 16th century, scenes of pathos and sentiment, at first completely foreign to comedy, became its characteristic element. In this manner, the modern sentimental love plot took form, and by the middle of the 17th century romantic love became the indispensable theme of comedy throughout Europe, infiltrating even the hard comedy of the Restoration.

In England the classical style was successful principally in the hands of Ben Jonson, who was also the leading English proponent of the theory of humors. Jonson's *Every Man in his Humour* (1598), *Volpone* (1606), *Epicoene, or the Silent Woman* (1609), and *The Alchemist* (1610) guaranteed the ancient forms a certain viability, the consequence of which may be seen in the comedy of the Restoration and in such belated versions of the classic style as Oscar Wilde's *The Importance of Being Earnest* (1895). But Terentian comedy was thematically too limited, and Plautine comedy too bawdy, to outlast the Renaissance. After the essential character of the classical style had been vitiated, it gave way easily to the vogue for three-act romantic comedy in the style of Lope de Vega, so that in Italian comedy of the later 17th century, as earlier in England, girls were most often seen disguised as boys, scenes of love were prominently featured, swords were regularly unsheathed in the second act, and Spanish *pundonor* played a critical role in practically every plot.

Spanish Comedy. At the beginning of the 17th century the Spanish theater was in much the same situation as the theater in England had been a generation earlier. Drama in Spain was a popular art, rooted in native traditions, and expressive of national aspirations and ideals that were often exaggerated in literature in proportion to their neglect in the realities of the times. By about 1590 the modest troupes of actors, such as that of Lope de Rueda, that had roamed the Spanish countryside playing *pasos* and *entremeses*, became established in several cities, most strongly in Madrid. The theaters, *corrales de comedia*, were at first simple structures set up in courtyards under the windows of adjoining houses, with a rude parterre to accommodate the general public. Plays were given by daylight on a bare stage against a backdrop that served a multitude of purposes, in a manner not far removed from the style of Elizabethan staging.

In the last decade of the 16th century, Lope de Vega (1562–1635) almost single-handedly fixed the forms of Spanish drama for the future. In the course of a long career in the theater, Lope endowed it with a repertory of plays of many kinds, perhaps as many as 1,500, although less than 500 are extant. The *comedia*, as he devised it, was a three-act play with the climax in the second act. It was written in various forms of verse that flowed smoothly into one another in accordance with the changing moods of the action. The subject matter was drawn from every possible source, but regardless of the subject, plot and characterization followed the same general outlines. The result was a complex, extravagant, and frankly theatrical genre, which blended seriousness with comedy, and breathed a peculiarly Spanish atmosphere of piety and ferocity, a strong sense of justice and individual dignity, and unquestioning faith in the rightness of the medieval world structure. The basic form was cloak-and-sword comedy, *comedia de capa y espada*. This usually involved an amorous intrigue, complicated by questions of honor, jealousy, and revenge. The main plot concerned the fortunes of the amorous *galán,* a young cavalier, while the indispensable underplot took account of the parallel fortunes of his witty valet, the *gracioso,* whose common sense made a foil to his master's extravagance.

In this chivalric matrix were molded all the other forms of Spanish *comedia*, including the heroic comedy derived from "historical" sources, and even the peasant drama and the religious plays. Lope's enormous productivity obviously precluded anything like meticulous workmanship. A great many of his plays have interchangeable parts, and the disadvantages of mass production are also evident in the work of those who followed in his path—Juan Ruiz de Alarcón (c.1581–1639), Tirso de Molina (1571–1648), Francisco de Rojas Zorilla (1607–1648), and the greatest of these, Pedro Calderón de la Barca (1600–1681). With the death of Calderón, the golden age of Spanish drama came to an end. Dramatists became monotonously repetitive, and at last had to turn to French classical sources for inspiration. It was not until the latter half of the 19th century that the Spanish spirit in the drama once again found voice.

Lope left many fine plays, but no masterpieces. Certain of his plays—*Peribáñez, El mejor alcalde el rey, El castigo sin venganza, La selva sin amor,* and *Fuente Ovejuna*—are often singled out, for special reasons. Among his successors there were many who left plays of distinction. *Don Gil de las calzas verdes* and *El vergonzoso en palacio,* both by Tirso de

Molina, are first-rate comedies; and his *El burlador de Sevilla* forms, together with José Zorrilla y Moral's *Don Juan Tenorio* (1844), the basis of the Don Juan theme in the drama. Among the many distinguished works of Calderón, *El mágico prodigioso*, *El príncipe constante*, and *La dama duende* are certainly noteworthy, and *La vida es sueño* (*Life is a Dream*, q.v.) must be numbered among the great masterpieces of dramatic art.

French Comedy. The influence of Spanish *comedia* upon French comedy is to some extent overshadowed by the contribution of the Italian *farceurs*, who were more or less established in Paris ever since the Gelosi troupe first visited the Hôtel de Bourgogne in 1571. Pierre Corneille, however, initiated the French comedic style in imitation of the Spanish. His early comedies were not particularly influential, but his comic masterpiece, *Le Menteur* (1643), adapted from Alarcón's *La verdad sospechosa*, set a style. It was to this play that Molière, by his own admission, owed his inspiration for *Le Misanthrope*.

Jean Baptiste Poquelin, called Molière (1622–1673), survived a frustrated ambition to be a tragedian and, after a long exile (1645–1658) with a secondary company in the provinces, emerged in Paris in 1658 as the author of the brilliant farce *L'étourdi* (first produced in Lyon in 1655). He followed this at once with *Les précieuses ridicules* (q.v.), and its success resulted in the devoted patronage of Louis XIV, for whom he wrote a long series of elaborate court entertainments and many farces. The great Molière comedies, however—*L'école des femmes* (1662), *Don Juan* (q.v.), *Tartuffe* (q.v.), *Le Misanthrope* (1666), *L'Avare* (q.v.), and even the farces *Georges Dandin* (1668) and *Le bourgeois gentilhomme* (q.v.)—were of a curiously serious turn. In these plays, perhaps for the first time, broad comedy was consciously used in a frame designed to provoke thought as well as laughter. Molière wrote close to the borders of the Roman style, but the effect is not at all Terentian, and far from Plautine. His plots are obviously contrived, but his characters —the miser, the gull, the hypocrite, the amorous *senex*, the henpecked husband—are sentient beings who reveal their inner life in all its complexity.

In view of the highly artificial genre he developed, Molière's extraordinary realism is astonishing. Because of it, his comedies converge sharply on the tragic, for the spectacle of a man making an ass of himself is funny only if we do not take him seriously. Doubtless the audience once laughed heartily at *Le Misanthrope* and *Georges Dandin*, but time has revised these plays. It takes a singularly objective spectator to laugh at them now, and even in the time of Molière people were uncomfortably conscious of the poignancy of these characterizations. No great powers of penetration are required to see the relation of *Tartuffe* to the black comedy of the 20th century.

With *Les précieuses ridicules* and *L'école des femmes*, Molière defined two relatively new genres: comedy of manners and comedy of character. Paul Scarron (1610–1660) had already brought comedy indoors—as far, at least, as the bedroom. Molière set *Tartuffe*, *Les femmes savantes*, and *Le Misanthrope* in the living room. With these plays, comedy moved in off the sidewalk and ceased to be a public spectacle. It now became possible to play an intimate scene with realism, and with this new intimacy regular comedy began to take on a new sensibility.

Sensibility entered the 17th century drama by way of the pastoral writers and the early novelists, Georges de Scudéry (1601–1667) and Gautier de La Calprenède (1614–1663). In England the hard comedy of George Etherege and William Congreve was based on the idea that the principal human faculty is the intellect, an organ not subject to sentiment. It was this classic conception that gave the comedy of the Restoration its peculiar flavor, and also limited its possibilities. In the drama, by the end of the 17th century, the reign of the intellect had all but run its course. In the next era, it was the heart, not the mind, that gained supremacy over the human spirit, and sensibility ruled the stage.

6. Restoration Comedy

The French influence is apparent in English Restoration comedy, but not the French spirit. In Restoration comedy, style is everything. The ruthless pursuit of wealth and pleasure is excusable in a man of fashion, provided it be done with grace; and the basest dishonesty is allowable in a man of wit, who thus inherits the values of the clever slave of Latin comedy. Morality plays no part in this artificial world, but there is a golden mean to be observed in rascality—a mean that corresponds to a standard of taste. Thus the pitiless egotism of the Mirabells and Dorimants of Congreve and Etherege is held up as a model for admiration, but the bumbling efforts of the Witwouds and the excesses of the Fopling Flutters earn only ridicule, and sheer villainy is beneath contempt.

The Restoration wits imitated Molière in all outward matters, but they could not, in their political environment, imitate his warmth or his gaiety. Of the more distinguished writers of this period, time has dealt most charitably with the work of John Vanbrugh (1664–1726), William Wycherley (1640–1716), and William Congreve (1670–1729). All three wrote in a highly artificial and consciously theatrical style, remote from any sort of reality; and all three suffer from an inclination to demonstrate superhuman ingenuity in plotting. Nevertheless, George Etherege (c. 1635–1691) in *The Man of Mode* (1676), Vanbrugh in *The Relapse* (1696), and Congreve in *Love for Love* (q.v.) and *The Way of the World* (q.v.) provided the English stage with authentic masterpieces of stylish comedy; and in *The Country Wife* (1675) and *The Plain Dealer* (1676) Wycherley bequeathed to us two very useful plays. It is only, however, when they are touched with some warmth of sensibility that any of these plays comes to life. George Farquhar's *The Beaux' Stratagem* (1707), by far the most humane of the Restoration comedies, is already tinged with romantic color, and it presages the later masterpieces of the Restoration style—Goldsmith's *She Stoops to Conquer* (q.v.) and Sheridan's *The School for Scandal* (q.v.). With these two plays the period of English greatness in the theater comes, for a time, to a close. It was not until almost a century later that the English dramatic spirit once again manifested itself in the work of Wilde, Shaw, and Galsworthy.

7. Modern Realism

The 18th century marked the end of the Renaissance tradition in the drama. The last manifestations of this tradition in comedy may be studied in the very extensive work of Carlo Goldoni (q.v.), who effectively reformed the Italian stage by substituting tolerably realistic comedies with detailed characterization for the worn-out routines of the *commedia dell'arte*. The height of his success in Venice was reached with *Il Bugiardo* (1750), *La bottegha del caffè* (1750), and *La Locandiera* (1751), generally accounted his masterpiece. But in spite of his early success, the times were against Goldoni. He had not the greatness of Molière, but rather a quick eye for the passing world and its absurdities. The cataclysmic changes of the later 18th century put his talents in the shade, and, after the French Revolution of 1789, the tide of comedy turned in a quite different direction.

The history of the drama in the course of the 19th century is substantially the history of realism. About the middle of the 18th century, Denis Diderot (q.v.) pointed out in the novel *Les bijoux indiscrets* (1748) and the essay *Dorval et moi* (1757) that for some time tragedy had not been a living art. He proposed a substitute, *le genre sérieux*, that would deal seriously and convincingly with matters of genuine concern in contemporary life in a form that produced a complete illusion of reality. Diderot, however, was not talented as a playwright. He produced some plays—*Le fils naturel* (1757) and *Le père de famille* (performed 1761)—but it remained for others to develop the serious drama he proposed. In 1765, Michel Sedaine (1719–1797) effectively launched the new style with *Le philosophe sans le savoir*, a prose play in five acts. It was the first serious play in the history of the drama that was in no sense a poem, and the first modern play to deal seriously with a topic of current social interest. For lack of a better word, it was called a *drame*. About a half century later, Émile Augier (1820–1889) further advanced the cause of the new style with *Le gendre de Monsieur Poirier* (1854), a four-act play in prose on much the same subject as Sedaine's *drame*—the reciprocal relations of the middle class and the nobility. The overwhelming success of this play ushered in the drama of social problems, and the thesis play, the most important dramatic development of the next generation.

The steps through which the realistic tendencies of this type of drama reached their culmination in the last years of the 19th century began, strangely enough, with the innovations of Eugène Scribe (1791–1861), a professional showman with no interest in reform. Scribe crystallized the technique of the "well-made play," a smooth and logically constructed dramatic structure in five acts, with strong climaxes, sustained suspense, and a happy outcome. *Le verre d'eau* (1840) and *La bataille de dames* (1851) are good examples. The application of the Scribean technique to problems of a domestic and social nature gave rise to a form of drama that culminated in the discussion or demonstration of a thesis. This genre was developed widely in the latter half of the 19th century, principally by Augier and Alexandre Dumas *fils* (1824–1895) in a series of social plays, among which Dumas' *Le demi-monde* (1855) and *La question d'argent* (1857) and Augier's *Les Effrontés* (1861) are especially noteworthy.

The reaction of Émile Zola (1840–1902) and his followers to the artificiality of these "salon plays" resulted in the naturalist movement and the "slice of life" type of drama. This new genre aimed at the presentation of real-life situations, mostly of a sordid nature, without plot, and without embellishments of any sort, and also without moralizing comments on the part of the author or his *raisonneur* (his spokesman in the play). The actor-manager André Antoine (q.v.) provided the naturalist drama with a home in the Théâtre Libre, which he established in Paris in 1887. But the movement in itself was short lived, and its effects were felt abroad more strongly than in France.

The new realism actually made its mark in France through the work of Henry Becque, (1837–1899), who did not consider himself a naturalist. With *Les Corbeaux* (1882) and *La Parisienne* (1885), Becque initiated a tradition of bitter comedy, *comédie rosse*, which pointed the way for the tragic farce of the 20th century, as it is exemplified in the plays of Jean Anouilh (q.v.). The crusading spirit of Zola, who had vainly aspired to teach the "bitter science of life" in the theater, bore fruit in the grim social studies of Eugène Brieux (1858–1932)—*Les trois filles de M. Dupont* (1897), *La robe rouge* (1900), *Les avariés* (1902), and *La Maternité* (1903); in the social drama of Gerhart Hauptmann; and eventually in the comedies of George Bernard Shaw and John Galsworthy, both of whom threw in their lot with the naturalists, though their styles were of a totally different order.

The salon dramatists were moralists who concentrated on the consequences to an individual of his aberrations from the established standards of the middle class. The naturalists, however—in an age that produced Darwin and Marx and the positivism of Auguste Comte—burned with a strong sense of social justice, and they focused their plays sharply on the life of the lower classes, brutalized by poverty and ignorance. It was inevitable that social standards themselves should come under attack in these circumstances, and the stage for the first time assumed importance as an instrument of social discussion and a means of social reform.

8. German Romanticism

The bourgeois drama in the meantime was undergoing a convergent development in Germany. With *Miss Sara Sampson* (1755)—a play for which he was indebted to George Lillo's *The London Merchant* (1731) on the one hand, and to Richardson's novel *Clarissa Harlowe* (q.v.) on the other—Gotthold Lessing (1729–1781) had long before attempted to find a basis for tragedy in modern times. Johann Christoph Friedrich von Schiller (1759–1805) made a vain effort along similar lines with his play *Kabale und Liebe* (1784). But the German temper in these times was not capable of adjusting the conditions of tragedy to a bourgeois environment. Romanticism was very much in the air. Goethe (1749–1832) initiated the *Sturm und Drang* literature with a Shakespearean imitation, *Götz von Berlichingen* (1773), and Schiller followed this with *Die Räuber* (1781), in much the same romantic strain. Schiller then went on to develop the modern history play with *Don Carlos* (1787), *Wallenstein* (1798–1799), *Maria Stuart* (1800), and *Wilhelm Tell* (1804). Thus neither of the great German dramatists felt much inclined to deal seriously with contemporary issues on the stage. Indeed, the development of the bourgeois drama suffered a severe setback with the immense popularity of August Friedrich von Kotzebue (1761–1819), Schiller's contemporary, whose 200 plays flooded Europe in melodramatic sentimentality. After the immense success of his *Menschenhass und Reue* (1789), it was a good half century before anything approaching tragic austerity could be achieved on social subjects.

The pioneer in social drama was Friedrich Hebbel (1813–1863). In 1843, while Scribe was still at the height of his popularity, Hebbel was in Paris putting together *Maria Magdalena* (1844), which he hoped would fulfill the conditions for a modern tragedy along social lines. The story was drawn from life, and concerned the tragic inability of an upright man to keep pace with the times. Hebbel's idea of the tragic hero as a casualty of the dialectic progress of history was Hegelian. Its dramatic possibilities were enormous. It allowed the dramatist to give heroic magnitude to the sufferings of ordinary persons by virtue of their association with the clash of world movements, so that in their passion was seen reflected the passion of humanity. In these terms the tragedy of a carpenter or a salesman might acquire the scale that formerly was the exclusive attribute of kings and heroes. This idea became the basis of modern tragedy. It was the underlying idea of the great series of social dramas that Ibsen was to write in the next generation, and, of course, the basis for plays such as Arthur Miller's *Death of a Salesman* (1949).

9. Naturalism

By 1906 the successful writers of the *Théâtre Libre* were all absorbed in the commercial theater, and even Becque seemed old-fashioned. But the naturalistic mode, considered as a stage in the development of 19th century realism, had a long and varied career throughout Europe and in the United States. The most influential naturalist manifesto was contributed not by a French critic, but by the Swedish dramatist August Strindberg (1849–1912), whose famous preface to *Miss Julie* (1888) was published just seven years after Zola's *Le naturalisme au théâtre* (1881). In Germany the naturalist movement began with *Die Familie Selicke* (1890), written by Arno Holz (1863–1929) and Johannes Schlaf (1862–1941), and mightily developed by Gerhart Hauptmann (1862–1946) in a series of remarkable social plays—*Einsame Menschen* (1891; *Lonely Lives*), *Die Weber* (1892; *The Weavers*), and *Fuhrmann Henschel* (1898) among them. In Italy, naturalism took the form of *verismo*, a movement developed by Giovanni Verga (1840–1922), Luigi Chiarelli (1884–1947), and Luigi Pirandello (1867–1936). In England the principal proponent of naturalism was John Galsworthy (1867–1933); *The Silver Box* (1906), *Strife* (1909), and *Justice* (1910) are among the finest plays in this style. In Ireland naturalism resulted in a magnificent series of plays from John Millington Synge's *The Playboy of the Western World* (1907) to Sean O'Casey's *Juno and the Paycock* (1924).

To the United States, long preoccupied with Scribean plots and various brands of melodrama, naturalism came like a breath of fresh air. Eugene O'Neill (1888–1953) was the first American dramatist to take up naturalism in a significant fashion. Although he experimented with symbolist and expressionist techniques—*The Emperor Jones* (1920) and *The Hairy Ape* (1922)—he was successful chiefly with plays in the naturalist manner—*Beyond the Horizon* (1920), *Anna Christie* (1921), *Desire under the Elms* (1924), *Strange Interlude* (1928), and *The Iceman Cometh* (1946). Almost all the important American writers of his generation and the next were under strong naturalist influence—Maxwell Anderson (1888–1959), Elmer Rice (1892–1967), Clifford Odets (1906–1963), John Steinbeck (1902–1968), and Lillian Hellman (1905–   ). But through the dialectic of literary trends, symbolism—which originated in the 1880's in reaction to naturalism—eventually made common cause with its antithesis. The consequence is a style which alternates or blends realism and symbolism in understandable fashion, as in the work of Thornton Wilder, Tennessee Williams, and Arthur Miller, or enigmatically, in the manner of Edward Albee or the English playwright Harold Pinter.

10. Ibsen and Symbolism

In spite of its vast influence on 20th century drama, naturalism was not the principal agency in the reform of the European theater at the end of the 19th century. It was through the genius of the Norwegian Henrik Ibsen (1828–1906), and his later contemporary August Strindberg (1859–1912), that the new spirit of the age was ultimately transmitted to the 20th century. Ibsen began writing as a realist in the style of Augier and Dumas, which he perfected. *A Doll's House* (1879) and *Ghosts* (1881) belong as much to the tradition of Scribe as to the newer drama; both are well-made plays, carefully contrived, and thoroughly improbable. It was the violence of the attack on the hitherto sacred institution of the family that principally distinguished these plays from the thesis-drama of Dumas. The series of social dramas that followed—*An Enemy of the People* (1882), *The Wild Duck* (1884), and *Rosmersholm* (1886)—more clearly demonstrated Ibsen's true position as a dramatist. He had as highly developed a sense of social justice as Zola or Brieux, but he was scarcely interested in social reform. He was, as he often asserted, principally a poet. His work, mainly comedic in its tendency, is a contemplation of the human condition in all its absurdity and its pathos, but in a period of swift social transition, he had no panacea to offer for the ills of humanity. He was, if anything, an anarchist. Ibsen brought the 19th century social drama to its perfection, but he made a new departure only in his early plays, *Brand* (q.v.) and *Peer Gynt* (q.v.), and in 1892, 25 years after *Peer Gynt*, in *The Master Builder* (q.v.). These plays foreshadow the vogue of the symbolist movement that is associated with Maurice Maeterlinck (1862–1949) and his *La princesse Maleine* (1889), *L'Intruse* (1890), and *Intérieur* (1894).

The new direction that drama was to pursue in the last years of the 19th century, in fact, took its orientation from the symbolist poets

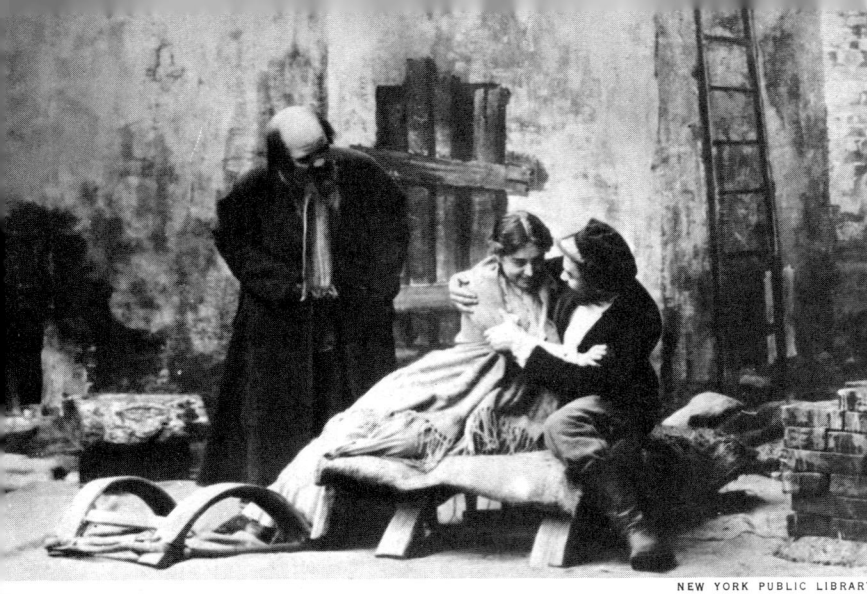

MODERN RUSSIA'S greatest realistic play is Gorky's *The Lower Depths*. It was first produced by the celebrated Moscow Art Theater in 1902.

NEW YORK PUBLIC LIBRARY

who followed in the wake of Baudelaire, and from the movements associated with postimpressionism in art. In the last years of the 19th century all the major European dramatists turned to symbolism in an attempt to reach a higher and more inward reality than naturalism could command. The best that was done in this area was, apart from the work of Ibsen, Hauptmann's *Hannele* (1893) and *The Sunken Bell* (1896), Wedekind's *Die Erdgeist* (1895) and its sequel, *Pandora's Box* (1903), Synge's *Riders to the Sea* (1904), and Yeats' *The Land of Heart's Desire* (1894). Nevertheless, next to naturalism, symbolism is by all odds the most important single influence on current dramatic art. Its effects may be seen everywhere in contemporary drama, and above all, in the plays of Jean Giraudoux (1882–1944), by far the most gifted dramatist of the period between World Wars I and II. Its most extreme expression, however, is to be found in the later plays of August Strindberg (1849–1912), whose work resulted in a whole new school of drama.

Strindberg began his dramatic career with *Master Olof* (1872), a powerful historical drama, then turned to naturalism with *Miss Julie* (1888). He had already indicated his postimpressionist tendencies with *The Father* (1887) and *Creditors* (1888), and he returned to this seminaturalistic style in *Easter* (1900), and *The Dance of Death* (1900–1901), violent and exaggerated representations of a reality that is not quite of this world. In 1898 he finished the first part of *To Damascus*, a play that broke completely new ground in the drama and, with *The Dream Play* (1902), laid the basis for the expressionist drama of the 1920's. But while the German expressionists—Georg Kaiser (1878–1945), Reinhard Sorge (1892–1916), Franz Werfel (1890–1945), and Fritz von Unruh—inherited the fantastic technique, the terror, and the anguish of Strindberg, German expressionism had its optimistic side. Its sense of spiritual renewal after the disaster of World War I developed naturally into a spirit of positive social reform. This is manifested in the plays of Ernst Toller (1893–1939) and Walter Hasenclever (1890–1940), in which the spirit that gave rise to the theater of Brecht is already perceptible.

Bertolt Brecht (1898–1956) began his dramatic career with *Drums in the Night* (1922), a bitterly realistic postwar play. The "epic" style, which he developed later with the cooperation of the director Erwin Piscator, was characterized by the conscious manipulation of the dramatic illusion through the interpolation of nondramatic material in such a way as to prevent the audience from losing itself in the play so completely as to be immune from external suggestion. By periodically alienating the audience from the principal action, the author could design a play so as to form a bridge toward reality rather than an escape from it. The result of this theory was an important refinement in the technique of the thesis-play; and the consequent transformation of the drama, into a powerful vehicle for propaganda, the very antithesis of the drama of art for art's sake that the symbolists were promoting. All of Brecht's important plays are exemplary fables in which the thematic element is sharply distinguished from the doctrinal passages. Brecht's socialist orientation came to light initially in his first great success, *The Three-Penny Opera* (1928), with music by Kurt Weill. A series of Marxist-influenced plays followed, some in the same musical idiom, and all of them with a bitter anti–middle class bias—*Mother Courage and Her Children, The Life of Galileo, The Good Woman of Setzuan* (all written in the 1930's) and *The Caucasian Chalk Circle* (1945). These plays, examples of the use of realistic technique in a consciously unrealistic way, have exerted widespread influence particularly in England and the United States.

11. Modern Russian Drama

Realism in the last decades of the 19th century had its fullest development in Russia. Russian drama is relatively new. It had its beginnings in the time of Peter the Great (1672–1725) and was first established, as an arm of the state, to perpetuate his greatness. The national drama made a modest debut in 1749 with a tragedy written in Russian by Aleksandr Sumarokov (1718–1777). But while the Russian theater, administered officially from St. Petersburg, encouraged great actors, it did not encourage genius in its writers. The first great play by a Russian author was a bitter comedy in the manner of *Le Misanthrope, Gore ot uma* (1824), usually translated as *Woe from Wit*, by

Aleksandr Griboyedov (1795–1829). Both Aleksandr Pushkin (1799–1837) and his successor in the romantic genre, Mikhail Lermontov (1814–1841), took Shakespeare and Schiller as their models, but their plays did not readily reach the stage. Pushkin's *Boris Godunov* was composed in 1825 but did not pass the censor until 1870; Lermontov's masterpiece, *The Masquerade,* written in 1835, waited fully a century for its first production. Nikolai Gogol (1809–1852) was the first great Russian dramatist to have a success in the theater in his own lifetime. His *Revizor (The Inspector General)* was written in 1835 and produced the following year. It marked a turning point in the Russian drama. Barely 50 years separate Gogol from Chekhov. These years span the full development of the Russian theater—they were the years of Ostrovsky, Turgenev, and Tolstoy.

Aleksandr Nikolayevich Ostrovsky (1823–1886) was the first professional playwright in Russia, and the first to devote himself to a serious exposition of Russian life. In the more than 50 plays he wrote during his long career—among which *The Bankrupt* (1850), *Don't Sit in Another's Sleigh* (1853), *Poverty Is No Disgrace* (1854), and *The Storm* (1860) are certainly noteworthy—middle-class Russia for the first time saw itself reflected in the theater. However, it was very likely from the work of Ivan Turgenev (1818–1883) that Anton Chekhov took his departure as a dramatist. Turgenev, though primarily a novelist, gave the Russian stage several of its finest plays, among them *A Month in the Country* (1850), his masterpiece. Like Turgenev, Anton Chekhov (q.v.) expressed himself most naturally in the narrative medium. His first long play, *Ivanov* (1889), had a great but undeserved success, and did much to put the author on the wrong track. But the success of *The Seagull* in its production by the Moscow Art Theater in 1897 showed him where his talent lay, and in *Uncle Vanya* in 1899, *The Three Sisters* in 1901, and *The Cherry Orchard* in 1904 he brought the realistic genre to its highest perfection. The essence of Chekhov's developed technique was to suggest the extraordinary in the drama of ordinary things, to indicate, through a meticulously objective representation of the perceptible, what the eye itself cannot perceive, the inner life of people, through which is expressed the movements of a soul beyond the soul of man, the world soul itself.

It was a desire to achieve something of this sort that motivated Leo Tolstoy (1828–1910) to write *The Power of Darkness* (1888), his dramatic masterpiece. But powerful as it is, this study of peasant life is perhaps too deeply involved with Tolstoy's philosophic convictions to have universality. Something of the sort may be said also of the dramatic works of Maksim Gorky (q.v.). His masterpiece in the theater, *The Lower Depths* (1902), is doubtless one of the strongest plays ever written in the realistic mode, yet it is somewhat marred by the melodramatic tendencies, not only of the author of the Russian drama in general.

After Gorky the Russian theater produced no more masterpieces. Under the Soviet regime, the theater was necessarily considered more than ever an arm of the state, and drama not enlisted in the socialist cause was likely to be decried as formalistic and reactionary. Even the best of the revolutionary playwrights—Valentin Katayev, Mikhail A. Bulgakov (1891–1940), Aleksandr Afinogenov (1904–1941), Konstantin Simonov—produced nothing of interest to the West, and a similar judgment must be passed on the later playwrights Aleksei Arbuzov, Aleksandr Volodin, and Aleksandr Shtein. The greatness of the Russian theater, for the time being, lies largely in its past.

12. Modern Italian Drama

The greatness of modern Italian drama seems to be more or less concentrated in the work of Luigi Pirandello (1867–1936), but Italy has produced a number of distinguished playwrights in the past 100 years. Between the time of Goldoni (1707–1793) and the time of Verga (1840–1922) there was no important Italian drama. Verga was the principal proponent of *verismo*, the Italian version of naturalism. His plays about Sicilian life, *Cavalleria rusticana* (1884) and *La Lupa* (1896), opened the way for dramatists of talent who concentrated on the Sicilian scene—Luigi Capuana (1839–1915) and Nino Martoglio (1870–1921). This firmly rooted drama contrasted strongly with the empty pretentiousness of Gabrielle D'Annunzio (1863–1938), whose plays *La figlia di Jorio* (1904), *La Gioconda* (1898), and *Francesca da Rimini* (1902) amply attest the poverty of Italian drama after the unification of Italy in 1870. A new spirit in Italian drama was initiated by Luigi Chiarelli (1884–1947). His play *The Mask and the Face* (1916), described by its author as "*un grottesco in tre atti,*" gave its name to the theater of the grotesque, of which Piermaria Rosso di San Secondo (1887–1956), Luigi Antonelli (1882–1942), and Enrico Cavacchioli (1885–1954) are important representatives. At the core of the grotesque theater, as well as of much that followed it in Italy, is unquestionably the spirit of Ibsen; but this influence is felt in a peculiarly Italian way, and is complicated by the rigorous naturalism of Zola, and also by the native tendency to tell, above all, a good story. These tendencies are especially perceptible in the work of Luigi Pirandello.

Pirandello brought to the theater a developed skill as a writer of short stories, many of which he himself adapted for the stage. Since many of his plays were thus, in the main, twice-told tales, it was inevitable that he should seek out progressively novel ways of presenting his material. His early plays show him to have been strongly under the influence of the *veristi*, and of these plays the best is perhaps *Liolà* (1916), a realistic peasant idyll. *Così è (se vi pare)* (1917; *Right You Are if You Think You Are*) marked the beginning of his almost morbid obsession with the problem of truth and the impossibility of attaining any sort of certainty in this life. *Six Characters in Search of an Author* (1921) and *Tonight We Improvise* (1930) are examples of the use of expressionistic techniques to translate a sordid tale into enigmatic, even mystical, drama. It is interesting to compare these plays with *Vestire gl'ignudi* (1922) and *Non si sa come* (1934), which arrive at somewhat similar conclusions in less spectacular fashion. *Enrico IV* (1922) is Pirandello's masterpiece and demonstrates the author's skill in transforming a commonplace story into something magically suggestive. It shares with Calderón's *La vida es sueño* a profoundly significant metaphysical conception that transcends the ordinary limits of the theater.

Of the later Italian dramatists, probably the most important is Ugo Betti (1892–1953, q.v.). The best-known example of his style is *Corruzione al palazzo di giustizia* (1949); but *La regina e gli insorti* (1951) is certainly noteworthy for the delicacy and the lyrical quality of the characterization.

13. Modern Spanish Drama

The drama languished in Spain from the close of its golden age to the end of the 19th century. Classicism, predominantly French classicism, was chiefly influential under the Bourbon kings of Spain, but as European styles changed, Spanish drama changed with them. Nothing very original is to be found in the work of José Echegaray (1832–1916), the outstanding Spanish dramatist at the beginning of the 20th century. The new realism was represented by Benito Pérez Galdós (1843–1920), whose *La loca de la casa* (1893) was clearly written under naturalist influences. Later in the 1890's, Spanish drama took a stride forward with the social satires of Jacinto Benavente (1866–1954).

In the next decades all the new literary currents of Europe were reflected in the Spanish theater. The Spanish counterpart of Italian *verismo* was represented by a series of studies of Spanish life that included the sparkling, but obviously prettified, comedies of the Quintero brothers and the brooding dramas of Jacinto Grau (1877–1958). Symbolism was well represented in the drama of Gregorio Martínez Sierra (1881–1947), and in a totally different way in the *esperpentos* (grotesque satires) of Ramón del Valle Inclán (1866–1936). Valle Inclán's *Las luzes de Bohemia* (1924) and *Los cuernos de Don Friolera* (1921) are good examples. Without doubt, however, the finest achievement of the modern Spanish theater, and the most original, is the work of Federico García Lorca (1899–1936), especially the three great tragedies *Bodas de sangre* (1933; *Blood Wedding*, q.v.), *Yerma* (1934), and *La casa de Bernarda Alba* (1936).

14. 20th Century Trends

In the period following World War I, the means of communication were such that, save for some countries in eastern Europe, Western drama became truly international. Even before that time, the style of drama was much more significant than its national provenience. Thus many of the plays of Bernard Shaw—in some ways the most important dramatist of the time—were seen first outside of Britain, and it was only when his fame was firmly established abroad that British audiences could be persuaded to take him seriously.

George Bernard Shaw (1856–1950) stands curiously outside the traditions of European drama. His influence has been immense, but he has left no school. Unlike Oscar Wilde (1854–1900), whose sources are easily traceable to the drama of the second French Empire on the one hand, and to the works of English Restoration wits on the other, Shaw took his departure from popular sources, chiefly 19th century melodrama and extravaganza. Working within these forms, Shaw thought of himself primarily as a social propagandist and an Ibsenist, and his plays were theoretically designed to demonstrate a thesis. But aside from the generally socialist and anti-idealist tendencies that he shared with the avant-garde of his day, it is sometimes difficult to say what this thesis is. Doubtless his orientation was melioristic along Fabian lines; in his economic interpretation of morals and conventions he shows himself to be a Marxist; and he proclaimed loudly and often his mission as a reformer. But after *Heartbreak House* (q.v.), his plays betray a growing disillusionment both with humanity and with socialism; and it is demonstrable that his comedies, even as early as *The Devil's Disciple* (1897) and *Captain Brassbound's Conversion* (1900), have an undercurrent of bitterness that borders on the tragic. The most complete statement of the philosophic position toward which he was working during the earlier part of his preposterously long career is to be found in *Man and Superman* (q.v.). In this four-act play, with its preface, its interpolated discussion scene, and its appendix, Shaw defines evolution in terms of the aspiration of the Life Force, a concept adapted from Bergson and Lamarck. To this idea he gave a very full interpretation in *Back to Methuselah* (1921), which he regarded as his masterpiece. It is, however, in his less ambitious works, such as *Arms and the Man* (1894), *You Never Can Tell* (1896), *Candida* (q.v.), *Androcles and the Lion* (1912), *The Doctor's Dilemma* (1906), *Pygmalion* (1913), and *Saint Joan* (1923), that he survives, in a theater that inclines to less polite and more violent satire.

The most vociferous, though by no means the most significant influence on contemporary drama comes from Dadaist and surrealistic writers, who having cast their lot with the symbolists,

NATURALISM in American drama is represented by Eugene O'Neill's *Long Day's Journey Into Night*.

GJON MILI

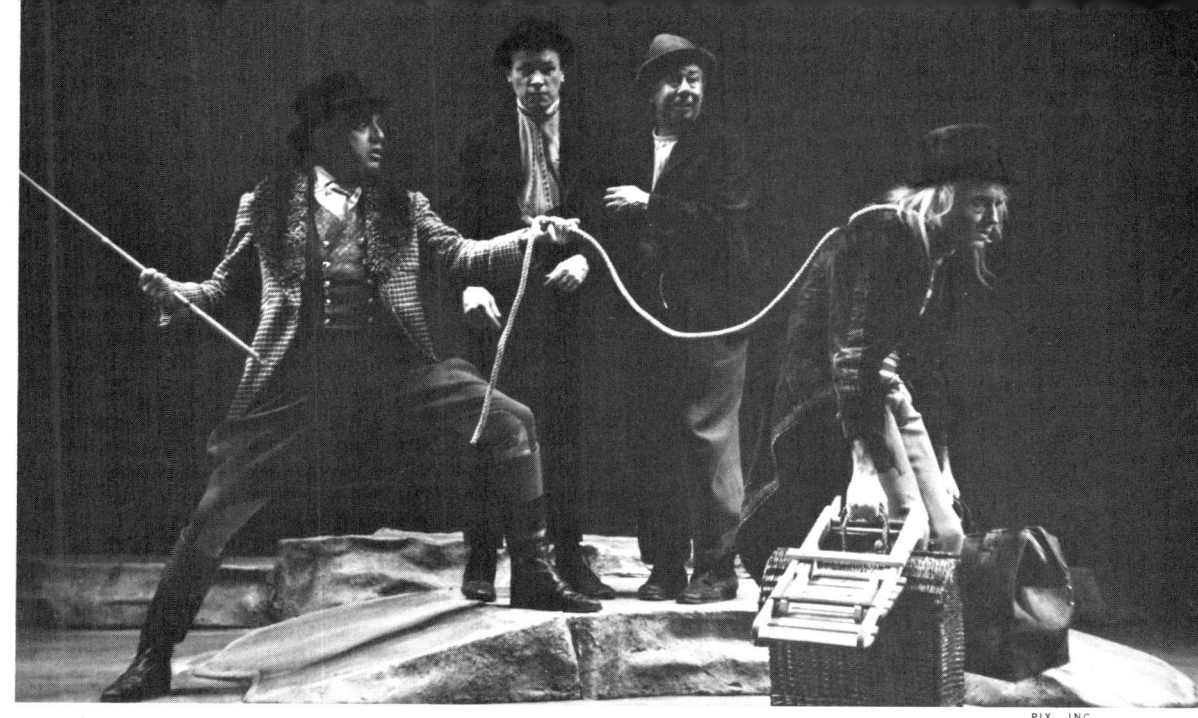

In the mid-20th century, Samuel Beckett's *Waiting for Godot* was an example of the "theater of the absurd."

claim not merely the aggressive tendencies that marked their beginnings, but also significant mystical complexes that usually defy explanation. The origins of these attitudes may be sought in primitivistic reactions of considerable antiquity. It is usual, however, to find a point of origin for the modern "theater of the absurd" in the *Ubu Roi* (produced as a puppet play in 1888 and with live actors in 1896) of Alfred Jarry (1873–1907). *Ubu,* in spite of its extravagance and its extraordinary language, has a thoroughly conventional middle-class viewpoint, and apart from a certain comic mischievousness, it has little in common with Dada. The writers generally lumped together as representatives of the "theater of the absurd"—Eugène Ionesco, Arthur Adamov, Samuel Beckett, and Jean Genet—differ very widely from one another in their approach to the drama and also in their techniques. They have in common the marked antipathy to the ideals and conventions of middle-class society that generally characterizes modern art, as well as a resolutely pessimistic attitude toward the future. Their work therefore implies a destructive tendency that is quite different from Shaw's melioristic approach to contemporary problems. None of these writers appears to have a positive orientation. Whether consciously or not, they reflect, except for Genet, the social attitudes of a philosopher of the type of Herbert Marcuse more clearly than the ideas of Antonin Artaud, with whose theories they are sometimes associated. See also ABSURD.

Antonin Artaud (1896–1948) declared that he derived the inspiration for the critical essays published as *Le théâtre et son double* (1938) from the Eastern theater, specifically the theater of the Balinese dancers. In fact, his theoretical basis may be found in the ideas of Flaubert and Mallarmé, who had dreamed, the one of a novel without subject, the other of drama that approximated ritual. To the idea of drama independent of plot or language, Artaud added the concept of a theater colored principally by cruelty (which he considered a fundamental human trait), having the function of purging the natural ferocity that civilized life inhibits. This catharsis would not be achieved through anything resembling an intellectual experience, but through a purely visceral reaction.

The psychological and sociological connotations of these ideas were immediately apparent in the postwar world, but their usefulness in the theater was not clear until Jean Genet demonstrated their possibilities in a series of imaginative, but entirely enigmatic, plays of quasi-ritualistic character—*Les Bonnes* (1947), *Le Balcon* (1957), and *Les Nègres* (1959). But even before these plays had demonstrated their value at the box office, gifted writers such as Tennessee Williams had sensed the dramatic utility of the outrageous, and following his lead, the younger dramatists of England and America hastened to develop a form of violent drama that looks chiefly to the element of shock and indecency for its effects, precisely as Artaud had counseled. A number of interesting plays tossed about in the wake of the wave of spiritual malaise that characterized the middle years of the 20th century, among them John Osborne's *Look Back in Anger* (1956), Harold Pinter's *The Caretaker* (1959) and *The Homecoming* (1965), Edward Albee's *Who's Afraid of Virginia Woolf?* (1962), and Jean Claude van Itallie's short play *Motel* (1966; one of bill of three one-act plays called *America Hurrah*). In *Motel,* amid a truly impressive display of obscenity, the characters smash up the set and throw it at the audience.

Since the school of playwriting that stems from the theories of Artaud generally rejects any appeal to the intellectual faculty as decadent, the question of meaning is not relevant to this type of play—at the most such plays suggest a mood. The plays of Samuel Beckett, although the author's symbols are sometimes impenetrable, are generally amenable to rational interpretation. It is rather in his technique that Beckett demonstrates his inventiveness. This is often a matter of dramatizing a metaphor in a striking way, so that his plays are full of interesting conceits that invite interpretation. In *Endgame* (1958), the old people live in garbage cans; in *Play* (1963) the characters are imprisoned in jars; in *Waiting for Godot* (1955), the two tramps are imprisoned by hope. These plays have no conflict, complication, or special conclusion; presumably they might go on forever. They are, indeed, examples of an essentially nondramatic technique of playwriting. No play conceived along these lines is capable of the progression that is usually considered indispensable to drama, and this characteristic gives these bitter comedies their special *cachet*.

The plays of Eugène Ionesco cover a wider area than those of Beckett or Genet, and have a more provisional character. Ionesco specializes in the *reductio ad absurdum* of conventional behavior and speech. His plays are comedies of manners developed in an atmosphere of surrealism, and their relation to the techniques of avant-garde painting in the 1930's is tolerably clear. *The Bald Soprano* (1950), subtitled an "anti-play," is in fact an interesting tissue of nonsense with affinities to the medieval satirical nonsense verses called *coq-à-l'âne*. *The Lesson* (1951) is of much the same sort; but *The Chairs* (1952) is an *exemplum* that shows, with a certain pathos, the futility of communication. *Le tueur sans gages* (1959) and *Rhinocéros* (1960) are strong fantasies, though not particularly profound. In *Le roi se meurt* (1963), played in English as *Exit the King*, Ionesco seems to have come closer to the style of Genet in an attempt to escape the limitations he found were inherent in his former style.

If these plays speak for the confusion and the bitterness of an uncertain time, the plays of Jean Giraudoux (1882–1944) represent the clear, imaginative, and supremely rational tradition that has come down from the age of Montaigne and Molière. Giraudoux's *La guerre de Troie n'aura pas lieu* (1935; *Tiger at the Gates*), *Intermezzo* (1933; *The Enchanted*), *Ondine* (1938), and *La Folle de Chaillot* (1945), characteristic examples, are tinged with Maeterlinckian symbolism, but saved from its excesses by the incomparable wit of the author. They belong to an elegant tradition that seems infinitely remote from the hysteria of the 1960's, but their popularity in those troubled years might be considered a source of hope for the future of the theater.

It is, nevertheless, to experiments along the lines of postimpressionist painting and contemporary music that the modern drama owes both its vigor and its obvious lack of direction. After 1950 the commercial theater in the United States, and even in Britain, became too expensive to support anything in the nature of a speculation. The new trends in drama therefore took shape principally in little theaters in out-of-the-way places. In such circumstances a good deal of meaningless rubbish was produced and listened to with the respect ordinarily reserved for higher things. Nevertheless it was in the little theaters that the vitality of post World War II drama seemed to be concentrated, and it was in the insurgent rather than the established playwrights that the hope of the theater was centered in these years of transition.

Oriental Drama

Like Western drama, the drama of Asia originated as an elaboration of liturgical practices. However, Asian drama developed along different lines. Eastern drama in general is based on the concept of *sangita*, the threefold art of music, dance, and poetry fused into a single artistic entity. The emphasis is consequently on performance rather than on the intellectual significance of the subject matter. Asian actors long ago rejected realistic presentation in favor of abstraction and symbolism. Accordingly, when in the 19th century, Western influence began to be felt in the Asian theater, the result was not in the nature of an assimilation, but of a complete break with native tradition. Thus in modern times the classical theater in Eastern countries subsists as a national heritage side by side with the developing techniques of a new drama patterned after European practice but strongly colored by local habit and taste.

15. India

India is the ultimate source of the Asian theater. The pervasive influence of Indian drama is largely attributable to the proselytizing tendencies of the Buddhist pilgrims who, after their gradual expulsion from India, wandered throughout Asia carrying with them their art and their literature. But while the Indian influence on dance and drama continues to be felt everywhere in the East, in India itself the Muslim invasions of the 12th to the 15th centuries effectively inhibited the development of the drama, and in the 18th and 19th centuries, British rule all but put an end to native art. Although the indigenous arts of India were later encouraged, the most highly developed expression of the Indian spirit in the drama is to be found, not in India proper, but in Bali, Thailand, Cambodia, Ceylon, and Indonesia.

In the basic, and very ancient, treatise on Indian drama, the *Nāṭyaśāstra* (3d century A.D.) no distinction is made between dance and drama. Indian dance is dramatic, and dramatic works are invariably arranged so that they develop naturally into episodes of dance. This is partly because of the nature of the subject matter, which is largely supernatural. The three main sources of dramatic material are the great religious epics, the *Rāmāyana* (q.v.) and the *Mahābhārata* (q.v.), and the later legends of Krishna. To these sources is traceable the bulk of the thematic material around which the Indian drama developed, from the northern *Ram Lila*, which is performed yearly in Delhi, to the *kathakali* dances of south India and the dance dramas of related countries.

The Sanskrit drama had its principal development between the 3d and the 8th centuries A.D. It is to this remote period that the three most famous playwrights of India belong —Kālidāsa, Bhasa, and Sudraka—as well as the majority of the 500 extant Sanskrit plays. These plays were originally staged at court, for the

Kathakali, the ancient dance drama of south India, is a principal source of thematic material for Indian drama.

learned drama in India was an urban activity, quite distinct from the folk plays of the villages. Some of the well-known Sanskrit plays, such as *Śakuntalā* (q.v.) and *The Little Clay Cart* (also called *The Toy Cart*) are not far from Western standards and have been translated and widely performed in Europe and America, but the larger part of this literature is hardly accessible outside of India.

Although some realistic properties are used, representation in the Sanskrit theater is in the highest degree symbolic. The principals speak in Sanskrit, a language comprehensible only to the learned. Abstract ideas are represented by colors, and the actors manage a complex repertory of stylized gestures that supplement, explain, and extend the spoken word. There are 24 basic *mudras* (hand gestures), 13 movements for the head, and 32 for the feet, and each has its more or less specific significance. Emotion is signified through vocal pitch and intonation: comic and erotic speeches are delivered in a deep voice; heroic passages in the treble. All this is underscored musically, both vocally and instrumentally, but principally through the use of the drum, the indispensable accompaniment of dramatic action.

The Sanskrit play is an acted poem. Its design is in large part attributable to the circumstances of production, which favor a type of drama that exploits to the full the emotional possibilities of each confrontation of characters. Sanskrit drama has neither much interest in, nor any means of elaborating, the circumstances through which dramatic situations are brought about. The recital of an event has no interest for the poet, no matter how important or marvelous it may be. It is the effect on the characters that interests him. They are voluble in expressing their feelings in the various situations of the play, but indifferent as to how they arrived at them.

Sanskrit plays are never tragic. In Indian drama, man is not subject to external fate. He is what he has made of himself in his past lives, and the drama invites him to justify his past in the present. The play therefore radiates confidence in the universal scheme of things, and in the capacity of men to overcome through their own efforts the obstacles to felicity that life provides. In all cases, good triumphs over evil, and every play has a happy ending.

In the 12th century a shift in the focus of Indian worship put Krishna at the center of the pantheon. A consequence was the proliferation of a vast dramatic literature that centers on the story of Krishna, the mischievous cowherd, and his adoring milkmaids and his favorite love, Radha. In this manner a new and profoundly stimulating erotic element came into the drama. The literary masterpiece in this genre is the *Gītāgōvinda* (*The Song of the Divine Cowherd*) by Jayadeva (q.v.), a play that had an immense influence on Indian literature. The result of the Krishna worship, however, was to restrict the permissible moods of Indian drama to love in its physical and spiritual aspects; and the character relationships through which this mood could be evoked were eventually limited to five, all of them of erotic nature. These limitations necessarily put a heavy restraint on the development of Indian drama. The consequence was to inhibit the drama, and to stimulate the dance, through which a more direct appeal to the senses could be made along the permissible lines.

The terms *bhava* and *rasa*, the understanding of which is essential in any discussion of Indian drama, are singularly elusive for the Western mind. The spectrum of feelings that can properly be represented by actors is traditionally limited to nine—love, laughter, pathos, anger, energy, fear, disgust, wonder, quietude. These are the *bhavas*. *Rasa* means taste, or flavor. It is neither feeling nor emotion, but the mood evoked by the artistic exhibition of feeling or emotion; a mood, impersonal, generalized, and without empathy, that is savored as pure aestheticism—the taste of the play. *Rasa* thus defines the pleasure of the spectator who has witnessed the transformation of emotion into art. Each *rasa* has therefore a special quality depending on the emotion that evokes it. The nine *rasas* correspond with the nine *bhavas*. The strict classification of permissible stimuli and the consequent reactions gave rise to a shaping principle entirely foreign to Western dramaturgy. It is on its success in developing the appropriate *rasa* that the value of a play depends, not at all on the logic or the significance of the events represented. These ideas are fundamental in all branches of Asian drama with the exception of the Chinese.

16. China

Chinese drama is completely outside the Indian sphere of influence. It is based, like the drama of India, on the trinitarian concept of *sangita*, but it differs essentially from Indian theater in the minimal reliance it places on dance. Dance is at the very core of the Indian spirit: in the beginning Siva initiated the world rhythm on his hand drum, dancing to its beat until all the world came into being. But in China, during the period that the art of drama principally developed, dancing was not cultivated as a court entertainment, nor did the Chinese favor the type of poetic exaltation that dance expresses and arouses. The Chinese spirit is not mystical, but practical, and its drama reflects this attitude; in the plays, the spiritual Taoist and the Buddhist priest are comic figures. The general tone of Chinese drama is Confucian, that is to say, agnostic, secular, high-minded, moralistic, and businesslike. Chinese drama is not much involved with the loves and combats of the gods. Its chief preoccupation is with human questions.

The origins of Chinese drama in antiquity are traceable to festivals and ceremonies that were apparently accompanied by song and dance. In T'ang times the emperor Ming Huang (reigned 713–756 A.D.) established the celebrated Academy of the Pear Orchard for the training of young singers and actors. The foundation of the popular Peking opera, the *ching hsi*, is however more directly related to a type of erudite music drama called *k'un ch'ü*, which had its origins in the Yüan dynasty (1271–1368 A.D.). This style reached a high point of refinement under imperial patronage in Soochow during the reigns (1661–1722 and 1736–1796) of K'ang Hsi and Ch'ien Lung, and came to an abrupt end with the T'ai-p'ing Rebellion of 1853. The rise of the *ching hsi* style of drama dates from this period.

The *ching hsi*—*ching* means capital; *hsi* means drama—is popular in its appeal. It draws its plots from such popular novels and romances as *The Romance of the Three Kingdoms* and *The Water's Edge* (or *The Water Margin*), capacious works representing compilations of tales handed down for generations, which picture an antique past in terms of the traditional patterns of virtue. Since these tales deal with characters entirely familiar to an urban audience, any originality by way of plot or characterization is more likely to be resisted than welcomed. The 500 plays of the *ching hsi* repertory celebrate the deeds of heroes, their wars, revolts, and feats of arms, especially during the period of the Three Kingdoms (220–265 A.D.). The dramatic adaptations were made, not by men of letters, but by actors, who apparently cherished their anonymity as writers. These plays can therefore hardly be considered as independent works of art. They furnish merely the blueprint for a production that integrates speech and action with music and poetry in a single operatic complex.

Chinese opera has four main roles, the male (*sheng*), the female (*tan*), the "painted face" (*ching*)—representing personages of unusual masculinity such as warriors, bandits, and ministers of vital temper—and the clown (*ch'ou*). These characters portray standard personalities of abstract character. Each has its own peculiar gait, gestures, and vocal habit. There is no attempt at individual characterization, nor any need for it. Instead, the actor is required to show his skill in demonstrating minutely, and with perfect formality, the ideal characteristics of the type-character he represents. From the time of Ch'ien Lung until quite recently female parts were played by men, and some of the great stars of the Chinese theater —Mei Lan-fang (1894–1961), for example— devoted their talents to female impersonation.

The Chinese actor is an adept, the product of long years of rigorous discipline. Ideally, he requires nothing but his art in order to give a performance. In practice, he is elaborately costumed and made-up and has a number of assistants, musicians, and stage attendants, all of them singularly self-effacing instrumentalities, who are, in a sense, invisible, and are therefore released from the need for any sort of formality whether they are working on the stage or not. The actor is primarily a singer, but one whose skill as acrobat and mime is quite as important as his vocal ability. His movements are precisely coordinated with the vocal rhythms of song and declamation, and the entire perform-

IN CHINESE OPERA, the popular theater of China, acting styles are dictated by many years of tradition.

PHOTO PIC, FROM RAPHO-GUILLUMETTE

Japanese No drama, in which actors wear traditional masks, developed from a dance form in the 14th century.

ance is regulated by the orchestra leader, whose drum and redwood clappers *(pang-tsu)* give the pulse of the play. It is this texture of sound and movement, transformed through poetry into a high fantasy, that is the real goal of the playwright. The lines spoken by the individual characters, and the logical unfolding of the plot, are secondary concerns.

The willingness of the audience to enter imaginatively into the story determines, to a great extent, the nature of the *ching hsi* performance, as well as its extraordinary breadth of dramaturgic possibility. The stage is bare, except for a square carpet. There is no front curtain, nor any scenic decoration except a gaudy backdrop, the property of the principal actor and the visible measure of his current affluence. All entrances are made right stage, and all exits to the left. An ordinary wooden table and two straight-backed chairs are all that is necessary for the enactment of the most complicated scenes, battles by land and sea, the conquest of cities, storms, tempests, and hair-breadth rescues. By placing a chair on top of the table, the stage attendant creates a dizzying precipice, which he helps the actor to scale; a cloth hung between the chairs represents a bed; a horse is symbolized by a whip in the actor's hand (the attendant relieves him of it when he dismounts); a black flag represents the wind. In combat, the defeated character walks off the stage; if he is killed, he crosses his eyes and falls back into the arms of the waiting attendant. With such techniques there is no limit to what can be represented on the stage.

On the other hand, the most rigid tradition dictates every detail of the performance. The actor's movements are drawn from a long and complex glossary of permissible gestures. Through his appearance, the movements of his limbs, and the manipulation of his sleeves—the *tan* actor has 39 prescribed sleeve movements, each with its precise signification—the actor commands a vocabulary of symbols that extends and interprets his words and his song. As in the Sanskrit drama of India, this vocabulary is indispensable to the performance. Dramatic dialogue does not imitate ordinary speech.

Except for the clowns, who are permitted to speak in *pai-hua*, the ordinary Peking dialect, the actor's speeches are inflated with honorific terminology far above the level of civil communication, and the actors aim at a rhythmic intonation that draws out certain syllables and raises or lowers the pitch of the voice in special modulations that make his words incomprehensible.

While the actors thus observe the strictest formality, the audience is seldom attentive. There is incessant chatter in the auditorium. Tea is constantly served. Until recently it was customary for the actor to be offered some refreshment before embarking on an important aria. Thus in *Ssu Lang Visits His Mother,* Ssu Lang is traditionally offered tea by the stage attendant after reciting the exposition, which affects him deeply, before he launches into the famous song that opens the action of the play.

The fortunes of this celebrated play may serve as an example of the fate of much of the 19th century repertory in contemporary China. Beginning as a provincial entertainment sometime in the 18th century, this play was first staged in Peking in 1874 with improvements by the noted actor T'ung Chih. The great T'an Hsin-p'ei arranged it as an opera in Peking style. In this form it became the most popular play in the *ching hsi* repertory, and provided Mei Lan-fang with one of his most famous roles, Princess Iron Mirror. In 1949, *Ssu Lang* all but vanished from the stage, for the reason that its theme, which puts family loyalty ahead of national allegiance, was considered incompatible with Marxist principles. Much the same fate befell *The Butterfly Dream,* which deals comically with the inconstancy of women, a theme inappropriate to the new feminism of China.

The beginning of Western style theater in China dates from 1907, when *Camille* (q.v.) and *Uncle Tom's Cabin* were adapted for the Chinese stage. The new genre was called "talking drama" *(hua chü)*. There was, however, at that time no language available for the interpretation of such plays. The Peking vernacular was considered too vulgar for use as an artistic vehicle;

while the written language was deemed too exclusive for a popular audience. In 1919, when the "literary revolution" caused the vernacular to be adopted for all literary purposes, Western-style drama became possible, and with it came an approximation to Western realism. In China, as in Japan, it was Ibsen who really opened the way to a new national drama involving the reappraisal of social values, and he has been much imitated. But the *ching hsi* must still be considered the chief contribution of China to the history of the drama.

17. Japan

The dance and drama of Japan at the present time are the result of an uninterrupted tradition of 13 centuries. The oldest extant dance forms are the *bugaku* and *gagaku* dances, highly aristocratic forms performed only at court. The No drama is some 500 years old. Kabuki began in the early 17th century, in the Genroku period. Following the Meiji Restoration (1868), Westernizing influences in the theater resulted in a transitional genre called Shimpa, an attempt to adapt Kabuki methods to the European style. In 1924, after earlier efforts to establish it had failed, "new drama" (*shingeki*) began in a small theater in downtown Tokyo. This was a complete departure from the traditional Japanese forms. Here, under influences chiefly from the Moscow Art Theater, Western drama was played in relatively faithful translation, particularly the plays of Ibsen, Chekhov, and Shaw. World War II put a temporary end to this activity, but during the American occupation the new drama returned, this time to stay. But while no nation has shown greater interest or greater ingenuity in adapting itself to foreign ways, the new drama in Japan remains essentially Japanese.

No means "accomplishment" or "ability." The No drama is the result of the development in the early 14th century of a dance form called *sarugaku-no* at the hands of the actor Kanami (1333–1394), and his son Zeami Motokiyo (1363–1443). Kanami was the head of a troupe that performed at the Kasuga shrine in Nara. As a result of the patronage of the shogun Yoshimitsu (1358–1408), this troupe was established in the shogun's palace, and its style became influential throughout Japan.

Zeami was a writer as well as an actor of distinction. Of the 241 plays that exist in this genre, 100 are attributed to him. He also left a treatise on the art of acting called the *Kadensho* (*The Book of the Handing Down of the Flower*), supposedly addressed to his son. This is the theoretical basis of the No drama.

For Zeami the art of the theater has as its goal the revelation that results from the distillation of experience into its essential forms. Like other arts that developed under the influence of Zen, the drama aims at the attainment of that inner quietude that is the consequence of the transcendence of self, and the awareness of the unity of all things. For the artist, this involves a state of effortless virtuosity without any trace of personal exhibitionism; for the dramatic production, it involves an austere economy of means.

The plot material of the No plays is usually lurid and melodramatic in the extreme, and well illustrates the Japanese taste for the remote and strange, but no part of it is represented on the stage. What is performed is a limpid distillation of the events in question. The play thus conveys the emotional essence of long-forgotten things, now transformed into something quintessential and pure.

The special flavor of No drama is called *yugen*, a term from Zen literature that signifies "what lies below the surface." What the Zen poet and the Zen painter perceive as the essence of experience, the flower, is what the actor seeks to transmit through the No performance. This performance attains a very high degree of refinement through the simplest means. The stage, roofed over and made of polished cedar, is itself a musical instrument, resonant to the stamp of the foot. On the back wall is painted a pine tree, reminiscent of the pines behind the stage at the Kasuga shrine. A railed gallery (*hashigakari*) leads to the dressing room, its opening screened by a curtain lifted from below to admit the actor. Backstage, behind a low railing, sits a small orchestra consisting of three drums and a flute. At right stage sits a chorus of 10 or 12 men in 2 rows.

Most No plays have only two important roles. The principal actor is called the *shite*; the secondary character, the *waki*. Each may have followers (*tsure*). Dramatically, the two characters are not opposed, and usually develop no conflict. In the rare cases when they clash, their confrontation dissolves into a dance by the *shite*. Where Western drama seeks to create an illusion of reality, No deliberately aims at an effect of unreality. The No character is conceived, and the No actor moves, in such a way as to suggest the insubstantiality of the appearance. The transit of the actor to and across the stage is so slow as hardly to suggest movement. The sense of place is important; but there is no sense of time, so that the play takes place without dimension. The scene is evoked through a complex symbolism. The fan in the actor's hand may represent a sword, a tray, or falling snow. The language is archaic, courtly, and inflected in such a way as to be comprehensible only to the scholar. The actors' faces are either masked or completely expressionless, so that the characters seem like dream figures moving imperceptibly through a world beyond reality, bloodless, without will or individuality, the memories of people rather than the people themselves.

The other traditional forms of Japanese drama, the doll theater and the Kabuki, are intimately related to the No, and equally romantic, but they are frankly popular forms in which everything is represented that in the No theater is suppressed.

In the 16th century there existed a popular style of declamation, called *joruri*, in which dramatic episodes of a historical nature were chanted to the accompaniment of a three-stringed banjo, the *samisen*. Late in the century, a *joruri* performer and his accompanist were added to a puppet show established in Osaka. A century later, under the management of the gifted *joruri* performer Gidayu Takemoto (1651–1714), the Osaka puppets enjoyed such fame as to attract the services of the playwright Monzaemon Chikamatsu, the first professional dramatist in Japan. The greatness of the puppet theater, later called Bunraku after one of its managers, dates from this time.

Chikamatsu's plays were written in the form

of narratives intended for declamation by the *joruri* performer, with episodes of dialogue mimed by the puppets, interspersed with lyrical passages of great beauty accompanied by the *samisen*. The plots were mainly of two sorts—history plays, such as *The Battle of Coxinga* (1715), and domestic tragedies, such as *The Love-Suicide at Amijima* (1720). In the latter half of the 17th century, the Kabuki troupe at Osaka felt the competition of the puppets so keenly that it was judged necessary to imitate the methods of the doll theater and to borrow its scripts for the use of live actors.

The Kabuki was essentially an actors' theater, but its plots were drawn from the same sources, and adapted by the same writers, as in the doll theater. Until the great Chikamatsu made his influence felt in the puppet theater, writers had no great status in the Kabuki troupe. They were considered servants, like the black-veiled stage attendants. Until 1680 no author's name appeared on a playbill. It was Chikamatsu who established the Kabuki play as a literary genre.

By 1663 the *joruri* performer and his *samisen* player were firmly established on the Kabuki stage, and thenceforth the entire performance was synchronized to the rhythms of the *samisen*, just as in the doll theater. As early as 1703 the puppets had realistic sets, and in the course of the next 50 years, they acquired elevators, trap lifts, and a revolving stage, mechanical marvels the Kabuki actors hastened to adapt or to surpass. In the fervor of competition, the actors went so far as to ape the acting style of the puppets, adopting the stylized gait of dolls, and a vocal technique patterned after the dialogue style of the *joruri* performer.

From the time of Chikamatsu, plots and plays shuttled back and forth between the puppet theater and its live counterpart. The elaborate feud between the Minamoto clan and the Taira, the story of the Soga brothers, the history of the Forty-Seven Loyal Ronin, and *Sugawara's Secrets of Calligraphy* kept puppets and actors busy for centuries. The moral tendency of these plays was the celebration of the feudal virtues, especially those encouraged by the Tokugawa regime—loyalty, obedience, self-sacrifice, the duty of revenge, and the paramount sense of obligation. The typical situation of serious drama is one of divided loyalty, as between love and honor. Such dilemmas are invariably resolved in terms of the heroic affirmation of social obligation as man's highest duty, but the result is never happy as in Western drama patterned along similar lines. In the Kabuki, man's fate is tragic. It is generally death that brings about the necessary equilibrium of right and wrong. Even this is a provisional solution, for the idea of *inga*, the Japanese equivalent of the Buddhist *karma*, involves the inescapable consequences of evildoing in future incarnations in the form of an evil destiny against which the individual is powerless to struggle.

While the No drama rigorously excluded comic effects, save by way of interludes (Kyogen), the Kabuki writers had no compunction about introducing broad comic effects into serious scenes, nor did they hesitate to join together anachronistically and illogically whatever they deemed useful in putting together a dramatic action. Apart from the illustration of accepted ethical standards, the Kabuki writer felt little of the artistic responsibility that dignifies the Western writer in the high periods of Western drama. From a dramatic viewpoint, the Kabuki theater is bounded on the one side by Chikamatsu, on the other by the greatest of his successors Mokuami Kawatake (1816–1893). With the exception of the works of these two authors, Kabuki plays give no inkling of the relation of drama to contemporary life. The world of Kabuki is a fantastic wonderland, the marvels of which may be contemplated with the equanimity reserved for an art that approaches closely an ideal of art for art's sake. See also ORIENTAL THEATER.

MAURICE VALENCY, *Columbia University*

Bibliography

Anderson, John, *The American Theatre* (New York 1938).
Bentley, Gerald E., *The Jacobean and Caroline Stage*, 5 vols. (New York 1941–1956).
Bernbaum, Ernest, *The Drama of Sensibility* (Boston and New York 1915).
Bieber, Margarete, *The History of Greek and Roman Theatre*, 2d ed. (Princeton 1961).
Bowers, Faubion, *Theatre in the East* (New York and London 1956).
Bowra, Cecil M., *Sophoclean Tragedy* (New York and London 1965).
Chambers, Edmund K., *The Medieval Stage*, 2 vols. (London 1903).
Chambers, Edmund K., *William Shakespeare: A Study of Facts and Problems*, 2 vols. (New York 1930).
Clark, Barrett, ed., *European Theories of the Drama* (New York 1947).
Ernst, Earle, *The Kabuki Theatre* (London 1956).
Esslin, Martin, *The Theatre of the Absurd* (New York 1961).
Guicharnaud, Jacques, and Guicharnaud, June, *Modern French Theatre* (New Haven, Conn., 1967).
Hamilton, Edith, tr., *Three Greek Plays* (New York 1937).
Harrison, Jane E., *Ancient Art and Ritual* (New York 1913).
Hauser, Arnold, *The Social History of Art*, tr. by Arnold Hauser and Stanley Godman, 2 vols. (New York 1951).
Herrick, Marvin T., *Italian Comedy in the Renaissance* (Urbana, Ill., 1960).
Hunningher, Benjamin, *The Origin of the Theater* (London 1955).
Keith, Arthur B., *The Sanskrit Drama* (London and New York 1924).
Lea, Kathleen M., *Italian Popular Comedy*, 2 vols. (New York 1962).
Murray, Gilbert, *Euripides and His Age*, 2d ed. (London and New York 1946).
Rennert, H. A., *The Spanish Stage in the Time of Lope de Vega* (New York 1909).
Robinson, Lennox, *The Irish Theatre* (London 1939).
Scott, Adolphe C., *The Classical Theatre of China* (London and New York 1957).
Stuart, Donald C., *The Development of Dramatic Art* (New York 1928).
Summers, Montague, *The Restoration Theatre* (New York 1934).
Thomson, George D., *Aeschylus and Athens* (London 1941).
Valency, Maurice, *The Breaking String: The Plays of Anton Chekhov* (New York and London 1966).
Valency, Maurice, *The Flower and the Castle: An Introduction to Modern Drama* (New York 1964).
Varneke, Boris V., *A History of the Russian Theatre, 17th–19th Centuries*, tr. by Boris Brasol (New York 1951).
Waley, Arthur D., *The Nō Plays of Japan*, 2d ed. (London 1950).

For Specialized Study

Aristotle, *On the Art of Poetry*, tr. by Ingram Bywater (London 1909).
Bab, Julius, *Das Theater der Gegenwart, Geschichte der dramatischen Bühne seit 1870* (Leipzig 1928).
Cohen, Gustave, *Le théâtre en France au moyen-âge*, 2 vols. (Paris 1931).
Doumic, René, *De Scribe à Ibsen* (Paris 1893).
Ewen, Frederic, *Bertolt Brecht* (New York 1967).
Lamm, Martin, *August Strindberg* (Stockholm 1928).
Martino, Pierre, *Le naturalisme français* (Paris 1923).
Scherer, Jacques, *La dramaturgie classique en France* (Paris 1955).
Tilgher, Adriano, *Studi sul teatro contemporaneo*, 3d ed. (Rome 1928).
Tilley, Arthur, *Molière* (New York 1921).

DRAMA CRITICISM. See CRITICISM, DRAMA.

DRAMATIC ARTS. See ACTING; COSTUME, THEATRICAL; MAKE-UP; MOTION PICTURES; PLAY PRODUCTION; THEATER.

DRAMATIC MONOLOGUE, in literature, any speech of some duration uttered by one person, usually in a dramatically climactic situation. Broadly defined, it includes the soliloquy in drama—a discourse delivered by an actor who is either alone on stage or acts as though he were alone. Such soliloquies were common in Greek, Roman, and Renaissance drama.

As a special literary form, the dramatic monologue is a poem in which a single character speaks to an identifiable but silent person at a climactic moment in the speaker's life. The circumstances surrounding the situation are made clear by implication in the poem, and through this knowledge the reader understands supposedly hidden aspects of the speaker's character. Thus the dramatic monologue reveals "a soul in action."

The dramatic monologue was virtually established as a literary form by Robert Browning in the 19th century, as in *My Last Duchess* and *Andrea del Sarto*, although examples in English can be found as early as the Anglo-Saxon poems *The Wanderer* and *The Seafarer*. Many poets have used the dramatic monologue with distinction, including Tennyson, Robert Frost, Edwin Arlington Robinson, Carl Sandburg, and T. S. Eliot.

C. HUGH HOLMAN
Coauthor of "A Handbook to Literature"

DRANG NACH OSTEN, dräng näKH ōs'tən, is a concept used in Slavic, French, and English works to indicate German eastward expansion in Europe. A German phrase, it means "Drive to the East," and refers primarily to: (1) German eastward expansion from 900 to 1500 (by the Teutonic Knights and the Hanseatic League and by migrations); (2) Austrian expansion into the Balkans after 1683; (3) German-Polish relations, 1815–1914; (4) German ambitions in the Middle East, 1889–1914; (5) German and Austrian plans to dominate Europe, 1914–1918; and (6) Nazi plans and aggressions, 1933–1945.

HENRY CORD MEYER
University of California at Irvine

DRAPER, Henry (1837–1882), American physician and amateur astronomer, who first successfully photographed the spectrum of a star. He was born in Prince Edward county, Va., on March 7, 1837, the second son of the chemist John W. Draper. Draper became a professor of medicine at New York University, but his main interest was astronomy, particularly celestial photography. He took some fine early photographs of the moon, stars, and star clusters.

Although William Huggins had attempted to photograph stellar spectra as early as 1862, Draper was the first, in 1872, to obtain satisfactory results. In 1880 he obtained the first direct photograph of a nebula, that in Orion, and 18 months later he also photographed its spectrum. In 1881 he and Huggins independently photographed for the first time the spectrum of a comet. He died in New York on Nov. 20, 1882.

BRIAN G. MARSDEN
Smithsonian Astrophysical Observatory

DRAPER, John William (1811–1882), American scientist, who made contributions to photochemistry and photography. He was born in St. Helens, England, on May 5, 1811, studied at the University of London, and emigrated to the United States in 1832. Draper completed medical studies at the University of Pennsylvania in 1836 and joined the New York University medical school, of which he was president from 1850 to 1873. A founder of the American Chemical Society, he was elected its first president in 1876. He died at Hastings-on-Hudson, N. Y., on Jan. 4, 1882.

Draper's experiments in photochemistry in 1841 showed that only light that is absorbed can produce chemical reaction. He found that the amount of reaction is proportional to exposure time at constant illumination, and that the rate of reaction is proportional to the intensity of the absorbed light (Draper's law). He also noted that heated solids begin to show a red glow at 525° C (977° F); as the temperature increases the glow includes more of the spectrum, ultimately resulting in the emission of white light.

Draper improved the Daguerre process of photography, enabling him to make the first satisfactory photographic portrait (1840). He made the first photograph of the moon (1840), obtained the first spectral photograph of a star (the sun, in 1844), and pioneered in making photomicrographs (first published in 1856).

AARON J. IHDE, *University of Wisconsin*

DRAPER, Paul (c. 1911–   ), American dancer, who established his own dance form by combining elements of ballet and tap dancing. A nephew of the monologist Ruth Draper, he was born in Florence, Italy, of American parents, on Oct. 25, about 1911. As a boy he lived in London, then in the United States, leading a very unsettled life until he decided to become a dancer.

Draper made his stage debut in London in 1932, but he did not develop his famous "ballet-tap" style until he returned to the United States and studied traditional ballet at the American School of Ballet in New York City. From 1940 to 1948 he toured with harmonica virtuoso Larry Adler, and he later taught dancing at major studios and published articles in *Dance Magazine*. Draper created all his own choreography and sometimes performed it without musical accompaniment. Among his satirical sketches are *A Sharp Character* and *Sonata for Tap Dancer*.

DRAPER, Ruth (1884–1956), American monologist, who was famous for her versatility and her original repertoire. She was born in New York City on Dec. 2, 1884, the granddaughter of Charles A. Dana, editor of the New York *Sun*. In 1915 she made her debut as an actress in the play *A Lady's Name* in New York City, and a year later she began performing her unique one-woman show. Her success as a monologist really began with her triumphant London debut in 1920. She gave a command performance for the British royal family in 1926 and during her career performed on every continent. She died in New York City on Dec. 30, 1956.

In her 37 monologues, which she wrote herself, Miss Draper portrayed 58 different roles, assuming each with remarkable empathy and keen insight. Her most famous stage pieces include *The Italian Lesson, At an English House Party,* and *Three Generations*.

DRAPERY AND CURTAINS are pieces of material arranged to hang in soft or tailored folds, used as interior furnishings. Although curtains are commonly called draperies, the two words are not synonymous. Drapery is a relatively stationary arrangement of loosely, often gracefully hung cloth that is usually decorative. It may or may not perform a function. It is used most frequently as a kind of wall hanging but may also be placed over a table. The term "drapery" may also be used in relation to clothing (see CLOTHING; DRESS). Curtains usually have a function: they shut off or hide something, such as an alcove, doorway, or window, or give protection from cold, heat, or glare. Frequently they may be drawn back or up when necessary.

Development of Drapery and Curtains. In ancient civilizations, which were generally located in warm climates and whose buildings had few windows, drapery and curtains as items of interior furnishings are relatively rare. There is literary mention, however, of wall hangings in ancient temples, and curtains were probably used to shut off doorways in Roman houses.

Medieval ivory carvings and illuminated manuscripts show curtains hanging from rods between two columns supporting a lintel or arch to form an alcove. The cold damp castles and churches of the time were often decorated with and made more comfortable by drapery or some other form of hanging on their walls. The small, deepset, often unglazed windows were generally curtainless and might be closed by shutters.

Gradually, curtains came to be hung from the ceiling around beds. By the 15th century, wealthy households had huge carved-wood beds supporting a tester, or canopy, which consisted of a roof and ornamental border formed by a stiff cornice board or a valance of softly arranged fabric. From the tester hung voluminous curtains, which in daytime were drawn back from the center to the corner posts and at night were let down to form a warm private bedroom.

During the Renaissance and baroque periods, as textiles became more plentiful and dwellings developed from fortified castles into ostentatious palaces, drapery and curtains were especially sumptuous. Rich Italian velvets, silk damasks, or silk brocades were hung on walls and occasionally at windows. Probably the most elaborate curtains were those on state beds, such as the curtained beds designed by Daniel Marot, from which it was customary in the 17th century for the nobility to receive visitors. Layers of curtains hung from a cornice board ornamented with swags, fringe, or plumes and could be tied back

FOUR STYLES OF CURTAINS

Lined curtains over sheer curtains, falling from a cornice board, are appropriate for a formal room. The sheer curtains, which cover the window, offer privacy and reduce glare.

Nontransparent curtains, lined or unlined, with a pleated heading, may be both dramatic and practical. They are often used over large windows or walls in rooms of modern design.

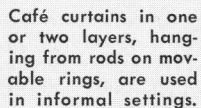

Sheer, ruffled curtains with tiebacks suit country houses and informal rooms in traditional styles.

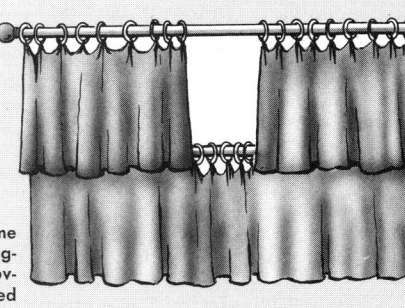

Café curtains in one or two layers, hanging from rods on movable rings, are used in informal settings.

BED CURTAINS, as in this 18th century example from Osterley Park, England, provided warmth and privacy.

LOUIS H. FROHMAN

separately with beautiful tasseled silk ropes. In less pretentious establishments where beds were often built into an alcove in the wall, curtains sometimes were hung at the opening.

In portraits by Holbein, Titian, Honthorst, and Van Dyck, figures are posed against rich drapery, which is often arranged for decorative effect across a pillar or balustrade, or framing a landscape. Northern European interiors by Holbein and Vermeer show Oriental rugs draped over tables or drawn aside to frame a room. De Hooch's paintings of middle-class Dutch households show plain thin curtains hung in vertical folds over large glazed windows.

In the more delicate and intimate rooms of the rococo period—as shown in the paintings of French and Italian interiors by Boucher and Longhi—and of the more austere neoclassical period, the fabric of drapery and curtains was generally of lighter weight and color than previously. Pastel silks and printed cottons were popular. Drapery was seldom used on walls, which were usually painted or papered, but it sometimes decorated dressing tables, mirrors, and sofas. Bed curtains were still rather ornate, but smaller in scale. Sometimes, on beds with no footposts, they hung only at the head of the bed. On some beds set parallel to the wall with no posts, curtains hung from a small central canopy separate from the bed and could also surround a portable bath.

Windows were frequently curtained, often elaborately. Sometimes two or more layers of curtains of different materials were used to create a rich effect. Some could be pulled back; others were stationary. They hung from rods, which often had ornamental ends or were covered by a cornice board or a valance with ruffles, pleats, swags, or jabots. Curtains also were hung over doors. During the French Empire and English Regency periods, which continued the neoclassical style, window curtains became simpler and more tailored. Illustrations of drapery and curtains appear in books of English furniture by Chippendale, who was noted for rococo design, and by Sheraton and George Smith, who worked in the neoclassical style.

In the display-conscious Victorian period, drapery and curtains, like most other furnishings, were overdone. Heavy fringed velvet and brocade curtains hung from doorways and windows, often over curtains of lace; shawls and other pieces of fabric were draped over tables and pianos. In contrast to the Victorian period, the 20th century has tended toward a functionalism that frequently makes use of much simpler materials and styles.

Curtains in Contemporary Interiors. Curtains today are made in a variety of fabrics and styles and are usually designed to add to the beauty of a room. There are three basic types: sheer, unlined nontransparent, and lined.

Sheer, usually transparent curtains may be made of such materials as cotton, linen, and silk or of longwearing nylon, Orlon, Dacron, saran, or fiber glass, in a variety of weaves and in plain colors or prints. Sheer curtains should be very full and, if they are to hang straight, should have a double hem and weight at the bottom. They are often used under heavier curtains to soften the light and provide privacy. Sheer curtains with ruffles and tiebacks may be used alone to provide a "country" or feminine atmosphere.

Unlined nontransparent curtains are made of cotton, linen, or a synthetic fabric, in a variety of textures. They may be used for slightly more dramatic effects than are possible with sheer curtains and are cheaper and simpler to care for than lined curtains.

Sheer and other unlined curtains are often gathered along a curtain rod through a hem at the top. Sometimes they are only half as long as the window and are hung from the rod on rings, in one or two tiers, forming a *café curtain*. *Casement curtains* for casement windows must be hung on the inside window trim or wall if the window opens out and on the window frame itself if the window opens in.

Heavy, lined curtains are probably the most commonly used. They are made of a variety of fabrics, particularly of rich materials such as fine linen or silk damask, and are lined to give them more body and to protect them from sunlight and dirt. They may be used to frame or hide a view or to absorb sound. They may be decorated with braid, fringe, or tassels and may be hung from under a cornice board or valance, thus adding elegance to a high-ceilinged room. If the cornice or valance extends above or beyond the window frame, it makes the window appear taller or wider. Curtains may be hooked to traverse rods and drawn, with the heading (the part above the rod) in French-, cartridge-, or box pleats to control the way the curtain hangs.

MARY JEAN ALEXANDER
Author of "Decorating Made Simple"

Further Reading: Alexander, Mary J., *Decorating Made Simple* (New York 1964); Faulkner, Ray, and Faulkner, Sarah, *Inside Today's Home*, rev. ed. (New York 1960); Obst, Frances M., *Art and Design for Home Living* (New York 1963); Whiton, Sherrill, *Elements of Interior Design and Decoration*, 3d ed. (Philadelphia 1964).

DRAPIER LETTERS, drā'pē-ər, a series of letters published in 1724 by Jonathan Swift (q.v.) over the signature "M. B. Drapier." In 1722 the Duchess of Kendal sold a patent to William Wood to produce copper coinage for Ireland. Swift's letters, written in the character of a Dublin draper, prophesied that Wood's halfpence would ruin the Irish and advised them to shun the coinage. A committee of inquiry recommended that the amount to be coined should be reduced, but Swift's letters had aroused such a storm that Wood lost the patent entirely. He was compensated with a pension.

DRAUGHTS. See CHECKERS.

DRAVA, drä'vä, one of the main right-bank tributaries of the Danube River. The Drava (German, *Drau*) rises in the Tyrol near the Austrian-Italian border and flows eastward past Villach and Klagenfurt, entering Yugoslavia northwest of Maribor. Continuing eastward, it is joined by the Mura (Mur) river at Legrad, whence it becomes, except for one short distance, the border between Yugoslavia and Hungary until it reaches Miholjac. Here it turns southeast past Osijek to join the Danube.

About 450 miles (725 km) long, the Drava is navigable by river steamers for only 100 miles (160 km) above the Danube, but barges carrying wood and coal travel an additional 200 miles (320 km).

BARBARA JELAVICH and CHARLES JELAVICH
Indiana University

DRAVIDIAN, drə-vid'ē-ən. The Dravidian languages are spoken in a great unbroken area of southern India, in northern Ceylon, in many patches in the wilder parts of central India as far north as the Ganges, and in an isolated patch far to the northwest of Baluchistan (a part of Pakistan). The total number of speakers as of 1961 was about 110 million, making the Dravidian family fifth or sixth among the language families of the world in number of speakers.

At present, 21 languages are known to belong to the family, and one or two more may still be discovered. On the whole, the languages are hardly more differentiated than are the Romance languages or the Germanic languages, and identification of a language as Dravidian on the basis of morphology, syntax, and vocabulary is easy.

Subfamilies. The southernmost languages, Tamil and Malayalam, are very closely related, the latter having diverged from the former only in the 9th and 10th centuries A. D. They belong to the South Dravidian subfamily. Very closely related to these two are the two Nilgiri languages, Toda and Kota, Toda being the most aberrant of all the Dravidian languages in its phonetics. Kodagu, which is spoken in Coorg between the Malayalam and the Kannada areas, is also closely related to these four languages. Kannada, spoken in Mysore state, belongs in the same subfamily as the preceding five languages. Tulu in the Mangalore area on the Malabar coast is separate from the South Dravidian subfamily, as is Telugu, spoken to the north of the Tamil area on the east coast. In central India, Kolami, Naiki, Parji, and Ollari form a subfamily. Gondi is a group of closely related dialects also spoken in central India. Linked to Gondi, in central India also, are Konda, Pengo, Manda, and finally Kui and Kuwi, which show some relationship to Telugu. The North Dravidian subfamily includes Brahui in Baluchistan, and Kurukh (Oraon) and Malto, which are very closely related to one another and are spoken to the north of the Kui-speaking areas.

Among the Dravidian languages, Tamil, Malayalam, Kannada, and Telugu have extensive literatures, the early records of Tamil reaching back 2,000 years. Because of these old records, much that is archaic Dravidian is preserved in Old Tamil. However, by no means all of the features of Old Tamil are archaic, and archaic Dravidian features are in some instances preserved in the nonliterary Central Dravidian languages, some very interesting features of the verb morphology showing up especially well in Kui.

Syntax. The Dravidian languages are suffixal and agglutinative in type, with a mild tendency toward fusion of morphemes. Their major form classes are nouns and verbs. The nouns are declined for number and case. Most of the languages have a gender system based on a distinction between beings "of high rank" and beings or things not of high rank. In many of the languages nouns can add the same person and number suffixes that are found in the verb paradigms, thus forming one-word sentences with such meanings as *It is a tiger* or *I am a Kui.* The verb system of many of the languages includes a negative paradigm. Also, each of the verb paradigms contains an adjective form which can precede a noun and may be translated by such phrases as *who came, whom I saw,* or the like. There are many nonfinite verb forms that may be strung together in chronological series ended by a finite verb form: *He, having boxed and having wrestled, rested.* This last morphological and syntactic feature in Dravidian may be the source of a similar type of construction in Indo-Aryan, the Sanskrit "gerund."

General Characteristics. The Dravidian languages provided the Indo-Aryan languages of North India with many words for plants, animals, and objects peculiar to the Indian scene, as well as with some that are more general in scope. Some of the peculiarities of the phonetic makeup of the Indo-Aryan languages, such as retroflex consonants, are in part due to Dravidian influence, as are some of their morphological and syntactic features.

Excavations of the long-dead cities of the Indus Valley (Harappa) civilization have yielded many short, still undeciphered inscriptions. The most promising language family in which to look for clues has seemed to be Dravidian. So far, however, this guess has led nowhere.

Connections linking the Dravidian family to other families have been sought, but none have been established. In one obvious direction, the languages of Southeast Asia and Indonesia seem to be ruled out by their general character and by other connections that have been established for them. See also INDIA—*4. Languages;* KANARESE; TAMIL; TELUGU.

MURRAY B. EMENEAU
University of California at Berkeley

Further Reading: Bloch, Jules, *Structure grammaticale des langues dravidiennes* (Paris 1946); Burrow, T., and Emeneau, M. B., *A Dravidian Etymological Dictionary* (Oxford 1961); Caldwell, Robert, *A Comparative Grammar of the Dravidian Family of Languages,* 3d ed. (London 1913); Grierson, G. A., *Linguistic Survey of India,* vol. 4 (Calcutta 1906).

DRAWBRIDGE. See BRIDGE—*3. Movable Bridges* (Bascule).

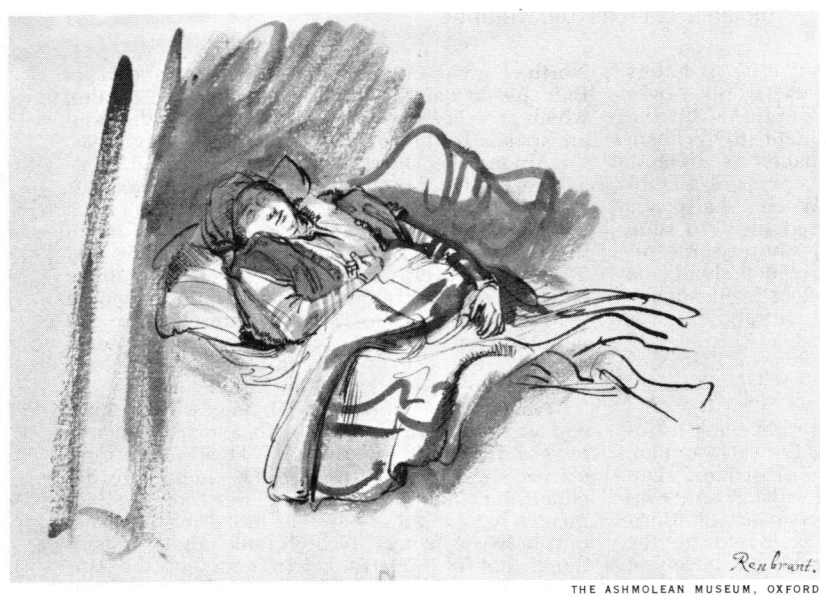

REMBRANDT'S sketch *Saskia in Bed* was drawn with a brush and quill pen in bister.

THE ASHMOLEAN MUSEUM, OXFORD

DRAWING. In English, to draw means literally to trace or delineate, implying that a drawing is an image represented purely in line and therefore monochromatic. In this sense, drawing is closely related to writing, since both involve graphic notation and significant linear configurations; indeed, the tools of drawing and writing have generally been identical. In other languages, however, the word for drawing—*disegno* (Italian), *dessin* (French)—includes the concept of design in a broader sense, the full range of visual composition.

In its complexity, drawing includes the varieties of artistic representation encompassed by both these definitions. A drawing may be simply a line or a series of lines, or it may be an image as fully developed as a painting.

Techniques and Media. Drawing media can be broadly divided into two categories: dry and wet. In the dry media—including chalks, charcoal, crayons, graphite, and metalpoint—the drawing instrument itself carries its own pigment, leaving its own mark. In the wet media the various inks and washes are applied with a separate implement, usually pen or brush.

Wet Media. Although inks of many different colors have been used by draftsmen, black and brown inks have been the favorite choices throughout the history of drawing. The most important inks, varying in tone according to their primary ingredients, are carbon, iron gall, and bister. Black carbon inks, which date back at least to ancient Egypt and China, are prepared by combining carbon particles obtained from soot or charcoal in an aqueous binding medium. Such inks afford the most absolute graphic potential, making a jet-black mark. Diluted with water, they yield clear gray washes. Iron gall inks, however, have been more popular in European drawing and especially in writing. Prepared from the acids of gallnuts, these inks are of a grayish purple color, but with age they turn a deep brown. The acidity of iron gall inks can have a corrosive effect on paper, so that in many old master drawings the paper has been eaten away along portions of the ink lines. Bister, even more popular with European draftsmen, is a lighter brown ink prepared from soluble tars extracted from wood soot.

Until the early 19th century the quill pen was the principal writing implement in Europe and the type most frequently used in drawing. Cut from the quills of geese, swans, ravens, or crows, these pens were versatile instruments that were capable of producing a varied, flexible, and graceful line. Although historically more ancient, pens made from reed or cane were not so popular with medieval illuminators or Renaissance and post-Renaissance draftsmen. The blunter nib of the reed pen makes a broader, less flexible stroke than the quill, and hence it is more suitable to a bold and vigorous manner of drawing.

The steel pen point, developed at the end of the 18th century and in mass production by the middle of the 19th century, displaced the hand-cut quill as the basic writing implement in Europe. By the end of the 19th century it had also become the favorite pen of artists. Convenient and available in a variety of points, the steel pen produces a crisp, clean line, hard yet flexible. Its sharp point, however, requires a paper of smooth and uniform surface, free of fibrous particles that might catch the nib.

Brushes are also used as instruments for applying ink. Varying in quality, they can be at once broader and more flexible than the pen. Occasionally they are the primary drawing tools, dipped into the undiluted ink and applied directly to the paper. But more frequently they serve to supplement an initial design executed with pen or pencil. The ink is diluted, and areas of wash are applied to the drawing, indicating middle tones and shadows.

The chiaroscuro drawing is executed in a variety of wet media—pen and brush, ink, wash, and opaque white watercolor—on tinted paper, either dyed in manufacture or specially coated. The ground provides a basic middle tone; the darker lines and washes and the white heightening complete the monochrome spectrum. The resulting design is pictorially rich, approaching painting in the fullness of its effect.

Dry Media. The dry media vary according to the sources of the pigment and the nature of the binding agent. The quality of the line left by the instrument depends on the friction between the medium and the ground on which it is applied. The texture of the surface abrades the drawing point or edge, picking up small particles of pigment and thereby creating the line or tone.

Charcoal, which is manufactured by the slow carbonizing of sticks of wood, is an extremely friable material that crumbles readily when drawn across any textured surface. A broad medium unsuited to fine line drawing, it is ideal for covering wide areas and has a rich tonal range—from the palest gray to pure black, depending on the pressure of application.

Historically, the most significant dry medium has been natural chalk. It is found in several colors, but black, white, and reddish chalks are most often used in old master drawings. The particular quality of the chalk depends in part on the deposit from which it is cut. Generally, however, red chalks tend to be harder than black and have been preferred therefore for a neater line and more precise manner of draftsmanship. Artists have often combined several colors of chalk in a single drawing to produce a pictorially rich image, not unlike the chiaroscuro drawings in wet media.

Artificially prepared chalks and pastels are fabricated by mixing a paste of powdered pigments and water-soluble binding agents; this paste is then formed into sticks and dried. Crayons are made in a similar fashion but with an oleaginous binder; their fatty substance leaves a rather different mark than chalk, firmer and chromatically more intense and hence less susceptible of subtle gradation.

The medium of metalpoint is suited to an extremely fine and delicate manner of drawing. The implement itself is a stylus made of metal —most commonly lead, often silver, and occasionally gold. When drawn across a specially prepared surface, usually a tinted ground, the stylus leaves a delicate line. But the metalpoint is not responsive to variations in pressure, and

PISANELLO'S pen and ink sketch *Head of a Horse*.
THE BETTMAN ARCHIVE

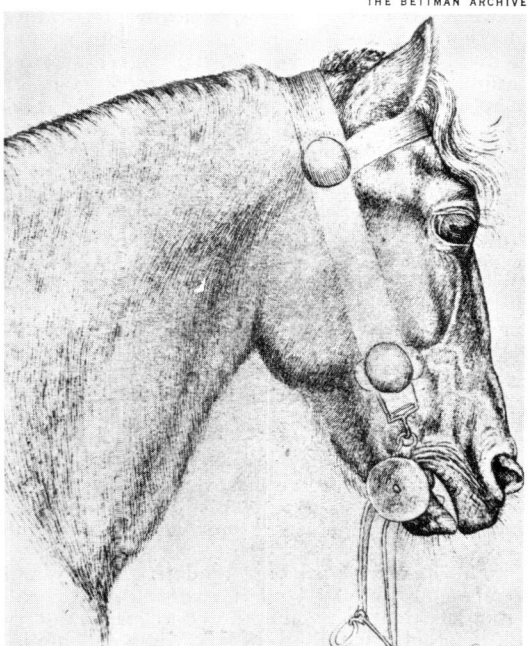

THE METROPOLITAN MUSEUM OF ART

MICHELANGELO'S preliminary sketches done in red chalk for *Libyan Sibyl* fresco in the Sistine Chapel.

its line is basically uniform. Popular in the late Middle Ages and early Renaissance, the medium has been little favored since the 16th century.

The modern graphite pencil, in extensive use since the late 17th century, might be considered the successor to the metalpoint. Closer to chalk in its friability, however, it is a much more pliable medium than metalpoint, with a greater chromatic and textural adaptability.

Function. Throughout the history of postmedieval art, at least until the 20th century, drawing has been a technically ancillary, although essential, activity. It has served many purposes; but, unlike paintings, drawings were not often made as ends in themselves, as finished works of art. One of drawing's primary functions has been as a means of recording and preserving visual knowledge. Its other main function has been to serve in the preparation of other works of art—painting, sculpture, or architecture.

Drawings for Reference. In medieval art, drawing was the fundamental carrier of visual traditions. Pictorial formulas and iconographic types were recorded in drawings and collected in albums that became part of the working material of the studio. From such a collection of *exempla*, or simile drawings, the artist could select the appropriate model for the task at hand. Each page of such a model book generally contained several motifs, distributed over the surface so as to maintain the clarity of each. The linework of the drawing was characteristically simple, intent on preserving the basic pattern. The most famous of these model books is the 13th century album of Villard de Honnecourt.

The tradition of the model book continued through the 18th century, although the character of the drawings changed considerably. Toward the end of the 14th century, studies after

Chalk studies in red, black, and white by Watteau.

nature were incorporated in the albums. These studies—as exemplified by the beautiful drawings of birds and animals by the early Renaissance painter Pisanello—preserve a different kind of visual knowledge, based on the direct observation of nature rather than on earlier prototypes.

In the late 15th century in Italy drawing was further developed as a means of preserving knowledge gained in the new investigation of nature. The study of human anatomy was initiated by artists during this era, and drawing was the indispensable means in this experience. In the anatomical drawings of Leonardo da Vinci the eye and hand of the artist combine to decipher intricate organic forms and to record the new knowledge with clarity.

Preparatory Drawings. Simile drawings and studies of nature by their very purpose were intended to be preserved for future reference. Preparatory drawings, however, were in a sense consumed as they served their function and were replaced by the finished work of art they helped create.

In medieval and early Renaissance mural decorations, preparatory drawings were done directly on the wall. The design was sketched first with chalk or charcoal and then fixed, the basic lines retraced with a brush—usually with a red-ocher color called *sinopia* in Italian. This drawing would eventually disappear beneath the layer of fine plaster to which the colors were applied.

Not until about 1400 did paper become cheap enough to allow the artist to use it freely as a ground for dispensable drawings. In the Middle Ages the artist might work out his first ideas on wax tablets that could be reworked and reused for each new project. As paper became more plentiful, however, it replaced the wax tablet and expensive parchment and vellum as the common drawing ground, and in the course of the 15th century new approaches to drawing and new categories of drawing evolved.

The artist could now experiment in drawing, working out his ideas in many small-scale sketches on paper, slowly developing them until he was satisfied with a final composition. By their very nature, these sketches are tentative, open statements, freely executed. Through their meandering lines the draftsman explores the possibilities of various solutions. In the course of such exploration, new unforeseen ideas are discovered, and sketching thus becomes a seminal experience in artistic creation. Leonardo da Vinci, if not the first artist to utilize this approach, was the first fully to comprehend the great potential and theoretical implications of the process.

In the second half of the 15th century in Italy, drawing on paper also came to replace the preliminary *sinopia* drawing in the preparation of fresco decorations. Instead of drawing directly onto the wall, the artist now prepared a cartoon (*cartone* in Italian), a full-size, carefully executed drawing on large pieces of heavy paper. The entire composition was thus elaborated in drawing and then transferred to the wall.

In the procedure evolved during the Renaissance, between the first rough sketches and the finished cartoon lay a series of intermediary studies of the composition as a whole and of the various details—in particular, studies of the human figure, drawings made from a living model or from sculpture. Exercises in drawing the human form became, in the 16th century, the fundamental educational experience of the young artist, and even today life drawing is a standard feature of most art school curriculums.

Another category of drawing related to the preparation of painting is the *modello,* or presentation drawing—a finished small-scale design intended to give the patron some idea of the final composition. These drawings vary in technique; often they are chiaroscuro designs, but they might also be executed in chalk or pen and ink.

It is impossible to distinguish absolutely between drawings with a specifically preparatory function and those done apparently with no immediate end in view. Casual sketches after nature, for example, may inspire more complex pictorial ideas and thus participate in the preparatory process. Furthermore, an artist's stock of drawings served as a record of his experiences, as a source of new ideas, and in this way even the most random notation might eventually become as functional as a medieval simile drawing.

Style. The style of a drawing is the product of several related factors: the particular medium, the function of the drawing, the draftsman's personality, and his general style. Most immediately, the style depends upon the response of the medium to the movements and pressures of the guiding hand; in turn, the hand of the practiced draftsman is aware of the peculiar nature of the medium—its expressive potential and technical limits—and moves accordingly. This reciprocity determines the quality of the individual line as well as the combinations of lines creating the significant patterns of the design.

The lines of a drawing rendered quickly and spontaneously will record the very speed of execution in their flow and direction and attest to the energetic handling of the drawing implement. Conversely, a line drawn slowly and with care will express the deliberation and control behind it. The pace of such a line—the rhythm of its variations and its changes in direction—will reflect the measured character of the draftsman's hand.

Stylistic differences are not purely idiosyncratic, however. The intention of the draftsman and the purpose of his drawing significantly affect style. If a drawing is intended to preserve a maximum of factual information—as in anatomical and nature studies, portrait drawings, and perspective constructions—it will be executed rather carefully; the linework will tend toward a certain preciseness, and tonal gradations will be deliberately controlled. The contours of a drawing intended to convey a different message, a more impressionistic effect, will be more open; patterns of light and shade may be bolder and the execution freer and more suggestive.

In such pictorial effects the paper itself plays an especially important role, contributing the essential element of light. Open, interrupted contours allow the light background surface to flow from solid object to surrounding space. The result is an overall unity that is by implication atmospheric, pervading the entire design.

Closed contours or dense patterns of linear hatching tend to isolate the objects rendered and set them against the background, rather than within it. This concentration on the physical autonomy of form may be considered a sculptural rather than a pictorial mode of drawing.

The particular configuration of lines, the critical determinant of graphic style, may depend very closely on a drawing's preparatory function. Preparatory drawings for engravings or woodcut, for example, are generally executed in pen and ink, since the print depends entirely on clear linear patterns for its effects. The linework of the drawing that is to be transferred to the copperplate or wood block is therefore crisp and regular.

The style of preparatory drawings for paintings will naturally relate to the style of the projected painting as well as to the particular technical procedures to be followed. Drawings leading up to a cartoon are usually highly articulated; since the cartoon itself will be transferred directly to the painting surface, the contours must be precisely delineated. This sense of precision is evident in the preliminary drawings and especially in studies intended to clarify details.

Painters for whom the cartoon is not an essential step in the production of a picture have generally tended to create preparatory drawings that are more open and pictorial, unconcerned with fixing the contours of the design before the actual painting.

Theory and Aesthetics. Art theory since the 15th century has recognized the central role of drawing in the processes of artistic creation. Italian artists of the early Renaissance proclaimed drawing to be the foundation of the arts of painting and sculpture, and it is significant that theory and drawing developed together during this period. Each in its own way expressed the general concern with finding a rational basis for art in mathematical principles. The perspective construction underlying painting in the Renaissance was important in both practice and theory: as a technical guide in the construction of spatial illusion and as evidence of painting's intimate connection with geometry.

Art theory developed in Italy especially in those centers, Florence and Rome, where the traditions of fresco painting and the use of the cartoon were strongest. Hence the technical significance of drawing in actual studio procedure was echoed in theoretical programs. Giorgio Vasari, the 16th century artist and biographer, declared drawing to be the "father" of the three arts of painting, sculpture, and architecture. Drawing became the fundamental unifying element in the trinity of the "fine arts."

This attitude was strengthened by certain trends in Renaissance philosophy, specifically the Neoplatonic concept of genius, and discussions of drawing acquired more metaphysical connotations. Federico Zuccaro, an artist and writer of the late Renaissance, distinguished two different but related realms of drawing: interior *(disegno interno)* and exterior *(disegno esterno)*. The latter signified drawing in the traditional aesthetic sense, while the former referred not to any actual design but to the idea, divinely inspired, in the mind of the artist. Drawing thus came to be recognized as a direct expression of the artist's imagination. The sketch, in particular, was highly valued as the revelation of genius, the immediate record of the moment of inspiration; its rapid delineation preserved in its spontaneity the excitement of the poetic imagination suddenly inspired.

A corollary of this unusually high valuation of drawing in art theory was the development of drawing collections. Among the earliest significant and systematic collections was that assembled by Vasari, intended as visual documentation for his biographies of the Italian artists. Vasari mounted his drawings in elaborately decorated frames, isolating them for aesthetic contemplation and thereby elevating even the most cursory sketch to the level of a finished work of art.

The 18th century was the great age of collection and connoisseurship. The aesthetic traditions and attitudes of the preceding 200 years were assimilated, reformulated, and given new impetus. The connoisseur delighted in the exam-

Pencil drawing of Mme. Hayard by Ingres (a detail).
FOGG ART MUSEUM

MUSEUM OF MODERN ART
Pencil and wash study by Picasso for *Guernica*.

ination of a drawing, considered the most intimate form of artistic creation. Drawing was believed a surer guide to the artist's personal style than painting, which by its finish obscured the most revealing—because unstudied—traits of its creator. In its informality a drawing afforded a revelation of the workings of the artist's imagination; as a direct link between mind and hand, it revealed the very steps of the creative process.

These attitudes continue to inform the critical appreciation of drawing in our own day. The calligraphy of the draftsman is considered, like handwriting, a key to his personality. But in the 20th century the distinction between drawing and painting is no longer as insistent. The development of modern styles of painting, with their stress on spontaneity and open process, has witnessed the application to painting of creative approaches and critical concepts hitherto applied primarily to drawing.

DAVID ROSAND, *Columbia University*

Bibliography

Catalogs of art museum collections are a major source of information on masters of drawing and individual works. Of particular importance are the catalogs of the Royal Library at Windsor Castle, the Department of Prints and Drawings in the British Museum, and the Fogg Art Museum, Cambridge, Mass.
Berenson, Bernard, *The Drawings of the Florentine Painters* (Chicago 1938).
Blake, Vernon, *The Art and Craft of Drawing* (London 1927).
Borsook, Eve, *The Mural Painters of Tuscany* (London 1960).
Hill, Edward, *The Language of Drawing* (Englewood Cliffs, N.J., 1966).
Hutter, Heribert, *Drawing: History and Technique* (London 1968).
McGraw-Hill, "Drawing," *Encyclopedia of World Art*, vol. 4 (New York 1961).
Mendelowitz, Daniel M., *Drawing* (New York 1967).
Pope, Arthur, *The Language of Painting and Drawing* (Cambridge, Mass., 1949).
Reitlinger, Henry S., *Old Master Drawings, a Handbook for Amateurs and Collectors* (London 1922).
Rosenberg, Jakob, *Great Draughtsmen from Pisanello to Picasso* (Cambridge, Mass., 1959).
Scheller, Robert W., *A Survey of Medieval Model Books* (Haarlem, the Netherlands, 1963).
Tietze, Hans, *European Master Drawings in the United States* (New York 1947).
Tietze, Hans, and Tietze-Conrat, Erika, *The Drawings of the Venetian Painters in the 15th and 16th Centuries* (New York 1944).
Tolnay, Charles de, *History and Technique of Old Master Drawings* (New York 1943).
Watrous, James, *The Craft of Old-Master Drawings* (Madison, Wis., 1957).

DRAWING, Engineering, the representation of the ideas of the architect, designer, and engineer through a standard graphic language of lines, geometric shapes, and symbols. Because the draftsman uses a number of mechanical instruments in engineering drawing, it is often called *mechanical drawing*. Engineering drawings are used mostly to communicate the ideas of the architect, designer, and engineer to the manufacturer and assembler, but they are also used in illustrations for the layman. In engineering drawing there are two fundamental methods of shape representation: pictorial and orthographic.

PICTORIAL DRAWING

One of the most common ways of representing an object, particularly for and by the layman, is by a pictorial drawing. In this type of drawing the object is shown three-dimensionally, similar to the way it appears to the eye. The television set in Fig. 1. is drawn pictorially. Generally, pictorial drawing has limited value in the fabrication of objects, but it is widely used for display, general design, and technical illustrations. There are three types of pictorial drawings: axonometric, oblique, and perspective.

Axonometric Projection. Of the three types of axonometric projection, *isometric* is the most commonly used because it is the easiest to draw. While *dimetric* and *trimetric* drawings usually are more pleasing to the eye than isometric drawings, the difference does not usually warrant the additional time required to make them.

Isometric Projection. In isometric drawings, objects must be visualized so that an axis is formed at one corner of the object. (See Fig. 2.) The height, width, and depth (H, W, D) axis lines are set 120° apart. Where the edges of an object are mutually perpendicular, as in the case of the illustrated television set, they will fall in the drawing on the isometric axis or on lines parallel to the axis lines.

The primary advantage of isometric drawing is that all measurements are easily made, in the desired scale, on the appropriate *isometric lines* (lines on or parallel to the axis lines). Conse-

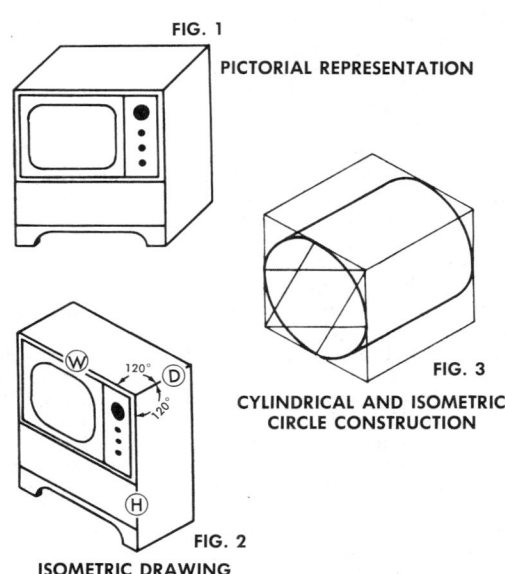

FIG. 1
PICTORIAL REPRESENTATION

FIG. 3
CYLINDRICAL AND ISOMETRIC CIRCLE CONSTRUCTION

FIG. 2
ISOMETRIC DRAWING

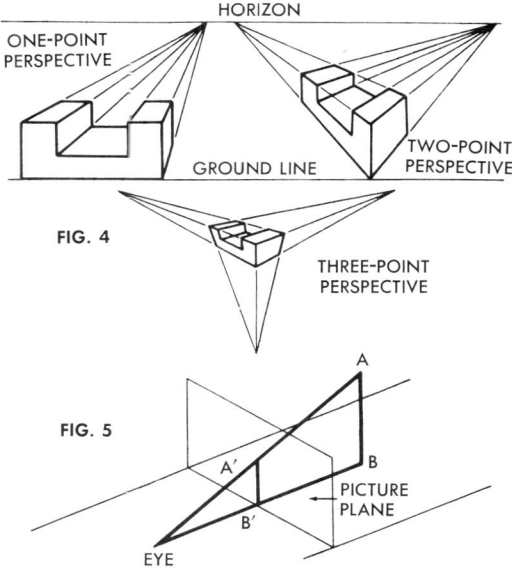

FIG. 4

FIG. 5

one half the full size, is more common. The television set in Fig. 1. is a cabinet drawing.

Perspective Drawing. The most difficult to draw of all the pictorial drawings is perspective. Perspective drawing is used extensively in architectural work, since it is a representation which depicts more nearly the object as an observer sees it. For example, as rails on a railroad track seem to converge, the further away they are from the eye, the receding parallel edges of an object are represented by lines that converge in a perspective drawing. Vanishing points are used to direct the receding lines. Depending on how the object is viewed, the drawing may have a one-, two-, or three-point perspective. (See Fig. 4.) In a perspective drawing the lines of sight intersect the picture plane in line with the object. (See Fig. 5.)

ORTHOGRAPHIC PROJECTION

Orthographic views are derived by imagining that the eye of the observer is at an infinite distance from the object so that the lines of sight are

quently, the size of an object can be ascertained by measuring the height, width, and depth on the extension of the axes. Measurements for the location of other lines and geometric shapes that make up the object must be made on isometric lines.

Some objects, such as cylinders, do not have mutually perpendicular edges. They require the construction of *nonisometric lines* (lines not on or parallel to the axis lines) and *isometric circles*. The ends of cylinders, for example, are drawn as isometric circles and require a unique four-centered construction. (See Fig. 3.) Arcs and semicircles are drawn using appropriate portions of an isometric circle.

Dimetric and Trimetric Projections. The basic difference between these and isometric projection is in the axis angle. In isometric projection, all three of the angles are equal (120°), in dimetric projection two of its angles are equal. In trimetric projection, all the axis angles are different. Also, depending on the object and the angles used, the axis lines are foreshortened in various ratios.

Oblique Projection. An object that has most of its important detail on one of its sides can be shown better in an oblique drawing than in an axonometric drawing. In oblique projection the principal side is placed parallel to the picture plane and perpendicular to the line of sight. The television set in Fig. 1. is an oblique drawing. Oblique projection permits the primary surface and the surfaces parallel to it to be drawn in their true size (to scale) and shape. Depending on other desirable features to be shown, the receding axis is drawn to the left or right and up or down at an angle between 0° and 90° with the horizontal axis.

There are two types of oblique drawings: *cavalier* and *cabinet*. In a cavalier drawing the receding axis is usually drawn at a 45° angle to the picture plane and is extended to the full depth. Since the full depth often makes the proportions of the object appear distorted, cabinet drawing, in which the depth is drawn to only

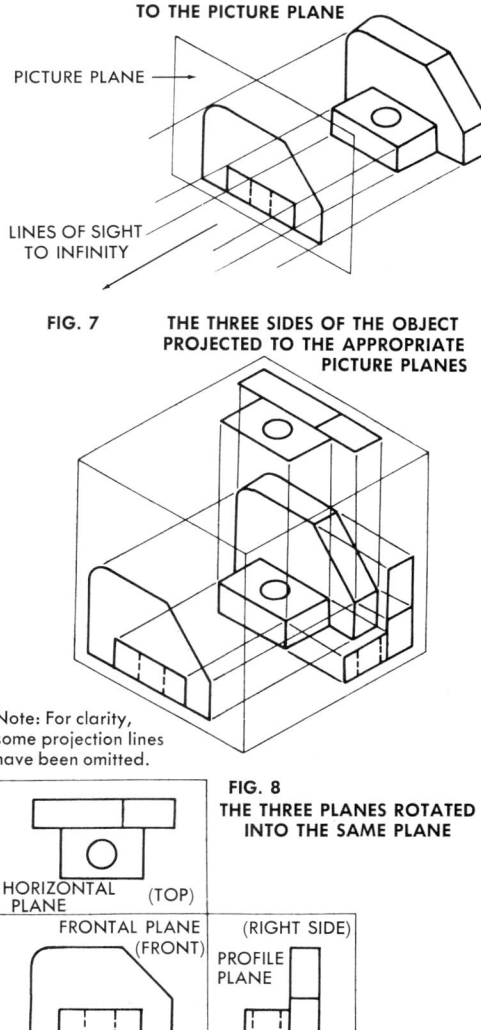

FIG. 6 LINES OF SIGHT AND PROJECTION TO THE PICTURE PLANE

FIG. 7 THE THREE SIDES OF THE OBJECT PROJECTED TO THE APPROPRIATE PICTURE PLANES

Note: For clarity, some projection lines have been omitted.

FIG. 8 THE THREE PLANES ROTATED INTO THE SAME PLANE

perpendicular to the object and to the picture plane. (See Fig. 6.) The points at which the lines of sight intersect the picture plane are then connected to form an image of the object in true size and shape. Drawings of the other sides of the object can be made in the same way on picture planes placed parallel to each side. (See Fig. 7.) The different sides, when represented in mutually perpendicular picture planes, can be rotated into one plane while maintaining their particular relationships to each other. (See Fig. 8.) Usually it is necessary to draw only three or fewer views to illustrate an object adequately. While three views are common, the number of views necessary to illustrate is determined by the complexity of the object. Objects that have little thickness, such as sprockets and gaskets, can be represented in a single view. Cylindrical objects usually require only two views.

In orthographic drawing the object is represented by solid lines, called *visible object lines*, and broken lines, called, *invisible object lines*. Each view of the object must show all edges. When these edges are visible to the viewer, they are drawn as solid lines, and where invisible edges exist, they are represented by broken lines. (See Fig. 8.)

Auxiliary Views. Occasionally an object has an inclined, or slanted, surface that must be shown in its true size and shape. Projection to any one of the principal planes will not provide this effect because the surface is not parallel to any of the planes. Therefore it is necessary to introduce an auxiliary picture plane that is parallel to the inclined surface. The projection lines are then perpendicular to the plane, and a true size and shape representation of the surface is possible. (See Fig. 9.) The size and shape of these inclined surfaces are obtained from measurements in those

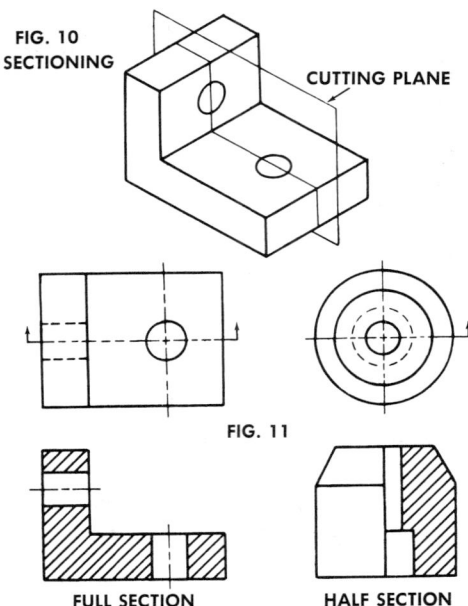

FIG. 10 SECTIONING

FIG. 11

FULL SECTION   HALF SECTION

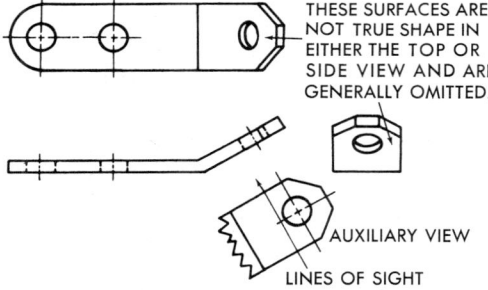

FIG. 9   AUXILIARY PROJECTION

THESE SURFACES ARE NOT TRUE SHAPE IN EITHER THE TOP OR SIDE VIEW AND ARE GENERALLY OMITTED.

AUXILIARY VIEW
LINES OF SIGHT

views where true line lengths can be determined. Generally, an auxiliary view depicts only the inclined surface without attempting to illustrate the remaining portion, which then does not appear in its true shape.

Sectional Views. Many manufactured objects contain unusual internal shapes that cannot be shown adequately through the use of "invisible" lines. In such instances, a sectional view is created. Sectional views are obtained by passing an imaginary cutting plane through the object where the internal ambiguity exists. (See Fig. 10.) The internal shape of the object along this cutting plane is then projected onto a picture plane in the same way that other orthographic views are derived.

On the drawing itself, the internal solid areas passed through by the cutting plane are designated with *crosshatching* or *section lining*. These are closely spaced solid lines drawn on an angle (usually 45°). When a material is specified for the object, a standard symbol may be used instead of the conventional section lining. The areas that are open spaces are left clear. Hidden edges are not represented.

In sectional drawings, one of the normal views (top, front, or side) is replaced by the sectional view. Very often assembly drawings contain sectional views to show more clearly how an object is assembled.

Depending on where the cutting plane is made to pass, various types of sectional representations are obtained: full section, half section, revolved and removed section, offset section or broken-out section. (See Fig. 11.)

Dimensioning. The manufacture of any item requires that specific and exact dimensions be given to each part in a way that is clear and concise. Both fractional and decimal numbering

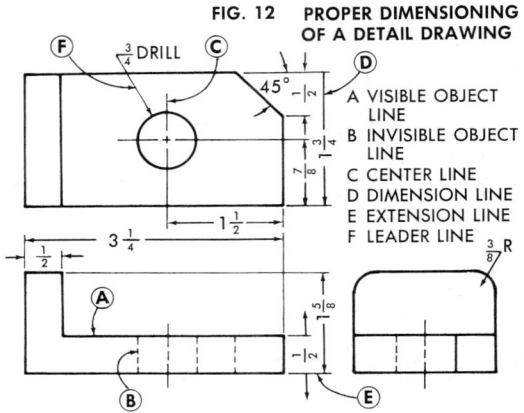

FIG. 12   PROPER DIMENSIONING OF A DETAIL DRAWING

A VISIBLE OBJECT LINE
B INVISIBLE OBJECT LINE
C CENTER LINE
D DIMENSION LINE
E EXTENSION LINE
F LEADER LINE

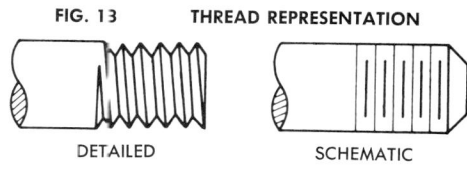

FIG. 13   THREAD REPRESENTATION
DETAILED   SCHEMATIC

systems are used, and unless measurements are given in feet and inches, the inch mark (″) is omitted. Dimensions are situated on *dimension lines* so that they can be read from the horizontal or on the right side of the drawing. (See Fig. 12.) Measurements for circular shapes are given in diameters, and for arcs in radii. Locating the center of such objects is done from center lines and from edges of the object. *Notes* and *leaders* are also used to specify dimensional information that cannot be specified conventionally.

Alphabet of Lines. As part of the graphic language, a number of different lines and line weights are employed. Most of them are illustrated in Fig. 12.

Production Drawings. Production, or working, drawings are of two types: *detail* and *assembly*. They are used in product fabrication. A detail drawing contains all of the essential information required to manufacture the individual part, while the assembly drawing depicts how all the parts are interrelated and how each part functions within the product.

Fastening Devices. The assembly of most products requires the use of fastening devices such as screws, nails, rivets, washers, and pins, which must be illustrated. Screw and screw threads, for example, are numerous and diverse in both construction and use. The most common thread profile is the *American National*. (See Fig. 13.) It is available in three series: National Coarse (NC), National Fine (NF), and National Extra Fine (NEF). The series designation represents the number of threads per inch and the diameter of the shaft. The degree of tightness between two mating parts is the *class of fit* of a thread. On a drawing the screw thread is designated by a note, such as ¼–20 NC–1A. This is interpreted as:

¼ nominal size (diameter in inches)
20 number of threads per inch
NC thread series (National Coarse)
1A class of fit

With this information the draftsman can make either a detailed or schematic representation of the threads.

Drafting Tools. The draftsman uses a number of tools to make the various drawings. Drawing boards, T squares, and triangles are used in making various vertical, horizontal, and angular lines. Compasses are used for drawing circles and arcs. Dividers and scales are used for measurements. Templates and other aids are used to produce an accurate engineering drawing.

MARSHALL A. BUTLER
Montclair State College, N. J.

Further Reading: French, Thomas E., and Vierck, Charles J., *Fundamentals of Engineering Drawing* (New York 1966); Giachino, Joseph W., and Beukema, Henry J., *Engineering: Technical Drafting and Graphics* (Chicago 1966); Hoelscher, Randolph P., and Springer, Clifford H., *Engineering Drawing and Geometry* (New York 1961).

DRAWING, Mechanical. See DRAWING, ENGINEERING.

DRAYTON, Michael (1563–1631), English poet, who wrote a large body of work in a great variety of poetic styles. He was not a major poet, but his achievements give him a position of more than merely historical interest.

Life. Drayton was born at Hartshill, in Shakespeare's native county of Warwickshire, but little more is known of his early life. He served as a page in the household of Sir Henry Goodere and seems not to have attended a university. After going to London he wrote briefly for the stage, but little of his dramatic work has survived. Throughout most of his productive life he benefited from the generosity of noble patrons, chief among them Lucy, Countess of Bedford. His acquaintances in London literary circles included Shakespeare, Jonson, Chapman, Walton, and Selden. Drayton died in London and was buried in Westminster Abbey.

Works. Drayton's poetry is essentially Elizabethan in style and conception, although some response to new poetic fashions may be noted in his work after 1612. His earliest publication, *The Harmony of the Church* (1591), a series of metrical paraphrases of the Scriptures, was followed by a group of eclogues, *Idea: The Shepherd's Garland* (1593); a sonnet sequence, *Idea's Mirror* (1594); a historical epic, *Mortimeriados* (1596; revised and published as *The Barons' Wars*, 1603); and a set of fictional letters, *England's Heroical Epistles* (1597).

In 1605, Drayton published his *Poems Lyric and Pastoral*, including the stirring *Ballad of Agincourt*, and in 1612 the first part of his massive *Polyolbion*, a topographical poem celebrating the English countryside and its history and legends. He continued to write sonnets, including the exquisite one beginning "Since there's no help, come let us kiss and part," which dates from 1619. The completed *Polyolbion* appeared in 1622, and his folkloristic fairy poem *Nymphidia* in 1627. In the verse epistle *Of Poets and Poetry* (1627), Drayton expressed judgments on his artistic predecessors and contemporaries.

FRANK J. WARNKE, *Coeditor of
"Seventeenth Century Prose and Poetry"*

Further Reading: Elton, Oliver, *Michael Drayton: A Critical Study* (London 1905); Newdigate, Bernard H., *Michael Drayton and His Circle* (New York 1941).

DRAYTON, William Henry (1742–1779), American Revolutionary leader. Descended from two prominent South Carolina families, he was born near Charleston, S. C., in September 1742, and was educated in England. He defended British colonial policy after his return to South Carolina, but later became an advocate of independence. He was suspended from the governor's council of South Carolina in 1775 for protesting British appointments to posts in the colony, and as chief justice of South Carolina in 1776–1779 he actively stirred the Carolinas to revolution. Drayton also was president of the provincial congress of South Carolina (1775) and a member of the Continental Congress (1778–1779). He died in Philadelphia on Sept. 3, 1779.

John Drayton (1766–1822), his son, was twice governor of South Carolina (1800–1802 and 1808–1810) and was a federal judge from 1812 to 1822. He was influential in establishing South Carolina College (now the University of South Carolina). He completed and published his father's memoirs of the American Revolutionary period (1821).

DREAM ALLEGORY, a medieval poetic convention that was used to present symbolic visions to give them authority and plausibility. *The Romance of the Rose, The Pearl, Piers Plowman,* and Chaucer's *Parliament of Fowls* are typical works that use the "framing" device of a dreamer-hero who lies down to rest and then sees the allegorical vision in his sleep. The dreams have prophetic meaning, according to Biblical tradition and on the authority of Macrobius' *Commentary on the Dream of Scipio* (about 400 A.D.), an influential medieval work.

The usual setting of a dream allegory of love is the outdoors in springtime. Through the dreamer's vision we enter a fictional world with a natural transition in consciousness. Certain works, such as Bunyan's *Pilgrim's Progress,* point specifically to a dream; others, such as Dante's *Divine Comedy,* only suggest it. Dream allegory survives today more as an atmosphere, as in Kafka's *Metamorphosis,* than as a specific psychological device. See also ALLEGORY.

ANGUS FLETCHER, *Author of*
"Allegory: The Theory of a Symbolic Mode"

DREAM OF THE RED CHAMBER is the title of a great Chinese novel written in the 18th century by Ts'ao Hsüeh-ch'in. Like *War and Peace* and *The Tale of Genji,* the *Dream of the Red Chamber* is a prodigious detailing of an entire civilization. The characters, especially Chia Pao-yü, the princely hero surrounded by adoring women, are described with such psychological truth that the huge novel comes to possess a hallucinatory reality, and the final downfall of Pao-yü as he vanishes into the mists wearing the robes of a Buddhist monk comes to the reader as a personal tragedy. There are some 400 characters, all sharply distinguished and made memorable by the novelist's remarkable insight into human character.

Ts'ao Hsüeh-ch'in (also called Ts'ao Chan) came from a distinguished Chinese family long connected with the Manchu army and the court. Born about 1719, he grew up in Nanking, where his grandfather, who held the lucrative post of silk commissioner and was well-known as a bibliophile and a poet, held a small court of his own. Two of the grandfather's daughters had married into the ruling family, and when the emperor visited Nanking, he would stay in the Ts'ao family palace. Ts'ao Hsüeh-ch'in grew up in luxury, but the family fortunes dwindled after the grandfather's death.

When he was about 30 and living in Peking, Ts'ao Hsüeh-ch'in began to write a poetic drama describing the decay of a great family, evidently his own. This idea was later abandoned, and the drama was converted into a novel that was left unfinished at his death on the eve of the Chinese New Year in 1763. He had written 80 chapters, and from his notes others constructed the remaining 40 chapters. The first complete edition was printed in 1791.

The title *Dream of the Red Chamber* is a direct translation from the Chinese title *Hung Lou Mêng.* It has been translated in part by Bancroft Joly (1892–1893), Wang Chichen (1958), and Fritz Kuhn (1958).

ROBERT PAYNE
Editor of "The White Pony, an Anthology
of Chinese Poetry"

Further Reading: Wu Shih-ch'ang, *On the Red Chamber Dream* (London 1961).

DREAMS are ordinarily sequences of images that are experienced by the mind during sleep. For thousands of years they were regarded as divine visitations or prophecies, wanderings of the soul, or even actual events. Only in the late 19th century were dreams first scrutinized carefully and systematically.

Freud. The first comprehensive scientific study of dreams was begun by Sigmund Freud (q.v.), the founder of psychoanalysis, in the 1890's. It culminated in the publication of Freud's *Die Traumdeutung* (1900; Eng. tr., *The Interpretation of Dreams,* 1913). This volume, revised and enlarged several times during Freud's life, remains the classic in the field. Following a scholarly survey of previous literature on dreams, it presents Freud's views on their functions, sources, and formation, and describes a method of interpreting them.

According to Freud, dreams have two principal functions: to attempt to fulfill repressed, unconscious wishes, mainly sexual and aggressive in character, and to guard sleep. Because the expression of reprehensible sexual and aggressive desires, even in fantasy, is almost certain to arouse anxiety in the sleeper and thus awaken him, the wishes must express themselves in disguised form in order to protect sleep. Such a disguise is accomplished by distorting the underlying dream thoughts in various ways: by condensation, the fusing of various dream thoughts in a single image; by displacement of a disturbing emotion from its source to a neutral object; and by symbolization. The result is a distorted and symbolic representation (what Freud termed the *manifest content* of the dream) of an unconscious wish (the *latent content*). The disguise is not always perfectly effective, however, and anxiety dreams do occur. In fact, most dreams that are remembered are unpleasant; thus dreams often do not succeed in their function of protecting sleep.

Freud held that the contents of dreams consist of memories but that the stimulus for a dream is always an unconscious wish that has its origin in childhood. To identify the infantile wish one must unravel the distortions and decode the symbols, in addition to winnowing out the *secondary elaboration,* material introduced by the dreamer in the process of remembering the dream in order to increase its coherence. The interpretation is accomplished by dividing the dream into its constituent parts; then the subject reports whatever he immediately associates with each of the elements. By this free association, the dream as it is remembered is translated into the latent dream thoughts. Freud considered dreams "the royal road to the unconscious," and the interpretation of dreams is one of the chief tools used by psychoanalysts in the treatment of patients.

Jung. A second illustrious investigator of dreams was Carl Jung (q.v.). Like Freud, Jung analyzed the dreams of his patients in order to explore the otherwise inaccessible regions of the unconscious mind, and he too believed that dreams are largely symbolic. Jung's view of the function of dreams—compensation for aspects of the dreamer's personality that have been neglected in his conscious life—does not differ substantially from Freud's wish-fulfillment theory. The principal difference between their theories is that, whereas Freud ascribed dreams to infantile wishes, Jung held that they originate in the inborn thought patterns (or *archetypes*) of a racial unconscious common to all mankind. These archetypes are symbolically represented in dreams not for disguise but because they can express themselves only through symbols. For Jung, dreams attempt to reveal rather than to conceal what is in the unconscious mind. Because archetypes are imperfectly realized in dreams, one must find all possible meanings of an archetypal symbol to arrive at the true meaning of a dream. Jungians make much use of mythology, comparative religion, and history in interpreting symbols.

Physiology of Dreaming—REM Sleep. Although Freud and Jung, by subjecting dreams to scientific study, were instrumental in salvaging them from the superstitions that had surrounded them, their influence was largely limited to the use of dream interpretation in psychoanalysis. Dreams were not studied in the scientific laboratory on any large scale until 1953, when Nathaniel Kleitman and Eugene Aserinsky, at the University of Chicago, reported a momentous observation they had made while watching the eye movements of sleepers. They observed that series of bursts of rapid eye movements occurred about four to six times during the night. The first such rapid eye movement (REM) period took place about an hour after the beginning of sleep and lasted from five to ten minutes. Succeeding REM periods occurred at intervals of about 90 minutes each and lasted progressively longer, the last occupying about 30 minutes. About one fifth of an adult's typical sleep is REM sleep; the percentage is much higher in infants and perhaps somewhat lower in the elderly. Animals of many kinds also have REM periods during their sleep.

Suspecting a correlation of eye movements with dreaming, Kleitman and Aserinsky awakened subjects during REM periods and asked them whether they had been dreaming. In a large majority of such awakenings, the subjects said that they had been dreaming and proceeded to relate their dreams. When a subject was awakened while his eyes were quiescent, he could rarely remember a dream. Kleitman and Aserinsky concluded that rapid eye movements are an objective sign of dreaming. Thus, although investigators still had to rely upon the dreamer's verbal report to learn the content of his dream, the process of dreaming could now be studied objectively under laboratory conditions.

This discovery stimulated extensive research on the physiological aspects of REM sleep. Among the earliest discoveries was that of a characteristic brain wave pattern accompanying REM sleep. This pattern is distinguished by fast, low-voltage waves, not unlike those that occur in the waking state but very different from the slower, high-voltage waves of non-REM sleep. During REM sleep, breathing and pulse rates are more irregular than during non-REM sleep, suggesting emotional disturbance; there is a relaxation of the head and neck muscles; and, in men, the penis becomes partially or fully erect. This last observation has been interpreted by some investigators as supporting Freud's contention that many dreams are sexual in character.

Studies of the relationship of the subject matter of dreams to physiological changes during REM periods have not established any close correlations. Although early investigations indicated that the pattern of eye movements is correlated with the directions in which the dreamer dreams he is looking, recent evidence raises serious doubt concerning this "scanning" hypothesis.

Moreover, there is now fairly strong evidence that dreaming can sometimes occur during non-REM periods. This suggests that dreaming may be more or less continuous during sleep, but that conditions for the recall of dreams are more favorable following REM awakenings than otherwise. In any case, the prevailing view is that rapid eye movements are not an objective sign of all dreaming, but that they reliably indicate when a dream is most likely to be remembered.

The Need to Dream. The discovery of a stage of sleep during which most dreaming seems to take place made it interesting to see what would happen when a sleeping person was deprived of REM sleep. This was accomplished by awakening subjects whenever their eyes began to move. Depriving a person of REM periods for several consecutive nights affects sleep in two ways. First, the number of times the eyes begin to move during the night is greatly increased. This means that the subject has to be awakened more often on each successive night of REM deprivation in order to obliterate REM sleep. Second, when the subject is finally allowed to sleep undisturbed, the proportion of time spent in REM sleep is greatly increased for several nights until the deficit is made up.

These two findings indicate that there is an imperious demand for REM sleep. Because REM sleep usually accompanies dreaming, it was also concluded from these studies that there is a strong need to dream. If dreaming is a kind of safety valve permitting the discharge of tensions from unfulfilled wishes, as Freud said, or is compensatory for neglected aspects of the personality, as Jung believed, then REM deprivation should cause the REM-deprived person to manifest disturbed waking behavior as the deprivation continues night after night. Early studies of prolonged REM deprivation seemed to support this inference dramatically. The waking behavior of some subjects underwent striking abnormal changes. It was assumed that if REM deprivation were continued long enough, the subject would become insane. However, later studies with prolonged deprivation have not confirmed the degree of the behavioral changes noted earlier; so this basic question is not settled. There is definitely a need for REM sleep, but whether there is also a need to dream is still in doubt.

Remembering Dreams. By using an electroencephalograph to monitor sleep during the night and by awakening subjects during REM periods, it has been conclusively established that everyone normally dreams every night. Even a person who has never in his life remembered a dream will do so if he is awakened during a REM period.

It is believed that dreams are remembered more accurately immediately after awakening during the night than they are in the morning. For example, color in dreams has been reported as much more often recalled after laboratory awakenings than on the following mornings. It has been suggested that dreams are always in color but that the color is forgotten by morning. No one has yet determined the meaning of color in dreams or its possible relationship to personality traits.

It is uncertain to what extent dreams collected under laboratory conditions are truly representative of normal dream life. That the experimental setting influences what a subject dreams about for the first few nights he sleeps in the laboratory is indicated by dream references to the experiment and the sleep laboratory, but the effect soon wears off. However, laboratory dreams appear to be more prosaic than those remembered under home conditions. This may be due to selective recall of the more dramatic dreams at home, to an inhibitory effect exercised by the laboratory situation, or to both factors.

Analysis of Dreams. New methods of collecting dreams have given rise to new methods of analyzing them. The Freudian method of free association and the Jungian method of amplification are suitable to psychoanalysis, where the analyst has lengthy contact with the patient and much information about him. However, these methods are less well adapted to analyzing large numbers of dreams collected from nonpatient populations.

The principal method employed in analyzing reported dreams, whether collected in the laboratory or at home, is content analysis. This consists of classifying the various elements that appear in dreams. Most dreams contain references to people, animals, and physical objects with which the dreamer interacts. These elements are divided into classes such as males and females; familiar persons and strangers; aggressive, friendly, and sexual interactions; and objects such as conveyances, buildings, implements, clothing, and so forth. Content analysis can be used to determine similarities and differences among groups of people differing in age, sex, ethnic background, and mental and physical health. For example, it has been found that male dreamers dream much more about other males than about females, whereas women dream about equally often of both sexes. Male dreamers have proportionately more aggressive and fewer friendly interactions with other males in their dreams, and fewer aggressive and more friendly interactions with females. Female dreamers, on the other hand, have about equal proportions of aggression and friendliness with males and with females. In another study, it was shown that a distinctive feature of male mental patients' dreams is a high proportion of hostility toward females.

Other experiments have involved the use of content analysis and the electroencephalograph to study the effects on dreams of films shown just prior to sleep. Presentations of stimuli such as names of persons known to the dreamer have been made during REM periods to determine how such stimuli affect dream content. Experiments on mental telepathy have also been facilitated by the electroencephalographic method of retrieving dreams during the night.

Understanding of dreams has been greatly advanced in the 20th century by the analytic work of Freud and Jung and the discovery of REM sleep by Kleitman and Aserinsky. No longer are dreams regarded as messages sent by gods or ancestors. Today they are being studied scientifically to learn more about man's nature.

CALVIN S. HALL
University of California, Santa Cruz

Bibliography
Freud, Sigmund, *The Standard Edition of the Complete Psychological Works of Sigmund Freud:* vols. 4-5, *The Interpretation of Dreams,* tr. and ed. by James Strachey (New York and London 1953).
Hall, Calvin S., *The Meaning of Dreams* (New York 1966).
Hall, Calvin S., and Van de Castle, Robert L., *The Content Analysis of Dreams* (New York 1966).
Jung, Carl G., *Collected Works:* vol. 8, *The Structure and Dynamics of the Psyche,* tr. by Richard F. C. Hull, ed. by Herbert Read and others (New York 1960).
Kleitman, Nathaniel, *Sleep and Wakefulness,* rev. ed. (Chicago 1963).

DRED SCOTT CASE, formally *Scott v. Sandford,* a decision of the U. S. Supreme Court on March 6, 1857, which involved the freedom of a slave and, in the process of decision, considered such questions as slavery in the territories and the status of persons of African descent. In denying Scott his freedom all nine justices delivered opinions, and accordingly there is some doubt as to just what the court did decide.

Background. In 1832, John Emerson, an army surgeon of St. Louis, Mo., purchased the Negro slave Dred Scott. Scott accompanied Emerson to posts in Missouri, Illinois, and the Minnesota territory. In Minnesota he married, and his wife gave birth to their first child in free territory. Scott then returned with Emerson to St. Louis, and after the latter's death in 1843, he sought freedom for himself and his family, first unsuccessfully through purchase and then in the Missouri courts, beginning in 1846.

The Case in Court. Scott's lawyers maintained that residency in the free state of Illinois had liberated him, as had his stay in Minnesota, according to a provision of the Missouri Compromise (q.v.) of 1820 prohibiting slavery in territories north of 36°30' north latitude. The attorneys for Mrs. Emerson, who had inherited Scott, countered that he was subject to Missouri law upon his return to the state. After losing the initial trial, Scott won a retrial, but the latter verdict was overruled by the state supreme court in 1852.

Undaunted, Scott's lawyers succeeded in shifting the case into the federal district court in 1853. With Mrs. Emerson's remarriage, the administration of her late husband's estate was turned over to her brother, John Sanford of New York. Scott, asserting Missouri citizenship, sued Sanford for assault, and Sanford (his name is misspelled in the reports) became the defendant in the famous Dred Scott case.

Sanford's lawyers challenged the federal court's jurisdiction on the basis that Scott could not be a citizen because he was descended from Africans sold into slavery. Judge Robert Wells upheld Scott's claim to citizenship; yet his charge to the jury was such that it found Sanford not guilty and Scott still Sanford's slave.

This verdict in 1854 caused Scott's counsel to move for a writ of error to the U. S. Supreme Court. Due to a backlog of business the case was not heard until February 1856, and in December it was reargued by decision of the court on a point involving Scott's citizenship.

Political Controvery. As a legal quest for freedom, *Scott v. Sandford* had numerous precedents before the Supreme Court, dating back to 1806. What made this case so controversial were the political circumstances surrounding it. The question of congressional authority to prohibit slavery in the territories, once considered settled by the Missouri Compromise, had been reopened by the acquisition of land from Mexico and the polarization of proslavery and antislavery forces in Congress. The Compromise of 1850 and the Kansas-Nebraska Act (qq.v.), which repealed the Missouri Compromise, only intensified the debate. The violence in Kansas between proslavery and antislavery factions known as "Bleeding Kansas" brought matters to the boiling point, and some politicians looked to the Supreme Court to produce a solution where Congress had failed.

Among those who sought a definitive pronouncement was the president-elect of 1856,

James Buchanan. In his inaugural address on March 4, 1857, Buchanan predicted that the Supreme Court would shortly lay to rest the question of slavery in the territories. Two days later the Dred Scott case was decided, but the issue remained unsettled.

Maneuvering on the Court. Buchanan's prediction was promoted not only by advance information but also by his personal appeal to Justice Robert Grier, a fellow Pennsylvanian, to agree that the court should act as final arbiter of the great political questions. The court apparently had been ready to decide the case on the basis of an 1851 precedent, *Strader* v. *Graham,* which simply meant adherence to findings of state courts when a slave's status was involved, and Justice Samuel Nelson was to deliver this opinion. As matters turned out, however, the nine justices wrote individual opinions considering different aspects of the case. The crucial step of attempting to settle the political crisis seems to have been taken because of Grier's vote, but the announced intention of Justices John McLean and Benjamin R. Curtis to dissent from the original plan of following *Strader* v. *Graham* and raise the substantive question was instrumental in causing this change of mind.

The Opinions. Chief Justice Roger B. Taney's opinion, delivered as that of the court, is the most controversial. He maintained that the federal courts lacked jurisdiction because no Negro could be a citizen under the Constitution. Nevertheless, Taney considered all aspects of Scott's case. Because the due process clause of the 5th Amendment protected the right of slaveowners to bring their property into the territories, the antislavery clause of the Missouri Compromise was void. Furthermore, residence in Illinois had not freed Scott because his voluntary return to Missouri made him subject to that state's law.

Nelson and five other justices wrote opinions sustaining Scott's servitude and agreeing in varying degrees with Taney. The two dissenters also differed in their emphasis. McLean held that Scott was free because of his residence in both Illinois and Minnesota, while Curtis, in what essentially was a point-by-point refutation of Taney's opinion, stressed Scott's stay in Minnesota and the authority of Congress to prohibit slavery in the territories.

Implications. *Scott* v. *Sandford* determined the status of Dred Scott, but was inconclusive on the relevant controversies. However, most people believed the court had sustained the proslavery position. Accordingly, the infant Republican party, which was based on opposition to the extension of slavery, vigorously attacked the decision and the court. Proslavery elements in the Democratic party supported the decision, and many Democrats who favored Stephen A. Douglas' popular sovereignty doctrine left the party. (Douglas himself remained loyal.)

In this sense the Dred Scott case, rather than smoothing political controversy, accentuated it and indirectly helped bring on the Civil War. As for the central figure in the controversy, Scott was manumitted with his family on May 26, 1857, after the death of Sanford, but he died of consumption in St. Louis on Sept. 17, 1858.

DONALD M. ROPER
State University College, New Paltz, N. Y.

Further Reading: Hopkins, Vincent C., *Dred Scott's Case* (New York 1951); Kutler, Stanley I., *The Dred Scott Decision: Law or Politics?* (Boston 1967).

DREDGE, a barge or other vessel equipped for digging mud, sand, rock, and other deposits from the bottoms of waterways. The major purpose of dredging is to maintain clear channels for water transportation, which is essential for the movement of bulk cargoes. Dredging is necessary because rivers deposit silt and because ocean currents deposit sand, blocking channels or making them too shallow for navigation.

Dredging is also used to widen and deepen navigation channels, to dig canals, such as the Suez Canal and the Panama Canal, and to mine under water for sand, gravel, gold, tin, and other minerals.

History. Before the invention of mechanical means to dredge, dikes were built to confine streams so that their currents would be strong enough to carry away sediment and to scour the channel. Also, especially in Europe, tidal basins were built to fill at high tide and to hold the water until low tide so that the flow would scour the channel.

The first primitive dredging equipment was a large leather bag attached to a strong iron hoop (spoon) at the end of a long pole. Dredging with spoon and bag was done by the Chinese and Assyrians to clear their canals, and this method was used for centuries in the Netherlands, England, Italy, and France. For dredging the canals and ditches of the Netherlands, the hoop was forced into the soft bottom material and brought to the surface by means of the long pole, a suspending rope, and a sweep-pole in the boat.

Another dredging method, practiced as early as 1400, was to use a harrow or plow suspended from the bottom of a boat. The harrow loosened the bottom material of harbor entrances so that it would be carried away by the tide.

About 1600 the Dutch developed the "Amsterdam mudmill," entirely made of wood. It consisted of a scow with an inclined gutter or trough through the middle. Silt was moved up the trough by means of boards fitted across it on an endless chain that was driven by a treadmill. Five horses, two pulling and three resting, supplied the power. The Amsterdam mudmill, usable only in quiet waters, could dig to depths of 10 to 15 feet (3–4.5 meters). It could remove 400 tons of mud per day, which was a remarkable production record for a 2-horsepower dredge.

The first recorded use of a bucket dredge, which has an endless chain fitted with buckets instead of boards, was for deepening the Maas River in the Netherlands in 1623. In this kind of mudmill, copper buckets were kept in motion on the chain by using manpower. Later, horsepower was used.

Mudmills were in general use in Europe until the mid-1800's—even after the invention of the steam engine, which made possible the construction of the steam dredge. The first steam dredge, built in 1796, was used in Sunderland Harbor in England. Oliver Evans, an American, built the first steam dredge with a bucket chain in 1805.

In more recent times, steam engines and internal combustion engines have been used to provide the mechanical power for dredging equipment. Another method, first used in the 19th century, is to use pumps to suck up the sand or mud. The Mississippi and Orinoco river entrances and Maracaibo Harbor, for example, are kept open by seagoing dredges that suck up a mixture of bottom material and water and discharge it into the river or ocean currents.

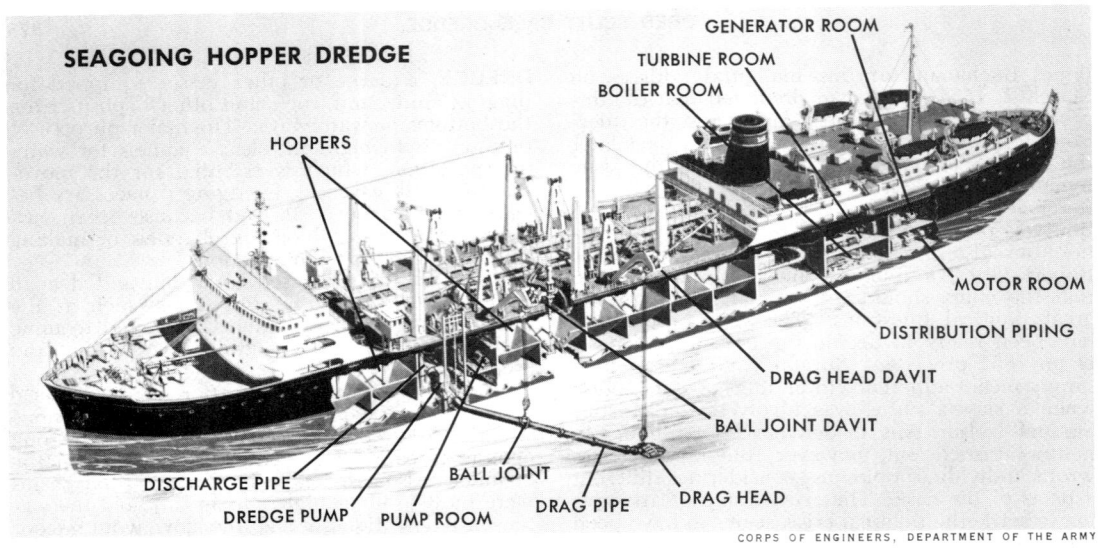

A complete dredging unit in itself, the seagoing hopper dredge collects and discharges sediment hydraulically.

How a Dredge Works. Typically, a dredge is a barge or vessel with some sort of scoop to pick up material and a derricklike mechanism to lift the scoop with its load and to dump it. A complete dredging unit usually consists of the dredge itself, dump scows, tugs to transport the dump scows, a motor launch, fuel and water supply scows, and a derrick to set anchors.

After a dredge is floated over the place where the work is to be done, it is held in position by heavy posts, called *spuds*, that descend through openings in the dredge and rest on the bottom of the waterway. There are usually three spuds, two at the scoop end and one at the stern of the dredge. The spuds, which may reach a length of 70 feet (21 meters), are made of timbers, sometimes 40 inches (102 cm) square, or of extra-heavy pipe. Spuds are pointed to penetrate hard bottoms, and they are fitted with shoes of various areas for soft bottoms. In very soft bottoms, where spuds are ineffective, the dredge is held in position solely by anchors and lines.

After the dredge has removed all of the material that it can reach, the spuds are raised, and the dredge is moved ahead 5 to 10 feet (1.5–3 meters) to the next position by pulling on anchor lines, by placing the dipper ahead and drawing in on it, or by using a tug.

TYPES OF DREDGES

Dredges are of two general classes: *intermittent* and *continuous*. The intermittent class, which includes dipper and grab dredges, operates a single bucket or scoop and alternately digs and lifts the load. The continuous class, including ladder, hydraulic (or suction), and scouring dredges, digs continuously, raising the material at the same time.

Dipper Dredge. The dipper dredge, which digs in the same way as the steam shovel on land, has a single bucket, called a dipper, attached to a long handle. The bucket, usually equipped with teeth, is most effective in firm material, such as compacted sand, clay, or soft layered rock. A dipper dredge can remove 5,000 to 10,000 cubic yards (2,820–7,650 cu meters) of sand per 24-hour day, using a bucket with a capacity of 9 cubic yards (6.9 cu meters). The larger dredges can dredge to a depth of 50 feet (15 meters).

Grab Dredge. The grab dredge has a single bucket suspended by chain or cable from the end of a swinging boom. The bucket has two or more shells or jaws that close and open to load and discharge it. When the bucket has two shells, it is called a *clamshell bucket;* when it has three or more jaws, it is called an *orange-peel bucket.*

The bucket is lowered to the bottom open; its weight causes it to bite into the bottom material and to fill as it is raised and closes. This type of dredge is used primarily for soft material into which the bucket can sink readily. It can be used to dig to great depths simply by increasing the length of the chain or cable.

Ladder Dredge. The ladder dredge consists of a series of small buckets forming an endless chain that moves around an inclined frame called a *ladder*. One end of the ladder is hinged to the dredge superstructure, and the other end is lowered to the bottom. The buckets, which have a capacity up to a cubic yard (0.76 cu meter), receive their loads as they pass the lower end of the ladder and scrape along in the bottom. They discharge their loads into chutes or onto con-

The dipper dredge is most effective in firm material.

DREDGE DIVISION, ELLICOTT MACHINE CORPORATION

veyor belts as they pass over the tumbler at the upper end of the ladder.

Hydraulic Dredge. The hydraulic dredge sucks up material from the bottom by means of a ladder-mounted suction pipe connected to a powerful suction pump. There are two types of hydraulic dredges. In the *swinging-ladder* type, the ladder pivots about the bow of the dredge, which is held stationary by spuds. In the more usual *swinging-dredge* type, the ladder can only be raised or lowered, so the entire dredge is swung about one of two spuds at a time at the stern by using anchors and wires set out from each side and ahead of the dredge. The dredge or the ladder is rotated in order to dig over a broad area.

The dredged material is pumped through a floating line to the shore and from there through shore pipe to the area being filled. Hydraulic dredges, which can pump material to locations as far away as about 10,000 feet (3,000 meters) without booster pumps, are the most economical means of dredging.

Scouring Dredge. The scouring dredge has a submersible harrow or plow that stirs up light, silty bottoms and bars so that the river or ocean currents carry the material to a location where it is unobjectionable.

Seagoing Hopper Dredge. The seagoing hopper dredge has a hull like that of an ocean vessel. This self-propelled dredge is equipped with all of the special apparatus required for dredging material hydraulically, discharging the dredged material into its hoppers, and transporting it to a disposal site at sea, or ashore on occasion. The bottom material is raised by dredge pumps through drag arms, which are part of the suction assembly. The upper ends of the drag arms are connected to the ship, and the lower ends have drags for contact with the bottom. The drag arms are raised and lowered, as required, by hoisting tackle and winches.

The seagoing hopper dredge operates with the drag arms trailing as it moves slowly ahead as a vessel under its own power. Sometimes it operates in a stationary position when dredging for fill material. As pumping continues, the solid particles of material settle in the hoppers, and the excess water passes overboard through troughs. When the hoppers are filled, the drag arms are raised, and the dredge then proceeds at full speed to the dispersal area where the hoppers are emptied.

The largest dredge in the United States is the *Essayons* ("We will try"), named after the motto of the Corps of Engineers, United States Army, which operates it. This seagoing hopper dredge can hold 8,200 cubic yards (6,270 cu meters) of material in its hoppers. The largest dredge in the world is the *Zulia*, owned and operated by Venezuela. It has a 10,000-cubic-yard (7,650-cu-meter) hopper capacity.

J. P. GROENENDYKE, JR.
Consulting Engineer

Bibliography

Dekker, P. M., *Dredging and Dredging Appliances* (New York 1950).
McDaniel, Allan B., *Excavation: Machinery, Methods and Costs* (New York 1919).
Massey, George B., *Engineering of Excavation* (New York 1923).
Simon, Fred L., *Dredging Engineering* (New York 1920).
United States Army, Corps of Engineers, *The Hopper Dredge, Its History, Development and Operation* (Washington 1954).
Veen, Johan van, *Dredge, Drain, Reclaim: The Art of a Nation*, 3d ed. (The Hague 1950).

DREES, drās, **Willem** (1886–), Dutch political leader. He was born on July 5, 1886, in Amsterdam and joined the Dutch Socialist party at an early age. Elected alderman of The Hague in 1913, he entered parliament in 1933 and became leader of his party in the Second Chamber in 1939. When the Germans invaded his country in 1940, he was sent to a concentration camp. Released in 1941, he joined the Dutch resistance.

In 1945, Drees became minister of social affairs and played a decisive role in shaping the social security system. In 1946 he helped to form a non-Marxist Labor party that was to become the basis of his own government in 1948. As prime minister (1948–1958), Drees had to deal with the nationalist revolution in the East Indian colonies, and he was responsible for the transfer of sovereignty to Indonesia in 1949. His European policy strongly favored economic integration. When the Labor government fell in 1958, Drees withdrew from active politics.

JACOB W. SMIT, *Columbia University*

DREISER, drī'sər, **Theodore** (1871–1945), American novelist, who was a pioneer of naturalism in American writing. He sought to free the novel both from Victorian notions of decorum and from the "realistic" literary theory that the novelist's task is simply to reproduce "ordinary" life. Such Dreiser novels as *Sister Carrie* and *An American Tragedy* were both important indictments of the American dream of worldly success and acute appraisals of the individual's agony in a modern, industrialized urban society.

Dreiser defied conventional morality and thus allied himself with the naturalists, who were attacking the canons of a more genteel tradition and addressing themselves to new social problems. Dreiser's naturalism derived from a mechanistic concept of life that sees man as the victim of instincts, social forces, economics, and chance. His philosophy was strongly influenced by Herbert Spencer, who had popularized Darwin's theory of evolution and applied the biological laws of survival to life in the anonymous streets of the city. Dreiser was also influenced by Balzac, often thought to be the precursor of French naturalism.

There is no critical consensus about Dreiser's stature as a novelist. At his best he wrote with

Theodore Dreiser

CULVER

great power; the attention to detail he learned as a reporter served him well when he tried to evoke the urban settings characteristic of his fiction. On the other hand, Dreiser's diction is often annoyingly verbose, and his attempts to explain the psychology of his characters are clumsy and unconvincing. In his later years he moved toward a vague mysticism that emphasized "the endless drag toward nothingness" and that further obscured the point of view in his work.

Life. Dreiser was born in Sullivan, Ind., on Aug. 27, 1871, the ninth of the ten Dreiser children who survived into adulthood. His father was a German immigrant and a Roman Catholic; his mother, the daughter of Mennonites of Czech background. The grim poverty of his childhood, his father's stern Catholicism, and the chronic misadventures of his brothers and sisters were important agents in shaping his naturalistic vision.

In the 1860's Dreiser's father had attempted to establish his own woolen mill, but it was destroyed by fire, and from that point on the family lived a precarious existence. During his childhood, Dreiser lived in numerous towns in Indiana and for a brief time in Chicago. His schooling was erratic, but through the patronage of a former teacher he was able to spend the year 1889–1890 at the University of Indiana.

Dreiser worked at odd jobs before beginning to write for the Chicago *Globe*, in 1892. He soon moved to a better position with the St. Louis *Globe-Democrat*, and subsequently was a reporter for papers in Pittsburgh and New York. In 1895, with the support of his brother Paul (Paul Dresser, a successful songwriter), he began to edit his own magazine, *Ev'ry Month*, but gave this up in 1897 to work as a free-lance writer. In 1898 he married Sara White, a schoolteacher.

In 1899, encouraged by a friend, the editor Arthur Henry, Dreiser began to write the novel *Sister Carrie*. Frank Norris, then a reader for Doubleday, Page & Co., accepted the novel for publication. With its appearance in 1900 began one of the great legends of American literature. Frank Doubleday, the president of the publishing company, returned from a European holiday, read the novel, and immediately disapproved of it; his wife felt even more strongly that it was unsuitable for publication. Consequently, the firm obeyed the letter but not the spirit of their contract; they made no attempt to promote the work, and although 1,000 copies were printed, fewer than 500 were sold.

This disappointment, the death of his parents, the difficulties his brothers and sisters were encountering, the unhappiness of his marriage, and a quarrel with his brother Paul all combined to drive Dreiser to the verge of suicide. In the next few years he worked at a variety of literary jobs, and by 1910 was earning $10,000 a year as editor of three women's magazines. Throughout the remainder of his life he continued to write short stories, plays, poems, travel books, novels, and memoirs. After Sara's death in 1942, he married Helen Richardson, who had long been his companion. Dreiser died in Hollywood, Calif., on Dec. 28, 1945.

Writings. The hallmarks of Dreiser's private life are clearly visible in his fiction. His poverty-stricken childhood unquestionably accounts for the fascination that wealth and power held for him, and he often found inspiration for his plots in his own experiences or those of his brothers and sisters.

Sister Carrie, which was based on the life of one of his sisters, retells the ageless story of an innocent young girl who goes to the city and loses her virtue. It was judged "obscene" by some of its readers, chiefly because Carrie is unpunished for her transgressions and feels no guilt for her conduct. At the conclusion of the novel she is alone and lonely, but this, Dreiser seems to urge, is the condition of the world, particularly the condition of the big city, and not the wages of sin.

Much the same kind of criticism was leveled at *Jennie Gerhardt*, Dreiser's second novel, which did not appear until 1911. It is the story of another of Dreiser's sisters and, like *Sister Carrie*, is a criticism of society more than an indictment of a "fallen woman."

The Financier (1912), *The Titan* (1914), and *The Stoic* (posthumously published in 1947) —the so-called "Cowperwood" trilogy—are minor novels. In *The "Genius"* (1915), an autobiographical novel, Dreiser attempts to equate the longing for sexual satisfaction with the longing for financial success.

The same theme is present in Dreiser's best and most famous novel, *An American Tragedy* (1925). Based on the Gillette-Brown murder case of 1906, it is the story of a young man who sets out to gain entry into the enchanted world of the American dream of success. Driven by passion and ignorance, however, he "accidentally" murders a young woman in order to improve his situation and is executed for the crime. But Dreiser makes it clear that a materialistic society is as much to blame as the murderer himself. See also AMERICAN TRAGEDY.

Dreiser published three books dealing with his travels in Russia and the United States, and an impressive autobiography, *A Book About Myself* (1922). His plays were collected as *Plays of the Natural and Supernatural* (1916) and *The Hand of the Potter* (1918); his short stories appeared in *Free and Other Stories* (1918) and *Chains* (1927); and his poems were collected under the title *Moods, Cadenced and Declaimed* (1926).

DAVID GALLOWAY
Case Western Reserve University

Further Reading: Elias, Robert G., *Theodore Dreiser: Apostle of Nature* (New York 1949); Gerber, Philip, *Theodore Dreiser* (New York 1964); Matthiessen, Francis O., *Theodore Dreiser* (New York 1951).

DRENTHE, dren'tə, is a province in the northeast of the Netherlands, whose boundary on the east forms part of the border with West Germany. It has an area of 1,023 square miles (2,649 sq km). The province consists of a low, undulating plateau, which rises toward the east to the ridge of the Hondsrug plateau. Much of its heathland and peat bogs have been reclaimed, though 30% of the province is classified as waste.

Several small towns, chiefly servicing centers for the surrounding farmlands, include Assen, the administrative center of the province; Meppel, a small port linked by canal to the IJsselmeer; Hoogeveen, an industrial town; and Emmen.

Originally a countship, the area became a part of the bishopric of Utrecht in 1046. In 1536 it passed to the Habsburg Empire under Charles V. It joined the Dutch Republic at the end of the 16th century. Ruled by France from 1795 to 1813, it became a province in the kingdom of the Netherlands in 1814. Population: (1965) 342,280.

F. J. MONKHOUSE
Author of "Geography of Northwestern Europe"

DRESDEN, drās'dən, is a city in the German Democratic Republic (East Germany) and the capital of the administrative district (*Bezirk*) of Dresden. It lies on the Elbe River, 19 miles (30 km) from the Czechoslovak border and 100 miles (160 km) southeast of Berlin. Almost completely destroyed by bombing in World War II, it has since been rebuilt. Today Dresden is a manufacturing center of great importance and is the third-largest city in East Germany. It is an important railroad junction for Saxony and is closely linked with Berlin and Prague. The Elbe is navigable for barges of medium size and the traffic on it is considerable

Dresden's somewhat belated development as a center of manufacturing industry in the 19th century was assisted by the dense population and large market in the Saxon plain, by the ease of land transportation, and the navigability of the Elbe. The vicinity of the city, however, is lacking in most of the raw materials and fuels necessary for modern industry. The coalfields of the nearby Erzgebirge are very small, and heavy industry is almost completely absent from the city. Instead, manufacture is concentrated in goods to which skilled labor contributes the chief value. Foremost among these are precision-engineered products, cameras, and optical equipment. Other industries include the manufacture of electronic equipment, fine quality printing, and food processing. Much of Dresden's industry lies along the Elbe Valley, to the east and west of the city proper, where transportation by river, road, and rail is most highly developed.

JOHN LA DUE
DRESDEN'S 18th century Zwinger, built as a palace forecourt, was restored as a museum and art gallery.

The Historic Capital. As the capital of the duchy and later the kingdom of Saxony, which was one of the more important of the German principalities, Dresden was a flourishing artistic center. In the early 18th century the manufacture of fine porcelain was established at Meissen, 12 miles (19 km) to the north, and much of the product was marketed in the city as "Dresden" china. The painter Bernardo Bellotto was engaged as court artist by the king of Saxony in the 18th century and left a collection of pictures of the city. Dresden was also a major center of music and drama, and its opera was one of the most renowned in Europe. The Saxon kings contributed greatly to the planning and embellishment of the city that earned it the reputation of being the "Florence of the Elbe."

The city as it existed until it was almost totally destroyed by bombing in 1945 was largely the creation of the 18th and 19th centuries. On the south bank of the Elbe lay the Altstadt, or Old City, an area of prevailingly baroque character. The Altstadt was noted for the number of its baroque churches, very few of which survived the bombing, and for the rococo Zwinger, built as the forecourt of a palace, which has been restored as a museum and art gallery. Its collections of paintings and porcelain are among the finest in the world. The paintings include Raphael's *Sistine Madonna* and large numbers of works by other Italian, Flemish, and Dutch masters.

The palace of the Saxon kings, which lay beside the Elbe, was greatly altered in the late 19th century and was extensively damaged in World War II. Today most of the ruins of the Altstadt have been cleared; very wide streets have been laid out, flanked by multistoried blocks of offices and apartment houses. The new architecture in the Old City is functional but plain to the point of ugliness.

The New City lies north of the river. It developed in the 19th century into an important residential and industrial suburb. At that time Dresden also expanded southward into the low hills that border the Erzgebirge.

History. Dresden was founded early in the 13th century, by German settlers from the west, on the site of a Slav village. It guarded an important crossing of the Elbe and grew into a small commercial town during the Middle Ages. Dresden belonged at first to the margraves of Meissen; it was then occupied in turn by the kings of Bohemia and the margraves of Brandenburg but was ultimately incorporated into Saxony. It was the capital of Saxony from the 16th century until 1871, when Saxony ceased to be a separate political entity. Dresden's strategic position on the Elbe caused it to play an important role in many military campaigns, and the city was severely damaged on several occasions prior to its near-destruction in World War II.

The District. The administrative district (*Bezirk*) of which Dresden is the capital is the most southeasterly in East Germany. It covers an area of 2,601 square miles (6,738 sq km) and includes much of the middle Elbe Valley as well as the eastern Erzgebirge. The plain that makes up the northern part of the district is rich farmland, but the southern half consists of forested hills that are of little agricultural value. The chief towns, apart from Dresden, are quite small. They include Pirna, Meissen, Freital, Zittau, Görlitz, and Bautzen. Most of them have light industries, chiefly textiles.

Population: of the city (1966 est.) 504,000; of the district (1965 est.) 1,887,000.

NORMAN G. POUNDS
Indiana University

DRESDEN PORCELAIN. See MEISSEN PORCELAIN.

DRESS

Dress is a reflection of the culture of a period. In the 18th century, as seen in this painting (1731) by Jean François de Troy, costume was influenced by the refinement and rococo elegance of the French court. The ladies wear contouches having Watteau pleats. The gentlemen are in elaborately decorated collarless coats with wide skirts.

STAATLICHEN SCHLÖSSER UND GÄRTEN, BERLIN

CONTENTS

Section	Page
Introduction	378
Ancient Civilizations	380
Mesopotamia	380
The Steppes and Persia	380
Egypt	380
Crete	381
Greece	381
Rome	381
Western Civilization	382
Middle Ages	382
Early Modern Period	383
Recent Period	385
Pre-Columbian Civilizations	389
Middle America	389
Andes	390
Eastern Civilizations	390
North Africa and the Middle East	390
India	391
The Far East	392

DRESS is an inclusive term for garments, jewelry, cosmetics, and hairdressing. It is here considered as an aspect of the culture of civilized peoples; in this sense the term "dress" may be used interchangeably with the term "costume." For a discussion of dress in an anthropological context, see the article CLOTHING.

Dress is influenced by geographical factors, such as climate and available materials; by technological developments, such as weaving methods; and by historical events, including war, trade patterns, and religious movements. Dress is also affected by its functions—protection, preservation of modesty, adornment, and indication of status. Concern with the last two functions leads to most of the complex and artistic refinements of dress. The history of the dress of civilized people, including changes in fashion—the predominant style of a particular group at a particular time—reveals the interplay of all these influences.

Geographical, Technological, and Historical Influences. Draped garments originated in warm river valleys, where the peoples of early agricultural civilizations first learned to raise fiber crops and to weave. They found it more comfortable to wear rectangles of cloth wrapped loosely around the body—the predecessors of kilts, togas, saris, and such garments—than to wear animal skins. Tailored clothes were first devised by the hunters and herdsmen of cool forests and steppes. Using bone needles and sinews, they adjusted the shape of animal hides more closely to the form of the human body in an effort to make warm, fitted coats and trousers.

Among technological advances affecting dress was the early narrow loom. It produced a narrow strip of cloth, which could be made into a sacklike garment. Sleeve pieces might be added to allow freedom of movement. The underarm seam was left open or was closed with a square insert to make a narrow sleeve, a development that led to the shaped armhole. To gain width, at first a straight strip was inserted at each side; it was soon modified by the material-saving practice of cutting the strip on the diagonal.

Other technological advances included the 16th century stocking frame and the 19th century sewing machine. The former produced trim knitted stockings to replace clumsy hose sewn out of cloth. To outdo the poor, who could barely afford one pair, the rich wore two pairs, one gartered up, the other wrinkling down to the boot tops. The sewing machine, used at first in factories to mass-produce army uniforms, made it possible eventually to copy the expensive handmade dress of the upper classes at a price within reach of industrial workers.

Dress is also affected by the materials available. Early fabrics were wool and linen, both washable. Wool came in various natural colors and took dye well. Cool linen, worn in warmer climates, was harder to dye and therefore was often left natural or bleached white. Silk, which originated in China, was brought by traders along the Silk Route across Asia to Greece and Rome and eventually was produced in Byzantium and in Muslim cities, whence it was traded to medieval Europe, especially after the Crusades. Gloriously colored and patterned, silk was highly prized for use in the handsomest expensive garments.

Cotton was the basic fabric of China, southeastern Asia, and the pre-Columbian civilizations of the Western Hemisphere. It did not begin to be important in European dress, however, until various trading companies imported it from India in the 17th century. The cool, washable, colorfast textile, printed with exquisite designs in

FASHION

Above: A 16th century painting by Hans Holbein the Younger shows Lady Jane Seymour wearing an elaborately ornamented gown of rich fabric which features massively draped sleeves and tight bodice.

Above: Faithfully recorded in this tapestry is French high fashion of 1450. It was typified by a wire-supported headdress and a high-necked, fur-lined garment cinched by a belt slightly below the armpits.

Photos (above) by Francis G. Mayer

Above: Mid-17th century costumes, designed to conceal the figure, were boned, padded, draped, and, as in the large lace ruff which is shown, wire-supported. The portrait, by Emanuel de Witte, is of Duchess Magdalena.

Permanent collection, Brooklyn Museum

Two dresses designed by Worth. *Above:* A visiting dress of 1886; *right:* a dinner dress of 1896.

The Metropolitan Museum of Art

Left: Typical gown from 18th century French fashion plate.

FASHION

Right: This 1911 dress, with its brilliant color, high waist, and casual lines, epitomizes the Paul Poiret style.

Above: In 1925 Jean Patou changed the fashion silhouette by eliminating the waist and raising the hemline.

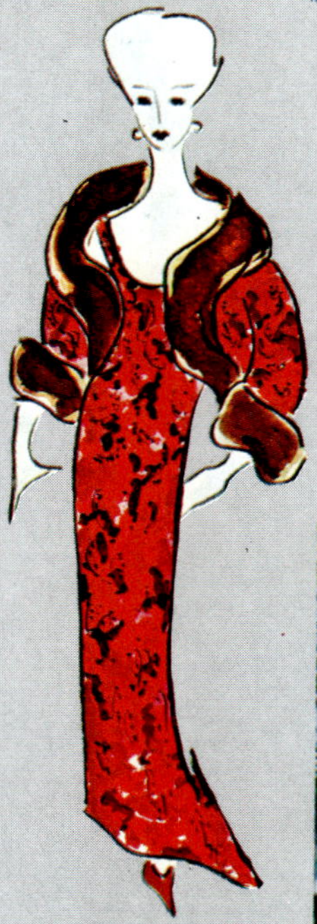

Molyneux, who settled in England after World War I, designed simple, charming clothes. Two 1934 outfits are shown: *Below left:* Wool cape-suit with nutria; *below right:* Linenlike, tweed-lined "duster" over jersey.

(Top left) French Reproduction Rights, Inc., courtesy The Metropolitan Museum of Art; (top right) The Metropolitan Museum of Art; (center) Arnold Scaasi; (bottom left) Condé Nast Publications, Inc.; (bottom right) Saks Fifth Avenue

Above: A 1962 dinner dress by Scaasi. Long and slim, it is typical of the period when easier fitting clothes became popular.

Above: The Spanish influence is apparent in this two-piece ensemble which was designed by Anne Fogarty in 1963. It combines a sleeveless dress with an embroidered bolero jacket.

natural dyes, was admired by all, but the French government forbade its import or production after a shipment in 1685 ruined the wool market. Cotton manufacturing flourished, however, in England, and by the end of the 18th century France was producing splendid wood-block cotton prints. In the 19th century the invention of fabric printing by copper roller and of aniline dyes made attractive cottons readily available.

The 20th century has seen the invention of synthetic fabrics such as nylon. Variously drip dry, nonshrinkable, and stain- and moth-resistant, they are more practical and often cheaper than natural fabrics. Synthetics had been refined to meet the needs of war, but they also put attractive, easily cared for clothing within reach of all.

New materials and techniques constantly appear. Garments may be made of extruded, or nonwoven, material, such as "paper" for throwaway dresses, and Pellon for stiffening. Other nonwoven materials include vinyl for waterproof raincoats and boots and Corfam for washable shoes. Some nonwoven materials may be molded to shape, and their seams, pockets, and zipper closings may be bonded, or sealed by heat. Combinations of natural and synthetic materials may be bonded together for lightweight warmth. Such developments could bring an end to the era of woven cloth, tailoring, and buttons.

Other influences on dress include such historical forces as war, contact with foreign peoples, and the temper of the times. Wars not only occasion technological changes, as with factory-made clothes in the 19th century, but may directly influence changes in fashion—for example, the shortening of skirts and the wearing of trousers by women in military service or in factories in World Wars I and II. The Manchu conquest of China changed the dress of that country, and the colonial expansion of Europe caused many non-Western peoples to adopt their rulers' dress. Christianity's traditional emphasis on poverty and the spirit was reflected in the sober, modest dress of early medieval Europe and Puritan England, while in exuberant, affluent secular societies—as in the Roman Empire or Renaissance Europe, or in the 1920's—dress emphasized physical attractiveness, freedom, and rich display.

Dress as Adornment and Indication of Status. Whether or not garments are needed for protection, in all civilizations dress is worn for modesty, to enhance the appearance of the wearer, and to proclaim his place in society, including rank, occupation, age, sex, place of origin, marital status, and religion. For example, about 4,000 years ago in the warm Indus Valley, an assured little dancing girl from Harappa felt well-dressed wearing only bracelets, knowingly massed, a necklace, and well-coiffed hair. Nor did the proud Maya nobles of Central America need many garments for protection, but they wore elaborate headdresses, decorated gaiters, and much jewelry, besides tattooing their bodies, artificially shaping their heads, filing their teeth, and crossing their eyes.

Whatever the climate, eminent personages dress primarily for beauty, display, and symbolic value, with little regard for the practical purposes and cost that must concern ordinary men. Cost may depend on the rarity, quality, or quantity of materials used, or the skill, taste, and labor required to assemble them. Among such conspicuous luxuries, for example, are the embroidered squares on a Chinese mandarin's gown, the feathered cape of an Aztec warrior, the jeweled doublet of a Renaissance noble, the lace collar of a 17th century courtier, and the rich furs and diamonds of a 20th century film star. Jewelry has the added advantage of being a form of investment, especially in unstable societies. A medieval king's crowns and regalia or a peasant woman's coin necklace may represent a large part of their owner's fortune.

The eminent frequently wear more garments than ordinary men both for display and for the aesthetic effect of superimposed colors and textures. Whether such garments add to the wearer's comfort, as do boots and gloves in northern lands, or detract from it, as did the stays, petticoats, and shoes of 19th century Englishwomen in India, is secondary. One of the earliest and most enduring examples of the conspicuous use of unnecessary garments is the enormously extended, hanging outer sleeve that originated on overcoats in ancient Persia, was brought back to Europe by the Crusaders, and persisted in the dress of 16th century Palatinate landgraves and of Turkish officials as late as the 19th century.

The eminent may also seek beauty and show status by adopting new fashions in dress. This procedure is relatively uncommon in the leisurely, rural, non-Western world, where fashion changes slowly; both the rich Indian princess and the poor villager wear their saris according to the custom of centuries. In the West, however, with its large number of urban centers, easy communications, and relatively high standard of living, changes in fashion are frequent and are exploited for their aesthetic and symbolic effect. The example for a new style may be set by a group, such as the French court or the "jet set," or by a prominent individual, as, for example, Louis XIV, who introduced high-heeled shoes to increase his height; the dancer Irene Castle, who popularized bobbed hair; or the fashion designer Courrèges, who introduced white boots for women. New fashions are spread through the example set by the upper classes, who frequently travel and often buy clothes seasonally in London, Paris, Rome, and New York. New styles are also popularized through fashion magazines, and theater, motion pictures, and television.

The eminent who adopt a new style show that they can afford a complete change in wardrobe in contrast to the average man, who must make do with the garments he has. The less eminent, however, generally try to imitate their superiors, with the result that the dress once characteristic of superior status loses its significance and is therefore abandoned by social leaders, although it may persist among certain groups as a stylized anachronism. The eminent must then find some other way to distinguish themselves.

One of the earliest examples of stylized anachronism is the purple stripe (*clavus*) on the Roman tunic. It originally proclaimed Roman citizenship, but since by the 1st century A.D. it was worn by everyone, including the lowest servants, it lost its significance and was adopted in proud humility by Christians, who considered themselves "the servants of the servants of God." The daily costume of ladies and gentlemen in the late Middle Ages persists in present-day academic dress and in many religious habits. The horizontal rows of braid on the coat of a courtier of Louis XIV, which had become part of a lackey's livery by the time of Louis XV, linger on in the horizontal stripes on the vest of a valet in French farce.

Today the tailcoat, once associated with gentlemen, is becoming the uniform of symphony orchestras and headwaiters.

Fashions may also rise in the social scale. Lace, for example, was first worn in France by peasants, who were taught to make it by nuns, before it was taken over by the courtiers of Louis XIV. During the French Revolution, trousers, previously worn only by sailors and farmers, were adopted by young English gentlemen sympathetic to the revolution, who were thrown out of clubs or dismissed by universities (or marked absent) for wearing such unsuitable attire in place of breeches. Today, on occasion, a similar reaction may greet men without neckties and women in slacks.

Generally, however, in contemporary Western society, where secularism, industrialization, democracy, and prosperity tend to reduce formality and obliterate social distinctions, dress is worn more for comfort and to symbolize equality than for adornment or to show status. This revolution in taste, accelerated after World War II, is reflected in the current attitude that in dress "anything goes." Sports clothes are gradually replacing more formal wear; the term "dress shirt," for instance, no longer means an evening shirt but merely a long-sleeved, closed-collared garment in contrast to a sports shirt. As the sexes more and more share the same activities, they more and more resemble each other in appearance. Girls wear trousers and tights; boys wear long hair and jewelry. These changes in attitude, combined with new technological developments, may result in the decline of the conventional attire established in the West in the 19th and early 20th century and lead to a whole new era in dress.

ANCIENT CIVILIZATIONS

In the ancient world, dress was of two basic kinds, suitable for two different climates and types of society—the fitted leather garments of the nomadic warrior-herdsmen of the cold Asian steppes and the draped woven clothing of the settled peoples of warm Mesopotamia and the Mediterranean. As the nomads pushed south, east, and west, the two varieties of dress intermixed, and eventually fitted fabric garments became the basic dress of Western Europe.

Mesopotamia. Bas-reliefs, statues, and cylinder seals from such Sumerian cities as Kish, Lagash, and Ur in southern Mesopotamia (before 2000 B.C.) and neighboring Mari indicate that Sumerian male dress consisted of two principal garments, a skirt and a shawl. The skirt (*kaunakes*) was originally a shaggy goatskin or sheepskin wrapped around the waist in parallel overlapping lines, with a pendant tail. Although this style was long retained for religious use, for general use the kaunakes came to be woven of wool into which tufts of animal hair were inserted. Later, the tufts were replaced by rosettes and checks woven into wool and also into linen and silk. Eventually, the garment became a tunic, or shirt. The shawl, wound around the body and carried over the left shoulder, was also first of hide and later copied in patterned fabric, trimmed with jewels, fringe, balls, and braids.

Sumerian women wore similar but longer garments covering the torso. Men and women went barefoot and (except for priests, who were shaven) wore long hair. The women's hair was often wound up into huge elaborations, some of which may have been wigs. Both sexes wore admirable jewelry—gold and jeweled hair ornaments and the *fibula* (shoulder clasp).

The succeeding Babylonian civilization (beginning about the 18th century B.C.) continued Sumerian styles of dress, much enriched and sophisticated, as it did other aspects of Sumerian culture. Basic Assyrian dress (14th to 7th century B.C.) was a short-sleeved shirt, dyed for laymen, bleached for priests. Nobles, priests, and women wore it full length and added a mantle, which for women covered the head. The mantle of kings and priests was a deeply fringed garment wound around the body in a spiral and, for the king, belted to hold a dagger. To indicate rank, the eminent also wore fringed aprons in back and fringed scarfs, curled their long hair and beard, and displayed gold bracelets and necklaces. Women were veiled according to law about 1200 B.C. Noblemen wore sandals, and soldiers, shown in bas-reliefs at Nimrud, Nineveh, and Khorsabad, wore leggings and boots.

The Steppes and Persia. Such nomadic warrior-herdsmen from the Eurasian steppes as the Scythians (who were roughly contemporary with the Assyrians) and, later, the Sarmatians, developed fitted leather or fur garments suggested by the natural shape of the hides. They wore a long-sleeved tunic seamed at the shoulder, trousers tucked into high boots, a sleeved overgarment, and a pointed hood or a cap with side flaps. They also fashioned superb gold work, which sheathed their armor and was sewn in animal and floral motifs on their clothes, and fine gold jewelry set with exotic gems from Siberian mines.

The costume of the Persians, who rose to prominence in the 6th century B.C., was developed from the dress their nomadic ancestors brought to the Iranian plateau. It included a long-sleeved, fitted cloth coat, open in front, and a *candys*, or collared overcoat with ribbon ties, slung on the shoulders with sleeves hanging—a fashion that indicated status and influenced the extended sleeves of medieval European dress. From these garments derived both the European coat and the *caftan*, a long fitted coat worn throughout the Middle East. Another basic item of Persian dress was wide trousers, later introduced to the West by Venetian traders. Feet were shod in boots and shoes, often with heels, which made walking more comfortable in the hilly Persian terrain, and with upturned toes. Nobles copied Assyrian hair styles and wore a high cylinder-shaped, or a soft, round-topped, felt hat. Women's dress was similar to male dress, except that their coats were closed and longer, and they wore long veils.

According to the fashions of the Sassanian period (3d to 7th century A.D.), enormously widened trouser flapped, ribbons fluttered, and hair puffed under headdresses that changed with the taste of each monarch. Richly dyed patterned silks from China, traded at Samarkand and Bukhara, were copied by Sassanian weavers.

Egypt. Dress among the ancient Egyptians, whose civilization was approximately contemporaneous with that of Mesopotamia, is revealed in tomb paintings, statues, and glazed tiles. It was based on a short wrapped loincloth, or kilt, for men and a *kalasiris* (a long, close-fitting sheath) for women, strapped over the shoulders. Both sexes wore a mantle that was knotted in front. In time, the Egyptians wore several layers of garments of different lengths and weights, and the kalasiris, in the New Empire, became a

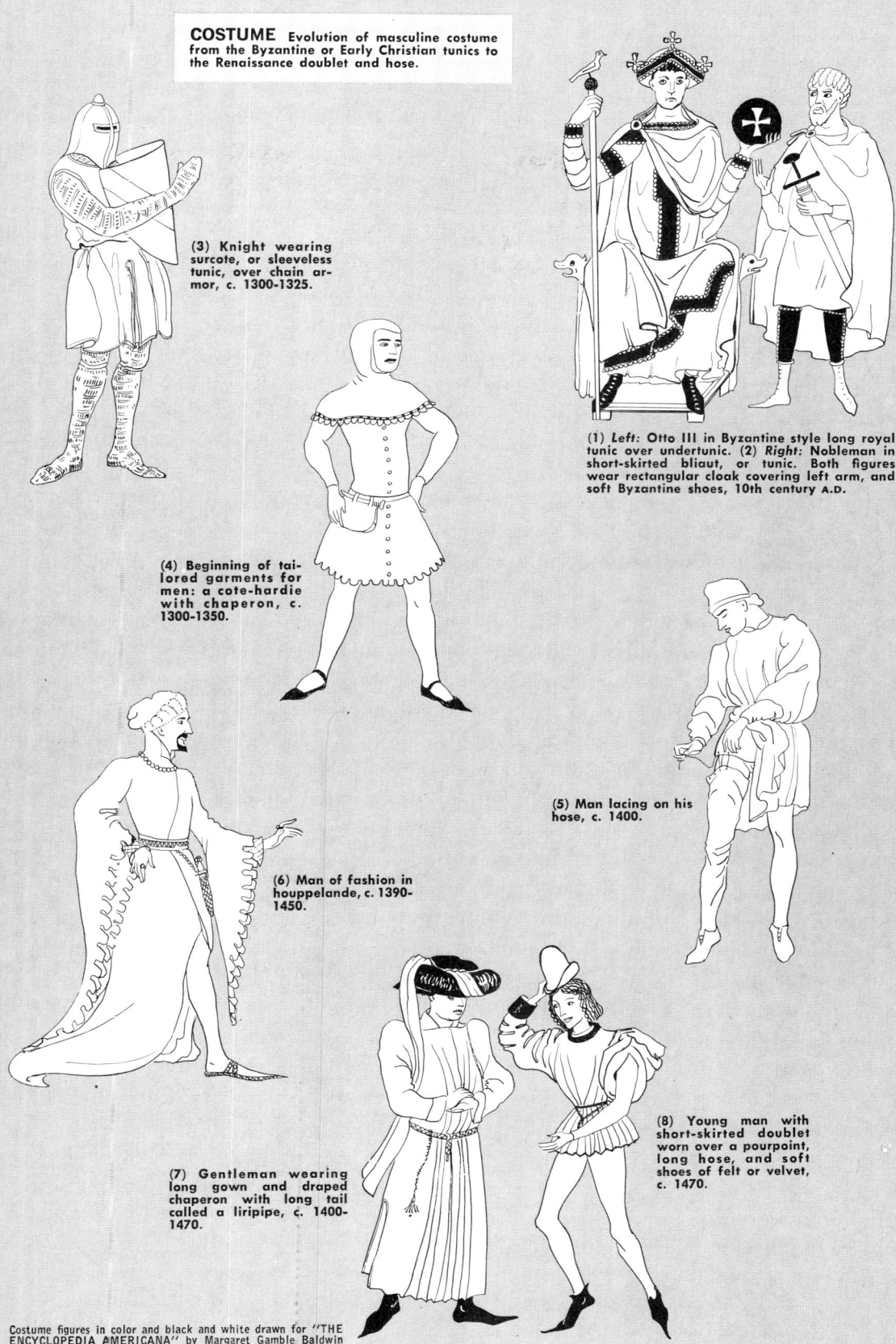

COSTUME Children were dressed like their parents until the late 18th century (1) (2) (3) (4). From stiff formal styles (4) there was a sudden change to simplicity (5). The Victorian age again brought tight adult styles (6) (7). During the Edwardian period sailor suits were popular for small boys (8) and, in a modified form, for girls as well. Since 1910 children's clothes have been designed specifically for children (9) (10).

(1) c. 1200-1300
(2) c. 1570-1588
(3) c. 1655-1670
(4) c. 1730-1745
(5) c. 1775-1790
(6) c. 1840-1860
(7) c. 1850-1865
(8) c. 1890-1910
(9) c. 1925-1930
(10) c. 1950

sleeved shirt for both men and women. The most common material in all periods was linen, usually white. Decoration was provided by elaborate pleating, bead-netting, appliqué, and superb collars and necklaces of blue glazed beads, semiprecious stones, and gold. Flowers and cosmetics also added color. The Egyptians were a cleanly people, and both sexes wore their hair clipped, later shaved, under black wigs. The skulls of aristocratic girls, such as Queen Nefertiti, were deformed from birth to elongate the back of the head. Soldiers wore quilted garments until the New Empire, when they adopted coats of mail sent as tribute by Syria.

Symbols of rank were important. The pharaoh wore a double crown, signifying his overlordship of Upper and Lower Egypt, decorated with a uraeus (rearing viper) as a sign of royalty and an *ankh* (a looped cross) as a symbol of life. He carried a crook, a flail, and an animal-headed staff. Over the centuries, details of dress of royalty in one dynasty, granted or adopted as honorifics, became the dress of the nobility in a later dynasty and eventually that of commoners.

Crete. Under the influence of contemporary Egypt and Mesopotamia, Cretan, or Minoan, civilization evolved the most individual and elaborate dress of all antiquity, especially for women. Examples are shown by bronze, ivory, and clay statuettes, in wall paintings from palaces at Knossos and Tiryns, and in bas-reliefs on vessels and sarcophagi.

Cretan women wore a short, tightly laced jacket leaving the breasts bare, a very tight wide belt with snake-like rolled edges, and a stiffened bell-shaped skirt (a version of the old Sumerian kaunakes), composed of parallel strips or of layers of flounces. All these garments were of leather. Hair was worn long under a high headdress. Cretan men wore a tight belt, an apron or kilt, and boots. They might add a shaped mantle and a hood or *petesus* (wide-brimmed hat) to cover their long hair.

Greece. From the Homeric age (about 1000 B.C.) to the Hellenistic age (ending 1st century B.C.), Greek dress was noted for graceful simplicity, which allowed the sport-loving Greeks maximum freedom. It consisted of two basic draped rectangles worn variously by both men and women—a shirtlike garment (the Dorian *peplos* and the Ionian *chiton*) and a wrap (the *himation* and the *chlamys*).

The Dorian peplos, worn by all women on the Greek mainland until the 6th century B.C., and by some later, was a relatively narrow rectangle folded on the left side, often opening on the right, and caught on the shoulders and bloused over a belt. The upper edge was turned down in a deep overfold which could be held under the belt or raised to cover the head. The peplos, of colorfully dyed wool, was heavy and closefitting.

The Ionian chiton, of Phoenician origin, was worn by men and women in Greek cities in Asia Minor before it reached the Greek mainland about the 6th century B.C. It was made of two wide pieces of fabric sewn up the right side and sewn or caught along the upper edge from the neck to each wrist. The chiton, girdled in various ways, was at first long and was later shortened for younger men. The material was white linen, often gauzy or creped and sometimes patterned in purple, that fell in flowing folds or pleats, shown on vases and in statues and bas-reliefs.

A Persian statue of silver (right) showing a pointed hood and an overcoat worn over a fitted tunic and trousers (6th century B.C.).
STAATLICHE MUSEEN ZU BERLIN

Stone statuette (below) of bare-breasted Cretan goddess, with a cinched waist, a skirt with rows of flounces, and tiered headdress.

FITZWILLIAM MUSEUM, CAMBRIDGE, ENGLAND

Basalt statue (left) of a Sumerian priest wearing a kaunakes, a shaggy wrap-around skirt (about 2600 B.C.).
AUTHENTICATED NEWS

The himation, worn by married women and by men, was a large woolen rectangle often patterned or embroidered, with weighted corners that allowed it to be gracefully draped around the body. Dorian men and, later, some Athenians might wear the himation only and be considered properly attired, while the chiton alone was considered informal. Other wraps included the man's chlamys, a small wool rectangle of Macedonian origin pinned at the right shoulder, sometimes his only garment.

Men's hair, originally long, later was worn shorter. Peasants and travelers wore the *pilos*, or Phrygian bonnet derived from the Scythians, and the broad-brimmed petasus. Women's hair was bundled up in back and bound with nets, fillets, and pins, sometimes with a diadem or a hat rising to a point. Jewelry, such as gold fibulae, was worn chiefly by women.

Both sexes went barefoot at home. Later, men wore sandals, or high boots for hunting and travel. Peasants and workers swathed their feet and legs in hide or cloth. Soldiers wore armor of hide or bronze consisting of a tight molded corselet over the chiton, a helmet, often crested, and greaves.

Rome. Roman dress (about 700 B.C. to about 500 A.D.) was, like that of Greece, based on two draped garments—a tunic (man's *tunica* or woman's *stola*), and a wrap (*toga* or *pallium*). The man's tunica, roughly equivalent to the Greek chiton but directly derived from the Etruscan predecessors of the Romans, was girded up to the knee. Originally sleeveless, of white or

Egyptian pharaoh and his wife (*above*) wear pleated linen and jeweled collars (18th dynasty). A replica of a Greek relief (*below*) shows figures wearing draped chitons and chlamyses or cloaks (5th century B. C.).

natural wool, it was later cut with short sleeves and was of linen or cotton or of leather for workmen. A long-sleeved, floor-length version (*tunica talaris*) was worn chiefly by actors. Rank was indicated by *clavi*, or purple bands of different widths on the shoulders of the tunica. The tunica alone was worn by gentlemen indoors, by workmen everywhere.

Gentlemen did not appear in public without a wrap. The characteristic wrap of the Roman citizen, forbidden to slaves and exiles, was the woolen toga, similar to the Greek himation but elliptical rather than rectangular and carefully draped around the body under the right arm and over the left. The toga of the emperor was purple, that of the rich, white, that of the poor, natural wool. Other wraps were the pallium (*palla*), a large rectangle also like the Greek himation, and the hooded, bell-shaped, weatherproof *paenula*, derived from the Etruscans, which was more convenient than the toga and eventually replaced it.

In the house, women wore a stola, over which they added another stola for formal occasions. One had sleeves; both were long and girdled once or twice; outdoors, women added a palla and a veil.

Footwear included *soleae* (slippers) or *soccae* (light shoes) in the house. On the street men wore leather *calcei* and soldiers wore hobnailed *caligae*, both strapped to varying heights.

As Rome became more deeply involved in foreign conquest and trade, foreign influences appeared in dress. Romans began to adopt Eastern luxuries, such as brilliant silk, cosmetics, elaborate hairdressing for the women, and gold jewelry. They also took over various practical barbarian garments; for example, the Gallo-Roman *cucullus* (hood with small cape) and *braccae* (trousers). Braccae were traditionally despised by Mesopotamian and Mediterranean peoples as the dress of uncultivated conquerors and were at first forbidden in Rome. However, they were worn by soldiers in cold outlying garrisons, and by the 5th century A.D., as the barbarians gained control of the empire, they were accepted in Rome itself. Barbarian influence also affected the Roman tunica, which developed into the wide-cut, wide-sleeved, long, ungirdled *dalmatica*, introduced from Dalmatia by the 3d century A.D. The dalmatica was popular among early Christians, especially among the Copts of Egypt, who decorated it with superbly colored tapestry-woven insets and borders in place of the clavi. The dalmatica or another tunic was often worn over the basic tunic.

WESTERN CIVILIZATION

Western dress evolved from the draped garments of the classical peoples and the fitted garments of the barbarians, as the two groups fused under the late Roman Empire and in the early Middle Ages. Dress was relatively static and utilitarian in those unsettled times. Then, as the wealth and social complexity of Europe increased and its horizons expanded, dress became more luxurious, ornamental, and class-conscious and was marked by more and more rapid changes in fashion. Trends in the 20th century suggest a return to more egalitarian, comfortable garments suitable for industrialized mass societies.

Middle Ages—Byzantine and Early Medieval Period. Early medieval dress was basically Roman, modified by the costume of the barbarian peoples of northern Europe and of the Byzantine Empire in the east. Mosaics at Ravenna show the dress of the court of the 6th century Byzantine emperor Justinian—a full length tunica talaris, whose sleeves covered the hands, and a chlamys (mantle) caught by a fibula on the right shoulder and decorated with two *tablions* (embroidered squares) on the front and back edge. Some items of Byzantine dress retained by the clergy into modern times include the dalmatic, the paenula (chasuble and cope), and an abbreviated form of the pallium (which became the insigne of an archbishop). Byzantine garments were of fine silk damask and brocade, in brilliant colors with metallic threads. The Byzantines had originally obtained these fabrics from China but learned to make them themselves after the Sassanid rulers of Persia in the 6th century blocked the Silk Route.

The barbarian nomads, who eventually settled in small agricultural villages in western Europe, wore shaped garments of fur, leather, and wool. Wool was woven in herringbone and diaper patterns by the Scandinavians (as discovered in burial barrows and ships) and in bright-colored checks and stripes by the Celts. Men wore a sleeveless smock, later a sleeved tunic, often over a shirt, and a mantle. Particularly interesting are the various combinations of garments that covered their legs and feet, including long trousers (some Scandinavian examples had feet attached), knee breeches, cross gartering with or without leg wrappings, *pedules* (leather or cloth sock-boots), *chausses* (fabric hose), and fine leather shoes. For armor they wore a ring-mail tunic, later also covering legs and head.

The woman's basic costume was a narrow-sleeved, ankle-length *kirtle* (tunic), often worn over a linen *chemise* (shirt), to which in public were added a loose, wide-sleeved, shorter kirtle, a mantle, and a veil over loose or braided hair. Decoration for both sexes was supplied by *orphreys* (woven bands of trimming) and by gold and bronze jewelry—large fibulae, *torques* (hinged collars), and twisted bracelets—with enamel, gems, or filigree. Both orphreys and jewelry used interlaced animal and ribbon forms, originally of magical significance, as shown in Irish illuminated manuscripts.

11th to 13th Centuries. The dress of peasants, scratching a living out of the soil, changed little. The costume of the nobility, however, was altered by Eastern influence from the 11th to the 13th century as a result of Italian trade, the Norman conquest of Muslim Sicily, and the Crusades. In sculpture, ivory carving, and illuminated manuscripts, clothes became more fitted, with interest shifting from the leg covering to the sleeve. The *bliaut*, a long, fitted gown often worn by both men and women in place of the old loose tunic, had funnel-shaped or trailing sleeves over the hand in the Byzantine manner and stressed the hip and belly according to Oriental taste. Over the bliaut or over a knight's *hauberk* (tunic of chain mail) might go a sleeveless *surcoat*, which later was emblazoned with a knight's coat of arms. Such superimposition of garments was especially striking in the relatively sophisticated court dress of cosmopolitan Spain. Other Eastern importations included the turban, rich silks, the fleur-de-lis motif, diagonal neck closings, single lapels, and the hanging unused sleeve on the 13th century *garde-corps* (overcoat).

The man's tunic became the shorter, tighter *pourpoint*, produced by tailors, who organized into guilds in the 12th century, and there were longer, better fitting hose of stretch wool reaching to short drawers. Gloves appeared, and the toes of shoes lengthened. Married women began to bundle up their hair and cover it with increasingly important *coifs* (close-fitting linen caps), pill-box caps, and jeweled *crispines* (nets), worn with veils and *wimples* (linen around the chin and neck) and *barbettes* (chin straps). Men wore a variety of coifs, berets, brimmed hats, cowls, and hoods, often one on top of the other. The point of the cowl and hood developed into a *liripipe*, or long tippett.

14th and 15th Centuries. Late medieval and early Renaissance dress became more exaggerated and luxurious, reflecting the increasing emphasis on wealth, manners, and the fine arts at such princely courts as those of Philip the Good of Burgundy and Lorenzo de' Medici in Florence. Rulers tried in vain to impose sumptuary laws restricting extravagance in dress, especially among the newly rich bourgeoisie, who attempted to outdo the nobility in splendor. Garments were made in fabrics ranging from the fine linen and wool produced by Italian and Flemish towns to costly silk damasks, velvets, and metallic brocades, which Italian weavers had learned to make from Byzantine and Muslim craftsmen. Later, as a result of the Italian wars and the French invasion of Italy, these luxury fabrics were made in France by Italian immigrants. The Germans copied Italian fabrics by printing designs with wood blocks. Fabric was also decorated with heraldic devices, by now codified and inherited. The bourgeoisie sought the same effect by wearing *particolor*, or *motley*, garments, with, for example, one leg red and the other striped yellow and black. Motley, along with *dagging* (scalloped edges), was eventually worn only as livery.

Men generally wore short garments, although the long garments of the preceding period were retained by royalty, the clergy, members of the professions, and the elderly, and for ceremonial occasions, as may still be seen in present-day coronation robes, judicial and academic dress, and the habits of religious orders. The pourpoint became the short padded *doublet* with extravagantly wide shoulders and often a wide or very long, hanging sleeve, revealing the tight sleeve of a *cotte* (undergarment). Long hose laced to the doublet and joined by a codpiece were worn in place of short hose and breeches or drawers. Over the pourpoint men wore a *cotehardie* (a progressively shorter, boat-necked overgarment laced or fastened by a row of tiny buttons) or, on formal occasions, a *houppelande* (an open gown of Franco–Flemish origin, varying from knee length to more than floor length). The houppelande's high collar, carefully belted pleats, and prominent sleeves—funnel-shaped or hanging to the ground with dagged edges—were later taken over by the cotehardie. Men's hair was first bobbed and rolled and then worn long. New headgear included the *chaperon* (a low turban formed from winding the elongated liripipe of the hood around the crown), tall Burgundian caps, and plain Italian felt caps. *Poulaines* (shoes with ridiculously long pointed toes often chained to the knee), which were deplored by the church because they made it difficult to kneel in prayer, were protected from mud by wooden clogs. Armor, worn without a surcoat, was now made completely of plate, often beautifully chased or inlaid.

The woman's kirtle (cotte) was tight fitted and belted, with a narrow sleeve and liripipe. Over it went a long cotehardie or a surcoat, which was deeply cut away at the sides, with fur edges or a stomacher of fur and a stiffened band at the hips to carry the weight of a full gored skirt. The more formal woman's houppelande was a robe with a wide, low V-neck, a wide belt just under the bust, and an extremely long gored skirt, which, held up by the wearer or an attendant, revealed the skirt of the cotte beneath. Hair was drawn back from the brow and hidden under a high, pointed, veiled *hennin* or a wide-horned *atours*, giving a hairless effect. Paintings of the Italian Renaissance show a more modest neckline, separate sleeves, which were fenestrated (slashed) to show puffs of white underlinen, and hair, often bleached blond, displayed under small caps, twists of veiling, binding, or rolls.

Early Modern Period—16th Century. Late 15th and early 16th century dress, depicted in Hol-

Byzantine courtiers (left) in a 6th century mosaic; and sculpture of a shepherd (12th century); a French lady in a surcoat (14th century); and a Dutch lady in houppeland and horned headdress (15th century).

bein portraits and German woodcuts, showed a sobriety and solidity characteristic of the Protestant, mercantile bourgeoisie. The tall, willowy silhouette that complemented the vertical late Gothic style became shorter and broader, paralleling the horizontal tendency of Renaissance design. Fabrics were plain and dark and were slashed in the German-Swiss manner, revealing puffed undergarments, to emphasize width.

The close-fitting, vestlike male doublet had narrow, later wide, slashed sleeves and *bases* (short cartridge-pleated skirts), both of which were tied on. The neckline was first low and square, showing a fine embroidered and pleated linen shirt, and later rose to a small collar over which the shirt collar, sometimes fluted, turned down in a *falling band*. The *jerkin*, or jacket, which replaced the cotehardie, was fuller than the doublet. It had a wide sailor collar, often of fur, and was either sleeveless or had wide slashed sleeves. Cloaks also had wide collars. Hose reached the waist, then divided into upper stocks, consisting of *canions* (close-fitting, slashed breeches) fastened to nether stocks (stockings). Shoes were open in back, with wide, slashed toes. Men had moustaches and beards and long hair, wore various brimmed hats, many with brooches and plumes, and carried swords.

A woman's gown consisted of a bodice sewn to a skirt and having separate, interchangeable sleeves. The bodice was first square with a wide square neck, often filled in with a pleated or fluted high-collared linen tucker; it later became more pointed and rose to a high collar over which appeared a fluted linen chemise collar. The funnel-shaped outer sleeves, often fur-lined, turned back to show contrasting narrow, puffed, and tied undersleeves. An overskirt was tucked up, or later opened in an inverted "V," to show a contrasting underskirt. From a chain at the waist hung purses, rosaries, mirrors, or pomanders —a fashion that long continued. Heads were covered with fitted lappeted hoods of heavy dark material edged with white folds or ruching. This costume lingers as the dress of playing-card queens.

In the latter half of the 16th century, European dress was affected by the rigid formality of Spain, as padding, slashing and puffing, *ruffs*, and *farthingales* (stiffened underskirts) distorted the figure. Colors brightened, and rich silks and velvets were often embroidered with silk, gold, or pearls. Clothes were trimmed with *picadills* (tabbed edges), stuffed rolls at the armhole, and lace, which spread from Italy to northern Europe under the influence of Catherine de Médicis, queen of France.

The doublet developed a long rigid torso, later swollen by *bombast* (padding) into a *peascod* belly, and its skirt was reduced to a picadill edge. Bombast also inflated the sleeves to a "leg o'mutton" shape. The falling band became a pleated, wired, or starched ruff, and matching linen adorned the wrist. Upper stocks grew into short, heavily padded and slashed *trunk hose* (French hose or round hose), often worn above close-fitting canions or tucked into loose, padded, knee-length *slops* (*galligaskins* or *venetians*). Woven stockings were replaced by gartered, knitted silk stockings. Capes and *mandilions* (sleeveless, sideless jackets) were slung diagonally over a shoulder. Shoes developed a tongue, square toes, and high heels. Hair lengthened under high-crowned or wide-brimmed hats, worn both indoors and out.

Women's dress, as seen in portraits of Queen Elizabeth I and her ladies, outdid men's in rigidity, padding, and ornate sleeves. Long, corsetlike bodices pointed in a deep "V." The fluted high collars of tuckers and chemises became narrow ruffs over open tuckers and then widened into cartwheels, with a nearly bare bosom below, or they increased into high, stiff, lace-edged fans framing the head. Bell-shaped skirts over Spanish farthingales later became squared and ankle-length as they were further extended by French sausage-rolls at the hips. Hair showed under a neat French hood, flattened and dipped at the center of the forehead. Later, hair was dressed over rolls and mounts, padded with false hair, and caught up in back in a *caul* (net) to avoid the ruff, the whole decorated with pearls and feathers. Women wore hats similar to men's and carried stiff fans. Both sexes displayed ornate gold, gem-studded jewelry—necklaces, brooches, and—for men as well as women—chains, earrings, and rings. Men and women carried embroidered gloves and wore black half-masks to conceal their identity while taking part in court masques and ballets.

17th Century. In the first half of the 17th century the exaggerated stiff Spanish influence was replaced by more graceful flowing fashions influenced by the easy military styles of the Flemish and Swedish armies fighting the Thirty Years' War. The period was marked by long locks, lace, and leather, as seen in Van Dyck portraits of elegant, satin-clad English Cavaliers and in paintings of somber Dutch and Flemish burghers by Rembrandt, Rubens, Hals, and Vermeer.

The man's tight doublet lost its padding and became easier in fit. It eventually was cut in one piece with its skirt, which was slit into overlapping panels that gradually became shorter, and it had set-in sleeves turned back at the wrist, suggesting a cuff. The shirt showed through button-edged slits in the body of the doublet, and it bloused below the short skirts and the sleeves. The stiff ruff gave way to falling bands, plain-edged for the Puritans or scalloped lace for the Cavaliers. The collarless jerkin was often a laced-up military garment of leather, sleeveless or with contrasting sleeves. Trunk hose, now relegated to livery, were replaced by loose, unpadded breeches, which slipped low on the hips and were cut short or caught at the knee. Both the doublet and breeches were profusely trimmed with matching ribbons and lace.

Men wore two pairs of expensive colored silk stockings, wrinkled down to show the pair underneath, and they protected the stockings with lace-trimmed linen boothose. Their spurred boots had wide tops folded down to hold boothose, stockings, garters, and hems of breeches. Boots were usually worn, although there were also heavy, square-cut, high-heeled shoes with rosettes of ribbon or lace on the instep. Long loose military cassocks (coats) and cloaks were tied diagonally and worn with the swashbuckling, broad-brimmed, cocked and plumed hats, typical of the long-locked Cavaliers, or with the stiff, narrow-brimmed, high-crowned hats of the close-cropped Puritans (Roundheads). Beards were reduced to pointed Vandykes.

Women's dress softened as the bodice shortened and widened, and the skirt fell in rich folds over petticoats instead of a farthingale. Sometimes a loose open robe set over the bodice was draped up over a lighter-colored underskirt. The neckline moved below the shoulder, and the ruff became a falling band and finally a gauzy kerchief. A full slashed or "leg o' mutton" sleeve was tied with a rosetted ribbon on the upper arm and finished with a lace cuff at the wrist or a blousing linen undersleeve at the elbow. In addition, there were lace-trimmed aprons, short-waisted jackets, and cloaks. Hair, drawn back into a bun, with loose side curls lengthening as the shoulders were bared, was covered indoors only by a kerchief. Outdoors, hoods and high-crowned hats were worn. Pearls replaced gold jewelry.

During the second half of the 17th century and the first decade of the 18th, the sumptuous, dignified costumes that complemented the baroque splendor of the court of Louis XIV at Versailles were copied at lesser courts all over Europe. French influence spread through the first fashion periodical, *Mercure galant* (1672–1728), and through fine engraved plates, such as those by the Bonnart family. Court costumes were made of French silk and lace and manufactured according to strict standards under royal patronage until the revocation of the Edict of Nantes (1685) caused the French silkweavers, mostly Protestant, to flee to England. Extremely popular for informal and bourgeois costumes were the washable *indiennes* (printed cottons from India), which, along with furs from the New World, were imported by royal patent.

In the 1660's the male costume, which included the very short, open doublet over the bloused shirt and *rhinegraves* (petticoat breeches or full pantaloons) trimmed at waist and hem with loops of ribbon, gave the effect of several tiers of ruffles. In the 1670's there appeared the basic costume of the next century—a solid-color collarless coat (derived from the military cassock) with slender, thigh-length, later wide, knee-length, skirts and a wide-cuffed sleeves; waistcoat (derived from the doublet); shirt with neckcloth (formerly the falling band) and ruffled cuffs; *culottes* (close-fitting knee breeches derived from rhinegraves) made to match the coat or of black velvet; stockings; and buckled shoes instead of boots. Cloaks were used only for bad weather. Faces were clean-shaven under heavy *periwigs* with long corkscrew curls. Hats—*tricornes* (low-crowned, wide brimmed hats with cocked brims) decorated with braid and ostrich plumes—were carried if they did not fit over the huge wigs. Gentlemen also carried walking sticks.

The female silhouette again became rigid and was exaggeratedly tall, lank, and angular. The tightly corseted bodice had a long uncluttered line, extending from a wide, lace-draped neckline, through a "V"-shaped opening filled by embroidery or brocade, to a deep center point. The heavy overskirt was pleated onto the bodice, as was the full sleeve, and was draped back into a bustle and train over a contrasting underskirt supported by *panniers* (hoops), which flattened the figure in front and back and extended the sides. Under the pious influence of Mme. de Maintenon the pale colors of Louis XIV's early reign gave way to dark brocade. Hair was curved widely at the sides, with a bun in back covered by a delicate cap, which in the 1690's became the tall pleated-lace *fontage*. Hooded capes were worn outdoors. Kid gloves, parasols, masks, and beautifully painted folding fans were important accessories. Both men and women used rouge, powder, tiny black patches, and scent.

These styles, created by the aristocracy and bourgeoisie, were copied in modified form by the peasants, who retained them, with regional differences, long after the upper classes had adopted new fashions.

Recent Period—18th Century. For most of the 18th century the French court continued to set fashion, followed after a time lag of months, years, or decades by the rest of Europe and the New World. With the death of Louis XIV the

Sketch by Holbein (*above left*) showing early Renaissance dress. (*Right*) Doublet, trunk hose, and canions, depicted in an anonymous painting of *Sir Walter Raleigh and His Son* (c. 1590).

Dutch burghers (*above*) wearing lace, from *Burgomaster Dirk Bas Jacobs* by D. Santvoort (1635). (*Right*) Dress in the English style and frac and breeches, in *The Morning Walk* (1785) by Gainsborough.

heavy, rigid dignity of late baroque court dress gave way to the light, graceful, vivacious rococo style of Louis XV, familiar in the paintings of Watteau, Fragonard, Boucher, and Chardin. Influenced by Rousseau's enthusiasm for nature, dress developed a delicate simplicity, especially in more rurally-oriented England, as reflected in portraits by Gainsborough, Reynolds, and Romney. This tendency was increased in the 1780's, when Europe was swept by a wave of Anglomania, characterized by plainer, more masculine styles. Concurrent with these developments, an increased emphasis on walking and riding and on bourgeois domestic life led to the differentiation of formal and informal clothing. Also, children's clothes, as a result of Rousseau and the taste for simplicity, were no longer copies of adult garments but were specially designed soft shirts, trousers, and white dresses.

The man's collarless coat, with wide skirts (buttoned back for riding) and wide sleeves with buttoned-back cuffs (the origin of buttons on modern jacket sleeves), gradually evolved into the slender, narrow sleeved *frac* (swallow-tailed frock coat) with a standing collar. The waistcoat, often beautifully embroidered, followed the shape of the coat. The shirt was finished by ruffled cuffs and a variety of neckcloths, such as the flowing *steinkirk*, the pleated *stock*, the ruffled *jabot*, and the knotted *cravat*. Culottes, exposed by the frac, were bias cut for better fit. Overgarments included capes, coachmen's coats with multiple short capes, and, later, the double-breasted English *redingote* (riding coat). Standardized versions of these garments gradually became the brilliant military uniforms of the period. The full-bottomed, powdered wig, a messy nuisance to active men, was gradually relegated to older men and professional men, such as judges, who still wear it in England. Most gentlemen wore a small powdered wig caught at the nape in a black bow, pigtail, or other arrangement or dressed their own hair to look like a wig. Tricorne hats, tasseled canes, quizzing glasses, huge muffs, pocketwatches, and jeweled, painted, or enameled snuffboxes and buttons all contributed to the elegance of a gentleman's costume. Swords, which became unfashionable as they were adopted by servants, were finally relegated to the court.

For most of the period the pointed bodice of the woman's gown changed little from that of the 17th century. The low neck was veiled by a delicate *fichu* (scarf) or edged by ruching. The sleeves had an important cuff at the elbow, later a ruffle. The skirt silhouette, however, changed greatly. The rigid, panniered bustle and train gave way to a loose, ankle-length, usually open *contouche* (sacque) with a *Watteau pleat* from the back of the shoulders flowing into the skirt. The quilted or embroidered underskirt was supported by the new, funnel-shaped farthingale. The *robe à la française*, similar but with a trailing skirt, was for court wear. When the lilting farthingale, worn by women of every class, became so huge that it would not pass through doors, it was succeeded by stately, more maneuverable panniers, which widened the hips to as much as six feet but could either be angled or raised by hand through slits in the skirt. Later the shorter *polonaise*, with the overskirt looped up to the back, was worn for walking. Fabrics were usually patterned silk for court wear, printed cotton for the country.

Skirt styles were balanced by changing hair styles. The graceful farthingale was topped by neat little heads of clipped powdered hair, surmounted, if the wearer was elderly or bourgeois, by a tiny lappeted muslin cap. Pretty hoods, flat straw shepherdess hats, and tricornes were worn outdoors. The wide panniers, however, were balanced by towering, padded arrangements of false hair, three feet high, including such decorations as mobcaps, garlands, feathers, or perhaps a full-rigged ship. Between dressings, which required half a day's work by a professional male hairdresser every three weeks, they became verminous. Hoods, such as the gauzy *Thérèse* or hooped *calash*, or various hats were worn outdoors with wide cloaks or short jackets.

The English influence of the 1780's introduced a new gown, often of white muslin. It was short waisted, with a long narrow sleeve, a bouffant kerchief at the neck, and a trailing skirt without panniers, its fullness drawn to the back in a bustle. With this softened style hair lost its padding and fell into a *hérisson* (hedgehog) of massed ringlets worn with large English leghorns (flat straw hats) or high-crowned, masculine beavers. These narrower dresses were covered by masculine greatcoats and Orientally-inspired coat gowns. Throughout the period, shoes and stockings became lighter in weight and color, and fans, black throatbands, scarves, gloves, drawstring purses, parasols, and canes were important accessories.

19th Century. French Directoire and Empire fashions (about 1790–1820) expressed the exhilarating sense of freedom, sometimes degenerating into unkemptness and license, that accompanied the French Revolution. However, the elegant, meticulous simplicity of tailoring and linen insisted on by the English dandy Beau Brummell ensured England's preeminence in male fashion into the 20th century.

The frac, blazing with metallic embroidery, and aristocratic satin culottes were gradually restricted to court and military dress. They were superseded by plain, high-collared coats with lapels, squared-off waists, and tails at the back and by tight, light-colored *pantaloons* of stockinet or doeskin, first knee length with boots or garters, then strapped under the foot with shoes. Waistcoats shortened to square-cut vests worn over shirts with high, soft collars tied with an elaborate neckcloth or stiffened cravat. Overcoats resembled skirted coats. Natural hair, worn short, was combed forward in shaggy locks under the English beaver round hat with high conical or stovepipe crown, although *bicornes* were prescribed for court and the army.

Women's fashions reflected the classical spirit that inspired the Revolution and Napoleon and influenced all the arts of the time. Following the lead of such Parisian beauties as Mme. Récamier and the Empress Josephine, women wore a simple white muslin dress that was basically a narrow tube with a drawstring at the neck and just under the bust and with short puffed sleeves. Color was provided by pastel sashes and bright matching long gloves and ballet slippers or, during the Empire period, by colored tunics and narrow overskirts. Undergarments were reduced to one petticoat or simply pink tights. During a series of cold winters beginning in 1810, long narrow sleeves were added, and the muslin dress became a coat dress of heavier fabric. Overgarments included large shawls, *spencers* (short jackets), *pelisse robes* (fitted coat dresses), and redingotes.

After the Napoleonic Wars, European dress reflected the materialism, conservatism, and romantic sentimentalism that reached a peak in the Victorian age. As a result of the Industrial Revolution, cheap, factory-made cloth was sewn by machine into ready-made, mass-produced clothes, especially for men. Women's clothes, still usually made by seamstresses, were inspired by French examples exhibited at international expositions or in fashion periodicals or translated into paper patterns, often accompanied by the specified dress lengths. As commerce became increasingly important in bourgeois-dominated society, clothing became more utilitarian and severe both for men and for women working in offices. Special clothes were devised for rain, using Charles Macintosh's invention of waterproof fabric, and for sports.

From the 1820's to the 1850's men's garments had a shapely elegance. Tight-waisted, wide-shouldered coats included the formal, open tail coat, the everyday frock coat (a knee-length,

Empire fashion (*left*) featured the puffed-sleeve, high-waisted dress and, for men, a high-collared coat and tight pantaloons.

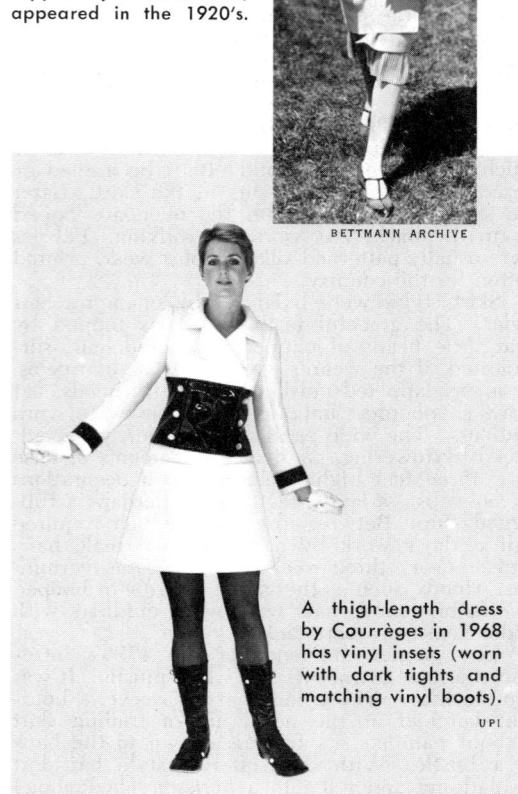

French town dress (*above*) of the 1860's has tight waist and a hoop skirt.

Shorter skirts and the boyish silhouette (*right*), topped by a cloche hat, appeared in the 1920's.

A thigh-length dress by Courrèges in 1968 has vinyl insets (worn with dark tights and matching vinyl boots).

skirted, double-breasted closed coat with a shoulder cape), both in dark colors, and a variety of morning coats and sport coats in loud checks and plaids. Two contrasting vests were worn over shirts with stiff detachable collars and dark cravats. Only artists and dandies affected a negligently loose, open-necked blouse. Pantaloons became easier-fitting cloth trousers worn with high soft black Wellington boots.

In the 1860's coat, vest, and trousers became a shapeless, tubular, black suit, the forerunner of the loose, somber sack suit still considered standard business dress. Capeless frock coats (Prince Alberts) and tailcoats remained for formal day and evening dress. The cravat had become a necktie, and Wellingtons were replaced by stiff laced or buttoned boots. There was a variety of overcoats. Hats included the formal black silk top hat, the stiff, dome-crowned bowler (derby), the soft-crowned Homburg, the flat-crowned porkpie, and visored sports caps. Hair was often plastered down with Macassar oil, and most faces were adorned with moustaches or beards.

In the 1820's women's dress changed dramatically. The waist of the vividly colored silk gown dropped to normal above a flaring, ankle-length skirt (supported by starched ruffles or hip and bustle pads) that was balanced by a horizontal neckline widened by immense collars and leg o' mutton sleeves with projecting wings. The neckline might be open or filled with a linen tucker or a fichu-like *canezou*. Hair was bunched high under great hats laden with feathers and loops of ribbon. Footgear included white stockings and black ballet slippers or laced shoes.

From the 1840's to the 1860's women, personifying the demure, helpless, sentimental heroines of Victorian novels, wore soft gowns with sloping shoulders, fichu-like bands, tightly corseted waists, and skirts billowing ever wider over layers of full petticoats or later a bell-shaped crinoline (hoop skirt). The swaying crinoline revealed lace-edged *pantalettes* (long, separated tubes) that were the first underdrawers for women. High-necked, muted day dresses had long narrow sleeves belling out over full white linen undersleeves. Lacy, flounced, white evening dresses, as painted by Winterhalter, were bare shouldered with short sleeves. Like the furniture of the period, such dresses were overdecorated with tassels, gimp, fringe, beads, flowers, and bows. Hair was modestly looped down over the ears, later massed at the nape, and concealed by a bonnet. Out of doors the figure was swathed in full, knee-length cloaks and coats. The fashion of the period was set by Worth, dressmaker to Empress Eugénie and the founder of *haute couture* (high fashion houses).

Amelia Bloomer's introduction of full Turkish trousers under short skirts was rejected as too radical a reform, but more conservative practical garments for sports and travel gradually appeared —short walking dresses, bathing dresses, white shirtwaists (developed from the *canezou*) and skirts, and tailored suits popularized by Alexandra, Princess of Wales. In the 1870's and 1880's crinolines disappeared, and skirt fullness was bunched back into a bustle. In the 1890's, under the influence of the English actress Lily Langtry and the American Gibson Girl, women displayed elegant "hour glass" figures set off by collars boned to the ears, leg o' mutton sleeves, and trailing skirts. Hair was piled high in a pompadour under a stiff sailor or wide-brimmed "Merry Widow" hat.

20th Century. Dress in the 20th century has tended toward simplicity, comfort, and informality. Men's costumes remained relatively unchanged until after World War II. There were, however, such innovations as trouser cuffs, soft-collared shirts, Fair Isle sweaters, and suède shoes, all introduced by the Prince of Wales (Edward VIII), and blue jeans and loud-patterned, open-necked sport shirts, popularized by American films.

Women's costume, however, changed radically. By 1914, under such influences as the costumes of the modern dancer Isadora Duncan and the Ballets Russes, the patrons of the Paris couture, then at its height, were abandoning rigid corsets for the soft draped clothes of Paul Poiret and the revolutionary bias-cut crepes of Madeleine Vionnet. After World War I women's dress became easy, straight, and practical, paralleling the functionalism of architecture and reflecting the sense of freedom and vitality characteristic of the newly emancipated woman. In an effort to achieve a boyish silhouette, women bobbed their hair, flattened their figures, dropped their waistlines to the hip, and raised their skirts to the knee, above flesh-colored silk stockings and pumps. Gabriel Chanel's delightful, simple little jersey dresses (easily copied in factories) and ropes of fake pearls began the downfall of the couture. The silhouette of the 1930's continued to be tubular, with a natural waistline and longer skirts. Such American fashions as the shirtwaist dress were popular. During World War II, shoulders were square, and slim skirts rose to the knee. As servants vanished and women went into factories, slacks appeared for informal wear.

In 1947, in reaction to wartime austerity and the standardization of military uniforms, the French designer Christian Dior introduced the feminine New Look, characterized by an emphasis on bust and hip and by full, calf-length skirts over stiff petticoats. Italian designers for men began to make looser suits with more drape, ruffled shirts, and pointed shoes. By the late 1950's these styles were modified; dresses, often sleeveless, resembled short, shapeless sacks, and many men adopted the Madison Avenue, or Ivy League, naturally-cut grey flannel slack suit, worn with button-down shirts and "sincere" (quiet) neckties. Many men also gave up vests and wore much shorter overcoats. The sober dinner jacket, which had replaced the tailcoat for evening, was worn in lurid colors, chiefly by jazz bands. For sports both sexes wore bright colored "separates"—shirts, sweaters, jackets, shorts, or slacks—of American or Italian design.

The 1960's saw striking changes in the whole pattern of Western dress. While conventional styles still lingered, the tendency for people of all ages and social levels was to follow the lead of nonconformist, middle-class youth, who adopted strikingly colored, flamboyantly cut styles. The inspiration for this movement came from England, where the young either affected an Edwardian elegance (the Mods) or a black leather, metal-studded toughness (the Rockers). Young English designers such as Mary Quant, who introduced *miniskirts* and who covered legs in vivid or patterned tights and in boots, and Tuffin and Foale, who stressed the long-sleeved, lace-trimmed granny look, created inexpensive mass-produced clothes for the young mass-market shoppers along London's Carnaby Street. Men appeared in shaped trousers; high-collared, long-skirted, close-fitted Mao or Nehru jackets (the latter adapted from official Indian dress); and turtleneck jerseys with medallions, or colored or ruffled shirts. These styles were quickly adopted by the clothing industry in the United States. Concurrently, the great Paris houses of custom-made clothes lost their preeminence. In order to compete with England and the United States, some adopted Carnaby Street fashions, and many opened boutiques that sold ready-to-wear clothes.

PRE-COLUMBIAN CIVILIZATIONS

In the pre-Columbian civilizations of Middle and South America the basic articles of Indian dress were rectangular garments secured by knots or pins and marvelously enriched by brilliantly colored, patterned fabrics, elaborate headdresses, and jewelry. After the arrival of the Spanish in the 16th century, more and more Indians adopted Western dress, especially in the 20th century, but ancient traditions and regional differences may still be seen.

Middle America. The austere Olmec of eastern Mexico developed such religious motifs as the baby-faced man-jaguar, seen in the colossal stone heads of La Venta, and the feathered serpent of their other sculpture. These motifs, transmitted by the Olmec along with their brine-soaked, quilted cotton armor and such costumes of the neighboring Totonac and Huastec as wearing tall caps, piercing their ears and noses to hold ornaments, and tattooing their bodies, appear in the sculpture, frescoes, and codices of other people from the Valley of Mexico to Peru.

A sequence of related civilizations in the Valley of Mexico—Teotihuacán, Toltec, and Aztec—shows a basic similarity of dress. Aztec men wore a *maxtli* (kilt or loincloth), a *poncho* (a long, horizontally worn rectangle with a neck-slit), and, if eminent, a high headdress topped by feathers and open cotton bolls. Knights wore the Olmec quilted, brine stiffened armor (adopted by the Spaniards as cooler than steel armor). Women dressed in a *huipil* (sleeveless shirt), a *cueitl* (skirt), and a *quisqueme* (a square with a neckslit and embroidered edges, worn cater-

Maya priests with elaborate headdresses and jaguar skins, from a fresco (c. 800 A.D.) in Bonampak, Mexico. *PEABODY MUSEUM, HARVARD UNIVERSITY*

corner). Their hair was braided with colored material and wound round their head.

Aztec garments were of native maguey or, for the eminent, of tribute cotton from the Mixtec, patterned by expert weaving, tie-dyeing, or embroidery. Feathers, also obtained by tribute, were knotted together or to cloth, to make gorgeous mosaic capes for the nobles. Necklaces, bracelets, and ear, nose, and lip ornaments were made of gold, silver, or copper by techniques derived from the Indians of the Andes and were embellished with shells, turquoise, and jade. Faces and bodies were painted. Clothes, hair, and jewelry showed status, especially military achievement.

Among the Maya, contemporaries of the peoples of the Valley of Mexico, who flourished in Guatemala, Honduras, and Yucatán, men of rank wore either a belted loincloth with a long narrow apron or short trousers, a jaguar skin cape, decorated gaiters, and sandals. Women usually wore a skirt and cape or, occasionally, a loose white gown. Aristocrats of both sexes wore much jewelry and attempted to achieve the ideal of an artificially flattened forehead and an exaggeratedly humped nose, crossed eyes, tattooing, and teeth filed and inlaid with precious stones. The effect was enhanced by a tall hat or a high plumed or feathered headdress.

Andes. Before 200 B.C. the coastal Chavín people, a part of a sequence of Andean civilizations, were weaving local cotton and making feather capes and headdresses, net bags, and gold jewelry. Later, the coastal people of Paracas and Nazca wove cotton and, from the highlands, the wool of alpacas, llamas, and vicuñas, into mantles, fringed ponchos, kilts, wraparound skirts, turbans, headbands, hairnets, and bags, such as those discovered in the Paracas Necropolis. The textiles, of unsurpassed quality, were woven and decorated by every known technique except printing. The highland people of Tiahuanaco were also skilled weavers, and the coastal Mochica made fine gold jewelry and painted or tattooed their bodies, as seen in their pottery.

The dress of the Incas, heirs to these earlier civilizations, is known chiefly through Spanish accounts. The clothing of nobles was woven in vivid patterns by skilled "Chosen Women" of the Inca ruler. Men wore loincloths, ponchos, cloaks, sandals, and unique square caps of material suggestive of Oriental rugs. They carried handsome, double-woven shoulder bags to hold amulets and coca leaves, and their rank was indicated by headdresses, collars, and large cylindrical earplugs. Warriors, painted black for battle, wore quilted armor. Women wore a girdled, anklelength garment (either a tunic or a wraparound pinned on the shoulder) and a mantle fastened by a *topo* (pin) with a curved cutting edge that was used for handwork. Their long hair was covered by a headband and a large folded cloth.

EASTERN CIVILIZATIONS

The dress of Eastern civilizations developed from the intermixture of the shaped garments of the Asian nomads and Chinese, the draped garments of Indians and southeast Asians, and the garments formed of sewn strips characteristic of the Japanese. Eastern dress reflected great artistic and technological skill but was slow to change. As Western technology and standards spread to the East, Eastern dress began to be replaced by Western clothing, both for economic reasons and for the prestige it gave its wearer.

North Africa and the Middle East. Traditional dress in the Muslim lands of North Africa and the Middle East was derived from the fitted garments of ancient Persia combined with a variety of loose overgarments. In public the outline of the figure was concealed, in keeping with Muslim traditions of modesty, as well as for protection against the harsh conditions of steppe and desert. Great wealth and taste, however, might be expended on the quality of the fabric, trimming, and jewelry. Details of dress are given on Muslim ceramics, in illuminated manuscripts, and in the accounts of Western observers.

In the settled areas of North Africa and the Middle East, men generally wore a high-necked, long-sleeved tunic, or shirt, falling outside trousers, either full or tight, fastened at the ankle. Over this attire might go a tunic, jacket, or coat, or one or two vests of varying lengths. In the eastern Ottoman Empire and Persia, gentlemen in public added the Persian caftan, a long fitted coat often of rich embroidery or metallic brocade. It had a standing collar, overlapping skirt, and narrow sleeves (sometimes extended over the hands), and was bound by a sash, into which might be thrust a scimitar or dagger.

For outdoor wear, all classes added an outer robe. In Persia it was the fitted overcoat with hanging sleeves; in other areas it was a long, loose, unbelted garment, such as the open *binish*, the closed *djibbah*, the hooded *djellaba*, or the hooded, striped *burnous*. Footgear was usually sandals or heelless leather slippers (often with Persian upturned toes) easily removed at home and in the mosque. One type of headgear was the *turban*, of Hindu origin, consisting of many yards of fabric wound round the head or around a cap or *fez*. The drape, color, and ornament indicated the status of the wearer. Another type of headgear was the fez, or tarboosh, a truncated, usually tasseled, felt cone, of Persian origin. In 1925, Turkey prohibited wearing the fez, but it is still worn in other areas, often with Western suits.

In Arabia, Mesopotamia, Palestine, and Egypt, a loose, flowing costume of Semitic origin evolved, which was more suited to desert conditions than the fitted dress of the Persians. The basic garment was a *thobe* (shirt), long, full, unbelted, and usually white. Over it, on ceremonial occasions, the upper classes added an *aba*, a long, voluminous open robe. This distinctive garment was made of two lengths of camel's hair sewn together horizontally across the back, folded forward to make a wide front opening, and then sewn across the shoulders. There were slits for the arms, which were nevertheless covered by the fullness of the garment. The upper section of the aba might be elegantly woven and embroidered in vertical lines. Hair was long, and headgear consisted of a skullcap under a large square of cotton folded diagonally and large enough to be drawn across the face in a sandstorm. It was secured by a rope of black wool or camel's hair.

Muslim city women of status dressed luxuriously in the secluded women's quarters of their homes. Their basic costume consisted of a fine silk, linen, or muslin shirt, a long vest or short bodice, a sash, and velvet, brocade, silk, or muslin *shalwar* (pantaloons). They might fit closely or be enormously wide and long; in Turkey even when gathered at the ankle or drawn up to the knee they still dragged on the floor. In the eastern Ottoman Empire and in Persia, women added at least one *yelek* (the female caftan). It was of rich fabric, cut low in front to reveal the varied materials of the garments beneath, and fastened up the front, the buttons bursting, or left unbuttoned, over a full, accentuated abdomen. An open, sleeveless coat might be worn over it. A low-slung sash emphasized the hips. In Arabia, Mesopotamia, and Egypt, however, instead of these Persian-derived garments, women wore a thobe (long wide tunic) of silk or of blue cotton.

Women wore their hair long or braided, under a turban in Turkey and Persia, or with a jeweled pillbox or white muslin veil. Feet were bare or were covered with delicate leather slippers or, for Bedouins, with orange boots. Much use was made of cosmetics, including eye shadow and henna to tint hair and stain nails and the soles of the feet. Bedouin women tattoed tribal marks in indigo on their foreheads. Women wore quantities of jewelry—diamonds and pearls, gold and silver bangles, and earrings and necklaces dripping coins.

Outdoors a lady was swathed in a voluminous *chadar* (dark cloak), *baracan* (shawl), or aba. To this was added a *haik* or *yashmak* (veil), a garment of non-Arab origin, which hid all but the eyes. These garments set off respectable women from freer, working-class women, who might wear only a dark wrap-around garment, or countrywomen, such as the Bedouins, who wore no veil. The veil was forbidden in Turkey in 1928 and is now discarded, along with the rest of traditional dress, by many city women.

India. In the warm Indian subcontinent, traditional Hindu dress reflected a religion whose sensuous aspects celebrated the body. Religious sculpture and wall paintings, dating from the 2d century B.C. to the 13th century A.D., show voluptuous divinities in luxurious costume that emphasizes the infinite capacity of the body for assuming graceful postures. The male figures generally have some drapery about the hips and sometimes a shoulder scarf. The female figures wear an enormous jeweled girdle, slung low on the hips to reveal the umbilicus; the girdle sometimes holds a brief skirtlike garment or drapery at the back. Such coverings and an occasional scarf and tight bodice often appear as transparent material indicated by no more than faint, almost indistinguishable lines. Both male and female divinities are laden with jewelry—immense headdresses, ornate collars, strings of beads, hollow neck decorations, and bracelets for the arms, wrists, and ankles. Turbans also appear.

According to Hindu religious writings, however, ordinary mortals were expected to dress more modestly. From ancient times the basic garment of India has been a long strip of cloth—the man's *dhoti* and the woman's *sari*—wrapped around the lower part of the body. The ends of the dhoti are drawn through the legs and tucked into the waist to form loose drawers. The exact arrangement and the material used indicate the wearer's origin and status. In addition, men wear a chadar (scarf), tied about the waist or thrown over the shoulder, and a turban and sandals.

The sari envelops the lower part of the body, is often pleated in front, and is brought up across the bust and over the left shoulder. It may be drawn over the hair, which is combed back in a knot. The sari has infinite variety, both in the manner of drapery and in material, which ranges from the pale silks of Bengal with silver and gold thread borders to the coarse, vivid tie-dyed cottons of Rajputana and the embroidered, mirror-encrusted cottons of Sind and Punjab. A poor woman may wear only a sari but a richer woman will wear a petticoat beneath it and a *choli* (a tight, short- or elbow-sleeved bodice stopping under the bust). Women in Rajputana add a long pleated skirt.

Such Hindu garments are more prevalent in southern India than in the north, where, as a result of Muslim invasions from the 10th to 16th century, Muslim fitted clothes and standards of modesty were introduced. Muslim men wear a long-sleeved *kurta* (tunic), or shirt, hanging outside *pajamas* (loose or tight trousers). Over these may go a caftanlike *jama* or *choga*, with a standing collar of Chinese influence carried down to ties at the waist, and a long vest or, for scholars and officials, a long loose open robe with short sleeves. A turban or fez covers the head, and red leather shoes with upturned toes protect the feet. Examples of such dress may be seen in exquisite illuminated manuscripts, of Persian inspiration, painted at the Mughul court.

In the north, many Hindus of all classes added the kurta to their dhoti, and Hindu gentlemen attached to the Mughul court wholly adopted Muslim dress. From it emerged the official costume of modern India—an *achkan* (or *sherwani*, a knee-length fitted coat with a standing collar, white in summer and black in winter) over white *jodhpurs* (trousers loose at the hip and tight from the knee down) and a folded cotton cap symbolic of the Congress party.

Muslim women in India wear the kurta, trousers, a short jacket or a caftan, and a scarf. Many add the Indian sari, and some adopt the pleated skirt and choli of Rajputana. In public, Muslim women are bundled from head to foot in a *burka*, which has a trellised or mesh section through which they see and breathe.

Indian influence is strong in most of Southeast Asia, where the basic garment for men and women is a vividly colored, wrapped skirt—

EASTERN DRESS includes (left to right) pantaloons on Persian woman (c. 16th century); a kimono on an 18th century Japanese actor; sheer drapery and jeweled girdle on carved figure from India (c. 13th century).

called in different areas a *sarong, longyi, panung,* or *sampot*. With it is worn some sort of jacket, blouse, or shirt, usually outside the skirt. Sometimes women also wear a scarf. In Indochina, traditionally influenced by Chinese styles, peasants wear dark jackets and trousers, while ladies prefer the *ao-dai*, a tightly fitting, long-sleeved high-collared, long dress, with a narrow skirt slit to the waist on both sides, worn over black pajamas.

The Far East—China. Long isolated from other civilizations, China developed a unique form of shaped silk garment that later influenced the dress of Korea and Japan. Unlike the narrow cotton and linen looms of Asian peasants, which produced shoulder-seamed tunics with set-in sleeves, the wide Chinese silk looms, patronized by royalty, allowed the full sleeve and skirt of one half of a gown to be cut all in one piece, front and back. Two such shaped pieces were then stitched together to make a garment having under-arm and center-back seams. A wedge-shaped panel attached to the front edge of the left piece overlapped the right piece and was fastened diagonally to the right piece from throat to underarm seam by characteristic ribbon ties (later loops and knots). At first the neckline was a low "V" like that of a Japanese kimono. Later, a standing "mandarin" collar was added.

Such gowns (*p'ao*), worn by both gentlemen and ladies during the Han period (202 B.C.–220 A.D.), continued for centuries to be characteristic Chinese dress. Bas reliefs, ceramic, jade, and ivory figurines, and paintings on silk show ribbon-girdled gowns loosely flowing about the feet and hiding the hands in wide, long sleeves, reflecting the Confucian emphasis on modesty and circumspection. Gradually certain colors and woven or embroidered designs were established for ceremonial use to show rank. Ladies wore narrow stoles and extra drapery around the hips and dressed their hair high with combs, pins, and flowers. They covered their faces with white rice powder and affected tiny rouged mouths and plucked, thin-painted brows. From an early age, ladies' feet were bound and encased in tiny embroidered shoes to give a teetering walk considered sexually attractive and indicating that they need not work. Both men and women grew long fingernails, guarded by gold or jade shields, another indication of leisure, and carried fans. Men wore stiff black hats with winglike projections.

From 300 B.C., trousers, tunics, and boots—the costume of nomads from Central Asia who constantly threatened China's borders—were worn by the Chinese for riding. Cotton trousers and jackets, front- or side-fastened, became the dress of peasants of both sexes. These garments were generally blue in most regions but were of a lustrous black on the southern coast. Since the Chinese had no wool, in cold weather they wore many layers of silk- or cotton-padded garments, removing them layer by layer as spring approached. Footgear consisted of white socks and cloth slippers. Men's hair was long, wound into a topknot; women's hair was drawn smoothly back into a knot. For outdoor work both sexes wore wide straw hats.

By the Ming period (1368–1644) the Han gown had become shorter and more severe in cut and was worn over trousers by both sexes. A jacket or loose open coat, with or without sleeves, might be worn over the gown. Ladies added a pleated skirt under the gown on formal occasions. When the Manchus, fierce nomadic warriors, conquered China in 1644, they allowed ordinary citizens to retain their traditional costume, except that men had to adopt the Manchu queue. Chinese officials and their wives, however, had to wear Manchu dress. The Manchus had already modified the Chinese gown, familiar as tribute, into the caftan, which was close fitting at the waist, with slit skirts for riding. It had long narrow sleeves ending in "horse-hoof" cuffs over the hands, an indication of status, similar to the

Korean men in stovepipe hats and high-waisted coats watching a dancer (from a painting c. 1800).

Persian extended sleeve. Costume indicated rank, according to a code based on Ming tradition, prescribing color (yellow for the emperor, stone blue for mandarins), design (embroidered within "Mandarin squares" on the chest and the back of the gown), and ornamental buttons on the crown of a round hat, which often had an upturned fur brim.

In the 20th century the Manchu gown, tightened, shortened, and sleeveless, worn with high heels, evolved into the Chinese city woman's *cheong sam* or *chipao*; upper-class men adopted Western dress. Under the Communists, standard attire is a worker's front-fastened jacket and trousers in blue or grey.

Korean dress was a modification of the Chinese. Men wore white *paji* (wide, high-waisted trousers tied at the knee or ankle), a *chogori* (short jacket), and a *tsurumagi* (overcoat) with extremely long sleeves. A tall stovepipe hat of black horsehair and bamboo protected the coiled topknot of hair worn by married men. Women wore full trousers, a very short jacket, and a full, high-waisted skirt, all of which were colored for maidens and white for matrons.

Japan. During its early history, Japan adopted Chinese culture, directly or through Korea, including styles of dress. Basic garments were a short tunic or jacket and full trousers, which continued for centuries to be the attire of peasants and servants. In the 7th century the nobility adopted the silk *kimono* (gown), from the Chinese *p'ao* or its Korean variant, for court wear. A painting of the pro-Chinese Prince Shotoku shows him in a long brocade coat (the Korean *tsurumagi*) worn over long trousers with a handsome belt, sword, and wallet. Court ladies wore long, high-necked gowns with long hanging sleeves over trousers. Both sexes used face powder and rouge, and blackened their teeth.

During the Heian period (8th–12th century) elaborate court dress developed, based on Chinese principles of rank indicated by color and design.

Men wore several dark kimonos, fastened on the right, with long, wide sleeves and elaborate girdles, and *hakama* (full, skirtlike trousers) gathered at the ankles. Kimono sleeves and hakama could be shortened by cords to allow for free movement, during uprisings, for example. Similarly, the *kamishimo* (stiff garments with winglike extensions), later worn by nobles and samurai over the kimono, could be shrugged off for combat. Heads were shaved almost bare and covered with black lacquered silk hats with stiff projections.

Beautiful and talented women dominated the court of the late Heian, or Fujiwara, period (9th–12th century). Scrolls illustrating Lady Murasaki's *Tales of Genji* show delicate ladies in 12 or more airy layers of enormously wide, long kimonos, tied in front with a narrow *obi* (sash) and trailing over full scarlet hakama, with their unbound hair, often artificially lengthened by added hair, streaming down behind them. Enormous care was spent by both men and women to achieve the right color harmonies of the silks, woven under imperial supervision, according to the season or as inspired by a poem.

Eventually, as Japan became more militaristic and nationalistic, dress became somewhat simpler. During the Tokugawa period (17th–19th century), men and women wore a floor-length kimono made of 6 strips of 18-inch cloth basted together (to be taken apart for cleaning). It had a roll collar, a "V" neck closing on the right, and hanging sleeves sewed partly up the sides to be used as pockets. Beneath the kimono was an under kimono, with a shirt and loincloth for men and petticoats for women. The kimono was held in place by a wide obi elaborately tied in back. The cotton or silk materials for these garments, as seen in woodcuts of the time, were exquisitely printed or embroidered with striking naturalistic designs. For outdoor and formal wear, a *haori*, a knee-length black silk coat, printed with white *mon* (family crests), was worn over the kimono. Court ceremonial also required dark silk hakama. Footgear consisted of white cotton *tabi* (mitten-socks) and, for outdoor wear, sandals or clogs. Women's hair was lacquered into elaborate shapes and ornamented with combs, pins, and flowers.

Peasants wore cotton trousers or white loincloths and *happi* (short coats). Happi designs, usually white on indigo, identified one's occupation. Women added aprons and often kerchiefs. Both sexes wore sandals, straw raincoats, and wide straw hats. Traditional dress is often worn in villages, for ceremonies, or at home, and is preserved in No and Kabuki theater.

See also COSMETICS; COSTUME, ECCLESIASTICAL; COSTUME, THEATRICAL; HAIRDRESSING; JEWELRY; and the Index entry *Dress*.

MILLIA DAVENPORT
Author of "The Book of Costume"

Bibliography

Boehn, Max von, *Modes and Manners* (Philadelphia 1936).
Boucher, François, *Twenty Thousand Years of Fashion* (New York 1966).
Contini, Mila, *Fashion from Ancient Egypt to the Present Day*, ed. by James Laver (New York and London 1965).
Davenport, Millia, *The Book of Costume* (New York 1948).
Leloir, Maurice, *Histoire du costume*, 5 vols. (Paris 1935–1949).
Laver, James, *Taste and Fashion* (London 1945).
Tilke, Max, *Le costume en Orient* (Berlin 1922).

Marie Dressler

DRESSLER, dres'lər, **Marie** (1869–1934), Canadian-born American actress, whose great bulk, large mobile face, and robust sense of the ridiculous made her a comedy favorite on the stage and in films. She was born Leila Koerber in Cobourg, Ontario, on Nov. 9, 1869, and took the name "Marie Dressler" when she began a career on the American stage in 1883. She appeared in music halls with Weber and Fields, Lillian Russell, and other stars at the turn of the century, and introduced and made famous the song *Heaven Will Protect the Working Girl.*

Miss Dressler was an instantaneous success in her first film, *Tillie's Punctured Romance* (1914), but her screen career then went into a decline until sound was introduced. She regained stardom in such films as *The Divine Lady* (1929), *The Vagabond Lover* (1929), *Anna Christie* (1930), and *Min and Bill* (1931), for which she won an Academy Award as best actress. Her last successes were *Tugboat Annie* (1933) and *Dinner at Eight* (1933). She died in Santa Barbara, Calif., on July 28, 1934.

HOWARD SUBER
University of California at Los Angeles

DREW, Charles Richard (1904–1950), American surgeon, who developed techniques for processing and storing blood plasma for use in transfusions. He was born in Washington, D.C., on June 3, 1904. He graduated from Amherst College in 1926 and received an M.D. from McGill University in 1933. From 1938 to 1940 he was a fellow in surgery at Columbia University, where he received a Ph.D. in medical science (1940) with a dissertation on blood preservation.

At the start of World War II, Drew worked on blood-transfusion programs for the French and British armies, for which he developed techniques for processing and storing liquid plasma. In 1941 he became director of an American Red Cross program for the U.S. armed forces, developing techniques for using dried instead of liquid plasma. He resigned after only three months, following an armed forces ruling that Caucasian and non-Caucasian blood would have to be stored separately. He was fatally injured in an automobile accident near Burlington, N.C., on April 1, 1950.

DREW, Daniel (1797–1879), American capitalist, who engaged in notorious stock market speculations. His lack of business ethics was typical of the post-Civil War era of American business expansion. Drew was born in Carmel, N.Y., on July 29, 1797, and grew up on his father's farm with little education. At 15 he began his career, driving livestock to New York City from upper New York state and later from the Middle West. In 1834 he entered the steamboat business on the Hudson River.

Having built up his capital, he turned to stockbrokerage in 1844. He became interested in the stock of the Erie Railroad for speculative purposes. As director and treasurer of the company, he used his position to further his stock manipulations. With his associates Jim Fisk and Jay Gould, he engaged in an unscrupulous struggle (1866–1868) with Cornelius Vanderbilt, who was determined to control the line. The scale of business dishonesty in this contest, unchecked by the courts or the state legislature, caused a public outcry. In 1870 he was outmaneuvered on the stock market by Fisk and Gould and the panic of 1873 completed his ruin. He declared bankruptcy and never regained his wealth.

Before his losses he had built Methodist churches and founded the Drew Theological Seminary in Madison, N.J., and the Drew Seminary for Young Ladies at Carmel, N.Y. He died in New York City on Sept. 18, 1879.

ELEANOR S. BRUCHEY, Michigan State University

DREW, John (1853–1927), American actor, the leading matinee idol of his time, who after establishing his reputation in classical roles, became world-famous for his suave performances in drawing-room comedies. He was born in Philadelphia, Pa., on Nov. 13, 1853, the son of two celebrated actor-managers—John Drew and Louisa Lane Drew. His sister, Georgiana Drew Barrymore, was the wife of the actor Maurice Barrymore and the mother of Lionel, Ethel, and John Barrymore. A founding member of the Players Club (1888), Drew served as its president for many years. He died in San Francisco, Calif., on July 9, 1927.

Career. Drew made his stage debut in 1873 at his mother's theater as Plumper in *Cool as a Cucumber*. In 1875 he joined Augustin Daly's company, making his first New York appearance in *The Big Bonanza*. Subsequently he played with Edwin Booth in *Hamlet* and with Joseph Jefferson in *Rip Van Winkle*. In 1878–1879 he toured with his brother-in-law Maurice Barrymore. From 1879 to 1892 he was with Daly's new company, playing opposite Ada Rehan, and was acclaimed in Daly's New York and London productions of *The School for Scandal, As You Like It, Twelfth Night*, and *The Taming of the Shrew*. His Petruchio in *The Taming of the Shrew* was a particular triumph.

From 1892 to 1915, Drew was under the management of Charles Frohman, who starred him in *The Masked Ball* (1892) with Maude Adams. Ethel Barrymore made her New York debut with Drew in *Rosemary* (1896), and Lionel Barrymore won fame in a supporting role with Drew in *The Mummy and the Hummingbird* (1902). One of Drew's most memorable later performances was in *The Circle* (1921–1923). He last appeared on the stage in 1927.

MYRON MATLAW, Queens College of the
City University of New York

DREXEL, Anthony Joseph (1826–1893), American banker and philanthropist, who founded the Drexel Institute of Technology in Philadelphia. He was born in Philadelphia on Sept. 13, 1826, and at the age of 13 began work in his father's banking house. He became a partner at 21. When his father died in 1863, Drexel became the guiding influence in the firm. Facing the vast investment opportunities after the Civil War, the firm changed its business to investment brokerage and expanded, with connections in San Francisco, New York, London, and Paris. Drexel added to his own fortune by real estate investments in Philadelphia and its environs. He also was co-owner of the Philadelphia *Public Ledger*.

The most important of Drexel's many philanthropies was establishing the Drexel Institute with a gift of $3 million. It opened in 1892, offering courses in technology to all, regardless of race, religion, sex, or social class. Tuition was low, there were scholarships, and night classes were held. Public lectures and concerts were also provided.

Drexel never held public office, but he was one of the small group of businessmen who were influential in the administration of President Grant. He died in Carlsbad, Bohemia, on June 30, 1893.

Eleanor S. Bruchey
Michigan State University

DREXEL, Katharine (1858–1955), American philanthropist, who founded the Sisters of the Blessed Sacrament for Indians and Colored People. A daughter of Francis Anthony Drexel, international banker, she was born in Philadelphia, Pa., on Nov. 26, 1858. After her father's death in 1885 she determined to devote the bulk of her inheritance to the education of American Indians and Negroes.

Under the guidance of Bishop James O'Connor of Omaha and Archbishop Patrick Ryan of Philadelphia, she founded the Sisters of the Blessed Sacrament in 1891. She established and maintained schools and convents throughout the United States, and in 1915 she founded Xavier University in New Orleans, La. At her death in Cornwells Heights, Pa., on March 3, 1955, her order numbered over 500 sisters with 63 schools. She had donated over $20 million to preparing American Negroes and Indians as citizens.

Sister M. Ann Nicola, S. B. S.
St. Elizabeth's Convent, Cornwells Heights, Pa.

DREXEL INSTITUTE OF TECHNOLOGY is a private, nonsectarian, coeducational institution of higher education located in Philadelphia, Pa. Founded in 1891 by the Philadelphia banker and philanthropist Anthony J. Drexel, it opened in 1892 as the Drexel Institute of Art, Science, and Industry; its present name was adopted in 1936.

The institute comprises seven units: colleges of engineering, science, business administration, and home economics; a graduate school of library science; an evening college; and a division of humanities and social sciences, which awards no degrees but serves the undergraduate colleges. All undergraduate and some graduate students may elect a plan alternating class work with periods of employment in business or industry. Drexel's total enrollment grew from about 3,000 students in 1950 to more than 11,000 in the late 1960's.

John Tully, *Drexel Institute of Technology*

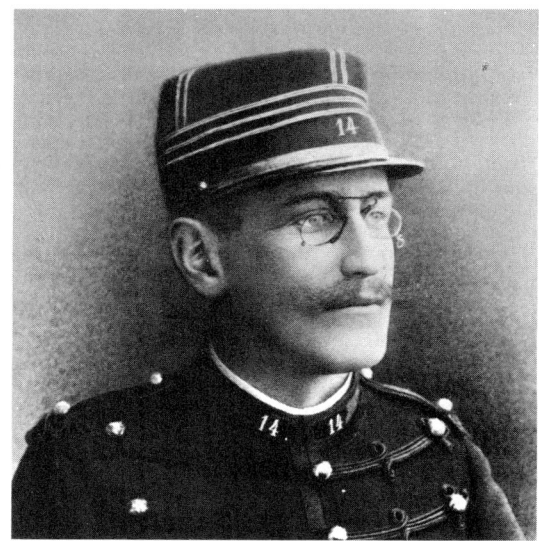

Alfred Dreyfus

DREYFUS, drā-füs', **Alfred** (1859–1935), French army officer, who became the central figure of a famous scandal that reflected social and political conflicts in France. Dreyfus was born on Oct. 9, 1859, in Mulhouse, Alsace, into a prosperous Jewish family. When Alsace was annexed by Germany in 1871, he went to France to live. An army officer at 21, Dreyfus had been assigned to the general staff by 1894 and appeared to have begun a successful career.

At this time the French attached considerable importance to the army; hope of recovering the lost provinces of Alsace and Lorraine had not been abandoned, and the French still feared Germany. Many looked to the army for leadership in reestablishing France's greatness and contrasted the military leaders with the politicians, who were often corrupt and ineffective. The groups that dominated the high posts in the army were sometimes guilty of anti-Semitism during the late 19th century.

The "Bordereau." The "Dreyfus affair" began in September 1894, when a scrap of wastepaper was removed from the wastebasket of the German military attaché in Paris. This paper, which came to be known as the *bordereau*, or "memorandum," was an unsigned letter promising information about various military matters, some of which were highly secret. Everyone, including Gen. Auguste Mercier, the minister of war, assumed that some well-informed officer was betraying secrets to the Germans. Dreyfus was arrested on Oct. 15, 1894, when it was discovered that his handwriting was similar to that on the *bordereau*.

General Mercier thought that only a conviction would maintain the army's good reputation. He instructed the counterespionage section of the ministry of war to compile a secret file of evidence that could not be used in open court. This evidence was then shown to the judges but not to Dreyfus' lawyer. In spite of his claims of innocence, Dreyfus was found guilty and sentenced to life imprisonment on Devil's Island. The fact that he was Jewish, with connections in Alsace—an area under German control—may have encouraged belief in his guilt.

The Role of Major Esterhazy. In May 1896 further evidence suggested that the German mili-

395

tary attaché was communicating with another French officer, Maj. Marie Charles Esterhazy. The new head of counterespionage, Lt. Col. Georges Picquart, found that Esterhazy's writing strongly resembled that of the *bordereau*. Picquart's superiors were reluctant to reconsider Dreyfus' position and reassigned Picquart to Tunisia in an effort to keep him quiet.

Dreyfus' brother Mathieu had taken up the cause, however, and had by now convinced many people that there was something odd about his brother's case. By October 1897, Esterhazy's name was being mentioned publicly, and it was impossible to avoid bringing him to trial. Military officials were still convinced of Dreyfus' guilt because more incriminating material had been added to the secret file; they therefore assisted Esterhazy, who was acquitted in January 1898. Émile Zola, the novelist immediately published a newspaper article entitled *"J'accuse"* (I accuse"), which charged the authorities with conspiring to imprison Dreyfus, an innocent man, and to free a traitor, Esterhazy.

Dreyfus' Second Trial. As excitement over the affair rose, many thought that there was a Jewish conspiracy seeking to humiliate the French Army and nation, while others, sympathetic to Dreyfus, believed that arrogant military leaders were trying to protect themselves and to resist civil authority. As it became clear that the Roman Catholic Church was opposed to a retrial, the old quarrel of separation of church and state was revived.

Public interest in the case reached new heights when one of the most vital documents in the secret file on Dreyfus proved to be a forgery. Maj. Hubert J. Henry, an intelligence officer, admitted the forgery and then committed suicide, on Aug. 31, 1898. Esterhazy, his intrigues in danger of being revealed, fled from France. After delays, Dreyfus was brought from Devil's Island to Rennes for a new court-martial, which began on Aug. 7, 1899. The trial was long, rambling, and complicated, and the verdict was confusing. Dreyfus was found guilty by a majority of the court, but with extenuating circumstances. He was then persuaded to accept a pardon from the President of France. In 1904, further forgeries were discovered in the evidence against Dreyfus, and in 1906 the court of cassation quashed the Rennes verdict and reinstated Dreyfus in the army. He was also awarded the Legion of Honor.

Later Life. After serving in World War I, Dreyfus retired as a lieutenant colonel. He died in Paris on July 12, 1935. For years after the affair officially ended, many people believed in Dreyfus' guilt and maintained that secret incriminating evidence existed. Some thought that a mysterious and unidentified officer was the traitor. The most likely explanation is that Esterhazy wrote the *bordereau*, but that he was in a position to give only the most general information about the military subjects mentioned. The affair grew to such dimensions because it illuminated many of the traditional divisions within France and because Dreyfus' conviction violated the sense of justice of many of the people.

DOUGLAS JOHNSON
University of Birmingham, England

Further Reading: Chapman, Guy, *The Dreyfus Case* (London 1955); Johnson, Douglas, *France and the Dreyfus Affair* (New York 1966); Schechter, Betty, *The Dreyfus Affair* (Boston 1965).

DRIESCH, drēsh, **Hans Adolf Eduard** (1867–1941), German experimental biologist and philosopher, who contributed to the development of embryology and was a leading advocate of vitalism. In 1891, Driesch began to study sea urchin eggs. He demonstrated that part of an early embryo could develop into a complete organism, smaller than normal size. This discovery not only was an important contribution to embryology but also directed attention to the role of experiment in studying the development of organisms.

During his early work, Driesch was a mechanist. His work on the development of the sea urchin, however, gradually led him to adopt the philosophy of vitalism (q.v.) and eventually to give up science and become a philosopher. Driesch believed that a nonmaterial agency that he called "entelechy" was the basis of life and individuality and controlled embryonic development. He expounded his vitalistic theories in several books, including *The Science and Philosophy of the Organism* (1908).

Driesch was born in Kreuznach, Germany, on Oct. 28, 1867. He studied at the universities of Freiburg, Munich, and Jena and did research at the Zoological Station of Naples from 1891 to 1900. Later, he was a professor of philosophy at the universities of Heidelberg, Cologne, and Leipzig. He died in Leipzig on April 17, 1941.

ELDON J. GARDNER, *Utah State University*

DRILL, a stout, short-tailed monkey that lives in the tropical rain forests of west central Africa. The drill (*Mandrillus leucophaeus*) is closely related to the mandrill (*M. sphinx*); like the mandrill, it sleeps in trees during the night and forages for food both on the ground and in trees during the day. Both species travel in large groups and feed mainly on fruit, nuts, and small animals.

Although drills have the same habits and general body structure as mandrills, they are somewhat smaller and have slightly longer tails. Also, the coloring of the male drill differs from that of the male mandrill. The male drill has a jet black face, a white beard, and an olive-green body, while the male mandrill has a lacquer-red nose, prominent vivid blue facial swellings near the nose, a yellow beard, and a dark-gray coat.

JOHN R. NAPIER
Author of "A Handbook of Living Primates"

DRILL, any of several small marine snails that feed on bivalves and other snails by boring a hole through the victim's shell. Boring is accomplished by the tiny radulae, or ribbon of teeth, in the snail's mouth. Once a round hole is filed through the victim's shell, the drill extends its proboscis into the animal's soft body and draws out the flesh.

The Atlantic oyster drill (*Urosalpinx cinerea*), which is only about 1 inch (25 mm) long, is a major pest of oysters; one drill can destroy several dozen young oysters in a week. Although native to the Atlantic coast of the United States, the species was accidentally introduced on the Pacific coast. Drills are difficult to eliminate, but sometimes the adults can be lured into traps and destroyed. The female lays dozens of small eggs, each protected by a leathery capsule, among rocks and oyster shells.

R. TUCKER ABBOTT
Academy of Natural Sciences of Philadelphia

DRILL, a cutting tool used to make or to enlarge holes in metal, wood, plastic or other solid materials. Most drills are rotary drills. They produce holes by rotating about their longitudinal axis while at the same time moving axially through the material being drilled. A few drills, also called punches, are percussive and are used with a hammer to make holes. A succession of rapid hammer blows drives the drill into the workpiece. These percussive types of drills are used on hard, brittle, abrasive materials, such as concrete and rock.

Drills are powered by hand or machine. They consist of three parts: a point, a body, and a shank.

Point. At one end of a drill is the point. As the drill moves into the workpiece, the point cuts away small chips. The point on a twist drill is cone-shaped. It has one or more straight cutting edges at the intersection of one edge of each body flute. Thus a two-fluted drill has two cutting edges.

The points of some woodworking drills, or bits, consist of a pointed screw. The points of rock drills, such as the diamond drill, consist of particles of a hard abrasive embedded at the end of a metal tube. Abrasives commonly used for this purpose are particles of tungsten carbide, boron nitride, silicon carbide, and industrial diamonds. The advantage of using a tube-shaped drill rather than a solid one for the drill body is that a smaller amount of the material being drilled has to be abraded away since the tube leaves a solid core that can be mechanically removed in a solid piece.

When the point of a drill gets dull from usage, the cutting edges are sharpened by regrinding. Each sharpening reduces the length of the drill from a few thousandths of an inch to as much as $1/16$ inch (0.16 cm) in the case of an extremely worn drill.

Shank. The shank of a drill is at the driving end of the drill. Its main function is to transmit the torque necessary to rotate the drill and the force necessary to feed the drill into the workpiece. It may have any of various shapes—cylindrical, tapered, splined, or rectangular. The two most common types of shanks used on industrial twist drills are the tapered and the straight, or solid, cylinder.

Body. The center, and major, portion of a drill is the body. The body often contains flutes that run from the point to the shank. Flutes are straight or helical channels through which the

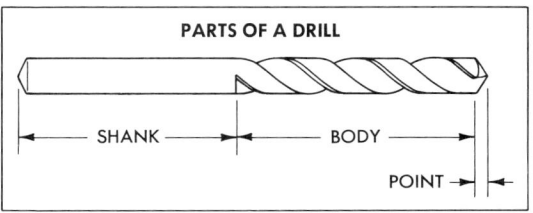

chips or cuttings from the bottom of the drilled hole move to the surface of the workpiece. The actual cutting of the workpiece is done at the point of the drill and not along the fluted body of the drill.

Drilling Machines. *Drill presses* are motor-driven drilling machines used to operate industrial drills. The name is also used to denote the entire machine, including the cutting tool. Small hand or portable drilling machines are called *electric drills* or simply *drills*. They are used mostly in home shops. Drill presses are generally classified according to their weight, position, number of spindles, and means of feeding the drill into the workpiece. The speed of the drill usually decreases with the hardness of the material being drilled. The larger the diameter of the drill, generally the faster it is fed per rotation of the drill.

TWIST DRILLS

The most common types of drills used in manufacturing plants to drill holes in metal, wood, and plastics are twist drills. The name derives from the fact that the flutes of the drill are twisted in the form of a helix about its longitudinal axis. In the larger-sized drills the helix is formed by actually twisting a straight-fluted bar, but in the smaller drills, the helix is formed by machining the flutes in a solid cylindrical bar with a milling cutter. The most common helix angle of the twist drill is 30°. The cross section of a twist drill closely resembles a dumbbell with a very short connecting member. This connecting member is called the *web*.

Among the most common types of twist drills used in industry, in addition to the straight-shank and taper-shank drills, are core drills, center drills, and gun drills.

Core Drills. Core drills are three-fluted drills. They are used for enlarging cast, forged, or punched holes. They cannot be used to originate holes.

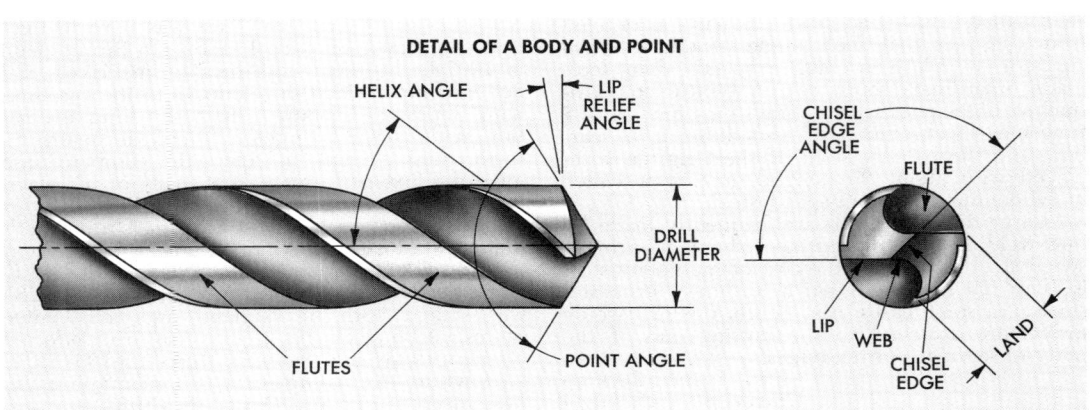

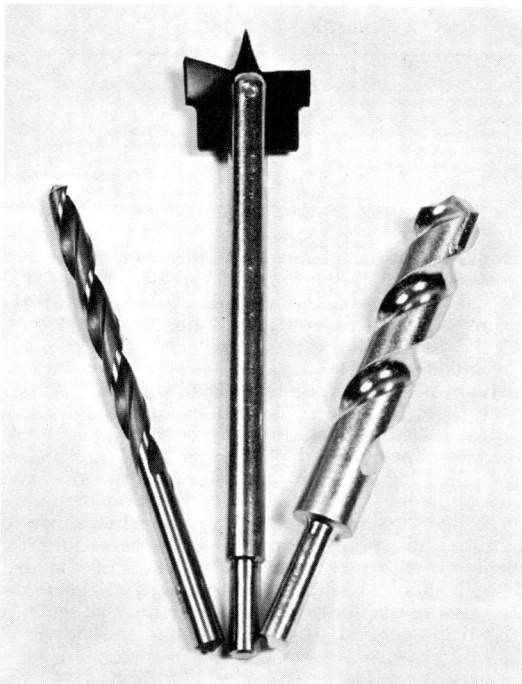

BLACK & DECKER MFG. CO.

SPECIAL DRILLS are designed for originating and enlarging holes in a variety of materials. From left to right are drills for working metal, wood and masonry.

Center Drills. Center holes in workpieces are often made with center drills. They have both a drill portion and an adjacent countersink portion. The countersink is used to flare the end of the drilled hole in the workpiece so that it may be held between conical ends during subsequent machining and grinding.

Gun Drills. Gun drills are straight-fluted drills that are used for drilling deep holes (the depth of the hole is generally greater than about 10 times the diameter of the drill). Gun drills usually have cutting-fluid passages running longitudinally through the body to both cool the cutting edges and flush out the chips as the drill moves into the workpiece.

Drill Materials. The home-shop and cheaper twist drills are made of inexpensive carbon tool steel. The most common material used to make the commercial twist drills is a type of high alloy steel called high-speed steel. Its name is derived from the fact that tools made of this material can cut at relatively higher speeds than tools made of ordinary tool steel. A typical composition of high-speed steel (tungsten type) is 18% tungsten, 4% chromium, 1% vanadium, 0.75% carbon, and the balance iron. If the tungsten is replaced with about 8% molybdenum, it is called molybdenum type high-speed steel.

Large-diameter drills are frequently made by butt-welding a structural steel shank to a high-speed steel body since the cost of high alloy steel is 10 to 20 times as great as ordinary structural steels. In some cases, cast nonferrous or carbide inserts are attached to the cutting end of the body to serve as cutting edges.

JOSEPH DATSKO
University of Michigan

DRILL, Military, the training of soldiers to respond automatically to command, so that they will perform their duties in battle despite danger or disturbance. It involves the practice and rehearsal of prescribed movements to weld individual soldiers into a team, and seeks to develop self-control, discipline, and immediate obedience.

Close-order drill consists of formal marching movements for parades and ceremonies. *Extended-order drill*, sometimes called *combat drill*, emphasizes the more flexible movements required on the battlefield. Live ammunition may be used to accustom troops to combat conditions.

All training, whether in rifle marksmanship or in tank battle formations, is regarded as drill. The regular meetings of Reservists and National Guardsmen, whether they are combat troops preparing for antiriot duties or public relations officers planning a recruiting campaign, are called drills.

Modern drill emerged from the introduction of firearms in warfare. The musket was difficult to load and fire and was highly inaccurate. In order to gain effectiveness, soldiers had to fire in unison (volleys). This required them to load their pieces, an intricate process, simultaneously. A series of commands led the men of a unit through the numerous steps of loading, aiming, and firing. The ability of troops to perform these actions in the presence of the enemy depended on their having been thoroughly drilled.

In the 17th and 18th centuries, all the formal movements of troops on the battlefield also required teamwork. Soldiers were usually from the least educated classes, so constant practice and rehearsal were necessary. A severe, perfectionist drillmaster is still called a "martinet," after Jean Martinet, inspector general of infantry in France under Louis XIV.

Improvements in the accuracy and range of weapons and the development of new forms of warfare that stress individual initiative and flexibility have largely outmoded close-order drill. But a howitzer crew still is drilled to achieve smooth teamwork and rapid execution of a prescribed series of actions. In peacetime exhibitions of marching and rifle handling in unison, special drill teams demonstrate adeptness in complex movements, even though these movements have little direct relationship to battle.

MARTIN BLUMENSON
Author of "The Duel for France"

DRINKWATER, John (1882–1937), English playwright and poet, who is best known for his play *Abraham Lincoln* (1918). He was born in Leytonstone, Essex, on June 1, 1882. In Birmingham in 1907 he helped found the Pilgrim Players, the acting company that developed into the Birmingham Repertory Theatre. He had a long association with the Birmingham "Rep" as actor, director, and general manager; the company also gave the first performances of many of his plays. He died in London on March 25, 1937.

In addition to *Abraham Lincoln*, Drinkwater's important historical dramas are *Mary Stuart* (1922), *Oliver Cromwell* (1923), and *Robert E. Lee* (1923). His comedy *Bird in Hand* (1928) was staged both in England and the United States. Among his books of verse are *Collected Poems* (1923) and *Summer Harvest* (1934). He also wrote two volumes of autobiography: *Inheritance* (1931) and *Discovery* (1932).

DRIVE, in psychology, an internal condition that arouses, sustains, and directs the activity of an organism. Such a condition forms a necessary link between stimulus and response. The concept of drive was adopted to explain and integrate a phenomenon previously explained in terms of such notions as hunger, thirst, and pain.

Physiological and Acquired Drives. Drives are conventionally divided into two types, physiological (or primary) and acquired (or secondary). Most physiological drives are continually recurring metabolic conditions based on organic needs such as those for air, water, food, rest, and (in the higher species) constant internal temperature. A physiological drive in any species is common to all or nearly all individuals of the species; estimates of the number of such drives in human beings vary, ranging up to about 12. Acquired drives, although based on physiological drives, are the products of learning. Hence they are more common, and characteristically less closely related to physiological drives, among the higher species.

The first American psychologist to use the term "drive" was Robert Woodworth, who proposed the concept in 1918 as analogous to the energy needed to drive a machine. Later psychologists distinguished various physiological drives according to their goals, or incentives, and attempted to measure their relative strengths. In 1943, Clark Hull introduced the hypothesis of a general drive that, when present, reinforces all of an organism's responses to stimuli. Such a drive, the existence of which is indicated by physiological and anatomical evidence, is distinguished from specific drives, which reinforce only such responses as satisfy specific needs.

The first comprehensive theoretical treatment of acquired drives appeared in *Social Learning and Imitation* (1941), by John Dollard and Neal Miller. The authors held that acquired drives are directed toward goals that the individual has learned to utilize for or to identify with the satisfaction of physiological drives.

The concept of the acquired drive is most often employed in explaining the process of socialization among human beings. In modern society, socialization generally involves the substitution of stimulation by acquired drives for stimulation by physiological drives. An illustration is the custom of eating at set times during the day rather than waiting for a deficiency of glucose in the bloodstream or for the onset of hunger pangs. An acquired drive of some sort is usually invoked in accounting for such behavior as working for money, seeking power, or seeking security.

Drives and Learning Theory. Since the 1940's, the role of learning in the motivation of human behavior has been one of the most extensively researched and discussed areas in psychology, and the number of acquired drives that have been postulated is almost infinite. It is not entirely clear, however, whether the concept of the acquired drive is necessary. It is obviously related to the learning process by which neutral objects and ideas gain rewarding power by association with valued goals. Thus the phenomena now explained by the concept of the acquired drive may perhaps be explained more economically by the principles of association learning theory.

MICHAEL G. ROTHENBERG
Columbia University

DROESHOUT, drōōs'hout, **Martin** (1601–c. 1650), English engraver, whose portrait of William Shakespeare accompanied the First Folio (1623), the first edition of Shakespeare's works. Droeshout is thought to have been born in London in April 1601, but the place of birth is uncertain. He is believed to have been the son of the engraver Michiel Droeshout, who probably trained him in his craft. Although Ben Jonson praised Droeshout's portrait of Shakespeare as "true to life," it is unlikely that Droeshout executed the famous engraving until after Shakespeare's death in 1616. Droeshout's work included other portraits and book decorations.

DROGHEDA, drô'ə-də, an urban district and seaport in County Louth, Ireland, is on the Boyne River, 4 miles (6 km) from its mouth in Drogheda Bay. It is one of Ireland's largest towns. Drogheda manufactures cement, footwear, linen, cotton, and beer and is also a thriving market town. The port has a considerable trade with Britain.

Founded by the Danes in 911, Drogheda was taken by the Normans and became an important center of English rule. Irish parliaments were frequently held in the town; in 1494 a parliament there enacted the hated Poynings' law, which declared all future laws invalid unless ratified by the English privy council. The town figured largely in the wars of the 17th century and was held by a garrison of 3,000 Royalists against Cromwell in 1649. When it was finally taken by Cromwell that year, the defenders were all killed or transported to Barbados. In 1690, Drogheda surrendered to William III the day after the Battle of the Boyne, fought 3 miles (5 km) to the west. Population: (1966) 17,823.

THOMAS FITZGERALD
Department of Education, Dublin

DRÔME, drōm, is a department of southeastern France, in the western and southwestern portion of what was the province of Dauphiné. It is bounded on the west by the Rhône River. Drôme has an area of 2,533 square miles (6,560 sq km). The department seat is Valence.

Physiographically, the department is divided into three distinct belts: the Alps proper in the east, the pre-Alps in the center, and the Rhône Valley in the west. A number of streams flow westward through Drôme to join the Rhône; the most important are the Isère, the Drôme, and the Aygues. The northern part of the department is rainier and greener than the south, and it lacks a distinct dry season. Toward the south the summers are very hot and arid, and the landscape's hues reflect the drier climate. The population grows steadily sparser toward the east and the more mountainous terrain.

Drôme produces olives, wine, and fruit and manufactures textiles, felt hats, and shoes. Montélimar is noted for its nougat (a nut confection). Considerable hydroelectric power is generated at Montélimar, at the southwestern border (Donzère-Mondragon), and along the lower Isère. Population: (1962) 304,227.

HOMER PRICE, *Hunter College*

DROMEDARY. See CAMEL.

DRONE, a male honeybee, which is stingless and does not share in the general work of the hive: hence, figuratively, an unproductive idler.

DRONE FLY, a widely distributed species (*Eristalis tenax*) of hover fly (family Syrphidae). The adult is yellow and brown, with a patterned abdomen, and resembles the drone of the honeybee. Often seen on leaves or feeding on the nectar and pollen of flowers, it is generally mistaken for a bee, but it has no sting, cannot bite, and is quite harmless. Adult drone flies often hibernate, and they may then be discovered indoors in large numbers, crowded into small crevices.

The larva of the drone fly is aquatic but breathes air. It takes in air through two openings (spiracles) located at the end of a long telescopic breathing tube, which is kept at the surface of the water. Because of the presence of this tube, which looks like a tail, the larva is known as the rat-tailed maggot. It feeds on any animal or vegetable debris and also takes in dissolved organic substances from the water. It lives in foul water of all kinds, such as stagnant pools, tanks, or cisterns, and in the organic seepage from heaps of farmyard manure and vegetable garbage.

HAROLD OLDROYD
British Museum (Natural History), London

DRONGO, drong'gō, any of a family of about 20 species of birds possibly related to the Old World flycatchers. Drongos are most common in Southeast Asia, but they also occur in southern Africa, the Malay archipelago, and northeastern Australia. The king crow (*Dicrurus macrocercus*) of India is a typical species.

Varying in size from 8 to 14 inches (20–35 cm), drongos are typically iridescent black and have long, deeply forked tails. Their beaks are heavy, arched, and slightly hooked at the tip, and their nostrils are covered with long bristles. Some drongos have extravagantly ornamental feathers, such as shaggy head crests or long, racketlike tail feathers.

Drongos frequent forest canopies and edges, wooded savannas, and cultivated fields at altitudes from sea level to 10,000 feet (3,000 meters). They are pugnacious in defending their nests and aggressive in seeking food. They feed almost exclusively on insects, catching many of them on the wing. Some species of drongos associate with cattle and monkeys in order to catch the insects that are usually near these animals. The calls of most drongos are noisy and harsh, but some species can mimic the melodious calls of other birds.

The drongo nest is a shallow saucer of twigs, grass, and lichen, held together with cobwebs. The female lays 3 to 4 eggs that are usually speckled white. Both sexes care for the young.

Drongos are classified in two genera: *Dicrurus* and *Chaetorhynchus* in the family Dicruridae of the order Passeriformes.

CARL WELTY
Beloit College

DROP FORGING. See FORGE, FORGING, AND FORGING MACHINES.

DROPOUT, a person who leaves school before completing a course of study. Such students, particularly those who drop out of high school, face serious handicaps in finding jobs. See CAREER PLANNING; EDUCATION—6. *Secondary Education*

DROPSY is a term sometimes applied to the accumulation of fluid in the body. The condition is more commonly known as *edema*. See EDEMA.

DROSERA. See SUNDEW.

DROSHKY, drosh'kē, a small, low, four-wheeled open carriage used by the Russians. It is uncovered. A bench runs down the middle of the body. The driver straddles the bench, and the passengers ride either straddling it or side by side, resting their feet on bars below. The wheels are covered by mudguards.

The name "droshky" is applied also to several other types of two- or four-wheeled vehicles used in the Soviet Union as well as in other countries.

DROSOMETER. See DEW.

DROSOPHILA, drō-sof'a-la, is a genus of fruit flies, sometimes called *wine flies* or *vinegar flies*, found primarily in tropical regions. Though only a small proportion of the nearly 800 species are native to temperate areas, *Drosophila* can survive and even breed through the winter in indoor habitats throughout the world.

Drosophila larvae feed, most commonly, on decaying fruit and vegetables. The adults are about ⅛ inch (3 mm) long and have one pair of broad wings, feathery antennae, and usually bright red eyes. The *Drosophila* life cycle is about two weeks per generation.

D. melanogaster, a species that is used in genetics research, can be bred in small glass jars containing raw oatmeal wetted with a suspension of brewer's yeast (100 grams of yeast to 600 cc of water).

HAROLD OLDROYD
British Museum (Natural History), London

Common drongo

DROSTE-HÜLSHOFF, dros'tə hüls'hōf, **Baroness Annette Elisabeth von** (1797–1848), German writer, who is considered Germany's finest woman poet. She was born into a noble Catholic family of Westphalia on Jan. 10, 1797, at the Hülshoff mansion near Münster. After her father's death in 1826, she moved with her mother to Rüschhaus, a small estate near Hülshoff. Her first book of poems appeared in 1838. In 1841 she spent a year at the castle of her brother-in-law, Joseph, Baron von Lassberg, in Meersberg near Lake Constance. There she became deeply infatuated with the writer Levin Schücking, who later wrote and appreciative biography, *Annette von Droste* (1862). The success of a second volume of lyrics and ballads, which appeared in 1844, enabled her to buy a small cottage near Meersburg, where she spent her last years in poor health. She died at Meersburg on May 24, 1848.

Annette von Droste-Hülshoff wrote in regional and Catholic traditions. However, although she upheld the standards of her aristocratic past, she was keenly aware of the dissolution of the old order, which began in her lifetime. As a writer of such epic ballads as *Die Schlacht im Loener Bruch*, she followed somewhat in the English romantic tradition of Sir Walter Scott. However, in her nature lyrics, she disdained all sentimentality, and relied instead on earthy words or scientific description. Her most personal poetic confession is contained in *Das geistliche Jahr* (completed in 1839, but published posthumously in 1851), a devotional book, which nevertheless voices many religious doubts.

Of her narrative prose, the novella *Die Judenbuche* (1842) achieved far-reaching fame. This realistic tale of guilt and retribution, set in Westphalia, tells how the murderer of a Jewish tradesman is finally punished through divine justice. The best edition of Annette Droste-Hülshoff's complete works appeared in 4 volumes in 1925–1930.

ERNST ROSE
Author of "A History of German Literature"

Further Reading: Droste-Hülshoff, Annette von, *The Jews' Beech Tree*, tr. by Angel Flores in *Nineteenth Century German Tales* (New York 1959); Mare, Margaret L., *Annette von Droste-Hülshoff*, including many translations of her poems (Lincoln, Nebr., 1965).

DROUAIS, drōō-e′, **François Hubert** (1727–1775), French portrait painter. He was born in Paris and spent his life there, receiving his earliest training from his father Hubert Drouais (1699–1767), a competent miniaturist, and later studying under such noted artists as Boucher. In 1756 Drouais became court painter to Louis XV, and in 1758 he was admitted to the Royal Academy. He exhibited regularly in the Paris Salon from 1755 until his death in Paris in 1775.

Drouais' sitters ranged from famous actresses (Mme. Favart) and courtesans (Mme. du Barry and Mme. de Pompadour) to the entire royal family. Children were featured in his work, their noble birth never obscured by such guises as gypsy costume or pastoral setting. These picturesque contrivances, like the assumption of mythological roles by court ladies, were recurrent elements in his art. Drouais' earlier works were delicately and skillfully handled, but his popularity caused him to become increasingly superficial.

Jean Germain Drouais (1763–1788), François' son, was also a painter.

JANICE K. JOHNSON, *Art Gallery of Ontario*

DROUGHT, drout, is a deficiency of water in the ground, streams, lakes, and reservoirs, resulting from a prolonged deficiency of rain and snow melt. It causes damage to crops and depletion of the water supply. No precise definition of the term is acceptable to all persons and interests adversely affected by drought. A month of below-normal precipitation may not have any important effect on water supply in reservoirs; but if it occurs when crops are just emerging from the ground, crop damage can be severe. Thus, farmers might call the condition a drought while city dwellers might not.

Drought is insidious. Its effects can take firm hold of the economy before the people realize what is happening. A few weeks of pleasant weather are generally welcome, but they may so deplete the groundwater that only a quick change to rainy weather can prevent ill effects. People tend to be optimistic and assume that the rains will surely come. Government officials responsible for water and food supplies may also fail to recognize the gravity of the situation until it is too late for effective countermeasures.

The Nature of Drought. Drought is essentially an imbalance of the hydrologic cycle. In this cycle, water vapor enters the atmosphere by evaporation from oceans, lakes, and ground surfaces and by transpiration from plants. Water is returned to the earth in the form of rain or snow. Some of it recharges the soil moisture, some accumulates in bodies of water, and some runs off to the oceans. Thus, drought can result simply from a deficiency in precipitation over a period of time, or it may be caused or intensified by excessive evaporation and transpiration.

The normal difference between precipitation and evapotranspiration (evaporation plus transpiration) is a measure of the dryness or wetness of a climate. In this sense desert areas, with a great excess of evapotranspiration over precipitation, are in perpetual drought. Some areas have drought in one season of the year, and other areas have a year-round water surplus that is discharged through streams and rivers. However, the economy of any region tends to be closely adjusted to normal climatic conditions, so that it is more practical to confine the term drought to abnormally dry periods. A drought in Cairo, Egypt, where the normal annual precipitation is 1.1 inches (27.9 mm), is vastly different from a drought in New Orleans, La., where 64 inches (1,626 mm), is expected annually.

An *index of meteorological drought* has been devised in an attempt to make the definition more meaningful in relation to a local economy. The index is based upon actual precipitation as compared to the amount of precipitation required. The latter depends upon the amount of moisture already in the ground, the amount of rainfall that can be absorbed, the runoff in streams, and the evapotranspiration. The index varies from above +4 (extreme wetness) to below −4 (extreme drought) and is computed for each month.

Causes of Drought. Explaining the causes of drought is one of the most intractable problems in the science of meteorology, even though many direct causes are recognized. Aside from the obvious statement that drought results from lack of precipitation, it is known that drought is intensified by high temperature, strong wind, and low humidity, all of which increase the loss of moisture by evapotranspiration. One important cause of drought is a shifting of normal cyclone

DROUGHT affecting northeastern United States, drying up parts of the Delaware River (l.) in 1965, was caused by northwesterly winds moving unusually far south and pushing moist air out to sea.

(low-pressure storm system) tracks across a region, leaving some areas in the region without their normal precipitation for protracted periods. Associated with the shifting of storm tracks is a tendency for the affected area to be dominated by high-pressure systems in which the air sinks and is warmed by compression, preventing condensation and precipitation. This is the cause of the perpetual droughts in the great deserts of the earth. However, although shifting storm tracks and persistent highs are reocgnized causes of drought, it is not known why they happen, when they can be expected, or when they will end.

Another recognizable cause of drought is abnormally low sea-surface temperatures. For example, on the west coast of Peru there is usually little precipitation except in the feeble form of drizzle. Low sea-surface temperatures off the coast stabilize the atmosphere so that the vertical air currents needed to produce appreciable precipitation are suppressed. On the rare occasions when warmer water from equatorial regions moves southward along the coast of Peru, the rainfall becomes disastrously heavy. Any region situated downwind from the ocean is likely to suffer from below-normal precipitation if the ocean temperatures are below normal.

There are other causes of drought that are plausible or only suspected. Any attempt at a scientific explanation must recognize that several causative factors, each of small effect and relatively independent of the others, may happen to act simultaneously. It has been found that annual rainfall varies from year to year in the same manner as a random variable (a quantity whose variation is controlled by a number of independent factors). Thus, drought may be a random process, predictable only to the extent that the individual causes can be predicted months ahead of time. Such predictions are not yet possible.

Controlling Drought. Lacking sufficient knowledge of the causes of drought and the ability to predict them, man is in no position to devise effective means of control. Although it is possible in certain circumstances to increase natural precipitation by seeding clouds with materials such as dry ice and silver iodide, this method is useless unless rain-bearing clouds are present. A drought is characterized by lower than normal humidity at cloud level, less frequent occurrences of precipitation, and less precipitation when it does occur. Conceivably, a small improvement might be achieved by attempting to increase the amount of rain in the relatively rare instances when some rain actually is falling.

Man in fact may be inadvertently affecting natural rainfall by the ever-increasing amount of pollution he puts into the atmosphere. Some of the particulate pollutants can act as nuclei for condensation of water vapor, with two possible but opposite consequences: an increase of precipitation where natural nuclei are scarce, or a decrease resulting from the formation of too many tiny cloud droplets that cannot conglomerate into raindrops. Local effects of man's activity have already been observed. For example, the rainfall at La Porte, Ind., has steadily increased over the years as industrial activity in the nearby Chicago area has expanded. It is believed that the heat produced by the industries is directly responsible for the increase.

By far the greatest effort is concentrated on controlling the effects of drought instead of on controlling drought itself. In the great (1962–1966) drought in the northeastern United States, for example, the reservoirs supplying water to New York City fell to dangerously low levels. The Hudson River was tapped and its polluted water purified, thereby supplementing the water supply by about 10% of the normal requirement. Residents were asked to conserve water, and other water-saving measures were required.

Irrigation and mulching, commonly practiced in the agriculture of semiarid climates, may be adopted as emergency measures during a drought in more humid climates. Irrigation is not likely to be successful, however, partly because the necessary piping and ditches take time to construct, but mostly because the streams dry up and the water supply from wells diminishes as the water table level in the ground lowers.

Adaptations. Plants and trees in semiarid climates have become adapted to survival during the dry season of the year. In general, the adaptation is accomplished by dormancy or by protective coatings on the leaves to reduce transpiration. Desert plants have deep, extensive roots and a minimum of transpiration. Seeds of desert flowers will not germinate until, after a period of months or years, a heavy rainstorm thoroughly soaks the upper several inches of the ground. When the desert soil is sufficiently moist, the seeds germinate, quickly grow to maturity, and produce flowers and new seeds before the soil moisture has been lost by evaporation.

Droughts in the Past. There is no doubt that drought has been a recurrent weather phenomenon since the time when, early in the history of the planet earth, the primitive atmosphere evolved into the atmosphere of today. The history of droughts for many thousands of years past is recorded in the sedimentation of the earth's surface and in deposits on the floor of the oceans. Tree rings in living trees are an especially useful record of fluctuations in annual precipitation for the past 3,000 years. For even more remote times, fossil trees can be used. The thickness of an annual ring is governed primarily by the availability of moisture. However, both sedimentation and tree rings are affected by other processes in addition to drought, so that their interpretation requires expert knowledge plus some assumptions. Since drought is a complex phenomenon, involving not only rainfall but also ground moisture supply and other factors, there can be no certainty of the occurrence and severity of a drought without adequate firsthand observations, and these are generally available only for the past 100 years.

Long-period variations in rainfall can lead to decades, centuries, or millenniums that are drier or wetter than usual. For example, indirect evidence indicates that a marked deficiency occurred in Britain and Sweden from about the 25th century B.C. to the 22d century B.C. and that this deficiency moved to central Europe in the period of the 23d to the 21st century B.C. (Accurate observations of rainfall are available for too short a time to permit assessment of any long-period, or "secular," trends that may be in progress at the present time.)

In the United States after the Civil War, settlers in large numbers spread throughout the area between the Mississippi River and the Rocky Mountains, claimed homesteads, and began farming and cattle raising. All went well in years when the rainfall was ample, but about every 5 to 10 years there was a drought lasting one or more years. The farmers, dependent upon a maximum yield, were in some years forced by the thousands to give up their property and move elsewhere. Even a minor drought could cause the cattle growers to send most of their stock to market, glutting the market and depressing prices to low levels. Nevertheless, in World War I, cultivation and grazing of the land in this region (particularly the semiarid part known as the Great Plains) were extended in response to the high prices available at that time. They continued to be extended in the 1920's, when rainfall was usually adequate, but overcultivation and overgrazing removed most of the tough grasses that had protected the land from erosion.

Then came the great drought of the 1930's. Topsoil was picked up by the wind, carried eastward in dense "black blizzards," and deposited all over the eastern and southeastern United States. Combined with the economic depression of the 1930's, this drought brought financial disaster to most of the farmers. Many of them, penniless, emigrated as best they could to California and other places where life seemed better. The "Dust Bowl" of this period, comprising parts of the Texas Panhandle, western Oklahoma, southwestern Kansas, and southeastern Colorado, became a vast wilderness of loose dust scoured from the ground and carried by the wind.

Drought Disasters Today. Great as the Dust Bowl disaster was, nearly all of the people survived, but such is not the case when drought strikes a heavily populated region where people are completely dependent for each year's food supply on the crops produced in that year. China and India are especially vulnerable. Seemingly slight deficiencies of rainfall or slight delays in the onset of the summer monsoon rains will diminish the agricultural production to the point of famine. Of all weather hazards, drought is clearly the greatest killer, although it does not strike with sudden spectacular violence. A single drought-produced famine cost a million lives in India and several million in China. A six-year drought in northern Africa, particularly in the West African countries of Senegal, Mauritania, Mali, Upper Volta, Niger, and Chad, was partially alleviated in rains in 1974, but by that time tens of thousands of people and millions of cattle and other livestock had died. See also CLIMATE; DESERT.

JAMES E. MILLER
New York University

DROWNING, droun'ing, is suffocation caused by the presence of water or another liquid in the lungs. Drowning is one of the leading causes of accidental deaths (see ACCIDENTS—*Drownings*). Although it occurs most often in deep water, it may also occur in only a few inches of water, as in a bathtub.

Shortly after water enters the lungs, the body tissues are deprived of oxygen, and carbon dioxide accumulates in the body. The increased carbon dioxide stimulates the respiratory centers of the brain, which produce an increase in the rate and depth of respiratory movements. The rate of heartbeat is also increased, and the veins in the neck become prominent. Within a few minutes, however, both the respiratory movements and the heartbeat slow down. Death usually occurs if the victim remains submerged for more than 5 minutes. When a person is rescued, he must immediately be given artificial respiration. See ARTIFICIAL RESPIRATION.

DROYSEN, droi'zən, **Johann Gustav** (1808–1884), German historian. He was born on July 6, 1808, at Treptow in Prussian Pomerania. After studying classical philology and history, he taught at Kiel, Jena, and Berlin. In early publications on Greek history and Alexander the Great, Droysen developed the concept of "Hellenism" (the diffusion of Greek influence in the Mediterranean and Middle Eastern world, from Alexander to Augustus). His basic work on historiography, *Grundrisse der Historik* (1868), reflects the influences of Hegel and of German idealism.

At Kiel, Droysen supported the anti-Danish cause of the duchies of Schleswig and Holstein. After the 1848 revolution began he was elected to the Frankfurt Parliament and became secretary of its constitutional committee and editor of the parliamentary debates. When the Prussian king declined the crown offered by the Parliament in 1849, Droysen withdrew from politics.

Thereafter, Droysen concentrated on studies in Prussian history, based primarily on original sources. He also stimulated publication of the writings and political correspondence of Frederick the Great. He died in Berlin on June 19, 1884.

HENRY CORD MEYER
University of California at Irvine

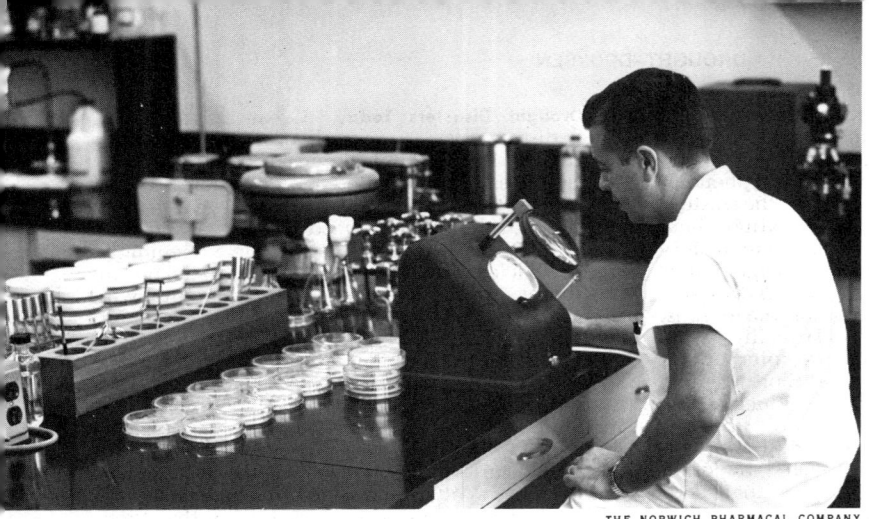

A technician in a pharmacology laboratory examines fungus cultures on which a potential antifungal compound has been tested to determine whether the compound is effective in inhibiting the fungus growth.

THE NORWICH PHARMACAL COMPANY

DRUG, a chemical agent that is used therapeutically to treat disease. More broadly, a drug may be defined as any chemical agent that affects living protoplasm. Few substances would escape this definition, however, and the term "drug" is usually used in its narrower sense to refer to a chemical whose specific purpose is the treatment of a disease.

CONTENTS

Section	Page	Section	Page
1. Sources and Uses of Drugs	404	4. Factors Influencing Drug Action	409
2. Drugs and Their Effects	405	5. Drug Toxicity	409
Chemotherapeutic Drugs	405	6. Drug Tolerance, Dependence, and Addiction	410
Pharmacodynamic Drugs	406	7. Government Regulations Concerning Drugs	410
3. Drug Administration, Absorption, and Excretion	408		

Drugs provide the basis of the practice of modern medicine. In 1900, man's life expectancy in the United States was 47 years; in the early 1980's it was over 70 years. Part of this great increase in life expectancy has been the result of the discovery of new drugs and their introduction into medicine.

The art of preparing, compounding, and dispensing drugs is known as *pharmacy*, while the study of the physical and chemical properties, absorption, fate, excretion, effects, and mode of action of drugs in the body is called *pharmacology*. The study of the use of drugs in the treatment of disease is called *therapeutics*.

1. Sources and Uses of Drugs

The number of drugs used today is vast and is steadily increasing as new drugs are developed and new uses are found for old drugs.

Sources. Several drugs still used by doctors, such as the active principle in aspirin, have been used clinically for many hundreds of years. Many drugs, including digitalis, cocaine, morphine, and others, are of plant origin. At first, drugs were often rather crude, and pharmacognosy, the branch of pharmacology that deals with the physical characteristics of crude drugs, came to focus on the study of the botanical sources of drugs.

Drugs may also be obtained from animal or mineral sources. Many hormone preparations, for example, are obtained from animal tissue, and many drugs contain minerals, such as sodium, potassium, and iron, essential for the proper functioning of the body. Drugs of plant, animal, or mineral sources are still being introduced into medicine.

Most modern drugs, however, are synthetic. Even drugs, such as the salicylates, that can be obtained from natural sources are now often wholly made synthetically because of the resulting greater purity or lower manufacturing costs. Other naturally occurring drugs, such as many of the penicillins, are produced by partial chemical synthesis from some simpler biological compound. The great advantage of synthetic and semisynthetic drugs is that minor changes in the structure of the drug can be made during the synthetic process, and these changes may enhance or modify the therapeutic response to the drug.

Uses. The main purpose of the use of drugs is to cure disease or correct a disorder. Chemotherapeutic drugs, such as the antibiotics, the sulfa drugs, and the antimalarial drugs, fight infection by acting directly on disease-causing invading organisms, either immobilizing or killing them. Some chemotherapeutic drugs are also used to suppress or prevent infection. The use of quinacrine (also called atabrine) to suppress overt clinical attacks of malaria during World War II is a prime example of the preventive use of a chemotherapeutic agent.

Pharmacodynamic drugs, on the other hand, do not fight infection but cure disease by affecting the systems of the body. Atropine, for example, blocks the transmission of impulses from nerves to muscles and glands in the wall of the stomach and intestines and thus greatly reduces movement of the gastrointestinal system and the secretion of gastric juices, with a consequent beneficial action in cases of peptic ulcer.

A third class of drugs includes those drugs that are used diagnostically to determine whether or not disease is present. For example, a large and abrupt fall in blood pressure following the intravenous injection of phentolamine (a drug that blocks some of the effects of epinephrine and norepinephrine—hormones produced by the adrenal gland) into a person indicates the presence of pheochromocytoma, a cancer of the cells of the adrenal medulla. Other drugs are used to prevent disease, to counteract poisons, or to modify the effects of another drug. See also Toxicology—*Treatment;* Vaccines and Vaccination.

2. Drugs and Their Effects

Although the exact way in which some drugs act is not clearly understood, the main effects of the various chemotherapeutic and pharmacodynamic drugs are known.

CHEMOTHERAPEUTIC DRUGS

The chemotherapeutic agents used to fight and kill invading organisms that cause infection fall into several broad classes depending on the type of infection that they combat.

Classes of Chemotherapeutic Drugs—Antibiotics. Antibiotics are substances derived from one living microorganism that are used to attack and eventually to kill other microorganisms. They are produced by various species of microorganisms, including bacteria, fungi, and actinomyces. Many hundreds of antibiotics have been isolated, but only a fraction of these have been developed to the stage where they are useful in the treatment of infections. Nevertheless, a vast number of antibiotics are now available, and their introduction and widespread use since the 1940's represent perhaps the most dramatic event in modern medicine.

The golden age of antimicrobial therapy started in 1941. Penicillin was discovered by Alexander Fleming in London in 1929, but it was 1941 before the brilliant research of a group of investigators, led by Sir Howard W. Florey in Oxford, England, enabled penicillin to be produced in quantities sufficient to permit clinical trials. A vast research program undertaken in the United States by governmental, university, and industrial laboratories made possible the commercial manufacture of large quantities of the antibiotic in time to save untold numbers of lives during World War II.

Penicillin is highly effective against a vast number of disease-causing microorganisms. Unfortunately, however, two drawbacks appeared soon after the use of the original preparation, known as penicillin G. First, penicillin G is unstable in the acidic stomach contents and so cannot be given reliably by mouth. This drawback was subsequently overcome by chemically modifying the structure of the parent drug. The second and major drawback to penicillin therapy is that many of the microorganisms originally sensitive to the antibiotic lose their sensitivity to it —that is, they acquire resistance to the drug. Furthermore, some microorganisms appear to be naturally resistant to the drug. Both the acquired and natural bacterial resistance to penicillin occur because the resistant microorganisms produce an enzyme called penicillinase that destroys the antibiotic before it can act therapeutically. Fortunately, bacterial resistance can be overcome, at least partly, by using modified penicillins, such as oxacillin, that are resistant to destruction by penicillinase. Very often, however, the microorganisms in time again acquire resistance to penicillin even in its modified form, and some other antibiotic has to be used to treat the infection.

Bacterial resistance occurs with all antibiotics. Fortunately, cross-resistance is not usual, however. This means that a population of organisms that has become resistant to penicillin through repeated exposure to it will probably not have become resistant to an antibiotic from an entirely different group, such as streptomycin, and infections may then be successfully treated with this second antibiotic. However, if the population is then exposed to streptomycin for a long time, it may eventually acquire resistance to this drug as well. The population might still be sensitive to a third and fourth class of antibiotics, however, and for this reason, there is a continuing search for new antibiotics.

The effectiveness of penicillin in the treatment of certain types of infection was the prime stimulus for the search for other types of antibiotics. The search led in 1943 to the discovery by Selman A. Waksman and his co-workers of a strain of actinomycetes (filamentous bacteria, often parasitic in mammals) in the soil that produced a potent antimicrobial substance they named streptomycin. Streptomycin was found to combat a large number of infections that were unaffected by penicillin. Although its therapeutical usefulness has been restricted in recent years by the discovery of other antimicrobial agents, streptomycin is still widely used in the treatment of tuberculosis.

The success of penicillin and streptomycin prompted the systematic screening of soil specimens from all over the world in an effort to find more antibiotics. One result of this work was the introduction in 1948 of a new class of antibiotic agents called tetracyclines. The tetracyclines are effective against a wide range of infections and so are called broad-spectrum antibiotics. They are the drugs of choice for the treatment of psittacosis, one of the few viral diseases susceptible to antibiotic treatment. Other antimicrobial agents include chloramphenicol, which is particularly effective against typhoid fever but which has many dangerous effects that make its use in other diseases highly questionable; nystatin, which is useful in treating fungal infections; and many other agents, including erythromycin and cephalosporin.

Sulfa Drugs. The sulfa drugs were the first effective chemotherapeutic agents to be employed systematically for the prevention and cure of bacteria infections in man. Although compounds containing sulfonamide groups had been prepared at the beginning of the 20th century, credit for the discovery of the chemotherapeutic value of sulfa drugs belongs to Gerhard Domagk, who was awarded the 1938 Nobel Prize in physiology or medicine for his discovery. The considerable medical and public health importance of the discovery and the subsequent widespread use of sulfa drugs were quickly reflected in the sharp decline in morbidity and mortality figures for infectious diseases. Before the advent of penicillin, the sulfonamides were the mainstay of antibacterial chemotherapy. Although they have been replaced to a large extent by the antibiotics, they continue to occupy an important, though small, place in modern medicine.

Antimalarial Drugs. Various malaria-causing parasites of the genus *Plasmodium* are transmitted to man by mosquitoes. Antimalarial drugs have been developed to fight malarial infections in several different ways. Primaquine, for example, is a causal prophylactic, or preventive, drug that kills the malarial parasites almost immediately after they are injected by the mosquito; primaquine may also effect a radical cure, completely ridding the body of the parasites. Other agents, such as chloroquine, which is one of the most generally useful of the antimalarial drugs, do not prevent initial infection but do stop the multiplication of the parasites within the red corpuscles of the blood and thus keep the infected individual free of the characteristic recurring bouts of malarial fever. Quinine—the first drug widely used to treat malaria—is today rarely employed alone as an antimalarial agent except in those parts of the world where the new antimalarial drugs are not available.

After prolonged exposure to antimalarial drugs, the population of malarial parasites acquires a certain degree of resistance to the drug, and now there are several parts of the world where programs aimed at the mass suppression of malaria have resulted in the appearance of drug-resistant strains of *Plasmodium*.

Antituberculosis Drugs. The antituberculosis drugs are the keystone of the management of all forms of tuberculosis in man. In fact, the use of antituberculosis drugs has so altered the treatment of tuberculosis that the need for sanatorium care has been strikingly reduced, and today many tuberculosis patients may be treated at home by general physicians after a stay of only about four to six weeks in a hospital. The first clinically effective drug to be available for the treatment of tuberculosis was the antibiotic streptomycin. Unfortunately, its usefulness was severely limited by the emergence of organisms resistant to it and by its toxic reactions, particularly deafness and inner ear damage. In the 1940's paraminosalicylic acid was first employed in the treatment of tuberculosis, but it was soon found that, used alone, it was inferior to streptomycin. More recently, several effective tuberculostatic drugs (drugs that inhibit the growth of tuberculosis-causing bacteria without killing them) and tuberculocidal drugs (drugs that kill tuberculosis-causing bacteria) have been introduced. Isoniazid, introduced in 1952, proved more potent than any other known drug against tuberculosis.

The main problem in the treatment of tuberculosis is the emergence of drug resistance in the bacteria. Since there is little cross-resistance between the various classes of tuberculostatic drugs, however, satisfactory control of the disease can usually be obtained by using combinations of two or more antituberculosis drugs.

Antiviral Drugs. Chemotherapeutic agents are now available to treat most infective diseases, to some extent at least. Prominent exceptions are diseases caused by small viruses that enter host cells and use the mechanisms in the host cell to multiply. Selective chemical attack on the viruses without simultaneous destruction of the host cell is especially difficult to achieve. Nevertheless, progress is being made in the development of antiviral drugs.

Others. Other chemotherapeutic agents include the drugs used to treat leprosy, protozoan-caused amebiasis, and worm infections. There has been much research on the development of drugs to treat tumors. Although many drugs have been used in the care of malignant diseases, the majority are very toxic and cause unpleasant and dangerous side effects. The best results have been obtained with drugs used to treat the leukemias.

How Chemotherapeutic Agents Work. Antimicrobial chemotherapeutic agents may, for practical purposes, be divided into two groups: *bacteriostatic agents*, which act by stopping bacterial growth and thus perhaps allow the person's own defense mechanisms to kill the invading bacteria; and *bactericidal agents*, which act by killing the bacteria. The sulfonamides, the tetracyclines, and paraminosalicylic acid are primarily bacteriostatic, while penicillin and streptomycin are primarily bactericidal. The exact way in which some chemotherapeutic agents act is now clear. Penicillin, for example, acts on the bacterial cell wall to inhibit the formation of mucopeptides. When the bacteria then multiply, no new cell wall is produced and the newly formed bacteria are left in an extremely vulnerable, moribund state. Other agents, such as nystatin, exert a detergent effect on the cell membrane. The tetracyclines and the streptomycins interfere with protein synthesis in bacteria, and other antibiotic agents (such as griseofulvin) affect nucleic acid metabolism.

PHARMACODYNAMIC DRUGS

In contrast to the chemotherapeutic agents, which attack only the invading microorganisms and have no direct effect on the infected person, the pharmacodynamic agents, forming the second major group of drugs, work by altering the physiological and biochemical responses of various systems of the body.

Central Nervous System. Three main categories of drugs act on the central nervous system. The first category contains the general central nervous system depressants, such as the general anesthetic drugs, ether, and the barbiturates and other hypnotics and sedatives. These drugs depress all tissue that conducts nerve impulses. The second category is formed by the general central nervous system stimulants. These stimulants include strychnine, which is not used much in modern medicine; amphetamine, which is used in the treatment of certain nervous disorders; and caffeine, which is used to counteract sluggish functioning of the central nervous system.

The third group contains those drugs that selectively modify some function of the central nervous system. Included in this group are the anticonvulsants; the skeletal muscle relaxants, which act on the central nervous system; narcotic-analgesics; and analgesic-antipyretics. The analgesic-antipyretic aspirin, for example, reduces fever by specifically affecting nerve cells in the region of the brain called the hypothalamus. Also included in the third category of central nervous system drugs is the large number of drugs used to treat psychiatric disorders. These drugs are known as psychopharmacological drugs.

Psychopharmacological drugs produce specific changes in the mood and behavior of individuals, although it is not clear how they work to produce these effects. Some of the psychopharmacological drugs, such as the benzodiazepines (Valium, Librium) and some barbiturate and nonbarbiturate sedatives, are used to treat anxiety and neurotic conditions, while others are used to treat depression, and still others, such as the tranquilizer chlorpromazine and its phenothiazine analogs, are used primarily in the treatment of psychoses and have been responsible for revolutionary changes in the treatment of psychiatric disorders. Since 1953 the use of the psychopharmacological drugs has greatly changed the care of the mentally ill and enabled many to return home and work after a comparatively short hospital stay. See also DRUGS IN PSYCHIATRY.

Peripheral Nervous System. Drugs that affect the peripheral nervous system are either local anesthetics, which block conduction in nerve trunks, or drugs that modify the transmission of nerve impulses from nerve endings to the muscle they supply. Local anesthetics block conduction when they are applied locally to a nerve trunk. They stabilize the nerve membrane and thus prevent it from transmitting a nerve impulse from one part of nerve to another.

Drugs that affect transmission at the junction between a nerve and muscle act in several different ways. Some paralyze the muscle or gland supplied by the nerve. For example, atropine paralyzes certain muscles in the eye and so dilates the pupil; similarly, curare paralyzes the muscle responsible for bodily movement. Such drugs block transmission of the nerve impulse by preventing acetylcholine, a chemical released by the end of the nerve, from activating the muscles supplied by the nerve. In contrast to the drugs that block acetylcholine activity, a second group of drugs mimic acetylcholine and have a stimulant action at the junction. For example, the alkaloid pilocarpine, when applied locally to the eye, causes constriction of the pupil. The eye becomes temporarily fixed for near vision because pilocarpine mimics acetylcholine, the natural transmitter, at certain junctions between nerve and muscle in the eye. Other drugs may block transmission or may act as artificial transmitters at other junctions where the normal transmitter released by the nerve is not acetylcholine but is epinephrine or norepinephrine. A third group of drugs, such as parathion and malathion, enhances the activity of the normal transmitter that is released. These drugs, known as anticholinesterases prevent the destruction of acetylcholine released at the nerve endings. As a result, the transmitter persists in the junction region for a much longer time than normal and produces an exaggerated response of the muscle or gland cell that the nerve supplies.

Circulatory System. Many of the drugs that ultimately affect the circulatory system may act primarily on the autonomic nervous system. For example, such drugs as epinephrine and ephedrine, which cause the blood vessels to constrict by exciting junctions in the sympathetic division of the autonomic nervous system, effectively raise blood pressure, while drugs that block transmission at these junctions lower blood pressure. Similarly, changes in the heart rate can be effected by drugs that act on the autonomic nervous system. Atropine, for example, blocks the chemical released at the junction between the heart muscle and the nerve endings of the parasympathetic system (another part of the autonomic system) and thus increases the heart rate.

In addition to the drugs that affect the heart through the nervous system, many drugs act directly on the heart muscle itself. For example, digitalis, which is widely used in the treatment of heart failure, acts directly on the heart muscle to increase its force of contraction. Antiarrhythmic drugs (such as quinidine) depress the heart muscle and are particularly useful in treating disturbance of heart rate and rhythm.

Patients with high blood pressure are given many different antihypertensive drugs that lower blood pressure. These drugs act in a variety of ways: sedatives, such as the barbiturates, lower blood pressure by relieving anxiety; rauwolfia alkaloids, such as reserpine, lower blood pressure by tranquilizing the patient and preventing blood vessel constriction; other drugs, such as hexamethonium, block transmission of other nerve impulses and also lower the blood pressure. The benzothidiazide diuretics are also used to treat hypertension. The exact way these and other antihypertensive drugs act is not well understood, however.

Other drugs that affect the circulatory system include vasodilators, such as the nitrites, which are used to treat angina pectoris, and the anticoagulants heparin, coumarin, and their derivatives, which are used in thromboembolic diseases to delay blood clotting. Several other drugs have been tried in cases of atherosclerosis to lower cholesterol levels and prevent the occlusion of arteries.

Excretory System. The kidneys play an extremely important role in maintaining both the volume and the composition of body fluids and in excreting waste products from the body. Drugs that alter renal, or kidney, function are therefore extremely important. Drugs that increase the flow of urine are classified as diuretics, while drugs that decrease urine flow are antidiuretics.

Perhaps the most effective and useful of all diuretic drugs are the organic mercurials and the thiazides, a new class of diuretic drugs. These diuretics act directly on the tubules of the kidney to prevent the reabsorption of sodium. Salt is therefore excreted in the urine and it pulls with it large volumes of water. Recent diuretic discoveries include drugs that antagonize aldosterone—a steroid secreted by the adrenal cortex that influences the electrolyte and water balance of the body—causing an increase in urine flow. The major clinical use of diuretics is in the treatment of edema associated with heart failure or with cirrhosis of the liver.

The antidiuretic hormone (vasopressin) secreted by the posterior pituitary gland promotes the maximal reabsorption of water by the kidney tubules and so decreases the flow of urine. An antidiuretic hormone obtained from cattle is used to reduce urine flow in diseases such as diabetes insipidus.

In addition to reabsorbing water and salt from the kidney tubules and so preventing their excess loss in urine, the kidneys also excrete and reabsorb organic compounds. Probenecid, for example, prevents the secretion of the organic acid penicillin into the urine; as a result penicillin remains in the bloodstream longer, and a greater therapeutic effect is obtained.

Gastrointestinal System. Cathartics, drugs that promote defecation, are important agents acting on the gastrointestinal tract. Cathartics are extensively misused by the general population, and the physician is faced with the problem of chronic abuse of cathartics more frequently than he is required to prescribe them. Nevertheless, when properly used, cathartics have an important place in medicine. They are valuable in cases of drug and food poisoning and in certain cases of infestation with intestinal worms. They serve the obvious purpose of eliminating the parasites or toxic substance.

Stimulant cathartics, such as cascara sagrada, act directly to increase the motor activity of the intestinal tract; saline cathartics, such as milk of magnesia, are salts that are slowly absorbed from the digestive tract and retain water in the intestinal lumen; bulk-acting cathartics, such as bran, enhance the peristaltic movement of the intestines; and lubricant cathartics, such as mineral oil, merely facilitate defecation by softening and lubricating the feces.

Drugs known as antacids and digestants also act on the gastrointestinal tract. Antacids neutralize or remove excess acid from the gastric tract and are useful in treating cases of peptic ulcer or excess hydrochloric acid secretion by the stomach. Digestants, such as bile and hydrochloric acid, are used to promote digestion when these substances are secreted by the body in amounts lower than normal.

Endocrine System. The endocrine, or ductless, glands of the body produce various chemicals known as hormones. These hormones are released into the blood and carried to distant parts of the body where they produce their effects. These effects are vital to the proper functioning of the body. When an endocrine gland secretes an insufficient amount of hormone into the bloodstream, additional hormone obtained from another source may be given to the patient to restore his normal hormonal balance. In diabetes insipidus, for example, where the insulin secretion by the pancreas is not sufficient to meet the body's needs, a daily injection of insulin prepared from pigs or cows can restore the patient to normal. Similarly, myxedema, a disease associated with the degeneration and atrophy of the thyroid gland, can be treated by giving thyroid hormone obtained usually from pigs. Extracts of the two parathyroid hormones: the parathyroid hormone and calcitonin, both of which are important in the regulation and maintenance of bones, may also be given in cases of decreased parathyroid gland functioning.

The anterior pituitary gland produces at least six hormones: the growth hormone, which has been used to treat dwarfism; prolactin, which stimulates milk secretion but which has not yet been used in medicine; and four others that influence the functioning of the gonads, the thyroid gland, and the adrenal cortex. The posterior pituitary secretes at least two hormones used in medicine: vasopressin, the antidiuretic hormone; and oxytocin, used in obstetrics to induce labor and control postpartum bleeding.

The corticosteroids produced by the adrenal cortex have numerous and diverse biochemical and physiological actions. Some, called the glucocorticoids, affect carbohydrate, fat, and protein metabolism, while others, called the mineralcorticoids (such as aldosterone) primarily affect electrolyte balance in the body. Addison's disease, in which there is insufficient secretion of the adrenal cortex hormones, can be adequately treated by administering the needed hormones.

The male sex hormones, called androgens, are secreted by the testes. They control the changes of puberty and the sexual functioning of the male. Androgens are used in medicine to treat deficient hormone secretion by the testes.

Various female sex hormones, known as estrogens, are secreted by the ovaries and are largely responsible for the changes that take place at puberty in females. In unusual conditions, when the ovaries never develop, and puberty does not occur, and in all women after menopause, the functions of the ovaries are absent or diminished. Estrogen therapy at the appropriate time can bring about the events of puberty in the first group and control some of the symptoms of menopause. Progesterone, another hormone produced by the ovaries, is important in the control of pregnancy and the menstrual cycle and is used to treat several reproductive disorders.

It is not always necessary to use the hormone itself to correct a hormonal deficiency. Many synthetic compounds have proved more useful in therapy than have the hormones themselves. These compounds sometimes resemble the hormones chemically, but often they do not. Diethylstilbestrol, for example, duplicates the reactions of estrogen, but resembles it only remotely.

Finally, there is a group of drugs that interfere with the normal hormonal balance of the body. An excellent example is furnished by the estrogens. The presence of the estrogenic hormones in the blood inhibits the pituitary gland from releasing the hormones that control the activity of the gonads and thus prevents ovulation. This is the basis for the action of many of the oral contraceptives (combinations of an estrogen and a drug resembling progesterone).

3. Drug Administration, Absorption, and Excretion

The most convenient way to administer drugs is by mouth. The numerous pills, elixirs, and "medicines" with which most people are familiar testify to this fact. However, some drugs are not absorbed from the gastrointestinal tract at all, and others are absorbed so irregularly that, when given by mouth, they can present a hazard to life. If not enough of a drug is absorbed, the disease against which the drug is given is undertreated; if, on the other hand, too much of a drug is absorbed, toxic reactions associated with drug overdosage may result. Such drugs are therefore injected into the body either directly into the bloodstream or more commonly into the muscle from which they are subsequently slowly absorbed into the blood and distributed throughout the body. Some drugs are applied topically; atropine, for example, may be dropped directly on the eye to widen the pupil. Still other drugs may be absorbed through the mucous membranes in the mouth or in the rectum.

Whatever the site of administration, the drug usually has to be carried by the blood to its site of action in the body. All drug absorption depends on the solubility of the drug. The more soluble a drug is, the more rapidly it will be absorbed. The rate at which a tablet disintegrates or local factors, such as the acidity of the drug's environment, influence drug absorption. When a drug is absorbed from a mucosal surface or from an intramuscular or subcutaneous injection, clearly the greater the area of exposure, the more rapidly the drug is absorbed. Increased blood flow, produced by the local application of heat or by other drugs speeds absorption. The rate of gastric emptying is also important. For example, many fatty foods that slow down the rate of stomach emptying will slow down the rate at which alcohol is absorbed into the bloodstream; alcohol therefore remains longer in the stomach, where it is less rapidly absorbed than from the small intestine.

After a drug has been absorbed or injected into the bloodstream, it must still pass through various body compartments to reach its site of action. Many drugs, particularly those that are ionized, find it very difficult to pass from the blood to the brain; some blood-brain barrier seems to exist. For this reason, when local or rapid drug effects on the brain are desired, as in acute central nervous infections, drugs are sometimes injected directly into the spinal subarachnoid space (the space between two of the protective layers surrounding the spinal cord).

Drugs may accumulate in various areas of the body as a result of binding, dissolving in fats, or active transport into cells. The beneficial action of these trapped drugs is not lost, however, for the site of accumulation serves as a storage depot from which the drug is gradually released over a period of time to maintain a long therapeutic response.

Some drugs have to be transformed in the body into a compound that is therapeutically active. For example, prontosil—the first of the sulfa drugs to be used medically—is itself inactive and must be converted to the active compound sulfanilamide before it can exert its effect.

The most important organ for drug excretion is the kidney. Some drugs, particularly polar compounds, such as penicillin, are eliminated from the body unchanged. Less polar, more fat-soluble drugs are usually not eliminated until they are first metabolized to more polar, less fat-soluble compounds. Excretion of drugs by the kidney involves both passive filtration of the blood into the glomeruli of the kidney and an active, complex process of reabsorption and secretion by the kidney tubules.

Some drugs are excreted in the feces because they have not been completely absorbed after being taken in by mouth or because they have been excreted in the bile. Other drugs, mainly the anesthetic gases and vapors, are eliminated by the lungs. Drug excretion in milk also occurs; the drugs thus excreted are potential sources of toxic effects to the nursing infant.

4. Factors Influencing Drug Action

Various factors influence or modify the effects of drugs in the body. Children, for example, are overreactive to certain drugs, particularly those that change the water and electrolyte balance in the body and those that produce stimulation or depression of the central nervous system. This is why beverages containing caffeine are often forbidden to very young children.

The weight of a person is also an important factor modifying drug action. In general, the heavier a person is, the larger is the amount of drug required to obtain a given therapeutic effect. In addition, an obese individual may respond to a drug differently than a more muscular individual of the same weight.

Women are thought to be more susceptible to the effects of some drugs than men. Pregnancy, in particular, presents a special situation involving drug use. Special caution in the administration and dosage of drugs is required at this time because the uterus or fetus might be adversely affected by a drug given for therapeutic reasons to the mother. A wise precaution, therefore, is to avoid the use of drugs as much as possible during pregnancy. The soundness of this advice was highlighted in the early 1960's by the thalidomide disaster, in which several thousand babies in Europe were born deformed because their mothers took the drug, for which there was no pressing medical need.

The route of administration of a drug may also affect its action in the body. Clearly a drug given intravenously will produce its effects much more rapidly and with smaller doses than the same drug given by mouth. The time of administration is also an important consideration. Absorption usually proceeds more rapidly if the stomach and upper portion of the intestinal tract are free of food; in fact, the same amount of drug that is active before a meal may be ineffective if given after eating.

Of particular importance is the fact that the effects of a drug may be modified by the prior administration of another drug. The dose of the anticoagulant bishydroxycoumarin, for example, must be reduced when large amounts of salicylates are to be given at the same time and may have to be increased if barbiturates are given at the same time. Two or more drugs, each having approximately the same therapeutic effect, may act additively and are often prescribed together in a single mixture. This, however, often leads to confusion, and it is nearly always preferable to treat an illness with a single drug rather than a drug mixture. For example, if a patient receiving a medicine containing three drugs has a severe allergic reaction to the mixture, all three drugs must be withheld until the single offending drug is found. The time required for this may well prejudice the patient's well-being. Had single drugs been used in the first place, the drug responsible for the allergy would have been readily identified, and one of the other two drugs could have been used immediately.

Genetic factors are also important in many cases. As a result of a genetic deficiency in one of the enzyme systems of the red blood cells, Negroes are much more likely to develop anemia following antimalarial treatment with primaquine than are Caucasians.

5. Drug Toxicity

No drug is free of toxic effects. This factor is what ultimately limits the usefulness of drugs. Some of the untoward effects of drugs are trivial and can be readily tolerated. Others, however, are serious and may even be fatal. Some toxic effects of drugs are merely extensions of the drug's therapeutic effects. For example, too much insulin may lower the blood sugar in a diabetic so far as to cause coma and eventually death if the condition is untreated.

With many drugs, it is almost impossible to avoid toxic effects completely. For example, the beneficial effects of digitalis are obtained with amounts that are only slightly below those that produce the first signs of toxicity and may be less than half the amount that can produce death. This is why drugs never should be taken except under the guidance of a physician. A physician is aware of the potential hazards of a drug and is prepared to act promptly if toxicity occurs. Furthermore, the physician is aware that many of the toxic effects produced by drugs are unexpected, bizarre, and often not clearly related to the taking of a drug; for example, it is still not clear why the sedative thalidomide causes babies to be born without arms and legs. The thalidomide tragedy also revealed that some drugs may have little or no toxic effects on an adult but may severely damage a fetus or a newly born baby.

Many people suffer from drug allergy—one of the most serious problems of pharmacology. Penicillin, for example, is an extremely safe drug for most people, but it produces hypersensitivity reactions in about 15% of the American population. In some cases the reaction is so serious that it is necessary to forbid the future use of penicillin because of the risk of death. Drug allergy takes many different forms: skin reactions varying from a mild rash to severe dermatitis; blistering of the skin; a severe fall in blood pressure resembling shock; and even a degeneration of parts of the blood vessels or of any organ of the body.

The kidney and the liver are particularly prone to the toxic effects of drugs because drugs tend to become concentrated in these organs. For example, as the kidney concentrates the fluids filtered into the glomeruli from the blood, certain sparingly soluble substances may precipitate and cause undesirable effects; intrarenal precipitation of the sulfonamides, for example, is the major cause of the toxicity of these agents.

One class of untoward reactions to the antibiotics is superinfection. Superinfection occurs when an antibiotic kills not only the microorganisms responsible for the original infection but also the microbes that, without harming an individual, normally inhabit the mouth, gut, urinary tract, or air tubes and lungs. These areas may then be invaded by other foreign microorganisms that cause disease. Superinfection, which is relatively common, is potentially dangerous because the organisms responsible for the new diseases are often insensitive to antibiotics.

6. Drug Tolerance, Dependence, and Addiction

When a drug is taken repeatedly over a prolonged period of time, drug tolerance develops, and larger and larger doses of the drug must be taken in order to obtain the therapeutic effect produced by the original small dose. The mechanisms by which drug tolerance develops is known in some cases. Repeated ingestion of barbiturates, for example, activates the enzyme system in the liver that destroys barbiturates. The result is that a given dose of barbiturates is destroyed more and more quickly in the body, and the time that an individual is kept asleep decreases. Unfortunately, tolerance to the hypnotic and sedative effects of barbiturates does not seem to increase the lethal dose. With other drugs, on the other hand, tolerance for the lethal dose may also develop. Thus an individual who has acquired tolerance to cocaine or morphine may take several times the amount that would be lethal to an ordinary individual. When a drug is not taken for some time, tolerance disappears.

As mentioned above for the barbiturates, tolerance does not appear equally toward all reactions of a drug. The morphine addict, for example, may soon become tolerant to the central effects of the narcotic and may experience little or none of the euphoria that he once did, but the same degree of tolerance does not develop toward the effects of morphine on smooth muscle, and even a highly tolerant user of morphine or heroin continues to have pinpoint pupils and to be constipated. Cross-tolerance to the effects of related drugs may also develop.

The repeated administration of some drugs that cause profound changes in the central nervous system and in behavior may lead to drug dependence. These drugs include opiates, barbiturates, amphetamines, alcohol, cocaine, and various psychopharmacological agents. These drugs often lead to psychic dependence, that is, a drive or craving that requires periodic administration of the drug for pleasure. Some of the drugs also produce physical dependence so that when the drug is no longer given, physical symptoms, known as "a withdrawal syndrome," occur. Abrupt withdrawal of some central depressants—for example, the barbiturates—may produce effects so severe as to cause death.

Drug addiction has been defined as the compulsive use of a drug in greater amounts than are used in ordinary therapeutic practice or are acceptable in social custom, and that is harmful to the individual, to society, or to both. This subject is discussed in detail in the article DRUG ADDICTION AND ABUSE.

7. Government Regulations Concerning Drugs

The U. S. drug laws give the federal government the right and duty to prevent the manufacture of an unsafe or ineffective drug. The Food and Drug Administration (FDA) is the federal agency responsible for the enforcement of the drug laws.

At the beginning of the 20th century, many physicians in the United States became concerned about the increasing degree to which preservatives, some of which were harmful, were being added to food, and about the rising extent to which patent medicines of questionable value were being sold. They also worried that even proven medicines were being marketed in an adulterated or even decomposed state so that their potency and therapeutic efficacy were unreliable. Many pure food and drug bills were therefore introduced into Congress; the movement culminated, on June 30, 1906, in passage of the Pure Food and Drug Act, which made it illegal to manufacture or introduce an adulterated or misbranded food or drug anywhere in the United States.

The 1906 law represented a major step forward and ensured the purity of drugs, but it did not, surprisingly, guarantee that drugs were safe to use. A disaster, in which over a hundred people died as a result of taking an elixir of sulfonamide dissolved in the highly toxic diethyl glycol, resulted in the passage in 1938 of the Food, Drug, and Cosmetic Act, which required manufacturers to test their new drugs for safety and to report the test findings to the FDA. Although this act required new drugs to be proved safe, it still did not require proof of therapeutic efficacy. Worried by the ever-increasing consumer drug bill, Congress passed the Drug Amendments Act in 1962. This act requires a manufacturer to demonstrate the efficacy of a drug as well as its safety. This law and subsequent amendments apply not only to new drugs but to all drugs introduced since 1938. Through these laws, drugs found to be too dangerous in proportion to their therapeutic worth can now be removed from the market.

Narcotic agents and some related drugs are under special government control. The Harrison Narcotic Act of 1914, the Federal Marihuana Regulations of 1937, and the Narcotics Manufacturing Act of 1960—all enforced by the Bureau of Narcotics in the U. S. Treasury Department—control the medical uses and interstate traffic in opium, cocaine, marihuana, and a variety of pharmacological agents.

J. MURDOCH RITCHIE
Yale University School of Medicine

Bibliography

Bloom, Barry, and Ullyot, Glenn E., eds., *Drug Discovery: Science and Development in a Changing Society* (American Chemical Society 1971).
Clarke, Frank H., ed., *How Modern Medicines Are Developed* (Futura Publications 1977).
Fixx, James F., ed., *Drugs* (Arno 1971).
Gilman, Alfred G., Goodman, Louis S., and Gilman, Alfred, *The Pharmacological Basis of Therapeutics*, 6th ed. (Macmillan 1980).
Grabowski, Henry G., *Drug Regulation and Innovation* (American Enterprise Institute 1976).
Reekie, Duncan W., and Weber, Michael H., *Profits, Politics and Drugs* (Holmes and Meier 1979).

DRUG ADDICTION AND ABUSE. It is very likely that every society has had mood-changing drugs and that there have always been individuals who used them in ways that were not socially approved. In this sense, drug abuse, the socially nonsanctioned use of a drug, is universal and as old as history. Which behaviors are called drug abuse varies from culture to culture and from time to time within the same culture. Since laws do not always correspond to prevalent social attitudes, there may be times when users of an illegal drug are not considered to be drug abusers (for example, the people who drank alcoholic beverages in the United States during Prohibition). From a pharmacological viewpoint, attitudes toward drugs are often inconsistent or irrational. Some drugs may be totally outlawed, while others with similar actions are made generally available and may be self-administered with full social approval.

The repeated use of some drugs can lead to a *dependence* on the drug, in which the effects of the drug or the conditions associated with its use are felt by the users to be necessary for their well-being. Dependence may vary in intensity from a mild inclination to a strong craving or compulsion to use the drug. Severe dependence may result in a type of behavior characterized by a preoccupation with the procurement and use of the drug. This type of behavior is also known as *compulsive drug use*, and since a severe dependence on any self-administered drug is generally not socially approved, the term is usually synonymous with *compulsive drug abuse*. One obvious exception is the use of tobacco, where social acceptance is so complete that even heavy compulsive use, which is damaging to the user's health, is commonly not considered to be drug abuse.

The term *drug addiction* has been defined in many ways, but in this article it is used to mean a behavioral pattern of compulsive drug use characterized by an overwhelming involvement with the procurement and use of the drug and the high tendency of the user to relapse to drug use after a period of abstinence. It is synonymous with *intensive* or *severe drug dependence*. Contrary to popular belief, drug addiction is not the same as physical dependence on a drug. *Physical dependence* is a physiological or biochemical condition produced by the administration of a drug to the extent that a characteristic pattern of signs and symptoms appears when the drug is withdrawn and disappears when the drug is administered again. Physical dependence can be produced by a wide variety of drugs that are used in everyday medical practice. Some drugs that produce physical dependence are not pleasant to take and are neither abused nor used compulsively. Also, not all withdrawal symptoms are associated with a craving for the drug that produced the physical dependence.

Drugs can be categorized into nine major groups, based primarily on pharmacological considerations such as similarity of effects, mechanisms of action, cross-tolerance, and cross-dependence. They are (1) opioids, including opium, morphine, codeine, heroin, methadone, and meperidine; (2) sedatives, including alcohol and antianxiety agents, which depress the central nervous system (CNS); (3) cocaine and amphetamine-like drugs, which stimulate the CNS; (4) cannabinoids, including both natural forms (found in marijuana) and certain synthetics; (5) nicotine; (6) psychedelics or hallucinogens, including LSD, mescaline, and psilocybin; (7) arylcyclohexylamines (phencyclidine and related compounds); (8) inhalants, including nitrous oxide, ether, and toluene; and (9) a miscellaneous group made up of substances contained in tea and coffee (caffeine), betel nuts, kava, and other plant products.

This article discusses the abuse of opioids, CNS depressants, CNS stimulants, psychedelics, and arylcyclohexylamines. Additional information on drugs in these groups will be found in articles on specific drugs, such as AMPHETAMINE, BARBITURATE, HEROIN, and MORPHINE. Alcohol, the most important sedative and the most important of all addictive drugs, is discussed separately in ALCOHOLISM. For information on caffeine, the cannabinoids, and nicotine, see CAFFEINE, MARIJUANA, and SMOKING AND HEALTH.

OPIOIDS (NARCOTIC ANALGESICS)

The opioids commonly referred to as narcotics are opium; purified alkaloids obtained from opium, such as morphine and codeine; derivatives of morphine, such as heroin; and the synthetic morphine-like drugs, such as meperidine (Demerol) and methadone (Dolophine). More than 15 opioids are clinically available in the United States and elsewhere.

Major scientific advances have shown that the opioids exert their effects by interacting with very specific sites, or *opioid receptors*, on nerve cells. These receptors normally are activated by polypeptides, substances produced by certain nerve cells. Because they originate within the body, these substances are known as *endogenous opioids*. The two major categories of endogenous opioids are the enkephalins, consisting of short (5-amino acid) polypeptides, and the endorphins, larger polypeptides ranging in size from 13 to 31 amino acids.

There are several kinds of opioid receptors. Formerly, most of the known opioid drugs were much like morphine; all of them acted on the same kind of receptor. All of these classic opioids show cross-tolerance and cross-dependence—that is, tolerance to one drug includes tolerance to the others. Withdrawal symptoms due to physical dependence on one drug can be prevented by the use of any of the others. For example, addicts who stop using heroin will not suffer withdrawal symptoms if they use morphine. Newer opioid drugs such as pentazocine and butorphanol do not have all of the properties of morphine. They have morphine-like subjective effects, but they do not suppress the morphine withdrawal syndrome and may even antagonize the effects of morphine and precipitate withdrawal. These new opioid drugs appear to exert their effects on a distinct kind of opioid receptor.

Among the major factors that play a role in determining whether individuals will self-administer opioids are availability, curiosity, and influence of friends. It is not known, however, why some people repeat the experience and others do not, and why some, but not all, of those people who do repeat the experience become compulsive users. It is clear, though, that availability is important, for the incidence of compulsive opioid use is several times higher among doctors and nurses than among the general population. Among U. S. military personnel in Vietnam, heroin use increased dramatically in 1970 when pure heroin became easily available. By mid-1971, 42% of Army enlisted men had experimented with heroin, and about half of these had become physically dependent at some point.

History. The use of opium anteceded written history. For centuries it was used primarily for medicinal purposes, first in Asia and later in Europe. In Europe it was not until in the 18th century that opium was used for its psychological effects. This section deals only with the development of opiate abuse in the United States. The historical development of opiate abuse throughout the world is discussed under OPIUM.

Opium smoking was introduced into the United States in the early 1800's, but the use of opium by injection did not become common until after the Civil War. Until about 1900, opiates were sold in general stores and could be purchased without a prescription. About one in every 400 people was using opiates regularly, and scientists were already attempting to find a substitute that would not cause physical dependence. It was hoped that heroin, a morphine derivative introduced in 1898, would become such a drug, but it soon became obvious that heroin, like opium and morphine, causes physical dependence and is just as likely to lead to compulsive use.

During the early 1900's most of the users were women who were given opiates for medical reasons. No criminal activity and little social hardship were associated with the use of the drugs. The passage of the Harrison Narcotic Act in 1914 was the first attempt on a national scale to reduce the extent of opiate dependence by restricting the availability of the drugs to legitimate medical needs. This restriction was quite successful in dramatically reducing the number of individuals using opiates, but one of the costs of this reduction was that those users who were unable to tolerate permanent abstinence from opiates were forced to obtain the drugs through illegal channels. By the mid-1920's the population of opiate users gradually shifted from women with medical problems to individuals who were willing to risk the severe legal penalties attached to narcotics use. At about this time, also, the intravenous use of opiates began to spread. Opiate use became more popular among criminals, and as the cost of illegal opiates increased, it became more common for opiate users to commit crimes to obtain the money needed for the drugs.

As the illegal traffic became centered in the poorer sections of large cities, the ethnic composition of the opiate-using population changed to reflect the makeup of the groups living in those areas. By the mid-1950's the problem of opiate addiction, primarily of heroin addiction, was largely a black, Puerto Rican, and Mexican-American problem. During the 1960's, however, the use of opiates increased among the youth of the affluent middle class.

By the mid-1960's it was apparent that the official estimates of 58,000 opiate addicts, based on Federal Bureau of Narcotics files, were gross underestimates. More realistic estimates, based on newer statistical methods, indicated that at the peak of the epidemic of the early 1970's there may have been more than 500,000 regular heroin users and addicts. Estimates of active heroin users declined from about 1975 to 1980. Then the figures for overdose deaths, emergency-room visits, new admissions to treatment programs, and other indicators began to turn upward, accompanied by reports that large supplies of potent heroin were being smuggled in from Iran, Afghanistan, and Indochina.

Effects on the Mind and Body. Opioids exert their major effects on the nervous system and gastrointestinal tract, inducing a state of indifference to pain and anxiety. For some people, opioids seem to reduce fatigue, alleviate depression, and reduce interest in sexual activity. For some users, the major effect is euphoria, an unusual sense of well-being.

If an opioid is used repeatedly several times a day for more than a few days, the user developes tolerance to and physical dependence on the drug. Tolerance refers to the need to use more of the drug to get the same effect obtained when the drug was first used. Physical dependence on opioids varies in severity according to the quantity and length of time used. With daily use, significant dependence can develop within two to three weeks. However, by using an opioid antagonist it is possible to demonstrate that low levels of physical dependence begin with the first dose.

The signs and symptoms of morphine or heroin withdrawal (abstinence) appear within a few hours after the last dose and reach their peak intensity within 24 to 72 hours. They then gradually subside over a period of four to six days. These signs and symptoms include runny nose and eyes, anxiety, restlessness, yawning, profuse sweating, insomnia, and generalized body aches. When the physical dependence is severe, nausea, vomiting, dilated pupils, gooseflesh, loss of appetite, diarrhea, abdominal cramps, kicking movements of the legs, and increases in body temperature, blood pressure, and rate of respiration are also involved. With longer acting opioids, such as methadone, withdrawal has a slower onset and lasts longer.

Unlike alcohol or barbiturates, narcotics do not cause obvious incoordination, slurred speech, or a staggering gait. Those who obtain opioids through legal channels are able to work productively and live relatively normal lives. However, even when given access to legitimate supplies, many individuals with antisocial tendencies continue to commit crimes. Prolonged use of opioids does not appear to injure the body, but even in ideal circumstances chronic use may cause problems. Tolerance does not develop with equal rapidity to all of the effects caused by the drugs, so that sexual interest and bowel activity may remain diminished long after the user is relatively tolerant to many of the other effects. Young opioid users have a tendency to use the drugs intravenously, often disregarding the basic procedures for sterilizing their implements. Such practices introduce viruses and bacteria into the body and may lead to bacterial endocarditis, hepatitis, lung abscesses, and septicemia. In addition to possible death from such diseases, fatalities may result from overdoses of the drug or from allergic reactions to the drug or to the materials used to adulterate it.

Even those who do not develop physical problems may acquire major psychological and social difficulties as a result of their continued use of short-acting opioids. Regardless of the initial reasons for using an opioid (pain, tension, depression, or a desire for euphoria), the drugs will simultaneously reduce a number of psycho-

PERCENTAGES OF RESPONDENTS REPORTING NONMEDICAL DRUG USE IN A U.S. NATIONAL SURVEY

Age	12–17		18–25		Over 25	
	Ever used	Last 30 days	Ever used	Last 30 days	Ever used	Last 30 days
Heroin	0.5	Less than 0.5	3.5	Less than 0.5	1.0	Less than 0.5
Analgesics	3.2	0.6	11.8	1.0	2.7	Less than 0.5
Alcohol	70.3	37.2	95.3	75.9	91.5	61.3
Sedatives	3.2	1.1	17.0	2.8	3.5	Less than 0.5
Tranquilizers	4.1	0.6	15.8	2.1	3.1	Less than 0.5
Stimulants	3.4	1.2	18.2	3.5	5.8	0.5
Cocaine	5.4	1.4	27.5	9.3	4.3	0.9
Hallucinogens	7.0	2.2	25.1	4.4	4.5	Less than 0.5
Marijuana	31.0	16.7	68.2	35.4	19.6	6.0
Cigarettes	54.1	12.1	82.8	42.6	83.0	36.9
Inhalants	10.0	2.0	16.5	1.2	3.9	0.5

Source: 1980 report of National Institute on Drug Abuse. All responses concerning standard medicines (sedatives, tranquilizers) indicate nonmedical, or nonprescribed use.

logical and physiological tensions. Repeated self-administration of a drug to reduce these tensions causes a form of self-conditioning that reinforces the likelihood of repeating the drug-using behavior when these tensions recur. Physical dependence develops with repeated use, and a new tension—withdrawal distress—occurs each time a drug is not used. After a time, the drug users may lose the ability to discriminate among the various tensions. No longer able to tell pain from anxiety, anger, depression, or withdrawal distress, they know only that an opioid will quickly and completely make them feel "normal." Thus, the drug may take on magical properties as the users become convinced that it solves all of their problems. Some experts believe that it is primarily this repeated relief of withdrawal distress that makes a user become an addict. In addition, the withdrawal distress can be "conditioned" to the environment in which it occurs. It is conceivable, therefore, that persons who have stopped using narcotics may feel as if they are having withdrawal symptoms when they return to the circumstances under which they had used them. Thus, conditioning may play a role in the repeated relapses that seem to characterize narcotics addicts.

Social Implications of Narcotics Use. Medical problems and impairment of social functioning can occur even when opioids are obtained from legal channels. Many users become so involved with experiencing the drug's effect that they are unable or unwilling to carry out normal activities. When the drugs must be obtained by trickery from legal sources or entirely through illegal sources, the impact on the users' self-image and social adjustment is profound. Those who obtain drugs from illicit sources begin to restrict their social contacts to other drug users. This association increases the number of illegal sources available to them and ensures that police action against one source will not leave them without a supply. Even individuals who were not antisocial prior to becoming drug users learn to rationalize any illegal act they commit to obtain the drugs or the money needed to buy them. Selling drugs, forging checks and prescriptions, stealing, and prostitution are the most common offenses among addicts, whereas crimes of violence are less commonly committed.

The amount of time spent to obtain money and purchase drugs from illegal sources is so great that little time is left for other activities. Those who become compulsive drug users before acquiring an education or a vocational skill find it difficult to hold jobs because of the uncertainty of their drug supply and not, as is commonly believed, because of the effects of the drugs. Once addicts have prison records or reputations as unreliable employees, their vocational problems become even more difficult to resolve. There is considerable individual variability. Some Americans hold jobs even when using illegal drugs. Others continue to commit crimes even when provided with legal opioids.

Treatment. Since there is no single reason for beginning to use drugs, for continuing their use, and for relapsing after withdrawal, and no single pattern of use, treatment must be tailored to meet the needs and problems of the individual. Physical dependence on opioids is relatively easy to manage using the principle of cross-dependence. In the most commonly used treatment, methadone is substituted for morphine or heroin and gradually withdrawn over a period of one to three weeks. The methadone withdrawal syndrome lasts longer than that of morphine, but it is much less severe. Newer nonopioid drugs, such as clonidine, have been tested for treatment of opioid withdrawal.

Preventing a relapse or helping compulsive drug users become productive and law-abiding members of the community is much more difficult than treating physical dependence on drugs. The traditional approaches, such as group therapy or individual psychotherapy during or after prolonged hospitalization, have been effective for only a few patients. In the United States it has not been possible to deter relapses reliably by imposing harsh penalties or prolonged periods of imprisonment or commitment to other institutions. Studies indicate that most institutionalized narcotics users return to the use of narcotics during the first year following their release, even when they are supervised and regularly tested to determine whether they are using drugs. However, harsh penalties and strict supervision are reported to be effective in other cultures.

Several distinct approaches to treatment with very different perspectives on the basic problem are now in use. The methadone-maintenance approach takes the view that for a prolonged period after withdrawal, the addict experiences a persistent sense of abnormality—a "hunger" for narcotics. Methadone, the same long-acting synthetic drug that can be used to treat the withdrawal syndrome, seems to alleviate this feeling and permit productive social functioning. Patients who receive daily doses of methadone are physically dependent on the drug, but because it is so long-acting they do not experience the repetitive sequence of narcotic effect followed by withdrawal distress. They often become so tolerant that they hardly feel the methadone. Furthermore, since methadone can induce a marked cross-tolerance to other narcotics, patients who take large doses of methadone regularly cannot feel the effects of drugs like morphine or heroin.

The therapeutic-community approach views the users as emotionally immature individuals who require a period of intensive reeducation to achieve the maturity needed to live productively without drugs. The addicts are expected to accomplish this living for a period of months or years in a community operated and controlled by former drug users who can understand and help correct their behavior. The first such self-regulating community devoted to the rehabilitation of drug users was Synanon, founded in California in 1958. Numerous organizations of this kind operate in the United States, and the idea of using former drug addicts as therapists has been incorporated into some nonresidential treatment approaches.

Another approach involves the use of opioid antagonists, such as naltrexone, which prevent opioids from activating opioid receptors in the nervous system. Individuals who are given opioid antagonists regularly will not feel the effects of opioids and will not become physically dependent on them even if they use them regularly. It is possible that addicts treated with opioid antagonists will eliminate their conditioned tendencies to use opioids since the opioids will not produce their usual effects. In any event, the use of antagonists will prevent the development of physical dependence, and this alone may prove useful in long-term rehabilitation. In the United States the treatment of opioid dependence has emphasized providing several alternatives in the hope that one or another will meet the needs of a given individual. Studies indicate that, while some people are able to quit without help, treatment for those who seek it does have some positive effects. In general, there is a decreasing preoccupation with total abstinence itself and an increased interest in finding the best ways to help the opiate user become a law-abiding productive member of society.

CENTRAL-NERVOUS-SYSTEM GENERAL DEPRESSANTS

Among the many drugs categorized as central-nervous-system general depressants are alcohol and the sedative-hypnotics, such as the barbiturates and certain drugs to reduce anxiety. Other categorizations would consider alcohol and the benzodiazepine antianxiety agents separately. Colloquially, the sedative-hypnotics are known mostly as "goof balls," "downs," and "yellow jackets."

Some individuals take general depressants to augment or modify the effects of other drugs. For example, a person may take a depressant to induce sleep after having taken an amphetamine. Alcoholics may use depressants to prevent alcoholic withdrawal symptoms, while heroin users sometimes take them to increase the sense of intoxication when the quality of available heroin is poor. Central-nervous-system depressants are often properly prescribed to relieve anxiety or to induce sleep. But they can be used excessively and without proper supervision, and such use can gradually lead to compulsive abuse and dependence. Some people who use depressants strive primarily to obtain relief of anxiety or of insomnia; others use enough of them to be constantly intoxicated.

The accompanying table provides a crude estimate of the percentage of people who use sedative-hypnotics without medical supervision. But there is no reliable way of knowing how many users are psychologically or physically dependent on the drugs. Judging from the tons of these drugs manufactured each year, it must be inferred that their abuse is considerably more prevalent than the abuse of opioids.

History. Dependence on alcohol is probably the oldest form of drug dependence. Dependence on the sedative-hypnotics is a relatively recent development. The hypnotic (sleep-inducing) effects of chloral hydrate were first recognized in 1869; paraldehyde was first used medically in 1882; and the first hypnotic barbiturate, barbital, was introduced in 1903. Since then, many new chemicals with similar actions have become available. Many of the newer agents are used mainly for daytime sedation or anxiety reduction rather than for the induction of sleep. Compulsive use of paraldehyde, chloral hydrate, and the barbiturates was recognized in the 1920's. Careful studies of physical dependence on barbiturates were not conducted until the 1950's.

The first attempts to deal with the problem of sedative-hypnotic dependence involved the synthesis of drugs with different chemical structures in the hope that these newer drugs would not be abused and would not cause a barbiturate type of physical dependence. But just as the use of short-acting barbiturates had displaced chloral hydrate and paraldehyde as the popular drugs of abuse, these newer, nonbarbiturate sedative-hypnotics and tranquilizers are displacing the barbiturates.

In the United States, federal laws passed in 1965 increased the penalties for illegal manufacture and sale of sedative-hypnotics, stimulants, and hallucinogens. In 1970 these agents were all included in a major drug-law reorganization, the Controlled Substances Act. These laws may have reduced the availability of some drugs, but they have had little impact on the social adjustment and behavioral patterns of compulsive users of central-nervous-system depressants.

Effects on the Mind and Body. The effects of sedative-hypnotics are similar in many ways to those of alcohol. Low doses usually produce relaxation and decreased anxiety; higher doses produce drowsiness. Even if people can stay awake, they may appear confused and show poor judgment and loss of emotional control. Slurred speech, a staggering gait, muscular incoordination, and nystagmus (rapid involuntary eye movements) are also characteristic effects. Although alcohol and the sedative-hypnotics are all depressants of the nervous system, low or moderate doses can produce an effect that resembles stimulation. The individual may become euphoric and more active, and show a decrease in inhibitions. Very high doses produce coma and death due to respiratory failure.

The chronic use of sedatives or alcohol can produce both tolerance and physical dependence. Tolerance to these differs from that produced by opioids in that tolerance to large doses, which cause serious respiratory depression and death, is much less. The degree of physical dependence induced by sedatives varies according to the size of the dose and the length of time the person has taken the drug. As with alcohol, it is possible to use small doses intermittently over a prolonged period without producing physical dependence.

The withdrawal syndrome that occurs when sedative-hypnotics or alcohol are abruptly stopped begins with anxiety, restlessness, tremors, and insomnia. In severe cases, the individual may have convulsions and a delirium characterized by disorientation, hallucinations, and fever. The full-blown alcohol withdrawal syndrome is called delirium tremens (D.T.'s), but the withdrawal syndrome is virtually the same whether the drug is a barbiturate, alcohol, meprobamate, or other sedative. Because there is little cross-dependence between the sedative/alcohol drugs and narcotic analgesics, even large amounts of opioids will not prevent withdrawal symptoms in individuals dependent on barbiturates. It is possible that each time a sedative-hypnotic agent relieves withdrawal distress, there is a reinforcement of the drug-taking, as has been postulated for the opioids.

The newer benzodiazepine antianxiety agents (such as Librium, Valium, and Dalmane) share certain properties with the older sedatives. Their differences are also significant, in that the benzodiazepines may act on specific receptors in the brain and are less likely to cause overdose deaths. However, there is cross-tolerance and cross-dependence between the antianxiety agents and the older sedatives, and the withdrawal syndromes are similar.

Treatment. The treatment of compulsive use of sedative-hypnotics usually begins with the gradual withdrawal of the drug under medical supervision. Cross-dependence occurs between drugs in this group so that it is possible, for example, to substitute pentobarbital for glutethimide or a benzodiazepine such as diazepam (Valium) for alcohol.

Withdrawal of the drug is only the first step. Numerous studies have been made on the treatment of alcoholism and the long-term outcome of such treatment, but few on how sedative-hypnotics addicts respond to different types of postwithdrawal treatment. It is generally believed that the relapse rate is quite high.

Research on sedative-hypnotic dependence has attempted to determine why the same type of withdrawal syndrome is produced by so varied a group of drugs; what long-term changes are produced by the chronic use of such agents; what physical, psychological, and social factors contribute to the development of compulsive use; and how best to treat the user once the drug is withdrawn. None of these questions has been answered with certainty.

CENTRAL-NERVOUS-SYSTEM STIMULANTS

The central-nervous-system stimulants include the amphetamines (Benzedrine, Dexedrine), cocaine, and related drugs. Colloquially, amphetamines are known as "pep pills," "bennies," "dexies," or "ups," while cocaine is known as "coke" or "snow." Amphetamines or methamphetamine when used intravenously are called "speed."

History. The compulsive use of cocaine in Europe was described only 30 years after the drug was first isolated from the leaf of the coca plant in 1859. The compulsive use of amphetamines was well known less than 20 years after their stimulant properties had been recognized in 1933.

For many years after amphetamines were first marketed, self-administration was limited mainly to long-distance truck drivers who used them to stay awake and to depressed persons who took too many diet pills containing amphetamines in order to lift their spirits. During the 1960's, however, the use of amphetamine and related drugs increased to the point where it briefly rivaled heroin addiction as an important social problem. Very large doses of both oral and intravenous amphetamines were used by young adults who took them to produce euphoria. With increased controls on production under the 1970 federal legislation, illicit use of amphetamines declined. However, in the early 1970's cocaine use began to increase sharply, and by the end of the decade it had become one of the common drugs of abuse among young adults.

Amphetamine and methamphetamine are still being manufactured by illegal laboratories, and, although the price of cocaine is extremely high, the beginning of the 1980's did not suggest a trend toward decreased use.

Effects on the Mind and Body. The effects of cocaine or amphetaminelike drugs on the mind and body depend on the dose, who is taking them, how they are taken (orally, by inhalation, or by injection), and the circumstances under which they are taken. In relatively low doses, these drugs suppress appetite, improve one's mood, and restore to near normal levels the performance of one who is overcome with fatigue.

Given intravenously, amphetamines and cocaine produce similar effects. There is a very sudden pleasurable sensation that is often called a "flash" or "rush." By any route, high doses of amphetamines and cocaine can induce a marked elevation of mood, increased energy, talkativeness, unrealistic optimism, and a decreased need for sleep. Many people, however, feel anxious and agitated when they take too much of such drugs, and irritability and suspiciousness may develop.

When first used, amphetamines and cocaine produce an increased heart rate and an elevated blood pressure. With amphetamines, eventually considerable tolerance develops to these effects on the heart and the blood vessels as well as to the effects on one's mood. To continue to experience the effect on mood, users often have to increase their dosage. In some cases, users have ingested more than 1,000 mg of amphetamines a day for months at a time. The average dose given for weight reduction is 30 mg per day. Tolerance to the psychological effects of cocaine does not appear to occur.

Users of amphetamines or cocaine may stay up continuously for several days, stop using the drug, and then fall into a deep exhausted sleep lasting one or more days. Even after discontinuing the drug, some users find it extremely difficult to function normally without using amphetamines. Although it is not necessary to administer any medications to prevent a life-threatening or painful withdrawal syndrome, many users who abruptly discontinue using amphetamines experience profound psychological depression. Some continue using the drug to avoid this feeling.

Both the amphetamines and cocaine, when taken by any route, are potentially toxic. Some users become irritable and have a tendency to repeat certain behavior patterns. Others develop a psychotic syndrome characterized by delusions of persecution (paranoid ideation) and auditory or visual hallucinations.

HALLUCINOGENS

The drugs classified as hallucinogens include some of the oldest and some of the newest drugs known to man. Psilocybin, which is found in certain mushrooms, was in use by Indians when the Spanish conquerors first arrived in Mexico. On the other hand, lysergic acid diethylamide (LSD) was synthesized in 1938, and some of the newer agents, such as 2.5-Dimethoxy-4-methylamphetamine (DOM, colloquially known as STP), were not discovered until the 1960's.

The patterns of psychedelic self-administration in the United States are quite varied. There are many young people and mature adults who seem to accept the general values of society and yet experiment with LSD, mescaline, and similar agents, as indicated in the table. The overwhelming majority of these people do not continue to use these drugs but return to the use of more conventional drugs, such as alcohol and marijuana.

Reports in the 1960's that LSD may increase the number of broken chromosomes in the white blood cells may have contributed to the decline in popularity of these drugs. Other drugs as well as ordinary viral infections also break chromosomes. In contrast to the risk of chromosome damage, which remains unconfirmed, there is little question that the unsupervised use of LSD entails the risk of serious psychiatric difficulties. In addition, the laws against the manufacture and distribution of these drugs make it difficult for users to obtain supplies of uncontaminated drugs.

Effects on the Mind and Body. Although the term "hallucinogen" has been used to refer to these drugs, their effects are more subtle and involve far more than hallucinations. They cause dilated pupils and increases in blood pressure, temperature, and pulse rate. At low or moderate doses, such drugs alter both mood and perception. Familiar objects, situations, and relationships may seem novel, and the mood may vary from a sense of tranquillity to intense anxiety or panic. Higher doses usually produce visual or auditory hallucinations, or both.

The psychedelics as a class do not induce physical dependence, although considerable tolerance does develop. There is cross-tolerance between LSD, mescaline, and psilocybin. These drugs seem to have similar actions in the nervous system. There is no cross-tolerance between these psychedelics and the cannabinoids or the arylcyclohexylamines.

Daily use of psychedelics is quite uncommon; an overwhelming compulsion to take them does not occur. In this sense, addiction does not occur. See also HALLUCINOGEN.

ARYLCYCLOHEXYLAMINES (PHENCYCLIDINE AND RELATED DRUGS)

Phencyclidine was first used in the 1950's as an anesthetic for animals. It was also used for humans, but because some patients experienced delirium when they awoke, such use was discontinued. It was abused briefly in the 1960's, but because of severe side effects it did not achieve any substantial popularity. It was reintroduced in the 1970's as a drug to be "snorted" (inhaled) or smoked. This route of administration gave the user greater control over the dose, and the use of phencyclidine spread rapidly. Phencyclidine has a number of street names: "PCP," "peace pill," "hog," and "angel dust."

Although it is still used as a veterinary anesthetic, phencyclidine is relatively easy to synthesize, and the drug used by people comes mostly from illicit laboratories. A number of derivatives of phencyclidine have been synthesized and have similar actions. Although high doses of phencyclidine and related compounds produce hallucinations, the overall effects and the mechanisms of actions are quite distinct from those of LSD and related psychedelics, and the arylcyclohexylamines appear to represent a distinct pharmacological category. By 1977, 14% of 18- to 25-year-olds had reported some experience with phencyclidine.

Effects on the Mind and Body. In humans, small doses produce a sense of intoxication, with staggering gait, slurred speech, and nystagmus, much like that observed with alcoholic intoxication, except that numbness of the extremities, sweating, and sometimes muscular rigidity and a blank stare also may occur. Users may also experience drowsiness, disorganized thoughts, and changes in body image. Depending on dose, there may be amnesia for the episode or hostile and bizarre actions. At high dosage there is stupor and coma—often with the eyes open and muscular rigidity. At very high doses the coma is prolonged, and convulsions may occur. Few drugs induce so wide a range of subjective effects. Intoxication with phencyclidine can mimic a variety of psychiatric disorders, including schizophrenia and manic-depressive disorder, and such psychotic states may last for weeks.

Intoxication with phencyclidine can last many hours, but a typical "high" lasts four to six hours. The mechanism of its action on the brain is still unknown. With chronic use, some tolerance develops to the behavioral and toxic effects of phencyclidine, and withdrawal may be accompanied by vague complaints about craving. Chronic users have reported speech, memory, and thinking impairments lasting as long as a year after stopping, and some researchers believe that it is likely that chronic PCP use induces some form of brain damage.

JEROME H. JAFFE
University of Connecticut Health Center

Bibliography

Brecher, Edward M., *Licit and Illicit Drugs* (Little 1972).
Dupont, Robert I., Goldstein, Avram, and O'Donnell, John, eds., *Handbook on Drug Abuse* (National Institute on Drug Abuse 1979).
Jaffe, Jerome H., "Drug Addiction and Drug Abuse," in *The Pharmacological Basis of Therapeutics*, ed. by Alfred Goodman Gilman, Louis S. Goodman, and Alfred Gilman, 6th ed. (Macmillan 1980).
Jaffe, Jerome H., and Martin, William R., "Opioid Analgesics and Antagonists," in *The Pharmacological Basis of Therapeutics*, ed. by Alfred Goodman Gilman, Louis S. Goodman, and Alfred Gilman, 6th ed. (Macmillan 1980).
Jaffe, Jerome H., Petersen, Robert, and Hodgson, Ray, *Addictions: Issues and Answers* (Harper 1980).
Lettieri, Dan J., Sayers, Mollie, and Pearson, Helen Wallenstein, eds., *Theories on Drug Abuse: Selected Contemporary Perspectives* (National Institute on Drug Abuse 1980).
Platt, Jerome J., and Labate, Christina, *Heroin Addiction: Theory, Research, and Treatment* (Wiley 1976).

DRUGS IN PSYCHIATRY, drugs that are used either alone or in conjunction with psychotherapy to treat psychiatric illnesses. The medical treatment of psychiatric illness is based on a firm conviction that the patient's behavior is in fact a symptom of an illness and not simply a variant of acceptable behavior in society. The study of drug effects on mental processes is called psychopharmacology.

Certain patterns of disease with mental manifestations are biologically characteristic of humans. The use of drugs to treat these disease patterns is directed either at alleviating symptoms or at inhibiting or stopping the underlying disease processes. Diseases that have purely psychological causes, but appear in ways that disturb society or distress the individual, are often treated with nonspecific remedies that either sedate or alert the individual. For all mental illnesses with specific biological causes, psychopharmacologists seek to develop drugs that change the biological functioning of the individual so that the symptoms of disease either do not occur or have a lesser impact on his or her life and behavior.

The use of drugs in the treatment of psychiatric illness is not a denial of the importance of psychological or social factors in the causation or pattern of a disease. Drug treatment of psychiatric illness is based on the principle that the human nervous system is always a chemical-biological system. Some psychiatric treatment systems—for example, psychoanalysis—do not utilize drug treatment. Some mental health experts feel that the use of drugs is only for the control of patients and not their treatment.

Nonspecific drugs, such as barbiturates (sedatives) or amphetamines (stimulants), primarily affect the individual's state of consciousness. They do not have specific actions on disturbed thought or mood. In larger doses these drugs have toxic actions on the nervous system and may produce symptoms of psychiatric illness.

It is well established that a number of psychiatric drugs have specific effects not only in changing pathologic thought patterns toward normality, but also in changing mood and behavior. These specific psychopharmacological agents include antipsychotics for psychoses, antidepressants for depression, sedative antianxiety agents for anxiety, and a mood stabilizer for mood disorders. See accompanying table.

Antipsychotic Drugs. A psychopharmacological revolution occurred in the early 1950's with the discovery and application of the antipsychotic drug chlorpromazine (examples of trade names are Thorazine and Largactil). It was noted by the French physicians H. Laborit, J. P. L. Delay, and P. Deniker that chlorpromazine seemed to have specific effects on the symptoms of schizophrenia, one of the major causes of psychiatric disability.

Chlorpromazine and other drugs of the chemical class of phenothiazines are called neuroleptics. Other compounds with different chemical structures (for example, the butyrophenones) have been found to share the therapeutic properties of the phenothiazines. These drugs as a class have been variously called ataraxics, neuroleptics, antischizophrenics, tranquilizers, antipsychotics, and many other names. The modern term antipsychotics seems to be most clearly descriptive. The drugs do not always tranquilize. Sometimes they will alert a retarded patient; thus the term tranquilizer is inappropriate. Because they seem to affect most psychoses, antischizophrenic is too limited a term. Neuroleptic is also widely used as a descriptive term.

Biochemical Theory of Psychosis. Impulses traveling along nerves are electrochemical in nature. The substances that are released by nerves to signal the next nerve in the network are called neurotransmitters. The most widely held theory of the biomedical basis of schizophrenia is that the disease is a sign of an underlying disturbance in the release and uptake of the neurotransmitter chemical dopamine at nerve endings in some areas of the central nervous system. All presently used antipsychotic drugs interfere with dopamine transmission. This biochemical theory of psychosis is at best only a partial explanation and is constantly being refined.

Apparent Effects. When given to a psychotic patient, antipsychotic drugs—over the course of days or weeks—change the aberrant thought process and behavior characteristic of schizophrenia and other psychoses. All the drugs are sedating. The sedation, indifference to stimuli, and immobilization, observed as effects of reserpine (a drug derived from the Indian plant *Rauwolfia serpentina*, a folk remedy for insanity), gave rise to the term "tranquilization" in medicine. Although indifference to stimuli may be contributory to the apparent reduction of illness, it is not the most desired therapeutic effect.

Administration of antipsychotic drugs reduces most of the symptoms of schizophrenia—hallucinations, disorder of thought pattern, bizarre thinking, paranoia, inappropriate response, and distorted sense of self. The drugs are also effective in the treatment of the mania (excitement, expansiveness, euphoria) of manic-depressive illness and in the psychoses associated with transient or permanent brain damage (organic brain syndromes).

The widespread use of antipsychotic drugs has been associated with a marked decrease in the number of hospitalized schizophrenics, because many of these patients can live outside the hospital when treated with drugs. In fact, 75% to 80% of schizophrenics can be successfully treated with antipsychotic drugs. Some patients require only short three- to six-month courses of treatment, though others need longer-term treatment—for several years or even for life.

PSYCHOTROPIC DRUGS

Official or Generic Name	Chemical Type	Some Trade Names
ANTIPSYCHOTICS		
haloperidol	Butyrophenone	Haldol
loxapine	dibenzoxazepine	Loxitane
molindone	dihydroindolone	Moban
chlorpromazine	aliphatic phenothiazine	Thorazine
fluphenazine	piperazine phenothiazine	Prolixin
thioridazine	piperadine phenothiazine	Mellaril
thiothixine	thioxanthene	Navane
ANTIDEPRESSANTS		
imipramine	tricyclic	Tofranil
amitriptyline	tricyclic	Elavil
phenelzine	MAOI	Nardil
tranylcypromine	MAOI	Parnate
MOOD STABILIZER		
lithium	lithium	Lithane
ANTIANXIETY DRUGS		
diazepam	benzodiazepine	Valium
chlordiazepoxide	benzodiazepine	Librium
meprobamate	carbamate	Miltown

Side Effects. All antipsychotic drugs produce side effects that may limit their usefulness. All can cause a "masked" facial expression, tremor, and slow movements that resemble those associated with Parkinson's disease. Some effects persist only as long as the drug is used. Other side effects appear after prolonged use of antipsychotics and may be permanent.

Temporary effects include sleepiness, Parkinsonian movements, feelings of stiffness, symptoms of automatic nervous system block, low blood pressure, dryness of mouth, and disturbances in temperature regulation. Other transient effects include increased sun sensitivity, decrease in white blood cells, impairment in sexual function, and jaundice. All these effects disappear when the drug is stopped.

A different set of side effects may continue after an antipsychotic drug is stopped. Tardive dyskinesia is an often irreversible movement disorder associated with antipsychotic drug use. The first signs are often involuntary mouth and tongue movements in a "fly catching" pattern. The disease may progress to writhing movements of the limbs and trunk. Tardive dyskinesia occurs most frequently in older patients with a history of chronic antipsychotic drug use. In contrast to the usual development of side effects, the disease will often appear when dosage of the drug is reduced and may go away when the dosage is increased. If the drug is stopped, the movement disorder continues. This side effect may be permanently disfiguring or, in rare cases, fatal.

It is thought that tardive dyskinesia is a result of supersensitivity, or rebound overresponsiveness, to dopamine occurring after a long-term deprivation of dopamine at the nerve endings when the dopamine-blocking drug is taken away.

There is no known satisfactory treatment of tardive dyskinesia. To avoid this complication the antipsychotic drugs should be used only when medically necessary. Preventive measures are based on a supposition that the least drug exposure is the safest. These measures include reduction of dosage, or drug-free periods (drug holidays). However, many patients cannot function successfully unless they take an antipsychotic drug, and for them the risk of developing tardive dyskinesia is outweighed by the therapeutic effects of the drug.

Antidepressant Drugs. Severe depression, often a time-limited disease (lasting about six months) characterized by a blue mood, lack of energy, reduced concentration, anxiety, sleep disorder, and despair, is presumed to have a biological basis. Because depression can lead to suicide, vigorous treatment often is necessary. Antidepressant drugs and electroconvulsive therapy (ECT) are the most effective treatments.

Psychotherapy is used in conjunction with drugs in the treatment of depression and is often helpful to the patient. Psychotherapy without drugs is useful in the milder depressions.

Theory of Depression. One widely held theory of depression is that it is the result of certain reduced neurotransmitter activity in the brain. Neurotransmitters such as the biogenic amines norepinephrine and serotonin are either diminished in quantity or action in the brain. This hypothesis, the "biogenic amine theory of depression," widely held since the early 1960's, is only a partial explanation of depression. It is likely that other neurotransmitters and hormones are also involved in depressive illness.

Tricyclics. In the early 1960's, R. Kuhn, a Swiss psychiatrist, noticed that certain drugs that chemically resembled the phenothiazine antipsychotics did not have antipsychotic effects, but after a few weeks of administration seemed to relieve depression. This group of drugs, known as the tricyclic antidepressants, are now widely used to treat depression. Imipramine (Tofranil) and amitriptyline (Elavil) are examples.

The exact mechanism of action of the tricyclics is unknown but is probably related to the fact that they block the reuptake of norepinephrine and serotonin in nerve endings, thus increasing their levels at the endings. All the tricyclic antidepressant drugs also have blocking actions on the parasympathetic nervous system that cause constipation, dryness of the mouth, and decreased sweating.

The drugs are not stimulants. In fact, even when single doses are given to patients they cause sedation, sleep, low blood pressure, dryness of mouth, constipation, and other signs of "slowing" of body functions. Despite this paradoxical "depressant" action of the tricyclics, there is a mood change and activation of depressed patients after a few weeks on tricyclic medication. Sleep is improved, and anxiety and ruminations are diminished.

Overdoses of the tricyclic antidepressants are often deadly. These drugs have a narrow therapeutic ratio—that is, the treatment dose is not much less than a toxic dose. For that reason they must be given with care to suicidal patients, often only in a hospital.

Monoamine Oxidase Inhibitors. Another group of antidepressant drugs is the monoamine oxidase inhibitors: drugs such as phenelzine (Nardil) and tranylcypromine (Parnate). These compounds prevent the destruction of amines by preventing the action of an enzyme, monoamine oxidase, that normally destroys the neurotransmitters norepinephrine, dopamine, and serotonin. The net effect of these drugs is thus similar to the actions of the tricyclic antidepressants, but the way they achieve that end is different. Like the tricyclics, monoamine oxidase inhibitors (MAOI's) also lower blood pressure. Unlike the tricyclics, however, they often have a simulating, rather than sedating, effect.

These drugs have been somewhat limited in their use because they have many drug and food interactions that may be dangerous to the patient. In 1963 an English pharmacist noticed that a patient who ate cheddar cheese while taking an MAOI had severe headaches. This observation led to experiments that showed that aged cheese and other foods high in naturally occurring amines—for example, tyramine—could often cause serious acute rise in blood pressure in MAOI-treated patients.

Ordinarily the body protects itself from the blood-pressure-increasing effects of high amine foods such as aged cheese, pickled herring, aged meat, red wine, and yeast by the activity of monoamine oxidase in the gastrointestinal tract. When the antidepressant MAOI's are given, this natural protection is blocked; thus previously innocuous foods can cause high blood pressure, headaches, or even strokes.

Drugs such as meperidine (Demerol), a narcotic, or over-the-counter cold remedies (Neo-Synephrine, Sudafed) can also interact with the MAOI's to cause high blood pressure or high fever.

With appropriate care the MAOI's can be used safely to treat depressions resistant to the tricyclic antidepressants.

Other Drugs Used in Depression. Other drugs sometimes used in treating depression, such as the antipsychotic agents, the sedative drugs, or stimulants such as amphetamine, are of limited usefulness and are rarely appropriate or effective treatments.

Electroconvulsive Therapy (ECT). Working by an unknown mechanism, ECT is an effective treatment for depression and may be the treatment of choice for some patients. Legal restrictions have limited the applications of ECT in some areas of the United States, but it is at times the only treatment that can relieve depression in some patients.

Mood Stabilizer—Lithium. Another major psychiatric illness, manic-depressive illness, can be both prevented and treated with the use of lithium. In 1949, James Cade, an Australian psychiatrist, discovered that lithium salts reversed the manic or excited phase of manic-depressive illness. Extensive studies in Scandinavia demonstrated that regular use of lithium prevented mania in patients with this disease. It also appeared to have some effect on the recurrent depressions that also occur in the illness. Lithium, although a simple ion, appears to have profound biological effects not only in mental illness but also in a number of other pathological states.

Unlike the other psychopharmacological agents, lithium has relatively little mental effect when given to normal persons. It is only slightly sedating and does not interfere with normal functions. However, when given to manic patients, it provides a striking and specific reduction of excitement, grandiosity, paranoia, aggressiveness, loose associations, and flight of ideas. The full effect is not immediate but may take several days of medication to become apparent. In the initial treatment, lithium may be used in conjunction with antipsychotic drugs such as haloperidol (Haldol) or chlorpromazine (Thorazine, Largactil).

Because lithium is a potentially toxic drug, its use must be monitored by measurement of the concentration of lithium in the blood. Periodic blood samples are drawn from patients, and an attempt is made to adjust drug dosage to maintain a blood concentration of about 0.6 to 1.2 milliequivalents of ion per liter of blood. (Milliequivalents are a measure of concentration of molecules in the body fluids.) Patients with manic-depressive illness often are maintained for many years on prophylactic doses of lithium. Such treatment has been shown to markedly reduce the incidence of illness and hospitalization and allows patients to lead normal lives.

Lithium also has been used in the treatment of aggressive disorders, thyroid disease, and the reduced white-cell count seen in patients who are being treated for cancer. Many other therapeutic claims—such as the treatment of migraine headaches—have been made for lithium, but the full potential of its therapeutic uses is yet to be found.

Lithium has effects on amine neurotransmitters in the brain and also substitutes for sodium in the membranes of nerves. Its exact mechanism of action is not known.

Side Effects. Lithium, well tolerated in most patients, can cause fine tremors, increased white blood cells, increased thirst and urination, and thyroid disorders. In some patients, it may cause permanent kidney damage, but so far this has been a rare event.

Antianxiety Drugs. Anxiety is a frequently occurring normal state as well as a symptom of disease. Anxiety has been called the cardinal symptom of neurosis and may produce physical as well as mental symptoms. When anxiety interferes with work or social functions to the detriment of the individual, it may be appropriate to treat this symptom with drugs. Many individuals treat their own anxieties themselves with alcohol or marijuana. The professional treatment of anxiety states is accomplished with sedative antianxiety agents (also called anxiolytic agents or minor tranquilizers).

How Antianxiety Agents Work. The antianxiety agents work by unknown mechanisms that may involve neurotransmitters such as gamma aminobutyric acid (GABA) or amines, such as norepinephrine. Specific pharmacological receptors in the brain have been identified for diazepam (Valium). These receptors may play a role in producing the symptoms of anxiety.

Phenobarbital and Meprobamate. Phenobarbital, a long-acting barbiturate, was the first of these drugs to achieve wide usage. The discovery of meprobamate (Miltown, Equanil) by F. M. Berger opened up a new era in the treatment of chronic and acute anxiety. However, meprobamate was not much different from the barbiturates.

Benzodiazepines. The introduction of the benzodiazepines (Librium, Valium) increased the use of antianxiety agents. These drugs were effective, relatively nontoxic, well tolerated, and fulfilled an apparent long-standing need of physicians and patients. They quickly became the most widely prescribed of all medications and a center of public controversy because of their possible overuse.

Other agents in the benzodiazepine group are used as hypnotics (sleeping pills). The major advantage of these over other hypnotics is that they have a wide margin of safety and cannot be easily used as suicide drugs.

Side Effects and Tolerance. Antianxiety agents are used effectively in short courses of treatment. They may cause oversedation in some persons and can cause physical and psychological dependence. If they are used for prolonged periods they lose their effectiveness—that is, the patient develops tolerance.

Propranolol. There has been some success in treating anxiety with agents such as propranolol (Inderal) that block the sympathetic part of the autonomic nervous system. These drugs are still used only experimentally to treat anxiety.

Future Outlook. As knowledge about the biological basis of mental illness increases, many additional psychopharmacological agents will be introduced. Drug treatment in psychiatry is already fully accepted practice. Its specificity and effectiveness are likely to improve.

ROBERT BYCK, M. D.
Yale University School of Medicine

Further Reading: Ayd, F. J., Jr., and Blackwell, B., eds., *Discoveries in Biological Psychiatry* (Lippincott 1970); Byck, R., "Drugs and Psychiatric Disorders," in *The Pharmacological Basis of Therapeutics*, 5th ed., ed. by L. Goodman and A. Gilman (Macmillan 1975); Caldwell, A. E., *Origins of Psychopharmacology: From CPZ to LSD* (Thomas 1970); Lipton, M. A., DiMascio, A., and Killam, K. F., eds., *Psychopharmacology: A Generation of Progress* (Raven Press 1978).

DRUIDS, drōō'ədz, a religious order among the ancient Celts of Gaul, Britain, and Ireland. Information about the druids comes largely from Greek and Latin literature and ancient Irish literary tradition. A highly fictitious, if picturesque, conception of the druids was developed during the 18th and 19th centuries, particularly in connection with ideas about the "noble savage." Contemporary studies in comparative primitive religion classify the druids in the general category of Eurasian magician-sages.

The word "druid" comes from *druides,* a Gaulish (Celtic) word repeated by ancient Greek and Latin writers. Independently, it is known from Old Irish in the form *druí,* of which *druid* is the plural form. It survived in Welsh, another Celtic tongue, but only as a bird name, *dryw,* meaning "wren." The ancient meaning is obscure. The stem *dru-wid* has been explained as "deep knowledge" or "knowledge of the oak."

Druids in Gaul and Britain. The oldest reference to the druids is from an anonymous Greek source, about 200 B.C., in which druids are spoken of as "philosophers" among the barbarian Celts. The principal classical sources are later, however, and include Julius Caesar and the three Greek writers, Diodorus Siculus, Strabo, and Athenaeus. Each of these seems to have relied almost entirely on the now lost writings of the Greek philosopher Posidonius (135?–50 B.C.). Although an accurate observer of the barbarians, Posidonius saw the druids through the concepts of his own Stoic philosophy and ascribed to them, as to other barbarian sages, idealized intellectual attainments far beyond their range of cultural experience. In the 1st century B.C. the druids were part of that Celtic life in Gaul that still practiced sacrifice and headhunting.

Drawing on classical sources as a whole, one can reasonably conclude that the druids formed an order of magician-sages and that they were the authoritative class in Celtic society. Recruits to the druidical order were drawn from among children of the aristocratic warrior class. They were trained for many years in schools of oral learning. The reason the druids did not employ writing was probably not to safeguard their lore, as alleged by Caesar, but to continue a sacred tradition that the art of writing would impair.

Druidical functions included arbitration, pronouncements on matters of public policy, enchantment, divination, and sacrifice. The Roman historian Pliny, in his *Natural History,* described the druidical rite of cutting mistletoe from an oak and also mentioned the ritual sacrifice of a pair of white bulls. The Greek historian Diodorus indicated that no sacrifices were undertaken without the druids.

Caesar speaks only of the druids, but the other authors, relying on Posidonius, also mention seers (*vates*) and bards (*bardoi*). It is not known how clearly delineated the functions of these various practitioners may have been; it is possible that all of them were druids in a wide sense. The seers seem to have been mainly concerned with prognostication, to which human sacrifice was sometimes a means, and the bards specialized in the composition and allocution of verse and eulogy in song.

The druids appear to have enjoyed extratribal privileges enabling them to travel at large, and Caesar states that they held an annual gathering at a holy place in the territory of the Carnutes in central Gaul. Caesar's further comment that druidism was thought to have originated in Britain, and that diligent students traveled there, is believed no more than indicative that Britain had remained a stronghold still beyond the reach of Rome. The only specific reference to druids encountered by the Romans when they invaded Britain is in connection with the assault on Mona (Anglesey) in 61 A.D. under the command of Seutonius Paulinus.

In Gaul, the druids rapidly lost influence with the advance of Roman arms, and they suffered suppression as a seditious influence. But numerous Gallo-Roman altars and shrines and various inscriptions show that cult functionaries of lesser standing continued throughout the pagan period of the Roman Empire.

Irish Druids. Information on the druids in Ireland derives from the oral literary tradition that continued among the Irish from pagan into Christian times. From the 8th century on, much druidical lore was written down in Irish monasteries by monks who had also received their training at the hands of poets and men of letters in the native schools. The Irish evidence supports in most particulars the information contained in classical sources, and being much fuller and less self-conscious, it permits many important observations in terms of comparative institutions. In Ireland the druids took precedence over king and warriors. They were recruited as in Gaul, attended schools of oral learning, and were concerned with prognostication, enchantment, and sacrifice. Church influence naturally suppressed much information on sacrifice and cult practice.

In Ireland, at least some druids were householders and warriors, in contrast to Caesar's statement to the contrary regarding Gaulish druids. Women druids are also mentioned in Irish lore, although their role, apart from powers of spell casting, stands in some doubt. Women on the Continent enjoyed comparable, or even greater, offices. According to the Roman historian Tacitus, the migrating Celtic tribe known as the Bructeri was led by the prophetess Veleda, whose Celtic name is cognate with Irish forms implying "inspired sight."

Bards continued long in Ireland as the performers of spoken prose and verse. Among the most interesting aspects of Irish druidism was emphasis on powers of shape shifting and on incantation and trance. A druid, gorged on bull's flesh and wrapped in its hide, delivered oracles for the choosing of a new king for Tara. There are also descriptions of druids' dress incorporating bird skins and wings, endowed with powers of ascent, that indicate shamanistic elements known from a wide Eurasian comparative field.

It is impossible to determine which Irish druidical practices were insular and which derived from Continental druidism. However, there are many parallels in cult practice, social institutions, terminology, and even literary form between the pre-Christian Irish tradition and other Indo-European traditions, particularly Hindu and Italic. Druidism in Gaul and Ireland, as doubtless once elsewhere in the Celtic realms, adopted many strange elements while retaining its essential function of sustaining by magical means the prosperity of tribe and land. See also CELTIC PEOPLES.

T. G. E. POWELL, *University of Liverpool*

Further Reading: Kendrick, T. D., *The Druids* (London 1928); Piggott, Stuart, *The Druids* (London 1968); Powell, T. G. E., *The Celts* (London 1958).

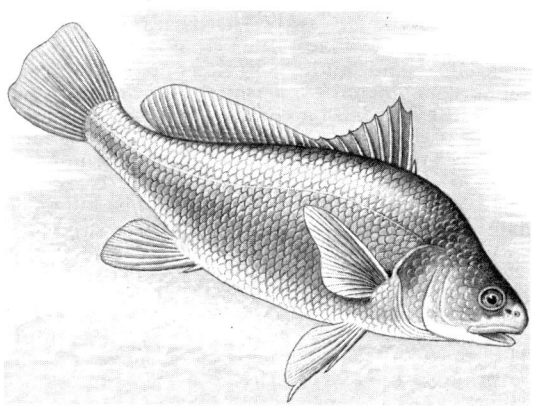

Freshwater drum (*Aplodinotus grunniens*)

DRUM, any fish of the family Sciaenidae. The family includes somewhat less than 200 species, many of which are important food fishes in many parts of the world. The common name "drum" and another frequently used term—croaker—refer to the croaking noise produced by these fish.

The characteristic croaking noise of drums is produced by the drumming muscles attached to the sides of the swim bladder. The walls of the bladder expand and contract rapidly and the bladder acts as a resonating chamber. The noise level of a school of drums increases during the breeding season and also changes from day to night, but the function of the sound is not well understood.

Drums are found throughout the world in tropical and temperate shallow waters of continental shelves, usually over sandy or muddy bottoms. Some species and the young of many species will also live in brackish water estuaries, and one species is found in freshwater.

All drums have several characteristics in common: their dorsal fin is deeply notched between the spiny and soft portions and may even be divided into two parts; the continuous lateral line extends onto the caudal fin; the head and body are covered with thin, usually slightly ctenoid, or toothed, scales; the bones of the top of the skull are cavernous; and the chin is usually equipped with pores or barbels.

Drums vary greatly in size; most are between 1 and 5 feet (0.3–1.5 meters) long and weigh from 2 to 20 pounds (1–9 kg). Some species, however, reach much larger sizes; for example, the totuava (*Cynoscion macdonaldi*) of the Gulf of California may attain a weight of over 200 pounds (90 kg). Drums usually feed on small invertebrates, but some large drums also eat other fishes.

Drums make up the family Sciaenidae of the order Percomorphi. See also CROAKER.

JAMES C. TYLER
The Academy of Natural Sciences of Philadelphia

DRUM, a musical instrument of the percussion family, made of skin stretched over one or both ends of a cylindrical frame or hollow vessel to produce sounds when struck. The name applies to such instruments used in Western symphony orchestras, as well as to more primitive instruments of similar construction used in many parts of the world in cultural and religious ceremonies or to accompany singing and dancing.

Kettledrum. The most important drum in the symphony orchestra is the kettledrum, or *tympanum*, a single-skinned drum tuned to a specific pitch. It is made of a large, bowl-shaped copper "kettle," and the tension of the skin, or head, can be adjusted either manually or mechanically to permit pitch changes. Struck with sticks having various felt or sponge heads, it can produce different tone effects. Kettledrums originated in the Middle East, where they were carried in pairs by players on horseback. They were introduced to Europe at the time of the Crusades and into the symphony orchestra during the 18th century, when they were palyed in pairs tuned to tonic and dominant pitches. In modern orchestras, three or more kettledrums are usually used.

Beethoven (1770–1827) was the first composer to vary the tuning of kettledrums from the conventional tonic-dominant. Hector Berlioz (1803–1869) was probably the first to call for a change of tuning during a single movement. Béla Bartók (1881–1945) made use of the glissando—a rapid, slurring effect made possible only by mechanical tuning.

Other Drums. The other drums of the orchestra have two skins and are of indefinite pitch. The tension of their skins is maintained by cords or rods that stretch from skin to skin and can be tightened or loosened. Among these drums are the snare ("side") drum, the tenor drum, and the bass drum.

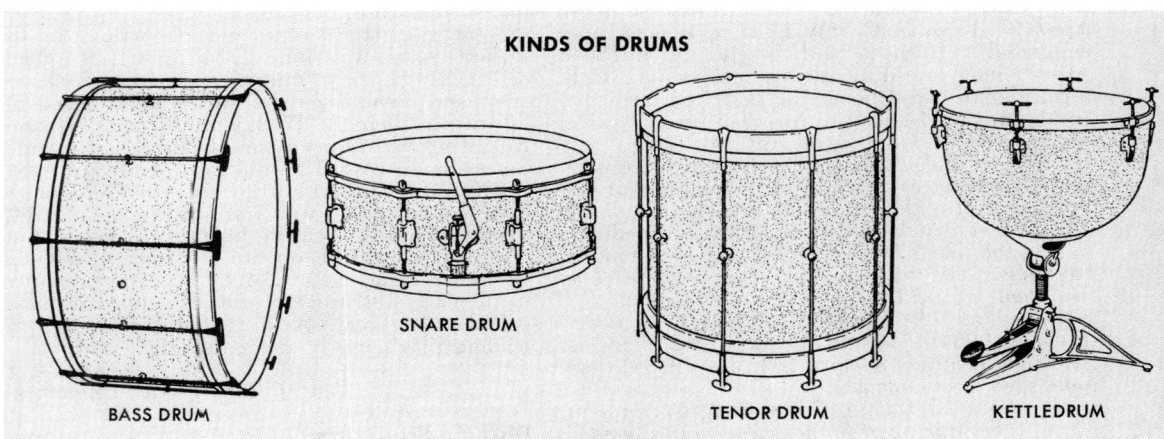

KINDS OF DRUMS

BASS DRUM — SNARE DRUM — TENOR DRUM — KETTLEDRUM

The *snare drum* gets its name from its characteristic rattling tone created by snares—gut or metal strings, stretched tightly across the lower drumhead. The upper head is struck with wooden sticks, frequently in "rolls," or rhythmic trills, that are difficult to perform. Eighteenth century composers used the snare drum primarily to create special effects, but it has become standard equipment in modern orchestras.

The *tenor drum* is a larger version of the snare drum without the snares. Its tone is dull and muffled, and it is used principally in the fife and drum corps.

The *bass drum* is the biggest member of the drum family. Held vertically by a marching player or standing on a frame in the orchestra, it is struck on one or both heads.

A combination of drums and cymbals called a *trap set* is used in popular music and jazz. The drummer is seated and beats the bass drum with a foot pedal, keeping his arms free to play the other drums and the cymbals.

The *tambourine* is a drum made from a wooden hoop with a single head stretched over the top and has "jingles," or small cymbal-like pieces of metal, attached to its frame. It can be shaken or played with the fingers. See also BONGO DRUMS.

SHIRLEY FLEMING, *Editor of "Musical America"*

DRUMLIN, drum'lən, a smoothly rounded, elongated or oval hill consisting of unstratified boulder clay or glacial till. Such hills were formed beneath the great ice sheets of the last glacial period, which ended approximately 10,000 years ago. The drumlins were formed in the ground moraine near the end of the ice sheets, when the ice at the base of the sheets became so loaded with rocks and clay that it stopped moving. The deposits were then overridden by the overlying clear glacial ice and were left behind when the ice retreated.

Drumlins are commonly about a half mile (less than 1 km) long and 100 to 200 feet (30–60 meters) high. The longer axis parallels the direction of glacial movement. Some of the islands in Boston harbor are drumlins. Drumlins also are abundant north and south of Lake Ontario and in eastern Wisconsin.

MARSHALL KAY, *Columbia University*

DRUMMOND, drum'ənd, **William Henry** (1854–1907), Canadian poet, who is known chiefly for his dialect poems about the *habitant* and *voyageur* backwoodsmen. Drummond was born on April 13, 1854, in County Leitrim, Ireland, and emigrated to Canada with his family in 1864. After taking an M. D. degree at Bishop's College, Lennoxville, Quebec, he practiced medicine in Montreal and taught at McGill University. He died in Cobalt, Ontario, on April 6, 1907.

In his dialect verse Drummond portrayed with sympathy and humor the quaintness of expression and outlook of rural French Canadians. The dialect that he uses is an invented medium, raising the patois to a literary language of unique freshness. His volumes of verse include *The Habitant ...* (1897), *Johnny Courteau ...* (1901), and *The Voyageur* (1905). *The Great Fight* (1908), *Poetical Works* (1912), and a selection, *Habitant Poems* (1926 and 1959), were published posthumously.

MICHAEL GNAROWSKI, *Coeditor of "The Making of Modern Poetry in Canada"*

DRUMMOND OF HAWTHORNDEN, drum'ənd, hô'thôrn-dən, **William** (1585–1649), Scottish poet, translator, and author of prose works. Drummond's notes on conversations with the poet-dramatist Ben Jonson constitute the only intimate record of Jonson's personality. Born at Hawthornden, Scotland, on Dec. 13, 1585, Drummond studied law at the universities of Paris and Bourges. In 1610 he succeeded his father as laird of Hawthornden, where he was visited by Ben Jonson during the winter of 1618–1619. He died at Hawthornden on Dec. 4, 1649.

A linguist, Drummond translated poetry from three Romance languages and was among the first Scottish poets to write exclusively in English. His outstanding works include *Tears on the Death of Meliades* (1613), an elegy on Prince Henry (son of James I); *Poems* (1616), commemorating his deceased fiancée, Mary Cunningham of Barns; and *The Cypress Grove* (1623), a collection of prose meditations. His poem *Forth Feasting* (1617) reflected his ardent royalist views.

DRUMMONDVILLE, drum'ənd-vil, a city in southeastern Quebec, Canada, is on the St. Francis River, 63 miles (100 km) northeast of Montreal. Its principal manufactured products are artificial silk, textiles, clothing, lumber, pencils, heavy machinery, paper boxes, and electrical accessories. A radio transmitting and receiving station for overseas messages is located here.

Drummondville was founded in 1815 by Maj. Gen. Frederick George Heriot and named for Sir Gordon Drummond, then commander in chief in Canada. Population: 27,347.

DRUNKENNESS. See ALCOHOLISM.

DRUPE. See FRUIT—*Fleshy Fruits*.

DRURY LANE THEATRE, droor'ē, one of the oldest and most famous theaters in the world. It is situated, perversely, in Catherine Street, London, and merely backs on Drury Lane.

Originally called the Theatre Royal, "Drury Lane" was built by Thomas Killigrew under a direct patent from Charles II that granted Killigrew the right "to erect a Company of Players which shall be Our own Company." The lease was dated 1661, and the theater opened in 1663. The royal livery is still worn by the footmen at Drury Lane Theatre.

Drury Lane was repeatedly destroyed or damaged by fire, but it has always been near its present site. Its best-known playwright in its earliest years was John Dryden, and its chief actor was Thomas Betterton. David Garrick, as actor and co-manager, began the finest phase of his career there in 1742 with *Richard III* and *King Lear*, but Drury Lane Theatre was too large for really successful productions of Shakespeare.

It was at Drury Lane, in 1777, that Sheridan's *School for Scandal* was first acted and, in 1814, that Edmund Kean made his famous debut. But it was through the operas of Michael William Balfe that Drury Lane Theatre kept its popularity in the early 19th century, and through the musical plays of Ivor Novello that it continued as a leading playhouse in the mid-20th century.

ALAN DENT
Author of "Mrs. Patrick Campbell"

DRUSE. See DRUZE.

DRUSUS, Marcus Livius (died 109 B.C.), Roman aristocrat. Tribune in 122 B.C., he undermined the popularity of Gaius Gracchus by proposing to establish 12 colonies in Italy with free land allotments. Drusus became consul in 112 and campaigned against the Scordisci in Thrace. He died while serving as censor in 109.

His son, also named Marcus Livius Drusus, (died 91 B.C.), similarly manipulated popular legislation in the interests of the aristocracy. As tribune in 91, he sponsored a reform program that included grain distribution and colonization. More important, he proposed expansion of the Senate and senatorial control of the judiciary. The proposals aroused opposition, driving Drusus to more extreme measures. His effort to enfranchise Italians cost him much support. The Senate annulled his measures, and Drusus was treacherously slain late in 91. The murder helped spur the great Italian rebellion of 90–88.

ERICH S. GRUEN
University of California at Berkeley

DRUSUS, Nero Claudius (38–9 B.C.), Roman general. He was the son of Tiberius Claudius Nero and Livia, but three days before his birth his mother married Octavian, (later the Emperor Augustus), having divorced Nero. His elder brother became the emperor Tiberius. Drusus married Antonia Minor, a daughter of Mark Antony. They had three children, Germanicus, Livilla, and the future emperor Claudius.

In 13 B.C., Drusus became governor of the three Gauls, and in the following year he invaded Germany. By 11 B.C. he had penetrated as far as the Weser River, and in the year 9 B.C., when he was consul, he reached the Elbe. In the same year Drusus was killed in a fall from a horse. He and his descendants were given the name Germanicus. At the peak of his career he was Rome's most popular general, but his policy of extending the Roman frontier to the Elbe was later abandoned.

ARTHER FERRILL, *University of Washington*

DRUSUS CAESAR (c. 11 B.C.–23 A.D.), Roman consul, was the son of Emperor Tiberius and Vipsania. He married Livilla, the sister of Germanicus. After Germanicus' death, Drusus Caesar became the heir-designate of Tiberius. He became consul in 15 A.D. and was commander in Illyricum from 17 to 20. He was consul again in 21.

Drusus Caesar died in 23, at an early age. Tradition says that he was poisoned by his wife Livilla, who wanted to marry Tiberius' minister, Sejanus. In 31, Livilla starved herself to death after she was charged with the crime. Drusus Caesar was a forceful man, intemperate, sometimes violent and cruel, but with a sense of humor and good military judgment.

ARTHER FERRILL, *University of Washington*

DRUZE, a member of a religious sect, related to the Ismaili Muslims, living in the mountains of Syria, Lebanon, and Israel. The Druzes (also *Druses*) number about 200,000.

The sect originated in the time of al-Hakim, the 6th imam of the Fatimid dynasty of Egypt and North Africa, who ruled between 996 and 1021. Al-Hakim was a strange man, noted both for his generosity and moralizing and for his cruelty. He disappeared in 1021 in mysterious circumstances, presumably having been murdered. As imam of the Fatimids, he was, according to Ismaili doctrine, the divinely appointed leader, guide, and guardian of the faith. In later life he claimed he was an incarnation of the Divine itself and began to propagate this belief through missionaries. There grew up a cult of al-Hakim, of which the Druze faith is the continuation.

The name of the sect comes from al-Darazi, who was the first to proclaim the cult publicly. He laid emphasis upon the esoteric truth taught by the cult and exalted al-Hakim to the status of a supernatural being.

Hamza Ibn Ali. The man who gave form to the Druze faith was Hamza Ibn Ali, al-Darazi's contemporary and rival. Al-Darazi had considered al-Hakim to be the incarnation of the principle of creative Divine Reason always present in the world and had spoken of him as imam or leader. Hamza, however, went beyond this established Ismaili theology. He viewed al-Hakim as identical with the Divine itself, as the very indefinable and ineffable One to whom even the creative Divine Reason is subordinate. He taught that the One had always been present in the world through a series of past incarnations, of which al-Hakim was the last and the one who would initiate the Day of Judgment. He claimed for himself the role of imam, the principal servant of the One, who would lead men to truth.

Hamza's teaching emphasized immediate and direct communication with the One as a living presence; hence the Druzes call themselves Muwahhidun (Monotheists, or "Oners"). Hamza denigrated the Prophet Mohammed and Ali, both of whom he considered teachers of false doctrines. Hence the Druzes were considered heretics. They were persecuted in Egypt, and the Druze community was able to sustain itself only in the mountains of Syria and Lebanon.

Beliefs and Practices of the Sect. Although the Druzes consider the Bible and the Koran inspired books, they have a Scripture of their own that supersedes these. It is composed of 111 pastoral letters by Druze leaders, under the title *Rasail al-Hikma* (*Discourses on Wisdom*). The Druzes in time became a closed community having its own law, prohibiting either conversion or apostasy, forbidding marriage with outsiders, and keeping its principal doctrines secret. The community is divided into two groups—the *uqqal*, or initiates into the secrets of the faith, and the *juhhal*, who are not initiated.

Outsiders may attend community religious services on Thursday evenings, but the secret ritual of the group is never performed before a non-Druze. The basic moral code consists of seven commandments enunciated by Hamza, the most important being always to speak the truth. Druze belief, however, permits dissimulation about one's religion in a hostile environment.

The Druzes have been an important factor in the history of Syria. At times they have ruled independent states in the area and have offered strong resistance to any who sought to subdue them. As late as the 1920's they staged a major armed uprising against the French mandate authorities. At present there are many Druzes in the United States, where they have gone to escape religious and political difficulties in Syria.

CHARLES J. ADAMS, *McGill University*

DRY CELL. See BATTERY, ELECTRIC—*Dry Primary Cells.*

DRY CLEANING, also written *drycleaning,* is the process of washing fabrics with liquids other than water. Dry cleaning solvents dissolve oily and fatty substances that are not soluble in water. These solvents do not swell natural fibers as water does. Such swelling is one of the major causes of shrinkage.

History. Archaeological discoveries have revealed the existence of dry cleaning in the Mycenaean civilization (1600–1100 B.C.). Mention of dry cleaning was included on clay tablets that listed more than 100 occupations. Grease-absorbent earths may have been used.

Turpentine has long been known as a good spotting agent for grease stains. In 1690 an anonymous writer stated, "Oil of turpentine will make rosin crumble away." In 1716 a French book about arts and crafts, *Secrets concernant les arts et métiers,* described a "special secret for removing grease and oil spots from silk stuff." It said, "One rubs the spots on the silk with spirits of turpentine, this spirit evaporates and takes with it the oil in the spot."

Dry cleaning as we know it today was not really practiced until the birth of the chemical industry in the 1800's, when such solvents as benzine (from petroleum), benzol (from coal tar), naphtha, and gasoline initially became available.

The first commercial dry cleaning plant was probably opened by the Jolly-Belin organization in Paris about 1845. After visits to this plant, J. Pullar of Perth, Scotland, and W. Spindler of Berlin returned to their native countries and introduced dry cleaning. Dry cleaning then began to spread throughout Europe.

Dry cleaning became widespread in America by 1910. The exact date that it became established initially is not known. In the 1920's valet shops or press shops became common in the United States. These shops sent clothing out to be cleaned. Garments were returned to the shops for finishing or pressing. This type of service has to a great extent been replaced by shops with small dry cleaning plants. In the 1930's many laundries added dry cleaning departments, and gradually dry cleaning has become the predominant service.

Dry cleaning grew from a $55 million industry in the United States in 1919 to a slightly less than $2 billion industry in 1959. In the late 1960's the industry's estimated volume was $2.8 billion. This amount included the earnings of the 36,000 to 37,000 dry cleaning plants in the United States.

Dry cleaning is classified as "small business" in the United States. Most plants can be maintained by three to five persons. Even smaller family-operated plants are not uncommon. There are also many large dry cleaning plants that employ 150 to 200 persons.

Solvents. Gasoline was the main solvent used in the United States in the early 20th century. But gasoline and the other petroleum derivatives used then were highly flammable and explosive. From 1921 to 1925 the National Institute of Dyers and Cleaners, now known as the National Institute of Drycleaning, conducted research to find a safer solvent. The solvent that was developed, with a minimum flash point of 100°F (38°C), was named Stoddard solvent in honor of the institute's president, W. J. Stoddard, who had been a prime mover in its development. This solvent is also known as white spirits in Britain. It is the petroleum solvent generally used today.

Synthetic solvents have since been developed. Perc (perchlorethylene) is the principal synthetic solvent. It is nonflammable and has greatly helped the growth of dry cleaning plants in well-populated areas. Most of the smaller dry cleaning plants in the United States use synthetic solvents, although petroleum-base solvents are still widely used and have certain cleaning advantages.

Dry Cleaning Procedures. Garments to be dry-cleaned are inspected upon arrival at the plant for spots, stains, items left in pockets, tears, and special instructions from the customer. They are then tagged for identification by the marker, who also removes buttons, belts, shoulder pads and fragile ornaments that require special handling or that cannot be cleaned. The clothing is next sorted according to fabric type, color, and construction. Each garment is sent through the plant with tags bearing special handling instructions.

After classification, clothing goes to the cleaning department where it is placed in the perforated revolving cylinder of a washer containing the dry cleaning solvent. A special detergent is added to the solvent. The solvent dissolves the oily, greasy soils, and the detergent loosens and suspends the remaining insoluble soils. The dirty solvent passes from the washer cylinder through a filtration system where insoluble soils are removed. The solvent itself is periodically distilled to remove soluble soils.

Most of the solvent is removed from the garments by centrifugal force during the spinning cycle of the washer. Drying then takes place in a tumbler or in a special drying cabinet where the last traces of the solvent are eliminated.

Garments are handled next by the spotter, one of the most highly skilled men in a dry cleaning plant. He identifies and removes stains by using a variety of chemicals, tamping the fabric with a brush, and flushing it with a special steam-air gun. The spotter must be able to identify fibers in order to remove stains effectively without damaging the fabric or dye. Some plants maintain a separate wet cleaning department to which garments are sent by the spotter when dry cleaning and spotting have not been sufficient.

Garments are next sent to the finishing department. A variety of equipment, ranging from small puff irons to body-sized steam-air forms apply steam to soften the fabric, remove wrinkles, and restore shape.

Then each garment is inspected. Ornaments removed before cleaning are replaced. Some dry cleaning plants also perform minor repairs and alterations. The clothes are then assembled into individual customer orders and are placed in protective bags for delivery to the customer.

Essentially the same procedures are followed the dry cleaning of many textile items other than clothing, such as draperies, table linens, blankets, and small rugs. Leather garments are dry-cleaned also, but the dry cleaning of leather requires special skills, and most dry cleaners send such articles to leather cleaners.

In 1959, small dry cleaning establishments with coin-operated machines were introduced. The small complete dry cleaning units hold 8 pounds (3.6 kg). The customer or an attendant loads and unloads the garments.

VAN SIGWORTH
National Institute of Drycleaning

FLOATING DRY DOCK (above) and graving dock (right) are two types of structures used for providing workmen with access to the underwater parts of large ships' hulls.

DRY DOCK, a concave structure in which a ship is supported out of water on blocks so that maintenance and repair work can be done on its underside. A *graving dock* is a walled basin built into the shore; a *floating dry dock* is a buoyant structure that can be lowered and raised in the water to receive and lift a ship. Both kinds of dry docks can be filled with water and emptied.

GRAVING DOCK

In docking a ship within a graving dock, the basin is filled with water, the ship is floated into the dock, and then an entrance gate is closed. As the water is removed by pumping, the ship settles on blocks on the dock floor. The blocks support the ship while maintenance and repair work is done, utilizing mechanical and electrical service outlets and hoisting equipment on the periphery of the dock. After repair work is completed, the dock is flooded, the gate is opened, and the ship is floated out.

Emptying and Filling Systems. A graving dock (see illustration) has two sidewalls that have tunnels and openings for water flow in emptying and filling the basin; an additional means of filling often is provided by openings in the entrance gate. The water flow is regulated by electrically or hydraulically operated sluice gates and gate valves. Pumps located in one sidewall usually empty the basin in 1.5 to 2.5 hours. Filling takes about 1 hour.

Entrance Gate. The floating-caisson entrance gate, the commonest type in the United States, has ballast tanks for lowering and raising it in dock seats. Caisson gates that slide or roll into position are commonly used in England.

Ship Positioning Equipment. Power capstans and cables, placed at intervals around the periphery of the basin, are used to maneuver a ship into position over the blocks before the dock is unwatered. One capstan can pull a load as great as 30,000 pounds (13,600 kg).

Blocks. After a ship is properly centered in the dock and the water is removed, the ship settles on blocks previously arranged so that they conform to the hull profile of the ship being docked. One line of blocks, called keelblocks, is located along the dock centerline; other lines of blocks, called bilge blocks, are located off the centerline. The blocks, which are made of wood, cast iron, and steel, rise 3.5 to 5.5 feet (1–1.6 meters) above the dock floor. Besides supporting the dead weight of the ship they provide a level base and give workmen access to the underside of the ship.

Service Outlets and Hoisting Equipment. Along the service altar, outlets are located in groups to supply electric lighting and power, steam compressed air, fresh and salt water, and gases for metal-cutting torches. These outlets are connected to flexible lines to carry the services to work locations on the ship.

All heavy materials for a dry-docked ship are handled by cranes that operate from tracks along the dock sidewalls. A traveling crane has a lifting capacity in the range from 20 to 75 tons (18–68 metric tons).

Design and Construction. The design of a graving dock strongly depends on the rock and soil conditions at the site. Bearing piles are needed if there are soft materials below the floor. Where water is present in the soil, provisions must be made for resisting or relieving the water pressure on the underside of the dock floor.

Graving docks are constructed either in open excavations or by underwater concreting. Open excavations are kept dry by the combined use of wells, well points, and pumps. Underwater concreting, used where it is not feasible to exclude water from the site, requires lowering of special formwork to receive concrete through large pipes called tremies.

History. The Phoenicians and Egyptians repaired a small vessel by bringing it into a cove at high tide and allowing it to settle on the bottom at ebb tide. The Greeks sometimes floated a vessel into an excavation made on the shore and then built an earth dam across the entrance and removed the water in the basin.

The first graving dock in England, built at Portsmouth in 1495, had crude entrance gates and also timber walls backed with stone. In the United States, durable stone-masonry dry docks were in use by 1840, and several timber docks were built in the 1850–1900 period. Reinforced concrete is used for building most modern graving docks.

FLOATING DRY DOCK

A floating dry dock basically consists of a bottom pontoon and two sidewalls subdivided into compartments to provide stability while lifting ships. It is lowered in the water to accommodate ship entry by flooding the compartments, and it is raised by pumping the water out.

Floating dry docks normally are towed from place to place and are operated at a berth alongside a pier or wharf where they can be supplied with mechanical and electrical services. Some military dry docks that are self-propelled have living quarters, electrical and mechanical services, and traveling cranes on board.

Types. A single-section floating dry dock, which either has open ends or has one closed end and one gated end, has two single-section sidewalls. Its main advantages are rigidity, simplicity, and the use of only one pumping plant.

A multisection floating dry dock has two multisection sidewalls. Separate sections, each about the same length, are joined to form a single dry dock that has the required total length and lifting capacity. Each section has its own buoyancy chambers, ballast compartments, and pumping plant. Some multisection steel dry docks are capable of lifting a battleship.

History. Floating dry docks made of wood and shaped like a hull were in use by 1785; they apparently were first made from sterns cut off from hulls. Floating dry docks made of iron were introduced about 1860. During World War II, many timber and steel, and some concrete, dry docks were built to meet military needs. Modern floating dry docks most commonly are made of steel.

JAMES R. AYERS and RALPH C. STOKES
Formerly, U. S. Navy Bureau of Yards and Docks

Bibliography

Abbett, Robert W., *American Civil Engineering Practice*, vol. 2 (New York 1956).
Cornick, Henry F., *Dock and Harbour Engineering*, vol. 1 (London 1958).
Du-Plat-Taylor, F. M. G., *Design, Construction and Maintenance of Docks, Wharves and Piers*, 3d ed. (London 1949).
Quinn, Alonzo DeF., *Design and Construction of Ports and Marine Structures* (New York 1961).

DRY FARMING is the production of crops without irrigation in semiarid climates or areas of limited rainfall. Dry farming, because of moisture limitations, is a specialized system of farming involving many soil management and crop production practices not followed in irrigated or in humid areas. Under dry farming a vigorously growing crop uses up all the available water from the root zone by the time of harvesting.

The boundaries marking dry farming regions from those of humid farming and desert areas are not clear-cut because of modifying factors such as soil characteristics, rainfall distribution, and temperature. In general, dry farming in the cooler climates is practiced in the 10- to 20-inch (25- to 50-mm) rainfall belts, whereas in warmer climates, areas having as much as 30 inches (75 mm) of annual precipitation are classified as dry farming regions. Actually, slightly more than one quarter of the earth's surface receives 10 to 20 inches (25 to 50 mm) of precipitation annually. Dry farming is widely practiced in Argentina, South Africa, southern Australia, Manchuria, Outer Mongolia, the Soviet Union, the Prairie provinces of Canada, and in many parts of the western United States.

HISTORY

Dry farming has long been practiced in many arid and semiarid regions of the world. In the dry lands of ancient Greece and Italy, farmers found that they could conserve the moisture of the soil by plowing the land to keep the surface layers powdery. Despite these efforts, dry farming produced only limited crop yields and it was not until the mid-19th century that dry farming methods were developed sufficiently to cultivate crops on a large scale in the vast plains of the dry temperate regions. This article deals with the development of dry farming practices in the western United States; these practices were subsequently adapted to or independently developed for similar regions.

The first North Americans to grow crops extensively on dry lands were the early settlers in Utah who, about 1865, began developing special techniques for growing crops on arid land. Within 15 to 20 years dry farming became an established system in many of the unirrigated portions of that state. Dry land cultivation in California and the Pacific Northwest commenced about 1870. Colonization of much of the semiarid parts of Kansas and Nebraska was attempted without success in the 1880's. Only after three decades did this vast plains area become more or less permanently settled.

Today, dry farming in the western part of the United States embraces an area of 450,000 square miles (1,165,500 sq km), approximately two thirds or 300,000 square miles (777,000 sq km) of which is tillable agricultural land of potentially great productive capacity. The dominant cash crop in this region is wheat.

In 1900, the U. S. Department of Agriculture initiated a series of botanical and ecological investigations in the dry farming areas of the Great Plains. These developments paralleled a bitterness over whether the plains should continue primarily as a ranch country. Secretary of Agriculture James Wilson and others became concerned over the plight of settlers pouring into the Great Plains region, as they were without training suited to the area, and there existed no body of information on which to plan and build a stable agriculture. This need served as the impetus for the establishment of the Office of Dry Land Agriculture in 1906 as a part of the U. S. Department of Agriculture. Soon thereafter, arrangements were completed for cooperative investigations at six existing state substations, and for the establishment of federal dry land stations where no state facilities were available.

In the years that followed, these publicly supported federal and state research centers had a profound influence on the development and stabilization of dry farming operations in the Western states. Many practical and theoretical problems found answers. First, emphasis was placed on gathering information on the relationship among moisture storage, seasonal crop conditions, and crop yields; on an evaluation of the importance of timely tillage and tillage methods in connection with the fallow operation and seed bed preparation; on the influence of previous crops on the yield of succeeding crops; and on an evaluation of the limitations and potentialities of the area for crop production. Continuous and comprehensive climatological observations were recorded and have served as a positive index in characterizing the semiarid areas with respect to their agricultural potentialities.

The introduction, development, and use of crop varieties adapted to the hazardous environment of the dry farming region have been an early and continuing function of experimental stations. As a result of this endeavor, higher yielding crop varieties better able to withstand drought, winter injury, insect and disease infestations, and other hazards are being introduced for dry land farming each year. Breeding and adaptation studies have not been limited to the extensively grown grain crops, but significant accomplishments have been made with forages, grasses, small fruits, vegetables, and trees.

MODERN PRACTICES

Choice of Crops. Crops grown under dry land conditions are not ordinarily more efficient in the use of water than the same crops grown under more humid conditions. Under dry land conditions, the humidity of the air is usually low and water loss by transpiration and evaporation is high; hence more water is frequently required to produce a unit of dry matter. It follows, then, that crops best adapted to dry land are those that make their maximum growth when climatic conditions are not too severe. The general displacement of spring wheat by winter wheat in those dry land areas where both are adapted is a striking example of this principle. Winter wheat is usually mature before the hottest part of the summer, whereas spring wheat most frequently matures under much more severe conditions.

Although wheat is by far the most important crop in the dry farming areas of the United States, crops other than wheat also are grown extensively. For example, oats, barley, corn, and flax are grown extensively in the northeastern section of the Great Plains, while corn and oats are raised in the east-central region, sorghum and cotton are grown in the southern region, and other small grains and range grasses are grown in the western areas.

Grasses and legumes have been unable to compete on an economical basis with wheat and other grain crops on cultivated dry land soils. Legumes and grasses leave the soil in a very dry condition and have a high water requirement that considerably limits their use and adaptability to dry farming systems. For example, the agronomist Arthur C. Dillman found in western South Dakota that 430 pounds of water were required to produce one pound of spring wheat, whereas 798 pounds of water were required to produce one pound of alfalfa.

Soil Moisture Problem. Water is generally the principal limiting factor in crop production in the dry farming areas. Contrary to early theories, which presupposed that water rises from the water table or deep subsoil by capillary movement to help support plant growth, it has now been well established that surface soil water from precipitation is the primary source of water for growing crops.

A successful dry farming system is based on the most efficient use of available precipitation. Losses of water through transpiration by weeds and by runoff are two major water-conserving factors that can be largely controlled by the farmer. Weeds are controlled through conventional methods of tillage, weed sprays, and clean seed. Runoff control, however, is more difficult. Runoff occurs during heavy or torrential rains in most dry land areas. In the northern Great Plains and in areas west of the continental divide, considerable water is lost in runoff from melting snows since the soil surface is often frozen when the snow begins to melt. The maintenance of crop residues and a loose, rough condition at the soil surface have been the most effective means of controlling or alleviating runoff losses. Strip cropping and terracing have also been effective.

The selection of a crop from the standpoint of its seasonal moisture requirements, timeliness of seeding, and cultivating the soil at the proper time are all important considerations in the maximum utilization of stored moisture. The quantity of water available to a particular crop may be augmented to some extent by growing it after a crop that does not exhaust the water supply of the soil. Row crops such as corn and potatoes usually do not utilize all of the available soil moisture; hence crops that follow are favored by this residual moisture. The greatest supply of moisture can be carried over from one year to the next by means of summer fallow.

Summer Fallow. Not until the development and widespread use of the summer fallow practice was dry farming a stabilized and economically successful enterprise. Summer fallow as applied to dry farming areas refers to keeping the land free of vegetation during one crop season in order to store moisture for crop production during the next. The most common method of handling fallow is to permit the stubble from a crop to stand over winter, to plow the soil in the spring before weeds have removed much water, and to keep the land free of weeds but in a condition to absorb rains during the summer.

The extent to which the summer fallow practice is used in dry farming areas depends largely on its effect on the quantity, economy, and stability of production. These factors are in turn affected by other considerations, such as the type of farming practiced, the type of soil, the kind of crops grown, the competition afforded by replacement crops, the weed control needed and afforded and erosion hazards. In a small grain farming system, an increase of 100% in acre yield on fallowed land makes the use of fallow almost imperative. Fallow is still a desirable practice when the increase falls considerably below 100% because keeping part of the land fallow and part in crop is cheaper than to grow a crop on all of the land. The use of fallow has other advantages. Production tends to be stabilized, as complete crop failures under a fallow system of farming are less frequent even though production totals may be unaffected. Weeds, plant diseases, and insects can usually be more effectively controlled under a system of farming where land is fallowed periodically.

While the summer fallow practice is a means of storing water in the soil for crops that follow, it is very inefficient from the standpoint of moisture conservation. Usually, only about 20% to 25% of the rainfall that comes during the fallow season is stored in the soil for future crop use.

Water losses by evaporation from clean tilled fallow land are extremely high. Although small amounts are lost as runoff, water losses through transpiration in weeds are often large.

Fertility Problem. In their uncultivated state, dry land soils have been described as being rich in nitrogen and other plant nutrients. With cultivation and crop production, however, over a period of some 50 to 75 years, the organic matter levels of these soils have been steadily dwindling. It is estimated that only about two thirds of the original quantities remain today. With the decline in the level of organic matter, the supplies of nitrogen, phosphorus, and other nutrients for crop growth have become less abundant. In the heavier rainfall areas and during certain years in the drier sections of the dry farming areas, the use of nitrogen fertilizer on certain crops and soils has now become a profitable practice. As the dry farming areas of the United States become older agriculturally, fertilizer usage will become more widespread and essential to the productivity of these soils.

Wind and Water Erosion. Wind erosion is an ever-present problem confronting the dry land farmer, and if allowed to proceed unabated, it becomes a national problem. The threat of soil blowing has become steadily greater as more and more land has been brought under cultivation. During periods of drought, the problem becomes particularly acute. Since the advent of the dust bowl in the early and middle 1930's, a considerable number of practices have come into usage for the prevention or the alleviation of widespread soil blowing. In many areas, cropped and fallowed strips are arranged alternately in a direction perpendicular to the prevailing wind. This practice does not ensure control in itself and additional resistance to wind action is attained when fallowed soils are covered with a crop residue or with clods of soil. Ridged soils also check soil drifting. Deep cultivation for ridging and bringing moist clods to the surface is often an effective practice on land where the loss of soil has already started. This method is recommended only when other practices have failed to give adequate protection against wind erosion. Because of light precipitation, water erosion is not so important a factor in dry farming areas as in humid areas.

CHESTER E. EVANS
*Chief, North Plains Branch
Soil and Water Conservation Research Division
Agricultural Research Service
U.S. Department of Agriculture*

Further Reading: Gregor, H. F., "Push to the Desert: California's Arid Lands," *Science*, vol. 129, pp. 1329–1339 (Washington 1959); U. S. Department of Agriculture, "Conserving Soil Moisture" and "The Northern Great Plains, the Winter Wheat and Grazing Region, and the Southern Plains Region," *Soil, the 1957 Yearbook of Agriculture* (Washington 1957).

DRY ICE is a common term for solid carbon dioxide. Its name arises from the fact that at normal pressures the substance sublimes (goes directly from a solid to a gas), instead of melting, and leaves no liquid residue. Dry ice should be handled with great care because it is extremely cold and can cause severe burns.

Dry ice is a good refrigerant and is widely used for shipping perishable goods over long distances. It can produce much lower temperatures than ordinary ice and occupies less space because it is more dense. It has good lasting qualities for shipping because it is surrounded by a heavy layer of gas that acts as insulation. Dry ice mixed with ether, chloroform, or acetone produces a solution that reaches temperatures as low as $-77°C$ ($-106°F$), and such solutions are used as cooling baths in laboratories. Dry ice is also used for carbonating beverages and for producing an inert atmosphere.

Carbon dioxide is stored and shipped as a liquid in tanks at pressures approaching 75.2 kg/sq cm (1073 lb/sq inch). In the production of dry ice the liquid carbon dioxide is withdrawn from the tank and allowed to evaporate at normal pressure in a porous bag or similar apparatus. The rapid evaporation absorbs so much heat that part of the liquid freezes. At this stage the frozen liquid looks somewhat like snow but has a temperature of $-78.5°C$ ($-109°F$). The flaky material is compressed into blocks and sold commercially as dry ice.

OTTO W. NITZ, *Stout State University, Wis.*

DRY POINT. See ENGRAVING; ETCHING.

DRY ROT is a type of wood decay that is caused by fungi. It is mainly confined to structural timbers, floorboards, and other wooden structures that are in contact with damp ground. Wood affected by dry rot usually becomes brown and may sound hollow when tapped. In advanced stages, the wood cracks perpendicularly to the grain, forming cubes that may shatter or crumble. Although coniferous wood seems to decay more rapidly than hardwood, the rate of decay is largely influenced by the moisture and temperature of the surroundings. Warmth and dampness encourage the growth of the fungi.

Cause. The most common cause of dry rot in the United States is the fungus *Poria incrassata*. In Europe the major cause is *Merulius lacrymans*. Both fungi belong to the class Basidiomycetes and are characterized by pores on the undersurface of the fruiting body. The fruiting body, or sporophore, ranges in color from orange to purplish black.

Dry rot fungi do not attack living trees, only dead wood. They spread by means of airborne spores or creeping threads, called hyphae, that penetrate the wood. Irregularly shaped brown or gray masses of hyphae spread through cracks in the wood and transport water and nutrients from the wood to the growing fungus.

Dry rot decay in oak wood.

U. S. DEPARTMENT OF AGRICULTURE

Prevention. Once a wooden structure is infected with dry rot fungi, it cannot be treated and must be replaced with good timber. The best way of preventing dry rot is to follow sound building practices, such as placing untreated wood at least 18 inches (45 cm) from the ground and avoiding conditions where moisture can accumulate. Removing all wooden debris from beneath buildings is also helpful in preventing dry rot.

Applying fungicide to the surface of a wooden structure is seldom effective, since the fungus inside the wood will not be killed. Fence posts, telephone poles, and railroad ties can be treated by impregnating them with creosote. This treatment is not used for building timber because of the offensive odor of creosote and because the methods required for proper treatment would increase costs. Inorganic salts, such as zinc chloride, are sometimes useful in protecting construction timber against dry rot fungi.

JERRY T. WALKER, *Brooklyn Botanic Garden*

DRY TORTUGAS, tôr-tōō′gəz, a group of seven keys (islands) in the Gulf of Mexico, 68 miles (109 km) west of Key West, Fla. They are part of Monroe county, Florida. Their total area is 75 square miles (194 sq. km). On Garden Key is the unfinished bulk of Fort Jefferson, and on Loggerhead Key there is a lighthouse. The other islands are sand or coral reefs, with sparse growth and no fresh water.

The Dry Tortugas were designated a national monument in 1935. The bird rookeries on the island, where sooty and noddy terns breed, were made a federal reservation in 1908. The only residents of the islands are representatives of the National Park Service, who act as guides to visitors. The only access is by charter flight or boat from Key West, and visitors must carry their own food and water.

Fort Jefferson was begun in 1846 but never completed. During the Civil War it was used as a Union prison. Dr. Samuel A. Mudd, a Virginia physician, was imprisoned there in 1865 for giving medical aid to John Wilkes Booth after Booth assassinated Lincoln. Mudd was pardoned by President Andrew Johnson in 1869 for his service in a yellow fever epidemic in the islands.

The islands were discovered in 1513 by Juan Ponce de León, who named them Tortugas for the turtles he found. Later visitors, finding no water, called them Dry Tortugas. They were annexed to the United States with Florida in 1819.

JAMES G. EBERHARDT
Florida Keys Junior College

DRYADS, drī′ədz, in Greek mythology, the nymphs of trees and woods. These nymphs (also called *hamadryads*) were usually pictured as rustic huntresses or shepherdesses, crowned with oak leaves. Sometimes they were shown armed with axes to protect the oak trees, which were sacred to them. The dryads were mortal; when a tree died, so did the dryad inhabiting it.

DRYBURGH ABBEY, drī′bə-rə, is in southeastern Scotland, in the county of Berwick, on the Tweed River, 4 miles (6 km) east of Melrose. Sir Walter Scott, the novelist and poet, is buried in the abbey church. The abbey, founded in 1150, is now in ruins. Its final purchaser, Lord Glenconner, presented it to the nation in 1918.

John Dryden (from a portrait by Sir Godfrey Kneller).

NATIONAL PORTRAIT GALLERY, LONDON

DRYDEN, drī′dən, **John** (1631–1700), English poet, dramatist, and critic. The greatest writer of the Restoration period and a not unworthy successor to Shakespeare and Milton, Dryden was the true founder of English literary criticism and the formulator of a new style of poetic expression, the heroic couplet.

LIFE

Early Years. He was born at Aldwinkle All Saints, Northamptonshire, on Aug. 9, 1631, of "gentle" but not wealthy parents of Puritan persuasion. He was educated at Westminster School (about 1644–1649) and, Trinity College, Cambridge (1650–1655). After leaving the university, he held a small government post for a short time (1656–1658) under Secretary of State John Thurloe. While still at school (1649) he had had his first verses printed, an elegy on Lord Hastings; ten years later he brought out his more ambitious stanzas on the death of Oliver Cromwell. As soon as Charles II returned to England, Dryden hurried out his welcoming *Astraea Redux* (1660), followed by a *Panegyrick* on the coronation (1661). No doubt at this time he was in monetary difficulties, and very probably there is truth in the statement that the publisher Henry Herringman "kept him in his House" in return for his engaging in hackwork. Soon, however, he became friendly with Sir Robert Howard, son of the 1st Earl of Berkshire, who apparently gave him "plenty, ease and liberty to write" and whose sister, Lady Elizabeth, he married in 1663.

Road to Success. With the Restoration came the reopening of the theaters, and quite naturally the young poet turned to the stage in search of fame and profit. After a false start with *The Wild Gallant* (produced in 1663)—possibly merely the reworking of an early play by Richard Brome—he and Sir Robert Howard won resounding success in serious drama with their joint effort, *The Indian Queen* (1664), while Dryden himself showed his comic power in *The Rival Ladies* (published in 1664). In 1665 came the plague, followed by the Great Fire (1666), and Dryden, like the young William Shakespeare two generations before, now found himself denied access to the theater. Apparently, with many other Londoners, he retired to the country; at the Earl of Berkshire's estate he occupied himself with writing *Annus Mirabilis* (published 1667) and *Of Dramatick Poesy, an Essay* (published 1668). At the same time he must have been engaged on *Secret-Love, or the Maiden Queen,* which was ready for production almost immediately after the playhouses were opened again in 1667. This won instant esteem; Charles II liked it so much that he called it "his Play," and there is reason to believe that the King himself and one of his mistresses may have been the models for the gay lovers, Celadon and Florimel. Now came a long series of other popular dramas, both comic and serious. By the year 1668, Dryden was firmly established in reputation and finances; the King's company gave him a contract whereby he received one-and-a-quarter shares in the theater on consideration of his providing three plays a year, while court approval and monetary support came from his appointment as poet laureate and, two years later, as historiographer royal.

Political Controversy. The way, of course, was not always smooth. In 1671 he was held up to scorn as Bayes in the witty *Rehearsal* by the 2d Duke of Buckingham (George Villiers), while two years later he became involved in a rather indecorous controversy with the dramatist Elkanah Settle. Maybe this controversy helped him to modify his own views; maybe he had grown tired of the style of serious drama that he himself had largely been responsible for creating and of which the outstanding example was his *Conquest of Granada by the Spaniards,* 2 parts (1670; 1671); at any rate, he now gradually began to abandon this style, and in *All for Love, or The World Well Lost* (produced 1677) he wrote a blank verse tragedy confessedly inspired by Shakespeare. These and numerous other plays written up to 1681 placed him without question at the head of contemporary dramatists.

The year 1681 introduced him to a fresh sphere of activity. The atmosphere was vibrant with political excitement, and Dryden stepped forward as the chief literary supporter of the court party and the Tories against the Whigs led by the Earl of Shaftesbury. His magnificently incisive satirical poem *Absalom and Achitophel,* appeared late in 1681, and in the next year came *The Medall,* so entitled to cast ridicule on the Whigs, who had had a medal struck to commemorate Shaftesbury's acquittal on a charge of high treason. Naturally, these biting invectives were not allowed to pass unchallenged by the opposite party. Both Settle and Thomas Shadwell were ranged on the other side, and the latter's *Medal of John Bayes* (1682) was a bitter attack on Dryden's person and beliefs. In reply came Dryden's mordant *Mac Flecknoe, or A Satyr upon the True-Blew-Protestant Poet,* T.S. (1682), in which Shadwell was pilloried amid rousing laughter, and the second part (1682) of *Absalom and Achitophel,* wherein Dryden's two rivals were bitterly castigated as Og and Doeg. Nahum Tate wrote the second part of *Absalom and Achitophel,* but Dryden was responsible for a large section of it and probably revised Tate's work.

Religious Convictions. No doubt this immersion in political and religious controversy served to make Dryden search more deeply in his own heart, and the result is to be seen in *Religio Laici* (1682). The Puritanism of his family had never made a great impression on him, and he had very easily become an Anglican at the Restoration; at the same time his attachment to that church can never have been profound, and—as he confessed—he had always been "naturally inclined to Scepticism in Philosophy." *Religio Laici* shows him still unwilling to give himself to faith:

> For MY Salvation must its Doom receive
> Not from what OTHERS, but what *I* believe.

Nevertheless, the poem indicates a new soul-searching, and it is obvious that, while Dryden still struggled to rest his religion upon his own reason, he was groping forward toward an acceptance of mystical belief.

It is not unsurprising, therefore, that he entered the Roman Catholic Church in 1685, when the Catholic James II succeeded Charles II. Perhaps he may have been influenced somewhat by the new king's affiliations, but everything points to its having been a genuine conversion. Within a short time Dryden produced his poetic apologia, *The Hind and the Panther,* in which the "Milk white Hind," the pure, unsullied Catholic Church, is set above and apart from " the bloudy Bear, an Independent Beast," "the bristl'd Baptist Boar" and the Anglican "Panther."

Later Works. The year after the publication of this poem the Catholic monarchy was gone, and Dryden, deprived of his laureateship in 1689, entered a time of economic difficulty. Returning to the theater, he won some success, but nothing like that which had greeted his early dramas; in any case, the theaters themselves were in a bad way and had not so much to offer as they had during Charles' golden days. With his usual adaptability, however, Dryden discovered a fresh field of activity in poetic translation. His Juvenal and Persius (in which he associated himself with collaborators) appeared in 1693, his Virgil in 1697. Three years later came the *Fables, Ancient and Modern,* episodes culled from Homer, Ovid, Boccaccio, and Chaucer. Worn out and tired, Dryden died in London on Aug. 9, 1700, on the night of the third performance of his *Secular Masque,* a piece incorporated in Sir John Vanbrugh's prose version of John Fletcher's play *The Pilgrim.*

DRYDEN—THE MAN AND THE WRITER

The Man. In his life, as in his poetry, Dryden seems to have taken the middle course. Although he was the associate of many of the rakish aristocratic wits of the time, he does not appear to have permitted himself to become, like them, debauched. His modesty is spoken of by contemporaries, and there are references that show that, despite the prominent position he took in the conversational group that haunted Will's Coffeehouse, he was not rapier-quick in repartee. Perhaps we may think of him moving among his lighter companions, a somewhat stout, heavy figure of a man with ruddy cheeks, in part assured in spirit because of his unquestioned attainments and in part with what he himself styled his "natural diffidence."

The Dramatist. As a dramatist, Dryden is important but not truly great. His early comedies in some ways anticipate the kind of drama—the comedy of manners—in which Sir George Etherege and William Congreve were to excel, but he did not possess their light touch and easy dalliance. When his scenes are compared to theirs, a certain roughness becomes apparent, and he produced no comedy so worthy of modern revival as Etherege's *Man of Mode* or Congreve's *Way of the World.* In writing serious plays, he found himself in an age incapable of truly appreciating tragic intensity; and for the most part he exploited the heroic play, with its simple conflict between love and honor, its exotic atmosphere, and its artificiality in plot and sentiment intensified by its dialogue in rhymed couplets. In a sense, the heroic play was an attempt to do in England what Pierre Corneille and Jean Baptiste Racine were currently doing in France; but the English genius, unlike the French, could not create masterpieces in this style, and Shakespeare's influence was too close and too strong to permit the dramatists to cultivate the style in its purity. Apart from that, Dryden, while he had a blunt theatrical skill, did not possess the power of entering deeply into character; he was too much a personality himself to put his being into others. Even when he turned from the rhymed heroic play to "imitation" of Shakespeare, his *All for Love* exhibited structural power but hardly any real animation in the persons he put on the stage.

The Critic. In dramatic appreciation, however, Dryden excelled, and Samuel Johnson was fully justified in calling him "the father of English criticism." All through his life he displayed a consistent quality: confronted by a problem in creative expression, he set out to consider the aspects of that problem, to weigh conflicting elements, and to base his creative approach upon a sound foundation of critical thought. It is this quality which invests his prose prefaces and essays with an incisive interest—an interest, indeed, very similar to that of George Bernard Shaw's prefaces, the difference being that, where Shaw was most intent upon sociological ideas, Dryden was almost always intent upon literary form. The argumentation in these writings is by no means consistent, for Dryden was great enough to be willing to change his mind, but this perhaps adds to, rather than detracts from, their appeal. In one thing, however, he was consistent: he had a profound admiration for certain great writers of the past, Chaucer and Shakespeare in particular, and his penetrating judgments concerning their works are alert and profound.

In such writings, Dryden became one of the chief founders of modern prose style—logical, exact, based on the exercise of reason rather than on the excitement of emotion. He belonged to a time when scientific thought was being born; and science, for its advancement, requires a clear, logical form of expression. One of the aims of the Royal Society was to develop and cultivate a prose style of this kind, and Dryden was elected one of the society's earliest fellows in 1662. As prose writing proceeded from 1668 into the 18th century the impress of Dryden is clearly apparent.

The Poet. It is, however, on his verse that Dryden's fame must ultimately rest. Much of this verse may, at first glance, seem uninteresting when compared with the rapture of the romantic poets; all of it, written by a man whose constant intellectual home was Will's Coffeehouse, may be found lacking in that love of nature taught us later by the Lakeland poet, William Wordsworth; yet further reading, with a consequent understanding of what he aimed to accomplish and why, must serve to convince us that he was, indeed, one of the great masters of English poetry and possessed of an authentic inspiration. He did not live in a lyrical age, but the songs included in his plays show a mastery, a sensitivity, and a rhythmical variety peculiarly effective. Lines such as "No, no, poor suffering heart, no Change endeavour" and "Hark, hark, the Waters fall, fall, fall" testify to his keen ear for musical values, an in this musical approach he stands alongside the Italian poet Pietro Metastasio who, through his operatic writings in the 18th century, made himself the lyric master of Europe. It is love of music that gives exquisite quality to Dryden's most ambitious essay in this kind, *Alexander's Feast* (1697), a lyric in form and inspirational force worthy to vie with any.

Most of his verse, however, is written in simpler measures and depends upon an intellectual rather than an emotional approach. His name will always be associated with the heroic couplet, a type of verse form that requires some comment. During the years immediately before the outbreak of the Civil War in 1642, one of the chief trends in poetry was the development and cultivation of the so-called metaphysical style. In the hands of minor versifiers this was being carried to absurdity, with forced conceits, constant straining after novelty, exaggerated and fanciful comparisons, a general lack of precision, and frequent lapses in taste. Like nearly all young poets, Dryden started with the imitation of bad models, and his lines on Lord Hastings display all the current faults:

> Was there no milder way but the Small Pox,
> The very filth'ness of Pandora's Box?
> So many Spots, like *naeves*, our Venus soil?
> One Jewel set off with so many a Foil?
> Blisters with pride swell'd, which thro' 's
>   flesh did sprout
> Like Rose-buds, stuck i' th' Lilly-skin about.

It is a measure of his greatness and of his acute perception that almost immediately after writing these lines he began to aim, not at a chastening of this style, but at the cultivation of a completely different form. At first he did not seem able to determine whether the quatrains popularized by Sir William Davenant or the simpler couplets would best serve his needs and the needs of the time; his Stanza's on Cromwell of 1659 are quatrains, and even as late as 1667 his *Annus Mirabilis* not only adopted that form but was prefaced by the statement that he had ever judged quatrains "more noble and of greater dignity both for the Sound and the Number than any other Verse in use amongst us." Gradually, however, he came to realize that the balanced couplet was best suited to his purpose—and that purpose was designed to rid poetry of extravagance and to substitute a rational for an emotional approach. In the critical essay introducing *Annus Mirabilis* he makes his aims clear: "The Composition of all Poems," he argues, "is or ought to be of wit"; wit, "like a nimble Spaniel, beats over and ranges through the field of Memory till it springs the Quarry it hunted after," so that "the first happiness of the Poet's Imagination is properly Invention, or finding of the Thought"; then comes Fancy, which varies and molds "that Thought as the Judgment represents it proper to the subject"; and, finally, Elocution shapes the poems through "the Art of clothing and adorning that Thought so found and varied, in apt, significant and sounding words." The whole account of poetic composition indicates clearly that Dryden sought for intellectual strength and rational precision in form.

He himself was sufficiently close to the Elizabethans never to proceed so far in the framing of these verses as Alexander Pope was later to do. While his whole tendency was toward the epigrammatic, exact, and balanced couplet, he yet permitted himself considerable freedom. There is something almost feminine in Pope's delicate touch; in Dryden we always have the impression of masculinity and boldness. Pope achieves his best effects by subtle underemphasis; Dryden's best effects are gained by downright methods, as in the well-known portrait of Zimri (the Duke of Buckingham) in *Absalom and Achitophel:*

> In the first Rank of these did Zimri stand:
> A man so various, that he seem'd to be
> Not one, but all Mankind's Epitome:
> Stiff in Opinions, always in the wrong;
> Was Everything by starts, and Nothing long:
> But, in the course of one revolving Moon,
> Was Chymist, Fidler, States-man, and Buffoon.

To those reared on romantic poetry, Dryden's style may at first seem unappealing; yet even a slight familiarity with his verses and a general appreciation of his critical views demonstrate that although he deliberately cut himself off from many fields of poetic inspiration, he richly harvested those of his own choice. Wordsworth may soar far higher than Dryden but Dryden's flight is steadier. The romantic poets adored extremes; Dryden is the poet of measure, balance, and accomplished taste.

ALLARDYCE NICOLL
Author of "Dryden and His Poetry"

Bibliography

Dryden's Works are available in various editions, including Bredvold, Louis I., ed., *The Best of Dryden* (New York 1933); Day, Cyrus L., ed., *The Songs* (New York 1967); Elloway, David R., ed., *Dryden's Satire* (New York 1967); Noyes, George R., ed., *Poetical Works*, rev. and enl. ed. (Boston 1950); Ward, Charles E., ed. and comp., *The Letters* (Durham, N. C., 1942).

Aden, John M., ed., *Critical Opinions of John Dryden* (New York 1963).
Eliot, T. S., *John Dryden* (New York 1932).
Bredvold, Louis I., *The Intellectual Milieu of John Dryden* (Ann Arbor, Mich., 1935).
Hoffman, Arthur W., *John Dryden's Imagery* (Gainesville, Fla., 1962).
Macdonald, Hugh, *John Dryden, a Bibliography* (London 1939).
Miner, Earl R., *Dryden's Poetry* (Bloomington, Ind., 1967).
Nicoll, Allardyce, *Dryden and His Poetry* (New York 1967).
Pendlebury, Bevis J., *Dryden's Heroic Plays* (New York 1967).
Scott, Walter, *Life of Dryden*, ed. by Bernard Kreissman (Lincoln, Nebr., 1963).
Swedenberg, Hugh T., Jr., *Essential Articles for the Study of John Dryden* (Hamden, Conn., 1966).
Van Doren, Mark, *John Dryden: A Study of His Poetry* (Magnolia, Mass., 1960).
Ward, Charles E., *Life of John Dryden* (Chapel Hill, N. C., 1961).

DRYDEN, drī'dən, a town in southwestern Ontario, Canada, is about 180 miles (289 km) northwest of Fort William. It is a distributing center for a region in which lumbering, mining, and agriculture are important. Numerous lakes attract tourists and sportsmen. Dryden manufactures pulp and paper and chemicals and has a specialized printing plant. Population: 6,640.

DRYOPITHECUS, drī-ə-pith'ə-kəs, is a genus of fossil apes. *Dryopithecus* apes ranged over Europe, Asia, and Africa during the early or middle Miocene to the Pliocene, that is, from 5 to 20 million years ago. They were the ancestors of chimpanzees and gorillas. *Dryopithecus* gives a clear idea of the ape grade of organization that probably preceded the hominid level of organization.

Seven species (including findings known as *Proconsul, Sivapithecus,* and *Kenyapithecus*) are classified in the genus *Dryopithecus*. Some were slightly smaller than pygmy chimpanzees, while others were the size of gorillas. The only known skull is lightly built with a more or less globular braincase. The forehead and jaws do not protrude much, and there are no brow ridges. Although the cranial capacity of *Dryopithecus* apes cannot be accurately determined, it was probably about 100 to 400 cc, a volume similar to that of living apes of equivalent bulk. The braincast indicates that *Dryopithecus* was more monkeylike than apelike, however. The unspecialized postcranial skeleton shows no walking or arm-over-arm swinging specializations.

The teeth of *Dryopithecus* differ from those of living apes in several ways. In *Dryopithecus* the lower incisors are relatively smaller than in living apes and closer to one another, whereas the canines may be the same size or smaller than those of living apes. The molars are generally lower-crowned than in chimpanzees or gorillas, and they increase in size from the first to the third, also unlike modern apes. As in living apes, however, the most anterior lower premolar has a shearing edge.

FREDERICK S. SZALAY
The American Museum of Natural History

DRYOPTERIS. See FERN.

DRYSDALE, drīz'dāl, **Don** (1936–   ), American baseball pitcher, who established a major league record by holding the opposition scoreless through six consecutive complete games and a total of 58 consecutive innings in 1968. Relying on a sinking fast ball and a slider, the 6-foot 6-inch right-hander of the Los Angeles Dodgers bettered the complete game mark of five set by Guy Harris White of the Chicago White Sox in 1904 and passed Walter Johnson's consecutive inning record of 56 made for Washington in 1913.

Donald Scott Drysdale was born in Van Nuys, Calif., on July 23, 1936. He began his major league career in 1956 with the Brooklyn Dodgers. He received the Cy Young Award as the outstanding major league pitcher in 1962, when he won 25 games and lost 9. In striking out 210 batters in 1965, he set a National League mark of 200 or more strikeouts in six seasons. He retired in 1969 with a career record of 209 wins and 166 losses.

BILL BRADDOCK
New York "Times"

DRYSDALE, drīz'dāl, **Russell** (1912–   ), Australian painter, whose landscapes of the remote "outback" territory established him as one of Australia's leading artists. George Russell Drysdale was born in Bognor Regis, Sussex, England, on Feb. 7, 1912, but from about age 11 he lived in Australia, where members of his family had been pioneers for several generations. He attended grammar school in Victoria, but serious eye trouble forced him to forsake his studies in 1929. By 1935 he had already lost the sight of one eye; nevertheless, he began to study painting, in Melbourne.

After additional study in London and Paris, Drysdale returned to Australia in 1939 and set out to produce his "own vision of the land" in his landscapes of Australia. His paintings all express strong nationalistic sentiment. Drysdale collaborated with the Australian zoologist and explorer Jock Marshall on the book *Journey Among Men* (1962).

DUAL CITIZENSHIP. See CITIZENSHIP.

DUALISM is any theory that the world or some part of it, such as man, consists of two things or of two essentially different kinds of thing. This is often expressed by speaking of "two worlds"; for example, the world of mind and the world of matter, or the world of appearance and the world of reality.

Dualistic Theories. Dualistic theories have been common in the history of religious and philosophical thought. One of the earliest relates to the origin of good and evil: if evil is not original and eternal but merely subsidiary to good, there is, properly speaking, no dualism; but there is a dualism if there are two ultimate, irreducible principles, good and evil, as Zoroaster probably taught about the 6th century B.C. Similarly, Manichaeism, which arose in the 3d century A.D., involved the notion of a primeval conflict between two ultimate principles—light and darkness.

In Chinese Taoism, on the other hand, the division between yin (a passive, weak, negative cosmic force) and yang (an active, strong, positive cosmic force) was not a real dualism but merely a superficial opposition, since even the important, dualistically inclined 11th century thinker Ch'eng Yi regarded yin and yang as merely two aspects of the Way, which existed formlessly before them. According to this school of thought, everything is produced by the interaction of yin and yang, but they are not ultimate.

In early Greek philosophy, the Pythagoreans developed 10 pairs of opposites, such as odd and even, male and female. All these pairs fell under, and were presumably reduced to, a single contrast between the two principles of Limit and the Unlimited. This conception is perhaps the earliest instance of an ontological reduction leading to two basic categories for the description of the cosmos; it illustrates the fact that philosophical dualism is normally the outcome of a drive toward simplification, a drive that would lead on to monism (q.v.) if it were not blocked by the obstacle of what seems to a given thinker or school of thought to be a radical difference in the nature of things. Even the dualism of the Pythagoreans seems to have been immediately challenged by the monist Parmenides with arguments to show that there is, after all, only a single reality.

In modern philosophy, the most influential dualism has been Descartes' opposition between mind and matter, probably because it expressed in a precise philosophical form the age-old view held by common sense. Although Greek philosophers, especially Anaxagoras, had given mind an important place as a being distinct from matter, Descartes' formulation of the "mind-body problem" remained standard after the 17th century until it was attacked as a "category-mistake" by Gilbert Ryle in his *Concept of Mind* (1949).

In Descartes' view, mind and body are different substances (entities that could conceivably exist even if all else were destroyed), and a person is therefore a compound. More precisely, his view was that the world is divided into a single *res extensa* ("extended substance," or matter) and a number of entities, each of which is a *res cogitans* (a "thinking substance," or mind). Thus, Descartes does not maintain that there are really, or ultimately, only two things (a position sometimes called *substantival dualism*), but holds that there are just two ultimate kinds of substance or attributes of substances (*attributive dualism*). In fact, substantival dualism is inherently unattractive because there seems no good reason, once two ultimate substances (or even two within any kind) have been admitted, not to allow a greater number; whereas attributive dualism seems genuinely economical, because any abandonment of it in favor of a greater number (pluralism; q.v.) of basic attributes would let in whole new realms of being.

Other Uses of the Term "Dualism." The label "dualism" may be more loosely applied to philosophical systems, such as those of Plato and Kant, where one wants to refer to a fundamental contrast that is strongly stressed by a thinker but is not necessarily meant to include everything there is. In this sense one can speak of Plato's dualism, because a central feature of his thought is the separation of the eternal world of Forms, which can be known by the mind, from the fluctuating and transitory world of particulars, which appear to the senses. Likewise, Kant can be said to present a dualism, in that he makes a distinction between the noumenal and the phenomenal world.

Other highly significant dichotomies, such as God and Nature, reason and emotion, fact and value, the actual and the possible, time and eternity, may also be termed "dualisms." Such bifurcations seem at first to offer neat solutions to problems, but each gives rise to the insoluble problem of how, once the two realms are separated, to interrelate them again. How, for instance, once God is divorced from the natural world, can He be said to act in Nature?

ROLAND HALL
University of York, England

DUANE, doō-ān′, **James** (1733–1797), American political leader. He was born in New York City on Feb. 6, 1733. A conservative during the pre-Revolutionary period, he nevertheless became a member of the New York patriot committee in 1774 and was one of the authors of a resolution calling for the First Continental Congress. Elected to that body, he helped prepare the statement of American rights of 1774 but favored continued union with Britain.

As a member of Congress during most of the Revolutionary War, Duane favored a strong central government. He urged creation of separate departments of war, finance, and foreign affairs. As mayor of New York City (1784–1789) he reconstructed the city's municipal administration. From 1789 until he retired in 1794 he was a federal judge for the district of New York. He died in Schenectady, N.Y., on Feb. 1, 1797.

DON HIGGINBOTHAM
University of North Carolina

DUARTE. See EDWARD, king of Portugal.

DU BARRY, dü bȧ-rē′, **Countess** (1743–1793), mistress of King Louis XV of France. She was born Jeanne Bécu, the illegitimate child of a lower-middle-class woman, on Aug. 19, 1743, in Valcouleurs. After a convent education she served a brief apprenticeship to a milliner. At 17, under the name of Mlle. Vaubernier, she became the mistress of Jean du Barry, who earned his living by providing pretty women for young nobles. He brought Jeanne, a girl of fabulous

Countess du Barry (portrait by Marie Vigée-Lebrun)

beauty, to Louis XV's attention and arranged, at the King's insistence, to procure for Jeanne the social credentials necessary to be presented at court as Louis' official mistress. Legitimate birth and a husband who issued from an unbroken line of nobility since 1400 were required; du Barry therefore obligingly invented a deceased legal father for Jeanne and in 1768 married her to his brother Guillaume, Count du Barry.

Royal Mistress. In the eight months between Jeanne's marriage and her presentation at court in 1769, there was intrigue at Versailles for and against the presentation. Although there was some connection between these intrigues and the rivalry of the Choiseul and Richelieu factions, Choiseul's dismissal from the ministry in 1770 was not even partially a direct result of Mme. du Barry's presentation. During her six years of extraordinarily generous and good-natured tenure as royal mistress, du Barry took little part in politics. She was, nevertheless, banished to the abbey at Pont-aux-Dames after Louis XV's death in 1774. Two years later she was permitted to reside at Louveciennes.

Later Years. Mme. du Barry formed a serious attachment in 1781 with an old friend, the Duke de Brissac, which endured until he was murdered by a mob during the revolution in September 1792. He was decapitated and his head was thrown through the open window of Mme. du Barry's salon, where it came to rest at her feet. She had made several trips to England in 1791, ostensibly to recover jewels stolen from her but perhaps in the royalist cause. After her husband's death she sailed for England again, seeking refuge. While in London, she contributed 200,000 livres for émigré relief and gave an equal sum to the royalist Duke de Rohan-Chabot in France.

Returning to France in March 1793, Mme. du Barry found herself outlawed and her property placed under seal. A warrant for her arrest was signed by the Committee of Public Safety, and she was executed in Paris on Dec. 8, 1793.

LIONEL ROTHKRUG, *University of Michigan*

DU BARTAS, dü bàr-tàs', **Seigneur** (1544–1590), French poet, who introduced the religious epic in France. Guillaume de Salluste, Seigneur du Bartas, was born at Montfort, Gascony, and studied law in Toulouse. A Huguenot, he was encouraged to write religious verse by Jeanne d'Albret, queen of Navarre. In 1580 he became gentleman in waiting to her son, Henry of Navarre (later Henry IV of France), who occasionally sent him on diplomatic missions. In 1587 he was knighted by James VI of Scotland. Du Bartas died at Condom near his estate.

Du Bartas and other Protestant poets were disciples of Pierre de Ronsard, but whereas Ronsard and the Pléiade group imitated the literary themes and forms of pagan antiquity, the Protestants turned to the Bible. Du Bartas' verse includes the moral epics *Judith, Le triomphe de la foi,* and *Uranie,* all of which are in the collection *La muse chrétienne* (1574). For a time his fame rivaled Ronsard's, especially for *La semaine ou la création du monde* (1578), an ambitious epic divided into seven "days," describing the Creation. This had over 30 editions in six years and was translated into several languages; Joshua Sylvester's English translation influenced Milton's *Paradise Lost.* Du Bartas completed only half of a sequel, *La seconde semaine* (on Biblical history up to the birth of Christ).

Du Bartas was imitated and praised abroad, but he was soon forgotten in France. His noble and grandiose conceptions are seldom matched by the execution; prolix, deficient in taste and technique, he cataloged facts monotonously in bombastic or precious verse and invented outlandish new words.

EDWIN JAHIEL, *University of Illinois*

DUBBO, dub'ō, is a town in New South Wales, Australia, on the Macquarie River, 180 miles (290 km) northwest of Sydney. Dubbo is an important regional rail junction and the crossroads of two major highways. Wheat, cattle, and wool, the chief products of the area, are sold at markets in Dubbo and processed in the town. "Dubbo" is an aborigines' corruption of the name of R. V. Dulhunty, a settler of the 1830's. Dubbo became a village in 1849 and a municipality in 1872. Population: (1966) 15,568.

DUBČEK, do͞ob'chek, **Alexander** (1921–), Czechoslovak political leader. Becoming first secretary of the Communist party in 1968, he presided over the widespread popular movement to "de-Stalinize" and "democratize" communism in Czechslovakia.

Dubček was born on Nov. 27, 1921, in Uhrovec in western Slovakia. In 1925 his father moved the family to the USSR, where young Dubček attended school and worked in an industrial cooperative organized by his father and other Czechoslovaks. The family returned to Czechoslovakia in 1938, and a year later Dubček, then studying to become an engineer, joined the illegal Communist party. In 1944 he participated with Slovak guerilas in the uprising against the Nazi puppet regime in Slovakia.

His steady rise through the ranks of the party in Slovakia began in 1949, and from 1955 to 1958 he attended the advanced political school of the Soviet Communist party in Moscow. In 1960–1962 he was elected a secretary of the central committee and a member of the presidium of the Czech party as well as of its Slovak wing, becoming first secretary of the latter in 1963. On Jan. 5, 1968, he succeeded Antonín Novotný as first secretary of the Czechoslovak party, the first Slovak to hold this post. He firmly resisted Soviet pressure to halt the party's liberalizing reforms. During the resulting occupation of Czechoslovakia by Warsaw Pact armies in August 1968, he was imprisoned; he then resumed his functions under Soviet surveillance. He lost his post as first secretary in 1969.

JOSEPH F. ZACEK
State University of New York at Albany

DU BELLAY, dü be-lā′, **Guillaume** (1491–1543), French diplomat and historian. Born near Montmirail, France, du Bellay, Seigneur de Langey, received a scholastic education at the Sorbonne in Paris and later continued his studies in Italy. After service as a soldier in Flanders and Italy, he was sent on his first important diplomatic mission, to Italy, in 1526–1527. For the next 10 years he was involved in negotiations in England and Germany.

To further the alliance of Francis I with Henry VIII of England, du Bellay persuaded the Sorbonne to decide in favor of Henry's divorce in 1530. In Germany he pushed for a council to restore unity in the church. Named governor of Turin in 1537, he became governor of the whole of Piedmont in 1540. He died at St.-Symphorien-en-Laye on Jan. 9, 1543. Rabelais, who was du Bellay's physician and secretary from 1540, describes his death in *Gargantua and Pantagruel.*

In 1524, du Bellay had begun his major literary work, *Ogdoades,* a history of the reign of Francis I. He collected eyewitness accounts from people at court and had friends make extracts of important documents. The work was probably never completed, but sections of it were incorporated by his brother Martin into his *Mémoires.*

FREDRIC L. CHEYETTE, *Amherst College*

DU BELLAY, dü be-lā′, **Jean** (1492–1560), French prelate and diplomat. A younger brother of Guillaume du Bellay and cousin of the poet Joachim du Bellay, he was a major figure in the French humanist movement. In 1529 he joined Guillaume Budé in founding the Collège de France, and he became a patron of Rabelais, who wrote *Pantagruel* at his request. He himself wrote treatises, poems, and epigrams.

After studying law, du Bellay entered the church and became bishop of Bayonne in 1524 and of Paris in 1532. Sent on a number of diplomatic missions by King Francis I, he played a conciliating role in the early years of the Reformation; he tried unsuccessfully to arrange an accommodation between Pope Clement VII and Henry VIII of England over the latter's divorce and appealed, equally unsuccessfully, for a general council of the church to end the breach with the Protestants. Also an important royal administrator, in 1536 he held the post of lieutenant general in Champagne and Picardy.

Like other prelates, du Bellay accumulated many benefices, including the archbishopric of Bordeaux (1544–1553). He became a cardinal in 1535. After the death of Francis I (1547), he retired to Rome, where he was a serious contender for the papacy in 1555. He died in Rome on Feb. 16, 1560.

FREDRIC L. CHEYETTE, *Amherst College*

DU BELLAY, Joachim. See BELLAY.

DUBINSKY, dōō-bĭn′skē, **David** (1892–1982), American labor leader, who built the International Ladies' Garment Workers' Union from a membership of 45,000 in 1932 to over 450,000 in 1966, when he retired. He was born in Brest-Litovsk, Russian Poland, on Feb. 22, 1892. Arrested several times for union activity, he was sent to Siberia, escaped, was amnestied, and went to the United States in 1911.

Dubinsky joined the Cutters Union Local 10 of the ILGWU in New York City and was active in the socialist and cooperative movements. By 1921 he had become manager of Local 10. After a disastrous strike in 1926, provoked by a strong Communist element within the ILGWU, had left the union almost powerless, Dubinsky became national secretary-treasurer in 1929 and president in 1932, and crushed the Communists.

Within two years, through Dubinsky's effective use of the National Industrial Recovery Act, the union organized thousands of workers throughout the United States and turned a million-dollar deficit into an $850,000 surplus. In negotiations, he considered the women's garment industry as a unit. He stabilized the industry and raised the workers' standard of living.

Dubinsky became a power nationally as a vice president of the American Federation of Labor. He pioneered in welfare unionism that built health, cultural, and social elements into the trade union movement. He developed labor union political action and encouraged aid to the community by the labor movement. Dubinsky died in New York City on Sept. 17, 1982.

HARVEY L. FRIEDMAN
University of Massachusetts

DUBLIN, a city in central Georgia, the seat of Laurens county, is about 130 miles (310 km) southeast of Atlanta. Plywood, wooden rims, bats and handles, sashes and doors, furniture, kitchen cabinets, wall coverings, concrete blocks, toys, woolens, and shirts are manufactured. There are meat-packing, cottonseed oil, and peanut-crushing plants.

Dublin was incorporated in 1812. It has a mayor-council government. Population: 16,083.

DUBLIN, a small county on the east coast of Ireland, with an area of 355 square miles (920 sq km), includes the urban concentrations of Dublin city and Dun Laoghaire borough. Other towns are Clondalkin, west of the city, and Balbriggan, Skerries, and Swords, to the north.

County Dublin is an area of striking natural contrasts. On the southwest of Dublin city rises the northern rim of the Wicklow hills. On the north and west are low-lying fertile plains, suited to the fattening of cattle. The northern area bordering the sea is an intensive farming area, with the big city market at its doorstep. The farms here are small; large farms predominate in the rest of the county.

Balbriggan produces linen, cotton goods, and hosiery. Clondalkin makes paper and tiles. Swords is a developing manufacturing area making felts and machinery. Skerries has a fishing fleet and is a popular seaside resort. St. Patrick's Island, about a mile from Skerries, once housed a medieval monastery, plundered by the Vikings in 795. Population: (1981), including Dublin city and Dun Laoghaire borough, 1,001,985.

THOMAS FITZGERALD
Department of Education, Dublin

THE FOUR COURTS, on the northern quays of the Liffey River, houses the Irish Law Courts. The 18th century building, designed by James Gandon, was largely destroyed during the fighting of 1922 but was carefully restored later.

PICTORIAL PARADE

DUBLIN, dub′lən, capital of the Republic of Ireland, is the cultural, educational, and economic center of the nation. It has been the scene of many dramatic and significant events in Irish history. The city is situated near the middle of the country's east coast, on the Irish Sea, about 70 miles (110 km) west of Holyhead, Wales. The city grew up at the mouth of the Liffey River, where the river was fordable and there was access from the sea between the chain of hills in the south and the wide plains to the north. The place was called *Dubh-Linn* (Dark Pool) by the Gaelic natives because of the peat-colored waters of the Liffey.

Dublin is a city of many natural splendors. Fringed by golden beaches, its setting just north of the blue Wicklow hills is most attractive. It has always been a residential city; its wide streets, magnificent old buildings, and lovely parks give it a character all its own. Since Ireland achieved independence from Britain in 1922, Dublin has also become an industrial city.

Historic Dublin. Dublin is remarkable for the number of its public monuments. The main artery, O'Connell Street, starts at the Charles Stewart Parnell monument, commemorating the great parliamentary leader of the latter half of the 19th century, and runs southward to the O'Connell monument, the city's tribute to Daniel O'Connell, the "Liberator," who secured emancipation for the country's Roman Catholic majority in the first half of the 19th century. O'Connell Bridge, over the Liffey, leads to Westmoreland Street, a short wide street opening into College Green.

College Green is the architectural heart of the city, with the splendid Bank of Ireland building facing the façade of Trinity College. On the left stands the statue of Thomas Moore, whose beautiful and patriotic lyrics helped preserve the soul of Ireland in the dark days following the failure of the insurrection of 1798. On guard over the entrance to Trinity College are statues of Trinity's illustrious alumni, Oliver Goldsmith and Edmund Burke.

The Bank of Ireland, a fine porticoed building begun in 1729 and completed in 1794, was formerly the seat of the Patriot Parliament, which came to an untimely end with the Act of Union in 1800. Henry Grattan, one of the noble figures of the time, is represented by a statue near the former Parliament House, which so often echoed to his oratory. Beyond the Grattan statue in Dame Street, a monument by Edward Delaney has been erected to commemorate Thomas Davis, the leader of last century's "Young Ireland" movement.

Dublin's most attractive buildings include the Custom House (1790) and the Four Courts (1785), facing the river, and the General Post Office (1818) in O'Connell Street, all of which suffered damage during the War of Independence (1919–1921) and the Civil War that followed. Of the new buildings the most notable is An Busáras, the central bus station, situated near the Custom House and providing a remarkable contrast in architectural styles. The Custom House and the Four Courts were designed by James Gandon. The General Post Office was the headquarters of the Irish Volunteers in the Easter Rebellion of 1916. It was here that Padraic Pearse read the declaration of the Irish Republic. Other notable buildings are Dublin Castle, dating from the 13th century; the City Hall (1769–1779); the Mansion House, official residence of the Lord Mayor since 1715; Leinster House (1745), now housing Dáil Éireann (the Irish Parliament); and the King's Inns, where the Supreme Court holds its sittings.

Ancient Churches. Dublin is unique in having two medieval cathedrals within a few hundred yards of each other. Christ Church Cathedral was founded in 1038 by Sitric, the Danish king of Dublin. The first Norman archbishop of Dublin, Archbishop Comyn, built St. Patrick's Cathedral just outside the city walls in 1192. Both cathedrals, which are now Protestant, underwent extensive restoration in the 19th century.

In Christ Church may be seen the tomb of Strongbow, the great Norman knight, and his wife Eva, daughter of the Leinster king who brought in the Norman invaders and cemented their friendship by marrying his daughter to Strongbow. Jonathan Swift (1666–1745), one of Dublin's great writers, was dean of St. Patrick's for 30 years and lies buried there where, in the words he wrote for his epitaph, "savage indignation can no longer rend his heart."

St. Michan's, near the Four Courts, was built in the 17th century on the site of a much older

O'CONNELL BRIDGE, wider than it is long, attracts crowds of Sunday strollers. The bridge crosses the Liffey River and leads directly into O'Connell Street, Dublin's spacious main thoroughfare running north to Parnell Square.

LOUIS GOLDMAN, FROM RAPHO GUILLUMETTE

Danish church. It has a remarkable vault in which have been preserved for centuries bodies which have not decomposed—a "nun" and a "crusader" can be seen by visitors to the vault.

St. Werburgh's Church near ancient Christchurch Place was built in the 12th century and is one of the oldest in the city. It contains the Geraldine (FitzGerald) monument, the oldest of the city's memorials. In its vaults lie the remains of the 19th century patriot Lord Edward FitzGerald. St. Audoen's Church in High Street was founded by the Normans. It has a beautiful Norman font and an old Celtic cross; nearby is St. Audoen's Arch, built in 1215, the last surviving gate of the ancient city walls. St. Catherine's Church in Thomas Street stands on the site of the old Abbey of St. Thomas, named after St. Thomas à Becket. It was here that Robert Emmet was executed after the failure of his rebellion in 1803.

Owing to severe penal laws against the practice of their religion after the Reformation, Catholics were not permitted to build churches until the last century. The classical Pro-Cathedral (1815–1825) in Marlborough Street is the most imposing of the churches they did build.

Education and Cultural Life. Dublin has two famous university institutions, Trinity College and University College. Trinity College was founded by Queen Elizabeth I in 1591 and is the only college of the University of Dublin. It has been almost exclusively Protestant from its beginning but now admits Catholics to its staff and student body. Trinity incorporates a magnificent library, including a new building contrasting pleasantly with the older buildings on its splendid campus in the heart of Dublin. Visitors from all over the world come to the college library to see the Book of Kells (q.v.), a beautifully illuminated gospel book of the 8th century.

University College, now a constituent college of the National University of Ireland, traces its descent from the Catholic University founded in the last century by Cardinal Newman. It has sister colleges in Cork and Galway, both of which are over a century old. University College never had an adequate campus before the late 1960's, when it began to move to a new site at Belfield on the coast road south. The Irish government has announced a decision to merge the two colleges, Trinity and University, in one University of Dublin.

Dublin has five schools of medicine; three colleges of higher technology, which provide courses in commerce, engineering, architecture, and kindred faculties; and four training colleges for primary teachers. There are two music schools, the Royal Irish Academy of Music and the Municipal School of Music, as well as a college of art. The Royal Dublin Society is a long-established institution holding two shows annually, the spring show catering to agriculture and industry, and the horse show in August, an equestrian event which draws people to Dublin from many parts of the world.

The National Library of Ireland in Kildare Street is situated beside Leinster House. It has a fine collection of books on many subjects and specializes in books of Irish interest. Marsh's Library, near St. Patrick's Cathedral, was established in 1707, and its original bookcases are still in use. Sir Chester Beatty bequeathed to the nation the library which bears his name. It is particularly rich in items of Byzantine and Oriental interest. The Royal Dublin Society possesses a fine library, and there is a law library in the Four Courts. There are also many municipal libraries scattered throughout the city.

The National Museum in Kildare Street displays valuable exhibits of gold ornaments of great antiquity. Adjoining the museum, the National Gallery of Art has a fine collection of paintings. The Municipal Art Gallery in Parnell Square concentrates largely on modern art.

Parks. Phoenix Park, one of the largest and loveliest city parks in Europe, encloses an area of 1,760 acres (700 hectares). Here, in a beautiful setting, are the Zoological Gardens, one of the oldest zoos in the world, famous for its breeding of lions. At Glasnevin in the northwest part of the city is the long-established Botanic Gardens, which has many excellent features, including the Alpine House, Rock Gardens, and rare pine trees. St. Stephen's Green, another of Dublin's beautiful parks, is just south of College Green. It is adjacent to many streets of fine old Georgian houses, many of which are being replaced by modern multistoried buildings.

Theaters, Literature, and Communications. Dublin has made a special niche for itself in the world of the theater, mainly due to the famous Abbey Theatre. This theater was founded in 1904 by W. B. Yeats and Lady Gregory with funds provided by an Englishwoman, Miss Annie Horniman. Great dramatists, Yeats, J. M. Synge, and Sean O'Casey, made it internationally famous, and many of its actors and actresses, Barry Fitzgerald, Maire O'Neill, Sara Allgood, and F. J. McCormick, are among the immortals of the stage. The theater burned down in 1951 and was rebuilt from a design by Michael Scott. (See Abbey Theatre.)

Among great literary figures who were born in Dublin and whose residences may be discovered there are Richard Brinsley Sheridan (1751–1816), Oscar Wilde (1854–1900), George Bernard Shaw (1856–1950), and James Joyce (1882–1941).

Dublin journalism is represented by three morning, two evening, and two Sunday newspapers. The *Irish Times* is a long-established paper of excellent quality; the *Irish Independent* has the largest circulation; the *Irish Press*, the baby of these three morning papers, was founded in support of the ruling Government party, Fianna Fáil.

Television and radio are under monopoly control. The Radio Television Authority, composed of members appointed by the government under an act of the Dáil, has a reasonable measure of control over programs presented for listeners and viewers.

The Economy. Dublin offers great natural advantages to the industrialist. It is close to the big British market and all Irish rail and road communications radiate from Dublin. As a result of these advantages, Dublin has outgrown the rest of the country. To remedy the imbalance the government devised a series of incentives to encourage industries in the more remote areas of the country. Nevertheless, Dublin is becoming more industrialized every year. Most of the new industries are small and highly specialized and have been established chiefly by English and American industrialists. Some of Dublin's better known products are beer, stout, and whiskey, clothing and footwear, textiles, fertilizers, and chemicals. There are also large engineering works and automobile assembly plants.

Tourism is one of the major Irish industries, second only to agriculture in the country's balance of trade. Dublin, as the capital, takes the lion's share of the profits of tourism. Dublin Airport, at Collinstown on the north side of the city, is the home of Aer Lingus, the Irish Air Lines. The city is also an important financial center, its most important bank being the Bank of Ireland. The central bank, established by the government, directs credit control, takes part in research and statistical operations, the management of government securities, and establishment of a local money market. The Dublin Stock Exchange is on Anglesea Street.

Urban and Suburban Developments. Recent developments in the city include the building of a large concentration of flats for workers in the area of Ballymun on Dublin's western fringe. This is the largest of the many new built-up areas that have had a depressing effect on the city's center by gradually denuding it of population. The middle class moves out to row houses in the suburbs while the working population shifts from broken-down tenements to modern flats in the outskirts.

Dublin has many attractive suburbs. Dun Laoghaire is the port of call for passenger vessels from Holyhead across the Irish Sea. It has a fine harbor and the coast road stretches southward to the ancient town of Dalkey, now largely a dormitory of Dublin. Dun Laoghaire, Blackrock, and Dalkey form a local government unit distinct from the city proper. On the north side of the estuary of the Liffey, Clontarf, Dollymount, Sutton, and Howth delight native and visitor. The Hill of Howth is one of the loveliest spots in Ireland. Westward, too, is the picturesque village of Lucan, home of Patrick Sarsfield, leader of the Irish at the Battle of the Boyne in 1690.

Government. The government of the city is in the hands of the lord mayor, aldermen, and councillors of the City of Dublin, an ancient body whose first charter dates from 1171. The executive power rests largely in the hands of the city manager acting in consultation with the corporation and under the authority of the state. The corporation deals with all matters of local interest—housing, libraries, roads, streets, water, and sanitation—and it has a subcommittee with wide powers in educational matters.

History. The city of Dublin owes its origin to the Danes, who saw the value of the Liffey estuary as a trading center. The native Irish living in Dublin, who were converted to Christianity by St. Patrick in the 5th century, resisted the Danish inroads, but a Danish fortress built about 841 was the real beginning of the city. A Viking named Ivar succeeded to the rule of Dublin in 871, and the new city quickly developed as capital of a small kingdom closely associated with the Gaelic Leinstermen to the south. The combined forces of Danes and Leinstermen were defeated by Brian Boru, King of Munster and of Ireland, at the Battle of Clontarf in 1014. After this battle the power of Danish Dublin began to weaken and the Danes were gradually absorbed into the Gaelic population.

Under English Rule 13th to 20th Century. In 1170, Dermot Mac Murrough, King of Leinster, persuaded a group of Norman barons from Wales to

THE CUSTOM HOUSE stands in the distance, behind freighters along the south bank of the Liffey River.

EWING GALLOWAY

PHOENIX PARK is one of the most beautiful city parks in Europe, displaying many notable features. The home of the president of the Republic of Ireland is surrounded by fine lawns.

IRISH INTERNATIONAL AIRLINES

invade Ireland in order to restore him to his kingdom from which he had been outlawed. The Normans captured and held Dublin in the name of Henry II, King of England. Dublin then became the center of English authority in Ireland. Dublin Castle, built in the early 13th century, remained the impregnable bastion of English rule for 700 years.

By the end of the 17th century Dublin was in a state of decay, due to the ravages of the religious wars of 1640 and 1690. But the 18th century saw a wonderful renaissance. The city grew greatly in population, in trade, and in manufacture, and the period of Dublin's architectural glory began, with fine houses and wide streets spreading chiefly north and south.

Dublin became the seat of an independent parliament and the city flourished in the last two decades of the 18th century. But with the abolition of the Irish Parliament by the Act of Union of 1800 a slow decay again set in. The country-wide famines of the 19th century brought the starving peasantry to Dublin in large numbers. Here they crowded together in the fine but deteriorating old houses and generated what came to be known as the worst slums in Europe.

Easter Rebellion and After. The lot of the people slowly improved in the final decades of the 19th century and the beginning of the 20th century. In 1913, however, agitation by the workers for a proper living standard led to riots and bloodshed in the streets. From this turmoil developed the Citizen Army which was trained to use arms against the British regime. This army was the force that played such a leading role in Dublin's most historic week, Easter Week of 1916, when the Citizen Army and the Irish Volunteers took advantage of Britain's war in Europe to raise the banner of armed rebellion in the streets.

The rebels occupied strategic positions in the city on Easter Monday, April 24, 1916, and made the General Post Office their headquarters. The British pinned them down with artillery and machine-gun fire and shelled the buildings on O'Connell Street from a gunboat in the Liffey. By Saturday, Dublin's Easter Week rising was over. Its leaders, including Padraic Pearse, were subsequently executed by the British.

The executions crystallized anti-British feeling in the country. The rebel Sinn Fein party won an overwhelming victory in the General Election of 1918. On Jan. 21, 1919, in Dublin's Mansion House, the Irish declared their independence. Guerrilla warfare between the Irish Republican Army (I.R.A.) and British forces continued for two years. On May 25, 1921, the Irish took the Custom House, the center of British administration, and burned it. A truce was arranged in July and after protracted negotiations a treaty was signed in London. The terms of the peace treaty were not acceptable to all parties. They received the approval of the Dail by a small majority. Opponents and supporters of the treaty then fought a civil war, which ended on April 30, 1923.

In June 1932 a Eucharistic Congress was held in Dublin to celebrate the 1,500th anniversary of St. Patrick's coming to Ireland. More than a million people attended the solemn high mass in Phoenix Park. Another historic Dublin event was the inauguration of Douglas Hyde as first president of Ireland in 1938. Population (1966): 568,271.

THOMAS FITZGERALD
Department of Education, Dublin

Further Reading Guiness, Desmond, *Portrait of Dublin* (New York 1967); Pritchett, V. S., and Hofer, E., *Dublin: A Portrait* (New York 1967).

DUBLIN, University of, dub'lən, a state-supported coeducational university located in Dublin, Ireland. Founded in 1591 under a charter granted by Queen Elizabeth I, it received large grants from King James I. Its attendance was restricted to members of the Church of England. Building began with Trinity College; although the charter allowed for other colleges, none was ever built, and the names "University of Dublin" and "Trinity College, Dublin" are practically interchangeable. Catholics were first allowed to study for degrees in 1793, and in 1871 all remaining religious restrictions were removed. Women were first admitted in 1904.

Trinity College receives more than half its financial support from the Irish ministry of education, and it has three representatives in the Irish senate. In the late 1960's its faculty numbered about 300, and its total enrollment was more than 3,500. The library, which in 1801 was made a legal deposit library entitled to receive one copy of every book published in the United Kingdom, includes a major collection of ancient and medieval Irish manuscripts, among them the Book of Kells.

Trinity College is to be distinguished from University College, Dublin, a nonsectarian institution that enrolls twice as many students. However, a plan calling for a merger of the two colleges was approved late in 1968 by the Irish national assembly. According to this plan the union of the two colleges, which were to be fully merged by 1969, would be known as the University of Dublin. Each college would keep its own liberal arts faculty; biological sciences, medicine, and law would be taught at Trinity College, and business, engineering, and the physical sciences at University College.

CLIFTON L. HALL, *University of Tennessee*

DUBLINERS, dub'lə-nərz, is a book of 15 short stories by James Joyce (q.v.), written between 1904 and 1907 and published in 1914. The stories are aimed at exposing Dublin as a center of spiritual paralysis, although Joyce's scorn is usually tempered with compassion. The stories are in chronological order: the first three deal with childhood, the next four with adolescence, four with maturity, and three with public life. The last story, *The Dead*—one of the world's great short stories—provides an epilogue uniting "all the living and the dead."

The stories are unified by a common background and common theme—escape. The most remarkable feature of *Dubliners* is the way in which every detail contributes to meaning and every symbol suggests a deeper vision of reality.

Joyce's own life and that of his family form the basis for most of the stories. He is the small boy of *Araby*, his brother Stanislaus is the model for Mr. Duffy in *A Painful Case*, and *The Dead* involves experience of three generations of Joyce's family.

JAMES S. ATHERTON
Author of "The Books at the Wake"

DUBOIS, dü-bwä', **Eugène** (1858–1940), Dutch anatomist, who discovered Java man. Marie Eugène François Thomas Dubois was born in Eisden, Limburg, Netherlands, on Jan. 28, 1858. He studied medicine at the University of Amsterdam, where he became a lecturer in anatomy in 1886. Fascinated by the problem of human descent and convinced that a truly primitive fossil of an ape-man was to be found in the East Indies, he resigned his university post to become an army surgeon in the Dutch Indies.

In 1891, near Trinil, Java, Dubois discovered a skullcap and a thighbone of a fossil man. The thighbone indicated that the man had walked upright, but the skullcap indicated that he had a brain intermediate in size between the brains of apes and man. Therefore, Dubois called his find *Pithecanthropus erectus* (upright ape-man). His interpretation of *Pithecanthropus* as a human ancestor aroused an intense controversy, and Dubois withdrew his finds from all examination for some years. In 1922 he published a description of the Wadjak remains he had found 33 years before in Java. These represented a modern type of man, somewhat resembling the Australian aborigines. Dubois died at Bedelaer, Netherlands, on or about December 16, 1940.

CLIFFORD J. JOLLY, *New York University*

DUBOIS, dü-bwä', **Guillaume** (1656–1723), French cardinal, who rose from almost total obscurity to become France's chief minister. He was born on Sept. 6, 1656, in Brive-la-Gaillarde and was educated in a monastery there. He became the tutor of Philippe d'Orléans, Duke de Chartres and later Duke d'Orléans.

Ambitious and unscrupulous, Dubois earned his pupil's affection by unseemly indulgence and won royal favor when he arranged the Duke's marriage to Mlle. de Blois, a legitimated natural daughter of Louis XIV. Dubois later became secretary to Philippe, who, on becoming regent for Louis XV in 1715, appointed Dubois a councillor of state. He made Dubois foreign minister in 1718.

Dubois worked to defend the Peace of Utrecht and opposed the expansionist plans of Giulio Alberoni, Spain's chief minister. Dubois achieved his goals through the Triple Alliance with Britain and the Netherlands (1717) and by compelling Alberoni's dismissal through military intervention (1719). Dubois extracted from the regent the archbishopric of Cambrai in 1720, and in 1721, through bribes, influence, and support of the papal position against the Jansenists, he won a cardinal's hat. The next year he was appointed France's first minister. Despite his faults, Dubois rendered important service to France, bringing peace to his country. He died on Aug. 10, 1723, at Versailles.

LIONEL ROTHKRUG, *University of Michigan*

DU BOIS, dü-bwä', **Guy Pène** (1884–1958), American painter. He was born in Brooklyn, N.Y., on Jan. 4, 1884, and studied art in New York City with William Chase and Robert Henri. From 1924 to 1930 he painted in France, and his paintings reflect the influence of Forain and Steinlen.

A socially conscious artist and a follower of the "ashcan school" (q.v.), Du Bois painted scenes of city life, restaurants, night clubs, and a few outdoor views, and achieved a satirical effect by using doll-like figures and a direct, precise style. Examples of his paintings appear in leading American museums, and he is also represented by murals on a horse-racing theme in the post office at Saratoga Springs, N.Y.

Du Bois' autobiography, *Artists Say the Silliest Things*, was published in 1940. He died in Boston, Mass., on July 18, 1958.

DUBOIS, dü-bwä′, **Paul** (1829–1905), French sculptor. He was born at Nogent-sur-Seine on July 18, 1829. After attending the École des Beaux-Arts, he continued his studies in Italy, where his exposure to the classical eloquence of Renaissance sculpture strongly influenced his work. Among his important early pieces are *The Florentine Singer* and a *Virgin with Child*.

Dubois' later works include the tomb of General Lamoricière in the cathedral of Nantes, with its four powerful allegorical figures in bronze, representing Courage, Faith, Meditation, and Charity. His most famous sculpture is the equestrian statue of Joan of Arc, which stands before the cathedral of Reims. This work best expresses the qualities of heroism and spiritual strength that Dubois sought to embody in much of his sculpture. He also made fine portrait busts, including one of the great chemist Louis Pasteur. From 1878 to 1905, Dubois was director of the École des Beaux-Arts. He died in Paris on May 2, 1905.

DUBOIS, dü-bwä′, **Pierre** (c.1250–c.1320), French lawyer and pamphleteer. Probably Norman by birth, he studied at Paris under Thomas Aquinas and Siger of Brabant and then took up law. For most of his life he practiced at Coutances, where by 1302 he had become royal advocate. He represented Coutances in the assemblies summoned by King Philip IV in 1302 to consider the royal charges against Pope Boniface VIII, and in 1308 to hear the charges against the Knights Templar. On both occasions Dubois wrote pamphlets in support of the King's cause.

His most famous tract, *De recuperatione Terre Sancte* (*The Recovery of the Holy Land*), written around 1306, is a compendium of many of the radical ideas current in France at the time; in it Dubois attacked the secular clergy, defended the Friars Minor, and vigorously championed the authority of the King of France. Part 1, addressed to King Edward I of England, called for a new crusade to rescue the Holy Land from the Saracens. To promote this venture, the Church was to be reformed, peace was to be sworn by all Christians, and a permanent board of arbitration was to be established to settle disputes between sovereign princes. The crusade would be financed by confiscating clerical property, reforming the monasteries, and placing the papal states under French royal administration. Part 2, addressed to Philip IV, called for French hegemony over Europe and the Byzantine Empire.

FREDRIC L. CHEYETTE, *Amherst College*

DUBOIS, dü-bwä, **Théodore** (1837–1924), French composer, organist, and teacher, who wrote operas, chamber music, and symphonic works but is best known for his melodic religious compositions. Clément François Théodore Dubois was born on Aug. 24, 1837, in Rosnay, France. He studied at the Paris Conservatory, where he won the Prix de Rome in 1861. He spent some time in Italy, returning to Paris in 1866 to become choirmaster of the Church of Ste. Clotilde. There his most celebrated work, the oratorio *Les sept paroles du Christ* (*The Seven Last Words of Christ*), was first performed in 1867. From 1871 he was associated with the Paris Conservatory, first as teacher of harmony and from 1896 to 1904 as director. Meanwhile, in 1877, he had succeeded Saint-Saëns as organist at the Church of the Madeleine in Paris. Dubois died in Paris on June 11, 1924.

DUBOIS, dōō-bois, **W.E.B.** (1868–1963), American educator and writer, who led the modern American Negro movement for full equality. William Edward Burghardt DuBois was born in Great Barrington, Mass., on Feb. 23, 1868, of mixed French, Dutch, and African parentage. He went to Fisk University (A.B. 1888) and then to Harvard (A.B., 1890; M.A., 1891; Ph.D., 1895). After studying in Berlin, DuBois taught at Wilberforce College and then was professor of sociology at Atlanta University for 13 years (1897–1910). While there, he published his best book, *The Philadelphia Negro: A Social Study* (1899), and the annual *Atlanta University Publications*, which he conceived as a factual base for enlightened social policy on the Negro. He also sought to train the "talented tenth" of his people to be leaders in the struggle for equality.

Originally favoring the compromises in the famous speech of Booker T. Washington (q.v.) in Atlanta in 1895, DuBois became impatient with gradualism and, with other educated Negroes, began to demand equality immediately, not in some clouded future. Deeply resenting Washington's views and his power among both blacks and whites, DuBois, in 1910, eagerly joined the biracial National Association for the Advancement of Colored People (NAACP) as director of research and editor of its periodical, the *Crisis*.

Soon DuBois became the Negro's most influential spokesman. He made his editor's desk a podium for his changing ideas: first, cooperation with well-disposed white or biracial groups working for racial justice; then, association with colored peoples elsewhere (Pan-African congresses); and finally, under the impact of the Depression, creation of a self-sufficient Negro community—a program that led to DuBois' abrupt departure from the NAACP in 1934.

A second career emerged after World War II. After a decade (1934–1944) back at Atlanta University and four years (1944–1948) with a working desk at the NAACP, DuBois, an admirer of the Soviet Union, joined the worldwide peace movement and advocated the spread of socialism. He became alienated from the United States. He won a Lenin Peace Prize in 1959. In 1961 he joined the American Communist Party, then emigrated to Ghana. He died in Accra, a Ghanaian citizen, on Aug. 27, 1963. DuBois' *Souls of Black Folk* (1903), a minor classic, is partly autobiographical.

FRANCIS L. BRODERICK
Chancellor, University of Massachusetts

Further Reading: Broderick, Francis L., *W. E. B. DuBois: Negro Leader in a Time of Crisis* (Stanford, Calif., 1959).

DU BOIS, dōō bois′, a city in western Pennsylvania, is in Clearfield county, 75 miles (120 km) northeast of Pittsburgh. It is in a hunting and fishing region of the Allegheny plateau. The city's industries include bituminous mines, railroad workshops, machine shops, electronics works, silk and lumber mills, woodworking shops, and breweries. Brick and tile products, china, rubber goods, and automobile batteries and springs also are produced. The Du Bois Undergraduate Center of Pennsylvania State University is here.

The community was settled in 1812 and was named for John Du Bois, an early settler. It was incorporated as a borough in 1881 and as a city in 1914. The commission form of government was adopted in 1951. Population: 9,290.

DU BOIS-REYMOND, dü-bwä′ rā-môn′, **Emil** (1818–1896), German physiologist, who studied the electrical properties of animal tissues. Du Bois-Reymond was born in Berlin on Nov. 7, 1818. He studied anatomy and physiology at the University of Berlin under Johannes Müller, one of the founders of modern physiology. After writing his graduation thesis on electric fishes, Du Bois-Reymond became interested in the electrical properties of animal tissues. In 1840 he began to refine old instruments and invent new ones with which he might detect the passage of tiny currents of electricity in nerve and muscle tissue. One of his inventions, a type of induction coil, is still used.

Using the improved instruments, Du Bois-Reymond showed that a nerve impulse is accompanied by a change in the electrical condition of the nerve. This finding was, in a way, a return to the idea of "animal electricity," introduced earlier by Luigi Galvani and subsequently mysticized by Franz Mesmer. However, Du Bois-Reymond's ideas, accompanied by accurate measurements, upset vitalism by showing that even the subtle action of nerves was amenable to physical study with instruments that were similar to those used to measure electric currents in wires.

In 1858, Du Bois-Reymond became professor of physiology at the University of Berlin. Although popular with students, he offended many conservative colleagues by his materialistic views and his championship of controversial beliefs. He was an early supporter of Charles Darwin's theory of evolution by natural selection. Du Bois-Reymond died in Berlin on Dec. 26, 1896.

Isaac Asimov
Boston University School of Medicine

DUBOS, doo-bōs′, **René Jules** (1901–1982), American bacteriologist, who made important contributions to the study of bacterial diseases and the role of environment in health and disease. In 1930, Dubos, in collaboration with O. T. Avery, isolated a soil bacterium that contained an enzyme capable of decomposing the capsular polysaccharide of type III pneumococci (the bacteria that cause lobar pneumonia in man). They extracted the enzyme and found that it was effective in treating pneumococci infections in various animals.

Dubos' most outstanding work came in 1939, when he isolated a crystalline substance— tyrothricin—capable of destroying certain gram-positive organisms (organisms, such as streptococci, that are stained by Gram's reagent). Tyrothricin proved effective in treating some bacterial infections in man and animals, but it was found to be too toxic for widespread use. Its discovery was important, however, because it was the first antibiotic commercially produced and used. Dubos' work undoubtedly influenced Selman Waksman's studies of other soil bacteria capable of producing antibiotics—work that culminated in the discovery of streptomycin.

After World War II, Dubos became interested in the influences of environment on man. His studies on microbial flora indigenous to the human body showed the interaction of microorganisms, host, and environment. From the 1960's on, Dubos was best known for his widely read articles and books dealing with man's effect on his own environment.

Dubos was born in St.-Brice, France, on Feb. 20, 1901. After graduating from the Institut National Agronomique in Paris, he worked for two years at the International Institute of Agriculture in Rome. In 1924 he went to the United States and received his Ph.D. from Rutgers University in 1927. Except for two years at Harvard's Medical School, Dubos' entire scientific career was spent at Rockefeller Institute for Medical Research and its successor, Rockefeller University, in New York City. He died in New York City on Feb. 20, 1982.

L. R. C. Agnew*
University of California, Los Angeles

DUBROVNIK, doo′brŏv-nēk, a city in Yugoslavia, in southern Dalmatia in the republic of Croatia. It lies on the Adriatic coast at the base of Mt. Srdj (Mt. Sergius), a rugged limestone mountain that overlooks Dubrovnik. The Italian name for the city is *Ragusa*.

Dubrovnik is one of the principal tourist attractions of Yugoslavia. A medieval walled city, it has not changed much since it was restored following an earthquake in 1667. It is situated on a promontory, and the city walls, which are 9 to 12 feet (2.5–3.5 meters) thick, rise from the water's edge. From the top of the walls one obtains an excellent view of the entire city. The main street (Stradum) is lined on either side with impressive late Renaissance buildings. The very narrow, winding side streets are lined with attractive old houses. The most important architectural monuments are the Benedictine and Franciscan convents, the churches of Sveti Spas and St. Vlaho (the patron saint of Dubrovnik), the Sponza Palace, housing the city museum and state archives, and the famous Rector's Palace (15th century).

Every summer Dubrovnik sponsors a music festival featuring performers from all the European countries and the United States. It also has impressive theater productions, at times by foreign companies; the productions of Shakespeare's *Hamlet* on the walls of Fort Lovrijenac, just outside the city walls, are well known.

The city can be reached by rail from Belgrade and Zagreb by way of Sarajevo, by air direct from most European countries, by ship from Brindisi in Italy or Rijeka in Yugoslavia, and by a modern highway that runs the length of the Adriatic coast.

In addition to tourism, Dubrovnik, through its nearby deepwater port of Gruz, serves as an outlet for the goods produced in the region. The principal products are wood, olives, grapes, milk, and cheese. Dubrovnik's busy marketplace, attracts villagers from the surrounding area.

History. Dubrovnik was founded at the end of the 7th century by Roman refugees from the old Greek town of Epidaurus (present-day Cavtat, just south of Dubrovnik), when the latter was overrun by the first Slavic invaders. Subsequently, the Slavs merged with the Latin elements in Dubrovnik. It became a fortified walled city under Byzantine protection. In 1205 it fell to Venice and thereafter was under the nominal control of the Venetians (1205–1358), Hungarians (1358–1526), and Turks.

By paying a yearly tribute to the Turks and through skillful diplomacy, Dubrovnik was able to establish and maintain its status as an independent republic until 1808, when Napoleon seized it. At the Congress of Vienna in 1815, Dubrovnik, as a part of Dalmatia, was incorpo-

DUBROVNIK, the old walled city, juts out into the Adriatic Sea off Yugoslavia's Dalmatian coast. The mercantile fleet that sailed from this harbor was one of the Mediterranean's largest in the 16th and 17th centuries.

SCHUGAR, FROM MONKMEYER

rated into the Habsburg Empire. Since 1918 it has been a part of Croatia, within the Yugoslav state, except for the period of the German-Italian occupation (1941–1944).

The greatest period in Dubrovnik's history was 1400 to 1800. At one time the city controlled the coastal area from Boka Kotorska (the Gulf of Kotor) in the south to Ston in the north. Although the city was always overshadowed by Venice, its fleets sailed throughout the Mediterranean and to England and America. The city was also the intellectual center for the South Slavs for centuries. Its most famous citizens were the Renaissance playwright Marin Držić (1508–1567), the poet Ivan Gundulić (1588–1636), and the mathematician-philosopher Rudjer Bošković (1711–1787). Even today the citizens of Dubrovnik are known for their strong pride in their city and their local patriotism. The city has a cosmopolitan air that reflects its extensive Mediterranean and European connections. Population: (1968 est.) 25,000.

BARBARA JELAVICH and CHARLES JELAVICH
Indiana University

DUBUFFET, dü-bü-fe', **Jean** (1901–   ), French painter, whose deliberate, sophisticated style achieves the kind of unself-conscious beauty found in the crudest art forms—graffiti scratched or drawn on walls and the art of children and the insane.

Dubuffet was born on July 31, 1901, at Le Havre, and studied painting for only a few months in 1918 at the Académie Julian in Paris. Beset by doubts about the value of art and culture, he abandoned painting from 1924 to 1930 and again from 1933 to 1942. During these fallow periods he operated a winery, traveled, served in the French meteorological service, and indulged his interest in music.

Dubuffet's work is done in named series of paintings related to one another in subject and technique. The *Metro* series of 1943 is drawn in a childlike style that has a lightly satirical effect. In the *Corps de dame* series of 1949–1950 he combined heavy textural surfaces (incorporating sand, plaster, and cinders) with grotesquely misshapen figures of women. Other series are of cows, Arabs (inspired by trips to the Sahara), and landscapes. Several nonobjective series resemble the intricate textural patterns of old walls.

LORETTA GRELLNER
Lecturer, Chicago Public School Art Society

Further Reading: Selz, Peter, *The Work of Jean Dubuffet* (New York 1962); Trucchi, Lorenzo, ed., *Jean Dubuffet* (New York 1965).

DUBUQUE, də-būk', a city in eastern Iowa, the seat of Dubuque county, is situated on the Mississippi River opposite the Wisconsin-Illinois state line, about 150 miles (240 km) northeast of Des Moines. It is a trading center and a river port for a rich farming area and has important industries. Agricultural machinery is manufactured in the city, and there are large meat-packing, metalworking, and woodworking plants. The business and industrial sections of the city lie along the river under rocky bluffs that rise to a height of 300 feet (90 meters). The residential section occupies the higher level.

The University of Dubuque, a coeducational institution founded in 1852 and related to the United Presbyterian Church, has a college of liberal arts and a theological seminary. The city is also the home of three Roman Catholic institutions: Loras College for men, which includes the Seminary of St. Pius X; Clarke College for women; and Mount St. Bernard Seminary, a theological school. Wartburg Theological Seminary of the American Lutheran Church is also in Dubuque.

The first settler on the site of the city was Julien Dubuque, a French Canadian who arrived in 1788 and obtained permission from the Indians to mine lead. Intensive settlement began in 1833, after the treaty that ended the Black Hawk War (q.v.). The area was then part of the Territory of Wisconsin, and when Dubuque county was created in 1834, the new settlement became the county seat. It was organized as a city in 1837 and received a charter from the new Territory of Iowa in 1841. In the mid-19th century, Dubuque was an important lumbering center, sending great log rafts down the Mississippi.

Government is by council and city manager. Population: 62,321.

DU CANGE, dü känzh', **Sieur** (1610–1688), French historian and philologist. He was born Charles du Fresne, in Amiens, on Dec. 18, 1610. (Sieur du Cange was his title as lord of his paternal estates.) After attending the Jesuit college in Amiens, he studied law and was admitted to practice in Paris in 1631. Meeting with discouragement in his profession, he returned to Amiens and devoted himself to historical and linguistic studies. He died in Paris on Oct. 23, 1688.

Du Cange's facility with languages and his indefatigable research enabled him to digest a vast amount of material that formed the bases of his writings. His two works of most enduring importance to students of the Middle Ages are his dictionaries of Latin and Greek, *Glossarium ad scriptores mediae et infimae Latinitatis* (1678) and *Glossarium ad scriptores mediae et infimae Graecitatis* (1688).

DUCAS, dū'kəs, was the name of a Byzantine family of great prominence. Andronicus Ducas, who scored brilliant victories over the Arabs during the reign (886–912) of Emperor Leo VI, was the first important member of the family. His popularity led to accusations that he wanted to seize the throne. Rebelling in 906, he fled to the Arabs in 907 and became a Muslim.

Constantine, his son, followed him into exile, but eventually he returned to Constantinople and Leo made him general commander of the troops. Constantine was killed in 913 while attempting to seize the throne. His son Gregory and apparently all the other male members of the family were destroyed.

In 1059 another Constantine Ducas became emperor and ruled until his death in 1068. The family of this Ducas was related, probably through the female line, to the Ducas family of the 9th century. In 1071 the son of Constantine Ducas was put on the throne as Michael VII; he was deposed in 1078.

Neither Constantine nor Michael Ducas distinguished himself as a ruler, and no other Ducas ascended the throne. The Ducas family, however, continued to be powerful and influential to the very end of the empire. Irene, the wife of Alexius I Comnenus, was a Ducas, and there was a famous historian named Ducas in the 15th century.

PETER CHARANIS
Rutgers—The State University (N.J.)

DUCAS, dū'kəs, Byzantine historian of the 15th century A.D. He was related to the imperial family of that name, but little is known about his background or career. He served as secretary to the Genoese podesta of Phocaea in Asia Minor; visited Demotika in Thrace, where he witnessed the preparations of the Ottomans for their assault on Constantinople; advocated the union of the Greek and Roman churches; and, following the fall of Constantinople in 1453, entered the service of the Gattilusio family of Lesbos.

The fame of Ducas rests primarily on his *History*, written some time after 1462, a principal source for the study of the growth of Ottoman power and the fall of Byzantium. It covers the period from 1341 to the capture of Lesbos by the Ottomans in 1462, but is detailed in its exposition of events for only the years after 1391.

PETER CHARANIS
Rutgers—The State University (N.J.)

DUCASSE, Isidore Lucien. See LAUTRÉAMONT.

DUCASSE, dü-kȧs', **Roger** (1873–1954), French composer. Jean Jules Aimable Roger Ducasse (also known as *Roger-Ducasse*) was born in Bordeaux on April 18, 1873. At the age of 19 he entered the Paris Conservatory, where he studied with Gabriel Fauré. In 1902, Ducasse's cantata *Alcyone* won the second Prix de Rome. He was appointed inspector of singing instruction in the municipal schools of Paris in 1909, and in 1913 was promoted to inspector general of singing instruction in the city's schools, a post he held until his death. In 1935 he succeeded Paul Dukas as professor of composition at the Conservatory, but he resigned when France fell to the Germans in 1940. Ducasse died at Taillan (near Bordeaux) on July 20, 1954.

Ducasse composed symphonies, symphonic poems, choral works, motets, piano pieces, the *mimodrame* (pantomime) *Orphée* (1913), and the comic opera *Cantegril* (1931). His music is characterized by an elegant and imaginative use of classic discipline and harmonic innovation.

DUCAT, duk'ət, is the name given to several types of medieval and early modern gold and silver coins. The earliest ducats were silver coins struck in the duchy (Italian, *ducato;* hence the name of the coin) of Apulia by the kings of southern Italy, Roger II (reigned 1102–1154) and William I (reigned 1154–1166).

Venice struck ducats of silver from 1202 and of gold from 1284. The latter weighed about 0.12 oz (3.5 grams) and rapidly became the most important gold money in the eastern trade. Imitations were struck in Rome, Rhodes, Syria, and even India, and the ducat served as the model for the *cruzado* of Portugal (1457) and the *excelente* of Spain (1497). Venice struck the coin until the end of its republic (1797), and elsewhere imitations were still being minted about 1840.

DAVID HERLIHY, *University of Wisconsin*

DUCCIO DI BUONINSEGNA, dōōt'chō dē bwô-nēn-sä'nyä (1255?–?1319), Italian painter, who transformed the highly decorative conventions of the prevailing Italo-Byzantine style into a reasoned and coherent pictorial system, imbued with a new grace and a hint of naturalism. Combined with his uncommonly fine execution, these qualities have given Duccio a place among the greatest painters of the Western tradition. His work provided the foundation for the great Sienese school of painting of the 14th and 15th centuries.

Little is known of Duccio's life. In 1285 he was commissioned to paint a *Madonna* for the Church of Santa Maria Novella in Florence; this is almost certainly the *Rucellai Madonna* now in the Uffizi Gallery, Florence. There still exists the contract of Oct. 9, 1308, for Duccio's great masterpiece, the *Maestà*, an altarpiece for the Cathedral of Siena, whose main panel is now in the cathedral's museum. The 18 small panels of the predella below the main panel are divided among the National Gallery in London, the National Gallery in Washington, D.C., the Staatliche Museen in Berlin, and other museums.

The "Maestà." Duccio's only signed and undeniably documented work is *Maestà* (1311). The main panel, 12 feet long, was originally a single wood panel painted on both sides. The front and back were cut apart in the 18th century.

The front panel shows the Madonna and Child enthroned, flanked by rows of saints and bishops. This great crowd, which was new to Italian painting, recalls the entourage of a royal court and may have been suggested by some source in northern European art, which frequently reflected aspects of feudal life. Although Duccio's rows of flat figures merely overlay to suggest spatial depth, the figures are slightly more naturalistic than the angels in the earlier *Rucellai Madonna*.

The reverse of the *Maestà* is made up of 26 small scenes from the Passion of Christ, remarkable for their concise lyricism of form and mood. Their elegant style is derived from late Byzantine art, but something of the classical decorum of Nicola Pisano and the Gothic vigor and naturalism of Giovanni Pisano can also be discerned in the thoughtfully varied moods suitable to the different episodes. The sinuous gold hem that marks Christ's robe may be traced to the French Gothic, but Duccio characteristically uses it for both decorative and narrative purposes. Similarly, the attempted rendering of interior space may owe something to the more realistic style of contemporary Roman painters, and Duccio carefully repeats an interior setting when a sequence of episodes occurs in one place. This meticulous recreation of his subject and an unprecedented facility for visually coherent composition are innovations of the greatest importance.

BARRY HANNEGAN
University of Virginia

Further Reading: Brandi, Cesare, *Duccio* (Florence 1951); Carli, Enzo, *Duccio* (Milan 1952); DeWald, Ernest, *Italian Painting, 1200–1600* (New York 1961); Edgell, George, *A History of Sienese Painting* (New York 1932); Weigelt, Curt, *Sienese Painting of the Trecento* (New York 1930).

DU CERCEAU, dü ser-sō′, a family of French architects and designers of architectural decoration, who were prominent in the 16th and 17th centuries. The most important members of the family are Jacques I (1510?–?1585), his sons Baptiste (1544?–1590) and Jacques II (1550?–1614), and Baptiste's son Jean (1585?–?1649). The main influence of the du Cerceaus was in decorative design rather than in the more substantial aspects of architecture. Their broken and twisted pediments, curved doors, ornamental roofs, and richly complicated rustication had a lasting influence on the art of French interior decoration.

Jacques I, the founder of the family, added "du Cerceau" to the family name, Androuet (dropped by later members of the family). He is famous mainly for his books of engravings of architecture and architectural design. His most notable buildings, the châteaus of Charleval and Verneuil, are both now destroyed. After a trip to Italy in 1533 he published his first book, engravings of ancient arches and monuments, in 1549. His first book of original architectural designs, *Livre d'architecture* (1559), dedicated to Henry II, brought him into favor at court. From 1560 he worked for the Duchess of Ferrara, for whom he altered the Château of Montargis. In the 1570's he worked for Charles IX and enjoyed the patronage of Catherine de' Medici.

Jacques II designed the Hôtel de Mayenne (?1605) in Paris. Baptiste was the probable designer of the Hôtel Lamoignon (1584), which has crudely detailed giant orders and abrupt changes of scale but is relatively severe com-

Duccio di Buoninsegna's *Rucellai Madonna*

pared with the work of Jacques I. Baptiste's son, Jean, became architect to Louis XIII in 1617. He built the Hôtel de Sully and reconstructed the Port au Change.

BRUCE ALLSOPP
University of Newcastle upon Tyne

DU CHAILLU, dü shà-yü′, **Paul Belloni** (1831?–1903), French-American explorer and author, who made important discoveries about the zoology, ethnology, and geography of Africa. He was born probably in Paris in the early 1830's. He spent several years in Gabon and went to the United States in 1852, where he became a citizen.

From 1856 to 1859 he traveled alone in equatorial Africa, penetrating the interior of Gabon and exploring the Muni and Ogooué rivers. He was the first modern Westerner to see live gorillas. His popular account of the expedition, *Exploration and Adventures in Equatorial Africa* (1861), was vivid but unscientific. Although widely criticized initially, his discoveries were later substantially verified. In 1863–1865, Du Chaillu further explored Gabon and visited the Pygmies of the equatorial forest. His *A Journey to Ashango-land* (1867) was based on more scientific study.

In 1871 he began a series of visits to Scandinavia, about which he wrote a popular travel book, *The Land of the Midnight Sun* (1881), and a detailed study of the Vikings, *The Viking Age* (1889). Du Chaillu went to Russia in 1901. He died in St. Petersburg (now Leningrad) on April 30, 1903.

HARRISON M. WRIGHT, *Swarthmore College*

DUCHAMP, dü-shäN′, **Marcel** (1887–1968), French-American painter whose controversial works stimulated major trends in 20th century art —futurism, Dadaism, surrealism, and pop art. His small body of work was produced mostly before 1925, when he abandoned art to pursue other interests, primarily chess.

Duchamp was born at Blainville, France, on July 28, 1887, the younger brother of the artists Raymond Duchamp-Villon and Jacques Villon. He began to paint around 1909. In 1911 he did *Nude Descending a Staircase, No. 1* (Philadelphia Museum of Art). Essentially a cubist painter at this time, Duchamp was already evolving a form of expressionism that emphasized action, mood, and personality. His most famous work, *Nude Descending a Staircase, No. 2* (1912; Philadelphia Museum of Art), outraged the public in 1913 when it was exhibited at the Armory Show (q.v.) in New York.

After 1912, Duchamp created a series of paintings of "sex-machines," satirical translations of sensuous or romantic themes into forms suggestive of modern biology or engineering. Among the major works of this kind are *The King and Queen Surrounded by Swift Nudes* (1912), *Bride* (1913), and *The Bride Stripped Bare by Her Bachelors, Even* (1915–1923; also known as *The Large Glass*), all in the Philadelphia Museum of Art.

By 1915, Duchamp had almost ceased painting, but his "ready-made" sculpture introduced two of the major innovations of modern sculpture —mobile work and the use of found objects. One of his first moving sculptures was *Bicycle Wheel*, mounted on a high wooden stool (1913, original lost; 3d version, 1951, Museum of Modern Art, New York). His "ready-made, aided," named *L. H. O. O. Q.* (1919; private collection, New York) is a photographic reproduction of the Mona Lisa, to which he added a moustache and a goatee. Duchamp became an American citizen in 1955. He died in Paris on Oct. 1, 1968.

H. H. ARNASON
The Solomon R. Guggenheim Foundation

Further Reading: *NOT SEEN and/or LESS SEEN of/by MARCEL DUCHAMP/RROSE SELAVY, 1904–64* (New York 1965); Lebel, Robert, *Marcel Duchamp* (New York 1959); Tomkins, Calvin, *The World of Marcel Duchamp* (New York 1966).

DUCHAMP-VILLON, dü-shäN′ vē-yôN′, **Raymond** (1876–1918), French sculptor, who was the most successful of the sculptors embracing cubist principles in the early 20th century. The brother of the painters Marcel Duchamp and Jacques Villon, Duchamp-Villon was born in Paris on Nov. 5, 1876. He left the study of medicine for sculpture about 1900. Rodin's influence was strong in his work until about 1905, when he began to draw on the more classical style of Maillol.

After 1910, twisted figures and a new angularity appeared in Duchamp-Villon's art. A key work in his career is the portrait bust *Baudelaire* (1911), in which a cubist emphasis on geometric forms and simplified planes is apparent. Many of his major works were produced just before World War I, including the relief *The Lovers* (1913) and a bronze statue, *The Horse* (1914). In the latter work, his most famous, he achieved a synthesis of cubist and futurist styles that is reminiscent of a similar blending of the two styles in Marcel Duchamp's *Nude Descending a Staircase*. Duchamp-Villon died at Cannes on Oct. 7, 1918.

WILLIAM GERDTS
University of Maryland

DUCHESNE, dü-shân′, **André** (1584–1640), French geographer and historian, who is often called the "father of French history" because of his work in collecting and analyzing historical documents. Born in L'Île-Bouchard, Touraine, in May 1584, he was a native of the same district as Richelieu, who made him royal historian and geographer. His 59 folio volumes of manuscript extracts now in the Bibliothèque Nationale, as well as his two dozen or so printed works, are more valuable for what they tell us about lost documents than for any intrinsic merit.

Some of Duchesne's projects, including *Historiae Francorum scriptores* (5 vols., 1636–1649) and *Histoire des cardinaux français* (2 vols., 1660–1666), were continued posthumously and published by his son François. André also published editions of Abelard, Alain Chartier, and Étienne Pasquier, as well as a translation of Juvenal's *Satires*. He died in a carriage accident near Paris on May 30, 1640.

LIONEL ROTHKRUG, *University of Michigan*

DUCHESNE, dü-shân′, **Louis Marie Olivier** (1843–1922), French Roman Catholic scholar and ecclesiastic. He was born in St.-Servan, France, on Sept. 13, 1843. Duchesne studied theology in Rome and Christian archaeology and the history of the early church as a student of G. B. de Rossi. After his ordination in 1867, he taught at the École St. Charles de St. Brieuc, studied at the École des Hautes Études in Paris, and went on a scholarly expedition to Mt. Athos and Asia Minor in 1874–1876.

In 1877, Duchesne accepted the chair of church history at the Institut Catholique de Paris, where he taught until 1885. When serious criticism was raised against his lectures because of his strictly scientific methods, he became maître de conférences in the École des Hautes Études (1885–1895). In 1895 he became the director of the French School of Archaeology in Rome, where he remained until his death on April 21, 1922. Among his many works are *Liber Pontificalis en Gaule au VIe siècle* (1882) and *Les origines du culte chrétien* (1889).

MARK VANDERHEYDEN, *Rider College, N. J.*

DUCHESS OF MALFI, mal′fē, a verse tragedy by the English playwright John Webster (q.v.), first acted in 1613 or 1614 and frequently revived. The play, derived from events involving Giovanna, duchess of Amalfi from 1490 to about 1513, tells how the widowed duchess, against the will of her brothers—a cardinal and a duke (Ferdinand)—secretly marries her steward Antonio. The marriage is revealed by Bosola, a servant of the duchess in Ferdinand's pay. The husband and wife flee, but she is captured, imprisoned, and strangled. The fourth act, in which she dies, is outstanding among 17th century presentations of suffering. Act V shows the madness and remorse of Ferdinand and the deaths of both brothers and of Bosola and Antonio.

Webster's poetry is eloquent and the motivations of his characters subtle, with an avoidance of plain statement. Ferdinand's incestuous attachment to his sister is hinted at but never made explicit; the duchess' love is ambivalently presented as genuine yet rash; and Bosola mingles cruelty and resentment with an unexpected display of remorse.

CLIFFORD LEECH
Author of "John Webster: A Critical Study"

A pair of mallards. The mallard is a river duck found in North America, Europe, and Asia.

DUCK

DUCK, any of a group of heavy-bodied, short-legged, web-footed swimming birds closely related to geese. Ducks nest in all major aquatic environments of the world except the Antarctic.

Wild ducks have long been favorite game birds. Because they are hunted for sport, food, and feathers, they have considerable economic as well as aesthetic value. To safeguard wild populations, various conservation measures have been widely adopted. These include the establishment of breeding and wintering refuges and limitations on hunting.

Ducks also have been domesticated for many centuries and are raised commercially for their meat and eggs. In the United States, ducks are raised mainly for their meat, but in some other countries, such as England, they are favored for their eggs. Duck meat is dark, rich in iron and the B vitamins, and fattier than chicken or turkey meat.

DESCRIPTION

Ducks range from 12 to 24 inches (30–60 cm) in length and from 1 to 16 pounds (0.5–7 kg) in weight. They have broad, shallow bodies, long necks, large heads, and flat, flexible bills that are edged on the sides either with lamella (plates) or serrations ("teeth"). Their legs are placed far to each side. When walking, ducks alternately place each foot inward toward the center of gravity, producing a waddling motion. They take off laboriously on relatively small, long, and narrow wings.

Ducks are covered with down and dense plumage that consists of many short, broad feathers. The feathers are waterproofed by oil secreted by the uropygial gland, a gland found at the base of the tail feathers. Unlike geese, ducks also often have a wing speculum, or brightly colored patch, that differs in color from the surrounding area. The males, known as *drakes,* are usually more colorful than the females.

Unlike geese, which molt annually, ducks molt twice a year. The females molt partially in the late winter and then molt completely in the summer after breeding. While the female is incubating the eggs, the male sheds his colorful plumage for dull plumage, known as eclipse plumage. After some time, he again molts and regains his more colorful feathers. Both sexes are flightless for several weeks during their complete molt.

KINDS OF DUCKS

Ducks belong to the family Anatidae of the order Anseriformes. The term "duck" is usually applied to members of the subfamily Anatinae and the names "goose" and "swan" to members of the Anserinae subfamily. However, some members of the Anserinae subfamily are referred to as "ducks" because they have evolved ducklike habits and body shape. These include the peculiar freckled duck (*Stictonetta naevosa*) of Australia and the whistling, or tree, ducks.

Whistling Ducks. Tree ducks, or whistling ducks, are primitive, small, swanlike birds. They are found in tropical and temperate regions throughout the world. The fulvous whistling duck (*Dendrocygna bicolor*) has one of the most unique distributions of any bird. It is found on every continent except Australia and surprisingly does not vary in color or size on the various continents. Some whistling ducks nest in tree holes, but most nest in marsh plants over water.

True Ducks. Ducks of the subfamily Anatinae, or true ducks, are divided into 7 tribes.

Tadornini. The tribe Tadornini includes the most primitive and gooselike tribe of ducks. It contains seven species of shelducks and eight of sheldgeese (which are really ducks). It is represented on all the continents except North America. The shelducks are relatively large and colorful ducks with an iridescent, colorful patch of feathers on the wing and contrasting patterns of black, white, and brown.

The best known shelduck is the common shelduck (*Tadorna tadorna*) of Eurasia, but other shelducks are found throughout the Old World. The sheldgeese are found mainly in South America. Steamer ducks are massive diving ducks usually classified in this tribe. There are 3 species: two are marine and flightless, while one can fly and occurs on deep inland lakes of Patagonia.

River Ducks. The best known and most typi-

Mandarin duck
GEORGE FORSS, FROM NATIONAL AUDUBON SOCIETY

ARTHUR AMBLER, FROM NATIONAL AUDUBON SOCIETY
Male European sheldrake

PAUL JOHNSGARD, FROM NATIONAL AUDUBON SOCIETY
Male ruddy duck

cal of the true ducks are the river ducks. They are often known as "dabbling ducks" because they feed from the surface of the water by dipping their bills and heads into the water for food. Though associated with water, they walk on land more easily than do most other ducks, and they usually nest on land. This group of 36 species is found throughout the world, and some species, such as the mallard (*Anas platyrhynchos*), are found in North America, Europe, and Asia.

Other river ducks include the teals, shovellers, widgeons, and pintails. The association of closely related species has apparently led to the evolution of diverse color patterns and complex courtship displays that serve to help the species identify one another, thus preventing hybridization. Young river, or dabbling, ducks feed mostly on insects and aquatic crustaceans for the first several weeks. After that they increase the amount of vegetation and seeds in their diets, and as adults their main foods are seeds and aquatic foliage.

Perching Ducks. Closely related to the dabbling ducks, perching ducks are primarily tropical and subtropical in distribution. They spend much of their time perching in forest trees near water. They are characterized by a patch of color on the wing, by metallic coloration, and often by brilliantly colored bills and plumage. They are diverse in form and include the dabblerlike, beautiful South American ringed teal (*Calonetta leucophrys*) and Brazilian duck (*Amazonetta brasiliensis*) of South America, the heavy-bodied Muscovy (*Cairina moschata*), the large, awkward-looking spur-winged goose (*Plectropterus gambensis*) of Africa, and the smallest of waterfowl—the cotton teal, or pygmy goose (*Nettapus coromandelianus*), found in India and Australia. The best-known perching ducks and the most beautiful of all ducks are two northern tree-nesting species: the Carolina, or North American, wood duck (*Aix sponsa*) and the mandarin duck (*A. galericulata*) of Asia.

Pochards. Inland diving ducks, known as pochards, are a diverse group found on all continents. They are freshwater ducks that favor shallow lakes and marshes rich in submerged plants as well as in vegetation above the water level. The canvasback (*Aythya vallisineria*) of North America is a well-known pochard that is a favorite with hunters of the prairie marshes of North America and is considered a delicacy.

Another group of pochards includes the scaup. Scaup are compact diving birds that usually have black heads and white backs. They are abundant and are represented by one or more species on all continents except South America.

Sea Ducks. Sea ducks are skilled divers that nest on freshwater lakes of the Northern Hemisphere but often winter along the seacoasts. The tribe is divided into several subgroups: eiders, scoters, goldeneyes, and mergansers. All are limited to the Northern Hemisphere, except for the rare Brazilian merganser (*Mergus octosetaceous*) and the now extinct Auckland Island merganser (*M. australis*). The mergansers, specialized for eating fish, have tubular bills with serrated edges that they use to hold their prey.

Stiff-Tailed Ducks. Stiff-tailed ducks comprise a distinctive tribe that includes most of the ruddy ducks of the genus *Oxyura*. Stiff-tailed ducks occur on every continent. They are stocky ducks with thick necks, large heads, heavy, often blue, bills, and legs set so far back that the ducks have difficulty walking. Their tails are usually long and stiff and carried nearly vertically. Stiff-tailed ducks are skillful divers, but they favor shallow, densely vegetated marshes as do pochards. All the stifftails have air sacs, and some produce sound by drumming their bills on an inflated neck or chest. All stifftails occasionally lay their eggs in the nests of other water birds.

There are several unique species that are generally considered atypical member of this tribe. The musk duck (*Biziura lobata*) of Australia is a massive diving duck. The male is at least twice

Male lesser scaup

RUSS KINNE, FROM PHOTO RESEARCHERS

Pekin duck

GRANT HEILMAN

Hooded merganser

ALLAN D. CRUICKSHANK, FROM NATIONAL AUDUBON SOCIETY

the size of the female and has a large leather lobe hanging from under his bill. The parasitic black-headed duck (*Heteronetta atricapilla*) of South America is another unusual duck classified with the stiff-tailed ducks, although it resembles a teal and feeds on seeds.

Torrent Duck. The torrent duck (*Merganetta armata*) is a species whose relation to other ducks is uncertain, and it is usually classified in a separate tribe. The torrent duck is unique in its adaptation to the torrential streams of the South American Andes. It dives and feeds on insect larvae, and even the young have amazing skill at swimming in very fast-moving water.

BEHAVIOR

Flight and Migration. Ducks are strong fliers. They have relatively small wings for their body weight and have a rapid wing beat. They regularly fly from 35 to 50 miles (55–80 km) per hour, but speeds of 60 to 70 miles (95–110 km) per hour have been recorded. Their altitude depends on the weather and the aim of the flight. Migrating ducks fly at altitudes of 500 to 8,000 feet (150–1,525 meters), but most ducks fly at 3,000 to 5,000 feet (900–1,525 meters).

Ducks are noted for their spectacular, long-range migrations. They migrate in response to severe climatic conditions, such as cold or drought. Migration is common in high latitudes, especially in the Northern Hemisphere, where the migrations are climate-controlled and usually involve movements during favorable following winds. The ducks remain in the north until pushed south in mass migrations that take a large percentage of the population 1,000 to 1,500 miles (1,600–8,000 km) southward within a few days. Migrations are erratic in the Southern Hemisphere desert marshes where water levels vary dramatically.

The routes traveled by migrating ducks have been observed and studied by the recovery of banded, or marked, birds. The routes tend to follow major topographic features, such as coastlines, rivers, and mountain ranges. The resulting broad flight lanes are called *flyways*. Four flyways—Atlantic, Mississippi, Central, and Pacific—occur in North America.

Although little work has been done on the methods of navigation used by ducks, it is believed that ducks use the position of the sun and stars as well as topography for orientation. Young ducks instinctively migrate in certain directions, whether or not adults are in the flock.

Feeding. Dabbling ducks feed from the surface of the water. They usually feed in shallow marshes and lakes on seeds, tubers, and other vegetative parts of plants, as well as on insects and other invertebrates. In very shallow water, they submerge only their bills and strain out small food organisms. As the depth of the water increases, they submerge their heads and finally turn upside down in an attempt to find food. Some dabbling ducks will also eat cultivated grains, causing considerable damage. They also feed on flooded crops such as rice.

Inland diving ducks (pochards) dive in depths of 3 to 20 feet (1–6 meters) of water to obtain bottom-dwelling invertebrates and the vegetative parts of submerged plants. Sea ducks pursue larger bottom-dwelling mollusks and some fish. Some sea ducks have been caught in fishermen's nets at depths of 150 to 180 feet (45–55 meters). Such deep-diving sea ducks may use their wings in diving, but most ducks do not.

Reproduction—Courtship. The reproductive cycle of ducks has been best studied among Northern Hemisphere ducks. Dabbling ducks pair in the early winter prior to migration, but sea ducks and inland diving ducks court later. All may still be actively courting during the migration or on breeding areas. The courtship displays of ducks are among the most spectacular in birds. Males of most species display in groups. Generally, but not in every case, the display takes place in the presence of a female. The male's display is often characterized by his conspicuous colors, by movements of his head, wings, or tail, and by feather erection. His calls are whistles and grunts. Females have limited vocalizations but avoid unwanted males by being aggressive or by flying away. Males pursuing an unmated female often gather in groups of 15 or more and form high-flying maneuvering courtship flights.

Pair bonds are constantly tested and probably exchanged until a firm seasonal pair is established. (Ducks, unlike geese, form pair bonds for only one season, and they rarely establish family units.) After the pairs are established, copulation takes place on water in isolated areas. Females of some species will accept as many mates as they can attract.

Nesting. Although island-nesting species, such as eiders, are highly social in their nesting, most pairs segregate on nesting areas. The males are aggressive and usually like to have a space between pairs.

Dabbling ducks and some sea and inland diving ducks nest on land, usually within several hundred feet of water. Inland diving ducks regularly nest in vegetation above the water, while most perching ducks and some sea ducks nest in tree holes. Females construct the nests from materials near at hand; they do not carry construction materials to the nest.

Although some ducks have weak maternal drives and desert their nests and young, only one duck—the black-headed duck (*Heteronetta atricapilla*) of temperate South America—is fully parasitic. It apparently never nests but lays its eggs in the nests of any marsh bird. The young stay there only until they are dry and then leave the nest and feed and care for themselves.

The Eggs. The first egg is laid during the first or second day of nest building, and most species lay at intervals of 1 to 1½ days until the clutch is complete. Clutch size varies from 4 to 12, but even more eggs may be found in a nest when several females lay in the same nest. The incubation period, timed from the laying of the last egg until its hatching, varies from 21 to 35 days. In all true ducks, the female alone incubates the eggs, but in whistling ducks, the males incubate the eggs. Female ducks leave the nest once or twice a day so that they may drink and feed.

Many animals prey on duck eggs in the nest. Ground-dwelling ducks commonly lose 60% to 85% of their clutches, while ducks that nest over water or in tree holes are more successful. Females commonly renest until a brood is produced.

Care of the Young. At hatching time, the females begin an incessant "kukking" call. When the young are dry, the female may encourage their departure from the nest by leaving the nest herself and then calling. Young ducks in tree holes will jump from any height to this call. The broods remain intact until the young can fly, that is, for about 5 to 9 weeks, depending on the species. Predation, storms, and straying accounts for losses of ⅓ to ½ of the ducks in a brood before they attain flight.

Following one or more nesting attempts, the female may be thin and ragged, and some can hardly fly. A differential sex ratio among adult ducks implies that female ducks suffer high mortality during the nesting period. Singly or in groups, they shed their flight feather and develop their winter plumage.

In the colder climates the males usually do not help care for the young but desert the female as soon as the clutch is complete. Many move hundreds of miles to lakes where they molt into their dull eclipse plumage and become flightless. In the tropics, the males more often remain with the females and brood.

DOMESTIC DUCKS

Ducks are raised commercially for meat and eggs. A few species, such as the silver-crested duck, are also raised as ornamental species. The domesticated breeds are derived from two wild species: the mallard of the Northern Hemisphere and the Muscovy of South America. Muscovies are used on a small scale, but they have limited egg production. Most commercial varieties are derived from mallard stock. The varieties may be three times the size of the wild birds and of many colors.

White varieties are preferred for meat production. The White Pekin is favored in North America, especially on Long Island where 60% of the ducks raised in the United States are produced. White Pekins reach a market weight of 7 pounds in 8 weeks. Most are marketed as ducklings at 7 to 8 weeks of age. Another variety, the White Aylesbury, is favored in England where it was developed, but it has low egg production.

Most commercial egg producers use the khaki-colored Campbell ducks, which have produced averages of 365 eggs per year (chickens rarely reach 300 eggs a year). Duck eggs are artificially incubated. Muscovies have an incubation period of 35 days, while mallards require only 28 days.

Domesticated ducks are fed diets rich in protein. They may also be given antibiotics, since diseases can cause heavy losses in large commercial operations. Botulism, caused by the bacterium *Clostridium botulinum*, and fowl cholera, caused by *Pasturella* bacteria, are diseases that may result when sanitation is poor. Virus hepatitis is another serious disease of ducks, but vaccine that reduces mortality is now available.

MILTON W. WELLER, *Iowa State University*

DUCK, fabric. See CANVAS.

DUCKBILL, also called *duck-billed platypus.* See PLATYPUS.

DUCKING STOOL, an instrument of punishment used from the 15th to the 18th century for minor offenders, particularly quarrelsome women. The ducking stool consisted of a seat attached to a pole and mounted on a support in such a way that a person strapped to the seat could be lowered into water. The punishment was a public spectacle, and the offender was ducked many times. A similar device, called a cucking stool, was used to punish scolds and dishonest tradesmen. In this instance the culprit was tied to a chair and exposed to public ridicule.

These methods of punishment were widespread in England and Germany and were brought to New England in the 17th century by the colonists. They were not practiced in most of the Latin countries. The rationale for them was similar to that for the pillory and stocks. The emphasis was on public shaming rather than on physical pain or harm to the offender. It was expected that shaming would prevent the recurrence of the offense and warn others.

ERIKA BOURGUIGNON, *The Ohio State University*

Lesser duckweed (Lemna minor)
HUGH SPENCER, FROM NATIONAL AUDUBON SOCIETY

DUCKWEED is a family of small aquatic flowering plants with no distinct stems or leaf structures. The plant body (thallus) consists of one or more green flattened or rounded fronds that float on the surface of the water and serve as leaves. Of the four genera in the family (Lemnaceae), *Wolffia* and *Wolffiella* lack roots; *Lemna*, the duckweed proper, has one root protruding from the bottom of each plant, and *Spirodella* has two or more roots.

Duckweeds range in size from 2/100 to 4/10 inch (0.5–10 mm) and include the smallest known flowering plant, *Wolffia arrhiza*. Though other species also occasionally reproduce by means of tiny flowers produced on the frond, most reproduction is by budding, or forming new plants, on the margins or at the bases of the fronds.

Duckweeds are widespread through the temperate and tropical regions of the world. They often occur as a floating green covering on small lakes, ponds, or ditches, and they serve as food for waterfowl, especially mallard ducks. In temperate climates, duckweeds survive the winter as buds that sink beneath the pond bottom.

CHARLES W. REIMER
The Academy of Natural Sciences, Philadelphia

DUCKWORTH, Sir John Thomas (1748–1817), British admiral. During his 52 years of service he was court-martialed three times and won a gold medal. Duckworth was born at Leatherhead, Surrey, on Feb. 28, 1748. He saw active service at the Battle of Quiberon Bay (Nov. 20, 1759) when he was 11. Held responsible for the accidental death of five men in a transport off Rhode Island on Jan. 18, 1777, he was court-martialed but acquitted. A retrial was ordered, but again Duckworth was found not guilty.

Specially commended in command of H. M. S. *Orion* at Lord Howe's victory over the French off Ushant on June 1, 1794, Duckworth received one of the commemorative gold medals struck to mark the occasion. On April 5, 1800, off Cádiz, the capture of a Spanish convoy brought him an estimated £75,000 in prize money.

On Feb. 6, 1806, Duckworth's victory over a superior French fleet off Santo Domingo earned him a pension of £1,000 a year and the freedom of the city of London. In 1807, ordered to dictate terms to Turkey, he forced the Dardanelles, but through lack of wind he had to withdraw.

Duckworth was created a baronet on Nov. 2, 1813. He died while commander in chief at Plymouth on Aug. 31, 1817.

B. B. SCHOFIELD, *Vice Admiral, Royal Navy Author of "British Sea-Power"*

DUCLOS, Jacques (1896–1975), French Communist leader. He was born at Louey, France, on Oct. 2, 1896. A member of the French Communist party from the time of its formation in 1920, he rose to the top ranks of the party, serving as a member of the central committee and as secretary of the political bureau. Elected to the Chamber of Deputies from Paris, he served as a deputy from 1926 to 1939 and as vice president of the chamber from 1936 to 1939.

When the Communist party refused to support France's war with Germany in 1939, Duclos went into hiding to escape arrest. Subsequently, under the German occupation, he helped direct the party's underground apparatus. After the war he served again in parliament from 1945 to 1958, and was elected senator in 1959 and 1968.

From 1950 to 1953, Duclos served as acting secretary general of the Communist party and led it in its militant anti-American phase. In 1969 he became a candidate for the presidency, opposing Georges Pompidou. He wrote *À l'assaut du ciel* (1961) and *Avenir de la démocratie* (1962). He died in Paris on April 25, 1975.

JOEL COLTON, *Duke University*

DUCOMMUN, Élie (1833–1906), Swiss journalist and pacifist, who shared the Nobel Peace Prize in 1902 with Charles Albert Gobat. Ducommun was born in Geneva, Switzerland, on Feb. 19, 1833. After serving as editor in chief of the newspaper *Revue de Genève*, he moved to Bern, where he edited *Der Fortschritt*. Widely known for his liberal ideas and for his activities on behalf of peace—he took part in the first of a series of peace conferences in 1889—he was commissioned by the Congress of Rome in 1891 to organize the International Bureau of Peace at Bern, and he became honorary secretary of the permanent bureau. He won the Nobel Prize for his work in creating this organization. Ducommun died in Bern on Dec. 7, 1906.

Among Ducommun's books on peace are *L'oeuvre de la paix* (1893), *La programme pratique des amis de la paix* (1897), and *Précis historique du mouvement en faveur de la paix* (1899).

DUCOS DU HAURON, Louis Arthur (1837–1920), French physicist, who pioneered in color photography. He was born in Langon, Gironde, France. In his *Couleurs en Photographie* (1869) he described methods of three-color photography. He pointed out that the three colors used in printing the pictures must be complementary to the red, green, and blue filters used in making the negatives. This is the basis of all subtractive three-color photography.

Ducos du Hauron later described a three-color camera with mirrors for making the three negatives with one exposure; a viewing instrument that superimposed red, green, and blue transparencies to produce a color image; and a screenplate process of color photography that was perfected in 1907 by Auguste and Louis Jean Lumière. In 1897 he patented the making of red, green, and blue negatives with three separately sensitized emulsions coated over each other. Several modern films developed from this process.

Ducos du Hauron was ahead of his time and was unable to perfect any of his processes. He died in Agen, France, in 1920.

C. B. NEBLETTE, *Author of "Photography: Its Materials and Processes"*

DUCTILITY is the ability of a material to withstand deformation without fracturing. Children's modeling clay, plasticine, is an example of a highly ductile material. The term "ductility" is most often used, however, in reference to the ability of a metal to withstand plastic working without fracture.

The ductility of a material may be measured by the percentage of plastic elongation or reduction in a cross-sectional area of a rod or wire when it is subjected to a tensile load until it fractures. The greater the elongation or the greater the reduction in area at the point of fracture, the greater the ductility of the material. For example, if a rod of a ductile material, such as putty, is pulled at both ends, the putty will flow, producing a piece that is longer than the original, but also smaller in diameter. The percentage of length increase is called *elongation*, and the percentage of decrease in diameter at the fracture point is referred to as *reduction in area*. When the application of a tensile force to a plastic rod causes fracture, it is usually termed "ductile fracture."

Plastic deformation of a metal crystal occurs through the movement and interaction of dislocations, which slip by block movement along certain crystallographic planes that are called *slip planes* and, in certain characteristic directions, *slip directions*. (See Dislocation.) Generally, the slip process is very complex, and the behavior of the material is not always predictable. For example, a metal may be brittle under tension but ductile under hydrostatic compression; or a material may be ductile if a load is applied slowly but brittle if the load is applied suddenly, as on impact.

Douglas V. Keller, Jr., *Syracuse University*

DUCTLESS GLANDS. See Endocrine Glands.

DU DEFFAND, dü de-fän', **Marquise** (1697–1780), French intellectual, who is noted for her salon and for her correspondence with Voltaire, Horace Walpole, d'Alembert, the Duchess de Choiseul, Hénault, and other notables.

Marie Anne de Vichy-Chamrond was born of a noble family at the Château de Chamrond, in Burgundy, on Dec. 25, 1697. A precocious rationalist, she even preached irreligion to her companions in the fashionable convent where she was educated. Soon after her marriage to the Marquis du Deffand in 1719, she left him and led a brilliant and uninhibited life typical of the Regency period. Highly intelligent and witty, but with a very pessimistic outlook on life, Mme. du Deffand made her Paris salon the meeting place for well-known figures in the social and intellectual world, but her circle never became a literary clique.

When she became blind in 1753, Mme. du Deffand employed as her companion Mlle. de Lespinasse, but in 1754, after a spectacular quarrel, Mlle. du Lespinasse set up a rival salon. When Mme. du Deffand was nearly 70, she experienced the first passion of her life, for Horace Walpole, 20 years her junior. Their peculiar, bittersweet relationship lasted until her death, in Paris, on Sept. 24, 1780. She left Walpole all her papers, which have been published in various editions.

Edwin Jahiel, *University of Illinois*

DUDEVANT, Baroness. See Sand, George.

DUDLEY, Sir Edmund (1462?–1510), English political leader, who discovered and tapped the sources of private wealth in England for the benefit of the Tudor monarchy. Dudley attended Oxford and studied law at Gray's Inn. In 1504 he became speaker of the House of Commons, King Henry VII's chosen spokesman in that chamber. Thereafter, Dudley and Sir Richard Empson worked with Henry to reduce the power of unruly barons and enrich the royal treasury.

The two men acted as a special subcommittee of the Privy Council, entering into recognizances with the barons to keep the peace. The result was greater law and order as well as greatly increased revenues for Dudley and the King. The two councillors also acted as a court, summoning men to appear before them and levying fines. It is believed that they had special authority in 1508–1509 to enforce criminal laws.

By the end of Henry VII's reign (1509), Dudley was rich and despised by the baronial class. When Henry died, Dudley called his friends to arms, ostensibly to protect the new King, Henry VIII. But Dudley's enemies charged him with wanting to harm the King. One of Henry's first acts was to arrest and try Dudley and Empson. Both were convicted, attainted by Parliament, and beheaded on Tower Hill, on Aug. 18, 1510. The outcome did not, however, put an end to their methods or goals, which subsequently were regarded as definitively Tudor.

While in the Tower, Dudley wrote *The Tree of Commonwealth*, an allegory that defended absolute monarchy and contained the germs of an anticlerical theory of government.

Stuart E. Prall, *Queens College, New York*

DUDLEY, Joseph (1647–1720), American colonial governor. He was born in Roxbury, Mass., the son of Thomas Dudley (q.v.). A member of the Massachusetts General Court (1673–1684), he served as temporary governor of the colony in 1685–1686 and then became chief justice of the superior court under Gov. Edmund Andros. Dudley was jailed by the colonists in their uprising against Andros in 1689 but was released on royal order and appointed chief justice of New York. In England from 1693 to 1702, he served in Parliament and was governor of the Isle of Wight. As governor of Massachusetts (1702–1715), he led his administration in a struggle with the General Court over the royal prerogative, which he stoutly defended. Dudley died in Roxbury on April 2, 1720.

George D. Langdon, Jr., *Vassar College*

DUDLEY, Thomas (1576–1653), American colonial governor. Born in Northhampton, England, the son of an army captain who was killed in action, he was brought up in the household of the Earl of Northampton. He served in the army in France and as steward to the Earl of Lincoln.

Influenced by Puritan teachings, Dudley became a leader in the Massachusetts Bay Company and sailed on the *Arabella* for New England in 1630. He held numerous high offices in Massachusetts and was elected governor four times between 1634 and 1650. A founder of Harvard College, Dudley as governor signed the college charter in 1650. Vigorous in enforcing Puritan law, he was more unyielding than John Winthrop, with whom he often disagreed. He died in Roxbury, Mass., on July 31, 1653.

George D. Langdon, Jr., *Vassar College*

DUE PROCESS OF LAW is a central concept of Anglo-American constitutional history. It is generally traced to the Latin phrase *per legem terrae* (by the law of the land) in the Magna Carta (q.v.) of 1215. In chapter 39 of that document King John promised: "No free man shall be arrested, or imprisoned, or disseized, or outlawed, or exiled, or in any way molested; nor will we proceed against him, unless by the lawful judgment of his peers or by the law of the land." Magna Carta was periodically confirmed by succeeding sovereigns, and in a statute of 1354, reign of Edward III, the phrase "due process of law" first appears: "That no man of what estate or condition that he be, shall be put out of land or tenement, nor taken, nor imprisoned, nor disinherited, nor put to death, without being brought in answer by due process of law."

While none of these documents specified what was meant by law of the land, or due process, some indication is supplied by the Petition of Right of 1628, which prayed that "freemen be imprisoned or detained only by the law of the land, or by due process of law, and not by the King's special command without any charge." It was the English understanding of due process that Daniel Webster undertook to summarize in 1819 in his argument in the Dartmouth College case (q.v.), where he spoke of due process as "the general law; a law, which hears before it condemns; which proceeds upon inquiry, and renders judgment only after trial," so that "every citizen shall hold his life, liberty, property, and immunities, under the protection of the general rules which govern society."

The Fifth Amendment. Due process of law was written into the U. S. Constitution when the Bill of Rights (q.v.) was adopted in 1791. The 5th Amendment, among other guarantees, provided that no person should be "deprived of life, liberty, or property, without due process of law." The U. S. Supreme Court held in *Barron* v. *Baltimore* (1833) that this clause was a limitation only on the federal government, not the states.

In practice, the due process requirement of the 5th Amendment has had comparatively little importance. In federal criminal trials it is pushed into the background by the other, more specific guarantees of the Bill of Rights, such as the 4th Amendment protection against unreasonable searches and seizures, the 5th Amendment guarantee against self-incrimination, and the 6th Amendment right to the assistance of counsel. As a protection for property rights, due process is partially overshadowed by another 5th Amendment provision—namely, that private property shall not be taken for public use without just compensation. Nevertheless, due process has been useful in imposing general standards of fairness on government administrative proceedings, requiring notice, fair hearing, and opportunity for judicial review where personal or property rights are affected by administative action. Due process also applies to military justice, though here again it is a general obligation, backstopping the more specific provisions of the Bill of Rights and the Uniform Code of Military Justice. See COURT-MARTIAL.

The 14th Amendment. It was not until the due process obligation was extended to the states by the 14th Amendment that its potentialities were realized. Actually, the drafters of the amendment had no great expectations for the due process clause, because it had been of little consequence in the 5th Amendment. Their attention was concentrated rather on the preceding clause, which forbids the abridgement of the privileges and immunities of citizens of the United States. As it turned out, however, in the very first ruling by the Supreme Court on the 14th Amendment, the Slaughterhouse cases (q.v.) (1873), the privileges and immunities clause was interpreted so narrowly as to render it practically meaningless. On the other hand, the 14th Amendment due process clause has come to be the source of more constitutional law than any other language in the Constitution.

Substantive Due Process. The initial expectation that the due process clause would provide procedural protection for the liberty and property rights of the newly freed slaves was almost completely confounded. Instead, due process achieved very quickly a remarkable success in an entirely different role, the protection of the property rights of businesses and corporations against regulation by state legislatures.

To be sure, the Supreme Court did for a time, as in the Slaughterhouse cases and *Munn* v. *Illinois* (1877), reject efforts to project it into judging the merits of regulatory legislation. In the Munn case, the court refused to interfere with legislative fixing of the rates charged by grain elevators, with Chief Justice Morrison R. Waite remarking that for the correction of legislative abuses "the people must resort to the polls, not to the courts." But 10 years later, while upholding a state prohibition act in *Mugler* v. *Kansas* (1887), the court asserted that there were limits on state exercise of the police power, and that the due process clause required the court to "look at the substance of things, whenever they enter upon an inquiry whether the legislature has transcended the limits of its authority." Thus substantive due process was born, though it was not until *Allgeyer* v. *Louisiana* (1897) that the court actually set aside a state law on this ground.

During the half century from 1887 to 1937, substantive due process was the Supreme Court's most distinctive contribution to American constitutional law. The liberty protected by the due process clause was interpreted to include freedom of contract, and laissez-faire became a constitutional dogma by which the Supreme Court presumed to judge the wisdom of dozens of state regulatory statutes. In *Lochner* v. *New York* (1905) it invalidated a 10-hour law for bakers. In *Adkins* v. *Children's Hospital* (1923) it held minimum wages for women unconstitutional. In *Burns Baking Co.* v. *Bryan* (1924) it struck down a law regulating weight of loaves of bread.

It was this assumption of judicial veto power over state legislation that was one of the principal factors in public rejection of the court under the New Deal. The first judicial signal of reversal of doctrine came in *Nebbia* v. *New York* (1934), when the court upheld the price-fixing of milk. Approval of both state and federal minimum wage statutes followed in 1937 and 1941. In fact, the court so completely abandoned substantive due process in the late 1940's and the 1950's that it withdrew entirely from reviewing state economic legislation, even on the broad grounds of reasonableness. Thus the court came full circle back to the Munn position that the appeal against legislative errors in the field of economic regulation is to the polls, not the courts.

Due Process and State Judicial Proceedings. Surprisingly, the Supreme Court proved much more reluctant to assume responsibility for assuring procedural due process in state court actions, with which it was charged by the 14th Amendment, than it had been to undertake substantive due process review of state regulatory legislation, where its authority was much more dubious.

The court's initial assumption was that the 14th Amendment gave it only the right to enforce the basic and traditional requirements of jurisdiction, notice, and hearing in state judicial proceedings. For three quarters of a century the court firmly rejected the contention that the specific protections of the 4th through the 8th amendments, applicable to trial procedures in federal courts, had been made binding on state courts by the 14th Amendment. In a series of noteworthy decisions—*Hurtado* v. *California* (1884), *Maxwell* v. *Dow* (1900), *Twining* v. *New Jersey* (1908)—the court held that the states were not obliged to enforce the grand jury indictment, jury trial, or self-incrimination requirements of the Bill of Rights. The court's view was that it would not be wise to bind the states to any fixed set of procedures in criminal cases; they should be free to adapt their legal institutions to new situations.

In the Maxwell case, Justice John M. Harlan, dissenting, bitterly contrasted the court's differing practice with respect to substantive and procedural due process and charged that for the court "the protection of private property is of more consequence than the protection of the life and liberty of the citizen." He contended that the drafters of the due process clause had intended to "incorporate" and impose on the states the same restrictions that the 4th through the 8th amendments imposed on the federal courts. But his colleagues rejected this argument and asserted that the test of state procedures was whether they were in accord with the fundamental principles of liberty and justice that inhere in the very idea of free government. Justice Benjamin N. Cardozo gave the "ordered liberty" view its classic formulation in *Palko* v. *Connecticut* (1937).

The "incorporationists," however, did not give up. In *Adamson* v. *California* (1947), led by Justice Hugo L. Black, they lacked only one vote to overturn the "ordered liberty" standard. A significant breakthrough came in *Wolf* v. *Colorado* (1949), where the Court unanimously agreed that the states were forbidden by the 14th Amendment to conduct unreasonable searches and seizures. However, a majority of the court declined to apply to the states the "exclusionary rule" utilized in federal courts to enforce the 4th Amendment, a rule that provides that evidence secured illegally is inadmissible in court.

During the 1950's the court found it increasingly difficult to rationalize this dual system of constitutional standards for criminal justice under which state courts would admit illegally secured evidence, fail to provide counsel for defendants unable to hire them, or compel self-incrimination. Finally, in *Mapp* v. *Ohio* (1961), the court capitulated, overruled the Wolf decision, and held evidence secured by illegal searches and seizures inadmissible. In prompt succession most of the other provisions of the 4th through the 8th amendments were also brought into effect in the states. The most noteworthy rulings in this series were *Gideon* v. *Wainwright* (1963), which required state courts to provide counsel for defendants in criminal cases, and *Duncan* v. *Louisiana* (1968), which overruled *Maxwell* v. *Dow* and held that the 6th Amendment required the availability of jury trial in the states except for petty crimes.

The due process clause has also been the foundation for the Supreme Court's concern with police investigative methods in the pretrial period. In *Escobedo* v. *Illinois* (1964) the court held that a suspect taken into police custody for questioning about a crime must be given an opportunity to consult a lawyer. Two years later, *Miranda* v. *Arizona* (1966) held that incommunicado police detention is inherently coercive and that confessions obtained without informing the suspects of their right to remain silent and to see counsel cannot be used in court.

The First Amendment. Though the Supreme Court quickly read into the due process clause a protection for liberty of contracts that is nowhere mentioned in the Constitution, it did not discover until 1925 that the 1st Amendment protections of free speech and press were embodied in the "liberty" guaranteed by the 14th Amendment and so protected against state infringement. As late as 1922, the court had held that the Constitution did not impose on the states any duty to recognize the right of free speech. But in *Gitlow* v. *New York* (1925) the court abruptly announced: "We may and do assume that freedom of speech and of the press ... are among the fundamental rights and 'liberties' protected by the due process clause of the 14th Amendment from impairment by the States."

In 1940 the court, in *Cantwell* v. *Connecticut*, for the first time brought the freedom of religion guarantee of the 1st Amendment into effect upon the states. Justice Owen J. Roberts explained that the fundamental concept of "liberty" embodied in the 14th Amendment embraces all the liberties guaranteed by the 1st Amendment. Logically, the court in *Everson* v. *Board of Education* (1947) made the establishment of religion provision applicable to the states.

Conclusion. It is thus the due process clause that has given the Supreme Court its major responsibility for enforcing the basic freedoms of the American democratic system. Particularly since the 1940's the court, in some of its most significant decisions, has repeatedly construed state restrictions affecting the liberty to speak, to print, to assemble, to organize, to demonstrate, to worship. It is the due process clause that has given the court many of its most difficult problems in reconciling the competing claims of freedom and order.

In short, the due process clause has had a curious history. It has had two major uses, neither of which may have been foreseen by its framers. First, it was given a novel substantive interpretation that authorized the Supreme Court to act like a superlegislature in reviewing state economic regulation. When the New Deal brought this phase to an end, due process reappeared in an even greater role as the powerful instrument by which the libertarian language of the Bill of Rights was made effective throughout the nation.

C. HERMAN PRITCHETT
Author of "The American Constitution"

Further Reading: Griswold, Erwin N., *The Fifth Amendment Today* (Cambridge, Mass., 1955); Pritchett, C. Herman, *The American Constitution* (New York 1968).

AARON BURR fires a fatal shot at Alexander Hamilton in an old print of the duel fought on July 11, 1804, at Weehawken, N. J. Hamilton's friends claimed that he did not fire at Burr, but shot aimlessly into the air.

DUEL, a form of combat between two persons usually armed with lethal weapons and fought in the presence of witnesses according to a certain ceremony and a strict code of law or honor.

Dueling was unknown in the ancient world, and its origins can be traced back no further than 501 A.D., when Gundobad, king of the Burgundians, legally established the trial by combat, or judicial duel. This was to provide an alternative form of justice, or "Judgement of God," to the ordeal or the oath. Many defendants, to avoid trial by ordeal, had chosen to take an oath, and had then committed perjury.

Gundobad decided that they "might as well risk their bodies as their souls." Accordingly he prescribed that "whenever two Burgundians are at variance, if the plaintiff shall declare that he is ready to maintain, sword in hand, the truth of what he advances, and the defendant does not then acquiesce, it shall be lawful for them to decide the controversy by dint of sword." Gundobad's example was followed all over western Europe, and "Trial by Battel" became an accepted part of the medieval theory of justice.

In theory these judicial duels had to be fought in person, but women, invalids, and old men were exempted, and gradually a whole class of proxy fighters known as "champions" came into existence. During a proxy duel the principals were kept out of sight with ropes around their necks. At the end of the combat the defeated champion had his hand chopped off, and the principal worsted by proxy was hanged.

Judicial Duels. The first recorded trial by combat after Gundobad's pronouncement took place in 590. Eventually the frequency of judicial duels led to the publication of various edicts intended to regulate them. The most famous edict was the Truce of God (1041), prohibiting duels from Wednesday to Monday, these days having been consecrated by Christ's Passion. Trial by combat, although very common in Europe, was unknown in England before the Norman Conquest (1066), after which it soon became common practice in both civil and criminal actions. The first notable case in England was the duel at Salisbury in 1096 between William Count d'Eu and Godefroy Baynard, who had accused the count of conspiring against William II of England. Worsted in the fight, the count was promptly emasculated and his eyes put out.

In England, trial by combat remained the only honorable means of deciding a matter of right until the reign of Henry II, who instituted the alternative of trial by jury. Even then, judicial duels continued to be fought occasionally, and the right to choose trial by combat lingered on as part of English law until the early 19th century. In 1817 a certain Abraham Thornton, charged with murder, claimed the right to "wage his battle." As no one could be found to fight for the victim, Thornton was acquitted. Soon afterward, on March 22, 1819, Parliament abolished the right to appeal to the "Judgement of God," and with it the judicial duel.

Chivalric Duels. Springing from the judicial duel, and existing concurrently with it for several centuries, was the so-called duel of chivalry. In chivalric duels two knights, generally on horseback and always with much ceremonial, engaged in single combat to settle differences of law, possession, or honor. The first chivalric encounter may have been the combat in 858, near Strasbourg, between the Carolingian emperor Charles the Bald and his brother Louis II of Germany. Certainly by the 12th century, knighthood was generally established in France, Spain, and England, along with the duel of chivalry.

The Roman Catholic Church, largely because jurisprudence of the sword interfered with that of the altar, condemned the duel of chivalry at the councils of Valence, Limoges, and Trent. Several popes excommunicated all sovereigns who allowed dueling to take place in their realms. But the church's authority was constantly flouted. King Edward III of England even challenged French King Philip to a duel in 1340. Gradually, however, the duel of chivalry disappeared, as mounted knights were made militarily obsolete by unmounted archers. The last mounted encounter held in England was probably in 1492, when Sir James Parker and Sir Hugh Vaughan met in mortal combat at a tournament in Richmond. Henceforth duels were fought with less pomp and ceremony, between gentlemen rather than between knights, and as private encounters rather than public battles.

Dueling Codes. The development of the "duel

of honor"—a fair fight in private between two combatants armed with equal weapons—was a considerable step in the direction of humanity and law, superseding the murderous assaults that had become everyday occurrences in 15th century Europe. But if the duel was to become an established institution, the rules governing it had to be universally understood and strictly enforced. Hence the multiplicity of treatises, attempting to regulate every circumstance of the duel, that were published from the 16th to the 19th centuries. Offenses were classified, from the slap or slur to the most heinous of all insults—"giving the lie" (accusing another man of lying). Instructions were given the would-be duelist on the sending of a challenge or "cartel," the selection of seconds, and the choice of weapons. The first dueling codes were formulated in the 16th century by Andrea Alciati and other Italian theoreticians. The greatest fencing masters also were found in Italy at that time.

The choice of weapons in continental Europe lay with the offended party or challenger, but in English-speaking countries it was with the offender or challenged party. Occasionally, unusual weapons were proposed. The 18th century Italian charlatan Cagliostro challenged a physician to a duel with two pills, one lethal, the other harmless. Billiard balls were the weapons used in a fatal duel fought in France in 1843. But swords and pistols were the usual arms chosen. The sword was the customary weapon from the 16th to the 18th century, and the pistol in the 18th and 19th centuries.

Continental Europe. The vogue for dueling spread to France as a result of the Italian campaigns of Charles VIII and Louis XII in the late 15th and early 16th centuries, and the practice soon became widespread. Francis I did nothing to discourage the fashion. On the countrary, he himself issued a bombastic challenge to Charles V. Francis' successor, Henry II, whose reign was ushered in by the famous duel between the Lord of Jarnac and François de La Chastaigneraye, was too weak to impose any check on dueling. Henry IV issued several edicts against dueling, but these were not enforced. It has been calculated that during Henry's reign (1589–1610) no fewer than 4,000 men were killed in affairs of honor. By the middle of the 17th century, dueling had become such an essential part of the life of the French nobility that even Louis XIV was unable to stamp it out. A court of honor that he set up to decide disputes peacefully soon lost its novelty. Louis' celebrated *Édit des duels* (1679), prescribing capital punishment for all duelists and their seconds, remained a dead letter.

During the 18th century, dueling continued to flourish in France. It was a period of famous swordsmen—like the Duc de Richelieu and Saint-Évremont, who gave his name to a thrust he devised, and the mysterious Chevalier d'Éon. With the French Revolution, dueling, as a relic of the *ancien régime*, fell into disfavor, but it revived under the Directory and the Empire. The 19th century witnessed a spate of political duels as well as countless affairs of honor, but after World War I dueling in France declined sharply. It is now almost nonexistent.

From France, the dueling cult spread eastward to Russia, where it was practiced enthusiastically until the Russian Revolution. Two of the country's greatest writers, Pushkin and Lermontov, lost their lives in affairs of honor.

Germany, too, followed the French lead, although most of the duels there were between university students, especially members of the exclusive Korps, or student societies. During the 19th century, however, the duel in Germany gave place to the *Mensur,* a form of duel in which thrusting with the sword was forbidden and protective clothing was devised to prevent any injury beyond "decorative" facial cuts.

Britain and the United States. In England dueling was little known before the 17th century and never became as prevalent as in France. No English king felt compelled to condemn the practice until 1613, when James I issued his *Proclamation Against Private Challenges and Combats*. But dueling continued to flourish until the Civil War in England, when there was a sharp decline. It recovered all its prestige with the Restoration. One of the most famous and terrible duels of all time was fought in 1712 in Hyde Park, London, where the Duke of Hamilton and Lord Mohun hacked each other to death.

In the early 19th century great excitement was caused by two highly publicized encounters —between George Canning, the foreign secretary, and Viscount Castlereagh, the secretary for war, in 1809, and between the Duke of Wellington and the Earl of Winchester in 1829. After a series of fatal duels, an Anti-Dueling Association was founded in 1843. The following year, with encouragement from Queen Victoria, the war office made dueling between army officers a punishable offense. This action, combined with public pressure and the obvious determination of judges and juries to convict duelists of murder, succeeded in suppressing dueling in Britain by the middle of the 19th century.

Dueling, a European practice, never really found favor across the Atlantic. In 1832, de Tocqueville reported that "in America one only fights to kill." Public opinion in America was generally opposed to dueling, but whereas European governments were perpetually legislating against the practice, few states in America instituted measures to restrain it. The most famous of all American duels was undoubtedly the encounter in 1804 between two famous political leaders, Alexander Hamilton and Aaron Burr, in which Hamilton was fatally wounded. Almost as famous was the pistol duel in 1806 in which Gen. Andrew Jackson killed Charles Dickinson after being wounded himself in the chest. A duel with knives, fought in 1827 near Natchez, Miss., between Major Wright and James Bowie, made famous that classic American weapon, the bowie knife.

During the 1830's and 1840's the South witnessed most of the duels fought in the United States, but with the discovery of gold in the Sacramento Valley in 1848 dueling moved westward. Even in California, however, it incurred public hostility, and by the end of the century it had virtually disappeared from the United States.

Today, with the exception of a few undercover duels fought by students in German Korps, some lighthearted affairs at England's ancient universities, and occasional encounters in France conducted with the minimum of risk and the maximum of publicity, the duel is dead. It was killed, not so much by legislation as by press ridicule, public disapproval, and a more humane attitude to the conduct of social relations.

ROBERT BALDICK, *Oxford University*
Author of "The Duel"

DUERO RIVER. See DOURO RIVER.

DU FAY, dü fä´, **Charles François de Cisternay** (1698–1739), French scientist, remembered chiefly for his contributions to the theory of electricity. Du Fay was born in Paris on Sept. 14, 1698. At the time he began experimenting with electricity, it was known that non-electrified objects were attracted by substances such as glass and amber that had been electrified by rubbing, but it was thought that electrified objects repelled each other. Du Fay discovered in 1733 that electrified glass was attracted by electrified amber, and he concluded that there were two electricities—vitreous (from glass and similar substances) and resinous (from amber and similar substances)—each of which attracted the other but was self-repelling. From this theory Benjamin Franklin later developed the concepts of positive and negative electricity.

Du Fay also investigated the efficiency of the French dyeing industry. His theory that particles of dyestuff lodged in pores of a fabric was later disproved, but he introduced methods of lasting value for testing dyes by boiling dyed fabrics with chemicals. He died in Paris on July 16, 1739.

W. A. SMEATON, *University College, London*

DUFAY, dü-fä´, **Guillaume** (c. 1400–1474), Flemish composer of church and secular music, who is considered the most important composer of the mid-15th century in western Europe. Probably born in Hainaut (now in Belgium), he was educated at Cambrai, France, and became a priest. From 1428 to 1437 he sang in the papal choir at Rome. Returning to France, he obtained a degree at the Sorbonne about 1442 and then instructed the son of the Duke of Burgundy in music. He went back to Cambrai in 1445 and held the post of canon there and at Mons. Dufay died at Cambrai on Nov. 27, 1474.

An innovator and a master of the art of counterpoint, Dufay attempted to break away from the extravagant musical style of the period that preceded him. He contributed significantly to the development of the polyphonic mass and also composed motets, magnificats, and 3-part chansons, for which he is particularly famous.

DUFEK, dōō´fek, **George John** (1903–1977), American naval officer and polar explorer, who was the first American to set foot on the South Pole (in 1956). He was born in Rockford, Ill., on Feb. 10. 1903. Dufek graduated from the U. S. Naval Academy in 1925 and remained in the Navy until he retired in 1959. During World War II he was an aviator before taking command of the escort carrier *Bogue*. In the Korean War he commanded the aircraft carrier *Antietam*.

Dufek made four trips to Antarctica, the first as a navigator under Adm. Richard E. Byrd in 1939. He led a group of ships in Byrd's 1946–1947 expedition (Operation Highjump). In 1948, Dufek visited weather stations in the Arctic. Promoted to rear admiral, he commanded Task Force 43 in Operation Deepfreeze (1955–1959) and constructed seven Antarctic air and logistic bases in support of the International Geophysical Year (1957–1958). On Oct. 31, 1956, he flew to the South Pole with a crew of six in a Navy plane and planted the American flag there. Dufek wrote *Operation Deepfreeze* (1957) and *Through the Frozen Frontier* (1959). He died in Bethesda, Md., on Feb. 10, 1977.

DUFF, Alexander (1806–1878), Scottish Presbyterian missionary. He was born at Auchnahyle, Perthshire, Scotland, on April 26, 1806, and was educated at St. Andrews University. He was ordained in 1829 and was the first missionary sent to India from the General Assembly of the Church of Scotland. A promoter of the extension of European ways to India, he opened a successful school at Calcutta where Indians could study literature, arts, and sciences as they were taught in England, as well as the Bible.

Duff assisted in establishing the University of Calcutta during his last stay in India (1856–1864). His numerous writings reflect his intimate knowledge of India. He returned permanently to Scotland in 1864 and devoted his energies to the spread of interest in missions. He died at Edinburgh on Feb. 12, 1878.

POWEL MILLS DAWLEY
General Theological Seminary, New York

DUFF, Sir Lyman Poore (1865–1955), chief justice of Canada. He was born in Meaford, Ontario, on Jan. 7, 1865, and graduated from the University of Toronto (B. A., 1887; LL. B., 1889). After a successful practice in Victoria, he was appointed a puisne judge of the supreme court of British Columbia in 1904 and a justice of the supreme court of Canada in 1906. He was chief justice from 1933 until he retired in 1944. He died in Ottawa on April 26, 1955.

In his almost 40 years on the supreme court, Duff's important constitutional judgments were generally in conformity with those of the privy council (formerly the highest court of appeal). On the whole he supported provincial authority. In the case of the Dominion Insurance Act of 1916, for example, he argued that the Canadian Parliament should not encroach on the matters entrusted to provincial legislatures. Of Duff's other public duties, the most significant was the chairmanship of the royal commission of 1931–1932 on transportation problems.

G. DE T. GLAZEBROOK
Author of "A Short History of Canada"

DUFF ISLANDS, ten islets of the Solomon Islands in the Southwest Pacific. They were discovered in 1606 and were named for a missionary ship that visited the islands in 1797. Population: (1963 est.) 400.

DUFFERIN AND AVA, duf´ər-in, ä´və, **1st Marquess of** (1826–1902), British diplomat. He was born Frederick Temple Blackwood, in Florence, Italy, on June 21, 1826, and succeeded to a barony in the Irish peerage in 1841. Educated at Oxford, he first distinguished himself as the author of *Letters from High Latitudes* (1857), describing a voyage to Iceland. His earliest important diplomatic success came in 1860 as a British representative in the six-power negotiations at Constantinople over the massacre of Christians in Syria. Created an earl in 1871, he became governor general of Canada the following year and served ably in that position. After leaving Canada in 1878, he served successively as ambassador to Russia and to Turkey, as viceroy of India, and as ambassador to Italy and to France. He was created marquess of Dufferin and Ava in 1888. Lord Dufferin died in Clandeboye, Ireland, on Feb. 12, 1902.

DU FRESNE, Charles. See DU CANGE, SIEUR.

DUFY often painted the rich and fashionable at play. *Deauville Racetrack* was done in 1929.

NELSON GALLERY, ATKINS MUSEUM, KANSAS CITY

DUFY, dü-fē', **Raoul** (1877–1953), French painter, who began as one of the major artists of the Fauve group but later evolved a personal style that combined the boldness and bright color of Fauvism with the decorative brilliance of such 18th century French painters as Boucher and Fragonard.

Dufy was born at Le Havre on June 3, 1877. In 1900 he enrolled at the École Nationale des Beaux-Arts in Paris. After 1902, when he met Matisse and the other artists who came to be known as "Les Fauves," Dufy began to abandon his late-impressionist manner in favor of solid, strong colors, large shapes, and simplified forms. He exhibited his works with the Fauves in the 1906 Salon d'Automne.

Dufy's Fauve style already incorporated the dynamic and rhythmic calligraphy that gradually came to dominate his art. His line, which became ever more facile and elegant, continued the tradition of Ingres and Constantin Guys. Like Guys, Dufy favored scenes of amusement and luxury—racetracks, yachting harbors, and sailing regattas. Other favorite subjects were anemones, musical instruments (often as homages to Mozart), and streets gaily decorated with flags and banners. Although Dufy never stopped painting in oils, his rapid linear "handwriting" eventually found its freest expression in watercolor.

In addition to his easel paintings, Dufy created murals for the Jardin des Plantes and the Palais de Chaillot. For the Palace of Electricity at the Universal Exposition in Paris in 1937, he painted a huge decorative panel, 11 yards (10 meters) high and 65 yards (59 meters) long. Dufy was also active as a printmaker, a book illustrator, and a designer of textiles, ceramics, and ballet sets and costumes. In 1952 he was awarded the grand prize (French painting section) in the Venice Biennale, and in the same year a large retrospective exhibition of his work was held in Geneva. He died at Forcalquier, France, on March 23, 1953.

JEAN DUFY (1888–1964), Raoul's brother, was also a painter. Influenced chiefly by Raoul, but also by Cézanne and Picasso, Jean's work is representational, and much of it is indistinguishable from Raoul's. Jean painted watercolors, gouaches, and oils and also designed china for the Haviland company.

WILLIAM GERDTS
University of Maryland

Further Reading: Cogniat, Raymond, *Dufy*, tr. by Thomas L. Callow (New York 1962); Lassaigne, Jacques, *Dufy*, tr. by James Emmons (Cleveland, Ohio, 1954).

DUGHET, dü-gē', **Gaspard** (1615–1675), Italian painter of classical landscapes in the manner of Poussin. He is generally believed to have been the first artist to represent storms. Although he was widely known in his own day and achieved immense popularity in the 18th century, his work now is felt to be derived too much from formulas and to lack personal force.

Dughet was born in Rome, on June 7, 1615, the son of a French painter who had settled in Italy. From about 1630 to 1633 he studied with his brother-in-law Nicolas Poussin, who so influenced his style that Dughet was often called Gaspard-Poussin.

When he was already an established painter, Dughet discovered the landscapes of Claude Lorrain, and he added the warm light of that artist to the classical style of Poussin in his late works. He died in Rome, on May 25, 1675. Dughet's paintings are displayed in many Italian museums, as well as in the Louvre (Paris) and English galleries.

DUGONG, dōō′gong, a large marine mammal that lives in warm waters along the shores of the Indian Ocean and the western Pacific. It reaches 12 feet (3.5 meters) in length and more than 600 pounds (270 kg) in weight, with a heavy skeleton and much body fat. The forelimbs are modified into flippers; there are no hind limbs; and the tail fin—which is the primary source of propulsive power—is broad and notched. The brownish to grayish skin is almost hairless except for some stiff bristles around the muzzle. Both jaws are bent sharply downward at the front, and in males the single pair of upper incisor teeth are formed into tusks.

Dugongs live in shallow coastal waters, alone or in small groups, apparently never going out to sea, rarely entering fresh water, and never coming onto land. They feed on marine grasses and algae, swallowing them almost whole. There seems to be no distinct breeding season. Usually a single young is born after a gestation period of about 11 months, and it nurses underwater at the pair of pectoral (chest) teats.

Dugongs, which are continually hunted for their fat and meat, have been greatly reduced in numbers. There is only one species (*Dugong dugon*), the sole surviving member of the family Dugongidae. The related Steller's sea cow, of the Bering Sea, has been exterminated by man. Dugongs and manatees make up the order Sirenia, which may be related to the elephants.

WALTER A. SHEPPE, JR., *University of Zambia*

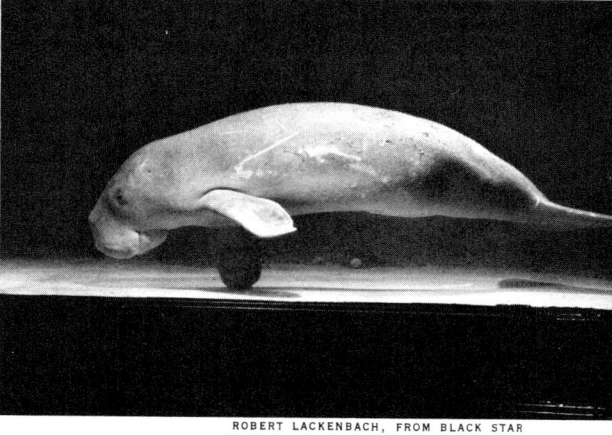

ROBERT LACKENBACH, FROM BLACK STAR
Dugong

DU GUESCLIN, dü ge-klaN′, **Bertrand** (c. 1320–1380), French military commander. He was ugly, brutal, and conceited and had no great abilities as a general. But he was punctilious in his respect for the code of chivalry and became a symbol of honor and chivalric prowess.

He was born near Dinan about 1320. Little is known about his early life. After being knighted in 1357, he entered the service of King Charles V of France. Du Guesclin won his most brilliant victory at Cocherel on May 16, 1364, when he defeated the troops of King Charles II of Navarre and ended Navarre's threat to Charles V. He was less fortunate in Brittany, where he went to support Charles of Blois in a civil war. In September 1364 at Auray, Du Guesclin's troops were defeated, he himself was captured, and his lord Charles was killed. After being ransomed, Du Guesclin attempted to rid the center of France from the scourge of unemployed mercenary soldiers who were pillaging the countryside. At first he tried to lead them off on a crusade against the Turks; finally he succeeded in luring many to Spain to fight for Henry of Trastámara against Pedro the Cruel. At Nájera, Du Guesclin was again defeated and captured, and Charles V was forced to ransom him.

In 1370, with the English troops burning the countryside around Paris, Charles V appointed Du Guesclin *connétable* of France. Lacking troops and money, the King imposed a strategy of harassment and avoiding pitched battles. The English troops, though they devastated the countryside, could thus accomplish no lasting victories. Careful negotiations by others allowed Du Guesclin to reconquer much of southwestern France almost without a blow. He died on July 13, 1380, during the siege of Châteauneuf-de-Randon.

FREDRICK L. CHEYETTE, *Amherst College*

DUGUIT, dü-gē′, **Léon** (1859–1928), French legal and political theorist, who challenged the validity of analytical jurisprudence, which looked upon law as deriving from a single source of authority —the sovereign. In his view, law arises out of social relationships.

Born in Libourne, Gironde, France, on Feb. 4, 1859, Duguit studied law at Bordeaux, where he taught for most of his career and where he died on Dec. 18, 1928. The most complete exposition of his views is *Traité de droit constitutionnel* (3d ed., 3 vols., 1927–1930).

Duguit's theories can best be understood as a reaction against the view of law as a creation of the state. He saw the state as a social need, an institution whose justification lies in man's social interdependence. Law is not a necessary emanation from the sovereign but arises from the needs of men in a given society at a given time. The state and the sovereign are subject to the rule of law because the state is an instrument for furthering social life.

Duguit was not explicit on the critical issue of how a society should resolve different perceptions of social need. However, his work was an important corrective to views of the state that overemphasized logical structure and political security at the expense of other social needs.

ARTHUR VON MEHREN
Harvard University Law School

DUHAMEL, dü-à-mel′, **Georges** (1884–1966), French author, many of whose works express a profound concern with the spiritual and physical sufferings of man and his often ineffectual struggles to surmount them. He was born in Paris on June 30, 1884. After studying medicine at the University of Paris, he joined the Abbaye group of poets, who lived at Créteil, near Paris. During World War I he served as an army surgeon. Later, using the name Denis Thévenin, he wrote two books about the sufferings of the wounded at the front: *Vie des martyrs* (1917; Eng. tr., *The New Book of Martyrs*, 1918) and *Civilisation* (1918; Eng. tr., 1919), for which he received the Prix Goncourt.

Following the war, Duhamel began his 5-volume novel *Cycle de Salavin* (1920–1932; Eng. tr., 1936), about a man whose fear of life thwarts his search for happiness. Perhaps his best-known work is the 10-volume cyclical novel

Chronique des Pasquiers (1933–1945; Eng. tr., 1937–1946), the fictional history of a middle-class Parisian family. Duhamel also wrote plays and collections of essays, including *Scènes de la vie future* (1930; Engl. tr., *America: The Menace*, 1931), an attack on what he regarded as the dehumanizing overindustrialization of American civilization. Duhamel died in Valmondois, France, on April 13, 1966.

HARRY T. MOORE
Author of "Twentieth Century French Literature"

DUHEM, dü-em', **Pierre Maurice Marie** (1861–1916), French physicist, philosopher, and historian of science. In his *Traité d'énergétique* (1911) he applied the theory of heat to the whole of physics. In his *Aim and Structure of Physical Theory* (1906) he argued that theory ought to correlate and classify experimental laws rather than explain them, and he showed that as means to theoretical certainty the ideal of experimental induction and the crucial falsifying experiment were alike utopian.

In his *Études sur Léonard de Vinci* (1906–1913) and *Le système du monde* (1913), Duhem sought to show the continuity of science in the slow accumulation of experimental laws and in the evolution of theory.

Duhem was born in Paris on June 10, 1861, and was educated there at Collège Stanislas and the École Normale Supérieure. He died at Cabrespine on Sept. 14, 1916.

NIALL MARTIN, *University College, London*

DUIKER, dī'kər, a small antelope ranging from 14 to 18 inches (36–47 cm) in height and from 11 to 143 pounds (5–65 kg) in weight. The duiker tribe (Cephalophini) is the most homogeneous and widespread of the African antelopes, being found everywhere south of the Sahara where suitable cover occurs.

All but one species are classified in the genus *Cephalophus*, which is characterized by short, straight, back-slanted horns in both sexes, a tuft of hair between the ears, a rounded back, heavy hindquarters, and short legs; the most distinctive feature, however, is a preorbital gland in an elongated slit on either side of the muzzle. All are forest or bush dwellers and browsers or mixed feeders. The blue duiker (*Cephalophus monticola*) is the most widespread and, at 14 inches (36 cm) high, the smallest member of the genus; the goat-sized yellow-backed duiker (*C. silvicultor*) is the largest.

The gray duiker (*Sylvicapra grimmia*) differs from the members of the genus *Cephalophus* in having more upright, comparatively long horns, up to 7 inches (18 cm) in length, which usually occur only in the males. It is remarkably adaptable to diverse habitats, from savanna to mountaintops (though not to dense forest), and has an extremely varied diet, which includes even flesh and human excrement around villages.

Duikers are solitary and strongly territorial and inhabit limited areas. Most are active in twilight or at night, bedding down by day in close concealment. These traits enable duikers to flourish in settled areas long after other game has been shot out. If discovered, a duiker bolts in a dodging run and "dives" into the nearest cover; hence the name "duiker," which means "diver" in Afrikaans.

The aromatic secretion of the preorbital glands is apparently important in courtship; in the gray duiker, for instance, the climax to the buck's prancing sexual display comes when the pair rub their preorbital glands together, after which the male attempts to mount.

RICHARD D. ESTES, *Museum of Comparative Zoology, Harvard University*

DUISBURG, düs'boorkH, is an industrial city and river port in West Germany, in the state of North Rhine-Westphalia. It lies on the east bank of the Rhine River close to its junction with the Ruhr, 15 miles (24 km) north of Düsseldorf. The industrial centers of Ruhrort, Meiderich, and Hamborn are within the city.

Duisburg is a major West German center of the iron-smelting and steelmaking industries. It also has shipbuilding, engineering, and chemical industries. The city is one of the busiest ports in the Rhineland.

Duisburg was settled at least as early as the 9th century and grew during the Middle Ages into a small commercial city. Ruhrort was established in the same period. In the 19th century both cities became important manufacturing centers of the Ruhr area and also, together, its leading port. Duisburg and Ruhrort were merged in 1908, and the city's boundaries were further extended in 1929. Population: (1965 est.) 487,000.

NORMAN J. G. POUNDS, *Indiana University*

DUJARDIN, dü-zhàr-daN', **Felix** (1801–1860), French zoologist, who studied the morphology of protozoa and established a system of protozoan classification that is still useful today.

In 1841, Dujardin published *Infusoria: The Physiology and Classification of These Animals...*, in which he showed that protozoa, or infusoria as they were then known, are composed of a homogeneous mass that does not have any organ systems. He called this mass "sarcode"; it later became known as "protoplasm." Dujardin then classified protozoa on the basis of their organelles of locomotion. He divided them into three groups: those with contractile extensions (rhizopods), those with flagellae (flagellates), and those with cilia (ciliates). Dujardin's classification repudiated the work of the German zoologist C. G. Ehrenberg, who in 1838 had proposed a classification system for protozoa based on the erroneous assumption that they had organ systems like those of higher animals.

Gray duiker
ARTHUR W. AMBLER, FROM NATIONAL AUDUBON SOCIETY

Dujardin was born in Tours, France, on April 5, 1801. Mostly self-taught, he was interested in engineering, mathematics, optics, and chemistry, and only later in the biological sciences. After a brief period on the faculty of the University of Toulouse, he became professor of botany and zoology at the University of Rennes in 1841. He held this post until his death in Rennes, on April 8, 1860.

MORRIS SOLOTORVSKY
Coauthor of "Three Centuries of Microbiology"

DUJARDIN, dü-zhȧr-daN′, **Karel** (1622–1678), Dutch painter, whose most characteristic works are Italianate landscapes, often peopled with shepherds and peasants. He also painted portraits, genre scenes, and religious and mythological subjects.

Dujardin was born in Amsterdam in 1622, the son of an artist. He studied under Nicolas Berchem, a painter of landscapes in the Italian manner, and this, together with a trip he made to Italy as a young man, were the formative influences on his style. When he returned from Italy in 1652, he worked in Amsterdam and at The Hague In 1674 he returned to Italy, living for a time in Rome and then in Venice, where he died on Nov. 20, 1678.

Among Dujardin's best-known works are *Italian Landscape: Morning* and *Italian Landscape: Evening* (both in the Dahlem Museum, Berlin); *Charlatans* and *Christ on the Cross Between Two Thieves* (both in the Louvre, Paris); and *Allegory on the Vanity of Human Life* (Royal Museum, Copenhagen).

DUKAS, dü-kȧ′, **Paul** (1865–1935), French composer, who wrote the popular orchestral scherzo *L'apprenti sorcier* (*The Sorcerer's Apprentice*). He was born in Paris on Oct. 1, 1865. From 1882 to 1889 he studied at the Paris Conservatory, where he won a Prix de Rome (2d prize) for composition. He first made his mark as a composer in 1892 with the performance of his overture to Corneille's drama *Polyeucte*. This was followed in 1896 by the Symphony in C Major. In 1897, Dukas produced his best-known work, the lively, rhythmic, superbly orchestrated *Sorcerer's Apprentice*. It is based on a ballad by Goethe that tells how a sorcerer's apprentice gets into difficulties when he tries to apply his master's magic.

Dukas' Sonata in E Flat Minor (1901) and the *Variations, Interlude, and Finale on a Theme by Rameau* (1903) are among the most important 20th century French works for piano. He wrote one opera, *Ariane et Barbe-Bleue*, with libretto by Maeterlinck, which was first produced at the Opéra Comique in 1907. It is a masterpiece of the French lyric theater. His ballet *La Péri* (1912) is another work that reveals his gift for brilliant instrumentation and his effective use of impressionistic tone color.

Dukas composed relatively little, partly because he was involved in many different musical activities and partly because he was intensely self-critical and wanted posterity to have only his best work. An excellent teacher, for many years he was professor of composition at the Paris Conservatory and the École Normale de Musique. He was also music critic for several reviews in Paris, notably the *Gazette des beaux-arts*. Dukas died in Paris on May 17, 1935.

GILBERT CHASE, *Tulane University*

DUKE, James Buchanan (1856–1925), American industrialist and philanthropist, who formed the American Tobacco Company and established the Duke Endowment. He was born on the outskirts of Durham, N. C., on Dec. 23, 1856. In his boyhood, with his older brother, Benjamin, he labored long and hard under the direction of their father, Washington Duke, in preparing, packaging, transporting, and selling smoking tobacco. The center of their operations for eight years after the Civil War was the family farm. Eventually prospering, "Mr. Wash," "Ben," and "Buck" (James B.) moved into Durham in 1873, soon built a factory, and began operating under the firm name of W. Duke, Sons and Company.

The bright-leaf tobacco of the region bore a high reputation for flavor, and the Dukes met local competition. James B. Duke decided in 1881 that the firm should concentrate on cigarettes. Three years later he opened a branch in New York City. Wide-awake salesmanship, strategic price cuts, heavy advertising, and mechanization (the Bonsack cigarette machine) gained for Duke a clear advantage over all competitors.

Industry Expansion. By 1890, Duke had convinced his four main rivals to combine with him to form the American Tobacco Company, capitalized at $25 million. This "tobacco trust" headed by Duke made great profits in selling Duke of Durham, Sweet Caporal, and many other cigarette brands. It also moved during the next two decades to control other segments of the industry: chewing tobacco, smoking tobacco, snuff, cigars, manufacturing supplies, and distribution outlets. The combination had reached a capitalization of $235 million and control of 80% of the industry when in 1907 the federal government brought suit under the Sherman Antitrust Act. In 1911 the U. S. Supreme Court ordered the company to dissolve and reorganize. Ironically, Duke's assistance was needed to effect the reorganization.

Later Years. Hydroelectric power projects in North Carolina, South Carolina, and Quebec absorbed Duke's interest in his later years. His invested tobacco wealth greatly expanded the cotton textile industry. This led to the creation of the Southern Power System, subsequently the Duke Power Company.

Over a period of 30 years, Washington, Benjamin N., and James B. Duke gave hundreds of thousands of dollars each to develop Methodist-related Trinity College in Durham. Before his death in New York City on Oct. 10, 1925, James B. Duke established the Duke Endowment. It has appropriated more than $265 million in the Carolinas to various institutions.

STUART NOBLIN
North Carolina State University at Raleigh

DUKE, a title of nobility that is found in many parts of Europe, most notably in England, where the title was not known until the 14th century. Derived originally from the Latin word *dux* (leader), the title implied important civil and military responsibilities in the late Roman and Byzantine empires.

In Lombard Italy the numerous dukes were clan chieftains. They were often very powerful. Yet only two of the Lombard dukedoms (Spoleto and Benevento) became permanent territorial units. In another use of the title in Italy, the duke, or *doge*, of Venice was the chief executive of the town, usually elected for life.

The title was more important in medieval Europe north of the Alps, where it became associated with tribal names. In Charlemagne's empire the basic local officer was the count, but by 900 there were a number of powerful dukes ruling large areas that correspond roughly to regions once settled by a specific tribe. Thus Aquitaine has pre-Roman origins; Saxony, Bavaria, Swabia, and Burgundy reflect 6th century Germanic settlement; and Normandy dates from early 10th century Norse settlement. Despite the tribal names for the duchies, most medieval dukes were not members of the ancient tribe and some were appointees of the king. In the later Middle Ages the title began to proliferate and the dukes derived their power only from their feudal position.

The last important dukes in Europe outside Germany were the 15th century dukes of Burgundy who unified the Netherlands and ruled vast territories between France and Germany.

JOHN HENNEMAN, *McMaster University*

DUKE UNIVERSITY is a private coeducational university located in Durham, N.C. It traces its history to 1838, when a group of Methodists and Friends in Randolph county, N. C., founded the Union Institute; this became Trinity College in 1859. Duke University was created in 1924 by the trust indenture of James B. Duke (q.v.), which provided for its establishment as the chief beneficiary of the Duke Endowment. Trinity became the nucleus and undergraduate men's college of the new university. Duke now also comprises a women's college, a graduate school, and schools of law, divinity, medicine, forestry, nursing, engineering, and business.

Special institutes include the World Rule of Law Center, the Commonwealth Studies Center, the Center for the Study of Aging, the Population Studies Center, and the Cardiac Research Center. With North Carolina State University and the University of North Carolina, Duke participates in the Research Triangle of North Carolina and the Triangle Nuclear Laboratory. Other research facilities include Duke Hospital, Duke Forest, a marine laboratory, a parapsychology laboratory, and a general library housing nearly 2 million volumes and manuscript collections of more than 4 million items. Duke's enrollment is approximately 7,500.

JOSEPH MARTIN, *Duke University*

DUKHOBORS. See DOUKHOBORS.

DULAC, dü-làk′, **Edmund** (1882–1953), French-born English artist, who created vivid and charming illustrations for traditional fairy tales. He was born in Toulouse on Oct. 22, 1882. After studying at Toulouse University, he attended the Toulouse Art School and in 1904 and 1905 exhibited portraits at the Paris Salon. He also participated in private art shows in London from 1907 to 1918. In 1912 he became a British subject. He died in London on May 25, 1953.

Dulac's fairy-tale illustrations were published in such works as *Hans Andersen's Snow Queen and Other Tales* (1912) and *Edmund Dulac's Fairy Book* (1916). He also illustrated *The Arabian Nights* (1907), Shakespeare's *The Tempest* (1908), *The Rubaiyat of Omar Khayyam* (1909), and *Treasure Island* (1927). In addition, Dulac designed the King's Poetry Prize medal and the coronation stamp of George VI.

DULANY, dōō-lā′nē, **Daniel** (1685–1753), American colonial political leader. He was born in Queens (later Leix), Ireland. Dulany went to Maryland in 1703, arriving penniless, but soon became a wealthy planter and a practicing lawyer. A member of the Maryland assembly from about 1722 to 1732, he at first opposed the proprietary government for not providing the colonists with the benefits of English laws. He died in Annapolis, Md., on Dec. 5, 1753.

DANIEL DULANY (1722–1797), his son, increased the family's fortune and prestige. He was born in Annapolis on June 28, 1722, was educated in England, and became a lawyer. He served in the Maryland assembly and on the governor's council. The younger Dulany is chiefly remembered for his *Considerations on the Propriety of Imposing Taxes in the British Colonies* (1765), the most influential pamphlet written in opposition to the Stamp Act. However, in a controversy with Charles Carroll, he defended the governor's right to impose certain fees. During the Revolutionary War, Dulany remained neutral. He died in Baltimore on March 17, 1797.

DON HIGGINBOTHAM
University of North Carolina

DULCIMER, dul′sə-mər, an ancient musical instrument, known in Persia and Arabia, possibly first introduced into Europe by the Crusaders. The dulcimer consists of a set of strings stretched over a rectangular or trapezoidal soundboard or box. It is set on a table and played with small hammers. The dulcimer played by Hungarian gypsy bands is called a *cimbalom*.

DULLES, dul′əs, **Allen Welsh** (1893–1969), American lawyer, diplomat, and public official. He was born in Watertown, N.Y., on April 7, 1893. He received B.A. (1914) and M.A. (1916) degrees from Princeton and an LL.B. (1926) from George Washington University. Entering diplomatic service in 1916, he was legation secretary in Vienna. After the United States entered World War I, Dulles was sent to Bern, Switzerland, where he established liaison with informants in the Balkans and in Austria–Hungary, and in 1918 he was a member of the American peace commission in Paris. From 1922 to 1926 he was chief of the State Department's Near Eastern Affairs division in Washington. He then retired to private law practice but took part in several international conferences over the next decade.

During World War II, while serving with the Office of Strategic Services (OSS) in Switzerland, Dulles guided the sensitive, top-secret negotiations that led to the Nazi surrender in northern Italy. After the war he again practiced law, but in 1947 he took part in writing, for President Truman, an analysis of the newly established Central Intelligence Agency (CIA). Asked to help implement the document, Dulles returned to government service, first as the CIA's deputy director (1951–1953) and then as its director (1953–1961). Eisenhower's secretary of state, John Foster Dulles, was his brother.

In 1963 and 1964, Dulles was on the President's Commission on the Assassination of President Kennedy. He wrote *The Craft of Intelligence* (1963) and *The Secret Surrender* (1966). Dulles died in Washington, D. C., on Jan. 29, 1969.

DONALD B. JOHNSON, *University of Iowa*

DULLES, dul'əs, **John Foster** (1888–1959), American diplomat and public official. As secretary of state (1953–1959) during the administration of President Dwight D. Eisenhower, he insisted that the United States stand firm against the threat of Communist aggression.

Earlier Career. Dulles was born in Washington, D.C., on Feb. 25, 1888, the son of the Rev. Allen Macy Dulles and Edith Foster Dulles. He was a grandson of John Watson Foster, who served as secretary of state under Benjamin Harrison, and a nephew of Robert Lansing, one of Woodrow Wilson's secretaries of state. As a young man, Dulles was attracted to the ministry, but in 1907 his grandfather took him to the Hague Conference, where Dulles, then only 19, served as secretary to the Chinese delegation. This marked the beginning of a career in international law and diplomacy spanning 52 years.

Dulles was educated at Princeton (B.A., 1908), the Sorbonne (Paris), and George Washington University (LL.B., 1911). He was admitted to the New York bar in 1911 and joined the law firm of Sullivan and Cromwell in New York City. During World War I he served with the War Trade Board, and in 1919 he was counsel to the United States delegation to the Reparations Commission at Versailles. He then rejoined Sullivan and Cromwell and soon became one of the nation's leading international lawyers and a financial adviser to several foreign governments.

He was a United States delegate to the San Francisco Conference in 1945 and to the United Nations General Assembly in 1946, 1947, 1948, and 1950. He also served as special adviser to the secretary of state at the Councils of Foreign Ministers in London (1945), Moscow (1947), and Paris (1949). In July 1949 he was appointed by Gov. Thomas E. Dewey of New York to fill a vacancy in the U.S. Senate, but he lost the seat in a special election in November. In 1951, as a representative of President Harry S Truman, with the rank of ambassador, he was chief negotiator of the peace treaty with Japan.

Secretary of State. On Jan. 21, 1953, Dulles entered the Eisenhower cabinet as secretary of state. He occupied that post until serious illness compelled him to resign on April 15, 1959. He died in Washington on May 24, 1959.

Dulles' 60 trips abroad and nearly 500,000 miles (800,000 km) of flying to and from conferences during his six years in office made him the most traveled of all American secretaries of state up to his time. He was also the most controversial. In a magazine article published in 1956, he was quoted as saying that the Eisenhower administration had walked three times to the "brink of war" and that the ability to get to the verge and yet sidestep war was a "necessary art" of diplomacy. These statements at once became issues of intensive debate. He also coined the phrase "massive retaliation" in a reference to the role of atomic weapons as the mainstay of the West's defense against attack.

Throughout his tour of service, Dulles tended to define political problems in moral terms. In his view, communism was a moral evil; therefore it was wrong to compromise with it; and, because it was evil, the forces of righteousness would inevitably triumph. He successfully insisted on quick action in the U.N. Assembly to halt the Anglo-French and Israeli armed attacks on Egypt in the fall of 1956. Following his deepest conviction, he always stood ready to put the full

John Foster Dulles

force of American power behind any free country menaced by aggression, and he clearly believed that the Soviet Union and Communist China should never be permitted to misjudge the determination of the United States to defend the world's freedom. After his resignation, many of his critics joined his supporters in praising him for his personal courage and for his contribution of firmness and resolution to the Western alliance,

MALCOLM MOOS
President, University of Minnesota

DULONG, dü-lôn', **Pierre Louis** (1785–1838), French chemist and physicist. Dulong was born in Rouen on Feb. 12, 1785. Trained as a physician, he early turned to teaching physics and chemistry, and in 1811 he joined the distinguished group of scientists who met at Claude Louis Berthollet's laboratory in Arcueil.

Dulong's first important work, the discovery of the explosive nitrogen trichloride, cost him an eye and two fingers in 1812. In 1816 he discovered hypophosphorous acid. He then began to work with Alexis Thérèse Petit, and in 1818 they were awarded a prize by the Academy of Sciences for their research on thermal expansion and temperature measurement. Their most important work followed in 1819, when they discovered that for most solid elements the product of the atomic weight and specific heat is constant. Dulong died in Paris on July 18, 1838.

W. A. SMEATON, *University College, London*

DULUTH, dü-lüt', **Daniel Greysolon** (1639–1710), French soldier and fur trader. Duluth, or Du Luth, or Dulhut, was born in St-Germain-Laval, France. Having sojourned twice in Canada, he went there to stay in 1674. His first trading expedition (1678) led him to the western end of Lake Superior, where he concluded an alliance with local Indian chiefs and encouraged them to trade with the French. The city of Duluth, Minn., is named for him.

Duluth took possession of the Sioux territory in the name of the king of France and returned to Quebec in 1681. In 1696 he was made commander of Fort Frontenac (now Kingston, Ontario). Duluth died in Montreal on Feb. 26, 1710.

MICHEL BRUNET, *University of Montreal*

DULUTH, Minn., looking toward the ship canal and the Aerial Lift Bridge, with Lake Superior in the distance. The round building near the ship canal is the Arena-Auditorium, completed in 1966.

DULUTH CHAMBER OF COMMERCE

DULUTH, də-lōōth′, a city in northeastern Minnesota, is the third-largest city of the state. It is situated at the western end of Lake Superior, 140 miles (225 km) northeast of Minneapolis. With the neighboring city of Superior, Wis., it forms the western terminus of the Great Lakes–St. Lawrence Seaway.

Because of its advantageous location near iron-ore ranges and vast grain fields, the port of Duluth-Superior ranks high among United States ports in tonnage shipped. Vessels from many nations find their way to this midcontinent seaport. Passing through the ship canal and under the Aerial Lift Bridge, 227 feet (70 meters) high, they reach the natural harbor formed by the 9-mile (14-km) peninsula called Minnesota Point. Foreign ships come mostly for the grain that is loaded from huge grain elevators lining the harbor. The long, slim Great Lakes carrier ships bring in coal, and for the return trip down the lakes they take on iron ore and taconite.

The Economy. Besides heavy industries, including iron- and steelmaking, cement production, and oil refining, Duluth has light industries such as meat packing, brewing, wood-products processing, and textile manufacture. Newer industries have also developed in the city, including publishing, electronics manufacturing, and Oriental food processing. Duluth has a large U.S. air base, a Coast Guard station, and an international airport. The National Water Quality Laboratory is an important federal laboratory for freshwater research.

Tourism. Situated at the edge of the northern wilderness (the city is actually invaded by bears during occasional dry summers), Duluth has many scenic attractions for tourists. It has been called the "Air-Conditioned City" because it possesses resources that are becoming increasingly scarce elsewhere—clean fresh air and pure cold water. Beginning at Duluth, one can drive along the majestic north shore of Lake Superior for 155 miles (250 km) to the Canadian border. Or the motorist can follow the famous Skyline Parkway for 20 miles (32 km) along a high terrace above the city and take the St. Louis River Road to rugged Jay Cooke State Park. The nearby canoe country, which offers summer recreation, also provides excellent ski and snowmobile terrain for winter vacationists.

Education and Cultural Life. Duluth is the home of the College of St. Scholastica, established by the Benedictine Sisters in 1912, and of the Duluth Campus of the University of Minnesota, which enrolls some 5,000 students. A vocational high school, the Duluth Area Institute of Technology, was completed in 1968. The Duluth Playhouse began offering plays in 1912 and is the nation's oldest civic theater. Duluth has a symphony orchestra, organized in 1932, as well as the Duluth Art Institute and the St. Louis County Historical Society and Museum.

Residents and visitors enjoy the Duluth Zoo, the Chisholm Museum (for children), and Leif Erikson Park, where an authentic replica of a Viking ship is on display. On the university campus are the Tweed Art Gallery and the Alworth Planetarium. The Arena-Auditorium, completed in 1966, offers good facilities for conventions and for sporting and cultural events.

History. The Sioux Indians, who first inhabited northern Minnesota, were displaced by the Chippewa (Ojibway) at about the time the first French explorers and fur traders came to the region. A French voyageur, Daniel Greysolon, Sieur du Luth (or Dulhut) visited the site in 1679, and the city was later named for him. A large bronze statue of du Luth by the noted sculptor Jacques Lipchitz now stands on the Duluth Campus of the University of Minnesota.

As the early fur trade developed, a trading post was established in 1792 in the area called Fond du Lac, where the St. Louis River enters the bay of Lake Superior. In 1817 the post was taken over by fur merchant John Jacob Astor for his rapidly expanding American Fur Company. The early fur traders were followed by lumbermen, and in 1856 the town of Duluth was founded.

The first railroad reached Duluth in 1870, the same year that Duluth became a city. The following year the ship canal was cut through Minnesota Point, and as mining developed in the 1880's, the city began to grow rapidly.

In 1956 the mayor-council form of government was adopted, to replace the previous commission form of government. Population of the city, 92,811; of the Duluth-Superior metropolitan area, 266,650.

RUDOLPH JOHNSON, *University of Minnesota*

DUMA, doo'mə, is the name of the popularly elected chamber of the Russian legislature during the brief era of constitutional monarchy, 1905–1917. The Russian word connotes *"thought"* and had been applied to various deliberative bodies throughout Russian history. Russian emperors stubbornly resisted the principle of an imperial consultative Duma until the revolution of 1905 forced Nicholas II to agree to a national assembly with genuine legislative powers.

The October Manifesto of 1905 proclaimed as an "immutable rule" that no law should be promulgated without the approval of a State Duma. But the restricted powers finally reserved to the Duma by the Fundamental Law of April 23 (New Style, May 6), 1906, disappointed both moderate and radical public opinion. Fully one third of the national budget was placed beyond the jurisdiction of the Duma. The emperor enjoyed an absolute veto over legislative bills and could prorogue or dissolve the Duma as long as he announced the election date for a new Duma.

First and Second Dumas. Despite an electoral law that was less than democratic, the First Duma, which convened in April (New Style, May) 1906, was far more liberal than the government had anticipated. Over 200 peasant delegates were elected out of a total chamber of 524; they proved to be sympathetic to the Duma's most radical ideas rather than the conservative bulwark that the government had hoped for. A unanimous resolution was quickly presented to the government demanding direct and equal voting for Duma members by the entire electorate; abolition of the legislature's conservative upper chamber; and land reforms based on expropriation of large estates.

Nicholas II dissolved the Duma in July 1906 and appointed a vigorous bureaucrat, Pyotr Stolypin, to help convene a more cooperative Duma. Party lines in the Second Duma were more sharply drawn than in the first, with numerous extremists at both ends of the political spectrum and with a majority objectionable to the government. The Second Duma, seated in February (New Style, March) 1907, was dissolved in June 1907, as the government illegally issued a restrictive new electoral law.

Third and Fourth Dumas. Elections under the new law resulted in a Duma with fewer peasant and worker representatives and a majority amenable to most of the government's program. Stolypin's land reforms were passed by the Duma but, to the government's chagrin, had to be introduced under an "emergency powers" clause of the Fundamental Law after rejection by the conservative upper chamber. The Third Duma served its full legal term of five years and was succeeded by an even more conservative Fourth Duma in November 1912.

Although the Fourth Duma pledged its loyalty at the beginning of World War I, it later became sharply critical of the government and was dissolved by Nicholas II at the same time as the February (New Style, March) Revolution in 1917 was dissolving the governmental structure. Despite its shortcomings, the Duma had become a public forum for criticism of the government and represented progress in the political evolution of Russia away from bureaucratic autocracy.

PETER CZAP, JR., *Amherst College*

Further Reading: Charques, Richard, *The Twilight of Imperial Russia* (New York 1965).

DUMAGUETE, doō-mä-gä'tä, in the Philippines, is the capital and chief port of Negros Oriental province, on Negros Island. It enjoys a typhoon-free location, 424 miles (682 km) southeast of Manila and 80 miles (130 km) southwest of the city of Cebu. The city is situated between the Mindanao Sea and Tañon Strait, through which interisland shipping is channeled from the Visayan Sea. Dumaguete's harbor also accommodates foreign freighters loading copra, sugar, abaca products, and corn. An airport for domestic lines lies 3 miles (4.8 km) north of the city. To the west, slopes rise to 6,185 feet (1,885 meters) at the extinct Magaso volcano.

The principal language of Dumaguete is Cebuano. Silliman University, at the city's northern border, is the leading institution of higher education in the Visayan Islands. Population: (1966) of the municipal district, 42,643.

LEONARD CASPER, *Boston College*

DUMAS, dü-mä', **Alexandre** (1802–1870), called *Dumas père*, French writer, who is the most universally read of all French novelists. His critics have often been severe with his novels for their unsophisticated style and their loosely connected string of adventures, which strain belief; and they have found fault with the author for his lack of interest in the nuances of psychological analysis. But undemanding readers continue to relive in imagination the thrilling incidents of *The Three Musketeers* and *The Count of Monte Cristo*. Thackeray called Dumas "Alexander the Great," and the 20th century British historian D. W. Brogan described him as "a great creator of the vision of France held by foreigners."

Life. Alexandre Davy de La Pailleterie Dumas was born at Villers-Cotterêts, France, on July 24, 1802. His grandfather was a French nobleman who had settled in Santo Domingo (now the Dominican Republic); his grandmother, Marie Dumas, was a Negro woman of that island. Their natural son, Alexandre's father (who took the name Dumas), became one of Napoleon's generals. Because General Dumas' death in 1806 left his family penniless, Alexandre's education was neglected. However, he read books of history and developed a passion for the conspiracies, dark plottings, and cruel

Alexandre Dumas père (the elder)

GRANGER COLLECTION

or heroic feats of the 16th and early 17th centuries. His good penmanship earned him a modest position as a lawyer's clerk; then, obsessed by dreams of a literary career, he began to write for the stage, which the romantic rebels of Paris were then attempting to conquer. His first play, *Henri III et sa cour* (1829), scored a resounding success, and he went on to write additional plays and the many historical novels that brought him fame and an enormous fortune.

Dumas lived adventurously. He took part in the revolution of July 1830; he caught cholera during the epidemic of 1832, survived it, and traveled in Italy to recuperate. (His travel books are among the liveliest of the 19th century, blending vivid descriptions of the real life with fictitious incidents stranger than truth.)

Always careless about money, Dumas lavished huge sums on an imposing number of mistresses, on his friends, and on fatuous buildings and art works, often chosen with little discrimination. He finished his life debt-ridden, bankrupt, but still cheerful. Alexandre Dumas *fils* (q.v.), his son by one of his mistresses, had meanwhile started his career as a dramatist and as a moralist; he was concerned about the dire social consequences of adultery and the evils brought upon illegitimate children by their carefree parents. Dumas *fils* attempted to remonstrate with his father and convince him that he should reform, but to no avail. To the end, which came on Dec. 5, 1870, at Puys, near Dieppe, Dumas *père* had no fear of death. "I shall tell her a story," he said to a friend, "and she will be kind to me."

Plays. French audiences, far enough removed in time from the French Revolution and the Empire to delight in plots of violence, revenge, and fierce loves, were ready to accept Dumas' dramatic works. He followed *Henri III et sa cour* with several more plays of the same type. In *Antony* (1831) he depicted the wife of an army officer who for several months had resisted the advances of the irresistible young Dumas. *Tour de Nesle* (1832), concerning the secret debauches of Marguerite of Burgundy, remains one of the most successful melodramas on the French stage. *Kean* (1836), which starred the most famous actor of the time, Frédérick Lemaître, is a skillfully written drama about Edmund Kean, the great English actor of the romantic period; Jean-Paul Sartre adapted and modernized the play in 1954.

Novels. It was as a historical novelist, a French Sir Walter Scott, that Dumas scored his greatest triumphs. He was among the first, along with Balzac and Eugène Sue, to grasp the full possibilities of the *roman feuilleton* (serial novel). His enormous literary production, in which he was assisted by collaborators who read memoirs and volumes of history in order to provide him with themes and episodes, brought him a huge fortune. His chief collaborator was Auguste Maquet, a history teacher who also wrote novels and plays on his own.

From Dumas' score of long novels, those that survive and are often retranslated and republished include *The Three Musketeers* (1843–1844) and its sequel, *Twenty Years After* (1845); *The Count of Monte Cristo* (1844); and *La reine Margot* (1845), which, set in the reign of Charles IX, depicts the massacre of St. Bartholomew's Day (1572).

Dumas had a flair for re-creating the atmosphere of history, especially of the French religious wars, the conspiracies and duels of the reign of Louis XIII, and the romantic swashbuckling of such historical personages as D'Artagnan (q.v.). Dumas rearranged the facts, supplemented them with imaginary people and events, and breathed life into the actors of past dramas. To Dumas, history was a nail on which he could hang his novels and, unlike Scott or Balzac, he never yielded to the temptation of overlong descriptions or dissertations on the significance of his stories. Bernard Shaw declared, "The elder Dumas was what Gounod called Mozart, a summit of art. Nobody ever could, or did, or will improve on Dumas' romances and plays." See also COUNT OF MONTE CRISTO; THREE MUSKETEERS.

HENRI PEYRE, *Yale University*

Further Reading: Maurois, André, *The Titans,* tr. by Gerald Hopkins (New York 1957).

DUMAS, dü-må', **Alexandre** (1824–1895), called *Dumas fils,* French writer, who is most famous as the author of the play commonly called *Camille* (q.v.). His many plays enjoyed great success in France in the second half of the 19th century and were widely read in Russia, England, and the Scandinavian countries. Although his own life was not above reproach, he felt it his duty to preach a stern morality in his plays, and, like all plays with too obvious a didactic purpose, they tend to be heavy-handed and lacking in humor and poetical suggestion.

Dumas was born in Paris on July 27, 1824, the illegitimate son of Alexandre Dumas *Père* (q.v.) and a seamstress he had seduced when he arrived in Paris as a young man. Dumas *fils* never forgave his father for the profligate life he led. He inherited his father's dramatic talent, but cultivated it with more arduous reflection and a more searching critical spirit. After Dumas *fils* was elected to the French Academy in 1874, he never ceased assigning a moral purpose to literature. He died at Marly-le-Roi on Nov. 27, 1895.

Writings. In 1848, Dumas scored a wide success with his novel *La dame aux camélias,* which in 1852 he turned into the play of the same name. (It is best known in English as *Camille.*) During the Second Empire he became convinced that European society was becoming more corrupt as it became wealthier, and he wrote turgid prefaces to his plays to make their moral intentions more

Alexandre Dumas *fils* (the younger)

GRANGER COLLECTION

obvious. He stood against the emancipation of women, against prostitution and adultery, and for the sacredness of the marriage bond.

Dumas' most striking plays, after *Camille*, were *Le demi-monde* (1855), in which he vituperated against women who were content to be *déclassées*; *La question d'argent* (1857), a satire on greedy financiers; *Le fils naturel* (1858); and *Francillon* (1887), a plea for husbands no less than wives to be bound by the law of fidelity. His plays mix a realistic portrayal of life, which had already invaded the novel, with an indefatigable moral purpose.

HENRI PEYRE
Yale University

Further Reading: Maurois, André, *The Titans*, tr. by Gerald Hopkins (New York 1957); Taylor, Frank A., *The Theatre of Dumas Fils* (New York 1937).

DUMAS, dü-mà', **Jean Baptiste André** (1800–1884), French organic chemist whose work revolutionized organic theory. He was born in Alais, France, on July 16, 1800. He was apprenticed to an apothecary whom he accompanied to Geneva in 1816. There he received an excellent education in botany and chemistry. With Charles Coindet, Dumas introduced the use of iodine for treating goiter. He collaborated with J. L. Prévost in investigating blood and reproduction.

Dumas went to Paris in 1823 and joined the faculty of the École Polytechnique, where in 1832 he founded the first teaching chemistry laboratory in France. In 1834, he discovered that chlorine could replace hydrogen in hydrocarbons. This contradicted Berzelius' theory that chemical combination depended on the electrical states of the constituent atoms. Dumas' law of substitutions led to a reconsideration of the theory of organic compounds and paved the way for the theory of types proposed by Charles Gerhardt and Auguste Laurent. Dumas also isolated a number of important organic substances, including anthracene (1831) and chloroform (1834). He died at Cannes on April 11, 1884.

L. PEARCE WILLIAMS
Cornell University

DUMAS, dü-mà', **Jean Daniel** (1721–1792), French field marshal, who held important commands in the French and Indian War. He was born in Montauban, Gascony, on Feb. 24, 1721. He received a captain's commission in the French army in 1742 and went to Canada in 1750, serving in various parts of North America.

In the battle near Fort Duquesne, Pa., on July 9, 1755, when the French surprised the British under Gen. Edward Braddock, Dumas succeeded to the command after his superior was killed, and led his troops to victory. He then became commandant at Fort Duquesne. Dumas was named inspector general of the marine troops in Canada in 1759, and on September 13 of that year he led the right wing of the French army that was defeated by the British outside the city of Quebec. He returned to France in 1760 and from 1766 to 1768 was governor of the island colony of Mauritius. Dumas was promoted to field marshal in 1780. He died in 1792.

DU MAURIER, doo mô'rē-ā, **Daphne** (1907–), English writer, noted in particular for such best-selling suspense novels as *Rebecca* (1938) and *My Cousin Rachel* (1952), both of which were made into successful motion pictures. She was born in London on May 13, 1907, the daughter of Sir Gerald du Maurier (q.v.), the actor and theater producer. She published her first novel, *The Loving Spirit*, in 1931. In 1932 she married Sir Frederick A. M. Browning.

Among Daphne du Maurier's suspense fiction are *Jamaica Inn* (1936), about smugglers on the Cornish coast; *The Scapegoat* (1957), about two men who look alike and exchange identities; and *The Flight of the Falcon* (1965), set in Italy. She also wrote plays, including *The Years Between* (1945) and *September Tide* (1948), and published *Kiss Me Again Stranger* (1953), a collection of stories; *The du Mauriers* (1937), a fictionalized family history; and *Gerald: A Portrait* (1934), a biography of her father.

DU MAURIER, doo mô'rē-ā, **George** (1834–1896), English artist and writer, who became famous both for his satirical illustrations of the foibles of Victorian high and middle-class society and for two novels, *Peter Ibbetson* and *Trilby*.

Life. George Louis Palmella Busson du Maurier was born in Paris on March 6, 1834. After the death of his father, who had wanted him to be a chemist, du Maurier studied art in Paris and later at Antwerp, where he lost the sight of his left eye. On his return to London in 1860, he began to submit drawings to *Punch*, the famous English comic periodical, becoming a regular contributor in 1864. He also did illustrations for books by such authors as Thackeray, Henry James, and Meredith, until his failing eyesight late in life led him to give up drawing as a career and attempt novel writing. He produced three novels—*Peter Ibbetson* (1891) and *Trilby* (1894), both highly successful, and *The Martian* (1896). Du Maurier died in London on Oct. 6, 1896.

Works. Du Maurier himself illustrated *Peter Ibbetson* and *Trilby*, which draw heavily on his recollections of his early childhood and his youthful bohemian days as an art student. *Peter Ibbetson* was subsequently produced as a play (1915), as an opera (1931), with music by Deems Taylor, and as a motion picture (1935). However, *Trilby*, the story of an artist's model hypnotized by the villian Svengali, was du Maurier's most popular work. It was dramatized in 1895 and was filmed three times.

NORTON B. CROWELL, *University of New Mexico*

DU MAURIER, doo mô'rē-ā, **Sir Gerald** (1873–1934), English actor and theater manager, who was a dynamic figure in the English theater in the early 1900's, particularly as a champion of naturalistic acting. The son of the writer George du Maurier, Gerald Hubert Edward Busson du Maurier was born in Hampstead on March 26, 1873. He made his stage debut in 1894 and his first major success in 1902 in J. M. Barrie's *The Admirable Crichton*. In 1904 he portrayed Captain Hook and Mr. Darling in Barrie's *Peter Pan* and in 1906 played his most famous role, the lead in Ernest W. Hornung's *Raffles*.

After becoming a theater manager in 1910, du Maurier produced plays that included Barrie's *A Kiss for Cinderella* (1916) and *Dear Brutus* (1917) and Cyril McNeile's *Bulldog Drummond* (1921). He died on April 11, 1934, in London. His daughter, Daphne du Maurier, published a biography of him that year.

DUMBARTON. See DUNBARTON.

DUMBARTON OAKS, dum'bär-tən, is a large estate in the Georgetown section of Washington, D. C. The Dumbarton Oaks Conference was held at the estate in 1944 to draft the basic plan for the United Nations organization. See DUMBARTON OAKS CONFERENCE.

The original part of the Dumbarton Oaks house was built in 1801 on property then called The Rock of Dumbarton. The estate was acquired in 1920 by Mr. and Mrs. Robert Woods Bliss, who renamed it Dumbarton Oaks. They landscaped the grounds and added two wings to the house for their collection of Byzantine and medieval books and objects of art.

This collection formed the nucleus of the Dunbarton Oaks Research Library and Collection, which the Blisses conveyed to Harvard University in 1940 as a research center, along with part of the grounds. The remaining 27 acres of the estate were given to the District of Columbia as a public park.

Two new wings were added to the Dumbarton Oaks house in 1963—a pavilion, designed by Philip Johnson to house the Robert Woods Bliss Collection of Pre-Columbian Art, and the Garden Library, containing 10,000 volumes on gardening that had been collected by Mrs. Bliss. The 12 acres of formal gardens are open to the public.

DUMBARTON OAKS CONFERENCE, dum'bärtən, was the international meeting in which the first blueprint of the organization of the United Nations was prepared. Held in 1944 by the major Allied powers of World War II, the conference was conducted in two separate phases at Dumbarton Oaks in Washington, D. C.

The first phase (August 21–September 28) was attended by the representatives of the Soviet Union, the United Kingdom, and the United States; the second phase (September 29–October 7), by representatives of China, the United Kingdom, and the United States. This arrangement served to respect Soviet neutrality in the war against Japan.

The conferees adopted a set of proposals, based on a United States draft project, for the structure of a general international organization that eventually became the United Nations. Under these Dumbarton Oaks proposals, the primary purpose of the organization was to maintain international peace and security. The key body in the organization was to be the Security Council, on which the "Big Five"—China, France, the Soviet Union, the United Kingdom, and the United States—were to be permanently represented.

A number of knotty questions, however, remained unresolved and became the subject of negotiations in later conferences at Yalta and San Francisco. One problem concerned the Soviet demand that all 16 Soviet republics be admitted to the new organization as full-fledged members. Also, the conferees at Dumbarton Oaks could not agree on the voting procedure in the Security Council, the future status of territories under League of Nations mandates, and whether or not to restructure the Permanent Court of International Justice. See also UNITED NATIONS.

SERGIO BARZANTI
Fairleigh Dickinson University

DUMDUM BULLET. See BULLET—*Types of Bullet.*

DUMFRIES, dum-frēs', a county of southern Scotland, is on the border of England at the northeast end of the Solway Firth. It is sometimes known as *Dumfriesshire.* The county is essentially agricultural and pastoral. The principal rivers are the Nith, the Annan, and the Esk. The northern portions, although high and exposed, afford good pasture for sheep and cattle. The southern half is undulating land that produces oats, turnips, barley, and potatoes. Much of this portion is wooded.

Dumfries, the county town, and Annan have light industries. Langholm produces tweed. There is a nuclear generating plant at Chapelcross. Gretna Green, on the English border, is famous as a place where eloping couples go to be married.

Traces of hill forts and roads remain from Roman times. The Ruthwell Cross, believed to date from the 8th century, is preserved in the church at Ruthwell. The ruins of Caerlaverock Castle date from the late 13th century.

The poet Robert Burns lived and died in the town of Dumfries. Thomas Carlyle was born in Ecclefechan. Population: (1966) 88,940.

D. B. HORN, *University of Edinburgh*

DUMFRIES, dum-frēs', a royal burgh in southern Scotland and the county town of Dumfries, is situated on the Nith River about 7 miles (11 km) from its mouth on the Solway Firth. Its principal industrial products are canned milk, rubber goods, plastics, and synthetic fibers. Dumfries also has important livestock markets and is a major retail center. The manufacture of tweed, hosiery, and knitwear, for which the town was famous in the 19th century, has dwindled.

The Mid Steeple (built 1707), the former town hall, is the finest of Dumfries' public buildings and provides a dignified background for the ceremonies that draw visitors to the annual Guid Nychburris (Good Neighbors) celebration. The Church of the Greyfriars, where (in 1306) Robert Bruce is said to have murdered John Comyn the Younger (the Red Comyn), one of his rivals for the Scottish crown, is an attraction. The Martyrs' Monument commemorates the Scottish Covenanters, who had a headquarters in Dumfries in the 17th century. The poet Robert Burns resided in Dumfries in his later years and died there. His house is now a museum. A mausoleum, to which Burns' body was moved in 1815, is nearby.

Four bridges span the Nith to Maxwelltown, in Kirkcudbright. One, for pedestrian use only, is traditionally said to have been built by Devorguila Baliol, mother of John de Baliol, the Scottish king from 1292 to 1296. It probably dates only from the 15th century.

The boundaries of Dumfries were extended in 1929 to include Maxwelltown. Population: (1966) 28,450.

D. B. HORN, *University of Edinburgh*

DUMMER, dum'ər, **Jeremiah** (1645–1718), American silversmith, who is also believed to have been the first native-born portrait painter in colonial America. Dummer was born in Newbury, Mass., on Sept. 14, 1645. He was apprenticed in Boston, to the mint master John Hull in 1659 and he established his own shop there about 1667. Dummer was one of the finest silversmiths in colonial New England. Examples of his work are exhibited in collections of silver at the Boston Museum of Fine Arts and at the Metropolitan Museum, New York City. Dummer died in Boston on May 25, 1718.

Dummer's signature was discovered in 1921 on portraits of himself and his wife that had been attributed to the English portrait painter Sir Godfrey Kneller. In 1929, his signature was discovered on portraits of John Coney and his wife, Dummer's sister-in-law.

DUMMER, dum'ər, **Jeremiah** (c. 1679–1739), American colonial agent. He was born in Boston and educated at Harvard, where, according to President Increase Mather, he was the best scholar of his time. Dummer studied in Europe and received a Ph.D. degree from the University of Utrecht in 1703. He settled in England in 1708 and became involved in English politics.

In 1710 he was appointed colonial agent for Massachusetts and, in 1712, for Connecticut also. Dummer was successful in obtaining support from Elihu Yale and others for founding a college in New Haven. Like other colonial agents, however, he found his task of trying to reconcile colonial interests with English policy frustrating and difficult. In 1721 the Massachusetts House voted his dismissal, and Connecticut dismissed him as its agent in 1730. He died in Plaistow, England, on May 19, 1739.

GEORGE D. LANGDON, JR., *Vassar College*

DUMMER'S WAR, dum'ərz, an Indian war across the Maine-Canada boundary in 1724 and 1725. Named for the acting governor of Massachusetts, William Dummer, it was inspired by English and French conflicts over settlement.

Concerned by the thrust of English settlement across the Kennebec River from Maine, the French authorities in Canada turned to their Indian allies to disrupt the English advance into Canadian lands ceded to England by the Treaty of Utrecht in 1713. Acting through Catholic missionaries, and in particular Father Sebastian Râle, who lived with the Norridgewock tribe, the French gave the Indians weapons and advised them to resist English settlement.

The Indians attacked and burned two English settlements, and the English responded by destroying the Norridgewock village on the Kennebec and killing Râle. The Indians sued for peace in 1725 and agreed to recognize King George I. In turn, the English promised to establish government trading posts near the Indian settlements, and peace was established.

GEORGE D. LANGDON, JR., *Vassar College*

DUMONT, Alberto Santos. See SANTOS-DUMONT, ALBERTO.

DUMONT, dü-môn', **François** (1751–1831), French miniature painter. He was born at Lunéville on Jan. 7, 1751, and studied with Jean Girardet. From 1784 to 1788 he worked in Rome. When he returned to France he was elected to the Academy and given an apartment in the Louvre. Dumont painted many of the most important people of his time, including Louis XVI, Marie Antoinette, Louis XVIII, and Charles X. Many of Dumont's works are in the Louvre and in the J. Pierpont Morgan collection in New York. He died in Paris on Aug. 27, 1831.

Dumont's sons, Aristide and Bias, became painters, and his brother Tony was also a painter of miniatures.

DUMONT, dü-môn', **Gabriel** (1838–1906), Canadian rebel. A métis (half French, half Indian), he was born at Red River, Rupert's Land (now in Northwest Territories). Although he did not take part in the Red River Rebellion in 1870, he subsequently joined the métis who migrated to the Saskatchewan Valley. In 1884 he and others invited Louis Riel, in refuge in Montana, to organize the métis and the established white inhabitants of Saskatchewan, who were struggling against the Ottawa government and recent white settlers.

When Riel resorted to force and set up a provisional government in 1885, he named Dumont commander of his militia. After humiliating the federal forces at Duck Lake (March 26) and Fish Creek (April 24), the rebels were crushed at Batoche on May 12. Dumont fled to Montana. Following an amnesty, he returned to Canada. He died near Batoche, Saskatchewan, on May 19, 1906.

MICHEL BRUNET, *University of Montreal*

DUMONT D'URVILLE, dü-môn' dür-vēl', **Jules Sébastien César** (1790–1842), French naval officer and explorer. He was born at Condé-sur-Noireau, Calvados, France, on May 23, 1790. He entered the navy as an apprentice in 1807.

While on a hydrographic survey in the Mediterranean Sea in 1819–1820, Dumont d'Urville recognized the significance of the *Venus de Milo*, a statue that had been discovered on the Greek island of Melos. He was influential in having the statue acquired by the Louvre.

From 1822 to 1825 he served under Louis Duperrey aboard the *Coquille* on an expedition to the Pacific Ocean and around the world. As commander of the same ship, renamed the *Astrolabe*, Dumont d'Urville returned to the western Pacific to search for the ill-fated La Pérouse expedition in 1826. He returned to France in 1829 and in 1830 transported France's King Charles X to exile in England.

Dumont d'Urville in 1837 began a voyage to explore the Antarctic region, assess whaling potential, and search for new islands in the western Pacific. His ships *Astrolabe* and *Zélée* sailed through the Straits of Magellan and along the margins of Antarctic ice, discovering Louis Philippe Peninsula and Joinville Island in 1838. He then explored the southwest Pacific before sailing to Tasmania and south to Antarctica. In 1840 he discovered a portion of the Antarctic coast and named it Adélie Coast for his wife. He died in a train wreck near Paris on May 8, 1842.

HOWARD J. CRITCHFIELD
Western Washington State College

DUMORTIERITE, doō-môr'tē-ə-rīt, is a borosilicate of aluminum and iron, used in the manufacture of high-grade porcelain. It is named in honor of the French paleontologist Eugène Dumortier. The mineral usually is found in schists and gneisses in fibrous or columnar aggregates, and less commonly in pegmatite dikes; good crystals are rare. It ranges from blue and greenish blue to violet and pink. Notable deposits of dumortierite are located in France, the island of Madagascar, Brazil, and Mexico; and in California and Nevada, where it is mined.

Composition, $(Al,Fe)_7O_3(BO_3)(SiO_4)_3$; hardness, 7; specific gravity, 3.26–3.36; crystal system, orthorhombic.

GEORGE SWITZER, *Smithsonian Institution*

DUMOULIN, dü-mōō-laN′, **Charles** (1500–1566), French legal scholar, known as "the prince of legists," who was one of the most versatile and controversial scholars of the 16th century. Born in Paris, he studied law at the universities of Poitiers and Orléans and practiced in the municipal government and the *parlement* of Paris. He devoted his major writings to the defense of the French monarchy and a national church. His first book, a commentary on the customary law of Paris published in 1539, established him as an authority on feudal law. Later he published commentaries on the other provincial customs as steps toward the creation of a national code.

Dumoulin's conversion to Protestantism in 1542 turned his interests to canon law, and 10 years later he issued an attack on the papacy so radical that he had to go into exile. For more than four years he traveled, visiting Protestant friends, stirring up more religious controversy, and teaching at French and German universities. Back in Paris, he continued his religious attacks, notably in his pamphlets of 1564 against the Jesuits and the Council of Trent. By this time he also had turned against the Protestants because of their "seditious" role in provoking the religious wars that had broken out in 1562. A Catholic once more, he remained a doctrinaire Gallican and an arch-nationalist. Dumoulin died in Paris on Dec. 27, 1566.

Donald R. Kelley
State University of New York at Binghamton

DUMOURIEZ, dü-mōō-ryā′, **Charles François** (1739–1823), French general and diplomat, who deserted his country during the wars of the French Revolution. He was born on Jan. 25, 1739, in Cambrai, and entered the army in 1758. Dumouriez' military career before the French Revolution was punctuated by a series of intrigues and adventures. Promotions came quickly after he sided with the revolutionaries, and he was made a lieutenant general in 1792. The same year he was appointed minister of foreign affairs and advocated war with Austria.

Occupation of Belgium. When war came later in 1792, Dumouriez rejoined the army and helped check the invading Prussian forces at Valmy in September 1792. He then took command of the Army of the North and provided the National Convention (the revolutionary government) with a great victory at Jemappes, Belgium, on November 6, subsequently occupying the country. Dumouriez thus became the French Revolution's first military hero. Taking advantage of his enormous power and prestige, he tried to dominate affairs in Belgium, but his ambitions were blocked by a suspicious French government, which established tight control over the occupation forces. This humiliation climaxed Dumouriez' hostility toward a government whose radicalism he despised.

Desertion. After the defeat of his badly weakened army at Neerwinden on March 18, 1793, he withdrew from Belgium and entered secret negotiations with the Austrians, hoping they would help him disperse the National Convention. When his army refused to move, he deserted to the Austrians. Settling in England, he ended his life as a minor figure in the world of European counterrevolution. He died at Turville Park, England, on March 11, 1823.

Isser Woloch
University of California at Los Angeles

DUN & BRADSTREET, INC., is the oldest and largest mercantile agency in the world. The company is best known for collecting, analyzing, and disseminating credit information to businesses. This information is contained in the *Reference Book* and the *Analytical Report*, which "rate" millions of businesses by capital and credit.

Through acquisitions, D & B has expanded into related businesses. Using electronic data-processing equipment and its immense storehouse of financial information, the company provides industry with over 60 publications and services in economics, marketing, credit, finance, education, and research. The Reuben H. Donnelley Corporation, which it acquired in 1961, publishes classified telephone directories and business magazines and offers direct mail and marketing services. Moody's Investors Service, Inc., acquired in 1962, publishes financial manuals and provides investment advisory services.

Dun & Bradstreet is based in New York and has branches throughout the United States. It dates from 1841, when Lewis Tappan, a pioneer credit executive, founded the Mercantile Agency. The present name was adopted in 1933 in an amalgamation of two credit information bureaus, R. C. Dun and Company and the Bradstreet Company.

Donald E. Fischer, *University of Connecticut*

DUN LAOGHAIRE, dun lâ′rə, a borough in county Dublin, Ireland, is a port and seaside resort on the south shore of Dublin Bay, 7 miles (11 km) southeast of Dublin. It is the chief port for the passenger and mail steamer service running to Holyhead, Wales. The harbor is one of Ireland's finest. Dun Laoghaire is the center of Irish yachting.

The name of the borough derives from the dun, or fort, built here by Laoghaire, a 5th century Irish king. It was renamed Kingston in 1821 on a visit by King George IV, but the original name was restored in 1922. Population: (1961) 47,803.

DUNANT, dü-näN′, **Jean Henri** (1828–1910), Swiss humanitarian and founder of the Red Cross movement. Born in Geneva on May 8, 1828, he early became active in the World Evangelical Alliance and promoted the World Alliance of Young Men's Christian Associations. He ministered to the wounded following the Battle of Solferino (1859) and later wrote *Un souvenir de Solférino* (1862), proposing the organizing of volunteers for battlefield service to the wounded. This led to the Geneva Convention of 1864, the first international treaty with a humanitarian goal. Dunant later worked in Paris on humanitarian projects, aiding prisoners and the wounded in the Franco-Prussian War (1870–1871), during which the Red Cross movement became famous.

In 1871, Dunant proposed a universal alliance to prevent war through arbitration by an international court. He then lived in obscurity until 1895, when a journalist discovered him in Heiden, Switzerland. Here, until his death on Oct. 30, 1910, he conducted a huge correspondence to promote international unity; much of the success of the Hague conferences of 1899 and 1907 is credited to him. In 1901 he shared with Frédéric Passy the first Nobel Peace Prize. See also Red Cross.

Violet K. Libby, *Author of "Henry Dunant"*

DUNBAR, dun'bär, **Paul Laurence** (1872–1906), American black poet and novelist, who is best known for the dialect verse and stories by which he first gained recognition. He later proved his competence in standard verse and tried to escape the racial tag completely in novels dealing primarily with white characters.

Dunbar was born in Dayton, Ohio, on June 27, 1872. His *Lyrics of Lowly Life* (1896), which combined the best verse from his *Oak and Ivy* (1893) and *Majors and Minors* (1895), catapulted him to fame. In this verse and later in his many short stories, he employed stereotyped Negro dialect of the antebellum South. His later volumes of poetry include *Lyrics of Love and Laughter* (1903), *Lyrics of Sunshine and Shadow* (1905), and *Complete Poems* (1913). His short stories were collected in *Folks from Dixie* (1898), *The Strength of Gideon and Other Stories* (1900), *In Old Plantation Days* (1903), and *The Heart of Happy Hollow* (1904).

Dunbar's novels with white characters in a white people's world are *The Uncalled* (1898), *The Love of Landry* (1900), and *The Fanatics* (1901). *The Sport of the Gods* (1902), his novel dealing with Negroes, argues that the Southern Negro is unadaptable to urban culture. Dunbar died in Dayton, on Feb. 8 or 9, 1906.

BLYDEN JACKSON, *University of North Carolina*

Further Reading: Brawley, William, *Paul Lawrence Dunbar: Poet of His People* (Chapel Hill, N. C., 1936).

DUNBAR, dun'bär, **William** (1460?–1521), Scottish poet, who was perhaps the most important poet of Scotland in the early Renaissance. He is often compared with Chaucer, but although Dunbar had Chaucer's technical dexterity, he lacked his narrative ability and broad human sympathy.

Most of Dunbar's biography must be hesitantly inferred from his poems. He was probably born in East Lothian, perhaps the propertyless younger son of a good family. He probably graduated from St. Andrew's University in 1479 and was probably a priest. From 1501 to 1513 he received various payments, for unknown services, recorded in the royal treasurer's accounts. His death has been put as early as 1513 but, possibly living on a benefice of the kind he often solicited, he may have survived to write a doubtfully attributed poem in 1520.

Writings. A bitter and disappointed man, Dunbar carried to perfection the art of the begging poem. He was frequently passed over for offices and pensions and, as a result, in a number of his poems he suffered the humiliation of pleading for favors from his king, James IV of Scotland. These poems attract, however, because of their flashes of grotesque humor and savage satire.

Dunbar's resentment doubtless accounts for his acid, tough, often immensely comic poems on court and town life, friars, and women. His most scathing poem on women is *The Tretis of the Tua Mariit Wemen and the Wedo* (*The Treatise of the Two Married Women and the Widow*), written in unrhymed alliterative verse. This form was by that time somewhat old-fashioned, but Dunbar manipulated it brilliantly. *The Flyting (Flaying) of Dunbar and Kennedie* displays his skill in ferocious personal abuse.

Dunbar also wrote a wide range of serious meditative poems, from lamentation at the inevitability of death to exultation in the Resurrection of Christ. The orthodox ideas are expressed in competent, though not always inspired, verse.

More effective are *Lament for the Makaris* (Makers, that is, poets) and his Christmas hymn *Of the Nativity of Christ*. On occasion, as in his mock dirge parodying the Office of the Dead, his wild and extravagant gusto at the expense of serious religion contrasts sharply with the tone of his devotional poems and suggests that his piety was largely a matter of convention.

Dunbar was also a craftsman-practitioner of so-called "courtly" verse. *The Thrissill and the Rois* (*The Thistle and the Rose*), celebrating the marriage (Aug. 8, 1503) of James IV to the English princess Margaret Tudor, is a polished heraldic allegory in which the thistle stands for James and the rose for Margaret. Similarly, *The Goldyn Targe (Shield)* is a brilliant, though conventional, allegory on how reason defended the poet from love.

DAVID F. C. COLDWELL
Southern Methodist University

Further Reading: Baxter, J. W., *William Dunbar: A Biographical Study* (Edinburgh 1952); Scott, Tom, *Dunbar: A Critical Exposition of the Poems* (New York 1966).

DUNBAR, dun'bär, an industrial city in west central West Virginia, in Kanawha county, is on the Kanawha River, 7 miles (11km) west of Charleston, of which it is a suburb. The surrounding area has gas and oil wells. Dunbar produces farm machinery, wire products, and glass. The city was incorporated in 1921. It is administered by a mayor and council. Population: 9,285.

DUNBARTON, dun-bärt'ən, a county in west central Scotland, extends westward from Glasgow along the Clyde River and then north along the western shore of Loch Lomond to the Highlands around Ben Vorlich (altitude 3,092 feet, or 940 meters). A detached portion of the county, east of Glasgow, includes the new town of Cumbernauld and remnants of the Roman Antonine Wall.

The county's farm produce, chiefly sheep, cattle, and oats, finds a ready market in Glasgow and communities along the Firth of Clyde. The main industries are shipbuilding and engineering. Clydebank is the chief industrial center.

The county town is Dumbarton, 10 miles (16 km) northwest of Glasgow. It marked the western end of the Antonine Wall and later controlled a main route to the Highlands. It received a royal charter in 1922. Population: (1966) of the county, 207,500; of Dumbarton town, 26,340.

C. J. BARTLETT, *University of Dundee*

DUNCAN I (c.1001–1040), king of Scots, was "the gracious Duncan" of Shakespeare's *Macbeth*. Contrary to the Celtic practice whereby the ablest male of the royal house was held to have the best claim to succession and often asserted it by violence, Duncan succeeded his grandfather Malcolm II (died 1034) without a contest. But his reign became a struggle against rivals.

In 1039–1040, Duncan suffered heavy losses in an unsuccessful siege of Durham and was defeated twice by his cousin Thorfinn, Jarl (earl) of Orkney, under whom Norse power in Scotland reached its greatest extent. Thorfinn may have advanced a claim to the throne. Macbeth, Mormaer (subking) of Moray, certainly did. On Aug. 14, 1040, Macbeth killed Duncan at Pitgaveny, near Elgin. Macbeth's deed can be regarded as a natural reaction to a tenure not based on established custom.

GORDON DONALDSON, *University of Edinburgh*

DUNCAN, Isadora (1878–1927), American dancer, who did more than any other person to bring about the revolution that took place in dance during the early years of the 20th century. A visionary innovator of what came to be called "modern dance," she performed at a time when ballet had become stultifyingly mechanical. Her free movements, modeled after motions she observed in nature, showed that dance could be the natural expression of the human body and emotions. An advocate of unconventional living, she practiced free love, presenting a constant challenge to Victorian mores.

Dora Angela Duncan was born in San Francisco on May 27, 1878. At an early age she began to dance in the unconventional, nonformalized way for which she became famous, and she was teaching neighborhood children when she was six. All her life she was an inspiring teacher, but she lacked the patience to codify a method.

After a brief stint in the theater and unsuccessful recitals in Chicago and New York, Miss Duncan went to London. The Tanagra figurines in the British Museum inspired her to adopt the Greek chiton and bare feet as the freest, most expressive dance costume. Her first successful performances were presented in Budapest (1903), Berlin (1904), and London and New York (1908).

Miss Duncan's early work, of which *Primavera* is a typical example, was primarily lyrical. However, after her two children, Deirdre and Patrick, were accidentally drowned in 1913, she frequently turned to tragic and heroic themes, principally to the music of such composers as Beethoven and Wagner.

In 1921 she was invited to establish a school of the dance in the Soviet Union, similar to those she had already established in Germany and France. She stayed for several years in Russia, where her work had a profound effect on the choreographer Michel Fokine. In 1922 she married the Russian poet Sergei Esenin, but it was a brief, disastrous union, and the couple separated. After 1923 her career became erratic. Miss Duncan died at Nice, France, on Sept. 14, 1927, accidentally strangled when a scarf that she was wearing became tangled in the wheels of an automobile.

DORIS HERING
"Dance Magazine"

Further Reading: Savinio, Alberto, *Isadora Duncan* (Rizzoli Intl. 1979); Schneider, Ilya I., *Isadora Duncan: The Russian Years*, tr. by David Magarshack (1969; reprint, Da Capo 1981).

DUNCAN, a city in southern Oklahoma, the seat of Stephens county, is 85 miles (137 km) southwest of Oklahoma City. Cotton, oats, wheat, and pecans are the principal crops of the surrounding region; beef and dairy cattle and poultry are raised. There are many oil wells in the area. The city's major industries are oil refining and the manufacture of oilfield supplies and of asphalt.

Duncan was founded in 1892, when Oklahoma was Indian Territory. It was organized as a town in 1900 and in 1910 adopted the commission form of government. Since 1920, Duncan has been governed by a city manager and council. Population: 22,517.

DUNCAN PHYFE FURNITURE. See PHYFE, DUNCAN.

DUNCIAD, The, dun′sē-ad, a mock-epic by Alexander Pope. Composed of 1,700 lines in heroic couplets, the poem satirizes moral and intellectual stupidity, or "Dulness," as the negation of man's most noble aspects. Many recent critics, contradicting earlier estimates of the work as splenetic and poorly organized, consider it to be Pope's crowning achievement, profoundly serious and adequately unified.

History. The embryo of *The Dunciad*, a satire on contemporary writers, was conceived and partly written by 1725. Pope was prompted to finish this first version by the appearance in 1726 of Lewis Theobald's *Shakespeare Restored*, a pedantic examination of the texts of Shakespeare's plays. Theobald's incidental revelation of Pope's inaccurate editing of Shakespeare inspired Pope, urged on by Swift, to attack all forms of "Dulness" in literature. The first three books of *The Dunciad*, published anonymously in 1728, roused a storm of angry letters and pamphlets, and in 1729, Pope replied with *The Dunciad Variorum*, a burlesque of scholarship in general and of Theobald's in particular. A fourth book, *The New Dunciad*, was published separately in 1742. In 1743 the four books were combined, at which time Colley Cibber, the actor and dramatist, replaced Theobald as King of the Dunces.

Critique. Although *The Dunciad* is full of specific references to Pope's contemporaries, it is much more than a mere outlet of personal spleen. Underlying it is the concept defined in Pope's *Essay on Man*: man is in a middle state of chaos between thought and passion, beast and angel, and must subjugate the beast. The characters in the final version of *The Dunciad* are not merely the pedants and poetasters of Pope's day but symbols of eternal forms of moral and intellectual stupidity, who, by worshiping "Dulness," have given in to vanity, jealousy, ambition, and venality, and lowered themselves to the level of beasts.

By means of its epic framework and its many echoes of Virgil, Homer, and, above all, Milton, *The Dunciad* contrasts the beautiful innocence and fertility of true nature and the moral seriousness of the Christian intellectual tradition with the evil and sterile ugliness produced by hack writers whose careless incompetence subverts both the cultural and the natural order. These devices, combined with repeated images equating light with goodness and essential being, and darkness with evil and destruction, operate throughout all four books. They help to unify the poem and, by reminding the reader constantly of *Paradise Lost*, relate the evil of the Dunces' actions to that of Satan's war with God, and show that the morality and sanity of the world are at stake.

GEORGIA DUNBAR, Hofstra University

Further Reading: Erskine-Hill, Howard, *Pope: The Dunciad* (Dynamic Learning Corp. 1972); Rogers, Robert W., *The Major Satires of Alexander Pope* (Univ. of Ill. Press 1955); Williams, Aubrey L., *Pope's Dunciad: A Study of Its Meaning* (1955; reprint, Shoe String 1968).

DUNDALK, dun′dôk, is an unincorporated community in north central Maryland, in Baltimore county, on the Patapsco River. It is just southeast of Baltimore, of which it is a suburb. Dundalk has some industry but is chiefly a residential center for workers employed in Baltimore. The community is under the jurisdiction of Baltimore county. Population: 71,293.

DUNDAS, dun-das', **Henry** (1742-1811), British political leader, who is remembered as the trusted lieutenant of William Pitt the Younger and as the uncrowned king of Scotland. He was born in Edinburgh on April 28, 1742, and educated at Edinburgh University. After a brief career in law he was elected to Parliament in 1774 and soon became a follower of Pitt. Dundas was a good debater in Commons, but his basic political strength was control of the government patronage in Scotland.

Dundas was home secretary from 1791 to 1794 and secretary of war from 1794 to 1801. As secretary of war he had the chief voice in planning Britain's first campaigns in the Napoleonic Wars. When Pitt resigned office in 1801, Dundas resigned, too, and accepted a peerage as Viscount Melville in 1802. He returned to the cabinet as first lord of the admiralty in Pitt's last government (1804–1806), only to be accused of malversation as treasurer of the navy 20 years earlier and impeached. He was acquitted of all charges but never held office again. Dundas died in Edinburgh on April 28, 1811.

D. B. HORN, *University of Edinburgh*

DUNDAS, dun'dəs, a town in southwestern Ontario, Canada, is an industrial center and retail distribution point. It also serves as a residential suburb of Hamilton, 2 miles (3.2 km) to the east, where about a third of Dundas' labor force is employed. Dundas' principal manufactures are machine tools, furniture, store fixtures, showcases, and textiles. The town was incorporated in 1847. Population: 19,586.

DUNDAS STRAIT, dun'dəs, is a channel in northern Australia that connects Van Diemen Gulf with the Timor and Arafura seas. About 18 miles (29 km) wide, the strait separates Melville Island from Coburg Peninsula.

DUNDEE, Viscount of. See GRAHAM, JOHN.

DUNDEE, dun-dē', the third-largest city in Scotland, lies in a semicircle on the north bank of the Firth of Tay about 40 miles (65 km) north of Edinburgh. A royal burgh and a "county of city," with county status, Dundee is second only to Glasgow as a manufacturing center in Scotland. Few of Dundee's ancient buildings remain, the most notable being the rebuilt 15th century tower adjoining the City Churches, a mid-19th century building housing three parish churches.

Dundee is popularly known as "the city of jute, jam, and journalism." It is the principal British producer of jute and once led the world in jute production. Marmalade was first made in Dundee, and the city is now known for its production of preserves and confectionery. Its "journalism" fame stems from the fact that Dundee is an important publishing center for national magazines and local newspapers.

Since World War II, Dundee's economy has been diversified with light electrical and engineering industries. The city is also a port on the North Sea and has a small shipyard. The Firth of Tay, about 2 miles (3 km) wide at Dundee, is spanned by the longest bridges in Britain—a highway bridge, opened in 1966, and a railway bridge.

The University of Dundee, chartered in 1967, is an outgrowth of the university college founded there in 1881. The Duncan of Jordanstone College of Art, a technical college, and a college of education are also in Dundee.

Created a royal burgh in 1200, Dundee became an important town in the Middle Ages. In Scotland's wars with England, the city, as a seaport, was always vulnerable. After the English assault of 1651, it made no important contributions to the Scottish economy until the 19th century. Population: (1966) 184,870.

C. J. BARTLETT, *University of Dundee*

DUNDEE's Old Steeple, 180 feet high, is an historic landmark. Its construction dates from the 15th century.

DUNDONALD, 10th Earl of. See COCHRANE, THOMAS.

DUNE, a windblown embankment of sand-size sediment. Dunes may form in any climate zone, but they are especially important and extensive in the arid deserts and semiarid steppes that cover 26% of the earth's land area. Dunes also are found along oceanic coastal areas and along lake shores.

Quartz sand is the most common dune material; in typical dunes, such as those of the Egyptian desert, the particles range from 0.004 to 0.008 inches (0.2–0.4 mm) in diameter. Dunes of medium-grade gypsum sand are found in the White Sands region of New Mexico, whereas calcite sands are the dominant dune material on atolls and other coral islands.

Large pyramidal or star-shaped dunes up to 500 feet (150 meters) high are found in deserts where winds come alternately from many directions and with roughly the same intensity. In the Rub al-Khali Desert of the Arabian peninsula, sigmoidal (S-shaped) dunes up to 300 feet (90 meters) high occur where winds of equal intensity blow from opposite directions. Dominantly one-direction winds may form *transverse dunes* with long axes at right angles to the wind. Individual crescent-shaped transverse dunes (with points downwind from the main mass) are called *barchan dunes.* They may be up to 100 feet (30 meters) high. Where many barchanlike dunes have merged, the result is a huge, migrating sand mass called a *sand sea.*

Under the same wind conditions, rates of migration of barchan dunes vary with their size. Thus, in the coastal desert of southern Peru, barchan dunes 3 feet (nearly 1 meter) high migrate about 100 feet (30 meters) per year, whereas dunes 22 feet (7 meters) high migrate about 30 feet (9 meters) per year.

Longitudinal desert dunes are oriented parallel to the dominant wind. The largest reported dunes of this type are the 700-foot (200-meter) seif, or sword, dunes of the Iranian desert.

In coastal areas, the presence of a sparse grass and shrub vegetation favors growth of *coastal blowout dunes;* they are crescent-shaped transverse dunes with the points of their crescents in a windward direction. Irregular dune ridges that run more or less parallel to the coastline are usually found on the backshore, where they have been partially or completely stabilized by vegetation. Longitudinal dunes in coastal regions take the form of low, parallel streamers of sand extending landward from the backshore.

WARREN E. YASSO
Teachers College, Columbia University

DUNEDIN, dun-ē′dən, a city in New Zealand, is at the head of Otago Harbour on the southeastern coast of South Island. It is the second-largest city of South Island and the chief shipping and industrial center of Otago provincial district. Industries include the processing of agricultural and pastoral products, brewing, chemical and fertilizer production, engineering, and the manufacture of consumer goods. Principal exports through the port of Dunedin and nearby Port Chalmers are wool and frozen meat. Major imports are petroleum products, fertilizers, and steel.

The commercial district of Dunedin lies along the waterfront below residential areas that rise on numerous hills. The University of Otago (founded in 1869), a teacher training college, art galleries, museums, and numerous public parks are located in the city.

Scottish immigrants settled Dunedin in 1848 and gave it the Gaelic name for Edinburgh. The settlement grew rapidly following the discovery of gold in the area in the 1860's. Population: (1966) urban area, 108,734; city, 77,149.

HOWARD J. CRITCHFIELD
Western Washington State College

DUNFERMLINE, dun-fûrm′lin, a royal and parliamentary burgh in Fife, Scotland, situated about 12 miles (20 km) northwest of Edinburgh across the Firth of Forth. The town grew up around the abbey church, founded by Malcolm III MacDuncan. Malcolm was married at Dunfermline in 1607. After her death, his wife was canonized as St. Margaret. The abbey was the burial place of several Scottish kings, including King Robert the Bruce. Adjoining the abbey was the royal palace, now in ruins, which continued to be a residence of the Scots royal family until the union of the crowns (1603). Charles I was born there in 1600.

The prosperity of modern Dunfermline rests on its linen industry and engineering works and the collieries that surround it. Andrew Carnegie, (1835–1919), the American industrialist and philanthropist, was born in Dunfermline, the descendant of a radical family of weavers. He presented a public library, hall, and baths to his birthplace and made it the headquarters for some of his charitable trusts. He also gave its citizens Pittencrieff Park and Glen, which protected the abbey and palace with open space and provided a superb recreation ground.

Dunfermline's boundaries were extended in 1911 to include the naval base of Rosyth on the Firth of Forth. The opening of the Forth Road Bridge in 1964 gave new impetus to the town's development. Population: (1966) 46,790.

D. B. HORN, *University of Edinburgh*

DUNG BEETLE, any of a large family of beetles found throughout the world and named for their habit of burrowing into dung and sometimes rolling it into balls. The beetles place their eggs in the dung, which serves as food for both the larvae and the adults.

Dung beetles have oval, usually black bodies that vary in size from ¼ inch (6 mm) to nearly 1 inch (25 mm). One of the best-known species is the dorbeetle. See also DORBEETLE.

DUNHAM, dun′əm, **Katherine** (1910–   ), American dancer, choreographer, and teacher, who made effective theater of primitive and urban Negro dance. An anthropologist as well as an artist, Miss Dunham used her expert knowledge of the cultural heritages of Afro-Caribbean, Afro-Brazilian, and other peoples as the basis for her dance techniques and to provide material for her choreography.

Miss Dunham was born in Joliet, Ill., and earned a B. A. and an M. A. in anthropology at the University of Chicago. While studying, she formed a small dance group with other Negro artists, and, encouraged by the choreographer Ruth Page, they performed at the Chicago Civic Opera and in concerts. A Rosenwald fellowship enabled her to make the first of several trips to the West Indies to study native dances and folklore. From this material she developed a repertoire of dances, and in 1940 she and her company made their New York debut in a series of concerts that established her as a major figure in the world of dance. Subsequently she appeared as dancer and actress in such Broadway musicals as *Cabin in the Sky* (1940) and *Carib Song* (1945); in films, including *Carnival of Rhythm* (1941) and *Star-Spangled Rhythm* (1942); and in her own revues. With her company she toured in the United States, Mexico, and Europe.

Miss Dunham's dances of primitive origin include *Shango,* dealing with voodoo; *Bahiana,* a Brazilian seduction dance; *L'Ag'Ya,* a dance drama culminating in a fighting dance; and *Rites du Passage,* concerned with the evoking of magical forces. Among her dances of the urbanized Negro are *Flaming Youth 1927, Blues,* and *Ragtime.* They use much African pelvic movement as well as American social dance forms. Many were staged by John Pratt, her husband.

Miss Dunham opened her own school in New York City and in 1963 choreographed dances for the Metropolitan Opera production of *Aïda*. She also lectured at American universities and at the Royal Anthropological Society in London. She published many articles and two autobiographical books—*Journey to Accompong* (1946) and *Touch of Innocence* (1959).

WALTER TERRY
Author of "The Ballet Companion"

DUNITE, dōō'nīt, is a dark igneous rock of the peridotite group. The peridotites consist chiefly of varying proportions of the minerals olivine (a magnesium iron silicate) and pyroxene, with very little feldspar present. Dunite, in particular, is almost wholly olivine and contains no feldspar. The rock occurs in solid granular masses, often in association with the important chromium ore, chromite. Platinum is found associated with chromite in some dunite rocks.

DUNKARDS, dung'kərdz, a name commonly applied to a group of Protestant sects originating in Germany and now located in the United States. The name refers to the practice of baptism by immersion. The largest group of Dunkards is the Church of the Brethren. See also GERMAN BAPTIST BRETHREN.

DUNKIRK, dun'kûrk, is a city in northern France, in Nord department, in what was once the province of Flanders. It lies on the coast near the Belgian border, at the eastern end of the Strait of Dover, the body of water that connects the English Channel with the North Sea.

Dunkirk (French, *Dunkerque*) is the principal seaport for the nearby cities of Lille, Tourcoing, Roubaix, and the other industrial centers of the densely settled Nord district, which is one of the major industrial regions of France. It ranks as France's third port in tonnage handled and first in the amount of coal and minerals imported. Its busy harbor has over 6 miles (10 km) of wharves.

Dunkirk is also a major industrial city, with important shipyards and a large oil-refining capacity. It is the site of one of the six big coastal iron and steel works that were established in the Common Market countries in the middle 1960's.

History. A very old stronghold city, Dunkirk (literally "church among the dunes") has weathered many sieges, battles, and bombardments. It was ruled successively by the Burgundians, Spaniards, and English. In 1658 the English and French defeated the Spaniards at Dunkirk, and thereafter the city reverted permanently to France. In the 17th century it was a center for piracy, and in the 18th century it became an object of dispute between the French and the English; the English wanted its fortifications destroyed.

In World War I, Dunkirk, which was a major naval base, suffered severe damage. During World War II, from May 29 to June 2, 1940, the city was completely surrounded by German forces and became the scene of historic and almost miraculous evacuation of Allied troops to England by a flotilla of warships and commercial, fishing, and pleasure vessels, large and small. Despite withering fire from the German air force, about 350,000 troops, of whom more than 100,000 were remnants of the defeated French and Belgians, were saved. On June 4, when the Germans captured the city, only about 40,000 Allied troops were left.

Later, Dunkirk suffered heavy bombings and more destruction in the land fighting that preceded its fall to the Allies on May 9, 1945. About 85% of the city was completely destroyed by the end of the war. Since then it has been rebuilt as a spacious modern city. The port was renovated and considerably enlarged in the years immediately following World War II. Population: (1962) 26,197.

HOMER PRICE, *Hunter College*

DUNKIRK, dun'kûrk, a city in southwestern New York, in Chautauqua county, is situated on Lake Erie, 41 miles (66 km) southwest of Buffalo. Dunkirk has an excellent harbor, protected by a breakwater. It is a port of entry, and there is extensive trade with Great Lakes ports. The city's chief manufactured products are stainless steel, oil-refining machinery, radiators and boilers, marine motors, valves, shovels and hoes, glass reflectors and bowls, and silk gloves. It is the center of an agricultural region.

Dunkirk was settled in the first decade of the 19th century. It was incorporated as a village in 1837 and received a city charter in 1880. Government is by mayor and council. Population: 15,310.

DUNLAP, William (1766–1839), American playwright, theater manager, painter, and historian. He was born in Perth Amboy, N. J., on Feb. 19, 1766, and was blinded in one eye from a boyhood accident. He studied painting at home and from 1784 to 1789 worked with the American painter Benjamin West in London, where he developed a strong interest in the theater. His comedy *The Father* was produced in 1789 in New York City. In 1796 he bought an interest in a New York theater firm, which produced his plays. Theatrical ventures, painting, editing, and writing occupied him for the rest of his life. He died in New York City on Sept. 28, 1839.

Dunlap has been called America's first professional playwright. His many plays include *Leicester* (1794) and *André* (1798). Among his historical works is *The History of the American Theatre* (1832).

DUNLOP, John Boyd (1840–1921), Scottish inventor of the first commercially successful pneumatic tire. He was born in Dreghorn, Ayrshire, on Feb. 5, 1840. While a veterinary surgeon in Belfast, Ireland, he conceived the idea of a cushion of air to reduce the vibration of the solid rubber tires of his son's tricycle. Robert William Thomson had been issued a British patent in 1845 for a pneumatic tire, but it had found little application.

In 1888, Dunlop was given a British patent for an all-rubber inner tube, covered by a canvas jacket with a rubber tread. Flaps in the jacket were rubber-cemented to the wheel. He began commercial production in 1890, and his company soon obtained other patents for fastening the tire to the wheel by wires in the tire edges which engaged in a wheel rim. Dunlop died in Dublin, Ireland, on Oct. 23, 1921.

ROBERT S. WOODBURY
Massachusetts Institute of Technology

DUNMORE, dun-môr', **Earl of** (1732–1809), British colonial governor in America. He was born John Murray, in Scotland, the eldest son of a Scottish peer. He served in the British Army until he succeeded to his father's title and estates in 1756. In 1770, Dunmore was appointed governor of New York; after serving for 11 months, he became governor of Virginia.

Flexible in following royal instructions, Dunmore was at first a popular governor. He encouraged western settlement—thereby bringing on the so-called Lord Dunmore's War with the Shawnee Indians, in which chief Cornstalk was defeated. However, growing hostility in Virginia toward England made Dunmore's position difficult, and when he convened the Assembly in June 1775 to consider Lord North's conciliatory proposals, a rebellion ensued. Dunmore fled to a British man-of-war. He appealed to his old enemy Cornstalk to take up arms against the rebels, and he proclaimed the slaves in the colony free. Before returning to England he launched attacks on the Virginia coast and set fire to Norfolk. Dunmore later served as governor of the Bahamas. He died in Ramsgate, England, in May 1809.

GEORGE D. LANGDON, JR., *Vassar College*

DUNMORE, a borough in northeastern Pennsylvania, is in Lackawanna county, east of Scranton, in an anthracite region. The community was settled in 1783 and named Buckstown. It was renamed in 1840 in honor of a visiting son of the 5th Earl of Dunmore, who promised to raise money in England to build a railroad through the town. The railroad never was built. The borough, incorporated in 1862, has a mayor-council form of government. Population: 16,781.

DUNNE, Finley Peter (1867–1936), American political satirist, best known for his "Mr. Dooley" essays in newspapers and periodicals. Born in Chicago on July 10, 1867, Dunne became a reporter for various Chicago papers and from 1897 to 1900 edited the Chicago *Journal*. In 1900 he was invited by William C. Whitney to edit the New York *Morning Telegraph*. In 1911, Dunne retired and lived in relative obscurity. He died in New York on April 24, 1936.

Mr. Dooley, a skeptical Chicago Irish bartender, often delivered his political, social, and philosophical comments to his gullible friend Mr. Hennessey. Through Mr. Dooley, Dunne attacked corruption in government, big business, and American imperialism (especially during the Spanish-American War). Dunne's humanitarian outlook put him on the side of reform, but he was not a political radical.

Mr. Dooley may be seen as a descendant of James Russell Lowell's Hosea Biglow (see BIGLOW PAPERS), but instead of a rural Yankee, an urban Irishman plays the shrewd philosopher. Mr. Dooley's pronouncements, delivered in a thick Irish brogue, became enormously popular and were widely reprinted and repeated. The pieces remain readable for their wit and wisdom; each is a polished little dialogue often winding up with a pithy statement. The first collection, *Mr. Dooley in Peace and War* (1898), was followed by several more volumes, ending with *Mr. Dooley on Making a Will and Other Necessary Evils* (1919).

JEROME STERN, *Florida State University*

Further Reading: Ellis, Elmer, *Mr. Dooley's America* (New York 1941).

DUNNING, John Ray (1907–1975), American nuclear physicist who is best known for his historic measurement of the energy released from the fission of natural uranium and for showing that separated U-235 would fission under neutron bombardment. He was born in Shelby, Nebr., on Sept. 24, 1907, graduated from Nebraska Wesleyan University in 1929, and received his Ph. D. from Columbia University in 1934. He continued at Columbia, where he became a professor of physics in 1946 and dean of the school of engineering and applied science in 1950.

Dunning laid the foundation for much of the early development of nuclear physics in the United States. In 1939 he measured the energy released from uranium fission, and in 1940 he and Alfred Nier showed that the isotope U-235 would fission. That same year, he and his colleagues invented the gas diffusion system for separating U-235 from uranium ore. He directed much of the work leading to the production of U-235 at facilities in Oak Ridge, Tenn., Ohio, and Kentucky. He also served as scientific director for the construction of a 385-million-volt synchrocyclotron at Irvington-on-Hudson, N. Y. He died in Key Biscayne, Fla., on Aug. 25, 1975.

ROBERT A. HARPER, *Columbia University*

DUNNING, William Archibald (1857–1922), American historian. He was born in Plainfield, N. J., on May 12, 1857. He spent almost 45 years at Columbia University as student (Ph. D., 1885) and professor, becoming the university's first Lieber professor of history and political philosophy in 1904.

In his writings Dunning was the first historian to provide a thorough, scholarly, and dispassionate study of the Reconstruction Period. His outstanding works in this field are *Essays on the Civil War and Reconstruction* (1897; rev. ed., 1904), in which he held that the Reconstruction acts were political rather than economic, and *Reconstruction: Political and Economic, 1865–1877*, in which the North is scrutinized as well as the South. Dunning also wrote *History of Political Theories, Ancient and Mediaeval* (3 vols., 1902–1920). He died on Aug. 25, 1922.

DUNNVILLE, a town in southern Ontario, Canada, is on the Grand River, about 5 miles (8 km) north of Lake Erie. Among its manufactures are knitted goods, draperies and tapestries, sashes and doors, and wire fencing. The community grew after its site was chosen in 1827 as a terminus of a feeder to the Welland Canal. Dunnville was incorporated as a village in 1860 and as a town in 1900. Population: 11,353.

DUNOIS, dü-nwà', **Count de** (c. 1403–1468), French soldier, who was one of Charles VII's most famous military leaders. He was the illegitimate son of Mariette d'Enghien and Louis, Duke d'Orléans, and was named Jean. He was widely known as *le Bâtard d'Orléans*.

His military prowess was first recognized when he delivered the town of Montargis from the English in 1427. In 1428–1429 he took part in the defense of Orléans against the Duke of Bedford and helped induce the Dauphin Charles (the future Charles VII) to accept the aid of Joan of Arc. He fought beside Joan before the walls of Paris in August 1429 but could not prevent her capture. After Charles' coronation in 1429, Jean joined in the reconquest of northern France. He was created Count de Dunois in 1439.

Dunois' military reputation and royal (though illegitimate) blood made him an important figure in several plots and rebellions. In 1440 he joined the Duke d'Alençon, the Dauphin Louis, and others in a revolt known as the *Praguerie*, but Charles bribed him into defecting. In 1461 he joined the *Ligue du bien public* (League of the Public Weal) against the former Dauphin, now King Louis XI. He returned to Louis' favor in 1465. He died on Nov. 24, 1468, at L'Hay.

FREDRIC L. CHEYETTE, *Amherst College*

DUNS SCOTUS, dunz skŏt'əs, **John** (1265/1266–1308), Scottish theologian and philosopher, known as the Subtle Doctor. He was born in Duns, Berwickshire, Scotland. He entered the Franciscan order at the age of 15 and was ordained a priest in 1291. Scotus seems to have studied in Paris from 1293 to 1296 and to have returned to England to lecture on the *Sentences* of Peter Lombard at Oxford. In 1302 he was teaching at Paris, but was banished in June 1303 for his support of Pope Boniface VIII against King Philip IV (the Fair) of France. In 1304 he again taught in Paris and became regent master of theology in 1305.

Toward the end of 1307, Scotus was transferred to Cologne, where he died suddenly on Nov. 8, 1308. His remains are buried in the choir of the Franciscan church in Cologne. Scotus is venerated as a saint within the Franciscan order, but the cult is not universally recognized.

The canon of Scotus' work has long been uncertain, partly because his works, which include treatises on grammar, logic, metaphysics, and theology, have come down to us mainly in reports written by his pupils, often with additions of the reporter's own composition. Recent studies have proved that certain works long attributed to Scotus are definitely spurious. The *Opus Oxoniense* and *Reportata Parisiensia*, his commentaries on the *Sentences* of Peter Lombard, are undoubtedly authentic and constitute, together with the *Quaestiones quodlibetales* and the *De primo principio*, the best source of Scotus' doctrine. Other authentic works are his various commentaries on Aristotle's logic, the *Quaestiones in libros Aristotelis de anima*, left incomplete, the *Collationes Oxonienses* and *Collationes Parisienses*, and the *Quaestiones subtilissimae in metaphysicam Aristotelis* (the first nine books only). The authenticity of the *Theoremata* is still under discussion.

Scotus' works were edited by Luke Wadding (12 vols., Lyon 1639) and reprinted by L. Vivès (26 vols., Paris 1891–1895). A commission of Franciscan scholars, headed by Father Charles Balić, is preparing a critical edition of all Scotus' works, *Opera omnia, studio et Cura Commissionis scotisticae ad fidem cadicum edita* (Vatican City 1950–). By 1963 seven volumes of his works were completed.

Scotist Philosophy. Scotus is the leader of the Franciscan school of philosophy and theology, just as St. Thomas Aquinas is the leader of the Dominican school. Powerful thinker that he was, he attempted to harmonize Augustinianism and Thomism into a superior synthesis that would overcome the contrast between the two systems and make up for their deficiencies. For this reason criticism occupies an important place in his writings. Such criticism is directed not against Thomistic doctrines alone but against Augustinian doctrines as well. Because of his depth of thought and sharpness of mind, Scotus' place as philosopher and theologian is among the highest.

In philosophy, he maintains that the proper object of the human intellect is being as being and not merely the essence of material things, as Aquinas teaches. The concept of being is univocal, which means that it can be predicated in the same way both of God and of creatures, prescinding from their intrinsic modes of being, such as finiteness and infinity. Thus Scotist univocity leaves intact the metaphysical transcendence of God.

Scotus accepts the theory that matter and form are the substantial principles of material bodies. Yet he departs from Aquinas in saying that prime matter is not pure potentiality. Matter has an act of its own, the act of being matter, independently of form. To assure the objectivity of our universal concepts, Scotus elaborates the theory of the common nature (*natura communis*) as a distinct "formality" that exists singularly in concrete things and becomes universal in the intellect. While the common nature—for example, humanity—makes a thing belong to a particular species, the principle of individuation, or that which distinguishes one individual from the rest within the same species, is for Scotus a positive perfection which he calls *haecceitas*, or "thisness."

According to Scotus, there are two forms in man, the form of corporeity (*forma corporeitatis*) and the soul. The form of corporeity is the ultimate disposition of matter that enables it to receive the soul, and remains in the body even after the soul's departure. Scotus refuses to consider intellect and will as faculties really distinct from the soul, as Aquinas teaches. Between the soul and its faculties, as well as between the faculties themselves, he admits only a "formal" distinction (*distinctio formalis a parte rei*). This distinction obtains between entities or formalities that exist in one and the same thing but are neither really distinct nor formally identical. Scotus holds that the immortality of the soul is known by faith, and that no strict metaphysical demonstration of it is possible. The natural reason can only produce "probable and persuasive arguments" for the support of this doctrine.

Scotus argues to the existence of God from efficiency, finality, and the degrees of perfection, taking as his starting point the possibility of things rather than their actual existence. The possibility of things is a metaphysical truth; their actual existence is only a fact of contingent experience. For him, radical infinity is the attribute that best distinguishes God from creatures and constitutes Him in his absolute unicity and perfection. It represents also the climax of his metaphysical proof for God's existence. Creation is primarily an act of the will of God, so that things exist and are true and good because God wills them. However, God wills always "in a most rational and orderly way."

Ethics and Theology. Scotus' ethics is an attempt to show that goodness and duty are meaningful only inasmuch as they are related to supreme goodness and duty. Against Aquinas, he admits the possibility of morally indifferent acts in the concrete. He also maintains that only those of the Ten Commandments that concern our duties toward God belong to the natural law in the strict sense. The other commandments belong to the natural law taken in a broad sense.

The theology of Scotus centers on the notion of God as love. Creation is the effect of God's love, inasmuch as He communicates His goodness to creatures so that they will love Him freely. Sanctifying grace is identical with the infused virtue of charity and has its seat in the will. The sacraments are not the physical cause of grace, although they really produce grace. Because of his theory of the superiority of the will over the intellect, Scotus asserts that man's heavenly happiness will consist primarily in the love of God.

Divine love shines particularly in the Incarnation of the Word, which, according to Scotus, would have taken place even if Adam had not sinned. For Christ is the archetype, the center and end of the universe both as man and as God, and His Incarnation could not have been determined by the original sin. Redemption is also a work of love. Yet, in Scotus' view, the merits of Christ are only infinite in a broader sense.

Although several of Scotus' doctrines have gained wide recognition even among theologians outside his school, his name has gone down in history as closely associated with the doctrine of the Immaculate Conception, of which he became the champion.

BERNARDINO M. BONANSEA, O. F. M.
The Catholic University of America

Further Reading: Bettoni, Efrem, *Duns Scotus: The Basic Principles of His Philosophy*, tr. and ed. by Bernardino Bonansea (Washington 1961); Copleston, Frederick C., *A History of Philosophy*, vol. 2 pp. 476–551 (Westminster, Md., 1950); Gilson, Étienne H., *Jean Duns Scot* (Paris 1952); Ryan, John K., and Bonansea, Bernardino M., eds., *John Duns Scotus, 1265–1965*, vol. 3 of *Studies in Philosophy and the History of Philosophy* (Washington 1965).

DUNSANY, dun-sā′nē, **Lord** (1878–1957), Irish writer, whose fiction, poems, and plays blend realism and fantasy. He was born Edward John Moreton Drax Plunkett, in London, on July 24, 1878, and was educated at Eton and Sandhurst. In 1899, on the death of his father, he became the 18th Baron Dunsany. In addition to being a writer, Lord Dunsany was a distinguished sportsman and chess player. In 1940–1941 he served as Byron professor of English literature at the University of Athens.

Lord Dunsany, a self-confessed dreamer and spinner of fantasies, was a prolific writer of short stories, novels, plays, poetry, and memoirs. He published his first volume of short stories, *The Gods of Pegana*, in 1905; his first play, *The Glittering Gate*, was produced by the Abbey Theatre, Dublin, in 1909. *The Gods of the Mountains*, a mixture of ironic humor and grotesque horror, was moderately successful when acted in London in 1911 and at the Abbey Theatre in 1929. Another stage fantasy, *If*, had a long run in London in 1921, partly because the cast included two highly popular English players, Gladys Cooper and Henry Ainley. A one-act play popular with amateur groups is *A Night at an Inn* (1916).

Lord Dunsany's best novel is probably *The Charwoman's Shadow* (1926). Among his volumes of verse is *Fifty Poems* (1930), and his autobiographical writings include *The Sirens Wake* (1945).

Lord Dunsany's Oriental allegories and artificial mythologies did not attract the general public. His plays and stories begin far better than they end, which may account for his having never achieved notable success either in Dublin or London. The best books on the Abbey Theatre have only the most fleeting and cursory mention of his plays, though a few were acted there. He died in Dublin on Oct. 25, 1957.

ALAN DENT
Author of "Mrs. Patrick Campbell"

DUNSTABLE, dun′stə-bəl, **John** (died 1453), English composer. Described in an astronomical treatise as a "musician to the Duke of Bedford," he may have been a native of the town of Dunstable in Bedfordshire. He evidently spent much of his life in France, presumably in the service of the Duke, who was the brother of King Henry V of England.

Dunstable seems to have enjoyed considerable fame as a composer and musical innovator, and his compositions had a major influence on music in France. His works, chiefly masses and motets, were collected in the eighth volume of *Musica Britannica* (1953), which also includes two chansons, *Puisque m'amour* and *O rosa bella*, that are believed to be his. He was also well versed in astronomy and mathematics. Dunstable died in London on Dec. 24, 1453.

DUNSTAN, dun′stən, **Saint** (c.910–988), English monk and archbishop of Canterbury. Dunstan was born near Glastonbury, England. He was educated by Irish monks at Glastonbury and lived for a time in the household of his uncle, the archbishop of Canterbury. Brought to the attention of King Athelstan because of his learning, he served for a brief period at court but left because of the jealousy of courtiers. He became a Benedictine monk at Glastonbury and retired to a hermitage nearby. There he worked as a scribe, illuminating many manuscripts, and as a silversmith and a composer. In 943 he was made abbot of Glastonbury by King Edmund.

As counselor to kings from Athelstan to Æthelred II, Dunstan became the first of a long line of ecclesiastical statesmen. Exiled by King Edwy, he spent two years in Ghent, where he became familiar with the Continental monastic reform movement initiated at the Abbey of Cluny. Recalled to England in 957 by King Edgar, he became his chief minister and was largely responsible for the legislation of that reign. Under Edgar he became bishop of Worcester and of London successively and then archbishop of Canterbury in 961.

Dunstan introduced the Cluniac reform into English monasteries and, with the aid of Saints Æthelwold of Winchester and Oswald of York, corrected many clerical abuses. Shortly after the death of King Edward the Martyr in 978, Dunstan retired to Canterbury, where he taught in the cathedral school until his death on May 19, 988. His feast is observed on May 19.

SISTER ALPHONSUS MARIE SAWKINS, I. H. M.
Marygrove College, Detroit

DUODECIMAL SYSTEM, dōō-ə-des′ə-məl, a system of notation for real numbers that is based on the number 12. It is similar to the decimal system, with 12 replacing 10 as a base.

Historical Background. In the 18th and 19th centuries, Charles XII of Sweden, the Count de Buffon, Isaac Pitman, and Herbert Spencer were among those who advocated adoption of the duodecimal system. In the 20th century there has been a resurgence of interest. Duodecimal societies, such as the Duodecimal Society of America (founded in 1944), sprang up in the United States and abroad, publishing literature on the advantages of the base 12 system.

Since 12 has six divisors—1,2,3,4,6, and 12—some commonly occurring fractions have a simpler duodecimal form than the corresponding decimal form. Also, use of base 12 introduces a consistency between numeration and metrology. Eggs, for example, are sold by the dozen, and a foot is 12 inches.

The main objections to the adoption of the duodecimal system are the cost and labor of converting from the decimal system. Also, high-speed electronic computation makes advantages of the duodecimal system relatively minor.

Number Systems. The duodecimal system is one of many positional systems of numeration. In such systems, the base, or radix, b, can be any positive integer other than 1. Numerals used for whole numbers less than the base are called *digits.* There are b different digits in a system base b. Thus, if $b = 2$, the digits are 0 and 1. If $b = 12$, the digits are $0, 1, \ldots, 9, t, e$ (t corresponding to ten, and e corresponding to eleven). The value of a digit depends upon its position in the numeral. Any whole number can be written uniquely in base b as:

$$d_n \ldots d_2 d_1 d_0 = d_n b^n + \ldots + d_2 b^2 + d_1 b + d_0 \quad (1)$$

where the $d_n, d_1, d_2 \ldots$ represent any one of the digits from 0 to $b - 1$. For example, $314_{12} = 3(12)^2 + 1(12) + 4$. A number between 0 and 1 can be written as:

$$.d_1 d_2 d_3 \ldots = d_1 b^{-1} + d_2 b^{-2} + d_3 b^{-3} \ldots \quad (2)$$

For example, $.15_{12} = 1(12)^{-1} + 5(12)^{-2}$. Note that the base number is designated by a subscript written in the 10 scale.

Conversion. To convert an integer from base 10 to base 12, successive division is performed by 12. The duodecimal digits are the ascending vertical array of remainders. For example, $359_{10} = [d_2 d_1 d_0]_{12} = 25e$ since

$359 \div 12 = 29$; remainder $e = d_0$
$29 \div 12 = 2$; remainder $5 = d_1$
$2 \div 12 = 0$; remainder $2 = d_2$.

To convert a decimal fraction from base 10 to base 12, successive multiplication is performed by 12, with whole numbers being detached. The duodecimal digits are the descending vertical array of whole numbers. For example $.125_{10} = [.d_1 d_2]_{12} = .16_{12}$ since $.125 \times 12 = 1.500$; $1 = d_1$
$.500 \times 12 = 6.000$; $6 = d_2$.
In changing numbers from base 12 to base 10, expansions (1) and (2) can be used. For example, $e8.6_{12} = e(12)^1 + 8(12)^0 + 6(12)^{-1}{}_{10} = 140.5_{10}$.

Operations. Rules of base 10 arithmetic apply to duodecimal arithmetic, although the addition and multiplication tables for base 12 are different from the tables for base 10. The equation $e + 1 = 10_{12}$ is important for carrying in addition and for borrowing in subtraction. For example, $1e + 2t = 49_{12}$.
For the units column,
$t + e = (t - 1) + (e + 1)$
$= (9) + (10)$
$= 9$, and carry 1.
For the twelves column,
$2 + 1$, and carry of $1 = 4$.
See also NUMBER SYSTEMS AND NOTATIONS.

LOUISE GRINSTEIN
Kingsborough Community College, N. Y.

Further Reading: Andrews, F. Emerson, *New Numbers* (New York 1964); Terry, George S., *Duodecimal Arithmetic* (New York 1938).

DUODENUM, the first segment of the small intestine. See INTESTINE.

DUPANLOUP, dü-pän-lōō′, **Félix Antoine Philibert** (1802–1878), French Roman Catholic bishop of Orléans. The illegitimate son of a peasant, Anne Dechosal, he was born at St.-Félix, in Savoy, on Jan. 3, 1802. He was ordained a priest in 1825 and served as curate in Paris and director of the Seminary of St. Nicholas (1837–1845), where he gained fame for his new educational methods and for his deathbed reconciliation of Talleyrand to the faith.

Named bishop of Orléans in 1849, Dupanloup became nationally prominent both as a defender of the church against anticlericalism and as a proponent of liberal ideas within the church. He was elected to the French Academy in 1854. Though he was a staunch defender of the temporal power of the papacy and admitted the doctrine of papal infallibility, he opposed its definition as inopportune at the First Vatican Council (1869–1870). He was elected to the French National Assembly (1871) and the Senate (1875). He died at Lacombe (Isère) on Oct. 11, 1878.

JOHN T. FORD, C. S. C.
Catholic University of America

DUPARC, dü-pàrk′, **Henri** (1848–1933), French composer, who is best known for his dramatic and sensitive songs based on the poems of major contemporary French poets. These songs, influenced by Schubert's lieder, constituted the high point of vocal expression in French music in the late 19th century.

Marie Eugène Henri Fouques-Duparc was born in Paris on Jan. 21, 1848. Inspired by César Franck, under whom he studied piano at the Jesuit College of Vaugirard from 1872 to 1875, Duparc made music his career. A perfectionist, Duparc destroyed much of his work, and after a serious nervous disorder he stopped composing altogether in 1885. The small volume of his work that remains, in addition to his songs, includes the symphonic poem *Lenore* (1875), the orchestral nocturne *Aux étoiles* (1910), and a motet for three voices, *Benedicat vobis Dominus* (1882). Duparc died on Feb. 12, 1933, at Mont-de-Marsan.

DUPIN, Amandine Aurore Lucie. See SAND, GEORGE.

DU PIN, dü paṅ′, **Louis Ellies** (1657–1719), French priest and church historian. Du Pin (or *Dupin*) was born in Paris on June 17, 1657. He received his doctorate in theology at the Sorbonne in 1684. Two years later he began to publish *Bibliothèque universelle des auteurs ecclésiastiques* (1686–1691), a history of Christian literature, which was severely criticized by Bishop Bossuet and others and resulted in a censure by the archbishop of Paris in 1691. However, Du Pin eventually completed the work under another title. In 1713 he refused to submit to Clement XI's bull *Unigenitus*, on the doctrine of Jansenism; he was suspected of unorthodox beliefs and was temporarily exiled to Châtellerault. Du Pin also attempted to establish a dialogue between the Anglican and Roman Catholic churches through a correspondence with William Wake, archbishop of Canterbury. He died in Paris, on June 6, 1719.

MARK VANDERHEYDEN, *Rider College*

DUPLEIX, dü-pleks′, **Marquis** (1697–1763), French colonial administrator in India. Joseph François Dupleix was born in Landrecies, France, on Jan. 1, 1697. After voyages to India and America, he was appointed in 1721 to the superior council of the French East India Company at Pondicherry. Ten years later he was made superintendent of the French settlement at Chandernagore, and in 1742 he was appointed governor-general of French establishments in India.

During the War of the Austrian Succession (1740–1748) between France and Britain, Dupleix undertook military action against the British in India in the hope of expanding the French territories there. With the aid of the French fleet he took Madras and withstood a British siege of Pondicherry. However, the Peace of Aix-la-Chapelle (1748) nullified his gains. He exploited political divisions among contending Indian princes but was outmaneuvered by the British under the brilliant leadership of Robert Clive (q.v.). Dupleix was replaced in 1754 and returned, discredited, to France. He died in obscurity in Paris on Nov. 10, 1763.

WALTER HAUSER, *University of Virginia*

DUPLESSIS, dü-ple-sē', **Maurice Le Noblet** (1890–1959), Canadian political leader, who was premier of Quebec in 1936–1939 and 1944–1959. He was born in Trois-Rivières, Quebec, on April 20, 1890. After studying law at Laval University, he was called to the bar in 1913. In 1927 he was elected as a Conservative to the Quebec legislature and by 1933 was provincial party leader.

Duplessis and the new party he formed, the Union Nationale, won a large majority in the 1936 elections. As premier, he championed provincial autonomy, realizing that the centralizing policies of the federal government disquieted many French-speaking Quebecers. The Liberals won in Quebec in 1939, but Duplessis, profiting from French-Canadian opposition to federal Liberal war policies, regained power in 1944. He held that the federal government's financial policies unjustly restricted provincial initiatives. When, in 1954, Quebec instituted an income tax, the Canadian government was forced to review and modify its fiscal policies.

Duplessis' authoritarianism, mixing a clan chief's guile with an enlightened despot's assurance, became legendary, but he was not a dictator. Although toward the end of his life events had clearly passed him by, he contributed importantly to Quebec's evolution. He died in Schefferville, Quebec, on Sept. 7, 1959.

MICHEL BRUNET, *University of Montreal*

DUPLESSIS MORNAY, dü-ple-sē' môr-nā', **Philippe** (1549–1623), French Huguenot leader, theologian, and soldier. He was born in Buhy, Normandy, on Nov. 5, 1549. As an influential Huguenot he advocated an anti-Spanish policy and French support of the Dutch insurgents in the Spanish Netherlands. This fact made him a target for attack by the Catholic party in France, and he narrowly escaped the St. Bartholomew's Day massacre in 1572 and fled to England.

In behalf of Henry of Navarre, who sought the French throne, Mornay carried out important missions to England and the Netherlands from 1578 to 1581. On Henry's accession in 1589, Mornay was rewarded with the governorship of Saumur. When Henry became a Roman Catholic their friendship waned.

His publication of *De l'institution, usage et doctrine du saint sacrement de l'Eucharistie* (1598), a controversial work on the institution and doctrine of the sacrament of the Eucharist, led to a public debate in 1600 with Jacques Duperron, bishop of Évreux, into which Mornay believed he had been ensnared by the King. After the religious wars broke out again in 1621, Mornay retired to his castle at La-Forêt-sur-Sèvre, where he died on Nov. 11, 1623.

JAMES H. SMYLIE
Union Theological Seminary, Richmond, Va.

DUPLICATING MACHINES are devices for producing large numbers of copies of printed, typed, handwritten, or drawn matter from specially prepared masters. They are widely used in business, industry, schools, and other organizations. There are three principal types of duplicating machines: spirit process duplicators, stencil duplicators, and offset duplicators.

Spirit Process Duplicators. One of the earliest duplicating machines, and the most widely used of the machines, is the spirit process duplicator. The master copy is prepared by typing, writing, or drawing on the face of a master unit (a sheet of master paper and a sheet of spirit carbon). This results in a negative image in carbon deposits on the back of the master. The master is placed image-side-up on the drum of the duplicator. Each time the drum rotates, a sheet of copy paper, moistened with spirit fluid, is pressed against the master by the drum and the impression roller. The spirit fluid dissolves a minute quantity of the aniline dye which is on the carbon sheet, transferring it to the copy paper. Thus a positive image is produced on the paper. Up to five colors can be duplicated at the same time from a single master that is prepared with different spirit carbon sheets.

Modern spirit masters can produce from 5 to 350 copies. Some are capable of producing as many as 500 copies. Production speeds range up to 120 copies a minute. Spirit duplicators produce the lowest cost dry copies. Masters may be stored and used again until the carbon is depleted. Recharging permits them to be used without limit.

Stencil Duplicators. The production of copies by stencil duplicators, also called mimeograph machines, requires cutting a master, or stencil, which is a sheet of fibrous tissue with a wax coating that is impervious to ink. The master is cut by typing or by writing or drawing with a pointed stylus that pushes aside the coating so that ink can flow through the tissue. The stencil is placed on the duplicator cylinder, which is covered with an ink-saturated pad. When the impression roller pushes copy paper against the stencil cylinder, ink is forced through the fibrous tissue in the cut areas onto the paper.

Stencils can be used to produce from 1,000 to 10,000 copies. Stencils from which the ink has been removed may be stored and reused.

Offset Duplicators. Copies made by offset duplicators most closely resemble commercial printing. Offset duplicators can be used to reproduce halftone photographs as well as line copy. Paper masters are imaged by printing, typing, or drawing. Metal masters are usually imaged by photographic methods. The master is placed on a cylinder of the offset machine. Water, which is applied by a roller, adheres to the master except in the areas of the oil base ink image. The wet master is then inked again by another set of rollers. The ink adheres only to the image areas previously inked. A rubber blanket cylinder then receives a negative image in ink from the master to the blanket. Still another set of rollers presses the copy paper against the blanket, and a positive image is offset, or printed, on the paper.

Offset duplicators operate at high speeds (8,000 or more copies an hour) and have long runs (250 to over 2,500 copies from paper masters and up to 50,000 copies from metal masters).

W. T. WHITEHEAD
Bell & Howell Company

DU PONT, dōō-pont, is the name of a family that has been identified with American industry for more than 150 years. The family's full name is *du Pont de Nemours*. Members of the family founded and managed a company, bearing their name, that first manufactured gunpowder, and later synthetic textile fibers, plastics, and other chemical products, and became one of the principal industrial enterprises in the United States.

The company's full name is E. I. du Pont de Nemours & Company. In short form, the company now refers to itself as "Du Pont." The first company president who was not related to the du Pont family took office in 1940.

Du Ponts have been active also in military and naval affairs, state and national politics, various other public services, and philanthropy.

PIERRE SAMUEL DU PONT (1739–1817), born in Paris, was a French economist. Disenchanted by the militarism and absolutism of the French monarchy, he turned to the physiocratic school of economics, which preached economic and individual freedom. He was closely associated with François Quesnay, leader of the new school. He was also a protégé of Turgot, Louis XVI's minister of finance. Through him, Pierre Samuel became editor of the government's *Journal of Agriculture, Commerce and Finance* in 1765 and inspector general of commerce in 1774. When Turgot left office, du Pont retired temporarily, but he returned to public service in 1778.

During the early phase of the French Revolution, Pierre Samuel was active in the States General and then the Constituent Assembly, of which he was twice elected president. As the revolution grew more violent and radical, du Pont lost sympathy with it and was briefly imprisoned for his views. During this period he was in the printing and publishing business. After continued difficulties with the Jacobins, du Pont in 1799 emigrated to America, where he hoped to found a new colony on the Ohio River.

The colonization project failed to develop, and du Pont returned to France in 1802. He became secretary of the provisional government after Napoleon's downfall. When Napoleon returned to France in 1815, Pierre Samuel again fled to America, where his sons were citizens.

VICTOR MARIE DU PONT (1767–1827), elder son of Pierre Samuel, was born in Paris but became an American manufacturer. He entered the French diplomatic service in 1787 and was first stationed in Charleston, S.C. When Franco-American relations deteriorated after the XYZ Affair in 1798, Victor Marie returned to France. He settled permanently in the United States in 1800 and was associated with the family firm in an export-import business and other projects. In 1809 he joined his brother Éleuthère Irénée at Wilmington, where he managed the latter's woolen mills. He served as a captain of Delaware volunteers in the War of 1812, was a member of the Delaware legislature, and was a director of the Bank of the United States in Philadelphia.

SAMUEL FRANCIS DU PONT (1803–1865), son of Victor Marie, was born at Bergen Point, N.J., and became an American naval officer. He was appointed a midshipman in the Navy by President Madison in 1815. By 1842 he had risen to commander, and in 1845 he helped organize the administration of the new U.S. Naval Academy. Transferred to the Pacific in the same year, he served on the *Congress*. During the Mexican War he commanded the *Cyane* in operations along the California coast. He was appointed flag officer in 1861 and took command of the South Atlantic blockading squadron. In November, cooperating with Gen. Thomas Sherman's land forces, he took Port Royal, S.C. To enforce the blockade he established some 14 stations along the coast. Promoted to rear admiral in 1862, he led an unsuccessful attack on Charleston, S.C., in April 1863. Relieved of command, he went on inactive duty for the rest of the war.

ÉLEUTHÈRE IRÉNÉE DU PONT (1771–1834), born in Paris, the younger son of Pierre Samuel, established an American gunpowder firm that grew into the present diversified Du Pont company. A student of the chemist Antoine Lavoisier (q.v.), Éleuthère learned gunpowder manufacture in the French government's mills at Essonne. In 1791 he took charge of his father's printing and publishing house in Paris, and in 1799 he emigrated to the United States with his father. He was impressed by the poor quality of gunpowder manufactured in America and suggested that the family add this business to those it was considering. His father was skeptical, but in 1801, with active interest from the French government, the son organized a company to manufacture military and sporting gunpowder. The firm was capitalized at $36,000, and 11 of the 36 shares were held by the family firm, du Pont Père, Fils et Cie. Operations began on the banks of Brandywine Creek near Wilmington, Del., in 1802. The first powder was sold through Victor Marie's office in New York. Over opposition from an American investor in the venture, the firm was named E. I. du Pont de Nemours & Company.

Éleuthère Irénée guided his company through steady growth. His high-quality gunpowder was in demand by the U.S. government and the American Fur Company, among other customers. By the late 1820's some 140 employees were producing 800,000 barrels of gunpowder a year.

Éleuthère Irénée served as director of the Bank of the United States in Philadelphia and was inconspicuously active in politics. When he died, management of the company passed to his son-in-law, Antoine Bidermann, who had worked closely with the founder for many years.

ALFRED VICTOR DU PONT (1798–1856), the eldest son of Éleuthère Irénée, took over leadership of the family company from Antoine Bidermann, his brother-in-law, in 1837. The company was free from debt and growing. Alfred Victor was trained in chemistry and was most interested in the technical aspects of powder making. He also proved himself a good business administrator. One of his important contributions was to systematize and expedite the shipping of gunpowder. He brought barrel makers to the Brandywine and had a powder magazine and dock erected on the Delaware River above Wilmington. He made other improvements in the conduct of the business and the quality of the product, besides guiding the firm's response to the rapid growth of demand for gunpowder generated by the Mexican War. In 1850 he turned leadership of the business over to his brother Henry.

HENRY DU PONT (1812–1889), another son of Éleuthère Irénée, was head of the Du Pont company from 1850 to 1889 and presided over some of its most important developments. He was trained at West Point for a military career but resigned his commission in 1834, a year after graduation, to satisfy his father's request that he master the black powder business. Succeeding his brother Alfred Victor, Henry was the leader in the family partnership for nearly 40 years.

The technical developments of this period were largely the work of his nephew Lammot du Pont (1831–1884). Among other things, Lammot was responsible for the development of an effective blasting powder made from low-cost Peruvian nitrate and a more effective propellant black powder suited for use in rifled cannons. Lammot later led the company's movement into the dynamite business. Henry organized the sales and other business activity to market these products.

During the Civil War, Henry was appointed a major general by the governor of Delaware and also worked effectively to keep the state on the Union side. His company supplied the government with 4 million pounds of powder of all kinds and did so without profiteering. At the end of the conflict, government surplus gunpowder threatened the commercial black powder market. "General" Henry, faced by this situation and the emergence of numerous price-cutting powder producers, was active in forming the Gunpowder Trade Association in 1872. The leading members —the Du Pont firm, Laflin & Rand Company, and the Hazard Company—divided the country into sales areas, and agreed upon sales quotas for each member. Similar agreements were being made in other industries plagued by overproduction and price cutting.

In 1876 the Du Pont firm purchased the Hazard Company and was acquiring other, smaller firms. Du Pont and Laflin & Rand were the industry leaders and, directly or through controlled companies, they were jointly interested in most of the explosives manufacturers of the country.

Henry du Pont made no effort to get into the promising but dangerous business of manufacturing dynamite, a new high explosive. However, through the company's interest in the California Powder Company, he found himself in the dynamite field. The Repauno Chemical Company, two thirds owned by Du Pont and one third by Laflin & Rand, was formed in 1880. Lammot du Pont became its president. Repauno soon purchased a Cleveland dynamite plant, which became the Hercules Powder Company with the same officers and stockholders as Repauno. Lammot resigned from the family company to devote his full time to Repauno. When he was killed in an accident at the works in 1884, the Du Pont company acquired his Repauno stock and integrated dynamite production into its other activities.

Henry du Pont was long active in Republican politics in Delaware and was a presidential elector in every election from 1868 to 1888 with only one exception. He clung to old ways in conducting his business but proved a shrewd business leader in his chosen field.

EUGENE DU PONT (1840–1902), grandson of the company's founder, Éleuthère Irénée, directed the company from 1889 to 1899 as it made further progress. He contributed to it a practical powderman's approach to production and a practical businessman's emphasis on organization and efficiency. During his administration the innumerable sales agencies of the company were reduced to 10 branch offices selling directly to dealers, a larger home office was established in Wilmington, and activities formerly conducted in New York and Philadelphia were centralized in company headquarters. New facilities were built on the Delaware River to handle bulk powder shipments. The family company continued as a partnership, and the partners continued to conduct their lives to serve the company.

HENRY ALGERNON DU PONT (1838–1926), eldest son of Henry du Pont, was a soldier and legislator. Graduated from the U.S. Military Academy in 1861 at the head of his class, Henry A. du Pont had a distinguished record in the Civil War. After varied service he was appointed in 1864 chief of artillery in the department of West Virginia. He received the Congressional Medal of Honor for extraordinary gallantry at Cedar Creek, Va., on Oct. 19, 1864. He resigned from the Army in 1875. From 1877 to 1899 he was president and general manager of the Wilmington & Norfolk Railroad. Under his cousin Eugene, he was one of the principal partners in the Du Pont firm. When the firm was incorporated in 1899, be became a vice president and was active in this capacity until 1902. He served two terms as U.S. senator from Delaware (1906–1917) and headed the Senate Military Committee from 1911 to 1913.

ALFRED IRÉNÉE DU PONT (1864–1935), grandson of Alfred Victor, proved himself an able black-powder man and made numerous technical improvements that increased the quality, uniformity, and safety of gunpowder manufacture. Educated at the Massachusetts Institute of Technology, he entered the family business in 1887. He was sent to Europe to study smokeless powder manufacture. His investigation contributed to the firm's successful entry into this field in 1894.

When Eugene du Pont died in 1902, Alfred was the youngest partner in the family concern. The other partners were seriously considering sale of the company to Laflin & Rand, but Alfred was determined to keep the business in the family. He interested his cousins Thomas Coleman du Pont and Pierre Samuel du Pont in joining this effort, which proved successful. A new company, the E. I. du Pont de Nemours Powder Company, was incorporated in 1903. It included most of the members of the Gunpowder Trade Association and existed until 1915 when its properties were transferred to the present corporation.

Alfred became vice president and general manager of Du Pont's manufacturing departments. He was a talented individual but apparently not an outstanding business administrator. Eventually he ran into difficulty with his cousins and became inactive in the company after 1915 when a syndicate headed by Pierre Samuel purchased Coleman's stock.

Alfred at one time owned several Delaware newspapers and used them to oppose the election of Thomas Coleman du Pont and Henry A. du Pont to the U.S. Senate. From 1926 to his death in 1935 he lived in Florida, where he engaged in banking, real estate, and philanthropy.

THOMAS COLEMAN DU PONT (1863–1930), another grandson of Alfred Victor, served as president of the firm from 1902 to 1915. Known as Coleman, he graduated from the Massachusetts Institute of Technology, worked in his father's Kentucky coal mines, and was active in street railway reorganizations and the steel business before joining his cousins Alfred and Pierre in the purchase of the Du Pont company in 1902.

During his presidency the company underwent major changes. It acquired Laflin & Rand, Du Pont's largest competitor, in 1902. A committee system of management, capped by executive and financial committees, was introduced.

Research was expanded, with the Eastern Laboratory at Repauno, N.J. (1902), concentrating on dynamite while the Experimental Station on Brandywine Creek near Wilmington specialized in black powder and the new smokeless powder. In 1907 the government instituted antitrust proceedings against Du Pont, with the result in 1912 that the company was forced to transfer some of its industrial powder facilities to the Hercules Powder Company and the Atlas Powder Company.

Coleman was active in various business fields. He acquired a controlling interest in the Equitable Life Assurance Society and eventually turned it into a mutual company, selling his stock to policyholders. After retiring from the Du Pont company, he invested in hotels and office buildings. He also built a major highway from Wilmington to the Maryland state line and presented it to the state in 1924. He was appointed to the U.S. Senate in 1921 to fill an unexpired term and was elected to the Senate in 1924.

PIERRE SAMUEL DU PONT (1870–1954), another grandson of Alfred Victor, was president of E. I. du Pont de Nemours & Co. from 1915 to 1919 and chairman of the board from 1919 to 1940. He graduated from the Massachusetts Institute of Technology in 1890. Working with his cousin Francis Gurney du Pont a few years later, Pierre helped to develop Du Pont's smokeless powder. He was later active in the steel business before joining Coleman du Pont and Alfred Irénée du Pont in the purchase of the Du Pont company in 1902. First as treasurer, then as acting president during Coleman's illness, and finally as president of Du Pont, Pierre was responsible for many of the administrative, organizational, and product policies that underlie the present prominence of the company.

A syndicate headed by Pierre acquired Coleman's stock in 1915, and Alfred Irénée also ceased to be active in company affairs. The new management was confronted with heavy demands for powder to fight World War I. The company produced—among other things—some 1.3 billion pounds of smokeless powder for the war effort. The gross capital employed in the business rose from $83.5 million to $309 million, while the number of employees increased from 5,300 to 85,000.

In an effort to utilize the large resources developed to meet war needs, Pierre and his associates developed a plan for diversification of the company's products, based on its expertise in nitrocellulose, a key ingredient of explosives but also suitable for commercial products. By 1919 the firm was moving into varied but related products such as chemicals, paint and varnish, celluloid, and artificial leather. Under Pierre the family-run company had been transformed into a professionally managed corporation where family members had to meet high managerial standards.

Pierre's secretary, John J. Raskob, interested Du Pont in the General Motors Corporation, created by the brilliant but erratic William C. Durant. The first investments were made in 1917. When Durant ran into trouble in 1920, Du Pont funds met the crisis. Pierre personally took charge of GM, and from 1920 to 1923 he served as president of the automobile company. His successor in this post, Alfred P. Sloan, Jr., continued the successful work that made Du Pont's GM investment an important asset to its stockholders.

IRÉNÉE DU PONT (1876–1963), succeeded his brother, Pierre Samuel, as Du Pont's president in 1919, continued as president until 1926, and then served as vice chairman until 1940. He graduated from Massachusetts Institute of Technology in 1897 and received an M. S. in 1898. When his brother Pierre and their cousins Alfred Irénée and Coleman assumed control of the Du Pont company in 1902, Irénée joined them. He became a director two years later, manager of the development department in 1908, and vice president in 1914. As general manager after Alfred Irénée, he was responsible for sales as well as manufacturing. He remained a key figure after a syndicate headed by Pierre Samuel took over the company in 1915. During his presidency the decentralized multidivisional structure of the company was perfected.

During the years Irénée was president and vice chairman, the company moved rapidly ahead in new fields. Employing its own research and by agreement with French producers who held patents and process rights, the Du Pont company moved into rayon and cellophane production. Its Duco enamel found wide acceptance in the automobile industry, and in 1925 research on synthetic rubber commenced. In these and other areas, the company built a high-quality, diversified line of products based on its expertise in chemistry and manufacturing.

LAMMOT DU PONT (1880–1952), brother of Pierre Samuel and Irénée, became Du Pont's president in 1926 and retained the post until 1940. From 1940 to 1948 he was chairman of the company's board. He graduated from Massachusetts Institute of Technology in 1901 with a degree in civil engineering. In 1902 he joined the Du Pont company as it entered its new phase of development under Alfred, Pierre, and Coleman du Pont. By 1913, Lammot was general superintendent of the black powder department, and two years later he participated in the syndicate headed by Pierre to purchase Coleman's stock. He became successively a director and vice president. During World War I he headed the department that planned the company's postwar diversification program and supervised the resulting research in dyes, paints, and plastics. When his brother Irénée became president in 1919, Lammot became chairman of the policy-making executive committee.

During his presidency the company continued its commercial development of research-based products and extended its commitment to pure research. Among the new products introduced during the 1930's were the synthetic rubber neoprene; a plastic, Lucite; and the synthetic textile fiber nylon. In 1941 another synthetic fiber, Dacron, was produced.

Lammot accepted the U. S. government's invitation for the Du Pont firm to participate in the atomic development program of World War II. He was active in planning the Hanford Engineer Works near Pasco, Wash., which produced plutonium, one of the basic elements of the atomic bomb. He was a director of General Motors Corporation from 1918 to 1946 and chairman of its board from 1929 to 1937.

ARTHUR M. JOHNSON, *Harvard University*
Author of *"Government-Business Relations"*

Further Reading: Carr, William H. A., *The du Ponts of Delaware* (New York 1964); Dorian, Max, *The du Ponts* (Boston 1962); Saricks, Ambrose, *Pierre Samuel du Pont de Nemours* (Lawrence, Kans., 1966).

DUPONT DE L'EURE, dü-pôn' də lûr', **Jacques Charles** (1767–1855), French lawyer and legislator. He was born in Neubourg, France, on Feb. 27, 1767, and was trained as a lawyer. He entered the Normandy legislature when the French Revolution began in 1789 and also held legal posts in Normandy before serving (1798–1799) as a member of the Council of Five Hundred, the lower house of the French legislature during the Directory (1795–1799).

He left Paris for several years to return to legal work and became the president of the court of Rouen in 1812. Elected to the Chamber of Deputies in 1814, he was its vice president when Napoleon returned to France during the Hundred Days (1815). After Napoleon's defeat at Waterloo, Dupont de l'Eure drew up a proclamation stating that the country would only accept a government that guaranteed the "rights of man."

A member of the republican opposition until Louis Philippe became king in 1830, Dupont de l'Eure served as minister of justice for a short time before rejoining the opposition. He headed the provisional government briefly following the Revolution of 1848 but lost his seat in the Chamber of Deputies in 1849 when extremist views became more popular than his moderate republicanism. He died at Rouge-Perriers on March 2, 1855.

DUPRAT, dü-prà', **Antoine** (1463–1535), French cardinal, who, as chancellor of France, was the chief statesman during the early reign of Francis I. He was born in Issoire on Jan. 17, 1463. He was named first president of the Parlement of Paris in 1507 and chancellor one week after the accession of Francis I in 1515. He remained chancellor until his death, at Nantouillet, on July 9, 1535.

The King's trusted servant, Duprat negotiated the Concordat of Bologna (1516) with Pope Leo X, by which the French crown gained greater control over church appointments in France. As head of the council of regency during the Italian campaign of 1524–1525 and during the King's imprisonment in Spain in 1525–1526, he was held responsible by the public for the political disasters that followed.

Duprat profited greatly from the concordat. He was named archbishop of Sens in 1525 and added to the revenues of this office those of the abbey of St.-Benoît-sur-Loire. He was named cardinal in 1527.
FREDERIC L. CHEYETTE, *Amherst College*

DUPRÈ, dü-prà', **Giovanni** (1817–1882), Italian sculptor, in whose works the neoclassical style is mixed with a degree of naturalism that gives them a distinctive vitality. The son of a woodcarver, he was born in Siena, on March 1, 1817. He studied in Florence with Lorenzo Bartolini but was largely self-taught. Among his early works are *The Death of Abel* (1842; Hermitage, Leningrad); *Cain* (1844; Pitti, Florence), which was commissioned by the Grand Duchess Maria of Russia; and *Giotto* (1845; Uffizi, Florence).

In 1856 he visited Rome, where the monument to Pius VI by Antonio Canova influenced him to work in a more neoclassical style. The effect is apparent in his *Sappho* (1857; Galleria Nazionale d'Arte Moderna, Rome). His other works include the *Pietà* in the cemetery at Siena and a statue of St. Francis in the Assisi cathedral. He died in Florence on Jan. 10, 1882.

DUPRÉ, dü-prā', **Jules** (1811–1889), French painter, who was one of the Barbizon school of romantic landscape artists. He excelled in portraying the dramatic, gloomy, and desolate aspects of nature, especially in his late seascapes.

Dupré was born in Nantes on April 5, 1811, and began his career decorating porcelain in his father's factory. In 1830 he went to Paris, where his work was soon accepted into the annual Salons. The paintings of John Constable influenced him greatly during a visit to England in 1834, and the influence of 17th century Dutch landscape painters is also apparent.

Many of Dupré's late paintings are views of the ocean under heavy, gloomy skies. His works include *The Large Oak* and a *Self Portrait* (both in the Louvre, Paris); and *The Hay Wagon* (Metropolitan Museum of Art, New York City). He died at L'Isle-Adam on Oct. 6, 1889.

DUPRÉ, dü-prā', **Marcel** (1886–1971), French organ virtuoso and composer, noted for his genius for improvisation. He was born in Rouen on May 3, 1886, and received his musical training at the Paris Conservatory. A precocious musician, he gave his first public organ recital in 1896, became a church organist in Rouen at the age of 12, and had an oratorio, *Le songe de Jacob*, performed when he was 15.

From 1916 to 1922, Dupré substituted for the ailing Louis Vierne as organist at the Cathedral of Notre Dame in Paris, and he performed the complete organ works of J. S. Bach from memory in ten recitals at the Paris Conservatory in 1920. In 1937 he succeeded Charles Widor as head organist at the Church of St. Sulpice in Paris, and from 1954 to 1956 he was director of the Paris Conservatory. Dupré composed choral, organ, and piano pieces and published works on organ music. He died in Meudon, France, May 30, 1971.

DUPUY, dü-pü-ē', **Charles Alexandre** (1851–1923), French premier, who played a leading role in the Dreyfus affair. He was born at Le Puy on Nov. 5, 1851, and was a teacher before turning to politics. Elected to the Chamber of Deputies in 1885, he became minister of public instruction in 1892. He was premier for the first time in 1893, and later in 1894–1895 and 1898–1899. Dupuy won fame for his calm remark, "Gentlemen, the session will continue," after a bomb was thrown by an anarchist in the chamber of Deputies on Dec. 9, 1893, when Dupuy was president of the Chamber.

His second and third premierships coincided with two crises of the Dreyfus affair (see DREYFUS, ALFRED). Dreyfus was arrested and convicted during Dupuy's second term. In his last premiership, the reopening of the Dreyfus case caused demonstrations, and Dupuy, who was criticized for his lack of energy in defending republican institutions, was forced to resign. He was elected to the Senate in 1900 and served until his death on July 23, 1923, at Ille-sur-Têt.
DOUGLAS JOHNSON
University of Birmingham, England

DUQUESNE, dü-kân', **Abraham** (1610–1688), French naval commander, whose greatest exploits were against the Spanish and Dutch. Born in Dieppe, he became a sailor as a boy. He distinguished himself in the Thirty Years' War at Guetaria (1638), Coruña (1639), and Barcelona (1643).

After the death of Richelieu and Louis XIII, however, the French virtually abandoned their navy, and Duquesne sought employment abroad. He chose Sweden and, as vice admiral from 1643–1645, defeated the Danes in several engagements. Returning to France, he remained loyal to the crown during the Fronde (q.v.). Commanding several ships equipped at his own expense in 1650, Duquesne blockaded Bordeaux and compelled the rebel city to surrender. Anne of Austria, regent for Louis XIV, then promoted him to squadron leader.

Defeat of the Dutch. Duquesne's greatest fame followed the naval reorganization begun in 1668. During the Dutch War (1672–1679), his French forces routed the Dutch near Catania, Sicily, in April 1676. Adm. Michel de Ruyter was killed and most of the enemy fleet was burned, thereby securing France's command of the Mediterranean. His last engagements were the bombardments of Tripoli (1681), Algiers (1682), and Genoa (1684).

In 1681, Louis XIV made Duquesne a marquis and gave him an estate near Étampes for his services. Duquesne refused to renounce Calvinism despite promises of promotion, but his reputation protected him after the revocation of the Edict of Nantes (1685) stripped French Protestants of their rights. He died in Paris on Feb. 2, 1688.

LIONEL ROTHKRUG, *University of Michigan*

DUQUESNE, doo-kān', an industrial city in southwestern Pennsylvania, in Allegheny county, is on the Monongahela River, about 10 miles (16 km) southeast of Pittsburgh. One of the largest steel manufacturing plants in the United States is situated here. Duquesne was laid out in 1885 by the Duquesne Steel Company, which later was taken over by Andrew Carnegie. It was incorporated as a borough in 1891 and as a city in 1910. Government is by commission. Population: 10,094.

DUQUESNE, Fort. See FRENCH AND INDIAN WAR; PITTSBURGH—*History*.

DUQUESNE UNIVERSITY, doo-kān', is a coeducational Roman Catholic university located in Pittsburgh, Pa. Founded in 1878 by the Holy Ghost Fathers, it was first named Pittsburgh Catholic College of the Holy Ghost; in 1935 it adopted its current name in honor of the Marquis Duquesne de Menneville, the governor general of Canada under whom the first Catholic observances were brought to western Pennsylvania.

Duquesne comprises a college of liberal arts and sciences; schools of business administration, education, law, music, nursing, and pharmacy; and a graduate school offering master's degrees in many areas and doctorates in several. It was the first university to offer a doctoral program in phenomenological psychology. Its Institute of African Affairs offers major concentration in African languages. Enrollment grew from about 3,600 in 1950 to about 7,000 in the late 1960's.

J. A. LAURITIS, *Duquesne University*

DUQUESNOY, dü-ke-nwȧ', **François** (1594–1646), Flemish sculptor, whose works are in a relatively classical, conservative manner within the general baroque style. He is sometimes called *François Flamand* or *Il Fiammingo*. Most of Duquesnoy's work is in marble, bronze, or terra-cotta, but he also did small ivory figures and reliefs and was celebrated for his lifelike nudes of children.

Duquesnoy was born in Brussels and was taught sculpture by his father. About 1620 he settled in Italy, where, under the patronage of Pope Urban VIII, he carved the groups of children that adorn the canopy above the main altar at St. Peter's, as well as his two largest and best-known works, *St. Susanna* (1628–1633; Santa Maria di Loreto, Rome) and *St. Andrew* (1630–1640; St. Peter's). In 1642 he was called to France by Louis XIII, but he died on the journey, at Leghorn, Italy, on July 12, 1646.

DURALUMIN. See ALUMINUM—*High Purity*.

DURAM, thoo-rouN', **José de Santa Rita** (c. 1737–1784), Brazilian poet, whose long descriptive poem *Caramúru* ranks as a national epic in Brazil. His name is also spelled *Durão*.

He was born near Mariana in the state of Minas Gerais. He received his early education at a Jesuit college in Rio de Janeiro and later studied theology at the University of Coimbra, Portugal. Duram joined the Augustinian order in 1756. Forced into temporary exile because of his liberal views, he traveled in Spain and Italy. In 1778 he accepted a post at the University of Coimbra. He died in Lisbon on Jan. 24, 1784.

Caramúru is based on the story of Diego Alvarez Correa, surnamed "Caramúru," the legendary hero of Bahia. Written in 10 cantos, the poem vividly describes Indian life and the scenery of South America. It was originally published in Lisbon in 1781 and appeared in French in 1829. Duram destroyed most of his other works.

DURAN, dü-rän', **Carolus** (1837–1917), French painter, who did portraits of socially prominent contemporaries. His name is also written *Carolus-Duran*. Born Charles Auguste Émile Durand, at Lille on July 4, 1837, he studied at Paris, at Rome, and in Spain, where the works of Velázquez were a major inspiration to him. He first aroused attention in Paris in 1865 when his *Evening Prayer* was exhibited at the Salon. The following year one of his major works, *The Assassinated*, was a great success at the Salon.

Duran's portraits ultimately made his reputation. Among the best are *Lady with a Glove* (1869), *Portrait of Madame Criozette on Horseback* (1875), *Émile de Girardin* (1875), and *Comtesse de Vandal* (1879). In 1878 he painted *The Glory of Marie de Médicis*, a ceiling decoration now in the Louvre, which, like his other large compositions, is less successful than his portraits. He died in Paris on Feb. 18, 1917.

DURANCE RIVER, dü-räns', in southeastern France. It rises in the Alps near Briançon, in the department of Hautes-Alpes, and flows about 180 miles (290 km) southwest and then west to join the Rhône River 2 miles (3 km) southwest of Avignon. The lower course of the Durance is extensively used for irrigation. A tributary, the Verdon, is tapped for an ambitious development project, the Canal de Provence, which provides water for the burgeoning population of southern Provence, for the industrial growth of the Marseille-Aix area, and for many thousand acres of newly irrigated land in Bouches-du-Rhône and western Var. The upper Durance has been exploited for hydroelectric power.

HOMER PRICE, *Hunter College*

DURAND, dū-rand', **Asher Brown** (1796–1886), American engraver and painter, who was the foremost American engraver of the early 19th century. He is best known today as one of the leading painters of the Hudson River school.

Durand was born in Jefferson Village (now Maplewood), N. J., on Aug. 21, 1796, of a family of French Huguenot ancestry. In 1812 he was apprenticed to the engraver Peter Maverick of New York and in 1816 became Maverick's partner. When painter John Trumbull engaged the firm to engrave his *Signing of the Declaration of Independence* in 1820, he insisted that Durand execute it. The engraving established Durand's reputation, and, because of jealousy, Maverick dissolved their partnership.

In the late 1830's, Durand abandoned engraving for painting, concentrating primarily on landscapes. His careful, faithful scenic depictions were painted directly from nature—an unusual practice in that period. His most famous painting, *Kindred Spirits* (1849; New York Public Library), shows William Cullen Bryant and Thomas Cole conversing in a wild landscape setting.

Durand was a founding member of the National Academy of Design and served as its second president from 1845 to 1861. In 1869 he retired to his birthplace, where he died on Sept. 17, 1886.

NICOLAI CIKOVSKY, JR.
University of Texas

Further Reading: Durand, John, *Life and Times of Asher Brown Durand* (1894; reprint, Da Capo 1970).

DURANGO, doo-räng'gō, an interior state of northwestern Mexico, is the fourth-largest Mexican state, covering 46,196 square miles (119,648 square km), but is not densely populated. The western part, dominated by the Sierra Madre Occidental, is a mountainous region of moderate precipitation, forested in pine and oak. East of the sierra is a central zone of subhumid scrub and grasslands devoted to ranching and farming. The northeastern half of the state is predominantly steppe and desert, except for a few areas of irrigated land, the most important of which is the Laguna district. Here, waters from the Nazas River make possible the cultivation of cotton, wheat, corn (maize), alfalfa, grapes, and other irrigated crops.

The territory that now constitutes Durango was the core of the colonial Reino de Nueva Vizcaya, a region explored and settled in the mid-1500's, primarily in connection with mining and missionary activities. Mining and ranching are the mainstays of the economy, although farming and lumbering are becoming important. Durango generally ranks second among Mexican states in metals production; it produces most of the nation's iron ore, much of its gold, and silver, cinnabar, lead, copper, and other minerals.

The state's industrial facilities (which stress the processing of minerals, foodstuffs, and pine forest products) are concentrated near the largest cities, which include the capital city of Durango in the south and Gómez Palacio and Ciudad Lerdo, both in the Laguna district. National highways and railroads provide good connections to the north, northeast, and southeast, but the Durango-to-Mazatlán highway is the only surface route across the Sierra Madre to the Pacific. Population: (1978 est.) 1,273,160.

DONALD D. BRAND
The University of Texas at Austin

DURANGO, doo-räng'gō, a city of northwestern Mexico, is some 500 miles (800 km) northwest of Mexico City. Its name is officially *Victoria de Durango*. The city is situated at an elevation of over 6,300 feet (1,900 meters) in the fertile Guadiana Valley in the southern part of Durango state, of which it is the capital and largest city.

Durango is a commercial and industrial center in a farming and ranching area with a mining and lumbering hinterland. On the northern outskirts is the Cerro de Mercado, a large hill of hematite that assays at about 62% pure iron and is the chief Mexican source of iron ore. Local industries include foundries, textile mills, food-processing, mineral-reduction, and forest product plants, glass works, and tobacco factories. Durango is also an important road and rail hub; it is on Inter-American Highway. The city was founded in 1563 and is the seat of the state university. Population: (1977 est.) 209,014.

DONALD D. BRAND, *The University of Texas*

DURANT, doo-rant', **Will** (1885–1981), American historian. William James Durant was born on Nov. 5, 1885, in North Adams, Mass. After studying at St. Peter's College in Jersey City (B. A., 1907) and Columbia (Ph. D., 1917), he taught and directed an adult education program in New York. In 1926, Durant astonished the publishing world when his book *The Story of Philosophy* became a bestseller. Thereafter he devoted himself exclusively to writing.

Some minor works followed, including a novel, *Transition* (1927). In 1935 he published *Our Oriental Heritage*, the first volume in the series *The Story of Civilization*. The 10th volume, *Rousseau and Revolution*, won a Pulitzer Prize in 1968. The 11th and final volume, *The Age of Napoleon*, appeared in 1975. In an enthusiastic, lucid narrative style, he appraises the human feelings of his leading characters and stresses their passionate natures. Critics recognized his knowledge of cultural history but complained of his sweeping, often outdated generalizations, his reliance on sometimes dubious secondary works, and his avoidance of controversial subjects.

Durant died in Los Angeles, Calif., on Nov. 7, 1981. His wife, Ariel (1898–1981), died two weeks earlier, on October 25. She was coauthor of the last five volumes of *The Story of Civilization* series and of their last book, *A Dual Biography* (1977).

BERTRAM WYATT-BROWN
Case Western Reserve University

DURANT, doo-rant', **William Crapo** (1861–1947), American manufacturer, who was a leading organizer of the automobile industry. He was born in Boston on Dec. 8, 1861, but grew up and attended school in Flint, Mich. At the age of 25 he organized the Durant-Dort Carriage Company in Flint, which attained an annual production of 150,000 vehicles. In 1905 he founded the Buick Motor Car Company and in 1908 the General Motors firm, which in two years acquired the Cadillac, Oakland, and Oldsmobile enterprises.

Durant came into complete control of General Motors by 1915 and the same year set up the Chevrolet Motor Company, which three years later was absorbed by General Motors. He lost control of General Motors in 1920 but the next year organized Durant Motors, Inc., which was less successful than his earlier ventures. In his later years he manufactured rayon and speculated in real estate.

Concerned over disregard of the prohibition law and other laws, Durant collected enforcement plans from police, prosecutors, and judges in 1928, and initiated a contest in which 23,000 persons sought a $25,000 prize for the best plan. His book, *Law Observance,* published in 1929, details these efforts. Durant died in New York City on March 18, 1947.

COURTNEY R. HALL
Author, "History of American Industrial Science"

DURANTE, də-ran'tē, **Jimmy** (1893–1980), American comedian, whose trademarks were a raspy voice (both speaking and singing), a battered hat, a strut like a penguin's, and an oversized nose that earned him the nickname "Schnozzola." James Francis Durante was born of immigrant Italian parents on the Lower East Side of New York City on Feb. 10, 1893. He started in show business at the age of 17 as a ragtime piano player in a Coney Island saloon. In 1916 he formed a five-man jazz band, and in 1919 he organized a nightclub and vaudeville act with Eddie Jackson and Lou Clayton. As one feature of the act, Durante, a slight man of almost boundless energy, tore a piano apart.

Durante was closely identified with such songs as *I'm Jimmy, the Well-Dressed Man, Inka, Dinka, Doo, Did You Ever Get the Feelin' That You Wanted to Go, Still You Have the Feelin' That You Wanted to Stay?,* and, in later years, Kurt Weill's *September Song.* He was perhaps as well known for such quips as "Everybody wants to get inta da act," "I've gotta million of 'em," and "I'm mortified."

Durante appeared on the Broadway stage in such musicals as *Show Girl* (1929), *Strike Me Pink* (1933), *Jumbo* (1935), and *Red, Hot and Blue* (1936). Beginning in 1930 he made such motion pictures as *Ziegfeld Follies* (1946), *Billy Rose's Jumbo* (1962), and *It's a Mad, Mad, Mad, Mad World* (1963). In the 1940's he had his own radio show and in the 1950's his own television program. He died in Santa Monica, Calif., on Jan. 29, 1980.

DURANTI, doō-rän'tē, **William** (died 1296), medieval canonist and liturgist. Born in Puymisson, Provence, between 1230 and 1237, he studied law at Bologna and later taught there and at Modena. Duranti held various posts in the Roman Curia. He was known during the later Middle Ages as the "Speculator" from his treatise *Speculum iudicale,* used for centuries as a guide in civil and ecclesiastical courts.

Duranti was appointed bishop of Mende in 1285 but did not take possession of his see until 1291. In 1295 he returned to administrative duties in Rome, where he died in 1296. His name also appears in the Latinized form *Gulielmus Durandus,* and he is sometimes referred to as "Duranti the Elder" to distinguish him from his nephew William Duranti, who succeeded him as bishop of Mende.

DAMIEN BLAHER, O. F. M.
Holy Name College, Washington, D. C.

DURAS, dü-rà', **Marguerite** (1914–   ), French author, one of the postexistentialist "New Wave" novelists. She was born Marguerite Donnadieu at Gia Dinh, Indochina (now Vietnam), on April 4, 1914. She studied law at the Sorbonne, Paris, and worked at the ministry of colonies from 1935 to 1941. Several of her books have been translated into English, including *Sea Wall* (1950; Eng. tr., 1952), set in Indochina; a psychological romantic novel, *Sailor from Gibraltar* (1952; Eng. tr., 1967); *Little Horses of Tarquinia* (1953; Eng. tr., 1960), which explores the obstacles that impede human relationships; and *India Song* (1973; Eng. tr., 1976). She wrote the screenplay for the film *Hiroshima, Mon Amour* (1959), in which past and present are merged in the emotions of the characters.

DURAZZO. See DURRËS.

D'URBAN, dûr'bən, **Sir Benjamin** (1777–1849), British general and colonial administrator. He entered the British Army in 1793. During the Napoleonic Wars, D'Urban served in Spain as a quartermaster general and helped reorganize the Portuguese Army. He was knighted in 1815. In 1820 he was made governor of Antigua in the Caribbean. In 1824 he transferred to Demerara and Essequibo, which later combined with Berdice to form British Guiana, of which he became the first governor in 1831.

D'Urban was appointed governor of the Cape of Good Hope in 1833. He occupied Natal, where the town of Port Natal was renamed Durban for him. Under D'Urban, slavery was abolished, legislative and municipal councils were established, and the colony expanded. At the same time, the British troops were fighting the Kaffirs. In this period the trek of the Dutch Boers out of the British-controlled area began. In the British territory, D'Urban called for equal treatment of all inhabitants, Dutch and English, Kaffir, Zulu, and Bantu. Recalled in 1837, D'Urban was assigned the military command of Canada in 1847. He held this post until his death in Montreal on May 25, 1849.

HELEN M. BAILEY, *East Los Angeles College*

Jimmy Durante starred in almost every medium of show business—nightclubs, Broadway musicals, movies, and TV.

CULVER PICTURES

DURBAN'S fine beaches and warm winter climate have made it a popular resort. Behind the beaches, swimming pools, hotels, and sports fields have been built.

SATOUR

DURBAN, dûr′bən, is the busiest seaport in the Republic of South Africa. It is the largest city in Natal province and the third-largest city in the country. Located in the eastern part of Natal, Durban overlooks the Indian Ocean. It lies south of the Umgeni River, on the north shore of the virtually landlocked Bay of Natal.

Harbor. The Bay of Natal is the best natural harbor in South Africa, but it was the last site developed by Europeans, partly because of the presence of the Bantu peoples and partly because of the nature of the harbor entrance. Enclosing the harbor on the south is a row of dense, shrub-covered hills called the Bluff. More than 200 feet (60 meters) high, the Bluff diverts the long-shore current and causes sand to accumulate across the mouth of the bay. However, by constant dredging and reclamation of the marshy bayhead area, an excellent port has been developed.

On the northern side of the harbor is the Back Beach, a sand-covered area 20 feet (6 meters) above sea level, which makes a superb beach and serves as a major recreation facility. The Back Beach terminates in the Point, which forms one side of the narrow harbor entrance (the other is the tip of the Bluff). The enclosed harbor has ample modern wharves as well as a large drydock, floating dock, manganese loader, and the largest grain elevator in South Africa.

Economy. Durban's great growth has been due primarily to its function as the principal cargo port of the country. It serves as the main outlet for the most richly endowed and most fully developed part of South Africa. The city's major exports include coal, manganese, chrome, grain, sugar, wool, and hides.

The growth of trade has stimulated industrial and commercial development. Durban is the center of Natal's sugar-growing and sugar-refining industry. Industries in the city also produce textiles, soap, fertilizer, paint, automobiles, and rubber.

The City. Durban covers an area of about 93 square miles (240 sq km), extending 6 or 7 miles (10 or 11 km) inland beyond the Berea, a ridge of hills 400 to 500 feet (120–150 meters) high. The Berea surrounds the center of the city and provides the best residential sites in Durban. Industrial and commercial areas have been developed on the more level land and the reclaimed areas of the harbor district. Continuing growth and expansion have forced the city to acquire both residential and industrial sites to the north and south.

Durban is an attractive city, especially noted for the great variety of flowering trees and shrubs that adorn its streets and parks. Buildings of note include the Natal Settlers Old House Museum, a replica of the 1849 homestead at that site; the Old Fort, dating from 1842 and now a national museum; and the Warriors' Gate. One of the two branches of the University of Natal is located in Durban.

The city has an excellent year-round climate, which, added to the attractive beaches and other recreational facilities, makes it one of the most popular resorts in South Africa. During the winter months, May to August, the climate is uniform and exhilarating, with the daily temperature averaging about 60°F (15°C). In the summer months the heat is tropical but at no time excessive. Rainfall averages 40 inches (100 cm) annually, with the maximum during the summer months.

History. Durban dates from 1824, when a party of 25 people, under the command of Lt. Francis Farewell, established a settlement they called Port Natal. The town was laid out and the name changed to Durban in 1835. Its growth was slow but steady until it became the chief port for the Transvaal after the discovery of gold in 1866. The railroad linking Durban with Johannesburg was completed in 1895, and from then on the growth of the port and city of Durban has been rapid. Population: (1960) 560,010.

EDWARD J. MILES, *University of Vermont*

DURBAR, dûr′bär, was a term used in India for the council chamber of a ruler and, by derivation, for an administrative council or a formal state ceremony. The word comes from the Persian *darbar*, meaning "house," "court," or "audience hall." The British adopted the term, and under the British raj great ceremonial "durbars" were held on state occasions. A durbar of great magnificence was held at Delhi when Queen Victoria became empress of India.

DÜRER, dü′rər, **Albrecht** (1471–1528), German artist, who is considered the first northern European artist to combine Italian Renaissance ideas and forms with the late Gothic art of the north. Dürer was the first northern Renaissance man, a master of theory as well as of painting and graphics. Though he wished to be equally proficient in all fields, he was best known for his prints. The Italians celebrated him for his greatness in graphic work, and Erasmus referred to him as the Apelles of black lines because, like that most famous painter of classical Greece, Dürer made visible, things invisible—for example, death. Dürer's contributions to the techniques of woodcut and engraving, as well as his imagery, opened up new realms to graphic artists, and his pursuit of theoretical understanding altered the course of northern art.

Early Life and Apprenticeship. Dürer was born in Nuremberg on May 21, 1471. His father, a goldsmith, had come from Hungary to Nuremberg in 1455 and there married Barbara Holper, his master's daughter. Albrecht was apprenticed to his father at about age 14. This training in the working of metal and the use of tools laid the groundwork for his skill in engraving. He also absorbed the great Netherlandish tradition in which his father had been trained. Dürer already represented himself as a self-assured young boy in the precise and meticulous silverpoint *Self-Portrait at Age 13* (1484; Albertina, Vienna), which combines the careful and accurate rendering of details characteristic of northern art with a sensitivity that reveals his own precocious talent.

The young Dürer preferred drawing and painting to goldsmithing, so in 1486 he was apprenticed to the painter Michael Wolgemut. In Wolgemut's busy shop Dürer learned the fundamentals not only of drawing and painting but of woodcut as well. The workshop was actively producing books in which illustrations had great importance, not only in size but in dramatic force and illusionism. Impressions of woodcuts were made, not by hand, but in the presses used for movable type, with a resulting increase in clarity that allowed more complex designs. Dürer may have aided in preparing some illustrations in Hartmann Schedel's *Nuremberg Chronicle* (1493), and he would have seen works by the foremost printmakers of the time, among them the Housebook Master (also known as the Master of the Amsterdam Cabinet), Martin Schongauer, and Italian artists.

Wanderjahre. In 1490, Dürer left on his *Wanderjahre,* the period of travel that was a customary part of the education of young artists. He may have gone first to the northwest to see the Housebook Master working in the middle Rhine area, and then perhaps to the Netherlands. But the main aim of the trip was to visit Martin Schongauer in Colmar. On his arrival there in 1492, however, he learned that the master had died. Schongauer's brothers welcomed Dürer and no doubt made available to him prints and drawings in the workshop. The precise treatment of line and the perfectly controlled design of Schongauer's engravings, in direct contrast to the blurred line and atmospheric space of the Housebook Master's drypoints, had a lasting influence on Dürer's graphic style.

Dürer soon went on to Basel to stay with another Schongauer brother, who conducted a goldsmith workshop there. In Basel, a center of graphic production and book publishing, Dürer made many contacts and contributed a signed woodcut for the title page of an edition of the *Letters of St. Jerome,* representing the saint in his study curing the lion. The success of this print probably led to other commissions in Basel, and he continued to work for publishers in Strasbourg, where he went in the fall of 1493.

First Trip to Italy. Dürer was called home from Strasbourg for a prearranged marriage to Agnes Frey, on July 7, 1494. The *Self-Portrait with Eryngium* (1493; Louvre, Paris) was probably intended as an engagement picture. He inscribed above it: "My affairs will go as ordained on high." But not long after his marriage, in the fall of 1494, Dürer set out alone for his first trip to Italy. This visit to Italy enabled him to see his good friend Willibald Pirckheimer, who had introduced Dürer to humanist thought and classical literature and who was then studying in Padua. Even before his trip Dürer had seen and copied mythological subjects and studies of nudes by Andrea Mantegna and Antonio Pollaiuolo at a time when few northern artists were concerned with such subjects.

Dürer spent most of this first trip in Venice. There he may have met Jacopo de'Barbari, whose figures, constructed according to geometrical methods, inspired Dürer to a lifelong study of human proportions and forced one basis for his theoretical writings. In Venice, Dürer made drawings of exotic figures and animals and did nature studies. He never directly copied classical monuments, but he knew them from the works of Italian artists. He may also have met Gentile Bellini, and some of his drawings indicate a knowledge of the work of Leonardo and his followers.

The development of Dürer's artistic vision during his Italian experience can be seen in his treatment of landscape. An early watercolor, *Landscape with Wire-Drawing Mill* (about 1489; Kupferstichkabinett, Berlin), is a carefully detailed document of a particular locale. But the *Castle of Trent* (1495; British Museum, London), done probably on his way home through the Alps, shows a new and unified concept in which details have been subordinated to the whole view, and *Wehlsch Pirg* (c. 1495; Ashmolean Museum, Oxford) has an atmospheric treatment of extraordinary breadth.

Nuremberg. Dürer returned to Nuremberg by the summer of 1495, and before his second trip to Italy, in 1505, he produced a large number of prints and paintings. In 1496 he began his first great series, *The Apocalypse,* published in 1498. He personally undertook all aspects of its production—design, cutting, printing, and publishing. In the 15 large, full-page woodcut illustrations with text on the back, Dürer perfected and refined what he had learned of woodcut in Wolgemut's shop and from Schongauer's engraving style. He depicted the miraculous events in the most literal way, yet conveyed the force of the dramatic and mystic visions in the Book of Revelation. Also from this period are seven woodcuts of the *Large Passion* (before 1500) sold as individual prints, and 17 woodcuts for the *Life of the Virgin* (before 1505).

Dürer used the medium of engraving for subjects that reflected his theoretical interests. From about 1500 his concern for the problems of proportion and perspective increased, probably through fresh contacts with Italian works and study of Vitruvius. The *Adam and Eve* (1504) brought to a high point of refinement both his engraving technique and the construction by geometrical methods of male and female figures of perfect proportion and classic beauty. But his figures are set against a dense German forest alive with animals of allegorical meaning, and there are typically Gothic allusions to the medieval doctrine of the four humors. Dürer's other concern, perspective, is reflected in the engraving of the *Nativity* (1504) and the painting of the *Adoration of the Magi* (1505). The *Paumgärtner Altarpiece* (about 1501–1502; Alte Pinakothek, Munich), shows a balanced emphasis on both perspective and proportion.

Throughout his career Dürer produced portraits of family, friends, and patrons. During this period he painted *Frederick the Wise* (about 1496; Deutsches Museum, Berlin), his own father (1497; known only in replicas, one in the National Gallery, London), the Tucher portraits (1499; in Kassel and Weimar), and *Oswolt Krell* (1499; Alte Pinakothek, Munich). He also painted two important self-portraits (1498; Prado, Madrid; and 1500, Alte Pinakothek, Munich).

Second Italian Trip. In 1505, Dürer drew *Crowned Death on a Thin Horse* (British Museum, London), perhaps inspired by the plague epidemic, which is considered the immediate cause of Dürer's departure for Italy in the summer or fall of 1505. By this time he was mature and successful, esteemed mainly for his graphic work. After a stop in Augsburg, he went on to Venice, where he wished to develop his painting style. Although his prints were much admired, he complained that painters criticized his style as not "antique" enough. Only Giovanni Bellini, now an old man, praised him.

Dürer's highest achievement at this time was the *Feast of the Rose Garlands* (1506; State Gallery, Prague), ordered by the German merchants in Venice. In this work he combined the richness of Venetian color with the monumentality of Italian compositions. He also painted *Christ Among the Doctors* (1506; Thyssen Collection, Lugano); *Virgin with the Siskin* (1506); and the *Portrait of a Young Woman* (1506–1507), in which new tonal unity and softness of color are evident. (The last two are in the Deutsches Museum, Berlin.)

Late Career. Dürer returned to Nuremberg in February 1507. Two painted panels of *Adam and Eve* (1507; Prado, Madrid) show a new standard of beauty in their more elongated figures and fluid treatment. For some years he continued to concentrate on painting, producing the *Martyrdom of the Ten Thousand* (1508; Gemäldegalerie, Vienna) and the *Assumption and Coronation of the Virgin* (1509), to which Grünewald added four panels in 1512. Dürer's central panel was burned in 1729 and is known today only through a copy made in the 17th century.

Dürer experimented with drypoint in three works of 1512, but by 1513 he was concentrating on engraving. Three large prints that he next produced were among his most ambitious works. Now called "Master Engravings," they were not issued as a set but are related in that they typify three virtuous ways of life as understood by the medieval scholastics: *Knight, Death and the Devil* (1513) represents the active Christian warrior; *St. Jerome* (1514) shows the contemplative life of a scholar in his study; and *Melencolia I* (1514) depicts the despairing creative genius unable to use her divine gifts because she is conscious of her limitations.

In a charcoal drawing of his mother (1514; Kupferstichkabinett, Berlin), Dürer conveyed a more personal, tender message. His engraved *St. Anthony* (1519) has a cubistlike simplicity. During this time Dürer also explored the etching technique in six works, experimenting with mood and mysterious lighting effects.

Dürer was also busy with time-consuming enterprises for Emperor Maximilian I: a huge woodcut, 11½ feet by 9¾ feet (3.5 by 2.97 meters), *Triumphal Arch* (1515–1517); and the companion *Triumphal Procession* (unfinished), in which complex designs done in flat, decorative style glorify the Emperor. Dürer also provided marginal ink drawings for the *Prayer Book of Maximilian*, which was left incomplete at the Emperor's death in 1519. Dürer then was faced with the possible loss of his imperial pension.

Seeking to confirm his stipend with the new emperor, Charles V, as well as to find new markets for his work, Dürer set off in July 1520 with his wife on a visit to the Netherlands. He recorded his impressions of the land in a silverpoint sketchbook of 27 drawings. The trip was not a financial success, but he saw the great works of the past and met fellow artists. His vast curiosity led Dürer on an expedition to see a giant whale that had been washed ashore in Zeeland. He arrived too late to see the whale, but he may have contracted on this excursion the malaria that was eventually to be fatal.

In the Netherlands, Dürer met Erasmus and drew his portrait in charcoal. He had already expressed interest in Luther's teachings and owned several of his works, and in Luther and Erasmus he seemed to find answers to the anxious questions about faith that he himself was confronting, though he never broke with his Catholic patrons.

Dürer returned to Nuremberg in July 1521 and produced a number of portrait engravings, including *Cardinal Albrecht of Brandenberg* (1523); *Willibald Pirckheimer* (1524); and finally *Erasmus of Rotterdam* (1526), with a setting reminiscent of Flemish portrayals of St. Jerome. Among his late painted portraits are the powerful *Hieronymus Holzschuher* (1526; Deutsches Museum, Berlin) and *Johann Kleberger* (1526; Gemäldegalerie, Vienna).

The so-called "Four Apostles" remain the greatest testament of Dürer's faith at the end of his life. Dürer originally intended them as part of an altarpiece in the Venetian style, but he only completed two wings (1526; Alte Pinakothek, Munich), which he presented to the town council of Nuremberg. The four monumental figures pictured (two are not Apostles) fill the entire space and forcefully project their presence through expression alone. These panels are the highest achievement of Dürer's search for greater simplicity in his late works.

Theoretical Writings. Dürer died in Nuremberg on April 6, 1528. At his death, his theoretical treatises were not completed, but some were already published. *Underweysung der Messung . . .*, a treatise on perspective, came out in 1525. Two years later his work on fortification of towns, *Etliche Underricht zu Befestigung der Stett . . .*, was published, and the four books on human proportion, *Vier Bücher von menschlicher Proportion*, in incomplete form, appeared in 1528. In these works Dürer calls for an art based on scholarly

DÜRER'S portrait of his mother, a charcoal drawing made in 1514, is one of many portraits of family, friends, and patrons in various media.

ADAM AND EVE, an engraving Dürer made in 1504, sets figures of classical beauty against a dense forest in the German landscape tradition.

principles, and he was the first northern artist brought up in the medieval craft tradition to redefine the arts in this way. He was especially concerned with the training of young apprentices, for he felt that if they were taught with methods that emphasized only craft and technique they would grow up in ignorance, "as a wild, unpruned tree."

According to Dürer, capturing the beauty of the human body is the most significant aim of art, but this cannot be realized without knowledge of proportion and anatomy, and only through geometry can true beauty be known. Dürer's call for scientific methods was a radical departure from medieval treatises, which generally offered a schematic guide for representing figures embodying moral values. Contrary to Italian theorists like Alberti, Dürer accepted the variety of forms found in nature—the normal, the ugly, even the monstrous, as in his engraving the *Monstrous Pig* (1496). The artist is obliged to represent nature, not as it should be, but as it is, for art is embedded in nature and must be extracted from it by combining artistic genius with high technical skill.

Dürer was the first artist to care enough for his individual creations to sign sketches as well as more finished works. He was also the first to be so concerned with his own image that he recorded himself in numerous works. His concept of the artistic genius as inspired by God led him to identify himself with Christ, as in the self-portrait of 1500, not as a blasphemous gesture but in tribute to the source of his creative powers. He also portrayed himself in the drawing *Man of Sorrows* (1522; Kunsthalle, Bremen), a reflection of the ill health and agony of questioning he was experiencing at the time. But his religious faith remained strong, and he was especially preoccupied with salvation and the torment and loneliness of Christ, which he expressed in scenes of the Passion. Throughout his life, Dürer also maintained a strong belief in the power of cosmic forces, and even of dreams, in which he saw fearful portents of troubled times (*Dream*, watercolor, 1525; Kunsthistorisches Museum, Vienna); and he continued to invest death with form and substance, in the tradition of the medieval Dance of Death.

Dürer was immersed in the great realistic tradition of Netherlandish art and the mysticism of German art, but he also sought to encompass the monumental and idealizing tendencies of the Italian Renaissance. Though he failed to achieve a true synthesis, the vitality and expressive force of his art make him one of the greatest artists of all times.

LOLA B. GELLMAN
Vassar College

Bibliography

Conway, William M., ed., *The Writings of Albrecht Dürer* (New York 1958).
Dodgson, Campbell, *Dürer Drawings in Colour, Line and Wash . . . in the Albertina* (London 1928).
Friedländer, Max J., *Albrecht Dürer* (Leipzig 1921).
Fry, Roger, ed., *Albrecht Dürer, Records of the Journey to Venice and the Low Countries* (Boston 1913).
Hind, Arthur M., *Albrecht Dürer; His Engravings and Woodcuts* (New York 1911).
Kurth, Willi, ed., *The Complete Woodcuts of Albrecht Dürer* (London 1927; reprinted, New York 1946).
Levey, Michael, *Dürer* (New York 1964).
Panofsky, Erwin, *The Life and Art of Albrecht Dürer*, 2 vols. (Princeton 1943).
Schilling, Edmund, *Dürer's Drawings and Watercolors* (New York 1949).
Waetzold, Wilhelm, *Dürer and His Times* (New York 1950).

DURESS, do͞o-res′, in law, means force, or threats that induce a person to act in a way that is contrary to his own wishes. A confession in a criminal case, if induced by physical assaults, took place under duress and thus may be disregarded by the court. To enable the person alleging duress to avoid responsibility for his act, the pressure must have been so severe that it forced him to comply with demands to which he would not yield otherwise. Thus, a "shotgun wedding," a marriage under compulsion because of pregnancy, can be annulled or set aside.

Contracts executed under duress are not binding. Whether a case is actually one of duress is a matter to be determined by a jury, depending also on such surrounding circumstances as age, sex, capacity, situation, and relation of the parties. For example, a person who protests his innocence may nevertheless have entered into a contract in settlement of a claim for alleged embezzlements. If he was induced by threats of prosecution by another party, the case was one of duress, and the contract may be avoided by the person coerced.

Contracts made under duress are voidable, but not void, and later may be ratified voluntarily by the individuals who were wrongfully compelled to execute them.

SAMUEL G. KLING, *Author of "The Complete Guide to Everyday Law"*

D'URFÉ, dür-fā′, **Honoré** (1567–1625), French writer, who is best known for his 5-volume pastoral romance, *L'Astrée* (1607–1627). He was born on Feb. 11, 1567, of a noble family at Marseille and was educated at the Jesuit Collège de Tournon. He fought on the side of the Holy League in the French religious wars. After its defeat, he entered the Duke of Savoy's service. He died on June 1, 1625, at Villefranche.

L'Astrée, the most important of d'Urfé's works, is a prose romance influenced by Italian and Spanish pastorals. Set in 5th century Auvergne, it relates the loves and trials of the shepherd Celadon and the shepherdess Astrée. Its subtle discussions of love had a great influence on France culture in his day. Though d'Urfé died before finishing the lengthy work, his secretary, Balthazar Baro, completed it from d'Urfé's notes. *Sireine* (1596), a pastoral poem, and *Epîtres morales* (1598), a prose work, are among d'Urfé's other published writings.

D'URFEY, dûr′fē, **Thomas** (1653–1723), English dramatist and songwriter of the Restoration period, popularly called *Tom Durfey*. He was born at Exeter, Devonshire. His first play, the tragedy *The Siege of Memphis; or, the Ambitious Queen*, was produced at the King's Theatre in 1676. He also wrote such popular comedies as *The Fond Husband* (1676) and *Comical History of Don Quixote* (1694–1696), issued in three parts.

Many of the vivacious songs with which D'Urfey embellished his plays were set to music. A well-known collection of his lyrics, *Wit and Mirth; or, Pills to Purge Melancholy*, was published in 1684. D'Urfey's verses were praised by the poet Alexander Pope but ridiculed by the satirist Thomas Brown and the essayist Jeremy Collier. Although many of D'Urfey's songs have survived, his 25 plays quickly lost their popularity. He died in poverty in London on Feb. 26, 1723.

DURGA, do͞or′gä, in the Hindu religion, is either one of the consorts of Shiva (Śiva) or one of the forms of Devi (q.v.), the chief consort of Shiva and the mother goddess and creative spirit of Hinduism. Shiva is one of the two principal gods of contemporary Hinduism, the other being Vishnu (Visnu). Durga is militant and noted for her power. Although well-disposed toward mankind, she is fierce in her treatment of the forces of evil. She can be contrasted in appearance with Kali, her counterpart: Kali is represented as grotesque, whereas Durga is depicted as a woman of celestial beauty.

Durga's principal feats in Hindu legend have to do with the slaying of demons during her descents to earth in various incarnations, or avatars. She was created from the flames of rage that leapt from the gods' mouths after they had been driven out of the celestial kingdom by Mahisa, a buffalo demon. The gods each gave Durga a weapon of combat—Vishnu a discus, Shiva a trident, and Surya a flaming dart—and Durga went to the Vindhya mountains, where she met and killed Mahisa after a violent struggle.

In iconography, Durga is represented wearing a crown and numerous jewels, with a weapon in each of her many arms. She steps down upon the body of a vanquished demon from her steed, a lion, who tears at the demon's body with its claws. As with Kali, the chief center for contemporary worship of Durga is in Bengal. Durga is celebrated at the Durgapuja, a great festival held during the fall.

CHARLES S. J. WHITE
University of Pennsylvania

DURHAM, dûr′əm, **1st Earl of** (1792–1840), British imperial reformer and governor of Canada. He was born John George Lambton, in London, on April 12, 1792. He entered Parliament in 1813. An aristocrat by temperament and background, a democrat by conviction (called "Radical Jack"), he played a leading role in drafting and urging the parliamentary reform bill of 1832. He was of first rank among the now victorious Whig-Liberal forces, but bad health forced him to resign as lord privy seal in 1833 (although he was ambassador to Russia in 1835–1837). Following the rebellions of 1837 in Upper and Lower Canada, he agreed to deal with the colonies' problems for the Melbourne Whig government in Britain.

Durham's Report. In May 1838, Durham arrived in Canada as governor-in-chief and high commissioner. He resigned his post in September and left in November after a quarrel with the Melbourne ministry. But in this brief span he did much to restore tranquillity in Canada and to shape its future through his *Report on the Affairs of British North America* (1839).

The report, in advocating "responsible government" for the colonists, had consequences far beyond Canada in promoting self-government in the British Empire. For Canada, Durham's report analyzed grievances in remarkable depth and detail, recommended many practical improvements, and particularly urged union of the Canadas, French and English, and the granting of responsible government to allow the colonists to manage their own internal affairs on the British ministerial model. Durham died on July 28, 1840, at Cowes, Isle of Wight.

J. M. S. CARELESS, *University of Toronto*

DURHAM, dur'əm, is a maritime county of northeastern England with a coastline on the North Sea between the rivers Tyne and Tees. The Wear River crosses the county from the Pennine Hills to the sea at Sunderland.

Durham's industrial prosperity was founded on coal mining, shipbuilding, iron and steel making, and heavy engineering. The first two have seriously declined in importance. Many mines, especially in western Durham, are worked out. New employment and housing for former miners have been found in more prosperous eastern areas and in "new towns" such as Peterlee and Newton Aycliffe, where new light industries have been developed. There are large steel works at Consett in north Durham. Agriculture is diversified, with stock raising in the Pennine valleys and dairy farming in the eastern lowlands.

The administrative center of the county is Durham city. Durham University was founded in 1832 and originally installed in the castle in that city. The county's residential college for further education is in Lambton Castle near the town of Chester-le-Street.

Notable buildings in Durham county are Washington Old Hall, home of George Washington's ancestors; Raby Castle, a splendid 14th century stronghold; and the Bowes Museum of Arts at Barnard Castle in southwestern Durham.

The Local Goverment Act of 1972 transferred parts of Durham to the county of Tyne and Wear and the county of Cleveland. It also reduced the county's area from 1,015 square miles (2,629 sq km) to 941 square miles (2,436 sq km). Population: (1979 est.) 603,200.

DURHAM, dur'əm, seat of Durham county, England, is an ancient borough 15 miles (24 km) south of Newcastle upon Tyne. The oldest part of Durham is perched on a lofty sandstone peninsula formed by a hairpin turn of the Wear River. Here are the Norman castle, now used by parts of Durham University, the Norman cathedral, and some pleasant 17th and 18th century secular buildings. The modern built-up areas of the city lie across the river. Durham's population is engaged chiefly in the local government, distributive trades, and professional services.

Durham Cathedral, begun in 1093, wears its great age well. Noteworthy are its incised columns and Chapel of the Nine Altars. For centuries the bishops of Durham represented the king in the north of England. The last of these prince-bishops founded the university (1832) by endowing it with the castle and considerable revenue. A valuable recent addition to the university is the Gulbenkian Museum of Art and Archaeology. Population: (1975 est.) 86,500.

GORDON STOKES
Author of "English Place-Names"

DURHAM, dur'əm, a city in north central North Carolina, the seat of Durham county, is 20 miles (32 km) northwest of Raleigh. It is an important industrial and educational center. Situated in the greatest tobacco-growing area in the world, Durham produces about 20% of the cigarettes made in the United States. Nearly 50 million pounds (22.6 million kg) of tobacco is sold each year on the Durham market. The city also manufactures cotton textiles and hosiery, machinery, containers, chemicals, proprietary medicines, furniture, lumber products, building materials, flour, and food for livestock.

BRITISH TRAVEL ASSOCIATION
DURHAM'S Norman cathedral, begun toward the end of the 11th century, rises above the city's Wear River.

The area was first settled by Scotch-Irish and English in 1750. By 1850 there were two villages of fewer than 100 inhabitants each: Durhamville, the present downtown Durham, and Prattsburg, 2 miles (3 km) to the east. When William Pratt, a landowner in Prattsburg, refused to grant a right of way for a railroad station, Dr. Bartlett Durham's offer of 4 acres of land at Durhamville for this purpose was accepted.

The railroad encouraged growth, and industrial development began shortly before the Civil War with the discovery that the soil would produce a fine bright tobacco. Early tobacco factories were operated by John Green and William T. Blackwell, whose product was called "Bull Durham," and by Washington Duke and his sons Brodie, James B., and Benjamin N. The Dukes were the first to mechanize the industry, and in 1881 they began making cigarettes. Their enterprise became the American Tobacco Company.

The philanthropy of the Duke family was largely responsible for making Durham an important educational and medical center. Trinity College, which dated from 1851, became Duke University in 1924, established by James B. Duke with the Duke endowment. The Duke Medical Center is a research and teaching institution. The city is also the site of North Carolina College at Durham.

South of Durham is the 5,000-acre Research Triangle Park, organized in 1959 as an industrial and governmental research center. It is situated in the triangular area formed by Duke University, North Carolina State University at Raleigh, and the University of North Carolina at Chapel Hill.

Durham, incorporated in 1869, is governed by a council and manager. Population: 100,538.

GEORGE R. LINDER
Durham City-County Public Library

DURHAM, University of, dur'əm, a private coeducational university located in Durham, England. It was established in 1832 by an act of Parliament. Originally endowed by revenues of the Church of England, it is now largely supported by government grants. Extension courses were instituted in 1871, and women were first admitted as students in 1896. Durham was federated with King's College in Newcastle upon Tyne until 1963, when the latter became the University of Newcastle upon Tyne.

The University of Durham comprises faculties of arts, divinity, education, music, and science. It includes nine residential colleges and one noncollegiate society. In addition, two foreign colleges are affiliated to Durham: Codrington College, in Barbados, and Fourah Bay College, in Freetown, Sierra Leone. The university maintains an institute of education, a business research unit, and the Gulbenkian Museum for Oriental Art and Archaeology. Durham's enrollment in 1960 was about 1,500; within a decade it had doubled to about 3,000.

DURIAN, doo'rē-ən, the name applied to the fruit of the Malaysian tree *Durio zibethinus* of the bombax family (Bombacaceae) and to the tree itself. The fruit, despite its offensive odor, is prized for its delicious pulp.

Durian trees, which grow to a maximum of 150 feet (45 meters) high, occur in the southern areas of the Philippines and from western New Guinea through Malaya. They are sometimes found in fairly pure stands in northeastern Sumatra, the Celebes, and the Moluccas. Durians have been successfully introduced into Vietnam, Cambodia, Thailand, Burma, Ceylon, and southern India.

The durian, infrequently cultivated, is in an early stage of domestication, and little effort has been made to improve the fruit by breeding and selection. To a limited extent, trees with superior fruits are propagated by budding in order to retain the desired qualities, but propagation is usually accomplished by seed. For this reason, the quality of the fruit varies to a great extent.

The large, round or ovoid, spiny fruits may reach 8 inches (20 cm) in diameter. They have a tough rind that seldom splits open even after the fruit has fallen from a great height. The spines are often very sharp, making it painful to handle the fruit by any portion other than its stalk.

The edible part of the fruit is the pulpy material (aril) that surrounds the seeds. It is commonly eaten fresh, but it is also used as an ingredient of cakes and ice cream or preserved in sugar solution and mixed with spices as a relish. Durian seeds—roasted, fried, or boiled—are also eaten.

Lawrence Erbe
University of Southern Louisiana

Fruit of the durian tree, native to Southeast Asia.
T. H. EVERETT

DURKHEIM, dür-kem', **Émile** (1858–1917), French sociologist, who was one of the founders and leading figures of modern sociology. He was born in Épinal, France, not far from Strasbourg, on April 15, 1858, the son of a distinguished Jewish family. After graduating from the École Normale Supérieure in Paris in 1882, he began teaching philosophy and law. In 1887, at the University of Bordeaux, he taught the first course in sociology in France, and in 1896 he received the first chair in sociology. He later went from Bordeaux to the University of Paris, where he became professor of sociology and education. Durkheim died in Paris on Nov. 12, 1917.

One of Durkheim's principal concerns was to establish a properly scientific method for the study of society. The object of sociological research, in his view, is society as a realm of unique social facts. A basic theme in his writings is the importance of social order or cohesion in society. His concern was to understand the basis of social stability. In his earliest major work, *The Division of Labor in Society* (1893; Eng. tr., 1960), he addresses himself to this problem by contrasting two types of society—the primitive, "mechanically" organized society and the more modern, "organically" functioning society. Each type is based on external pressures that foster cohesion. In the primitive society, cohesion is based on a common or collective conscience, while in the modern society it is based on an integration of special functions and roles. Durkheim believed the change to the more advanced form was caused by increases in population density.

In *Suicide: A Study in Sociology* (1897; Eng. tr., 1951), Durkheim demonstrated how suicide rates reflect variations in social stability. Societies that tend to foster higher rates of suicide are separated into three classes—altruistic, egoistic, and anomic. The anomic is characterized by anomie, which is reflected in the individual by a sense of dislocation and anxiety. It is the fundamental type for modern societies and occurs in the presence of major economic changes, such as depressions or periods of sudden increases in wealth.

Durkheim's last major work, *The Elementary Forms of the Religious Life* (1915; Eng. tr., 1954), again stressed the importance of collective representations. These collective forms were a reality independent of consciousness. Religion was the clearest expression of these forms. The oneness of society was necessarily related to the sacred or religious functions. The stability of society is dependent, therefore, upon a stability of beliefs and values that are both sacred and profane.

John M. Goering
Washington University, St. Louis

DUROCHER də-rō'shər, **Leo Ernest** (1906–), American baseball player and manager. He was born in West Springfield, Mass., on July 27, 1906. He played a year each in Atlanta and St. Paul and two years with the New York Yankees before being sold to Cincinnati in 1930. He moved to the St. Louis Cardinals in 1933 and became key man of the "Gas House gang" that defeated Detroit in the 1934 World Series. A cocky, fiery player, he was nicknamed "Lippy."

Traded to the Brooklyn Dodgers in October 1937, Durocher became captain in 1938 and manager 1939–1946, and 1948; he won the pennant in 1941. In 1947 he was suspended for the season by Commissioner Albert Chandler for "cumulated unpleasant incidents," which he did not fully explain.

From 1948 to 1955, Durocher managed the New York Giants, taking two pennants (1951 and 1954) and winning the 1954 World Series. He entered television in 1955 but returned to baseball as coach of the Los Angeles Dodgers from 1961 to 1964. Named manager of the Chicago Cubs in 1965, Durocher led them from tenth place in 1966 to third in 1967.

BOB MCCORMICK, *Associated Features Inc.*

DURRELL, dŭr'əl, **Lawrence** (1912–), Anglo-Irish author, who wrote the tetralogy *The Alexandria Quartet—Justine* (1957), *Balthazar* (1958), *Mountolive* (1958), and *Clea* (1960). Set in Alexandria, Egypt, the *Quartet* explores the varied and complex aspects of human love, telling essentially the same story from various viewpoints in the different volumes. The work, written in rich, rhythmic prose, is regarded by some critics as a major contribution to 20th century English literature.

Durrell was born of Irish parents in the Himalayan region of India, on Feb. 27, 1912, and was taken to England as a youngster. An indifferent student, he attended numerous schools, finally quitting his studies to take on odd jobs, including that of jazz pianist in a London nightclub.

Shortly after moving to Corfu in 1935, he began a long and fruitful correspondence with Henry Miller, who became his mentor. In 1938, Durrell published *The Black Book*, a novel that foreshadowed many elements of the *Quartet*. From 1941 to 1956 he held various official and diplomatic posts in the Middle East and Mediterranean area, using his experiences as the subject matter for such works as *Bitter Lemons* (1957), a travel book on Cyprus, and *Tunc* (1968), a psychological adventure story set in London, Istanbul, and Athens. He also wrote plays, including *Acte* (1962).

HARRY T. MOORE, *Southern Illinois University*

DÜRRENMATT, dür'ən-mät, **Friedrich** (1921–), Swiss playwright and novelist, whose work has affinities with black humor and the theater of the absurd, but whose taut, ironic idiom is uniquely his own. In all his works, he exploits the subtle convergences of fantasy and reality, of the comic and the grotesque.

Dürrenmatt was born in Konolfingen, near Bern, on Jan. 5, 1921, and was educated at the universities of Bern and Zürich. His first play, *Der Blinde*, was produced in 1948, but he reached a much larger audience when *Die Ehe des Herrn Mississippi* (1952) was produced in New York in 1958 as *Fools Are Passing Through*. His most widely known stage work is the tragic farce *Der Besuch der alten Dame* (1956), successfully staged in New York as *The Visit* (1958).

Dürrenmatt's novels include *Der Richter und sein Henker* (1952; Eng. tr., *The Judge and His Hangman*, 1955); *Der Verdacht* (1953; Eng. tr., *The Quarry*, 1962); *Grieche sucht Griechen* (1955); *Die Panne* (1956; Eng. tr., *The Dangerous Game*, 1960); and *Das Versprechen* (1958; Eng. tr., *The Pledge*, 1959).

DAVID GALLOWAY, *Author of "The Absurd Hero"*

DURRËS, door'rəs, a seaport in Albania, is on the Adriatic coast, about 19 miles (30 km) from Tiranë. Durrës (Italian, *Durazzo*) is Albania's principal port. Its harbor installations, destroyed by the German Army in 1944, were rebuilt and improved after the war. A railroad links the port with Tiranë and Elbasan. There was also considerable industrial development in the region after the war. Flour, clothing, cigarettes, rubber, salt, and bricks are produced.

The first city on this site, Epidamnus, was founded by Greek colonists in the 7th century B.C. It later came under Roman rule and was renamed Dyrrachium. It was the terminus of the military highway, the Via Egnatia, that led overland to Salonika. With the decline of Roman power, the area was invaded repeatedly. The city was held by Ostrogoths, Bulgarians, Normans, Byzantine Greeks, Serbians, and Venetians before it fell to the Ottoman Turks in 1501.

When an independent Albanian state was established in 1912, Durrës was its first capital. In World War I it was occupied first by the Austrians and then by the Italians, who left in 1920. In 1939, at the beginning of World War II, the Italians returned and launched an invasion of Albania through this port. By the late 1950's the port had assumed political importance. Isolated from its immediate neighbors, both Communist and non-Communist, Albania depended on its sea communications with its one ally, China, and on its trade with such states as Italy. Population: (1963 est.) 45,935.

BARBARA JELAVICH and CHARLES JELAVICH
Indiana University

DURYEA, door'yā, **Charles Edgar** (1861–1938), American automobile manufacturer who, with his brother J. Frank Duryea (1870–1967), built the first commercially successful cars in the United States. Duryea was born in Canton, Ill., on Dec. 15, 1861. He and his brother were bicycle mechanics when they decided to build a car. The bicycle craze had developed mechanical elements essential for cars.

The Duryeas ushered in the automobile era in America with their two-cycle, one-cylinder car, which was driven in Springfield, Mass., on Sept. 21, 1893. Their second car (1894), a four-cycle, two-cylinder automobile, received great publicity when it won the Chicago *Times-Herald* race on Nov. 28, 1895. Their fifth car (1894) had many features of modern automobiles: a gear shift for three speeds forward and one reverse, a water-jacketed, four-cylinder engine with electric ignition, a bevel gear differential, and a rigid front axle with steering knuckles. The Duryea motor wagon company, established in 1895, made 13 cars in 1896. Duryea died in Philadelphia, Pa., on Sept. 28, 1938.

ROBERT S. WOODBURY
Massachusetts Institute of Technology

DUSE, doo′zə, **Eleonora** (1859–1924), Italian actress, who, with Sarah Bernhardt (q.v.), ruled the stage in the 19th and early 20th century. Duse was born in Vigevano on Oct. 3, 1859, into a theatrical family, and began acting at the age of four. She first caught the attention of the public when she played Juliet at Verona when she was 14. In 1878 she went to Naples, where she won critical acclaim for her interpretations of Ophelia, Electra in Alfieri's *Oreste,* and the title role in Zola's *Thérèse Raquin.*

When she saw Bernhardt perform in 1882, Duse was encouraged to abandon roles that bored her and repertory she found stale for more demanding parts in new French plays, particularly by Dumas *fils.* She formed her own troupe, which, after 1890, toured throughout Europe and the United States. Duse was idolized everywhere for her stirring performances in such plays as Dumas' *La dame aux camélias,* Sardou's *Fédora,* Goldoni's *La Locandiera,* Pinero's *Second Mrs. Tanqueray,* and Ibsen's *Doll's House, Rosmersholm, Hedda Gabler,* and *Lady from the Sea.*

In 1897, Duse fell in love with the tempestuous, talented Italian poet Gabriele D'Annunzio (q.v.), who wrote showy parts for her and whose plays, especially *Francesca da Rimini* (1902), she helped to succeed. D'Annunzio fictionalized their mutually stimulating affair in his novel *Il fuoco* (1900).

In 1909, Duse, plagued by illness, retired, but financial need frequently forced her to return to the stage. Her last New York appearance, in 1923, was in her favorite Ibsen play, *Lady from the Sea.* She died in Pittsburgh, Pa., on April 21, 1924, while on tour.

Style. Duse is inevitably contrasted with Bernhardt. While "the divine Sarah" was a flamboyant, histrionic actress, always playing Bernhardt no matter what the role, "the Duse" was simple, lacking apparent artifice. Her underplaying, her thorough comprehension of the psychological motives of the women she played, her skill in adapting her face, walk, voice, and gestures to each new role resulted in the subordination of her personality to that of the character. As Duse observed, she did not "act" her roles; she "lived" them. Partly from her underacting technique springs the predominant contemporary American style of acting. Despite Duse's habitual restraint, her emotional evocation was unbounded. Time, prodded by George Bernard Shaw, has given Duse the nod over Bernhardt.

J. SHERWOOD WEBER, *Pratt Institute*

DUSHAN, Stephen. See STEPHEN DUSHAN.

DUSHANBE, doo-shán′bə, in the USSR, is the capital of the Tadzhik republic, in Central Asia. The city is situated in a valley at the foot of the Gissar (Hissar) Mountains, an outlying range of the Tien Shan system, at the junction of two railroad lines and several highways. Dushanbe is the industrial, cultural, and transport center of the Tadzhik republic. It accounts for about one third of the republic's manufacturing output. Most of the industries are based on the agricultural products of the surrounding countryside. Among the industries are cotton milling, garment and leather goods manufacturing, meat packing, and wine making.

Dushanbe has a multinational population, but the two main groups are the Tadzhiks and the Russians. The city is the seat of Tadzhik University and the Tadzhik Academy of Sciences. It also has a Tadzhik opera and ballet, and Tadzhik and Russian drama theaters. Dushanbe is a city of broad, straight streets and pastel-colored buildings. The height of the latter is limited to two or three stories because of earthquakes.

The city was founded in 1925 on the site of the village of Dushanbe or Dushambe, a name meaning "Monday," for the day on which the market was held there. The city was named Stalinabad from 1929 to 1961. It then reverted to its original name. Population: (1971 est.) 388,000.

THEODORE SHABAD
Editor of "Soviet Geography"

DUSSEK, doo′sek, **Jan Ladislav** (1760–1812), Czech pianist and composer. His name is also spelled *Dušek* or *Dusík.* He was born in Čáslav, Bohemia, on Feb. 12, 1760, and became a pupil of Karl Philipp Emanuel Bach in Hamburg. He achieved fame not only as a pianist but also as a virtuoso of the newly invented harmonica.

Most of his compositions are piano works, but he also wrote an opera, *The Captive of Spilberg,* produced in London in 1798; incidental music for Richard Brinsley Sheridan's play *Pizarro* (1799); chamber music; 6 harp sonatinas; and songs. Dussek died at St.-Germain-en-Laye, France, on March 20, 1812.

DÜSSELDORF, düs′əl-dôrf, is an industrial city in West Germany. Lying on the east bank of the Rhine River, 21 miles (34 km) northwest of Cologne, it is the capital of the state of North Rhine-Westphalia.

Though situated well to the south of the Ruhr coalfield, it owes its growth in the 19th and 20th centuries largely to the expansion of heavy industry in the Ruhr area. It was never a center of the primary metal industries, but it developed very important machine-construction and metal-fabricating industries. Many of these are controlled by the iron and steelmaking concerns in the Ruhr, which supply most of the raw materials. Düsseldorf, cleaner and more spacious than the cities of the Ruhr, contains the business headquarters of several Ruhr companies.

Düsseldorf is also a river port, though its docks are less extensive than those of Neuss on the opposite bank of the Rhine. The city also serves as a shopping, banking, and cultural center for the industrialized lower Rhineland.

The city was founded in the 13th century and became the capital of the county of Berg. It was long overshadowed by its neighbor Cologne. In 1805 it became the capital of Napoleon's grand duchy of Berg, and in 1815 it was added to the kingdom of Prussia. Its modern industrial growth began in the mid-19th century, when shipping on the Rhine developed and railways linked it with the rapidly developing industries of the Ruhr.

Düsseldorf has a famous academy of art which produced its own school of painting in the 19th century. A few 18th century buildings, as well as a medieval church and Renaissance city hall, have survived in the modern city, which was largely rebuilt after damage in World War II; but the palace of the electors palatine was destroyed by fire in 1872. The city center is now distinguished by its wide streets, squares, and parks, which make it one of the most dignified of industrial cities. Population: (1971) 660,963.

NORMAN J. G. POUNDS, *Indiana University*

DUST is composed of tiny particles of many kinds of solid materials. The particles have diameters of less than 0.0025 millimeters (0.0001 inches); a million typical dust particles would have a total volume equal to about one grain of sand. The particles consist of minerals, organic matter, soot, radioactive materials, and salt from evaporated sea spray. In relatively pure air there are fewer than 500 particles of dust per cubic centimeter (1 cc = 0.06 cu inches), whereas dirty air may contain more than 50,000 particles per cc. Inside a house where there is much activity, the concentration of organic dust alone may reach 100,000 particles per cc; the particles include bacteria, spores, and bits of cotton, wool, wood, and hair, in addition to the usual amounts of soot and minerals.

Sources. Natural sources of dust are volcanoes, dry land areas, sea spray, forest fires, meteorites, plant spores, and bacteria. Man also contributes great amounts of dust to the atmosphere, directly and indirectly By cultivating semiarid land and thus removing wild grasses whose roots stabilize the soil, he has exposed dry soil to the wind and created recurrent dust bowls. Smoke from industry and from burning refuse and radioactive materials from nuclear explosions are among man's direct contributions to atmospheric dust.

Distribution. The average number of dust particles suspended in the open atmosphere is about 15,000 per cc over land areas and 200 per cc over the oceans. The particles are mostly minerals. Concentrations decrease upward; at heights of more than 50,000 feet (15,000 meters) there may be only 5 to 35 particles per cc. Over dry, wind-swept land surfaces the concentration sometimes is great enough to reduce visibility to a few yards. Dust and smoke haze over cities may reduce visibility to a mile or so.

The frictional drag of wind on dust particles is proportional to the square of their diameter; the force of gravity on them is proportional to the cube of their diameter. Thus, the smaller the particle is, the more effective is wind drag in carrying it aloft and holding it in suspension. Very small particles may remain aloft for years. Particles larger than 0.004 mm in diameter fall out of the atmosphere in a short time.

Measurement. Dust concentrations can be measured with the Aitken dust counter, a chamber in which a sample of air is collected, mixed with moist pure air, and forced to expand by suction. The expanding air cools, and droplets of water condense on the dust particles. The droplets settle on a plate and are counted under a microscope. Dust concentration also can be determined by exposing a plate covered by an oil film that collects the particles, or by drawing air through a porous material that retains them. Rough estimations of dust content can be made from the degree of visibility through the atmosphere (when fog is absent) and from the intensity of the colors of sunrise and sunset.

Beneficial Effects. Dust is both beneficial and harmful. If there were no dust in the atmosphere, much less rain and snow would fall, because dust particles are the nuclei on which are formed the water droplets and ice crystals of clouds. In order for water vapor to condense in the absence of dust, the relative humidity would have to be very much greater than 100%. Two kinds of particles may be distinguished. *Hygroscopic nuclei* are soluble particles that can convert water vapor into liquid water droplets at less than 100% humidity. *Sublimation nuclei* are nonsoluble particles on which water vapor is deposited in the form of ice.

The beauty of sunsets is due to the scattering of light by dust particles. Blue light is scattered more than red light, giving the glorious reds and oranges of sunset. For a short time at sunset, the blue of the sky merges with the red near the sun, producing the delicate "purple light." A major volcanic eruption injects many very fine particles into the high atmosphere. These particles persist for a year or more and create extremely colorful sunsets.

Harmful Effects. The time and money spent on ridding homes, offices, streets, and clothing of their accumulated dust is incalculable. Dust inhaled in normal quantities is ejected by the lungs, but in greater concentration it may accumulate instead. This leads to such diseases as silicosis, which occurs among workers exposed to silica dust produced by grinding and drilling operations, and which in turn may result in tuberculosis. In addition, radioactive dust from nuclear explosions continually falls to earth or is washed down by rain. It presents a potential danger of overexposure to radioactivity, especially to those radioactive substances that are absorbed and retained by the body. Finally, dust storms remove valuable topsoil and reduce the productivity of farmlands.

Control. To control dust, streets are sprinkled in dry weather, air conditioners are used to filter indoor air, and, in periods of severe drought, farmlands may be deep-plowed to bring hard clay up to cover the topsoil. In industries where workers or machinery are adversely affected, dust can be filtered at the source where it is produced, or workers may wear protective masks. The ultimate effects on human health of dusts produced by modern industry, transportation, and agriculture are not yet well known. Dust is but one of the many pollutants that are by-products of man's increasing standard of living and are at the same time a threat to his survival.

JAMES E. MILLER
New York University

DUST BOWL is a popular term describing a region of 150,000 square miles (390,000 sq km) in southwestern Kansas, southeastern Colorado, northeastern New Mexico, and the Oklahoma and Texas panhandles, which was devastated by drought in 1933–1939. It is an area of low annual rainfall (15 inches, or 381 mm) and of light soils and is swept each spring by high winds.

Stock raising predominated in the area until World War I, when high grain prices encouraged farmers to plow up millions of acres of grassland for winter wheat. A long drought set in during the 1930's, the Depression years in the United States. The winds blowing over dry bare fields piled sand in dunes, some 30 feet (9 meters) high. Roads and fences were covered, houses and barns were banked with sand, and pasture grasses were choked. Lighter silt accumulated in dust clouds, some of which were 5 miles (8 km) high, forming "black blizzards" that swept to the Atlantic coast. Counties in the dust bowl lost 60% of their population through migration.

The resulting large-scale wind erosion was a new agricultural problem, but government agencies moved to aid in land salvage. The federal Soil Conservation Service and local soil conservation districts set up demonstration projects to teach farm rehabilitation methods. Millions of acres were restored to grass. Rows of trees were planted to check wind and hold the soil. Farmers were encouraged to allow half their cultivated land to lie fallow each year, storing moisture in the subsoil for the next year's crop. Drought-resistant cover crops, in strips alternating with fallow land, checked the wind. Contour plowing and terracing helped hold rainwater.

By 1941 the dust bowl had been rehabilitated. But prosperity and plentiful rains in the World War II years enticed farmers again to plow up grasslands and plant wheat. A long drought in the 1950's augured a return of the dust bowl. In 1956, Congress approved the Great Plains program to restore several million acres of wheat land to grass. The Soil Bank plan paid farmers to retire grain lands. Increased irrigation provided moisture for drought periods. Farmers learned that to prevent dust bowl conditions the soil must not be denuded and moisture must be stored to carry crops through dry periods.

ARRELL M. GIBSON, *University of Oklahoma*

DUST CLOUD THEORY. See COSMOLOGY; SOLAR SYSTEM.

DUST DEVIL, a whirling funnel of sand and dust that occurs in the heat of the day, as a result of strong convection, in hot and dusty regions such as tropical deserts. Although the funnel of a dust devil is no more than a few yards in diameter, it may extend upward 2,000 to 3,000 feet (600–900 meters). The whirlwinds move at a rate of 5 to 30 miles (8–48 km) an hour.

DUSTIN, dus'tin, **Hannah** (born 1659), American frontier heroine. She was born in Haverhill, Mass., on Dec. 23, 1659. Indians attacked Haverhill on March 16, 1697, killed some 40 persons including Mrs. Dustin's week-old child, and carried her and her nurse into captivity. Guarded by an Indian party of two men, three women, and seven children, the captives were being taken to a large Indian village when they halted for the night at an island six miles (10 km) above present-day Concord, N. H. Samuel Lennardson, a young English captive, helped Mrs. Dustin kill all the Indians in their sleep except a squaw and a small boy, who escaped. She then scalped the dead to have proof of her exploit. After an arduous journey, the two women and Lennardson returned to Haverhill, where Mrs. Dustin rejoined her husband Thomas and their seven surviving children. The circumstances of her death are unknown.

DUSTY MILLER is a name commonly applied to a number of plants that are densely covered with a white woolly coating of matted hairs. One species, *Artemisia stelleriana*, is also called "beach wormwood" and "old woman." It belongs to the composite family (Compositae) and is a perennial plant about 2 feet (60 cm) tall with feathery leaves and small heads of flowers. Originally native to Asia, it is planted in gardens as a border plant. Two other composites also known as dusty miller are *Centaurea cineraria* and *Senecio cineraria*. Another plant known as dusty miller is *Lycknis coronaria*, which belongs to the pink family (Caryphyllaceae). It is also known as the "rose campion" and the "mullein pink."

SYDNEY C. BAUSOR
California State College, Pa.

DUSUN, dōō'sən, the largest ethnic group indigenous to the state of Sabah (formerly North Borneo) in Malaysia. Sabah natives did not traditionally call themselves by this name. The term was applied to them by invading Malays and was later adopted by the British during the colonial period (1877–1963). The term is now widely used even in Bornean literature.

An agricultural people, the Dusun are of the Malay race and speak a variety of closely related Malayo–Polynesian dialects. There are well over 145,000 Dusun, most of whom are animists, although approximately 25% are listed as Christians and 7% as Muslims.

Dusun villages are found primarily in the coastal, interior plain, and hill regions of western Sabah. In the former two regions, irrigated rice is the staple crop, while in the hills dry rice is cultivated. Multifamily longhouses are typical of Dusun communities in northern Sabah, while single-family dwellings occur in coastal and inland plain areas. Traditionally the village was the largest political unit. After 1963 all Dusun communities were integrated into the state of Sabah.

ALFRED BACON HUDSON
Michigan State University

DUTCH ART AND ARCHITECTURE. See NETHERLANDS—*Cultural Life* (Art).

DUTCH CHURCH. See REFORMED CHURCH IN AMERICA—*Netherlands Reformed Church.*

DUTCH EAST INDIA COMPANY. See EAST INDIA COMPANIES.

DUTCH EAST INDIES. See INDONESIA.

DUTCH ELM DISEASE is a serious fungus disease responsible for the destruction of thousands of American elm trees. The disease was first noticed in the Netherlands around 1920 and was discovered in the United States near Cleveland in 1930. Today it is found from the east coast to the Rocky Mountains and from the Southern states into Canada.

The disease, which is caused by the fungus *Ceratocystis ulmi*, is characterized by wilting leaves and browning of the vascular tissue beneath the bark. The fungus is transmitted from diseased to healthy trees by two bark beetles, the native bark beetle and the lesser European bark beetle, during their feeding activities. It is also spread underground between the roots of trees.

Once a tree is infected, the fungal spores move rapidly throughout the tree's water-conducting system, plugging the vessels and producing toxic substances. Wilting may be confined to only a few branches or may develop throughout the entire canopy. Once diseased, a tree will not recover, although a large tree may survive for several years.

The successful control of Dutch elm disease is seldom achieved unless communities faithfully execute a sanitation program, destroying all trees that are diseased or are suspected of being diseased. Spraying healthy trees with insecticide to control the bark beetles also helps prevent the spread of the disease. In addition, some elm species are more resistant to the disease than the American elm.

JERRY T. WALKER
Brooklyn Botanic Garden

DUTCH LANGUAGE, a West Germanic language, as are English and German. Some scholars recognize Old Dutch, of the period from about 400 to 1100 A.D., as the oldest form of the language, and all scholars agree that "Middle Dutch" is the proper name for the language that flourished from about 1100 to 1500. An important body of literature, both poetry and prose, was created during this period. Until the end of the 15th century, the language of the people was called *diets* or *duuts,* as distinguished from the language of the church, which was Latin, and the modern English word "Dutch" is derived from *diets* (*duuts*). At the end of the 15th century the language acquired its modern name —*Nederlands.*

Modern Dutch. The earlier forms of modern Dutch can be traced back to the 17th century and even to the 16th, but the literary language did not achieve a standard form until the 18th century. The great 17th century poet Joost van den Vondel wrote in a language that differs as much from modern Dutch as Shakespeare's language does from modern English.

Both its structure and its vocabulary show modern Dutch to be a Germanic language, but it is simpler than German because many inflectional endings were dropped, especially for the cases of nouns. As a result of several spelling reforms, Dutch spelling is much simpler than English spelling.

The standard language of the Netherlands is called Algemeen Beschaafd Nederlands (Standard Educated Dutch). Standard Dutch developed mainly from the language spoken in Amsterdam and other cities of the old province of Holland, with some elements from the south, especially from Brabant, so that the Dutch sometimes call their language *Hollands.* Modern dialects in the Netherlands include Gronings, Drents, Limburgs, Oost-Hollands, West-Vlaams, and Brabants.

The speaker of German or English would have little difficulty with the grammar of the Dutch language and would immediately recognize such words as *man* (man), *drie* (three), *warm* (warm), *school* (school), *ijs* (ice), *hand* (hand), and *melk* (milk), but there are many common words that are quite different, such as *mooi* (pretty), *kwaad* (bad), *leuk* (nice), *heus* (really), *fooi* (tip), *fiets* (bicycle), and *raam* (window). Also unfamiliar are some of the Dutch diphthongs, such as *ij* (ī), *eu* (û), and *ui* (oi); characteristic consonants that are difficult to pronounce are *g* (KH) and *sch* (SKH).

Dutch-Speaking Peoples. There are over 17 million speakers of Dutch; 12 million live in the Netherlands; and 5 million live in Belgium, where they speak Flemish. Numerous other speakers of Dutch are scattered throughout the world, in such places as the Netherlands territory of Surinam. Afrikaans (q.v.), the language spoken by the Afrikaners of South Africa, is an independent language that developed from Dutch during the 17th century and represents even further simplification of the original language. See also FLEMISH LANGUAGE.

SEYMOUR L. FLAXMAN, *City College of the City University of New York*

DUTCH NEW GUINEA. See NEW GUINEA.

DUTCH REFORMED CHURCH. See REFORMED CHURCH IN AMERICA.

DUTCH WARS, the name given to the three wars of the 17th century between England and the Netherlands. Of the three wars at least the first two were primarily the result of commercial rivalry. Dutch control of the East Indies, predominance in seaborne trade and North Sea fishery, and virtual monopoly of the distribution of English exports aroused English hostility. The Dutch sought protection in the principle of the free seas, but the English claimed sovereignty over the seas, demanding recognition of their right to search Dutch ships and compensation for Dutch fishing activities.

Oliver Cromwell initially saw the Dutch anti-Orangist government as an ally for the English Commonwealth, because he feared the Orange-Stuart connection (William II of Orange married Mary Stuart in 1641). But when plans for an Anglo-Dutch union failed, he gave way to the anti-Dutch demands of the English trading interests. A protectionist Navigation Act, prohibiting the carriage of English goods in Dutch ships, was passed in October 1651, and in May 1652 war began.

First Dutch War (1652–1654). It soon became apparent that the Dutch fleet was not capable of simultaneously fighting the English and protecting seaborne trade in the North Sea. The trading province of Holland pushed through peace negotiations, which resulted in the Peace of Westminster (April 1654). The main issues were left undecided, but the province of Holland, in a separate Act of Seclusion, promised Cromwell to exclude the house of Orange from office.

Second Dutch War (1665–1667). The restoration of Charles II in England (1660) did not improve Anglo-Dutch relations. In 1664 the English seized possessions of the Dutch West Indies Company in West Africa and North America, and war began in 1665. The Dutch navy defeated the English repeatedly and penetrated the Thames estuary. The Peace of Breda (July 1667) defined the rights of neutral trade as the Dutch demanded and softened the interpretation of the Navigation Act. The Dutch kept Surinam but ceded New Netherland to the English.

Third Dutch War (1672–1674). The initiative for the third war came from Louis XIV, who saw Dutch power as an obstacle to French expansion in the Spanish Netherlands. In 1670 he concluded the secret Treaty of Dover with Charles II against the Dutch. The French attacked in March 1672 and occupied much of the republic. But the Dutch fleet won all its battles with the English. The desperate situation in the republic had brought William III of Orange to power as stadholder, but he refused to negotiate with either enemy. Opposition to Charles II in Parliament led to the Second Peace of Westminster (February 1674); the English dropped their pretension to sovereignty of the seas and conceded free fishery rights to the Dutch.

English trading interests had wanted to settle their problems with the Dutch out of fear of France. The Franco-Dutch war, its course affected less by the English withdrawal than by the formation of a European coalition against France (1673), continued until 1678–1679 (Treaty of Nijmegen). Anglo-Dutch relations improved steadily. After the accession of William of Orange to the English throne in 1688, the Anglo-Dutch alliance was to become the mainstay of the coalitions against Louis XIV.

JACOB W. SMIT, *Columbia University*

DUTCH WEST INDIA COMPANY. Incorporated in 1621 by a charter from the States-General of the Netherlands, the Dutch West India Company was granted a monopoly over Dutch trade along the Atlantic coasts of Africa and the Americas. Its central purpose was to regulate the contraband trade with Spanish and Portuguese America, especially in supplying Negro slaves. Distinctions between piracy, trade, and war were unclear in the mercantilist era, and the company's history was largely one of strife.

In 1624 the Dutch West India Company took Bahia (now Salvador), Brazil, but soon lost it. In 1628 the company's coffers were swelled by Piet Hein's capture of a Spanish silver fleet off Cuba. The establishment of trading posts followed. Pernambuco (now Recife), Brazil, was held from 1630 to 1654. Curaçao, taken from Spain in 1634, became the center of Dutch West Indian trade. Other posts included St. Eustatius, Bonaire, Aruba, Saba, and St. Martin.

The North American colony of New Netherland dated from an earlier company's establishment of Fort Nassau (Fort Orange), now the site of Albany, N.Y., and of the New Amsterdam trading post, now New York City. The Dutch West India Company in 1624 sent 30 Walloon families to New Amsterdam. Settlements were started in the Hudson, Mohawk, and Connecticut valleys and on Long Island, and in 1637 Peter Stuyvesant captured New Sweden in the Delaware Valley.

Although agriculture and shipbuilding were developed, the company's directors were more interested in the fur and slave trade and in booty taken from Spaniards. Wars cost the company dearly. In 1650 part of Long Island was lost to the English. In 1661 all Dutch claims to Brazil were relinquished. In 1664 the English fleet forced New Amsterdam to surrender—an event not wholly unwelcomed by the settlers, who by now were of many ethnic origins and were disenchanted with the feudal-manorial patroon system imposed on them. By the Peace of Breda (1667) the company received Surinam (Dutch Guiana) in exchange for the lost North American holdings. The company was dissolved in 1674 and reorganized in 1675. For over a century it traded with Surinam and the West Indies.

RANDALL M. EVANSON
Wisconsin State University, Oshkosh

DUTCH WEST INDIES. See NETHERLANDS ANTILLES.

DUTCHMAN'S BREECHES, brich'əz, a low-growing, herbaceous perennial with flowers resembling Dutch pantaloons. Each flower has two small sepals, two pairs of petals, and two spurs, or saclike projections, extending from the base of the two outer petals. The flowers are white and are borne in a cluster of 4 to 10 blossoms.

The delicate compound leaves of the plant arise from a bulblike tuber in the soil. The leaves are composed of 3 parts that are divided into linear lobes. The flowering shoot, like the leaves, arises from the underground tuber.

The Dutchman's breeches is native to the northeastern United States, where it grows on wooded hills and rocky slopes. It is known botanically as *Dicentra cucullaria* and belongs to the fumitory family (Fumariaceae).

SYDNEY C. BAUSOR
California State College, Pa.

Dutchman's pipe (*Aristolochia durior*)

DUTCHMAN'S PIPE, a woody vine named for its S-shaped, tubular flowers, which somewhat resemble a long-stemmed Dutch pipe. The tubular portion of each flower is greenish and is about 1 to 1½ inches (25 to 38 mm) long. Surrounding the open end of the flower is a 3-lobed, purplish rim.

The flowers appear singly or in twos or threes and arise from the leaf axils, the upper angles between the leaves and the stem. The leaves of the vine are heart shaped and may reach a width of 15 inches (38 cm), although they are usually smaller.

The Dutchman's pipe is known botanically as *Aristolochia durior*, and it is a member of the birthwort family (Aristolochiaceae). The vine is native to the eastern United States and is sometimes cultivated for use as an arbor or pergola cover.

SYDNEY C. BAUSOR
California State College, Pa.

Dutchman's breeches (*Dicentra cucullaria*)

DUTOURD, cü-toor', **Jean** (1920–   ), French writer, who won the Prix Interallié for his ribald satire on French middle-class society, *Au bon beurre* (1952), translated into English as *The Best Butter* (1955). Dutourd was born in Paris on Jan. 14, 1920. He studied philosophy at the Sorbonne and served in the Resistance in World War II. Later, working as a journalist, he began writing satires as an avocation, achieving international popularity with his fantasy *Une tête de chien* (1949), published in English as *A Dog's Head* (1951). Among his other books are a collection of satirical versions of popular stories, *The Last of the Redskins* (Eng. tr., 1965); and *The Horrors of Love* (Eng tr., 1967), a novel in dialogue form.

DUTRA, doo'trə, **Eurico Gaspar** (1885–1974), president of Brazil. He was born on May 18, 1885, in Cuiabá, Mato Grosso, Brazil. A professional soldier, he became minister of war in 1936. Early in World War II he was considered an Axis sympathizer, but in 1942, Brazil enlisted on the Allied side. Elected president in December 1945, the colorless Dutra replaced the clever dictator Getulio Vargas in January 1946.

His government was more democratic than that of Vargas, even though Dutra was backed by the army. Freedom of the press was allowed, and the federal government was decentralized. His chief political problem was the Communist party, which was outlawed by his government. Brazil's inflationary economy was Dutra's major concern. He tried in many ways to improve conditions. In 1951 he was succeeded by Vargas. He died in Rio de Janeiro on June 11, 1974.

HELEN MILLER BAILEY
East Los Angeles College

DUTT, dôt, **Michael Madhu Sudan** (1824–1873), Bengali poet, who was one of the creators of modern Bengali literature. He was born in Sagandari, Bengal, India, on Jan. 25, 1824, and studied at Hindu College in Calcutta.

Dutt's first poems were in English, the best known being *The Captive Ladies* (1848). Its lukewarm reception in Calcutta literary circles convinced him to turn to his native Bengali for poetic expression. His first attempts in Bengali were dramas dating from 1858. His fame in Bengali literature rests on his epic *Meghanad-Badh* (1861; *The Fall of Meghanad*), based on an episode from the *Ramayana*, and on his numerous sonnets, the first examples of that genre in Bengali. Fluent in 10 European and Indian languages, he borrowed freely from both traditions. His revolt against conventionality and verbosity that then burdened Bengali poetry marks him as one of the most innovative of 19th century Indian poets.

In 1862, Dutt went to England to prepare himself for the bar at Grey's Inn. He returned to Calcutta in 1867 and practiced law there until his death on June 29, 1873.

CARLO COPPOLA, *Oakland University, Mich.*

DUTT, dôt, **Toru** (1856–1877), the first Indian woman to write significant poetry in English. Born on March 4, 1856, in Calcutta, she received her early education from her father and between 1869 and 1873 studied in France and England.

Returning to India, she published her translations of French poetry, *A Sheaf Gleaned in French Fields* (1875), and set herself to learning Sanskrit in order to translate from that language into English. Her Sanskrit translations were posthumously published in 1882. Although her translations and her own poetry have certain defects of metrics and diction, her narrative passages and descriptions of nature often equal the best in Western romantic poetry. Toru Dutt died of tuberculosis in Calcutta on Aug. 30, 1877, at the age of 21.

CARLO COPPOLA, *Oakland University, Mich.*

DUTTON, Edward Payson (1831–1923), American publisher, who founded the publishing firm of E. P. Dutton and Co. He was born on Jan. 4, 1831, in Keene, N.H., and educated in Boston. From 1852 he was a partner in the Boston bookselling firm of Ide and Dutton, which he later reorganized as E. P. Dutton and Co.

Dutton bought the Boston retail firm of Ticknor and Fields and the bookselling business of the General Protestant Episcopal Sunday School Union and Church Book Society of New York in 1864 and moved his headquarters to New York City in 1869. In 1904 he acquired the U. S. rights to Everyman's Library (low-priced reprints of world classics) from the English publisher J. M. Dent. Dutton died in Ridgefield, Conn., on Sept. 6, 1923.

DUTTON, Ira Barnes (1843–1931), American Roman Catholic missionary among the lepers on the Hawaiian island of Molokai. He was born in Stowe, Vt., on April 27, 1843. As a young man he was a clerk, newspaperman, soldier, distillery superintendent, railroad freight agent, and government claims investigator. During the Civil War he was a Union Army lieutenant.

Dutton became a Catholic in 1883 and for 20 months lived in the Trappist monastery at Gethsemane, Ky., taking the name Brother Joseph. In 1886 he went to Molokai to help Father Damien (q.v.) care for the lepers. Later he joined the lay order of St. Francis (Third Order Secular). After Father Damien's death in 1888, Brother Joseph became administrative assistant of the leper colony and founded the Baldwin Home for men and boys. He died in Honolulu on March 26, 1931.

MARION A. HABIG, O.F.M.
St. Augustine Friary, Chicago, Ill.

DUTY. The term "duty" covers a family of related concepts. The central notion is that an act is one's duty if and only if it is wrong not to perform it. A *legal duty* is more specifically an act that must be performed on pain of being subject to criminal punishment or civil suit, except when certain defenses can be made. A *moral duty* is some act, failure to perform which renders one properly liable to condemnation or punishment, except when a valid excuse can be offered. People also commonly speak of the duties of a position or role (for example, duties to parents), meaning partly actions that are duties in a legal or moral sense as a consequence of the position or role, and partly the recognized functions of that position or role.

The concept of moral duty is one of the basic notions in Western ethical thinking. Moral duty is generally conceived to be distinct from matters of custom or manners and to be independent of the commands, wishes, or approval of anyone (except possibly God).

Rather, an act is one's duty if and only if the desirability of its performance, and disapproval for failure to perform it (except with excuse), can be given a justification of the kind appropriate in ethics.

Many philosophers think that moral duty cannot be given rational justification in any way comparable to the rational justification possible for statements in mathematics, logic, or the empirical sciences. But this contention is one that concerns most other ethical concepts as well, and it is not discussed here.

It has sometimes been said that there is a duty only if there is a very strong moral obligation; but the generally accepted view is that duties may differ in stringency from the very weak to the very strong. It has also been argued that it is correct to say something is one's duty only if one prefers not to perform it; but this again is not generally accepted, although the concept of duty would probably never have been formed if people were uniformly interested in doing what, from an objective point of view, it is best that they do. It is sometimes said that duty is properly spoken of only in connection with some office or relationship (for example, one's duties toward one's children); but this does not correspond to ordinary usage, which does not prohibit saying it is one's duty to do what one can to end racial discrimination, irrespective of any "office" beyond being a human being or citizen. Some writers have not found it necessary to distinguish duty from the desirable; but it is obvious that there are things that may be regarded as desirable to do (for example, to learn to play the violin for relaxation) that are not matters of duty.

Toward a General Concept. One's duty may sometimes be to do any one of several things, such as to pay a debt by check or to pay it in cash. In this case one does not say it is his duty to do some specific one of these, although one says it is *right* to do any one of them. On the other hand it is never one's duty to perform incompatible tasks. In this respect duty seems to differ from an obligation, for it seems correct to say that one has an obligation both, say, to purchase something his child needs, and also to assist a close friend in a financial emergency, even if he cannot do both. With this fact in mind, some writers identify one's moral duty with whatever act will most adequately satisfy all one's obligations in a given situation.

The concept of duty is further complicated by the fact that most people think (1) that individuals, because of misinformation about the facts or for some other cause, have mistaken views about what their duty is, and ought to try to find what their real duty is; and also (2) that individuals cannot be blamed for failing to do their real duty, if they have done what they thought was their duty and otherwise have shown a conscientious desire to meet all their obligations; that is, they are considered to have done their duty even if they have not done their real duty. These facts have led some philosophers to distinguish two or more senses of moral duty (or concepts of duty).

It is agreed that it is never one's duty to do the impossible, but some qualifications are needed. Obviously, some act can be one's real duty in the above sense, even if ignorance of it prevents doing it. Also, it is never an excuse to say that one's defects of character rendered a certain act impossible, and therefore that it was not one's duty. It has been widely debated whether it is possible to do more than one's duty (works of supererogation), but today it is generally held that it is—that there are some acts it is desirable and admirable to do, although one cannot properly be condemned for failure to perform them.

Among the acts that are generally thought to be obligatory, and to be duties when there is no countervailing obligation, are the following types: to avoid injuring people, to do good, to improve oneself, to keep one's promises, to repair injuries done to others, to show one's gratitude for benefits, and to see justice done.

Other Concepts. Whether this general concept of duty, common among educated people in the Western world, is universal is open to question. Possibly some peoples have no ethical concepts at all. Certainly some primitive peoples do not have exactly the concept of duty here delineated. Even in 18th century British thought, some philosophers identified duty only with what man is obliged to do for the sake of his own future happiness, in view of God's commands and expected punishments. And in Jewish and early Christian thinking generally, the concept of duty is closely intertwined with the notion of God's law and demands on men, and God's threat of punishment for disobedience.

The philosopher Immanuel Kant, in the late 18th century, gave renewed emphasis to the early Stoic notion of duty as the law of reason, distinguishing the concept sharply from divine commands; and practically all modern philosophical writers emphasize the general concept of duty approximately as formulated above, distinguishing it (except for a few theologians) from all theological ideas. But even where this concept is present in other cultures, past or present, it may not play a role in philosophical thinking comparable to its role in the Western world today; thus Plato and Aristotle, for example, say practically nothing about it, directing their energies to determining what kind of life is worth living, and what kind of person is a good or virtuous one.

Some Gestalt psychologists hold that the concept that acts are obligatory or required deserves special psychological attention and have attempted to develop this concept into a theory. Psychoanalysts and learning theorists, many of whom also have a special interest in ethical phenomena, have confined their theoretical activities to an attempt to explain the experience of guilt. Any adequate general psychological theory about the formation of beliefs and attitudes must include the formation of convictions about duty. See also ETHICS.

RICHARD B. BRANDT
Author of "Ethical Theory"

DUTY. See CUSTOMS DUTIES; TARIFF.

DUUN, doōn, **Olav** (1876–1939); Norwegian novelist. He was born in Namdalen on Nov. 21, 1876. After working on his father's farm for several years, he became a schoolteacher.

Duun used his native Namdalen as the scene of all his novels, which he wrote in *Landsmaal*, the literary language used for a fusion of peasant dialects. His books are notable for their beauty of style, skill in characterization, and richness of local color. Their main theme is man's struggle with destructive forces—but those within himself and those in his environment.

Duun's major work, *Juvikfolke* (1918–1923; Eng. tr., *The People of Juvik,* 1930–1935), a cycle of six novels, traces the fortunes of a family through a century of change, dramatizing the conflict between the old culture and the new. He died in Botne, Norway, on Sept. 13, 1939.

DUVALL, dōō-val′, **Robert** (1931–   ), American actor, known for his wide range of characterizations. He was born on Jan. 5, 1931, in San Diego, Calif. He received a bachelor's degree in drama from Principia College, Ill., and studied acting at New York City's Neighborhood Playhouse. One of his most notable stage roles was Eddie Carbone in *A View from the Bridge,* which he first played in 1957. As a result he won lead roles in many television dramas.

Duvall made his film debut as the feebleminded Boo Ridley in *To Kill a Mockingbird* (1962). Subsequently, he often appeared in "character" or strong supporting roles, as well as leading roles. His films include *M*A*S*H* (1970); *The Godfather* (1972); *The Great Santini* (1980); *Tender Mercies* (1983), for which he won an Academy Award as best actor; and *The Natural* (1984). He also directed the documentaries *We're Not the Jet Set* (1977) and *Angelo, My Love* (1983).

DUVALIER, dü-vȧ-lyā′, **François** (1907–1971), president of Haiti. He was born in Port-au-Prince, Haiti, on April 14, 1907, of middle-class black parents. In 1934 he graduated from medical school and for a decade practiced medicine.

Despite his marriage into a mulatto family, he became identified as a champion of the underprivileged blacks in their struggle against the mulatto elite. He joined forces with political leader Dumarsais Estimé, who espoused the black cause. After Estimé became president in 1946, he appointed Duvalier successively director general of public health, assistant secretary of labor, and finally secretary of labor. Estimé was ousted, however, in 1950 by Paul Magloire, commander of the Haitian guard, and Duvalier left office.

When Magloire was forced from office in 1956, Duvalier emerged as a presidential candidate. Handling himself astutely during the chaotic first half of 1957, he gained an overwhelming majority in the September elections and was inaugurated on Oct. 22, 1957.

Although it could not be expected that Haiti would move rapidly toward model democracy, most observers expected Duvalier, in keeping with his past career, to institute social and economic programs to aid the lower classes. On the contrary, his regime was corruption-ridden, terroristic, and authoritarian to an extreme degree. In 1964 he drew up a new constitution, establishing a lifetime presidency for himself.

His championing the blacks led only to the suppression of the mulattoes. His failure to curb the bribery of his officials led to the cancellation of U. S. economic aid programs, and the institution of a personal and brutal secret police force, the Ton-Ton-Macoute, discouraged political opposition and disastrously affected the tourist trade. Haiti's gross national product, the lowest in all Latin America, declined further during Duvalier's regime, which ended with his death in Port-au-Prince on April 21, 1971. He was succeeded by his 19-year-old son, Jean-Claude.

Karl M. Schmitt, *University of Texas*

DUVEEN, dōō-vēn′, **Baron** (1869–1939), English art dealer and connoisseur, who influenced the formation of famous art collections in the United States. He was born Joseph Duveen, at Hull, England, on Oct. 14, 1869, the son of Sir Joel Joseph Duveen, founder of Duveen Brothers, dealers in fine china, furniture, silver, and works of art. At the age of 17, Duveen went to work in the New York branch of the family firm. By 1914 he was dealing primarily in European paintings and sculptures, and his patrons included the American collectors Henry C. Frick, Andrew Mellon, Joseph E. Widener, Benjamin Altman, and Henry Huntington.

Duveen, who made generous contributions of works of art to English galleries and donated to the British Museum the addition that houses the Elgin Marbles, was knighted in 1919 and created 1st Baron Duveen of Millbank in 1933. He died in London, on May 25, 1939. His observations on various contemporary artists were published as *Thirty Years of British Art* (1930).

Loretta Grellner
Lecturer, Chicago Public School Art Society

Further Reading: Behrman, Samuel N., *Duveen* (1952; reprint, Crown 1982); Duveen, James Henry, *The Rise of the House of Duveen* (Knopf 1957).

DUVENECK, dōō′vȧ-nek, **Frank** (1848–1919), American painter, sculptor, and educator, who is best-known as a teacher of other painters. He was born Frank Decker on Oct. 9, 1848, in Covington, Ky. He took his stepfather's name when his mother remarried after his father's death. As a youth, Duveneck worked for a decorator of churches in Cincinnati, Ohio, and then studied at the Royal Academy in Munich, Germany.

After his return to the United States in 1873, Duveneck executed some portrait commissions and held a successful exhibition of his paintings in Boston. He went back to Europe in 1875, and in 1878 he started an art school in Munich, which he moved to Florence, Italy, the following year. In 1888 he returned to Cincinnati, where he taught at the Cincinnati Art Academy. Duveneck died in Cincinnati on Jan. 3, 1919.

DUVERGIER DE HAURANNE, dü-ver-zhyā′ dȧ ō-ràn′, **Jean** (1581–1643), French theologian. He was born at Bayonne, France. His study of theology was begun at the Sorbonne and continued at Louvain. His close friendship with Cornelius Jansen was cemented in Paris and Bayonne, where for 12 years they studied Scripture and the writings of the church fathers seeking the doctrinal bases of a reform of the Roman Catholic Church from within. During this time Duvergier was made a canon of the Bayonne cathedral. He later received an honorary abbacy at Brienne and was known thereafter as the Abbé de Saint-Cyran.

His reputation for learning and eloquence brought him an invitation to preach at Port-Royal in Paris, a convent of Cistercian nuns known for its austere rule under Angélique Arnauld (1591–1661). It counted many prominent personages among its supporters. When Saint-Cyran was appointed its spiritual director, Port-Royal became the headquarters of Jansenism (see Jansenism). He completely devoted himself to the cause in his later years. His intransigence made him many enemies, including the Jesuits whom he denounced in his books and speeches for casuistry. He incurred the enmity of Cardinal Richelieu for attacks on his foreign policy, and his continued relations with Jansen. Intending to prove Saint-Cyran guilty of heresy, Richelieu had him thrown into prison in 1638. Saint-Cyran remained in prison until Richelieu's death in 1642, but died in Paris on Oct. 11, 1643, eight months after his liberation.

JULIE KERNAN
Translator of "Port-Royal," by Marc Escholier

DUVEYRIER, dü-vā-ryā´, **Henri** (1840–1892), French explorer of the Sahara, whose explorations paved the way for French penetration of the area. He was born in Paris on Feb. 28, 1840. He decided at an early age to explore Africa, and after a preliminary trip to Algeria in 1857 he secured the support and assistance of the explorer Heinrich Barth.

After extensive scientific preparations, Duveyrier traveled in the Sahara almost continuously from 1859 to 1861. He returned to France broken in health. His major work was *Les Touareg du Nord* (1864), a methodical and scientific description of the geology, geography, commercial produce, and ethnology of the areas he had visited. The book was a spur to French activity in the Sahara and of great value to other explorers.

In later years Duveyrier occasionally traveled in the desert, but he was largely restricted to writing and to promoting the development of the Sahara from France. His enthusiasm for the Tuareg and his optimism about Saharan commerce were notable. On April 25, 1892, at Sèvres, he committed suicide.

HARRISON M. WRIGHT, *Swarthmore College*

DU VIGNEAUD, dōō vēn´yō, **Vincent** (1901–1978), American biochemist, who contributed to the understanding of vitamins, hormones, and metabolic reactions. Born in Chicago on May 18, 1901, he studied organic chemistry at the University of Illinois (M. S., 1924) and biochemistry at the University of Rochester (Ph. D., 1927). Following further studies in biochemistry, he held professorships at the University of Illinois (1930–1932), George Washington Medical School (1932–1938), and Cornell University Medical School, serving as biochemistry department chairman at the two latter schools.

His research was almost always associated with biologically important organic sulfur compounds, from his early explanation of the role of the amino acid cystine in the insulin molecule to his synthesis of polypeptide hormones. He was particularly interested in the relation between chemical structure and physiological function.

During the 1930's, du Vigneaud recognized the importance of active methyl groups in methionine, choline, and related compounds. Using deuterium (heavy hydorgen), he studied the process of transmethylation (transfer of CH_3 groups between compounds) in biological systems. In 1942 he established the structure of biotin, a compound that had caused much confusion in vitamin studies. The next year chemists at Merck Laboratories synthesized this sulfur-containing compound, using a procedure suggested by du Vigneaud. Later he studied the chemistry of penicillin and in 1946 was successful in preparing crystals of synthetic penicillin G.

Du Vigneaud was awarded the 1955 Nobel Prize in chemistry for his synthesis of oxytocin, the polypeptide hormone produced by the posterior lobe of the pituitary gland and capable of causing contraction of the uterus. His laboratory also synthesized vasopressin, a similar pituitary hormone that causes elevation of the blood pressure. Du Vigneaud wrote *A Trail of Research in Sulfur Chemistry and Metabolism and Related Fields* (1952). He died in White Plains, N. Y., on Dec. 11, 1978.

AARON J. IHDE, *University of Wisconsin*

DUXBURY, duks´ber-ē, is a residential town in southeastern Massachusetts, in Plymouth county, on an arm of Plymouth Bay of the Atlantic Ocean, about 30 miles (48 km) southeast of Boston. It was founded about 1624, when Myles Standish, William Brewster, John Alden, and others from Plymouth Colony, 5 miles (8 km) to the south, went to the area. Alden's house is still standing. Duxbury was incorporated in 1637. Government is by town meeting and selectmen. Population: 11,807.

DVINA RIVER, Northern, dvyi-nà´, in the USSR, in northern European Russia. It is 450 miles (750 km) long. The Northern Dvina is formed at the town of Veliki Ustyug ("The Great Mouth of the Yug") by the confluence of two great headstreams, the Sukhona, which is 349 miles (562 km) long, and the Yug, 356 miles (574 km) long. After a short course of about 40 miles (64 km), the Northern Dvina receives a third major tributary, the Vychegda, 700 miles (1,130 km) long, at Kotlas. The river then flows generally northwest in a broad valley through the northern forest, reaching the White Sea at Archangel, where it forms a great delta.

The abundant stream flow is of relatively little significance for navigation because the Northern Dvina traverses a sparsely populated lumbering region and is icebound from November to April. It is used for the floating of logs during the summer and for fisheries. An old canal, suitable only for small barges, connects the upper reaches of the Sukhona with the Sheksna River, part of the Volga-Baltic waterway.

THEODORE SHABAD
Editor of "Soviet Geography"

DVINA RIVER, Western, dvyi-nà´, in the USSR, flowing first southwest, then west and northwest through European Russia, Belorussia, and Latvia to the Baltic Sea. The river has a length of 635 miles (1,020 km) from its source in the Valdai Hills to its delta at Riga. In addition to Riga, the principal towns along its banks are Vitebsk and Polotsk in Belorussia and Daugavpils in Latvia. The river is known as the *Daugava* in Latvia.

During the ice-free season, which lasts from April to December, the Western Dvina is used for the floating of timber. The rapids in the river limit navigation. Shipping conditions have been improved and the river's hydroelectric potential has been utilized by the construction of two dams in Latvia. The 68,000-kw station at Kegums first went into operation in 1939 and it was rebuilt in 1945 after destruction in World War II. The 825,000-kw Plavinas plant, located at the new town of Stucka, was opened in 1965. Additional hydroelectric facilities, expected to yield at least 1 million kilowatts, are planned for the Western Dvina.

THEODORE SHABAD
Editor of "Soviet Geography"

DVINSK. See DAUGAVPILS.

DVOŘÁK, dvôr′zhäk, **Antonín** (1841–1904), Bohemian composer, who wrote brilliant, moving works that brought international recognition of the musical genius of the Czechs. Often ranked with such composers as his contemporaries Brahms and Tchaikovsky, Dvořák produced a large body of music, marked by great lyricism, superb orchestration, and exciting rhythms.

During Dvořák's lifetime, Bohemia was still a part of the Austrian Empire, and Bohemian patriots were striving for cultural as well as political independence from Habsburg rule. Consequently, much of Dvořák's music has a strongly "national" flavor. Following the lead of his predecessor and compatriot, Bedřich Smetana, and eventually surpassing him, Dvořák sought to embody his country's spirit in his music.

Life. Antonín Dvořák was born at Nelahozeves, not far from Prague, on Sept. 8, 1841. His father, an innkeeper and butcher, expected his son to carry on the business. However, the boy showed such musical talent that when he was 16, he was sent to Prague to attend the organ school there. Beginning about 1860, Dvořák taught music, composed, and played the viola in several orchestras, including that of the National Theater in Prague. In 1873 he became organist at St. Adalbert's church in Prague. In the same year he married Anna Čermaková, a singer.

Dvořák's first successful composition was *Hymnus* (1873), for chorus and orchestra. His music became increasingly popular, and in 1875 he won a grant from the Austrian government. At about this time, also, Brahms took an active interest in Dvořák's music. This marked a turning point in the career of Dvořák, who was soon being internationally acclaimed. In 1884, on the first of several triumphant trips to England, he conducted his *Stabat Mater* (1877) in London. He also visited Germany often and Russia once.

Dvořák's fame also reached the United States, and in 1892 he was appointed head of the National Conservatory of Music in New York City. During his highly successful American stay, he wrote his best-known work, the symphony *From the New World* (1893). In 1895, overcome by homesickness, he returned to Bohemia, where he continued to compose and teach, becoming director of the Prague Conservatory in 1901. Dvořák died in Prague on May 1, 1904.

Music. In Bohemia, during Dvořák's formative years, Czech folk music was heard mainly on village greens. The music performed in concert halls was frequently of German or Austrian origin, and Dvořák's early compositions reflect the influence of such composers as Beethoven, Schubert, Wagner, and Brahms. Gradually, however, inspired by the example of Smetana and impelled by his own ardent patriotism, Dvořák began to draw, frequently though not exclusively, on the folk idiom of Bohemia. He occasionally combined folk tunes with his own lyric melodies.

A versatile and prolific composer, Dvořák wrote in virtually all the musical genres. Among his famous orchestral works are the *Symphonic Variations* (1877), the spirited *Slavonic Dances* (1878, 1886), and the *Scherzo capriccioso* (1883). He also wrote nine symphonies, which have now been renumbered from the traditional order to the order of actual composition, between 1865 and 1893. Previously unnumbered and posthumously published are Symphony No. 1 in C Minor; Symphony No. 2 in B Flat Major; Symphony No. 3 in E Flat Major; and Symphony

Antonín Dvořák

No. 4 in D Minor. The renumbered works are Symphony No. 5 in F Major (formerly No. 3); Symphony No. 6 in D Major (formerly No. 1); Symphony No. 7 in D Minor (formerly No. 2); Symphony No. 8 in G Major (formerly No. 4); and Symphony No. 9 in E Minor, *From the New World* (formerly No. 5). Although Symphony No. 8 and Symphony No. 9 are the most frequently played, many critics regard Symphony No. 6 and Symphony No. 7 as artistically greater achievements.

Many themes from the famous *New World* Symphony, as well as from the String Quartet in F Major (1893), the String Quintet in E Flat Major (1893), and the great Cello Concerto in B Minor (1895), all composed in the United States, were long thought to have had their origins in Negro spirituals. Actually, however, Negro spirituals have many melodic and rhythmic features in common with the folk music of Bohemia, a fact of which Dvořák was aware and which he brilliantly utilized in these works.

In addition to orchestral compositions and such chamber works as the outstanding Piano Quintet in A Major (1887), Dvořák wrote piano music, songs, choral pieces, and operas. His works for piano include numerous waltzes, mazurkas, and the well-known humoresque in G Flat Major (1894). Among his famous songs are the *Moravian Duets* (1876) and, from the set entitled *Gypsy Songs* (1880), *Songs My Mother Taught Me*. Of Dvořák's eight major choral works, the *Requiem Mass* (1890) is perhaps the most impressive. He also composed 11 operas, which did not meet with the same success as his other works. Among his operas are *The Peasant a Rogue* (1877), *Jacobin* (1887; revised 1897), and *Rusalka* (1900).

Gervase Hughes
Author of "Dvořák, His Life and Music"

Bibliography

Clapham, John, *Antonín Dvořák, Musician and Craftsman* (London 1966).
Hoffmeister, Karel, *Antonín Dvořák*, ed. and tr. by Rosa Newmarch (London 1928).
Hughes, Gervase, *Dvořák, His Life and Music* (London and New York 1967).
Purdy, Claire L., *Antonín Dvořák, Composer from Bohemia* (New York 1950).
Sourek, Otakar, *Antonín Dvořák, His Life and Work* (London 1952).

DWARF, a person of extremely short stature, below 4 feet 4 inches (1.3 meters) for adult men. Dwarfs, who are disproportionate in build and deformed, are distinguished from midgets, who are normally proportioned but pathologically short. Neither is to be confused with Pygmies. See also DWARFISM; PYGMIES.

In History. Dwarfs and midgets have often served as court jesters, circus performers, and entertainers. Their presence has been recorded in the art of many periods. Examples are found in ancient Egyptian graphic arts and statuary (for example, the dwarf Shumhotep, whose statue in the Cairo Museum dates from the 5th dynasty), in the paintings of Pompeii, and most particularly in the paintings of the Spanish masters of the 17th century. Velázquez created several portraits of dwarfs, including the portrait of Antonio Inglès (standing next to a dog, thus indicating the man's short stature) and that of the female dwarf María Barbola in his great painting *Las meninas* (*The Maids of Honor*) at the Prado Museum in Madrid. One of the most famous dwarfs was the 19th century French painter Toulouse-Lautrec.

Some of the famous midgets whose identity is on record are Jeffrey Hudson, of the court of Charles I of England, and Nicholas Ferry, the jester of King Stanislas of Poland whose adult height was 36 inches (91 cm). One of the best-known midgets of recent times was Charles Sherwood Stratton (Tom Thumb), who measured 38 inches (97 cm) and who was made famous as a circus performer by P. T. Barnum. A female midget, Princess Floh, was 32 inches (81 cm) tall.

In Folklore and Literature. Mythical beings of short stature, gifted with supernatural powers, appear in the folklore of many peoples. In Nordic mythology they are guardians of subterranean treasures. They were thus associated with mineral wealth and work in precious metals. A reflection of this theme is seen in the tale of Snow White and the Seven Dwarfs. Other examples of dwarfs in European folklore and mythology are fairies, trolls (which appear both as dwarfs and as giants), gnomes (a term invented by the 16th century Swiss physician Paracelsus, referring to their hidden knowledge), and in Irish folklore, leprechauns.

Beliefs and tales concerning these demonic beings date from pre-Christian times; more recently dwarfs have been reduced to the status of characters in children's tales. In addition to the dwarfs of Snow White, there are the magical figure of Rumpelstiltskin and the midget Tom Thumb. Many such beings are found in folk tales collected by Jacob and Wilhelm Grimm.

Dwarfs appear also in the folklore of other peoples. They are known as the *azizan* (little people of the forest) among the Fon of Dahomey and as the *mmoetia* (forest dwarfs) among the Ashanti (Ghana), both in West Africa.

Dwarfs have been used as characters by various writers: fairies by Shakespeare (*A Midsummer Night's Dream*), trolls by Henrik Ibsen (*Peer Gynt*), and metalworking dwarfs by Richard Wagner (Fafner and Fasold, in *Siegfried*). Swift introduced a whole population of little people, the Lilliputians, in *Gulliver's Travels*. Various contemporary writers, such as Katherine Anne Porter and Günter Grass, have also used dwarfs as symbolic figures.

ERIKA BOURGUIGNON
The Ohio State University

DWARF STAR is a term commonly applied to main-sequence stars fainter than absolute magnitude $+1$. These bodies include the sun and the majority of stars that fall in the main sequence on the Hertzsprung-Russell spectrum-luminosity diagram. Danish astronomer Ejnar Hertzsprung first used the term to contrast low-luminosity red stars with the much larger high-luminosity red giants.

DWARFISM, dwôr′fizm, is the condition in which a person is far below normal size and lacks the capacity for normal growth. Dwarfism also occurs in plants as well as animals. In humans, it may be due to many different causes, some of which are inherited and others of which are acquired.

Inherited Disorders. One inherited type of dwarfism occurs in mongolism, a disorder that is also characterized by mental deficiency, atypical facial appearance, and abnormalities of the hands and feet. Achondroplasia is another inherited disorder characterized by dwarfism. Achondroplastic dwarfs have short arms and legs, normal trunks, and normal mentalities. In gargoylism, dwarfism is accompanied by mental deficiency and gross distortions of the skeleton, skull, and skin.

In cretinism, the person is both dwarfed and mentally defective. Another inherited type of dwarfism occurs in Turner's syndrome, which is also characterized by the virtual absence of sex glands, a failure to undergo puberty, and abnormalities of the blood vessels and skin.

Acquired Disorders. Among the many serious diseases that may cause dwarfism are chronic kidney disease (nephritis), diseases in which the body fails to absorb food normally (cystic fibrosis and celiac disease), simple malnutrition early in life, and heart and lung diseases that are associated with a low concentration of oxygen in the blood. Generally, the type of dwarfism caused by these diseases may be cured only by the successful treatment of the underlying disorder.

Greatest medical interest has centered on the potentially treatable type of dwarfism known as *pituitary dwarfism*. Usually, this type of dwarfism occurs when the pituitary gland does not secrete sufficient amounts of growth hormone. The underlying cause may be a lesion in the base of the brain (the hypothalamus) or in the pituitary gland itself, but usually no anatomical abnormality can be found. In African pygmies it has been found that pituitary dwarfism may occur even when the amount of growth hormone secreted is not below normal levels. The growth hormone is defective in some way and in other cases the tissues that are stimulated by the hormone (primarily the skeleton) fail to respond normally.

Pituitary dwarfism is usually noticed within the first year of life. As the child develops, its face remains immature and doll-like and its trunk remains pudgy. However, the skeletal proportions are normal and intelligence is average or above average. The treatment of pituitary dwarfism entails the administration of purified human growth hormone that is extracted from pituitary glands obtained in surgery or at autopsies. Generally, patients respond to the treatment by growing 3 inches per year faster than their rate of growth before treatment. No other form of dwarfism responds to the administration of growth hormone.

NICHOLAS P. CHRISTY, M. D.
The Roosevelt Hospital, New York

DWARKA, dwär′kä, a town in India, in Amreli district of Gujarat state, is one of the seven sacred centers of Hinduism in the country. Dwarka is closely associated with the cult of Krishna and has a temple dedicated to him. Many pilgrims visit the town, which lies at the western end of the Kathiawar Peninsula on the shores of the Arabian Sea and is a convenient port of call on the sea route between Karachi and Bombay.

As a seaport, Dwarka exports ghee (clarified butter), millet, salt, and oilseeds. Its chief manufacture is cement. Population: (1961) 11,912.

DWIGHT, John (c.1640–1703), English potter, who is often considered the father of the English pottery industry. Few facts about his life are known definitely. He was born about 1640 and was registrar to the bishop of Chester in 1661. In 1671 he obtained a patent for the "Mistery of Transparent Earthenware, commonly knowne by the Names of Porcelaine or China, and Persian Ware, as also the Misterie of the Stone Ware vulgarly called Cologne Ware." The patent was renewed in 1684, but Dwight was involved in several lawsuits over his rights before his death in 1703.

Dwight's pottery was in Fulham, a section of London, and his descendants operated it until 1862. Because his gray stoneware jugs closely resemble German wine jugs, he is thought to have employed German potters. His busts and statuettes, although translucent in the thin parts, are not true "porcelaine." Examples of his work are in the Victoria and Albert Museum.

DWIGHT, Timothy (1752–1817), American Congregational clergyman, theologian, and college administrator. A grandson of Jonathan Edwards, he was born in Northampton, Mass., on May 14, 1752. Dwight graduated from Yale in 1769 and was a popular tutor there from 1771 to 1777. During the American Revolution he served as an army chaplain for a year, before returning to Northampton to become a farm manager, preacher, teacher, and state legislator. After being ordained in 1783, he served the Greenfield Hill (Conn.) congregation.

From 1795 until his death in New Haven on Jan. 11, 1817, Dwight was president of Yale. He overcame religious indifference and unbelief among the students by eloquent argument and became one of the leaders of the "Second Great Awakening," or religious revival, in America.

Failing eyesight did not prevent him from writing and publishing. His sermons at Yale Chapel, *Theology Explained and Defended* (1818), constitute his most important and popular work. In his moderate Calvinism and Edwardsean theology, the accent was on human agency and activism. He made a sharp distinction between revealed and natural religion and gave unprecedented importance to a "system of duties" to be performed by the Christian. Dwight's other writings earned him a place among the "Hartford Wits," an informal literary group with strong Federalist leanings who satirized the political scene. Among these works are *The Conquest of Canaan* (1785), an epic about American independence and development; *The Triumph of Infidelity* (1788), an abusive polemic against contemporary infidels; and *Greenfield Hill* (1794), a poem urging moral improvement.

JAMES H. SMYLIE
Union Theological Seminary, Richmond, Va.

DWIGHT, Timothy (1828–1916), American Congregational clergyman, scholar, and president of Yale. A descendant of Jonathan Edwards and grandson of Timothy Dwight (president of Yale from 1795 to 1817), he was born in Norwich, Conn., on Nov. 16, 1828. He graduated from Yale in 1849 and studied at Bonn and Berlin in 1856–1858. In 1858, Dwight became professor of sacred literature at Yale Divinity School, earning a reputation as a New Testament scholar. He served on the American committee for the revision of the King James Bible, which published the American Standard Bible in 1901. He also translated Godet's *Commentary on the Gospel of John* (1886).

Dwight was elected president of Yale in 1886 and served until his retirement in 1899. During his presidency the college was rechartered as a university and greatly expanded its physical facilities and educational program. Dwight died in New Haven, Conn., on May 26, 1916.

JAMES H. SMYLIE
Union Theological Seminary, Richmond, Va.

DYAK. See DAYAK.

DYCE, dīs, **Alexander** (1798–1869), Scottish scholar and editor, who published scholarly editions of the works of Shakespeare and other Elizabethan dramatists. He was born in Edinburgh on June 30, 1798. After graduating from Oxford in 1819, he entered the Anglican ministry but resigned his curacy in 1825 to devote his time to literature. His reputation as a brilliant scholar was established with his editions of the works of William Collins (1827), John Webster (1830), Thomas Middleton (1840), Beaumont and Fletcher (1843–1846), and Christopher Marlowe (1850).

Dyce's 9-volume edition of Shakespeare (1857; rev. ed., 1864–1867), with its annotations and its textual criticism, was an important contribution to Shakespearean scholarship. His commentaries on other editions were equally acute. He died in London on May 15, 1869.

DYCE, dīs, **William** (1806–1864), Scottish painter and muralist, who was a forerunner of the English pre-Raphaelite school. He was born at Aberdeen on Sept. 19, 1806, and studied art at Edinburgh and at the Royal Academy of Art in London. Dyce's style was influenced by the Italian Renaissance murals that he studied during visits to Rome in 1825 and 1827, and by the German "Nazarene" painters then working in Rome. His first exhibited work was *Bacchus Nursed by the Nymphs of Nysa*, shown at the Royal Academy in London in 1827.

From 1830 to 1837, Dyce worked in Edinburgh, primarily as a portraitist. In 1844 he was one of the winners of the competition to do murals for the Houses of Parliament. In the House of Lords he painted the *Baptism of Ethelbert* and an unfinished series on Arthurian legend for the queen's robing room. On commission by Prince Albert he did a mural entitled *Neptune Giving the Empire of the Sea to Britannia*, at Osborne, Queen Victoria's residence in Scotland. Dyce died in London on Feb. 14, 1864.

LORETTA GRELLNER
Lecturer, Chicago Public School Art Society

DYCK, Sir Anthony Van. See VAN DYCK, SIR ANTHONY.

HAND DYEING in the 18th century at the famous Gobelin works near Paris. The fabric is carried into and out of the dyeing vat by the hand-operated rollers.

DYE is matter used to impart color to other materials by dyeing. Dyes are used to color natural fibers, such as cotton, wool, silk, and linen, and synthetic fibers, such as nylon, cellulose acetate, and polyester. They are also used on other types of substances, such as leather, wood, food, paper, and in photography. Dyes for home use are the same as those used in industry, and they are applied by the same methods.

Dyes and Other Colored Substances. Not all colored compounds will behave as dyes; for example, indigo and cochineal are dyes, but red iron oxide and ultramarine are not. In the dyeing process a solution of the dye is made, and the material to be dyed, called the *substrate,* is put in the solution. Colored matter from the solution is transferred to the substrate by the process of *absorption;* the removal of the dye from the solution is called *exhaustion.* This is a general description of all dyeing processes. For a particular case *dyeing assistants* are added to the dye solution to facilitate the interaction of a particular type of dye with the substrate. Typical dyeing assistants include acids, alkalis, and wetting agents. Red iron oxide and ultramarine are examples of *pigments*. These substances are not suitable for dyeing processes but may be used to color other materials by simple mixing or pigmentation as, for example, with lipstick, paints, plastics, and rubber.

The process of absorption of a dye by a substrate implies that there is a chemical or physical interaction between the material and the dye molecules, leading to the formation of bonds. The behavior of a dye is thus dependent both on its chemical structure and on the structure of the substrate.

The Color of Dyes. Different molecular systems absorb light at different energy levels or wavelengths. Which wavelengths are absorbed and which are reflected determine the color of an object. In terms of color in dyes, the absorption of the light energy depends on the dye's acting as an optical filter on a molecular scale. The part of the dye molecule that is primarily responsible for this action is called the *chromogen*. Normally a chromogen is part of a molecule that bears substituent groups that modify the light absorption in various ways, so that a variety of shades may be obtained from a given chromogen. Thus, much of the history of dye production is concerned with the preparation of different chromogens.

The light-absorption characteristics that give organic dyes their color arise from the electron structures of the dyes. An atmosphere of delocalized electrons associated with the conjugated system of the dye molecules determines the dye color. Absorption of light energy depends upon the energy level of the electrons with which it interacts, so that different chemical structures lead to different colors.

Delocalized electrons are also involved in the development of the intermolecular forces of attraction, known as *dispersion forces*, that bind dye molecules to fabrics. Other kinds of intermolecular forces are also thought to be involved in binding dye molecules to fabric substrates. Such forces include coulombic or electrostatic forces between oppositely charged parts of molecules, hydrogen bonding, and hydrophobic bonding. The latter is a kind of interaction which arises from the special physical and chemical properties of water.

The study of light absorption by dyes has always aroused interest from the point of view of color prediction and calculation; light absorption by dyes has also been studied in terms of the photochemical reactions involved. The complexity of even simple dye molecules has prevented the development of a general theory relating color and molecular structure; however, a number of semiempirical relations between molecular structure and color have been developed that work well within a group of related compounds.

The calculation and prediction of colors is of great importance in industry, and a number of methods have been evolved that allow the relations inherent in color mixing to be calculated on analog or digital computers. These developments are bringing about great changes in all industries concerned with the use of color.

The Fastness of Dyes. The problems of color fastness during washing and on exposure to light have always represented a major challenge to color chemists. The absorption of most dyes by a substrate is a reversible process. In the dyeing process, after a certain period of time an equilibrium is set up in which the rate of absorption of the dye by the fiber is equaled by the rate of desorption (loss of dye by the fiber). When the dyed fiber is washed, a new equilibrium occurs, which means that there is a net desorption of dye and a loss in depth of shade with, perhaps, the staining of other articles. This process may be limited by making dyes with large molecules that diffuse slowly from the substrate during washing; by using dyes that form strong bonds with the substrate; and by using substances, such as azoic dyes, that form insoluble pigments that cannot wash out.

NATURAL DYES

From prehistoric times until the mid-1800's, when the first synthetic dye was developed, dyeing was done with natural dyes, such as indigo, saffron, and henna. A wide range of natural coloring matters were used. Some of them, such as madder root extract with an alum mordant, gave excellent results, while others were very poor.

Many of the natural coloring matters, such as logwood and madder, form slightly soluble complexes with the ions of transition metals. This is because they contain hydroxyl and other groups that can chelate such metal ions. The early dyers found that it was possible to pretreat the textiles, or "mordant" them, with various naturally occurring salts. The mordant forms a chelated complex on the fiber in the dyeing process. Alum, an aluminum sulfate compound, is a frequently used mordant.

The use of different salts with the same plant extract dyes was found to give rise to different colors, thus providing a wider variety of shades. The shade produced by such dyes is also affected by impurities in the water supply, so that in some cases a certain shade becomes associated with particular districts or even villages.

One of the most important of the natural dyes was the coloring matter contained in the leaves of indigo-bearing plants. (See INDIGO.) This substance is soluble in water but oxidizes to the insoluble pigment indigo. The pigment may then be reduced by various reducing agents, applied to the substrate from solution, and then reoxidized to produce a blue material. The preliminary reduction of the indigo is known as *vatting*; the dye is an early example of the vat dyes.

By the end of the 19th century a method for the commercial synthesis of indigo had been invented. Coupled with the synthesis of madder (the dye alizarin), this marked the effective end of natural dyes as commercial materials.

SYNTHETIC DYES

In 1856 at the Royal College of Chemistry in London the British chemist Sir William Henry Perkin attempted to synthesize quinine. As part of his research, Perkin oxidized aniline sulfate with potassium dichromate. Fortunately, as it turned out, Perkin's aniline contained some toluidine as an impurity, and consequently, from the black tar that he prepared, Perkin was able to extract the first synthetic dye, mauveine.

Basic Dyes. The first synthetic dyes fell into the class of basic dyes—that is, the colored molecules were cations (bearing a positive electrical charge). This type of dye is easily applied to materials, such as wool, silk, and nylon, that contain anionic groups (negative groups, such as carboxyl groups). Basic dyes may be employed for dyeing cellulosic materials, but because these materials contain few anionic groups, mordants must be used, which confer a negative charge to the fiber.

The commercial manufacture of mauveine in England marked the beginning of the organic chemical industry, although its technical life did not last more than a decade. It was superseded by a flood of new products from laboratories in England, France, and Germany. Other early basic dyes included magenta and rosaniline. Basic dyes are generally characterized by poor fastness to light and are relatively little used. However, modern developments have produced fast basic dyes which are of great importance in the dyeing of acrylic fibers.

BEFORE DYEING, raw fabric is run through a bath of hot soapy water for thorough cleaning and shrinking.

UNITED PIECE DYE WORKS

SINGEING a fabric by passing it rapidly through rows of open gas flame produces a smooth surface for dyeing. *UNITED PIECE DYE WORKS*

Acid Dyes. In 1862 it was observed that phenyl rosaniline could be treated with sulfuric acid under appropriate conditions to introduce the sulfonic acid group. The dyes thus formed are anionic and are therefore termed acid dyes. The acid dyes are water-soluble and do not suffer from many of the deficiencies of basic dyes. They are used on wool, silk, and some of the synthetic fibers.

Azo Dyes. The next major breakthrough came with the utilization of the diazo reaction in the formation of synthetic dyes in the late 1870's. The diazo reaction had been discovered by the German chemist Peter Griess in 1858, when he observed that aromatic amines ($R \cdot NH_2$) could be readily converted to diazonium compounds ($R \cdot N \equiv N \cdot Cl$) under appropriate conditions. Later it was found that diazonium compounds could be coupled with phenols and other aromatic molecules to form azo dyes ($R \cdot N = N \cdot ROH$).

More than 2 million azo dyes have been prepared since their discovery. The early ones possessed excellent properties for the dyeing of wool and silk but were of little value for cellulosic fabrics.

Some azo dyes are used with mordants. In this case, chelating metals are used with the dyes to achieve both light and wet fastness. Without the chelating group the azo group is open to photochemical attack and the chromogen can be destroyed. This possibility can be reduced considerably by incorporating a chelating system, usually the o-o' dihydroxy azo system, into the molecule to chelate a metal atom.

The involvement of the azo nitrogen atoms in the chelate system brings about considerable stabilization against chemical and photochemical activity and gives very good light fastness. In the dyeing of cellulosic materials the use of copper as a metallizing agent for o-o' dihydroxy azo direct dyes was developed to improve light fastness. On protein substrates such as wool, when chromium is used as the metallizing agent, high wet fastness, as well as light fastness, is also achieved, because the chromium atom reacts with the wool to give an effective chemical linkage between the dye and the fiber.

The old mordanting system of pretreatment of the fiber was unsuitable for the production demands of the 20th century, and two modified techniques were developed. In the *after-chrome process* the dye was exhausted onto the fiber and then chelated with the metal ions in an after-treatment in the same bath; in the *metachrome process* the dye and potassium dichromate were applied simultaneously. The dichromate was reduced by the wool to give trivalent chromium ions, which were chelated by the dye, which was absorbed at the same time.

Direct Dyes. By 1884, the German scientist P. Böttinger had completed investigation into the relationship between the chemical structure of a dye and its affinity, or *substantivity*, for cellulose; this research resulted in the introduction of the bis-azo dye, congo red. This was the first of a new class of direct dyes, which can be applied directly to cellulose without pretreatment of the fiber with a mordant.

Azoic Dyes. At this time attempts were made to synthesize an insoluble azo pigment directly on the fiber. An aromatic phenol was applied to cellulosic substrates, and after appropriate rinsing the fabric was treated with a diazonium salt solution to give a billiant pigmented material in which the pigment crystals were held in the fiber interstices. The first dye of this kind was vacanceine red, which was obtained by coupling β-naphthol with diazotized β-naphthylamine. There were few developments in this field until 1911, when Zitscher and Laska produced a naphthol of significantly higher substantivity.

Vat Dyes. From the research on indigo, derivatives of indigo were prepared, and a range of indigoid vat dyes was produced. In 1901 the German chemist René Bohn attempted to make the anthraquinone analogue of indigo by applying the indigo/sodamide fusion to the glycine derived from aminoanthraquinone. The result was a new multiple-ring quinonoid structure, indanthrone, which is a vat dye with vastly superior properties of wet and light fastness. Since that time, new synthetic vat dyes of comparable properties have been produced, so that fast dyeings on cellulosic fabrics can be produced over a wide range of shades.

Dyes for Man-made Fibers. Many new problems in dyeing arose with the emergence of the synthetic fiber industry in the 1920's. At that time cellulose acetate was established as a useful textile material, but its commercial future was jeopardized because it could not be satisfactorily dyed with the available dyes. The more recently fabricated fiber, polypropylene, has also presented this difficulty.

It was found that cellulose acetate could be dyed by simple aminoazo compounds with very low solubility in water, provided they could be satisfactorily dispersed in an aqueous dyebath. The production of satisfactory orange and red shades was easily achieved, but the complete solution to the problem only came about with the work of the British chemists Baddiley and Sheperdson, who prepared suitably dispersed aminoanthraquinone blue dyes. The *disperse dyes*, as this new class was called, are sparingly soluble in water and actually dye from solution.

Since the 1920's man-made fibers have been produced in increasing quantity and variety. By the mid-1960's the consumption of man-made fibers exceeded that of wool. For the most part these fibers are particularly suitable for dyeing with disperse dyes, and considerable advances have been made in improving the fastness of such dyes.

One of the consequences of using a weakly polar dye molecule, is that the un-ionized dye often possesses a significant vapor pressure. An example of such a dye is C. I. Disperse Orange

$$Cl-\underset{NO_2}{\bigcirc}-NH-\bigcirc-OCH_3$$

15. Althought this can give rise to the problem of *sublimation fastness*, in which the dye may vaporize during hot pressing treatments, it has also made possible the development of dry-heat dyeing processes, which utilize the volatility of the dye. Research has explored the possibility of a completely dry-vapor phase dyeing process. Improved sublimation fastness is achieved by the use of dyes of higher molecular weight or increased polarity. These dyes are more difficult to use in dyeing because they diffuse more slowly in the fiber. However, high-temperature (130–140°C) and pressure-dyeing processes and appropriate dyeing machinery have been developed to overcome this problem.

The color fastness requirements of the old cellulose acetate fibers were not stringent. This was not true of later fibers. Nylon, the next important synthetic fiber developed after cellulose acetate, can be dyed with either acid or disperse dyes. The acid dyes are used where fastness is required. However, polyester, polyacrylic, and polypropylene fibers required the development of new dyes to give fast results.

Polyester fibers cannot be dyed with ionic dyes, and since the polyester is a high-quality fiber, high fastness is required. The growing importance of this fiber has provided the main incentive for the development of sublimation-fast and wash-fast disperse dyes.

Polyacrylic fibers are anionic in character and may be dyed with both disperse (non-ionic) and basic (cationic) dyes. However, the fibers cannot be dyed at high temperatures, and fastness must therefore be achieved with the basic dyes. Until these synthetic fibers appeared, the basic dyes were declining in importance because of their poor light fastness. However, acrylic fibers possess the surprising property of giving dyeings of good light fastness with many basic dyes. This may be connected with the relatively high electrical conductivity of the polymer.

Polypropylene presents another problem; it is very readily dyed with disperse dyes, while ionic dyes show no significant substantivity for it. However, the disperse dyes are removed from polypropylene almost as easily as they are applied. There has been considerable research into the production of modified polypropylenes and suitable dyes. The most successful approach so far has been to incorporate into the polymer metal ions that can chelate with suitable dyes to produce a fast dyeing.

Metal Complex Dyes. The most significant developments in the period since 1945 have been the growing importance of 1:2 chromium complex dyes and the appearance of a completely new class of fiber reactive dyes. The 1:2 metal

UNITED PIECE DYE WORKS

THE DESIGN to be printed on fabric is engraved on copper rollers, a separate roller used for each color.

complex dyes, which contain two molecules of dye combined with one molecule of metal, are a logical development of the mordant dyes. It was found as early as 1925 that certain dyes that contained chelating groups formed soluble 1:1 complexes with chromium—that is, one molecule of dye combined with one atom of metal. These dyes could be applied under strongly acid conditions to give good dyeings on wool, and they were used fairly successfully over the next two decades.

Their development stimulated further work on the use of preformed metal complex dyes for wool, and by the 1940's investigations into the use of 1:2 complexes were fairly advanced. These dyes have a high substantivity, and in order to obtain sufficiently controllable dyeing rates, they must be applied in a nearly neutral dyebath. It was found that the application of the 1:2 metal complex dyes was simplified by the addition of weakly polar groups, such as sulfonamide and methylsulfonyl groups, in place of the usual sulfonic acid solubilizing groups.

The ranges of dyes of this type were carefully built up from selected dyes with compatible dyeing behavior and were probably the first range of dyes designed in this way. The previous approach had been to establish large ranges of dyes that were applied by the same general method, and from these ranges compatible groups could be selected by the users.

Fiber-Reactive Dyes. The reactive dyes, which began to be used commerically in 1956, are increasing in importance so rapidly that they may well become the most important class of dyes in the foreseeable future. All of the dyes that have been discussed so far are reversibly absorbed by the substrate in dyeing. The only exception is the mordant dyes, but even these can be recovered in an unchanged form by appropriate treatment, despite the possibility of chemical linkage between the metal atoms and the substrate. This is not true of the fiber-reactive dyes, which have

PRINTING a complex multicolored pattern may take up to ten rollers like this, each using a different dye.

UNITED PIECE DYE WORKS

a dye molecule bearing a labile atom or group; these dyes can form stable covalently bonded compounds between the colored residue of the dye and the fiber.

Fiber-reactive dyes were first investigated in 1894 by the British scientists C. F. Cross and E. J. Bevan, the discoverers of cellulose xanthate, which is an essential intermediate in the manufacture of viscose rayon. They observed that cellulose can be reacted with strong caustic soda to form a cellulose salt called soda cellulose and that this could be readily reacted with various acylating reagents. Proceeding from this starting point, Cross and Bevan synthesized an azo dye that was chemically linked to cellulose and was faster than the common azo dyes available at that time. However, their process was very complex and of little value industrially. The investigations of the British chemists I. D. Rattee and W. E. Stephen in 1953 produced a highly efficient reaction under mild conditions on the basis of a proper understanding of the physical chemistry of the system. These investigations have been intensively pursued in many countries with the result that fiber-reactive dyes constitute the most important class of dyes for cellulosic fibers.

The main target of current fiber-reactive dye research has been dyes for cellulosic fibers. This is the most important textile fiber, and prior to the development of fiber-reactive dyes it was the most difficult fiber to dye with a compatible dye range covering all shades. Direct cotton dyes based on the azo system were deficient in bright shades and good blues, while vat dyes based on quinone systems provided very poor reds.

There are two reasons for the very rapid expansion in the use of fiber-reactive dyes for cellulose. First, they are very easy to apply and are particularly suitable for application by low-cost, high-production methods. Second, their fastness to wet treatment depends only on the stability of the chemical linkage between the dye and the fiber. Thus, the chromogens—the part of the molecule that determines the dye color—may be selected according to their shade and their stability against direct chemical attack by light, bleach, and other substances. The chromogen may be of any suitable type, such as azo or anthraquinonoid; it may chelate metal atoms; it may even be cationic or non-ionic. Non-ionic reactive dyes have been developed for application to nylon by reaction with the amino groups it contains.

Research has been done on the development of fiber-reactive dyes for wool and nylon with some success. The achievement of high wet fastness on wool and nylon with a wide range of shades is possible using conventional dyes; consequently the technical incentive has been less than in the case of dyes for cellulose. Recent developments in minimum-care wool fabrics are creating the need for very fast wool dyes, and fiber-reactive dyes may well provide the solution to the problem. Current research on the production of fast dyes involves dyes that polymerize on the fiber but do not necessarily react with it.

IAN D. RATTEE
University of Leeds

Bibliography

Abrahart, Edward N., *Dyes and their Intermediates* (Pergamon 1969).
Adrosko, Rita J., *Natural Dyes and Home Dyeing* (Dover 1971).
Billmeyer, Fred W., and Saltzman, M., *Principles of Color Technology* (Wiley 1966).
Cockett, Sydney R., and Hilton, K. A., *Dyeing of Cellulosic Fibres and Related Processes* (Academic 1961).
Proud, Nora, *Textile Printing and Dyeing* (Reinhold 1965).
Robinson, Stuart, *History of Dyed Textiles* (MIT Press 1970).
Schmidlin, Hans U., *Preparation and Dyeing of Man-Made Fibers* (Reinhold 1963).
Whittaker, Croyden M., Wilcock, C. C., and Ashworth, J. L., eds., *Dyeing With Coal-Tar Dyestuffs* (Van Nostrand 1964).

DYER, dī'ər, **John** (1699?–1758), English poet. He was the son of a solicitor of Aberglasney, Carmarthenshire, Wales. Educated at Westminster, he first practiced law, later turned to the study of art, and entered the Anglican ministry in 1741. His best-known work, *Grongar Hill*, is a brief meditative poem, in which he gives a classical description of natural scenery. It was included as an "irregular ode" in a miscellany published by Richard Savage in 1726, and it was independently published in 1727. Dyer's *Ruins of Rome* (1740) resulted from a trip he made to Italy to study painting. In his lengthy four-part blank verse poem *The Fleece* (1757), written in the style of Virgil's *Georgics*, he applies the language of poetry to an unpoetic subject, the sheep and wool trade. Dyer died at Coningsby, Lincolnshire.

DYER, dī'ər, **Mary** (died 1660), American Quaker martyr. She went to Massachusetts in 1635 from Somersetshire, England, with her husband, William Dyer. She identified herself with Anne Hutchinson and her antinomian views, which stressed faith in God rather than obedience to moral, church, or state laws. In 1638, Mrs. Dyer and her husband followed Mrs. Hutchinson into banishment in Rhode Island, where William Dyer became one of the founders and leading citizens of Portsmouth.

Mrs. Dyer accompanied her husband to England in 1650, and while there she became a Quaker. She returned to New England in 1657 and along with other members of the Society of Friends began to travel through the area as a missionary proclaiming the gospel of the inner light.

In 1657 and 1658 harsh anti-Quaker laws were passed in Massachusetts. These included the death penalty for those who returned to the colony after banishment. Mary Dyer began to visit imprisoned Quakers in Massachusetts. She herself was imprisoned, released, and banished, but she returned in 1659 and was sentenced to death along with William Robinson and Marmaduke Stevenson. She gained a reprieve but returned again. Her purpose in refusing to remain in Rhode Island was to obtain the repeal of "unrighteous laws of banishment on pain of death" in Massachusetts.

Mary Dyer was finally hanged in Boston on June 1, 1660. "She hangs there as a flag," a bystander was heard to remark as her lifeless body hung from the gallows. After the martyrdom of Mary Dyer, there was only one other execution of Quakers in Boston.

JAMES H. SMYLIE
Union Theological Seminary, Richmond, Va.

DYERSBURG, dī′ərz-bûrg, is a city in northwestern Tennessee, the seat of Dyer county. It is situated on the North Fork of Forked Deer River, 77 miles (127 km) northeast of Memphis. Dyersburg is a trade, processing, and industrial center. The principal agricultural products include soybeans, cotton, and corn. Manufactures include canned foods, cottonseed oil, textiles, rubber products, and electric products.

Dyersburg was laid out in 1825 and was incorporated in 1850. Government is by a mayor and board of aldermen. Population: 15,856.

DYING GAUL, an ancient copy of a Greek sculpture, now in the Capitoline Museum in Rome. The statue, a masterly marble replica of a bronze original, was executed, probably early in the 3d century B.C., at Pergamum in Asia Minor. The subject, recognizable as a Gaul (or Galatian) by his bristly hair and twisted collar, reclines on his shield, his head bowed, his left hand resting on his right knee, the weight of his body supported by his right arm, which Michelangelo restored. The blood streaming from a wound in his right side is an especially marked bit of realism. The portrayal of anatomy is superb, and the style is vigorous.

The sculpture, sometimes called *The Dying Gladiator*, inspired part of Byron's poem *Childe Harold's Pilgrimage*.

DYK, dik, **Viktor** (1877–1931), Czech nationalist poet, playwright, and novelist. He was born on Dec. 31, 1877, in Pšovka, near Mělník, Bohemia (then a part of the Austrian Empire). As a young journalist he wrote anti-Austrian articles for Czech nationalist periodicals, for which activity he was imprisoned by the Austrians in 1917. After World War I, Dyk served the newly created Czech nation, first as a member of Parliament and then as a senator. He died at Lopud, near Dubrovnik, Yugoslavia, on May 14, 1931.

Dyk's writings reflect his fervent nationalism. His lyric poetry, the area of his greatest talent, is imbued with irony and satire, notably in the collection *Okno* (1920; *The Window*), inspired by his prison experience. His successful plays range from historical dramas to satirical comedies. His novels are the least successful of his creations.

DYKES, dīks, **John Bacchus** (1823–1876), English clergyman and composer of hymn tunes. He was born in Kingston-upon-Hull, England, on March 10, 1823. He was educated at Cambridge, where he distinguished himself as an amateur musician. In 1847 he entered holy orders and was appointed to the curacy of Malton, Yorkshire. He was appointed a minor canon and precentor of Durham Cathedral in 1849, and in 1862 was named vicar of St. Oswald's, Durham.

Dykes wrote numerous hymn tunes, many of which were published in *Hymns Ancient and Modern* (1861). He provided the musical settings for such hymns as *Lead, Kindly Light; Nearer, My God to Thee; Jesus, Lover of My Soul;* and *Holy, Holy, Holy.* Dykes died at Ticehurst, England, on Jan. 22, 1876.

DYLAN, dil′ən, **Bob** (1941–   ), American folk-rock singer and composer, whose antiestablishment songs were a rallying cry for the disaffected youth of the 1960's. Robert Zimmerman (he later took the name Dylan in honor of poet Dylan Thomas) was born in Duluth, Minn., on May 24, 1941. He briefly attended the University of Minnesota in 1960 and then went to New York City, where he met folk musician Woody Guthrie, his idol and greatest influence. After performing in Greenwich Village coffeehouses, Dylan, who played the guitar and harmonica, appeared at Carnegie Recital Hall in 1961. In 1962 he recorded his first album and wrote his lyrical *Blowin' in the Wind*—and his rise was meteoric.

Among Dylan's best-known compositions are *The Times They Are A-Changin'* (1964), *Mr. Tambourine Man* (1965), *Just Like a Woman* (1966), and *Lay Lady Lay* (1969). See also ROCK MUSIC.

DYING GAUL, a marble copy of the bronze original, exemplifies the realistic trend of Hellenistic art.

ALINARI, FROM ART REFERENCE BUREAU

DYNAMICS. See MECHANICS.

DYNAMISM, in general, is the belief that the appearances of and changes in material things are visible manifestations of an invisible force or power. In primitive religions it is the animistic belief in the sacred, mysterious powers inherent in all things and beings, which cause such phenomena as the motions of the heavens and the changes of the seasons.

In philosophy and science, dynamism takes many forms. To explain physical change, some pre-Socratic philosophers used such dynamic principles as the condensation and rarefaction of the elements, the binding force of love, and the separating power of strife. Others, notably atomists, explained all change as the result of the constant movement of indivisible atoms within the void. In the Socratic period there arose the notion of form as a dynamic constituent of things, especially of the soul as the form that gives a living body its living activity and of nature as the intrinsic source of activities of things.

Some dynamisms tend to concentrate on the interactions within the universe as a whole. Gravitation, the attraction of one mass for another, is a "force" explanation that is widely applied. Newton gave a mathematical expression to this mass-relationship, and, in general, the 16th, 17th, and 18th centuries saw many dynamisms of this kind. In Leibniz' explanation, all appearances are manifestations of simple, indivisible, unextended, and unalterable centers of force or activity called "monads," which are grouped in large numbers to form the things observed.

In modern physics, the notions that mass and energy are interchangeable and that the whole world consists of fields of force of varying intensities in varying locations are forms of dynamism. Modern biochemistry attempts to discover how the dynamic forces within atoms and molecules produce the activities characteristic of living things.

FRANCIS J. COLLINGWOOD
Marquette University

DYNAMITE is a powerful industrial explosive. It is widely used for underground coal mining, tunneling, and other applications requiring small boreholes.

History. Dynamite was discovered and named by the Swedish chemist Alfred Nobel in 1867. Nobel found that when nitroglycerin, which is very sensitive to shock, was absorbed in diatomaceous earth it became less sensitive to shock and was less likely to explode from impacts encountered in handling and shipping. However, it could still be readily exploded by a blasting cap. Because dynamite is both more powerful and less expensive, it quickly replaced black powder, which for centuries had been used both for blasting and gunpowder, as a blasting agent.

In 1875, Nobel recognized the need for a cohesive explosive that would detonate reliably underwater, and he gelatinized nitroglycerin by the addition of 7% nitrocellulose. "Blasting gelatin" is now little used in its original form, but it is a key ingredient of gelatin dynamite.

Composition. Modern dynamite is composed principally of glycerin-ethylene glycol nitrates, ammonium nitrate, sodium nitrate, and combustible pulps, such as wood meal, starch, rye flour, and sugarcane pith. It has a dry granular consistency.

Ethylene glycol nitrates are included in the formula because they form a low-freezing mixture with glycerin. Pure nitroglycerin freezes at 13° C (55° F), and when frozen, it is insensitive to a blasting cap. The mixture eliminates the hazard of a dynamite charge that fails to explode in cold weather.

Most dynamite is packaged in cylindrical paper cartridges ranging in diameter from 2 to 20 cm (0.8–8 inches) and in length from 20 to 91 cm (8–36 inches). Where the explosive needs to be used in long, rigid columns—for example, for generating earth vibrations in seismic prospecting—cardboard couplers are provided or the cartridges are made of plastic with threaded ends.

Reactions. In the detonation reaction, dynamite is converted essentially to carbon dioxide, nitrogen, and water vapor. The formation of poisonous carbon monoxide and nitrogen dioxide is kept at a safe level by a careful balance of the ratio of nitrates to pulps in those grades of dynamite intended for underground use.

The heat liberated by the explosion of dynamite amounts to 900 to 1,200 calories per gram, depending on the nitroglycerin content. With a high nitroglycerin content, the reaction produces a momentary pressure of almost 1,000,000 lb/sq inch (70,000 kg/sq cm) in a very intense shock wave that travels at a rate of several thousand feet per second. The resultant shattering effect is useful in breaking hard rock. On the other hand, a mixture of ammonium nitrate and pulps produces gas at a somewhat slower rate with a peak pressure near 60,000 lb/sq inch (4200 kg/sq cm); thus dynamite containing up to 80% of these ingredients is effective for mining coal in large pieces. Formulas high in ammonium nitrate and including some sodium chloride have been approved by the U. S. Bureau of Mines as "permissible" for use in coal mines because they produce a flame that is relatively brief and cool enough to avoid igniting a mixture of methane, coal dust, and air. Coal mine disasters have been relatively rare since permissible dynamite replaced black powder in mines.

Use with Other Blasting Agents. Dynamite is used to prime charges of nonnitroglycerin blasting agents that are more economical than dynamite for the large excavations required in the strip mining of coal, open-pit mining of metal ores, and rock quarrying. These agents are relatively safe in view of their insensitivity to mechanical impact or the explosion of a blasting cap. A reliable performance is assured by the use of a stick of dynamite with each charge.

A typical blast in such operations involves roughly 13,500 kg (30,000 lb) of explosive distributed among 25 to 50 large boreholes. If the holes are dry, they are loaded by blowing ammonium nitrate coated with fuel oil through a hose with compressed air. Where water is encountered, a "water gel" explosive may be used: it contains ammonium nitrate, TNT, or powdered aluminum, and 10% to 20% water gelatinized with a soluble gum. The use of nonnitroglycerin blasting composition is increasing.

HARRISON H. HOLMES
E. I. du Pont de Nemours & Co.

Further Reading: Cook, Melvin A., *The Science of High Explosives* (New York 1958); E. I. du Pont de Nemours & Co., *Blasters' Handbook* (Wilmington, Del., 1967).

DYNAMO. See GENERATORS, ELECTRIC.

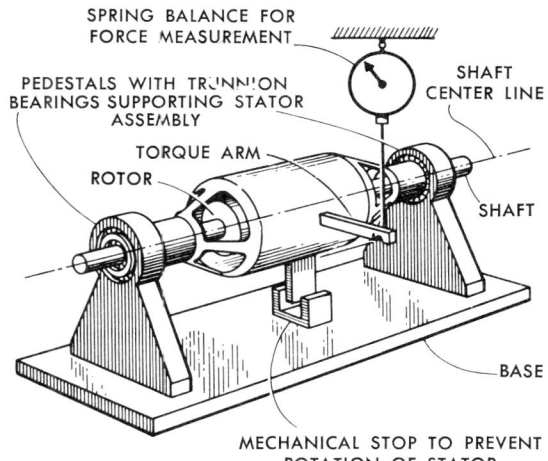

Direct-current electric dynamometer

DYNAMOMETER, dī-nə-mom′ə-tər, a device with a rotating shaft that is coupled to the shaft of a machine under test to measure the output torque or the required driving torque of the machine. The torque measured by the dynamometer is multiplied by the shaft angular velocity, measured by a tachometer, to compute the horsepower of the machine under test. Dynamometers are used to determine the torque and horsepower characteristics of electric motors, generators, internal combustion engines, gas turbines, and pumps.

Types. In some tests, the dynamometer absorbs the mechanical power output of a motor or other machine and yields a measurement of its output torque. In other tests, the dynamometer supplies mechanical power to the drive shaft of a generator or other machine and yields a measurement of its required driving torque.

The *direct-current* (dc) *dynamometer*, the most common type, can measure either output torque or driving torque. This dynamometer has a stationary frame, or stator, and a rotor that is connected to the rotor of the machine under test. When the dc dynamometer is used, mechanical power is converted to electrical power, and this power is consumed in an external loading device such as an array of resistors.

The *eddy-current dynamometer* and the *hydraulic dynamometer* can measure only output torque. These dynamometers consume mechanical power internally by converting it to heat and therefore require cooling systems.

Operation. The principle of operation of the dynamometer is based on Newton's third law of motion, which states that the forces of action and reaction are equal and coexistent. In motors and generators, for example, the torque developed by the armature current of the machine exerts an equal and opposite (reaction) torque on the machine frame. When a dynamometer is used to test such machines, its reaction torque is used as a measure of the tested machine's torque.

In tests with a dc dynamometer, the frame is suspended in trunnion bearings supported by pedestals (see figure). The bearing suspension allows the frame to rotate, but this rotation is limited to a few degrees by mechanical stops. Electric-power connections to the dynamometer are made through flexible cables. The force required to prevent frame rotation is usually measured by a spring balance or a lever-type balance working in a vertical direction. The reaction torque is this measured force multiplied by the torque arm length (the horizontal radial distance from the center line of the shaft to the point at which the force measurement was made).

Other Applications. The word "dynamometer" is also used to designate devices or structures that measure the linear reaction force developed by jet engines and rocket engines and to designate devices that measure the drag of ship model as they are towed in model tanks.

WALTER LaPIERRE, *Singer Company*

DYNAMOTOR, dī′nə-mō-tər, a rotating machine that accepts direct-current (dc) power at one voltage level and delivers it at another voltage level. In its simplest form it has one armature, two separate armature windings, and two separate commutators. One armature winding with its commutator operates as a constant-speed dc motor, and the other armature winding with its commutator operates as a dc generator. The motor section accepts dc power and provides the mechanical drive for the generator section. The generator section produces the dc output voltage. The stationary frame and field-pole structure of the dynamotor is like that of the usual dc dynamo (generator).

The dynamotor is used to obtain a constant-voltage dc supply from a dc power system having a voltage that is different from that required for a piece of equipment that must be supplied with power. It is thus used in a way that is analogous to the use of the transformer in alternating-current (ac) systems. Dynamotors have been used extensively as voltage sources for electronic equipment in aircraft.

WALTER LaPIERRE, *Singer Company*

DYNASTS, The, dī′nasts, a poetic drama by Thomas Hardy (q.v.) on the Napoleonic Wars of 1805–1815. In three parts (1, 1904; II, 1906; III, 1908), with 19 acts and 130 scenes, the play is intended not for the stage but for "mental performance."

Although Hardy uses historical personages and bases much of the action on historical episodes, he is primarily interested in giving a philosophic rather than a realistic account of the persons and events. He presents his own concept of the functioning of an "Immanent Will" in the world and his belief in "evolutionary meliorism"—this Immanent Will's growing awareness of itself. To this end he employs a group of characters he calls "phantom intelligences," who comment on the action and thus give the drama philosophic depth and epic breadth. Hardy's affirmation of evolutionary meliorism gives the play a positive note not usually found in most of his later writings.

MICHAEL TIMKO, *Queens College, New York*

DYNASTY, a succession of rulers of the same line or family. The word originally meant simply "sovereignty" or "power," but about the beginning of the 17th century it acquired the connotation of transmitted power, probably because in hierarchic societies power tended to perpetuate itself in groups or families. In contemporary American usage the term has been applied to wealthy or socially prominent families that have maintained their position for extended periods, and to families, such as the Adams family of Massachusetts, that have produced men of talent for several generations. The term has also been used to designate associated groups of wealthy persons in capitalist societies, constituting an alleged "power elite."

The intelligentsia of Victorian England had so many family interrelationships that it was regarded by some as dynastic. The author Leslie Stephen, for example, a protégé of Matthew Arnold, was the son-in-law of William Makepeace Thackeray and the father of Virginia Woolf.

DYNE, dīn, the unit of force in the centimeter-gram-second system of units. One dyne is the force required to give a mass of one gram an acceleration of one centimeter per second squared. Compared to other standard units of force, the dyne is extremely small: 100,000 dynes equals one newton (the unit of force in the meter-kilogram-second system), and about 445,000 dynes equals one pound. Therefore, the dyne is most often used by scientists rather than by engineers or laymen. See also METRIC SYSTEM.

DYRRACHIUM. See DURRËS.

DYSENTERY, dis'ən-ter-ē, is an infectious disease characterized by frequent loose stools, intestinal bleeding, and, in severe cases, intestinal ulceration. There are two major types of dysentery, caused by two different types of organisms—bacteria and amebas. The bacterial, or bacillary, form is caused almost entirely by bacteria of the genus *Shigella* and is sometimes known as "shigellosis." The amebic form, known as "amebic dysentery" or "amebiasis," is caused by the ameba *Endamoeba histolytica*.

Both the bacterial and amebic forms of dysentery are usually spread by food or water that is contaminated with the fecal matter of infected individuals. Both disorders may occur in epidemic form when individuals are crowded into small areas where there is poor sanitation, and outbreaks of dysentery are frequent in unsanitary prisoner-of-war camps, refugee camps, asylums, and military barracks. A tropical climate favors the spread of the disease primarily because of the abundance of insects that act as carriers of the disease-causing organisms and thus spread the infection.

Bacillary Dysentery. Bacillary dysentery has been known to man since ancient times, but its cause was unknown until 1898, when the Japanese physician Kiyoshi Shiga discovered the primary causative organism during an outbreak of the disease in that country. The organism was later named *Shigella shigae*. During World War I workers in the United States and Canada identified related forms—*S. flexneri, S. boydii,* and *S. sonnei*.

The incubation period for bacterial dysentery ranges from one to six days. The first symptom is the copious production of watery, sometimes blood-tinged stools. Other early symptoms include fever, cramps, and dehydration. In advanced stages of the disease, the stools are bloody and the bowel wall becomes ulcerated. If the disease is not treated, various complications may develop, including meningeal irritation, conjunctivitis, and arthritis.

Bacterial dysentery is usually treated with tetracycline, chlortetracycline (Aureomycin), oxytetracycline (Terramycin), and similar antibiotics. If the patient is severely dehydrated, fluids are administered to reestablish the body's fluid balance. In rare cases blood transfusions may be necessary to restore lost blood.

Amebic Dysentery. This form of dysentery is harder to treat than the bacterial form because the causative organism may occur in two different forms: a motile form and a cyst, or resting, form. The motile form produces acute amebic dysentery, with watery, blood-tinged stools, abdominal cramps, fever, and weakness. The cyst form produces chronic amebic dysentery, with intermitent diarrhea and some abdominal discomfort. Chronic amebic dysentery is more common than the acute form, and sometimes the symptoms are so mild that the person is not aware that he has the disease.

In treating both chronic and acute amebic dysentery, the drug emetine is injected, and either penicillin or succinylsulfathiazole (Sulfasuxidine) is given orally. In addition, the drug diiodohydroxyquin (Diodoquin) is administered orally for about three weeks, and carbarsone or fumagillin may then be given for the next 10 days. Although a complete cure can usually be achieved, relapses may occur, and therapy must be started again.

REAUMUR S. DONNALLY, M.D.
Washington (D. C.) Hospital Center

DYSLEXIA, dis-leks'ē-ə, a marked difficulty in learning to read. The term "dyslexia" is often applied to persons who habitually reverse the letters of words, reading "saw" for "was," for example; or reverse the letters themselves, reading "b" for "d" and "p" for "q." These people may also perceive words upside down as well as backward. For example, they may read the word "OIL" as the number "710."

Dyslexia is regarded by some authorities as a definite neurological or psychological disorder with characteristic symptoms and specifiable causes. Most of these authorities include the combination of illegible handwriting and poor spelling, together with average or above average intelligence, among the symptoms of dyslexia. Some include general dyssymbolia, the inability to formulate thoughts into language, as a symptom of dyslexia, and others limit dyslexic symptoms to problems of translating and combining symbols into concepts. Still others include as dyslexics poor readers who also have difficulties with hand-eye coordination. This poor coordination, they feel, accounts for the distorted handwriting, poor spelling, and evidence of neurological disorders that may be associated with dyslexia.

Among the causes suggested for dyslexia are brain damage and inherited neurological abnormalities not associated with brain damage. Environmental factors, such as poor teaching, are also regarded as possible causes.

Many researchers and practitioners question the use of the term "dyslexia." While they agree that individual symptoms and combinations of symptoms may exist in both good and poor readers, they still refuse to use the term for two reasons. First, few professionals seem to agree on the proper use of the term, and second, even when there is agreement, the term has little or no relevance to treatment.

S. ALAN COHEN, *Yeshiva University*

DYSMENORRHEA is the discomfort sometimes associated with menstruation. See MENSTRUATION.

DYSON, dī'sən, **Sir Frank Watson** (1868–1939), British astronomer, who studied the motions and distributions of the stars. He was born at Ashby, Lincolnshire, on Jan. 8, 1868, and was educated at Bradford Grammar School and Trinity College, Cambridge. In 1894 he became chief assistant at the Royal Observatory at Greenwich and reworked the star positions measured by Stephen Groombridge some 80 years earlier. The proper motions that he determined proved invaluable for studies on stellar distribution. He also measured the spectrum of the solar corona and chromosphere at three total eclipses.

In 1906 he was appointed astronomer royal for Scotland. In 1910 he returned to Greenwich as astronomer royal, a position he held until he retired in 1933. At Greenwich he inaugurated important programs of stellar parallax measurement and photographic photometry and greatly improved the time service. With Sir Richard Woolley he wrote *Eclipses of the Sun and Moon* (1937).

Dyson was knighted in 1915. He died during a voyage from Australia on May 25, 1939.

BRIAN G. MARSDEN
Smithsonian Astrophysical Observatory

DYSPEPSIA is the medical term for indigestion. See INDIGESTION.

DYSPNEA, disp'nē-ə, is the sensation that occurs when a person experiences difficulty in breathing. A person suffering dyspnea often complains that he is out of breath or that he cannot get enough air. Dyspnea is often a sign of a serious underlying disease. It is a particularly distressing symptom because of the emotional impact produced when a person feels that vital function of breathing is somehow in jeopardy.

Types. Under some circumstances dyspnea may occur normally. This type, known as *physiologic dyspnea*, occurs in normal people who have exercised too strenuously. The amount of activity required to produce dyspnea varies greatly, from the severe exertion required of a conditioned athlete to the relatively minor activities performed by elderly or obese people who are in poor physical condition.

Pathologic dyspnea may be due to a wide variety of diseases. Among the most serious of these diseases are disorders of the heart, of the lungs, of the red blood cells, and of the muscles and nerves associated with the process of breathing. In addition, dyspnea may be associated with certain emotional disorders.

Causes. There are four basic respiratory factors that may be involved in the onset of dyspnea. One factor is an inadequate supply of oxygen, which may be due to a reduced amount of oxygen in the air or to an obstruction in one of the air passages to the lungs. Dyspnea may also be induced by an impairment in the distribution of inhaled air throughout a large portion of the lung so that the normal oxygenation of the blood cannot be fully accomplished. An impairment in the diffusion of oxygen through the lung membrane into the blood may also result in dyspnea. This type of impairment may be due to abnormalities in the lung membrane or to a reduction in the amount of blood flowing through the lung tissue. Lastly, dyspnea may result from defects in the movement of the chest wall or in the flexibility of the lung itself so that the ventilatory function of the lung is reduced.

Any of these four factors may upset the normal concentrations of oxygen and carbon dioxide in the blood. Once the concentration of oxygen falls too low or that of carbon dioxide rises too high, the brain's respiratory centers are stimulated and they, in turn, produce an increase in both the rate and depth of breathing. This increase leads to dyspnea.

However, there are physiological factors other than these four respiratory conditions that may lead to changes in respiration. Prominent among these factors are changes in the acidity of the blood, which may be due to metabolic abnormalities such as those occurring in kidney disease and diabetes mellitus.

RALPH TOMPSETT, M. D.
Baylor University Medical Center

DYSPROSIUM, dis-prō'zē-əm, is a soft silver metallic element (symbol Dy). It is one of the rare-earth metals. Dysprosium was discovered in 1886 by the French chemist Paul Émile Lecoq de Boisbaudran. The name comes from the Greek word *dysprositos*, meaning "hard to get at."

Uses. There are few uses for pure dysprosium. However, some uses are now being made of the metal in nuclear control applications because of its high neutron absorption cross section and high melting point.

Properties. The atomic number of dysprosium is 66, and its atomic weight is 162.50. The element has a large number of isotopes ranging from ^{149}Dy to ^{167}Dy, the most abundant being ^{164}Dy, ^{162}Dy, and ^{163}Dy. Dysprosium has a valence of +3. Its density is 8.536 grams/cu cm (0.307 lb/cu inch), and it crystallizes in the hexagonal close-packed system. The melting point of the element is 1407° C (2564° F), and the boiling point is 2873° C (5203° F).

Occurrence and Preparation. Dysprosium occurs in the minerals bastnaesite and monazite, as well as in a variety of other minerals common to rare-earth metals. Pure dysprosium is isolated from the rest of the rare-earth family through a very complex series of fractional crystallizations to an anhydrous chloride or fluoride. The chloride or fluoride is then either electrolyzed or reacted with calcium at high temperature in a vacuum furnace. The excess calcium and calcium halide are are vaporized, leaving the pure metal.

DOUGLAS V. KELLER, JR.
Syracuse University

DYSTROPHY. See MUSCULAR DYSTROPHY.

DZERZHINSK, dyer-zhinsk', is a city in the USSR, in Gorky oblast of the Russian SFSR. It is situated on the left bank of the Oka River, 20 miles (32 km) west of the city of Gorky. During the 1930's this area was selected as the site of a vast complex of chemical plants producing phosphate and nitrogen fertilizers, synthetic fibers, insecticides, caustic soda, and other chemicals.

Apatite from the Kola Peninsula and coal from the Moscow Basin long served as the main raw materials for the chemical industry. After the development of natural gas fields in the USSR in the late 1950's and the 1960's, the chemical industry of Dzerzhinsk shifted increasingly to the use of gas and the production of petrochemicals. Power for the city's industries is supplied by a coal-fed power plant at Igumnovo, just east of Dzerzhinsk, and by the 520,-

000-kw Gorky hydroelectric station, opened in 1955 at Gorodets on the Volga River.

Originally known as Rastyapino, the city was renamed in 1929 for Soviet leader Feliks Dzerzhinsky. Population: (1967 est.) 201,000.

THEODORE SHABAD
Editor of "Soviet Geography"

DZERZHINSKY, dyēr-zhĕn'skē, **Feliks Edmundovich** (1877–1926), one of the founding fathers of the Soviet state. He was born on Sept. 11, 1877, in Vilna province, into a family of Polish gentry. He became a socialist in 1895 and was repeatedly arrested and exiled by the czarist police. As a member of the Communist party's central committee he played an important part in the Bolshevik seizure of power in November 1917.

This enigmatic, forceful man held a number of important posts in the new Communist regime, but his name is usually associated with the founding of the secret police (Cheka, or OGPU after 1922), which he headed from December 1917 until his death. He was also minister of the interior after 1919. In his last years he devoted himself primarily to economic matters, becoming minister of transport in 1921 and, in 1924, chairman of the supreme economic council. He died on July 20, 1926, in Moscow.

GEORGE W. SIMMONDS, *Wayne State University*

DZHAMBUL, jäm-bool', is the capital of Dzhambul oblast in the USSR, in southern Kazakhstan. It is situated in a cotton- and sugar beet-growing oasis along the Turksib (Turkestan-Siberia) railroad and the Talas River. The city has a fertilizer plant, which was expanded greatly in the 1960's as a result of the exploitation of phosphate deposits in the Karatau Mountains to the northwest. A large coal-burning power station was opened in 1967.

Dzhambul is on the site of the trading center of Taraz, which flourished from the 7th century until its destruction in the 13th century by the hordes of Genghis Khan. A new settlement, known as Aulie-Ata, was established in the late 18th century by the emirs of Kokand. It fell to the Russians in 1864. The present name, commemorating a Kazakh poet, dates from 1938. Dzhambul oblast, which covers an area of 55,830 square miles (144,600 sq km), is largely desert, with a few cultivated oases along its southern margins. Population: (1967 est.) of the city, 158,000; of the oblast, 736,000.

THEODORE SHABAD
Editor of "Soviet Geography"

DZHUGDZHUR MOUNTAINS, joog-joor', a rugged mountain range in the Russian republic of the USSR. It stretches for over 300 miles (480 km) along the coast of the Sea of Okhotsk from the Uchur to the Ulya rivers. The range has a sharp alpine relief, with peaks reaching over 7,000 feet (2,100 meters) above sea level, or from 4,000 to 6,000 feet (1,200–1,800 meters) above the galley bottoms. The range separates the rivers that drain into the Sea of Okhotsk from those that drain into the Aldan and Lena rivers. In the north the range ends in the Yudomo-Maya plateau; in the south it merges with the Stanovoi range.

According to the Soviet geographer L. S. Berg, the Dzhugdzhur (or Aldan) range is tectonically a southern extension of the Verkhoyansk range, but S. P. Suslov considers it to be sharply distinguished both geologically and tectonically. The range consists chiefly of Mesozoic extrusives, such as diabases and andesites. The Precambrian gneisses and crystalline schists, common to the Stanovoi range, are rare, while the Paleozoic marine sedimentaries characteristic of the Verkhoyansk complex are also missing.

W. A. DOUGLAS JACKSON
University of Washington

DZUNGARIA, dzŏŏng-gär'ē-ə, is a geographical region in western China, situated in Sinkiang-Uigur autonomous region (Sinkiang), between the Tien Shan and Altai mountain systems. It is a desert ringed by a belt of grasslands and oases at the foot of enclosing mountains. Among the oases is Urumchi, the capital of Sinkiang. One of the mountain ranges separating Dzungaria from the Soviet Union is the Dzungarian Ala Tau, the northernmost outlier of the Tien Shan system. It rises to 16,550 feet (5,044 meters) in snow-covered peaks. At the eastern end of this range, on the Soviet-Chinese border, lies a series of mountain passes known as the Dzungarian Gates.

About 35% of the people are nomadic herders, chiefly Kazakhs and Mongols. The sedentary population of the agricultural oases includes Uigurs (35%), Chinese (17%), and Chinese Muslims (10%). The major mineral resource is petroleum. Its discovery at Karamai in 1955 spurred the Communist Chinese to speed up both the development of the area and the extension of the railroad to the region.

Among the nomads from central Asia were the Dzungars, a Mongol tribe generally identified with the "eastern wing" (*Dzungar* in Mongolian) of the Kalmyks, or western Mongols. They ruled all of Sinkiang in the 17th century but were unable to resist the advance of the Chinese, who gained control of the area in the mid-18th century. Since 1954 most of Dzungaria has been part of Sinkiang's Ili Kazakh autonomous district, with its capital at Kuldja. Population: (1953) 1,500,000.

THEODORE SHABAD
Author of "China's Changing Map"

DZUNGARS, dzŏŏn'gärz, a western Mongol (Oyrat) tribal confederation that in the 17th and early 18th centuries ruled a Central Asian empire centering on Dzungaria, a region now part of western China.

During the 15th and 16th centuries, various confederations of Oyrat tribes terrorized their Central Asian neighbors. At the beginning of the 17th century one such group moved west to the lower Volga River, where they became known as Kalmyks. Those remaining in Dzungaria, the Dzungars, formed a militant confederation. In the north and west the Dzungars came into conflict with the Russians in Siberia and with the Kazakhs in Kazakhstan. In the east they encountered China and its eastern Mongol allies.

The Dzungars' control over the trade corridor between Russia and China gave them their place in history. From 1635 to 1758 they warred with Russia and China and also fought the Kazakhs over pasturage. After the death of their leader Galdan Khan in 1697, Dzungar power waned, and after defeat by Chinese forces in 1758 much of their population was annihilated.

ELIZABETH E. BACON
Michigan State University

	EARLY NORTH SEMITIC	PHOENICIAN	EARLY GREEK	CLASSICAL GREEK	ETRUSCAN Early	ETRUSCAN Classical	EARLY LATIN	CLASSICAL LATIN
E	ᗐ	ᗐ	ꓘ	E	ꓘ	ꓘ	ꓘ	E
	CURSIVE MAJUSCULE (ROMAN)	CURSIVE MINUSCULE (ROMAN)	ANGLO-IRISH MAJUSCULE	CAROLINE MINUSCULE	VENETIAN MINUSCULE (ITALIC)		N. ITALIAN MINUSCULE (ROMAN)	
	⊢	₤	e	e	e		e	

A. C. SYLVESTER, CAMBRIDGE, ENGLAND

DEVELOPMENT OF THE LETTER E is illustrated in the above chart, beginning with the early North Semitic letter. The evolution of the majuscule (capital) E is shown at the top; that of the minuscule (lowercase) at bottom.

E, ē, is the fifth letter in the English alphabet, as it is in the other West European alphabets (see ALPHABET). It was also the fifth character in the original (North Semitic) alphabet as well as in the Greek, Latin, and Etruscan alphabets, the prototypes of the modern Western alphabet. In the ancient North Semitic alphabets, as in the modern Hebrew, the letter *e* was a consonant, having the phonetic value of the aspirant *h,* and was called *he.* The ancient meaning of *he,* if indeed it had one, has been conjectured to be "a lattice window." However, the form of the letter in old Semitic alphabets suggests this less clearly than does the Cretan symbol with which it is often compared.

When the Greeks took over the North Semitic alphabet, *he* became *epsilon;* in some varieties of the Greek alphabet, and in the Greek classical alphabet derived from these, *epsilon* was adopted to represent the short *e,* while the Semitic *heth* or *het* (see H) was adopted to denote the long *e* or *ēta.* In other Greek alphabets, *epsilon* was adopted in order to represent both the short and the long *e.*

The Etruscan and the Latin alphabets, descendants of the Greek alphabet, used the letter *e* (*epsilon*) with no distinction between the long and short vowels. In the Latin alphabet, the Greek *ēta* (H), descended from the North Semitic *heth* or *het,* was used (as it is used in modern Western alphabets) to express the aspirate *h.* While the capital E is, generally speaking, the Latin monumental letter (for development of its form from the original, see the headpiece to this article), the development of handwriting from the 3d century A.D. favored the rounding of the character, resulting in the minuscule *e.* See also PALEOGRAPHY.

Pronunciation. The name and phonetic value of *e* in Latin and all the West European languages except English are actually "eh" (as it is in the standard international alphabet). In English, its chief pronunciation, as well as its name, is that of the sound in such words as *he, me,* or *be*—that is, the sound of the Continental *i;* but in such words as *men, credit,* and *rectify,* the letter *e* sounds like the Continental *e.* In the British pronunciation of *Derby* and *clerk* the phonetic value of *er* is *ar.*

In Middle English, the final *e* was usually pronounced, but in Modern English *e* in the final position is mute, though it generally lengthens the preceding vowel (compare, for instance, *mat* with *mate* or *lob* with *lobe*). E following *c* or *g* generally softens these letters (as in *face* or *rage* as compared with *rag*). In final *es, e* is not pronounced except after sibilants (as in *classes, races,* or *boxes*); and in final *ed,* the *d* is often pronounced "t" and the *e* usually is silent (see D).

The combination of *e* and other vowels expresses various sounds: *ea* may sound like "ee" (as in the present tense of the verb *read* or in the noun *sea*) or the Continental *e* (as in the past tense of the verb *read* or in the noun *lead* but not the verb *lead*). *Ei* may sound like "ee" (as in *receive*), like long *i* (as in *seismic*), or like long *a* (as in the verb or noun *seine*). *Ie* sometimes has the value of short *e* (as in *friend*). *Eo* is generally a long *e* (as in *people*), but there are exceptions (as in *surgeon*); *oe* usually has the phonetic value of short *e* (as in *foetid*), though it sometimes has the value of long *e* (as in *foetus*). *Eu* and *ew* have generally the phonetic value of *iu* (as in *Europe, euphonic, ewe,* or *new,* the last of which, however, is generally pronounced "noo" in the United States); *ue* may have the sound of short *e* (as in *guest*) or of "oo" or "yoo" (as in *pursue*). *Ey* may sound like "ee" (as in *key*) like long *a* (as in *prey*), or long *i* (as in *eye*).

Frequency of Occurrence. E is used more often than any other English letter. Compared with the other English vowels, its frequency of occurrence is as follows: 1,000 to 728 for *a;* 1,000 to 704 for *i;* 1,000 to 672 for *o;* and 1,000 to 296 for *u.* The main reason for this is that in many Modern English words, *e* has replaced the vowels *i, o, a,* or *u* of Old English words (as in Modern English *seep* from Old English *sipian,* or Modern English *when* from Old English *hwanne*).

E as a Symbol. In music, E is the third note of the natural scale of *C* and the fifth semitone in the chromatic scale. In the fixed system of solmization, E is called *mi* and is the third tone of the C major scale. E is a frequently employed keynote.

In chemistry, E stands for einsteinium. In physics, it may stand for "electron," "electric field strength," or "energy." In mathematics, *e* is the symbol of an irrational number whose approximate value is 2.7182818.

In school or college grading systems, E represents either the lowest passing mark or a conditional grade, although in some systems it represents failure. In still other systems, E may stand for "excellent."

DAVID DIRINGER
Author of "The Alphabet"

Further Reading: See the bibliography for ALPHABET.

e, in mathematics, is an irrational number (2.718281828459 . . .) with important applications in science. It is also called *Euler's number* for Leonhard Euler who introduced it in his *Introductio in analysin infinitorum* (1748).

Many processes in nature have the following characteristic: the rate of change of a quantity depends on the amount of the quantity present. The quantity may be the number of bacteria on a dish, an amount of radioactive material, or the strength of an electric current. In each case the basic equation describing the situation is $dy/dt = ky$, where k is the "rate constant" describing how fast the quantity changes. This equation has only one solution: $y = Ae^{kt}$, where A is a constant depending on initial conditions. Such behavior is called *exponential growth* (k positive) or *exponential decay* (k negative). The exponential function e^{kt} occurs in nearly all fields of physics and chemistry. Thus tables of powers of e, and also logarithms to the base e (called *natural logarithms*), are in wide use.

Euler's number may be defined by the expression $e = \lim (1 + 1/n)^n$ as n becomes indefinitely large. Alternatively, $e = 1 + 1/1! + 1/2! + \ldots$. Complex numbers may be written in the form $re^{i\theta}$, where $e^{i\theta} = \cos\theta + i\sin\theta$. Euler was the first to relate the numbers e, π, and i through the rather simple equation, $e^{i\pi} + 1 = 0$.

J. DAVID TEAL, *Tougaloo College*

E PLURIBUS UNUM, ē ploor'ə-bəs ū'nəm, Latin phrase meaning "from the many, one," used as a motto on the Great Seal of the United States, referring to the Union of the states. It has been traced to Vergil's poem *Moretum*. It appeared on the design for the United States seal prepared by Philadelphia artist Pierre Eugène du Simitière in 1776. The Continental Congress did not approve this design. The Great Seal of the United States, adopted on June 20, 1782, and designed mainly by William Barton, retained the motto on a scroll held in the eagle's beak. The motto appears on the seals of the President, the Senate, the Supreme Court, and the State and Treasury departments; on U.S. coins and the dollar bill; on the flag of North Dakota, and on the seals of Michigan and Wisconsin.

EA, ā'ä, was a Babylonian god, the father of Marduk, and was identified with the earth, whose Sumerian name was Enki. Ea first appears about 2200 B.C. as the patron god of the city of Eridu, one of the most ancient towns in the valley of the Euphrates, but later he became a universal deity ruling the waters surrounding the world. He became the patron deity of healers and magicians and of arts and crafts.

Ea was worshiped under the symbol of a monster, half fish and half goat. Many stories were told about his feats and how through cleverness or even deceit he was able to accomplish great deeds. In the Akkadian creation epic, Ea appears, together with Anu and Enlil, as one of a triad ruling the cosmos. He is also mentioned in a stele of Nabonidus, a ruler of Babylon in the 6th century B.C. Afterward, Ea shared the fate of other Babylonian deities and is remembered only in oracles and incantations.

RICHARD N. FRYE
Author of "The Heritage of Persia"

EADS, ēdz, **James Buchanan** (1820–1887), American engineer, who designed the first important steel bridge in the United States. Eads was born in Lawrenceburg, Ind., on May 23, 1820. He left school at age 13 to work on Mississippi River steamboats, and in 1842 he organized a company to salvage wrecked river vessels. This venture was a great financial success and displayed his genius for hydraulics and mechanics. An interlude in the glass-manufacturing business brought him heavy financial losses, however, and he returned to river work.

During the Civil War, Eads designed and built river gunboats for the Union. After the war he guided a company that was formed to build a bridge across the Mississippi at St. Louis. Congress required spans so high and wide that most engineers considered the project hopeless, but Eads' ingenuity prevailed. The bridge, completed in 1874, is still in use.

In 1875, Eads undertook a project to open the mouth of the Mississippi, which had become choked with mud and silt. He devised a system of jetties that concentrated the flow to make the river current itself remove the mud and silt. The project was completed in 1879. His last interest, a railway to carry ships across the Isthmus of Tehuantepec, Mexico, never came to fruition. Eads died in Nassau, Bahama Islands, on March 8, 1887.

PAUL B. TRESCOTT
Miami University, Oxford, Ohio

EAGLE, any of a diverse group of about 55 species of flesh-eating diurnal birds of prey that occur on all continents except Antarctica.

Large, spectacular eagles (especially the sea eagles, harpies, and large booted eagles) are becoming rare. They are killed by farmers and gamekeepers, who shoot them or put out poisoned carrion as bait. They are also in demand by falconers (see FALCONRY), zoos, and trophy collectors. In addition, the reproductive success of eagles may be impaired by pesticide poisoning. These artificial pressures, plus natural mortality and the eagles' low reproduction rate, place many species in serious danger of extinction.

Description and Behavior. Eagles vary in size. Ayres' eagle (*Hieraetus dubius*) is 16½ inches (42 cm) long, while the harpy (*Harpia harpyja*), the monkey-eating eagle (*Pithecophaga jefferyi*), and Steller's sea eagle (*Haliaeetus pelagicus*) are 36 to 40 inches (90–100 cm) long—among the largest of flying birds.

Eagles have long, massive, hooked bills and powerful toes with long, curved claws. Their eyes, although located laterally, are directed forward, thus allowing good binocular depth perception. Their wings are broad, and their breast muscles are powerfully developed. Most species are various shades of brown, black, or gray, but some are white or streaked on the underside or have light markings on the head, shoulders, wings, or tail.

The relative length of an eagle's wings and tail and the covering of its legs vary with the habitat and food habits of the species. Species that inhabit forests generally have relatively short wings and long tails that permit them to maneuver among the trees. Open country eagles, on the other hand, have relatively long wings enabling them to soar in search of prey. Species that feed mostly on birds or mammals have feathered tarsi (lower parts of the leg), while snake and fish eaters have unfeathered, heavily-scaled tarsi and rough-soled toes that allow them to get a firm grip on slippery prey.

Most eagles hunt while soaring although some species watch for their prey from a high perch. Feeding territories are very large, up to 16 square miles (41 sq. km.) for large species that may range great distances for food. Eagles usually dive at their victims at an oblique angle and rely on surprise and strength rather than speed or agility. They capture a variety of live vertebrates, but most also take some carrion and are not above robbing other predators. The eagle usually captures its prey on the ground and may then carry it off to eat it elsewhere.

Reproduction and Life Cycle. Eagles nest both on seacoasts and on inland mountains, usually in tall trees or in high cliffs. The nest is a massive structure of sizable sticks lined with leaves and grass. Eagles may use the same nest for many years, adding to it each year; in fact, one nest in Ohio was used for 36 years and weighed almost 1 ton (0.9 metric ton).

Eagles lay only one or two light brown eggs, spotted and splotched with black. Both parents incubate the eggs for relatively long periods, up to 49 days in the larger species. Both parents feed the downy young, which remain in the nest as long as 130 days before fledging. In the larger eagle species the entire reproductive cycle may last more than 12 months, so that successful breeding may take place only once every other year. Although eagles are slow to reach reproductive age, they are long-lived.

KINDS OF EAGLES

Eagles do not constitute a single natural unit of classification. They are classified, along with kites, hawks, Old World vultures, and harriers, in the family Accipitridae of the order Falconiformes. Eagles are divided into four groups: sea and fish eagles (subfamily Milviinae), serpent eagles (subfamily Circaetinae), harpies and booted (or true) eagles (subfamily Accipitrinae).

Sea and Fishing Eagles. Sea and fishing eagles are very large species found on seacoasts or inland waters throughout most of the world. They have massive bills, scaled tarsi, and wedge-shaped tails in most species. They feed largely by diving at fish near the surface, but they also take mammals, birds, and reptiles, and they do feed on carrion. Sea and fishing eagles include the American bald eagle (*Haliaeetus leucocephalus*), the European white-tailed sea eagle (*H. albicilla*), Steller's sea eagle (*H. pelagicus*) of northeast Asia, the tropical African fish eagle (*H. vocifer*), and the freshwater fishing eagles (*Ichthyophaga*) of southern Asia.

Serpent Eagles. Serpent eagles, which are medium-sized and stocky, prey on reptiles. They are found only in the Old World and include the widespread harrier eagles (*Ciraetus*) of Africa, Asia, and southern Europe, the long-tailed serpent eagles (*Dryotriorchis* and *Eutriorchis*) of the rain forests of central Africa and Madagascar, and the crested serpent eagles of southeast Asia (*Spilornis*). In serpent eagles the head and neck are thickly feathered, and the legs and short toes are armored—adaptations that help the eagles in capturing their dangerous and elusive prey. Serpent eagles inhabit open and lightly forested country where they soar for long periods or watch for potential prey from high perches. They kill a snake by crushing its head in their bill and then swallow it whole.

The chunky, black and chestnut bateleur (*Terathopius ecaudatus*), found over the grasslands and forests of Africa, is the most striking and unusual species of the serpent eagle group. The bateleur has remarkably long wings and almost no tail. Its face has bare, bright red skin. In flight the bateleur eagle rocks from side to side and performs acrobatics. When it dives for prey, it is fast and noisy.

Harpies. The harpies include four huge, broad-winged, long-tailed eagles that inhabit the tropical rain forests of New Guinea, the Philippines, and northern South America. The most spectacular harpy is the rare monkey-eating eagle (*Pithecophaga jefferyi*) of the Philippines. It has a ruff of pointed erectile feathers around its face, a narrow highly arched bill, massive feet, and sharp talons capable of tearing apart monkeys, dogs, pigs, or poultry. The harpy eagle (*Harpia harpyja*) of South America, similar to the monkey-eating eagle, preys on Capuchin monkeys, sloths, and large macaw parrots. Both species nest in very high trees, and mounds of prey bones often accumulate under the nests.

Booted Eagles. Booted eagles (*Aquila, Hieraetus, Spizaetus,* and related genera) are a cosmopolitan group of eagles whose legs are feathered to the toes. Several booted eagles, especially the small crested eagles (*Spizaetus*) in Africa, have elongated crown feathers. The trim, graceful Old World hawk eagles (*Hieraetus*) are long-winged,

JEANNE WHITE, FROM NATIONAL AUDUBON SOCIETY

GOLDEN EAGLE was originally found in many mountainous areas of North America. It has been exterminated through much of its range, including the eastern U.S.

open country bird predators. The true eagles (*Aquila*) hunt in open country even if they nest in forests. They include the holarctic golden eagle (*Aquila chrysaetus*) and the Eurasian imperial eagle (*A. helica*). The true eagles are dark brown or black with golden or white feathering on the head, nape, shoulders, and base of the tail. They fly low often over open countryside hunting for birds and small mammals. They also often harass other birds to give up their own prey, and they eat carrion.

EAGLE IN SYMBOLISM

The grandeur of eagles has inspired men since the Paleolithic (Old Stone Age), when drawings of eagles first appeared in European caves. Eagles symbolize power, courage, freedom, and immortality and have long been used as national, military, and heraldic emblems and as symbols in religion.

The single- or double-headed eagle served as an emblem of the might and unity of empire for Belshazzar of Babylon, the Caesars, Charlemagne, many Holy Roman and Byzantine emperors, Napoleon, the Russian czars, and many Austrian emperors. An eagle devouring a serpent on the national seal of Mexico symbolizes the triumph of good over evil. In 1782 the United States adopted as the central motif of the seal of the United States a spread-winged bald eagle brandishing the arrows of war and the olive branch of peace to represent the strength and liberty of the nation. Eagles also appeared on the coins of many countries; the U. S. $10 gold piece had an eagle emblem. The heraldic eagle, an emblem of victory, courage, and royalty, appeared in Sumerian, Persian, and Egyptian battle ensigns and on the standard ("aquila") of the Roman legion.

In many ancient religions the eagle symbolized the protective strength of the deities and was the companion of the chief gods. Some North American Indians used the eagle as a symbol of ancestral immortality on their totem poles. In Hebrew and Christian religions the eagle represents the flight of the soul to heaven and the fulfillment of the messianic promise.

GEORGE E. WATSON, *Smithsonian Institution*

Further Reading: Brown, Leslie, and Amadon, Dean, *Eagles, Hawks, and Falcons of the World* (New York 1968).

EAGLE PASS is a city in southwestern Texas, the seat of Maverick county, on the Rio Grande 135 miles (217 km) southwest of San Antonio. It is opposite the city of Piedras Negras, Mexico, and is a port of entry. Its industries include a fluorspar and a barite plant, clothing factories, and a vegetable-packing enterprise.

The city traces its origin to the establishment of Fort Duncan in 1849 near a smuggler's crossing of the Rio Grande that was known as Paso del Aquila (Pass of the Eagle). The fort protected emigrants bound for the California gold fields, and a settlement that grew up around it was called California Camp. From this, the city of Eagle Pass developed. Government is by a city manager and council. Population: 21,407.

EAKER, ā'kər, **Ira Clarence** (1896–), American general and pioneer military aviator, who was a major air commander in World War II. Born at Field Creek, Texas, on April 13, 1896, he joined the U. S. Army in 1917 and became a pilot in its Air Service. He served 10 years on the main air staffs between 1923 and 1940. He also participated in a 6-month goodwill flight through Latin America (1926–1927) and in the endurance flight of the *Question Mark* (1929), and made the first transcontinental instrument flight (1936).

After observing air combat in Britain in 1941, Eaker returned there in 1942, selected bases for the U. S. 8th Air Force, organized VIII Bomber Command, and on August 17 led the first U. S. heavy bomber attack flown from England (against Rouen-Sotteville, France). Taking command of the 8th Air Force on Dec. 1, 1942, he directed daylight precision bombing of German strategic targets. From Jan. 15, 1944, he headed the Mediterranean Allied Air Forces, and in June 1944 held the first shuttle-bombing mission from Italy to the USSR. From April 1945 to June 1947 he served as deputy commanding general, U. S. Army Air Forces. He retired as a lieutenant general, U. S. Air Force, in 1947, and became an aircraft industry executive.

With Gen. H. H. Arnold he was coauthor of three books: *This Flying Game* (1936), *Winged Warfare* (1941), and *Army Flyer* (1942).

JOHN W. CARPENTER, III
Lt. Gen., USAF; Commander, Air University

PHILIP GENDREAU

BALD EAGLE, best known of North American eagles, is depicted on the Great Seal of the United States.

THOMAS EAKINS'
The Agnew Clinic.

UNIVERSITY OF PENNSYLVANIA

EAKINS, ā′kins, **Thomas Cowperthwait** (1844–1916), American painter, who was the foremost realist in 19th century American art.

Early Career. Almost all Eakins' life was passed in Philadelphia, where he was born on July 25, 1844. He studied drawing at the Pennsylvania Academy of the Fine Arts and anatomy at Jefferson Medical College. Going to Paris in 1866, he had three years of rigorous academic training at the École des Beaux-Arts under Jean Léon Gérôme. In 1869 he went to Spain, where he first saw the work of the 17th century Spanish painters, especially Velázquez, who thenceforth was his greatest admiration. He returned to Philadelphia in 1870 and occupied a studio in his father's house.

Eakins began to paint the life around him—portraits; scenes of sailing, rowing, and hunting in the city and its environs, which furnished him opportunities to picture the human body in action; and domestic genre depicting his family and friends, entirely realistic but pervaded with reserved, intense feeling. The chief work of this period is *The Gross Clinic* (1875; Jefferson Medical College), showing the famous surgeon Samuel D. Gross operating before his students. The powerful realism of this work shocked the public but established Eakins' reputation as a leader of a new naturalism.

Next to painting, Eakins' chief interests were anatomy and mathematics. An expert photographer, in 1844 he collaborated with Eadweard Muybridge in photographing human and animal locomotion. A born teacher, he became an instructor at the Pennsylvania Academy in 1876, and in 1882 was appointed its director. He based his curriculum on the thorough study of the nude, including anatomy and dissection, and on scientific perspective—innovations that revolutionized American art teaching. But his insistence on the nude scandalized the authorities, and in 1886 he was forced to resign. The majority of his male students seceded and started the Art Students League of Philadelphia, which lasted six or seven years, with Eakins as its unpaid head.

Late Portraits. The Academy affair and the lack of popular success for his painting undoubtedly account for the fact that in his early 40's Eakins began to devote himself almost entirely to portraiture. His sitters were mostly his friends, his students, and individuals who interested him, particularly scientists, musicians, fellow artists, and the Catholic clergy. His uncompromising realism, his strong sense of character, his mastery of the structure of the head, body, and hands, his psychological penetration, and the essential vitality of his portrayals made him the most mature and powerful American portraitist of his time. But he never achieved worldly success, and almost all of his portraits were labors of love. After many years of neglect, he received a small flurry of honors before he died, in Philadelphia, on June 25, 1916.

Eakins' Contribution. Eakins' art, based primarily on the human figure, possessed a power and substance, and a sculptural sense of form, beyond that of any other contemporary American artist. The limitations of his environment, combined with his own realism, unquestionably prevented the full realization of his potentialities as a plastic designer. But his contribution to American art was monumental, for he was the first major artist of the post-Civil War period to create a strong and profound art from the realities of American life.

LLOYD GOODRICH
Author of "Thomas Eakins"

Further Reading: Goodrich, Lloyd, *Thomas Eakins: His Life and Work* (New York 1933); Porter, Fairfield, *Thomas Eakins* (New York 1959); Schendler, Sylvan, *Eakins* (Boston 1967).

EAMES, ēmz, **Charles** (1907–1978), American designer, best known for his form-fitting chairs, manufactured by mass-production techniques. He also designed other furniture, toys, and buildings. Eames was born on June 17, 1907, in St. Louis, Mo. He studied architecture there at Washington University, and at Cranbrook Academy of Art, Bloomfield Hills, Mich., under Eliel Saarinen. In 1940, Eames and Eero Saarinen won first prizes in both major categories (storage and seating) in the organic furniture competition sponsored by the Museum of Modern Art in New York. Their chair, a molded plywood shell with foam rubber padding, introduced a novel method of

Swivel base chair and ottoman by Charles Eames.

articulating aluminum legs to the thin wood shell by means of a rubber-weld joint.

Applying the same principles of leg joining and molding in plywood or fiberglass, Eames developed a series of chairs for the Herman Miller Company during the 1940's and 1950's. His most famous design was a soft leather-upholstered swivel tilt lounge chair and ottoman. He was elected to the American Academy and Institute of Arts and Letters in 1977. He died in St. Louis on Aug. 21, 1978.

JOSEPH ARONSON, *Author of "The New Encyclopedia of Furniture"*

EAMES, āmz, **Emma** (1865–1952), American operatic soprano, whose singing, though not considered highly dramatic, showed remarkable technical command and fine vocal quality. She was born of American parents in Shanghai, China, on Aug. 13, 1865. The family settled in the United States in 1870. Emma studied music in Boston and later in Paris.

Miss Eames made her operatic debut at the Paris Opéra in March 1889 as Juliette in Gounod's *Roméo et Juliette*. In 1890 she created the role of Colombe in Saint-Saëns' unsuccessful opera *Ascanio*, and in 1891 she made her London debut at Covent Garden and her New York debut at the Metropolitan Opera House. She also sang with other leading opera companies in Europe and America. She published her autobiography, *Some Memories and Reflections*, in 1927. She died in New York City on June 13, 1952.

EAMES, ēmz, **Wilberforce** (1855–1937), American bibliographer, who specialized in early American books. He was born on Oct. 12, 1855, in Newark, N. J., and was self-educated. From 1885 he worked at the Lenox Library in New York City, where he became librarian in 1893. In 1895, when the Lenox became a part of the New York Public Library, Eames was named bibliographer. He died in New York on Dec. 6, 1937.

Eames edited volumes 15–20 of Joseph Sabin's *Dictionary of Books Relating to America* (1885–1892) and other scholarly books, including *Humble Requests of Governor Winthrop and Company, 1630* (1905). Among his own writings are *Bibliographic Notes on Eliot's Indian Bible* (1890) and a bibliographic account of early New England catechisms (1898).

EAR, the special sense organ concerned primarily with hearing. The ear also provides the organism with information concerning the orientation, or position, of the head so that the organism can maintain its equilibrium, or balance. Ears are generally not found in invertebrates, although many insects have specialized structures for detecting vibrations. Some invertebrates also have special structures that help them in maintaining their equilibrium.

The ear's function in hearing is to convert sound waves into nerve impulses. These impulses are then transmitted to certain areas of the brain, where they are perceived and interpreted as sounds.

In humans, the ear consists of three major parts: the outer ear, the middle ear, and the inner ear. Sound waves entering the outer ear travel through the ear canal to the eardrum, the thin membrane stretched across the inner end of the canal. Changes in air pressure inside the canal cause the eardrum to vibrate, and these vibrations are transmitted to a chain of three tiny bones, called ossicles, which are located in the middle ear. These three bones conduct the vibrations across the middle ear and transmit them to a thin membrane, known as the oval window, which separates the air-filled middle ear from the fluid-filled inner ear. In the inner ear, a spiral-shaped structure, called the cochlea, houses the essential organ of hearing, the organ of Corti, which rests on a very sensitive membrane known as the basilar membrane. When the basilar membrane vibrates, tiny sensory hair cells inside the organ of Corti are bent, and this bending of the hair cells stimulates the transmission of nerve impulses to the brain.

STRUCTURE OF THE HUMAN EAR

Outer Ear. The outer, or external, ear consists of two basic structures: the flexible, roughly oval-shaped appendage attached to the head; and the ear canal, or *meatus*, leading to the middle ear. The external flap, called the *auricle* or *pinna*, is made up of fibrous cartilage covered with skin, and it is relatively insensitive to feeling or pain. The size and shape of the pinna may vary greatly from one person to another, but its basic structure does not change. Although many vertebrate animals can direct the pinna toward a source of sound, human beings have very few muscles attached to the pinna and are limited in their ability to move it. Whereas a horse or dog can rotate its pinna to locate a sound, a man must turn his whole head.

The tube known as the ear canal is slightly less than one inch (25 mm) long, and it varies from an almost cylindrical shape to a narrow slit. Near the pinna, the wall of the ear canal is made up of cartilage, but as it enters the head, the wall is made of bone. Sometimes the entrance of the ear canal may be partly closed by hairs that point outward and by a waxy secretion known as cerumen. The ear canal terminates at the eardrum, the thin, tough, flexible tympanic membrane, which stretches somewhat diagonally across the ear canal to separate the outer ear from the middle ear. Attaching the tympanic membrane to the bony wall of the ear canal is a ring of tough, fibrous tissue.

Middle Ear. The middle ear is a narrow, air-filled cleft in the temporal bone, one of the flat bones that form the skull, and it extends from the eardrum to the bony wall of the inner ear.

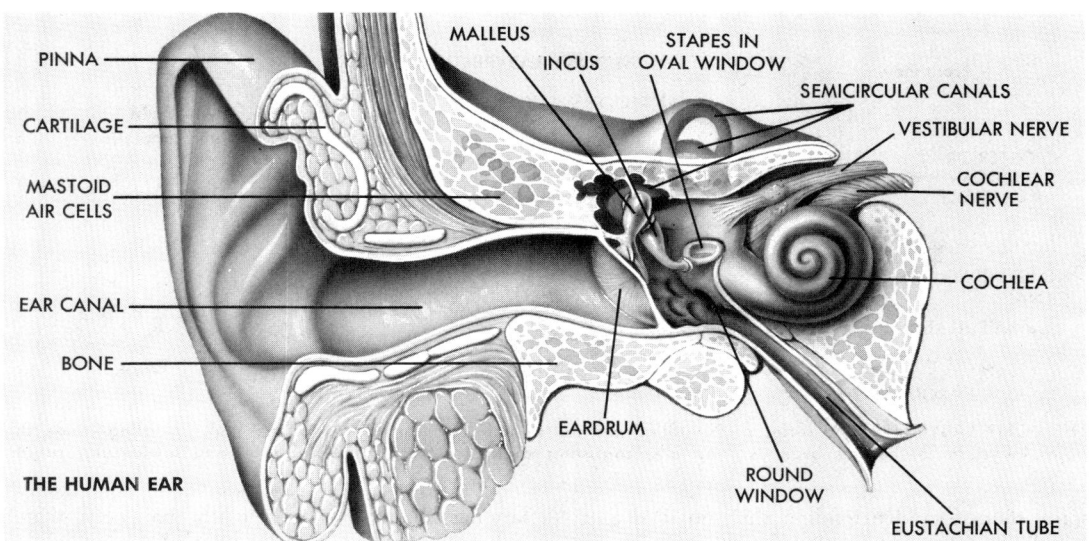
THE HUMAN EAR

The middle ear contains two openings, one to the mastoid air cells of the temporal bone, and another to the *Eustachian tube,* a narrow canal that runs from the middle ear cavity to the back of the nose. The function of the Eustachian tube is to equalize the air pressure between the middle ear and the outside.

Although the eardrum is so thin that it is translucent, it is made up of three separate layers: an outer skin, a central fibrous membrane, and an inner lining of mucous membrane. Attached to the eardrum by its "handle" is the hammer-shaped *malleus,* the first of the chain of three tiny bones, or ossicles, of the middle ear. Together with a small muscle, the *tensor tympani,* which is attached to the eardrum, the malleus exerts a slight pull on the eardrum, making it somewhat cone-shaped like the cone of a loudspeaker. The round head of the malleus fits snugly into a socketlike concavity in the second tiny bone, which is called the *incus,* or *anvil.* This bone narrows to a long, curving tip, which ends near the center of the middle ear cavity and touches the third bone of the chain, the stirrup-shaped *stapes.* The curved upper part of the stapes lies nearly perpendicular to the long tip of the incus, and the flat footplate of the stapes fits into the *oval window,* the membrane that forms one of the boundaries between the middle ear and the inner ear. The other boundary is a similar membrane-covered opening called the *round window.* Connecting the footplate of the stapes to the oval window is a small ligament, the *annular ligament,* and connecting the neck of the stapes to the wall of the middle ear cavity is the tiny *stapedius muscle,* the smallest muscle in the human body.

Inner Ear. The inner ear, or labyrinth, consists of two parts, the *bony labyrinth* and the *membranous labyrinth.* The bony labyrinth is a complex series of chambers lying within the temporal bone of the skull and containing a fluid called *perilymph.* Floating within this fluid is the membranous labyrinth, a series of fluid-filled ducts and sacs whose shapes conform closely to the shape of the bony labyrinth. The membranous labyrinth consists of three types of structures: the three semicircular canals, each with an enlarged end, or *ampulla,* containing the sensory hair cells; the snail-shaped *cochlea;* and two sacs called the *saccule* and the *utricle,* which lie in a chamber known as the *vestibule.* The ducts and sacs of the membranous labyrinth are filled with *endolymphatic fluid.* The semicircular canals play little or no part in hearing, but together with the saccule and utricle they provide information about the movement of the head and its orientation in space.

The structure concerned with hearing is the cochlea, which is shaped like a snail shell that winds two and a half times around a conical central axis. From the base to the tip, the cochlea is nearly 1½ inches (about 35 mm) long. Extending the length of the cochlea, and dividing it into two separate galleries, is the *basilar membrane.* The upper gallery is called the *vestibular gallery* or the *scala vestibuli,* and the lower gallery is known as the *tympanic gallery* or the *scala tympani.* The basilar membrane is attached on one side of the cochlea to a bony shelf, called the *spiral lamina,* and on the other side to a spiral ligament. Near the base end of the cochlea, the vestibular gallery is separated from the middle ear by the oval window, and the tympanic gallery is separated from the middle ear by the round window. The basilar membrane stops just short of the tip of the cochlea, leaving a small opening between the two galleries.

The vestibular gallery is itself divided into two parts by a membrane that runs the length of the cochlea. This membrane, called *Reissner's membrane,* extends from the upper edge of the spiral lamina diagonally upward to the outer wall of the cochlear duct. The channel created by this membrane is known as the *scala media.* Thus, a cross section of the cochlea shows three separate ducts: the vestibular above, the scala media in the middle, and the tympanic below.

Both the vestibular and tympanic ducts are filled with perilymph, but the scala media contains endolymph. At the base of the cochlea, the vestibular gallery opens into the vestibule, and the fluid within the two chambers is continuous. The tympanic gallery does not open into the vestibule. The endolymph in the scala media connects with the fluid of the saccule at the base end of the cochlea, but at the other end the scala media tapers to a blind end.

The hearing organ, the *organ of Corti,* lies within the scala media and is attached to the upper, or vestibular, side of the basilar membrane. The organ of Corti, like the cochlea, is

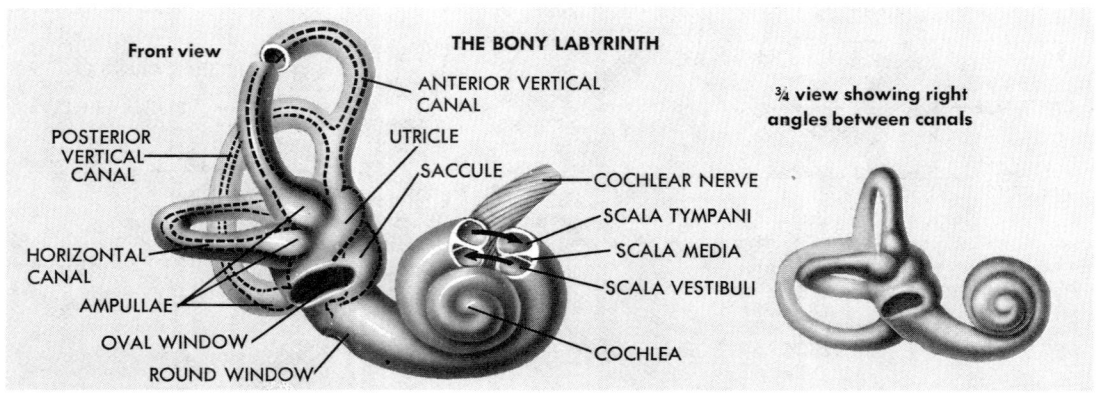

THE BONY LABYRINTH is a series of fluid-filled chambers in the temporal bone of the skull. Floating inside the bony labyrinth is the membranous labyrinth, consisting of the cochlea, utricle, saccule, and semicircular canals.

spiral-shaped, and extending through it is a triangular tunnel. The tunnel is formed by two rows of pillars, or rods. On one side of the tunnel is a row of about 3,000 hair cells, called the inner hair cells. On the other side of the tunnel are about 20,000 outer hair cells arranged in three rows. The cells that support the hair cells rest on the movable basilar membrane. The upper ends of the hair cells pass through a delicate netlike membrane known as the *reticular lamina* and are embedded in the thick, jellylike *tectorial membrane*. Nerve fibers extending from the bottom ends of the hair cells join like strands of a rope to form the cochlear portion of the nerve that leads to the brain. Similar nerve fibers from the vestibular apparatus form the vestibular branch of this nerve, which is called the auditory nerve.

TRANSMISSION AND PERCEPTION OF SOUND

When a sound wave strikes the outer ear, part of the sound is reflected, or scattered, and part is conducted into the ear canal, where it strikes the eardrum. The eardrum yields easily before the wave and is driven inward; whereupon the malleus and the incus, which rotate together as a kind of lever, push the stapes more deeply into the oval window of the inner ear. Because the area of the eardrum is about 30 times that of the footplate of the stapes, and because all the energy that the eardrum collects is transmitted to the stapes, the pressure of the stapes on the oval window is 30 times greater than the original pressure on the eardrum. This increase in pressure is needed because the eardrum receives its push from the highly compressible air, but as the energy moves on into the middle and inner ear, the stapes must transfer the energy into the almost incompressible perilymph.

When the perilymph in the vestibular gallery is pushed inward by the movement of the stapes, the flexible basilar membrane bulges into the tympanic gallery, which, in turn, causes the round window to bulge outward into the middle ear cavity. The basilar membrane can also be set in motion by vibrations transmitted by the bones of the head. Although bone conduction is not as efficient as air conduction, it may play an important part in hearing if the normal conduction route (air conduction) is obstructed, damaged, or diseased.

Since the triangular tunnel formed by the rods of the organ of Corti give stiffness to that section of the basilar membrane, the organ of Corti rocks as a unit, pivoting on the spiral lamina. The hairs (cilia) of the hair cells, which are embedded in the tectorial membrane, are thereupon bent by the shearing force exerted by the tectorial membrane, which, because it is stiffened by fibers attached to the spiral lamina, can only flap rather stiffly. Thus, the organ of Corti and the tectorial membrane slide against each other as they move up and down together, and it is this sliding action that bends the hairs of the hair cells.

Located near the bases of the hair cells are the endings of about 27,000 nerve fibers. Although the number of nerve fiber endings is approximately equivalent to the number of hair cells, the fibers and hair cells are not connected to each other in a one-to-one ratio. The interconnections between the hair cells and fibers are complicated and overlapping, especially for the outer hair cells. As the hairs are bent, nerve impulses are stimulated in the nerve fibers, but the exact mechanism by which the bending hairs produce the electrical impulses in the nerve fibers is not known. One theory is that the stria vascularis, a network of capillaries and small blood vessels lining the outer wall of the scala media, may maintain an electrical charge in the scala media and that some of the current may leak through the organ of Corti. There is some evidence that the amount of current passing through the organ of Corti is changed by the passage of a sound wave and that this change in the current may initiate the nerve impulses.

Because of the changing stiffness of the basilar membrane from one end of the cochlea to the other, the cochlea acts as a mechanical analyzer of sound. For high-frequency sounds, only the narrow basal end of the membrane (near the stapes) vibrates. For medium frequencies, the part of the membrane in the middle turn of the cochlea vibrates more vigorously than the part near the base, and for low frequencies the whole membrane vibrates, but the greatest vibration is at or near the tip of the cochlea. Thus the cochlea is able to transform frequencies into locations of vibration on the basilar membrane, and the sensation of pitch depends on which part of the basilar membrane is made to vibrate.

BALANCE AND ORIENTATION

The structures concerned with equilibrium, or the static sense, are the three semicircular canals and the two small sacs in the vestibule— the *utricle* and the *saccule*. These structures provide information concerning the orientation of the head, enabling man to maintain his equilibrium.

The three semicircular canals are roughly at right angles to one another, two standing vertically and one lying horizontally. Each semicircular duct has an enlargement, or ampulla, which houses the sensory hair cells. The hairs of the hair cells project into a gelatinous mass, called the *cupula*. When the head is turned from side to side, the horizontal lateral canal rotates, but its endolymphatic fluid lags behind, and the hairs of the hair cells are bent by being driven through the relatively stationary fluid. In a similar manner, the vertical anterior and posterior canals respond to movements of the head in the other planes. As in the cochlea of the ear, the bending of the hairs stimulates the transmission of nerve impulses to the brain. The hair cells may also be stimulated by irrigating the ear canal with warm or cold water, as well as by movement of the head. Thus, under such temperature stimulation a person has the sensation of moving or turning even though he is standing still.

In both the utricle and the saccule, the sensory receptor is called a *macula*. It is an oval thickening of the vestibule wall, with the sensitive hair cells on its surface and nerve fibers extending from the bases of the hair cells. The hair cells protrude into a thin gelatinous pad that contains lime crystals called *otoliths*. The plane of the macula in the utricle is like that of the horizontal semicircular canal, while that of the macula of the saccule is at right angles to it. When the head is tilted, the force of gravity causes the lime crystals to come into contact with the hair cells, which then initiate nerve impulses to the brain. Acceleration causes a similar response.

DISEASES OF THE EAR

The outer ear and its ear canal are subject to all of the various infections, cysts, and other disorders that affect the skin. In addition, an accumulation of wax (cerumen) in the ear canal may serve to immobilize the eardrum, causing a partial loss of hearing. Clearing of the ear canal by a physician usually restores full hearing. A hearing loss may also occur if the eardrum becomes perforated. Perforation of the eardrum may result from infection or from a sudden change in air pressure, such as may be caused by a nearby explosion, or from the insertion of a sharp object into the ear canal. Sometimes a perforated eardrum heals naturally, but sometimes it remains perforated permanently. Some surgeons have developed techniques for repairing perforated eardrums through grafting or inducing the growth of epithelium to fill the opening.

A very mild, temporary hearing impairment may occur if the pressure of the air filling the middle ear through the Eustachian tube is not kept in balance with the air pressure in the ear canal. This condition, known medically as *aerotitis media*, commonly occurs in people who descend from high to low altitudes. It can be prevented or corrected by yawning or swallowing, which causes the Eustachian tube to open so that the air pressure in the middle ear cavity becomes equalized with that of the environment. Sometimes, when a person has a cold, the Eustachian tube may be blocked or swollen by inflammation and it may not be sufficiently open to ventilate the middle ear. In such cases, medical help may be necessary to relieve the pressure by forcing air through the Eustachian tube.

Any infection of the middle ear is known as *otitis media*, and the microorganisms commonly involved are *Streptococcus* bacteria. The microorganisms enter the middle ear through the Eustachian tube, and the resulting pus of the infection may invade nearby structures, including the facial nerve, the mastoid bone, the inner ear, and even the brain. Antibiotics and sulfa drugs may relieve the symptoms, but unless the pus is drained, complications may result. By constricting the movement of the middle ear structures, chronic otitis media can cause permanent impairment of hearing.

The development of a growth in the bony wall of the middle ear is known as *otosclerosis*. In about 10% of the cases, the growth causes the footplate of the stapes to become rigidly fixed in the oval window, thus preventing the stapes from passing sound vibrations to the inner ear. As time goes on, the resultant hearing loss worsens, and in severe cases surgery may be required. Several types of operations are used in an effort to correct otosclerosis. In one operation, known as a fenestration operation, a new opening is made in the vestibule so that sound waves can pass to it from the middle ear. In another oper-

SOUND WAVES traveling through the air enter the ear canal and are transmitted by the eardrum and the bones of the middle ear to the cochlea of the inner ear. In the scala media of the cochlea, the waves stimulate the organ of Corti hair cells. The hair cells then transmit nerve impulses along the cochlear nerve to the brain.

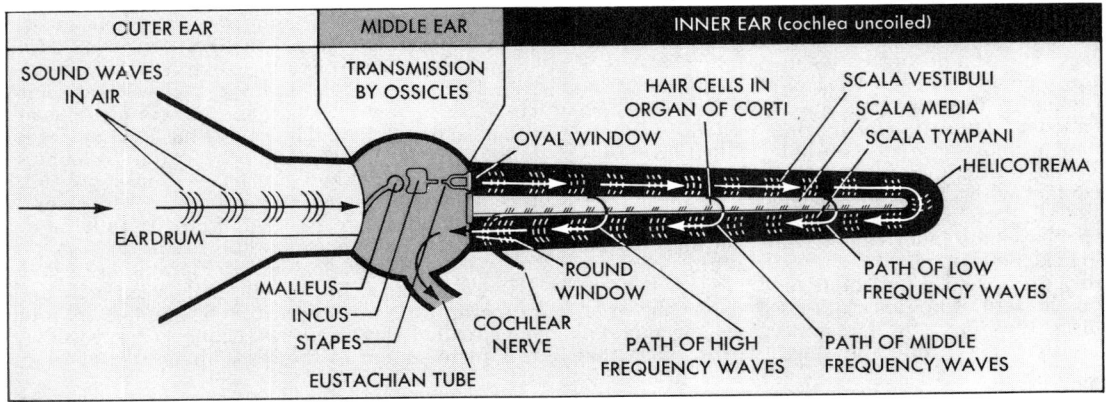

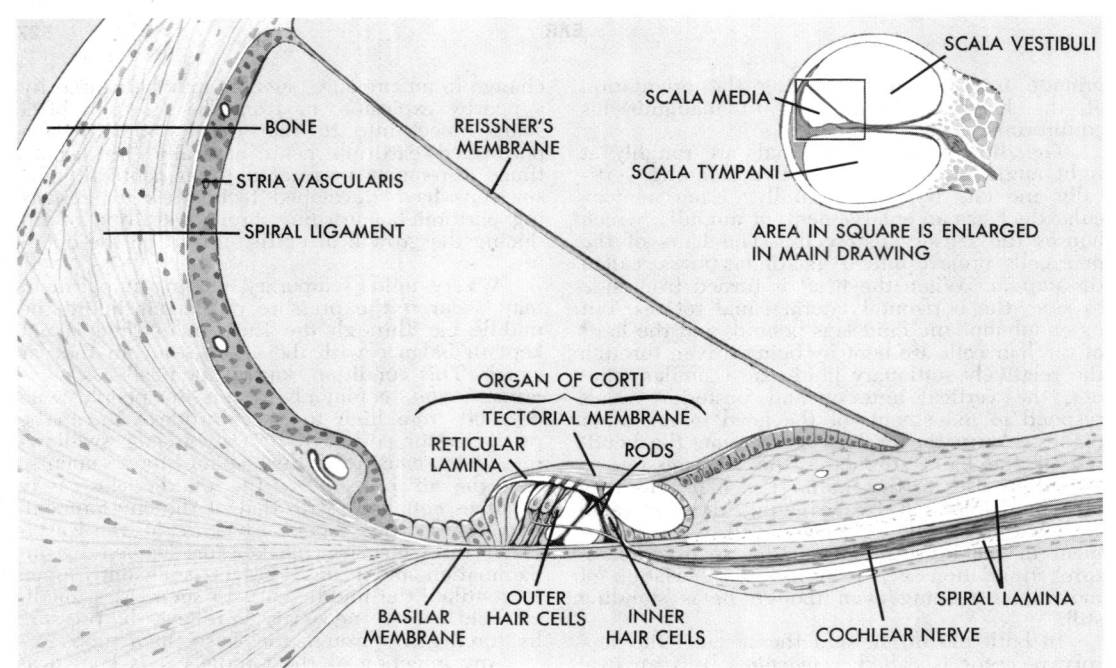

THE ORGAN OF CORTI is located in the scala media where it rests on the basilar membrane. When the organ of Corti and the tectorial membrane slide against each other the hairs of the hair cells are bent back and forth, initiating nerve impulses to the brain.

ation, called stapes mobilization, the stapes is freed from its rigid position. In a third operation, called stapedectomy, the stapes may be removed and replaced by an artificial device to conduct sound vibrations to the fluid of the inner ear. See also DEAFNESS.

In the inner ear, a disturbance of the pressure of the fluids in the labyrinth may cause vertigo (dizziness) or head noises (tinnitus). A severe case of labyrinth involvement, causing loss of equilibrium, nausea, and deafness, is known as *Ménière's disease*.

A fairly common disorder that becomes evident in middle age, and that progresses as the person becomes older, is *presbycusis*. It is a progressive degeneration of the sensory hair cells of the organ of Corti in the cochlea, and it is usually accompanied by some hearing loss for high tones. The amplification of sounds by a hearing aid can partially compensate for the sensory-neural hearing loss in presbycusis.

COMPARATIVE ANATOMY

Although some invertebrates have a tympanic organ that is receptive to sound waves, this structure is not found in the head. In insects it may be located on the abdomen, the thorax, or the legs, and it appears to be in no way related to the mammalian ear. Most equilibrium, or static, organs in invertebrates consist of a hollow sac, called a *statocyst*, which contains hair cells and one or more granules of lime, called *statoliths*. When the animal moves, the statoliths come in contact with the sensory hair cells.

All vertebrates have a structure that corresponds to the inner ear of man. During embryological development, the ear structure originates in a thickened patch of tissue that can be seen on the fetus through a microscope. As the organism develops, the area becomes invaginated (pushed in) inside the skull, with a duct that sometimes remains open to the surface of the head. The pocket that is formed by the invagination develops ridges, which become the semicircular canals. The pocket itself becomes the utricle, and it is pinched off to form the saccule and another structure, the *lagena*, which in higher vertebrates becomes the cochlea.

Fish. Experiments have shown that some fish may be able to hear, although little is known about their ability to differentiate among various sounds. Fish do not have an outer ear or a middle ear, and their inner ear is mainly concerned with equilibrium. In the most highly developed fish, and bony teleosts, the membranous labyrinth is filled with endolymph, and the ducts contain small lime crystals—the otoliths. Some of the cartilaginous elasmobranchs (sharks, rays, and related fish) have an open canal, called an invagination canal, leading from the surface of the head to the saccule, which is filled with sea water. In some sharks, grains of sand, rather than otoliths, are found in the saccule.

All cartilaginous and bony fish have three semicircular canals—a utricle, a saccule, and a lagena—which grow out of the saccule. The primitive hagfish and lamprey eels (cyclostomes) have the simplest static organs, consisting of a single doughnut-shaped structure that corresponds to the utricle and the two vertical semicircular canals of the higher vertebrates. In all fish, each semicircular canal has an enlarged ampulla that houses a sensory patch containing the hair cells. When the fish changes position, the otoliths or grains of sand are moved against the hair cells, which are thereby stimulated to transmit nerve impulses to the brain.

Amphibians and Reptiles. In amphibians a middle ear is formed from a gill cleft or spiracle, and an eardrum covers the external opening. A long bone, called the *columella*, connects the eardrum to a plate similar to the stapes bone in mammals.

This plate fits into an opening in the inner ear. The lagena, an outgrowth of the saccule, becomes more differentiated in amphibians than in fish and it begins to take on the characteristics of a cochlea.

In reptiles the eardrum is depressed into the skull, and the opening is covered by scales. The lagena and the basilar papilla, a second saccular outgrowth, unite in a kind of elongated cochlear structure. A basilar membrane divides the lagena into two parts, both of which, like the cochlea, are filled with fluid. The Eustachian tube connects with the pharynx. The columella has developed into three distinct parts, and the stapes fits into a membrane-covered window. Crocodiles have outer flaps that suggest the pinnas of higher animals, and their inner ears are spirally wound, as in mammals. In the snake, the columella is directly attached to the skull, suggesting that snakes hear only by bone conduction.

Birds. Birds have an open outer ear canal, but it is curved to protect the eardrum, and in owls the canal is covered by an external movable flap. A columella connects the eardrum with a window to the inner ear. An organ of Corti is located in the lagena, which begins to resemble the mammalian cochlea except that the upper and lower galleries of the lagena, formed by the basilar membrane, are not connected with each other at the tip of the structure.

Mammals. Mammals have the most highly developed ears. In addition to the external pinna, they have three separate bones replacing the columella, and the utricle and saccule are more distinctly separated, with a small communicating duct between them. Most important, the lagena has extended to become the spiral cochlea, and the added length of the organ of Corti permits the hearing of a wider range of frequencies.

Although all mammals have a spiral-shaped cochlea, the length and number of turns of the cochlea vary among different species. In man the cochlea is nearly 1½ inches (about 35 mm) long and turns two and a half times. In the elephant it is 2.3 inches (60 mm) long and winds two and a half turns, and in the guinea pig it is only ⅗ of an inch (18 mm) long and winds four times. The guinea pig's cochlea is a thin shell of bone protruding into a large cavity, whereas in man and most other large mammals it is embedded in hard bone. The accessibility of the guinea pig's cochlea is a major factor in its frequent use in physiological studies.

Mammals with large middle ears and cochleas respond best to relatively low frequency sounds, while the very small animals, such as mice and bats, respond best to high frequency sounds. For example, humans hear sounds ranging from frequencies of 20 to 20,000 cycles per second, while the common brown bat's hearing may extend to frequencies above 90,000 cycles per second.

S. S. STEVENS, *Harvard University*

Bibliography

Adams, L. Everett A., and Eddy, Samuel, *Comparative Anatomy: An Introduction to the Vertebrate* (New York 1949).
Davis, Hallowell, and Silverman, S. Richard, eds., *Hearing and Deafness*, rev. ed. (New York 1960).
Stevens, S. S., Warshofsky, Fred, and the Editors of Life, *Sound and Hearing* (New York 1965).
Stevens, S. S., and Davis, Hallowell, *Hearing: Its Psychology and Physiology* (New York 1938).
Von Békésy, Georg, *Experiments in Hearing* (New York 1960).
Wever, Ernest G., and Lawrence, Merle, *Physiological Acoustics* (Princeton 1954).

EAR SHELL. See ABALONE.

EARACHE. Most earaches are due to infections in the middle ear, the part of the ear between the eardrum and the inner ear. However, they may also be caused by accumulations of ear wax, a foreign body, or infections in the auditory canal, the tube leading from the outside to the eardrum. Occasionally, an earache occurs as referred pain from the mouth or jaw. For example, a severe toothache may also sometimes be felt as pain in the ear.

Infections in the middle ear, known medically as *otitis media*, are usually caused by streptococci or staphylococci bacteria. The bacteria enter the middle ear chamber through the Eustachian tube, a narrow canal that connects the middle ear with the back of the throat. By coughing, sneezing, or changing the air pressure in the middle ear (as in diving or flying), bacteria-laden particles from the throat may be carried into the middle ear. Shortly after the infection starts, the eardrum becomes inflamed and very painful. As pus accumulates inside the middle ear chamber, it presses upon the eardrum, creating a sense of fullness in the ear and sometimes producing a temporary loss of hearing.

The treatment of an earache depends upon the underlying cause. When ear wax or a foreign body is present, it must be removed; in most cases, the material is lodged so deeply in the auditory canal that it must be removed by a doctor.

Infections of the middle ear can be successfully treated by the administration of antibiotics, and the treatment should be started promptly to prevent complications, such as perforation of the eardrum or mastoiditis. A perforated eardrum may lead to chronic infections of the middle ear; it can be repaired through surgery. Mastoiditis is an infection in the part of the skull bone directly behind the ear. Most often, the infection can be effectively treated with antibiotics, but in some cases it is necessary to remove part of the bone (mastoidectomy).

REAUMUR S. DONNALLY, M. D.
Washington Hospital Center

EARHART, âr'härt, **Amelia** (1898–?1937), American flyer, who was the first woman to make a solo flight across the Atlantic Ocean. She was born in Atchison, Kans., on July 24, 1898, the daughter of a railroad attorney, and attended Ogontz School in Rydal, Pa., and Columbia University. Learning to fly in California, she took up aviation as a hobby. While she was employed as a settlement worker in Boston, she was chosen to be a passenger on the trimotor *Friendship*, piloted by Wilmer Stultz, which flew from Newfoundland to Wales, landing at Burry Port on June 18, 1928. She thus became the first woman passenger on a transatlantic flight. Thereafter Miss Earhart made a career of flying. After a series of record flights, she made a solo transatlantic flight from Harbour Grace, Newfoundland, to Ireland in 1932, and in 1935 she flew the first solo from Hawaii to the American mainland.

Miss Earhart flew from Miami, Fla., in June 1937, with Frederick J. Noonan as navigator, to attempt the first round-the-world flight near the equator. After taking off on July 1 from New Guinea for Howland Island in the Pacific, she vanished. A great naval search failed to locate her, and it was assumed that she had been lost at sea.

Amelia Earhart
WIDE WORLD

Later, the mystery of her fate grew, with hints that she and Noonan were taken and perhaps killed by the Japanese. The theory rests mainly on the word of some U. S. Army veterans and natives of Saipan, suggesting that the pair had been imprisoned on that island, then under Japanese administration.

Miss Earhart married George Palmer Putnam, a publisher, in 1931. She wrote three books about her flights.

C. R. ROSEBERRY
Author of "The Challenging Skies"

EARL, the oldest English title of nobility, ranked in the modern peerage between marquess and viscount. The dignity is equivalent to the continental European "count." The wife of an earl bears the title of countess.

The word "earl" is related etymologically to the Norse and Danish word *jarl,* meaning hereditary chieftain. Originally it meant simply a nobleman, one who possessed five hides (or about 600 acres) of land. From the reign of King Alfred (871–899) certain of these noblemen received responsibility for governing the various administrative districts, or shires, into which England was being divided. These royal officials were known as *ealdormen* until the reign of Canute (1016–1035), when the title of earl was created for them. In Anglo-Saxon England each ealdorman served with the local bishop and sheriff as one of the presidents of the shire court.

The jurisdictions of the Anglo-Saxon ealdormen were not coterminous with the counties, and before the Norman Conquest there were always fewer ealdormen than there were shires. In fact, the number of earls had so diminished and their individual powers so increased by 1066 that they virtually controlled the central government. William the Conqueror recognized the dangers of this system, and it was he who equated the earldoms with the counties. From his time the office became more and more an honor, rather than an administrative position. In 1328 the first earldom (that of March) that did not carry a county jurisdiction was created.

In modern Britain the heir of a duke or marquess receives the courtesy title of earl.

JOHN FERGUSON, *Smith College*

EARL MARSHAL, the eighth in rank of the great officers of state in Britain. He attends the sovereign at the opening and closing of Parliament, arranges coronations and other state functions, and determines processional order. The earl marshal is also the head of the Heralds' College, which has sole authority to grant arms in Britain. The office has been filled by the dukes of Norfolk since 1677.

The functions of the earl marshal derive from those of the marshal, a household officer under Norman and Plantagenet kings, whose duties included service at the court of chivalry. The present office was first granted by Richard II in 1386 to Thomas Mowbray, Earl of Nottingham, from whom the Howards, later dukes of Norfolk, trace their descent.

EARLE, John (c. 1601–1665), English bishop and writer, who is best known for his *Microcosmographie, or, a Peece of the World discovered in Essayes and Characters* (1628), a witty and perceptive series of essays and character sketches. Probably a native of York, Earle was educated at Oxford, where he became a fellow of Merton College in 1619 and proctor of the university in 1631. In 1641 he was appointed tutor to Prince Charles (later King Charles II), whom he joined in France in 1651 during the Civil War.

After the Restoration, Earle returned to England and became dean of Westminster in 1660, bishop of Worcester in 1662, and bishop of Salisbury in 1663. He died at Oxford on Nov. 17, 1665.

EARLE, Ralph (1751–1801), American painter, whose portraits, consciously modeled after those of John Singleton Copley, have a ruggedly provincial style that places them among the most distinctive American work of the late 18th century.

Earle (also spelled *Earl*) was born in Worcester County, Mass., on May 11, 1751. By 1775 he was working in New Haven, Conn., where he painted a portrait of Roger Sherman (Yale University Art Gallery). A Loyalist, Earle fled to London in 1778, where he studied with Benjamin West, an experience that increased his facility but did not significantly affect his style. He returned to America in 1785 and resumed his itinerant practice in New York and New England. He died at Bolton, Conn., on Aug. 16, 1801.

Among Earle's other portraits are *William Carpenter* and *Mary Carpenter* (both 1779; Worcester Art Museum), *Lady Williams and Child* (1783; Metropolitan Museum, New York), and *Daniel Boardman* (1789; National Gallery, Washington, D. C.).

CHARLES H. ELAM
Editor of "The Peale Family"

Further Reading: Sawitzky, William, *Ralph Earl* (New York 1945).

EARLY, John (1786–1873), American Methodist clergyman and bishop. He was born in Bedford county, Va., on Jan. 1, 1786, and became an itinerant Methodist minister about 1807. Concerned for the welfare of the Negro people, he was active in exploring the possibilities for their return to Africa and was president of the Colonization Society in Lynchburg in 1825. In 1830, Early was one of the founders of Randolph-Macon College.

Early preferred to remain in the ministry. In 1844 he assumed an active part in the conference that separated the Methodist Episcopal Church South from the northern Methodists, and he became a bishop in the Southern body in 1854. He retired in 1866. Early died at Lynchburg, Va., on Nov. 5, 1873.

POWEL MILLS DAWLEY
General Theological Seminary, New York

EARLY, ûr'lē, Jubal Anderson (1816–1894), American Confederate general, who is famous for his daring advance on Washington in 1864. He was born in Franklin county, Va., on Nov. 3, 1816. He was graduated from the U. S. Military Academy at West Point in 1837, served briefly in the Seminole War, and then resigned. For the next 23 years, except for service in the Mexican War, Early was a lawyer in Rocky Mount, Va.

Early opposed secession, but when the Civil War came, he sided with his state. At the First Battle of Bull Run (Manassas), Early, then a colonel, led the brigade whose arrival won the day for the South. Promoted to brigadier general, he was in the battles of the Army of Northern Virginia. He fought as a brigade commander at the Second Battle of Bull Run (Second Manassas) and at Antietam and as a division commander at Fredericksburg. As a major general, he fought in the Chancellorsville Campaign and at Gettysburg, the Wilderness, and Spotsylvania.

In June 1864, Early, now a lieutenant general, was sent to clear Union forces from the Shenandoah Valley. He accomplished this and, with only 14,000 men, crossed the Potomac, won a victory at the Monocacy River on July 9, and marched toward Washington. Early's purpose was not to capture the city but to relieve Northern pressure on Petersburg. Exaggerated reports of his strength caused consternation. Union troops rushed to Washington. Early withdrew, his mission accomplished. His outnumbered forces were beaten by Maj. Gen. Philip H. Sheridan at the Battle of Cedar Creek on Oct. 19, 1864.

After the war, Early went to Mexico, thence to Canada, but returned to practice law in Lynchburg, Va., where he died on March 2, 1894.

JOSEPH B. MITCHELL
Author of "Decisive Battles of the Civil War"

EARP, ûrp, Wyatt (1848–1929), American gunfighter. He was born in Monmouth, Ill., on March 19, 1848. Lean and ordinary in appearance he was 6 feet tall and weighed 150 pounds. In the cow capitals of Kansas he was employed to help keep the peace. His two brothers hung out with him, so that the Earp boys made a sort of natural gang. In his Kansas days, Earp seemed mild and straightforward, but later in Arizona the brothers became a part of Western lore.

The classic gunfight at the O. K. Corral in Tombstone, Ariz., was in part a fight between sheepmen and cattlemen, but it may have been set off by an excess of alcohol in Ike Clanton's system. On the Earps' side was the picturesque consumptive, John H. (Doc) Holliday. Within 60 seconds, three of Clanton's associates were killed and Earp's two brothers were wounded. About half of Tombstone wanted to lynch the Earps and Holliday, but a coroner's jury refused to hold them. Was it murder, or did the Earps save Tombstone from the outlawry of the Clantons? Scholars still disagree. Earp survived several other gunfights, subsequently settled in California, and died in Los Angeles on Jan. 13, 1929.

JOE B. FRANTZ, *University of Texas*

EARRINGS are ear ornaments usually suspended by a curved hook through a hole pierced in the earlobe. Many present-day earrings are made for unpierced lobes and are held in place by a spring clip or a screw device. Earrings have been made since prehistoric times, and, except in parts of the Orient, they have been almost exclusively a form of feminine adornment. In addition to earrings there have been other types of ear ornamentation; for example, some primitive tribes use earplugs to distend the lobes.

Ancient Types. One of the earliest records of earrings, in Genesis, indicates that the earrings belonging to Jacob's family were valued as a talisman or amulet. The earliest surviving earrings, discovered at Ur in Mesopotamia and dating to about 3500 B. C., are large hollow tapered hoops. Egyptian earrings of this time were made of gold and silver combined with such stones as amethyst, turquoise, garnet, and jasper. The hoop earring also appeared in the earliest Greek period (2500–1600 B. C.). During the late Minoan and Mycenaean periods (1600–1100 B. C.) the ends of the earrings were wound into spirals, which came to represent horns when a conical addition transformed the ring into the shape of a bull's head. A more elaborate form was a crescent with a scalloped edge and granular decoration.

In the great age of Greece (600–475 B. C.), when gold was plentiful, workmanship became increasingly expert, with the result that there were many different shapes and considerable elaboration. For example, the plain boat shape of earlier earrings assumed the form of a real boat containing a human figure or various animals. The pendant earring, popular in late classical times (475–330 B. C.), consisted of complex shoulder-length objects with dangling chains, rosettes, or other forms suspended from a large decorated disk. Studlike earrings were formed by disks on either side of the lobe connected by an interlinking tube.

The Etruscans (7th to 5th centuries B. C.) made gold earrings with delicate filigree work often inlaid with stones. A style introduced late in the period consisted of a tubular ring with an animal-head finial. Roman jewelry derived from Etruscan and Hellenistic prototypes. Plain hoop earrings continued to be worn, as did those with animal finials, but more typical was a ball type —a hemisphere suspended on a hook. This was later superseded by a pendant earring consisting of a bezel-set stone suspended from another stone, or a stone set above a horizontal bar holding pendant stones.

Byzantine and Medieval Types. Byzantine earrings were basically Roman styles in a much elaborated form: cascades of flashing gems in long pendants are typical of the Byzantine love of ostentation. During the medieval period in northern Europe earrings were rarely more than a simple metal ring, perhaps with a bead of colored glass attached. Earrings disappeared during the later medieval period when women wore their hair in long braids or covered their heads.

Renaissance and Later Types. The renewed interest in antiquity during the Renaissance brought earrings into favor once more as a form of personal adornment. However, extreme elaboration was concentrated mainly upon such pieces as necklaces, brooches, and belts, and earrings were usually simple pendants of gold occasionally enriched with enamel or with drop pearls. The complexity of contemporary headdresses probably hindered any elaboration, and throughout the 17th century—and well into the 18th century—the drop pearl was by far the most popular earring. It was also a popular male adornment (worn singly); that worn by Charles I of England when he went to the scaffold still survives.

The 18th century saw the development of girandole earrings, large stones having from three to five pendants of diamonds, or of the increasingly popular artificial gems called "pastes." By the end of the century the settings had become extremely refined and elegant. The size and style of 18th century earrings were wholly dependent upon the dictates of fashion that in 1774 positively prohibited the wearing of earrings. In the early 19th century, earrings of enamel, facet-cut steel, and Wedgwood cameos were followed by simple gold earrings set with pearls, cabochon stones, or diamonds in such naturalistic settings as flowers or birds.

The Victorian period was one of endless search for novelty, and all manner of materials (jet, coral, hair) and subject matter (locomotives, horseshoes) were used. Copies of medieval and Renaissance jewels and imposing suites of large, brightly colored stones were replaced in the 1880's by diamonds and pearls in simple silver settings or by earrings of carved jet or ivory. Further simplicity was encouraged by the aesthetic movement at the end of the Victorian period, and most earrings were small and discreet.

The disappearance of the craftsman goldsmith and the emergence of the designer resulted in the introduction of new and imaginative techniques and styles for earrings, particularly in mass-produced costume jewelry, much of which was made for unpierced ears. The 20th century also saw the introduction of platinum as a setting for precious gems. During the 1920's, long pendant earrings reflected an Oriental influence. In the 1930's, clips of cultured pearls (or imitation pearls) enjoyed a long popularity.

The development of plastics after World War II gave unlimited scope to the inventiveness of earring designers, who created brightly colored earrings of all shapes and sizes. Also, ear piercing, which had lost popularity after World War I, returned to favor.

The Orient. Large circular earrings of both bronze and gold were made in India before the 1st century B.C. Later styles include intricate gold filigree earrings of the pendant type and drops composed of pearls and precious gems. A Chinese painting of the 7th century A.D. shows women wearing hoop earrings, and the pendant type, ornamented with pearls and stones after the Indian fashion, were worn during the T'ang dynasty (618–906 A.D.).

Pre-Columbian America. Central and South American Indians of the pre-Columbian period made ear ornaments of pure gold, using anthropomorphic and zoomorphic forms, at times combined, for example, when divinities with human figures and animal heads were represented. The Pre-Columbians also made disk-type earplugs of such materials as shell inlaid with turquoise, attached to the earlobe by a wooden rod.

KAY STANILAND, *Gallery of English Costume Platt Hall, Manchester, England*

Further Reading: Bradford, Ernle B. S., *Four Centuries of European Jewellery* (London 1953); Evans, Joan, *History of Jewellery, 1100–1870* (London 1953); Flower, Margaret, *Victorian Jewellery* (London 1951); Higgins, Reynold A., *Greek and Roman Jewellery* (London 1961).

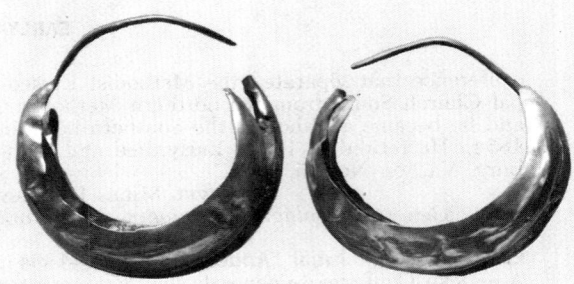

THE METROPOLITAN MUSEUM OF ART

Sumerian gold earrings, 3500-2800 B.C.

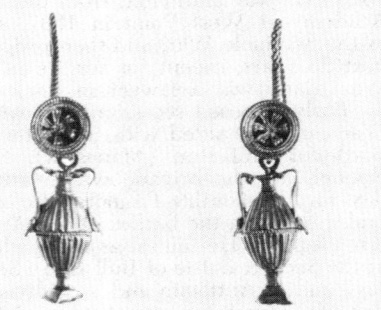

THE BOSTON MUSEUM OF FINE ARTS

Etruscan gold earrings, 4th century B.C.

THE BOSTON MUSEUM OF FINE ARTS

Greek gold earrings, 3d century B.C.

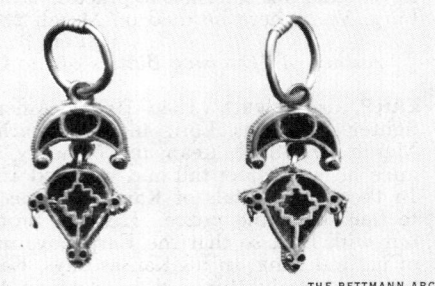

THE BETTMANN ARCHIVE

Byzantine gold earrings, 6th century A.D.

THE BROOKLYN MUSEUM

Peruvian gold ear spools, pre-Columbian.

EARTH

CONTENTS

Section	Page	Section	Page
1. The Earth as a Planet	534	Chemical Composition	537
Shape and Size	534	Heat in the Interior	538
Gravity	534	Hydrosphere and Atmosphere	539
Motions	535	**3. Geomagnetism**	540
Satellites	536	Properties	540
Tides	536	Origin of the Field	540
The Space Environment	536	Polarity Reversals	540
2. Structure and Composition of the Earth	536	**4. History of the Earth**	541
Structure of the Interior	536	Origin of the Earth	541
		Large-Scale Changes	541

EARTH. The earth, the home of all known life, is a satellite of the star called the sun. It is the third planet from the sun in order of distance, completing one orbit every 365.25 days at an average distance from the sun of about 92.9 million miles (149 million km). The earth consists mainly of heavier elements such as iron, silicon, and aluminum. It is enveloped by an atmosphere consisting primarily of nitrogen and oxygen, with smaller amounts of carbon dioxide and water vapor.

The earth is spherical in shape, with an average diameter of about 7,910 miles (12,740 km), except for a slight flattening at the poles due to the centrifugal force of its daily rotation. It has one major natural satellite, or moon, which is large enough—2,160 miles (3,378 km) in diameter—for the earth and the moon sometimes to be called a two-planet system.

The total surface area of the earth is 197 million square miles (510 million sq km), of which 59 million square miles (153 million sq km)—29% of the total area—is land. The rest of the earth is covered by oceans or seas to an average depth of nearly 3 miles (5 km). The land area is divided into 6 major continental bodies: Eurasia, Africa, North America, South America, Australia, and Antarctica.

Development of the Study of the Earth. The earliest known image that men had of the earth was that it was a flat, rigid platform at the center of the universe. The sun, the moon, the stars, and the planets all seemed to revolve around this platform. As early as the 6th century B.C., however, some Greek thinkers such as Pythagoras had progressed far enough beyond this simple image to realize that the earth might be a sphere. That is, they noticed that distant ships appear to drop below the horizon, that for an observer traveling north or south the positions of the stars seem to change relative to the horizon, and that in lunar eclipses the earth's shadow is curved.

Thus, about 250 B.C., the Greek astronomer Eratosthenes estimated the size of the earth by noting that when the sun was vertically overhead at Syene in southern Egypt, it was 7° south of the zenith at Alexandria in northern Egypt. Using this angle and the known distance between the two cities, he calculated the earth's radius and obtained a figure that was surprisingly accurate for its time. The concept of a spherical earth was not widely accepted until the Renaissance, however. Other Greek astronomers had similarly modern ideas about the nature of the earth in space. Aristarchus, for example, pro-

CROSS SECTION OF THE EARTH

From the surface of the earth to the center of the planet is a distance of about 3,950 miles (6,360 km). The weight of the overlying material produces pressures of about 54.5 million pounds per square inch (50.3 grams per sq cm) at the center. The diagram below indicates the dimensions of the major divisions of the earth: a core of iron (in both a solid and a molten state), a mantle of iron and dense rock, and a thin outer crust of complex and varied rock materials.

CRUST 20 MILES THICK
MOHOROVICIC DISCONTINUITY
MANTLE (DENSE ROCK)
INTERFACE AT 2,158 - MILE RADIUS
OUTER CORE (MOLTEN IRON)
INTERFACE AT 808 - MILE RADIUS
INNER CORE (IRON SOLIDIFIED BY PRESSURE)

Geophysicists may sometimes make another division of the outer portion of the earth. Thus, a rigid lithosphere consisting of the crust and the upper mantle is said to float on a softer, more deformable lower portion of the mantle.

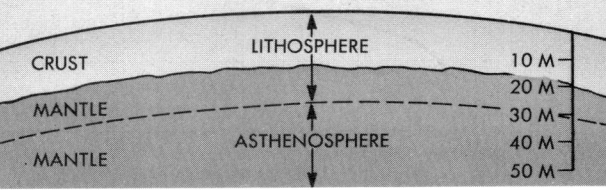

posed in the 3d century B.C. that the earth is only one of a family of planets revolving around the sun. But again, this heliocentric view was not generally accepted until the 17th century, following the work of Nicolaus Copernicus, Johannes Kepler, and Galileo Galilei.

The study of the earth continued to develop in a fragmented fashion. This happened partly because each of the earth sciences was long confined within the limitations of its original techniques. Thus, *geodesy*—the study of the shape of the earth—developed from the land surveying and measuring techniques of geometry; and *geology*—the study of rocks, minerals, fossils, and the forces that shape the earth's surface—began as the simple study of land features. *Geophysics*—the application of the methods of physics to the study of the earth—originated with the precise physical theories of geomagnetism and gravity of William Gilbert and Isaac Newton, but for some time the necessary data were lacking for further progress in this field.

Since the beginning of the 20th century, however, the development of new scientific instruments and their application in ships, airplanes, and satellites have overcome earlier limitations. The various earth sciences have been brought together in more united studies of the earth as a whole. The outer atmosphere and the ocean floors are no longer inaccessible. *Geochemistry* has been added to the earth sciences; high-pressure and high-temperature experiments are helping to interpret observations that seismologists make of the earth's interior. Studies of radioactivity and geomagnetism are providing a time scale and a history of old rocks.

The earlier fragmentation of earth sciences is indicated by the lack of a general theory that can account for worldwide geological processes. Thus, the standard doctrine in geology textbooks has been that the continents are forever fixed in one place, as if on a rigid platform. Now it is becoming apparent that scientists, by this long insistence that the earth is rigid, may have created a stumbling block to the understanding of many data. There is strong evidence that the continents are, in fact, slowly drifting about on the earth's surface. Until basic considerations of this nature are settled it cannot be said that men have a real understanding of the planet on which they live. A great change in thinking is required, from which a new and united science of the earth appears to be emerging. The terms *geoscience* and *geonomy* have been proposed for this unified study of the earth.

1. The Earth as a Planet

The earth will be described as a planet of the sun before its structure and geophysical processes are discussed in greater detail. This description includes the dimensions and motions of the earth, and its gravitational relationships.

Shape and Size. The fact that the earth has an approximately spherical shape was realized by some men as long ago as the days of ancient Greece. They were able to make rough calculations of the radius of this sphere by determining the separation of two stations, or points of observation, that lay on the same meridian. Later, more extensive surveys showed that the length of a degree of latitude varies with the latitude, indicating that the earth deviates from a perfectly spherical shape. Newton accounted for this by demonstrating that the centrifugal force of the earth's rotation should cause it to bulge at the equator.

Today it is known that the earth is an oblate spheroid, with an equatorial radius a that is longer than its polar radius b. (Oblateness is defined by the formula $(a - b)/a$.) A combination of geodetic and astronomical methods has been employed to determine what are now the internationally accepted values for these quantities: a is 3,963.338 miles (6,379.388 km), b is 3,946.887 miles (6,351.912 km), and therefore the oblateness is 0.003367, or approximately 1/298. The total surface area of the spheroid is 197 million square miles (510 million sq km), of which 59 million square miles (153 million sq km) is land.

It is interesting to note that the meter was first defined as being one 10-millionth the distance from the pole to the equator, as measured along the earth's surface. Therefore the average value of a degree of latitude is 10 million meters (10,000 km) divided by 90°, or about 111 km (about 69 miles).

The mass of this spheroid is close to 6.6×10^{21} tons (6×10^{24} kg), and its average density is 344.7 pounds per cubic foot (5.52 grams per cu cm). By astronomical methods the earth's moment of inertia has been determined as $0.334 MR^2$, where M is the earth's total mass and R is its radius. For a uniform sphere the value of the moment of inertia would be $0.4 MR^2$; this discrepancy indicates that the earth becomes denser toward its center—an observation that agrees with the low value of 2.87 obtained for the average density of surface rocks, compared to the average for the earth as a whole.

Gravity. Newton's law of gravitation states that if two particles of masses m_1 and m_2 are at a distance r from each other, each particle attracts the other particle with a force Gm_1m_2/r^2. (G is the constant of gravitation; it has been measured in the laboratory by comparing the force exerted on one mass by another with the attraction exerted on that mass by the earth. The latest value is 6.668×10^{-8}, in the metric system.)

Thus, if M is the mass of the earth and R is its radius, the weight W of a body of mass m on the surface of the earth is $W = mg = GMm/R^2$, where g is the weight of a unit mass or the acceleration due to gravity. R can be measured

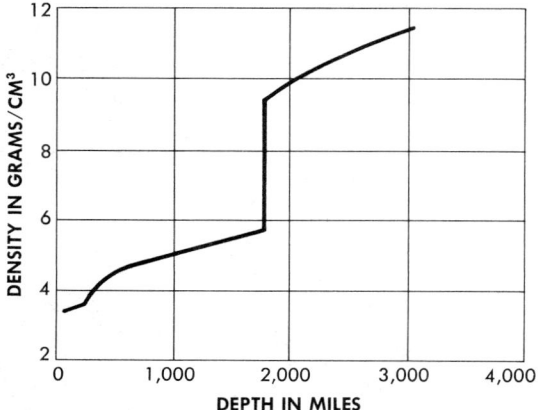

DENSITY OF THE EARTH increases sharply at the core-mantle interface. Such information is gained from studies of seismic waves generated by earthquakes.

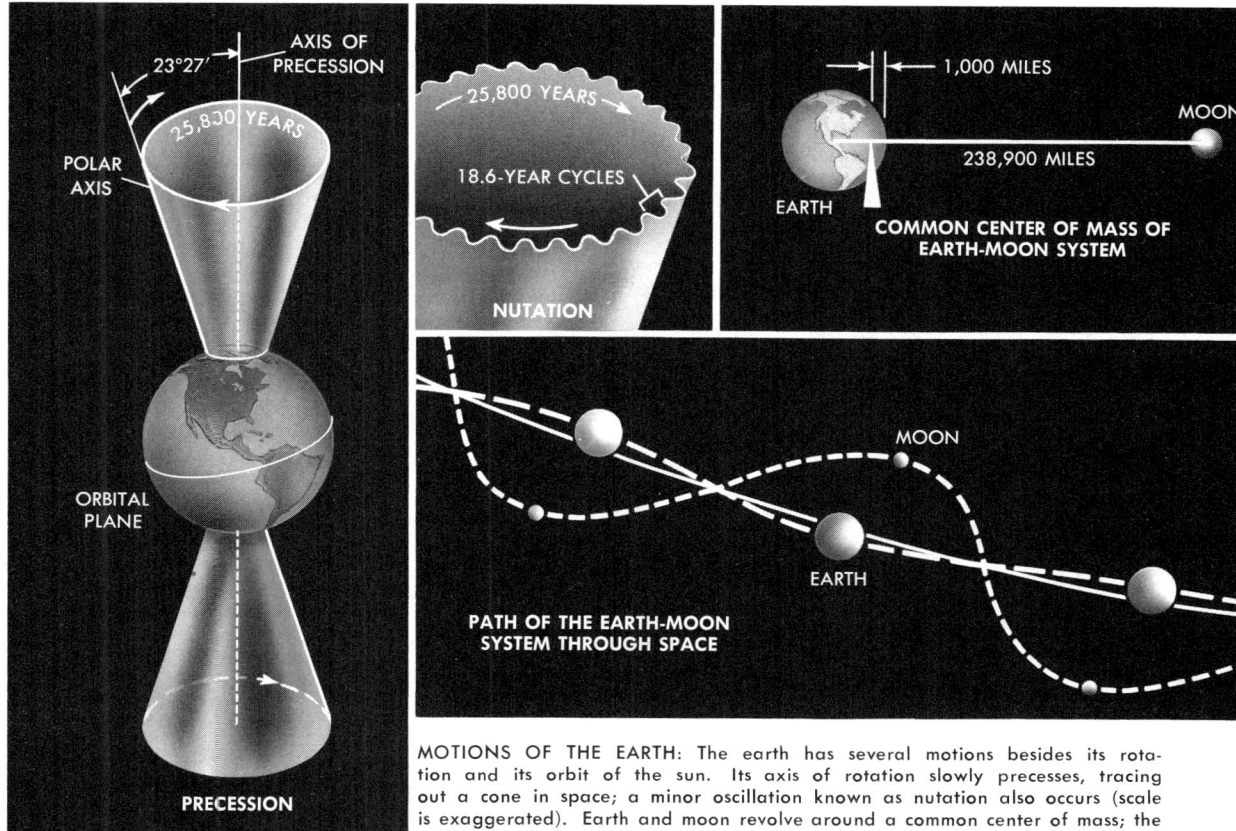

MOTIONS OF THE EARTH: The earth has several motions besides its rotation and its orbit of the sun. Its axis of rotation slowly precesses, tracing out a cone in space; a minor oscillation known as nutation also occurs (scale is exaggerated). Earth and moon revolve around a common center of mass; the path of this center around the sun is the solid line seen in the lower diagram.

very accurately, and g also has been measured for many places on the earth's surface. Because the earth is a spheroid and because of the centrifugal force caused by its rotation, the value of g depends upon the latitude. At sea level at the equator it is about 32.09 feet (978.04 cm) per second per second, whereas at the poles it is about 32.26 feet (983.28 cm) per second per second. (By international agreement, the relationship between the acceleration due to gravity g and the latitude Φ is $g = 978.049$ $(1 + 0.0052884 \sin^2\Phi - 0.0000059 \sin^2 2\Phi)$.)

The value g, of course, may vary from this calculated value at any place because of differences in elevation above or below sea level and because of local irregularities in the density of rocks in the neighboring crust or mantle. The difference between a measured and calculated value is called an *anomaly*, and maps of gravity anomalies are useful guides to underground structures and are used in prospecting. For example, salt domes beneath the earth's surface, which often carry oil, are low in density and are marked by negative anomalies.

Motions—Revolution. The earth completes one revolution of the sun in 365.25 days. It follows an elliptical orbit with a maximum radius (aphelion) of 94.6 million miles (152 million km), and a minimum radius (perihelion) of 91.3 million miles (147 million km). The mean distance of the sun from the earth therefore is about 92.9 million miles (149 million km); this distance is called the *astronomical unit*. The mean linear velocity of the earth in its orbit is 18.5 miles (29.8 km) per second.

Rotation. The earth rotates about its axis at a mean linear velocity of about 0.29 miles (0.46 km) per second (at the equator). The axis is tilted at an angle of 23°27' with respect to the plane of the earth's orbit; this tilt is the major cause of the variation in the seasons on earth. The time it takes the earth to complete one rotation about its axis with respect to a fixed star is known as a *sidereal day*. The sidereal day is shorter by 1 part in 365 than the *mean solar day*, which is the average time between successive passages of the sun across the same meridian on earth. The length of the sidereal day in mean solar time is 23 hours 56 minutes 4 seconds.

The earth does not rotate on its axis quite regularly, however. The length of the day changes in three small ways: a regular slowing down of the earth's rate of rotation, seasonal variations, and irregular changes in the earth's orbit. The gradual slowing of the earth's rate of rotation is considered to be due to the loss of energy in tidal action and the subsequent dissipation of this energy as a slight heating of the sea. The loss has been estimated from studies of ancient eclipses to amount to a lengthening of the day by about 0.03 milliseconds per year at present; this implies that the day formerly was much shorter. The seasonal changes are very small and can be attributed to the effects of changes in ice sheet and glacier coverage as well as in atmospheric and oceanic circulation. The irregular changes also are small and are measured in thousandths of a second per year. For a long time they were a puzzle, but they are now attributed to changes in the pattern of convection in the earth's liquid core.

Precession of the Equinoxes. It might be expected that the direction of the axis of rotation of a spinning body such as the earth would remain fixed in space. However, the gravitational attraction of other bodies—especially the moon and the sun—causes the earth's axis to move. The motion, known as the precession of the equinoxes, is such that the axis traces out a cone in space. As a result the celestial poles—the extension of the earth's axis to the celestial sphere—appear to move slowly in a circle through the constellations in the celestial polar regions. One such circle is completed every 25,800 years. Because of this motion, accounts of the stars given by ancient writers no longer fit the present sky, and ancient observatories and monuments such as the pyramids of Egypt no longer point to the stars on which these structures were oriented when they were built.

Nutation and Chandler Wobble. Superimposed on the precession of the equinoxes are two other motions of smaller amplitude. One of them is a minor regular oscillation of the earth's axis called the nutation, with a period of 18.6 years. This motion amounts to about 9" of arc and is caused by a periodic variation in the angle of the moon's path with respect to the earth's equator. The other motion, called the Chandler wobble, causes the earth to move about its axis with a variable period of about 440 days.

Satellites. The earth has one natural satellite, or moon, which is 81 times less massive than the earth and has a diameter that is about ¼ of the earths' diameter. Nevertheless, it is far larger in proportion to the earth than is the satellite of any other planet in the solar system; hence, the earth-moon system sometimes is called a binary, or two-planet, system. The moon revolves about the earth in an orbit with a mean radius of 238,900 miles (384,400 km) and a sidereal period of about 27⅓ days. (Actually, the earth and the moon revolve around a common center of mass that, because of the earth's larger size, lies more than 1,000 miles (1,600 km) below the earth's surface.)

There are theoretical reasons for supposing that the earth may have other natural satellites, although obviously they must be very small. That is, there are two stable libration points (points of orbital equilibrium) in the gravitational system formed by the earth and the moon. Clouds of cosmic dust could accumulate at these points and remain in stable orbit. A sighting of such clouds was first reported in 1961 by a Polish astronomer, Kazimierz Kordylewski, and other sightings have since been made.

Tides. The sun and the moon cause tides on the earth, chiefly affecting the sea. In the open ocean the vertical range of such tides is only a few feet. Coasts, however, may experience tides that reach a maximum of about 60 feet (18 meters) in places such as the Bay of Fundy and Ungava Bay on Canada's east coast. The earth's land areas also are distorted by tides, but land tides are hard to detect and amount to less than a foot.

The Space Environment. Life on earth depends on the electromagnetic radiation emitted by the sun. About two calories of solar energy fall on each square centimeter of the earth's atmospheric surface each minute. This energy supports photosynthesis in plants, drives the air currents, and maintains the hydrologic cycle. Some of the radiation reaches the earth's surface, some is absorbed by the atmosphere, and some is reflected back into space. A variety of energetic particles from the sun—the *solar wind*—and from other celestial sources also interacts with the earth's atmosphere and with its radiation belts. In addition, about one ton of matter is introduced into the atmosphere every day by meteors.

2. Structure and Composition of the Earth

The earth's structure may conveniently be discussed in terms of the planet's interior (including the crust); its oceans, or hydrosphere; and its atmosphere (including the zones of radiation that surround the earth). Primary attention is given here to the body of the planet itself. See also ATMOSPHERE; OCEANOGRAPHY; VAN ALLEN RADIATION BELTS.

STRUCTURE OF THE INTERIOR

The earth is symmetrically arranged in three major concentric spheres called the *core*, the *mantle*, and the *crust*. Pressures rise steadily inside the earth because of the weight of overlying rock. Thus, pressure at the outer boundary of the core reaches 1.37 million atmospheres, and at the center of the earth it reaches 3.7 million atmospheres. (One atmosphere equals 14.7 pounds per square inch, or 13.6 grams per sq cm.)

Seismic Studies. Nearly all the knowledge that scientists have of the deep interior of the earth has been gained through study of the seismic waves generated by large earthquakes. Subsidiary information comes from study of the earth's geomagnetic and gravitational fields, from a knowledge of the earth's moment of inertia, and from comparisons with meteorites and with simulated systems in the laboratory that are thought likely to resemble conditions deep in the earth.

Stresses that build up slowly within the earth are relieved from time to time by the fracturing and movement of the rocks of the crust. Seismic waves radiate through the earth from the source, or *focus*, of such earthquakes. Most of these shocks are small and have only local effects, but large shocks release more energy than a hydrogen bomb does. These large shocks send waves throughout the earth that are recorded at seismological stations, of which there are several hundred in all parts of the world. The very largest earthquakes cause the earth to vibrate like a bell for several hours, with a fundamental period of vibration of 54 minutes.

Two kinds of seismic waves, called *body waves*, travel through the interior: primary or P waves, which are compressional in nature and arrive first at a recording station; and secondary or S waves, which are transverse and arrive later. Other waves, called long or *L waves*, travel more slowly around the surface of the earth. Besides traveling directly through the earth from focus to observatory, body waves also may be reflected and refracted at the earth's surface and at interior interfaces. Quake records at stations far from the focus therefore are made complex by the arrival of many pulses of energy that have traveled by different paths.

The velocities of the two kinds of body waves depend upon the densities and the elastic properties of the materials through which they travel.

(The moment of inertia of the earth also depends upon the distribution of these densities.) Quake observations thus can be used to determine the probable densities and elastic constants for all parts of the earth (except for some uncertainty about the innermost core). Since 1903 the International Association of Seismology has collected data on earthquakes. Geophysicists have interpreted these data to give a fairly complete picture of the earth's interior, even though the problem is complicated because velocities of seismic waves increase with depth and their paths curve inward.

Interfaces. There is one great discontinuity in the earth's interior: the boundary between the mantle and the core, which was detected in 1913 by the German-American geophysicist Beno Gutenberg at a depth of 1,800 miles (2,898 km) below the surface of the earth. The core therefore has an average radius of 2,158 miles (3,473 km)—ignoring flattening—and constitutes nearly 55% of the earth's radius. The outer parts of the core do not transmit S waves. Since this nontransmission is universally characteristic of liquids, it is assumed that the outer core is probably molten iron. (The mantle, on the other hand, is dense rock.) Another interface bounds what is known as the inner core, which has a radius of 808 miles (1,300 km) and is probably iron solidified by extreme pressure.

In his studies of a 1909 earthquake, Croatian geologist Andrija Mohorovičić discovered another boundary at a shallow depth, between the crust and the mantle; this is now known as the *Mohorovicic discontinuity*. Further investigations—chiefly using the echoes of waves generated by small explosions—have shown that under the continents the structure of the crust is very complex and averages 20 miles (35 km) in thickness. Under the ocean floors, however, it is more uniform and has three layers that total only about 3 miles (5 km) in thickness. This difference between oceanic and continental crust is sharp and important. The continental blocks rise abruptly 3 miles (5 km) above the ocean floors at the continental slopes, and their "roots" also protrude much deeper into the mantle. The continents are high because they are light, and they are underlain by crust of different structure and composition from that of the ocean floors.

Asthenosphere and Lithosphere. The core, the crust, and the mantle are apparently of quite different compositions, but within the upper mantle and the crust another differentiation can be made, based on differences of physical state at different depths. That is, a lower portion of the mantle, because of temperature and pressure conditions there, is believed to be softer and more easily deformed. This layer, the asthenosphere, begins at a depth of 30 to 60 miles (50–100 km), and its bottom grades slowly into a rigid lower mantle at a depth of several hundred miles.

The layer of rigid rocks above the asthenosphere is called the lithosphere. It includes both the crust and the uppermost part of the mantle. The lithosphere thus may be regarded as a brittle skin floating on the slightly viscous layer of the asthenosphere, somewhat as ice floats on a frozen lake. The existence of a deformable asthenosphere was suspected in the 19th century when geodetic and gravitational observations showed that mountains are not extra loads supported by a rigid earth, but that instead they are supported by deep roots of light rock. This idea was strengthened when it was noticed that regions such as Scandinavia and northern Canada, which until about 10,000 years ago had been covered for a long time by ice sheets, are rising at rates up to 0.4 inch (1 cm) per year. Apparently the land is floating upward in response to the loss of the great loads of ice.

The asthenosphere has attracted much recent interest because of the discovery of seismic methods for studying it and of the realization that if continents drift they must do so by the motion of plates of the lithosphere sliding over the asthenosphere. There is no such motion at the Mohorovicic discontinuity at the base of the crust.

CHEMICAL COMPOSITION

The study of the earth's chemical constitution started, naturally enough, with analyses of the surface rocks of the continental crust. These rocks are very diverse, but petrologists and geochemists have shown that most of the rocks are silicates and that only a few elements actually are abundant. These elements are oxygen, silicon, aluminum, iron, magnesium, calcium, sodium, and potassium. There are smaller quantities of titanium, phosphorus, hydrogen, and a very few other elements; all the rest occur in negligible amounts except in the occasional ore bodies that are found.

Crust. The structure of the rocks of the continental crust is very complex, because they have repeatedly been eroded, carried about, and transformed by mountain building and igneous intrusion. The depths of the crust are now being investigated by explosion seismology and by drilling. The bottom of the crust has not yet been reached by such drilling, but beyond some increase in iron and magnesium content and hence in density, the lower crust is not thought to be very different from the top. Surface rocks give some idea of the nature of the earth's chemistry as a whole, but they certainly are not typical, because their density is far too low.

The oceanic crust is quite different from the continental crust. The U. S. Project Mohole to drill a deep hole right through the ocean floor was abandoned, but other information—obtained by drilling shorter holes, by dredging, and by seismic investigations—has made the composition of the three layers of the oceanic crust fairly certain. The uppermost layer, layer 1, consists of unconsolidated sediments or muds deposited particle by particle, washed in by sudden rushes of dense turbidity currents down the continental slopes or carried along by slow deep currents. These sediments are very young and occur only in thin and sporadic layers near the central ridges of the oceans, but they increase in thickness and maximum age towards the continents (which suggests that the oceans are spreading away from the central ridges). Layer 2, the middle layer, is about 1 mile (1.6 km) thick and seems to be a uniform layer of basalt that perhaps was formed at the central ridges on the ocean floor. Layer 3, the lowest layer, seems to be a few miles thick and to consist of the rock called serpentine; it could be a hydrated form of the rock of the uppermost mantle. The ocean floor thus can be regarded merely as the somewhat altered mantle on which a very thin veneer of basalt lavas and sediments has accumulated. It is considerably denser than the continental crust and has none of its complex structures.

Mantle and Core. Any discussion of the chemistry of the earth's deep interior is handicapped by the impossibility of collecting samples. Mining and drilling operations, as previously stated, have not even penetrated the crust. Lavas and other igneous rocks come from unknown but probably fairly shallow depths of a few tens of miles.

Comparisons can provide clues, however. The spectroscopic studies made of the sun and other stars, for example, reveal that they consist largely of hydrogen and helium and some other gases, but also present are the same heavy elements as are found in meteorites and in terrestrial rocks. In cosmic terms, the commonest heavier elements (in order of decreasing abundance) are iron, sulfur, aluminum, carbon, silicon, magnesium, calcium, sodium, nickel, and phosphorus. Apart from the loss of gases that is inevitable in small bodies with weak gravitational fields, such as the earth, it appears that the whole universe is rather uniform. Therefore it is probable that the earth's interior also is made of the commonest heavy elements.

Iron, for example, is the commonest heavy element, and the density and other physical properties of iron fit the determined properties of the earth's core. Theoretical considerations of temperature and pressure suggest that in the outer core the iron probably is liquid, but that the higher pressures of the inner core might cause it to be solid. Lesser amounts of nickel and other common elements are likely to be present in solution.

It has long been suspected that meteorites can also provide important clues to the composition of the earth's interior, since they may be representative of the material commonly present in the days when the solar system was first being formed. Two chief kinds of meteorites fall to earth: nickel-iron meteorites, which are considered to approximate the composition of the core; and the much more numerous meteorites composed of magnesium and iron silicates, which may correspond to the composition of the mantle. Thus, the mineral olivine (a combination of Mg_2SiO_4 and Fe_2SiO_4), which is abundant in meteorites, has properties that fit the determined properties of the mantle. Another likely constituent is pyroxene (a combination of $MgSiO_3$ and $FeSiO_3$).

Two refinements in instrumentation have produced support for the suggestion that these common minerals compose the mantle. For one, it has become possible to study the behavior of minerals at the high temperatures and pressures prevailing at depths of several hundred miles; the Carnegie Institution of Washington and the Australian National University have been leaders in this work. At certain temperature and pressure levels, appropriate mixtures of the silicates mentioned above change their crystal structures to denser forms—in particular, altering from normal olivine to another crystal form called spinel, and then dissociating into still denser forms of the constituent oxides. The other refinement is that new networks of seismological stations are yielding more precise knowledge of the layers in the upper mantle with the aid of computers. It has been shown that sudden increases in density occur at levels corresponding to the phase changes that are observed in the laboratory. From these results it may be concluded that the lower mantle probably is richer in iron, is permanently rigid, and is relatively uniform. The upper mantle is more variable in composition. Olivine is an easily deformed mineral, which makes the probable mobility of the upper layers of the mantle easier to understand.

HEAT IN THE INTERIOR

The most likely source of heat in the earth's interior is the decay of radioactive elements. No direct methods have been proposed for measuring temperatures within the earth, but there are reasonable indirect arguments that can suggest temperature limits. Near the surface of the earth, for example, the temperature rises rather rapidly downward in mines and drill holes. This temperature gradient varies between 29° and 58°F per mile (10°–20°C per km) of depth. If this is multiplied by the thermal conductivity of the surrounding rocks—a constant property measured in the laboratory for each material—the product is the quantity of heat flowing out of the earth. This value does not vary greatly; it amounts to an average of 1.2×10^{-6} calories per square centimeter per second—only a small fraction of the heat derived from the sun. If such surface gradients continued downward, however, temperatures of thousands of degrees would be reached at depths of only hundreds of miles. All rocks would certainly melt in spite of the high pressures at such depths. Since it is known from seismic wave studies that rocks are not in a liquid state at these depths, temperatures must in fact rise more slowly there than they do near the surface.

The earth's heat derives, as stated, from the decay of naturally radioactive elements, espe-

Two kinds of seismic waves travel through the earth: compressional primary waves, which arrive first at recording stations; and transverse secondary waves, which arrive later. They may be reflected and refracted several times at the surface and at interior interfaces.

PATHS OF SEISMIC WAVES THROUGH THE EARTH

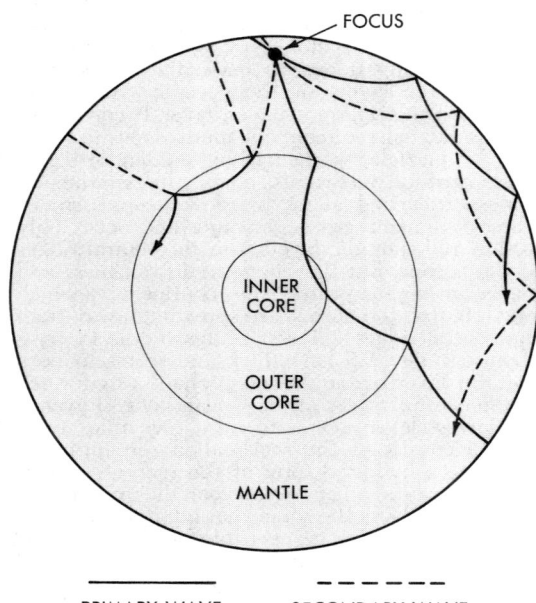

PRIMARY WAVE   SECONDARY WAVE

cially uranium and thorium. If these elements are concentrated upward near the surface (and this appears likely on chemical grounds), the lower temperature gradients at greater depths could be explained by a decreasing radioactive-element content in the mantle. In addition, because uranium and thorium tend to be concentrated in siliceous rocks such as granite, it was supposed that the heat flow through the basaltic ocean floors would be much less than through the granitic continents. Measurements have shown that this is not the case, however, and it was therefore argued that the mantle under the ocean basins must be enriched in radioactive elements. This in turn was held to be a strong argument against continental drift, until it was pointed out that a continent in effect warms the mantle beneath it. After the continent has been carried away by drift, the uncovered mantle gives off this excess heat for tens of millions of years; this process tends to equalize temperatures between continents and ocean floors.

Estimates of temperatures in the deep interior are, in fact, educated guesses that depend on estimates of the increase in melting point with increasing pressure. For example, it is thought that the temperature at the core-mantle boundary is about 5400°F (3000°C) and that at the center of the earth it is perhaps 7300°F (4000°C). Radiative transfer should play an important role in the earth's interior. At low temperatures silicates are good insulators, but with a rise in temperature they become transparent to radiation; and it is likely that the lower mantle is hot enough to conduct heat readily for this reason. The process has the double effect of conveying heat away from the core and of keeping the temperature of the lower mantle below the melting point of its materials; the core itself is of molten metal and is not transparent to radiation. The loss of heat through the mantle maintains convection currents in the earth's interior that in turn generate the geomagnetic field discussed below.

In the upper mantle, where the temperature is lower, silicates cease to be good conductors, and heat accumulates; but before the melting point is reached the silicates lose their rigidity—a process assisted by the changes in phase from oxides to spinels to olivines—and become capable of flow. This does not constitute proof that the asthenosphere in the upper mantle can flow and that it has its own convection currents, but at least it makes the mechanism plausible as a cause of continental drift.

HYDROSPHERE AND ATMOSPHERE

Some mention should also be made of the earth's hydrosphere (its waters and glacial ice) and its envelope of gases, although these are discussed more fully in separate articles. The hydrosphere weighs about 3.11×10^{21} pounds (1.41×10^{25} grams), or 0.03% of the earth's total weight, while the atmosphere weighs about 1.12×10^{19} pounds (5.1×10^{21} grams), or 0.0001% of the earth's weight. The oceans constitute 98% of the whole hydrosphere and cover 70.8% of the earth's surface; they have an estimated average depth of nearly 12,500 feet (3,800 meters). Ocean water varies greatly in salinity, but the composition of the dissolved salts is constant. Sodium and chlorine are by far the most abundant elements among these salts, but the sea also has appreciable quantities of mag-

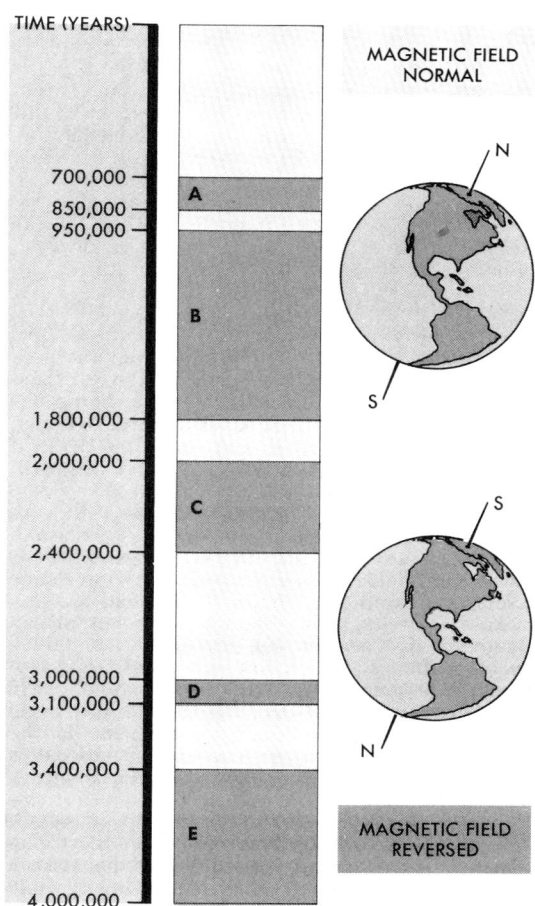

Studies of rock magnetism showed that the earth's magnetic field has reversed itself many times. The timescale ratios of the reversals correspond to the width ratios of the pattern of reversed magnetic strips found on either side of mid-ocean ridges. This suggests that the ocean floors are spreading because of an upwelling of material at the ridges.

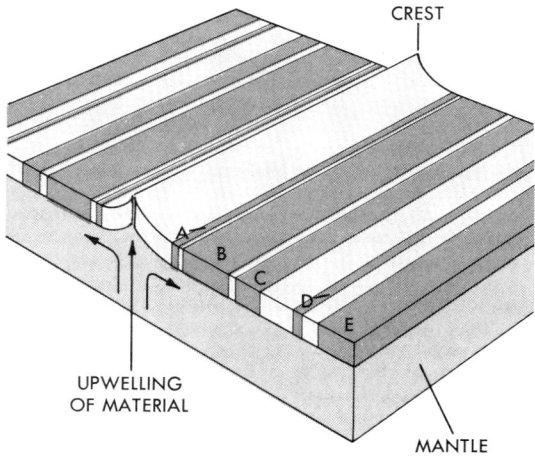

nesium, sulfur, calcium, potassium, and bromine in solution, besides traces of many other elements.

The atmosphere also is constant in composition to a height of 60 miles (100 km); it consists primarily of nitrogen and oxygen, with lesser amounts of argon, carbon dioxide, and other gases. Above this, however, the ionosphere (and the much higher Van Allen radiation belts surrounding the earth in space) consist of free electrons and ionized atoms and molecules. These zones conduct electricity, trap radiation, give rise to the aurora, and have important effects in controlling radio waves and the amount of solar radiation that reaches the earth's surface.

3. Geomagnetism

The early English physicist William Gilbert demonstrated in 1600 that the geomagnetic field of the earth is similar to the field of a magnetized sphere. Subsequent observations have borne out his view that the earth behaves as a big magnet, but they have indicated that its magnetic field is not quite regular and that it fluctuates with time.

Properties. In the first half of the 19th century the German mathematician Karl Friedrich Gauss demonstrated that the earth generates its own main field internally, and that only some minor and rapid fluctuations in the field are due to solar activity. This main field is not placed symmetrically within the earth. A magnetic needle points in a direction that usually is a few degrees east or west of true, or geographic, north, depending on the observer's longitude; this angle is known as the *angle of declination*. If the needle is free to move vertically, it also dips downward at an angle known as the *angle of inclination*. The dip is not vertical at the geographic poles but at the magnetic dip poles—one of which was over Bathurst Island in the Canadian Arctic Ocean and the other near the coast of Antarctica south of New Zealand in the late 1960's. The poles are not exactly opposite to each other geographically, nor are they stationary.

The earth's field can be compared to that of a dipole magnet in the earth that neither passes through the earth's center nor points along the axis of rotation. The north dip pole is moving northwest at an average rate of 5 miles (8 km) per year. It seems probable that the magnetic field nevertheless is loosely coupled to the axis of rotation, so that over many centuries it would be seen to have a mean position oriented along the earth's axis.

The strength and direction of the earth's magnetic field have been mapped in detail by nonmagnetic ships and their towed instruments, by aircraft, and by observations on land. The patterns of the maps show irregularities that either are very large or are very small; there are no anomalies of intermediate size. The small anomalies have been found to be caused by permanent magnetization of geological features within the crust, the temperature of which is below the *Curie point*—the temperature at which ferromagnetic materials lose their permanent magnetization. The large anomalies, which apparently are formed in the earth's core, move slowly westward at a rate of about 0.3° per year.

Origin of the Field. These properties of the geomagnetic field are puzzling. The earth cannot be a huge permanent magnet; it is much too hot. All magnetic substances lose their magnetism above the Curie point, which never is more than a few hundred degrees centigrade. Nor could a permanent magnet shift about as the earth's field does. The generally accepted answer is that the earth is a dynamo; it has been demonstrated that the main magnetic field could be caused by electric currents flowing in the fluid, metallic core. The escape of heat generated by the decay of small amounts of radioactive elements could maintain convection currents in the core, rather like currents in a pot boiling on a stove. The convection currents would carry the electric currents that generate the earth's field and produce the large anomalies and motions of the field. (The lack of irregularities of intermediate size is ascribed to the absence of any magnetic influence in the mantle, which is both solid and above the Curie point.)

The small anomalies related to geological features are due to a phenomenon called *rock magnetism*. When a melt of iron-rich lava such as basalt solidifies and cools below its Curie point in a magnetic field, grains of iron oxides in the solidified melt retain a slight but easily measured magnetization along the direction of the field at the time of solidification. (The same property can be observed in some sedimentary rocks.) This means that measurements made today can determine the direction in which the earth's field lay in past times.

One important piece of information provided by such study of many lavas formed in the recent past is that their directions of magnetization are scattered but that their average value coincides with the present field. This evidence supports the view that the dynamo in the core has a mean position symmetrically arranged around the rotational axis; it also suggests that by the averaging of several determinations, the orientation of old rocks and their geographical latitude at time of formation can be found. This is the basis of the study of *paleomagnetism*.

Polarity Reversals. Work on rock magnetism also has shown, surprisingly, that the earth's magnetic field has reversed its polarity many times. This happens irregularly and for reasons that are not fully understood. All that can be said is that the phenomenon is conceivable in terms of the dynamo theory. The reversals in polarity were discovered as early as 1906, but they have attracted much attention only since it has become possible to date young lavas by measuring radioactive decay. Using the potassium-argon method, geophysicists have established the time scale for the past 5 million years; the periods are irregular, but are the same for every site sampled.

The ratios of this time scale have been found in two other connections since 1965. Thus, it has been shown that if the magnetization is measured at close intervals along undisturbed cores of sediments taken in the ocean floors, the cores show reversals at depths that are in the same ratios to each other as are the ratios of the time scale. This can be readily understood if it is assumed that ocean floors were deposited uniformly and each layer has preserved the polarity of its time of deposition. Even more remarkable are the magnetic patterns found over ocean floors. The patterns consist of very regular strips that run parallel to mid-ocean ridges and are arranged symmetrically on either side of them. It has been established that the widths of the successive strips, when measured outward from the ridges, are in the same ratios to one another as are the timescale ratios found in rock magnetism.

As a result of these discoveries it has been proposed as an explanation by various scientists that the ocean floor is being generated by upwelling at mid-ocean ridges, that the basalt in layer 2 of the crust is being imprinted magnetically with the polarity of the geomagnetic field at the time of upwelling, and that the whole ocean floor is being carried away in either direction from the ridges at uniform velocities. Therefore the widths of the strips of anomalies correspond to the periods between successive reversals of the field. This is strong evidence for continental drift, and it also provides a precise way to determine the recent motions of continental blocks.

4. History of the Earth

The subject of the earth's history may be divided into two broad areas: the origin of the earth (and hence of the solar system), and the nature of the large-scale processes that have shaped the earth since its original formation. For a detailed account of geological eras of the past, see GEOLOGY and related articles.

ORIGIN OF THE EARTH

The solar system is remarkably regular in several ways. The planets all revolve around the sun in the same direction; their orbital planes do not differ greatly from the plane of the ecliptic; the sun, the moon, and most of the planets rotate about their axes in the same direction as the planets revolve around the sun; and the succession of the mean distances of the planets from the sun follows a rather simple mathematical relationship (see BODE'S LAW). Such regularity very strongly indicates that all the members of the solar system had a common origin.

One of the first attempts to determine scientifically the time of the earth's origin was made by the English astronomer Edmund Halley (1656–1742), who noted that the rivers of the world carry small quantities of dissolved sodium salts to the oceans. The total estimated salt in the oceans, divided by the rate of addition, suggested that the oceans are at least several hundred million years old. Geologists arrived at a similar figure by considering the great thickness of sedimentary strata and the long evolutionary sequence of the fossils they contain.

On the other hand, before the discovery of radioactivity it was believed that the earth could be warm only if it had had a hot origin and had cooled to its present condition. Physicists doubted whether this process could have taken more than a few tens of millions of years. After 1896, however, the discovery of radioactive isotopes with half-lives of 1 to 10 billion years at once lengthened this time estimate by providing a continuing source of heat within the earth. It also yielded the best means of estimating the earth's age. That is, the age of a rock containing a known amount of radioactive isotope can be calculated from the time required to generate the amount of end product (of radioactive decay) also present in the rock. Such determinations have shown that the oldest continental rocks are about 3.5 billion years old. Meteorites seem to have been formed about 4.5 billion years ago.

Another time estimate is indicated by the shrift toward the red in the spectra of light from distant galaxies. The spectra indicate that the galaxies are rushing away from our own Milky Way galaxy at velocities proportional to their distances, and that hence the universe is expanding. If this assumption is correct, the universe may have had an explosive origin calculated to be about 5.5 billion years ago.

These figures place limits on the age of the earth, and a more subtle argument gives a precise figure within these ultimate limits. The single isotope of thorium and the two isotopes of uranium all decay to lead, but to three different isotopes of lead; therefore, lead from different sources differs in composition depending on its history. It has been shown by this means that all the lead in the earth and in meteorites is likely to have had a uniform composition and hence to have derived from a common source about 4.5 billion years ago. This figure is generally accepted as the age of the earth.

For 200 years, views about the nature of the solar system's formation have vacillated between two theories: the *collision theory* (cataclysmic) and the *nebular theory* (evolutionary). The 18th century French naturalist Buffon first proposed one version of the collision theory—that the sun and another star collided to form the planets. It has been decided, however, that the hot gases produced by such a collision would have escaped the sun's gravity and would not have condensed into bodies as small as planets. Catastrophic theories therefore have been abandoned.

The alternative nebular theory of the French astronomer Pierre Laplace (1749–1827)—actually first proposed by the German philosopher Immanuel Kant—was that the sun cooled from a gas cloud, or nebula, and that in cooling it shed rings that coalesced eventually to form the planets. This theory was not adequate as originally stated, but it has since been revised by the 20th century scientists. The German physicist Carl von Weizsäcker, for example, proposed in 1944 that the solar system was formed from a vast cloud of dust and gas. The sun heated the central portions of the cloud, driving the gases and volatile elements outward. Gravitational instabilities subsequently caused the cloud to form into planets; those closer to the sun were smaller and denser, and those farther away retained a higher proportion of light substances. With various modifications, the nebular hypothesis is generally accepted today.

The earth, then, coalesced about 4.5 billion years ago from a cold dust cloud. Warmed by the heat of the sun and by internal heat generated from its own radioactive elements, the earth may have become partially molten, enabling the materials of the core and the mantle to differentiate and the radioactive elements to collect near the surface. The earth probably lost all its free water and gases at that time, and has generated its present hydrosphere and atmosphere by later volcanic action. It seems evident that the continental crust has risen to the surface like froth at the surface of a boiling pot, but at the present time it is not agreed whether most of the crust formed early or whether it accumulated steadily throughout the earth's history.

LARGE-SCALE CHANGES

The general similarity of rocks of all ages suggests that the earth's surface has changed only slowly and slightly, relatively speaking, since the earth first formed, and that the earth as a whole has been stable. Earthquakes, volcanoes, and erosion processes testify to the steady change of the surface. Geologists have shown that rocks formed below the seas are now high in mountains and that mountain chains have been raised repeatedly at different places and then worn away. Great regions such as the Colorado plateau in North America have been elevated from time to time without any evidence of the compression and folding seen in mountains. The cause of these changes has been much debated and can be discussed only briefly here.

The oldest suggestion is the contraction hypothesis, which holds that the earth is shrinking by cooling and that this process pushes up successive mountain systems like wrinkles on a drying apple. The discovery of a radioactive heating within the earth has made this theory difficult to accept.

The opposite view—that the earth is expanding—has also been advocated. While this might explain the origin of some ocean basins, it does not provide a reason for mountain building. Furthermore, no cause for an expanding earth has been put forward.

The remaining important theory—continental drift—has had a long history, during most of which it had little support. Since 1965, however, it has emerged as the only hypothesis capable of explaining terrestrial phenomena in detail. Older arguments for continental drift can be regarded as inconclusive. Among them are the arguments used by German geologist Alfred Wegener in 1912, such as the correspondence in shape and geology between opposite coasts of the Atlantic Ocean; the attempts to measure continental motions directly; arguments about isostasy (q.v.) and the need for a horizontal flow of rock to compensate for postglacial uplift; discussions about possible mechanisms of drift; and biological debates about the distribution of plants and animals. The new arguments that led most earth scientists to accept continental drift in the 1960's involve paleomagnetism, ocean floor spreading, the discovery of many large faults with horizontal offsets of hundreds of miles (including a new variety called transform faults), and a demonstration that the distribution and direction of earthquakes can be explained by a certain pattern of drift.

The particular version of continental motion now being accepted uses the observation that all important earthquakes lie along narrow belts. The belts divide the lithosphere into six large plates and a few small ones. Each pair of plates moves by rotation about an axis, and the plates move apart because of upwelling and spreading of the sea floor between them. They come together along mountains and deep ocean trenches, where one plate of the lithosphere overrides another, forcing the lower plate back into the lithosphere. Magnetic imprinting of the ocean floors provides a key—rather like the growth rings on a tree stump—that is enabling geophysicists to determine the time of the opening of the Atlantic and Indian oceans and to work out the former positions of the continents for several ten millions of years. During this period the Pacific Ocean has been shrinking; and the continents around it are overriding the Pacific floor, producing peripheral mountains, island arcs, and deep trenches.

Paleomagnetism suggests that drift is not new but that it has operated intermittently throughout most of geological time. It has been proposed that the dominant process that is molding the earth's surface has been the slow growth and disappearance of ocean basins. The first sign of a new ocean is considered to be an uplift and rifting of crustal material, an outpouring of lava, and the start of spreading—as in the East Africa rift valleys, the Red Sea, and the Gulf of Aden. Gradually the ocean widens along its central ridge, as is happening to the Atlantic Ocean. The coasts are undisturbed, but great deltas and shelves of sediments accumulate there. This growth is compensated by shrinking elsewhere, as is happening around the margins of the Pacific Ocean. Eventually an ocean closes up, building mountains from the sedimentary rocks on its coasts. This is the stage of the Mediterranean Sea and Himalayan regions today. Thus, according to this view, great mountains mark the former site of vanished oceans.

The energy to create these slow but vast changes can come only from the earth's original and radioactive heat. This heat can escape from the core by convection currents and through the lower mantle by radiation, and it tends to produce near-melting in the asthenosphere. This generates shallow convection currents in the asthenosphere that rise, splitting the lithosphere apart beneath mid-ocean ridges. The currents spread slowly sideways and descend again beneath mountains and trenches. The earth's asthenosphere thus behaves somewhat like a shallow boiling pot, except that in the case of the earth a "skin" cools and becomes brittle on the surface.

There does not appear to be any reason why these processes should change rapidly. Natural radioactivity should suffice to maintain convection and continental drift for many millions or billions of years, perhaps until after mankind and all the planets and creatures known today are extinct. Ultimately, astronomers believe, the sun itself will go through a short period of rapid expansion before final cooling. When this happens, the earth will be pulled into the sun's fiery embrace and be consumed.

See also ATMOSPHERE; CLIMATE; CONTINENT; GEOCHRONOLOGY; GEODESY; GEOLOGY; GEOMAGNETISM; GEOPHYSICS; METEOROLOGY; OCEAN; OCEANOGRAPHY; SOLAR SYSTEM.

J. T. WILSON
University of Toronto

Bibliography

Adams, Frank D., *The Birth and Development of the Geological Sciences* (Magnolia, Mass., 1954).
Beiser, Arthur, *The Earth* (New York 1968).
Gaskell, Thomas F., *The Earth's Mantle* (London and New York 1967).
Holmes, Arthur, *Principles of Physical Geology*, 2d ed. (New York 1965).
Hurley, Patrick M., ed., *Advances in Earth Sciences* (Cambridge, Mass., 1966).
Jacobs, J. A., Russell, R. D., and Wilson, J. T., *Physics and Geology* (New York 1969).
Jeffreys, Harold, *The Earth: Its Origin, History, and Physical Constitution*, 4th ed. (New York 1959).
Kuiper, Gerard P., ed., *The Earth as a Planet* (The Solar System, Vol. II) (Chicago 1954).
Munk, Walter H., and Macdonald, G. H. F., *The Rotation of the Earth* (New York 1961).
Phinney, Robert A., *History of the Earth's Crust* (Princeton, N. J., 1968).
Runcorn, S. K., *The Mantle of the Earth and Terrestrial Planets* (New York 1967).
Strahler, Arthur N., *The Earth Sciences* (New York 1963).
Takeuchi, H., Uyeda, S., and Kanamori, H., *Debate About the Earth* (San Francisco 1967).
Wegener, Alfred, *The Origin of Continents and Oceans*, trans. of 4th ed. by John Biram (New York 1966).

EARTH INDUCTOR of the observatory type. The hand-operated crank that spins the wire coil is at the right.
U. S. COAST AND GEODETIC SURVEY

EARTH INDUCTOR, an instrument used in magnetic observatories and in magnetic surveys for measuring the dip, or inclination, of the earth's magnetic field at a given site. In most geomagnetic work the earth inductor has replaced the dipping needle (q.v.), or dip circle, because of its far greater accuracy and precision.

The instrument consists of a coil of wire mounted on a spindle so that it can be spun by a hand-operated crank and flexible cable. The direction of the axis of rotation can be adjusted horizontally and vertically until it is exactly parallel with the direction of the earth's magnetic field. When thus adjusted, the spinning coil does not intersect any lines of the field, and no voltage is induced.

To detect the voltage generated when the coil is not aligned with the magnetic field, the coil windings are connected to a two-segment commutator mounted on the spindle shaft. The electrical circuit is completed through the commutator brushes and a galvanometer of high sensitivity. The galvanometer must be within about 3 feet (1 meter) of the earth inductor so that the operator may easily observe its deflection, but it must not contain a large permanent magnet such as the one found in most laboratory galvanometers. Instead, an astatic galvanometer is used, having two small bar magnets, with opposite polarities, mounted a few centimeters apart on a vertical rod that is suspended by a fine quartz fiber. This kind of mounting reduces the effects of the magnetic field on the galvanometer. The current generated by the spinning coil of the earth inductor is fed through a set of coils that are fixed adjacent to the suspended magnets.

The coil assembly of the earth inductor is mounted in a yoke to which is attached a precisely divided vertical circle for measuring angles. Two readings of the circle are required. One is made with the coil stationary and adjusted so that its axis is exactly vertical, as indicated by a sensitive spirit level permanently placed inside the coil form. The other reading is made after adjusting the inclination angle of the spinning coil until no voltage is generated. The difference between the two readings is a measure of the magnetic dip at the given site. The accuracy obtainable with an observatory earth inductor is about 3 to 5 seconds of arc. A smaller model designed to operate on a tripod for field work has an accuracy of about 15 seconds.

J. H. Nelson, *U.S. Coast and Geodetic Survey*

EARTH PILLAR, in geology, a tower of earth or soft rock. Earth pillars are created chiefly by the action of rain in washing away fine material that surrounds a mass of heavier material in steep slopes. Frequently a large rock remains on top of the pillar, protecting the material directly beneath it from rain. Pillars carved into fantastic shapes in western North America are sometimes called *hoodoos*. Pillars not weathered to slender columns are termed *outliers*.

Earth pillars occur most commonly in areas where precipitation is infrequent and highly concentrated when it does occur. In the United States, Colorado's Garden of the Gods contains interesting examples. The troglodytic dwellings near Erciyaş Dağı in Turkey are carved into earth pillars of volcanic materials.

EARTHENWARE is any nonvitreous pottery, sun-dried or fired, glazed or unglazed. When fired to temperatures above approximately 1250°C, clay vitrifies or fuses and becomes nonporous stoneware or porcelain. Earthenware is any pottery fired at temperatures below this, or merely sun-dried. It is dried but not fired, it retains its tendency to turn again to mud when wet. Fired to temperatures of 500°C or above, earthenware loses this property of returning to mud and becomes hard and brittle. Fired earthenware is porous, however, and liquids stored in it seep through to the outside of the container, where evaporation causes a slight cooling effect. To prevent seepage, earthenware may be glazed. See also Pottery—*Nonvitreous Pottery*.

EARTHLY PARADISE, a poem by the English poet, craftsman, and designer William Morris (q.v.), published in three volumes (1868–1870). It consists of a prologue, an epilogue, lyric interludes, and 24 narrative poems that are largely retellings, inspired by Chaucer's *Canterbury Tales*, of classical and medieval tales. *The Earthly Paradise* is Morris' longest (42,000 lines) and most important work.

Morris conceived the frame for his tales on a large and romantic scale. The prologue tells of a band of Norsemen who escape a land ravaged by the Black Death by sailing in search of the fabled Earthly Paradise, an exquisite and eternal place, far off in the Western seas. Unsuccessful in their search, they arrive, as old men, at a strange, nameless isle inhabited by descendants of the ancient Greeks. There they are greeted hospitably and invited to feast with their hosts twice each month for a year, with the Greeks and the wanderers telling stories alternately. The hosts tell 12 stories from Greek mythology, including *Atalanta's Race*, *Cupid and Psyche*, and *The Love of Alcestis*. The wanderers relate 12 tales from Norse legend, among them *Ogier the Dane*, *The Loves of Gudrun*, and *The Fostering of Aslaug*. Lyric interludes link the pairs of narratives. In the epilogue, Morris pays tribute to Chaucer as his master.

The tales, though overlong and slow-paced, are moving in their increasingly fateful mood. Throughout is an awareness of the brevity of life and the imminence of death, reminiscent of Anglo-Saxon poetry. Morris thought of himself as "the idle singer of an empty day," who sang for those who "Grudge every minute as it passes by,/Made the more mindful that the sweet days die."

Norton B. Crowell, *University of New Mexico*

Ruins left by quake that shook several towns of western Sicily in January 1968 are searched for survivors.

EARTHQUAKE, a shaking of the ground caused by the breaking and shifting of subterranean rock under immense pressure. The vibrations that constitute an earthquake are at times sufficiently severe to damage or destroy man-made structures and to effect visible changes in the earth's surface. Often the vibrations are felt by people but cause no destruction. In the great majority of cases their existence is known only through records of their passage obtained on instruments called seismographs, designed to register this kind of ground movement.

When earthquake waves are recorded by seismographs at distant points, the patterns indicate that the waves originated within a limited region, called the *focus* of the earthquake. It is thought that many foci are in the range of 30 miles (50 km) in length and breadth, but a few of the largest may measure up to 500 or 600 miles (800 to 960 km). Foci have been located at depths down to a little more than $\frac{1}{10}$ of the earth's radius (about 400 miles, or 640 km). An important question for seismologists is why they are no deeper.

Magnitudes. How to express the size of an earthquake has always been a problem. In 1935 a scale based on instrument records was devised by U. S. seismologist Charles F. Richter. He ascribed to each earthquake a number called its magnitude, an index of the quake's energy at its source. According to this scale, an earthquake of magnitude 2.5 has an energy of less than 10^{17} ergs (about the amount of energy released by burning 100 gallons, or 3,800 liters, of gasoline). Such microtremors occur very frequently. An earthquake of magnitude 4.5 (10^{20} ergs) can cause some very local minor damage, while one of magnitude 6 is potentially quite destructive. About 100 quakes of magnitude 6 or higher occur each year. A magnitude of 7 (10^{25} ergs) or higher represents a major earthquake; there may be about 25 such quakes in a year. Only 1 or 2 earthquakes per year have a magnitude of 8 or higher. The most powerful earthquakes that have thus far been recorded by seismological instruments have had a magnitude of 8.6 on the Richter scale.

CAUSES OF EARTHQUAKES

Early peoples believed that the earth was fixed in space, and that the sun, moon, and stars rotated around it. They naturally concluded that the earth must be fixed on some support, and earthquakes were then quite reasonably attributed to movements in that support. In Japan at one time the support was believed to be a great spider, and later a giant catfish. In Mongolia and the Celebes it was believed to be a hog; in India, a gigantic mole; in some parts of South America, a whale; and among some of the North American Indians, a giant tortoise.

Aristotle, working with the four elements of the universe as conceived in his time—air, earth, fire, and water—pictured large masses of air or gases contained in subterranean cavities and heated to the point that they struggled to escape. This struggle and occasional escape, he believed, caused the shaking of the ground that produced earthquakes. Aristotle further expounded the idea that, prior to an earthquake, the atmosphere becomes stifling because the air has been forced or taken into earth cavities in abnormal amounts. This led to the notion that the stuffiness that sometimes accompanies high humidity was a warning of an impending earthquake. The idea that there is such a thing as "earthquake weather" has persisted to this day, although there is no basis in scientific fact for the belief.

It is now recognized that the cause of earthquakes is intimately related to a universal mobility of the earth's surface. There is ample evidence of the existence of forces constantly at work molding the skin of the globe, although the origin of those forces is not known. Evidence is supplied by the data of structural and

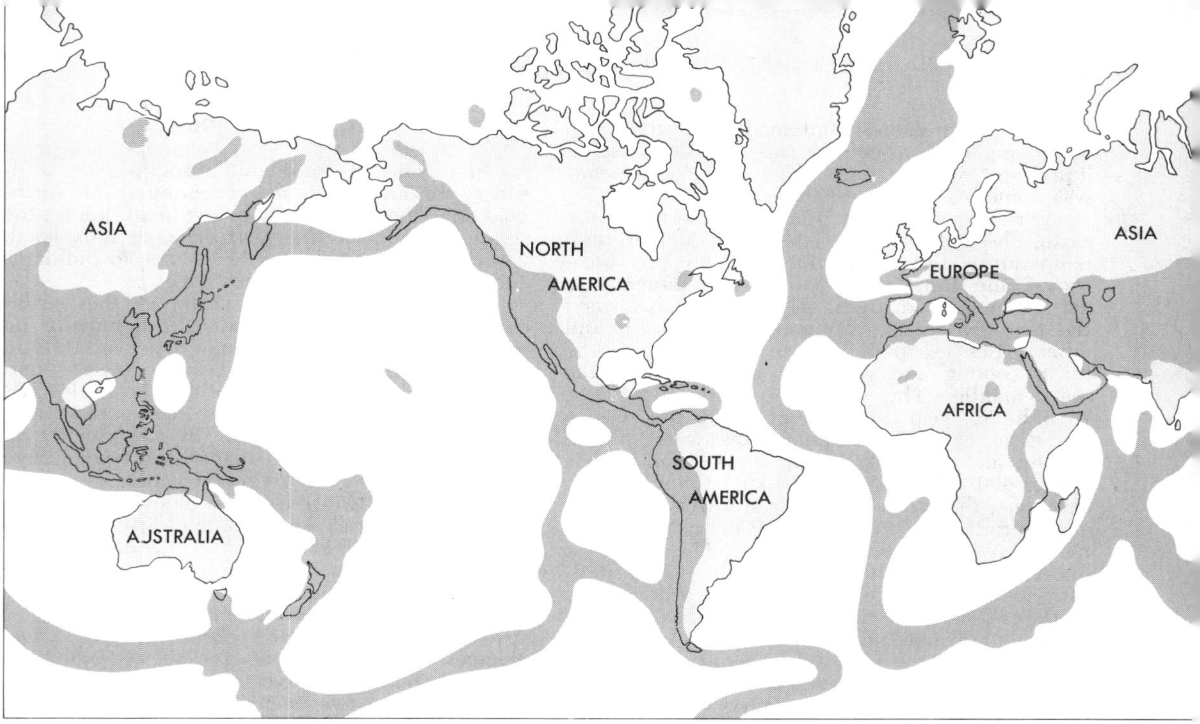

Quake zones of the Pacific Ocean, the Mediterranean area, and Asia release 95% of the world's seismic energy.

historical geology. Thus, every mountain range in the world today consists in large part of sedimentary rocks that were at one time formations on the bottom of an ocean. Theories concerning the ultimate causes of the mobility of the earth's crust have had their origin, for the most part, in attempts to explain mountain making.

Boiling of the Mantle. For half a century, it was generally believed that faulting causes earthquakes. A classic example often cited was California's San Andreas fault, along which a 20-foot (6-meter) displacement occurred at the time of the San Francisco earthquake of April 18, 1906. This hypothesis, however, together with related requirements that earthquake foci occur in rocks of the earth's crust, was upset by new measurements made in the 1960's. Seismologists obtained funds when large quantities of money were allocated to search for means of detecting underground nuclear explosions. This made possible a rapid increase in the number and quality of earthquake measurements through the use of sophisticated modern technology. Computer processing, in particular, was used to cope with the enormous statistical problems of determining location and depth of focus for thousands of quakes each year.

It now appears that an overwhelming portion of the world's earthquakes have their foci in the earth's mantle. Faulting in the crust is a secondary phenomenon; it is damage produced as the crust is deformed by mantle movement. A new hypothesis has been offered to meet the situation. It suggests that the upper mantle is, in effect, boiling, as great masses of steam form and move slowly upward (at a rate of only a few centimeters a year, because of the enormous viscosity of the mantle). The steam and other materials eventually appear at the surface. This hypothesis assumes that the earth's mantle is neither solid, liquid, nor gaseous, but a very hot, random mixture of atoms and molecules, pre-

SEISMOGRAPH RECORDING of the quake that struck Alaska in March 1964 shows the severity of the tremors, which reached a magnitude of 8.5 on the Richter scale.

CALIFORNIA INSTITUTE OF TECHNOLOGY

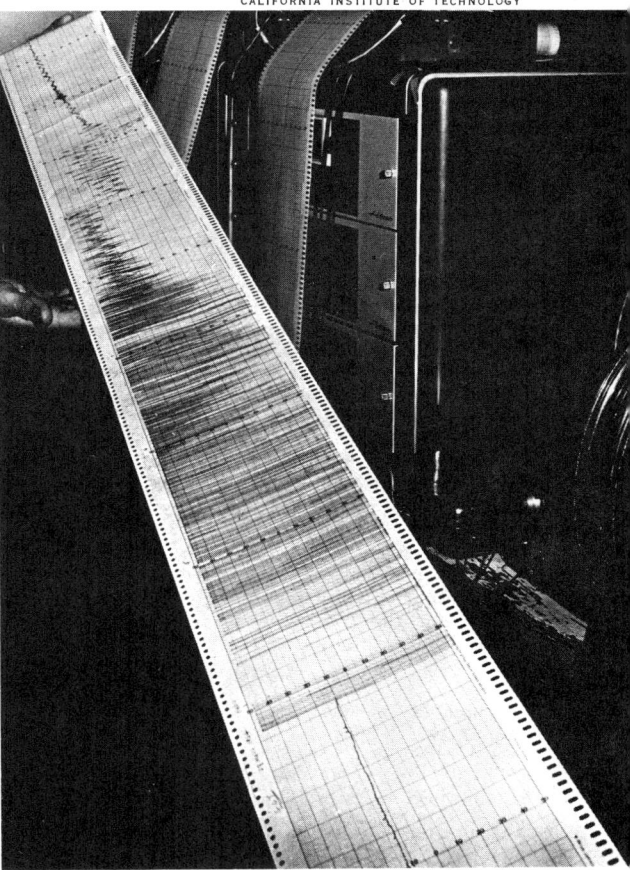

vented by pressure-maintained viscosity from combining to form components of either a solid, liquid, or gaseous state. The name *soliqueous* was coined to designate this state.

Very early in the process of forming the earth, the outside material—which was at high temperature but under little or no pressure—cooled and formed compounds and minerals as gases, liquids, and solids. These materials formed the primitive crust. Components of steam and other gases escaped with magma through the crust, cooling and removing material from the outer mantle. This process is continuing today. In 5 billion years it has brought to the surface the gases of the atmosphere, the water of the oceans, and the rocks of the crust, from a zone 300 to 400 miles (480 to 640 km) thick. Within this zone, the escape of material lowers pressures and permits the formation of more gases and magma, which in turn move out. The process is like a very slow boiling of extremely viscous stuff. Movements are jerky, and each slip produces an earthquake. Below this zone, there has been no movement of material since the earth was formed. The boiling of the mantle is reflected in volcanic activity and the continuous heaving and settling of the crust to form and renew the world's mountains. The ultimate source of energy is primeval heat.

DISTRIBUTION OF EARTHQUAKES

On the average, it is likely that each year there will be one great earthquake, 10 major earthquakes, 100 destructive shocks, 1,000 damaging shocks, 10,000 minor strong shocks, and 100,000 minor shocks. If the very smallest shocks are included, it is likely that the total may be well over a million. On the other hand, one great earthquake may release more energy than the energy released by all the rest of the year's quakes added together.

Roughly 80% of the seismic energy of the world is released in a belt that girdles the Pacific Ocean. A secondary belt, starting in the Mediterranean area and running roughly eastward across Asia, is the scene of earthquakes that represent over 15% of the seismic energy of the world. This leaves less than 5% for the rest of the globe. There are few areas, however, that have not experienced earthquakes, and there have been some very large quakes at places remote from the major belts. Entire regions that are otherwise comparatively quiet may have short periods of unusual high activity. The northeastern region of the United States, for example, is one of these areas.

In general, any region that has had earthquakes in the past may expect them in the future. There may be a lapse between large earthquakes in any area as the strain builds up, but repetitions of previous shocks will inevitably occur. Eight great earthquakes, which represented nearly 25% of the total energy released by quakes since 1900, were located as follows:

Date	Magnitude	Place	Latitude and longitude
Jan. 31, 1906	8.6	Colombia	1° N, 82° W
Aug. 17, 1906	8.4	Chile	33° S, 72° W
Jan. 3, 1911	8.4	Tien Shan Mountains, Asia	44° N, 78° E
Dec. 16, 1920	8.5	Kansu, China	36° N, 105° E
Mar. 2, 1933	8.5	Japan	39° N, 145° E
Aug. 15, 1950	8.6	China	29° N, 97° E
May 22, 1960	8.4	Chile	38° S, 73.5° W
Mar. 27, 1964	8.5	Alaska	61° N, 148° W

EFFECTS OF EARTHQUAKES

In regions of considerable ruggedness, landslides are an inevitable concomitant of earthquakes. They are usually of two main kinds: the simple slump, and the avalanche, or rock flood. Either may be extremely destructive to buildings and human life in populated areas.

Abrupt changes in the level of the earth's surface have been observed at the time of an earthquake. Following a major shock in 1899 in the vicinity of Yakutat Bay, Alaska, it was found that portions of the sea floor had been elevated 50 feet (15 meters). There have also been noticeable horizontal shifts. In the vicinity of San Francisco in 1906, roads and fences were offset by as much as 20 feet (6 meters).

Submarine landslides sometimes have important effects as well. At the time of a severe earthquake in 1929 off the Grand Banks in the North Atlantic Ocean, 12 submarine cables were broken in 28 places by what was believed to have been a gigantic flow of bottom material.

Tsunamis. Submarine landslides or level changes sometimes disturb the ocean to such an extent that a great wave is started out across its surface. The wave is great in the sense of involving large masses of water and having distances of hundreds of miles from crest to crest, but ordinarily it is much too small to be seen in the open ocean. As it approaches a shelving shore, however, there is usually, at first, a pronounced withdrawal of water from the shore—sometimes so slow as to be like an extremely low tide. Then the water returns. Sometimes it comes slowly, sometimes more rapidly, but in any case, the tremendous energy in the wave piles the water higher and higher until it overflows the land with irresistible force. The great seismic sea waves, or tsunamis, are popularly known as tidal waves, although they have nothing to do with ordinary ocean tides.

One of the greatest tsunamis on record is the one that, on Oct. 6, 1737, broke 210 feet (64 meters) in height on the coast of Cape Lopatka, on the southern tip of Kamchatka Peninsula, Siberia. Severe earthquakes off the Aleutian Islands have caused several tsunamis along Hawaiian shores. Such waves have been known to travel as fast as 350 to 500 miles (560 to 800 km) an hour.

Quake-Caused Fires. When an earthquake occurs near a modern city, fire is often a much more destructive agent than the tremors themselves in causing loss of life and property damage. If water mains and fire-fighting equipment are rendered useless, the fires burned unchecked. Thus, in San Francisco, the earthquake of Apr. 18, 1906, was estimated to have caused property damage of about $20 million, whereas the fire that followed caused damage estimated at $40 million. In one of the major catastrophes of modern times, the earthquake of Sept. 1, 1923, near Yokohama and Tokyo, Japan, it was estimated that 95% of the property loss came from fire. Tokyo was nearly 50 miles (80 km) from the source of the quake, but fires started simultaneously in over 200 different places and within 48 hours had gutted 65% of the city. Yokohama, a city of 750,000 persons at that time, was burned to the ground.

Incorrect Ideas About Earthquakes. There are, on the other hand, a number of incorrect notions about what happens during an earthquake. One

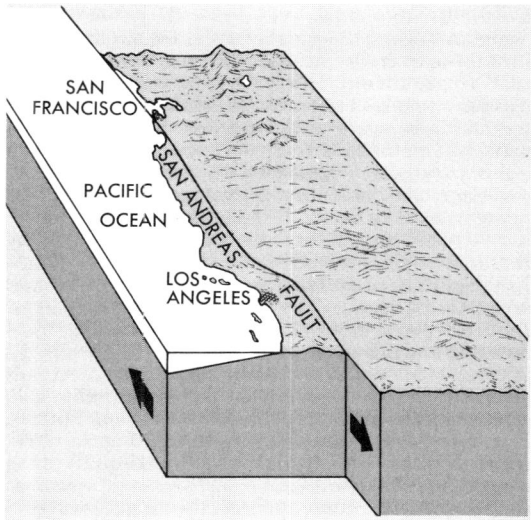

SAN ANDREAS FAULT runs for about 600 miles (950 km) through California's coastal region. Its western side always moves northward in relation to the eastern side. Aerial view (right) shows movements in one area.

U. S. GEOLOGICAL SURVEY

of the most popular of the old wives' tales that have survived for centuries is that sometimes the ground yawns open, swallowing people, houses, and whole villages, then closes awesomely and leaves behind no trace. Actually, unconsolidated sands and clays will sometimes be sufficiently shaken to cause them to slump down slopes and leave cracks near the heads of small slides, or to fall away from beneath hard-surfaced roads, which thereupon crack and break up when left unsupported. There is not one single authenticated case, however, of the earth's solid crust opening into bottomless cracks and swallowing anything. Another popular fantasy that has no basis in fact is that in some way the tremors of earthquakes sometimes bring with them great flashes of fire from the interior of the earth. Such reports have been traced variously to electrical short circuits, meteor swarms, and thunderstorms in the vicinity of the quake.

Earthquake Sounds. As an earthquake occurs, there are frequently vibrations in the ground that disturb the air in such a way as to produce sounds within the range of human hearing. These earthquake sounds have been variously described, but they are usually low and booming. Very near the source of an earthquake the sound sometimes includes sharp snaps that suggest the tearing apart of great blocks of rock. Farther away, the sounds have been likened to heavy vehicles passing rapidly over hard roads, the dragging of heavy boxes over the floor, a loud but distant clap of thunder, an explosion, and the boom of a distant cannon. Earthquakes are accompanied by sound in a very large number of cases, if not in all.

As a rule, the beginning of the sound precedes the first shock to be felt, the largest sound accompanies the greatest shaking, and the end of the sound coincides with the end of the shaking. There are many exceptions, but it is difficult to assemble reliable statistics on a phenomenon of this kind. Anyone who has experienced a severe or even a moderate earthquake knows that the confused impressions that result are so mingled as to render uncertain the subsequent attempts to untangle and classify them.

EARTHQUAKE WAVES

The vibrations in the earth that produce the shaking of an earthquake are not simple things. They are in the form of waves of several kinds. The waves are transmitted by the displacement of particles, which in turn shove against and displace particles next to them and cause the advance of the disturbance.

Kinds of Waves. One kind of wave advances by a pushing and pulling of particles in its path as they move back and forth along the direction of the wave's travel. The technical designation for this wave is *longitudinal wave*. Less impressive but just as acceptable technically is the designation *push-pull wave*.

Another kind of wave advances by shaking particles in its path so that they move in a direction at right angles to the direction in which the wave advances. This kind of wave has several designations, such as *shear wave* (because it advances by means of a shearing displacement of the particles in its path) and *transverse wave* (because particles in its path move transversely to the direction of the wave). The wave is just as recognizable, however, under the name *shake wave*. Push-pull and shake waves travel through the interior of the earth.

A third general class of waves, analogous to waves on water, travels only on the surface of the earth. There are at least two and possibly three different kinds of *surface waves* that have been identified thus far.

Movement of Waves. When a break occurs in the earth's crust, push-pull and shake waves are generated simultaneously. They immediately start out in all directions from the point of origin, but at different speeds. The push-pull wave is the faster, and reaches distant points first. As a result, before its exact physical nature was understood, it was called simply the *primary*

SAN FRANCISCO after the 1906 earthquake. Fire-fighting equipment was rendered useless by the tremor, and the fire that followed was still more destructive.

ROAD IN JAPAN is split in half by a tremor that hit the northern part of the country in May 1968, killing more than 40 people and injuring hundreds of others.

wave. By the same token, the shake wave that came in second was called the *secondary wave.* From these names came the symbols P and S that are commonly used for the waves. Surface waves, because they are the longest of the different kinds, were given the symbol L. Surface waves sometimes stretch out as much as 100 miles (160 km) from crest to crest.

After the earthquake waves start simultaneously from a focus, P gains progressively on S. A place 100 miles (160 km) away is reached by P 20 seconds before S gets there. At a place 1,000 miles (1,610 km) away, P is 2 minutes and 40 seconds ahead of S and 4 minutes ahead of L. At 2,000 miles (3,220 km), P leads S by 4 minutes and 52 seconds, and at 7,175 miles (11,550 km) P leads S by a full 12 minutes. At this distance L is more than a half hour behind P.

In addition to traveling at different speeds, P and S waves differ in another important respect: P can travel in a solid, a liquid, or a gas. The push-pull wave in air and water is a sound wave. In contrast, the shake wave S can exist only in materials that resist attempts to shear—that is, attempts to distort them or change their shape. Such materials do not include liquids and gases. This fact has an important bearing on seismological information about the earth's central core.

RECORDING OF EARTHQUAKES

The principal instrument used by the seismologist is the seismograph, the name of which derives from Greek words meaning "earthquake" and "to write." The main function of a seismograph is to record vibrations in the ground. The most modern form of seismograph is, basically, a weight suspended by springs in such a way that its inertia tends to keep it still when the ground moves under it. The weight, in some cases, is free to move only up and down for registration of vertical ground motion. In other cases, it is free to move in one horizontal direction. A complete set of instruments consists of one that records north-south movements, one for east-west movements, and one for vertical motion.

Attached to the weight in a seismograph are armatures around which are wrapped coils. When the base moves relative to the weight (or the reverse), a small electrical current is generated. The current is conducted to a galvanometer and causes its mirror to move back and forth. A light beam reflected from this mirror is focused on a drum around which is wrapped a sheet of photographic paper. The paper is changed and developed every 24 hours. The drum rotates and moves sideways, so that a continuous line is drawn on it by the light beam. Contacts on a clock cause marks to be placed on this continuous line once every minute. Then, if ground vibrations disturb the instrument, they are translated into displacements of the continuous line on the photographic paper, and time marks are available to determine the exact instant at which the vibrations began.

For example, suppose that an earthquake has an origin that is fairly well known from surface evidence or distribution of its surface effects. The distances from that point of origin to various seismograph stations that recorded the vibrations are therefore known, and it is possible to make timetables for the intervals between the P and S earthquake waves, as well as other waves, as they reach known distances.

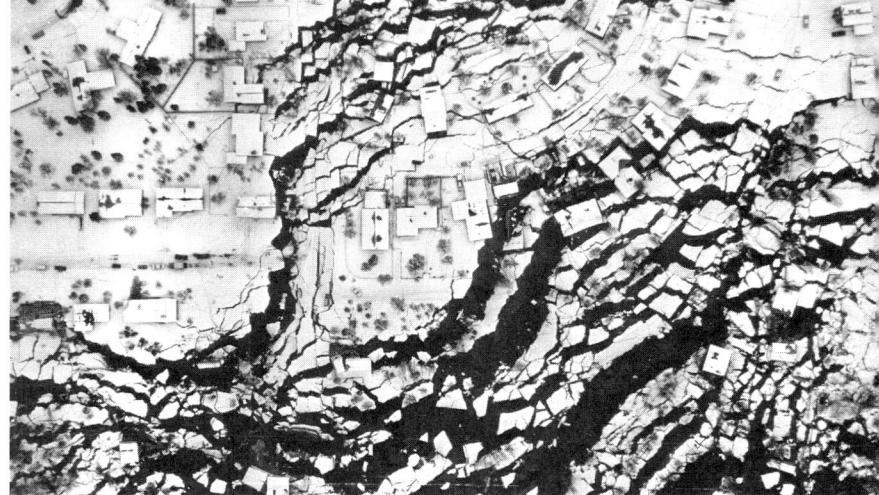

THE DESTRUCTIVE POWER of earthquakes is vividly apparent in these photographs. One side of a street in Anchorage (*top*) fell 10 feet (3 meters) in the 1964 quake; damage in the nearby Turnagain area (*middle*) is viewed from the air. The walls of many adobe houses in Huacho, Peru, collapsed after an earthquake late in 1966 (*bottom*).

(TOP) WIDE WORLD; (MIDDLE) U. S. ARMY, ALASKA MOHAWK PHOTOGRAPHY; (BOTTOM) UPI

AN EARTHQUAKE IS LOCATED by computing its distance from each seismograph station that recorded the quake. An arc of appropriate radius is drawn around each station; the quake lies where the arcs intersect.

SAMPLE TIMETABLE FOR P AND S

Distance from source		Travel time of P		Travel time of S	
Miles	Kilometers	Min	Sec	Min	Sec
100	160	. .	27	. .	47
1,000	1,610	3	20	6	0
2,000	3,220	5	56	10	48
3,000	4,830	8	0	14	30
4,000	6,440	9	50	17	50
5,000	8,050	11	26	20	51
6,000	9,660	12	43	23	27
7,000	11,270	13	50	25	39

Such tables as these are essential tools of the seismologist. They are based entirely on experience. When the records of a station, which are ordinarily changed daily, show an earthquake with P and S clearly evident, the observer determines the intervals between them. By using the interval table, he can find at once the distance to which those intervals apply. For example, if he observes that S arrives 8 minutes after P, he concludes from the table that the earthquake was 4,000 miles (6,440 km) away. He then notes that P arrived at, say, 12 minutes and 22 seconds after 4 A. M. From the travel timetable, it appears that P requires 9 minutes and 50 seconds to travel 4,000 miles. It therefore started that length of time before it reached the station in question, so the time of the earthquake at its source was 4:12:22—9:50, or 4:02:32—that is, it occurred 2 minutes and 32 seconds after 4 A. M.

This process is carried through by all seismograph stations that record a quake. The times that they compute for the instant of the quake should, of course, be in close agreement. Arcs drawn on the globe about each station, with radii equal to the computed distances, intersect at or near the center of the disturbance, and the earthquake is thereby located.

As the waves from an earthquake are traced outward at successively more distant stations, it is found that something happens at just beyond 7,000 miles (11,270 km) from the earthquake's source. The first recorded waves fail to conform to the schedule established up to that point for P. The P wave is late. Worst of all, S disappears or grows so weak that it is lost. It can be shown that P waves that reach a surface point about 7,000 miles from an earthquake have had to penetrate close to 1,800 miles (2,800 km) into the interior of the earth. This is not the depth

SAMPLE TABLE FOR P AND S

Distance from source		Time interval between P and S S minus P	
Miles	Kilometers	Minutes	Seconds
100	160	0	20
1,000	1,610	2	40
2,000	3,220	4	52
3,000	4,830	6	30
4,000	6,440	8	0
5,000	8,050	9	25
6,000	9,660	10	44
7,000	11,270	11	49

In addition to this information, the seismograph station records would show the exact time of day at which these waves reached the different stations. By working backward it is possible to figure the instant at which P and S waves were together—that is, the time of the earthquake at its source of focus. The intervals between waves can then be supplemented by the time it took them to reach the different distances.

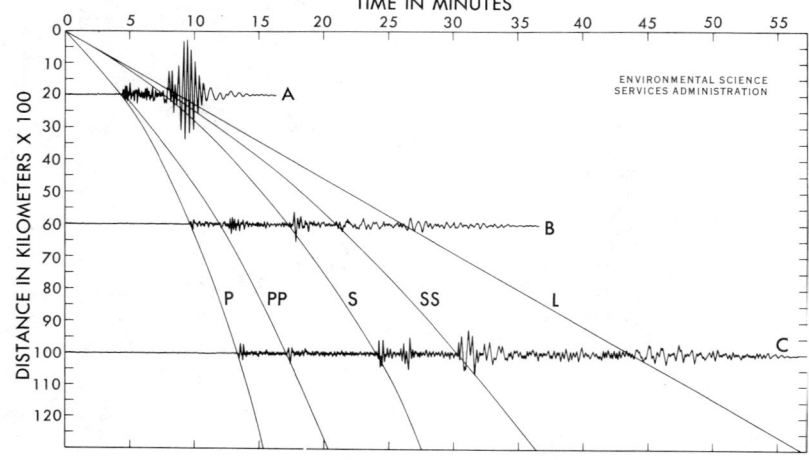

THREE SEISMOGRAMS made at progressively greater distances from a tremor are superimposed on a graph where the P, S, and L waves of the tremor are plotted, to illustrate the effect of distance on the patterns of the recordings. The patterns agree with the time-distance curves of waves.

PORTABLE SEISMIC FIELD STATIONS (*above*) are taken to sites of major quakes to monitor aftershocks. Seismometer was placed in a Colorado cave (*right*) to study the effects of a 1967 underground nuclear test.

penetrated by a chord of the earth's sphere—that is, the shortest path—because the actual path of the waves is slightly curved; the waves follow the path of shortest time rather than that of shortest distance.

From the strange case of the late P wave and the missing S wave, it is learned that the earth has a definite core that begins 1,800 miles below the surface. Whatever its chemical composition, the core is in a condition that will not transmit a shake wave. That is, it is either a gas or a liquid or of such low rigidity that it takes most of the shake out of the S wave and at the same time takes some of the push out of the P wave.

L. DON LEET, *Harvard University*

Further Reading: Bolt, Bruce A., *Earthquakes: A Primer* (W. H. Freeman 1978); Hodgson, John H., *Earthquakes and Earth Structure* (Prentice-Hall 1964); Leet, L. Don, and others, *Physical Geology*, 5th ed. (Prentice-Hall 1978); Oakeshott, G. B., *Volcanoes and Earthquakes* (McGraw 1976); Verney, Peter, *The Earthquake Handbook* (Paddington Press 1979).

MAJOR EARTHQUAKES

856, December—Corinth, Greece: an estimated 45,000 lives lost.

1290, Sept. 27—Chihli (Hopei), China: about 100,000 people killed.

1556, Jan. 24—Shensi, China: up to 800,000 die.

1703, Dec. 30—Edo (now Tokyo), Japan: 200,000 lose lives.

1737, Oct. 11—Calcutta, India: an estimated 300,000 people killed.

1755, Nov. 1—Lisbon, Portugal: 60,000 perish in what was probably the most violent earthquake in historic time.

1883, Aug. 26–28—Netherlands Indies: eruption of Krakatoa; violent explosions destroy two thirds of island; sea waves occur as far away as Cape Horn, and possibly England; estimated 36,000 die.

1891, Oct. 28—Mino and Owari provinces (near Nagoya), Japan: 7,500 killed, 200,000 houses destroyed; classic surface evidence of the break in the crust that caused the earthquake.

1897, June 12—Assam, India: felt over an area of 1,750,000 square miles; scientific reports on this and the Mino-Owari earthquakes represent the beginnings of modern seismology.

1902, May 8—Martinique, West Indies. Mt. Pelée erupts and wipes out city of St.-Pierre; 40,000 dead.

1906, April 18—San Francisco, Calif.: about 500 killed as earthquake and fires destroy center of city.

1908, Dec. 28—Messina, Sicily: about 85,000 killed; city totally destroyed.

1920, Dec. 16—Kansu, China: great landslides caused and about 100,000 killed.

1923, Sept. 1—Japan: Yokohama completely destroyed and Tokyo about 50% destroyed; 95,000 die.

1935, May 31—Quetta, India: an estimated 50,000 die.

1939, Jan. 24—Chile: some 50,000 square miles razed; 30,000 people killed.

1939, Dec. 27—Northern Turkey: severe quakes destroy city of Erzincan; about 100,000 casualties.

1949, Aug. 5—Ecuador: about 6,000 killed; 50 towns razed.

1950, Aug. 15—India: earthquake affects 30,000 square miles in Assam, 20,000–30,000 killed.

1960, Feb. 29–March 1—Agadir, Morocco: earthquakes, tidal waves, and fire destroy 80% of city; estimated 12,000 die.

1962, Sept. 1—Iran: earthquake kills more than 12,000.

1964, March 27—Southern Alaska: earthquake lifts 25,000 sq mi of coastal area; leaves 114 dead.

1968, Aug. 31–Sept. 1—Iran: 18,000 to 20,000 killed in Khurasan province by severe quakes.

1970, May 31—Peru: estimated 70,000 killed, 600,000 homeless; city of Yungay buried by avalanche.

1972, Dec. 23—Managua, Nicaragua: earthquakes destroy the city, killing over 10,000 and injuring 10,000.

1976, Feb. 4—Guatemala: earthquake in area of Guatemala City leaves estimated 23,000 dead, 75,000 injured.

1976, July 28—Northern China: earthquake centered in area bordered by Tangshan, Peking, and Tientsin leaves 655,237 dead and 779,000 injured.

1976, Aug. 17—Philippines: earthquake and tidal wave leave estimated 8,000 dead in southern Mindanao.

1976, Nov. 24—Eastern Turkey: quakes leave 4,000 to 6,000 dead and 250,000 homeless in Van Province.

1978, Sept. 17—Eastern Iran: severe quakes destroy city of Tabas; at least 25,000 killed.

1980, Nov. 23—Southern Italy: earthquake and aftershocks destroy several towns; estimated 4,500 dead.

1981, July 28—Southeastern Iran: earthquake in province of Kerman leaves estimated 8,000 dead.

1982, Dec. 13—Northern Yemen: estimated 3,000 killed and 400,000 left homeless as earthquake destroys 21 villages and heavily damages 274 others.

EARTHSHINE is the dim glow sometimes seen on the crescent moon, on the portion of the face that is not lit by the sun. This glow is sunlight being reflected by the earth onto the moon and is equivalent to moonlight on earth.

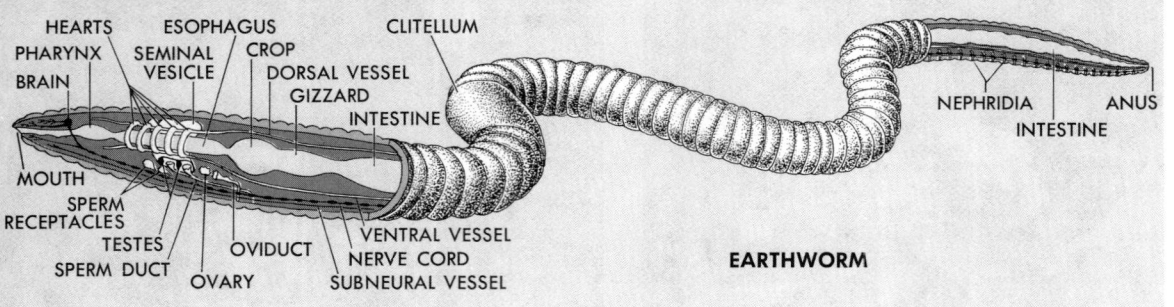

Diagram of an earthworm showing elements of the reproductive, circulatory, nervous, and alimentary systems.

EARTHWORM, any of the terrestrial worms (class Oligochaeta, phylum Annelida) characterized by conspicuous segmentation of the body and the absence of a head. The common night crawler (*Lumbricus terrestris*), is undoubtedly the best-known species. Except for size and occasional color differences, all earthworms look much like this species. Small species of earthworms may measure less than 1 inch (2.5 cm) long, whereas giant species, like *Megascolices australis* from Australia, have been recorded up to 10 feet (3 meters) in length and about 1 inch (2.5 cm) in diameter.

Earthworms occur wherever adequate moisture and food and acceptable soil are found. In good habitats, high population densities are attained: in parts of the Netherlands and New Zealand, for example, there may be as many as 6 million earthworms per acre (nearly 15 million per hectare).

When numerous, earthworms are important geologic agents. They carry the organic materials they have eaten far below the surface; they bring soil passed through the digestive tract to the surface and deposit it as castings—thus helping to create topsoil—and their burrows help air and water to penetrate the soil. Most of this activity occurs in the upper foot (30 cm) or so of the soil, but burrows as deep as 20 feet (6 meters) have been recorded. As much as 40 tons of earth per acre (90 metric tons per hectare) is brought to the surface each year where earthworm populations are maximal.

Earthworms are usually most active in the spring and fall in temperate regions, hibernating in the winter and estivating in the summer.

Body Wall. The body is composed of from about 50 to over 500 similar segments. The well-developed muscles of the body wall are of two types: an outer layer of circular muscles and an inner layer of longitudinal, or lengthwise, muscles. Contraction of the circular muscles squeezes and elongates the body; contraction of the longitudinal muscles shortens it. By contracting and relaxing its muscle layers the worm induces peristaltic waves that propel it forward. Chitinous hairlike structures, called setae, are thrust out to increase friction and aid in movement.

Digestive Tract and Coelom. Contained within the body, like a tube within a tube, is the digestive tract. It is separated from the body wall by a fluid-filled cavity, called the coelom. The coelom is divided into compartments at each segment by partitions called septa.

Circulatory System. Earthworms have well-developed circulatory systems, some containing hemoglobin pigment for oxygen transport. The dorsal blood vessel, lying above the digestive tract, generally serves to propel blood forward by peristaltic contractions. A ventral blood vessel, lying below the digestive tract, serves as the main distributing vessel. The two main vessels are connected by sets of distributing and collecting vessels in each segment. Connective vessels in the esophageal region that are able to pulsate and pump blood are referred to as "hearts."

Nervous System. A dorsal ganglion ("brain") lies above the pharynx. Two circumpharyngeal connectives attach the dorsal ganglion to the subpharyngeal ganglion, lying below the pharynx. A ventral nerve cord, containing a ganglion in each segment, runs from the subpharyngeal ganglion to the rear of the body.

Respiration and Excretion. As a rule, earthworms lack special respiratory organs. Small blood capillaries lie close to the cuticle, or body covering, allowing the circulating blood to obtain oxygen and give off carbon dioxide through the moist body surface.

In nearly every body segment there is one—in some species there are several—pair of long, coiled tubes, called nephridia, used for excretion.

Regeneration. The common night crawler has about 150 body segments. If no more than 10 front segments are cut off, 4 or 5 new ones may be regenerated, or regrown; if at least 35 front segments are left intact, a new posterior may be regrown. A cut after the 11th and before the 36th segment is almost always fatal.

Reproduction. Earthworms are hermaphroditic—that is, each individual possesses both male (testes) and female (ovaries) reproductive organs. Sperm and egg cells are released and mature in the coelom, where the sperm cells enter special pouches called seminal vesicles, or sperm sacs. Similarly formed pouches, called ovisacs, in which the egg cells mature, are sometimes also present. Mature sperm and egg cells are conveyed to body openings (genital pores) by a duct system.

A mutual exchange of sperm occurs during copulation, the sperm being temporarily stored in cavities called seminal receptacles. In sexually mature worms, the body wall of several of the forward segments is thickened by gland cells, forming a more or less conspicuous girdle known as the clitellum. The clitellum secretes bandlike cocoons for some weeks or months after copulation. Sperm and several eggs are placed in each cocoon, but relatively few eggs develop. In *Lumbricus* only a single worm emerges from each cocoon after two or three months of development. The young worm matures in about six months, depending on temperature and moisture. Some species live ten years or more.

PAUL A. MEGLITSCH
Drake University

Further Reading: Stephenson, John, *The Oligochaeta* (Oxford 1930); Satchell, J. E., "Earthworm Biology and Soil Fertility," *Soils and Fertilizers*, vol. 21, pp. 209–219 (Farnham Royal, England, 1958).

U. S. DEPARTMENT OF AGRICULTURE
Earwig

EARWIG, a slender insect of the order Dermaptera, with a pair of forcepslike cerci, or pincers, at the tip of the abdomen. If an earwig is handled, the cerci may grip the skin, but they are not able to pierce it. Possibly the cerci are used to assist in folding the very complicated hind wings, which are semicircular, with supportive veins radiating out in fanlike fashion. When folded, the hind wing is packed way underneath the fore wing, which is reduced to a short, leathery cover. Earwigs rarely fly, perhaps because it is so difficult to stow away the wings. Some wingless earwigs parasitize bats and rats.

It has been suggested that the name "earwig" may be a corruption of "ear wing," a reference to the peculiar type of wing. More commonly, it is believed that the name is derived from the habit attributed to these insects of crawling into the ears of sleeping people. Though now generally discredited as an old superstition, this idea is not without some grounds. Earwigs are nocturnal creatures and spend the day concealed in crevices. They display a reflex orientation (thigmotaxis) to tactile stimuli, or touch, that compels them to squeeze into narrow spaces.

Earwigs have chewing mouthparts and eat either animal or vegetable food. Some forms are predatory and will catch flies and other insects, but earwigs are chiefly scavengers of decaying material. They occasionally feed on living plants and may cause some damage in gardens or greenhouses. A nonpesticide method of control is to clear away plant debris under which the earwigs can hide and then to set up "earwig traps," consisting of flowerpots lightly stuffed with straw, into which the earwigs will crawl at night.

The reproduction of earwigs is of special interest because they practice an elementary form of maternal care. The female lays her eggs in a burrow in the ground and guards them until they hatch, even turning them over from time to time. The young, called nymphs, pass through four to six stages, or instars, before reaching maturity.

There are over 1,000 species of earwigs in the world, 20 of which occur in North America. The native American earwigs, however, are seldom seen. The most familiar European earwig, *Forficula auricularia*, has been introduced by man into the United States, where it is likely to become a minor horticultural pest as it is in Europe.

HAROLD OLDROYD
British Museum (Natural History), London

EARWORM. See CORN EARWORM.

EASEMENT, in law, is the right to make some limited use of another person's land for a specific purpose, or the right to have another person refrain from making certain uses of his own land. An easement involving the privilege of doing acts on lands owned by another is sometimes called an *affirmative easement*, while one consisting of a deprivation of the right of an owner to use his own land as freely as he otherwise could is called a *negative easement*.

Examples of rights frequently included in affirmative easements are the right to pass over another's land (known as a right of way); the right to pollute air over another's land; the right to have buildings supported by another's land; and the maintenance of aqueducts, drains, and sewers on another's property. Examples of negative easements are the assurance that the owner of adjacent land will refrain from obstructing light and air; the right not to have another person's buildings overhang one's adjoining land; and the suspension or modification of water rights between neighboring landowners.

Easements are generally classified as *appurtenant* or *in gross*. An easement that is incidental to the ownership of a piece of land and conducive to its beneficial use is known as appurtenant to that land. An easement that consists simply of a personal right to make a limited use of another's land, without reference to the ownership of a particular piece of land by the owner of the easement, is called in gross. Land to which an appurtenant easement is attached is called the *dominant* tenement or estate, while land that is in some manner burdened by the existence of an easement is called the *servient* tenement or estate. The dominant and servient tenements are usually adjacent to each other, but this is not an absolute requirement.

An easement is usually created by an express grant, but it may also arise from an express reservation, an implied grant or reservation, an adverse use of another's land for a certain period (called *prescription*), the operation of a statute (such as proceedings under the power of *eminent domain*), or an act or representation by the owner of land that precludes him from denying the existence of an easement (called *estoppel*). An easement by grant must generally be in writing, and sometimes must be by an instrument under seal. An easement by reservation is created when a person conveys a portion of his land, reserving certain privileges in it for the benefit of neighboring land retained by him.

An easement by *implied* grant (for the benefit of land conveyed) or by *implied* reservation (for the benefit of land retained) arises when the circumstances are such that the law presumes an intention on the part of the grantor and the grantee that such an easement shall exist.

An easement by prescription may be acquired by making a certain use of land (such as for a right of way) without the owner's permission for a prescribed period of time. An example of an easement by estoppel is the right of way on land retained by a grantor when the grantor, in conveying an adjacent parcel, described it as bounded by a road that is nonexistent.

An easement can be extinguished by the cessation of the purpose for which it was created, by the vesting of title to the dominant and servient tenements in the same person, by express release, or by abandonment.

RICHARD L. HIRSHBERG, *Attorney at Law*

EAST, Edward Murray (1879–1938), American geneticist, who helped develop hybrid corn. It had long been known that crosses between purebred varieties of corn frequently yielded a hybrid strain that was larger and more vigorous than either of the parent varieties. This phenomenon is called *hybrid vigor,* or *heterosis.* One theory to account for it is that each purebred strain has certain (but different) weaknesses and that in the hybrid each weakness inherited from one side is neutralized by a corresponding strength from the other side. Then, too, two different genes on a chromosome pair sometimes produce a cell chemistry better adapted to certain situations than would either gene present as an identical pair.

The first major application of heterosis came in 1910 when East, in collaboration with the American botanist George H. Shull, crossed inbred varieties of corn (maize) and produced hybrid strains with many desirable qualities such as high yield, disease resistance, straight stalks, and well-shaped ears. This hybrid corn was not only useful in itself, but it set the pattern for other applications of heterosis that have served to increase mankind's food supply.

East was born in Du Quoin, Ill., on Oct. 4, 1879, and was educated at the University of Illinois. After spending four years at the Connecticut agricultural experiment station, he joined the faculty at Harvard University in 1909 and became a professor in 1914. In the 1920's he warned mankind of the necessity of population control. East died in Boston on Nov. 9, 1938.

ISAAC ASIMOV
Boston University School of Medicine

EAST AFRICA is the general term for the region of Africa comprising Kenya, Uganda, and Tanzania. The area is coextensive with the territory of the former British East Africa. It is differentiated from "eastern Africa," which also includes Ethiopia, Somalia, Rwanda, Burundi, and Mozambique (Portuguese East Africa).

East Africa has a total population of about 28 million. The people are primarily Africans, but there are large European, Indian, and Arab minorities. Although East Africa is an area of great cultural heterogeneity, Swahili is widely spoken and is considered a lingua franca.

Most of East Africa is a plateau lying 3,000 to 4,500 feet (900–1,400 meters) above sea level. The site of some of the world's most magnificent scenery, the region is dominated by several of the highest peaks in Africa, including Mt. Kilimanjaro (19,565 feet, or 5,963 meters). The eastern and western branches of the Great Rift Valley cross East Africa and contain several large lakes, such as Rudolf and Albert.

After World War I the British colonial government attempted to promote closer union among the territories of East Africa, and the region was united economically through a system of joint services. African nationalists opposed any form of union, however, fearing that it would be dominated by European settlers. Nationalists began to work toward an East African federation only as independence under African rule neared. Tanganyika achieved independence on Dec. 1, 1961, Uganda on Oct. 9, 1962, and Kenya and Zanzibar in December 1963. Tanganyika and Zanzibar united to form Tanzania in 1964. See also BRITISH EAST AFRICA.

L. GRAY COWAN, *Columbia University*

EAST AFRICAN COMMUNITY, an intergovermntal grouping of Kenya, Uganda, and Tanzania, established to speed the development of an East African common market. The Community was inaugurated, with headquarters at Arusha, Tanzania, on Dec. 1, 1967. It succeeded the East African Common Services Organization (EACSO), which was established in 1961 to coordinate the economic affairs of East Africa.

The East African Community (EAC) instituted a common customs tariff, and trade restrictions among the three states were banned except for a transfer tax system, which enables a member state with a trade deficit to impose a transfer tax on other member states. The EAC also established an area development bank and took over the services previously performed by EACSO. The Community's ruling organs are the East African Authority, consisting of the presidents of the member states; ministerial councils; and the East African Legislative Assembly.

EAST AFRICAN HIGH COMMISSION. See BRITISH EAST AFRICA.

EAST ANGLIA, ang′glē-ə, in England, was an independent kingdom in the early Anglo-Saxon period, comprising what is now Norfolk, Suffolk, and part of Cambridgeshire. In modern usage the term occasionally excludes Cambridgeshire or includes other adjacent counties.

East Anglia was one of the most important early kingdoms, but lack of written sources makes it impossible to discern more than the outline of its history. It was settled in the 5th century A.D. by Angles, Saxons, and perhaps Frisians. From about 500 a people of Swedish descent, probably from northern Jutland, appeared there, and some of them may have founded the royal house. To what extent the Celts who had inhabited the area in Roman times survived the invasions is uncertain.

Little is known of the kings of East Anglia until Redwald, who reigned from about 600 to some time between 616 and 627. For a time he was overlord of all England south of the Humber. The wealth of the royal house in the early 7th century is attested by the treasure found at Sutton Hoo (q.v.). The permanent establishment of Christianity in East Anglia dates from the arrival of the first bishop, Felix, in about 630. Archaeological evidence suggests considerable economic development from the later 7th century.

Repeated invasions by Penda, king of Mercia, in the mid-7th century appear to have reduced the power of the East Anglian kings, and thereafter they were often under the overlordship of others. From 841, East Anglia was invaded by the Danes, who in 870 killed King Edmund (St. Edmund). Danes subsequently settled there, and Danish rulers controlled the kingdom from about 880 until their subjection to Edward the Elder in 917 brought East Anglia's independence to an end.

J. CAMPBELL, *Oxford University*

EAST ANGUS, a town in southern Quebec, Canada, on the St. Francis River, is about 95 miles (153 km) east of Montreal. Pulp and paper, bags, sashes and doors, and bricks are manufactured. The town was incorporated in 1912 and named for William Angus, who built the first paper mill here in 1882. Population: 4,016.

EAST ASIA is the term that after World War II was preferred by scholars for the region formerly called the "Far East." The countries usually included in this region are Japan, Korea, and China (mainland and Taiwan). East Asia is the cultural region where the Chinese Confucianist civilization has predominated, although there are distinct variations of this civilization in Korea and Japan, stemming from separate early developments.

The region has a varied climate, ranging from continental in North China to marine in Japan and tropical in South China. The East Asian economy is predominantly agricultural, with rice, vegetables, fish, pork, and soybean products the major elements of the diet.

JAMES R. SHIRLEY
Northern Illinois University

EAST CAPE is a cape on the east coast of North Island, New Zealand. It extends to about 178° E longitude and is the easternmost point of North Island and of New Zealand. The cape has a lighthouse.

EAST CHICAGO is a city in northwestern Indiana, in Lake county, on Indiana Harbor, 2 miles (3 km) east of the city limits of Chicago. The city is an important port. Indiana Harbor canal provides an extensive system of docks within the city limits.

East Chicago is situated in the important Calumet industrial area. It has steel mills and foundries, oil and metal refineries, railroad car and equipment shops, and plants that manufacture chemicals, heavy industrial equipment, and men's clothing.

The title to the land upon which East Chicago stands passed from the United States government to the state of Indiana in 1853. The community was incorporated as a village in 1885 and received a city charter in 1893. Government is by a mayor and council. Population: 39,786.

EAST CHINA SEA. See CHINA SEAS.

EAST CLEVELAND is a city in northeastern Ohio, in Cuyahoga county, near Lake Erie. It is a residential suburb of Cleveland, which adjoins it on the west, but it has varied industries. The Warner-Swasey Observatory of Case Western Reserve University is situated here.

East Cleveland (which should not be confused with a village of the same name that was annexed to Cleveland in 1872) was settled in 1801 and set off as a township in 1805. Collamer and the hamlet of East Cleveland were incorporated as the village of East Cleveland in 1895. A city charter was approved in 1918. Government is by council and city manager. Population: 36,957.

EAST DETROIT, di-troit', is a city in southeastern Michigan, in Macomb county, about 7 miles (11 km) northeast of downtown Detroit, of which it is a residential suburb. It is 3 miles (5 km) west of Lake St. Clair. Automobile and marine parts are manufactured here.

The site was first settled in 1827. In 1925 the community was incorporated as the village of Halfway, so named because of its situation halfway between Mt. Clemens and Detroit. It was incorporated as the city of East Detroit in 1928. The city is administered by a city manager and council. Population: 38,280.

EAST GERMANY. See GERMANY.

EAST GRAND RAPIDS is a residential city in western Michigan, adjoining Grand Rapids. About 95% of the residents own their own homes. There are no industries. It was settled in 1834 and incorporated as a village in 1891 and as a city in 1927. Government is by commission and city manager. Population: 10,914.

EAST GREENLAND CURRENT, a cold ocean current that flows from the Arctic Ocean southward east of Greenland through the Greenland Sea and the Denmark Strait into the North Atlantic. It carries numerous icebergs into the Atlantic.

EAST HAMPTON is a town in southeastern New York, at the eastern end of Long Island, about 100 miles east of New York City. The town, on the Atlantic Ocean, is a resort, fishing, and farming area that comprises the incorporated village of East Hampton (population: 1,886) and the communities of Amagansett, The Springs, Montauk, Wainscott, and part of Sag Harbor.

The house made famous by John Howard Payne in *Home, Sweet Home* is owned and maintained by the village of East Hampton. Clinton Academy erected in 1784, the first academy chartered in New York state, is now a museum. Guild Hall is a cultural center that features exhibits and a permanent art collection and houses the John Drew Memorial Theater. The East Hampton Free Library, organized in 1897, contains the Pennypacker Collection of books and documents.

The town area was settled in 1648 and was first called Maidstone. The village of East Hampton was incorporated in 1920 and is governed by a mayor and a board of trustees. Population: 14,029.

EAST HARTFORD, a town in central Connecticut, is situated on the Connecticut River directly opposite Hartford. It is a major center for the manufacture of aircraft engines. Other principal industries are steel fabrication and the manufacture of paper, stamp and die plates, and candy; the storage and distribution of bulk oil, and the growing and processing of tobacco.

The first settler on the site was John Crow, in 1639. In the 18th century the community became a manufacturing center. An iron mill was operating in 1747, and the first powder mill in America was built on the Hockanum River in 1775. By 1823, East Hartford had a woolen mill, two glass factories, eight powder mills, a hat factory, and several gristmills and sawmills.

East Hartford was incorporated in 1783. Until 1929, government was by town meeting and selectmen. After several changes, a strong mayor-council form of government was adopted. Population: 52,563.

RALPH SECORD
East Hartford Public Library

EAST HAVEN is a town in southern Connecticut, in New Haven county. It is situated 3 miles (5 km) east of New Haven, just north of Long Island Sound. The town is primarily a residential suburb. Some fruits and vegetables are raised in the area. The town includes Lake Saltonstall, the site of the first iron mill in the state. East Haven was incorporated in 1785. Government is by representative town meeting. Population: 25,028.

EAST INDIA COMPANIES were trading companies chartered by European countries in the 17th and 18th centuries to enhance their economic and political power. The lure of profits from spices and gems, and later tea, cotton, and silk, attracted adventurers to the Far East. The actions of these companies resulted in conflict with one another and with local rulers.

Portuguese navigators were the first Europeans to reach the East Indies. In the decades after Vasco da Gama's voyage to India in 1498 the Portuguese placed agents in Socotra, Goa, Malacca, and Canton; reached Banda, the Moluccas, Java, Siam, Formosa, and Japan; and leased Macao. Profits were dissipated by huge payrolls, graft, enemy attacks, and Lisbon's decline as a market.

English penetration of the Indian Ocean began with contact in 1583 with the Mogul emperor Akbar. Despite disastrous expeditions to India in 1591 and Cathay (North China) in 1596, the East India Company was formed in 1600—an event influenced by the raising of the price of pepper by the Portuguese and Dutch.

Dutch activity in the Orient dates from the same period. By 1602, when the States-General of the Netherlands chartered the Dutch East India Company (Oostindische Vereenigde Maatschappij), more than 60 Dutch vessels had sailed to the Far East, fighting the local populations, the Portuguese, and one another. The charter sought to regulate and protect Dutch commerce while promoting the war with Spain. It granted the company a trade monopoly, free customs passage, and authority to raise an army and navy, erect forts, colonize, make war and peace, sign treaties, coin money, and administer justice. The Dutch soon had factors in Banda, Tidore, the Moluccas, Ambon (Amboina), and Japan. They drove the Portuguese from Ceylon and Malacca and began a colony at the Cape of Good Hope.

Spread of Dutch Influence. Trouble between the Dutch and the English erupted in Java when an English fleet, urged by a local sultan, attacked Jacarta (present-day Djakarta). Dutch governor Jan Pieterszoon Coen (q.v.) ejected the English and established his capital there, renaming the city Batavia. A 1619 merger of the Dutch and English companies was aborted by a Dutch massacre of the English on Ambon in 1623. Dutch aggression finally left the English with only a post at Bantam. Dutch influence spread to Sumatra, Siam, Bengal, and the Persian Gulf. In 1669, at its zenith, the Dutch East India Company had 150 merchantmen, 40 warships, and 10,000 soldiers.

Political and military burdens, however, contributed to the company's decline. Local agents lined their pockets. In 1795 the Capetown colony was occupied by the British (to keep it from Napoleon), and they never left. In 1798 the British took Ceylon, and the Netherlands government took over the remaining company holdings.

The English in India. While the Dutch were taking over the East Indies, the English moved into India. Their first east coast factory (trading station) was at Masulipatam (1611). On the west coast, contact with Emperor Jahangir in 1609 was undone by Portuguese intrigues, but retaliation came in 1612 when two English ships defeated a Portuguese fleet off Swally. Jahangir promptly authorized a factory at Surat.

Rival traders plagued the company in the 17th century. The Assada Merchants, licensed in 1635, counterfeited and resorted to piracy, for which all English were blamed. Oliver Cromwell reasserted the East India Company's monopoly, but interlopers created problems, the weavers' guilds in Britain opposed cotton imports, and James II, a major shareholder, was deposed. A rival Scottish company failed, but in 1698 Parliament chartered a new rival company. The two companies were merged in 1702 into the United Company, which became history's largest trading group. In addition to strife with the Portuguese and Dutch, it met competition from the Ostend Company (formed by the Holy Roman emperor in 1722), the Danish East India Company (1729), and the Swedish East India Company (1731).

Mercantilist Warfare. The formation in 1664 by Jean Baptiste Colbert of the French East India Company (Compagnie des Indes Orientales) signaled a century of mercantilist warfare. The French in 1669 got a foothold at Masulipatam and São Thomé. Ejected from the latter by the Dutch, they moved to Pondicherry. By 1690 they were in Chandernagore, Surat, Balasore, and Kasimbazar (Cossimbazar); later they entered Calicut and Mahé. In 1719 the French East India Company and other colonial companies were united into the Compagnie des Indes; the collapse of John Law's financial scheme (see MISSISSIPPI BUBBLE) almost destroyed the company, and reorganization followed in 1722. In that year Joseph François Dupleix arrived in Pondicherry and challenged British primacy in India. The War of the Austrian Succession spilled over into India in 1744, but French successes were reversed by the Treaty of Aix-la-Chapelle.

Hostilities did not end, however, for the French and English backed opposing factions in a local war. Robert Clive defeated the French at Arcot (1751) and the Maratha nawab Sirajud-Daula at Plassey (1757). By 1761 French power was ended; the French firm dissolved in 1769.

Civil and Military Burdens. By this time India was largely in the hands of the British East India Company, as a result of chance as much as of design. The company's primary aim was trade, not conquest, and during its first century there was little interference in internal affairs. Despite reluctance to administer a country divided by religion, language, and political intrigues, the East India Company filled the vacuum created by the decay of the Mogul Empire. Attacks by rival Europeans and harassment by local princes made defense necessary. Increased piracy, Persian invasions, the rampage of the Marathas, and the Black Hole and Patna massacres forced the company to unify India through use of arms. Clive's victories gave the company control of Bengal and a buffer state in Oudh. Questions of sovereignty and politics at home led to partial governmental control with the Regulating Act of 1773. Another war with the French and Marathas ended with English hegemony.

The Indians paid for disorder with the loss of sovereignty, but the East India Company paid for power with heavy civil and military burdens and the frustrations of coping with poverty, suttee, infanticide, thuggee, caste, racial and religious disunity, and the sometimes barbarous activities of its own employees. The company's end came in 1858 when the Sepoy Mutiny precipitated British intervention and India passed to the crown.

RANDALL M. EVANSON
Wisconsin State University, Oshkosh

EAST INDIES. See INDONESIA, REPUBLIC OF.

EAST KILBRIDE, kil'brīd, the largest of Scotland's New Towns, is a burgh 8 miles (13 km) southeast of Glasgow. Formerly a village, it was developed under the New Towns Act of 1946 and by the late 1960's had more than 100 industrial firms, manufacturing a wide range of products. It is also the site of the National Engineering Laboratory of Britain's Department of Scientific and Industrial Research.

East Kilbride is well situated to provide manufactures for Scotland, Northern Ireland, and northern England, and it was recognized as a major growth area in the 1965 regional plan for central Scotland. One of the modern features of the burgh is a traffic-free shopping area. East Kilbride has a high proportion of low-rental housing, which has helped reduce overcrowding in Glasgow, but—along with an unusually large school population—it has taxed the town's resources. Plans for striking a more satisfactory housing balance have been given priority. Population: (1966) 47,490.

C. J. BARTLETT
University of Dundee

EAST LANSING is a city in south central Michigan, in Ingham county, on the Red Cedar River. It adjoins Lansing, of which it is a residential suburb, and is 80 miles (129 km) northwest of Detroit.

East Lansing is the seat of Michigan State University, a 4-year coeducational institution. Originally chartered in 1855 as the Agricultural College of the State of Michigan and later called Michigan State University of Agriculture and Applied Sciences, it was the first state agricultural college in the United States. There is no industry in East Lansing, and the activities of the community are centered around the university. Grain, sugar beets, and livestock are raised in the surrounding area.

The first settler came to the area now within the city limits in 1849. East Lansing received its city charter in 1907. Since 1944 it has been governed by a council and city manager. Population: 48,309.

EAST LIVERPOOL, a city in eastern Ohio, in Columbiana county, is on the Ohio River, 95 miles (155 km) southeast of Cleveland. The manufacture of ceramic products, such as general ware, electrical porcelain and pottery supplies, is the principal industry. The pottery industry was founded by James Bennett in 1840. He built a one-kiln pottery and began making yellow and Rockingham ware. White ware was produced first in 1860. The clays are obtained principally from Florida, Kentucky, North Carolina, and England. East Liverpool also produces cartons, paving, steel lining, building and fire brick, and sewer pipe. There are machine shops, foundries, and ice cream and ice plants.

The city was settled in 1795 and incorporated in 1834. Government is by mayor and council. Population: 16,687.

EAST LONDON is a city in South Africa, in the southeastern part of Cape province. It is situated on the Indian Ocean, at the mouth of the Buffalo River. The city is South Africa's fourth-largest port in terms of tonnage and the only river port in the country.

East London is the commercial center for a large hinterland that includes parts of Orange Free State and Cape provinces, Lesotho, and the Transkei. Its major exports are wool, meat, fruits, and dairy products. Some industry has been attracted to the city, which has good rail and road connections to the interior.

The area first attained importance in 1847 when it was used as a supply base during the Kaffir wars. The town and port were established the following year. Use of the harbor was restricted by silting until breakwaters were built in the 1870's. Dredging operations are still carried on to maintain sufficient depth for cargo ships. Population: (1960) 113,746.

EDWARD J. MILES
University of Vermont

EAST LONGMEADOW is a town in southwestern Massachusetts, in Hampden county, 5 miles (8 km) southeast of Springfield. It is a residential community with some manufacturing. It was detached from Longmeadow (founded 1644) in 1894. The community is governed by town meeting with three elected selectmen. Population: 12,905.

EAST LOTHIAN, lō'thē-ən, is a county in southeastern Scotland, east of Edinburgh, between the Firth of Forth and the Lammermuir Hills. The coastal strip is a cultivated plain that produces grain, turnips, and potatoes. The southern uplands are pastoral, but woodlands are expanding. Stock raising and market gardening are important. Haddington, the county town, has a grain market and a number of light engineering industries.

East Lothian includes several islands, notably the Bass Rock, which has been a fortress and prison and a lighthouse site. It is now a bird sanctuary. On the hill of Traprain Law a hoard of silver, dating from about the 4th century A.D., believed to be the plunder of a raid by the Romans, was discovered in 1919. The feudal castles of Dirleton, Tantallon, and Hailes are noteworthy.

Oliver Cromwell defeated the Scots at Dunbar in 1650, and Prince Charles Edward Stuart routed the Hanoverian forces at Prestonpans in 1745, in the Rising of the Forty-five. John Knox, the religious reformer, was born in or near Haddington about 1515. Population (1961): 52,653.

D. B. HORN
University of Edinburgh

EAST LYNNE is a novel by the English author Mrs. Henry Wood, published in 1861. A highly sentimental and melodramatic work of little artistic value, it was extraordinarily popular both in its original form and in the stage version, also by Mrs. Wood, which was first produced in 1861.

The heroine, Lady Isabel Vane, mistakenly doubts her husband's fidelity and leaves him for another man several years after her marriage. Later she returns in disguise as nurse to her own children. She ultimately discovers that she had wrongly suspected her husband and, broken in spirit and in health, dies after receiving his forgiveness on her death bed. The expression "Next week, East Lynne" eventually became a sarcastic response to any excessive display of sentiment.

EAST MASSAPEQUA, mas-ə-pē′kwə, is an unincorporated community in southeastern New York, in Nassau county, near the southern shore of Long Island. The community, which is part of Oyster Bay township, is about 30 miles (48 km) southeast of downtown New York City. East Massapequa is primarily a residential center. Population: 13,987.

EAST MEADOW, an unincorporated area of Nassau county in southeastern New York, is in Hempstead Township on western Long Island, 4 miles (6 km) southeast of Mineola and about 23 miles (37 km) east of New York City. East Meadow is a residential community. Population: 39,317.

EAST MILLCREEK, an unincorporated area of Salt Lake county, in northern Utah, is a residential suburb of Salt Lake City, about 10 miles (16 km) southeast of the center of the city. It was settled by Mormon pioneers in 1847. Population: 24,150.

EAST MOLINE, mō-lēn′, is a city in northwestern Illinois, in Rock Island county, on the Mississippi River. It is a part of the metropolitan area that includes Rock Island and Moline, Ill., and Davenport, Iowa. Farm implements are manufactured here. East Moline is governed by a mayor and council. Population: 20,907.

EAST NORTHPORT, an unincorporated area of Huntington township in southeastern New York, is in Suffolk county on the north shore of Long Island, just southeast of Northport and about 40 miles (68 km) east of New York City. It is a residential community. Population: 20,187.

EAST ORANGE is a city in northeastern New Jersey, in Essex county, bordering Newark on the west. It is a residential suburb of Newark and New York City and is the largest of the four Oranges (Orange, West Orange, South Orange, and East Orange).

Industries in East Orange include photo enlarging and the manufacture of hydrants, waterworks supplies, audiovisual equipment, and plastic tubes. The city is a major insurance center, with home, branch, and regional offices of more than 65 companies. It is the seat of Upsala College, a 4-year coeducational institution founded in 1893, and of the East Orange Veterans' Hospital.

Citizens of Newark first settled the area in 1678. Until 1863, East Orange was part of the city of Orange; in that year it was incorporated as a separate township. In 1899 it was chartered as a city. It has a mayor-council form of government. Population: 77,690.

LEARNED T. BULMAN
East Orange Public Library

EAST PALO ALTO, a city in San Mateo county, California, on the west shore of San Francisco Bay, adjacent to Palo Alto. The city contains steel, paper, and chemical plants and is the site of Nairobi College for blacks. The city was incorporated in 1983. Government is by a mayor and council. Population: 18,191.

EAST PEORIA, pē-ôr′ē-ə, an industrial city in north central Illinois, in Tazewell county, is on the Illinois River, opposite Peoria, of which it is a suburb. It is 60 miles (96 km) north of Springfield. The manufacture of tractors is the chief industry of East Peoria. Fort Creve Coeur State Park, site of the first French fort in Illinois, is just south of the city at Creve Coeur. East Peoria was incorporated in 1919 and is governed by a commission. Population: 22,385.

EAST POINT, a city in northwest central Georgia, in Fulton county, is 6 miles (10 km) southwest of Atlanta. Its manufactured products include textiles, machinery, commercial fertilizers, and chemicals. In the Civil War it was a key point in the Confederate defenses of Atlanta when the army of Gen. William T. Sherman besieged the city in 1864. Government is by mayor and council. Population: 37,486.

EAST PROVIDENCE, a city in eastern Rhode Island, is in Providence county, on the east bank of the Providence and Seekonk rivers, opposite Providence. The principal industries are chemicals, fabricated metals, machinery, electronics, jewelry, plastics, printing, and paper. There are also oil-storage facilities and trucking terminals.

The Emma Pendleton Bradley Hospital, one of the world's first neuropsychiatric hospitals for children, is in the city. Thomas Willett, the first mayor of New York City, resided in East Providence in his later years and is buried in Little Neck Cemetery in the Riverside section of the city.

East Providence originally was part of Plymouth Colony, Massachusetts. Later it became part of Rehoboth, Mass., and in 1812 of Seekonk, Mass. To settle a dispute over the location of the state border, a section of Seekonk was annexed to Rhode Island in 1862 and was named East Providence. Government is by council-manager. Population: 50,980.

VIRGINIA B. CONNER
Anne Ide Fuller Library

EAST PRUSSIA, prush′ə, a former province of Germany on the Baltic Sea, was partitioned between Poland and the Soviet Union after World War II. On the eve of the war, East Prussia (German, *Ostpreussen*) was an area of about 14,283 square miles (36,992 sq km), with a population of about 2.5 million. It is a low-lying, heavily forested area, thickly covered with glacial deposits and studded with lakes. Its chief economic activities are shipbuilding, lumbering, fishing, farming, and stock raising. Lignite and amber are mined.

Early History. The name "Prussia" comes from Borussi or Prussi, the name of a Baltic tribe that was either assimilated or exterminated by the Germans and the Slavs in the Middle Ages. In 1226 the Teutonic (German) Knights were asked by Conrad of Masovia, a Polish prince who ruled the middle Vistula River basin, to help drive back the pagan Prussi. The Knights obliged and kept East Prussia for themselves. They not only built castles to control the country but also introduced German settlers and developed ports.

In 1466 the Poles secured for themselves part of the territory, but the remainder continued to be ruled, under the nominal sovereignty of Poland, by the grand masters of the Teutonic Knights. In 1525 the last grand master, Albert of Brandenburg, secularized the lands of the Knights and made them hereditary in his own family. In 1619, the Knights' former territory was inherited by the elector of Brandenburg, and

EAST PRUSSIA IN 1929

in 1657, Polish sovereignty over it was ended by the Treaty of Wehlau.

In 1701, Elector Frederick III of Brandenburg assumed the title of Frederick I, King of Prussia. During the partition of Poland in 1772, the area between East Prussia and Pomerania, sometimes known as West Prussia, was annexed by Prussia, together with those parts of East Prussia that Poland had governed since the 15th century.

Modern History. East Prussia remained part of Prussia until the revival of Poland in 1918. The Treaty of Versailles made minor boundary changes, giving Poland part of West Prussia (the so-called Polish Corridor) and providing for a plebiscite in certain areas of mixed population in southern East Prussia, which elected to remain in Germany. Lithuania incorporated Memel, a small strip of territory north of the Niemen River.

In 1945 the Potsdam Conference confirmed decisions concerning East Prussia that had been reached during Allied war conferences. East Prussia was partitioned by a west-east line from roughly Braniewo (Braunsberg) to Gołdap, with the Soviet Union taking the area to the north and Poland occupying that to the south.

NORMAN J. G. POUNDS
Indiana University

EAST RIDGE, a town in southeastern Tennessee, in Hamilton county, is situated just south of Chattanooga, of which it is a residential suburb. It was incorporated in 1921. Government is by mayor and commission. Population: 21,236.

EAST RIVER, in New York City, a strait connecting Long Island Sound on the north and upper New York Bay to the south. It is about 16 miles (25 km) long and varies in width from about 1,000 yards (915 meters) to 3 miles (5 km). Manhattan Island (the borough of Manhattan) forms the west shore and Long Island (the boroughs of Queens and Brooklyn) the east shore. The Harlem River enters from the west near the north end of the East River. Welfare, Randall's, Ward's, Rikers, and North Brother islands are in the East River. Various types of city institutions are situated on these islands.

A part of the river between Ward's Island and Long Island is called Hell Gate, because of reefs that formerly were a danger to navigation. The reefs were blasted away, and large vessels operating between New York and New England ports and along the coast now use the passage. The Brooklyn, Manhattan, Williamsburg, Queensboro, and Triborough bridges, for vehicular traffic, and the Hell Gate railroad bridge span the East River, and several subway tunnels and the Queens-Midtown vehicular tunnel have been built under it.

EAST ROCKAWAY is a village in southeastern New York, on Long Island, about 20 miles (32 km) east of New York City. It is a commuter residential center on the Rockaway peninsula, fronting on Hewlett Bay.

The first settlement was grouped around a grist mill built in 1688. The mill has been moved from its original site to a village park and is a museum sponsored by the Old Grist Mill Historical Society of East Rockaway. The village of East Rockaway was incorporated in 1900 and is governed by a mayor and board of trustees. Population: 10,917.

EAST ST. LOUIS, a city in southwestern Illinois, in St. Clair county, is on the east bank of the Mississippi River opposite St. Louis, Mo., to which it is connected by four bridges. The city is an important industrial center. Steel, oil refinery equipment, machinery, gasoline, brick and tile, pigments, and meat products are among the principal manufactures. East St. Louis is also a livestock center. The surrounding area is agricultural, with rich bottomlands, and there are also valuable rock quarries.

One of the best-known memorials in Illinois is the Cahokia Courthouse, situated on the outskirts of the city, which draws thousands of tourists. Built about 1837, it is believed to be the oldest courthouse west of the Allegheny Mountains. Parks College of Aeronautical Technology of St. Louis University is near the city and offers tours of its facilities. East St. Louis has more than 1,500 acres (607 hectares) of parks.

The first permanent settler on the site was Capt. James Piggott, who established a ferry service across the Mississippi about 1795. The village of Illinoistown was platted near the ferry in 1817. The name was changed to East St. Louis in 1861, and the community was incorporated as a city in 1865. Since 1917 it has had a commission form of government. Population: 55,200.

EUGENIA MCCLINTON
Public Library, East St. Louis, Ill.

EASTBOURNE, ēst′bôrn, a county borough in southern Sussex, England, is on the English Channel, 52 miles (84 km) southeast of London. It is a resort center with parks and gardens and a 3-mile (6-km) promenade along the terraced sea front. Devonshire Park is named for William Cavendish, 7th Duke of Devonshire and chief landowner in the area, who was largely responsible for development of the town late in the 19th century.

The Old Town, the original settlement, is 1 mile (2 km) inland and has a 12th century parish church. Eastbourne was incorporated in 1883. Population: (1961) 154,296.

EASTER, the principal Christian feast day, celebrates the Resurrection of Jesus Christ. Most Christian churches in the West observe Easter on the first Sunday after the full moon that comes on or after the vernal equinox (March 21). Thus, Easter falls within a 35-day period between March 22 and April 25, inclusive. The date of Easter in some Eastern churches may vary from the Western date.

Origin of the Name. The origin of the English word "Easter" is uncertain. In the 8th century, the Venerable Bede proposed that it was derived from the name of an Anglo-Saxon goddess of spring, Eostre. This view has long been popular, but another explanation has been offered. In the early church, Easter week was called *hebdomada alba* ("white week"), because of the white garments worn by those baptized at Easter. The plural of white was later misunderstood as the plural of dawn and so translated into Old High German as *eostarum*, from which the English word "Easter" was derived.

In the Romance and some other languages, the word for Easter is derived from the Hebrew *Pesach* (Passover) through its Greek transliteration *Pascha*. Recent Biblical and liturgical usage has employed the noun "Pasch" and the adjective "Paschal" in speaking of the Christian celebration.

History and Date. The history of Easter, as well as its theological and liturgical significance, is rooted in the Old Testament. In the Book of Exodus, "Passover" refers not only to the Angel of Death "passing over" the houses of the Jews in Egypt but also to Israel's deliverance from servitude—the exodus from Egypt and the entrance into the Promised Land. The Jewish Passover feast joined the theme of gratitude for divine deliverance with a spring harvest feast in which the first produce of the year was offered to God. Since Christ was crucified during Passover, the Christian commemoration of His death not only coincided with Passover, but also incorporated elements of the Jewish feast. Thus Easter is the Christian Passover.

Passover, which was celebrated on the 14th day of Nisan in the Jewish lunar calendar, could fall on any day of the week. Some early Christians, called Quartodecimans, observed Easter on the 14th Nisan. However, most Christians felt that Easter should always be observed on a Sunday, the weekly celebration of the Resurrection. The attempt to impose the Sunday observance on the Quartodecimans led to heated controversies in the 2d century. Eventually, it was decided at the Council of Nicaea (325) that Easter be observed on the Sunday after both the 14th Nisan and the vernal equinox.

While the date of Passover (and Easter) was calculated according to a fixed date in a lunar calendar, it had to be expressed as a variable date in the imperial or Julian solar calendar, which most Christians followed in daily life. It was obviously desirable to devise a long-range list of future dates according to a predetermined pattern or cycle in the solar calendar. Devising such a cycle proved extremely complicated for the methods then available. Various cycles (of 16, 19, 84, even of 532 years) were constructed in various places and resulted in further controversies, lasting until the 9th century, about the date of Easter. A further divergence in the date of Easter began in 1582 with the introduction of the Gregorian calendar, which some countries were slow in adopting.

Easter is now uniformly observed by Western churches; however, Easter may still fall on a different date in those Eastern churches that use a different method of calculation. The proposal of a perpetual calendar, in which each date falls on the same day of the week every year and in which Easter would fall on a fixed Sunday, presents no theological difficulty.

Theological-Liturgical Significance. The central theme of Easter is the celebration of the death, Resurrection, and Ascension of Christ, and the sending of the Holy Spirit to the church. The richness of this theme was gradually expanded into a protracted period of liturgical celebration. Thus the weeks immediately preceding and immediately following Easter were times of special devotion. Eventually, Easter was preceded by an extended period of preparation (Lent) and followed by a 50-day period of celebration (Eastertide or Paschaltide) that lasted until Pentecost.

Easter is envisioned not merely as a commemoration of a past event but also as a manifestation of Christ's death and Resurrection to new life shared by those believing in Him. Hence Easter was an appropriate time for the administration of baptism, which symbolizes the baptized person's deliverance from evil and rising to a new life in Christ. Because prospective converts or catechumens needed to receive instruction prior to their baptism, the Lenten season was devoted to catechetical instruction. Lent was also associated with Christ's 40-day fast and His Passion and was observed as a penitential period.

In the early church, every Sunday began with a vigil service consisting of scriptural readings and responses, but the vigil of Easter attained a special solemnity that it still retains in Catholic and Orthodox liturgies. In the modern Roman liturgy, for example, the Easter vigil begins at the church entrance with the blessing of a newly kindled fire. This serves to light the Paschal candle and the candles carried in procession into the darkened church. The symbolism of light reminds the worshipers that the risen Christ is the light of the world overcoming death and the darkness of evil. Then the deacon chants the *Exsultet*, which recalls God's deliverance of His people in times past; a similar theme is found in the Scripture readings that follow. Next comes the blessing of the baptismal font, followed by the baptism of catechumens and the renewal of baptismal vows by those present. Finally, at midnight there is the celebration of the Easter Eucharist. In the early church the newly baptized were clothed in white garments to symbolize their deliverance from the darkness of sin through the light of the risen Christ.

The Protestant observance of Easter has varied through the centuries. Some churches have always given a special place to Easter. Other denominations, particularly those influenced by Puritanism, once tended to reject any special observance. In the United States the observance of Easter became more prominent during the Civil War, when Easter Sunday was set aside as a day of remembrance for those who had died in that war.

In the 20th century, Easter has received considerable emphasis in American Protestant churches as a commemoration of Christ's Resurrection, a confirmation of Christian faith, and an expression of the joyous character of Christian belief. In many churches Easter is the culmination of a series of services held during Lent and especially during Holy Week, when Communion services are held on Maundy Thursday in commemoration of the Last Supper and Good Friday services recall the Crucifixion. Many churches hold an outdoor service at dawn on Easter in re-enactment of the Gospel narrative of the discovery of Christ's Resurrection. This sunrise service aptly symbolizes the end of darkness and the awakening of hope among Christians. Frequently, the Holy Week and Easter services are interdenominational.

Popular Customs. Many customs have become associated with Easter at different times and places. Some customs are popular dramatizations of the Gospel accounts of Christ's Passion and Resurrection. A Palm Sunday procession reenacting Christ's entry into Jerusalem is common and is a part of some official liturgies. In some places it is customary to reenact other events, such as the Crucifixion, the burial, and the visitation of the tomb. During the Middle Ages such dramatizations evolved into complete plays, some of which are still performed today.

The origins of some customs and their association with Easter are not always easily determined. Some customs may be adaptations of practices originally associated with pagan spring festivals or with local folklore. However, such practices can prevail without any explicit connection being recognized. Eggs, for example, are central to a variety of Easter customs. A number of explanations have been suggested. Formerly, eggs were forbidden during the Lenten fast but could again be eaten at Easter. Thus, decorated eggs could symbolize the end of the penitential season and the beginning of joyful celebration. Also, eggs, as traditional symbols of life and creation, suggest the Resurrection. Likewise, eggs, colored like the rays of the returning sun or the northern lights, symbolize the return of spring. In any case, it has become customary in many places to decorate and exchange eggs at Easter; sometimes, eggs are blessed in church. Also egg rolling and egg hunting have become traditional in some places, such as at the White House in Washington, D.C. The most elaborate custom developed in imperial Russia, where the nobility exchanged egg-shaped curios made of precious materials and decorated with jewels.

Associated with Easter in popular lore are flowers, particularly the lily, and also animals. The rabbit, an ancient symbol of fertility, and the chicken are popularly portrayed as laying eggs in nests prepared for them or hiding eggs for children to find. In some places, it is customary to prepare butter or baked goods shaped like lambs. The lamb signifies the natural fecundity of spring while also symbolizing the "Lamb of God," the crucified and risen Christ.

Thus, throughout the customs associated with Easter, there is a blending or interplay of symbols of spring with the religious significance of the Resurrection. Such a blending is found more generally in Easter itself. It is both an occasion marking the beginning of spring by preparing special foods and wearing new or distinctive apparel and also the feast when the Christian reaffirms his basic faith in Christ.

JOHN T. FORD, C. S. C.
Catholic University of America

Further Reading: Bouyer, Louis, *The Paschal Mystery*, tr. by Sister Mary Benoit (Chicago 1951); Dix, Gregory, *The Shape of the Liturgy* (Naperville, Ill., 1964); Hole, Christina, *Easter and Its Customs: A Brief Study* (Clifton, N. J., 1961).

EASTER ISLAND is a small, barren, isolated island in the Pacific Ocean, situated at latitude 27°08'37"S and longitude 109°26'10"W. The easternmost outpost of Polynesia, it lies 1,100 miles (1,750 km) east of lonely Pitcairn Island and 2,200 miles (3,500 km) off the coast of Chile, of which it is a dependency. In 1968 the native population was about 1,000, in addition to a few Chilean officials.

Of volcanic origin without coral reef, the roughly triangular island measures about 14 by 7 miles (23 by 11 km), with an extinct volcano near each corner, the highest rising about 1,800 feet (550 meters) above sea level. The rough lava coast is predominantly high and precipitous, without any harbor but with a sandy beach at Anakena Bay on the north shore. There are no streams, but some prehistoric wells with brackish water are located near the coast, and there are also three partly overgrown freshwater crater lakes, the largest of which, in the deep caldron of Rano Kao, measures nearly 1 mile (1.6 km) in diameter.

The climate is subtropical, with dry and steady southeasterly trade winds in the summer, and heavy rainfall averaging nearly 50 inches (1.3 meters) in the winter. At the time of European discovery, seabirds were the only fauna apart from the chickens, rats, and lizards introduced by the aboriginal natives. Today there are numerous flies and cockroaches, as well as semiwild cats and a species of hawk; the domesticated animals include horses, sheep, pigs, and some cattle. The flora, too, was poor; the island was mainly covered by native grasses, which have in modern times been replaced by European species. With the exception of a small forest of toro-miro trees (*Sophora toromiro*) surviving in the Rano Kao crater until recently, the early Europeans found only small clusters of such shrubs as *Triumfetta semitriloba*, *Thespesia populnea*, *Santalum*, and *Sapindus saponaria*. Aboriginal culture was above all based on sweet potatoes (*Ipomoea batatas*); other cultivated plants included sugarcane (*Saccharum officinarum*), gourd (*Lagenaria siceraria*), banana (*Musa sapientum*), totora (*Scirpus riparius*), and paper mulberry (*Broussonetia papyrifera*). Today eucalyptus and coconut palms have been planted in several places.

Modern History. Easter Island remained unknown to Europeans until accidentally hit upon in 1722 by the Dutch admiral Jakob Roggeveen, who named it after his day of discovery, Easter Sunday. The native names for the island are Rapa Nui and Te-Pito-o-te-Henua, the latter meaning "the navel of the world." A rediscovery was made in 1770 by the Spanish captain Felipe González, who named the island San Carlos. Subsequent visitors were James Cook in 1774 and the Comte de La Pérouse in 1786.

During the following century a number of vessels made brief calls without much affecting the native culture, but in 1862 a flotilla of Peruvian slave raiders carried away some 1,000 natives, about one third of the population, including the last king and the *tangata rongo-rongo* (learned men), to work on the guano islands off Peru. Nearly all died within a year; the 15 who survived the return voyage brought back to Easter Island a smallpox epidemic that killed all but 111 of the total island population. In 1864 the first missionaries settled on the island, and they brought the entire population together in Hangaroa village on the west coast. Apart from the

EASTER ISLAND is famous for its prehistoric statues on the slope of Rano Raraku, an extinct volcano. More than 600 statues have been found.

efforts of this Roman Catholic mission, the island was entirely neglected until Chile, in 1888, took formal possession. Chile leased over four fifths of the island to a British wool-growing company, reserving for the natives the remainder of the land around the village. In 1954 the Chilean government turned over the island and the sheep range to naval administration.

Strong efforts have been made to fight the serious epidemics of influenza and the exceptionally high rate of leprosy among the natives, and the island has a hospital and a leper settlement.

For some time the only regular contact with the mainland was provided by a naval vessel that visited the island once a year in January to load wool and unload necessities; but in 1967 an airport was opened, and since then tourists have begun to swarm to the island.

Archaeology. Easter Island is famous for numerous colossal stone statues of prehistoric origin which have been the source of much guesswork and wild speculation. A systematic survey of the surface archaeology was made in 1914 by a private British expedition led by Katherine Scoresby Routledge, and was continued in 1934–1935 by a Franco-Belgian expedition with Henri Lavachery as archaeologist and Alfred Métraux as ethnologist. In 1955-1956 a private Norwegian expedition, organized and led by Thor Heyerdahl and with Edwin N. Ferdon, William Mulloy, Arne Skjölsvold, and Carlyle S. Smith as archaeologists, conducted the first organized excavations with radiocarbon datings and pollen borings, a work resumed in 1960 by Mulloy and others.

It appears that by 380 A.D. (with a possible margin either way of 100 years) the island already had an extensive population engaged in reshaping a natural fissure between two ancient lava flows to form a defensive ditch nearly 2 miles (3 km) long, 12 feet (4 meters) deep, and about 40 feet (12 meters) wide, which protected the access to the cliff-girded plateau of Poike. At this time the island was wooded with several plant species that were subsequently exterminated. The earliest stone constructions on the island differed from the subsequent island *ahu* both in shape and masonry technique. Elevated platforms were built of huge basalt blocks of irregular size and shape, put together in such a way that the visible part of each stone was smoothly polished and shaped to fit its neighbor precisely without the use of cement. The strategic positions and conventionalized technique indicate partly defensive and partly ceremonial functions in this first phase. This highly specialized stonework and associated statues of the same early period are strongly reminiscent of characteristic features in pre-Inca sites of northwestern South America.

Archaeology also reveals a very distinct second cultural phase. A new wave of immigrants reached the island and demolished all the former fitted-masonry walls to rebuild them as *ahus*, ceremonial bases for the huge homogeneous monuments characteristic of this second period. Former statues were demolished and used as filling in the crude architecture of the newcomers. The *ahus* were given a long, vertical retaining wall facing the sea, with secondary wings on the flanks, and with an originally stepped inland side subsequently filled with boulders to form a sloping incline leading down to a ceremonial court. Secondary burial vaults were added. Most *ahus* carried 4 to 6 giant statues, or fewer, but Ahu Tongariki carried 15.

The giant *moai* (statues) of the second epoch differed from the smaller statues of the first epoch in being of a homogeneous and local style, all being carved from the yellowish tuff of the Rano Raraku volcano. Unfinished statues in the quarry reveal that the fronts and sides were finished with crude basalt hand picks. The statues were then temporarily raised in pits to have their backs completed before they were dragged to destinations all over the island. They were raised onto *ahus* by wedging countless small stones underneath the statues and prying them upward with poles. Below the tall heads the statues had full-length torsos ending in flat, flaring bases without legs. The arms are long and slender, with hands bent and fingers close together on each side of the masculine member. Female statues are rare. Not until erected on an *ahu* did statues receive eyes and a large cylindrical *pukao* or topknot of red tuff on the head. More than 600 statues are known, measuring usually from 12 to 25 feet (4 to 8 meters) in height. The largest statue raised on an *ahu* measures 32 feet (10 meters) high, weighs about 50 tons, and once carried a 10-ton topknot. The largest one standing in a pit measures 40 feet (12 meters) high, and the largest unfinished statue in the quarry, 69 feet (21 meters). The largest topknot measures 600 cubic feet (17 cu meters) and weighs roughly 30 tons.

Even the secular dwellings of Easter Island's early periods differed completely from those of all other islands in Polynesia. One type comprised circular stone houses with core-filled masonry walls, conical thatch roofs, and entrances through the ceilings. Another type included low lenticular stone houses with cribwork at the corners and with corbeled slab roofs covered by earth. Whereas stone houses of any form are unknown on all other Pacific islands, both these house types are typical of the Titicaca area of southern Peru and northern Bolivia and Chile, on the mainland nearest Easter Island. There, as on Easter Island, the stone houses are generally clustered together as contiguous-room villages, another feature unknown elsewhere in Polynesia. Toward the end of the second cultural epoch, lenticular huts of a previously existing type, with cut stone foundations, curved ridgepoles, and arching walls of sticks covered by totora reeds, became the prevalent dwelling structures.

About 1680 A. D. a civil war between the second-epoch stone sculptors and the arriving Polynesians started an era of decadence and cannibalism on the island, during which all statues were overthrown from the *ahus*, the last falling in 1840. During this period the natives frequently abandoned their haycock-shaped reed houses and found refuge in large caves, and even now family treasures are preserved in secret caves supposedly protected by spirits called *aku-akus*.

The victorious Polynesians, who probably arrived from the Marquesas Islands, confined their own art to wood carving and lava sculptures, the ever-repeated motifs being long-eared, half-decayed men with goatees, and birdmen. They retain vivid traditional memories of their ingenious predecessors, who are referred to as "long-ears" because of their habit of enlarging the ear lobes. Their main cult center was a semisubterranean mountain village, Orongo, where an annual birdman was proclaimed after a swimming competition to find the first egg of the *manu tara* birds.

Strange wooden tablets with incised inscriptions were found in the hands of the 19th century natives, who carried them while reciting religious chants but were unable to read or write the script. The tablets are still undeciphered, despite occasional claims to the contrary.

All immigrants to Easter Island have arrived by sea. Theories of a submerged continent are contrary to available evidence, as paved prehistoric roads lead to landing places on the present coastline.

THOR HEYERDAHL, *Head, Norwegian Archaeological Expedition to Easter Island*

Bibliography

Ferdon, Edwin, *One Man's Log* (London 1966).
Heyerdahl, Thor, *Aku-aku* (Chicago 1958).
Heyerdahl, Thor, and others, *Reports of the Norwegian Archaeological Expedition to Easter Island*: vol. 1, *Archaeology of Easter Island*; vol. 2, *Miscellaneous Papers*; vol. 3, *Art of Easter Island* (London and Chicago 1961–1968).
Métraux, Alfred, *Ethnology of Easter Island* (Honolulu 1940).
Routledge, Katherine S., *The Mystery of Easter Island* (London 1919).

EASTER RISING, in Irish history, the climax in 1916 of a long series of revolutionary struggles in Ireland. The outbreak of World War I in 1914 furnished an opportunity for revolt against English rule. Three local forces combined to make the rising possible: (1) the Irish Republican Brotherhood, which was responsible for the military planning and whose leaders included Tom Clarke, the last of the Fenians (q.v.), and Patrick Pearse; (2) the Irish Volunteers, numbering about 16,000, led by Eoin MacNeill and Pearse and armed with German weapons smuggled into the country at Howth in July 1914; and (3) the Citizen Army of about 200, formed by James Connolly from the Dublin workers after the collapse of the 1913 general strike.

Prelude. Pearse, the main inspiration of the rising, realized that it had no chance of ultimate success, but he hoped that if it could be sustained for two or three weeks, world opinion—and especially American opinion—would be mobilized on behalf of Ireland. Yet even for that limited goal two conditions were necessary and neither was fulfilled. One was the acquisition of additional arms from Germany; the other was that the rising should be nationwide.

To obtain weapons, Sir Roger Casement (q.v.) had gone to Germany in 1914. He gradually became convinced that sufficient German aid would not be forthcoming, and in April 1916 he returned to Ireland in a U-boat to urge that the rising be canceled. On Good Friday, April 21, he was arrested soon after landing at Banna Strand in Kerry and was sent to London. The Germans actually did send a ship, the *Aud*, with a cargo of obsolete Russian rifles, but the British admiralty had broken the German naval code and intercepted the *Aud* off the coast of Kerry.

When news of Casement's capture reached MacNeill, he canceled the mobilization of the Volunteers ordered for Easter Sunday. Despite the confusion, Pearse, Connolly, and Clarke were resolved to proceed with the rising—but it had to be postponed one day and was limited in operation to Dublin.

Revolt. On Easter Monday, April 24, about 1,500 Volunteers and 200 men from the Citizen Army seized key points in Dublin. From headquarters at the General Post Office they issued a proclamation, written by Pearse, that established an Irish republic and a provisional government. Pearse was declared president and commander in chief. The proclamation was signed by seven men—Clarke, Pearse, Connolly, Thomas MacDonagh, Sean MacDermott, Eamonn Ceannt, and Joseph Plunkett—each of whom was signing his own death warrant.

The insurgents fought with bravery and chivalry, but they had no artillery and were heavily outnumbered. Within 48 hours some 5,000 British soldiers were in Dublin. Artillery battered the rebel positions; their ammunition was soon exhausted; and after six days Pearse surrendered, on Saturday, April 29.

About 450 people were killed in the rising and more than 2,500 wounded. Most were civilians. Some 56 Volunteers and 130 British soldiers died. Much of Dublin was destroyed. Between May 3 and 12, 15 leaders of the rising were shot, and 75 others were condemned to death (their sentences were later commuted). About 2,000 Irishmen were deported to England.

The rising had been unpopular in Dublin, but the protracted executions caused a revulsion. As Pearse had foreseen, the leaders became martyrs. Casement's execution in London on August 3 intensified the sentiment. In the next election (1918), Sinn Féin (Republicans) swept the country, and on Jan. 21, 1919, the republic was again proclaimed. After 30 months of fighting, the British evacuated southern Ireland in 1922 and handed over the government to the Free State. The rising was vindicated.

GIOVANNI COSTIGAN, *University of Washington*

EASTERN CHURCHES, Catholic, those churches in union with the pope of Rome that have retained their ancient and distinctive liturgies and rites, laws and customs. These churches originated some time between the apostolic age and the 6th century, when they were organized in the eastern Byzantine portion of the Roman Empire, in Persia, and in Armenia. Within this territorial area the patriarchates of Alexandria, Antioch, and Constantinople came to exert great influence over surrounding territories. The neighboring communities adopted the customs of the patriarchates and thus evolved five basic rites or liturgical families: Alexandrian, Antiochene (or West Syrian), Byzantine, East Syrian, and Armenian. Ultimately, all Eastern churches can be traced to these rites.

Estrangement between the Eastern and Western churches began in 431, when the Persian church separated itself from the rest of the churches due to the Nestorian controversy. Twenty years later the Christological controversy over Monophysitism also split the church; the Alexandrian, Antiochene, and Armenian churches rejected the Christological doctrine of the Council of Chalcedon (451) in favor of the Monophysite teaching and they too left the main body. By the 5th century, the "orthodox" or "right-teaching" church included only the Roman and Byzantine churches. When, after 1054, the Byzantine Rite churches no longer recognized union with Rome, it may be said that the Eastern Catholic churches, as such, had ceased to exist with, perhaps, the exception of the Italo-Albanians in Sicily and southern Italy, who remained in union with Rome, and the Maronites.

The Eastern Catholic churches, therefore, are more exactly defined as those groups of Orthodox, Nestorian, and Monophysite churches that reunited with Rome from the 12th to the 20th century. In recognizing the primacy of the pope, however, they did not adopt Roman customs but retained their Eastern traditions.

This gradual process of reunion began in 1198 when, through contact with the Crusaders, some Monophysite Armenians in Syria formed the Armenian Catholic Church. Reunion on a large scale was attempted by the Eastern churches and the Roman Church at the councils of Lyon (1274) and Florence (1439), but these unions were of short duration.

After the Eastern churches (Orthodox, Nestorian, and Monophysite) fell under Muslim rule in the 15th century, Rome realized the difficulties involved in large-scale reunion and changed its tactics. Missionary orders, such as the Capuchins, Jesuits, Franciscans, and Dominicans were encouraged, at least implicitly, to proselytize among the Eastern Christians. In addition, Unia, the movement to attract splinter groups to unite to Rome, was launched in the Middle East and western Russia. The Unia movement was to some extent successful: the Chaldeans, or Nestorians, entered into union with Rome in 1552; the largest group to reunite was the Ukrainians and White Russians whose metropolitan, Michael Ragoza, and bishops formed the Union of Brest-Litovsk in 1595 to petition Rome for reunion. A Syrian Catholic Church was developed in 1663, and the Arab-speaking Melchites united with Rome in 1729; and the Catholic Coptic Church dates from 1895. A more recent union was effected in 1930, when the Jacobite Indian Syrians became a new Catholic Church, the Malankar.

Rite and Ethnic Group	Eastern Catholics
Alexandrian	
Coptic	82,894
Ethiopian	59,215
Antiochene	
Malankar	124,433
Maronite	850,000
Syrian	80,000
Armenian	97,000
Byzantine	
Albanian	400
Bulgarian	9,480
Georgian	10,000
Greek	2,872
Hungarian	250,000
Italo-Albanian	70,000
Melchite	397,611
Rumanian	1,572,979
Russian	3,000
Ruthenian	778,555
Slovak	305,645
Ukrainian	4,340,000
White Russian	35,000
Yugoslavian	56,000
Chaldean	
Chaldean	190,000
Malabar	1,349,360

Source: *Oriente Cattolico: Cenni storici e statistiche* (Rome 1962)

EASTERN CATHOLICS IN NORTH AMERICA

The approximately 800,000 Eastern Catholics in the United States and the 220,000 in Canada represent 11 ethnic groups and 8 rites. The majority are of Slavic origin and use the Byzantine Rite. Most of the Eastern Catholics migrated to North America in the latter part of the 19th century. At first they were deprived of their own bishops and, contrary to their ancient tradition, were forced to accept a celibate clergy. As a result, many of them turned to the Orthodox Church; it is estimated that 400,000—or more than 60% of the faithful of the American Russian Orthodox Church—converted from Eastern Catholicism. Diminution in their number also resulted from the insufficient numbers of priests available to serve them and from intermarriage between Latin and Eastern Catholics. The contemporary Eastern Churches in the U. S., however, are attempting to adapt the ancient customs, especially in the use of the vernacular in the liturgy, to meet the needs of the modern generation.

The Ukrainians, Ruthenians (the U. S. group embraces Ruthenians, Slovaks, Hungarians, and Croatians of the Byzantine Rite), Maronites, and Melchites have their own bishops. The Ukrainian eparchies (dioceses) are in Philadelphia, Chicago, and Stamford, Conn.; the Ruthenian eparchies are in Pittsburgh and Passaic, N. J.; the Maronite bishop resides in Detroit; and the Melchite prelate resides in Boston. The remaining Eastern Catholic groups—Armenians, Chaldeans, Italo-Albanians, Rumanians, Russians, Syrians, and White Russians—are governed by local Latin Ordinaries.

GEORGE A. MALONEY, S. J.
Fordham University

Further Reading: Attwater, Donald, *The Christian Churches of the East*, 2 vols., rev. ed. (Milwaukee 1961–1962); King, Archdale A., *The Rites of Eastern Christendom*, 2 vols. (London 1950).

EASTERN EMPIRE. See BYZANTINE EMPIRE.

EASTERN ORTHODOX CHURCH. See ORTHODOX EASTERN CHURCH.

EASTERN QUESTION, the term used to describe the problems in European diplomacy caused by the decline of the Ottoman Empire and the subsequent revolt of its subject Christian people. Until the end of the 17th century the Ottoman Empire had been a constant threat to Europe, but the failure of the second Ottoman assault on Vienna in 1683 had marked the turn of the tide. Thereafter the empire lost territory to both Russia and Austria. By the Treaty of Karlowitz (1699) Austria received most of Hungary, Transylvania, Croatia, and Slavonia; Poland and Venice also gained Ottoman territory.

In the 18th century the greatest acquisitions of Ottoman territory were made by Russia, particularly during the reign of Catherine the Great. By the Treaty of Kuchuk Kainarji (1774), Russia also gained the right to intervene in behalf of the Christian inhabitants of the Ottoman possessions of Wallachia and Moldavia, and it was later to claim that the agreement gave it a special position in regard to all the Christian inhabitants of the empire.

Great Power Interests. The decline of Ottoman military power was paralleled by the internal decay of the state. By the beginning of the 19th century the danger existed that the empire would simply fall apart. Because of the strategic location of the Ottoman territories, the great powers were concerned about their fate.

After 1815 the three states chiefly involved in Ottoman affairs were Russia, Britain, and Austria. Both Austria and Britain feared that Russia, because of its close relations with the people of the Balkan peninsula—through their common Orthodox religion and the fact that the majority of the Balkan peoples were Slavic—would gain control of the area. Britain believed that such an eventuality would endanger its communications with its empire; and Austria did not wish to be surrounded by Russian-controlled lands to the south and east in addition to the ones in the north. Although the Russian government did not have direct designs on the Balkan peninsula, it was concerned over the fate of the Turkish Straits, the exit from the Black Sea to the Mediterranean. There was also sympathy for the Christian people under Muslim rule.

Crises. Throughout the 19th century a series of crises, centering chiefly on the Balkan area, often brought the powers to the brink of war. In general, Britain and Austria supported the maintenance of the Ottoman Empire; Russia was more willing to accept the formation of national states. The first successful revolt of a Christian nation against the empire was that of Serbia (1804–1815). The second revolution, that of the Greeks, had far wider European repercussions. In 1821 revolts broke out in both the Morea (Peloponnesus) and the Danubian principalities (Wallachia and Moldavia). Although they defeated the movement in the Danubian principalities, the Turkish armies were not able to put down the rebellion in the Greek lands. In 1826 and 1827, Russia, France, and Britain together attempted to settle the question. In 1828, Russia and the Ottoman Empire went to war over other matters. Russian armies marched into the Balkans and almost reached Constantinople. By the Treaty of Adrianople (1829), Russia was awarded the mouth of the Danube, as well as a protectorship over Serbia and the Danubian principalities. Greece was to be an autonomous state. In 1830 a small but independent Greek state was established, and Serbia was declared autonomous.

In the 1830's the chief problem in the Middle East was the attempt of Mohammed (Mehmet) Ali, the pasha of Egypt and a vassal of the Turkish sultan, and his son Ibrahim to set up a strong Egyptian state including Syria. In 1833 the Ottoman Empire was forced to accept an alliance with Russia by the Treaty of Unkiar Skelessi to gain support against Egypt. In the later 1830's the great powers intervened to protect the sultan against his rebellious vassal. In 1841 the Convention of the Straits was concluded; it put the Turkish Straits under international control for the first time.

Crimean War. The principal conflict in the 19th century involving the Eastern Question was the Crimean War (1853–1856) in which Britain, France, the Ottoman Empire, and Sardinia-Piedmont fought Russia in an attempt to check the extension of Russian influence over the empire. After an allied invasion of the Crimea and the capture of the fortress of Sevastopol, Russia was forced to accept the allied terms. By the Peace of Paris (1856) the Black Sea was demilitarized; Russia lost southern Bessarabia (acquired in 1812) and gave up its claim to an exclusive protectorate over the Balkan Christians.

Balkan Conflicts. The 1870's represented another period of intense crisis. In 1875 a revolt against Ottoman rule broke out in Bosnia-Herzegovina, followed in 1876 by an uprising in Bulgaria. Also in 1876, Serbia and Montenegro became involved in a war with the Ottoman Empire. After the great powers failed to negotiate a settlement, Russia in 1877 again conducted a successful campaign against the empire. In March 1878, by the Treaty of San Stefano, the Russians won a very advantageous peace, which upset the balance of power in the Balkans. Under the pressure of the other powers, Russia was forced to submit this agreement to revision at the Congress of Berlin (June–July, 1878). The congress established a Bulgarian state, smaller than the one created by Russia in the Treaty of San Stefano. It confirmed the independence of Rumania, Serbia, and Montenegro.

Between 1878 and 1908 crises occurred over Bulgaria, Macedonia, and Armenia and over the full annexation by Austria-Hungary of Bosnia-Herzegovina, which had been under Habsburg administration since 1878. But no major territorial change in the Balkans occurred until 1912. At that time Greece, Montenegro, Serbia, and Bulgaria joined in a war against the Ottoman Empire, which they quickly defeated. In a quarrel over the spoils, Bulgaria became involved in a war with its neighbors. As a result of these two Balkan wars, the major portion of Macedonia was divided between Greece and Serbia, although Bulgaria received an outlet on the Aegean. Rumania gained part of Dobrudja, and an independent Albania was established. Thus by the beginning of World War I the Ottoman Empire had lost its European possessions, and successor states had been established in the Balkans. See also BALKANS—*4. History.*

BARBARA JELAVICH AND CHARLES JELAVICH
Indiana University

Further Reading: Anderson, Matthew Smith, *The Eastern Question* (London 1966).

EASTERN RITE. See EASTERN CHURCHES, CATHOLIC.

EASTERN STAR, Order of the, a fraternal society associated with Freemasonry and composed of Master Masons, their wives, daughters, mothers, widows, and sisters. The order is dedicated to serving people in need, to social enjoyment and to promoting civic interests. It gives Eastern Star Training Awards for Religious Leadership, to needy students; makes contributions to the International Peace Garden (a memorial at the boundary between North Dakota and Manitoba), and the International Eastern Star Temple, Washington, D.C.; and aids cancer research. Eastern Star Grand Chapters maintain homes for the aged and for orphaned children of members. Local chapters, in addition to providing assistance to the projects mentioned, pursue a number of their own private charities.

The beginning of the Order of the Eastern Star is not known, although records indicate that a similar organization existed in France during the 18th century. It was introduced in the United States by Rob Morris of La Grange, Ky., an ardent Mason, teacher, poet, lawyer, minister, and philosopher, who wrote the first ritual in 1850 and who revised and published it in 1865 as *The Rosary of the Eastern Star*.

The General Grand Chapter, organized in 1876, has headquarters in Washington, D.C. It exercises jurisdiction over 14,000 chapter in the United States, Canada, and many other countries. By the late 1960's membership in the Order of the Eastern Star totaled almost 3,000,000.

MAMIE LANDER
Order of the Eastern Star

EASTERN TOWNSHIPS, a region in southeastern Quebec, Canada, comprising a large portion of the territory between the St. Lawrence River and the United States border. The French form of the name is Les Cantons de l'Est. The region extends from Dorchester county in the northeast to Missisquoi county in the southwest, and includes 13 other counties. The total area of Eastern Townships is about 9,120 square miles (23,610 sq km).

Mines in Drummond and Megantic counties yield a major share of the world's asbestos. Sheep raising, fruit growing, and maple sugar production are also important in the area. Manufacturing centers produce pulp and paper, textiles, machinery and furniture.

The region was surveyed in 1791, when the English land laws superseded French seigneurial tenure in Lower Canada. The name "Eastern Townships" was used to distinguish the tract from the Western Townships west of Montreal. The land was originally occupied by settlers of British stock, but now a majority of the population is French-speaking.

EASTHAMPTON, ēst'hamp-tən, a town in central Massachusetts, in Hampshire county, is 12 miles (19 km) northwest of Springfield. It is situated in a farming region. Printing is an important industry, and the city produces textiles, clothing, men's furnishings, rubber goods, rubber thread, felt, elastic webbing, brushes, castings, metal doors, and household chemicals. Williston Academy, a school for boys, is located here.

Easthampton was settled in 1664. The settlement was almost destroyed by the Indians in the spring of 1704. It was incorporated as a town in 1809. It has a town meeting form of government. Population: 15,580.

EASTLAKE, Sir Charles Lock (1793–1865), English painter and author, who was the first director of London's National Gallery. He was born in Plymouth, England, on Nov. 17, 1793, and studied in London with Benjamin Haydon, a painter of historical subjects, and at the Royal Academy. In 1815, Eastlake painted *Bonaparte on Board the Bellerophon* from sketches made while Napoleon was held prisoner on shipboard in Plymouth harbor. From 1816 to 1830 he lived in Italy, where he made use of the Italian landscape in such pictures as *Lord Byron's Dream* (1829).

As keeper (1843–1847) of the National Gallery and later as its first director (1855–1865), Eastlake was largely responsible for assembling the gallery's great Italian collection. He was knighted in 1850 when he became president of the Royal Academy. His best-known book is *Materials for the History of Oil Painting* (1847). Eastlake died at Pisa, Italy, on Dec. 24, 1865.

EASTLAKE is a city in northeastern Ohio, in Lake county, just south of Lake Erie. It is situated 16 miles (26 km) northeast of downtown Cleveland, of which it is a residential suburb.

The surrounding area was first settled about 1850. Eastlake was incorporated as a city in 1948. It has a mayor-council form of government. Population: 22,104.

EASTLAND, James Oliver (1904–   ), American political leader. He was born in Doddsville, Miss., on Nov. 28, 1904. Educated at the University of Mississippi, Vanderbilt University, and the University of Alabama, he was admitted to the bar in 1927. He was a member of the Mississippi House of Representatives from 1928 to 1932.

Appointed to the U.S. Senate to fill a vacancy in 1941, he served for three months. In 1942 he was elected to the Senate as a Democrat from Mississippi and was regularly reelected thereafter. As a member of the Senate Judiciary Committee, which has jurisdiction over civil rights bills as well as over the federal courts, Eastland consistently opposed civil rights legislation and denounced the Supreme Court for its 1954 decision outlawing segregation in the public schools. In 1956 he became chairman of the Judiciary Committee under seniority rule, and in 1972 he was elected president pro tempore of the Senate.

EASTMAN, Charles Alexander (1858–1939), American physician and writer. A Wahpeton (Santee) Sioux, he was born in Redwood Falls, Minn. His Indian name was Ohiyesa. He graduated from Dartmouth (1887) and took his medical degree at Boston University (1890). For the next three years he was physician at Pine Ridge Agency, S. Dak., the first Indian to hold such a position. A witness to much of the Ghost Dance excitement, he was among the first to visit the scene of the Wounded Knee massacre.

In 1891, Eastman married the poet Elaine Goodale. After a brief period of private practice, he was active in YMCA and Boy Scout work. His great contribution was in interpreting Indians and whites to each other. Among his many writings are *The Soul of the Indian* (1911) and *From the Deep Woods to Civilization* (1916). Eastman died in Detroit on Jan. 8, 1939.

EDGAR I. STEWART
Eastern Washington State College

EASTMAN, George (1854–1932), American industrialist and philanthropist, who popularized photography. Eastman was born in Waterville, N.Y., on July 12, 1854, and began photography as a hobby while a bookkeeper in a bank in Rochester. In 1879 he devised an improved machine for applying gelatin emulsion to glass to make dry photographic plates, and shortly afterward he began manufacturing them. The business prospered, but it was clear that it would remain small as long as the market was confined to a few amateur and professional photographers.

Eastman, aware of the need for a simple procedure for taking pictures, took the first steps toward making photography available to everyone. He introduced flexible film in 1884 and a simple box camera, the Kodak, in 1889. The new film and camera, backed by aggressive advertising, made Kodak a household word. More than 100,000 of his cameras were sold in the first two years, an unprecedented achievement in the photographic industry.

After making many improvements both in cameras and in films, Eastman reorganized his business as the Eastman Kodak Co. in Rochester in 1892. By the turn of the century it employed over 3,000 persons throughout the world.

Eastman was a pioneer in the exploitation of foreign markets, the spending of large sums of money for industrial research, large-scale advertising, and organized marketing. He also pioneered in establishing health services, retirement plans, and profit-sharing plans for employees.

Eastman's gifts to education began with $50 to the Mechanics Institute, now the Rochester Institute of Technology, in 1887. In later years he gave more than $75 million to the Massachusetts Institute of Technology, the University of Rochester, Hampton Institute, and Tuskegee Institute, and for the establishment of dental dispensaries in many countries. He provided funds for the Eastman School of Music at the University of Rochester and contributed liberally to the university's schools of medicine and of dentistry.

Suffering from an incurable disease, Eastman took his own life on March 14, 1932, in Rochester.

C. B. NEBLETTE, Author of
"Photography: Its Materials and Processes"

EASTMAN, Max (1883–1969), American writer and editor, who for many years was an influential leader of liberal opinion in the United States. He was born at Canandaigua, N.Y., on Jan. 4, 1883. After graduating from Williams College, he continued his studies at Columbia University, where he taught from 1907 to 1911. He edited two socialist magazines, the *Masses* (1913–1917) and the *Liberator* (1918–1923). Though he was a member of the Communist party until 1923, he became critical of Stalinism and eventually published such anti-Communist books as *The End of Socialism in Russia* (1937), *Marxism: Is It a Science?* (1940), and *Reflections on the Failure of Socialism* (1955).

Among Eastman's nonpolitical works are his popular *Enjoyment of Poetry* (1913) and two autobiographical books, *Enjoyment of Living* (1948) and *Love and Revolution* (1965). He also published volumes of poetry and translated works by Pushkin, Marx, and Trotsky. He died in Bridgetown, Barbados, on March 25, 1969.

EASTMAN SCHOOL OF MUSIC. See ROCHESTER, UNIVERSITY OF.

EASTON, a city in eastern Pennsylvania, the seat of Northampton county, is situated at the confluence of the Delaware and Lehigh rivers, about 50 miles (80 km) north of Philadelphia. It is part of the Allentown-Bethlehem-Easton metropolitan area. Easton is a residential city in a rich farming area. Its industries make machinery, textiles, electrical products, chemicals and chemical products, paper, and food products.

In the center of the city is a great square, which was created to the specifications of Thomas Penn, who gave the land for the town. The first courthouse was located here, and the city's activity still centers around the square. It is the site of a farm market that dates to colonial times.

Easton is the home of Lafayette College. Historic buildings are the First United Church of Christ, which was used as a hospital during the American Revolution, and the home of George Taylor, a signer of the Declaration of Independence. The Easton Area Public Library, which was founded in 1811, has a flag made by the women of Easton for the occasion of the reading of the Declaration of Independence in the center square on July 8, 1776. The Northampton County Historical and Genealogical Society building has notable collections.

Easton was laid out in 1752. It was incorporated as a borough in 1789 and as a city in 1866. Government is by mayor and council. Population: 26,027.

JANE S. MOYER
Easton Area Public Library

EASTPORT, a city in eastern Maine, in Washington county, shares with the nearby town of Lubec the distinction of being the easternmost community in the United States. It is situated about 130 miles (211 km) east of Bangor, on Moose Island in Passamaquoddy Bay of the Atlantic Ocean. There is a fine harbor kept free of ice throughout the year by the 25-foot (7.6-meter) tides. A causeway connects the city with the mainland.

Eastport is popular with summer visitors and offers facilities for deep-sea fishing. The principal industries are fishing, sardine canning, the production of fish meal and chemicals from fish scales, and textile manufacturing. Near the city are the buildings of Quoddy Village, built in 1935 for a federal project to build dams that would utilize the high tides for power production. The project was later abandoned.

Eastport was settled about 1780. In the War of 1812 it was captured by the British and was not returned to United States control until 1818. Government is by council and manager. Population: 1,982.

EASTVIEW, a city in eastern Ontario, Canada, is surrounded by the city of Ottawa. It is situated on the east bank of the Rideau River, a tributary of the Ottawa River. Eastview has plants that make brick and tile and also has iron and steel works. The first settlement on the site, made in 1824, was called Janesville. The name was changed to Eastview about 1900. It was incorporated as a town in 1912. As the city of Ottawa expanded around and beyond the town, Eastview retained its identity. It was incorporated as a city in 1963. Population: 24,269.

EATON, ē'tən, **Cyrus Stephen** (1883–1979), American industrialist and financier. He was born in Pugwash, Nova Scotia, Canada, on Dec. 27, 1883, and went to the United States in 1900, becoming a citizen in 1913. After attending McMaster University in Toronto, he was persuaded by John D. Rockefeller, whom he had met while working at a hotel, to enter business instead of the ministry. His success in completing some business transactions for Rockefeller led him to build a series of power plants in Manitoba. With the ensuing profits he began developing interests in steel, rubber, railroads, and investment banking.

Eaton's reputation as a financier rests largely on organizing Republic Steel into the nation's third-largest steel producer. After losing most of his fortune in the Great Depression, Eaton founded a second business empire. A maverick of the financial world, he attacked Wall Street's dominance of the securities market, forcing utility and railroad companies to submit securities issues to competitive bidding. He helped finance Kaiser-Frazer's entry into the automobile industry and became a major shareholder in the Chesapeake & Ohio Railway. At one time he was a director of some 40 companies in which he had holdings.

An occasional writer on public affairs, Eaton in 1955 converted his home in Pugwash into a center at which scholars and scientists might exchange views on science and public policy in the nuclear age. One of the Pugwash conferences concluded that "misuse of nuclear energy could lead to the annihilation of mankind." Alarmed, Eaton visited the USSR and eastern Europe, met Nikita Khrushchev, and became an outspoken advocate of ending the nuclear arms race. The USSR awarded him the Lenin Prize in 1960. Eaton died at Acadia Farm, near Cleveland, Ohio, on May 9, 1979.

ROBERT L. DANIEL, *Ohio University*

EATON, Dorman Bridgman (1823–1899), American lawyer and public official, who was a leader in the struggle to establish the merit system for civil service employees. He was born in Hardwick, Vt., on June 27, 1823. After graduating from the University of Vermont (1848) and Harvard Law School (1850), he settled in New York City.

Concerned over civic reform, Eaton helped topple "Boss" William M. Tweed's political machine and drafted legislation reorganizing city departments. As chairman of the first U.S. Civil Service Commission (1873–1875) he worked to end the political spoils system. He shares with Carl Schurz and George W. Curtis the credit for getting the federal merit system established in the Pendleton Act (1883). Eaton served again as chairman of the U.S. Civil Service Commission (1883–1886). He died in New York City on Dec. 23, 1899.

DAVID LINDSEY
California State College at Los Angeles

EATON, John (1829–1906), American educator. He was born on Dec. 5, 1829, in Sutton, N.H. After graduating from Dartmouth College in 1854, he became superintendent of schools in Toledo, Ohio. He then attended Andover Theological Seminary, where he was ordained in 1861. A chaplain in the Civil War, he was chosen to supervise the Negro slaves freed by the Union Army; he was appointed colonel of a Negro regiment in 1863 and brigadier general in 1865.

In 1870, Eaton was appointed U.S. commissioner of education. In this office he did much to promote public education, winning congressional support for the Bureau of Education and urging federal aid to schools. After resigning in 1886, he served as president of Marietta College until 1891 and of Sheldon Jackson College from 1895 to 1899. In 1900, Eaton supervised the establishment of public schools in Puerto Rico. He died in Washington, D.C., on Feb. 9, 1906.

CLIFTON L. HALL, *University of Tennessee*

EATON, John Henry (1790–1856), American lawyer, political leader, and diplomat, who was secretary of war in Andrew Jackson's first cabinet. His second marriage to a woman considered socially unacceptable by some Washingtonians caused the dissolution of the cabinet and contributed to the estrangement between Jackson and Vice President John C. Calhoun.

Eaton was born in Halifax, N.C., on June 18, 1790. After attending the University of North Carolina, he studied law and settled in Franklin, Tenn. There he practiced law and became friendly with Jackson, whose ward, Myra Lewis, he married. He served in the War of 1812 and in 1817 completed a eulogistic biography of Jackson, begun by John Reid.

From 1818 to 1829, Eaton represented Tennessee in the U.S. Senate. Now a widower, he married Margaret O'Neill early in 1829 and shortly afterward was appointed secretary of war by Jackson, for whom he had campaigned in 1828. He resigned from the cabinet in 1831, and ran unsuccessfully for the Senate in 1833. From 1834 to 1836 he served as governor of Florida and from then until 1840 as minister to Spain. Eaton's refusal to support Martin Van Buren in the latter's 1836 presidential campaign resulted in a breach with Jackson and the close of his own political career. He remained in Washington, D.C., until his death there on Nov. 17, 1856.

Eaton's second wife, Margaret (Peggy) O'Neill, or O'Neale (1796–1879), was the daughter of a Washington innkeeper. Her first husband, John B. Timberlake, a Navy purser, committed suicide in 1828. Because of gossip connecting her with Eaton before her first husband's death, the wives of other cabinet members and Mrs. Calhoun, the Vice President's wife, refused to receive her socially. Although Jackson supported the couple, Eaton resigned his cabinet post. Jackson then reorganized his cabinet, eliminating three Calhoun supporters. The "Eaton affair" contributed to his decision to support Van Buren, not Calhoun, as his successor.

Mrs. Eaton, who possessed considerable charm, enjoyed a social success while her husband was minister to Spain. After his death she married Antonio Buchignani, a young Italian dancing master, but he ran off with her granddaughter, and they were subsequently divorced.

EATON, Theophilus (1590–1658), American colonist, who was a principal founder and lifelong governor of New Haven colony. He was born in Stony Stratford, England, and became a successful London merchant. He was deputy governor of the Eastland Company and served Charles I as an agent in Denmark.

A Puritan, Eaton was one of the original patentees of the Massachusetts Bay Company. In 1647 he and John Davenport (q.v.) led a group of emigrants to New England. Declining to settle within the existing colonies, they established in 1638 a new colony, later named New Haven, at Quinnipiac in Connecticut. Eaton was elected governor in 1639 and reelected thereafter every year until his death in New Haven on Jan. 7, 1658.

Both Eaton and Davenport were strict interpreters of Puritan orthodoxy, and New Haven became the most rigorous of the Puritan colonies. Their legal code, drawn up in 1655, became known as the Connecticut "blue laws."

GEORGE D. LANGDON, JR., *Vassar College*

EATON, ē'tən, **William** (1764–1811), American army officer, who developed the type of mobile desert warfare later employed by T. E. Lawrence ("Lawrence of Arabia") in World War I and by Field Marshal Harold Alexander in World War II. Eaton was born in Woodstock, Conn., on Feb. 23, 1764. Entering the U.S. Army as a captain in 1792, he fought against the Indians in Ohio and Georgia. In 1799 he became U.S. consul at Tunis where he negotiated a new treaty.

Eaton returned to the Mediterranean, with the title of naval agent, in 1804 during the Tripolitan War and undertook a military campaign to restore the rightful ruler to the throne of Tripoli. Commanding a force of mercenaries, unreliable Arab cavalry, and a squad of U.S. Marines, he marched 600 miles (965 km) across the Libyan desert from Alexandria to Derna, which he captured on April 27, 1805—a feat commemorated in the *Marine Hymn*. He held the town against Navy orders until June 12 after a peace had been made with the pasha of Tripoli. Eaton returned home a hero but soon after became involved in the alleged conspiracy of Aaron Burr. He died in Brimfield, Mass., on June 1, 1811.

NOEL B. GERSON, *Author (under the pseudonym Samuel Edwards) of "Barbary General"*

EAU CLAIRE, ō klâr, a city in west central Wisconsin, situated at the confluence of the Eau Claire and Chippewa rivers, 165 miles (266 km) northwest of Madison. It is the seat of Eau Claire county. Eau Claire is a commercial and industrial center in the heart of a dairying area and is a gateway to the Indian Head region, a vacation center known for its excellent fishing.

The chief industries of the city are printing, electronics, meat-packing, brewing, and the manufacture of rubber tires, culverts, machine-shop products, and paper. Eau Claire is the seat of a branch of the University of Wisconsin, the Eau Claire Technical Institute, and two small religious colleges. The Paul Bunyan Camp at Carson Park is a facsimile of an early lumber camp.

Eau Claire was settled in the 1840's and developed as a logging center. It was incorporated in 1872. The city's name means "clear water" in French. Government is by city manager. Population: 51,509.

DORIS E. FRIEDMAN, *Eau Claire Public Library*

EBAN, ē'bän, **Abba** (1915–   ), Israeli diplomat, political leader, and scholar. He was born on Feb. 2, 1915, in Cape Town, South Africa. Taken to England as a child, Eban studied classics and Oriental languages at Cambridge University, where in 1938 he became a tutor at Pembroke College. Rising to the rank of major in the British Army during World War II, he served in the Middle East and in 1944 was named director of the language program at the Middle East Arabic Center in Jerusalem.

Eban first came to public notice at the United Nations, where he brilliantly led the delegation of Israel's provisional government, becoming his country's first permanent representative in May 1949. He held this post, and also, after September 1950, that of Israel's ambassador to the United States, until 1959. A member of the ruling Mapai (Israel's Labor party), Eban was elected to the Knesset (legislature) in 1959, becoming minister of education and culture in June 1960 and deputy prime minister in Levi Eshkol's first government (1963–1965). He served as foreign minister from January 1966 until May 1974.

While his reputation as a politician never matched his reputation for eloquence and diplomacy, Eban was regarded as one of the ablest of the younger generation of Israeli leaders. His major United Nations speeches appeared in *The Voice of Israel* (1957) and *The Tide of Nationalism* (1958).

J. C. HUREWITZ, *Columbia University*

EBBINGHAUS, eb'ing-hous, **Hermann** (1850–1909), German experimental psychologist, who is best known for his studies of memory. He was born in Barmen, Germany, on Jan. 24, 1850, and studied at the University of Bonn, receiving his Ph.D. in 1873. Between 1880 and 1909, Ebbinghaus taught psychology and philosophy at the universities of Berlin, Breslau, and Halle, founding psychological laboratories at Berlin and Breslau. He died in Halle on Feb. 26, 1909.

Most of Ebbinghaus' research concerned rote learning and memory. In *Memory: A Contribution to Experimental Psychology* (1885; Eng. tr., 1913), he demonstrated that learning and memory could be investigated by quantitative methods, thus helping to divorce psychology from philosophy and initiating a major shift in psychological research, away from sensation and perception and toward learning. Techniques and materials that he designed are still in use, notably the "nonsense syllable" used in memory studies. Ebbinghaus also studied color vision.

MICHAEL G. ROTHENBERG, *Columbia University*

EBERHART, e'bər-härt, **Richard** (1904–   ), American poet, who was considered one of the major lyric voices of the 20th century. He was born in Austin, Minn., on April 5, 1904, and studied at Dartmouth College and Cambridge University. He was a professor of English and poet-in-residence at Dartmouth from 1956 until his retirement in 1971, when he became professor emeritus. He also served as the first president of the Poets' Theatre in Cambridge, Mass., in 1950–1951. From 1959 to 1961 he was poetry consultant to the Library of Congress.

Eberhart's verse, though some critics consider it uneven, at its best contains stunning imagery and significant philosophical speculation. Some of his most notable individual poems are *The Groundhog; Seals, Terns, Time;* and *The Horse Chestnut*. He also published several collections of his poetry, and his dramatic verse appeared in *Collected Verse Plays* (1962).

Eberhart shared the Bollingen Prize in Poetry in 1962. He won the Pulitzer Prize in poetry in 1966 for *Selected Poems, 1930–1965* and the National Book Award for poetry in 1977 for *Collected Poems, 1930–1976*.

EBERS, ā′bərs, **Georg Moritz** (1837–1898), German Egyptologist and novelist. He was born in Berlin on March 1, 1837. After studying law and archaeology, he became professor of Egyptology at Leipzig University (1870–1889).

Ebers gave his name to a famous medical papyrus of the 16th century B.C. that he acquired in Luxor in 1873 and published two years later. The Ebers Papyrus, which is a reference manual for physicians, provides proof of the relatively advanced nature of Egyptian medicine.

His historical novels and a two-volume work on his travels in Egypt were very successful, arousing great public interest in the ancient Middle East. Ebers' collected works were published in 25 volumes (1893–1897). He died in Tutzing, Germany, on Aug. 7, 1898.

RICHARD A. PARKER, *Brown University*

EBERT, ā′bərt, **Friedrich** (1871–1925), first president of the German Weimar Republic. He was born in Heidelberg on Feb. 4, 1871. He left his saddler's trade in 1893 to become editor of the newspaper *Bremer Bürgerzeitung*. An energetic trade unionist and a persuasive orator, he rose to leadership in the Bremen Social Democratic party and was elected a city councilman in 1900. In 1905 he became a member of his party's central committee and moved to Berlin. He was elected to the Reichstag in 1912 and succeeded the founder of the party, August Bebel, as party leader in 1913.

Social Democratic policies during World War I were significantly influenced by Ebert, who became leader of the party caucus in the Reichstag in 1916. He supported Prince Max von Baden's efforts in October 1918 to reform the monarchy. When the Kaiser fled, Ebert assumed the chancellorship on Nov. 9, 1918, and he became cochairman of the Council of People's Commissars the following day. The Weimar National Assembly elected him president of the republic in 1919, and he held this office until his death.

Conservatives and reactionaries never forgave Ebert for his support of the workers' strikes in January 1918, while Communists and other left extremists attacked him for his cooperation with German army units in suppressing the "Spartacist Revolt" of Jan. 5 to 15, 1919. But he survived the abortive Kapp putsch (March 1920), and he alerted the army when Hitler attempted to stage his coup in Munich in November 1923.

Ebert was a moderate Marxist who devoted his efforts to practical party affairs and avoided divisive theoretical disputes. During his political career he fostered social legislation, worked for woman suffrage, and sought broader educational opportunities for the masses. His practicality and self-confidence won the respect and support of moderate bourgeois parties. As president, he led Germany through a difficult period, in which he held the young republic together. He died in Berlin on Feb. 28, 1925.

HENRY CORD MEYER
University of California at Irvine

Further Reading: Ryder, A. J., *The German Revolution of 1918* (London 1967).

EBIONITES, ē′bē-ə-nīts, a dissident Judeo-Christian sect of the early Christian era. The Ebionites formed one of the various groups that refused to accept Saint Paul's view that circumcision and observance of the Mosaic Law were unnecessary for the baptized Christian. Their name most likely derives, not from a legendary founder called Ebion, but from the Semitic word *ebionim* (poor men). They may have adopted it to symbolize their asceticism, but it was used as a taunt by opponents to deride the meagerness of their theology.

Jesus, according to Ebionite belief, was not the son of God. They differed among themselves on the question of his virgin birth, some asserting and others denying it. All agreed that, although not divine, he was the anointed Messiah. This rank he won by his singularly punctilious observance of the Law of Moses, for which God rewarded him by public accolade during his Baptism by John in the Jordan. The Ebionites were enjoined to follow Jesus' example, accepting both circumcision and Baptism, and following both the Law and Gospel as ways of salvation. They stood at the opposite pole from the Marcionites, who repudiated all Jewish attachments, even the ancient Scriptures.

The Ebionites had their own collection of sacred writings. The Old Testament they used was said to be neither the Hebrew original nor one of the Greek translations circulated among Christians but the Greek version of Symmachus, who, according to the church historian Eusebius, was an Ebionite. Paul's letters they disdained as writings of an apostate. They seem to have had none of the standard Gospels but circulated a "Gospel according to the Hebrews," probably a heavily edited version of Matthew.

The Ebionites are mentioned somewhat tolerantly by Justin Martyr (though not by name) about 160 A.D. Later they are discussed rather acidly by such early Christian writers as Tertullian, Irenaeus, Hippolytus, and Eusebius. The descriptions suggest that they had disagreements among themselves (some were apparently Gnostics) and that they impinged only remotely upon orthodox Christianity up to the 4th century, after which they faded from view.

JAMES T. BURTCHAELL, C.S.C.
Notre Dame University

EBLA, eb′lə, an ancient city of Syria, identified with Tell Mardikh, 34 miles (55 km) southwest of Aleppo. Beginning excavation in 1964, Italian archaeologists uncovered occupation levels from about 2900 B.C. (Early Bronze I) to Byzantine times (Mardikh VIII). Of these, the Mardikh IIB1 level, with its royal palace (Palace G) and its archive of cuneiform clay tablets, is the most important.

The many documents and letters from Ebla reveal that it had perhaps 250,000 inhabitants, that it headed a state administered by 12,000 officials, and that it had far-flung trade and territorial ambitions. The sequence of early rulers— Igrish-Khalam, Irkab-Damu, Ar-Ennum Ibrium, Ibbi-Sippish, and Dubukhu-Ada—formed a dynasty lasting probably from about 2400 to 2250 B.C., though the absolute dates of none are known. The conflagration that destroyed Mardikh IIB1 was probably the work of Naram-Sin of Akkad, who boasted of having destroyed Ebla. Though the city was rebuilt and flourished between 2000 and 1800 B.C. (Mardikh IIIA), it never regained its former prestige. However, most of the fortifications and temples discovered there date from this period.

Ebla ruled substantial territory nearby, but the farthest limits of its control are difficult to set.

Sometimes they stretched to the Euphrates at Carchemish to the northeast and at Mari (Tell Hariri) to the southeast. King Iblul-Il of Mari (though himself undated) was contemporary with Ar-Ennum of Ebla. The control of caravan routes through these cities and westward to the Syrian coast and the Taurus made Ebla an important trading center, especially for textiles, both locally manufactured and imported. Much of the archive is concerned with textile trade, though accounts of agriculture and the administration of the city wards also were kept.

Until the discovery that the Ebla archive was written in an archaic Semitic language (now called Eblaite or Palaeo-Canaanite), the seminomadic Amorites were thought to have been the first Semitic stock to colonize Syria, about 2000 B.C. The Ebla texts indicate that Syria had an advanced Semitic urban society as early as the mid-3d millennium B.C

Mythological and other texts were originally much publicized as throwing light on Hebrew origins and biblical themes. But reassessment has shown that Ebla myths were largely translations of Sumerian ones and that the religion was essentially Syrian, centered on the cults of the gods of grain (Dagan), sun (Sippish), pestilence (Rasap), and love (Eshtar). Though Palestinian cities are claimed by some scholars as identified in commercial texts, the only significant connection with the Bible is linguistic, Eblaite illuminating some difficult Hebrew readings.

WILLIAM CULICAN, *University of Melbourne*

Further Reading: Matthiae, Paolo, *Ebla, an Empire Rediscovered* (Hodder and Staughton 1980); Pettinato, Giovanni, *The Archives of Ebla: An Empire Inscribed in Clay* (Doubleday 1981).

EBONY, eb'ə-nē, the blackish heartwood (nonliving central portion) of a number of species of tropical Asian and African trees of the genus *Diospyros* of the ebony family (Ebenaceae). The finest ebony is obtained from the macassar ebony tree (*Diospyros ebenum*), native to Sri Lanka, southern India, and Malaysia, and the Mauritius ebony (*D. reticulata*), from Mauritius.

Fine ebony is extremely hard, heavy, fine grained, and jet black in color; more commonly, it is patterned with brown stripes or mottling. The deep black color results from deposits of tannins and other by-products from the living part of the trunk. Ebony is used in carvings, cabinetwork, inlays, and other applications.

The most important commercial source of ebony is the macassar ebony, which grows to 50 feet (15 meters) high and bears narrow leathery evergreen leaves, 2 to 6 inches (5–15 cm) long. Each tree bears separate male and female flowers, greenish yellow in color. The fruit is a rounded berry, about 1 inch (2.5 cm) in diameter.

The closely related American persimmon (*D. virginiana*), well known for its large edible fruits, also is utilized for its heavy, hard wood, which is sometimes called American ebony. The Jamaica ebony (*Brya ebenus*), of the pea family (Leguminosae), native to the West Indies, yields a hard, durable wood also known as cocus wood, granadillo, or American ebony. Calamander, a very hard black-mottled wood similar to ebony, is obtained from *D. quaesita* of Sri Lanka and several other species of *Diospyros*.

RICHARD S. COWAN
Smithsonian Institution

EBRO River, ā'vrō, the largest river of northern Spain. It is about 580 miles (930 km) long. Rising in the mountains of Santander, it flows southeast into the Mediterranean between the Pyrenees and Iberian ranges. Its major tributaries from the Pyrenees are the Arga, Ega, Aragón, and Segre. The Jalón is the chief tributary from the Iberian mountains.

The Ebro cuts through the coastal ranges in a series of gorges, so that seagoing vessels cannot go upstream above Tortosa, although small vessels can proceed as far as Tudela. Since Moorish times, irrigation has been practiced along the river's most important valleys. Today, more than 35 major dams have expanded the irrigated land to over 919,715 acres (372,210 hectares).

JAMES M. HOUSTON
Hertford College, Oxford University

EÇA DE QUEIROZ, ā'sə thə kā-ē-rôsh', **José Maria** (1845–1900), Portuguese author, who was the outstanding master of the modern Portuguese novel. Eça de Queiroz (Queirós) was born in Póvoa de Varzim on Nov. 25, 1845. He studied law at the University of Coimbra and spent most of his life in the Portuguese consular service in Cuba, England, and Paris, where he died on Aug. 16, 1900.

As a member of the literary reform group called the Generation of 1870, Eça de Queiroz wanted to replace the oratorical, conventional, and (to him) hypocritical Portuguese tradition with a literature dealing realistically with the issues of life. His romantic early writings, collected as *Prosas bárbaras* (published posthumously, 1905), showed an entirely new prose style—lyrical, ironic, melodious, full of subtle insinuations—that eventually revolutionized Portuguese prose. In 1871 he and Ramalho Ortigão began to write and publish a monthly journal, *As Farpas* (1873–1883), which mordantly satirized Portuguese life.

Eça's first major effort was the novel *O crime do Padre Amaro* (three versions, 1875–1880), which used the love affair of a priest to expose the corruption of the provincial clergy. *O Primo Basílio* (1878) focuses, through a Flaubertian case of adultery, on the middle class of Lisbon. Eça's analysis of society was completed with *Os Maias* (1888), in which an incident of incest is used to take the upper strata of Lisbon to task. Eça's stark naturalism, devastating sarcasm, and novel prose style provoked bitter attacks, and he was called the "Portuguese Zola."

Eça's naturalism was only a phase. In *O Mandarim*, a Faustian novelette published in 1880, he had already moved on to a new and original aesthetic form in which observed reality is subordinated to the free flight of imagination. In *A Relíquia* (1887), a delightful picaresque story of cupidity and religious hypocrisy, he constantly intertwines opposites—caricature and truth, crudeness and lyricism, irreverence and piety, fancy and reality. In the posthumously published *A ilustre Casa de Ramires* (1900), *A Cidade e as Serras* (1901), and *A correspondência de Fradique Mendes* (1900), without renouncing his caustic attitude, he turns his eyes with tenderness on Portugal's past. An aesthete disillusioned with city life, he rhapsodizes about the bucolic simplicity of the peasants and the countryside.

ERNESTO G. DA CAL
Author of "Lengua y Estilo de Eça de Queiroz"

ÉCARTÉ, ā-kär-tā', is a card game for two players, widely played for high stakes by French and English society during the 19th century. A pack of 32 cards is used, all cards below the seven having been removed from a standard deck. Each suit ranks in the following order: king (high), queen, jack, ace, 10, 9, 8, 7. Players cut for deal; the one with the highest card deals. Dealer gives 5 cards to each player, 3 and 2 at a time, and turns up the next card as trump. This card is never dealt. If the card turned up is a king, dealer scores 1 point immediately. During play the object of each player is to win the majority of tricks.

After the deal, nondealer may *stand* and lead, if satisfied with his hand. Or he may *propose*, that is, offer a chance for each player to improve his hand by exchanging some cards for new ones in the pack. Dealer may *refuse* the proposal and demand a lead, or *accept* it, in which case he deals from the pack as many cards as both players discard. Again, nondealer may stand or propose and, if he proposes, dealer may refuse or accept. This continues until nondealer chooses to lead or is forced to do so, or until not enough cards remain in the pack to take care of the discards. In the latter case the hand is played out anyway.

Nondealer always leads to the first trick, and the winner of each trick leads to the next. The trick (two cards) is won by the highest card of the suit led or by a trump. Second hand must follow suit if able and must play a higher card than the lead if possible. If neither is possible, second hand can play any card.

If nondealer stands after the original deal, he must win at least 3 tricks in the play or else his opponent gets 2 points. Nondealer gets 1 point for taking 3 (or 4) tricks. Likewise, if dealer initiates play by refusing the first proposal, he has to win 3 tricks to earn 1 point; otherwise nondealer gets 2 points. After the second group of cards is dealt, either player gets 1 point by taking 3 or 4 tricks; there is no penalty for failure. A player gets 2 points for winning all 5 tricks (a *vole*), except that no player may earn more than 2 points in the play of any one hand. If either player has the king of trumps, he scores 1 point if he announces it before playing to the first trick. Game is 5 points.

FRANK K. PERKINS, *Boston "Herald"*

ECBATANA, ek-bat'ən-ə, the Greek name for the capital of the ancient empire of the Medes, at modern Hamadan, Iran. The Old Persian name was *Hangmatana*, "the place of gathering." Herodotus says Ecbatana was founded about 678 B.C. by Deïoces and also credits Deïoces with the establishment of the Median dynasty, but both statements are questionable. The city may have been built by Phraortes, the son of Deïoces, who also probably founded the Median empire.

Ecbatana remained the summer capital of Cyrus the Great of Persia and his son Cambyses in the 6th century B.C. According to the Bible (Ezra 6:2), the imperial records of Cyrus' time were kept here. The city was noted for its splendor and luxury. Herodotus, in the 5th century B.C., described it as having seven concentric walls, the inner walls rising above the outer, since the city was on a hill. Each wall was of a different color.

RICHARD N. FRYE
Author of "The Heritage of Persia"

ECCENTRICITY, in mathematics. See ELLIPSE.

ECCLES, ek'əlz, **Sir John Carew** (1903–   ), Australian physiologist, who was awarded the 1963 Nobel Prize in physiology or medicine for his research on the fundamental transmission of nerve impulses. He shared the award with Alan L. Hodgkin and Andrew F. Huxley. Eccles' work in neurophysiology is basic to knowledge of how neurons interact with each other, especially in explaining integrated movements and their pathological alterations, and to eventual understanding of higher functions of the brain.

Contributions to Science. Eccles' first investigations, done at Oxford University in collaboration with the famous neurophysiologist Sir Charles Sherrington, dealt with the reflex properties of the spinal cord. Eccles and Sherrington based their analysis of reflexes on the operation of the contacts between nerve cells in the spinal cord— the synaptic junctions, which were thought to involve inhibitory and excitatory mechanisms. Eccles first developed a theory that electrical currents passing from the terminal of one neuron across the cleft of the synapse excited or inhibited the discharge of the next neuron. This theory seemed attractive at the time, because the nerve impulse was known to be electrical in nature. However, it was later shown by researchers that the synaptic junction between nerve fibers and the muscle fibers operated by means of a chemical transmitter called acetylcholine, which is released in small amounts to bring about activation of the muscle fiber membrane.

Using this knowledge, Eccles and his colleagues were able to record synaptic transmission in the large motoneuron cell bodies within the spinal cords of cats. These recordings were made by glass microelectrodes inserted in the nerve cells, permitting the cells to remain viable and functioning. By this and other ingenious techniques, it was shown that the synapses on the motoneurons did not operate electrically but by means of at least two different transmitter substances. One of these substances, as yet unknown, brings about excitation of the action-potential discharge of the neurons; the other brings about inhibition. Later, Eccles and his colleagues extended the principles upward in the nervous system to include studies of synapses in parts of the brain, specifically in the dorsal nuclei, the hippocampus, and the cerebellum.

Life. Eccles was born in Melbourne, Australia, on Jan. 27, 1903. He received bachelor of medicine and science degrees from the University of Melbourne in 1925, and then was a Rhodes Scholar at Oxford, where he took his Ph. D. degree in 1929. He was a fellow of Exeter from 1927 to 1932 and of Magdalen College, Oxford, from 1931 to 1937. Returning to Australia, he served as director of the Kanematsu Memorial Institute of Pathology in Sydney for eight years. From 1944 to 1951 he was professor of physiology at the University of Otago, Dunedin, New Zealand, and then became professor of physiology at the Australian National University in Canberra. He was knighted in 1958 and received the Royal Medal in 1962.

Eccles' monographs include *Reflex Activity of the Spinal Cord* (1932, written in collaboration); *The Neurophysiological Basis of Mind* (1953); *The Physiology of Nerve Cells* (1957), and *Physiology of Synapses* (1964).

SIDNEY OCHS, *Indiana University*

ECCLES, ek'əlz, **Marriner Stoddard** (1890–1977), American financier and business executive, who served as chairman of the Federal Reserve Board. He was born in Logan, Utah, on Sept. 9, 1890, one of 22 children of David Eccles, who built a fortune in banking, insurance, and other enterprises. Eccles attended Brigham Young College and served two years as a Mormon missionary in Scotland before organizing the Eccles Investment Co. in 1916.

In 1928, Eccles became president of the First Security Corporation, operating banks in Utah, Idaho, and Wyoming. An advocate of government spending to combat the depression, he was appointed assistant secretary of the treasury in 1934. He headed the Federal Reserve System from 1936 to 1948. He died in Salt Lake City, Utah, on Dec. 18, 1977.

ECCLESIA, i-klē'zē-ə, the basic sovereign assembly of citizens in ancient Greek city-states, especially Athens, where the term seems to have originated. The assembly developed out of the gatherings of armed men in early times to ratify the decisions of the king and must have survived in some form through the period of aristocratic control. In Athens, however, it was of little importance until the early 6th century B. C., when Solon granted membership to all adult male citizens. After the reforms of Cleisthenes at the end of the 6th century B. C., it became Athens' most important political body.

The *ecclesia* elected and directed the magistrates; legislated on matters of all types; and in certain serious cases had judicial powers. It met at least 40 times a year, usually on the Pnyx hill. The proportion of citizens usually attending was probably relatively small; the quorum for an ostracism was 6,000, perhaps one sixth of those eligible. Early in the 4th century B. C. payment for attendance was introduced.

Meetings were called and the agenda prepared by the Council of Five Hundred. Supervision lay with the *prytaneis*, a standing committee of 50, in the 5th century and with the *proedroi*, a group of 9, in the 4th century. One member was chosen by lot as chairman. Although technically only matters introduced by the Council could be acted upon, any citizen had the right to speak on them, and the latitude allowed for amendment and substitution was so great that in effect anyone could make a proposal. The only real check was the threat of prosecution for introducing an illegal motion (*graphe paranomon*), although it was not until the end of the 5th century B. C. that a separate body of law was set up to which enactments of the assembly were expected to conform. Voting was by a show of hands, except for ostracism, and a simple majority of those present prevailed. Rapid reversals of policy were possible because the composition of successive assemblies could change, and the latest decision was binding.

Similar assemblies in other city-states had different names, although the use of the name *ecclesia* became more and more widespread. In states less democratic than Athens membership was often limited by setting up property qualifications, and the assembly's powers were limited by the council and magistrates. In early Christian times, *ecclesia* came to be applied to meetings of the faithful and so grew to mean "church."

DONALD W. BRADEEN
University of Cincinnati

ECCLESIASTES, Book of, i-klē-zē-as'tēz, one of the "wisdom" books of the Old Testament. Called in Hebrew Koheleth, or "The Preacher," it is a collection of observations on human life, very skeptical and disillusioned in tone and content, unlike the rest of the Hebrew sacred books. While it is attributed to King Solomon (986?–933 B. C.), it is most unlikely that the book was written or compiled by Solomon; the vocabulary and style do not belong to the 10th century, nor do its prevailing views. Skepticism was not an unknown attitude in ancient Semitic thought, or in ancient Greek or Latin, but the amount and degree of unbelief here is overwhelming. Its theme is announced in the opening lines: "Vanity of vanities, says the Preacher, vanity of vanities! All is vanity."

Modern scholars are inclined to attribute this skeptical outlook to the influence of popular Greek philosophy, chiefly Epicurean, in the period following the catastrophic end of the Peloponnesian War (404 B. C.), from which ancient Greece never recovered. The negative attitude of Greeks toward Jewish religion is reflected in pagan ridicule quoted in the Book of Wisdom and I Maccabees, both found in the Apocrypha (q.v.). Not all Jews reacted against paganism; some under the Ptolemies and Seleucids, adopted the skeptical outlook of their conquerors—a skepticism from which the 25-year Maccabean War delivered the nation as a whole.

If the Book of Ecclesiastes comes from the 3d century (about 225 B. C.), it takes on a special meaning: it affirms what is left of the Jewish faith in God at a time when appearances were against it, especially the belief in divine rewards for fidelity, for trust in God and obedience to His commandments.

The book represents the last stand of a heroic soul who would not yield to utter skepticism. In a world of disbelief and ridicule of the older religions, this Jew and his readers clung firmly to their belief in God and obedience to His laws. His conclusion is summed up in 12:13, "The end of the matter; all has been heard. Fear God, and keep his commandments; for this is the whole duty of man."

Most editors and commentators recognize a number of passages in the book as having been composed in poetic form. (See, for example, the new translations in the Revised Standard Version and the Jerusalem Bible.) Some editors print the whole text as poetic; but the rules of Hebrew poetry, that is, parallelism and stress, do not cover the whole work. It seems probable that the author selected passages of poetic composition from his own or some earlier writing and wove them into his journal, or daybook, in which he set down his experiences and convictions about human life and destiny.

Theme. As in most "wisdom" books, a few subjects are repeated, with slight variations. The main theme is the emptiness and injustice of life, the folly of striving for permanent achievement, wealth, health, and comfortable living. God has made all things, but He has not decreed that all men shall be successful or happy or that any life shall achieve permanent results. Even the achievement of wisdom is futile—just as futile as the eager pursuit of pleasure. The same fate overtakes the wise man and the fool (2:12–17), an observation that led to the confession, tragic for a seeker of wisdom, "So I hated life."

One of the author's convictions is that for

everything there is a time (3:1–8), a view that is held today by many who believe that ethical behavior is conditioned by changing circumstances: there are no absolute standards. But Koheleth does not go that far. Human behavior is variable, but the commandments of God stand fast. His skeptical theism supports the ancient principle: "Shall God send good, and not evil?" God never promised to send only happiness, success, pleasure, or abundance.

This suggests the conclusion that God knows best, and always provides what is best for human beings. Only Koheleth does not quite say it. His God is still mysterious, like the God of the prophet, "a God who hidest thyself" (Isaiah 45:15); but the wise man does not invoke him as "God of Israel, the Savior." The appeal to a final judgment in the last verse of the book is a warning, not a promise, and some editors think it a later addition to the work.

Koheleth has no eschatology. He lived at a time when the old faith was still dominant among those who professed and practiced it; but the day was nearing when the crises of persecution and threatened annihilation, and the valiant uprising of the Maccabees against overwhelming odds, would open a new course of development, the messianic or eschatological hope, destined to characterize Judaism ever afterward. Koheleth lived scarcely fifty years before this new dawn with its fresh ideas and their courageous supporters, eventually known as the Pharisees.

Canonicity. By the time the canon of the Hebrew Bible was defined, at the Council of Jamnia, about 90 A.D., there were many Jews who opposed the admission of Koheleth to the list of sacred, or inspired, books (see BIBLE—*1. Canon of the Old Testament*). Even later still it was challenged; some rabbis held that it did not "defile the hands," a curious way of intimating that the book was not inspired because the customary ceremonial washing of the hands after taking up a sacred book was unnecessary. (See Mishnah, *Yadaim* 3:5.) As late as 389 A.D., St. Jerome knew Jews who wished the book had not survived. The admission of the book to the sacred Canon was probably due to the final conclusion at the end of chapter 12, and its attribution to Solomon.

Ecclesiastes is one of the five Old Testament books called the Megilloth, or scrolls, read at appropriate Jewish festivals. Its use in the liturgy is on the third day of Sukkoth (Tabernacles), the traditional Jewish harvest feast. It is read as a reminder of the brief and transitory nature of human life; as a warning against reliance on prosperity, wealth, and property, which are evanescent; and as an admonition to remember that true happiness consists solely in obedience to God's commandments, whatever misfortunes overtake one. That is also the teaching of Judith and other contemporary works: God may save "by many or by few," or He may choose not to save at all. We are in His hands and must obey His will. Upon this stern creed were nurtured the heroes of Israel in ancient times.

Greek Influence. Koheleth's attempt to combine Greek ideas with Hebrew did not prove widely successful. In spite of some infiltration, the effects of the Jewish war (165–142 B.C.) and the rejection of syncretism with the surrounding cults resulted in a strong revulsion against paganism. The introduction of Greek studies into the Jewish schools came much later, and even then did not introduce fundamental changes in Jewish faith or doctrine. Koheleth's belief that "the earth remains for ever" (1:4) states the usual Greek and Roman idea of the universe, sharply contrasting with the Hebrew view that the universe had been created in time and presumably would have a conclusion, though the belief was not always clearly expressed. The Stoics believed in recurrent universes, and poets took up the theme and foretold a new Tiryns and Mycenae, another Troy and Trojan War, another Hector and Achilles. Thus Ecclesiastes 3:15 reads: "That which is, already has been; that which is to be, already has been; and God seeks what has been driven away." If the world is eternal and if there is a limited number of possible events, recurrence is inevitable.

But these echoes of Greek popular thought are merely tags, not systematic, even though some modern writers have endeavored to trace the explicit influence of Epicureanism, Stoicism, and Cyrenaicism. Koheleth can scarcely have studied in a Greek school or deeply pondered the works of the Greek philosophers. Then as today, however, it was possible to hold views that were influenced by scientists and philosophers, without knowing their systems in detail. The popular philosophy of the Hellenistic age was ubiquitous. The final conclusions of Koheleth—for example, that it is best never to be born (4:3), and that the resurrection of the dead is biologically impossible—are merely echoes of the new philosophy of skepticism, which had taken its texts from the early poets, such as Homer and Euripides. The popular belief that there was no remembrance in the grave or communication with God or the heavenly deities was written on countless funerary monuments and tombs in the age of Hellenism and the early Roman Empire.

Some scholars have found traces of influence from Egyptian religious lore. But the parallels are not wholly convincing. Moreover, the traditional opposition of the Hebrews to Egyptian beliefs and practices make such borrowing unlikely. The best way to study Ecclesiastes—or any ancient book—is in the light of the historical times and background of the author. Severe theological judgments based on standards of doctrine, Jewish or Christian, in far later centuries, only obscure the book's positive statements. Koheleth reflects his own time.

Attempts have been made to attribute Koheleth to two, three, or more authors or later editors who undertook to erase the author's unbelief. He has been called the greatest (almost the only) heretic in ancient Hebrew literature, and doubtless he roused opposition even from some in his own time. But the evidence for plural authorship is not clear, and the probability is that Koheleth did not mind setting forth his negative views. It is fortunate for the students of the Bible today that we have such a book, at least to set up as a foil against which the later developments can be studied.

FREDERICK C. GRANT
Union Theological Seminary, N.Y.

Bibliography

Gordis, Robert, *Koheleth, the Man and His World* (New York 1951).
Jastrow, Morris, *A Gentle Cynic* (Philadelphia 1918).
McNeile, Alan H., *Introduction to Ecclesiastes* (London 1904).
Rankin, O. S., "Ecclesiastes," *Interpreter's Bible*, vol. 5 (New York 1956).

ECCLESIASTICAL ARCHITECTURE. See CATHEDRALS AND CHURCHES.

ECCLESIASTICAL ART. See articles on specific subjects, such as BYZANTINE ART AND ARCHITECTURE; MANUSCRIPTS, ILLUMINATED; STAINED GLASS.

ECCLESIASTICAL COMMISSIONERS, a body that managed the estates and revenues of the Church of England from 1835 to 1948. In 1835, Sir Robert Peel, as prime minister, appointed a commission to reorganize dioceses and espiscopal finances, to reduce the size of cathedral chapters, and to abolish sinecures, nepotism, pluralism, and nonresidence. In 1836 the commission was established as a permanent corporation by an act of Parliament. As a corporation the commission was given the power to hold and purchase land and to plan the reorganization and redistribution of ecclesiastical revenues.

Members of the commission included all the archbishops and bishops of the Church of England, such officials as the lord chancellor and the chancellor of the exchequer, and other laymen of the Church of England appointed by the crown and the archbishop of Canterbury. The commission was to make an annual report to Parliament. In 1948 the Ecclesiastical Commissioners were replaced by the Church Commissioners for England, who continued discharging the responsibilities of trusteeship and the financial administration of the Anglican Church and its parishes.

JAMES H. SMYLIE
Union Theological Seminary, Richmond, Va.

ECCLESIASTICAL COSTUME. See COSTUME, ECCLESIASTICAL.

ECCLESIASTICUS, i-klē-zē-as'ti-kəs, is a book written in the tradition of the Old Testament wisdom literature by Jesus ben Eleazar ben Sira, or Sirach. It is sometimes referred to as *Sirach*. The book is classified among the Old Testament apocrypha by most Protestants, although it is accepted as canonical by Roman Catholics and recognized by the tradition of the Eastern Orthodox Church. (See BIBLE—*1. Canon of the Old Testament*.) The Latin title, Ecclesiasticus, which means "ecclesiastical," first appears in the writings of Cyprian of Carthage (died 258), and it suggests that the book was read in the early church.

The book was originally written in Hebrew in Jerusalem about 200–180 B.C., and was translated into Greek some time after 132 B.C. by the author's grandson. In his prologue the translator informs us that he undertook the work "for the benefit of those living abroad who wish to acquire wisdom and are disposed to live according to the standards of the Law."

Text. The text of the work presents difficult problems. The Hebrew version, although known to St. Jerome and quoted in early Jewish sources, was lost to the Western world until the end of the 19th century. Since then, several discoveries have yielded about two thirds of the original Hebrew text: parts of five different manuscripts were discovered among the treasures of the genizah (a storeroom for worn-out manuscripts) of the Karaite synagogue in Old Cairo; a fragmentary scroll containing chapters 39–44 was found in the excavations at Masada in 1963–1964; and a few fragments have been excavated from Cave 2 near Khirbet Qumran. The Hebrew text has several glosses, with many retroversions to the early Syriac version, which itself was translated from the Hebrew.

The Greek form of the text represents the original Hebrew, but it also contains several corrupt renderings. The Old Latin translation (from the Greek) adopted by St. Jerome for the Vulgate Bible has several expansions in it. Hence any modern translation is forced to weigh all the evidence from the Hebrew text and the ancient versions if it intends to be a scientific and accurate rendering.

Author. From the book itself we learn that ben Sira was a wisdom teacher, or scribe (*sopher:* 50:27; 51:23), resident in Jerusalem, and he has left a description of himself and his profession in 39:1-16. He was very conscious of his mission as a wisdom teacher (24:30-34), and his work is a compendium of Old Testament wisdom teaching. He used the phraseology of earlier Biblical works, especially Proverbs and Psalms, to express his thought and wrote in the manner of "anthological composition." But he was no mere theorist; he speaks also of his travels (34:11), and his observations reveal his broad experience of the world he lived in.

Contents. The contents of the book are so diversified and loosely structured that any division of the work is somewhat artificial. Many scholars have indicated a division into three parts. The first two begin with long poems in praise of wisdom (1:1-20; 24:1-29). The third begins with a hymn praising God's works in nature (42:15).

The general style is that of the proverb, or *mashal*, which embodies varied aspects of truth, based upon both traditional teaching and experience. Ordinarily there are two hemistichs to each unit, following the pattern of Hebrew parallelism, and the units are usually bunched together when they treat of a particular theme; for example: wisdom (1:1-30; 4:11-19; 6:18-37; 14:20 to 15:10; 19:17-26; 24:1-31); humility (3:17-29); friendship (6:5-17; 9:10-16; 11:29 to 14:2; 22:19-26; 36:18 to 37:15); women (9:1-9; 25:13 to 26:18; 42:9-14); Providence (32:14 to 33:18; 40:1 to 41:13). Toward the end of the book various literary forms are employed: hymns (42:15 to 43:33, on the greatness of God's works in nature; 39:12-35, in praise of God the creator; 24:3-29, on Wisdom's praise of herself; 44:1 to 50:24, in praise of the fathers); psalm of thanksgiving (51:1-12); lamentation (36:1-17).

Doctrine. The teaching of Sirach represents the point of view of a traditionalist in Palestine at the turn of the 2d century B.C., before the process of Hellenization reached the stage of persecution that marked the reign of the Seleucid ruler Antiochus IV Epiphanes (died 163 B.C.). Without being explicitly anti-Hellenistic (but see 36:1-17), the work is a stern reminder to fellow Jews of the ideals and practices of their religion.

The direction of the author's teaching can be seen from the fact that he explicitly identifies wisdom with the Law of Moses (chap. 24). The eternal and divine origin of wisdom was proclaimed in Proverbs 8:22-31. Wisdom was often personified in the Bible; thus it is described as being commanded by the Creator to take up a dwelling in Jacob, an inheritance in Israel (24:8). Wisdom, which is beyond the normal attainment of creatures (Job 28:1-28), is to be acquired by observing the Law. Its beginning was already recognized in the "fear of the Lord" (Proverbs 1:7; Job 28:28). Sirach develops and concretizes this theme in the observance of the Law.

For Sirach, divine retribution is a basic fact in life. He warns against "senseless men" who argue that God is not concerned about them (16:17ff.); they will surely be punished: "Great as his mercy is his punishment; he judges men, each according to his deeds" (16:12). He refuses to be scandalized by the apparent prosperity of sinners (11:14ff.) or by the affliction of the poor: "call no man happy before his death, for by how he ends, a man is known" (11:28).

Nevertheless, he says nothing about retribution in the next life. He holds the same view of the next world and of death as his Jewish predecessors (38:16–23; 41:1–4). After death, men (both good and evil) are to lead a more or less miserable existence in the nether world (Sheol), so vividly described by Job (10:21–22) and in Ecclesiastes (9:10). Therefore, the divine honor demands that the scales of justice be balanced in this life. In view of the intimations of a blessed immortality in Psalms 49 and 73, and of the doctrine of bodily resurrection in Daniel 12:2, Sirach's conservative attitude on the question is somewhat surprising. All the more admirable is his spirit of faith and acceptance in the face of death (41:1–4).

Although Sirach does not open new paths in theology, his work is a valuable summary of, and witness to, Jewish piety in the period before the Christian era.

ROLAND E. MURPHY, O. CARM.
Catholic University of America

Bibliography
Box, George H., and Oesterley, W. O. E., "Sirach," *The Apocrypha and Pseudepigrapha of the Old Testament*, pp. 268–517 (Oxford 1931).
DiLella, Alexander, *The Hebrew Text of Sirach: A Text-Critical and Historical Study* (The Hague 1966).
Duesberg, H., *Les scribes inspirés*, 2d ed. (Maredsous, Belgium, 1966).
Hartman, Louis F., "Sirach in Hebrew and Greek," *Catholic Biblical Quarterly*, vol. 23, pp. 443–451 (Washington 1961).
Smend, R., *Die Weisheit des Jesus Sirach* (Berlin 1906).

ECCLESIOLOGY, ik-lē-zē-ol'ə-jē, is the branch of Christian theology concerned with a systematic study of the church. The fundamental concern in ecclesiology is the relationship between the church's visible, organizational structure and its invisible, or spiritual, reality. The New Testament writers did not attempt a systematic theological presentation on the church; rather they spoke from their experience of the church as a community of believers, using terms such as the "Kingdom of God" and the "Mystical Body." Similarly, patristic and Scholastic treatments of the church are not systematic analyses but considerations of specific aspects. The first formal treatises on ecclesiology appeared in the late medieval period.

By the time of the Reformation, two trends in ecclesiology are recognizable: Protestant ecclesiology emphasized the church's spiritual nature, while Catholic ecclesiology stressed visible structure. Modern trends seem to be directed toward development of an ecclesiology that integrates these two aspects of the nature of the church.

JOHN T. FORD, C. S. C.
Catholic University of America

ECDYSIS, ek'də-səs, the process of casting off the outer layer of the skin. See MOLTING.

ECHEGARAY Y EIZAGUIRRE, ā-chä-gä-rä'ē ē e-ē-thä-gēr'rä, **José** (1832–1916), Spanish dramatist, who was the outstanding playwright of Spain in the last decades of the 19th century. He was born in Madrid on April 19, 1832, and was professor of mathematics in Madrid from 1854 to 1868. In 1868 he was elected to the Cortes, and he served in a number of government posts until 1874, when he published *El libro talonario*, the first of his more than 60 plays. In 1904 he shared the Nobel Prize for literature with Frédéric Mistral. He died in Madrid on Sept. 14, 1916.

Echegaray's earliest plays, such as *La esposa del vengador* (1874), were romantic, but he was increasingly influenced by Ibsen, and his most famous dramas are "problem" plays, such as *O locura o santidad* (1877; Eng. tr., *Madman or Saint*, 1912) and *El gran Galeoto* (1881; Eng. tr., *The World and His Wife*, 1908).

ECHEVERIA, ech-ə-və-rē'ə, is a genus of low-growing succulent plants of the orpine family (Crassulaceae). Members of the genus have relatively large, flat, fleshy leaves that are often arranged on a short stem in the form of a rosette. Their flowers are borne in long clusters and are symmetrical in the number and arrangement of their floral parts. There are five fused sepals, five petals that are fused into a tube, two whorls or five stamens each, and five pistils. One of the most widely grown species is *Echeveria metallica*, which has purplish leaves with a metallic sheen. Another popular species is *E. secunda*, which has pale green, red-tipped leaves. Both species are grown as potted plants and as edgings.

SIDNEY C. BAUSOR
California State College, Pa.

ECHEVERRÍA, ā-chā-ver-rē'ä, **Esteban** (1805–1851), Argentine poet, who introduced romanticism into South American literature. He was born in Buenos Aires and lived from 1826 to 1830 in Paris, where he was exposed to European liberal political theory. Returning to Argentina, he opposed the dictator Juan Manuel de Rosas and in 1838 was exiled to Montevideo, Uruguay, where he died.

Although Echeverría was more talented as a prose writer, his greatest influence was as a romantic national poet. His most famous poem, *La cautiva*, included in *Rimas* (1837), idealizes the Argentine pampas. Other works include the poem *Elvira* (1832), the verse collection *Los consuelos* (1834), and the novella *El matadero* (1837).

ECHEVERRÍA ÁLVAREZ, ā-chā-ve-rē'ə äl'vä-räs, **Luis** (1922–   ), president of Mexico. He was born on Jan. 17, 1922, and received a law degree from the National University of Mexico. He joined Mexico's ruling Institutional Revolutionary party (PRI) in 1946 and served the party as press director. Beginning in 1952 he held a series of government posts of increasing importance, culminating in 1964 with his appointment as minister of the interior. Echeverría held this key office until October 1969, when he was nominated as the PRI presidential candidate in the 1970 election.

Although nomination by the dominant PRI assures election in Mexico, Echeverría campaigned extensively, pledging to continue the basically centrist policies of the incumbent, Gustavo Díaz Ordaz. Echeverría won by a landslide and began his six-year term on Dec. 1, 1970.

Echidna
R. VAN NOSTRAND, FROM NATIONAL AUDUBON SOCIETY

ECHIDNA, i-kid'nə, the *spiny anteater,* a primitive egg-laying mammal of Australia and New Guinea. Echidnas range from 14 to 32 inches (35–77 cm) in length and from 5½ to 22 pounds (2.5–10 kg) in weight. Their fur, which is mixed with white, yellowish, or black spines, varies from brownish to black in color. The jaws lack teeth, and the sensitive muzzle is long and hairless. The mouth is small, being wide enough only for the protrusion of the long sticky tongue.

Echidnas have strong legs and powerful claws and are able to bury themselves in the ground with remarkable rapidity. They feed almost entirely on ants and termites, which they obtain by digging up the insects' nests.

The female lays a single egg into a pouch that develops on the belly in the breeding season. The young (about ½-inch, or 13 mm, long) hatches after 10 days and stays in the pouch for 6 to 8 weeks, until its spines appear. It feeds by sucking milk from two special areas— the mammary areolae—of the female's skin, where the ducts from the milk glands open to the outside.

The echidnas make up the family Tachyglossidae of the order Monotremata. Two species (*Tachyglossus aculeatus* and *T. setosus*) are found in Australia; *T. setosus* is confined to Tasmania and some of the nearby islands. In addition to *T. aculeatus,* three species of echidnas (*Zaglossus bruijni, Z. bartoni,* and *Z. bubuensis*) occur in New Guinea.

A. G. LYNE, *Author of "Marsupials and Monotremes of Australia"*

ECHINOCACTUS. See CACTUS—*Varieties.*

ECHINOCEREUS, ek-ə-nō-sē'rē-əs, is a genus of about 50 species of cacti found in the western United States and Mexico. Members of the genus are known as *hedgehog cacti.* They are mostly desert plants, but some are found in brush and on hillsides from sea level to an elevation of 10,000 feet (3,000 meters). They are also sometimes cultivated for their attractive flowers.

Hedgehog cacti are generally globe-shaped or cylinder-shaped and are found low and prostrate or sometimes pendant. They are spiny and have day-blooming flowers on the sides near the top of the branches. The flowers are large and either bell- or funnel-shaped; they may be scarlet, purple, yellow, white, or brownish green. The fruit of some hedgehog cactus species is edible.

ECHINODERM, i-kī'nə-dûrm, any member of the exclusively marine phylum Echinodermata, containing the starfish, brittle stars, sea urchins, sea cucumbers, crinoids, and several large fossil groups. Echinoderms often occur in immense numbers and are most abundant in the warmer seas and shallow water. They are also found in the deepest parts of the ocean and in polar seas.

Echinoderms, except for a few pelagic sea cucumbers, are bottom dwellers but vary greatly in habits and ecological roles. Crinoids feed on detritus and plankton, which are trapped in mucus and carried along special grooves to the mouth. Sea cucumbers are also detritus eaters, but they use a circle of tentacles around the mouth to collect their food.

Starfish have no jaws but are carnivorous. They swallow worms and similar prey animals whole; in the case of colonial animals or large clams or oysters that cannot be swallowed, the starfish extrudes its stomach and envelopes the soft parts of its prey, digesting it externally.

Brittle stars have teeth around the mouth and feed on detritus and small organisms. Sea urchins, which may be either mainly herbivorous, mainly carnivorous, or scavengers, use a complex jaw mechanism (Aristotle's lantern) for crushing their food.

Structure. Most echinoderms are radially symmetrical, with five (or multiples of five) similar parts regularly arranged around a central point. In some groups, notably the sea urchins and sea cucumbers, the symmetry becomes biradial—a combination of radial and bilateral (matching right and left sides) symmetries.

The echinoderm's body wall contains calcareous (stony) plates, spines, or spicules. These skeletal structures, or ossicles, may be separated by connective tissue to form a flexible body wall, as in starfish and sea cucumbers, or fused together to form a firm test, or shell, as in the sea urchins.

Echinoderms are headless, and their diffuse, uncentralized nervous system lacks a brain. The circulatory (haemal) system consists of a system of coelomic sinuses, or body cavities, and is generally poorly developed. The fluid of this system, moved by action of hairlike cilia, is believed to carry digested food to all parts of the body. There are no excretory organs. Excretion is accomplished by the diffusion of dissolved wastes through the body wall or by special amoebocyte cells in the coelom (main body cavity) that engulf wastes and carry them to the outside. Respiratory arrangements vary within the groups but basically consist of the exchange of gases through the body wall and tube feet.

Ambulacral System. The ambulacral, or water vascular, system occurs in all echinoderms. It is a hydraulic system of fluid-filled canals that functions in locomotion, in grasping prey or substrate, and in respiration. Water enters the system through the sievelike madreporite (water pore) and passes down the stone canal into the ring canal circling the mouth. The ring canal gives rise to the spokelike radial canals, which possess numerous branches called lateral canals. The lateral canals, each equipped with a valve, lead into the external tube feet, or podia. The internal ends of the podia are expanded into bulblike ampullae.

In starfish and crinoids, the podia project into depressions, called ambulacral grooves, running along each arm. Body surface areas penetra-

ECHINODERMS include the starfish (*left*), sea urchins (*top right*), and sand dollars (*bottom right*), among other forms. The living sea urchin is covered with movable spines, which are missing from the skeleton. Living sand dollars are covered with very short spines. Certain starfish prey upon sea urchins and sand dollars.

CLASSIFICATION OF ECHINODERMS

The phylum Echinodermata is divided into two subphyla, the Eleutherozoa and the Pelmatazoa. All living forms except the Crinoidea belong to the Eleutherozoa.

SUBPHYLUM ELEUTHEROZOA

This group comprises stalkless free-living forms that normally lie on one side or live with the oral surface downward.

Class Asteroidea. This class of echinoderms comprises the familiar starfish. The arms are not sharply set off from the central disc, and each arm has an open ambulacral groove. Asteroids, worldwide in distribution, prefer rocky coasts, but some occur in deep water. Pincerlike structures, called pedicellariae, found among the body spines, are used to clean the body surface and to attack small invaders. Starfish first appeared in the Ordovician period, nearly 500 million years ago. Five orders are recognized, two of which are entirely extinct.

Class Ophiuroidea. The ophiuroids, or brittle stars, have slender, agile arms supported by skeletal ossicles (vertebrae) that either permit twining and grasping movements or restrict motion to the horizontal plane. Although abundant, brittle stars are inconspicuous, hiding under rocks or living in the sand. They are found in polar and tropical seas, in shallow or deep water. The most remarkable forms are the basket stars, with repeatedly branching arms. The class, comprising some 1,600 living species, first appeared in the Mississipian period about 350 million years ago.

Class Echinoidea. The echinoids are characterized by a firm, compact test, or shell, and many movable spines. The class is divided into two subclasses: the radially symmetrical Regularia, which includes the hemispherical to globose sea urchins, and the biradially or bilaterally symmetrical Irregularia, which includes the disclike sand dollars and the more convex heart urchins. The highly developed Aristotle's lantern of sea urchins pumps coelomic fluid in and out of the gills (little bushy outgrowths around the mouth) for respiratory exchange. Echinoids first appeared in the Ordovician period. There are about 850 living species.

Class Holothuroidea. The holothuroids, or sea cucumbers, are elongate leathery animals generally preferring shallow tropical waters, but some occur in the cold depths. Sea cucumbers are not obviously radial, as they normally lie with one ambulacral field down; this ventral surface is modified for locomotion, while the dorsal (upper) surface bears sense organs. Sea cucumbers are commonly bottom dwellers, but some members of the order Elasipoda are floating pelagic forms. A unique feature of many sea cucumbers is the "respiratory tree" attached to the hindgut: water is pumped through the anus into the tree for respiratory exchange. Sea cucumbers first appeared in the Ordovician period. About 500 living species are known.

SUBPHYLUM PELMATAZOA

This group, which includes one living class and four extinct classes, contains those echinoderms that live attached to the bottom, at least temporarily, by an aboral (lower surface) stalk.

Class Crinoidea. This class includes the stalked sea lilies and the free-living feather stars; the latter are attached as juveniles but break free as they mature. Crinoids are gregarious: sea lilies occur in crowded submarine gardens, and as many as 10,000 feather stars have been taken in a single haul. Unlike most echinoderms, the crinoids prefer cold water and are most abundant in the cold ocean depths or in cold oceans. The class Crinoidea contains about 600 living species, all belonging to the order Articulata. The first crinoids appeared in the Cambrian period, about 600 million years ago, and more than 5,000 extinct species are known.

Fossil Classes. Four of the five classes of the subphylum Pelmatazoa are wholly extinct. The class Heterostelea appeared in the Cambrian period, about 600 million years ago, and became extinct in the lower Silurian, some 440 million years ago. The Heterostelea, lacking radial symmetry and typically without arms, are the most primitive echinoderms. The class Edrioasteroidea also appeared in the Cambrian, but persisted until the lower Carboniferous (Mississippian), some 350 million years ago. They were disclike forms, free living or attached aborally, with five ambulacral fields on the oral surface. The classes Cystidea and Blastoidea appeared in the Ordovician period, about 500 million years ago, and became extinct during the Permian, some 225 million years ago. The Cystidea were usually without pentamerous radial symmetry, actually having only three ambulacral fields that were divided to form five. They possessed slender armlike structures known as brachioles. The Blastoidea were bud-shaped, had pentamerous radial symmetry, and, like the Cystidea, possessed brachioles.

ted by the podia are known as ambulacral fields.

The closing of the valve in a lateral canal makes the ampulla-podium appendage a closed cylinder. Contraction of muscles in the walls of the ampulla is then able to force water into the podium, extending it. Muscles in the podial wall bend the podium or pull in the center of its tip to form a suction cup. Movements of the podia are used for locomotion or food handling, as well as for attaching the animal to the bottom.

Development. The symmetrical relationships of the echinoderms are unique. They typically begin as free-swimming, bilaterally symmetrical larvae that eventually undergo a profound metamorphosis. They change from a bilateral symmetry to a radial symmetry usually centered around a top-to-bottom axis. The coelom (main body cavity) becomes greatly altered, giving rise to the ambulacral system and a complex set of coelomic cavities, or sinuses. Five radial canals and five radial coelomic sinuses, which form the basis for the characteristic five-part symmetry of the adult, develop from the central ring structures of these two systems. Starfish, brittle stars, and crinoids develop five radially arranged arms into which extend the radial canals, coelomic sinuses, and other parts.

PAUL A. MEGLITSCH
Drake University, Des Moines, Iowa

Further Reading: Hyman, Libbie H., *The Invertebrates:* vol. 4, *Echinodermata* (New York 1955).

ECHINOID, a member of the echinoderm class Echinoidea, which includes sea urchins, sand dollars, and heart urchins. See ECHINODERM.

ECHIUROID ek-ē-yōō'roid, any of a small group of unsegmented, burrowing marine worms found throughout temperate and tropical regions. Echiuroids, which make up the phylum Echiuroidea, are distinguished by their highly mobile, bilobed proboscis (tubular extension from the forward end of the body), which they use as a tactile organ, for getting food, and for locomotion.

An echiuroid worm has a stout, sausage-shaped body equipped with a pair of strong setae used in burrowing. It is usually green, red, or brown. The digestive tube is thin-walled, coiled, and convoluted. A short dorsal blood vessel functions as a heart. The dorsal vessel is connected to a long ventral blood vessel in the region of the proboscis, and a blood sinus around the digestive tube returns the worm's colorless blood to the dorsal vessel. Nephridia are used for excretion. A ventral nerve cord, in which no segmented ganglia can be seen, connects with a nerve ring at the forward end of the body, but there is little evidence of a brain.

Germ cells are released from the gonads of both sexes into the body cavity, where they mature. They then are shed into the sea, where fertilization occurs, and the young pass through a larval stage. In one genus—*Bonellia*—the mode of sexual determination is unusual: a larva developing alone always becomes a female, while a larva developing near a female becomes a dwarf parasitic male.

PAUL A. MEGLITSCH, *Drake University*

ECHO, ek'ō, in classical mythology, was a mountain nymph. As servant to Hera, she was persuaded by Zeus to distract his wife with endless chatter. Hera deprived her of speech, condemning her to repeat only the last syllable of every word she heard. Echo fell in love with the beautiful Narcissus, but unable to declare her love, she pined away until nothing was left but her voice. Another legend told of her rejecting Pan's love. In his wrath he drove the shepherds to tear her apart, but each of the parts retained the power to speak.

ECHO, a sound reflected from a surface distant from the sound source. When a person lets out a brief shout at a steep cliff, for example, he first hears the sound traveling directly to his ears and a little later hears the sound bounced back from the cliff. A person can distinguish an echo from the emitted sound only if the reflecting surface is more than about 30 feet (9 meters) away.

A rough estimate of the distance to a reflecting surface can be made by measuring the time from the emission of the sound to the arrival of the echo and by using the equation $d = vt/2$, where d is the distance in feet, v is 1,100 feet (335 meters) per second (speed of sound in air), and t is the time in seconds.

Bats, porpoises, and some other animals find their way by emitting high-frequency sounds and listening for echoes bounced off obstacles. Echolocation as expertly practiced by bats and porpoises also enables them to find their prey. Man makes use of echolocation to detect objects under water, in the air, and in space. See also ANIMAL BEHAVIOR; BAT; RADAR—*1. Principles;* SOUND—*Reflection of Sound;* ULTRASONICS.

ECHO SOUNDING. See SOUNDINGS.

ECHTERNACH, eкн'tər-näкн, is a small town in Luxembourg, situated on the right bank of the Sûre (Sauer) River (which here forms the border with West Germany), 8 miles (13 km) above its confluence with the Moselle. The winding valley of the Sûre, affording picturesque scenery, attracts numerous tourists, for whom Echternach, with its several hotels, is a convenient center. The town began as a Roman settlement and later grew around a 7th century Benedictine priory; surviving buildings include a 15th century town hall. Population: (1960) 3,389.

F. J. MONKHOUSE
Author of "Geography of Northwestern Europe"

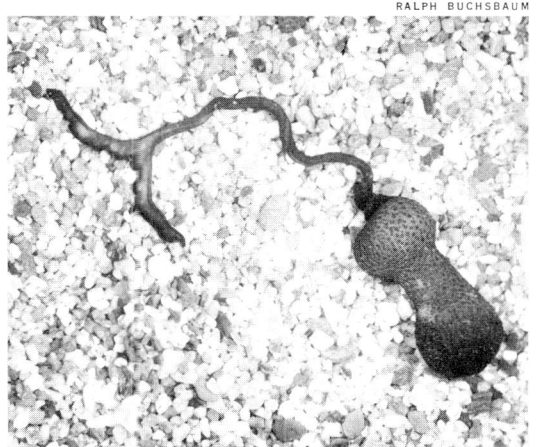

FEMALE ECHIUROID of the genus *Bonellia*. The males of this genus live as parasites on or within the females.

RALPH BUCHSBAUM

ECK, ek, **Johann** (1486–1543), German Catholic theologian, who was Martin Luther's principal opponent. His real name was Johann Maier, but he adopted the name *Eccius,* Latinized from Egg, the Swabian village where he was born on Nov. 13, 1486. After studies in Heidelberg, Tübingen, Cologne, and Freiburg and ordination to the priesthood in 1508, Eck began in 1510 his lifelong career as professor of theology in Ingolstadt. His treatise on predestination and his liberal opinion favoring the morality of a 5% rate of interest gained him an early reputation and brought him into friendly contact with Luther.

Eck's critical remarks on Luther's 95 theses on indulgences led to the Leipzig Disputation of 1519, in which Eck defended man's free cooperation with God's grace against Luther's colleague Carlstadt. When Luther argued that the special authority of the bishop of Rome was a manmade ordinance, Eck answered that the councils and Church Fathers saw the pope's authority as given by Christ. This drove Luther to question the authority of ecumenical councils and to assert Scripture as the only source of doctrine.

In Rome in 1520, Eck helped compose *Exsurge Domine,* Pope Leo X's condemnation of 41 propositions from Luther's early writings. Eck was commissioned to publish the condemnation throughout Germany. In the 1520's he wrote erudite treatises against Luther, defending papal authority, confession, purgatory, and the sacrifice of the Mass. His *Enchiridion,* which saw 91 editions from 1525 to 1600, was a presentation of the main Protestant articles with a refutation from Scripture and the Fathers. In 1530 at Augsburg and 1541 at Regensburg, Eck represented the Catholic side in unsuccessful colloquies seeking agreement with the Protestants.

Eck clearly saw the need of reform in the church and urged the Pope to call synods in order to rouse the lethargic bishops. He underscored the abuses in preaching, clerical conduct, indulgences, and the benefice system that needed correction. In Ingolstadt he spent 10 years as the zealous pastor of the Church of Our Lady. Five volumes of his sermons appeared in the 1530's, and his largely unsuccessful translation of the Bible into German came out in 1537. He died in Ingolstadt on Feb. 10, 1543.

JARED WICKS, S. J.
Bellarmine School of Theology, North Aurora, Ill.

ECKENER, ek'ə-nər, **Hugo** (1868–1954), German aeronautical engineer and airship pioneer. He was born in Flensburg, Germany, on Aug. 10, 1868. In the early 1900's he joined Count von Zeppelin's firm and helped develop the rigid airship. The company built 5 commercial airships, which transported some 37,250 passengers on almost 1,600 flights before World War I. During World War I, Eckener trained airship pilots and directed the construction of 88 Zeppelins for the Germany Navy.

After Zeppelin's death, Eckener returned to commercial airships in November 1918. He commanded the ZR-3, built for the U. S. Navy as a war reparations payment, when it was flown across the Atlantic from Germany to Lakehurst, N. J. (The airship was renamed the *Los Angeles.*) He also piloted the *Graf Zeppelin* in its 1929 flight around the world and commanded it in its polar exploration flight of 1931.

In 1937, Eckener commanded the *Hindenburg* when it burned at Lakehurst, N. J., on May 6, with heavy loss of life. This tragedy, which might have been averted if the United States had not refused to sell the safer helium gas to other countries, virtually ended rigid airship travel as well as military use of airships.

After World War II, Eckener became a consultant for the Goodyear Tire and Rubber Company, but he returned to Germany in 1948 to head a machinery plant. He died at Friedrichshafen, Germany, on Aug. 14, 1954.

ROBERT S. WOODBURY
Massachusetts Institute of Technology

ECKERMANN, ek'ər-män, **Johann Peter** (1792–1854), German author, best known as a literary assistant and close friend of Goethe. Eckermann was born at Winsen, Hannover (now part of Lower Saxony), on Sept. 21, 1792. After attracting Goethe's interest wtih his *Beiträge zur Poesie mit besonderer Hinweisung auf Goethe* (1823), he moved to Weimar to become the poet's literary assistant. After Goethe's death in 1832, Eckermann was responsible for the publication of his literary remains (1832–1833) and, with Friedrich Wilhelm Riemer, of his complete works (40 vols., 1839–1840). Eckermann died at Weimar on Dec. 3, 1854.

Eckermann's most important work was *Gespräche mit Goethe in den Letzten Jahren seines Lebens* (3 vols., 1836–1848; Eng. tr., *Conversations with Goethe,* 1850), which records the essence of Goethe's thought and character during the last years of his life. Eckermann also published two volumes of poetry (1821, 1838).

ECKHART, ek'härt, **Johann** (c.1260–1328), German Dominican theologian and writer, who is regarded as the founder of mysticism in Germany. He is often called *Meister Eckhart;* his name is sometimes spelled *Johannes Eckart.*

Born at Hochheim in Thuringia, Eckhart joined the Dominican order at Erfurt, where sometime between 1290 and 1298 he was prior. Shortly after, he became vicar of Thuringia. In 1300 he went to Paris to study and there became a master of theology. Elected provincial of the Dominican province of Saxony in 1303, he served two terms. He returned to Paris to lecture in 1320; later he taught at Strasbourg and in 1323 returned to Cologne to become regent of the Dominican house of studies.

Eckhart was a prolific writer. He wrote in Latin for the educated and preached in German for the illiterate. As a preacher he attracted huge audiences. At that time German had few philosophical or theological terms, and Eckhart coined many new words.

In Eckhart's later years, the papacy was engaged in a violent struggle with King Louis IV of Bavaria over the disputed election of the Holy Roman emperor in 1314. Louis denounced Pope John XXII as a heretic and demanded his deposition; in turn, the Pope excommunicated him. The Dominicans published the bull throughout Germany, thereby enraging the partisans of the king. The friars were driven out of some cities, and their monasteries were burned.

During this period the archbishop of Cologne was Henry II of Virneburg, a fanatic who wanted to destroy the Dominicans. He appointed a commission consisting of two Franciscan spirituals, both enemies of Eckhart, to try the Meister for heresy. They cited him before their tribunal on Sept. 26, 1326. Although he denied their jurisdiction, they declared him guilty of heresy on 100 counts. Eckhart appealed to the Pope, who ordered the archbishop to forward all documents to Avignon. To defend his teaching, Eckhart went to that city. Soon after the hearings began, he fell ill, and returned to Cologne, where he died a few months later, in 1328.

After his death, the papal commission dismissed 71 of the charges, many of which were gross distortions. The commission found 17 statements were heretical and 11 others "temerarious but capable of being explained in an orthodox sense." Eckhart was not declared a heretic because he had publicly declared, months before the trial began, that he would submit to any judgment by the church on his teaching.

Influenced by Neoplatonism and by Thomas Aquinas, Meister Eckhart's theology is complex. Like all mystics, he strains common theological terminology to convey his experiences. The highest form of the mystical life is union with God, and Eckhart demands a complete "laying bare" of the soul as a prerequisite for this union. The contact with God takes place in the inmost part of the soul, its highest part, the source of divine life. It is essentially intellectual and transcends human imagery. Union or identification with Christ, the Mediator, makes possible the return of the soul to God.

Eckhart's teaching was not pantheistic, although he was accused of it. Among those he influenced were Heinrich Suso and the mystics Johannes Tauler and Jan van Ruysbroeck.
WILLIAM R. BONNIWELL, O. P.
Priory of St. Vincent Ferrer, New York

ECKHEL, ek'əl, **Joseph Hilarius** (1737–1798), Austrian historian and numismatist, who founded scientific numismatics. He was born in Enzersfeld, Lower Austria, on Jan. 13, 1737. He became a member of the Society of Jesus in 1751 and was ordained in 1764.

Eckhel became interested in coins while teaching at a school where there was a collection of ancient Greek coins. In 1772 he abandoned teaching because of illness, and he subsequently devoted himself to the study of numismatics and archaeology. In 1774 he became director of the numismatic section of the Imperial Museum in Vienna, and in 1776 he was appointed professor of antiquities at the University of Vienna. He published many works on coins and gems, but his greatest work was *Doctrina nummorum veterum* (8 vols., 1792–1798; addenda, 1826). He died in Vienna on May 16, 1798.

ECLAMPSIA, e-klamp'sē-ə, is a rare disorder that occurs only in pregnant women and is characterized by high blood pressure, edema (swelling), excessive weight gain, convulsions, and the presence of albumin in the urine. Eclampsia occurs during the last 10 weeks of pregnancy and is most common in young women having their first babies. The cause is unknown.

Early symptoms of eclampsia can usually be detected through regular prenatal checkups. When a doctor finds that a pregnant woman has developed high blood pressure and puffiness of the face, ankles, and fingers, along with other symptoms, he immediately sends her to the hospital. In the hospital she is given sedatives and other drugs that nearly always prevent the onset of convulsions. She is also given drugs to reduce her blood pressure and increase her urine output. In most cases the patient soon improves, and labor begins spontaneously. With the birth of the baby, eclampsia usually disappears.

In those cases where the patient does not respond to treatment, the pregnancy is terminated by breaking the amniotic sac (bag of waters), administering drugs to induce labor, or performing a cesarean section. If convulsions have already started, the pregnancy is terminated as soon as the seizures stop.
J. P. GREENHILL, M. D.
Cook County Graduate School of Medicine

ECLECTICISM, e-klek'tə-siz-əm, in philosophy and the arts, is the selection of elements from a diversity of sources to create a new approach or style. The term is derived from the Greek word *eklegein* (to select or choose).

Philosophy. A philosophical system is said to be eclectic if its heterogeneous doctrines are logically incompatible or otherwise antagonistic. Eclectic systems, as distinguished from syncretistic systems, which also combine diverse ideas, generally do not try seriously to reconcile opposing concepts or show an underlying unity of thought. They are thus vulnerable to the charge of inconsistency, and the term "eclectic" is frequently used unfavorably.

Philosophical eclecticism usually develops when there are several conflicting systems of thought. In the 2d century B. C. the skeptical approach of Carneades to the established Greek schools of philosophy gave rise to an eclectic spirit among such Greek philosophers as Panaetius of Rhodes and Posidonius of Apamea. Most Roman philosophers, especially Cicero and such Neoplatonists as Iamblichus, variously combined elements from Stoicism, Platonism, Pythagoreanism, and Cynicism.

Renaissance humanists were eclectic in their mixture of Christian and classical ideas, with the exception of Pico della Mirandola, who attempted to synthesize the doctrines of previous thinkers according to the Platonic theory that they were all faulty glimpses of a perfect truth. In modern times, major philosophers tend to be eclectic in their consideration of various traditions, such as rationalism and empiricism; but they generally go on, like Leibniz and Spinoza, to a syncretistic attempt at reconciliation. More specifically eclectic philosophers include Christian Wolff and Moses Mendelssohn in the 18th century and, in the 19th, Victor Cousin (q. v.), who coined the term. Such speculative literary figures as Coleridge, Carlyle, Pater, Emerson, and Thoreau may also be considered eclectics.

The Arts. In the arts the term "eclecticism" is applied to a school or trend that draws on many aesthetic styles to produce works that, if not harmonious or beautiful in the classical sense, are at least novel. (Victorian architecture, for example, is called eclectic because it drew on such past styles as classical and Gothic.) The word may be used unfavorably, as in the case of Saint-Saëns, who is called eclectic in that his music draws indiscriminately from many aesthetically incompatible styles. Milton and other Mannerist poets are sometimes praised for their eclecticism in the sense that they have combined diverse styles with artistic success. Eclecticism is often associated with decadence, as in the case of the "decadent" school of such writers as J. K. Huysmans.
F. X. J. COLEMAN, *University of Pittsburgh*

TOTAL ECLIPSE OF THE SUN reveals structural details of the solar chromosphere and corona in a dramatic fashion. An overexposed image of the planet Venus is seen at the right of the photograph, taken in Bolivia in 1966.

HIGH ALTITUDE OBSERVATORY, BOULDER, COLORADO

ECLIPSE, i-klips'. In astronomy, an eclipse is said to occur when one celestial body enters the shadow of another body, or when it is hidden temporarily—either partially or totally—by another body.

Kinds of Eclipses. A *solar eclipse* takes place when the moon passes in front of and obscures the sun's disk; a *lunar eclipse* takes place when the moon enters the shadow of the earth. Because the sun and the moon dominate the sky and are close enough to be seen as disks, such eclipses are impressive natural phenomena. It is usually these events that are thought of, therefore, when speaking of eclipses.

Other celestial bodies also take part in eclipses, however. The other planets of the solar system sometimes pass behind the sun. The planets Mercury and Venus sometimes cross in front of it as well, because their orbits lie inside the orbit of the earth. Similarly, a number of planets have satellites, and these pass in front of and are eclipsed by their primaries. The earth's moon eclipses many stars as it moves across the sky. In all of these instances, however, the word "eclipse" ordinarily is not used, because of the great disparity between the apparent sizes of the bodies involved. Instead, the passage of one celestial body in front of a much larger body is called a *transit*, and the eclipse of a body of very small apparent size by a much larger or nearer body is called an *occultation*.

It should also be mentioned that beyond the solar system, when the orbital plane of a binary star system is seen nearly edge-on from the earth, the two stars that make up the system may be said to eclipse or occult one another reciprocally. Such star systems are called *eclipsing binaries*. The present article does not discuss the phenomena of eclipsing binaries, occultations, or transits; it is concerned only with eclipses of the sun and of the moon. See also BINARY STAR; OCCULTATION; TRANSIT.

History of Eclipse Observations. The earliest astronomical studies were intermingled with astrological concepts, and it was only natural that the spectacular phenomena of solar and lunar eclipses were taken by ancient civilizations to signify divine warnings to humanity. In the Mesopotamian region, for example, celestial phenomena such as eclipses were observed regularly, both for calendar computation and for religious purposes. One of the first eclipses to be observed with real precision was recorded in Babylonia in 721 B.C.; such early records of lunar and solar eclipses have even today found use in modern computations of lunar motions. The Chaldeans, in fact, commonly are credited with the discovery of the *saros*, a time cycle of about 18 years in which almost identical eclipses of the sun and moon are repeated.

Observations of eclipses and attempts at forecasts are found in records of ancient China, and it would also seem that the Mayan civilization in Guatemala and the Yucatán peninsula reached a remarkable level of astronomical knowledge. Mayan computations of time were very elaborate, and the Maya had tables for forecasting solar and lunar eclipses.

The first serious attempts to develop a scientific understanding of eclipses are found in ancient Greece, especially in the works of Hipparchus and of the later Alexandrian astronomer Ptolemy (2d century A.D.). Ptolemy's *Almagest* became the basic astronomical text for centuries thereafter, although scientists such as the 9th century Arab astronomer al-Battani improved somewhat on the calculations of precise locations and motions of celestial bodies through observing eclipses. Christopher Columbus, in his fourth journey along the northern coast of South Amer-

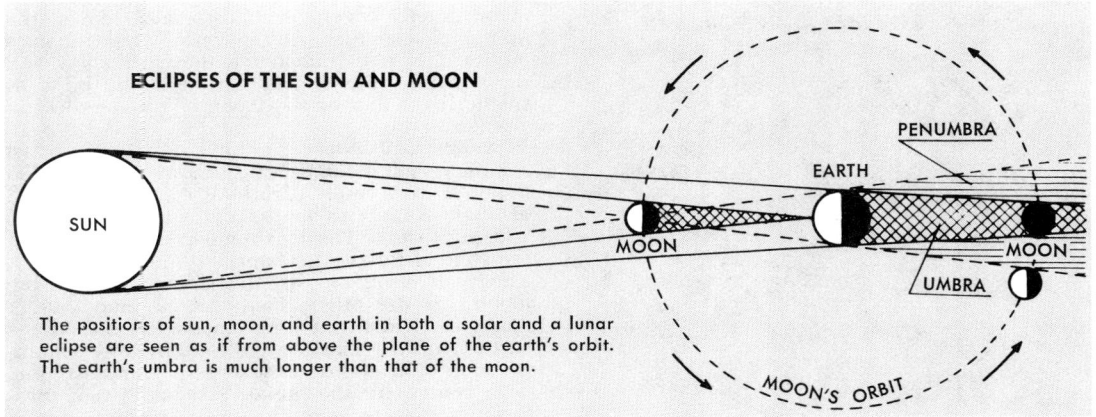

ECLIPSES OF THE SUN AND MOON

The positions of sun, moon, and earth in both a solar and a lunar eclipse are seen as if from above the plane of the earth's orbit. The earth's umbra is much longer than that of the moon.

ica, made use of the *Ephemeris* (tables of observed positions of celestial bodies) of the 15th century German astronomer Regiomontanus to predict a lunar eclipse on Feb. 29, 1504, in order to avoid a dangerous conflict with Indians. Jesuit missionaries who traveled to China about 1600 taught the Chinese how to use eclipse observations to calculate longitudes.

It was not until the 16th and 17th centuries, however, that the mechanics of eclipses were firmly established on a theoretical basis by the work of Johannes Kepler, Galileo, Isaac Newton, and other scientists. Their work determined the laws of motion and of gravitation that govern the orbits of the sun, the moon, the earth, and all other celestial bodies.

Galileo also is of interest in the history of eclipse observations for having discovered in 1610 the four brightest moons of Jupiter. This discovery aroused hopes that through observing the eclipses of these satellites it would be possible to determine differences in longitude around the earth by comparing local times of observation with those forecast by the ephemerides (astronomical tables). The ephemerides were still very inexact, however, as a result of imperfect knowledge of the satellites' motions and the inaccuracy of the clocks in use at that time. The proposed method therefore was not able to yield sufficiently reliable results.

On the other hand, the observations of the eclipses of Jupiter's moons gave the Danish astronomer Ole Rømer the opportunity, in 1675, to establish that light takes time to travel. Rømer had noticed that the intervals between successive eclipses of a satellite of Jupiter were regularly shorter when Jupiter and the earth approached each other, and that the intervals increased when the planets moved away from each other. From this he deduced that light has a finite velocity; and, using the observed time differences in the eclipses and the known distances between Jupiter and the earth, he was able to make the first good estimate of this velocity.

The astronomical tables of today—*The American Ephemeris, The Nautical Almanac,* and *Connaissance des Temps,* for example—provide all the basic information about the eclipses that will occur in a given year for some years in advance. The most outstanding work of this nature is the *Canon der Finsternisse* of the Austrian astronomer Theodor von Oppolzer, published in 1887, which contains a list of details on all the eclipses of the sun and the moon that have occurred and will occur between 1208 B.C. and 2162 A.D. It also contains a series of clear diagrams representing the zones of totality for solar eclipses in that period.

WHEN ECLIPSES OCCUR

In any one year, the minimum possible number of eclipses that can occur is two, and both of these would be solar eclipses. The maximum number is seven eclipses, five of the sun and two of the moon. The most recent year in which this maximum occurred was in 1935, and it will occur again in 2160.

Nodes of the Moon's Orbit. In order for an eclipse of the sun or the moon to take place, the sun, the moon, and the earth all must be on the same plane. In a solar eclipse, the sun must project the cone of the moon's shadow, or *umbra,* onto the earth's surface. In a lunar eclipse, the earth's umbra must envelop the moon. If the three bodies always remained on the same plane, an eclipse of the sun would occur at every new moon, and a lunar eclipse would occur at every full moon. This, of course, is not what happens. The reason is that the moon's orbit around the earth is inclined about 5° 9' to the ecliptic (the plane of the earth's orbit). Solar and lunar eclipses therefore can occur only when the new moon or the full moon is at one of the two *nodes,* or points of intersection, of the moon's orbit with the ecliptic.

If the two nodes of the lunar orbit were fixed, eclipses would still take place in a short and regular cycle. Because the moon is perturbed by other celestial bodies, however, the nodes of its orbit are not fixed. Instead they move with a retrograde motion—that is, from east to west—with respect to the earth, and they complete a revolution of the earth in 18.6 years.

Shadow Lengths. There is a further restriction on the occurrence of solar eclipses. The shadow projected by the moon toward the earth must indeed reach the earth's surface. The diameter of the sun is 400.7 times the diameter of the moon. From the known distances between the earth, the sun, and the moon, it can be calculated that the mean length of the moon's umbra is less than the mean distance of the moon from the earth. On this basis, the moon's shadow could not reach the earth at all. Because of the eccentricities of the orbits of the earth and the moon, however, the moon is nearer to the earth than

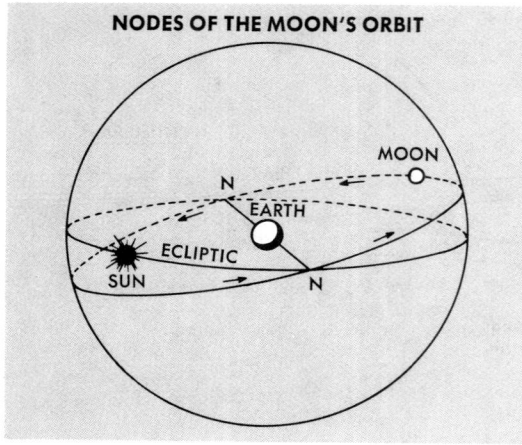

The two nodes, N, of the moon's orbit are the points where the orbit intersects with the ecliptic. Their positions shift, completing a revolution of the earth in 18.6 years. A solar or lunar eclipse can occur only when the new or full moon is at one of these nodes.

this mean distance much of the time. Its shadow can reach at least limited portions of the earth's surface.

The diameter of the earth's shadow at the distance of the moon, on the other hand, is about 2.65 times the diameter of the moon. Again, because of the eccentricity of the earth's orbit, the length of the earth's shadow and hence its diameter at the distance of the moon varies, but only by a few miles.

Cycle of Eclipses. Eclipses having similar characteristics (with respect to orbital relationships) take place in a cycle of about 18 years—the period of time that the Chaldeans called a saros. More precisely, the period is 6,585.32 days, the time that it takes nodes of the moon's orbit to complete one full circuit of the earth. The saros is exactly 223 times the length of the lunar month (the period of 29.5306 days from one new moon to the next). As for the sun, it takes 346.62 days, or one *eclipse year*, to return to the same node; and precisely 19 of these eclipse years are equal to 6,585.78 days. It can be noted that the period of 223 lunar months and the period of 19 eclipse years are almost exactly equal. This means that at the end of each saros the sun, the moon, and the nodes of the moon's orbit will be in almost identical positions, and that the sequence of eclipses will be repeated with only very small differences. Because of the rotation of the earth and because the zone of totality for solar eclipses is quite limited, however, the average time interval between two successive total solar eclipses at a given place on earth is about 360 years.

SOLAR ECLIPSES

An eclipse of the sun can occur only at new moon and when the moon is close enough to the earth for the vertex of its umbra to reach the earth's surface. Because of the respective sizes of the sun and the moon and their distances from the earth, their apparent diameters in the sky are almost the same. An observer of a solar eclipse, if he is located within the limited zone of totality, therefore sees the dark disk of the moon exactly cover, or almost exactly cover, the luminous solar disk. If the vertex of the moon's umbra does not quite touch the earth, however, the apparent diameter of the moon will be a bit smaller than that of the moon. This is called an *annular eclipse*.

Length and Extent. A total eclipse may last from a very few minutes up to a maximum of 7.5 minutes, as a result of orbital eccentricities and of slight variations in the diameters of the sun and the moon. The maximum possible extent of the zone of totality is about 170 miles (270 km). The *penumbra*, or partial shadow, cast by the moon, on the other hand, has a much wider diameter than the umbra. In the regions of the earth's surface that are covered by the penumbra, the solar eclipse is seen as a *partial eclipse*. The center of the lunar disk does not pass through the center of the solar disk in a partial eclipse; the maximum phase of the eclipse is described in terms of the ratio between the minimum width of the solar crescent and the diameter of the sun.

In the zone of total eclipse the umbra of the moon shifts from west to east—the same direction as the earth rotates—with a velocity of about 0.6 mile (1 km) per second. If this figure is combined with the velocity of rotation at different latitudes, it can be calculated that the umbra moves across the earth's surface with a relative velocity ranging from about 0.3 to 1.2 miles (0.5–2 km) per second.

An eclipse is described as a sequence of *contacts*. Thus, the first contact takes place when the disk of the moon, in its apparent motion from west to east, meets the west limb of the sun. About 75 minutes later there is a second contact, of the east limb of the moon with the sun's east limb; this is the beginning of the short phase of totality. The third contact occurs when the west limb of the moon leaves the west limb of the sun; and, again about 75 minutes later, there is a fourth and last contact when the west limb of the moon leaves the east limb of the solar disk, and the eclipse is over.

Appearance. In a partial eclipse there are no effects to be observed except the eclipse itself. A total eclipse presents a spectacle, however, that has aroused the admiration of men since the most ancient times. A rapid approach of the moon's umbra and the increasing darkness of the sky prepare observers for the moment when total eclipse begins. At that moment a relative darkness begins, somewhat like a night when a full moon is shining. Some fractions of a second before total eclipse, the so-called *Baily beads* can be seen. These dots of light are produced either by mountains that at the moment are on the limb of the moon or by the effect of diffraction. At the moment of total eclipse, the brilliant red solar chromosphere appears around the moon's dark disk. It is interrupted here and there by more or less extended high red flames. These flames are *prominences* that penetrate the silvery corona; the corona, in turn spreads to a great distance from the sun, its long streamers curved at the poles. The form and the appearance of the corona vary with the 11-year cycle of the sun's sunspot activity.

Scientific Importance. From a scientific viewpoint the study of total eclipses of the sun is very important for two major reasons. First, the stages of the eclipse can be precisely observed so that the times obtained can be compared with those forecast by calculations. The differences between these values can serve to verify and eventually to improve on the theories of the motions of the moon and of the earth. Second, in the brief moments when total eclipse takes place, the sun's chromosphere and corona can be studied in detail without the interference of the glaring light of the solar photosphere. Although the invention of the coronagraph (q.v.) and of monochromatic filters by the French astrophysicist Bernard F. Lyot, has somewhat diminished the importance of solar physics research that can be conducted through eclipse studies, the investigations of the chromosphere and the corona that eclipses make possible are still of value.

The most remarkable advances in the scientific study of solar eclipses began in the middle of the 19th century with the development of photographic and spectrographic techniques. Today, cameras of great focal length are used in order that the eclipsed sun and the corona can form large images on the resulting photographic plates. The light intensity of the various regions of the corona can be studied in this way, and the coronal polarization and constitution can be determined. By using spectroscopes—or better still, by using prism or grating spectrographs—it has been possible to study the spectra of the chromosphere and of the corona.

In the 1898 solar eclipse (which was visible in Italy), the English astronomers J. N. Lockyer and Arthur Fowler photographed the *flash spectrum* (the emission spectrum of the chromosphere). In the same eclipse the U.S. astronomer William W. Campbell employed, for the first time, a moving plate method he had invented. In this method, a narrow slit is placed in front of a moving photographic plate so that only a narrow strip of the solar spectrum is recorded on the plate. By giving the plate a uniform motion in a direction perpendicular to the slit at the instant the flash spectrum appeared, Campbell obtained a record of the various phases of its transformation, from the absorption spectrum to the emission spectrum.

Two astronomical tests of the theory of relativity make use of the sun and solar eclipses. In one method, the shift of the spectral lines of the sun toward the red end of the spectrum and the deflection of luminous rays in its gravitational field are observed and analyzed. In the second method, cameras of great focal length are used to photograph an eclipse of the sun, but stars in the immediate vicinity of the sun are included in the photographs. The camera is left in position, and in two or three months the same stars are photographed after the sun has moved away from that region of the sky. By comparing the photographs with precise measurements of the coordinates of these stars, it is possible to calculate the apparent shift in position of the stars that was caused by the sun's deflection of their rays. Several tests already have brilliantly confirmed the theory of relativity.

Observation. In order to observe a solar eclipse, it is necessary to be in the limited zone of totality. This may occur in the remotest regions of the earth. The principal observatories of the world have prepared numerous expeditions to such regions. Much work and meticulous care are required for the selection and equipping of observing stations. Radio telescopes are among the numerous complicated instruments being used. They serve to determine the variations in density of the different radio wavelengths being emitted by various regions of the sun as the eclipse progresses.

Amateur astronomers also have organized cruises to study solar eclipses. Interesting photographs of the eclipses can be made with good photographic or motion picture cameras, and simple prism or grating spectroscopes can be used in the observation of the flash spectrum. On a simpler level, naked-eye observations can be made of the phases of an eclipse by the use of smoked glasses or neutrally tinted glasses.

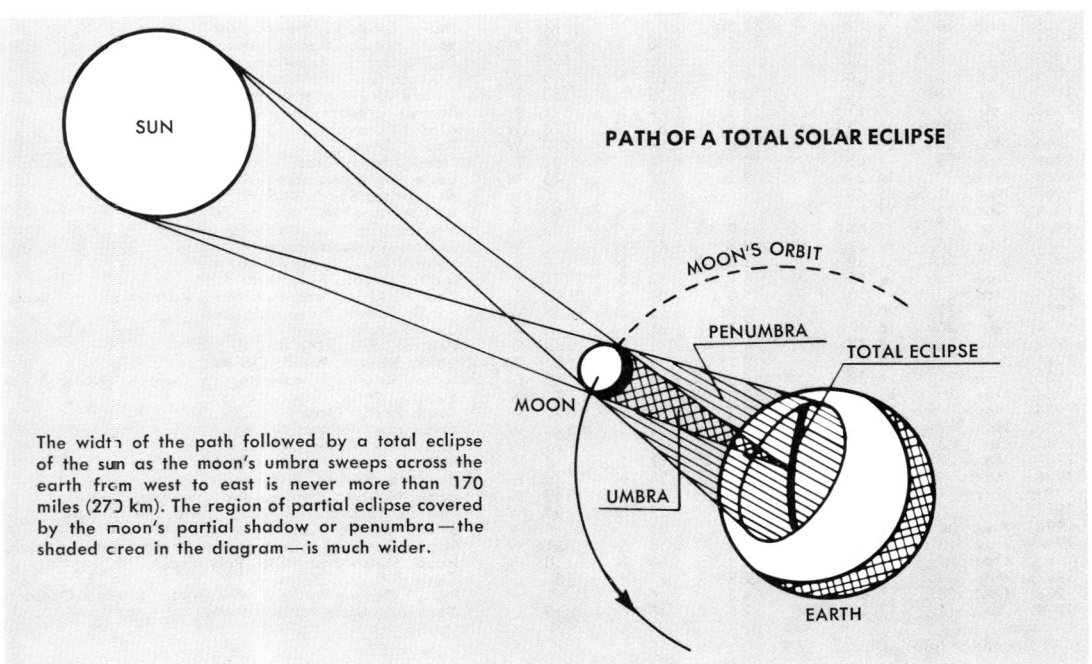

The width of the path followed by a total eclipse of the sun as the moon's umbra sweeps across the earth from west to east is never more than 170 miles (270 km). The region of partial eclipse covered by the moon's partial shadow or penumbra—the shaded area in the diagram—is much wider.

TOTAL ECLIPSES OF THE SUN IN THE 20TH CENTURY

Solar eclipses in the 20th century that have a total phase, however brief, are listed below. The first column is the date at the point on the earth's surface where the eclipse is central at noon. The second column gives the Greenwich Mean Time of the conjunction (in longitude) of the sun and the moon; the third column gives the number of minutes of total eclipse at the most favored site. The fourth and fifth columns give the latitude and longitude of the site where the eclipse is central at noon, and the final column indicates the path of the total eclipse.

Date of eclipse	Greenwich mean time (in hours and minutes)	Maximum duration of totality (in minutes)	Locality of eclipse latitude	longitude	Course of moon's shadow
1901, May 18	5 38	6.7	2° S	97° E	Sumatra, Borneo, New Guinea.
1903, Sept. 21	4 30	2.3	70 S	101 E	Indian Ocean, Antarctic Ocean.
1904, Sept. 9	21 08	6.3	5 S	133 W	Polynesia, Pacific Ocean.
1905, Aug. 30	13 13	4.0	45 N	12 W	Canada, Spain, Egypt.
1907, Jan. 14	5 57	2.6	39 N	89 E	Russia, China, Siberia.
1908, Jan. 3	21 44	4.5	12 S	145 W	Polynesia, Pacific Ocean.
1908,* Dec. 23	11 49	0.4	53 S	3 E	South Atlantic Ocean.
1909, June 17	23 29	0.5	88 N	173 W	Siberia, Arctic Ocean, Greenland.
1911, April 28	22 26	5.4	1 S	155 W	Australia, Polynesia, Pacific Ocean.
1912,* April 17	11 40	0.2	46 N	1 W	Spain, France, Germany, Russia.
1912, Oct. 10	13 41	2.2	35 S	33 W	Ecuador, Peru, Brazil.
1914, Aug. 21	12 27	2.4	71 N	2 E	Scandinavia, Russia, Persia.
1916, Feb. 3	16 06	2.9	16 N	62 W	Pacific Ocean, Panama, Venezuela, West Indies.
1918, June 8	22 03	2.5	51 N	152 W	Pacific Ocean, United States.
1919, May 29	13 12	6.9	4 N	18 W	Peru, Brazil, Central Africa.
1921, Oct. 1	12 26	..	84 S	19 W	Antarctic Ocean.
1922, Sept. 21	4 38	6.4	12 S	106 E	Indian Ocean, Australia.
1923, Sept. 10	20 53	3.8	38 N	128 W	Pacific Ocean, United States, West Indies.
1925, Jan. 24	14 46	3.3	42 N	44 W	United States, Atlantic Ocean.
1926, Jan. 14	6 35	4.4	10 S	82 E	Central Africa, Sumatra, Borneo, South America.
1927,* Jan. 3	20 29	0.1	52 S	125 W	Pacific Ocean, South America.
1927, June 29	6 32	1.0	78 N	84 W	England, Scandinavia, Siberia.
1928, May 19	13 14	..	50 S	30 E	At sunset; Antarctic Ocean.
1929, May 9	6 32	5.5	1 S	89 E	Sumatra, Malay peninsula, Borneo.
1930,* April 28	19 10	0.2	45 N	113 W	United States, Canada.
1930, Oct. 21	21 47	2.2	36 S	155 W	Pacific Ocean, Patagonia.
1932, Aug. 31	19 55	1.9	78 N	109 W	Canada, United States.
1934, Feb. 14	0 44	2.0	19 N	168 E	Borneo, Celebes, Pacific Ocean.
1936, June 19	5 15	2.7	56 N	101 E	Greece, USSR, Siberia.
1937, June 8	20 43	7.3	10 N	131 W	Pacific Ocean, Peru.
1938, May 29	14 00	4.3	52 S	27 W	South Atlantic Ocean, Antarctic Ocean.
1940, Oct. 1	12 41	5.9	19 S	16 W	Colombia, Brazil, South Africa.
1941, Sept. 21	4 39	3.7	30 N	114 E	Central Asia, Pacific Ocean.
1943, Feb. 4	23 31	2.8	47 N	176 W	Hokkaido, Pacific Ocean, Alaska.
1944, Jan. 25	15 25	4.4	7 S	49 W	Peru, Brazil, North Africa.
1945,* Jan. 14	5 07	0.0	51 S	108 E	South Atlantic Ocean, Indian Ocean.
1945, July 9	13 36	1.4	70 N	20 W	United States, Canada, Scandinavia, Russia.
1947, May 20	13 44	5.6	2 S	25 W	Argentina, Paraguay, Brazil, Central Africa.
1948,* May 9	2 31	0.2	44 N	138 E	China, Hokkaido, Pacific Ocean.
1948, Nov. 1	6 03	2.2	37 S	82 E	Central Africa, Indian Ocean.
1950, Sept. 12	3 29	..	34 N	115 W	At sunset; Arctic Ocean, Siberia.
1952, Feb. 25	9 17	3.5	22 N	39 E	Central Africa, Arabia, Central Asia.
1954, June 30	12 27	2.7	62 N	5 W	United States, Canada, Scandinavia, USSR.
1955, June 20	4 12	7.3	15 N	117 E	India, Thailand, Philippines.
1956, June 8	21 30	4.9	40 S	141 W	South Pacific Ocean, Antarctic Ocean.
1958, Oct. 12	20 52	5.4	26 S	139 W	Pacific Ocean, Argentina.
1959, Oct. 2	12 31	3.3	23 N	6 W	Atlantic Ocean, Morocco, Central Africa, Ethiopia.
1961, Feb. 15	8 11	2.9	53 N	53 E	France, Italy, Austria, Siberia.
1962, Feb. 5	0 11	4.3	4 S	179 E	Borneo, Celebes, New Guinea, Polynesia.
1963, July 20	20 43	1.8	62 N	126 W	Alaska, Canada.
1965, May 30	21 14	5.6	4 S	137 W	Pacific Ocean.
1966,* May 20	9 43	0.1	41 N	31 E	North Africa, Greece, Asia Minor, Central Asia.
1966, Nov. 12	14 27	2.2	38 S	43 W	Chile, Argentina, Brazil.
1967, Nov. 2	5 48	..	54 N	15 W	At sunrise; South Atlantic Ocean.
1968, Sept. 22	11 09	..	42 N	90 E	At sunset; USSR, Novaya Zemlya.
1970, Mar. 7	17 43	3.9	25 N	88 W	Mexico, Yucatán peninsula.
1972, July 10	19 39	2.8	67 N	111 W	Alaska, Canada, Labrador.
1973, June 30	11 39	7.2	19 N	6 E	Venezuela, Central Africa.
1974, June 20	4 56	5.4	32 S	107 E	Indian Ocean, Southwest Australia.
1976, Oct. 23	5 10	5.0	31 S	95 E	Central Africa, Indian Ocean, Australia.
1977, Oct. 12	20 31	2.9	16 N	127 W	Pacific Ocean, Venezuela.
1979, Feb. 26	16 47	3.0	61 N	77 W	United States, Canada.
1980, Feb. 16	8 52	4.4	1 N	48 E	Central Africa, India, China.
1981, July 31	3 53	2.2	54 N	127 E	USSR, Siberia, Pacific Ocean.
1983, June 11	4 38	5.5	7 S	11 E	Indian Ocean, Sumatra, New Guinea, Pacific Ocean.
1984,* May 30	16 48	0.0	38 N	74 W	Mexico, United States.
1984, Nov. 22	22 57	2.2	39 S	170 E	South Pacific Ocean.
1985, Nov. 12	14 20	..	52 S	146 W	At sunrise; Antarctic Ocean.
1986, Oct. 3	18 55	..	66 N	26 W	At sunrise; Arctic Ocean.
1987, Mar. 29	12 45	0.4	17 S	6 W	Atlantic Ocean, Central Africa.
1988, Mar. 18	2 03	4.1	28 N	146 E	Sumatra, Borneo, Philippines.
1990, July 22	2 54	2.7	73 N	142 E	USSR, Novaya Zemlya, Arctic Ocean, Siberia.
1991, July 11	19 06	7.2	22 N	105 W	Mexico, Yucatán peninsula, Venezuela, Brazil.
1992, June 30	12 19	5.5	26 S	5 W	South Atlantic Ocean.
1994, Nov. 3	13 36	4.6	36 S	31 W	Pacific Ocean, South America, South Atlantic Ocean.
1995, Oct. 24	4 37	2.4	10 N	110 E	India, Malay peninsula, Polynesia.
1997, Mar. 9	1 15	2.9	71 N	154 E	Central Asia, Siberia.
1998, Feb. 26	11 08	4.5	6 N	81 W	Pacific Ocean, Panama, Venezuela, Atlantic Ocean.
1999, Aug. 11	17 27	2.6	46 N	18 E	Germany, USSR, China, India.

* Annular total eclipses.

LUNAR ECLIPSE is photographed over the dome of the U. S. Capitol in 1968. As the full moon rises, it is covered slowly by the cone of the earth's umbra.

LUNAR ECLIPSES

A lunar eclipse occurs only when the moon is full and is at or in the region of one of the nodes of its orbit. The same sequence of contacts that takes place during a solar eclipse (between the lunar and the solar disks) is observed during a lunar eclipse as the earth's shadow passes across the face of the moon. The period of total eclipse can last, at the most, up to one hour and 40 minutes. A partial eclipse of the moon takes place when the moon enters the cone of the earth's penumbra. In general, however, the decrease of light in the full moon during a partial eclipse is so slight that it is not noticed by the naked eye.

When the disk of the moon enters the earth's umbra a total eclipse begins. In contrast to a solar eclipse it is difficult to determine the times of contact precisely, however, because the earth's atmosphere in part diffuses and in part refracts the solar rays passing through it. These effects of the atmosphere explain why the disk of the moon, even during total eclipse, continues to be seen in a more or less reddish light and does not totally disappear in the earth's shadow. The intensity and homogeneity of the reddish light depend on whether the rays of the sun traverse a more or less cloudy atmosphere as the eclipse progresses.

Scientific Importance. From the point of view of the advancement of astronomical knowledge, total eclipses of the sun are more important than lunar eclipses. Because the moments of contact in an eclipse of the moon cannot be established with any great precision, it is not possible to make use of such eclipses in further calculations of lunar motions. In past centuries, the forecasts of lunar eclipses given in astronomical tables were used by navigators and others to determine the differences in longitude between different localities on earth or at sea. The imperfections of the tables and the difficulties in determining local time with sufficient accuracy, however, have not made such determinations very precise. Today, with the availability of modern radio devices, eclipses of the moon no longer are used for these purposes.

GIORGIO ABETTI
University of Florence

Further Reading: Abetti, Giorgio, *History of Astronomy*, tr. by Betty Burr Abetti (New York 1952); Baker, Robert H., *Astronomy*, 8th ed. (Princeton, N. J., 1964); Oppolzer, Theodor von, *Canon of Eclipses*, tr. by Owen Gingerich (New York 1962).

A few minutes before totality in the 1968 eclipse (left), part of the moon is shaded only by the earth's penumbra. At totality (right) the moon has a reddish color, produced by diffusion of sunlight through the earth's atmosphere.

ECLIPTIC, i-klip′tik, the apparent path that the sun traces on the celestial sphere. This path is actually the projection of the earth's orbital plane onto the celestial sphere. The intersection points of the celestial equator (the projection of the earth's equator onto the celestial sphere) and the ecliptic are called the equinoxes.

The inclination of the ecliptic to the celestial equator at these intersection points is called the *obliquity of the ecliptic*. Its value presently is about 23° 27′, but it is decreasing at the rate of 0.75′ per century. The decrease results from the combined action of the moon and the sun in aligning the earth's rotation axes perpendicular with the orbital plane. See also CELESTIAL SPHERE; DAY.

LAURENCE W. FREDRICK
University of Virginia

ECLOGUE, ek′log, a type of pastoral poem. The term was first applied, in ancient Greek literature, to a varied selection of poems. It was later used to refer to Virgil's pastoral poems, the *Bucolica*, and from that time it signified a formal type of pastoral poem written in the form of a dialogue or soliloquy. The term can be applied to any dramatic poem, with little action, written in dialogue or soliloquy form.

The most common eclogue types involve one or more rustics, usually shepherds, perhaps engaged in a dialogue about their flocks or mistresses, lamenting over a dead shepherd, or singing a courting song. Examples of eclogues in English literature are Edmund Spenser's *The Shepheardes Calendar* (1579), which contains an eclogue for each month; Christopher Marlowe's *The Passionate Shepherd to His Love* (1599), which begins with the line, "Come live with me and be my love"; and John Milton's *Lycidas* (1638).

ÉCOLE NATIONALE SUPÉRIEURE DES BEAUX-ARTS, the greatest school of fine arts in France and one of the greatest in the world. Located in Paris, it developed out of two 17th century institutions. The first of these, the École Académique, was founded in 1648 by Louis XIV at the instigation of Cardinal Mazarin; later it came under the direction of the Académie Royale de Peinture et de Sculpture, also founded in 1648 by Charles le Brun, painter to the King. The second institution was the École de l'Académie d'Architecture, founded in 1671 by Jean Baptiste Colbert, a minister of Louis XIV. The two schools were united in 1795.

The Écoles des Beaux-Arts is administered by the Académie des Beaux-Arts, one of the five learned societies forming the Institut de France (q.v.). Coeducational, it admits foreign as well as French students; enrollment totals about 3,500. Tuition is free to all students who pass the rigorous entrance examination. The usual course of study lasts three years and entails lectures and studio practice. There are three departments of instruction: painting and graphic arts, sculpture, and architecture (possibly the most famous). The faculty, which numbers about 40, includes some of the most eminent French artists. The best French students, along with many from other schools, compete annually for the Prix de Rome, a scholarship for advanced study at the Académie de France in Rome. The École des Beaux-Arts has strongly influenced American art.

CLIFTON L. HALL, *University of Tennessee*

ECOLOGY, i-kol′ə-jē, the study of the relationship of plants and animals to their environment, of the relationship of plants and animals to one another, and of the influence of man on the ecosystem. The word *ecology* is derived from the Greek word *oikos*, meaning house or place to live, and from the word *logos*, meaning science or study. The word was first promulgated by the German naturalist Ernst Haeckel in 1869 and used by Charles Darwin shortly thereafter, but it was in limited use even earlier as evidenced by the writings of the American naturalist and poet Henry David Thoreau.

In recent years, many people have become aware of man's abuse of his environment, and the words environment and ecology have become public bywords. Often, however, the two words are confused. The environment of man includes both physical, or abiotic (nonliving), components and biological, or biotic, components. The physical attributes of our environment are the subject of such fields as geophysics, meteorology, climatology, hydrology, oceanography, and economics, while the biological characteristics of our environment are investigated in the sciences of anthropology, sociology, and biology, including the ecology of organisms.

Man pollutes the air he breathes and the water he drinks. His concern with the problem of pollution may be purely an environmental issue rather than an ecological issue in that he wants clean, noncorrosive air and water and is concerned mainly with the quality of the physical environment. (For a discussion of current pollution problems, see AIR POLLUTION; ENVIRONMENT; WATER POLLUTION.) If, however, the focus of his concern becomes the plants and animals that are contaminated, then the issue with which he is dealing is ecological. Some of our current problems—dust in the air, climate change, noise and sonic booms, and manmade earthquakes—are primarily environmental, but the majority and by far the most complex of our problems—eutrophication of lakes, DDT in the ecosystem, lead or mercury poisoning of man and animals, nitrates in well waters, and the influence of climate change on agricultural production—are of an ecological nature.

The ultimate challenge to man is to manage the surface of the earth in such a way as to keep it green and vital, to maintain the magnificent diversity of life, and to preserve the inherent stability of the system in the face of climate change or disease and insect infestation. Man has had to create monocultures of wheat, corn, rice, or sugarcane in order to increase the productivity of the land to feed the people of the world. Man has learned to release great reserves of energy, to build machines, and to create vast quantities of exotic products, including plastics and automobiles. In this way, man has violated and contradicted nature. Yet man himself is inexorably and utterly dependent on nature and is a direct product of biological evolution. He must learn to maintain a reasonable balance and blend of nature with nonnature based on the facts of ecology.

THE BIOSPHERE AND ITS PARTS

The biosphere is the thin outer shell of the earth that contains life. Generally, the biosphere includes the soils and surface rocks of the world, the oceans, seas, lakes, rivers, streams, and other bodies of water, and the lower atmo-

PLANT SUCCESSION IN AN ABANDONED FIELD

In the first stage of plant succession, the field is covered with grasses and weeds (*upper left*). In the second stage, seedlings and saplings start to develop on the grass and weed cover (*upper right*); and by the third stage, the field is fully stocked with trees (*center right*). In a typical climax stage of plant succession, the area is filled with mixed hardwoods (*lower right*).

U. S. FOREST SERVICE PHOTOS

sphere, particularly the troposphere and the stratosphere and ionosphere as far as they contain organisms.

Ecosystem. The ecologist views the biosphere as broken down into a series of subunits that he terms *ecosystems*. An ecosystem is a unit of landscape, including its biotic (living) components and its abiotic (nonliving) physical components. The biotic and abiotic parts of an ecosystem are inexorably intermixed and intertwined. Through nearly three billion years of evolution, the living and nonliving characteristics of the earth's surface have slowly evolved together from the primordial rocks that originally formed the earth's crust. For example, oxygen in the earth's atmosphere is a direct consequence of photosynthesis by the green plants of the world, and yet all animal life and plant decay requires oxygen.

An ecosystem may be a pond, meadow, forest, sand dune, bog, or even a small aquarium. In particular, it is the complex of interactions of all the organisms with their physical environment and with one another. We can speak of the entire planet earth as an ecosystem; it is the ultimate ecosystem with which we are primarily concerned. The term, however, is generally used to refer to parts of the biosphere, such as a forest. A forest considered as an ecosystem is not simply a stand of trees, but is a complex of soil, air, and water, of climate and minerals, of bacteria, viruses, fungi, grasses, herbs, and trees, of insects, reptiles, amphibians, birds, and mammals.

The dynamics of an ecosystem involve the flow of matter and energy and include the birth, growth, death, and decay of all organisms. An ecosystem is composed of four primary constituents: (1) the abiotic portion that includes the flow of energy through the system, the flow of nutrients, water, and gases, and the concentrations of organic and inorganic substances in the

MAJOR BIOMES OF THE WORLD

TUNDRA

Tundra lies between the farthest limit of trees and the region of snow or ice, frozen ground, and low temperatures; it also occurs above the timberline in high mountains (alpine tundra). The tundra is perhaps the most dynamic and extreme of all biomes having enormous seasonal and daily variations of microclimate, and consequently much frost action in the soil. The vegetation is low, dwarfed, and often matlike, and includes a large proportion of grasses and sedges.

In the alpine tundra, the summer sunshine is intense and rich in ultraviolet, the winds are prevalent, and the precipitation highly variable; during the remainder of the year, precipitation is mainly snow with the snow accumulation patterns strongly affecting the vegetation pattern.

In the Arctic and Antarctic, the growing season is short, and summer light is continuous. Total snowfall is low, but the surface is snow-covered most of the winter. The arctic vegetation surface is characterized by a mosaic of polygonal patterns formed as a result of massive vertical ice wedges going down into the ground. In the arctic tundra many animals remain active throughout the year, including caribou (reindeer in Eurasia), musk ox, arctic hare, arctic fox, arctic owl, lemming, ptarmigan, and others. Dipterous insects and their larvae play an especially important role as grass consumers in the Arctic. The total number of plant and animal species is relatively very low in the Arctic, the number of migratory birds that visit the Arctic during the short summer is quite large.

NORTHERN CONIFEROUS FOREST

The northern coniferous or boreal forests are the evergreen trees stretching in broad belts across North America and Eurasia just south of the tundra. Evidence seems to indicate that the northern border of the boreal forest coincides with the southern boundary of arctic air mass trajectories during the summer months. The northern coniferous climax forest is characterized by spruces, firs, pines, and in places by tamarack and hemlock. The climate of the region is only slightly less severe than that of the alpine tundra. Following fires, plant succession goes from grasses to bracken fern to blueberry and to stands of aspen and birch. Lakes and bogs are abundant in the coniferous forest biome and represent unique ecosystems within themselves.

In contrast to the tundra, the primary productivity of the evergreen forest is high and therefore it is one of the great lumber producing regions of the world. Along the west coast of North America in the vicinity of Puget Sound, the northern coniferous forest has high precipitation, greatly enhanced by fog, and here we find western hemlock, western arborvitae, grand fir, and Douglas fir. Because of the high humidity, evapotranspiration from the forest is low and growth is abundant, provided sufficient sunlight is available. South along the coast into California, redwood forests predominate; and north along the coast of Canada and Alaska, Sitka spruce is common.

Animals of the northern coniferous biome include moose, deer, bear, snowshoe hare, lynx, bobcat, squirrels, chipmunks, moles, shrews, grouse, chickadees, siskins, crossbills, woodpeckers, warblers, and migratory birds. Some of the animals eat the broad-leaved shrubs and herbs of the forest floor, while others depend on conifer seeds for food.

TEMPERATE DECIDUOUS FOREST

Temperate deciduous forest biome occupies a region of more moderate climate. It is a region of abundant evenly distributed rainfall with warm summers and cold winters. Because the leaves fall from the trees in the autumn, the understory of the deciduous forest has a complex flora that flowers and fruits in the spring and has a well-developed herb and shrub layer.

The deciduous forest of North America has many important subdivisions, such as the beech-maple of the north central region, the beech-basswood of Wisconsin and Minnesota, the oak-hickory of the central and southern regions, and a mixed deciduous forest type of the Appalachian mountains. Between the northern coniferous forest and the temperate deciduous forest there are many regions of mixed vegetation where usually the local edaphic (soil type) situation determines the climax community type. Animals in this forest include deer, bear, squirrel, fox, bobcat, and many birds such as the vireo, wood thrush, tufted titmouse, ovenbird, woodpeckers, and warblers.

EVERGREEN FOREST

The broad-leaved evergreen forest takes over to the south of the temperate deciduous forest. Rainfall is abundant in this area, and temperatures are warmer in the winter than they are farther north. Plants that dominate the evergreen forest, which in North America is limited primarily to Florida and sections along the Gulf and Atlantic coasts, are live oaks, magnolias, bays, hollies, figs, palms, vines, and epiphytes (plants that take moisture and nutrients from the air and rain and usually grow on other plants). Although some of the plants are related to tropical species, none of the birds or mammals found in the region are tropical in origin, indicating that Florida has not had an easy land bridge to the south.

TEMPERATE GRASSLAND

The temperate grassland covers a vast area of the central portion of the United States and Canada, Uru-

---

system; (2) the primary producers, largely green plants; (3) the consumers, which include the herbivores, carnivores, and omnivores; and (4) the decomposers, which include heterotrophic organisms, such as bacteria and fungi, that break down protoplasm into its simpler components.

Within the larger ecosystem of the planet earth, there are two broad categories of ecosystems—terrestrial and aquatic. Each of these is further divided into subunits. Hence within the aquatic ecosystems we have freshwater and marine, or salt water, ecosystems. The terrestrial ecosystems are classified according to their dominant type of vegetation (grasses, shrubs, trees and so on); these subunits are called *biomes*. European ecologists often use the term *major life zone* for biome.

Biome. The major biomes, sometimes referred to as plant provinces, of the world are the tundra; taiga, or northern coniferous forest; temperate deciduous and rain forest; temperate grassland; chaparral; desert; tropical rain forest; tropical grassland and savanna; and mountain vegetation. Broadly speaking, these biomes are latitudinal zones that are encountered successively in moving from the poles to the equator, except for the mountain vegetation biome that changes its character according to the altitude of the mountain.

The animals associated with each biome are generally different, although there is considerable overlap of some animals from one biome to the next. Certain rodents, mammals, birds, or insects inhabit both the desert and the chaparral or the taiga and the tundra, but in general, the animals of one biome are quite distinct from the animals of other biomes.

Communities and Ecotones. The biomes of the world are further subdivided into smaller units known as *communities*. For example, the tundra biome is divided into alpine tundra and arctic tundra; the desert biome is divided into the creosote bush desert and the sagebrush desert. Even further subdivision is necessary when one considers the vegetative regions in more detail. Obviously, biomes are not entities that have absolutely sharp boundaries; rather, there are transition zones, known as *ecotones*, between any two biomes. There is the tundra-coniferous forest ecotone of northern Alaska and Canada, the coniferous-deciduous forest ecotone of the northen United States and southern Canada, the coniferous forest and prairie grassland ecotone of the central United States, the oak-pine ecotone in the southeastern United States, and many others.

Succession in an Ecosystem. When a vegetation type is disturbed by fire, wind, flood, disease, insects, or other forces, including the plow or the saw, the plants begin to repair the damage through the long and slow process of plant succession. The orderly change of an ecosystem from pioneer stages to more mature communities is called *ecological succession*. The plant and

MAJOR BIOMES OF THE WORLD, continued

guay, Argentina, and the steppes of Russia. It is a region of persistent wind and moderate to low precipitation—30 to 10 inches (75–25 cm) per year. In this respect, the grasslands do not differ so much from the cold tundra which also has low precipitation and frozen soil limiting available moisture. The grassland biome is divided into areas of tall grass, mixed grass, short grass, and bunchgrass prairies, depending on the amount of rainfall. The grasslands often become very dry during the summer and autumn, and some of the grasses have roots that penetrate the soil 6 feet (1.8 meters) or more seeking moisture.

Some of the grasses, such as big bluestem, buffalo grass, and wheatgrass have a network of rhizomes that help bind the soil. Little bluestem, June grass, and needlegrass grow in clumps. The various grasses compete with one another by growing at different times of the spring, summer, or autumn. Needlegrass, wheatgrass, and bluegrass grow early in the spring and set seed in early summer, become semidormant during hot weather, but resume growing during autumn. The bluestems, buffalo grass, and grama grass grow throughout the summer. True indicators of the grassland biome are some of the forbs, such as thistle, tumbleweed, and sunflower.

The animals of the grasslands are either of the running and clustering type, such as the buffalo or antelope, or of the burrowing type, such as ground squirrels, prairie dogs, and gophers. Birds of the North American grassland are prairie chickens, meadowlarks, longspurs, horned larks, and rodent-eating hawks.

Many animals, including birds, not naturally found in the high plains grasslands of western Kansas and eastern Colorado are now found there because of man's activities. Opossum, raccoon, cardinal, and others find it easy to move from grainfield to grainfield and from farm pond to farm pond and hence to span the "great American desert" as the high plains of North America were once called.

SAVANNA

The tropical savanna is a grassland of warm regions with annual rainfall 40 to 60 inches (1.0–1.5 meters) and a pronounced dry season when fires are frequent. The fires are an important factor in maintaining the savanna in grass; they burn the shrubs, thus returning nutrients to the soil and giving the grasses more light. (Fire may also have played a more significant role in the maintenance of the North American grasslands than many people suspect.) The scattered trees of the African savanna are acacias, baobab trees, euphorbias, and palms. The giraffe with its long neck, has evolved to feed on these tall trees and thereby not compete with the antelope, wildebeest, and zebra, which browse on the grasses of the region. Lions, hyenas, and other animals feed off grazing animals and top off the food chain in this ecosystem.

DESERT

The deserts of the world generally occur where the annual rainfall is under 10 inches (25 cm). Three types of plants are found in desert areas: annuals that are dormant during the driest season and grow during the wet season; succulents, such as cacti and euphorbias, that store water; and shrubs with small, thick leaves that may be shed during the dry season. Some of the plants of the American desert include the creosote bush, sagebrush, prickly pear, saguaro, and palo verde. Desert reptiles and insects are protected from excessive moisture loss by thick, impervious skin or by waxy surfaces. During midday heat, the desert reptiles most often stay in the shade of a plant, the rodents remain in burrows in the cooler ground, and the desert birds stay inside large saguaro.

CHAPARRAL

The chaparral is a zone of stunted trees and shrubs that often abuts the desert. It is a region of hot, dry summers. There is, however, adequate winter rainfall. Typical trees and shrubs of the region—chamiso and manzanita—have hard, thick evergreen leaves. Mule deer and many birds inhabit the chaparral during the wet season in addition to the wood rats, chipmunks, lizards, wrentits, and towhees found there during all seasons.

TROPICAL RAIN FOREST

The tropical rain forest occupies low-lying areas near the equator where the annual rainfall exceeds 80 to 90 inches (2.0–2.3 meters). There are usually one or more dry periods, and if the dry periods are long, the evergreen forest becomes deciduous. The number of animal and plant species found in the tropical rain forest is probably greater than anywhere else in the world.

The trees are tall with many vines climbing their trunks and with vast numbers of epiphytes growing amid the vast canopy high above the ground. A large number of diverse species of animals live in the canopy. The dark interior of the rain forest, however, tends to be relatively open and with fewer animals. The trees have shallow roots; the rate of turnover of nutrients is rapid; and the rain forest has a high productivity.

Often, when the rain forest is replaced by cultivated fields, the productivity drops, and the land deteriorates rapidly. The lateritic soil (reddish soils formed by rock decay and having a high content of iron oxides and aluminum hydroxides) typical of rain forests, leech out and become baked as hard as brick in the sun, and neither forest nor crops will grow.

---

animal community that is the end result of growth within the limits of the physical habitat is referred to as the *climax community*. If a forest is cut over, the land revegetates progressively from grasses to herbs to shrubs to trees until the climax for the particular locale is reestablished. If climate limits the final stable form of the plant and animal community, then it is known as a *climatic climax*. If soil or underlying substrate limit the community structure, then it is an *edaphic climax*.

Habitat and Niche. The *habitat* of an organism is the place where it lives—for example, the forest floor, a sand dune, a bog, a rock surface, or the stomach of a deer. The concept of the niche that a plant or animal occupies is more difficult to describe. The *niche* of an organism is its status or position within an ecosystem. The ecological niche of an organism includes not only where it lives but also its complex relationship to all other organisms of the habitat. For example, a woodpecker occupies a hole in a tree, flies through the air, and moves up and down tree trunks searching for insects. The habitat of the woodpecker is the woodland. But, in addition, the woodpecker occupies a particular position in the woodland community of plants and animals. This position is partially determined by the woodpecker's place in the food chain—that is, by its special food requirements (namely, beetles and grubs) and by the predators that attack and feed on it. The woodpecker's niche is also determined by its position within the intricate behavioral web of all other animals of the habitat. The totality of these factors defines the position or niche that the woodpecker may occupy in the woodland community of organisms. Other organisms in the community, such as cottontail rabbits, squirrels, or snakes, occupy entirely different niches within the woodland.

ORGANISMS AND THEIR PHYSICAL ENVIRONMENT

Plants and animals are integrated with the physical characteristics of the earth. They have evolved within the earth's gravitational, electrical, and magnetic fields and have learned to live amid the elemental constituents of its surface.

Water, plus the elements nitrogen, phosphorus, carbon, oxygen, and magnesium, are all necessary to life as are energy and a proper temperature. The earth's primordial atmosphere was composed of nitrogen, hydrogen, carbon dioxide, and water vapor, but lacked oxygen and ozone. Gradually amino acids and large protein molecules were formed, and life on earth began. Once green algae that could photosynthesize (that is, use the carbon dioxide and water of the atmosphere and in the presence of sunlight and its own chlorophyll synthesize foodstuffs and give off oxygen) evolved, then oxygen was gradually released to the air. Then, through photochemical reactions, ozone was formed. Oxygen and ozone, together with water vapor, then screened the organisms on the earth's surface from the actinic ultraviolet radiation from the sun.

Under this protective screen, the first land plants emerged during late Silurian times, some 420 million years ago. With them evolved many species of spiders, mites, and wingless insects that began to breathe air. Life then spread rapidly across the land as the oxygen-rich atmosphere permitted large amounts of organic respiration to occur. The production of oxygen by photosynthesis and the consumption of oxygen by respiration were in balance.

The earth's atmosphere as we know it today is the consequence of hundreds of millions of years of slow evolution between plants, animals, and the atmosphere. Plants take up carbon dioxide to manufacture carbohydrates by means of photosynthesis. The oxygen released is consumed in respiration by bacterial decay or organic debris and by animal respiration. But for all of this to occur the surface temperature of the earth had to be compatible with the kinetics of life's chemistry. An earth that is too hot would burn up its organic forms, and on an earth that is too cold life could not function. Energy is constantly flowing from the sun, a high temperature source, to the earth's surface and back out into the cosmic cold of space, a very low temperature sink. Energy flow is necessary for life on earth. The constant flow of radiation from the sun created order from disorder and organic forms from inorganic substance, and gradually the temperature of the earth stabilized at a level at which life could evolve.

Life is action, motion, and work. Energy is the ability to do work; all living things consume energy. Plants and animals exchange energy with their environment in the form of radiation, by convection and conduction of heat from air or water, by the evaporation or condensation of water, and by chemical reactions. Some organisms, specifically the green plants and green sulfur bacteria, are *autotrophs*, or primary producers, that photosynthesize, using sunlight to form energy-rich compounds, such as carbohydrates, from carbon dioxide or from hydrogen sulfide. A second class of organisms—the *heterotrophs*, or secondary producers—derive their energy from the food produced by the autotrophs; this class includes all animals, bacteria, and fungi.

Photosynthesis. Through the process of photosynthesis, green plants provide both foodstuff for other organisms and the oxygen needed by animals and plants. Photosynthesis in green plants is a very complex process that depends on a large number of green chlorophyll molecules to cooperate in harvesting light quanta for the formation of high-energy chemical compounds. The basic chemical reaction that occurs is written

$$6CO_2 + 6H_2O \xrightarrow{112 \text{ kcal}} C_6H_{12}O_6 + 6O_2$$

This equation indicates which ingredients enter into the photosynthetic process—carbon dioxide and water—and which products emerge from the process—carbohydrate and oxygen. It also tells us that 112,000 calories of light energy absorbed by chlorophyll converts 6 moles of carbon dioxide and water into 1 mole of carbohydrate and 6 moles of oxygen. A single chlorophyll molecule cannot carry out photosynthesis by itself; approximately 2,400 chlorophyll molecules must work cooperatively as a single machine to channel whatever energy is absorbed into the reaction center. Similarly, a single quantum of light will produce no reaction, but eight quanta absorbed anywhere simultaneously in the set of 2,400 chlorophyll molecules will make the photosynthetic process work. Moreover, the light must be within a certain frequency and wavelength range if photosynthesis is to occur.

In addition to these requirements, plants must also have nitrogen for the formation of amino acids, carbon for carbohydrates and proteins, as well as phosphorus, calcium, magnesium, iron, and other elements for the food products they form. If the organisms are to continue to live generation after generation, the nutrients, once used, must be returned to the soil and be used over and over again. The use and reuse of many of these elements are discussed in terms of cycles.

Use of Solar Radiation. A great deal of sunlight —about 35.6×10^{20} calories—is incident on the earth's surface each day. Of this amount, only about 19.0×10^{20} calories per day is incident on the ground. This is equivalent to about 6.95×10^{23} calories per year or about 136 kilocalories (kcal) per cm^2 on the average ground surface—a tremendous amount of energy. However, the distribution of this energy over the globe is very uneven, with the greatest amount (200 kcal per cm^2 per year) reaching the ground in desert regions and the least amount (60 to 80 kcal per cm^2 per year) in polar regions.

The quantity of solar radiation incident on tropical regions varies only a little from January to June, but in polar regions there is darkness much of the winter and sunlight nearly twenty-four hours a day during the summer. Temperate regions of the world, where much of the food is grown, receive from 100 to 140 kcal per cm^2 per year, and a substantial fraction of this is received during the winter when temperatures are too low for much plant growth. Moreover, of the solar radiation reaching the ground, only about 25% is contained in the wavelength span of photosynthetic activity.

Estimates made of the gross production of one acre of corn field during one growing season of 100 days show that of the total incident solar radiation (2,043 million kcal), 44.4% was consumed by the evaporation of water and 54.4% (including 0.4% for respiration) was reflected or dissipated as heat, leaving only 1.2% (25.3 million kcal) for net primary plant production. Other examples indicate similar findings—a perennial grass-herb old field in southern Michigan has a net production efficiency of 1.05%; Lake Mendota in Wisconsin showed a primary production of 0.27%, and Cedar Bog Lake in Minnesota, 0.39%. It is evident that of the total solar radiation incident on the earth's surface, only about 0.3% to 1.2% of the energy goes into net primary productivity. The exact percentage varies with the region, of course, with the desert having a very low net primary production efficiency, and coniferous forests and tropical rain forests having higher production efficiency.

Vast numbers of animals derive energy from plants and build some of the plant biomass into their own bodies. The efficiency with which the energy stored in plant cytoplasm is transferred to animal protoplasm is 10% to 15%.

Carbon Cycle. In photosynthesis, plants take in carbon dioxide from the air and assimilate the carbon into carbohydrates, proteins, fats, and other compounds. Through their respiration,

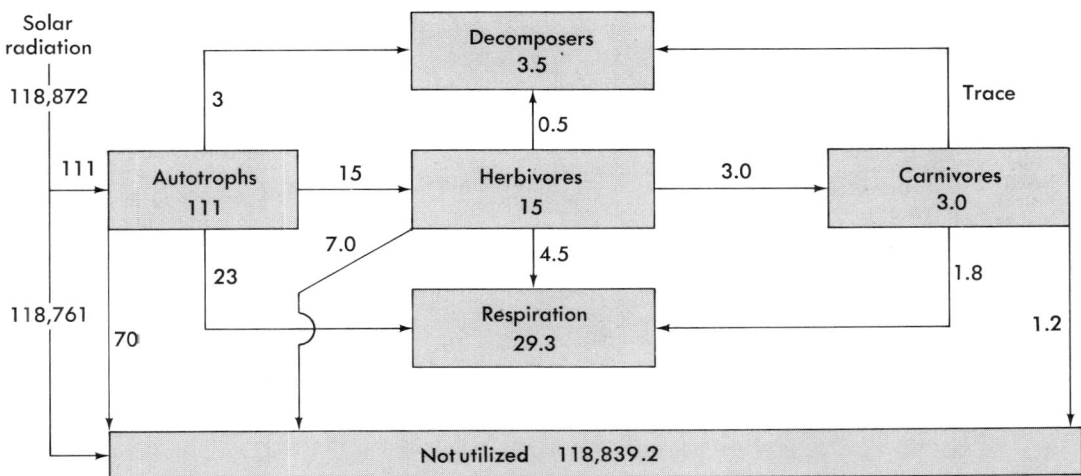

FLOW OF ENERGY, given in calories per square centimeter per year, in the food chain of Cedar Bog Lake in Minnesota. Solar radiation incident on autotrophs passes to decomposers and herbivores and then to carnivores.

plants also give off carbon dioxide, thus returning some of the assimilated carbon to the atmosphere. However, most of the carbon bound up in carbohydrates must return to the air through the decomposition of living matter—either the plants themselves or other organisms to which the carbohydrates have passed in the food chain. Carbon is also released to the atmosphere in the form of carbon monoxide (CO) and carbon dioxide (CO_2) when wood, oil, or coal are burned. Carbon is also released through the weathering of limestone rocks, which are formed by the mixing and compacting of clay and calcium carbonate ($CaCO_3$) released by aquatic plants in alkaline water as a by-product of photosynthesis. Not all carbon in the ecosystem is kept in the cycle, however; some is locked up in the fossil fuels (coal, oil, etc.), and some remains in the shells of mollusks that are bound into carbonate rocks.

Normally there is an approximate balance between the amount of carbon dioxide in the atmosphere and that in the oceans and lakes of the world, between which there is a constant flow by diffusion and precipitation. A single liter (1.06 quarts) of rain water contains 0.3 cc of CO_2, which combines with water (H_2O) to form carbonic acid (H_2CO_3) in a reaction that is reversible. The carbonic acid molecules can then break down to hydrogen ions (H^+) and bicarbonate ions (HCO_3^-), which in turn can break down further into more hydrogen ions and carbonate ions (CO_3^-) as

$$H_2O + CO_2 \rightleftarrows H_2CO_3 \rightarrow H^+ + HCO_3^- \rightarrow H^+ + CO_3^-$$

There is more carbonate present in acidic water (high pH) and more bicarbonate in alkaline (low pH) water. The degree of alkalinity or acidity of the water and the carbon dioxide content of the atmosphere function to drive the reaction system in one direction or the other. Man speeds up the process of exchange by burning huge quantities of fossil fuels and releasing carbon dioxide into the atmosphere. The increased carbon dioxide in the atmosphere leads to potential climate change through its effect on heat balance of the earth.

Nitrogen Cycle. The nitrogen cycle is necessary to life and is very complex. Plants need nitrogen to construct amino acids, which are a part of all food chains and all living systems. Even though the earth's atmosphere is 80% nitrogen and acts as a huge reservoir for this important element, plants are not able to use the nitrogen directly from the atmosphere since nitrogen is a relatively inert gas. Nitrogen must be fixed into nitrates (NO_3), nitrites (NO_2), or ammonia (NH_3) before it can be used by plants and other living forms. Nitrogen is fixed by bacteria or blue-green algae and by lightning discharges into the atmosphere. It is estimated that electrochemical action generates approximately 35 milligrams of nitrates per square meter per year, while biological processes create between 150 and 700 milligrams of nitrates per square meter per year.

The capacity to convert free nitrogen into the useful nitrate form is thought to be limited to the following organisms: free-living bacteria, symbiotic nodule bacteria on the roots of legume plants; free-living or symbiotic blue-green algae, and a few other microorganisms. Bacteria—specifically, denitrifying bacteria—are also responsible for returning nitrogen to the atmosphere; plants and animals cannot release it directly.

Energy is required to advance from simple molecules to more complex ones, such as from nitrates to nitrites to ammonia to amino acids to proteins. The energy for this process comes primarily from sunlight acting on green plants. Likewise, when protoplasm of proteins are broken down by the process of bacterial or fungal decomposition, energy is released in the form of heat to the decomposers.

In order to maintain agricultural production, increasing amounts of nitrogen fertilizers are put onto farmers' fields with the consequence that greater amounts of nitrates are washing off the land into the rivers, streams, lakes, and ponds, and also into wells. The nitrates and phosphates that concentrate in lakes and ponds cause serious eutrophication problems. See EUTROPHICATION. Moreover, there is increasing concern with the fate of nitrate in the soil, which may get into well waters. Infants and some livestock such as cattle have become ill and sometimes died after drinking well water containing nitrates.

Phosphorus Cycle. Phosphorus is also an essential constituent of protoplasm. In other words, molecules of protein, acids, and fats that make up protoplasm cannot be built without phosphorus as well as nitrogen and carbon. The phosphorus cycle seems simpler than the nitrogen

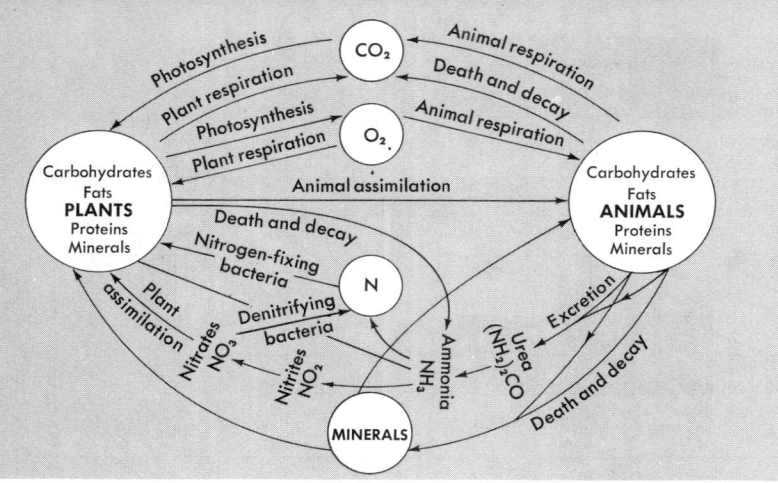

CARBON DIOXIDE, OXYGEN, AND NITROGEN CYCLES

Oxygen, nitrogen, and carbon dioxide from the atmosphere and minerals from the soil move to and from plants and animals through the processes of respiration, photosynthesis, assimilation, excretion, and death and decay, as indicated by the arrows in this drawing.

cycle. The great reserve bank for phosphorus is not the air but the rocks and sediment of the earth. Plants require phosphorus for nutrition in the form of orthophosphate ions. From the plants, the phosphorus passes to animals. Bacterial and fungal decomposers acting on plant and animal matter function to return phosphates to soil, water, and sediment. Phosphorus apparently does not cycle very evenly within the earth ecosystem, and much is constantly dissolved into waters and washed into the sea where it is deposited amid the sediments.

Energy Exchange. The thing that makes all living organisms "go" is the flow of energy from and back to their physical environment.

All surfaces radiate energy in relation to the temperature of the surface, and all organisms live in a complex radiation environment. A plant or animal out of doors during daylight may receive many streams of incident radiation, including direct sunlight, scattered skylight, light reflected off the ground and nearby objects, and radiant heat emitted by the soil surface, by rocks and plants, by the water vapor and carbon dioxide of the atmosphere, and by the bases of clouds. Each plant or animal absorbs a certain fraction of the incident radiation, reflects some of it, and in some cases, such as tree leaves, transmits some.

Air flowing over the surface of a plant or animal will cool or warm it by convection. A boundary layer of air, across which there are temperature and moisture gradients, adheres to all surfaces. In the region that lies beyond the boundary layer the air moves freely and carries whatever heat is conducted to or from the animal surface. Hence, convection is a combination of heat conduction across the stationary boundary layer and mass transport of heat by air movement beyond the boundary layer. When wind blows across the organism, it reduces the thickness of the boundary layer, and there is an increase in the rate of heat exchange or moisture loss.

The thickness of the boundary layer is related to the diameter or width of the plant or animal surface and to the wind speed. If a plant or animal is resting on a rock or on soil that is colder than it is, heat is conducted from the plant or animal into the rock or soil; if, on the other hand, the organism is colder than the surface upon which it rests, energy is conducted to the organism.

Many animals can sweat; all plants transpire; and all animals lose moisture by breathing. The moisture loss is always converted from liquid water within the organism to water vapor. It requires 580 calories per gram to change water from liquid to vapor at 30° C (86° F). Hence, moisture loss by breathing, sweating, or transpiration represents an effective evaporative cooling that helps an organism avoid overheating.

Over extended periods of time all plants and animals must receive neither more or less energy than they lose; otherwise, they will all get hotter and hotter and perish by heat, or colder and colder and perish by cold. This fact demands that a plant or animal have a balanced energy budget, expressed by the following equation:

$$\text{Energy In} = \text{Energy Out}$$

In other words,

$$\text{Metabolism} + \text{Radiation Absorbed} = \text{Radiation Emitted} + \text{Convection} + \text{Conduction} + \text{Evaporation}$$

When this expression is written out in mathematical form, it shows explicitly how each of the environmental factors—radiation, air temperature, wind, and humidity—enters into the exchange of energy between the organism and its environment. At any moment, the surface temperature of a plant or animal must assume a value that balances the energy budget so that as much energy is coming in as is going out. If any single factor changes, then a new value of surface temperature is necessary for a balanced energy budget. This equation provides the only way of understanding the intricate interactions between the climatic factors of the environment and the organism, because a change in any one factor necessitates a readjustment of all terms in the system to a new equilibrium.

Using man as an example will clarify the equation. An active adult human has a metabolic rate of about 263 watts. In addition he receives sunlight or radiant heat from the environment; for example, the walls of a room at 77° F (25° C) emit about 720 watts. Hence, an active adult in a room has a total power input of 720 + 263 or nearly 1,000 watts of energy. Unless this energy is dissipated, he will overheat and perish. Approximately 46%, or 460 watts, will be dissipated with the evaporation of water, mainly in the lungs, which is expelled by breathing. The remaining 54%, or 540 watts, is lost by radiation emitted by the skin or clothing surface and by convection to the cooler air near the body.

Temperature Control in Plants. During the day, sunlit leaves are frequently 5° to 15° C (41°–59° F) above air temperature, and transpirational

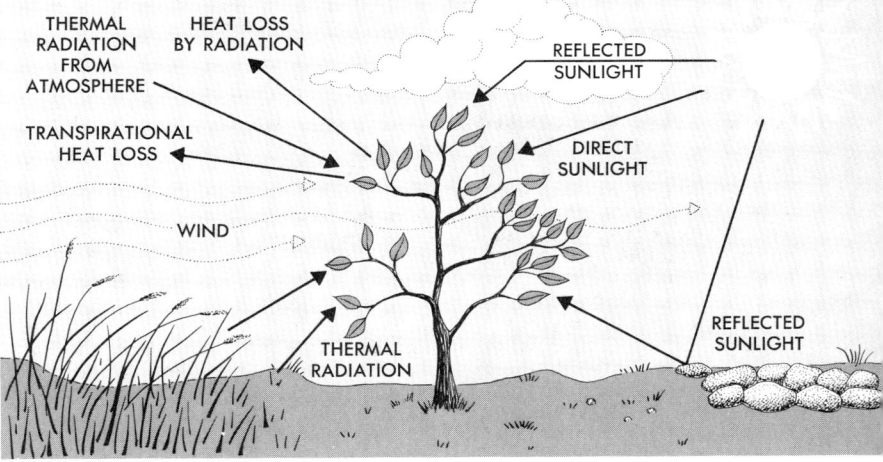

EXCHANGE OF ENERGY BETWEEN A PLANT AND ITS ENVIRONMENT

Thermal radiation, wind, and direct and reflected sunlight transfer energy to a plant, and a plant's heat loss through radiation and transpiration returns energy to the environment. Although these various processes may not operate at the same instant, a balanced energy exchange is maintained.

cooling keeps them from being 20° to 30° C (68°–86° F) above air temperature. Shaded leaves, on the other hand, are often 2° to 3° C (36°–38° F) below air temperature due to transpirational cooling. At night, leaf temperatures drop nearly to air temperatures or a few degrees below. Small leaves tend to have their temperatures strongly coupled to the air temperature. This is an advantage for the small leaves of desert plants, which, if they were large, would be very hot and cause the plant proteins to denature.

If a plant can use a lot of water and has a low resistance to water loss, it will stay cool by evaporation cooling. A plant may have its leaves in a vertical orientation, present only a small area for absorbing incident sunlight at midday and thereby keep its temperature down by absorbing as little radiation as possible. Thus, a plant leaf, depending on its characteristics, can use the mechanisms of radiation, convection, and transpiration to regulate its temperature in the hot summer sun.

Temperature Control in Animals. The energy budget of an animal surface is almost the same as for plant leaves. The surface of an animal adjusts to a temperature such that the energy of the animal is in equilibrium with its surroundings. For *homeotherms*, that is, animals with fixed body temperatures, the energy budget must keep the body temperature at the correct level. Birds, for example, keep their body temperatures between 37° and 39° C (98.6°–102° F), and man keeps his at 37° C (98.6° F). Homeotherms control their energy budgets by changing their metabolic rate, their respiratory and evaporative water loss, and their insulation by fur, feathers, or clothing.

Poikilotherms, on the other hand, permit their body temperatures to vary over a vast temperature range. They have little insulation by fur or feathers, little moisture loss, and low metabolic rates. The poikilotherms usually regulate their energy budget by changing their position within the environment—that is, from sun to shade, wind to no wind, above ground to below ground, or by migration. The desert iguana can withstand a body temperature as low as 37° F (3° C) and as high as 113° F (45° C). Many insects can withstand temperatures far below freezing and thereby survive cold winters.

RELATIONSHIPS BETWEEN ORGANISMS

Ecologists are interested not only in the flow of energy through an ecosystem but also in the complex interrelationships of all organisms within a community.

Food Chain and Food Web. One of the easiest ways to understand the interrelationships of organisms in a community is to study which organisms eat which other organisms. The simplest direct-line relationship from the primary producer—a green plant—to a herbivore to a carnivore is the *food chain*. There are many food chains within any single ecosystem, and there are many cross linkages from one food chain to another, so that an entire *food web* for a community of organisms results.

The following are two food chains that are interconnected to form a simple food web:

Canada blue grass ⟶ Meadow vole ⟶ Least weasel
Goldenrod ⟶ Red-legged grasshopper ⟶ short-tailed shrew ⟶ Barred owl

As shown here, the grasshopper and the vole are each at the second trophic, or feeding, level; the weasel and shrew are at the third trophic level; and the owl is at the fourth trophic level—the top of the food web.

In another example, the seabird shag eats herring, which is at the top of a food web of nine or more food chains, all of which originate with diatoms and flagellates, the primary producers in the oceans. Three examples of these food chains are the following:

diatom ⟶ copepod ⟶ sand eel ⟶ herring ⟶ shag
flagellate ⟶ crustacean ⟶ crustacean ⟶ herring ⟶ shag
diatom ⟶ barnacle larva ⟶ arrow worm ⟶ herring ⟶ shag

Food chains are usually quite short, seldom exceeding four or five consumers. Usually there are many more animals at the second trophic level than at the third, and more at the third than at the fourth. Organisms at all levels of the food web die and decay. The bodies of all dead plants and animals are returned to the soil through the action of decomposers, mainly bacteria, fungi, and microorganisms.

Man is in a unique place in the earth's food webs. He is omnivorous and operates on several trophic levels, eating plants, insects, mammals, birds, fish, and other organisms. Man also often shortens the food chain and reduces the number of organisms in the system in order to achieve increased productivity of a certain organism.

One important ecological principle that man violates in order to produce food for himself is the principle that diversity in nature appears to produce stability of an ecosystem. The close, cooperative, interacting structure of the many kinds of plants and animals in an ecosystem produces an inherent stability and an inertia to catastrophic change. Climate may fluctuate—wet to dry or cold to hot—or insects may invade the community, or a virus may infect a species, or other forces may develop, but because of the complexity and diversity of the ecosystem, none of these factors will by itself destroy the ecosystem.

Violating this principle, man plants large fields of corn and only corn. Then when a virus, fungus, or insect begins to attack the corn, it runs rampant through the crop. The simplified monoculture ecosystem is destroyed and the corn crop is in ruin. A monoculture is highly unstable and susceptible to damage by climate, insects, or disease. Man must have monoculture for food, but the cost of maintenance for stability and productivity is very high indeed.

Types of Species Interaction. The interaction of species within an ecosystem is a necessary and essential property of the plant and animal community. There are several different basic types of interaction: *neutralism*, in which neither species affects the other; *competition*, in which the two species are vying for the same space, water, air, sunshine, nutrients, etc.; *mutualism*, in which the two species need each other for survival; *protocooperation*, in which both species benefit but neither is necessary to the other; *commensalism*, in which one species is affected but the other is not; *amensalism*, in which one species is inhibited by the other but the reverse is not true; *parasitism*, in which one species lives on or within the other and benefits at the expense of the other; and *predation*, in which one species attacks the other and needs it for food. The word *symbiosis* is often used in the same sense as mutualism. See COMMENSALISM; PARASITISM; SYMBIOSIS.

POPULATION DYNAMICS

The numbers of plants or animals in a population change with time. Sometimes the changes in population densities are sudden and explosive; at other times they are gradual. Often changes are related to seasonal events, such as the emergence of houseflies in the spring and their rapid die-off in the autumn.

The rate of growth of an animal population depends on the birthrate, the natural death rate, the predator-prey relationships, the food supply, parasitic activity, infection by bacteria, and other factors, such as climatic changes. Some animals are strongly territorial and will not let others of their species occupy the same territory, thus quickly limiting the population density of the species. Animal populations cannot increase indefinitely. Some factor limits the growth, and the growth curve of most populations results in a sigmoid S-shaped curve.

Many animals manage to keep their population below the level at which they would begin to starve. Often when a bird population is increasing rapidly, there will be fewer eggs laid and fewer hatchlings. On the other hand, the enormous density of passenger pigeons in early America was thought to have been the very stimulus that maintained reproduction of the pigeon. When the population of passenger pigeons was reduced by man, it suddenly went below the self-sustaining size and extinction of the species resulted from lack of social stimulus.

An explosive increase of population occurs when predators are removed. When the mountain lions of the Kaibab Plateau in northern Arizona were killed by man, there was an enormous increase in the deer population. When the opossum was introduced to New Zealand, where it had no natural enemies, its population increased to devastating proportions. The prickly pear cactus increased abundantly when accidentally introduced to Queensland, Australia, and nearly destroyed the cattle industry there. Then a moth caterpillar that devoured the plant was introduced and the cactus population diminished to a tolerable level.

The predator-prey relationship is always a complicated one. The activity of the predator generates a defensive response in the prey, such as increased ability to hide or to avoid the predator. The predator population will then drop and the prey population will increase. But then it becomes easier for the predator to encounter the more abundant prey, and the cycle swings the other way. Many animal populations undergo strong cyclic changes in this way.

HISTORY AND BRANCHES OF ECOLOGY

Birth of Ecology. Much of biological science was natural history before the 20th century, and a considerable body of ecological knowledge accrued despite the fact that ecology was not then consciously recognized as a distinct science. Charles Darwin, the Swiss-American naturalist Louis Agassiz, the American Henry Baldwin Ward, and English naturalist Edward Forbes, and many other great biologists contributed much ecological knowledge prior to 1900, and conditions by that time were ripe for ecology to become a distinct scientific discipline. In fact, ecology is sometimes referred to as scientific natural history. The French naturalist Count Georges Louis Leclerc Buffon emphasized in his writings the interrelationships of organisms. French pioneer physiologist René Réaumur reported in 1735 on the relationship between the flowering of plants and the mean daily shade temperature. This led later directly to C. H. Merriam's 1894 publication concerning life zones for plants and animals, and even later to A. D. Hopkins' bioclimatic law published in 1920.

20th Century Development. By the beginning of the 20th century, plant ecology grew at a more rapid pace than did animal ecology. The study of plants was often more convenient than the study of animals because plants do not migrate and move about.

During the 1920's, a number of important works in the field of population ecology concerning the biology of death, human biology, and the biology of population growth were published. The field of human ecology received great impetus with the publication of Ellsworth Huntington's *Civilization and Climate*. Also during the 1920's, paleoecology, with most of the emphasis concerned with paleobotany, began to emerge as an active field of ecology. Charles Elton, the British ecologist, published several significant books on animal ecology that gave emphasis to ecological principles, in particular to food-chains, nutrient cycles, food niches, and the pyramid of numbers.

By the 1940's the field of population ecology began to emerge as a quantitative, analytical subject. Prior to that time the ecologists had worked with species and their distributions, but finally they began to ask important questions concerning 'How many?' and "Why?" Much of the motivation for doing this was an interest in the economics of insect populations as they affected agricultural production.

After World War II, ecology became very much more quantitative, and the emphasis was on physiological ecology with concern for mechanisms. Principles of physics and chemistry were brought in as an integral part of ecology, and mathematics became a useful tool. The advent of the computer made possible the handling of large amounts of data, and the quantitative aspects of ecological thought grew quickly.

Branches of Ecology. As with any science, ecology is divided into various subdivisions and fields. Autecology is the study of an individual organism or species in relation to its environment and to other species. Synecology is the study of a community of organisms such as a forest; this subdivision is sometimes further divided into population ecology, community ecology, and ecosystem ecology. Other branches of ecology include marine ecology, freshwater ecology, and terrestrial ecology.

The study of man in relation to his environment, including the relationships among men or groups of people, is called human ecology. The study of animal-borne diseases of man is in the realm of medical ecology or public health ecology. Many animals, such as lice, flies, ticks, and rodents, act as intermediate hosts to infectious diseases of man. In order to deal with malaria one must manage the populations of mosquitoes, and this demands knowledge concerning the ecology of the mosquito.

Present Trends and Future Needs. Today we are on the threshold of an exciting new era for ecology in which the full spectrum of knowledge from molecular biology through physiology and community dynamics is used in the fabric of ecological theory. Life involves all systems—both the biotic and the abiotic—and almost by definition ecology is the complete holistic science.

Man dominates the world ecosystem in a very selfish manner by exploiting the resources of the earth and by abusing the air, water, and soil. Yet eventually he will discover that he must live in a compatible manner with the myriad of other organisms on earth and to regard the environment as a very fragile womb. It is by means of human ecology, a knitting together of sociology, demography, human geography, urban planning, landscape architecture, design, etc., that man gains a perspective concerning himself in the exotic world he has created. Concepts of energy flow, cycling of nutrients and materials, diversity and stability, monoculture and instability, and geometrical growth of populations are fundamental ecological principles by which man must live and by which he must manage the earth.

DAVID M. GATES
Missouri Botanical Garden

Bibliography
Allee, Warder C., Emerson, A. E., Park, O., Park, T., and Schmidt, K. P., *Principles of Animal Ecology* (Philadelphia 1949).
Billings, William D., *Plants and the Ecosystem* (Belmont, Calif., 1964).
Kormondy, Edward J., *Concepts of Ecology* (Englewood Cliffs, N. J., 1969).
Odum, Eugene P., *Fundamentals of Ecology* (Philadelphia 1959).
Smith, Robert L., *Ecology and Field Biology* (New York 1966).

ECOLOGY, Human, i-kol'ə-jē, a social science that studies the relationships between man and his environment. The ecological study of man may be divided into two fields: *human ecology proper*, which studies the relationships between human biological factors and the natural environment, and *social ecology*, which studies the relationships among natural environment, population, technology, and society.

HUMAN ECOLOGY PROPER

In studying man's adaptation to the natural environment, the human ecologist is concerned with the entire hominid line, from the 1.5 million-year-old, Pygmy-like *Australopithecus* to modern man, *Homo sapiens sapiens*. For example, studying temperature adaptation, he finds that the hominids are tropical-adapted creatures that cannot survive without clothing at temperatures lower than 25° to 27° C (77° to 81° F). Colder temperatures require either genetic or cultural adaptation. Various forms of clothing were developed early in hominid history, but the possibility of physical adaptations remains. Research has tentatively established the presence of possible genetic adaptations among certain living tribal groups. The Australian aborigines, for example, may have the capacity to withdraw blood from circulation near the skin, thereby conserving heat during exposure. The Eskimo may be able to increase metabolism rapidly, thus increasing the supply of heat. However, clothing, shelter, and individual adjustments were more important than genes in adapting to climate.

Adjustments to environment accomplished during the life of individuals are studied under several categories. *Acclimatization* refers to momentary adjustments, such as adjustments in blood flow to regulate heat; it is found in all populations, although some populations, as noted, may have special genetically determined capabilities. *Acclimation* refers to more gradual processes taking place in the individual during a lifetime of exposure to particular environmental factors. For example, Indians living at very high altitudes in the Andes have larger lungs resulting from a lifetime of deeper breathing. *Habituation* refers to routine behavioral adjustments to environment, such as fanning or lassitude.

Man's teeth and his digestive system indicate that the hominids were omnivorous during most of their evolution. However, under different environmental and cultural conditions, men have adopted different diets. During the Paleolithic period, or Old Stone Age, the reliance upon meat was heavy, but with the development of food production during the Neolithic, or New Stone Age, vegetable foods increased in importance. The diets of many peasant peoples have been short of meat-derived protein ever since. The coming of agriculture meant that the elite attained richer diets, but the poor generally fell below the standards of tribal hunter-gatherers.

Medical ecology is concerned with epidemics and the environmental basis of disease. The popular belief that a microbial disease can be eliminated by a specific poison invented to destroy the infectious microorganism is an oversimplified view. Despite great strides in medicine, infection rates for many diseases have not dropped. Some infectious diseases become more harmless because of evolutionary changes in the microorganism itself; others disappear under changed social circumstances, even without medical intervention. After World War I the incidence of tuberculosis rose and fell with monetary inflation, since the disease is closely related to general physical well-being as induced by changing social and economic conditions.

The physical environment surrounding man is becoming increasingly contaminated as a result of insecticides, food additives, industrial wastes, emissions from internal combustion engines, and agricultural fertilizers. Many pollutants affect man directly, as in respiratory diseases and cancer. In other cases, the effects are indirect, as in salinization of soil by improper irrigation.

The salient factor in human ecology is the increasing take-over of the natural world by human agencies in a state of high technology. The idea that natural resources are there to be exploited must give way to a view that emphasizes a greater balance or partnership with nature.

SOCIAL ECOLOGY

Both anthropologists and sociologists have studied the relationships among population, natural environment, technology, and society.

Anthropological Ecology. The concepts of anthropological ecology derive from 19th century German ethnic geographers, such as Friedrich Ratzel, who pointed out that man's relationships to environment are conditioned by technology and that parts of culture can be explained by a knowledge of the relationships between technology and environment. Anthropologists, in their ecological studies, have been concerned primarily with past civilizations and with tribal people, and with the wide variety of technical and economic adaptations to given environments. In the southwestern desert of North America, Navajo Indians became sheepherders, Pueblo Indians were corn farmers, and Shoshone were collectors of wild food. Thus, available natural resources do not necessarily determine particular cultural adaptations: man can make a choice.

On the other hand, if a specific resource is relied upon extensively, this fact may condition the entire course of development. The Egyptian use of the Nile is an example. The decision to develop agriculture in a narrow, annually flooded strip in a desert permitted the population to build up in a small space; the compact population, plus the task of controlling the waters, led to bureaucratic structures that influenced every aspect of Egyptian civilization.

A classic study in which anthropologists discovered a significant relationship between certain biological and cultural processes involved in environmental adaptation was that concerning the "sickle-cell" disease, an inheritable condition of the hemoglobin (red) blood cells. Found in many African populations, the sickle-cell disease was once thought to be a racial trait of Negroid peoples. It was discovered, however, that the frequency of the disease was greatest in populations living in agricultural areas with high incidence of malaria. The disease, although lethal if inherited from both parents, confers virtual immunity to malaria if inherited from only one parent. Consequently, it tended to confer adaptability on populations exposed to malaria. Thus a cultural trait, agriculture, set in motion conditions that led to a buildup of a mutated gene in particular populations.

A close relationship has developed between ecology and studies of cultural evolution. The American anthropologist Julian Steward has shown that, given similar natural resources and levels of technology, the development of widely separated peoples will bear close resemblance.

Sociological Ecology. Sociological ecology developed in the 1920's at the University of Chicago, where sociologists produced a series of studies illustrating the use of ecological principles in charting population and cultural movements in a modern city. One approach used in this work was based on concepts borrowed from natural ecology. Thus the concept of "succession," referring to the replacement in the natural environment of one plant species by another, was applied to human social or economic groups. These natural ecology principles were combined with the principles of "social morphology" as defined by the French sociologist Émile Durkheim. Social morphology concerns the relationships of size, density, and spatial distribution of the population to the separation of functions in a society. Common to both approaches was a concern with competition as the moving force in the environment.

Modern sociological ecology bases its study of the development and form of an urban community on both approaches. There is an emphasis upon spatial distribution insofar as it relates to the overall balance of activities and groups within a city. Economic pressures and competition are still the driving forces for the distribution or movement of people, goods, and services throughout various areas of a city.

Research has shown that the American city has about five concentric zones. The business district is at the center, and outside of this is a zone for light manufacturing and recreation. The latter may also contain an area of cheap lodgings. The next three zones are areas of residence: the first for working people; then middle-income groups; and finally the suburbs. The residential areas closest to the center of the city tend to resemble ghettos. Each population group strives to invade the adjacent and more desirable zone. However, despite the replacement or succession of groups, the social characteristics of the zones remain the same and are therefore felt to be "natural areas."

Much research has been devoted to demonstrating statistical relationships between the location and characteristics of these natural areas and the characteristics of their residents. For example, alcoholism and delinquency are much more common in areas adjacent to the city center and decline toward the suburbs; however, pockets of exceptions, based on special cultural changes, often occur. High rates of schizophrenic disease are associated with forms of social disorganization. Bad housing is associated with the comparatively poor health of the residents.

Some sociological ecologists have also investigated natural-resource utilization by agrarian peoples. A characteristic problem concerns the extent to which people display "rationality" in their use of resources, that is, balancing the need for the resource, the cost of developing it, and the need for conservation. Such studies contribute to our knowledge of how man can utilize nature without destroying it in the process. See also ANTHROPOLOGY; CULTURE; ECOLOGY.

JOHN W. BENNETT, *Washington University*

Further Reading: Dubos, René, *Man Adapting* (New Haven 1965); Hawley, Amos H., *Human Ecology* (New York 1950); Steward, Julian H., *The Theory of Culture Change* (Urbana, Ill., 1955).

ECONOMETRICS, i-kon-ə-me′triks, is the study of economics as a science with the help of rigorous methods, especially mathematics and statistics. The term came into use after the organization in 1930 of the Econometric Society, an international society for the advancement of economic theory in its relation to statistics and mathematics. The society's membership, widely spread over the world, includes many leading economists and some distinguished mathematicians and statisticians.

Historical Background. Of mathematical contributions to economics, those now regarded as important began with Antoine Augustin Cournot's *Recherches sur les principes mathématiques de la théorie des richesses*, published in 1838. His treatments, with the help of calculus, of monopoly, duopoly, and taxation are notable, though much revised by later writers. In the next decade another Frenchman, Jules Dupuit, engineer and inspector of roads and bridges, developed a money measure of what he called the *utilité* of public works and the effects of tolls. Later, Alfred Marshall drew heavily on the ideas of Dupuit and Cournot, renaming Dupuit's *utilité* "consumers' surplus."

Before the end of the 19th century Léon Walras, Vilfredo Pareto, Francis Ysidro Edgeworth, Irving Fisher, and others had made mathematical contributions to economic theory. These for the most part involved no mathematics more advanced than elementary calculus. But Edgeworth's discovery in the 1890's that imposition of a tax on a commodity, to be paid by the seller, may under some reasonably plausible circumstances lead to a reduction in price both of this and of a related commodity requires more advanced mathematics for its full understanding. Edgeworth's conclusion was considered unsound by many economists of the time as flying in the face of common sense, but it has since been vindicated and extended. Edwin R. A. Seligman, in his widely used *Shifting and Incidence of Taxation* (1899), attempted to refute Edgeworth on this point and used his paradox to condemn mathematics in economics, but later he admitted that Edgeworth was right. Mathematics has yielded surprising new qualitative results in this case and in others treated by later econometricians.

Econometric Investigations. The demand, cost, and supply curves familiar to economists are inadequate for dealing with more than one commodity at a time, since curves are well suited to represent functions only of a single variable. For as few as two related commodities the demand relations of the prices to the quantities involve four variables, and the analogue of the demand curve is a two-dimensional surface in four-dimensional space. Supply relations are represented by another such surface, intersecting the first in point. The direction of motion of this point as a result of shifts of demand or supply caused by taxes or other changes cannot easily be followed by geometrical or other intuition, and all these questions involving related commodities seem to require the use of partial derivatives of implicit functions and the theory of definite quadratic forms for their elucidation. Besides these mathematical subjects, a few 20th century economists have used differential equations and the calculus of variations to deal with mineral economics, the economic distribution in time of use of water in hydroelectric reservoirs, and speculation. The study of dynamic variations in the economy has led to the use of still other branches of higher mathematics.

The econometric movement includes both deductive work of this kind and factual studies. Factual studies by econometricians tend to proceed from general economic theory and to attempt to verify or disprove these hypotheses or to make them numerically definite. Thus such investigations form a more closely knit group than a great mass of disconnected studies of a descriptive or historical type that are not bound by any strong links with economic theory. The factual studies are usually statistical, and the great advances in mathematical statistics are having an impact on them.

HAROLD HOTELLING
University of North Carolina

Bibliography
Christ, Carl F., and others, *Measurement in Economics* (Stanford, Calif., 1963).
Fisher, Franklin M., *Identification Problems in Econometrics* (New York 1966).
Econometric Society, *Econometrica* (New Haven, Conn., quarterly).
Goldberger, Arthur S., *Econometric Theory* (New York 1964).
Johnston, John, *Econometric Methods* (New York 1963).
Klein, Lawrence R., *Introduction to Econometrics* (Englewood Cliffs, N. J., 1962).
Tintner, Gerhard, *Econometrics* (New York 1952).
Wold, Herman, ed., *Econometric Model Building* (New York 1964).

ECONOMIC AND SOCIAL COUNCIL, a major organization of the United Nations responsible for promoting international cooperation in economic, social, educational, health, and related matters.

The council is composed of 27 member nations of the United Nations elected by the UN General Assembly, 9 each for 3-year terms. Each member has one vote, and decisions are made by a majority of the members present and voting. The council normally holds two regular sessions every year—a spring session at the UN headquarters in New York and a summer session at the Palais des Nations in Geneva, Switzerland.

The council is aided in its work by several expert bodies called functional commissions, such as the commission on Transportation and Communications, Population, Human Rights, and the Status of Women. There are also several special bodies under the council's direction; these include the Permanent Central Opium Board and the United Nations Children's Fund (UNICEF).

Since many international economic problems can best be dealt with on a regional basis, the council has established four regional economic commissions: the economic commissions for Europe, for Asia and the Far East, for Latin America, and for Africa.

The council also serves as the coordinating agency for numerous intergovernmental and nongovernmental organizations concerned with matters within the council's competence. Among the well-known organizations that have established relationships with the council are the International Labor Organization, the World Health Organization, the International Chamber of Commerce, and the International Confederation of Free Trade Unions.

ECONOMIC COOPERATION ADMINISTRATION, an agency established in 1947 to administer United States contributions to the Marshall Plan. See UNITED STATES—*20. International Relations and Diplomacy* (Marshall Plan).

ECONOMIC DEVELOPMENT is a process that transforms a stagnant society with a low average real income into one in which incomes rise more or less continuously as technology is embodied in accumulating capital.

Economists, perhaps oversimplifying, measure economic development by income—the sum of valued goods and services flowing to an individual or a country. Differences can then be indicated by comparing annual per capita income. At the close of the 1970's, income in the less-developed countries commonly averaged between $200 and $1,000 per person per year, while in northern Europe and the United States incomes averaged $10,000.

Modern Western economic development began in the Renaissance, when Europe was in the process of organizing into national states, but it evolved slowly. A flood of industrial and agricultural developments began in the mid-18th century and produced a remarkable acceleration of the development process. During the 19th century the spread of a continuously advancing technology—and the conversion of the economies of Europe and North America to the market system (exchange of goods and services)—raised incomes to levels beyond any in history.

Since the end of World War II there has been a revival of interest in economic development, focusing on the needs of non-Western countries that failed to make the economic transformation along with Europe, North America, Australia, and South Africa in the two preceding centuries. The end of colonialism and the establishment of new nations in Asia and Africa after World War II stimulated an uneven economic development reminiscent of Europe's earlier experience.

One evaluation of the economic backwardness of the new countries holds that they are at an early stage of a multistage process and may reasonably expect to reach the later stages just as the advanced Western countries did. But their experiences in the 1950's and 1960's indicate that the "inevitable" advanced stages may be some time away. Their changes ranged from rapid economic progress (as in Thailand and Taiwan) to retrogression (as in Indonesia in the 1960's and Burma and Ethiopia in the 1970's).

The Development Process. The process of economic development encompasses changes in the quality and composition of production inputs, the technology by which the inputs are combined, and the final goods and services (outputs) produced. Inputs at first are predominantly direct labor and the products of nature, such as coffee beans or iron ore. Later there is a gradual substitution of capital for labor. Although the total number of hours worked per family per week may not decline, the quality of labor changes. Developed labor, embodying more training and education, is more skilled and productive.

Much of the change in technology may be a response to the availability of new inputs—for instance, as cheaper European capital became available in the 19th century, the United States chose to build railroads rather than more canals. Some changes come because old inputs grow in value in alternative uses (the rise in wages and the invention of dough mixers caused the disappearance of hand-kneaded bread from U.S. markets). But much of the changing technology is autonomous and may be inconsistent with the resource needs of the time. This is often the case with internationally "borrowed" technology—for example, the adoption of American capital-using, laborsaving machinery in India, where capital is scarce and labor is plentiful.

The composition of output changes in response to changing income and tastes. As incomes rise, a smaller proportion of a family's money is spent on food and a larger proportion on education, travel, and medical care. The changing costs of producing particular goods and services also bring about changes—for example, fewer domestic servants and more factory-made dishwashing machines.

Effects on People. Life expectancy, the family system, and the percentage of farm jobs differ considerably between the advanced and the less-developed countries. The more developed countries are healthier because of better medical care and improved sanitation. Life expectancy may be 35 to 40 years in some African countries and over 70 years in northern Europe.

Changes occur in the family system as the center of social life changes. In less-developed countries, people live together in "extended families" of three and four generations; in advanced countries, the common household unit is a couple and their children.

In less-developed countries the proportion of the population that is rural and dependent upon farming is likely to be between 50% and 90%. In the United States it is only about 3%.

Why the United States Progressed. After careful statistical analysis of the economic development of the United States, it has been found that accumulation of capital itself accounts for only a decidedly minor fraction of the rise in per capita income since the 1860's. What then is responsible for the phenomenal economic progress of the country? The answer lies in elements such as:

(1) Change in the kind of capital accumulated, embodying a new, more productive technology.

(2) Increase in human capital, embodying education.

(3) Improvement in the output from given inputs, reflecting the economic advantage of a larger scale. (The U.S. economy is from 10 to 15 times larger than it was in the 1860's.)

(4) Change in the way resources are combined, using new technology that does not require new capital—such as better organization of production and more efficient specialization.

(5) Switches in production to new goods that can be produced more economically.

To put these diverse elements into a mold called "capital accumulation" may encourage belief that development can be purchased as if it were machinery. In reality, personal and social transformations are probably more important for successful national development.

BARRIERS TO TECHNOLOGICAL CHANGE

If technological change is so important, why do not aspiring developing countries adopt the technology of the West that is all but free for the asking? Borrowed technology encounters barriers of demand, barriers of supply, and institutional barriers.

Barriers of Demand. In some cases economies are too small to warrant investments that must be made on a large scale. In other cases potential investments do not appear profitable by themselves, because of lack of adequate demand, but could be profitable if at the same time other investments were going forward to generate a new demand for these outputs. The practice of making uncoordinated investment decisions could account for such barriers.

Barriers of Supply. Because of the lack of local supplies of some of the required inputs, the costs of production remain high for many goods with potentially favorable conditions of production in less-developed countries. To satisfy diverse supply needs, at an economically practical cost, may require a broad multi-industry investment program that would strain the local supply of skills and capital. A special case of the supply barrier is the difficulty of satisfying the rising food needs of a growing urban labor force. Unless there is a large and productive investment in agriculture, investments in industry, facing rising labor costs to cover the high cost of food, will prove unprofitable, and further industrial development may be discouraged.

Institutional Barriers. Many institutional problems arise. Unless a country's economy is directed in detail by central authority (as in Albania or Cuba), development depends on replacing traditional controls over productive resources with market control. An example of such change is "land reform" to remove land from feudal (nonmarket) control and to subject it to the social demand for its use that is usually commanded through the market. Some "reforms" are designed to change control in the opposite way—from market control to legalized protection from the market for a favored group of landholders. In these and numerous other cases, the institutional barriers to economic development are not simply the results of backwardness or stupidity. They may reflect the priority given to other social objectives that conflict with the goal of economic development.

The process of self-sustaining economic growth requires institutions conducive to continuous change. Much of the world's experience shows that successful development has generally occurred when it has been possible for individual innovators to acquire control over the needed resources without appealing directly to central governmental authority. Even so, freedom for entrepreneurs does not now have universal appeal for aspiring less-developed countries. The drawbacks to decentralizing control over resources for new projects include the unpredictability of the results and the politically unpopular distribution of social costs that may be imposed on the established influential classes. In addition, development may visibly enrich individual innovators who may be social pariahs.

The most important successful exception to an individualistic growth system is the Soviet Union, which demonstrates that a centralized economy can grow when a leadership group sets rapid economic development sufficiently high among its goals.

ECONOMIC DEVELOPMENT POLICIES

Rapid economic development is not the only goal of government, even in less-developed countries, and the combination of policies adopted and implemented is a compromise among competing goals. Four policies are considered here.

(1) Economic development may be based on a policy of expanding export trade in commodities in which the aspiring country has a known comparative advantage or on an ability to produce more cheaply than others. Expansion of the export industries is limited only by the country's own resources and the capacity of the world market to absorb the new supply. General dependence of developing countries on export expansion would cause prices of the goods they export to fall and prices of the goods they import to rise, thus reducing the potential benefits of the policy. In addition, the growth of one or a few such industries might fail to encourage development in the rest of the economy. Also, there may be an emotional objection to a colonial form of economic dependence on the rest of the world and to what is regarded as a lopsided dependence on the production and export of primary goods (such as minerals and crops).

(2) The export-based growth strategy may be modified to a policy of exporting manufactured goods that require much labor and little capital to take advantage of a surplus labor supply. The success of such a strategy depends on the willingness of the great foreign markets to accept such imports. It works for Puerto Rico because of a special political relationship with the United States. It is also important in the development of some of the most successful of the developing countries in the Pacific, including South Korea, Taiwan, Hong Kong, and Singapore.

With these exceptions, this is not, however, the main direction of world development strategy. More common has been the policy of import-substitution industrialization. Based on a home market assured by an existing flow of imports, domestic industries are established behind high tariffs or import prohibition. With guranteed markets, it is possible to introduce industries that have much or little promise of producing locally at costs competitive with the displaced imports. In this way, governments may assure industrialization where it is a high-priority objective. The further such a policy is pursued, however, the greater become the social costs of industrialization; the most efficient industries are established first, and more extensive industrialization brings into production higher-cost industries. Some countries, such as Brazil, in which this strategy has been carried furthest have altered course to encourage their industries to become competitive in the world market and to increase participation in world trade.

(3) The policy of political-economic integration (the elimination of trade barriers among specific groups of countries to gain benefits of international specialization) is pursued in the form of customs unions, free trade associations, more far-reaching economic unions, political federation, and even political unification. Integration permits the expansion of a country's lowest-cost industries to the extent of the integrated market's capacity before the next best choice of industries (next highest cost relative to world market costs) must be introduced.

(4) On another dimension are policies that are characterized as "instruments," such as the use of some form of centralized planning and the use of government power to alter institutions and social attitudes that are significant for development. See also ECONOMIC PLANNING.

RICHARD S. WECKSTEIN, *Brandeis University*

ECONOMIC GEOLOGY. See GEOLOGY—*The History of Geology* (Economic Geology).

ECONOMIC INDICATORS. See BUSINESS INDICATORS.

ECONOMIC PLANNING is the conscious control of economic activity in order to achieve certain goals. Discussions of economic planning are usually confined to consideration of the activities of national governments. This article is similarly limited in scope. Nevertheless, economic planning is also practiced by state and local governments and by all private enterprises.

Much government intervention in economic life is justified by certain inherent "failures" of the market. For instance, the typical individual will not voluntarily offer to buy his fair share of sidewalks, mosquito control, or national defense, because he knows that he will receive the benefits anyway. Further, the market cannot be relied upon to accomplish efficiently and equitably large shifts in resources such as are necessary in time of war.

The market system also fails, although less dramatically, where benefits or losses to society are not reflected in an industry's profits. Without a good educational system, the costs of training labor would be much higher for industry, and the level of social life would suffer. But because these benefits to society do not show up in the profits of educational institutions, private education tends to be much smaller in scope than is warranted from a social point of view. So a need arises for government and foundation support.

When industries pollute air and water or destroy forests, the losses to society are not subtracted from private profits. These industries therefore have everything to gain by pursuing "antisocial" activities—except insofar as the government steps in to stop them.

The natural operation of the competitive system results in extreme unevenness in distribution of income. Governments have always felt impelled to assist, in varying forms, the poorer strata of the population.

HISTORICAL BACKGROUND

Economic planning on a piecemeal basis has been practiced as long as nation states have existed. The construction of large-scale irrigation projects many millennia ago in the Middle East and Far East represented state planning in the cradles of world civilization.

In the United States, tariffs were used until World War I to protect domestic industry and thereby encourage industrialization. The gift of public land was used extensively to influence many facets of American development in the 19th century: to stimulate the development of the West by encouraging farming (the Homestead Act of 1862) and railroad building, and to induce the states to support institutions of higher learning (the Morrill Land Grant Act of 1862).

Economic planning has become much more pervasive in the second half of the 20th century. For the Soviet Union (since 1917) and other Communist nations, such planning was virtually necessitated by nationalization of all means of production and, in many areas, the elimination of price-market mechanisms. In the West, economic planning has come about more slowly. It resulted from at least three factors:

(1) Global or macroeconomic theory (economic analysis concerned with the general level of income and output) has advanced significantly, particularly after John Maynard Keynes published his *General Theory of Employment, Interest, and Money* (1936). The theoretical developments were translated into forms usable by economic policymakers as a result of rapid advances in national-income accounting, input-output analysis, and econometric projection techniques.

(2) The worldwide Great Depression of the 1930's and World War II gave impetus to economic planning. The Great Depression proved conclusively that free market mechanisms are at times inadequate to guarantee the levels of employment, stability, and security that modern civilization demands. World War II affirmed the need for a government "steering wheel" and forced wider government participation in economic life.

(3) Concern with national welfare objectives and problems of underdeveloped nations has turned attention to problems of a long-run nature, such as economic growth and population control.

STEPS IN PLANNING

Western economic planning involves at least three major steps.

(1) The government or planning board must establish its major *goals* or *objectives*, and assign relative priorities among these goals. Priorities are necessary because the goals may conflict with each other or the plan may not work out as conceived. Typical major goals of many nations have been a high rate of economic growth, low level of unemployment, price and wage stability, high rate of investment, rapid increase in standard of living, redistribution of economic activity, and favorable balance of payments. The conflict between goals is illustrated by full employment and price stability: as a nation approaches full employment, prices rise.

(2) The goals have to be translated into explicit, quantitative, and, so far as possible, consistent targets, called *target variables*. The target variables may be identical with the goals, but this is not necessarily so.

If consistency among targets is to be achieved, an econometric model may be needed. Such a model is a set of equations and constraints that specify, as completely as possible, the determinants of the target variables, usually including interrelationships among target variables. A change in any important economic variable affects most other variables—and the resulting changes affect still other variables. These interrelationships are so complicated that they cannot be envisaged mentally. So they are set forth in a series of equations that can be solved simultaneously for the precise values of each variable. Although useful, these models suffer because economic relationships usually cannot be specified anywhere as precisely as relationships in physical sciences.

(3) *Instrument variables*, or *controls*, must be selected and used to carry out the plan. Examples of instrument variables under capitalism are: open-market operations (buying or selling of securities) by the central bank to change the interest rate; changes in the exchange rate or the level of tariffs to rectify the balance of payments; and changes in income taxes to alter consumer spending.

General controls affect all activities of a certain type. During inflation a government might impose an overall wage or price freeze, run a budgetary surplus, or force an increase in the interest rate. *Selective controls* directed toward the same end would be consumer credit restraints, price limits only on food and rent, and reduced government spending on education.

Automatic controls, also called *stabilizers*, go into action without special legislative or administrative action. So, in a recession, when more spending is needed, the unemployed automatically get jobless pay, which tends to maintain spending. During inflation the progressivity of the income tax provides for higher effective rates of taxation when these rates are needed to dampen personal expenditures. *Discretionary controls* require legislative action, such as raising the whole income tax rate schedule or introducing a surtax.

Direct controls usually work against the market. Most of them are negative or prohibitive. Direct controls include acreage limitations on farmer, quotas on imports, maximum prices or wages, rationing, or restraints on consumer credit. Positive direct controls include compulsory education and compulsory military service. Direct controls are personal and coercive, but they afford precision and reliability. By use of the draft, a government is able to get the exact number of soldiers needed. Direct controls make possible large and quick shifts of resources.

Indirect controls work through the market by affecting the profitability of various activities or by affecting aggregate expenditures. Instead of compelling people to send their children to school, the state could either levy a special tax on those who don't send their children or give a bonus to those who do. Higher pay in military service could substitute for the draft. Unlike direct controls, indirect controls do not put individual markets out of balance. Indirect controls leave individuals free to choose among alternatives—they simply change the data on which decisions are made. This is politically and psychologically more satisfactory and avoids excessive unpleasant bureaucratic controls by government.

CAPITALIST CASE STUDIES

Although many differences of detail can be enumerated, the United States, the Netherlands, and France are fairly representative of a planning spectrum in the Western capitalist nations.

United States. The U.S. government limits its economic planning largely to pursuing fiscal and monetary policies designed to stabilize the economy in the short run. It aims at a rate of economic activity high enough so that unemployment does not rise above, say, 4% or 5% of the labor force and yet not so high as to induce inflation of more than a few percent per year. In the 1960's these policies also were geared toward rectifying the U.S. balance-of-payments deficit. Stabilization policy is legally rooted in the Employment Act of 1946, which explicitly recognized the federal government's responsibility in this area and created a Council of Economic Advisers to assist the president in formulating policies.

The Netherlands. The Netherlands also plans for stability. A central planning bureau makes recommendations based on an econometric model consisting of 36 variables and equations. The Dutch directly control the wage level. In this respect they differ from most Western capitalist nations.

France. French planning since World War II has been the most extensive of Western capitalist nations. Its target variables go beyond short-run stability and equilibrium in the balance of payments. Steps have been taken to achieve a high rate of economic growth, to modernize industry, to influence regional development, and to increase the ratio in consumption of public to private goods.

The French planning apparatus includes not only government experts but also representatives of major industries and labor unions. This "consensus planning" also has the support of major economic groups. Econometric projections and the use of input-output tables supplement the expertise of participants. The final plan, as approved by parliament, usually for four years, establishes growth rates for the economy and its sectors and output targets for industries. Targets are not broken down by enterprise, and no one is forced to achieve a specific goal. However, since the goal of the overall plan is maximum output consistent with full employment and stability, it is in the interest of entrepreneurs to try to achieve the levels of output implied for their firms. Because its goals are not compulsory, French planning is called "indicative"; Soviet-type planning is "imperative."

SOVIET-TYPE CENTRAL PLANNING

A vast difference exists between Western capitalist planning and the type of planning that, at least up to the mid-1960's, characterized the Soviet and eastern European economies (with the exception of Yugoslavia). These are centrally planned economies. Virtually all economic activity is planned, often in great detail, by agencies of the central governments. Direct controls usually circumvent or substitute for market mechanisms. Private enterprise virtually no longer exists except in agriculture, and all means of production are owned by the state.

Under central planning the government directly determines the levels of consumption, saving, and investment, fixes prices and wages, balances trade, and maintains employment at as high a level as possible. The direct determination of these and other goals and target variables eliminates the need for the large arsenal of instrument variables by which capitalist nations manipulate markets to induce the private sector to fulfill national objectives.

The general direction the Soviet-type economy is to take is set forth in plans that cover periods of from 3 to 20 years. Major goals of these plans have been high rates of economic growth and radical restructuring of the economies, primarily away from agriculture and toward industry. Annual plans are fitted into longer-run plans. They are the basis of binding instructions handed down to production, distribution, and administrative organizations.

Production and Supply. Basically, two kinds of plans are established: production plans and supply plans. The production plans result from interchange of information between the central planning agencies and the industrial ministries and enterprises subordinated to them. These plans establish the outputs of each plant and the inputs required by them. The final plan is legally binding upon the enterprise.

The supply plans arrange in great detail for distribution of the total output of a large percentage of individual enterprises to other enterprises, which use them either as inputs or sell them to distributors or final consumers. Planners strive to make the output of each commodity —say, steel—in the production plan just equal to the amount required as inputs by all users. The amounts usually do not balance at first instance, and adjustments are complicated by indirect effects that are not easily envisaged. If, for example, the planned demand for steel exceeds planned output, additional output must be scheduled—so steel producers need more coal; coal producers need more machinery; machinery producers need more steel.

These repercussions could be quickly estimated if operational input-output tables were available to planners, but that is not the case. Instead, adjustments are made manually, laboriously, by means of *material balances* for thousands of commodities. Material balances are accounts that list all sources of a commodity on one side of a page and all uses on the other. The time of many planners is devoted to this balancing activity. In addition, planners spend much time supervising the production and allocation of supplies—activities that are handled relatively cheaply and painlessly by market mechanisms in the West.

The centrally planned economies rely on market mechanisms in two sectors: to allocate labor (by differential wages) and to distribute consumer goods. No market in the true sense of the word exists, however, in the allocation of producer goods and raw materials. These are largely allocated (rationed) directly. The absence of markets, along with the resulting irrational price systems, leaves up to the planners the further problem of having to determine, often by makeshift means, efficient methods of producing, of distributing new investment resources, and of trading with other nations.

Reforms. These problems of how to balance output and input and how to produce, invest, and trade efficiently led to reforms throughout the Soviet bloc beginning in the mid-1960's. The more radical reforms (Hungary and Czechoslovakia took the biggest steps) decentralized the setting of many prices. With more rational prices, it becomes possible to eliminate most output targets and to make "profits" the goal of plant management. It also becomes possible to allow decentralized market allocation of most supplies. Enterprises were given greater freedom in making and financing investment decisions. The more radical reforms presage a big shift away from direct physical controls and toward the use of indirect controls.

Yugoslavia began decentralizing earlier, in 1950, and presently may be as dependent on free-market mechanisms and indirect controls as many capitalist economies. Yugoslavia also has innovated in a major way by introducing worker control of enterprises and profit sharing in them. Although the degree of control that workers actually exercise over managers apparently varies from plant to plant, no one would deny that they have considerable power in a large part of the economy.

FRANKLYN D. HOLZMAN, *Tufts University*
Author of "Soviet Taxation: The Fiscal and Monetary Problems of a Planned Economy"

Further Reading: Grossman, Gregory, *Economic Systems* (Englewood Cliffs, N. J., 1967); Kirschen, E. S., and others, *Economic Policy in Our Times*, Vols. I–III (Chicago 1964); Köhler, Heinz, *Welfare and Planning* (New York 1966); United Nations, *Economic Survey of Europe in 1962*, Part II (Geneva 1965).

ECONOMIC SYSTEMS are forms of social organization for producing goods and services and determining how they will be distributed. See CAPITALISM; COMMUNISM; FASCISM; MARXISM; SOCIALISM.

ECONOMIC UNION is, broadly, a form of economic cooperation among nations. In a narrower sense, an economic union exists when two or more nations establish free mutual trade, a common external tariff, easy movement of money, goods, and labor among member countries, and common monetary, fiscal, and social policies. This is one step less than complete economic integration, in which all member countries are under a single economic policy. Political unification sometimes follows economic integration and is often the ultimate aim of those who propose economic union.

In the broader sense, an economic union may be a customs union (q.v.), a common market (q.v.) or any grouping of nations for a single economic purpose, such as the Universal Postal Union or multinational airlines such as the Scandinavian Airlines System of Denmark, Norway, and Sweden.

Since World War II. As a result of the tariff wars of the 1930's, the Great Depression, and the terrible destruction of World War II, Europe was in economic chaos in 1945. The dream of a united Europe, common long before the war, began to take on more reality as Europe's broken economy was ministered to by a host of agencies that treated all Europe as an economic unit.

In 1951, France, West Germany, Italy, Belgium, the Netherlands, and Luxembourg (the last three linked since 1948 in an economic union called Benelux, q.v.) formed the European Coal and Steel Community (ECSC). Highly successful, it was followed in 1957 by the European Atomic Energy Community (EAEC or Euratom) and the European Economic Community (EEC), popularly called the Common Market. All members derived considerable benefit from their economic integration.

Britain, whose attempts to enter the Common Market were frustrated by France, promoted formation of the European Free Trade Association (EFTA) in 1960. The members, sometimes called the Outer Seven, were Austria, Britain, Denmark, Norway, Portugal, Sweden, and Switzerland.

The example of the Common Market prompted establishment of economic unions in other regions. The Central American Common Market (CACM) was founded in 1960 among Central American states, and the East African Common Market in 1967 among Kenya, Uganda, and Tanzania. Also in 1967, the Latin American states undertook to form a Latin American Common Market by 1970 to replace the Latin American Free Trade Association (LAFTA, established in 1960) and complement the Alliance for Progress (formed in 1961). Another economic union, the Association of Southeast Asian Nations (ASEAN), was formed in 1967.

Earlier Forms. Many forms of economic union have existed. In one form, called colonial customs assimilation, colonies joined the economic system of the mother country (see COLONIALISM; MERCANTILISM). With independence, former colonies were protected by preferential tariffs, as in the British Commonwealth and French Community. Several customs unions appeared in the 19th century, including the Zollverein (q.v.) in 1834 that led to unification of Germany. In the late 19th century, rising nationalism reduced the appeal of economic union.

SERGIO BARZANTI
Fairleigh Dickinson University

ECONOMIC WARFARE, essentially economic manipulation by a government for its own purposes, has varied meanings and is used to denote different types of competition among nations. During war, or in preparation for possible war, economic warfare means economic measures used against a present or potential enemy.

In peacetime, economic warfare can mean using tariffs, import quotas, export subsidies, and other governmental programs, including even foreign aid, to advance a country's international economic and financial position. Also bilateral reciprocity treaties and special trade arrangements that operate against third parties, the extension of credit, and even private financing, may sometimes be called economic warfare.

World War I. During World War I the British government found that its blockade of enemy ports, to be effective, must also limit shipping to neutral ports. The "Navicert" system was developed, under which "innocent" goods were authorized shipment to neutral ports through the blockade. Goods that would be of military importance in enemy hands were labeled contraband, and the British stopped their shipment.

World War II. A more extensive and effective system was developed in World War II. The British established a ministry of economic warfare, whose mission was described in this official definition: "The aim of economic warfare is so to disorganize the enemy's economy as to prevent him from carrying on the war. Its effectiveness in any war in which this country may be engaged will vary inversely with the degree of self-sufficiency which the enemy has attained, and/or the facilities he has, and can maintain, for securing supplies from neighboring countries, and directly with the extent to which (1) his imports must be transported across seas which can be controlled by His Majesty's ships, (2) his industry and centres of storage, production, manufacture and distribution are vulnerable to attack from the air, and (3) opportunities arise for interfering with his exports."

When the United States entered the war a counterpart organization was established, eventually named the Foreign Economic Administration. The London blockade committee had members from these two organizations, the British foreign office, and the U.S. Department of State. The Washington machinery had similar committees.

Early in the war the British signed trade agreements with the European neutrals, assuring the neutrals of an adequate flow of those supplies that could be secured only from Allied countries. Particularly important to the European neutrals were food supplies and petroleum from overseas sources. In return for this so-called basic ration, the European neutrals agreed to sell to the Allies certain needed raw materials. It was also possible through the Supply Purchase Agreements, implementing the trade agreements, to exert pressure on the neutrals to stop shipment of strategic materials to Germany.

An economic blockade was maintained to prevent shipment by sea of strategic goods from neutrals to the Germans, and the old Navicert system was reestablished. Since sea blockade could not prevent overland shipment from European neutrals to the Germans, firms that traded with the enemy were blacklisted. Where this was ineffective and the raw materials were important, the Allies bought the materials in the neutral countries to keep them from Germany.

The Germans were dependent upon imports for all ferroalloys essential in the production of steel. To a great degree, these alloys are interchangeable. Mercury was secured from Italy, manganese from the German-occupied Ukraine, nickel from occupied Norway, chrome from Turkey, and wolfram (tungsten) from Spain and Portugal. The fortunes of war denied to the Germans manganese from the Ukraine and mercury from Italy. By diplomatic arrangements, Turkish chrome was denied Germany; sabotage was used to stop the shipment of Norwegian nickel; economic pressure—the stoppage of petroleum and the slowing of food shipments to Spain and Portugal—resulted in the slowing and stopping of wolfram shipment from the Iberian Peninsula. Thus the Allies dried up all Germany's sources of ferroalloys.

Precision products, such as ball bearings, were sorely needed by the German air force and could be purchased in Sweden and Switzerland. To stop this traffic, the blacklist was used, as were contracts to buy producers' total output.

Peacetime Applications. Economic warfare can be employed in peacetime for several purposes. In the League of Nations, between the world wars, the concept of economic sanctions was adopted. In order to prevent or stop any war, sanctions were to be imposed on the aggressor, cutting off his international trade completely or for selected vital items, and thus forcing him to make peace. After Italy attacked Ethiopia, economic sanctions were imposed in 1935, but they failed because some nations would not stop trading with Italy.

The United Nations imposed similar selective economic sanctions on South Africa in 1963 and on Rhodesia in 1966, banning the supply of arms and petroleum and, in the latter case, the purchase of Rhodesian exports. As a few countries disregarded these sanctions, they too were ineffective (see SANCTIONS, INTERNATIONAL).

Just before the United States entered World War II, while technically neutral, it embargoed shipment of strategic materials to Japan and Germany, but continued supplying them to Britain, thus using economic warfare to assist a prospective ally. During the Cold War (q.v.) the United States maintained general or partial embargoes against most Communist countries, the object being to deny strategic materials to potential enemies. The effect of an embargo over a long period, however, is that the deprived country develops its own resources or substitutes, or finds other sources of supply (see EMBARGO).

Foreign aid has also been an important Cold War implement, used by the United States to strengthen its allies and to contain Communist pressure, and used by the USSR to destroy what it considered encirclement. Large amounts of goods and money have been used covertly, as well, to strengthen local Communists so that they could subvert their national governments.

ROYDEN DANGERFIELD, *University of Illinois*

Bibliography
Allen, Robert L., *Soviet Economic Warfare* (Washington 1960).
Gordon, David, and Dangerfield, R., *The Hidden Weapon: The History of Economic Warfare* (New York 1947).
Hirschman, Albert O., *National Power and the Structure of Foreign Trade* (Berkeley, Calif., 1945).
Medlicott, William N., *The Economic Blockade*, vol. 1 *History of the Second World War* (London and New York 1952).
Wu, Yuan-li, *Economic Warfare* (Englewood Cliffs, N. J., 1952).

CHOICES: Economics involves choices. Each household, for example, may spend its income as it sees fit.

ECONOMICS is a social science that analyzes the utilization and allocation of available resources among competing uses. Economics involves choices. These choices determine, for example, what a household will consume, what a firm will produce, and how people will spend their time on work, education, and leisure. Thus economics deals with important aspects of everybody's life.

1. Introduction

Economics would be a trivial subject if humans had so few wants or if resources were so abundant that keeping everyone satisfied at all times would not exhaust available resources. But such is not the case. In all societies, as far as is known, resources have been scarce relative to human wants.

Technological progress helps to relieve scarcities. Synthetic rubber freed the world from dependence on natural rubber, and rayon and nylon ended dependence on cotton. But while relieving the world of one scarcity, technological progress often aggravates another or creates new ones. Uranium became scarce when people learned how to use it to generate atomic energy, and even clean air became scarce in modern cities after gasoline-powered automobiles filled the streets.

There always have been and probably always will be scarcities. Households, firms, and government constantly find it necessary to husband all available resources—that is, to manage them prudently, to economize. The term "economy" derives from the Greek words *oikos* (house) and *nemein* (to manage).

Forms of Organization. There are two pure forms of economic organization, the centrally planned economy and the free-enterprise economy. The centrally planned economy operates much like an army. A top command decides what should be done, and orders filter down to the platoon level, becoming increasingly specific and detailed on their way. Nothing is supposed to be done without an order to do it, and any order is supposed to be carried out without question.

A free-enterprise economy consists of households and firms that are free to do as they please. There is private property of consumers' goods as well as of producers' goods, and private property carries the right to buy and sell. Firms sell consumers' goods to households and producers' goods to other firms. Households sell productive services—their labor, for example—to firms. Buying and selling constitute markets, and prices are formed in such markets according to demand and supply.

Neither the centrally planned economy nor the free-enterprise economy is ever found in a pure form. The Soviet Union is not a pure centrally planned economy, for Soviet consumers are free to decide how to spend their income, and consumers' goods may be privately owned. The United States is not a pure free-enterprise economy, for the government owns and operates the post offices, schools, and veterans hospitals. Not all prices are established according to demand and supply. Public utility rates, for example, are fixed by government.

Both the Soviet Union and the United States, then, are mixed economies. But it remains true that the Soviet mix leans heavily toward the centrally planned economy, while the mix in countries such as Australia, Britain, Canada,

Sweden, Denmark, the United States, and West Germany leans heavily toward the free-enterprise economy.

Allocation of Resources. How does a free-enterprise economy allocate its resources? The economist distinguishes five kinds of allocation that determine how goods get produced and distributed.

(1) *Allocation of Consumers' Goods Among Households.* In a free-enterprise economy no government agency sees to it that a household receives a certain product—for example, an automobile. The profit motive and the price system are trusted to see to that.

Each household is free to spend its income as it sees fit and to borrow funds if it can find a lender. If automobiles are important enough to the household, it will be willing to spend part of its funds on them. Manufacturers may then find it profitable to produce automobiles and ship them to potential buyers—at a price.

No government agency fixes the price of that automobile, yet its level is far from accidental. The price must be low enough to induce the household to buy, otherwise the automobile firms will not find enough demand to justify mass production. On the other hand, the price must be high enough to cover the costs of production, transportation, and distribution and still leave a profit at least as high as the same capital could have earned in other industries. Innumerable things remain unproduced because the lowest price at which they could be produced would be too high, and too few people would be willing to spend their incomes on them.

(2) *Allocation of Producers' Goods Among Firms.* In a free-enterprise economy no government agency makes certain that, for example, each automobile firm gets all the steel it needs. Again the profit motive and the price system are trusted to see to that. Like other firms, the automobile firm is free to spend its funds as it sees fit. If steel is useful enough to it, the automobile firm will be willing to spend part of its funds on steel. Steel firms, in turn, find it profitable to produce steel and ship it to automobile firms—at a price.

The level of the steel price is not accidental. The price must be low enough to discourage the automobile firms from switching to a competitive material—aluminum, magnesium, fiber glass, or plastic. Yet it must be high enough to cover the costs of production, transportation, and distribution, still leaving a profit at least as high as the same capital could have earned in other industries.

(3) *Allocation of Labor Among Firms.* How does a firm—for example, an automobile manufacturer—obtain the labor it needs? Again, no government agency assigns workmen in a free-enterprise economy. Incentives are trusted to do the job.

If labor is useful to the automobile manufacturer, the firm will be willing to spend funds on labor. Men and women then find it worthwhile to seek employment in the automobile industry—at a certain wage rate.

That wage rate is not fixed by a government agency but by collective bargaining between the manufacturer and a labor union. The rate must be low enough to keep the manufacturer from automating its plants so thoroughly that too many members of the labor union become unemployed. But the rate must be high enough to keep the workers from leaving for other firms offering better pay.

CONTENTS

Section	Page	Section	Page
1. **Introduction**	602	Post-Keynesians: Input-Output Economics	610
Forms of Organization	602	Growth Economics	611
Allocation of Resources	603	4. **Mathematical Economics in Action**	611
Government Role	603	Practice of Keynesian Economics	612
The Problem of Waste	603	Components of a Keynesian Model	612
2. **The Method of Economics**	604	Working Out the Model	612
Scientific Approach	604	How to Use the Model	613
Branches	605	Need for Information	613
3. **History of Economics**	605	5. **Economics as a Career**	613
Mercantilists	605	Requirements	613
Physiocrats	606	Specialization	614
Classicists	606	Employment	614
Marxists	608	Opportunities	614
Neoclassicists	608		
Keynesians	610		

For broad views of economics, see:

Econometrics
Economic Development
Economic Planning
Income
Industry
Welfare Economics

For information on major fields or on specialized subjects, see:

Accounting
Advertising
Banks and Banking
Collective Bargaining
Consumer Protection
Cooperatives
Corporation
Federal Reserve System
Finance
Industrial Management
Insurance
Interstate Commerce
Labor Unions
Marketing
Personnel Management
Public Utility
Trade

For information on terms, concepts, and historical developments in economics, see:

Antitrust Laws
Automation
Balance of Payments
Balance of Trade
Barter
Bimetallism
Black Market
Break-Even Point
Budget, Business
Budget, Family
Budget, Government
Business Cycles
Business Indicators
Capital
Capitalism
Cartel
Communism
Competition
Consumption
Cost of Living
Credit
Currency
Debt
Devaluation
Diminishing Returns
Division of Labor
Free Enterprise
Free Trade
Futures Trading
Gold Standard
Great Depression
Guild
Index Numbers
Industrial Production Index
Industrial Revolution
Inflation
Interest
Investments
Labor
Laissez Faire
Land
Marxism
Mercantilism
Money
Monopoly
Pension
Poverty
Prices
Production
Profits
Rent
Savings
Single Tax
Social Security
Socialism
Stock Exchange
Supply and Demand
Tariff
Tax
Unemployment
Value
Wages
Wealth

---

(4) *Allocation of Time.* How do labor households allocate their time among possible uses? A number of decisions must be made by individuals.

If a man decides to work, should he enter the automobile industry or some other industry? How many hours per week should he work? In 1920 the average U. S. wage earner worked 50 hours a week; 45 years later, the average workweek—determined in varying degrees by the worker, employer, and government—had declined to slightly over 40 hours.

Should a youth drop out of high school or stay on and get a diploma? The trend is toward staying in school. Of all U. S. males from 14 to 19 years of age, 52% were working in 1920 but only 45% in 1965, according to Stanley Lebergott, *Manpower in Economic Growth*, quoted by the U. S. Department of Commerce, Bureau of the Census, in *Long Term Economic Growth* (1966).

How soon should a workingman retire? Of all United States males 65 years of age and older, 56% were working in 1920, but exactly half that percentage, 28%, were working in 1965, according to Lebergott and the Department of Commerce.

Should a wife stay home or join the labor force? An increasing percentage of U. S. women have elected over the years to join the labor force. Of all United States females 14 years of age and older, 23% were working in 1920 and 38% in 1965.

The net result of all these trends, upward and downward, has been negligible. Of the total U. S. population 14 years of age and older, 56% were working in 1920 and 58% in 1965.

(5) **Investment for the Future.** An important problem is that of allocating available resources between the needs of the moment and the needs of the future. For example, households may save —that is, deprive themselves of present consumption in order to be that much better off in the future. And firms may invest—that is, construct or buy durable producers' goods, such as a new factory, the productive contributions of which lie chiefly in the future. Or firms may search for new mineral deposits, new synthetics, or new drugs. The search may be in vain, and the payoff—if there is one—may lie in the distant future.

Nations vary in the amount they invest in the future. As for investment in physical capital, the United States is a bit on the low side in comparison with, for example, Japan and West Germany. Gross investment in the United States from 1960 to 1964 was slightly under 17% of the gross national product—the country's total output of goods and services. This percentage has changed little since the period 1920–1929, when it was slightly over 17%.

Another important kind of investment in the future—one that does not show in national income accounts—is investment in a man's knowledge and training. Such investment is often called investment in human capital. A person who goes to college devotes resources available at a given time to the needs of the future. In the United States, higher education enrollment in the population 18 to 21 years of age rose from 8% in 1920 to 44% in 1965. Such a change in 45 years constituted a massive investment in human capital and was unmatched by any other country in the world.

Government Role. Many resources are allocated by government. In the United States, for example, states provide the bulk of higher education. The federal government allocates resources to postal services, defense, and space research, among other things. Funds for such allocation are provided partly by taxation and partly by government borrowing.

The Problem of Waste. Society does not always accept the allocation of resources resulting from the profit motive and the price system. A free-enterprise economy allocates resources to gambling, prostitution, marijuana, and organized crime as well as to the production of houses, pharmaceuticals, electrical appliances, and books. Also, a free-enterprise economy may fail to utilize the resources it has. During the Depression of the 1930's, for example, one man out of three in the United States or in Germany was out of work. At the start of the 1970's, Negro unemployment in the United States ran much higher than white unemployment. Waste is not confined to mature economies—Gunnar Myrdal, in *Asian Drama* (1968), found a massive waste of resources in India.

An economist can analyze waste of resources and find out whether something could be done to eliminate it but not whether or not something *should* be done. The economist is like a physician: He can diagnose troubles and indicate a possible cure, but the ultimate decision is the patient's own.

2. The Method of Economics

Economics has become a science rather than a clash of opinions, but this does not mean that economics now knows all the answers. On the contrary, the best modern economists are much less pleased with themselves than was one of the best classical economists, John Stuart Mill, who wrote in his *Principles of Political Economy* in 1848: "Happily, there is nothing in the laws of value which remains for the present or any future writer to clear up; the theory of the subject is complete." Modern economists are less glib and chatty than their predecessors and more devoted to long, hard thinking and to painstaking measurement. They still have their predecessors' preference for simple hypotheses, but they have seen too many such hypotheses to be willing to embrace wholeheartedly any single one of them.

Scientific Approach. Like medicine or engineering, economics is a rigorous discipline. Hard thinking has produced hypotheses, and those hypotheses have been tested by empirical observation and, where possible, by careful measurement. When the results turned out to be inconsistent with the hypotheses, more hard thinking came up with new hypotheses. The method of economics, then, is no different from the methods of other sciences.

If economics has been progressing slowly it is, perhaps, because of some difficulties that are peculiar to it. (1) Economics cannot conduct controlled experiments as physics and biology can. No household, firm, or government would be willing to let itself be run by an economist motivated by nothing but idle curiosity. The subject matter of economics is too close to the pocketbook for such experimentation to be practicable. (2) Even an economist kept out of control of consumption, production, and budgets is not always allowed to measure these things. The subject matter of economics is too close to the privacy of households, firms, and government. (3) Even an economist permitted to measure everything going on cannot be sure that people behave in the same way when he watches them as when he does not. For these three reasons economists envy physicists and biologists, and progress in economics has been slow.

Nevertheless, there has been progress, and each approach has contributed to it. Some economists have specialized in economic history and have described the rise and fall of economic institutions such as guilds, slavery, tariffs, free trade, the gold standard, and industrialism. Some have specialized in statistics and tried to establish fundamental relationships between economic quantities—prices and the quantity of money, consumption and income, investment and the rate of interest, demand and price. Some economists, such as David Ricardo and Léon Walras, have been pure theorists concentrating on the formulation of hypotheses and leaving the testing of them to others. About 1930 *econometrics* emerged as an attempt to integrate economic theory, mathematics, and statistics.

Branches of Economics. Basically, economists may look at the economy from two angles. They may look at the details or they may look at the whole, ignoring the details.

Microeconomics deals with small segments of the economy such as a household, a firm, or an industry. For example, microeconomics analyzes household decisions to consume, to save, and to work. Or microeconomics analyzes a firm's decision to absorb inputs, produce and sell outputs, fix prices, and advertise.

Macroeconomics deals with large aggregates such as national output, national income, national saving, and national investment. For example, macroeconomics analyzes unemployment, inflation, the balance of trade, and national income distribution.

Basic economics is the hard core of economic theory. *Applied* economics is the use of such theory to illuminate specific problems, some of which are political. For example, how can government action promote growth, combat inflation, reduce a balance-of-payments deficit, eliminate poverty, or finance a war?

3. History of Economics

Expression of economic thinking appeared in the ancient world. They included, for instance, the philosophic declarations of Plato and Aristotle. Churchmen in the Middle Ages also contributed thoughts on economic matters, particularly as they related to ethics. But the first scraps of economic analysis—organized thinking on the subject—date only from the 17th century.

The history of economics since that time may be divided into seven principal schools—mercantilists, physiocrats, classicists, Marxists, neoclassicists, Keynesians, and post-Keynesians. Obviously, however, the history of economics can be compressed into a mere seven schools only by allowing for some diversity within each school.

THE MERCANTILISTS

Organized economic analysis, even though fragmentary, began in the 1600's when the new European sovereign powers, as successors to the feudal barons, were worrying about war and unemployment. They had become engaged in a succession of armaments races and wars. In addition, agrarian technology had changed profoundly, destroying the old relations between lords and peasants and flooding the new national states with destitute beggars and vagrants.

Advisers, some appointed by governments and some self-appointed, produced the system of economic doctrine now called "mercantilism." One mercantilist, Andrew Yarranton, put his goals into the title of his book: *England's Improvement by Sea and Land, to Outdo the Dutch without Fighting, to Pay Debts without Moneys, to Set to Work all the Poor of England* (1677).

The mercantilists were issuing advice at a time when nations encountered a series of emergencies. As might be expected under the circumstances, the mercantilists gave short-run policy advice. In fact, their advice shows striking resemblance to short-run national policies in the 1930's, when governments were also worrying about war and unemployment.

INVESTMENT: In a free-enterprise economy, industry may spend its funds as it chooses. A firm may invest for the future by searching for new drugs. The pay-off—if there is one—may lie in the distant future.

Mercantilism derives its name from its emphasis on trade, especially foreign trade. The foremost advice given by the mercantilists was to gain a so-called favorable balance of trade—a surplus of exports over imports. Imports, the merchantilists held, should be discouraged or, better, fully controlled through quantitative restrictions. Mercantilists contended that industries producing import substitutes should be encouraged and, if necessary, subsidized. Exports, too, should be encouraged and, if necessary, subsidized.

The argument for such protectionism was twofold. (1) Because foreign sources of supply might prove inaccessible in wartime, a nation should not make itself too dependent on them. The most intelligent mercantilists saw that power and profits might clash, at least in the short run. (2) Protectionism might be a quick way to reduce unemployment. Export creates domestic employment, but import does not. Also, an export surplus would have to be paid for by foreigners in specie and so would increase domestic liquidity, lubricate the wheels of business, and reduce unemployment.

It was precisely their awareness of unemployment that made the mercantilists' ideas so hard

RESOURCES: Resources are scarce relative to human wants. There always have been and probably always will be scarcities. Industry, impelled by the profit motive, seeks a resource—petroleum—on Alaska's North Slope.

to grasp for classicists and neoclassicists, who always assume full employment. It is the same awareness of unemployment that makes the mercantilists look so sensible to Keynesians.

THE PHYSIOCRATS

François Quesnay, in his *Tableau économique* (1758), was the first to offer a well-specified model of the economy. Basically, said this French economist, founder of the physiocratic school, there are only three inputs—land, labor, and capital. Labor and capital are reproducible and will not earn more income than necessary to reproduce them. Labor gets an income necessary to reproduce the workingman's ability to work, and capital gets what is necessary for replacing the capitalist's stock plus what is necessary to make him take the risk. Consequently, wages, depreciation, and interest are gross income, but the net income from labor and capital is zero.

Land is different. Land is irreproducible but lasts forever, and any income from it is therefore a net income, a *produit net*. Quesnay assumed complete separation of ownership and control in agriculture. Landlords owned the land, and farmers cultivated it. To Quesnay, there were three classes in the economy—landlords, farmers, and all the people engaged in nonagricultural pursuits. He glorified farmers by calling them "productive." He called nonagriculturists "sterile" without implying that they were useless. In economics, as elsewhere, labels mean much, and the physiocratic doctrine was no doubt rejected by many who simply disliked those labels.

Quesnay's lasting contribution to economics is his vision of the general interdependence of industries. He saw how this interdependence manifests itself in circular flows of output and income among landlords, farmers, and nonagriculturists. Landlords receive their rent from the farmers and spend it on produce and manufactures. Farmers receive revenue from selling produce and spend it on rent and on tools and consumers' goods purchased from nonagriculturists. In turn, nonagriculturists receive revenue from selling tools and consumers' goods and spend it on produce for themselves. Quesnay depicted these flows in his *Tableau*.

The importance of his *Tableau* is threefold. (1) He established the tradition of reducing the myriad transactions in the economy to a few income and output flows. Karl Marx and John Maynard Keynes went on from there. (2) Having reduced the entire economy to a few income and output flows, Quesnay found that the temptation to measure them was irresistible and tried to collect income and output data for the French economy. Thus Quesnay was the first econometrician, and modern national income accounting and input-output tables descend from his work. (3) Quesnay's economic table implicitly poses the question, "Under which conditions will the economy be in equilibrium?" If too much income is being generated, the economy will suffer from shortages and inflation. If too little is being generated, the economy will suffer from bulging inventories and unemployment. See also PHYSIOCRATS; QUESNAY, FRANÇOIS. For accounts of others in the school, see also DU PONT—*Pierre Samuel du Pont;* TURGOT, ANNE ROBERT JACQUES.

THE CLASSICISTS

The dominant English writers on economics in the last quarter of the 18th and the first half of the 19th century made up the classical school. The most prominent names are Adam Smith, Thomas R. Malthus, and David Ricardo.

Smith and a Free Economy. Adam Smith, in *An Inquiry into the Nature and Causes of the Wealth of Nations* (1776), saw the economy as an interplay of selfish interests that paradoxically produced highly desirable social results. Assuming that everyone is left free to pursue his own interest without any interference from the government, said Smith, households will spend their incomes on the goods most desired, and firms will produce the goods most in demand, because such goods will carry a high profit margin. As more and more businessmen are attracted by the high profits, however, competition will drive down the price of the goods. How far? Down to the point where price just covers the cost of production plus a normal return to capital. At that point no more businessmen are attracted to the industry, and the industry is in equilibrium. Adam Smith vividly painted the picture of a free economy in which all the most desired goods would be produced and sold at the lowest possible price.

Smith's style was impressionistic and fluent, and as a result he was highly influential. He cast doubts on the wisdom of the mercantilist regimentation of the British economy and paved the way for free trade, finally adopted in 1846.

Malthus and Subsistence. Thomas Robert Malthus is best known for his *Essay on the Principles of Population*. In its first edition in 1798, Malthus restated the 200-year-old idea that population would tend to grow more rapidly than the means of subsistence and would be held in check only by infant disease, plague, famine, and war. This idea was first stated, fully developed, by Giovanni Botero in his *Della ragion di stato* (1589). Malthus merely added seeming precision to it by saying that population would tend to grow according to a geometric progression (a, ar, ar^2, ..., where $r > 1$), while, on the contrary, the means of subsistence would tend to grow according to an arithmetic progression (a, $a + d$, $a + 2d$, .., where $d > 0$). This formulation is an excellent example of mathematics ill employed by an economist, for it is futile to try to formulate independent laws for the behavior of two very interdependent quantities.

In the second edition of his *Essay* (1803), Malthus added the idea that besides infant disease, plague, famine, and war—called "positive" checks—there were "negative" checks as well. The negative checks consisted of voluntary action such as late marriages and sexual restraint in marriage. The negative checks deprive the theory of much of its seeming precision. Only in the skillful hands of Ricardo did the Malthusian scraps of thought become a genuine theory of wages—an explanation of the relationship of population to the subsistence minimum.

Malthus did, however, have other and better ideas. He saw the possibility that too much thrift might reduce aggregate consumption demand and create overproduction and unemployment. In this sense he was a forerunner of John Maynard Keynes.

Ricardo's Theories. Of the three leading English classicists, David Ricardo was the most profound thinker. In contrast to the impressionism of Adam Smith and Malthus, his theories were derived logically from well-specified assumptions.

In his *Principles of Political Economy and Taxation* (1817), Ricardo formulated the law of diminishing returns. This law, which was to become one of the cornerstones of economics, says that if more and more doses of labor and capital inputs combined are applied to a given quantity of land, the additions to output will get smaller and smaller. Ricardo explained that if too many labor-capital doses get crowded on the best part of the land, the last dose on this *intensive margin* of cultivation contributes little. Or, he said, if additional doses are employed on poorer and poorer parts of the land, the last dose on this *extensive margin* of cultivation again contributes little.

Next, Ricardo wanted to explain the price of one output relative to another, often called the relative price of an output. In two masterly strokes Ricardo reduced the determinants of relative price in a three-input economy (land, labor, and capital) to just one input, labor. The first stroke was to eliminate land by watching either the intensive or the extensive margin of cultivation. Here at the margin, where it was not worthwhile to employ more labor and capital because they would contribute no more than what they cost, there was nothing left for rent. And the margin is where prices get determined, for price must cover the cost of producing under the least favorable circumstances, not merely the cost of producing under more favorable circumstances. Rent, therefore, was out of the picture.

Ricardo's second masterly stroke was to assume that the useful life of capital goods is the same in all industries, and that labor and capital combine in the same proportions in all industries. Then it became possible for Ricardo to say that relative prices are determined by the relative amounts of labor incorporated in the goods. If it took twice as much labor to produce one good as another, then under Ricardo's assumption it would also take twice as much capital to do so (for labor and capital combined in the same proportions in all industries). Consequently the first good would have a price twice as high as that of the other good.

This statement was a big advance toward an explanation of relative prices, but one difficulty remained. Clearly the quantity of labor incorporated in a good would depend on where the margin of cultivation was. In a sparsely populated country the margin has not been pushed very far, and the required quantity of labor is low. In a densely populated country the margin already has been pushed very far out, and the required quantity of labor is high.

How could Ricardo determine his margin of cultivation? He could do so by borrowing a leaf from Malthus' book. He said that the real wage rate—the basket of goods that the money wage rate will buy—would have to be high enough "to enable the laborers, one with another, to subsist and to perpetuate their race, without either increase or diminution"—a biological constant. If the real wage rate were higher than the subsistence minimum, he said, population would rise and depress the real wage rate because land would become scarcer. And if the real wage rate were lower than the subsistence minimum, population would fall and thus raise the real wage rate because land would become less scarce.

In a very similar way Ricardo determined the rate of return on capital as a minimum constituting, as he said, "an adequate compensation for their [the farmer's and the manufacturer's] trouble, and the risk which they must necessarily encounter in employing their capital productively." For if the rate of return were higher than that minimum, capital accumulation would rise and depress the rate of return, again because land was becoming scarcer. And if the rate of return were lower than the minimum, capital accumulation would fall and thus raise the rate of return, again because the scarcity of land would be somewhat relieved.

Now everything falls into place. The margin is established at the point where land will yield just enough to give labor and capital each its minimum. The Ricardian model succeeds in determining the margin and with it the population and capital accumulation an economy can support. But if an attempt were made to force an economy to support more people than that, only misery and starvation would result. Consequently Ricardo warned against all social security programs. His warnings earned economics the title of "that dismal science."

There has always been a tendency to judge a theory by its political implications, and Ricardo's did not prove immune to this. Because his theory led to such repugnant political conclusions, it was widely rejected. Worse still, economic theory as such was widely rejected.

For accounts of other leaders in the Classical School, see also HUME, DAVID; McCULLOCH, JOHN RAMSAY; MILL, JOHN STUART; SENIOR, NASSAU WILLIAM.

THE MARXISTS

Karl Marx the economist, as distinguished from Karl Marx the historian, sociologist, pamphleteer, organizer, and journalist, was interested exclusively in the long-run working mechanism of capitalism that would result in its ultimate breakdown. He never offered any blueprint for a socialist economy.

Marx, in *Das Kapital* (1867), like Quesnay, and more clearly than Ricardo, saw the general interdependence of industries, and he simplified things as far as he could without losing sight of that interdependence. His economy has only two industries—one for producers' goods and a second for consumers' goods.

Each industry absorbs two inputs, producers' goods and labor. Assume a_1 to be the man hours absorbed in producing one unit of producers' goods. Let a_2 be the man hours absorbed in producing one unit of consumers' goods. Let b_1 be the producers' goods absorbed in producing one unit of producers' goods. And let b_2 be producers' goods absorbed in producing one unit of consumers' goods. The useful life of all producers' goods is assumed to be one year.

Marx differs from Ricardo by leaving out land and diminishing returns. But like Ricardo, he had a labor theory of value. It is not quite clear whether Marx considered his labor theory of value merely a definition of value—and in that case there could be no argument—or whether he believed, as had Ricardo, that the relative prices of producers' and consumers' goods would tend under free competition to be in proportion to the relative (direct plus indirect) labor embodiments of producers' and consumers' goods. If he believed the latter, he was as right or as wrong as Ricardo had been. He was right if either the rate of return on capital equaled zero or if labor and capital combined in the same proportions in producers' and consumers' goods—that is, $a_1/b_1 = a_2/b_2$. He was wrong in all other cases.

Right or wrong, Marx was not after a mere theory of relative prices. He wanted to formulate the proposition that as capital accumulation goes on, as it must, then the rate of return on capital will fall, and the real wage rate—meaning the money wage rate divided by the price of consumers' goods—will also fall. If this were true, capitalism would inevitably destroy itself from within by generating so much misery and unrest that workers would overthrow it by force.

For a long time the majority of economists judged a theory by its political implications, and they found the Marxian vision of capitalism destroying itself from within particularly repugnant, so they chose to ignore Marx. When enough time had passed to permit empirical testing of the Marxian proposition, it turned out that Marx the theorist had been a poor forecaster. True, accumulation had continued and capital had been growing much more rapidly than labor. But neither the rate of return on capital nor the real wage rate had fallen.

On the contrary, the rate of return on capital has remained constant—in the United States, around 9% annually for the first half of the 20th century. Also, the real wage rate went up, not down. Total compensation per working hour for U. S. manufacturing workers, expressed in terms of dollars of the purchasing power a dollar had in 1957, went up from 46 cents in 1889 to $2.55 in 1963, a more than fivefold increase in 74 years. These historical facts of a constant return to capital and a rising real wage rate have been well simulated by modern economic models built by Jan Tinbergen (1942) and Robert M. Solow (1956).

Discredited by the facts and superseded by superior theory, Marx was all but forgotten by economists, and testing him on his own ground was delayed until Paul A. Samuelson of the Massachusetts Institute of Technology, writing in the *American Economic Review* in 1957, reconstructed the Marxian model in terms of linear algebra. Samuelson showed that neither constant nor progressing technology permits a falling rate of return on capital to be accompanied by a falling real wage rate. Samuelson's test is an excellent example of the fact that once an argument has been recast in mathematical form, errors in it can be detected much more easily.

Not only the economists forgot Marx. Most socialists forgot him, too, and became preoccupied with problems of strategy. Was revolution or reform the best way of approaching socialism? Few socialists were interested in economic theory, and fewer still were able to use the Marxian model, let alone add to it. One who did so was Rosa Luxemburg who, in her *Die Akkumulation des Kapitals* (1912), attempted an economic explanation of imperialism.

See also MARX, KARL; MARXISM—*Marx's Economic Theory*.

THE NEOCLASSICISTS

The neoclassicists were classicists in the sense that they, too, derived their results logically from well-specified axioms. But both their axioms and their results differed from those of the classicists, and they were much less policy-oriented.

Three neoclassicists—William Stanley Jevons of England, Carl Menger of Austria, and Léon Walras, who was born in France and taught at the University of Lausanne in Switzerland—almost simultaneously in the early 1870's formulated a counterpart to Ricardo's law of diminishing returns. The counterpart was the law of diminishing marginal utility, which said that if more and more output is consumed by an individual, the additions to his utility will get smaller and smaller. The discovery of the law of diminishing marginal utility opened the way to an analysis of consumption, governing demand, as a needed counterpart to the classical analysis of production, governing supply.

Insights of Walras. One of the neoclassicists, Walras, went further. While Jevons and Menger kept trifling with partial relationships and insisting on expressing such relationships in terms of "cause" and "effect," Walras took his cue from Quesnay and went to work on the general interdependence of industries and households. Walras set forth his views in *Éléments d'économie politique pure* (1874). He considered the gen-

PRICES: Firms produce and ship steel to customers—for a price. The price must be low enough to restrain customers from switching to a competitive material, but high enough to cover costs and leave a profit.

eral case of an economy with m outputs, n inputs, and s households. Here, the principal variables were: quantities of outputs supplied by industries and demanded by households, quantities of inputs supplied by households and demanded by industries, and prices of all outputs and inputs. From these variables Walras formed new ones. The cost per unit of output of an industry, for example, would be price of first input times quantity of it absorbed per unit of output of the industry plus price of second input times quantity of it absorbed per unit of output of the industry plus ... and so on.

Having defined all his economic variables, Walras tried to say in mathematical form all that could be said about them. For example, in a stationary economy saving is zero, so any household must break even. But this means that its income must equal its consumption expenditure. Next Walras wrote demand and supply functions for output and input. He wrote household demand for output as a function of prices and the marginal utility of output, subject to the budget constraint that, for each household, income equals consumption expenditure. What about the supply of output? Under pure competition all profit over and above normal return to capital will be washed away, so the price of output of an industry must equal the cost per unit of output of that industry, as defined above. At that price industry will supply what all the s households are demanding.

As for inputs, Walras wrote industry demand for an input as the input-output coefficient for that input in first output times first output plus the input-output coefficient for that input in second output times second output plus ... and so on. What about the supply of input? Walras wrote household supply of input as a function of prices and the marginal disutility of providing input, subject again to the budget constraint that, for each household, income equals consumption expenditure.

All that now remained for Walras to do was to express the condition that demand equals supply. For the entire economy to be in equilibrium, this condition would have to be satisfied in every output market and every input market.

Having written in mathematical form all the statements he could think of, Walras counted his equations and found them to be one short of the number of his variables. He then took an arbitrary price, called the *numéraire,* and divided all his price equations by that price. This would convert all his price equations into statements about prices relative to the *numéraire,* thus reducing the number of variables by one. Now the numbers of equations and variables were equal, and Walras thought he was finished. Had he been a better mathematician, he would have known that such an equality between the numbers of equations and variables does not guarantee the existence and uniqueness of positive and real solutions for all variables. But Walras' deficiencies have since been remedied, chiefly by the Princeton mathematician John von Neumann, writing in the journal *Review of Economic Studies* in 1945 and 1946.

Walras' greatness, unaffected by such deficiencies, is to have seen the futility in looking for "cause" and "effect" between economic variables. All his variables were determined simultaneously within his system of simultaneous equations. To Ricardo, cost had been the "cause" of price. But Walras showed that cost was composed of input prices and input quantities absorbed, and all prices and quantities were determined simultaneously. To Menger, on the other hand, marginal utility was the "cause" of price. Walras showed that marginal utility is not determined until the margin of consumption is determined, and that margin gets determined simultaneously with everything else in the system.

Walras was not understood by his contemporaries. To a friend he wrote, "If one wants to harvest quickly, one must plant carrots and salads; if one has the ambition to plant oaks, one must have the sense to tell oneself: My grandchildren will owe me this shade." Readers of the current leading economics journals, such as the *American Economic Review, Quarterly Journal of Economics,* or *Economic Journal*—as well as readers of the highly technical *Econometrica* and *Review of Economic Studies*—will see how much the grandchildren and great grandchildren owe Walras.

In Britain and the United States, Walras was virtually unknown until 1954, when his work was finally translated into English.

Other Neoclassicists. The best known neoclassicist in the Anglo-Saxon countries was Alfred Marshall, Cambridge professor and author of *Principles of Economics* (1890). Marshall analyzed cost and demand more carefully than had been done before and pioneered the theory of the firm and the industry. But he always looked at one thing at a time and never tried to bring everything together in an all-embracing equilibrium, as Walras had done.

Less well known by their contemporaries—but now considered of greater stature than Marshall—were the Swede Knut Wicksell, author of *Lectures on Political Economy* (1901–1906), and the American Irving Fisher, who wrote *Nature of Capital and Income* (1906) and *The Rate of Interest* (1907). Wicksell and Fisher each offered a brilliant contribution to what had been the weakest part of Walrus' performance—the theory of capital and interest.

Another neoclassical student of the firm and the industry, but very different from Marshall, was Joseph Alois Schumpeter, who was born and taught in Austria and moved on to Germany and then the United States. In his *Theorie der wirtschaftlichen Entwicklung* (1912, translated 1934) and *Business Cycles* (1939), Schumpeter examined the long-run implications of profit maximization and found them to be something like this: If exploration uncovered new mineral deposits, if chemical and biological research created new synthetics or new drugs, if consumers developed new preferences or—even better—could be persuaded by advertising to adopt new preferences, new profit opportunities would open up and there would be rich rewards for the first firm that exploited the new opportunities.

For a while, the exclusive right to unusual mineral deposits, to patents, or to trademarks may protect the innovator's high rate of return. But eventually others will invade the field. The invader is unlikely to be a new firm, for such a firm would lack the retained earnings and the large depreciation allowances that are such important sources of finance. It would also lack easy access to the stock market.

Most innovation, invasion, and counterinvasion hides behind the facades of established, large corporations. Yet the serenity of those facades is deceptive. Behind them are not only the rich rewards accruing to the first firm that exploits the new opportunities. There is also the steady erosion of those rewards by powerful invaders. If the rich rewards are the carrot, the erosion of them is the stick. Like the proverbial donkey, capitalism is spurred on by the stick no less than by the carrot.

Schumpeter's theory of growth is broad and sweeping, written in a style reminiscent of Adam Smith. Schumpeter is the first economist to build his analysis around the modern large corporation rather than around the small Marshallian proprietorship. In this sense he was the first to analyze the aggressive and dynamic capitalism found in the United States, Germany, and Japan in the 20th century. One of his policy conclusions was that the large corporation should not be bothered with antitrust action, for technological advance and invasion by giant rivals could be trusted to erode all monopoly positions.

See also CLARK, JOHN BATES; FISHER, IRVING; JEVONS, WILLIAM STANLEY; MARSHALL, ALFRED; MENGER, KARL; SCHUMPETER, JOSEPH A.; WALRAS, LÉON; WICKSELL, KNUT.

THE KEYNESIANS

No 20th century economist has been as influential as John Maynard Keynes, who published *The General Theory of Employment, Interest, and Money* in England in 1936. Keynes fundamentally changed the thinking of economists as well as the practices of governments.

The basic idea of Keynesian economics is quite simple. In a way, Keynesian economics is nothing but the law of demand and supply extended to the economy at large. But while older economics used the law of demand and supply to explain the price of a particular commodity, Keynesian economics uses it to explain national output and inflation.

Actually, the law of demand and supply had been extended to the economy at large before Keynes, most clearly by two Swedish economists—Knut Wicksell in *Geldzins und Güterpreise* (1898) and his disciple Erik Lindahl, in *Penningpolitikens medel* (1930). But Wicksell and Lindahl were hidden behind their language barrier, so the extension of the law of demand and supply became generally accepted in its English-language, Keynesian form.

Keynes explained how aggregate demand is generated and how it determines national output. He also explained how government can affect the level of national output and employment through appropriate monetary and fiscal policy. But while most younger Anglo-Saxon economists had become Keynesians by the outbreak of World War II, Keynesianism did not become practical U. S. policy until two decades later. See also KEYNES, JOHN MAYNARD, and the section, *Mathematical Economics in Action,* in this article.

THE POST-KEYNESIANS: INPUT-OUTPUT ECONOMICS

Keynes had asked and answered questions of paramount importance, but on others he had been silent. One question left unanswered was the determination of the composition of national output in detail, industry by industry.

Such a determination required econometrics, which is the study of economics with the help of mathematics and statistics. Walras probably never thought of putting his model of the interdependence of industries to practical use by estimating its structural constants empirically. Wassily Leontief of Harvard University did so in 1941 in *The Structure of American Economy, 1919–1929.* Before Leontief could succeed in such a venture, drastic simplification of the Walrasian model was necessary. All supply limitations had to be ignored and all nonindustry demand had to be made a constant, thus ignoring specifically the relationship between household demand and household income. Even so, Leontief's accomplishment is a majestic one.

The input-output model compiled by the U. S. Department of Commerce has 81 industries in it, but the working principle behind all such models can be illustrated by an economy having only two industries in it, each producing a single product. Let the industries be manufacturing and agriculture, producing manufactures and produce, respectively. The table below shows input and output for such a two-industry, two-product economy.

Input-Output Table for a Two-Industry Economy Expressed in Physical Units of Output

From \ Into	Manu-facturing	Agriculture	Household consumption	Total
Manufacturing[1]	—	20	40	60
Agriculture[2]	24	—	16	40

[1] Absorbs 0.4 units of agricultural produce as input per unit of manufacturing output. [2] Absorbs 0.5 units of manufactures as input of agricultural output.

Manufactures are absorbed by households for purposes of consumption. Assume that the number needed for this purpose is 40. Manufactures are also absorbed by agriculture in the form of inputs, such as fuels and implements. Assume that for each unit of output of produce, agriculture will absorb 0.5 units of manufactures as inputs. Produce is absorbed by households for purposes of consumption. Let the number needed for this purpose be 16. Produce is absorbed by the manufacturing industry as an input, such as cotton and hides. For each unit of output of manufactures let 0.4 units of produce be absorbed as inputs. Under these assumptions, what will the outputs of the two industries have to be?

The answer is that the economy must produce 60 units of manufactures and 40 units of produce. Of the 60 units of manufactures, households take 40, so there are 20 left. Since each of the 40 units of produce requires 0.5 units of manufactures as input, agriculture will need exactly those remaining 20 units.

Agriculture produces 40 units. Households take 16 of these, so there are 24 left. Since each of the 60 units of manufactures requires 0.4 units of produce as input, manufacturing will need exactly those remaining 24 units.

This simple input-output model has only two industries and therefore only two interindustry transactions. But if the number of industries were raised, the number of interindustry transactions would rise much faster. A model with three industries would have six interindustry transactions. A model with four industries would have 12 interindustry transactions. When there are n industries there will be $n^2 - n$ interindustry transactions. Mapping all the $n^2 - n$ interindustry transactions and finding all the $n^2 - n$ empirical input-output coefficients may become a major econometric project necessitating the use of high-speed digital computers. For example, the input-output table published by the U. S. Department of Commerce breaks down the U. S. economy into 81 industries. Consequently it has 6,480 interindustry transactions and 6,480 empirical input-output coefficients.

Most advanced nations now possess input-output tables of this magnitude. In the Soviet Union and the eastern European countries input-output tables have become an important instrument of central economic planning.

THE POST-KEYNESIANS: GROWTH ECONOMICS

Medieval economies were stationary, but slow growth was brought about by the geographical discoveries in the late 15th century and by technological progress in agriculture beginning in the 16th century. However, it was not until industrialization that economies began to grow as rapidly as 3% or more per year.

Industrialization flourished in the early 19th century. Yet, with the exception of Marx, 19th century economics is the economics of the stationary state. And the Marxian speculations about the growth and decay of capitalist economies were not borne out by later economic developments.

Keynes, too, left unanswered the question of how the rate of growth of national output was determined. The simple Keynesian model was a short-run model that left net investment unexplained. As soon as economists tried to explain net investment they were forced to allow for growth. Several possible motives may cause businessmen to add to their capital stock, but the most important must surely be the growth of output over time.

In the 1940's, Evsey D. Domar, an American, and Roy F. Harrod, an Englishman, examining a purely private economy, discovered a delicate dynamic balance based on two constants. The first constant is the Keynesian propensity to consume. Assume, for example, that households always consume nine tenths of net national output. The second constant is the capital coefficient defined as the number of dollars' worth of capital stock it takes to produce $1 worth of output per year. Assume, for example, that it take $4 worth of capital stock to produce $1 worth of output.

If in such an economy the output in year 1 is 100, how large must output be in year 2? It must be 102.5, and it is easy to see why this answer is correct. Out of an output of 100, consumers will consume 90%, or 90. If firms expect output to rise from 100 in year 1 to 102.5 in year 2, and their capital coefficient is 4, their capital stock must rise from 400 in year 1 to 410 in year 2—that is, by 10. But the increase in capital stock is net investment, so consumption demand 90 and investment demand 10 will add up to output of 100 in year 1.

The Domar-Harrod model of growth is extremely crude. John von Neumann, in a 1945–1946 restatement of Walras, offered a far more sophisticated growth model, the full implications of which are still being investigated by economists. Neither the Domar-Harrod model nor the von Neumann model included technological progress, which must be a key factor in the growth process. Nevertheless the Domar-Harrod model remains a simple and beautiful illustration of how economists have put motion into their models. Once it has been decided to go from the analysis of the stationary state to the analysis of motion, refinement is not too difficult.

4. Mathematical Economics in Action

Whether studying the firm, industry, or the economy at large, a modern economist likes to arrange his thoughts in the form of a model. By a model is meant the complete specification of the variables used, the relationships between them, and the constants used to express those relationships. A model may be formulated in mathematical or nonmathematical terms.

Can mathematics do anything that cannot be done verbally? Clearly not, for mathematics is taught verbally, with each new word defined as it is introduced. But just because bulldozers can do nothing that could not be done by teaspoons, it does not follow that one should always use teaspoons. Like a bulldozer, mathematics is a very powerful and often a very economical tool. It is unrivaled in solving complicated problems, such as those involved in large-scale input-output systems, where solutions came within reach only after the development of large electronic digital computers.

Mathematics contributes to the clarity and safety with which any problem is solved, whether complicated or not. Trying to reason one's way through modern economics in purely verbal form would be both inefficient and risky—inefficient, because finding the ultimate solution would take much longer; risky, because errors in reasoning are much more likely to occur and are much more difficult to detect in verbal than in mathematical form. Moreover, mathematics facilitates communication among economists, statisticians, and computers.

Mathematics, furthermore, has an immense aesthetic appeal. In no other language can one express oneself with such precision, richness, generality, and elegance—and yet with such compactness and economy.

As a result of all this, mathematics has become as indispensable in theoretical and practical economics as in chemistry or physics.

Practice of Keynesian Economics. Keynesian economics provides an example of how a modern economist builds up the components of his model and puts them together in order to draw precise quantitative conclusions.

Like Adam Smith and David Ricardo, John Maynard Keynes fundamentally changed the thinking of economists and, with some delay, the practices of government. Keynes' ideas were practiced as early as the late 1940's by the Australian, British, and Scandinavian governments but were not embraced by the United States and West German governments until the 1960's.

Keynesian economics—the law of demand and supply applied to the economy at large—explains national output and inflation. It can tell how governments could steer national output in a desired direction—upward if there is unemployment and slack in the economy, or downward if the economy is coming too close to capacity and shows signs of inflation. The U. S. government has practiced such steering. Upward steering came in the form of the income tax rate reductions enacted in 1964. The success of the tax cuts in reducing unemployment at long last brought practical recognition to Keynesian economics in the United States. Four years later, downward steering came in the form of an income tax surcharge enacted to combat inflation.

Components of a Keynesian Model. The core of a Keynesian model deals with how demand is generated and how it determines national output. That core is most easily understood in simple algebraic terms. The first decision a Keynesian model-builder must make is how many variables and constants he wants to include in his model. The following variables and constants are needed to show the essence of a Keynesian model.

Variables
C = consumption demand
R = tax revenue
X = net national output
Y = net national money income
y = disposable net national money income

Constants
A, B, and c = structural constants
G = government demand for goods and services
I = net investment
P = price of net national output
t = marginal tax rate

Working Out the Model. The first and largest item in the demand for national output is consumption demand. In the United States, for example, about seven tenths of net national output is claimed for consumption. Consumption demand is chiefly determined by income after tax, so it is necessary to clarify the concepts "income" and "tax." Net national money income is defined as the money value of net national output:

$$Y = PX$$

where Y is net national money income, P is the average price of net national output, and X is net national output itself.

Next, disposable net national money income is defined as net national money income after tax:

$$y = Y - R$$

where y is disposable net national money income, Y is net national money income as before, and R is tax revenue from all taxes—federal, state, and local.

Tax revenue R must now be examined. The important fact here is that the U. S. Congress does not legislate tax revenue, for in the tradition of the Western world, going back to the Magna Carta and the American Revolution, taxes are collected according to statute, and statute defines tax base and tax rate. The tax base of income taxes is income. The tax base of property and real estate taxes is assets. The tax base of sales taxes is final sales value. Since both assets and final sales value tend to vary directly with net national money income, it is possible as a first approximation to say that tax revenue is determined by net national money income:

$$R = B + tY$$

where R is tax revenue as before; B is a constant whose sign and size indicate whether the tax system is progressive, proportional, or regressive; t is the marginal tax rate; and Y, as before, is net national money income. If B is negative, the tax system is a progressive one—that is, tax revenue grows more rapidly than income. If B is zero, the tax system is a proportional one, that is, tax revenue grows exactly as rapidly as income. If B is positive, the tax system is a regressive one—that is, tax revenue grows less rapidly than income. For countries such as the United States and West Germany it is safe to assume that B is either zero or negative.

With the "income" and "tax" concepts thus clarified, the next step is to deal with consumption demand. It is a temptation to say that consumption demand is simply determined by disposable net national money income y. But econometric tests have shown that disposable net national real income y/P is a better explanation than y, so an economist would rather say that consumption demand is determined by disposable net national real income:

$$C = A + cy/P$$

where C is consumption demand; A is a structural constant that is normally positive; c is what Keynes called the marginal propensity to consume—that is, the fraction of additional income that will be spent on consumption. For example, if people spend 90 cents out of an additional dollar's worth of disposable net national real income, the marginal propensity to consume is said to be 0.90.

More refined explanations of consumption demand could be written. It has been shown, for example, that the interest rate, assets, and the permanence of income may also affect consumption demand, but in this first approximation those items are ignored.

In the United States net investment—that is, the increase of capital stock such as plant, equipment, houses, and inventory—claims slightly less than one tenth of net national output, and government purchases of goods and services claim slightly more than two tenths. How do Keynesians include net investment and government purchases in their model? Usually these two items—call them I and G—are simply considered constants. The justification for treating net investment I as a constant is that net investment is a result of long-range planning by business, while the Keynesian model is a model for the short run. The justification for treating government purchases G as a constant is that such purchases are for the most part made for noneconomic purposes, especially defense. They are simply outside the proper realm of the economist.

The demand for national output, then, is the sum of consumption demand, net investment demand, and government demand, or $C + I + G$. Of these, I and G are constants, while C is a variable. All that remains is to express the Keynesian version of the law of demand and supply. The key to it is inventory. Inventory is always watched by the businessman. If demand exceeds output, inventory will decrease, and this is a signal for him to raise output. And if demand is short of output, inventory will increase, and that is a signal to reduce output. There is, then, a persistent tendency for demand and output to be equal:

$$C + I + G = X$$

How to Use the Model. Using the components of his model as building blocks, the economist now puts all his equations together. To solve the Keynesian model for its net national output X, the economist inserts the first four equations into the fifth and finds:

$$X = \frac{A + G + I - cB/P}{1 - c(1 - t)}$$

How is the economist to interpret this solution for output? Two observations are important.

(1) The solution shows which level of output would generate exactly the demand needed to absorb it—no more, no less. Such a level of output may or may not be feasible. As long as output as determined by this solution is comfortably below capacity, the solution is clearly feasible. And because of the inventory mechanism previously described, output cannot for long differ from demand, so the solution is highly relevant, too. Indeed, demand may generate a level of output far below capacity, as it did in the Great Depression. Keynesian economics was born under the influence of that disaster—and is ideally suited to analyze it.

But the opposite extreme also may occur. Demand may be so strong that it could be met only by a level of output beyond the capacity of the economy. In that case the output solution developed here is not feasible. By definition, output cannot exceed capacity. In trying to catch up with demand, the individual businessman will try to add to his plant, equipment, and labor force. But he can succeed only at the expense of other businessmen. In such an "overheated" economy, prices and wage rates tend to rise. The U. S. Civil War, both world wars, and the Korean and Vietnam wars produced such inflation. Although in such situations this output solution is not feasible, it may still help us see possible remedies.

(2) The solution of the Keynesian model teaches government how to steer national output in a desired direction—upward if there is unemployment and slack in the economy and downward if the economy is coming too close to capacity and shows signs of inflation.

In the output solution developed here, both the tax rate t and government demand G occur. What influence do t and G have upon net national output X? In practice both c and t lie between zero and one, and B is either zero or negative. Thanks to these facts the economist can say that raising government demand G will raise output X, and that reducing the marginal tax rate t will do the same. Once the numerical values of all constants are known, the economist can also say precisely by how much output X would rise.

Need for Information. There is more to Keynesian economics than such simple armchair algebra. Applying it in practice demands full numerical information about the economy's structural constants such as the propensity to consume c and the marginal tax rate t. Application also demands precise information about current levels of net investment, government purchases, and so on. It is not surprising, therefore, that parallel with the rise of Keynesian economics there has been a steady improvement of the national income and output information collected and published by the governments of the United States and other industrialized countries.

5. Economics as a Career

It follows from the definition of economics that an economist is a social scientist who analyzes the utilization and allocation of available resources among possible uses. He may engage in some of the hard thinking on the frontiers of knowledge, or in some of the careful measuring that tests the hypotheses of the thinkers. Or, more likely, behind the frontier he may simply apply known and tested hypotheses to particular problems of business or government.

Requirements. What makes a good economist? Whatever he does, an economist should have a thorough training in economic theory, mathematics, and statistics, and the better universities offer such training. An economist must be on guard against provincialism. Some knowledge of the world outside his own country will protect him from provincialism in space, and he needs such protection, for both business and government are deeply involved in the world economy. Some knowledge of economic and political history will protect the economist from provincialism in time and will condition him always to expect change and always instinctively to be looking for basic long-run forces under the surface of things.

But above all an economist should have a feel for human beings. Statistical observations of them can be designed and interpreted only by an observer who has imagination to see the incentives and constraints, the hopes and frustrations, under which the observed humans are performing.

Specialization. Major universities now stress specialization within economics less than they once did. Special courses in transportation, public utilities, land economics, the tariff history of the United States, and the like are giving way to basic courses in mathematics, econometrics, operations research, activity analysis, and so on, teaching the student the tools of the trade rather than the specific results of economic inquiry into particular problems.

There are good reasons for this approach. For one thing, the highly technical training in the tools used today is simply quite time-consuming. For another, in a changing world no economics student knows where his career will lead, and the more basic his training is, the better his chance of being useful almost anywhere. Also, universities do and should respond to market demand, and it is quite apparent that the candidate in basic mathematical economics is more in demand than the candidate in nonmathematical economics applied to some particular field.

Employment. Where do economists operate? The answer is found in the National Register of Scientific and Technical Personnel, a program of the National Science Foundation. To be included in this register an economist has to be known to some professional society such as the American Economic Association, to respond to the National Science Foundation questionnaire, to report an earned master's degree or equivalent experience, and to designate some branch of economics as his field of greatest special competence. The register reported in 1964 that about 45% of economists were employed by educational institutions, 35% by industry and business, and 11% by the federal government. Others were employed in smaller numbers by nonprofit organizations, government agencies other than federal, and by the military services. About 2% of economists were self-employed.

Opportunities and Outlook. The best single measure of opportunities is salary. The increasing complexity of business and government has increased the demand for economists. As a result, economists' salaries were found second to none— and equal to those of statisticians and physicists —among the 12 professions in the National Register of Scientific and Technical Personnel.

Business and government are expected to become even more complex, and it appears difficult to foresee anything other than a steadily expanding demand for economists at above-average salaries, as well as an accelerated demand for economists to train economists.

HANS BREMS, *University of Illinois*
Author of "Quantitative Economic Theory"

Bibliography

Alchian, Armen A., and Allen, William R., *Economic Forces at Work* (Indianapolis, Ind., 1977).
Bach, George L., *Economics*, 5th ed. (Englewood Cliffs, N. J., 1966).
Bator, Francis M., *The Question of Government Spending* (New York 1960).
Bergson, Abram, *Planning and Productivity Under Soviet Socialism* (New York 1968).
Boulding, Kenneth E., *Principles of Economic Policy* (Englewood Cliffs, N. J., 1958).
Galbraith, John K., *The New Industrial State*, 3d ed. (New York 1979).
Galenson, Walter, *A Primer on Employment and Wages* (New York 1966).
Heller, Walter W., *The Economy: Old Myths and New Realities* (New York 1976).
Kuznets, Simon, *Modern Economic Growth, Rate, Structure, and Spread* (New Haven, Conn., 1966).
Marshall, Alfred, *Principles of Economics*, 9th ed., 2 vols. (New York 1961).
Mill, John Stuart, *Principles of Political Economy*, ed. by W. J. Ashley (New York 1965).
Phelps, Edmund S., ed., *The Goal of Economic Growth* (New York 1962).
Samuelson, Paul A., *Economics*, 9th ed. (New York 1973).
Schumpeter, Joseph A., *Ten Great Economists From Marx to Keynes* (New York 1951).
Senior, Nassau William, *An Outline of the Science of Political Economy* (New York 1965).
Smith, Adam, *An Inquiry into the Nature and Causes of the Wealth of Nations*, 2 vols., ed. by Edwin Cannan (Chicago 1976).
Soule, George, *Ideas of the Great Economists* (New York 1955).
Timbergen, Jan, *Development Planning* (New York 1967).

Specialized Study

Brems, Hans, *Quantitative Economic Theory* (New York 1968).
Commons, John R., and associates, *History of Labor in the United States*, 4 vols. (New York 1918–1935).
Dorfman, Robert, Samuelson, Paul A., and Solow, Robert M., *Linear Programming and Economic Analysis* (New York 1958).
Keynes, John Maynard, *The General Theory of Employment, Interest, and Money* (New York 1936).
Klein, Lawrence R., *The Keynesian Revolution* (New York 1964).
Koopmans, Tjalling C., *Three Essays on the State of Economic Science* (New York 1957).
Leontief, Wassily, *Structure, System, and Economic Policy* (New York 1977).
Mitchell, Wesley C., *What Happens During Business Cycles, a Progress Report* (New York 1951).
Myrdal, Gunnar, *Asian Drama, an Inquiry into the Poverty of Nations*, 3 vols. (New York 1968).
Pigou, Arthur Cecil, *The Economics of Welfare*, 4th ed. (New York 1932).
Ricardo, David, *Works and Correspondence*, ed. by Piero Sraffa, 10 vols. (New York 1951–1952).
Samuelson, Paul A., *Foundations of Economic Analysis* (New York 1965).
Schumpeter, Joseph A., *History of Economic Analysis* (New York 1954).
Tinbergen, Jan, *On the Theory of Economic Policy* (Amsterdam, Netherlands, 1963).
Walras, Léon, *Elements of Pure Economics*, tr. by William Jaffé (New York 1969).

ECORSE, ē′kôrs, is a city in southeastern Michigan, in Wayne county, on the Detroit River, 7 miles (11 km) south of Detroit. Its principal manufactured products are steel, chemicals, automobile parts, garage doors, and tools.

The site was settled in 1812 as Grandport, and the community was incorporated as the village of Ecorse in 1903. The name was derived from a small stream in the city, which the French explorers called Rivière aux Écorces (meaning "bark") because the bark of the trees along its shores was used by the Indians to build canoes. Ecorse, incorporated as a city in 1941, is governed by a mayor and council. Population: 14,447.

ECTODERM. See EMBRYOLOGY—*Formation of Primary Germ Layers.*

ECTOMORPH. See BODY TYPE.

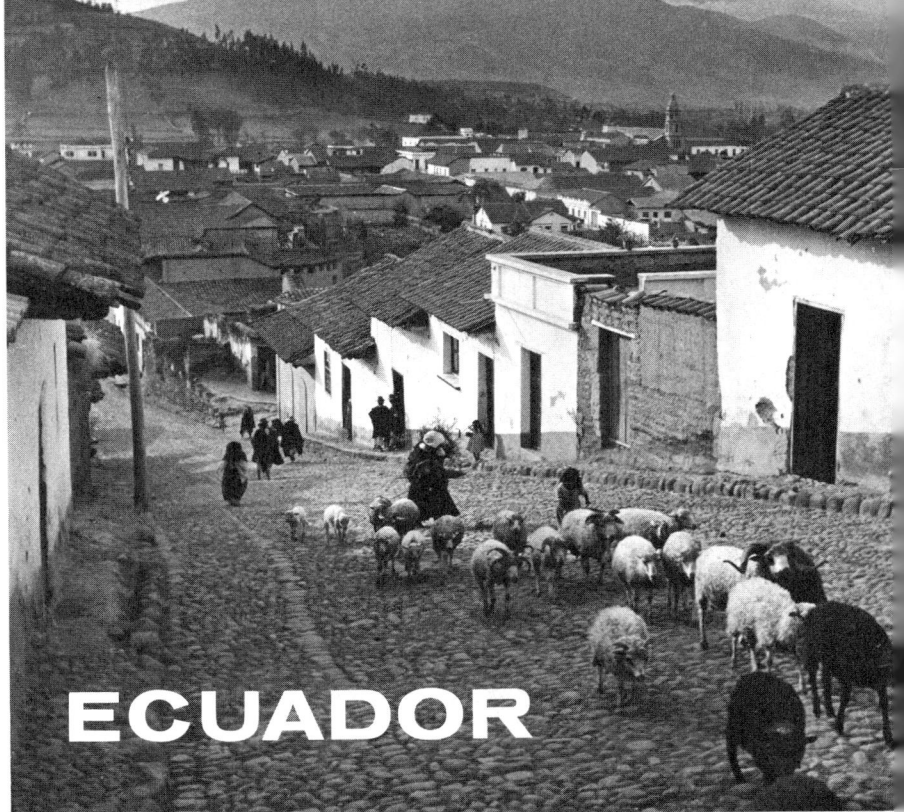

RURAL LIFE encroaches on the towns in Ecuador's Andean highland. At Otavalo, a mountain community near Quito, Indians drive sheep up a cobblestoned street.

ECUADOR

CARL FRANK

Coat of Arms of Ecuador

CONTENTS

Section	Page	Section	Page
1. The People	616	Petroleum and Mining	619
The Cities	616	Transportation and Communications	619
Rural Ecuador	616		
The Indians	616	4. Education and Cultural Life	619
2. The Land	618		
3. The Economy	618	5. Government and Politics	620
Agriculture	618		
Foreign Trade	619	6. History	621

INFORMATION HIGHLIGHTS

Official Name: República del Ecuador.
Head of State: President.
Head of Government: President.
Legislature: Unicameral Chamber of Representatives of 69 members, popularly elected for five-year terms.
Area: 109,483 square miles (283,561 sq km).
Highest Elevation: Mt. Chimborazo, 20,577 feet (6,272 meters).
Population: (1962 census) 4,585,472; (1967 estimate) 5,508,000.
Capital: Quito (estimated 1965 population, 402,000).
Major City: Guayaquil (estimated 1965 population, 652,000).
Major Language: Spanish.
Major Religion: Roman Catholic.
Monetary Unit: Sucre (100 centavos).
Weights and Measures: Metric system (official) and local measures.
Flag: Upper half, yellow; lower half, two horizontal bars (blue above red); national coat of arms at center. See also FLAG.
National Anthem: *Salve, o patria* (Hail, O Fatherland!)

ECUADOR, ek'wə-dôr, is one of the so-called Andean republics that line South America's Pacific coast. It is bisected by twin ranges of the Andes chain and is situated on the equator, from which it derives its name. Its geography, its people, and its history are quite distinctive; yet in the inequities of its social structure and the instability of its politics, it may be considered the classic example of a turbulent Latin American republic.

The country has sharply defined geographic regions. From east to west they are: the Oriente, a sparsely populated territory east of the Andes; the Andean highlands, called the *sierra*; the coastal region, a plain extending from the Pacific to the Andean foothills; and the Galápagos Islands (q.v.), an archipelago some 600 miles (960 km) west of the Ecuadorian coast, inhabited by picturesque wildlife but by very few people. The Galápagos and the Oriente are of marginal importance in national life. The fundamental fact of Ecuadorian existence is the contrast, and often the conflict, between coast and *sierra*, reflected not only in the geography but also in the nature of economic activities, ways of life, religious beliefs, ethnology, and political identification.

PATCHWORK FARMS cover the valley floor and inch up the precipitous sides of a volcano south of Quito.

1. The People

Each of the two major regions is dominated by a great city: Quito, the national capital, is in the *sierra,* and Guayaquil, the country's major port and largest city, is in the coastal area. In the 1820's, at the end of the colonial period, less than 10% of the population lived on the coast, an area plagued by tropical diseases such as malaria and yellow fever. By the mid-1960's, the coastal population exceeded that of the *sierra.* The total national population doubled in the 25 years from 1940 to 1965 and was increasing at a high annual rate of from 3% to 3.5% during the 1960's.

The Cities. Eight or nine provincial capitals have populations of more than 10,000, but fast-growing Quito (nearing half a million in the late 1960's) and faster-growing Guayaquil (nearing 700,000) dominate urban life in Ecuador. The third-largest urban center is Cuenca, a *sierra* city of perhaps 75,000 that prides itself on the richness of its cultural life and is sometimes referred to as the "Athens of Ecuador."

The favored class in Ecuadorian urban life—of European culture and, principally, of European ancestry—includes at most only 10% of the population. Upward social mobility is possible in the dynamic social and economic life of Guayaquil. It is more difficult in Quito, where an upper-class social position does not necessarily signify the possession of great wealth. The lower classes in the cities and towns, while generally literate and participant in national political life, live at a very low economic level and, particularly in the *sierra,* are most definitely regarded as social inferiors by members of the upper class. See also GUAYAQUIL; QUITO; CUENCA.

Rural Ecuador. Despite the growth of the cities, the population of Ecuador remains predominantly rural and agricultural. In the *sierra* the land is held principally in large estates, which are worked by a resident Indian labor force, although there are some autonomous Indian villages. On the coast, where the subordination of the lower classes is less severe, many rural residents farm unoccupied lands on their own, while others depend on fishing; the larger coastal landholdings usually produce commercial crops for export, in contrast to the haciendas of the *sierra,* which mainly produce food crops for domestic consumption.

The rural masses of the coast, though largely of Indian origin, no longer partake of traditional Indian cultural patterns, and the population contains a heavy Negro admixture, while the *sierra* remains predominantly Indian. These cultural differences, as well as divergent economic interests, add to the rivalry between the two areas.

The Indians. As elsewhere in Latin America, an Indian is defined less by his racial background than by his way of life. A man who goes barefoot or wears rope-soled sandals, subsists at a low level on a traditional diet, lives in a hut, and sleeps on the floor is usually branded as an Indian. Although only 15% of all Ecuadorians speak Indian languages (mostly Quechua), at least a third of the population would be called Indians under the common social definition.

Here and there, small groups have managed to maintain their distinctiveness—the headhunting Jívaros of the Oriente; the sheep-owning, black-robed Saraguros; the Colorados, who plaster their helmet-shaped haircuts with ocher; and the industrious Otavalans, who weave cloth and trade it all over South America. The Otavalans have shown that it is possible for Indians to adapt successfully to the conditions of the modern world without losing their character as Indians, but most Ecuadorian Indians continue to live at a semi-human level of abject poverty and virtual serfdom.

Religion. Most Ecuadorians are Roman Catholics. Catholic practice is much stronger in the *sierra* than on the coast, and the religious question is still important in politics.

Customs. Ecuadorian diet is based on the corn-beans-potatoes complex, with rice and seafood more common on the coast. Standard European dress is worn in the cities; highland Indian men normally wear a fedora and a woolen poncho over cotton shirt and pants.

Health. Average levels of health and well-being are extremely low, with conditions worse in the *sierra* than on the coast, and much worse for Indians than for whites. In 1967 the average life expectancy was 52 years, somewhat below the middle of the range for Latin American countries; infant mortality, at 94 per thousand, was especially high despite considerable improvement since World War II. There was a ratio of one physician to 5,000 Ecuadorians (as compared with one to 670 persons in Argentina). Rural hospital facilities are limited at best, and are virtually nonexistent in many parts of the *Sierra.*

ECUADOR Map Index

Total Population
5,508,000

PROVINCES

Province	Population	Ref
Azuay	274,642	C 7
Bolívar	131,651	C 5
Cañar	112,733	C 6
Carchi	94,649	D 3
Chimborazo	276,568	D 5
Cotopaxi	154,971	D 4
El Oro	160,650	C 7
Esmeraldas	124,881	C 3
Guayas	979,223	B 6
Imbabura	174,039	D 3
Loja	285,448	C 8
Los Ríos	250,062	C 5
Manabí	612,542	B 5
Morona-Santiago	25,503	D 6
Napo	24,253	E 4
Pastaza	13,693	E 5
Pichincha	587,835	D 4
Tungurahua	178,709	D 5
Zamora-Chinchipe	11,464	D 8

CITIES and TOWNS

Alamor, 1,370........B 8
Alausí, 6,676........D 6
Ambato, 53,372........D 5
Arenillas, 3,925........B 7
Atuntaqui, 8,759........D 3
Azogues, 8,075........D 6
Baba, 693........C 5
Babahoyo, 16,444........C 5
Bahía de Caráquez, 8,845........B 4
Balao, 1,415........C 6
Balsas, 688........B 7
Balzar, 6,588........C 5
Baños, 3,782........D 5
Biblián, 1,791........C 6
Bolívar, 410........B 3
Bucay, 2,072........C 6
Cajabamba, 2,094........D 5
Calceta, 4,946........B 4
Cañar, 4,935........C 6
Canoa, 588........B 4
Canuto, 912........C 4
Cariamanga, 5,381........C 8
Catacocha, 3,796........C 8
Catarama, 2,424........C 5
Cayambe, 8,101........E 3
Cayo, 713........B 5
Cazaderos, 565........B 8
Celica, 3,467........C 8
Chinca, 224........C 3
Chone, 12,832........C 4
Chunchi, 2,388........D 6
Cojimíes, 1,538........B 3
Colonche, 470........B 6
Concepción, 390........D 2
Cotacachi, 4,314........D 3
Cuenca, 60,402........C 6
Daule, 7,428........C 5
El Ángel, 4,009........D 3
El Corazón, 1,118........C 5
El Pun, 612........E 4
Esmeraldas, 33,403........B 2
Flavio Alfaro, 813........C 4
Gima, 188........C 7
Girón, 1,914........C 7
Gonzanamá, 1,363........C 8
Gualaceo, 3,065........D 6
Gualaquiza, 635........D 7
Guale, 980........B 5
Guamote, 2,640........D 5
Guano, 4,455........D 5
Guaranda, 9,900........C 5
Guayaquil, 651,542........B 6
Ibarra, 25,835........D 3
Jambelí, 317........B 7
Jipijapa, 13,367........B 5
Latacunga, 14,855........D 4
Loja, 26,785........C 7
Los Andes, 307........E 3
Macará, 5,027........C 8
Macas, 1,355........D 6
Machachi, 3,951........D 4
Machala, 29,036........C 7
Manglaralto, 799........B 5
Manta, 33,622........B 4
Manú, 334........C 7
Méndez, 527........D 6
Milagro, 28,148........C 6
Molleturo, 463........C 6
Montecristi, 4,540........B 5
Nanegal, 321........D 3
Naranjal, 2,982........C 6
Nuevo Rocafuerte, 435........G 4
Oña, 452........C 7
Otavalo, 8,630........D 3
Pacto, 547........D 3
Paján, 1,818........B 5
Pasaje, 13,215........C 7
Paute, 1,511........D 6
Pedernales, 610........B 3
Pelileo, 2,545........D 5
Pillaro, 2,714........D 5
Piñas, 3,344........C 7
Playas, 5,067........B 6
Portoviejo, 32,228........B 5
Posorja, 2,086........B 6
Pueblovjejo, 1,541........C 5
Puerto Baquerizo, G 9
Puerto López, 2,220........B 5
Pujilí, 2,534........D 4
Puyo, 2,290........E 5
Quevedo, 20,602........C 5
Quito (cap.), 401,811........D 4
Riobamba, 41,625........D 5
Rioverde, 177........C 2
Rocafuerte, 4,349........B 4
Rosa Zárate, 1,662........C 3
Salinas, 5,460........A 6
San Francisco, 518........B 3
San Gabriel, 6,803........E 3
Sangolquí, 5,501........D 4
San Lorenzo, 575........D 2
San Miguel, 2,410........C 5
San Miguel de Salcedo, 3,442........D 5
Santa Ana, 3,940........B 5
Santa Elena, 4,241........B 6
Santa Isabel, 1,602........C 7
Santa Lucia, 1,717........B 5
Santa Rosa, 8,935........C 7
Santo Domingo de los Colorados, 6,951........C 4
Saquisilí, 2,344........D 4
Saraguro, 1,562........C 7
Sigsig, 1,228........D 7
Sucre, 2,578........B 5
Suscal, 385........C 6
Tabacundo, 2,009........D 3
Tabiazo, 207........C 3
Tachina, 902........C 3
Tena, 1,029........E 4
Tixán, 1,581........D 6
Tufiño, 632........D 3
Tulcán, 16,448........E 3
Valdez, 3,358........C 2
Viche, 230........C 3
Vinces, 5,901........C 5
Yacuambí, 405........D 7
Yaguachi, 2,996........C 6
Zamora, 1,030........C 8
Zapotillo, 460........B 8
Zaruma, 9,000........C 7
Zumba, 485........C 8

OTHER FEATURES

Aguarico (river)........F 4
Ancón de Sardinas (bay)........C 2
Antisana (mt.)........D 4
Blanco (river)........C 3
Bobonaza (river)........F 6
Cayambe (mt.)........E 3
Chimborazo (mt.)........D 5
Chira (river)........B 8
Coca (river)........E 4
Conambo (river)........F 5
Cóndor, Cordillera del (mts.)........D 8
Cononaco (river)........G 5
Cotopaxi (mt.)........D 4
Curaray (river)........F 5
Daule (river)........C 4
Esmeraldas (river)........C 3
Galápagos (isls.), 2,391........G 7
Guaillabamba (river)........D 3
Jambelí (channel)........C 7
Jubones (river)........C 7
Mira (river)........D 2
Nangaritza (river)........D 8
Napo (river)........E 4
Pastaza (river)........E 5
Paute (river)........D 6
Puná (isl.), 5,459........B 6
Putumayo (river)........G 3
Puyango (river)........C 7
San Miguel (river)........F 3
Tumbes (river)........B 8
Zamora (river)........D 7

Total population—1967 official estimate; capital & Guayaquil—1965 official estimate; other pops.—1962 final census.

GUAYAQUIL, Ecuador's largest urban center and chief port, is in the republic's tropical coastal lowlands.

The average daily per capita intake of 2,100 calories and 50 grams of protein was below the "subsistence" level established by international organizations in the public health field.

2. The Land

The line of the equator runs a few miles north of Quito, leaving most of the nation's territory in the Southern Hemisphere. Despite its equinoctial location, Ecuador is fortunate in its climate, its highlands being comfortable because of their great elevation and its tropical coastal area being cooled by the Peru (or Humboldt) Current.

The Sierra. The *sierra* region includes about one fourth of the nation's land area. It consists of the Western and Eastern Cordilleras of the Andes, together with the valleys and plateaus lying between the two. The highest of the country's peaks is Mt. Chimborazo—at 20,577 feet (6,272 meters) it is higher than any mountain in North America. Several of the mountains—Sangay, Tunguragua, and Cotopaxi—are active volcanos. The intermontane valleys provide rich agricultural land, and the hills around Quito are green. The frequent rains in the *sierra* (averaging nearly 50 inches, or 125 cm, a year at Quito) contribute to a propitious climate for agriculture, and virtually all grains, fruits, and vegetables that can be grown in temperate zones are cultivated in the year-round growing season of the *sierra*. The flora and fauna are typical of the central Andes, varying greatly according to altitude and the amount of rainfall in each locality.

The thinness of the atmosphere—Quito lies at an altitude of almost 10,000 feet (3,000 meters)—provides a bracing climate, with a wide variation in temperature over a 24-hour period.

The Coast. In the coastal zone, which occupies another fourth of Ecuador's territory, tropical and subtropical commercial crops predominate. The climate is hotter than that of the *sierra* throughout the year, but it never reaches the unbearable heat and humidity found elsewhere in the tropics at this latitude. The rainy season from the end of December to the end of April, which is called winter, is actually slightly warmer than the so-called summer from May to December. Although there are scattered patches of desert and some ranges of low hills, the coastal region is generally well-watered and flat. Vegetation ranges from tropical rain forests to palm-studded grasslands and to cactus and brush. Reptile specimens are numerous.

The major river system is that of the Guayas, in the south central part of the country. Guayaquil, the principal port of entry, is on the Guayas River, 30 miles (48 km) from its mouth.

The Oriente. The jungle region east of the Andes that is called the Oriente covers about half of the country's land area. Although the Oriente has a variety of trees that could profitably be exploited for their woods, sap, nuts, and berries, very little in the way of gathering activities exists. The region is inhabited only by handfuls of nomadic and savage Indians, hopefully pursued by large numbers of foreign missionaries, ethnologists, and linguists.

3. The Economy

The major features of the Ecuadorian economy reveal the usual regional dichotomy. In the *sierra*, food production continues to absorb the largest single element of the labor force, while the need for many manufactured goods is met by a substantial handcraft sector, organized on the basis of a traditional apprentice system. On the coast, factory-made goods are the rule.

Business attitudes and practices also vary between the two regions, with the tendency for investment funds in the *sierra* to go into land, urban real estate, and other low-risk ventures, while on the coast more dynamic attitudes prevail. The most influential economic interests are thus the large landowners in the highlands and the banking and export-import entrepreneurs of the coast.

Manufacturing activities are those typical of a less-developed country: the production of articles of prime necessity—processed foods, beer, soft drinks, cigarettes, matches, clothing, building materials—for the domestic market behind a protective tariff wall.

Agriculture. Only about 5% of the total land surface of the country is actually put to productive use, about half of it for crops and half for grazing. Most of the land is in forest or jungles, but much unused land remains that could easily be brought into cultivation, especially in the coastal provinces.

In the mid-1960's, less than 1% of all Ecuadorian landholding units controlled half of all the land in production. In the *sierra* the large haciendas usually occupy the better lands in the valleys, while small private plots farmed by Indian owners are precariously situated on mountain slopes. Only a fraction of the hacienda land is actually farmed—by unskilled Indians who either are paid a few cents a day or exchange their labor for the right to be allowed to continue working their own small plots. The *hacendado* is more anxious to keep his costs low than to achieve maximum production.

Agriculture on the coast is more rational and sometimes depends on seasonally hired labor, often of migrant workers from the *sierra*. Bananas are the dominant crop. There are more small and medium-sized market-oriented farmers on the coast, and some land is worked directly by foreign corporations. An agrarian-reform law of 1973 provides that private ownership of farmland requires both adequate production and observance of social responsibilities.

Foreign Trade. Frequent unfavorable trade balances, because of dependence on agricultural exports, have been eliminated since development of the petroleum industry in the 1970's. Exports of crude oil in 1973 were over 71 million barrels—the second largest in South America, next to Venezuela. Ecuador's principal trading partner is the United States, which normally buys more than a third of its exports and furnishes about a third of its imports.

Ecuador's four most important agricultural exports are bananas, coffee, cacao, and sugar. From 1900 to 1914, Ecuador led the world in cacao production. After World War II, bananas were developed as a major export crop, and Ecuador had become the world's leading banana producer by 1963. Forest products are important, and Ecuador leads the world in production of balsa wood.

Almost all of Ecuador's imports and more than half of its imports pass through the port of Guayaquil. Guayaquil interests once blocked the development of other ports, but docking facilities at Manta and Esmeraldas have been improved.

Minerals. Gold, silver, lead, sulfur, and copper are produced, but the most important mineral is petroleum. Crude oil has been produced in the coastal provinces since the early 1900's by foreign companies, but the most productive fields were discovered in the Oriente region in the 1960's. Oil reserves are estimated at 2.5 billion barrels. Production in 1973 totaled 76.2 million barrels (third among South American countries, after Venezuela and Argentina). Oil is conveyed by a 300-mile (480-km) pipeline across the Andes to the port of Esmeraldas.

Ecuador became a full member of the Organization of Petroleum Exporting Countries (OPEC) in 1973 and supported policies that greatly raised the price of oil. Petroleum revenues totaled about $3 billion annually by the mid-1970's and were contributing to the government's investment in hundreds of projects. By 1974 the state corporation CEPE had acquired 25% ownership of the Texaco-Gulf consortium properties.

Transportation and Communications. The country's transportation network is substandard but is being improved. A railway completed in 1908 extends from Quito to Guayaquil and San Lorenzo, but poor maintenance and obsolete equipment—especially after the line was nationalized in 1944—have left it in poor condition. Paved highways link the *sierra* valleys with Guayaquil and other coastal cities. The Pan American Highway, which follows a north-south highland route, and the Quito-Guayaquil highway, completed in the mid-1960's, are subject to damage from rockslides in the rainy season. A good system of domestic airlines serves all medium-size and large cities, and international carriers serve Quito and Guayaquil. Telephones and telecommunications networks are up to international standards.

4. Education and Cultural Life

Ecuador's system of public education is inadequate. About a third of the adult population is illiterate, a proportion that is declining, but very slowly.

Elementary Education. The lack of public schools and teachers, especially in the rural areas, is notorious, and one of the most frequent occurrences in Ecuadorian politics is a strike of teachers trying to secure payment of back salaries. The constitution of 1967 provides that at least 30% of the national budget must be devoted to education—a difficult goal, since it would require a doubling of previous expenditures. Most schools are operated by the national government; municipal and private schools also exist, but their curriculums must conform to government regulations.

Higher Education. There are four public universities in the country—in Quito, Quayaquil, Cuenca, and Loja. Central University in Quito, the most important, schedules classes so that they can be attended on a part-time basis by students holding jobs during normal working hours. The part-time nature of the commitment of both students and professors to the university weakens the educational process considerably, as do the perpetual political activity of student activists and the political interference in faculty appointments. Despite the country's need for technicians, most students at Central University specialize in law and the humanities. Many affluent Ecuadorians continue to send their children overseas for their higher education.

Literature and the Arts. The cultural heroes of Ecuador are two literary figures: Eugenio de Santa Cruz y Espejo, an Ecuadorian of mixed ancestry whose writings in the late colonial period made him a precursor of national independence; and Juan Montalvo, the liberal writer of the late 19th century known for his polemics against the dictator Gabriel García Moreno. Leading figures in contemporary national literature are Benjamín Carrión (named ambassador to Mexico in the late 1960's), whose own book about García Moreno cast the strong man in a more favorable light; and Jorge Icaza, whose novel *Huasipungo* (1934) sympathetically described the hopeless misery of Ecuadorian Indians driven to rise in forlorn revolt against their oppressors.

Ecuadorian painting in the colonial era was devoted to religious themes, treated in the baroque manner, and much artistic effort was ex-

COFFEE BEANS, harvested inland, arrive at Guayaquil to await shipment down the Guayas River for export.

JERRY FRANK

INDIANS, who are deft weavers, display woven mats for sale in the market place at Otavalo, in northern Ecuador.

pended on church decoration. Today Ecuadorian painters generally work under the influence of contemporary Western European schools, although a tendency does exist for the realistic depiction of national and Indian themes in a style reminiscent of that of the Mexican revolutionary school.

A distinctive Ecuadorian national music employs Indian instruments such as the *rondador*, or panpipes. Small local bands and street musicians are common. The plaintive melodies of the *sanjuanito*, a popular highland dance, are evocative of the special charm of the people of the *sierra*.

5. Government and Politics

The governmental institutions of Ecuador have long been similar to those in the rest of Latin America and, in a superficial way, to those in the United States. By the time the constitution of 1979 had come into effect, the country had had at least 18 constitutions since gaining its independence from the Spanish in 1822. Through most of its history, the political process of the Ecuadorian republic has been neither very stable nor controlled by constitutional provisions.

National Government. The three-man military junta that took control of the government in 1976 promised to restore to Ecuador a genuine representative democracy as soon as possible. In April 1979 a new Congress and president were elected, and in August of that year a new constitution went into effect. In place of the previous Congress with its Chamber of Deputies elected for two-year terms, a Senate elected for four-year terms, and a president also elected for a four-year term, the new constitution called for a president and a 69-member unicameral Congress called the Chamber of Representatives, both popularly elected for five-year terms.

Traditionally the legislature has played a secondary role, spending its time principally on maneuvers aimed at gaining partisan advantage, while the president has been left to run the government. The president appoints an advisory cabinet of ministers whose number varies (it numbered 14 in 1982).

The judiciary plays a marginal political role, as often occurs where the legal heritage does not derive from the Anglo-Saxon common-law tradition.

PRESIDENTS OF ECUADOR FROM 1934

1934–1935	José María Velasco Ibarra
1935	Antonio Pons
1935–1937	Federico Páez
1937–1938	Alberto Enríquez
1938–1939	Aurelio Mosquera Narváez
1940–1944	Carlos Alberto Arroyo del Río
1944–1947	José María Velasco Ibarra
1948–1952	Galo Plaza Lasso
1952–1956	José María Velasco Ibarra
1956–1960	Camilo Ponce Enríquez
1960–1961	José María Velasco Ibarra
1961–1963	Carlos Julio Arosemena Monroy
1963–1966	Government by junta
1966–1968	Otto Arosemena Gómez
1968–1972	José María Velasco Ibarra
1972–1976	Guillermo Rodríguez Lara
1976–1979	Alfredo Poveda Burbano
1979–1981	Jaime Roldós Aguilera
1981–1984	Osvaldo Hurtado Larrea
1984–	León Febres Cordero Rivadeneira

Local Government. The country is divided into 20 provinces, one of which is the Galápagos Islands. The latter is administered by the Ministry of National Defense. The other provinces are administered by a governor appointed by the central government. Municipal councils are elected in urban communities, and the provincial capitals have elected mayors.

The Politics of Instability. A crucial feature of the Ecuadorian system is that while all Ecuadorian citizens over 18 may vote in the elections, not all people born in Ecuador are citizens; to be a citizen one has to be able to read and write. This means that almost half the population (and nearly all of the impoverished Indians of the *sierra*) are not citizens in their own country and are unrepresented in its government. Thus, Ecuadorian politics is the preserve of the social elite of upper-class whites, together with the mestizo masses of the towns and cities. Within these segments of the national society, politics is turbulent. Governments have fallen so frequently that the average length of presidential terms has been two and a half years, not the four years stipulated.

In general, three techniques are used to bring down a government before the end of its legal term. One is the seizure of power by the military, usually after a worked-up public opinion insistently demands that the military intervene. (Normally, in such cases the officers transfer the government to a civilian provisional president or supervise the holding of new elections, without attempting to perpetuate themselves in office.) The second technique is the mounting of demonstrations, usually spearheaded by the university

HISTORICAL HIGHLIGHTS

1534	Spanish city of Quito was founded by Sebastián de Benalcázar (Dec. 6).
1767	Jesuits were expelled from Ecuador.
1822	Independence forces defeated Spaniards in Battle of Pichincha (May 24).
1830	Ecuador seceded from federation of Gran Colombia.
1845	Dictatorship of General Juan José Flores ended.
1852	Slavery abolished.
1875	Conservative dictator Gabriel García Moreno assassinated after 16 years in power (Aug. 6).
1895	Conservative-Liberal civil war won by Liberals under Flavio Eloy Alfaro.
1908	Quito-Guayaquil railway was inaugurated.
1912	Eloy Alfaro was killed (January).
1925	Young military officers revolted (July), seized power, and attempted to reform political and economic systems.
1942	After its defeat by a Peruvian invading force, Ecuador accepted terms of Rio Protocol (January) awarding large eastern territory to Peru.

students, which disrupt national life and make it impossible for the government to function. The third technique is the special weapon of the mercantile interests in Guayaquil, who often resort to it when government attempts to impose new taxes disadvantageous to them. This is the general strike, which closes down the port and thus dries up the chief source of government revenue, its import duties.

Sometimes all three techniques are used in combination, the merchants and bankers of Guayaquil striking and calling on students to demonstrate, with the army stepping in to seize power after official repression of the initial student demonstrations has resulted in loss of life, an escalation of the violence, and general public disgust with the government.

Parties and Personalities. The major traditional parties in Ecuador are the Conservatives and the Radical Liberals. The Conservatives are strongest in the *sierra* and have a political orientation based on a traditional, strongly Roman Catholic view of the world. The Radical Liberals, who have more influence on the coast, tend to be a party of professionals and businessmen; they are equally a party of the elite but have a secular (though not antireligious) orientation and are somewhat more progressive than the Conservatives. The two traditional parties were joined in 1924 by the Socialist party of Ecuador (PSE), a party of intellectuals that has some union support and frequently works in coalition with the Radical Liberals. The tiny Communist party was splintered and generally ineffectual throughout the 1960's. There is also an extremist party of the right called the ARNE.

Ideological and personalist movements are of considerable importance in Ecuador. In fact, presidents are more often political independents with their own personal followings than they are natural leaders of the traditional parties. The "Velasquistas"—supporters of the populist leader José María Velasco Ibarra—have been particularly numerous, and former presidents Camilo Ponce Enríquez, Carlos Julio Arosemena Monroy, and Otto Arosemena Goméz also have had large followings. This welter of parties and groups makes it virtually impossible to establish coherent long-run majorities.

6. History

The country that is now Ecuador was on the margin of the Inca empire, which was centered on Cuzco in the Peruvian *sierra* and was conquered by the Incas only a few decades before the arrival of the Spanish conquistadors in 1531. The Inca policy of creating a homogeneous empire by imposing the use of the Quechua language and transferring populations from one area to another had thus not completely taken effect there, although Quito, the ancient center of an Indian "kingdom," had been transformed into the capital of the Incas' northern province.

The Colonial Era. When the Spaniards landed, a war was in progress over the succession to the Inca imperial throne. Atahualpa, the claimant who ruled at Quito, defeated his rival in 1532, only to be imprisoned later in the year (and subsequently executed) by Francisco Pizarro. On Dec. 6, 1534, Sebastián de Benalcázar, who had mopped up the remnants of Inca resistance in the north, founded the new Spanish city of Quito at the site of the old. (The anniversary of this event is still enthusiastically celebrated in Quito.) The

ECUADOREAN GOVERNMENT TOURIST COMMISSION, QUITO
LEGISLATIVE PALACE in Quito displays on its facade carved panels of stone that depict Ecuador's history.

city became the seat of an *audiencia real*, a standard Spanish colonial form of local government, which was at times subordinate to the viceroyalty at Lima (1563–1710 and 1722–1739) and at times to the viceroyalty of New Granada, with its seat at Bogotá (1710–1722 and 1739–1822).

Under colonial rule, a rather degenerate version of late medieval feudalism was transferred to Ecuador. Under the *encomienda* system, Spaniards were granted large estates and total control of the Indians resident on these lands in return for services to the crown, which included a promise to Christianize the natives. However, the obligations that limited the feudal lord in Europe were weak or absent in Ecuador, the king was far away, and the Indian population was docile. Only the Roman Catholic Church attempted —intermittently—to protect the Indians. Impatience with this sporadic ecclesiastical interference, together with the anticlericalism of the age of Enlightenment, resulted in the expulsion of the Jesuits from the country in 1767.

Subsequently, loyalist resistance to the viceroys sent out by Napoleon's puppet government of Spain evolved into an independence movement, and Ecuadorian forces fought under Simón Bolívar for the liberation of the Andean countries. A crucial defeat of the Spaniards by independence forces commanded by Antonio José de Sucre took place at Pichincha, near Quito, on May 24, 1822.

Republican Ecuador: The First Hundred Years. After independence was won, three of the countries liberated by Bolívar—present-day Colombia, Venezuela, and Ecuador—joined in the Federation of Gran Colombia, but local ambitions and resentments led to Ecuador's secession from the federation in 1830. The early decades of Ecuador's separate existence were an age of military adventurers, the most prominent of whom was Juan José Flores, formerly a general in Bolívar's army. Separation from Spain brought no change in the social structure; the upper-class elite continued to be dominant, unhampered even by the limited controls that had been imposed by the Spanish authorities, and the lower-class majority was exploited to an even greater degree.

Stability and a coherent policy of government were brought to Ecuador under the Conservative dictatorship of Gabriel García Moreno, who dominated the country from 1859 until his murder in 1875. Conservatives regard García Moreno as the greatest representative of the Conservative

INDEPENDENCE PLAZA in downtown Quito centers on a monument commemorating heroes of the independence movement. The Government Palace at the right houses offices of Ecuador's president.

CARL FRANK

tradition, stressing his promotion of education and trade. Liberals are more inclined to remember him as an arbitrary dictator and religious fanatic, who permitted only practicing Catholics to be Ecuadorian citizens.

The strong man's death was followed by 20 years of confusion, from which Flavio Eloy Alfaro emerged triumphant in 1895, after leading a Liberal army to victory in a brief civil war. Alfaro's progressive and anticlerical policies were carried on, after his murder in 1912, by his collaborator Gen. Leonidas Plaza Gutiérrez.

During and immediately after World War I the Ecuadorian economy boomed, largely as a result of the growth of its international trade. The era marked the emergence of Guayaquil as a dominant force in the country's economy and politics. By the mid-1920's, however, conditions had deteriorated as a result of a combination of inflation and the destruction by an insect pest of much of the key export crop (cacao). The army seized power in July 1925. The junta that took office tried to effect changes, including land reforms, but sophisticated upper-class politicians easily blocked these efforts. The only reforms that survived were the establishment of a central bank as the only bank of issue and the linking of the sucre to the U. S. dollar instead of to the pound sterling.

The Modern Era. The years of turbulence that followed were marked by the rise to prominence of José María Velasco Ibarra, who was to take office as president in 1934, 1944, 1952, 1960, and 1968. He completed only one of his first four terms—that of 1952–1956—the others being brought to an end by military coups or popular revolts, or both. A stirring orator whose words seemed to reflect the innermost dreams of the Ecuadorian masses, Velasco also built support through heavy spending on public works. Erratic and incoherent in his ideas and policies, Velasco was supported at one time or another by all groups, from the Communists to the Conservatives and the Guayaquil bankers, although, as each of his administrations degenerated into chaos, his support tended to melt away.

A major event of this period was the 1941 invasion of Ecuador by the Peruvians, who claimed territory in the Ecuadorian Oriente on the basis of a rather dubious interpretation of administrative boundaries during the colonial period. The ill-prepared Ecuadorian army was quickly defeated. The major American powers, preoccupied by World War II and unwilling to see a protracted dispute in South America, brought pressure on President Carlos Arroyo del Río to sign the Protocol of Rio de Janeiro of January 1942. Under its terms, Ecuador surrendered to Peru a tract of land on the Amazon that, though sparsely populated, was equal in area to all of the country's remaining territory. The episode left a legacy of popular resentment directed against Peru, against the powers (Argentina, Brazil, Chile, and the United States) that guaranteed the agreement, against the inter-American system in general, and against all political figures then prominent. The lingering bitterness still flares into occasional acts of violence.

During a new period of prosperity induced by the boom in banana exports after World War II, three presidents in succession managed to serve out their terms peacefully: Galo Plaza Lasso (1948–1952), Velasco Ibarra (1952–1956), and Camilo Ponce Enríquez (1956–1960). After 1960, however, Ecuador returned to the previous chaotic pattern of civil and political discord. Several presidents failed to complete their terms, and the country was under military control much of the time after 1963.

Velasco Ibarra was elected to an unprecedented fifth term as president in 1968. In June 1970 he suspended Congress and assumed dictatorial powers. In February 1972 he was overthrown in a military coup, and Gen. Guillermo Rodríquez Lara seized power. He was forced out of office in January 1976 when a military junta led by Vice Adm. Alfredo Poveda Burbano took command. In April 1979, Jaime Roldós Aguilera was elected president, and in August another of Ecuador's many constitutions came into effect. President Roldós was killed in an airplane crash in May 1981 and was succeeded by Vice President Osvaldo Hurtado Larrea. In 1984, León Febres Cordero Rivadeneira became president.

MARTIN C. NEEDLER[*], *University of New Mexico*

Further Reading: Aviles, J. J., *Ecuador* (Gordon Press 1977); Hurtado, Osvaldo, *Political Power in Ecuador*, tr. by Nick D. Mills (Univ. of N. Mex. Press 1981); Linke, Lilo, *Ecuador: Country of Contrasts* (Gordon Press 1976); Pike, Frederick B., *The United States and the Andean Republics* (Harvard Univ. Press 1977).

ECUMENICAL MOVEMENT, ek-yə-men′i-kəl, an attempt on the part of the divided Christian churches of the world to recognize their essential unity and to move toward new concord and reunion. The word "ecumenical" comes from the Greek word for "the inhabited earth," but in current usage it is ordinarily linked to the specific Christian spirit, movement, and set of organizations that seek religious reconciliation.

The process by which the churches came to be divided has taken almost 1,000 years. The year 1054 is the traditional date for the beginning of the schism between Eastern and Western churches that has lasted up to the present day. Early in the 16th century the Western church was split as a consequence of attempts to reform it during the period known as the Protestant Reformation. That schism has also not been overcome. Meanwhile, for over 450 years, Protestantism itself has been divided.

Prehistory of the Modern Movement. While most efforts to overcome division have occurred in the 20th century, the previous four centuries saw sporadic pioneering attempts. Many of the original Protestant groups made efforts at first to reestablish contact with Roman Catholics. The Lutherans' Augsburg Confession of 1530 was regarded as a document that was open-ended toward Roman Catholicism and Reformed Protestantism. The Reformed Churches of Germany and Switzerland, under the leadership of John Calvin and Ulrich Zwingli, made more strenuous efforts than the Lutherans to establish a united Protestantism. After the middle of the 16th century there was little positive contact between Protestants and Catholics, and Protestants themselves settled down in patterns of division.

Pioneering efforts through the centuries took a variety of forms. Some tried through scholarly efforts to find a simple essence of Christianity on which men of goodwill could agree. Others of a more mystical or pietistic bent tended to downgrade doctrinal differences and to devalue partisan controversy. Similarly, late 18th and early 19th century revivalists in Britain and America were often willing to play down their differences in efforts to gain converts and to shape a Christian society.

Less successful were political schemes, like the Prussian Union of 1817, which was more or less imposed on Lutherans and Reformed parties. In the United States the 19th century saw highly successful voluntary efforts, like the great outburst of cooperative societies for reform, education, and missions. The Evangelical Alliance of 1846 united these forces on an international scale. Some new church groups like the Disciples of Christ tried to uphold an ecumenical ideal through their desire to reincarnate what they believed to be primitive (and thus united) Christianity. The British Anglican Oxford Movement (about 1840) stimulated an increase of interest in the doctrine of the church and an expression of regard for its continuity and unity.

The 20th Century Movement. Modern transportation and communication helped make the global ecumenical movement possible, just as pressures from a secular world helped make it necessary. The most comprehensive unitive organization is the World Council of Churches. It was formed, after a delay occasioned by World War II, in Amsterdam in 1948. By 1968, when its fourth assembly met in Uppsala, Sweden, it numbered over 230 church bodies, including most of the major Protestant, Anglican, and Orthodox churches of the world. Roman Catholicism was interested in but not integrated into this organization.

The World Council of Churches was the product of a number of streams and strains. One derives from the World Missionary Conference at Edinburgh in 1910, the event from which modern ecumenism measures its anniversaries. In 1961 the International Missionary Conference, an extension of the original meeting, joined forces with the World Council of Churches. A second strain came from the world churches' efforts to work and serve together. This part of the movement was called Life and Work and met in two great conferences, at Stockholm in 1926 and at Oxford in 1937.

Many Christians were uneasy, however, about unitive efforts based on anything short of doctrinal consensus or at least of profound discussion of valid differences. Out of their concern the Faith and Order movement was born. Faith and Order held four world conferences, beginning in 1927 at Lausanne. By the late 1960's Faith and Order was also integrated into the World Council of Churches. The formal entrance of the Eastern Orthodox churches of Russia, Bulgaria, Poland, and Rumania in 1961 enhanced and complicated the W. C. C.'s life, since tens of millions from Communist nations were now represented.

Roman Catholicism and Ecumenism. During the 19th century most efforts on the part of Roman Catholics to find concord with Protestants and Orthodox were frustrated. Thus Pope Leo XIII in 1896 denied the validity of Anglican orders, cutting off positive contact with what many had seen to be a "bridge church." Roman Catholicism did, however, begin to develop relationships with Orthodoxy during the pontificates of Leo XIII and Pius XI.

During the years between World Wars I and II, groups like Una Sancta and Die Sammlung in Germany and similar ones in France gave new expression to Catholic interest in Protestants. Protestant-Catholic minority resistance to totalitarian regimes further drew the churches together.

So far as the general public was concerned, the greatest ecumenical figure was Pope John XXIII, who created a Secretariat for Promoting Christian Unity and in 1961 convoked the Second Vatican Council, whose agenda included Christian unity themes. The later three sessions of the Council, in particular, made it clear that the Catholics of the world wanted to move closer to Protestants and the Orthodox in every way. Since that time, all over the world, there have been conversations, cooperative activities, and kinds of shared worship that could not have been envisioned a decade earlier.

Ongoing Efforts. In the United States many mergers have occurred within denominational families among Protestants. Hundreds of state and local councils of churches have arisen to develop service projects, social action, common worship, and theological discussions. On a higher level, the National Council of Churches of Christ in the United States of America, formed in 1950, incorporates such concerns.

MARTIN E. MARTY
University of Chicago

Further Reading: Bea, Augustine, *The Unity of Christians* (New York 1963); Rouse, Ruth, and Neil, S. C., *A History of the Ecumenical Movement, 1517–1948*, 2d ed. (Philadelphia 1967).

ECZEMA

ECZEMA, ek'sə-mə, is a rather vague term used to describe an inflammation of the skin. Usually the term "eczema" is used interchangeably with "dermatitis," but "eczema" is sometimes reserved for an inflammation whose cause is not known. See also DERMATITIS.

Although there are several different types of eczema, they all produce the same basic changes in the skin. In the acute stage of eczema, fluid accumulates in the epidermis, both within and between the epidermal cells. Blisters are formed, and although they are often microscopic, they may occasionally be visible to the naked eye. The blisters, along with the increased amount of fluid between the cells, produce the characteristic moist, or weeping, surface of the skin.

Another symptom of eczema is a reddish skin color, which is due to the dilation (widening) of the blood vessels near the skin surface. In addition, the skin appears slightly swollen. As the condition continues, the epidermis thickens and the skin becomes scaly or flaky.

Types. *Seborrheic eczema* occurs most commonly on the scalp, where it is manifested as severe dandruff. On the face, chest, and in the body folds it appears as a reddish rash that is sometimes covered with yellowish scales. In *nummular eczema,* coin-sized eczematous patches appear on the arms and legs. This type of eczema is most common in people with dry skin.

Infantile eczema, which occurs only in infants, is often due to friction on an area of skin that has been dried out by too frequent bathing. This type of eczema is particularly apt to occur in winter. Sometimes infants also develop seborrheic eczema, which usually involves the scalp, producing the condition often known as "cradle cap."

Treatment. In cases of eczema where weeping is prominent, wet dressings are the best type of therapy. Not only does the wet cloth have a cleansing action, but the evaporation of water from the dressing produces a cooling sensation. This cooling alleviates any itching and also helps constrict the skin's blood vessels. The wet dressings should be removed, remoistened, and reapplied every 5 minutes for 1 to 2 hours. This should be repeated three or four times a day. During the intervals between dressings, various creams, lotions, or pastes may be applied to the skin. Once the eczema has stopped weeping, the condition may be controlled with ointments or creams, especially those containing anti-inflammatory agents.

STEPHEN E. SILVER, M. D.
Montefiore Hospital, New York City

EDAM

EDAM, ā-däm', is a town in the Netherlands, in the province of North Holland, 13 miles (21 km) northeast of Amsterdam, near the shores of the IJsselmeer. It is the marketing center for the well-known red-crusted Edam cheese. Industries include the making of earthenware, jute sacking, clothing, paper, and plastics.

From the 14th to the late 16th century Edam was an important port and shipbuilding center. But the construction of sluices to check flooding caused the harbor to silt up, and Edam is now an inland town. Its large Church of St. Nicholas (14th century) was rebuilt after a disastrous fire in 1602 destroyed much of the town; there is also an 18th century town hall. Population: (1960) 14,440.

F. J. MONKHOUSE, *University of Maryland*

EDDAS

EDDAS, ed'əz, two classic works of Old Icelandic literature: the *Elder Edda,* or *Poetic Edda,* also known as *Sæmundur· Edda;* and the *Younger Edda,* or *Prose Edda,* also called the *Snorra Edda.* They rank among the outstanding works of world literature.

Historical Background. Neither the author nor the compiler of the *Poetic Edda* is known. Scholars differ widely on the age of the individual poems, but most appear to date from the 8th to the 12th centuries A. D., the largest number falling into the latter part of that period. The poems making up the *Poetic Edda* were preserved in oral form until after 1100, when they began to be recorded. The majority were probably set down between 1150 and 1250.

The *Prose Edda,* on the other hand, is known to date from the first quarter of the 13th century. It is the work of Snorri Sturluson (1179–1241), an Icelandic poet and historian.

The meaning of "Edda," a name originally applied only to the *Prose Edda,* is obscure. Some scholars feel that the term is identical with the word "great-grandmother" that occurs in the poem *Rigsþula* in the *Prose Edda.* Others believe that it is derived from *óðr* (poem, poetry) and means "poetics." Still others associate the term with Oddi, the great center of learning in southern Iceland, where Snorri grew up and was educated, which would give the meaning "The Book of Oddi." This interpretation is the most widely accepted.

The Poetic Edda. Most of the Eddic poems, often referred to as lays, are preserved in a 13th century Icelandic vellum manuscript, known as the *Codex Regius* (Royal Manuscript). In 1643 this treasure was acquired by the Icelandic bishop Brynjólfur Sveinsson, who sent it to King Frederick III of Denmark. It was returned to Iceland on April 21, 1971.

Bishop Sveinsson and other Icelandic scholars and antiquarians of the time were already familiar with the contents of the *Prose Edda* of Snorri. They felt that Snorri had used some of the poems contained in the newly discovered manuscript (which they rightly believed to be an earlier *Edda*) as the source for the sections of his work dealings with mythology. Bishop Sveinsson attributed the manuscript to Sæmundur the Learned (1056–1133), the founder of a famed school at Oddi and renowned for his learning and his supposed mastery of magic. Actually, Sæmundur was neither the author nor the compiler of the collection. However, the name *Sæmundur Edda* is still used, although *Poetic Edda* is widely preferred.

Place of Origin. The place of origin of the Eddic poems has long been hotly debated. Three locations are suggested: Iceland; Norway, from which most Icelanders originally came; and the Norse settlements in the British Isles originating in the 8th century. However, since the poems have been preserved only in Iceland, it is reasonable to assume that even those that may have originated elsewhere were subsequently cast in an Icelandic mold.

Poetical Style. Alliteration is a basic principle in the Eddic poems, linking the verse lines together. The poems are composed in three stanzaic forms. These are *fornyrðislag* (epic measure), consisting of eight verse lines of four syllables each, which may, however, vary; *málaháttr* (speech measure), which also has eight verse lines, but of five syllables each; and *ljóða-*

háttr (chart measure), composed of six verse lines varying from four to eight syllables.

The uncomplicated verse forms of the Eddic poems are matched by a corresponding terseness and simplicity in language. The poems differ in subject matter and mood, yet the verse forms and diction almost consistently and strikingly fit the elevated themes.

Contents. The Eddic poems deal with Old Norse mythology, moral teachings, and heroic legends. The unknown compiler arranged the poems generally in this order, linking them with explanatory passages.

The *Poetic Edda* opens dramatically with the Völuspá (The Sibyl's Prophecy). In this poem an inspired seeress speaks in haunting, mystical tones to both gods and men, revealing the Old Norse concept of the beginning of the world and of its approaching end, the ultimate engulfing destiny of deities and mortals alike. However, she envisions a glorious new world rising on the ruins of the old. The poem's grandeur and sweep of vision attest to the imaginative power of the unknown poet.

Foremost among the didactic poems is *Hávamál* (The Words of the High One). The High One is Óðinn, or Odin, the chief Scandinavian god and the fountainhead of wisdom. This poem is the principal direct source of our information about the Old Norse view of life. In it, rules of social conduct and basic ethical precepts are expressed in terse and simple language. By ascribing his words to Óðinn, the poet adds weight and sanctity to his counsels. The realism of the Norsemen, their fatalism, and their heroism are memorably conveyed. To them, the attainment of good repute was the most desirable and lasting thing in life.

Of the Eddic poems about individual gods, *Þrymskviða* (The Lay of Þrymr) is especially noteworthy for its racy humor and narrative excellence. It relates how Þór (Thor), the god of thunder, regains his famous hammer, which had been stolen by the giants, the archenemies of the gods. The masterful portrayal of Þór impersonating Freyja (Freya), the goddess of love, as a ruse to trick the giants into returning his hammer, is highly amusing.

Several poems, or lays, in the *Poetic Edda* deal with ancient legendary German and Scandinavian heroes and heroines. Among the specially significant cycles of poems are *Helgakviða Hundingsbana* (The Lay of Helgi Hundingsbani) and *Sigurðarkviða Fáfnisbana* (The Lay of Sigurd Fáfnisbana), which are an older version of the German *Nibelungenlied*.

The Prose Edda. That Snorri Sturluson wrote the *Prose Edda* is undisputed, since he is specifically mentioned as its author in the oldest extant manuscript of this work, dating from about 1300. This copy of the *Prose Edda*, one of the four main manuscripts of the work, is now in Uppsala, Sweden.

Purpose. The *Prose Edda* was written as a textbook for young *skalds*, the name by which medieval Scandinavian court poets were known. Snorri admirably achieved his aim, and the work remains the authoritative source of technical information on skaldic verse, an extensive branch of Old Icelandic literature consisting of songs and poems in praise of kings and chieftains.

The earliest known skalds, from the 9th and 10th centuries, were Norwegian. From the middle of the 10th century to the end of the 13th century, however, Icelanders dominated the art of skaldic poetry and excelled in it.

Contents. The *Prose Edda* consists of three principal sections. The first part, *Gylfaginning* (The Beguiling of Gylfi), covers the same ground as the Sibyl's Prophecy of the *Poetic Edda*, corroborating the theory that Snorri drew extensively on his knowledge of the *Poetic Edda* as well as on other sources. Snorri's work, however, gives a more detailed picture of the cosmogony and the mythology of the ancient Scandinavians than that found in the older *Edda*. The origin of the world, the creation of man, and the life and ultimate fate of the gods are treated in both prose and verse in the form of a dialogue between Gylfi, a legendary Swedish king, and Óðinn himself, who was also the god of poetry. Snorri's style is brilliantly varied, ranging from pungent humor to high tragedy. His mastery of narrative style, along with the interesting subject matter, have made the *Gylfaginning* widely popular.

The *Gylfaginning* forms a logical introduction to the next section, *Skáldskaparmál* (Poetic Diction), for knowledge of Nordic mythology and heroic legends was essential for anyone who wanted to become an accomplished skald. Thus, after the presentation of content comes a discussion of the diction for expressing poetic ideas in the skaldic tradition. Among the most interesting phenomena of skaldic poetic diction discussed by Snorri are the *kenningar* (kennings), metaphorical and descriptive expressions produced by combining two or more words. For example, "shield" becomes "moon of the ship" (*tungl skipsins*), since shields were hung along the gunwales of Viking ships. Snorri gives many examples of kennings from earlier masters of the skaldic craft. Such circumlocutions add to the pictorial quality of skaldic verse. Unfortunately, however, the kennings are often so complex that they become veritable riddles, and skaldic poetry, generally, has much greater historical and cultural than literary value.

The third section, *Háttatal* (Enumeration of Meters), was composed by Snorri in honor of his royal friends King Hákon Hákonarsson and Earl Skúli Bárðarson of Norway. It consists of 102 stanzas, each of which illustrates a different metrical form. Snorri has also inserted definitions and informative comments. *Háttatal* impressively reveals his mastery of skaldic meters, which were often highly intricate.

Influence of the Eddas. The Eddas have been extensively translated and their influence has been far-reaching, notably on German and Scandinavian literature. The *Poetic Edda* particularly, with its rich treasure of ancient Germanic and Scandinavian lore, has provided poets, such as Thomas Gray and William Morris, with themes for important works of their own.

In the field of music the German composer Richard Wagner found inspiration for his famous operatic cycle *Der Ring des Nibelungen* in the medieval Germanic epic *Nibelungenlied*, which was derived in part from the *Poetic Edda*.

RICHARD BECK
Editor of "Icelandic Poems and Stories"

Further Reading: Hollander, Lee M., tr., *The Poetic Edda* (Austin, Texas, 1928, rev. ed., 1962); Hollander, Lee M., *The Skalds* (Princeton 1945); Ker, William Paton, *Epic and Romance* (London 1897; 2d ed., 1908); Phillpotts, Bertha S., *Edda and Saga* (New York 1931); Sturluson, Snorri, *The Prose Edda*, tr. by Jean I. Young (Philadelphia 1955).

EDDINGTON, ed'ing-tən, **Sir Arthur Stanley** (1882–1944), British astronomer, who first explained the mechanism for the transport of energy from the interior of a star to its surface. Eddington was born at Kendal, Westmorland, on Dec. 28, 1882, and was educated at Owens College, Manchester, and Trinity College, Cambridge. In 1906, as chief assistant at the Royal Observatory at Greenwich, he planned and executed observations with the Cookson floating zenith telescope to determine the small variations in the positions of the earth's poles, and the constant of aberration.

In 1907, by studying the observed motions of the stars, he greatly extended the findings of the Dutch astronomer Jacobus Kapteyn concerning the existence of "star streams"—the apparent preferential motion of the stars toward two opposite points in space, caused by the movement of the solar system in space. He succeeded George H. Darwin as Plumian Professor of Astronomy at Cambridge in 1913 and the following year became director of the Cambridge Observatory. He held these positions until his death in Cambridge on Nov. 22, 1944. He was knighted in 1930 and awarded the Order of Merit in 1938.

Work. In *Stellar Movements and the Structure of the Universe* (1914), Eddington laid the groundwork for the discipline of stellar dynamics In 1916 he began his pioneering work establishing that in a star energy is transported by radiation—not by convection as had been thought previously—from the interior of the star to its surface. His discovery that the luminosity of a giant or main-sequence star depends almost exclusively on its mass was of outstanding importance, necessitating a complete revision of ideas on stellar evolution. In *The Internal Constitution of the stars* (1926) he also included a study of the reflection effect in close eclipsing binaries and a demonstration that the light variations of Cepheids are due to periodic pulsations, accounting for the observed relationship between luminosity and variation period.

Eddington also worked extensively on relativity theory, and his new generalization of geometry, presented in *The Mathematical Theory of Relativity* (1923), is of fundamental theoretical significance. His observations of the deflection of starlight around the sun during the 1919 total eclipse provided an important test of general relativity. Later he attempted to unify relativity theory and quantum theory and to derive values of physical constants, such as the gravitational constant and the mass of the electron, entirely by theoretical means and by the assumption of conversion constants. These highly controversial investigations were presented in *Relativity Theory of Protons and Electrons* (1936), *The Combination of Relativity Theory and Quantum Theory* (1943), and *Fundamental Theory* (1946, posthumously).

Eddington was a gifted expositor, as is evidenced equally by his theoretical works, his more popular works (*Space, Time and Gravitation,* 1920; *Stars and Atoms,* 1927; and *The Expanding Universe,* 1938), and his philosophical writings (*The Nature of the Physical World,* 1928; *New Pathways in Science,* 1935; and *Philosophy of Physical Science,* 1939).

Further Reading: Dingle, Herbert, *Sources of Eddington's Philosophy* (New York 1954).

BRIAN G. MARSDEN
Smithsonian Astrophysical Observatory

EDDY, Mary Baker (1821–1910), American religious leader, founder of the Church of Christ, Scientist, and author of the Christian Science textbook, *Science and Health with Key to the Scriptures.* The subject of sharp controversy in her own day, she is now recognized as a pioneer of modern spiritual healing, but her position as a Christian thinker is still variously estimated. Mrs. Eddy herself urged that her life and her works be submitted to the New Testament test "By their fruits ye shall know them" (Matthew 7:20), and any responsible estimate of her must be determined by one's understanding of Christian Science.

Life. Mary Morse Baker, the daughter of a farmer, was born at Bow, near Concord, N. H., on July 16, 1821. Because of her poor health her education was sporadic, but she received valuable mental stimulus and guidance from her elder brother Albert, a brilliant student at Dartmouth. Although deeply religious, she was also independent and early took issue with her father's strict Calvinism. Largely because of the sense of New Testament Christianity she imbibed from her mother, she found it impossible to accept the doctrine that most of the human race had been born to inevitable damnation. A sharp confrontation on this issue with the minister of the Congregational Church at Sanbornton Bridge (now Tilton), N. H., when she was 17, resulted surprisingly in her being accepted into membership despite her doctrinal protest.

In 1843, Mary Baker married George Washington Glover, a contractor and builder. He died in 1844, and for several years she was oppressed by increasing invalidism, enforced separation from her son George, and other misfortunes. In 1853 she married Daniel Patterson, an itinerant dentist, but the marriage proved unsuccessful, and she obtained a divorce in 1873.

In 1866 her years of illness came to an abrupt climax when she was critically injured by a fall and restored suddenly to health while reading in the Bible of one of Jesus' healings (Matthew 9:1–8). This was the genesis of Christian Science. The remainder of her long life was given to study, writing, healing, teaching, and finally to organizing and guiding the Church of Christ, Scientist. In 1877 she married Asa Gilbert Eddy, a practitioner of Christian Science healing. One of her last acts, when she was 87, was the founding of the international daily newspaper the *Christian Science Monitor* in 1908. She died in Chestnut Hill, Mass., on Dec. 3, 1910, leaving behind her a church with nearly 100,000 members.

Thought. During her years of invalidism Mrs. Eddy's faith in orthodox medicine had waned, and she had sought relief through homeopathy, hydropathy, and other systems then popular. Gradually she came to the conclusion that all disease was mental rather than physical. This was confirmed by her experience in the early 1860's with a healer named Phineas P. Quimby, in Portland, Me. For several years she identified Quimby's methods with those of Jesus, but she later repudiated them as a form of hypnosis wholly unrelated to genuine Christian healing.

All her life Mrs. Eddy had turned to the Bible for comfort, guidance, and spiritual light. Following her 1866 healing she devoted three years to an intensive study of the Scriptures in an effort to understand better the divine law underlying the phenomenon of spiritual healing. The result was the metaphysical system she named Christian

Science and set forth in *Science and Health,* first published in 1875. Looking to the activist faith of St. Paul rather than to the detached idealism of Plato or Berkeley, she held to her conviction that spirit alone is real, but she made this faith the basis for a transformation of life rather than an idealization of it.

Mrs. Eddy's writings define God as Spirit, Mind, Soul, Principle, Life, Truth, and Love, and they define man as His son, made in His image and likeness. Jesus Christ, in being impelled by no other will or mind than that of his divine Father, is seen as the prototype of a regenerated humanity, lifted above deceptive material appearances to the recognition and demonstration of true spiritual being. All Christians can approximate the example of Jesus to the degree that they understandingly follow St. Paul's command: "Be not conformed to this world: but be ye transformed by the renewing of your mind, that ye may prove what is that good, and acceptable, and perfect, will of God" (Romans 12:2). Healing in this context is an integral part of Christian regeneration, the natural result of drawing closer to God. Theology becomes a study, a discipline, to be put to the proof in daily life.

Mrs. Eddy repeatedly revised *Science and Health* with the aim of making its teaching clearer and more broadly applicable to the ills and evils of human life. She also wrote a number of other books, among them *Unity of Good* (1891), the autobiography *Retrospection and Introspection* (1891), *Manual of the Mother Church, the First Church of Christ, Scientist, in Boston, Massachusetts* (1895), and *Miscellaneous Writings* (1896).

Church. Mrs. Eddy had hoped at first that the Christian churches would accept her "discovery," but she met with intense opposition. She soon concluded that she must "organize a church designed to commemorate the word and works of our Master, which should reinstate primitive Christianity and its lost element of healing" (*Church Manual,* p. 17). The Christian Scientists' Association was formed in 1876, and the Church of Christ, Scientist, was first chartered in 1879. In 1892 the church was reorganized in its present form. See CHRISTIAN SCIENTISTS.

Besides the *Christian Science Monitor,* Mrs. Eddy founded a monthly magazine, the *Christian Science Journal* (1883); the first Christian Science Reading Room (1888); and the Christian Science Publishing Society and Christian Science boards of lectureship and education (all founded in 1898). One of her most striking departures from tradition was the substitution, in 1895, of a "lesson-sermon" for a sermon preached from the pulpit. These weekly lessons, composed of related passages from the Bible and *Science and Health* on such topics as "God," "Man," and "Reality," are studied during the week by Christian Scientists individually and then read aloud in all branch churches on Sunday by two elected "readers." The Bible and *Science and Health* thus constitute the dual, impersonal pastor of the Church of Christ, Scientist.

Mrs. Eddy's last two years were devoted largely to putting the church on a basis that would not require her continued personal presence. Within the strong structural framework established by the *Church Manual,* she provided for the democratic development of the branch churches. Since the denomination has no clergy, the emphasis falls naturally on lay responsibility

© 1929 RENEWED 1957 CHRISTIAN SCIENCE PUBLISHING SOCIETY, ALL RIGHTS RESERVED

Mary Baker Eddy

or individual witnessing to truth. Mrs. Eddy wrote in 1903, "What I am remains to be proved by the good I do." This pragmatic concern still characterizes Christian Science a century after its inception.

J. BUROUGHS STOKES
The First Church of Christ, Scientist

Further Reading: Beasley, Norman, *Mary Baker Eddy* (New York 1963); Peel, Robert, *Mary Baker Eddy: The Years of Discovery* (New York 1966); Smith, Clifford P., *Historical Sketches, from the Life of Mary Baker Eddy and the History of Christian Science* (Boston 1941).

EDDY CURRENTS are electric currents that flow in any conductor subjected to a magnetic field that is changing in intensity or direction or moving with respect to the conductor. Their occurrence is explainable by Faraday's law of electromagnetic induction, which states that a changing magnetic field is surrounded by an electric field proportional to the rate of change. The electric field generates eddy currents in a conductor, and these currents flow in such a direction as to oppose the change in the magnetic field (Lenz's law).

Eddy currents attenuate a changing magnetic field as it penetrates a conductor, oppose the motion of a conductor in a magnetic field by a braking force proportional to its velocity, and produce heat in a conductor. One or more of these effects are put to useful purposes in damping oscillations in delicate instruments, braking trains smoothly, hardening and forging steel, forming and cutting metals by means of intense pulsed magnetic fields, and heating by induction.

In transformers, inductors, motors, and generators, eddy currents are undesirable because they cause energy loss and produce heating in magnetic cores exposed to alternating current. To reduce eddy currents, armatures are made of thin varnish-insulated laminations, sintered oxide-coated granules, or nonconducting magnetic materials such as ferrites.

HENRY H. KOLM
Massachusetts Institute of Technology

Edelweiss
T. H. EVERETT

EDELWEISS, ād'əl-wīs, is a popular low-growing perennial plant native to the Alps and the Himalayas. Edelweiss ranges in height from 4 to 12 inches (10–30 cm) and is cultivated in gardens for its white, woolly, alternate lance-shaped leaves and its creeping stems. The white hairy growth on the upper surface of the leaves gradually wears off as the plant matures, but the hairs on the undersurface remain all season long. The flower heads are small yellow disks about ¼ inch (6 mm) across. Directly underneath each flower are whitish leaflike structures.

The edelweiss is known botanically as *Leontopodium alpinum,* and it belongs to the composite family (Compositae). It grows best in poor soil in the full sun and is often grown in rock gardens. Propagation is accomplished by simply dividing the plant in late summer.

DONALD WYMAN
Arnold Arboretum, Harvard University

EDEMA, i-dēm'ə, is an abnormal swelling in any of the body tissues due to the accumulation of watery fluid around the cells. Edema is not a disease itself but is a symptom of some disorder. Local edema is often caused by bruises, fractures, sprains, cuts, infections, sunburn, frostbite, insect bites, and chemical irritations. In each case, the site of the injury becomes puffy, swollen, and filled with fluid. This reaction is due to changes in the permeability of the capillaries in the area, resulting in the seepage of blood serum from the tiny blood vessels into the surrounding tissues.

Generalized, or systemic, edema, also sometimes known as dropsy, is characterized by puffiness or swelling in more than one part of the body. This type of edema may be caused by an increase in the body's retention of water, which occurs in kidney disease and occasionally during pregnancy. The toxic effects of certain drugs and poisons may also result in an accumulation of fluid in the body tissues.

When edema occurs in certain body organs and cavities, it usually indicates a serious disease. Pulmonary edema, which is an accumulation of serous fluid in the lungs, generally indicates heart failure, and kidney, or renal, edema may be due to nephritis. The accumulation of fluid in the abdominal cavity is known as ascites, and it is often a manifestation of cirrhosis, circulatory disease, or kidney failure.

JEFFREY WENIG
ENDO Laboratories

EDEN, Sir Anthony, 1st Earl of Avon (1897–1977), British prime minister in 1955–1957. He was born near Bishop Auckland, Durham, England, on June 12, 1897. He received his education at Eton and Oxford. After service in World War I, he entered Parliament as a Conservative in 1923. He was parliamentary secretary at the foreign office from 1926 to 1929 and then served as undersecretary for foreign affairs from 1931 to 1933.

After a year as lord privy seal, he became minister for League of Nations affairs in 1935 and was foreign secretary from 1935 to 1938, when he resigned. After less than a year out of office he served, successively, as dominion affairs secretary (1939–1940), secretary for war (1940), foreign secretary again (1940–1945 and 1951–1955), and prime minister (1955–1957).

Eden's early public reputation was enhanced by his elegant appearance and his support for the League of Nations. His resignation in 1938 involved issues that were by no means clear-cut: the differences between Eden and Prime Minister Neville Chamberlain over negotiations with Mussolini were concerned with timing rather than fundamental policy and also involved the personal strains resulting from Chamberlain's tendency to bypass Eden in policy making.

After his resignation Eden was reluctant to join in outright opposition to Chamberlain's "appeasement" policy and (with Winston Churchill) rejoined the government shortly after the outbreak of war in 1939. His reputation as an opponent of appeasement protected Eden from the blame received by most of Chamberlain's colleagues, and he played a major role in Churchill's government, formed in 1940.

Prime Minister. After 1945, Eden was recognized as Churchill's heir apparent, and his accession to the prime ministership on Churchill's retirement in April 1955 was automatic. Eden's long association with foreign affairs made him a diplomat rather than a politician: his major successes (for example, his part in the Indochina settlement in Geneva in 1954) were in diplomatic initiatives. The narrowness of his political experience and his unfamiliarity with political maneuverings may explain his lack of impact as prime minister.

Anthony Eden, 1st Earl of Avon

WIDE WORLD

He gained the reputation of "interfering" in the work of his colleagues, and his role in the Anglo-French Suez expedition of 1956 found few defenders. The expedition eventually resulted in Britain's withdrawal from Egypt, without compensation for losses caused by the nationalization of the Suez Canal. Eden's critics emphasized the folly of acting in defiance of United States and United Nations opinion and without regard for Britain's precarious economic position. They also criticized his allegedly "dictatorial" methods in resorting to force without adequate consultation of his colleagues. Eden's position in the Conservative party was seriously damaged by the Suez episode, but his resignation in January 1957 was on genuine grounds of ill health. He had been knighted in 1954 and was created 1st Earl of Avon in 1961.

Eden died in Salisbury, Wiltshire, England, on Jan. 14, 1977. He was a skilled diplomat of undoubted integrity, whose political skill was not always adequate to the circumstances in which he had to act. He published his memoirs in three volumes: *Full Circle* (1960), *Facing the Dictators* (1962) and *The Reckoning* (1965).

A. J. BEATTIE, *London School of Economics*

EDEN, Garden of, the setting for one of the two Biblical creation narratives in Genesis: "And the Lord God planted a garden in Eden, in the east; and there he put the man whom he had formed. And out of the ground the Lord God made to grow every tree that is pleasant to the sight and good for food, the tree of life also in the midst of the garden, and the tree of the knowledge of good and evil" (Genesis 2:8–9).

In the Mesopotamian myths that form the story's background, Eden is a wilderness within which an enclosed oasis is created for man. In the dry and somewhat barren Middle East, one of the favorite images of luxury is that of a park, shaded by heavy foliage and well watered by streams. Though it is a theological tale, the creation narrative does offer some indication of locale. A river arises in Eden to irrigate the garden, where it divides into four streams: the Pishon, the Gihon, the Tigris, and the Euphrates. The first two, otherwise unknown, are said to water the lands of Havilah (probably Arabia) and Cush (possibly in lower Mesopotamia). The garden is thus situated by the storyteller somewhere in present day Iraq.

Among the flora in the garden in Eden are the tree of life and the tree of the knowledge of good and evil. In the symbolism of the Genesis tale, man and woman (Adam and Eve) eat the forbidden fruit of the latter tree (sin) and forfeit the fruit of the tree of life. Thus, the story shows that death is not God's creation but is due to man's loss of innocence.

Subsequent Biblical literature draws on the Hebrew meaning of "Eden" (delight) and on its Greek translation (paradise). It is spoken of as the garden *of* Eden rather than *in* Eden, and is sometimes called the garden of God (Ezekiel 28:13). Later extra-Biblical writings state that Eden was created in heaven before the earth was made (Apocalypse of Baruch; IV Esdras). Futuristic texts, such as Revelation 2:7, look to a new heavenly Eden in the final days: "To him who conquers I will grant to eat of the tree of life, which is in the paradise of God."

JAMES T. BURTCHAELL, C. S. C
Notre Dame University

EDENTATE, ē-den′tāt, any of an order of mammals found exclusively in North and South America. There are about 30 living species, including sloths, armadillos, anteaters, and pichiciegos, ranging from Kansas (common armadillo) to Patagonia (pichiciego). The order evolved in South America during the Tertiary period. Among the many extinct forms were giants that roamed the savannas of Argentina and Brazil.

Edentates vary widely in appearance. Some are only 6 inches (15 cm) long, while others reach a length of 48 inches (120 cm). Sloths and anteaters are hairy, while armadillos and pichiciegos are covered with bony plates. Although the term "edentate" means "without teeth," only the anteaters are really toothless, and some armadillos have up to 100 teeth. The edentate's cheek teeth lack enamel; they also have open roots and grow continuously. All edentates lack true canine or incisor teeth.

The behavior of edentates also varies. Most edentates are solitary except at the mating season, but armadillos may associate in family groups. Most edentates bear one or two young, but the common armadillo may have up to 12 embryos from a single egg. Sloths are vegetarians, while anteaters feed on insects and termites, and armadillos are omnivorous.

FERNANDO DIAS DE AVILA-PIRES
Museu Nacional, Rio de Janeiro

EDENTON, ē′dən-tən, a town in northeastern North Carolina, the seat of Chowan county, is situated on a bay of Albemarle Sound near the mouth of the Chowan River. It is the business center of an agricultural area where corn, peanuts, soybeans, and tobacco are raised. The area is undergoing industrial development. Major economic activities are commercial fishing, peanut processing, and the manufacture of textiles, farm machinery, and boats.

Edenton is noted for its many examples of distinctive architecture of the colonial period and later. Among these are the Cupola House (1725), St. Paul's Church (begun in 1736), the James Iredell house (about 1759), the Chowan county courthouse (1767), the Barker house (about 1782), and 35 other buildings dating from 1740 to 1860 in the town and the county.

Edenton was the third town created in North Carolina. It was laid out in 1712 and named for the colonial governor Charles Eden in 1721. It was incorporated in 1722 and was the first "metropolis" (capital) of the colony. In the "Edenton Tea Party" on Oct. 25, 1774, 51 women signed resolutions endorsing the actions of the rebel colonial assembly that had committed North Carolina to the cause of the American Revolution. This is believed to be the earliest purely political activity by American women.

Edenton is governed by a mayor and council through an administrator. Population: 5,264.

ELIZABETH V. MOORE
Edenton Historical Commission

EDER, ā′dər, **Josef Maria** (1855–1944), Austrian chemist who is best known for his contributions to the development of photography. Eder was born in Krems on March 16, 1855. In one of his first experimental works he explained the chemical actions of chromates on the gelatin used in photographic emulsions. In 1883 he invented a silver chloride emulsion for transparencies and for development in the artificial light used in copying. For making film sensitive to green light, he recommended using erythrosine instead of eosine. His theory of the ripening process of photographic emulsions assumed intermediate products of silver salt reduction down to the metal as active centers.

While a professor in Vienna, Eder founded and directed an institute for graphic arts. In addition to writing many books on photography, he published a handbook of spectroscopy (with Eduard Valenta). Eder died in Kitzbühel, Austria, on Oct. 18, 1944.

EDUARD FARBER, *Editor of "Great Chemists"*

EDERLE, ā'dər-lē, **Gertrude Caroline** (1906–), American swimmer, who was the first woman to swim the English Channel. She was born in New York City on Oct. 23, 1906. The daughter of a west side butcher, she learned to swim at Highlands, N. J. Between 1921 and 1925 she held 29 amateur national and world records. In 1922 she broke seven world records in one afternoon at Brighton Beach, N. Y. A member of the U. S. Olympic team in 1924, she helped win a gold medal in the 400-meter freestyle relay.

On Aug. 6, 1926, Trudy Ederle swam the English Channel from Cape Gris-Nez, France, to Kingsdown, England, completing the 35 miles in 14 hours and 31 minutes, thus breaking the existing men's record. She received a ticker tape parade in New York City on her return. Included among her many honors was the Helms Foundation Hall of Fame award (1953).

NEIL AMDUR, *New York "Times"*

EDESSA, ä'thä-sä, a city in northern Greece, is the capital of the Macedonian department of Pella. Situated high above the coastal plain of the Thermaic Gulf, it commands an extensive view. Edessa controls the only route leading westward from the coastal plain into the upland plain of Phlorina, from which roads lead into Albania and Yugoslavia. A river, called in antiquity Skirtos ("the leaper"), cascades through the town. A disastrous flooding of the river caused the Emperor Justinian I (reigned 527–565) to cut a new bed through the town.

A leading city of the ancient Macedonian kingdom, although probably not identical with its old capital, Aegae, Edessa gave its name to cities founded in Asia by Alexander the Great. As a station on the Via Egnatia, the great road used in Roman and medieval times to connect the Adriatic coast and Constantinople, Edessa was a prize held during various periods by Romans, Goths, Byzantines, Crusaders, Bulgars, Serbs, and Turks. Population: (1961) 15,534.

N. G. L. HAMMOND, *University of Bristol*

EDESSA, ē-des'ə, is the former name of Urfa (q.v.), a city situated in southeastern Turkey in the plain lying between the Euphrates (Firat) and Tigris (Dicle) rivers. Urfa province, of which the city is the capital, is a barren, arid region patchily cultivated for the production of wheat, fruits, and vines.

Since ancient times, the city has been an important station on the northern route connecting the Mediterranean with the East. In the middle of the 2d millennium B. C. it was dominated by the powerful Hurrian-Mitannian kingdoms, and it was subsequently occupied by the Hittites, Arameans, and Assyrians. To the Greeks it was known as Orrhoë, but the name was changed to Edessa (in recollection of a Macedonian city) when the city became the capital of the Seleucid kingdom of Osrohene (Arabic, Ruha) at the end of the 4th century B. C. In the middle of the 2d century B. C. the Aramean principality of the Abgars arose here, serving as a buffer state between the Persian East and the Roman West.

In the 5th century A. D., Edessa became the center of the Eastern (Nestorian) Syrian Church. It was an important seat of Christian learning, from which missionaries spread the doctrine throughout the East. It was taken in 637 by the Arabs, under whose rule it played the role of a frontier city in wars with the Byzantines. The latter recaptured it in 1030, only to lose it again to the Seljuk Turks in 1087. In 1098 the Crusader Baldwin of Boulogne established the county of Edessa, but this met its end at the hands of the Zangid atabegs in 1144. The city and its region passed to the Ayyubids and then to the Mamluks. The latter were defeated by Selim I in 1516, when, along with the rest of their lands, Edessa became Ottoman territory.

JOHN R. WALSH, *University of Edinburgh*

EDFU. See IDFU.

EDGAR (943–975), king of the Anglo-Saxons, was one of the most powerful kings of 10th century England and a great patron of reformed monasticism. The younger son of King Edmund (q.v.), he became king of Mercia and of Northumbria in 957. On the death of his brother Edwy in 959 he succeeded to Wessex also, thus becoming king of all England.

Edgar promoted Dunstan, Æthelwold, and Oswald to bishoprics and supported them in reforming and endowing monasteries. The number of reformed monasteries rose in his reign from one or two to more than 20. These were important not only for religious reasons but also for the extension of royal power. The interdependence of church and state was symbolized by Edgar's coronation at Bath in 973.

The secular history of Edgar's reign is obscure. A number of the rulers of Wales and Scotland acknowledged Edgar's supremacy in 973 at Chester. His laws suggest a developing legal and administrative system. Important reforms were made in the minting and controlling of the currency. Edgar died on July 8, 975.

J. CAMPBELL, *Oxford University*

EDGAR, Sir James David (1841–1899), Canadian public official and author. He was born in Hatley, Lower Canada (Quebec), on Aug. 10, 1841, and was admitted to the bar of Upper Canada (Ontario) in 1864. He served as a Liberal from Monck in the Canadian House of Commons from 1872 to 1874, acting as his party's chief whip during the parliamentary crisis in 1873 that led to the fall of Prime Minister John Macdonald's government.

Returned in 1884 to Parliament, where he represented West Ontario until his death, Edgar was largely responsible for the passage of the Canadian Copyright Act of 1889. He was a leading Liberal in the House, becoming its speaker in 1896. Edgar wrote *This Canada of Ours and Other Poems* (1893) and *Canada and Its Capital* (1898). In 1898 he was created a Knight Commander of St. Michael and St. George. Edgar died in Toronto on July 31, 1899.

EDGAR THE ÆTHELING, a'the-ling (died 1125 or later), was the only English prince to survive the Norman Conquest. Edgar was the son of Edward the Ætheling and grandson of King Edmund Ironside. His hereditary claim to the English throne was pressed in an attempt to make him king after the death of Harold at the Battle of Hastings in 1066. However, he submitted to William the Conqueror and after 1074 was fairly influential in the Anglo-Norman state.

Edgar's sister married King Malcolm III of Scotland about 1069, and in 1097, Edgar led an expedition that made her son Edgar king there. He also participated in the First Crusade. A friend of Robert, Duke of Normandy, he was captured fighting for him against Henry I of England at Tinchebray (Tinchebrai) in 1106. Henry pardoned him, and he was still alive about 1125.

J. CAMPBELL, *Oxford University*

EDGARTOWN, ed'gər-toun, a town in southeastern Massachusetts, is on the eastern shore of the island of Martha's Vineyard, on an inlet of Nantucket Sound, 30 miles (48 km) southeast of New Bedford. It is the seat of Dukes county. Edgartown is a summer resort and a fishing and yachting center. The Dukes County Historical Society is here. The *Vineyard Gazette,* founded in 1846 and published in Edgartown, is one of the best-known weekly newspapers in the United States.

Edgartown was settled in 1642. It was incorporated in 1671 and named for Edgar, the infant son of James II of England. Edgartown was one of the first whaling ports in New England and was the site of a large sperm-oil candle factory in the whaling period. Government is by town meeting. Population: 2,204.

EDGE, Walter Evans (1873–1956), American public official. He was born in Philadelphia on Nov. 20, 1873, and began his working life as a printer's devil in Atlantic City, N. J. Later he was successful in advertising, banking, and other lines of business.

Edge served as a Republican member of the New Jersey Assembly in 1910 and then as a state senator (1911–1916), becoming Republican Senate leader in 1912 and president of the Senate in 1915. He spearheaded a drive for state workmen's compensation legislation. He was governor of New Jersey from 1917 to 1919, resigning to enter the U. S. Senate, where he championed legislation that established the federal Bureau of the Budget. Edge remained in the Senate until 1929 when he resigned to become ambassador to France (1929–1933). Again elected governor of New Jersey in 1943, he served until 1947. He died in New York on Oct. 29, 1956.

EDGEWORTH, Maria (1767–1849), English novelist, who strongly influenced the development of the 19th century novel. She was vastly popular in her own time in England, throughout Europe, and in the United States. Like her contemporary Jane Austen, she specialized in the domestic novel. Jane Austen is much the greater artist. However, Maria Edgeworth, though limited by her didacticsm, extended the range of the novel into social strata previously unexplored, especially by women authors. In her Irish stories she initiated the regional novel and became the model for such writers as Scott and Cooper.

Life. Maria Edgeworth was born in Blackbourton, Oxfordshire, England, on Jan. 1, 1767, one of 22 children of Richard Lovell Edgeworth (q.v.). Her long and happy life was dominated by her admiration for her father, whose mind was steeped in 18th century progressivism and utilitarianism, and by her close family ties. Apart from tours of England, France, and Scotland, Maria, from the age of 15, lived at the family estate at Edgeworthstown, county Longford, Ireland. She died there on May 22, 1849.

Works. Maria Edgeworth's tales began as "wee, wee stories" to entertain her brothers and sisters and also as practical illustrations of the theories that she and her father jointly published in *Practical Education* (1798). She developed these theories, which express her father-collaborator's belief in moral and social improvement through education—and in fiction as the vehicle for such education—in *The Parent's Assistant* (1796–1800), *Early Lessons* (1801–1825), *Moral Tales for Young People* (1801), and *Popular Tales* (1804). The titles of such children's stories as *Simple Susan* and *Lazy Laurence* bespeak their didacticism; yet their delighted understanding of children has made them minor classics.

The aims and methods of her children's tales were maintained in her fiction for adults. Each novel forms a moral diagram in which the characters are divided into good and bad types, with the bad always getting retribution and the good always being rewarded. Yet, again, her powers of observation break through the didacticism, in her portraits of fashionable society in *Tales of Fashionable Life* (1st series, 1809; 2d series, 1812) and in such brilliant character sketches as Lady Delacour in the novel *Belinda* (1801) and Lady Davenant in *Helen* (1830), her last novel. Her greatest work, *Castle Rackrent* (1800), traces the gradual ruination of an Irish family during the course of several generations, as seen through the eyes of an old retainer. Irish material, lovingly and humorously realized, set her imagination free. Even the didacticism of Maria Edgeworth has a freshness and ingenuousness that continues, within its limits, to make her work appealing to many readers.

INGA-STINA EWBANK
University of Liverpool, England

Further Reading: Hare, Augustus, ed., *The Life and Letters of Maria Edgeworth* (London 1894); Newby, Percy Howard, *Maria Edgeworth* (Denver, Colo., 1950).

EDGEWORTH, Richard Lovell (1744–1817), English educational theorist and author, who strongly influenced the writings of his daughter, the novelist Maria Edgeworth (q.v.). He was born at Bath on May 31, 1744, attended Corpus Christi College, Oxford, and later studied law. An admirer of the educational theories of Rousseau, he visited Paris in 1771 and presented his son Richard to Rousseau as an embodiment of the precepts of *Émile.* Edgeworth, who was married four times and was the father of 22 children, settled on his family estate in Edgeworthstown, Ireland, in 1782. An amateur inventor, he made pioneer experiments in telegraphic communication. He died at Edgeworthstown on June 13, 1817.

Edgeworth's *Practical Education* (1798), written in collaboration with Maria, is based on Rousseauean principles. He also wrote *Poetry Explained for Young People* (1802) and *Essays on Professional Education* (1809).

EDICT OF NANTES, ē'dikt, näNt, a proclamation signed at Nantes, France, on April 13, 1598, by King Henry IV granting a broad measure of religious liberty, civil rights, and security to his Calvinist subjects, called Huguenots (q. v.). Although Huguenots formed only a small proportion of the total French population, they held approximately 100 fortified towns, a fact that lent weight to their demands.

The edict contained 92 general articles, signed on April 13, 1598; 56 particular "secret" articles, signed on May 2; and 3 secret briefs (*brevets*). The general and particular articles granted freedom of conscience to the Huguenots, but most of the clauses favorable to them were based on older edicts and treaties revoked in the course of the wars of religion of the 16th century. Thus, the Huguenots were permitted by the Edict of Nantes to hold public worship freely wherever they had earlier been accorded that right by the Edict of Poitiers (1577) and the treaties of Nérac (1579) and Fleix (1580), and in two towns in every bailiwick (*bailliage*). Where the 1577 edict had banned Protestant services within a radius of 10 leagues from Paris, however, the Edict of Nantes applied that restriction for only 5 leagues. Protestant worship was restricted to specified *lieux d'exercice*, and any increase in the number of Huguenot strongholds was strictly forbidden. The edict also guaranteed the Huguenots complete social and political equality: it gave them rights to trade freely, to inherit property, and to hold political meetings; admitted them to all schools, universities, and hospitals; and made them eligible to serve as members of all councils and assemblies. They were exempted from arrears of taxes and promised restitution of all property lost during the wars. The three secret *brevets* granted subsidies to the Huguenots in the amount of 248,000 crowns annually.

After Henry's assassination in 1610, the religious and political position of the Huguenots became once more precarious. Their political rights as well as the strongholds were taken away in 1629 by the Edict of Alais issued by Louis XIII on the advice of Cardinal de Richelieu. Their religious liberties were abrogated by Louis XIV when he revoked the Edict of Nantes on Oct. 18, 1685.

MICHAEL V. GANNON, *University of Florida*

EDINA, ē-dī'nə, is a village in southwestern Minnesota, in Hennepin county, immediately southwest of Minneapolis. The village is primarily a residential suburb but has many business and commercial establishments. It was incorporated in 1888. The village of Morningside was annexed in 1966. Edina has a council-manager government. Population: 46,073.

EDINBURG, ed'ən-bûrg, a city in southeastern Texas, the seat of Hidalgo county, is 50 miles (80 km) northwest of Brownsville. It is the trade center for an agricultural region and is one of the largest citrus fruit-shipping points in Texas. Pan American College, a 4-year state-supported institution founded in 1927, is in Edinburg. The city was incorporated in 1911. Government is by manager and council. Population: 24,075.

EDINBURGH, Duke of, prince consort of Queen Elizabeth II of England. See PHILIP, DUKE OF EDINBURGH.

EDINBURGH, ed'ən-bər-ə, the historic capital of Scotland, lies along the south shore of the Firth of Forth in southeastern Scotland. It is one of the four largest Scottish cities—second only to Glasgow in size—and like the other three it has county status as a "county of city." It is also a royal burgh and the county town of Midlothian. Edinburgh is about 40 miles (65 km) east of Glasgow and 344 miles (553 km) northwest of London. The life of the city is dominated by the professions. Edinburgh is the seat of the Scottish supreme courts and headquarters of the Church of Scotland. It has long been famous as a scholastic and medical center.

Leith is Edinburgh's seaport on the Firth of Forth. From this point the land rises irregularly to the top of Castle Rock, which is 445 feet (125 meters) above sea level. Beyond lie the nearer slopes of the Pentland Hills. The "old town" section of Edinburgh occupies the top and sides of a natural ridge, dropping gradually to the east between Edinburgh Castle and Holyrood Palace. North, across a deep ravine is the "new town" based on Princes Street.

The picturesque old town gives an impression of a medieval city because of its narrow passageways, which are known as "pends" and "closes," its many-storied dwellings called "lands," and its quaint stairs, turrets, and crow-stepped gables. The new town, built like the older one of locally quarried stone, is in many respects the finest example of 18th century town planning in the world. Except for prestige buildings, most new construction since 1918 has been of brick—particularly the suburban housing.

Places of Interest. Much the most ancient and conspicuous building in Edinburgh is the castle, of which the oldest part is St. Margaret's Chapel, a tiny Romanesque church dating probably from early in the 12th century. David II's tower, a massive defensive work, was built in the 14th century. Other castle buildings include the banqueting hall, with its magnificent hammer-beam roof, and the private apartments occupied in the 16th century by the Scottish royal family.

JOHN KNOX, the Scottish religious reformer, lived in this Edinburgh house, built about 1550 on High Street.

BRITISH TRAVEL ASSOCIATION

Edinburgh Castle (left) dominates the city. Princes Street (right) is bordered by handsome gardens (center).

These include the room in which Mary Queen of Scots in 1566 was delivered of her son, James VI of Scotland, who became also King James I of England. Opposite the banqueting hall is the Scottish National War Memorial commemorating Scotland's part in World Wars I and II.

The broad street leading from the castle eastward to Holyrood Palace is known at the castle end as Lawnmarket; then it becomes High Street and, approaching the palace, Canongate. Nearly a mile long, this link between castle and palace is popularly called the Royal Mile.

Holyrood Abbey, near Holyrood Palace, was founded by David I in 1128, although its ruined church dates mainly from the 13th century. Holyrood Palace includes a 16th century tower where Mary Queen of Scots lived. Charles II added to this tower a century later and thus created a massive quadrangle. The medieval timbered houses of the burghers in the High Street and Canongate have disappeared, but thanks partly to recent refurbishing, much of the 16th and 17th century character of the old town remains.

John Knox's House (about 1550) and Gladstone's Land (16th century, rebuilt 1620–1634) are perhaps the best-known dwellings. St. Giles Cathedral, the original parish church, is easily recognized by its 15th century openwork lantern tower. The finest individual building in the new town is certainly the General Register House designed by Robert Adam in 1772 to be the public record office of Scotland. Perhaps the most notable of the numerous buildings erected since 1945 are those housing the University of Edinburgh around George Square.

Squares and Parks. Charlotte Square, planned by Adam in 1791, is the most admired and least altered of many squares and crescents. Much the most extensive park is the Queen's Park, which stretches from Holyrood across the 823-foot (250-meter) summit of the hill called Arthur's Seat to Duddingston, where there is a bird sanctuary. In the center of the town the whole area between Princes Street, which is open to the south, and the castle is occupied by public gardens.

In East Princes Street Gardens is the handsome memorial to Scotland's great novelist and poet Sir Walter Scott. The Scott Monument, erected in the early 1840's, has a graceful 200-foot (60-meter) Gothic spire above a statue of Scott and his dog Maida. Separating the East and West Princes Street Gardens is the Mound, formed from excavations for the new town, providing a connection between the old town and the new. At the north end of this street are two art galleries, the gallery of the Royal Scottish Academy and the National Gallery. The latter has a distinguished collection of paintings of the Dutch, French, British, and Italian schools.

The Edinburgh Zoo, where animals are housed as far as possible in natural conditions, covers a large area. The Botanic Gardens, with newly rebuilt hothouses and a famous arboretum and rock garden, lie to the north of the new town.

Education and Cultural Life. The University of Edinburgh was founded by royal charter in 1582 as a liberal arts college with a divinity school attached. It added faculties of medicine and law in the 17th and 18th centuries and became one of the leading universities of the world under the noted historian William Robertson, who was its principal from 1762 to 1793. Its medical school attracted many American students, who later helped found some of the first U. S. medical schools. Equally renowned was the university's teaching in philosophy and the sciences.

More recently, a second university has been created in Edinburgh by upgrading the former Heriot-Watt (technical) College to become Heriot-Watt University.

The oldest Edinburgh school is the Royal High School. In the Middle Ages the school was attached to Holyrood Abbey, but from the 16th century onward it was run by the town council. The Edinburgh Merchant Company administers four schools. Other schools for boys and girls include fee-paying secondary schools and several English-type public schools—for example, Fettes for boys and St. George's for girls. Most of Edinburgh's children, however, are educated at excellent primary and secondary schools controlled by the town council.

The town has two internationally known libraries, the National Library of Scotland and the Edinburgh University Library, as well as the Edinburgh Public Library. The last has an Edinburgh room, devoted to local history. The town council also maintains a whole group of specialized museums—for example, a Museum of Childhood. The General Register House contains the public records of Scotland and has built up an extensive collection of family papers. The leading museums are the Royal Scottish Museum, exhibiting principally art and technology, and the National Museum of Antiquities of Scotland.

The Scottish National Orchestra and Reid Orchestra give concerts in season, and there are other frequent musical performances. Eighteenth century St. Cecilia's Hall has been equipped with a collection of early harpsichords. There are two theaters in Edinburgh, one commercial and the other operated by the town council as a repertory theater. The small experimental Traverse Theatre presents avant-garde productions. The annual Edinburgh Festival, primarily a festival of music, has established the city internationally as a music and cultural center.

One morning paper, the *Scotsman*, with a distinguished history, and an associated evening paper, the *Evening News*, are published daily. Other newspapers are also widely read. For radio and television, Edinburgh is served by the British Broadcasting Corporation and Scottish Television networks.

The Economy. Banking, insurance, and finance are Edinburgh's leading businesses. Most Scottish banks and insurance companies have their head offices in Edinburgh, though effective control has largely been transferred to London. Brewing and printing are also long established, and papermaking is carried on in the vicinity. More recently, various rubber and engineering works have been established in the city; there has also been a sensational expansion in the electronics industry. From its early days Edinburgh was more a commercial than an industrial city, and Princes Street shops, though many are now owned by multiple (chain) stores, are still famous.

Leith docks, which have been extended and developed, are reasonably busy, especially with grain imports. Edinburgh is linked with London by three main railway lines: the east coast line, which has been built up as a trunk route; the midland, which has been downgraded and threatened with closure; and the west coast, which is monopolized by Glasgow passengers. If, as seems likely, the Glasgow-London line is electrified and the east coast route downgraded, Edinburgh passengers will have to travel by the longer, less reliable, and more congested west coast route. This will matter less, however, because of the rapid development of air transport facilities that provide transportation to points within the United Kingdom.

Urban Development and Problems. The town council has been anxious that the city's expansion should not be uncontrolled and haphazard. Critics have alleged that this policy has slowed development more than is necessary or desirable. More serious has been the British government's refusal to recognize Edinburgh as a "development area"; industrialists looking for a site naturally prefer one where they may obtain maximum financial assistance from the government. A number of firms, long established in Edinburgh and anxious to expand their capacity to produce, have moved outside of the city. The prefabricated temporary houses erected at the end of World War II have been replaced by permanent housing, and land available for housing within the city boundaries is now virtually exhausted.

Much has been done to bring schools and hospitals up to the best contemporary standards. The complete rebuilding on its present site of the historic Royal Infirmary will be another outstanding example of this modernization. The town council also has on hand several large-scale developments in various parts of the town involving demolition of substandard property, provision of new roads and facilities, and segregation of pedestrian and motor traffic.

Old and new Edinburgh were surrounded in the 18th century by suburbs, some of them—like Corstorphine and Colinton—already old centers of population. In the 19th and early 20th centuries there was a good deal of row housing built along the radial roads, while prosperous citizens erected handsome suburban mansions within easy reach of the city. Since 1918 there has been further expansion in all directions. Already a substantial part of the working population commutes daily from beyond the city boundaries, a practice that seems likely to increase. Formerly, suburban railways were used; now nearly all commuters come by bus or car. Within the city the town council provides a reasonably efficient bus service. Express buses run regularly to many Scottish and English towns.

Government. For purposes of local government the city is divided into wards. A town council or corporation, the members of which are elected for three years, with a third of them retiring each year, conducts the city's business. Members are unpaid, and each serves on a number of committees charged with specific functions—for example, in finance, education, or water supply. In recent years the line of division between members of the corporation has become much more political. Nearly all belong either to the majority Progressive party or to one of the minority parties, Labour or Scottish Nationalist.

Each year some councillors who have served with distinction are appointed by their colleagues as bailies and act as magistrates in the burgh court and as chairmen of the corporation committees. The chief magistrate, elected by the councillors, is lord provost. He presides at meetings of the council and takes precedence as first citizen within the city. Permanent officials, such as the town clerk, city chamberlain, and city architect, act as advisers and executive officers to the various committees.

History. Edinburgh's name is often wrongly linked with the 7th century Northumbrian king Edwin. Actually, 6th century Britons called the place Din Eidyn. When the Saxon invaders came, they translated Din, meaning "fortified town," to Saxon "burgh." The town's situation so near the border with England made it unsuitable as a royal residence, but it was one of the original "four burghs" out of which grew the Convention of Royal Burghs, which has been described as the oldest surviving representative institution in Europe. By the mid-14th century, Edinburgh had become in fact the capital of Scotland and the usual meeting place of the Scottish parliament. When James V set up the College of Justice (1532) and Protestantism was established (1560), Edinburgh became the normal meeting place of the supreme courts of state and church.

James VI's departure to London in 1603 to rule in England involved loss of prestige, but not of prosperity, for Edinburgh. It was at this time that Heriot's Hospital and Parliament House were built. The union of the parliaments in 1707 was a more serious blow to the city's prestige than the union of the crowns, but by the middle of the 18th century Edinburgh had become one of the cultural capitals of Europe. Eminent writers and scholars, physicians and surgeons, historians and philosophers, economists and sociologists jostled each other in the High Street and settled themselves in the new town.

The end of Edinburgh's golden age may be dated with the death of Sir Walter Scott in 1832, but the town has continued to produce eminent scholars, novelists and other literary men, scientists, physicians, and surgeons. It was in Edinburgh, for example, that James Simpson first experimented with anesthetics and Joseph Lister with antiseptics. The *Edinburgh Review*, for many years the most influential journal published in the United Kingdom, did more for the cause of reform than any other 19th century periodical. *Blackwood's Magazine*, also published in Edinburgh, represented the opposite or Tory point of view and survived its greater competitor. In the 19th century, Edinburgh also continued to be the ecclesiastical capital of Scotland. Here the Presbyterian Church underwent the Disruption of 1843, and here its two principal branches were reunited in 1929.

The old unrepresentative town council was reformed by the Municipal Corporation Act of 1834–1835, and instead of the town council electing Edinburgh's member of Parliament the franchise was slowly extended to include virtually every adult. Since 1885 a secretary for Scotland has had his headquarters in Edinburgh, and civil servants have been moved from London to Edinburgh to assist him. This process has done something to revive the political importance of the city, but the rise of the Scottish Nationalist party shows that steps toward decentralization are no longer regarded as adequate answers to Scottish demands for effective self-government. Population: (1966) 462,340.

DAVID B. HORN, *University of Edinburgh*

Further Reading: Horn, D. B., *Short History of the University of Edinburgh* (Edinburgh 1967); Keir, D. E., ed., *City of Edinburgh* (Edinburgh 1966); Lindsay, Ian, *Georgian Edinburgh* (Edinburgh 1948); Youngson, A. J., *Making of Classical Edinburgh* (Edinburgh 1966).

EDINBURGH, University of, ed'ən-bur-ə, a private coeducational university located in Edinburgh, Scotland. Chartered by King James VI in 1582, it was founded by the town council of Edinburgh and opened for instruction in 1583 as the "Tounis College." In 1621 an Act of Confirmation by the Scottish Parliament ensured the college, then known as the College of James VI, the rights and privileges of the three older Scottish universities. After that date it gradually came to be known as the University of Edinburgh.

The university first consisted of a liberal arts college and a divinity school. Faculties of law and medicine were added in the early 18th century; the faculty of medicine soon established an international reputation. Faculties of music and science were created in 1893, and faculties of social sciences and veterinary medicine were added in the 1960's. Women students were first admitted to the university in 1889.

The Edinburgh town council exercised almost complete control of the university until 1858, when the Universities Act ensured its autonomy. A Senatus Academicus, consisting of the professors and other members of the faculty, now governs the university's academic affairs, while financial and administrative concerns are controlled by the University Court. The university derives most of its support from parliamentary grants.

As the first British city university, the University of Edinburgh has exercised considerable influence on the development of universities in Britain. It was taken as a model by the founders of the University of London, and several important medical schools in North America were founded by Edinburgh graduates. In the late 1960's the university's enrollment exceeded 10,-000 students, and its library contained more than 1 million volumes and periodicals.

DAVID B. HORN, *University of Edinburgh*

EDINBURGH REVIEW, ed'ən-bur-ə, the first of the great critical periodicals of the 19th century. It was founded by Francis Jeffrey, Sydney Smith, Francis Horner, and Henry Brougham, and first appeared in October 1802. After the first number, which was edited by Smith, the magazine was edited by Jeffrey for 27 years. It ceased publication in 1929.

The *Edinburgh Review* became extremely influential. Its vigorous, outspoken editorial policy was slanted politically against the Tories and strongly biased against various literary groups and figures. In its early years, it was particularly noted for its attacks on the Lake poets, including Robert Southey and William Wordsworth. An article by Henry Brougham criticizing Byron's *Hours of Idleness* (1807) provoked Byron's famous satire *English Bards and Scotch Reviewers* (1809). Among the notable contributors to the publication were Macaulay, Carlyle, Hazlitt, and Arnold.

EDIRNE, e-dir'ne, is the second-largest city of European Turkey and capital of the province of Edirne. It is situated in the Thracian plain, near the frontiers of Bulgaria and Greece. Edirne is a trade and agricultural center, and manufactures cotton goods and silk. Until 1930 the city was generally known as *Adrianople*. At that time the Turkish government requested foreign post offices to address the city as Edirne, a name used domestically since early Ottoman times.

The city was the capital of the Ottoman Empire from 1362 to 1453. Edirne has lost its former distinction, but it still possesses several beautiful mosques, including those of Selim (designed by the great Turkish architect Sinan) and Bayezid II. Population: (1965) with environs, 78,161. See also ADRIANOPLE.

J. R. WALSH, *University of Edinburgh*

EDISON'S LABORATORY was moved from Menlo Park, N. J. to Greenfield Village in Dearborn, Mich., in 1929. It has been restored and houses models of his inventions. A statue of Edison by James Earle Fraser is at left.

HENRY FORD MUSEUM, DEARBORN, MICH.

EDISON, Thomas Alva (1847–1931), American inventor and pioneer industrialist. Rough-hewn and self-educated, Edison rose to become a folk hero in his day and one of the most prolific inventors of all time. During his lifetime more than a thousand American patents were granted on work of his own or of teams under his supervision. Three of his inventions—the phonograph, a practical incandescent light and electric system, and a moving picture camera—helped found giant industries that were to change the life and leisure of the world. Besides being an inventor, Edison was a manufacturer, a businessman, and a founder of organized research as well as one of the most colorful and paradoxical personalities of the late 19th and early 20th centuries.

Edison was married twice. In 1871 he married Mary G. Stilwell, and two years after her death in 1884 he married Mina Miller. He had three children by each of his wives.

EARLY LIFE

Edison was born in Milan, Ohio, on Feb. 11, 1847. He was the seventh and last child of Samuel and Nancy (Elliott) Edison. His ancestry was Dutch-English on his father's side and Scotch-Yankee on his mother's. When Edison was born, his father was a prosperous shingle manufacturer in Milan, Ohio. When he was 7 years old, however, a collapse of the family fortunes forced Samuel Edison to move his family to Port Huron, Mich., where they were to live in adequate but poorer circumstances.

Education. During childhood Edison learned eagerly by asking questions and discovering things for himself. Unable to adapt himself to the routine of school, however, he quit three months after beginning when his teacher called him "addled." His mother, a former teacher, then continued his education at home. When he was 9 years old, she gave him a primer on physics that described scientific experiments he could perform himself. He read this avidly but challenged every statement in it until he had tested it personally. The next year he set up a chemical laboratory in his cellar.

First Jobs. Needing more money for chemicals and apparatus, Edison got a job as a newspaper and candy salesman on the Grand Trunk Railway when he was 12 years old. To avoid wasting time he moved his cellar laboratory to the baggage car and read in the public library during layovers in Detroit. When he was 15, he bought a printing press and edited and printed a small local newspaper, the *Weekly Herald*, in the same baggage car.

One morning when young Edison was trying to climb onto a moving train, a trainman helped him aboard by grasping his ears. He later attributed to this incident the beginning of the deafness that was to increase through his life—an affliction that cut off many personal associations but undoubtedly helped him concentrate on his work. A history of the symptoms, however, indicates that his deafness was probably largely an aftereffect of an earlier attack of scarlet fever.

In 1863, at the age of 16, Edison learned telegraphy, and for the next four years he roamed the Middle West as an operator. It was during these years that he first dreamed of becoming an inventor. This ambition was fired to action in 1868 when, employed by the Western Union Telegraph Company in Boston, he read *Experimental Researches in Electricity* by Michael Faraday—a great experimenter whose background seemed similar to his own.

Early Inventions. Edison filed papers for his first invention, an electric vote recorder, in October 1868 and received a patent on June 1, 1869. Finding no buyer, he formed the policy he was to follow the rest of his life: he would never attempt to invent anything unless he was sure there was a commercial demand for it. His first patent under this new rule was for improvements on a stock ticker. Although he sold this, he did not receive enough money to pay the expenses he had incurred.

Hoping to change his fortune, he went to New York in 1869. Arriving penniless, he visited Laws' Gold Indicator Company, where friends invited him to study the instruments and to sleep in the battery room. The indicator, invented by S. S. Laws, was an electric device that transmitted changes in gold prices to subscribers. Edison's big chance came one day when the central transmitter broke down. Quickly spotting the trouble, he had the device running within two hours. Laws gave him a job and soon made him manager at the then high salary of $300 a month. Edison lost this position through a merger, but his fortune was to soar again. Late in 1870 he received $40,000 from the head of the combined company for improvements he made on the stock ticker.

636

Diplex and Quadruplex Telegraphs. With this sudden wealth Edison equipped a shop in Newark, N.J., and began manufacturing tickers. By now his reputation as a "young wonder," able to rectify defects in the devices of others, had spread. Promoters brought him their problems. One was an automatic telegraph invented by G. D. Little, good in principle but sometimes sluggish and indistinct in operation. Backed by another $40,000, Edison put the telegraph in good working order and opened a shop to manufacture the machine. In 1873 he devised a "diplex" telegraph with which two messages could be sent simultaneously over one wire in the same direction. It was a variation of the "duplex" of J. B. Stearns, with which messages could be sent simultaneously in opposite directions. In 1874 he combined the diplex with the duplex to make a "quadruplex" which was able to carry four simultaneous messages over one wire.

MENLO PARK

Bored with manufacturing and no longer able to handle alone the ideas that filled his mind, Edison moved in 1876 to Menlo Park, N.J., where he established the world's first "invention factory" —a well-equipped and ably staffed laboratory dedicated solely to testing, improving, and inventing useful products for pay. Forerunner of the modern industrial research laboratory, this unique institution was itself one of Edison's greatest inventions and was to play a leading part in his subsequent achievements. The first important product to come from Edison's invention factory was the carbon telephone transmitter (1877–1878), a device that extended greatly the clarity and range of Bell's original system.

Phonograph. The second product of the Menlo Park laboratory was the phonograph (1877), Edison's favorite invention and considered to be his only completely original one. The idea for it came to him while he was trying to improve a telegraph repeater. In this device a paraffin-coated paper tape was drawn at high speed through a receiving instrument where a stylus or needle embossed it with the dots and dashes of an incoming message. The embossed tape was then fed into a transmitting instrument, where another stylus followed the indentations and so repeated the message.

Once, when racing through a repeater, a tape gave off a noise that sounded to Edison like "a light, musical, rhythmical sound, resembling human talk heard indistinctly." This set him thinking. What would happen if he connected a telephone diaphragm to the embossing needle in place of the telegraph arm? Could he thus impress on the tape the subtler vibrations of the human voice and so produce recording that could talk back intelligibly?

His first attempts were made with a simple adaptation of the telegraph repeater. Then he tried devices using grooved cylinders of wax and chalk, and finally of metal covered with tinfoil, instead of the tape. Into an improved machine using tinfoil, and before a small group of witnesses, he recited *Mary Had a Little Lamb*. When a stylus was run over the indented foil, all were dumbfounded to recognize Edison's high-pitched voice almost perfectly reproduced. Although the subsequent early phonographs were harsh-sounding and crude, throngs came to hear them, and the popular press began hailing Edison as a "magician" and "wizard."

EDISON NATIONAL HISTORIC SITE, NATIONAL PARK SERVICE
THE YOUNG EDISON is shown with the phonograph he invented in 1877. The machine used a tinfoil record.

Electric Lighting Industry. In 1878, Edison began the enterprise for which he is best known— the commercial introduction of the incandescent lamp. He did not invent this lamp, but he did devise and manufacture the first lamp and electrical distributing system that could be operated economically together—a feat more important than the invention of the lamp itself in promoting the general use of electricity.

Unlike previous investigators in the field of electric lighting, Edison envisioned not merely a lamp but a complete lighting system that could compete with the popular gaslight of the day. The key to such a system, he believed, was a lamp having a high-resistance, hairlike "filament," instead of the low-resistance wires and rods used by rival inventors. In October 1879, after thousands of experiments, he made such a lamp, using carbonized thread that burned for 40 hours. The next year he made lamps suitable for commercial use with filaments of bamboo. With the help of Francis R. Upton, the mathematician in his employ, Edison also devised dynamos, the feeder-and-main system, and later a three-wire system— each of which cut the cost of supplying electricity.

On Sept. 4, 1882, Edison opened his first commercial central station on Pearl Street, New York City, with about 85 customers and some 400 lamps wired in the circuits. Modest in size but revolutionary in idea, this station marked the beginning of the electric lighting industry in America.

Although this and other Edison stations built during the next dozen years demonstrated conclusively that the distribution and sale of electricity from central stations were commercially possible, the dependence of these stations on low-voltage direct current severely limited their range and size. An alternating-current power and lighting system patented in 1888 by his onetime employee Nikola Tesla (q.v.) and promoted by George Westinghouse (q.v.) broke these limitations, but Edison obstinately opposed its use. Alternating current, he maintained, was not only dangerous but commercially impractical, and he would never permit its use in any company that bore his name. Ironically, it was the final adoption of this a-c system—against Edison's will—that was to establish Edison's fame by making his dream of universal light and power come true.

Besides devising lamps and equipment for his lighting system, Edison organized numerous companies to manufacture them. In 1889 these companies, together with the patent-holding Edison Electric Light Company and the Sprague Electric Railway and Motor Company, were joined to form the Edison General Electric Company. In 1892 this firm joined with its biggest rival, the Thomson-Houston Electric Company, to create the General Electric Company. Apart from inventing, Edison thus helped found what became one of the world's largest industrial manufacturing concerns.

Edison Effect. In March 1883, while experimenting with his lamp, Edison made his only discovery in pure science. He had inserted a vertical wire in the space between the legs of the horseshoe-shaped filament lamp. When this wire was connected to the positive side of the circuit, a current flowed between it and the filament; when connected to the negative side, none flowed. Seeing no practical use for the phenomenon, he put it aside. Later called the "Edison effect," it was explained in 1897 by the British physicist J. J. Thomson as due to an emission of electrons, and in 1904 it was adapted by J. A. Fleming to produce the first vacuum valve to detect radio waves.

WEST ORANGE

In 1887, Edison moved from Menlo Park to West Orange, N.J., where he built a larger and more modern laboratory for collective invention. From this, among other things, came improved phonographs and records; dictating machines; a fluoroscope; a moving-picture camera and a peepshow device, the Kinetoscope, for viewing its pictures; the iron-alkaline storage battery; magnetic methods for separating low-grade iron ore; and methods for manufacturing chemicals and cement. Edison spent his later years trying to obtain rubber economically from domestic plants. He died in West Orange on Oct. 18, 1931.

Honors. Edison was awarded a special Congressional gold medal in 1928 for his many contributions to the nation's welfare. In 1929, Henry Ford restored his Menlo Park laboratory at Greenfield Village, Dearborn, Mich., and in 1962 his West Orange laboratory and his nearby home, Glenmont, were dedicated jointly as the Edison National Historic Site. Both are open to the public. In 1960, Edison was elected to the Hall of Fame for Great Americans at New York University.

KENNETH M. SWEZEY
*Technical Adviser on "Edison,"
by Matthew Josephson*

Bibliography
Bryan, George S., *Edison, the Man and His Work* (New York 1926).
Burlingame, Roger, *Engines of Democracy* (New York 1940).
Crowther, James G., *Famous American Men of Science* (New York 1937).
Dyer, Frank L., and others, *Edison, His Life and Inventions*, rev. ed., 2 vols. (New York 1929).
Josephson, Matthew, *Edison* (New York 1959).
MacLaren, Malcolm, *The Rise of the Electrical Industry During the Nineteenth Century* (Princeton 1943).
Passer, Harold C., *The Electrical Manufacturers, 1875–1900* (Cambridge, Mass., 1953).

EDISON, a township in central New Jersey, in Middlesex county, is situated 15 miles (24 km) southwest of Newark, near the Raritan River. It is an industrial and residential community. The manufacture of plastics and chemicals are its principal industries.

Edison includes the village of Menlo Park, where Thomas A. Edison established a laboratory in 1876 (see also EDISON, THOMAS ALVA—*Menlo Park*). Edison State Park at Menlo Park includes the Edison Memorial Tower, which was built near the site of the laboratory. The tower, 129-feet (39 meters) in height, contains many devices made by the inventor.

Incorporated as the township of Raritan in 1870, the community was renamed Edison in 1954. It has a mayor-council form of government. Population: 70,193.

EDITING. See BOOK—*2. Publishing and Selling* (Editorial Procedures); CAREER PLANNING—*Professional and Administrative Jobs* (Editors).

EDMAN, Irwin (1896–1954), American philosopher, who popularized philosophical concepts in books, general magazine articles, and radio forums. He was born in New York City on Nov. 28, 1896, and took a doctorate in philosophy at Columbia University in 1920. He became a lecturer at Columbia in 1918, professor in 1935, and head of the philosophy department in 1945. He died in New York City on Sept. 4, 1954.

Edman's philosophy combined the pragmatism of James and Dewey with Platonism and an emphasis on aesthetics. He was also an outstanding authority on the philosophy of George Santayana, whose works he edited in 1936. Edman's most widely read books were the semiautobiographical *Philosopher's Holiday* (1938) and its sequel, *Philosopher's Quest* (1947). In *Fountainheads of Freedom* (1941) he expressed his faith in democracy. Other publications included *Arts and the Man* (1939) and *John Dewey* (1954).

EDMONDS, Walter Dumaux (1903–   ), American historical novelist, whose work combines historical accuracy with lively characterization and vivid description, in an entertaining narrative style. Edmonds was born on July 15, 1903, in Boonville, N.Y. In Charles Townsend Copeland's writing course at Harvard he discovered his major subject matter, the history of New York State.

Edmonds' first novel, *Rome Haul* (1929), dealing with life in New York in the late 1850's, was well received and was dramatized by Marc Connelly and F. B. Elser as *The Farmer Takes a Wife* (1934). Edmonds' best-known novel, *Drums Along the Mohawk* (1936), tells of events in the Mohawk Valley during the American Revolution. Other fiction works include *Erie Water* (1933), *Mostly Canallers* (short stories, 1934), and *Chad Hanna* (1940). He also wrote such nonfiction books as *The First Hundred Years* (1948), a history of the Oneida Community (q.v.), and *The Musket and the Cross* (1968), a historical account of the struggle of France and England for North America between 1609 and 1689.

Edmonds also wrote numerous children's books. His first, *The Matchlock Gun* (1941), received the Newbery Award in 1942. *Hound Dog Moses and the Promised Land* (1944) won the Boys' Club of America Award.

JEROME STERN
Florida State University

EDMONTON, ed'mən-tən, a city in central Alberta, Canada, is the capital of the province and the fifth-largest city in the nation. Situated 350 miles (560 km) north of the United States border, it is the gateway to the Canadian north and a key to the development of the rich resources of that region, which extends beyond the Arctic Circle

Edmonton is a rapidly growing distribution, communications, manufacturing, and educational center. Its new skyline of high-rise towers above the steep wooded banks of the North Saskatchewan River startles visitors who have expected a flat, prairie frontier town. The invigorating climate, with a mean temperature in summer of 61°F (17°C) and a winter mean of 13°F (11°C), and with a light, dry snowfall that averages 7 inches (178 mm) annually, permits construction to continue all the year.

The city's population increased about 400% in the two decades after World War II. A vast program of planning envisions a corporate area of about 300 square miles (775 sq km) to accommodate a projected population of one million by the year 2000. A civic center has been built in the heart of the city. A program of freeway and bridge construction and a rail system of rapid transit have been undertaken.

The Economy. Edmonton's historic economic base was agriculture, and the city remains the farming, dairying, poultry, egg, and meat capital of Alberta. Agricultural products are collected, processed, and distributed in the city, which is also a center for agricultural implements and supplies. However, Edmonton's economy has changed with changes in the economic base of the province, where mineral production has taken first place.

The discovery of the Leduc oil field, about 20 miles (32 km) south of Edmonton, in 1947, made the city the center of Canada's oil industry. Thousands of oil wells and the Athabasca oil sands, the largest known oil reservoir in the world, lie in the city's sphere of influence. Edmonton is the major oil refinery center of western Canada. From the city two major pipelines pump 80% of Canada's oil east and west across the nation. Gas lines reach Montreal and California.

Half of the manufacturing in Alberta is concentrated in Edmonton. Petrochemical, plastics, metal refining, and steel industries crowd the area known as Chemical Valley.

Two new railroad lines connect the city with the North. One of several airports that serve Edmonton, the Industrial Airport (Canada's first licensed field, from which bush pilots began to fly to the remote North before 1920) is one of the busiest in Canada, largely because of the increase in the volume of traffic to the frontier.

Education and Cultural Life. The University of Alberta has its principal campus in Edmonton, and a second campus is scheduled to open in 1973. The Northern Alberta Institute of Technology trains young students and retrains adults who have been displaced by automation in industry. The Centennial Library is the center of the citywide system of branch libraries, which innovated bookmobile service before 1920. There are many symphony, opera, little theater, dance, music, and film groups.

Recreation and Places of Interest. A novel feature of recreation in Edmonton is a network of community leagues in various sports that involve half the families in the city. In the hundreds of

G. HUNTER, FROM NATIONAL FILM BOARD OF CANADA
EDMONTON'S City Hall typifies the architecture of the city's massive post-World War II building boom.

acres of parks are scores of skating rinks and playing fields and more than a dozen golf courses.

As the capital of Alberta, Edmonton has an impressive array of buildings housing the provincial government, including the legislative building and four large office buildings. A federal office building was erected in 1955.

Of special interest are the Provincial Museum and Archives; the site of the home of John Walter, an Edmonton pioneer; the Historical Building; Fort Edmonton; the Jubilee Auditorium; the Storyland Valley Zoo; Elk Island Park; and the Alberta Game Farm.

Government. Edmonton is governed by an elected mayor and aldermen. A commission board administers the various civic departments and all utilities except natural gas. Property taxes and utility profits are the major sources of revenue.

History. Fort Edmonton was established on the north side of the North Saskatchewan River in 1795 by the Hudson's Bay Company as a strategic point on the principal exploration and fur-trading route across Canada. The first post was destroyed by Indians in 1807, but a larger fort was erected in 1820. Stragglers from the goldfields in British Columbia settled on the site of the city in the mid-1860's.

The Canadian Pacific Railroad reached Strathcona on the south bank of the river in 1891, and in 1892, Edmonton was incorporated as a town, with a population of 700. Rapid growth began in 1897 and 1898, when thousands who attempted the dangerous overland route to the Klondike goldfields (approximately on the line of the present Alaska Highway) turned back to settle in Edmonton.

Edmonton was incorporated as a city in 1904, a year before Alberta became a province, and was merged with Strathcona in 1912. Population: (1961) 281,027; (1966) 376,925; (1971) 438,152; (1976) 461,361; (1981) 532,246.

H. L. PAWSON
Public Relations Director, City of Edmonton

EDMUND I (921–946), king of the Anglo-Saxons, was the son of Edward the Elder. He succeeded his half brother Athelstan as king in 939. Soon afterward the Norse king Olaf Guthfrithson occupied York and much of Northumbria and in 940 forced Edmund to concede to him the northeast Midlands also. But in 942 and 944, Edmund regained the lost lands and in 945 was able to fight a successful campaign in Strathclyde, in the far northwest.

Edmund's reign was important in the regeneration of the English church. He made the reformer Oda archbishop of Canterbury (942) and Dunstan abbot of Glastonbury (about 940); Glastonbury became the first reformed monastery in England. Edmund's laws indicate attempts to improve the administration of justice. He was murdered by an outlaw at Pucclechurch (Gloucestershire) on May 26, 946.

J. CAMPBELL, *Oxford University*

EDMUND II (died 1016), called Edmund Ironside, king of the Anglo-Saxons, whose brief reign is remembered for his stand against the Danish invasion of England. In early 1015 he rebelled against his father, King Æthelred II, but joined him in resisting the invasion of the Danish leader Canute later that year. In April 1016, Æthelred died, and Edmund, his eldest surviving son, was immediately elected king of England. But soon afterward a larger assembly accepted Canute as king in opposition to Edmund.

In the resulting war against Canute and his Danish and English supporters, Edmund gained several successes but was defeated at Assandun (Ashdon, or possibly Ashingdon, Essex). An agreement was then concluded at Alney (Gloucestershire) whereby Edmund was to rule England south of the Thames and Canute the lands to the north. A tradition that the rivals fought in single combat at Alney is unsubstantiated. Edmund died on Nov. 30, 1016, probably at Oxford.

J. CAMPBELL, *Oxford University*

EDMUND OF ABINGDON, ab'ing-dən, **Saint** (c. 1175–1240), English prelate and scholar. He was born at Abingdon, near Oxford, and later studied in Paris. After lecturing in arts at Paris and Oxford, he studied theology in Paris and again taught at Oxford. In 1222 he was appointed treasurer at Salisbury Cathedral and in 1227, at the request of Pope Gregory IX, he preached the Sixth Crusade in England.

Edmund was elected archbishop of Canterbury in 1233 and consecrated the following year. During his episcopate he engaged in stormy disputes with King Henry III. He forced the King to exclude foreign advisers from his council and championed the national church against excessive papal and clercial taxation. Perhaps in an endeavor to release himself from Edmund's control, the King requested a papal legate in 1237. In the same year Edmund went to Rome to plead his cause against the King. He also tried to check the King's practice of leaving benefices unoccupied to collect the revenues, but he was not supported by Pope Gregory.

In 1240, while on his way to Rome to attend a general council called by the Pope, Edmund stopped in Pontigny, France. Unwell, he retired to nearby Soisy, where he died on Nov. 16, 1240. His feast is celebrated on November 16.

SISTER ALPHONSUS MARIE SAWKINS, I. H. M.
Marygrove College, Detroit

EDMUND THE MARTYR, Saint (c. 841–870), king of East Anglia. He was born in Saxony, the son of King Alkmund and Queen Scivare, and was adopted in 854 by King Offa of East Anglia as his heir. He succeeded Offa as king in 854 at the age of 14. On Christmas Day 855, he was crowned and anointed by Humbert, bishop of Hulme, probably at Bures St. Mary, Suffolk.

Edmund was a virtuous and wise ruler. In 870 the Danes invaded England, perhaps to avenge the death of one of their pirates. The invaders spent the winter on the island of Sheppey. Edmund was residing in Suffolk at the time, possibly in the village of Hoxne. Captured by the Danes, he either refused their terms, which included renouncement of the faith, or gave himself up to prevent further attacks on his people. In 870, at or near Hoxne, he was bound to a tree, shot with arrows, and finally beheaded. He was buried at the Benedictine settlement of Bury St. Edmunds, which was named in his honor. His tomb became a famous shrine in the Middle Ages. His feast is November 20.

SISTER ALPHONSUS MARIE SAWKINS, I. H. M.
Marygrove College, Detroit

EDMUNDS, George Franklin (1828–1919), American political leader. He was born in Richmond, Vt., on Feb. 1, 1828. Privately educated, he was admitted to the Vermont bar in 1849 and began law practice at Burlington. He served in the state house of representatives (1845–1859) and state senate (1861–1862). An active Republican at the outbreak of the Civil War, he engineered a union of Republicans and "War Democrats" in a statewide convention to adopt his resolutions in support of the Union.

Appointed to fill a U. S. Senate vacancy in April 1866, Edmunds hastened to Washington to cast his first vote with the majority to override President Andrew Johnson's veto of the Civil Rights Act of 1866. A senator for the next quarter century, he helped arrange the impeachment trial of President Johnson, contributed much to the Ku Klux Klan Act of 1871 and the Civil Rights Act of 1875, served as a member of the electoral commission to decide the disputed Hayes-Tilden presidential election of 1876, drafted the Edmunds Act for the suppression of polygamy in Utah (1883), served as president *pro tempore* of the Senate, and wrote much of the antitrust legislation adopted as the Sherman Act in 1890. Reformers supported him for president in 1884, but he failed to win the Republican nomination. Resigning from the Senate in 1890, he established a law practice in Philadelphia. He died in Pasadena, Calif., on Feb. 27, 1919.

DAVID LINDSEY
California State College at Los Angeles

EDMUNDSTON, ed'mənd-stən, is a city in northwestern New Brunswick, Canada, at the junction of the Madawaska and Saint John rivers, 130 miles (209 km) northwest of Fredericton. The Saint John River here forms the boundary with the United States. Pulp production is the chief industry; shirts, shoes, and gloves also are manufactured. Edmundston is also a railroad center.

Settled by Acadian refugees on the site of an Indian village, it was first called Petit Sault (Little Falls) for the rapids of the Madawaska River but was renamed in 1850 after Sir Edmund Head, governor of New Brunswick. It was incorporated in 1905. Population: 12,044.

EDO, e'dō, a people inhabiting the area west of the Niger River in the Mid-West state of southern Nigeria. Numbering over 500,000, they speak a language belonging to the Kwa subfamily of the Congo-Kordofanian family.

The Edo are primarily farmers. Their principal food crops are yams and cocoyams, and palm oil products are an important agricultural export. In the early 1960's many Edo workers were attracted to the newly established oil and other industrial enterprises in and near their region.

Originally an offshoot of the Yoruba peoples to the west, the Edo created a strong centralized state in the 12th century. Known as Benin, it expanded by conquest and treaty into the powerful kingdom found by the Portuguese in the late 15th century. The oba (king), his elaborate court, and a complex government were located in Benin city, which was favorably compared with major European cities by visitors in the 17th century. Internal dissension, the diversion of the prosperous slave trade to other areas, and the growth of powerful rival states brought about the decline of the kingdom of Benin after the 18th century. But Benin's former glory is reflected in its art, such as the famous Benin bronze castings. Today, Benin is the capital of the Mid-West state.

ROBERT A. LYSTAD, *The Johns Hopkins University*

EDO PERIOD, e-dō, an era of Japanese history, from 1603 to 1867, when Japan was ruled by the Tokugawa shogunate in Edo (present-day Tokyo). In 1600, Tokugawa Ieyasu, the most powerful daimyo in Japan, emerged victorious over his rivals at the Battle of Sekigahara, and in 1603 he received the title of shogun (q.v.) from the politically impotent emperor in Kyoto. The Tokugawa family thenceforth held land that produced approximately one quarter of the nation's rice yield; directly administered a number of important cities and other key economic and strategic locations; and exercised military hegemony over some 260 daimyos (q.v.), all of whom ruled their own nearly autonomous provincial domains.

After a period of adjustment, the Tokugawa shogunate became a highly conservative regime. Politically, it sought to prevent the formation of potentially dangerous daimyo leagues; socially, it attempted to maintain sharp class divisions among the samurai (q.v.), peasants, artisans, and merchants; and intellectually, it utilized Neo-Confucianism to inculcate values deemed appropriate for a hierarchically structured, predominantly agrarian state. Moreover, in order to restrict and control overseas trade, to prevent further political and military entanglement with European countries, and to proscribe Christianity, the shogunate instituted a national seclusion policy that limited foreign contact to dealings with the Dutch and Chinese at Nagasaki.

Despite these measures aimed at sustaining an unchanging national order, there was considerable economic and commercial growth during the Edo period. Merchants prospered and gave rise to Japan's first bourgeois culture in the great urban centers of Edo, Osaka, and Kyoto. Western scientific knowledge and ideas also filtered in through the Dutch. Incapable of meeting the challenge of a renewal of Western intrusion in the 1850's, the shogunate finally succumbed to the pressures of a coalition of samurai who effected the Meiji Restoration in 1868.

H. PAUL VARLEY, *Columbia University*

EDOMITES, ēd'ə-mīts, a Semitic tribe that inhabited the area southeast of the Dead Sea from the 12th to the 6th century B.C. About the beginning of the Iron Age, a major migration of Semitic peoples dispossessed the nomads in the lands to the east of the Jordan River and to the southeast of the Dead Sea. The migrants then settled down as separate tribes: Amorites, Ammonites, Moabites, and (south of the Zered watercourse) Edomites. The Edomites encircled the plain of Seir with a series of stout stone fortresses and established Sela, Bozra, and Teiman as principal towns. Edom developed a flourishing agriculture.

The Edomites were frequently involved in conflicts with the Hebrews, who had been hostile ever since they were refused transit privileges through Edom during their migration from Egypt to Palestine (Numbers 20:14–21). Later the Hebrews continually struggled for possession of the rich iron and copper mines in the Arabah Valley and the seaport of Elath (modern Aqaba) on the Gulf of Akabah. Israel under King David annexed Edom and expelled King Hadad. The Edomites later revolted, were again subjugated, and finally won their freedom, in 735 B.C., from Ahaz, king of Judah.

Edom fell into a decline and eventually came under the control of the Babylonians in the 6th century B.C. By the 4th century B.C., the Edomites were themselves displaced from their original territory by the stronger Nabataeans. Some stayed on and were absorbed, other clans joined those who had already pushed north into the parts of Judah vacated because of the Babylonian Exile (see BABYLONIAN CAPTIVITY), and still others crossed to the west of the Arabah Valley, where in Greek times they were known as Idumaeans.

JAMES T. BURTCHAELL, C.S.C.
Notre Dame University, Indiana

EDTA, or ethylenediamine tetraacetic acid, is an organic chelating agent. It is used in the treatment of feed water for steam boilers, in the analysis of metal ions in water solutions, and in certain rust removers, metal cleaners, and boiler scale removers. It is especially useful for determining the concentration of calcium or magnesium ions in hard water and for preventing boiler scale formation.

EDTA is usually used as the sodium salt of the acid, which has the structure:

$$\begin{array}{c}
\text{(1)} \quad \overset{O}{\underset{\|}{C}} \quad H \qquad\qquad\qquad\qquad H \quad \overset{O}{\underset{\|}{C}} \quad \text{(5)} \\
Na^+\!-\!O\!-\!C\!-\!C \qquad\qquad\qquad C\!-\!C\!-\!O\!-\!Na^+ \\
H \quad \text{(3)}\; H\;\; H\; \text{(4)} \quad H \\
N\!-\!C\!-\!C\!-\!N \\
H\;\; H \\
\text{(2)} \quad H \qquad\qquad\qquad\qquad H \quad\quad \text{(6)} \\
Na^+\!-\!O\!-\!C\!-\!C \qquad\qquad\qquad C\!-\!C\!-\!O\!-\!Na^+ \\
\underset{O}{\overset{\|}{}}\quad H \qquad\qquad\qquad H\;\; \underset{O}{\overset{\|}{}}
\end{array}$$

The salt ion has negative charges at positions (1), (2), (5), and (6). There are unshared electron pairs at positions (3) and (4).

Metal ions are strongly attracted to positions (1), (3), (4), and (5), and in some cases to (2) and (6). This creates complex chelated, or clawlike, structures that may involve as many as five rings about one metal ion. These chelated structures are soluble but tie up metal ions so that scale formation cannot occur.

OTTO W. NITZ
Stout State University, Wisconsin

PRESCHOOL STUDENT divides objects into matching sets preliminary to learning basic rules of arithmetic.

EDUCATION

CONTENTS

Section	Page	Section	Page
1. **History of Education**	644	Orthopedic and Other Health Problems	700
The Ancient World	645	Behavioral Deviations	701
The Middle Ages and Renaissance	646	9. **Educational Administration**	703
The Reformation Period	647	10. **Educational Psychology**	707
The 17th–19th Centuries	648	Relationships to General Psychology and the Curriculum	708
The 20th Century	650	Relationships to the Field of Learning	710
2. **Philosophy of Education**	652	Applications to Instruction	714
Educational and Social Philosophy	652	11. **Educational Measurement**	715
Development of Major Themes in Educational Philosophy	653	Kinds of Tests	717
		Test Validity	718
Worldwide Trends and Issues	655	Interpreting Test Scores	718
3. **Education Around the World**	657	Uses of Tests	721
4. **Primary Education**	667	12. **Educational Research**	722
5. **Intermediate Education**	673	13. **Instructional Technology**	727
6. **Secondary Education**	678	New Terminology	727
7. **Post-Secondary Education**	684	Historical Development	728
8. **Education of Exceptional Children**	693	Facilities and Applications	730
The Gifted	694	Developments and Prospects	734
The Mentally Retarded	696	14. **Careers in Education**	735
The Physically Handicapped	697	15. **Glossary of Educational Terms**	737

EDUCATION. In its broadest meaning, education is any process by which an individual gains knowledge or insight, or develops attitudes or skills. *Formal education* is acquired through organized study or instruction, as in a school or college. *Informal education* arises from day-to-day experiences or through relatively unplanned or undirected contacts with communications media, such as books, periodicals, motion pictures, radio, or television.

The function of education is both social and individual. Its social function is to help each individual become a more effective member of society by passing along to him the collective experience of the past and present. Its individual function is to enable him to lead a more satisfying and productive life by preparing him to handle new experiences successfully.

"Education" is also the name given to that science or branch of study that deals historically and contemporaneously with the principles and practices of teaching and learning. The present article constitutes a survey of education in this sense of the term.

The outline of this 98-page article is shown in the table of contents above. Although each section is a logical unit, many sections are interrelated. For example, the sections on the philosophy of education and the history of education complement each other. The discussion of primary education necessarily meshes with the description of the next level, intermediate education, and intermediate with secondary. Cross-references in each section direct the reader to relevant discussions in other sections.

In addition, many articles in other parts of the encyclopedia extend the discussion of education. For example, the history of all levels of education in major countries is summarized in the country articles—for instance, in GREAT BRITAIN AND NORTHERN IRELAND—*Education*. A special topic in the history of education is surveyed in COEDUCATION.

Additional information on the philosophy of education may be found in entries on great theorists such as Plato, John Amos Comenius, Jean Jacques Rousseau, and John Dewey.

Section 3 of this article entitled *Education Around the World* describes the school systems of representative countries. Each country article has a section or sections on the educational system—for example, CANADA—*Elementary and Secondary Education, Higher Education, Vocational and Adult Education,* and *Government Aid to Education.* Exchanges of students, teachers, and scientists among nations, and other programs to promote world understanding through cultural exchange, are discussed in INTERNATIONAL EDUCATION. That article also covers comparative studies of educational systems.

Section 4. *Primary Education* focuses on the school program that starts with grade 1. In a broad sense, however, primary schooling also encompasses programs for children too young for the first grade. Such programs are described in the separate articles HEAD START PROGRAM, KINDERGARTEN, NURSERY SCHOOLS, and PRESCHOOL EDUCATION.

Information pertinent to levels of schooling from elementary through high school can be found in the separate article CURRICULUM. This article describes such plans as the activity and core curriculums. Areas of instruction and methods of teaching are covered in such entries as CITIZENSHIP EDUCATION, PHYSICAL EDUCATION, READING, SEX EDUCATION, SOCIAL STUDIES, and VOCATIONAL EDUCATION.

The discussion of higher education in section 7 is supplemented by the major article COLLEGES AND UNIVERSITIES, which covers such topics as programs, costs, admissions policies, and history. Also pertinent are the article JUNIOR AND COMMUNITY COLLEGES and other entries such as COSTUME, ACADEMIC and DEGREE. Hundreds of colleges and universities around the world have individual entries. The broad topic of post-secondary education gets additional treatment in ADULT EDUCATION.

Section 8 deals with special programs for varieties of exceptional students—first the gifted and then the handicapped. Additional facts on special education can be found in the entries BLINDNESS and DEAFNESS.

From the discussions of educational psychology and measurement the reader can go to such entries as CHILD DEVELOPMENT and LEARNING. The problem of describing and measuring intellectual ability is treated in the articles INTELLIGENCE and TESTING.

Cross-references at suitable points in this article direct the reader to relevant articles in other volumes. The *Glossary of Educational Terms* also supplies many references. The index in Volume 30 offers a complete listing of entries on education.

The reader who wants to continue his investigation beyond the limits of the encyclopedia will find selected books listed at the end of each major article.

STUART ROSNER/STOCK, BOSTON

Graduate students in archaeology investigate layers of soil, and bag and label findings at an urban "dig."

A relief from a Roman tomb found in Trier, Germany, depicts a teacher and his students in a Roman school.

1. History of Education

Schools as we know them in the late 20th century are of fairly recent origin. Not until the late 19th century were universal primary or elementary systems of education effectively established in some European countries and North America. Very few pupils then moved on to second level schools, and even fewer ever reached the third, or university, level of education.

During the 20th century, particularly since 1945, there has been an enormous expansion of public education. Compulsory schooling lasting from eight to ten years is a fact in most European countries including the USSR, in North America, many parts of the Commonwealth of Nations, and Japan. Elsewhere governments are striving to attain this goal. In many industrialized countries all children attend some kind of second level school to prepare for more education, a profession, or a job in industry or commerce. Opportunities for secondary education in low-income countries lag far behind those in the industrialized nations, but they are growing. Everywhere, since 1945, the proportion of young people attending universities or other institutions of higher education has increased considerably.

UNESCO reports on school enrollments show both the progress made in the 20th century and the need for further expansion of education. In 1950, for example, UNESCO found that in more than 100 countries less than half the school-age population was enrolled in school. Thirty years later the number of these countries had been reduced to fewer than 50.

Changes have also taken place in the material equipment used in education. To be sure, all over the world teachers stand (or sit) with a blackboard behind them and rows of children at desks in front of them. "Chalk and talk" are often the main ingredients of teaching. That schools everywhere tend to look alike is not surprising because their common origin lies in man's command of language and in the many inventions that made it possible for him to accumulate knowledge and pass it on from one generation to the next. Cave paintings, rock carvings, hieroglyphics, ideograms, alphabets, pens, pencils, paper, and printed books illustrate the growth in man's power to accumulate and disseminate information. Modern technology has provided sound recordings, films, and videotapes. Film and slide projectors, radio sets, closed-circuit TV equipment, tape recorders, videocassette recorders, computers, and programmed learning machines are among the devices that have been introduced into schools to improve instruction and extend the range of information passed on to the younger generation.

So great, indeed, has been the explosion of man's knowledge that everywhere one of the most serious problems facing teachers is that of selecting, from an enormous stock of information, what is worth preserving and handing down. Each society makes a decision on the basis of its educational aims. Consequently, national systems differ in important respects. A broad distinction may be drawn, however, between those schools whose principal task is to conserve cherished traditions and those that are regarded as agents of individual and social change. The European educational tradition, based on Plato's rejection of change as undesirable, is broadly conservative. The schools of the United States have been influenced by pragmatic philosophers such as John Dewey, and many educators believe that the schools should be agents of social improvement. In fact schools serve both functions. During some stages of history they have been a dynamic element; at other periods, they have been unduly conservative. Their changing role can best be understood through a study of the many historical ingredients that have made national school systems what they are today.

It is impossible to make a sharp separation between the history of education and the philosophy of education. What the schools have done often reflects what influential thinkers have said they ought to do. On the other hand, many practical problems prevent the full carrying out of any theory of education. Moreover, the schools have been influenced by traditions built up over centuries of experience. This section therefore focuses on history, while another section concentrates on theories (see section *Philosophy of Education*).

ANCIENT WORLD

Modern schools, wherever they are found, owe much to the institutions established in the ancient societies of China, India, and Greece. From them have developed present-day systems, most of which retain the aim of educating individuals for a restricted range of social roles.

China. The ancient Chinese system selected and trained people for public service as state officials. In the 2d century B.C. the schools prepared candidates for carefully graded competitive examinations. Success at each succeeding level qualified a candidate for a higher rank in the civil service.

In village elementary school pupils were taught the three R's. At the second and higher stages pupils learned Chinese history, law, mathematics, finance, military affairs, and agriculture as well as ceremonial etiquette and dancing. Classical literature, particularly the works of Confucius, dominated the curriculum. Rules of behavior for sons, wives, and daughters and for kings and ministers of state were laid down in great detail.

The classics had to be learned by heart—perhaps because of language difficulties. Picture words or ideograms form the written language, and some 1,500 of them have to be memorized in order to read a Chinese newspaper. The scholar must know the meaning of many thousand more ideograms. Since many spoken languages or dialects of China bear little relation to the official written language, Mandarin, education had a bookish character.

Many features of this system of schools made it a conservative force. Respect for the past and for elders, learning by heart, careful selection of candidates for high office, reverence for teacher and parent, and the authority of sacred texts fostered by the schools—all these helped to prevent change and to maintain a hierarchical social structure. In spite of these limitations, the methods of selecting civil servants in France, Britain, and elsewhere by public competitive examinations— and the concepts of public service associated with the bureaucracies in these countries—owe much to the Chinese examination system and code of behavior.

India. Ancient Hindu education was based upon the sacred Vedas, the oldest of which are said to have been composed about 1200 B.C. According to Vedic literature, God is everywhere and has to be worshiped through nature. The position of the sacred cow in India need only be mentioned to illustrate some conservative features of Hindu education.

The caste system, closely linked as it is with education, also inhibits change and divides society on the basis of heredity and occupation. Many subdivisions grew out of the four original castes—Brahmans, who were priests and teachers; Kshatriyas, who were warriors and rulers; Vaisyas, who were merchants and traders; and Sudras, who were the artisans and laborers. Caste training was planned to prepare individuals for their jobs in life. Writing and arithmetic and some legendary lore were taught to all classes except the lowest. Members of the warrior caste were trained in martial discipline and the customs of the society. Brahmans studied the sacred Vedas, religious practices, and national traditions.

Parishads, or collegiate institutions of learning, attracted many thousands of students to open-air gatherings, but the house of the *guru* (priest-teacher) was the most important educational center. Here, over a period of some 12 years, worthy students from many parts of the country received an all-round education as members of the household. Physical health and moral virtue were cultivated through constant and close contact between teacher and taught. Teaching was by the oral method, and the Vedas were memorized. Writing was practiced in the sand, but when the pupil had acquired some skill he wrote on palm leaves with an iron point.

This method of teaching and learning was necessarily authoritarian and depended heavily on memory. Today the tradition persists among Indian students, who are able to commit whole textbooks to memory for examination purposes. The effects of caste and religion on Hindu education, combined with the oral tradition of teaching, the lack of technical aids, and the content and authority of the Vedas tend to favor the transmission of slowly accumulated knowledge rather than to encourage individual initiative and creativity. Consequently—in spite of possessing before the Arabs themselves the so-called Arabic system of numeration with all its advantages for computation—the Hindus were many centuries behind Europeans in the development of astronomy and the scientific instruments needed for precise measuring.

During the 6th century B.C., Buddha rejected caste and wandered up and down the Ganges Valley teaching that all men are equal and that life is full of pain and sorrow from which escape is possible through the right kind of education. The followers of Buddha established monasteries or temples to educate the masses. Emphasis was on character training and the cultivation of the mind through meditation. Strict rules were laid down about taking life, telling lies, dressing, eating and drinking, and singing and dancing. Scant attention was paid to physical education.

Greece. Greek education, in contrast, paid great attention to physical training. Its contribution to educational theory and practice was, however, its emphasis on the all-round development of individuals insofar as this was compatible with social stability and well-being. Its purpose was to develop moral freedom and a love of knowledge for its own sake so that people could think for themselves and act responsibly, particularly in affairs of state. The political needs of an elitist society were strongly emphasized.

The two best-known Greek educational theorists were Plato and Aristotle. Plato's *Republic* took Sparta as the model of an ideal society in which the workers were simply to learn a suitable trade, the warriors were to learn music and gymnastics, and guardians were to be trained in philosophy, the sciences, and metaphysics. These philosopher-kings were to rule what Plato hoped would be a stable, unchanging society. The society Aristotle had in mind was a democratic city-state in which a minority enjoyed the rights of citizenship. Education, as a branch of politics, was only for prospective citizens whose potential was to be developed through physical, moral, and intellectual training in that order. The end of education was moral virtue, and the achievement of virtue ought to be the goal of society.

Spartan Schools. Down to about 150 B.C., the most famous systems of education were those of Sparta and Athens. The schools of Sparta were run by the state for the purpose of making each eligible individual the ideal soldier—physically perfect, courageous, and willing to obey the laws without question. From birth, children were under the supervision of the state. For the first seven years of life they were given a hardy training by their mothers. From the age of 7 to 11 was a period of elementary education when boys went to school during the day for physical education and games. At the age of 12 they went to boarding schools, and at 15 they began a 4-year course of military service.

There was very little intellectual training in Spartan education. It contained elements of reading and writing, but the curriculum consisted chiefly of military drill, hunting, riding, swimming, scoutcraft, and hard work under the careful supervision of older boys and adults. National songs, dances, and poems were taught. Conditions in the boarding schools were hard in order to make boys tough and brave. Discipline was harsh and flogging frequent. Not until they were 30 could men become citizens or warriors; at this age they were obliged to marry. Girls stayed at home, and though trained like the boys to wrestle, run, and throw the discus, their role was to bear strong soldier sons.

Not surprisingly, this limited kind of education sowed the seeds of its own and society's destruction. Yet the Spartan schools have been influential. Conditions of life in an English boarding school are often Spartan in some respects. In the past, Eton, Harrow, and other famous "public" schools put great emphasis on games in the hope that leadership qualities would be developed on the playing fields.

Athenian Schools. The schools of Athens were different from those of Sparta. Although physical education was emphasized, the chief aim of education was aesthetic—to develop a cultured soul in a graceful body. At first, Athenian education remained private, aristocratic, and for the wealthy, but as time went by most parents sent their boys to school. The fundamentals of the curriculum were gymnastics and music—the former for the body, the latter for the soul. Between the ages of 7 and 14 boys went to the *palaistra* for physical education and to music schools for musical and simple literary instruction. For the majority, education stopped at 14; only sons of the wealthy went further. In the gymnasium they were taught different sports—wrestling, boxing, the long jump, running, and discus throwing—and took part in some of the social and cultural activities of civil life. Later, special military service education was introduced for youths between 18 and 20.

A new form of Athenian education developed in the 5th and 4th centuries B.C. It arose in part through criticism by men such as Aristophanes, Plato, and Isocrates of existing education in Athens. The Sophists were the pioneers of this new type of education. They were teachers who introduced the lecture method of teaching and who elaborated rhetoric and oratory. One group trained young people in the art of public speaking. Isocrates, who was the most successful of these rhetorical teachers, did much to make Athens the intellectual center of the world. The other group trained young people to discuss and debate ethical questions in an organized manner. The most famous of these philosophical schools were Plato's Academy and Aristotle's Lyceum.

Thus, in the second phase of Athenian education, a previous emphasis on physical education gave way to an approach that involved intellect, aesthetic awareness, and moral consciousness.

The traditions of this period have been very influential. A little over a century after Aristotle's death the habits and customs of the Greeks were coloring the lives of Persians, Jews, Egyptians, and Romans. Alexandria became the most outstanding of the new centers of learning that derived their inspiration from Athens.

Jewish Schools. Prior to this Hellenistic period, Jewish education had been based on the view that the God of the Jews was a moral and national God who regulated His dealings with His people on the basis of moral principles. Education was consequently intended to make men wise by training them to know and follow the laws of Moses and to understand national history. Teaching was primarily the responsibility of parents. Paradoxically, the Jews adopted a Hellenic institution—the school—to protect them from Greek influence.

Rome. Roman education also felt the impact of Greek culture. Down to 250 B.C., Rome knew no Greek influence; from 250 B.C. to 146 B.C., Greek influence began and gradually increased; and from 146 B.C. to the fall of the empire the culture of Rome was virtually Graeco-Roman. Little is known of the first period except that education was provided in the home, was very practical, and aimed at forming the good citizen through the study of war, politics, law, and oratory.

After Greece became a Roman possession in 146 B.C., scholars, books, and art treasures were taken to Rome. A new form of education emerged, which nevertheless retained its practical purpose. The elementary school, which taught the three R's, could be entered at the age of 6 or 7. Discipline was severe, and corporal punishment was common. Boys could enter grammar school at the age of 12. Grammar and literature were stressed, and while at first Greek learning was popular, Latin literature later gained in prestige. Still later, arithmetic, music, geometry, and astronomy were introduced. After completing the grammar school at about 16 years of age, a boy could proceed either to military service or the rhetorical school, where he learned to be a lawyer or statesman.

With the decline of the empire, the value of this kind of training diminished. Education became formal and artificial, but still served as a model for Europe. Many centuries had to elapse before the schools could again serve as agents of social change.

THE MIDDLE AGES AND RENAISSANCE

For centuries after the fall of Rome, education in Christian Europe was exclusively in the hands of the clergy. Learning was restricted and fixed in accordance with the interests and dogmas of the church. Secular literature was regarded with great suspicion in the monastic schools until the 11th century. Subsequently, it had to be painfully rediscovered as part of the renaissance of secular learning, which was accompanied by an explosion of scientific knowledge and innumerable social, economic, and political innovations.

The Beginning of the New Learning. The revival of learning in Europe dates from approximately 1000 A.D. The cities of Italy, and later those in northern Europe, began to attract students for the study of medicine, law, and theology in their universities. The universities in Bologna, Paris, and Oxford became models for the rest of Europe.

There were differences of emphasis, but a common starting point was the two-stage liberal arts curriculum: the trivium—grammar, rhetoric, and dialectics (or logic)—and the *quadrivium*—music, arithmetic, geometry, and astronomy. Another feature of the early universities was the role of lecturers. At a time when printing from movable type was still unknown and manuscripts were rare, a teacher who combined knowledge and a gift of exposition attracted students from all over Europe to hear him. The tradition of the lecture in university teaching remains strong.

Out of the revival of learning arose two tendencies. One was a move toward national differences in education, and the second was a move away from the domination of the church in educational matters. Man rather than God became central to humanist doctrines, which emerged first in Italy in the 14th and 15th centuries and later in northern Europe. Erasmus, born in 1466 in Rotterdam, believed that the classics would aid rather than hinder moral training. His admiration for the aristocratic social and political institutions of the ancients made him use them as models for the modern world, so that his educational proposals were not geared to the needs of ordinary working and middle-class men and women. He failed to recognize that Latin as a medium of instruction and classical literature as content were not enough to make a useful curriculum. Yet his criticisms of schools make him an influential figure in educational history.

Subsequently, humanism and conservative religion became more sharply contrasting, and as time went on classical and scientific humanism emerged. These dichotomies—together with the older one between education for an elite and training for the masses—have dominated educational debate from the Renaissance on. The religious-secular issue has influenced control of the schools; classics-science controversies have affected curriculum policies.

THE REFORMATION PERIOD

Protestant School Reforms. Within the sphere of church-related education the Reformation had momentous consequences. After Martin Luther broke with the Roman Catholic Church early in the 16th century, one of his concerns was to reconstruct education. He translated the Bible into German so that the common people could study it. He proposed that the new church and municipal authorities take over the schools. He wanted schooling to be provided at public expense for all children, regardless of sex or social class. His broader curriculum was to include languages, history, singing, and mathematics.

Protestant princes and scholars in Germany responded to Luther's demands. City and town universities and higher schools were established, but popular schooling developed more slowly. When the idea that a humanistic culture must depend on the writings of Greece and Rome became fixed, formalism developed and the schools were not able to respond to the needs of society.

The influence of another 16th century Protestant leader, John Calvin, spread from Geneva to France, Holland, England, Scotland, and America. He recognized the importance of schools as agents of religion and made their central purpose knowledge of the word of God. The vernacular and secular subjects were introduced as handmaidens to this aim.

In Scotland these educational ideals were most fully realized. John Knox proposed that every church in a town of any size should appoint a schoolmaster to teach grammar and Latin. The universities were to be the pinnacle of a system that would enable a clever pupil—whether rich or poor—to learn to read, go on to the town grammar school to study grammar and Latin for three years, and then attend a higher school or a college for logic, rhetoric, and the ancient languages. He would complete his studies in dialectics, mathematics, and natural philosophy at the university.

Catholic Education. Roman Catholic educators responded to the educational challenge of Protestantism. The Jesuit system of education was pioneered by a Spanish nobleman, Ignatius of Loyola. In 1534 his Society of Jesus was formed to combat heresy and to promote the interests of the Catholic Church through higher education. The system of schools was organized on military lines under the control of a general of the society, responsible only to the pope. A strong organization was established all through Italy, Portugal, Spain, France, and Belgium.

Jesuit schools and colleges catered to an elite. Lower schools lasted six years. Students entered at the age of 10 or 12, and the curriculum stressed Latin and Greek grammar and literature. Higher studies for three years followed. Higher education included philosophy, rhetoric, dialectics, and some metaphysics. Beyond this there were two advanced courses: a 4-year course in theology that prepared students to preach, or a 6-year course in philosophy that trained teachers. The curriculum changed slowly, and not until 1832 were subjects such as history, geography, elementary mathematics, and science added. Teaching methods were thorough. They depended on oral

UNIVERSITY OF PARIS instructor leads scholars in a discussion, in this engraving from about 1400.

THE BETTMANN ARCHIVE

THE MEDIEVAL MONASTERY schools were important centers of education during the Middle Ages. Chief subjects of instruction were church music and Latin.

THE BETTMANN ARCHIVE

questioning, memorization, and competition. Teachers were chosen with care, and their preparation was superior to that of most teachers of that period.

Although at first the Jesuit system was ahead of its time, as generations went by its inflexibility and lack of interest in individual needs made it a conservative force. Many of its features were incorporated into national systems, such as the French, when secular nationalistic movements closed down the Jesuit schools.

To offset the educational monopoly of the Jesuits, two teaching congregations—the Order of the Oratory of Jesus and the congregation of Port Royal—set up schools of a different style. The Oratorians and the Port Royalists believed in the doctrine of original sin; consequently, they thought education should watch over the behavior of the individual and train his mind. The Little Schools of Port Royal, organized in France in 1646, had a short life, yet the principles on which they were run remain influential. They admitted girls as well as boys, and their classes were small. These schools intentionally did not compete with university-oriented secondary schools. Great emphasis was placed on French language and literature. Competition was played down. Finally, the personal qualities of the teacher were rated more important than his knowledge of subject matter. His teaching was to be based on his intimate understanding of the nature (or psychology) of children and on the needs of each of them. Methods of teaching emphasized the value of play. There was less concern with the rules of grammar than with the ability of young people to translate from one language to another.

The Oratorians, too, were innovators in that their schools were child-centered and placed less emphasis on intellectual development than had previously been the case. Their influence persists in many modern nonreligious progressive movement in education.

THE 17TH TO 19TH CENTURIES

Following the Reformation came a period marked by the planning of national systems of education. Trends in the 17th and 18th centuries can be illustrated by the ideas of a 17th century Bohemian educator, John Amos Comenius.

Comenius' Influence. One of the greatest of educational thinkers, Comenius received invitations from Sweden and England to advise on educational policy. His position on schooling was near to that of Luther. He advocated a system of universal education that would meet the needs of rich and poor, boys and girls, nobles and commoners, and townsmen and villagers. He held that instruction should fit the child and not the reverse. His curriculum was to embrace all useful knowledge, which, he argued, came not through words but things. His book, *The World in Pictures*, attempted to present visually all the fundamental activities of life. For many years it was the only school book with pictures.

Comenius was a great educational innovator. He wanted to extend education to everyone, and he wanted a far wider curriculum. He refused to regard learning the classics as of central educational importance. He proposed new, more active methods of teaching and learning.

Colonial American School Laws. As early as 1642 and 1647, in colonial America, the Massachusetts Bay Colony passed laws requiring townships to teach the three R's, build elementary schools, and establish high schools. The laws were never fully effective, but they show realization of the need to educate all citizens.

Prussian Legislation. In Prussia laws relating to the compulsory attendance of children (in schools) were passed between 1713 and 1717. They provided eventually for a centrally organized and financed system of schools. Later, part-time teaching was made illegal, and finally a teacher training school was set up at Stettin. In 1737, regulations were issued dealing with the construction, maintenance, and fiscal management of schools. By 1740 some 1,800 schools had been established. Between this date and 1786 more educational laws were passed relating to compulsory attendance (boys and girls between the ages of 5 and 13 were to attend), and to curriculums, textbooks, fees, grants, and the licensing of teachers.

Other achievements in Prussia during the 18th century were the establishment of an examination system for the academic secondary schools, the taking over by the state of schools and universities from the control of the church, and the creation of teacher training centers. Nineteenth century observers of the Prussian system admired many aspects of it. Others pointed to practical deficiencies in equipment and to the narrow age of children who were included.

JOHANN HEINRICH PESTA-LOZZI (1746–1827), Swiss educational reformer, teaching in one of the humanitarian school-orphanages that he founded.

THE BETTMANN ARCHIVE

French Plans for Universal Education. Toward the end of the 18th century many plans for universal systems of national education were proposed in France, reflecting the broad views of Comenius. One important motive was to get rid of church control. A famous plan was proposed in 1763 by an opponent of the Jesuits, Louis de La Chalotais. The secularization of education was his chief aim. He argued that the church should abandon to state schools the teaching of morals and the control of purely human studies. Schools should prepare students for practical and professional life. The core of the curriculum should be the natural sciences. French rather than Latin should be studied, and modern history should be made important.

In many respects La Chalotais anticipated policies of free and compulsory education put forward during the Revolutionary period in France. Many schemes were drawn up, but that which the Marquis de Condorcet presented to the Legislative Assembly in 1792 offers a basis for discussing 19th century educational developments not only in France but in many other countries. Condorcet envisaged a school system that would make education as equal and as universal as possible. He proposed five stages: primary schools, secondary schools, institutes, *lycées,* and the National Society of Arts and Sciences.

The first stage was to enable individuals to know their rights and be capable of performing their duties. Every village of 400 inhabitants was to have a school providing a 4-year course for children from 6 years of age to 10. The curriculum was to consist of the three R's, elementary surveying, industrial techniques, rules of conduct, and physical education.

Secondary schools were to be established first in towns or districts with 4,000 or more inhabitants. Ultimately, this stage was to be made available to all. The curriculum was to include mathematics, natural history, applied chemistry, ethics, social science, elementary commerce, and possibly a foreign language. The course was to last three years.

The third stage, which was to last from 13 years of age to 18, was to be provided in 110 institutes. The curriculum—emphasizing science and practical subjects—was to teach students what they needed to know in order to function as effective citizens and to give them a professional education.

There were to be nine *lycées* to train professional men and future scholars. One person in 1,600 was thought to be capable of benefiting from a *lycée* course.

The National Society of Arts and Science, as the fifth stage, was to be composed entirely of scholars and was to be free from any government control, with absolute liberty of opinion. The society was to organize lectures and meetings open to the public in Paris and the provinces.

The object of this selective system of schools was to provide a minimum education for all and to pick out—irrespective of wealth—and train an aristocracy of talent for positions of national leadership. To this end primary and higher education were to be free and scholarships were to enable poor but deserving pupils to attend an institute and a lycée. In the United States, Thomas Jefferson submitted almost identical proposals for his own state of Virginia.

Emergence of a Three-Level System. In fact, a three-level system of education began to emerge in most countries of Europe and in America. The first level was for all children, continuing for some up to the age of about 14. At the second level, a proportion of young people went either to academic schools (for the few) or to vocational schools. Students who successfully completed a full course at an academic school were qualified to attend universities and other institutions of higher learning.

The characteristics of the second and third levels varied considerably from one country to another, but two issues were universal. One concerned the variety of schools at the second level of education. The second issue was the extent to which science should find a place in the curriculum of the academic schools in the face of the heavy emphasis on the classical languages and, after these, on modern languages.

In England, elementary education was offered first in charity schools, which later adopted the monitorial system of self-teaching. Then church schools developed with the help of government money. Finally, after about 1870, elementary schools were financed and run by local school boards. Secondary schools were for the most part private until 1902. To the great "public" schools such as St. Paul's, Winchester, Harrow, Eton, and Charterhouse were added in the 19th century a great many more "public" schools for the sons of the growing middle classes. Matthew

Arnold, while an English school inspector, deplored the absence of state secondary schools.

In France the revolutionary government failed to establish a system of universal education. But the education law of 1833 placed an obligation on each local community to maintain an elementary school. The *communes* failed to finance these schools, and only much later was universal compulsory and lay elementary education achieved. Academic secondary schools, known as *lycées*, were established by Napoleon. They were state maintained and controlled, prepared students for the universities, and placed great emphasis on classical studies. Throughout the century educational authorities debated the position of science in the curriculum.

In Germany elementary schools for pupils between the ages of 6 and 14 developed. A second, or middle, level of education also emerged, divided into academic schools and a variety of nonacademic vocational schools. Access to the university could be obtained only through the academic school—the *Gymnasium*. Efforts to reduce the classical emphasis led to the growth of *Realschulen*, which provided a somewhat more practical curriculum. Technical studies were offered in a variety of different technical schools.

Many critics of the system maintained that the schools were too closely geared to growing manpower needs. Certainly personnel were prepared for positions at all levels within the German bureaucracy.

Patterns similar to the German one grew up in the Scandinavian countries, Austria, Yugoslavia, the Netherlands, and some other countries during the 19th century.

Developments in the United States took still another form. The principle of local, "common" elementary schools was widely accepted by about 1850 as a result of the work of such men as Horace Mann. The growth of local public schools continued at a rapid rate, and private schools declined. The public schools were more nonsectarian in outlook and control than European schools. They were intended primarily to provide a common background for young Americans whose parents came from many different national and social backgrounds. A striking feature of U.S. education was the rise of public high schools and the enormously rapid growth in their enrollments after 1870. This pressure of numbers made adjustments in the curriculum very necessary. Emphasis on classical language studies declined, and an already present practicalism gained ground. This foreshadowed a radically new conception of curriculum organization that emerged in the early 20th century. It involved the selection of material on the basis of the problems that students were likely to face when they left school rather than on a choice of subjects from among the traditional or new disciplines.

THE 20TH CENTURY

Toward the close of the 19th century the emphasis in education in various countries differed. The French schools were noted for their attention to intellectual development based on principles of logical, rational thinking derived from Descartes. The German schools, influenced by Hegel and by Wilhelm von Humboldt's concept of liberal education, stressed another, more intuitional, form of intellectualism. One influence of men such as Thomas Arnold of Rugby School was that the English secondary schools felt that moral character was more important than intellectualism. In the United States the needs of democracy faced with an influx of millions of immigrants were given priority.

In spite of these differences of emphasis, the Aristotelian dichotomy between general education and practical training dominated most of 19th century thinking and forms of organization. For the most part, educators in Europe firmly believed that the classics, mathematics, and modern languages should form the core of a sound general education. Technical subjects and vocational training were relegated to separate schools of less prestige, under different administrative control, and offering no preparation for students who wanted to go on to a university. Even the pure natural sciences were admitted with reluctance to the curriculum of the academic secondary schools. As the schools began to serve more pupils, however, the need for curriculum reform became more pressing. The 20th century, therefore, has been a period of debate over structural changes in the school system and directions for curriculum reform.

Reforms After World War I. World War I was a landmark in school reform. Immediately after its conclusion and during the 1920's reformers in France, under the leadership of Paul Langevin, campaigned unsuccessfully for an *école unique*—a secondary school for all children from 11 to 15 that would have a curriculum more suited to the times. In Germany plans to establish similar comprehensive secondary schools (*Einheitsschulen*) were put forth under the Weimar Republic, but they never materialized. Obstacles included economic conditions, the built-in opposition of the academics, and the policies of the Hitler period. In England, after 1902, free places were made available in the academic secondary schools for clever 11-year-old elementary school pupils, many of whom came from working-class backgrounds. Educational opportunity was in fact extended without radical changes in the organization of the second level school system.

In most systems the primary schools or first level of education for children from 5 (as in England), 6 (in France and Germany), or 7 (in Scandinavia and the USSR) to either 10, 11, or 12 years of age was unified for all children in the publicly maintained schools. Differentiation of school types at the second level of education was still very much the general pattern of organization up to World War II except in the United States and the Soviet Union. In the United States some school systems had an 8-year common elementary school followed by a 4-year high school with academic and vocational tracks. Others had primary school, followed by an intermediate or junior high school, and then a 3-year senior high school. The Soviet authorities were establishing a common 10-year school based on seven years of compulsory education.

The curriculums of the different types of second level schools in Europe varied considerably. The academic secondary schools of Europe (the *lycée* in France, the *Gymnasium* in Germany, Scandinavia, Austria, and the Netherlands) still strongly emphasized classical languages. In English grammar schools, where the curriculum was made up of a very restricted number of subjects, Greek was on the decline, and Latin, although important still, became less popular compared with history, modern languages, and English. Vocational schools in Europe offered a core of

An early public school, in Colrain, Mass., opens for instruction in 1812. Local public schools grew rapidly in 19th century America.

general subjects, with an increasing proportion of time devoted to technical and commercial subjects as the course progressed. Some of these courses were intended to train young people for a specific occupation. Students in the French vocational schools were trained for an enormously wide range of jobs at various levels within the occupational structure. In England, educators firmly kept vocational training out of the schools at the second level. Such training was reserved for part-time evening classes in institutions of further education. In the USSR a 10-year common school was set up, but after the 1930's great attention was paid to studies that would prepare students for training in science and technology at the third level of education.

In general the interwar period in Europe was one of much discussion about changes in the second stage of education but of little achievement.

Programs After World War II. After World War II, programs to reform the second level again stressed the need for a common or comprehensive secondary school. The Labour party in Britain pressed this form of organization on the Local Educational Authorities under the 1944 Education Act, which made possible a wide range of organizational choices. In France the Langevin-Wallon committee also proposed comprehensive second level schooling. Reform proposals were submitted frequently to the parliament with no success until comprehensive reform legislation was passed under the regime of President de Gaulle in 1959. In practice the proposals to have a 2-year period of orientation and guidance for pupils entering the second level of education did not work out very well. The power and prestige of the *lycée* teachers effectively prevented radical changes in the curriculum in these first two years.

Sweden's reforms of 1962—a 9-year comprehensive school followed by increasingly differentiated programs of study—were based on extensive research but nevertheless met considerable opposition. Norway was also able to legislate for a somewhat similar kind of comprehensive school. In Germany postwar reforms included the Bremen and Rahmen plans, which were intended to postpone by one year the age at which children made a choice of an academic or vocational track. The same principle of postponing selection lay behind reforms in the Netherlands and Denmark.

The difficulties of making proposals for reform effective in practice are immense. Educational change is opposed by vested interests within education, by some political parties, often by groups of parents, and sometimes by churches.

There is no doubt that postwar opinion has moved toward the belief that educational opportunity should not be based on the social class background or family income of pupils. The belief that ability alone should determine the level a pupil reaches in the educational system is now widely accepted. This ideal has led people to propose common second level schools and more widely useful curriculums. Pressures have increased to provide higher education for a larger proportion of young people.

Some of the problems of education can be illustrated by the experience of Soviet educators with curriculum change. The program was overloaded, heavily biased toward science and technology, and highly academic in emphasis. Reform movements culminating in the 1958 education law attempted to redress the balance between intellectual and manual training. It was hoped that stressing vocational tasks would produce general education suited to a 20th century Communist society. Learning about the activities of industry, agriculture, and commerce was expected to give children an all-around education that would enable them to be worthy citizens. Similar hopes lie behind many educational proposals put forward in the United States.

Indeed, one of the major dilemmas for educators in the latter part of the 20th century was finding a way to break down the centuries-old dichotomy between education and training; intellectual pursuits retained high prestige, and manual work was frequently despised. The other task was to provide equality of educational opportunity for boys and girls irrespective of race, social class background, and economic position.

These issues had not been resolved even in the wealthier nations, and they plagued the developing countries, whose systems of education were for the most part copies from those of Europe. The imperial powers transplanted, as a matter of policy (in the case of France) or be-

2. Philosophy of Education

The philosophy of education—ideas about what education ought to do and how to do it—can never be neatly separated from the history of education. The same names, from Plato to John Dewey, occur in debates over what the schools should achieve and in reports of what the schools have, in fact, accomplished. Still it is important to pick out for special study some of the major themes that have been set up as goals for education. This section can be read in conjunction with section *1. History of Education* to balance educational aims against practices.

EDUCATIONAL PHILOSOPHY AND SOCIAL PHILOSOPHY

The aims of education can be derived from the writings of social philosophers. Most of them have had something to say, either directly or implicity, about education. Philosophers have examined man's relationship to society and analyzed the role that education ought to play in preparing young people to enter adult society and to participate in it. Different patterns of belief have emerged from these writings and have given rise to further discussion and debate. A number of issues are perennial. The kind of answers given to the questions these issues raise largely determine the aims of education. Historical and national philosophical traditions have influenced the answers and no single philosophy can serve as the source of social and educational aims.

Each philosophy of education represents a coherent pattern of beliefs or theories about education and its relationships to man and society. This pattern provides general guidelines for establishing educational systems. One task of the philosopher of education is constantly to examine the assumptions on which his view of education's roles is based; he looks for inconsistencies and strives to reformulate his concepts so as to achieve greater coherence and logical consistency. In order to do so he has to examine the terminology of educational discussion and make meaningful the words used. How can we educate for "democracy" or "freedom" or "economic betterment" unless we know what is meant by the terms used? How can we develop wiser and better individuals unless we have a clear notion of what constitutes the "good and wise person"? How can we work toward the achievement of any educational aims unless we know what these are and can accept them and understand them within a framework of social, political, and economic goals? In other words, any philosophy of education should be examined in the light of relevant social-philosophical and social-psychological theories. Broadly speaking, some philosophers have stressed the importance of society and provided social-centered aims for education, while other philosophers have emphasized child-centered aims. It is the task of philosophers of education to make clear not only the aims of education but their relationship with other social ideals.

Beliefs About Man and Society. Through the ages most philosophers have supported their highest aspirations about man and the society in which he lives by saying that they were based on knowledge and understanding. Consequently, they and their followers have argued that what man hopes for in terms of his own development and in terms of his way of living with other

RURAL AMERICAN SCHOOLHOUSE of the late 19th century typically accommodated all grades in one room.
SY SEIDMAN

cause they saw no real alternative (in the case of Britain), institutions from their own countries. Consequently, the schools in territories formerly in the French Empire resemble in most details those of France. Schools in countries that were parts of the British Empire are like the schools of England. Such schools may or may not meet the needs of independent countries, which range from teaching adults reading to training doctors and scientists. The models that educators can follow seem to be numerous—at least superficially—but in reality the European prototypes resemble each other in many respects. A new model to which many people now turn is the school system of the United States, both for organization and for curriculums at the three levels of education. This model suggests prospects that the schools will act as agents of desirable change and will work for the best possible development of all children—whether rich or poor, gifted or slow. History shows, however, how difficult it is to realize the highest ideals of men through the schools.

BRIAN HOLMES, *University of London*

Bibliography

Bowen, James, *A History of Western Education*, 3 vols. (St. Martin's 1972–1981).
Boyd, William, and King, Edward J., *The History of Western Education*, 11th ed. (Barnes & Noble 1980).
Connell, W. F., *A History of Education in the 20th Century World* (Teachers College Press 1981).
Cremin, Lawrence A., *American Education: The National Experience, 1783–1896* (Harper 1980).
Evans, Gillian, *Learning in Medieval Times* (Longmans 1974).
Galt, Howard S., *A History of Chinese Educational Institutions* (Heinman 1951).
Gwynne-Thomas, E. H., *A Concise History of Education to 1900* (Univ. Press of America 1981).
Laurie, Simon S., *Historical Survey of Pre-Christian Education* (1900; reprint, Gordon Press 1977).
Marrou, Henri I., *History of Education in Antiquity* (1956; reprint, Univ. of Wis. Press 1982).
Meyer, Adolphe E., *Educational History of the Western World*, 2d ed. (McGraw 1972).
Mookerji, Radhakumud, *Ancient Indian Education*, 5th ed. (Orient Book Distributors 1974).
Neuberg, Victor E., ed. *Eighteenth Century Education: Selected Sources* (Biblio Distribution 1983).
Perkinson, Henry J., ed., *Two Hundred Years of American Educational Thought* (Longmans 1980).
Reeder, D. A., ed., *Urban Education in the 19th Century* (St. Martin's 1978).
Rusk, Robert R., and Scotland, James, *Doctrines of the Great Educators*, 5th ed. (St. Martin's 1979).
Stone, Lawrence, ed., *Schooling and Society: Studies in the History of Education* (Johns Hopkins 1976).
Ulich, Robert, *Education of Nations: A Comparison in Historical Perspective* (Harvard Univ. Press 1967).
Woodward, W. H., ed., *Studies in Education During the Age of the Renaissance* (Teachers College Press 1967).

people are not merely matters of opinion but are based on truths that can be discovered by proper methods on enquiry.

To be sure, opinions have differed about man, society, and knowledge. Is man naturally good or bad? Is he born with certain abilities that can be developed but not changed? Or does the environment in which he grows up determine what kind of man he is, how clever he becomes, and how much he is able to learn? Are all men born equal? Or are some from birth better and cleverer than others? Can only a few men perform certain tasks, or do all men have the capacity to do all things? These questions are still being debated. Since the 18th century, however, there has been a movement of opinion toward the principle that all men are equal, or ought to be treated as equal.

Views about man and his abilities are closely correlated in the writings of philosophers with their views about society and how its affairs should be conducted. Is the "good" society one that ought not to change very much? Or is social change good in itself? Is the best society one in which each person knows his job, fits into his own niche, is happy to do so, and remains there most of his life? Or is the good society one in which individuals are able to move freely from one job to another and can compete for better paid jobs with higher status and prestige? Is the good society one in which a few wise and knowledgeable men—the elite—offer political and cultural leadership? Or ought all men and women to participate actively in the political and cultural life of the society in which they live? Are all men equally capable of becoming leaders? Should leaders inherit from their fathers their position in society? Or should members of any elite be elected to that position? Or should they become members of it by virtue of their superior abilities and knowledge?

The organization of schools depends very much on the answers given. Debates have been endless but the movement toward accepting democratic ideals has been gaining momentum. The peoples of the world expect to participate actively in government. Increasingly they resent kings and princes whose positions are based on the accident of birth. Moreover age, with its accumulated experience and wisdom, is no longer held in the esteem it once was as a criterion of leadership. Technical ability and professional knowledge are replacing qualities previously held in high regard as criteria for positions of social leadership. The democratization of education has consequently become a major aim.

Beliefs About Knowledge. Knowledge is still important. What is it? Who can acquire it? And in what ways can it be taught and learned? Is it a matter simply of rational thinking? Or can knowledge only be acquired by looking at, touching, hearing, or smelling—that is, by observing? Is man's mind or brain the source of his knowledge, or does it depend in the first instance upon his senses? Many philosophers, of course, would argue that both his mind and his senses are involved in learning.

Concepts of this world differ too. For some philosophers it is made of bricks and mortar—of things that can be weighed, measured, and molded to man's needs. It is a world of atoms whose behavior can be studied, and this material world is the one we know. On the other hand, some thinkers have argued that the important and knowable world is the world of ideas and ideals. These do not change and, once known, make wise and good action possible. For many centuries both the materialists and the idealists tended to believe that, in a world of change, men could know those things that did not change. The materialists study indestructible atoms or their parts; the idealists study those ideas that persist and that inform all aspects of our lives.

Sources of Authority. These questions and the answers given to them about the nature of man and society and the nature of knowledge have profoundly influenced the aims of education. Two major sources of authority should be mentioned. The first is religious belief which has almost always been considered a source of truth and wisdom. Primitive religions have many gods who interfere directly in the lives of the people. World religions such as Christianity, Buddhism, and Islam appeal to sacred books as the basis of worthwhile knowledge. Prophets and priests have from time to time interpreted this knowledge afresh, but the basic ideas have remained the same. Each of these religions has given rise to a system of beliefs that includes, as one important element, aims for education.

The second source of authority is man himself. Humanism gives man responsibility for his knowledge; no source outside himself can provide it. To be sure, in observing or thinking about a real world around him he has to depend on carefully developed techniques in order to learn all about it. Nevertheless, according to this view man's knowledge of himself and the society in which he lives does not depend on divine revelation, or sacred books, or the interpretations of specially selected persons. Knowledge can, in theory at least, be acquired by all men. This is the faith of the scientist, and it has become increasingly important since the applications of scientific knowledge to our everyday lives have become so obvious and numerous.

DEVELOPMENT OF MAJOR THEMES IN EDUCATIONAL PHILOSOPHY

A study of the history of educational ideas, of course, shows how many strands have contributed to present thinking and debates in the field of education. Broad patterns of development can, however, be traced by referring to major figures in philosophy. Special attention will be given to the ideas that have influenced the theory and practice of education in Europe and the Americas, but important aims in education can be found in Buddhism, Islam, Hinduism, and Confucianism.

Greek Influences. European-American traditions in education are usually taken to spring from the writings of the classical Greek philosophers, notably Plato and Aristotle. Perhaps of the two, Plato's views on education throw the more light on modern aims of education and current controversies about them. Plato's *Republic* offers a blueprint for the "good" society. Individuals within it inherit from their parents abilities that can and should be developed through education. The all-around development—aesthetic, moral, physical, and intellectual—of individuals according to their individual abilities has long been, and remains, an important aim of education. According to Plato, however, only a few children have the innate potential to benefit from education. These few, the philosopher-kings, should be educated for social responsibility and leadership. Their source of knowledge is a form of intuition. The rest of the people should be trained to perform happily their allotted tasks in a stable society.

Aristotle shared Plato's views in thinking that education should prepare citizens to participate actively in civic affairs. He emphasized logic as the source of knowledge and restricted the content of education to the liberal arts. Education was for the few persons who would constitute his democratic society. The rest, the majority, should be prepared for the manual work.

Developments in Europe. For many centuries in Europe, elitist education remained a strong tradition. The emphasis given to moral, aesthetic, physical, or intellectual development varied, but under the influence of Christian leaders great attention was paid to moral and intellectual education. The aim of education then was to develop a good man and a clever one. Goodness was related to Christian or Judaic ethics; cleverness to theories of knowledge that laid great stress on logic and rhetoric. Aristotelian views still dominated the aims of schooling. Even when humanism began to emerge again after the Middle Ages the emphasis of men such as Erasmus was on the classical writings of Greek and Roman scholars. The curriculum remained largely the seven liberal arts.

The Renaissance and the Reformation. The Renaissance and the Reformation were important turning points in the history of ideas and in the aims of education. The first reintroduced Platonic and other Greek traditions in addition to that of Aristotle. The second was significant because Luther and Calvin, in challenging the power of the Roman Catholic Church, turned from revelation as the fundamental source of knowledge to the written word—the Bible—which all could understand if they were able to read. To be sure, the idea of a moral elite persisted, but the possibility emerged that man could redeem himself through his good works.

The 17th and 18th Centuries. The 17th and 18th centuries witnessed the flowering of two important movements that profoundly influenced the aims of education. The first may be ascribed to the Bohemian scholar Comenius, who extended enormously the range of information he regarded as relevant in education. He also thought that knowledge should be made much more widely available. Moreover, he placed great emphasis on observation as a way of learning, in contrast to the importance the tradition of Aristotle placed on logical thinking. Comenius was religious, a member of a Protestant group, but the tradition in education that he helped to create was taken over by humanists. In some cases these thinkers not only rejected religion as the basis of the aims of education but turned away from the classical curriculum to one more firmly based in the "new" sciences—the physics of Galileo, the chemistry of Boyle, and the mathematics of Descartes, Leibniz, and Newton.

The 18th century encyclopedists stressed that education should open the minds of all people to a broad range of knowledge. With John Milton, the 17th century English poet and philosopher, they stressed the civic purpose of education. Education should, for Milton, prepare a man "to perform generously and magnanimously the offices both public and private of peace and war." In France during the revolutionary period, Condorcet urged the National Assembly to promote education that would enable all citizens to know their rights and to discharge their duties and responsibilities in a democratic society.

Thomas Jefferson in the newly created United States advocated similar aims for education. He thought, of course, that a republican form of government was best. But he did not regard all men as equal except before the law. He maintained that there was a natural aristocracy of talent. The aim of education should be not only to provide the masses with a basic civic education but also to select the talented members of society and train them for leadership.

The other important movement of the 17th and 18th centuries was the growth of nationalism in education. Through the 18th century the authority of the Roman Catholic Church in western Europe and the temporal power of the Holy Roman Empire had helped to set a pattern of education that was, with small but important differences, common to the continent as a whole. The aims were similar; the content and methods of teaching were largely the same.

The political breakup of the Holy Roman Empire was accompanied by greater cultural diversity. Associated with the desire to extend educational provisions more widely was the view that schooling ought to be provided in the vernacular, the language of the people. In France, Descartes helped give French education a unique flavor by writing in the vernacular. His own philosophical ideas, which represented a radical break with tradition, were incorporated into French schools. As a result, French schools developed characteristics that distinguish them sharply from English, German, or Russian schools.

The 19th and 20th Centuries. These movements toward encyclopedic knowledge and the participation of all in the processes of democracy effectively presaged the introduction of mass education and the development of national systems of education. If the 17th and 18th centuries were the seedbed of ideas, the 19th and 20th have been centuries of educational achievement as far as the mass of people are concerned. During the 19th century distinctive national traditions began to emerge. Among the most important are those of France, Germany, England, the United States, and the Soviet Union.

France. The aims of French education during the 19th century remained similar to those enunciated by Condorcet: to provide education for the masses that would enable them to participate effectively in democratic government; to educate members of the elite drawn from the masses for positions of leadership in politics and administration. From Descartes came the view that the best way to prepare Frenchmen for their role in society was through an education that would train them to think clearly, logically, and analytically and would enable them to express their thoughts succinctly. Another aim, expressed by Napoleon, was that a corps of educationists should be built up who were independent of political pressures. The hope was that state *lycées* should educate the elite while local or community elementary schools trained the masses and picked out those pupils who were capable of benefiting themselves and their country by going on to the *lycée*.

Germany. One of the aims of German education was to allow scholars to pursue their studies in freedom—at the price of noninvolvement in politics. At the same time the needs of a growing bureaucracy and the commercial and industrial activities of 19th century Germany had to be met. One aim of German education, consequently, was to educate people for various positions in a differentiated, hierarchical, and industrializing society.

Another aim was to develop the intellectual and academic competence of an elite group. Here the influence of the German philosopher Hegel can be observed. He gave German concepts of scholarship a content of permanent ideas that transcend and yet motivate social processes and individual behavior. Through a heavy emphasis on classical languages, the elite were to penetrate behind appearances to the inner meaning of society and the world. Similarities in the content of education in the French *lycée* and the German *Gymnasium* should not be taken to mean that these schools are based on similar theories of knowledge. The analytical rationalism of Descartes is a far cry from the historicism of Hegel. Both systems, however, can be said to stress intellectual development.

England. English aims of education in the 19th century, on the contrary, stressed moral qualities. Thomas Arnold of Rugby School is regarded as one of the main architects of these aims. They were derived from his concepts of Christianity: a form of ecumenism that took a good deal of the theology and dogma out of church practice. Another base on which he built his theory of education was his concept, derived from John Locke, of the kind of person a gentleman should be and how he should behave. Locke's English gentleman valued leisure above work, was politically minded yet tolerant, and based his knowledge not so much on rational argument as on his observations of the world around him. Arnold, as a practical schoolmaster, established in English education the belief that the good boy or girl, the individual of character, is valued more than the clever person. The gifted amateur became more highly prized than the competent professional. Character training, became the most important aim of education in the "public" schools of 19th century England.

United States. Philosophers in the United States drew together strands from England, France, and Germany and created their own brand of educational theory. The ideas of Jefferson, influenced by French thinkers, have been noted. The American tradition included notions drawn from the English Dissenters who, like Milton, gave the practical pursuits of life an importance not accorded to them by most continental Europeans. In the 18th century, Benjamin Franklin was the American spokesman of practicalism in education, and this emphasis has remained entrenched in American educational aims.

Practicalism could not easily be reconciled with the scholasticism and concepts of academic research taken to the United States from Germany during the 19th century. Many Americans took advanced degrees at German universities and returned impressed by German scholarship and research. During the second half of the century American philosophy was strongly Hegelian. Some of the new American universities owed much of their character to German influences.

Yet another philosophical school of thought influenced Americans during this half century of enormously rapid growth and change. This was the social Darwinism of Herbert Spencer. He applied to social institutions Darwin's theory that those organisms best adapted to their environment survive. The less well adapted perish. Out of this tradition, pragmatism grew as a philosophy of life and education in the United States. It drew into itself the practical aims of Franklin, the political and social aims of Jefferson and Horace Mann, and the social reconstructionism of John Dewey. Perhaps for the first time educational theorists suggested that schools should be direct agents of social change. Traditional aims, from Plato onward, have tended to accord to education the conservative role of transmitting from one generation to the next the accumulated knowledge and wisdom of society. Some pragmatists suggested that the schools could, and should, solve the problems of society by changing or reconstructing it. The schools were, in short, to be the initiators of change.

Commitment to democratic forms of government has characterized the pragmatists. There has also been a commitment to mass participation in the processes of government, backed by an education for democracy. For a leading pragmatist, John Dewey, education should release in individuals their intelligence so as to make democracy work. His aim was to enable individuals to cooperate intelligently in problem-solving situations. The practical implications of his position include a belief that education should be continued for all individuals for as long as possible. The content of such education cannot remain fixed. It must constantly be in process of change, selection being based on the information young people and adults need in order to solve intelligently the problems they face. A further implication of the pragmatic position is that knowledge, however acquired, is never absolute. We "know" something only in a particular situation. Democracy, for example, takes different forms in France, Britain, and the United States. Action is good or bad only in the light of the circumstances under which it is performed. In short, the relativism of Dewey's pragmatism makes itself felt in some of the aims Americans hold for education. Yet in important respects they cling to a traditional belief in the social and economic function of education.

The Soviet Union. Soviet philosophers, working from a different theoretical viewpoint, are also anxious to bring education into a close relationship with life. For them, following Karl Marx, the basis of life is the relationships men and women establish in a factory, on a farm, or in an office. Education consequently should be closely linked with the productive life of society, and schools should train individuals to participate actively in useful work. Only in this way can a truly Communist society be built up. Individuals in this society must be educated in a way that will ensure their all-around development—moral, aesthetic, physical, and mental. Education should inculcate attitudes that will make for harmonious relations between manual workers and intellectuals. Indeed, the crux of the Soviet educationists' case is that any separation between manual training and a so-called liberal education is false. Only through education for, and participation in, work can a person be truly educated. This view, incidentally, is similar to one advanced by John Dewey, who said that a sound general education should be provided through vocational studies.

WORLDWIDE TRENDS AND ISSUES

A survey of the aims of education in Europe and the Americas reveals a measure of consensus. Education should be provided for all children as a human right. It should prepare them for political and economic life. It should continue virtually throughout a person's life and ensure his all-around development. Only if these ends are reached can the quality of society be improved. National differences are largely a matter of emphasis on how these personal and social aims ought to be achieved.

The religious basis of educational aims remains strong in many schools, but emphasis on man's reason and on the possibility of his being educated to behave rationally increases. Ideas of what constitutes rationality vary from one culture to another, depending on the philosophical traditions of the society. Some understanding of the assumptions behind these traditions can be gained by studying representative writers. Plato and Aristotle offer a frame of reference against which European philosophies of education can be seen as a whole. Descartes and Condorcet offer a basis for understanding French aims. Hegel may be taken as one spokesman of German liberal education. John Locke and Thomas Arnold offer a rationale against which present debates in English education may be understood. In the United States, Benjamin Franklin, Thomas Jefferson, and John Dewey are representatives of a continuing tradition.

It should be noted, of course, that selected philosophers do not state fully the aims of the educational systems they have influenced. Present-day aims are frequently expressed in educational legislation or in national institutions. Priorities in education are reflected in major educational laws and in the budget provided for schooling. Careful study of laws and policies makes it possible to discern the philosophical assumptions from which the aims of education in a country are derived.

For example, the United Nations Declaration of Human Rights placed an obligation on member nations to provide universal primary education free of charge and to offer secondary and vocational education on the basis of the ability of children to benefit from it and not on the ability of their parents to pay for it. This declaration of intention was widely accepted. Many newly independent nations and many older countries wrote appropriate clauses into their constitutions or into major educational legislation. Apart from the economic difficulties of implementing such policies, questions of reconciling traditional non-Western educational aims with those of Europe and the Americas have arisen.

In Islamic countries, for example, Western Hellenic-Judaic-Christian philosophies have to be reconciled with the principles laid down in the Koran. The purposes of traditional Muslim education were to teach people the precepts of faith and to help them gain God's favor by living according to His commands in this world and by preparing for the life hereafter. Thus there were strongly theoretical and practical aspects involved in Muslim education. The fact that in practice much rote learning of the Koran goes on in Koranic schools tells rather little about the stated aims of Muslim education.

Buddhism finds its inspiration in the Pali texts, which provide distinct aims for education. Among these are the need to dispel spiritual ignorance and hence suffering. Steps in the path to knowledge include an acceptance of Buddhist principles, a determination to be unselfish, and a sincere desire to eliminate unwholesome tendencies and to think and behave correctly.

The writings of Confucius also provide aims for education. Moral values were central to his view of education's purpose. Benevolence, filial piety, righteousness, propriety, and wisdom are important values.

In summary, it may be said that in most of the great historical traditions, whether religious or secular, aims for education have been expressed by philosophers of distinction or prophets of renown. A philosophy of education includes a coherent set of statements about man and his society.

Modern philosophers of education have spent a great deal of time analyzing the meaning of words used in education. "Authority," "discipline," "individuality," "democracy," and "subject matter" are among the terms that have been considered in great detail. This analytical approach of philosophers of education is somewhat different from the methods of earlier times. Traditionally, scholars in the field commented on the educational ideas of great thinkers, showed how consistent or inconsistent the ideas were, and discussed the relevance of these ideas to current life. Thus, until the second half of the 20th century, most courses in the philosophy of education might more appropriately have been termed "the history of educational ideas." In the 1960's scholars turned away from this approach toward the hard-nosed, systematic study of educational terms in a carefully structured frame of reference.

These trends are not surprising. Even economic and political questions about education lead to theoretical questions. If a country's budget allows it to educate only some of its people, then the issue becomes which people to put first. Without a philosophy of education few questions in education are meaningful. It is the task of philosophers to make them meaningful.

BRIAN HOLMES, *University of London*

Bibliography

Apple, Michael, and Weis, Lois, eds., *Ideology and Practice in Schooling* (Temple Univ. Press 1983).
Barrow, Robin, *Plato and Education* (Routledge & Kegan 1976).
Brent, Allen, *Philosophy and Educational Foundations* (Allen Unwin 1983).
Brubacher, John, *On the Philosophy of Higher Education* (1977; reprint, Jossey-Bass 1982).
Cole, Percival R., *A History of Educational Thought* (1931; reprint, Greenwood 1972).
Dewey, John, *Democracy and Education* (1916; reprint, Darby Books 1982).
Garforth, Frank W., *John Stuart Mill's Theory of Education* (Barnes & Noble Imports 1979).
Hu, C. T., ed., *Chinese Education Under Communism*, 2d ed. (Teachers College Press 1974).
Kneller, George F., *Movements of Thought in Modern Education* (Wiley 1984).
Lord, Carnes, *Education and Culture in the Political Thought of Aristotle* (Cornell Univ. Press 1982).
Okafor, Festus C., ed., *Philosophy of Education and Third World Perspective* (Brunswick Pub. 1981).
Peden, C., and Chipman, D., eds., *Critical Issues in Philosophy of Education* (Univ. Press of America 1979).
Perkinson, H. J., *Since Socrates: Studies in the History of Western Educational Thought* (Longmans 1980).
Peters, R. S., ed., *The Philosophy of Education* (Oxford Univ. Press 1973).
Phenix, Philip H., *Education and the Common Good* (1961; reprint, Greenwood 1977).
Price, Ronald F., *Marx and Education in Russia and China* (Rowman 1977).
Soltis, Jonas F., *Philosophy of Education Since Mid-Century* (Teachers College Press 1981).

Burmese children learning to read. They are pupils at a state primary school located in a small town in Burma.

UNITED NATIONS

3. Education Around the World

A country's network of schools, public and private, at all levels from primary to university, makes up the nation's system of education. In the broad sense, a national system of education also includes libraries, museums, publishers, and all other agencies that transmit knowledge and skills to the people. To say that a country has a national system of education does not necessarily mean that there is one fixed organization for all schools and agencies or that all educational activities are directed by a nationwide authority. Britain, the United States, and Switzerland, for example, do not have centralized educational administrations. However, the presence of a unified aim helps to consolidate the schools in these countries into what may be safely described as a national system. In regard to the question of fixed organization, an American scholar in the field of comparative education, I. L. Kandel, pointed out that no national system of schools "has reached a stage of equilibrium; all are in a state of becoming."

The discipline that studies educational systems around the world is comparative education. The analysis of comparisons and contrasts in the schools of various nations can help educators find solutions to educational problems in their own country. Comparative studies also help international cooperation efforts to promote education.

UNESCO's surveys of world education include descriptions of the educational systems of some 200 countries and territories. It is obviously not possible to summarize the features of all of these systems in this article. The following pages, therefore, will present sketches of the general backgrounds, outlines, and some of the outstanding features of the school systems of a number of representative nations.

Britain. Prior to the 19th century, education in Great Britain had made its greatest impact on the secondary and university levels. The grammar schools and the public schools (for example, Eton, Harrow, and Rugby), as well as Oxford and Cambridge universities, prepared young men for leadership in all branches of British society. Toward the close of the 18th century, especially in connection with religious activities, attention began to be paid to the need of educating young children. However, it was not until some decades later, when philanthropists tried to rescue children from some of the evils accompanying the Industrial Revolution, that specific steps were taken to provide more opportunities for elementary schooling. As the 19th century progressed, three forces were engaged in raising the level of primary education—church people, humanitarians, and political reformers.

All these efforts, however, proved to be far from adequate. Accordingly, Parliament passed the Forster Act (1870), which set up local school boards to take charge of publicly maintained schools. Parallel to this law was the Education (Scotland) Act of 1872. With the establishment of a system of schools, it was now possible to elaborate and to refine its administration and organization. Other basic laws were then passed, such as the Board of Education Act (1899), which created the forerunner of the national Department of Education and Science; the Education Act of 1902, which organized the Local Education Authority to replace the local school board; the Fisher Act (1918), which made school attendance compulsory between the ages of 5 and 14; and the Butler Act (1944), which established the present educational system of England and Wales. Laws similar to these were enacted in Scotland and Northern Ireland, taking into account differences in traditions.

The educational enterprise in Britain is administered by means of three separate systems—one for England and Wales, under the Department of Education and Science in London; one for Scotland, under the Scottish Education Department in Edinburgh; and one for Northern Ireland, under a Department of Education in Belfast. These administrative systems are a result of historical circumstances, religious developments, and cultural heritages.

The British approach to public education is based on the principle of decentralized administration. The financing of schools, appointment of teachers, organization of instruction, and other educational functions are performed by the Local Education Authorities (L.E.A). Another characteristic is the existence of voluntary, or denominational, schools which obtain funds for

657

A student of Britain's Open University does an experiment at home. The Open University gives many persons who otherwise would be denied the opportunity a chance to work for an academic degree.

THE OPEN UNIVERSITY

teachers' salaries, teaching materials, and building services from the L.E.A. and in return are subject to supervision of secular instruction. A third type is the independent school, which does not receive any financial aid from the Department of Education or from the L.E.A. The internationally renowned "public schools" (which would be called private or independent in American terminology) belong in this category, although as secondary schools they may receive public grants and are therefore subject to inspection by the Department of Education.

The British school system provides free education, including books and necessary supplies, to all children from 5 to 16. By the mid-1980's more than 90 percent of all children were attending free, publicly maintained secondary schools.

Primary education, which goes on until the age of 11, consists of nursery schools or classes that are voluntary for children aged 2 to 5; infant schools for children aged 5 to 7; and junior schools, for children aged 7 to 11. In addition, there are many primary schools that take care of the educational needs of youngsters of all ages between 5 and 11. About half of the primary schools belong to the voluntary variety; that is, they are denominational schools that receive some aid from the L.E.A. As a result, it may be said that England and Wales support a dual system of schools.

Secondary education, free to all since the Butler Act of 1944, consists of three types: secondary grammar, mainly for those pupils who intend to go to the university; secondary modern, which dates from the Fisher Act of 1918, for those who desire a general education that does not lead to the university; and secondary technical, for those interested in vocational training. There are also bilateral and multilateral secondary schools that combine, respectively, two or three of the school types. One of the significant problems in current secondary education is the question of the comprehensive secondary school, an institution that combines the three types into a single unit furnishing to the pupils a common core of learning experience with provision for specialized interests. Comprehensive schools have been opened in increasing numbers, especially in London. Besides these publicly maintained secondary schools, there are voluntary secondary schools, the famous public schools, and a variety of independent schools. While these schools are visited by government inspectors, they must be regarded as private in the American sense of the term because pupils are usually obliged to pay tuition.

The L.E.A.'s are also required to provide special schools for physically and mentally handicapped children, as well as such ancillary services as school health inspection and service, school meals, and school milk. Moreover, they are responsible for the organization of further education until the age of 18 in the form of part-time county colleges, vocational courses of various kinds, and the leisure-time Youth Service. This further education will, under proper conditions, become compulsory for all those who leave school at the age of 16 in order to work. Still another responsibility of the L.E.A.'s is the provision of religious worship and religious instruction in all schools receiving public funds. However, all religious instruction in the county schools (corresponding to the American public schools) must be nondenominational in nature and based upon a nonsectarian *Agreed Syllabus* drawn up by representatives of religious groups of the area, the teachers, and the L.E.A.

Qualifications for teachers in publicly maintained schools are subject to the approval of the national Department of Education. Primary teacher education, as a rule, is carried on in colleges of education in cooperation with the departments of education in the universities. Secondary school teachers obtain academic training generally at the university, after which they usually study for a year in a university department of education. All teachers in publicly maintained schools are engaged by the L.E.A., are paid according to a national scale, and are eligible, if they are employed full time, for pensions.

British universities are financed by private endowment and, since 1919, also by funds from the national government through the University Grants Committee. Among the major developments in higher learning in the 1970's and early 1980's were the increase in the number of institutions, the success of the Open University (mostly instruction at home), and the growing influence of the Council for National Academic Awards in granting nonuniversity degrees. National financial difficulties made it necessary to impose tuition fees on foreign students.

France. The French educational tradition stems from the Jules Ferry laws of the 1880's, which established free, compulsory, and secular education; the law of 1902, which set up the seven-year secondary school; the law of 1904, which suppressed the Catholic teaching congregations; and the law of 1936, which raised the age of compulsory attendance from 13 to 14. The tendency toward educational reform in France is of special interest. One important change, brought about by Jean Zay, minister of national education in 1937, made easier the transition from primary to secondary education. The well-publicized attempt by Paul Langevin and Henri Wallon after World War II to introduce progressive practices and compulsory education up to 18 called forth much opposition. The Delbos Bill of 1949, which incorporated the proposed reforms in compromise form, was never enacted into law, chiefly because of opposition by Communists.

Probably the most momentous event in recent French educational history was the crisis of 1968, when violent university student demonstrations led to the decentralization of higher education, an increase in the number of institutions, and the concentration of power in councils controlled by students and faculty. The 1968 reform reversed the policy of centralization inaugurated by Napoleon I a century and a half earlier.

The French educational system draws its aims and ideals from the Revolution of 1789, the Ferry reforms of the 1880's, and the national constitutions of 1946 and 1958. Public education is free, compulsory, and accessible to all. Religious education is not permitted in public schools, but it can be arranged by parents on Wednesdays, when the schools are closed. Teachers in private schools may receive state salaries if they are qualified, follow the regular curriculums, and are supervised by public authorities.

Of great significance for the French school system was the Haby Reform, enacted into law in 1975. The Haby Reform strengthens the principle of decentralization by stressing the rights of all children to express their individuality, attain maximum development, and prepare for a productive place in society. Emphasis is laid on the equalization of opportunity, a common core curriculum, universal access to secondary education, instructional options for specialized needs, and school councils in which teachers, parents, and pupils participate. The law went into effect in 1977, and its provisions were put into practice gradually. Another indication of change was the establishment in 1978 of the Ministry of Universities, whereby higher education became independent of the Ministry of National Education.

Preprimary education is offered optionally to children aged 2 to 6 in *écoles maternelles, jardins d'enfants,* and *classes enfantines.* Compulsory attendance, for ages 6 to 16, comprises a five-year primary course in three stages and four years in a secondary *collège.* The advanced cycle of secondary education, three to five years in length, leads to a *baccalauréat,* which is required for admission to a university or higher technical school. Higher education is organized in three cycles, two to seven years in length, ending in diplomas (*licence, maîtrise*) and doctorates. The highest awards are the state doctorate and the competitive *agrégation,* the teaching license for advanced secondary schools and higher institutions.

The Ministry of National Education functions mainly as a coordinating and fund-disbursing body. In the spirit of decentralization, administration and supervision are under the direction of 27 regional areas (*académies*), each headed by a rector appointed by the minister.

The Netherlands. The Dutch educational tradition may be traced primarily to the activities of the Reformed Church in the 17th century, when an effort was made to set up a system of universal education. The first modern school law, however, dates from 1801, when the government laid down the principle that each parish had the right to open and maintain schools. All through the 19th century there was a debate between the proponents of denominational schools and those of nondenominational schools. The law of 1920 ended the controversy by declaring that denominational schools were fully equal with state schools, both types being eligible for public funds. The resultant decentralization is certainly unique in western Europe. The private school, in return for public funds, must provide a curriculum and a period of instruction equivalent to those offered by the public schools.

The function of the Ministry of Education and Sciences is only to supervise the quality of the educational work, while the actual administration is within the jurisdiction of the local authorities. An Educational Council advises the ministry on all important general questions.

Compulsory school attendance is from 6 through 16 years. The Dutch school system is free and consists of a two-year preprimary school, a six-year primary school, three types of secondary schools of four to six years' duration (preuniversity, general, and vocational), and three- to eight-year higher education programs in universities and professional schools. Provisions are made for handicapped pupils and for those with particular interests and skills. The higher degrees are *doctorandus* (master's), *ingenieur* (engineering or agricultural), *meester* (law), and *doctor* (dissertation required). In 1980, because of financial problems, the Dutch government imposed a limitation on length of attendance in universities to discourage perennial students and those who must repeat courses.

French schoolgirls walking between classes at a modern lycée, or public secondary school, in Nîmes. DE WYS

Switzerland. Swiss elementary education is free and compulsory, controlled by the cantons and half cantons, which also administer secondary and higher education. The federal government assists in financing and administers the institutes of technology in Zürich and Lausanne.

Each canton administers its schools through a Department of Education. Compulsory elementary attendance varies from six to nine years, although in most cantons children are required to attend school for at least eight years. The school systems, as a rule, consist of a two-year preschool, a primary school of four to six years, lower and higher levels of secondary school (three to nine years, according to a student's ability), and higher education in universities and technical and other professional schools.

Swiss higher education comprises the German-language cantonal universities of Basel, Bern, and Zürich; the French-language cantonal universities of Geneva, Lausanne, and Neuchâtel; the bilingual (French and German) cantonal university of Fribourg; the St. Gallen Graduate School of Economics, Law, Business, and Public Administration (German); the federal technological institutes in Lausanne (French) and Zürich (German); and cantonal and regional colleges. Medical study and nursing education are under the direction of the Swiss Red Cross.

Germany. Following World War II, Germany was divided into four occupation zones and ultimately into two separate territories: the German Federal Republic (West Germany), made up of ten states (*Länder*); and the German Democratic Republic (East Germany). Berlin, which is not officially a part of either republic, was likewise divided into west and east sectors, with corresponding political affinities. Accordingly, there emerged two distinct systems of education in Germany.

Article 7 of the constitution of the German Federal Republic (1949) left educational administration and control in the hands of the *Länder*, thus making for a decentralized school system. On the other hand, a tendency toward some uniformity in educational practice emerged, primarily as a result of the Permanent Conference of the Ministers of Education. This group began meeting in 1948 to discuss common problems in education and to achieve interstate cooperation, though without legal powers.

The West German states established centralized school systems of their own, each of them under the direction of a Ministry of Education. Each state, in turn, was divided into city counties and rural counties, with their school superintendents appointed by the minister of education. Local school boards, selected by the local governing bodies, were given some role to play in the administration of schools, but not the powers of American school boards. Curriculums, supervision, and the appointment and salaries of teachers remained the function of the state government, while the local authority was given responsibility for the construction and maintenance of school buildings, the procurement of equipment, and the health and welfare of the school children. The financing of the schools, for the most part, was divided between the *Länder* and the local authorities. In general, the school system in West Germany was founded on the 8-year primary school, which was linked to the middle school and to various types of secondary schools, such as the *Gymnasium* and the *Oberrealschule*, emphasizing, respectively, classical and scientific-mathematical subjects. Transition to upper elementary, lower elementary (middle), or standard secondary education was placed at the end of the fourth year of primary instruction. Also included in the system of education were different levels of vocational and technical schools, advanced schools in such fields as theology and the arts, and the universities.

While the West German republic established a relatively decentralized system of education, the East German republic set up a highly centralized system with respect to administration, organization, supervision, curriculums, and methods of instruction. From the point of view of ideology, education in East Germany was taken over completely by the Communists, who ensured that the teachers, courses of study, and textbooks would reflect the values and aims of Marxism, as in the Soviet Union.

USSR. One of the first steps in setting up a school system after the Russian Revolution of 1917 was the inauguration of a campaign to eradicate illiteracy. After experimenting for some years with the progressive practices in vogue in the United States and western Europe, the school authorities of the Soviet Union decided in the middle 1930's to abandon them. In the following period, the teaching of scientific and technical subjects was intensified, with the result that the Union of Soviet Socialist Republics (USSR) became one of the leading nations in developing scientists and engineers.

The educational system of the USSR is under the control of the Communist party, which seeks to propagate Communist ideology on all school levels. A major aim is to continue raising the level of literacy. According to the USSR census of 1939, 81.2% of the people (with the exception of children under the age of nine) were literate. By the 1960's, the Soviet government claimed that the rate of adult literacy had risen to 90 to 95%. The Soviet definition of literacy, however, appears to be broader than that accepted by many other nations.

The general elementary and secondary schools are administered by the Ministry of Education

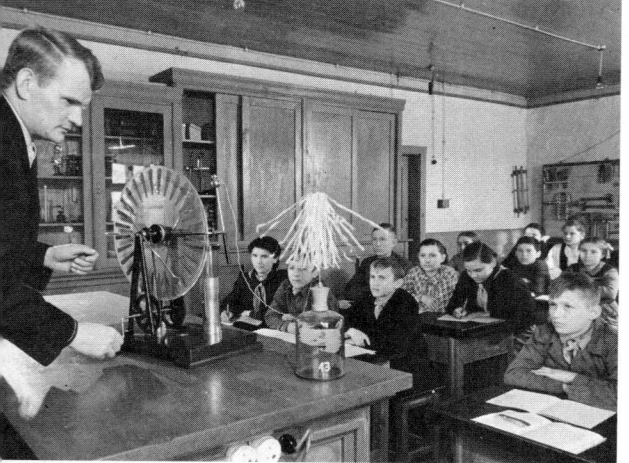

PICTORIAL PARADE

Russian instructor demonstrates the properties of static electricity in the school of a collective farm.

The university in Frankfurt, West Germany, was named for the poet Goethe, the city's most famous son.

of the USSR. While the republics have some freedom of action with certain aspects of schooling, the ministries of education of the various republics tend to follow the lead of the Russian Soviet Federated Socialist Republic in all essential educational matters. In addition, the Central Committee of the Communist Party and its constituent divisions are always on the alert to see that the schools throughout the Soviet Union adhere to the ideology and policies of the party. Higher education and specialized secondary education are under a centralized ministry. The higher education ministry controls and supervises the universities, technical institutes, and other higher educational institutions, and also is in charge of the middle-level specialized and technical schools. It likewise shares control, with the appropriate ministries, of all other higher educational institutions, such as teachers' institutes, medical schools, agricultural institutes, and arts institutes.

Soviet education consists of two types—general, and technical or specialized. Apart from preschool, children normally start at about 7. Prior to 1952 three kinds of schools prevailed: primary, a four-year course; incomplete middle, a seven-year course; and complete middle, a 10-year course. In 1952 the government adopted a universal compulsory program with a 10-year course of study. In 1958 another year was added to allow for work experience as an integral part of the educational program. The educational system returned to the 10-year program in 1964; however, the emphasis on work experience was retained. The general schools also provide part-time and rural evening instruction for young people already employed. The specialized school system consists of the *tekhnikum* (middle special school), which prepares for certain trades and professions; the labor reserve schools; and the normal schools. In addition, there are 60 universities and numerous other schools of equivalent grade. The universities, the vast majority of which were founded after 1917, are supplemented by over 700 technological and other professional institutes. The Soviet success in launching space satellites is generally attributed to the pervasive program of scientific and technical training.

The higher educational system within the USSR has attracted students from Asia, Africa, and Latin America, particularly from the developing countries.

All through the system, the natural sciences and mathematics are given special emphasis. In other respects, however, the Soviet curriculum is similar, as a general rule, to the standard course of study in effect in the various countries of Europe. The basic difference lies in the fact that in the Soviet school each subject, whether it be science, mathematics, a branch of culture, or social studies, is influenced by the ideology of the Communist party.

Japan. The traditional school system of Japan before the end of World War II was based on the

A Japanese elementary school drawing class enjoys a field trip on which the pupils draw landscapes.

Indian children in the primary class of a girls' school in Jaipur. Public schools are under state control.

Imperial Rescript of 1890. This decree stressed moral qualities, filial piety, and devotion to the emperor and the nation. Later, the school system was modified by an emphasis on scientific, technical, and commercial studies designed to achieve the modernization of Japan. Virtually all Japanese children were enrolled in school, and the entire system was controlled by the state. Acceptance of State Shinto was mandatory in all Japanese schools, and the "cult of the Emperor" powerfully reinforced the nationalistic and militaristic aims of the nation's leaders.

After World War II, education moved in a new direction. The constitution of 1946 specifies that education is to be free and compulsory. It removes religious education from the curriculum, and guarantees academic freedom. These and other changes in the traditional Japanese policy are reflections, to an important degree, of the impact of educational ideas from the United States.

The new system of schools, which was inaugurated in 1947, consists of a six-year elementary school, a three-year middle or junior high school, a three-year senior high school, and a four-year college. There also are junior colleges with two- or three-year courses and postgraduate schools. Administration is not so centralized as formerly; local boards of education, established under the law of 1948, administer public elementary and secondary schools in their districts.

When Japan became free of U.S. military occupation, many of the post-World War II educational reforms were discontinued. However, during the 1970's and 1980's, the technical, industrial, and commercial success of Japan prompted international interest in its educational system.

India. During the early years of British rule in India, formal education was furnished by missionary and other private schools and by the traditional schools in many of the villages. Such schooling was generally available only to the children of the more affluent. In 1781, Warren Hastings, governor general of the East India Company which then ruled British India, established the Calcutta Madrasah to prepare young Muslims for government positions. Ten years later the Banaras Sanskrit College was founded to accomplish the same purpose for Hindus. Controversy broke out between the "Orientalists," who favored training in Sanskrit and Oriental literature, and the "Filtrationists," who believed that the modern culture of the West, as reflected in the English tradition, should be studied, and that the benefits of this program would "filter down" to the masses. Thomas Babington Macaulay, later one of England's most distinguished men of letters, in his famous Minute of 1835 helped to carry the day for the study of English and Western learning. The 1854 Dispatch of Sir Charles Wood, an authority on Indian questions, called for a greatly extended educational program, including grants-in-aid to private schools, but the positive results were very limited. However, in 1857, three modern universities were founded at Calcutta, Bombay, and Madras.

British India offered little or no formal education for the masses. The village schools were inadequate; the country was too poor to provide a free public school system, and the villagers were rarely able to pay fees, although sometimes produce or goods were accepted as payment. The result was that when India gained its independence in 1947, more than 80 per cent of the population was illiterate. Secondary schools served primarily the few pupils who went on to a more advanced education. Both secondary and higher education were generally conducted in English, in contrast to the use of local languages in primary schools.

Critics of the educational system of British India pointed out that it served only the social elite, that the education provided was too academic and literary and not in keeping with the real needs of India, and that a diploma was too often simply a means to a government position rather than a sign of a good education.

Consequently, Mohandas K. Gandhi and other Indian leaders developed an educational program in 1937 known as the Wardha Scheme, later referred to simply as Basic Education. This plan

Village schools in India have increased rapidly since the country attained independence from Britain.

called for education organized around certain basic crafts. Students were to obtain the necessary manual skill in a particular craft and learn practical arithmetic and the history and social significance of that craft. Basic Education thus was devised to avoid the frustrating situation in which the student received an academic education without having the opportunity to put it to use. Traditional Indian cultural values were not to be sacrificed in Basic Education, and the student was expected to be trained in such a manner that on graduation he would be adjusted to his environment and would possess a skill that would provide his living and benefit the national economy. Progress in putting this plan into effect was interrupted by World War II, but after India achieved its independence in 1947, the central government and each of the state governments adopted the principles of Basic Education.

India has been heavily preoccupied with the problem of setting up a satisfactory school system and of reducing the prevalent illiteracy. The public schools are under the direction of the individual states, with an elected minister of education responsible to the state legislature, and a professional director of public instruction in charge. The Central Ministry of Education coordinates and guides educational activities, provides information on education, and controls the institutions of higher education and of scientific and technical education. There is a Central Advisory Board of Education composed of the central minister of education, the state ministers of education, and a number of experts.

The Indian school system comprises primary education (four to six years), which is compulsory for five years; secondary education (middle school, high school, and technical and vocational schools); and higher education.

India has more than 120 general and specialized universities that provide professional training. The language of instruction may be Hindi (the national language), English, or a regional tongue. Language teaching remains a national problem, as does ethnic and religious equality, in this multilingual and multicultural nation.

Latin America. During the 300 years of Latin America's colonial history, formal education was provided mainly by Catholic religious orders and limited largely to the white population. Revolutions against Spanish and Portuguese rule in the 19th century resulted in political independence and an influx of educational ideas from Europe and North America. The subsequent formation of the various national school systems arose, in large measure, from the contributions of such great 19th century educational leaders as Domingo Faustino Sarmiento of Argentina, José Pedro Varela of Uruguay, and Justo Sierra of Mexico. The principles and practices of elementary education in the United States, secondary education in France, and vocational and technical instruction in Germany were combined and refashioned into school systems serving increasing numbers of students. One important result of the educational reforms of the 19th century was the emergence of constitutional provisions for free, secular, compulsory schooling.

The educational problems of Latin America include the prevalence of illiteracy, the need to assimilate vast numbers of people of non-European origin, the complex geographical situation that necessitates overcoming difficulties in rural ar-

UNITED NATIONS

A Honduran teacher, using an abacus designed by UNESCO, gives arithmetic lesson to her primary class.

eas, the constantly changing political situation, the need for well-trained teachers, and student unrest on the secondary and higher levels. These problems, especially illiteracy and ethnic assimilation, reached into the 1980's. Efforts are being made for improvement—for example, Mexico's opening of rural boarding schools in 1980 to reduce migration to overcrowded cities.

Canada. Since the British North America Act of 1867, education in Canada has been fully controlled by the 10 provinces. Among the functions of the federal government are the education of Eskimos and Indians, administration of public education for the Northwest and Yukon territories, and collection of school statistics. The federal government also provides grants for vocational education and—upon recommendation by a Royal Commission in 1951—

A Canadian Eskimo class learning to read English at a small schoolhouse in the Northwest Territories.

ANNAN

makes grants to universities and colleges. Provincial departments are headed by ministers of education, assisted by deputies with professional training in the field. Supervision is carried on by departmental inspectors. The administration of local schools is effected through elected school boards, which are responsible for employing teachers, constructing and maintaining buildings, and providing educational equipment. The school boards also engage professional educators to perform the duties of actual school administration. The province of Quebec maintains two school systems, one for the French-speaking Roman Catholic majority and one for the Protestants and other religious groups.

During the 1970's, Canada inaugurated programs for multicultural education to reflect its varied population. Considerably more stress was laid on bilingual education, while in Quebec the French-speaking majority sought to make its language the dominant one in the province. In many organizational respects, the Canadian school system is quite similar to that of the United States.

United States. The educational traditions of the United States may be traced to the home countries of the early colonists: England, Scotland, Holland, France, and Spain. In the later decades of the period of colonization, as well as during the 19th century, influences from Germany, Switzerland, and the Scandinavian countries also helped to shape the American school system. During the 20th century, the situation has been reversed, with many countries of Europe and other continents borrowing educational ideas and practices from the United States.

The salient features of the school system of the United States are: the absence of a national administration, each of the 50 states controlling and directing its own schools; a single educational ladder by which a pupil may advance from one school level to another; the lack of fees in elementary and secondary education and, in some cases, in higher education; the separation of church and state in educational affairs; and compulsory school attendance, often until the age of 16. The basic aim of education in the United States is to make it possible for all boys and girls to develop, as far as capacities permit, into well-rounded, well-informed citizens.

The federal government includes a cabinet-level Department of Education for the purpose of collecting educational statistics, issuing various kinds of surveys and reports, advising state and local school authorities (upon invitation), and supervising the expenditure of certain funds as specified by law. In addition, the federal government is concerned with the school system of the District of Columbia, the service schools (West Point, Annapolis, and the Air Force and Coast Guard academies), education of Indians, schools in outlying territories, and the exchange of both teachers and students with those of foreign countries.

Education in the United States is carried on by 50 school systems, each of which is under the control of a state legislature. In spite of this diversity, there are many unifying tendencies in American education. Most states direct their schools by means of a central board of education that is made up of lay persons, but the administrative work is under the direction of an elected or appointed superintendent or commissioner of schools. He is aided by a staff of supervisors and specialists, and often sets up and enforces standards for curriculum, attendance, and the qualifications and efficiency of teachers. Local, especially urban, areas may be allowed their own criteria, but these must meet the minimum state requirements. Private schools usually have leeway in choosing their teachers and textbooks and in planning their curriculums, but they usually are obliged to meet standards set by the states.

Public schools are financed by state and local authorities. Most of their funds come from property taxes. In addition, the schools have for many years received federal aid for special purposes such as vocational training and school lunches. After World War II, there was a movement to have the national government provide funds to equalize educational opportunities among all the states. This movement reached a decisive point in 1965 when Congress approved a major program of federal support for the schools.

In each community or rural area there is a school board, elected or appointed, which chooses the superintendent of schools, controls educational policy, and performs other pertinent functions. The larger cities generally have a staff of specialists, supervisors, and assistants to help the superintendent administer school affairs.

Many school systems have public kindergartens, but formal schooling as a rule begins at the age of 6 or 7. The traditional organization is an eight-year elementary school followed by a four-year high school. Starting in the 1900's, this plan gave way in more than half of the country's schools to a division of the high school into junior and senior divisions. In one plan a six-year elementary school is followed by a three-year junior high school and a three-year senior high school. A six-six plan and other variations have been introduced. Some school districts now have an intermediate, or middle, school between the primary grades and the high school.

Special schools serve handicapped children, young people who want to train for vocations, and adults who want to take courses in their free time. Many states and cities have established two-year public colleges to serve both adults and young people. These junior, or community, colleges are a specific feature of education in the United States and are found in few other countries.

Higher education is offered by private and public institutions. All states and many cities support public colleges and universities. There are many public and private technical and professional schools.

Many significant issues face American education. One of them is how to provide equal opportunity for all pupils to obtain the schooling that meets their particular abilities and needs. A second problem involves the segregation of black children in separate schools. In May 1954 the U.S. Supreme Court declared that segregation in the public schools was unconstitutional because it violated the principle of "equal protection of the laws" for all citizens as stated in the 14th Amendment. On the 10th anniversary of the decision, less than 2% of the black children in the 11 Southern states were attending integrated schools. Nevertheless, the Southern and border states had made significant progress toward complying with the ruling. By 1965 the great majority of school districts had announced their intention to maintain some integrated classrooms. In the North, *de facto* segregation was recognized as an urgent problem, particularly in the cities. Delegates to the 1965 White House Conference on Education reported that the American people had not fully committed themselves to integrating their schools.

The educational problems and issues facing the United States during the 1970's and early 1980's included racial and ethnic equalization, the financing of public schools, and church-state-school relations. As in previous periods, criticism was common, especially of teacher education and efficiency and achievement by pupils in elementary and high schools. Special attention in public discussions and controversies, in the legislatures, and in the courts was given to sex discrimination, bilingual education, provisions for handicapped pupils, and the lowering of standardized test scores in relation to college admissions.

Compulsory Education Laws. Compulsory education is an old concept. From ancient times societies have enjoined parents or other elders to instruct children in basic information and rules of conduct. Compulsory attendance laws requiring children to attend specified schools for a certain number of years are chiefly a modern development. In Europe compulsory attendance laws date from the 16th and 17th centuries. In America a pioneering move toward compulsory education was part of the school policy of Massachusetts in 1642. However, compulsory attendance laws were not widely adopted and enforced in the United States until the early years of the 20th century.

After World War II most countries of the world enacted compulsory education laws. The accompanying table shows the age limits and total years required for a number of representative countries. In some countries, actual school attendance is far behind the intent of the law. On the other hand, some nations provide more years of public education than the minimum required.

The data for some countries show a range of limits and total years required. In the United States, for example, each of the 50 states can set its own limits. The most common age range is from 7 to 16. Many states allow exemptions from attendance for reasons such as physical disability. In all states pupils can leave school before the statutory upper age limit if they need to go to work. Usually they must have reached a minimum age, usually 16, and must have completed a required number of grades.

Worldwide Educational Problems. A convenient way to identify the pressing problems of education on a worldwide scale is to take note of the questions discussed at the annual International Conference on Public Education, convened each summer since World War II in Geneva, Switzerland, under the sponsorship of UNESCO's International Bureau of Education. Among the topics have been the teaching of reading, raising the level of primary and secondary teacher training, increasing the length of compulsory attendance, the equalization of educational opportunity in the secondary schools, the availability of education to women, the improvement of teachers' salaries, the proper financing of education, the teaching of mathematics, and the inspection of schools.

Not all of these problems are of immediate crucial significance to each of the approximately 60 nations participating, but they indicate common educational interests and concerns all over the world. Several other problems have also been studied by individual countries, groups of nations, and UNESCO itself. These include the teaching of history in a manner calculated to increase international understanding on the part of pupils, the offering of suitable educational opportunities to adults, the liquida-

COMPULSORY EDUCATION REQUIREMENTS IN SELECTED COUNTRIES

	Age Limits	Years Required		Age Limits	Years Required
AFRICA			Israel	5–15	9
Algeria	6–14	8	Japan	6–15	9
Congo	6–16	10	Korea, North	7–15	8
Egypt	6–12	6	Korea, South	6–12	6
Ghana	6–16	10	Philippines	7–13	6
Liberia	6–16	10	Sri Lanka	5–15	10
Libya	6–15	9	Syria	6–11	6
South Africa	7–16	7–9	Thailand	7–15	7
Zimbabwe	7–15	8	Turkey	6–14	5
NORTH AMERICA			Vietnam	6–11	5
Canada	6–16	8–10	**EUROPE**		
Cuba	6–14	6	Austria	6–15	9
Mexico	6–14	6	Belgium	6–14	8
United States	7–16	10	Bulgaria	7–15	8
SOUTH AMERICA			Czechoslovakia	6–15	9
Argentina	6–14	7	Denmark	7–16	9
Bolivia	6–14	8	France	6–16	10
Brazil	7–14	8	Germany, West	6–15	9
Chile	6–13	8	Greece	6–12	6
Colombia	6–12	5	Italy	6–14	8
Ecuador	6–14	6	Norway	7–16	9
Paraguay	7–14	6	Poland	7–17	8
Peru	6–15	9	Romania	6–16	10
Uruguay	6–14	6	Spain	6–16	10
Venezuela	7–14	6	Sweden	7–16	9
ASIA			Switzerland	7–16	8, 9
Afghanistan	7–15	8	USSR	7–17	10
Bangladesh	5–10	5	United Kingdom	5–16	11
Hong Kong	6–12	6	**OCEANIA**		
India	6–11	5	Australia	6–16	9, 10
Indonesia	7–13	6	New Zealand	6–15	9
Iran	6–14	8			
Iraq	6–12	6			

Source: UNESCO, *Statistical Yearbook*.

tion of illiteracy, and the organization of schools in such a manner as to give persons of all races and religions equal access to educational programs.

Illiteracy has come under close international scrutiny, especially since World War II. UNESCO has led the attack on illiteracy by conducting surveys to find the extent of the problem and by organizing programs to teach reading and writing to children and adults.

New problems affecting education in many countries have begun to command increasing attention. One of these is the interrelationship of teacher education, salaries, and social status. With the shortage of teachers all over the world after World War II, it became evident that the role of the teacher in school and in society would have to be reexamined if chaos were to be averted in certain national school systems. In some countries, such as Italy and the United States, teachers went on strike in order to gain better salaries and teaching conditions. Although this problem has not been solved, some improvements have gone into effect in a number of countries. But the solution of the teacher shortage is not yet in sight in many parts of the world. Contributing in a large measure to this situation is the rising birth rate, particularly in the developing countries.

Juvenile delinquency and crime are important educational and social problems in various countries, including the United States, the USSR, and Britain. The rapid changes and perplexing uncertainties deriving from World War II and its aftermath have been mentioned from time to time as helping to bring about this state of affairs. Attempts are being made in the various countries suffering from juvenile delinquency to strengthen the school system and youth service work and to attack this problem from other angles. Another issue is the apparent race among such nations as Britain, the United States, and the USSR to train the most and the best scientists and engineers. This condition is doubtless due to the persistence of the cold war and the recent developments in atomic and nuclear physics. The emphasis on the teaching of science has caused some educators in these countries to sound a warning that the cultural and social fields of study are being seriously neglected. Other crucial problems involve the education of ethnic minorities; the expansion of secondary and higher education for all people; the needs of the newer nations, especially of Asia and Africa; the expansion and improvement of adult education (also called "lifelong" or "recurrent"); the employment of secondary-school and higher-education graduates; and equal opportunities in education for women and minorities. The role of UNESCO was seriously questioned by some countries, which claimed that it was tendentious and politicized.

See also sections *1. History of Education; 2. Philosophy of Education;* and education sections of country articles, for example, CHINA—*4. Education;* INDIA—*5. Education;* and JAPAN—*6. Education.*

WILLIAM W. BRICKMAN
University of Pennsylvania

Bibliography

Altbach, Philip G., and others, eds., *Comparative Education* (Macmillan 1982).
Clignet, Remi, *Liberty and Equality in the Educational Process: A Comparative Sociology of Education* (Wiley 1974).
Connell, William F., *A History of Education in the Twentieth Century World* (Teachers College Press 1981).
Elvin, Lionel, ed., *The Educational Systems in the European Community: A Guide* (Humanities Press 1981).
Eurich, Nell P., *Systems of Higher Education in Twelve Countries: A Comparative View* (Praeger 1981).
Fraser, Stewart E., and Brickman, William W., eds., *A History of International and Comparative Education: Nineteenth Century Documents* (Scott 1968).
Ignas, Edward, and Corsini, Raymond J., eds., *Comparative Educational Systems* (Peacock 1981).
King, Edmund J., *Other Schools and Ours: Comparative Studies for Today,* 4th ed. (Holt 1973).
Newcombe, Norman, *Europe at School* (Methuen 1977).
Organization for Economic Cooperation and Development (OECD), *Compulsory Education in a Changing World* (OECD 1983).
Ringer, Fritz K., *Education and Society in Modern Europe* (Ind. Univ. Press 1979).
Titmus, Colin, *Strategies for Adult Education: Practices in Western Europe* (Cambridge Book 1981).
UNESCO, *World Guide to Higher Education: A Comparative Survey of Systems, Degrees and Qualifications,* 2d ed. (Bowker 1982).

FUJIHIRA, FROM MONKMEYER

Congolese schoolgirls attending a health class at a secondary school in Ladja, Democratic Republic of Congo.

Children at a day nursery in New York City learn new skills while enjoying the task of constructing simple objects.

IRENE BAYER, FROM MONKMEYER

4. Primary Education

Primary or elementary education generally denotes the basic or introductory schooling that young children receive, usually starting at 6 years of age and continuing to 10 or 12. The ages of starting and stopping vary. In some countries preschool education in nursery schools or kindergartens precedes the 1st grade. Some school systems end primary training as early as the 5th grade, after which children who are continuing their education go on to a middle school. In other systems, the break between the elementary and secondary schools comes after the 7th or 8th grade.

Primary education can be called the most universal and significant level of formal education in that far more of the world's people get schooling at this level than at the secondary and higher levels. UNESCO reports state that in Latin America about 75% of children in school are enrolled at the first or elementary level, about 19% at the second level, and about 6% at the third level. In Asia about 67% are enrolled at the first level, 28% at the second, and 5% at the third. In Africa the corresponding figures are 80%, 18%, and 2%. Highly developed nations such as the United States have a more even distribution between the first and second levels, but in general nearly half of their children in school are enrolled at the elementary level.

The purposes of primary education are influenced by the proportion of children a country is educating at higher levels. Where primary schooling is the first and last formal education children get, the paramount aim is to teach basic skills such as reading, writing, and simple arithmetic. Raising the literacy rate may be a major endeavor. The schools may also give time to such areas as history, citizenship, and health. In the developed nations, where a large share of children go on to secondary schools, the primary schools still teach fundamental skills. They are also concerned, however, with preparing students to continue up the educational ladder to high school and college. They may, for example, introduce children to the study of sciences and foreign languages. The schools also can afford to give time to areas such as art and music with the aim of enriching the child's background.

This article gives brief descriptions of the elementary school systems of the United States, Canada, and western Europe. Additional information can be found in the education sections of articles on individual countries.

UNITED STATES

Colonial Period. Public elementary education in colonial New England was an outgrowth of the Reformation. The Puritans who settled along the New England coast were determined that children should receive sufficient education to insure their ability to read the Bible and to participate in religious services. When it was evident that some parents and masters of apprentices were neglecting this responsibility, the colony of Massachusetts in 1642 passed a law directing the officials of each town to ascertain, from time to time, if parents and masters were attending to their educational duties; if children were being trained "in learning and labor and other employments profitable to the Commonwealth"; and if children were being taught "to read and understand the principles of religion and the capital laws of the country." Officials were empowered to impose fines for noncompliance.

In 1647 another law was passed directing that every town having 50 householders should at once appoint a teacher of reading and writing, and provide for his wages in such manner as that town might determine; and that every town having 100 householders must provide a (Latin) grammar school to fit youths for the university. For the first time among English-speaking people the right of the state to require communities to establish and maintain schools was determined. The Massachusetts laws of 1642 and 1647, together with the laws of 1634 and 1638 providing for the equalized and compulsory taxation of all for all town charges, represent the very foundation stones upon which the American system of public education has been constructed. This legislation established a precedent for school management and support which survived the separation of church and state and influenced the development of education throughout the United States.

In the middle colonies the early schools were associated with religious sects. Unlike New England, no sect was in a majority. It was felt that church control by each denomination was the most satisfactory arrangement, and no appeal was made to the colonial government for financial support. The result was a policy of leaving education to private and parochial effort, a policy that later was to retard the development of free public schools. Each denomination did as it wished. Except in the cities where private pay schools were operated, education was largely in the nature of rudimentary and religious instruction. Apprenticeship training for orphans and the children of the poor was also given.

In the Southern colonies education at public expense was regarded as a form of charity. As in England, education was not considered a concern of the state, and the Anglican Church in the South did not give any great attention to it.

Instruction in the New England colonial schools was dominated by a religious purpose. Catechisms were in common use. The *New England Primer* (q.v.), a little volume of somber reading material, appeared in 1690. Over 3 million copies were sold during the period of its use. Teachers were selected primarily for their soundness in the faith. School hours were long and discipline severe. Individual methods of instruction were universally followed, each child coming to the teacher's desk to recite. Instruction in reading, arithmetic, and writing predominated.

19th Century. After the Revolutionary War a new political motive for education developed, which in time entirely superseded the old religious motive. While the Constitution does not mention education, Washington, Jefferson, and others stressed the need for general education in a democratic form of government. Gradually a system of national land grants for public schools developed, the basis of the permanent school funds in all of the states west of the Alleghenies. A new educational consciousness was awakened. In many cities, school societies were formed to obtain funds for the establishment and support of free elementary schools.

The introduction of the Lancasterian monitorial system of instruction in the early 1800's contributed greatly to the extension of elementary education. Briefly, the plan provided for the instruction of a group of the brightest pupils, known as monitors, who in turn taught a designated number of pupils, usually ten. The plan became highly systematized. Detailed manuals of instruction were developed and rigidly adhered to. Used at first only for reading and the catechism, the plan was soon extended to writing, arithmetic, spelling, and even the higher branches of learning. From 200 to 1,000 pupils were assembled in large halls, with a monitor in charge of the instruction of each row. While the plan was mechanical and militaristic, it exerted an important influence in awakening public interest in elementary education. It made possible the instruction of large groups of pupils by a single teacher. Scores of elementary schools established between 1806 and 1830 were known as "Lancasterian schools."

During this period the "infant school" idea developed. Strangely enough, in most cities children were expected to be able to read at the time they entered the typical public elementary school. Such instruction was expected of the home or the dame school, the latter a neighborhood gathering of children under a privately employed woman as tutor. With the development of elementary schools the need for primary education became apparent. At first a separate school, the infant school eventually became a department of the developing elementary school.

The 19th century was a period of emerging concepts of public education. By 1850 the principle of providing an elementary school education for all children at public expense had been accepted in the Northern states. Successive struggles were made to secure adequate tax support, to eliminate the pauper-school idea (pauper schools were charity schools maintained at public expense), to make the schools entirely free, to establish school supervision, to eliminate sectarianism, and to extend the system. Horace Mann (q.v.) was a great educational leader of this period. Through his annual reports to the Massachusetts State Board of Education, his *Common School Journal,* and his addresses he influenced greatly the development of education. Henry Barnard (q.v.), the first United States commissioner of education (1867–1870) and editor of the *American Journal of Education,* also stands out as a conspicuous leader during the formative period of American education.

The elementary schools of the early national period (1789–1815) emphasized the three R's. Noah Webster's *American Spelling Book,* William H. McGuffey's *Readers (Eclectic Readers),* Lindley Murray's *English Grammar,* and Jedediah Morse's *Elements of Geography* were the popular texts. These early textbooks and their imitators firmly fixed reading, spelling, word analysis, declamation, and ciphering as the fundamental subjects of instruction. In the city elementary schools arithmetic, grammar, geography, history of the United States, and civics were additional subjects. Between 1840 and 1850 most of the larger schools organized their pupils into seven, eight, or nine grades, in accordance with the Prussian graded school system described by Horace Mann in his 7th annual report (1844).

The teachers of early schools of the 1840's and 1850's were not professionally trained. Although the first American state normal school was established in Lexington, Mass., in 1839, there were but 11 such schools in 1860, all of which were located in eight Northern states. There were few professional books for teachers. The best teachers were graduates of the academies, but the great majority of teachers had little education beyond the schools that they themselves taught. Terms were short, salaries low, and the teacher "boarded around." Until the introduction of graded schools, teaching was conducted on an individual basis. Oral instruction predominated, with one pupil at a time reciting to the master. Schoolhouses were poorly constructed and equipped. The chief aim of instruction was knowledge through memorization.

European Influences. The early schools of the United States represented largely a native development of educational ideas transplanted from England. Nevertheless, other European influences were felt in the 18th century and grew to be of major importance in the 19th century. In 1779, Thomas Jefferson tried unsuccessfully to establish a complete system of public education for Virginia, based on current French ideas. He proposed a free elementary school for every community, a series of regional secondary schools, and a state college.

In 1762, Jean Jacques Rousseau published *Émile* (q.v.), a vigorous attack on the formalism of the time in education, religion, and manners. Rousseau championed a natural development of the child's personality through carefully directed concrete experiences. Freedom of action rather

MONTESSORI SCHOOL in Stamford, Conn., employs special educational methods emphasizing freedom of expression.

than inhibition, expression rather than repression, were the keynotes of his philosophy. The teacher is a guide, not a taskmaster. Among those most deeply influenced by Rousseau's ideas was Johann Heinrich Pestalozzi (q.v.).

Pestalozzi is often referred to as the father of modern elementary education. He believed that the development of a rich sensory background was necessary in order that definitions and abstract statements of books might be really meaningful. He felt that real and genuine knowledge was derived through first-hand experiences. Objects, field trips, and directed observations were used to provide sensory experiences. Pestalozzi's influence was widespread; many educators visited his schools in Switzerland, and many read *How Gertrude Teaches Her Children* (1801), an exposition of his methods. The object-teaching technique, which was introduced into the United States about 1850, was one manifestation of Pestalozzi's influence.

Johann Friedrich Herbart (q.v.) and Friedrich Froebel (q.v.) studied Pestalozzi's work and carried it still further. Herbart, a German scholar and professor of philosophy at Königsberg and Götingen, developed a system of pedagogy based upon the psychological principles underlying the work of Pestalozzi. His "five formal steps" in the presentation of subject matter (preparation, presentation, association, systematization, and application) vastly influenced educational practice in the latter half of the 19th century.

Froebel introduced the kindergarten idea in 1837 with the opening of a children's school in Blankenburg, Germany, in which plays, games, songs, and occupations involving self-activity characterized the instruction. Given wider notice through the writings of Baroness Bertha von Marenholtz-Bülow, Froebel's movement spread rapidly over Europe and America in the 1880's and 1890's. It gave new emphasis to natural but directed self-activity toward educational, social, and moral ends.

Other important influences from Europe were those of Herbert Spencer (q.v.), whose essay "What Knowledge Is of Most Worth?" (1859) led to a new emphasis upon the study of science, and Philipp Emanuel von Fellenberg (q.v.), who introduced manual training as a phase of education.

As a result of these influences, the elementary school course of study was vastly improved, both in content and method. Leaders in this liberalizing movement in education in the United States were William T. Harris (q.v.), federal commissioner of education from 1889 to 1906, and Col. Francis W. Parker (q.v.), head of the Cook county normal school in Chicago from 1883 to 1899. Harris' annual reports interpreted and justified the school as a social institution. Colonel Parker utilized the contributions of European educators to reorganize and improve elementary education. By the turn of the 20th century the elementary school had become a typically American institution.

Changing Elementary School Practices. In the early 1900's, major social and economic changes in American life began to gather increased momentum. Advancement in scientific knowledge and industrial development was rapid. The home and church began to lose much of their force as educative agencies. The American people looked to public education to meet the challenge of a rapidly changing civilization. School enrollments increased by geometric proportions, and public education became one of the greatest enterprises in the nation. The public elementary school became in truth a training ground for all the children of all the people.

While school administrators were concerned largely with rapidly increasing enrollments, educational philosophers were concerned with curriculum studies to meet the increased responsibilities of the public school. The old theory of mental discipline, which had justified so much curriculum content of doubtful utility, was seriously questioned. A task was not "good for the mind" simply because it was arduous or distasteful. Furthermore, society was constantly changing, and education had to accept the responsibility of orienting the child to a changing world. Social and economic changes were making new demands upon individual initiative, integrity, and development. It was at this time that the work of John Dewey (q.v.) began to attract attention.

Dewey, who is frequently referred to as the foremost educational philosopher in America, believed that the school should be life, not a preparation for life. Society should be interpreted to the child through his daily living in the classroom, which acts as a miniature society. Growth takes place as the child engages in purposeful activities that are genuine and meaningful to him. The teacher functions as an intelligent director of these activities. Accordingly, in the experimental school which Dewey directed (1896–1904) at the University of Chicago no definite curriculums of school subjects were set up. The content and skills of the usual studies were developed out of the children's life activities. The life of the school was characterized by purposeful activity of the children directed by the teacher toward worthwhile goals.

In his writings Dewey constantly sought to elaborate his concept of education as "a reconstruction or reorganization of meaningful experience by means of creative intelligence applied in purposeful activity." His publications include *School and Society* (1899), *The Child and the Curriculum* (1902), *How We Think* (1909), and *Democracy and Education* (1916). It is generally conceded that Dewey laid the foundations of a new philosophy of education that affected and still affects the whole structure of American education, especially at the elementary school level. Dewey's writings and lectures influenced thousands of educators, who sought to put into practice in varying degrees his concept of the educational process. Outstanding among Dewey's followers was William Heard Kilpatrick, who, through his *Foundations of Method* (1925) and other publications and through his lectures to thousands of teachers at Teachers College, Columbia University, was instrumental in making the Dewey philosophy operative in the classroom.

Varying practices make it difficult to describe a typical elementary school of the 1930's and 1940's. There were relatively few ultraprogressive or ultraconservative schools. Nevertheless, the elementary schoolroom that emerged during this period was by and large a different place from the classroom of 1900, not only in equipment, but in curriculum content and teaching methods as well. Underlying these external changes was the new concept of the nature and purpose of elementary education—a concept that owed much to the pioneer work of John Dewey and his followers.

Concepts of Elementary Education. In the modern elementary school, democracy is seen as a way of life rather than merely a form of government. Through the maintenance of a democratic atmosphere in the classroom, the teacher strives to encourage the child, from the first grade on, to learn to respect the rights of others, to accept responsibility, to do his share of the work, and to act unselfishly and cooperatively as a member of a social group.

Policies are discussed and adopted rather than enunciated autocratically. Pupils learn under teacher guidance to make their own rules for conduct in the classroom, in the assembly, and on the playground. They learn citizenship by practicing its duties and responsibilities in their immediate social group. Thus, a spirit of constructive participation in social living is developed through the normal activities of daily living in the classroom.

Another characteristic of the richer concept of democracy that pervades the classroom is the spirit of respect for the personality of the child. His abilities and interests are recognized in the establishment of learning goals and the development of experiences. Each child learns that he can and should make his contribution to the learning progress of the group. The variety and flexibility of the school program make it possible for each child to earn some desirable type of recognition. Efforts are made to redirect thwarted personalities and restrict antisocial attitudes.

Another development is an emphasis on child study. In order to meet more effectively the needs and interests of the learner, the teacher must know not only the materials of instruction, but also the nature of the child being taught.

In addition, modern teachers emphasize the active nature of the learning process, as contrasted with a passive absorption of information. Actually, it is purposeful activity, not activity *per se*, that is the dominant characteristic of the newer school practices. The child not only learns by "doing," but he "does," because he experiences a felt need or purpose for accomplishing the task at hand. Thus, a good teacher is one who can stimulate worthy purposes and can direct pupil activity along lines that will result in maximum pupil growth intellectually, morally, physically, and artistically.

Unit Plan. In an endeavor to organize the learning experiences of elementary school children around worthy purposes, teaching units have been widely adopted. While the term "unit" has various interpretations, it is generally understood to mean a series of activities engaged in by pupils under teacher direction to carry out some project or solve some problem.

The typical unit involves six phases. These are by no means successive steps in a cycle, but rather aspects of a continuous process, and several of them may be carried out simultaneously. The phases are: (1) exploration and stimulation of interests and formulation of purpose; (2) planning and organization of methods of work; (3) acquiring skills and doing research to obtain needed information; (4) preparation of reports,

Fourth graders work on a math problem using Cuisenaire rods, which help illustrate basic mathematical concepts.

ELIZABETH CREWS/STOCK, BOSTON

exhibits, and similar projects for presentation to the class; (5) sharing the outcomes of the study; (6) evaluation of learning progress in terms of skills and knowledge acquired and growth in understandings and attitudes.

Several controversies have grown out of the use of the unit plan. One concerns the extent to which pupils should participate in planning learning experiences. A second touches on the proper place of traditional subject divisions. A third relates to how much drill is needed for mastering essential facts and skills.

Unit teaching has led to the use of a wide variety of learning materials. For example, a student no longer uses a single textbook for each subject. Instead, he is encouraged to read widely, but discriminately, and with a purpose.

The typical elementary classroom is a workshop for learning. Tables and chairs are movable, permitting arrangements for class work, group projects, or games. Modern classrooms often have activity centers equipped for special projects. Many schools provide computers and audiovisual equipment such as television sets, record players, and videocassette recorders.

Criticisms of Education. The developments in elementary school teaching in the 1940's and 1950's led to more and more outspoken charges that American education was becoming soft and ineffectual. The activity program was criticized as being harmful to the traditional educational values of systematic and sequential learning and exact and exacting studies.

Some critics blamed John Dewey for weakening traditional education. Actually, Dewey's ideas were misunderstood and misapplied. His emphasis on self-discipline as the only satisfactory type of control was interpreted to mean no discipline at all. His reliance on the child's interests as the motivating forces in learning was misunderstood to mean that the child should be allowed to do as he pleased.

Such extremes of "progressive education" were found in relatively few schools. Yet their effect was to shake public confidence in the nature and quality of the elementary school program. Not only were the aims and methodology of American education questioned, but also the curriculum and the preparation of teachers.

After the Soviet Union launched Sputnik I in October 1957, the seething criticism of American schools boiled over. It was a rude shock to Americans to be outdistanced in the space race, and, unfairly or not, the schools were blamed. From all sides came demands for changes in curriculums, methods, and requirements, including higher standards, more training in science and mathematics, better provisions for bright students and harder study for all, and improved instruction in foreign languages. While some of the extreme criticisms of American education seemed unjustified, there was considerable agreement that it did need strengthening. Observers felt that standards of achievement were too low in too many schools and that the majority of schools needed to raise the level of their instruction.

A direct result of the controversy was the passage of the National Defense Education Act of 1958. This act marked the beginning of a multimillion dollar program of federal aid to education, designed to strengthen instruction in science, mathematics, and foreign languages; to provide facilities and equipment for newer instructional aids, such as television and language laboratories; and to extend financial aid to college students.

In the 1960's the "pursuit of excellence" became a rallying cry for American educators. Schools hastened to examine their curriculums and academic requirements. Programs for gifted pupils were introduced on a wide scale. Foreign language instruction was begun in the elementary grades, especially in urban areas. Programs in mathematics and science were reorganized, with higher standards of accomplishment stressed.

However, in the late 1960's and early 1970's a decrease in federal funds for education coincided with a trend toward more permissiveness in the schools. As a result, 20 years after Sputnik, American schools again were accused of providing inadequate education. Critics pointed to a decline in standardized test scores as evidence that students were not acquiring basic skills at the elementary and secondary levels. A "back-to-basics" movement among parents and educators called for a return to traditional teaching methods and subject matter. Many states developed competency tests to ensure that graduating students had learned these fundamental skills.

Instructional Aids and Practices. Beginning in the 1950's, increased concern over education resulted in the adoption of a number of new instructional aids and practices. These ranged from the introduction of new methods of teaching mathematics to the use of instructional technology in the schools. In the 1950's and 1960's grants from private foundations and federal aid provided funds for experimentation with television teaching. Later, the microelectronics revolution made the computer more accessible to the classroom.

Sharp differences of opinion greeted the introduction of programmed learning and the use of teaching machines. These mechanical devices for self-teaching lead students by short, easy steps through material to be learned, with each step requiring a student decision and action. A typical machine is equipped with a keyboard, a visual display, and audio devices. It poses a question or problem through words or pictures. Students are able to check their responses, advancing to the next question if correct or practicing further if incorrect.

An important factor in the success of teaching machine instruction is the programming of the material. The sequence of small steps must be carefully organized and the questions carefully phrased. The machine is not a substitute for the teacher, but it does enable students to work independently and to test their mastery of a subject immediately. See also section *Instructional Technology;* AUDIOVISUAL EDUCATION.

In the 1960's, widespread interest developed in team teaching as a way to make more effective use of teaching personnel. While the plan takes many forms, its basic characteristic is that two or more teachers, who work in close cooperation, are assigned the responsibility for all or a part of the instruction of the same group of pupils. The plan offers great possibilities for effective ability grouping. For example, while a specialist in reading offers remedial instruction to a small group of pupils, the other members of the team can carry on their regular work. For bright pupils, tutorial or independent study can be arranged.

Like team teaching, the nongraded primary unit is a relatively new practice in elementary education. Introduced in Milwaukee in 1942, the plan spread to some 40 to 50 communities in the 1950's and grew rapidly thereafter.

Briefly, the plan provides for grouping children beyond the kindergarten and below the fourth grade in what is called a primary unit. The work of this unit may be completed in two, three, or if necessary, four years. In some instances the same teacher stays with a group throughout the period; in others, teachers change yearly.

Two reasons for adopting the plan are often cited. One is the difficulty of providing for individual differences in regular graded schools. The other is dissatisfaction with nonpromotion as a stimulus to achievement.

Extensive changes in the point of view, content, and methodology of mathematics instruction have taken place in the elementary and higher grades. In the "new mathematics" that emerged in the 1960's, the conceptual aspect of mathematics and the *why* of the computation were stressed to give a better understanding of the basic principles involved. While computation remained important, the amount of time spent on drill was reduced, and pupils were taught to manipulate abstract concepts. Subsequently, the new mathematics was criticized for not adequately emphasizing computational skills. The 1970's was marked by a return to the teaching of basic skills as well as increased use of calculators and computers in mathematics classes. See also NEW MATHEMATICS.

The "look-say" method of teaching reading, in which the pupil learns words by simple recognition rather than by alphabetical composition, was hailed in the 1920's as a natural approach, on a sound psychological basis, to learning how to read. This method was subjected to growing criticism in the 1940's and 1950's as wasteful and ineffective, and several books, such as Rudolph Flesch's *Why Johnny Can't Read* (1955), led many parents to insist that their children be taught the sound of letters and letter combinations. The criticism resulted in an increased use of the older phonetic approach to teaching word recognition and meaning, and the discussion of reading techniques abated somewhat. See also READING.

Teaching Staff. Up to World War II, the supply of teachers was not a serious problem. However, after the war began, qualified men and women left the profession for military service and defense jobs, and a teacher shortage developed. The shortage reached its most acute stage in 1946–1947, when one out of every seven teachers was practicing on a substandard certificate—that is, with no degree or a two-year degree. However, the problem became less and less acute. In 1966, 13.5% of elementary and secondary teachers had not earned a bachelor's degree. Today all the states require a bachelor's degree for initial certification as a teacher. The pupil-teacher ratio in public elementary and secondary schools is about 20 pupils per teacher.

Enrollment Trends. The ratio of children enrolled in school to all children of school age (5 to 17 years, inclusive) increased steadily in the United States after 1870, and by the late 1970's it had reached about 95%. The total number of pupils enrolled in school also increased. An exception was during a short period in the late 1930's, when there was a decrease in the pupils entering school because of a lower birthrate in the Depression years.

In the early 1940's the birthrate began to rise sharply. As a result, during the 1950's there was an increase of more than a million pupils a year in elementary school enrollments. By the late 1960's, approximately 32,000,000 children were enrolled in public elementary schools, and 4,600,000 were attending private and parochial elementary schools.

The early 1970's, however, saw a reversal in the trend toward increased enrollment, particularly in elementary education. In 1970, elementary enrollment totaled more than 37 million pupils. From then on, a steady decline ensued, to 31.2 million in 1980, but this was expected to reverse in the mid-1980's.

Expenditures for Education. Increasing enrollments, higher construction costs, and improved salaries for teachers have resulted in a tremendous increase in educational costs. Between 1953–1954 and 1983–1984, annual total expenditures for education at all levels in the United States increased from $13.9 billion to $230 billion. During this period, current expenditures for public elementary and secondary education grew from $8.7 billion to $124.7 billion a year. Approximately two thirds of these amounts were spent for elementary education (kindergarten through grade 8).

In terms of per capita school expenditures (the amount of money spent per person, both pupils and nonpupils), Alaska ranked first in the early 1980's, with about $1,320. Mississippi ranked last, with $317. The national average per capita school expenditure in 1981 was $451. It appeared inevitable that the cost of education would increase in the inflationary economy of the 1980's. However, the public and the federal government seemed increasingly resistant to larger outlays.

Federal Aid to Education. For many years the federal government has contributed in one way or another to the support of schools—for example, through the school lunch program. During and after World War II, the government followed a policy of direct aid to schools in areas where military or other federal activities overburdened the schools by sudden crowding. Two laws enacted in 1950 authorized aid for operating schools and for building new facilities in "federally affected areas." In 1979, on the elementary-secondary level, this assistance amounted to some $780 million dollars, an increase of 7.3% over the preceding year.

With the passage of the Elementary and Secondary Education Act of 1965, a broad program of federal financial aid was instituted. This law authorized spending more than $1 billion a year to support programs for children from low-income families. To make aid available on the broadest possible basis, the framers of the law provided that funds be given to programs serving children in both public and private schools, rather than to the schools directly. Funds were to be allocated and controlled by public agencies.

CANADA

Education in Canada is largely the responsibility of the provinces. Each province has a system of education that is administered by a department of education, headed by a cabinet minister. There is a chief superintendent of education in each province, who directs the inspectorial or supervisory staff, which, in turn, acts as a liaison group between the department of education on the one hand and the teachers, principals, and local school authorities on the other. Elementary school supervisors are attached to a local area and are responsible for some 70 to 100 classrooms.

The typical Canadian school organization, except in French-speaking Quebec, is an 8–4 system, like that in the United States. Quebec has a dual system of public and private education. The Roman Catholic parochial schools offer differentiated programs of studies for boys and girls in a seven-year elementary school (*école primaire élémentaire*). This is followed by a variety of specialized schools that provide academic, vocational, or preprofessional education.

In Canadian elementary schools the emphasis is on fundamental subjects (reading, writing, arithmetic, health education, and social studies), with varying additions of science, arts and crafts, music, home economics, and shopwork. Attendance is compulsory from the age of 7 or 8 to 14. In the rural areas, many pupils discontinue their formal education at the completion of elementary school.

The percentage of the elementary school-age population attending school in Canada is among the highest in the world. Virtually 100% of Canadian children of elementary school age are enrolled in school. One result of such high attendance is Canada's low illiteracy rate—less than 3% of the population.

In Quebec, the language issue poses a serious educational problem. In 1977 the Quebec government introduced legislation requiring the children of recent immigrants to attend French-language schools, an action that angered English-speaking residents.

WESTERN EUROPE

The typical elementary program in European countries, while subject to variations, is a 6-year course. At its completion, a selective process takes place, usually by means of examinations. The less capable pupils go into higher elementary schools, sometimes referred to as intermediate schools, which in turn may lead into special vocational institutions. However, these higher elementary schools constitute terminal education for many pupils, especially those with unfavorable economic and social backgrounds.

The more capable students attend 6- to 8-year secondary schools, and frequently continue to the universities. Elementary education is compulsory and free, and the percentage of literacy is generally high. Parochial schools share a large part of the educational effort, and, in some predominantly Roman Catholic countries, receive state support.

Administration in European schools is strongly centralized. Teachers are civil servants, and national school inspectors supervise local schools. However, there is some evidence of a movement toward more local autonomy. For example, the schools of West Germany—reorganized after World War II, largely under American guidance —are now somewhat more decentralized.

In the elementary schools of Europe, the emphasis is on fundamental subjects, although attention is also given both to developing powers of observation and self-expression and to encouraging creative talent in the arts and crafts and in music. The higher elementary school, corresponding roughly to the American junior high school, offers instruction in foreign languages, mathematics, and sciences.

Elementary teachers usually receive their preparation in normal schools designed especially for them. Although their training is intensive and thorough, they do not have the extensive academic background required of secondary school teachers, who are predominantly university graduates. The proportion of men to women in teaching is much higher in Europe than in the United States.

While European schools are traditionally conservative and "subject-centered," there is a growing interest in new teaching methods based on modern theories of the psychology of learning. In addition, the democratic structure of American public education is more fully understood and appreciated by European educators than was formerly the case. This changing viewpoint is reflected in current planning for more general extension of educational opportunities, especially on the postelementary school level.

See also sections *Education Around the World* and *Intermediate Education*; separate articles CURRICULUM; HEAD START PROGRAM; KINDERGARTEN; NURSERY SCHOOL; READING; and education sections of country articles—for example, CANADA—*Elementary and Secondary Education*; JAPAN—*Education*; UNITED STATES—*Education*.

EDWARD ALVEY, JR.*
*Mary Washington College
of the University of Virginia*

Bibliography

Althouse, Rosemary, *The Young Child: Learning with Understanding* (Teachers College Press 1981).
Callahan, Joseph F., and Clark, Leonard H., *Teaching in the Elementary School: Planning for Competence* (Macmillan 1977).
Carin, Arthur A., and Sund, Robert B., *Teaching Modern Science*, 3d ed. (Merrill 1980).
Cryan, John, and Surbeck, Elaine, *Early Childhood Education: Foundations for Lifelong Learning* (Phi Delta Kappa 1979).
Dearden, R. F., *Problems in Primary Education* (Routledge & Kegan 1976).
Decker, Cecil A., and Decker, John R., *Planning and Administering Early Childhood Programs*, 2d ed. (Merrill 1980).
Doyle, Walter, and Good, Thomas L., eds., *Focus on Teaching: Readings from the Elementary School Journal* (Univ. of Chicago Press 1983).
Hawes, H. W., *Planning the Primary School Curriculum in Developing Countries* (Unipub 1979).
Hike, Eileen V., *Elementary Education as a Profession* (R & E Research Assocs. 1981).
Jarolimek, John, and Foster, Clifford E., *Teaching and Learning in the Elementary School*, 2d ed. (Macmillan 1981).
Ragan, W. B., and Shepard, G. D., *Modern Elementary Curriculum*, 5th ed. (Holt 1977).
Rodgers, Frederick A., *Curriculum and Instruction in the Elementary School* (Macmillan 1975).
UNESCO, *The Child's First Learning Environment* (Unipub 1981).

5. Intermediate Education

Educators use the term "intermediate education" in different ways; here it refers to education for boys and girls who are roughly 10 to 15 years old. In the United States this level of schooling usually includes grades 5 through 9. It is preceded by primary education and followed by secondary education.

Schools for these "in-between" years take many forms. A 13-year-old in the United States, for instance, may be enrolled in an elementary school, a junior high school, a middle school, or a junior-senior high school.

A mathematics class in an English primary school teaches children how to add, subtract, and divide by having them pour water back and forth between various containers.

Approximately one third of the intermediate schools in the United States enroll grades 7, 8, and 9 and are usually called junior high schools. Another third, most often called middle schools, enrolls grades 6–7–8 or 5–6–7–8. Almost one quarter of the intermediate schools contain grades 7 and 8 and may be labeled either junior high or middle schools. The remainder of the schools have some other grade-level combination, including the junior-senior high school, which houses grades 7 through 12. The grade levels found in an intermediate-school building may vary from year to year, as school officials try to match the number of students at various levels with the available building space.

COMMON ELEMENTS

Despite this variety of names and grade-level groupings, intermediate education has a number of common characteristics. First, its position between primary and secondary education gives it mixed purposes. It must continue instruction in basic skills and knowledge (general education) that is emphasized in primary schools and also begin the specialized preparation for college or vocation that is the main business of secondary schools.

Second, this position of "between-ness" also affects the teaching staff. Because few colleges prepare teachers specifically for this level, intermediate schools employ both elementary and secondary teachers. Many elementary teachers enter teaching because they like to work with children; their training stresses understanding young people and adapting education to meet their needs. Secondary teachers are more apt to enter the profession because they enjoy a particular school subject; their preparation focuses on ways to stimulate in young people a similar love for the field of study. Of course, successful teachers enjoy both aspects of their work, but such differences in background may make it difficult for intermediate-school faculty members to agree on school programs.

Third, intermediate education is unique because its students are in a state of transition between childhood and adulthood. The changes that accompany adolescence take place at different rates in different children. Girls tend to mature earlier than boys, and all of a young person's characteristics do not mature at the same rate. Thus, there are greater differences among intermediate students than at any other level. See also ADOLESCENCE; CHILD DEVELOPMENT.

The rapid changes that accompany adolescence sometimes are upsetting to boys and girls. They need the advice and assistance provided by understanding adults at a time when, because they are striving for independence, they may have difficulty talking things over with their parents.

Young people today reach puberty or physical maturity at an earlier age than their parents or grandparents did. Moreover, television, radio, and popular magazines and books give them a more sophisticated knowledge of the world. This leads some educators to suggest that younger children be admitted to the intermediate school unit. Others say that this only aggravates the problem and that children of 9 or 10 should be kept away from older children, who might introduce them to undesirable forms of adolescent behavior, such as experimenting with drugs. Whether to adjust school organization to students' earlier sophistication or to try to counteract it is an unresolved issue.

In summary, the special character of intermediate education stems both from its position between primary and secondary education and from the nature of the students served. At the very time they are being transformed from child to adult status, intermediate students are encountering an educational program that is shifting in emphasis from general education to specialized preparation. Perhaps the common elements of intermediate education can best be summed up in one word: *transition*.

ILLUSTRATIVE PROGRAMS

The U.S. Junior High School. The first institution designed especially for students in transition was the junior high school, which appeared in the early 1900's. In most cases it was created by combining some of the upper grades from the elementary school with the lowest grade from the high school. Eventually a junior high of grades 7, 8, and 9 became the most prevalent combination, although junior high schools with grades 7–8 or 6–7–8 are not uncommon.

Most students are about 11 or 12 when they enter junior high. Actually, their intermediate education begins in the upper elementary school, where most of their studies are centered in one classroom with one teacher. In this "self-contained classroom" an elementary teacher has the same students most of the school day and provides instruction in reading, mathematics, language arts, social studies, and science. Students may go to specialized teachers for such subjects as art, music, and physical education.

Junior high schools vary in many ways, but it is useful to take as an example a city junior high school enrolling more than 1,000 pupils from several neighboring elementary schools. Students are divided into several "schools-within-a-school" or "houses," each containing about 375 students representing all three grade levels (7, 8, 9). Most of the classes and activities of a "house" take place in one area of the building, making it easier for students to become acquainted with one another and with their teachers.

Seventh Grade. Seventh graders may spend a little over two hours each day with one teacher in a class labeled "English–Social Studies." This teacher also serves as the homeroom adviser, helping students learn their way around the new school, recording their attendance, guiding their participation in student government, and the like. Having one teacher for this "block-time" class helps students to make the transition from the self-contained elementary program to the one-teacher-per-subject teaching common in junior and senior high.

Members of the guidance department, who are especially prepared to understand students' psychological and social problems, help block-time teachers advise their students. They also work directly with students who have problems that are too complicated for the classroom teacher.

Teaching both English and social studies, the block-time teacher can relate the two subjects whenever appropriate. For example, the class might add social-studies terms to its spelling lists and read Pearl Buck's *The Big Wave* while studying Japan.

Some block-time teachers plan their programs in cooperation with art and music teachers. Courses that combine these subjects are known as "humanities" in some schools.

Other teachers may involve the students more directly in planning and carrying out the course. Teacher and students cooperatively select a few major problems to study, such as "Achieving Peace in a Nuclear Age," "Choosing a Career," or "Drugs and the Teenager." Much work is done in small committees, and students evaluate their own progress. Courses that combine all the above characteristics are labeled "core" in some schools.

In this illustrative school, students change classes for mathematics, science, physical education, art, music, home economics, and industrial arts. Physical education meets three times a week. The other two days the students take art during the first semester and music the second. Home economics and industrial arts also are half-year subjects. All students take the same courses, except that some of the better students study a foreign language while the remainder take a course in reading.

English–social studies classes usually contain boys and girls of varied abilities, but students are frequently sectioned by ability in mathematics and science. Thus a student who is good in mathematics may be in the top section in that subject but in a lower section in science. In physical education, pupils may be sorted according to their strength and coordination.

Students with mental or physical handicaps are "mainstreamed" into classes offering them a reasonable chance to succeed. Special education teachers give them extra help as needed and also suggest to other teachers how they can assist the handicapped students in their classes.

Teachers sometimes vary the work given to different students within a class. For example, an especially capable student may be excused from doing the regular homework in order to carry out a special project. Or a class may be divided into small groups to work cooperatively on different skills or topics.

The student activities program also provides for individual differences. A large school ordinarily has many clubs and interest groups, a student council, a number of school publications, marching and concert bands, choruses, interscholastic athletic teams, and other activities.

Eighth Grade. The eighth-grade program is very similar, except that English and social studies are taught by separate teachers. Homeroom groups meet for a few minutes at the beginning and end of each day for taking attendance and carrying out other routines. A homeroom also meets for a full period once a week to conduct student-council business and to discuss such topics as how to improve study habits and boy-girl relations. Members of the guidance staff participate in many homeroom meetings, especially near the end of the year when students are selecting ninth-grade courses.

Most eighth graders take the same courses, but advanced students may take the foreign-language course normally offered to ninth graders or introductory physical science instead of the usual science course. Top sections in mathematics study more algebra than other groups and do more advanced work with computers.

Ninth Grade. Although housed in the junior high school, the ninth grade functions much like a part of the high school. The time spent on each subject is determined by high school regulations; ninth-grade credits are counted toward high school graduation; and courses are selected according to high school requirements for major and minor sequences. High school teachers also have a strong voice in the content of ninth-grade courses, especially in such fields as foreign languages and mathematics, where sequence of study is very important. Some ninth-grade students even participate in the high school interscholastic athletics program.

English, social studies, science, mathematics, and physical education are required of all ninth-grade students. Advanced science students may take biology, and the better mathematics students may take a course in advanced mathematics. Electives include art, music, several foreign languages, personal (not business) typing, computers, and introductory vocational courses.

The U.S. Middle School. The term "middle school" may be applied properly to any school that provides intermediate education. The same school might be called a middle school in one community, a junior high in another, and an intermediate school in a third. But since the 1960's an attempt has been made to limit the term "middle school" to one that begins with grade 5 or 6 and excludes grade 9. The number of middle schools has increased rapidly.

Middle schools, too, differ in many ways. An example of a middle school is one located in a suburban school system organized on a 5–3–4 pattern; that is, five years of elementary school, three of middle school, and four of high school.

Conducting a science experiment helps junior high school students learn laboratory skills and scientific method.

Here, too, intermediate education actually begins in the previous school; in this case, in the fifth grade of small neighborhood elementary schools. Instruction is "semi-departmentalized" —that is, the student has a homeroom teacher for English, social studies, and science but leaves this classroom twice a day for instruction in reading and in mathematics. Students are placed in a reading or mathematics group according to their skill in that subject, regardless of which homeroom they come from.

The School Building. In their sixth year, students enter the middle school. In a modern suburban school system the middle school might occupy a building with several clusters of classrooms radiating from a central "learning resources center." In addition to the usual library materials, the center circulates films, filmstrips, tapes, records, videotapes, and computer programs. Individual study carrels take the place of some of the usual library tables, and small seminar rooms for groups of 15 or fewer are available. Similar individual and small group study areas are found throughout the building.

In each classroom cluster a smaller learning-resources center houses materials and equipment needed for instruction in those classrooms. Folding walls between classrooms open so that as many as 125 students may hear the same lecture or view the same film. When the walls are closed, each classroom holds approximately 30 students, but movable room dividers or portable screens may be used to subdivide the space further. Thus room space is adjusted to fit the size of the learning group.

Teams of Teachers. At each grade level, instruction in English, social studies, science, and mathematics is provided in large blocks of time by "interdisciplinary" teams of four teachers. Sometimes a reading center is added to the team, especially for sixth graders. Teams share the services of guidance specialists, clerical aides, and instructional materials specialists.

Instruction by the team varies with the unit under study, with some presentations given to large groups of, say, 125 students; much work is done in the usual size classes of 25 to 30; and occasional small-group projects are held that involve 2 to 10 students.

All the students and teachers of a team may be involved in special projects, such as several days of school camping, a campaign to improve student behavior in the lunchroom, or a simulation of international trade.

Grouping of Students. Students are not sectioned by ability. Instead, teaching teams work with temporary groups based on ability, interest, or some other factor. With the emphasis on individualized learning, students spend some time in carrels working with individualized learning materials or computers to improve reading, writing, spelling, and thinking skills. As students demonstrate their ability to learn without immediate teacher supervision, they may be given increasing amounts of independent study time.

Guidance. Each student is assigned a teacher "adviser," who takes a special interest in that student's progress throughout the middle-school years. The adviser and a group of 15–20 students meet frequently to discuss common problems, improve study skills, share experiences, and conduct school business. Thus the adviser serves a guidance role similar to the core teacher or homeroom teacher in a junior high school.

Guidance specialists help teacher advisers determine the learning potential of each student, advise them on how to counsel students experiencing the ordinary problems of growing up, work directly with students who have more acute personal or learning problems, and refer unusual cases to other specialists such as the school psychologist or the speech therapist.

Exploration. Courses in art, music, industrial arts, and home economics are required of all students during their first year in the middle school. Thereafter they select from a variety of short-term "minicourses," clubs, and independent study opportunities. The intent is to help students investigate or explore a variety of possible interests. Hence this portion of the program often is called the "exploratory" program.

Student activities in the middle school are adapted to a younger age group than the junior high. Instead of varsity-type interscholastic athletics, there are "intramural" contests in a variety of sports. Emphasis is on participation for all, rather than on grooming a select few for high school performance. In place of dances, where dating is expected, social events feature activities appealing to different maturity levels.

The entire middle-school program is designed to use time, space, teacher talents, student grouping, and learning resources flexibly to meet individual needs of students.

Summary of U.S. Programs. The unique characteristics of intermediate education in U.S. schools are evident in both the preceding illustrations. General education is provided through required courses, sometimes combined in block-time courses like English–social studies or correlated by interdisciplinary teams. Adjustments for individual differences include ability grouping in some subjects, individual and small-group assignments, elective courses, and student activities.

In both illustrations, electives and student activities provide some specialized preparation for college or career, but specific vocational courses are found only in the ninth grade of the junior high school.

Junior high homeroom and block-time teachers, their work coordinated and supported by the guidance department, help students with the personal and social problems of growing up. In the middle school, guidance specialists work through the teacher advisers and also meet regularly with interdisciplinary teams.

Although the junior high has been depicted as rather conventional and the middle school as more modern, this is not necessarily the case. School systems that reorganized during the first half of this century tended to adopt the junior high pattern. Junior high schools today retain many features that were considered innovations at that time, such as block-time classes, exploratory courses designed to give students a sample of the studies available in high school, student activities programs, and the special shops and laboratories that usually were not available to intermediate students in the older eight-year elementary school. If established today, an intermediate school is likely to embody current innovations characteristic of the middle school, such as interdisciplinary teams, advisory programs, minicourses, individualized instruction, and the latest electronic means of instruction. The time of its birth influences the nature of a school's program.

Intermediate Education in Europe, the Soviet Union, and China. The future of a European child is profoundly affected by decisions made during the intermediate years. Those that have a good primary-school record may be admitted at age 10, 11, or 12 to one of the highly selective college-preparatory schools, such as the English "secondary grammar school," the German *Gymnasium*, the French *lycée*, or the Italian *liceo classico* or *liceo scientifico*. Less capable students and those not interested in college may prepare for middle-level positions in business, industry, or public service in a "secondary technical school" in England, a *Realschule* in Germany, a *lycée technique* in France, or any of the Italian institutes in agriculture, tourism, aeronautics, and the like. Children with lesser abilities or ambitions may attend a "secondary modern school," a *collège d'enseignement général*, or the upper division of a French or German elementary school. Sometimes all three programs are found under one roof, as in an English "bilateral school" or a French *collège d'enseignement secondaire*.

Programs vary in length. Those geared for college entrance are the longest and most difficult, terminating with rigorous examinations in a student's late teens. Some secondary schools are divided into upper and lower divisions, but separate junior high or middle schools are not common.

Segregating youngsters at such an early age has long been criticized as undemocratic, and the difficulty of transferring from one program to another works a hardship on children who change their minds or whose talents are slow in developing. Also, shortages in certain types of manpower make it mandatory that young people take advanced training. In response, educators in many countries are studying children's interests and abilities during the intermediate years and encouraging able students to continue their studies. Also, differences between programs have been reduced and transfer has been made easier. Italy has gone even further and established the *scuola media unificata* (unified middle school), which offers the same program to all students in grades 6 through 8. Distinctions that are based on vocational goal also are eliminated in the English "comprehensive secondary school."

In the Soviet Union, most boys and girls receive primary, intermediate, and secondary education in the same school. The "junior secondary" program includes grades 4 through 8. At the end of these five years, a committee of teachers recommends which of several secondary programs is best for the student, taking into account the student's record, examination scores, and input from parents and teachers.

In the People's Republic of China, intermediate education is provided in a three-year "junior middle school" that is similar to the American junior high school. It is followed by another three-year institution, the "senior middle school."

During the intermediate years, students in these countries often study 10 or more subjects at the same time, although some courses meet only one or two periods per week. Many students begin one or more foreign languages at this level, but otherwise there are relatively few electives. Ability grouping is practiced in many western European schools but officially frowned on in the Soviet Union. In addition to national differences, programs in many countries vary considerably from community to community, often with pronounced contrasts between rural and urban schools.

In all these countries, as in the United States, intermediate education programs emphasize the general education considered essential in that community or nation, and some provision is made for the vast individual differences that characterize this age group. Specialized preparation for college or career usually begins at this level, although specific vocational training is not emphasized.

See also EDUCATION—*Primary Education; Secondary Education.*

GORDON F. VARS
Kent State University

Bibliography

Alexander, William M., and George, Paul S., *The Exemplary Middle School* (Holt 1981).
Eichhorn, Donald H., *The Middle School* (Center for Applied Research in Education 1966).
Gruhn, William T., and Douglass, Harl R., *The Modern Junior High School*, 3d ed. (Ronald 1971).
Lipsitz, Joan, *Successful Schools for Young Adolescents* (Transaction, Inc. 1984).
Lounsbury, John H., and Vars, Gordon F., *A Curriculum for the Middle School Years* (Harper 1978).
National Middle School Association, *Middle School Journal* (quarterly).
Van Til, William, Vars, Gordon F., and Lounsbury, John H., *Modern Education for the Junior High School Years*, 2d ed. (Bobbs 1967).

Performing in a pep band at basketball games is one of many school-sponsored social activities participated in by high school students.

DOREEN E. PUGH/PHOTO RESEARCHERS

6. Secondary Education

In most countries secondary education is the second level of formal schooling, falling between the primary-elementary level and the specialized higher study offered by colleges and universities. Details of school organization vary from country to country and within countries, and some areas have intermediate or middle schools (see section 5. *Intermediate Education*). Broadly speaking, however, secondary education is the program of schooling designed for adolescent youth of 12 or 14 to 18 or 19 years of age. UNESCO surveys of world education take the 14-to-19 age range as the second level of schooling.

UNESCO's data on schooling in different countries show a great variation in the percentage of young people attending secondary school. Another outstanding fact is the dropout rate, after primary school. In Africa, 78% of children of primary school age are enrolled in school, but only 21% of children of secondary school age. In Asia, 85% of primary school age children and 35% of secondary school age children are enrolled. In Latin America, nearly 100% of the primary age group and 44% of the secondary group are in school. The highly industrialized nations such as Britain, Canada, and the United States, on the other hand, are much closer to the goal of having all children attend school through the secondary level. In the United States, for example, 99% of children in the 7-to-13 age group are enrolled in school, and 98% of the 14-to-15 group. Some drop out at around age 15, but 91% of the 16-to-17 group are enrolled in schools.

The fundamental functions and purposes of secondary schools are generally the same throughout the nations of the world: to prepare the young to live effectively and properly as adults in that society; to develop the intellectual powers of the young and transmit the knowledge and wisdom of the society to the new generation; to perpetuate the basic beliefs, value systems, and socially approved modes of behavior; to develop the powers and capabilities of the young so that they may realize their potentialities and advance the life of the social group. Practical considerations, however, have a great deal to do with the actual programs offered by secondary schools. In developing nations much of the money available for education may have to be allotted to primary schooling. Most of what is left for secondary schools may be used to train technicians who can help expand industry and agriculture and to prepare teachers to staff the elementary schools. The developed nations train many technicians and most teachers at the college level, and these nations can afford much more extensive programs for secondary students. In all countries, one of the functions of secondary schools is to prepare young people for college study. However, the number of students going on to the third level is far greater in the industrialized than in the developing countries.

U. S. SECONDARY SCHOOLS

Over a period of 250 years the American people built up a system of public secondary education that is still almost unique among the nations of the world. The American secondary school is a comprehensive educational institution that attempts to provide opportunities for youths to pursue various types of educational programs with meaning and significance for their intellectual development or career interests.

The concept of universal opportunity for secondary education irrespective of career plans, intellectual capabilities, sex, socioeconomic status of the family, or other factors was for a long time unique to the United States. Educators call this a "unitary" or "unilateral" system of schools in which pupils may progress uninterruptedly from the first year of study through secondary school to collegiate or other postsecondary institutions of learning. In most other countries of the world the system of schools after primary or elementary education has been a multilateral system in which young people are segregated into different types of schools on the basis of various noneducational factors. To counter this, France, for example, has made an effort to democratize the educational system so that all levels of training would be harmonized into a single unified system that would vary to meet the particular needs of students.

Frequently the program of secondary education in the United States is divided into two parts—the first two or three years may be offered in a junior high school or in an intermediate or middle school, and the last three or four years in what is commonly called a high school. In many countries, however, "high school" refers to a more advanced institution, comparable to a junior college in the United States.

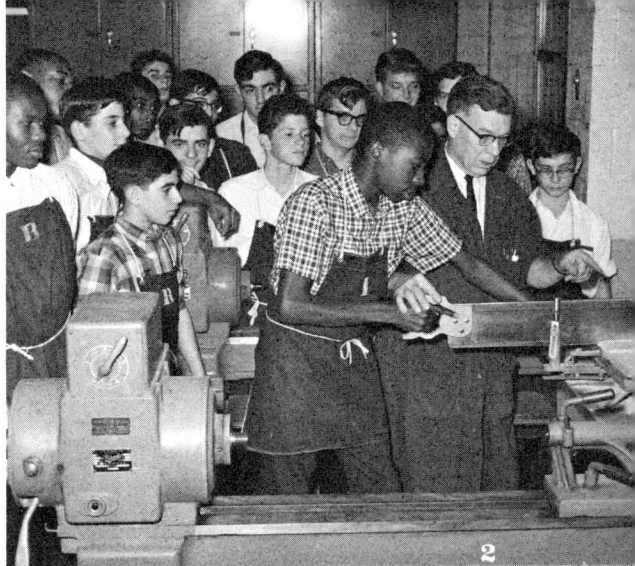

SHOP CLASS in a secondary school in New York City. The students are learning the proper use of a backsaw.

BOARD OF EDUCATION, NEW YORK CITY

Early Secondary Schools in the United States. The first formal educational institution in what is now the United States was the Boston Latin School, established by the Puritans in the Massachusetts Bay Colony. It is also regarded as the country's first secondary school. Its establishment preceded the founding of Harvard College by one year and the establishment of any system of formal education at the primary school level by almost a decade. The early colonists were imitating, in part, the type of grammar school they were familiar with in England. Those English schools were established by churches and were intended principally to teach young boys who were to become divinity students. The Boston Latin School, which still exists, was devoted primarily to the study of Greek and Latin and was designed to assist the boys in passing the entrance examinations for Harvard College.

The Latin grammar school, however, only existed in a few of the more important towns in the New England and Middle Atlantic colonies. By 1700 there were 26 identifiable Latin grammar schools in the New England colonies.

Later, private-venture schools were established by individuals in which instruction was offered in the practical arts as well as in academic subjects. The major advance in this area, however, was made by Benjamin Franklin who led the development of a new type of secondary school and opened a new era in education in the American colonies. In 1749 he published a pamphlet proposing the establishment of an academy for the education of youth in Pennsylvania. Franklin envisioned a secondary school in which instruction would be given in the English langauge, writing, history, mathematics, science, gardening, agriculture, commerce, bookkeeping, geography, and drawing. Latin and Greek were also to be offered to serve the youth who might later seek entrance to college. Although the academy, which formally opened in 1751, was never able to offer such a broad program of education, it and its imitators became the dominant type of institution of secondary education for more than 100 years. Replacing the classical institutions, academies were established throughout the new nation. It is estimated that in 1850, at the height of their popularity, there were 6,085 academies enrolling 263,096 pupils.

The program of the academies varied greatly, depending in large part on the educational wishes of the people who established it or the citizens of the community. Those pupils wishing to enter college could pursue subjects designed for this purpose; other students were enrolled in more rudimentary courses, often those of practical value. But by the latter part of the 19th century the academy was being superseded by a distinctly American institution—the public high school.

The Public High School. The first public high school in the United States was established by the Boston School Committee in 1821. At first this school was referred to as the English Classical School, but in 1824 it was renamed the English High School. This marked the original use of the term "high school" in America.

Although this new institution was to become the preeminent secondary school of the United States and one of the most exceptional educational institutions of the world, initial progress in its establishment was relatively slow.

The Committee of Ten. In 1892 the National Education Association appointed a national committee known as the Committee on Secondary School Studies, or the Committee of Ten. The primary responsibility of the committee was to bring about some uniformity among the colleges and, in turn, to establish guides for instruction in secondary school subjects and to standardize them, and to improve the quality of instruction. The committee quickly determined that the basic question was to determine the function of the high school and to plan a suitable program for fulfilling that function. They envisioned an academic program of particular benefit to a small proportion of students who planned to continue their education. This caused great controversy, for many principals and superintendents in the public school systems insisted that the schools had to be more practical and serve more fully the educational needs of all young persons.

The next 25 years brought a succession of committees appointed by the National Education Association to study the education program of the schools, with particular reference to the secondary school and its place in the educational stream. The culmination of the work of these committees was the report, *Cardinal Principles of Secondary Education*, issued in 1918 by the Commission on the Reorganization of Secondary Education. The commission proposed seven objectives that have remained the most widely accepted functions and purposes of the secondary school: health, command of fundamental processes, worthy home membership, vocation, citizenship, worthy use of leisure, and ethical character. Of course, it was the belief and recommendation of all who supported these principles that approved courses in these areas should be fully acceptable for admission to college.

During the years 1903–1918 the true character of the present-day program of secondary education emerged and the United States committed itself to the concept of a unitary system of education, equally accessible to all, that would enable pupils to progress without interruption from the first grade through graduate school. There was to be no multilateral or multipartite system of schools at the secondary level that would result in doors closed to higher institutions and hence to the professions and learned occupations. The principal efforts of educators since the second decade of the 20th century, therefore, has been to develop a program of secondary schooling that would fullfill adequately this broad concept of the basic functions of secondary education.

Rapid Growth of Public High Schools. Beginning with the last part of the 19th century, public secondary schools in the United States entered a period of phenomenal growth. A special study in 1904 by the U.S. commissioner of education stated that 321 public high schools had been established by 1860 and 3,526 by 1890; by 1900 there were 6,005 schools with 519,251 pupils enrolled. Further statistics show that in 1930 there were 23,930 public secondary schools with an enrollment of 4,399,422; in 1950 there were 24,542 serving 5,724,621 pupils; and in 1980 the number was estimated to be 20,563, with 13,700,000 pupils. In addition, a considerable number of private secondary schools operated during these years. Although accurate statistics are not readily available, in 1950 it was reported that there were 3,331 such schools with an enrollment of 672,363; in 1980 it was estimated that slightly less than 2,220 nonpublic schools existed, enrolling 1,400,000 pupils.

ORGANIZATION OF SECONDARY SCHOOLS

Some variation exists among the local school systems of the United States in the way they organize and structure the various levels of schooling. Traditionally, the 8–4 plan of school organization (8 years of elementary and 4 years of secondary school) has prevailed. Many educational leaders have felt, however, that the total number of years of secondary school should be extended. This led to the establishment of the junior high school as the lower part of a 6-year program of secondary education. In the 1960's a movement developed to redesignate the first part of the program as a middle school, often encompassing grades five through eight.

A further aspect of the reorganization of the secondary school system is an effort to abolish grade designations. But the division of schooling into levels still is based on the number of years that a child would typically devote to the program. However, in the ungraded type of elementary or secondary school, sharp grade distinctions are abolished within a level of schooling, and the pupil is placed in a group corresponding to his achievement level in a particular subject field.

One possible development in the ungraded system would permit a child in the elementary school to advance to the secondary school whenever he has reached the level of achievement that would enable him to carry successfully such a program. Most school systems are reluctant to promote pupils to the next school level on an individual basis; administrators have insisted that, regardless of achievement, the child spend a minimum number of years in each level before he can be promoted or graduated.

Types of Secondary Schools. Secondary schools in the United States can be classified in three major categories according to program.

A *high school* may encompass grades 9 through 12 or 10 through 12, and it may be one of several types. A *comprehensive school*, which is open to all youths of a community or attendance area, offers a broad program of academic, practical, prevocational, and vocational education. A *general school* is similarly open, but it offers a more limited program because of its size or the nature of the school population. Frequently excluded is an extensive program of prevocational and vocational courses or advanced courses in specialized academic subjects. A *vocational school* is for students of a community who are interested in its specialized area of training. It offers a program of general education but also has an extensive program of prevocational and vocational courses. A *specialized high school* is for pupils with special capabilities who are qualified to concentrate in a particular area of study. Usually these are high schools for the academically, musically, artistically, or mechanically talented. An *academic*, or *limited comprehensive*, *school* is one open to all pupils of the district or attendance area, but which does not offer a comprehensive program of education because of the nature of the student body. The emphasis is on academic and college preparatory courses.

The *6-year high school* (grades 7 through 12) is found in smaller communities. Because of its small enrollment and teaching staff, it is usually restricted in scope.

A *junior high school* is usually made up of grades 7 through 9. A *general junior high school* is open to all pupils of the attendance area and offers an adequate program fulfilling the first level of secondary education. A *restricted general junior high school* offers a somewhat more limited program of education with few choices available, and a limited number of practical courses.

Many school districts have adult or evening high schools. These usually are ungraded schools that offer a restricted program of high school subjects, primarily to enable persons who did not complete the regular high school course to obtain a diploma. They usually serve adults who are past the normal secondary school age. Instruction may be given by correspondence or television, as

Driver education pupils use push-button responders to answer questions on a film strip of a car accident.

AETNA LIFE & CASUALTY

A student model poses for a high school art class. Some secondary schools require students to take a minimum number of art courses.

A. DEVANEY

well as in classroom situations. See also ADULT EDUCATION.

ENROLLMENT AND GRADUATION RATES

Attendance in Secondary Schools. The efforts of the American people to make secondary schooling truly universal and equally available to all youth are illustrated by the fact that enrollments in public secondary schools, grades 9 through 12, doubled in each decade from 1900 to 1930. By 1930, more than half the young people of the nation were attending secondary schools. During the ensuing decades the growth was still remarkable. Secondary school enrollment began to decline gradually after 1977.

Of the adolescents who attend school, approximately 90% are enrolled in public secondary schools and the remaining 10% in nonpublic schools, either private or parochial. There are more than 20,000 public secondary schools of various types throughout the United States. The number of nonpublic secondary schools is estimated at 2,220. There are more than a million teachers employed in secondary schools.

Enrollments expanded because of population growth and the fact that more students remain in secondary schools until graduation. Census reports show that in 1900 only slightly more than 30% of all young people 15, 16, and 17 years of age were enrolled in any kind of formal school program but that by the 1980's, at least 90% of this age group were enrolled in school.

Graduation Rates. The extent to which young people have formally completed the program of secondary schooling has paralleled the increase in attendance rates. In the early part of the 20th century it was estimated that as few as 10% of the school-age population graduated from a formal program of secondary education. By the 1930's the figure had increased to approximately one third, and in the mid-1940's at least half of all the young people were graduating from secondary schools. By the start of the 1980's the graduation rate had risen to nearly 75%. This record is unequaled in any other country. However, the democratization of other systems of education has enabled more and more children throughout the world to complete secondary education.

In the United States about 50% of high school graduates enter an institution of higher education, and a considerable number enter noncollegiate postsecondary schools.

SECONDARY EDUCATION PROGRAMS

The American secondary school provides three important types of programs: the course program of school subjects; a program of student activities, sometimes designated as extracurricular activities; and an array of specialized services for the student body.

The School Subjects. By far the most significant and extensive aspect of the program of a secondary school is its course offerings. A large, comprehensive secondary school may offer as many as 150 to 200 separate subjects. For example, the course program of a high school often offers, in addition to the traditional academic subjects, courses as diverse as homemaking, driver education, health, and the fine arts. Moreover, a comprehensive high school might offer at least two and as many as five levels of work in subjects required of all pupils, such as English, biology, or American history.

Smaller high schools, some with enrollments as low as 100 to 200 pupils, cannot offer more than 30 to 50 different subjects. High schools in the middle range of enrollments (300 to 800) usually offer all the basic courses in each subject area, but few of the specialized courses of an advanced or vocational nature.

Senior high schools serving large numbers of students who plan to enter college often offer few courses in the practical arts or in vocational subjects. On the other hand, secondary schools whose students do not intend to enter college do not offer an extensive program of advanced courses in foreign language, mathematics, or science, although they do offer the basic required courses and some elective courses in these areas of study.

Extracurricular Activities. The high school in the United States is unique in the large number of extracurricular activities it sponsors and directs. These include interscholastic and intramural athletics, music and drama groups, a variety of clubs either related to the subject areas or to service and special interest groups, school publications, a student council that assists in the control and management of the school, school dances and other social affairs, and various specialized activities. Most secondary schools make provisions for fostering wholesome social development of the pupils through a variety of programs and activities.

PHYSICAL EDUCATION CLASS in high school has girls performing calisthenics in the school gymnasium.

Pupil Services. The educational program also encompasses such services as guidance and counseling, health care, school lunches, and library facilities. These programs contribute in important ways to the education of boys and girls.

Most school systems offer special programs for pupils with exceptional educational needs, such as the mentally retarded, the physically handicapped, and the emotionally disturbed.

Courses of Study. In all but the small high schools, planned subject sequences or major fields of study are established by the school authorities. A comprehensive senior high school usually offers a college preparatory course of study, a general course, a business course, a homemaking course, and a trade, industrial, or vocational course. In rural areas, an agricultural course may also be offered, and in some schools it may be possible to pursue a specialized course in music or in art. Students choose the particular high school course they wish to pursue. Minimum requirements for graduation from the secondary school are prescribed by local school authorities and the state department of education. The minimum for a 4-year program of education is generally 16 units of credit or 160 semester hours.

Most high schools specify certain subject requirements that must be met by all students. Usually they require that all pupils take an English course each year, often a minimum of two or three years in the social sciences, one year in mathematics, and one year in science. Almost all secondary schools require physical education. Some schools set additional requirements in music, art, or sometimes in homemaking or the industrial arts. Within each of these specified subject fields, students may choose the particular subject or class section of the subject they will take to fullfill the requirement, often with the assistance and recommendation of the school's counseling staff.

Junior high schools usually specify most of the subjects that pupils must take, allowing few elective subjects. This program usually includes courses in English, social sciences, mathematics, science, industrial arts or homemaking, music, art, and physical education.

In addition to these general requirements for graduation, additional requirements are prescribed for each of the planned programs. For example, many schools require students electing the college preparatory course to take a foreign langauge for at least two and often for three or four years. The amount of mathematics and science required is also increased for these students. In the business course, extensive work is required in typing, bookkeeping, office practice, and other appropriate subjects. In the vocational course practical experience as well as subject matter is required in the appropriate trade or occupational field.

Specialized High Schools. Some large school systems have established a few specialized high schools, along with a large number of comprehensive high schools. These specialized high schools include those especially designed for the study of music, art, business, particularly trades and industrial occupations, and the advanced academic subjects. High schools for music and art, for example, are found in New York City and Newark, N. J., as well as in other large cities. New York City has a special high school for business and one for the academically talented, the Bronx High School of Science. Philadelphia has a high school for boys and one for girls who rank high in academic ability. In Detroit, Cass Technical High School offers advanced programs in music, engineering, and architecture as well as in the academic disciplines. Specialized vocational schools exist in many large cities.

Students enrolled in these specialized schools, even those of a vocational nature, must fullfill the same general requirements for graduation as do students of other high schools in the city.

Educational authorities throughout the United States endeavor to offer the kind of course program that meets as fully as possible the educational needs of its student body.

New Directions in the Secondary Program. Beginning in the late 1950's, three major developments occurred in the program of secondary education in the United States: revisions in the course content of many subjects; provisions for much greater individualization of instruction; and new methods and procedures in teaching.

Curriculum Developments. The tremendous expansion of knowledge, the desire for greater study in depth of specialized areas and the necessity for updating the content of many subjects have resulted in major efforts to revise the content and instructional methods in a number of subject fields. Science and mathematics were, not surprisingly, the first to be extensively revised. The movement was later extended to include the fields of English, foreign languages, social sciences, health, industrial arts, and, to some extent, business and vocational subjects. In fact the entire program of the secondary school, including such courses as music, art, and physical education, has also benefited from significant national efforts to improve instruction. Frequently these course revisions have been fostered through substantial grants by government agencies to national curriculum planning commissions in the various subject fields. Some local school systems have adopted in their entirety the course content, curriculum plans, and teaching materials developed by these commissions; others have drawn extensively on the work of these groups in carrying on their own course revisions. See also CURRICULUM.

Individualization of Instruction. Many secondary schools have undergone administrative reorganization to enable the staff to provide greater individualization of instruction. These new procedures and practices include a more flexible type of class scheduling that enables the teaching staff to vary the nature and type of instruction. Provisions are often made for self-directed and independent study on the part of the pupils. Basic material may be presented to a large group and supplemented by seminar or small-group discussions.

Grouping, sectioning, and tracking procedures have also been introduced in the schools, including experimentation with an ungraded school system. The development of alternate course programs, often designated as "tracks," which students can select on the basis of their achievement levels or career plans, and opportunities for selected students to engage in independent research and laboratory activities have led to increased individualization.

Many secondary schools have introduced advanced courses in the basic disciplines that are comparable to courses traditionally offered in the first year of college or university. This practice enables students to obtain college credit by examination or to begin college work at an advanced level.

In the vocational and prevocational fields there has been considerable expansion in the programs offered in the secondary schools. This development has enabled students to select from a much wider range of courses. Substantial amounts of federal funds have been appropriated for the support of these new programs in vocational education.

A number of secondary schools in urban areas have developed special programs for youths who have not achieved success in school and who are likely to drop out before graduation. These special programs provide a greater opportunity for vocational preparation through cooperative work programs in industry and business. Special instruction to overcome deficiencies in the basic scholastic skills is also provided.

Developments in Instruction. The most noticeable change in teaching methods and procedures has been the extensive introduction of resource materials, including the use of motion pictures, television, filmstrips, slide projectors, audio recording equipment, videocassette recorders (VCRs) and videodiscs, and simulation games. In addition, there has been considerable experimentation with various types of self-study and self-directive learning devices, such as programmed teaching machines or texts, computers to assist pupils in using learning resources or to provide instruction, guides and learning activity materials for directing study activities, and more extensive use of library reference materials. See also section *Instructional Technology;* and separate article AUDIOVISUAL EDUCATION.

Secondary schools increasingly have established learning resource centers, usually organized on the basis of subject fields. For example, a social science resource center has available in one location many or all of the types of learning resources—textbooks, periodicals, and audiovisual materials—that would be most useful to the students engaged in this particular study. The main library has continued to serve as the central core of resource material of all kinds.

In their instruction, teachers try to place more emphasis on helping students develop concepts and understand fundamental principles of a particular area of study. They make increasing use of pupil participation in the discovery and formulation of concepts, principles, and generalizations.

See also sections *Education Around the World, Primary Education,* and *Intermediate Education;* also the separate articles BUSINESS EDUCATION; CURRICULUM; INDEPENDENT STUDY; VOCATIONAL EDUCATION; and education sections of country articles—for example, CANADA—*Elementary and Secondary Education;* GREAT BRITAIN AND NORTHERN IRELAND—*Education;* JAPAN—*Education.*

GALEN SAYLOR
The University of Nebraska

Bibliography
Alexander, William M., and Saylor, Galen, *Modern Secondary Education* (Rinehart 1959).
Armstrong, David G., and Savage, Tom V., *Secondary Education: An Introduction* (Macmillan 1983).
Callahan, Joseph F., and Clark, Leonard H., *Teaching in the Middle and Secondary School,* 2d ed. (Macmillan 1982).
Conant, James B., *The American High School Today* (McGraw 1959).
Grambs, Jean D., and Carr, John C., *Modern Methods in Secondary Education,* 4th ed. (Holt 1979).
Hargreaves, David H., *The Challenge for the Comprehensive School: Culture, Curriculum, and Community* (Routledge & Kegan 1982).
Hughes, M. G., ed., *Secondary School Administration: A Management Approach,* 2d ed. (Pergamon 1974).
Trump, J. Lloyd, and Miller, Delmas F., *Secondary School Curriculum Improvement,* 3d ed. (Allyn 1979).
Unruh, G., and Alexander, W., *Innovations in Secondary Education,* 2d ed. (Holt 1974).
Wilbur, Franklin P., and Chapman, David W., *College Courses in the High School* (National Assoc. of Principals 1978).
UNESCO, *Youth and the Changing Secondary School* (Unipub 1974).

A high school science teacher guides a student in examining a slide through a microscope.

JEAN B. HOLLYMAN/PHOTO RESEARCHERS

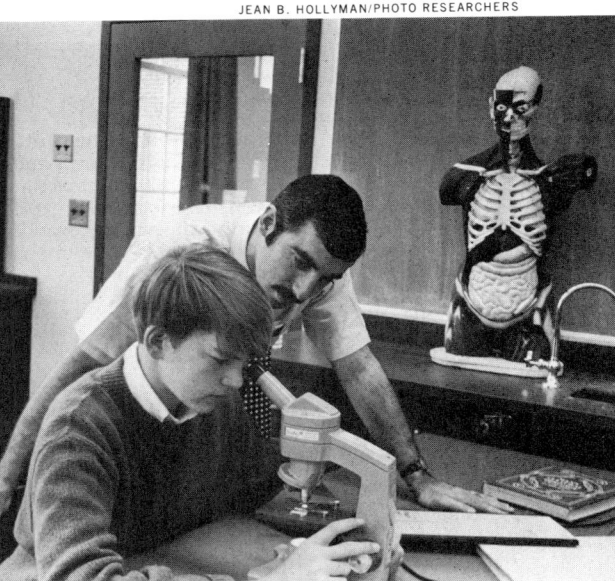

College science class in session in one of the lecture theaters of the University of Toronto, Canada.

7. Post-Secondary Education

Post-secondary education includes a great variety of programs beyond the level of the secondary schools. UNESCO reports on world education combine data on colleges, universities, higher technical schools, teacher training schools, theological schools, and many other specialized institutions under the heading Education at the Third Level. Various forms of adult education may also be included in programs at this level. A more restricted term, *higher education*, is used to mean regular enrollment in colleges and universities. Education at the higher level is available to only a small minority of the people of the world. For example, college and university enrollment is about 32 per thousand of the total population in the United States, 9 per thousand in Japan, 8 in France, 6 in Britain, 5 in West Germany, and 3 in Latin America.

In the simplest societies there is no higher education; everyone learns all that is known in the tribal heritage of skill and lore. In more developed cultures, knowledge outruns the memory and skill of any individual; specialists arise—potters, weavers, canoe builders, navigators, traders, priests, sages, artists, storytellers. The systematic mastering of such specialties foreshadows the higher education that sustains civilized living. Even tribes and nations ignorant of writing have developed forms of higher education. The Incas of Peru required sons and daughters of the nobility to reside in the capital in order to learn, not only the more exacting handicrafts and special skills such as weaving and warfare, but the art of government and the keeping of accounts by means of knotted cords. In New Zealand the Maori imposed upon young nobles a long training in memorizing an extensive body of tradition, genealogy, theology and philosophy, poetry, ritual, strategy, and—whether successfully or not—telepathy.

Thus higher education begins wherever a select minority is instructed in special branches of knowledge that are acquired only by concentrated effort. The ancient Egyptian theocracy, the palace sages and wandering teachers of ancient India, the scribes of Sumeria—all devoted themselves to the increase and transmission of learning. Without higher education civilized living is impossible, whether knowledge be imparted under the open sky, in temples, among guilds of architects or navigators, in secret societies, or in publicly maintained schools.

It is since the 18th century that higher education has come to denote formal study in a university or college on completion of secondary school preparation. In this modern sense higher education dates from the establishment of Germany's University of Halle in 1694. More precise outlines of the modern university were achieved by the University of Göttingen some 50 years later and by the University of Berlin, reorganized in 1810. This closer delineation of the nature, purposes, and structure of the university had to wait upon corresponding developments in the secondary school, which were not formalized until the first decades of the 19th century. Although the first great public schools in England were established in the 12th and 13th centuries and the Boston Latin School (1635) anticipated early public secondary education in America, the average age of the students at institutions like Oxford, Cambridge, and Harvard, even in the 18th century, was low, and the type of studies pursued fell short of modern concepts of higher education. Modern university and secondary education is hardly more than two and a half centuries old. Its roots, however, go back to antiquity; the precedents for higher education may be found in ancient China, India, and Egypt, as well as in Greece and Rome.

ANCIENT WORLD

China. The existence of schools is recorded in China even before 1000 B.C. The common people were taught only what was essential for their daily life. For the nobility the curriculum included ritual, music, archery charioteering, mathematics, and writing. Writing was a mystical art reserved for those who were to govern.

Under the Han dynasty (200 B.C.–220 A.D.), centers were developed for training youths for public service; in 125 B.C. a College of Doctors of Classics began with 50 students and grew shortly to 30,000. The famed civil service examinations were initiated in the Sui dynasty (590–618 A.D.). Examinations appear to have been a Chinese invention. Under the succeeding T'ang dynasty they were organized and expanded in scope to include not only classics and poetry but also history and current events. A National Academy at Changan was thronged with students; among them were scholars from Central Asia, Korea, and Japan. In the Sung dynasty (960–1279 A.D.) both private and public schools flourished at a high level of scholarship. In T'ang and subsequent periods the printing of encyclopedias and reference works was accompanied by intensive development of philology, geography, law, mathematics, and historical criticism.

Until the establishment of universities of the Occidental pattern in the 19th century, Chinese higher education centered in two main objectives, each with its own procedures: training for public office, largely based on Confucian and allied classics; and preparation for the Buddhist priesthood, which was confined to monasteries. General education occurred in locally maintained village schools and in guilds that trained apprentices. For higher education the individual student had to find a tutor, or enter one of the various grades of government schools that led to the great higher institutions at the capital. China stands among the pioneers of higher education. See also CHINA—*Education.*

India. India's brilliant intellectual traditions were perpetuated—from ancient times to the present—by the memorization of passages from the Vedas, Brāhmaṇas, Upanishads, and other religious and philosophical classics. Complete mastery of the Vedas traditionally required 48 years of study. Higher learning remained a practical monopoly of the Brahman caste, which maintained its power largely through the need of the less privileged castes for the Brahmans' services. The Sanskrit schools of early times gradually expanded their curriculums and divided into separate schools: literature, law, astronomy, medicine. The lower castes found instruction in practical matters at the simple schools of the villages. Under the Buddhist emperor Asoka (reigned c. 274–232 B.C.), Buddhist monasteries promoted education and systematically trained missionaries. In northwestern India, where Alexander had established centers of Greek culture, there was systematic higher education of missionaries, who spread Buddhism and higher learning—notably tinged with Greek influence in the fine arts—throughout central and eastern Asia. This diffusion of learning and the arts constitutes one of the great events of human history.

The feeling of ancient Indian scholars that history is better left unrecorded makes it difficult to fill in the details of time and place in the long story of higher education in India. The Chinese pilgrim Hsuan Tsang recorded details of education and of other aspects of India's civilization in the 7th century A.D. He described the university at Nalanda, where advanced studies were accessible to those who passed rigid entrance examinations (usual age, 20). Some 1,500 teachers lectured to about 8,500 students, with approximately 100 lectures daily on as many subjects. The various ranks of scholars were distinguished by titles roughly analogous to academic degrees. Both Brahmanic and Buddhist studies were fostered. Other universities, with approximate dates of establishment, or of their known flourishing, include Valabhi (6th century), Vikramasila with its Central Hall and six related colleges (10th century), Jagaddala (11th century), Odantapuri (dates uncertain), Mithila (11th century?), and Nadia (15th century). Whatever the uncertainties of detail, the rich literature and accumulated learning of India testify to millennia of specialized study in a rich culture that centered in religious and philosophical interests.

Egypt. In Egypt specialized education can be traced to the 3d millennium B.C., when the pharaohs began to rule in accordance with legal codes that influenced the moral and political philosophies of the Hebrews and Greeks. The sacred text was *The Book of the Dead*, a collection of maxims and rites to be mastered in anticipation of the Day of Judgment. The Egyptians developed hieroglyphic writing, mathematics, astronomy and other sciences, music, and the plastic arts; and they often are credited with greater contributions to learning, prior to 500 B.C., than any other people. The nearest approach to universities probably was found at the temples of Heliopolis, Thebes, and Memphis. Save that medicine was taught at the temples of Saïs and Heliopolis, little is known of education for the professions.

With the rise of Hellenistic culture, libraries, museums, archives, and other centers of learning were established in Egypt, culminating in the 700,000-volume library at Alexandria, founded by Ptolemy I Soter (reigned 304–283 B.C.). The city remained a truly international center of learning even after the library was burned in 47 B.C.

Greece. Developments in Greece after 500 B.C. were highly significant for modern advanced education, largely as a result of the teaching of such philosophic schools as the Sophists. Learning was less highly organized and controlled than in Egypt; students gathered around great teachers without benefit of formal organization or government sponsorship. The School of Pythagoras, Plato's Academy, Aristotle's Lyceum, and the rhetorical schools of Isocrates—often cited as forerunners of medieval universities—were conducted in what might be called converted residences, quite inferior physically to the elaborate structures of the Ptolemies. Unlike the 1st century B.C., Greece had nothing like the Alexandrian Library or the government-supported academies of the Jews. Yet nowhere was scholarly effort more intense and more significant for the future than among the Greek and Ionian peoples. Scholars were free—at least until the 3d century B.C.—to follow the light of the intellect wherever it might lead. Students and teachers were self-governing and were generally responsible only to each other; the state reserved the right to curb only such teachings as were deemed subversive. Subsequently state control tightened, and advanced education was held to fairly rigid norms. The ephebic college, for example, which included selected men of 18 to 20, evolved from an informal civic institution to a fashionable military academy catering to an aristocratic elite.

In the Hellenistic era (after 300 B.C.), advanced education developed along two main lines: the one under state aegis; the other typified by Epicurus' school called The Gardens and the school of Zeno, which was held in a portico, or *stoa*—hence the name Stoics. Such schools as these, taken collectively, have been termed figuratively the "University of Athens." There were, however, no licensed faculty members, no examinations, and no granting of degrees or licenses. Although teachers on the higher levels were held in great esteem, they were exposed to heavy political pressures on occasion: Socrates was condemned to death, Plato and Aristotle had to flee

Students attend an outdoor class at one of the autonomous institutes that compose the Universities of Paris.

abroad, and many "gymnasiarchs" were ostracized on the flimsiest charges.

Higher learning in Greece was based on concepts of the proper use of leisure time; *schola* meant "leisure," or the activities of a freeman directed to the fullest appreciation of life. Hence the term, "liberal" education, from the Latin *liber* meaning "free," in contrast to "vocational" or "professional" education, which prepared men to earn a living.

Athens was the leading center of advanced education from the 5th century B. C. until the 6th century A. D., when the Emperor Justinian banned (529) "pagan" teaching throughout the Roman Empire and closed the Platonic Academy at Athens. During this period in the Greco-Roman world, the content of higher education became universal in scope. This inclusive view of education ultimately led the Roman scholar Marcus Terentius Varro (116–27 B. C.) to classify learning into nine liberal arts, which were to form the basis of the medieval trivium (logic, grammar, rhetoric) and quadrivium (music, arithmetic, geometry, and astronomy). Varro included medicine and architecture as well. In the 2d century A. D., instruction became somewhat more formalized when the Roman emperor Marcus Aurelius endowed five chairs at Athens: one for rhetoric, and one each for Platonism, Aristotelianism, Epicureanism, and Stoicism—reflecting the further fact that no one school ever became dominant in Greece. See also GREECE—*History of Greece to 330 A.D.*

Rome. In Rome higher education began with Greek influence, as Greek aims, content, and methods spread to Rome in the 3d and 2d centuries B. C. Schools of Greek—later Latin—rhetoric initiated the tradition of higher learning. Advanced education centered in civics, politics, and family living, with a view to participation in public affairs.

Higher education in Rome was professional rather than "leisurely" in the Greek sense. The emphasis shifted from dialectics to memory and imitation, although a wide variety of subjects was provided; and such men as Cicero (106–43 B. C.) went to Athens or elsewhere in search of a truly liberal education. Influenced by the writings of Cicero, and later by the rhetorician Quintilian (latter half of the 1st century A. D.), the Romans concentrated on oratory; to that end they utilized Varro's nine liberal arts plus philosophy and literature. Influenced also by teachers of the quality of Polybius (2d century B. C.), Varro, and Plutarch (46?–?120 A. D.), Roman higher learning developed a humanistic character, which declined as imperial authoritarianism increased.

MEDIEVAL AND MODERN EUROPE

As Christianity spread throughout the Roman Empire, the Christians at first combined their theology with Hellenistic philosophy, especially under the tutelage of such Eastern church fathers as Justin Martyr, Clement of Alexandria, and Origen (2d and 3d centuries A. D.). Subsequently, under Jerome and Augustine (4th–5th century A. D.) and Gregory I (540?–604), Christian teaching broke sharply with pagan tradition. Greek and Roman learning was condemned by the Christian emperors as subversive, and Aristotelian teaching, at least, disappeared for centuries into the Arab world. St. Augustine cautioned Christians against "enjoyment" of secular knowledge as an end in itself, although he also provided a liberal estimate of the usefulness of Greek and Roman knowledge to sincere Christians. For centuries thereafter intellectuals regarded secular knowledge with attitudes that ran the gamut from sympathetic toleration to outright rejection.

In the 6th century Cassiodorus, who with Boethius was a major transmitter of classical learning to medieval times, wrote a syllabus of sacred and secular education, the *Institutiones divinarum et humanarum litterarum*, intended for the guidance of monks in their studies. Besides offering advice for the study of the Scriptures, the *Institutiones* included a discussion of the liberal arts, which provided a major basis for the system of liberal arts studies in the Middle Ages.

Monastic and Cathedral Schools. The collapse of the Roman Empire under the barbarian invasions of the 5th and 6th centuries left education to the church, and the monastic and episcopal schools were hard put to continue any tradition worthy of the name of higher education. Under Charlemagne, however, in the late 8th and early 9th centuries, formal education received powerful governmental support. Charlemagne appointed the noted scholar Alcuin (735–804), of the cathedral school at York, as head of the leading palace school at Aachen (Aix-la-Chapelle) that was later conducted by the illustrious Johannes Scotus Erigena (815?–?877) in the reign of Charles the Bald. The Carolingian rulers also decreed that every monastery and cathedral should maintain a school. In no sense, however, were these schools comparable to the universities that developed in later centuries. The monasteries did not advance learning, but they preserved it to some degree; and an incalculable debt is owed to the intrepid monks and teachers who cultivated learning in the cloisters and faithfully copied thousands of manuscripts in an age when priceless creations of civilization were being put to the torch or carried off as loot. The disintegration of the Carolingian empire and the political disorders of the late 9th and 10th centuries left the monks as almost the sole custodians of the intellectual traditions of the West.

By the end of the 11th century, the cathedral schools had emerged as an intellectual vanguard. They led the 12th century educational renaissance and became the nuclei of the later universities. Usually a chancellor presided over a cathedral school, appointed by the bishop of the diocese. Under papal authority he enjoyed the exclusive right to grant teaching licenses (*licentiae docendi*). For a time the authority of the cathedral schools and the power of their chancellors in educational matters were practically unquestioned throughout Europe. As teaching and learning spread beyond the individual cathedral schools, the *studium generale* developed. This was a place of general study, where students from many parts of Europe would assemble in one specially renowned cathedral school. These centers of learning were the embryos of the medieval universities. A *studium* always included at least one of the higher faculties—law, medicine, arts, theology. The faculty of medicine at the *studium* in Salerno, Italy, for example, developed into a European center.

First Universities. The revival of higher learning in Europe was signalized by the organization of student corporations at the *studium* in Bologna (c. 1158) and the organization of teaching masters in Paris. The Bologna *studium* was renowned for legal studies; that of Paris, for arts and theology. The word *universitas* denoted a corporation or guild; teachers and students used the existing model of the guild as their pattern of organization. Thus, as medieval higher education developed, two important types of "universities" emerged: (1) the university of students, exemplified at Bologna; and (2) the university of masters, for which Paris was the model. In time the terms *studium generale* and *universitas* became synonymous. The immediate stimulus for the organization of these guilds was the desire of students to pursue studies at levels beyond those provided in the cathedral schools, so that they might become teachers in such schools or join the ranks of accomplished churchmen, officials, and professionals. There was also a rising demand for more freedom and unity in the pursuit of learning.

The times favored the rising universities. Towns and principalities throughout the Continent had instituted formal measures of security and control, to ensure profitable trading and safe travel. The Crusades and contacts with Arabs and Jews in Spain had made much ancient knowledge accessible in western Europe. A good education became an important means to preferment in the church and in the state.

The legal position of medieval universities enhanced their viability. Jurisdictional disputes between "town and gown" led popes and secular monarchs to grant special privileges to the universities. In Paris the crown gave university masters the right to suspend lectures in protest against injustices perpetrated by town officials. Several times during the 13th century the pope intervened on behalf of a university. In Italy, a decree of Frederick I in 1158 provided that in legal proceedings against the scholars of Bologna the defendants might be "given the option of being cited before their own master or before the bishop." Measures also were taken to enforce better conduct on the students: in 1230, Henry III directed that students at Oxford and Cambridge be subject to the immediate authority of a master. Since a student was thus responsible to a member of the university, the legal autonomy of the university was implied. In general, the masters' "union" seized control of teaching licenses from the chancellors by claiming the exclusive right to accept or refuse candidates and by requiring enlisted members to obey "union" rules. When political or ecclesiastical interference grew unbearable, or when prices soared, students and teachers declared "cessations," followed by "dispersions." The former resembled the modern sitdown strikes; in the latter case, thousands of consumers moved away from local markets.

Formation of Colleges. The college originated at Paris as a hospice endowed to provide board and lodging for poor scholars. In time, especially at Oxford and Cambridge, individual colleges became the real centers of educational endeavor, with their own buildings and endowments, though they continued legally within the universities. There were some 70 colleges at the University of Paris before 1500; but with the revolution, at the end of the 18th century, the university began to absorb them, and today only such fragments or names as the Sorbonne remain. At Oxford and Cambridge the colleges are still central to university life, although financial determinants have effected increasing centralization. The emphasis on college organization eventually spread to the New World also, in greatly modified form.

England and Scotland. Established as a *studium generale* around 1168, Oxford was named in a public document in 1214. Cambridge came into being about 1209; disturbances at Oxford caused lectures to be suspended and a number of scholars migrated to Cambridge. In Scotland, universities were founded at St. Andrews about 1411, at Glasgow about 1451, at Aberdeen in 1494, and at Edinburgh in 1583. French rather than English influences characterized developments in Scotland. The college system was not adopted for lack of endowments. All four of the Scottish universities became renowned. By 1800 the University of Edinburgh had such a reputation for scholarship that many Englishmen completed their education there.

In the 19th century the dominance of Oxford and Cambridge was challenged by the rise of the great civic universities such as London, Manchester, and Birmingham. During the 17th and 18th centuries much of the progress in higher learning, especially in science, commerce, and trade, had occurred in academies and private societies outside the universities; on the whole, the dons of Oxford and Cambridge had avoided the so-called material aspects of learning. Following the lead of the 18th century German universities, and responding to the public will for increased opportunity for higher education, Britain's new civic universities quickly acquired recognition—not only in technological fields but also in the fine and liberal arts. See also GREAT BRITAIN AND NORTHERN IRELAND—*Education*.

France. In France higher education rested on its laurels until the Napoleonic educational laws of 1806 and 1808 established the "University of France," which was not a university, but a name given to the whole system of French education. Under a "grand master" who enjoyed almost absolute power, the French educational system soon became perhaps the most centralized in Europe. The country was divided into educational-political units called "academies," each headed by a university. Thus modern French universities, unlike those in other countries, have jurisdiction over much of the schooling above the elementary level, and the rector of the university wields great political and educational power within his district.

Higher learning in France is bulwarked by a well-defined system of higher schools, institutes, and conservatories. The 13 autonomous units of the University of Paris, including the Sorbonne, enroll some 250,000 students—making it one of the largest universities in the world. Scholarship standards in French universities are uniform, partly because of the integral educational philosophy that established and maintains them, and partly because of the highly developed system of national government examinations for entrance into the professions. In 1968, French students, notably at Paris, rebelled against what they considered the inflexibility of the country's educational system. In October of that year the National Assembly passed a law shifting the control of universities from the minister of education to councils elected by faculty and students. See also FRANCE—*Education*.

Germany. German universities forged ahead of the French in the 18th century with the founding of the universities of Halle (1694), Göttingen (1737), and Erlangen (1743). At the new German universities, systematic lectures displaced textual exposition, seminars superseded disputations, the German language replaced Latin, and freedom of research and instruction—*Lehr- und Lernfreiheit*—prevailed. Modern science and philosophy were studied, and the arts faculty was placed on an equal footing with theology, medicine, and law. At Berlin (1810), under the vigorous leadership of Wilhelm von Humboldt, all manner of subjects were investigated jointly by students and teachers. Lectures were subject to critical questioning and analysis by the hearers; laboratory experimentation replaced pure conceptualization and conjecture; theology, philosophy, and traditional learning were put to the test of inner consistency. Scholars produced by this system—the historian Leopold von Ranke, the philosophers Georg W. F. Hegel and Arthur Schopenhauer, Justus von Liebig the chemist and Hermann L. F. von Helmholtz the physicist, the psychologists Gustav Theodor Fechner and Wilhelm Wundt, Karl Friedrich Gauss the mathematician, and the philologists Jacob and Wilhelm Grimm—raised university standards to heights that elicited admiration and emulation the world over. The University of Berlin pioneered in the training of experts and researchers rather than teachers. Small wonder that universities in Britain, the United States, Scandinavia, and Europe generally, as well as far-off Japan, accepted Berlin as an exemplar of the new spirit of higher education. See also GERMANY—*West Germany* (Education) and *East Germany* (Education).

LATIN AMERICA AND CANADA

Latin America. In the New World the Spaniards established universities in Santo Domingo, Peru (San Marcos), and Mexico (the Royal and Pontifical University)—all by 1551. Thus by the time Harvard was established in 1636, higher learning in Latin America was nearly a century old. Patterned largely on the University of Salamanca in Spain, these institutions were feudal and ecclesiastical in spirit; the curriculum was based on the seven pillars of knowledge—theology, sacred Scriptures, canon law, jurisprudence, the arts, rhetoric, and grammar. The level of scholarship was not impressive until the arrival of the Jesuits near the close of the 16th century; and after their expulsion in 1767 many institutions either sank into oblivion or were converted into state secondary schools.

Since the 16th century, the vicissitudes of politics have repeatedly affected the fate of Latin American universities; for example, in the 19th century the National University of Mexico was closed and reopened at least three times because of clashes among social groups, the church, and the state. In contemporary Latin America, university teachers and students continue much more responsive to political decisions—and contribute more actively to their formulation—than in the United States or Canada. See also LATIN AMERICA—*Education* (Higher Education); and sections on education in articles on the individual Latin American countries.

Canada. Canada, settled originally by the French, came under British control in 1760. In 1783 some 70,000 Loyalists entered from the United States, and from that time agitation for establishment of a university increased. In 1802 a royal charter was granted to King's College at Windsor. In 1827, King's College of Toronto was instituted by royal charter, but religious disputes and financial problems delayed the actual opening until 1843. A new charter mitigated the religious requirements for directors of the college, and in 1849 and 1850 legislation converted King's College into the secularized University of Toronto. In protest, the University of Trinity College was founded in 1851. It followed Oxford and Cambridge closely: the dons had to subscribe to the Thirty-nine Articles of the Anglican Church, and remain celibate. Some of these features were continued even when Trinity became affiliated with the public University of Toronto in 1903.

Most of the more than 50 universities in Canada are privately endowed. However, nearly all the provinces have publicly supported universities generally comparable to U.S. state universities. Colleges, many affiliated with a university, provide additional education opportunities. All these institutions experienced sharp enrollment increases after 1960.

Laval University (1852), in Quebec, and the University of Montreal (1876) are modeled after the University of Paris and require secondary school preparation equivalent to that of the French *collège* or *lycée*. Dalhousie (1818) and Queens University (1841), which are now nonsectarian, reflect Scottish and Presbyterian influences; McGill (1821) also inherits a Scottish tradition. In 1923, King's College at Windsor—except for its divinity school—became affiliated with Dalhousie. The other universities, British-inspired, are mostly nonsectarian. Following Britain's example, the national government of Canada has adopted a program of direct grants to universities.

The French of Quebec have maintained their cultural and linguistic identity; and the Roman Catholic Church has continued to exert a powerful influence on all education in French-speaking Canada. In general, however, the conditions of higher education in Canada resemble those prevalent in the United States. See also CANADA—*Higher Education*.

UNITED STATES

Colonial Institutions. Higher education was inaugurated in the British colonies in America in 1636, when the General Court of Massachusetts Bay Colony authorized the establishment of a college to "advance learning and perpetuate it to posterity, dreading to leave an illiterate ministry to the churches, when our present ministers shall lie in the dust." Late in 1637 it was decided to locate the college across the Charles River from Boston, at "Newetowne," which was appropriately renamed Cambridge; and in 1639 the infant institution was given the name Harvard College in memory of a young clergyman, John Harvard of neighboring Charlestown, who had died the year before, leaving his books and a sum of money to the school.

More than 50 years elapsed before a second institution, William and Mary College, was established (1693) at Williamsburg, Va., and named in honor of the British sovereigns who granted the charter. Like Harvard, it was designed to train ministers, with a special stipulation that youths were to be taught to spread the Christian Gospel among the Indians. Yale was founded as the Collegiate School at Killingworth, Conn., in 1701, moved to New Haven in 1716, and took the name of Yale College two years later in honor of its English benefactor Elihu Yale. The declared purpose of the institution was to fit the youth of the colony "for Publick employment both in Church & Civil State." The Congregational ministers who founded it were motivated, in part at least, by concern over the increase of theological liberalism at Harvard.

By 1770 there were 10 collegiate institutions in the colonies, and from this time on the number increased steadily, both before and after the revolution. The University of Pennsylvania, which began as the Charity School in Philadelphia in 1740, was converted into an academy (with Benjamin Franklin as first president of the trustees) in 1751 and chartered as the College and Academy of Philadelphia in 1755. The Pennsylvania legislature changed the name to the University of the State of Pennsylvania in 1779 (shortened to University of Pennsylvania in 1791), making it the first institution in the United States to be officially styled a university.

Princeton, chartered as the College of New Jersey in 1746, opened at Elizabeth the following year, moved to Newark some months later, and to Princeton in 1756, though the name Princeton University was not officially taken until 1896. Washington and Lee, Virginia's second collegiate institution, began in 1749 as Augusta Academy and was known as Liberty Hall Academy from 1776 to 1798, when it became Washington Academy after George Washington made a gift of $50,000. The name Lee was added in 1871 after the death of Robert E. Lee, who was president of the institution from 1865 to 1870.

Other members of the first 10 were: Columbia, chartered as King's College in 1754; Brown, founded as Rhode Island College in 1764; Rutgers, chartered as Queen's College in 1766; and Dartmouth (1769).

Concerning education in the colonies, certain generalizations may be made. Religion was the strongest determinant of purpose and content, especially Puritanism in New England. Although influenced in largest part by the colleges at Oxford and Cambridge, early practices revealed a

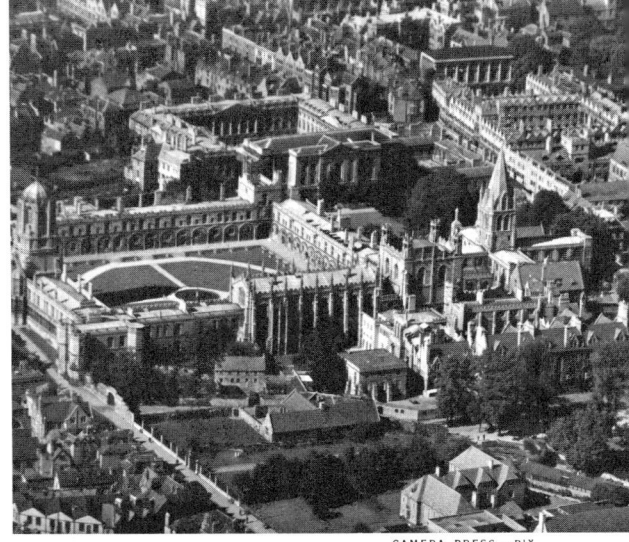

OXFORD UNIVERSITY in an aerial photograph showing Christ Church College (*left*) and Oxford Cathedral.

desire on the part of colonists to foster a system of higher learning that would be independent of the Old World and contribute spiritually and materially to colonial progress. The level of learning in the colleges was no higher than that of modern secondary schools until well into the 18th century. (Educational standards were such that Yale records tell of a seven-year-old scholar who passed the entrance examinations.) Harvard was for a long time little more than a one-man college; and William and Mary was for at least 50 years really no more than a grammar school. The general tenor of cultural attitudes was conservative.

Princeton and Pennsylvania grew out of a different tradition. Although Princeton represented the desire of New Jersey Presbyterians to establish an institution of their own for the training of the ministry, the college was founded not by the church but by the colonial government. This event mirrored the prevailing conviction in New Jersey (and other colonies) that the conservatism of New England was not suited to the newly created colony; it was also an example of a gradual movement away from dependence upon the church for the advancement of learning, and presaged the type of civic interest that later engendered state universities. The University of Pennsylvania evolved not so much out of a religious emphasis as out of the realism of such men as Benjamin Franklin, who showed a more intense interest in science and society, rather than theology and classical languages, as determinants of courses of study. The transition from religious, classical, and European emphases to concern for the social, political, and economic needs of the new nation was most evident in its early phases at this university, exemplified by the founding in 1765 of the first medical school in the country.

Early Federal Action. In the first years of the republic George Washington and others, notably James Madison, Thomas Jefferson, and the two Adamses, proposed the establishment of a national university in the District of Columbia. Washington bequeathed part of his fortune to the project, expressing deep concern in his will that so many of the nation's youth felt it necessary to go to Europe for their advanced education "before they had imbibed any adequate ideas of the happiness of their own." He advocated a plan to spread systematic ideas through all parts of this rising empire, thereby to do away with local attachments and State prejudices...." With considerable prescience Washington foresaw that the funds upon which much of the nation's higher learning depended would in the future be "too narrow to command the ablest professors" and that national aid was therefore imperative. But despite the impoverishment of many of the country's colleges with the ravages of the Revolutionary War, Washington's advice and offer of material aid went unheeded.

The cold reception given the proposal for a national university, and the refusal on the part of Congress even to mention education in the Constitution, did not mean that the federal government was uninterested in higher learning. As early as 1785, Congress enacted the Land Ordinance, providing in part for the encouragement and support of publicly controlled educational institutions. This ordinance laid the foundation for the future land-grant colleges, and at the same time placed public education clearly under the control of individual states.

Growth of Private Institutions. The early colonial colleges imitated their European counterparts, which had depended on royal or church sponsorship for their birth and life. But as the United States came of age, local and immediate circumstances determined the course of higher education. At first, the close union of educational leaders, church, and state made it possible to maintain church-founded institutions even after the churches alone could no longer carry the financial burden. But after the Dartmouth College case in 1819, public and private education began to take separate roads. Stimulated by the Supreme Court decision guaranteeing private ownership of institutions of learning against public encroachment, any individual or association with sufficient means could found a college and obtain a state charter.

The private institutions founded before the close of the Revolution, with the exception of Rutgers, have continued as such, but usually with marked relaxation of their sectarian character. Others that date from the 18th century may be classed with them: Georgetown University (1789) was established by Roman Catholics at Whitemarsh, Md. (now in the District of Columbia); Williams (1793) was established privately as a nondenominational school at Williamstown, Mass.; Bowdoin (1794) at Brunswick, Me., also was nonsectarian, as was Middlebury (1800) in Vermont. Union College (1795) at Schenectady, N. Y., was created by a "union" of several denominations.

The settlement of the Middle West was marked by the establishment of numerous private denominational schools patterned after Harvard, Yale, and Princeton both in their organization and in the desire to produce an educated clergy. Eastern colleges and churches provided inspiration and a measure of financial support. The Civil War eliminated many of the weaker institutions in the Midwest and especially in the South. In Ohio alone, 26 of the 43 existing colleges closed at this time. Among those that survived this trying period in the Midwest were Western Reserve (1826), now in Cleveland, first located at Hudson, Ohio; Oberlin College (1834) at Oberlin, Ohio; DePauw University (1832) at Greencastle, Ind.; Wabash College (1832) at Crawfordsville, Ind.; Illinois College (1829) at Jacksonville, Ill.; and Knox College (founded in 1836 as Prairie College) at Galesburg, Ill.

Roman Catholics, seeking to propagate their own faith and learning, had established 14 permanent colleges before the Civil War. These included St. Louis University (1832), the University of Notre Dame (1844) in Indiana, Fordham University (1846) in New York City, and Seton Hall (1861) in South Orange, N. J.

Colleges for women also appeared before the Civil War: Troy (N. Y.) Seminary was founded by Emma Willard in 1821; Mount Holyoke (South Hadley, Mass.) opened in 1837. Georgia Female College (now Wesleyan College) was started at Macon in 1836; Oxford (Ohio) College for Women in 1852; and Ohio Wesleyan Female College at Delaware, Ohio, in 1853. A majority of these institutions fell decidedly short of the academic standards provided for men, but Vassar College (incorporated 1861, opened 1865) set high intellectual standards from the start. Oberlin College was a pioneer in coeducation of a high order. See also COEDUCATION.

Even before emancipation, higher education of Negroes had been advocated, and in 1854 the Pennsylvania General Assembly sanctioned the establishment of Ashmun Institute (near Oxford, Pa.), which changed its name in 1866 to Lincoln University. After the Civil War, with northern missionary support, Negroes organized various institutions of higher learning. Among them Fisk University (1866) at Nashville, Tenn., Howard University (1867) at Washington, D. C., and Tuskegee Institute (1881) in Alabama are outstanding. Of these, Howard was the first to establish undergraduate, graduate, and professional schools under one organization.

During the 19th century, accelerating technological development prompted the establishment of specialized institutions of higher learning. Rensselaer Polytechnic Institute (1824) at Troy, N. Y.; Massachusetts Institute of Technology (1861) at Cambridge, Mass.; and California Institute of Technology (1891) at Pasadena, Calif., are outstanding examples of institutions specializing in scientific and technical education.

Private institutions continue to outnumber public colleges and universities in the United States, although public institutions enroll more than two thirds of the nation's advanced students. The marked heterogeneity of all these institutions, as to scholarly standards and academic customs, reflects that of American culture with its freedom of thought and movement. Characteristic of all institutions, however, is the division of studies into roughly standardized units or credit hours (about 45 lectures or class meetings per course of 3 credit hours), and the requirement of 120 such credit hours for the B. A. or B. S. degree. The significance and comparability of credit hours earned in different institutions, or in different fields of study within the same institution, remain open to debate.

Colleges have also organized voluntary associations for evaluating and standardizing educational practices. These associations regularly send evaluation teams, composed of professors from various schools, to individual colleges. On the basis of such evaluations, the association rates the college under investigation as "accredited" or as falling short of the informal standards that have been applied. Notable is the fact that these regional associations include both private colleges and state universities.

Of the hundreds of institutions of higher learning that were founded after 1865, a very considerable number were the result of individual philanthropy. These include some of the greatest American universities: Johns Hopkins (1876), Stanford (1885), the University of Chicago (1890), and Duke University (1924). Taxation of private fortunes and rising costs have made it increasingly difficult for private philanthropy to provide for a major university.

State Universities. Although the University of Georgia was chartered in 1785, it did not open until 1801, and the first state university actually to operate was North Carolina (chartered 1789, opened 1795). By 1860, six of the original 13 states had their own universities, and there were 17 state institutions in all. The Morrill Act (1862), granting land to the loyal states for the endowment of agricultural colleges, greatly accelerated the movement; and by 1956 every state in the Union was maintaining at least one state-supported institution of higher learning.

The land-grant colleges and the agricultural and mechanical institutions quickly took the lead in industrial, vocational, and agricultural education. Sooner or later they transcended their original aims, and provided also for the more traditional courses of study. With aid from federal departments (notably Agriculture, Labor, and Commerce), direct appropriations of state tax monies, and frequent private endowments, the state universities eventually came to include some of America's outstanding institutions of higher learning. The most recent aspect of the movement appears in the general addition of liberal arts content to the curriculums of numerous state-supported normal colleges which previously had been limited to the training of teachers for public school systems.

Graduate Schools. The graduate school is another feature that must be understood to grasp the pattern of American higher education. Students enter the colleges with less secondary preparation than in many other countries; hence the graduate schools must assume major responsibility for advanced studies. The need for concentrated study in specialized fields at the graduate level was recognized early at Johns Hopkins, Chicago, and Catholic University, while Clark University (1887) was at first exclusively a graduate institution.

Enrollment in graduate schools, totaling less than 100 in all institutions in 1870, more than doubled in each succeeding decade, and by the late 1970's the total had risen to more than a million. In 1983, 300,000 students received the master's degree and 33,000 were awarded doctorates—a sharp increase over the 59,000 master's and 9,000 doctor's degrees awarded in 1956.

Undergraduate Curriculums. As the bachelor's degree forfeited its position as the terminus of higher education, the curriculum of undergraduate colleges changed significantly. The democratization of higher education, the rise of state universities, and the spread of the philosophy of pragmatism all increased the freedom of students to choose what they were to study. After 1869 the trend was away from fixed curriculums toward elective programs, under the assumption that (1) the college student was old enough to decide what was good for him; (2) political and economic freedom called for freedom in educational experiences; and (3) traditional subjects

Fieldwork provides graduate students in chemical engineering with valuable practical experience.

were out of tune with scientific and social advances. President Charles W. Eliot of Harvard led the way in the elective movement, in the face of much criticism. During the 1930's specialization was stressed increasingly; during the following decades the tendency away from rigidly prescribed courses and toward a wide range of elective choice was noticeably increased.

The 20th Century. The rapid increase in the number of colleges between the Civil War and World War I brought chaos in standards of student selection, content of courses, and teaching quality and methods. Until the 1890's, American scholarship was regarded as immature, and well-to-do parents sent their sons to Europe for a university education, while European scholars were not attracted to America until the turn of the century. There was therefore a lack of cross-fertilization between European and American scholars. Only a few colleges were established in the 1920's, and the economic depression of the 1930's effected the demise of many of the weaker institutions. Student enrollment, however, continued to increase: in 1900 there were 238,000 students in American colleges and universities; in 1920, 531,000; and in 1930, 1 million.

Government financing of college education for war veterans effected a tremendous increase in enrollments after 1945. The postwar baby boom and higher college attendance among women and minorities caused enrollments to soar during the 1960's and 1970's. Although enrollment was expected to peak in the 1970's owing to a decline in births after 1964, the total number of college students continued to rise in the 1980's.

Other weighty factors affecting the whole course of higher education were (1) raising of the school-leaving age; (2) later entrance into employment; (3) increase in the level of educational accomplishment required by employers; (4) the concept of high school training as general rather than specialized; and (5) increased prestige of the college degree as an educational goal. Colleges were confronted by many dilemmas: overexpanded student bodies; economic inflation without proportionate increases in fees; the necessity of deciding whether private institutions should accept government aid that might lead to official control; persisting problems of discrimination based on economic status, race, or social standing, in a time when all classes of society were demanding higher education; and the necessity of curriculum revision in the face of changing demands.

Problems Facing Higher Education. American institutions of higher education are among the finest in the world, and they continue to make major contributions to the advancement of learning everywhere. In recent years, however, many of their perennial problems have been greatly exacerbated, and new problems have arisen in the wake of social and political upheavals.

Perennial problems include financial support, political autonomy, and curricular integrity. Even in the richest country in the world, the United States, colleges and universities find it increasingly hard to meet rising costs. Many institutions depend more and more on special aid from industry, private foundations, and the federal government. Although such financial support does not normally carry with it direct controls, reliance on outside funds nonetheless affects political autonomy and academic freedom by fostering certain types of inquiry (for example, science and technology) and neglecting others (for example, the humanities).

Autonomy and freedom in higher education are also beset by other troubles. The fact that colleges and universities take a greater interest in community life means that their members not only scrutinize but also actively engage in the many conflicts that rage on the public scene. Opponents of this kind of engagement often condemn an entire institution for the activities of some of its members and, in many cases, seek to curtail both autonomy and freedom.

Curricular offerings are likewise affected. As institutions of higher education become more socially concerned and enroll more and more students from varied backgrounds, they feel the need to relate their courses more directly to the cultural milieus of their students.

The problem, then, is how to maintain political autonomy, academic freedom, and curricular integrity in the face of conflicting social pressures on the university.

The period of the late 1960's will go down in educational history as one of student confrontations led by small dedicated groups. Their grievances were many. Some "activists"—students and faculty alike—completely rejected the form of American society and called for total revolution. Others wanted to abandon such values as competition, hard work, and material success for a style of life that is passive, withdrawn, peaceful, and cooperative. Another group of activists centered its attack on racial discrimination, especially in educational institutions, where such minorities as blacks, Mexican-Americans, and Puerto Ricans were barely represented on faculties and governing boards. These groups were united in one set of aims: to win greater recognition of their presence in the university community; to gain representation on faculty committees and governing boards; and to secure the right of self-determination in all matters affecting their educational welfare.

In the 1970's and after, however, following the U.S. withdrawal from Vietnam and the end of the war, the unrest of the 1960's, with its riots and disorders, gave way to a more conservative attitude among students and a greater emphasis on academic achievement. Nevertheless, certain problems remain that higher education has solved only in part: To what extent shall students be allowed to participate in the formation and administration of university policies? To what extent shall universities and colleges adopt new courses of study that are directly relevant to the needs of minority groups and to economically disadvantaged students? (Specifically, shall there be departments of ethnic studies devoted entirely to Afro-American, Negro-American, Mexican-American, or American Indian cultural contributions?) How best will the universities train future teachers and researchers, and retain existing ones, for such studies?

But the most persistent problem facing higher education is the ever-increasing cost. For example, average tuition, room, and board in some private universities rose from about $4,400 in 1975 to nearly $14,000 in 1985. As a result, it became increasingly difficult for many Americans to receive a post-secondary education.

See also COLLEGES AND UNIVERSITIES; COSTUME, ACADEMIC; DEGREE; JUNIOR AND COMMUNITY COLLEGES; UNITED STATES—*Education;* articles on special areas, such as ADULT EDUCATION, LEGAL EDUCATION, MEDICAL EDUCATION. See also the Index entry *Education: Higher.*

GEORGE F. KNELLER, *University of California*

Bibliography

Altbach, Philip, *Comparative Higher Education Abroad: Bibliography and Analysis* (Interbook Inc. 1976).
Altbach, Philip, and Berdahl, Robert, eds., *Higher Education in American Society* (Prometheus 1981).
Anderson, R. E., *Strategic Policy Changes at Private Colleges* (Teachers College Press 1977).
Bacca, M. C., and Stein, R. H., *Ethical Principles, Practices, and Problems in Higher Education* (C. C. Thomas 1983).
Bender, David R., *Learning Resources and the Instructional Program in Community Colleges* (Shoe String 1980).
Bienayme, Alain, *Systems of Higher Education: France* (Interbook Inc. 1978).
Boardman, Francis, *Institutions of Higher Learning in the Middle East* (Middle East Institute 1977).
Bok, Derek, *Beyond the Ivory Tower: Social Responsibilities of the Modern University* (Harvard Univ. Press 1982).
Kneller, George F., *The Education of the Mexican Nation* (1951; reprint, Octagon 1973).
Knowles, Asa S., ed., *The International Encyclopedia of Higher Education,* 10 vols. (Jossey-Bass 1977).
Levine, A., *When Dreams and Heroes Died: A Portrait of Today's College Students* (Jossey-Bass 1980).
Mayhew, L. B., *The Carnegie Commission on Higher Education: A Critical Analysis of the Reports and Recommendations* (Jossey-Bass 1974).
Medsker, L., and Tillery, D., *Breaking the Access Barrier: A Profile of Two-Year Colleges* (McGraw 1971).
Neave, Guy, *Patterns of Equality: New Structures in European Higher Education* (Humanities 1976).
Portman, David N., ed., *Early Reform in American Higher Education* (Nelson-Hall 1972).
Trivett, D. A., *Goals for Higher Education: Definitions and Directives* (Amer. Assoc. for Higher Educ. 1973).
Van Alstyne, C., and Coldren, S., *Financing Higher Education* (American Fed. of Teachers 1977).
Veysey, L. R., *The Emergence of the American University* (Univ. of Chicago Press 1965).
Willie, C. V., and Edmonds, R. R., eds., *Black Colleges in America: Challenge, Development, Survival* (Teachers College Press 1978).
World Guide to Higher Education: A Comparative Survey of Systems, Degrees, and Qualifications (Unipub 1976).

ACCELERATED STUDENTS in a primary school in Pittsburgh are given advanced instruction in human anatomy. Such schools give special attention to students who can advance more rapidly than other pupils in the class.

FORD FOUNDATION

8. The Education of Exceptional Children

In the field of education, the phrase "exceptional children" encompasses children with many kinds of disabilities as well as children of outstanding ability. The exceptional characteristics of such children generally prevent them from benefiting by general education programs in any degree commensurate with their potentials, and special programs must be designed to prevent the waste of their abilities.

BACKGROUND

Although the concept of exceptionality is relatively recent in education, dating from the latter half of the 19th century, an awareness of the existence of handicapped persons and of differences in abilities is older than history. One of the earliest references to the gifted is in Plato's *Republic*, where positions, authorities, and responsibilities were assigned according to each individual's ability to discharge them. However, man was well into the 20th century before anything approaching a systematic attempt was made to identify the gifted and to construct an educational program for them.

The treatment of the handicapped is dealt with in many early writings, including the Bible. It has varied markedly from one society and one age to another, depending on the prevalent philosophy. In many early societies handicapped persons were rejected for reasons of group survival or because they were thought to be possessed by devils. Evicted from the family group and abandoned by the tribe, often in infancy, they usually died quickly of exposure, starvation, or attacks by wild animals.

In the Middle Ages many handicapped persons found their way into the courts of noblemen and kings, where they acted as personal servants or as jesters providing entertainment and diversion. In later periods they were often imprisoned in asylums and provided with minimal care. In some societies, as among the American Indians, the mentally retarded or emotionally disturbed were considered children of the gods. As such, they could move freely from tribe to tribe, were safe from attack, and were freely provided for.

None of these ways of treating the handicapped was in any way educational, and none recognized the value of the handicapped as individuals. In general, they were considered to be subhuman and devoid of feelings, with little or no potential for contribution to either their own or the common welfare.

The notion of educating the handicapped had its ultimate source in the philosophic theory of the worth and equality of all men. This belief, which first appeared in the Middle Ages, led to the rejection of the idea of the divine right of kings and rulers and to the several revolutions that took place in France, Germany, Italy, and other western European countries, as well as in the Americas. One of its natural consequences was the development of educational programs for handicapped children. Only through education could the worth of the handicapped individual be demonstrated, and only by appropriate training could his handicap be offset. Education was the road to equality.

The intellectually superior did not profit by this philosophical movement. No special educational programs were designed for them, as such programs would only enhance their abilities to apply their intelligence and would thus accentuate their deviation from the norm.

Programs for the Handicapped. Not all the handicapped groups received educational attention simultaneously. However, educational programs for the mentally retarded and for children with physical or sensory disabilities all originated within a 50– to 100–year period beginning in the latter half of the 18th century. During this period Louis Braille developed his methods of reading and writing for the blind; methods of teaching deaf people the use and understanding of speech were developed into a systematic instructional approach; and foundations were laid for training programs for the mentally retarded.

French educators and physicians figured importantly in these early developments, although contributions were also made by Belgians, Swiss, Italians, and others. Movements spread quickly from one country to another. Institutions for educating the mentally retarded appeared in the United States in the 1860's, and broad laws relating to the care and treatment of this group began to be passed in the United States and in England early in the 20th century. By this time the public schools were also assuming responsibility, so that before World War I almost every large metropolis offered programs for most of the handicapped groups. State and federal departments of education began to institute bureaus for handicapped children to provide leadership in developing and administering these programs. Along with these organizations came standards to determine admissions to the programs and allotments of special support funds.

After World War I, programs for the physically and sensorially handicapped increased rap-

693

Modern instructional aids can help a determined learner overcome even the constraints of a wheelchair. A physically handicapped student learns to operate a computer.

© ALEC DUNCAN/TAURUS PHOTOS

idly. Public school programs expanded, and legislation was passed to provide the handicapped with such added services as vocational rehabilitation counseling. However, not until after World War II was there rapid growth of programs for the mentally retarded, the emotionally disturbed, the socially maladjusted, and those with learning disabilities.

The most significant U.S. legislation for the handicapped is the Education for All Handicapped Children Act, passed in 1975 and administered by the U.S. Department of Education. The act, which became effective in 1977, established the right of every disabled child to a free public education. The states were mandated to seek out such children and to provide them with an appropriate education—that is, a program tailored to the individual child. Rather than allowing exceptional children to "sink or swim" in standard school programs, the schools are required to develop an individualized educational plan for each handicapped student.

The classification, treatment, and care of exceptional children in the United States are essentially representative of those in almost all of the more advanced nations of the world. Although the services may be provided by various agencies from one country to another, the programs are very similar. The one major exception is the USSR, where certain officially promulgated scientific views deny the existence of the less acute forms of mental retardation that are caused by genetic, cultural, or social factors. The Soviet schools provide special programs for the physically and sensorially handicapped and for those children whose mental retardation is pathologically caused, as by brain injuries or by glandular disorders; but no such programs are provided for children for whose retardation no medical cause can be determined. In practice, however, differences in ability are recognized. Children that do poorly in school are placed in jobs at early ages, while gifted students are encouraged to continue their educations through graduate school if this appears appropriate.

Classification. An exceptional child is one that deviates significantly from the norm either intellectually, sensorially, emotionally, physically, behaviorally, or in his ability to communicate. The child is not termed exceptional if the deviation has no significant effect on his ability to profit by standard school curricula; thus children with minor or correctable disabilities—the mildly mentally retarded, the slightly hard-of-hearing, those that require glasses to correct their vision, and those with minor orthopedic handicaps—are not considered exceptional.

The educational definition of the exceptional child is clearly comparative and somewhat arbitrary; for this reason, estimates of the numbers of such children vary markedly from one study to another, depending on the definitions used.

Although such divisions are unsound in terms of treatment and education, exceptional children may be divided for purposes of discussion into various groups: intellectual deviates (mentally retarded and gifted), the physically and sensorially disabled (those with visual, aural, orthopedic, and certain speech handicaps), and behavioral deviates (those with behavior disorders and other speech handicaps). A number of subgroups have recently been added to these categories: to the physically and sensorially disabled group, children with brain injuries, minimal brain damage, and minimal cerebral dysfunctioning; to the behavioral deviates, children with learning disabilities.

The newer subgroups suggest a change in the criteria for determining educational groupings in this field. Whereas the older classifications are based primarily on physical, medical, and psychiatric characteristics, the more recent ones are based on behavioral characteristics and on educational needs. Where this trend will lead—if it truly exists—and what implications it holds for future grouping, education, and treatment can be determined only by time. Meanwhile it is necessary to discuss the education of exceptional children in terms of the traditional groupings.

THE GIFTED

Definitions of the gifted vary according to the degree of giftedness taken to be critical. Thus, if the intelligence quotient (IQ) is used as the criterion, the cutoff points proposed vary widely from one authority to another, ranging from 115 to 180; most cutoff points in actual use fall between IQ's of 125 and 135. Many educators feel that the IQ alone is not a valid indicator of exceptional ability. Certainly, a difference of a few points would not justify labeling one student "average" and another "superior." See also INTELLIGENCE.

Giftedness is characteristically defined as superior ability to deal with relationships and abstract ideas; such ability is thought of by some as "intelligence," by others as "creativity." Some authorities are concerned with more specific talents or aptitudes; these exist not only in the fine arts, where they are perhaps most easily recognized, but also in such areas as dramatics, mechanics, and mathematics.

In general, the schools classify as gifted those children that score in the superior range on intelligence tests and that also show outstanding learning skills. Programs for such children did not appear in the public schools until the early 20th century; even now, in spite of the many efforts to promote such programs and of the tremendous waste of talent that takes place in their absence, classes for the gifted are relatively few. Probably the greatest impetus to the development of these programs in the United States was the Soviet launching of Sputnik I in 1957, but even this impetus soon waned. Most gifted children are still educated in regular classes with no special provisions; more often than not, they are never even identified as gifted. They generally move through the grades with relatively little difficulty, tend to be above-average students, are usually well-adjusted and physically capable, and are often leaders of their classmates and popular with their teachers. A substantial proportion enter college, where many graduate in the top quarters of their classes.

Existing public school programs for the gifted may take any of several forms—tracking, homogeneous grouping, special ancillary services, acceleration, and enrichment. Although these programs are not mutually exclusive in their characteristics, each can easily be distinguished from the others.

Tracking Programs. These programs usually call for special classes. The gifted children may be identified early in school and special classes provided throughout the school years. In other cases the program may begin in a later grade and then may or may not continue. It may also encompass all course work or may be limited to a single area of study.

Tracking programs usually attempt to define the children's educational needs and to provide appropriate experiences in addition to the traditional requirements for graduation and for admission to college. Certain areas tend to receive special emphasis, particularly advanced mathematics and the physical and social sciences. The children are encouraged to do much of their work through independent research and study; they often prepare reports and projects the results of which are shared with the rest of the class. The teacher of such a class functions primarily as a sort of catalyst for learning, an advisor and an educational resource for the students.

Homogeneous Grouping. In this method, children in each grade are divided into separate classes, each of which is more or less homogeneous in terms of the children's achievements and abilities. Because such groupings change from year to year, and because special programs of this type do not ordinarily provide for the development of curricula other than the general curriculum, homogeneous grouping is often ineffective as a means of providing for the gifted. Its primary advantage is that it theoretically enables the teacher to provide instruction more nearly suited to each child's learning level. Whether supplementary instruction or special areas of study are introduced for the gifted pupils depends almost entirely on the individual teacher.

Special Ancillary Services. Some school systems employ special teachers that provide supplementary instruction for children that need it or that may derive particular benefit from it. For the gifted they may provide special instruction in a regular school subject, with the purpose of encouraging the students to go beyond the level reached in the regular class. They may also provide instruction in special subjects that are not ordinarily provided at certain levels, such as foreign languages. Such teachers may also encourage gifted students to undertake independent study by formulating special projects; in such cases the teachers may offer suggestions, point out possible alternate methods, and provide additional resources. See also INDEPENDENT STUDY.

Another kind of ancillary service is the assignment of a guidance counselor to work with the gifted pupils. The counselor talks over problems with the children, guides them into the most appropriate courses, and helps them to take maximum advantage of the learning opportunities offered by the school. Like homogeneous grouping, ancillary services seldom provide either a curriculum specifically designed for gifted pupils or the continuity that may be essential to the effectiveness of such programs.

Acceleration. The oldest type of educational programming for the gifted, acceleration, has also probably been the most widely used, but it is almost universally frowned upon by modern educators. Its operation is simplicity itself, requiring not even the identification or diagnosis of the gifted student. Each child is simply grouped with his equals in terms of academic achievement, and he moves through the grades as quickly as he can learn the required subjects. In such systems it is not unusual for highly gifted children to graduate from high school and to enter college at 12, 13, or 14 years of age.

Acceleration has been attacked as disregarding the child's social and physical maturity; while he may be able to do the schoolwork creditably, he may have no social peers and may be unable to participate in athletic activities. Despite this drawback, which has led to its partial abandonment, acceleration has far from vanished from the educational scene. Many students that grow bored, for whatever reasons, with traditional programs find ways to accelerate themselves, particularly in secondary school. They may register for heavier course loads, take special competency examinations, or attend summer schools. By such means they may condense their entire secondary school careers into a period of only one or two years.

A few universities continue to encourage acceleration. Some universities select students of high potential during their early years in high school and enroll them in special programs that enable them to complete their last two years of high school and four years of college in a total of four years. Many of these students then continue their educations in graduate school, returning to society with professional training at dates earlier than would otherwise be possible.

Enrichment. This approach to the education of the gifted calls for them to do independent and guided study in order to broaden their understanding of the material being dealt with in class. Although enrichment is seldom made into a systematic method, it is now by far the most widely advocated and practiced solution to this problem. Again the way in which the program is conducted depends almost exclusively on the individual teacher, who is expected to adjust his instruction to provide for the needs of every child in the class. As with some of the other programs for the gifted, this kind seldom uses unusual curricula; it rests on the assumption that the content of education is well defined and essentially the same for all children.

Other Methods. In addition to these relatively formal kinds of educational programs for the gifted, less organized provisions of many sorts are being made, especially in secondary schools. Special courses in such subjects as chemistry, physics, mathematics, history, and creative writing are growing more and more common. Student counselors are increasingly aware of gifted students and are not only advising them about enrolling in formal programs but also recommending valuable experiences—especially in the fine arts—that are available through participation in various community programs. In the large cities, especially, many opportunities in painting, sculpture, music, dance, and so forth not only are available but are systematically brought to the attention of able students.

Private, state, and community colleges are also becoming involved in the education of the gifted high school student. Many university courses are offered to those that are capable of participating, and special summer session programs are available for students that do not live in the immediate vicinity. The purpose of these programs is not simply to accelerate able students, allowing them to complete their educations earlier, but to graduate more competent students with fuller and better-rounded educations.

A survey of present practices reveals many opportunities for gifted students, of which most are not formalized or systematic. This freedom may be beneficial. Formal programs often grow overly rigid and restrictive. Gifted persons tend to be diverse and original, with highly individual educational needs. While approaches to the problem of their education will vary as widely as the school systems themselves, there are certain steps toward the solution that ought to be taken universally: the development of an awareness of the problem, a willingness to plan programs for individuals, and the organization of systematic programs of identification and evaluation of gifted students. These are the prerequisites to providing appropriate education for each one.

THE MENTALLY RETARDED

Definitions of "mentally retarded," as of "gifted," vary from one authority to another, but the phrase is generally considered to refer to the lowest 3% of the population in terms of IQ. Educators divide the mentally retarded into three broad groups: the educable, the trainable, and the custodial. Because mental retardation is a problem relating to learning, and the schools are the only places where learning abilities are systematically measured and compared, the educable mentally retarded largely blend into the general population at adulthood. Regardless of their degree of success in earning a living and avoiding trouble of various sorts, they are rarely thought of as mentally retarded. Only the more severely retarded, the trainable and the custodial, remain recognizable, their deviations being greater.

Educable Mentally Retarded. Children in this group, who constitute about 85% of the mentally retarded, have the potential to learn sufficient academic skills and knowledge, vocational tools, and social understanding to direct their social, personal, and economic activities independently as adults. They are generally accepted by the public schools on the basis of their scores on intelligence tests, their IQ's ranging roughly from 50 to 80.

There are a number of common misconceptions concerning the characteristics of the educable mentally retarded: their physical and motor development, their ability to reason and to learn, their tendency toward misbehavior and delinquency, and so on. In most such respects they are, of course, anything but homogeneous, but certain general tendencies may be discerned. Their physical and motor development tends to be somewhat retarded (although not as much as their intellectual development), which makes programs designed to provide compensatory activities and learning in these areas impractical. Within the limitations imposed by their experiences and level of intelligence, they can be taught to learn and reason efficiently.

Social behavior in the educable mentally retarded, as in general, seems more closely related to environment than to intelligence. Because most children in this group come from homes in the high-delinquency areas of their communities, their delinquency rate would be expected to be above average. But appropriate educational programs have been found to affect this sort of behavior, and in good programs these children are often found to be delinquent significantly less frequently than other children in their neighborhoods.

The earliest educational programs for this group were organized in institutions about the middle of the 19th century; not until the 1890's were public school programs instituted. Because adequate diagnostic instruments were generally available only after 1916, these early classes undoubtedly included many children who were not mentally retarded but whose progress in school was unsatisfactory for some other reason.

The number of classes for the mentally retarded increased slowly but steadily until World War II; from 1945 to the present there have been dramatic increases every year. States have enacted improved laws in education, specifically including the mentally retarded, and in many states special provisions for these children have been made mandatory. In the late 1950's the federal government became involved, enacting legislation to encourage research and the training of teachers and administrators in this field. The most important legislation was the Education for All Handicapped Children Act, which Congress passed in 1975.

The early public school programs for this group were housed in special schools and centers patterned on institutional schools. These have gradually vanished, and the usual procedure today is to house one to three such classes in a

With the help of attention-getting pictures, educable retarded children in a New York City classroom are taught to identify the correct names for food and clothing.

© ABRAHAM MENASHE/PHOTO RESEARCHERS

regular school, preferably the one the children normally would have attended. Thus the children can attend school in as natural a setting as possible, and there are opportunities for them to participate with normal children in activities in which they can take part on relatively equal terms.

Programs for the educable mentally retarded are usually divided into four levels: primary, elementary, and junior and senior high schools. Initial emphasis is placed on preschool, readiness, and beginning reading and arithmetic skills. Later, instruction in the skills is continued, and appropriate experiences in the physical and social sciences, art music, and physical education are gradually included. The applications, meanings, and interrelations of the various learnings are stressed much more heavily than is usual in general education. At the junior high school level a broad survey of industrial arts is introduced. At the end of this level the children's academic achievements typically range from the 3d-grade to the 5th-grade level.

The senior high school program is the most highly individualized. It generally has two related emphases: on practice in the application and use of learned skills and knowledge, and on preparation for the world of work. The students study occupational areas and visit industries to observe the performances required in specific jobs. Some students are given general job training followed by work-study programs, which allow deficiencies that show up in practice to be corrected in the related school program. Others are taught specific vocations in a vocational school, enabling them to move directly into the higher skilled trades.

Trainable Mentally Retarded. Mental retardation in children at the educable level may have various causes, among which environmental factors play a part. At the trainable level, however, postnatal environment seldom has an important causative effect, and children at this level (who constitute about 12% of all mentally retarded) come almost equally from all socioeconomic levels. Among the most common causes of their retardation are trauma (brain injury), disease of the child or mother during or just before pregnancy, blood incompatibility, and genetic characteristics effecting glandular imbalances, with resulting effects on the brain. The IQ's of these children generally range from 30 to 50.

Classes for these children were instituted in a few communities before World War II, but programs were not developed throughout the United States until well into the 1950's. The impetus for this development came not from educators but from associations of parents working through state legislatures.

The trainable mentally retarded, by definition, will always require supervision and direction. Nevertheless, they can learn a great deal in the way of independence, self-help, and contribution within a protected environment. Programs for the younger children in this group emphasize independence and self-help activities; later the emphasis shifts to contributory activities such as ordinary domestic tasks. In some communities this stage is followed by a protected workshop where the children learn more formal occupational activities. Some few are then placed in spots in industry where adequate, sympathetic supervision will be provided. Most of the trainable mentally retarded remain in the protected workshop and work on contract jobs or help produce selected objects to be sold at special sales or on the open market.

Custodial Mentally Retarded. Children in this group are not a responsibility of the public schools and are customarily kept at home or placed in institutions. A few institutions are conducting research on operant conditioning techniques in training. These techniques frequently involve rewarding the child for each instance of desirable behavior (see CONDITIONING). It has been found that many children so trained can learn, particularly in the area of self-care, skills sufficient to reduce significantly the amount of supervision and attention they need.

THE PHYSICALLY AND SENSORIALLY HANDICAPPED

This category includes such diverse groups as the visually handicapped, the aurally handicapped, those with orthopedic handicaps or some other health problems, and those with certain speech handicaps. A discrete educational program is required for each of these groups.

It is often said that the blind have less difficulty educationally than the deaf, because the former can learn effective oral communication skills at a very early age. Vocationally, however, the reverse is true; despite all the work of educators and vocational rehabilitation counselors, the blind are still less employable than the deaf.

The educability and employability of the orthopedically handicapped depend largely on the nature and severity of the handicap. Those with sufficient intelligence and oral communication can be provided with educational programs relatively easily, whether at home, in a school, or in a hospital. Vocational programs depend on the individual's physical and motor skills and sometimes on his ability to use a prosthesis (such as an artificial arm or leg), as well as on his intellectual ability to perform any job for which he may be physically suited.

Visually Handicapped. For educational purposes, the visually handicapped are divided into two distinct groups: the partially sighted and the blind. The partially sighted are those who have visual acuity ranging from 20/70 (with which what could normally be seen at 70 feet can be seen at 20 feet) to 20/200 in the better eye after all possible medical, surgical, and optical correction. The blind have visual acuity of 20/200 or less. Many can use their vision to distinguish light from dark, to make out large objects, and to find their way about and travel, but it is insufficient for general educational use.

The definitions of these groups are based on visual acuity, but other factors can be important in planning for the placement of a child. Among them is the child's ability actually to use his vision and to interpret what he sees. Another important consideration is whether the condition is progressive, so that the child will have less vision in the future than he has at present.

Programs for the blind were initiated earlier than those for the partially sighted; the first residential school for the blind was established in Boston in 1832. The major programs are still located in residential settings, although some significant ones have been developed in public schools, especially since 1950. The major programs for the partially sighted, which originated about 1900, have consistently been in the public schools.

Partially Sighted. The curriculum for the partially sighted differs from the general curriculum in only a few respects. The primary differences involve adaptations of materials, use of special materials and equipment, and different methods of organization for instruction.

AURALLY HANDICAPPED CHILD learns that nasal sounds of "moon" cause vibrations that can be felt.
IRENE BAYER, FROM MONKMEYER

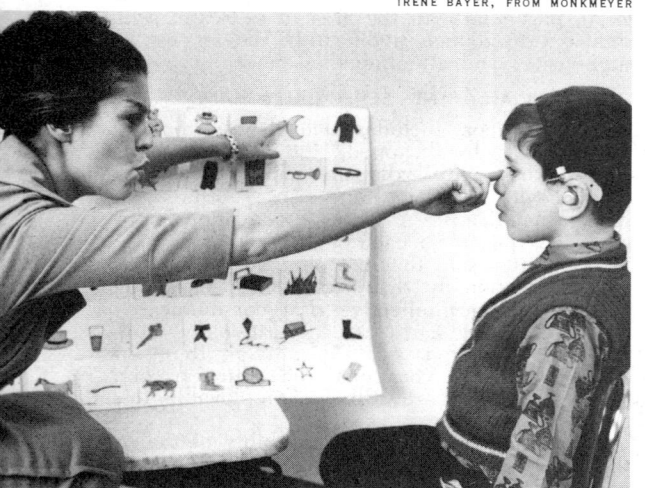

Because partially sighted children have difficulty in using many standard instructional materials, other materials of larger size, with larger type, or of different nature are usually substituted. Classroom lighting must be good, so that the children can use their limited vision optimally. Desks and other furniture should be light in color, and sharp color contrasts between woodwork and walls should be avoided. Chalk boards are usually green or beige, with chalk of contrasting colors. The children may use special editions of books printed with very large type. Where such books are unavailable, large magnifying glasses of special design for use in reading may be employed. In other cases the instructional material may be recorded on magnetic tapes or on long-playing records. Materials that the children can handle and feel may be substituted for more conventional ones, such as pictures.

At first, most programs for the partially sighted were housed in special classrooms where the children received all their instruction. Because the incidence of the disability is small, such segregated classes usually included pupils at a number of grade levels, and instruction was conducted much as in a one-room rural school. This arrangement has now largely been displaced by a number of organizational structures that more or less integrate the partially sighted with normal students. One method enrolls the children in special classes but provides for them to attend normal classes in subjects that require little or no use of close vision. A second method enrolls the children in normal classes; for instruction in areas requiring the use of close vision the children go to a resource room where a specially trained teacher and special instructional materials are available. A third method also enrolls each partially sighted child in a normal class but gives the special instructional materials to the teacher of that class; in addition, a resource teacher visits the class regularly to advise and to provide necessary tutorial help.

Blind. Most blind children are educated in special schools or classes, although some integration is occurring at all levels. Where alternative programs are available, each child is evaluated individually to determine the program most beneficial for him.

Classes for the blind require much greater adjustments in materials and methods than do those for the partially sighted. No visual materials are usable, no matter how large, and instruction must be conducted exclusively through the other senses. Braille (a system by which letters are represented by raised dots) is used for reading and writing; relief maps and globes, figures, and models are used in teaching geography, history, science, and mathematics. When Braille materials and magnetic tapes and long-playing records are not available, readers must be employed.

The curriculum for the blind is essentially the same as that for normal children. A significant addition in some of the better programs is instruction in traveling skills. Until fairly recently, particularly in residential schools, great emphasis was placed on training in a few highly restricted trades; the image of the blind piano tuner is a typical example. Today it is recognized that the blind can become widely employable, and educational programs are therefore

SPEECH THERAPY is often necessary for hard-of-hearing children. In picture at left, the child's mother watches through one-way mirror.

less specific. The greatest problem remaining is to convince employers of the potentials and skills of the blind. See also BLINDNESS.

Aurally Handicapped. The disability of children with hearing handicaps is a matter of oral communication—of both understanding and being understood. This handicap is especially acute in school, where most instruction is normally oral.

Education of the deaf requires one of the longest preparatory programs for the teacher, and it demands high competency in the profession. The teacher not only must have mastered general education but must also be effective as a teacher of speech, language, and speechreading (lipreading) and as a speech pathologist and must have a basic understanding of audiology. For purposes of education, the aurally handicapped— like the visually handicapped—are divided into two groups, the hard-of-hearing and the deaf.

Hard-of-Hearing. Whether a hearing loss affects a child's ability to benefit from normal instruction depends on several factors. Among these are the degree of loss, the range of hearing affected by the loss (which may be within or outside the voice range), and the age at which the loss occurred. The education of the hard-of-hearing is largely substitutive, remedial, and compensatory. After appropriate help has been provided and necessary skills acquired, these children usually can participate effectively with normal students. In addition to the normal curriculum, their education may include the fitting and use of hearing aids, auditory training, lipreading, and speech and language.

Modern hearing aids have little resemblance to early models. They are not only much smaller and easier to carry but, more important, they amplify more; some will selectively amplify the sounds in an especially important range. As a result, many children that would once have been seriously handicapped can now function as normal persons.

Auditory training may be essential in cases where the child has never heard, or has heard only partially and imperfectly for some time. Such training enables the child to hear, to distinguish between, to understand, and to relate sounds. Because speech and language are learned by imitation, a child who has had little aural stimulation must have it provided systematically through amplifications and the use of alternate experiences—such as reading—if he is to gain proficiency in these skills.

Even modern hearing aids cannot compensate for more severe hearing losses. Children thus disabled are taught speechreading so that they can add visual cues to partially heard ones. Thus they are better able to grasp the content of oral communication.

Deaf. For educational purposes, this group is divided into two subgroups: the congenitally deaf, who were born without hearing, and the adventitiously deaf, who lost their hearing after birth and usually after acquiring speech and language. Because oral communication is so important socially, the adventitiously deaf tend to be much better off than the congenitally deaf. Educating the adventitiously deaf involves helping them to maintain and improve their language skills and to learn to understand oral communication primarily through visual means—by speechreading, observing attitudes and gestures, and so forth. Educating the congenitally deaf is much more difficult, as it calls for artificial development of speech and language in children that have never heard their own utterances and can never compare them with the speech of others.

It is generally accepted that educational programs for the deaf ought to start in the preschool period (before age 6). The sooner the child is introduced to speech and language instruction, the better is the chance that he will eventually be able to use oral communication effectively. First the child must learn that there is a relationship between certain movements of the face, mouth, lips, and tongue of his teacher and various objects and actions in his environment. Then he learns to associate specific speech movements with specific objects and actions. Finally he learns to form these words, speaking them aloud when necessary, and to recognize them in print. Speech, reading of print, and speechreading are usually taught in relation to one another rather than separately.

At one time, most deaf persons learned to communicate only by signing (using sign language) and finger spelling. Signing is an inexact method of communication that often uses single

SPECIAL EQUIPMENT is essential in educating the blind; this relief globe helps in learning geography.

MARY ELEANOR BROWNING, FROM DPI

gestures to convey whole thoughts; however, it is faster than finger spelling, which spells out each word and fits it into a linguistic context. To combine speed of communication with sufficient accuracy, most deaf people that use manual communication employ both methods at once.

The acceptance of the oral method of teaching the deaf was accompanied by considerable controversy, and manual methods have by no means been abandoned. Most schools today teach oral communication, at least initially. Residential schools with children that have been unable to learn speech also have departments where manual instruction is used, and the children in such schools tend to communicate manually with each other because it is easier and more accurate. The usefulness of speechreading in English is limited by the number of sounds that are produced in apparently similar ways, as well as by the sounds that are produced in ways that are hidden within the speaker's mouth or throat.

The curriculum for deaf children resembles that for normal children except for the added emphasis on oral communication skills. In many communities, deaf children that have received some special training are integrated into the regular school programs. In such cases, they ought to be seated so that they can easily observe the teacher's face as he talks, and care must be taken to ensure that they understand discussions, explanations, and assignments. In addition, an itinerant teacher ought to be provided to explain to the faculty the limitations of the students, as well as what aids can be provided, and to work directly with the students to maintain and improve their oral communication skills. See also DEAFNESS.

ORTHOPEDIC AND OTHER HEALTH PROBLEMS

Children with various health problems that fit into no other classification are usually included in programs for the orthopedically handicapped. During the early 20th century about half of the children enrolled in these programs had heart malfunctions of one type or another or were "in delicate health" and had to have their physical activity restricted to some extent. With the advance of medical, psychological, and educational knowledge most children with such handicaps have been placed in regular educational programs.

Today many fewer children in this category are assigned to special schools and classes. Not only individuals but entire groups of children have been integrated with regular programs. For instance, a few large cities had special schools for epileptic children. These schools may have reflected some assumption about needs vaguely ascribed to the children, but they derived in large part from the general educator's fear and lack of understanding of the disease. Such schools have now vanished, and epileptic seizures in schoolchildren are now generally controlled by modern medication. Similarly, "fresh air rooms" and schools were once commonly provided for children suffering from malnutrition or "delicate health" or recuperating from some such disease as tuberculosis. The children were provided with rest periods, a balanced lunch, and supplementary snacks. They also got plenty of fresh air: the windows of the rooms were kept open, and the children wore their outdoor clothing at all times. These classes and schools no longer exist.

Another large group of disabled children was eliminated following the introduction of the first polio vaccine in 1955. The population of crippled children in the schools was so greatly diminished that special classes for them became anachronistic; today it is generally accepted that a wheelchair or a pair of crutches need not exclude a child from the regular classroom, and the number of crippled children that truly need special programs has become very small.

Programs for orthopedically handicapped children have much the same content as the general curriculum. Certain adaptations and additions of rooms and materials are provided to enable the children to participate physically. Such programs also provide for occupational therapy, physiotherapy, and corrective physical education to help the children improve their physical capabilities. Because a large percentage of these children have cerebral palsy, which causes a high incidence of speech problems, a speech therapy program is almost always provided.

When rooms were specially designed for the orthopedically handicapped they differed markedly from the usual classroom. Conventionally, the desks in public schools were fastened to the floor in carefully aligned rows, an arrangement which could not accommodate wheelchairs or walkers and made difficulties even for children with crutches. Thus rooms for the orthopedically handicapped were designed so that all the furniture could be moved. In modern schools, special provisions of this sort are incorporated into the general design of the school. Ramps are provided in addition to stairs, and elevators are built if second floors are to be used. Halls and doorways are made wide so that wheelchairs can be moved about easily. Halls are free of projections, and stair and hall railings are recessed so as to aid children in moving about without constituting a hazard. Other special provisions include additional rooms for speech therapy, physic therapy, and occupational therapy.

Speech Handicapped. Children with speech handicaps caused by physical problems are properly included in the class of children with physical handicaps. The primary physical causes of speech handicaps are cerebral palsy, cleft lip, and cleft palate.

Children with cerebral palsy often have difficulty with muscular control and coordination of the mouth, tongue, and lips, making proper articulation difficult; they may have problems of breath control and rhythm as well. The intelligibility of their speech may thus be very poor for several reasons, and a great deal of intensive work may be required to correct it.

The child with a repaired cleft lip may have difficulty because of the relative immobility of the upper lip; cleft palate, which entails an opening between the mouth and the nasal cavity, causes inability to make plosives (such as "p" and "b") and certain other sounds correctly. In dealing with problems of this sort, the work of the speech and hearing therapist must often be coordinated with dental, surgical, and prosthetic treatments and prescriptions. Speech therapists usually work as itinerant teachers, providing the children—either individually or in small groups—with regular instruction and exercises. Children receiving speech therapy leave the classroom regularly—usually once a day—to work with the therapist for a few minutes. This program continues until the child can communicate effectively or until no further improvement can reasonably be expected. See also CEREBRAL PALSY; CLEFT PALATE; SPEECH DEFECTS.

BEHAVIORAL DEVIATIONS

Broadly defined, children with behavioral deviations include all exceptional children, but those ordinarily grouped under this heading are children whose deviations seem not to be caused by intellectual, physical, or sensory abnormalities. The two most commonly recognized subgroups are children with behavioral disorders and children with speech handicaps that are not physical in origin. A third group, identified relatively recently, is becoming important in education; it consists of children with so-called learning disabilities, which may actually encompass a multiplicity of problems.

Behavioral Disorders. Children in this group have, over the years, been variously designated as emotionally disturbed, as social deviates, or as truants, delinquents, or discipline problems. Most such terms have been discarded by educators because they are imprecise, prejudicial, and without meaningful implication for the process of education. The term "behavioral disorders" is becoming more and more widely accepted to describe all children that cannot be tolerated in the regular classroom, regardless of the cause of their behavior.

In short, children with behavioral disorders are those whose behavior deviates so much as to interfere seriously with their education. In many cases their behavior is also disruptive, adversely affecting the education of other children in the class. Usually such behavior is extroverted and aggressive: the child may speak out, argue, fight, tease, mock, and generally disrupt the normal learning activities. However, children with behavioral disorders are sometimes so withdrawn as to appear completely unaware of their environments. Such a child does not disrupt normal classroom activities and discipline, but he needs help fully as much as a disruptive child.

No universally accepted program of treatment for such children has been designed. However, the main objective of all programs is of course to change the child's behavior so that he can participate in regular classes. The treatment may involve psychotherapy, operant conditioning, or changes in the curriculum.

The curriculum approach is the most widely used. It appears to be of greatest value with children that come from lower social and economic backgrounds. For these children the traditional college preparatory program often has little meaning, and they may consequently apply themselves poorly and achieve little. This lack of success, combined with the apparent meaninglessness of the learning activities, often induces a dislike for education and a frustration that can lead to aggressive behavior. In such cases, changes in the contents of the educational program designed to relate the learning activities to the child's daily experiences often result in a change in the child's attitude and in his consequent behavior. This is particularly true if such changes are tried in the early grades.

The psychotherapeutic approach to behavioral disorders has been in use for the longest time. Although it comprises programs based on several different theories, the theories generally share the assumptions that children with behavioral disorders have emotional problems; that these problems often originate outside the school; that they are often of long standing; and that, if the children can be brought to understand their problems and the causes of their behavior, they will be able to cope with the problems more effectively and to improve their behavior accordingly.

Many persons may be involved in the psychotherapeutic treatment program, including the psychiatrist, the psychologist, the social worker, and the special class teacher. Many school systems employ consulting psychiatrists, whose function is to diagnose problems and to provide some treatment for children with severe emotional disturbances. For acute problems requiring long-term therapy, the psychiatrist may refer the child and his parents to a community guidance clinic, advise them to consult a private psychiatrist, or recommend residential treatment. The psychologist performs evaluations, provides psychotherapy, and works with teachers, helping them to provide the acceptance and understanding these children often require. The social worker provides a liaison between the school and the children's homes, working with the children and their parents and teachers. Special-class teachers have been trained to understand the problems and behavior of these children and to provide a learning environment as therapeutic as possible. The emphasis in therapy is on behavioral changes rather than on academic skills, although the experience of success in a learning activity is often very therapeutic in itself. In any case, instruction can be a very important part of the treatment program, and the teacher must consequently be competent in his profession as well as understanding (though not necessarily tolerant) of deviant behavior.

The most recently developed approach to the treatment of behavioral disorders, which shows excellent potential for success, is based on operant conditioning. The goals of programs of this type are highly defined in terms of the child's behavior, academic learning, assumption of responsibility, and so forth. Every desired form of behavior is analyzed into its smallest component parts; both child and teacher are aware of each successive step; and the child is immediately rewarded for all positive behavior, regardless of how small it is. He is then encouraged to progress to the next step. Rewards may consist of such things as small pieces of candy, or check marks or chips that may be accumulated and turned in for larger rewards (such as food or toys).

The objective of such programs is to teach the child the value of appropriate and acceptable behavior. The system of tangible rewards starts the child in the right direction, but, after he has progressed sufficiently, material incentives may be successfully replaced by conventional social rewards—a pat on the back, a word of approval, or a smile.

Nonphysical Speech Handicaps. The most common single speech handicap, which accounts for more than 50% of all speech defects, is faulty articulation; this includes substitutions of sounds, such as "th" for "s" ("thing" for "sing") and "w" for "l" ("way" for "lay"), and omissions of sounds (as in "pay" for "play"). Another important speech handicap is stammering. Other problems of this type arise from speech patterns peculiar to isolated groups or areas when children from such backgrounds move to other communities or sections of the country.

Because speech, which is learned by imitation, is often not fully developed by the time children start school, speech programs for early childhood consist mainly of providing the children with a good model. Every teacher must have good, accurate speech and enunciation. Speech therapists can help by teaching the children to articulate sounds correctly.

Speech instruction as such is usually provided by an itinerant speech and hearing therapist, who works not only with the articulation of sounds but also with pronunciation, enunciation, and language skills. Depending on the specific problem, the work may be conducted on an individual basis or with a small group of children who share the same problem and require the same instruction. Ordinarily, each speech and hearing therapist works with children at many grade levels and at many different schools. Therapy sessions are usually short, lasting only a few minutes, and take place once or twice a week. Children with more acute problems may be seen more often. A child may receive therapy of this sort for a period ranging from a few months to several years. An alternative method, now being tried out by some school systems, is known as a "block" approach. Programs of this sort call for each therapist to see a small group of children intensively for a period of approximately six weeks, then to begin with a new group of children. Which approach achieves better results with more children is still undetermined.

Regardless of the approach used, the therapist often consults with the classroom teacher; in this way the speech instruction can be made more meaningful by being related to activities that go on in the regular classroom. In addition, the classroom teacher can be instructed in the objectives of speech training and in the ways in which essential practice can be included in normal classwork, thus making the speech instruction continuous and also increasing the chances of success. See also LISPING; SPEECH DEFECTS.

Learning Disabilities. This recently identified area is currently receiving a great deal of attention. It has long been known that many children fail to learn to read well under normal instructional procedures; other children have difficulty with arithmetic. Those children that cannot attain proficiency in such skills even with normal remedial help are considered as having learning disabilities.

The two primary theories of the causation of these disabilities attribute them to brain injury or to psycholinguistic deficiency. These theories have engendered several different types of programs.

One kind of program calls for reducing extraneous, or nonmeaningful, stimuli or for raising the stimulus value of the learning material, so that the children are less easily distracted. In such programs pictures and other irrelevant materials are often removed from the classroom; walls may be painted neutral colors and windows frosted. In extreme cases each child may be isolated from the others by clinical screens or by placing him in a cubicle. The instructional materials may be changed analogously by removing illustrations and by offering the materials in small discrete units (a sentence, a word, or a problem at a time). Emphasis may be focused on the material by increasing the heaviness of the lines or by using colors. A commonly successful technique is to have the child perform some physical activity in conjunction with and related to the learning activity.

Another kind of program requires each child to participate actively in a sequence of physical and psychological developmental activities. The purpose is to ensure the formation of the normal neural pathways essential to continued development and to future learning. Programs of this kind are based on the theory that, if a child misses any in the sequence of activities that children normally experience, the development of his learning ability will be inhibited. The omission of certain sensory experiences presumed to be essential to certain stages of development theoretically leaves some normal neural pathways unformed. These programs therefore consist of providing the child with appropriate experiences to promote the formation of the needed synapses.

A third kind of program aims to strengthen the child's perceptual skills, particularly in the area of vision, so that he will understand accurately what he sees. Here perception is defined as the attaching of appropriate meaning to sensation. If a child does not respond to the important aspects of a situation—the foreground of a picture or the meaningful aspects of an activity—he has a perceptual disturbance and must be taught to distinguish the important from the unimportant. This discrimination is induced by first suppressing extraneous stimuli and then gradually reintroducing them as the child learns to tolerate and to disregard them.

A fourth kind of program is designed to strengthen deficient psycholinguistic areas. Such programs rest on the notion that communication involves three processes—decoding, association, and encoding. Decoding is the understanding of sensory (especially visual and auditory) signals; association is the attaching of appropriate meanings and relationships to the signals, and the formulation of a reply in accordance with them; encoding is the expression (in words, gestures, and so forth) of thoughts or ideas. A deficiency in any of these processes theoretically results in a learning disability; thus the program aims to identify the area of weakness and to strengthen it, on the assumption that when the area is effectively operational the child will be able to learn more efficiently.

Each of these programs has had significant success with some children. As with the other areas of the education of exceptional children, one of the greatest needs in the area of learning disabilities is improvement of differential diagnoses, so that the most beneficial program can be designed for each child for whom regular education cannot adequately provide.

G. ORVILLE JOHNSON
The Ohio State University

Bibliography

Blake, Kathryn, *Educating Exceptional Pupils: An Introduction to Contemporary Practices* (Addison-Wesley 1981).
Brill, Richard G., *The Education of the Deaf* (Gaullaudet College 1974)
Brolin, D.E., and Kokaska, C.J., *Career Education for Handicapped Children and Youth* (Merrill 1979).
Cronbach, L.J., and Snow, R.E., *Aptitudes and Instructional Methods* (Irvington 1977).
Deno, E., ed., *Instructional Alternatives for Exceptional Children* (Council for Exceptional Children 1975).
Doyle, Phyllis B., et al, *Helping the Severely Handicapped Child: A Guide for Parents and Teachers* (Crowell 1979).
Gallagher, James J., *Teaching the Gifted Child*, 2d ed. (Allyn & Bacon 1975).
Griffiths, Anita, *Teaching the Dyslexic Child* (Academic Therapy Publications 1978).
Hare, Betty A., and others, *Teaching Young Handicapped Children* (Grune 1977).
Hart, Verna, *Mainstreaming Children with Special Needs* (Longman 1980).
Koegel, Robert L., and others, *Educating and Understanding Autistic Children* (College-Hill 1981).
Smith, Sally L., *No Easy Answers: Teaching the Learning Disabled Child* (Little 1979).
Stanley, Julian C., and others, eds., *The Gifted and the Creative: A Fifty Year Perspective* (Johns Hopkins Univ. Press 1977).

9. Educational Administration

The public schools of the United States are administered by 50 state systems and more than 10,000 local school districts. This plan stands in marked contrast to the administrative systems of countries that have all public education directed by a national ministry. This section concentrates on the United States. Information on other systems can be found in section 3. *Education Around the World* and in the education sections of country articles.

Role of the Federal Government. The federal government in the United States does not control public education, but it has wide influence. Federal influence on the schools has developed gradually and often in indirect ways. The Constitution of the United States does not mention education. Because the 10th Amendment reserves to the states or to the people powers not expressly delegated to the United States by the Constitution, education has generally been conceived to be the prerogative of the states, and most public education in the United States is carried on by local school boards acting under state laws. Nevertheless, the "general welfare" clause and other clauses of the Constitution have served as warrants and guides for the development of numerous federal activities in education.

The role of the federal government in education was greatly increased by the National Defense Education Act of 1958 and the Elementary and Secondary Education Act of 1965. The former provided funds to stimulate education in the sciences. The latter provided for direct aid to school districts in such forms as funds for textbooks and library materials. These two bills and other federal programs of the 1960's marked a great departure in federal involvement in education. However, most of these programs were to be administered through state or local educational agencies, thereby retaining the traditional emphasis on local control of education.

Earlier forms of federal aid were rather incidental, such as the land grant program initiated in the Ordinance of 1785 and confirmed in the Northwest Ordinance of 1787. Most of the states admitted to the Union since 1789 have been given land grants for education under similar legislation. Since Civil War days, Congress also has appropriated money for vocational education, beginning with the Morrill Act of 1862, which initiated the land-grant college movement. Later acts of Congress strengthened these agricultural and mechanical colleges.

Originally, money for the support of these schools came from the sale of land. Subsequently, direct money grants replaced grants of land. In making these grants, Congress did not provide for any continuing control over the recipient institutions, although it did indicate the subjects that should be emphasized. As a result, land-grant colleges are operated, for the most part, under state auspices.

In 1914, in the Smith-Lever Act, the federal government initiated a policy of matching funds with states, colleges, or local schools for vocational programs. The Smith-Hughes Act of 1917 made funds available for vocational education in high schools under specified conditions. The federal government thereby has influenced educational policy in developing the fields of agriculture, home economics, and trades and industries at the high school levels, as well as in the training of teachers in these areas.

During the Depression other acts with educational aspects, although of a temporary nature, such as the Civilian Conservation Corps (1933), the National Youth Administration (1935), and many others, contributed greatly to the welfare of the nation. The role of the federal government in educating the veterans of World Wars I and II, the Korean War, and the Vietnam conflict also marked a significant level of federal participation in education. However, the government did not appreciably influence the educational policies and programs of the schools that the veterans elected to attend.

The 1954 Supreme Court decision requiring the desegregation of public schools and later decisions on its implementation also increased the federal role in education on the local level. Because the federal government has exerted pressure on local areas to desegregate schools and also enforces the Supreme Court decisions, it is necessarily becoming more and more involved in the administrative details of the local school.

Many federal activities in education, including the distribution of federal air, are centered in the U.S. Department of Education, created in

1979 to replace the Office of Education (founded 1867). Originally mandated to collect statistics and publish information, the office came to have much wider—though still indirect—influence. The present department is concerned with promoting equal access to education and improving educational quality. Because of the local control of public schools, the department does not have direct authority over them. The secretary of education is not comparable to the minister of education in a country with centralized control. See also EDUCATION, DEPARTMENT OF.

Role of the States. The generally accepted opinion in the United States is that formal education is legally a state function. The state can and does delegate this function to other educational agencies, but does not thereby escape responsibility for providing and supervising the units it has created. Actually, the need for schools was so self-evident that local schools antedated state provisions for them. Moreover, it has been impossible and undesirable for the state to operate and administer directly the schools of the commonwealth. Consequently, education is largely a local enterprise with a minimum of state control and supervision.

Every state has a central education agency, usually consisting of a state board of education, a state superintendent of schools, and a state department of education. However, no two states have identical arrangements for the organization and administration of the schools. Strong central education agencies are to be found in only a few states. State administration of the educational services has been called the weakest aspect of the American educational system, and less attention has been paid to the improvement of the central state agency than to the more efficient operation of the local unit.

The state central agencies have been largely regulatory; their objective has been the maintenance of a minimum program by the local units. However, as the program features have been enlarged the states have assumed more financial responsibility, and, of necessity, extended their controls. Most states now have regulations and standards regarding most aspects of school operations, such as courses of study, textbooks, teacher certificates, compulsory attendance of pupils, length of the school term, the school census, transportation of pupils, health of pupils, school architecture, and the auditing of funds. There is, of course, the danger that state minimum standards become local maximum standards. In many respects the state office has the ideal position for educational leadership; it is far enough from the local scene to be objective in its appraisal, far enough from the people to be respected, and potent enough to influence new legislation.

There is a growing feeling among educators that the central state agency should spend more time on research and less time on actual supervision. More supervision can be shifted to the local units as they are enlarged and strengthened. Research is needed to provide a proper standard for the evaluation of the actual operations of the local units, to demonstrate their comparative accomplishments, and to indicate their most pressing needs. Most controversies can be settled only by research, which remains the most neglected aspect of most state operations.

Unfortunately, many central state education agencies are still involved in partisan politics. In many instances the state superintendents of public instruction are elected on partisan ballots in national and state elections and their salaries and qualifications are detailed in state statutes. It is extremely difficult to get able leaders under these circumstances. Authorities are quite generally agreed that the chief state school official should be selected by the state school board after a careful study of the qualifications of several highly recommended individuals. The salary should also be set by the state board so that it will attract and retain the services of the best qualified person.

The best manner of choosing competent members of a state board of education is still controversial. If the board selects the chief state school official and determines educational policy under legislative mandate, it is clearly a very important instrument of government. A state board made up wholly or in part of ex officio members who have other pressing official duties is no longer considered desirable. The presence of professional educators in an ex officio status has proved to be very embarrassing to the chief state school official. In the main, educators are agreed that appointment by the governor, with the approval of one or the other house of the state legislature, is a workable plan. At any rate, this is the usual procedure. In recent years there has been some experimentation in a few states with the election by the general public of the members of the state board of education. For a number of reasons such innovations are extremely difficult in the larger states, though they may have some merit in smaller states where devoted public servants are better known and where campaigns are less expensive.

Few states have adequate state departments of education. If the personnel is limited in number, and untrained and untried in service, the department is ineffective. Low salaries, feeling of insecurity in office, and the necessity for political sponsorship are too much in evidence. Inefficiency at this level influences the work of the local public school. In most states there are local school offices that command far more respect and salary and afford far more opportunities for genuine leadership. Fortunately, considerable progress is being made in the effort to make the state appointments professional and to give them civil service or comparable classification.

Despite shortcomings the states have done much in recent years to bring about the reorganization of their schools, such as providing state aid for transportation, and new school buildings, and requiring an approved minimum program. A great deal of progress is being made every year in all sections of the United States.

Local School District Organization and Administration. The local school district organization is, in final analysis, the main determinant of the educational product. State and federal services exist, for the most part, to advance the educational program at this level.

Over the years, the states have followed a policy of consolidating school districts. In 1940 there were more than 100,000 school districts in the nation, and nearly all were separately structured and administered. Gradually the total number of school districts diminished to less than 15,000, and other levels of government began to assume greater responsibility for educational matters. However, the number of local school districts varies greatly from state to state. Geography is partially responsible for the number of districts maintained by a state, but tradition is also a factor.

Consolidating the districts into relatively larger units serves to more nearly equalize the tax burden and offers the opportunity to improve the educational program as well. The small district often offers only a very meager elementary school program with inadequate facilities, taught by poorly trained and poorly paid teachers. The consolidated or unified school district frequently maintains cosmopolitan high schools under well-qualified teachers; occasionally it operates a junior college that takes the pupils through the 14th grade free of tuition.

Intermediate School District Organization and Administration. In most states there is an intermediate school district, usually the county district. In these states there are county superintendents of schools and, frequently, county boards of education. The intermediate districts are frequently regarded as virtual extensions of the state school office. In many states, county superintendents are elected on partisan ballots at general elections. Although initially the superintendents were, in the main, performing clerical functions, their offices are taking on more important duties. Frequently, the superintendents are now instrumental in stimulating the reorganization of local units, in supervising the minimum program required by the state, and in furnishing special services of various sorts, such as transportation, health, guidance, and audiovisual aids.

The Evolution of School Administration. As is commonly known, the earliest colonial schools were administered by the community as a whole, through the medium of the "town meetings" and by the selectmen who managed town affairs in the intervals between meetings. Apart from the local schools, the beginning of the legal basis for the administration of American schools was the Massachusetts law of 1642, which authorized the selectmen to charge parents with the responsibility of teaching their children their letters, the catechism, and the capital laws of the state. As time passed, the procedures of the town meeting did not suffice, and it became the practice to appoint or to elect special committees of laymen to supervise the schools, to select teachers, and to propose necessary taxation to raise school revenue. These special committees came to be recognized as having the sole responsibility for the management of the schools. The provision for such committees, or school boards, became a legal requirement in Massachusetts with the laws of 1789 and 1827. These boards were empowered to exercise general supervision over the schools. Before the middle of the 19th century the idea of a separate school board for public school management had become generally accepted throughout the country. In time, in most localities, it was deemed expedient to set up the school committee completely independent of political control. This is the prevailing practice today, with some notable exceptions.

Naturally, as the cities expanded, the complexities of school administration multiplied until scrutiny of all the details was beyond the power of a school board. It became customary then to appoint subcommittees and to designate individuals to specific tasks. This was the beginning of the standing-committee arrangement that persists to this day, especially in the large city boards of education. Nevertheless, these standing committees could not do the work involved in executing policies. The problems of financing, housing, staffing, and supervising schools led some school committees to appoint a secretary, a treasurer, a clerk, or a building inspector to help in specific areas of administration. Principals were sometimes made superintendents over groups of schools, usually acting only in advisory capacities to the school board, and with little administration authority.

The mounting complexities of administration and the attendant laborious and time-consuming efforts required of the school board members led to the creation of the office of superintendent, for the complex problems of management were quite beyond the capabilities of the lay part-time board member. It is doubtful that any business of the magnitude of the large city systems could have functioned under the conditions then prevailing in the schools; there was no responsible head; there was every opportunity to evade responsibility, and with inefficiency there was a constant tendency to corruption. Most authorities list Buffalo, N. Y., and Louisville, Ky., in 1837, as having the first city school superintendents. Other cities soon followed until, by the time of the Civil War, nearly all large cities in the United States had established the office. Some school boards, however, were reluctant—as some still are—to relinquish administrative and supervisory functions.

It must be admitted that the early superintendents contributed, in some measure, to the slow development of the superintendency. No doubt they were responsible in many instances for the chief problem that plagues their successors; namely, the lack of unity of control over all aspects of the school system. It is generally conceded that many of the early superintendents were scholars, who had more interest in instruction than in the executive phases of administration. Many of them did not understand school financing, the school plant, or other noninstructional aspects of administration. To many of them there was a sharp line of demarcation between the intellectual and the business affairs of the school system. One authority, Arthur Bernard Moehlman, concludes, "Thus, the unfortunate organization of the executive activity into areas of 'instruction' and 'business' was due probably as much to the belief and attitudes of the superintendents as to the boards of education, a perfect example of the serious errors that result from the absence of sound theory." (*School Administration;* ..., Boston 1951.) The unitary conception of school administration is of recent origin. In fact, dual and multiple organizations are still in evidence, especially in the large city systems. Vestiges of the committee system are also common; many a superintendent must still explain things to a committee and then help the committee explain them again to the board before he can get his proposals to the attention of the board as a whole.

As the complexities of administration increased, especially in the great city systems, the superintendent began to enjoy greater respect. The board members became less inclined to get involved in the details of administration and more inclined to select persons of experience to cope with the complex problems that came to their attention. Gradually, the superintendent was given increased responsibility for selecting and assigning the teaching staff for the supervision of instruction, for the procedures of pupil personnel, for grading schools and classifying pupils, for courses of study, for the finance and building programs, and for public relations. Since the turn of the century professional courses have done much to advance the cause of efficient school administration, especially the unitary conception of school administration. Men and women now come to their administrative positions with theoretical training as well as with practical experience; they know what the authorities think best, and they recognize outmoded practices. Numerous theses and dissertations for postgraduate degrees deal with the practical problems of administration. These works constitute a never-ending source of suggestions and inspiration. The professors of such courses have become known as authorities, and they do not hesitate to take their graduate students into the field with them. Surveys are to this day the best single source of suggestions for the improvement of administrative practices.

Unfortunately, until very recent times, the emphasis in school administration has been upon the material and mechanical aspects. Until well into the 20th century the forms of organization received most attention; stress was placed upon the size of school boards, the reduction and abolition of standing committees, the fiscal policies, and the consolidation of schools. During the second and third decades of this century the scientific movement became uppermost, and much time was devoted to perfecting standardized tests, making age-grade studies, studying the optimum size of classes, rating teachers, rating school buildings, and establishing uniform business practices.

Trends in Educational Organization and Administration. In the traditional school organization there is almost complete separation of planning and performance. The plans are the work of the superintendents, associate superintendents, and principals, who send their instructions down the line of authority to the teachers and pupils. In recent years there has been a shift away from the traditional line-and-staff organization and toward cooperative group-planning schemes. The central ideas in the reformation are to substitute leadership for authority and to implement participatory group study and decision in policy formation on the part of the teachers, parents, and pupils. Oftentimes, the change is not so much in the way the system is reorganized as in the manner in which it is used. Even within traditional patterns there is evidence of many new elements, such as advisory councils, workshops, and conferences, as well as increased committee activity of various sorts.

However, it should be noted that final responsibility for the educational enterprise cannot be shifted from the legally designated officials. Advisory and consultative services should be extended as far as possible, but the ultimate responsibility for administrative decisions cannot be delegated. The efficient administrator suggests, encourages, develops, and secures, "areas of agreement" among staff members. The able superintendent or principal is one who can motivate and direct the staff members in their legitimate professional activities, without having them encroach upon his final authority. There should be loyalty both up and down the line, a two-way street where ideas flow back and forth. This two-way interchange of recommendations and suggestions for the improvement of the school is now recognized as the responsibility of the whole staff.

Democracy and Educational Administration. Inasmuch as schools are the seedbeds for democracy, they must be administered democratically. But emphasis on democratic educational leadership has not always characterized the preparation of educational administrators. Many of the earlier school administrators were benevolent despots and autocrats. Later, the scientific movement in education envisioned the successful school administrator as an expert who operated at a level beyond teacher or lay criticism. In more recent years these somewhat aristocratic and mechanistic conceptions of school administration have come under severe criticism. Prospective school administrators today are being taught democratic techniques in theory and, to a degree, in practice. They are learning the group process of arriving at decisions and the techniques of releasing creative abilities inherent in individuals and groups. They are taught how to enlist the parents and the pupils in programs of appraisal, modification, and improvement. Administrators are learning to regard the school system as a community resource and not as an empire apart from the workaday world.

In the final analysis the administration of the schools will not improve a great deal until the public has greater understanding of, and greater appreciation for, the role of the public schools in American democracy. The public schools are the very center of American life. Other schools, private and parochial, have their proper place in American life, but the public school is the hub of democracy. Under the principle of reciprocity, democracy countenances schools sponsored and supported by minority groups, but the entire public has a special obligation to the common public school. Traditions peculiar to sects, classes, and minority groups may be preserved, oftentimes to the advantage of the public, in church and other private schools, but the common heritage is the primary responsibility of the American public school. It is doubtful if any other institution in American life is so influential on all citizens; it is the one major institution, aside from the federal government, that binds the population together. Its proper administration constitutes one of the greatest challenges in America.

See also education sections of country articles: for example, CANADA—*Education;* CHILE—*Education;* UNITED STATES—*Education.*

JOHN T. WAHLQUIST, *Author of "The Administration of Public Education"*

Bibliography

Baron, George, and Howell, D.A., *The Government and Management of Schools* (Humanities 1974).
Barr, Rebecca, and Dreeben, Robert, *How Schools Work* (Univ. of Chicago Press 1983).
Campbell, Roald F. Cunningham, L.L., and McPhee, R.F., *The Organization and Control of American Schools* (Merrill 1980).
Getzels, Jacob W., and others, *Educational Administration as a Social Process* (Harper 1968).
Gorton, Richard A., *School Administration and Supervision: Leadership Challenges and Opportunities,* 2d ed. (William C. Brown 1982).
Hanson, Mark E., *Educational Administration and Organizational Behavior* (Allyn 1978).
Knezevich, Stephen, *Administration of Public Education* (Harper 1983).
Morphet, Edgar, and others, *Educational Organization and Administration: Concepts, Practices and Issues,* 4th ed. (Prentice-Hall 1982).
Poster, Cyril, *School Decision-Making* (Heinemann Educ. Books Inc. 1976).
Silver, Paula, *Educational Administration: Theoretical Perspectives on Practice and Research* (Harper 1983).

A SCHOOL COUNSELOR confers with a student. Such counselors, often specially trained in psychology, advise students about their personal problems, as well as matters bearing on their education.

A. DEVANEY, INC., N. Y.

10. Educational Psychology

Educational psychology is concerned with finding and applying principles and techniques that promote efficiency in instruction. Because its primary focus is on curriculum objectives and instructional methods, educational psychology is much concerned with the principles of learning. However, efficient learning also depends on a satisfactory "learning climate" that takes into consideration the learner's physical, social, and mental well-being, his motives, attitudes, and values, his personality characteristics, his unique abilities, and the like. Consequently, educational psychologists try to use information about all these matters so that the student may realize his potential more fully than he could without such assistance. Because educational psychology relies on the scientific method to find and apply knowledge in these areas, it is regarded as an applied science.

DEVELOPMENT OF THE FIELD

Much early thinking in educational psychology was done by philosophers. By the 4th century B.C., Aristotle and others had proposed that the learning of rhetoric involved three elements: nature (ability and temperament), art (categories, definitions, and rules), and exercise (practice in imitating the best models known). Descartes, Locke, Kant, Bergson, and other philosophers made interesting speculations on the mind, character, will, and the relationship between mind and body. Some 18th century philosophers held that the mind has a few principal faculties, such as thinking, feeling, willing, and memorizing. This "faculty psychology" led to the doctrine of "formal discipline," which recommended that the faculties be strengthened by appropriate exercises as a part of the school curriculum. Preoccupation with exercises or "drill" thus came to characterize education.

Educational psychology as such began with Johann Heinrich Pestalozzi, whose opposition to the conventional curriculum was determined by his interest in child development. In the school he opened at Yverdon, Switzerland, in 1805, Pestalozzi tried to "psychologize education." Unlike those who subscribed to formal discipline, he was uncommitted to Latin as the chief subject of instruction, and he studied methods of teaching the new subjects of arithmetic, geometry, nature study, drawing, and music. Looking to nature for the principles to use in teaching, he advocated that children observe nature directly and use counting and naming activities as sources of information. Geography was taught by direct observation of the surrounding valley: the children made relief maps of what they saw.

This trend away from the older curriculum, rote memory, and drill was continued by the progressive education movement of John Dewey. Dewey's insistence on the importance of varied experience, of emotional adjustment, and of social effectiveness lastingly influenced American education. Dewey's impact was probably strengthened by the fact that psychology had played a role in teacher training in America from the very beginning. The first normal school, in Lexington, Mass., had a course in "mental philosophy" that covered elementary psychology. In 1863 the normal school at Oswego, N.Y., offered a course in "child study," and in the late 19th century almost all normal schools offered courses in educational psychology.

The first formal psychological laboratory was established by Wilhelm Wundt at the University of Leipzig in 1879. Wundt's empirical approach to the study of human behavior had important consequences for educational psychology, leading to quantitative studies of learning and forgetting, such as those by the German psychologist Hermann Ebbinghaus. As early as 1880, Granville Stanley Hall, who had studied with Wundt and was a founder of laboratory psychology in the United States, showed American teachers how data on growth and development could be used by them in their work.

Edward Lee Thorndike's textbook *Educational Psychology* (1903) marked the beginning of the modern period. Thorndike, who had studied with William James, had a wide range of interests that could be investigated by the newer laboratory methods. Especially notable was an experiment in which, studying problem-solving ability in animals and children, he found considerable similarity in their learning processes. His observations established the importance in learning of motivation, repetition, and reward, which he concluded to be the basic elements in trial-and-error learning.

Thorndike's descriptions of the learning process were pioneering efforts. But, even in comparatively simple learning situations such as he explored, the matters of motivation, repetition, and reward are proving more complex and interdependent than he realized. Learning theory is having trouble in developing conceptual systems that are internally consistent and have high levels of generality. Although Thorndike's early views of learning have limited applications in some areas of teaching, they are inadequate to the more complex demands of classroom instruction.

RELATIONSHIPS TO GENERAL PSYCHOLOGY AND THE CURRICULUM

Educational and General Psychology. Because educational psychology drew most of its early principles from general psychology, it has often been considered merely a technical application of general psychology. This view was more appropriate several decades ago than it is now. Since 1935, educational psychologists have done extensive research in the areas of genetic and child psychology, the psychology of adolescence, individual differences, mental hygiene, guidance procedures, learning, tests and measurements, personality, thinking, reasoning, and problem-solving. It is clearly no longer true that educational psychologists are simply technicians who apply principles discovered by general psychologists. They still draw on the findings of general psychology, but when it holds no solutions for their problems, they proceed to do their own research.

Whereas the general psychologist often deals with theoretical problems involving relatively simple behavior, the educational psychologist usually deals with practical problems involving very complex behavior. As a result, research in educational psychology is more fragmented and lends itself less readily to neat systematic formulations. For this reason, many do not consider educational psychology a discipline. If, however, a discipline is defined as a specific field in which vigorous scientific research is being conducted, then educational psychology may be called a discipline. Its level of complexity prevents it from formulating general laws as readily as less complex disciplines can, but such formulations are not inherently impossible. Professional educational psychologists at the larger graduate schools (as opposed to teachers and administrators) are considerably interested in the theoretical and systematic problems associated with learning. How soon educational psychology formulates its own basic laws may depend on how efficiently researchers, teachers, and administrators learn to cooperate. A comparison of textbooks in educational psychology reveals serious disagreement among educational psychologists as to what subjects their field ought to include; but there are many topics that all would include, and the field can ultimately be unified around these uncontested areas.

Psychology has had more impact on education in the United States than in Britain, where teacher training places less emphasis on basic principles of general psychology. Because of these loose ties between psychology and education, the term "educational psychologist" in Britain usually refers not to an educator with a broad background in behavioral science but to a person trained for specialized work in the area of adjustment problems, counseling, and guidance.

Role in the Curriculum. Educational psychology plays a dual role with respect to the curriculum. It is both a part of the curriculum and one of the major shapers of the curriculum. As a subject, educational psychology has achieved high status. In many colleges it has become a major area of instruction. Most programs of teacher education require educational psychology as a preliminary undergraduate course, and courses in many aspects of the field are offered for graduate credit. As a shaper of the curriculum, educational psychology exercises its influence through the thousands of teachers who were exposed to courses in the field while preparing for their careers. Opinions of prominent educational psychologists and findings in educational research influence both curriculum content and curriculum methods. Many large universities have well-financed research facilities that permit the testing of hypotheses important to the development of educational psychology as an applied science and as part of the curriculum.

A major curriculum problem of educational psychology is that of determining the content of a basic required course in the field, which includes so many topics that not all can be covered in the first year. Experts disagree as to which areas should be excluded. Some schools permit students to elect one or two courses, according to preference, from a group of five or six basic undergraduate courses in educational psychology. In schools requiring that the field be covered in two courses, the usual method is to teach the psychology of learning in one course and child development in the other. This reflects the conviction of most educational psychologists of the basic importance of these two topics.

PROBLEMS IN DOING RESEARCH

The development of both the theoretical and practical aspects of educational psychology rests on actual tests of specific hypotheses. One problem in this complex area is that so many factors may enter simultaneously into the situation that it is difficult to set up a meaningful experiment. One way to solve this problem is to compare two groups that are identical in all respects except for the one under study (the control group method). Another way is through analysis of variance, a complex statistical procedure designed to interpret results when a number of variables are operating simultaneously. Both methods presuppose accurate measurement of the conditions being studied and of the effects produced. Sometimes, when experiments are designed so that exact measurements are possible, the conditions no longer resemble the situation that the experiment was intended to investigate. Theoretical researchers face this problem less frequently than those doing research that they wish to apply in the classroom.

Another troublesome problem is presented by the motivation variable. If some subject is taught in the usual manner and then in some novel way, it is frequently found that students respond better to the new method. The superior results, however, may be due to nothing more profound than that both teacher and students find almost any new method more interesting than older methods and are temporarily more highly motivated. Only after the novelty has worn off can it be reliably judged whether the new method is truly superior.

A similar problem in judging the effectiveness of a new method may arise for an entirely different reason. Assume that a group of students take a test in some subject and that those who do poorly on the test are brought together in an experimental remedial program. After several sessions with the program the students are again tested. Even if all have improved significantly, this does not prove that the remedial program is successful. To the extent that the students guessed on the earlier test, those who scored low on it may have been simply unlucky in guessing. Since it is statistically unlikely that the same students will be unlucky two times in succession, their scores will usually improve when they are retested whether or not they have been exposed to any remedial program. Research workers in educational psychology must take care to avoid both the motivational trap and the statistical trap; otherwise they may find that every instructional innovation or remedial method is "successful." See also Section *11. Educational Measurement.*

COMPREHENSIVE THEORIES OF BEHAVIOR

The goal of theorists and system builders in any science is to find a theory or "model" that accounts for all phenomena that are observed in the field. The success of chemists in finding the elements that compose all matter has encouraged others to seek similar order in their own fields. Yet, despite the accumulation of facts, the behavioral sciences, including educational psychology, have not yet arrived at comprehensive theories that can do for them what the discovery of elements and the periodic table have done for chemistry. Instead, there are a number of competing theories, none of which fully accounts for all the behavior to be explained. Traditional theories of human behavior will be briefly reviewed here before the current situation is evaluated.

Faculty Psychology. In the 19th century, before experimental psychology began, there were two theories of mind. One, faculty psychology, assumed that the mind comprised a few basic faculties—such as feeling, thinking, and willing—and a number of subdivisions such as memory and imagination. Attempts by 19th century anatomists to find the precise locus of each faculty led to an elaborate system of phrenology and to a concept of school as a place to exercise or drill the faculties. Although research contradicted the claims of the phrenologists, more recent experiments by the American psychologists L. L. Thurstone and R. B. Cattell reflect a continuing interest in classifying human abilities. The modern approach is based on findings made when tests of many different kinds are given to many different individuals. Tests that correlate with each other form clusters of ability; these clusters provide foundations for various lists of "primary" or "basic" abilities. Using such correlations, Thurstone tentatively identified seven "primary mental abilities" as presumably underlying much behavior. Confirmation of the existence of a few such basic potentialities might be helpful to educational psychologists working in the areas of training and guidance. There has thus been a renewed interest in faculty psychology in this much more sophisticated form.

Association Theory. The other theory prominent in the 19th century was association theory. This opposing theory denied inborn faculties of the mind, holding that the mind's content is determined by ideas originating in sense impressions. These ideas become associated with each other according to such principles as similarity, contrast, and contiguity. All mental activity was to be understood in terms of association of ideas. The work of Hermann Ebbinghaus on memorizing series of nonsense syllables was in the tradition of association theory.

Psychoanalysis. The psychoanalytic views of Sigmund Freud were presented in lectures attended by American psychologists and educators as early as 1909. Freud's influence was so great that even today the layman is apt to equate psychology with psychoanalysis. Central to Freud's theories is his concept of the unconscious. It is assumed that wishes inhibited in childhood are driven out of awareness into the unconscious, where they remain influential. Such unconscious impulses may be expressed in socially acceptable behavior, such as scientific or artistic activity, or in dreams or slips of speech that may reveal the contents of the unconscious. The method of free association was designed to help reveal unconscious wishes, which presumably caused tensions.

Such wishes were assumed to be almost always sexual, even in childhood. The prominence of sex in Freud's theories delayed their acceptance, and studies of early childhood sought alternative explanations of human behavior. In the United States the growing emphasis on child psychology and clinical psychology in the 1950's multiplied opportunities to apply psychoanalytic principles in education, while traditional opposition to them was reduced by greater frankness about sex. Because psychoanalytic theories are difficult to test, the usefulness of many has yet to be determined. Psychoanalysis is now generally regarded as a set of valuable hypotheses about certain rather special forms of behavior. Its controversial nature has motivated its opponents to search for more satisfactory approaches to both child psychology and clinical psychology.

Stimulus-Response Psychology. A fourth theory of behavior, stimulus-response psychology, originated in the work of I. P. Pavlov on conditioned responses in dogs. The fact that behavior can be conditioned by environmental variables was drawn upon heavily by John B. Watson, who, in 1913, founded behaviorism in the United States. This school of psychology, which arose partially in reaction to the introspective method used at that time to study emotion and consciousness, held that such studies were unnecessary; it proposed to make psychology objective by studying behavior exclusively.

Behaviorism as a system has lost some of its force, but its emphasis on objective methods is consistent with current stimulus-response theory. Stimulus-response psychology, for example, views all behavior as responses to stimuli, and it examines stimuli and responses as the beginnings and ends of causal chains. The American psychologist B. F. Skinner and his followers studied reinforcement contingencies—conditions under which stimulus-response associations are strengthened or weakened. An event is termed "reinforcing" if it strengthens a response preceding it. As with behaviorism, there is no concern with whether such an event is pleasurable, as this could be determined only by introspection. All behavior studied is thus described in terms of external events that can be shown to affect learning.

Not every stimulus-response psychologist joins Skinner in completely excluding motivation and

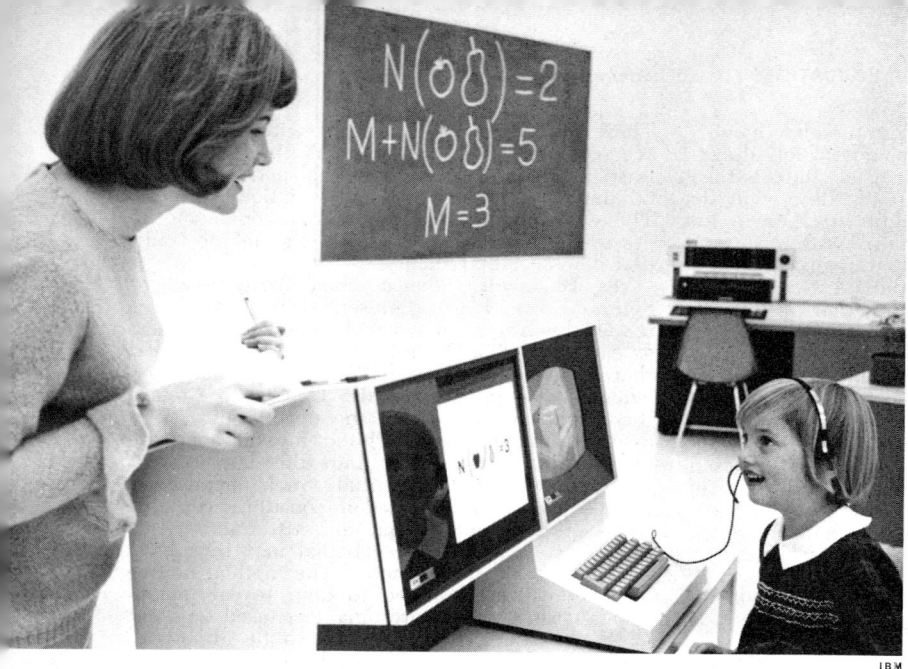

NEW TEACHING METHODS are a concern of educational psychology. Here a computer presents a "new math" problem on a viewing screen; the pupil responds by typing the answer on the keyboard.

other "inner states" from consideration, but those that are concerned with these states or "intervening variables" are straying from the path of classical behaviorism. It should be noted that some early stimulus-response psychologists, including Edward L. Thorndike, came to the stimulus-response position apparently through association theory rather than through behaviorism. Many contemporary stimulus-response psychologists have entered the field of behavioral engineering in industry and education.

Gestalt Psychology. Gestalt psychology had its origins in Germany between 1912 and 1917. Max Wertheimer and his colleagues were dissatisfied by the descriptions of learning provided by association theory, behaviorism, and stimulus-response psychology. These theories viewed learning as a gradual accumulation of small response tendencies that ultimately combine to form an entire "chain" or complex response. The German psychologists chose the word *Gestalt*, meaning "figure" or "pattern," to reflect their belief that learning is an organization of components into a totality that is more than the sum of the constituent bits and pieces. They reached this conclusion by observing problem-solving behavior in apes and men, who, after initial inspections of problems, often solve them suddenly, without benefit of trial and error or piecemeal learning. These "insightful" solutions are taken as evidence that learning is not additive, as association theory and stimulus-response behaviorism contend, but holistic or patterned.

Perception of relationships is important in some kinds of learning, and Gestalt psychologists maintain that stimulus-response chains play little part in the attainment of insight. They draw support from studies of perception that reveal that unfamiliar objects are perceived as totalities and that their details are noticed later: the brain does not perceive minute details first and then add them together so as to perceive the entire object. Gestalt psychologists recommend that educational procedures emphasize the organization of materials so as to stimulate insight into meaningful relationships. Drill and rote memory procedures, more consistent with piecemeal or incremental learning theories, are rejected.

Current Trends in Theory. None of the "comprehensive theories" is as comprehensive as its proponents claim. Because each has furthered our understanding in certain limited areas of behavior or perception, the theoretical positions taken by educational psychologists tend to reflect the areas in which they work. In the areas of child psychology, mental hygiene, and behavior problems, psychoanalytic formulations are prominent. Stimulus-response behaviorism illuminates the acquisition of facts and the shaping of fairly simple forms of behavior. With regard to complex thinking and problem solving, Gestalt formulations stressing organization and insight are most helpful. But the psychologist who works in many of these areas is likely to perceive the need to be flexible and to use ideas from each of these theories when they are helpful. No one theoretical system is sufficiently comprehensive to solve all the problems of educational psychology.

Today there is a growing tendency to limit theories to much smaller systems, or "models," which try to account for just a few phenomena. Examples include various theories of short-term memory, of long-term memory, of attitude and motive formation, of role playing, and of cognitive development. The more accurate knowledge resulting from current research in these highly limited areas should provide a foundation for comprehensive theories of the future that will be much more substantial than past or present ones.

Although the early comprehensive theories or "schools of psychology" have decided limitations, they have been valuable in various ways. They have provided rallying points and clearinghouses for psychologists of similar views, promoting research and the exchange of information. In addition, these explicit formulations of ideas under formal labels have given their opponents something tangible to oppose and thus galvanized them into constructive action in attempts to refute such theories and, if possible, to replace them with more plausible systems.

RELATIONSHIP TO THE FIELD OF LEARNING

The psychology of learning concerns all forms of relatively permanent behavioral change that result from experience. Since education attempts to modify behavior in planned directions by careful exposure to certain kinds of experience, it is clear that studies of learning should profoundly influence instructional techniques. Indeed, the psychology of learning was the core of educational psychology a few decades ago.

Since 1940, however, textbooks in educational psychology have given less space to learning. The reason is twofold. First, there is much more emphasis today on the development of the whole child and less exclusive preoccupation with his intellectual growth. Thus textbooks now give more attention to topics such as personality development, mental hygiene, guidance, and the like. Second, it has become clear that "laws" of learning cannot always be applied in programs of instruction. Current learning experiments usually avoid the danger of being too ambitious by studying very limited areas of behavior under highly controlled laboratory conditions. While this is probably the best way to build a systematic body of knowledge in the field, it has little immediate bearing on learning problems in the classroom. As a result, professional "learning theorists" and educational psychologists concerned with classroom techniques have tended to go their separate ways, and a wide gap has opened. Some learning theorists say that they have no interest in the practical applications of their theories. Others maintain that the history of science shows the formulation of basic laws to be the best way of handling practical problems. Contending that "there is nothing as practical as a good theory," they seek basic laws as the first step toward ultimate application of theories of learning.

Problems of Application. Even if learning theorists eventually succeed in formulating acceptable basic laws, there will sometimes be formidable obstacles to their application to problems of educational psychology. It may often be necessary to analyze the skills and the subject matter to be taught into the psychological processes that the educational psychologist wishes to establish in the student. This "job analysis" approach to teaching has already been used to train industrial workers. Analyses of this kind, though difficult, may be necessary to clarify the relationship between the language of learning theories and the practical problems facing the student and the teacher.

The gravest problem in applying theories of learning is that of dealing with the many different conditions under which learning takes place or fails to take place. Schools typically have little control over many of the conditions influencing learning, which include personality, adjustment, health, academic aptitude, personal values, motivation, socioeconomic background, teacher-pupil relationship, classroom "climate," environmental distractions, physical maturity, mental maturity, social maturity, and many others. The educational psychologist cannot study each of these variables for each of his pupils. Thus it is hardly surprising that conflicting results have been reported when different learning techniques have been used by different teachers for different students in different situations.

To illustrate the point further: familiar learning principles state that meaningful memory is superior to rote memory, that learning distributed over many periods is superior to learning massed in one period, that transfer of learning takes place if the new task is similar to the old, that memory is impaired if certain experiences intervene between learning and testing, that environmental distractions impair learning, that competition and awareness of the purpose of a task facilitate learning, that studying a task as a whole is superior to studying it piecemeal, that active learning is superior to passive learning, and that directed or guided learning is superior to unguided or incidental learning. Each of these principles holds under certain conditions of learning and fails under others. We are presently aware of only a few of the conditions that determine their degree of validity.

It is apparent that there is no universally dependable principle of learning. Much progress can be made by abandoning attempts to determine whether such principles are "true" or "false" and instead engaging in "conditional thinking." The relevant questions are, "Under what conditions is meaningful memory superior to rote memory, and under what conditions is it inferior?"—and so on for all the other learning principles. This approach emphasizes the fact that the effects of an instructional technique can hardly be predicted unless the conditions under which it is to be used have been studied carefully in detail.

The educational psychologist must accept this imperfect state of affairs. Fortunately, he can experiment with different techniques and retain those that produce the best results—a recommendation made by some learning theorists who have few theories to contribute at the moment. A considerable body of literature exists concerning procedures that seem effective much of the time. An instructor need not wait for further research before noting the conditions under which each instructional technique appears to succeed or fail in his own institution. Most teaching techniques now in use have evolved in this way.

Reinforcement. One principle not mentioned above lends itself particularly well to this pragmatic approach and comes as close to consistent reliability as any known principle of learning. This is the "law of effect" first systematically investigated by Thorndike and termed the "principle of reinforcement" by Clark Hull and B. F. Skinner. It holds that a response is strengthened by immediate reinforcement. Unlike earlier theories that tried to equate reinforcement with pleasurable states or tension reduction, Skinner's purely empirical approach, bypassing unconfirmable inferred states, identifies as a reinforcer anything—immediately following the behavior—that calls out the behavior with increased frequency. Just as a rat is encouraged to press a lever in a Skinner box if consistently given food as soon as the lever is pressed, so a child may be encouraged to repeat desired behavior if rewarded immediately after the behavior occurs. With a child, the word "good" may be as reinforcing as a piece of candy; a correct response by an adult using a teaching machine may be reinforced by permitting him to go on to the next frame. But even the principle of reinforcement is not completely dependable, because what is reinforcing today may not be so tomorrow. Yet the principle's reliability under most conditions of learning and its relative independence from troublesome theoretical considerations make it one of the most useful tools in the technology of teaching. As Skinner has pointed out, the technique can even be used to encourage discovery learning and creativity at early ages—once they have taken place in such a way that reinforcement is possible. See also LEARNING.

MOTIVATION

Because learning often does not take place without motivation, the study of motivation is sometimes regarded as integral to the topic of learning. The satisfaction of physiological (primary) needs, such as those for food and water, provides the motive for some kinds of learning. Learned (secondary) needs, such as those for association with others and for recognition, are no less important because they are learned rather than inherited. The educational psychologist is interested in the distinction between primary and secondary needs mostly because secondary needs differ considerably from child to child according to their varying cultural origins. Thus it has frequently been reported that verbal approval and other social reinforcements are effective with middle-class children, while their age-mates from lower socioeconomic classes may require tangible reinforcement such as toys or candy. Tangible reinforcement also seems particularly important when pupils are disturbed, retarded, very young, or disadvantaged. Knowledge of the nature and significance of such individual differences is important in constructing effective learning situations in the schools.

Motivational Patterns. The sources of some kinds of motivation are in doubt. There is evidence, for example, that the level of stimulation necessary for well-being varies widely from one person to another. Why some require exposure to rich and varied stimulation and others require far less is understood only partially as a product of early experience. It is important to note that the "natural" state of the organism is not passive. Even people with relatively low optimum levels of stimulation are highly motivated to avoid passivity and to seek activity and new experience. Such motives can be used to advance learning.

Certain basic motivational patterns have consequences for many different kinds of behavior. Their importance may be illustrated by the difference between a person who is threat-oriented (dependent and afraid of failure, with low motivation to achieve) and one who is goal-oriented (relatively independent and unafraid of failure, with high achievement motivation). One's orientation depends partially on the reinforcements that follow early attempts to achieve goals. One is more likely to be goal-oriented if his attempts are usually rewarded than if they usually incur negative reinforcements, which can produce a trauma that can impair future opportunities for learning for many years. Psychologists working with very young pupils play an important part in determining each pupil's orientation in the learning situation. With older students, whose motivational patterns cannot be readily changed, it appears that threat-oriented students learn more when instruction is highly structured and directive and when goals are clearly attainable. Goal-oriented students appear to learn more from challenging and somewhat ambiguous situations in which success is not certain.

There is evidence that factors associated with national culture also influence motivation. The average motivations of groups of students in various countries have been found to vary significantly, with the differences correlating with the prevalence of themes related to achievement appearing in the textbooks used in the respective national school systems. Whether superior motivation derives from the greater number of these themes in textbooks or from the cultural patterns that produce such textbooks is not clear. In either case, achievement motivation is clearly learned and is, therefore, teachable.

Motivational Devices. Such observations underline the importance of student expectation or "set" as a factor in motivation. Less often cited is the importance of the teacher's expectation. It has long been assumed that teachers should avoid hostility and should encourage students. Only recently has it been confirmed that a teacher's expectations concerning individual students affect his behavior so as to bring about the expected behavior in the students. Thus when teachers were falsely told that certain students had exceptionally high IQ's, subsequent tests showed that the performances of these students rose significantly—as if in fulfillment of the teachers' expectations. A study of exactly how teachers interact with students whom they consider exceptional should reveal valuable motivational techniques.

An increasingly important motivational device, "ego involvement," entails relating subject matter to the interests of the students. Genuine ego involvement seems to have been difficult in the 1950's, when many college students showed apathy toward the educational process. Since the middle 1960's, however, there has been an almost unprecedented awakening of student concern with college education. There has arisen a "student culture" that no longer passively reflects the interests, attitudes, and values of the society as a whole. Student needs have become "demands," and organizations to attain student goals have arisen on many campuses. Virtually every large U.S. campus has felt the impact of this revolution, and activity has been increasing on smaller campuses and in many secondary schools. Students in Europe and South America appear to be similarly militant, and there are stirrings even behind the iron curtain.

Students in the United States generally seem inclined to regard the status quo, or "establishment," with suspicion; to regard older persons as representatives of the establishment; to do more thinking on their own; to demand that their courses be relevant to important current issues; to seek recognition as individuals rather than submerging their individuality within conventional organizations; to learn how to store facts and information; and to express themselves freely on important matters. The new student culture cannot be ignored: it challenges old methods in education and calls for the exploration of new ones. Although some regard it as a temporary aberration in student behavior, the strength of the movement will almost surely force modifications of the educational process to make it conform to student demands. A number of universities and colleges have already made changes in their curricula in response to student requests. In France the government has begun to respond to student demands that may effect the most profound changes in the French educational system since the Napoleonic era. If students continue to be vigorously motivated by their present concerns, educational psychologists may have to evolve new and more appropriate goals and procedures.

MATURATION AND DEVELOPMENT

The study of human maturation and development is a large area including child psychology and the psychology of adolescence. The method used most frequently is the genetic or developmental approach, which seeks to understand an individual's behavior by carefully studying his earlier experiences and stages of growth, often as far back as birth. In 1891, G. Stanley Hall founded a journal for the publication of research dealing with children, and in 1904 he published his book *Adolescence*, thus completing observations on a wide range of ages. Later, detailed observations and photographic records of children of various ages were made by Arnold Gesell and others at the Yale Clinic of Child Development. Developmental "norms" were published to indicate the expected or "normal" progression, year by year, of several forms of behavior. Although such norms can be used in a very rough way to determine activities appropriate for students of various ages, their use by persons untrained to allow for individual differences has caused problems in the home and the educational system. When used carefully, such norms might apprise a teacher that a wait of a few additional months might enable a pupil to accomplish more with less difficulty. This is particularly true of tasks requiring locomotion and perceptual-motor coordination, as these activities may be severely limited by factors of physiology or maturation.

This waiting strategy is less appropriate for tasks requiring higher thought processes, since research shows the importance of exposing even very young children to a variety of stimulating experiences. For years, parents at the upper socioeconomic and educational levels have sought preschool training for their children. Only recently, however, has there been solid evidence of the importance of early opportunities to learn. A recent study found that approximately half of all growth in human intelligence occurs between birth and the age of 4, roughly another 30% between 4 and 8, and the rest between 8 and 17, at which age the development of basic intelligence is nearly complete in most persons. Studies of animal behavior confirm the great importance of early experience. Dogs and monkeys deprived of normal stimuli early in life show behavioral abnormalities from which they never fully recover. Rats raised in stimulating environments develop cerebral cortexes heavier and denser and containing larger quantities of important enzymes than the cortexes of littermates raised in drab environments. If environment has its greatest effect on intelligence during the period of most rapid development, then by the time a child enters school he has already passed the most crucial stage, and the possible contribution of the educational system is seriously limited. These findings lend impetus to the developing American social concern for the disadvantaged or culturally deprived child.

To cope with the educational crisis in U.S. cities, crash programs are being established by urban centers at many institutions of learning, and the federal government is responding through the Office of Educational Opportunity and through grants to support local attempts to provide stimulating early environments. Only recently, with the advent of the Head Start Program, has there been any attempt to provide continuing preschool education on a massive scale. The New York State Board of Regents has called for free schooling by 1978 for all 3- and 4-year-olds whose parents seek such help, and the Carnegie Corporation is experimenting with sending public school teachers into disadvantaged homes to tutor mothers and very young children.

In Israel, research released by the department of education at Tel Aviv University indicates a similar concern, finding the preschool years to be critical for the child's perceptions, sense of security, individual development, basic elements of abstract thinking, attitudes, and style of intellectual performance. Experiments there indicate the possibility during the preschool period of significantly raising the IQ's of culturally deprived children.

The current emphasis on preschool education has been accompanied by a revival of interest in the work of Maria Montessori, an Italian physician who worked with undisciplined and untrained children in the slums of Rome about the turn of the century. Her methods, which stress individual attention to each child, are practiced not only in the many Montessori schools in the United States but also in the Head Start Program and inner-city programs. They are popular with parents and teachers who feel that most schools are too informal and underemphasize the conventional curriculum. This reaction against progressive education may reflect a trend. The Institute of Preschool Education in Moscow has been conducting preschool training programs resembling the Montessori method: the learning experience is highly structured, and the child is given considerable guidance in the pursuit of specific educational goals. A shortage of qualified preschool teachers has prevented general adoption of the program in the USSR thus far.

Parallel with this renewed interest in the Montessori method is an awakening of interest in the work of the Swiss psychologist Jean Piaget. For decades, Piaget studied children's understanding of the world and of morals as well as their numerical and spatial concepts. His work received much attention in Europe after World War II, but until the 1960's few American psychologists saw its relevance to educational problems. Piaget holds that perceptual and intellectual development depend not only on learning and maturation but also on a distinctive third process involving autonomous reorganization of behavior. Like Gesell, Piaget described for children at each age level the forms of behavior, language, and thought that he believed characteristic. His detailed studies of language and higher thought processes in children are frequently consulted by those interested in problems of curriculum and training.

The rapid growth of juvenile crime in the United States has revived interest in how values are taught to the young. The importance of parents and teachers as models has not been examined adequately, the research required being very difficult. One study of how "conscience" develops suggests the need for careful work in this area. Preschool boys were observed alone in situations where they had been forbidden to do certain things they enjoyed. Those that "resisted temptation" more frequently had warm, interested fathers than did those that disobeyed. This supports the theory that if a child genuinely likes a person he will be more apt to identify with him and to internalize his values. The implications of this study for pupil-teacher relationships are obvious but largely untested, although research shows that very few college programs or college teachers have any measurable impact on student values. Educational psychology is assisted in this area by studies in social psychology of attitude formation and attitude change.

THE INITIAL TEACHING ALPHABET figures in various experimental techniques for teaching reading.

APPLICATIONS TO INSTRUCTION

Methods of Teaching. Much information on what might be termed the "technology of instruction" is available on methods of teaching specific subjects such as foreign languages, arithmetic and mathematics, reading, writing, spelling, and the sciences. The suggestions stem in part from theoretical considerations but mostly from practical experiences of teachers and research workers, who do not always agree as to the best methods. Variations in the ages, abilities, and backgrounds of students often require that specific methods be modified or replaced. Even so, several important general trends can be discerned.

One such trend is that of teaching subjects at earlier and earlier ages. In the past, "readiness" to learn a subject was usually seen in terms of physiological or maturational factors on which the teacher had to wait before learning could take place. Today, this notion is yielding to the realization that a child's readiness often depends less on his chronological age than on the training he has had and the teaching methods used.

Readiness for certain subjects is less important than readiness for learning experiences of certain kinds, and the challenge is to translate subjects into learning opportunities that can be seized at much earlier ages. An example is provided by the "new mathematics." The traditional expression of mathematical concepts in formal terms, such as equations, often—even with older students —led to rote manipulation of mathematical operations without true understanding of their principles. This led to the notion that basic mathematical thinking was beyond the reach of grade school pupils. Now it appears that the basic ideas of science and mathematics can be expressed in terms understandable to such pupils. Thus, set theory was seen as a college subject until its basic usefulness for understanding mathematics became apparent. Now it is being taught successfully in grade school, precisely because it is based on logical considerations that can be understood early in life. Likewise, the principles of topology, usually considered a college subject, can be applied correctly by fourth-grade students who are taught games that require their use. The teaching of fractions is often delayed until the fourth grade or beyond, and even then many students handle the operations mechanically and with little understanding; but, if the meaning of fractions and the reasons for their manipulation are expressed logically, second-graders can usually master them readily.

It is believed that the grasping of abstract concepts is excellent preparation for the more formal work that follows, and it may help dispel the emotional trauma that has repelled so many people from science and mathematics. Because abstract concepts are difficult for children in early grades to handle, workers in mathematics and the social and physical sciences are seeking ways of making abstractions concrete so that they can be grasped intuitively. Such work has been supported by the National Science Foundation and others. Related research has shown that able junior high school pupils can do advanced college work in such sciences as anthropology, physics, chemistry, physiology, and psychology. Consequently, secondary science and mathematics courses have been considerably upgraded.

The trend to lower the ages at which subjects are taught clearly covers all levels of education; it also extends throughout most of the curriculum and includes many subjects. Whether the child is "ready" to read is now considered less relevant than whether the teacher is ready with an approach suited to the child's abilities. Not long ago the age of 6 or 7 was considered the proper time to learn reading. Methods now available are successful with many 3-year-olds, and a computerized "talking typewriter" has succeeded with even younger children. Spelling, writing, and other skills are susceptible to similar approaches.

A second trend, toward learning how to learn, needs special emphasis. Subjects are important not only for their information but also as opportunities for learning how to think about and to understand events and how to find out more about them. Students who simply memorize procedures, facts, and generalizations within each area may never develop techniques of learning that are useful in many fields. The effects of studying one subject are more likely to transfer to other situations if processes of discovery and inductive reasoning are stressed: if teachers in each area challenge students with questions and allow them to make discoveries and solve important problems, the students will learn how to learn. Work with both animal and human subjects has shown that those experienced in solving problems in a wide variety of situations are more apt to solve new problems. Many teachers are still preoccupied with subject matter as such, but its value as a vehicle for learning how to learn is increasingly recognized. Fortunately, this trend dovetails nicely with the current emphasis on relevance of subject matter to the problems of everyday life.

Automated Instruction. By the broadest reasonable definition, automated instruction would include all devices that automatically present educational materials to students. These include motion pictures and television, each of which has been hailed as a possible replacement for the teacher. In fact, each is now usually used to supplement rather than to replace personal instruction. The same is true of audio tapes, which are now being used extensively in high school and college language laboratories.

Programmed instruction uses teaching machines, computers, or books printed in such a way as to perform some of the functions of teaching machines. The subject matter is presented in a sequence of short units or frames, each containing information and a question that must be answered before moving to the next frame. Such a sequence, called a program, is often presented by a teaching machine, which instantly indicates whether the student's answer is correct. The development of teaching machines, begun by the American psychologist Sidney L. Pressey in the 1920's, was continued by B. F. Skinner and others after World War II. All programmed systems are designed to advance the student's knowledge in steps so small that he is unlikely to make an error, a method supposed to maximize his learning efficiency. Such systems have relieved many instructors of the tedium of teaching introductory concepts and vocabulary required for more advanced work.

Programmed instruction has been criticized on several grounds. Programs are difficult to prepare and are unavailable in some fields. Good students are often bored by the frame-to-frame approach and may learn more slowly than with conventional methods. Some say the method fragments subjects into facts and fails to challenge students to think about issues and unexplored problems. One recent improvement is branching programming, which allows brighter students to bypass large sets of frames; at the same time it gives error-prone students remedial instruction. When certain errors are made, the student is directed to special sets of frames that branch out from the main sequence and return to it when the remedial sequence has been completed. Because branching programs must be designed on the basis of current theories of learning, they may provoke controversy between Skinnerian behaviorists and followers of Piaget, whose theories reject the reinforcement process as the typical method of learning. This conflict is likely to be of increasing importance in both theoretical and applied areas of educational psychology.

Branching programming has been adapted to computers, in which entire courses can be stored, to provide computer-assisted instruction (CAI). The computer diagnoses the student's problems at each step and suggests appropriate remedies. Automated instruction, although it has had an important impact on education, has been used primarily as a supplement for conventional methods of teaching, not as a replacement for them.

Experiments conducted at Moscow University reveal an interest in teaching methods similar to programmed instruction. With elementary geometry, for example, the material to be taught is analyzed in detail so as to promote the error-free formation of concepts by students. Students respond to materials handed to them on cards—the equivalents of frames. Occasional errors are corrected by standard remedial routines similar to those of branching programming. See also section *Instructional Technology;* COMPUTERS—*Computer-Assisted Instruction;* TEACHING MACHINE.

FURTHER PROBLEMS

Recently there have been rapid increases in the number of students to be educated, in knowledge to be assimilated, in student and urban unrest, and in the financial problems of public and private education. Educational psychologists, caught in a number of crosscurrents, face many dilemmas. They must cope with pressure for curriculum changes from those who say that certain subjects should be taught earlier; that all subjects should be made more relevant to common problems of life, especially those of minority groups; that students should participate more in curriculum design; that more emphasis should be placed on discussion and problem-solving proportionately to lectures, and more on "inquiry training," "discovery methods," and "creativity" proportionally to facts; that educators should not shrink from teaching basic values; and that more attention should be given to overall adjustment, not only intellectual development.

Each of these suggestions raises problems of method. Should all subjects be taught earlier just because they can be? How much earlier? What are the pros and cons of teaching subjects as early as possible? How can courses be made more relevant and yet avoid overpopularization? Can students make realistic and constructive suggestions about the curriculum? What is the best balance between facts and discovery methods? Between lectures and problem approaches? How can basic values be taught without danger of indoctrination? Is there a distinction between education and indoctrination? If so, what is it?

Teachers are currently in the uneasy position of having to reconcile contradictory demands. They are exposed to research urging that they devote as much attention as possible to the needs of individual pupils, and they are simultaneously pressured by financial considerations to teach as many students as they can. Thus the main problem for the educational psychologist is to determine the optimal resolution of this conflict and to ensure the finest educational system that can be constructed with the resources available.

RALPH H. TURNER, *Oberlin College*

Bibliography

Biehler, Robert F., ed., *Psychology Applied to Education*, 2d ed. (Houghton 1978).
Blair, Glenn M., and others, *Educational Psychology*, 4th ed. (Macmillan 1975).
Cronbach, Lee J., *Educational Psychology*, 3d ed. (Harcourt 1977).
Gage, N.L., and Berliner, David C., *Educational Psychology*, 2d ed. (Houghton 1979).
Hamachek, Don E., *Psychology in Teaching, Learning, and Growth*, 2d ed. (Allyn 1979).
Lindgren, Henry C., *Educational Psychology in the Classroom*, 6th ed. (Oxford 1980).

11. Educational Measurement

The indispensability of testing in education is emphasized by the constantly growing demand that the output of our educational systems be objectively evaluated. Educational measurement may be broadly understood to include evaluation by means other than the use of tests, but this discussion will concentrate on educational testing.

DEVELOPMENT

Educational testing is traceable to ancient and medieval times. Most of the known yearly instances of testing involved oral examinations or tests of the essay type in which the individual responded to questions presented in written form. Modern educational measurement did not emerge, however, until the 20th century, when standardized tests first appeared in the United States.

The development of standardized tests was gradual. In the early 1800's every New England town had a school committee, one of the func-

CODING TEST requires student to substitute symbols for numbers; it tests coordination and learning speed.

tions of which was to make an annual examination. The committee visited the classrooms and questioned the students, who thus "stood the oral examination." The many weaknesses of this plan led Horace Mann in 1837 to press for improvement in the evaluative process. As a result of his leadership, the Boston School Committee in 1845 used printed examinations for the first time. This method of testing was such a departure from the old oral examination that it was not accepted without great controversy.

Although the tests proposed and developed under Mann's influence would not meet present criteria for standardized tests, they had many of the characteristics of modern tests. They sampled the curriculum more widely than the oral tests of the time; they were far more objective, in the sense that they could be graded by different people with only minor discrepancies; and they made use of existing statistical techniques for tabulating the results. Two notable later advances in the development of standardized tests were the establishment of the New York State Regents' Examination in 1865 and the founding of the College Entrance Examination Board in 1900.

The 20th Century. In 1905 the French psychologists Alfred Binet and Théodore Simon published the Binet-Simon Intelligence Scale, which inaugurated a new era in mental testing. The scoring of the Binet-Simon Scale was relatively objective, but a degree of subjectivity remained. Objectivity in the scoring was advanced by the American psychologists Lewis M. Terman, whose handbook *The Measurement of Intelligence* accompanied the Stanford Revision of the Binet-Simon Test (1916), and Rudolf Pintner, who later prepared a "Supplementary Guide" for the scoring of the Stanford Revision.

One of the great pioneers in the field of measurement was the American psychologist Edward L. Thorndike. His *Introduction to the Theory of Mental and Social Measurement* (1904) was the first major textbook on educational measurement, and his *Scale for Handwriting of Children* (1910) was a major contribution to the to the cause of objectivity in testing. This test derived its scoring technique from that of George Fisher, an English schoolmaster, who in 1864 had tackled the problem of subjectivity in grading papers by constructing a series of scales consisting of sample questions with answers given to serve as guides in grading the responses of students. The decade following 1910 was marked by the spread of objective testing. For instance, objective arithmetic tests were published by the American educators John C. Stone in 1908 and Stuart A. Courtis in 1909.

About 1914, Arthur S. Otis, working under Terman's direction, developed a group test of intelligence that, although derived in many respects from the Stanford Revision of the Binet-Simon Test, made important innovations. Otis was probably the first to make substantial use of multiple-choice questions with completely objective scoring stencils; he also developed many statistical techniques for dealing with the resulting data.

Otis' work was given great impetus by the U. S. Army's use of psychological examinations during World War I. He himself spent the war years as one of a team responsible for developing the Army Alpha Test, of which his group test was the precursor, and its nonlanguage equivalent, the Army Beta. The Army's successful use of psychological tests opened the floodgates, and, stimulated additionally by the growing popularity of school surveys, the number of mental ability and achievement tests developed and used in the United States increased astronomically in the decade following the war. They were especially widely used to test schoolchildren, as the precedent of examining children to determine their levels of achievement and intelligence had long since been established.

The Stanford Achievement Test, which appeared in 1923, was the first major standardized achievement test to cover the curriculum comprehensively. This test was simple to administer and was objectively scored. It provided national age norms drawn from a more or less representative population of 1,500 children, thus facilitating the comparison of any individual performance with the average. These norms were later revised to incorporate geographical variations more correctly.

Analysis. In the late 19th century the English scientist Sir Francis Galton laid the foundations for the statistical analysis of test results, introducing the idea of the correlation coefficient—a mathematically precise expression of the strength of relationship between any two sets of data. Methods of analysis were greatly advanced by Galton's student, Karl Pearson. Truman Kelley, an American psychologist who was one of the authors of the Stanford Achievement Test, was influential in applying statistical methods to the analysis of test data. His *Statistical Method* (1924) is now considered a classic text. In 1925, Otis published his *Statistical Method in Educational Measurement*, which, though less profound than Kelley's volume, probably had much more influence on the statistical analysis of test scores. In addition to discussing various ways of interpreting test scores, Otis provided simple devices for analyzing them.

From these early beginnings, testing, both educational and psychological, became an accepted part of the school program. Today very few pupils proceed through the grades without taking one or more tests of achievement or intelligence along the way.

KINDS OF TESTS

The number and variety of standardized tests now being used are both very great. However, the bulk of testing in the public schools involves one or another of three major kinds of tests: achievement tests, ability tests, and personality inventories of various kinds.

Achievement Tests. The earliest tests used in the public schools were achievement tests. Comprehensive achievement batteries such as the Stanford, Metropolitan, or California achievement tests still account for the largest single block of testing done. Each constituent test, though developed within the battery form, can be used separately; in addition, especially at the secondary level, standardized tests are now widely available in such subjects as algebra, science, social studies, and English. The cooperative tests published by the Educational Testing Service, and the Evaluation and Adjustment Series published by Harcourt, Brace & World, Inc., are among the most widely used.

Within the domain of achievement testing there has been a strong movement in recent years away from simple factual tests and toward measures of higher mental abilities. The *Taxonomy of Educational Objectives* (ed. by Benjamin S. Bloom, 1956) sets forth a hierarchy of mental abilities that starts with the acquisition of knowledge and continues through comprehension, application, analysis, synthesis, and evaluation, each being a step higher and more complicated than the one before. It has proven very difficult to develop tests to measure these higher mental abilities, partly because the curriculums in common use tend to emphasize rote learning and partly because the abilities may easily be confused: an answer that may represent evaluation in one testing situation will represent merely the acquisition of knowledge in another if it merely repeats an evaluation put forth by an instructor during his teaching.

Ability Tests. The prototype of all ability tests was the Binet-Simon Intelligence Scale, which purported to test general intelligence. Such tests may be called intelligence tests, mental ability tests, aptitude tests, readiness tests, or prognostic tests; in any case, their purpose is to measure some underlying ability, either general mental ability or some specific ability regarded as prerequisite for success in some field. Such tests, which are indispensable in school administration, enjoy tremendous and increasing popularity. See also INTELLIGENCE.

Personality Inventories. The third major class of standardized tests is smaller but still very substantial. It includes a wide variety of instruments intended to quantify individual interests or to define and measure certain other aspects of personality. Nearly all of these inventories are of the "self-report" type, in which the subject tells things about himself but can, without penalty, withhold from the examiner any information he wishes. Because the validity of these measures depends almost entirely on the subject's honesty, some psychologists prefer not to call them "tests," restricting that term to tests of maximum performance, in which each question has an objectively correct answer. Some devices have been built into personality inventories to detect subjects who are deliberately trying to mislead, but these devices are not foolproof. Nevertheless, if used with care, such inventories can be of great assistance in counseling and guidance. See also MENTAL TESTS; VOCATIONAL GUIDANCE.

Kinds of Test Questions. Some fields, such as spelling and arithmetic, lend themselves naturally to tests that can be graded quite objectively: there is ordinarily only one correct way to answer an arithmetic problem or to spell a word. In other fields the oldest and most basic kind of item is the essay, or free-response, question. Unfortunately, answers to such questions cannot be graded objectively. For this reason, fill-in, or completion, questions, which allow more objectivity in scoring, came into considerable use in early achievement and intelligence tests. Yet even these questions were less easy to score and less objective than was desirable, and they have largely been displaced by multiple-choice items, in which a partial statement ("stem") or a question is followed by a number (usually four or five) of choices of which only one is correct. Because such items lend themselves to a wide variety of scoring procedures, including scoring by machine, they are now the kind most widely used on objective tests.

Virtually all items designed for scoring by machine are derived from the multiple-choice format. Variations on this format include multiple-response items, on which the subject is to choose more than one answer; negative multiple-choice items, on which the subject is to choose the worst answer; items on which one choice involves a combination or rejection of previous choices; items on which the subject is to evaluate a statement along a scale of truthfulness; matching questions; category items, on which a single set of choices is used for a number of questions; and so on. In most instances, but not always, true-false items can be considered another variation of multiple-choice questions. New kinds of items are being developed constantly.

BUILDING A BRIDGE in imitation of the tester, this child is being tested for her imitative ability.

HAYS, FROM MONKMEYER

COPYING A DESIGN with blocks, this student is being tested for abilities to visualize and organize.

Some are modifications of the multiple-choice type; others depart from it in allowing an escape of some sort from the "these-or-nothing" situation posed by a limited number of choices.

True-false and multiple-choice items have certain weaknesses. One is that some questions have more than one correct answer; another is that, through carelessness on the part of the test designer, the most completely correct answer may not appear. Consequently, the directions for such items should (but often do not) read, "From the choices given, choose the answer that is most nearly correct." Even so, great care must be taken in grading the test results to avoid penalizing a bright student who is occasionally rightly dissatisfied with all the answers offered.

TEST VALIDITY

The most important property of any test is its validity, or the degree to which it measures what it is supposed to measure. For a predictive test, the obvious means of determining its validity is to compare the subjects' test scores with their subsequent performances, provided that these can somehow be quantified; such a comparison reflects the test's *empirical validity*. Clearly, tests are not valid in general, only in specific situations and for specific purposes. Similarly, one test may be more valid than another, but none is absolutely valid.

Validity is not as simple a matter as it may seem. That a test is called a reading test and does indeed involve reading does not mean that it truly measures the subject's reading ability. It may, in fact, be simply a series of paragraphs and questions dealing with material of common knowledge, perhaps in social studies or science, so that it becomes in effect an achievement test. A good way to judge whether a test is indeed a reading test is to see whether the questions can be answered without reading the material presented. If so, the test is not a test of reading at all; if its stated purpose is to test reading ability, it is not valid.

To protect themselves against the charge of lack of validity, the authors and publishers of achievement tests make detailed studies of the contents of courses and make each test conform to the content of the relevant course as closely as possible. When this is done skillfully, the test has relatively high *content validity*. However, test validity unfortunately does not depend solely on content. The type of item used, the adequacy of the directions, the suitability of the answering method to the population tested, the administration of the test, and the attitudes toward testing of those who take the test and of those who administer it—all affect the ultimate validity of the test. For example, if one wants to know whether a student can solve a certain arithmetic problem, the most direct test is simply to compare his answer with the correct one. But this method, while completely objective, cannot practically be scored by machine. Contrariwise, a test consisting of multiple-choice questions may encourage the subject to estimate or guess; the actual solution of the problems becomes less essential.

Valid test items generally share certain characteristics. They should, within reason, be passed by greater percentages of older students and of abler students. Items too difficult or too easy to discriminate effectively are usually discarded as a waste of space and time.

The validity of standardized tests is often attacked on the ground that they put too much emphasis on speed in answering. Generally, however, such tests progress from relatively easy to relatively hard questions; thus the questions not answered for want of time are the ones that would least often be correctly answered anyway, and subjects' scores would usually be little affected if the subjects were allowed additional time for answering.

The validity of specific test results is related to the quality and appropriateness of the instruction in evaluation received by the teachers who administer the tests. A survey of the situation in the late 1960's indicated great room for improvement in training teachers as evaluators.

INTERPRETING TEST SCORES

In the scoring of any test the first outcome is ordinarily a raw score, usually the number of items answered correctly. Such scores have no intrinsic meaning; to understand their significance, it is necessary to compare them with norms of some sort. Standardized tests are generally provided with norms based on previous performances on the tests by presumably representative samples of students of appropriate age or grade.

National Norms. Most standardized tests are now accompanied by norms more or less representative of all individuals of a given grade or age in the entire nation. National norms have certain drawbacks: none can ever be based on a truly random sample, because communities cannot be forced to participate; furthermore, there is no clear-cut agreement on the best method of obtaining norms. Even so, national norms are constantly improving. Computers are making possible ever more extensive sampling: the norms for the first Stanford Achievement Test in 1923 were based on a sample of 1,500 subjects, whereas those for the 1964 edition of the test involved testing, under fairly severe statistical controls, of 800,000 children, some from each of the 50 states. In addition, the growing use of stratified random samples is a means of increasing the true representativeness of the norms.

EXAMPLES OF ACHIEVEMENT TESTS

Reproduced on this page are sample items from a group of achievement tests used in U.S. schools to measure how much students have learned about basic subjects. The samples show the kinds of questions asked and the ways students record their answers. Questions range from easy to difficult. The reading and science tests use multiple-choice questions. The language test calls for marking one of three choices and writing in a correct word where needed. The arithmetic computation test requires that the student work each example and write in his answer. Similar tests are provided for word knowledge, spelling, language skills such as using a dictionary, arithmetic problem solving, and social studies information and skills. The whole group of tests is called a battery.

READING

DIRECTIONS

Read each story. Then read each question below the story. Find the best answer to the question and put a cross through the letter in front of the answer you have chosen. Certain questions refer to particular words in the story. These words can be found in the lines which have the stars (★) beside them. Study the sample below and notice how the questions have been marked.

SAMPLE

★ Frank has a good hobby. He collects stamps. He has stamps from many different places. Of course, he has many United States stamps. He saves them from the letters he gets from his Aunt Carrie in Texas and his Cousin Jack in Ohio. But Frank also has stamps from foreign countries.

A Frank's Aunt Carrie lives in —
   [a] Ohio   [b] New York
   [c] Africa   [✗] Texas

B In this story, the word saves means —
   [e] rescues   [f] protects
   [✗] keeps   [h] prevents

LANGUAGE

Part A Usage

DIRECTIONS

In each of the sentences below, one word is underlined and is written in **heavy black letters**. Read each sentence carefully. If you think the underlined word is the correct word to use, put a cross through the R (for right). If you think it is incorrect, mark the W (for wrong) and write the correct word on the line at the right. If you are not sure whether the underlined word is correct or incorrect, mark the DK (for don't know). Notice how the samples have been answered.

SAMPLE A She was **too** tired to go............. [✗] [W] [DK] _____ A

SAMPLE B I wonder who **give** me this present...... [R] [✗] [DK] _____gave_____ B

ARITHMETIC COMPUTATION

DIRECTIONS: Work each example in the space provided with the example. Copy your answers in the column marked "ANSWERS" at the right. Reduce all improper fractions to mixed numbers, and all answers to simplest terms. Study the sample item carefully. It has been worked for you and the answer has been entered in the answer column.

SAMPLE Add

```
  2 0
+ 1 6
  3 6
```

ANSWERS

S ___36_____

SCIENCE

DIRECTIONS

This is a test of what you know about science. For each question there are four possible answers. Read each question carefully and decide which one of the answers is best. Put a cross through the letter in front of the answer you have chosen. Study the sample below. The right answer has been marked for you.

SAMPLE An animal with fur is the —   [✗] bear   [b] robin   [c] fish   [d] turtle

FROM METROPOLITAN ACHIEVEMENT TESTS: INTERMEDIATE BATTERY, FORM A. COPYRIGHT © 1958 BY HARCOURT, BRACE & WORLD, INC., NEW YORK. ALL RIGHTS RESERVED. REPRODUCED BY PERMISSION.

Local Norms. National norms are less appropriate for some purposes than local norms which have the advantage that an individual's scores on tests in different subjects can easily be compared with one another, and with intelligence test scores, because all the norms are based on the same group studying the same curriculum. However, local norms are no substitute for national norms when the goal is to evaluate individual performance in relation to a very large (and therefore more representative) population.

Application of Norms. In addition to being categorized according to the samples on which they are based, norms vary according to the criteria they provide for the evaluation of individual performances. Some norms are based on the average performances for various grades or ages; if a child's performance on a reading test employing such norms equals the average for the 6th grade then he is scored as reading at the 6th-grade level, regardless of the grade to which he belongs. Intervening values are obtained by interpolation. Such scores have serious drawbacks due to variations in rates of development from one individual to another, from one subject to another, and from one stage of learning to another.

Deviation Norms. The most useful type of norm is that which reflects various levels of performance for others of the same grade or age as the individual or group being tested. Such norms, sometimes called deviation norms, allow each individual's performance to be ranked with respect to the performances of his age- or grade-mates.

The most familiar kind of deviation norm is the percentile rank. A raw score's percentile rank equals the percentage of subjects whose scores on the test are lower than or equal to that score. Thus if a test score of 78 equals or exceeds the raw scores of 45% of the students taking the test, it corresponds to a percentile rank of 45. Percentile ranks have one serious drawback. The distribution of scores on any good test generally follows, at least roughly, the normal curve of distribution; this means that scores tend to be bunched in the middle of the distribution and strung out at the extremes. For this reason, a percentile rank difference of 10 represents a much smaller and less meaningful difference in raw score at the middle of the distribution than it does at an extreme. For instance, the difference between percentile ranks of 1 and 3 often reflects a difference in raw scores greater than that reflected by the difference between percentile ranks of 40 and 60.

In order to surmount this difficulty, various other kinds of deviation norms were devised. One was the deviation IQ, first suggested by Arthur S. Otis in the early 1920's. As it is now generally defined, the deviation IQ is a standard score with a mean of 100 and a standard deviation of 16. In less technical terms, this ordinarily means that the raw score average is converted to 100 and that (for instance) a score corresponding to the 84th percentile rank becomes 116, while one corresponding to the 16th percentile rank becomes 84. A child's normalized score is most accurate when his age corresponds most precisely to the age on which the norms are based.

During World War II, the U. S. Air Force introduced a simple kind of deviation norm based on the *stanine*, a unit of distribution the nature of which is indicated by the accompanying illustration. Scores normalized on this basis range from 1 to 9, with an average of 5; because the distance from the upper limit of one stanine to that of the next one above it is always the same (stanines 1 and 9 being slight and deliberate exceptions for convenience) the stanine units are equal: a specific difference in stanines at any point in the range is equal to the same difference at any other point. Norms based on stanines are coming into wider and wider use for the interpretation of scores on ability and achievement tests, because of their simplicity and because they are well adapted to the comparison of scores on one test with those on another (as on an ability test and an achievement test) in simple graphic terms.

A growing emphasis on "individual progress" has stimulated changes in curriculums and school administration designed to allow each student to move through school at his own pace. Because of these trends, it is often unclear to what norm a student's test performance ought to be compared. The student's age remains a fundamental consideration, but he cannot fairly be compared with other students of the same age whose educational experience may be much less or much greater. Because the "individual progress curriculum" retains the idea of systematic and cumulative instruction, especially within such basic subjects as reading and mathematics, it is still possible to compare an individual student with others whose educational experience has been essentially the same. For these reasons, it is logical to expect a growing use of norms based on samples that are uniform with respect to both age and educational experience.

A basic issue involved in all testing concerns the extent to which schools should share test information with parents. This, of course, is a matter of opinion, but it hardly seems justifiable in a democracy for a school to measure a student's learning (or potential to learn) without sharing the results with the persons who

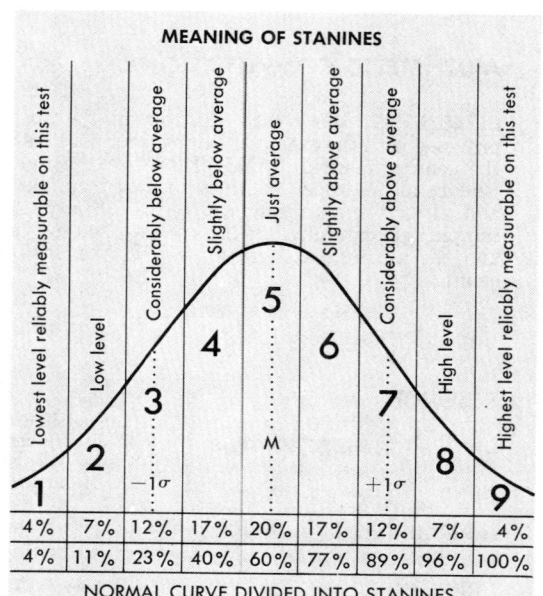

NORMAL CURVE DIVIDED INTO STANINES

are most directly involved and most likely to be in a position to further the educational process by insisting on performance that is commensurate with ability.

USES OF TESTS

The most important function of the educational process is to lead each child systematically and logically through a body of subject matter to the point at which he has developed enough basic learning skill and mastered enough material to permit him to make a sensible decision about his vocation. Tests are virtually indispensable for the efficient performance of this function.

Testing in the Public Schools. The use of tests by the public schools begins for many students before formal schooling itself. For example, tests are being used effectively in connection with the Head Start Program, which precedes kindergarten in many communities and precedes 1st grade in almost all. In addition, tests are used as criteria for the admission to school of many children who would otherwise be barred by age standards even though they are intellectually capable of doing schoolwork. Some of the instruments used for this purpose are not standardized tests in the usual sense of the word; instead they constitute a kind of standardized interview procedure intended to assess the child's emotional maturity as well as his intellectual ability to handle the work.

Group intelligence tests have been used successfully in kindergarten and 1st grade for many years. Examples include the Pintner-Cunningham Primary Mental Test, first published in 1923 and revised several times since, and the Kuhlmann-Anderson Intelligence Tests, published in 1927. The proper administration of such tests requires considerable skill; the administrator should study the directions carefully, and the tests should be administered to groups smaller than the average class: 10 to 15 children is optimal. The correlations of these intelligence tests with the Stanford-Binet Test are slightly variable but generally high.

Tests play an important role in determining promotion policies. Readiness tests are used very extensively late in kindergarten to identify those students who are ready for 1st grade. These tests combine aspects of achievement tests and intelligence tests; they attempt to assess certain knowledges, skills, and intellectual abilities that have been found to be important for normal progress in 1st grade. National norms are provided for these tests, usually in terms of IQ's, percentile ranks, or stanines, but such norms are less useful in the early grades than they are later. School programs, entrance age, and the general level of learning ability—conditioned as it may be by the environment from which the students come—all vary greatly from one community to another; thus it is highly desirable to establish local norms wherever possible. Each community should conduct its own studies to find the cutoff score that will best eliminate those unqualified for 1st grade without penalizing the abler students.

Although retardation as an administrative policy has diminished greatly, and only a very small percentage of students are held back at each grade level, some communities now designate certain grades as "holding grades," in which some youngsters are encouraged to stay back a year in order to gain maturity before

STANFORD-BINET I. Q. TEST for fifth grade includes "Plan-of-Search" test measuring ability to plan.

moving to the next higher level. More and more primary schools are ungraded, allowing students to progress as they are able and to take as long as four years for three years' work. These are not simply other methods of "holding back" the pupils but rather efforts to encourage intellectual development at the rate best suited to each student. The information essential in determining readiness for each major advance in the progression toward the end of the primary block is provided by tests. Certain critical evaluation points are advisable, as at the end of 6th grade and at the end of 8th or 9th grade, depending on the organization of the school. Standardized tests especially if carefully chosen, administered, and interpreted, can greatly improve the effectiveness of fully ungraded schools by providing the essential quality control without which such plans are likely to fail.

Test results tend to be surprisingly stable and dependable, especially when cumulative test results for several years are available and when ability measures are combined with measures of skill development for a composite score of learning aptitude. Very few students would be improperly placed at the high school level if the decisions concerning their placement were made at the end of 6th grade on the basis of a systematic cumulative testing program beginning in the early grades.

Testing Disadvantaged Children. It is often said that intelligence and achievement tests are unfair to children that come from socioeconomically deprived homes and communities. On the contrary, tests are the most dependable means of determining each student's functional learning ability. Achievement tests will in fact measure each child's status accurately if the child can read well enough to understand the test items and is not handicapped by the time limits imposed. Partly for this reason, the most important test for any child is probably a reading test, which reveals the extent to which the child can use his reading ability in the total learning process as well as in taking written tests in other subjects. Ability tests are usually designed to minimize the student's dependence on his reading skill: at the lower elementary levels such tests often contain dictated or diagrammatic material to which the child can react without reading, while in ability tests at higher levels the difficulty of the vocabulary is controlled, unless the test is designed to measure some facet of reading ability.

If the students in elementary grades are to meet certain minimal standards, even in an ungraded curriculum, it is important to measure the levels at which the students function, regardless of their socioeconomic backgrounds, so that instruction may be tailored to each student's level of development. Not testing students who come from culturally deprived environments would necessitate subjective judgments of their abilities and achievements. If the students are tested with the tests most appropriate to their levels of development, then at least some objective data are available as a basis on which to make plans for instruction.

The learning status of the child as measured by an achievement test does not necessarily correspond to the grade assignment that would be best for him according to his innate ability to learn. Therefore it is essential that the results of school achievement tests be compared with those of tests of school learning ability. The danger of ability testing of disadvantaged children is that the results, viewed uncritically, may be taken as permanent and definitive, whereas in fact they represent a situation that may change dramatically over a period of months or years. However, it is the IQ that changes, not the innate ability; IQ's can be raised, but innate ability cannot. Most of the opposition to the testing of disadvantaged children has arisen because teachers and administrators often overlook the possibilities of change.

Testing and Instruction. Tests can be used in many ways as guides to the improvement of instruction. They can serve to identify pupils with specific learning disabilities; additional analytical and diagnostic tests can then help the teacher to determine the particular nature of the problems and to provide adequate remedial instruction.

Tests are clearly valuable not only because they reflect the student's knowledge but because they reveal what he does not know. Such information can help the teacher to review and to organize his subject material more effectively. In some fields an item-by-item analysis of test results will identify particular knowledges and skills that have not been mastered by the class as a whole; the teacher can then consider the need for review.

Another way in which tests are valuable is as reflections of the quality of education in the school. Systematic standardized tests provide a means of determining the quality of a school's instructional program; their absence can lead to undetected deterioration of the quality of education in the school.

College Entrance Examinations. Certain tests are widely used as bases for determining admissions to colleges. This field is dominated by the College Entrance Examination Board, which was founded about 1900; its instruments include a scholastic aptitude test, measuring numerical ability and verbal ability, and various achievement tests in subjects that may be chosen by the student or required by various colleges. Another college admissions test, somewhat differently organized, is the American College Test. Each of these tests is a so-called "secure" examination: new forms are made up each year, and students are admitted to the examination rooms only after prepayment of a fee and proper identification. Test results are centrally processed and then forwarded to colleges stipulated by the students. Many colleges that do not use either of these two formal examinations employ their own private batteries of admission tests, consisting of various combinations of published standardized test materials.

One value of these tests is that they discourage students from attending colleges at which they have little chance to succeed. Undoubtedly there are cases in which students have been barred from colleges at which they could have succeeded, but few students have actually been compelled by low scores on such tests to forgo college education entirely.

In general, college entrance examinations predict college success with less accuracy than might be expected. The most obvious reason for this is that college success depends not solely on a student's ability but also on his determination and adaptability. Another reason is that the use of such tests narrows the range of ability among students who are admitted by rejecting most of the students with lower scores. This narrowing tends to lower the correlation between the test itself and any criterion of success in college. Finally, the predictive accuracy of such tests can be assessed usually only by comparison with grade point averages, and such subjective measures leave much to be desired as indexes of the value of entrance examinations. See also INTELLIGENCE; INTERESTS AND THEIR MEASUREMENT.

WALTER N. DUROST
University of New Hampshire

Bibliography

Ebel, Robert L., *Essentials of Educational Measurement*, 3d ed. (Prentice-Hall 1979).
Ebel, Robert L., *Practical Problems in Educational Measurement* (Heath 1980).
Gronlund, Norman E., *Measurement and Evaluation in Teaching*, 4th ed. (Macmillan 1981).
Mehrens, William A., and Lehmann, Irvin J., *Standardized Tests in Education*, 3d ed. (Holt 1980).
Noll, Victor H., and others, *Introduction to Educational Measurement*, 4th ed. (Houghton 1979).
Payne, David A., *The Assessment of Learning: Cognitive and Affective* (Heath 1974).
Popham, W. James, *Criterion-Referenced Measurement* (Prentice-Hall 1978).
Thorndike, R.L., and Hagen, E.P., *Measurement and Evaluation in Psychology and Education* (Wiley 1977).
Thorndike, Robert L., ed., *Educational Measurement*, 2d ed. (American Council on Educ. 1971).
Tyler, Ralph W., and Wolf, Richard M., *Crucial Issues in Testing* (McCutchan 1974).
Wargo, Michael J., and Green, Donald R., eds., *Achievement Testing of Disadvantaged and Minority Students* (Calif. Test Bureau/McGraw 1978).

12. Educational Research

Research in education comprises all methods of gathering knowledge about the processes and conditions of education. Research seeks to systematize knowledge in the field of education, its final goal being a comprehensive theory that orders, unifies, and explains not only educational data but also subordinate theories, laws, and generalizations within the field. With such a comprehensive theory, educators could work systematically to improve educational methods.

Educational research includes studies of many kinds: historical, logical, descriptive-survey, philosophical, developmental, clinical, growth, case, cross-cultural, and experimental. It has borrowed from the methods and findings of such disciplines as history, sociology, anthropology, political science, economics, psychology, and social psychology. Despite this great diversity, many educational investigations merely accumulate masses of data and do little to build a system of organized knowledge about education. Systematized knowledge is built when research is designed to test specific propositions, whether of great generality, such as supposed laws of human learning, or of limited concern, such as theories about the difference in effectiveness of two different methods of teaching.

Educational Propositions. Any comprehensive theory of education must rest fundamentally on data: the number of students attending a school, for instance, which may determine the school's share in the distribution of state funds. On data of various sorts may be erected propositions, or laws, relating two or more variables or relating conditions to consequences. There are two basic kinds of laws: nomothetic propositions, which hold in every instance and permit exact predictions to be made; and statistical propositions, which are accurate within varying limits.

Most propositions in the field of educational research are statistical. For example, given certain test data and information about grades attained in high school, it can be predicted that 90 of the top 100 students in a group of 1,000 would maintain a passing average in a certain college, and that increasingly smaller percentages would do so for hundreds selected in descending order. But such predictions are approximate, and within each hundred it cannot be certainly predicted which students would succeed and which would fail.

A similar example is provided by a battery of tests developed in World War II to choose among candidates for pilot training. Candidates were ranked in nine groups called "stanines." If the number of pilots needed was small, only those in the top stanine might be admitted to training; about 95% of them would survive primary training. If the need was greater, candidates might be admitted from lower stanines, in which success rates were lower. Results showed that the correlation of success on the test battery with success in pilot training was only a moderate 0.49; nevertheless, the use of the battery in candidate selection made the cost of producing one successful pilot $15,000 less than it had been with any other method.

Nomothetic propositions are harder to illustrate. When lengthy research on public school principals failed to relate effectiveness as a principal to experience, level of training, or several measures of personality variables, an in-service training program to improve the effectiveness of a group of 36 principals was designed upon propositions adapted from perceptual psychology. These propositions were: (1) if a group of individuals is placed in a low-threat situation where they can regard themselves and their problems as subjects, their perceptions of themselves and of their situation will change; and (2) if their perceptions change, then their behavior will change, first within the group and later in other situations. The results of the experiment indicated that these propositions were correct. Whether the propositions could qualify, however, as nomothetic would depend heavily on the qualities of the teachers or consultants, the duration of the training, the characteristics of the subjects, and other variables.

DEVELOPMENT OF EDUCATIONAL RESEARCH

Before 1900, educational research was largely deductive, imitating mathematics and logic. Its principles were derived from physiology, psychology, and philosophy, particularly ethics. In this century its methods have grown increasingly empirical, and it has borrowed more and more from a much wider variety of fields.

Empirical answers to educational questions were almost unknown until the 1890's. Philosophers through the ages had proposed educational systems elaborated from axioms that were either self-evident or drawn from other disciplines. Several developments, beginning about 1860, laid the foundation for modern educational research. Darwin's theory that individual variations eventually led to new species or to extinction of species stimulated Sir Francis Galton's studies of human variability, which in turn led to the development of statistical tools for describing central tendency, variability, and concomitant variation. Experimental work in psychology also began in the 1860's.

United States—Developments to 1950. American educational research has grown rapidly since 1890. Its techniques have multiplied, it has been heavily subsidized, and its influence has spread to countries all around the world.

The objective testing of educational practices began in 1897 with a study of the possibility of spending less time on spelling. Questionnaires were practically unknown until the 1890's, when G. Stanley Hall developed a series on children and educational topics. One of the first curriculum studies was done in 1893; its conclusion was that the college preparatory program in the high schools of the time, with its emphasis on mathematics, science, and English, was not only excellent preparation for college but also the best possible preparation for life for students whose parents could afford to send them to high school but not to college.

Psychological and educational tests underwent great development during the early decades of the 20th century. The first book on mental measurement was published in 1904, and the Binet-Simon individual intelligence test appeared in France the next year. The Stone Arithmetic Test in 1908 was the first standardized achievement test; it was followed rapidly by tests in almost all academic areas. The mass intelligence testing done with the U.S. Army Alpha and Beta tests during World War I produced data of lasting influence. These test results documented on a mass scale the consequences of poor schooling and culturally impoverished environments.

The development of tests and the need to use them prompted the establishment of "research bureaus" by cities, state departments of education, and universities. These bureaus served many purposes. Many were organized to give educational tests; many carried on censuslike collection of data; some conducted institutional studies; and others carried out assignments for chief administrators. In addition to the research bureaus, both the National Education Association and the American Council on Education began stimulating and conducting research during this period, and many other associations established research units.

Another trend that began about 1910 was the school survey movement. School systems and later entire states were subjected to methodical surveys and assessments. Data were collected on administration, buildings, teachers and teaching, curricula, and pupil populations. Sweeping changes were often recommended. Later, system-wide surveys were often required before state money was released for construction of new school buildings.

Many of the trends begun in the first quarter of the century continued during the second. Tests multiplied in both number and variety. In 1938 a series of *Mental Measurements Yearbooks* was begun under the editorship of Oscar K. Buros; the books that have appeared in this series contain expert critical appraisals of most published commercial tests, reviews of books and monographs on testing, and a comprehensive index and directory. Another important influence in testing, the Educational Testing Service, was organized in 1948.

The American Educational Research Association (founded in 1915) began in 1931 to publish the *Review of Educational Research*, which summarizes research under 15 major topics in 3-year cycles. The AERA also sponsors the *Encyclopedia of Educational Research*, which appears every 10 years.

William A. McCall's *How to Experiment in Education* (1923) was the first treatment of experimental design in education. It was followed in the next few years by comprehensive treatments of educational research and, in 1935, by Sir Ronald Fisher's *Design of Experiments*. Fisher introduced to the statistical analysis of agricultural research the techniques of analysis of variance and covariance, which were soon widely adapted to educational research.

Meanwhile, educational research methods and results were being subjected to severe criticism. Critics argued that problems were often poorly defined, that concepts were often vague in contrast to those in the physical sciences, that experimental procedures and techniques were often faulty, that measuring instruments often failed to meet minimal standards, and that researchers had failed to grasp theoretical ideas properly.

Developments Since 1950. Educational research in the United States has been accelerated by a number of developments that began about 1950. Many foundations have heavily subsidized educational innovation and research. An example was the Cooperative Program in School Administration (1950–1955), subsidized by the Kellogg Foundation. Cooperative centers were established at eight universities, with subcenters at dozens of other schools. Every phase of school administration was analyzed by school administrators and professors of school administration and other disciplines. One result was the University Council for Educational Administration, including most universities that give the doctorate in educational administration; the council stimulates research and dissemination activities.

The years since 1950 have marked the rise to prominence of the computer. Applications of factor analysis that once required hundreds of hours with desk calculators are now practicable. The computer also allows routine use of fairly complicated experimental designs involving analysis of variance and covariance. (Early experimenters attempted to control all possible sources of variation except the experimental independent variable. Changes in the dependent variable were then attributed to changes in the independent variable. The computer makes possible statistical controls for some sources of extraneous error. For example, if there is a variation of a year or more in mean mental age from school to school in a large-scale experiment on achievement, covariance analysis can remove that part of the variance in achievement attributable to the difference in mental age between schools.) The computer can simultaneously assess the influences of several independent variables on the dependent variable. It has also begun to reduce dependence on experiments with small samples.

There have also been advances in the conceptual basis of educational research. In 1963 the AERA published the *Handbook of Research on Teaching*. One section of this book, "Experimental and Quasi-Experimental Designs for Research," by Donald T. Campbell and Julian C. Stanley, has profoundly influenced experimental research. This research had been plagued by problems of internal and external validity—internally, by alternative possible explanations of results, and externally, by the problem of identifying the population about which experimental findings can be generalized. The authors systematically examine 16 experimental designs with regard to 12 common threats to internal and external validity.

Probably the most important development of the period since 1950, however, has been the entry of various government agencies into subsidizing educational research, development, and dissemination activities, and the training of educational researchers. The U.S. Office of Education (USOE), later the Department of Education, has been especially active in this area. In 1954, under the Cooperative Research Act, the USOE was empowered to contract for specific research projects with state departments of education, universities, and colleges. Other funds were earmarked for research programs in foreign-language teaching, vocational education, education of the handicapped, new media, and library improvement. The National Institutes of Health and National Institute of Mental Health also supported some educational research.

One of the most interesting of early USOE-funded projects dealt with the characteristics and styles of elementary school principals. Principals were recruited at centers around the country, and each was inducted as principal of the simulated "Whitman School" through movies, board regulations, a doctoral study, and other data. After a day of orientation, each spent four days coping with various administrative duties. Data collected from their home schools and combined with tests they took at the center resulted in the book *Administrative Performance and Personality* (1962), by John K. Hemphill and others. A second interesting study, concentrating on kindergarten children, concluded that their self-concepts, inferred by trained observers from picture-story tests and structured play, could be used to predict success in academic tasks at least as well as their scores on intelligence tests could.

In the belief that more rapid and unified progress could be made if organized units were established within particular areas, the USOE began channeling funds to a number of research and development centers organized usually by individual universities. One activity of these centers is the publication of technical papers. Later, a number of regional education laboratories were organized by groups made up of city school systems, state departments of education, universities, colleges, and other educational groups. These laboratories were intended to perform research, development, and dissemination.

Growing criticism of the managerial capabilities of the USOE led to the creation in 1972 of the National Institute of Education (NIE). The NIE took over responsibility for most federal educational research. It both conducts and funds long-term research and development programs.

Another development was the entry of industry into education-related enterprises. General Electric, IBM, Xerox, and other firms contracted to assess federal educational investments or to study further educational needs and resources.

An advance in the dissemination of educational information was gained with the establishment by the USOE of the Educational Resources Information Center (ERIC). ERIC comprises a nationwide information network consisting of a central staff at the NIE and 16 clearinghouses located in or near universities throughout the United States. Each clearinghouse focuses on a specific field of education; for example, the University of Oregon is responsible for the area of educational management. ERIC publishes *Resources in Education*, a monthly journal of abstracts listing recent research reports; an index to education journals; and a directory of ERIC microfiche collections.

The Educational Research Service (ERS) is a nonprofit agency established in 1973 to conduct research on educational management and policy. It is sponsored by seven management organizations, including the national associations of elementary and secondary school principals.

Educational Research in Other Countries. Although the intellectual backgrounds of educational research were located largely in Europe, especially in Britain, Germany, and France, such research has developed more slowly in countries other than the United States and is often modeled on work done there. Information on educational research in other countries is available in the *Review of Educational Research* and in the *World Survey of Education*.

The most centralized educational research is that done in the USSR, where it is the responsibility of the Academy of Pedagogical Sciences. The periodical *Soviet Education* is the best American source of information on Soviet educational research. Research areas are planned several years in advance, and results are usually reported as statements without supporting evidence.

A significant West German study, reported in the late 1950's, concluded that a large proportion of children who failed did so because they began school too early and not because of any mental deficiency. Research in the early 1960's focused on political education. One study concluded that political education would be effective only when democracy was practiced out of school and when the school administrators and teachers were conscious of serving a democracy. Many teachers feared that political education would impair student performance of fundamental tasks and would jeopardize certain long-established school traditions and the authority of the teacher. About 30% of a sample of high school students reported a commitment to democracy, while 20% continued to support authoritarianism in government.

Swiss educational research is most notable for the work of the psychologist Jean Piaget (q.v.). Although Piaget has profoundly influenced educational research in the United States, he seems to have had little effect on other researchers in Switzerland. In Scandinavia, recent research has dealt with independent work in secondary schools, with instructional methods in English and mathematics, with scholastic achievement at various levels, with factor-analytical techniques, and with various uses of educational measurement.

The English-speaking countries—Canada, New Zealand, and Australia, as well as the United Kingdom—all have broad programs of educational research. While the call in the United States is for more rigor in education, studies from these countries, with their high standards and exclusiveness, indicate that talent is wasted and that admissions are influenced by standards other than ability.

Two non-European countries with advanced programs of educational research are Israel and Japan. Much Israeli research is conducted by the Henrietta Szold Institute, founded in 1942 to promote child welfare by research, publication, and advisory work. Research has been directed to the solution of immediate practical problems. Special experimental programs have been set up to remedy the deficiencies of Israeli children from Oriental countries, who perform less well on intelligence and achievement tests than Israeli children from Europe. Educational research in Japan covers a very broad scope. Topics studied, research methods, and even research instruments are similar to those used in the United States.

Many other countries support some educational research. Interest in and output from research are increasing in Poland, and more rapidly in Yugoslavia. Educational research is beginning in Spain, in the Latin American countries, and in some of the former British colonies in Africa.

RECENT METHODS AND FINDINGS

Educational research may be categorized in many ways: (1) as historical, philosophical (or logical), diagnostic, experimental, comparative (or cross-cultural), or normative-survey; (2) by the method used in collecting data, as interview research, questionnaire research, observation research, or testing research; (3) by the method used to analyze data, as analytical research or statistical research—and, if statistical, as descriptive or inferential; and (4) in experimental research, by the experimental or quasi-experimental design used and by the analysis-of-variance model used to analyze the data.

The traditional tools of educational research —the questionnaire, interview, test, scale, and observation schedule—have been elaborated and refined. It is now generally accepted that each must be demonstrably reliable and valid. By reliability is meant that the technique used tends to measure, rank, or categorize the subjects consistently; by validity is meant the extent to which the technique measures what it is supposed to measure. The educational researcher has also learned how to sample and how to get a return from his sample high enough so that he can be reasonably confident of his results.

Prompted by criticism focusing on theoretical inadequacies, educational researchers have introduced theoretical formulations in many aspects of education. The educational psychologist has used learning theories for some time. More recently, theories have been proposed for teaching, for curricula, for supervision, and for school administration. These theories have been based on techniques and findings in the fields of social psychology, sociology, and political science. Researchers have also used the techniques of systems analysis, game theory, decision theory, simulated situations, and the case method for both training and research. Specific methods drawing on procedures developed in other fields include the application of computers to studies of learning theory and of instructional theory; the probing of biochemical influences on memory and learning; and the application of perceptual psychology to the understanding and modification of measured intelligence, academic achievement, teaching style, and administrative behavior.

One of the more important fields of research has been sociometry, the study of social relationships within peer groups. By asking subjects to name their peers for specific activities, researchers can find social isolates, leaders, stars, and cliques, and can define operationally such terms as "prejudice," "leadership," and "democracy." Other sociometric techniques include the semantic differential, a way of measuring the connotative meanings of concepts, and the Q-sort technique, in which the subject describes himself or a peer by sorting a set of 60 to 150 related items into a given number of piles ranging from most like himself to least like himself.

Still other innovations include advances in the understanding of intelligence and of creativity, and the development of a variety of observational systems and research that are making it possible at last to define effective teaching in terms of observable consequences. Finally, tape recorders, both audio and video, have become essential equipment for much educational research, and both still and motion pictures are widely used.

Recent Findings. The most significant recent research in education has been in the form not of single studies but of cumulative work in areas of great importance. Some such work has dealt with the malleability of human nature and the educative impact on its development of the entire environment. Certain findings indicate that the experiences of children during the first months and years of life are even more crucial to later cognitive development than they are to emotional development.

Among the outstanding individual researches was the "Eight Year Study," in which students graduating from 30 "progressive" high schools in the years 1936 to 1939 were followed through a variety of colleges and compared with students from conventional high schools who were similar in age, sex, family background, intelligence, and other respects that might influence success in college. Although the students from the progressive schools had spent less time in high school on academic subjects, they equaled or excelled the corresponding students in most academic areas in college and far excelled them in nonacademic activities. Students from the most progressive schools excelled corresponding students from traditional schools by even wider margins than did those from moderately progressive schools. Other projects showed similar superiority for pupils in progressive elementary schools.

Other important studies reached these conclusions: (1) Pupils will probably make more progress if promoted with their age-mates than if kept back in the hope that they can be coerced into meeting grade standards. Thus a slow reader is more likely to be further retarded than to be accelerated by nonpromotion. (2) Code emphasis programs (using phonics, linguistics, the initial teaching alphabet, and the like) enable children to recognize words better at the end of each of the first three grades than do programs involving basal readers emphasizing meaning and recognition of whole words. (3) Women, on the whole, make more effective elementary school principals than do men. This last finding was demonstrated by three major research projects on school administration conducted between 1955 and 1966.

PRESENT STATUS OF EDUCATIONAL RESEARCH

Educational research has reached its adolescence. Mountains of data have accumulated on almost every aspect of education. In many areas, research has indicated approaches that would considerably raise present standards. Many statistical propositions about education are available, and a few nomothetic propositions are on the horizon. Promising beginnings have been made in developing theories of learning, teaching, curriculum, and school administration.

Educational research is constantly improving its techniques. Researchers are being trained almost fast enough to meet needs. Computers are used increasingly to handle tedious calculations. Through research and development centers, ERIC, and regional education laboratories, means are at hand for disseminating research findings.

Unfortunately, Americans tend to ignore the results of educational research, and the findings mentioned above have been largely ignored. Progressive education is lagging. Hundreds of school systems, through nonpromotion policies, further retard their pupils. Every year the proportion of female elementary school principals decreases. And the study of reading instruction failed to find a single researcher whose position had been changed by the results of his research.

On the other hand, educational innovations no longer require 50 to 65 years to be generally accepted. Some of the new national curriculum programs, for example, have been adopted by most schools in a decade or less. What is needed now is adequate testing of innovations followed by rapid dissemination and acceptance of findings. Such an ideal seems possible in the near future.

VYNCE A. HINES, *University of Florida*

Bibliography

Ary, Donald, and others, *Introduction to Research in Education*, 2d ed. (Holt 1979).
Connecting Worlds: A Survey of Developments in Educational Research in Latin America (Unipub 1981).
De Landscheere, G., *Empirical Research in Education* (Unipub 1983).
Dershimer, R.A., *The Federal Government and Educational R & D* (Heath 1976).
Fraas, John W., *Basic Concepts in Educational Research* (Univ. Press of America 1983).
Good, Thomas L., and Brophy, Jere E., *Looking in Classrooms*, 2d ed. (Harper, 1973).
Hopkins, Charles D., *Understanding Educational Research: An Inquiry Approach*, 2d ed. (Merrill 1980).
International Directory of Higher Education Research Institutions (Unipub 1982).
Lindenmann, Walter K., *Attitude and Opinion Research*, 2d ed. (Council for Advancement and Support of Education 1981).
Mitzel, Harold, ed., *Encyclopedia of Educational Research*, 4 vols., 5th ed. (Macmillan 1982).
National Institute of Education, *Education Research: Limits and Opportunities* (National Council for Education Research 1977).
Sax, Gilbert, *Foundations of Educational Research*, 2d ed. (Prentice-Hall 1979).
Van Dalen, Deobold B., *Understanding Educational Research*, 4th ed. (McGraw-1978).

A language laboratory enables students to listen and respond to tapes of conversation in a foreign tongue.

13. Instructional Technology

Instructional technology incorporates those tools and materials that present, support, and reinforce teaching. The devices used range from the pad and pencil to the computer. The use of technology in education started long ago, when the slate was introduced as a supplement to books and lectures. The slate gave way to the blackboard and the chalkboard. From such beginnings came thousands of tools and devices to help teachers teach.

Advances in instructional technology have been made in many countries. The first public television broadcast originated in London in 1936, and educational television is now widespread throughout all Britain. Magnetic audio tape, the predecessor of videotape, was developed in Germany. In the 1960's, educational television broadcasts were inaugurated in Sweden and Israel, among other places, and were also part of the regular programming in West and East Germany, France, and the Soviet Union. Instructional technology is developing in all regions of the world—Africa, Latin America, and Asia—as well as the industrialized countries. Experiments using educational television and radio have been undertaken in the less industrialized countries often under the leadership of the United States. Computers have aided education in Germany and the Soviet Union for many years.

The post-World War II electronic revolution, which was advanced in the 1970's with the invention of the microchip, accelerated the introduction of instructional technology into classrooms. At first, single devices were used to accomplish small tasks within the education programs: a tape recorder, for example, recorded a panel discussion to be replayed later in the classroom. Educators soon found that they could accomplish more with greater flexibility by combining several pieces of equipment into a package or system. Thus a teacher added a filmstrip, slides, or a motion picture to a tape recording to serve a more clearly defined educational aim.

Today's instructional technology is a combination of hardware, software, and application procedures (or techniques of use). The hardware is equipment, such as computers, cameras, cables, and electronic facilities—the devices on which materials are used. The software consists of textbooks or other printed items, filmstrips, motion pictures, videotapes, videodiscs, phonodiscs, audiotapes, and computer programs—the stored information to be presented by means of the hardware. The techniques of use include planning for specific learning aims or objectives, matching the software to the aims, and matching the learners to both the aims and the software. This systematic procedure chooses each ingredient in the instructional package because it, and others selected to go with it, can achieve an educational goal better than any other combination available at reasonable cost.

TERMINOLOGY

New words and phrases, and new meanings for old ones, have evolved in the field of instructional technology. Some of the new terms include: carrel, learning laboratory, educational media center (or learning resources center), programmed instruction, teaching machine, instructional and educational television, videorecording (videocassette recorder and videodisc), microcomputer, and computer-assisted instruction.

Carrel. A carrel is a private or semiprivate facility for students to use for study. Generally, carrels are located in a library, in classrooms, or in study areas. A table partitioned with panel dividers can serve to create individual spaces for this purpose. Several carrels may be arranged along a wall, either attached or freestanding, or grouped in a cluster. They can be equipped to accommodate a variety of learning resources, such as tape recorders, phonographs, or microcomputers. The growing trend is to equip each station electronically so that prerecorded lessons, programs, and other resources can be transmitted to them.

Learning Laboratory. A learning laboratory is a place set aside for student activity, containing such hardware for learning as audio recorders, videocassette recorders (VCRs), television sets, projectors, and microcomputers. It also has software available for individual use, sometimes under direct control of a teacher. It can have limited or expandable capabilities and can be mobile or permanent. A simple kind of laboratory provides for student listening stations (as in language learning) to which the teacher electronically sends a taped lesson selected at a console or selected by the student. Other laboratories may emphasize individual study using software provided as an automated audiovisual presentation or a microcomputer program. Early learning laboratories were set up for language learning, but nearly any subject can now be learned in a laboratory.

Educational Media Center. A media center is an area where a range of information sources, associated equipment, and services from the staff are accessible to students and teachers. Educational media include motion pictures, television, books and other printed materials, computer-based instruction, graphic and photographic materials, sound recordings, and three-dimensional objects.

Programmed Instruction. Programmed instruction is information presented in a highly organized step-by-step sequence accompanied by questions to be answered, problems to be solved, or exercises to be performed. It is organized in such a way as to permit the student to respond and to proceed on the basis of that response if correct, or to reconsider and correct it if wrong. Reinforcement and knowledge of performance are provided after each response.

Teaching Machine. A teaching machine is a device that presents programmed instruction to the learner through words or pictures or both and provides for learner response through visual display, a keyboard, and audio provisions for listening or recording. In a less structured sense, any media device that presents information for learning may be considered a teaching machine. These vary from partially programmed arrangements to straight nonprogrammed approaches. Audio and videorecorders, microcomputers, and many other devices fall into this category.

Instructional and Educational Television. Instructional television (ITV) refers to those television programs designed and scheduled expressly for use with specific classes or groups for particular learning situations. These programs originate in a studio or classroom with a teacher, or from videorecordings and films.

Educational television (ETV), a broader term, covers general use of television in schools or in homes. ETV programs are transmitted by VHF (very high frequency or UHF (ultrahigh frequency) or low-power (2,500 Mhz) transmission for limited-area reception; or by direct cable or microwave relay, which link a studio or other origination source to classrooms in the same building or in different buildings or to homes. Closed-circuit television is a system in which programs are distributed only to those receivers that are directly connected to the origination point by cable or microwave. Open circuit refers to broadcast situations where programs are radiated for reception by any viewer within range of the station.

Videorecording. Television programs are recorded in two major ways: videotape and videodisc. Videotape is the same magnetic tape used in audio recordings, with magnetic particles that are arranged in patterns corresponding to the information being recorded. Videotape is most often contained in cassettes for ease and convenience of handling. It is recorded and played on videocassette recorders (VCR's). The videodisc stores information as transparent or reflecting spots on a plastic disc, using a laser beam to record and to play back the information. Both of these video recording systems are used extensively as tools of instructional technology.

Microcomputer. The microcomputer (or personal computer) is an extremely small and very efficient version of larger computers that became available after the mid-20th century. Its evolution depended on the invention of various microelectronics components—particularly the microprocessor, a silicon chip that processes data and controls a computer's components.

Using magnetic discs and tapes to store instructional programs, the microcomputer can present complete sequences or courses of instruction for students.

Computer-Assisted Instruction. Computer-assisted instruction (CAI) refers to the instructional uses made of a computer. The computer stores information and can be programmed to supply it to students in different patterns either according to a prestructured plan or in a random way based on student responses and needs. It also can be programmed to evaluate student responses and even to "converse" with learners.

HISTORICAL DEVELOPMENT

The promise of a successful alliance between visual aids and instruction appeared early. The magic lantern, an early type of projector and one of the oldest devices, was demonstrated in Rome in 1646 by Athanasius Kircher. It was not until the middle of the 19th century, however, that educators were urged to use this aid in their classrooms. The modern counterpart of this device is now known as the opaque projector.

Compared to other, more familiar, aids to instruction, such as textbooks, maps, and charts, the magic lantern was expensive. The asking price of one of the least expensive of the early lanterns was $25, according to an 1874 catalog listing; the more refined stereopticon might cost as much as $325. Cost of accessories, as well as initial cost, discouraged early school use of this mechanical-optical aid.

As other audiovisual devices were introduced in the 19th and 20th centuries—the phonograph, filmstrip, and slide projectors, the opaque projector, and the silent and then sound projectors—problems followed that proved to be even more difficult to solve than cost. These devices had been developed separately, and each experienced difficulties in respect to theories of usage, availability of suitable materials, and trained personnel. For example, the first films used in schools at the turn of the century were silent theatrical, industrial, or government films, none of which had been made expressly to aid instruction in schools. Their use was limited because of the lack of low-priced portable projection equipment and of safe nonflammable film, but especially because of the controversial quality of film content.

Later, film and equipment companies were formed to capitalize on the growing recognition that films with specific educational content and low-priced projection were needed. While some of these companies contributed to the spreading acceptance of educational films, the success of these efforts to produce substantial film collections was spotty. Many of these commercial educational film producers failed because of educators' low opinion of the theatrical films and because of a general lack of coordination between educational and commercial interests.

One of the more important commercial efforts to help provide answers to the problems educational films had experienced was Electrical Research Products, Inc. ERPI produced sound-on-disc attachments for 35-mm silent projectors and specialized in portable sound projectors. It created a nontheatrical film producing unit that engaged educators to act as advisers on productions. During the 1930's and 1940's, under an agreement with the University of Chicago, ERPI produced some of the finest educational films then available.

Radio as an instructional tool was strongest in the decade preceding World War II. It was used as early as 1929 in Ohio to broadcast stories, current-events programs, and special features to all grades, and was strong in many other city school systems.

The Impact of World War II. By the end of World War II, school departments of audiovisual instruction had been established on several levels, and studies of the effects of audiovisual instruction had been reported. In addition, teacher preparation courses at the university level and professional organizations and journals for these new specialists had been established.

During and immediately following the war, demands for audiovisual equipment and techniques intensified. The scattered commercial and educational developments that had occurred could not satisfy the needs created by World War II. Moreover, a great number of servicemen, trained in the armed forces to teach a variety of special skills and information, became readily available. And, while the military did not solve all the problems audiovisual education had experienced, it did use many of the known devices and techniques more efficiently than the schools had done. In addition, it directed focus on another aspect of this kind of instruction—the learner and how he learns from the new media. The success of the various training programs that the armed forces produced has been attributed to the standardization of curricula and the widespread publicity and distribution of available material made possible by generous funding.

Wire and then tape audio recorders found an especially useful application in teaching Morse code and foreign languages during World War II. Used in combination with texts and recordings of foreign languages, the audio recording equipment made possible playback of the trainees' own practice with the language and increased their proficiency. This development was the beginning of the language laboratory movement, which has had two consequences: the improvement of the teaching and learning of languages, and the development of learning laboratories used for teaching in most of the academic disciplines in secondary schools and colleges.

In the late 1940's and 1950's more sophisticated pieces of equipment were developed, including television, teaching machines, and programmed learning.

© JEAN-CLAUDE LEJEUNE/STOCK, BOSTON

Audiovisual resource centers provide for individualized study through a wide range of instructional equipment.

Instruction via commercial television became popular in the 1950's through such programs as Frank Baxter's lectures on Shakespeare from Los Angeles, and later by the nationally broadcast *Continental Classroom*. In the mid-1950's, Pittsburgh, St. Louis, and Chicago pioneered successfully with educational television.

The system developed in Washington county, Maryland, represents one of the earliest and broadest explorations into wide use of closed-circuit instructional television. Beginning in 1956 this experiment focused on providing instruction in the basic subject areas as self-contained presentations rather than as merely supplementary ones. The telecasting that began with eight Washington county schools eventually included all schools in the county district. Joining education and industry, the operation involved four organizations: the Chesapeake and Potomac Telephone Company of Maryland and the Bell Laboratories, which developed the coaxial cable system of communication for bringing telecasts to classrooms; the Radio-Electronics-Television Manufacturers Association (later called the Electronic Industries Association), which procured all the studio and other equipment used; and the Fund for the Advancement of Education, which underwrote the cost of designing, training staff, and operating the project. Sophisticated and easy-to-use videorecording equipment and techniques have replaced scheduled TV broadcasts as the primary way to use TV for educational and instructional applications. In the late 1970's Washington county discontinued distributing TV lessons by cable and now issues videorecordings and films from a central library of materials.

Acceptance of teaching machines was hindered by the fact that development of equipment items outpaced the instructional materials used on them. Either there were no programs or they were uninteresting to the learner. After the initial impetus given to teaching machines and programmed learning, the movement reached a pla-

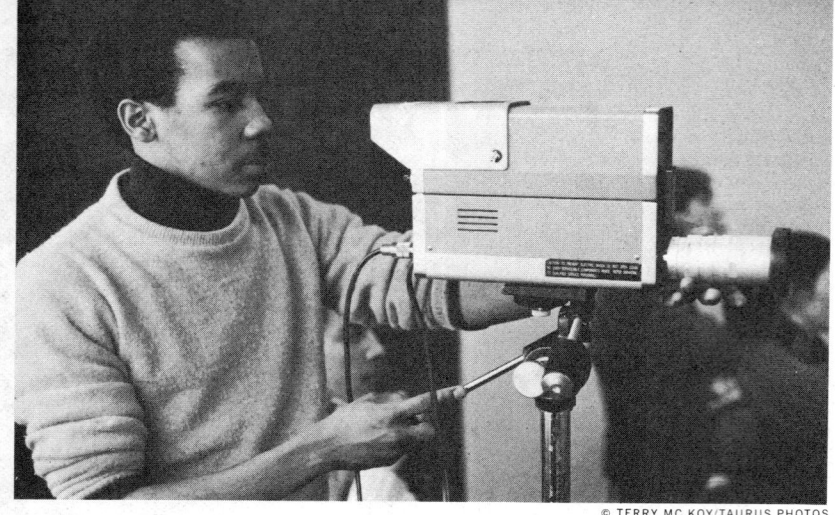

Some high-school and college courses provide students with the opportunity to gain firsthand experience using video equipment.

© TERRY MC KOY/TAURUS PHOTOS

teau, but research and restudy to develop and perfect better programming formats and more flexible equipment continued.

Technological developments in the miniaturization of electronic circuitry, especially the microchip, permitted the production of individual devices that interact with and reinforce individual learning, with or without a teacher's supervision. At present, a great variety of materials, devices, and facilities are available in an almost confusing number of combinations. The most useful device seems to be the microcomputer, particularly in combination with such other items as a projector, audiorecorder, or television display. The real hope for the proper use of instructional technology is the adequate development of systems of both hardware and software in complementary combinations.

FACILITIES AND APPLICATIONS

The trend in the use of instructional technology in the field of education is to provide electronic facilities for a wide range of functions. Although no single communications or instructional system will adequately serve all situations, more and more electronic control of presentation is occurring. The best approach to one learning situation might be facilities to support cooperative teaching and large group instruction. Individual study spaces and carrels for self-directed learning from computers and other presentation devices might be best for another situation. The communications technology offers a variety of devices and techniques that can be employed individually and in combinations to meet differing requirements.

Characteristics and applications of some of the major systems are described below.

Learning Laboratories. Learning laboratories are used for a variety of purposes that reach far beyond foreign-language instruction, which was their first application. Among the learning experiences that these facilities make available are passive listening or viewing, audio-active participation, media-directed activities, and computer-assisted instruction.

(1) Passive listening and viewing occurs in student carrels equipped with headphones, screens for TV or projected visual images, and appropriate selection and volume controls. Most often the students can select their own listening or viewing material.

(2) Audio-active participation allows the students to hear their voices and to assess the spoken words, phrases, or sentences. This is particularly useful for language study.

(3) Media-directed activities occur at a learning station where the students receive directions from a workbook, an audiovisual instructional package such as a photo slide and audio tape presentation, or a videorecorded instructional sequence. The students follow instructions without need for a teacher and can be tested by the media at the end of a sequence. Simple scientific experiments can be conducted by the students at such a station or carrel.

(4) Computer-assisted instruction uses a computer terminal or complete microcomputer at a learning station. Typically the terminal consists of a keyboard, a video display screen, and a disc or tape recording/playback unit. The students interact with the instructional program by typing on the keyboard and reading the input and output on the screen. Paper printers and audio devices can be added to use more sophisticated instructional programs.

The layouts of learning laboratories take a variety of forms, according to the instructional needs, space, funds, and resourcefulness and creativity of the designer. They range from a very simple installation to complete individual learning environments. Some of the various types of these facilities are mobile listening carts; mobile laboratories; complete and permanently installed laboratories; perimeter laboratories, where the booths are located around the walls of the classroom, leaving the center of the room free for regular activities; and electronic classrooms equipped with special tables that can be converted into learning-laboratory stations. Hinged tops cover built-in cavities, so that part of the working surface can be raised to provide access to equipment controls and at the same time provide an acoustical barrier and visual isolation. Conventional classroom activities can be carried on when tabletops are down.

Uses of Computers. Three forces have helped to make the computer one of the most useful tools of instructional technology. The ability of educators to organize knowledge so that it is more easily learned was enhanced by the trials of programmed instruction. The miniaturization of electronic components has made small but very powerful microcomputers available at reasonable cost. And simplified computer programming languages allow anyone to write programs that instruct. As a result, microcomputers are being used in most American schools and colleges.

Computer literacy courses, which introduce students to the functions of computers, often are offered in elementary schools.

© ROBERT KNOWLES/BLACK STAR

One of the most important areas of study with the computer is the computer itself—to make the student "computer literate." Computer literacy is the study of what makes up a computer, what functions it can perform, how one can use it for work or play, and how to program it. Some colleges are requiring each student to have a microcomputer, and most schools and colleges teach computer literacy.

Experiments have shown that children as young as two and one-half years can usefully operate a computer. Many elementary schools introduce students to computers, since the computer is often a familiar household object. Indeed, the prevalence of the microcomputer in American homes and work places has often forced its introduction in the schools.

Computer-assisted instruction (CAI) has proved to be especially successful in simulating actual situations involving problem-solving experiences. For example, sophisticated chemistry experiments can be "performed" on a computer. For a specific experiment, the student uses a typewriter to give the computer the necessary data (input) concerning desired quantities of chemicals and temperatures required. The student then directs the computer in the steps of the process. The computer interprets and reports the results of such inputs.

The student can ask the computer what the results will be when the quantities of chemicals and temperatures are varied in many different combinations. The computer will instantly perform these complicated calculations and return the information to the student within seconds after the input has been completed.

Computers can assist instruction in other ways. The student terminal station may be employed as a calculating device or laboratory instrument in classrooms where physics and mathematics are taught. Students can then carry on computations that would be far beyond the capability of ordinary calculating machines. The computer can also be programmed to function as a record depository containing student performance data and student history. Subsequent performances can be retrieved for purposes of guidance, conferences, and so forth. Further, the computer can receive and evaluate a learner's homework. Finally, the computer may serve as a nerve center and control device to expedite the use of multiple audio or visual displays that assist the learner in mastering the information presented.

A number of accessory applications indicate that the same computer facilities can be used for other learning requirements. One such instance is audio response service, an accessory that makes it possible for learners to interrogate the computer's memory and to be answered in structured audible sentences rather than in conventional computer printout. Voice-actuated computer programs are becoming increasingly common as electronic engineers perfect this capability.

In universities, computers are used increasingly for research. Administration and accounting functions are also performed by computers in most schools and colleges. Administrative uses of the computer in education include college registration, as well as record keeping of all kinds. Most colleges and schools would be severely hampered if they did not have both a central computer facility and remote computer centers, used for a great variety of activities, ranging from class scheduling and teacher assignments to budgeting and the recording of student grades.

The computer, however, should not be considered a replacement for the teacher; nor is it expected that learners will sit at computer terminals for long periods of time. CAI is rather a potentially valuable technology and methodology of instruction, one of many pertinent resources available to the teacher.

Applications of Television. At its best, educational television provides the most efficient and best-planned program that can be arranged by a team of teachers, learning psychologists, and audiovisual specialists, working together with knowledgeable production crews. And in its strictest instructional application, the television program uses appropriate film clips, demonstrations, laboratory experiments, flat pictures, and other resource materials in the proper instructional design to be effective.

Television can perform related educational functions that are not necessarily instructional. Where an internal coaxial cable distribution system is employed, it can also transmit data as part of an information retrieval system. For example, a library reference service can be initiated to service a number of inquiry stations located in various departments in a school. Also, administrative and counseling information can be sent over the television cable from central records depositories to appropriate offices.

Television receivers in schools generally are like consumer sets, with 21- or 23-inch screens.

One receiver for every 15 or 20 students is desirable, although special applications may require different treatment. Study halls and auditoriums used for television viewing might require as many as 20 receivers. This creates problems of location of the sets for easy viewing, keeping all receivers properly tuned, providing understandable audio, and isolating the viewers from the distraction of seeing multiple images. One solution is the use of projection television units that provide a single large image on a screen.

Most areas of the United States are served by public television stations. These stations provide some instructional programs for the schools; in fact, several of the stations are licensed to school districts. More than 70% of school districts have instructional TV programming available. But two factors have caused the amount of such programming to decline: the schools have been unable to bear the high costs of TV production; and better, less expensive, TV recording devices have been developed.

In addition, a major barrier to the successful use of television in schools has been the lock-step requirements of programming for broadcast. All classes or interested groups have had to view a particular program at a specific time that might be inconvenient for the teachers.

Video Recording. Videocassette recorders and videodiscs have gone far to correct this. Substantial cost reductions and compact, lightweight designs have made it feasible for many schools to put videocassette recorders into specific classrooms, to install remote units for recording classroom activities from a distance, and to establish special units that travel outside the school, taping speeches, interviews, and documentaries for later classroom playback.

Videocassette recorders can be used for a variety of subject matter. In speech classes, students can present short addresses and record them on the magnetic tape. The teacher can play back the recording, which includes both the visual and the audio. Slow-motion replay and single still-frame reproduction features are available on some machines.

In science classes, instead of repeating the same experiment for four or five classes during a single day, the teacher can plan a single presentation and record it on tape. With this technique, the teacher can review and edit the presentation. Experiments and demonstrations involving hazardous, highly inflammable, or radioactive materials can be isolated and recorded without students being present.

A major challenge to the social-studies teacher is to stimulate constructive discussion. With videocassette recorders, students and teachers can record open-ended, dramatized situations leading to discussion.

In physical-education classes, it has been customary to photograph the posture of individual students. Such techniques result only in static visuals. The videocassette machine can record posture aspects in motion to permit a more objective diagnosis of defects as a basis for recommending correctional exercises. Coaches often use television cameras connected to a videocassette machine to record sequences directly from the athletic field for replay in the locker room. Players can correct techniques or play formations that they employed minutes before.

Finally, on occasion, almost every school has need for professional visits by community servants, such as policeman, fireman, or nurse. The ability to record their presentations or interviews results in a collection of valuable resource materials that can be reproduced as desired to meet the needs of the school.

In some cases it may not be desirable to bring video equipment into classrooms. Occasionally the recorder, camera, and technical personnel may disturb the rapport between the teacher and the students. To overcome this problem, cameras may be positioned temporarily or installed permanently to observe a scene or particular action through remote control. With such facilities, no special personnel are needed in the classroom. Properly installed, video equipment can easily record up to 2,000 feet (600 meters) away from the source. Greater distances can be accommodated through the addition of special amplifiers.

Remote videorecording has been used with great success in teacher-training programs; laboratory observation; closed-circuit central videotaping, which makes it possible to centrally tape proceedings involving a variety of activities; off-the-air recording, through which broadcasts can be preserved for later replay over the internal closed-circuit system; orientation sessions; special faculty meetings; and field applications. The light weight and small size of the videorecorders encourage mobility, eliminating the necessity for trucks. Battery sources or automobiles equipped with auxiliary generators permit taping in locations where local plug-in power is not conveniently available.

Instructional Television Fixed Service (ITFS). In 1963 the Federal Communications Commission (FCC) established the Instructional Television Fixed Service (ITFS), which uses 20 frequencies in the 2,500-megahertz band. Since these frequencies are substantially higher than standard VHF and UHF channels, they require special antennae (dishes) that are usually placed on the roof of the school or other buildings to receive and transmit line-of-sight signals. In a sense, this telecasting ability is similar to cablecasting because the signals cannot be freely received on standard TV receivers. ITFS provides a means for the transmission of instructional materials and other educational applications on channels other than those regularly used for TV broadcasts.

Hundreds of ITFS systems are used for instruction throughout America, increasing the uses of TV for education. The more than 400 school buildings of San Diego County, Calif., are linked together by ITFS, one of the largest such systems in the world.

Satellites. The communications technology that has revolutionized worldwide communication is the fixed orbital satellite. Educators have come to depend on satellite communications to bring current events and major telecasts from around the world into the classroom. Satellite technology has also permitted the economical distribution of instruction and other education services to remote villages in the Alaskan tundra and in the Appalachian and Rocky Mountain regions of the United States. See also COMMUNICATIONS SATELLITE.

Telecommunications. Although a literal definition of telecommunications is communicating at a distance, the term has come to mean the use of electronics to communicate. A variety of telecommunication systems have greatly advanced instructional technology. The "conference call" has become popular in industry and in some schools as an effective method of exchanging information and ideas. It is a simple procedure to schedule verbal communications between two or more points on a telephone network. When conventional headphone-microphone combinations are used, conference calls are restricted to individuals at each terminal point or extension. To overcome this limitation, portable amplification units can boost voice reproduction levels so that everyone in the audience can clearly hear the speaker from the remote location, and an extension microphone permits audience members to participate in the conversations.

As a result of these advances, schools have developed telelecture systems that bring guest lecturers into the classrooms by telephone, permitting two-way conversations with distinguished scholars, scientists, statesmen, inventors, and other leaders.

By means of a telelecture system, guest lecturers talk to audiences without ever leaving their offices, laboratories, or homes.

Over the years numbers of hospitalized and homebound children have been able to participate in classroom activities via two-way audio employing ordinary telephone lines. Facilities in the classroom and at the learner locations are simple audio intercom units. With his own set, the shut-in child hears every word spoken in the classroom and may recite in return. The portable classroom component brings his voice clearly and distinctly to the teacher and every member of the class.

Another advance in telecommunications is the electrowriter. This device permits an instructor to write, draw, solve problems, or present information in any other graphic way to audiences in remote locations. The equipment, in conjunction with telelecture service, allows two-way verbal interchange between students and the instructor and reproduces simultaneously any written or drawn material created by the instructor. For two-way graphic communications, both the instructor's location and the classroom involved are equipped with an electrowriter transceiver—a self-contained unit that sends and receives handwritten messages.

Certain types of telecommunications are not feasible in all instances. Cost of conventional transmission of television signals for a telelecture on coaxial cables, through microwave links or by satellite, is prohibitive to schools when long distances are involved. An alternative is audiographic conferencing. This is an audio conference that is augmented by the use of such visual technologies as slow-scan TV, facsimile, computer graphics, electronic blackboards, or remotely controlled projection equipment. In slow-scan TV the television camera records sequential images for transmission over ordinary telephone lines. Every 30 to 45 seconds a new image is picked up by the camera and transmitted progressively to the receiving location or locations. The special television receiver presents an image for 30 to 45 seconds while it is accumulating the elements of the next image being transmitted. When all of the components of the new image have been received, the composite visual is exposed on the screen until it is replaced by subsequent transmission.

Although this system provides only still images, it does make it possible to transmit relatively complex scenes, reproductions of photographs, and so forth, at the same line-charge as for telephonic communication.

© GLYN CLOYD

Computers can be programmed to supply information on a topic, ask questions, and evaluate student responses.

Facsimile. Several items now available are capable of transmitting written, typed, or printed material, as well as drawings and photographs, over ordinary telephone lines. These devices are known as facsimile machines. It is only necessary to install one facsimile transmitter-receiver at each point. The insertion of copy in one of the machines will allow progressive transmission of the material, so that an identical copy is reproduced at the receiving location in a matter of minutes. An advantage of this facsimile transmission is that there is no opportunity for inaccurate reproduction, as occurs when a document is manually reproduced on a typewriter.

Information-handling systems can be designed to meet almost any information need. But certain system combinations and components are especially responsive to the demands of public schools.

Microfilm. Microfilm cameras in the library, guidance suite, and administration area make it quick and simple to record data permanently on films. Master record prints, along with duplicate films for routine purposes, can dispose of the bulk of original paper from which the information was recorded.

The various film formats available produce a perplexing storage problem. Both 16-mm and 35-mm reel or cartridge films are widely used. Also available are aperture cards containing film inserts that are designed for machine processing, microfiche (a small sheet of film) in two popular sizes, and transparent plastic jackets into which separate microfilm frames can be progressively inserted for cumulative record purposes. Certain formats are particularly adapted for specific applications.

ERIC. In 1964 the U.S. Office of Education (now the Department of Education) activated a significant project called ERIC (Educational Resources Information Center). Its purpose is to facilitate and coordinate information storage and retrieval efforts in all areas of educational research. To implement this goal, subcenters or clearinghouses were established in different parts of the country to acquire, encode, and synopsize current materials. The task included searching for published as well as nonpublished documents, addresses, letters, and other pertinent items that should be made available to the educational community without the usual time delay occasioned through conventional publication and communications channels.

Center specialists screen documents for inclusion in the ERIC-central system. If a resource is deemed acceptable, it is summarized in 250 words. A document to be entered into the master system is indexed, and both the abstract and the index terms are combined on an ERIC resume form, which becomes the key description of the document. This information and the entire document are copied on microfiche.

The microfiche format accommodates reductions of up to 60 pages of printed copy, visuals, or tables. Reports can be reproduced in full size or in enlarged form from such films, and the substantial physical reduction of information makes it feasible to store innumerable reports in a very small space. ERIC-central can provide upon request and at a nominal fee hard-copy reproduction or microfiche of any of the reports. To make known what is available, the center publishes a monthly index of these reports.

The ERIC system has introduced the computer disc recording as another means of distributing its documents and reports. Many of the individual centers make their information available on floppy discs as well as microfiche.

DEVELOPMENTS AND PROSPECTS

Nearly every aspect of instructional technology has been affected by the miniaturization of electronics and the resulting development of microcomputer technology. Just as the microcomputer is pervasive in American consumer products, it offers the most capability for the improvement of communications in education when coupled with a variety of other audiovisual devices.

As television technology improves to include digital processing of signals, stereo sound, and truly high-definition TV, it promises to become the heart of the home communication system, in company with the microcomputer. This will hasten its dominant role in school and college classrooms. The historic trend for technology used in education to be first proven and adopted in the consumer market in the United States will continue.

Study carrels are being transformed more and more into electronic learning stations. The home study and learning center may, in fact, challenge the classroom as the primary place for learning by the turn of the century. Instructional packages in the form of videorecordings or computer software are making learning an activity that can occur anywhere. The instruction itself is "portable."

Knowledge organized in learnable form continues to be a primary need for the educational system. Good software for computer-assisted instruction, effective TV lessons and courses, and well-organized instructional materials of all kinds continue to be the most needed aspects of the educational system.

The schools are dependent on their information resources as never before. The media center, with its array of audiovisual and print materials and devices, continues to be an activity at the heart of the instructional process.

Transmitting data has become almost as important as recording and storing it. More and more information is being passed along within a building or between buildings, states, and regions. Schools are increasingly involved in communications tie-ins to process properly their day-to-day business transactions: accounting, guidance, food services, inventory, and other functions. A number of schools that were using on-line time sharing services for computer-assisted instruction are now concentrating on using microcomputers dispersed in the classrooms under individual teacher control. Even more are participating in networks to exchange information and experience between staff members, and between students. The growth of national information networks linking microcomputer users, videotext and teletext services, and myriad other information activities offers even more opportunities for educational improvement.

The variety of components of instructional and communications technology that is available stresses the importance of integrated planning at every level and in every area.

Through the use of modern technology, any school, no matter how small or how remote from population centers, can be tied in through an appropriate network to share in the benefits of new developments. Such systems are very much in demand. Virtually every state in the United States has a network plan on paper. States such as South Carolina, Connecticut, and Wisconsin have networks ranging from telephone nets to television nets to computer nets among the schools. Some states have banded together to form regional networks, and other states are making innovative uses of existing networks. As these networks grow and interconnect, it is possible to visualize a nationwide system of such facilities. See also AUDIOVISUAL EDUCATION; COMPUTER.

PHILIP LEWIS
Instructional Dynamics Incorporated
HOWARD B. HITCHENS, *Vanitch*

Bibliography

Anderson, Charnel, *Technology in American Education 1650–1900* (National Educ. Assoc. 1962).
Bransford, Louis, and Hitchens, Howard B., *Adoption of Technological Innovations in Education* (National Institute of Educ. 1984).
Dirr, Peter J., and Pedone, Ronald J., *Uses of Television For Instruction 1976–1977* (Corp. for Public Broadcasting 1979).
Heinich, Robert, Molenda, Michael, and Russell, James D., *Instructional Media and the New Technologies of Instruction* (Wiley 1982).
Informational Technology and Its Impact on American Education Report of Office of Technology Assessment, U.S. Congress (Wiley 1982).
Ingle, Henry T., Hitchens, Howard B., and Harris, Eileen, *Advanced Communication and Information Technology for Education and Training: Status and Prospects* (UNESCO Report 1983).
Lumsdaine, A.A., and Glaser, Robert, eds., *Teaching Machines and Programmed Learning: A Source Book* (National Educ. Assoc., Dept. of Audiovisual Instruction 1960).
Martin, James, *Telematic Society: A Challenge For Tomorrow* (Prentice-Hall 1982).
Olgren, Christine H., and Parker, Lorne A., *Teleconferencing Technology and Applications* (Artech House 1983).
Saettler, Paul, *A History of Instructional Technology* (McGraw 1968).

14. Careers in Education

Teaching is one of the biggest occupations in the United States. Between 3 and 4 million full-time teachers are employed in elementary and secondary schools and colleges and universities. Teaching is the largest professional field for women and the second largest (after engineering) for men.

For many years after World War II, teaching on all levels was regarded as a growing profession. However, as the birthrate declined after the mid-1970's, it became evident that there would be more and more competition for teaching positions, with preference being given to persons with greater training and experience.

Professional Careers. More than 1.5 million teachers, most of whom are women, work with preschool and elementary school children in public and private schools. Nursery school teachers are in demand to work with children who are three to four years old. Kindergarten programs are designed for children who are approximately five years of age. Teachers at this level guide experiences with play, music, art, stories, and poetry and provide introductions to language, social studies, science, and numbers.

Kindergarten programs are not found in all school systems; nursery schools are even less common. There is, however, growing demand for these programs within the public schools.

The elementary school offers many employment opportunities. In many school systems this level includes children from grade 1 through grade 6, though some systems add grades 7 and 8, and other combinations of grades exist.

Most elementary teachers are responsible for the same students throughout the school day. The teacher may be the only one who works with the class. In other cases, he or she teaches several subjects and furnishes leadership for special teachers who come into the classroom for one or more periods each day or week. In some schools teachers in the upper elementary grades teach several groups in one or more subjects.

Some school systems employ special teachers in the fields of art, music, physical education, industrial arts, foreign languages, and homemaking. These teachers either help the regular classroom teacher present a lesson or take over the class for specified periods of time.

More than 1 million teachers are employed in junior and senior high schools, with numbers of men and women nearly equal. In junior high schools, and even more in high schools, teaching is usually departmentalized. An instructor may concentrate on one specialty, such as English, Spanish, or biology, or perhaps teach two related subjects, such as mathematics and general science or English and history. Teachers of art, music, home economics, industrial arts, and physical education usually do all or most of their work in their specialized fields.

Concern for children who have unusual learning problems has opened many new career opportunities in special education. Instructors are needed to teach children who are visually handicapped, deaf or hard-of-hearing, speech impaired, crippled or with other special health problems, emotionally and socially maladjusted, or mentally retarded. Another special field provides expanded programs for gifted children.

Over half a million teachers—nearly 65% of them men—serve in colleges and universities. This total includes teachers in junior or community colleges, with two-year programs.

Four-year colleges and universities offer teaching opportunities in all fields of scholarship. The college teacher is required to be a specialist in his or her subject area. Typically, the beginning instructor must work upward through the successive ranks of assistant professor, associate professor, and professor. Other posts include department chairman and dean. Promotion depends on excellence in the teacher's chosen field as demonstrated by teaching, research, and publication of books and articles.

Many opportunities for careers in education exist for those who wish to support teachers in their efforts with pupils. The school librarian, for example, manages the library, helps pupils use it, and assists teachers in their reading and research assignments. Other persons make contributions through pupil personnel positions. Guidance counselors advise students, and school psychologists aid students with problems too complex for the skills of the counselor. School social workers try to define and solve problems growing out of the home or neighborhood environment. School nurses administer first-aid treatment and conduct health programs.

Many career opportunities exist in the broad field of educational administration and supervision. The chief administrator for any school district is the superintendent. Among his many responsibilities are appointment of teachers and other school personnel, supervision of the curriculum, maintenance of all school property, and projection of future plans. In small districts the superintendent may personally oversee each of these responsibilities, but in larger districts many supervisory and administrative personnel may be employed to head departments. Opportunities exist for positions as associate superintendent, assistant superintendent, and instructional supervisors.

The principalships of elementary, junior high, or senior high school offer other opportunities. The principal is the chief executive of a school and, at the direction of the superintendent, is responsible for its operation. In larger schools the position of assistant principal is common. Colleges employ many administrators to handle academic and business operations.

Rewarding careers exist, and the number has increased considerably, in the field of educational media. These include preparation and use of audiovisual materials such as films and tapes; development of published aids, including textbooks; and writing, producing, and teaching for educational television.

Qualifications for Professional Careers. In the United States all who seek to be teachers must have college training. In every state, public school teachers must have certificates and the minimum requirements for certification include a bachelor's degree.

In all college programs for teacher preparation the emphasis in the first two years is on a liberal arts education. During the next two years prospective elementary teachers study child development and methods courses in their several areas of teaching responsibility. The usual program includes a period of student teaching. The requirements for certification for nursery school and kindergarten teachers are similar, but the emphasis within the professional courses is on early childhood education.

Students preparing to teach in the secondary schools will, in the third or fourth year of college, usually study educational psychology and methods of teaching in their particular fields. A period of student teaching also is required. The major portion of preparation is spent in the field of specialization. Candidates for high school teaching usually spend more time on one field of specialization than students who are preparing for elementary school posts. In several states a fifth year of study is required for certification as a secondary teacher; in those cases the master's degree is usually required for qualification.

The positions of supervisor, principal, or superintendent demand at least the master's degree and some years of classroom teaching. A growing number of districts require the doctoral degree for superintendents.

In most states special requirements have been established for librarians, counselors, and special education teachers. In many cases the master's degree is required. Some states have certification standards for school nurses, psychologists, and social workers.

There has been increasing agreement among states on the recognition of out-of-state teaching certificates. However, a certificate may not be acceptable everywhere; some local school districts have requirements for teachers beyond those of state certification. Certification within a given state is usually assured by the completion of the teacher education program by a college or university of that state.

Those who plan to teach at the college level need the master's degree as a minimum entering credential. In many institutions the teacher must be well on the way toward the doctorate to be considered for appointment and must earn that degree before being considered for any rank above that of instructor.

Teachers in certain state-supported junior colleges must meet state certification standards. In those cases a sequence of courses in professional education is required as well as the master's degree in the subject field. Most colleges set their own standards for appointment.

Range of Income. Average salaries for teachers in the U.S. public elementary and secondary schools increased from about $2,700 in the late 1940's to about $20,000 in the mid-1980's. However, teacher incomes differ greatly from state to state and from district to district. Average salaries in the 50 states in the mid-1980's ranged from a low of about $15,000 in the lowest-paying states, to about $25,000 in the higher-paying states, to a maximum of about $34,000 in Alaska, the highest-paying state.

Some elementary and secondary schools offer pay increments for teachers who gain advanced degrees. A significant increase can be received by the teacher who moves to a school system that credits his experience and has a higher salary schedule; accepts an administrative, supervisory, or special teaching assignment; or transfers to the junior college or college level.

At the college level, average salaries range from about $16,000 for instructors in small colleges to more than $30,000 for professors in major universities. Salaries tend to be lowest in teachers colleges and highest in universities. On the whole, pay is lower in private than in public institutions, though top-ranked private universities pay premium salaries. Faculty members in medical, dental, and law schools usually receive higher salaries than teachers of the same rank in other schools.

Teachers are usually paid for an academic year of about 9 months. Most college teachers (and many below the college level) may add to their income by teaching in summer sessions. Additional opportunities for supplemental income increase as a faculty member gains recognition. Insurance and retirement plans are very attractive in most colleges and in many school systems. Colleges and school systems may give teachers time off for travel and study.

Top salaries and benefits go to teachers who have gained tenure status by completing a specified length of satisfactory service. A teacher with tenure can be removed only through legal proceedings.

Auxiliary Personnel. More and more, especially in schools in metropolitan areas, public school teachers are being assisted by auxiliary personnel. These fall into two categories: school volunteers and paraprofessionals.

School volunteers, as the term implies, are not paid for their services. Often they are retired or nonworking persons, who bring a resource of personal experience and activity into the classroom. School volunteers help the teacher with nonprofessional chores and give guidance and counseling to individual students or groups of students. They also serve to inform the community about school activities and problems.

Paraprofessional personnel, who are paid for their services, often do work that formerly had been done by certified teachers. Their duties may be in the classroom, as part of the health program of the school, or as family workers who go into the home to help and advise both students and parents. Some paraprofessional personnel need no special training. However, a number of positions, such as educational associate and auxiliary trainer, require as many as 60 college credits and in-service training.

Sources of Information. Information on school districts and certification requirements within a given state is available from each state department of education in the state capital.

Information on elementary and secondary teacher preparation, standards, and opportunities may be obtained from: United States Department of Education, Washington, D.C.; American Federation of Teachers (AFT), Washington, D.C.; National Council for Accreditation of Teacher Education, Washington, D.C.; and National Education Association (NEA), Washington, D.C.

Sources of information on teaching and research opportunities at the college level include: United States Department of Education; American Association of University Professors (AAUP), Washington, D.C.; and American Council on Education, Washington, D.C.

RAY E. BRUCE*
The University of Georgia

Bibliography

Hartbarger, Neil, *Your Career in Teaching* (Arco 1979).
Hilsum, Sidney, and Start, K.B., *Promotion and Careers in Teaching* (Humanities 1974).
Leavitt, Guy P., *Teach with Success*, rev. ed. (Standard Publishing Co. 1978).
Lyons, Geoffrey, *Teacher Careers and Career Perceptions* (Humanities 1981).
McDaniel, T.R., *The Teacher's Profession: Essays on Becoming an Educator* (Univ. Press of America 1982).
Richey, Robert W., *Preparing for a Career in Education* (McGraw 1974).

15. Glossary of Educational Terms

In this glossary, cross references in CAPITALS AND SMALL CAPITALS direct the reader to separate articles that give fuller information on the subject. Cross references to other terms in this glossary are in *italics*.

Academic Freedom.—The right of a teacher to teach or of a learner to study without unreasonable restraint, fear of reprisal, or loss of standing. See also ACADEMIC FREEDOM.

Academy.—The name of Plato's school in ancient Greece; a term now used to designate secondary schools, usually private ones. The American academy was the precursor of the public high school. See also EDUCATION—*Secondary Education*.

Acceleration.—A system that permits gifted children to advance more rapidly than others of the same age. In the United States, many schools offer special curriculum enrichment instead of placing such children in a more advanced age group. See also EDUCATION—*Education of Exceptional Children*.

Accreditation.—A system of evaluating institutions to ensure that they meet certain standards. In the United States this is done both by the individual states and by regional associations of schools and colleges. In many other countries the central government is responsible for establishing standards of education. See also ACCREDITATION OF SCHOOLS AND COLLEGES.

Achievement Test.—An examination designed to determine how much an individual, or group of individuals, has learned about a certain subject. It is usually standardized in content, administration, and scoring. See also ACHIEVEMENT TESTS; EDUCATION—*Measurement*.

Adult Education.—Formal and informal education for the mature person. Its purposes may be to complete basic schooling, gain specific advanced skills, or explore a new area of interest. See also ADULT EDUCATION.

Advanced Placement Program.—A program that gives qualified high school students the opportunity to study at the college level in certain fields. The term may be used to include early admission to college.

Alternative School.—A school that offers nontraditional education programs, often in an informal setting. Developed in the 1960's, the schools frequently serve disaffected or dropout-prone students.

Apprenticeship.—A feature of vocational education; it gives young people practical experience in a trade supplemented by related school instruction. See also APPRENTICESHIP; VOCATIONAL EDUCATION.

Aptitude Test.—A standardized test designed to predict success in a certain course of study or field of work. It differs from an achievement test in attempting to predict future competence rather than to assess present knowledge. See also APTITUDE TESTS; EDUCATION—*Educational Measurement*.

Audiovisual Education.—Teaching with supplementary aids such as films, slides, television, tape recordings, and models. See also AUDIOVISUAL EDUCATION; EDUCATION—*Instructional Technology*.

Bachelor's Degree.—A degree given after successful completion of three or four years of college or university work. Originally, the degree indicated that a person had fulfilled certain preliminary requirements toward the master's or doctor's degree. See also DEGREE.

Basic Skills.—Standard school subjects, such as reading, writing, and arithmetic, stressed by some educators in response to a perceived decline in student competency. See also *Competency-Based Education*.

Bilingual Instruction.—Teaching in two languages, necessary when the language of the school is different from the one used at home. This occurs in countries where two language groups live in close proximity or in certain cities where a sizable proportion of a school's enrollment includes foreigners or speakers of a foreign language.

Board of Education.—In the United States the educational authority that oversees the public schools of a community. The state board of education provides partial funds for the support of local schools and formulates overall educational policy for the state. See also EDUCATION—*Administration*.

Business Education.—Originally, training in such skills as office practice including bookkeeping; the field now extends to the graduate level and includes electronic data processing, corporate management, and economic theory. See also BUSINESS EDUCATION.

Carnegie Unit.—A standard of measurement for secondary school work set up by the Carnegie Foundation for the Advancement of Teaching. A unit constitutes the study of a subject for one year for a minimum of 120 hours. Colleges can require that applicants have completed a number of units (often 15).

Certification of Teachers.—The system by which teachers are licensed to teach in the public school system. In the United States, certification is granted by the state boards of education.

Coeducation.—Education of both sexes in the same institution of learning with the same instructors. The practice is almost universal in U.S. public elementary and secondary schools, and it is increasing in colleges and universities. See also COEDUCATION.

College.—In most countries, an institution offering education beyond the secondary school level. It usually offers a 4-year program leading to a bachelor's degree. In France, a *collège* is a secondary school preparing students for the baccalaureate examination. See also COLLEGES AND UNIVERSITIES.

College Entrance Examination Board.—A U.S. organization, founded in 1900, that provides standards for uniformity in the administration of college entrance examinations, and thus in high school preparation. It sponsors a scholastic aptitude test and various achievement tests that must be taken by the majority of college applicants.

Commencement.—The occasion at which college and university students receive a degree in recognition of having completed a prescribed course of study. The term is often used synonymously with graduation.

Commercial Course.—Business education and vocational training often included in high schools in the United States. It is distinguished from the academic course taken by students who plan to attend college.

Community College.—A 2-year college, designed to serve a local community, that offers an educational program beyond the 12th grade. See also JUNIOR COLLEGE.

Comparative Education.—The study and comparison of educational theory and practice in two or more countries. See also INTERNATIONAL EDUCATION.

Compensatory Education.—Special classes and tutoring to bring disadvantaged children and others to the level of their peers. Project Head Start, for example, serves preschool children. Many colleges and universities have programs to assist and encourage persons of college potential.

Competency-Based Education.—An academic curriculum that requires students to master certain basic skills. As part of this program, *competency tests* often are given to ensure that students have learned the skills designated for their level.

Compulsory Education.—The requirement in the laws of many countries that children attend school for a specified number of years. See also EDUCATION—*Education Around the World*.

Computer-Assisted Instruction.—The use of electronic computers in teaching, for example, to present questions and answers and record the student's progress. See also COMPUTERS—*Computer-Assisted Instruction*; EDUCATION—*Instructional Technology*.

Consumer Education.—Education that aims at making people more intelligent and discriminating consumers of goods and services. See also CONSUMER EDUCATION.

Continuing Education.—Formal educational activity engaged in by persons at a later age, as the completion by an adult of a high school course. See also ADULT EDUCATION.

Core Curriculum.—A program built around a central theme—for example, a social problem. Standard school subjects are used as components. See also CURRICULUM.

Correspondence Study.—A system of instruction by which students receive lessons by mail from a special school or a branch of a university. See also CORRESPONDENCE SCHOOLS AND COURSES.

Counseling.—Assistance, or guidance, given by specialists in such areas of student welfare as course planning, vocations, social relationships, and mental health.

Curriculum.—The learning opportunities provided by a school. In the broadest sense this includes both the systematic courses prescribed for certification or graduation and the informal learning programs provided by the school. See also CURRICULUM.

Decentralization.—In school administration, breaking large public school districts, particularly in cities, into neighborhood units. The purpose is to give the people of a neighborhood more control over their schools.

Degree.—A title given by a college or university to one who has completed a prescribed course of study. See also DEGREE.

Desegregation.—The elimination of racial segregation in educational institutions. In 1954 the U.S. Supreme Court made it illegal for states to maintain separate schools for blacks and whites.

Development Education.—The study of the methods by which educational systems can be modernized, particularly in developing nations. See also INTERNATIONAL EDUCATION.

Diagnostic Test.—A written test given to discover the strengths and weaknesses of students in a particular area of learning or portion of a subject.

Diploma.—An official document given to graduates of a school or college as evidence of their having completed a course of study.

Disadvantaged Student.—One who has not received at home the minimal advantages to prepare him for school. Such students are often given special help.

Dissertation.—A relatively extensive piece of writing presenting an independent and original contribution to knowledge, as required for the doctor's degree; often used interchangeably with *thesis*.

District.—The basic administrative unit in the U.S. public school system. Each district elects a board to oversee the schools of the area. See also EDUCATION—*Administration*.

Doctor's Degree.—The highest academic degree. Completion of a specified course of study, submission of a dissertation, and oral and written examinations are required of all candidates. See also DEGREE.

Dropout.—A student who leaves school before completing a course of study—usually applied to students who do not complete high school and due to their age are not legally required to do so. Vocational training and other special programs have helped numbers of these students complete their education and increase their employment capability.

Elementary Education.—The first level of schooling, preceding intermediate or secondary schooling. It aims to teach the fundamental skills of education—reading, writing, and arithmetic—as well as to develop the child intellectually, socially, and emotionally. See also EDUCATION—*Primary Education*.

Examination.—A set of questions, either written or oral, designed to determine a student's achievement in a certain area. Objective examinations require single, brief answers; essay examinations allow the student to give in written form the answers to certain questions or to discuss broad topics.

Extension Education.—A program of education for persons not regularly enrolled as students in an educational institution, often given after school hours or by correspondence. See also AGRICULTURAL EDUCATION; EXTENSION EDUCATION.

Extracurricular Activities.—School activities outside the traditional curriculum, including athletics, school publications, clubs, and social activities. Some educators consider these part of the curriculum. See also CURRICULUM.

Foreign Exchange Programs.—Programs run by governments and private institutions, giving students and teachers the opportunity to study or teach abroad. Many colleges and universities provide scholarships for foreign students.

General Education.—A broad program of studies designed for all persons regardless of their vocational intentions; for example, courses in literature, history, and general science.

Graded School.—An organizational system by which students are placed in groups according to age. Individual school systems differ, but in the United States a common pattern offers 12 years of schooling: 5 to 6 years of elementary school, 3 or 4 of middle or intermediate school, and 3 or 4 years of high school.

Grades.—See *Marks*.

Graduate Education.—A course of study leading to a master's or doctor's degree. See also COLLEGES AND UNIVERSITIES.

Grouping.—The assignment of pupils to class sections. It may be done on a homogeneous basis, according to a specific criterion such as academic performance, or on a heterogeneous basis, in which pupils of differing levels of competence are placed together within the same section.

Handicapped, Education of the.—Special programs in a public or private school system for children who are physically, mentally, or socially handicapped. See also BLINDNESS; DEAFNESS; EDUCATION—*Education of Exceptional Children*.

Headmaster.—See *Principal*.

Head Start Program.—A program initiated in 1965 as part of the U.S. antipoverty program to provide preschool learning experience, medical facilities, and social services to disadvantaged children. See also HEAD START PROGRAM.

High School.—Traditionally, a 4-year secondary school comprising grades 9 through 12, but often a 3-year school (grades 10 through 12) following a junior high school (grades 7, 8, and 9). See also EDUCATION—*Secondary Education*.

Higher Education.—The formal education program provided by colleges, graduate schools, and professional institutions. See also COLLEGES AND UNIVERSITIES.

Home Economics.—Study of topics related to home and family, such as nutrition. See also HOME ECONOMICS.

Home Study.—Education arranged for independent study at home, especially for adults. See also CORRESPONDENCE SCHOOLS AND COURSES.

Homework.—Lessons assigned for students to prepare at home in preparation for the next class.

Illiteracy.—The inability to read or write a simple message in any language. *Functional illiteracy* refers to the failure to read with understanding a newspaper article or simple written instructions. See also ILLITERACY.

Independent Study.—A program in secondary schools and colleges to encourage students to work individually, for example on independent research projects. See also INDEPENDENT STUDY.

Individualized Instruction.—A curriculum tailored to the needs of an individual, which attempts to provide him with the learning experiences having greatest value for him, often within the structure of independent study.

Industrial Arts Education.—A phase of general education designed to familiarize all students with materials, tools, and industrial processes. See also INDUSTRIAL ARTS EDUCATION.

Intelligence Test.—A test that attempts to measure intellectual ability of a child and his likeliness to succeed in schoolwork. See also INTELLIGENCE.

Interdisciplinary Curriculum.—An integrated or core curriculum unifying two or more subjects, for example, history and English.

Intermediate School.—See *Middle School*.

International Education.—A term denoting cultural and educational relations among nations as well as exchange of teachers, students, and educational materials. See also INTERNATIONAL EDUCATION.

Internship.—See *Student Teaching and Internship*.

Junior College.—An institution offering two years of education beyond high school, often called a community college. See also JUNIOR AND COMMUNITY COLLEGES.

Junior High School.—A division of the school system that usually includes grades 7, 8, and 9, regarded as a transition between elementary school and high school. See also EDUCATION—*Secondary Education*.

Kindergarten.—An educational program for children between the ages of 4 and 6, intended to prepare them for the first grade. See also KINDERGARTEN.

Laboratory School.—A school attached to a college or university for testing educational ideas. A notable example is the University of Chicago Elementary School founded in 1896 by John Dewey.

Land-Grant Colleges.—Institutions of higher learning in the United States established under authority of the Morrill Act of 1862, which provided the states with federal land to be sold to support colleges. See also COLLEGES, LAND-GRANT.

Language Arts.—Subjects on the elementary and secondary level aimed at improving the student's ability to communicate—for example, through compositions, public speaking, and dramatics.

Learning Disability.—A physical or psychological impediment to learning. Various programs are available for learning-disabled children. See also EDUCATION—*Education of Exceptional Children*.

Learning Laboratory.—A room containing a system of tape recorders, headphones, and microphones connected to a control console and used for the transmission of taped lessons. See also EDUCATION—*Educational Technology*.

Liberal Arts.—Studies intended to impart general knowledge and help develop broad intellectual abilities, as distinguished from technical, professional, and scientific studies. Chief among liberal arts subjects are language, literature, philosophy, and history. In the medieval universities the Seven Liberal Arts were grammar, rhetoric, logic, arithmetic, geometry, astronomy, and music. See also LIBERAL EDUCATION.

Lyceum.—A system of adult education popular in 19th century America. See also LYCEUM.

Mainstreaming.—The policy of integrating handicapped children into the regular classroom. Mainstreaming is required by federal law whenever feasible.

Marks.—A system of notations, also called grades, used by the teacher to report and record the student's progress in school subjects. Numbers or letter scores are used. See also GRADING AND MARKING.

Master's Degree.—An academic degree awarded to holders of the bachelor's degree who completed one or two years of graduate study. See also DEGREE.

Mental Retardation.—A marked limitation of intelligence in an individual due to deficient mental development. It is most often caused by damage to the nervous system or by inherited factors. See also MENTAL RETARDATION.

Middle School.—A school offering intermediate education, usually comprising grades 5 through 7. The middle, or intermediate, school provides a transition from the elementary school to the high school. See also EDUCATION—*Intermediate Education*.

Military School.—A privately operated, preparatory school for boys that emphasizes military organization and discipline.

Montessori Method.—A teaching method developed early in the 20th century by Maria Montessori. It is used principally on the kindergarten and grade-school level and emphasizes freedom of expression and creativity rather than formal instruction. See also MONTESSORI, MARIA; MONTESSORI METHOD.

Night School.—Evening courses offered by a college or high school, especially for working people.

Nongraded School.—An organizational plan that eliminates or minimizes formal grade structure. In this system a child is assigned to a subgroup in accordance with his capabilities, and he moves from one level of study to the next at his own pace instead of being promoted at the end of the year.

Normal School.—In France and the United States, originally a 2-year college to prepare students for elementary school teaching. Normal schools in the United States have changed to 4-year teachers colleges.

Norms.—The average scores made on tests that have been administered to a large number of students over a wide geographical area and against which the scores of students later tested may be compared. See also EDUCATION—*Educational Measurement*.

Nursery School.—A school for children under five years of age. See also NURSERY SCHOOL.

Parent-Teacher Association.—An organization intended to promote home and school cooperation in the education of children. Most parent-teacher groups in the United States are affiliated with the National Congress of Parents and Teachers. See also PARENT-TEACHER ASSOCIATIONS.

Parochial School.—A school supported by a religious body.

Phonics.—A method of teaching reading, spelling, and pronunciation by the sound value of letters and syllables. See also READING.

Preschool Education.—The informal education of the child from birth until school age. The term is sometimes applied to nursery schools and kindergartens. See also PRESCHOOL EDUCATION.

Principal.—The chief administrative officer of an elementary school, middle school, junior high, or high school. The chief supervisor of a private school is usually called a *headmaster*.

Private School.—A school that is financed and operated by a nongovernmental organization.

Professor.—A member of a college or university faculty above the rank of instructor. Most institutions of higher learning recognize three professorial ranks: assistant professor, associate professor, and professor.

Programmed Instruction.—A teaching method that presents subject matter in a sequence of carefully prepared steps. Each step requires the learner to make a response before going on to the next item. Programs can be presented in book form or can be used with teaching machines. See also EDUCATION—*Instructional Technology*.

Progressive Education.—A term used to indicate certain theories and practices in 20th century education, often associated with the philosophy of education formulated by John Dewey and his followers. They emphasize the child's own interests and activities and advocate participation of the child in the learning process, as opposed to traditional practices that relied on more passive, rote techniques.

Promotion.—The practice whereby students normally progress each year from one age-grade level to the next. To be promoted, the student must meet specific requirements set by the school. Advanced students are sometimes permitted to "skip" a grade. Failing students are required to repeat a grade.

Provost.—A high-ranking administrative officer in a university, often concerned in his duties with the enforcement of college regulations.

Public School.—In the United States and many other countries, a tax-supported elementary or secondary school operated by the local government and open to all children. In England, the public school is a private, endowed secondary school that prepares students for the university; Eton and Harrow are famous examples.

Reading Readiness.—A child's ability to begin instruction in reading. Some children begin reading later than others because their experience has been narrow or their language background limited. By the age of 6, most children are ready to learn how to read. See also READING.

Released Time.—Time during the school week regularly allotted to students for special activities or study, as for religious instruction from their churches.

Remedial Education.—The application of special teaching techniques that are designed to overcome difficulties in learning, such as difficulty in forming concepts or faulty study habits.

Retardation.—The practice of requiring that failing pupils repeat a grade in school. Retardation offers extra time for slow learners or those whose attendance has been irregular. It is also believed to permit better psychological adjustment for immature children.

Scholarships and Fellowships.—Grants of money that are awarded to an individual to support his studies or creative activities, usually by a college, foundation, or governmental agency. See also FULBRIGHT SCHOLARSHIP; SCHOLARSHIPS.

School District.—See *District*.

Secondary School.—A school at the level of education between the elementary school and college, often called *high school*. See also EDUCATION—*Secondary Education*.

Sex Education.—Instruction in the physiological, psychological, and sociological aspects of human sexuality. Sex education in the public schools has become a controversial issue. See also SEX EDUCATION.

Special Education.—Special programs and facilities for children with exceptional capacities or deficiencies, such as gifted or handicapped pupils.

Speech Education.—Training in oral language skills. On the elementary and secondary level, special emphasis is given to the speech arts, such as voice and diction, phonetics, oral interpretation, and public speaking. Specialized therapy is often available for speech defectives.

Standardized Tests.—Tests administered under uniform conditions and designed to evaluate intelligence, achievement, or personality. The interpretative standards, or norms, are based on scores made by a large number of students from a variety of schools.

Student Government.—The management of certain student affairs by the students themselves through an elected body. A student governing body may, for example, be empowered to formulate dress codes or discipline disruptive students.

Student Teaching and Internship.—Supervised teaching by students enrolled in a teacher-training program. A student teacher is usually assigned by his college to a specific school and class for a certain number of hours for a semester. The term *internship* is used when the practice teacher is a college graduate who teaches several classes and is paid by the school district.

Summer School.—Classes held in summer enabling students to make up schoolwork or accelerate their educational program.

Superintendent.—The chief officer of a school system, usually appointed by the board of education. The superintendent of schools is typically in charge of both the business aspects and the instructional programs of the school system. He is likely to be responsible for selecting teaching personnel and maintaining community relations.

Teachers Colleges and Training.—A teachers college offers a 4-year liberal arts program and grants a bachelor's degree. Teacher education includes a general academic background, specialized studies, and extensive familiarization with teaching procedures. Many teachers receive their preparation in liberal arts colleges and universities.

Teaching Load.—The total obligations connected with a teacher's classwork. It is usually measured by the number of classes taught per day and the total number of students enrolled in those classes.

Teaching Machines.—Machines that present programmed instruction to the learner through words or pictures, and to which the learner is able to respond, as by keyboard. See EDUCATION—*Instructional Technology*.

Tenure.—Permanent employment granted to teachers after a probationary period, often of three to five years. Teachers with tenure may not be dismissed without the school officials or school board showing good cause for its action.

Textbooks.—Books used in the study of a subject or course, usually containing an orderly presentation of the subject. They are often accompanied by tests, exercises, and other instructional aids for the teacher.

Transcript.—An official record of a student's educational achievement in a particular institution.

Technical Education.—The teaching of the knowledge, skills, and attitudes necessary to the practice of one of a cluster of closely related trades, occupations, or professions. See also TECHNICAL EDUCATION.

Team Teaching.—Teaching by two or more staff members who plan and carry out cooperatively the educational program of a class of pupils. The team may consist of different categories of staff personnel.

Tuition.—A fee set for instruction in a college or private school, often based on the number of courses or credit hours taken. See also COLLEGES AND UNIVERSITIES—*College Costs*.

Underachievement.—Performance in school work that does not measure up to a student's capabilities.

University.—An institution of higher learning offering graduate as well as undergraduate education. A university typically includes a number of colleges and professional schools. See also COLLEGES AND UNIVERSITIES.

Vocational Education.—The preparation of young people and adults for skilled trades and semiprofessional careers. It is most frequently offered at the high school or junior college level. See also VOCATIONAL EDUCATION.

Work Study Plan.—A plan by which students alternate periods of on-campus academic study with periods of full-time paid employment. Such an arrangement enables many students to pursue higher education who otherwise would be financially unable to do so.

EDUCATION, Department of, an executive department of the U. S. government that is responsible for federal programs in support of education. It is the 13th cabinet-level agency. Its major function is to establish policy and administer and coordinate federal educational assistance funds.

The Department of Education, known as ED, was created by legislation proposed by President Carter. On Sept. 27, 1979, Congress passed the Department of Education Organization Act, signed into law on Oct. 17, 1979. The first secretary, Shirley M. Hufstedler, was sworn into office on the following December 6, and the department was officially established on May 7, 1980.

In general, the Department of Education assumed the responsibilities of the Office of Education, which had been a component of the Department of Health, Education, and Welfare (HEW). Under the act, HEW was redesignated the Department of Health and Human Services. Basically, education in the United States is a state and local function, and the act passed by Congress strongly reaffirmed decentralized control, stating that "the establishment of the Department of Education shall not ... diminish the responsibility for education which is reserved to the states and the local school systems and other instrumentalities of the states."

The Department of Education conducts about 150 programs that endeavor to reflect the educational needs of most Americans. The purpose of these programs is to attain two goals. First, the department aims to guarantee that students of all ages enrolled in schools, colleges, or vocational centers have equal access to the best possible education. The second goal is to improve the quality of education for every student.

The funds for most programs are distributed to the states as formula grants—that is, the amounts are determined by formulas based on the number of students in various special categories. The states then redistribute the funds to local districts under departmental approved plans. This approach reaffirms the principle of state and local control of education.

Duties of the Secretary. The secretary advises the president on federal education plans, policies, and programs. In addition to supervising departmental staff in executing approved programs, goals, and objectives, the secretary carries out certain responsibilities related to four federally aided corporations: the American Printing House for the Blind, Lexington, Ky.; Gallaudet College for assisting the deaf, in Washington, D. C.; Howard University, Washington, D. C.; and the National Technical Institute for the Deaf, which is part of the Rochester (N. Y.) Institute of Technology. The secretary is assisted by an undersecretary, an inspector general, a general counsel, assistant secretaries, and other administrative personnel.

Elementary and Secondary Education. The Office of Elementary and Secondary Education administers programs that provide extra services that children need to succeed in school but that states and communities cannot themselves offer because they lack the resources. The office's largest program is for disadvantaged children, authorized under Title I of the Elementary and Secondary Education Act of 1965.

The Office of Elementary and Secondary Education also administers funds provided by the Indian Education Act, which aims to meet the special educational and cultural needs of Indian students. In addition there are programs to assist school desegregation, either voluntary or court ordered, to aid school districts affected by federal activities that overburden local tax sources and to assist districts struck by natural disasters.

Education for the Handicapped. The responsibility for helping states to give handicapped children the best education to meet their needs lies with the Office of Special Education and Rehabilitative Services. Since the mid-1960's, various federal laws have increased the rights of handicapped children, whether blind, deaf, autistic, or otherwise disabled, to a free public education.

Of particular importance among these laws is the Education for All Handicapped Children Act, passed in 1975. This act requires states receiving federal aid to locate, evaluate, and provide individual learning programs for disabled children. In addition, the Office of Special Education and Rehabilitative Services is in charge of federal funds for vocational training for the disabled, mostly adults.

Bilingual Education. Among the major problems confronting American education is the large number of children for whom English is not a native language. Programs for educating these children are administered by the Office of Bilingual Education and Minority Languages Affairs. Under the programs, children are instructed in their own languages as they learn to speak and understand English. Both languages are used to teach basic skills, such as reading and writing. These skills are then applied to English, which gradually becomes the principal classroom language.

Non-Public Education. The Office of Non-Public Education is the only federal agency to ensure that children and teachers in about 20,000 private schools in the United States, both independent and church-related, receive all services to which they are entitled under federal programs. As necessary, the office proposes to the secretary needed changes in laws, regulations, or policies that will implement the equitable administration of these programs in relation to non-public schools.

Educating Dependents of Military Personnel Abroad. The United States has military forces stationed around the world, and the children of such personnel must be provided with educational opportunities equal to those they would receive at home. Formerly the sole responsibility of the Department of Defense, schools for children of overseas military personnel are now administered by the Department of Education through its Office of Education for Overseas Dependents.

Postsecondary Education. The Office of Postsecondary Education administers federal financial programs, such as loans, grants, and jobs, to assist college students or postsecondary vocational trainees. The office also offers academic support programs for disadvantaged college students and provides funds to graduate and professional schools to recruit more women and minorities and to assist in paying tuition and other costs.

Vocational and Adult Education. Through the Office of Vocational and Adult Education, the federal government helps states and communities provide specialized training for young people and adults so that they may acquire marketable skills. Some 17 million persons are enrolled in such training programs. Other services include the support of remedial help, such as improving proficiency in English and upgrading other skills, and career counseling.

Educational Research. The Office of Educational Research and Improvement conducts research and demonstration programs to improve education from preschool through graduate school. Such research includes studies on how children and adults learn, the nature of teaching, and how schools and colleges can improve the management of their resources. The office of Educational Research and Improvement also deals with libraries, museums, and educational programming by media.

Civil Rights. The Office for Civil Rights is responsible for educational institutions complying with four landmark laws against discrimination. These laws are: Title VI of the 1964 Civil Rights Act, prohibiting discrimination on the basis of race, color, and national origin; Title IX of the 1972 Education Amendments, prohibiting discrimination on the basis of sex; Section 504 of the 1973 Rehabilitation Act, prohibiting discrimination on the basis of handicap; and the 1975 Age Discrimination Act, prohibiting discrimination on the basis of age.

EDUCATION, Office of, formerly a division of the federal Department of Health, Education, and Welfare (HEW). Under legislation enacted in 1979, the functions of the Office of Education were assumed by the cabinet-level Department of Education. (HEW was redesignated the Department of Health and Human Services.)

The Office of Education was founded in 1867 as an independent Department of Education "for the purpose of collecting such statistics and facts as shall show the condition and progress of education in the several States and Territories, and of diffusing such information respecting the organization and management of schools and school systems, and methods of teaching, as shall aid the people of the United States in the establishment and maintenance of efficient school systems, and otherwise promote the cause of education throughout the country."

In 1869 the Department of Education was attached to the Department of Interior and was renamed the Office of Education. In 1870 its name was changed to Bureau of Education. In 1929 the name Office of Education was restored. In 1939 the office was transferred to the newly created Federal Security Agency. In 1953 it was incorporated in the newly established Department of Health, Education, and Welfare.

UNITED STATES COMMISSIONERS OF EDUCATION

Henry Barnard, 1867–1870; John Eaton, 1870–1886; N. H. R. Dawson, 1886–1889; William T. Harris, 1889–1906; Elmer E. Brown, 1906–1911; Philander P. Claxton, 1911–1921; John J. Tigert, 1921–1928; William J. Cooper, 1929–1933; George F. Zook, 1933–1934; John W. Studebaker, 1934–1948; Earl James McGrath, 1949–1953; Lee M. Thurston, 1953; Samuel Miller Brownell, 1953–1956; Lawrence Gridley Derthick, 1956–1961; Sterling M. McMurrin, 1961–1962; Francis Keppel, 1962–1965; Harold Howe II, 1965–1968; James E. Allen, Jr., 1969–1970; Sidney P. Marland, Jr., 1970–1973; John R. Ottina, 1973–1974; Virginia Y. Trotter (Assistant Secretary for Education), 1974–1977; Ernest L. Boyer, 1977–1979.

EDUCATION OF HENRY ADAMS, an autobiography by the American man of letters Henry Adams. It was first printed privately in 1907 and published posthumously in 1918. The work, which proceeds from the assumption that the individual's true education begins with birth and terminates only at death, is acclaimed as one of the greatest autobiographies in American literature and an important landmark in intellectual history.

Polarization of opposites haunts *The Education*. Adams saw the world in contrasts—country and city, paternal fiber and maternal sympathy, elitism and mass democracy. Accordingly, he conceived of this work, subtitled *A Study in 20th Century Multiplicity*, as a complement to his earlier *Mont-Saint-Michel and Chartres* (private printing, 1904; published, 1913), subtitled *A Study in 13th Century Unity*.

One of the most famous chapters in *The Education*—"The Virgin and the Dynamo"—is on this larger contrasting theme suggested by the subtitles. In it, Adams claims that the symbolic figure of the Virgin Mary was the unifying force in the life of medieval man. He contrasts this unity with the effect of the dynamo (mechanical force, technology) on the life of 20th century man, claiming that the symbolic figure of the dynamo creates "multiplicity" (fragmentation, unordered complexity) in modern life. In looking back, Adams found that his humanistic formal education had been inadequate in preparing him for the multiplicity of 20th century life and that future man must be better prepared, if disaster, including complete impersonalization and moral disintegration, is to be avoided.

The Education is notable not only for its theory of history and for its profound interpretation of the modern American, but also as a portrayal of a highly intellectual descendant of the Adams family, the most enduring political family in the United States. The work studies all of Adams' life between 1839 and 1905, except the period around the time of his marriage (1872–1885), which ended in the tragic suicide of his wife. Much of the later part of the book, dealing with his life in Washington, D. C., where he made his permanent home, is devoted to a careful study of political power.

HENRY WASSER, *Author of*
"The Scientific Thought of Henry Adams"

EDWARD I (1239–1307), king of England, was known as the English Justinian because of his brilliance as a lawgiver. Edward was born at Westminister on June 17 or 18, 1239. Little is known of his early years apart from the fact that, as the eldest of more than a dozen children born to Henry III and Eleanor of Provence, he received vast tracts of land in Wales, western England, and Gascony. When he was 15, he was married to Eleanor, the half sister of Alfonso X of Castile.

Youth. After 1255, Edward became the focus of royalist resistance to a group of barons, ultimately led by Simon de Montfort. These nobles were trying to purge the king's advisers and rule England themselves. In the ensuing struggle, Edward suffered military defeat at Lewes on May 14, 1264, and was later imprisoned at Dover. But he soon escaped, regrouped his forces, and defeated the barons so completely by 1266 that the rest of the weak-willed Henry's reign passed peacefully.

With England calmed, Edward looked for new triumphs. Moved by genuine piety, a desire for fame, and the insistence of Louis IX (St. Louis) of France, who backed up his exhortations with a large loan, Edward agreed in 1268 to join Louis' second crusade against the Muslims. Lord Edward arrived at Aigues-Mortes, the port of embarkation, at the appointed time two years later, but he discovered that Louis had already set sail for Tunis. When Edward reached Tunis, he found the French army decimated by fever and the saint-king dead, and assured that the situation there was irretrievable, he departed for Acre. There his forces proved too meagre to make headway against the Muslims. At length, in the summer of 1272, learning that his aged father was about to die, Edward reluctantly started home. Two years later, following his unopposed succession on Henry's death, he finally reached London and was crowned on Aug. 19, 1274.

Early Kingship. During the next 16 years Edward laid the foundation for his reputation as a diplomat, jurist, and administrator. His relations with the King of France were bedeviled by complications arising from a settlement between St. Louis and Henry III, and in 1279 he and Philip III of France met at Amiens to settle their differences; in return for a large parcel of land, which included Agen and the Agenais, and confirmation of Queen Eleanor's recent inheritance of Ponthieu, Edward abandoned any pretensions to Normandy. He also spent the years 1286–1289 on the Continent in successful effort to achieve a pacification of Europe.

At home, Edward suppressed the principality of Wales by 1283 and executed the last independent prince for treason. Thereafter the title "Prince of Wales" was customarily, though not inevitably, bestowed on the heir apparent to the English crown. He completed his work there by constructing strong castles and introducing the shire system and English common law.

Edward was determined to create a strong central government, and to do so he realized he had to modify the effect of England's confusing, occasionally contradictory, and largely unwritten common law. His accomplishments were to attain specificity in the laws of real property, to attract foreign merchants by providing prompt and speedy settlement of disputes about debts, and to recover lost royal rights from usurping barons. He also defined and separated the jurisdictions of the various royal courts and initiated proceedings in equity as opposed to trial by the restrictive conventions of common law. Edward's statutes were not intended to be antifeudal, but taken as a whole they put an end to the divisive political effects of feudal tenure.

Edward was not unwilling to share the burden of governing. Drawing on the Roman law principle that what concerns all ought to have the consent of all and on precedents from his father's reign, he encouraged the development of Parliament as a forum for redressing grievances, securing assent to the collection of taxes, and judging the temper of his people. Although the Model Parliament of 1295 was not the first parliament in English history, it does mark the point at which that institution became a permanent part of English governmental machinery.

Later Reign. Crises at home and abroad marked the last years of Edward's reign. In 1294 the Welsh rose in revolt. Edward subdued them before the end of the next summer, but about the same time France and Scotland joined in alliance against England. Before the year's end, war with France erupted and swelled into a war with Scotland, and intolerable financial strains led to a resurgence of baronial opposition.

By 1306 the aging monarch had made peace with France, conquered Scotland, and pacified his nobles, but the nationalistic Scots soon rebelled again. Edward advanced toward Scotland, but weakened by an attack of dysentery, he died at Burgh-on-Sands, near Carlisle, on July 7, 1307. His death and the succession of his fourth son, Edward of Caernarvon, ended a period of brilliant consolidation of the English nation.

Description. Edward was tall and thin—amply justifying the description "Longshanks"—with blond hair that darkened before it turned white in old age. He was regarded by his countrymen as a great king, respected for physical courage and wisdom. By his first wife, Eleanor, he had ten children, and by Margaret of France, whom he married on Sept. 10, 1299, three others.

JOHN FERGUSON, *Smith College*

Further Reading: Plucknett, Theodore F. T., *Legislation of Edward I* (New York and London 1949); Powicke, Frederick M., *King Henry III and the Lord Edward* (New York and London 1947); Stones, Edward Lionel Gregory, *Edward I* (New York and London 1968).

EDWARD II (1284–1327), king of England, misruled for 20 years and was deposed and murdered in captivity. Edward was born at Caernarvon, Wales, on April 25, 1284, the youngest child but only surviving son of Edward I and Eleanor of Castile. Edward II was a total disappointment to his masterful and warlike father. He was an athlete but no warrior. Unintelligent, unsociable except among intimates, very indolent, he was delighted to leave government to others. Thus the exercise of royal power and patronage by subordinates during his reign became a recurrent cause of political crisis. He also inherited a dangerous legacy: an interminable war to conquer Scotland, huge debts, and resentful barons.

Accession and Opposition. On becoming king (July 8, 1307), Edward reversed his father's policies. All vigor went out of the prosecution of the Scottish war; his father's chief minister was imprisoned; and his own favorite, Piers (Peter) Gaveston, exiled by Edward I, was immediately recalled. Gaveston caused the first major crisis. He had ability, but his lack of wisdom alienated all groups of barons, and the old opponents of Edward I combined with the moderates. In 1310 their coalition imposed on Edward a council of "lords ordainers," which enacted, in 1311, ordinances banishing Gaveston and other Royal supporters and seriously restricting the King's personal authority. When Gaveston rejoined the King, the barons pursued the hated favorite and murdered him (June 1312). Their act temporarily split the government of the "ordainers," but the disastrous defeat that Edward suffered in Scotland in June 1314 (Battle of Bannockburn) again put him at the mercy of the opposition.

Civil War. After Bannockburn the Scots ravaged northern England with impunity and also invaded Ireland. Famine and lawlessness added to England's wretchedness. In 1321 civil war was provoked by the self-serving schemes of Edward's current favorite, Hugh Despenser the Younger (see DESPENSERS). Again Edward's enemies combined with the moderates to secure the exile of Hugh and of his father (August 1321). But feuds between Thomas, Earl of Lancaster, the leader of the opposition, and his allies soon allowed Edward to counterattack. A rising of Welsh loyalists neutralized the forces of the Despensers' enemies among the Welsh marcher lords, and the other enemy forces, led by Lancaster, were trapped in Yorkshire.

Capture and Deposition. Edward and the Despensers wasted their victory. Their wholesale execution and dispossession of their opponents started a reign of terror, and the government they set up was too corrupt and too unpopular to last. When Edward's estranged and embittered wife, Isabella (q.v.), landed at Harwich on Sept. 24, 1326, she met virtually no resistance. From all parts of the country supporters flocked to her camp; London rose in her favor; and most of the King's officials and retainers deserted him.

Edward fled to the Despenser lordship of Glamorgan in South Wales, where he was captured on November 16. A threat to dispossess his dynasty forced him to abdicate in favor of his heir, Edward III, whose reign started on Jan. 25, 1327. The deposed King was imprisoned at Berkeley Castle, rescued for a brief time, and then returned and murdered by his captors, on Sept. 21, 1327.

Edward's overthrow and violent death weakened the authority of the English monarchy and left memories that contributed to monarchical instability until the end of the 15th century.

E. B. FRYDE
University College of Wales, Aberystwyth

Further Reading: Johnstone, Hilda, *Edward of Carnarvon* (Manchester, England, 1946); Tout, Thomas Frederick, *The Place of the Reign of Edward II in English History*, 2d ed. (Manchester, England, 1936).

EDWARD III (1312–1377), king of England, whose forceful assertion of a claim to the French throne inaugurated the series of battles known as the Hundred Years' War. His reign was a period of brilliant military achievement.

Early Years. Edward was born at Windsor on Nov. 13, 1312, the elder son of Edward II and Isabella of France, through whom he and subsequent kings of England laid claim to the throne of France. Richard de Bury tutored the young prince, but Edward's formal education must have been limited. Nevertheless, it is known that he could read and write.

At 14, having already assumed the titles Earl of Chester, Count of Ponthieu, and Duke of Aquitaine, but not Prince of Wales, Edward became keeper of England during his father's absence abroad. The next year his mother enmeshed him in her machinations leading to the deposition and murder of the King.

Edward ascended the throne on Jan. 25, 1327, and was formally crowned at Westminster on January 29. For more than three years, however, Isabella and her paramour, Roger Mortimer, used him as a puppet to legitimize their own despotic government. Meanwhile, on Jan. 24, 1328, Edward was married to Philippa of Hainault (Hainaut), who bore him seven sons and five daughters.

A palace revolution in October 1330 began Edward's actual rule. He surprised and captured Mortimer at Nottingham, executed him for treason, and forced the dowager queen into retirement. He then turned to a conquest of France.

War with France. England declared war on France in 1337. Hostilities began two years later, and on Jan. 26, 1340, after a brief, indecisive foray into the Low Countries, Edward proclaimed himself king of France at Ghent. From 1340 until a disastrous campaign in 1359–1360, which was to have led to his coronation at Reims, the English monarch's armies moved from victory to victory—Sluis (1340), Crécy (1346), and Poitiers (1356), where King John II of France himself was captured. To celebrate his triumphs, Edward inaugurated the Order of the Garter, in emulation of King Arthur's Knights of the Round Table.

At home, however, government had not proceeded smoothly. In a major constitutional crisis, the King dismissed the archbishop of Canterbury as chancellor (1340) and, taking an unprecedented step, appointed a layman to replace him in that office. This was followed in 1345 by the bankruptcy of the Bardi and Peruzzi houses, the crown's financial agents. In 1348 the Black Death, the worst outbreak of plague since the 6th century, struck England, and within two years it carried off 20% of the population.

These disasters, coupled with military reverses, led Edward to make peace with France at Brétigny in May 1360. In return for France's cession of territory, including Gascony, Poitou, Agenais, Périgord, Quercy, and Limousin, and payment of £500,000 for the French King's ransom, Edward promised to renounce his claims to the throne of France and to other French territory, but he did not honor this pledge.

Last Years. An extremely lethal outbreak of plague in 1360–1361 marked the beginning of the downward curve of Edward's career. On the Continent his Breton and Flemish allies deserted him, and at home the Scots made an alliance with France against England (1371). Queen Philippa died in 1369, and Edward, rapidly becoming senile, fell under the influence of a grasping mistress, Alice Perrers. In the same year, war with France was resumed. Reverses followed, and by 1375, England held only Calais and the coast between Bordeaux and Bayonne.

In 1376 the King's eldest son, Edward the Black Prince (q.v.), died, leaving a child of only 10 years (the future Richard II) to inherit the throne. Edward himself died at Sheen (now Richmond), on June 21, 1377, forsaken by all save Dame Alice, who removed the rings from his fingers before she fled, and a single priest.

In spite of Edward's decline during the last years of his reign, the glories of his military victories were never obscured. However costly to Englishmen in the long run, his conquests were a source of pride to them for centuries to come. Edward left four sons, two of whom (John of Gaunt and Edmund) founded the rival dynasties of Lancaster and York.

JOHN FERGUSON, *Smith College*

Further Reading: Longman, William, *The History of the Life and Times of Edward III*, 2 vols. (London 1869); Nicholson, Ranald, *Edward III and the Scots* (New York and London 1965).

EDWARD IV (1442–1483), king of England, who established the house of York after the Lancastrian King Henry VI was deposed.

Youth. Edward Plantagenet was born at Rouen, France, on April 28, 1442, the eldest son of Richard, Duke of York, and his wife, Cecily Neville. In his father's lifetime, Edward was entitled Earl of March. He was too young to participate in York's attempts to gain control of Henry VI's council, the last of which resulted in the first Battle of St. Albans (1455), which started the Wars of the Roses.

In 1459, when York was routed at Ludlow and forced to take sanctuary in Ireland, Edward fled to Calais with the Neville Earls of Salisbury and Warwick. Early in 1460 they crossed to England and raised an army that defeated the royal forces and captured Henry at Northampton (July 10). When York returned from Ireland shortly thereafter to demand the crown as the legitimate heir of King Edward III, Edward of March was said to have joined other Yorkists in opposing the demand. York's arguments, nevertheless, overwhelmed the reluctant lords, and they agreed that he might become king after Henry's death.

On Dec. 30, 1460, a Lancastrian army defeated and killed York at Wakefield and went on to rescue Henry from his Yorkist captors at the second Battle of St. Albans (Feb. 17, 1461). Edward, who meanwhile had defeated a Lancastrian force at Mortimer's Cross, in the west of England, rushed to relieve Warwick in London. On March 1, 1461, Warwick and a small junta in self-defense declared Edward king. He acceded on March 4 and secured his throne by a decisive victory at Towton, Yorkshire, on March 29. He was crowned on June 28.

Reign. Edward, who was only 19, was not initially a free agent. His dependence, particularly on Warwick, was disclosed by his granting many vital offices to the Neville family. In 1464, however, his privately arranged wedding to Elizabeth Woodville, the widow and daughter of former enemies, signaled his intention to be master. Warwick tried to recover his influence by detaining Edward in 1469, but the King soon freed himself, and Warwick was forced into exile. In order to retrieve his fortunes, Warwick allowed himself to be persuaded by Louis XI of France to make an alliance with Henry VI's queen, Margaret of Anjou. Edward was unprepared for Warwick's subsequent invasion or for the treachery of his own brother George, Duke of Clarence, who joined forces with Warwick. Edward took refuge in Flanders, while Warwick freed Henry VI and restored him to the throne (Oct. 3, 1470).

Edward's return was assisted by his brother-in-law Charles, Duke of Burgundy, who was unwilling to see England under French influence. After an unopposed landing in Yorkshire, Edward rapidly formed an army that defeated and killed Warwick at Barnet (April 24, 1471). He thus regained charge of the country. Another force under Margaret, belatedly invading from France, was destroyed at Tewkesbury (May 4), and the murder of Henry VI on May 21 completed the elimination of Edward's foremost enemies.

After Tewkesbury, Edward enjoyed general acceptance as king. Even close associates of Queen Margaret, such as the future Cardinal Morton, entered his service. Although ruthless when necessary, Edward was naturally tolerant, and his proven military prowess and charm won him popular regard; the fatalistic English were easily reconciled to the removal of the unkingly Henry VI. The nation, moreover, was enjoying greater prosperity as its wool exports rose.

Edward's popularity was enhanced by his fiscal program, which anticipated that of Henry VII. His foreign policy was generally peaceful. A short campaign in France in 1475 ended with Louis XI's promise of a pension (Treaty of Picquigny), and an attack on Scotland in 1482 secured the recovery of Berwick-on-Tweed. Otherwise, Edward "lived on his own" by reorganizing royal rents under the control of the "chamber," a domestic department that bypassed the antiquated processes of the Exchequer. Parliaments consequently became infrequent and were well disposed toward him. Although he made few new laws, he took close interest in preserving public order and once sat on King's Bench himself. Had he not died at the early age of 40 (at Westminster, on April 9, 1483), Edward might well be regarded as one of England's most capable and successful kings.

See also HENRY VI; YORK, DUKES OF.

R. L. STOREY
University of Nottingham, England
Author of *"The End of the House of Lancaster"*

EDWARD V (1470–1483), king of England, was the elder of two young sons of Edward IV who are believed to have been murdered in the Tower of London after the usurpation of Richard III.

Edward was born at Westminster on Nov. 2, 1470. From 1473 he lived at Ludlow, in the Welsh marches. He succeeded to the throne on his father's death, but three weeks later, on April 30, 1483, he was seized en route to London by his uncle Richard, Duke of Gloucester.

In order to forestall any attempt by the queen dowager and her kinsmen, the Woodvilles and Greys, to gain control of the government, Gloucester assumed authority as the young King's protector. He tightened his grip further by removing prominent councillors of Edward IV whom he distrusted. Gloucester next declared that Edward V was a bastard because his parent's marriage was irregular. He then usurped the crown and ruled as Richard III from June 26, 1483.

Edward V and his brother Richard, Duke of York, were imprisoned in the Tower, and there is no proof of their survival after 1483. Rumors that Richard III had murdered his nephews were then circulating in England and abroad, and it is likely they were killed about July 1, 1483.

R. L. STOREY
University of Nottingham, England

EDWARD VI (1537–1553), was the last Tudor king of England. He died when he was 15. Edward was born at Hampton Court on Oct. 12, 1537, the only son of Henry VIII, by his wife Jane Seymour. He was a good student, particularly of religion, but he was fragile and over-earnest. He succeeded to the throne when he was only 9. Henry VIII's will had provided for rule by a "Council," but Edward's uncle Edward Seymour, Earl of Hertford, forced himself on the new king as protector and, as Duke of Somerset, assumed control. Somerset's weaknesses as a leader were not compensated by any degree of religious toleration or social justice (both he and the King were narrowly Protestant), and as a result Kett's Rebellion (q.v.) and other discontents soon provided John Dudley, Earl of Warwick and the son of Sir Edmund Dudley (q.v.), an opportunity to depose Somerset and take charge of the King and kingdom.

The tyrannical and corrupt Warwick, who soon became duke of Northumberland, gained a marked influence over the young King. Northumberland consolidated his power by crushing his opposition, and after making peace with France and Scotland, he turned his attention—and the King's—to Protestant purification of the Church of England. Anticipating the King's death, he persuaded Edward to will the crown to Lady Jane Grey, wife of Northumberland's son, Guild-

Edward VI of England (portrait after Holbein)

Edward VII of England

ford. When Edward died, at Greenwich on July 6, 1553, Lady Jane succeeded to the throne, but within nine days the council rallied to Mary Tudor (see MARY I, queen of England).

Edward was largely the puppet of his protectors, but his journal shows that he was aware of corruption in his government and misery among his subjects. Had he survived, England's religious development almost certainly would have been far less libertarian than it was.

STUART E. PRALL, *Queens College, New York*

EDWARD VII (1841–1910), king of the United Kingdom of Great Britain and Ireland. Eldest son and second child of Queen Victoria and Prince Albert, Prince Albert Edward was born at Buckingham Palace, London, on Nov. 9, 1841. No English monarch served so long an apprenticeship as heir to the throne (Victoria reigned until January 1901), yet few have begun their reign so inexperienced in affairs of state.

Edward's education was rigidly and exhaustively planned with two aims: to enable him to rule in what was expected to be a time of revolution and antimonarchical feeling, and to produce in him a replica of his highly educated father. In fact, Edward was to become king at a time when the popularity of the English monarchy was high. He was not studious like his father (although excellent at languages), and he showed little interest in games, a fact that owed much to his childhood isolation from companions other than his family. In 1859, Edward became the first Prince of Wales ever to attend Oxford as an undergraduate, but his real interests lay in military affairs, in which, however, he was never allowed to play more than a ceremonial role. His exclusion from affairs of state was almost complete. Despite repeated requests by her ministers, Victoria allowed her heir access to none but the merest glimpse of state papers.

The Prince was a sensitive, affectionate youth, whose harsh upbringing provided few emotional satisfactions. Following Victoria's virtual retirement from social engagements after Albert's death in 1861, Edward gladly filled her place in London society. In 1863 he was married to Princess Alexandra, eldest daughter of King Christian IX of Denmark. Although the marriage was harmonious, it did little to mitigate the Prince's zest for pursuit of pleasure, and his liaisons with famous beauties in England and on the Continent often caused gossip and scandal.

His interest in politics was neither great nor sustained; he had strong pro-Danish and pro-French prejudices in foreign affairs, and as monarch strongly supported Admiral Fisher's unpopular naval reforms. He became king on Jan. 22, 1901, at the age of 59, conscious of political inexperience and bearing the effects of a near-fatal attack of typhoid in 1871. He played little part in the crises of his reign (for example, the Commons-Lords conflict of 1909–1911 and worsening Anglo-German relations) and was in this sense a model constitutional monarch. He was anxious to further peace at home and abroad, and his European tours and popularity at home genuinely helped these ends. He died at Buckingham Palace, after a reign of just over 9 years, on May 6, 1910.

A. J. BEATTIE, *London School of Economics*

Further Reading: Magnus, Philip, *King Edward the Seventh* (New York 1964).

EDWARD VIII (1894–1972), king of the United Kingdom of Great Britain and Northern Ireland, who abdicated his throne in order to marry Mrs. Wallis Simpson, a divorced American woman. Prince Edward Albert Christian George Andrew Patrick David was born at Richmond Park, in Surrey, England, on June 23, 1894, the eldest son of George V and Queen Mary. His childhood associations were mostly with the royal family, under his father's rather rigid influence. He preferred life as a cadet at the Royal Naval College to his early education under private tutors or his sojourn at Oxford from 1912 to 1914. Appointed a midshipman in 1911, he advanced to admiral of the fleet in 1936.

In 1914, when World War I broke out, he was appointed 2d lieutenant in the 1st Battalion of the Grenadier Guards. He was aide-de-camp in France to the commander in chief of the British Expeditionary Forces, on active service, although, to his great disappointment, his position as Prince of Wales and heir to the throne precluded his being sent to the front lines. In 1916 he served in Italy, France, and Egypt.

EDWARD VIII with his bride, Mrs. Wallis Simpson. To marry her, he abdicated the British throne in 1936.

After the war, the Prince of Wales became a popular national figure through his participation in royal ceremonial duties, and was also most effective on goodwill missions to other parts of the world. His reputation with the press as a man sympathetic to social reform caused discomfort to his father, who believed the crown should be politically impartial. The Prince had little interest in politics, but he was moved by mass unemployment and poverty, and he pressed, always in a private capacity, for reform.

On his accession to the throne on Jan. 20, 1936, Edward VIII hoped to make the public image of the monarchy accord with his view of changed social attitudes. But in November 1936 he told Prime Minister Stanley Baldwin of his wish to marry Mrs. Simpson, who had been twice divorced. The cabinet refused to support the King because the marriage would have been incompatible with his position as head of the Church of England. Because persistence would have caused a major political crisis, Edward was forced to choose between his throne and "the woman I love," as he said in his speech announcing his abdication on Dec. 11, 1936. Succeeded by his brother the Duke of York (as George VI), he was henceforth H. R. H. Prince Edward, Duke of Windsor.

After their marriage on June 3, 1937, the Duke and Duchess of Windsor resided chiefly in France. From 1940 to 1945 he was governor of the Bahama Islands. He died in Paris on May 28, 1972.

A. J. Beattie, *London School of Economics*

EDWARD (1391–1438), king of Portugal from 1433 to 1438. Edward (Portuguese, *Duarte*) was the son of King John I of Portugal and Philippa of Lancaster. Distinguished for his learning, he was the author of a treatise, *O leal conselhiero* (*The Loyal Counselor*). He appointed Fernão Lopes court historian; today the surviving chronicles of that great historian are a primary source of medieval Portuguese history.

Edward encouraged his brother Prince Henry the Navigator, who initiated the Portuguese overseas empire. In 1437, during his reign, the Portuguese were defeated trying to seize Tangier from the Moors. Edward died at Tomar on Sept. 9, 1438, and was succeeded by his son Alfonso V.

EDWARD (1330–1376), prince of Wales, called the *Black Prince*, was one of England's greatest soldiers in the Hundred Years' War. He was the eldest son and heir apparent of King Edward III, but he died one year before his father.

The Black Prince was born at the royal manor of Woodstock, Oxfordshire, on June 15, 1330. He was created Earl of Chester at the age of 3, Duke of Cornwall at 7, and Prince of Wales at 13. From an early age he was trained in both statecraft and warfare, but his talents proved to be mainly in the latter. (His epithet "Black Prince" may reflect the terror he inspired in the French, but it probably refers to the color of his armor.)

Edward first distinguished himself in battle when he was 16. He shared his father's victory at Crécy in 1346 and participated in a successful siege of Calais the next year. In 1355 he assumed command in France and a year later led his armies to a stunning victory at Poitiers, a pivotal battle at which he captured King John II of France and proved the superiority of his unmounted archers over France's mounted knights.

In July 1362, some 15 months after he had married Joan, the twice-wed Countess of Kent, Edward became Prince of Aquitaine. The next year he and Joan sailed for France, where they remained for eight years. As head of the English domains in southwestern France, Edward showed little administrative ability. He failed to unify the factious nobility; his sumptuous court outran the revenues of the principality; and his frequent demands for money at meetings of the three estates of the principality displeased all his subjects. In 1367 he led an invasion of Spain and defeated a Spanish army at Nájera, but a year later his French subjects rebelled. Edward restored order after sacking Limoges in 1370, but sickness and grief over the death of his older son forced him to retire in 1371. He returned to England, surrendering Aquitaine to his father.

Edward lived his last years as a semi-invalid in retirement at Berkhampstead, going to Westminster occasionally and apparently intervening in the Good Parliament in 1376 to make sure that the crown would pass without opposition to his second son, Richard of Bordeaux (later King Richard II). Edward died of dysentery at Westminster on June 8, 1376.

Seldom cruel, often generous, no patron of the arts or learning, but very extravagant, Edward personified the chivalric knight. His venture into government failed, but his successes in foreign wars increased Englishmen's consciousness of their individuality and national identity.

John Ferguson, *Smith College*

EDWARD (1453–1471), Prince of Wales, was the only child of King Henry VI of England and his queen, Margaret of Anjou. Edward was born at Westminster, England, on Oct. 13, 1453, two months after the onset of his father's mental collapse. After Henry's recovery, when control of his government consequently returned to his favorites from the hands of Richard, Duke of York, Edward was created Prince of Wales (March 15, 1454). Margaret took him to Scotland after the decisive Yorkist victory at Towton, which confirmed the accession of York's son as Edward IV, and in 1463 to France, where the castle of Koeur, in Lorraine, became the home of the Lancastrian court. There, in 1468–1469, Sir John Fortescue, Henry VI's former chief justice, wrote for Edward's instruction the unique account of the contemporary English constitution, *De laudibus legum Angliae*, cast as a dialogue between the Prince and Fortescue, who asserted that as the future king of England Edward should learn its laws.

Edward accompanied the invading force led by Margaret that was trapped and destroyed by Edward IV at Tewkesbury on May 4, 1471. He was killed either in the battle or, according to some accounts, after his capture. With the subsequent murder of Henry VI, the direct line of the royal house of Lancaster was brought to an end.

R. L. STOREY
University of Nottingham, England

EDWARD II, a verse play by the English dramatist Christopher Marlowe (q.v.), written probably in 1591. One of the major Elizabethan plays on an English historical theme, it influenced Shakespeare's *King Richard the Second*, which likewise traces a king's path from misgovernment through his abdication and murder. An adaptation of Marlowe's play by Bertolt Brecht and Lion Feuchtwanger (1924) was translated into English and produced in London in 1968.

King Edward antagonizes the barons through his infatuation with the low-born Gaveston, and, led by Mortimer, the barons overthrow the king. Edward's queen, Isabella, is for a long time faithful to her husband but is won over to Mortimer's side and shares his guilt in the king's brutal murder. Mortimer and Isabella are overthrown when Edward's son assumes power.

The interest is centered on the personal relationships of Edward, Isabella, Mortimer, and Gaveston. Edward is depicted as weak and irresponsible, but the humiliations heaped on him make him a tragic figure.

CLIFFORD LEECH, *Editor of "Marlowe: A Collection of Critical Essays"*

EDWARD, Lake, a freshwater lake in the western Great Rift Valley in East Africa on the Uganda-Congo (Kinshasa) border. The smallest of the great lakes of East Africa, Lake Edward, also called *Edward Nyanza*, is 830 square miles (2,-150 sq km) in area and lies 2,995 feet (913 meters) above sea level. The lake's only outlet is the Semliki River, which flows north to Lake Albert and then to the Nile. Lake Edward was discovered in 1877 by Henry M. Stanley. Lake Edward is noted for its rich fish and bird life. Its swampy southern shores are famous for their hippopotamuses.

HUGH C. BROOKS
St. John's University, N. Y.

EDWARD THE CONFESSOR (died 1066) was king of England during the unsettled period immediately before the Norman Conquest. Edward was born about 1003, the son of Æthelred the Unready and Emma of Normandy. When the Danes overran England in 1013, the family fled to Normandy, but Edward was the nominal leader of the deputation that negotiated Æthelred's return to power in 1014. During the reigns of Canute (1016–1035) and Harold Harefoot (1035–1040), Edward was again an exile, but in the reign of Hardecanute (1040–1042) he was recalled, apparently to be established as heir presumptive (1041).

Reign. In 1042, Edward succeeded to a kingdom divided between the great earls Siward of Northumbria, Leofric of Mercia, and Godwin of Wessex. Godwin was the most powerful of the three—his sons were already establishing earldoms of their own—and in 1045, Edward married Godwin's daughter Edith. He had already asserted his power in 1043 by greatly reducing his mother's, with the blessing of all three earls. By 1049, Edward's preference for foreign nobles and prelates had led to coolness between him and the house of Godwin. In that year he exiled Sweyn, Godwin's eldest son, for various crimes; in 1051, after overcoming an attempt at armed coercion, he exiled the remaining male members of the family and sent Edith to a nunnery.

However, the kingdom was not secured. Godwin and his family returned and recovered their position in 1052, and many of the King's foreign favorites were exiled. Godwin died in 1053, but his sons increased their power, and on the death of Siward in 1055, one of them, Tostig, became earl of Northumbria. Ten years later violent rebellion broke out in Northumbria. The rebels elected Morcar, a grandson of Leofric of Mercia, earl in Tostig's place and invaded England as far south as Northampton. King Edward was forced to agree to Morcar's appointment.

During Edward's reign major foreign wars were avoided, but the security of England was constantly endangered. Wales, which was unified under Gruffydd ap Llywelyn, presented a serious threat until Harold, son of Godwin, reduced it in 1063. Gruffydd had frequently allied himself with the rebellious Alfgar, son of Leofric of Mercia, and once (1058) had had the support of a great Norwegian fleet. Malcolm, king of Scotland, was not overly grateful for the help he had received against Macbeth, for in 1061 he ravaged Northumbria.

Succession. Many claimants were waiting to succeed the childless Edward. Abroad there were Magnus and later Harold Hardrada of Norway, Sewyn of Denmark, and William of Normandy; and at home, Harold, son of Godwin, and Edward, the King's own nephew, son of his deceased elder brother, Edmund Ironside. Harold succeeded the day after Edward's death at Westminster on Jan. 5, 1066, but he died fighting Norman conquerers at Hastings the following October.

Edward the Confessor enjoyed a posthumous reputation for saintliness and religious preoccupation—he was canonized in 1161—for which there is no contemporary evidence. His charity seems to have been limited to his foundation of Westminster Abbey, which was consecrated in 1065. The ecclesiastical history of his reign is mainly a succession of disputes over preferments.

ALISTAIR CAMPBELL, *Oxford University*

EDWARD THE ELDER (died 924), king of the Anglo-Saxons, extended to nearly all of England south of the Humber River the kingdom left by his father, Alfred the Great.

Battles with the Danes. Edward first appears in history in 893, when he defeated the Danes at Farnham and, helped by Earl Æthelred of Mercia, forced them to agree to leave the south of England. When Edward succeeded to the throne in 899, he had to face a rebellion by Æthelwold, the son of Alfred's brother Æthelred. Æthelwold, who was allied with the Danes of Northumbria and East Anglia, fell in the Battle of the Holme in 902, and seven undisturbed years followed. Peace was confirmed with the East Anglian and Northumbrian Danes about 906 (Treaty of Tiddingford), but Edward was undoubtedly planning the reconquest of the vast area left in Danish hands at the end of Alfred's wars.

Reconquest of Danish England. In 909, Edward sent a combined West Saxon and Mercian army to ravage Northumbria. The Danes retaliated in 910 with an invasion of English Mercia, but ultimately their forces were destroyed at the Battle of Tettenhall. In 911, Æthelred of Mercia died, and Æthelflaed, his widow, became a vigorous supporter of the West Saxon advance. In 914 the West Saxons' plans for extending their kingdom were delayed by a serious invasion of Vikings from Brittany, but by building fortresses to cover their positions and delivering well-timed attacks, Edward and Æthelflaed practically obliterated Danish power south of the Humber by the time of Æthelflaed's death in 918. Edward completed the job in the same year and incorporated English Mercia into the West Saxon kingdom.

While Edward was dealing with invaders in the south, the Northumbrian Danes, who had offered submission to Æthelflaed before her death, fell prey to an Irish Scandinavian, Raegnald, who established a kingdom at York. Nevertheless, Raegnald, together with Ealdred, who represented the last vestige of English power in Northumbria, and several Celtic monarchs formally submitted to Edward about 920, and the last years of Edward's reign were peaceful. He died in 924.

ALISTAIR CAMPBELL
Oxford University

EDWARD THE MARTYR (962?–978 or 979), king of the Anglo-Saxons, whose reign was marked by an "antimonastic reaction." Edward succeeded his father, Edgar (q.v.), as king in 975. He may have been illegitimate, and there was opposition to him from the beginning.

Attacks were launched by Ælfhere, Ealdorman of Mercia, and others on monasteries that had been founded during Edgar's reign. These attacks may have been expressions of hostility to Edward, because such great monastic founders as Dunstan were among the King's leading supporters.

On March 18, 978 (or possibly 979), Edward was murdered while visiting his stepmother, Ælfthryth, and his half brother, Æthelred, at Corfe (Dorset). It is uncertain who was responsible, but it is clear that the murder was in the interest of Æthelred, who became king after Edward's death (see ÆTHELRED II). Within a generation Edward was venerated as a saint.

J. CAMPBELL
Oxford University

EDWARDS, Jonathan (1703–1758), American theologian, philosopher, and Congregational minister. His writings show him to have been one of the most profound and original thinkers in America. His sermons stimulated the religious revival known as the Great Awakening.

Edwards was born in East Windsor, Conn., on Oct. 5, 1703, the only son among the eleven children born to Timothy and Esther Stoddard Edwards. His father, a minister, provided the precocious boy's only education until he entered Yale College in his 13th year. After his graduation from Yale in 1720, Edwards underwent a religious conversion and decided upon the ministry as a career. He served briefly as the minister of a church in New York City and in 1724 returned to Yale to become a tutor in the college. Two years later he was invited to be an assistant to his grandfather, Solomon Stoddard, minister of the church in Northampton, Mass., and a preeminent figure among the New England clergy. In 1727, Edwards married Sarah Pierrepont. The couple had 12 children, including the theologian and educator Jonathan Edwards, Jr.

In 1729, when Stoddard died at the age of 85, Edwards became the senior minister of the church in Northampton. In 1731 he was invited to deliver a public lecture in Boston, giving the grandson of the famous Stoddard his first exposure to the ecclesiastical aristocracy of New England. His address, "God Glorified in the Work of Redemption," immediately established his reputation as a warm and intelligent expositor of the Puritan faith.

In 1735 the evangelical ardor of his preaching was finally rewarded in Northampton with a revival. Edwards' own informal history of this revival, *A Faithful Narrative of the Surprising Work of God* (1737), was the most influential of his many books to be published in his own lifetime. It came to be used as a handbook by evangelical ministers during later revivals.

The Great Awakening. In 1740, after a "dead" period in religion, a vast revival known as the Great Awakening aroused the religious spirit of the greater part of New England. While Edwards was not the sole initiator of the Awakening, his preaching was very largely instrumental in its first vivid successes. The Great Awakening lasted several years, during which there was widespread fanatical religious activity. Persons were subject to direct visions of God or Satan, and religious meetings were frequently disrupted by unintelligible shrieking and violent body movements on the part of the worshipers. The proper moral and spiritual governance of the towns and villages became a deeply felt concern. It was to a congregation affected in this manner that Edwards preached his famous "Sinners in the Hands of an Angry God" (1741), the sermon that has made him known as a purveyor of severe maledictions.

It would be far from the truth, however, to assume that this kind of preaching gives a correct picture of the man. From his childhood Edwards was concerned with complicated philosophical questions and scientific investigations, as is evidenced by his astonishingly accurate study of the flying spider written in his 11th or 12th year. His study at Yale brought him under the influence of the British philosopher John Locke, for whom experience, and not innate ideas, was the starting point for serious thinking. This meant for Edwards that the truth of theological assertions was not to be found in the free speculation of the mind but in the actual experience of that with which the assertions dealt. The goodness of God, for example, cannot be believed simply because someone says God is good; it can only be believed if one experiences the goodness of God.

From the enormous quantity of miscellaneous and unpublished notes that continued to collect in Edwards' study, we know that behind the busy pastor and preacher there was always the philosopher objectively studying the world around him. As a result of these reflections he sharply questioned much of the activity in the Great Awakening. In a series of sermons preached in 1742 he noted how urgent it was that Christians be able to tell gold from dross in religious experience. These sermons were later published as the *Treatise on Religious Affections* (1746), the finest volume ever to come from Edwards' pen but too subtle in the confusing aftermath of the Great Awakening to heal the divisiveness that had sprung up in his congregation.

Later Years. Several years later Edwards revealed another conclusion of his thinking, one that had much more effect on his career. In *An Humble Inquiry* (1749) he reversed the position his grandfather Stoddard had taken some 50 years earlier—that church membership ought to be open to anyone desiring salvation. Edwards had decided that a man's profession of faith could not be accepted unless his life gave some visible evidence that God's grace was at work in it. This was more than the increasingly prosperous Americans of the mid-18th century thought was necessary to determine the validity of their righteousness. After a bitter controversy, the church voted overwhelmingly to remove Edwards from his office in the year 1750.

Edwards spent most of the remaining eight years of his life as a missionary to the Indians in the western Massachusetts village of Stockbridge. In spite of the many hardships brought upon his family in this primitive setting, he managed to publish several important books, chief among them *Freedom of the Will* (1754), a summary of his lifelong reflection on this problem. In this book, the heart of Edwards' theological and philosophical thinking is to be found.

In 1757 he became president of the College of New Jersey (now Princeton University). He died in Princeton on March 22, 1758.

Philosophy. Edwards showed that the will is not a separate faculty of the mind but is connected indissolubly to the intellect. A man does not perceive by means of his intellect what is the greatest good and then decide whether he will choose accordingly; rather, he chooses at once whatever he may understand to be the greatest good. Therefore, to say that the will is as the greatest apparent good is means that the will always immediately follows the intellect or understanding.

It follows from this that if man can do only that which appears to his understanding as the greatest good, then God, if He is to move man at all, must become man's most apparent good. This led Edwards to a distinctive doctrine of Christ. In his sermons, especially, he presented Christ as though He were God's attempt to bring himself movingly before the understanding of man. Edwards wanted people to see that within the darkness of the human condition Christ's unvarying resolve to serve and forgive others can

THE ART MUSEUM, PRINCETON UNIVERSITY
Jonathan Edwards (portrait by Henry Augustus Loop)

manifest itself vividly to the understanding as the most apparent good.

The other consequence of this doctrine of the will was Edwards' conclusion that if the intellect and the will are not to be separated, then the true nature of the inner man will manifest itself in the actions of the outer man. One can tell from what a man does, in other words, what for him is the most apparent good. To the enlightened observer it can be determined whether a man has seized on God, or on something else, as his most apparent good.

It is this latter point that struck Edwards with such force during the Great Awakening when so frequently there were violent inner experiences of God while outer expressions of it in the lives of the believers were so rare. In his *Treatise on Religious Affections* he attempted to develop a reliable series of signs by which truly gracious affections, or feelings, might be distinguished from those which have no grace in them. Edwards never thought that one man could be the final judge of another in this matter, but he was persuaded that the church, by means of a charitable and reasonable discernment, could exercise this judgment. It was his expression of this opinion that led to his dismissal in 1750.

One of Edwards' most striking convictions was that the American settlement would become the place where the Kingdom of Christ would have its first foothold. From America true spiritual enlightenment would be spread throughout the world, along with perfect peace and justice. As he revealed in the *History of the Work of Redemption* (1737), a book that chronicles divine and human affairs from the creation to the end of history in the final judgment, he thought in the 1730's that the Kingdom might come at any moment. Edwards never lost his certainty that God was working out His redemption within the context of human history, but he apparently felt after the excesses of the Great Awakening that the arrival of the Kingdom of Christ was being withheld for another time and another place.

Edwards' immediate followers had much less imagination and theological wisdom than he, and his work was taken as the basis for a rigid orthodoxy—precisely what Edwards himself was trying to avoid. As a result, the "Edwardean" school of theologians made only a limited impact on religious thought in the 19th century. They were concerned chiefly to show that the thought of Edwards was essentially consistent with that of the 16th century reformer John Calvin.

Resurgence of Interest. In the 20th century Edwards has been treated as a thinker of very great originality. Beginning with Perry Miller's book on Edwards in 1949, there has been a revival of interest in his writings. Some scholars have judged him to be one of the several great geniuses in American literary history. Some have seen in his work the foundation for a genuinely American theology inasmuch as he gave central place to one's experience of the present factual world. Still later, several scholars emphasized in Edwards' thought his understanding of America as a civilization that exists for the salvation of the world. Edwards believed that the American "plantation" was but a stage in the development of the ultimate society, that Americans as a people were on the long journey toward this final chapter of history. A somewhat secularized version of this view of America is still celebrated by political leaders and official philosophers.

JAMES CARSE, *New York University*

Bibliography
Editions of Edwards' works include *Works of President Edwards*, ed. by S. Austin, 4 vols. (New York 1843); *Works of Jonathan Edwards*, ed. by Perry Miller; vol. 1, *Freedom of the Will;* vol. 2, *Religious Affections* (New Haven, Conn., 1957–). Selections and individual works include *Jonathan Edwards, Representative Selections*, ed. by Clarence H. Faust and Thomas H. Johnson (New York 1962); *The Nature of True Virtue*, ed. by William K. Frankena (Ann Arbor, Mich., 1962); *The Philosophy of Jonathan Edwards from His Private Notebooks*, ed. by Harvey G. Townsend (Eugene, Oreg., 1955).
Carse, James P., *Jonathan Edwards and the Visibility of God* (New York 1967).
Cherry, Conrad, *The Theology of Jonathan Edwards: A Reappraisal* (New York 1966).
Miller, Perry, *Jonathan Edwards* (New York 1949).

EDWARDS, Jonathan, Jr. (1745–1801), American Congregational minister, son of the famous New England theologian Jonathan Edwards. He was born in Northampton, Mass., on May 26, 1745, and graduated from the College of New Jersey (Princeton) in 1765. He studied theology under Joseph Bellamy and was ordained to the Congregational ministry in 1769. Edwards served the White Haven Church in New Haven, Conn., until 1795 when he was dismissed in a controversy over the "Halfway Covenant" (q.v.) and the baptism of the children of nonprofessing members. In 1799 he became president of Union College, in Schenectady, N.Y. He died there on Aug. 1, 1801.

Edwards' most important theological contribution was his advocacy of the "governmental" theory of Hugo Grotius, the 16th century Dutch scholar, who attempted to explain the Atonement of Christ in legal terms. Edwards maintained the theory in two works: *On the Necessity of the Atonement, and Its Consistency with Free Grace and Forgiveness* (1785) and *The Salvation of All Men Strictly Examined* (1789).

JAMES H. SMYLIE
Union Theological Seminary, Richmond, Va.

EDWARDS PLATEAU, in southwestern Texas, is geographically a southeastern extension of the Great Plains. It is bounded on the southeast and east by the Balcones Escarpment, which extends to the vicinity of San Antonio and Austin, and on the south by the Rio Grande. On the west, the canyon of the Pecos River separates it from the Stockton Plateau, regarded as topographically a part of the Edwards Plateau. The elevation of the Edwards Plateau varies from about 3,000 feet (900 meters) at the edge of the Llano Estacado (Staked Plain) in the north to about 1,000 feet (300 meters) in the east.

EDWARDSVILLE, ed'wərdz-vil, a city in southwestern Illinois, the seat of Madison county, is 17 miles (27 km) northeast of East St. Louis, Ill. It is situated in a region where coal mining, farming, and dairying are carried on. A branch of Southern Illinois University is here.

Edwardsville was founded in 1805 and named for Ninian Edwards, a governor of Illinois Territory and later of the state. It was incorporated in 1837 and was chartered as a city in 1872. Government is by mayor and council. Population: 12,460.

EDWIN (584 or 585–633), Anglo-Saxon king of Northumbria, was responsible for the introduction of Christianity in that kingdom. The son of Ælle (Ælla), king of Deira, Edwin was driven into exile by Æthelfrith, king of Bernicia, who gained control of Deira. In 616, Redwald, king of East Anglia, defeated Æthelfrith and established Edwin on the throne of Northumbria (comprising both Bernicia and Deira). According to the historian Bede, Edwin subsequently became overlord of all Britain except Kent and was the first English king with such wide authority.

About 619 (or perhaps 625), Edwin married the Kentish princess Æthelburh. A Christian, she brought to Northumbria the Italian missionary Paulinus, who in 627 converted Edwin and many of his people. On Oct. 12, 633, Edwin was defeated and killed by Cadwallon of Gwynedd and Penda of Mercia at Hatfield Chase.

J. CAMPBELL, *Oxford University*

EDWY, ed'wē (942?–959), king of the Anglo-Saxons. The little that is known of his reign suggests that he was too young and too ill-advised to rule successfully. Edwy was the elder son of King Edmund (q.v.) and became king in 955 in succession to Eadred. Shortly thereafter he drove Dunstan, then abbot of Glastonbury, into exile because (so it was later said) Dunstan had stopped him from misbehaving at the coronation feast. Nevertheless Edwy appears to have been generous to churches and monasteries.

In 957, Mercia and Northumbria rejected Edwy's authority and elected his brother Edgar as their king. There obviously was much political tension in the reign, but its causes and details are largely unknown. There is inconclusive evidence that Edwy separated from his wife Aelfgifu in 958 because they were too closely related. He died on Oct. 1, 959.

J. CAMPBELL, *Oxford University*

EECKHOUT, āk'hout, **Gerbrand van den** (1621–1674), Dutch painter, whose style reflects the influence of Rembrandt, his teacher. Eeckhout, like Rembrandt, took many of his subjects from the Bible.

He was born in Amsterdam, on Aug. 19, 1621, and studied with Rembrandt from 1635 to 1640. His paintings are characterized by the bright palette and rich colors that are typical of

American freshwater eel (*Anguilla rostrata*)

NEW JERSEY DIVISION OF FISH AND GAME

Rembrandt's work before 1640. Eeckhout was also influenced by the meticulous styles of the Dutch painters Gerard Terborch and Peter de Hooch, particularly in his genre paintings. Among his works are *Isaac Blessing Jacob* and *Sodom and Gomorrah* (both at the Metropolitan Museum, New York); *Resting Huntsman* and *Woman Taken in Adultery* (both at the Rijksmuseum, Amsterdam); *Anne Consecrating Her Son to the Lord* (Louvre, Paris); and *Four Chiefs of the Wine Guild* (National Gallery, London). Eeckhout died in Amsterdam, on Sept. 29, 1674.

EEDEN, ā'dən, **Frederik van** (1860–1932), Dutch writer, psychotherapist, and social reformer. He was born at Haarlem on April 3, 1860. After studying medicine at Amsterdam and in France, he settled at Bussum, where he attempted to establish a communal farming colony called Walden. In 1885 he cofounded the Dutch literary journal *De nieuwe gids*. Eeden became a Roman Catholic in 1922. He died on June 16, 1932, at Bussum.

Eeden's best-known work is his symbolic fairy tale *De kleine Johannes* (1887; Eng. tr., *Little Johannes*, 1895). He also wrote novels, poems, plays, and sociological treatises. Among his most important writings are *Van de koele meren des doods* (1900; Eng. tr., *The Deeps of Deliverance*, 1902), a novel reflecting his mystical ideas; and his 3-volume philosophical poem *Het lied van schijn en wezen* 1895–1922). His plays include *De heks van Haarlem* (1915).

EEL, any of a large order of elongate, cylindrical fish with long dorsal and anal fins. The American eel, *Anguilla rostrata*, is typical of the group.

There are 20 to 26 families of true eels consisting of several hundred very diverse species found in the order Anguilliformes, or Apodes. One family lives in fresh water, but most families are marine; some live in shallow tropical oceanic waters, while others occur in cold deep sea waters. The group includes, besides the freshwater eels (Anguillidae), the morays (Muraenidae), conger eels (Congridae), snake eels (Ophichthidae), snipe eels (Nemichthyidae), and many other marine groups.

The name "eel" has also been applied to many other fishes that are shaped like eels but are quite distinct fishes that are neither true eels nor related to one another. Among these are swamp eels (Synbranchidae), mastacembelid eels (Mastacembelidae), gymnotid eels (Gymnotidae), and electric eels (Electrophoridae). The name "eel" is also given to lampreys—primitive, round-mouthed, jawless vertebrates. The long cylindrical, eel-like shape of many of these fishes undoubtedly results from the fact that they are burrowing or crevice-dwelling fish.

All true eels share the same general body shape and lack pelvic fins. Many eels also lack scales, while in others the scales are so embedded that they appear to be absent. Eels vary in color. Deep-sea and freshwater eels are usually steel-gray or brown, while inshore tropical eels range from green or chocolate to pale colors. The inshore eels also often have variously colored marbling and spots of different sizes. Many eels change color during their life-span; for example, the freshwater eels of North America and Europe change color several times during their lives in relation to their reproductive cycle and migration.

Eels spawn in the sea and go through a characteristic development. The eggs hatch into transparent, strongly-compressed, ribbon-like, deep-bodied larvae known as *leptocephali*. These larvae drift about near the ocean surface and feed on minute organisms. When they grow to a sufficient length, they stop feeding. They then undergo metamorphosis and gradually change, becoming small replicas of adult eels.

The various marine eels live all their lives in the sea and do not carry out extensive migration. They feed on fishes, crabs, and other invertebrates. Some, like the snake eels and the conger eels, are most often found in shallow waters, while others, like the snubnosed eel (family Simenchelidae) and the snipe eels, prefer deeper waters. Some snubnosed eels and some snake eels are parasitic, boring into other fishes and feeding on them. See also CONGER EEL; MORAY.

Freshwater eels feed on living insects and other invertebrates as well as on fishes and frogs; they also scavenge for dead material. The American eel has an average weight of about 7 to 8 pounds (3.1–3.6 kg) but it may reach a maximum of 15 pounds (6.8 kg). Its average length is about 36 inches (90 cm), but it may measure 50 inches (1.2 meters).

Migration. The annual appearance of large numbers of small eels, or elvers, in the coastal streams of North America and Europe in May and

June and the movements toward the sea of the strangely colored adult freshwater eels in the fall have always aroused considerable interest. Freshwater eels are catadromous—that is, the adults move down to the sea to spawn and die, and the young eventually return to freshwater and live there most of their lives.

In the early 1900's, Johannes Schmidt, a Danish biologist, became intrigued with the migration of eels and tried to find the exact spawning site of those freshwater eels that spawned in the Atlantic. He noted the size of young eels captured at various localities in the Atlantic Ocean. Since he found that the smallest eels were always taken in the Sargasso Sea between Bermuda and the West Indies, he concluded that adult European and American freshwater eels go to the Sargasso Sea to spawn. He also concluded that ocean currents carry the developing young back to the mouth of freshwater streams in Europe and North America.

Schmidt believed that the adults from Europe and the adults from North America, thought to be two distinct species, spawned in separate locations in the Sargasso Sea area and that the young later moved to their respective coasts. It has been suggested more recently that these eels are not distinct species, but that the differences between the European and North American forms are the result of the differing development that the young undergo while reaching the two coasts, and the differences that develop as they mature in the freshwaters of the two continents. The North American eel takes about one year to travel up the coast and enter its freshwater habitat, while the European eel takes three years for its homeward trip.

Commercial Importance. Eels from freshwater have long been a substantial food item in Europe, but they are not so popular in North America, where most people find them too oily and rich. Smoked eels, on the other hand, are popular in North America also, even though they are still rich. Some saltwater eels, such as morays and conger eels, are eaten in various parts of the world, but to a far lesser extent than freshwater eels.

E. J. Crossman, *University of Toronto*

EELGRASS, any of several kinds of submerged aquatic plants. Freshwater eelgrass (*Vallisneria americana*), also known as tapegrass or wild celery, is found mostly in shallow water in lakes and slow-moving streams in the eastern United States. Ribbonlike leaves arise in clusters from nodes buried in the mud. Small, white female flowers occur on long thin stalks, while male flowers are inconspicuous at the leaf base. The leaves, fruit, and fleshy stems are important food sources for waterfowl.

The common saltwater plant *Zostera marina* is also called eelgrass or grass wrack. It is found along the east and west coasts of the United States on muddy intertidal flats. The plant has flattened stems with long grasslike leaves and male and female flowers on the same stalk. This species is also an important food for waterfowl, especially for the American brant.

Another saltwater plant—*Thalassia testudinum*—found in the shallow waters of Florida, the Gulf Coast, and the West Indies, is also commonly called eelgrass or turtle grass.

Charles W. Reimer
Academy of Natural Sciences of Philadelphia

EELPOUT, ēl'pout, any of a family of small marine fishes that inhabit cold littoral waters of the Northern Hemisphere. They occur from the very cold shallow waters down to a depth of one mile. A few species also are found off South Africa, but these are rarely caught. Eelpouts are of little economic importance.

Most eelpouts grow to a length of less than 18 inches (45 cm). The ocean pout (*Macrozoarces americanus*) may grow to a length of 3½ feet (105 cm) and a weight of 12 pounds (5.5 kg), but specimens over 2½ feet (75 cm) are rare. Eelpouts are moderately slender and eel-like. They usually have smooth, scaleless bodies; if they do have scales, the scales are only weakly developed. The anal fin and often the dorsal fin are joined to the caudal fin to form one long continuous fin, When pelvic fins are present, they are small, soft-rayed, and jugular (in the throat region). Eelpouts vary from blackish or reddish brown to yellowish or gray. Some species are mottled, and some are banded. An eelpout's underside is usually brownish or grayish and lighter than the upper surface.

A. W. AMBLER, FROM NATIONAL AUDUBON SOCIETY

OCEAN POUT (*Macrozoarces americanus*) is found in shallow Atlantic waters from Labrador to Delaware.

Some eelpouts, such as the European species *Zoarces viviparus*, are viviparous, and the female bears up to 40 live young. Other species, such as the ocean pout, are oviparous, depositing eggs in large gelatinous masses. One female can produce as many as 4,200 eggs, which are about ¼ inch (6–7 mm) each in diameter. The parents guard the eggs for 2–3 months until hatching.

Eelpouts belong to the family Zoarcidae of the order Percomorphi.

W. B. Scott, *University of Toronto*

EFATE, e-fä'tā, is the principal island of the New Hebrides, an island group and an Anglo-French condominium in the Southwest Pacific, east of Australia. Efate (French, *Vaté*), formerly called *Sandwich Island*, lies 155 miles (250 km) southeast of Espiritu Santo, the largest and westernmost island of the group. Vila, the capital of the New Hebrides, is an important port, on Mele Bay, on the southwest coast of Efate. Havannah, on the northwest coast, is the other chief commercial city and port. It was developed during World War II, when the New Hebrides was used as a military base by the Free French.

The northern part of Efate is hilly, and the island's plantations, which produce copra, coffee, and cacao, are located mostly in the southern lowlands. Sandalwood is also produced.

EFENDI, e-fen′dē, is a Turkish title of address meaning "lord" or "master." In early Ottoman usage, *efendi* (also *effendi*) was a title restricted to the sovereign and to the nobility. It was applied to the judicial classes in the mid-16th century and still later to all men of learning. By the mid-19th century it was the general form of polite address. By a law of 1934 it was replaced by *bey* in official usage.

JOHN R. WALSH, *University of Edinburgh*

EFFICIENCY is generally defined as the ratio of useful output to input. For example, a machine described as 80% efficient would have an available output of 80 units of energy or power for every 100 units of input. Typical efficiencies for some common types of engines are: electric motor, 80%–95%; steam engine, 50%–85%; internal-combustion engine at low speeds, 75%–90%, and at high speeds, 50%–70%; and ramjet, 90%. Conservation of energy implies that the efficiency is never greater than one (100%).

In thermodynamics, the concept of efficiency is refined, and a more stringent fundamental limit on the efficiency is derived. It is necessary first to define two abstract types of systems. The first is a *work source*—a system in which energy can be transformed and stored in mechanical, electrical, or chemical form. An example is a frictionless spring, which stores mechanical work in the form of elastic potential energy. The second type of system is a *heat reservoir* (such as an infinitely large body of water), which can absorb or deliver heat without changing its own temperature T.

A classic problem of thermodynamics involves two heat reservoirs at temperatures T_1 and T_2 ($T_1 > T_2$) and a single work source. The goal is to remove a certain amount of heat Q_1 from the hotter reservoir and to convert the largest possible fraction of this energy to work W, delivering the remainder ($Q_2 = Q_1 - W$) as heat to the cooler reservoir. The efficiency ε of this process is the useful output W divided by the input Q_1, or $\varepsilon = W/Q_1$. For a steam locomotive the steam boiler is the hot reservoir, the ambient atmosphere is the cold reservoir, and the work source is the system of pistons and valves that are activated by steam and that eventually turn the locomotive wheels.

A fundamental result of thermodynamics is that all reversible processes by which the above goal may be accomplished exhibit precisely the same efficiency; this universal efficiency is

$$\varepsilon_{\max} = (T_1 - T_2)/T_1.$$

A reversible process is one in which no energy is lost because of frictional or viscous dissipation. (Technically, it is a sequence of equilibrium states that can be traversed at constant entropy.) Since all real processes involve some dissipation, $\varepsilon_{\max}$ is the limiting efficiency that could in principle be approached, but never exceeded, by real machines. For a real system such as a locomotive, the overall efficiency should include a measure of the effectiveness with which the coal is utilized to heat the steam boiler, but this preliminary phase is omitted from the thermodynamic definition. Hence the thermodynamic efficiency is not always the economically significant factor.

Carnot Cycle. It is conventional to represent the concept of thermodynamic efficiency by a particular model of an engine, called a Carnot cycle, using an ideal gas. Here, the ideal gas extracts heat from the hot reservoir and delivers it to the cold reservoir by isothermal expansion and compression, respectively. It delivers work to the work source by isentropic expansion, and it finally returns to its initial state. This model can be calculated in detail, and it exhibits the efficiency $\varepsilon_{\max}$. See also THERMODYNAMICS.

HERBERT CALLEN, *University of Pennsylvania*

EFFIGY, ef′ə-jē, an image of a particular person or of a mythical or supernatural being. An effigy serves to fulfill symbolically the role of the person it represents. Thus effigies of persons who have incurred animosity are burned or hanged in public. In England an effigy of Guy Fawkes is paraded and burned on November 5 to commemorate the discovery of the Gunpowder Plot of 1610.

Effigy mounds in the shape of birds and animals were frequently used in American Indian burials about 2,000 years ago. Such mounds probably had religious significance. One of the most famous is the Great Serpent Mound, in southern Ohio, which extends for more than 1,000 feet (300 meters) and represents a snake with open jaws. See also MOUND BUILDERS AND MOUNDS.

Effigies appear in Etruscan tomb sculpture dating from the 6th or 5th century B. C. The main development of tomb carving, however, dates from the 11th century slab tombs of France and northern Europe, characterized by full-length, reclining figures in low relief. After the 13th century the relief became higher and the carving more detailed, and the architecturally sculptured sarcophagus replaced the slab tomb. The highest development of effigy sculpture was during the Italian Renaissance. Notable here were the tombs of the Medici, designed by Michelangelo (1521 and 1534), in the Church of San Lorenzo in Florence. The use of heavily sculptured, ornate effigies spread through Europe until the 18th century, when again they fell into disuse.

PRISCILLA C. WARD
American Museum of Natural History

EFFLORESCENCE, in chemistry, is the process by which certain crystalline compounds lose water on exposure to air. This occurs when the vapor pressure of the water of crystallization of the hydrated compound exceeds the partial pressure of the water vapor of the air. The loss of water results in the formation of a powder on the surface of the crystals. The most familiar example of efflorescence is found in common washing soda, $Na_2CO_3 \cdot 10H_2O$. The glassy crystals of the washing soda (sodium carbonate) become white and powdery in air.

Deliquescence is the opposite of efflorescence. In this phenomenon a compound absorbs moisture from the air and gradually becomes liquid.

EGADI ISLANDS, ȧ′gä-dē, an island group in the Mediterranean Sea, off the westernmost part of Sicily, that was the scene of the final naval battle between Rome and Carthage during the First Punic War (264–241 B.C.). The islands were known in ancient times as the Aegates. The three largest islands in the group are Favignana, Levanzo, and Marettimo (ancient Aegusa, Phorbantia, and Hiera).

The Egadi Islands are near the sites of Lilybaeum and Drepana (modern Marsala and Trapani), which were among the last Punic strongholds on the island of Sicily. Rome equipped and trained a fleet through loans from its wealthiest citizens and was in the midst of a siege of the Sicilian bases when Carthage hastily outfitted a fleet in an attempt to relieve Hamilcar Barca and his beleaguered forces. Despite inclement weather, the Roman commander, G. Lutatius Catulus, decided to fight when the Punic ships approached the Egadi Islands rather than allow the ships to relieve Hamilcar's forces. The Romans lost about a dozen ships, while 50 of the enemy vessels were sunk and 70 were captured.

The Egadi Islands are rocky, mountainous, and dotted with caves, some of which contain Paleolithic art treasures. The highest elevation, 2,244 feet (684 meters), is on the island of Marettimo. The islanders, living primarily in small coastal villages, make their living fishing for tuna and anchovy. Population: (1966) 6,071.

RICHARD E. MITCHELL, *University of Illinois*

EGAN, Patrick (1841–1919), Irish nationalist, who was prominent in Irish-American politics. He was born in Ballymahon, Longford, on Aug. 13, 1841. Egan became a successful Dublin businessman and treasurer of the National Land League before going to the United States in 1883. He settled in Nebraska, where he succeeded in a variety of business ventures.

From 1884 to 1886, Egan was president of the Irish National League of America, established to support Parnell's home rule efforts. In protest against President Cleveland's free-trade policy, which he considered pro-British, and in an effort to build an Irish-American power base in the Republican party, Egan supported the presidential ambitions of James G. Blaine in 1884 and of Benjamin Harrison in 1888. But his power manipulations in both the league and the party encouraged division in the faction-prone Irish-American nationalist movement. Harrison appointed Egan minister to Chile. Egan died in New York City on Sept. 30, 1919.

LAWRENCE J. MCCAFFREY
University of Maine

EGAÑA, ā-gä′nyä, **Juan** (1768–1836), Chilean lawyer, writer, and patriot. He was born in Lima, Peru, on Oct. 31, 1768. After receiving a law degree from San Marcos University in Lima, he went to Chile to establish a practice. There he participated in the independence movement of 1810 against Spain. In 1811 he drew up a declaration of rights that called for a federation of Spanish American states. He was also a cofounder of the first 1812 Chilean newspaper, *Aurora*.

After Chile won its independence in 1818, Egaña helped establish the National Institute of Education. After the fall of the Bernardo O'Higgins government in 1923, Egaña presided over the constituent congress and drafted the national constitution of 1823. This short-lived document created a "supreme director" for the country and gave him and the chamber of deputies unusual power over private business and morals. Egaña maintained an active writing career until his death in Santiago on April 29, 1836.

HELEN M. BAILEY
East Los Angeles College

EGBERT, eg′bərt (died 839), king of the West Saxons, whose reign marked an important stage in the rise of Wessex to dominance in England. Egbert was a member of a remote branch of the royal family of Wessex, where his first attempt to make himself king failed. He was driven into exile in Gaul about 789 and gained the throne of Wessex only in 802.

In 825, Egbert defeated the Mercians at Ellendun (Wroughton, Wiltshire), and in 829 he made himself king of Mercia. For a year or so he had authority, either directly or as overlord, over all England. Mercia quickly regained its independence, but Wessex retained the lands in the southeast (Essex, Kent, Surrey, and Sussex) that had been seized from Mercian control in 825. These gains, which brought with them control over the see of Canterbury, were crucial for the future greatness of Wessex. Egbert also defeated the Britons of Cornwall in 815 and an invading army of Britons and Danes in 838.

J. CAMPBELL, *Oxford University*

EGER, e′gər, is a city in northern Hungary, 64 miles (103 km) northeast of Budapest. It lies on the Eger River, a right bank tributary of the Tisza, and on the southern margin of the mountains of northern Hungary. Eger is a manufacturing town with mechanical engineering and food and tobacco processing industries. It is also the center of an important wine producing region and is the capital of Heves county.

The city, set amid the rolling foothills between the Matra and the Bükk massifs, is one of the most attractive in Hungary. It was an important medieval town and the seat of a bishop. It served as a frontier fortress during the Turkish wars, and was held by the Turks from 1596 to 1687. It failed to grow as rapidly as other towns during the 19th century because the railway from Budapest to northeastern Hungary was built across the flatter land south of the city.

Eger has remained an old city with many monuments to its historic past. It has been called the "Hungarian Rome" because of the number of religious foundations there. Population: (1965) 42,716.

NORMAN J. G. POUNDS, *Indiana University*

EGG, Augustus Leopold (1816–1863), English painter, whose subjects are primarily historical anecdotes and scenes from literary classics. He was born in London on May 2, 1816, and studied at the Royal Academy, where he exhibited for the first time in 1838. His works include *Queen Elizabeth Discovers She Is No Longer Young* (1848), *Peter the Great Sees Catherine for the First Time* (1850), *The Life and Death of Buckingham* (1855), a triptych on the *Fate of a Faithless Wife* (1858), and scenes from works by Shakespeare, Thackeray, and Sir Walter Scott.

Egg was a close friend of Charles Dickens and Wilkie Collins, with whom he visited Italy in 1853. He was also a noted amateur actor. Egg died in Algiers on March 26, 1863.

EGG, or *ovum*, the female reproductive cell, germ cell, or gamete from which the new individual arises. In common usage, the term refers most specifically to the bird egg; more generally, it includes the eggs of reptiles, amphibians, fish, and insects that develop outside the mother's body. Wider connotations embrace female germ cells throughout the animal and plant kingdoms, except among the simplest (unicellular) organisms, in many of which male and female gametes are alike in size and form. In addition, the word "egg" is used to signify the internally developing embryo (as in humans and other mammals) up to the stage of the blastocyst and sometimes even beyond.

KINDS OF EGGS

Animals are often distinguished as oviparous, viviparous, or ovoviviparous. In *oviparous* animals, such as many frogs and fishes, the egg undergoes both fertilization and development after it is laid. In *viviparous* animals, which include all mammals except the egg-laying platypus and echidna, the egg is fertilized and rapidly develops into an embryo within the mother's body; the embryo is then nurtured within the mother's body and is born as a living young. In *ovoviviparous* animals, a less well-defined group, the egg is fertilized within the mother's body and is either laid containing an embryo, as in birds and many insects, or hatches just before laying, as in some snakes; the young hatched internally may receive some nourishment from the mother before birth, as in some salamanders.

Bird Eggs. The largest bird eggs known are those of the extinct *Aepyornis*: these eggs measured 13 inches (33 cm) long by 9½ inches (24 cm) wide and could hold 2 gallons (7.5 liters) of liquid. Of the living birds, the largest eggs are those laid by the ostrich: these are 7×5 inches (18×13 cm) in size, 3 pounds (1.3 kg) in weight, and can hold 3 quarts (2.8 liters) of liquid. The smallest eggs, those of the hummingbird, are the size of a pea and weigh about $\frac{1}{30}$ ounce (1 gram).

Domestication has increased the number of eggs laid; hens and ducks occasionally approach 365 eggs in one year. Highly productive hens can lay about 300 pounds (135 kg) of eggs in a lifetime, which is equivalent to about 70 times their body weight. High production also depends on the practice of removing eggs from the nest each day. Such regular removal increases by about ten times the numbers of eggs laid by pheasants, mallard ducks, and canaries.

Eggs of Other Vertebrates. Eggs of sizes between hen and ostrich eggs are produced by some other vertebrates, notably the bigger reptiles and sharks. In numbers of eggs, some reptiles equal or exceed the hen: thus, tortoises and turtles may lay as many as 200 to 300 eggs in a single clutch; some species, in addition, lay several times a year. Much larger numbers are usually encountered in animals producing small eggs. The bullfrog sheds 10,000 to 25,000 eggs in one season, and some fishes produce prodigious numbers: 28 million in the ocean sunfish, 5 to 20 million in the freshwater eel. Sunfish and eels broadcast their eggs on the surface waters of the ocean; by contrast, fishes that provide parental care—nest building (sticklebacks), mouth incubation (some catfish), or abdominal brood pouches (seahorses, pipefishes)—produce far fewer eggs. The eggs of ocean sunfish and eels are buoyant and float at the surface: they are termed *pelagic*. *Demersal* eggs, such as those of most river fishes, rapidly sink to the bottom.

EGGS AS FOOD

Hen eggs are a major article of diet in most developed countries; average consumption varies between 1 and 7 eggs per capita per week, the highest rates being in Canada and the United States. Also eaten, though in much lower numbers, are the eggs of duck, goose, guinea fowl, and turkey. See also POULTRY—*4. Industry*.

In some areas, depending on fashion, convenience, or abundance, eggs of many wild species are esteemed. Similarly, the eggs of creatures other than birds are used as food: these include those of crocodiles, turtles, fish—notably sturgeon (caviar), Chinook salmon, cod, shad, and herring—and sea urchins.

Composition. Hen eggs consist of about 66% water and 34% solids, the solids being ⅔ organic matter and ⅓ inorganic matter. The main organic components are proteins (12%), lipids (10.5%), and carbohydrates (1%).

The yolk is much more complex than the albumen, and its organic matter consists of ⅔ lipids, ⅓ proteins, and a trace of carbohydrates; it represents the main food store for the developing chick. The albumen—which is 88% water and 10.6% proteins plus small amounts of carbohydrates, minerals, and pigments—is chiefly important as a source of water (and of water-soluble vitamins).

Nutritive Value. The nutritive value of adequately cooked hen eggs is high and can meet most needs for maintenance, growth, reproduction, and lactation in man. As a sole source of nutrient, raw egg is unsatisfactory for most animals, owing to the low digestibility of raw albumen and the harmful effect of an albumen component called avidin. Avidin, which is destroyed by cooking, combines with and inactivates biotin, a growth factor of the vitamin B complex, resulting in skin sores, muscle pain, loss of appetite, and other symptoms.

The contents of eggs from well-nourished hens are rich in fat-soluble and water-soluble vitamins (except ascorbic acid, or vitamin C) and in essential minerals (except calcium); they have proteins of high biological value and provide the essential fatty acids.

The energy value of the contents of hen eggs is about 160 calories per 100 grams (3.5 ounces)—there are 75 to 80 calories per standard egg. Duck eggs, because of their higher fat content, yield about 200 calories per 100 grams.

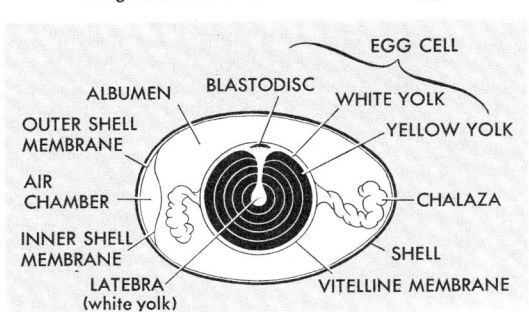

Diagrammatic section of a chicken egg.

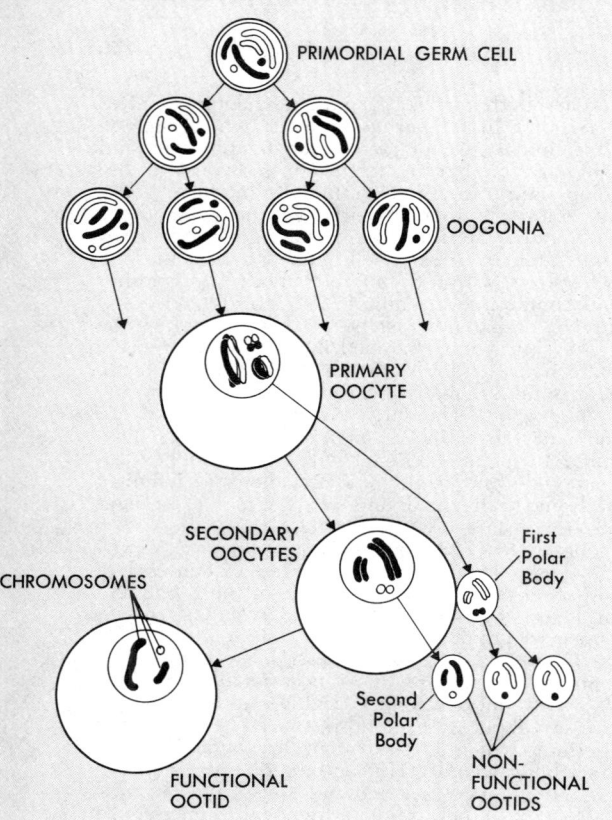

OOGENESIS in mammals. Primordial germ cells, formed in the embryo, multiply at sexual maturity to become oogonia. Oogonia grow into primary oocytes. Two meiotic (or chromosome-reducing) divisions then follow. Primary oocytes become secondary oocytes; secondary oocytes become ootids, with only one of each four possible able to function as a mature egg.

The eggs of the monotremes—the platypus and the echidna—are the largest mammalian eggs, averaging ½ to 1 inch (13-25 mm) in diameter. All other mammals (like most marine invertebrates) have minute eggs, the diameters ranging from 50 to 250 microns (about two thousandths to ten thousandths of an inch). The human egg measures about 100 microns (four thousandths of an inch). A single egg is usually released from the human ovary in each menstrual cycle; in the lifetime of an average woman about 480 eggs become available for fertilization. The ovaries at birth contain between them several hundred thousand eggs, but most degenerate in the ovary.

EGG STRUCTURE

The egg is a single cell. It is generally larger than somatic (body) cells, but its essential nature is the same: a mass of cytoplasm containing a nucleus and organelles—such as mitochondria, Golgi bodies, plastids (in plants), and ribosomes—surrounded by a delicate plasma membrane. In addition, the egg usually carries nutrient stores (deutoplasm, or yolk) for the developing embryo.

Eggs with much yolk (birds, reptiles) are called *megalecithal*; those with moderate amounts of yolk (amphibians), *medialecithal*; and those with little yolk (most marine invertebrates, higher mammals), *miolecithal*. In birds and reptile eggs, the yolk is so large that the living cytoplasmic component, from which the embryo will develop, appears as a small flat "blastodisc" on the surface of the yolk. Yolk in miolecithal and medialecithal eggs takes different forms: droplets, granules, or crystalloids of protein, lipid, starch, or glycogen, evenly dispersed or grouped in various ways, the form and pattern being distinctive for the species.

Egg Coatings. Eggs are commonly surrounded by investments, or coatings, of different kinds; those of higher mammals have a tough transparent coat of mucoprotein; those of many amphibians and marine invertebrates have a thick layer of jelly. Elasmobranchs (cartilaginous fishes such as sharks) produce eggs in flexible tubes ("candles") or tough horny cases. Snake eggs have leathery or membranous shells, while in alligators and crocodiles the eggs are hard-shelled.

Construction of the Bird Egg. As formed in the ovary, the bird egg has a circular blastodisc (embryo-forming portion), whose nucleus (germinal vesicle) contains the chromosomes, and a yolk body made up of concentric layers of yellow and white yolk, with a pool of white yolk (the latebra) in the middle. After leaving the ovary, the egg passes into the albumen-secreting region of the oviduct and becomes covered with the albumen layers. The albumen is composed of both viscous liquid and gelatinous semisolid. Two ropelike strands (chalazae) consisting of semisolid albumen extend through the liquid albumen at each end of the egg; they become twisted with rotation of the egg and tend to keep the yolk at the center.

As the yolk moves down the oviduct and enters the isthmus, it receives close-fitting egg and shell membranes. Initially, the membranes are in apposition with each other, but soon after laying, a space called the air cell appears between them, usually at the blunt end of the egg.

The shell is added in the uterus, the last part of the oviduct; it is formed by deposition of calcium salts on the matrix provided by the shell membrane, and its numerous microscopic pores allow gaseous exchange between the egg and the outside. A very thin layer of protein, the cuticle, is applied to the shell just before the egg leaves the uterus.

OOGENESIS AND MEIOSIS

Oogenesis is the process of formation and development of the mature egg, or female gamete. The female gamete is typically a *haploid* cell, that is, it has half the diploid, or characteristic, number of chromosomes for the species.

Reduction to the haploid number takes place in meiosis, a special type of cell division. In most organisms, meiosis consists of two successive divisions and may occur in gamete maturation (as in most metazoans, multicelled animals), immediately after fertilization (as in some algae), or in the division of the spore parent cell (as in other algae, ferns, conifers, and flowering plants).

In simpler organisms, the derivation of the egg appears to be directly from somatic (body) cells; thus, in the alga *Ulva* gametes of both sexes are formed from seemingly any cell of the thallus (plant body), and in sponges, ameboid interstitial cells are transformed into gametes.

Oogenesis in Plants. In most plants, including many algae, there are two generations—the sporophyte and gametophyte—in each reproductive cycle. The sporophyte generation produces spores

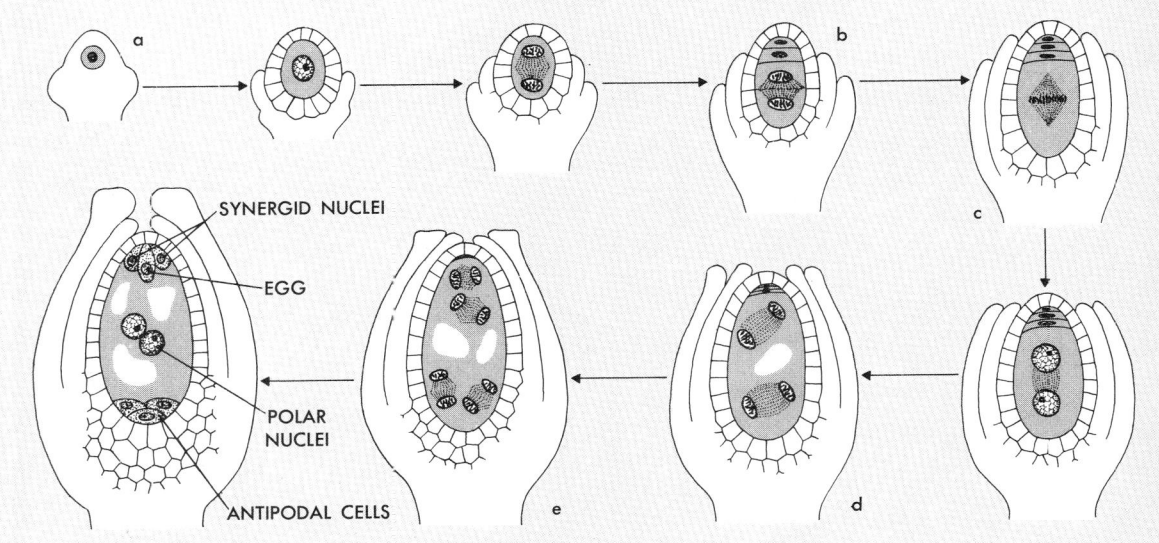

EGG CELL DEVELOPMENT in flowering plants. The megaspore mother cell (a) undergoes meiotic (chromosome-reducing) division to produce four megaspores (b), three of which degenerate. The nucleus of the fourth megaspore, or megagametophyte, divides three times (c, d, e), to produce eight nuclei, one of which is the egg.

by meiotic division of the spore parent cell; these spores then germinate and grow into the haploid gametophyte generation. The gametophyte generation, by mitotic, or ordinary, cell division, produces the gametes.

Many lower plants, like ferns, show the two generations as clearly separate and different forms, but in the higher plants, the female plant (megagametophyte) of the gametophyte generation does not have a separate existence.

In gymnosperms (conifers and others), the sporophyte generation (trees) produces cones containing ovules ("young seeds"). A special cell, the megaspore mother cell, within each ovule undergoes meiosis, dividing into four megaspores. Three of the four megaspores regress, but the fourth enlarges to form the megagametophyte, in which several archegonia (female sex organs) differentiate. Each archegonium contains a megagamete, or egg cell.

In angiosperms (flowering plants), the megaspore mother cell also undergoes meiosis to produce most commonly four megaspores, with three degenerating and the fourth forming the oval-shaped megagametophyte. The nucleus of this single-celled haploid megagametophyte undergoes three mitotic divisions by which eight nuclei are derived, four at each end of the cell. One nucleus from each group moves to the center of the megagametophyte cell, now also called the embryo sac; these two nuclei are known as polar nuclei and are involved in the formation of the endosperm, or food store, of the seed. Cell walls then form about each remaining nucleus in the two groups, producing at one end three antipodal cells and at the other two synergids and the egg cell. The synergids are usually involved in the transmission of the pollen (male) nuclei during fertilization; the function of the antipodal cells is uncertain.

Oogenesis in Higher Animals. In most metazoans, special ovarian cells, called oogonia, divide mitotically many times to produce a host of cells known as oocytes. The oocytes, nourished by surrounding cells (nurse cells, follicle cells), grow enormously in size, partly by increase in the amount of cytoplasm and partly by accumulation of yolk. When growth is complete, the oocyte undergoes maturation, which involves meiosis, or divisions that reduce the number of chromosomes.

In the first meiotic division, homologous ("matching") chromosomes of the primary oocyte (an oocyte derived from the oogonia) exchange parts and separate into two groups. In most metazoans, one of these groups is extruded from the oocyte in a small mass of cytoplasm called the first polar body. After extrusion of the first polar body, the oocyte is termed a secondary oocyte.

In the second meiotic division, the two halves (chromatids) of each chromosome in the secondary oocyte are separated to form two groups, one of which passes out of the oocyte in the second polar body. In the process, the secondary oocyte becomes an ootid and the chromatids develop into chromosomes.

Generally, the polar bodies degenerate and play no part in embryonic development. In insects and some other animals, polar groups of chromosomes, rather than polar bodies, are formed, but these too regress and disappear.

FERTILIZATION AND CLEAVAGE

The essential step in fertilization is the union of two nuclei, or chromosome groups; union reestablishes diploidy (characteristic number of chromosomes), generally entails recombination of genes from unrelated sources, and commonly provides a mechanism of sex determination. In angiosperms, uniquely, normal fertilization involves two male nuclei; one unites with the egg-cell nucleus to form the zygote ("embryo") nucleus, and the other with the polar nuclei to form the triploid nucleus of the endosperm (the food store in the seed).

After fertilization, in most organisms, the egg undergoes a series of cell divisions known as cleavage. Typically, cleavage involves subdivision without increase in total mass. As it proceeds, it is increasingly accompanied by differentiation, so that the embryo gradually takes shape and cells come to differ in structure and function. The cleavage phase ends when growth and differentiation supersede.

Cleavage patterns differ and are in part determined by an innate polarity (differentiation of major regions) and in part by the presence of yolk. Miolecithal eggs with homogeneously distributed yolk show *holoblastic* cleavage, which produces separate cells of equal size; megalecithal eggs undergo *meroblastic* cleavage, in which the initial subdivision of the cytoplasm is incomplete and the cells are not fully separated. Medialecithal eggs, and miolecithal eggs with uneven yolk distribution, cleave holoblastically, but cells vary in size, the larger ones containing the bulk of the yolk.

PARTHENOGENESIS AND APOMIXIS

Parthenogenesis usually denotes development of a plant or animal from an egg without fertilization. Apomixis implies development without union of male and female nuclei (amphimixis = fertilization). The two terms are essentially synonymous by these definitions; some authorities, however, would include in apomixis vegetative reproduction, numerous forms of which occur in plants but only a few in animals.

Parthenogenesis may be natural or artificial. The natural variety includes:

(1) Cyclic parthenogenesis (aphid *Tetraneura*). Females lay eggs that develop without fertilization into young that are all females. This process continues for a number of successive generations from spring to fall. At the approach of winter, however, both males and females are produced and eggs are fertilized. After overwintering, these eggs hatch in the spring to produce only females.

(2) Haploid parthenogenesis (rotifers, many insects). In bees, fertilized eggs develop into diploid females (queens, workers), while unfertilized eggs form haploid males (drones).

(3) Paedogenesis (gall midge *Miastor*). Under certain environmental conditions, precocious development takes place in the ovaries of the larvae, and a new generation of larvae is formed from the unfertilized eggs. As these larvae grow, they consume the mother larvae and in due course themselves fall victim to the next generation of larvae developing within them.

(4) Pseudogamy (nematode worm *Rhabditis*). Copulation occurs, followed by sperm entry into the egg, but fertilization is not completed. There is no union of nuclei, the sperm nucleus degenerates, and development proceeds with only the egg nucleus.

Artificial parthenogenesis concerns development initiated by experimental means, such as pricking the egg with a needle or treating it with acid solutions. Mature sea urchins and frogs can sometimes be obtained in this way, but development with most animals is very limited.

C. R. AUSTIN, *Cambridge University*

Bibliography

Austin, Colin R., *The Mammalian Egg* (Oxford 1961).
Blandau, R. J., "Biology of Eggs and Implantation," *Sex and Internal Secretions*, ed. by W. C. Young (Baltimore 1961).
Costello, Donald P., and others, *Methods for Obtaining and Handling Marine Eggs and Embryos* (Woods Hole, Mass., 1957).
Goin, Coleman J., and Goin, O. B., *Introduction to Herpetology* (San Francisco and London 1962).
Lagler, K. F., Bardach, J. E., and Miller, R. R., *Ichthyology* (New York 1962).
McLean, Robert C., and Ivimey-Cook, Walter R., *Textbook of Theoretical Botany*, 2 vols. (London and New York 1951-1956).
Pincus, Gregory, *The Eggs of Mammals* (New York 1936).
Romanoff, Alexis L., and Romanoff, Anastasia J., *The Avian Egg* (New York 1949).
White, Michael J. D., *Animal Cytology and Evolution* (London 1954).
Wilde, J. de, "Reproduction," *The Physiology of Insecta*, ed. by M. Rockstein (New York and London 1964).

EGGLESTON, Edward (1837–1902), American novelist and historical writer, whose stories of the Middle West were early examples of realism in American literature. He was born in Vevay, Ind., on Dec. 10, 1837. He toured the West as a Bible agent and Methodist minister until 1866, when he became associate editor of the juvenile magazine *Little Corporal* in Evanston, Ill. In 1870 he joined the staff of the *Independent* in New York City, and in 1871 he became editor of *Hearth and Home*, the magazine that serialized his first adult novel, *The Hoosier Schoolmaster* (1871). After serving from 1874 to 1879 as pastor of the Church of the Christian Endeavor in Brooklyn, N. Y., he devoted himself entirely to writing.

Eggleston's works include *Roxy* (1878); *The Hoosier Schoolboy* (1883); *Duffels* (1893), a volume of short stories; and several books on American cultural history. He died at Lake George, N. Y., on Sept. 2, 1902.

EGGPLANT is the name of a widely cultivated herb (*Solanum melongena*), of the potato or nightshade family (Solanaceae) and of its large, glossy, usually dark purple fruit. The eggplant fruit, botanically a berry, grows to about 1 foot (30 cm) in length. On an equal-weight basis, its nutritional value (protein, calories, minerals) is similar to that of tomatoes, except that it is much poorer in vitamin A and lower in ascorbic acid.

The eggplant, native to India, has been cultivated for about 4,000 years. It is one of the most important vegetable crops of China, Japan, and India. It is a staple vegetable in the Mediterranean and Balkan areas. In the United States,

Eggplant

BURPEE SEEDS

however, the eggplant is the least important of the 22 principal vegetable crops.

Well-drained, fertile, loamy soil rich in organic matter is ideal for growing eggplant, which requires high temperatures for its cultivation. The fruits are edible from the time they are about one-third grown, and better yields will be obtained if the fruits are harvested before they reach maximum size.

LAWRENCE ERBE
University of Southwestern Louisiana

EGILL SKALLAGRÍMSSON, ā'yid-əl skäd'əl-ägrēms-sôn (c. 910–c. 990), was an Icelandic Viking warrior and skaldic poet, whose life story and poetry are the basis of *Egill's Saga*, a medieval Icelandic narrative of uncertain origin.

Egill was born into a noble Norwegian family that had settled in Iceland after trying in vain to resist King Harold Fairhair's unification of Norway. About 948, Egill was captured at what is now York, England, by King Harold's son, Eric Bloodaxe. To regain his freedom, he recited the lengthy poem *Höfuðlausn*, which he composed overnight, ostensibly in praise of Eric. The poem, written in short, rhyming lines, was the first of its kind in Icelandic or Norse literature, but it reveals less of Egill's poetic genius and technical skill than his later unrhymed, metrical poems, *Sonatorrek* (about 961), a lament for his two dead sons, and *Arinbjarnarkviða* (962), a long poem celebrating his best friend, the Viking Arinbjörn.

EGINHARD. See EINHARD.

EGK, ek, **Werner** (1901–1983), German composer, whose musical style employs modern rhythmic and harmonic techniques and whose melodies convey the flavor of German folk songs. Werner Mayer (he adopted the name Egk much later) was born in Auchsesheim, near Augsburg, on May 17, 1901. He studied music in Munich, where he became musical director of a puppet theater in 1920. After living in Italy in 1925–1928, he returned to Germany to follow a career as conductor and composer. He conducted the Berlin Staatsoper in 1936–1940 and directed the Hochschule für Musik in West Berlin in 1950–1953. He died in Inning, West Germany, on July 10, 1983.

As a composer, he achieved his greatest success with such works as the operas *Die Zaubergeige* (1935), *Peer Gynt* (1938), and *Der Revisor* (1957), and the ballets *Joan von Zarissa* (1939) and *Abraxas* (1948). His choral music and orchestral works include *Französische Suite* (1949) and *Variations on a Caribbean Theme* (1960).

EGLANTINE, eg'lən-tīn, is a type of rose valued for its fragrant foliage. The eglantine, also commonly called "sweetbriar," is native to Europe but has become naturalized in North America, where it grows wild in rocky pastures.

The eglantine, which is known botanically as *Rosa eglanteria*, develops into a bush about 6 feet (1.8 meters) tall. Its flowers are pink and about 1½ inches (38 mm) across. They ripen into red fruits about ½ inch (13 mm) in diameter. The eglantine's leaves usually consist of 7 small, oval, toothed leaflets. On the underside of each leaflet is a dense, hairy, glandular coating. When the leaflets are rubbed, the glands release a sweet-smelling substance. Another feature of the eglantine is the presence of strong hooked thorns mainly below the stipules at the base of each petiole, or leaf stem.
SIDNEY C. BAUSOR, *California State College, Pa.*

EGLEVSKY, eg-lev'skē, **André** (1917–1977), Russian-American dancer, one of the finest classical ballet dancers of the 20th century. Despite his square shoulders and muscular physique, Eglevsky became famous for the catlike ease of his leaps and for pirouettes that begin at peak speed and gradually fade into stillness.

Eglevsky was born in Moscow, on Dec. 21, 1917. His family fled to Nice, France, during the Russian Revolution, and it was there and in Paris that he received most of his training. When he was 15, he made his debut as soloist with Colonel de Basil's ballet company, but he soon moved to the Ballet Russe de Monte Carlo, where he attracted international attention. In the following years he appeared with such companies as the various Ballets Russes, the American Ballet Theatre, and the Marquis de Cuevas' International Ballet. In 1950, Eglevsky, who had become a citizen of the United States in 1939, joined the New York City Ballet as principal male dancer, partnering, among others, ballerina Maria Tallchief. In 1958 he started his own school and ballet company. He died in Elmira, N. Y., on Dec. 4, 1977.
DORIS HERING, *"Dance Magazine"*

EGMONT, eKH'mônt, **Count of** (1522–1568), Netherlands political leader. He was born on Nov. 18, 1522, in La Hamaide, Hainaut. Lamoral (Lamoraal), as he was named, was a member of an ancient noble house, whose title of Egmont he later inherited. He performed military and government service for the Habsburg emperor Charles V and achieved military fame for his role in the victories over the French at St. Quentin (1557) and Gravelines (1558) under Philip II of Spain. In 1559 he was appointed governor of Flanders and Artois and a member of the Council of State of the Netherlands.

After 1559, Philip II's attempts to strengthen Spanish control of the Netherlands aroused increasing resentment among the native nobility. Egmont, together with William of Orange and the Count of Hoorn (Horn), took the lead in a League of Grandees, demanding reforms that would make the Council of State a real governing body. They also called for cancellation of Philip's plan to reorganize the bishoprics (which would further diminish the nobility's influence). The League succeeded in removing Cardinal Granvelle, Philip's adviser, from the Council of State (1564), but Egmont's mission to Spain in 1565 failed to produce the desired reforms.

Philip II's rigorous persecution of the Protestants in the Netherlands had also become a political issue. Although none of the noblemen of the League were Protestants, they demanded toleration. Even so, they were religiously conservative, a fact that became clear when the more radical lesser nobility rebelled in 1566, secretly encouraged by William of Orange. Egmont, himself a Roman Catholic, tried to quell the rebellion in his provinces.

The revolt was crushed in 1567 and William fled the country. But Egmont, despite the fact that his name had been implicated in the rebellion, remained, and he was arrested by the new governor, the Duke of Alva, on Sept. 9, 1567. During his trial, his privileges as a noblemen were openly violated, and his execution (in Brussels, on June 5, 1568) was judicial murder.

The historical Egmont bore no resemblance to the hero of Goethe's tragedy of the same name. The real Egmont was a typical example of the 16th century nobleman, who was torn between the ideal of feudal independence and loyalty to his king.

JACOB W. SMIT, *Columbia University*

EGMONT, eg′mont, is a prose play by Johann Wolfgang von Goethe (q.v.), written from 1775 to 1787. It was published in 1788 and was first performed in Weimar in 1791. In 1810, Beethoven wrote an overture and incidental music for it.

Egmont, which spanned both Goethe's "storm and stress" and classical periods, is primarily based upon Famianus Strado's account in *De bello Belgico* (1651) of the execution of Lamoral, Count of Egmont, and of Philip of Montmorency, Count of Hoorn. The executions, in the Brussels marketplace on June 5, 1568, led to the uprising of the Netherlands against Spanish rule.

Goethe eliminated the figure of Hoorn from the play and changed the historical Egmont into a dashing young cavalier, who leads a charmed existence as a man of the people and is beloved of Klärchen, a sweet girl of the lower classes. Goethe's hero blindly trusts to fate in his role as defender of his people against Spanish tyranny, and is not even deterred by the arrival of a stern new governor of the Netherlands, the Duke of Alba. Egmont is at last imprisoned by Alba and, shortly before his execution, has a vision of himself as liberator of his country. Although this operatic ending is not fully convincing, *Egmont* remains one of Goethe's most highly unified and skillfully executed dramatic works.

ERNST ROSE
Author of "A History of German Literature"

EGMONT, Mount, eg′mont, an extinct volcano on North Island, New Zealand. Noted for its beauty, Mt. Egmont, named Taranaki by the Maoris, has been called the "Fujiyama of New Zealand." Its symmetrical cone rises to a snow-capped peak of 8,260 feet (2,517 meters).

Lush pastures, forming one of the most productive farming areas of the world, are located on the lower slopes of the volcano. A forest belt rises above the pasture region.

EGO, ē′gō, in classical psychoanalysis, that portion of the personality that mediates between an individual's biological drives and the obstacles to those drives that are presented either directly or indirectly by the environment. Of the other uses of the term, the most important is that current in analytical psychology, which defines the ego (from Latin *ego*, meaning "I") as the individual's awareness of his continuing selfhood. The functions of the ego, which has both conscious and preconscious components, comprise sensory perception, thinking (including distinguishing between objective and subjective reality), memory, and voluntary motor control.

The concept of the ego was first developed by Sigmund Freud around 1895, but it was clarified in its present form only with the publication of Freud's *The Ego and the Id* in 1923. Freud held that personality consists of three portions: the *id*, the *ego*, and the *superego*. The id, which is the reservoir of biological impulses, constitutes the entire personality of the infant at birth. Its principle of operation, to guard the person from painful tension, is termed the *pleasure principle*. Inevitable frustrations of the id, together with what the child learns from his encounters with external reality, generate the ego, which is essentially a mechanism to minimize frustrations of the biological drives in the long run. It operates according to the *reality principle*. Freud held that the ego had no energy of its own, its dynamics originating in the id. The superego comprises the *conscience*, a partly conscious system of introjected moral inhibitions, and the *ego-ideal*, the source of the individual's standards for his own behavior. Like external reality, from which it derives, the superego often presents obstacles to the satisfaction of biological drives. In general, the function of the ego is to find ways in which such drives can be satisfied within the limitations imposed by the conscience, so as to relieve physical tensions without incurring guilt.

The ego adopts various means to perform its task. Most commonly, the discharge of an impulse originating in the id is simply postponed until the situation is suited to it. In many cases, however, such an impulse can never be discharged directly, and the ego must utilize one of many defense mechanisms in order to protect itself from conflict. It may succeed in transforming the impulse so that it may be expressed without danger to the individual; otherwise, the impulse may be repressed, in which case its psychic energy accumulates as tension within the personality. When such tensions become excessive, because of deficiency in the ego or external circumstances, neurosis or psychosis result.

Later psychologists have altered or abandoned Freud's conception of the ego. Some neo-Freudians consider the ego in some sense autonomous and maintain that it functions sometimes to satisfy its own needs, not exclusively those of the id. Among non-Freudian conceptions of the ego, that of the social psychologists Muzafer Sherif and Hadley Cantril defines it as a set of attitudes such as "what I think of myself, what I value, what is mine and what I identify with." Gordon Allport, a psychologist of personality, distinguished the ego as a process from the ego as an object of knowledge, anticipating the distinction by a later writer (Isidor Chein) between the ego and the self. See also PSYCHOANALYSIS.

AUSTIN E. GRIGG, *University of Richmond*

EGOISM, ē′gō-iz-əm, is a theory of human nature that may be stated in psychological terms (each person seeks to promote his own good) or in ethical terms (each person ought to promote his own good). Egoism stands in contrast to *altruism* (q.v.), which also has a psychological form (each person seeks to promote the good of others) and an ethical form (each person ought to promote the good of others). Egoism should be distinguished from *egotism*, which means vanity.

Historical Background. Egoism is compatible with a variety of views about what is good. Historically, however, it has been closely associated with various forms of hedonism, which defines the good as pleasure in some form. The roots of egoism lie, therefore, in Greek thought, particularly in the individualism, subjectivism, and relativism of Sophist thought and in the hedonist doctrines of the Cyrenaics and Epicureans. In classical and in Christian thought, no major philosophical conflict was seen between egoism and altruism, because no sharp distinctions were drawn between the good for an individual, the good of the natural and social orders, and, simply, the good. See also CYRENAICS; EPICUREANISM; SOPHISTS.

Hobbes. It was Thomas Hobbes (q. v.), in the 17th century, who first raised the problem of a conflict between egoism and altruism. He rejected the Platonic, Aristotelian, and Christian idea that the good for each individual coincides with the pursuit of the highest good, and claimed that all human action is motivated by the will to self-preservation and to power over others. According to Hobbes, even actions that seem altruistic are always motivated by some underlying egoism. Hobbes' view of human nature was accepted by Bernard Mandeville, La Rochefoucauld, the French Encyclopedists, and by many 20th century psychologists, particularly Freud and his followers.

Responses to Hobbes. Attempts to answer Hobbes gave rise to the "selfishness controversy" beginning in the 18th century. Replies to Hobbes followed three main lines. One, initiated by Richard Cumberland (q.v.), accepted psychological egoism but said that ethical altruism is one of the chief means by which man advances his own good, a view developed later by the utilitarians Jeremy Bentham and John Stuart Mill. A second response to Hobbes' egoism (also initiated by Cumberland, and defended by Thomas Reid and Richard Price, among others), said that ethical altruism can be known by reason to be as natural to man as psychological egoism. The third response to Hobbes, by Shaftesbury, Francis Hutcheson, David Hume, Adam Smith, and others said that since psychological altruism is true and psychological egoism is false, ethical altruism is a better theory than ethical egoism.

Modern Attitudes. Henry Sidgwick, writing in the late 19th century, was the first ethical analyst in the contemporary sense. He argued that there is no logical transition from psychological facts alone to normative ethical conclusions. Both ethical altruism and ethical egoism rest upon intuition, are logically independent, and are irreconcilable without some appeal to theology.

The development of analytical attitudes and techniques has led in two different but related directions. Some contemporary writers argue that when the concepts are clarified, it can be shown that ethical egoism is faulty on logical or ethical grounds. Others, however, tend to see the history of egoism as a history of confusion, and they have set out to clarify the issues by locating the problem in the nature of language.

BERNARD PEACH
Duke University

Bibliography

Frankena, William K., *Ethics* (Englewood Cliffs, N. J., 1963).
Hall, Everett W., *Modern Science and Human Values* (New York 1966).
MacIntyre, Alasdair, *A Short History of Ethics* (New York 1966).
MacIntyre, Alasdair, "Egoism and Altruism," *Encyclopedia of Philosophy* (New York 1967).
Sidgwick, Henry, *Outlines of the History of Ethics*, 6th ed. (London 1931).
Sidgwick, Henry, *Methods of Ethics*, 7th ed. (London 1922).

JACK DERMID

Common egret

EGRET, ē′grət, any of a group of herons, usually white, characterized during the breeding season by elaborate filamentous plumes on the back. These plumes, called "aigrettes," are erected during mating displays.

Egrets occur in a variety of wetland habitats throughout the temperate and tropical zones. They are found in fresh- and saltwater marshes, in shallow lakes and lagoons, and in damp meadows. The largest-sized species, the great, or common, egret (*Egretta alba*) is found on all continents except Antarctica, and one species has colonized remote islands and atolls in the Indian and Pacific oceans. During the last part of the 19th century, egret feathers were widely used in millinery, and populations of some species were threatened, especially in North America. Egrets are now protected by strict conservation laws.

Egrets are long-legged, long-necked wading birds, 20 to 41 inches (50-100 cm) tall. They are slender-bodied but have relatively long, broad wings. The bill is long and daggerlike, and the neck is folded onto the shoulders in an S shape when the bird is at rest or in flight. The legs trail behind in flight. All egrets have pure white plumage, but three true egrets also have dark bluish gray or mottled color phases.

The egret's diet consists of fishes, frogs, salamanders, snakes, small mammals, worms, and crustaceans. Occasionally egrets associate with large herbivores, especially cattle, and feed on insects the mammals stir up. During the breeding season, egrets form rookeries occasionally numbering thousands. The nest, a platform of sticks and twigs, is placed on the ground or in a tree. Both sexes incubate the three to six pale bluish eggs and care for the young.

True egrets make up the genus *Egretta* in the family Ardeidae, but the name "egret" is also used for other herons with plainer plumes.

GEORGE E. WATSON, *Smithsonian Institution*